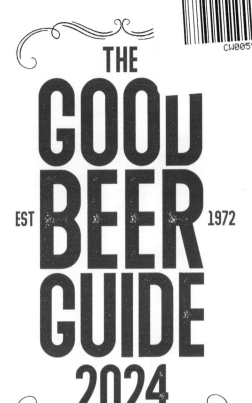

THE GOOD BEER GUIDE 2024

EST 1972

MANAGING EDITOR
Emma Haines

EDITORS
Katie Button, Alan Murphy, Claire-Michelle Taverner-Pearson

PROJECT ASSISTANCE
Stewart Campbell

SALES & MARKETING
Toby Langdon

CAMRA BOOKS

Special thanks to the 155,000 CAMRA members who carried out research for the pub entries; the Campaign's Regional Directors and Area Organisers, who co-ordinated the pub entries; the Campaign's Brewery Liaison Coordinators and Brewery Liaison Officers, who carried out research for the brewery entries; Rick Pickup for assistance coordinating the brewery entries; Alex Presland for technical support; Iain Barker, Christine Beatty and Simon Mather at AMA Dataset; Bruce Dickinson, Edward Stewart-Lockhart and the Phantom Music Team, Paul Ainsworth, Maddy Hardman, Roger Protz, Michael Slaughter, Adrian Tierney-Jones and Camilla Weddell for supplying articles, images and information for the Guide; Geoff Strawbridge for proofreading assistance; all CAMRA's staff and CAMRA's National Executive for their help and support. In memory of Chris Gillette.

Thanks also to the publicans, breweries, CAMRA members and others who have kindly contributed their photographs.

Photo credits: [Key: t = top; b = bottom; c = centre; l = left; r = right] p4 Mike MacGregor; p5 John McMurtrie; p9 (l) simon noh/Unsplash; (r) christian chen/Unsplash; p10 (tr) Michael Slaughter; p12 (br) monica di loxley/Unsplash; p13 (bl) jon parry/Unsplash; (cr) meritt thomas/Unsplash; p15 (cl) Ivan Radic/Flickr CC BY 2.0; p926 David Pritchard; p927 Martyn Smith/Flickr CC BY 2.0; p931 (t) Bob Smith; p932 George Greenaway; p933 (bl) Dennis W Jones; (tr) Peter Down; (br) Stuart McMahon; p934 (t) Stuart McMahon; (br) Stuart McMahon; p935 (tl) Stuart McMahon; (tr) Sarah Crawford; (b) Stuart McMahon

Design: Cover art: Phantom Music. Jacket designs: Jack Pemberton/Stuart Crouch Creative.

Colour and extra mono pages: Dale Tomlinson.

Production: Database, maps, typesetting of listings and indexes: AMA Dataset Ltd, Preston.

Printing: Printed and bound in the UK by CPI William Clowes, Beccles, Suffolk.

Published by the Campaign for Real Ale Ltd, 230 Hatfield Road, St Albans, Herts, AL1 4LW. www.camra.org.uk

Beerwolf Books, Falmouth, Cornwall (p278). Photo: Timara Easter

CONTENTS

3

ABOUT THE GOOD BEER GUIDE

Your Guide to the best pubs and beer in the UK.

For more than five decades, the *Good Beer Guide* has been a comprehensive guide to the UK's breweries, their ales and the best outlets to find them in around the country.

There may be other pub guides out there, but this book is different. Where other guides might have a small editorial board pulling together entries, the *Good Beer Guide* has a huge volunteer team, based around the country, all regularly using their local pubs, trying out the beers on offer and recommending the best of them to other beer- and pub-lovers.

We strive hard to ensure that all areas of the country are covered. Each county or region has a listing allocation based on a scientific calculation of its population, number of licensed premises and levels of tourism. As a result, the Guide's reach is unparalleled.

The *Good Beer Guide* is also proudly independent. Inclusion in this book is dependent on merit, not on payment. No pubs or breweries paid to be in this book.

VOLUNTEER INVOLVEMENT

CAMRA has more than 150,000 members across more than 200 branches around the UK. It's within these branches that entries are democratically selected. All members are invited to rate beers served to them via the National Beer Scoring System (see p936). These scores are used by branches to identify pubs consistently serving the best real ale. Not only is the quality of the cask beer monitored, but also factors that could affect the range on offer, and the overall standard of the pub, such as change of ownership or management.

While the core purpose of the Guide is to seek out quality real ale, it also considers other things such as history, architecture, food, family and disabled facilities, gardens and special events (such as beer festivals). The pub listings you find in these pages paint a full picture of what you can expect before you embark on a trip to visit them.

The listings are checked many times before publication, to ensure they are accurate and up to date.

BREWERY LISTINGS

The *Good Beer Guide* includes a comprehensive listing of the more than 1,800 breweries currently operating in the UK – not just those producing real ale – and their core cask-conditioned beers available.

Each one is appointed a local CAMRA volunteer as soon as they come on stream. These volunteer officers regularly keep in touch with the brewery to stay abreast of what's being brewed and developments that may be taking place.

A REGIONAL GUIDE

The Guide features pub and brewery listings together, by county within regions, making it easier for you to find local beers and where to drink them, plus information about the breweries that produce them.

OPENING HOURS

Opening hours are not listed in the Guide as they are subject to significant change. Please phone ahead if you are travelling.

A fine selection of ales on the bar at the Phoenix, Dundee.

SANCTUARY

My day job is one of the best on the planet. Not only do I get to perform and travel around the world, but I also get to brew and taste beers all around the globe as I do so, which is why I take such pleasure in writing the foreword for this latest edition of the *Good Beer Guide*.

As a born-in-1958 'vintage human', my student days were full of the growing movement pushing back against the soulless corporate brews of the '70s, and the beginning of what is now called 'craft brewing'. You hold in your hands a voyage of discovery not just through a wonderful world of traditional ales and brewers, but also a lens through which to observe the web of history that weaves around the fabric of that almost unique institution – the British pub. Every beer has a story to tell, and every pub … well … if the walls could speak what dramas have unfolded under the oak beamed roofs? It is easy to forget that the roots of our pub culture go back for centuries, and perhaps we have been guilty of taking them for granted.

This guide is a clarion call to get involved, to go local, to preserve humanity and courtesy in our pubs, not have them turned into mere alcohol cash machines. The preservation of our nooks and crannies, our snugs and sofas, the right to quiet enjoyment of a pint without screaming over piped music, is something to be cherished.

Ironically, for me as a musician, the sound of silence and human conversation is a scarce commodity. The pub can be a place of contemplation as well as a place of celebration. Pub landlords need to be let off the leash by their corporate masters to bring an individual and personal touch to their pub. Luckily this guide will show you the way but, as in all things, what we do not support will surely atrophy.

I write this thousands of miles away from England. When I return in 36 hours' time, I will go to my local. They will pour my pint as I stick my head through the door, and say "welcome back… where have you been?"

Good company, good beer, and good luck to you all!

Bruce Dickinson

PS. As some of you know I just celebrated my own 'craft brewing' anniversary after a decade of blissful Trooper beer collaborations with my great friends at Robinsons Brewery in Stockport. We have made some great beers together, some of which can be found in their pub estate which stretches from the Lake District to North Wales and in the big towns and cities of the North West – hopefully some of which can be found in this guide!

Bruce Dickinson is the lead singer of **Iron Maiden**, one of the most successful metal bands in the world. He is also a celebrated writer, broadcaster, fencer and aviator. He has been brewing Trooper beer in collaboration with Robinsons Brewery of Stockport since 2013.

REAL TROOPERS

As we follow on from celebrating 50 years of the Campaign in 2021, and 50 years of publishing the *Good Beer Guide* in 2022, there's much to be excited about as we enter the next half century. There is also plenty of hard work to be done to ensure the future of the UK's beer, cider and pubs trade.

We've well and truly hit our stride with festivals once again, with huge success across the country at local events, as well as with our flagship event, the Great British Beer Festival. Despite continued building work and renovations at Olympia London, our volunteers were as hard-working and dedicated as ever, and succeeded in delivering a brilliant event, showcasing the best of UK cask, craft, cider and perry, as well as wines, gins and plenty of entertainment. The event saw the return of the Champion Beer of Britain after an extended hiatus due to the pandemic affecting judging processes, and the second iteration of the Homebrew Competition that highlights the best up and coming brewers across the country.

THE DIGITAL AGE

Volunteers and staff have been collaborating this year on setting out CAMRA's digital future, ensuring all the tools the Campaign has are available in the most effective and user-friendly way. One of the most illustrious feathers in CAMRA's cap is our Learn & Discover platform,

and this year there has been an incredible amount of work put in to make it as accessible as possible. The last 12 months have seen fantastic written, video and audio content added to the platform from the leading voices in beer and cider, including David Jesudason, Rachel Hendry, Jonny Garrett, Gabe Cook and Hollie Stephens.

The What's Brewing online platform goes from strength to strength, with regular columns from *50 Years of CAMRA* author Laura Hadland, and Matthew Curtis, author of *Modern British Beer*. Plus, the sixth series of the *Pubs. Pints. People.* podcast has entertained listeners across the globe, from Australia to the United States.

CAMPAIGNING SUCCESSES

As ever, there has been plenty for us to be raising our voices about. The top priority has been addressing the parallel cost of living and cost of business crises – resulting in high-profile campaigning to secure vital energy bill and business rate support. Throughout the year we have used our unique voice as consumers,

Join CAMRA at the Great British Beer Festival

rather than licensees, to tell Government about the nightmare situation many people find themselves in: wanting to support their local pubs and clubs, but not having the disposable income to do so.

Each time we have asked our membership to email their MPs about issues ranging from Small Brewers Relief, cider tax and High Street Rental Auctions, they have answered the call with gusto. We have also seen members organising in their numbers to celebrate another Summer of Pub campaign, with mini-festivals, tap takeovers and pub quizzes galore taking place over the summer months.

Desi Pubs was published in June to great acclaim.

We've also been looking inwards. Following discussion in the beer and pub industry about tackling discrimination, CAMRA set up an Inclusion, Diversity and Equality Review Group to ensure members and non-members do not suffer discrimination and feel safe and welcome within the organisation and at its events. The Group's report, packed with recommendations for the coming years, was launched at our April 2023 Members' Weekend.

PUTTING THE PINT IN PRINT

Our publishing arm CAMRA Books began the year with the *Good Beer Yearbook 2023*, an ambitious new publication that took a closer look at the contemporary world of beer, highlighting the developments, innovations, people, trends, concerns and causes for celebration that are having an impact on the modern beer scene. The book features a whole host of award-winning voices including Annabel Smith, Roger Protz and Emma Inch.

One of the most exciting books to come from us this year has been *Desi Pubs* by David Jesudason. First established in the 1960s to break the racist colour bar, which saw many

non-white customers refused service, Desi Pubs have since evolved into a modern-day celebration of multiculturalism. To celebrate the launch of the book, Meantime Brewing Company brewed a very special beer – Desi Pale. *Desi Pubs* was picked up across the UK press as a groundbreaking book, and we're proud to have been able to support David as he told this story.

Another story at the heart of what CAMRA does is that of cask beer, and this summer Des de Moor has brought that to print. *CASK* introduces cask-conditioned ale to a new generation, explaining why it's still important and what distinguishes it from other beer. Des examines the history of cask in detail, explores why it has survived and explains why it remains this country's greatest gift to the world of beer.

CONTINUING THE STORY

This 51st edition of the Guide is the perfect opportunity for CAMRA to reaffirm its commitment to campaigning on behalf of consumers across the UK. Through events, education and socialising with one another, our membership can ensure that our pubs and clubs, breweries and cider producers thrive for at least another 50 years to come.

In the words of Iron Maiden's Bruce Dickinson on the 1983 track *The Trooper*: "You'd better stand: there's no turning back."

Nik Antona, *National Chairman*

LIVE BEER, LIVE MUSIC!

Pubs and music have always gone together, whether it was pub rock, or standing around the old Joanna having a good old ding-dong, or just a bunch of spotty youths setting up their gear in order to sing the pop hits of the day. In the 19th century, the music hall came out of pubs and if you walk around any high street at the weekend you're sure to hear some band pumping out 'Alright Now' or some other evergreen from a small platform located in a corner of a pub.

Without pubs there would have been no punk rock and none of the subsequent musical styles that emerged out of the energy and creativity of punk. There wouldn't have been a BrewDog either, but that's a discussion for another time.

PUB ROCK

Towards the mid-1970s, a musical movement emerged that, for want of a better name, was called pub rock basically because bands such as Ducks Deluxe, Dr Feelgood and Kilburn and the High Roads (a certain Ian Dury was the singer) played in pubs. It was as simple as that and the energetic and uncomplicated character of pub rock, which emerged as a kind of reaction against overblown, extravagant, rock histrionics from the likes of Genesis, Yes and Rick Wakeman and his knights on ice, was the catalyst for punk.

Bands that went on to great success often played early gigs in pubs, such as the Arctic Monkeys who apparently debuted at the Grapes in Sheffield, while the Grade II-listed Hare & Hounds in Birmingham saw UB40's first ever gig. Bragging rights though must go to the Driftwood Spars at Trevaunance Cove in Cornwall, where Queen played in 1971 before they hit the big time. Allegedly the person who ran the venue at first refused to pay the band because he thought they were rubbish. Mind you, looking at the ad for the Queen gig and other bands throughout the August week then, I wonder whatever happened to the Hairy Magpies.

'Not many people know that Queen played here, but they should!' says Natasha Brown, Weddings and Events coordinator at the Driftwood Spars. 'You can still see the ticket in the main bar along with loads of other trinkets that had stories attached, many of which match our beer names.'

The pub, which has its own brewery so that you will be sure of such award-winners like Alfie's Revenge, still puts on music for its regular Sunday sessions with all sorts being played.

Queen played the Driftwood Spars, Trevaunance Cove, Cornwall, in 1971 before they hit the big time.

'We have solo acoustic guitar sessions, cajun jams, blues, rock, pop, open mic, opera,' says Natasha. 'We even had a band that tap-danced along as a part of their music! It brings a great atmosphere, shows off great talent and brings the community together. Most of our sessions are free to attend, which is a bonus.'

MUSIC BELONGS IN PUBS

This is the beauty of music in modern-day pubs, booking organisers can be as eclectic as they like or otherwise specialise in certain genres. They can book groups that write their own songs and perhaps one day might be found playing at Glastonbury, or turn to cover bands that rock out their audiences with familiar classics, as is the case of a couple of pubs near me most weekends in Exeter. Pubs also offer young, unsigned bands a helping hand, a stage and an audience, whether it's 100 or mum, dad and a couple of lads from school. The main thing about all of this is that music belongs in pubs, as Pete Tiley from the award-winning Salutation in Gloucestershire told me.

'Despite the fact that it often doesn't generate a lot of extra profit once you've paid the musicians, I have live music in the pub for three main reasons,' he says. 'The first is that I often combine it with another event to drive incremental sales. For example, if we had a BBQ or food night or a beer festival then I would often use live music as a way of driving sales for the food or extra beer. I also have live music because it can draw in new audiences to the pub that may have previously never been in before. Assuming they like the pub then hopefully they come back for other events/nights. Finally I have live music because I personally enjoy it. I love the atmosphere it creates and I also like to use it as a treat for my regulars.'

GOOD BEER, GOOD MUSIC

Having put up with indifferent beers during my time reviewing gigs in pubs when I was a music journalist, it goes without saying that a decent pint is a requisite when you're listening to say a folk band fiddling away in the back room of a pub.

'I think the idea of going to a pub and drinking good beer and listening to music is very appealing,' says Simon Webster, CEO of Thornbridge Brewery, whose Greystones pub in Sheffield is an essential part of the local music scene. 'I think, when we started, having good beer at a music venue was unheard of and the Greystones has managed to build that reputation for both things and we get gig-goers coming from far and wide to enjoy a few pints of Jaipur and a night listening to their favourite band.'

These bands have included the likes of Wilko Johnson, T'Pau, China Crisis and Richard Hawley, who lives nearby and drinks in the pub. 'Music is hugely important to the pub,' adds Simon. 'When we opened the pub in 2010 it had a back room that had a glitterball and pool table and was rather sad. Historically it had hosted folk music in the past with the likes of Ralph McTell and Billy Connolly, so we wanted to bring those days back and we did that from day one.'

Pubs and bars keep the fire of live music going.

CONNECTING PEOPLE

As is the case with pubs in general, those that host music nights still find it tough. Music licensing can be expensive and venues in the middle of residential areas can be the subject of noise complaints. Yet there are still those pubs and bars that keep the fire of live music going, connecting people, entertaining people and above all providing good beer to get you through the dullest of jazz acts.

'I think that's ultimately what draws me to live music pubs and why I host it in my own one,' says Pete Tiley. 'It amplifies the connectedness I feel with others and it heightens that shared experience in the unique shared space that a pub provides.'

In other words, pub music rocks.

Adrian Tierney-Jones is an award-winning journalist who writes about beer, cider, travel and pubs for various magazines and newspapers. He is also the author of many books on these subjects, including *United Kingdom of Beer*. Follow him on Twitter @ATJbeer

PUB HERITAGE

The nation's pub heritage has always been important to CAMRA – our initial Articles of Association included 'to campaign for the retention... of the traditional British pub'. The late 1970s was a time when threats to historic buildings, including pubs, became many and various, leading to the formation of a national Pub Preservation Group in 1979, which has evolved into the present-day Pub Heritage Group (PHG).

It wasn't until 1997 that we published our first *National Inventory of Historic Pub Interiors*, which was the product of research over many years. The focus then, as now, was on interiors that have either been largely intact for a long time or display features that are rare or exceptional. The initial list totalled 179 pubs (some sadly no longer with us) and was soon joined by *Regional Inventories*, covering the next tier of interiors in terms of historic importance.

STAR RATINGS

Just recently, we've moved to a single National Inventory with entries graded at three levels. Three Star pubs have stayed wholly or largely intact for the past 50 years or retain rooms or features that are truly rare or exceptional or display a combination of the two. They total around 300. Two Star pubs have interiors where the intactness, rarity and exceptional features are somewhat lower. One Star pubs either have readily identifiable historic layouts or retain rooms or features of special interest, but more significant changes are allowable than for the first two categories.

PROMOTION AND PROTECTION

PHG is not just about producing lists. We campaign hard both to promote and to protect these precious assets. The main vehicles for promotion are our many publications and our website. Over the years we have published heritage pub guides covering all regions of the country plus our flagship *Britain's Best Real Heritage Pubs*. The website catalogues all inventory-listed pubs with detailed descriptions and copious photographs, along with other information about heritage pubs.

The Garden Gate, Leeds, widely acclaimed as 'the jewel in the crown' of historic pub architecture in Yorkshire, is currently closed and at risk.

Protection involves campaigning to resist unwanted changes or closure threats to heritage pubs and getting as many of them as possible statutorily listed by Historic England. Although we have inevitably lost a few pubs to closure or unsympathetic alteration, we have also had many successes, with some pubs 'coming back from the dead', much to our delight. Recent examples include the Red Lion, Ampney St Peter, Gloucestershire, the Castle, Macclesfield, the Zetland, Middlesbrough, and the Vines, Liverpool. However, others are, at the time of writing, causing us great concern – two Yorkshire pubs, the Garden Gate, Leeds, and the New Beehive, Bradford, in particular.

CONNECTING WITH HISTORY

There can be little doubt that the idea of the 'traditional' pub is hugely appealing and bound up with a sense of Britishness. Stepping into one somehow connects us with a bit of history and, if the interior has heritage importance, then so much the better. Happily, most Inventory pubs serve real ale and many are featured in this book (look out for the ★ symbol), so please enjoy both the beer and the surroundings on your visits.

For more information on the Pub Heritage Group and the work CAMRA undertakes to promote and protect historic pubs, please visit **pubheritage.camra.org.uk**. Publications can be purchased at **shop1.camra.org.uk**

CAMRA'S BEER STYLES

We are very lucky in the UK to enjoy a rich variety of traditional beer styles developed by brewers over the past few hundred years. The number of brewers brewing international recipes and experimenting with new styles means that there are ever more beers to choose from. Such a wide range of styles, names and variations can be a little overwhelming, so CAMRA have cut through the jargon and have come up with 12 beer style categories to help you navigate the choices at the bar.

Over the next few pages, we take you through the beer style categories, with advice on some of the flavour profiles you can expect.

1. Milds
up to and including 4% ABV

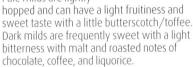

Look: There are two types of mild: light/pale milds, and dark milds. Milds can be dark brown to black to pale amber or even gold.

Taste: Light drinking and not very hoppy. Pale milds are lightly hopped and can have a light fruitiness and sweet taste with a little butterscotch/toffee. Dark milds are frequently sweet with a light bitterness with malt and roasted notes of chocolate, coffee, and liquorice.

Scottish 60 shillings or Scottish light beer also fits into this category and can be dark brown to black in colour with flavours of malt with butterscotch/toffee notes.

2. Session Bitters
up to and including 4.3% ABV

Look: Amber to dark brown in colour.

Taste: Bitterness can range from light to strong. These are 'traditional bitters' with a thin to average body, a malt character with noticeable hops; typically earthy, spicy and peppery, they can also be floral or piny. Fruitiness, sometimes citrus, can be present.

3. Premium Bitters
4.4%–6.4% ABV

Look: Usually amber to dark brown in colour.

Taste: Premium bitters are traditionally stronger bitters with an average to thick body. They have medium to strong malt flavour with noticeable hops; typically earthy, spicy and peppery, they can also be floral, piny, or citrus. Fruitiness can be medium to strong.

Stronger bitters can have estery notes such as pear drops, and the bitterness can range from medium to strong.

4. Session Pale, Blond & Golden Ales
up to and including 4.3% ABV

Look: Pale ales are dark gold to amber in colour. Blond ales are straw to golden in colour.

Taste: These are refreshing, light-drinking beers. Malt flavours are light in character, with hop flavours more noticeable and varying from earthy or spicy to citrus and tropical.

Pale ales can be fruitier than a session bitter. Malt is minimal with low to moderate fruit flavours. Hops again can vary but will not have a strong citrus character. Golden ales have pronounced fruity, citrus hop notes and can have strong bitterness.

5. **Premium Pale, Blond & Golden Ales**: 4.4%–6.4% ABV

Look: Pale ales are dark gold to amber. Blond and golden ales are straw to gold in colour.

Taste: These beers are refreshing but fuller-bodied than the session varieties. Malt is light to medium in character and not dominant. Fruit can vary from minimal to strong and is often citrus or tropical. Hops are noticeable and vary from earthy and spicy to citrus.

6. **British & New World IPAs** 5.5% ABV and above

Look: British IPAs are usually amber to pale brown. New World IPAs are straw to pale brown. Black IPAs are typically dark brown or black.

Taste: These are strong, hoppy beers. The finish is long and complex.

British IPAs often have a biscuit malt aroma and peppery, spicy, earthy, piny or floral hop notes. New World IPAs are noticeably fruitier with citrus, tropical or white wine flavours. The malt tends to make less of an impact. Black IPAs have a lighter roasted character which complements rather than dominating the hops and fruit in the flavour profile.

7. **Brown & Red Ales, Old Ales & Strong Milds**: up to 6.4% ABV

Look: Darker in colour, from deep red to dark brown.

Taste: These beers tend to have malty notes.

Brown ales have malt to the fore, often with roasted, smoky or nut-like flavours. Hops are sometimes evident, and they can have a moderately bitter or dry finish. Fruity flavours such as raisins or sultanas can be present. American brown ales tend to be much fruitier, sometimes with pronounced bittering.

Red ales have malt to the fore, often with roast or nutty flavours. Rye can be present, creating a balanced tartness. American red ales are fruitier and hoppier. Strong milds and unaged old ales have a light to rich malt character, sometimes with caramel and fruit notes such as raisins and sultanas.

8. **Session Stouts & Porters** up to and including 4.9% ABV

Look: Dark ruby to jet black.

Taste: Stouts are typically black and less hopped than porters. Their flavour and aroma results from the roasted grain malts, for example chocolate, caramel and coffee notes. They have minimal hop and fruit notes. There are several different types of stout brewed, each with a slightly different flavour profile. These include dry stouts, oyster stouts, oatmeal stouts and milk stouts.

Porters also have roasted notes of coffee or chocolate but are balanced by a hoppy character.

9. **Strong Stouts & Porters**
5% ABV and above

Look: Dark ruby to jet black.

Taste: Grain, burnt fruit, fresh leather, espresso coffee, bitter chocolate, molasses and liquorice notes. Warming alcohol is often noticeable due to the high alcohol content. These are stronger, dry versions of the session varieties, usually with a smoother, fuller mouthfeel. Flavours range from sweet to dry but with a rich, full body.

Imperial stouts and Baltic (or Imperial) porters are deep and complex with roast grain, burnt fruit and fresh leather notes.

10. **Barley Wines & Strong Ales**
6.5% ABV and above

Look: Pale gold, amber, ruby to black.

Taste: Strong beer used to be produced to allow it to be kept, particularly to provide beer when it was too warm to brew. Many of the beers in this category are still aged before selling, leading to wine-like notes. They are rich, complex, and full-bodied with noticeable alcohol, but can vary from dry to sweet. Bitterness can be medium to strong.

11. **Speciality Beers**:
differently produced

Look: Varies.

Taste: Differently produced speciality beers are those brewed with non-standard ingredients or techniques, as opposed to flavoured speciality beers, which have flavour added. Non-conventional ingredients and techniques are only limited by the brewer's imagination. They can include styles such as Pilsners, Vienna lagers, Märzen, dark lagers and Kölsch, wheat beers, sours, saisons, wood-aged and smoked beers.

12. **Speciality Beers**: flavoured

Look: Varies.

Taste: Flavoured speciality beers are beers with a flavour added. They can be similar to other styles in that any beer style can be adapted by a flavour addition to become a speciality beer. They include fruit beers or beers brewed with herbs, spices or other culinary ingredients. The latter can include ginger, coriander, mint, elderflower or ingredients such as honey, coffee, chocolate, vanilla or fortified wines and spirits.

The character of a base beer will influence the final taste of a fruit beer but the wide range of fruit available to brewers means that tastes can vary from sour (typical of lemons and some cherries), to bitter (such as bergamot), through to sweet (such as mango or strawberry).

To help you find your favourite beers more easily we now include beer style information next to each beer listed in the brewery section of the Guide. Please see the inside back cover for more information, or the CAMRA website **camra.org.uk/learn-discover**

PUBS, PINTS AND PEOPLE

We're all about Pubs, Pints and People so see how just three of the campaigns that CAMRA has run this year are supporting pubs, clubs, brewers, cider makers and of course consumers.

PUBS

In 2017, CAMRA won landmark protection for pubs in England. Converting or demolishing a pub now requires planning permission, giving local people a vital chance to have their say. This year, that work has come under threat as the Government's latest levelling up plans proposed stripping this protection away from high street pubs.

A new government proposal gives permitted development rights for vacant high street pubs, which could see developers convert them with no way for communities to have their say.

Plans for 'High Street Rental Auctions' are designed to regenerate high streets by giving Councils the power to auction off a lease for commercial properties that have been vacant for more than a year. Campaigners often see popular pubs closed to their communities and left to decay, as owners try to make the case to planning authorities that a once thriving business is not viable – and therefore ripe for a profitable housing conversion – so at first glance this looked like a welcome opportunity to see pubs brought back into use.

However, buried in the detail were some concerning proposals.

The Government's consultation included plans to allow pubs to be converted for the length of the lease without the need for planning permission, divided up into multiple units, and gutted of their bars, cellars or other important fittings. There would be no obligation to reinstate the pubs fittings at the end of the lease – in fact at that point developers would be able to apply to make the conversion permanent. Any high street pub that had been closed for over a year would be up for grabs, even listed buildings.

We responded quickly, and CAMRA's members sent thousands of emails to their MPs, asking them to ensure that communities would keep their right to the planning process before a pub can be converted. Our campaigning so far has seen questions asked in Parliament, letters sent to the Minister and calls for an investigation by the Select Committee, and an extension to the consultation has been announced. All promising signs, as we continue the campaign to keep pubs protected.

PINTS

In 2021 CAMRA celebrated the introduction of one of our flagship campaigning policies, as Rishi Sunak – then Chancellor – announced that a new, lower rate of tax would be created for beer and cider served on draught.

For the first time, our tax system would recognise the unique status of pubs and social clubs as community spaces and go some way to levelling the playing field between the price of beer sold on draught in social settings and cheap supermarket alcohol consumed at home.

But good news about taxes is never simple. Several new campaigning issues were created between this announcement and the implementation of the new tax system.

Initially, the new rate would only apply to containers over 40L. This would have seriously disadvantaged the smallest producers, as independent brewers commonly supply their beer in 4.5-gallon casks, or 30L kegs, and small cider producers often use a 20L 'Bag-in-Box' for distribution. We successfully campaigned for this to be lowered to 20L and supported the campaigning of organizations like the Society of Independent Brewers (SIBA) as they called for the same thing.

At first, the Government announced that the lower rate would only be applied in England, Scotland, and Wales – leaving out pub-goers in Northern Ireland. We kept up pressure on the Government, reminding them that they had an obligation to support pubs throughout the UK. Under the new 'Windsor Framework' the new draught rate will apply across England, Scotland, Wales and Northern Ireland.

Finally, we got to see a draft of the legislation that would create the new draught duty rate. CAMRA's policy experts soon realised that the exact wording made it fraud to decant a draught duty paid product into a container for consumption off the premises – in other words, they made it illegal to buy a takeaway pint. Here we won an important concession that allows businesses that mainly sell takeaway beer to continue to operate under the old tax system, meaning that bottle shops offering refills won't be forced out of business. Despite extensive campaigning from CAMRA and the industry, the Treasury hasn't yet agreed with any of the proposed solutions for letting pubs make occasional takeaway sales, and this will be a key issue for us as we look towards next year.

Despite extensive campaigning, the Treasury have not yet agreed with any of the proposed solutions for letting pubs make occasional takeaway sales.

PEOPLE

CAMRA's campaigning isn't all legislative technicalities about tax. Once you get down to it, it's people that make change happen, which is why it's important that we also make sure we're a welcoming organisation that values our members.

This year, we completed the first phase of work on our Inclusivity, Diversity and Equality Review. The review was carried out by a group of experts recruited from our membership who set out to learn what aspects of the Campaign members enjoy and find the areas where we have room for improvement. Some had never volunteered with CAMRA before while others were veteran campaigners. Some brought a unique understanding of CAMRA's (admittedly complex) internal processes while others bought lived experience of some of the issues the group aimed to tackle.

Having commissioned a survey of CAMRA's entire membership, they also held a series of consultation sessions where they heard from the myriad of groups that drive CAMRA's work through their expertise. The findings were then presented at our annual Members' Weekend and Conference where members had the chance to hear first-hand about how CAMRA can work better for everyone.

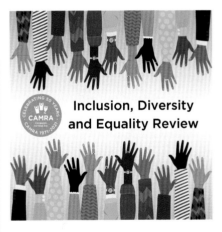

Inclusion, Diversity and Equality Review

We've already created new materials for use at the 180+ CAMRA beer festivals that run each year, and other recommendations from the Review will be rolled out in the coming months, including new branch roles, extra training opportunities, better and more accessible communication, and more open recruitment so that everyone has a chance to volunteer in every area of the Campaign.

Building on those specific recommendations and policies, culture change within the Campaign will ensure that everyone feels welcomed into the CAMRA family, and we can all drink to that. Cheers!

To find out more about CAMRA's campaigning activities please visit **camra.org.uk/take-action**

KEY MAP

The Guide is divided into 14 geographical regions. Within each region individual chapters cover the county or authority areas indicated on the map below. Each county area is listed alphabetically within the region, with pub listings first, followed by brewery listings. Numerous changes to administrative boundaries mean that some county areas are approximate only. Please see the contents list on p3 for a full breakdown of regions and areas.

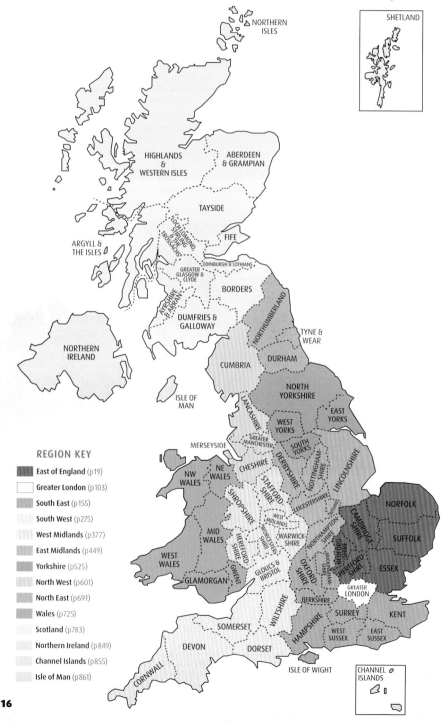

REGION KEY

- East of England (p19)
- Greater London (p103)
- South East (p155)
- South West (p275)
- West Midlands (p377)
- East Midlands (p449)
- Yorkshire (p525)
- North West (p601)
- North East (p691)
- Wales (p725)
- Scotland (p783)
- Northern Ireland (p849)
- Channel Islands (p855)
- Isle of Man (p861)

England

East of England

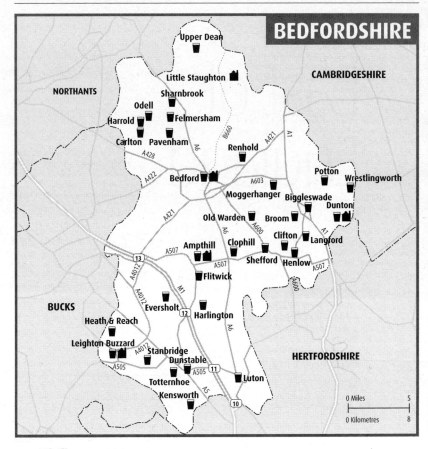

BEDFORDSHIRE

Ampthill

Albion

36 Dunstable Street, MK45 2JT
☎ (01525) 643126
Everards Beacon Hill, Tiger; 3 changing beers (sourced nationally; often Everards) Ⓗ
A proper narrow-fronted Victorian pub, which includes one large bar and various handpumps serving two regular and three to four guest cask ales from Everards and other national breweries. There are two craft keg beer taps. There's a small 'snug' meeting room and secluded patio garden towards the rear. A varied selection of local clubs and groups are supported.
🏠🏵🕮🖵(42,44) ♣ ♫

Bedford

Burnaby Arms Ⓛ ✅

66 Stanley Street, MK41 7RU (in Prime Ministers area N of town centre)
☎ 07923 140210 ⊕ theburnabyarmsbedford.co.uk
Brewpoint Origin Pale Ale, Legacy Golden Ale, DNA Amber Ale Ⓗ
A traditional street-corner pub with a single bar at the front and a step down to the larger drinking area. It is in the increasingly popular Prime Ministers area (formerly known as Black Tom) of Victorian terrace houses and acts as the centre for various community activities throughout the year. A variety of board games and a book swap are on offer, while a good range of spirits is also available.
🏠🏵♣🖵(10) 🐾 🏵

Castle Ⓛ

17 Newnham Street, MK40 3JR
☎ (01234) 353295 ⊕ castlebedford.co.uk
Brewpoint Origin Pale Ale; 4 changing beers (sourced nationally; often Black Sheep, St Austell, Timothy Taylor) Ⓗ
Lively town pub with a pleasant walled patio garden, five minutes from the town centre and convenient for the Bedford Blues rugby ground. Lunches and light evening meals are served. Current guest beers with tasting notes are listed on the website and social media. A guesthouse behind the pub provides five en-suite bedrooms. Open mic features on a Monday evening, quiz monthly. A former local CAMRA Pub of the Year.
🏠🏵🍴🕮◐♿♣P🖵🏵🛜 ♫

Devonshire Arms Ⓛ ✅

32 Dudley Street, MK40 3TB (1 mile E of town centre S of A4280)
☎ (01234) 301170 ⊕ devonshirearmsbedford.co.uk
6 changing beers (sourced nationally; often Adnams, Brewpoint, St Austell) Ⓗ
Pleasant late-Victorian pub in a residential area, a Wells house for over 125 years. The front bar has bare floorboards and an open fire, while there is a separate rear bar. The garden has a gazebo for smokers and a non-smoking paved area covered by a marquee in winter. Beer and cider festivals are held twice a year. A range of wines is sold by the glass or bottle. A former local CAMRA Pub of the Year, and Town Pub of the Year 2022.
Q🏠🏵♣🖵(4) 🛜 ♫

Pilgrim's Progress ⊘
42 Midland Road, MK40 1QB
☎ (01234) 363751
Greene King Abbot; Ruddles Best Bitter; Sharp's Doom Bar; 6 changing beers (sourced nationally) Ⓗ
Photographs and architectural drawings show the building in its former life as a furniture store before conversion to a Wetherspoon hotel. The bar is divided into five distinct areas on the ground floor and a mezzanine gives access to the upper (non-smoking) outside area with a garden below. Across from the pedestrianised shopping area, it attracts a wide age range and is a good place from which to see the world go by. Suspended trombones mark Glenn Miller's time in Bedford. ♿❀🛋🌳❄🚆🚌🛜

Three Cups Ⓛ
45 Newnham Street, MK40 3JR (200yds S of A4280 near rugby ground)
☎ (01234) 352153
Greene King IPA; 7 changing beers (sourced nationally; often Greene King, Kelchner, Leighton Buzzard) Ⓗ
Comfortable inn dating from the 1770s, owned by Greene King but operated by the Kelchner brewery and offering Kelchner and other microbrewery beers and Saxby's cider. Food is available through a local street-food vendor. Old wood panelling helps retain some of the pub's original character. An attractive garden offers extra seating under cover plus a large terrestrial TV for major sporting events. It is an easy walk from the town centre and close to Bedford Blues rugby ground. ❀🍴🚆🌳🛜🎵

Wellington Arms 🍸
40-42 Wellington Street, MK40 2JX (N of town centre)
☎ 07340 116919
8 changing beers (sourced regionally) Ⓗ
The Welly has been an essential part of the local real ale scene for many years. Now free of the Banks & Taylor tie, full use is being made of the freedom to get beers from a wider range of breweries. Breweriana on display include a wide selection of pumpclips, including some from now closed breweries. A selection of Belgian and other beers is kept in the fridge. Local CAMRA Pub of the Year 2023 and well worth searching out. ❀🌳🎵

White Horse Ⓛ ⊘
84 Newnham Avenue, MK41 9PX
☎ (01234) 409306 🌐 thewhitehorsebedford.co.uk
Brewpoint Origin Pale Ale, Legacy Golden Ale; 2 changing beers (sourced nationally; often Black Sheep, St Austell) Ⓗ
Three seating areas, all with their own style, are served from a single bar. The regular Tuesday quizzes are popular. Musical events are advertised on Facebook. Food is freshly cooked to order, with a choice of roasts on Sunday, but it is wise to book ahead for Sunday and Tuesday evenings. The beer and wine selection is complemented by a wide choice of gins.
♿❀🛋🌳🚆(4)🌳🛜🎵

Biggleswade

Crown Hotel ⊘
23 High Street, SG18 0JE
☎ (01767) 310510
Greene King Abbot; Ruddles Best Bitter; Sharp's Doom Bar; 3 changing beers (sourced nationally) Ⓗ
A substantial 2017 conversion of a 1793 coaching inn which provides the usual good value food and drink associated with the Wetherspoon brand. Nine hotel bedrooms are also available. The walls of the bar are adorned with pictures of local interest. There is usually an eclectic range of ales available and tasting sessions are held on the eve of Wetherspoon beer festivals. Real ales are delivered to the bar by a Flojet system. The large open-plan drinking area is complemented by an outdoor patio. ♿❀🛋🌳❄🚆(73,74)🛜

Wheatsheaf ⊘
5 Lawrence Road, SG18 0LS
☎ (01767) 222220
Fuller's London Pride; Greene King IPA Ⓗ
Built in 1873, this unspoilt, single-room, back-street pub has now featured in the Guide for 21 editions. Ales at a reasonable price are one attraction, others are the friendly atmosphere, traditional pub games, sport — particularly horse racing and football —on the two TV screens and an attractive garden at the rear with a great play area for children. Although the beer range isn't extensive the landlord's prize-winning cellarmanship always ensures an excellent pint.
♿❀🚆♣🚌(73,188) 🐾🛜

Broom

Cock ★ ⊘
23 High Street, SG18 9NA
☎ (01767) 314411 🌐 thecockinnbroom.com
Black Sheep Best Bitter; Fuller's London Pride; Greene King Abbot; 3 changing beers (sourced nationally; often Tring, Woodforde's) Ⓖ
This Grade II-listed Rural Pub of the Year has been identified by CAMRA as having a nationally important historic pub interior. The pub has three rooms off a central corridor, one of which has darts and Northamptonshire skittles, beyond which is the cellar from which all drinks are served. An extensive outside drinking area leads to a field for camping, with access to cold water and toilets. Three apartments are available across the pub yard. Three Apple Cottage ciders are served. Q♿❀🛋🌳♣♠🚆(200)🌳🛜🎵

Carlton

Fox Ⓛ
High Street, MK43 7LA (off Turvey Rd, S of village centre)
☎ (01234) 720235 🌐 thefoxatcarlton.pub
Eagle IPA; Timothy Taylor Landlord; 2 changing beers (sourced regionally; often Buntingford, Potbelly, Tring) Ⓗ
A charming, thatched community pub with a warm welcome and an attractive garden popular with families. Guest beers are often from local microbreweries. Good-value, home-cooked lunches are served Tuesday to Sunday and evening meals Tuesday to Saturday. There is a regular Thursday evening quiz. Spring and summer bank holiday festivals are held using an outbuilding as an additional bar, with a sausage and cider festival in April and a gin festival in June. Local CAMRA Pub of the Year 2022. Q♿❀🛋♣♠🚆(25)🌳🛜🎵

REAL ALE BREWERIES	
Brewhouse & Kitchen 🍺	Bedford
Brewpoint 🍺	Bedford
Crown 🍺	Little Staughton
Kelchner	Ampthill
Leighton Buzzard 🍺	Leighton Buzzard
March Hare 🍺	Dunton

Clifton

Admiral
1 Broad Street, SG17 5RJ
☎ (01462) 811069
5 changing beers (sourced nationally; often Brains, Harvey's) Ⓗ

Friendly single-room local dating to 1867, serving five ales and bottled craft beers. Maritime memorabilia decorates the interior where a wood-burning stove keeps the cold away in winter. Board games and darts are available and sport is shown on a mid-size, unobtrusive TV. Pub quizzes and live music events are run, as well as an annual beer festival in June. Food offerings include bangers & mash and burger nights midweek, fish & chips Fridays, and Sunday roasts.
🌑🏵◑♣🚇(9A,9B)🐾🛜♪

Clophill

Stone Jug ♀ Ⓛ
10 Back Street, MK45 4BY (500yds off A6 at N end of village) TL083381
☎ (01525) 860526 🌐 stonejug.co.uk
Shepherd Neame Spitfire; 4 changing beers (sourced regionally; often 3 Brewers of St. Albans, Buntingford, Vale) Ⓗ

Originally three 16th-century cottages, this popular village local has an L-shaped bar serving two drinking areas and a family/function room. Excellent home-made lunches are available Tuesday to Saturday. Changing beers are usually from local microbreweries. Picnic benches at the front and a rear patio garden offer outdoor drinking space in fine weather. Parking can be difficult at busy times. A good refreshment stop for the nearby Greensand Ridge Walk. Local CAMRA Country Pub of the Year 2023. Q🌑🏵◑♣P🚇(44,81)🐾

Dunstable

Gary Cooper Ⓛ ✅
Grove Park, Court Drive, LU5 4GP
☎ (01582) 471452
Greene King Abbot; Ruddles Best Bitter; Sharp's Doom Bar; 7 changing beers Ⓗ

A large, airy, modern Wetherspoon bar serving a selection of up to seven guest ales. The usual range of JDW craft beer is also well stocked. Situated in Grove Park leisure area, not far from the Grove Theatre, its large outdoor patio area overlooks the Grove House gardens with many bus routes stopping nearby. Named after the Hollywood star, Gary Cooper, who attended the local grammar school in 1910-13. The pub gets busy on Friday and Saturday nights. 🌑◑🖐🚇🛜

Globe
43 Winfield Street, LU6 1LS
☎ (01582) 512300
5 changing beers (sourced locally) Ⓗ

Popular beer destination and community local where the handpumps boast a good range of four ever-changing microbrewery beers, plus a real cider and perry. A range of Belgian beers are also available. Bare boards, barstools, breweriana and a famous plank at the end of the bar create a traditional town pub atmosphere buzzing with conversation. Dog (and people) friendly. A former Local and County Pub of the Year.
Q🌑🖐♣🚇(F70,F77)🐾🛜♪

Victoria Ⓛ
69 West Street, LU6 1ST
☎ (01582) 662682

House beer (by Tring); 4 changing beers (sourced nationally) Ⓗ

The Victoria is a popular town-centre pub near the Police Station on West Street. It usually offers three varying ales from microbreweries plus a house beer from the local Tring brewery. Darts, dominoes and crib are popular as well as televised sports in the bar. There is a completely separate function room available next to the rear courtyard. 🌑🏵♣🚇🐾🛜♪

Dunton

March Hare ♀ Ⓛ
34 High Street, SG18 8RN
☎ (01767) 318121
Digfield Chiffchaff; March Hare BGB; Oakham Inferno; 3 changing beers (sourced nationally; often Nene Valley, Otter, Titanic) Ⓗ

This local CAMRA Pub of the Year offers up to six constantly changing real ales in excellent condition, one from the on-site brewery. A roaring open fire greets the customer in winter while the garden is a popular drinking area when the weather permits. Comfortable seating is available throughout, and the pub walls are adorned with brewery mirrors, historical pictures of Dunton and framed jigsaws of brewery drays. Beer festivals and social events are well supported. Apple Cottage Cider is always available. 🌑🏵♣🍴♿🚇(188,189)🐾🛜♪

Eversholt

Green Man
Church End, MK17 9DU
☎ (01525) 288111 🌐 thegreenmaneversholt.co.uk
Timothy Taylor Landlord; 1 changing beer (sourced nationally; often Roman Way) Ⓗ

A genuine free house in Church End, one of the many 'Ends' that make up the village of Eversholt. It features flagstone floors, exposed brick fireplaces and has a large patio/garden. Freshly prepared, good-quality food is served in the bar and the separate restaurant (not Sun eve). Conveniently placed for the nearby and popular tourist attractions of Woburn. Closed all day Monday.
🌑🏵◑♿P🐾🛜♪

Felmersham

Sun Ⓛ
Grange Road, MK43 7EU
☎ (01234) 781355 🌐 thesunfelmersham.com
Eagle IPA; 2 changing beers (sourced regionally; often Kelchner, Potbelly) Ⓗ

Pretty, thatched community pub with a family-friendly rear garden, convenient for visits to the historic parish church and a nature reserve across the river. Guest beers are often from local microbreweries. The creative food menu includes rotisserie-cooked chicken, hand-cut chips and seasonal ingredients from local producers. There is also a monthly food and drink theme night. The dining room can accommodate up to 40. Two B&B rooms available. Local CAMRA Cider Pub of the Year and Lockdown Hero 2020. 🌑🏵🛏◑♿♣♠P🚇(50)🐾🛜

Flitwick

Crown
Station Road, MK45 1LA
☎ (01525) 713737 🌐 crownflitwick.co.uk
4 changing beers (sourced nationally) Ⓗ

Large and thriving two-bar pub where the tenants are extremely keen on their real ales, with four changing ales and a craft keg beer usually available. The front bar has TV, jukebox, pool, darts and Saturday evening music nights. There is a large garden with a patio, children's play area and even table tennis. Pizzas are available every evening except Sundays, and Sunday lunches are served. ⮕❀❉◑◔❦⬥♣🅿🍴(2,200)●🛜♪

Harlington

Old Sun

34 Sundon Road, LU5 6LS

☎ 07468 617866

Adnams Ghost Ship; St Austell Tribute, Proper Job; Timothy Taylor Landlord 🅷

A traditional half-timbered, Grade II-listed pub which is a short walk from the railway station. The pub dates back to at least 1785 and has two bars, both featuring sports TVs, plus an upper level side room. There is a pleasant garden and patio and an outside bar in summer. It hosts beer festivals on bank holidays in May and August.
Q⮕❀❉⬥🅿🍴(X42)●🛜♪

Harrold

Oakley Arms 🅛

98 High Street, MK43 7BH (next to Harrold Institute)

☎ (01234) 720166 ⊕ theoakleyharrold.co.uk

Tring Ridgeway; 1 changing beer (sourced regionally; often Tring) 🅷

Attractive, 400-year-old village inn with a modest bar and large lounge. There is no car park, but street parking nearby is not usually difficult. There are various seating areas including a private dining room for up to 10, and board games are available. The menu varies daily according to what is in season. Food is prepared to order with a preference for locally sourced ingredients. The ales are usually from Tring or other local microbreweries. ⮕❀◑◔🍴(25,26)●🛜

Heath & Reach

Axe & Compass 🅛

Leighton Road, LU7 0AA

☎ (01525) 237394 ⊕ theaxeandcompass.pub

2 changing beers (sourced nationally) 🅷

This village community pub has been a free house since 2014. The older front bar, with its low beams, is a lounge and dining area while the rear public bar has gaming machines, pool table and a TV screen. The large garden includes a children's play area. Regularly appearing guest beers mostly come from local breweries such as Tring, Vale and Leighton Buzzard. Accommodation is available in a separate lodge. ⮕❀❉◑♣🍴🅿🍴(150)●🛜

Henlow

Engineers Arms 🅛 ✅

68 High Street, SG16 6AA

☎ (01462) 812284 ⊕ engineersarms.co.uk

10 changing beers (sourced nationally; often Cotleigh, Grainstore, Tring) 🅷

Multi-award winning Cider Pub of the Year serving up to 10 continually changing ales along with real perries and ciders (typically Sandford Orchards and Seacider). A quiet front bar has an open fireplace, brewery and distillery memorabilia and local pictures while the rest of the pub is sport oriented with several dedicated TV screens. Poker, quiz and board game nights, karaoke, live bands, pub outings and tap takeovers ensure that there is something for everyone. Covered outdoor seating is available. Q⮕❀❉⬥♣🍴🅿🍴(9B,74)●🛜♪

Old Transporter Ale House 🅛

300 Hitchin Road, SG16 6DP

☎ (01462) 817410 ⊕ theoldtransporter.co.uk

4 changing beers (sourced nationally; often Potbelly, Tring) 🅖

Single-room beer house near RAF Henlow boasting a friendly and welcoming atmosphere with transport-themed décor and outdoor seating in a delightful marquee area. Real ale is served direct from barrels set up behind the bar and real cider is occasionally available. A choice of small snacks is offered. The pub houses a local darts team and has a widescreen TV for sporting events. Live music, quizzes, raffles and mini beer festivals feature occasionally. Community Pub of the Year. ⮕♣🍴(9b,74)●🛜♪

Kensworth

Farmer's Boy

216 Common Road, LU6 2PJ

☎ (01582) 872207 ⊕ farmersboykensworth.co.uk

Fuller's London Pride; Gale's HSB; 2 changing beers (sourced nationally; often Fuller's) 🅷

Located at the Whipsnade Zoo end of the village, this traditional 19th-century pub has several dining and dining areas. The attractive windows were installed in the 1930s when the pub was bought by Mann, Crossman & Paulin. Popular for food, with pub classics available in different portion sizes. It has a large selection of board games. Children and pets are made welcome. ⮕❀◑◔⬥🅿🍴(X31)●🛜♪

Langford

Plough

77 Church Street, SG18 9QA

☎ (01462) 700348

Greene King Abbot; Timothy Taylor Landlord; 1 changing beer (sourced nationally; often Caledonian, Fyne, Oakham) 🅷

The last pub in Langford, it is popular with dog walkers, ramblers, cyclists and others who appreciate a well-kept pint. The pub supports pool, darts, football and pétanque teams and is the meeting place for many local clubs and societies. At the side is a large, well-furnished garden where the September beer festival is held. Quiz nights on Thursdays and live music on Saturdays are both popular. The landlord is a CAMRA member who elevated previous pubs to the Guide. ⮕❀♣🍴(74)●🛜♪

Leighton Buzzard

Bald Buzzard Micropub 🅛

6 Hockliffe Street, LU7 1HJ

☎ 07538 903753

3 changing beers (sourced nationally) 🅖

Popular micropub that first opened its doors back in 2015. It provides the discerning beer enthusiast with a superb selection of ales and ciders. Its seating layout encourages conversation, with a bespoke chiller room, and four KeyKeg dispensers serving an ever-changing selection of keg and cask beers not normally found locally. Four ciders are available, with a large selection of bottled and canned craft beers. ⮕❀⬥♣🍴🅿🍴(F70,F77)●

Black Lion 🍺

20 High Street, LU7 1EA

☎ (01525) 853725 ⊕ blacklionlb.com

Draught Bass; Nethergate Suffolk County Best Bitter; Vale VPA; 5 changing beers (sourced nationally) 🅷

Traditional alehouse with 17th-century origins featuring exposed beams, wooden floors and an open fire. Eight handpumps often feature beers from North Cotswold, Slater's and Purity, including four keg beers. Eight changing real ciders are available and an impressive bottled and canned beer menu features continental and British beers. There is a large paved garden with separate gin bar. Bar snacks are served and customers are welcome to bring their own lunches. Local CAMRA Pub of the Year 2015-2022. Q ☜ ✿ ❍ ◖ ♣ ● ☐ (F70,F77) ✿

Leighton Buzzard Brewing Company Brewery Tap ⅃

Unit 31, Harmill Industrial Estate, Grovebury Road, LU7 4FF (2nd left from Grovebury Rd)
☎ 07538 903753 ⊕ leightonbuzzardbrewing.co.uk
6 changing beers (sourced locally; often Kelchner, Leighton Buzzard) Ⓖ
The brewery tap of Leighton Buzzard Brewing Company. The brewery's beers are dispensed directly from casks in the cool room, with bottles available to drink on the premises and to take home. A good range of real cider and guest ales are also served. Brewery comedy nights and live music Saturdays usually take place once per month between March and December (check website for details), often with with local food offerings.
☜ ⅃ ♣ ● P ⊟ ☐ (D1) ✿ ☂ ♪

Swan Hotel ⊘

50 High Street, LU7 1EA
☎ (01525) 380170
Greene King Abbot; Ruddles Best Bitter; Sharp's Doom Bar; 4 changing beers (sourced nationally) Ⓗ
Dating from the 17th century, this former coaching inn is a Leighton Buzzard High Street landmark and was renovated by Wetherspoon. With good value food and 39 guest rooms the Swan is busy for much of the week. Friendly service comes from one long bar serving two rooms, a conservatory and a courtyard. Guest beers may feature local microbreweries and real cider is available in summer months. Families are welcome until 11pm. Events include biannual beer festivals.
Q ☜ ✿ ✉ ❍ ◖ ⅃ ● ☐ (F70,F77) ☂

Luton

Black Horse ⅃

23 Hastings Street, LU1 5BE
4 changing beers (sourced nationally; often Leighton Buzzard, Oakham, Tring) Ⓗ
Characterful back-street pub near Luton town centre. The pub is popular with music fans with DJ nights and live bands a big feature on Saturday nights, late closing at weekends. There is a large, covered outdoor seating area for smokers. Very popular on Luton Town matchdays as it is the closest ale pub to the Kenilworth Road ground.
☜ ✿ ♣ ● P ☐ ✿ ♪

Bricklayers Arms

16-18 High Town Road, LU2 0DD
☎ (01582) 611017
6 changing beers (sourced nationally; often Oakham) Ⓗ
Quirky pub in the High Town that has been run by the same landlady for over 30 years. There are sports TVs in both bars and a popular quiz night is held every Monday. The six handpumps serve a variety of guest beers with a choice of light, amber and, usually, a mild. Draft Belgian beers and real ciders are also available. The extension of the outdoor drinking area is a bonus on Luton Town match days. ✿ ☰ ● ☐ (14) ✿ ☂

Globe ⊘

26 Union Street, LU1 3AN
☎ (01582) 482259
3 changing beers (sourced nationally) Ⓗ
Friendly and homely street-corner local, just off Luton town centre. The L-shaped single bar offers three constantly changing beers from micro and regional breweries, it also stages occasional beer festivals. Sport is shown on several TVs. Food is served on Saturday matchdays and roasts on Sunday lunchtimes. There is an enclosed patio area with a function room to the rear of the small car park. ☜ ✿ ◖ ⚹ ☰ ♣ P ✿ ☂ ♪

Great Northern

63 Bute Street, LU1 2EY
☎ (01582) 729311
St Austell Tribute Ⓗ
This may be the smallest pub in Luton. Its name was changed in the 1860s when the Great Northern Railway was built right on its doorstep. It still retains green Victorian wall tiles and a table featuring quirky brass pint glass holders at each corner. St Austell Tribute is regularly served. The front door opens onto a pedestrianised area of the Hat District. ☰ ♣ ✿ ☂

White House ⅃ ⊘

1 Bridge Street, LU1 2NB
☎ (01582) 454608
Greene King Abbot; Ruddles Best Bitter; Sharp's Doom Bar; 6 changing beers (sourced nationally) Ⓗ
A large, two-bar, town-centre Wetherspoon pub with the usual keenly priced food and drinks. There are six different guest ales on both the two separate bars. Local ales often include something from Tring or Kelchner breweries. This bright and clean pub in the Galaxy Centre has a large outdoor drinking area facing St Georges Square. Q ☜ ✿ ❍ ◖ ⚹ ☰ ☐ ☂

Moggerhanger

Guinea ⅃ ⊘

Bedford Road, MK44 3RG
☎ (01767) 640388 ⊕ guineamoggerhanger.co.uk
Brewpoint Origin Pale Ale, DNA Amber Ale; 2 changing beers (sourced regionally) Ⓗ
Large 18th-century village pub with beamed ceilings, in a prominent position at the heart of the village. There is a garden at the front and car parks at the side and rear. The main bar has a drinking area and two areas beyond for diners. A separate games bar has hood skittles and darts. There is a regular quiz on Thursday. Freshly prepared food is available daily (not Sun eve).
Q ☜ ✿ ❍ ◖ ⚹ ♣ P ☐ ✿ ☂ ♪

Odell

Bell

81 High Street, MK43 7AS
☎ (01234) 910850 ⊕ thebellinodell.co.uk
Greene King IPA, Abbot; 3 changing beers (sourced nationally; often Ruddles) Ⓗ
Handsome thatched village pub with a large garden, near the River Great Ouse. A popular stop for walkers with the Harrold-Odell Country Park just down the lane. Sympathetic refurbishment and a series of linked but distinct seating areas help retain a traditional pub atmosphere. Good value, quality food includes a Sunday roast, steak and chips Monday evening and pie and chips Tuesday. Tea and cakes are available all day. Local CAMRA Lockdown Hero 2020. Q ☜ ✿ ✉ ❍ ◖ P ☐ (25) ✿ ☂ ♪

Old Warden

Hare & Hounds L
The Village, SG18 9HQ
☎ (01767) 627225 ⊕ hareandhoundsoldwarden.com
Brewpoint Origin Pale Ale, DNA Amber Ale; 1 changing beer (sourced regionally; often Brewpoint) ⊞
Pub-restaurant in a charming thatched village. The car park entrance leads into the main bar and dining rooms beyond. Follow the corridor or enter through the front door to find the second bar and cosy rooms harking back to village times past. Good-quality meals include light bite lunchtime options, traditional roast on Sunday and evening meals with daily specials. It holds a spring bank holiday beer and music festival. One mile walk to the Shuttleworth aircraft and vehicle collection and Swiss Garden. Q ⑤ ❀ ◑ P ❀ 중 ♪

Pavenham

Cock
High Street, MK43 7NJ
☎ (01234) 822834 ⊕ thecockatpavenham.co.uk
Marston's 61 Deep, Wainwright, Pedigree; 1 changing beer (sourced nationally; often Brakspear, Courage) ⊞
A friendly village pub with a warm welcome and a choice of cask ales. The bar has a late Art Deco look, mirrored in the pub sign outside. The large rear garden connects through a rear gate to the Ouse Valley Way and John Bunyan Trail public footpaths. Food is not served on a regular basis, but there are occasional food events such as pie nights. ⑤ ❀ ♣ P ♒ (25,29) ❀ 중

Potton

Rising Sun L ✔
11 Everton Road, SG19 2PA
☎ (01767) 260231 ⊕ risingsunpotton.co.uk
Brewpoint DNA Amber Ale; Fuller's London Pride; Timothy Taylor Landlord; 4 changing beers (sourced nationally; often Black Sheep, Fyne, Ossett) ⊞
Licensed as a beer house in 1836, this spacious family-run pub is popular with diners, for its locally sourced and home-cooked food, and with drinkers, for some of the less common beers usually served. Both current and future ales are itemised on the pub's comprehensive website and each beer has tasting notes and ABV listed. The comfortable interior has several distinct seating areas as well as an upstairs function room with a west-facing roof terrace. ⑤ ❀ ◑ A P ♒ (189,190) ❀ 중 ♪

Renhold

Polhill Arms
25 Wilden Road, MK41 0JP (at Salph End)
☎ (01234) 771398 ⊕ polhillarms.co.uk
Hardys & Hansons Bitter; Morland Old Speckled Hen; 2 changing beers (sourced nationally; often Greene King, St Austell) ⊞
Family-friendly village local with a welcoming atmosphere. It has a large garden, children's play area and restaurant. An interesting collection of pub and brewery artefacts and airship memorabilia is displayed. Traditional pub food and bar snacks are served, including fish & chips (no food Sun or Mon eves). There are regular quiz nights and live music, and skittles is popular. ⑤ ❀ ◑ ♣ P ♒ (27) ❀ 중 ♪

Sharnbrook

Swan with Two Nicks L
38 High Street, MK44 1PF
☎ (01234) 781585 ⊕ swanwithtwonicks.com
Adnams Southwold Bitter; Brewpoint DNA Amber Ale; 1 changing beer (often Black Sheep, Brewpoint) ⊞
Friendly village pub with an attractive, enclosed rear courtyard and patio garden. Home-cooked quality lunches and evening meals are served, using locally sourced ingredients where possible and including daily specials and home-made pies. A selection of award-winning wines is available by the glass or bottle. A good base for local walks and nature reserves near the River Great Ouse. Walking and cycling groups welcome. ⑤ ❀ ◑ P ♒ ❀ 중 ♪

Shefford

Brewery Tap L
14 Northbridge Street, SG17 5DH
☎ (01462) 628448
3 Brewers of St Albans Shefford Bitter, Dragon Slayer; 4 changing beers (sourced nationally) ⊞
Primarily a drinkers' pub with a divided open-plan bar area featuring wood panelling and decorated with breweriana. A smaller family area to the rear offers more tables. Sandwiches, toasties and other light lunches are served, with breakfast available at weekends. There is a weekly quiz, and occasional live music or charity fundraising events. The large rear garden with seating is heated on cool evenings. Car park access is through an archway beside the pub. ⑤ ❀ ◑ ♣ P ♒ ❀ 중 ♪

Stanbridge

Five Bells
Station Road, LU7 9JF
☎ (01525) 210224 ⊕ fivebellsstanbridge.co.uk
Fuller's London Pride; Gale's Seafarers Ale, HSB; 1 changing beer (sourced nationally) ⊞
A Fuller's-owned country pub with wooden floors, real fire, cosy snug and 'mind your head' low beams. It has a separate 80-seater restaurant in the 18th-century wing which can be used for weddings and other functions. It is set in extensive and attractive grounds and named after the nearby church which once had five bells but now has six. Three regular Fuller's/Gale's beers are served with an occasional guest ale from the Fuller's portfolio. ⑤ ❀ ◑ ₠ ♣ P ♒ (F77) ❀ 중 ♪

Totternhoe

Cross Keys
Castle Hill Road, LU6 2DA
☎ (01525) 220434 ⊕ thecrosskeys.pub
Greene King IPA; 1 changing beer (sourced nationally; often Timothy Taylor) ⊞
Attractive thatched Grade II-listed building dating from 1433. It is a great place to relax and unwind, with a glorious damson orchard and wide views over Ivinghoe Beacon and the Vale of Aylesbury. The guest beers rotate weekly from a list chosen by the locals. In the warmer months basket meals and barbecue food are served in the garden. Dogs are welcome in the public bar. Q ⑤ ❀ ◑ ♣ P ♒ (61) ❀

Old Farm Inn
16 Church Road, LU6 1RE
☎ (01582) 674053 ⊕ theoldfarminn.co.uk
Dark Star Hophead; Fuller's London Pride; Gale's HSB; 1 changing beer (sourced nationally) ⊞

Charming village pub in the conservation area of Church End, boasting two inglenooks. Dogs are welcome in the front bar and there is a child-friendly garden. Quizzes are held on alternate Thursdays. Tasty home-cooked food is served including popular Sunday roasts (no food Sun eve or all day Mon). Beer festivals held in May and August.
🛏️⊛◑&♣♠P�(61) 🌑🐾

Upper Dean

Three Compasses ✅
High Street, PE28 0NE (S of village on road to Melchbourne)
☎ (01234) 708346 ⊕ thethreecompasses.co.uk
Greene King IPA; St Austell Tribute; Timothy Taylor Landlord Ⓗ

Attractive thatched and partly-boarded pub on the southern edge of the village. The main bar is to the left of the entrance with a games area behind. A small lounge bar on the right is used mainly for dining, and there is a large garden at the rear. Since reopening the pub several years ago, the current owners have successfully created a popular rural venue for food and drink. A former local CAMRA Most Improved Pub.
🛏️⊛◑♠P�(28) 🌑🐾♪

Wrestlingworth

Chequers
43 High Street, SG19 2EP
☎ (01767) 631818 ⊕ thechequerswestoning.co.uk
3 changing beers (sourced nationally; often Adnams, Greene King, Hardys & Hansons) Ⓗ

Friendly family-run Grade II-listed pub, parts of which date from the late 17th century. Popular with villagers, community groups, ramblers, bikers and cyclists as well as those who enjoy well-kept ales and home-made meals. Two open fires in the main bar and dining area create a welcoming atmosphere during the colder months and the south-facing exterior is a suntrap during the summer. An area directly across from the entrance has a TV for sport, and a dartboard.
🛏️⊛◑♣P�(188,189) 🌑🐾♪

Breweries

A-B InBev
Porter Tun House, 500 Capability Green, Luton, LU1 3LS
☎ (01582) 391166 ⊕ inbev.com

No real ale.

Brewhouse & Kitchen SIBA
🍽 **115 High Street, Bedford, MK40 1NU**
☎ (01234) 342931 ⊕ brewhouseandkitchen.com/bedford

Part of the Brewhouse & Kitchen chain, producing its own range of award-winning keg and cask beers. Senior brewer Paul offers weekly brewing experience days, and beer, gin and whisky masterclasses are available.

Brewpoint (Wells & Co) SIBA
Cut Throat Lane, Bedford, MK41 7FY
☎ (01234) 244444 ⊕ brewpoint.co.uk

⊛Brewpoint was launched in 2020 by Wells & Co, which has brewed in Bedford since 1876. The Brewpoint complex also houses the company head office and features conference and meeting rooms, a brewery shop

and a taproom/restaurant, plus beer garden. Beers are also brewed for the Charles Wells brand, but not all are cask-conditioned. ‼🍽◆⚭

Origin Pale Ale (ABV 3.7%) BLOND
Legacy Golden Ale (ABV 4.1%) GOLD
DNA Amber Ale (ABV 4.3%) BITTER

Crown
🍽 **Crown, Green End, Little Staughton, MK44 2BU**
☎ (01234) 376260 ⊕ thecrownstaughton.com

Brewing began in 2017 in a building behind the Crown public house. The brewery is owned and run by the landlord of the Crown, with the beers only being produced for the pub and local events. ◆

Eagle
Havelock Street, Bedford, MK40 4LU
☎ (01234) 272766 ⊕ eaglebrewery.co.uk

Founded in 1876 and remained with the Wells Family until 2017, when the brewery and its brands were acquired by Marston's, and renamed Eagle Brewery. It brewed Young's beers after the closure of the Ram Brewery in 2007 and the popular Bedfordshire Ale, Eagle IPA. In late 2022 the brewery was sold to SA Damm and all production of cask beers transferred to other breweries in the Carlsberg Marston's Brewing Co.

Kelchner SIBA
Unit D, The Sidings, Station Road, Ampthill, MK45 2QY
☎ 07508 305754 ✉ kelchnerbrewery@gmail.com

Kelchner began brewing began in 2018. Beers tend to be themed on local features and Luton Town FC. The brewery is keen to support various local community organisations. ‼🍽LIVE

Half Nelson (ABV 3.8%) GOLD
James Blonde (ABV 3.9%) BLOND
Local is Lekker (ABV 3.9%) GOLD
Ampthill Gold (ABV 4.1%) GOLD
Hat Trick (ABV 4.1%) GOLD
Masquerade (ABV 4.3%) RED
Full Nelson (ABV 4.5%) GOLD
IPA (ABV 4.5%) PALE
Parklife (ABV 4.5%) BITTER
After Dark (ABV 4.8%) PALE
Ammetelle (ABV 5%) STOUT

Leighton Buzzard SIBA
Unit 23, Harmill Industrial Estate, Grovebury Road, Leighton Buzzard, LU7 4FF
☎ (01525) 839153 ⊕ leightonbuzzardbrewing.co.uk

The first brewery to operate in Leighton Buzzard for more than 100 years. Established in 2014, the brewery changed hands in 2019. ‼🍽◆⚭

Golden Buzzard (ABV 4.1%) GOLD
Bavarian Dragon (ABV 4.2%) GOLD
Best Buzzard (ABV 4.3%) BITTER
Restoration Ale (ABV 4.6%) BITTER

March Hare
🍽 **34 High Street, Dunton, SG18 8RN**
☎ (01767) 318121

Brewing commenced in 2022. Head brewer John is an award-winning homebrewer and has been brewing since he was 15. Beer styles include traditional bitters, stouts, porters, milds and golden ales with occasional specials recreated from historic recipes.

L○CALe

Many entries in the Guide refer to pubs' support for CAMRA's LocAle scheme. The ⌷ symbol is used where a pub has LocAle accreditation. The aim of the scheme is to get publicans to stock at least one cask beer that comes from a local brewery, usually no more than 30 miles away.

The aim is a simple one: to cut down on 'beer miles'. Research by CAMRA shows that food and drink transport accounts for 25 per cent of all HGV vehicle miles in Britain. Taking into account the miles that ingredients have travelled on top of distribution journeys, an imported lager produced by a multi-national brewery could have notched up more than 24,000 'beer miles' by the time it reaches a pub.

Supporters of LocAle point out that £10 spent on locally-supplied goods generates £25 for the local economy. Keeping trade local helps enterprises, creates more economic activity and jobs, and makes other services more viable. The scheme also generates consumer support for local breweries.

Support for LocAle has grown at a rapid pace since it was created in 2007. It's been embraced by pubs and CAMRA branches throughout England and has now crossed the borders into Scotland and Wales.

For more information, see camra.org.uk/locale

What is CAMRA LocAle?

- An initiative that promotes pubs which sell locally-brewed real ale
- The scheme builds on a growing consumer demand for quality local produce and an increased awareness of 'green' issues

Everyone benefits from local pubs stocking locally brewed real ale...

- Public houses, as stocking local real ales can increase pub visits
- Consumers, who enjoy greater beer choice and locally brewed beer
- Local brewers, who gain from increased sales and get better feedback from consumers
- The local economy, because more money is spent and retained in the local economy
- The environment, due to fewer 'beer miles' resulting in less road congestion and pollution
- Tourism, due to an increased sense of local identity and pride – let's celebrate what makes our locality different

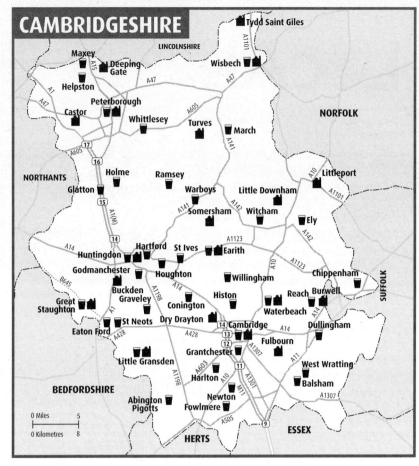

CAMBRIDGESHIRE

Abington Pigotts

Pig & Abbot
High Street, SG8 0SD (off A505 through Litlington)
☎ (01763) 853515 🌐 pigandabbot.co.uk
Adnams Southwold Bitter; Fuller's London Pride; 2 changing beers (often Mighty Oak, Woodforde's) Ⓗ
This Queen Anne-period pub in a surprisingly remote part of the south Cambridgeshire countryside offers a warm welcome. The interior has exposed oak beams and two fires, including a large inglenook with wood-burning stove. A comfortable restaurant offers home-made traditional pub food and specialises in fresh fish & chips, steak & kidney puddings, and pies. Two guest beers are stocked, often including offerings from Burton Bridge, Humpty Dumpty, Mighty Oak, Timothy Taylor or Woodforde's. A fomer local CAMRA Pub of the Year.
Q ♿ 🛏 ❀ ◑ ♣ ♠ P ❀

Balsham

Bell Inn
2 West Wickham Road, CB21 4DZ
☎ (01223) 892999
Greene King IPA; 3 changing beers Ⓗ
Popular community two-bar pub. The public bar has a jukebox, pub games and TV; and the wood-panelled lounge bar has tables for diners or drinkers. Tasty home-made pub food is served at affordable prices, with food vans on Mondays. The changing ales always include a mild or other dark beer, and the selection of ciders often includes a locally produced one. The large rear beer garden has cosy sheds to house customers in less clement weather. Local CAMRA dark beer Pub of the Year 2022. Q ♿ 🛏 ❀ ◑ ♣ ♠ ● P 🚪 (19) ❀ 🛜 ♪

Cambridge

Alexandra Arms
22 Gwydir Street, CB1 2LL
☎ (01223) 324441 🌐 thealexcambridge.com
4 changing beers Ⓗ
This back-street corner pub has been refurbished in a modern style. Three distinct areas span two levels inside, with wooden flooring and plenty of tables. The attractive enclosed garden has a garden room which can be booked for functions, along with covered booths. A Greene King local hero pub that is mainly free of tie. Guest beers frequently feature local breweries alongside Greene King beers. Food is home-made and includes burgers with buns from a local bakery.
🛏 ❀ ◑ ● 🚪 (Citi 2) ❀ 🛜

Calverley's Brewery Tap Ⓛ
23A Hooper Street, CB1 2NZ
☎ 07769 537342 🌐 calverleys.com
Changing beers (often Calverley's)

Close to Mill Road, the brewery was established in a former stable in 2013. Open for on-sales Tuesday to Friday evenings and all day Saturday, it offers a wide selection of live beer from keg, cans for off-sales, local real ciders and occasionally cask beer. A taproom constructed in 2020 provides more seating, and frees up more space in the brewery, allowing a wider beer range. Pizzas are delivered from a nearby restaurant. Q☻▷&●🖨(Citi 2) ☻

Cambridge Blue

85-87 Gwydir Street, CB1 2LG
☎ (01223) 471680 ⊕ cambridge.pub/the-blue
Nene Valley Manhattan Project Ⓗ; Tring Citra Session Ⓖ; 14 changing beers Ⓗ/Ⓖ
Popular pub in the Mill Road 'beer quarter', with two bars and an extension leading to its sizeable garden with heated marquee in winter. Breweriana and pumpclips adorn walls and ceiling. Up to 14 beers from microbreweries nationwide are served on handpump or by gravity. Gluten-free beer usually available, as well as several ciders and perries and a large selection of international bottled beers. Its main beer festival is held in June. Food consists of a range of burgers.
☻❀◑&●🖨(Citi 2) ☻🎧

Champion of the Thames

68 King Street, CB1 1LN
☎ (01223) 351464 ⊕ thechampionofthethames.com
Greene King IPA, Abbot; 3 changing beers Ⓗ
Small, two-room, city-centre pub with a welcoming atmosphere. The oarsman after whom the pub is named is commemorated in the etched windows. Wood-panelled with wooden floors, fixed benches and a part-glazed partition between the rooms, the pub has been identified by CAMRA as having a historic interior of regional importance. The chatter of customers predominates. Q❀♣🖨☻🎧

Devonshire Arms Ⓛ

1 Devonshire Road, CB1 2BH
☎ (01223) 316610
6 changing beers (sourced locally) Ⓗ
Rescued from decline and reopened in 2010 as Milton brewery's first pub in Cambridge. A wide range of Milton beers is always stocked including dark and strong ales, plus guest beers. Larger inside than appears from the road, with outside seating at both front and rear, the pub retains a traditional feel which attracts a wide mixture of customers. A beer festival coinciding with Mill Road winter fair is held in early December.
☻❀◑≒♣●🖨☻🎧♪

Elm Tree

16A Orchard Street, CB1 1JT
☎ (01223) 322553 ⊕ elmtreecambridge.co.uk
Brewpoint Origin Pale Ale, DNA Amber Ale; 5 changing beers (sourced nationally; often Brewpoint) Ⓗ
Back-street pub close to Parker's Piece, owned by Charles Wells. The short bar is near the entrance, with seating around and beyond. Decorated with breweriana, quirky bric-a-brac, photos and Belgian flags. Charles Wells have three of the seven handpumps, with the others offering changing guests and generally including a dark beer. A cider is also served. Complementing these is a menu of around 40 bottled Belgian beers. There is regular live music. Local CAMRA city community Pub of the Year 2022. ☻♣🖨☻🎧♪

Free Press

7 Prospect Row, CB1 1DU
☎ (01223) 368337 ⊕ freepresscambridge.com

Greene King IPA, Abbot; Timothy Taylor Landlord; 4 changing beers Ⓗ
Friendly, intimate pub serving high-quality food and great beer. A pub since 1834, it just survived the 1970s Kite area redevelopment. Identified by CAMRA as having a regionally important historic pub interior, only the tiny snug is original; the rest is a loving reconstruction. A walled garden is at the rear. the pub is named after a Temperance movement newspaper that lasted for just one edition. The press room in the garden is a recent addition. ☻❀◑♣🖨☻🎧

Geldart 🍸 Ⓛ ✔

1 Ainsworth Street, CB1 2PF
☎ (01223) 314264 ⊕ the-geldart.co.uk
Adnams Ghost Ship; Oakham Citra; St Austell Tribute; 5 changing beers (sourced nationally) Ⓗ
Tucked away in the back streets with diners and live music to one side, a drinkers bar to the other, and an enclosed patio garden. A music and film theme dominates with musical instruments as handpumps and menus on 12-inch vinyl discs. It has a good reputation for its food and real ales. There are six beers, cider, and a selection of malt whiskies and rums. Changing guest beers often include a locally sourced dark beer. Live music events are frequently held. ☻❀◑●☻🎧♪

Haymakers Ⓛ

54 High Street, CB4 1NG
☎ (01223) 311077
Milton Pegasus; 5 changing beers (often Milton) Ⓗ
Milton brewery's second of three Cambridge pubs, popular with locals and employees from the nearby science park. There are drinking areas either side of the door plus a snug. Dark wood and warm colours abound. A good-sized beer garden is behind, as well as the largest pub cycle park in Cambridge. Eight real ales, including at least one dark and guests, are on offer, plus real ciders or perries and Moravka unpasteurised lager. Local CAMRA Pub of the Year 2021 and city LocAle Pub of the Year 2022. ☻❀◑&♣●🖨☻🎧♪

Live & Let Live

40 Mawson Road, CB1 2EA
☎ (01223) 460261

REAL ALE BREWERIES

Bowler's Deeping Gate
Burwell Burwell
Calverley's ✦ Cambridge
Cambridge 🍺 Cambridge
Castor Castor
Downham Isle ✦ Littleport
Draycott Buckden
Elgood's Wisbech
Grafham Great Staughton
IVO Somersham
Lord Conrad's Dry Drayton
Mile Tree Peterborough
Milton ✦ Waterbeach
Moonshine Fulbourn
Oakham Peterborough
Oakham (2nd Site) 🍺 Peterborough
Papworth ✦ Earith
Pastore ✦ Waterbeach
Rocket Great Staughton
Secret Project Turves (NEW)
Son of Sid Little Gransden (brewing suspended)
Three Blind Mice Little Downham
Tydd Steam Tydd Saint Giles
Wheatsheaf ✦ Huntingdon (NEW)
Xtreme Peterborough

Oakham Citra; 5 changing beers H
An unassuming Victorian street-corner local just off Mill Road. With a single wood-panelled bar area and a small snug furnished with simple wooden tables and chairs plus a few bar-stools at one end of the long bar counter, this is a pub made for conversation. There is a wood-burner in the fireplace. The six handpumps regularly feature Oakham and Nethergate beers. The 10 keg taps feature both unusual and well-known beers. The six still ciders include some real ones. ⇌♣🍴🚪🌕🛜

Maypole L
20A Portugal Place, CB5 8AF
☎ (01223) 352999 ⊕ maypolefreehouse.co.uk
Changing beers H
The Maypole has been in the capable hands of the Castiglione family since 1982, initially as tenants, latterly as owners. Showcasing quality beers won the landlord the local CAMRA branch's first Real Ale Champion award. Up to 16 ever-changing beers are served, more during festivals, including LocAles, with micros predominating. It has a busy front bar and quieter back bar downstairs plus a function room upstairs, and large covered patio outside. Food focuses on home-cooked Italian dishes and English pub classics. 🌕🕛🚪🛜

Queen Edith L
Wulfstan Way, CB1 8QN
☎ (01223) 318536
Milton Justinian, Pegasus, Sparta, Minerva, Nero; 3 changing beers H
The third of Cambridge's Milton brewery pubs, built after the demolition of a pub of the same name at the rear of the site. The style is mock Georgian inside and out. The larger bar to the left of the entrance has large windows on two sides and a wood-burning stove. The other bar has wooden booths down one side. Regular and changing Milton beers are served plus guests. Local and County CAMRA Pub of the Year 2022.
Q🐾🌕🕛🍴♣🚪🛜

Royal Standard L
292 Mill Road, CB1 3NL
☎ (01223) 569065 ⊕ cambridge.pub/royal-standard
4 changing beers H
A well-designed renovation of a former two-bar Victorian local that had not been a pub for some time. Popular with the local population, with a single bar to the front of the entrance with seating on either side. To the right there is access to the partly covered and heated patio. there is a selection of three or four draught beers and many ciders, plus keg beers which frequently include locals. Greek food available to eat in or take out. Local CAMRA Cider Pub of the Year. 🌕🕛♿🍴🚪(Citi2)🌕🛜

Chippenham

Tharp Arms
46 High Street, CB7 5PR
☎ (01638) 720234
Woodforde's Wherry; 2 changing beers H
Georgian pub that takes its name after a local eminent family who lived at Chippenham Park. A straightforward village pub with two bar rooms and a further room to the rear. The pub is frequented by the popular village cricket team as well as others further afield. The pub was purchased in 2014 by the community who are keen to support local brewers. It is a Grade II-listed building and is also listed as an Asset of Community Value. 🌕🕛♣P

Conington

White Swan
Elsworth Road, CB23 4LN
☎ (01954) 267251 ⊕ thewhiteswanconington.co.uk
Adnams Southwold Bitter, Ghost Ship G; **1 changing beer** H
Classic destination village pub. The 19th-century building is fronted by a large lawn and children's play area. A permanent marquee allows alfresco drinking in all weathers. The main bar has a tiled floor and a brick fireplace occupied by a fine cast-iron stove. The wheelchair friendly bar is notably lower than usual. Two of the three ales are served by gravity. Owned by Conington Pub Co and run free of tie since being sold by Greene King in 2013. Q🐾🌕🕛♣🚪P🌕🛜

Dullingham

Boot L
18 Brinkley Road, CB8 9UW
☎ (01638) 507327 ⊕ thebootdullingham.co.uk
Adnams Southwold Bitter; 3 changing beers (sourced regionally) G
Traditional village inn rescued by a regular in 2000 after Greene King thought it non-viable. It is now a welcoming community local with several darts, crib and pétanque teams. Home pub of the village cricket team and a veterans football team. Ales are served direct from casks in the cellar. Lunchtime food served, and fish & chips on Wednesday evenings. Children welcome until 8pm. Live music nights and at least one beer festival are held. One mile from Dulllingham railway station. 🐾🌕🕛♣P🌕♫

Earith

Crystal Ship L
32 Earith Business Park, PE28 3QF
☎ (01487) 740634 ⊕ papworthbrewery.com
11 changing beers (sourced locally; often Papworth) G
This is the Papworth brewery tap, housed in an industrial unit adjacent to the brewery. It is open for indoor and outdoor drinking, serving up to 11 changing Papworth ales and a guest ale, alongside ciders, wines and spirits. Pizzas are available on Thursday and Saturday evenings. Occasional events (classic cars, quizzes, live music, food and drink tastings etc) are held – see their Facebook page for details. There is also a bottle shop where a range of Papworth beers and Cromwell ciders can be purchased. Q♿🅰♣P🌕🛜♫

Eaton Ford

Barley Mow ✓
27 Crosshall Road, PE19 7AB
☎ (01480) 474435
Greene King IPA, Abbot; 2 changing beers (often St Austell, Timothy Taylor) H
Simple, one-bar community pub with a wide variety of activities focused on the regulars, plus live music events and seasonal celebrations. The decor is a mix of plaster, brick and wood panel and a long service counter dominates the centre of the bar. Images of past pub social events adorn the walls. There is a garden room and large beer garden with an extensive children's play area. The two changing beers are not normally from the Greene King range. 🐾🌕🕛♣P🚪(905)🌕🛜♫

Ely

3At3 Real Ale & Craft Beer Café

3 Three Cups Walk, CB7 4AN (passageway off top end of Fore Hill)

☎ (01353) 659916 🌐 3at3craftbeer.co.uk

6 changing beers (sourced locally) Ⓗ

The 3At3 Real Ale & Craft Beer Café is on Three Cups Walk, a small passageway off the top end of Fore Hill. It offers six regularly changing draught craft beers, local ciders and wines in a café terrace setting. No food served at time of writing but customers can bring their own. The bottle shop stocks over 150 different bottled real ales from local micro breweries as well as local ciders and wines from the local Elysian Vineyard. ✿🎔🕭🍺🐾🍽️🌐

Drayman's Son 🍷 Ⓛ

29A Forehill, CB7 4AA

☎ (01353) 662920 🌐 draymansely.com

12 changing beers (sourced nationally; often Three Blind Mice) Ⓖ

Small, welcoming micropub in former shop premises nostalgically themed with old railway and enamel signs. Drinks are generally delivered to your table. Twelve ales are generally available – six on gravity, five KeyKeg and a craft lager on keg – mostly sourced from Three Blind Mice and microbreweries. Over 20 ciders are available, many sourced locally. The cellar is in a temperature-controlled back room. Local CAMRA Pub of the Year and Cider Pub of the Year 2023. 🍴🚲🍺🚆🐾🌐

West End House ✅

16 West End, CB6 3AY

☎ (01353) 662907 🌐 westendhouseely.co.uk

Adnams Broadside; Sharp's Doom Bar; 2 changing beers Ⓗ

The Westie is a local drinkers pub in a small community area, a short distance from the cathedral and Oliver Cromwell's House. It is a snug pub with low ceilings, and has four distinct drinking areas and an enclosed patio area. There is a fireplace that is used in the winter which adds to the atmosphere. In the summer local bands sometimes perform. It is an excellent pub for all your moods, welcoming and dog friendly. ✿🍴🐾🌐

Fowlmere

Chequers

High Street, SG8 7SR

☎ (01763) 209333 🌐 thechequersfowlmere.co.uk

4 changing beers (sourced regionally; often Nene Valley) Ⓗ

Once a 16th century coaching inn, this pub has a lovely quirky feel to it. A comfortable bar complete with open fire is adjacent to a large conservatory, with stairs leading to a galleried dining area. Other areas are dedicated to Samuel Pepys, who stayed here in 1660. The pub sign commemorates the 339th fighter group of the USAF who were based nearby. One regular bitter from Nene Valley Brewery is served, with up to three, usually interesting, guest beers. Q🌞😺🍴🍺P🚆(31)🐾🌐

Glatton

Addison Arms Ⓛ

Sawtry Road, PE28 5RZ

☎ (01487) 830410 🌐 addison-arms.co.uk

Digfield Fools Nook; Greene King Abbot; house beer (by Digfield) Ⓗ

A Grade II-listed pub named after the playwright and politician Joseph Addison (co-founder of The Spectator), who was a relative of the first landlord. A welcoming pub offering three real ales, two usually sourced from the local Digfield brewery. There are two rooms: a bar and a larger lounge where the handpumps are located. The large beer garden is popular in the summer months. The kitchen underwent a major refurbishment in April 2023 prior to relaunching its food service. Q🌞😺🍴🍺P🚆(904)🐾🌐

Godmanchester

Comrades Club

58 Cambridge Street, PE29 2AY

☎ (01480) 453991 🌐 comradesclubgodmanchester.co.uk

Sharp's Doom Bar; 2 changing beers (sourced regionally) Ⓗ

The Comrades Club (Working Men's & Social Club) which started life in 1920 for the Comrades of the Great War, is a respected and established member of the Godmanchester community and is committed to providing members, their families and visitors with the very best facilities, services and entertainment. It often stocks beers from the north of England as well as national favourites. Bar bingo and karaoke on Friday nights, cash bingo on Tuesday and Friday (available to members and non-members). ♿🐾P🎵

Grantchester

Blue Ball Inn

57 Broadway, CB3 9NQ

☎ (01223) 846004 🌐 blueballgrantchester.co.uk

Adnams Southwold Bitter; Woodforde's Wherry; 2 changing beers (sourced regionally) Ⓗ

Built in 1893 over the cellar of the 1767 original that was lost in a fire, this cosy, authentic local retains its original two-bar layout and many old fittings. It has been identified by CAMRA as having a historic interior of regional importance. No TV, no games machines: good beer, good conversation and traditional pub games are the order of the day. The name commemorates the landing opposite of a hot-air balloon in 1785. Q🌞😺🍴🍺🚆(18,118)🐾🌐

Graveley

Three Horseshoes

23 High Street, PE19 6PL

☎ (01480) 700320 🌐 thethreehorseshoesgraveley.co.uk

2 changing beers (sourced regionally) Ⓗ

A late addition to the village, the pub was built in the early 20th century after the other village pubs closed or burnt down. WWII Graveley Airbase was used by bomber squadrons until 1946. Two changing real ales are from regional or microbreweries. Food is served lunchtime and evening, with a popular carvery on Sunday lunchtime. Quiz nights and a meat raffle are held on Sunday evening. Q🌞😺🍴♿🐾P🌐

Great Staughton

White Hart

56 The Highway, PE19 5DA (on B645)

☎ (01480) 861131

Batemans XB, XXXB; 1 changing beer Ⓗ

Passing through the narrow entrance of this fine small former coaching inn, dating back to 1630, takes you back to the days of horse-drawn coaches. It has been extended and altered, but still warrants a Grade II listing. As well as the main bar there is a small pool room at the front of the pub and a restaurant at the rear. Traditional pub food is served at lunchtime Thursday to Sunday, and in the evening on Saturday. Q🌞😺🍴P🐾🌐🎵

Harlton

Hare & Hounds

60 High Street, CB23 1ES
☎ (01223) 264698 ⊕ hareandhoundsharlton.co.uk
3 changing beers Ⓗ
Thatched single-bar 18th-century country pub with half-timbered walls, a beamed ceiling and a large fireplace. The large garden has views over the countryside, plus a children's play area and pétanque pitch. The pub has been owned by a community interest company since 2017. Three changing beers come mainly from local breweries and regional brands. Cider and perry include locally produced ones. Home-cooked food has a strong reputation, especially Sunday lunch. Quiz night on Sunday, bridge on Tuesday and cribbage on Thursday. Local CAMRA Cider Pub of the Year 2022.
Q✿🕏⊛◑♣👜P🛏🕏(75)🌸🛜♪

Hartford

King of the Belgians 🍷 Ⓛ

27 Main Street, PE29 1XU (on the old village high street, parallel to the B1514 from Huntingdon to St Ives)
☎ (01480) 52030 ⊕ kingofthebelgians.com
4 changing beers (sourced locally; often Digfield, Nene Valley, St Austell) Ⓗ
A 16th-century pub which actively supports local charities. It hosts a beer festival in May and another in late August, with all profits going to local good causes. An ever-changing selection of four real ales, ciders and good-value food is served every day. The public bar is characterised by its low oak beams and a copper-topped bar, and there is a peaceful separate dining area. There are regular quizzes, games nights and monthly open mic, themed food and bring-your-own cheese nights. Local CAMRA Pub of the Year and Cambridgeshire Cider Pub of the Year 2023. Q✿🕏⊛◑♣👜P🛏🌸🛜♪

Helpston

Bluebell Ⓛ

10 Woodgate, PE6 7ED
☎ (01733) 252394 ⊕ bluebellhelpston.co.uk
Adnams Ghost Ship; Hopshackle Special Bitter; 2 changing beers (often 8 Sail, Church End, Woodforde's) Ⓗ
Quiet 17th-century stone village pub, extensively refurbished in 2014, with the main entrance at the side. There are two wood-panelled bars, a number of dining areas, and a snug named after local poet John Clare who worked in the pub as a pot boy and lived next door. It serves beers from Adnams and the local Hopshackle brewery, plus two rotating guest beers from breweries around the country. Good-value food is served lunchtime and evenings. Q✿🕏🚪◑♣♣👜P🛏🌸🛜

Histon

King William IV

8 Church Street, CB24 9EP
☎ (01223) 233930 ⊕ kingbillhiston.co.uk
Buntingford Polar Star; Fuller's London Pride; Sharp's Doom Bar; St Austell Tribute; 1 changing beer (sourced regionally) Ⓗ
Characterful pub known as the King Bill. The L-shaped lounge comprises an old front section and newer extension. The front section has exposed timbers, a brick-built open fire at one end and a wood-burner at the other. A narrow doorway beside the main fireplace leads to the former games room which now contains more seating. It serves four regular ales from St Austell, Sharps,

Fuller's and Buntingford, with a changing guest. Local CAMRA rural LocAle Pub of the Year 2022.
🕏⊛◑♣P🛏🌸🛜

Red Lion Ⓛ ✓

27 High Street, CB24 9JD
☎ (01223) 564437 ⊕ theredlionhiston.co.uk
Adnams Ghost Ship; Barsham B.O.B; Oakham Citra; 6 changing beers (sourced regionally) Ⓗ
Two-bar free house adorned with a wonderful collection of breweriana and historical photos. The nine handpumps are in the right-hand bar which is quieter and child-free. It holds two beer festivals each year, the Easter aperitif and the main event in September, which raise money for local charities. The left-hand bar is family and dog friendly. The large beer garden has an accommodation block at the rear of the premises and there's an outside pizza shed.
Q✿🕏⊛🚪◑♣👜P🛏🌸🛜♪

Holme

Admiral Wells Ⓛ

41 Station Rd, PE7 3PH (Jct of B660 and Yaxley Rd)
☎ (01487) 831214 ⊕ admiralwells.co.uk
Adnams Southwold Bitter, Ghost Ship; Digfield Fools Nook; 1 changing beer (often Adnams, Wadworth) Ⓗ
Officially the lowest level pub in the UK, this Victorian inn was named after one of Nelson's pallbearers. It has two bar/lounge areas in a modern style, a conservatory and a function room at the rear. Outside is a beer garden at the front, a marquee with a bar in summer and a children's play area. A large car park is to the side. Four ales are available with one from the local Digfield brewery.
Q✿🕏⊛◑♣👜P🌸🛜

Houghton

Three Horseshoes ✓

St Ives Road, PE28 2BE (off A1123)
☎ (01480) 462410 ⊕ threehorseshoesinnhoughton.co.uk
Greene King IPA; Sharp's Doom Bar; 1 changing beer (often Milton) Ⓖ
Characterful Grade II-listed 17th-century building in a picturesque village that is popular with locals as well as walkers and cyclists. The lane opposite leads to the river and the historic Houghton Mill. There are two bar areas and plenty of space for diners. The real ales, which always include one from a local brewery, are served by gravity dispense from a tap room behind the bar. Home-cooked food is available every day (except Mon and Tue in winter months). Q✿🕏⊛🚪◑ÅP🛏🌸♪

Huntingdon

Old Bridge Hotel Ⓛ ✓

1 High Street, PE29 3TQ (at S end of High St on ring road, by river)
☎ (01480) 424300 ⊕ huntsbridge.com
3 changing beers (sourced locally; often Adnams, Lacons, Nene Valley) Ⓗ
An ivy-clad hotel in an 18th-century former private bank at the southern end of the High Street with a prominent position on the banks of the River Great Ouse. Enjoy imaginative and high-quality food in the Terrace Restaurant, the covered patio and the garden area, or simply relax with a drink in the bar or lounge. The award-winning Old Bridge Wine Shop offers wine tasting as a diversion and the bus station is a short walk away.
Q✿🕏⊛🚪◑Å P🛏🌸🛜

Little Gransden

Chequers 🅛
71 Main Road, SG19 3DW
☎ (01767) 677348 ⊕ chequersgransden.co.uk
Lacons Legacy; Milton Nero; 1 changing beer (sourced locally) 🅗

Village pub owned and run by the same family for over 70 years (and in this Guide for 29). The unspoilt middle bar, with its wooden benches and roaring fire, is a favourite spot to pick up on the local gossip. When brewing, the pub's Son of Sid brewhouse supplies the pub and local beer festivals. Home-made pizzas are available on Friday nights (booking essential). Winner of numerous CAMRA awards and finalist for the National CAMRA Pub of the Year 2018. Q❀🅙♪🅐♿🅿🖵🖩❀❖🏵

March

Rose & Crown 🅛
41 St Peters Road, PE15 9NA
☎ (01354) 652077
St Austell Tribute; 4 changing beers (often Adnams, St Austell, Tydd Steam) 🅗

150-year-old traditional community pub with two carpeted rooms, low-beamed ceilings and a real fire in the main bar. Ale lovers prepared to make the walk away from the town centre will receive a warm welcome. Normally five real ales are on offer from mainly small breweries, with at least one St Austell beer, and a large selection of gins and single malt whiskies. Good-quality food is available lunchtimes and evenings. Quiz night is Thursday. Received a '10 years in the Guide' award in 2023. Q❀🅙♪🅿🖵(33,46)🏵♪

Ship Inn 🅛
1 Nene Parade, PE15 8TD
☎ (01354) 607878
Woodforde's Wherry; 3 changing beers (often Church End, Lacons, Tydd Steam) 🅗

Thatched Grade II-listed riverside pub built in 1680, with extensive riverside moorings. It reopened in 2010 as a free house after a major refit. The unusual carved beams are said to have 'fallen off a barge' during the building of Ely Cathedral. A quaint wobbly floor and wall lead to the toilets and a small games room. Friendly and welcoming, the Ship is a Guide regular and winner of CAMRA Gold Awards in 2012 and 2019. Q☙🅙❀♣🖵(33,46)❖❀♪

Maxey

Blue Bell 🅛
39 High Street, PE6 9EE
☎ (01778) 348182
Abbeydale Absolution; Fuller's London Pride, ESB; Oakham Bishops Farewell; 5 changing beers (sourced regionally; often Grainstore, Ossett, Woodforde's) 🅗

Originally a limestone barn, the building was converted many years ago and reflects its rural setting. Paraphernalia of country life adorn the stone walls and shelves of the two-roomed interior. Nine handpumps dispense a range of quality ales from large and small breweries far and wide. The pub is a popular meeting place for several groups including birdwatchers and golfers. A former local CAMRA Pub of the Year and Gold Award winner. Q❀♣🖵(22,413)❀❀🏵

Newton

Queen's Head
Fowlmere Road, CB22 7PG
☎ (01223) 870436 ⊕ queensheadnewton.co.uk

Adnams Southwold Bitter; 2 changing beers (sourced regionally) 🅖

This village local is one of only a handful of pubs to have appeared in every edition of the Guide, and a list of landlords displayed in the public bar has only 18 entries since 1729. Adnams Bitter and up to three other beers are available from the stillage directly behind the bar. A monthly Saturday bistro night and Wednesday night food vans have been added to the traditional soup and sandwiches, and an expanded menu is available Thursday-Saturday evenings and on Sundays. Q❀🅙♪♣♿🖵(31)❀🏵

Peterborough

Blue Bell 🍷 🅛
6 The Green, Werrington, PE4 6RU
☎ (01733) 571264
Elgood's Cambridge Bitter; 3 changing beers (often Dark Star, Fuller's, Hop Back) 🅗

An 1890s pub on the village green with a light, airy front bar and comfortable lounge restaurant serving meals from an extensive menu. It has a large garden with an outdoor bar, lots of seating and family pods. It serves possibly the best Elgood's beer in the city, and interesting guest ales from a restricted list. There is regular live entertainment and darts, pool and cribbage are played. Sunday is quiz night. Winner of local Gold Award in 2022 and City Pub of the Year 2023. Q❀🅙♿♣♿🖵(1)❀♪♫

Brewery Tap 🅛
80 Westgate, PE1 2AA
☎ (01733) 358500 ⊕ thebrewery-tap.com
Oakham JHB, Inferno, Citra, Scarlet Macaw, Bishops Farewell; 1 changing beer (sourced regionally) 🅗

Housed in a former 1930s Labour Exchange, this brewpub, close to bus and railway stations, claims to be one of Europe's largest. The small craft brewery, where limited-edition beers are brewed, can be seen through large windows, and a mezzanine floor area with some brewing artefacts is incorporated into the pub's modern design. The ales usually on offer are mainly from the Oakham range. Thai food is served, with live music and late closing at weekends and open mic night on Sundays. ☙❀🅙≢♣🖵🖩❀♪

Bumble Inn
46 Westgate, PE1 1RE
⊕ thebimbleinn.wordpress.com
5 changing beers (sourced regionally; often Marble, North Riding (Brewery), Rooster's) 🅗

This micropub opened in 2016 in a former chemist's shop. Minimalist in style, it has five handpumps dispensing quality ales from far and wide, so expect the unusual from regional and national brewers. Taster paddles of three third-pints are available. A small selection of wines, spirits and soft drinks are also sold, plus two craft keg beers, two ciders, and rare bottled and canned beers. Nepalese food is available to order from next door. A former local CAMRA Pub of the Year. ≢♣🖵🏵

Charters 🅛
Town Bridge, PE1 1FP (down steps at Town Bridge)
☎ (01733) 315700 ⊕ charters-bar.com
Oakham JHB, Inferno, Citra, Bishops Farewell; 4 changing beers (often Nene Valley) 🅗/🅖

This converted Dutch grain barge from circa 1907 sits on the River Nene near the city centre. An oriental restaurant is on the upper deck and food is also served in the bar. The large garden, with covered areas, a bar and landing stage for boats, is popular in summer. Up to 10 ales are available, plus ciders. Live music plays most weekends, outside the pub in summer. Close to the Nene Valley Railway. Local CAMRA Gold Award winner in 2023. ☺❀◑♣♠P🖵(1,3) ❀🛜♪

Coalheavers Arms L

5 Park Street, Woodston, PE2 9BH
☎ (01733) 565664
Tydd Steam Barn Ale; 5 changing beers (sourced locally; often Hop Back, Lacons, Zest) H
This small, one-roomed, friendly back-street community pub dates back to the 1850s. The only Peterborough pub to be bombed in World War II. Serves up to six mostly local guest ales plus craft beer. Well-attended beer festivals are held twice a year and the large garden is popular in the summer with families. Food available on match days including chips, burgers, pies etc. It can be very busy on football match days. Monthly vinyl night on second Friday of each month. Q☺❀♣P🖵(5,6)❀🛜♪

Draper's Arms L

29-31 Cowgate, PE1 1LZ
☎ (01733) 847570
Brewsters Hophead; Grainstore Ten Fifty; Greene King Abbot; Ruddles Best Bitter; Sharp's Doom Bar; Titanic Plum Porter; 5 changing beers (often Brewsters, Grainstore, Newby Wyke) H
A converted former draper's shop, built in 1899 and one of the two Wetherspoon pubs in the city. The beer range, with many from local microbreweries, is dispensed through 12 handpumps. The interior is broken up, with intimate wood-panelled spaces and dividers, and there is a new roof terrace. Food is served all day and regular beer and cider festivals are held throughout the year. Wednesday is quiz night. A regular top 10 real ale pub within the company chain. Q☺❀◑♣⇋♠🖵🛜

Frothblowers L

78 Storrington Way, Werrington, PE4 6QP
☎ 07756 066503 ⊕ frothblowers.site
7 changing beers (sourced regionally; often Brewsters, Hopshackle, Tydd Steam) H
This micropub is easily accessed by bus from the city centre. It has five handpumps and more beers available in the cellar, with at least 25 ciders and bottled beers. Alcohol-free beers are available. A hub of the local community, activities include tap takeovers, acoustic music, bus tours, a summer cycling club and a knitting club. A regular local CAMRA award-winner, including Cider Pub of the Year 2023. Cash only.
☺❀♣♠P🖵(1) ❀♪

Hand & Heart ★ L

12 Highbury Street, PE1 3BE
☎ (01733) 564653
6 changing beers (sourced regionally; often Brewsters, Rockingham, Tydd Steam) H
Rebuilt in 1938, this Art Deco-style community local has been identified by CAMRA as having a nationally important historic pub interior. A drinking corridor connects the rear room to the main public bar, with its war memorial and real fire. Up to six handpumped ales are served, with more from the cellar. The range is eclectic and forever changing. Beer festivals with live music are held in the large garden. A Guide regular for over 10 years and former CAMRA local and county Pub of the Year. Q☺❀♠🖵(1,62)❀♪

Ostrich Inn L

17 North Street, PE1 2RA
☎ 07307 195560 ⊕ ostrichinnpeterborough.com
5 changing beers (sourced regionally; often Nene Valley, Thornbridge, Tiny Rebel) H

Refurbished in 2009, the pub reopened with its original name restored. A U-shaped bar in this one-room pub has up to five regularly changing beers on offer, many from local breweries, alongside craft keg and KeyKeg lines. A large gin selection is also available. There is live music up to four evenings a week. The small enclosed patio is a suntrap. Popular when Peterborough FC are playing at home. A former local CAMRA City Pub of the Year.
☺❀◑♣⇋♠P🖵❀♪

Palmerston Arms L

82 Oundle Road, PE2 9PA
☎ (01733) 565865
Batemans Gold, XXXB H/G**; Castle Rock Harvest Pale; 4 changing beers (sourced regionally; often Lacons, Ossett, St Austell)** G
Popular 400-year old listed stone-built locals' pub. Owned by Batemans, two of their beers are rotated alongside four or more other real ales, including from Oakham Ales or Nene Valley brewery. Traditional cider, perries and an extensive range of malt whiskies are available. Most beers are served straight from the cellar which can be seen through a large glass screen. Rolls and a variety of snacks available. It can be busy on football match days. ❀♣♠🖵(1,24)❀🛜

Ploughman L

1 Staniland Way, Werrington, PE4 6NA
☎ (01733) 327696
6 changing beers (sourced regionally; often Blue Monkey, Castor, Tiny Rebel) H
This thriving community free house serves up to six real ales including regular LocAles and unusual ales from far and wide, with a large selection of ciders, craft beers and over 50 gins. With two separate bars, the pub is well established on the local entertainment scene and features live music every weekend. The pub is an outstanding fundraiser for local charities, and hosts a popular beer festival in July. A former local CAMRA Pub of the Year. ☺❀♣♠P🖵(1,22.)♪

Wonky Donkey L

102C High Street, Fletton, PE2 8DR
☎ 07919 470635
Dancing Duck Abduction; 4 changing beers (sourced locally; often Digfield, Mile Tree, Tydd Steam) H/G
Housed in two rooms of a former florist's, this is Peterborough's latest micropub, situated in a previously pub-free area. It usually offers five beers, many straight from the cask, mostly LocAles, and also stocks a large range of ciders, wines and gins, along with several quality bottled lagers. Themed evenings include pop-up food nights. The pub regularly helps to brew house specials with local brewery Mile Tree. A local CAMRA Gold Award recipient in 2021. ☺♦♣♠🖵(5)❀♪

Woolpack ✓

29 North Street, Stanground, PE2 8HR (in old part of Stanground village by River Nene)
☎ (01733) 753544 ⊕ thewoolpack.pub
Timothy Taylor Landlord; 3 changing beers (sourced regionally; often Nene Valley, Ossett, Tydd Steam) H
Originally built in 1711, a medieval wall remains in the garden and the old barn used to be the village mortuary (last used in the 1850s). The covered beer garden is used for live music and leads to the old River Nene, with boat moorings available. The L-shaped bar has TVs and a dartboard and is adorned with old photos and prints. At least two guest beers are available. The pub is on the city Green Wheel cycle route. A former local CAMRA Pub of the Year. Q☺❀◑♣♠❀🛜♪

Yard of Ale
72 Oundle Road, PE2 9PA
☎ (01733) 348000 🌐 theyardofalepub.co.uk
Sharp's Doom Bar; house beer (by Digfield); 4 changing beers (often Rooster's, Tydd Steam) Ⓗ
Built on land that was part of the nearby Palmerston Arms stable yard, this 120 year-old pub was refurbished and reopened in early 2017. Tastefully decorated in shades of grey with a warm wooden bar and surround, the large open-plan single room is split into four distinct areas by the central supporting structure. Entertainment includes sports TV, darts, pool and live music most weekends. A large beer garden with pizza oven operates in the summer months. A former local CAMRA LocAle Pub of the Year. 🕭😋♣👜🖳(1)🛜🎵

Ramsey

Angel
76 High Street, PE26 1BS
☎ (01487) 711968
Adnams Ghost Ship; Greene King Abbot; 2 changing beers (often Lacons, Orkney, Tydd Steam) Ⓗ
This traditional brick-built two-room pub was refurbished in 2019. The main bar area contains two dartboards, jukebox, pool table and plenty of seating and is accessed from the rear car park and beer garden. Friendly staff and locals make this a great venue to enjoy a drink or two with a LocAle always being available, usually from Tydd Steam. Cheap rolls are available from the bar at weekends. 🕭😋♣P🖳(31)😋🛜

Reach

Dyke's End
8 Fair Green, CB25 0JD
☎ (01638) 743816 🌐 dykesendreach.co.uk
Woodforde's Wherry; 2 changing beers (sourced regionally) Ⓗ
Quintessential village pub. The interior has a cosy, food-free taproom and a larger dining area serving freshly prepared meals. Photos and art of local interest adorn the walls. The front garden overlooks the village green where the Reach Fair takes place on the early May bank holiday Monday. Its cask ales are sourced from small and medium-sized regional breweries, sometimes including the nearby Moonshine brewery.
Q🕭😋◑♿♣P🖳(11)😋🛜🎵

St Ives

Nelson's Head Ⓛ
Merryland, PE27 5ED
☎ (01480) 494454 🌐 nelsonsheadstives.co.uk
Greene King IPA, Abbot; Oakham JHB; Timothy Taylor Landlord Ⓗ
This popular pub is located in a picturesque narrow street in the town centre. Alongside the beers from Greene King there are two other regular beers. The interior has two distinct areas and there is a large outdoor patio area. Lunchtime food is available daily. On Sunday afternoons there are live bands from 3pm and the pub gets very busy. 😋◑🐾😋🛜🎵

St Neots

Ale Taster
25 Russell Street, PE19 1BA
☎ (01480) 581368
4 changing beers (sourced regionally) Ⓖ
A small back-street pub in the style of a micropub. It features up to three changing beers served from a stillage behind the bar. Also available are up to nine real ciders and perry. The owners source beer and cider from local producers as much as possible and are happy to chat about their beers. Three large fridges display a wide selection of bottled beers from around the world. The pub encourages conversation, with quiet background music and no electronic machines, and traditional bar games can be played. Q🕭😋♣👜P🖳(905)😋

Pig 'n' Falcon Ⓛ
9 New Street, PE19 1AE (town centre behind Barretts department store)
☎ 07951 785678 🌐 pignfalcon.co.uk
6 changing beers (sourced locally; often Nene Valley, Potbelly, Three Blind Mice) Ⓖ
This busy town-centre pub has up to six real ales, focusing on microbreweries and unusual beers including milds, porters and stouts. It has a good range of bottled ciders, UK and foreign bottled beers including Trappist ales, and several real ciders. Beer festivals are held throughout the year. Live blues and rock nights are hosted on Wednesday, Friday, Saturday and Sunday. Outside is a large, imaginatively created covered and heated beer garden. Three Blind Mice beers are real ale served in KegKegs. 🕭😋👜🖳(905)😋🎵

Weeping Ash ✓
15 New Street, PE19 1AD (N of town centre)
☎ (01480) 408330
Greene King Abbot; Ruddles Best Bitter; 6 changing beers Ⓗ
This Wetherspoon conversion of the old Victorian town post office is named after a large Weeping Ash tree that once stood on the site before the post office was built. A large, open, wood-panelled bar area with period decor leads to separate dining areas and an outdoor patio at the rear. It features lots of local history and postal memorabilia, and one long bar with a mural above depicting the local area. 🕭😋♿♣(905)🛜

Warboys

Royal Oak ✓
70 Mill Green, PE28 2SB
☎ (01487) 824848
Fuller's London Pride; 1 changing beer (sourced nationally) Ⓗ
This popular village pub reopened in 2022. There is a large main bar and a separate dining room. Outside there is a large beer garden at the front of the pub. One regular and one changing real ale are always available. The pub offers a good selection of traditional pub food cooked to order, and Sunday roasts. 🕭😋◑♣P🖳😋🛜🎵

Waterbeach

Sun Inn ✓
Chapel Street, CB25 9HR
☎ (01223) 861254
3 changing beers Ⓗ
Traditional pub overlooking the village green. The cosy lounge is dominated by a huge fireplace surrounded by bottles and rustic bric-a-brac, while the simply appointed public bar, with its woodblock floor, is always lively. There is a small meeting room and a function room upstairs that hosts gigs. An annual beer and music festival is held over the early May bank holiday weekend. The list of changing guest beers is interesting and includes local ales and often a dark ale. 🕭😋◑♿≉♣👜🖳(9)😋🛜🎵

West Wratting

Chestnut Tree
1 Mill Road, CB21 5LT
☎ (01223) 290384
Greene King IPA; 3 changing beers Ⓗ
Impressive two-bar Victorian-style pub, with modern
extensions creating a roomy interior. The lounge to the
right is mainly set out for dining, while to the left is a
comfortably furnished public bar with a pool table. This
friendly pub hosts darts, pool and pétanque teams and a
small lending library. Free of tie since the present owners
bought it in 2012, its three changing beers are mainly
from micros, including local suppliers. Local CAMRA Rural
Pub of the Year 2023. Q☺️❀◑♣🅿️🚌(19)❀🐾🛜

Whittlesey

Boat Inn Ⓛ
2 Ramsey Road, PE7 1DR
☎ (01733) 202488 ⊕ quinnboatinn.wordpress.com
**4 changing beers (sourced regionally; often Parkway,
Tydd Steam, Wychwood)** Ⓗ/Ⓖ
This corner pub consists of two rooms: a public bar with
sports TV, and a cosy lounge. A large number of
traditional ciders and perries supplement the real ales,
some of which are served direct from the cask. A whisky
club meets here on the second Friday of the month and
organises regular trips to tasting events. Outside is a
pétanque terrain which is used by dancers at the Straw
Bear Festival in January. A large car park is to the rear.
☺️❀🛏️&♣●🅿️🚌(31)❀🛜🎵

Letter B Ⓛ
53-57 Church Street, PE7 1DE
☎ (01733) 206975 ⊕ theletterb.co.uk
**Sharp's Atlantic; 4 changing beers (often Digfield,
Nene Valley)** Ⓗ
This 200-year-old pub has two bars, a small side room
with a bar billards table and decked rear patio area. Over
recent years the cider range has expanded rapidly to
complement the five real ales. A beer festival is held in
January during the Straw Bear Festival weekend, which is
popular with locals and visitors. The pub has won
numerous local CAMRA awards including county and
cider Pub of the Year. Accommodation is sometimes
available. Q☺️❀◑♣🚌(31,33)❀🛜🎵

Willingham

Bank Micropub
9 High Street, CB24 5ES
☎ (01954) 200045 ⊕ thebankmicropub.co.uk
3 changing beers Ⓖ
Formerly a village bank, this single-room micropub has a
short bar rescued from a closed Cambridge pub. Its walls
are decorated with photos of local interest. A wide range
of beers are available, direct from the cask, from
membrane keg or more. There is also a fridge well-
stocked with cans. Ciders include local Foxhay in bottles.
The Bank offers a warm welcome and the casual visitor is
certain to be included in local conversation. Q♣●🛢️🚌❀

Wisbech

Potting Shed
Mile Tree Lane, PE13 4TR
☎ (01945) 585044 ⊕ thesecretgardentouringpark.co.uk
**Mile Tree Mosaica, Larksong; 2 changing beers
(sourced locally; often Mile Tree, Xtreme)** Ⓗ
This modern, oak-framed building, on the grounds of a
family-run horticultural business and campsite, has an

open, airy, vaulted roof and a stone floor complete with
central log burner. Drinkers are well catered for in a
relaxed, friendly atmosphere with quality ales from Mile
Tree brewery, who were once based here. The well-
stocked on-site bottle shop sells spirits distilled here by
Fen Spirits. There are patio heaters outside, and music is
planned for most Fridays and Saturdays.
☺️❀🛏️◑&🅰️●🅿️🎵

Witcham

White Horse
7 Silver Street, CB6 2LF (1 mile from A142 jct, then first
left)
☎ (01353) 777999
**2 changing beers (sourced regionally; often
Grainstore, Rocket Ales, Wolf)** Ⓗ
Popular, family-friendly village pub with a constantly
changing selection of real ales, mostly from East Anglia.
As well as the main bar, there is a dining area and pool
table area. Witcham village is famous for hosting the
annual world pea-shooting championship, normally on
the second weekend in July. The pub sign is unique,
depicting the current world champion in battle dress
astride a white horse, with pea shooter held aloft.
Q☺️❀◑♣🚌🛜🎵

Breweries

Bowler's SIBA
**84 Lincoln Road, Deeping Gate, Peterborough,
PE6 9BB** ☎ 07480 064147 ⊕ bowlers.beer

⊠ Established in 2019, supplying many pubs, restaurants
and beer festivals both locally and nationally in cask. It
also brews bottled ales and supplies a number of beer
and farm shops in the region. Regional SIBA award
winners for several of its beers. ◆LIVE

The Duke (ABV 3.9%) BITTER
Sundance (ABV 4.5%) GOLD
Brown Derby (ABV 4.8%) BROWN
Trusty Steed (ABV 5.5%) IPA

BrewBoard SIBA
**Unit B3, Button End Industrial Estate, Harston,
CB22 7GX**
☎ (01223) 872131 ⊕ brewboard.co.uk
Founded in 2017. Now brewing with 150-hectolitre
plant. No real ale. 🍴🍺◆

Burwell
Burwell, CB25 0HQ ☎ 07788 311908
⊕ burwellbrewery.com

⊠ Richard Dolphin and Paul Belton established Burwell
Brewery in 2019 in a purpose-built timber brewery at the
bottom of Richard's garden. The plant, recently upgraded
to 2.5-barrels, together with four conditioning tanks and
produces beer in cask, bottle and bag-in-box. 🍴◆

Beer Fuggled Best Bitter (ABV 4%) BITTER
Priory Wood Rauch (ABV 4%) BROWN
Judy's Hole Chocolate Porter (ABV 4.5%) PORTER
Margaret's Field Amber (ABV 5%) PALE
Moulin D'Etienne Wit Bier (ABV 5%) SPECIALITY
Stefans' Mü¥hle Weiss Bier (ABV 5%) SPECIALITY
Sunshine Pale Ale (ABV 5%) PALE
Double Beer Fuggled Special Bitter (ABV 5.5%)
BITTER

Absolutely Beer Fuggled Extra Special Bitter (ABV 6.5%) STRONG

Calverley's SIBA

23a Hooper Street, Cambridge, CB1 2NZ
☎ (01223) 312370 ☎ 07769 537342
⊕ calverleys.com

⊙Brewery started 2013 by brothers Sam and Tom Calverley. It is located in a converted stable yard close to the city centre. The brewery is open to the public for on and off-sales (Thursday-Saturday). A large proportion of production is sold onsite, and local pubs are also supplied. Most beers are keg (various styles), but the brewery remains committed to cask ale. ‼️🍺◆

Porter (ABV 5.1%) PORTER

Cambridge

🍺 1 King Street, Cambridge, CB1 1LH
☎ (01223) 858155 ⊕ thecambridgebrewhouse.com

⊗ Brewing began in 2013 at the onsite microbrewery in the Cambridge Brew House. ◆

Castor SIBA

Castor, PE5 7AX
☎ (01733) 380337 ⊕ castorales.co.uk

This three-barrel brewery, established in 2009, is located in a specially converted outhouse in the garden of the founder brewer. Several local outlets feature the beers as well as many national beer festivals. ‼️◆

Roman Gold (ABV 3.7%) GOLD
Hopping Toad (ABV 4.1%) GOLD
Roman Mosaic (ABV 4.2%) GOLD

Downham Isle

19 Main Street, Littleport, CB6 1PH
☎ (01353) 864795 ☎ 07732 927479
⊕ downhamislebrewery.co.uk

Downham Isle Brewery opened 2016 in Little Downham, in the north eastern Cambridgeshire fens. Brewing real and craft ales, the customer base spans the Isle of Ely, Cambridge and Dusseldorf! Artisan, small batch brewing methods are used. The brewery moved to premises in Littleport in 2021. Normally four core ales are brewed, both cask and bottle conditioned. ‼️🍺◆LIVE🍃

Main Street Citra (ABV 3.5%) IPA
Goose Ely (ABV 3.7%) PALE
Main Street Best Bitter (ABV 4.4%) BITTER
Duneham Ale (ABV 4.8%) BITTER

Draycott

Low Farm, 30 Mill Road, Buckden, PE19 5SS
☎ (01480) 812404 ☎ 07740 374710
⊕ draycottbrewery.co.uk

⊗ The brewery was set up by Jon and Jane Draycott in 2009, and is located in an old farm complex. Focus is on bottle-conditioned beers which are available in a one-pint, traditionally-shaped bottle. Four regular beers are available, along with a cask beer brewed for the Grafham Trout pub, or to order. A seasonal ale made with local wild hops is also produced. LIVE

Elgood's SIBA

North Brink Brewery, Wisbech, PE13 1LW
☎ (01945) 583160 ⊕ elgoods-brewery.co.uk

⊗ The North Brink brewery was established in 1795. Owned by the Elgood family since 1878, the fifth generation are now involved in running the business. Elgood's has approximately 30 tied pubs within a 50-mile radius of the brewery and a substantial free trade. Lambic-style beers are produced using the brewery's old open cooling trays as fermenting vessels. Off-sales are available all year round from the shop in the brewery office when the visitor centre is closed. ‼️🍺◆

Black Dog (ABV 3.6%) MILD
Black-red mild with liquorice and chocolate. Dry roasty finish.
Cambridge Bitter (ABV 3.8%) BITTER
Fruit and malt on the nose with increasing hops and balancing malt on the palate. Dry finish.
Cambridge Gold (ABV 3.9%) BLOND
Blackberry Porter (ABV 4.5%) SPECIALITY
Plum Porter (ABV 4.5%) SPECIALITY

Grafham

The Orchard Garden Farm, The Town, Great Staughton, PE19 5BA ☎ 07590 836241
⊕ grafhambrewing.co

Grafham Brewing Co is a five-barrel brewery that began commercial production in 2019. In 2022 the brewery moved from Grafham to Great Staughton.

Hodders Panama (ABV 4.8%) PALE
Sunken Church (ABV 4.8%) PALE

IVO SIBA

10 Church Street, Somersham, PE28 3EG ☎ 07823 400369 ⊕ ivobrewery.co.uk

Established in 2020, IVO Brewery is run by two friends and neighbours, Charlie Abbott and Jason Jones, both successful homebrewers. Every beer is naturally fined and vegan-friendly. Despite being a small brewery, a core range is brewed with occasional and on-demand specials. All are available bottle-conditioned with some also in cask, and the remainder in keg (dependent on the style). ◆LIVE V

Car Park Cuddle (ABV 3.8%) PALE
No Man (ABV 4.5%) STOUT
She Keeps It Nice (ABV 4.5%) PALE
Evening Brown (ABV 5%) BROWN
Heavy on the Chips (ABV 6%) PORTER

Jesus College

Jesus College, Cambridge, CB5 8BL

In-house brewery for Jesus College at the University of Cambridge. Beers are produced for college use only and are not available to the general public.

Lord Conrad's

Unit 21, Dry Drayton Industrial Estate, Scotland Road, Dry Drayton, CB23 8AT ☎ 07736 739700
⊕ lordconradsbrewery.co.uk

⊗ Lord Conrad's was established in 2007 and moved to Dry Drayton in 2011, using a 2.5-barrel plant. One permanent outlet is supplied, the Black Horse, Dry Drayton, along with other local free houses and beer festivals. The brewery adheres strongly to green principles, using low energy systems, recycled materials and local ingredients. All beers are available cask-conditoned and bottle-conditioned with a varying selection available in keg. ‼️🍺LIVE

Hedgerow Hop (ABV 3.7%) BITTER

Spiffing Wheeze (ABV 3.9%) PALE
A-Bomb (ABV 4%) GOLD
Big Bad Wolf (ABV 4%) PALE
Fools Gold (ABV 4%) PALE
Slap N'Tickle (ABV 4.3%) BLOND
Horny Goat (ABV 4.8%) SPECIALITY
Self Isolation (ABV 5%) PALE
Stubble Burner (ABV 5%) BLOND

Mile Tree SIBA

29 Alfric Square, Woodston, Peterborough, PE2 7JP
☎ 07858 930363 ⊕ miletreebrewery.co.uk

⌧ Mile Tree was established in 2012 at the Secret
Garden Touring Park in Wisbech, and moved to
Peterborough in 2018. Beer is brewed on a five-barrel
plant. It serves the local area and beer festivals. ♦LIVE

Meadowgold (ABV 3.8%) GOLD
Mosaica (ABV 4.2%) GOLD
Larksong (ABV 4.5%) BITTER
Wildwood (ABV 4.9%) GOLD
Porter (ABV 5.2%) PORTER
Winter Ale (ABV 6%) OLD

Milton SIBA

Pegasus House, Pembroke Avenue, Waterbeach,
CB25 9PY
☎ (01223) 862067 ⊕ miltonbrewery.co.uk

⌧ The brewery has grown steadily since it was founded
in 1999, moving to larger premises in Waterbeach in
2012. It now operates three pubs in Cambridge through a
sister company. In 2016 a separate brand, Beach
Brewery, was created to market unpasteurised and
unfiltered keg beers. Since 2021 the brewery has an
outdoor taproom (open on a seasonal basis). !! ◆

Minotaur (ABV 3.3%) MILD
A dark ruby mild with liquorice and raisin fruit
throughout. Light dry finish.
Dionysus (ABV 3.6%) BITTER
Yellow bitter with good balance of biscuity malt and
citrus hop. Some malt and hops linger on long dry
aftertaste.
Justinian (ABV 3.9%) BITTER
Straw-coloured bitter with pink grapefruit hop character
and light malt softness. Very dry finish.
Pegasus (ABV 4.1%) BITTER
Malty, amber, medium-bodied bitter with faint hops.
Bittersweet aftertaste.
Sparta (ABV 4.3%) BITTER
A yellow/gold bitter with floral hops, kiwi fruit and
balancing malt softness which fades to leave a long dry
finish.
Minerva (ABV 4.6%) GOLD
Nero (ABV 5%) STOUT
A complex black beer comprising a blend of milk
chocolate, raisins and liquorice. Roast malt and fruit
completes the experience.
Cyclops (ABV 5.3%) BITTER
Marcus Aurelius (ABV 7.5%) STOUT
A powerful black brew brimming with raisins and
liquorice. Big balanced finish.

Moonshine

Hill Farm, Shelford Road, Fulbourn, CB21 5EQ
☎ 07906 066794

Office: 28 Radegund Road, Cambridge, CB1 3RS
⊕ moonshinebrewery.co.uk

⌧ Established in 2004, the brewery produces up to 20
barrels a week. Locally-produced ingredients are used,
including water from the brewery's own well, and barley
grown on the farm where the brewery is based. CAMRA
beer festivals are supplied throughout the country, with
30 local outlets supplied direct. ♦LIVE

Trumpington Tipple (ABV 3.6%) BITTER
Cambridge Pale Ale (ABV 3.8%) PALE
Shelford Crier (ABV 3.9%) BITTER
Cambridge Best Bitter (ABV 4.1%) BITTER
Heavenly Matter (ABV 4.1%) GOLD
Black Hole Stout (ABV 5%) STOUT
Cellarman's Stout (ABV 6%) STOUT
Chocolate Orange Stout (ABV 6.7%) SPECIALITY

Oakham SIBA

2 Maxwell Road, Woodston, Peterborough, PE2 7JB
☎ (01733) 370500

Second Site: Brewery Tap, 80 Westgate,
Peterborough, PE1 2AA ⊕ oakhamales.com

⌧ Established in 1993 in Oakham, the brewery moved to
Peterborough in 1998. Its main production site is a 75-
barrel plant in the Woodston area of the city. The six-
barrel 'Westgate' plant at the Brewery Tap pub
recommenced brewing in 2023. Five permanent beers
are supplied along with monthly seasonals. Additionally
around eight 'cask aged' beers are brewed every year.
!! ➤ ◆LIVE

JHB (ABV 3.8%) GOLD
Hoppy yellow golden ale with bags of citrus hop. An
underlying sweet maltiness ebbs away as the citrus hop
prevails.
Inferno (ABV 4%) GOLD
The citrus hop character of this straw coloured brew
begins on the nose and builds in intensity on the palate.
Clean, dry, citrus finish.
Citra (ABV 4.2%) GOLD
Robust golden ale with explosive grapefruit and lemony
hop. A scattering of sweet malt provides contrast to the
hop bitterness.
Bishops Farewell (ABV 4.6%) GOLD
Mouth-filling yellow beer with uncompromising zesty
citrus hop, softened by undertones of malt, delivering a
big-hearted bittersweet palate.
Green Devil (ABV 6%) IPA
Powerful premium golden ale with soaring citrus hop
deepening in the mouth progressing into an unrelenting
dry hoppy finish.

Papworth SIBA

24 Earith Business Park, Meadow Drove, Earith,
PE28 3QF
☎ (01487) 842442 ☎ 07835 845797
⊕ papworthbrewery.com

Brewing began in 2014 in Papworth Everard. The
brewery moved to new premises in Earith in 2017 and
acquired an 11-barrel plant, significantly increasing its
production. A brewery tap and bottle shop, the Crystal
Ship, opened in 2020 and can be found at Unit 32, Earith
Business Park. !! ➤ LIVE ◆

Mild Thing (ABV 3.5%) MILD
Mad Jack (ABV 3.8%) BITTER
The Whitfield Citrabolt (ABV 3.8%) GOLD
Whispering Grass (ABV 3.8%) BITTER
Fen Skater (ABV 4%) PALE
Crystal Ship (ABV 4.2%) BITTER
Half Nelson (ABV 4.2%) PALE
Old Riverport Stout (ABV 4.5%) STOUT
Red Kite (ABV 4.7%) BITTER
Off the Lip (ABV 5%) IPA
Robin Goodfellow (ABV 5.4%) BITTER

Pass the Porter (ABV 5.5%) PORTER
Koura (ABV 5.7%) SPECIALITY
Saison d'Etre (ABV 6%) SPECIALITY

Pastore

Unit 2 Convent Drive, Waterbeach, CB25 9QT
⊕ pastorebrewing.com

⊠ Founded in 2019, Pastore Brewing & Blending specialise in mixed-fermentation sour and wild ales. Pastore (Pas-tor-ray) is Italian for shepherd, in honour of the brewer's Italian family. It ties rustic, wild brewing with a modern, semi-urban setting, making new-age fresh, fruited weisses, as well as barrel-aged old saisons. ‼ ⌷ ◆LIVE ◢

Rocket

The Orchard, Garden Farm, The Town, Great Staughton, PE19 5BE ☎ 07747 617527
✉ info@rocket-ales.com

Originally using spare capacity at King's Cliffe Brewery, Rocket Ales relocated to its own site in 2017 and brews five core ales and a changing range of specials.

Black Knight (ABV 3.7%) MILD
Congreve IPA (ABV 3.9%) IPA
Rapier (ABV 3.9%) IPA
Sidewinder (ABV 3.9%) PALE
Bloodhound (ABV 4.2%) PALE

Secret Project (NEW)

March Road, Turves, PE7 2DW ☎ 07429 185333
✉ secretprojectbrew@gmail.com

A microbrewery in Cambridgeshire, specialising in hoppy craft beer. Only limited run single batches are brewed, so please contact the brewery for details of current range.

Son of Sid

≣ **Chequers, 71 Main Road, Little Gransden, SG19 3DW**
☎ (01767) 677348 ⊕ sonofsid.co.uk

⊠ Son of Sid was established in 2007. The three-barrel plant is situated in a room at the back of the pub and can be viewed from a window in the lounge bar. It is named after the father of the current landlord, who ran the pub for over 40 years. His son has carried the business on as a family-run enterprise. Beer is sold in the pub and at local beer festivals. Brewing is currently suspended. ‼ ⌷LIVE

Three Blind Mice SIBA

Unit W10, Black Bank Business Park, Black Bank Road, Little Downham, CB6 2UA
☎ (01353) 864438 ☎ 07912 875825
✉ mice@threeblindmicebrewery.com

Award-winning 16-barrel brewery, established in 2014. The name comes from the three owners/brewers, who reckoned they didn't have a clue what they were doing when they first started brewing. Beer is supplied regularly to the Drayman's Son, Ely, plus other outlets in Ely, Cambridgeshire and further afield. ◆

Lonely Snake (ABV 3.5%) GOLD
Gold session ale with a fruity aroma, a sustained sweet fruitiness and a short-lived gentle balance of hops and malt.
Old Brown Mouse (ABV 4.2%) BITTER
A ruby brown beer with light fruity malt aromas, a sweetish malty palate and a light malt finish.
Juice Rocket (ABV 4.5%) PALE

Hazy pale ale with citrus hop aroma supported by sweet malt in the mouth. Sweet fruity finish with mellow hop.
Milk Worm (ABV 5.3%) PORTER
Rocket Nun (ABV 5.5%) IPA

Tydd Steam SIBA

Manor Barn, Kirkgate, Tydd Saint Giles, PE13 5NE
☎ (01945) 871020 ☎ 07932 726552
⊕ tyddsteam.co.uk

⊠ Established in 2007 in a converted agricultural barn, the brewery is named after two farm steam engines. A 15-barrel plant was installed in 2011. Around 70 outlets are supplied direct. ‼◆LIVE

Barn Ale (ABV 3.9%) BITTER
A golden bitter that has good biscuity malt aroma and flavour, balanced by spicy hops. Long, dry, fairly astringent finish.
Scoundrel (ABV 4%) BITTER
A dry pale amber bitter with a gentle malty and hoppy aroma, plenty of hop bitterness with fruity hints in the taste and a persistent dry aftertaste.
Piston Bob (ABV 4.6%) BITTER
Amber bitter with malt and faint hop aroma, a malty flavour balanced by hops and fruit then a dry finish.

Wheatsheaf (NEW) SIBA

17 Halcyon Court, St Margarets Way, Huntingdon, PE29 6DG ⊕ wheatsheafbrewery.co.uk

Founded in 2022, Wheatsheaf Brewery produces handcrafted ales. All the beer is unfined and made in small batches using only quality natural ingredients. A mix of traditional and modern brewing techniques are used. The onsite taproom is generally open the last Saturday of the month. LIVE ◢

Supernova (ABV 4%) GOLD
Unlocked (ABV 4.5%) BITTER
Oracle (ABV 4.8%) GOLD
Mockingbird (ABV 5%) STOUT

Wylde Sky SIBA

Unit 8a, The Grip, Hadstock Road, Linton, CB21 4XN
☎ (01223) 778350 ⊕ wyldeskybrewing.com

⊠ Established in 2018, the brewery uses 10-barrel plant to brew small batches of innovative beers in a range of styles from around the world. All beers are unfined, unfiltered and unpasteurised. A number of outlets are supplied in the area and its taproom is open Thursday-Sunday (some seasonal variations). ‼ ⌷◆◢

Xtreme

Unit 21/22, Alfric Square, Peterborough, PE2 7JP
☎ 07825 680932 ⊕ xtremeales.com

⊠ The Hunt brothers took over Xtreme Ales in 2020. The core range of ales is retained, along with some of the popular seasonals, but a number of new brews have also been added. Its award-winning beers can be found locally and at national beer festivals. ‼◆

PiXie APA (ABV 3.7%) PALE
Xplorer Pale Ale (ABV 4.1%) PALE
Pigeon Ale (ABV 4.3%) PALE
Red FoX (ABV 4.5%) RED
Strawberry Xtreme (ABV 4.5%) STOUT
OatiX Stout (ABV 4.6%) STOUT
Special Bitter (ABV 5%) BITTER
Triple Hop Xtra-IPA (ABV 5%) GOLD
Xporter (ABV 6%) PORTER
SaXquatch (ABV 8.6%) OLD

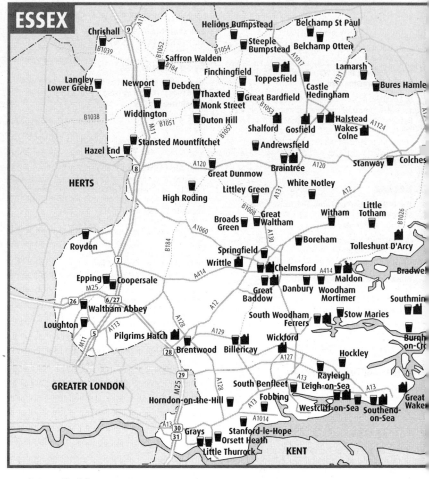

ESSEX

Andrewsfield

Millibar ⑤
Stebbing Airfield, New Pasture Lane, CM6 3TH
(accessed by a track beside the runway, nr Stebbing Green) TL689248
☎ 07923 981900 ● andrewsfield.com/andrewsfield-millibar
Bishop Nick Ridley's Rite Ⓗ
The manager of the bar at this local flying school is keen on local supply and has installed Ridley's Rite from Bishop Nick brewery as his sole ale. There is also a range of Bishop Nick bottled beers. Home cooked food is served every day. The bar and clubhouse area display flying memorabilia. The training airfield is a small grass strip dominated by single-engine Cessna aircraft, a Mustang III and B17 Meteor IIIs, and trial flying lessons are available. The public are welcome in the bar, and it stays open until 11pm if there are customers.
Q ☎ ⊛ ⑴ P ♣ 🖕

Belchamp Otten

Red Lion ⑤
Fowes Lane, CO10 7BQ (on a small single track lane, signed by the duck pond) TL799415
☎ (01787) 278301
Adnams Southwold Bitter; 2 changing beers (sourced nationally) Ⓗ

Lovely local inn on the Suffok and Essex border, hidden away in the smallest of the Belchamps. The owner and his friendly Labrador provide a warm welcome, and there is an open fire in winter. The pub does not currently serve food, but has delivery arrangements with local takeaway restaurants. It has darts and a pool table, and occasional events are run. The local area boasts excellent views and there are good walks and cycle rides from here. ☎ ⊛ ♣ P ♣ 🖕

Belchamp St Paul

Half Moon
Cole Green, CO10 7DP TL792423
☎ (01787) 277402 ● halfmoonbelchamp.co.uk
3 changing beers (sourced nationally) Ⓗ
Beautiful, friendly, thatched pub dating from about 1685, situated opposite the village green. Three real ales are available with guest beers changing regularly, and often supplied by local breweries. This rural venue is popular with locals and has an excellent choice of freshly-made and locally sourced bar and restaurant meals with an ever-changing seasonal menu (no food Sun eve or Mon). In the past, it provided one of the locations for the first Lovejoy TV series, and has hanging baskets, original wooden beams, a real log fire and low ceilings in places.
Q ☎ ⊛ ⑴ 氏 ♣ P 🖕

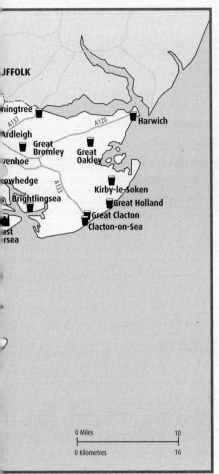

0 Miles   10
0 Kilometres   16

Oakham, and the pub is part of the Oakademy. The bar service is efficient and friendly. Good-quality, home-made food is available selected lunchtimes and evenings, with a curry night on Wednesday. A collection of tankards hangs from the ceiling. There is a cosy and attractive courtyard garden. ✿❶Ġ⩲P🚲(100)🛜

Railway

1 High Street, CM12 9BE

☎ (01277) 652173 ⊕ therailwaybillericay.co.uk

Dark Star Hophead; Wibblers Dengie IPA; 3 changing beers (sourced nationally) 🅷

Friendly pub with a welcoming atmosphere, which earns its tag line: Number 1 in the High Street. It has served over 940 different real ales and won several local CAMRA awards. Guest beers are updated on social media. Regular events include a quiz, charity days and league darts. This community-oriented venue has a beer garden outside, and an open fire indoors during winter. Traditional bar games include shove-ha'penny with real ha'pennies. Live music is played one Sunday afternoon a month and karaoke on the second Sunday of the month. ➳✿Ġ⩲♣P🚲(100,9) 🌶🛜♫

Boreham

Queen's Head 🅛

Church Road, CM3 3EG

☎ (01245) 467298

Timothy Taylor Landlord; 3 changing beers (sourced nationally) 🅷

Dating from the 16th century and run by the same family for over 20 years, this friendly pub is tucked away just past the church. There are two contrasting bars: one with bench seating for darts, dominoes and crib; the other for dining. A wooden conservatory has been added, leading to the garden; this offers a lovely area with picnic benches to enjoy food and drink in a tranquil setting. Home-cooked fare is served Wednesday to Sunday. Bank holiday beer festivals are held at Easter and in August. Local CAMRA Pub of the Year 2022. ➳✿❶♣●P🚲(71,371) 🌶🛜♫

Billericay

Billericay Brewing Co. Shop & Micropub

52 Chapel Street, CM12 9LS

☎ (01277) 500121 ⊕ billericaybrewing.co.uk

Billericay Zeppelin, Blonde, Dickie; 1 changing beer (sourced locally; often Billericay) Ⓖ

This brewery tap micropub is next door to the brewery. It serves up to four ales on gravity, mostly from Billericay brewery, plus two other beers on KeyKeg. Seating is on high stools next to solid wooden tables with outdoor seating available as well. It is also a beer shop with bottles from Billericay and other breweries, and foreign beers. The shop is usually open for off sales from 10am Tuesday to Saturday. Beer festivals held several times a year; see social media for details. ➳✿⩲♣●🚲(100,222) 🌶🛜

Coach & Horses 🅛

36 Chapel Street, CM12 9LU

☎ (01277) 622873 ⊕ thecoachandhorses.org

Adnams Broadside; Mighty Oak Maldon Gold; Oakham Citra; Wibblers Dengie IPA; 1 changing beer (sourced nationally) 🅷

Close to the High Street, this welcoming pub with an inviting atmosphere has appeared in this Guide for over 20 years. Five ales are served, with one always from

REAL ALE BREWERIES

Billericay 🍺 Billericay
Bishop Nick Braintree
Black Box ⬧ Southend on Sea
Brentwood ⬧ Pilgrims Hatch
Brewhouse & Kitchen 🍺 Chelmsford (NEW)
Chelmsford ⬧ Great Baddow
Colchester Wakes Colne
Courtyard ⬧ Gosfield
Crouch Vale ⬧ South Woodham Ferrers
Datum Attitude Tolleshunt D'Arcy (NEW)
Fallen Angel Writtle
George's Great Wakering
JackRabbit Ardleigh
Leigh on Sea ⬧ Leigh on Sea
Mersea Island East Mersea
Mighty Oak ⬧ Maldon
Moody Goose 🍺 Braintree
Neolithic Bradwell
Other Monkey ⬧ Colchester
Posh Boys ⬧ Wickford
Pumphouse Community ⬧ Toppesfield
Shalford Shalford
St Botolphs Colchester
Watson's Colchester
WHARF Colchester (NEW)
White Hart 🍺 Halstead
Wibblers ⬧ Southminster

41

Braintree

King William IV 🅛
114 London Road, CM77 7PU
☎ 07830 283033 ⊕ kingwilliamiv.co.uk
4 changing beers (sourced nationally) Ⓖ
Friendly, traditional, free house serving up to four real ales, usually featuring Essex microbreweries, plus an interesting selection of ciders. There is a main bar and a small back bar. A large patio area with picnic tables and extensive gardens are used to host many functions throughout the year, including beer festivals and musical events. This is a traditional drinking pub that does not offer cooked meals. The Moody Goose brewery is located in the pub grounds, and at least one of their ales is usually available in warmer months.
Q❀🐾P🖵(70,370) ❀ ♫

Picture Palace ✅
Fairfield Road, CM7 3HA
☎ (01376) 550255
Greene King Abbot; Ruddles Best Bitter; Sharp's Doom Bar; 3 changing beers (sourced nationally) Ⓗ
The first cinema in Braintree, the Picture Palace was built in 1912, and was replaced by the Embassy in 1930. Now a spacious Wetherspoon pub, it retains the character of a picture house with the floor sloping down to the long curved bar at the front, where the stage used to be. It has a large TV screen above it, and some eye-catching Art Deco installations. Additional TVs give a choice of channels. Close to the bus and train stations.
🕏◑♿≷🖵🛜

Brentwood

Rising Sun ✅
144 Ongar Road, CM15 9DJ (on A128, at Western Rd jct)
☎ (01277) 227400
Greene King IPA; Sharp's Atlantic; Timothy Taylor Landlord; 2 changing beers (sourced nationally) Ⓗ
Good community local with five real ales, extensively refurbished and extended in 2020. A charity quiz is held on Monday evenings. Five handpumps in the saloon bar dispense three regular ales plus two guests. Outside there is a covered heated smokers' area and a patio garden. Food service – including pizzas – starts when the pub opens and finishes an hour before closing time. Children are not permitted in the bars, but well-behaved children are allowed in the outdoor covered, heated area. ❀◑🐾P🖵(21,71)❀🛜♫

Victoria Arms 🍷
50 Ongar Road, CM15 9AX (On A128)
☎ (01277) 201187
Adnams Ghost Ship; Crouch Vale Brewers Gold; Harvey's Sussex Best Bitter; 3 changing beers (sourced nationally) Ⓗ
Pleasant and comfortable Gray & Sons pub with a friendly atmosphere. Unusually for the area, there is normally a Harvey's beer on tap, as well as Ghost Ship and three changing ales. There are several TV screens which mostly show sports matches, and an outside smoking area. Cribbage and other card games are played. Local CAMRA Pub of the Year 2021 and 2023. ❀🐾P🖵(498,21)♫

Brightlingsea

Railway Tavern 🍷 🅛
58 Station Road, CO7 0DT
⊕ alesattherails.co.uk
Crouch Vale Essex Boys Best Bitter; 2 changing beers (sourced nationally) Ⓗ

Local CAMRA Pub of the Year 2020 and 2023, this recently-refurbished traditional local has a number of bar areas and a covered garden. Ales are kept in excellent condition, making it popular with visitors to the area, as well as with locals. Regular functions including music and party events are advertised on their Facebook page.
Q🕏❀🐾🖵(62) ❀

Broads Green

Walnut Tree 🅛 ✅
CM3 1DT
☎ (01245) 360222
Bishop Nick Ridley's Rite; Timothy Taylor Landlord Ⓖ
Formerly a dairy, this red-brick Victorian pub overlooking the green, has been identified by CAMRA as having a nationally important historic pub interior. The front door opens into what was the bottle and jug but is now a small snug. To the left is a wood-panelled public bar, little-changed since it was built in 1888, right is the saloon bar. The half-cellar has gravity-served beers. Outside there is seating in front of the pub, with a large family garden to the side and rear. The landlord concentrates on his beers and maintains a traditional atmosphere, so no food offering. Q🕏❀🜨♣P❀🛜

Bures Hamlet

Eight Bells 🅛
6 Colchester Road, CO8 5AE (on B1508)
☎ (01787) 227354
Greene King IPA, Abbot; Timothy Taylor Landlord; 3 changing beers (sourced nationally) Ⓗ
A real gem, this is a traditional village pub with a long-serving landlord of over 40 years. It has three separate drinking and dining areas, served by a large bar. Traditional pub food is available daily, with a roast on Sunday. There is a separate function area. It is 200 yards from the Stour Valley Footpath and only two minutes' stroll from Bures station, and walkers and cyclists are always welcome. Q🕏❀◑♿≷(Bures)P🖵(754)❀ 🛜

Burnham-on-Crouch

Queen's Head
26 Providence, CM0 8JU
☎ (01621) 502422
Chelmsford Cool Bay; Mighty Oak Captain Bob; 2 changing beers (sourced nationally) Ⓗ
A true locals' pub just off the High Street, owned by Gray & Sons. It is frequently busy, with a good and varied range of beers and ciders. The basic no-frills interior is warmed in winter by a log-burning stove. The pool table is a popular feature. The small sheltered garden to the rear of the pub provides a delightful outside space with a heated smoking area. Beer festivals are hosted on the August bank holiday, and there are regular music nights and quiz nights. Burnham-on-Crouch railway station is 15 minutes' walk away. 🕏◑🐾🖵(31)❀🛜♫

Castle Hedingham

Bell 🅛
10 St James Street, CO9 3EJ (on main road through village)
☎ (01787) 460350 ⊕ hedinghambell.co.uk
3 changing beers (sourced locally) Ⓖ
Owned by Gray & Sons, this 15th-century coaching inn has two main bars, alongside small rooms for drinking and dining, and a nice outside area to enjoy in fine weather. Beer is cask dispensed and summer and winter beer festivals are held. Local musicians play on most

Friday evenings and Sunday is quiz night. Locally sourced food includes Turkish specials prepared in a wood-fired stone oven, and Wednesday evening features a fish barbecue menu in summer months.
Q☺☜❄◐♿▲♣P🖬🖳(89) ♥🐾🎵

Chelmsford

Ale House 🄻
24-26 Viaduct Road, CM1 1TS
☎ (01245) 260535 ⊕ the-ale-house-chelmsford.co.uk
9 changing beers (sourced nationally) 🄷
A unique bar in Chelmsford, located under the arches at the railway station. It has one of the widest beer ranges in Essex with nine continuously-changing ales, always including dark and stronger beers, plus six real ciders and at least eight craft keg. There are also imported lagers on tap and a wide range of bottled beers from around the world. No food, but customers are welcome to bring their own, or order a takeaway; plates and cutlery can be provided. Quizzes are held on the last Sunday of each month. Regular beer festivals are held.
☺☜❄♿▲♣●🐾♥🎵

Hop Beer Shop 🄻
173 Moulsham Street, CM2 0LD
☎ (01245) 353570
4 changing beers (sourced nationally) 🄶
Essex's first micropub; four beers are served by gravity, with local breweries always represented alongside interesting beers from around the country, with usually a stout or porter and a golden beer. There are also craft keg beers, around 100 bottled beers from local and international breweries, and bottled cider (not all real), which may be drunk there or purchased to take home. A former local CAMRA Pub of the Year, and Cider Pub of the Year on several occasions. Close to many bus routes.
Q●🐾🖳♥

Orange Tree 🄻
6 Lower Anchor Street, CM2 0AS
☎ (01245) 262664
Chelmsford Cool Bay; Colchester Sweeney Todd; Mighty Oak Oscar Wilde, Captain Bob; 4 changing beers (sourced nationally) 🄷
The Orange Tree is one of the best real ale pubs in Chelmsford and was local CAMRA Pub of the Year 2014, 2015 and 2020. A second pub for Max and Jess, who also run the Queen's Head in Boreham. This is a place for conversation and meeting friends. Refurbishment in 2015 has made the separate public and saloon bars both much larger. A great range of beers is served, always something for food. Lunchtime food is served, with a themed food night on Thursday. Close to many bus routes. ☺☜❄◐♿▲♣●P🖬🐾♥

Railway Tavern 🄻
63 Duke Street, CM1 1LW
☎ (01245) 280679
Dartmoor Best; Red Fox IPA; 6 changing beers (sourced nationally) 🄷
A Tardis-like corner pub, right outside Chelmsford rail station and close to bus station. Not surprisingly, a railway theme dominates. The interior is long and narrow, with banks of hand pumps at opposite ends of the central bar counter. Craft beers and over 50 different gins are also sold. There is a small enclosed garden where you can listen to the station announcements and marvel at the ever-changing mural. The pub may stay open later on summer Sundays. Former local CAMRA Pub of the Year. ❄♣🖬🐾♥

Woolpack
23 Mildmay Road, CM2 0DN
☎ (01245) 633344 ⊕ thewoolpackchelmsford.co.uk
Hardys & Hansons Bitter; 7 changing beers (sourced nationally) 🄷
It is an easy walk from the town centre to this award-winning, friendly Victorian local. Five to seven changing beers are usually on offer. There are three rooms, with a lounge area overlooking the large outside courtyard garden with covered areas. Darts and a pool table are in a smaller room. A beer festival is held in the garden over Easter weekend. Close to many bus routes.
☜❄◐♿♣P🖳🎵

Chrishall

Red Cow 🅥
11 High Street, SG8 8RN (N of B1039) TL446393
☎ (01763) 838792 ⊕ theredcow.com
Adnams Southwold Bitter; Woodforde's Wherry; 2 changing beers (sourced nationally) 🄷
Thatched 14th-century inn in a small village near the Cambridgeshire/Hertfordshire border, with guest beers usually from East Anglia. Situated on the Icknield Way, the pub is a popular stop-off for ramblers. It has a good reputation for food, served in the tiled bar or restaurant which are separated by original open timbering. Quality accommodation is available in the renovated barn alongside the pub. A shop established in the car park provides the village with essential supplies. One corner of the bar has a small tuck shop. Q☺☜❄🛏◐P🐾♥🎵

Clacton-on-Sea

Moon & Starfish
1 Marine Parade East, CO15 1PT
☎ (01255) 222998
Greene King Abbot; Ruddles Best Bitter; Sharp's Doom Bar; 6 changing beers (sourced nationally) 🄷
This Wetherspoon pub is situated opposite Clacton's famous pier and Venetian bridge and handily placed for the town centre and memorial gardens, with the railway station within easy walking distance. Six pumps are always available, with changing guest ales. An outside seating area provides excellent views of the Clacton air show and the carnival procession, both held in August.
Q☺☜◐♿❄●🖳♥

Old Lifeboat House
39 Marine Parade East, CO15 6AD
☎ (01255) 476799
Greene King Abbot; St Austell Proper Job; 3 changing beers (sourced nationally); often Greene King, Colchester, St Austell) 🄷
This family-run pub is a favourite with locals. Up to five ales are available, regularly including local brews from Colchester, Mauldons and Mighty Oak, alongside numerous ciders and perries. Local CAMRA Pub of the Year 2012, 2013 and 2014 and Cider Pub of the Year 2015, the pub has been in this Guide regularly for more than a decade. Two darts teams play on Monday or Thursday. Food is available Wednesday evening, and occasionally at other times, though hours vary so check before travelling. ☺☜♿❄♣●🖬🖳♥🎵

Colchester

Ale House 🄻
82 Butt Road, CO3 3DA
☎ (01206) 573464 ⊕ thealehousecolchester.co.uk
8 changing beers (sourced nationally) 🄷 /🄶

43

A genuine free house just outside the city centre. A wide range of ales are on offer, including at least one dark, dispensed via a mixture of handpump and gravity, along with a range of ciders. Darts and TV sports are available, along with regular quiz and folk nights. The pub has won many CAMRA awards under the friendly landlady. There is a large walled garden to the rear which was a saviour during the pandemic. ❀⇌(Town)♣●🚪(S6,S7)🛜

British Grenadier

67 Military Road, CO1 2AP
☎ 07832 215118
4 changing beers (sourced nationally) Ⓗ
This welcoming local pub, run by a knowledgeable publican, has featured in the Guide for over 15 years. This is a traditional Victorian two-bar pub with a pool table in the small rear bar and a dartboard in the main bar, which is heated by an open fire in the winter months. A changing range of local, regional and nationally sourced beers and ciders is served via handpumps.
🌀❀&⇌(Town)♣●🛢🚪🐾🛜

Fat Cat Ⓛ

65 Butt Road, CO3 3BZ (head away from the city centre, past the police station, pub is on right)
☎ (01206) 577990 ⊕ fatcatcolchester.co.uk
6 changing beers (sourced nationally) Ⓖ
A popular single-bar, split-level establishment, just outside of the city centre, with an open fire and the city's smallest beer garden. A variety of ales are sold on gravity from the central tap room, with a selection of Belgian beers also available. A recent refurbishment has given the pub an upstairs area and balcony. Sunday roasts are available, along with a variety of food during the week.
🌀❀◑&⇌(Town)♣🚪🐾🛜♫

Magnet

134 North Station Road, CO1 1UZ
☎ 07707 399131 ⊕ themagnetpub.co.uk
3 changing beers (sourced nationally) Ⓗ
Independent micropub on the site of the old Norfolk pub, close to Colchester (North) station. Its name honours the achievements of Colchester-born William Gilberd. Three changing ales are on offer with a selection of interesting craft beers, ciders and locally-produced spirits. The pub has a relaxed atmosphere and a westerly-facing suntrap courtyard garden. 🌀❀⇌♣●P🚪🐾🛜

New Inn Ⓛ

36 Chapel Street South, CO2 7AX
☎ (01206) 522412 ⊕ theoldnewinnpub.co.uk
4 changing beers (sourced regionally) Ⓗ
With a quiet, comfortable saloon bar and an open public bar featuring music, TV sports, and friendly conversation, this is a venue of two halves. Both bars have log burners for the winter and the garden comes to life in the summer. A traditional roast is served on a Sunday with food also available Tuesday to Saturday. A function room for groups is available.
🌀❀◑&⇌(Town)♣●P🚪(S6,S7)🐾🛜

Odd One Out Ⓛ

28 Mersea Road, CO2 7ET
☎ 07976 985083
Colchester Metropolis, Number One; 5 changing beers (sourced nationally) Ⓗ
This multi-award-winning pub features two bars and a back room for customers to enjoy and has been identified by CAMRA as having a regionally important historic pub interior. It offers at least two beers from Colchester brewery and a range of changing guest ales over seven handpumps, as well as a varied selection of ciders. There is a large, landscaped rear garden allowing

for a quiet pint outdoors. Check Facebook for details of regular evening quizzes, impromptu music sessions and barbecues. Q🌀❀⇌(Town)●🚪(8,S8)🐾🛜♫

Purple Dog Ⓛ ✅

42 Eld Lane, CO1 1LS
☎ (01206) 564995 ⊕ purpledogs.touchtakeaway.net/menu
Adnams Ghost Ship; Fuller's London Pride; 4 changing beers (sourced regionally) Ⓗ
Corner pub in the town centre with an outdoor drinking area and wooden beams. One of the oldest pubs in Colchester, it dates back to 1647. Six handpumps provide mainly regional beers alongside the usual town-centre pub offerings. An extensive menu, which is complemented by changing special dishes, is available daily. The pub hosts regular music events (DJs with occasional bands) and a monthly quiz night.
🌀❀◑⇌(Town)🚪🛜

Three Wise Monkeys Ⓛ

60 High Street, CO1 1DN
☎ (01206) 543014 ⊕ threewisemonkeyscolchester.com
Colchester Metropolis, Number One; Greene King Yardbird; house beer (by Greene King); 1 changing beer (sourced nationally) Ⓗ
Centrally-located, multi-level pub on the High Street, near Colchester Castle. The ground floor houses a spacious bar area, serving a range of local and national beers (including from the neighbouring brewery) via both handpump and keg lines. The venue hosts regular beer festivals and quiz nights. Meals are served daily with a focus on smokehouse style food. Live music and club nights regularly take place on the top floor. There is also a basement bar with a speakeasy vibe.
❀◑&⇌(Town)🚪🐾🛜♫

Victoria Inn Ⓛ

10 North Station Road, CO1 1RB
☎ (01206) 514510 ⊕ victoriainncolchester.co.uk
Colchester Metropolis; 5 changing beers (sourced nationally) Ⓗ
Multi-award-winning pub and current local CAMRA Cider Pub of the Year. It has three distinct seating areas, including a lively rear bar and a traditional pub area with low tables and a fire in winter. Two regular beers from Colchester brewery and three other constantly-changing beers sourced nationally are available. Six to nine real ciders are on most of the time. A pleasant courtyard style area is a suntrap in summer. Live music is played every other Sunday evening. ❀⇌♣●🚪🐾🛜♫

Coopersale

Garnon Bushes ✅

13 Coopersale Common, CM16 7QS
☎ (01992) 560211 ⊕ garnonbushespub.com
Courage Best Bitter; Timothy Taylor Landlord; 1 changing beer (sourced nationally) Ⓗ
Situated on the edge of Epping Forest and on the Essex Way, the pub dates back to the 17th Century and has flagged floors and low beams. It was fully refurbished in 2013 and redecorated during lockdown. The menu is varied and there is pleasant outdoor seating. The Mozzino Scooter Club meets here and there is space for a pre-booked overnight stop with a campervan.
🌀❀◑●P🚪🐾

Theydon Oak Ⓛ

9 Coopersale Street, CM16 7QJ (1 mile S of Coopersale, on the left at a jct)
☎ (01992) 572618 ⊕ thetheydonoak.co.uk
Fuller's London Pride; 4 changing beers (sourced regionally) Ⓗ

Located on the outskirts of Epping, this quaint pub has an open fire, comfortable seating and plenty of room to relax. The outside patio area has been constructed with easy access from the bar and is ideal for smoking customers, whilst inside tasty food is served in the seated area and good beer at the bar.
Q🐴❀◐◑♣P🚌(381) 📶♫

Danbury

Cricketers Arms

Penny Royal Road, CM3 4ED
☎ (01245) 222022 🌐 cricketersarmsdanbury.com
Shepherd Neame Whitstable Bay Pale Ale, Spitfire, Bishops Finger; 1 changing beer (sourced nationally; often Shepherd Neame) [H]
This 400-year-old building has been a pub for about 200 years. It has had a modern refurbishment, with a public bar, main bar, lounge and dining room, and a function room available. A beer festival is held each year in July, and there are monthly quiz nights. Close to National Trust's Danbury Common and Danbury Country Park, it is popular with ramblers and cyclists. Towels and bar snacks are available for dogs. Q🐴❀◐◑♿♣P🚌(336,31)🐾📶♫

Debden

Plough [L]

High Street, CB11 3LE
☎ (01799) 541899 🌐 theploughatdebden.co.uk
3 changing beers (sourced regionally) [H]
The sole remaining village pub, it has a restaurant and garden and has been revitalised by a young, energetic couple. It offers a warm and friendly welcome. An interesting and varied range of local beers is available alongside an extensive food menu. The pub is an important social centre for this village and the surrounding area, and a good base for walkers and cyclists. A monthly quiz night is normally held on the third Wednesday. Q🐴❀◐◑P🚌(6,313)♫

Duton Hill

Three Horseshoes [L]

CM6 2DX (1 mile W of B184) TL606268
☎ (01371) 870681 🌐 the-shoes.co.uk
Mighty Oak Maldon Gold; 2 changing beers (sourced nationally) [H]
Outstanding village local with a garden, wildlife pond and terrace overlooking the Chelmer Valley and farmland. The landlord often hosts a weekend of open-air theatre in July. A millennium beacon in the garden, breweriana and a remarkable collection of Butlins memorabilia are features. A beer festival is usually held on the late spring bank holiday in the Duton Hill Den. Look for the pub sign depicting a famous painting, Our Blacksmith, by former local resident Sir George Clausen. Local and parish newspapers are available.
🐴❀♿♣P🚌(313) 🐾

Epping

Forest Gate Inn [L]

111 Bell Common, CM16 4DZ (turn off the main B1393 road opp the Bell Hotel)
☎ (01992) 572312 🌐 forestgateinnepping.co.uk
Adnams Southwold Bitter, Broadside; Bishop Nick Ridley's Rite [H]; 1 changing beer [H]/[G]
On the edge of Epping Forest, the pub is in a 17th-century building, with low ceilings and flagstone floors, run by the same family for 50 years. It is popular with locals, walkers and their dogs. Hot pub meals and soups are available in the bar, as well as in Haywards Restaurant next door, which has a B&B. There is a large grassed seating area. It is about a mile's walk from the town centre and its London Underground station.
Q🐴❀🛏◐◑P🚌🐾📶

Finchingfield

Finchingfield Lion 🏆 [L]

6 Church Hill, CM7 4NN (on B1053, opp guildhall)
☎ (01371) 810400 🌐 thefinchingfieldlion.co.uk
3 changing beers (sourced regionally) [H]
A 15th-century coaching inn, just up the hill from the pond of this famously picturesque village. A friendly local with a warm atmosphere, it has a heavily-beamed bar area with an open fire, and a separate restaurant and function room. There is also a garden for better weather. Popular with cyclists, walkers and locals; families are also welcome. There are normally four beers on from different local breweries including Mauldons, Green Jack, and Wibblers. The food menu features only pizzas with old favourites and some interesting variations. Local CAMRA Pub of the Year 2023. Q🐴❀◐◑♣P🚌🐾📶♫

Fobbing

White Lion ✔

1 Lion Hill, SS17 9JR (nr B1420)
☎ (01375) 673281 🌐 thewhitelionfobbing.co.uk
Greene King IPA; St Austell Tribute; Sharp's Doom Bar; Wadworth 6X [H]
Attractive hilltop pub in a 15th-century building that was originally used as a chandlery, making sails for ships that used the nearby wharf. It was licensed to sell alcohol in 1605. This traditional village local has home-cooked food and a large beer garden which includes a small bar. The famous author Daniel Defoe and Peasants' Revolt leader Jack Straw reputedly frequented the pub.
❀◐P🚌(11,374) 📶

Grays

Theobald Arms

Kings Walk, RM17 6HR (6-8 mins' walk down High St from Grays rail and bus stations)
☎ (01375) 372253
4 changing beers (sourced nationally) [H]
Genuine, traditional pub with a public bar that has an unusual hexagonal pool table. The changing selection of four guest beers features local independent breweries, and a range of British bottled beers is also stocked. Lunchtime meals are served Monday to Friday. There are old stables and an enclosed patio at the rear. Darts and cards are played. Local CAMRA Pub of the Year 2022.
❀◐♿≠♣P🚌

Wharf

Wharf Road South, RM17 6SZ (S of A126)
TQ6085077578
☎ (01375) 374633 🌐 thewharfgrays.co.uk
Adnams Ghost Ship; Sharp's Doom Bar; 3 changing beers (sourced regionally) [H]
Reopened in 2021 under new ownership after renovation, this Grade II-listed, wood-panelled old riverside pub is below the River Thames wall in new housing development. Up to 3 changing beers may be available. Hot food is served every day, including a Sunday carvery. There is a quiz on Monday from 8pm, karaoke on Tuesday, Wednesday board games and card games, a Friday DJ or live music and Saturday open mic. The first Sunday of the month is bingo.
🐴❀◐◑♿P🚌🐾📶♫

Great Baddow

Chelmsford Brew Co Taproom
Brewery Fields, Church Street, CM2 7LE
☎ (01245) 476267 ⊕ chelmsfordbrewco.co.uk
3 changing beers (sourced locally; often Chelmsford) ℍ
Located on a small industrial estate in Great Baddow, south of the city. The Tap Room is part of the brewery, just behind the brewery shop, with comfortable seating and several benches to relax on. The seating layout lends itself to good conversation and a pleasant atmosphere. A selection of the brewery's beers is always available and an occasional guest in cask. Q❧☞♠P🚪(C7,31)🎵

Great Bardfield

Bell Inn 𝕃
Dunmow Road, CM7 4SA
☎ 07506 661989
1 changing beer (often Bishop Nick) ℍ
A friendly local with a warm welcome. It has a beamed bar and restaurant area, with an open fire and a separate public bar with TV and darts. There's a pool table, and an outside patio area. Good-value, locally sourced food is available. It is linked to the Great Bardfield artists, and is a refreshment stop on the Dunwich Dynamo cycle trip. Closing time may vary; if the outside lights are on, then the pub is open. ❧❀◗♣🚪❀🎵

Great Bromley

Cross Inn
Ardleigh Road, CO7 7TL
☎ (01206) 621772 ⊕ greatbromleycross.pub
2 changing beers (sourced nationally) ℍ
A remote country inn, which is an absolute gem, and well worth a visit, this pub was saved by the community in 2016 after much campaigning and fundraising. It now also hosts the Post Office, coffee shop and library. It was formerly the home of Frank Goddard, a British heavyweight boxing champion. Recently refurbished throughout and the toilets extended, with disabled access by radar key 24 hours per day. Hours vary, so check before travelling. ❀&♠P🚪❀🎵

Great Clacton

Ship ✅
2 Valley Road, CO15 4AR (on B1027)
☎ (01255) 475889
St Austell Proper Job; Timothy Taylor Landlord; 1 changing beer (sourced nationally) ℍ
Returning to the Guide after a few years' absence with a new family at the helm, this local pub is situated in the oldest building in Great Clacton after St John's church. The building dates back to the 16th century, becoming an alehouse in about 1709, and tales of smugglers' tunnels are numerous. Popular with diners, with about half of the pub used for dining, those only visiting for a drink are made just as welcome. The large garden at the rear includes a secure children's play area. ❧❀◗&P🚪❀🎵

Great Dunmow

Angel & Harp 𝕃
Church End, CM6 2AD (on B1057)
☎ (01371) 859259 ⊕ angelandharp.co.uk
Nethergate Augustinian Ale; 2 changing beers (sourced regionally) ℍ
A refurbished pub and restaurant with a substantial garden area and a patio. The pub runs occasional beer festivals, usually at Easter and in September. Local ales regularly feature as guest beers. This pub is on the north-east side of Great Dunmow and accommodates families and large parties, although the drinking area around the bar is small. Q❧❀◗&P❀🎵

Great Holland

Ship Inn
Rectory Road, CO13 0JP
☎ (01255) 679262 ⊕ shipinngreatholland.co.uk
Greene King Abbot; 2 changing beers (sourced regionally) ℍ
Hidden away in the long-ago-bypassed heart of the old village of Great Holland, this pub was saved by the community purchasing it, since its closure by previous owners during the pandemic. Food has recently been introduced and they have hopes of introducing a community shop in part of the premises. Beers are well-kept and many events are held which are popular and well supported. Various local footpaths allow pleasant round trip walks to the seafront and back. There is a car park to rear. ❧❀◗♣P🚪❀🎵

Great Oakley

Maybush Inn 𝕃
Farm Road, CO12 5AL (nr B1414)
☎ (01255) 880123 ⊕ maybushinn.co.uk
Courage Directors; house beer (by Eagle); 1 changing beer (sourced nationally) ℍ
Since being saved by its locals in 2016, this community-owned pub has kept its ales in excellent condition and was local CAMRA Pub of the Year 2022. A quiet beer garden to the rear is a great location in summer. Various activities such as quizzes, bingo, crib and music every week are enjoyed and supported by the community. A beer festival to mark the anniversary of the pub opening is held annually. An extremely welcoming and friendly village local. Q❧❀♣♠🚪❀🎵

Great Waltham

Rose & Crown 𝕃
Minnows End, Chelmsford Road, CM3 1AG
☎ (01245) 360359 ⊕ roseandcrowngreatwaltham.co.uk
Bishop Nick 1555; Greene King IPA; 1 changing beer (sourced nationally) ℍ
A rural pub with a traditional bar, a separate snug seating 10, and a small function room The Old Office. The 22-seat restaurant serves home cooking, focusing on local produce, with a discount on food for those with NHS ID. There is a patio area and a new outside decking area. Jazz nights are hosted on the 4th Wednesday of each month and an open mic night on the 3rd Monday. Q❧◗P🚪(70,C1)❀🎵

Halstead

Courtyard Tap 𝕃
24 Trinity Street, CO9 1JA (on A131)
☎ 07713 433131
3 changing beers (sourced locally)
Halstead's first micropub was previously a shop in the town centre. It comprises two rooms with a garden which is a suntrap in summer. As the Gosfield brewery tap, it specialises in its own beers, offered on a changing basis, served direct from cask and in bottles, as well as regular guests and two ciders. With a lively and enthusiastic staff, it attracts a wide range of customers. Q❧❀♠🚪❀🎵

Dog Inn [L]

37 Hedingham Road, CO9 2DB (on A1124)
☎ (01787) 477774
5 changing beers (sourced nationally) [H]
Welcoming, traditional local pub with two bars, close to the town centre. The public bar has a TV with sports and the comfortable saloon has a real fire. Five changing beers are on tap, often from local microbreweries. A large beer garden at the rear is perfect for the summer. The pub has regular live music. En-suite B&B rooms are also available. 🐴❀🛏♣P🚌(88,89)🐾📶♫

White Hart Inn [L]

15 High Street, CO9 2AA (on A131)
☎ (01787) 475657 🌐 whitehartinnhalstead.co.uk
White Hart Halstead Bitter, Golden Hart; 2 changing beers (sourced nationally) [H]
The White Hart, in the centre of the town, is one of the oldest coaching inns in Essex, with parts dating back to the 13th century. It has its own brewery and gin distillery in the old stables at the rear of the premises; the distillery produces London Dry and Hop Gins. Ales sold include those from its own brewery as well as local and national beers. Comfortable en-suite bedrooms and traditional home-cooked food, including Sunday roasts are also on offer. 🐴❀🛏◐◑P🚌🐾📶

Harwich

New Bell Inn [L]

Outpart Eastward, CO12 3EN
☎ (01255) 503545 🌐 thenewbell.co.uk
Greene King IPA; Mighty Oak Oscar Wilde; 2 changing beers (sourced regionally) [H]
There is a hint to its history of this 18th-century pub before you enter, with a blue plaque marking the nearby burning of a martyr. A regular mild from Mighty Oak, which is much-loved by the locals, is complemented by a changing guest real ale and cider line-up. The pub has always been a community favourite, and many local groups meet here. There is a secret walled garden for sunny weekends and summer evenings, and a small car park opposite. Q🐴❀◐🚆(Town)♣●P🚌🐾📶♫

Hazel End

Three Horseshoes

CM23 1HB
☎ (01279) 813429 🌐 threehorseshoeshazelend.co.uk
Adnams Southwold Bitter; Sharp's Doom Bar; 1 changing beer (sourced nationally) [H]
A friendly pub opposite the cricket green. It has been completely renovated – a large extension has created more space to both eat and drink in comfort. Food includes an impressive fish menu. This is a good example of a once run-down premises transformed into a thriving, successful establishment. It has low ceilings, wooden beams and two wood-burning stoves. ❀◐◑▲P🐾

Helions Bumpstead

Three Horseshoes

Water Lane, CB9 7AL
☎ (01440) 730088 🌐 threehorseshoeshelions.co.uk
Adnams Southwold Bitter; 3 changing beers (sourced regionally) [H]
Village pub brought back to life by the Helions Bumpstead Community Benefit Society and reopened in 2021, having been closed for four years. Now managed by experienced local licensees, the pub is run on community principles with community events hosted. A mobile post office, refill provisions van, and a fruit and veg stall visits the car park on Thursday mornings. The pub is gaining a reputation for its restaurant. Runner-up in CAMRA's National Pub Saving Award in 2022. Q🐴❀◐◑♿♣P🚌(59)🐾

High Roding

Black Lion [L]

3 The Street, CM6 1NT (on the B184 Dunmow to Ongar road)
☎ (01371) 872847 🌐 theblacklionhighroding.co.uk
4 changing beers (sourced locally; often Colchester, New River) [H]/[G]
A striking, half-timbered, 14th-century building that was a coaching inn on the London-Norwich road, it has low ceilings and oak beams and a huge fire in the winter. The restaurant serves good locally-sourced food, with a popular roast on Sundays. There is a TV in the end bar, usually showing rugby on Saturdays. There is a pleasant courtyard garden and the pub runs tasting evenings throughout the year. Q🐴❀◐◑♿P🚌(17,18)🐾

Hockley

White Hart

274 Main Road, SS5 4NS (by B1013)
☎ (01702) 203438 🌐 whitehartockley.co.uk
3 changing beers (sourced nationally) [H]
Friendly village pub with a modern comfortable interior. A popular quiz night is held on the first Monday of the month. This old coaching inn has been integral to village life for over 200 years. It still retains its original sash windows, central open fire and horse brasses. Three changing guest ales are served, and occasional beer festivals are held in the function room. There is a huge rear garden with seating and a patio area, plus picnic tables at the front. 🐴❀◑♿🚆♣P🚌(7,8)📶

Horndon-on-the-Hill

Bell Inn

High Road, SS17 8LD (near centre of village, almost opp the Woolmarket and Orsett Rd)
☎ (01375) 642463 🌐 bell-inn.co.uk
Crouch Vale Brewers Gold; 3 changing beers (sourced nationally) [H]
Popular 15th-century coaching inn, where beamed bars feature wood panelling and carvings, run by the same family since 1938. Note the hot cross bun collection; a bun has been added every Good Friday for more than 100 years. One regular beer is on the bar, plus three guests, including ales from Essex breweries. The award-winning restaurant is open daily (booking advisable). Accommodation is available in 26 bedrooms.
Q🐴❀🛏◐◑♿P🚌(11)🐾📶

Kirby-le-Soken

Ship

35 Walton Road, CO13 0DT (on B1034)
☎ (01255) 679149 🌐 theshipkirbylesoken.co.uk
Adnams Southwold Bitter, Ghost Ship, Broadside; 3 changing beers (sourced nationally) [H]
Popular with drinkers and diners alike, this free house has a large beer garden to the rear, that contains a marquee used for various events, including an annual beer festival. An outside seating area to the front is much used in fine weather. Trays of three third-pints of cider are available. A wide selection of food is offered in the restaurant. Well-behaved dogs are welcome. Local CAMRA Pub of the Year 2021 and local CAMRA Cider Pub of the Year 2017, 2018 and 2023. Q🐴❀◐◑♣●P🚌🐾📶

Lamarsh

Lamarsh Lion
Bures Road, CO8 5EP (1¼ miles NW of Bures) TL892355
☎ (01787) 227007 ⏺ lamarshlion.co.uk
Woodforde's Wherry; 3 changing beers (sourced nationally) Ⓗ
This wonderfully restored community pub dates from the 14th century and continues to delight. Boasting both Constable and Gainsborough as former customers, whose paintings portrayed the outstanding views of the Stour Valley, it has gained the nickname The Painters' Pub. Close to the Stour Valley Footpath, it serves a daily food menu. Social events, including music, are hosted in its renovated interior. Q❄☆❀◑♿▲♣P❀🌫♪

Langley Lower Green

Bull
Park Lane, CB11 4SB TL437345
☎ (01279) 777307 ⏺ thebullpub.co.uk
Adnams Southwold Bitter; Bishop Nick Heresy; 2 changing beers (sourced regionally) Ⓗ
Classic Victorian village local with original cast-iron lattice windows, in a tiny isolated hamlet close to both Hertfordshire and Cambridgeshire. The pub has a loyal band of local regulars. There is an aquarium in the lounge bar. Occasional quiz nights are held. An annual beer festival takes place in September. Parties can pre-book food outside of normal service times, and regular food vans are available at weekends. ❄☆❀♣P❀🌫♪

Leigh-on-Sea

Legra Tap & Kitchen
1517 London Road, SS9 2SF (on A13)
☎ (01702) 478954 ⏺ legratapandkitchen.co.uk
Leigh on Sea Legra Pale; 3 changing beers (sourced nationally; often Leigh on Sea) Ⓗ
A joint venture between Leigh on Sea brewery and Black's Kitchen. This is a smart bar with a focus on beers from Leigh on Sea and other independent breweries. The food offering is fresh Asian-inspired street food, with roasts on Sunday. It is on bus routes and is walkable from Leigh-on-Sea Station. There is no customer parking (except for a disabled space, by prior arrangement). Both keg and cask beers are available with up to four real ales on handpump, 12 keg lines and three ciders. Popular quiz nights and other events are held. ❄☆❀◑●🚩(1,27)❀🌫

Leigh On Sea Brewery Tap Ⓛ
35 Progress Road, SS9 5PR (on Progress Rd Industrial Estate, N of the A127; behind an industrial unit reached by a signposted path to the right of the building)
☎ (01702) 817255 ⏺ leighonseabrewery.co.uk
8 changing beers (sourced locally; often Leigh on Sea) Ⓗ
A wide range of Leigh on Sea brewery beers are served in the taproom, through six cask and two KeyKeg lines plus two handpumps, including one-off specials brewed on the pilot kit. The decor features exposed brickwork, tall tables and a bar top of cockleshells. Occasional sporting events are shown on the TV, including international rugby. Regular music events and food pop-ups take place. Open Thursday to Saturday, and Sunday in the summer. Hours can change, so check their website or social media. ☆●🚩(20,9)❀🌫♪

Mayflower Ⓛ
5-6 High Street, Old Leigh, SS9 2EN (at far end of Old Leigh from railway station, behind the chip shop)
☎ (01702) 478535 ⏺ mayfloweroldleigh.com

Crouch Vale Brewers Gold; George's Cockleboats; St Austell Proper Job; 3 changing beers (sourced regionally) Ⓗ
Popular pub serving six real ales and one cider, most of which are locally brewed. One handpump is dedicated to a changing dark beer. The outdoor seating area has views across the Thames Estuary. Meals are served at lunchtime all week and in the evening Friday to Sunday – mainly fish & chips which are cooked in the adjoining restaurant. One wall lists the names of all who sailed on the Mayflower. Dogs and children are welcome. ❄☆◑♿➔P🚩(26)❀🌫

Little Thurrock

Traitors' Gate Ⓛ
40-42 Broadway, RM17 6EW (on A126)
☎ (01375) 372628 ⏺ traitorsgatepub.wordpress.com
Greene King Abbot; 3 changing beers (sourced regionally) Ⓗ
This pub has reverted to being run directly by the owner and has an established reputation for live bands on Fridays. The quieter, traditional end of the pub is to the right of the front bar. A covered garden/outdoor drinking area is accessible through the pub. Five handpumps are available, with four dispensing a varied selection of regional guest beers. The pub is not easy to find, due to the lack of external signage. ❄☆♿♣🚩(66)❀♪

Little Totham

Swan
School Road, CM9 8LB TL889117
☎ (01621) 331713 ⏺ theswanlittletotham.com
Crouch Vale Brewers Gold; Mighty Oak Captain Bob; St Austell Tribute; 3 changing beers (sourced regionally; often Adnams, Woodforde's) Ⓖ
A cosy three-roomed, cottage-style pub, dating from the 1600s and surrounded by beautiful countryside. It features a separate restaurant area with locally-sourced food available, and a snug. There is a good log fire in the inglenook fireplace in winter. Beers are served direct from the cask from the chilled cellar. It has child and dog-friendly enclosed front and large rear gardens. An annual beer festival is held over two weeks in June ending on Father's Day. Supporting the community, quiz nights raise funds for charity. Q❄☆❀◑♿▲♣P❀🌫♪

Littley Green

Compasses Ⓛ
CM3 1BU TL699172
☎ (01245) 362308 ⏺ compasseslittleygreen.co.uk
Bishop Nick Ridley's Rite; 5 changing beers Ⓖ
Formerly the Ridley's brewery tap, this is a picturesque Victorian country pub in a quiet hamlet. A wood-panelled bar has benches around the walls and a tiled floor. Beers are drawn directly from casks. It has a changing range of boxed cider from popular producers, not all real, and regular beer festivals are held throughout the year. Renowned filled huffers (giant baps) are available lunchtimes and evenings, plus other traditional dishes. There are seats and tables outside and in the large gardens. Accommodation comprises five high-quality rooms. Local and Essex CAMRA Cider Pub of the Year 2022 and 2023. Q❄☆❀◑●♣P🏠❀🌫

Loughton

Victoria Tavern ✓
165 Smarts Lane, IG10 4BP
☎ (020) 8508 1779 ⏺ thevictoriatavern.co.uk

Adnams Southwold Bitter; Sharp's Doom Bar; Timothy Taylor Landlord; 1 changing beer (sourced regionally) Ⓗ

This is an old-fashioned traditional pub that prides itself on real ale and inclusive conversation. It lies between Loughton and Epping Forest and is a 10 minute walk from Loughton tube station. It has a pleasant gated garden and the pub is used by locals and walkers; well-behaved dogs are welcome. It serves generous portions of fresh seasonal food and has no TV, just good ale, good food and good company. Q ⇄ ✿ ❁ ◑ P ⌹ 🛜

Maldon

Carpenters Arms

33 Gate Street, CM9 5QF

☎ (01621) 859896

Adnams Southwold Bitter; Crouch Vale Yakima Gold; Mighty Oak Oscar Wilde; 3 changing beers (sourced nationally) Ⓗ

A back-street gem at the top end of this historic town, this Gray's community pub with ancient low wooden beams offers a welcoming atmosphere. A pub since 1849, with parts dating to 1349, it was once the Gray's Maldon brewery tap. A wide range of ales and ciders are on offer, and an annual beer and cider festival is held. The pub also supports thriving darts and dominoes teams. Q ⇄ ✿ ❁ ♣ ◑ P ⌹ ❀ 🛜 ♪

Mighty Oak Tap Room

10 High Street, CM9 5PJ

☎ (01621) 853892 ⊕ micropubmaldon.uk

Mighty Oak Oscar Wilde, Maldon Gold, Kings, Captain Bob; 2 changing beers (sourced locally) Ⓖ

A cosy, welcoming micropub housed in 16th-century building serving Mighty Oak's range of award-winning beers from a chilled cellar behind the bar. The seating arrangements and welcome lack of piped music, TVs or fruit machines encourages conversation. An upstairs room has oak beams and comfy seating for a dozen or so people and is available for private functions/meetings. Acoustic live music sessions are held most Sundays. Q ♣ ◑ ⌹ ❀ 🛜 ♪

Queen Victoria

Spital Road, CM9 6ED

☎ (01621) 852923 ⊕ queenvictoriamaldon.co.uk

Adnams Southwold Bitter; Greene King Abbot; Mighty Oak Captain Bob; Red Fox Pucks; 3 changing beers (sourced nationally; often Elgood's, Wibblers) Ⓗ

A warm and friendly welcome awaits everyone to this Gray's pub. Extensive menus offer locally sourced, home-cooked meals, with vegetarian and vegan options; booking is recommended. Families are welcome throughout, with dogs permitted in the beer garden and public bar. Seasonal events are celebrated, together with beer festivals. Darts, dominoes and bar skittles are played. ⇄ ✿ ◑ ❁ ♣ ◑ P ⌹ (5,31A) ❀ 🛜

Rose & Crown ✅

109 High Street, CM9 5EP

☎ (01621) 852255

Greene King Abbot; Ruddles Best Bitter; Sharp's Doom Bar; 3 changing beers (sourced nationally) Ⓗ

Wetherspoon revitalised this historic 16th-century high street pub in 2015, adding an attractive airy extension to the rear housing a long marble bar with ample seating and an outside courtyard. Food is served all day. Children accompanied by an adult are welcome until 9pm. Sparklers are used on all beers. Q ⇄ ✿ ◑ ⌹ 🛜

Manningtree

Red Lion

42 South Street, CO11 1BG

☎ (01206) 391880 ⊕ redlionmanningtree.co.uk

Adnams Southwold Bitter; 2 changing beers (sourced regionally; often Colchester, Mighty Oak, Woodforde's) Ⓗ

This historic pub traces its origins back to 1603, but has seen many changes. More recently these have included improving the customer space available, modernisation of the toilets, and the addition of a small function room, all while maintaining the quality of their ales. Larger events such as Oktoberfest and live music take place in the large function room upstairs. The pub has a pizza restaurant to the rear, and is takeaway friendly. ⇄ ✿ ♣ ◑ ⌹ ❀ 🛜

Monk Street

Farmhouse Inn Ⓛ

Thaxted, CM6 2NR (off B184, 2 miles S of Thaxted)

TL614288

☎ (01371) 830864 ⊕ farmhouseinn.org

Greene King IPA; 2 changing beers (sourced locally) Ⓗ

Built in the 16th century, this former Dunmow brewery establishment has been enlarged to incorporate a restaurant and accommodation; the bar is in the original part of the building. The quiet hamlet here overlooks the Chelmer Valley, two miles from historic Thaxted. A disused well in the garden supplied Monk Street with water during World War II. There is a rear patio, front garden and a top field. ⇄ ✿ ◑◑ P ⌹ (313) ❀ 🛜 ♪

Newport

Coach & Horses ✅

Cambridge Road, CB11 3TR (on B1383)

☎ (01799) 540292

Adnams Southwold Bitter; Fuller's London Pride; 1 changing beer (sourced nationally) Ⓗ

An ex-coaching inn on the main road through Newport, on the north side of the village. This modernised pub has exposed beams and a welcoming and warm atmosphere. The pub can be used for functions and has an excellent kitchen serving great locally sourced food, featuring both traditional British and continental dishes. There's a large garden, suitable for families, with ample seating. Q ⇄ ✿ ◑ P ⌹ ❀ 🛜

Orsett Heath

Fox ✅

176-178 Heath Road, RM16 3AP (near A1013)

☎ (01375) 373861 ⊕ foxorsett.co.uk

Dartmoor Jail Ale; Greene King Abbot; 1 changing beer (sourced nationally) Ⓗ

Two-bar country pub with real fires, located between Orsett and Grays, with a large garden and outdoor drinking area. Two regular and one guest real ale, and good-value lunches are served. Popular with locals and visitors alike, regular charity fundraising events include quizzes and meal evenings, alongside live music at weekends. Breakfast is served on Saturday from 9.30am. ✿ ◑ ♣ P ⌹ (100,200) ❀ 🛜 ♪

Rayleigh

Crafty Casks

33 Eastwood Road, SS6 7JD

☎ (01268) 779516

4 changing beers (sourced locally) Ⓗ
A modern micropub with a constantly-rotating lineup of real ale – usually from local breweries – craft beer, wine, spirits, cider, cocktails and Prosecco. The bar has up to 25 taps in use, with four real ales, up to eight ciders and 13 keg beers – with Tiny Rebel beers featured as well as a strong dark beer. Regular events include live music. The pub is located just off Rayleigh High Street. ⇌☐(1,9)♫

Rowhedge

Olde Albion 🍷
High Street, CO5 7ES
☎ (01206) 728972
4 changing beers (sourced nationally) Ⓗ
The local CAMRA Pub of the Year for both 2022 and 2023. A free house on the waterfront, playing a substantial role in local village life. The pub serves an interesting range of changing ales, sourced nationally, from various breweries. There is usually a cheese board on Sundays, and a warming fire in cold weather. In summer there are tables and chairs on the greensward overlooking the River Colne. Occasional live music events are also hosted by the pub. ❀♣☐(S9)❀♠♫

Roydon

New Inn ✪
90 High Street, CM19 5EE
☎ (01279) 792225 ⊕ thenewinnroydon.co.uk
Adnams Broadside; Greene King IPA; Sharp's Doom Bar; 1 changing beer (sourced nationally) Ⓗ
The New Inn was built in the 18th century in the charming village of Roydon and retains many period features. It is a short walk from the station and the River Stort Navigation and welcomes walkers and boaters as well as a local clientele. It was nominated for 2020 Parliamentary Pub of the Year by the local MP. There is a large garden, with children's play area, and a beer festival each September. Barbecues are hosted on fine Friday evenings and a seniors' lunch on Wednesday. ❀◖▶⇌P❀♠♫

Saffron Walden

King's Arms Ⓛ
10 Market Hill, CB10 1HQ
☎ (01799) 522768 ⊕ thekingsarmssaffronwalden.co.uk
Adnams Southwold Bitter; Otter Bitter; Timothy Taylor Landlord; 2 changing beers (sourced nationally) Ⓗ
Venerable wooden-beamed, multi-roomed pub, just off the market square (market days are Tuesday and Saturday). It has welcoming log fires in cold weather and a pleasant patio for alfresco dining and drinking. A mild or dark beer is sometimes available in winter. There is live music at weekends and a monthly quiz. Food is served at lunchtimes. Q☎❀◖☐❀♠♫

Railway Arms Ⓛ ✪
Station Road, CB11 3HQ (300yds SE of war memorial)
☎ (01799) 619660 ⊕ railwayarms.co.uk
House beer (by Pumphouse Community); 5 changing beers (sourced regionally) Ⓗ
Victorian street-corner local, opposite the former Saffron Walden railway station, which closed in 1964 as part of the Beeching cuts. Community-owned, there has been significant renovation inside and out, much of it undertaken by volunteers. There is plenty of outside seating and tables in the garden and courtyard. Completely free of tie, it serves a range of beer styles exclusively from local breweries, a dark ale, craft beers

and a number of real ciders. Runner-up in CAMRA's National Pub Saving Award in 2021. Community defibrillator for public use on the outside wall. ☎❀♿◖🅿☐❀♠♫

South Benfleet

South Benfleet Social Club Ⓛ
8 Vicarage Hill, SS7 1PB (on jct with B1006 High Rd)
☎ (01268) 206159 ⊕ southbenfleetsocialclub.co.uk
3 changing beers Ⓗ/Ⓖ
A popular social club that is a huge asset to the community. A beer festival is held in May, and a good range of beers and ciders is always served. It is a former CAMRA East Anglia Regional Club of the Year and has been the local CAMRA Club of the Year for 10 years and counting. Games include pool and poker, with quiz nights, sport on TV and live music at weekends all adding to the ambience. CAMRA members and Guide holders are always welcome. ☎❀◖♿⇌(Benfleet)♣🅿☐(21,27)❀♠

South Woodham Ferrers

Tap Room 19
19 Haltwhistle Road, CM3 5ZA
☎ (01245) 322744 ⊕ crouchvale.co.uk/tap-room-19
Crouch Vale Blackwater Mild, Essex Boys Best Bitter, Brewers Gold, Yakima Gold; 2 changing beers (sourced locally; often Crouch Vale) Ⓖ
Tucked away on the town's Western Industrial Estate in front of the Crouch Vale brewery, it is about 10 minutes' walk through side streets from the railway station. Simply furnished, with understated decor, this is a welcome real ale oasis in a town with few other outlets. Beers are served from a taproom visible through windows at the rear of the bar. There is a small outdoor seating area to the front. A stop on the Crouch Valley Rail Ale Trail. Q☎❀♿⇌♣◖🅿☐(36)❀♠

Southend-on-Sea

Black Box Tap
18-19 Aviation Way, SS2 6UN (No.9 bus to Rockall bus stop then a 15-min walk)
☎ 07471 733719 ⊕ blackboxbrewery.co.uk
4 changing beers (sourced locally) Ⓗ
New-build brewery and tap room in Southend Airport Business Park. Five real ales are served on gravity and all have an aircraft theme. Bottled beers are available at the tap room or to take home. Bands often play on Saturday evenings and other events, like a quiz, Sunday BBQs in the spring and summer, and beer festivals are popular. Check social media for opening times. The tap room is also available for hire and functions. ❀🅿

Mawson's Ⓛ
781 Southchurch Road, SS1 2PP (on A13)
☎ (01702) 601781 ⊕ mawsonsmicro.com
George's Wallasea Wench, Cockleboats; 4 changing beers (sourced nationally) Ⓗ
This converted shop was Southend's first micropub and has up to six cask ales, with a least two from the local George's brewery. One real cider, three craft keg beers, one draught German pilsner and two draught ciders – one of which is Rocquette of Guernsey – are also sold. Set in the Southchurch village area, the bar has a large gallery of Laurel and Hardy pictures. Quiet music adds to happy conversation, with occasional live music and quiz nights. ☎♿⇌(East)◖☐☐(2,14)❀♠♫

Olde Trout Tavern

56 London Road, SS1 1NX (opp Sainsbury's, nr A13)
☎ (01702) 337000
House beer (by Wantsum); 2 changing beers (sourced nationally) ⊞

Modern town-centre ale bar close to the High Street and both train and bus stations. It offers three real ales, one of which is a house beer, Trout Ale, and one changing cider. The pub offers a loyalty card scheme. Open mic nights are held every other Thursday night with karaoke on first Saturday of the month. Quiz night is every Sunday night. Occasional beer festivals have been held.
◑➔(Victoria,Central) ♣⊟🎧♪

Southminster

Station Arms 🍸

39 Station Road, CM0 7EW (nr B1021/B1018 jct)
☎ (01621) 772225 🌐 thestationarms.co.uk
Adnams Southwold Bitter; 4 changing beers (sourced regionally; often Colchester, George's, Mighty Oak) ⊞

A traditional Essex weatherboarded pub that has featured in this Guide for over 30 years – testament to the standards of this welcoming and thriving community local. The comfortable bar area, with its open log fire, is decorated with railway and brewery memorabilia. An attractive courtyard is popular in fine weather and a barn with a wood-burning stove provides shelter if required. Live blues and folk music is hosted monthly. Various charity events take place during the year including a conker competition. Local CAMRA Pub of the Year 2023.
Q❀≄♣⊟♪

Wibblers Brewery Taproom & Kitchen ⃝L

Goldsands Road, CM0 7JW
☎ (01621) 772044 🌐 wibblers.co.uk/taproomkitchen
Wibblers Dengie IPA, Beneath The Embers, Crafty Stoat ⊞; **6 changing beers (sourced locally; often Wibblers)** ⊞/Ⓖ

The taproom is attached to a beautiful award-winning, restored medieval tithe barn, housing Wibblers brewery. A dining area for the extensive menu of home-cooked food, using mostly local produce, is in the extension. The bar is simply furnished and, weather permitting, you can sit outside in the countryside. The brewery and taproom host open days and various other events throughout the year, including televised rugby and themed food evenings. Southminster railway station is only five minutes' walk away. Q🐾❀◑♿♣⊖P⊟(31X)🎧➡️

Springfield

Endeavour 🍸 ⃝L

351 Springfield Road, CM2 6AW (on B1137)
☎ (01245) 257717
Mighty Oak Captain Bob; 4 changing beers (sourced nationally) ⊞

Cosy and friendly community pub about 25 minutes' walk (or on a direct bus route) from Chelmsford city centre. It has three separate rooms, with a quiet area on the left as you enter. There is a regularly-changing selection of cask ales, and home-cooked meals are served Thursday to Saturday. The pub hosts mini beer festivals, tap takeovers and regular charity events. Dog friendly, it has a suntrap garden. Local CAMRA Pub of the Year 2023. Q❀◑♣⊖⊟(C8,73)🎧➡️

Stanford-le-Hope

Rising Sun ⃝L ✅

Church Hill, SS17 0EU (opp church and nr A1014)
☎ (01375) 671097
5 changing beers (sourced nationally) ⊞

Much-improved two-bar traditional town pub in the shadow of the church. The five guest beers are mainly from independent breweries, including LocAle beers, and up to three ciders or perries are stocked. Regular monthly live music takes place, and beer festivals are held three times a year in spring, summer and winter, with the summer festival in the large rear garden. A cider festival is also held. The back bar is available for private functions. ❀≄♣♠P⊟🎧➡️♪

Stansted Mountfitchet

Rose & Crown ⃝L

31 Bentfield Green, CM24 8HX (½ mile W of B1383)
TL505256
☎ (01279) 812107 🌐 roseandcrownstansted.co.uk
2 changing beers (sourced regionally) ⊞

Family-run Victorian pub on rural edge of large village, with the welcoming atmosphere of a local. There is an interesting jukebox in the main bar. This free house has been modernised to provide one large bar and a snug at the side. A large variety of gins is stocked. There is a covered outside drinking area and a garden. Home-cooked food is served at weekends, with occasional food trucks. 🐾❀◑P⊟(7,7A)🎧➡️

Stanway

Live & Let Live ⃝L

12 Millers Lane, CO3 0PS (in a small lane, 100m off London Rd)
☎ (01206) 574071 🌐 theliveandletlive.co.uk
4 changing beers (sourced nationally) ⊞

A traditional, welcoming local that continues to delight, with a homely saloon bar and a public bar. The publicans regularly support local breweries and take great pride in the condition and quality of their real ales. The beers are competitively priced, as is the traditional home-cooked food, served most lunchtimes and evenings. The pub is renowned for its beer, sausage and pie festivals. Local CAMRA Town Pub of the Year in 2022.
Q🐾❀◑♣♠P⊟🎧➡️♪

Steeple Bumpstead

Fox & Hounds ⃝L

3 Chapel Street, CB9 7DQ (on B1057)
☎ (01440) 731810 🌐 foxinsteeple.co.uk
Greene King IPA; 4 changing beers (sourced nationally) ⊞

A 17th-century coaching inn in a picturesque village on the Essex/Suffolk border, featuring an open fire in the main bar, a courtyard rear garden and further seating at the front. On Wednesday evening a complimentary cheese board is offered, with reduced-price real ale and wine all evening. Live bands perform and quiz nights take place throughout the year. The outside barn has been converted into a games room.
Q🐾❀♣⊟(18) 🎧➡️♪

Stow Maries

Prince of Wales

Woodham Road, CM3 6SA
☎ (01621) 828971 🌐 prince-stowmaries.net
6 changing beers (sourced nationally) ⊞

This classic weatherboarded pub boasts several characterful drinking areas with open fires and an old bread oven. The extensive garden and courtyards provide plenty of options for outside drinking. Food is available, made with local produce where possible. Many special events are held including Burns Night, a firework display on the last Saturday in October and live music. A free comedy night with top West End acts takes place monthly. Q✤⏰🍴◑♿♣🅿🚲(503)🐾🐕🛜

Thaxted

Maypole ✅
31 Mill End, CM6 2LT (by B184)
☎ (01371) 831599 ● maypolethaxted.com
Eagle IPA; Timothy Taylor Landlord; 3 changing beers (sourced locally) Ⓗ
A warm welcome awaits at this redecorated pub. The current landlords took over in 2020 and are keen to support community activities. Regular musical events and quizzes are held along with occasional beer festivals. Home-cooked food is available every day, except Tuesday. The pub sits back from the main road and there is a rear car park and attractive garden with comfortable outdoor seating. ✤❀◑🅿🚲(313,314)🐾🛜♪

Toppesfield

Green Man Ⓛ
Church Lane, CO9 4DR
☎ (01787) 237418 ● thegreenmantoppesfield.com
2 changing beers (sourced nationally; often Pumphouse Community) Ⓗ
A community-owned local which hosts beer festivals and events throughout the year. It has two pool teams and darts is played in the public bar. PumpHouse Community brewery is next door. This village is the only place in the UK to have a pub, brewery and shop all owned by the community. Meals may need booking, and group pre-booking at lunchtime is possible on weekdays. Closing time depends on whether there are customers, check if intending to arrive late. ✤❀◑◐♿♣🅿🐾🛜♪

Waltham Abbey

Woodbine Inn ♜ Ⓛ ✅
Honey Lane, EN9 3QT
☎ (01992) 713050 ● thewoodbine.co.uk
Mighty Oak Oscar Wilde Ⓖ**; 4 changing beers (sourced locally; often Adnams, New River, Red Fox)** Ⓗ/Ⓖ
Multi award-winning pub in Epping Forest close to junction 26 of the M25. It concentrates on an extensive range of ever-changing local real ales and over 40 small-producer ciders. London Glider cider is produced on site. Food is homemade, with local sausages, ham and steak as specialities. Dogs are welcome in the main bar where there is bar billiards. The Ale Sampling Society and Comedy Club meet monthly. If arriving after mid evening phone ahead to check it will be open. National finalist for CAMRA Cider Pub of the Year 2019 and local Pub of the Year 2023. ✤◑♣◐🅿🚲(66,66A)🐾♪

Westcliff-on-Sea

Mile & a Third ♜
67 Hamlet Court Road, SS0 7EU
☎ (01702) 902120 ● mileandathird.com
2 changing beers (sourced nationally) Ⓖ
Micropub run by two beer managers from the Rochford Beer Festival. Two real ales served on gravity, with three real ciders. Eight keg lines offer beers from breweries like Neon Raptor, Polly's Brew, Verdant and Mikkeller. The

bottleshop has an interesting selection including sours and stouts. Music is a feature and is mainly played on vinyl. A pavement seating area offers additional space and four trees with fairy lights give the interior a quirky look, with hops around one. Local CAMRA Pub of the Year 2020-2023. ✤❀≈(Westcliff)♣◐🚇🚲(1,27)🐾🛜

West Road Tap
2 West Road, SS0 9DA
☎ (01702) 330647 ● westroadtap.com
3 changing beers (sourced nationally) Ⓖ
Near the Palace Theatre in Westcliff, this is a two-level micropub and bottle shop. The main bar, upstairs, serves up to two nationally sourced cask ales, and six KeyKeg beers. The downstairs bar, The Bunker, has six taps and both bars have an extensive fridge selection of craft beer in bottles and cans to drink in or take home. Two real ciders are available in boxes. The beer garden to the front is a suntrap. Children welcome until 7pm. Q✤❀≈(Westcliff)♣🚲(1,27)🐾

White Notley

Cross Keys Ⓛ
1 The Street, CM8 1RQ
☎ (01376) 583297 ● ckwn.co.uk
Adnams Southwold Bitter; 3 changing beers (sourced locally) Ⓗ
Traditional, beamed, Grade II-listed pub, dating from the 1700s, tastefully refurbished inside and out. It has two wooden-floored bars, plus a separate area which is used as a restaurant or occasional function room. A selection of home-cooked food is served, including a pizza menu on Monday from 3-8pm. Some interesting historical artwork and photos adorn the walls, with an intriguing comic history of the village on a frieze in the back corridor. Outside are a large garden and patio area. Q✤❀◑≈🅿🐾🛜♪

Widdington

Fleur de Lys Ⓛ
High Street, CB11 3SG TL538316
☎ (01799) 543280 ● thefleurdelys.co.uk
Timothy Taylor Landlord; Woodforde's Wherry; 2 changing beers (sourced nationally) Ⓗ
A welcoming 400-year-old village local which boasts a large open fireplace, beams and an attractive garden. A bar extension and new toilets were completed in 2021. This was the first pub to be saved from closure by the local branch of CAMRA after the branch's formation. Quality meals are offered with fresh local ingredients. The source of the River Cam and English Heritage site Prior's Hall Barn are both nearby. A range of real ciders is available. ✤❀◑♿♣◐🅿🚲(301)🐾

Witham

Battesford Court Ⓛ ✅
100-102 Newland Street, CM8 1AH
☎ (01376) 504080
Greene King Abbot; Ruddles Best Bitter; Sharp's Doom Bar; 5 changing beers (sourced nationally) Ⓗ
Large Wetherspoon conversion of a former hotel of the same name. The 16th-century building was previously the courthouse of the manor of Battesford. It has distinct areas with wood panelling and oak beams, and there is a family area. Up to five regional beers are served including something local, usually from Bishop Nick or Wibblers. The standard Wetherspoon food offering is available. Close to many bus routes. Q✤❀◑♿🚲🛜

White Hart Hotel ✓

Newland Street, CM8 2AF
☎ (01376) 512245 ⊕ whitehartinwitham.co.uk
Greene King IPA Ⓗ; 4 changing beers (sourced nationally; often Crouch Vale, Mighty Oak, St Austell) Ⓖ
Situated on the main street, this is a large, many-roomed, busy hotel. Up to five beers are served, with four beers on gravity in a separate cask ale bar with a temperature-controlled cabinet behind the bar. A self-tilting stillage is a notable feature. Three beer festivals are usually held annually, coinciding with St George's Day, the Witham Puppet Festival in September, and the Christmas period. Close to many bus routes.
✿🕮◑♠➡️Ⓟ🖼️🌐📶

Woolpack Inn Ⓛ ✓

7 Church Street, CM8 2JP
☎ (01376) 511195
Greene King IPA Ⓗ; Witham No Name Ⓖ; 2 changing beers (sourced locally) Ⓗ/Ⓖ
A traditional local pub, this is the only regular outlet for the Witham brewery, now based in Coggeshall. Set in a conservation area, the building probably dates from the 15th century. It has two rooms with low wooden beams and a real log fire in winter. Up to two guests ales, usually from the local area, are served predominantly on gravity. An extensive collection of glass soda syphon bottles is a notable feature. ➿♠🚃(40)🌐📶

Wivenhoe

Black Buoy

Black Buoy Hill, CO7 9BS
☎ (01206) 822425 ⊕ blackbuoy.co.uk
Colchester Number One; 5 changing beers (sourced nationally) Ⓗ
Friendly community pub that has won many local CAMRA awards. It has various areas for drinking or eating. There is a pleasant outside area with open and undercover areas, which is lit at night. The pub normally hosts popular beer festivals in spring and summer. Current and upcoming beers are displayed on their website which is regularly updated. It also hosts live music and poetry evenings. Q✿🕭🏵️◑👟♠Ⓟ🖼️(S1)🌐📶♫

Horse & Groom

55 The Cross, CO7 9QL (on B1028)
☎ (01206) 824928 ⊕ handgwivenhoe.co.uk
Adnams Southwold Bitter, Ghost Ship, Broadside; 3 changing beers (sourced nationally) Ⓗ
Welcoming and popular Adnams pub at the top end of Wivenhoe with public and lounge bars serving regular and seasonal Adnams beers. It has a pleasant atmosphere, allowing customers to enjoy conversation with their drink. The garden has an open area, with undercover seating when the weather is inclement. Dogs and children are welcome. A varied menu of excellent home-cooked food is available at lunchtimes. Regular entertainment includes music and comedy. There is also an excellent bus service to Colchester.
Q✿🕭◑👟♠Ⓟ🖼️(S1,74)🌐📶♫

Station Hotel

27 Station Road, CO7 9DH (on B1028)
☎ (01206) 822991
2 changing beers (sourced nationally) Ⓗ
Corner pub with an ever-changing beer choice, opposite the railway station, with various railway artefacts inside and very pleasant atmosphere and seating outside. Live music with local musicians often features, and there are occasional quiz nights. The pub is popular with rugby fans

with matches shown on TV. On Friday evening there is a food vendor outside, and demand is such it often sells out. The car park also houses the community chickens.
🏵️➿♠Ⓟ🖼️(S1)🌐📶

Woodham Mortimer

Hurdlemakers Arms

Post Office Road, CM9 6ST (off B1010)
☎ (01245) 225169 ⊕ hurdlemakersarms.co.uk
5 changing beers (often George's, Mighty Oak, Wibblers) Ⓗ
A Gray's house, this 400-year-old former farmhouse seamlessly blends restaurant with pub. Good food complements the beers. One area is dedicated to dining while a separate bar caters for drinkers. A huge beer garden with a play area and shady trees is ideal for families. Barbecues feature on summer weekends and a popular beer festival is held in late June. Functions are catered for in a marquee or Mortimer's barn.
Q✿🏵️◑👟♠Ⓟ🖼️🌐📶

Breweries

Billericay SIBA

🍴 **Essex Beer Shop, 54c Chapel Street, Billericay, CM12 9LS**
☎ (01277) 500121 ☎ 07788 373129
⊕ billericaybrewing.co.uk

With numerous regular beers and local distribution outlets, Billericay Brewing opened at its present site in 2014, using a 4.5-barrel plant. It has an adjacent micropub and well-stocked beer shop. The brewery hosts plenty of food and drink events and is dog friendly.
‼️🍺♦LIVE

Zeppelin (ABV 3.8%) BITTER
Blonde (ABV 4%) GOLD
Billericay Dickie (ABV 4.2%) BITTER
Vanilla Bark (ABV 4.3%) SPECIALITY
Woody's Bark (ABV 4.3%) STOUT
Rhythm Stick (ABV 4.8%) BITTER
Sex & Drugs & Rock & Roll (ABV 5%) PALE
Barista (ABV 5.9%) SPECIALITY
Chapel Street Porter (ABV 5.9%) PORTER
Chilli Porter (ABV 5.9%) SPECIALITY
Mayflower Gold (ABV 6.5%) IPA

Bishop Nick SIBA

33 East Street, Braintree, CM7 3JJ
☎ (01376) 349605 ⊕ bishopnick.com

⊠ Bishop Nick was launched in 2011 by Nelion Ridley, a member of the family that started Ridley's brewery near Chelmsford in 1842. In 2013 a new brewery was established in Braintree using a 20-barrel plant. 🍺♦

Ridley's Rite (ABV 3.6%) BITTER
Heresy (ABV 4%) GOLD
1555 (ABV 4.3%) BITTER
Devout (ABV 4.5%) STOUT
Martyr (ABV 5%) PALE
Divine (ABV 5.1%) BITTER

Black Box SIBA

18 Aviation Way, Southend on Sea, SS2 6UN ☎ 07471 733719 ⊕ blackboxbrewery.co.uk

⊠ Brewery and taproom on the airport industrial estate, with an aircraft theme. ♦

Ground Speed (ABV 3.8%) PALE
Landing Gear (ABV 3.8%) BITTER
Golden Wings (ABV 4%) GOLD
First Class (ABV 4.4%) PALE
Spruce Goose (ABV 4.4%) PALE
Bird Strike (ABV 4.8%) PORTER
Coffee & Vanilla Porter (ABV 4.8%) PORTER
Auto Pilot (ABV 5%) BITTER
Lost Luggage (ABV 5%) BITTER

Brentwood SIBA

Calcott Hall Farm, Ongar Road, Pilgrims Hatch, CM15 9HS
☎ (01277) 200483 ⊕ brentwoodbrewing.co.uk

⊗ Since its launch in 2006, Brentwood has steadily increased its capacity and distribution, relocating to a new purpose-built brewery unit in 2013 with a visitor centre. Seasonal and special beers are also available including more unusual beer styles under the Elephant School brand name. ‼️🍺♦LIVE GF ♦

IPA (ABV 3.7%) PALE
Marvellous Maple Mild (ABV 3.7%) SPECIALITY
Brentwood Legacy (ABV 4%) PALE
Best (ABV 4.2%) BITTER
Gold (ABV 4.3%) GOLD
Hope & Glory (ABV 4.5%) BITTER
Lumberjack (ABV 5.2%) BITTER
Chockwork Orange (ABV 6.5%) SPECIALITY

Brewed under the Elephant School brand name:
Aussie Blond (ABV 4%) BLOND
Mallophant (ABV 4.1%) STOUT
My Milk Stout Brings All The Bulls To The Yard (ABV 4.5%) STOUT

Brewhouse & Kitchen (NEW) SIBA

🏠 Anne Knight Building, Chelmsford, CM1 1LW

Part of the Brewhouse & Kitchen chain, producing its own range of beers. Carry outs and brewery experience days are offered.

Chelmsford

2 Brewery Fields, Church Street, Great Baddow, Chelmsford, CM2 7LE
☎ (01245) 476267 ⊕ chelmsfordbrewco.co.uk

Chelmsford Brew Co, established in 2017, is a family-owned brewery located in Great Baddow, near the former Baddow Brewery. A brewery shop and taproom is open Thursday-Saturday, and online orders are delivered free-of-charge to locations within 10 miles. 🍺♦

Blueshack Bitter (ABV 3.8%) BITTER
Cool Bay (ABV 3.9%) PALE
Port Jackson (ABV 4%) PORTER
Davy Dark (ABV 4.2%) MILD
Radio Wave (ABV 4.2%) PALE
Wild Coast (ABV 4.5%) IPA
Luxury Porter (ABV 4.6%) PORTER
Death of a Cowboy (ABV 4.7%) PALE
Mr Beard (ABV 5.2%) STOUT
Hand Grenade (ABV 5.3%) IPA

Colchester SIBA

Viaduct Brewhouse, Unit 16, Wakes Hall Business Centre, Wakes Colne, CO6 2DY
☎ (01787) 829422 ⊕ colchesterbrewery.com

⊗ Set up in 2012 by three friends, Tom Knox, Roger Clark and Andy Bone, using the double drop process. Popular during the early 20th century this process requires

additional brewing vessels in a two-tier system resulting in clean beer with pronounced flavours. ‼️🍺♦LIVE

AKA Pale (ABV 3.7%) PALE
Metropolis (ABV 3.9%) GOLD
Jack Spitty's Smuggler's Ale (ABV 4%) BITTER
Number One (ABV 4.1%) BITTER
Sweeney Todd (ABV 4.2%) BITTER
Brazilian Coffee & Vanilla Porter (ABV 4.6%) SPECIALITY
Cat's Whiskers (ABV 4.8%) STOUT
Old King Coel London Porter (ABV 5%) PORTER

Courtyard SIBA

Gosfield Cottage, The Street, Gosfield, CO9 1TP
☎ (01787) 475993 ☎ 07710 230662
⊕ courtyardbrewery.co.uk

Courtyard Brewery uses a six-barrel plant designed to perfectly fit into a 19th century coach house in the north Essex village of Gosfield. It is run by two brewers passionate about producing ales traditionally, but with a 21st century twist. ♦

IPA (ABV 3.8%) PALE
Gold (ABV 4.1%) GOLD
Dark (ABV 5%) PORTER

Crouch Vale SIBA

23 Haltwhistle Road, South Woodham Ferrers, CM3 5ZA
☎ (01245) 322744 ⊕ crouchvale.co.uk

⊗ Founded in 1981 by two CAMRA enthusiasts, Crouch Vale is well established as a major player in Essex brewing, having moved to larger premises in 2006. It supplies to various outlets as well as beer festivals throughout the region. One tied house, the Queen's Head in Chelmsford, is owned. ‼️🍺♦LIVE ♦

Blackwater Mild (ABV 3.7%) MILD
Malty, fruity and full with a deep-ruby colour and a dry roast character.
Essex Boys Best Bitter (ABV 3.8%) BITTER
Brewers Gold (ABV 4%) PALE
Golden pale ale with striking citrus hop alongside biscuity malt supported by a sweet fruitiness.
Yakima Gold (ABV 4.2%) GOLD
Creamy session golden ale with aromatic citrus hop and a touch of biscuity malt.
Amarillo (ABV 5%) GOLD

Datum Attitude (NEW)

Tollesbury Road, Tolleshunt D'Arcy, CM9 8UA
☎ 07498 218283 ⊕ datumattitude.co.uk

A family-run, small-batch craft brewery established in 2021, producing unfiltered and unfined vegan-friendly beers. LIVE V

Fallen Angel

Unit 21c, Reeds Farm Estate, Roxwell Road, Writtle, CM1 3ST
☎ (01245) 767220 ☎ 07572 614067
⊕ fallenangel-brewery.co.uk

Formerly known as the Broxbourne Brewery, the name changed to Fallen Angel in 2017. Brewing began in 2013 using a 12-barrel plant. A 15-barrel plant has been in operation since the brewery's move from Hertfordshire to Essex in 2015.

Ginger Beer (ABV 4%) SPECIALITY
Cowgirl Gold (ABV 4.2%) GOLD

Angry Ox Bitter (ABV 4.8%) BITTER
Fire in the Hole (ABV 4.9%) SPECIALITY
Black Death (ABV 5.2%) SPECIALITY

George's SIBA

Common Road, Great Wakering, SS3 0AG
☎ (01702) 826755 ☎ 07771 871255
⊕ georgesbrewery.com

⊠ George's Brewery and Hop Monster Brewing
Company (qv) are owned by the same brewer, using the
same plant. George's concentrates on traditional styles
and Hop Monster on the more unusual. ‼ ☛ ♦ LIVE

Wallasea Wench (ABV 3.6%) BITTER
Wakering Gold (ABV 3.8%) GOLD
Cockleboats (ABV 4%) BITTER
Empire (ABV 4%) BITTER
Figaro (ABV 4%) PALE
George's Best (ABV 4%) BITTER
Banshee Porter (ABV 4.4%) SPECIALITY
Broadsword (ABV 4.7%) BITTER
Excalibur (ABV 5.4%) GOLD
Merry Gentlemen (ABV 6%) OLD
Excalibur Reserve (ABV 7.2%) STRONG

Brewed under the Hop Monster Brewery name:
Rakau (ABV 4.2%) GOLD
Snake Oil Stout (ABV 5%) STOUT

JackRabbit

Prettyfields Dead Lane, Ardleigh, CO7 7PF ☎ 07506
596597 ⊕ jackrabbitbrewing.co.uk

JackRabbit Brewing Co was founded in 2019 by two beer
lovers with an aim to bring modern craft beer to the
Essex & Suffolk border. It offers a popular core range all
available in can and keg. Flagship cask pale ale is College
Hop-Out. New and special releases all year round. ☛

Leigh on Sea SIBA

35 Progress Road, Leigh on Sea, SS9 5PR
☎ (01702) 817255 ⊕ leighonseabrewery.co.uk

⊠ Established in 2017 to produce vegan-friendly beer,
which is unfiltered, unpasteurised and unfined (except
for Renown). Initially brewing on a one-barrel kit, it
rapidly progressed to a 10-barrel plant. Many of the
names of the beers are based on Leigh's maritime
heritage. The brewery has its own taproom, and has now
opened a pub, Legra Tap & Kitchen. ‼ ☛ ♦ V ⊘

Bawley Bitter (ABV 3.4%) BITTER
Legra Pale (ABV 3.8%) PALE
McFadden Mild (ABV 3.8%) MILD
Boys of England (ABV 3.9%) BITTER
Brhubarb (ABV 3.9%) SPECIALITY
Kursaal Gold (ABV 3.9%) GOLD
Renown (ABV 4%) STOUT
Six Little Ships (ABV 4.2%) BITTER
Beach Hut Brew (ABV 4.5%) PALE
Two Tree Island Red (ABV 4.5%) RED
Boatyard IPA (ABV 5%) PALE
Crowstone (ABV 5.5%) IPA
Cockle Row Spit (ABV 5.6%) IPA
SS9 (ABV 9%) STOUT

Mersea Island

Rewsalls Lane, East Mersea, CO5 8SX ☎ 07970
070399 ⊕ merseabrewery.co.uk

⊠ The brewery was established at Mersea Island
Vineyard in 2005. It supplies several local pubs on a
guest beer basis as well as beer festivals. It holds its own

festival of Essex-produced ales over the four-day Easter
weekend. The Cork 'n' Cap off sales and gift shop opened
in 2020. ☛ LIVE

Mersea Mud (ABV 3.8%) MILD
Yo Boy! (ABV 3.8%) BITTER
Gold (ABV 4.4%) SPECIALITY
Skippers (ABV 4.8%) BITTER
Oyster Stout (ABV 5%) STOUT

Mighty Oak

14b West Station Yard, Spital Road, Maldon, CM9 6TW
☎ (01621) 843713 ⊕ mightyoakbrewing.co.uk

⊠ Established in 1996, the Mighty Oak Brewery
produces 5000+ hectolitres of beer per year. Some 450
outlets across East Anglia and the South East are
supplied. Bottled ales are a recent addition. Its popular
annual free festive beer tasting day takes place in early
December. The Mighty Oak Brewery Tap can be found at
the top end of Maldon High Street. ‼ ☛ ♦ LIVE ⊘

Oscar Wilde (ABV 3.7%) MILD
Roasty dark mild with suggestions of forest fruits and
dark chocolate. A sweet taste yields to a more bitter
finish.
Captain Bob (ABV 3.8%) BITTER
Maldon Gold (ABV 3.8%) GOLD
Pale golden ale with a sharp citrus note moderated by
honey and biscuity malt.
Jake the Snake (ABV 4%) PALE
Old Man and the Sea (ABV 4.1%) STOUT
Gorgeous George (ABV 4.2%) BITTER
Kings (ABV 4.2%) GOLD
This yellow-gold beer is easy-drinking with a gentle
anchor of citrus hops and a slowly tapering malty sweet
background.
Cascade IPA (ABV 6.2%) IPA

Moody Goose

⬛ King William IV, 114 London Road, Braintree,
CM77 7PU ☎ 07595 911046
✉ info@moodygoosebrewery.co.uk

A three-barrel brewery, brewing approximately 15 times
a year. The beers are currently only available in the King
William IV, where the brewery is located, and select beer
festivals.

Neolithic

Bradwell, CM0 7PS ⊕ neolithicbrew.co.uk

Nanobrewery producing bottled beers and naturally
carbonated keg using hand-milled malt.

Other Monkey

5-6 Nicholas Street, Colchester, CO1 1LB
☎ (01206) 986446 ⊕ othermonkeybrewing.com

⊠ Other Monkey is located in the rear portion of the
Other Monkey Taproom and is visible to users of the pub.
The beer brewed is predominantly served on draught,
but cask is produced alongside this and served at the
taproom and the Three Wise Monkeys pub next door.
☛ ⊘

Pale Ale (ABV 4.4%) PALE

Posh Boys

Riverside House, 8 Lower Southend Road, Wickford,
SS11 8BB ☎ 07474 594379 ⊕ poshboysbrewery.com

⊠ Posh Boys is a small, independent craft brewery, set up by two friends and operating on a part-time basis. Beers are available in the taproom, local pubs and occasionally at festivals. ◆

The Blind Butler (ABV 4%) BITTER
The Blonde Maid (ABV 4%) BLOND
Room No. 6 (ABV 4.1%) BLOND
The Bowlers Hat (ABV 4.5%) BITTER
The Coachman (ABV 4.5%) BITTER
The Night Porter (ABV 4.5%) PORTER

Pumphouse Community

Green Man Barn, Church Lane, Toppesfield, CO9 4DR
☎ 07934 126592 ⊕ pumphousebrewery.co.uk

⊠ Pumphouse is a community-owned brewery. Established in 2015 it uses a two-barrel plant and specialises in session beers with occasional one-off, experimental brews. Pubs, clubs, special events and festivals are supplied within a 20-mile radius as well as its Green Man tap outlet. ⬛◆LIVE◆

Allied Amber (ABV 3.8%) BITTER
St Margaret's Ale (ABV 3.8%) BLOND
Gold (ABV 4.2%) GOLD
19 Elms (ABV 4.3%) BROWN
9th Havocs (ABV 4.3%) PALE

Redchurch

15-16 Mead Park Industrial Estate, Harlow, CM20 2SE
☎ (01279) 626895 ☎ 07836 762173
⊕ redchurch.beer

⊠ Established in 2011 using an eight-barrel plant in railway arches at Bethnal Green. In 2016 most of the production moved to Harlow, leaving only the taproom on site. It was purchased by new management in 2019, who closed the Bethnal Green taproom. In 2022 it was purchased by the Laine Brewing Co to expand Laine's current range and brewing capacity. Redchurch's range of ten core beers and seasonal specials is only available in keg and bottles. ‼⬛◆◆

St Botolphs

8 Gladwin Road, Colchester, CO2 7HS
☎ (01206) 511835 ✉ info@stbotolphsbrewery.co.uk

Brewing began in 2014. Its Belgian-style bottled beers can be found in pubs, farm shops, specialist beer shops, markets and food festivals in Essex and Suffolk.

Shalford SIBA

Killhogs Farm, Water Lane, Shalford, CM7 4QX
☎ (01371) 850925 ☎ 07749 658512
⊕ shalfordbrewery.co.uk

Shalford began brewing in 2007. More than 50 outlets are supplied direct. ◆LIVE

1319 Mild (ABV 3.7%) MILD
Barnfield Pale Ale (ABV 3.8%) PALE
Pale-coloured but full-flavoured, this is a traditional pale ale. Malt persists throughout, with bitterness becoming more dominant towards the end.
Braintree Market Ale (ABV 4%) BITTER
Levelly Gold (ABV 4%) GOLD
Stoneley Bitter (ABV 4.2%) BITTER
Dark amber session beer whose vivid hop character is supported by a juicy, malty body. A dry finish makes this beer very drinkable.
Hyde Bitter (ABV 4.7%) BITTER
Stronger version of Barnfield, with a similar but more assertive character.

Levelly Black (ABV 4.8%) STOUT
Rotten End (ABV 6.5%) STRONG

Watson's

Old Heath, Colchester, CO1 2HD ☎ 07804 641267
⊕ watsonsbrewery.co.uk

⊠ Small-batch home brewery, three firkins at a time, supplying local pubs and beer festivals with many one-off beers and a few regulars.

WHARF (NEW)

Upp Hall Farm, Salmons Lane, Colchester, CO6 1RY
☎ (01376) 563123 ⊕ wharfbrewing.co.uk

WHARF Brewery was founded in 2023 with the merger of three breweries, Red Fox, Harwich Town and Witham. WHARF brews at the former Red Fox brewery premises, where Witham and Harwich Town were cuckoo breweries using the same plant, and has a beer range derived from all three constituent parts. It sells to real ale pubs across the combined catchment area, supplies many beer festivals and puts on the Coggeshall Beer Festival at the beginning of September and the Harwich Redoubt Beer Festival at the end of July each year.

IPA (ABV 3.7%) BITTER
EPA 100 (ABV 3.8%) PALE
Leading Lights (ABV 3.8%) BITTER
Scruffy Mild (ABV 3.9%) MILD
Best Bitter (ABV 4%) BITTER
Pucks Folly (ABV 4.2%) GOLD
Redoubt Stout (ABV 4.2%) STOUT
No Name (ABV 4.3%) BITTER
Stone Pier (ABV 4.3%) GOLD
Parkeston Porter (ABV 4.5%) PORTER
Golden Boar (ABV 5%) GOLD
Wily Ol' Fox (ABV 5.2%) PALE

White Hart

⬛ **White Hart Hotel & Restaurant, 15 High Street, Halstead, CO9 2AP**
☎ (01787) 475657 ⊕ whitehartbrewery.co.uk

⊠ Brewing began in 2017 in old stables at the back of the White Hart. Both the brewery and pub are owned by father and son, Charles and Hugo Townsend. Beers are available in the pub and at local beer festivals.

Wibblers SIBA

Goldsands Road, Southminster, CM0 7JW
☎ (01621) 772044 ⊕ wibblers.com

⊠ Established in 2007, in 2009 it expanded to a 20-barrel plant. In 2016 it moved to new premises, housed in a medieval barn in Southminster with its own taproom. Craft beers and ciders are produced as well as seasonal specials. Numerous outlets are supplied throughout East Anglia in addition to exporting to Europe. It runs an annual Flocculation brewing event each August and hosts 'Be the Brewer' and brewery experience days. ‼⬛◆LIVE◆

Dengie IPA (ABV 3.6%) PALE
Apprentice (ABV 3.9%) BITTER
Dengie Dark (ABV 4%) MILD
Dengie Gold (ABV 4%) GOLD
Hop Black (ABV 4%) BITTER
Beneath The Embers (ABV 4.7%) PALE
Crafty Stoat (ABV 5.3%) STOUT

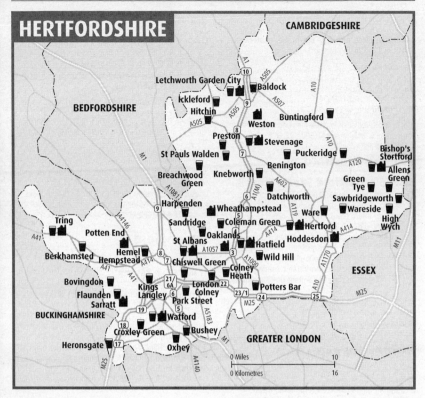

HERTFORDSHIRE

Allens Green

Queen's Head 🅛

CM21 0LS (turn up West Rd, Sawbridgeworth, at mini roundabout on main road, at T-jct turn right) TL455170
☎ (01279) 723393 ⊕ qhpub.co.uk
Fuller's London Pride; Mighty Oak Maldon Gold; 2 changing beers (sourced locally) 🅖
Popular village inn that reopened thanks to the efforts of a group of locals. It is well worth seeking out for a constantly changing range of about four beers. Hot snacks are available unless the pub is very busy. A frequently winner of local CAMRA Pub of the Year over the past decade and current regional Cider Pub of the Year. Q🕸🖤♿P🐾🎵

Baldock

Orange Tree 🅛 ✅

Norton Road, SG7 5AW
☎ (01462) 892341 ⊕ theorangetreebaldock.com
Greene King IPA, Abbot; Tring Mansion Mild; 9 changing beers (sourced nationally) 🅗
This 300-year-old multi-roomed pub is home to more than 10 local clubs and societies. The nine guests are all from small breweries, changed every weekend, and there are five local real ciders. There is a huge malt whisky collection on display as well as a a large vintage bottled beer collection. Good home-cooked food is available. Quiz nights on Tuesday, folk music on Wednesday. 🕸🖤◐♿♣♠♿P🚌🐾🎵♪

Benington

Lordship Arms 🍸

42 Whempstead Road, SG2 7BX

☎ (01438) 869665 ⊕ lordshiparms.com
Black Sheep Best Bitter; Crouch Vale Brewers Gold; Timothy Taylor Landlord; 6 changing beers (sourced nationally) 🅗
Under the same ownership since 1993, this pub is a repeat winner of local and county CAMRA awards including local CAMRA Pub of the Year in 2021 and 2023. The single bar is decorated with telephone memorabilia. The garden features floral displays to be enjoyed in the summer. Excellent fresh sandwiches and lunchtime snacks are served. There is a classic car gathering on the third Tuesday of each month from April to September. Winter Sunday hours can vary – call to check. Q🕸◐♿P🚌🐾

Berkhamsted

George Inn 🅛 ✅

261 High Street, HP4 1AB
☎ (01442) 874159 ⊕ thegeorgepubberkhamsted.co.uk
Wadworth 6X; 2 changing beers (sourced nationally; often Tring) 🅗
Situated close to Berkhamsted's town centre, this mid-17th century pub has a central island bar within a single room with bench window seating and high tables with stools. To the rear is a small, covered courtyard with a bar and cast-iron tables and chairs. Further back is a sloping garden with more table seating. Three well-kept hand-pulled beers are available. Food consists of sandwiches and cold cheese and meat sharing boards. Families and dogs are welcome. 🕸🖤🍴♿🚌(500,501)🐾

Rising Sun 🅛

1 Canal Side, George Street, HP4 2EG (at lock 55 on Grand Union Canal, from station follow the canal towards Hemel Hempstead)

☎ (01442) 864913

Tring Drop Bar Pale Ale; 3 changing beers (sourced nationally; often Adnams, Butcombe, Chiltern) 🍴
The Riser is a thriving canalside pub with plenty of outdoor space – a firm favourite of local hikers, dog walkers and cyclists. The recipient of many well-deserved CAMRA awards, it serves five well-kept real ales and 15-20 real ciders. It hosts many popular events including quiz nights, folk music afternoons, a cheese club and quarterly beer and cider festivals. A range of bar snacks is offered such as pork pies and a renowned ploughman's. ᗷ⊛≉♣●🚲(500,501)🐾🛜

Bishop's Stortford

Bishop's Stortford Sports Trust 🅛
Cricketfield Lane, CM23 2TD
☎ (01279) 654463 ⊕ bssportstrust.co.uk
6 changing beers (sourced locally; often New River, Hadham, Mauldons) 🍴
Everyone is welcome at this pub within a club – no membership required. Beer quality is driven by high turnover from the thirsty sports-playing members. Conversation flows in the comfortable seating area; the TV sports screens are usually muted. Outside drinking in summer comes with an attractive view. The venue is easily reached from town via Chantry Road, turning left at the end to see the grounds on the right. A recent regional CAMRA Club of Year winner. ᗷ⊛&P

Castle
38 Castle Street, CM23 3TG (up Newton Rd from South St and first left)
☎ (01279) 652578
2 changing beers (sourced regionally; often Hadham) 🍴
This family-run back-street local, established in 1840, is a real gem. The public bar adjoins a cosy snug with wooden settles, bookshelves and often a fireside cat. A south-facing patio is inviting in fair weather. The pub is hidden away in the old town and is well worth seeking out. Opening times may vary, so check first if travelling here. Q▶≉♣P🚲

Star 🅛 ⊘
7 Bridge Street, CM23 2JU
☎ (01279) 654211
5 changing beers (sourced regionally) 🍴
A 17th-century town-centre pub catering for all ages. It is busy on Friday and Saturday evenings with a young crowd, but at other times attracts a mixed clientele. Tuesday is quiz night. A quiet pint can be enjoyed on other evenings and at lunchtimes. Beers from local and regional breweries are offered on an ever-changing basis. Reasonably priced traditional pub food is freshly prepared throughout the day. ⊛◑≉●🚲🛜♫

Bovingdon

Bell 🅛 ⊘
79 High Street, HP3 0HP
☎ (01442) 832800 ⊕ bellbovingdon.co.uk
Tring Side Pocket for a Toad; Young's London Original; 3 changing beers (sourced nationally; often Timothy Taylor, Tring) 🍴
Friendly 18th-century village pub featuring an original front section consisting of a bar split over two levels, plus a snug with a dartboard. The large area to the back is often, but not exclusively, used for dining. Wood-burning stoves throughout provide additional winter cosiness. Outside is a garden terrace with pergola and a covered smoking area. The pub hosts a popular monthly charity

quiz, food-themed evenings and fortnightly open mic on Sundays. No food on Mondays.
Q ᗷ⊛◑♣P🚲(1,352) 🐾🛜

Breachwood Green

Red Lion ⊘
16 Chapel Road, SG4 8NU
☎ (01438) 833123 ⊕ redlionbreachwoodgreen.co.uk
Greene King Abbot; St Austell Tribute; Woodforde's Wherry; 1 changing beer (sourced nationally) 🍴
The pub – the only one in the village – attracts many locals as well as visitors from further afield. There is a TV showing main sporting events as well as a quiet dining area. The garden provides views of the countryside. It serves good home-made food and the guest beers are unusual for this area. It has its own darts, dominoes, football and cricket teams. Accommodation is available. ᗷ⊛≉◑♣●P🐾🛜

Buntingford

Crown
17 High Street, SG9 9AB
☎ (01763) 271422
3 changing beers (sourced nationally) 🍴
Town-centre pub with a large front bar, cosy back bar and large function room. Outside is a covered patio plus a secluded garden with pétanque piste. The pub serves fish & chips on Friday evenings and there is an acoustic music night on the third Monday of the month. The pub has been identified by CAMRA as having a regionally important historic pub interior.
Q ᗷ⊛◑♣🚲(386,331) 🐾♫

Bushey

Swan
25 Park Road, WD23 3EE
☎ (020) 8950 2256
Greene King Abbot; Timothy Taylor Landlord; Young's Bitter; 1 changing beer (sourced nationally; often Timothy Taylor, Black Sheep) 🍴
Located in a quiet side street in Bushey Village, this 150-year-old single-room Victorian local has bare floorboards and real fireplaces. Its walls are adorned with old photos, paintings and newspaper clippings of sporting events and life in Bushey. The TV screens show sports and a dartboard complements the range of bar games available. The pub serves four real ales, and hot snacks are available. It has picnic benches at the front. Access to the Ladies is via the garden at the back.
⊛♣🚲(142,258) 🐾🛜

REAL ALE BREWERIES

3 Brewers of St Albans ⚒ Hatfield
Belgian Brewer, The ⚒ Bishop's Stortford
Bowtie Watford
Crossover Blendery ⚒ Weston
Farr Brew ⚒ Wheathampstead
Garden City 🍺 Letchworth Garden City
Mad Squirrel ⚒ Potten End
McMullen Hertford
New River Hoddesdon
Oxhey Village Watford
Paradigm Sarratt
Pope's Yard Watford
Six Hills ⚒ Stevenage
Tring Tring
Two Bob Oaklands
White Hart Tap 🍺 St Albans (brewing suspended)

Chiswell Green

Three Hammers

210 Watford Road, AL2 3EA (on B4630, 1 mile N of jct 21A on M25)
☎ (01727) 846218
Fuller's London Pride; 4 changing beers (sourced nationally) ⊞
The oldest part of this former coaching inn and forge (hence the name) dates from the 15th and 16th centuries. Oak beams and an ornate bar front feature in the contemporary interior. A pleasant garden is situated alongside the main road. The five real ales include three ever-changing guests. Good-quality meals are served every day. There are regular beer festivals during the year and quiz nights on Sunday and Tuesday.
🏠◑♿Ⓟ🖳(321,724) 🌑🐾🛜

Coleman Green

John Bunyan

Coleman Green Lane, AL4 8ES (on country lane between B653 and B651) TL190126
☎ (01582) 832037 ⊕ johnbunyanpub.co.uk
McMullen AK Original Mild, Country Bitter; 1 changing beer (sourced nationally) ⊞
Fine, old-fashioned, family-run country pub dating back to 1932. It is named after the Baptist preacher (1628-1688) and author of The Pilgrim's Progress, who is believed to have stayed nearby. Walls and ceilings are festooned with china plates and jugs, with a roaring fire in winter. Well-behaved dogs are very welcome in the pub and the large garden. It is open from May to September every day including bank holidays, and also on Sunday evenings when the monthly quiz night held.
Q🏠◑♿♣Ⓟ🖳(366,610) 🌑🐾🛜

Colney Heath

Crooked Billet ℂ

88 High Street, AL4 0NP
☎ (01727) 822128 ⊕ thecrookedbilletpub.com
Fuller's London Pride; Tring Side Pocket for a Toad; Young's London Special ⊞
Popular and friendly cottage-style village pub dating back over 200 years. A genuine free house, it stocks three beers from national and regional breweries and micros. A wide selection of good-value home-made food is served lunchtimes and Friday and Saturday evenings. Summer barbeques and Saturday events are held occasionally. This is a favourite stop-off for walkers on the many local footpaths. Families are welcome in the bar until 9pm and in the large garden, where there is play equipment. ⏖🏠◑♣Ⓟ🖳(304)🐾

Croxley Green

Sportsman ℂ

2 Scots Hill, WD3 3AD (at A412 jct with the Green)
☎ (01923) 443360
6 changing beers (sourced nationally; often New River, Paradigm, Vale) ⊞
A family-run community pub with friendly, welcoming service, providing a traditional pub atmosphere in a modern context. It serves up to six ever-changing guest ales, mostly from smaller breweries both local and from further afield. Two craft keg beers are sourced from the local Paradigm brewery. The dartboard and pool table are in frequent use. A rear patio offers comfortable outdoor seating. Croxley tube station is a short walk away. ⏖🏠♣Ⓟ🖳(321)

Datchworth

Plough ℂ

5 Datchworth Green, SG3 6TL (on crossroads in centre of village)
☎ (01438) 813000
3 changing beers (sourced nationally) ⊞
Small, single-bar free house on the edge of Datchworth Green sporting an ever-changing selection of real ales including LocAle. This is a real locals' pub at the hub of the village and all are made to feel welcome. The 'secret' garden is a real suntrap in the summer months and features a well-used pétanque piste. Darts and pétanque teams meet here regularly. 🏠♣Ⓟ🖳(379)🌑🐾🛜

Flaunden

Green Dragon ✓

Flaunden Hill, HP3 0PP (from main road through village, follow signs towards Latimer) TL015008
☎ (01442) 832020 ⊕ greendragonflaunden.co.uk
Rebellion Smuggler, Overthrow; Timothy Taylor Landlord; Young's London Original; 2 changing beers (sourced nationally) ⊞
A 17th-century village pub containing an historic taproom, it has been identified by CAMRA as having a nationally important historic pub interior. The bar area features two distinct sections, with a wood-burning stove, exposed brickwork and wooden beams. A sizeable additional area is past the pizza oven to the back right. Food offerings include wood-fired pizza, trattoria, and Sunday lunch menus. Look out for the large, wooden green dragon's head in the substantial garden. A function room is for hire in separate building. Closed Mondays.
Q⏖🏠◑♿♣Ⓟ🐾🛜

Green Tye

Prince of Wales ℂ

Much Hadham, SG10 6JP (Green Tye is well signposted but sat nav is recommended) TL444184
☎ (01279) 842139 ⊕ thepow.co.uk
Abbeydale Moonshine; Wadworth Henry's IPA; 1 changing beer (sourced locally) ⊞
A traditional rural village local that is the centre of social life in the village. Opening hours are variable and the pub will stay open up to 11pm if there is custom, or meetings and other events taking place later in the evening. It is best to call in advance to make sure it is open. A beer festival is held over the May Day weekend.
Q⏖🏠♿Ⓟ🐾🛜

Harpenden

Cross Keys ℂ ✓

39 High Street, AL5 2SD (opp war memorial)
☎ (01582) 763989
Timothy Taylor Landlord; Tring Side Pocket for a Toad; 1 changing beer (sourced nationally; often Tring) ⊞
A warm welcome awaits you here at this two-bar pub, a regular entry in the Guide. It has retained its traditional charm, with a rare, fine pewter bar top, flagstone floors and oak-beamed ceiling. In spring and summer you can enjoy your pint in the large, secluded rear garden, and in autumn or winter savour your beer in front of the fire in the public bar. Q⏖🏠◑➔♣🖳🌑🛜

Marquis of Granby

31 Marquis Lane, AL5 5AE (at bottom of Crabtree Ln where it joins Marquis Ln)
☎ (01582) 713372 ⊕ omgmog.pub

Adnams Ghost Ship; Fuller's London Pride; Sharp's Doom Bar; 1 changing beer (sourced locally) Ⓗ
A pleasant neighbourhood local located by the River Lea. A guest changing beer from the Tring brewery range rotates with the regular beers. The pub is popular with diners who come to enjoy its lunchtime meals and evening sharing tapas platters. A morning café serves breakfasts, pastries and coffees at the weekend.
Q ☕ 🏠 ♿ ➔ ♣ P 🚭 ◆ 🐾 奈 ♪

Hatfield

Horse & Groom
21 Park Street, AL9 5AT
☎ (01707) 264765 ⊕ horseandgroom-oldhatfield.com
3 Brewers of St Albans Classic English Ale; Greene King Abbot; Timothy Taylor Landlord; 3 changing beers (sourced nationally) Ⓗ
In the heart of Old Hatfield, this Grade II-listed building is thought to house a priest hole. It serves up to six real ales, with beer festivals held during the year. Tuesday is Sausage & Mash night – purchase an ale for a free portion. Numerous buses run from nearby Hatfield station, and the public car park behind the nearby Great Northern pub. Access is via an alleyway.
Q ☕ 🏠 ♿ ➔ ♣ P 🚭 ◆ 🐾 奈 ♪

Hemel Hempstead

Full House Ⓛ ✅
128 Marlowes, HP1 1EZ (near bus interchange)
☎ (01442) 265512
Greene King IPA, Abbot; Sharp's Doom Bar; house beer (by Tring); 5 changing beers (sourced nationally; often Tring, Vale) Ⓗ
Spacious pub with extensive seating and decor reminiscent of its cinema past. It is worth a visit for its consistently good beer quality and wide range of changing beers, which are often local. The ciders on offer are Westons Old Rosie, Gwynt Y Ddraig Black Dragon, Cockeyed Pear Mania, and a rotating fruity cider, all from the box. There are five craft beers on keg, and many craft beers in bottles and cans. A recent local CAMRA Pub of the Year. Q ☕ 🏠 🌳 ♿ 🚭 奈

Monks Inn Ⓛ
31-32 The Square, Marlowes, HP1 1EP
☎ 07786 365225 ⊕ monksinn.uk
9 changing beers (sourced nationally; often Neptune, Titanic, Windsor & Eton) Ⓗ/Ⓖ
Town-centre micropub that has enhanced Hemel Hempstead's beer scene since opening in 2018. There is something for everyone here: six real ales on handpumps and three on gravity in a comprehensive range of styles, plus six real ciders and four craft keg beers. The small interior, converted from an old betting shop, is complemented by gazebos outside. You are welcome to bring in food from local eateries. Senior citizens discount available. ☕ 🏠 ♣ ◆ 🚭 奈

Heronsgate

Land of Liberty, Peace & Plenty 🍷 Ⓛ
Long Lane, WD3 5BS (J17 of M25, head W away from Rickmansworth, ¾ mile on right) TQ023949
☎ (01923) 282226 ⊕ landoflibertypub.com
6 changing beers (sourced nationally; often Redemption, Tring, XT) Ⓗ
Welcoming pub just off M25, popular with walkers, cyclists, locals and real ale enthusiasts. It has historic connections to the Chartists, who had a short-lived rural community nearby. Up to six microbrewery beers are usually offered covering a range of styles and strengths. Real ciders and a range of malt whiskies are also stocked. Beer festivals, tastings and charity events are held throughout the year. Bar snacks are available all day. There is a large outside pavilion for families.
❀ ♣ ◆ P 🚭 🚆 (R2) 🐾 奈

Hertford

Black Horse Ⓛ ✅
29-31 West Street, SG13 8EZ
☎ (01992) 583630 ⊕ theblackhorse.biz
6 changing beers (sourced nationally) Ⓗ
A community-focused, timbered free house, dating from 1642 and situated in one of Hertford's most attractive streets, near the start of the Cole Green Way. It serves six real ales from around the country, including one from Hertfordshire. The food menu features game and home-made curries, pies and daily specials. The well-kept garden includes a separate and safe childrens' area and a summer pizza oven. The pub has its own RFU-affiliated rugby team, and is handy for Hertford Town FC supporters. ☕ 🏠 ◆ ♣ 🚭 🐾 奈

Hertford Club
Lombard House, Bull Plain, SG14 1DT
☎ (01992) 421422 ⊕ hertford.club
3 changing beers (sourced nationally) Ⓗ
Dating from the 15th century with later additions, Lombard House, on the River Lea, was built as an English hall house and is one of the oldest buildings in Hertford. It has been the home of this private members' club since 1897. CAMRA members are welcome and may be signed in on production of a membership card. You will find two or three changing beers and real cider, which can be enjoyed in the delightful walled garden and riverside terrace. Home-cooked food is served at lunchtimes and on Friday evenings. ☕ 🏠 ◆ ➔ (East) ♣ ◆ 🚭 🚆 奈 ♪

Old Barge
2 The Folly, SG14 1QD (ask for Folly Island and you'll find the Old Barge)
☎ (01992) 581871 ⊕ theoldbarge.com
Marston's 61 Deep; 2 changing beers (sourced nationally) Ⓗ
A free house on Folly Island, pleasantly situated canalside on the River Lea, offering a selection of ales – sometimes including a dark brew – and a range of ciders and perries. Locally sourced home-cooked food is served all day, with roasts on Sundays. There is a music quiz on the last Thursday of the month. The Spring Fling music festival takes place on the second May bank holiday Monday. Look out for the annual duck race on Easter Monday. ☕ 🏠 ◆ ➔ (East) ♣ 🚭 奈

Old Cross Tavern Ⓛ
8 St Andrew Street, SG14 1JA
☎ (01992) 583133 ⊕ oldcrosstavern.com
Timothy Taylor Landlord; 5 changing beers (sourced nationally) Ⓗ
Superb town free house offering a friendly welcome. It serves up to six real ales from brewers large and small, usually including a dark beer of some distinction, and there is a fine choice of Belgian bottle-conditioned brews. Two beer festivals are held each year – one over a spring bank holiday weekend, the other in October. No TV or music here, just good old-fashioned conversation. Home-made pork pies and Scotch eggs are available.
Q ➔ (North) ♣ 🚭 (395) 🐾

High Wych

Rising Sun

High Wych Road, CM21 0HZ

☎ (01279) 724099

4 changing beers (often Oakham, Tring) [G]

Friendly village pub popular with locals and walkers. It has never used handpumps; the range of four or five beers, often featuring East Anglian breweries such as Tring, Adnams and Oakham, is served on gravity. Although recently refurbished, the original character has been preserved by means of a stone floor, attractive fireplace and wood panelling. The pub holds an annual vegetable competition. Parking is in the village hall car park opposite. Q❀♣P🚌(347)🐾

Hitchin

Albert

50 Walsworth Road, SG4 9SU

☎ (01462) 610237 🌐 thealbertpub.com

Tring Side Pocket for a Toad; 1 changing beer (sourced nationally) [H]

This charming pub has undergone a number of improvements since 2019 when it changed hands. It has been given a fresh, modern feel, and there is a patio area at the back. The addition of a kitchen has allowed it to serve excellent food (lunch and dinner Mon-Sat, Sun lunch only). It offers two real ales and five craft beers. There is a quiz night on Thursday and live music every Sunday. 👶❀◑🚆🚌🐾♫

Half Moon [L]

57 Queen Street, SG4 9TZ

☎ (01462) 453010 🌐 thehalfmoonhitchin.com

Adnams Southwold Bitter; Young's Bitter; 10 changing beers (sourced nationally) [H]

Friendly and welcoming one-bar pub dating from the 18th century. The two house ales and eight ever-changing guest ales ensure a variety of beer styles is always available from a range of breweries near and far, alongside a selection of traditional ciders. Bar snacks are also offered. The regular quiz and music nights are popular. and twice-yearly beer festivals are held. Local CAMRA Pub of the Year and Cider Pub of the Year 2022. 👶❀◑♣🍎P🍺🐾📶♫

Highlander [L]

45 Upper Tilehouse Street, SG5 2EF

☎ (01462) 454612 🌐 highlanderpubhitchin.co.uk

Greene King IPA; 3 changing beers (sourced nationally) [H]

This Grade II-listed free house is just out of the town centre on the Luton road. It has been run by multiple generations of the same family for the past 43 years. The dishes on the menu are reasonably priced and feature a fusion of traditional English pub grub and French bistro-style cooking, all created by the French chef using locally sourced ingredients. The pub holds monthly jazz nights. Q👶❀◑♿P🚌(100,101)🐾📶♫

Victoria

1 Ickleford Road, SG5 1TJ (E of town centre towards railway station)

☎ (01462) 432682 🌐 thevictoriahitchin.com

Greene King IPA, Abbot; 4 changing beers (sourced nationally) [H]

This busy community pub dating from 1865 hosts a range of events, from quiz nights and live music to comedy and cabaret as well as an annual beer and cider festival and the Vic Fest music festival. It offers two regular Greene King beers plus two guest beers. Good-value home-made modern British food is served every day, including Sunday roasts and regular pie nights. The historic barn is available for community use and live events. 👶❀◑♿♣🚌📶♫

Ickleford

Plume of Feathers ✔

Upper Green, SG5 3YD

☎ (01462) 455953

Greene King Abbot; Sharp's Doom Bar; Woodforde's Wherry; 1 changing beer (sourced nationally) [H]

The recently refurbished Plume of Feathers has been a traditional village pub since around 1762. It stands just off the Hitchin to Bedford bus route and it is reported to be the only pub that has a stream running through the cellar. Food is served from Tuesday to Sunday at lunch and dinner times. It has a secluded beer garden. 👶❀◑♣P🚌🐾

Kings Langley

Saracen's Head [L] ✔

47 High Street, WD4 9HU (on main road through village)

☎ (01923) 400144 🌐 saracensheadkingslangley.co.uk

Timothy Taylor Landlord; Tring Side Pocket for a Toad; 1 changing beer (sourced locally; often Tring) [H]

Dating from 1619 is this friendly, popular free house, consisting of a single bar with low ceilings and a large open fire. The well-stocked bar has a good choice of beers, and is noted for its selection of gins and whiskies. Food is served weekday lunchtimes, with reductions for senior citizens and 'bottomless brunch' days. Darts are played on Tuesdays and there is a large screen TV showing major sporting events. 👶❀◖🍎🚌(501,508)🐾📶

Knebworth

Lytton Arms

Park Lane, SG3 6QB

☎ (01438) 812312 🌐 thelyttonarms.co.uk

Abbeydale Daily Bread; Woodforde's Wherry; 5 changing beers (sourced nationally; often Brancaster) [H]

A 19th-century pub adjacent to the Knebworth House estate. It was built for Hawkes & Company of Bishop's Stortford, whose original logo is visible in the pub sign's ironwork. Four house beers are supplemented by a changing mix from regional breweries and micros. Good home-made food is available every day. Live music features on Friday evenings. Outside is an attractive decked patio and garden. 👶❀◑♣P🚌(44,45)🐾

Station

1 Station Approach, SG3 6AT

☎ (01438) 579504 🌐 stationpubknebworth.com

Shepherd Neame Spitfire; 3 changing beers (sourced nationally) [H]

An attractively refurbished pub next to the railway station. Now owned by the local parish council, it was reopened after a lengthy campaign that saved it from residential development. Four cask ales are available, covering a range of styles, and delicious food is served every day. 👶❀◑♿🚆P🐾📶

Letchworth Garden City

Garden City Brewery & Bar [L]

22 The Wynd, SG6 3EN

☎ 07939 401359 🌐 gardencitybrewery.co.uk

8 changing beers (sourced nationally) [G]

An award-winning, friendly, family-run brew-bar in a converted café on a charming pedestrianised street. All ales are served on gravity, normally four of the brewery's own, which are only available here, and four guest beers. There is also a large selection of local and other UK ciders. Locally produced bar snacks are on offer. Outside is a paved beer garden with a weatherproof awning. The bar has an events programme. It is a fve-minute walk from the station, with parking adjacent.
Q🐴❀♿🚆🍎P🐾📶♫

London Colney

Bull [L]
Barnet Road, AL2 1QU
☎ (01727) 823160 🌐 thebullpublondoncolney.co.uk
St Austell Tribute; Timothy Taylor Landlord; 2 changing beers (sourced nationally) [H]
A lovely 17th-century timbered building near the River Colne, offering a range of real ales. It has a cosy lounge featuring an original fireplace, and a large public bar with a dartboard and TV. Evening events include live music sessions. Good value home-made meals are served Monday to Saturday lunchtimes and evenings, with breakfast on Saturday and a roast on Sunday. Outside is a children's play area. ❀◐◑♣P🚌🐾📶♫

Oxhey

Railway Arms ✔
1 Aldenham Road, WD19 4AB
☎ 07976 647569 🌐 railwayarmsbushey.com
Greene King IPA, Abbot; 2 changing beers (sourced nationally; often Tring) [H]
Friendly and welcoming Victorian pub opposite Bushey station. The interior features railway memorabilia, befitting its name. Historically it was used as a masons' meeting house, as indicated by the coat of arms on the side of the pub. It is now a multi-screen sports venue showing a wide range, including Gaelic football. The public bar has a pool table and signed Watford FC shirts.
🐴❀🚆(Bushey) ⊖(Bushey) ♣P🚌🐾📶

Villiers Arms
108 Villiers Road, WD19 4AJ
☎ (01923) 448848
Timothy Taylor Landlord; 2 changing beers (sourced nationally; often Butcombe, Tring) [H]
Traditional family-run village pub, popular with the local community. The entrance leads straight into the single small bar, with a lounge area around the corner decorated with vintage advertising posters and other memorabilia. The pub is cosy in the evenings and has a light, airy feel in bright weather. The patio and beer garden provide extra space for the warmer months. Entertainment includes occasional live music and a regular quiz, normally on the first Monday of the month.
Q🐴❀🚆(Bushey) ⊖(Bushey) ♣🚌🐾📶

Park Street

Overdraught
86 Park Street, AL2 2JR
☎ (01727) 768221
Greene King IPA; 1 changing beer (sourced nationally) [H]
Traditional, family-friendly village pub situated on the old Roman Watling Street. The O.D., as it is known by locals, features a split level bar with beams, brass and a listed fireplace, and a range of sporting photographs adorning the walls. Meals are served daily, with food prepared from locally sourced produce. Poker is played on Tuesday evenings. There is a sizeable garden with children's play equipment and a pool table in the newly-built annex.
🐴❀◐◑♿🚆♣P🚌(652,655) 🐾📶♫

Potters Bar

Admiral Byng ✔
186-192 Darkes Lane, EN6 1AF (corner of Byng Drive)
☎ (01707) 645484
Greene King Abbot; Ruddles Best Bitter; Sharp's Doom Bar; 8 changing beers (sourced nationally) [H]
A friendly community Wetherspoon pub with a display of two model sailing ships and other memorabilia celebrating the exploits and death of Admiral Byng who was executed for 'failing to do his utmost' to save Minorca from falling to the French in 1756. (The family estate is located nearby.) It offers a good choice of real cider. In summer the frontage of the pub is opened onto the street, with additional seating provided.
🐴❀◐◑♿🚆♣🚌(84,610) 📶

Preston

Red Lion [L]
The Green, SG4 7UD (on the green at crossroads in village)
☎ (01462) 459585 🌐 theredlionpreston.co.uk
Timothy Taylor Landlord; 4 changing beers (sourced nationally) [H]
This attractive free house on the village green is the first community-owned pub in Britain. There is an ever-changing list of beers, many from small breweries. Fresh home-made meals are served, often using locally sourced ingredients (no food Sun eve and Mon). The pub hosts the village cricket teams. It has been voted local CAMRA Pub of the Year numerous times, as well as regional Pub of the Year in 2019, and received a CAMRA 50th anniversary golden award in 2021.
Q🐴❀◐◑♣🍎P🚌(88) 🐾📶♫

Puckeridge

White Hart [L]
Braughing Road, SG11 1RR
☎ (01920) 821309
McMullen AK Original Mild, Country Bitter; 1 changing beer (sourced nationally) [H]
A 14th-century pub that was named after the emblem of Richard II. Its many rooms include a dining room with a huge fireplace (ask about the story of the beam over it). The large garden has a children's play area and you will also find a thatched gazebo built around a tree in the car park. 🐴❀◐◑P🚌(386,331)🐾📶♫

St Albans

Garibaldi ✔
61 Albert Street, AL1 1RT
☎ (01727) 894745 🌐 garibaldistalbans.co.uk
Fuller's Oliver's Island, London Pride, ESB; Gale's HSB; 1 changing beer (sourced nationally) [H]
A fine example of a back-street local, in the heart of Sopwell near the cathedral. The landlord is a past winner of the Fuller's Master Cellarman award and serves an extensive range of Fuller's ales. Home-cooked food is available on Saturday and roasts on Sunday, with excellent service provided by friendly bar staff. This is a genuine community pub, supporting a variety of national and local good causes, and hosting bingo, music, darts nights and annual charity quizzes.
🐴❀◐◑♿🚆(Abbey) ♣🚌🐾📶♫

Great Northern L ✓

172 London Road, AL1 1PQ
☎ (01727) 730867 ⊕ greatnorthernpub.co.uk
Marston's Pedigree; 4 changing beers (sourced nationally) Ⓗ

This independent, Grade II-listed pub was reopened in 2015 after major renovation and serves a rotating range of cask beers, including at least one Hertfordshire ale. The menu features classic British dishes and roasts on Sundays. Quiz nights are held on Tuesday and music nights on the first Wednesday of each month. The pub hosts occasional brewery takeovers, and an annual summer beer festival is held in June/July, with other beer festivals taking place throughout the year. There is a large garden with a heated marquee.
⛄❀◑ὸ≉(City)●♜❀♠

Lower Red Lion L

34-36 Fishpool Street, AL3 4RX
☎ (01727) 855669 ⊕ thelowerredlion.co.uk
Tring Side Pocket for a Toad; 4 changing beers (sourced nationally) Ⓗ

Classic Grade II-listed pub located in a conservation area in one of the city's most picturesque streets. The Lower Red was an early champion of CAMRA's values in the real ale revival movement and continues to stock quality real ales, ciders and perries. Home-cooked food is sourced locally where possible and served at lunchtimes and weekday evenings. Beer festivals are held in May/June and August. ❀◑Ｐ♜❀♠

Mermaid

98 Hatfield Road, AL1 3RL
☎ (01727) 845700
Oakham Citra; 5 changing beers (sourced nationally) Ⓗ

Welcoming community pub with a diverse clientele, a short walk from the city centre and railway station. It serves an interesting and regularly changing choice of ales, usually including a stout or porter, plus ciders and bottled foreign beers. Beer festivals are held on the May Day and August bank holiday weekends, and a cider festival over the Spring bank holiday. Live music is performed on Sunday evenings. Outside is an impressive covered garden. Winner of several local CAMRA awards.
❀◑≉(City)♣●Ｐ❀♠

Portland Arms

63 Portland Street, AL3 4RA
☎ (01727) 851463 ⊕ portlandarmsstalbans.com
Fuller's London Pride, ESB; Gale's Seafarers Ale; 2 changing beers (sourced nationally) Ⓗ

Welcoming traditional community local, tucked away in a residential area, a short stroll from the city centre and handy for the cathedral and Verulamium Museum. The open fire, wood panelling and old pictures of St Albans give the pub a warm and cosy feel. It offers a variety of live music, quizzes and entertainment nights. Freshly-prepared, home-cooked meals are served using locally sourced ingredients. Q⛄❀◑ὸ≉(Abbey)♣Ｐ❀♠

Robin Hood ✓

126 Victoria Street, AL1 3TG
☎ (01727) 856459 ⊕ robin-hood-st-albans.co.uk
Harvey's Sussex Best Bitter; 2 changing beers (sourced nationally) Ⓗ

Friendly single-bar community pub handy for St Albans City station and popular with homeward-bound commuters. Real cider or perry is always available to complement the rotating beer range, reliably presented in excellent condition. A secluded garden to the rear offers summer enjoyment, while a selection of board games, table skittles and traditional jukebox provide

entertainment indoors. Folk music is played on Wednesday evenings. Local CAMRA Pub of the Year 2021. Closing times may vary. ⛄❀≉(City)♣●♜❀♠

Royston Social Club

12 College Road, AL1 5ND
☎ (01727) 853656
Fuller's London Pride; 3 changing beers (sourced nationally) Ⓗ

Friendly and long-established social club serving a part of St Albans with few other real ale options. A warm welcome awaits card-carrying CAMRA members who can use the bar facilities as guests, and the four well-kept cask beers usually include offerings from smaller local brewers. A large function room, complete with stage, complements a smaller drinking area with a traditional public bar atmosphere. Entertainment includes a jukebox, pool table and dartboards. CIU affiliated.
⛄❀ὸ♜❀♠

Six Bells L ✓

16-18 St Michael's Street, AL3 4SH
☎ (01727) 856945 ⊕ the-six-bells.com
Oakham JHB; Timothy Taylor Landlord; Tring Ridgeway; 3 changing beers (sourced regionally) Ⓗ

Characterful 16th-century pub located in the attractive St Michael's village, a short walk from the city centre and cathedral and close to Verulamium Museum and Roman Theatre. Three regular beers are offered, including at least one from Hertfordshire, plus three changing guests, often provided by Vale brewery. Traditional cider is available during the summer months. Good-quality home-cooked food is served daily, with themed food evenings on Thursdays once or twice a month. There is a pleasant outdoor covered patio. Notably dog friendly.
⛄❀◑♣Ｐ❀♠

Waterend Barn

Civic Close, St Peter's Street, AL1 3LE
☎ (01727) 814100
Greene King Abbot; Ruddles Best Bitter; Sharp's Doom Bar; 4 changing beers (sourced nationally) Ⓗ

These two characterful 16th- and 17th-century timber barns were dismantled and transported to St Albans from elsewhere in Hertfordshire in the early and middle 20th century, then joined together and run for many years as tea-rooms. Converted into a JD Wetherspoon pub in 2005, the timber construction is largely exposed to view and there are several drinking areas and a wide range of real ales on offer. Food is available all day, with early morning breakfasts. ⛄◑ὸ♜❀

White Hart Tap L ✓

4 Keyfield Terrace, AL1 1QJ
☎ (01727) 860974 ⊕ whiteharttap.co.uk
St Austell Tribute; Timothy Taylor Landlord, Boltmaker; Tring Side Pocket for a Toad; 2 changing beers (sourced nationally) Ⓗ

One-bar back-street local featuring two beers free of tie, including some from microbreweries. Good-value, home-cooked food is served at lunchtimes and on Monday to Sunday evenings, with roasts on Sunday (booking recommended) with occasional themed food nights. The Wednesday quiz night is popular locally; other attractions include summer barbecues and occasional beer festivals. There is a heated, covered smoking area outside, plus gazebos, and a public car park opposite the pub.
⛄❀◑ὸ≉(City)♣●♜❀

St Pauls Walden

Strathmore Arms L

London Road, SG4 8BT TL193222

☎ (01438) 871654 ⊕ thestrathmorearms.co.uk
Tring Side Pocket for a Toad; 4 changing beers (sourced nationally) Ⓗ
This traditional pub on the Bowes-Lyon estate in rural Hertfordshire has been serving drinkers since 1882. It offers a constantly changing list of guest beers, featuring little-known breweries. Unusual bottled beers are also sold, along with real ciders and perries. A regular in the Guide since 1981, the pub displays a full collection of Good Beer Guides going back to 1976. It has a separate snug. Pizza and pasta evening is Wednesday and gourmet food nights are held on occasion (booking essential). Q☾❀⊕❶Å♣P🚪❀ 🎵

Sandridge

Green Man ✔
31 High Street, AL4 9DD
☎ (01727) 854845 ⊕ greenmansandridge.co.uk
Greene King Abbot; Sharp's Atlantic; Tring Side Pocket for a Toad Ⓖ**; 1 changing beer (sourced nationally)** Ⓗ
This community pub in the centre of the village extends a warm welcome to beer drinkers, with all ales served directly from casks in the cellar located a few steps along from the bar. Traditional freshly cooked and locally sourced food is available at lunchtimes. A rear conservatory caters for small groups and the courtyard garden behind the pub boasts sunset countryside views. The pub holds a quiz every Monday night. Dogs are welcome. Q☾❀❶♣P❀ 🎵

Rose & Crown Ⓛ
24 High Street, AL4 9DA
☎ (01727) 859739 ⊕ roseandcrownpubsandridge.co.uk
Tring Ridgeway; 2 changing beers (sourced nationally) Ⓗ
A 17th-century inn located in the centre of Sandridge, on the doorstep of Heartwood Forest. The pub's traditional features of oak beams and inglenook fireplace are tastefully augmented with an abundance of seating and dining areas. There is a large car park to the rear and a garden where barbecues are regularly held. The pub also has a separate function room available for hire. Sunday roasts are served; booking in advance advised. Q☾❀❶&♣P🚪❀ 🎵

Sawbridgeworth

George IV
Knight Street, CM21 9AT
☎ (01279) 723527
McMullen AK Original Mild, Country Bitter, IPA Ⓗ
A friendly, community-led McMullen's pub off the main high street, near the town centre and railway station, with two bars and a pleasant paved garden. Food is not served but the landlady is happy for customers to bring their own – a nearby baker's is a popular choice. The local beer group, darts teams and bellringers meet here and charity quizzes are run frequently. Q☾❀&╋🚪(509,510) ❀

Stevenage

Broken Seal Tap Room
29B High Street, SG1 3AU (entrance Basils Rd at N end of High St)
☎ 07973 673040 ⊕ sixhillsbrewing.co.uk
3 changing beers (sourced nationally) Ⓖ
Stevenage's first brewpub opened in 2019 as the taproom for Bog Brew brewery, subsequently renamed as Six Hills brewery. Their beers are brewed on site and usually served via KeyKeg, though guest beers often

include two or three cask beers. A large range of bottled and canned beers are also available to drink in or take away. Q❀&❶🚪🎵

Tring

King's Arms Ⓛ
King Street, HP23 6BE (corner of Queen St and King St)
SP921111
☎ (01442) 823318 ⊕ kingsarmstring.co.uk
Tring Moongazing; 4 changing beers (sourced regionally; often Hook Norton, Leighton Buzzard, XT) Ⓗ
An 1830s building affectionately known as 'the pink pub' by locals for its fuchsia exterior. The pub offers a changing range of five real ales and one cider. Two real fires are welcoming in winter, and the outside heated patio and canopies provide extra space in the warmer months. Fantastic home-cooked cuisine is on offer. Children are welcome at all times.
Q☾❀❤❶&♣🚪(500,501) 🥾

Ware

Crooked Billet ✔
140 Musley Hill, SG12 7NL (via New Rd from High St)
☎ (01920) 462516
4 changing beers (sourced nationally) Ⓗ
Friendly gem of a traditional community pub, tastefully refurbished in 2021, well worth the 15-minute walk up New Road and Musley Hill from the town centre. Its two small bars feature TV sport and darts. It serves a varying range of two to three ales, often including a mild, porter or stout at weekends. Outside there are tables to the front and rear. ☾❀&♣🚪(395)❀ 🥾

Wareside

Chequers Ⓛ
Ware Road, SG12 7QY (on B1004)
☎ (01920) 467010 ⊕ chequerswareside.com
House beer (by Hadham); 1 changing beer (sourced regionally) Ⓗ
A rural free house dating from the 15th century, the Chequers was originally a coaching inn and has three distinct bars plus a restaurant. The rotating complement of three beers features local brewers and some from further afield. The house IPA is brewed exclusively for the pub by the local Hadham brewery. All food is home-made and there are extensive vegetarian/vegan options. Walkers and cyclists are welcome, making this a good base for a ramble. There are no games machines, no music, and no swearing allowed.
Q☾❶&♣❤P🚪(M3,M4) ❀ 🥾

Watford

Two Trees Micro
18 Vicarage Road, WD18 0EH (in the pedestrian area at NE end of Vicarage Rd) ⊕ twotreesmicro.com
3 changing beers (sourced nationally) Ⓗ
A recently opened small micropub with four handpumps serving three real ales and a cider, plus four craft keg beers. Due to licensing restrictions the bar closes at 10.30pm during the week and 9.30pm on Sunday (though it may open until later if people arrive by closing time). Closed on Mondays. Further restrictions may apply on Watford FC match days. There is a small outside drinking area to the front of the pub. Basic pub snacks are available. Q🥾(High Street)❤🚪

Wild Hill

Woodman ♈

45 Wildhill Road, AL9 6EA (between A1000 and B158)
TL264068
☎ (01707) 642618 ⊕ thewoodman.uk
Greene King IPA, Abbot; 4 changing beers (sourced nationally) 🅗

A friendly and unpretentious rural village pub that is extremely community orientated. It is a staunch supporter of real ale, serving up to six ales including four guests. Lined oversized glasses available on request. Good pub grub is served at lunchtimes (Mon-Sat only). Look for God's Waiting Room – a good spot for a cosy drink. The large garden is ideal in summer. Multiple winner of local and county CAMRA Pub of the Year.
🏚🌣♣P🐾🛜

Breweries

3 Brewers of St Albans SIBA

The Potato Shed, Symonds Hyde Farm, Symonds Hyde Lane, Hatfield, AL10 9BB
☎ (01707) 271636 ☎ 07941 854615
⊕ 3brewers.co.uk

⊗ Launched in 2013, the 3 Brewers uses water from its own borehole. Cask and keg beers are supplied to local pubs and clubs, with bottled beer and mini kegs sold direct from the brewery. The taproom is open Friday/Saturday (and Sunday during summer). A mezzanine level with extra seating is available and is regularly used by local artists for displays. Both the mezzanine and brewery are available for private hire. Brewery tours and membership are available and an annual music festival is held every September. ‼🍴♦

Golden English Ale (ABV 3.8%) GOLD
Copper (ABV 3.9%) BITTER
Classic English Ale (ABV 4%) BITTER
Three Brewers Blonde (ABV 4.2%) BLOND
Dunstable Giant (ABV 4.5%) BITTER
IPA (ABV 4.6%) PALE
Special English Ale (ABV 4.8%) BITTER

Contract brewed for B&T Brewery:
Shefford Bitter (ABV 3.8%) BITTER
A pale brown beer with a light hop aroma and a hoppy taste leading to a bitter finish.
Dragon Slayer (ABV 4.5%) GOLD
A golden beer with a malt and hop flavour and a bitter finish. More malty and less hoppy than is usual for a beer of this style.

Baron

Great Hormead, SG9 0PB
☎ (01763) 289924 ☎ 07936 357617
⊕ baronbrewing.co.uk

Launched in 2021, Baron Brewing is run by Jack Baron in the Hertfordshire countryside. The focus is on modern styles including heavily-hopped pale ales and IPAs, along with lagers and table beers. The 1,000-litre brewhouse allows experimentation and an ever-changing range of beers to be brewed including a number of collaborations with other well-known craft breweries. Currently beer is distributed in can and keg only but there are plans for cask in the future. The brewery taproom opened in 2022. There are plans for brewery experience days in the future along with a range of new beer styles. ♦

Belgian Brewer, The

Unit 11, The Links Business Centre, Raynham Road, Bishop's Stortford, CM23 5NZ
☎ (01279) 507515 ⊕ thebelgianbrewer.co.uk

Situated just outside Bishop's Stortford town centre, the Belgian Brewer is a small brewery and taproom. Established in 2018, it produces Belgian-style beers brewed to traditional Belgian methods using family recipes. Currently producing under 10,000 litres per month, demand is increasing, especially for its speciality fruit beers. The brewery has recently expanded to take on the premises next door to increase capacity and allow the creation of a function hall. ‼🍴♦LIVE♦

Bowtie

78 Church Road, Watford, WD17 4PU
⊕ bowtiebrewers.co.uk

A one-barrel nanobrewery founded in 2018 in a specially designed brewshed. Commercial brewing began in 2019, offering three ranges of small batch beers – traditional, craft and speciality. Beers are mostly available in bottles but cask-conditioned beer is occasionally produced. ♦LIVE

Buntingford

Greys Brewhouse, Therfield Road, Royston, SG8 9NW
☎ (01763) 250749 ☎ 07851 743799
⊕ buntingfordbrewery.com

⊗ Brewing commenced on the current site in 2005 and has expanded to a capacity of approx. 15 barrels per brew. Regular beers are brewed alongside seasonal/occasional brews, and various themed specials. An onsite well supplies water and malt is sourced from East Anglia. All liquid waste is treated in a reed bed. The brewery is located on a conservation farm, and a wide variety of bird life is visible from the brewhouse. The brewery is open to the public one day a month. ♦

Twitchell (ABV 3.8%) BITTER
Hurricane (ABV 4%) BITTER
Single Hop Varieties (ABV 4%) GOLD
Polar Star (ABV 4.4%) GOLD
Riwaka Station (ABV 4.8%) PALE

Creative Juices

Woodoaks Farm, Denham Way, Maple Cross, Rickmansworth, WD3 9XQ
☎ (01923) 771779
⊕ creativejuicesbrewingcompany.com

A craft brewery, taproom and beer garden that opened 2019 in a renovated dairy building, on a farm in Hertfordshire. Beers are unpasteurised and filtered and are either kegged or canned. No cask-conditioned ale is produced. ♦

Crossover Blendery

Lannock Manor Farm, Hitchin Road, Weston, Hitchin, SG4 7EE ⊕ crossoverblendery.co.uk

Founded in 2018, a small blendery operation producing 100% spontaneously-fermented beers aged in traditional vessels such as oak barrels. The aim is to source ingredients as close to the blendery as possible, working with farmers and growers directly, and promoting its produce through the beers. Taproom and shop opened in 2022 (see website for opening hours). ‼🍴♦♦

Farr Brew SIBA

Unit 7, The Courtyard, Samuels Farm, Coleman Green Lane, Wheathampstead, AL4 8ER ☎ 07967 998820 🌐 farrbrew.com

⊗ Farr Brew began brewing in 2014, expanding in 2016 with a new 10-barrel facility. Ecological and environmental concerns are at the forefront of everything Farr Brew creates. Community engagement includes hop-growing and most recently the launch of a home brewers competition. The brewery now runs six pubs around Hertfordshire: Reading Rooms, Wheathampstead; Rising Sun, Slip End; Red Cow, Harpenden; Eight Bells, Old Hatfield; Elephant & Castle, Amwell; and most recently Bull, Whitwell. ‼ ♦

Chief Jester (ABV 3.6%) PALE
Our Greatest Golden (ABV 4.1%) GOLD
Our Best Bitter (ABV 4.2%) BITTER
Our Most Perfect Pale (ABV 4.2%) PALE
Pride Pale (ABV 4.2%) PALE
Farr Afield (ABV 4.3%) BITTER
Black Listed IBA (ABV 4.5%) PALE
Farr & Away (ABV 4.5%) PALE
Farr Apart (ABV 4.8%) PALE
Rusty Stag (ABV 4.8%) BITTER
Fresh Start (ABV 4.9%) PALE
1492 (ABV 5%) GOLD
Porter (ABV 5%) PORTER

Garden City

22 The Wynd, Letchworth Garden City, SG6 3EN ☎ 07932 739558 🌐 gardencitybrewery.co.uk

⊗ A brewbar established in 2016 using a 2.5-barrel plant, serving a selection of its own ales plus guests on gravity. ♦

Lock 81

c/o Wishful Drinking, 124 High Street, Rickmansworth, WD3 1AB ☎ 07768 320 229 🌐 wishfuldrinking.co.uk

Named after the Batchworth lock on the Grand Union Canal at Rickmansworth. Name and beer recipes now owned by the owners of the Wishful Drinking bar in Rickmansworth and currently cuckoo brewing canned and KeyKeg beers at various sites.

McMullen SIBA IFBB

26 Old Cross, Hertford, SG14 1RD ☎ (01992) 584911 🌐 mcmullens.co.uk

McMullen, Hertfordshire's oldest, independent brewery, was founded in 1827. Its famous brew, AK, is traceable back to the 19th century. The 'Authentic Heritage' tag promotes its core beers. Additional seasonal ales are produced throughout the year, sometimes produced under the Rivertown Brewing name. A microbrewery supplements the main plant. Almost all 125 tied pubs, spread across South-East England, serve cask beer. ♦

AK Original Mild (ABV 3.7%) MILD
A pleasant mix of malt and hops leads to a distinctive, dry aftertaste.
Country Bitter (ABV 4.3%) BITTER
A full-bodied beer with a well-balanced mix of malt, hops and fruit throughout.
IPA (ABV 4.8%) PALE

Mad Squirrel SIBA

Unit 18, Boxted Farm, Berkhamsted Road, Potten End, HP1 2SG ☎ (01442) 256970 🌐 madsquirrelbrew.co.uk

⊗ Brewing began in 2010 on the outskirts of Hemel Hempstead. Since 2017 it has used a custom brew kit from the US, using water from an onsite borehole at Potten End. The brewery maintains an innovative outlook, introducing many specialised craft beers while maintaining a range of more traditional cask ales and beers. Output is distributed to venues throughout London and the South-East, including its own ever-increasing chain of Tap & Bottle shops. All beers are suitable for vegans. ‼ ♦ V

Mister Squirrel (ABV 4%) BITTER
Resolution (ABV 4.2%) GOLD
London Porter (ABV 5%) PORTER

New River SIBA

Unit 47, Hoddesdon Industrial Centre, Pindar Road, Hoddesdon, EN11 0FF ☎ (01992) 446200 🌐 newriverbrewery.co.uk

⊗ New River commenced brewing in 2015 on the banks of the New River in Hoddesdon, using a new 10-barrel plant. Many of its beer names are themed around the river. Its core range of ales is complemented by seasonal beers and one-off specials. ♦

London Tap (ABV 3.8%) PALE
Twin Spring (ABV 4%) GOLD
Riverbed Red (ABV 4.2%) BITTER
Blind Poet (ABV 4.5%) PORTER
Five Inch Drop (ABV 4.6%) PALE
Isle Of Rye Pale Ale (ABV 5.2%) PALE

Oxhey Village

14 Maxwell Rise, Watford, WD19 4DX ☎ 07470 422842 ✉ shaun@ruthandshaun.co.uk

Oxhey Village Brewery is a nanobrewery set up by five drinking companions, which began commercial brewing in 2019. Currently producing real ale in cask and craft beer in keg for a few local pubs and clubs. Additionally, small batches are available on request for events and beer festivals.

Paradigm

4d Green End Farm, 93a Church Lane, Sarratt, WD3 6HH ☎ (01923) 291215 🌐 paradigmbrewery.com

⊗ Founded by two friends, Neil Hodges and Rob Atkinson, Paradigm went into production in 2015. Its five-barrel plant is located in an industrial unit on a farm. One-off beers are also brewed. The brewery and beer names are based on corporate jargon and buzzwords. ‼ ♦ LIVE

Fake News (ABV 3.8%) PALE
Seven (ABV 3.8%) PALE
Holistic (ABV 4%) GOLD
Heads Up (ABV 4.1%) PALE
Golden session pale ale with a predominately bitter hop core balanced by a backdrop of malt and touches of fruit.
Win-win (ABV 4.2%) BITTER
Levelling-up (ABV 4.3%) PALE
Synergy (ABV 4.3%) BITTER
Black Friday (ABV 6%) MILD
Woke (ABV 6%) GOLD

Pope's Yard

Unit 12, Paramount Industrial Estate, Sandown Road, Watford, WD24 7XA
☎ **(01923) 224182** ⊕ **popesyard.co.uk**

Pope's Yard began commercial brewing in 2012 using a one-barrel plant. Two expansions since then, and three relocations, means it now operates a five-barrel plant for production and a one-barrel pilot plant. Some beers may be suitable for vegans. LIVE V

Lacerta (ABV 3.9%) PALE
Luminaire (ABV 3.9%) PALE
Bright Star (ABV 4.1%) PALE
Quartermaster (ABV 4.4%) BITTER
Club Hammer Stout (ABV 5.5%) STOUT

Six Hills SIBA

Rear of 29b High Street, Stevenage, SG1 3BG
☎ **07973 673040** ⊕ **sixhillsbrewing.co.uk**

⊗ Previously known as Bog Brew, Six Hills Brewing was established in 2017 and renamed in 2021. Beers are available at local beer festivals, freehouses, and the tap, located next to the brewery. It has expanded from a two-barrel plant to 2,500 litres per month capacity. There are several regular beers as well as seasonal specials. All beers are unfined and vegan. The brewery holds regular events (festivals/takeovers) throughout the year.
!! ☰ ♦ LIVE V ✿

Running with the Big Dog (ABV 4.7%) PALE

Tring SIBA

Dunsley Farm, London Road, Tring, HP23 6HA
☎ **(01442) 890721** ⊕ **tringbrewery.co.uk**

Founded in 1992, Tring Brewery revived the traditional art of brewing in the market town of Tring, which had been without a brewery for more than 50 years. It moved to its present site in 2010. It brews more than 130 barrels a week, producing an extensive core range of beers augmented by monthly and seasonal specials, most taking names from local myths and legends.
!! ☰ ♦ LIVE

Side Pocket for a Toad (ABV 3.6%) BITTER
Brock Bitter (ABV 3.7%) BITTER
Mansion Mild (ABV 3.7%) MILD
Citra Session (ABV 3.9%) PALE
Drop Bar Pale Ale (ABV 4%) PALE
Ridgeway (ABV 4%) BITTER
Moongazing (ABV 4.2%) BITTER
Pale Four (ABV 4.6%) GOLD
Tea Kettle Stout (ABV 4.7%) STOUT
Colley's Dog (ABV 5.2%) BITTER
Death or Glory (ABV 7.2%) BARLEY

Two Bob

Oaklands, AL9 9SG ☎ **07966 159643**
✉ **twobobbrewco@gmail.com**

Two Bob Brewing Co is a nanobrewery in North East Hertfordshire producing small-batch, hand-crafted ales using traditional methods and natural ingredients. ♦ LIVE

Gold (ABV 4.3%) GOLD
EPA (ABV 4.6%) IPA

White Hart Tap

▤ **White Hart Tap, 4 Keyfield Terrace, St Albans, AL1 1QJ**
☎ **(01727) 860974** ⊕ **whitetharttap.co.uk**

Brewing began in 2015. Beers are only available in the pub. Brewing is currently suspended.

Plough, Datchworth (Photo: Emma Haines)

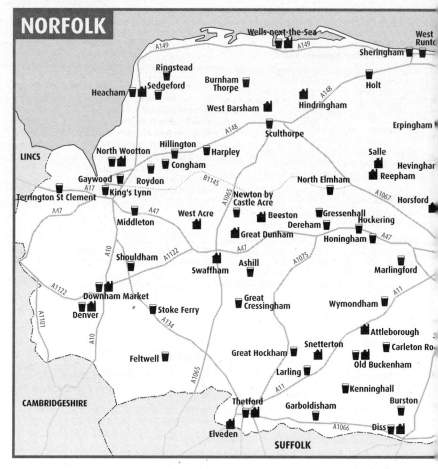

NORFOLK

Acle

Hermitage L

64 Old Road, NR13 3QP (on the A1064, 500yds from the A47 Acle roundabout)
☎ 07826 757733 ⊕ thehermitageacle.com
Adnams Ghost Ship H/G; 3 changing beers (sourced locally; often Green Jack, Mr Winter's) G
Food-led pub offering freshly prepared food and a good selection of ales, mainly sourced locally. It has an attractive courtyard garden and seperate areas leading off from the bar area, including a light and airy-west facing conservatory. The pub hosts various food-themed events throughout the year and live music plays in the courtyard during the warmer months. With friendly staff and locals, this pub is certainly worth the short walk from the village centre. Q❄☺❀❍◑ ÀP❏(X1,X11)❀ ❅ ♪

Ashill

White Hart Free House L ✅

Church Street, IP25 7AW (100yds from St Nicholas church)
☎ (01760) 622190 ⊕ ashillwhitehart.co.uk
6 changing beers (sourced regionally) H
Voted local CAMRA Pub of the Year for 2022 despite only reopening in October 2020, this pub has a warm and friendly atmosphere with a great choice of draught beers and home-cooked foods. The pub is a hub for the local community as well as a good place for visitors to stay to enjoy the local area. There is an EV charger available for those with electric vehicles. ❀❄❍◑❅P❀ ♪

Banningham

Crown Inn L ✅

Colby Road, NR11 7DY (N of B1145, 1 mile E of A140)
☎ (01263) 733534 ⊕ banninghamcrown.co.uk
Adnams Ghost Ship; Greene King IPA, Abbot; 4 changing beers (sourced nationally) H
Traditional 17th-century village inn, the original timbers in the bar area give it a warm atmosphere which is enhanced by a log fire in winter. Three permanent ales are supported by up to four guest beers from regional and microbreweries and a locally produced cider. Popular for its quality cuisine made using local produce. The patio, garden and barbecue areas are ideal for summer alfresco dining. Check the website for regular events, an annual music festival and seasonal opening times.
Q❄❍◑❅À❅P❏(18)❀ ❅

Burnham Thorpe

Lord Nelson

Walsingham Road, PE31 8HN (off B1355)
☎ (01328) 854988 ⊕ nelsonslocal.com
Changing beers (sourced regionally; often Woodforde's)

Carleton Rode

Carleton Rode Social Club
Jubilee Hall, Mill Road, NR16 1NQ
☎ 07507 035390
Adnams Southwold Bitter; 2 changing beers (sourced locally; often Moon Gazer) Ⓗ
A large social club on the outskirts of the village, serving three well-kept ales. It was extensively refurbished in 2020, and has active pool and darts teams, as well as a large garden. The first beer festival was held in May 2021, with potentially regular festivals planned. No food is served, but a pizza van visits. ❀&♣P

Catfield

Crown Inn Ⓛ
The Street, NR29 5AA (in centre of village, S of A149, E of Stalham)
☎ (01692) 580128 ⊕ catfieldcrown.co.uk
Greene King IPA; 3 changing beers (sourced locally) Ⓗ
This 300-year-old village inn, with a real fire in winter, is a local that is also a welcome oasis for Broads holidaymakers. Ales are usually sourced from local breweries, together with unusual imports from the West

A 17th century pub in the village where Nelson was born and the first pub to be named in his honour after the battle of the Nile (Abu Qir). It reopened in 2021 after a five year closure and is now owned by the Holkham Estate and run by Woodforde's brewery. The pub has been totally remodelled, but the original room with the settles survives. Beer is served from the adjoining bar. There is a large dining area and an extensive garden. All the beers are from Woodforde's. Q❀🕭⏲&P❀ 🛜

Burston

Crown Inn
Mill Road, IP22 5TW (on the green by crossroads in middle of village)
☎ (01379) 741257 ⊕ burstoncrown.com
Adnams Southwold Bitter Ⓗ/Ⓖ**; 4 changing beers (often Earl Soham, Grain, Tindall)** Ⓗ
Attractive 16th-century Grade II-listed pub featuring exposed beams, newspapers and log fire in the inglenook fireplace. It has two bars – the second with more table space – so the overall restaurant area is quite large. A popular food destination with locally sourced ingredients – booking is advised. Drinkers are welcome in the main bar. The garden has lots of outside seating, including a large, covered patio area. Live music plays on Sunday afternoons and there is an annnual Beer, Bikes and Bands festival. Q❀🕭⏲♣P❀🛜♫

REAL ALE BREWERIES

All Day ✦ Salle
Ampersand ✦ Diss
Barsham West Barsham
Beeston Beeston
Birdhouse Downham Market
Blimey! Norwich
Boudicca Horsford
Bull of the Woods Kirby Cane
Chalk Hill 🍺 Norwich
Dancing Men 🍺 Happisburgh
Drenchfoot Thetford
Duration ✦ West Acre
Elmtree Snetterton
Fat Cat Norwich
Fengate Hevingham
Fox 🍺 Heacham
Golden Triangle Norwich
Grain Harleston
Humpty Dumpty Reedham
Iceni Elveden
Lacons Great Yarmouth
Lynn North Wootton
Malt Coast Wells-next-the-Sea
Moon Gazer Hindringham
Mr Winter's Norwich
Opa Hay's Aldeby
Panther Reepham
People's Thorpe-next-Haddiscoe
Poppyland Cromer
Redwell ✦ Norwich: Trowse
S&P Horsford
St Andrews Brewhouse 🍺 Norwich
Steam Shed Swaffham
Stumptail Great Dunham
Tindall Seething
Tipple's Salhouse
Tombstone 🍺 Great Yarmouth
Two Rivers ✦ Denver
Wagtail Old Buckenham
Waveney 🍺 Earsham
Why Not Norwich
Wildcraft ✦ Smallburgh
Wolf Attleborough
Woodforde's Woodbastwick

Country. There is usually at least one dark ale available. Food includes home-made pub offerings, with local ingredients used where possible. There is a separate function/dining room and a secluded rear garden for the summer. Two holiday cottages are available. An annual beer festival is held in the summer, usually in July. Q ➤ ❀ 🍴 ◑ ♣ P 🚲 (10,6) ❀ 🛜

Chedgrave

White Horse ✓
5 Norwich Road, NR14 6ND
☎ (01508) 520250 ⊕ whitehorsechedgrave.co.uk
Adnams Southwold Bitter, Ghost Ship; Timothy Taylor Landlord; Young's Bitter Ⓗ
Friendly village pub with separate pub and restaurant facilities, a covered outdoor eating area and a large garden. Drinkers are well catered for with a range of five real ales, including Taylor's Landlord. Technically in Chedgrave, the pub is within easy walking distance of the holiday moorings in neighbouring Loddon. There is an active and varied social calendar including live music, a 40s evening, music festival and teddy bears' picnic. The pub hosts several clubs including pool, darts, running and bowls. ➤ ❀ ◑ ♿ ▲ ♣ P 🚲 (X22,146) ❀ 🛜

Congham

Anvil Inn
St Andrews Lane, PE32 1DU (off the B1153)
☎ (01485) 600625 ⊕ anvilcongham.co.uk
Greene King Abbot; 2 changing beers (sourced nationally) Ⓗ
This pub is a little off the beaten track, but worthwhile finding for its great home-made food. The bar is set in a large open-plan area and has three handpumps for ever-changing beers. Food is served in the bar area and in a separate restaurant which also doubles as a function room when required. Regular pub quizzes, charity bingo nights and live music make this a popular venue. A small campsite at the rear of the pub is a welcome new feature. Closed Mondays. ➤ ❀ ◑ ♿ ▲ ♣ P 🛜 ♫

Cromer

Red Lion Hotel Ⓛ
Brook Street, NR27 9HD (E of church on clifftop)
☎ (01263) 514964 ⊕ redlion-cromer.co.uk
8 changing beers (sourced locally) Ⓗ
Splendidly situated, with views of Cromer pier and the sea, the 19th-century Red Lion has retained many original features including panelling, a Victorian tiled floor and open wood fires. The work of local artists decorates the walls of the two bar areas. Up to six guest ales are usually served, often from local breweries such as Winter's and Green Jack. Beer festivals are held in the summer. The restaurant offers an extensive menu including breakfast. Accommodation is also available. Q ➤ ❀ 🍴 ◑ ♿ ▲ P 🚲 (CH1,X44) ❀ 🛜

Denver

Blackstone Engine Bar Ⓛ
95 Sluice Road, PE38 0DZ
☎ 07518 099868
Two Rivers Miners Mild, Hares Hopping, Kiwi Kick, Denver Diamond, Happy Hopper, Porters Pride; 3 changing beers (sourced locally) Ⓗ
The bar is located in the old workshop of the Denver Mill complex. The mighty Blackstone diesel engine that powered the mill is still in its original engine house and still in working condition, and you can see some of the

machinery which gives the bar its name. There is no food available but there is a reciprocal agreement with the café next door that you can take beer into the café or food into the bar. Local CAMRA Cider Pub of the Year 2019. Q ♣ P

Dereham

Cock ✓
28 Norwich Street, NR19 1BX
☎ (01362) 693393 ⊕ the-cock.co.uk
4 changing beers (sourced nationally) Ⓗ
This cosy pub has a front bar area with low beams and a large inglenook fireplace – complete with wood burner – which opens into a larger bar area with soft furnishings. To the rear is another room with additional seating and a dartboard. Outside to the rear is an attractive courtyard area with several tables and chairs. A separate room is available to hire for functions. Four changing beers from local and national breweries are served, alongside a range of snacks such as rolls and panini. Live music plays every Sunday afternoon. ➤ ❀ 🍴 ◑ ♿ ➤ ♣ P 🚲 ❀ 🛜 ♫

Diss

Ampersand Brew Tap ♈ Ⓛ
27-31 Sawmills Road, IP22 4GG
☎ (01379) 643944 ⊕ ampersandbrew.co
Ampersand The Cap Bitter; 4 changing beers (often Ampersand) Ⓗ
The brewery tap for Ampersand Brew Co. Three cask ales and up to 12 keg Ampersand ales and lagers are served. Food is from resident in-house food vendor Burger Jam. Sunday roasts are served, and a regular monthly Saturday brunch must be pre-booked. There are regular live music and DJ nights, a weekly bottle share and several special beer festival weekends organised throughout the year, including Oktoberfest. The brewery shop is open Monday to Friday, 10-5, and brewery tours and tastings can be booked. ◑ ♿ ❀ 🛜

Downham Market

Crown Hotel
12 Bridge Street, PE38 9DH
☎ (01366) 382322 ⊕ crowncoachinginn.com
Greene King IPA, Abbot; 2 changing beers (sourced nationally) Ⓗ
An unspoilt 16th-century coaching inn at the heart of the town. Entering through a room with a lovely staircase brings you to the bar with a beamed ceiling, panelled walls and large fireplaces. A good selection of ales is served. There is a restaurant, plenty of outside seating, and a separate function room that caters for parties and weddings. Accommodation is provided in 18 rooms, including family suites. Q ❀ 🍴 ◑ ➤ ♣ P 🚲 🛜

Whalebone Ⓛ ✓
58 Bridge Street, PE38 9DJ
☎ (01366) 381600
Adnams Ghost Ship; Greene King Abbot; Ruddles Best Bitter; Sharp's Doom Bar; 3 changing beers (sourced nationally) Ⓗ
This listed building, formerly the White Hart, is now part of the Wetherspoon chain. The pub has been extensively modified but retains the original façade. A large bar area leads to gardens at the rear and side. On the walls, heritage displays include whaling, drainage of the Fens, Horatio Nelson and replica whalebones. Look out for the unique carpet. There are regular beer and cider festivals plus occasional tap takeovers. Wheelchair access is available throughout. ➤ ❀ ◑ ➤ ♣ P 🚲 🛜

Earsham

Queen's Head ⓛ

Station Road, NR35 2TS (just W of Bungay)

☎ (01986) 892623

Waveney Lightweight, Welterweight; 2 changing beers (often Ampersand, Cloudwater) Ⓗ

Situated on Norfolk-Suffolk border, near Bungay, this busy 17th-century brewpub has a large front garden overlooking the village green. The main bar has flagstone floor, wooden beams and a large fireplace with a roaring fire in winter. It is home to the Waveney Brewing Co. There is a separate dining area serving food at lunchtimes (not Mon and Tue). The landlord has owned the pub since 1998. Four ales and at least one real cider are usually available. A previous local CAMRA Pub of the Year. Q❀🌳🔥◑⑃♿♣♠P🚃(580)❀📶

Erpingham

Spread Eagle ⓛ

Eagle Road, NR11 7QA (signposted off A140)

☎ (01263) 761938 ⊕ thespreadeagle.pub

Lacons Encore; Timothy Taylor Landlord; Woodforde's Wherry; 3 changing beers (sourced locally; often Lacons, Grain) Ⓗ

A traditional village-centre pub with a welcoming atmosphere. The main bar has two distinct areas, both with log stoves. There are three regular ales and three, mainly East Anglian guests. Food is served on Wednesday, Friday and Saturday evenings often by specialist high-quality caterers. A large function room, with TV and stove, overlooks the courtyard, and there is a beer garden for warmer days. Music evenings and events are held and there is an August bank holiday beer festival. Q❀🌳🔥♿♣P🚃(18,18A)❀📶

Feltwell

Wellington ⓛ

27-29 High Street, IP26 4AF

☎ (01842) 828224 ⊕ feltwellington.co.uk

3 changing beers (sourced nationally) Ⓗ

The Wellington reopened in 2014 after extensive refurbishment. There is a cosy lounge bar with a separate games room featuring pool and darts, and a 36-seat restaurant to the rear. One real cider is always on handpump. There is plenty of interesting memorabilia relating to the pub's namesake bomber. The pub is heavily involved with the local community and participates in the Meet Up Mondays initiative. On alternate weeks there are free movie screenings to provide a way for people to meet. 🌳❀◑♿♣♠P📶♫

Garboldisham

Fox Inn ⓛ

The Street, IP22 2RZ

☎ (01953) 688538 ⊕ garboldishamfox.co.uk

6 changing beers (sourced locally; often Lacons, Moon Gazer, Mr Winter's) Ⓗ

A 17th-century coaching inn near Bressingham Gardens and Banham Zoo. Bought by the local community to operate as a community pub, renovation work is ongoing. The pub serves ales from breweries such as Mr Winter's, Lacons, Norfolk Brewhouse and Wolf, and various Adnams ales from keg. Food such as pizza and souvlaki is available Friday and Saturday evening from various street food vendors see Twitter for constant updates. Sunday roasts are served and local ice cream is sold in tubs. Rumour has it that one of the pub ghosts is a black labrador. Q❀🌳🔥♿♣♠P❀📶

Gaywood

White Horse ⓛ

9 Wootton Road, PE30 4EZ

☎ 07776 061934

Fuller's London Pride; 1 changing beer (sourced nationally) Ⓗ

This popular local pub can be found near the Gaywood clock on the outskirts of King's Lynn. Since refurbishment in 2017 it has an open-plan one-roomed bar, with a number of TVs showing various sporting events. There is also a large sheltered seating and smoking area at the rear. Two beers are always available, generally from breweries from around the country. ❀♣P🚃(3,4)📶

Geldeston

Locks Inn ⓛ

Locks Lane, NR34 0HS (800yds along track from Station Rd)

☎ (01508) 830033 ⊕ thelocksinn.com

4 changing beers (sourced locally; often Lacons, People's, Wolf) Ⓗ

The Locks Inn, community owned with over 1,400 shareholders, is on the River Waveney, at the end of a long track off Station Road in Geldeston. It has large gardens and overnight moorings for boats. The original small main bar has low ceiling beams and a clay floor and is still lit by candlelight at night. Regular community events and beer festivals feature all year round at this truly community focused venue. Q❀🌳🔥◑♿♣♠P🚃❀♫

Gorleston

Dock Tavern ⓛ

Dock Tavern Lane, NR31 6PY (opp N side of Morrisons)

☎ (01493) 442255 ⊕ thedocktavern.com

5 changing beers (sourced nationally) Ⓗ

As its name suggest the Dock Tavern is close to the river, not far from the main shopping area. Subjected to flood damage many times, the various flood levels can be seen by the front door. The outside drinking area at the front has views of the river and docks. The pub has live music most weekends, and curry and quiz nights monthly, plus an annual charity music day. A warm welcoming pub with a lively friendly atmosphere. Q🌳❀◑♣🚃📶♫

New Entertainer 🍷 ⓛ

80 Pier Plain, NR31 6PG

☎ (01493) 300022

8 changing beers (sourced regionally; often Green Jack, St Austell, Woodforde's) Ⓗ

This traditional unusual pub with a unique curved frontage including original Lacons windows, has an interesting design and layout. A varied choice of beers is always on offer, with up to eight ales, often locally brewed. Recently refurbished inside, the pub has a loyal following and can get busy, with pool, darts and sports TV available, along with a monthly quiz. Please note that the main entrance is on Back Pier Plain. Local CAMRA Pub of the Year 2023. ❀♣🚃❀📶♫

Oddfellows Arms ⓛ

43 Cliff Hill, NR31 6DG

☎ 07876 545982 ⊕ oddiesgy.co.uk

5 changing beers (sourced locally; often Adnams, Grain) Ⓗ

Cosy two-bar back-street pub on Cliff Hill, a short distance from the harbour. Music and jam sessions are held on many Fridays, especially in summer, and there is plenty of jazz-themed memorabilia inside the pub. There are always three beers on offer, sometimes more, often from Norfolk breweries. There is a west-facing outdoor seating area at the front of the pub, and limited parking at the rear. This locals pub is worth seeking out. ☝☻&P☺☎♪

William Adams ⅃ ✅

176-177 High Street, NR31 6RG
☎ (01493) 600295
Greene King Abbot; Ruddles Best Bitter; Sharp's Doom Bar; 3 changing beers (sourced nationally; often Green Jack, Wolf, Woodforde's) ⊞
A new-build Wetherspoon pub on Gorleston High Street, this vibrant, busy town-centre pub is now very much part of the local social scene. The pub is named after William Adams, a famous Gorleston swimming instructor and lifesaver. It has one large open room with all the usual JDW facilities, including a pleasant outside enclosed seated area with designated smoking section. Note the outside area closes at 9pm. The decor depicts the famous local fishing industry and seaside themes. ☝☻◑&🚌(X1,X11) ☎

Great Cressingham

Olde Windmill Inn

Water End, IP25 6NN (off A1065 S of Swaffham)
☎ (01760) 756232 ⊕ oldewindmillinn.co.uk
Adnams Southwold Bitter, Broadside; Greene King IPA; 2 changing beers (sourced nationally) ⊞
Family run for three generations, the Windmill is a large rural pub and hotel, with a cosy feel despite its size. It offers a rolling range of beers including house beer Windy Miller – most ales are supplied by Purity. Real cider is also available. A popular food menu has something for everyone. The dining areas vary in size from a large conservatory to smaller, intimate rooms. Modern hotel accommodation is in separate buildings behind the pub. Q☝☻🛏◑&&♣●P☺

Great Hockham

Eagle ⅃ ✅

Harling Road, IP24 1NP
☎ (01953) 498893
Greene King IPA, Abbot; Morland Old Speckled Hen; 2 changing beers (sourced nationally) ⊞
Large family-friendly pub, set in a picturesque village close to Thetford Forest, with a longserving landlord at the helm. The main bar is separated from a games area by an open fire. Five real ales are available on handpump. Outdoor seating is provided at the front of the pub which is home to four pool teams and three darts teams. Quiz nights are held on alternate Wednesdays, and numerous other events are held regularly. ☝◑&P☺♪

Great Yarmouth

Blackfriars Tavern ⅃

94 Blackfriars Road, NR30 3BZ
☎ (01493) 331651
5 changing beers (sourced locally; often Barsham, Mr Winter's, Wolf) ⊞
Traditional village-style pub set in an urban conservation area, adjacent to both the best-preserved sections of the town wall and artwork by graffiti artist Banksy. Eight ever-changing real ales and over 10 real ciders are sourced from local breweries and producers. The pub also stocks over 100 bottled Belgian beers. Run by an enthusiastic landlord, the pub is known for its home-cooked pies and hearty meals (including vegetarian and vegan options). Stylishly decorated, with two seperate

bars with traditional games on tables plus two planted courtyards for outside drinking, the pub welcomes families, dogs and cyclists Q☝☻☺♣●P🚌(2)☺☎

King's Arms ⅃

229 Northgate Street, NR30 1BG
☎ (01493) 843736 ⊕ thekingsarmsgreatyarmouth.co.uk
Adnams Broadside; Woodforde's Wherry; 1 changing beer (sourced locally; often Humpty Dumpty, Tombstone) ⊞
Close to the minster, this welcoming pub with an excellent-value food menu has a single large room divided into different drinking areas. The friendly bar staff, landlord andlandlady provide a warm welcome. A comfortable seating area for diners has a real fire in winter. The large well-kept garden area is ideal for summer drinking and dining. Adnams Broadside and Woodforde's Wherry are complemented by a more local offering. It holds regular events, with live music at the weekends, and an annual August bank holiday beer festival features Norfolk ales and ciders. ☝☻◑&⇌P🚌☺☎♪

Lichfield Arms ⅃

116-117 Lichfield Road, NR31 0AB
☎ (01493) 302959
1 changing beer (sourced nationally; often Humpty Dumpty, Wolf) ⊞
A traditional community pub with a single large U-shaped bar, this popular back street local is worth seeking out when visiting the area. The long-serving landlord, who has been at the pub for 30 years, prides himself in serving one well kept ale. A dartboard and pool table feature, with various board games also available. The pub sponsors the local Wednesday real ale darts league. There is an outside area with seating for the warmer months. ☝☻&♣🚌☺

Red Herring ⅃

24-25 Havelock Road, NR30 3HQ (Havelock Rd is off St Peters Rd and is at the back of the Time & Tide museum)
☎ 07876 644742
4 changing beers (sourced nationally; often Green Jack, Lacons, Mighty Oak) ⊞
The Red Herring gets its name from the fish that were smoked in the nearby but now-closed smokehouses. The Herring has a dartboard, pool table and hosts a pool and darts team. The pub is close to the impressive medieval walls and to the award-winning Time & Tide museum. A regular entry in this Guide due to the long-serving landlord's passion for serving well-kept ales in a relaxing pub environment. No children or dogs allowed. Q☺♣🚌(2)

Tombstone Saloon Bar ⅃

6 George Street, NR30 1HR (on the NE corner of Hall Quay)
☎ 07584 504444 ⊕ tombstonebrewery.co.uk
Tombstone Arizona, Gunslinger ⊞/Ⓖ; **5 changing beers (sourced regionally; often Green Jack, Milestone, Moon Gazer)** Ⓖ
Well established as the tap for the on-site Tombstone brewery, this small Wild West-themed bar always showcases a wide range of mainly regional ales and beer styles. A regular entry in this Guide and winner of numerous CAMRA awards. The impressive range of ciders always includes some real ciders. Conversation rules, but there is unobtrusive TV and music. Frequent bus services stop outside and the bar is a short walk from Great Yarmouth Market Place. An annual Easter beer festival is held. Q☝⇌♣●P🚌☺♪

Gressenhall

White Swan

The Green, NR20 4DU

☎ (01362) 861296 ⊕ thewhiteswangressenhall.co.uk

Lacons Encore; 3 changing beers (sourced locally) ⊞
A community-owned pub overlooking the village green.
The stone-flagged rooms with rustic fittings and two
inglenook fireplaces serve as a multi-use area for dining
and casual drinking. Wall lights and agricultural pictures
adorn the walls. Outside, a covered patio overlooks an
enclosed garden with outdoor seating. An outside barn
has been converted into a separate room, complete with
wood-burning stove, for meetings and hire. Up to four
beers are on offer, sourced from East Anglian breweries.
Q ☎ ✿ ◑ ઙ ♣ ♠ P ☷ (21) ❀ 🛜 ♪

Harpley

Rose & Crown

Nethergate Street, PE31 6TW

☎ (01485) 521807 ⊕ roseandcrownharpley.co.uk

Woodforde's Wherry; 4 changing beers (sourced regionally) ⊞
Just off the A148 King's Lynn to Fakenham Road, this
attractive 17th-century pub offers guest ales from local
breweries. It features open bar areas with a stylish and
comfortable feel and has log fires in winter. Outside is an
enclosed beer garden for summer drinking. There is an
extensive menu serving excellent food, including one of
the best Sunday roasts around. The unspoilt village
provides pleasant walks and is close to Houghton Hall.
Local CAMRA Pub of the Year 2019.
Q ☎ ✿ ◑ P ☷ (48) ❀ 🛜

Heacham

Fox & Hounds Ⓛ

22 Station Road, PE31 7EX

☎ (01485) 570345

Fox Heacham Gold, Nelson's Blood, IPA; 1 changing beer (sourced nationally) ⊞
Popular with locals and visitors, this is the home of the
Fox brewery. There are eight beers on offer including a
selection from Fox, whose bottled beers are also sold,
plus a range of imported beers. The restaurant offers
beer recommendations to match the food. There is live
music on a Tuesday evenings (mainly blues) and a quiz
on Thursdays. Beer festivals are hosted throughout the
year. ☎ ✿ ◑ ઙ ♣ P ☷ (34,35) ❀ 🛜

Hillington

Ffolkes

Lynn Road, PE31 6BJ

☎ (01485) 600210 ⊕ ffolkes.org.uk

Adnams Ghost Ship; Moon Gazer Jigfoot; 1 changing beer (sourced nationally) ⊞
This family-run 300-year old former coaching inn was
extensively refurbished in 2017. Located just six miles
from King's Lynn and three miles from the Royal
Sandringham Estate, it provides a perfect base for
exploring North Norfolk. The Ffolkes has 25 bedrooms, an
outdoor adventure play area and an indoor games room.
There is an extensive menu and the popular street food
events are now a fixture. There are always several real
ales to choose from. The Ffolkes is part of the Norfolk
Passport scheme, offering a discount to cardholders.
☎ ✿ ⇔ ◑ ઙ P ❀ 🛜 ♪

Hockering

Victoria

The Street, NR20 3HL (in centre of village just off A47)

☎ (01603) 880507

Adnams Southwold Bitter, Ghost Ship; 1 changing beer (sourced nationally; often Moon Gazer, Humpty Dumpty) ⊞
Located just north of the A47 Norwich-Dereham road and
conveniently opposite the bus stop, this friendly pub
offers a warm Danish welcome. The guest beer is
normally from the Moon Gazer range. The large single L-
shaped bar has a widescreen TV at one end and a roaring
fire (in winter) at the other. Live music played on a
regular basis. ☎ ✿ ◑ P ☷ (A,B) ❀ 🛜

Holt

King's Head

19 High Street, NR25 6BN

☎ (01263) 712543 ⊕ kingsheadholt.org.uk

Adnams Ghost Ship; Moon Gazer Pintail, Nibbler; Woodforde's Wherry ⊞**; 2 changing beers (sourced nationally)** Ⓖ
Located in the historic Georgian town of Holt (rebuilt
after the medieval town was destroyed by fire in 1708)
the pub has an unusual sash bay window facing the High
Street. Four regular and two guest beers from regional
breweries can be enjoyed. The pub has two bars, a snug,
restaurant, garden and garden room, and food is served
all day. Easy access using local bus services and a
seasonal steam train which terminates at Holt station,
which has connecting bus services. ☎ ✿ ⇔ ◑ 🍴 ⬚ ❀ 🛜

Honingham

Buck Ⓛ

29 The Street, NR9 5BL

☎ (01603) 880393 ⊕ thehoninghambuck.co.uk

Lacons Encore, Legacy; 2 changing beers (sourced locally) ⊞
Dating back to 1789, this traditional one-bar village pub
has a separate restaurant area with an emphasis on
home-cooked food. An excellent menu of unusual dishes
is freshly cooked to order. The Buck has served Lacon's
real ales since the brewery bought it in 2015. Slate
floors, oak beams, a large fireplace and period furniture
enhance the image of a country pub. There is a large
garden with plenty of seating, and accommodation in
eight en-suite rooms. Q ☎ ✿ ⇔ ◑ ઙ P ☷ (4) ❀ 🛜

Kenninghall

Red Lion

East Church Street, NR16 2EP (opp parish church)

☎ (01953) 887849 ⊕ redlionkenninghall.co.uk

4 changing beers (sourced locally; often Black Sheep, Shortts, Timothy Taylor) ⊞
A beautifully restored pub dating from the early 16th
century with traditional bar and pine-panelled snug (one
of only two of its kind in East Anglia) adjacent to the 40-
seater restaurant in the style of old stables. It has been
identified by CAMRA as having a nationally important
historic pub interior. Good, wholesome home-cooked
food includes fresh fish on Fridays. Sunday roasts and
special boards all locally sourced where possible. Regular
live music and other community events are held.
☎ ◑ ઙ ❀ ♪

King's Lynn

Ferry Lane Social Club
Ferry Lane, PE30 1HN (off King St)
☎ (01553) 772239
4 changing beers (sourced nationally) Ⓖ
This welcoming club can be found at the end of a lane next to the departure point for the West Lynn Ferry. The bar looks over the river and there is a balcony where you can sit and enjoy the views. Five beers are on offer, from breweries near and far, alongside local cider from Sandringham. CAMRA members and visitors using this Guide are welcome, with a limit on the number of visits before being asked to join. Local CAMRA Club of the Year 2020-2023. ◀≉(Kings Lynn)♣

Live & Let Live Ⓛ
18 Windsor Road, PE30 5PL (off London Rd near Our Lady's Church)
☎ (01553) 764990
5 changing beers (sourced nationally) Ⓗ
This popular two-bar locals' pub has a small cosy lounge and a larger bar with a TV. Five beers are available, including a mild (rare for the area). Cider drinkers have a choice of ciders, normally including something from a local producer, and the pub was named local CAMRA Cider Pub of the Year 2020-2023. Live music is sometimes played in the public bar and various events are held to raise funds for charity. ≉(Kings Lynn)♣❀♫

Wenn's Chop & Ale House Ⓛ
9 Saturday Market Place, PE30 5DQ
☎ (01553) 772077 ⊕ thewenns.co.uk
Courage Directors; 2 changing beers (sourced regionally) Ⓗ
The Wenn's reverted to its former name after an extensive renovation in 2020. The remodelled interior has a number of separate rooms and there are also tables outside on the edge of Saturday Market Place. Beers are from local breweries and, despite its name, the menu offers traditional pub food and does not major on chops. There is pay parking opposite and round the corner. Highly rated accommodation is available. Q❦►✦◑&≉(Kings Lynn) ♣🏠❀🤍

Larling

Angel 🏆
NR16 2QU (1 mile SW from Snetterton racetrack, just of A11)
☎ (01953) 717963 ⊕ angel-larling.co.uk
Adnams Southwold Bitter; 4 changing beers (sourced nationally) Ⓗ
Five real ales plus a real cider are on handpump here, always including a mild. Over 100 whiskies are stocked, as well as 50 gins. The lounge and bar have real open fires, and there is a dining room which serves home-made fare in generous portions. A friendly atmosphere is enjoyed by locals, visitors, campers and rallyists who use the Angel's campsite. A popular long-running beer festival in August showcases over 80 real ales with live music. Local CAMRA Pub of the Year 2023. Q❦►✦◑&▲♣P🏠

Lessingham

Star Inn Ⓛ
Star Hill, NR12 0DN (just off B1159, corner of High Rd and Star Hill)
☎ (01692) 580510
Lacons Encore; 2 changing beers (sourced nationally) Ⓖ

A traditional, country pub with a friendly atmosphere. Three ales, including two guests, are served from the cask, as are up to three real ciders. The Star is popular for its high-quality meals made with carefully sourced ingredients and served in decent portions. Food may be enjoyed in the bar, a separate restaurant, or the spacious beer garden. Two en-suite double B&B rooms, refurbished in 2022, make this an excellent base to explore the local coast and enjoy the glorious sunsets in summer. Q❦✦◑▲♣●P🏠🚍(34)🤍🤍

Marlingford

Marlingford Bell Ⓛ
Bawburgh Road, NR9 5HX
☎ (01603) 880263 ⊕ thebellatmarlingford.co.uk
4 changing beers (sourced nationally) Ⓗ
This extended country village pub has a refurbished front bar with a wood-burning stove making it nice and cosy in winter. There are no regular beers – the changing ales come from Lacons, Winter's, Woodforde's and occasionally other small Norfolk breweries. One is dispensed on gravity. The large function and restaurant room with a separate bar at the rear opens on to a large garden. Quality, locally sourced food is made on the premises, and excellent bar menu dishes are served on biodegradable trays. Sunday roasts are popular (booking advised). Q❦❀◑&▲P🤍🤍

Martham

King's Arms Ⓛ
15 The Green, NR29 4PL
☎ (01493) 749156
3 changing beers (sourced nationally; often Adnams, St Peter's) Ⓗ
Traditional two-bar village pub located opposite the picturesque pond. The pub has a seperate dining area and good-value food is available. The landlord is also the chef. A welcoming fire awaits in the winter months, and a garden with childrens' play area for the warmer days. With three or more ales on offer the pub is very much a part of the social scene in the village and a friendly welcome awaits the visitor. Closed on Mondays except bank holidays. Q❦❀◑●P🚍(1,1A)🤍🤍

Middleton

Gate
Hill Road, Fair Green, PE32 1RW (N of A47, follow Fair Green signs)
☎ (01553) 840518
Greene King Abbot; Woodforde's Wherry; 1 changing beer (sourced nationally) Ⓗ
Although there is a pleasant dining room, this friendly family-run pub just off the A47 is still at heart a village local. The bar and semi-separate area with a jukebox and TV screen are used mainly by those who just want a drink. Food features seasonal produce and ingredients sourced from local suppliers. The pretty garden is popular in summer. The pub is closed on Mondays and Tuesdays. Q❦❀◑▲♣P🤍

Neatishead

White Horse Ⓛ
The Street, NR12 8AD
☎ (01692) 630828 ⊕ thewhitehorseinnneatishead.com
Woodforde's Wherry; 6 changing beers (sourced nationally) Ⓗ
Traditional village-centre pub with moorings a short walk away. There are two separate drinking areas. Six of the

seven cask ales are mainly from microbreweries across the UK, including from the in-house brewery. Up to seven craft keg beers are available. Meals are home-prepared with local produce a priority. There is a cosy restaurant area and a separate, larger, split-level restaurant beside the small courtyard. The beer garden lies at the rear. Q✿☻♿♣P🅿️☀️🛜

Newton by Castle Acre

George & Dragon
Swaffham Road, PE32 2BX (On A1065)
☎ (01760) 755623 ⊕ georgeatnewton.com
Adnams Ghost Ship; Woodforde's Wherry; 2 changing beers (sourced nationally) Ⓗ
The pub reopened in 2018 after a major refurbishment. Its wooden floor, exposed beams, comfortable seats and walls lined with old books gives it the air of a gentleman's club. The menu is interesting, with items such as a meat platter featuring potted rabbit and venison, as well as vegan options. There is a play area at the rear for children, and the Pig Shed Motel at the back caters for those who wish to stay. ➿✿🛏️◑P🅿️☀️🛜

North Elmham

Railway Arms
40 Station Road, NR20 5HH
☎ (01362) 668300 ⊕ therailwayarms.co.uk
2 changing beers (sourced regionally) Ⓗ
Situated in central Norfolk near the ancient remains of the Anglo-Saxon North Elmham Chapel, this is both a rural gem and a fine community pub. It has an L-shaped open bar with two real fires, together with a dining room off the main bar. The beers, all on handpump, usually come from microbreweries in Norfolk and Suffolk. Home-cooked meals using mainly locally sourced ingredients are available at lunchtime, and in the evening on Wednesday to Sunday. Q✿◑♿Å♣P🖵(21)☀️🛜♪

North Walsham

Hop In Ⓛ
2 Market Street, NR28 9BZ
☎ 07735 845983 ⊕ thehopin.co.uk
6 changing beers (sourced nationally) Ⓖ
Just around the corner from the marketplace, and owned and run by keen CAMRA members, this was Norfolk's first micropub. Six changing ales are served on gravity dispense plus a real cider. There is usually one dark beer available. In keeping with the micropub philosophy, there is no Wi-Fi, music or machines, just good conversation. There is a small seating area downstairs and more upstairs, plus a patio area outside. Q✿🌾🍽️🖵🐾☀️

North Wootton

Red Cat Hotel
Station Road, PE30 3QH (Station Rd is opp church of All Saints, where Nursery Ln joins Manor Rd)
☎ (01553) 631244 ⊕ redcathotel.com
Adnams Southwold Bitter; 1 changing beer (sourced nationally) Ⓗ
Built in 1898 and constructed in local gingerbread carrstone, this traditional village local offers two real ales. Nicely decorated and in a quiet location close to the Wash marshes, it has attractive gardens for summer drinks. Ask about the history of the namesake red cat – if you can believe it. The pub is near National Cycle Route 1, the Sandringham Estate and the west Norfolk coast. Q➿✿P🖵(3) ☀️🛜

Norwich

Alexandra Tavern
16 Stafford Street, NR2 3BB
☎ (01603) 627772 ⊕ alexandratavern.co.uk
4 changing beers (sourced locally) Ⓗ
Popular, bustling and friendly, this pub is a real gem sited just outside the city centre. The interior is brightly decorated, with the walls featuring pictures and articles of a nautical nature. The bar serves up to five changing beers from local breweries, and two real ciders. Food is served daily, with a good variety, including a soup menu. There is a dartboard and plenty of board games to choose from, with children welcome until early evening. Q➿✿◑♣♿🖵(19A,20) ☀️🛜

Artichoke
1 Magdalen Road, NR3 4LW
☎ (01603) 662807 ⊕ artichokepub.com
5 changing beers (sourced nationally; often Golden Triangle)
A 1930s flint building, originally decorated in the Brewers' Tudor style, with two circular bars with cone-shaped roofs (giving the pub its name), original Young's, Crawshay & Young's windows, parquet flooring and a long solid wood bar. Bought and significantly but sensitively refurbished by the owner of Golden Triangle Brewery in 2018, the bar now has eight handpumps offering two or three Golden Triangle beers, and a great selection of craft beers. There is outdoor seating in front and part-covered seating at the side. ✿♿♣🍴🖵☀️🛜

Beehive Ⓛ
30 Leopold Road, NR4 7PJ (between Unthank Rd and Newmarket Rd)
☎ (01603) 451628 ⊕ beehivepubnorwich.co.uk
Green Jack Golden Best; 5 changing beers (sourced nationally; often Oakham) Ⓗ
A friendly two-bar local with knowledgeable staff, featuring a comfortable lounge bar with sofas. The popular beer garden is used all year round and for charity barbecues during the summer months. A beer festival is held in late June with around 25 ales and ciders. There is a function room upstairs (available to hire) with a pool table. The pub has a regular fortnightly quiz on Wednesdays as well as regular themed food nights. A book swap library was established in 2021. Q➿✿♣🍴P🅿️☀️🛜

Brewery Tap Ⓛ
98-100 Lawson Road, NR3 4LF
☎ (01603) 413153 ⊕ fatcattap.co.uk
Oakham Bishops Farewell Ⓖ; Fat Cat Norwich Bitter, Tom Cat Ⓗ; 15 changing beers (sourced nationally) Ⓖ
Serving a huge range of real ales, ciders and quality keg beers from across the country, the Brewery Tap is a large single-bar pub in a 1970s building. Live music on Sundays complements a variety of events including tap takeovers, themed beer evenings and festivals, beer launches and community events. Loaded chips and other snacks are available. Lots of outside seating at front and mostly covered seating at the rear. The Fat Cat brewery is located in the same building. Q✿◑♿♣P🖵(11,12) ☀️🛜♪

Champion
101 Chapel Field Road, NR2 1SE
☎ (01603) 628148 ⊕ thechampionpub.com
Batemans Gold, XB, XXXB; 1 changing beer (sourced nationally) Ⓗ
Friendly L-shaped Bateman's pub, situated immediately adjacent to the main shopping mall in the city centre. A substantial section of the original city wall can be seen

from all aspects of this traditional corner pub. Sporting photographs of adorn the walls of the larger of the two drinking areas. There is a small outdoor area adjacent to the pub and a small function room is available. An acoustic music 'round' is hosted on Mondays.
&❍♣➡🦺🛜

Coach & Horses

82 Thorpe Road, NR1 1BA

☎ (01603) 477077 🌐 thecoachthorperoad.co.uk

Chalk Hill Tap Bitter, CHB, Gold, Dreadnought; 3 changing beers (sourced nationally) Ⓗ

Close to the station, this coaching inn, with its iconic balcony, is the home of the Chalk Hill brewery, and serves its full range of beers. Tours of the brewery are available by appointment. Excellent-value food is served along with Sandford cider. Sport, especially rugby, is shown on big screens, and the large fire is welcome in winter. Not far from the football ground, it gets busy before matches. There is lots of outside covered seating at the front. &❍♿🚃➡🦺🛜

Coach & Horses

51 Bethel Street, NR2 1NR

☎ (01603) 618522 🌐 thecoachandhorsesbethelstreet.co.uk

6 changing beers (sourced regionally) Ⓗ

Historic city-centre pub near the Theatre Royal, Market Place, and City Hall. The pub has a bright, welcoming bar with several separate seating areas including cosy alcoves, and a long part-covered patio garden area to one side. Although a Greene King house, it offers a well chosen selection of guest beers, and is a rare city centre outlet for dark ales. A bar billiards table is available. 🏃&❍♣🦺🛜

Cottage

9 Silver Road, NR3 4TB

☎ (01603) 464461 🌐 norwichcottage.com

6 changing beers (sourced nationally) Ⓗ

A large single-room pub with a lovely enclosed patio garden at the rear. Independently owned since 2019 by Richard and Ben, it has been refurbished to a high standard, with solid oak flooring, wood paneling, exposed brickwork and a copper bar top. The choices on the six handpumps include one locally sourced beer, and there is a selection of quality spirits and craft beers. Sunday roasts are served and there is an excellent burgers and tapas menu every evening (no food Mon). &❍♿♣🦺(10,10A) 🦺🛜♫

Duke of Wellington Ⓛ

91-93 Waterloo Road, NR3 1EG

☎ (01603) 441182 🌐 dukeofwellingtonnorwich.co.uk

Oakham JHB, Bishops Farewell Ⓖ**; Wolf Golden Jackal, Wolf Ale** Ⓗ**, Wolf in Sheep's Clothing; 8 changing beers (sourced nationally)** Ⓖ

This friendly pub serves a changing range of guest ales to complement the permanent beers (predominantly from Wolf brewery). The majority of which are served on gravity from a taproom behind the bar. The attractive enclosed rear garden/patio area hosts a beer festival in late August plus regular barbecues at weekends in summer. Events include monthly quiz evenings. Customers can bring in their own food or sample the filling and inexpensive pies and sausage rolls. &🚃♣🛒🦺(21) 🦺🛜

Fat Cat Ⓛ

49 West End Street, NR2 4NA

☎ (01603) 624364 🌐 fatcatpub.co.uk

Crouch Vale Yakima Gold; Fat Cat Norwich Bitter Ⓗ**, Marmalade; Greene King Abbot; Oakham Bishops**

Farewell, Green Devil Ⓖ**; 12 changing beers (sourced nationally)** Ⓗ/Ⓖ

Comfortable and traditional street-corner pub which from outside barely hints at the outstanding and extensive range of ales on offer; sourced from all over the UK. Ales from the Fat Cat range are served, plus real ciders and perries. Food is limited to pork pies. The interior is tiled, and has plenty of seating in two areas each side of the bar, and a small room at the rear. This is a superb example of what a real ale outlet should be, with excellent, friendly service. Twice CAMRA's National Pub of the Year. Q&🦺🛒🦺🛜

Fat Cat & Canary Ⓛ

101 Thorpe Road, NR1 1TR

☎ (01603) 436925

13 changing beers (sourced regionally; often Crouch Vale, Fat Cat, Oakham) Ⓗ/Ⓖ

Sister pub to the original Fat Cat, about a mile and a half from the centre of the city, the pub serves most of the Fat Cat brewery's ales, guests from around the UK, continental beers and real ciders. There is a small TV to the rear of the main bar, a large car park and terraces to the front and rear, the latter being heated. Home-made rolls are available and there are regular pop-up food vendors. Busy on Norwich City match days. 🏃&❍♿🛒🦺🛜

Garden House

1 Pembroke Road, NR2 3HD

☎ (01603) 628059

Brains SA; Oakham JHB Ⓗ**; 6 changing beers (sourced nationally)** Ⓗ/Ⓖ

This pub has two bar areas with extensive and comfortable seating and a separate pool room. An extensive garden at rear has covered and uncovered tables and seating, plus a TV for hardy sports addicts. Thre are always three ales on handpump – SA, JHB and Rev James – and at least six on gravity, sometimes 10 for special sporting events. An extensive range of ciders and keg and bottled beers are available. The landlord is always on the door to welcome guests. 🏃&♣🛒🦺🛜♫

Golden Star

57 Colegate, NR3 1DD

☎ (01603) 632447 🌐 goldenstarnorwich.co.uk

Greene King IPA, Abbot; 2 changing beers (sourced nationally) Ⓗ

A welcoming and relaxing pub with a main bar area and a second room to the left and behind the bar, hosting the bar billiards table, and occasional live music sessions. A quiz is held on Sunday evenings and a specials menu is served daily along with Sunday roasts, traditional pub meals and tapas. A wide selection of music is played, but unobtrusively. There is a small patio at the rear, and tables outside the front in summer. &❍♣🦺🛜♫

Jubilee Ⓛ

26 St Leonards Road, NR1 4BL

☎ (01603) 618734

4 changing beers (sourced regionally) Ⓗ

Attractive Victorian corner pub with a warm welcome. There are two bars, a comfortable conservatory and an enclosed patio garden. Many of the well-kept ales and craft beers are local. This popular venue, within easy reach of the city centre, is at the heart of the community and caters for all tastes, from sports fans to those who enjoy local history talks. Customers are welcome to bring in takeaway food, and there are regular Sunday roasts and occasional pop-up street-food fairs. 🏃&🚃♣🦺🛜

King's Arms

22 Hall Road, NR1 3HQ

☎ (01603) 477888 🌐 kingsarmsnorwich.co.uk

Batemans XB, Gold, XXXB; 6 changing beers (sourced regionally; often Tindall) 🄷

A friendly Batemans house close to the city centre, serving a wide range of guest ales to complement the Batemans beers, usually including a stout or porter and a mild. The guest brewery changes on a monthly basis. Real ciders are also stocked. Sausage rolls, pork pies and filled rolls are on the bar, but customers can bring in food from various nearby takeaways, with plates and condiments provided. Monthly quiz nights, poker evenings and live music take place. It gets busy on football match days. ❀♿♣🚌(39,40)🐾📶

King's Head L

42 Magdalen Street, NR3 1JE

🌐 kingsheadnorwich.com

8 changing beers (sourced regionally; often Elmtree, Mr Winter's, Tindall) 🄷

A traditional-style two-bar pub which offers up to eight quality real ales, mostly from local breweries but also selected guests from further away, plus two ciders. A mild or stout is usually available. No food is served except snacks, pork pies and pickled eggs, but customers can bring or order in their own, with plates and cutlery supplied. Bar billiards is well supported, with two teams in the local league. The pub supports fundraising for the On the Ball charity, and was a finalist for National Pub of the Year 2022. Q❀♣🍎🚆🚌🐾📶

Leopard L

98-100 Bull Close Road, NR3 1NQ

☎ (01603) 631111 🌐 theleopardpub.co.uk

6 changing beers (sourced nationally) 🄷

Welcoming single-bar local with a variety of changing ales. A house beer – Chin on Bar – is brewed by Mr Winter's, other regular breweries include Green Jack and Nene Valley. This traditional corner pub has a clean and bright bar area which gives a spacious feel, and a pleasant and quiet enclosed courtyard garden at the rear. Luca Pizza pop up is available from most Thursday evenings. Fortnightly quiz nights are on Wednesdays. ❀◗♿♣🚆🚌(10,10A)🐾📶

Lollards Pit L

69-71 Riverside Road, NR1 1SR

☎ (01603) 624675 🌐 lollardspit.com

Woodforde's Wherry; 5 changing beers (sourced nationally) 🄷

An attractive 17th-century inn, one of the first built outside the city walls, on the site of Lollards Pit, a place of execution for heretics for over 200 years. Guest ales are from local breweries, including Moon Gazer, Boudicca and Humpty Dumpty, with interesting offerings from further afield. The pub is close to the river and yacht station moorings, has a large patio garden at the rear and a real fire, and hosts local community groups and weekly quiz and bingo nights. ❀♿⇌♣🍎🚌🐾📶

Malt & Mardle

163 Magdalen Street, NR3 1NF

🌐 maltandmardle.co.uk

2 changing beers (sourced locally) 🄷

Norwich's first self-designated micropub, seating about 20 people in a single room, the Malt & Mardle was converted from retail use in 2021 by three friends who now run it. Two ales are served on gravity, alongside two KeyKeg beers, and there's a small bar at the front. Note that the pub is closed Monday and Tuesday and operate restricted hours when open. 'Mardle' is a Norfolk word for a relaxed conversation! Q❀♣🍎🚌🐾📶

Murderers

2-8 Timber Hill, NR1 3LB

☎ (01603) 621447 🌐 themurderers.co.uk

Wolf Edith Cavell; 9 changing beers (sourced nationally) 🄷

A busy city-centre pub that appeals to all sections of the public, with up to 10 real ales, including two permanent beers, one of which is the house Murderer's Ale (brewed by Wolf). Beer festivals feature in summer and autumn, with over 50 beers available, including many from local brewers. The upper area has a largescreen TV, making it a popular venue for viewing sporting events. There is a bar available for private hire, and a popular outside terrace. A traditional British menu is served in generous portions. ❀◖◗🍎🚌🐾📶♫

Plasterers Arms L

43 Cowgate, NR3 1SZ

☎ (01603) 440992 🌐 theplasterersarms.co.uk

Moon Gazer Pintail; 4 changing beers (sourced nationally) 🄷

A friendly corner local specialising in new and exciting breweries, with an ever-changing range of cask, keg, bottled and canned beers from around the country. Its motto is 'Drink less, drink better' and prices are by the half-pint to encourage sampling a variety of beers over drinking quantity. It offers tap takeovers, sport (with a big screen for more important events), excellent pizzas, breakfast at weekends and a Monday evening quiz. The pub also hosts a Fem.ale festival celebrating great women brewers. ❀◗♣🍎🚆🐾📶♫

Plough

58 St Benedict Street, NR2 4AR

☎ (01603) 661384 🌐 grainpubs.co.uk

5 changing beers (sourced nationally; often Grain) 🄷

A popular pub in one of the city's oldest areas, near the Norwich Arts Centre. One of two Grain brewery-owned outlets, it sells five ales, usually all from the brewery. The two-bar interior is fairly small, with wooden chairs and tables, and has an open fire in winter. The large Mediterranean-style courtyard garden is a fine place to spend a summer's evening. Craft beers are also served and there are barbecues in the summer. ❀♣🐾📶

Ribs of Beef L ✔

24 Wensum Street, NR3 1HY

☎ (01603) 619517 🌐 ribsofbeef.co.uk

Adnams Ghost Ship; Oakham Citra; Woodforde's Wherry; 4 changing beers (sourced nationally) 🄷

Traditional and well decorated pub overlooking the River Wensum. A row of nine handpumps dispense three regular ales and a selection of guests from quality local and non-local microbreweries, with two ciders and a variety of craft cans also available. Food is provided by pop-up kitchens. Relaxed and friendly, the pub has a room downstairs, a small riverside balcony, several tables outside at the rear, and tables on the street at the front. There is a regular Monday quiz, live music on most Sunday evenings and sporting fixtures are shown on TV. ❀◖◗🚌🐾📶♫

Rose Inn

235 Queens Road, NR1 3AE

☎ (01603) 623942 🌐 therosepubanddeli.co.uk

4 changing beers (sourced nationally) 🄷

Popular pub, close to both the Norwich City FC stadium and the city centre. The owner's passion for beer shows in the selection of four regularly changing real ales and six keg beers from some of the most exciting microbreweries around the country. There is also a selection of gins and wines from a local supplier. Stone-baked pizzas plus savoury pastries and cheeseboards are available from the in-house deli during food hours. A bar billiards table and team, regular quizzes, DJ nights, and a monthly curry night complete the mix. 🌐🍴🃏♿🅰️🅿️🚌❄️🛜

Rosebery

94 Rosebery Road, NR3 3AB
🌐 theroseberypubnorwich.co.uk
6 changing beers (sourced regionally) Ⓗ
A popular Victorian corner pub with large bright windows and high ceilings, decorated in modern tones. Up to six real ales are available, mostly sourced from local brewers, plus several real ciders. Further seating is outside at the front and in a pleasant gravelled and part-covered beer garden at the rear. Food is served daily and the pub offers an excellent Sunday roast. There is a popular quiz night on Tuesdays. B&B accommodation is available. 🌐🍴♿♣🍴🅿️(21)❄️🛜

Sir Toby's

182/183 Market Place, NR2 1NE
☎ 07786 993314 🌐 sirtobysbeers.co.uk
2 changing beers (sourced nationally) Ⓗ
This stall on Norwich Market sells two draught beers from KeyKeg and a large range of bottles and cans, including real ales and ciders, to drink on or off the premises. A small seating area is available, with views of the Guildhall and Gaol Hill, and food from other market stalls may be brought in and eaten. 🌐

Trafford Arms Ⓛ ✅

61 Grove Road, NR1 3RL
☎ (01603) 628466 🌐 traffordarms.co.uk
Adnams Ghost Ship; Lacons Encore; 8 changing beers (sourced regionally; often Barsham, Mr Winter's, Woodforde's) Ⓗ
This friendly local has a strong community feel and is open all day, every day. The pub offers a changing guest beer list including beers from Lacons, Oakham and Moon Gazer, and usually includes a dark beer. The February Valentine's beer festival is a major attraction, as is the regular quiz on the last Sunday of the month. Regular pop-up food is available. The pub is popular when Norwich City are at home! Q🌐🍴🃏🅿️(38,39)❄️🛜

Unthank Arms

149 Newmarket Street, NR2 2DR
☎ (01603) 631557 🌐 theunthankarms.com
3 changing beers (sourced nationally) Ⓗ
Lively, one-bar L-shaped corner pub with a spartan interior, popular with young clientele. One leg of the L is reserved for diners. Up to three real ales are available, mostly from established local breweries. Excellent food is also served in the upstairs bistro, and in the courtyard or garden. Breakfast is available at weekends, with a roast on Sundays including Norfolk beef and pork, chicken and home-made nut roast. Q🌐🍴🃏♿❄️🛜

Vine Ⓛ

7 Dove Street, NR2 1DE
☎ (01603) 627362 🌐 vinethai.co.uk
Fat Cat Tom Cat; Oakham JHB; 2 changing beers (sourced regionally) Ⓗ
Located just off the marketplace, this pub serves up to four quality ales, with traditional Thai cuisine served in the upstairs restaurant, although customers often eat downstairs in the bar area. A beer festival is held during the City of Ale festival. Quiz nights are every first Thursday of the month, and regular themed tastings take place. A good range of cider and bottled world beers is also available. Extra tables and chairs are set outside in the pedestrianised street, but there is no standing or sitting at the bar. Q🌐🍴🃏❄️

Warwick Arms

2 Warwick Street, NR2 3LD
☎ (01603) 627687 🌐 warwickarmsnorwich.co.uk
4 changing beers (sourced nationally) Ⓗ
A large, prominently-situated pub with a relaxed vibe and comfortable seating. There is a large main bar, a smaller snug room to one side and a spacious event space upstairs that can be boked at no charge for all manner of get-togethers. Ales are sourced from across the country and draught lagers include favourites as well as interesting craft beers. Wine and selection of cocktails are also available. Food, including tacos, burgers, pizza and churros, is available from pop-up providers on selected evenings. 🌐🍴🃏♿🍴🚌(25)

White Lion 🍷

73 Oak Street, NR3 3AQ
☎ (01603) 632333
7 changing beers (sourced nationally; often Bull of the Woods, Mr Winter's, Tindall) Ⓗ
A good and changing range of real ales from local and select national breweries is on sale here – often Mr Winter's, Tindall's, Bull of the Woods and Nene Valley. Eight to 10 ciders and perries are also sold. Food is varied and excellent value, using local produce and with daily specials. The traditional interior is split into three rooms, with a front and back bar and a room to the side with further seating and a bar billiards table. CAMRA East Anglia Cider Pub of the Year 2023 and Norfolk Pub of the Year 2023. Q🌐🃏🃏♣🍴🎱❄️🛜

Wig & Pen Ⓛ

6 St Martin-at-Palace Plain, NR3 1RN
☎ (01603) 625891 🌐 thewigandpen.com
5 changing beers (sourced nationally) Ⓗ
Pretty, beamed 17th-century free house with a spacious patio, immediately opposite the Bishop's Palace, and with an impressive view of Norwich Cathedral spire. Five ales are always available, all from local breweries. Good-quality food is served lunchtimes and evenings. This friendly pub is a short walk from Tombland, where there are bus stands for several bus routes, and is an ideal starting or stopping place for a walk along the river or in the Cathedral Close. Q🌐🍴🃏♿🍴🅿️❄️🛜

Old Buckenham

Ox & Plough

The Green, NR17 1RN (in centre of village overlooking green)
☎ (01953) 860970
Oakham JHB; Sharp's Doom Bar; Timothy Taylor Landlord; 3 changing beers (often Greene King, Ossett) Ⓗ
Family-friendly pub on one of the largest village greens in England. A community pub at the centre of village life, it has two open-plan drinking areas, one being quiet without TV or electronic games machines. The garden at front of pub overlooks the village green. Real ale is dispensed from three to five handpumps. A member of Oakham Academy, various changing Oakham ales are served, and Oakham Green Devil is the regular keg beer. Food is limited to bar snacks only. 🃏🌐♿♣🍴❄️🛜

Ringstead

Gin Trap Inn ✅

6 High Street, PE36 5JU
☎ (01485) 525264 🌐 thegintrapinn.co.uk
Adnams Ghost Ship; Greene King Abbot; Woodforde's Wherry; 1 changing beer (sourced nationally) Ⓗ

This attractive, whitewashed 17th-century coaching inn has been a pub since 1668. There is outside seating at the front and an enclosed garden to the rear. It has a split-level bar and a separate restaurant, although food is served throughout. Regular themed food evenings are hosted as well as live music nights. The main bar has a log-burning stove. The drinks menu features a range of some 100 different gins including the pub's own Gin Trap gin. ◐❀➿◖◗♿P❀❖♠

Roydon

Union Jack

30 Station Road, PE32 1AW (off A148)

☎ 07771 660439

Greene King Abbot; 3 changing beers (sourced nationally) ⊞

Popular with locals, this village pub has twice been local CAMRA Pub of the Year. The current landlord celebrated 20 years at the pub in 2022. Four handpumps dispense one regular and three changing ales, and beer festivals are held over the Easter and August bank holidays, usually featuring local breweries. There are occasional food nights, with live music each month, regular quizzes, and weekly support for darts, crib and dominoes. Outdoor seating is at the front. Q❀❖▲♣◗P☐(48)❀❖♠

Sculthorpe

Sculthorpe Mill

Lynn Road, NR21 9QG

☎ (01328) 633001 ⊕ sculthorpemill.uk

Greene King IPA; 2 changing beers (sourced locally; often Barsham, Greene King, Moon Gazer) ⊞

Large free-of-tie bar and restaurant, nicely situated beside the River Wensum in a former mill, south of the King's Lynn to Fakenham road. It has a large riverside area and outdoor kitchen, tables next to the mill pond, and was tastefully refurbished in 2021, when a snug bar was added over the mill race. Offering a choice of bar or à la carte menus, the pub is a winner of multiple awards for food, including the Michelin Bib Gourmand in 2022. A quiz held is every second Tuesday. ❀➿◖◗♣P❀❖♠

Sedgeford

King William IV

Heacham Road, PE36 5LU (off B1454)

☎ (01485) 571765 ⊕ thekingwilliamsedgeford.co.uk

Adnams Ghost Ship; Greene King Abbot; Woodforde's Wherry ⊞

A large well appointed village pub, popular for its locally produced food. Known by the locals as the King Willie, it has an excellent reputation for quality food but still retains a pub atmosphere that attracts local drinkers. There are two dog-friendly bars and a restaurant divided into four areas. A large garden at the rear has a superb outdoor covered drinking/dining area. Nine luxury rooms are available. Q❀◐➿◖◗♿P❀

Sheringham

Crown Inn ✓

East Cliff, NR26 8BQ

☎ (01263) 823213

Adnams Ghost Ship; Sharp's Doom Bar; Woodforde's Wherry; 1 changing beer (sourced locally; often Wolf) ⊞

This spacious pub next to the Sheringham Museum overlooks the beach. Two large lounges and a central bar serve up to five real ales and an extensive range of food, which is available throughout the day. There are meal

deal offers during the week in winter. An outside seating area facing the sea is popular in summer. Events are hosted, including live music on Saturday nights and a quiz on Monday evenings. Q❀◐❀◖◗♿≈♣P❀❖♠

Shouldham

King's Arms ⑃

The Green, PE33 0BY

☎ (01366) 347410 ⊕ kingsarmsshouldham.co.uk

2 changing beers (sourced nationally) Ⓖ

A four-time winner of the local CAMRA Pub of the Year award in recent years, the King's Arms is a community-owned business and also includes a café. The beer is served in lined glasses straight from the cask, with two or three choices usually available. Cider is also often on offer. Many community activities take place, from poetry evenings and live music to quiz nights. Details are chalked up on a noticeboard. ◐❀◖◗❀P☐☐(39)❀❖

Southrepps

Vernon Arms ✓

2 Church Street, NR11 8NP (NE of Thorpe Market off A149 Cromer-North Walsham road)

☎ (01263) 833355 ⊕ vernonarms.com

Adnams Southwold Bitter; Fat Cat Norwich Bitter; Greene King Abbot; 1 changing beer (sourced nationally) ⊞

A lively and welcoming village-centre local. The bar has a games area at one end and a log fire in winter at the other. The front terrace includes a heated, covered, smoking area and there is a garden at the rear. There are three regular ales and a guest, from mainly national breweries. Three separate dining areas serving meals which are prepared with locally sourced ingredients where possible – booking is advisable. Acoustic music sessions are held occasionally. ❀◖◗♿▲♣P☐(33)❀❖

Stoke Ferry

Blue Bell

Lynn Road, PE33 9SW

☎ (01366) 502204 ⊕ bluebellstokeferry.org

Greene King IPA; 1 changing beer (sourced nationally) ⊞

The Blue Bell officially reopened in July 2022 after a campaign by the local community to resurrect the village's only pub. A deal to buy the pub was completed in 2021 after a major fundraising and share option campaign. Much of the renovation work was completed by locals. The campaign was awarded CAMRA's National Pub Saving Award. There is also a licensed café operating from 9-4 Monday to Friday. ◐❀◖◗♿P❀❖

Strumpshaw

Shoulder of Mutton ⑃

9 Norwich Road, NR13 4NT (on Brundall-Lingwood road)

☎ (01603) 926530 ⊕ themuttonstrumpshaw.co.uk

Adnams Southwold Bitter, Ghost Ship; 3 changing beers (sourced nationally) ⊞

Traditional village pub with a friendly welcome, close to RSPB Buckenham and Strumpshaw Steam Museum. Moon Gazer Hare Today is the house beer, with Mr Winter's and Tindall's as regular guests. Three local ciders including Burnard's are also available. There is separate dining room which has a heated marquee extension, and patios at the rear overlook the courtyard, which has a pétanque court. Regular live music and events are held. ❀◖◗♿▲≈(Lingwood) ♣❀P☐(15A) ❀❖

Terrington St Clement

Wildfowler
28 Sutton Road, PE34 4PQ
☎ (01553) 828260 ⊕ facebook.com/
thewildfowlerterrington
Greene King IPA, Abbot; 2 changing beers (sourced regionally) Ⓗ
Stylish and friendly, this popular pub at the heart of the village came under new ownership in June 2022. The large spacious bar has a dining area for those wishing to partake of the excellent cuisine, but there is still plenty of room for those just wishing to pop in for a drink. In addition to the two regular beers there are always two guest beers on offer from local breweries. Theme nights and musical entertainment are held on a regular basis. ♿✿◑&P🚌(505) ❀ 🎵

Thetford

Black Horse Ⓛ
64 Magdalen Street, IP24 2BP
☎ (01842) 762717
Adnams Southwold Bitter; Greene King IPA; Woodforde's Wherry; 2 changing beers (sourced nationally) Ⓗ
A good no-nonsense town-centre pub offering a varying range of ales on five handpumps. It stages a popular annual St George's Day beer festival. The food is home-made and good both in quality and value – desserts are a feature – served in a small but pleasant eating area, which has now been extended with the addition of a marquee for outside dining. Look for the changing murals on the end wall. ✿◑&P

Red Lion Ⓛ ✔
Market Place, IP24 2AL
☎ (01842) 757210
Adnams Broadside; Greene King IPA, Abbot; 3 changing beers (sourced nationally) Ⓗ
On the market square, the Red Lion has had a varied history. It was opened by Lacons and the wall outside still retains its plaque, then it became a Portuguese restaurant, before becoming a Wetherspoon establishment. The decor features information about local history and attractions. There is often a dark ale on the bar. The pub has a variety of eating and drinking areas plus an outdoor space. ♿✿◑≈❀ 🛜

Thorpe Market

Gunton Arms Ⓛ ✔
Cromer Road, NR11 8TZ (signposted on W of A149 Cromer-North Walsham road SE of Thorpe Market)
☎ (01263) 832010 ⊕ theguntonarms.co.uk
Lacons Falcon Ale, Legacy; Woodforde's Wherry; 1 changing beer (sourced nationally) Ⓗ
A fine inn with magical vistas of Gunton Park and the deer herd. The cosy decor, comfortable furnishings and winter log fire create a warm country house atmosphere. The bar includes traditional pub games, and three East Anglian ales are supplemented by one craft brewery guest. First-class cuisine is served in three restaurants; the vaulted Elk Room hosts several dishes cooked on an open range (not Sun). In summer, a large beer garden provides alfresco dining. Sixteen luxurious rooms and suites complete this English gem. ✿🛏◑&▲♣P❀ 🛜

Suffield Arms
Station Road, NR11 8UE (signposted on main road S of Thorpe Market; head E on Station Rd)
☎ (01263) 586858 ⊕ suffieldarms.com

Grain ThreeOneSix; Lacons Encore, Falcon Ale; Woodforde's Wherry; 1 changing beer (sourced locally) Ⓗ
A rural pub with a large front bar, log fire and traditional games. The wood-panelled interior, decor and artwork are outstanding. Upstairs there is a comfortable saloon bar serving cocktails and an outside seating area overlooking the rear gardens. There are four regular ales and one guest plus a high quality bar menu. The restaurant at the rear features Mediterranean cuisine, a tapas bar and a secluded nook at the end. Gunton station is opposite, making this a perfect destination for the railway user. Q✿◑&▲≉(Gunton)♣P❀ 🛜

Thurne

Lion Inn Ⓛ
The Street, NR29 3AP (at end of Thurne Dyke, off A149 via Mill Ln and Repps Rd)
☎ (01692) 671806 ⊕ thelionatthurne.com
4 changing beers (sourced regionally; often Adnams, Humpty Dumpty, Mr Winter's) Ⓖ
Large country pub in a remote village near the River Ant at the end of Thurne Dyke. Plenty of moorings are available nearby for passing broads cruisers and the pub has a garden area with outside dining pods. Good value meals are available in the large restaurant or bar area. Four changing real ales on handpump include two brewed locally under the Pell & Co badge, real ciders and 14 kegs taps for craft offerings. Q♿✿◑&♣P🚌❀ 🛜

Trunch

Crown
Front Street, NR28 0AH
☎ (01263) 722341 ⊕ thecrownattrunch.co.uk
Batemans XB, Gold, XXXB; 3 changing beers (sourced nationally; often Batemans) Ⓗ
The Crown is set in the middle of a charming north Norfolk village with fine, old flint cottages, close to the coast. As Batemans' only pub in the area it offers an excellent choice of beers and a friendly atmosphere. Three Batemans beers are always available plus guests. The cider is from Inch's. There are regular quizzes, a comedy club, bingo and live music monthly. A beer festival is held over a weekend in summer. Pie and mash is the kitchen's speciality. Q✿◑&♣P🚌(5)❀ 🛜

Wells-next-the-Sea

Golden Fleece ✔
The Quay, NR23 1AH
☎ (01328) 710650 ⊕ goldenfleecewells.co.uk
3 changing beers (sourced locally; often Moon Gazer) Ⓗ
Flint-built pub situated on the picturesque quayside, with a small bar, plenty of seating and an upstairs restaurant. Mostly given over to diners in summer, there's a pleasant terrace at the rear, and a log burner in the main room in winter. There are three beers from Moon Gazer on the handpumps, and food is available (Wed-Sun). A good start or end for a walk to the fabulous beach, with iconic beach huts, about a mile away, the pub welcomes families and dogs. ♿✿◑♣🚌(36,46)❀ 🛜

West Runton

Village Inn
Water Lane, NR27 9QP
☎ (01263) 838000 ⊕ villageinnwestrunton.co.uk
4 changing beers (sourced locally; often Adnams, Moon Gazer) Ⓗ

A large inn a short distance from the station and the beach, set in pleasant gardens in the centre of this quiet coastal village. Up to five ales are stocked and rotated. Excellent home-cooked meals can be enjoyed in the dining areas or outside, where there is plenty of seating in the flint-walled garden. In the 1970s major rock bands such as Deep Purple played secret gigs at the Pavilion which was at the rear of the pub (sadly now demolished). Q❄✿❶❿▲⇌P🚲(44,CH1)❀🐕

Wymondham

Feathers

13 Town Green, NR18 0PN
☎ (01953) 605675
Adnams Southwold Bitter, Ghost Ship; Fuller's London Pride; St Austell Tribute; 2 changing beers (sourced locally) Ⓗ

Local community freehouse run by the same family for many decades, a short walk from the Market Cross, Wymondham Abbey and the Mid-Norfolk Railway. The L-shaped interior has open plan main bar and seating, with cosy alcoves and bar access to the side. Good-value meals are served. The patio garden has a large covered seating area and serving hatch for garden customers. In winter months Adnams Tally-Ho is available on gravity. Town Green car park (paid) is behind the pub.
Q❄✿❶⇌♣🚲(6) ❀🐕

Breweries

All Day

Salle Moor Farm, Wood Dalling Road, Salle, NR10 4SB
☎ (01603) 327656 ☎ 07825 604887
🌐 alldaybrewing.co.uk

⊗ Housed in a centuries old barn, the brewery has its own hop yard and an adjoining organic orchard. Many of the beers are barrel-aged, sours, or involve fruit grown at the brewery. They are available in the taproom and kitchen, along with vegan food, pizza and real cider. Home of the the Norfolk Hop Festival. ‼🍺♦LIVE🍏

Ampersand SIBA

27-31 Sawmills Road, Diss, IP22 4GG
☎ (01379) 643944 🌐 ampersandbrew.co

A small batch brewery established in 2017. Originally based on a family farm in South Norfolk, it relocated to Diss in 2021. 🍺🍏

Bidon (ABV 3.9%) BITTER
The Cap Bitter (ABV 3.9%) BITTER
On The Wing (ABV 4.5%) PALE
Cocow (ABV 4.8%) STOUT
Pulpit Pale (ABV 5%) PALE

Barsham SIBA

Estate Office, West Barsham, Fakenham, NR21 9NR
☎ (01328) 864459 ☎ 07920 181537
🌐 barshambrewery.co.uk

⊗ Barsham Brewery was purchased by the present brewers in 2017. Maris Otter is grown onsite and a private bore hole supplies water for the brewery. 🍺LIVE

Oaks (ABV 3.6%) BITTER
Balanced malty base with red fruit and hop adding contrast and depth. Gentle woodiness joined by a slowly growing bitterness.
Norfolk Topper (ABV 3.8%) BITTER

Lemon and grapefruit hoppiness mixes with almond bitterness to loom over an underlying maltiness. Grainy with a short drying finish.
Pilgrims Ale (ABV 4%) BLOND
B.O.B (ABV 4.3%) BITTER
Tawny-hued with a rich sweet maltiness that complements the toffee and red fruit baseline. Long-lasting, complex, bittersweet finish.
Stout Robin (ABV 4.6%) STOUT
A rich, creamy, caramel roastiness permeates aroma and taste. Vanilla jostles with Oxo for recognition in a soft, creamy melange.
Golden Close IPA (ABV 5%) PALE
Punchy hop signature in aroma and taste aided by a malty sweetness. Lemon, peach and grapefruit add complexity.

Beeston SIBA

Fransham Road Farm, Beeston, PE32 2LZ
☎ (01328) 700844 ☎ 07768 742763
🌐 beestonbrewery.co.uk

⊗ The brewery was established in 2006 in an old farm building using a five-barrel plant. Brewing water comes from a dedicated borehole and raw ingredients are sourced locally whenever possible. ‼♦LIVE

The Squirrels Nuts (ABV 3.5%) MILD
Cherry, chocolate and vanilla aroma. A malt and cherry sweetness comes to the fore but quickly fades. Short finish.
Worth the Wait (ABV 4.2%) BITTER
Hoppy throughout with a growing dryness. Complex and grainy with fruit notes, malt and understated bitterness.
Stirling (ABV 4.5%) BITTER
The Dry Road (ABV 4.8%) BITTER
Village Life (ABV 4.8%) BITTER
Copper-coloured with a nutty character. Malty throughout, a bittersweet background gives depth. Strong toffee apple finish.
On the Huh (ABV 5%) BITTER
A fruity raisin aroma. A bittersweet maltiness jousts with caramel and roast. A dry hoppiness adds to a strong finale.
Old Stoatwobbler (ABV 6%) STOUT

Contract brewed for Brancaster Brewery:
Best (ABV 3.8%) BITTER
Malthouse Bitter (ABV 4.2%) BITTER

Birdhouse

Revell Road, Downham Market, PE38 9SE ☎ 07858 628183 🌐 birdhousebrewery.co.uk

⊗ Birdhouse, a picobrewery, was established in 2019 by Paul Bird. It produces 150 bottle-conditioned beers per batch, making it one of the smallest breweries in the country. Beers are available in shops, local markets and online. ♦LIVE

Blimey!

Branksome House, 166 St Clements Hill, Norwich, NR3 1RS
☎ (01603) 449298 ☎ 07775 788299
✉ adriankbryan@googlemail.com

⊗ Brewing began in 2017.

Son of Pale Face (ABV 4%) GOLD
Eleven APA (ABV 4.5%) PALE
Solid orange citrus notes dominate aroma and taste. Full-bodied and robust with malt adding balance. Short, bittersweet finish.
Ten DDH APA Cryo (ABV 4.5%) PALE

The Pale Face (ABV 4.5%) GOLD
Thirteen (ABV 4.5%) GOLD
First Born IPA (ABV 5.2%) PALE

Boudicca

c/o S&P Brewery, The Homestead, Brewery Lane, Horsford, NR10 3GL ☎ 07864 321733

Office: 51 Bakers Street, Norwich, NR3 3AZ
⊕ boudiccabrewing.co.uk

⊠ Established in 2015, Boudicca was based on a North Norfolk estate until 2020. S&P (qv) are currently brewing its beers under contract until a new home is located. It is an award-winning brewery exclusively producing vegan beers and one gluten free, supplied to free trade outlets across East Anglia. ‼♦LIVE GF V

Bull of the Woods

Brook Farm, Kirby Cane, Bungay, NR35 2PJ
☎ (01508) 518080 ☎ 07833 702658
⊕ bullofthewoods.co.uk

⊠ The brewery began production in 2017. The brewery and shop are situated in the old milling barn on a family-owned farm. The head brewer gave up his tree surgery business to pursue his love of brewing real ale. The brewery goes from strength to strength and continues to expand its range of eclectic styles and seasonal favourites. Various brewery merchandise, along with a range of its bottled beers, are available in the shop. ☲♦LIVE

Rock Steady (ABV 3.8%) BITTER
Traditional malt and hop signature with the added complexity of walnut and quinine flowing through. Long, increasingly bitter finish.
Satan Session (ABV 3.8%) PALE
Hacienda (ABV 4%) PALE
Woodstock (ABV 4.2%) IPA
Vapour Trail (ABV 4.3%) PALE
Well-balanced with grapefruit and mandarin complementing a hoppy bittersweet base. Floral notes quickly fade in a long, drying finish.
Inca Gold (ABV 4.4%) GOLD
Pulsating lemon presence in aroma and taste looms over a balanced malt and hop foundation. A crisp, dry finish develops.
Twisted Wheel (ABV 4.5%) BITTER
Strong marmalade notes with sweet malty support slowly fade behind a crisp well-defined bitterness. Short, peppery ending.
Loaded (ABV 4.9%) PALE
Banjo Hill (ABV 5%) IPA
Shine a Light IPA (ABV 6.4%) IPA
Hop, apricot and toffee underpin a full bodied complex character. Bittersweet notes highlight a growing peppery dryness.

Chalk Hill

☰ Rosary Road, Norwich, NR1 4DA
☎ (01603) 477077 ⊕ thecoachthorperoad.co.uk

⊠ Chalk Hill began production in 1993 on a 15-barrel plant. It supplies local pubs and festivals. A small plant is used to brew experimental beers, which if popular become part of the regular range. ‼♦

Dancing Men

☰ Hill House Inn, The Hill, Happisburgh, NR12 0PW
☎ (01692) 650004 ☎ 07818 038768
⊕ hillhouseinn.co.uk

⊠ Brewing began in 2014 at the 16th century Hill House Inn on Happisburgh's fast-eroding clifftop. The microbrewery is named in honour of the Sir Arthur Conan Doyle Sherlock Holmes story, after he visited the pub in 1903. The five-barrel plant was acquired from Bees Brewery after its partial destruction in 2013. New recipes have been crafted using exclusive hops and barley including locally-grown Norfolk varieties. ‼♦

Drenchfoot

Unit 9, Hill Fort Close, Thetford, IP24 1HS

Office: 65 Vicarage Road, Thetford, IP24 2LW
⊕ drenchfoot.co.uk

Drenchfoot is a 400-litre microbrewery supplying pubs and bars in Norfolk and Suffolk. It sells bottles and polypins to the trade and direct to the public.

Dragon Slayer (ABV 3.6%) BITTER
Don't Panic (ABV 5%) IPA
To Pee or not to Pee (ABV 5.8%) IPA

Duration

Abbey Farm, River Road, West Acre, PE32 1UA
☎ (01760) 755436 ⊕ durationbeer.com

Situated at the historic West Acre Priory, Duration produces fresh beers, wild and blended farm-style ales. Beers are available in cans, keg and bottles. Its taproom is open Friday and Saturday afternoons. ‼☲♦LIVE ⚘

Elmtree SIBA EAB

Unit 10, Oakwood Industrial Estate, Harling Road, Snetterton, NR16 2JU
☎ (01953) 887065 ⊕ elmtreebeers.co.uk

⊠ Established in 2007, Elmtree brews on a six-barrel plant. More than 120 free trade outlets are supplied. Some of the strongest beers are only available in bottle-conditioned form. Bespoke beers for individual pubs are also brewed. ‼☲♦LIVE

Burston's Cuckoo (ABV 3.8%) GOLD
Assertive lemon hoppiness dominates a soft malty backdrop. A crisp bitterness gives definition to a slowly drying finale.
Bitter (ABV 4.2%) BITTER
Traditional malt and hop nose. Solid and well-balanced with a bittersweet hoppy maltiness throughout. Flowing crisp hoppy ending.
Norfolk's 80 Shilling Ale (ABV 4.5%) BITTER
Mixed fruit nose introduces a sweet fruity bitter with a bitter counterbalance. Short, drying finish.
Dark Horse Stout (ABV 5%) STOUT
Solid coffee and malt aroma. A cornucopia of vanilla, dark chocolate, and roast with a sweet foundation. Long strong finale.
Golden Pale Ale (ABV 5%) PALE
Sweet fruity aroma with hints of honey. Even handed mix of lemon and crisp hoppiness with a defined bittering finale.
Nightlight Mild (ABV 5.7%) MILD
A heavy mix of liquorice, roast and malt infuses aroma and first taste. A sweet spiciness slowly develops.

Fat Cat

98-100 Lawson Road, Norwich, NR3 4LF ☎ 07807 579517 ⊕ fatcatbrewery.co.uk

⊠ Established in 2005 by the owner of the 'Fat Cat' and 'Fat Cat & Canary' pubs, it is located in the same building as the Brewery Tap (separately owned). Beers are available in other outlets, mainly within Norwich and

Norfolk and also distributed by Small Beer of Lincoln.
♦LIVE

Norwich Bitter (ABV 3.8%) BITTER
Grapefruit on the nose. A strong hoppy bitterness with underlying maltiness adds depth and complexity. Softly drying finale.

Tabby (ABV 4%) BITTER

Tom Cat (ABV 4.1%) GOLD
A crisp citrus character with lemon, lime and orange in aroma and taste. Bitterness grows as cut grass hoppiness fades.

Milk Stout (ABV 4.6%) STOUT

Incredible Pale Ale (ABV 5.2%) PALE
Big hit of hoppiness with lemon and peach fruitiness. Background maltiness soon disappears under a level sustained bitterness. Full-bodied.

Marmalade (ABV 5.5%) BITTER
Orange and malt pervades both aroma and taste. A full-bodied mix of balanced flavours. A bittersweet finish with hoppiness.

Wild Cat IPA (ABV 6%) IPA

Fengate

Unit 3, Cobble Acre Park, Brick Kiln Road, Hevingham, NR10 5NL
☎ (01263) 479953 ☎ 07884 960697
✉ fengatebrewery@gmail.com

⊠ Fengate Brewery was established in 2019. Head brewer and owner Alistair brews a selection of traditional ales with a mix of new beer styles. Beers can be found in pubs and bottle shops in the surrounding area. ▶♦

Hudson's Bitter (ABV 3.6%) BITTER
3 Threads Smoked Porter (ABV 4%) PORTER
Cobble Acre Pale Ale (ABV 4.5%) PALE
West Coast IPA (ABV 4.8%) PALE
Extra Double Stout (ABV 9%) STOUT

Fox

▤ 22 Station Road, Heacham, PE31 7EX
☎ (01485) 570345 ⊕ foxbrewery.co.uk

⊠ Based in an old cottage adjacent to the Fox & Hounds pub, Fox Brewery was established in 2002 and now supplies around 30 outlets as well as the pub. A hop garden next to the brewery, trialled during 2009, has been enlarged. ‼▶♦LIVE

Heacham Gold (ABV 3.9%) GOLD
Red Knocker (ABV 3.9%) BITTER
Hop Across the Pond (ABV 4.2%) PALE
Cerberus Stout (ABV 4.5%) STOUT
Nelson's Blood (ABV 4.7%) SPECIALITY
Fox Grizzly Bear (ABV 4.8%) SPECIALITY
IPA (ABV 5.2%) PALE

Golden Triangle SIBA

Unit 9, Industrial Estate, Watton Road, Norwich, NR9 4BG
☎ (01603) 757763 ☎ 07976 281132
⊕ goldentriangle.co.uk

⊠ Golden Triangle, named after an area of Norwich, has been brewing modern, hop-forward ales on a 10-barrel plant since 2011. Brewing is on an occasional basis, with the beers mainly found in the brewery tap, the Artichoke, Norwich, which was purchased in 2018. ♦

Grain SIBA

South Farm, Tunbeck Road, Harleston, IP20 0BS
☎ (01986) 788884 ⊕ grainbrewery.co.uk

⊠ Grain Brewery was launched in 2006 by Geoff Wright and Phil Halls in a converted dairy in the Waveney Valley. It upgraded to an 18-barrel plant in 2012. Two pubs are owned: the Plough, Norwich, and the Spread Eagle, Ipswich. ‼▶♦LIVE

Oak (ABV 3.8%) BITTER
Good balance of malt, toffee and bittersweet fruitiness. Caramel in initial taste fades as biscuit and bitterness dominate the aftertaste.

ThreeOneSix (ABV 3.9%) PALE
Hop and grapefruit dominate throughout as an underlying bitterness slowly stifles a delicate malty echo. Crisp and well-defined.

Best Bitter (ABV 4.2%) BITTER
Brazil nut and malt introduce this well-balanced, complex bitter. Bittersweet caramel notes flourish before a gently-tapering malty finish.

Blackwood (ABV 4.5%) STOUT

Slate (ABV 6%) PORTER
Roast and dark fruits dominate throughout. Caramel and sweet malt add complexity and balance. Full-bodied with a short finish.

Lignum Vitae (ABV 6.5%) IPA
Orange, toffee and banana on the nose and first taste. A smooth, digestive sweetness adds depth as bitterness slowly grows.

Humpty Dumpty SIBA

Church Road, Reedham, NR13 3TZ
☎ (01493) 701818 ☎ 07843 248865
⊕ humptydumptybrewery.co.uk

⊠ Established in 1998, this 11-barrel, award-winning brewery continues to grow and expand its range of beers, including the Norfolk Broads Brewing series of occasional one-off brews. ‼▶♦LIVE

Little Sharpie (ABV 3.8%) PALE
Complex and smooth with a crisp bitterness underpinning a buttery biscuit follow through. Lemon hoppiness in a long, drying finish.

Branch Line Bitter (ABV 3.9%) BITTER

Lemon & Ginger (ABV 4%) SPECIALITY

Swallowtail (ABV 4%) PALE
Full-bodied marmalade and biscuit aroma with matching beginning. Grainy texture is enhanced by solid bitter notes flowing onward.

Broadland Sunrise (ABV 4.2%) BITTER

Red Mill (ABV 4.3%) BITTER
Full-bodied, robust and fruity. Coffee, dark fruits and caramel vie for dominance against a malty bitter base. Powerful rich ending.

Reedcutter (ABV 4.4%) GOLD
A sweet, malty beer; golden-hued with a gentle malt background. Smooth and full-bodied with a quick, gentle finish.

Cheltenham Flyer (ABV 4.6%) BITTER
A full-flavoured golden, earthy bitter with a long, grainy finish. A strong hop bitterness dominates throughout. Little evidence of malt.

EAPA (East Anglian Pale Ale) (ABV 4.6%) PALE
Amber gold with an orange marmalade nose. A bittersweet caramel beginning slowly dries out as malty nuances fade away.

Railway Sleeper (ABV 5%) OLD
A rich Christmas pudding aroma introduces this delightfully fruity brew. Malt, sultanas and raisins dominate a bittersweet backdrop. Full-bodied, smooth finish.

Iceni

The Walled Garden, Elveden Courtyard, London Road, Elveden, IP24 3TQ
☎ (01842) 878922 ☎ 07949 488113

Office: Iceni Brewery, 70 Risbygate Street, Bury St Edmunds, IP33 3AZ ✉ icenibrewe@aol.com

The Iceni Brewery is owned by Brendan Moore, who set it up in 1995. In 2020 a micropub, the Magic Hammer, opened. ♦LIVE

Fine Soft Day (ABV 4%) BITTER
Golden-hued with toffee notes throughout. A creamy, lightly-hopped backdrop softly sinks into a pleasant sweetness.

Lacons SIBA

The Courtyard, Main Cross Road, Great Yarmouth, NR30 3NZ
☎ (01493) 850578

Office: Cooke Road, Lowestoft, NR33 7NA
⊕ lacons.co.uk

⊠ Lacons Brewery has a rich history dating back to 1760, but was closed by Whitbread in the 1960s. It relaunched in 2013 and the Falcon Brewery is now nestled in a Courtyard in Great Yarmouth. Beers are available across East Anglia and use the original Lacons yeast strand. A range of monthly special heritage beers is also produced.
‼️ ⏂ ♦LIVE

Encore (ABV 3.8%) PALE
A solid hop backbone with strong citrus support. Sweetness subsides as a crisp dryness emerges in the long strong finale.

Legacy (ABV 4.4%) GOLD
Grapefruit and lemon nose and first taste where a crisp bitterness is also encountered. Some malt in a bitter finish.

Audit (ABV 8%) BARLEY
Honey, orange marmalade and maltiness define this full-bodied ale. Damson, toffee and a refreshing bitterness sharpens the palate.

Lynn

5 Hayfield Road, North Wootton, PE30 3PR ☎ 07706 187894 ⊕ lynnbrewery.co.uk

Lynn Brewery is an independent, family-owned brewery based in King's Lynn, making small-batch, hand bottled craft beer. It is passionately local, the grain used comes from a local malting group and all beers are inspired by, and named after, the people and places of Lynn.

Malt Coast

Branthill Farm, Wells-next-to-the-Sea, NR23 1SB
☎ 07881 378900 ⊕ maltcoast.com

Brewing began in 2016. It grows its own barley on the farm. ‼️ ⏂

Moon Gazer SIBA

Moon Gazer Barn, Harvest Lane, Hindringham, NR21 0PW
☎ (01328) 878495 ⊕ moongazerale.co.uk

⊠ Brewing began in 2012 using a 10-barrel plant. The brewery is owned and run by Rachel and David Holliday. Chalk-filtered water is used from the brewery's own well. ‼️♦

Jumper (ABV 3.9%) BITTER

Gentle hop character with supporting sweet malt and bitterness. Caramel swirls in and out as a dry edge develops.

Pintail (ABV 3.9%) PALE
Crisp lemon hoppiness flows through this well-balanced long lasting brew. Bitterness and light malty sweetness float in the background.

Jigfoot (ABV 4%) PALE
Orange peel and honey nose. Marmalade intro bolstered by well-defined bitterness. Initial sweetness fades into a sharp astringent bitterness.

Nibbler (ABV 4%) OLD
Roasty dark fruit nose flows through into the first taste. Increasing malt and caramel. Smooth grainy mouthfeel. Short bitter finish.

Bouchart (ABV 4.9%) MILD
Savoury smoky bacon character throughout. Bittersweet dark chocolate nuances give depth. A smooth and creamy finish with hints of blackcurrant.

Cheeky Jack (ABV 5%) PALE

Mr Winter's

8 Keelan Close, Norwich, NR6 6QZ
☎ (01603) 787820 ⊕ mrwintersbeers.co.uk

⊠ Winter's was established in 2001 by David Winter, who had previous success as a brewer for both Woodforde's and Chalk Hill breweries. Winter's has won many awards, with David now passing his brewing knowledge to his son, Mark, a multi award-winning brewer in his own right. The brewery rebranded as Mr Winter's in 2020. ⏂♦LIVE

Fusioneer (ABV 3.6%) MILD
Roast and dried fruit in both aroma and taste. Caramel, hazelnut and arrowroot add to a complex mix of flavours.

Twin Parallel (ABV 3.8%) PALE
Strong hop, grapefruit and apricot presence in aroma and taste. A bittersweet background gives depth and balance. Strong flowing finale.

Evolution APA (ABV 4%) GOLD
Clementine on the nose is followed by lemon and grapefruit in the body. Hoppy bitterness develops in a full-bodied finish.

Quantum Gold (ABV 4.1%) GOLD
A hint of hops in the aroma. Initial taste combines a dry bitterness with fruity apple. Fading dry bitter finish.

Tranquility (ABV 4.2%) BITTER
Sulphurous hoppy nose. Balanced hoppiness throughout with cereal and bitter orange providing contrast. Short ending with a bitter signature.

Rorschach (ABV 4.5%) STOUT
A smooth mouthfeel with a grainy edge. Roast dominates throughout balanced by malt, a bittersweet fruitiness and increasingly nutty finish.

Vanilla Latte (ABV 4.6%) SPECIALITY
Full on mix of coffee, vanilla and lactose with a smooth malty base. Continues to a long coffee crème ending.

Twisted Ladder (ABV 5%) PALE

Citrus Kiss IPA (ABV 6%) IPA
Strong citrus base with hop and malt in the background. Lemon and grapefruit continue as a bittersweet background provides depth.

Opa Hay's

Glencot, Wood Lane, Aldeby, NR34 0DA
☎ (01502) 679144 ☎ 07916 282729
✉ arnthengel@hotmail.co.uk

⊠ Opa Hay's began brewing in 2008. It is a small, family-run award winning brewery, taking its name from the brewer's great grandfather – a Brewmeister of Schleswig Holstein (northern Germany). Only traditional brewing methods are used, with ingredients that are, where possible, sourced locally. ♦LIVE

Panther EAB

Unit 1, Collers Way, Reepham, NR10 4SW ☎ 07766 558215 ⊕ pantherbrewery.co.uk

⊗ Panther began brewing in 2010 on an industrial estate near the old railway station, formerly the home of Reepham Brewery. ‼☷♦LIVE

Mild Panther (ABV 3.3%) MILD
Smooth, sweet base with contrasting dry cobnut notes and a gentle roastiness. Short clean finish with biscuit airs.
Ginger Panther (ABV 3.7%) SPECIALITY
Refreshingly clean ginger wheat beer with a distinct fiery kick. It contains all the ingredients of a Thai Curry.
Golden Panther (ABV 3.7%) GOLD
Refreshing orange and malt notes flow through this well-balanced, easy-drinking bitter. Hops and a soft bitterness add depth.
Honey Panther (ABV 4%) SPECIALITY
A gentle flowing brew with honey and malt throughout. Amber-coloured with a tapering bittersweet finale.
Red Panther (ABV 4.1%) RED
A distinctly malty nose with a nutty, bittersweet beginning. Rye, plum and caramel appear before a full-bodied hoppiness emerges.
American Pale Ale (ABV 4.4%) BLOND
Zesty lemon and hop character with a gentle sweet counterpoint. Light grapefruit notes bolster a short crisp finish.
Black Panther (ABV 4.5%) PORTER
Vanilla rum and raisin throughout. Strong supporting mix of caramel, malt and robust roastiness. Mellow and complex finish slowly sweetens.
Beast of the East (ABV 5.5%) IPA
A hoppy resinous bouquet with hints of sweetness. Earthy, peppery beginning with a hoppy backdrop. Long drying bitter citrus finish.

Pell & Co

White Horse Inn, The Street, Neatishead, NR12 8AD ☎ (01692) 630828 ⊕ thewhitehorseinnneatishead.com

⊗ Formerly known as Neatishead, production began in 2015 at the White Horse Inn. The brew kit can be viewed through glass from the restaurant. Beer is only available in the White Horse and the owner's other pub, the Lion, Thurne. A range of semi-regular beers is brewed with at least one ever-changing ale. Beer is currently being contract brewed by an unknown brewery.

People's

Mill House, Mill Lane, Thorpe-Next-Haddiscoe, Norwich, NR14 6PA ☎ (01508) 548706 ✉ peoplesbrewery@mail.com

⊗ A one-barrel brewery associated with the Queen's Head pub in Thurlton, which takes most of its draught output. Bottled beers are also available at Thurlton Community Shop.

Northdown Bitter (ABV 3.8%) BITTER
Raveningham Bitter (ABV 3.9%) BITTER
Thurlton Gold (ABV 4.2%) PALE
Norfolk Cascade (ABV 4.5%) GOLD
Northern Brewers (ABV 4.6%) BITTER

Poppyland

46 West Street, Cromer, NR27 9DS

☎ (01263) 515214 ☎ 07802 160558
⊕ poppylandbrewery.com

Established in 2012, the 2.5-barrel brewery specialises in unusual and innovative brews mainly using Norfolk malt. Foraged saisons a speciality. Beers are on sale at the brewery and at numerous specialist beer shops across East Anglia. Cask ales are available in some Norfolk and Norwich pubs. ☷LIVE

Redwell

Under the Arches, Bracondale, Trowse Millgate, Norwich, NR1 2EF ☎ (01603) 904990 ⊕ redwellbrewing.com

⊗ Redwell was started in 2013 by a group of beer lovers. It is now under new ownership and its Polish head brewer is Marcel Liput. The taproom accommodates up to 150 and the beer garden up to 300. Food is available most of the time. The brews are certified vegan, audited gluten-free, and are unfined and unfiltered. ‼☷GF V✦

S&P

Homestead, Brewery Lane, Horsford, NR10 3AN ☎ 07884 455425 ⊕ spbrewery.co.uk

⊗ Production commenced in 2013 using a 10-barrel plant constructed upon land once owned by prominent Norfolk brewers Steward & Patteson (1800-1965), hence the name. Locally-produced malts are used, as is water from the brewery's own borehole. ‼LIVE

Topaz Blonde (ABV 3.7%) BLOND
Apteryx (ABV 3.8%) GOLD
Tilt (ABV 3.8%) GOLD
Barrack Street Bitter (ABV 4%) BITTER
Blackberry Porter (ABV 4%) SPECIALITY
Rich blackberry notes in aroma and taste. Wide ranging and complex with dark chocolate and malty sweetness. Strong earthy finish.
First Light (ABV 4.1%) GOLD
Dennis (ABV 4.2%) BITTER
Fruit and malt, with some caramel, dominate aroma and taste. Full-bodied throughout with an increasingly bitter tail.
Eve's Drop (ABV 4.3%) BITTER
Darkest Hour (ABV 4.4%) STOUT
Deep dark roast notes dominate this singularly dry stout. Sweet biscuit notes fade in an increasingly bitter chocolate finish.
Marsha's Mood (ABV 4.4%) MILD
Beano (ABV 4.5%) STOUT
NASHA IPA (ABV 5%) PALE
Strong banana and grapefruit character throughout. A good balance of malt and hop with a bittersweet background. Rich and filling.

Contract brewed for Boudicca Brewery:
Queen of Hops (ABV 3.7%) PALE
A definitive grapefruit hoppiness dominates throughout. A backdrop of ginger and gentle grassiness appears before a growing dryness gains ascendancy.
Three Tails (ABV 3.9%) BITTER
A bitter backbone dominates throughout. Malt, grapefruit and pepper in the first taste fades as a dry bitterness slowly grows.
One for the Woad (ABV 4%) MILD
Golden Torc (ABV 4.3%) GOLD
Malty bouquet with a hint of grassy hop. Biscuity beginning with a growing zesty citrus background appears. Clean grapefruit finish.
The Red Queen (ABV 4.5%) RED

Malt, dark fruits and caramel in nose and taste.
Sweetness counters a growing hoppiness. Rye adds
contrast and depth.

Spiral Stout (ABV 4.6%) STOUT
Burnt toast on the nose and black malt in the taste
defines this traditional black and dry stout. Strong finish.

Prasto's Porter (ABV 5.2%) PORTER
Smooth and dark with molasses, malt and sweetness in
aroma and taste. A roast toffee edge with a drying finish.

St Andrews Brewhouse

⊟ **41 Saint Andrews Street, Norwich, NR2 4TP**
☎ **(01603) 305995** ☎ **07976 652410**
⊕ **standrewsbrewhouse.com**

⊠ A city centre brewpub opened in 2015 in the premises
formerly occupied by Delaney's Irish Bar. ‼◆

Steam Shed

The Old Train Shed, Station Street, Swaffham,
PE37 7HP ☎ **07387 005424**

Production began in 2021. Beer is available in casks,
polypins and bottles. Distribution is via local pubs and
farmers' markets. Brew capacity is circa 600 litres per
brew.

Stumptail

North Street, Great Dunham, Kings Lynn, PE32 2LR
☎ **(01328) 701042** ✉ **stumptail@btinternet.com**

⊠ Stumptail began commercial homebrewing in 2011
using a 100-litre plant. Bottle-conditioned beers are
produced with cask-conditioned versions brewed to
order, all to bespoke recipes. LIVE

Tindall

Toad Lane, Seething, Norwich, NR35 2EQ ☎ **07703
379116** ⊕ **tindallbrewery.com**

⊠ Tindall Ales began brewing in 1998. It was originally
based in Ditchingham but moved to its current location in
2001. Mike is passionate about brewing a new
generation of cask beer using the finest local ingredients,
whenever possible, and live yeast. ‼🚚◆

Best Bitter (ABV 3.7%) BITTER
Mild (ABV 3.7%) MILD
Soft malty, dark fruit bouquet. Balanced, with fig roll,
roast and a crisp, bitterness leading to a strong savoury
finish.

Liberator (ABV 3.8%) PALE
Golden-hued with a grapefruit and lemon hoppiness that
floats over a subtle maltiness. A bittersweet finish with
citrus notes.

Galaxy Dream (ABV 4%) BLOND
Seething Pint (ABV 4.3%) BITTER
Caramel Stout (ABV 4.5%) STOUT
Full on roast coffee and vanilla with caramel. Crisp, well-
defined taste with toffee adding complexity. Long finish
becomes dryer.

Tipple's

Unit 3, The Mill, Wood Green, Salhouse, NR13 6NY
☎ **(01603) 721310** ⊕ **tipplesbrewery.com**

⊠ Tipples was established in 2004 on a six-barrel brew
plant. In addition to a full range of cask ales, an extensive
range of bottled beers is produced, which can be found
in some farmers markets and supermarkets in Norfolk.
Bottled beers can now be ordered direct from the
brewery for delivery or collection. 🚚◆LIVE

Bowline (ABV 3.8%) BITTER
Malten Copper (ABV 4.4%) BITTER
Moonrocket (ABV 5%) BITTER
A complex golden brew. Malt, hop bitterness and a fruity
sweetness swirl around in an ever-changing
kaleidoscope of flavours.

Tombstone

⊟ **6 George Street, Great Yarmouth, NR30 1HR**
☎ **07584 504444** ⊕ **tombstonebrewery.co.uk**

⊠ Established in 2013, the brewery is run by former
homebrewer Paul Hodgson. The original brewery backed
onto the town cemetery, inspiring the name, but it has
now relocated to the rear of its brewery tap, the
Tombstone Saloon. Around 30 outlets are supplied
around Norwich. 🚚◆

Ale (ABV 3.7%) GOLD
Banana toffee aroma. Piquant bitter hoppy beginning
softened by a biscuity maltiness. Dry bitter finish.

Amarillo (ABV 3.8%) BITTER
Arizona (ABV 3.9%) BITTER
Malt and lemon nose. Initial lemongrass and sweet
biscuit beginning quickly fades. Sweet watery finish
enhanced by malt.

Texas Jack (ABV 4%) BITTER
Toffee apple and vanilla aroma. Caramel leads the
smooth complex mix of flavours. A bittersweet fruitiness
continues to the end.

Regulators (ABV 4.1%) GOLD
Gunslinger (ABV 4.3%) BITTER
Lone Rider (ABV 4.3%) OLD
Stagecoach (ABV 4.4%) OLD
A rich caramel and treacle aroma. Malt, roast and
caramel dominate a hoppy bittersweeet foundation.
Short increasingly dry finish.

Cherokee (ABV 4.5%) BITTER
Malty nose with plum and cherry. Initial mix of biscuit
and roasty bitterness gently changes to a slightly spicy
maltiness.

Santa Fe (ABV 5%) BITTER
Big Nose Kate (ABV 5.2%) BITTER
6 Shooter (ABV 6.6%) IPA

Brewed for Brunning & Price pub Co:
Blackfoot (ABV 4.8%) PORTER

Two Rivers SIBA

2 Sluice Bank, Denver, Downham Market, PE38 0EQ
☎ **07518 099868** ⊕ **denverbrewery.co.uk**

⊠ Established in 2012, bottled-conditioned ales have
been available since then, with cask ales being produced
since 2013. Experimental brews are also available on an
ad-hoc basis. The brewery also brews three house ales
for the Wellington, Feltwell, and will brew bottled or cask
ale on commission. The Blackstone Engine Bar at Denver
Windmill is the brewery's tap. ‼🚚◆LIVE🗝

Miners Mild (ABV 3.1%) MILD
Hares Hopping (ABV 4.1%) BITTER
Kiwi Kick (ABV 4.1%) GOLD
Denver Diamond (ABV 4.4%) BITTER
Happy Hopper (ABV 4.5%) PALE
Light citrus airs introduce a hop based beginning with
grapefruit notes. Biscuit arrives as a long dry finish takes
command.

Captain Manby (ABV 5%) BITTER
Porters Pride (ABV 5%) PORTER
Windmill Wheat (ABV 5%) SPECIALITY
Norfolk Stoat (ABV 5.8%) STOUT

Wagtail

New Barn Farm, Wilby Warrens, Old Buckenham, NR17 1PF
☎ (01953) 887133
✉ wagtailbrewery@btinternet.com

Wagtail Brewery went into full-time production in 2006. All beers are only available bottle-conditioned. This is a chemical-free brewery. No chemicals onsite and all cleaning is done with hot water and 'elbow grease'. LIVE

Waveney

▤ **Queen's Head, Station Road, Earsham, NR35 2TS**
☎ (01986) 892623 ✉ lyndahamps@aol.com

⊠ Established at the Queen's Head in 2004, the five-barrel brewery produces three beers, regularly available at the pub along with other free trade outlets. ♦

Why Not

95 Gordon Avenue, Norwich, NR7 0DR
☎ (01603) 300786 ⊕ thewhynotbrewery.co.uk

Why Not began brewing in 2005 on a 1.5-barrel plant originally located to the rear of the house of proprietor Colin Emms. In 2006 the brewery was extensively upgraded, doubling in capacity. In 2011 the brewery was moved to a new location and then again in 2022. LIVE

Wildcraft SIBA

Church Farm, Smallburgh, NR12 9NB
☎ (01603) 278054 ☎ 07584 308850
⊕ wildcraftbrewery.co.uk

⊠ Wildcraft was set up in 2016 and uses as many foraged and locally-sourced ingredients as possible, resulting in innovative and intriguing brews. In 2022, its continuing success resulted in a move to much larger premises to facilitate expansion. Its own malting barley is grown within 50 metres of the brewery. ‼▤GFV♦

Wild Eye P.A. (ABV 3.8%) PALE
Wild Norfolk (ABV 4.2%) PALE
Strong cut grass and citrus hop aroma. Full-bodied with lemon, sweet biscuit and a dry bitterness. Increasingly astringent finish.
Wild Caribbean (ABV 4.3%) GOLD
Wild Bill Hiccup (ABV 4.5%) BITTER
Wild Summer (ABV 4.5%) PALE
Wild Ride (ABV 5%) GOLD
Wild Stallion (ABV 5%) STOUT
Full on roastiness with black cherry, vanilla and burnt chestnut. A subtle sweet maltiness adds to the richness of flavour.
Wild Weekend (ABV 5%) PALE
Wild Wood (ABV 5.2%) STOUT
Wild Un-Bongo (ABV 5.8%) PALE
Wild One (ABV 8%) STOUT

Wolf SIBA

Decoy Farm, Old Norwich Road, Besthorpe, Attleborough, NR17 2LA
☎ (01953) 457775 ⊕ wolfbrewery.com

⊠ The brewery was founded in 1995 on a 20-barrel plant, which was upgraded to a 25-barrel plant in 2006. It moved to its current site in 2013. More than 300 outlets are supplied. ▤♦

Edith Cavell (ABV 3.7%) GOLD
Hoppy, peppery nose flows into taste. Malt, caramel and bitterness give depth. Crisp finish, hoppy edge.
Golden Jackal (ABV 3.7%) GOLD
Gentle lemon citrus aroma. A balanced mix of malt and hop with a crisp bitter tang. Burgeoning bitter swansong.
Wolf in Sheep's Clothing (ABV 3.7%) MILD
Robust mix of malt and caramel with crisp blackcurrant notes adding focus. Soft bittersweet undertones contribute to a smooth ending.
Lavender Honey (ABV 3.8%) SPECIALITY
Malty caramel aroma leads into a bittersweet beginning with background honey notes. A long drying finish.
Battle of Britain (ABV 3.9%) BITTER
Wolf Ale (ABV 3.9%) BITTER
Copper-coloured with a smooth mix of biscuit and hop. A growing grainy bitterness contrasts the long finale.
Lupus Lupus (ABV 4.2%) PALE
Hoppy throughout with malt and lemon. Increasing bitterness overcomes the initial sweetness although the beer is easy-drinking and balanced.
Sirius Dog Star (ABV 4.4%) RED
Rich tapestry of malt, roast and caramel with interwoven hop hints. Sweetness and bitterness provide a light but growing undercurrent.
Sly Wolf (ABV 4.4%) BLOND
Mad Wolf (ABV 4.7%) RED
Well-rounded, malty foundation with chocolate and chestnut support. A bittersweet hoppiness provides depth and balance. Full-bodied and lasting.
Granny Wouldn't Like It (ABV 4.8%) RED
Complex, with a malty bouquet. Increasing bitterness is softened by malt as a fruity sweetness adds depth.
Woild Moild (ABV 4.8%) MILD
Heavy and complex with malt, vine fruit, bitterness and roast notes vying for dominance. Increasingly dry finish.

Contract brewed for City of Cambridge Brewery:
Boathouse (ABV 3.7%) BITTER
Hobson's Choice (ABV 4.2%) GOLD
Atom Splitter (ABV 4.5%) GOLD
Parkers Piece (ABV 5%) PORTER

Woodforde's SIBA

Broadland Brewery, Woodbastwick, NR13 6SW
☎ (01603) 720353 ⊕ woodfordes.co.uk

⊠ Founded in 1981, Woodforde's is named after Parson Woodforde, the 18th century Norfolk diarist with a penchant for real ale. In 1989 the brewery moved to its current home at Woodbastwick. It has its own boreholes and brews using locally-grown Maris Otter. Further investment has increased capacity. The Fur & Feather is owned, serving as the tap and located next door to the brewery, along with the Lord Nelson, Burnham Thorpe. ‼▤♦LIVE

Wherry (ABV 3.8%) BITTER
A sweet biscuit base with strawberry and a contrasting hoppy bitterness. Long and well-balanced with a noticeable citrus encore.
Reedlighter (ABV 4%) PALE
Well-balanced hop and grapefruit backbone with a sweet biscuity undercurrent. Full-bodied with a pronounced bittersweet ending.
Bure Gold (ABV 4.3%) PALE
Singularly citrus throughout with a hop garland. Sweet biscuit floats in the background over a bitter footing.
Nelson's (ABV 4.5%) BITTER
Malt, hop and vine fruits dominate this full-bodied brew. Caramel and bitterness add depth and contrast.
Volt (ABV 4.5%) PALE
Rollicking mix of lemon, lime, hop and biscuit. Slightly astringent resinous notes add crispness and character.
Nog (ABV 4.6%) OLD
Full-bodied, with dark chocolate and roast provide the dominant aroma and taste. Hints of black cherry, raisin and caramel.

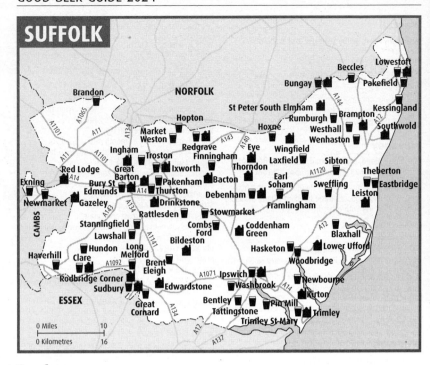

Beccles

Butchers Arms Ⓛ
51 London Road, NR34 9YT
☎ (01502) 712243
6 changing beers (sourced regionally; often Barsham, Mr Winter's, Wolf) Ⓗ
Situated a 10-minute walk from the town centre, this friendly pub serves up to six real ales, mainly from local breweries. Frequent quiz nights and community events are hosted. The interior, formerly with separate lounge and public bars, is now open plan. The bar and real fire remain, with a dartboard and pool tables in an extension. The rear garden has been refreshed and there is a patio with seating at the front. Local CAMRA Pub of the Year 2022. ⍟⛲◖▶♣🅿🚍(524)⛄🐾🎵

Caxton Club
Gaol Lane, NR34 9SJ
☎ (01502) 712829
4 changing beers (sourced nationally; often Greene King, Mauldons, Parkway) Ⓗ
Spacious club conveniently situated a short walk from bus and train stations and close to the town centre. All members and guests are warmly welcomed (a small charge is made to cover entertainment on Sat eve). It has a central bar, TV and darts room and a separate snooker room. There is also a large function room, a garden with children's play area, and a bowling green. Four real ales and traditional ciders are available. Assistance dogs only are allowed. ⍟⛲🐾♿🚲♣🛏🚍🎵

Ingate Ⓛ
108 Grove Road, NR34 9RE
☎ 07503 969220 ⊕ theingatefreehouse.co.uk
3 changing beers (sourced locally; often Green Jack, Lacons, Wolf) Ⓗ
Privately owned and popular two-bar free house serving the local community, a short walk from the town centre and train station. The lounge bar is furnished with tables, bar stools and sofas, and serves three real ales on handpump. The sports bar contains the dartboard and pool table – the pub's teams play in local leagues. Sports events are shown on large screens. The former car park is now a partially covered outdoor seating area. ⍟◖▶♿♣🚍⛄🐾🎵

Bentley

Case is Altered Ⓛ ✅
Capel Road, IP9 2DW
☎ (01473) 805575 ⊕ thecasepubbentley.co.uk
Adnams Southwold Bitter; 3 changing beers (sourced locally) Ⓗ
Owned and run by the local community, this pub has a single bar serving two drinking areas, a restaurant area with a wood-burning stove, and a pretty beer garden with plenty of seating. Various music evenings and themed food nights are hosted. Traditional pub games are played including darts, cards and dominoes. A quiz is held on the last Saturday of the month. Local artists' work is on display. Some of the produce used in the kitchen is grown by the local community. ⍟⛲◖▶♿♣🚍⛄🐾🎵

Blaxhall

Ship Ⓛ
School Road, IP12 2DY
☎ (01728) 688316 ⊕ blaxhallshipinn.co.uk
Adnams Southwold Bitter; Woodforde's Wherry; 3 changing beers Ⓗ
A cosy, two-roomed, 16th-century pub with a reputation for traditional singing in the bar. The menu offers a wide choice of home-made dishes and daily specials using locally sourced ingredients. A variety of live entertainment is on offer, including folk sessions (Mon afternoons), local bands, and storytelling, and the pub hosts a stage during the nearby Folk East festival weekend. Letting chalets are available beside the pub,

and there is camping nearby by arrangement. Dogs are welcome. Open all day, but book for breakfast in summer. ☋❀⇌◑♿⛺♣●P🚌🐾📶♫

Brandon

Ram 🄻 ✔

High Street, IP27 0AX

☎ (01842) 810275 🌐 ramhotel.co.uk

Greene King Abbot; 6 changing beers (sourced nationally) 🄷

Said to be one of the oldest surviving buildings in town, this attractive, Grade II-listed pub has some parts dating back 500 years. A wonderful log-burner greets you as enter this friendly, family-owned and run free house. It hosts regular club nights for the Iceni Car Club, Classic Vehicle Club, Model Engineering Club, Brandon Speakers Club, and the Champions Poker League.
☋❀⇌◑⛺⇌♣P🚌(86)

Brent Eleigh

Cock 🍷 ★ 🄻

Lavenham Road, CO10 9PB (on A1141)

☎ (01787) 247371

Adnams Southwold Bitter; Greene King Abbot; 2 changing beers (sourced locally; often Bishop Nick, Mauldons) 🄷

An unspoilt gem, deservedly recognised by CAMRA as having a nationally important historic pub interior. Conversation with the pub regulars in the two small bars is guaranteed. The main table in the public bar has been deeply etched with shove ha'penny grooves and a settle beside it has a 'pinch penny' cut into it. The snug bar is ideal for families. Home-cooked food is available.
Q❀⇌◑♣●P🐾📶♫

Bungay

Green Dragon 🄻

29 Broad Street, NR35 1EF

☎ (01986) 892681 🌐 greendragonbungay.co.uk

Green Dragon Chaucer Ale, Gold, Bridge Street Bitter, Strong Mild; 1 changing beer (sourced locally; often Green Dragon) 🄷

On the northern edge of town, this is home to the Green Dragon brewery. It is Bungay's only brewpub, with ales created in outbuildings adjacent to the car park at the rear of the property. It has a public bar and a separate spacious lounge with a side room where families are welcome, leading to a small enclosed garden surrounded by a hop hedge. Food is available Thursday to Saturday only. ☋❀◑⛺♣●P🚌🐾📶♫

Bury St Edmunds

Beerhouse 🄻

1 Tayfen Road, IP32 6BH

☎ (01284) 766415 🌐 burybeerhouse.co.uk

Brewshed Best Bitter; 7 changing beers (sourced nationally) 🄷

Traditional beer house in an unusual semi-circular Victorian building, handy for the nearby railway station, and refurbished with a modern feel. It serves beers from their own Brewshed brewery, which was relocated out of town in 2016, and also supplies four other local pubs owned by same company. Seven beer engines provide an ever-changing selection of well-kept real ales, plus three real ciders. Regular beer festivals and an annual cider festival are held. Major sporting events are shown a large screen, and there is an open fire in winter.
☋❀⇌●P🚌🐾📶

Dove 🄻

68 Hospital Road, IP33 3JU (5 mins' walk from town centre)

☎ (01284) 702787 🌐 thedovepub.co.uk

Woodforde's Wherry 🄷; changing beers 🄷/🄶

An early-Victorian back-street free house, just five minutes from the town centre. It has six handpumps, plus jugged ales brought up direct from the cellar, and also offers a selection of ciders. This is a genuinely traditional and basic pub, and the knowledgeable staff can advise on their ever-changing range of local ales. Twice winner of CAMRA Regional Pub of the Year and current local Pub of the Year. Q❀♣●P🚌🐾♫

Nutshell ★ 🄻 ✔

17 The Traverse, IP33 1BJ

☎ (01284) 764867 🌐 thenutshellpub.co.uk

Greene King IPA, Abbot 🄷

One of England's smallest pubs, with an interior measuring only 15ft by 7ft, and listed in the Guinness Book of Records. This Grade II-listed building dates from the mid-19th century and is a popular tourist attraction in the town. The main drinking area is crowded if there are more than six people in bar at one time. Good-quality Greene King Abbot and IPA are regularly available. A function room is upstairs. Q🚌

Oakes Barn 🄻 ✔

St Andrews Street South, IP33 3PH (opp Waitrose car park)

☎ (01284) 761592 🌐 oakesbarn.com

Oakham JHB; Woodforde's Wherry; 4 changing beers (sourced nationally) 🄷

REAL ALE BREWERIES

Adnams Southwold
Artefact Ixworth
Beccles Brampton
Biochemist Red Lodge
Brewshed Ingham
Briarbank ▤ Ipswich
Bruha ◆ Eye
Cabin Bildeston
Calvors Coddenham Green
Cliff Quay Debenham
Dove Street Ipswich
Drinkstone Drinkstone
Earl Soham Debenham
Green Dragon ▤ Bungay
Green Jack Lowestoft
Greene King Bury St Edmunds
Humber Doucy Bacton
Krafty Braumeister Leiston
Little Earth Project Edwardstone
Mauldons ◆ Sudbury
Mr Bees Trimley
Munson's ▤ Gazeley
Nethergate ◆ Rodbridge Corner
Old Cannon ▤ Bury St Edmunds
Old Felixstowe Kirton
Roughacre ◆ Clare
Shortts Thorndon
St Judes ▤ Ipswich
St Peter's ◆ St Peter South Elmham
Star Wing ◆ Redgrave
Stow Fen Bungay
Turnstone Wingfield
Uffa ▤ Lower Ufford
Watts & Co Debenham
Weird Sisters Great Barton

A real ale free house and social hub near the town centre, with some period features and historic links to the mediaeval town. Six real ales are always available, including one dark beer, alongside craft cider. Home-made food comprises lunchtime specials and snacks served all day, plus Sunday lunches on the first Sunday of month. There is an outside covered smoking area and open courtyard with seating. Regular events are held in the bar, and the upstairs function room is available to hire. ⏰☕⏰🅿️♣️🐾🚽⏰🎵

Old Cannon Brewery L

86 Cannon Street, IP33 1JR
☎ (01284) 768769 ⏰ oldcannonbrewery.co.uk
Adnams Southwold Bitter; Old Cannon Best Bitter, Gunner's Daughter; 3 changing beers (sourced nationally; often Mauldons, Timothy Taylor, Old Cannon) Ⓗ
This excellent brewpub is on the site of the original Cannon brewery. Both the brewpub and stable block date from mid-19th century and are Grade II listed. Now in private hands, it is a genuine free house. The beers are brewed on site and tours of the microbrewery are available (book ahead). Brewing in two copper vessels in the bar usually happens every Monday and Wednesday. The pub also serves good-quality food and offers comfortable accommodation. ⏰🛏️⏰🚆🅿️🐾🎵

Clare

Globe

10 Callis Street, CO10 8PX
☎ (01787) 278122 ⏰ globeclare.co.uk
Young's London Original; 3 changing beers (sourced nationally) Ⓗ
A phoenix risen from the ashes, the Globe reopened in 2013 after a 2-year closure. It is now a thriving local where beer and conversation dominate, and serves one well-kept regular beer and up to three changing guests. Live music plays every other Saturday night and live afternoon sessions happen every other Sunday. There is a separate pool room at the rear and a large garden for summer drinking. No food is served. Q⏰☕⏰♣️🅿️🚽⏰🎵

Roughacre Taproom

Clare Hall Barns, Cavendish Road, CO10 8PJ
☎ 07801 930091 ⏰ roughacre.com
6 changing beers (sourced locally; often Roughacre) Ⓖ
This cosy brewery taproom, located on the outskirts of the town, opened in 2021. Many of the house beers are available in bottles when not available on draught. It regularly hosts a wide variety of events such as Build a Beer Experience and food trucks. It is only open on Fridays and Saturdays. ⏰⏰🅿️

Combs Ford

Gladstone Arms L

2 Combs Road, IP14 2AP
☎ (01449) 771608 ⏰ gladstonearms.co.uk
Adnams Southwold Bitter, Broadside; Crouch Vale Brewers Gold; Fuller's London Pride; Sharp's Doom Bar; Woodforde's Wherry Ⓗ; 4 changing beers Ⓗ/Ⓖ
A large open-plan pub serving consistently good beer. The owners also operate the Dove Street Inn in Ipswich. Both pubs offer a similar beer range, with at least 12 real ales, including house beers brewed in Ipswich and a wide range of craft lagers, ciders and specialist foreign beers. Good-value snacks and meals are served, with vegetarian options. There are board games, sports TV and

regular live music. A beer festival is held here over the Easter weekend. There is a riverside garden to the rear. Q⏰☕⏰🅿️♣️🅿️(87,88)🐾⏰🎵

Debenham

Woolpack

49 High Street, IP14 6QN
☎ (01728) 860516
Earl Soham Victoria Bitter Ⓗ, Sir Roger's Porter Ⓖ; Fuller's London Pride; 1 changing beer (often Earl Soham) Ⓗ
A small one-bar pub with a wooden floor, accessed via steps up from the road. Until recent years it was still licensed as a beer house. Lots of horse brasses, village photographs and miniature bottles are on display in the bar area. Two TVs show terrestrial sport. Keenly priced homed-cooked food is available. The pub is home to darts than and hosts occasional live music, karaoke and quiz nights. There is a splendid view of the church from the patio to the rear – bell ringers meet here after practice sessions on Tuesdays. ⏰⏰⏰♣️🐾⏰🎵

Earl Soham

Victoria L

The Street, IP13 7RL (on A1120)
☎ (01728) 685758
Earl Soham Victoria Bitter; 2 changing beers (often Cliff Quay, Earl Soham) Ⓗ
A former traditional beer house that, despite refurbishment a few years ago, has changed little over the years. The two small bars are separated by a large fireplace with wood-burner. The menu is varied with home-cooked daily specials offered at lunchtimes and in the evening. The pub gets busy at weekends, when even a seat in the garden can be hard to find. Dogs and children are welcome. The Gents toilet is outside. Earl Soham brewery was originally located behind the pub. Q⏰☕⏰♣️🅿️🐾⏰🎵

Eastbridge

Eel's Foot L

Leiston Road, IP16 4SN (close to entrance to Minsmere nature reserve)
☎ (01728) 830154 ⏰ theeelsfootinn.co.uk
Adnams Southwold Bitter, Ghost Ship, Broadside; 2 changing beers (often Adnams) Ⓗ
Adjacent to the famous Minsmere nature reserve – where avocets and otters are notable local success stories – this pub is popular with ramblers and birdwatchers. It has a deserved reputation for locally sourced home-cooked food, with an extended and refurbished restaurant area leading out to a large terraced seating space for alfresco drinking and dining on summer days. Other recent improvements include an enlarged outdoor play area for children and en-suite accommodation. Traditional music sessions are held on Thursday evenings and live bands feature regularly. Q⏰☕⏰⏰🚼♣️🅿️🐾⏰🎵

Exning

White Horse ✅

23 Church Street, CB8 7EH
☎ (01638) 577323 ⏰ whitehorseexning.co.uk
3 changing beers Ⓗ
Mentioned in the Domesday Book, this fine, 300-year-old free house has been run by the same family since 1935. The pub retains much of its original character, with a public bar, cosy lounge and a separate restaurant

serving a good choice of home-cooked food. At least 10 real ales are rotated each week, and there is often cider on draught. A private room is available for hire. Q✿◑♣P🖵(11) ✿

Finningham

White Horse
Station Road, IP14 4TL
☎ (01449) 780243
Adnams Ghost Ship, Broadside; Greene King Abbot; 2 changing beers Ⓗ

Welcoming, traditional 15th-century village pub where conversation and good beer are the order of the day. The pub is timber framed, with many subsequent extensions, and bare floorboards, quarry tiles and stripped pine panelling add to the atmosphere. It is a popular stop-off point for walkers, cyclists and bikers, and it has informal camping and caravan pitches. Functions and events can be accommodated on request. A quiz is held on the last Sunday of every month. Inch's, Angry Orchard and Fire Dancer ciders are all available.
✿✿🅰♣P🖵(456,458) ✿ 🛜

Framlingham

Station Hotel Ⓛ
Station Road, IP13 9EE
☎ (01728) 723455 ⊕ thestationframlingham.com
Earl Soham Gannet Mild, Victoria Bitter, Brandeston Gold; 1 changing beer (often Earl Soham) Ⓗ

Cosy two-bar pub set in a former station buffet (although the branch line closed in 1963). Beers and a guest cider are dispensed from a set of Edwardian German silver handpumps. The pub has a long-standing reputation for good food, made with locally sourced ingredients and all prepared on the premises. The ever-changing menu is displayed on chalkboards. On Sundays, brunch and beers are available. The garden bar also has a wood-fired pizza oven. Children and dogs are welcome.
Q✿✿◑♥P🖵✿🛜

Great Cornard

Brook Inn
241 Bures Road, CO10 0JQ
☎ 07759 960051
5 changing beers (sourced nationally) Ⓗ

Friendly, welcoming country locals' pub, near the Suffolk/Essex border, with a beer garden and a good-sized car park. Formerly owned by Greene King but now independent, it offers a good range of up to five real ales on handpump. It has two bars, one with low-key TV for sports events, and also has bar billiards and pool tables, with teams in local leagues. Open mic music sessions are held on the third Sunday of each month.
✿✿🅰♣P🖵✿🛜

Hasketon

Turks Head ✔
Low Road, IP13 6JG
☎ (01394) 610343 ⊕ theturksheadhasketon.co.uk
Adnams Ghost Ship; Morland Old Speckled Hen; Woodforde's Wherry; 2 changing beers (sourced locally) Ⓗ

The pub has been much refurbished and extended in recent years but has retained its cosy, timber-framed bar with a large fireplace and wood-burner. A separate, large, modern restaurant and kitchen are located to the rear. Good food includes renowned Sunday lunches. Three to five changing beers are on handpump. An

annual beer festival is held in the summer. Events include quiz nights and themed food nights. The beautiful two-acre garden has seating and two pétanque pistes. ✿✿◑♣P✿🛜

Haverhill

Queen's Head
9 Queen Street, CB9 9DZ
☎ (01440) 702026
3 changing beers Ⓗ

Now Grade II-listed, this is the oldest building in town (dating from 1470). It survived the great fire of 1667, which destroyed most of the town, and still boasts its rare Crown Post roof. There is a good ambience in the three public rooms, and the beer is of a high quality. The pub's sign features the landlady. Q✿♿♣P🖵✿

Royal Exchange Ⓛ ✔
69 High Street, CB9 8AH
☎ (01440) 702155
Greene King IPA; Nethergate Suffolk County Best Bitter; 3 changing beers (sourced nationally; often Nethergate) Ⓗ

Friendly town-centre local with classic street-corner situation. The Greene King-managed house has been fully refurbished, with scrubbed floors and traditional furniture. It can be boisterous when live sport is shown on the five TVs – one of which is 3D (free goggles provided). A swift turnover on beer helps sustain the good quality. There is a large public car park behind the Arts Centre opposite. ✿♿♣🖵✿

Hopton

Vine
High Street, IP22 2QX
☎ (01953) 688581
Adnams Southwold Bitter; Greene King IPA, Abbot; Timothy Taylor Landlord; 5 changing beers (sourced locally; often Colchester, Lacons, Mauldons) Ⓗ

On the main road near the church, this village local has been revitalised since being taken over by the current landlord in 2013. Nine ales are available, including a selection of local and regional guests offered at reasonable prices. It also serves a variety of ciders. This welcoming pub, popular with locals and visitors, is a regular local CAMRA Pub of the Year.
✿✿♿♣♥P🖵(100) ✿🛜

Hoxne

Swan Inn of Hoxne
Low Street, IP21 5AS
☎ (01379) 668275 ⊕ theswaninnofhoxne.co.uk
Adnams Southwold Bitter, Ghost Ship; Fuller's London Pride; Timothy Taylor Landlord Ⓖ

This 15th-century pub reopened in 2016 after temporary closure and is now once again a thriving village local. It has a colourful history – it claims to be the former home of the Bishop of Norwich and later a brothel. There is a large open fire in the main bar and a wood-burner in the adjacent bar. The restaurant serves excellent home-cooked food, with an emphasis on local produce. There is a large garden at the rear. A beer festival is held in August. Buskers' night is Thursday. ✿✿◑♿♣P🖵✿🛜

Hundon

Rose & Crown
20 North Street, CO10 8ED (centre of village)
☎ (01440) 786261 ⊕ hundon-village.co.uk/roseandcrown

Sharp's Doom Bar; 3 changing beers (sourced nationally; often Fuller's, Mauldons, St Austell) ⊞
A traditional country pub comprising two bars with open fires. Home-cooked food is available Thursday to Sunday, including a popular Sunday lunchtime roast. The large beer garden has a patio to the side for alfresco dining, leading to a lawned area with a stage. An outside bar is used for weddings, parties, an annual community music festival (August bank holiday) and other events. The morris men gathering on St George's Day is enjoyed by all. Proud former winner of local CAMRA Community Pub of the Year. ⏷❀❶◗&♣P☺ ♠

Ipswich

Arbor House
43 High Street, IP3 3QL
☎ (01473) 219660 ⊕ thearborhouse.co.uk
Lacons Encore; Mauldons Suffolk Pride; 2 changing beers ⊞
A cosy and stylish single-bar pub located close to Ipswich Museum. Originally called the Arboretum, it was renamed in 2016 (the name derived from the nearby arboretum in Christchurch Park). There are usually three well-kept real ales available, at least one of which is a seasonal ale from a local brewer. The pub also offers an enclosed patio to rear of the bar and a function room upstairs. ⏷❀◗♣💷(116)☺♠

Dove Street Inn 🗓 ✅
76 St Helen's Street, IP4 2LA
☎ (01473) 211270 ⊕ dovestreetinn.co.uk
Adnams Broadside; Crouch Vale Brewers Gold; Fuller's London Pride; Greene King Abbot; Ruddles County ⊞; 7 changing beers (often Dove Street) ⊞/🄶
Popular multi-roomed pub with a wide selection of ales, continental beers and ciders. Some of the beers are brewed in the pub's own microbrewery. Home-cooked food and bar snacks are served at all times. Sports TV is frequently shown in the conservatory. Well-behaved dogs and children are welcome. A sister pub to The Gladstone Arms in Combs Ford. Also offers accommodation nearby. Last admission is 10.45pm.
⏷❀🛏◗&♣🛏💷(66)☺♠

Duke of York 🗓
212 Woodbridge Road, IP4 2QP
☎ (01473) 216007 ⊕ thegrandolddukeofyork.co.uk
6 changing beers ⊞
A pub with a large open-plan bar containing a pool table and various indoor seating areas, plus a large outside raised patio area to rear of a small car park. It offers a good selection of real ales from a variety of local brewers including some house beers, as well as a variety of bottled beers and craft beers. Regular live music sessions feature at weekends. ⏷❀◗&♣P💷(11,66)☺♠ ♫

Fat Cat ♟
288 Spring Road, IP4 5NL
☎ (01473) 726524 ⊕ fatcatipswich.co.uk
Adnams Southwold Bitter ⊞; Woodforde's Wherry; 14 changing beers 🄶
A highly popular multi-roomed drinking bar, free from intrusive background music and games machines. Up to 14 beers and five ciders are served from the taproom. Bar snacks include Scotch eggs and pasties cooked on the premises. An airy conservatory behind the main bar leads to a pretty garden that provides lots of extra space, especially on sunny afternoons. A monthly quiz is held. Frequently voted best pub in town by local CAMRA members. No under-16s. Q❀◗●🖥☺♠

Lord Nelson
81 Fore Street, IP4 1JZ
☎ (01473) 407510 ⊕ thenelsonipswich.co.uk
Adnams Southwold Bitter, Ghost Ship 🄶; 3 changing beers (often Adnams) ⊞
Cosy, timber-framed building dating from 17th century, just a short walk from the historic waterfront. The unusual gravity-dispense system incorporates old wooden casks to good effect and guarantees temperature-controlled real ales. Freshly prepared food is served daily, including specials. A small enclosed patio area to the rear is popular most of the year. Families and dogs are welcome. Quiz nights are held twice a month. A sister pub to the Red Lion in Manningtree and the Marlborough in Dedham. ⏷❀◗&♣☺♠

Spread Eagle 🗓
1-3 Fore Street, IP4 1JW
☎ (01473) 421858
Grain ThreeOneSix, Best Bitter, Slate, Lignum Vitae; 2 changing beers (often Grain) ⊞
A distinctive Grade II-listed building – the sole survivor of four pubs which once dominated this busy road junction – that was restored to a high standard a few years ago by Grain. They now offer up to six real ales on handpump, plus a selection of their own craft beers and some imported ones, and locally roasted coffee. Various events including occasional music sessions, regular quiz nights and an annual Octoberfest. The are is a secluded outside seating area. The pub is completely candlelit on Tuesday evenings. Q❀🖥☺♠

Steamboat Tavern ✅
78 New Cut West, IP2 8HW
☎ (01473) 601902 ⊕ thesteamboat.co.uk
4 changing beers ⊞
A popular historic riverside tavern which regularly features live music and offers good food prepared on the premises. The L-shaped bar services various drinking areas, including a recently refurbished beer garden. Music includes jazz on alternate Sundays and folk sessions on the third Thursday of the month, plus occasional blues and punk nights and an annual acoustic folk weekend. Local songwriters also play here monthly. ⏷❀◗♣☺♠♫

Woolpack ✅
1 Tuddenham Road, IP4 2SH
☎ (01473) 215862 ⊕ woolpack-ipswich.co.uk
Adnams Southwold Bitter, Ghost Ship; 2 changing beers ⊞
Popular three-bar tavern with a tiny snug at the front, flanked by a larger lounge and public bar. The more spacious back room is mostly used for dining. There are usually four beers on handpump. An interesting selection of high-quality home-cooked food is served all week (including breakfast). The menu includes specials, bar snacks and some vegetarian options. The pub hosts a regular Sunday night quiz and traditional music sessions. The patio area outside at the front is popular on sunny days. Q❀◗♣P🖥☺♠♫

Ixworth

Greyhound 🗓 ✅
49 High Street, IP31 2HJ
☎ (01359) 230887
Greene King IPA, Abbot; 3 changing beers (sourced nationally) ⊞
Situated on the village's attractive high street, this welcoming traditional inn has three bars, one of which is a lovely central snug. The heart of the building dates

back to Tudor times. Good-value lunches and early evening meals are served in the restaurant and include a bargain daily special. Dominoes, crib, darts and pool are all played in leagues and for charity fundraising. Quiz nights feature. Dogs and children are welcome. Q☺▧☀◑▶♣▶P♿(304,338)☙

Kessingland

Sailors Home L
302 Church Road, NR33 7SB
☎ (01502) 740245 ⊕ sailorshome.co.uk
Green Jack Golden Best, Gone Fishing ESB; 5 changing beers (sourced locally; often Green Jack, Lacons, Wolf) G
Situated on the seafront, with coastal views, this traditional pub is popular all year with locals, walkers and holidaymakers from nearby caravan parks and guesthouses. The interior has a mock-Tudor design with four adjoining rooms, one for diners serving good-value, home-cooked food, a large central bar area with a large TV screen, a games room and a side room. Up to seven ales and a regularly changing cider are served by gravity dispense. Boat hire is available for sea fishing trips.
☺☀◑▲♣▶P♿(99,146)☙🐾♪

Lawshall

Swan
The Street, IP29 4QA
☎ (01284) 828477 ⊕ swaninnlawshall.com
5 changing beers (sourced nationally; often Adnams, Colchester, Woodforde's) H
Set in the heart of rural Suffolk, this is a classic regional country pub. The beautiful 18th-century thatched building, with a low-beamed bar and inglenook fireplace, was lovingly restored in 2013 and is crammed full of period features. On the menu you will find all the traditional classics, together with few extra culinary delights. The large garden encourages children to play.
Q☺☀◑♣P☙🐾

Laxfield

King's Head (Low House) ★ L
Gorams Mill Lane, IP13 8DW (walk through churchyard and exit via lower street gate, pub is on right)
☎ (01986) 798395 ⊕ lowhouselaxfield.com
Earl Soham Albert Ale; Green Jack Golden Best; 2 changing beers (sourced locally; often Shortts) G
This timeless thatched building is a classic pub which is always worth a visit. The main room features listed high-back settles set around a small fireplace, with beers served on gravity direct from a small tap room to the rear. A separate dining room offers an interesting menu of locally sourced food, including a Sunday roast at lunchtime. It has an enclosed garden and patio to rear. Accommodation is available in an outside building.
Q☺☀▥♣P♿☙

Long Melford

Nethergate Brewery Tap L
Rodbridge Corner, CO10 9HJ
☎ (01787) 377087 ⊕ nethergate.co.uk
8 changing beers (sourced locally; often Nethergate) H
Nethergate brewery was founded in 1986 in Clare. This custom-built visitor centre and taproom opened in 2017 and is the third location they have operated from. The taproom has a bar with a range of Nethergate ales on draught, and a shop selling bottled beers, wines and

spirits. There is a window to view the brewery and tours can be booked. The members' club hosts regular events including beer festivals. Q☀♿P☜

Lowestoft

Plough & Sail
212 London Road South, NR33 0BB
☎ (01502) 566695
Greene King IPA; Sharp's Doom Bar; 4 changing beers (sourced nationally; often Green Jack, Mauldons, Mr Winter's) H
Set back off the street, with a small frontage, this friendly local is close to Lowestoft south beach and amenities. Inside is a long bar with wooden flooring and wood panelling throughout. TV screens show sporting events. A secluded enclosed courtyard with a canvas covered smoking area leads to a private function room. Live music and quiz evenings are regular attractions. Two permanent beers are available, plus up to four regularly changing beers from other breweries. ☀♣▥☜♪

Stanford Arms L
Stanford Street, NR32 2DD
☎ (01502) 574505 ⊕ stanfordarmslowestoft.co.uk
6 changing beers (sourced nationally; often Mr Winter's, Nene Valley, Three Blind Mice) H
This quality free house is within walking distance of Lowestoft train and bus stations and close to the football ground. The open-plan L-shaped bar is decorated with a fine collection of beer trays adorning the walls, and to the rear is a refurbished courtyard garden. The pub offers an exceptional range of cask and craft beers sourced from around the UK, plus bottled and canned beers from across Europe. There are regular quiz nights and live music most weekends. ☺☀◑●☙☜♪

Triangle Tavern L
29 St Peters Street, NR32 1QA
☎ (01502) 582711 ⊕ green-jack.com
Green Jack Golden Best, Trawlerboys Best Bitter, Lurcher Stout, Gone Fishing ESB, Mahseer IPA, Ripper Tripel H /G
This lively town-centre tavern is the brewery tap for Green Jack brewery. The parlour-style front bar is decorated with brewery memorabilia and CAMRA awards, and is home to live music most Friday evenings. A corridor leads to a back bar with a pool table and a jukebox. Alongside the full Green Jack range are real ciders, continental craft beers and occasional guest ales. Customers are welcome to bring in their own food for consumption in the pub. ☀⇆♣●▥☙☜♪

Market Weston

Mill L
Bury Road, IP22 2PD (on B1111)
☎ (01359) 221018
Adnams Southwold Bitter; 2 changing beers (sourced nationally; often Greene King, Lacons, St Austell) H
The Mill is a striking white brick- and flint-faced inn standing at a crossroads on the main B1111. It used to be the unofficial tap for Old Chimneys brewery and old pumpclips can still be seen behind the bar. It offers an excellent choice of beers, complemented by a good menu of home-cooked meals. Q☺☀◑♿♣P▥☙🐾♪

Newbourne

Fox Inn ✔
The Street, IP12 4NY
☎ (01473) 736307

Adnams Southwold Bitter; 3 changing beers ⓗ
A picturesque timber-framed, two-bar village local which is highly popular, not just with ramblers and cyclists, but also with discerning diners. The refurbished kitchen serves a wide range of home-cooked food, all locally sourced, with daily specials and vegetarian and gluten-free options. The restaurant has been considerably extended in sympathy with the orignal beer house building. The large garden includes a pond and a shed that houses an old skittle alley – the only one in Suffolk. Q🛆❀🕽🕽👜🖑🅿🚎(179)🐾🛜

Newmarket

Golden Lion ⓛ ✅
44 High Street, CB8 8LB
☎ (01638) 672040
Adnams Ghost Ship; Greene King Abbot; 7 changing beers ⓗ
A large, bustling, 18th-century Wetherspoon pub on the main high street. The name is thought to have originated from King Henry I, who was also known as the Lion of Justice. Knowledgeable and efficient staff serve up to seven real ales at any one time, including up to four guest ales. Real cider is also available. It is popular with the local horse racing community. Children are welcome until 9pm in the family area. 🛆❀🕽👜🖑⇌🅿🚎🛜

Pakefield

Oddfellows ⓛ
6 Nightingale Road, NR33 7AU
☎ (01502) 538415
House beer (by Green Jack); 4 changing beers (sourced locally; often Green Jack, Lacons, Woodforde's) ⓗ
Popular pub close to Pakefield's cliffs and the coastal heritage path. This small, cosy, pub has three open-plan areas including one for diners (booking advisable) with wood flooring and panelling throughout. The walls are adorned with pictures of old Pakefield and seafaring memorabilia. Sporting events are shown on TV screens. Up to five beers are usually available, including one or two from Green Jack brewery. Dogs are welcome, but not in the restaurant. 🛆❀🕽👜🚎🐾🛜

Pakenham

Fox ⓛ
The Street, IP31 2JU
☎ (01359) 230194 ⊕ pakenhamfox.co.uk
Mighty Oak Kings; 3 changing beers (sourced locally; often Elmtree, Shortts, Star Wing) ⓗ
Traditional 18th-century pub in a picturesque village. It has been restored beautifully and now features a handcrafted central bar. This free house serves four well-chosen ales that are sourced from local breweries, and four real ciders. The spacious beer garden has been extended and special events are often held there. Q🛆❀🕽👜🖑🖤🅿🚎(304,338)🐾🛜

Pin Mill

Butt & Oyster ✅
Pin Mill Road, IP9 1JW
☎ (01473) 780764
Adnams Southwold Bitter, Ghost Ship, Broadside; 1 changing beer (often Adnams) ⑄
Dating from the 17th century, this riverside pub enjoys a famous setting, with magnificent views of the Orwell estuary with its quay and historic coastal barges. Inside are three separate rooms connected via a flagstoned

corridor. High-backed settles and a wood-burner in the main taproom help to further recreate some old-world charm on cold winter days. The patio in front of the pub is often used by diners during busy sessions. Breakfast is served at weekends. Q🛆❀🕽👜🖑🖤🅿🚎(97,202)🐾🛜

Rattlesden

Five Bells ⓛ
High Street, IP30 0RA
☎ (01449) 737373
3 changing beers (sourced locally; often Earl Soham, Elgood's, Woodforde's) ⓗ
Set on the high road through a picturesque village, this is a fine traditional Suffolk drinking house – sadly few of its kind still survive. Three well-chosen ales on the bar are usually sourced direct from the breweries and often include a mild. The cosy single-room interior has a games area on a lower level and there is occasional live music. Pub games include shut-the-box and shove-ha'penny, plus pétanque in the garden in summer. Dogs are welcome. Q❀🖑🚎🐾♫

Redgrave

Cross Keys
The Street, IP22 1RW (on B1113)
☎ (01379) 779822 ⊕ crosskeysredgrave.co.uk
4 changing beers (sourced locally; often Earl Soham) ⓗ
The building dates from the late 16th or early 17th century, with later extensions and refronting. It was bought by the local community and reopened in 2018, and is now leased to a private landlord. It has a bar, a restaurant/lounge, and a snug area. The pleasant garden, with mature walnut trees, has seating and tables at the front, leading onto the Knoll (village green). 🛆❀🕽👜🖑🖤🅿🚎(304)🐾🛜

Rumburgh

Buck 🍷 ⓛ
Mill Road, IP19 0NT
☎ (01986) 785257 ⊕ rumburghbuck.co.uk
Adnams Southwold Bitter; 4 changing beers (sourced regionally; often Earl Soham, Lacons, Mighty Oak) ⓗ
Splendid, characterful inn that was originally the guesthouse for the Benedictine priory. It was extended some years ago and now has two dining areas, a public bar and games room around the historic core. The original bar is timber-framed with a flagstone floor. At the heart of village life, the pub hosts folk music evenings and is home to the Old Glory Molly Dancers. Good-quality meals are served featuring locally sourced produce (booking is advisable). Q🛆❀🕽🖏🖤🅿🛜🛜♫

Sibton

White Horse
Halesworth Road, IP17 2JJ
☎ (01728) 660337 ⊕ sibtonwhitehorseinn.co.uk
Adnams Southwold Bitter; 2 changing beers ⓗ
A charming and characterful 16th-century inn with lots of exposed timbers and a large fireplace with a wood-burner. There is a raised galley on one side of the main bar area. The large garden to the rear has a barbecue in the summer and a children's play area, and most of the kitchen's produce is grown here. There are various themed food evenings. There is a separate annex for accommodation, and the pub is a registered Caravan Club camping site. 🛆❀🕽🖏🖤🅿🐾🛜♫

Stanningfield

Red House 🅛

Bury Road, IP29 4RR
☎ (01284) 828330 ⊕ theredhousesuffolk.co.uk
Greene King IPA; 2 changing beers 🅗
This red-brick family-run free house is at the centre of the village in every sense. Its sign displays the red dress uniform of the Suffolk regiment. Good-value lunches and early evening meals are all home-cooked. The pub supports teams for darts, cribbage, and bar billiards, as well as hosting regular entertainment nights. There is a lovely garden at the rear. Car parking is available, plus a 10-bike parking space. 🌑🌞🕽♣🅿🚆(750,753)🐾📶

Stowmarket

Royal William 🅛

53 Union Street East, IP14 1HP
☎ (01449) 674553
Greene King IPA; 10 changing beers 🅖
An end-of-terrace back-street bar, tucked away down a narrow side street, just a short walk from the town centre and the nearby railway station. All ales are served by gravity dispense from the cellar behind the bar, with up to 10 beers and five ciders. Regular dominoes, darts and crib matches are played here. It has a games room and an outside smoking area. Sport is shown on TV and traditional music hosted monthly. Home-made bar snacks are often available. A winner of many local CAMRA awards. 🌑🌞🕽ᵭ🌿♣🍖🐾📶

Walnut

39 Violet Hill Road, IP14 1NE
☎ (01449) 401 6769 ⊕ the-walnut.square.site
6 changing beers 🅗
Refurbished by the current landlord and landlady in early 2019, this much-improved back-street pub now offers an ever-changing selection of real ales on handpump, along with ciders and craft beers. The beer menu regularly features some unusual choices for the town. Good-value snacks are available. The pub holds regular quiz and vinyl nights. There are two beer gardens, where children are allowed until 8pm. A former local CAMRA Pub of the Year. 🌑🌞ᵭ🌿🍖🚆🐾📶

Sudbury

Brewery Tap 🅛

21-23 East Street, CO10 2TP (200yds from market place)
☎ (01787) 370876 ⊕ thebrewerytapsudbury.co.uk
Mauldons Moletrap Bitter, Suffolk Pride, Black Adder 🅗**; 7 changing beers (sourced nationally)** 🅗/🅖
The Mauldons brewery tap is a haven for ale lovers. A good selection of Mauldons beers are always available, and these are complemented by a selection of national and locally sourced ales, with up to 10 at any one time on handpump and gravity. Some hearty snacks are available at lunchtimes, including pies and sandwiches. Beer festivals are held in April and October, and quiz, music and comedy nights are a regular feature in this traditional pub where conversation dominates. Q🌞ᵭᵭ🌿♣🍖🚆🐾

Sweffling

White Horse 🅛

Low Road, IP17 2BB (on B1119)
☎ (01728) 664178 ⊕ swefflingwhitehorse.co.uk
3 changing beers 🅖
A cosy two-room pub with a wood-burner and wood-fired range. Beers from local brewers are dispensed on gravity, served through a taproom door. Cider is also available, as well as fair trade, organic, locally produced bottled beers. Pub games include bar billiards, darts, crib and board games. Live music features twice a month. Local horse and trap rides may be available in summer. A former CAMRA East Anglian Pub of the Year, with a garden and a popular, award-winning campsite. Q🌑🌞🕽🏕Ⓐ♣🍖🅿🐾📶🎵

Tattingstone

Wheatsheaf 🅛

Church Road, IP9 2LY
☎ (01473) 805470 ⊕ wheatsheaftattingstone.com
3 changing beers (sourced locally) 🅖
Recently refurbished and extended pub, on the outskirts of this small village divided by the Alton Water Park reservoir. The large garden to the rear hosts a popular annual charity music and beer festival, plus a beetroot competition in June, and camping is available by arrangement. An ever-changing selection includes many from local brewers. Other live music and quiz nights are always popular, as are themed food evenings and Sunday roasts. The pub hosts local cribbage league matches and caters for private parties. 🌑🌞🕽Ⓐ♣🅿🚆(94,96)🐾📶

Theberton

Lion 🅛

The Street, IP16 4RU
☎ (01728) 830185 ⊕ thebertonlion.co.uk
Woodforde's Wherry; 2 changing beers (sourced locally) 🅗
A lively village bar with patio seating outside at the front, various seating areas inside and a large central fireplace. Many local pictures decorate the walls. The beer range is varied and a local beer club regularly meets in the bar. Real ciders in bottle are available all year round, including Giggler and Thistly Cross Traditional. Its outdoor toilets have been retained. It is located close to various popular coastal attractions, and log cabins are available to let. Opening hours may be extended during the summer. 🌑🌞🏕🕽ᵭ♣🍖🅿🐾📶

Thurston

Fox & Hounds 🅛

Barton Road, IP31 3QT
☎ (01359) 232228 ⊕ thurstonfoxandhounds.co.uk
Greene King IPA; 5 changing beers (sourced nationally; often Cliff Quay, Green Jack, Tring) 🅗
A popular pub in a listed building in the middle of the village, a short walk from the railway station. It serves good home-cooked food in a dining space within the public bar. A separate bar has been retained for pool and darts. The pub holds regular quiz nights and bingo with live music on bank holidays and special occasions. The pub also has its own golf society. 🌑🌞🏕🕽Ⓐ🚆🅿🐾📶🎵

Trimley St Mary

Mariners Freehouse

193 High Road, IP11 0TN
☎ (01394) 670444 ⊕ marinersfreehouse.co.uk
Adnams Southwold Bitter, Ghost Ship, Broadside; 3 changing beers 🅗
The name of this pub was changed in 2015 from the New Inn to the Three Mariners, to commemorate the

extraordinary feat of Sir Thomas Cavendish, who was born in the village. In July 1586 he set out with three ships and 123 men to circumnavigate the world, which he completed in May 1588. Inside the pub, various bright and airy drinking areas are set around a large central servery. There is a large beer garden to rear. Themed food nights and various live music sessions are hosted during the summer. Q ☼ ✿ ◑ ᕇ ᕦ ♣ P ☐ ⚲ 🌐 🎵

Troston

Bull Freehouse

The Street, IP31 1EW

☎ (01359) 269820 🌐 thebullfreehouse.com

Adnams Ghost Ship; 3 changing beers (sourced nationally) Ⓗ

Extensively refurbished and recently reopened, the Bull is now home to the Rascality microbrewery, which serves its own beers to the pub's customers. Bottles and growlers are also available to take away. Food is served five days a week, with plans to extend to seven days. The nice garden is ideal for alfresco dining and drinking on sunny days, or sit in the cosy bar and dining room inside. ☼ ✿ ᕦ ♣ P ☐ (332) ⚲

Washbrook

Brook Inn

Back Lane, IP8 3HR

☎ (01473) 730531 🌐 thebrookinnwashbrook.co.uk

Adnams Southwold Bitter; 2 changing beers Ⓗ

A spacious village pub that was purchased by a group of local residents in 2015. The public bar still retains a very traditional pub atmosphere, with a separate large and comfortable restaurant area for families. The menu features a lot of gluten-free options and also includes a good selection for vegetarians. There is an outside seating area and children's play area.
☼ ✿ ◑ P ☐ (95,96) ⚲

Wenhaston

Star Inn 🄻

Hall Road, IP19 9HF

☎ (01502) 478240 🌐 wenhastonstar.co.uk

Green Jack Golden Best; 5 changing beers (sourced regionally; often Colchester, Green Jack, Wolf) Ⓗ

Free house on the outskirts of the village, with a large garden and fine views of the Blyth valley. The pub has three small public rooms; the front bar is full of character with old enamel advertising signs and an open fire in winter. Good home-cooked food uses local produce (no food Sun and Mon). Beer festivals are held over the late May and August bank holiday weekends. Camping is available by prior arrangement.
Q ☼ ✿ ◑ ᕇ ♣ ● P ☐ (99A) ⚲ 🌐

Westhall

Racehorse Inn 🄻

Mill Common, IP19 8RQ

☎ (01502) 575665 🌐 westhallpub.com

5 changing beers (sourced locally; often Ampersand, Green Jack, Mr Winter's) Ⓗ/Ⓖ

This village free house, deep in rural Suffolk, is community owned and has a central bar with three interlinked rooms. Five real ales and one real cider are usually available. The pub is well supported by locals and food is now available daily. An open mic night is on the last Friday of the month. There are patio seating areas at the front and rear. Q ☼ ✿ ◑ ᕇ ᕦ ♣ ● P ☐ (524) ⚲ 🌐

Woodbridge

Angel 🄻

2 Theatre Street, IP12 4NE

☎ (01394) 382660 🌐 theangelwoodbridge.co.uk

Adnams Southwold Bitter; 5 changing beers Ⓗ

A lively and traditional two-bar drinking pub with beams and tiled floors. The regularly changing range of real ales is complemented by a massive selection of craft gins, with gin tasting sessions by arrangement. There is seating outside and a former stables to the rear. No regular meals are served but there is a wood-fired oven in the garden for pizzas. An open mic night is held on the second and fourth Wednesday of the month, plus a DJ every Saturday evening and other live music sessions.
☼ ✿ ≒ ♣ ● P ☐ ⚲ 🌐 🎵

Cherry Tree

73 Cumberland Street, IP12 4AG

☎ (01394) 384627 🌐 thecherrytreepub.co.uk

Adnams Southwold Bitter, Ghost Ship, Broadside; 1 changing beer (often Adnams) Ⓗ

A deceptively spacious family-friendly lounge bar/diner with a central servery and several distinct seating areas. The new kitchen provides popular, home-cooked food all day every day, starting with breakfast and including vegetarian and gluten-free options. Board games and cards are available to play and a quiz is often held on Thursday evenings. The large garden has children's play equipment. Accommodation is available in a converted barn. ☼ ✿ ✿ ◑ ≒ ♣ P ⚲ 🌐

Olde Bell & Steelyard

103 New Street, IP12 1DZ

☎ (01394) 382933

🌐 ye-olde-bell-and-steelyard.business.site

Greene King IPA, Abbot; 2 changing beers (often Greene King) Ⓗ

Large, family-friendly two-bar pub with oak beams and a separate function room. The ancient steelyard (a former cart weighbridge) still worked until it was hit by a lorry in 2018. It dates from 1650 and was on show at the Great Exhibition in 1851. Good home-cooked food is served. Traditional games include bar billiards, chess and bar skittles. Live rugby is often shown on TVs in the narrow side-bar. To the rear of the building is a heated and covered patio area and wheelchair access.
☼ ✿ ᕦ ♣ ● ☐ ⚲ 🌐 🎵

Breweries

Adnams SIBA

Sole Bay Brewery, East Green, Southwold, IP18 6JW

☎ (01502) 727200 🌐 adnams.co.uk

⊠ Adnams was founded in Southwold on the Suffolk coast in 1872, where it still brews today. It owns and manages eleven hotels, pubs and inns and has a number of partner pubs, as well as several retail stores. It remains an independent, values-based family business, committed to a sustainable future. ‼ ᕦ ♦

Southwold Bitter (ABV 3.7%) BITTER
Impressive, creamy, copper-coloured session bitter with lingering, earthy herbal hop, sweet nutty malt flavours, and hints of caramel and fruit.

Mosaic (ABV 4.1%) PALE
Impressive pale ale with citrus, tropical fruit and peach hop, quenching bitterness, subdued sweet malt and a balanced dry aftertaste.

Ghost Ship (ABV 4.5%) PALE

Vibrant pale ale with lingering orange, lemon, crisp hoppiness and biscuity sweetness. Great balance and easy-drinking.

Broadside (ABV 4.7%) RED
Rich, creamy, ruby brown beer. Malty and fruity throughout, balanced with hops in the mouth and ending fruity with sweet malt.

Artefact SIBA

Bridge Farm, Bury Road, Ixworth, IP31 2HX
⊕ artefactbrewing.co.uk

Artefact Brewing is a nanobrewery established in 2020. The brainchild of husband-and-wife team James and Kat Lawson-Philips, it operates from a cleverly converted shipping container in the village of Ixworth. Committed to a classic range using local and seasonal hops, the brewery also experiments and collaborates to produce new and interesting beers.

Dark Mild (ABV 3.2%) MILD
Session Pale Ale (ABV 3.8%) PALE
English Pale Ale (ABV 4.8%) PALE
Ixworth Blonde (ABV 4.8%) GOLD
Amber Haze IPA (ABV 6.2%) IPA

Beccles

The Studios, London Road, Beccles, Brampton, NR34 8DQ ☎ 07815 519576
✉ info@becclesbrewco.co.uk

⊠ The brewery has been in production since 2019 and is now run by one of the original owners with the assistance of family and friends. It has a production run three times a week, with a 700-litre capacity. Seven beers are regularly produced and can be found in local pubs. The beers are also available in bottle and mini-keg from the brewery and at the local Friday market in Beccles Town Centre. 🍺

Uncle Albert's (ABV 3%) MILD
Hodgkins Hop (ABV 3.6%) GOLD
Beautiful Sky (ABV 4.2%) PALE
Neil, Neil Orange Peel (ABV 4.2%) GOLD
Paint the Town Red (ABV 4.5%) RED
Boney's Island (ABV 4.6%) STOUT
Nelson's Tree (ABV 4.8%) BITTER

Biochemist

Boundary Road, Red Lodge, IP28 8JQ ☎ 07821 540237 ⊕ biochemistbrewery.com

Established in 2020, Biochemist Brewery is a part-time 100-litre nanobrewery producing small-batch core beers and an Experimental Series. Brews can be bought online or at local markets. Small batches of seasonal, dry ciders also produced.

Brewshed

Place Farm, Ingham, IP31 1NQ
☎ (01284) 848066 ⊕ brewshedbrewery.co.uk

⊠ Brewshed began brewing in 2011 using a five-barrel plant in buildings located behind the Beerhouse (one of its outlets). It's now located in the nearby village of Ingham, using a 12-barrel plant, resulting in greater capacity and a more modern beer range with two seasonal beers usually available, plus a number of unusual keg beers. It supplies its own five pubs plus a limited free trade. A dark beer is always available in cask with five beers minimum usually available. ♦

Pale (ABV 3.9%) PALE
Best Bitter (ABV 4.3%) BITTER

American Blonde (ABV 5.5%) BLOND

Briarbank SIBA

🍴 70 Fore Street, Ipswich, IP4 1LB
☎ (01473) 284000 ⊕ briarbank.org

The Briarbank Brewing Company was established in 2013, and is situated on the site of the old Lloyds Bank on Fore Street, Ipswich. The brewery is a two-barrel plant, and the bar above offers a core range of beers – including some speciality ales. 🍴♦

Bruha

Unit 4, Progress Way, Eye, IP23 7HU
☎ (01379) 882230 ⊕ bruhabrewing.co.uk

Originally known as Station 119, the brewery changed name in 2020 to Bruha Brewing. Established in 2014, it graduated to the current premises in Eye, Suffolk, in 2017. A 12-barrel brewhouse was installed in 2018. All the beers are unfiltered and have an emphasis on East Anglian malt. LIVE ♦

Session Pale (ABV 3.9%) PALE

Burnt Mill

Badley, Ipswich, IP6 8RS ☎ 07791 961974
⊕ burntmillbrewery.com

This farm brewery was created by Charles O'Reilly in 2016 and is set in a former grain shed. In 2017 Sophie de Ronde joined the brewing team as head brewer. All beers brewed to date have been unfiltered and are available in both KeyKeg and 440ml cans.

Cabin

44 Brooksfield, Bildeston, IP7 7EJ ☎ 07990 845855
⊕ cabinbrewery.co.uk

Owner and brewer Chris Smith has been brewing since 2013, with Cabin Ales available commercially since 2015. Demand soon outgrew the original plant and a new two-barrel kit was designed and installed in 2018.

Autumn Leaf (ABV 3.8%) BITTER
Chesn't (ABV 3.9%) BROWN
Gold Rush (ABV 4%) PALE
Mark's Gold (ABV 4%) PALE
Red Nek (ABV 4.3%) RED
Mary Celeste (ABV 4.5%) PALE
INNspiration (ABV 5%) PALE

Calvors

Home Farm, Coddenham Green, IP6 9UN
☎ (01449) 711055 ⊕ calvorsbrewery.com

Calvors Brewery was established in 2008 and brews three craft lagers, as well as cask-conditioned beers.

Lodestar Festival Ale (ABV 3.8%) GOLD
Smooth Hoperator (ABV 4%) PALE

Cliff Quay

Unit 1, Meadow Works, Kenton Road, Debenham, IP14 6RT
☎ (01728) 861213 ⊕ cliffquay.co.uk

⊠ Cliff Quay was established in 2008 by Jeremy Moss and John Bjornson (owner of Earl Soham Brewery) in part of the historic Tolly Cobbold brewery, Ipswich. In 2012 the brewery relocated to Debenham, a small, picturesque market town, due to redevelopment of the Cliff Quay brewery site. It now operates alongside Earl

Soham brewery, with shared production, offices and distribution facilities. !! �¶ ♦

Bitter (ABV 3.4%) BITTER
Pleasantly drinkable, well-balanced malty sweet bitter with a hint of caramel, followed by a sweet/malty aftertaste. A good flavour for such a low gravity beer.
Anchor Bitter (ABV 4%) BITTER
Black Jack Porter (ABV 4.2%) SPECIALITY
Unusual dark porter with a strong aniseed aroma and rich liquorice and aniseed flavours, reminiscent of old-fashioned sweets. The aftertaste is long and increasingly sweet.
Tolly Roger (ABV 4.2%) BITTER
Well-balanced, highly-drinkable, mid-gold summer beer with a bittersweet hoppiness, some biscuity flavours and hints of summer fruit.
Tumble Home (ABV 4.7%) BITTER
Aroma of marzipan and dried fruit. Flavour reminiscent of Amaretto, leading to a short, bitter, slightly spicy aftertaste.
Sea Dog (ABV 5.5%) GOLD
Dreadnought (ABV 6.5%) STRONG

Dove Street SIBA

82 St Helens Street, Ipswich, IP4 2LB
☎ (01473) 211270 ☎ 07880 707077
⊕ dovestreetbrewery.co.uk

⊗ Dove Street began brewing in 2011 using a 2.5-barrel plant in a garage opposite the Dove Street Inn. The pub, its sister pub and beer festivals are supplied. !!

Underwood Mild (ABV 3.2%) MILD
Gladstone Guzzler (ABV 3.6%) BLOND
Dove Gold (ABV 4%) PALE
Incredible Taste Fantastic Clarity (ABV 4%) GOLD
Dove Elder (ABV 4.1%) SPECIALITY
Apples & Pears (ABV 4.2%) PALE
Ed Porter (ABV 4.5%) PORTER
Thirsty Walker (ABV 4.6%) BITTER

Drinkstone

Rattlesden Road, Bury St Edmunds, IP30 9TL ☎ 07592 072140 ⊕ drinkstoneales.co.uk

Drinkstone Ales is a 100-litre, part-time nanobrewery owned by Colin Field, and based in his converted garage. It commenced brewing in 2021, supplying local outlets and festivals. It concentrates on traditional cask ale using only English malt and hops.

Bitter (ABV 3.8%) BITTER
Golden Ale (ABV 4%) GOLD
Farmers Ale (ABV 4.4%) RED
Road Apple Strong (ABV 5.2%) BITTER

Earl Soham SIBA

Meadow Works, Cross Green, Debenham, IP14 6RP
☎ (01728) 861213 ⊕ earlsohambrewery.co.uk

⊗ Earl Soham was set up behind the Victoria pub in 1984 and continued there until 2001 when the brewery relocated, moving again in 2013 to Debenham. Around 30 outlets are supplied and two pubs are owned. · !! ➶ ♦ LIVE

Gannet Mild (ABV 3.3%) MILD
A beautifully-balanced mild, sweet and fruity flavour with a lingering, coffee aftertaste.
Victoria Bitter (ABV 3.6%) BITTER
A light, fruity, amber session beer with a clean taste and a long, lingering hoppy aftertaste.
Elizabeth Ale (ABV 4%) BITTER

Sir Roger's Porter (ABV 4.2%) PORTER
Roast/coffee aroma and berry fruit introduce a full-bodied porter with roast/coffee flavours. Dry roast finish.
Albert Ale (ABV 4.4%) BITTER
Brandeston Gold (ABV 4.5%) GOLD
Popular beer brewed with local ingredients. Lovely sharp clean flavour, malty/hoppy and heavily laden with citrus fruit. Malty finish.

Green Dragon

⧉ 29 Broad Street, Bungay, NR35 1EF
☎ (01986) 892681 ⊕ greendragonbungay.co.uk

⊗ The locally-famed Green Dragon is Bungay's liveliest pub and brewery. Established in 1991 by brothers Robert and William Pickard, Green Dragon beer is brewed on site in an eight-barrel plant situated in a converted barn. !! ♦

Green Jack SIBA

Argyle Place, Love Road, Lowestoft, NR32 2NZ
☎ (01502) 562863 ☎ 07902 219459
⊕ green-jack.com

⊗ After 10 years at Oulton Broad, Green Jack moved to the Triangle Tavern, Lowestoft in 2003 and then to a nearby 35-barrel plant in 2009. One pub is owned and more than 150 outlets supplied. !! ♦ LIVE

Golden Best (ABV 3.8%) GOLD
Smooth, satisfying session golden ale with tangy citrus hops, well mixed with a malty sweetness, and a quenching bitter finish.
Nightingale (ABV 4%) BITTER
LGM1 (ABV 4.2%) PALE
Refreshing pale ale with bold citrus hop flavours and a well-defined malty base. Background sweetness fades slowly as bitterness expands.
Orange Wheat Beer (ABV 4.2%) SPECIALITY
Marmalade aroma with a hint of hops, leading to a well-balanced blend of sweetness, hops and citrus with a malt background. Mixed fruit flavours in the aftertaste.
Trawlerboys Best Bitter (ABV 4.6%) BITTER
Tawny premium bitter with sweet malt gently-balanced by caramel and fruit, and a gentle lingering hop bitterness providing contrast.
Lurcher Stout (ABV 4.8%) STOUT
Impressive creamy stout with spirited roast malt supported by a satisfying mix of hops and caramel. Lingering, roast bitter finish.
Red Herring (ABV 5%) SPECIALITY
Gone Fishing ESB (ABV 5.5%) BITTER
Full-bodied malty and fruity premium bitter with an amber glow and a background of hop flavours and caramel hints.
Mahseer IPA (ABV 5.8%) IPA
Pale amber brew with well-defined citrus hop, a background balance of malty sweetness and a lingering bittersweet finale.
Ripper (ABV 8.5%) BARLEY
Baltic Trader Export Stout (ABV 10.5%) STOUT
Worthog (ABV 11%) STRONG

Greene King

Westgate Brewery, Westgate Street, Bury St Edmunds, IP33 1QT
☎ (01284) 763222

Office: Abbot House, Westgate Street, Bury St Edmunds, IP33 1QT ⊕ greeneking.co.uk

⊗ Greene King has been brewing in the market town of Bury St Edmunds since 1799. It brews its beers using water drawn from artesian chalk wells below its brewhouse, as well as local East Anglian malt. Beers are also brewed under various brand names. The brewery has recently bought a significant number of pins in order to promote quality of beers at point of dispense. ‼ ☕ ◆ LIVE

IPA (ABV 3.6%) BITTER
Creamy, copper-coloured bitter with a meld of soft biscuity malt, hops, fruit and hints of caramel. Light, bitter, malty finish.
London Glory (ABV 4%) BITTER
Yardbird (ABV 4%) PALE
St Edmunds (ABV 4.2%) GOLD
Abbot (ABV 5%) BITTER
Mouth-filling premium bitter with sweet malt, caramel and redcurrant. Underpinning hop bitterness holds up well in a malty fruity finish.

Brewed for Taylor Walker:
1730 (ABV 4%) BITTER

Brewed under the Hardys & Hansons brand name:
Bitter (ABV 3.9%) BITTER
Olde Trip (ABV 4.3%) BITTER

Brewed under the Morland brand name:
Original Bitter (ABV 4%) BITTER
Old Golden Hen (ABV 4.1%) GOLD
Smooth, easy-drinking golden ale with fruity hop underpinned by a malty sweetness.
Old Speckled Hen (ABV 4.5%) BITTER
Light-bodied, ruby-brown, premium bitter with caramel, fruit and malt, touches of background hops and a developing gentle dryness.

Brewed under the Ruddles brand name:
Best Bitter (ABV 3.7%) BITTER
An amber/brown beer, strong on bitterness but with some initial sweetness, fruit and subtle, distinctive Bramling Cross hop. Dryness lingers in the aftertaste.

Humber Doucy SIBA

St Edmunds Garage, Broad Road, Bacton, Stowmarket, IP14 4HP
☎ (01449) 780151 ⊕ humberdoucybrew.co

Producing fresh, vegan-friendly beers from the heart of Suffolk, Humber Doucy started brewing in 2019 in an old MOT garage in Bacton. Brewery shop is located down the road within the Jeffries of Bacton Subaru Dealership. Beers are available nationwide and in pubs, shops and restaurants across East Anglia in bottles, cask and keg. ☕ LIVE V

King Slayer (ABV 3.6%) BITTER
Friday Street (ABV 4%) PALE
Pale Ale (ABV 4.4%) PALE
Nettle & Elderflower Saison (ABV 4.5%) SPECIALITY
Porter (ABV 5%) PORTER

Krafty Braumeister SIBA

Unit 4a, Eastlands Industrial Estate, Leiston, IP16 4LL
☎ 07508 435893 ⊕ kraftybraumeister.co.uk

Krafty Braumeister was established in 2018 and produces historic German beer styles, matured naturally in bottles and kegs.

Little Earth Project

Mill Green, Edwardstone, Sudbury, CO10 5PX
☎ (01787) 211118 ⊕ littleearthproject.com

Mill Green Brewery started in 2008, becoming Little Earth Project in 2016. Built on an old stable site, using local wood, reclaimed bricks, sheep wool and lime plaster. It has its own borehole, brewing liquor is heated using bio

and solar power, and its 3,000-litre storage is heated by solar panels, and a wood boiler. It creates innovative beers and sours. Most use local ingredients, and age in old wine barrels. About half is KeyKeg, the rest is bottled, with some cask available.

Mauldons SIBA

13 Church Field Road, Sudbury, CO10 2YA
☎ (01787) 311055 ⊕ mauldons.co.uk

Mauldons started brewing in Sudbury in 1795, was taken over by Greene King in the 1960s, and reopened by the Sims family in 2000. A new 30-barrel plant and brewery were built. After 19 years they retired and sold to local farming-based company, Heathpatch. It is planned that its barley and hops will be used in production. A new website was launched in 2020 (bottled and draught beer available online). Three pubs are owned, and more than 200 outlets supplied. ‼ ☕ ◆ LIVE ⚲

Pale Ale (ABV 3.6%) BITTER
Moletrap Bitter (ABV 3.8%) BITTER
Plum and toffee on the nose. A good balance of malt, hops and fruit, leading to an increasingly bitter aftertaste.
Ploughmans (ABV 3.9%) GOLD
Silver Adder (ABV 4.2%) BITTER
Light fruity aroma, dry hoppiness and citrus fruit with rich honey in the taste, and a long fruity sweet aftertaste. Refreshing and well-balanced.
225 (ABV 4.5%) PALE
Blackberry Porter (ABV 4.8%) SPECIALITY
Cherry Porter (ABV 4.8%) SPECIALITY
Suffolk Pride (ABV 4.8%) BITTER
A full-bodied, copper-coloured beer. A bubblegum nose leads to a spicy taste, with mild astringency in the aftertaste.
Black Adder (ABV 5.3%) STOUT
Full-bodied reddish black stout with roast malt throughout and, in the mouth, soft fruit with a scattering of caramel.

Mr Bees

Units D, Searsons Farm, Cordys Lane, Trimley, IP11 0UD ☎ 07503 773630 ⊕ mrbeesbrewery.co.uk

Mr Bees is based on the beautiful Suffolk Coast. All beers contain honey direct from the brewery's own beehives. All malted barley used comes from Suffolk and only English hops are used. Around 30 local outlets are supplied.

Best Bee-R (ABV 4%) BITTER
Beelightful (ABV 4.3%) BITTER
Black Bee (ABV 4.5%) STOUT

Munson's

🏠 **Chequers, The Green, Gazeley, CB8 8RF**
☎ (01638) 551511 ⊕ munsons.co.uk

Microbrewery at the Chequers, Gazeley, specialising in small-batch hoppy IPAs and Belgian-style beers.

Nethergate SIBA

Rodbridge Corner, Long Melford, CO10 9HJ
☎ (01787) 377087 ⊕ nethergate.co.uk

⊗ Nethergate was formed in 1986 in Clare, Suffolk and moved to its current site in 2017. It produces both traditional recipes and more modern beers and has recently added craft lager and low alcohol beer to its range. The establishment of a borehole means all the water comes directly from the chalk bed. In 2021 a still was added and local craft gins are now produced. Nethergate have now opened a shop in nearby Bury St Edmunds. !! ☰ ♦ ⏚

Melford Mild (ABV 3.7%) MILD
Venture (ABV 3.7%) GOLD
Refreshingly crisp golden ale with a firm citrus hop base throughout and a tapering soft sweet maltiness adding depth.
Umbel Ale (ABV 3.8%) SPECIALITY
Pleasant, easy-drinking bitter, infused with coriander, which dominates.
Suffolk County Best Bitter (ABV 4%) BITTER
Dark bitter with roast grain tones off-setting biscuity malt and powerful hoppy, bitter notes.
Stour Valley Gold (ABV 4.2%) GOLD
Augustinian Ale (ABV 4.5%) BITTER
A pale, refreshing, complex premium bitter. A fruity aroma leads to a bittersweet flavour and aftertaste with a predominance of citrus tones.
Old Growler (ABV 5%) PORTER
Robust dark brown porter with appealing bitter-sweet meld of roast malt, hop and caramel; sustained finish with developing hop bitterness.
Umbel Magna (ABV 5%) SPECIALITY
Old Growler flavoured with coriander. The spice is less dominant than in Umbel Ale, with some of the weight and body of the beer coming through.

Old Cannon

🛢 86 Cannon Street, Bury St Edmunds, IP33 1JR
☎ (01284) 768769 ⊕ oldcannonbrewery.co.uk

⊠ The St Edmunds Head pub opened in 1845 with its own brewery. Brewing ceased in 1917, and Greene King closed the pub in 1995. It reopened in 1999 as the Old Cannon Brewery, complete with a unique state-of-the-art brewery housed in the bar area. Other pubs in the chain are also supplied. At least six beers available at any one time. !! ♦

Old Chimneys

Office: Old Chimneys, The Street, Market Weston, IP22 2NZ
☎ (01359) 221411 ⊕ oldchimneysbrewery.com

Old Chimneys was established in 1995, moving to a converted farm building in 2001. In 2019 Alan Thomson ceased brewing at Market Weston to concentrate on collaborative brewing projects with other breweries. !! ♦ LIVE

Old Felixstowe

30 Falkenham Road, Kirton, Ipswich, IP10 0NW
☎ 07889 238784 ⊕ tofbc.co.uk

Brewing began in 2018 in an outhouse in Old Felixstowe. Following a move to Kirton, the brewery was upgraded to a two-barrel plant in 2020. Five core beers are produced, with seasonal specials. Beer is mostly available bottle-conditioned, but cask beers are provided to a handful of local pubs when capacity allows. Beers can be found at most local farmers markets and a selection of food and drink festivals. Free local delivery is also available. LIVE

> For we could not now take time for further search (to land our ship) our victuals being much spent especially our beer. **Log of the Mayflower**

Roughacre

Clare Hall Barns, Cavendish Road, Clare, CO10 8PJ
☎ 07801 930091 ⊕ roughacre.com

⊠ Established in 2018 by a passionate home brewer in Castle Camps, East Cambs. The brewery moved to Clare in West Suffolk in 2021. The brewery is run by a two-person team and now has a taproom and shop. It brews high quality, fine ales of character which range from classic amber ales and golden IPA, to Belgian-style Abbey Ale, and a dark coffee porter. The beers are now available in several local pubs. !! ☰ ♦ LIVE ⏚

Cavendish Red (ABV 3.8%) MILD
Ashdon Amber (ABV 4.4%) BITTER
Nighthawker Coffee Porter (ABV 4.6%) SPECIALITY
Three Counties East Anglian Best Bitter (ABV 4.6%) BITTER
Abbey Gold (ABV 5.2%) SPECIALITY
Mosquito IPA (ABV 5.2%) PALE
Saffron Sun (ABV 5.4%) SPECIALITY
Saints Reserve Premium English Ale (ABV 6.2%) BITTER

St Judes

🛢 2 Cardigan Street, Ipswich, IP1 3PF
☎ (01473) 413334 ☎ 07879 360879
⊕ stjudestavern.com

⊠ The 10-barrel brewery produces beer for the St Judes Brewery Tavern in Ipswich. It can also be found at some local festivals.

St Peter's SIBA

St Peter's Hall, St Peter South Elmham, NR35 1NQ
☎ (01986) 782322 ⊕ stpetersbrewery.co.uk

⊠ The brewery, built in 1996, is housed in traditional former agricultural buildings adjacent to moated, medieval St Peters Hall, dating from 1280. Brewing makes use of the water from an onsite bore hole combined with locally malted barley. Beer is distributed nationally across the UK and exported to more than 40 countries worldwide. !! ☰ ♦ ⏚

Organic Best (ABV 4.1%) BITTER
A very dry and bitter beer with a growing astringency. Pale brown in colour, it has a gentle hop aroma which makes the definitive bitterness surprising. One for the committed.
Ruby Red (ABV 4.3%) BITTER
Gold Dust (ABV 4.5%) GOLD
Plum Porter (ABV 4.6%) SPECIALITY
Citrus (ABV 4.7%) PALE
Fudge as well as grapefruit on the nose. A refreshing fruit flavour, with hints of grapefruit peel in the aftertaste.

Shortts SIBA

Shortts Farm, Thorndon, Eye, IP23 7LS ☎ 07900 268100 ⊕ shorttsfarmbrewery.com

An award-winning brewery established in 2012 by Matt Hammond on what has been the family farm for over a century. Ales are produced using carefully selected ingredients to create both traditional and more complex contemporary flavours. The beer names are based around a musical theme and can be found throughout East Anglia. LIVE

The Cure (ABV 3.6%) BITTER
Clean-tasting, copper-coloured, malty bitter. Sweetish malt and caramel with hints of fruit and a background hop bitterness.
Strummer (ABV 3.8%) BITTER

Amber bitter with hops supported by sweetish nutty malt and a gentle bitterness.

Two Tone (ABV 3.8%) MILD
Blondie (ABV 4%) PALE
Crisp gold-coloured ale with citrus hop and some background sweet malt which tapers as a light bitterness develops.
Rockabilly (ABV 4.3%) PALE
Skiffle (ABV 4.5%) BITTER
Copper-coloured premium bitter with light hop flavours jostling with sweet malt and a counterbalance of berry fruit.
Black Volt (ABV 4.8%) STOUT
Indie (ABV 4.8%) PALE
Mouth-filling amber-hued ale with a fruity aroma and fruity hop with hints of malt in the sweetish palate.
Darkside (ABV 5%) PORTER
Powerful porter with inviting roast malt and hop aroma then a booming roasty taste with biscuity caramel sweetness and hops.

Star Wing

Unit 6, Hall Farm, Church Road, Redgrave, IP22 1RJ
☎ (01379) 890586 ⊕ starwingbrewery.com

Brewing began in 2017 after converting an old sawmill into a brewery. Half an acre of hops have been planted with plans to grow more. Part of the sawmill has been converted into a taproom, which opened in 2019. Around 75 outlets are supplied direct. ⬤◆

Dawn on the Border (ABV 3.6%) PALE
Electric Trail (ABV 3.7%) PALE
Gospel Oak (ABV 3.8%) BITTER
Spire Light (ABV 4.2%) GOLD
Into the Woods (ABV 4.5%) PALE
Red at Night (ABV 4.5%) RED
Pesky Pilgrim (ABV 4.7%) BITTER
Four Acre Arcadia (ABV 5%) PALE
Stain Glass Blue (ABV 5.4%) PORTER

Stow Fen

Fenview, Flixton Road, Bungay, NR35 1PD ☎ 07775 279181 ✉ stowfenbrewingco@gmail.com

⊗ Stow Fen Brewing Co Ltd was established in 2020 by Paul Holland and Philip Gilham, the head brewer. Malts are from Branthill Farms in Wells-next-the-Sea, and all hops are from the UK. At present beers are all sold directly from the brewery.

Broad Water Gold (ABV 4.2%) GOLD
Angels Way Amber (ABV 4.4%) BITTER
Stock Bridge Best (ABV 4.6%) BITTER

Twisted Oak IPA (ABV 5%) IPA
Wolds ESB (ABV 5.8%) BITTER
Mouldings Porter (ABV 6.5%) PORTER

Turnstone

The Old Post Office, Vicarage Road, Wingfield, IP21 5RB ☎ 07807 262662
✉ turnstoneales@outlook.com

⊗ Turnstone Ales is a small home-based brewery set up in Kent in 2014 and relocated to Suffolk in 2020. Fining or filtering are not used and bottle-conditioned ales are available at local markets including Framlingham and Bury St Edmunds. LIVE

Uffa

⬤ White Lion Inn, Lower Street, Lower Ufford, IP13 6DW

☎ (01394) 460770

Uffa began brewing in 2011 using a 2.5-barrel plant. It is situated next to the White Lion pub in a converted coach house. ◆

Watts & Co

Gardeners Road, Debenham, IP14 6RX ☎ 07764 906886 ⊕ watts.fm

Watts and Co was established in 2015 and brew a range of traditional and modern beers from its tiny brewhouse in the heart of Suffolk. Each brew produces just 300 pints, with a range of traditional and modern beers, all handcrafted.

Weird Sisters

24, Timworth Heath Cottages, Great Barton, IP31 2QH
☎ 07827 923923

⊗ A nanobrewery established by a father and three daughters (the weird sisters) in 2018. The brewery has one core beer and mainly produces seasonal beers to mark the eight seasonal festivals of the wheel of the year. Beers can be found at festivals, morris dancing events and in specialist beer shops.

Slaphead (ABV 6.7%) IPA

A short history of the Good Beer Guide

The Good Beer Guide was first published in 1972 and was just 18 pages long. Rather than a printed and bound edition, it was just a collection of sheets of paper stapled together and posted out to CAMRA members. The first printed edition was published in 1974 and contained a comment on Watney's brewery that was considered libellous, causing the first print run to be pulped and the description for the brewery to be revised. There are a few copies of the first print run out there but they change hands for a fair amount of money.

There has been an edition of the Guide printed annually since 1974, meaning it is now in its 51st year. The longest serving editor was Roger Protz, who edited the Guide from 1978-1983 and 2000-2018. It has grown from 96 pages in 1974 to 944 pages for this edition, with 4,500 pubs listed and more than 1,800 breweries.

London's Best Beer, Pubs & Bars

Des De Moor

The essential guide to beer drinking in London, completely revised for 2022. Laid out by area, the book makes it simple to find the best London pubs and bars – serving the best British and world beers – and to explore the growing number of London breweries offering tours, taprooms and direct sales. Features tell you more about London's rich history of brewing and the city's vibrant modern brewing scene. The venue listings are fully illustrated, with detailed information on opening hours, local landmarks, and public transport links to make planning any excursion quick and easy. The book also includes a comprehensive listing of London breweries.

RRP: £16.99   **ISBN:** 978-1-85249-360-8

For this and other books on beer and pubs, visit CAMRA's online bookshop at **shop1.camra.org.uk** or call 01727 867201.

Discounts are available for CAMRA members.

Greater London

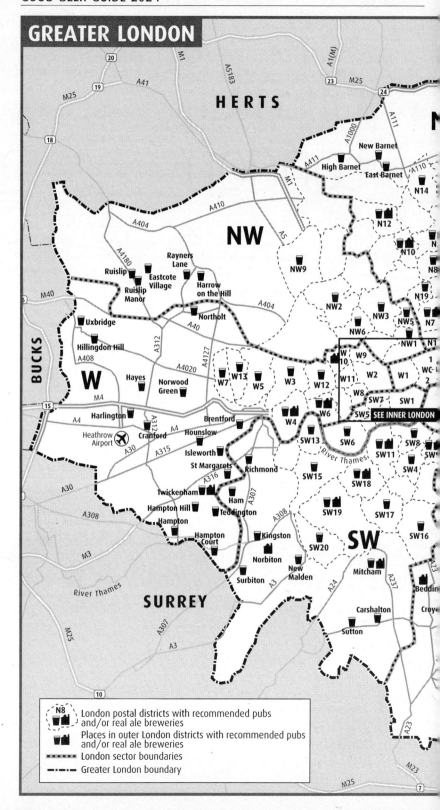

GREATER LONDON

ENGLAND

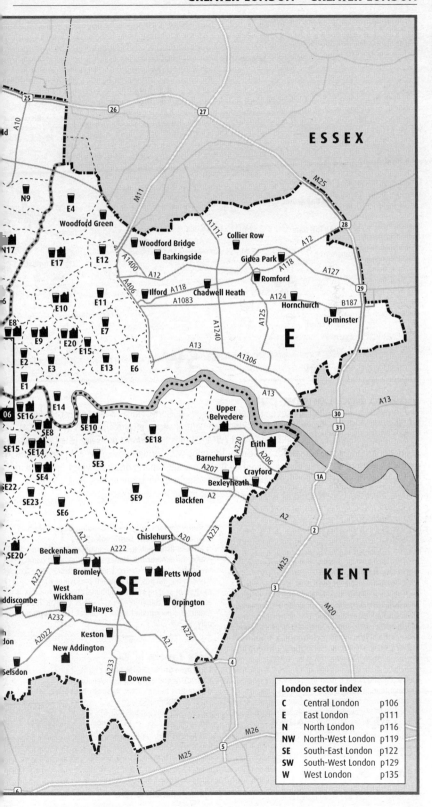

London sector index

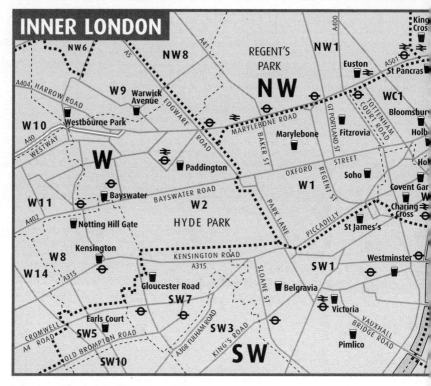

How to find London pubs

Greater London is divided into seven sectors: Central, East, North, North-West, South-East, South-West and West, reflecting postal boundaries. The Central sector includes the City (EC1 to EC4) and Holborn, Covent Garden and the Strand (WC1/2) plus W1, where pubs are listed in postal district order. In each of the other six sectors the pubs with London postcodes are listed first in postal district order (E1, E2 etc), followed by those in outer London districts, which are listed in alphabetical order (Barking, Chadwell Heath, etc) – see Greater London map. Postal district numbers can be found on every street name plate in the London postcode area.

CENTRAL LONDON
EC1: Clerkenwell

Sutton Arms
16 Great Sutton Street, EC1V 0DH
☎ (020) 7253 2462
3 changing beers (often Leigh on Sea, Ramsgate, Thornbridge) Ⓗ
A free house since 1991, this former Whitbread pub is named after 17th-century plutocrat Thomas Sutton who founded nearby Charterhouse. If you are looking for a traditional after-work bar, this is it – a corner pub with side bar and upstairs function room. Besides the three cask beers and KeyKeg from local breweries, there is a range of foreign bottled beers. A tap takeover is sometimes held for breweries outside London. Pies and sausage rolls are available. There is some outside seating. ⚲✿◐&⊖(Barbican)♣🗐❀🕏

EC1: Farringdon

Castle ⌊ ✓
34-35 Cowcross Street, EC1M 6DB
☎ (020) 7553 7621 ⊕ thecastlefarringdon.co.uk

Timothy Taylor Landlord; 2 changing beers (often Magic Rock, Orkney, Sambrook's) Ⓗ
A Grade II-listed pub to whose publican King George IV issued a pawnbroker's licence so that he could gamble his pocket watch on the cockfighting. It has a single bar, wooden floorboards and exposed brickwork, with a mixture of seating styles. Additional space to the rear is accessed by a couple of steps. There is a classic food menu, and background music is played. Card payment only. ◐&⇌⊖🗐🕏

Holy Tavern ⌊ ✓
55 Britton Street, EC1M 5UQ
☎ (020) 7490 4281 ⊕ theholytavern.com
4 changing beers (often Anspach & Hobday, St Peter's, Southwark) Ⓐ
The building housing this pub was built in 1719/20, with the frontage added in 1810. Originally a merchant's house, and then a workshop for the clock-making trades, it was converted to a pub – the Jerusalem Tavern – in 1996. The interior is a recreation of an 18th-century tavern, complete with real fire. The dispense is unusual, with beer from the cellar pumped by air pressure to emerge from fake cask ends behind the bar. Closed on Sundays. Q⚲◐⇌⊖🗐❀🕏

This ancient pub is located down an alley off Hatton Garden and can be hard to find the first time. The current building dates from the 18th century and has been identified by CAMRA as having a nationally important historic pub interior, with two bars and an upstairs function room, reached by a narrow staircase. There is often a beer from the wood available: check the website for details. Snacks such as toasties and sausage rolls are available. Closed at weekends.
Q❀≋(City Thameslink) ⊖(Chancery Lane/Farringdon) ♣●🗐🤁

EC1: Old Street

Old Fountain 🄻

3 Baldwin Street, EC1V 9NU
☎ (020) 7253 2970 ⊕ oldfountain.co.uk
4 changing beers (sourced nationally) Ⓗ
A privately owned free house, in the same family since 1964, and popular with workers from the nearby Silicon Roundabout. Adorned with stained glass windows at front and back, the split-level bar serves real ale as well as real cider and 20 keg lines, including Belgian and German beers. The roof terrace, with parasols and outdoor heaters, is an oasis in the city. A small menu, focused on pub classics and burgers, is served daily.
🖢❀🕽≋⊖♣●🗐🤁🛜

EC2: Liverpool Street

Lord Aberconway

73 Old Broad Street, EC2M 1QS
☎ (020) 7929 1743
Fuller's London Pride; St Austell Nicholson's Pale Ale; Sharp's Doom Bar; 2 changing beers (often Timothy Taylor, Titanic) Ⓗ
Popular with both city workers and tourists, this Victorian pub near Liverpool Street station has lovely traditional fittings, including some cosy booths. A Nicholson's establishment, it is named after a chairman of the old Metropolitan Railway. There is a traditional pub menu – check the website for availability times. In addition to the ground floor, there is also a gallery area used for dining. Terrestrial TV sports may be shown. 🕽≋⊖🗐🛜

EC3: Aldgate

Craft Beer Co.

29-31 Mitre Street, EC3A 5BZ
☎ (020) 7929 5112
House beer (by Kent); 2 changing beers Ⓗ
A city pub with wooden floorboards and bare brick walls adorned with mirrors from Bass and Burton breweries. There are high tables and stools in the upstairs bar and more seating downstairs. The 18 keg lines include cider, and a range of bottled beers is available. Scotch eggs are offered as bar snacks. Toilets are downstairs. The pub is closed but available for private hire at weekends.
≋(Fenchurch St) ⊖(Aldgate/Aldgate East) ●🗐🤁🛜

EC3: Gracechurch Street

Crosse Keys 🄻 ✅

7-12 Gracechurch Street, EC3V 0DR
☎ (020) 7623 4824
Fuller's London Pride; Greene King IPA, Abbot; Sharp's Doom Bar; changing beers (often Green Jack, Orkney, Sambrook's) Ⓗ
Housed in a grandiose building that used to be the headquarters of a banking corporation, this Wetherspoon pub is named after a coaching inn that was once nearby. Handpumps dispense up to 12 rotating guest ales and

Sir John Oldcastle ✅

29-35 Farringdon Road, EC1M 3JF
☎ (020) 7242 1013
Greene King IPA, Abbot; Sharp's Doom Bar; 3 changing beers (often Adnams, Rooster's, Titanic) Ⓗ
This Wetherspoon pub is named after the Sir John Oldcastle Tavern, which stood in the former grounds of Sir John's nearby mansion. John Oldcastle is thought to have been the model for Shakespeare's character, Falstaff. The pub has an L-shaped interior with plenty of seating in the usual mix of tables and booths. There are various interesting framed prints and photos of the local area around the premises. Q🖢🕽≋⊖🗐🛜

EC1: Hatton Garden

Craft Beer Co.

82 Leather Lane, EC1N 7TR
☎ (020) 7404 7049
House beer (by Kent); 4 changing beers (often DEYA, Exale) Ⓗ
In a Grade II-listed building with a glass ceiling and chandelier, the long bar of this popular pub offers several cask ales, 20 keg fonts and over 100 bottled beers, as well as bag-in-box real ales. Most seating is on high stools and it can get busy in the evenings with an after work crowd. A snack menu consists of crisps, nuts, olives and pork pies. Alternatively, pizza can be ordered in from next door. Closed at weekends.
🖢❀≋(Farringdon) ⊖(Chancery Lane/Farringdon) ●🗐🤁🛜

Olde Mitre ★ 🄻

1 Ely Court, Ely Place, EC1N 6SJ
☎ (020) 7405 4751 ⊕ yeoldemitreholborn.co.uk
Fuller's London Pride; 5 changing beers (often East London, Sambrook's, Windsor & Eton) Ⓗ

two ciders. The ales are listed on TV screens above the bar and are ordered by pump number. There are function rooms to the rear. A spiral staircase leads down to the toilets.
Q ⛲ ◑ ♿ ⇌ (Cannon St/Fenchurch St) ⊖ (Bank/Monument) 🚲 🛜

EC3: Tower Hill

Ship ✅

3 Hart Street, EC3R 7NB
☎ (020) 7702 4422 ⊕ shipec3.co.uk
Fuller's London Pride; St Austell Tribute; Timothy Taylor Landlord; 1 changing beer (often Adnams) Ⓗ
This cosy bar has a nautical theme. Seating is provided by tall bar stools alongside round tables and barrels. Look up to see the multitude of sailors' hats, each with a ship's name on its brim. With its opulent upstairs function room, the pub is closed but available for private hire at weekends. Bar snacks such as filled rolls are usually available. The Gents toilet is down a tightly spiralled staircase while the Ladies is upstairs. Background music is played.
⇌ (Fenchurch St) ⊖ (Tower Gateway/Tower Hill)
♣ 🚲 🐾 🛜

EC4: Cannon Street

Bell ✅

29 Bush Lane, EC4R 0AN
☎ (020) 7283 0029
Harvey's Sussex Best Bitter; Sharp's Doom Bar; Timothy Taylor Landlord Ⓗ
Copper pots and pans hang from the ceiling of this no-nonsense ex-Courage one-bar drinking house near Cannon Street station. A list of previous licensees going back centuries hangs on the back wall next to the photo of Sid James. Televised sports are quietly shown with tasteful background music gently playing. Food is mainly pie and mash, with the small upstairs dining area doubling up as a function room. Closed at weekends.
◑ ⇌ ⊖ 🚲 🛜

Pelt Trader

Arch 3, Dowgate Hill, EC4N 6AP
☎ (020) 7160 0253 ⊕ pelttrader.com

3 changing beers (often Burning Sky, Iron Pier, Redemption) Ⓐ
Nestled under an archway beneath Cannon Street station, this independent venue offers a variety of ales and a cider on cask, and up to 14 keg taps showcasing modern craft beer and cider. The archway has been a bar since 2013. Decorative mirrors and pictures portray pelt traders and a canoe hangs from the ceiling. Pizzas are available. Family and dog-friendly, the pub can get busy in the evenings with the city trade. Closed at weekends.
⛲ ❀ ◑ ⇌ ⊖ 🚲 🐾 🛜

EC4: Ludgate Circus

Old Bell ✅

95 Fleet Street, EC4Y 1DH
☎ (020) 7583 0070
St Austell Nicholson's Pale Ale; 4 changing beers (often Adnams, Fuller's, Titanic) Ⓗ
An M&B Nicholson's pub, said to have originated to cater for Wren's masons rebuilding St Bride's church after the fire of 1666. The crossed knife and fork in brass, set into the front threshold until the 1980s, was considered to be a sign for the illiterate workmen. The back of the pub looks out onto St Bride's churchyard and there is a little smoking space outside the door. Inside is a U-shaped bar and additional drinking area. Closed Sundays.
◑ ⇌ (City Thameslink) ⊖ (Blackfriars) 🍴 🚲 🛜

WC1: Bloomsbury

Swan ✅

7 Cosmo Place, WC1N 3AP
☎ (020) 7837 6223
Greene King IPA; Theakston Old Peculier; Timothy Taylor Landlord; 2 changing beers (sourced regionally; often Greene King, St Austell) Ⓗ
Popular, lively family-oriented venue nestled among the tourist hotels on Southampton Row, close to Great Ormond Street Children's Hospital. It has a single long room and tables out front on the pedestrianised passage. Six handpumps offer three to four regular real ales – Hammerton Penton Stout might alternate with Theakston Old Peculier – and up to three guests, many from London breweries. An extensive menu of pub grub and snacks is served all day. A large-screen TV shows live sports events. Q ⛲ ❀ ◑ ♿ ⊖ (Russell Square) 🚲 🐾 🛜

REAL ALE BREWERIES

Affinity ✦ SW9: Brixton
Anspach & Hobday ✦ Beddington
Battersea ✦ SW11: Battersea Power Station
Beerblefish ✦ E17: Walthamstow
Bexley ✦ Erith
Brew By Numbers ✦ SE10: North Greenwich
Brewhouse & Kitchen ⛽ E2: Hoxton
Brewhouse & Kitchen ⛽ N5: Highbury
Brick SE8: Deptford
Brixton ✦ SW9: Loughborough Junction
Brockley ✦ SE4: Brockley
Broken Drum Upper Belvedere
Clarkshaws ✦ SW9: Loughborough Junction
Cronx New Addington
Drop Project ✦ Mitcham
East London E10: Leyton
Five Points ✦ E8: London Fields
Forest Road ✦ SE14: South Bermondsey
Fuller's ✦ W4: Chiswick
Goodness ✦ N22: Wood Green
Hammerton ✦ N7: Barnsbury
Howling Hops ✦ E9: Hackney Wick

Kernel SE16: Bermondsey
London Beer Lab ✦ SW9: Loughborough Junction
London Brewing ✦ N12: North Finchley
Macintosh W6: Stamford Brook
Marlix Petts Wood
Muswell Hillbilly ✦ N10: Muswell Hill
Mutineers Bromley
Park ✦ Norbiton
Portobello W10: North Kensington
Redemption ✦ N17: Tottenham
Sambrook's ✦ SW18: Wandsworth
Signal ✦ Beddington
Signature ✦ E17: Walthamstow
Small Beer ✦ SE16: South Bermondsey
Southey ✦ SE20: Penge
Southwark ✦ SE1: Bermondsey
Spartan SE16: South Bermondsey (brewing suspended)
Tap East ⛽ E20: Stratford Westfield
Temple Brew House ⛽ WC2: Temple
Twickenham ✦ Twickenham
Up The Creek ⛽ SE10: Greenwich
Wild Card ✦ E17: Walthamstow
Wimbledon ✦ SW19: Colliers Wood

WC1: Holborn

Craft Beer Co.
168 High Holborn, WC1V 7AA
☎ (020) 7240 0431
Kent Pale; changing beers (sourced nationally) ⊞
Though in the ancient parish of St Giles, whose church featured in several of Hogarth's etchings including Gin Lane, this pub on the north-eastern edge of Covent Garden has a modern resonance. Over two levels, the sixth Craft Beer Co outlet would be more at home in Beer Street, with its many handpumps dispensing six or more ales from across the UK. There are frequent tap takeovers and Meet the Brewer events.
❀⊖(Covent Garden/Holborn) ☒

WC1: St Pancras

McGlynn's ⃝
1-5 Whidbourne Street, WC1H 8ET
☎ (020) 7916 9816 ∰ mcglynnsfreehouse.com
Southwark Bankside Blonde, Bermondsey Best; 1 changing beer (often Southwark) ⊞
A pleasant pub, located in a quiet side street, and one you might not expect to sell real ale, though they now have up to three regular beers, usually from Southwark brewery. The pub almost feels trapped in a welcoming time-warp with its eclectic selection of bric-a-brac, old Courage mirrors and unusual upright lighting on the bar. There is limited outside seating but plenty indoors as the pub is larger than it appears from the outside.
❀≉⊖(King's Cross St Pancras) ♣☒

Queen's Head ⃝
66 Acton Street, WC1X 9NB
☎ (020) 7713 5772 ∰ queensheadlondon.com
Redemption Trinity; 2 changing beers (sourced nationally) ⊞
Narrow, late-Georgian premises off Gray's Inn Road, with a single bar, a smoking patio at the rear and benches in front. The piano is used for jazz and blues on Thursdays and late Sunday afternoons. One handpump serves cider, with three more real ciders and a range of other draught and bottled beers in stock. Sharing snack platters are on offer at this comfortable pub frequented by locals and the occasional tourist. Local CAMRA Pub of the Year 2022.
❀◑≉⊖(King's Cross St Pancras) ♦☒☏♪

WC2: Chancery Lane

Seven Stars ★
53-54 Carey Street, WC2A 2JB
☎ (020) 7242 8521 ∰ thesevenstars1602.co.uk
Adnams Ghost Ship, Broadside; Dark Star Hophead ⊞
Dating from 1602 as the League of Seven Stars, a historical sobriquet for the seven provinces of the Netherlands, its decorative Victorian bar-back had led to it being identified by CAMRA as having a nationally important historic pub interior. The bar occupies the narrow space between two distinctive drinking areas, one named the Wig Box (the Royal Courts of Justice are nearby). The landlady – the legendary Roxy Beaujolais – serves gastronomic food. Resident cat, General often wears a legal ruffle. The toilets are accessible only via steep stairs.
Q◑≉(City Thameslink) ⊖(Chancery Lane/Temple) ☒☏

WC2: Charing Cross

Harp ♟ ⃝
47 Chandos Place, WC2N 4HS

☎ (020) 7836 0291 ∰ harpcoventgarden.com
Dark Star Hophead; Fuller's London Pride; Harvey's Sussex Best Bitter; 5 changing beers (sourced nationally) ⊞
Small, friendly, Fuller's pub where ciders and perries complement the fine beer range. Local CAMRA Pub of the Year again in 2023, during its time as a free house run by the late, legendary Binnie Walsh it was CAMRA National Pub of the Year 2010 – Greater London's only ever winner of this award. The narrow bar is adorned with mirrors and portraits. There is no intrusive music or TV and a cosy upstairs room provides a refuge from the throng. Q≉⊖♦☒☏

Lemon Tree ✔
4 Bedfordbury, WC2N 4BP
☎ (020) 7831 1391 ∰ lemontreecoventgarden.com
Harvey's Sussex Best Bitter; St Austell Tribute; 3 changing beers (often Adnams, Portobello, Sambrook's) ⊞
A one-bar pub next to the stage door of the Coliseum that is a favourite among locals, musicians and theatregoers. There is a large wall map of London from the 1700s. The Thai restaurant upstairs doubles as a function room. Look out for the pub entrance, slightly set back. In the choice of guest beers there is an emphasis on London brews, by popular demand. It is operated by All Our Bars, a small chain based in Edenbridge.
◑≉⊖☒☏

Ship & Shovell
1-3 Craven Passage, WC2N 5PH
☎ (020) 7839 1311 ∰ shipandshovell.co.uk
Hall & Woodhouse Badger Best Bitter, Fursty Ferret, Tanglefoot; 1 changing beer (often Hall & Woodhouse) ⊞
Almost beneath Charing Cross station, the two uniquely divided halves of this pub face each other across Craven Passage alleyway between Villiers Street and Craven Street. Acquired by Hall & Woodhouse in 1997, it is named after Admiral Sir Cloudesley Shovell whose fleet was grounded off the Scilly Isles in 1707, drowning him and 2,000 men. That catastrophe is believed to have inspired the Admiralty to offer the Longitude Prize for an accurate nautical timepiece. Q☾❀◑≉⊖☒❀☏

WC2: Covent Garden

Lamb & Flag
33 Rose Street, WC2E 9EB
☎ (020) 7497 9504 ∰ lambandflagcoventgarden.co.uk
Dark Star Hophead; Fuller's Oliver's Island, London Pride, ESB; Gale's Seafarers Ale; 2 changing beers (sourced nationally) ⊞
Owned by Fuller's since 2013, this Grade II-listed pub remains pleasant and traditional, without piped music or games machines. Tucked away up Rose Street from Garrick Street, it has a regionally important historic interior with two dark wood-panelled rooms, the rear one with an attractive fireplace and a connecting passage from the main bar on the ground floor. The upstairs bar and restaurant has table service only. Charles Dickens and Karl Marx were both regulars.
☾❀◑≉(Charing Cross) ⊖(Covent Garden/Leicester Sq) ❀☏♪

WC2: Holborn

Shakespeare's Head ✔
Africa House, 64-68 Kingsway, WC2B 6BG
☎ (020) 7404 8846

Greene King IPA, Abbot; Sharp's Doom Bar; 6 changing beers (often Twickenham, Windsor & Eton) ⊞

Large Wetherspoon bank conversion from 1998, named after a famous pub in the locality until the demolition of Wych Street over 100 years ago. It is usually busy with shoppers, tourists, local office workers and, during term time, students from the nearby London School of Economics. Here is a convenient place for a couple of pints after your cultural sojourn at the nearby Sir John Soane's Museum. Q ♿ ❀ ⑊ & ⊖ ⊟ ⬗

WC2: Temple

Devereux
20 Devereux Court, WC2R 3JJ
☎ (020) 7583 4530 ⊕ thedevereux.co.uk
Fuller's London Pride; 3 changing beers (often Adnams, St Austell, Timothy Taylor) ⊞

An attractive Grade II-listed pub built in 1844; part of the site was once the Grecian Coffee House. The comfortable lounge with wood panelling has a bar with five handpumps. Prints on the walls show local places of interest and historic figures, the judges and wigs reflecting proximity to the law courts. Upstairs is a restaurant, available for hire.
♿ ❀ & ⇌ (City Thameslink) ⊖ ♣ ⊟ ⬗

Edgar Wallace
40 Essex Street, WC2R 3JF
☎ (020) 7353 3120
3 changing beers (often Redemption, St Austell, Southwark) ⊞

Just off Fleet Street near the Royal Courts of Justice, this is a real gem of a one-room pub, with additional seating upstairs. The comfortable downstairs room, its walls and ceiling covered with beer mats and old advertising signs, has a fine wooden bar offering a range of rotating ales. This quiet pub allows no music, laptops, mobiles and so on. Good-value food is served all day, except on Friday evenings. Q ♿ ❀ ⑊ ⊖ ⊟ ❀

W1: Fitzrovia

Stag's Head 🄻
102 New Cavendish Street, W1W 6XW
☎ (020) 7580 8313
Fuller's London Pride; 1 changing beer (often Tring) ⊞

A smart, oak-panelled pub with an historic interior of regional importance, offering a friendly welcome to regulars and visitors alike. Rebuilt in the late 1930s by brewers William Younger, it has a marvellous Art Deco exterior, sporting a curved corner profile. Vertical drinking is assisted by unusual peninsular shelf projections to the bar and elsewhere. Sun lovers and smokers can relax on shaded benches outside. Traditional pub food is served at lunchtimes, with service extended on Sunday. ♿ ❀ ⑊ ⊖ (Great Portland St) ⊟

W1: Marylebone

Barley Mow ★
8 Dorset Street, W1U 6QW
☎ (020) 7487 4773 ⊕ barleymowlondon.co.uk
Fuller's London Pride; Sharp's Doom Bar; 4 changing beers (sourced nationally) ⊞

A Grade II-listed pub dating from 1791, identified by CAMRA as having a nationally important historic pub interior, most notably retaining two small drinking compartments fronting the main bar counter. Both bars, with their partly bare wood, partly carpeted floors, are furnished with upholstered pews, benches and stools. Original matchboard panelling displays prints of 18th-century Marylebone. Discreetly positioned screens and an eclectic selection of background music complete the ambience. Pieminister pies are served on weekday lunchtimes and until 9pm on Mondays and Tuesdays.
♿ ❀ ⑊ & ⇌ ⊖ (Baker St) ♣ ⊟ ⬗

Golden Eagle
59 Marylebone Lane, W1U 2NY
☎ (020) 7935 3228
Fuller's London Pride; St Austell Tribute; 2 changing beers (often Elgood's, Otter, Twickenham) ⊞

First licensed in 1842 and rebuilt in 1890, this single-bar pub is traditional in every way: small and cosy, with smart decor, a fine etched bar-back mirror and leaded windows. The historic interior is of some regional importance. Landlady Gina Vernon and her family celebrated 30 years here in 2021. Piano singalongs on Tuesday, Thursday and Friday evenings maintain the timeless atmosphere. Real ales are quality, not quantity. The pub has received local CAMRA awards several times.
& ⊖ (Bond St) ⊟ ♫

Jackalope
43 Weymouth Mews, W1G 7EQ
☎ (020) 3455 2871 ⊕ jackalopelondon.com
4 changing beers (often Adnams, East London, Five Points) ⊞

One of Marylebone's two remaining mews pubs, built in 1777 and Grade II listed, with a regionally important historic interior. The mirrors underneath the dividing beam allowed coachmen to observe when their passengers wanted to depart. Owned by Bloomsbury Leisure, operators of the Euston Tap, it has London's first Xiao Mian noodle kitchen downstairs, specialising in ramen dishes. A Jackalope is a cross between a jackrabbit and an antelope, a mythical creature of North American folklore.
♿ ⑊ ⊖ (Great Portland St/Regent's Park) ⊟ ❀ ⬗

W1: Soho

Dog & Duck ✅
18 Bateman Street, W1D 3AJ
☎ (020) 7494 0697
St Austell Nicholson's Pale Ale; Sharp's Doom Bar; 5 changing beers (often St Austell, Sharp's) ⊞

In the heart of Soho, this Grade II-listed M&B Nicholson's outlet, built in 1897, has been identified by CAMRA as having a nationally important historic pub interior. An elaborate mosaic depicts dogs and ducks, and wonderful advertising mirrors adorn the walls. The upstairs Orwell Bar can be hired for functions. The pub is small and so popular, especially with media people, that it is not just smokers who have to drink outside. The bar extends towards the Frith Street door.
⑊ ⊖ (Tottenham Court Rd) ⊟ ⬗

Lyric 🄻
37 Great Windmill Street, W1D 7LT
☎ (020) 7434 0604 ⊕ lyricsoho.co.uk
Harvey's Sussex Best Bitter; 8 changing beers (often Siren, Southwark) ⊞

A small, independently owned bar just off Shaftesbury Avenue, bay-fronted with a tiled, panelled interior, popular with local trade. Once two adjacent taverns, the Windmill and the Ham, it merged in the mid-18th century to form the Windmill & Ham, renamed in 1890 and rebuilt 16 years later. Alongside other draught beers, including London specialities, the cask ales come from a wide range of mainly small breweries nationwide, including Big Smoke. ♿ ⑊ ⊖ (Piccadilly Circus) ⊟ ❀ ⬗

Old Coffee House

49 Beak Street, W1F 9SF
☎ (020) 7437 2197
3 changing beers (sourced locally) Ⓗ
A large but cosy pub, close to the buzz of Carnaby Street. First licensed as the Silver Street Coffee House, it was rebuilt in 1894 and is now Grade II listed. The long bar and dark panelling are adorned with Watneys Red Barrel signage, brewery mirrors and sundry prints, posters, pictures and brassware. At lunchtimes you will find good-sized and reasonably priced portions of pub grub.
♿❄◐⊖(Piccadilly Circus)🚆🐾

Queen's Head Ⓛ ✅

15 Denman Street, W1D 7HN
☎ (020) 7437 1540 ⊕ queensheadpiccadilly.com
Fuller's London Pride; Sambrook's Wandle; 3 changing beers (often Dark Star, Gun, Sambrook's) Ⓗ
A rare West End free house with plenty of vertical drinking space below and a restaurant upstairs. The traditional feel is enhanced by an attractive bar-back and wall mirroring downstairs and an unusual leather-fronted bar in the restaurant. With its real ales, good-value pies and other pub food, including snacks and cheeseboards at the bar, this is a popular pub both for before and after theatre visits. ♿⊖(Piccadilly Circus)🚆🐾📶

EAST LONDON
E1: Shadwell

Sir Sydney Smith

22 Dock Street, E1 8JP
☎ (020) 7481 1766 ⊕ sirsydneysmith.co.uk
3 changing beers (often Greene King, Redemption, Ruddles) Ⓗ
Named after a British admiral from the Napoleonic wars, this traditional and comfortable pub is a short walk from St Katherine Docks, and not far from Wilton's Music Hall. It has a main bar, a back bar with bare brick walls, wooden flooring throughout and a dartboard. Burgers and pizzas are available. There are tables outside on the pavement. Closed on Sundays.
♿◐⇌(Fenchurch St) ⊖(Shadwell/Tower Gateway/ Tower Hill) ♣🚆🐾

E1: Spitalfields

Commercial Tavern

142 Commercial Street, E1 6NU
☎ (020) 3137 9563 ⊕ commercial-tavern.com
2 changing beers (often Burning Sky, Thornbridge, Tiny Rebel) Ⓗ
A Grade II-listed building with large windows, close to Shoreditch station and Brick Lane. It has been newly refurbished but retains a shabby chic style with a relaxed vibe. There are a few tables outside the front door. Cask ales are complemented by several KeyKeg beers and an extensive international bottled beer range. Pizzas are the food offering, served every day except Monday. The upstairs bar (open Wed-Sat) is available for private hire.
♿◐⇌(Liverpool St) ⊖(Liverpool St/Shoreditch High St)🚆🐾📶

Pride of Spitalfields Ⓛ

3 Heneage Street, E1 5LJ
☎ (020) 7247 8933
Crouch Vale Brewers Gold; Fuller's London Pride, ESB; Sharp's Doom Bar; 1 changing beer (sourced locally; often Five Points) Ⓗ
This back-street local is on a cobbled side street just off Brick Lane. A traditional pub, it is fairly small and can get

quite busy in the evenings with standing room only. It has an excellent atmosphere and there is a piano which customers sometimes play. Food is available weekday lunchtimes. The landlady has been there for a number of years and there is always a warm welcome.
♿◐⊖(Aldgate East/Shoreditch High St) 🚆🐾

E1: Wapping

Prospect of Whitby ✅

57 Wapping Wall, E1W 3SH
☎ (020) 7481 1095
Greene King IPA, Abbot; 4 changing beers (sourced nationally) Ⓗ
Grade II-listed Thames-side pub named after a coal boat. The current building is a 1777 rebuild of a 16th century one all but destroyed by fire. The interior has a flagstone floor and an unusual pewter bar top supported by wooden barrels. There are a further three rooms upstairs and a riverside beer garden. Popular with locals and tourists, it is often busy. The pub claims connections with Samuel Pepys and Charles Dickens.
♿❄◐♿⊖🚆(100,D3)🐾📶

Town of Ramsgate Ⓛ

62 Wapping High Street, E1W 2PN
☎ (020) 7481 8000 ⊕ townoframsgate.pub
Harvey's Sussex Best Bitter; Sharp's Doom Bar; Young's London Original; 1 changing beer (often Portobello) Ⓗ
This Grade II-listed pub has a long narrow bar area with comfortable seating and tables throughout. A riverside terrace can be found at the rear. The many references to Ramsgate include a magnificent large etched mirror to the left of the entrance, depicting the harbour. Weather watchers can check out the ornate barometer hanging on the wall. Food is served all day at weekends with a short break between lunch and dinner service on weekdays. A quiz is held on Monday evenings. ♿❄◐⊖🚆(100,D3)🐾

Turner's Old Star ✅

14 Watts Street, E1W 2QG
☎ (020) 3726 5371 ⊕ turnersoldstar.co.uk
3 changing beers (often Brockley, Redemption, Southwark) Ⓗ
A family-run, street-corner free house, named in honour of JMW Turner, the famous landscape painter who once owned the building. The red leather bench seats that abut the walls benefit from light shining through the multi-coloured stained-glass windows. A pool table and dartboard complement the two large TVs that show sporting events. Cooked breakfasts, then pie and chips comprise the food offering. A covered garden provides the location for occasional small beer festivals.
♿❄◐⊖♣🚆(100,D3)📶

E2: Bethnal Green

Camel Ⓛ ✅

277 Globe Road, E2 0JD
☎ 07305 470811 ⊕ thecamele2.co.uk
Sambrook's Wandle; 2 changing beers (often Adnams, Five Points, St Austell) Ⓗ
Small corner pub of a type becoming rare in London, boasting a noteworthy, tiled exterior. Run by an enthusiastic and welcoming landlady, the atmosphere is convivial. Space inside is limited but there are tables and chairs on the front pavement and a beer garden at the rear. The menu consists mostly of speciality pies and mash alongside burgers. Sport is occasionally shown on TV. A dark beer is usually available in winter.
♿❄◐⊖🚆🐾📶

King's Arms

11A Buckfast Street, E2 6EY

☎ (020) 7729 2627 ● thekingsarmspub.com

3 changing beers (often Five Points, Howling Hops, Siren) Ⓗ

A stylish back-street local serving four cask ales regularly, with five at the weekend. There are also a dozen keg beers, a large range of bottles and two ciders. There are no pumpclips; the beer menu is on the tables and on the wall. The food offering is Scotch eggs and tortillas with cheese or meat. There is some seating outside.

&●⊖(Bethnal Green/Shoreditch High St) ●🖥🐾🛜

E2: Cambridge Heath

Hare ⊘

505 Cambridge Heath Road, E2 9BU

☎ 07813 164634 ● theharee2.com

Fuller's London Pride; Timothy Taylor Landlord; 1 changing beer (often Five Points) Ⓗ

This traditional East End pub is a free house and has been run by the same landlord for 20 years. Sports oriented, with football matches and other sports shown on its screens, it has one bar with a pool table. Outside is a small area for smokers. The staff are welcoming and friendly. The landlord's model is a pub that sticks to its roots and remains a traditional boozer.

🐾⊖(Bethnal Green/Cambridge Heath) ♣🖥♫

E3: Bow

Eleanor Arms

460 Old Ford Road, E3 5JP

☎ (020) 8980 6992 ● eleanorarms.co.uk

Shepherd Neame Master Brew, Whitstable Bay Pale Ale; 2 changing beers (often Shepherd Neame) Ⓗ

Convenient for Victoria Park, canal users and the London Stadium, there has been a pub on this site since 1879. Traditional in style, with 1930s wood panelling, it features some interesting artwork and music-related decor. Traditional pub games are available, including shove-ha'penny and shut the box. Old Ford Jazz Club meets on a Sunday, and a 'non-Disco Disco' entertains on Friday/Saturday evenings. There is a beer garden to the rear. The pub opens from late afternoon on weekdays.

&🐾♣🖥(8) 🛜♫

Lord Tredegar

50 Lichfield Road, E3 5AL

☎ (020) 8983 0130 ● thelordtredegar.co.uk

3 changing beers (often Fyne, Kirkstall, Leigh on Sea) Ⓗ

A terraced pub that is larger within than the exterior suggests. A front bar and two smaller rooms on either side all have bare floorboards and comfortable furnishings. Two impressive fireplaces are still in use. At the back is a large conservatory with an open kitchen and a garden. Food is served from early evening and all day at weekends. Wheelchair users can access the pub via a ramp but the toilets are downstairs.

&🐾◐⊖(Mile End) ♣●🖥🐾🛜

E4: Chingford

King's Head Ⓛ ⊘

2B Kings Head Hill, E4 7EA

☎ (020) 8529 6283

Fuller's London Pride; St Austell Tribute; Sharp's Doom Bar; 4 changing beers (often Bishop Nick, East London, New River) Ⓗ

An old building that has been much extended, this Stonegate pub sells the widest range of real ales in the area and is often busy. Although there is only one bar, the interior is divided into several areas. At the back is a conservatory, garden and car park. Food, including options for canines, is served all day. Televised sporting events are occasionally shown in one area. Quizzes are held on Wednesday and Sunday nights.

&🐾◐&P🖥🐾🛜

E4: Highams Park

Stag & Lantern 🍸

11-12 The Broadway, E4 9LQ

☎ (020) 7998 8930 ● thestagandlantern.co.uk

3 changing beers Ⓗ

A welcoming and inclusive community-focused micropub, converted from shops in 2020. The inside is fairly small with stools made from beer casks. There is also seating outside in front of the premises. Takeaway beer is available. Craft beer, cider, bottles and cans are also available, including from the online shop. There are events such as quizzes. See the website for opening hours, current beer list and events. Closed Mondays and Tuesdays. Local CAMRA Pub of the Year 2023. Q🐾⊖🖥

E6: Upton Park

Boleyn Tavern ★

1 Barking Road, E6 1PW

☎ (020) 8472 2182 ● boleyntavern.co.uk

4 changing beers (often Shepherd Neame) Ⓗ

The former local to West Ham United football club's Boleyn ground closed after the team moved to the London Stadium but reopened in 2021 after a spectacular £1.5m restoration by Remarkable Pubs of the nationally important historic interior. Hand-crafted wooden screens with acid-etched cut glass have been recreated to restore the original seven-bar layout. The highlight is a massive coloured skylight in the rear dining area. The Grade II-listed building is floodlit at night, making it visible from a distance. &🐾◐&⊖🖥🛜

E7: Forest Gate

Holly Tree

141 Dames Road, E7 0DZ

☎ (020) 8221 9830 ● thehollytreepub.co.uk

Shepherd Neame Whitstable Bay Pale Ale, Spitfire; 2 changing beers (often Five Points) Ⓗ

A large community pub refurbished in 2019 by Remarkable Pubs in a traditional style, with an outside conservatory and spacious garden. Besides the beer and food menu, the single bar offers a real cider from Oliver's on handpump. A miniature train runs round the garden at weekends – see website for times – provided the weather is good, and accommodates riders of all ages, but note that children are not allowed in all areas of this family-friendly pub.

&🐾◐●⊖(Wanstead Park) ●🖥(58,308) 🐾🛜

E8: Hackney

Cock Tavern Ⓛ

315 Mare Street, E8 1EJ

● thecocktavern.co.uk

8 changing beers (sourced locally; often Howling Hops) Ⓗ

A bustling, friendly town-centre single-roomed pub with a small beer garden. There has been a pub called the Cock Tavern in Hackney since the 1650s. This one was built by Truman's in the 1930s. Eight of the 16 handpumps dispense a changing range of real ciders. A wide KeyKeg beer selection is also available. Food can be

brought in from outside, supplementing the range of pickled eggs available as snacks. Local CAMRA Cider Pub of the Year 2023.
⚲❀◗❍≷(Downs) ⊖(Central/Downs) ●🍴🚃❀🛜

Five Points Brewery Taproom 🅻
61 Mare Street, E8 4RG
☎ (020) 8533 7746 ⊕ fivepointsbrewing.co.uk
2 changing beers (often Five Points)
Based at the warehouse on Mare Street, this taproom has a vibrant atmosphere, with seating downstairs and on the mezzanine level as well as outside in the yard in the summer. There are 18 beers available from Five Points, mostly in keg format. The food offering is from ACE pizzas. You can also prebook a weekly brewery tour – see the website for dates and times.
⚲◗&⊖(Cambridge Heath) 🚃🛜

Hackney Tap
354 Mare Street, E8 1HR
☎ (020) 3026 4373 ⊕ hackneytap.com
3 changing beers (often Five Points, Hammerton, Rooster's) Ⓗ
This interesting building has been a town hall, a bank and a bookmakers. Original features are still in place: the panelling on the bar is from when it was a bank, and if you look up at the building on the outside you will see the logos from the previous incarnations. Besides the variety of changing cask beers, up to 20 keg choices are on offer, plus gyoza dumplings. Plenty of outside seating is available.
⚲❀◗❍≷(Downs) ⊖(Central/Downs) ●🚃🛜

Old Ship Inn
2 Sylvester Path, E8 1EN
☎ (020) 8986 2732 ⊕ oldshiphackney.com
2 changing beers (often Five Points) Ⓗ
This pub and kitchen is combined with a hotel. The main entrance in Sylvester Path is supplemented by an alleyway from Mare Street opposite Morning Lane. Two skylights generate a light and airy atmosphere. The walls are decorated with an eclectic mix of pictures, mirrors and an interesting Mermaid and Anchor artwork. Tables and chairs are plentiful alongside leather wall benches. One of the three handpumps dispenses a real cider. Food is served all day, with a short break in service on weekday afternoons.
🛏◗≷(Downs) ⊖(Central/Downs) ♣●🚃❀🛜

Pembury Tavern 🅻
90 Amhurst Road, E8 1JH
☎ (020) 8986 8597 ⊕ pemburytavern.co.uk
Five Points Pale, Railway Porter; 3 changing beers (sourced nationally; often Five Points) Ⓗ
A large corner pub with a friendly vibe, run by Five Points brewery. The spacious interior with wooden floors is comfortably furnished. Apart from cask beers, there are also 16 keg lines. Pizzas are available, with meat, vegetarian and vegan options. The pub is famous locally for its bar billiards table. There are quiz nights on Monday and occasional comedy nights. Check the website for upcoming events.
⚲◗&≷(Downs) ⊖(Central/Downs) ♣●🚃❀🛜

E9: Homerton

Chesham Arms
15 Mehetabel Road, E9 6DU
☎ (020) 8986 6717 ⊕ cheshamarms.com
4 changing beers (sourced nationally) Ⓗ
A lovely and friendly traditional back-street local that was saved from closure. It now sits at the heart of the community, with book swaps and occasional singalongs

at the piano. The cosy atmosphere inside is enhanced by two real fires. There is a large and attractive garden at the back. Four changing ales and one cider are on offer in winter; three and two respectively in the summer. Deliveries are available from Yard Sale Pizzas.
⚲❀◗⊖(Hackney Central) ♣●🚃❀🛜

E10: Leyton

Coach & Horses
391 High Road, E10 5NA
☎ (020) 8194 0332 ⊕ thecoachleyton.com
Mighty Oak Captain Bob; 5 changing beers (often East London, Purity, Sharp's) Ⓗ
A recently refurbished pub with a horseshoe bar. Some beers from London breweries are among those on the handpumps and 20 keg fonts. There is ample seating in the two rooms and rear beer garden. Monday is quiz night; Dungeons & Dragons games and Escape Room adventures are also played here, although you need to book ahead. The menu includes speciality burgers, pies and Sunday roasts. Sport is shown on multiple screens. The pub gets busy on Leyton Orient match days.
⚲❀◗⊖●🚃❀🛜♪

Leyton Orient Supporters Club 🅻
Breyer Group Stadium, Oliver Road, E10 5NF
☎ (020) 8988 8288 ⊕ orientsupporters.org
Mighty Oak Oscar Wilde Ⓖ; 10 changing beers Ⓗ
Multi award-winning club, previously a CAMRA national finalist, and current local CAMRA Club of the Year 2023. It is open on home match days (not during the matches) and for England football fixtures but also hosts four brewery tap takeovers every year. It can get extremely busy but the volunteer staff are efficient. On match days CAMRA members may need to show their membership card but other events are open to all. Q⚲❀⊖●🚃

E11: Leytonstone

North Star 🅻
24 Browning Road, E11 3AR
☎ 07747 010013 ⊕ thenorthstarpub.co.uk
East London Foundation Bitter; Oakham JHB; 4 changing beers (often Harvey's, Timothy Taylor) Ⓗ
A warm and welcoming atmosphere is guaranteed in this historic traditional glass-fronted pub in the Leytonstone Village Conservation Area. The varied selection of cask ales, keg and other drinks is dispensed in the smaller saloon bar and can be ordered from the public bar hatch. There is ample seating in the public bar, and outside in front and in the walled garden at the rear. Food is traditional Thai and stone-baked pizza. The pub is closed on Mondays in winter. ⚲❀◗⊖♣●

Northcote Arms 🅻
110 Grove Green Road, E11 4EL
☎ (020) 8518 7516 ⊕ northcotee11.com
2 changing beers (often East London, Redemption, Signature) Ⓗ
Traditional local pub with a strong community ethos. Identified by CAMRA as regionally important, the historic pub interior comprises five separate areas, comfortably furnished and served from a horseshoe bar. There are two gardens to the rear. Entertainment includes drag queens every Sunday evening as well as regular discos, singalongs, music bingo and live music. Burgers or hot dogs with vegan options are available (not Mon). Additional cask ales are on offer on days of Leyton Orient home games. ⚲❀◗⊖(Leyton)♣●🚃❀🛜♪

E11: Wanstead

George L ✔
159 High Street, E11 2RL
☎ (020) 8989 2921
Fuller's London Pride; Greene King Abbot; Ruddles Best Bitter; Sharp's Doom Bar; 8 changing beers (often East London, Sambrook's, Southwark) ⊞
A glass-fronted three-storey Victorian pub, originally the George & Dragon and then the George Hotel before acquisition by Wetherspoon in 1992. Spacious inside, it is spread over two levels but all the handpumps are on the main bar downstairs. Pictures of famous Georges adorn the walls. A car park and smoking area is at the rear. Three real ale festivals are held every year.
Q✿➸✿◑&☺🖶🛜

E12: Manor Park

Golden Fleece ✔
166 Capel Road, E12 5DB
☎ (020) 8478 0024
Greene King IPA, Abbot; 2 changing beers (often Greene King, New River, Southwark) ⊞
Busy in the summer, the pub's large garden is popular with families. The recently refurbished interior has a comfortable atmosphere. The pub is community focused with fun days for the family, and a jamming session for local musicians on alternate Friday evenings. Besides live sport on TV, other entertainment includes karaoke and a solo singer – see website for details. There is a varying food menu to suit all tastes. ➸✿◑&☺♣🖶🛜

E13: Plaistow

Black Lion ✔
59-61 High Street, E13 0AD
☎ (020) 8472 2351 ⊕ blacklionplaistow.co.uk
Mighty Oak Captain Bob; 3 changing beers (sourced nationally; often Adnams, Sharp's, Timothy Taylor) ⊞
Former coaching inn, rebuilt in 1747, with a split-level main bar and small back bar, both with beams and wood panelling. The back bar has its own door or can be accessed from the other bar via the serving area. The cobbled courtyard gives access to converted stables and outbuildings that house a function room, available for hire. The pub has had the same landlord for over 35 years and is still busy for West Ham home games.
➸✿◑♣☺🖶🛜

E14: Canary Wharf

Henry Addington ✔
22-28 Mackenzie Walk, E14 4PH
☎ (020) 7719 1114
St Austell Nicholson's Pale Ale; 6 changing beers (often Fuller's, Sharp's, Timothy Taylor) ⊞
A modern pub named after the man who, as Viscount Sidmouth, was Prime Minister (1801-4) and allowed the original Canary Wharf docks to be built. Located by the side of Middle Dock, below a modern office block, it is spacious, with a long bar and plenty of seating. Popular with the lunchtime and after work crowd, it offers good-value food and usually eight or nine cask ales from the Nicholson's seasonal range. ➸✿◑&☺🖶🛜

E15: Stratford

Olde Black Bull
13 Broadway, E15 4BQ
☎ (020) 8519 6720

2 changing beers (often Ringwood, St Austell, Woodforde's) ⊞
A friendly welcome awaits in this East End landmark, popular with shoppers thanks to its location opposite Stratford Mall. Ceiling-height etched windows illuminate the wood- and glass-panelled bar. Most of the floorspace is furnished with tables and chairs. Images of old Stratford complement Irish drink adverts. At the back is a small canopied garden with six picnic benches. Sports are shown on multiple TV screens. It gets busy here when West Ham United are at home.
✿➍⊖(Stratford/High St) 🛜

E17: Blackhorse Lane

Beerblefish Brewing Taproom L
Unit 2A-4, Uplands Business Park, E17 5QJ
☎ 07594 383195 ⊕ beerblefish.co.uk/taproom
4 changing beers (often Beerblefish)
A taproom in a former factory unit where you will be warmly welcomed. The beers are all brewed on the premises – some to old recipes which may contain unusual natural adjuncts. For amusement in addition to board games, there is a shuffleboard, a pool table with bias and a piano. Games night is Wednesday, but drop in for a drink anyway.
➸✿&⊖(Blackhorse Rd) ⬤P🖶🛜(158) ✿🛜

E17: Walthamstow

Olde Rose & Crown L ✔
53-55 Hoe Street, E17 4SA
☎ (020) 8509 3880 ⊕ yeolderoseandcrowntheatrepub.co.uk
4 changing beers (sourced nationally; often East London) ⊞
A spacious, welcoming community pub that, being free of tie, can surprise with the beers on offer. A theatre upstairs hosts regular events and a function room is downstairs. In the bar on the second Wednesday of the month is 78rpm record night; live bands may feature on other nights. Catering is split between two franchises with roasts Sunday lunchtimes and hot delights on other evenings. Local CAMRA Pub of the Year for 2022. Opens from mid-afternoon on weekdays.
➸✿◑⊖(Central) ♣⬤🖶✿🛜♫

E20: Stratford Westfield

Tap East L
7 International Square, Montfichet Road, E20 1EE
☎ (020) 8555 4467 ⊕ tapeast.co.uk
3 changing beers (often Tap East)
Opposite the Stratford International station entrance, this brewpub is furnished with sofas, high tables and chairs, with the brewery visible from the bar. Having West Ham's stadium nearby, it gets busy on match days, usually the only time for guest cask ales. A wide range of keg and bottled beers are available. There is no food but there are numerous eating places nearby. Major sporting events are shown on TV. Children are admitted but not dogs. Card payment only.
➸✿&⊖(Stratford/Stratford Intl) ⬤P🖶🛜

Barkingside

New Fairlop Oak ✔
Fencepiece Road, Fulwell Cross, IG6 2JP (on A123)
☎ (020) 8500 2217
Greene King Abbot; Ruddles Best Bitter; Sharp's Doom Bar; 7 changing beers (sourced nationally) ⊞
A Wetherspoon pub that puts customers and real ale first, with six handpulled guests waiting for eager patrons

ready to quench their thirst. It is named after an oak tree that was replanted in 1909; the original was one of Britain's largest trees and is thought to have been named by Queen Anne on a 1704 visit to the Fairlop Fair.
🗨👪🕪🧺❺(Fairlop) 🅿🚃🛜

Chadwell Heath

Eva Hart ✅
1128 High Road, RM6 4AH (on A118)
☎ (020) 8597 1069
Greene King Abbot; Ruddles Best Bitter; Sharp's Doom Bar; 7 changing beers (often Adnams, Big Penny, Fuller's) 🅷
Large and comfortable split-level Wetherspoon pub, divided into several distinct drinking areas. The building dates from 1892 and used to be the local police station. It is named after a local musical personality who was one of the longest-living survivors of the 1912 Titanic disaster; photographs and memorabilia are on display around the pub. Alcoholic drinks are served from 9am, food all day. Toilets (except accessible) are upstairs. Muted TVs show subtitles. Q🗨👪🕪🧺❺🅿🚃🛜

Collier Row

Colley Rowe Inn ✅
54-56 Collier Row Road, RM5 3PA (on B174)
☎ (01708) 760633
Greene King Abbot; Ruddles Best Bitter; Sharp's Doom Bar; 3 changing beers (sourced nationally) 🅷
Converted by Wetherspoon from two shops, the pub is close to six bus routes, giving easy access to and from Romford. It has a changing selection of guest ales and is often lively around the bar, but there are quieter alcoves at the rear. Alcoholic drinks are served from 9am. Food is served all day, every day and steak night is particularly popular. 🗨🕪🧺🚃🛜

Gidea Park

Gidea Park Micropub
236 Main Road, RM2 5HA (on A118)
Wibblers Apprentice 🅷; **6 changing beers (sourced nationally)** 🅶
Havering Borough and East London's second micropub opened in 2017 after winning a planning appeal for the change of use. Five to eight real ales from microbreweries are served (in all legal measures) from casks in the ground-floor cellar, alongside KeyKeg beers, real ciders, wines and gins. There are high and low tables and chairs, unusual spider lighting and an ever-growing display of pumpclips from beers sold here. Mobile phones should be silent. Local CAMRA Pub of the Year 2020. Q🗨👪🧺❺🚃(174,498)🌸🛜

Ship ✅
93 Main Road, RM2 5EL (on A118)
☎ (01708) 741571 🌐 theshipgideapark.co.uk
Greene King IPA; Sharp's Doom Bar; Timothy Taylor Landlord; 1 changing beer (sourced nationally) 🅷
More than 260 years old, this Grade II-listed split-level pub has extensive dark wood panelling, timber beams and huge fireplaces. The building is largely unchanged and has low ceilings in places – so duck or grouse! It is a family-run business with home-cooked food. Quiz nights are held on Thursday and live music is hosted on Saturday. Q🗨👪🕪❺🅿🚃(174,498)🌸🛜♪

Hornchurch

Hop Inn 🍷 🅻
122/124 North Street, RM11 1SU (at jct with Seymour Place)
☎ 07888 622532 🌐 hopinnhornchurch.co.uk
5 changing beers (sourced nationally) 🅶
Havering Borough's third micropub, opened in 2019, now has a snug room in the former Hop Shop off licence. Cask ales are dispensed from cooled cabinets behind the bar, KeyKeg beers, ciders and perry are served in all legal measures, plus craft beer cans and bottles, wines, gins and malt whiskies. No under-18s are admitted and mobile phones must be on silent! Local CAMRA Pub of the Year since 2021, twice Greater London regional winner and 2022 National Cider Pub of the Year. Closed on Mondays. Q❺(Emerson Park)🍃🌸🅿🚃🌸

J.J. Moon's
48-52 High Street, RM12 4UN (On A124)
☎ (01708) 478410
Greene King Abbot; Ruddles Best Bitter; Sharp's Doom Bar; 8 changing beers (sourced nationally) 🅷
A busy Wetherspoon pub, opened in 1993 and popular with all age groups, featuring a good variety of ales with an emphasis on breweries from London and the South East. Watercolour paintings of local scenes provide the main decoration, with the usual local historical interest panels to the rear. Families are welcome until evening, and alcoholic drinks are served from 9am. Silent TVs show subtitles. Q🗨🕪🧺❺(Emerson Park)🚃🛜

Ilford

Jono's ✅
37 Cranbrook Road, IG1 4PA (on A123)
☎ (020) 8514 6676
St Austell Tribute; 1 changing beer (sourced nationally) 🅷
A converted shop with an unusual style, just one minute's walk from the station. The front of the bar is in dark wood and the rear is half-timbered with a patch of thatch over the seating. Largescreen TVs and a projector show sports fixtures, and it can be noisy at times. There is live music on Friday and Saturday evenings. The bar staff are friendly and efficient. The second handpump sometimes has Marston's Wainwright or another cask ale. ❺🚃🛜♪

Romford

Moon & Stars ✅
99-103 South Street, RM1 1NX
☎ (01708) 730117
Greene King Abbot; Ruddles Best Bitter; Sharp's Doom Bar; 3 changing beers (sourced nationally) 🅷
Reopened with a new roof terrace and lift after a £1.1 million refurbishment in 2019, this Wetherspoon pub is close to the station and buses. Children are welcomed in the raised rear area until evening Friday and Saturday, but late during the week. Food is served from 8am. There are displays of local history on the walls. Toilets are upstairs (except accessible which require a key). It gets quite busy on Thursday and Friday evenings. 🗨👪🕪❺🚆❺🚃🛜

Upminster

Upminster TapRoom 🅻
1b Sunnyside Gardens, RM14 3DT (off St Mary's Lane)
☎ 07525 638440 🌐 aftervi.co.uk

Dark Star Hophead; 7 changing beers (sourced locally) G

Upminster and East London's first micropub, opened in a converted office in 2015 as a snack bar selling real ale before obtaining change of use on appeal. Its ownership changed in 2022. There are high tables, comfortable new chairs and benches. Up to eight cask ales, two KeyKeg beers, ciders and perry are served from the cool cellar, visible through the large window. Silence mobile phones or pay a fee for charity. Q♿☕❄️🕐👟♿⇄⊖👜🍴🚪🚲🎵

Woodford Bridge

Crown & Crooked Billet ✓
13 Cross Road, IG8 8BN (off B173)
☎ (020) 8502 9192
Fuller's London Pride; Sharp's Doom Bar; 3 changing beers (sourced nationally) H

Spacious multi-room pub overlooking the church spire and village green complete with large weeping willow tree and duckpond. Recently refurbished, it is clean and stylish, with wood beams and a conservatory, as well as plenty of outdoor seating, making for a pleasant venue in which to enjoy drinks and meals from an inviting menu. ♿❄️🕐👟♿P🚌(275,W14) 🐕🌳🎵

Woodford Green

Cricketers L
299-301 High Road, IG8 9HQ (on A1199)
☎ (020) 8504 2734
McMullen AK Original Mild, Country Bitter; 1 changing beer (sourced locally) H

Warm and friendly, and serving good-value food, this two-bar local has a dartboard in the public bar and plaques in the saloon for all 18 first class cricket counties, together with photographs of former MP Sir Winston Churchill, whose statue stands on the green almost opposite. There are tables on the front patio and a covered smoking area with seats at the rear. Boules is sometimes played on a pitch at the back. Q❄️🕐👟♣P🚌(179,W13) 🐕🌳

NORTH LONDON
N1: Hoxton

Wenlock Arms L
26 Wenlock Road, N1 7TA
☎ (020) 7608 3406 ⊕ wenlockarms.com
Mighty Oak Oscar Wilde; 7 changing beers (sourced nationally) H

Free house saved from closure by a vigorous local campaign. It features beers from small and medium-sized breweries across the UK, usually including a mild and subject to regular change. With one traditional cider, and a small snacks menu of toasties, Pieminister pies, baked Camembert and vegan sausage rolls, this is a truly welcoming street-corner local with an international reputation. Occasionally it serves beer from the in-house Block brewery in the cellar. ♿🕐👟♿⇄⊖(Old St) ♣👜🚲🌳🎵

N1: Islington

Earl of Essex
25 Danbury Street, N1 8LE
☎ (020) 7424 5828 ⊕ earlofessex.net
4 changing beers (often Five Points, Redemption) H

A craft beer house with an ever-changing list of cask beers from local and national breweries. Its own on-site brewery ceased operations some time ago. There is an impressive list of bottled and canned beers from the UK and abroad. A tasty food selection is served all day and, as with an increasing number of pubs, the use of pumpclips has been dropped and the beers on sale are listed on a large board. ❄️🕐👟♿⊖(Angel)👜🚲🌳

N1: King's Cross

Parcel Yard
King's Cross Railway Station, Euston Road, N1C 4AH
☎ (020) 7713 7258 ⊕ parcelyard.co.uk
Dark Star Hophead; Fuller's Oliver's Island, London Pride, ESB; 2 changing beers (sourced nationally) H

A large pub, up the stairs at the rear of the concourse, converted from the former station parcel office. It is used by local workers and commuters, and to host meetings. As well as bars on two levels, there are semi-private rooms converted from offices (available to book) and an indoor balcony. The decor is minimal and features rescued furniture. No music is played. Food, starting with breakfast, is served throughout the day. Wheelchair access is by lift. ♿❄️🕐👟⇄⊖(King's Cross St Pancras) ♣🚲🌳🎵

Scottish Stores ★ L
2-4 Caledonian Road, N1 9DU
☎ 07920 196603 ⊕ thescottishstores.co.uk
4 changing beers (often Hammerton) H

Identified by CAMRA as having a nationally important historic pub interior, this Grade II-listed pub, built in 1901, was the 2016 winner in the conservation category of the CAMRA National Pub Design Awards. Retaining an incredibly intact partitioned interior consisting of three separate bars, it is one of London's very few such survivals. Four handpumps offer a rotating selection of beers, some rarely seen in London. ❄️🕐⇄⊖(King's Cross St Pancras) 🚲🌳

N1: Newington Green

Lady Mildmay L
92 Mildmay Park, N1 4PR
☎ (020) 7241 6238 ⊕ ladymildmay.com
Five Points Best; 2 changing beers (often Five Points, Redemption) H

A large corner bar facing Newington Green, refurbished in 2015 when ownership moved to the current operator. That internal redecoration brought back the pub's original features. With its open kitchen, cosy fireplaces, sofas to lounge on and large windows to watch the world go by, this is a pleasant place to visit. The beers listed may change, but Five Points Best is close to being a regular, and others come mostly from London breweries. ♿🕐👟♿⊖(Canonbury) 👜🚲🌳

N1: Pentonville

King Charles I
55-57 Northdown Street, N1 9BL
☎ (020) 7837 7758 ⊕ kingcharles1st.co.uk
Southwark Routemaster Red; 3 changing beers (sourced nationally) H

Georgian building with a 1930s interior that has been identified by CAMRA as being of regional importance. The pub is small and cosy, containing knick-knacks and homely artefacts, and warmed by real fires in the winter. Food can be ordered at the bar or, during the day, from the Blue River café opposite. Live blues, folk and indie music can be impromptu or planned. Since 2015 the pub has been community-owned, with a 20-year lease shared by local residents and regulars. ❄️⇄⊖(King's Cross St Pancras) 👜🚲🌳🎵

N5: Canonbury

Snooty Fox 🗈
75 Grosvenor Avenue, N5 2NN
☎ (020) 7354 9532 ⊕ snootyfoxlondon.co.uk
Otter Ale; 3 changing beers (sourced nationally) ⊞
A vibrant community establishment with 1960s icons depicted throughout, serving up to four real ales. The airy bar features a 45rpm jukebox. A function room accommodates local groups and private dining, and outside there is a pleasant patio with seating. The kitchen serves quality modern British food and an excellent Sunday roast. A former local CAMRA Pub of the Year. ⍉❀➊⊖⊟♪

N7: Holloway

Lamb 🗈
54 Holloway Road, N7 8JL
☎ (020) 7619 9187 ⊕ thelambn7.co.uk
3 changing beers (often Five Points, Signature, Three Sods) ⊞
Highbury brewery's tap, taken over by Taylor Walker in 1912, later becoming the Flounder & Firkin before the demise of that chain. Three cask beers rotate, typically a best bitter and a pale ale alongside an amber, rye beer or porter from Redemption, Howling Hops, Five Points, Signature and many more local breweries. The beautiful interior has handsome wood panelling and skylights; the façade parades its painstakingly stripped back original green tiles. Live music is a speciality.
❀⑃≠⊖(Highbury & Islington) ⊟❀☏♪

N8: Crouch End

Small Beer
22 Topsfield Parade, Tottenham Lane, N8 8PT
☎ (020) 8350 0032 ⊕ smallbeern8.co.uk
3 changing beers (often Almasty, Two by Two, Vibrant Forest) ⊞
Occupying a converted shopfront in the middle of a busy high street, this is a cross between a brewery tap house and a rustic cocktail bar, with brick walls, wood floor, rustic tables and chairs and techno music in the background that is not overly intrusive. It has a comfortable, vibrant and inviting atmosphere and for a while was named after Henry Reader Williams (1822-97), in whose honour the nearby clock tower was built. Food comprises a variety of pizzas and desserts. Open daily at 4pm. ➊●⊟

N9: Lower Edmonton

Beehive
24 Little Bury Street, N9 9JZ
☎ (020) 8360 4358 ⊕ thebeehivebhp.co.uk
Greene King IPA; 4 changing beers (often Beerblefish, Mighty Oak, Vale) ⊞
Tucked away in semi-detached suburbia, this 1929 rebuild is now an imposing gastropub. A wide selection of food is on offer, including excellent Sunday roasts. Recently refurbished, the bar runs along most of the back wall. There is live entertainment on Friday or Saturday and a weekly quiz on Tuesdays. The garden houses an interesting selection of animals including pigs, goats, ducks and also an iguana only visible from the Gents. ⍉❀➊♣⊟(329,W8) ❀☏♪

Rising Sun ✅
240 Winchester Road, N9 9EF
☎ (020) 8807 1512 ⊕ therisingsunlondon.co.uk

Dark Star Hophead; 2 changing beers (often Adnams, St Austell, Vale) ⊞
A large, traditional back-street local with four Taylor Walker signs still fixed to the outside walls. It has a cosy bar on one side and a larger games room where pool and darts can be played. Darts league matches take place every week: men on Monday, women on Tuesday. You can choose your music from a jukebox. For outside drinking there is an enclosed area to the side of the pub and additional pavement seating at the front.
⍉❀♣⊡❀☏

N10: Muswell Hill

Mossy Well ✅
258 Muswell Hill Broadway, N10 3SH
☎ (020) 8444 2914
Greene King IPA, Abbot; Sharp's Doom Bar; 8 changing beers (often Redemption, Theakston) ⊞
A former Express Dairies tearoom and milk depot but a pub since 1984, reopened by Wetherspoon in 2015. Its name derives from the etymology of Muswell. Many internal features reflect its milky history. It is spacious inside, with a mezzanine floor and outdoor drinking areas at both front and back. Despite the size, it can be packed. Q⍉❀➊⑃⊟❀☏

N12: North Finchley

Bohemia ▾ 🗈
762-764 High Road, N12 9QH
☎ (020) 8446 0294 ⊕ thebohemia.co.uk
London Brewing Flying The Mags, London Lush, Beer Street, 100 Oysters Stout; 1 changing beer (sourced locally) ⊞
A large, lively brewpub on two levels, with large comfortable sofas in the front area and the brewery to view at the rear. Up to five of its cask ales, plus five real ciders, are served in one or two thirds measures. Table football and pinball complement a selection of board games. Quiz night is Tuesday, comedy night the second Thursday of the month and live jazz-funk-blues usually two Sundays a month. Local CAMRA Pub of the Year 2023. ⍉❀➊⑃⊖(Woodside Park)♣●⊟❀☏

Elephant Inn
283 Ballards Lane, N12 8NR
☎ (020) 8343 6110 ⊕ elephantinnfinchley.co.uk
Fuller's London Pride, ESB; 2 changing beers (often Arbor, Fuller's, Siren) ⊞
This fine wood-panelled pub has a regionally important historic interior, with three distinct areas round a U-shaped bar. The right bar has a pool table and shows sports TV; major events may be screened throughout the pub. The two guest ales are usually from the Fuller's portfolio. Bar food is served from the upstairs Thai restaurant. Outdoor areas include a huge wooden pergola on the front patio, with a courtyard at the rear. ⍉❀➊⑃⊖(West Finchley) ♣⊟❀☏

N14: Southgate

New Crown ✅
80-84 Chase Side, N14 5PH
☎ (020) 8882 8758
Greene King Abbot; Ruddles Best Bitter; Sharp's Doom Bar; 2 changing beers (often Redemption, Twickenham, Windsor & Eton) ⊞
There was an Old Crown on Chase Side until its demolition in the 1960s, hence the name. This large, well-established Wetherspoon pub is convenient for the tube, and four bus routes stop outside. Converted from a

Sainsbury's store more than 20 years ago, it has a single open-plan seating area. Up to two guest ales come from breweries across the country but with an emphasis on London brews whenever possible. Now celebrating 15 consecutive years in this Guide. Q ✿ ❄ ❍ & ⊖ ⚑ ☂

N16: Stoke Newington

Rochester Castle ✔

143-145 Stoke Newington High Street, N16 0NY
☎ (020) 7249 6016
Greene King IPA, Abbot; Sharp's Doom Bar; 6 changing beers (sourced nationally) ⊞
A Grade II-listed building, with an impressive frontage featuring some fine tiling and a large skylight at the back, this is a welcome outlet for cask beer and is now Wetherspoon's longest-trading venue. The pub here dates from 1702 as the Green Dragon, subsequently demolished and rebuilt by Richard Payne from Rochester (hence the name) although it was briefly the Tanners Hall in the 1980s. Among other features, note the four tiled wall fixtures, one for each season. ✿ ❄ ❍ ⊖ ⚑ ☂

N17: Tottenham

Antwerp Arms 𝕃

168-170 Church Road, N17 8AS (500yds from Sports Centre bus stop on High Rd)
☎ (020) 8216 9289 ⊕ antwerparms.co.uk
Redemption Pale Ale, Hopspur; 2 changing beers (often Redemption) ⊞
Tucked away in the historic and atmospheric Bruce Castle Park area, this Georgian building with beer garden is Tottenham's oldest working pub, serving the neighbourhood since 1822. Facing demolition in 2013, it was saved by the local community and CAMRA campaigners. Now owned as a community collective, it is in effect a permanent outlet for Redemption brewery beers. Food is served at limited times, so do check the pub website. ✿ ❄ ❍ ⊖ (White Hart Lane) ♣ ⚑ ☀ ☂ ♪

N19: Upper Holloway

Landseer Arms 𝕃

37 Landseer Road, N19 4JU
☎ (020) 7281 2569 ⊕ landseerarms.com
Hammerton N1; 4 changing beers (often Twickenham) ⊞
A Victorian pub, quite different from most of the places on nearby Holloway Road, and one that has been through many incarnations, eventually renamed after the artist whose works included the Trafalgar Square lions and the painting, Monarch of the Glen. The spacious interior includes a conservatory-style area on the other side of the bar, sometimes used for dining. There is plenty of pavement seating, with heaters and retractable awnings. ✿ ❄ ❍ & ⊖ ♣ ⚑ ☀ ☂ ♪

Shaftesbury Tavern 𝕃

534 Hornsey Road, N19 3QN
☎ (020) 7272 7950 ⊕ theshaftesburytavern.co.uk
3 changing beers (sourced locally) ⊞
A nice old venue, now operated by Remarkable Pubs and comprehensively restored since a 2014 refurbishment, with the former pool room turned into the restaurant area under a fine skylight. It has been identified by CAMRA as having a regionally important historic pub interior. Outside at the front there is seating on the terrace. Food comes from a predominantly Thai menu (not Sun), with some classics such as fish & chips and Sunday roasts. Quiz night is Tuesday. ✿ ❄ ❍ & ⊖ (Crouch Hill) ⚑ ☀ ☂

St John's Tavern

91 Junction Road, N19 5QU
☎ (020) 7272 1587 ⊕ stjohnstavern.com
Fuller's London Pride; 4 changing beers (sourced nationally) ⊞
Another piece of the real ale renaissance taking place in this part of London. Although the emphasis here is undeniably on food (hams hanging in the food preparation area are visible from the bar), this gastropub can have up to five real ales on at any one time and has room for those who just want to relax with a drink. The whole impression is one of space, helped by a large bar area and high ceilings. ❄ ❍ ⊖ (Archway) ♣ ⚑ ☂

N21: Winchmore Hill

Little Green Dragon

928 Green Lanes, N21 2AD
☎ (020) 8351 3530 ⊕ littlegreendragonenfield.com
4 changing beers (often Beerblefish, Five Points, New River) 𝔾
This micropub was voted Greater London Pub of the Year in 2018 and has been the local winner over five consecutive years. Meet the Brewer events are often held as well as regular music nights. Eclectic seating includes a church pew, bus seats and padded kegs, contributing to the friendly community atmosphere, with pavement seating or a small courtyard at the back for alfresco drinking. No excuses for missing your bus – electronic live times are displayed. Q ✿ ❄ ☀ ♣ ❍ ⚑ (125,329) ☀ ☂ ♪

N22: Wood Green

Prince

1 Finsbury Road, N22 8PA
☎ (020) 8888 6698 ⊕ theprincen22.co.uk
5 changing beers (often Five Points, Hammerton) ⊞
A handsome two-roomed venue occupying a prominent corner site, opposite the pleasant Finsbury Gardens and the New River Path, brought back to life in 2016. Up to five cask ales and nine keg beers come from small breweries across the UK and are listed on the website as they change regularly. Snacks are served weekday lunchtimes, and Japanese dishes in the evenings and all day at weekends. ❄ ❍ ≷ (Alexandra Palace) ⊖ ● ⚑ ♪

Westbury

57 Westbury Avenue, N22 6SA
☎ (020) 8889 2059 ⊕ westburyn22.co.uk
Timothy Taylor Landlord; 5 changing beers (often Goodness, Hammerton, Redemption) ⊞
Large, impressive corner pub taken over in 2014 by London Village Inns and extensively renovated as a pub and kitchen with lots of space, big windows throughout and heated outside seating. The wide range of beers includes a number from London breweries. Quiz night is Tuesday and there is live music on a Saturday. Payment is by card only. ✿ ❄ ❍ & ⊖ (Turnpike Lane) ● ⚑ ☂ ♪

East Barnet

Prince of Wales ✔

2 Church Hill Road, EN4 8TB
☎ (020) 8440 5392
Adnams Ghost Ship; Fuller's London Pride; Timothy Taylor Landlord; 1 changing beer (often Black Sheep, Sharp's) ⊞
Close to Oakhill Park, this pub serves three regular beers during the week with a guest ale normally available to enjoy at the weekend. Recently refurbished, the main bar leads through to a cosy area and then the garden,

which includes an attractive patio and a covered area for shade. There is also a raised terrace above street level at the front. Sports events are screened, Tuesday night is games night and a late-night DJ plays on Friday. ⛽🚲🍴👌♿⇌(Oakleigh Park) ♣P🚐☼

Enfield

Moon Under Water 🅻 ✅
115-117 Chase Side, EN2 6NN
☎ (020) 8366 9855
Greene King Abbot; Ruddles Best Bitter; Sharp's Doom Bar; 3 changing beers (often New River, Twickenham) Ⓗ
An early Wetherspoon pub in what had been the British School, opened in 1838 and closed in 1901, and later a public hall, a dairy, then a restaurant. The building has a church-like appearance with a stained-glass window allowing light to flood in on three sides. Popular with all age groups, it has a dedicated area for families and a patio garden space that used to be a car park. The beers are often local and London brews.
⛽🚲🍴👌♿⇌(Chase) 🍴🚐(191,W9) 🛜

Wonder 🅻
1 Batley Road, EN2 0JG
☎ (020) 8363 0202
McMullen AK Original Mild; 2 changing beers (often McMullen) Ⓗ
Recently redecorated old-fashioned two-bar local with a regionally important historic interior. The large public bar has a real fire, dartboard and a honky tonk piano for early Sunday evenings. Bands also play many Friday or Saturday nights. Some tables host board games such as backgammon, draughts and snakes & ladders. The seasonal ale might be a McMullen Rivertown beer. The car park has become an outside seating area.
🚲👌⇌(Gordon Hill) ♣🚐(191,W8) ☼🛜

High Barnet

Lord Nelson ✅
14 West End Lane, EN5 2SA
☎ (020) 8449 7249
Young's London Original, London Special; 1 changing beer (often Timothy Taylor, Young's) Ⓗ
A friendly and comfortable one-bar locals' pub hidden away off Wood Street. Full of bric-a-brac, it has a fabulous collection of novelty salt and pepper pots donated by customers returning from holiday. A guest beer may be available from the Marston's list. Fresh sandwiches are sometimes available while stock lasts. Tuesday night alternates between bingo and a quiz. Dogs are welcome provided they are on leads and off chairs. The pub often closes early on Thursdays. Q🚲♣🚐☼🛜

Olde Mitre Inne ✅
58 High Street, EN5 5SJ
☎ (020) 3674 3145
Greene King IPA, Abbot; Timothy Taylor Landlord; house beer (by House); 3 changing beers (often Oakham, Tring, Wantsum) Ⓗ
The oldest coaching inn in Barnet, there has been a pub here since 1553 and this Grade II-listed building oozes character and charm. It has beams, exposed brickwork, wood panelling and open fires. There are three separate drinking areas in the original building, then behind is a converted old stables and a large courtyard that has a retractable roof and a brick-built chiminea. Quiz night is Thursday with live music alternate Sundays. Families are welcome. ⛽🚲🍴👌⊖🍴🚐☼🛜

Olde Monken Holt ✅
193 High Street, EN5 5SU
☎ (020) 3674 3145
Greene King IPA, Abbot; 1 changing beer (often Greene King, Timothy Taylor) Ⓗ
At the northern end of the High Street, close to the site of the 1471 Battle of Barnet, this traditional Greene King tenanted pub dates from 1863. Locals mix with walkers dropping in after a stroll over the vast open space around Hadley. Well behaved dogs are welcome inside, in the recently refurbished beer garden at the back or within the additional seating area to the front. Many TVs at the rear of the pub show sport or news.
⛽🚲♣🚐(399) 🐾☼🛜🎵

New Barnet

Railway Bell ✅
13 East Barnet Road, EN4 8RR
☎ (020) 8449 1369
Courage Best Bitter, Directors; Greene King Abbot; Ruddles Best Bitter; Sharp's Doom Bar; 3 changing beers (often East London, Oakham, Twickenham) Ⓗ
A rarity for Wetherspoon's, this was not a conversion but had been a pub since the late 19th century. A recent massive refit, including a conservatory at the rear, gives it an airy and bright feeling, and families are welcome until late evening. The car park has gone, replaced by a larger garden that is now segregated between smoking and non-smoking, the latter with the benefit of astroturf.
Q⛽🚲🍴👌♿⇌🍴🚐🛜

NORTH-WEST LONDON
NW1: Camden Town

Camden Road Arms
102-106 Camden Road, NW1 9EA
☎ (020) 7485 4530
3 changing beers (often Siren) Ⓗ
Previously the Eagle, Rosie O'Grady's, Mac Bar and Grand Union, this huge pub was massively improved by the Draft House group in 2017 and twice since then by BrewDog. It has a horseshoe-shaped bar, eclectic lighting and comfortable seating, including armchairs, settees and semi-private booths. A board lists the various beers available; often one cask ale can be on offer at a bargain price until sold out. Full details of the food offerings are on the pub's website.
⛽🚲🍴👌⊖(Camden Rd/Town) 🚐☼🛜

Golden Lion 🅻
88 Royal College Street, NW1 0TH
☎ (020) 3915 3852 🌐 goldenlioncamden.com
Dark Star Hophead; Fuller's London Pride; Sambrook's Junction Ⓗ
A lovely and popular community pub, saved from closure in 2013; the licensee and the local community, supported by Camden Council, waged a long campaign to prevent its conversion into flats. This came to its final and excellent conclusion with the sitting tenant buying the building, which he now leases out. Tasteful decor complements the historic interior features identified by CAMRA as being regionally important, notably the mirrored bar-back. A real back-street community boozer.
⛽🚲🍴👌⊖(Camden Rd) ♣🚐☼🛜🎵

Tapping the Admiral 🍺 🅻
77 Castle Road, NW1 8SU
☎ (020) 7267 6118 🌐 tappingtheadmiral.com
House beer (by Redemption); 7 changing beers (sourced regionally) Ⓗ

A lively and enjoyable community venue where friendly, knowledgeable staff offer a warm welcome. Guest ales come mainly from local breweries. Great British food includes speciality home-made pies. Outside at the back is a well-designed, heated and covered beer garden. There is a popular Wednesday quiz and live traditional music on Thursday evening. Look out for monthly tap takeovers, pop-up events, and also the pub's cat, Nelson. Local CAMRA Pub of the Year 2023.
Q ✠ ❀ ◑ & ⊖ (Kentish Town West) ● ➡ ❀ ☎ ♪

NW1: Euston

Doric Arch Ⓛ
Euston Station Colonnade, 1 Eversholt Street, NW1 2DN
☎ (020) 7383 3359 ⊕ doric-arch.co.uk
Dark Star Hophead; Fuller's Oliver's Island, London Pride, ESB; 3 changing beers (sourced nationally) Ⓗ
Right next to Euston station, celebrating the arch wantonly demolished as part of its 'development', the pub is up a flight of stairs, with large picture windows below. It is used extensively by commuters, aided by the train times screen. Excellent staff are helpful and informative about the ales, including up to three guest beers. Railway memorabilias adorn the walls. Toilets are at basement level. ✠ ◑ ⇌ ⊖ (Euston/Euston Sq) ➡ ❀ ☎

Euston Tap Ⓛ
West & East Lodges, 190 Euston Road, NW1 2EF
☎ (020) 3137 8837 ⊕ eustontap.com
7 changing beers (often Five Points, Redemption) Ⓟ
Fronting the main station building, these impressive Grade II-listed Portland stone lodges, separated by a bus lane, are relics from the original 1830s station. The beers, mostly from smaller breweries, are pumped up to taps behind the bar. The small ground-floor spaces are augmented by seating up the wrought iron spiral staircases, where you will also find the toilets, and large heated drinking areas outside. The East Lodge opens later in the afternoon and its offering can vary, such as being the Cider Tap. ✠ ❀ ⇌ ⊖ (Euston/Euston Sq) ➡ ❀ ☎

NW2: Cricklewood

Beaten Docket ⊘
50-56 Cricklewood Broadway, NW2 3ET
☎ (020) 8450 2972
Greene King Abbot; Ruddles Best Bitter; 3 changing beers (sourced nationally) Ⓗ
A Wetherspoon pub named after a losing betting ticket; framed prints reflect the racing link, a feature of this area in the late 19th century. A series of booths to the left provide more intimate drinking areas while two TVs on silent mode offer either sport or rolling news. In summer, some of the doors and windows open more fully to create a pleasant atmosphere around the outside seating area to the front, which is open all year round.
Q ✠ ❀ ◑ & ⇌ ➡ ☎

NW3: Hampstead

Holly Bush
22 Holly Mount, NW3 6SG
☎ (020) 7435 2892 ⊕ hollybushhampstead.co.uk
Dark Star Hophead; Fuller's London Pride; Gale's HSB Ⓗ
A marvellous multi-roomed gem of a Fuller's pub at the top of steep steps leading from Heath Street. Sensitive refurbishment opened up rooms at the back some years ago, and there is also an upstairs dining room. However, the jewels of this pub are the main bar and the room, off

to the left as you enter, with the traditional open fire. On seeing them you will appreciate the Grade II listing and the pub's identification by CAMRA as having a regionally important historic pub interior.
✠ ❀ ◑ ⊖ ♣ ➡ (46,268) ❀ ☎

Magdala Ⓛ
2A South Hill Park, NW3 2SB
☎ (020) 7433 8322 ⊕ themagdala.co.uk
Big Smoke Solaris Session Pale Ale; Five Points Best; Harvey's Sussex Best Bitter; 4 changing beers (often By The Horns, Hammerton, Southwark) Ⓗ
Reopened as an independent pub after a long period under threat of permanent closure, the interior of this typical Charrington inter-war rebuild, with its wood panelling and green stained glass (identified by CAMRA as being regionally important), has undergone careful restoration. Named after Lord Napier of Magdala and dating back to 1885, outside here was where Ruth Ellis, the last woman hanged in England, shot her lover to death on Easter Sunday 1955, though alleged bullet marks on the façade are not authentic.
❀ ◑ ⊖ (Hampstead Heath) ➡ ❀

Old White Bear
1 Well Road, NW3 1LJ
☎ (020) 4553 0602 ⊕ theoldwhitebearhampstead.co.uk
Dark Star Hophead; Fuller's London Pride; Kirkstall Midnight Bell; Timothy Taylor Landlord Ⓗ
Now run by Northern Union Pubs, owned by the team behind Leeds brewery, this pub had been closed for nearly eight years until saved after another prolonged campaign by locals and CAMRA. The interior will be familiar to returning customers. The bar remains in a central position, with bar stools in front available for drinkers. The side rooms both have fireplaces, large wooden bench-style tables and banquette seating. A parquet floor extends throughout. ◑ ⊖ ➡ (46,268)

Spaniards Inn ⊘
Spaniards Road, NW3 7JJ
☎ (020) 8731 8406 ⊕ thespaniardshampstead.co.uk
Sharp's Doom Bar; Timothy Taylor Landlord; 1 changing beer (often Dark Star, Fuller's, St Austell) Ⓗ
A large, rambling inn with one bar and several rooms, some featuring wooden beams and low ceilings, making for a cosy atmosphere. Grade II listed, the building dates back to 1585, although it may not originally have been a pub. It is popular with walkers from the heath and so weekends can be extremely busy. Booking is recommended for meals. Drinkers may be directed to the large, heated garden if inside tables are booked for food.
Q ✠ ❀ ◑ ➡ ➡ (210,H3) ❀

NW5: Kentish Town

Lion & Unicorn Ⓛ
42 Gaisford Street, NW5 2ED
☎ (020) 7267 2304 ⊕ thelionandunicornnw5.co.uk
Young's London Original, London Special; 1 changing beer (often Redemption) Ⓗ
This popular community venue is a great favourite, with its genuine homely feel, open fire and comfortable seating. Run by friendly management and staff as a Geronimo-branded gastro-pub, its cask ale range features several breweries from the area. The front and back gardens have both won local and regional awards. A quiz is held on Sunday and comedy nights are hosted on occasion. Upstairs is the Giant Olive Theatre company; details of productions are available on the theatre's website. ✠ ❀ ◑ & ⇌ ⊖ ➡ ❀ ☎ ♪

Pineapple [L]
51 Leverton Street, NW5 2NX
☎ (020) 7284 4631 🌐 thepineapplepubnw5.com
House beer (by Marston's); 4 changing beers (sourced nationally) [H]
An authentic and friendly community venue, saved from closure by the locals, Grade II listed and identified by CAMRA as having a regionally important historic pub interior, notable for its mirrors and splendid bar-back. The front bar, with comfortable seating around tables, leads through to an informal conservatory overlooking the patio garden. The menu is Thai kitchen cuisine. Some of the beers come from across London and the range changes regularly as the pub is free of tie.
Q🚸❀◑🚆⊖🚌🐾📶

Southampton Arms
139 Highgate Road, NW5 1LE
🌐 thesouthamptonarms.co.uk
8 changing beers (sourced nationally) [H]
The pub does what it says on the sign outside: Ale, Cider, Meat. The 14 handpumps on and behind the bar serve almost equal numbers of ciders and different beers from microbreweries across the UK. Snacks include pork pies, roast pork baps, cheese and meat baps, plus veggie options. Music is played on vinyl only and the piano is in regular use. At the back is a secluded patio. Local CAMRA Cider Pub of the Year 2023.
❀◑🚆⊖(Gospel Oak/Kentish Town) 🍎🚌♫

NW6: Kilburn

Black Lion ★ [L]
274 Kilburn High Road, NW6 2BY
☎ (020) 3876 8204 🌐 blacklionkilburn.co.uk
Five Points Pale; London Brewing Beer Street [H]
A Grade II-listed building, identified by CAMRA as having a nationally important historic pub interior, this pub is worth a visit for its fantastic interior decor alone: a rich ceiling, original bar counter, island back bar, screen partition, etched and cut glass and decorative cornice. Cask beer and cider returned in 2022, after many years' absence, when London Village Inns, who already operated seven thriving and diverse pubs across London, took over and installed three handpumps.
🚸❀🛏◑⊖(Brondesbury/Kilburn) 🍎🚌🐾

NW6: Kilburn Park

Carlton Tavern
33 Carlton Vale, NW6 5EU
☎ (020) 7625 4760 🌐 carltontavern.co.uk
House beer (by Anspach & Hobday); 3 changing beers (often Big Smoke, Five Points, London Brewing) [H]
A site now famous nationally after the pub was demolished illegally and Westminster Council forced the developer to rebuild it brick by brick from its original plans. Much was salvaged from the wreckage of the old building, including tiles, bricks and the original bar and fireplaces, and some of the decorative ceilings were also rescued. Outside is a garden/patio area also used for dining in summer. Local CAMRA Pub of the Year 2022.
🚸❀◑⊖🚌🐾📶♫

NW9: Colindale

Moon Under Water ✔
10 Varley Parade, Edgware Road, NW9 6RR
☎ (020) 8200 7611
Greene King Abbot; Ruddles Best Bitter; 3 changing beers (often Sambrook's, Vale, Windsor & Eton) [H]
A large Wetherspoon pub converted from a Woolworth store in 1990. The rear is mainly for food or where well behaved children can sit with their parents while the front is the more traditional drinking and chatting area. Some of the changing cask beers and many of the craft beers on keg or in bottles will be from London breweries; the manager occasionally arranges Meet the London Brewer events. The silent TVs show either news or racing. Q🚸◑♿🚌(32,142)📶

Eastcote Village

Woodman ✔
Joel Street, HA5 2PR
☎ (020) 8868 0833 🌐 thewoodmanpinner.com
Rebellion IPA; Timothy Taylor Landlord; 1 changing beer (often Brains, Butcombe, Otter) [H]
A Grade II-listed, two-bar former Harman's pub dating from the 1640s, extended in 2005 and refurbished in 2021. Overlooking the Eastcote cricket club, it features a large function room with bar at the rear and a patio-style covered garden. On Sunday traditional roasts are available. Saturday evening meals are usually available from a changing food vendor in the pub garden.
🚸❀◑♿P🚌(282) 🐾♫

Harrow on the Hill

Castle ★
30 West Street, HA1 3EF
☎ (020) 8422 3155 🌐 castle-harrow.co.uk
Dark Star Hophead; Fuller's London Pride, ESB; 2 changing beers (often Dark Star, Fuller's, Thornbridge) [H]
A lively and friendly Fuller's house in the heart of historic Harrow-on-the-Hill. Built in 1901 and Grade II listed, it has been identified by CAMRA as having a nationally important historic pub interior. Reservations are recommended for Sunday lunchtimes. Three real coal fires help to keep the pub warm and cosy in the colder months and a secluded beer garden is popular during the summer. CAMRA's Harrow Pub of the Year 2022.
🚸❀◑♣🚌(258,H17) 🐾📶♫

Rayners Lane

Village Inn [L] ✔
402-408 Rayners Lane, HA5 5DY
☎ (020) 8868 8551
Greene King IPA, Abbot; Sharp's Doom Bar; Twickenham Naked Ladies; 5 changing beers [H]
A split-level, double-fronted shop conversion. The rear of the pub, accessed down a few steps, sports the traditional Wetherspoon booths, with a row of tables down the centre. A terraced area behind has a variety of large potted plants among the picnic tables. The front pavement has a few tables and chairs for that alfresco moment. There is a good cross-section of customers who mingle quite happily together. Alcoholic drinks are served from 9am. Q🚸❀◑♿⊖♣🚌📶

Ruislip

Hop & Vine
18 High Street, HA4 7AN
3 changing beers (sourced nationally) [G]
A micropub converted from a café, with seating at low tables with chairs and benches. The small bar counter in the right-hand corner dispenses real ales, keg beers and ciders from a temperature-controlled cellar room behind it. Bottled and canned beers, wines and spirits are also sold. Snacks are enhanced by cheeseboard and

charcuterie board options. The real ale choice increases to four or five at weekends, often with table service.
Q❀✿&⊖♣🖪🐾

Woodman ✓

Breakspear Road, HA4 7SE
☎ (01895) 635763 ∰ thewoodmanruislip.com
Fuller's London Pride; Rebellion IPA; Timothy Taylor Landlord; 1 changing beer (sourced nationally) Ⓗ
This cheerful and welcoming two-bar local close to Ruislip Lido and woods has been identified by CAMRA as having a nationally important historic pub interior. The cosy lounge bar is open-plan with a dartboard and games machine. The public bar is friendly and comfortable. Some of the outside seating is covered. A street food truck changes weekly, serving food on Friday evenings.
Q�✿◑&🖪(331) 🐾🛜♫

Ruislip Manor

J.J. Moon's ✓

12 Victoria Road, HA4 0AA
☎ (01895) 622373
Courage Directors; Greene King Abbot; Ruddles Best Bitter; Sharp's Doom Bar; Vale Gravitas; 7 changing beers (often Twickenham) Ⓗ
A large Wetherspoon pub conveniently located opposite the tube station. It is popular and often busy in the evening and at weekends. Food and beer alike are of good value, with the usual promotions. The pub hosts a weekly cellar dash and holds an annual Battle of the Brewery. At the rear is an elevated section leading to a small garden patio, while the front has a partitioned-off smoking area on the street. Q🌤✿◑&⊖🖪🛜

SOUTH-EAST LONDON
SE1: Bermondsey

Arch House

118 Druid Street, SE1 2HH
☎ (020) 8617 9510 ∰ anspachandhobday.com/the-arch-house
2 changing beers (often Anspach & Hobday) Ⓗ
Located within a railway arch along the Bermondsey Beer Mile, this venue was originally the home of the Anspach & Hobday brewery. Following the relocation of the main brewing operation to Croydon, the Arch House is now an enlarged pub space. Two of the brewery's cask ales are usually available along with up to 12 beers on tap – some dispensed from KeyKeg – and an extensive canned and bottled selection. Closed on Monday and Tuesday. ⊖🖪

SE1: Borough

King's Arms

65 Newcomen Street, SE1 1YT
☎ (020) 7407 1132 ∰ kingsarmsborough.co.uk
Harvey's Sussex Best Bitter; Purity Mad Goose; Timothy Taylor Landlord; 2 changing beers (often Five Points, Twickenham, Wantsum) Ⓗ
A popular, Grade II-listed, single-room pub with a traditional and comfortable interior, situated just off the busy Borough High Street. The striking external plaque above the entrance originally stood at the southern end of Old London Bridge and was rescued when all the buildings on the bridge were demolished in the mid-18th century. Five cask beers are usually available and traditional, mainly British, meals are served lunchtimes daily and evenings Monday-Saturday. A first floor function room is available for hire.
🌤✿◑⇌(London Bridge) ⊖🖪

Libertine ✓

125 Great Suffolk Street, SE1 1PQ
☎ (020) 7378 7877 ∰ thelibertine.co.uk
Harvey's Sussex Best Bitter; 2 changing beers (sourced regionally) Ⓗ
Originally a Whitbread house, this lively and spacious street-corner pub is popular with a mix of workers, locals and students. Pizza is the speciality on the food menu. Regular live music or DJ sessions are hosted and a weekly quiz is held on Tuesday. Major sporting events are shown and there is a dartboard in the front corner on a raised oche. The pub is closed on Sunday.
◑⇌(Elephant & Castle) ⊖♣🖪🛜♫

Royal Oak 🏆 ✓

44 Tabard Street, SE1 4JU
☎ (020) 7357 7173 ∰ royaloaklondon.co.uk
Harvey's Dark Mild, Sussex Best Bitter; house beer (by Harvey's); 2 changing beers (often Harvey's) Ⓗ
A charming, back-to-basics drinkers' pub separated into two sections by the bar counter and an off-sales hatch. This was the first London tied house of Sussex-based Harvey's brewery and is renowned for friendly and attentive service. The ales include seasonal brews, a mild, which is unusual for London, and several additional Harvey's bottled beers. The pub is something of a local institution with regulars coming from miles around to spend time here. Local CAMRA pub of the Year 2023.
🌤✿◑⇌(London Bridge) ⊖🖪🐾🛜♫

SE1: Borough Market

George ★ ✓

75-77 Borough High Street, SE1 1NH
☎ (020) 7407 2056
Greene King IPA; house beer (by Greene King); 3 changing beers (often Greene King, Southwark, Timothy Taylor) Ⓗ
This Grade-I listed, 17th-century hostelry is London's only surviving galleried coaching inn, now occupying one side of a courtyard that it originally surrounded. It has been identified by CAMRA as having a nationally important historic pub interior. There are multiple rooms to explore and the ground floor Parliament Bar, in particular, contains some of the country's oldest purpose-fitted pub woodwork and an 18th century one-handed clock. The building is owned by the National Trust and leased to Greene King. 🌤✿◑⇌⊖(London Bridge)🖪🛜

Market Porter

9 Stoney Street, SE1 9AA
☎ (020) 7407 2495 ∰ themarketporter.co.uk
Harvey's Sussex Best Bitter; 5 changing beers (sourced nationally) Ⓗ
This classic, rustic, Victorian market pub next to the famous Borough Market has a licence to open from 6am to 8.30am during the week, to accommodate the market workers from whom it gets its name. Popular with locals and visitors alike, it can get busy, with drinkers spilling out onto the street. An upstairs wood-panelled restaurant serves a changing seasonal menu mainly focused on British classic dishes. Card payments only.
🌤◑&⇌⊖(London Bridge) 🖪🛜

Old King's Head

King's Head Yard, 45-49 Borough High Street, SE1 1NA
☎ (020) 7407 1550 ∰ theoldkingshead.uk.com
Harvey's Sussex Best Bitter; St Austell Proper Job; 2 changing beers (sourced nationally) Ⓗ
A traditional hostelry down a narrow, cobbled lane off Borough High Street. Stained-glass windows hint at a

bygone era and the pictures adorning the walls tell the story of a pub, and an area, that has a rich history. The layout inside is simple, with an L-shaped bar in one corner usually offering four cask ales on handpump. The clientele is a mix of tourists, office workers and visitors to the nearby Borough Market.
◐&≉⊖(London Bridge) 🚌🛜

Rake
14 Winchester Walk, SE1 9AG
☎ (020) 7407 0557
2 changing beers (sourced nationally) Ⓗ
On the edge of Borough Market, this small speciality beer bar prides itself on offering a high-quality, varied beer selection, and over the years has become a real global destination for beer aficionados and brewers. The ever-changing cask ales are complemented by a comprehensive range of bottled beers, mainly from North America and Europe, plus a small range of wines and spirits. Beer festivals, brewery tap takeovers and other themed beer selections all feature.
Q✿&≉⊖(London Bridge) 🚌🛜

SE1: Lambeth North

Hercules
2 Kennington Road, SE1 7BL
☎ (020) 7920 9092 ⊕ thehercules.co.uk
Dark Star Hophead; Fuller's London Pride; 2 changing beers (sourced nationally) Ⓗ
Having operated as a variety of restaurants over the preceding years, the Hercules reverted back to a pub in 2019 under the ownership of Fuller's. The decor is contemporary, including exposed brickwork and large, modern chandeliers. There are bars on both the ground and first floors, the former serving cask beer and the latter featuring a large shuffleboard table. A separate meeting room is also available. Food is served all day.
✿◐≉(Waterloo) ⊖♣🚌

SE1: Southwark

Ring
72 Blackfriars Road, SE1 8HA
☎ (020) 7620 0811 ⊕ theringbarlondon.co.uk
Sharp's Doom Bar; 3 changing beers (often Southwark) Ⓗ
A traditonal English pub with a twist, this one-bar inn is named after a famous boxing arena that stood across Blackfriars Road from 1910 until it was destroyed by bombs in WWII. Pictures of the rich local boxing history adorn the walls, including some of a former professional boxer who ran the pub until 2001. Pavement/patio seating is available outside under awnings. Major sporting events on terrestrial TV are shown. Thai food is served lunchtimes and evenings on weekdays and all day on Saturday. Card payment only.
ᗡ✿◐≉(Waterloo/Waterloo East) ⊖🚌🛜

SE1: Waterloo

Hole in the Wall
5 Mepham Street, SE1 8SQ
☎ (020) 7928 6196
7 changing beers (often Big Smoke, Brew York, Southwark) Ⓗ
In a railway arch across the road from the main entrance to Waterloo station, this long-time family-owned free house and stalwart real ale outlet enjoys the comforting rumble of trains overhead. It has a small, cosy front bar, a larger bar to the rear showing sport on TV and a small, heated patio at the back. It can get particularly busy

when there's a rugby game at Twickenham. Irish folk music is played on Sundays.
ᗡ✿≉(Waterloo/Waterloo East) ⊖🚌🐾🛜♫

King's Arms Ⓛ
25 Roupell Street, SE1 8TB
☎ (020) 7207 0784 ⊕ thekingsarmslondon.co.uk
Adnams Southwold Bitter; house beer (by Sharp's); 6 changing beers (sourced nationally) Ⓗ
Tucked away in a street of Victorian terraced cottages often used for filming, this Grade II-listed pub has been identified by CAMRA as having a regionally important historic pub interior. The narrow public bar and small saloon at the front and side share a horseshoe-shaped bar and display old pictures. The larger rear conservatory, packed with bric-a-brac, serves Thai food lunchtimes and evenings on weekdays, and all day at weekends. Drinking is allowed outside on the pavement. Card payment only. ᗡ◐≉(Waterloo/Waterloo East)⊖🚌🐾

Waterloo Tap
Arch 147 Sutton Walk, SE1 7ES
☎ (020) 3455 7436 ⊕ waterlootap.com
5 changing beers (often Adnams, Iron Pier, Redemption) Ⓐ
Located in a railway arch on the pedestrian route between the South Bank attractions and Waterloo rail and tube stations, this bar, one of the small Tap chain, is often crowded but has additional covered seating outside at the front and a narrow patio area at the rear. The cask ales and a cider are dispensed from taps mounted centrally on the copper bar-back and are listed, together with up to 20 draught keg beers, on a blackboard above. Card payment only.
ᗡ✿&≉⊖🚌🐾🛜

SE3: Blackheath

Hare & Billet ✅
1A Eliot Cottages, Hare & Billet Road, SE3 0QJ
☎ (020) 8852 2352 ⊕ hareandbillet.com
House beer (by Greene King); 3 changing beers (often By The Horns, Cronx, Oakham) Ⓗ
An inn of this name has existed on the site since at least 1732, though the current building dates from the 19th century. The decor is contemporary, with stripped natural-finish wood cladding and bare floorboards. Plastic glasses may be used in the summer for outdoor drinking, with customers enjoying views over the heath's open expanse. The pub overlooks the Hare and Billet Pond with its abundance of aquatic avian wildlife. Card payment only. ᗡ◐&≉♣🚌(380)🐾🛜

SE3: Blackheath Standard

British Oak ✅
109 Old Dover Road, SE3 8SU
☎ (020) 8305 1781 ⊕ britishoakblackheath.com
Harvey's Sussex Best Bitter; 2 changing beers (often Adnams) Ⓗ
An imposing three-storey Victorian pub with a fine cast iron veranda across the first floor. The traditional public bar and the wood-panelled saloon remain unconnected, each having a separate external entrance. Identified by CAMRA as having a regionally important historic pub interior, this former Courage house appeared in a number of early editions of the Guide and makes a welcome return this year. The food offering majors on pies. Regular live music and open mic nights are hosted.
ᗡ✿◐♣🚌🛜♫

SE4: Brockley

Brockley Barge ✓
184 Brockley Road, SE4 2RR
☎ (020) 8694 7690
Greene King IPA, Abbot; Sharp's Doom Bar; 2 changing beers (often Portobello, Sambrook's, Twickenham) ⊞
A former Courage house, now part of the Wetherspoon chain, a stone's throw from the railway station. This is a popular, thriving hub with a clientele reflecting the vibrant local area. It is laid out in a semi-horseshoe shape with a variety of seating spaces and all facilities on the same level. A small courtyard to the south side is well used in the summer. The name recalls the former Croydon Canal, where the railway line now runs.
Q❄✿❍❹♿⚌⊖🚪🌭🛜

SE4: Crofton Park

London Beer Dispensary
389 Brockley Road, SE4 2PH
☎ (020) 8694 6962
3 changing beers (often Siren, Southey) ⊞
This former wine bar is one of the handful of Beer Dispensary outlets run by Penge-based Southey brewery. The beers were previously gravity-dispensed but the counter now sports a set of handpumps, one of which serves cider. Alongside a Southey beer are two changing guest beers, usually from microbreweries. The bar is popular with families; children are welcome until the evening. Food is available to order, in partnership with the pizzeria next door. ✿❹⚌🚪🌭🛜

SE5: Camberwell

Stormbird
25 Camberwell Church Street, SE5 8TR
☎ (020) 7708 4460
3 changing beers (sourced nationally) ⊞
The sister pub to the Hermit's Cave across the road, offering a slightly more contemporary feel and attracting a mixed but generally younger crowd. There is a huge array of beers of all types on the bar, including four changing cask ales and an extensive bottled and canned beer selection. The choice encompasses brews from the UK, continental Europe and the US. Draught beers are available in third-pint measures.
❹⚌⊖(Denmark Hill) 🚪🛜

SE5: Denmark Hill

Fox on the Hill ✓
149 Denmark Hill, SE5 8EH
☎ (020) 7738 4756
Greene King Abbot; Ruddles Best Bitter; Sharp's Doom Bar; 4 changing beers (often Southwark, Surrey Hills, Twickenham) ⊞
An attractive and imposing brick-built Wetherspoon pub opposite Ruskin Park. A series of rooms, with quiet alcoves and screened booths, surrounds a central bar area. Framed prints celebrate the numerous historic figures and notable thinkers who lived nearby, often lending their names to the streets. A lawn at the front affords views across to central London and there are large gardens across the rear. The pub is particularly popular when Dulwich Hamlet FC is playing at home.
✿❹❹♿⚌⊖🚪🛜

SE6: Bellingham

Fellowship Inn
Randlesdown Road, SE6 3BT (close to station)
☎ (020) 7138 1084 🌐 fellowshipinn.co.uk
House beer (by Anspach & Hobday); 2 changing beers (often Anspach & Hobday, Brockley, Five Points) ⊞
A spacious, Grade II-listed 1920s' improved public house built in mock-Tudor style and designed by FG Newnham, house architect of Barclay Perkins Brewery. Reopened in 2019 following a major restoration, it has been identified by CAMRA as having a nationally important historic pub interior. Many original features remain, including wood panelling, partitioning between the two bars, Tudor-arched fireplaces and the central bar counter. To the rear is a spacious function room and downstairs is the beautifully restored Art Deco cinema. ✿❹♿⚌♣🚪🎵

SE8: Deptford

Dog & Bell ⏸ ✓
116 Prince Street, SE8 3JD
☎ (020) 8692 5664
Fuller's London Pride; 4 changing beers (often Clarkshaws, Forest Road, Redemption) ⊞
A Guide stalwart for over 30 years, this welcoming traditional pub, on a pedestrianised side street, has recently been extended into the premises next door. A lively bar and real fire in winter attract a broad mix of clientele including locals, cyclists and those strolling along the nearby Thames Path. The cask ales are complemented by a selection of Belgian bottled beers, malt whiskies and simple, tasty meals. Regular beer festivals are often themed around the UK patron saints' days. ✿❹❹♿⚌♣🚪🌭🛜🎵

SE9: Eltham

Long Pond
110 Westmount Road, SE9 1UT
☎ (020) 8331 6767 🌐 thelongpond.co.uk
House beer (by Tonbridge); 4 changing beers (often Goacher's, Hop Fuzz, Mad Cat) Ⓖ
In a neighbourhood previously lacking a local pub, this popular micropub is named after the pond in nearby Eltham Park North. The mainly Kentish cask ales are served from a chilled stillage room. Wine, gins, malt whiskies and Dudda's Tun real cider or perry are also available, along with limited bar snacks. Seating is mainly high benches and tables, though the rear snug features low tables and chairs. Children and dogs are not admitted. Card payment strongly preferred.
Q♿⚌🚪(B16) 🎵

Park Tavern
45 Passey Place, SE9 5DA
☎ (020) 8850 3216 🌐 parktaverneltham.co.uk
6 changing beers (often Butcombe, Koomor, St Austell) ⊞
A free house since 2022, this traditional Victorian pub retains original Truman's brewery tiled frontage and signage. The compact interior has an L-shaped bar with stylish lamps and chandeliers. Etched windows feature elegant drapes; decorative plates and pictures line the walls. Light background music is played. Plenty of outdoor seating is available, including a covered and heated rear garden. It has an impressive selection of craft beers and lagers, whiskies and wine. Lunchtime meals are served, except on Sunday. Q✿❹⚌♣🚪🌭

Rusty Bucket
11 Court Yard, SE9 5PR
☎ 07776 145990 🌐 therustybucket.pub

2 changing beers (often Harvey's, Kent, Siren) Ⓖ
Opened along micropub lines in 2018, the pub retains the original frontage of the redeveloped Crown. Inside, the walls are half-panelled and brightly painted. The place is run by a couple of friends who are enthusiastic and knowledgeable about beers. The cask ales and some real ciders are dispensed from a walk-in chilled cellar cupboard. A large range of keg draught, bottled and canned beers is on offer. Live music sessions are held on Sunday. Card payment only. ✆ ♿ ♣ ● ⊟ ❀ ☆ 🎜

SE10: East Greenwich

River Ale House
131 Woolwich Road, SE10 0RJ
☎ 07963 127595 ⊕ theriveralehouse.com
6 changing beers (often Goacher's, Iron Pier, Kent) Ⓗ/Ⓖ
A multi-award winning hostelry in the micropub style, encompassing two rooms with a rustic feel and a ramp between them. The cask ales and ciders are dispensed from a chilled room behind the bar counter. Wines and spirits are also available. Pizzas are delivered in partnership with a nearby supplier. This friendly, family-run house has become a part of the local community and has also developed a wider following.
❀ ♿ �₮ (Westcombe Park) ♣ ● ⊟ ❀ ☆ 🎜

SE10: Greenwich

Morden Arms
1 Brand Street, SE10 8SP
☎ (020) 8858 2189
Sharp's Doom Bar; 3 changing beers (often Brockley, Iron Pier) Ⓗ
An ex-Courage corner house, now an eclectic independent pub with a strong orientation to recorded music, plus live music most weekends. Unpretentious, with no external pub sign or name even, this is one of a dying breed of back-street boozers in the area. It has a clientele of locals and music lovers. Cribbage night is Monday. The beer range is mainly from London breweries, with guest ales from further afield appearing occasionally. Cash payment only. ✆ ❀ ≏ ⊖ ♣ ⊟ ❀ ☆ 🎜

Plume of Feathers ✔
19 Park Vista, SE10 9LZ
☎ (020) 8858 1661 ⊕ plumeoffeathers-greenwich.co.uk
Harvey's Sussex Best Bitter; 2 changing beers (often Bexley, Brockley, Wantsum) Ⓗ
With parts dating from the late 17th century, this cosy and quiet historic pub sits opposite the northern wall of Greenwich Park, close to the National Maritime Museum. The maritime association is reflected inside with numerous interesting historical paintings and memorabilia. Outside is a pleasant rear garden area. Meals are served daily in both the bar and the separate rear restaurant. It has a loyal local following and is also popular with tourists and visitors.
✆ ❀ ◑ ≏ (Maze Hill) ⊖ (Cutty Sark) ⊟ ❀ ☆

SE11: Kennington

Old Red Lion
42 Kennington Park Road, SE11 4RS
☎ (020) 7735 4312 ⊕ theoldredlion.uk
Portobello Westway Pale Ale; 2 changing beers (sourced locally) Ⓗ
This Grade II-listed hostelry, now run by Portobello brewery, was rebuilt by Hoare and Co in about 1933 and designed in the Brewers' Tudor style by renowned inter-war pub architect Sydney C Clark. It has been identified

by CAMRA as having a regionally important historic pub interior. Retained original features include the central servery, low connecting doors between the two bars, exposed wooden beams, fireplace surrounds and glazed panels. Background music is often playing.
✆ ❀ ◑ ≏ (Elephant & Castle) ⊖ ⊟ ❀ ☆

SE14: New Cross

Royal Albert
460 New Cross Road, SE14 6TJ
☎ (020) 8692 3737 ⊕ royalalbertpub.co.uk
4 changing beers (often Five Points, Portobello, Southwark) Ⓗ
Now run by Portobello brewery, this Grade II-listed Victorian inn retains the original etched-glass windows and bar-back. The recently extended, spacious interior is furnished with wood panelling, ornate lamps and a mix of seating including chesterfield sofas. The open kitchen at the rear serves a selection of distinctive and enticing dishes. Monday is quiz night, comedy features every third Wednesday of the month and there is a live jazz session on Sunday evening. ✆ ❀ ◑ ≏ ⊖ ❀ ☆ 🎜

Shirker's Rest
9 Lewisham Way, SE14 6PP
☎ (020) 8091 4584 ⊕ theshirkersrest.co.uk
House beer (by Anspach & Hobday); **3 changing beers** (often Brockley, Burning Sky, Thornbridge) Ⓗ
A micropub opened in 2022, opposite Goldsmiths University, as a joint venture between popular local bloggers Deserter and pop-up pub specialists Camberwell Shark. Above the ground floor bar, an upstairs drinking area also hosts exhibitions and events showcasing local talent. There is limited outdoor seating. It offers seven craft beers on tap, bag-in-box cider, wine and spirits. Bar snacks are augmented by a free delivery arrangement with a local pizzeria. Card payments only.
❀ ◑ ♿ ⊖ (New Cross/New Cross Gate) ♣ ● ⊟ ❀ ☆

SE15: Nunhead

Ivy House
40 Stuart Road, SE15 3BE
☎ (020) 7277 8233 ⊕ ivyhousenunhead.co.uk
4 changing beers (often Brick, By The Horns, Southwark) Ⓗ
This spacious, 1930s, former Truman house was London's first community-owned pub. The largely unchanged, wood-panelled interior has been identified by CAMRA as being of regional historic importance. Behind the small front bar are two much larger rooms, one with a Tudor feel, the other having Art Deco detailing. Of particular note is the brown and white spittoon trough tiling, a feature of many inter-war Truman pubs. The venue's rich live music history continues to this day.
Q ✆ ❀ ◑ ♣ ⊞ (343,484) ❀ ☆ 🎜

SE16: Rotherhithe

Mayflower
117 Rotherhithe Street, SE16 4NF
☎ (020) 7237 4088 ⊕ mayflowerpub.co.uk
House beer (by Greene King); **5 changing beers** (often Bexley, St Austell) Ⓗ
This nautical-themed pub celebrates the Mayflower's historic journey to New England. Those with a family connection may sign their Descendants Book. The 16th-century tavern-style interior actually dates from 1957 but has been identified by CAMRA as having some regional historic importance. To the rear is a covered, wooden jetty over the River Thames. A popular place for tourists,

this is the only pub licensed to sell UK and US postage stamps. The house beer is the appropriately named Scurvy Ale. ✪🌢➊➋⊖●🔒🍴 (381,C10)

SE18: Plumstead Common

Plum Tree
154 Plumstead Common Road, SE18 2UL
☎ (020) 3556 0277
3 changing beers (often Arbor, Brew York, Bristol Beer Factory) 🅖
A micropub located in Birds Nest Hollow, as the area is locally known. Opened in 2019, the venue is now well settled into the local pub scene and conversation between locals and visitors is almost inevitable. The three changing cask ales and up to eight real ciders or perries are served on gravity dispense from a chilled cellar room. There are also seven craft beers on tap. To the rear is an outdoor drinking area. ✪♣●🔒

SE22: East Dulwich

East Dulwich Tavern
1 Lordship Lane, SE22 8EW
☎ (020) 8693 1316 ● eastdulwichtavern.com
4 changing beers (often Sambrook's, Twickenham, Volden) 🅗
An imposing, traditional building in a prominent corner position and operated by the Antic pub company. The spacious interior, with a mix of vintage and recycled decor, is classic boozer but in tune with the times and alive with customers. The kitchen menu is varied and of good quality. Previously a hotel, the upper storeys are now offices, although the first-floor masonic hall with its own bar, known as the Lodge, is available for hire and also hosts jazz concerts. 🌢✪➊➋♿≉♣🔒🍴�🎵

SE23: Forest Hill

Blythe Hill Tavern ★
319 Stanstead Road, SE23 1JB
☎ (020) 8690 5176 ● blythehilltavern.org.uk
Dark Star Hophead; Harvey's Sussex Best Bitter; Sharp's Sea Fury; 1 changing beer (often Adnams, Brockley, Timothy Taylor) 🅗
A multiple award-winning suburban pub with a longstanding licensee. This friendly Grade II-listed Victorian local has an unusual three-bar layout that has been identified by CAMRA as a nationally important historic pub interior. Alongside the cask beers are up to 13 ciders, many of them real. In two of the bars TV screens show sporting events, especially horse racing. Live traditional Irish music is played on Thursday evening. There is a spacious outdoor seating area at the rear. Q🌢➊➋♿≉(Catford/Catford Bridge) ●🔒😊🎵

Addiscombe

Claret & Ale
5 Bingham Corner, Lower Addiscombe Road, CRO 7AA
☎ (020) 8656 7452
Palmers IPA; 5 changing beers (often Palmers, Sambrook's, Twickenham) 🅗
This small, privately owned and friendly free house has regularly been local CAMRA Pub of the Year, and is making its 36th appearance in this Guide. It is a community pub where conversation is king, although sports are shown on silent screens. The changing beers often include another from Palmers; others are mainly from microbreweries all over the UK. A board facing the bar shows those beers that are on or are waiting in the cellar. ♿🔒😊🎵

Cricketers ✓
47 Shirley Road, CRO 7ER
☎ (020) 3654 9848 ● cricketersshirley.co.uk
Harvey's Sussex Best Bitter; Sharp's Doom Bar 🅗
Traditional community pub with a thriving darts following. The main bar boasts three screens for different sports and two real fires in winter, while the back area has a fourth screen and another fire. The floor and furniture were modernised in 2017, and the pub has capacity for guest ales to supplement the regular beers offered. 🌢🌢♿♣P🔒😊🎵♪

Barnehurst

Bird & Barrel 🅛
100 Barnehurst Road, DA7 6HG
House beer (by Bexley); 2 changing beers (sourced nationally; often Bexley) 🅗
A micropub opened in 2018 in a former tropical fish emporium. Owned by Cliff and Jane of Bexley brewery, it is in effect their brewery tap. A small one-roomer with a handful of standard-height tables, it has a covered, secluded beer garden at the back. House beer Hills & Holes commemorates the old name of the lane serving the station nearby. Three keg beers plus wines and spirits are also available. Last orders are 30 minutes before closing time. Q🌢🌢≉●🔒😊🎵

Beckenham

Bricklayers Arms
237 High Street, BR3 1BN
☎ (020) 8402 0007
St Austell Tribute, Proper Job; 2 changing beers (sourced nationally) 🅗
Traditional high-street pub providing a friendly welcome to a clientele of all ages. There is an open log fire in winter and a covered outdoor seating area with heaters and even a TV screen. The changing guest ales often reflect customers' recommendations. Occasional beer festivals are held. Live music is popular; both local and visiting bands play here. Live sports fixtures are also shown. Sunday hours apply on most bank holidays. 🌢🌢≉(Junction/Clock House) ♿(Junction) ♣🔒😊🎵♪

Bexleyheath

Furze Wren ✓
6 Market Place, Broadway Square, DA6 7DY
☎ (020) 8298 2590
Greene King Abbot; Ruddles Best Bitter; Sharp's Doom Bar; 7 changing beers (often Brains, Courage, Ringwood) 🅗
Spacious Wetherspoon pub named after a local bird, better known as the Dartford Warbler. It is at the heart of the shopping area, with buses serving every route through town, and attracts a wide clientele. Plenty of seating and large windows make it a great place to eat, drink and people-watch. Local history panels are displayed around the walls. Alcoholic drinks are served from 9am. No new admittance after 11pm. Q🌢🌢➊➋♿♣🔒😊

Kentish Belle
8 Pickford Lane, DA7 4QW
☎ (020) 3417 2050 ● thekentishbelle.com
7 changing beers (often Arbor, No Frills Joe, Thornbridge) 🅗
Located next to the station, Bexleyheath's first micropub has solid walnut furniture and a distinctly Art Deco feel. William Morris wallpaper is a nod to the artist who lived at the Red House, just under a mile away. Outdoor

seating is provided during the summer. Regular events include tap takeovers, quiz nights and mini-festivals.Various unusual beers, plus real cider and perry, are served by gravity from a chilled cellar room. Greater London CAMRA Cider Pub of the Year 2019.
Q ⓢ ⇌ ♣ ♠ P ⓓ ⯃ ❀ ♠

Long Haul ⓨ
149 Long Lane, DA7 5AE
☎ 07753 617874 ⊕ thelonghaul.co.uk
3 changing beers Ⓖ
Opened in 2020 in what had been a tattoo parlour in the local shopping area in Long Lane, this micropub is handy for the nearby Indian restaurant. Inside the bar counter is towards the back, with bench seating and standard tables provided. Usually there is also seating on the forecourt. Predominantly Kentish real ales and ciders are served from a rear chilled cellar room. Last orders are requested 30 minutes before closing time. Local CAMRA Pub of the Year 2022 and 2023. Q ❀ ♠ ⓓ ⯃ (301,401) ❀

Robin Hood & Little John Ⓛ
78 Lion Road, DA6 8PF
☎ (020) 8303 1128 ⊕ robinhoodbexleyheath.co.uk
Adnams Southwold Bitter; Bexley Bexley's Own Beer; Fuller's London Pride; Harvey's Sussex Best Bitter; 2 changing beers (often Bexley, Shepherd Neame, Westerham) Ⓗ
A back-street local dating from the 1830s, when it was surrounded by fields. Real ales come mostly from independent breweries, including Bexley. It has a good reputation for its home-cooked food at lunchtimes (no food Sun) with Italian specials, which can be eaten at tables made from old Singer sewing machines. A frequent local CAMRA Pub of the Year and regional winner three times, Ray and Katerina have been running it for 43 years. Over-21s only. Q ❀ ⓓ ⯃ (B13) ❀ ♪

Blackfen

Broken Drum Ⓛ
308 Westwood Lane, DA15 9PT
☎ 07803 131678 ⊕ thebrokendrum.co.uk
3 changing beers (sourced nationally) Ⓖ
A micropub named after an inn from Terry Pratchett's Discworld series – you can't beat it! Seating is a settle in each of the bay windows and a variety of tables and chairs, plus pavement tables and chairs for fair-weather drinking (until 8pm). With Cheesy Thursday the first Thursday of each month, occasional quizzes and excursions, this is a real community pub. It has won awards from both CAMRA and the Society for the Preservation of Beers from the Wood.
Q ⓢ ♣ ♠ P ⓓ ⯃ (51,132) ❀ ♠

Bromley

Partridge
194 High Street, BR1 1HE
☎ (020) 8464 7656 ⊕ partridgebromley.co.uk
Dark Star Hophead; Fuller's London Pride, ESB; Gale's HSB; 2 changing beers (often Butcombe, Fuller's) Ⓗ
Grade II-listed former NatWest bank, now a spacious Fuller's Ale & Pie house, retaining many original features including the high ceilings and chandeliers. There are two snug rooms off the long main bar, plus a small back patio. An upmarket food menu is offered, including vegetarian choices. Located by the Market Square, the pub is popular with shoppers and theatregoers for the nearby Churchill Theatre, as well as those drawn by its live music on Saturday evenings.
Q ⓢ ❀ ⓓ ⅋ ⇌ (North/South) ⯃ ❀ ♠ ♪

Red Lion ⊘
10 North Road, BR1 3LG
☎ (020) 8460 2691 ⊕ redlionbromley.co.uk
Greene King IPA, Abbot; Harvey's Sussex Best Bitter; 1 changing beer (often Black Sheep, Jennings, Oakham) Ⓗ
A traditional, well-kept hostelry in the quiet back streets just north of Bromley town centre, the Red Lion is well worth seeking out. Now in its 27th consecutive year in the Guide, this is the only pub in the borough to have featured in every edition since the local branch was formed in 2011. It retains many original features, including tiling, while an extensive library of books dominates one wall. Bar food consists of artisan pizzas.
Q ❀ ⓓ ⇌ (North) ♣ ⯃

Star & Garter
227 High Street, BR1 1NZ
⊕ starandgarterbromley.com
7 changing beers (often Bristol Beer Factory, Fyne, Siren) Ⓗ
A late 19th-century Grade II-listed pub, reopened in 2016 after more than two years' closure and offering real ale for the first time. The building has been completely refurbished and boasts eight handpumps, one of which frequently dispenses real cider. Real ales are usually from outside the mainstream, with local and regional microbreweries strongly represented. Customers are welcome to order in food from nearby takeaways. Local CAMRA Pub of the Year 2018-2020.
ⓢ ♠ ⇌ (North/South) ♠ ⯃ ❀ ♠

Chislehurst

Cockpit ⓨ
4 Royal Parade, BR7 6NR TQ443352
☎ 07946 100018 ⊕ thecockpitchislehurst.co.uk
House beer (by BritHop); 7 changing beers (sourced nationally) Ⓖ
Opened in 2020, this micropub has quickly proved to be a popular addition to the local community. A choice of real ales is available from small breweries from around the country. The deceptively spacious premises are shared with a florist and there is plenty of seating inside, as well as wooden panelling and exposed brickwork, plus more benches at the front. The pub name comes from the ancient cockpit situated nearby on Chislehurst Common. Local CAMRA Pub of the Year 2023. Q ⓢ ♠ ⯃ ❀

Crayford

Penny Farthing Ⓛ
3 Waterside, DA1 4JJ
☎ 07368 448446 ⊕ pennyfarthingcrayford.co.uk
4 changing beers (often Old Dairy, Wantsum, Whitstable) Ⓖ
Bexley's second micropub, opened in 2014. Ale and cider are served from a cold room with a viewing window. A charity fine is levied should your mobile phone ring. Kentish brewers feature mostly, with an increasing cider range supplementing Dudda's Tun and Westons. Pavement seating during summer overlooks a small riverside park. Usually open on bank holidays, it is a good venue to hold local public events. A former local CAMRA Pub of the Year and London regional runner-up.
Q ❀ ⇌ ♣ ♠ ⯃ ⅋ ❀

Croydon

Builders Arms
65 Leslie Park Road, CR0 6TP
☎ (020) 8654 1803 ⊕ buildersarmscroydon.co.uk

Dark Star Hophead; Fuller's London Pride, ESB; 1 changing beer (sourced locally) Ⓗ

A back-street community local opened in the 19th century, serving beers from the Fuller's range. The two bars each have their own character. The smaller public-style bar has a dartboard and a large screen TV showing sport. The larger saloon bar with comfortable seating also has sports TV and leads to a pleasant garden. Events include quiz night on a Tuesday.

⏴✿◑&≢(East) ⏪(Lebanon Rd) ♣🖳🐾🎵

Dog & Bull ✓

24 Surrey Street, CR0 1RG

☎ (020) 3971 5747 ⊕ dogandbullcroydon.co.uk

Young's London Original, London Special; 2 changing beers (sourced nationally) Ⓗ

With origins back in the 16th century, this Grade II-listed pub has an island bar and stained-glass windows. It is a favourite with local traders as well as visitors to the Surrey Street market. The large garden, an unexpected find in central Croydon, has been brought up to date with booths equipped with TV, large awnings and a bar and barbecue in the summer. The upstairs room is now a restaurant area.

⏴✿◑≢(East/West) ⏪(George St/Reeves Corner) ⊖(West) 🖳🐾

George Ⓛ ✓

17-21 George Street, CR0 1LA

☎ (020) 8649 9077

Greene King IPA, Abbot; Sharp's Doom Bar; Thornbridge Jaipur IPA; 11 changing beers (often Oakham, Surrey Hills) Ⓗ

A converted shop, this town-centre pub is named after a former Croydon coaching inn, the George & Dragon. The raised rear bar, with a ramp for access, is lined with booths and has six handpumps, often showcasing beers from breweries such as Surrey Hills, Oakham, and Thornbridge. The front bar offers a wider mix of beers, including real ales from local breweries and the Wetherspoon national range. The pub also hosts occasional tap takeovers.

⏴◑&≢(East/West) ⏪(George St/Reeves Corner) ⊖(West) 🖳🛜

Green Dragon Ⓛ ✓

58-60 High Street, CR0 1NA

☎ (020) 8667 0684

8 changing beers Ⓗ

This former bank building appeals to drinkers of all ages. The pub serves up to eight cask ales and other draught beers from local and national breweries. The food menu includes vegetarian and vegan options. The upstairs function room is available for hire and hosts weekly events such as quizzes and poker, and there are ukelele jam sessions on the first and third Sunday of the month.

⏴◑&≢(East/West) ⏪(George St/Reeves Corner) ⊖(West) ♣🖳🛜🎵

Royal Standard

1 Sheldon Street, CR0 1SS

☎ (020) 8680 3106 ⊕ royalstandardcroydon.co.uk

Dark Star Hophead; Fuller's London Pride, ESB; Gale's HSB Ⓗ

A street-corner local in the shadow of the Croydon flyover, making its 35th appearance in this Guide. This quiet retreat just south of the town centre has a single bar with four different drinking areas. Etched windows, wood panelling and owls feature throughout the pub. A small, secluded garden area is located across the road.

⏴✿◑⏪(Church St/George St) ♣🔶🖳🐾

Downe

Queen's Head Ⓛ ✓

25 High Street, BR6 7US TQ432616

☎ (01689) 852145 ⊕ queensheaddowne.com

Harvey's Sussex Best Bitter; 3 changing beers (often Bexley, Northdown, Westerham) Ⓗ

Attractive, traditional venue with open fireplaces, dating from 1565 and named following a visit to Downe by Queen Elizabeth I. There are several dining areas that offer a daily menu including home-made pies and specials. In the centre of this historic country village but less than 20 minutes by bus from Bromley or Orpington, it is popular all year round with walkers and visitors to nearby Down House, the home of Charles Darwin.

⏴✿◑♣🖳(146,R8) 🐾🛜🎵

Hayes

Real Ale Way Ⓛ

55 Station Approach, BR2 7EB

☎ 07446 897885

House beer (by Tonbridge); 9 changing beers (often Larkins, Mad Cat, Whitstable) Ⓖ

Opened in 2018, this family-owned micropub offers a welcome choice for local drinkers and rail commuters alike. It overlooks the entrance to Hayes station and numerous bus routes stop outside. Up to nine Kentish real ales are served from a cold room. The Kent theme extends to the wines and spirits, as well as to the bar snacks. The premises, once a bank and more recently an accountancy office, are quite large by micropub standards. Q≢🔶🖳🐾🎵

Keston

Greyhound ✓

Commonside, BR2 6BP TQ413646

☎ (01689) 856338 ⊕ greyhound.pub

Sharp's Doom Bar; Timothy Taylor Landlord; 4 changing beers (sourced nationally) Ⓗ

A popular local with an enthusiastic and welcoming landlord. It overlooks the common and is on walking routes including the London Outer Orbital Path, but is also easily accessed by bus from Bromley. The pub is at the heart of village life, with a crowded calendar of events, detailed in its newsletter. A beer festival is held during the Easter weekend, when up to 15 less well-known beers can be enjoyed.

Q⏴✿◑♣🔶🖳(146,246) 🐾🛜🎵

Orpington

Orpington Liberal Club Ⓛ

7 Station Road, BR6 0RZ

☎ (01689) 820882 ⊕ orpingtonliberalclub.co.uk

5 changing beers Ⓗ

Friendly club serving over 200 different cask ales every year, mainly from smaller breweries, across a range of beer styles. Real cider and bottled lower-alcohol and gluten-free beers are also available. Two real ale festivals are held each year. The club is a hub of the community, hosting many events in its spacious hall and supporting local charities. Regularly voted local CAMRA Club of the Year and a national finalist in 2020. A CAMRA/NULC card is required for entry.

Q⏴✿≢♣🔶P🖳🐾🛜🎵

Petts Wood

One Inn the Wood 🅛

209 Petts Wood Road, BR5 1LA

☎ 07799 535982 ⊕ oneinnthewood.co.uk

House beer (by Tonbridge); 4 changing beers (often Kent, Ramsgate, Tonbridge) 🅖

The first micropub in the area, opened in a former wine bar near the station in 2014, and winner of several CAMRA awards. Seating is on benches, with a large woodland backdrop dominating the left-hand wall. Beer is served from a glass-fronted cool room. Wine, gin and soft drinks are also sold, together with a range of mainly locally produced snacks. Families and dogs are welcome. Local CAMRA Pub of the Year 2022. Q⏚⪼≢●🖨🐾

Selsdon

Golden Ark

186 Addington Road, CR2 8LB

☎ (020) 8651 0700 ⊕ thegoldenark.co.uk

4 changing beers (sourced locally) 🅗

Croydon's first micropub, situated in Selsdon's main street, and offering a full range of alcoholic drinks. Bottled and canned beers and cider are also available for off-sales. Boards detailing the current beers are hung on the ceiling beam above the corner bar. The bar and some of the wooden tabletops have been artistically finished and artworks adorn the walls. The pub has won local CAMRA awards and has strong links with the community. ⏚⪾♣●🖨🐾🛜♪

South Croydon

Crown & Sceptre

32 Junction Road, CR2 6RB

☎ (020) 8688 8037 ⊕ crownandsceptresouthcroydon.co.uk

Dark Star Hophead; Fuller's London Pride, ESB; 2 changing beers (often Fuller's, Gale's) 🅗

A quiet, traditional side-street pub, with its name etched into one of the front windows. The single bar has been extended towards a patio at the rear. The walls carry pictures of local scenes and an impressive brewery mirror. A cabinet of trophies attests to the local golfing society's successes. The food leans towards pizza, although other dishes are available. ⏚🅐①⪾♣P🖨🐾🛜

West Wickham

Real Ale Way 🅛

75 Station Road, BR4 0PX

Larkins Pale; Tonbridge Traditional Ale; 5 changing beers 🅖

Opened in 2021, the second Real Ale Way micropub in Bromley borough operates in a similar manner to its sister in Hayes. Up to seven cask ales, almost all of which are sourced from smaller breweries in Kent, are dispensed by gravity from a cold room. A former soft furnishings shop, it has large windows, exposed floorboards and displays pictures by local artists to complement the contemporary interior. Q≢●🖨(119,194) 🐾🛜

SOUTH-WEST LONDON
SW1: Belgravia

Antelope

22-24 Eaton Terrace, SW1W 8EZ

☎ (020) 7824 8512 ⊕ antelope-eaton-terrace.co.uk

Fuller's London Pride, ESB; Gale's Seafarers Ale; 2 changing beers (often Dark Star, Fuller's) 🅗

Dating back to 1827, this Fuller's venue spent several years as an M&B Nicholson's pub until 2005. Original preserved features include etched-glass windows, a side room used as a snug, and the central bar. The upstairs bar and side room can be hired for functions. This is an upmarket house and the clientele consists mainly of local professionals. The pub plays cricket matches against the Churchill Arms in Notting Hill. Q⏚①●⊖(Sloane Sq)🖨🛜

Fox & Hounds ✅

29 Passmore Street, SW1W 8HR

☎ (020) 7730 6367 ⊕ foxandhoundssw1.co.uk

Young's London Original; 2 changing beers (often St Austell, Timothy Taylor) 🅗

Until 1998, the only remaining beer house (pub without a spirit license) in London, if not the country. The Beer Act 1830 allowed any ratepayer to set one up in their home on payment of a small fee and the estate landlord who granted the licence here in 1869, the future Duke of Westminster, was a temperance campaigner opposed to spirits. No music and no TVs. It is rumoured to be the pub where Coronation Street was devised. Q⊖(Sloane Sq) 🖨🐾🛜

Star Tavern

6 Belgrave Mews West, SW1X 8HT

☎ (020) 7235 3019 ⊕ star-tavern-belgravia.co.uk

Fuller's London Pride, ESB; 3 changing beers (often Butcombe, Dark Star, Wimbledon) 🅗

Down a mews, near embassies and rich in the history of the powerful and famous, this is rumoured to be where the Great Train Robbery was planned. A popular Fuller's pub where local residents, business people and embassy staff rub shoulders with casual visitors, it has featured in all 51 editions of this Guide. Beers from the wood may occasionally be served here and sometimes a special Fuller's beer can be found. Upstairs is a function room. ⏚①●⊖(Hyde Park Corner/Knightsbridge) ♣🖨🐾🛜

SW1: Pimlico

Cask Pub & Kitchen

6 Charlwood Street, SW1V 2EE

☎ (020) 7630 7225 ⊕ caskpubandkitchen.com

Changing beers (sourced nationally) 🅗

Formerly the Pimlico Tram, the Cask was converted to a beer destination 12 years ago by owners who have since also found renown for the Craft Beer Co chain. Tenhandpumps serve an ever-changing selection of real ales from microbreweries, and a vast range of bottled beers from the UK and around the world complements some unusual draught choices. Burgers feature on the weekday menu, with roasts on Sundays until late afternoon. A former local CAMRA Pub of the Year. ⏚🅐①≢(Victoria) ⊖🖨🐾🛜♪

SW1: St James's

Red Lion ★

2 Duke of York Street, SW1Y 6JP

☎ (020) 7321 0782 ⊕ redlionmayfair.co.uk

Fuller's Oliver's Island, London Pride, ESB; Gale's Seafarers Ale; 2 changing beers (often Fuller's) 🅗

Close to the upmarket shops in Jermyn Street, this is a deservedly celebrated little gem, worth visiting just for its historic pub interior, identified by CAMRA as nationally important and, in particular, its spectacular Victorian etched and cut mirrors and glass. The Grade II-listed building dates from 1821 and was given a new frontage in 1871. With little space inside, visitors often spill out onto the pavement. Beware of the precipitous steps down to the toilets. Food is served at lunchtimes only. ➰◀◑⊖(Green Park/Piccadilly Circus) 🚇❀🛜

SW1: Victoria

Wetherspoons ✅
Unit 5, Upper Concourse, Victoria Station, Terminus Place, SW1V 1JT
☎ (020) 7931 0445
Fuller's London Pride; Greene King IPA; Sharp's Doom Bar; 7 changing beers (often Adnams, Sambrook's, Windsor & Eton) Ⓗ
Above WHSmith, overlooking the station concourse and accessed mainly by escalators, this pub has a bright café bar atmosphere. Features include blue and cream tiling, two curved bars with marble-style tops and banquettes along the opposite side. TV screens show times of train departures. Note that British Transport Police sometimes close the bar when football fans are due.
Q➰◀◑&⇌⊖🚇🛜

Willow Walk Ⓛ ✅
25 Wilton Road, SW1V 1LW
☎ (020) 7828 2953
Greene King IPA; Sharp's Doom Bar; 6 changing beers (often East London, Portobello, Windsor & Eton) Ⓗ
Ground-floor Wetherspoon pub converted from a Woolworths in 1999, extending from opposite the eastern side entrance to Victoria station back to Vauxhall Bridge Road, with entrances on both streets. Some wood panelling, a fairly low ceiling and subdued lighting create a warm atmosphere. Friendly and attentive staff look after a mixed clientele including families. Some London-brewed guest beers are usually available. Alcoholic drinks are served from 9am. Q➰◀◑&⇌⊖🚇🛜

SW1: Westminster

Buckingham Arms
62 Petty France, SW1H 9EU
☎ (020) 7222 3386 🌐 buckinghamarms.com
Young's London Original, London Special; 3 changing beers (often Young's) Ⓗ
Said to have once been a hat shop, the Bell opened here in the 1720s and was renamed the Black Horse in the 1740s. Rebuilt in 1898, renamed again in 1901 and substantially renovated in recent years, it is another pub that has appeared in all 51 editions of this Guide. A mix of modern and traditional seats and tables, high and low, draws civil servants, visitors and the occasional MP. Open Sunday afternoons from the end of March through the summer. ➰◀◑⊖(St James's Park)🚇

Speaker ✅
46 Great Peter Street, SW1P 2HA
☎ (020) 7222 4589
Timothy Taylor Landlord; 4 changing beers (sourced nationally; often Hammerton, London Brewing, Sambrook's) Ⓗ
A friendly pine-panelled one-bar local decorated with parliamentary caricatures. Dating from 1729 or earlier, the Castle, renamed the Elephant & Castle around 1800 and the Speaker from 1999, was part of the Devil's Acre slum next to the world's first public gas works. The pub now welcomes local estate residents, office workers and the occasional MP, all of whom enjoy the attractive range of beers and the hot bagels. No music, TV or children. ⊖(St James's Park)🚇🛜

SW4: Clapham

King & Co
100 Clapham Park Road, SW4 7BZ
☎ (020) 7498 1971 🌐 thekingandco.uk
3 changing beers (often Adnams, Portobello, Twickenham) Ⓗ
Popular with the after-work crowd, this Portobello outlet in Clapham ticks all the boxes. Two real ciders and two or three real ales are served by genial staff in a buzzy atmosphere. Pop-up food enterprises take charge of the kitchen on a frequently changing basis. There are tables outside on the heated front terrace for alfresco drinking and eating when the weather is favourable.
➰❀◀◑⊖(Common) ●🚇❀🛜

Prince of Wales ✅
38 Old Town, SW4 0LB
☎ (020) 7622 4964 🌐 powsw4.com
Harvey's Sussex Best Bitter; Timothy Taylor Landlord; 1 changing beer (sourced nationally) Ⓗ
This is one of the few remaining drinkers' pubs in the Old Town area of Clapham and its interior has similarly ignored passing trends. Bric-a-brac adorns the ceiling and old prints and pictures line the walls. The falcon emblem of the pub's previous owners, the original Lacons brewery of Great Yarmouth, features in the charming tiled fireplace and on an exterior plaque. Bench tables outside the front are provided for alfresco drinking.
➰❀⊖(Common) 🚇❀🛜

SW5: Earls Court

King's Head
17 Hogarth Place, SW5 0QT
☎ (020) 7373 5239 🌐 kingsheadearlscourt.co.uk
Fuller's Oliver's Island, London Pride; 2 changing beers (often Fuller's, Robinson's) Ⓗ
A comfortable, friendly corner pub with a modernised interior, hidden away off the busy Earls Court Road; the building is a 1937 rebuild of the oldest (circa 17th century) licensed premises in the area. Seating is a mixture of high stools around tall tables. Three Fuller's cask ales are supplemented by a guest, usually from another local brewery. Upstairs is a separate dining room. Alcoholic drinks are served from 11am. On Monday evenings there is a quiz.
➰◑&⇌(West Brompton) ⊖🚇❀🛜

SW6: Fulham

Lillie Langtry ✅
19 Lillie Road, SW6 1UE
☎ (020) 3637 6690 🌐 thelillielangtry.co.uk
4 changing beers (often Park, Timothy Taylor, Twickenham) Ⓗ
Fulham's oldest surviving 19th-century pub, built in 1835 as the Lillie Arms and named after owner Sir John Scott Lillie. Originally a watering hole for the nearby Kensington Canal, later to become the West London Railway, it was renamed in 1979 after the famous actress and socialite who reputedly entertained many noblemen including Bertie, Prince of Wales. Real ales were introduced with the extensive 2016 refurbishment by Hippo Inns. ❀◀◑&⇌⊖(West Brompton)🚇❀🛜♫

SW6: Parsons Green

White Horse Ⓛ ✅
1-3 Parsons Green, SW6 4UL
☎ (020) 7736 2115 🌐 whitehorsesw6.com
6 changing beers Ⓗ

Destination Mitchells & Butlers pub that normally boasts five guest beers on handpump and an international selection of bottled beers. Regular beer and food matching events take place as well as beer festivals; the Old Ale Festival in late November has run for 38 years, with a stillage in the Coach House, normally reserved for dining. The pub can get busy when Chelsea FC are playing at home, but upstairs there is room to escape the crowds. Q♿☆✦❶⟊♿➘⊖(22,424)✿❄

SW7: Gloucester Road

Queen's Arms
30 Queen's Gate Mews, SW7 5QL
☎ (020) 7823 9293 ⊕ thequeensarmskensington.co.uk
St Austell Proper Job; Sharp's Doom Bar; Timothy Taylor Landlord; 3 changing beers (often Adnams, Harvey's, Hogs Back) Ⓗ
Lovely corner mews pub, discreetly tucked away off Queen's Gate, well worth seeking out for its real ales and its large range of interesting draught and bottled beers, malt whiskies and other spirits. Note the unusual curved doors. The clientele reflects the location: affluent locals, students from Imperial College and musicians from, and visitors to, the nearby Royal Albert Hall. It is wise to reserve a table. ⟊❶➘⊖❄❄

SW8: Battersea Park

Mason's Arms
169 Battersea Park Road, SW8 4BT
☎ (020) 7622 2007 ⊕ masons-arms-battersea.co.uk
Fuller's London Pride; 2 changing beers (often Dark Star, Fuller's) Ⓗ
Extensively refurbished in 2019, this stripped-back and opened-out Fuller's pub in a Grade II-listed bulding is almost opposite Battersea Park station and attracts a fairly young clientele. There is attractive floor tiling and glazed brickwork around the bar, which has has 23 draught lines (20 keg and three cask). The patio to the side is heated in winter for alfresco drinking. Information boards on a rear wall explain a range of brewing terms. Q♿☆✦❶❄➘≷(Park/Queenstown Rd) ⊖(Power Station) ❄♿❄♪

SW8: South Lambeth

Priory Arms Ⓛ
83 Lansdowne Way, SW8 2PB
☎ (020) 7622 1884 ⊕ theprioryarms.com
3 changing beers (often Anspach & Hobday, Kent) Ⓗ
Long-established free house with a modernised, split-level interior, attracting a youngish clientele. Microbreweries are well supported here, and there is a good choice of foreign and craft keg beers and ciders – usually including one from Snails Bank – as well as food inspired by the Dominican Republic's cuisine. The pub hosts occasional beer festivals. Board games are available and at the front is a small patio for smoking and outdoor drinking. Children are allowed until early evening. Card payment only. ✦❶⟊⊖(Stockwell)✦♿

Surprise
16 Southville, SW8 2PP
☎ (020) 7622 4623
Young's London Original; 1 changing beer (often Fuller's, Young's) Ⓗ
Tucked away next to Larkhall Park, this small, down-to-earth, L-shaped local with conservatory extension is the only building remaining from streets that were replaced by the park after WWII bomb damage. The back room walls display caricatures of former and regular

customers, while the middle section has old photographs of Battersea Power Station. Balls are available for the pétanque pitch beside the pub. There is an all-day pizza menu. ♿☆✦❶⟊⊖(Nine Elms/Wandsworth Rd)✦♿❄❄

SW9: Brixton

Craft Beer Co.
11-13 Brixton Station Road, SW9 8PA
☎ (020) 7274 8383
Changing beers (sourced nationally) Ⓗ
Close to Brixton market, this modern pub has a retro feel with hints of an American diner. Downstairs has red high stools and an industrial vibe while upstairs are bright blue bench seats, a tumbling blocks parquet floor, neon signs and enamel brewery advertisements from Belgium and France. London microbreweries are well represented among the draught and bottled beers, as are Belgian Trappists and Lambic. The pub gets busy when concerts are on at the nearby O2 Academy. ♿☆❄≷⊖♿♿❄❄

Trinity Arms
45 Trinity Gardens, SW9 8DR
☎ (020) 7274 4544 ⊕ trinityarms.co.uk
Young's London Original, London Special; 1 changing beer (sourced nationally; often Brick) Ⓗ
Something of a hidden gem in a quiet square just off Brixton's bustling high street, this attractive pub retains its tiled Young's façade, complete with the ram logo. Inside, a recent refurbishment has created a light and open interior with photographs of old Brixton. A function room is available upstairs. There is outdoor seating at the front and a pleasant patio at the rear with a fire pit. ♿☆✦❶❄➘⊖♿❄❄

SW11: Battersea Power Station

Battersea Brewery Tap Room Ⓛ
12-14 Arches Lane, SW11 8AB
☎ (020) 8161 2366 ⊕ batterseabrew.co.uk
Battersea Admiral Best Bitter; 1 changing beer (sourced regionally) Ⓗ
A must for the cask ale drinker visiting the Power Station complex, this taproom is located in a railway arch adjacent to its brewery. The decor on the ground and mezzanine floors has a suitably industrial feel with bare brick, exposed pipework and copper-topped tables. Food is limited to bar snacks such as chicken wings and toasties. In fine weather bench seating outside provides a good vantage point on Arches Lane, home to restaurants, a cinema and a theatre. ♿☆✦❶❄≷(Park) ⊖♿♿❄❄

SW11: Clapham Junction

Beehive ✓
197 St Johns Hill, SW11 1TH
☎ (020) 7450 1756 ⊕ beehivewandsworth.co.uk
Fuller's London Pride; 1 changing beer Ⓗ
This classic Fuller's local has maintained its traditional status while its new look gives it a fresh and inviting feel. The televisions show all sports. There is a great beer garden at the back and a suntrap patio at the front. The beers and drink selection is top notch and dogs are more than welcome. Look out for the wonderful 1898 housing survey map of south-west London; since then the Luftwaffe and town planners have altered things somewhat! ♿☆≷⊖♿❄❄

Eagle Ale House Ⓛ
104 Chatham Road, SW11 6HG
☎ (020) 7228 2328

Changing beers (often Downton, East London, Surrey Hills) H
A charming, cosy local, just off the busy Northcote Road, the Eagle is a bastion for microbrewery cask and KeyKeg beers from near and far. One handpump is kept for ciders and bottle coolers now feature continental classics including several Lambics. The garden benefits from a large heated shelter. Serveral TV screens come to life for major sporting events, with rugby dominating. Occasionally there is live music. Local CAMRA Pub of the Year again in 2022. Cash payment preferred.
❤✿🖵(319,G1) ❀ 🤍 ♪

SW13: Barnes

Red Lion
2 Castelnau, SW13 9RU
☎ (020) 8748 2984 ⊕ red-lion-barnes.co.uk
Fuller's London Pride, ESB; 3 changing beers (often Dark Star, Gale's) H
Large Victorian landmark establishment at the entrance to the Wetland Centre, comprising a front bar area and a spacious rear dining room with a mosaic domed ceiling light and an impressive fireplace. Outside is a covered patio, a large artificial grass garden, play area, two four-seater heated cabins and a bar in summer. Well-behaved dogs are welcome inside; children under 10 until early evening. Occasional beers come from Wimbledon and Park breweries. The pub has a Fuller's Master Cellarman award. Q❤✿🖤👶🖵❀🤍🛜

SW15: Putney

Bricklayer's Arms L
32 Waterman Street, SW15 1DD
☎ (020) 8246 5544 ⊕ bricklayers-arms.co.uk
Timothy Taylor Boltmaker, Landlord; 8 changing beers (often Five Points, Surrey Hills, Wimbledon) H
A back-street local dating from 1826 that clearly stands out in the otherwise strangely lacklustre Putney pub scene. Besides an interesting selection of real ales that are unusual for the area, often from microbreweries in London and the South East, it has traditional pub games and runs a cricket team. The pub is favoured by Fulham FC supporters and so the beer range may be depleted following home matches. It is also increasingly popular with families and younger drinkers.
❤✿🚆Θ(Bridge) ♣🖵❀🛜

Telegraph L
Putney Heath, SW15 3TU
☎ (020) 8194 2808
Timothy Taylor Landlord; house beer (by St Austell); 8 changing beers (often Adnams, Twickenham, Wimbledon) H
On the edge of Putney Heath this impressively refurbished pub has many distinct areas, with emphasis on food as well as up to 10 real ales, mostly locally brewed. The smart decor includes many prints and old London Underground posters as well as vintage maps and photographs. There is an extensive outdoor drinking area to enjoy in fine weather. It is on the site of the Putney Telegraph, part of the Admiralty Telegraph between London and Portsmouth, which operated from 1796 to 1848. ❤✿🖤👶🍴P🖵❀🛜

SW16: Streatham

Pratts & Payne
103 Streatham High Road, SW16 1HJ
☎ (020) 8677 1664 ⊕ prattsandpayne.co.uk

6 changing beers (often By The Horns, Sambrook's, Southwark) H
A large, high-ceilinged pub with a relaxed atmosphere and TV sports. Tables and chairs for dining are complemented by comfortable sofas and armchairs. Opened by Antic in 2012, its name commemorates the former Pratts department store and notorious former Streatham hostess, Cynthia Payne. Food is served Monday to Thursday evenings, and all day Friday and Saturday, with service finishing earlier on Sunday.
❤✿🖤👶🚆🖵❀🛜

Railway L ✓
2 Greyhound Lane, SW16 5SD
☎ (020) 8769 9448 ⊕ therailwaysw16.co.uk
Sambrook's Wandle; 4 changing beers (often Portobello, Southwark, Twickenham) H
Showcasing beers from London microbreweries, both cask and bottled, this busy two-bar community pub is close to Streatham Common station. The back bar, available for hire, is open in the afternoon as a popular tearoom. There is outside seating at the front and in the spacious rear enclosure. It hosts a quiz on Tuesdays, music nights and a popular monthly Sunday comedy night. Local CAMRA Pub of the Year in 2019 and 2021.
❤✿🖤👶🚆(Common) 🖵(60,118) ❀🛜

SW17: Summerstown

Phoenix
Plough Lane, SW17 0NR (behind the club shop at the main entrance off Coppermill Ln)
☎ (020) 3417 7338 ⊕ bythehorns.co.uk
3 changing beers (often By The Horns)
By The Horns brewery's London outlet is inside the new Cherry Red Records Stadium, home of AFC Wimbledon. Usually there will be one beer on, nearly always Stiff Upper Lip but sometimes Classic or, occasionally, Hopadelic. TV sport is shown and regular quiz nights are held. It is recommended that you check the fixture lists for both AFC Wimbledon and London Broncos Rugby League clubs before visiting, or telephone the pub, as the bar is not open to the public during matches.
❤👶🖵(493) ❀♪

SW17: Tooting

Antelope
76 Mitcham Road, SW17 9NG
☎ (020) 8672 3888 ⊕ theantelopepub.com
Sambrook's Wandle; Thornbridge Jaipur IPA; Volden Session Ale, Pale Ale; 3 changing beers (often Twickenham, Wimbledon) H
A large, lively Victorian community pub that has been identified by CAMRA as having a regionally important historic pub interior. It is currently decorated in the shabby-chic style typical of its operators, Antic. The main bar area, retaining some Barclay's signage, leads back to dining tables and the spacious Rankin Room that shows big-screen sports. Seating in the large back yard is part-covered and heated in winter. Regular events include live music and a quiz night. Sundays feature popular roasts and folk music in the afternoon. Children are welcome until mid-evening.
❤✿🖤👶🚆Θ(Broadway) 🖵❀🛜♪

SW18: Wandsworth

Cat's Back
86-88 Point Pleasant, SW18 1PP
☎ 07523 047335 ⊕ thecatsback.co.uk

Harvey's Sussex Best Bitter; 1 changing beer (often Harvey's) Ⓗ
As befits a pub owned by one of Britain's most traditional breweries, the Cat's Back has the feel of a back-street local, in an area dominated by new riverside residential developments. The upstairs room has recently been remodelled. Outdoors is a single bench on the pavement in front and a back garden with tables and chairs. In winter a real fire adds to the cosy atmosphere.
♨❀♿♣🚌🐾📶♫

Sambrook's Brewery Tap
40 Ram Street, SW18 1UD
☎ (020) 7228 0598 🌐 sambrooksbrewery.co.uk
Sambrook's Wandle, Pumphouse Pale, Junction; 2 changing beers (often Sambrook's) Ⓗ
Opened in 2021 within the historic site of the former Young's Ram brewery, the taproom here has outside seating in Bubbling Well Square and two inside bars – downstairs and upstairs – each with tall tables and stools as well as comfortable bench seating. Both bars have great views of large fermenting and conditioning tanks. On-site pizzas are provided by Crust Bros. The old Young's brewery coppers now form the centrepiece of a heritage centre and museum. ♨❀◑♿⇌(Town)🚌🐾📶

Spread Eagle ★
71 Wandsworth High Street, SW18 2PT
☎ (020) 8161 0038 🌐 spreadeaglewandsworth.co.uk
St Austell Proper Job; Young's London Original, London Special Ⓗ
With an historic pub interior identified by CAMRA as being of national importance, this opulent drinkers' establishment sits at the heart of Wandsworth opposite the former Young's brewery. Fine glass and woodwork include a full-height partition separating the ornate saloon bar from the plainer public bar to the left. Meals are served weekday lunchtimes only but paninis are available all day every day. The public bar can be hired for private functions. ♨⇄◑♿⇌(Town)🚌🐾📶

SW19: South Wimbledon

Sultan 🏆
78 Norman Road, SW19 1BT
☎ (020) 8544 9323
Hop Back GFB, Citra, Taiphoon, Entire Stout, Summer Lightning; 2 changing beers (often Downton, Hop Back) Ⓗ
Hop Back's London tied house is an attractive two-bar 1950s brick building identified by CAMRA as having a regionally important historic interior. Mostly carpeted, it has dark-wood walls, large tables with chairs, some fixed seating, settees in the conservatory and benches in the patio and outside. Up to four handpumps in the saloon bar dispense cider. Three-day beer festivals celebrate spring, summer and Christmas. Bottled Crop Circle and Taiphoon are gluten-free. Card payment only. Local CAMRA Pub of the Year 2023.
♨❀♿⇌(Haydons Rd) ⊖(Colliers Wood/South Wimbledon) ♣🚌🐾📶♫

SW19: Wimbledon

Hand in Hand Ⓛ
7 Crooked Billet, SW19 4RQ
☎ (020) 8946 5720 🌐 thehandinhandwimbledon.co.uk
Courage Directors; St Austell Proper Job; Young's London Original, London Special Ⓗ**; 3 changing beers (often Adnams, Young's)** Ⓗ/Ⓖ
Popular, dog-friendly establishment on the edge of Wimbledon Common with separate drinking areas and a variety of seating. At least three guest beers are regularly sold, usually from local breweries. Children are welcome in the family room. This is a great place to eat, either inside or on the front patio, with beer included in several recipes. There is poker on Monday, a quiz on Tuesday and occasional beer tastings and cellar tours.
Q♨❀◑♿♣🚌(200) 🐾📶

Wibbas Down Inn Ⓛ ✔
6-12 Gladstone Road, SW19 1QT
☎ (020) 8540 6788
Greene King IPA, Abbot; Oakham JHB; Sharp's Doom Bar; 12 changing beers Ⓗ
An enormous two-bar Wetherspoon pub stretching from Gladstone Road to Russell Road, unusual in that it was converted in 1995 from a Tesco supermarket. It is a favourite haunt for drinkers owing to its low prices and the back bar being well placed to serve the Wimbledon Theatre across the road. The guest beers change frequently and many are sourced from local breweries. Up to 50 beers are available at the frequent festivals. Food and coffee are served all day.
Q♨❀◑♿⇌⊖🚌📶

SW20: Raynes Park

Cavern
100 Coombe Lane, SW20 0AY
☎ (020) 8946 7980 🌐 thecavernfreehouse.co.uk
Sharp's Doom Bar; Wimbledon Common; 1 changing beer (often Wimbledon) Ⓗ
Opened in 1991 but with a 1960s rock'n'roll atmosphere successfully created by many photographs and posters, matched by the landlord's record selection and regular live music sessions. The floor is tiled but with carpeted seating corner areas. An original Gilbert Scott red telephone kiosk stands next to the door. A small room at the back has a pool table. The pub does not serve food but customers are welcome to bring in their own.
❀⇌♣🚌♫

Carshalton

Cryer Arts Centre Ⓛ
39 High Street, SM5 3BB
☎ (020) 8773 9390 🌐 cryerarts.co.uk
Surrey Hills Shere Drop; 2 changing beers (sourced nationally) Ⓗ
Formerly the Charles Cryer Theatre, the Cryer Arts Centre now combines arts events with the Spotlight Bar and Restaurant. A changing selection of cask ales is available on three handpumps, supplemented by a range of bottled and KeyKeg beers. An extra bar on the mezzanine floor is open when the theatre is in use and a room with its own small bar is available for hire.
♨◑⇌●🚌🐾📶♫

Hope 🏆 Ⓛ
48 West Street, SM5 2PR
☎ (020) 8240 1255 🌐 hopecarshalton.co.uk
Downton New Forest Ale; Windsor & Eton Knight of the Garter; 5 changing beers Ⓗ
A traditional pub in the heart of the Carshalton Conservation Area, owned by its regulars. Seven handpumps dispense cask ale in various styles, and up to four real ciders and a range of craft keg beers are served. Third-pint measures are available and a good range of bottled beer is stocked. A permanent marquee is available for private functions and regular beer festivals. Children are not admitted. Local CAMRA Pub of the Year 2023 and a former regional award winner.
Q❀◑♿⇌♣●P▯🚌🐾📶♫

Railway Tavern ✓
47 North Street, SM5 2HG
☎ 07710 476437 ● railwaytaverncarshalton.co.uk
Fuller's London Pride; 2 changing beers (sourced regionally; often Dark Star) Ⓗ
Street-corner community local close to the railway station, adorned with hanging baskets and with window boxes beneath the fine etched windows. Inside are a small U-shaped drinking area around a central bar, and a comfortable side area. The walls display various items of railway and brewery memorabilia. There is a regular 60s disco on Friday. ❁☰♣⎕❀🎵

Ham

New Inn
345 Petersham Road, TW10 7DB
☎ (020) 8940 9444
Adnams Broadside; Fuller's London Pride; Young's London Original; 2 changing beers (often Butcombe, Hook Norton, St Austell) Ⓗ
A traditional pub located in a prominent position at the corner of Ham Common. As the name implies, the New Inn replaced a previous pub: the White Hart, built in 1642. It is comfortable and relaxing, arranged around a central bar. Outdoor seating and tables are provided at the front overlooking the Green, and there is also a large, paved walled courtyard garden at the rear.
Q☰❁◗♿⎕(65,371)❀🛜

Kingston

Albion Ⓛ
45 Fairfield Road, KT1 2PY
☎ (020) 8541 1691 ● thealbionkingston.com
Big Smoke Solaris Session Pale Ale; 9 changing beers (often Big Smoke, Harvey's, Tiny Rebel) Ⓗ
Part of a chain that includes the Big Smoke brewery, serving ales mostly from small breweries nationwide and up to five changing ciders. Varnished wooden floors and comfortable wood-panelled seating areas extend to a rear patio garden with heaters, gin distillery and a glazed garden room available for hire. Music is from many vinyl LPs. Home-cooked food is served lunchtime and evenings (all day Fri-Sun). Board games are available and there is a Sunday night quiz. ☰❁◗♿☰●⎕❀🛜

Park Tavern
19 New Road, KT2 6AP
☎ (020) 8549 0361 ● perfectpub.co.uk
Fuller's London Pride; Young's London Original; 4 changing beers (sourced nationally) Ⓗ
This pub, close to Richmond Park, has been owned by the same family for over 30 years. Originally converted from two cottages, it is about 150 years old. The ceiling displays an impressive collection of pumpclips. A large screen TV shows all major sports, and cards and dominoes are played. Filled rolls are available at lunchtime. Besides seating outside at the front all year round, the rear garden is open in summer months. Children are welcome until early evening.
Q☰❁♣⎕(371)❀

Willoughby Arms Ⓛ
47 Willoughby Road, KT2 6LN
☎ (020) 8546 4236 ● thewilloughbyarms.com
4 changing beers (often Surrey Hills, Twickenham) Ⓗ
Friendly Victorian back-street premises, with a games and TV sports bar and a quieter lounge area. Upstairs is a soundproofed function room. Free of tie, it sources beers from smaller breweries. Pizzas and pies are cooked to order. The spacious garden includes heated beach huts

and a covered, heated and lit smoking area with a large TV screen. Quiz night is Sunday. Folk music is played on Monday nights. Local CAMRA Pub of the Year 2020.
Q☰❁♿♣⎕(371,K5)❀🛜

Wych Elm Ⓛ ✓
93 Elm Road, KT2 6HT
☎ (020) 8546 3271 ● thewychelmkingston.co.uk
Dark Star Hophead; Fuller's London Pride, ESB; 2 changing beers (often Dark Star) Ⓗ
Tucked away in a residential area, this is a delightful, warm and welcoming local pub. The guest ales are supplied by Asahi but one is often from another brewery. A Master Cellarman takes care of the beers. The food is traditional pub staples with a vegetarian option. There is a secluded garden, and log-burners are lit in winter. Some major sporting events are shown and parties and celebrations can be hosted. Charity quizzes, piano and wine evenings are also held. ☰❁◗☰⎕(K5)❀🛜

Mitcham

Windmill
40 Commonside West, CR4 4HA
☎ (020) 8685 0333
Young's London Original; 1 changing beer (often Courage, Sharp's, Shepherd Neame) Ⓗ
A warm, friendly, independent free house facing the common, with stained-glass windmills in attractive bow windows. This is very much a community pub, with TV for sports highlights, a dartboard, a regular quiz night and occasional live music. There is sometimes a second guest beer. Cocktail sausages and roast potatoes are served on Sundays. To the side is a spacious heated and covered patio with plenty of seating for smokers. Outside there is a convenient bus stop. ☰❁♣⎕❀🛜

New Malden

Watchman ♥ Ⓛ ✓
184 High Street, KT3 4ES
☎ (020) 8329 0450
Greene King IPA, Abbot; Sharp's Doom Bar; Twickenham Naked Ladies; 3 changing beers (sourced nationally) Ⓗ
A warm and friendly Wetherspoon pub in a former police station dating from the 1890s, named after the Royal Observer Corps member who operated an air raid siren on the roof during WWII. The bright interior includes a variety of seating, including booths and a dining area. The cask cellar is visible through a window in the passageway behind the bar. At least one guest beer is usually from a local brewery. Local CAMRA Pub of the Year 2023. Q☰❁◗♿☰⎕🛜

Richmond

Mitre
20 St Mary's Grove, TW9 1UY
☎ (020) 8940 1336 ● themitretw9.co.uk
Timothy Taylor Landlord; 6 changing beers (often Bristol Beer Factory, Burning Sky, Nightjar) Ⓗ
A traditional community free house off Sheen Road, originally built as a coach house in 1865 as part of the Church Estates. Church mitres feature in the leaded stained-glass windows. There is a decked area at the front and covered patio at the rear. Cask beers rotate from independent brewers outside the M25, with three handpumps dispensing cider or perry. Authentic Neapolitan style pizzas are cooked to order to eat in or take away Wednesday to Sunday.
☰❁◗☰(North Sheen)⊖●P⎕❀🎵

Roebuck

130 Richmond Hill, TW10 6RN

☎ (020) 8948 2329

Greene King IPA, Abbot; 3 changing beers (often Exeter, Oakham, Wimbledon) ⊞

Close to Richmond Park, this 280-year-old pub, rebuilt in 1741, commands the famous view over the Thames painted by Turner – the only view protected by Act of Parliament. Inside, there are a number of comfortable secluded areas and upstairs is a function room and bar for hire. Guest beers are on constant rotation and Weston's Old Rosie is a regular cider. Patrons can also use the outside terrace across the road (plastic glasses provided). ⓢⓄ&🖳(371)❁🛜

Surbiton

Antelope ⓛ

87 Maple Road, KT6 4AW

☎ (020) 8399 5565 ⊕ theantelope.co.uk

Big Smoke Solaris Session Pale Ale; 9 changing beers (sourced nationally; often Big Smoke) ⊞

The original home of the Big Smoke brewery, with two or three of its beers usually available in cask. The spacious split-level interior has a real log fire in winter and a covered, heated and lit courtyard behind, beyond which the old brewhouse now provides a dining or function room. Five changing ciders are usually sold. Home-cooked food includes Sunday roasts. Three beer festivals are held annually. A former local CAMRA Pub of the Year. ⓢ❁Ⓞ▶≠♠🖳🛜♪

Lamb ⓛ

73 Brighton Road, KT6 5NF

☎ (020) 8390 9229 ⊕ lambsurbiton.co.uk

Hop Back Summer Lightning; Surrey Hills Shere Drop; 2 changing beers (sourced nationally) ⊞

This small, family-run free house hosts many community events, especially those bringing people together through creativity. Live music often plays. Built in 1850 and formerly comprising four separate rooms and a small brewery, it retains the original horseshoe-shaped bar. Changing beers are usually from a microbrewery, sometimes local. Visiting local caterers serve evening food from the outdoor kitchen Wednesday to Sunday. To the rear is an extensive covered outdoor area. Children are welcome until early evening. ⓢ❁≠🖳🛜♪

Sutton

Little Windsor ⓥ

13 Greyhound Road, SM1 4BY

☎ (020) 8643 2574 ⊕ thelittlewindsor.uk

Fuller's London Pride, ESB ⊞

A small back-street corner local in the New Town area, east of Sutton town centre. The pub is popular with nearby residents, especially in the evening and at weekends, and sport is usually shown on TV. The L-shaped bar leads to a heated covered terrace and a garden on two levels. Children are welcome until early evening. ⓢ❁Ⓞ≠❁🛜

Moon on the Hill ⓥ

5-9 Hill Road, SM1 1DZ

☎ (020) 8643 1202

Greene King Abbot; Ruddles Best Bitter; Sharp's Doom Bar; 7 changing beers (sourced nationally) ⊞

Large, busy Wetherspoon conversion just off Sutton's main shopping street. The single bar serves a spacious ground floor area, and there is additional seating on raised and lower levels. There are two small rear patio areas and seating outside the front entrance. Guest beers

are sourced from a wide range of breweries. The pub hosts occasional beer festivals, and also Meet the Brewer and tap takeover events. ⓢ❁Ⓞ&≠🖳🛜

WEST LONDON
W2: Bayswater

Champion ⓥ

1 Wellington Terrace, W2 4LW

☎ (020) 7792 4527 ⊕ thechampionpub.co.uk

Adnams Ghost Ship; 4 changing beers (often By The Horns, Dark Star, Oakham) ⊞

The nearest pub to Kensington Palace, opposite the security-protected road on the northern side of Kensington Gardens. Built in 1838 and Grade II listed, it was refurbished in 2004 and spruced up more recently by owners Mitchells & Butlers. In warm weather the front windows are often opened into the bar with its tables and chairs and standing space. A plush basement area leads through to a sunken beer garden, with patio heaters lit in cold weather. ⓢ❁Ⓞ&⊖(Notting Hill Gate/Queensway) 🖳❁🛜

W2: Paddington

Bear

27 Spring Street, W2 1JA

☎ (020) 7262 3907 ⊕ thebearpaddington.com

6 changing beers (sourced nationally; often Titanic) ⊞

A welcome addition to the Paddington beer scene, this is the newest pub from the Craft Beer Co – the independent pub company owned by Martin Hayes and Peter Slezak. This former wine bar has been refurbished in an elegant spring green colour. Alongside the six real ales from small breweries, 29 craft beers are available on keg and an extensive range of Belgian bottled beers, alcohol-free beers and whiskies. The Den in the basement can seat about 25 people. ⓢⓄ≠⊖❁🛜

Mad Bishop & Bear

Upper Level, The Lawn, Paddington Station Concourse, W2 1HB

☎ (020) 7402 2441 ⊕ madbishopandbear.co.uk

Dark Star Hophead; Fuller's London Pride, ESB; 3 changing beers (sourced nationally) ⊞

Above the shopping complex just behind the station concourse, the modern pub interior features one long bar, railway memorabilia and train information screens. The raised areas can be hired for events and there are café-style seats outside. It can be quiet, even in the rush hour, but the bar could close early if football crowds are passing through. A former local CAMRA Pub of the Year and shortlisted several times. ⓢⓄ&≠⊖🖳❁🛜

Monkey Puzzle

30 Southwick Street, W2 1JQ

☎ (020) 7723 0143 ⊕ themonkeypuzzlepub.co.uk

Hall & Woodhouse Badger Best Bitter, Tanglefoot ⊞

A modern pub with a partially-heated beer garden on its Sussex Gardens side. It was built in 1969 on the ground floor of a residential high-rise development. The one long bar room has a raised eating area at the rear. Trade is mainly local, plus some tourists from the numerous hotels nearby. The food menu includes sausages from Biggles of Marylebone, 'the most acclaimed sausage maker in London', and Badger beer-battered cod. ❁Ⓞ≠⊖(Edgware Rd/Paddington) 🖳❁🛜

Victoria ★

10A Strathearn Place, W2 2NH

☎ (020) 7724 1191 ⊕ victoriapaddington.co.uk

Fuller's Oliver's Island [H]/[P], London Pride, ESB; 2 changing beers (often Dark Star, Thornbridge, Tiny Rebel) [H]
There is plenty to admire in this Grade II-listed mid-Victorian inn, popular with tourists and locals alike. It has been identified by CAMRA as having a nationally important historic pub interior, and includes ornately gilded mirrors above a crescent-shaped bar, painted tiles in wall niches and numerous portraits of Queen Victoria. The walls display cartoons, paperweights and a Silver Jubilee plate. Upstairs, via a spiral staircase, the Library and Theatre Bar provide extra space. Tuesday is quiz night. Several times a local CAMRA award runner-up.
Q🐴❀◑⇌⊖(Lancaster Gate/Paddington) 🚌🐾📶

W3: Acton

Red Lion & Pineapple ✔
281 High Street, W3 9BP
☎ (020) 8896 2248
Greene King IPA, Abbot; Sharp's Doom Bar; 6 changing beers (often Oakham, Twickenham) [H]
A Wetherspoon pub at the top of Acton Hill, formerly owned by Fuller's. Two pubs here were combined in 1906, hence the unique name. The larger room is home to the circular bar, surrounded by red and black tiles. The windows are large, with etched and stained tops, and the walls are decorated with historical photographs of Acton. The smaller room is mainly used by diners and families. The rear patio area was recently refurbished. Alcohol is served from 9am. Q🐴❀◑♿⊖(Town)🚌📶

West London Trades Union Club
33-35 High Street, W3 6ND
☎ (020) 8992 4557 🌐 wltuc.com
2 changing beers (often Nelson) [H]
A small, friendly club, run as a co-operative, that combines excellent beer with a busy cultural and social life. Two real ales are served from a variety of independent breweries, and particularly from the wide Nelson range. The Acton Community Theatre is upstairs and regular film shows are also held. The local CAMRA branch is an associate member; show a CAMRA membership card or this Guide for entry. Closed on most Saturdays – check website for exceptions.
Q🐴❀⊖(Central) 🚌🐾📶

W4: Chiswick

George IV
185 Chiswick High Road, W4 2DR
☎ (020) 8994 4624 🌐 georgeiv.co.uk
Fuller's London Pride, ESB; 3 changing beers (often Brew By Numbers, Sambrook's, Windsor & Eton) [H]
There has been an inn here in the heart of Chiswick since 1777 and the present inter-war pub is still reputed to have its own ghost, George. Inside, the different areas include the board game-themed mezzanine, while the Boston Room across the rear courtyard hosts activities including a comedy club. Regular music events are held on Friday and Saturday. Fuller's small-batch brews are often available, including a good variety of craft beers. Monday is quiz night.
🐴❀◑♿⊖(Turnham Green) ●🚌🐾📶♫

W5: Ealing

Questors Grapevine Bar [L] ✔
12 Mattock Lane, W5 5BQ
☎ (020) 8567 0011 🌐 questors.org.uk/grapevine
Fuller's London Pride; 2 changing beers [H]
A friendly theatre club bar near the centre of Ealing and Walpole Park, run by enthusiastic volunteers. CAMRA members and Questors theatre ticket holders are also welcome. Guest beers include some from local breweries, beer festivals are held twice-yearly and there are malt whisky tastings. Some books and the odd board game are available. Local CAMRA Club of the Year 2022, it won the CAMRA national award in 2012.
Q🐴❀♿⇌⊖(Broadway) ♣P🚌🐾📶

W6: Hammersmith

Andover Arms ✔
57 Aldensley Road, W6 0DL
☎ (020) 8748 2155 🌐 theandoverarmsw6.com
Fuller's London Pride; 2 changing beers (often Dark Star, Fuller's, Gale's) [H]
Hidden away in the back streets and with a rural feel about it, this popular and welcoming local has changed management since it was last in the Guide. The attractive panelled bar counter, with its elaborate bar-back, separates two areas furnished with an assortment of dining tables and chairs. There is now more attention to its kitchen offerings. Note that the pub is closed on Mondays and during the day on Tuesdays and Wednesdays. 🐴❀◑⊖(Ravenscourt Park)🚌🐾📶

Crabtree ✔
Rainville Road, W6 9HA
☎ (020) 7385 3929 🌐 thecrabtreew6.co.uk
Greene King IPA; 4 changing beers (sourced nationally) [H]
Spacious Thames-side pub in the back streets half a mile from Fulham football ground, rebuilt in 1898 by Sich's Lamb brewery of Chiswick. The split-level bar with restaurant at rear has a high-vaulted ceiling and some plush furniture including leather banquettes. A large patio/garden area overlooks the river and affords a view of the annual Varsity Boat Race; weeping willows and parasols provide shade. Occasional events include Meet the Brewer – see website and social media. Quiz night is Tuesday. 🐴❀◑🚌♫

Dove
19 Upper Mall, W6 9TA
☎ (020) 8748 9474 🌐 dovehammersmith.co.uk
Fuller's London Pride, ESB; 2 changing beers (often Dark Star, Fuller's) [H]
A Grade II-listed pub dating from the 1740s, identified by CAMRA as having a regionally important historic pub interior, overlooking the Thames and hence often crowded in summer. The likes of Dylan Thomas, Ernest Hemingway and Alec Guinness have enjoyed a pint or two here. Down off the main bar area, a tiny public bar holds the Guinness world record for the smallest bar area. The food service can be slow at busy times but is usually worth the wait.
🐴❀◑⊖(Ravenscourt Park) 🚌🐾📶

Prince of Wales Townhouse
73 Dalling Road, W6 0JD
☎ (020) 8563 1713 🌐 princeofwales-townhouse.co.uk
Big Smoke Solaris Session Pale Ale, Underworld; 3 changing beers (often Big Smoke, Harvey's, Laine) [H]
Just a little outside the centre of Hammersmith, this pub now belongs to the Big Smoke chain. Up to five ciders and 20 keg lines complement the cask beers. Besides the spacious, light and airy bar, there is is a covered and heated garden, featuring open-sided huts. The menu starts early with breakfast (alcoholic drinks served from 11am) and features pub favourites, sharers and more upmarket dishes from lunchtime until late evening.
🐴❀🛏◑♿⊖(Ravenscourt Park) ♣🚌🐾📶

William Morris Ⓛ ✓

2-4 King Street, W6 0QA
☎ (020) 8741 7175
Greene King Abbot; Ruddles Best Bitter; Sharp's Doom Bar; 7 changing beers Ⓗ

Close to Hammersmith's underground stations and Lyric Theatre, and not far from the Apollo music venue, this popular, modern Wetherspoon pub commemorates the Arts & Crafts designer who lived nearby. With entrances on both King Street and the pedestrianised Lyric Square, where there is terrace seating, the interior stretches in an L-shape, with the bar in the middle. Frequently changing interesting ales are usually on offer, often from smaller breweries. Alcoholic drinks are served from 9am.
🚫✹◑♿⊖🗔❤

W7: Hanwell

Dodo Micropub ♥ Ⓛ

52 Boston Road, W7 3TR
☎ (020) 8567 5959 ⊕ thedodomicropub.com
5 changing beers (sourced regionally) Ⓖ

A classic micropub shop conversion, opened in 2017. Up to five cask beers are served from a temperature-controlled cellar room at the rear, along with cider and wine. Beers almost always include some from local breweries. There is a small bar counter by the front door but table service is the order of the day. It hosts regular tap takeovers for local breweries and has arrangements with nearby street food vendors. Local CAMRA Pub of the Year 2023. Q🚫✹⊖♣🗔🚗❤🎵

Fox Ⓛ

Green Lane, W7 2PJ
☎ (020) 8567 0060 ⊕ thefoxpub.co.uk
Fuller's London Pride; St Austell Tribute; Timothy Taylor Landlord; 2 changing beers (often Five Points, Park) Ⓗ

Wonderful free house in the welcoming multicultural town of Hanwell, as popular with walkers, cyclists and other nearby canal users as with locals. Refurbishment in 2020 extended the pub into the garden, creating a large partly-covered outdoor seating area. It has a Thursday evening quiz and runs Easter and autumn beer festivals. Local CAMRA Pub of the Year on many occasions.
🚫✹◑♿♣🗔(195,E8) ❤🎵

Grosvenor Ⓛ

127 Oaklands Road, W7 2DT
☎ (020) 8840 0007
4 changing beers (often Ealing, Five Points, Twickenham) Ⓗ

A traditional local dating back to 1904, refurbished in 2014 without losing the features and charm of its historic pub interior, identified by CAMRA as regionally important. There is a main bar and a dining room section. A wide range of locally produced beers is available. Family-friendly, it has a congenial atmosphere and promotes local events. Jazz night is the second Tuesday of every month and there is an open mic night on the fourth Tuesday. A former local CAMRA Pub of the Year.
🚫✹◑♿♣🗔❤🎵

Viaduct ✓

221 Uxbridge Road, W7 3TD
☎ (020) 8567 5866 ⊕ viaduct-hanwell.co.uk
Dark Star Hophead; Fuller's London Pride, ESB; Gale's Seafarers Ale; 1 changing beer Ⓗ

A friendly Fuller's pub, much larger on the inside than it looks from the outside. A separate function room is available for hire when it is not being used for the Friday comedy nights. The pub was renamed around 1838 after the Wharncliffe Viaduct behind it, which was made famous as the first viaduct to carry a commercial electric telegraph. Ealing Hospital is also close by.
Q🚫✹◑♿⊖🗔❤❤🎵

W8: Kensington

Elephant & Castle ✓

40 Holland Street, W8 4LT
☎ (020) 7937 6382
Fuller's London Pride; St Austell Nicholson's Pale Ale; Sharp's Doom Bar; 3 changing beers (sourced nationally) Ⓗ

Tucked away north-east of Kensington Town Hall, this busy, cosy wood-panelled M&B Nicholson's pub was first licensed in 1865 as a beer house in what were originally two adjacent houses. It has been identified by CAMRA as having a regionally important historic pub interior: note the fine Charrington's bar-back. With its rural feel, it is a welcome refuge from the hurly-burly of Kensington High Street. Guest beers come from a wide range of breweries. Food, especially pies and sausages, is available all day, with a short break between lunch and dinner. 🚫✹◑⊖(High St)🗔❤❤

W8: Notting Hill Gate

Churchill Arms

119 Kensington Church Street, W8 7LN
☎ (020) 7727 4242 ⊕ churchillarmskensington.co.uk
Fuller's Oliver's Island, London Pride, ESB; 2 changing beers (often Fuller's) Ⓗ

A multi award-winning, deservedly popular pub, it has been identified by CAMRA as having a regionally important historic pub interior, including snob screens, now rare. Churchillian and Irish memorabilia are among the bric-a-brac suspended from the panelled ceiling. The Thai restaurant in the conservatory was one of the first in a London pub. Outside, at busy times, drinkers stand on the pavement below numerous hanging flower baskets; at Christmas, the tree decorations are something to behold. Q🚫◑⊖🗔❤❤

Windsor Castle ★ ✓

114 Campden Hill Road, W8 7AR
☎ (020) 7243 8797 ⊕ thewindsorcastlekensington.co.uk
Marston's Pedigree; Timothy Taylor Landlord; 4 changing beers Ⓗ

A back-street, Grade II-listed pub dating from 1830 and identified by CAMRA as having a nationally important historic pub interior. Sited on a corner, it contrasts an old-world rural feel with a modern upmarket service and menu style. The bar room is divided into four drinking areas separated by partitions that date from a 1933 refurbishment. The four rotating beers may include some interesting offerings. The courtyard beer garden to the rear boasts its own bar. Popular with local residents, workers and visitors to the capital. Q🚫✹◑⊖🗔❤❤

W9: Warwick Avenue

Warwick Castle ✓

6 Warwick Place, W9 2PX
☎ (020) 7266 0921 ⊕ warwickcastlemaidavale.com
Greene King IPA; house beer (by Hardys & Hansons); 2 changing beers (often Timothy Taylor) Ⓗ

With a dark green frontage blending with the rest of the terrace, this 1846 pub, featured in a 1927 painting by artist and illustrator Edward Ardizzone, is recognised by CAMRA as having a regionally important historic pub interior. Note the leaded windows with varied shades of coloured glass inserts. An interesting food menu offers a variety of dishes, including pub classics and roasts on Sundays. The clientele reflects the broad social mix of the area. 🚫🌮◐●🍴🐾❄

W9: Westbourne Park

Union Tavern 🄻
45 Woodfield Road, W9 2BA
☎ (020) 7286 1886 ⊕ union-tavern.co.uk
Dark Star Hophead; Fuller's London Pride; 2 changing beers (sourced locally; often Five Points) Ⓗ
Following a takeover by Fuller's this is now a part-tied beer house offering craft keg beers and cask ales produced within 30 miles and, with just one brewery exception, in London. The mainly young crowd enjoy various music nights and a Meet the Brewer event on the first Tuesday of the month. Good-value food is another attraction, with traditional Sunday lunches served. The canalside terrace comes into its own on a warm, sunny day. 🚫🌮◐●🚃🐾❄🎵

W12: Shepherds Bush

Central Bar ●
Unit 1, West 12 Centre, Shepherds Bush Green, W12 8PH
☎ (020) 8746 4290
Greene King IPA, Abbot; Sharp's Doom Bar; 4 changing beers (often Theakston, Thornbridge, Twickenham) Ⓗ
A Wetherspoon pub opened in 2002 on the upper floor of a new shopping centre. Access from the ground floor is via escalator or lift and through a wide entrance into a long bar area with large windows to the side overlooking the Green. It is named after the Central London Railway (or Tuppenny Tube), now the Central Line, which reached Shepherds Bush in 1900 when the Prince of Wales (later Edward VII) opened the station opposite.
Q🚫◐&≠⊖(Shepherd's Bush/Market) ●🚃❄

Crown & Sceptre
57 Melina Road, W12 9HY
☎ (020) 8746 0060 ⊕ crownandsceptreshepherdsbush.co.uk
Fuller's London Pride; 2 changing beers (often Dark Star, Fuller's, Tiny Rebel) Ⓗ
Well off the beaten track, this large 1866 corner pub is now an upmarket but welcoming Fuller's house, usually offering two real ales from their range and a third which may be a guest. Well-reputed Thai food is available and the comfortable garden is equipped with shelters and heaters. Weekly events include a Monday quiz night.
🚫🌮◐&🚃❄🎵

W13: Northfields

Owl & the Pussycat 🄻
106 Northfield Avenue, W13 9RT
⊕ markopaulo.co.uk
6 changing beers (often Ealing, Marko Paulo) Ⓗ
Unique to West London, this combination of microbrewery and pub has retained the atmosphere of the former bookshop. Drinkers can view the brewing process while avid readers can browse through the beer-related books and magazines. The owners also brew all the beers at Ealing brewing in Brentford. The ciders are often from Oliver's if not home-produced. In this small, friendly environment, conversation is all-important. Local CAMRA Pub of the Year 2022 and Cider Pub of the Year 2023. Q⊖(Northfields)🍃●🚃(E2,E3)❄

Brentford

Black Dog Beer House
17 Albany Road, TW8 0NF
☎ (020) 8568 5688 ⊕ blackdogbeerhouse.co.uk
4 changing beers (often Oakham, Ramsbury, Windsor & Eton) Ⓗ
This former Royal Brewery (Brentford) pub, rebuilt in its present form in 1901, has now become a neighbourhood favourite. The light, open L-shaped room has plenty of seating, no TV screens, music from classic vinyl LPs and an eclectic food menu. Chalkboards list the currently available real ales and ciders, and the 14 keg beers on tap. An in-house brewery, Fearless Nomad, is imminent. Local CAMRA Pub of the Year 2020. Note that it is closed on Tuesdays. 🌮◐≠🍃●🚃🐾❄❄

Express Tavern
56 Kew Bridge Road, TW8 0EW
☎ (020) 8560 8484 ⊕ expresstavern.co.uk
Big Smoke Solaris Session Pale Ale; Draught Bass; Harvey's Sussex Best Bitter; 7 changing beers (often Bristol Beer Factory, Rudgate, Thornbridge) Ⓗ
A local landmark since the 1800s, still featuring its illuminated external Bass signage, with Draught Bass remaining a fixture on the bar. It has been identified by CAMRA as having a regionally important historic pub interior. The small Chiswick Bar has 10 handpumps and the saloon/lounge bar has up to five ciders and perries on handpump and 10 craft keg taps. Music is played from vinyl LPs. Behind is a large, heated conservatory with TV screens. Outside is a spacious beer garden.
🚫🌮◐&≠(Kew Bridge) 🍃●🚃❄❄

Cranford

Queen's Head ★
123 High Street, TW5 9PB
☎ (020) 8897 0022 ⊕ queens-head-cranford.co.uk
Fuller's London Pride, ESB; 2 changing beers (often Adnams, St Austell) Ⓗ
Close to Heathrow Airport, this was among the first pubs bought by Fuller's brewery. Built in 1604 and rebuilt in the 1930s, it has been identified by CAMRA as having a nationally important historic pub interior, retaining its wooden beams, fireplaces, solid oak doors and wood panelling. Many photographs of old Cranford adorn the walls. There are two bars and a barn-style restaurant/function room. Changing beers are served in summer only. 🚫🌮◐🍃P🚃❄🎵

Hampton

Jolly Coopers 🍷
16 High Street, TW12 2SJ
☎ (020) 8979 3384 ⊕ squiffysrestaurant.co.uk
Courage Best Bitter; Hop Back Summer Lightning; 3 changing beers (often Ascot, Exeter, Park) Ⓗ
A traditional community pub with a proud heritage. A wall panel lists all the landlords since 1726 to the present incumbent who took over in 1986. The small horseshoe bar has five handpumps always in use, with a local guest beer. The walls are adorned with water jugs, pictures and local memorabilia. The on-site Squiffy's restaurant serves excellent tapas and traditional food; booking is essential for Sunday lunches. Outside is a covered patio. Local CAMRA Pub of the Year 2022 and 2023.
🚫🌮🍴◐&≠🍃🚃❄

Hampton Court

Mute Swan

3 Palace Gate, Hampton Court Road, KT8 9BN
☎ (020) 8941 5959 ⊕ muteswan.co.uk
House beer (by St Austell); 3 changing beers (often Ilkley, Surrey Hills, Twickenham) ⊞
This popular Brunning & Price pub opposite the palace gates draws locals and tourists alike. The main feature as you enter is the wrought iron spiral staircase up to a dining area (also accessible via normal stairs). Food is also served downstairs. Cask beers change frequently, with a cider on handpump during summer months. There is a log fire in the winter and no distracting TV screens. Seating and tables are available outside. No prams are allowed inside. Q◁▷≠♣♠🛏🅿️❀🎵

Hampton Hill

Roebuck

72 Hampton Road, TW12 1JN
☎ (020) 8255 8133 ⊕ roebuck-hamptonhill.co.uk
St Austell Tribute; Young's London Original; 2 changing beers (often Elgood's, Portobello, VOG/Vale of Glamorgan) ⊞
Comfortable street-corner, single bar Victorian pub, owned by an inveterate collector – obvious from the decor. Besides the wickerwork Harley Davidson, also look for Henry Cooper's boxing glove, vintage fruit machines, photos of Concorde's last flight and the wartime newspapers under glass on most of the tables. The small garden has a gazebo for smokers and there is a garden room available for hire. The real fire never goes out in winter. ❀≠(Fulwell)🅿️❀🎵

Harlington

White Hart

158 High Street, UB3 5DP
☎ (020) 8759 9608 ⊕ whitehartharlington.co.uk
Fuller's London Pride, ESB; 1 changing beer (often Dark Star, Fuller's, Gale's) ⊞
Large, Grade II-listed Fuller's pub standing proud at the north end of the village. It was refurbished in 2009 to improve facilities and create the welcoming feel now enjoyed by regulars and visitors from the nearby Heathrow Airport. The bar provides access to an open-plan space with soft seating, leading to an area favoured by diners. Local history is the theme of the wall displays. Quiz night is Thursday. Fuller's or Gale's seasonal ales are sometimes on the bar. ⋈❀◁▷🅿️❀🎵

Hayes

Botwell Inn ✓

25-29 Coldharbour Lane, UB3 3EB
☎ (020) 8848 3112
Greene King Abbot; Ruddles Best Bitter; Sharp's Doom Bar; 3 changing beers (often Adnams, Windsor & Eton) ⊞
Named after the hamlet of Botwell, now the location of Hayes town centre, this large Wetherspoon pub opened in 2000 following a shop conversion from furnishers S Moore & Son, with several areas for dining and drinking. There is a fenced paved area to the front and a patio at the rear with large market-type parasols with heaters. Several beer festivals are held annually. Q♿❀◁▷⇄⊖(Hayes & Harlington)🅿️🎵

Hillingdon Hill

Red Lion Hotel

Royal Lane, UB8 3QP
☎ (01895) 236860 ⊕ redlionhotelhillingdon.co.uk
Fuller's London Pride; 2 changing beers (often Dark Star, Fuller's) ⊞
A Grade II-listed pub more than 400 years old (refronted in 1800) with wood panelling, low ceilings and exposed beams. Part of the London Wall is claimed to be visible in the car park and it is believed that Charles I stayed here in 1646. The third handpump is often used to showcase Dark Star and other brewery ales. Q♿❀❀◁▷⚄🅿️🚫❀🎵

Hounslow

Moon Under Water ✓

84-86 Staines Road, TW3 3LF
☎ (020) 8572 7506
Greene King Abbot; Ruddles Best Bitter; Sharp's Doom Bar; 6 changing beers (often Portobello, Redemption, Twickenham) ⊞
Licensed from 9am, this is a 1991 Wetherspoon shop conversion still in original style, displaying many local history panels and photographs. A real ale oasis for beer lovers from the town and surrounding areas, it has been in this Guide for 22 consecutive years. Up to six guest ales come from across the country, with more at festival times when 11 handpumps are put to work. The regular cider is usually Weston's Old Rosie. Families are welcome during the day. Q♿❀◁▷&⊖(Central)🅿️❀🎵

Isleworth

Victoria Tavern

56 Worple Road, TW7 7HU
☎ (020) 8892 3385
Wadworth 6X; 1 changing beer (often Greene King, Hook Norton, Morland) ⊞
Built in 1902, this small, traditional back-street local comprises three rooms, two bars and a comfortable conservatory leading to an outside back patio area. One room is now reserved for special occasions or private functions. Live bands play on Saturday and Sunday evening. The pub is a short walk from Twickenham Stadium, but take note of parking restrictions on rugby days. Q♿❀&🅿️❀🎵

Northolt

Greenwood Hotel ★ 🅛 ✓

674 Whitton Avenue West, Wood End, UB5 4LA
☎ (020) 8423 6169
Greene King Abbot; Ruddles Best Bitter; Sharp's Doom Bar; 5 changing beers (often Redemption, Sambrook's, Twickenham) ⊞
This 1930s former Courage road house, identified by CAMRA as having a regionally important historic pub interior, was reopened by Wetherspoon's in 2016 after six years of closure. The pub has been sympathetically refurbished, honouring the Grade II-listed heritage features, including the original flooring, bar tops and light fittings. The old ballroom has been converted into a dining area. Twelve hotel rooms have also been added. Alcoholic drinks are served from 9am. Q♿❀◁▷&≠(Park)♣🅿️❀

Norwood Green

Plough

Tentelow Lane, UB2 4LG
☎ (020) 8574 7473 ⊕ ploughnorwoodgreen.com

ENGLAND

Fuller's London Pride; 1 changing beer (often Dark Star) 🅷

Dating back to circa 1650, this Grade II-listed building is Fuller's oldest tied house. With low, exposed beams, two real fires and a superb landlord who takes pride in both friendly service and a well-kept range of real ales and ciders, it offers traditional roasts alongside other dishes every day. Musicians entertain from time to time inside the pub as well as in the garden during the summer. There is patio seating at the front.
🏠⭐🌗♿♣👜🚃(120) 🌸🛜♪

St Margarets

Crown

174 Richmond Road, TW1 2NH
☎ (020) 8892 5896 🌐 crowntwickenham.co.uk
Harvey's Sussex Best Bitter; Surrey Hills Shere Drop; Young's London Original 🅷

A large pub dating from about 1730 and Grade II listed, with a substantial refurbishment enhancing the Georgian heritage of the original building. The Victorian hall at the back has been opened up for dining and the courtyard garden attractively remodelled. Inside are various seating areas and three fireplaces, one in the bar area with a real fire. Several windows and doors are original. Food is served throughout the day. 🏠⭐🌗♿🚃P🚃🌸🛜

Turk's Head

28 Winchester Road, TW1 1LF
☎ (020) 8892 1972 🌐 turksheadtwickenham.co.uk
Fuller's London Pride, ESB; 2 changing beers (often Dark Star, Fuller's, Twickenham) 🅷

A genuine local corner pub built in 1902 and famed for a scene in the Beatles film, A Hard Day's Night, where Ringo played darts. The Bearcat Comedy Club takes place on Saturday nights in the Winchester Hall, except in summer, and there is regular live music. The Jazz Sanctuary operates every other Thursday and the pub is included in London's Festival of Jazz. There is a covered garden area with plenty of seating.
Q🏠⭐🌗♿🚃🚃🌸🛜♪

Teddington

Abercorn Arms

76-78 Church Road, TW11 8EY
☎ (020) 3730 6602 🌐 theabercornarms.co.uk
Big Smoke Solaris Session Pale Ale, Underworld; Harvey's Sussex Best Bitter; 3 changing beers (often Five Points, Sambrook's, Surrey Hills) 🅷

Acquired by the Big Smoke brewery in their partnership with Punch Taverns and extensively refurbished in 2020, this pub has become popular with locals and with those visitors who can find it in its residential side street. Spacious inside and out, it offers good food all day and a wide range of ales, ciders and keg beers. Guest beers are often from small-batch UK breweries. Outside is a large, covered all-weather garden. Quiz night is Sunday.
Q🏠⭐🌗♿🚃♣👜🌸🛜♪

Masons Arms

41 Walpole Road, TW11 8PJ
☎ (020) 8977 6521 🌐 the-masons-arms.co.uk
Hop Back Summer Lightning; Sambrook's Junction; Vale Best IPA; 1 changing beer (often Buntingford, Hop Back, Portobello) 🅷

A small, friendly back-street community free house built in 1860, this is a beer-drinkers' haven, with bottles, pictures and pub memorabilia on display. Carpeting and comfortable seating create a cosy atmosphere. There is a log-burning stove, dartboard and a small secluded rear

patio. Music evenings include a bring-your-own-vinyl night on the third Tuesday of the month. The guest beer, sourced from a wide range of independent brewers, changes frequently. A former local CAMRA Pub of the Year. 🏠♿🚃♣👜🚃🌸🛜♪

Twickenham

Rifleman

7 Fourth Cross Road, TW2 5EL
☎ (020) 8255 0205
Harvey's Sussex Best Bitter; Twickenham Red Sky, Naked Ladies; Young's Bitter; 3 changing beers (often Hook Norton, Otter, Twickenham) 🅷

A traditional late-Victorian pub whose name commemorates rifleman Frank Edwards, a local resident, who dribbled a football across No Man's Land towards the German trench in WW1. A Twickenham Fine Ales house since 2019 and a community hub, it has a small beer garden, front patio, board games, TV sport and, on Thursdays, an open mic evening. Twickenham Stadium and Harlequins rugby clubs are a short walk away. Several bus routes are close.
Q⭐🚃(Strawberry Hill) ♣P🚃🌸🛜♪

White Swan ✅

Riverside, TW1 3DN
☎ (020) 8744 2951 🌐 whiteswantwickenham.co.uk
Otter Bitter; Twickenham Naked Ladies; 1 changing beer (often Dark Star, Gale's, Renegade) 🅷

A Grade II-listed building and award-winning traditional pub, built around 1690. Entry is via steps up to the first floor, where the bar has real fires and walls covered with rugby and other memorabilia. A small veranda/balcony and a triclinium (a three-sided room with window seats) afford views of the river and Eel Pie Island. Directly opposite is a covered beer garden (tides permitting), right on the water's edge. Quiz night is every Wednesday from September to April. Q🏠⭐🌗♿🚃🚃🌸🛜♪

Uxbridge

General Eliott

1 St John's Road, UB8 2UR
☎ (01895) 237385 🌐 generaleliottuxbridge.co.uk
Fuller's London Pride; St Austell Tribute; 1 changing beer (often Butcombe, St Austell, Tring) 🅷

One of six pubs in the country named after the teetotaller who defended Gibraltar from the Spanish in the late 18th century, this attractive, comfortable canalside pub dating from 1820 has a warm and friendly atmosphere. Refurbishment prior to lockdown included a new covered seating area next to the canal. A vegan menu is available. There is a Tuesday quiz, open mic on Thursdays and live music Friday and/or Saturday night.
🏠⭐🌗P🚃(3) 🌸🛜♪

Three Tuns ✅

24 High Street, UB8 1JN
☎ (01895) 233960
Greene King IPA, Abbot; house beer (by Greene King); 3 changing beers (often Greene King, Timothy Taylor, Tring) 🅷

A traditional high-street pub in a 350-year-old, Grade II-listed building. There is a small front bar and, down a few steps to the rear, a stone-flagged bar area, with a conservatory to one side. Outside are a small, covered patio at the back and tables to the front on the pedestrianised high street. Good quality food is served at lunchtimes and evenings, with the bar and food service attentive and friendly. 🏠⭐🌗😀🚃🌸🛜♪

Breweries

3 Locks (NEW)

Units N4 & N5, River Place, Hawley Wharf, Camden Town, London, NW1 8QG ⊕ 3locksbeer.com

Overlooking one of the eponymous Camden Locks, the brewery opened in 2022 in railway arches underneath the London Overground. Adjacent space is a planned shop. Founded by the owner of a brewery on the Greek island of Pathos, the initial range of a pale ale and a hefeweizen has been expanded to up to six. No cask ale. ◆

40FT SIBA

Bootyard, Abbot Street, Dalston, E8 3DP
☎ (020) 8126 6892

Office: The Printhouse, 18-20 Ashwin Street, Dalston, E8 3DL ⊕ 40ftbrewery.com

This six-barrel microbrewery was established in 2015 in two 20ft shipping containers. It has since expanded to a total of 150ft. Beers are produced for its taproom as well as pubs, bars, restaurants and off-licences. Output is in kegs and cans with cask specials for local beer festivals. ◆

Affinity

Grosvenor Arms, 17 Sidney Road, Brixton, SW9 0TP
☎ 07904 391807 ⊕ affinitybrewco.com

Established in 2016 in a container in Tottenham Hale and expanded in 2017 to the Bermondsey Beer Mile, 2020 saw the brewery start afresh in the basement of the Grosvenor Arms. Run as a separate business, cask, keg and canned beers are available in the pub and now quite widely. ◆

Grosvenor Gold (ABV 3.8%) GOLD

Anomaly

Glebe Gardens, Old Malden, KT3 5RU ☎ 07903 623993 ⊕ anomalybrewing.co.uk

Founded in 2017, beers started to appear at the end of 2018 brewed on a 100-litre home kit. Most production is available in bottles and cans but cask is sometimes available for pubs and at beer festivals. Old Belgian and English styles are the regular range.

Anspach & Hobday SIBA

Unit 11, Valley Point Industrial Estate, Beddington Farm Road, Beddington, CR0 4WP
☎ (020) 3302 9669 ⊕ anspachandhobday.com

⊗ Anspach & Hobday began brewing in 2014. In 2020 the brewery moved to a new site in Croydon. In 2022 following the success of its nitro-porter, London Black, the brewery expanded to a 24 barrel kit. The original site, the Arch House (on the Bermondsey Beer Mile), is now the home of its taproom and barrel-aged and sour beers. ‼ ▇ LIVE ◆

The Ordinary Bitter (ABV 3.7%) BITTER
Flavours of spicy and resinous hop overlaid with biscuit malt. A subtle bitterness and sweet malt emerge in the aftertaste.
The Patersbier (ABV 4.1%) SPECIALITY
The Smoked Brown (ABV 5.5%) SPECIALITY
Smoke, chocolate orange and caramel on nose and palate creates a well-balanced dark-brown beer with roasted malt and earthy hops.

The IPA (ABV 6%) IPA
A hoppy, bitter New World IPA, with lemons, grapefruit and spicy peppercorns overlaid by biscuit. Sweet biscuity, dry bitter finish.
The Porter (ABV 6.7%) PORTER
Roasted coffee notes throughout with caramel, dark fruit and hops in the flavour and lingering finish which is slightly dry.

Babel Beerhouse

▤ **1 Lewis Cubitt Walk, Kings Cross, N1C 4DL**
☎ (020) 8161 4446 ⊕ babelbeerhouse.com

Opened in 2019 as Little Creatures, it is the UK outpost of Australia's Little Creatures, and is ultimately owned by Kirin's Lion Group. Lion sold its UK brewing interests to Odyssey Inns in 2022, later renamed In Good Company. The brewpub has been renamed to Babel Beerhouse. Following a hiatus brewing resumed in 2023. No cask ale.

Battersea

12-14 Arches Lane, Battersea Power Station, Nine Elms, SW11 8AB
☎ (020) 8161 2366 ⊕ batterseabrew.co.uk

Opened in 2018, the brewery consists of two railway arches, one for the brewery and one for the taproom. A changing range of beers is produced in cask and keg available at the taproom and in pubs run by the brewery owners, the Mosaic Pub Company. ◆

Beavertown

Units 17 & 18, Lockwood Industrial Park, Mill Mead Road, Tottenham Hale, N17 9QP
☎ (020) 8525 9884

Ponders End: Unit 7, Ponders End Industrial Estate, 102 East Dock Lees Lane, Ponders End, London, EN3 7SR

Tottenham Hotspur Stadium: 748 High Road, Tottenham, London, N17 0AP
⊕ beavertownbrewery.com

⊠ Beavertown opened its Tottenham Hale site in 2014 after small beginings in De Beauvoir Town and Old Ford. A minority stake was sold to Heineken in 2018 and further investment saw the opening of 'Beaverworld' in Ponders End in 2020. Heineken completed 100% ownership in 2022. An onsite brewery and bar opened in the newly-built Tottenham Hotspur football ground in 2019 (access to ticket holders only). This beer is also available in the Corner Pin, Beavertown's pub opposite the stadium. No cask ale. ▇◆◆

Beerblefish SIBA

Unit 2A-4, Uplands Business Park, Blackhorse Lane, Walthamstow, E17 5QJ ☎ 07594 383195
⊕ beerblefish.co.uk

Starting at UBrew in Bermondsey in 2015, the Edmonton site began production in 2016. A move to Walthamstow occurred in 2021, to a site three times larger with a homely taproom. Capacity increased by subsequently buying the former Brew By Numbers kit. A series of hoppy pale ales and a range of Victorian heritage ales are available in cask, keg and bottles. LIVE ◆

Hoppy Little Fish (ABV 3.5%) PALE
Perfumed hoppy aroma with caramel and prune adding to a sweetish background. With a lingering, dry, bitter finish.
Hackney TNT (ABV 4%) RED

Edmonton Best Bitter (ABV 4.3%) BITTER
Amber-coloured, smooth, traditional bitter. Pears and citrus fruits overlay caramelised fudge. Spicy hops on the dryish bitter finish.

Pan Galactic Pale (ABV 4.6%) PALE
Amber, full-bodied beer with fruity tangerine notes with sweet biscuit. Aftertaste starts soft becoming bitter and dry. Floral, biscuity nose.

Blackbeerble Stout (ABV 5.2%) STOUT

1853 ESB (ABV 5.3%) BITTER
Sweet caramel flavour aroma and flavour with marmalade and a gentle developing spicy hoppiness becoming slightly bitter in the aftertaste.

1820 Porter (ABV 6.6%) PORTER
Aromas of Brettanomyces, roast and black treacle, which are also in the sweet caramelised fruity flavour. Spicy, dry, bitter finish.

1892 IPA (ABV 6.9%) IPA
Brett and marmalade aroma. Full-bodied with apricot, honey, caramelised orange and Brett. Strong spicy hoppy bitter orange builds in the finish.

Belleville

Unit 36, Jaggard Way, Wandsworth Common, SW12 8SG
☎ (020) 8675 4768 ⊕ bellevillebrewing.co.uk

Belleville began brewing in 2012. It was set up by a group of parents from a local primary school, after the success of the head brewer's efforts at homebrewing for a beer festival at the school. It specialises in American-style beers, with a core range and quarterly seasonals, available in keg and can. The taproom is a few units along from the brewery and offers the core range and current seasonals plus occasional guest beers. No cask ale. ‼◆⚲

Bexley SIBA

Unit 18, Manford Industrial Estate, Manor Road, Erith, DA8 2AJ
☎ (01322) 337368 ⊕ bexleybrewery.co.uk

Bexley Brewery was founded in 2014. Brewers Cliff and Jane Murphy produce regular, seasonal and experimental brews, all of which are gluten-free. The Bird & Barrel in Barnehurst, opened in 2018, replaced the taproom as the main source of the beers locally. ‼🍺◆GF⚲

Bursted Session Bitter (ABV 3.8%) BITTER
Hills & Holes Kent Pale (ABV 3.8%) PALE
Golden Acre (ABV 4%) GOLD
Smooth golden ale with citrus aroma. Flavour is of grapefruit, hops and a strong bitterness, continuing in the dry-fruity finish..

Bexley's Own Beer (ABV 4.2%) BITTER
Pale brown beer with a balance of fudge, floral hop, stone fruit and some bitterness growing in the dry finish.

Redhouse Premium (ABV 4.2%) BITTER
Malt aroma with orange marmalade, earthy hop notes. Bitter flavour, earthy and spicy hops, caramel malt sweetness. Long, bittersweet finish.

Idaho 7 Session IPA (ABV 4.4%) BITTER
Black Prince Porter (ABV 4.6%) PORTER
Creamy dark brown porter with treacle on the nose with hints of dark roast, cedar and fruit. Flavour has dark malt, damsons, citrus and toffee. Finish is dry with a little damson.

Anchor Bay IPA (ABV 4.8%) PALE
A deep golden beer with a fruity, spicy aroma, citrus taste and an astringent finish.

Spike Island Stout (ABV 5.3%) STOUT

Bianca Road

83-84 Enid Street, Bermondsey, SE16 3RA
☎ (020) 3221 1001 ⊕ biancaroad.com

After starting in 2016 in Peckham, the brewery moved to a bigger site in Bermondsey in 2017, and again in 2019 to two arches on the Bermondsey Beer Mile which incorporate the taproom (open Wed-Sun). Output is in keg and cans. ⚲

Big Penny

1 Priestley Way, Blackhorse Lane, Walthamstow, E17 6AL
☎ (020) 3700 1040 ⊕ bigpenny.co.uk

The Truman's Brewery name was revived in 2010 with a brewery established on Fish Island in 2013. A move to the former Crate brewery in Hackney Wick occoured in 2020 but they withdrew from brewing in 2022. A name change to Big Penny coincided with a start to contract brewing at Redchurch. Its Social Club taproom remains a major presence on the Blackhorse Beer Mile. No cask ale. ◆LIVE

Block

🏠 **Wenlock Arms, 26 Wenlock Road, Hoxton, London, N1 7TA**
☎ (020) 7608 3406 ⊕ wenlockarms.com

⊗ Block is based in the cellar of the award-winning Wenlock Arms. Launched at the end of 2016, the beer is available at the pub in cask and keg formats. Specials are available for local beer festivals.

Bohem

Unit 5, Littleline House, 41-43 West Road, Tottenham, N17 0RE
☎ (020) 8617 8350 ☎ 07455 502976
⊕ bohembrewery.com

Traditional Bohemian lagers, light and dark, brewed by Czech expats in North London. Beers are supplied widely, including the taproom near Bowes Park station. A second outlet was added in 2020, the Bohemia House in West Hampstead, replacing the former Czech club and specialising in Czech food to complement the beers. No cask ale. 🍺

Boxcar

Bethnal Green ⊕ boxcarbrewery.co.uk

After being located in Homerton for two years, Boxcar moved to Bethnal Green in 2019 opening a larger brewery and taproom. An ever-changing range of hoppy beers in keg and cans forms the majority of production, with cask sometimes available. Brewing is currently suspended. ⚲

Br3wery

253 Beckenham Road, Beckenham, BR3 4RP
☎ (020) 3793 2765 ⊕ br3wery.com

Established at home in 2019 producing bottle-conditioned beers, bigger batches of beer were later brewed at Birmingham Brewery. The current brewery opened in the shop in 2021 and produces a changing range of styles to drink onsite (part of the recently launched Local Brewery Loop). A new brewery nearby is planned. No cask ale. 🍺⚲

Brew By Numbers

Southern Warehouse, Morden Wharf, Morden Wharf Road, North Greenwich, SE10 0NU
☎ (020) 7237 9794 ⊕ bbno.co

Established in 2012, Brew by Numbers produces a wide range of styles with differing ingredients, leading to its eponymous numbering system, although this was simplified a few years ago. A new brewery was installed in 2021 at a site in North Greenwich, doubling as a taproom. The original taproom and pilot berwery along the Bermondsey Beer Mile closed during 2023. ▰LIVE ⬧

11 Session IPA (ABV 4.2%) GOLD
Pale gold beer. Strong fruity nose with green notes in the aroma and palate. Hops, fruit (mango, citrus) and some pine character in the biscuity sweet flavour with an underlying bitterness that lingers in the long astringent finish that becomes slightly spicy.

Brewdog (NEW)

Tower Hill: Unit 3, Minster Building, 21 Great Tower Street, Tower Hill, EC3N 5AR

Waterloo (NEW): Unit G, 01 The Sidings, Waterloo Station, Waterloo Road, SE1 7BH ⊕ brewdog.com

Established in 2007 by James Watt and Martin Dickie. Most of the production goes into cans and keg. The first Brewdog brewery outside of Ellon opened in Tower Hill in 2018. Another site opened in 2022 underneath the former Eurostar platforms at Waterloo station and claims to have the largest bar in London. More than 50 bars now exist in the UK. ⬧

Brewhouse & Kitchen SIBA

▮ 2a Corsica Street, Highbury, N5 1JJ
☎ (020) 7226 1026 ⊕ brewhouseandkitchen.com/highbury

Brewing began in 2015 in the open plan brewery at the rear of the pub, a former tram shed. Four cask beers are brewed to the chain's formula, named after local icons including the nearby Arsenal FC.

Brewhouse & Kitchen SIBA

▮ 397-400 Geffrye Street, Hoxton, E2 8HZ
☎ (020) 3861 8920 ⊕ brewhouseandkitchen.com/hoxton

Brewing began in 2018 in one of the arches under Hoxton Overground station. Four cask ales are brewed to the chain's formula, named after local icons including former land owner Sir Humphrey Starkey. It is opposite the relaunched Museum of the Home.

Brewhouse & Kitchen SIBA

▮ 5 Torrens Street, Angel, EC1V 1NQ
☎ (020) 7837 9421 ⊕ brewhouseandkitchen.com/islington

Brewing began in 2014 in the open plan brewery at the rear of the pub, the ground floor of the landmark office building by the Angel junction. Four cask beers are brewed to the chain's formula, named after local icons including former resident Charlie Chaplin and infamous estate agents Hotblack Desiato. Brewing suspended, to resume in 2024 after building refurbishment.

Brick

Units 13-14, Deptford Trading Estate, Blackhorse Road, Deptford, SE8 5HY
☎ (020) 3903 9441 ⊕ brickbrewery.co.uk

Established by owner and former homebrewer Ian Stewart in 2013. Due to continued expansion, the brewing operation relocated from Peckham to larger premises in nearby Deptford in 2017. The original Peckham railway arch site is retained as a brewery tap. Beside the core Foundation beers, frequent one-off and collaboration brews are produced throughout the year. ▰⬧

Peckham Pale (ABV 4.5%) GOLD
Well-balanced, refreshing hazy amber/gold-coloured beer with tropical fruits and sweet orange. Bready malt notes lead to a bitter finish.

Peckham Rye (ABV 4.7%) SPECIALITY
Citrus on the nose with dry, spicy characteristics, rich and full body. Medium bitterness balanced with rich, caramel flavours with residual sweetness.

Blackhorse (ABV 4.9%) STOUT
Smooth stout with sweet chocolate aroma. Dark bitter chocolate, sweet toffee and dark orange marmalade flavours. Lingering dry roastiness.

Extra Special Bitter (ABV 5.2%) BITTER
Ruby brown beer. Roasty chocolate notes throughout overlaid with raisins, toffee and marmalade. Dry roasty bitter finish with spicy hops.

Brixton

Arches 547 & 548, Brixton Station Road, Loughborough Junction, SW9 8PF
☎ (020) 3609 8880

Second Brewery: Units 1&2, Dylan Road Estate, Dylan Road, Milkwood Road, Loughborough Junction, London, SE24 0HL ⊕ brixtonbrewery.com

The brewery opened in 2013 in central Brixton with beer names and branding reflecting the local area. An investment by Heineken in 2017 enabled expansion into a nearby industrial unit. As of 2021 Brixton is now owned outright by Heineken. The original arch is used for seasonal and experimental brews and the adjacent arch houses the taproom. The bulk of production is in KeyKeg, cans and bottles. ‼▰⬧LIVE ⬧

Reliance Pale Ale (ABV 4.2%) PALE
Pale hazy gold beer with lemon zest and a growing bitterness. A little biscuit and apricot on the palate. Spicy hops finish.

Brockley SIBA

31 Harcourt Road, Brockley, SE4 2AJ
☎ (020) 8691 4380

Second brewery: Unit 28, Chiltonian Industrial Estate, Manor Lane, Hither Green, SE12 0TX
⊕ brockleybrewery.co.uk

The original SE4 brewery has been trading since 2013 and now focuses on core cask ales and single batch specials. In 2019, a new 20-barrel brewery was opened on the former site of the Chiltonian Biscuit factory in Hither Green. The brewery concentrates on brewing cask beers and supplying outlets across SE London. The whole range is vegan and available at the taprooms on both sites. ▰⬧V⬧

Pale Ale (ABV 4.1%) BITTER
Fragrant sweet nose leading to a hoppy citrus flavour. The aftertaste is sweet leading to a slightly bitter finish.

Red Ale (ABV 4.8%) RED
Smoky aroma on this well-balanced sweet, fruity, American-style red ale with growing spice overlaid with dry-roasted bitter character.

Broken Drum

Heron Hill, Upper Belvedere, DA17 5ER ☎ 07803 131678 ⊕ thebrokendrum.co.uk

Homebrewer that started trial brewing for the Broken Drum micropub in Blackfen, before going commercial in 2018. Brewed in small batches for the micropub and local beer festivals. All output is in cask.

Bullfinch

Arches 886 & 887, Rosendale Road, Herne Hill, SE24 9EH ☎ 07795 546630
⊕ thebullfinchbrewery.co.uk

Bullfinch began brewing in 2014 sharing with Anspach & Hobday in Bermondsey, but opened in Herne Hill in 2016 using a 2.5-barrel plant. The beers are available in the taproom, at its Bull & Finch bar, Gipsy Hill (which now has its own kit – the So What brewery) and increasingly in local pubs. ‼ ➡ LIVE ✦

Camden Town

Unit 1, Navigation Park, Morson Road, Ponders End, EN3 4TJ
☎ (020) 7485 1671

Second brewery: Arches 55-65, Wilkin Street Mews, Kentish Town, London, NW5 3NN
⊕ camdentownbrewery.com

⊠ Bought by A-B InBev in 2016. A modern, automated brewhouse situated in railway arches underneath Kentish Town West railway station with an onsite brewery tap. A second brewery in Ponders End opened in 2017, and is the main production site, with a large taproom open for special events. No cask ale. ‼ ✦

Clarkshaws

Arch 497, Ridgway Road, Loughborough Junction, SW9 7EX ☎ 07989 402687 ⊕ clarkshaws.co.uk

Established 2013, Clarkshaws is a small brewery focusing on using UK ingredients for its core beers, and reducing beer miles. The beers are suitable for vegans and vegetarians and are accredited by the Vegetarian Society. All beers are unfined and may be hazy. A small taproom operates on the premises for most of the year (check before travelling). V✦

Gorgon's Alive (ABV 4%) BITTER
Unfined, golden-coloured beer with spicy hops throughout. The flavour has hints of orange and peach with a dry bitterness.
Phoenix Rising (ABV 4%) BITTER
Tawny beer with a creamy toffee nose. Bananas, pineapple, hops and caramel flavours. Dryish, short, fruity biscuit finish.
Vegan Milk Stout (ABV 4.9%) STOUT
Coldharbour Hell Yeah Lager (ABV 5.3%)
SPECIALITY
Hops and mango notes that are also present on the flavour with some butterscotch. Dryish palate.
Hellhound IPA (ABV 5.5%) IPA
Spiced and citrus notes in this unfined amber beer with a bitterness in the flavour and finish, which is dry.

Coalition (NEW)

Office: Hill View Close, Purley, CR8 1AU
⊕ coalitionbrewing.co.uk

First brewed in 2015 at Hepworth in Sussex, later brewing has been undertaken at undisclosed breweries in London. 2023 saw brewing move to the newly installed Laine Brewery at the Ram, Wandsworth, formerly home to the SlyBeast Brewery. No cask ale.

Concrete Island

Pavilion Terrace, Wood Lane, Shepherd's Bush, W12 0HT ⊕ concreteislandbrewery.co.uk

Established as Small Beer Brewing in 2016, it was rebranded as Concrete Island Brewery in 2020. Run from a private flat in West London with a brew length of just 25 litres, it is one of the smallest commercial breweries. Unpasteurised and unfiltered beers are available in bottles. No cask ale.

Crate

White Building, Unit 7, Queens Yard, White Post Lane, Hackney Wick, E9 5EN ☎ 07547 695841
⊕ cratebrewery.com

Created as a brewpub and pizzeria in 2012, expansion later saw a move to the Brew Shed across the yard. Falling into administration in mid-2020, the Brew Shed was bought by Trumans (since closed) and Crate retreated back to the brewpub. The reduced range of four beers plus specials are available on keg and in bottles and cans. Beers are temporarily being brewed at Purity whilst the onsite brew kit is refurbished. No cask ale. ✦

Cronx SIBA

Unit 6, Vulcan Business Centre, Vulcan Way, New Addington, CR0 9UG
☎ (020) 3475 8848 ⊕ thecronx.com

Croydon-based microbrewery, opened in 2012, brewing a range of award-winning beers in cask, keg, bottles, cans and mini-kegs. Cronx has a dedicated bar within the Selhurst Park stadium which is open on Crystal Palace FC match days and has now opened a bar on Croydon High Street. ✦ LIVE

Standard (ABV 3.8%) BITTER
Easy-drinking brown bitter with sweetish fudge and spicy hoppiness notes throughout. Malty bitter finish with a dryness that remains.
Kotchin (ABV 3.9%) SPECIALITY
Grapefruity beer with pleasant hoppy notes. A little sweetness is balanced by a crisp bitter finish that grows on drinking.
Nektar (ABV 4.5%) PALE
Full-bodied, dark gold pale ale. Peach with citrus, sweet biscuit and floral hops, gently fade in the lingering bitter finish.
Pop Up! (ABV 5%) PALE
Smooth, amber APA with strong tropical and grapefruit throughout. Hoppy and bitter on the palate and dry finish.
Entire (ABV 5.2%) PORTER
Dark brown porter with chocolate roast in the aroma, flavour and finish. Fruit character is of caramelised raisins and plums.

Deviant & Dandy SIBA

Arches 184 & 185, Nursery Road, Hackney, E9 6PB
⊕ deviantanddandy.com

Initially cuckoo-brewed at Enfield Brewery for the Off Broadway bar in London Fields, Deviant & Dandy started brewing at its current premises in 2018 in railway arches under the London Overground. Beer is available in pubs, bars and at the onsite taproom (Thursday-Sunday). No cask ale. ✦

Distortion

647 Portslade Road, Battersea, SW8 3DH ☎ 07557 307452 ⊕ distortionbrewing.co.uk

⊗ Starting in the founder's garage in south London, the brewery was installed in a railway arch in 2020. The keg range is sold directly from serving tanks in the taproom (open Thursday-Sunday). No cask ale. ✦

Dog's Grandad

Arch 550, Brixton Station Road, Brixton, SW9 8PF ⊕ dogsgrandadbrewery.co.uk

Opened in 2021, the range of beers is available in keg at the taproom (Wednesday-Saturday), some local bars, and in cans from the website and bottle shops. Cask versions available to the trade. 🍽✦

Drop Project SIBA

Unit 8, Willow Business Centre, 17 Willow Lane, Mitcham, CR4 4NX ⊕ drop-project.co.uk

Drop Project began brewing at Missing Link in Sussex until brewing commenced at Mitcham in 2021. Beers are mostly available in keg and can, including regular collaboration brews with other breweries and groups, and a growing range in cask. ✦

East London SIBA

Unit 45, Fairways Business Centre, Lammas Road, Leyton, E10 7QB ☎ (020) 8539 0805 ⊕ eastlondonbrewing.com

East London Brewing Company is an award-winning, 25-barrel brewery established in 2011 by Stu and Claire. The brewery brews a core range of regular beers available in cask, keg, bottle and can. Regular specials are made, including an annual green-hopped beer each September, in collaboration with Walthamstow Beer (a collective of small-batch hop growers). 🍽✦LIVE

Pale Ale (ABV 4%) PALE
Amber beer with spicy hops, bitter lemon, tropical fruits and biscuit that are there in the dry aftertaste. Hoppy aroma.
Foundation Bitter (ABV 4.2%) BITTER
Dark amber bitter with nutty sweet caramel on the nose with naval orange and a little apricot. Finish has a hoppy, bitter spiciness.
Nightwatchman (ABV 4.5%) BROWN
Dark ruby-brown complex beer. Peach, caramelised fruit, toffee balanced by bitter, nutty and roasted malt flavours. Dry aftertaste.
Cowcatcher American Pale Ale (ABV 4.8%) PALE
Smooth pale ale. Sweet biscuit and hoppy citrusy notes on nose and palate. Long, dry finish of earthy bitter hops.
Jamboree (ABV 4.8%) BLOND
Hazy, blond beer with a lemon-sherbet nose. Slightly bitter with malt, orange and berries. Lasting, bitter, dry, citrus hoppy aftertaste.
Quadrant Oatmeal Stout (ABV 5.5%) STOUT
Roasty caramel malt, earthy and spicy hop notes. Sweet caramel malt, blackberry and bitter earthy hops flavour. Lingering, sweet, spiced fruitcake, bitterish finish.

Exale SIBA

Unit 2C, Uplands Business Park, Blackhorse Lane, Walthamstow, E17 5QJ ⊕ exalebrewing.com

Starting as Hale Brewery in Tottenham in 2017, expansion in 2019 saw a new brewery in Walthamstow and a new name. Most famous for Krankie, the Iron Brew sour. The core range and collaborations are available in keg and cans with cask ale being trialled in 2023. Its taproom (Thu-Sun) is one of the destinations on the Blackhorse Beer Mile. 🍽✦

Fearless Nomad

🏠 Black Dog Beer House, 17 Albany Road, Brentford, TW8 0NF
☎ (020) 8568 5688 ⊕ blackdogbeerhouse.co.uk/fearless-nomad

The Fearless Nomad Brewery is owned by Pete Brew who previously helped to set up the Big Smoke Brewery. Established in 2020, it is a small one-barrel brew plant producing a variety of different beers served in the Black Dog Beer House. Brewing is currently suspended and expansion plans cancelled while the business is appraised and future plans formulated.

Five Points SIBA

61 Mare Street, London Fields, Hackney, E8 4RG ☎ (020) 8533 7746 ⊕ fivepointsbrewing.co.uk

Five Points commenced brewing in 2013 in Hackney Downs. Crowdfunding in 2018 helped buy the Pembury Tavern. In 2020, the brewery moved into the existing warehouse facility in Mare Street. Crowdfunding in 2021 helped fund the addition of a taproom at Mare Street. Commitment to quality cask ale extends to a care scheme for stockists. 🍴LIVE✦

XPA (ABV 4%) GOLD
Grapefruit and biscuit aroma. Strong grapefruit, mango, hints of apricot over a biscuit flavour. A growing lingering bitterness, spicy character in the sweet aftertaste.
Best (ABV 4.1%) BITTER
Orange and sweet caramel aromas. Orange, apricot, caramelised fruit and fudge flavours. Sweet finish with hoppy spice and a developing bitterness.
Pale (ABV 4.4%) PALE
Earthy hops with tobacco hints and fruit sweet aroma. Tangerine, orange, nectarine fruit alongside honey notes in the spicy, bitter finish.
Railway Porter (ABV 4.8%) PORTER
Smoky, cocoa dominating porter with raisins, dark chocolate, plums and touch of marmalade. Lasting finish is bitter roasty dry and lingering.

Flat Iron Square

🏠 Flat Iron Square, 45 Southwark Street, Southwark, SE1 9HP ⊕ flatironsquare.co.uk/drink/our-beers

This brewpub opened in 2021 as St Felix, changing its name in 2022. Owned by Lagunitas (Heineken UK), exclusive beers are brewed for the site and possibly some of the Lagunitas range as well. No cask ale.

Forest Road SIBA

Unit 1a, Elizabeth Industrial Estate, Juno Way, South Bermondsey, SE14 5RW ⊕ forestroad.co.uk

Homebrewing at Forest Road, E8, at Van Eecke, Belgium, and Cropton (formerly C'84), Yorkshire, are all part of Forest Road's history before importing a brewery from San Francisco and setting up in South Bermondsey in 2021 with the onsite Emerald City taproom (open Thu and Fri evenings). Cask is more widely available now including at its recently acquired pub, the Quiet Night Inn, Westbourne Park, W11. ✦

Fourpure

Units 22 & 23, Bermondsey Trading Estate, Rotherhithe New Road, South Bermondsey, SE16 3LL ☎ (020) 3744 2141 ⊕ fourpure.com

Fourpure began brewing in 2013. In 2018 the brewery was bought by Lion of Australia, ultimately owned by Kirin of Japan, and again sold in 2022 to Odyssey Inns, later renamed to In Good Company. A substantial brewery tap opened along from the brewery in 2019, becoming a popular start (or end!) to the Bermondsey Beer Mile. No cask ale. ➤LIVE

Friendship Adventure SIBA

Unit G1, Coldharbour Works, 245a Coldharbour Lane, Loughborough Junction, SW9 8RR
🌐 friendship-adventure.com

Friendship Adventure began cuckoo-brewing at a range of breweries until its new brewery at Loughborough Junction opened in 2021. The popular onsite taproom (open Wednesday-Sunday) sells its wide range of keg beers. Canned beers are also available. No cask ale. ◆

Fuller's

Griffin Brewery, Chiswick Lane South, Chiswick, W4 2QB
☎ (020) 8996 2400 🌐 fullersbrewery.co.uk

⊠ The Griffin Brewery has stood for more than 360 years with the Fuller's name coming from the partnership formed in 1845. Gale's of Horndean was bought in 2005 and closed a year later. Dark Star of Sussex was bought in 2018 and closed in 2022 (Hophead is brewed at Chiswick, the other cask beers at Meantime). Fuller's sold its brewing interests to Asahi in 2019 but kept its pubs and hotels. ‼➤◆LIVE◆

Oliver's Island (ABV 3.8%) GOLD
Well-balanced golden ale with fruity aroma and flavour. Gentle bitter hoppiness balances a sweet, malty character flavour and short finish.
London Pride (ABV 4.1%) BITTER
Aromas of malt and hops. Well-balanced, smooth bitter with biscuity, orange citrus fruit flavour lingering into a bitter aftertaste.
Bengal Lancer (ABV 5%) PALE
Rich, creamy and well-balanced pale brown IPA with a gold hue. Hops with a dryish bitterness harmonise with the fruit and malty sweetness that linger into the aftertaste.
ESB (ABV 5.5%) BITTER
Caramelised malt and fruit aroma. Orange marmalade with hops, caramel and raisins in this strong brown bitter. Long, bitter, malty dry finish.
Brewed under the Dark Star brand name:
Hophead (ABV 3.8%) GOLD
A golden-coloured bitter with a fruity/hoppy aroma and a citrus/bitter taste and aftertaste. Flavours remain strong to the end.
Brewed under the Gale's brand name:
Seafarers Ale (ABV 3.6%) BITTER
A pale brown bitter, predominantly malty, with a refreshing balance of fruit and hops that lingers into the aftertaste where a dry bitterness unfolds.
HSB (ABV 4.8%) BITTER
Dates and dried fruit with spicy hops in the nose adding to the caramelised orange and treacle in the flavours. Malty throughout with a bittersweet finish.

German Kraft

Mercato Metropolitano, 42 Newington Causeway, Borough, SE1 6DR

Second Site: Mercato Metropolitano, 13a North Audley Street, Mayfair, London, W1K 6ZA

Third Site: Kraft Dalston, 130a Kingsland High Street, Dalston, London, E8 2LQ 🌐 germankraftbeer.com

Opening in 2017, to start with beer was imported from a German brewery in Bavaria (Steinbach Brau). In early 2018, the brewery officially opened near Elephant & Castle and beers were replicated onsite. The core range and seasonals reflect traditional German styles including lagering for four weeks. There are two further breweries with taprooms in Mayfair and Dalston with a bar (without a brewery) in Brixton. No cask ale. ◆

Gipsy Hill SIBA

Unit 8, Hamilton Road Industrial Estate, 160 Hamilton Road, West Norwood, SE27 9SF
☎ (020) 8761 9061 🌐 gipsyhillbrew.com

Gipsy Hill opened in 2014 at the same time and on the same site as London Beer Factory. It has since expanded into adjacent units and the taproom moved across the yard. A core range of four is supplemented by regular specials including AF options, available in keg and cans. Cask is occasionally produced. It has also brewed some barrel-aged beers. ◆LIVE◆

Goodness SIBA

5a Clarendon Yards, Coburg Road, Wood Green, N22 6TZ 🌐 thegoodnessbrew.co

⊠ A community-focused microbrewery, with taproom and event space, since 2019. The range consists of six core beers and various one-offs. All are unfiltered and vegan-friendly which are variously available as cask, keg or can. Wood Green Hopping City is brewed annually with hops grown by the local community. ➤V◆

Yes! Session IPA (ABV 4.5%) SPECIALITY
Notable citrus on the nose with mango, perfumed hops and biscuit taste. Finish starts bitter with a growing dryness.

Gorgeous

c/o 64 New Cavendish Street, Marylebone, W1G 8TB
☎ 07714 649988 🌐 gorgeousbrewery.com

⊠ Gorgeous inherited the brewing kit from London Brewing on the purchase of the Bull in Highgate in 2017. In 2018 a newly-built brewhouse at the rear of the pub came on stream but this was removed in 2022 at the insistence of the new pub owning company. Currently in storage until a new location is found with beers brewed elsewhere in the meantime. LIVE

Gravity Well

Unit 1, Compass West Industrial Estate, 33 West Road, Tottenham, N17 0XL ☎ 07833 226373
🌐 gravitywellbrewing.co.uk

Brewing started in 2018 in a railway arch in Leyton with a bigger taproom opening along the line in 2020. 2023 saw a move with new kit to Tottenham, into the same industrial estate as Redemption and the former OME brewery. The range of pale ales, sours and stouts (including double and imperial versions) is available in keg and cans. Cask is available for local beer festivals. ◆

Great Beyond (NEW) SIBA

416-418 Union Walk, Hoxton, E2 8HP
☎ (020) 3398 6471 🌐 greatbeyond.beer

Comprising three arches under the London Overground close to Hoxton Station; two arches contain the brewery, and one arch the comfy taproom (Wed-Sun). The seasoned brewers create a wide range of styles in keg and cans, available at the taproom and an increasing number of local bars. ◆

Hackney SIBA

Unit 10, Lockwood Way, Blackhorse Lane, Walthamstow, E17 5RB
☎ (020) 3489 9595 ⊕ hackneybrewery.co.uk

⊠ Founded in 2011 in Haggerston and relocated in 2021 to Walthamstow, the brewery and taproom are at the northern tip of the growing Blackhorse Beer Mile. The core range is available on keg and in cans supplemented by regular specials including monthly casks and collaborations. LIVE ◆

Hackney Church SIBA

Arches 16 & 17, Bohemia Place, Hackney, E8 1DU
☎ (020) 3795 8295 ⊕ hackneychurchbrew.co

Formerly known as St John at Hackney Brewery. Comprising two railway arches, the brewery is in one, the other being the atmospheric taproom. Available only from the taproom, for quality control, beers come from kegs or the tanks above the bar, or in bottles or cans for takeaway. All profits are used by the trust for worthy projects at the recently rebranded Hackney Church, the nearby parish church. No cask ale. ◆

Hammersmith (NEW)

Lower Ground Floor, 106 Fulham Palace Road, Hammersmith, W6 9PL
⊕ hammersmithbrewery.co.uk

Brewing started in 2019 in premises formerly used by the unconnected Hoppy Collie Brewery. Its basement taproom opened in 2022. The Italian brewer likes the darker beers, so stouts often appear on the menu along with hoppy pale ales. No cask ale. ◆

Hammerton SIBA

Units 8 & 9, Roman Way Industrial Estate, 149 Roman Way, Barnsbury, N7 8XH
☎ (020) 3302 5880 ⊕ hammertonbrewery.co.uk

⊠ Hammerton began brewing in London in 1868, but ceased in the 1950s, and was later demolished. In 2014, a member of the Hammerton family resurrected the name and opened a new brewery in Barnsbury. Expanded in 2019 after crowdfunding, the taproom is open Thursday-Saturday, complemented by its nearby bar, the House of Hammerton. ◆

N1 (ABV 4.1%) PALE
Biscuity sweet pale ale balanced by grapefruit, caramel and a building bitterness. Finish has a spicy character and is slightly dry.
Life on Mars (ABV 4.6%) RED
Ruby ale with roast, toffee and fruit aroma. Peppery hops, nutty roasty flavour with dark bitter marmalade. Dry lingering finish.
N7 (ABV 5.2%) PALE
Full-bodied pale ale. Sweet honey with honey, grapefruit, stone fruits, earthy hops, hint of apricot. Spicy, sweet finish overlaid dry bitterness.
Penton Oatmeal Stout (ABV 5.3%) STOUT
Sweet treacle and dark chocolate on the nose and rich palate. Developing dry bitter finish that lingers long and sweet.

Hiver

c/o 56 Stanworth Street, Bermondsey, SE1 3NY

☎ (020) 3198 9972 ⊕ hiverbeers.com

Beers are cuckoo brewed at Hepworth in Sussex using London urban honey. The taproom is on the often overlooked Maltby Street Market side of the Bermondsey Beer Mile. Beers are available in keg, bottles and can. No cask ale.

Howling Hops SIBA

Unit 9a, Queen's Yard, White Post Lane, Hackney Wick, E9 5EN
☎ (020) 3583 8262 ⊕ howlinghops.co.uk

⊠ Brewing began in 2012 at the Cock Tavern in Hackney, later opening a new brewery and tank bar in 2015 in Hackney Wick. Beers are widely available and cover many styles from pale ales with varying hops, sours and dark beers. Available in keg and cans with a growing range of cask. ◆

Husk SIBA

5, Unit F, The Factory Project, 33 Factory Road, Silvertown, E16 2HB ☎ 07803 271160
⊕ huskbrewing.com

Originally brewing in West Silvertown in 2015, 2023 saw a move to be part of the Factory Project, a creative work and event space in Silvertown itself. At the same time, a new brewery tap opened close to Canning Town station. Beers are available in keg and can with cask available on request. LIVE

Ignition

44a Sydenham Road, Sydenham, SE26 5QF
⊕ ignition.beer

Ignition is a not-for-profit small South London brewery, which employs and trains people with learning disabilities to brew beer. An onsite taproom opened in 2018 and provides staff with customer-facing experience. It puts on regular events. Beers, which are unfiltered, unpasteurised and suitable for vegans and vegetarians, are bottled for distribution or served from tanks in the taproom. LIVE V◆

Inkspot

Rookery Barn, The Rookery, 40 Streatham Common South, Streatham Common, SW16 3BX
☎ (020) 8679 7322 ☎ 07747 607803
⊕ theinkspotbrewery.com

Started in 2012 as Perfect Blend after a bar in Streatham, the brewery subsequently changed its name to Inkspot. Brewing began at its own premises in the middle of Streatham Common in 2018. Its Art & Craft bottle shops are the best places to find the beers along with when the taproom is open for 'shutters up' events. No cask ale. 🍺◆

Jawbone

Unit C, 1 Strawberry Vale, Twickenham, TW1 4RY
⊕ jawbonebrewing.com

Brewing commenced in 2020. Beer was initially available in cans, joined soon after by keg. The range of beers is available at the BrewDock taproom (open Thu-Sat) located next to a working boatyard by the River Thames. Cask ale is being trialled during 2023. ◆

Jiddlers Tipple

Office: Hornsey Park Road, Wood Green, N8 0JY
☎ 07966 527902 ⊕ jiddlerstipple.com

After using UBrew, 2019 saw output scaled up with brewing first at Birmingham Brewery and more recently at By The Horns and Goodness. The wide range of styles is available in keg and cans, sometimes on cask.

Kernel SIBA

Arch 11, Dockley Road Industrial Estate, Dockley Road, Bermondsey, SE16 3SF
☎ (020) 7231 4516

Office: 1 Spa Business Park, Spa Road, Bermondsey, SE16 4QT ⊕ thekernelbrewery.com

Kernel was established in 2009 by Evin O'Riordain and moved to larger premises in 2012 to keep up with demand. The brewery produces bottle-conditioned and keg beers, and has won many awards for its wide, ever-changing range. A new brewery tap, a few arches along, opened in 2020, and in 2022 it started to sell a different Kernel cask beer each week, now more widely available. ▰LIVE

Laine (NEW)

⊟ Ram, 68 Wandsworth High Street, Wandsworth, London, SW18 4LB

New brewing kit was installed by the Laine Pub Company in 2023 in the Ram, which formerly hosted SlyBeast Brewery. No Laine beers are produced here, the brewery is currently being used by the Coalition Brewery and its beers are available in the pub. No cask ale.

London Beer Factory

c/o The Barrel Project, 80 Druid Street, Bermondsey, SE1 2HQ ⊕ thelondonbeerfactory.com

London Beer Factory started brewing in 2014 on the same estate and at the same time as Gipsy Hill. This site was vacated during 2022 and brewing now takes place at an unknown location in Norfolk. The Barrel Project, along the Bermondsey Beer Mile, remains in use for fermenting and ageing beer. No cask ale.

London Beer Lab SIBA

Arch 283, Belinda Road, Loughborough Junction, Brixton, London, SW9 7DT
☎ (020) 8396 6517

Second site: Arch 41, Railway Arches, Nursery Road, Brixton, London, SW9 8BP ⊕ londonbeerlab.com

Opened in Brixton in 2013 as a bottle shop and homebrew supplies outlet, also offering brewing workshops and tastings. Commercial brewing began in Loughborough Junction in 2015 for larger batches with the shop focusing on small batch production and collaborations. ▰◆

Session IPA (ABV 4.2%) GOLD
Tip Top Citra (ABV 5%) PALE
Amber beer with citrus nose and flavour with some biscuity sweetness. The pithy bitter astringency builds in the bitter finish.

London Brewing SIBA

Bohemia, 762-764 High Road, North Finchley, N12 9QH
☎ (020) 8446 0294 ⊕ londonbrewing.com

⊠ London Brewing began brewing in 2011 at the Bull in Highgate. In 2014 it acquired its second pub, the Bohemia in North Finchley, at which brewing began in 2015 in a new 6.5-barrel brewhouse visible from the pub, becoming its sole location when the Bull was sold in

2016. The brewery endeavours to increase the range of cask ales. Beer is now widely available through pub chains and the free trade. ◆◆

London Lush (ABV 3.8%) BITTER
Earthy hoppiness on a sweet nose. Gentle hops, fruit and bitterness. Dry. slightly fruity finish with a fading spiciness.

Beer Street (ABV 4%) BITTER
Well-balanced, coppery brown best bitter with the hoppy bitterness underpinned by the caramelised malt character. Fruit is present throughout.

100 Oysters Stout (ABV 4.6%) STOUT
Dark chocolate and raisins on nose and palate, with roasty notes and dark plums. Dry roasty finish with fading spicy hops.

Long Arm

⊟ Long Arm, 20-26 Worship Street, Shoreditch, EC2A 2DX
☎ (020) 3873 4065 ⊕ longarmpub.co.uk

Opened in 2017, this brewery took over all Long Arm beers when brewing at the Ealing Park Tavern stopped. Beers are served onsite from tanks and in keg in the other 12 pubs in the ETM chain, the brewery's owners. No cask ale.

Macintosh

Stamford Brook Road, Stamford Brook, W6 0XH
⊕ macintoshales.com

Garage-based, 250-litre brewery, which went commercial in 2019, brewing once a week and nomadic brewing at various London breweries for larger batches. The two beers are available in cask, keg and bottle around North and East London.

Best Bitter (ABV 4.6%) BITTER
Pale Ale (ABV 4.6%) PALE

Magic Spells

c/o 24 Rigg Approach, Leyton, E10 7QN
☎ (020) 3475 1781 ⊕ magicspellsbrewery.co.uk

Magic Spells is owned and operated by Hare Wines. The onsite brewery was removed during 2021, with the beers now being brewed at an unknown brewery. Beer is available in cans and bottles. No cask ale.

Mammoth

Units DG02 3&4, Hackney Bridge, East Bay Lane, Hackney Wick, E15 2SJ ☎ 07970 927272
⊕ mammothbeer.com

Mammoth began brewing in 2021 and is located at the canal-side Hackney Bridge development for local enterprises. A brewery tap opened in Leytonstone in 2022 providing an outlet for the beers alongside regular appearances at the Hangar Bar at Hackney Bridge and the Rosemary Branch pub in Hoxton. No cask ale.

Marko Paulo

⊟ Owl & the Pussycat, 106 Northfield Avenue, Northfields, W13 9RT ⊕ markopaulo.co.uk

Brewing at the micropub was in parallel with the Ealing Brewery from 2016 until 2020, when brewing ceased. Ealing brewery itself ceased brewing in 2023 and brewing at the micropub was revived along with the Marko Paulo name. Beer is available at the micropub in cask and keg.

Marlix

Berger Close, Petts Wood, BR5 1HR ⊕ marlix.co.uk

⊗ Longtime friends Mark and Alex built a sizable garden shed to contain the brewery, after brewing beer together for the past 20 years, going commercial in 2020. Beers are available in cask, keg and bottles, with names based on the TV show The Young Ones. The range can be found in local micropubs and clubs. ♦

TPP (The People's Poet) (ABV 3.5%) BITTER
Kebab & Calculator (ABV 4.2%) PALE
Hazy light brown pale ale. Stone fruit on the nose with a building bitter taste. A lingering complex bitter/sweet aftertaste.
SPG (ABV 4.2%) SPECIALITY
Shut Up (ABV 4.7%) STOUT

Mash Paddle

92 Enid Street, Bermondsey, SE16 3RA
⊕ mashpaddlebrewery.com

Mash Paddle opened in 2022 in a railway arch along the Bermondsey Beer Mile as an incubator for startup brewers. A collection of small brewing kits allows customers to brew their own beers using supplied ingredients, tapping into the expert guidance onsite. Its own beers are also available from the taproom. No cask ale. ⬦

Meantime

Units 4 & 5, Lawrence Trading Estate, Blackwall Lane, North Greenwich, SE10 0AR
☎ (020) 8293 1111

Office: Norman House, 110-114 Norman Road, SE10 9EH ⊕ meantimebrewing.com

⊗ Founded in 2000, Meantime brews a range of continental-style beers widely available in keg, bottles and cans. In 2010 the brewery relocated to larger premises on the North Greenwich peninsula. Taken over by SABMiller in 2015 and subsequently by Asahi. In 2022, Meantime became the custodians of the remaining Dark Star cask beers, other than Hophead, when Asahi closed that brewery, acquired through its purchase of Fuller's. These beers are brewed on a newly installed cask production facility. ‼ 🏪 ♦ LIVE ⬦

Mellors

Trundleys Road, Deptford, SE8
⊕ mellorsbrewing.co.uk

Starting in 2021 in Harringay, a short-lived move to Suffolk saw Mellors back in London by the end of the year, Deptford this time. Small batches are brewed on the brewer's home kit and sometimes scaled up elsewhere, usually put into cans and sometimes into keg. No cask ale.

Mikkeller

🏢 **37-39 Exmouth Market, Clerkenwell, EC1R 4QL**
☎ (020) 3940 4991 ⊕ mikkellerbrewpublondon.com

Mikkeller of Denmark's second bar in London (sister bar to Mikkeller Shoreditch) opened in 2020 in collaboration with singer Rick Astley. Regular new beers appear in the brewpub and at the Shoreditch bar but a core range of favourites is emerging. No cask ale.

Mondo SIBA

86-92 Stewarts Road, Battersea, SW8 4UG

☎ (020) 7720 0782 ⊕ mondobeer.com

⊗ Mondo began brewing in 2015. Close to the rejuvenated Battersea Power Station complex, the onsite taproom (Wed-Sat) has 15 taps and showcases the wide range of beer styles brewed. The core, seasonal and occasional beers are available in keg and cans. Cask ale was trialled during 2023. ‼ ♦ ⬦

Muswell Hillbilly

4 Avenue Mews, Muswell Hill, N10 3NP ☎ 07920 554812 ⊕ muswellhillbillybrewers.co.uk

⊗ The founders of Muswell Hillbilly, originally homebrewers, acquired Mews premises in 2017. Brewing is in small batches, incorporating locally grown hops, with beers named after the local area. After the successful launch of a taproom in 2018, it took possession of a nearby unit in 2020, using a 500-litre brew kit. It is acquiring a fermenter to expand the range. ‼ 🏪 ⬦

Tetherdown Wheat Saison (ABV 5.1%) SPECIALITY
Funky, lemon nose and finish becoming dry, and slightly spicy. Honey is present in aroma and smooth flavour. Short finish.
IPA (ABV 5.3%) IPA
Tropical, orange, lemon and apricot fruit in aroma and flavour with a honey biscuit sweetness. Sweetness remains slightly bitter aftertaste.

Mutineers

London Lane, Bromley, BR1 4HE ⊕ mutineers.beer

Established in 2018, Mutineers brews in small batches using a 100-litre brew kit. Beers can be found locally and at beer festivals in cask and bottles.

Emu War (ABV 4.2%) IPA
Filibuster (ABV 4.2%) BITTER
Black Flag (ABV 4.5%) STOUT
Sky Pirate (ABV 4.8%) GOLD

Neckstamper SIBA

Unit 3, Cromwell Industrial Estate, Staffa Road, Leyton, E10 7QZ
☎ (020) 7018 1760 ☎ 07968 150075
⊕ neckstamper.com

Neckstamper began brewing in 2016 using a 10-barrel plant. Beers are all vegan-friendly and are available in keg and cans either at the taproom or locally. No cask ale. V⬦

Oddly

St John's Avenue, Friern Barnet, N11 3BX
✉ **hello@oddlybeer.com**

⊗ Originally founded on an island in the Thames at Hampton, it moved to be one of the three breweries in the Tottenham Brewery location during 2019 until later that year. Since then it has been brewing at home and using spare capacity at other breweries such as Muswell Hillbilly. ♦

Old Street

Unit 1, Queens Yard, White Post Lane, Hackney Wick, E9 5EN
☎ (020) 8525 9731 ⊕ oldstreetbrewery.com

Brewing began in 2013 at the Queen's Head pub in King's Cross. In 2018, the brewery moved to a railway arch near Bethnal Green underground station, with an onsite taproom. A second brewing site and onsite taproom was installed in Queens Yard, Hackney Wick in 2020. The Bethnal Green site was closed in late 2021. No cask ale. ◆

ORA SIBA

Unit 16a, Rosebery Industrial Park, Rosebery Avenue, Tottenham, N17 9SR ☎ 07703 563559
⊕ orabeer.com

Originally split between Italy and cuckoo brewing at Ubrew, Ora took over Brewheadz in Tottenham in 2019. A variety of hop-forward beers are brewed complemented with styles incorporating classic Italian ingredients such as lemons, balsamic vinegar and vanilla. No cask ale. ◆

Orbit SIBA

Arches 225 & 228, Fielding Street, Walworth, SE17 3HD
☎ (020) 7703 9092 ⊕ orbitbeers.com

Established in 2014 in a railway arch in Walworth, Orbit produces keg and bottled beers, focusing on traditional styles, especially continental European styles, supplemented by White Label specials. The design work and beer names relate to the founder's love of vinyl records. Cask is sometimes available in the new brewery tap in another railway arch across the street. **LIVE**

Park SIBA

Unit 7, Hampden Road, Norbiton, KT1 3LG
☎ (020) 8541 1887

Office: 38 St Georges Road, Kingston upon Thames, KT2 6DN ⊕ theparkbrewery.com

⊠ Founded in 2014, Park moved to larger premises in 2018. A wide variety of beers is now produced in cask, keg and cans, named after sites in nearby Richmond Park. The beers are unfined and sometimes experimental in their range of hops. !! ◆ LIVE ◆

Killcat Pale (ABV 3.7%) GOLD
Easy-drinking, straw-coloured golden ale. Citrus on nose and palate with the biscuity sweetness providing balance to the hoppy bitterness.
Amelia (ABV 4.2%) PALE
Pale gold. Aromas of biscuity malt and spicy hops. Dry-bitter and light with a grassy bitterness and a slight sweetness.
Gallows (ABV 4.5%) GOLD
Tropical fruit, orange and hop notes dominate. Malt is restrained with a gentle biscuit presence and growing bitterness. Well-balanced.
Spankers Hill IPA (ABV 6%) IPA
An amber-coloured, hoppy citrus dry golden ale with a similar finish and a touch of dry bitterness.

Perivale

Horsenden Farm, Horsenden Lane North, Perivale, UB6 7PQ ☎ 07892 409392 ⊕ perivale.beer

Established in 2019, the brewery is based at a farm looked after by the Friends of Horsenden Hill. As well as other events, monthly taproom openings are hosted, selling beers brewed with hops grown on the farm, and other local foraged ingredients, available in keg and bottles. No cask ale. ◆

Pillars SIBA

Unit 2, Ravenswood Industrial Estate, Shernhall Street, Walthamstow, E17 9HQ
☎ (020) 8521 5552 ⊕ pillarsbrewery.com

Brewing began in 2016 as an exclusively keg lager brewery. The range has been expanded over the years but still sticks to its lager roots. 2021 saw the introduction of 330ml stubby bottles. As well as the taproom, it runs the Untraditional Pub in the Crate development by St James Street station. No cask ale. ◆

Pinnora SIBA

Unit 2, rear of Jubilee Parade, Marsh Road, Pinner, HA5 1BB
☎ (0845) 744 2337 ⊕ pinnorabrewing.com

Family-run, craft brewery based in North West London. Refurbishment took place in 2021. The short four-hectolitre brew length means seasonal and an evolving series of craft beers. No cask ale. ◆

Portobello SIBA

Unit 6, Mitre Bridge Industrial Estate, Mitre Way, North Kensington, W10 6AU
☎ (020) 8969 2269 ⊕ portobellobrewing.com

⊠ Established in 2012, Portobello has since expanded into an adjacent unit and has a 7,500-hl capacity. The range of beers is available in cask with a similar range in keg, all widely available around London. The management of some pubs has been taken on in recent years, currently 19. ◆

Westway Pale Ale (ABV 3.8%) PALE
Easy-drinking pale ale with bitter grapefruit and tropical flavours overlaying a digestive biscuit sweetness. Lingering hoppy, bitter dry finish.
VPA (ABV 4%) PALE
Refreshing yellow best bitter with citrus fruit throughout and a little peppery hop and biscuit notes. Bitterness builds on drinking.
Star (ABV 4.3%) BITTER
Caramel toffee character throughout. Orange and apricot fruits in the flavour and notes of orange on nose. Spicy, dry, bitter finish.
Central Line Red (ABV 4.4%) RED
Ruby red beer. Creamy banana toffee base with caramel and hop bitterness. Long tapering finish with a nutty character.
Market Porter (ABV 4.6%) SPECIALITY
Rye porter with sweet chocolate and plums flavours. Finish of dry dark chocolate and a little fruit with some bitterness.
APA (ABV 5%) PALE
Full-bodied, straw-coloured strong ale. The honey sweetness and soft citrus fruit balanced by a bitter hops. Dry aftertaste.
Stiff Lip IPA (ABV 5%) PALE
Caramelised citrus, earthy hops and sweet honey notes. Apricot and mango flavours. Finish is sweet increasingly spicy. Aromas of sulphur malt and orange.

Pressure Drop SIBA

Unit 6, Lockwood Industrial Park, Mill Mead Road, Tottenham Hale, N17 9QP
☎ (020) 8801 0616 ⊕ pressuredropbrewing.co.uk

Run by three partners who were homebrewers but began commercial brewing in 2013, using a five-barrel plant and a small pilot kit. Moving to Tottenham in 2017, the original location is now a bar called the Experiment, operated with Verdant. Beers are mostly sold in KeyKeg and cans, cask versions are produced occasionally for beer festivals. **LIVE** ◆

Pretty Decent SIBA

Unit 10, Uplands Business Park, Blackhorse Lane, Walthamstow, E17 5QJ

☎ (020) 8638 6603 ⊕ prettydecentbeer.co

Brewing began in 2017 in a railway arch in Forest Gate, expanding into an adjacent taproom in 2021. Production now takes place in a new brewery and taproom in Walthamstow (opened 2022), part of the newly organised Blackhorse Beer Mile. Output is mostly keg and cans in a wide range of styles and includes alcohol-free options. Cask beer is available for local pubs and festivals on demand. A portion of profits is donated to local and international charities. ‼ ⬛ ♦ LIVE ⬦

Redemption SIBA

Unit 16, Compass West Industrial Estate, 33 West Road, Tottenham, N17 0XL

☎ (020) 8885 5227 ☎ 07919 416046
⊕ redemptionbrewing.co.uk

⊗ Redemption Brewing began in 2010 on a 12-barrel plant. In 2016 it moved into a larger unit with a 30-barrel plant. Most of the beer is supplied in cask to pubs in north and central London and to beer festivals. Keg, cans and bottles are also available, some being found in North London supermarket chains. Taproom opens before home games at the Tottenham Hotspur Stadium. ‼ ⬛ ♦ LIVE ⬦

Trinity (ABV 3%) GOLD
Refreshing golden ale where hops are noticeable alongside a biscuity sweetness and citrus notes. Sweet, dry, bitter, spicy lingering aftertaste.

Pale Ale (ABV 3.8%) PALE
Earthy hops, orange and apricot overlaid with a caramel sweetness on the palate lingering in the dry increasingly bitter finish.

Kazbek (ABV 4%) BLOND
Easy-drinking blonde beer with lemon in aroma and biscuity flavour. Spicy hops in the lingering dry bitter finish that builds.

Hopspur (ABV 4.5%) BITTER
Nicely-balanced, dark amber, premium bitter. Smooth with spicy hops, caramelised toffee, orange marmalade. Dry bitter finish.

Urban Dusk (ABV 4.6%) BITTER
Ruby-brown premium bitter. Chocolate notes throughout. Orange and sultana notes overlaid with dry roasty notes. Long, dry, spicy, bitter finish.

Fellowship Porter (ABV 5.1%) PORTER
Chocolate, hops and stone fruits on the nose and palate with toffee and sultanas. Malty, hoppy finish with liquorice allsorts.

Big Chief (ABV 5.5%) IPA
Amber IPA with biscuit and hops throughout. Grapefruit, lemon and resinous hops in the aroma and palate. Bittersweet dry finish.

Roundwood Project

Unit 24, Excelsior Studios, 17-19 Sunbeam Road, North Acton, NW10 6JP ☎ 07815 784704
⊕ theroundwoodproject.com

Brewing began in 2022 on a small scale selling bottled beers. The site is sometimes open for special events. No cask ale.

St Mary's

St Mary the Virgin, Elsworthy Road, Primrose Hill, NW3 3DJ
☎ (020) 7722 3238 ⊕ stmarysbrewery.co.uk

Based in the church crypt, this nanobrewery produces small-batch bottled beers sold at the adjacent farmers' market and on its website in aid of the church's youth projects. Larger batches may be produced elsewhere. The first pint was blessed by the Bishop of Edmonton and the names have an ecclesiastical theme. Brewing currently suspended pending a major restoration project in the church. No cask ale. LIVE

Salt

Unit 35.9 Cobalt, White Hart Triangle Estate, White Hart Avenue, Thamesmead, SE28 0GU
⊕ saltbeerfactory.co.uk

SALT Beer Factory of Saltaire bought the former Hop stuff brewery when it was put up for sale by Molson Coors in 2021. Four core keg beers are brewed here, widely available around London and the South East. No cask ale. ♦

Sambrook's SIBA

1 Bellwether Lane, The Ram Quarter, Wandsworth, SW18 1UR

☎ (020) 7228 0598 ⊕ sambrooksbrewery.co.uk

⊗ Sambrook's was founded in 2008 and supplies its award-winning ales throughout London. The range of beers is traditional in style and available in all formats but cask is the key focus. A move in 2021 saw a new brewery built in the redeveloped Young's Brewery complex in central Wandsworth, including the private Ram Brewery. This ensured centuries of continuous brewing on the site has been maintained. ‼ ⬛ ♦ LIVE ⬦

Wandle (ABV 3.8%) BITTER
Well-balanced bitter with sweetish malt character. Fruit, hops and hints of roast lead to a malty, dry, bitter aftertaste.

American Red (ABV 4.2%) BITTER
Fruity red beer with some chocolate notes in the palate. A developing dark chocolate on the spicy hoppy, dry finish.

Pumphouse Pale (ABV 4.2%) PALE
Aromas and flavours of honey, hops, citrus and apricot. Sweetness is balanced by a dry slight spicy bitterness that lingers.

APA (ABV 4.5%) PALE
A light-coloured refreshing smooth beer with hints of malt and fruit in the flavour.

Junction (ABV 4.5%) BITTER
Caramelised citrus, toffee, sultanas and hints of roasty chocolate throughout. Aroma is roasty, and slightly sweet. Dry, spicy bitter finish.

Powerhouse Porter (ABV 4.9%) PORTER
Ruby-brown sweetish porter with a pleasant roasted malt nose. Sweet chocolate, spicy marmalade, dark fruits and an underlying roasty bitterness.

Signal SIBA

Unit 8, Stirling Way, Beddington Farm Road, Beddington, CR0 4XN
☎ (020) 8684 6111 ⊕ signalbeerco.com

Starting in 2016, Signal's lager was the staple product in keg and cans. 2018 saw a refresh and a range of cask ale is now produced along with an increased variety of keg. Available at the taproom, its Cloud Nine bar at the O2 Arena in North Greenwich, and now regionally. ‼ ⬦

Absolutely Fuggled (ABV 4%) BITTER
Yellow-coloured, easy-drinking bitter with earthy hops and orangey fruit on the sweetish nose and biscuit flavour becoming bitter.

Sticky Hoppy Pudding (ABV 4.3%) SPECIALITY
Pale brown beer with a smooth mouthfeel. Distinct caramel and biscuit aroma and flavour with a little hop and fruit.

Signature SIBA

Unit 15, Uplands Business Park, Blackhorse Lane, Walthamstow, E17 5QJ
☎ (020) 7684 4664 ⊕ signaturebrew.co.uk

Starting off cuckoo brewing in 2011, crowdfunding saw brewing start in Leyton in 2015 followed by a move to Walthamstow in 2019. Aside from the core range, specials are brewed in collaboration with music artists. These are available in the onsite taproom, now selling cask, and its bars in Walthamstow and Haggerston.
☷◆LIVE◆

Roadie All-Night IPA (ABV 4.3%) GOLD
Hop-forward golden ale with lemon and grapefruit in aroma and flavour with a biscuity sweetness. Lingering, dry, bitter finish.

Backstage IPA (ABV 5.6%) IPA
Amber, unfined IPA with fruity hops and a bitterness, overlaid with some banana and biscuity malty notes. Lingering dry finish.

Nightliner Coffee Porter (ABV 5.7%) SPECIALITY
Smoky black porter with dark roast coffee dominating with hints of dark fruit, dark treacle and a dry toasty bitterness.

Small Beer SIBA

70-72 Verney Road, South Bermondsey, SE16 3DH
☎ (020) 7096 2353 ⊕ theoriginalsmallbeer.com

Small Beer was set up in 2017 as the world's first to specialise exclusively in the production of low strength beers (1.0%-2.7% ABV). The core range of five beers is widely available on keg, 350ml stubby bottles and now cans. One cask ale was introduced during 2022, including a green-hopped version, and is now regularly available at the taproom and a growing number of pubs in London as per the website map. ◆

Steam (ABV 2.7%) SPECIALITY

So What

🍴 Bull & Finch, 126 Gipsy Hill, Gipsy Hill, SE19 1PL
⊕ thebullandfinch.square.site

A nanobrewery was installed in the Bull & Finch in early 2022, a bar run by the Bullfinch brewery of Herne Hill. The intention was to revive old Bullfinch recipies in cask and keg under the Bull & Finch name and small batch wild and mixed fermentations under the So What name.

Southey

21 Southey Street, Penge, SE20 7JD
⊕ southeybrewing.co.uk

⊗ Southey took over the Late Knights brewery in 2017 in an old warehouse that has been an abattior and a candle factory. The vegan and unfiltered beers are available in the three Beer Dispensary bars, and in the onsite taproom (Wed-Sun). ◆V◆

Pale (ABV 3.8%) BITTER
Easy-drinking with a distinct bitter orange hoppy aroma. Orange, stone fruits and biscuity honey malt notes. Lingering bitter sweetness.

Best Bitter (ABV 4.5%) BITTER
Hazy, well-balanced pale brown premium bitter. Sweet caramel, malty biscuit overlaying tangerine, and some earthy hops. Dry, lingering bitter finish.

Oatmeal Stout (ABV 5.5%) STOUT
Smooth, rich stout with expresso coffee, dark chocolate and roasted malt in the flavour. Sweet honey notes in the aftertaste.

Southwark SIBA

46 Druid Street, Bermondsey, SE1 2EZ
☎ (020) 3302 4190 ⊕ southwarkbrewing.co.uk

⊗ Southwark opened in 2014 as the first cask-orientated brewery on the Bermondsey Beer Mile. The range of beers brings modern styles to cask, including a regularly changing, single hop beer, and is complemented by a small keg range. ☷◆LIVE◆

Bankside Blonde (ABV 3.8%) BLOND
Grapefruit and sweet biscuit in the aroma and flavour. A growing dry bitterness with peppery hops and some sweetness. Smooth.

Routemaster Red (ABV 3.8%) RED
Chocolate and caramelised fruits on aroma and flavour, where there are notes of bitter lemon, red berries and sweet toffee.

London Pale Ale (ABV 4%) PALE
Lime and melon, caramelised biscuit on the palate and aroma. Citrus and fruit finish. Dry, fruity and spicy bitter aftertaste.

Potters' Fields Porter (ABV 4%) PORTER
Raisins, prunes caramel, and bitter chocolate in the flavour with a hop bitterness, fading in the dry roast bitter aftertaste.

Mayflower (ABV 4.2%) GOLD
Citrus and tropical fruit dominates the flavour with honey and some spicy floral hop, which is also on the nose.

Bermondsey Best (ABV 4.4%) BITTER
Chocolate and earthy hops on aroma and palate with caramelised fruit and hazelnuts. Dry roasty finish and some hoppy bitterness.

Single Hop (ABV 5%) GOLD

Harvard (ABV 5.5%) IPA
Premium bitter with honey sweetness throughout. Orange and grapefruit marmalade aromas and flavours are prominent becoming bitter, dry and lingering.

Spartan SIBA

Arch 8, Almond Road, South Bermondsey, SE16 3LR
⊕ spartanbrewery.com

Spartan started brewing at UBrew in 2017, before moving in 2018 to premises on the Bermondsey Beer Mile vacated by Partizan Brewery. Cask, keg and can-conditioned beer is available and its taproom along the Bermondsey Beer Mile closed during 2023. Brewing is currently suspended. ☷

Tankleys

Beech Avenue, Sidcup, DA15 8NH ☎ 07901 333273
⊕ tankleysbrewery.com

Tankleys is a home-based brewery in Sidcup with a licence to brew larger batches at Beerblefish in Walthamstow. Its Australian brewer brews styles from modern takes on traditional through to avant garde, the Hawaiian Pizza Beer being particularly notable. Available in bottles and in cask locally and at beer festivals.

Tap East SIBA

🍴 7 International Square, Westfield Stratford City, Montfichet Road, Stratford, E20 1EE
☎ (020) 8555 4467 ⊕ tapeast.co.uk

⊗ Tap East is located in Westfield Stratford City shopping centre, opposite the entrance to Stratford International

Station. Brewing began in 2011 using a 2.5-barrel plant. One-off and collaborative beers with other breweries are also produced. Beers are available onsite or at the Utobeer stall and the Rake, both at Borough Market. 🍻♦

Temple Brew House

🍺 Temple Brew House, 46 Essex Street, Temple, WC2R 3JF
☎ (020) 7936 2536 ⊕ templebrewhouse.com/brewery

☺Originally opened in 2014 as the Essex Street Brewery, it reopened during 2022 after a two-year closure and rebranded to Temple Brew House, the name of the pub. Owned by the City Pub Group, the beers are available on cask and in keg at the pub. ‼♦

Three Hounds (NEW)

Three Hounds, 57 Beckenham Road, Beckenham, BR3 4PR
☎ (020) 3976 0028 ⊕ threehoundsbeerco.com

The long term ambition to open a brewery (either onsite or elsewhere) is still being worked on. Until then, the staff from the Three Hounds Bottle Shop help to brew their own beers at local breweries (eg Dogs Grandad and Affinity). Available in the bottle shop (cask and keg), including the Brewhouse Experiments range. 🍺♦

Tiny Vessel

Unit 505, Platts Eyot, Hampton, TW12 2HF ☎ 07888 730210 ⊕ tinyvessel.co.uk

⊠ Tiny Vessel is a 1.5-barrel brewery established in 2016 on Platts Eyot, an island on the River Thames near Hampton. All beers are unfiltered and unfined, mostly available bottled or in keg. At least one beer is usually available in bottle and keg (and sometimes in cask) in the Northumberland Arms, Brentford. LIVE

Twickenham SIBA

Unit 6, 18 Mereway Road, Twickenham, TW2 6RG
☎ (020) 8241 1825 ⊕ twickenham-fine-ales.co.uk

⊠ Established in 2004, Twickenham Fine Ales is London's oldest, independent, stand-alone brewery. Operating a 25-barrel plant, the styles are traditional with a modern twist and output is predominantly cask. It opens on match days for the rugby fans going to the nearby stadium. ‼🍺♦♦

Grandstand Bitter (ABV 3.8%) BITTER
Amber bitter with apricot and touch of orange fruits. Floral hops become spicier and bitter, balanced by a biscuity sweetness throughout.
Red Sky (ABV 4.1%) RED
Easy-drinking red ale with sweet citrus marmalade, chocolate, an increasing dryness and gentle spiciness which lingers in the finish.
Naked Ladies (ABV 4.4%) BLOND
Refreshing gold beer with honey sweetness throughout. Sweet grapefruit fading in the dryish finish with a growing spicy hoppy bitterness.

Two Tribes

Unit 4, Tileyard Studios, Tileyard Road, Barnsbury, N7 9AH
☎ (020) 3955 6782 ⊕ twotribes.co.uk

Brewing started in the old King's Brewery in Horsham in 2015, moving to its current London brewery north of King's Cross in 2018. It brews both onsite and using third parties. The name is based on the idea of collaboration.

Beers are sold around London, Horsham and Leeds as well as in its adjacent outdoor taproom with camp fires and 'live-fire' food plus music events. Active online sales offering for its cans with regular promotions. No cask ale. 🍺♦

Up The Creek

🍺 Up The Creek Comedy Club, 302 Creek Road, Greenwich, SE10 9SW
☎ (020) 8858 4581 ⊕ up-the-creek-brewery.co.uk

Up The Creek began brewing in 2018 (as Greenwich Brewery) using a three-barrel plant and is situated in the front part of the bar area of the Up the Creek Comedy Club. The beers are available in the bar and the range continues to be updated since the appointment of a new brewer in 2021. Entrance to the bar is restricted to event ticket holders only. LIVE

Urban Alchemy

York Road, New Barnet, EN5 1LJ ☎ 07894 452263
⊕ urban-alchemy-brewing.co.uk

⊠ Urban Alchemy started brewing commercially in 2019 and was established by a group of friends with years of brewing experience between them. A bespoke three-barrel plant is used. Beers are supplied to local pubs and beer festivals but are likely to be real ale in a KeyKeg, whilst cask may occasionally be produced. All beers are suitable for vegans. Bottle-conditioned beers are available for delivery. Brewing is currently suspended. LIVE V

Villages

21-22 Resolution Way, Deptford, SE8 4NT
☎ (020) 3489 1143 ☎ 07308 969667
⊕ villagesbrewery.com

Established in 2016 by brothers Archie and Louis Village who sold the business in 2022 and it is now a sister company to Backyard and Grasshopper breweries. Predominantly keg and canned beers although a cask beer is sometimes available at the taproom. 🍺♦

Volden SIBA

77 Malham Road, Forest Hill, SE23 1AH
☎ (020) 8684 4492 ⊕ volden.co.uk

⊠ Volden produces beer for the Antic Collective pubs. Originally taking over the Clarence & Fredericks brewery in Croydon in 2015, a new brewery was installed in Forest Hill in 2020 and it is hoped to commission this site during the currency of this Guide. Meanwhile, brewing is suspended and cask and keg beers are contract brewed at other breweries. ♦

Werewolf SIBA

Arch 87, Randolph Street, Camden Town, NW1 0SR
⊕ werewolfbeer.com

Starting at Little Creatures in Kings Cross and then brewing on its own nanobrewery in Kentish Town, 2022 saw the brewery open in a railway arch in Camden Town. The 'American brewery in London' includes a quirky theme park taproom with its own ghost train. No cask ale. ♦

Wild Card SIBA

Unit 2, Lockwood Way, Blackhorse Lane, Walthamstow, E17 5RB
☎ (020) 8935 5560 ⊕ wildcardbrewery.co.uk

Wild Card began brewing in 2013, initially using spare capacity at several breweries in and around London. After brewing since 2014 at its Ravenswood site, production moved to its Lockwood site in 2018. Cask ale was reintroduced during 2021 with great success. ⬛◆

Best (ABV 4.2%) BITTER
Victoria plums and malty coffee flavours overlaid with caramel and sultanas. Spicy, hoppy dry finish and a lingering gentle bitterness

Gold (ABV 4.2%) GOLD

Pale (ABV 4.3%) GOLD
Fruity nose and flavour of tropical grapefruit and peach. Sweet biscuit throughout becoming spicy and bitter in the fruity finish.

Wimbledon SIBA

Unit 8, College Fields Business Centre, 19 Prince Georges Road, Colliers Wood, SW19 2PT
☎ (020) 3674 9786 ⊕ wimbledonbrewery.com

Set up by Mark Gordon after a 23 year career in the City, Wimbledon began production in 2015, with former Young's and Fuller's brewer Derek Prentice at the helm of a brand new, 30-barrel plant. The brewery expanded in 2017 with two new 60-barrel fermenters, and further expanded in 2018 with an additional 60-barrel fermenter. Some beers are inspired by the original Wimbledon Brewery (destroyed by fire in 1889). Keg and canned beers are unfiltered, unpasteurised and vegan. ‼⬛◆LIVE V◆

Common Pale Ale (ABV 3.7%) BITTER
Well-balanced session bitter with hops, orange, biscuit and caramel on the nose and flavour. Long bitter and hoppy dry finish.

Copper Leaf (ABV 4%) RED
Red ale with sweet chocolate, dry roasty notes balanced by under-ripe plums, sultanas and burnt citrus. Gentle bitter dry finish.

SW19 (ABV 4%) BLOND

A strong hop presence, with hints of lemon and pineapple, balanced by malt flavours. A dry aftertaste developed.

Workshy

Cardigan Road, Richmond, TW10 6BW ☎ 07876 377594 ⊕ workshybrewing.co.uk

Workshy started using the facilities at UBrew in 2018 and brewed elsewhere when UBrew closed in 2019. The home kit was upgraded during 2021 and the beers now come from there. Available locally in keg and wider afield in cans. No cask ale.

Wrong Side of the Tracks

South Park Crescent, Catford, SE6 1JW ☎ 07493 499494 ⊕ wrongsideofthetracks.beer

A small-scale homebrewer selling bottled beers commercially to local bottle shops and from its webshop with delivery to the local area. After brewing was suspended in 2020, larger scale brewing was tried in late 2022 at Dog's Grandad resulting in the beer being available in keg and cans. No cask ale. Brewing is currently suspended.

Zerodegrees SIBA

⬛ **29-33 Montpelier Vale, Blackheath, SE3 0TJ**
☎ (020) 8852 5619 ⊕ zerodegrees.co.uk/blackheath

Started in 2000, this is the original of the chain of four brewpubs. A German computer-controlled plant produces unfiltered and unfined ales and lager served from storage tanks using air pressure. The core range remains a Czech pilsner, an American pale, a Mango golden ale and a changing monthly speciality. No cask ale. ◆◆

Carlton Tavern, NW6: Kilburn Park

South East

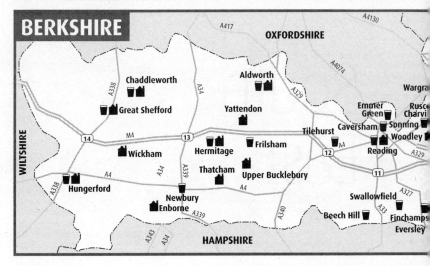

BERKSHIRE

OXFORDSHIRE

Aldworth

Bell Inn ♈ ★ 🄻
Bell Lane, RG8 9SE (250yds off B4009)
☎ (01635) 578272
Aldworth Five Giants; Arkell's 3B; Indigenous Baldrick; Rebellion Roasted Nuts; 3 changing beers (sourced locally; often Andwell) Ⓗ
This is a multi-generational family-run pub in its true sense, welcoming, inclusive, and sociable. The servery barely has room for the six handpumps, one dedicated to the on-site Aldworth brewing microbrewery. The expansive garden has ample outside seating. An extensive menu of filed rolls, hot soup and puddings is available lunchtimes only. A repeat winner of CAMRA National Pub of the Year, a perennial Guide entry, identifiedby CAMRA as having a nationally important historic pub interior. Local CAMRA County Pub of the Year 2023. Q ⽷ ❀ ⓓ ♣ ♥ P ❀

Beech Hill

Elm Tree
Beech Hill Road, RG7 2AZ SU6950364118
☎ (0118) 988 3505 ⊕ theelmtreebeechhill.co.uk
Ringwood Razorback; Timothy Taylor Landlord Ⓗ
Part pub, part restaurant, the Elm Tree is popular both with locals and visitors from further afield. Diners come to this gastro-pub to enjoy the quality food but drinkers are equally welcome at the bar. The cosy interior features open fires, wood beams and a central bar. The spectacular countryside views from the covered decking make alfresco dining a real pleasure during fine weather. May close early on Sunday if quiet. ⽷ ❀ ⓓ ♣ P ❀ 🎵

Binfield

Victoria Arms
Terrace Road North, RG42 5JA (100yds S of jct with Tilehurst Ln)
☎ (01344) 483856 ⊕ victoriaarmsbinfield.co.uk
Dark Star Hophead; Fuller's London Pride, ESB; 1 changing beer (sourced locally; often Elusive, Rebellion, Stardust) Ⓗ
This popular and busy Fuller's local is at the centre of the village community. In winter, an open fire warms the pub and in summer the terrace and garden offers some great outdoor space. There is an extensive traditional pub

menu, plus a children's menu and Sunday roasts on offer. The garden has a heated marquee which is available to hire for private functions. Recent local CAMRA Pub of the Year winner. ⽷ ❀ ⓓ ♣ P 🖵 (150) ❀ ❀ 🎵

Bracknell

Cannie Man 🄻 ✅
Bywood, RG12 7RF
⊕ cannieman.co.uk
Dartmoor Best; Sharp's Doom Bar; 3 changing beers (sourced nationally; often Hogs Back, Rebellion, Renegade) Ⓗ
An estate wet-led pub where good beer is given top priority with four handpumps serving a session bitter, a local ale and guests. Largescreen TVs in the L-shaped bar show sporting events and there is frequent live music. The landlady prides herself on offering a warm welcome to all. The pub supports many sports teams and its charity fundraising is legendary with recent campaigns resulting in a number of defibrillators being provided for the local community. ⽷ ❀ ♣ P 🖵 (171,172) ❀ ❀ 🎵

Newtown Pippin ♈ 🄻
Ralphs Ride, Harmans Water, RG12 9LR
☎ (01344) 426298 ⊕ thenewtownpippin.com
Bond Brews Best of British; Windsor & Eton Last Drop; 3 changing beers (sourced regionally; often Hogs Back) Ⓗ
A two-bar pub recently transformed into a true local asset that is highly valued by the community. Up to three real ales from local and regional breweries are served. Food is available daily and includes gluten-free and vegan options. Outside are patio areas with benches and a surrounding garden, allowing for alfresco dining and drinking. Regular quiz nights, live music and occasional beer festivals all contribute to the community atmosphere. A function room is available for hire. ⽷ ❀ ⓓ ♣ 🚌 🖵 ❀ 🎵

Old Manor 🄻 ✅
Grenville Place, RG12 1BP (at College roundabout jct with Church Rd)
☎ (01344) 304490
Greene King Abbot; Ruddles Best Bitter; Sharp's Doom Bar; 5 changing beers (sourced nationally; often Loddon, Rebellion, Windsor & Eton) Ⓗ

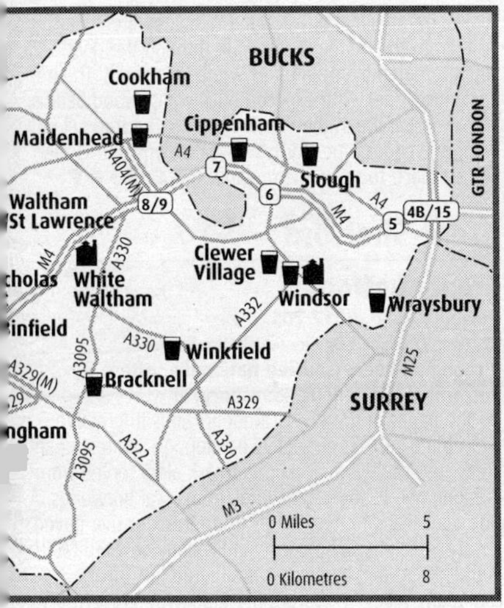

Wetherspoon pub occupying a building that dates from Tudor times and which contains several historic features. It is a favourite with locals and has been in the Guide for over 20 years. It has a variety of indoor and outdoor drinking areas, and an excellent range of regularly changing guest beers supplement their regular offerings, all served by the friendly, knowledgeable staff who are always welcome to suggestions for new beers. Parking on-site in a Pay & Display car park. ♘❀◑♿⇌P🚌📶

Caversham

Fox & Hounds L

51 Gosbrook Road, RG4 8BN
☎ 07915 540926 🌐 thefoxcaversham.com
6 changing beers (often Oakham, Siren, Wild Weather) H
A popular and lively community hub offering six changing beers and eight craft keg lines from local and independent breweries, plus up to four ciders and perries and a good selection of cans and bottles. It has extensive covered and heated outside areas. A blue plaque commemorates the day in 1960 that John Lennon and Paul McCartney performed here as the Nerk Twins. ♘❀◑♣●P🚌🐾📶♫

Chaddleworth

Ibex Inn L

Main Street, RG20 7ER (accessed from jct 14 of M4)
☎ (01488) 639052 🌐 ibexinn.com
3 changing beers (sourced locally; often Indigenous, Loose Cannon, White Horse) H
Cosy, characterful and inviting gastro-pub, situated in the tranquil countryside between Wantage and Newbury. It is popular with the surrounding villagers, as well as visiting walkers and cyclists, and offers comfortable and spacious en-suite accommodation. It is only 50 yards from the Indigenous microbrewery, which is a favoured local supplier. A former local CAMRA Community Pub of the Year. ♘❀🛏◑♿♣P🚏🐾📶♫

Charvil

Heron on the Ford ✔

Park Lane, RG10 0UE
☎ (0118) 934 0700 🌐 herononthetford.co.uk
Brakspear Gravity; 3 changing beers H
The Lands End was refurbished in 2018, including a new flag stone floor, and is now the Heron on the Ford. This spacious rural pub has a good-sized outside seating area and is under a mile from the bus stop on the old Bath Road. Sited by the ford across the River Loddon, walkers from Hurst can use the footbridge downstream but signs now dissuade drivers from using the ford. The garden includes a children's play area. ♘❀◑♿P🚌🐾📶♫

Cippenham

Barleycorn L

151 Lower Cippenham Lane, SL1 5DS
☎ (01628) 603115
Rebellion IPA; 3 changing beers H
Refurbished traditional single-bar pub that caters for a strong local following. Four guest beers always include one from Rebellion plus another from a local brewery. The other two are from national and local breweries, along with a summer offering of a real cider, plus a choice of fruit ciders. A large collection of bottles and jugs features around the walls. Occasional live music and two sports TVs provide the entertainment. The nearby public car park is free. Q❀♣P🚌(5)🐾📶♫

Clewer Village

Swan L

9 Mill Lane, SL4 5JG
☎ 07458 300026 🌐 theswanwindsor.co.uk
Windsor & Eton Guardsman; 2 changing beers (sourced nationally; often Windsor & Eton) H
Just 15 minutes' walk from Windsor town centre, this 18th-century village free house has been renovated following a closure of over three years. Purchased as a community interest company, it has become the hub of the village and now provides coffee mornings, cribbage, quiz nights, a cycle hub, occasional music and a book club. Major renovations are now completed, with a new kitchen offering freshly cooked food.
Q♘❀◑♿♣🚌(71,702)🐾📶♫

Cookham

Old Swan Uppers

The Pound, SL6 9QE

REAL ALE BREWERIES

Aldworth ▤ Aldworth (NEW)
Bond Brews Wokingham
Bucklebury Upper Bucklebury
Butts Great Shefford
Delphic Thatcham
Dolphin Woodley
Double-Barrelled ◆ Reading
Elusive ◆ Finchampstead
FutureState Reading
Hermitage Hermitage
Indie Rabble ▤ Windsor (NEW)
Indigenous Chaddleworth
INNformal Hungerford
Outhouse ▤ Wokingham
Renegade ◆ Yattendon
Siren ◆ Finchampstead
Stardust ◆ White Waltham
Swamp Bog Enborne
Two Cocks Enborne
Two Flints ◆ Windsor (NEW)
Wickham ▤ Wickham
Windsor & Eton ◆ Windsor
Zerodegrees ▤ ◆ Reading

☎ (01628) 523573 ⊕ theoldswanuppers.co.uk
Fuller's London Pride; Rebellion IPA Ⓗ
Friendly, cosy pub with flagstone floors and wood-burning stove. Its name stems from the ancient activity of 'Swan Upping' or marking of the swans on the River Thames. The front bar accommodates drinkers, with a separate restaurant and lounge to the rear. Food comes from a traditional pub menu (burgers, fish & chips, pies, steaks) and a tapas-style menu with a selection of around 20 plates. ❀◖➤P🍽(37)❀ 🍽 ⊛

Emmer Green

Black Horse
16 Kidmore End Road, RG4 8SE
☎ (0118) 947 4111
1 changing beer (sourced nationally; often Courage, Sharp's, Young's) Ⓗ
Well-kept two-bar local with a pool table and sports TV in its public bar, while the quieter lounge bar has a real fire. You can also sit outside the front, or in the enclosed rear patio. The pub moved to its present site before 1870, allegedly to remove temptation from the nearby chapel-goers at its original location in Old Peppard Road. In Victorian times the pub yard doubled as the local fire station. Q❀❀♣🍽❀ ⊛

Eversley

Tally Ho Ⓛ
Fleet Hill, RG27 0RR (on A327 jct with B3348)
☎ (0118) 973 2134
House beer (by Siren); 3 changing beers (sourced regionally; often Hogs Back, Stardust, Windsor & Eton) Ⓗ
Popular free house on the South Berkshire border, with extensive gardens and large car parks. The bar serves four changing local and regional real ales and cider. The pub is busy with diners at lunchtime and evenings but has plenty of seating in the bar, under the stretch tent, or in the garden. A warm welcome is extended to families with children, and dogs, who can explore the gardens and woods around the pub. Q❀❀◖&♣P❀ ⊛

Finchampstead

Elusive Brewing Tap Room Ⓛ
Unit 5, Marino Way, Hogwood Industrial Estate, RG40 4RF
☎ (0118) 973 2153 ⊕ elusivebrewing.com
Elusive Microball, Level Up, Oregon Trail, Spellbinder; 8 changing beers (sourced locally) Ⓗ
Small taproom for this award-winning and innovative microbrewery established in 2016 on an industrial estate. Seven KeyKeg taps and one handpull showcase their own excellent brews, and there are also many brewery collaborations and tap takeovers. During warmer months covered tables are set up outside. Retro video games can be played for free. Cans, bottles and growler-fills are available to take-away. Currently only open Friday and Saturday from noon to early evening. Card payment only. Q❀❀P🍽(3)❀ ⊛

Frilsham

Pot Kiln Ⓛ
Chapel Lane, RG18 0XX (on road between Yattendon and Bucklebury) SU552731
☎ (01635) 201366 ⊕ potkiln.org
Indigenous Chinwag, Tickety-Boo; house beer (by Renegade); 1 changing beer (sourced locally; often Indigenous) Ⓗ

Cosy and traditional British pub that is definitely worth a visit. From the moment you walk through the door, you're greeted by the friendly, welcoming staff. The pub has a rustic feel, with exposed brick walls, wood beams, and a roaring fire in the winter months. The tranquil pub garden overlooks the North Wessex Downs and is the perfect place to relax and unwind. Q❀➤◖&❀ ⊛

Great Shefford

Great Shefford Ⓛ
Newbury Road, RG17 7DS
☎ (01488) 648462 ⊕ thegreatshefford.com
4 changing beers (sourced nationally; often Butcombe, Indigenous, Ramsbury) Ⓗ
On the banks of the River Lambourn, this impressive, welcoming pub has distinctive bar, lounge and restaurant areas. The changing selection of cask ales, served from the long bar, includes favourites from local breweries. A side door leads to river views from an extensive paved terrace which has a barbecue and canopy-covered tables with lighting and heating. It is situated just off the Lambourn Valley Way, from the Ridgeway to Newbury, and provides a refreshing stop for walkers and cyclists. ❀❀◖&P🍽❀ ⊛♫

Hermitage

Fox Inn ✓
High Street, RG18 9RB (on B4009 at jct with Yattendon Rd)
☎ (01635) 200772 ⊕ thefoxhermitage.com
Renegade Good Old Boy; Sharp's Doom Bar; Timothy Taylor Landlord; Young's London Special Ⓗ
A popular, welcoming village pub in three converted artisan cottages dating from the 16th century. It has restaurant, bar and drinking/eating areas, with real fires in the latter two. The pub shares its name with the title of a book, The Fox, written by D.H. Lawrence, who lived in the village at the end of World War I. Traditional home-cooked food is served. Dogs are welcome except in the restaurant area. ❀❀◖♣P🍽(6,6A)❀ ⊛♫

Hungerford

John O'Gaunt Ⓛ
21 Bridge Street, RG17 0EG (30yds N of canal bridge)
☎ (01488) 683535 ⊕ john-o-gaunt-hungerford.co.uk
House beer (by INNformal); 7 changing beers (sourced regionally; often Elusive, INNformal, Siren) Ⓗ
A 16th-century free house serving ales from the nearby INNformal brewery. The wide drinks range also includes real ciders from Tutts Clump and Celtic Marches. There are stools and high tables near the bar, and in other parts of the pub tables of various sizes surround an open fire. Home-made steak and ale pie is a popular choice from the tempting menu. The outside tented area is especially lively in summer and during the annual Oktoberfest weekend. Q❀❀◖➤♣♣P🍽❀ ⊛

Hurst

Jolly Farmer Ⓛ
Davis Street, RG10 0TH
☎ (0118) 934 1881 ⊕ thejollyfarmerhurst.com
Rebellion IPA; St Austell Tribute; Timothy Taylor Landlord; 1 changing beer (sourced locally) Ⓗ
Now under the management of an experienced landlord, this pub lies on the B3030, between Winnersh and Hurst. Following extensive work, the garden now has several permanent undercover seating areas. The kitchen has

been greatly extended and serves Thai cuisine as well as an English menu. There is disabled access and a separate disabled toilet, and a large outside area and car park. Q❄✿❄🅿🚲(128,129) ☕🎵

Maidenhead

A Hoppy Place Maidenhead ▼ 🅛

Units 1-3, Trinity Place, Park Street, SL6 1TJ
☎ (01753) 206802 ⊕ ahoppyplace.co.uk
Siren Broken Dream Breakfast Stout; Stardust English Bitter; 3 changing beers 🅗
A beer emporium that opened in 2022, with four cask lines, 14 keg lines and more than 150 cans and bottles in the fridges. There is lots of seating inside, and more outside, as well as plenty of standing room. They offer 10% off all products with their 'A Hoppy Friend' membership card. Local CAMRA Pub of the Year 2023.
❄✿❄🚲🍴🅿☕🎵

Bear 🅛 ⊘

8-10 High Street, SL6 1QJ
☎ (01628) 763030
Greene King Abbot, IPA; Sharp's Doom Bar; 3 changing beers (sourced nationally) 🅗
A short walk from the town hall is this former coaching inn, which became a Wetherspoon in 2009. It has an open-plan bar with several different seating areas, including a licensed outside area to the front. There is additional seating on the upper floor. The 10 handpumps dispense up to six guest ales, many from local breweries. Ciders are also available. ❄✿🍴🚲🍴🎵

Craufurd Arms 🅛

15 Gringer Hill, SL6 7LY
☎ (01628) 675410 ⊕ craufurdarms.com
Rebellion IPA; 2 changing beers (sourced locally; often Stardust, Windsor & Eton) 🅗
This pint-sized local, just outside the town centre, is in a building dating back to the 1800s. It was the 50th community-owned pub to be established in the country and is well known for its friendly atmosphere and fine selection of local real and craft ales. The pub hosts a range of activities including live music, cribbage, darts and a quiz on Thursday night. Three TV screens show Sky and BT Sports. A former local CAMRA Pub of the Year.
❄✿🍴🎵(Furze Platt) ♣🅿🚲(9) ☕🎵

Maiden's Head 🅛

34 High Street, SL6 1QE
☎ (01628) 784786 ⊕ themaidenshead.co.uk
4 changing beers (often Rebellion, Stardust, Windsor & Eton) 🅗
Large single-room town-centre pub. It offers four constantly rotating guest ales, with an emphasis on local breweries, plus keg craft beers, as well as a range of world bottled beers. Food is served, including locally sourced beef burgers, chicken and wraps. It has separate seating areas inside, and a large beer garden at the back of the pub. Terrestrial TV shows some events, and live music is hosted at the weekend. Dogs are welcome outside. ❄✿🍴🚲🍴♣🚲☕🎵

North Star 🅛

91 Westborough Road, SL6 4AP
☎ (01628) 622711
Timothy Taylor Landlord; 2 changing beers (sourced locally; often New Wharf) 🅗
A friendly traditional back-street pub with two bars: a busy public bar with TV and darts, and a quiet lounge. It is an Asset of Community Value (ACV) and CAMRA accredited for serving consistently well-kept real ales, including a LocAle. Darts and cribbage are played, and

there is a quiz every other Thursday evening. Occasional live bands perform – phone for details. Outside, there is a patio area to the front of the pub. Q❄✿❄♣🚲(5)☕☕🎵

Newbury

Bowler's Arms

Enborne Street, Wash Common, RG14 6TW (between Enborne Lodge Ln and Wheatlands Ln)
☎ (01635) 47658 ⊕ thebowlersarms.co.uk
Fuller's London Pride; St Austell Tribute; Timothy Taylor Landlord 🅗
Located within Falkland Cricket Club, the modern, open-plan bar area is light, with views over the cricket pitch. Tables are well-spaced for a typical mix of drinkers, diners and community activities. A popular seasonal menu includes toasted sandwiches at lunchtimes. There are several TV screens for sporting events, and a pool table. Extensive outside seating, at ground and first floor levels, is available for warm days. This community asset enjoys an elevated position by a Civil War battlefield, with country footpaths nearby. ❄✿🍴🚲🍴♣🚲(2)☕

Cow & Cask 🅛

1 Inches Yard, Market Street, RG14 5DP (SE of pedestrian crossing at corner of Market St and Bartholomew St)
☎ 07517 658071
3 changing beers (sourced regionally; often Indigenous, Loddon, XT) 🅖
Berkshire's first micropub is small, friendly establishment where conversation flourishes. During a 2022 refit, the stillage and cask cooling system were updated. The selection from the new bottle cooler includes alcohol-free beers. Bag in box ciders and interesting local bottled beers are also available. The drinks choice and unique beers tally since the 2014 opening are chalked on a large blackboard. The quickest pedestrian access from the nearby railway station is through the new multi-storey car park. Q🍴♣🍴🚲(2)☕

Hatchet Inn 🅛 ⊘

12 Market Place, RG14 5BD
☎ (01635) 277560
Greene King Abbot; Ruddles Best Bitter; Sharp's Doom Bar; 5 changing beers (sourced nationally; often Loddon, Two Cocks) 🅗
This Grade II-listed Wetherspoon hotel, opened in 2011, overlooks the pedestrianised Market Place. To make space for a recent dining area extension, an expanded rear patio has shifted into the former car park, providing plenty of sheltered outside seating. Inside, ales are served from two sets of handpumps, positioned at each end of the bar, with boxed real cider in the fridge behind. Regular beer and cider festivals are held. Food, including breakfast, is available all day. Q❄✿🏨🍴🚲🍴♣🚲☕

King Charles Tavern

54 Cheap Street, RG14 5BX
☎ (01635) 36695 ⊕ kctavern.com
House beer (by Greene King); 7 changing beers (sourced nationally; often Greene King, Oakham, Vale) 🅗
This former local CAMRA Pub of the Year offers a comfortable and stylish interior consisting of three separate seating areas around a central bar. A house beer and an additional seven changing cask ales, sourced locally and nationally, are available. Home-made food is served at lunchtimes and evenings on weekdays, and a popular roast on Sundays. Quiz nights are held on the last Wednesday of each month. There is a small enclosed patio at the rear. ❄✿🍴🎵🚲☕☕

Lion ✅

39 West Street, RG14 1BD
☎ (01635) 528468 ⊕ thelionatnewbury.co.uk
Wadworth 6X, Horizon; 5 changing beers (sourced nationally; often Oakham, Rudgate, Tiny Rebel) 🅷
This friendly traditional local serves cask ales from Wadworth as well as offering up to four guest beers which are sourced nationally. Real cider is often available. Tex-Mex food is served until evening. Traditional pub games include darts. Sport is shown on a number of screens and there is a popular quiz night every Thursday, with occasional live music at weekends. There is an outside patio with a covered area. A former local CAMRA Pub of the Year. 🌂🏠❶🌮❄🍴🛏🐾🎧🎵

Lock, Stock & Barrel

104 Northbrook Street, RG14 1AA (in alleyway 20yds NW of canal bridge)
☎ (01635) 580550 ⊕ lockstockandbarrelnewbury.co.uk
Fuller's London Pride, ESB; 1 changing beer (sourced regionally; often Dark Star, Fuller's) 🅷
Located just off Newbury's main shopping street, next to the Kennet and Avon Canal, this is a popular, comfortably furnished pub with an open-plan interior. The extensive outdoor areas are particularly popular in fine weather, with views of Newbury Lock and St Nicolas Church. Seasonal beers from the Fuller's range are served. Traditional pub food is freshly cooked to order by the chef. There is regular live music and families are welcome until 9pm. 🌂🏠❶🌮♿🚆🛏🐾🎧🎵

Reading

Alehouse 🍷 🅛

2 Broad Street, RG1 2BH
☎ (0118) 950 8119
9 changing beers (sourced locally) 🅷
Popular drinking establishment that always leaves an impression on visitors with its quirky wooden fixtures and reclaimed wooden floor. As a champion of microbreweries, both local and further afield, rare and unusual ales are frequently found on the pumps. A selection of real ciders, perries and mead is also available. Often busy around the bar area, those wishing for a more peaceful drink can take advantage of the secluded snugs at the back of the pub. Local CAMRA Pub of the Year 2023. 🌂🚆⊖(Reading)🍴🛏🚌🐾

Allied Arms 🅛

57 St Mary's Butts, RG1 2LG
☎ (0118) 958 3323 ⊕ allied-arms.co.uk
Loddon Hullabaloo; 4 changing beers 🅷
A town-centre pub dating from around 1828, with two cosy bars entered through the side passage, not the front door. An enhanced range of up to 10 ales is available each weekend. The large walled garden is a popular refuge from the bustle of the town, with patio heaters for colder nights. A wide and interesting selection of music is available on the jukebox. The pub hosts a regular charity quiz. Card payments only.
🌂🌮🚆⊖(Reading)🛏🚌🐾🎧

Nag's Head 🅛

5 Russell Street, RG1 7XD
☎ 07765 880137 ⊕ thenagsheadreading.co.uk
12 changing beers 🅷
With a wide range of real ales, real cider and perry always on offer, visitors are sure to find something to their taste here. There is also a craft beer wall, with vessel and dispense clearly indicated on the adjacent blackboard. A selection of board games is available for those wanting to while away a few sociable hours. The

pub gets busy on Reading FC match days. A regular in CAMRA's National Pub of the Year awards.
🌂🏠❶🚆(West) ⊖(Reading) 🍴🛏🚌🐾🎧🎵

Park House (University of Reading) 🅛

Park House, Whiteknights Campus, RG6 6UR
☎ (0118) 378 5098
1 changing beer (often Rebellion, Siren, Titanic) 🅷
The university's old senior common room is open to the general public. Five ales are usually available (mostly LocAle) and an array of styles feature. It is a popular venue for the more mature university community and can get busy in the early evening. Visitors' vehicles are allowed on campus after 5pm Monday to Friday and all day at weekends – however, a regular bus service drops off inside the campus. Open from noon everyday. Card payment only. 🇶🌂🏠❶♿🍴🛏🚌(21,21A)🐾🎧

Retreat

8 St John's Street, RG1 4EH
☎ (0118) 957 2130 ⊕ theretreat.pub
Harvey's Sussex Best Bitter; 4 changing beers (often Butcombe, Sharp's) 🅷
This much-loved back-street boozer has been recently refurbished. A good range of real ales are squeezed onto the small bar – the landlord tends to concentrate on well-known regional brands, though there is a good range of more eclectic choices available in bottled form, including continental beers, as well as a number of ciders. The pub is renowned locally for regular live music and hosting local events. 🇶🌂🏠❶♿🚌🎵

Three Guineas

Station Approach, RG1 1LY
☎ (0118) 957 2743 ⊕ three-guineas.co.uk
Fuller's Oliver's Island, London Pride, ESB; Gale's Seafarers Ale; 4 changing beers (often Butcombe, Windsor & Eton) 🅷
Grade II-listed pub in the old ticket hall of Reading railway station. It was refurbished by Fuller's a few years ago and features ornate tiling, old railway memorabilia and a selection of classic clocks. There's a large outdoor seating area in front, but you cannot access the platforms directly, so make sure you leave enough time for your train! 🌂🏠❶♿🚆⊖(Reading)🚌🐾🎧

Ruscombe

Royal Oak 🅛

Ruscombe Lane, RG10 9JN (on B3024 E out of Twyford)
☎ (0118) 934 5190 ⊕ burattas.co.uk
Fuller's London Pride; 2 changing beers (sourced locally; often Loddon, Rebellion) 🅷
Also known as Buratta's, this lively pub-restaurant is noted for its food, but welcomes drinkers with a fine range of wines and up to three real ales. The open-plan area is divided between seating areas and dining space. At the rear of the restaurant is a bright conservatory overlooking a beautifully-kept garden. The interior is comfortably furnished and decorated with quirky objects and antiques; many are available for sale.
🇶🌂🏠❶♿🚆(Twyford) 🅿🛏(127,850) 🐾🎧

St Nicholas Hurst

Wheelwrights Arms ✅

Davis Way, RG10 0TR (off B3030 opp entrance to Dinton Pastures)
☎ (0118) 934 4100 ⊕ thewheelwrightsarms.co.uk
Wadworth Henry's IPA, Horizon, 6X; 2 changing beers (sourced nationally; often Wadworth) 🅷

A welcoming country pub frequented by dog walkers, families and cyclists visiting the nearby Dinton Pastures. The L-shaped bar is decorated with a cosy olde-worlde charm and leads to a more formal popular restaurant serving classic pub favourites and Sunday roasts. Wadworth real ales and still ciders are available. TV sport is shown inside or in the Stretch Tent in the winter, with gardens for summer relaxation. A regular quiz is held on Wednesdays. ⛲✿◑♿P🚃(128,129)✿🛜

Slough

Moon & Spoon L ✔

86 High Street, SL1 1EL
☎ (01753) 531650
Greene King Abbot; Ruddles Best Bitter; Sharp's Doom Bar; 4 changing beers 🅗
This Wetherspoon establishment has 12 handpumps offering three regulars beers, accompanied by up to four changing guest ales, including one from a local brewery. A couple of ciders are also usually available, often Old Rosie and Black Dragon. At the entrance is an eye-catching sculpture made of 1,148 spoons. The usual Wetherspoon all-day food menu is served. The rear of the pub has a cosy feel, with separate seating areas and an interesting ceiling light. ⛲◑♿⇌🚃(2,8)🛜

Sonning

Bull Inn

High Street, RG4 6UP (next to St Andrew's Church)
☎ (0118) 969 3901 ⊕ bullinnsonning.co.uk
Dark Star Hophead; Fuller's London Pride; Gale's HSB; 1 changing beer (sourced nationally) 🅗
This delightful, characterful, 16th-century pub is leased to Fuller's by the adjacent church. Most of the interior is set for dining, but there is a separate Village Bar drinking area, also used as a function room. The regular beers and changing guests are mainly from the Fuller's range. An excellent selection of quality food, from snacks to fine dining, is available daily. A good stop-off for those taking a walk alongside the Thames. Q⛲✿🚪◑P🚃✿🛜♪

Swallowfield

George & Dragon L

Church Road, RG7 1TJ
☎ (0118) 988 4432 ⊕ georgedragonpub.com
Siren Yu Lu; Timothy Taylor Landlord; 1 changing beer (often Siren) 🅗
Just outside Swallowfield centre itself, this Grade II-listed 17th-century pub was recently taken over by nearby Siren Craft Brew. The relaxed country gastro-pub serves Siren's own beers plus a guest ale, as well as excellent wines and good food. Tables are mainly set for dining but drinkers are more than welcome. ⛲✿◑P✿🛜

Tilehurst

Fox & Hounds

116 City Road, RG31 5SB
☎ (0118) 942 2982 ⊕ thefoxandhoundstilehurst.co.uk
2 changing beers 🅗/🅖
Right on the edge of Tilehurst, this low-beamed village pub is popular with locals from surrounding suburbia and visitors walking open fields to Sulham Woods via the dovecote tower at Nunhide Manor. It is worth visiting in all weathers, with darts and pool facilities, a garden gazebo, a conservatory and a recently-uncovered fireplace now containing a wood-burning stove. ⛲✿♿♣P🚃(33)🛜♪

Waltham St Lawrence

Bell L

The Street, RG10 0JJ
☎ (0118) 934 1788 ⊕ thebellwalthamstlawrence.co.uk
Loddon Hoppit; 4 changing beers (often Butts, Loose Cannon, Stardust) 🅗
A classic half-timbered 14th-century pub, bequeathed to the village in 1608 by Sir Ralph Newbury. It doubles as the village local and a quality restaurant, producing exceptionally good food from fresh seasonal ingredients, and promoting real ales from small independent breweries. They offer up to eight ciders and perries served from their cellar. You'll also find log fires in the winter and a good-sized beer garden for sunny summer days. Q⛲✿✿◑♣🚃(4A)✿🛜♪

Wargrave

Wargrave & District Snooker Club

Woodclyffe Hostel, Church Street, RG10 8EP
⊕ wargravesnooker.co.uk
2 changing beers 🅗
The club opens weekday evenings only and shares the building with the local library. The regularly changing beers reflect members' recommendations, with two on in the winter months and one in the summer. The TV's default is off, though the Six Nations and World Cup are exceptions. Visitors may show this Guide or CAMRA membership card for entry (£3 fee to use the snooker tables). Winner of local CAMRA Club of the Year for several years. ⇌♣P🚃(850)✿

Windsor

A Hoppy Place L

11 St Leonard's Road, SL4 3BN
☎ (01753) 206802 ⊕ ahoppyplace.co.uk
2 changing beers (sourced locally; often Stardust) 🅟
Windsor's first micropub, winner of the local CAMRA Pub of the Year in 2021 and 2022, and SIBA Best UK Craft Beer Retailer in 2021. It offers two casks, plus 11 keg lines, including a gluten-free option, and five fridges full of bottled and canned beer with a focus on local and international beers. The fridges are arranged by beer style, including one fridge for cider and many no-alcohol options. The pub has a canning machine to can cask and keg beer for takeaway while you wait. ✿◑⇌(Windsor & Eton Central)♣🚇🚃✿🛜

Carpenters Arms ✔

4 Market Street, SL4 1PB
☎ (01753) 863739
St Austell Nicholson's Pale Ale; Sharp's Doom Bar; 4 changing beers (sourced nationally) 🅗
Situated on a narrow cobbled street close to the castle, this excellent Nicholson's pub has been voted local CAMRA Pub of the Year several times. The elegantly decorated interior is on three levels, the lowest of which is reputed to house a passageway to the castle. Ashby's brewery tiles are on the floor by the entrance, harking back to the pub's former owners. The two regular beers are supplemented by four interesting guests, often including something dark. ⛲◑⇌(Windsor & Eton Central)🚃🛜

Corner House L

22 Sheet Street, SL4 1BG
☎ (01753) 862031 ⊕ thecornerhousepub.co.uk
Big Smoke Solaris Session Pale Ale; 9 changing beers (sourced nationally) 🅗
This Grade II-listed building, spread over two floors, was converted into a multi-screen sports venue in 2022. Beer

is not neglected, however, and 15 handpumps serve nine regularly changing real ales plus five ciders. These are supplemented by 10 keg lines. Diners are also well catered for with a good selection of traditional pub food. Many pub games are on offer upstairs where there is also a small, partly covered roof terrace. ✿◑≢(Windsor & Eton Central) ♣●🖥♣😷🛜🎵

Windsor & Eton Unit Four Brewery Tap 🅛

4 Vansittart Estate, Duke Street, SL4 1SE
☎ (01753) 392495 ● webrew.co.uk
Windsor & Eton Knight of the Garter, Windsor Knot, Guardsman; 5 changing beers (sourced regionally; often Windsor & Eton) 🅗
Newly opened in 2021, the new brewery taproom features eight handpumps dispensing six Windsor & Eton beers plus two guests and 22 keg lines. Cider is Devon Red and Fanny's Brambles by Sandford Orchards. The decor is modern, relaxing and includes a mezzanine floor and a stage for events. There is an interesting range of cans and bottles, as well as regular brewery tours. Tasty pub-style food is available.
🍽✿◑♿≢(Windsor & Eton Central) ●P🖥😷🛜

Windsor Trooper ✅

97 St Leonards Road, SL4 3BZ
☎ (01753) 670122 ● thewindsortrooper.com
Adnams Southwold Bitter; Oakham Citra; 3 changing beers (sourced regionally) 🅗
Popular pub within walking distance of Windsor town centre. It has been pleasantly refurbished in traditional style, with a collection of original brewery mirrors. Five cask beers are available plus nine traditional ciders. There is a large room at the rear that also serves as a function room and venue for Thursday night live music. Outside is a sizeable beer garden. Accommodation is available in nine en-suite rooms. Local CAMRA Cider Pub of the Year 2023.
✿🛏◑≢(Windsor & Eton Central) ●🖥😷🛜🎵

Winkfield

White Hart 🅛

Church Road, SL4 4SE (on A330 opp St Mary's Church)
☎ (01344) 882415 ● thewhitehartwinkfield.co.uk
Greene King Abbot; Rebellion IPA; Sharp's Doom Bar 🅗
This historic pub, once the parish courthouse, contains many original features, including a 250-year-old bread oven and a friendly ghost. It is now a genuine village pub with a comfortable bar, stone-paved floor and sofas close to a real fire and a separate dining room. The kitchen serves locally sourced home-made food – fish & chips on Fridays are very popular. The extensive garden can be enjoyed in warmer months. Dogs are allowed in the bar area. Closed Mondays. Q🍽✿◑♿P😷🛜

Wokingham

Crispin 🅛

45 Denmark Street, RG40 2AY (opp Denmark St car park)
☎ (0118) 978 0309
Hogs Back TEA; Rebellion Overthrow; 3 changing beers (sourced regionally; often Ascot, Rebellion, Stardust) 🅗
A traditional, cosy, real ale and cider pub named after the Patron saint of cobblers, championing LocAle and friendly conversation. Regular charity events are held and occasional beer festivals in the garden, which has covered seating. The pub does not serve food, but plates and cutlery are provided to consume your own food with a drink purchased from the bar. Closes early evening Sunday to Wednesday. 🍽✿😷≢♣🖥😷🛜🎵

Outhouse Brewery 🅛

Unit 4, Southgate House, Alexandra Court, RG40 2SL
● theouthousebrewery.com
4 changing beers (sourced locally; often Outhouse Wokingham)
Town-centre brewpub with the brewing equipment on display and new adjacent taproom with seating area. Outhouse brewery beers are served from a tap wall and are unfiltered and unpasteurised from membrane kegs, as listed on the beer blackboard. Bar staff are knowledgeable and will happily share the art of their brewing. Open at weekends and most weekday evenings. ✿♿≢🖥😷🛜

Wraysbury

Perseverance ✅

2 High Street, TW19 5DB
☎ (01784) 482375 ● thepercy.co.uk
Otter Ale; 2 changing beers 🅗
The comfortable pub is now free of tie. The larger front room has a piano and an inglenook fireplace with a real log fire. Another seating area with an open fire leads to the rear dining area, which has well-stocked bookshelves. The rear garden is delightful. Two guest ales are always varied and are from some of the more interesting breweries, both LocAle and around the country. Regular beer festivals are held. Quiz night is Thursday and live music plays on Sunday afternoons. Q🍽✿◑♣●P🖥(305) 😷🛜🎵

Breweries

Aldworth (NEW)

🍺 **Bell Inn, Aldworth, RG8 9SE**

Set up in late 2022 in an old barn behind the Bell (National Pub of the Year 2019). This nanobrewery is run by James Macaulay, son of the family who run the Bell. James trained as a brewer at West Berkshire Brewery (now rebranded as Renegade). The brewery has a capacity a 163 litres (approx 1 barrel or 4x9 gallon firkins) and is understood to be supplying the pub only.

Art Brew

c/o 120 Castle Street, Reading, RG1 7RJ ☎ 07881 783626 ✉ artbrewdevon@gmail.com

⊗ Brewing started in 2008 on the Jurassic Coast in Dorset before moving to Devon in 2016. In 2023, the brewery relocated to Reading at the Castle Tap, initiating the Count Me In Collective (CMIC). CMIC is a training partnership for people with barriers to work such as learning disabilities, autism or mental health difficulties. ◆LIVE

Bond Brews

Units 3 & 4, South Barns, Gardeners Green Farm, Heathlands Road, Wokingham, RG40 3AS
☎ (01344) 775450 ● bondbrews.co.uk

⊗ Bond Brews was established in 2015 using a six-barrel plant and produces a range of cask-conditioned and bottle-conditioned beers. Deliveries are made to pubs within a 30-mile radius and retail purchases are available from the brewery shop and online. Brewery tours and experience days are available by arrangement with the brewer. !! ▪ ◆ LIVE

Goldi-hops (ABV 3.9%) PALE
A golden-coloured, session pale ale with a fruit and hop aroma. Bramble and apple flavours lead to a lingering fruity, dry bitter aftertaste.

Best of British (ABV 4%) BITTER
Tawny-coloured session bitter, predominantly malty, hops and fruit aroma. Dried fruit, earthy caramel flavours lead to sweet nutty aftertaste.

Bengal Tiger (ABV 4.3%) PALE
A golden-coloured, session pale ale with a hoppy, fruity aroma. Initial fruity flavour leads to an earthy bitterness and a long, dry, bitter finish.

Railway Porter (ABV 4.5%) PORTER
A brown-coloured, session porter with roast malt and fruit aroma. Bitter and hoppy flavour with an earthy, peppery, bitter chocolate aftertaste.

Bucklebury SIBA

Broad Lane, Upper Bucklebury, RG7 6QJ ☎ 0783 4044468 ✉ info@buckleburybrewers.co.uk

A small-scale brewery which started production in 2020 using two 150-litre fermenting vessels. All the beers are unfiltered and unpasteurised. Beer in pressurised kegs is supplied to the Cottage Inn in the village, and bottled beers are supplied to local shops within a 10-15 mile radius of the brewery. LIVE

Butts

Northfield Farm, Wantage Road, Great Shefford, RG17 7BY
☎ (01488) 648133 ⊕ buttsbrewery.com

⊗ The brewery was set up in a converted barn in 1994. In 2002 the owners took the decision to become dedicated to organic production; all the beers brewed use organic malted barley and organic hops, and are certified by the Soil Association. ▪ ◆ LIVE

Jester (ABV 3.5%) BITTER
A pale brown session bitter with a hoppy aroma and a hint of fruit. The taste balances malt, hops, fruit and bitterness with a hoppy aftertaste.

Traditional (ABV 4%) BITTER
Pale brown session bitter with citrus hop aroma and flavours. A long, dry aftertaste is dominated by fruity hops.

Barbus Barbus (ABV 4.6%) GOLD
Premium golden ale with fruity hop aroma and hint of malt. Hops dominate the taste and aftertaste followed by some fruitiness and bitterness,

Golden Brown (ABV 5%) BITTER

Delphic

26 The Martins, Thatcham, RG19 4FD ☎ 07595 386568 ⊕ delphicbrewing.com

Thatcham's first craft brewery was established in 2019 by head brewer Tom Broadbank. It is a 2.5-barrel plant providing regular, seasonal and collaboration beers to local pubs, clubs and festivals. Bottles and cans are also available through well-established, off-sales outlets in Berkshire and the online shop. ◆

Level Crossing (ABV 4.2%) BITTER
World's End (ABV 4.6%) PALE
Daydream Believer (ABV 5.4%) SPECIALITY

Dolphin SIBA

Woodley, RG5 4TL ☎ 07979 753391
⊕ dolphinbrewery.co.uk

A 130-litre brewery operating on a small scale from the garage of one of the brewers' parents. It produces bottled beers and occasional KeyKeg. It specialises in niche styles; sours, gose, saison and porters. LIVE

Double-Barrelled SIBA

Unit 20, Stadium Way, Tilehurst, Reading, RG30 6BX
☎ (0118) 942 8390 ⊕ doublebarrelled.co.uk

Brewing began in 2018 on a 15-barrel plant. The beer range is wide, concentrating on pale ales, IPAs and a lager, but also includes seasonal fruited sours and stouts. The production of barrel-aged beers began in 2021. The occasional cask-conditioned beer is available locally. The majority of beers are only brewed once, with regular collaborations. The taproom is large and welcoming, offering local street food at weekends. !! ▪ V ◆

Elusive SIBA

Units 3-5, Marino Way, Hogwood Lane Industrial Estate, Finchampstead, RG40 4RF
☎ (0118) 973 2153 ⊕ elusivebrewing.com

Award-winning Elusive Brewing is a five-barrel brewery, established in 2016. With a fermenting capacity of 41 barrels, it produces a diverse range of unfiltered and unpasteurised cask, KeyKeg and canned beers. It continues many brewery collaborations and tap takeovers. The taproom sells beers from the Elusive range and other breweries, plus related merchandise. ▪ ◆ ◆

Microball (ABV 3.7%) MILD
Level Up (ABV 5%) RED
Morrisman (ABV 5%) SPECIALITY
Overdrive (ABV 5.5%) IPA
Oregon Trail (ABV 5.8%) IPA
Spellbinder (ABV 6%) SPECIALITY

FutureState

Earley, Reading, RG6 5XF ⊕ futurestatebrew.com

A nanobrewery being run from the owner's domestic garage, producing a wide variety of beers and participating in many collaborative brews. It registered for commercial activity in 2020 and beer is only available through its web-based subscription club.

Hermitage

Heathwaite, Slanting Hill, Hermitage, RG18 9QG
☎ (01635) 200907 ☎ 07980 019484
⊕ hermitagebrewery.co.uk

⊗ Established in 2013 by semi-retired food science lecturer, Richard Marshall. After many years as a home brewer, the opportunity arose to go commercial. The 0.5-barrel brewery produces bottle-conditioned and some cask ales. Volumes vary, but is about 200 bottles per week. A range of six core beers and six seasonal and special brews are sold to local shops. Cask is sent to festivals and a few pubs along with polypins for events. Bespoke beers are occasionally produced by special request. ◆ LIVE

Indie Rabble (NEW)

▤ 26-27 The Arches, Alma Road, Windsor, SL4 1QZ
☎ 07426 839741 ⊕ indierabble.co.uk

A 20-hectolitre brewery and taproom in a railway arch beneath the track for Windsor & Eton Central Station. Opened in 2023, it produces a range of beers, including German-influenced lager, both hazy and bright pale ales, kettle sours and stouts.

Indigenous

Peacock Cottage, Main Street, Chaddleworth, RG20 7EH
☎ (01488) 505060 ⊕ indigenousbrewery.co.uk

⊗ An occasional and informal microbrewer for many years, Kevin Brady established Indigenous in 2014, increasing production using a 2.5-barrel plant. Availability is restricted to local pubs, shops and an increasing number of regional beer festivals. ‼🍺♦LIVE

Baldrick (ABV 3.4%) MILD
Chinwag (ABV 4%) BITTER
Forager's Gold (ABV 4%) GOLD
Summer Solstice (ABV 4.1%) PALE
Billy No Mates (ABV 4.2%) PALE
Frisky Mare (ABV 4.2%) GOLD
Silly Moo (ABV 4.2%) STOUT
Tickety-Boo (ABV 4.2%) GOLD
Nutcracker (ABV 4.5%) OLD
Old Cadger (ABV 4.5%) BITTER
Monocle (ABV 4.6%) STOUT
Moonstruck (ABV 4.8%) PORTER
Dark brown session porter with malt, chocolate and coffee aromas. Full mouthfeel of hops, caramel and fruit with a bitter finish.
Nosey Parker (ABV 5.5%) MILD
Strong ruby mild with a malt and toffee note aroma. Malt dominates the taste with a balanced malt and hop aftertaste.
AMMO Belle (ABV 5.6%) IPA
Amber New World IPA with fruit, hops and malt on the nose followed by some bitterness in the taste. Malty aftertaste joined by a fruity hoppiness.
Double Warp (ABV 5.8%) STOUT
Dark brown strong stout with malt aroma and coffee notes. Roasted, sweet, malt flavour finishes with a balanced aftertaste.

INNformal

14 Charnham Street, Hungerford, RG17 0ES
⊕ john-o-gaunt-hungerford.co.uk

⊗ The INNformal brewery was established in 2015 and moved to Hungerford in 2019 when it expanded to a four-barrel plant. A selection of the beers can always be found at its affiliated pub the John O'Gaunt Inn, Hungerford. ‼♦

INN Session (ABV 3.5%) PALE
INNHouse Bitter (ABV 4.1%) BITTER
INNDeep (ABV 5%) STOUT
INN Alcatraz (ABV 5.9%) IPA
InnDarkness (ABV 6%) PORTER
Alice Inn Wonderland (ABV 7.1%) STRONG

New Wharf SIBA

Hyde Farm, Marlow Road, Maidenhead, SL6 6PQ
☎ (01628) 634535 ⊕ newwharfbrewing.co.uk

A 20-barrel brewery, which was set up in 2017. After a pause in 2019-2020, it restarted brewing in 2021 with an updated core range of two keg beers plus a pilsner and with intentions to expand and add seasonal beers to the range.

Outhouse

🍴 **4 Southgate House, Alexandra Court, Denmark Street, Wokingham, RG40 2SL**
⊕ theouthousebrewery.com

⊗ Brewpub encompassing a 300-litre (1.8-barrel) nanobrewery, established in 2021. Beers are supplied in KeyKegs, are unfiltered and unpasteurised. The majority of production is dispensed at the pub, with occasional KeyKegs on sale at local pubs or beer festivals. New recipes are constantly being brewed, and older recipes tweaked. 🍺LIVE

Phantom

Unit 3, Meadow Road, Reading, RG1 8LB
⊕ phantombrew.com

A brewery located on the outskirts of Reading town centre, brewing an ever-changing range of KeyKeg beers in a variety of styles including hoppy pales, fruit sours and stouts. No beer is brewed all the time, but favourites turn up at regular intervals. ‼♦

Renegade SIBA

The Old Dairy, Frilsham Farm, Yattendon, RG18 0XT
☎ (01635) 767090 ⊕ renegadebrewery.co.uk

⊗ Formerly known as West Berkshire and under new ownership since late 2021, the brewery rebranded to Renegade in 2022. Originally established in 1995, it moved to new, purpose-built facilities in 2018 in a former dairy farm building covering 68,000sq ft (its fourth expansion). Capacity was increased tenfold to 60,000 hectolitres, complemented by a fully-automated bottling and canning line. The site includes a shop, taproom and kitchen. ‼🍺♦⬧

Mister Chubb's (ABV 3.4%) BITTER
A drinkable, balanced, session bitter. A malty caramel note dominates aroma and taste and is accompanied by a nutty bittersweetness and a hoppy aftertaste.
Maggs' Mild (ABV 3.5%) MILD
Silky, full-bodied, dark mild with a creamy head. Roast malt aroma is joined in the taste by caramel, sweetness and mild, fruity hoppiness. Aftertaste of roast malt with balancing bitterness.
Good Old Boy (ABV 4%) BITTER
Tawny-coloured session bitter with malty aroma, then a balanced flavour with hops and fruit, leading to a long, dry, bitter aftertaste.
Maharaja IPA (ABV 5.1%) PALE

Siren SIBA

Unit 1, Hogwood Lane Industrial Estate, Weller Drive, Finchampstead, RG40 4QZ
☎ (0118) 973 0929

Office: Siren Tap Yard, Alberto House, 18 Marino Way, Hogwood Lane Industrial Estate, Finchampstead, RG40 4RF ⊕ sirencraftbrew.com

⊗ Established in 2013, this is a state-of-the-art, 40-barrel craft brewery, which produces 70-100 unique beers every year. Beers are produced in cask, keg, KeyKeg, bottles and cans, and are distributed throughout the UK and Europe. The Tap Yard serves freshly-brewed beers, pizzas and hosts special events. Siren also own a country pub nearby in Swallowfield and will open a brew bar in Reading in 2023 just after its 10-year anniversary. ‼🍺♦GF V⬧

Yu Lu (ABV 3.6%) SPECIALITY
Memento (ABV 3.8%) BITTER
Lumina (ABV 4.2%) PALE

Broken Dream Breakfast Stout (ABV 6.5%)
SPECIALITY

Stardust SIBA

Unit 5, Howe Lane Farm Estate, Howe Lane, White Waltham, SL6 3JP
☎ (01628) 947325 ⊕ stardustbrewery.co.uk

⊠ An independent, family-owned and run brewery, Stardust was established in 2016 and capacity was increased to 12 barrels in 2023. Located in a unit on a small farm estate, there's a brewery shop and a small bar on-site plus an online shop offering local and national delivery. It supplies direct to trade outlets in Berkshire and surrounding counties, and further afield via distributors. ‼🍴♦🗲

Easy Pale Citra (ABV 3.8%) PALE
English Bitter (ABV 4%) BITTER
Just Stout (ABV 4.2%) STOUT
Optic (ABV 4.2%) GOLD
Roast Note (ABV 4.3%) BITTER
Saaz Pilsner (ABV 4.5%) SPECIALITY
PK3 (ABV 5.6%) IPA

Swamp Bog

Church Lane, Enborne, RG20 0HB
⊕ swampbogbrewery.com

⊠ Under the same ownership and sharing the same kit as Two Cocks brewery (qv) this microbrewery, based on the edge of Hampshire/Berkshire, specialises in long-lost craft beer recipes from a time before brewing giants existed. The passion is for taste, not profit; low volume rather than mass production.

Bottom Biter (ABV 3.6%) BITTER
Edge Hopper (ABV 4.2%) GOLD
Pixie Pee (ABV 5%) PALE
The Ferryman's Brew (ABV 5%) SPECIALITY

Two Cocks

Church Lane, Enborne, RG20 0HB
☎ (01635) 37777 ⊕ twococksbrewery.com

⊠ Under the same ownership and sharing the same kit as Swamp Bog brewery (qv), Two Cocks was established in 2011, after wild hops were found growing in the farm's hedgerows. A 180-feet deep borehole supplies water for the brewery. During the English Civil War, the first Battle of Newbury (1643) was fought on the surrounding land and most of the beer names refer to it in some way.

'Diamond Lil' (ABV 3.2%) GOLD
1643 Cavalier (ABV 3.8%) GOLD
1643 Leveller (ABV 3.8%) BITTER
1643 Musket Bitter (ABV 3.8%) BITTER
1643 Roundhead (ABV 4.2%) BITTER
1643 Puritan (ABV 4.5%) STOUT
1643 Viscount (ABV 5.6%) BITTER

Two Flints (NEW)

25-26 The Arches, Alma Road, Windsor, SL4 1QZ
☎ 07827 915308 ⊕ twoflintsbrewery.com

Brewery and taproom in a railway arch below the track from Windsor & Eton Central Station. The 20-hectolitre plant opened in 2022 and brews a range of keg and canned beers. The taproom is on two floors, with food trucks often outside. ‼♦

Wickham

🏠 **Five Bells, Baydon Road, Wickham, RG20 8HH**
☎ (01488) 657300 ⊕ fivebellswickham.co.uk

A brewpub which started in 2020, on the same site and using the kit as previously used by INNformal brewery, which moved to Hungerford in 2019. The brewhouse was built by the previous owners behind the Five Bells in 2015. A borehole in the pub garden supplies water for the 2.5-barrel plant and 0.5-barrel test kit.

Windsor & Eton SIBA

Unit 1, Vansittart Estate, Duke Street, Windsor, SL4 1SE
☎ (01753) 854075 ⊕ webrew.co.uk

⊠ Founded in 2010 by ex-Courage brewers, Windsor & Eton Brewery produces over 5,000 barrels per year — mainly for the pubs of London and Thames Valley from its 18-barrel, Burton-fabricated brewing plant. It has a Royal Warrant and strong sustainability credentials. In 2021 it opened a new taproom, featuring up to 22 different draft beers, and Young's last working dray (used as a stage when not delivering beer around Windsor). Beers are also produced under the Uprising brand name. ‼🍴♦LIVE🗲

Knight of the Garter (ABV 3.8%) GOLD
Session golden ale with a citrusy hop aroma, joined by some sweetness in the taste, followed by bitterness in the finish.
Windsor Knot (ABV 4%) BITTER
Guardsman (ABV 4.2%) BITTER
Eton Boatman (ABV 4.3%) GOLD
Session golden ale with tropical fruit and citrus hop aroma, continuing into the taste with some sweetness and subtle bitter finish.
Father Thames (ABV 4.8%) BITTER
Conqueror (ABV 5%) PALE
Dark brown ale with an aroma of dark malts and citrus hops. Malt dominates the taste with citrus and spice. Dry malty finish.

Zerodegrees SIBA

🏠 **9 Bridge Street, Reading, RG1 2LR**
☎ (0118) 959 7959 ⊕ zerodegrees.co.uk

After a period of temporary closure, brewing has restarted at the Reading branch of Zerodegrees (part of a chain of four brewpubs). It is only brewing Bohemian (a Czech lager) and a few specials. All other beers are brought in from other branches. 🍴🗲

A quart a day keeps the doctor away

A judicious labourer would probably always have some ale in his house, and have small beer for the general drink. There is no reason why he should not keep Christmas as well as the farmer; and when he is mowing, reaping, or is at any other hard work, a quart, or three pints, of really good fat ale a-day is by no means too much.
William Cobbett, Cottage Economy, 1822

BUCKINGHAMSHIRE

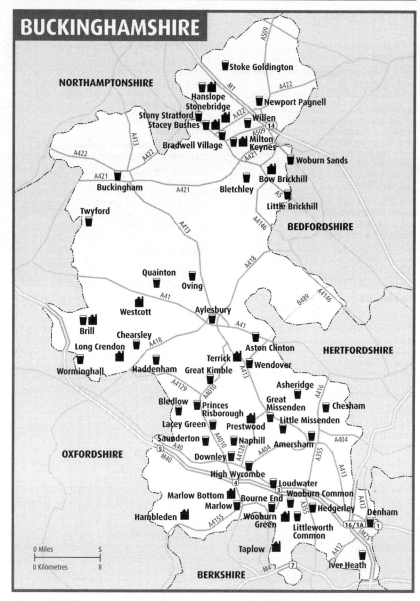

Amersham

Boot & Slipper ✓

2 Rickmansworth Road, HP6 5JN
☎ (01494) 727082
Greene King IPA; 5 changing beers (sourced nationally; often Rebellion, Timothy Taylor, Tring) ⊞
One of the most haunted pubs in Amersham on the Hill, this centuries-old building, owned by the Chef & Brewer chain, was refurbished in 2022. The central bar's six handpumps dispense well-kept beers with occasional unusual guests. The large restaurant occupies the entrance area and the rest of the pub has comfortable upholstered table seating. The large garden has extensive seating, including a sheltered, heated patio.
🛇❀🕭❶🕹�⇌⊖(Amersham) ₽♻(1,1A) 🐾♠

Asheridge

Blue Ball ᴸ

Asheridge Road, HP5 2UX
☎ (01494) 758263
Adnams Ghost Ship; Fuller's London Pride; Sharp's Doom Bar; Tring Side Pocket for a Toad ⊞
Dating from the late 17th century, this rural family pub is situated in a hamlet two miles north-west of Chesham. The L-shaped bar serves well-kept beers from four handpumps. There are two wood-burning stoves, one at each end of the main bar area. A restaurant serves good food at lunchtimes (no evening food is available). The extensive garden has seating, including a heated enclosure, with fine views over the adjacent valley.
🛇❀🕭❶♣₽🐾♠

Aston Clinton

Oak

119 Green End Street, HP22 5EU
☎ (01296) 630466 ⊕ oakastonclinton.co.uk
Fuller's London Pride; 1 changing beer (often Fuller's) Ⓗ
Large, pleasant and comfortable L-shaped bar with low beams, a wooden floor and plenty of seating. The pub boasts an extensive beer garden with attractive, leafy trees in season. While not completely separate, the tiled bar to the left operates like a public bar, full of local characters and chit-chat. The other areas of the bar are low-beamed and comfortable. ❀◑&P🚍(61,500)❀🐾

Aylesbury

Hop Pole Craft Beer & Grill Ⓛ

83 Bicester Road, HP19 9AZ (near Gatehouse Industrial Area)
☎ (01296) 482129
10 changing beers Ⓗ
Well worth a short stroll out of the town centre, this temple of beer regularly sports nine cask ales, including three or four guests among the Vale beers. There is also a good range of mostly Belgian bottled beers. It hosts a quiz on Tuesday night and also ukulele sessions on the second and fourth Wednesday of each month. There is also occasional live music at the weekend and seasonal beer festivals. Local CAMRA Pub of the Year 2022.
❀◑●🚍❀🐾♪

King's Head Ⓛ

Market Square, HP20 2RW
☎ (01296) 718812 ⊕ kingsheadaylesbury.co.uk
Chiltern Pale Ale, Beechwood Bitter; 3 changing beers Ⓗ
This is the oldest courtyard inn in England, complete with cobbles. Converted stables occupy one side. The magnificent building is owned by the National Trust. The bar is run by the Chiltern brewery as a de facto brewery tap – it has up to four Chiltern ales, two of which often change, and a guest beer, often a stout or porter in the winter months, and also often a cider. Beer festivals are held periodically. There is plenty of outside seating.
Q❀❀◑&≠●🚍🐾

White Hart ✅

Unit 4, Exchange Street, HP20 1UR
☎ (01296) 468440
Sharp's Doom Bar; 6 changing beers (sourced nationally) Ⓗ
Wetherspoon pub in a functional modern building on the site of the old cattle market and opposite the new Waterside Theatre. It is named after a pub that stood nearby, now long since demolished. A younger crowd frequents the pub at night, but during the day and early evening it attracts the usual Wetherspoons crowd as well as pre-theatre diners. It serves the usual Wetherspoons ale offering. ❀◑&≠●🚍🐾

Bledlow

Lions of Bledlow Ⓛ

Church End, HP27 9PE (from M40 jct 6 go through Chinnor to Bledlow village on B4009, take 2nd left through village on B4009, pub is signposted)
☎ (01844) 343345 ⊕ thelionsofbledlow.co.uk
5 changing beers (sourced locally; often Tring, Wadworth) Ⓗ
A charming 16th-century free house at the foot of the Chiltern Hills, between the Icknield Way and the Chinnor and Princes Risborough Steam Railways Line, popular with ramblers, dog walkers and cyclists. Its five handpumps offer a rotating variety of local, regional and natiional beers. Its interior, with traditional dark oak beams and quarry tiles, has been used as a location for ITV's Midsomer Murders detective series on several occasions. Q❀❀◑&P🚍❀🐾

Bourne End

KEG – Craft Beer Tasting Bar Ⓛ

12 Oakfield Road, SL8 5QN
☎ (01628) 529369 ⊕ kegcraftbeer.co.uk
2 changing beers (often Stardust)
Small and welcoming microbar just off the main road through the village. Named KEG after its owner, Kim E Georgiou, it offers two cask ales and seven craft keg beers. The bar is full pf bric-a-brac and plays music from the patron's eclectic vinyl collection. The bar is well worth a visit if you're in the area. There is limited seating outside and a car park nearby. ≠●🚍(36)🐾🐾

Brill

Pointer Ⓛ ✅

27 Church Street, HP18 9RT
☎ (01844) 238339 ⊕ thepointerbrill.co.uk
Vale Best IPA; house beer (by XT); 2 changing beers Ⓗ
Not only a destination eatery, this free house has also become a destination ale house, thanks to the skilled cellarwoman. Its four handpumps offer a reliable choice, which often features a stout or porter and another guest ale. An open-walled kitchen serves wonderful locally sourced food to a separate vaulted dining room. The pub supports the Brill beer festival in August.
Q❀❀◑≠●♣🚍🐾

Buckingham

Grand Junction ✅

13 High Street, MK18 1NT
☎ (01280) 731680 ⊕ thegrandjunctionbuckingham.co.uk
Fuller's London Pride; 1 changing beer (sourced locally; often Roman Way) Ⓗ
Closed for many years, then completely rebuilt by Oakman, the pub reopened in 2022 under its traditional name. The focus is on food, which is available from breakfast through to dinner, but drinkers are welcome, with one regular ale from the Fuller's list and one changing ale, often local. The large patio area has plenty of tables, benches and seats and is entered direclty from the street, giving level access to the large restaurant area and the Granary bar and function room.
❀❀◑&🚍(X5,X60) 🐾🐾

REAL ALE BREWERIES

Blackened Sun 🍻 Milton Keynes: Stacey Bushes
Boobytrap 🍻 Westcott
Brewhouse & Kitchen 🍺 Milton Keynes: Central
Bucks Star Milton Keynes: Stonebridge
Chiltern Terrick
Feisty Wooburn Green (NEW)
Grid Hanslope (NEW)
Hornes Milton Keynes: Bow Brickhill
Malt 🍻 Prestwood
moogBREW 🍻 Taplow
Old Luxters Hambleden
Rebellion 🍻 Marlow Bottom
Vale 🍻 Brill
XT 🍻 Long Crendon

King's Head Coffee & Gin Bar ✅

7 Market Hill, MK18 1JX

☎ (01280) 812442 ⊕ thekingsheadcoffeebar.com

Hornes Triple Goat Pale Ale; 1 changing beer (often Brains, Purity, Wadworth) Ⓗ

In the centre of Buckingham, this is a pleasant and comfortable pub with a hidden-away, sunny courtyard garden. As well as two real ales from the SIBA list and Old Rosie cider, it is a coffee, gin and cocktail bar with a buy-one get-one-free cocktail menu throughout the day. Its range of food menus from breakfast to evening offer a wide range; gluten-free and vegan needs are catered for. Although wheelchair-friendly, it has no disabled toilet. ♿❀◐🖶(X5,X60) ❀🛜♪

Mitre ▼

2 Mitre Street, MK18 1DW

☎ (01280) 813080 ⊕ themitrepub.co.uk

Timothy Taylor Boltmaker; 4 changing beers (sourced nationally; often Five Points, Harbour, Tring) Ⓗ

Buckingham's oldest pub is a stone-built free house dating from the 17th century. Its cosy and friendly atmosphere is enhanced by an open fire in winter. It offers changing and interesting beers – regularly including local ales – from five handpumps during winter months, with one replaced by still ciders in summertime. Large-screen TVs show major events, but live music also features regularly. A large stretch-tent covers the garden. Parking is on the street. Local CAMRA Pub of the Year 2023. ♿❀♣🖶❀🛜♪

Chearsley

Bell

Church Lane, HP18 0DJ

☎ (01844) 208077 ⊕ thebellchearsley.co.uk

Fuller's London Pride; Gale's Seafarers Ale; 2 changing beers Ⓗ

Attractive thatched pub on the edge of the village green, often featured in Midsomer Murders. The cosy interior has settles, flagstones, a real fire, and an interesting clock. The large garden is ideal for sunny summer days. This Fuller's house is well known both for its ales and for its good wholesome food. Q❀◐P🖶(110)

Chesham

Queen's Head 🄻

120 Church Street, HP5 1JD

☎ (01494) 778690 ⊕ queensheadchesham.co.uk

Fuller's London Pride, ESB; 3 changing beers (sourced nationally; often Dark Star, Gale's, Twickenham) Ⓗ

On Chesham's historic Church Street is this characterful 18th-century pub. It is divided into several distinct rooms: real fires warm the spacious lounge and public bar, which has a dartboard and beer-themed mini-library to keep you entertained, while another room to the rear, and the yard, provide further seating. Three changing ales often come from the Fuller's range, sometimes from far-flung breweries. Authentic Thai cuisine dominates the menu in both the pub and separate restaurant, and there is also currywurst. ♿❀◐&⊖(Chesham)♣P🖶❀🛜

Trekkers Bar & Bottleshop 🄻

2 High Street, HP5 1EP

☎ 07943 711501 ⊕ trekkersbars.co.uk

2 changing beers (sourced nationally; often Rebellion, Tring, Windsor & Eton) Ⓐ

Micropub in a former barbershop, named for its popularity with Chilterns walkers. Two cask ales are served, one from a local brewery, plus a real cider, nine craft beers, and a huge selection of bottles and cans to drink in or take away. If the cosy interior is busy, there are tables outside on Chesham's Market Square. Occasional live music and vinyl nights are hosted. Local CAMRA Best Newcomer in 2020. ♿❀&⊖(Chesham)●🖶(1,354)❀♪

Denham

Falcon Inn ✅

Village Road, UB9 5BE

☎ (01895) 832125 ⊕ falcondenham.com

Harviestoun Bitter & Twisted; St Austell Proper Job; Timothy Taylor Landlord; 2 changing beers (sourced regionally) Ⓗ

Small one-bar pub in Denham Village conservation area, overlooking the village green. Though the building dates from the 18th century it has a smart interior. The entrance has interesting old steps straight off the road. There is a lovely rear sunny garden. Good food is served lunchtimes and evenings, with bar snacks as well as a restaurant menu. Parking can be difficult, but there is easy access on foot from Denham station close by. High-quality accommodation is offered. Q❀🛏◐⇌🖶❀🛜♪

Green Man 🄻

Village Road, UB9 5BH

☎ (01895) 832760 ⊕ greenmandenham.co.uk

Rebellion IPA, Smuggler Ⓗ

This friendly free-of-tie inn has been sympathetically refurbished. The front bar has beams, a real fire and flagged floors, opening out into a large conservatory and well-tended beer garden and patio area, both with covered seating areas. The pub has a tempting food menu and is popular with diners and families as well as local drinkers. Historic Denham is a picturesque rural village, a pleasant stroll from the Colne Valley Country Park Visitor Centre. ♿❀◐⇌♣🖶❀🛜♪

Downley

De Spencer Arms

The Common, HP13 5YQ (across common from village on a flint track beyond end of Plomer Green Ln)

☎ (01494) 535317 ⊕ ledespencers.co.uk

Fuller's London Pride, ESB; 2 changing beers (sourced nationally) Ⓗ

A busy, friendly local on the edge of Downley Common, offering a warm welcome to all including walkers, dogs and children. The garden is a lovely area to sit during the summer months. The surrounding Area of Outstanding Natural Beauty offers many walks. There is car parking to the rear of the pub. ♿❀◐♣P🖶❀🛜♪

Great Kimble

Swan 🄻

Grove Lane, HP17 9TR

☎ (01844) 275288

Tring Side Pocket for a Toad, Moongazing; 2 changing beers (sourced locally) Ⓗ

A family-owned free house that dates back to the 18th century. It adjoins the children's playground on the green in this village at the foot of the Chiltern Hills, in excellent hiking, horse riding and cycling country. The back garden features a wood-fired pizza oven and barbecue. Sunday lunchtimes are popular. Opening times can vary during the week, as can the range of ales, especially in winter. ♿❀🛏◐&⇌(Little Kimble)♣P🖶(300)❀🛜♪

Great Missenden

George Ale House 🏆
94 High Street, HP16 0BG
☎ (01494) 865185
Harvey's Sussex Best Bitter; 3 changing beers (sourced nationally) Ⓗ
A pub with a really good atmosphere and ales that are always in excellent condition. It has three seating areas, some with comfortable sofas and real fires, and there is a small beer garden/patio at the back. There is no background music but sometimes on a Saturday evening there will be a group playing. Local CAMRA Pub of the Year 2023. Q❀☸≉♣♠P❄☺♫

Haddenham

Rising Sun Ⓛ ✅
9 Thame Road, HP17 8EN
☎ (01844) 291744 ⊕ risingsunhaddenham.co.uk
XT Four; 5 changing beers (sourced locally) Ⓗ
This bustling village pub boasts six real ales on handpumps, with favourites from XT brewery as well as unusual Animal Brewing Company creations, plus an ever-changing selection of guest ales, craft beers and ciders. The friendly locals inhabit an area to the left of the bar known as Compost Corner. With a landscaped garden, and treats on tap for canine companions, this family- and pooch-friendly pub blends the best of old and new seamlessly.
Q❀☸❄≉(Haddenham & Thame Parkway) ♠🚌(280) ☺🐾🛜

Hanslope

Club Hanslope
28 High Street, MK19 7LQ
☎ (01908) 510337 ⊕ theclubhanslope.co.uk
Adnams Ghost Ship; Draught Bass; 1 changing beer (sourced nationally; often Oakham, Potbelly, Timothy Taylor) Ⓗ
The original Hanslope Working Men's Club opened in 1898 and now welcomes everyone, including non-members for a nominal fee. The two downstairs rooms are designated the 'Bar' and the 'Lounge', serving two regular beers and a weekly-changing guest ale. Upstairs has a games room. It offers a wide range of community activities: children's events, discos, films, monthly bingo, live music, darts, Northants skittles, pool, cards and quizzes. The CIU-affiliated club also holds a weekend beer festival each Easter. ♿❀☸♣♠P🚌🛜♫

Cock Inn
35 High Street, MK19 7LQ
☎ (01908) 893741 ⊕ cock-inn.co.uk
Draught Bass; 1 changing beer (sourced nationally; often Timothy Taylor, Vale) Ⓗ
Popular local with a large single room that has a country-pub feel. The bar serves one regular and one guest ale, often from local breweries. It hosts a monthy supper club and food vans visit occasionally. There is a TV at one end and a real fire stove at the other, with plenty of tables and chairs in between. Customers enjoy regular quiz, bingo and poker nights, live music, and themed events such as a Halloween party. ♿❀☸🅍♿P🚌🛜♫

Hedgerley

White Horse Ⓛ
Village Lane, SL2 3UY (in old village, near church)
☎ (01753) 643225 ⊕ thewhitehorsehedgerley.co.uk

Rebellion IPA; 7 changing beers (often Mighty Oak, Oakham) Ⓖ
Local CAMRA Pub of the Year on numerous occasions, this village local offers an impressive range of real ales. New breweries often feature, as well as favourite ales from Oakham and Mighty Oak. Two craft beers and three real ciders/perries are also available. This classic pub has a well-tended garden and a heated, covered patio area. Regular beer festivals are held, the largest of which is over the Whitsun weekend and a must for real ale enthusiasts. Q☸❀🅍♣♠P❄☺🛜

High Wycombe

Rose & Crown Ⓛ ✅
Desborough Road, HP11 2PR
4 changing beers Ⓗ
This L-shaped pub next to the Eden shopping mall has steadily built up its real ale offering over the past few years and now has an extensive range. The pub holds an acoustic jam once a month and runs darts teams on Tuesday nights. Many sporting events are shown on two largescreen TVs. The bus station is close by.
❀♣🚌🛜♫

Iver Heath

Black Horse
95 Slough Road, SL0 0DH
☎ (01753) 652631 ⊕ theblackhorseiverheath.co.uk
Badger Best Bitter, Fursty Ferret, Tanglefoot Ⓗ
Refurbished by Hall & Woodhouse, this large pub/diner has a country-house feel with oak panelling and shelving packed with interesting books. There is a separate drinking area. A green oak timber conservatory restaurant opens on to a patio and garden. Meals and snacks, including vegetarian, are served all day. The Uxbridge to Slough bus stops outside (last bus approximately 8pm, also on Sun).
Q♿❀☸🅍♿P🚌(3) ☺🛜♫

Lacey Green

Black Horse
Main Road, HP27 0QU
☎ (01844) 345195 ⊕ theblackhorselg.co.uk
4 changing beers (sourced nationally) Ⓗ
Noted for its friendly atmosphere, this village pub in the heart of the Chilterns offers four cask ales, three of them changing regularly. Walkers, cyclists and children are welcome and there is a play area in the enclosed garden to the rear. Excellent, freshly-prepared, home-cooked food is available, including traditional Sunday lunch. Traditional pub games are also played. Well-behaved dogs are welcome in the bar and garden areas.
Q♿❀🅍♣P🚌☺🛜

Pink & Lily Ⓛ
Pink Road, Parslows Hillock, HP27 0RJ
☎ (01494) 489857 ⊕ pink-lily.com
Sharp's Doom Bar; 3 changing beers (sourced locally) Ⓗ
Family-owned pub in Parslows Hillock, a timeless hamlet in the heart of the Chilterns. It offers three regularly changing cask ales, mainly from local breweries. The historic Brooke Bar room is unmissable – it has been preserved as it was when World War I poet Rupert Brooke was a regular. The garden provides heated outdoor dining and a play area for children, as well as summer barbecues and interesting space-age dining pods. Q♿❀🅍♣P☺🛜

Little Brickhill

George Inn
Watling Street, MK17 9NB
☎ (01525) 261298 🌐 thegeorgelittlebrickhill.co.uk
2 changing beers (sourced nationally; often Cotleigh, Kirkstall, Nuttycombe) Ⓗ
This was the local of sports commentator John Motson, who enjoyed a pint here while watching a match the evening before his sad demise early in 2023. After major and tasteful refurbishment several years ago, two handpumps now face you as you enter, serving varying and well-kept beers in its bar area, which is for drinks only. Food is served at the tables beyond, and in the dining room and a large patio and garden, offering traditional British dishes with a slight Mediterranean twist, using quality seasonal produce.
Q 🕸 ֎ ◑ & P ✿ 🛜 ♪

Little Missenden

Crown Inn
HP7 0RD (off A413, between Amersham and Great Missenden)
☎ (01494) 862571 🌐 thecrownlittlemissenden.co.uk
Harvey's Sussex Best Bitter; 3 changing beers (sourced nationally; often Oakham, Otter, Timothy Taylor) Ⓗ
This stalwart of the Guide always offers a good pint and a warm welcome. The clientele includes a good mix of regulars and those passing through or enjoying some of the local walks. The landlord is a real ale enthusiast and often rotates his beers, so it is a good idea to check in advance if you are after a particular pint. The pub also has three en-suite rooms available.
Q 🕸 ֎ ⇦ ◑ ◆ P 🖵 (55) ✿ 🛜

Littleworth Common

Blackwood Arms
Common Lane, SL1 8PP SU937863
☎ (01753) 645672 🌐 theblackwoodarms.co.uk
Brakspear Gravity, Oxford Gold; Oakham Citra; 1 changing beer Ⓗ
A delightful Victorian country pub brought back to life by an enthusiastic couple after a long period of closure. It is close to Burnham Beeches and popular with walkers and diners. A large and attractive garden has plenty of seating, including a heated, covered area, and is well used in summer. In winter a roaring log fire burns. The pub is dog- and horse-friendly, with treats and hay provided. Closed on Mondays. Q 🕸 ֎ ◑ ♣ P ✿ 🛜 ♪

Loudwater

General Havelock
114 Kingsmead Road, HP11 1HZ
☎ (01494) 520391 🌐 generalhavelock.co.uk
Fuller's London Pride, ESB; Gale's Seafarers Ale; 1 changing beer Ⓗ
The General Havelock has been run by the same family since Fuller's acquired it in 1986, and remains popular with all age groups. The interior is adorned with an eclectic selection of bric-a-brac and antiques. There are four ales available at all times on handpump including a range of seasonal and guest beers. The pub has a cosy feel in the winter while the garden makes for a peaceful haven in summer. Thai food is served on Thursday and Saturday evenings. 🕸 ֎ ◑ ◆ P 🖵 (37B) ✿ 🛜

Marlow

Two Brewers Ⓛ ✅
St Peter Street, SL7 1NQ
☎ (01628) 484140
Rebellion IPA, Smuggler; 1 changing beer (often Rebellion) Ⓗ
Beautifully set on the banks of the Thames, down a quiet street a couple of minutes' walk from the bustling high street. A bright seating area at the front leads to a smaller snug area at a lower level to the right. A large terrace at the side of the pub gives space for outdoor drinking. The pub serves a selection of Rebellion regular beers in addition to its seasonal range.
🕸 ֎ ◑ & ⇦ 🖵 ✿ 🛜 ♪

Milton Keynes: Bletchley

Captain Ridley's Shooting Party ✅
183 Queensway, MK2 2ED
☎ (01908) 621020
Greene King Abbot; Ruddles Best Bitter; Sharp's Doom Bar; 4 changing beers (sourced nationally; often Hornes, Oakham, Tring) Ⓗ
Wetherspoon pub that celebrates Bletchley Park, the headquarters of Britain's famous World War II codebreakers, with many pictures, artefacts and features. The pub's name was used as cover for MI5 agents secretly checking Bletchley Park's suitability for the codebreakers. Twelve handpumps serve three regulars and four guests. The ground floor comprises one large bar with seating throughout. There is ample seating in front of the pub and a large patio garden at the rear. The small car park is free, with two electric car-charging bays.
🕸 ֎ & ⇌ (Bletchley) P 🖵 (5,6) 🛜

Milton Keynes: Bradwell Village

Victoria Inn
6 Vicarage Road, MK13 9AQ
☎ (01908) 312769
3 changing beers (sourced regionally; often Hornes, Vale, XT) Ⓗ
A cosy and traditional, recently refurbished 17th-century stone-built pub whose exposed beams, low ceilings and grey half-panelled walls offer a comfortable and relaxed atmosphere. The room on the right has a pool table and dartboard, while the left-hand room has two levels with tables and chairs and an open fireplace. Four handpumps on the bar greet you as you enter and serve regional beers. A paved terrace at the front has plenty of seating and a dog bowl. Q 🕸 ♣ 🖵 (33,33A) ✿ 🛜

Milton Keynes: Central

Wetherspoons Ⓛ ✅
201 Midsummer Boulevard, MK9 1EA
☎ (01908) 606074
Greene King Abbot; Ruddles Best Bitter; Sharp's Doom Bar; 6 changing beers (sourced nationally; often Arundel, Oakham, Tring) Ⓗ
Popular and easily accessible meeting place for many locals, including CAMRA members. Nine different handpumps serve a range of cask ales, several of them local, and there is a wide range of tap, canned and bottled craft beers. It has a single large, open bar with a small raised area. Plenty of tables and chairs also provide outside seating. Food from the usual Wetherspoon menu is served from early morning until late evening.
🕸 ֎ & ⇌ (Central) P 🖵 🛜

Milton Keynes: Stacey Bushes

Blackened Sun Brewery Tap 🅛

Unit 3, Heathfield, MK12 6HP
☎ (01908) 990242 ⊕ blackenedsunbrewing.co.uk
Blackened Sun Coven, Hédoné ⊞; 4 changing beers
(sourced locally; often Blackened Sun) ℗
The taproom of this award-winning microbrewery is on
an unpretentious industrial estate and has long tables,
bench seating and some stools. Six taps serve Blackened
Sun beers, sometimes including a collaboration brew. All
are real ales – naturally conditioned, unfined,
unpasteurised and unfiltered. Many are brewed with
Belgian yeasts and are usually vegan. Bottled house and
guest beers are also available, including for take-away;
growlers can be refilled. Under-18s are welcome until
8pm with an adult. Dogs are welcome. Q🅥🐕P🖥🚇(6)🌼

Milton Keynes: Stony Stratford

Stony Stratford Conservative Club

77 High Street, MK11 1AY
☎ (01908) 567105 ⊕ stonyconclub.co.uk
Brains Rev James Original; Vale VPA; 2 changing beers
(often Lister's, Phipps NBC, Roman Way) ⊞
Multi-roomed social club for Conservative Party
members. Card-carrying CAMRA members and those
with a current copy of this Guide are admitted as guests.
It offers up to four cask-conditioned ales, sometimes
local. Members enjoy regular events and activities,
including live music. Occasionally events open to the
general public are held and the restaurant/lounge is
available to the public at lunchtime when food is
available. The car park is restricted to members and their
guests; parking outside can be difficult.
🕭🕸🕘🚇♣P🖥(6,X60)🌼🔊♪

Milton Keynes: Willen

Ship Ashore

Granville Square, MK15 9JL
☎ (01908) 694360
Brains Rev James Original; Fuller's London Pride;
Timothy Taylor Landlord; 1 changing beer (sourced
nationally; often Rudgate) ⊞
Smart, modern Ember Inns pub on a residential estate
close to Willen Lake and its recreational facilities. The pub
comprises one large bar but pillars and half-walls give a
more intimate feel. There are three regular beers and a
changing guest ale, which are reduced in price on
Mondays and Thursdays. Food is served at lunchtime and
evenings, with a dedicated vegetarian/vegan menu.
Drinkers and diners are made equally welcome. The pub
hosts a weekly quiz. Outside is a small garden and free
parking. 🕸🕘🕭P🖥(1)🌼🔊

Naphill

Wheel ⊘

100 Main Road, HP14 4QA
☎ (01494) 562210 ⊕ thewheelnaphill.com
Greene King Abbot; Ruddles Best Bitter; 2 changing
beers ⊞
Friendly and popular local with a large garden, opposite
the village hall. It has two regular beers and two
changing beers. There are two bar areas and a space
used for dining towards the rear of the pub. Occasionally
sport is shown on TV. Dogs and muddy boots are
welcome. A regular in the Guide. Convenient for the 300
bus route. 🕸🕘♣P🖥🌼🔊

Newport Pagnell

Ousebank House

High Street, MK16 8AN
☎ (01908) 613604 ⊕ ousebankhouse.co.uk
Courage Directors; 2 changing beers (often Marston's,
Nelson, Phipps NBC) ⊞
Formerly the Royal British Legion Club, this 17th-century
building with a 19th-century extension is now a
community-owned pub. It has two bars: a front lounge
and the larger main bar. Friendly bar staff serve one
regular ale and two changing guests – these are rotating
beers from the Marstons stable, Phipps or more obscure
brews such as Nelson's Trafalgar. Food is only available
on Sundays. They also hold a drop-in monthly Armed
Forces and Veterans Breakfast. Current local CAMRA Club
of the Year. 🕭🕘🕵♣P🖥(21,C10)🌼🔊♪

Oving

Black Boy 🅛

Church Lane, HP22 4HN
☎ (01296) 641258 ⊕ theblackboyoving.co.uk
XT Four; 3 changing beers (sourced locally; often
Chiltern, Leighton Buzzard, XT) ⊞
Delightfully cosy 17th-century pub with a good
atmosphere and a roaring fire in winter. Summer visits
are also a treat with wonderful views across the local
countryside from the huge beer garden (from which hot
air balloons may occasionally be spotted). The drinking
areas have flagstone floors and wooden beams. The
carpeted restaurant opposite the bar serves good food
and is tastefully divided from the drinking area by a
wooden mesh around the archway. 🕭🕸🕘🕘♣P🌼🔊

Princes Risborough

Bird in Hand 🍷 🅛 ⊘

47 Station Road, HP27 9DE
☎ (01844) 345602 ⊕ birdinhandprincesrisborough.co.uk
Chiltern Beechwood Bitter; Thame Hoppiness; 2
changing beers ⊞
Thriving, welcoming community local in a residential
area near the station. The compact L-shaped bar is
supplemented by a beer garden and outside drinking
area. There is a reliably good selection of real ales on
handpump. The pub hosts various events, including
quizzes, and pop-up food stalls visit at weekends.
Parking can be tricky nearby. Local CAMRA County Pub of
the Year 2023. 🕸🚲♣🕘🖥(300)🌼🔊♪

Quainton

George & Dragon 🅛

32 The Green, HP22 4AR
☎ (01296) 655436 ⊕ georgeanddragonquinton.co.uk
4 changing beers (sourced locally) ⊞
Delightful free house with an adjoining coffee shop. It is
split between public and saloon bars, both offering
home-cooked food. The friendly public bar has darts, a
jukebox and a TV, while the saloon is dedicated to dining.
Four LocAles are served alongside two guests. Parts of
this well-maintained pub date back to the 1700s;
traditional features include inglenook fireplaces, beams
and a quarry-tiled floor. Regular beer festivals are held in
summer, overlooking the green, not far from the
windmill. 🕭🕸🕘🕵♣🕘P🖥(16)🌼🔊

Saunderton

Golden Cross

Wycombe Road, HP14 4HU

☎ (01494) 565974 ⊕ thegoldencrosspub.co.uk
Adnams Ghost Ship; 2 changing beers (sourced nationally) ⊞
A family-friendly village local, close to the station and on the main road between High Wycombe and Princes Risborough. It serves one regular and two ever-changing beers. It has a large garden with a children's play area. The pub is in an Area of Outstanding Natural Beauty, and is ideal for walks in the surrounding countryside.
🛆⊛◑≉♣🅿🚍(X30,130) 🌑🛜

Stoke Goldington

Lamb 🕑

16-20 High Street, MK16 8NR
☎ (01908) 551233
Tring Death or Glory; 2 changing beers (sourced regionally; often Oakham, Phipps NBC, Tring) ⊞
Family-run pub in a peaceful village between Milton Keynes and Northampton, offering a warm and friendly welcome. Its main bar has six handpumps, usually serving three ales and a cider, with a smaller room beyond, a restaurant bar and a large garden. Home-cooked food using local produce is available, including award-winning pies, with steak and ale a favourite. The pub has featured in the Guide for 22 consecutive years, winning many CAMRA awards, including local Pub of the Year several times. Q🛆⊛◑♿♣🅿🌑🛜

Twyford

Crown Inn

The Square, MK18 4EG
☎ (01296) 730216
2 changing beers ⊞
A freehold locals' pub central to the life of the village. The landlady has seen others pubs nearby decline and close, and has extended opening hours and increased food provision with the help of her family. The Crown is a deceptively large brick building opposite the village hall. A spacious bar area leads through to an even larger lounge/function area on the left. It serves one frequently changing beer from the barrel, and usually has seven different beers on during the week.
🛆⊛◑♿♣🚍(16) 🌑🛜♪

Wendover

King & Queen ✅

17 South Street, HP22 6EF
☎ (01296) 696872 ⊕ thekingandqueenwendover.co.uk
Timothy Taylor Landlord; Young's London Original; 1 changing beer ⊞
Situated just off the High Street, within easy reach of the station, this three-room village pub has a pleasant, homely ambience. It hosts occasional tap takeovers and events such as comedy nights. There is an impressive wall map of the local countryside in one room. A wood-burning fire helps to provide a warm winter welcome for cold walkers returning after exploring the nearby Chiltern Hills. Q🛆⊛♿≉🅿🚍🌑

Pack Horse

29 Tring Road, HP22 6NR
☎ (01296) 622075
Fuller's London Pride; 2 changing beers (often Fuller's) ⊞
A small, friendly village pub on the Ridgeway path. The building dates from 1769 and is located at the end of a terrace of thatched cottages named after Anne Boleyn (reportedly a gift from Henry VIII). It has been owned for over 50 years by the same family, who also run the White Swan, another Fuller's pub in the village, and offers a varied range of beers from the wider Fuller's portfolio. The pub has connections with nearby RAF Halton. ≉♣🚍

Woburn Sands

Station Tavern

146 Station Road, MK17 8SG
☎ (01908) 582495 ⊕ stationwoburnsands.co.uk
Phipps NBC India Pale Ale; 1 changing beer (sourced nationally; often Brains) ⊞
A friendly, traditional pub next to the station. It retains many original features, such as its horseshoe-shaped bar and railway memorabilia. Although it only has two handpumps the beer is always fresh and very drinkable. Its barn and covered courtyard both offer pleasant dining areas that can also be booked for private functions. The publicans received a local CAMRA award in 2022 for 36 years' service. Q🛆⊛◑♿≉🅿🚍(450)🌑🛜♪

Wooburn Common

Royal Standard 🕑 ✅

Wooburn Common Road, HP10 0JS (follow signs to Odds Farm)
☎ (01628) 521121 ⊕ theroyalstandard.biz
Hop Back Summer Lightning ⊞**; Timothy Taylor Landlord** ⊞/🇬**; 7 changing beers** ⊞
A warm welcome is guaranteed at this regular award-winning pub near Burnham Beeches and Cliveden House, set in the countryside and ideal for walks. It serves seven changing beers, some straight from the barrel, as well as real cider. A disused red phone box outside at the front has books that patrons can borrow. Q🛆⊛◑♿♣🅿🌑🛜

Worminghall

Clifden Arms 🕑

Clifden Road, HP18 9JR
☎ (01844) 338090 ⊕ theclifdenarms.co.uk
House beer (by Rebellion); 4 changing beers (sourced locally; often Chiltern, Vale, XT) ⊞
A characterful country local in a timber-framed building with brick noggin and a thatched roof. The older part is medieval, with a newer wing added in the 17th century. A restaurant offers a varied menu that is focused on local ingredients. The bar on the other side has comfy seating and a log fire. The regular beer is Rebellion IPA rebadged as Clifden IPA. Q🛆⊛🚲◑♣🅿🌑🛜♪

Breweries

Blackened Sun

3 Heathfield, Stacey Bushes, Milton Keynes, MK12 6HP ☎ 07963 529859
⊕ blackenedsunbrewing.co.uk

⊗ Blackened Sun began brewing in 2017 and is mainly focused on brewing beers using Belgian yeast. The brewery continues to diversify and innovate with its core range. It is involved in other brewing projects including a mixed fermentation programme and a project brewing with local home brewers ◆LIVE ⌀

Boobytrap

7b Upper Barn Farm, Bicester Road, Westcott, HP18 0JX
☎ (01296) 651755 ☎ 07811 437185
⊕ boobytrapbrewery.com

A five-barrel brewhouse and taproom established by chef Philip Baker in 2021 and producing beer in bottles and cans. ♦

Brewhouse & Kitchen SIBA

▤ 7 Savoy Crescent, Milton Keynes, MK9 3PU
☎ (01908) 049032 ⊕ brewhouseandkitchen.com/venue/milton-keynes

Known locally as 'The Upside Down' in reference to its inverted design, brewing is done in the round, perhaps a nod to the pub's location in Milton Keynes' Theatre District. The brewery's core beers are named after local heroes, history and place names. The brewery, like other Brewhouse & Kitchen breweries offers brewdays and beer sampling masterclasses. ♦

Bucks Star

23 Twizel Close, Stonebridge, Milton Keynes, MK13 0DX
☎ (01908) 590054 ⊕ buckinghamshirebeer.co.uk

A solar-powered brewery which opened in 2015 using a 10-barrel, purpose-built plant. Only organic malt is used and no sugars or syrups are added. The beers are unfiltered, vegan, and primarily available through Bucks Star's own zero-waste innovation (Growler Swap). This range of beers are conditioned inside reusable glass growlers, and are available at farmers' markets locally, and at various London locations. The brewery tap opened in the opposite unit in 2020. ‼ ▤LIVE V

Chiltern SIBA

Nash Lee Road, Terrick, HP17 0TQ
☎ (01296) 613647 ⊕ chilternbrewery.co.uk

⊗ Founded in 1980 and located on a working farm, Chiltern was one of the first microbreweries in the country and was expanded in 2023. Family-run, its emphasis has always been on producing natural, wholesome beers using the best British malt and hops (some grown in Buckinghamshire). Now run by the second generation, George and Tom, it supplies around 100 outlets including its tap, the King's Head, Aylesbury. Some bottled beers are suitable for vegans, and some are gluten-free. ▤♦LIVE GF V

Chiltern Pale Ale (ABV 3.7%) PALE
An amber, refreshing beer with a slight fruit aroma, leading to a good malt/bitter balance in the mouth. The aftertaste is bitter and dry.
Chiltern Black (ABV 3.9%) PORTER
Beechwood Bitter (ABV 4.3%) BITTER
This pale brown beer has a balanced butterscotch/toffee aroma, with a slight hop note. The taste balances bitterness and sweetness, leading to a long bitter finish.

Feisty (NEW)

The Stables at Gable Manor, Wooburn Common Road, Wooburn Green, HP10 0JS ⊕ feistybeerco.com

A nanobrewery in converted stables, which began brewing commercially in 2022 with a capacity of 53 litres or 0.65 barrels, but with plans to expand significantly. It currently produces EcoKegs, cans and occasional bottle-conditioned beers. It aims to specialise in higher ABV craft beers, stouts, and fruit-infused beers. Longer term it also aims to have one flagship cask-conditioned ale. It currently distributes to one or two local beer shops, taprooms and local markets. LIVE

Grid (NEW)

Unit 21, Cuckoo Hill Farm, Castlethorpe Road, Hanslope, MK19 7HQ

A nanobrewery which started in 2023 and is believed to be producing beer in KeyKegs.

Hornes SIBA

19b Station Road, Bow Brickhill, MK17 9JU
☎ (01908) 647724 ⊕ mkbeer.co.uk

A purpose-built, six-barrel brewery established in 2015 and producing a range of beers, several called Triple Goat after the three goats kept in a paddock at the brewery. Shop open by appointment only. Occasional events in the large garden. All beers are gluten-free. ▤♦GF

Featherstone Amber Ale (ABV 3.6%) BITTER
Dark Fox (ABV 3.8%) BITTER
Triple Goat Pale Ale (ABV 3.9%) PALE
Ryestone (ABV 4%) RED
Unlocked Hornes (ABV 4.3%) GOLD
Triple Goat Porter (ABV 4.6%) PORTER
Triple Goat IPA (ABV 5%) PALE

Malt SIBA

Collings Hanger Farm, 100 Wycombe Road, Prestwood, HP16 0HW
☎ (01494) 865063 ⊕ maltthebrewery.co.uk

⊗ Family-owned brewery, founded in 2012 using a 10-barrel plant. Based on a dairy farm in the heart of the Chiltern Hills, it has sustainability built into its brewing with spent grains going to feed the pigs on the farm and spent hops being composted. In-house deliveries are made to trade and direct customers in six surrounding counties. National distribution is through leading distributors and wholesalers. ‼▤♦◆

Moderation (ABV 3.4%) GOLD
Missenden Pale (ABV 3.6%) PALE
Starry Nights (ABV 4%) BITTER
Voyager (ABV 5%) PALE

moogBREW

Meads End, Ye Meads, Taplow, SL6 0DH ☎ 07941 241954 ⊕ moogbrew.co.uk

⊗ This nanobrewery was set up in 2016 and moved to new premises in 2019. Most of the production is keg, along with bottle-conditioned beer. Cask is available to local festivals and pubs on request. The focus of the brewery is to serve the local community through the onsite taproom and beer garden. Free home delivery is available locally. Visits to the brewery, and collections of off-sales, are by appointment outside opening times. ‼▤♦LIVE◆

Old Luxters

Old Luxters Vineyard, Dudley Lane, Hambleden, RG9 6JW
☎ (01491) 638330 ⊕ chilternvalley.co.uk

Situated in a 17th century barn beside the Chiltern Valley Vineyard, Old Luxters is a traditional brewery established in 1990 and awarded a Royal Warrant of Appointment in 2007. It produces a range of bottle-conditioned beers. ‼▤♦LIVE

Rebellion SIBA

Bencombe Farm, Marlow Bottom, SL7 3LT
☎ (01628) 476594 ⊕ rebellionbeer.co.uk

⊗ Established in 1993, Rebellion has grown steadily and relocated to its current site in 1999. It brews up to 100,000 pints per week, supplying around 600 trade customers within 30 miles alongside its retail shop, online store, drive-through and onsite Tap Yard. A three-barrel development brewery was installed in 2022 which enables it to brew small batches of a wider range of craft beer styles. The membership club now has around 4,500 active members. ‼️🍴♦️🔧

IPA (ABV 3.7%) BITTER
Copper-coloured bitter, sweet and malty, with resinous and red apple flavours. Caramel and fruit decline to leave a dry, bitter and malty finish.

Smuggler (ABV 4.2%) BITTER
A red-brown beer, well-bodied and bitter with an uncompromisingly dry, bitter finish.

Overthrow (ABV 4.3%) BLOND

Roasted Nuts (ABV 4.6%) BITTER

Vale SIBA

Tramway Business Park, Ludgershall Road, Brill, HP18 9TY
☎ (01844) 239237 🌐 valebrewery.co.uk

⊗ Established in 1995 initially in Haddenham, Vale moved to Brill in 2007. In 2010 it expanded to a 20-barrel brew plant. Four pubs are owned, including the Hop Pole, where sister brewery Aylesbury Brewhouse operated 2011-2019. When it closed, brewing moved back to Vale. In 2021, Phil and Mark Stevens decided it was time for a new set of brothers to take the reins, and sold the brewery to Joe and Jimmy Brouder. ‼️🍴♦️LIVE🔧

Brill Gold (ABV 3.5%) GOLD

Best IPA (ABV 3.7%) BITTER

This pale amber beer starts with a slight fruit aroma. This leads to a clean, bitter taste where hops and fruit dominate. The finish is long and bitter with a slight hop note.

VPA (Vale Pale Ale) (ABV 4.2%) PALE

Red Kite (ABV 4.3%) BITTER

Black Beauty Porter (ABV 4.4%) PORTER
A very dark ale, the initial aroma is malty. Roast malt dominates initially and is followed by a rich fruitiness, with some sweetness. The finish is increasingly hoppy and dry.

Gravitas (ABV 4.8%) PALE

XT SIBA

Unit 27, Notley Farm, Chearsley Road, Long Crendon, HP18 9ER
☎ (01844) 208310 🌐 xtbrewing.com

⊗ XT started brewing in 2011 using an 18-barrel plant. It supplies direct to pubs across southern England and the Midlands. The taproom and shop sell draught and bottled beers to drink in or take out. A range of limited edition, but ever-changing, one-off brews is produced under the Animal Brewing Co name. ‼️🍴♦️LIVE🔧

Four (ABV 3.8%) BITTER

Hop Kitty (ABV 3.9%) GOLD

One (ABV 4.2%) BLOND

Three (ABV 4.2%) PALE

Eight (ABV 4.5%) PORTER

Fifteen (ABV 4.5%) PALE

Squid Ink (ABV 5.5%) STOUT

Bird in Hand, Princes Risborough (Photo: Bob Smith)

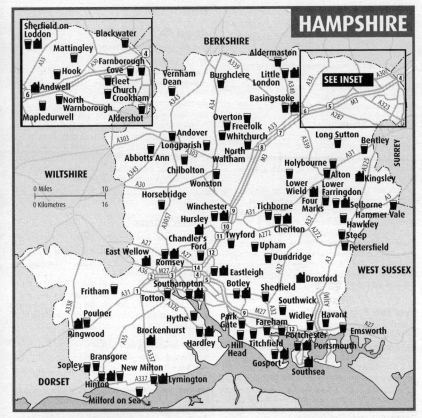

HAMPSHIRE

Please note: Ringwood Brewery renamed Best Bitter to Razorback but it is still available in some outlets as Best Bitter

Abbotts Ann

Eagle Inn 🅛
Duck Street, SP11 7BG
☎ (01264) 710339 🌐 theeagleinn.wordpress.com
Bowman Meon Valley Bitter; 2 changing beers (sourced locally) 🅗
Located in a picturesque village two miles south of Andover, this award-winning, well-loved pub run by a long-serving couple is at the heart of the community. The public bar has a pool table and there is a large skittle alley and function room at the back, which is available to hire. There is a pleasant landscaped rear beer garden. The core beer is supplemented by two changing beers, often local. A beer and cider festival is held in June. A selection of home-cooked food is available but please ring to confirm. A defibrillator is accessible.
🌐🍴♣P🚃(87)🐾🛜

Aldermaston

Aldermaston Recreational Society 🅛
Reading Road, RG7 4PR
☎ (0118) 982 4544 🌐 recsoc.co.uk
3 changing beers 🅗
On the Hampshire/Berkshire border, this sports and social club is on the site of the AWE facility, but operates independently. CAMRA members with a current card are welcome. There are play facilities on a grassy area outside, also used for drinking. Local ales are served from the three handpumps, two of which are in permanent

use. Live events feature plus a full food menu. Entry is via the West Gate of AWE with adjacent parking. The bus stop is a 10 minute walk away. 🌐🍴🍴♿♣P🚃♪

Aldershot

Garden Gate 🅛 ✅
2 Church Lane East, GU11 3BT
☎ (01252) 219717
Surrey Hills Ranmore; 1 changing beer (sourced regionally; often Courage, Young's) 🅗
Established in the mid-19th century, this conversation led pub remains at the heart of its local community. A single bar serves two distinct drinking areas, and a separate back room leads to a small patio. Three beers are generally on tap, including a house beer, Wobbly Gate, whose origin is a closely guarded secret. The well-attended Thursday night charity quiz funded the community defibrillator. The pub is a popular stop-off for dog walkers and is close to the railway station.
🌐🚅P🚃🐾

Alton

Eight Bells 🏆 🅛
33 Church Street, GU34 2DA
☎ (01420) 82417
Black Sheep Best Bitter; Flower Pots Perridge Pale, Pots Bitter; 1 changing beer (sourced nationally; often Longdog, Vale) 🅗

This Grade II-listed building, built in the 1640s, has been a pub since at least the 1840s. Frequently changing guest beers tend to be on the dark side. The main bar is a haven for good beer and conversation with a welcoming open fire in the winter months, while the back room has a TV only used for major sporting events. Outside is a paved seating area with colourful shrub borders in summer and a smoking shelter with an old well. Local CAMRA Pub of the Year 2023. Q❀✿❋➡️🚲(13)❀🐾🛜

Railway Arms Ⓛ

26 Anstey Road, GU34 2RB
☎ (01420) 542316
Triple fff Alton's Pride, Moondance; 5 changing beers (sourced nationally; often Ascot, Dorking, Triple fff) Ⓗ
Friendly pub close to the Watercress Line and mainline station. Owned by Triple fff brewery their beers, including seasonals, are supplemented by guest ales – often from local microbreweries. Real cider is from Seacider. The rear bar holds quiz nights and monthly music nights and is available for hire. The rear patio area incorporates a covered smoking area. There are tables outside at the front under a striking sculpture of a steam locomotive. Well-behaved dogs are welcome.
Q❀✿➡️♣️🚲(64,65) 🐾🛜♫

Ten Tun Tap House Ⓛ

1 Westbrook Walk, GU34 1HZ
☎ 07971 076657 🌐 tentuntaphouse.beer
4 changing beers (sourced nationally; often Siren, Steam Town, Thornbridge) Ⓗ
Four handpumps plus nine taps dispense real ale, craft keg and cider from around the country with local brews often available in this independent bar. The style is bare wood minimalist, with a buzz generated by the varied clientele and the jazzy background music. A recent extension has provided additional seating and a brewery is under construction. Local CAMRA Pub of the Year 2022 – an impressive achievement for a pub that opened just two days before the first Covid lockdown. ➡️🍴🚲🐾🛜

Andover

Andover Tap at the Lamb Ⓛ

21 Winchester Street, SP10 2EA
☎ (01264) 323961 🌐 theandovertap.co.uk
Longdog Bunny Chaser Ⓗ; 11 changing beers (often Unity) Ⓗ/🇰
The Lamb dates from the 17th century and now houses a joint venture between Wessex Spirits and the Andover Tap with each occupying half of the building. The Tap serves up to 12 beers – four on handpump, four on gravity dispense and four membrane keg – plus real cider. It comprises two rooms – a small front bar and a cosy back room. Families are welcome until evening and simple snacks are served. Special food and beer events are held regularly. Q✿🍴🚲🐾

Town Mills ✅

20 Bridge Street, SP10 1BL
☎ (01264) 332540 🌐 thetownmills.co.uk
Wadworth Henry's IPA, 6X; 2 changing beers (sourced regionally; often Wadworth) Ⓗ
Located in the town centre by the River Anton, this pub is in an historic mill with a working water wheel. There are several separate areas for dining and drinking including a comfy lounge upstairs. Pub games are played and a popular quiz is held weekly. The landscaped riverside garden is popular in summer. Beers from the Wadworth guest list are usually available. ✿❀◑&♣️P🚲🐾🛜♫

Basingstoke

Angel ✅

Unit R6, Lower Ground, Festival Place, RG21 7BB
☎ (01256) 854800
Greene King IPA, Abbot; Sharp's Doom Bar; 4 changing beers (often Andwell, Ascot, Longdog) Ⓗ
This is a smart, spacious Wetherspoon bar on the edge of the town's Festival Place restaurant quarter. It attracts a varied clientele – mainly the younger crowd in the evenings when ambient chatter combined with background music can make the pub quite lively. Lunchtimes are quieter, with customers from all age groups. Muted TVs show mainly news broadcasts. Food is served all day. Three resident beers and four guest ales are normally available. ✿❀◑&✿➡️🚲🛜

Queen's Arms Ⓛ

Bunnian Place, RG21 7JE (E of station)
☎ (01256) 465488 🌐 thequeensarmspub.co.uk
St Austell Tribute; Sharp's Doom Bar; 4 changing beers (sourced nationally) Ⓗ
Located close to Basingstoke rail station, this cosy corner-sited pub is handy for commuters and locals alike and serves a wide-ranging clientele. The choice of up to four guest beers is imaginative and the turnaround can be swift. Good-value food is available. During warmer weather the shady courtyard garden at the rear is a popular attraction. A beer festival is held annually and monthly quiz and weekly meat raffle feature.
Q✿◑➡️P🚲🛜♫

REAL ALE BREWERIES

Alfred's Winchester
Andwell Andwell
Bat Country East Wellow (NEW)
Botley ✦ Botley
Bowman Droxford
Brew Forest ✦ Lymington (NEW)
Brewhouse & Kitchen 🍴 Portsmouth
Brewhouse & Kitchen 🍴 ✦ Southampton
Brewhouse & Kitchen 🍴 Southsea
CrackleRock Botley
Crop 🍴 Portsmouth (NEW)
Dancing Man 🍴 Southampton
Drop The Anchor ✦ Hinton
Fallen Acorn ✦ Gosport
Flack Manor ✦ Romsey
Flower Pots Cheriton
Gilbert White's Selborne
Growling Gibbon Hursley
Irving Portsmouth
Little London Little London
Longdog ✦ Basingstoke
Maverick ✦ Kingsley (NEW)
Monkey 🍴 Lymington
Newtown Gosport
Pig Beer Brockenhurst
Queen Inn 🍴 Winchester
Red Cat Winchester (brewing suspended)
Ringwood Ringwood
Sherfield Village Sherfield on Loddon
Southsea Portsmouth
Staggeringly Good ✦ Southsea
Steam Town Eastleigh
Tap It ✦ Southampton
Triple fff Four Marks
Urban Island ✦ Portsmouth
Vibrant Forest ✦ Hardley

Bentley

Star Inn 🅛

Main Road, GU10 5LW

☎ (01420) 23184 ⊕ thestarinnbentley.com

Crafty Brewing LBB; Triple fff Moondance; 1 changing beer (sourced locally; often Crafty Brewing) 🅗

A free house under new management since 2021. The emphasis is on food, with tables laid up, but it retains a pub atmosphere serving mainly local beers. Fish specials feature on Friday and quiz night is the first Wednesday of the month. There is seating outside to the front and in a pleasant garden with a vine pergola at the rear. The bus stops are 100 yards away and in nearby Station Road.
Q🏠❀◐♣P🚲(65) 🐾🛜

Blackwater

Mr Bumble 🅛

19 London Road, GU17 9AP

☎ (01276) 32691

Fuller's London Pride; 3 changing beers (sourced regionally; often Ascot, Windsor & Eton) 🅗

Firmly a community local, Mr Bumble is located near the station and bus stops. The regular London Pride is accompanied by up to three guest ales. There is a large L-shaped bar with comfortable seating, tables and chairs. A few steps around the corner is a sports bar with darts and three pool tables. Widescreen TVs show major sporting events, and live music is staged on Thursday and Saturday. 🏠❀≈♣P🚲(3)🐾🛜♫

Botley

CrackleRock Tap Room 🅛

30A High Street, SO30 2EA (down alley beside Clarke Mews) SU5130213037

☎ 07733 232806 ⊕ cracklerock.co.uk

CrackleRock Verified, Fire Cracker, Gold Rush, Dark Destroyer, Crafty Shag, Crackatoa IPA; 2 changing beers (sourced locally; often Bowman, Steam Town, Urban Island) 🅗

A popular, cosy brewery tap, previously a bank, hidden down an alley off the High Street. The pub consists of a single L-shaped room split into several booths served by a bar with nine handpumps serving house beers and one guest, plus cider boxes in the summer. Four or six hole beer paddles of one-third pint glasses are available, plus gin, vodka and wine options. The brewery is located across the road, where the tap room was until 2018.
🅰♣🚲(3,49)🐾♫

Hidden Tap 🅛

Botley Mill, Mill Hill, SO30 2GB (immediate right on entering mill yard)

☎ 07909 337212 ⊕ botleybreweryltd.com

Botley HPA, Pommy Blonde, English IPA; 1 changing beer (sourced locally; often Botley, Bowman) 🅖

This small bar next to the brewery is plainly decorated with beer mats and has bar stools around the walls. It usually serves four beers direct from the cask, plus two real ciders from Meon Valley. Sparse seating indoors is compensated for by benches outside and tables placed by the wall that overlooks the River Hamble, where kingfishers can occasionally be spotted. Kayakers often paddle up the river and ring a bell to order drinks which are winched down in a wooden box. Closed Mondays and Tuesdays. Q❀◐🅰♣P🚲(3,49)🐾♫

Bransgore

Three Tuns ✅

Ringwood Road, BH23 8JH

☎ (01425) 672232 ⊕ threetunsinn.com

Otter Amber; Ringwood Razorback, Fortyniner; 1 changing beer (sourced nationally; often Crafty Brewing, Flack Manor) 🅗

This 17th-century thatched inn is situated on the edge of the New Forest National Park. It has a number of rooms including a snug with flagstone floor and wood-burner, and a restaurant. The large garden is used by a pétanque team based at the pub. A large barn and marquee can be hired for private functions. Dickies Dribble Cider from the nearby Harrow Wood Farm is served. A beer festival is held on the last weekend in September.
Q🏠❀◐🖑♣🅰♠P🐾🛜♫

Burghclere

Carpenters Arms ✅

Harts Lane, RG20 9JY

☎ (01635) 278251 ⊕ carpentersarms-burghclere.co.uk

Arkell's Wiltshire Gold, 3B; 1 changing beer 🅗

This village pub has lovely views over Watership Down and caters for walkers, families, dogs and drinkers enjoying its rural setting. Locally sourced food is served daily in the dedicated restaurant at the back, backing on to a large beer garden. There are three handpumps serving Arkell's beers. Q❀🚐◐P🚲(21,22)🐾

Chandler's Ford

Cleveland Bay ✅

1 Pilgrims Close, SO53 4ST

☎ (023) 8026 9814 ⊕ theclevelandbay.co.uk

Wadworth Horizon, 6X, Swordfish; 2 changing beers (sourced nationally; often Wadworth) 🅗

A welcoming pub located in Valley Park, at the edge of Chandler's Ford, one mile from Chandlers Ford railway station. Friendly and attentive staff serve good food and well kept Wadworth beers, with some guest ales in busier months. There is plenty of seating in several different areas around the pub and a roaring log fire in colder months. To the side is a large garden and a covered patio area plus a car park.
🏠❀◐♣P🚲(5,46)🐾🛜♫

Steel Tank Alehouse 🅛

1 The Central Precinct, Winchester Road, SO53 2GA

☎ 07895 584225 ⊕ thesteeltank.com

Gale's HSB; 6 changing beers (sourced nationally; often Eight Arch, Flower Pots) 🅗

A converted unit, previously a bank, the interior is furnished with a wooden bar and tables. Often busy, with a friendly atmosphere, it is a welcome addition to the town. Six handpumps are supplied from a cool-room behind the bar, with 10 keg taps for beers and ciders, and plenty of bottles and cans. The outdoor seating area has heaters. Conveniently located for public transport. Local CAMRA Pub of the Year 2019 and 2020. Closed Tuesdays and Wednesdays. Over 18s only.
Q🖑≈(Chandlers Ford)♣🖥🚲(1)🐾🛜

Cheriton

Flower Pots Inn 🅛

Brandy Mount, SO24 0QQ (¾ mile N of A272 Cheriton/Beauworth crossroads) SU5812928293

☎ (01962) 771318 ⊕ theflowerpots.co.uk

Flower Pots Perridge Pale, Pots Bitter, Buster's Best, Cheriton Porter, Goodens Gold, IPA; 1 changing beer (sourced locally; often Flower Pots) ⃤
A 19th-century pub in a pretty village bisected by the Rive Itchen and close to the site of a major Civil War battle. The original building contains three public rooms; an elegant extension houses the function room and garden bar. Flower Pots brewery is 50 yards away. No food Sunday to Tuesday evenings; Wednesday is Thai night. The rear garden affords views over countryside, and the National Trust property of Hinton Ampner is one mile away. Q❀☺✪❍⬥♣➡(67)❀🐾🛜

Chilbolton

Abbots Mitre
Village Street, SO20 6BA
☎ (01264) 860348 ⊕ abbotsmitre.co.uk
4 changing beers (sourced locally) ⊞
This is a lovely traditional local pub in a pretty rural village, with a spacious landscaped garden and covered outside terrace. The area is a walking and cycling haven, with nature reserves nearby. Beers rotate, and are mainly from local breweries such as Alfred's, Flower Pots and Flack Manor. There is an extensive food menu featuring locally-sourced produce with specials and themed food events. The pub has an external defibrillator.
Q❀☺✪❍P➡(15) 🐾🛜🎵

Church Crookham

Foresters
Aldershot Road, GU52 9EP
☎ (01252) 616503 ⊕ foresters-dining.co.uk
3 changing beers (sourced nationally; often Old Cannon) ⊞
This food-led pub, popular with dog walkers and families, has up to three changing real ales, often including Old Cannon. The single L-shaped bar is decorated in modern rustic style, with logs and solid wooden tables. The area to the left of the entrance is laid out for dining and contains a suspended fire pit. The remainder of the pub is more informal with a bookshelf to browse. The large beer garden has an attractive veranda. It will stay open later if busy. ❀✪❍⬥P🐾🛜

Wyvern
75 Aldershot Road, GU52 8JY
☎ (01252) 624772 ⊕ thewyvernpub.co.uk
Wadworth 6X; 4 changing beers (sourced nationally; often Theakston) ⊞
This community local can become lively at times, especially during sporting events, but is always family-friendly. Darts is played and there is a regular Thursday quiz night. Six screens show Premier League football and other sporting events. A sunny garden features heated beach huts. The pub has live music, often tribute acts, and supports local charities with fundraising events. A changing beer range is from a variety of breweries and often includes Theakston Old Peculier.
❀✪❍⬥♣P➡(10) 🐾🎵

Cove

Thatched Cottage
122 Prospect Road, GU14 8NU
☎ (01252) 444180 ⊕ thatchedcottagefarnborough.co.uk
3 changing beers (sourced regionally; often Ascot, Hogs Back, Vale) ⊞
Previously a private home, this thatched pub in the western suburbs of Farnborough has served its local

community for over 50 years. It was sympathetically refurbished, re-thatched and reopened as a free house in 2021 and prides itself on serving a wide range of locally sourced food and drink in a family-friendly setting. There are two distinct bar areas and a large garden. Three cask ales are generally on offer, with regular beers from Vale. Breakfast is available at the weekend. ❀✪❍P➡(10)🐾

Dundridge

Hampshire Bowman Ⓛ
Dundridge Lane, SO32 1GD (turn E off B3035 ½ mile N of Bishops Waltham then it's another 1½ miles)
SU5778218424
☎ (01489) 892940 ⊕ hampshirebowman.com
Bowman Swift One; Flower Pots Goodens Gold; Steam Town Barton; 2 changing beers (sourced regionally; often Andwell, Stonehenge, Hop Back) ⃤
A remote 18th-century pub, usually busy despite being hidden down a long narrow country lane. It typically serves five local ales direct from the cask, 10 real ciders and a variety of locally sourced food (not served Tue or Wed). It consists of a small brick-floored bar and larger dining room/bar, both decorated with various items including bows, beer jugs and a tricycle in the rafters. Outside is further seating in a large garden with children's play area. Q❀☺✪❍⬥♣P🐾🛜

Eastleigh

Steam Town Brew Co. Ⓛ
1 Bishopstoke Road, SO50 6AD
☎ (023) 8235 9139 ⊕ steamtown.co.uk
Steam Town Stoke Pale, Barton; 4 changing beers (sourced locally; often Steam Town) ⊞
A microbrewery and tap opened in 2017, running monthly brewery tours. The interior has an industrial feel with exposed pipework and a railway clock. A separate area, mainly for eating, has furniture from old train compartments, and upstairs is a function room. A continually changing beer range of four or more cask beers and a wide variety of craft-keg beers, ciders, bottles, and cans is served by the friendly bar staff. Food emphasis is on gourmet burgers and dirty fries.
☺✪❍⇌➡➡(2,3) 🐾🛜🎵

Emsworth

Blue Bell ✅
29 South Street, PO10 7EG
☎ (01243) 373394 ⊕ bluebellinnemsworth.co.uk
Sharp's Doom Bar; 2 changing beers (sourced nationally) ⊞
The pub was built in 1960 to replace a former Blue Bell (originally known as the Brewery Tap) the other side of the car park entrance. Sadly the brewery did not survive the relocation. Despite being a modern building, internally it has an olde-worlde feel with timber beams on the walls and ceiling. The relatively small bar is traditionally furnished and decorated with nautical memorabilia. ✪❍⇌➡(700)🛜

Coal Exchange
21 South Street, PO10 7EG
☎ (01243) 375866 ⊕ coalexchangeemsworth.co.uk
Dark Star Hophead; Fuller's London Pride; Gale's Seafarers Ale, HSB; 2 changing beers (sourced nationally; often Butcombe, Fuller's) ⊞
Originally a pork butchery and ale house, its proximity to Emsworth harbour made it a trading place between local farmers and merchants delivering coal by sea. The harbour is also at the end of a coastal walk from

Langstone. Somewhat unusual for a former Gale's pub it has a partly green tiled frontage still bearing that brewery's name. The single L-shaped bar has a mix of chairs, stools and pew-style seating. To the rear is a walled garden. ᏧᏇᏆᎧᏃᏅ(700)❀

Fareham

Crown ✓

40 West Street, PO16 0JW
☎ (01329) 241750
Greene King Abbot; Ruddles Best Bitter; Sharp's Doom Bar; 3 changing beers (sourced nationally) Ⓗ
This town-centre Wetherspoons situated in a former brewery, is in a pedestrianised street, convenient for the bus station and shopping centre. Wall-mounted portraits with brief histories of famous local figures add to the cosy atmosphere. There are two separate areas – the area away from the bar is set out with tables and chairs for diners. There are also two outdoor drinking areas. The usual beer and other festivals take place.
Q❀❀◑♦❡❒(3,69) ⚲

West Street Alehouse

164A West Street, PO16 0EH
☎ (023) 9435 0971
House beer (by Arundel); 2 changing beers (sourced regionally) Ⓗ
Fareham's first micropub opened in 2019, ideally situated as within walking distance of the bus and rail stations. In addition to the real ales, several craft beers and up to four ciders are available, all of which are listed on the TV screen. There is a bottle shop with local and foreign cans and bottles available for takeaway purchase. Customers are welcome to order food from nearby takeaways, and the pub will provide plates and cutlery.
Q❀❀❤❒❡❀

Farnborough

Goat in the Garden Ⓛ

21 Church Avenue, GU14 7AT
☎ 07920 153452
3 changing beers (sourced nationally; often Ascot, Church End) Ⓗ
Set in the affluent Farnborough Park area, the Goat in the Garden is an attractive bar, hidden away in the grounds of a small hotel, Melford House, but accessed via its own entrance. The single bar stocks up to four changing guest beers, sourced from mainly local breweries. The bar is a wonderful facility for residents of the hotel and their guests but everyone is warmly welcome to visit.
ᏧᏇ♣P❒(1) ⚲♪

Prince of Wales Ⓛ ✓

184 Rectory Road, GU14 8AL
☎ (01252) 545578
Bowman Swift One; Dark Star Hophead; Fuller's London Pride; house beer (by Ascot); 5 changing beers (sourced nationally; often Ascot, Hop Back) Ⓗ
This cosy free house has featured in the Guide for over 40 years. There is a central bar around which are several distinct but interconnected areas, with a wonderful wood-burning stove between the snug and adjacent seating area. Five guest beers, invariably including both dark and local beers, are served from the lower snug with regular offerings found on the front bar. Trestle tables at the front and back are popular in fine weather, while the back patio is covered and heated.
ᏧᏇᏃ(North) P❀ ⚲♪

Tilly Shilling ✓

Unit 2 to 5, Victoria Road, GU14 7PG
☎ (01252) 893560
Greene King Abbot; Ruddles Best Bitter; Sharp's Doom Bar; 5 changing beers (sourced nationally) Ⓗ
Modern town-centre Wetherspoon pub named after Beatrice Shilling, a celebrated engineer at the nearby former Royal Aircraft Establishment. Its aviation theme includes a row of airline seats and various Spitfire memorabilia. The large rectangular open-plan lounge features a glass frontage that opens in good weather, extending the pub on to the pavement. Ten handpumps leave lots of space for three regular and generally up to five guest beers. The toilets are all located downstairs in this pub. ᏧᏆᎧᏃ(Main)❒⚲

Fleet

Prince Arthur Ⓛ ✓

238 Fleet Road, GU51 4BX
☎ (01252) 622660
Greene King Abbot; Ruddles Best Bitter; Sharp's Doom Bar; 3 changing beers (sourced nationally; often Stonehenge, Twickenham, Windsor & Eton) Ⓗ
A traditionally designed Wetherspoon pub housed in a former grocery shop, more than 100 years old, with alcoves and wood surrounds. It is named after Prince Arthur, Duke of Connaught, who lived in Fleet in the 1890s when he was commander of Aldershot Garrison. Four or more different guest ales are on tap, including local ales supplied direct from breweries across Hampshire, Berkshire and Surrey. There are monthly tap takeovers from breweries local and further afield. The pub celebrated its 10th successive year in this Guide in 2022. Q❀❀❀◑❡(7,10)⚲

Freefolk

Watership Down Inn Ⓛ

Freefolk Priors, RG28 7NJ (just off B3400)
☎ (01256) 892254 ⊕ watershipdowninn.com
5 changing beers (sourced locally) Ⓗ
Built in 1840, this award-winning gastro-pub is known locally as the Jerry. The pub name celebrates author Richard Adams' book Watership Down, set in a local beauty spot of the same name. Outside is an extensive garden, patio and family area. Locally produced food features daily but booking is advised. The pub is popular with Test Valley walkers and cyclists. A famous gin distillery is nearby. Q❀❀❀◑P❒(76)❀ ⚲

Fritham

Royal Oak Ⓛ ✓

SO43 7HJ (W end of village down no through road)
SU2321614135
☎ (023) 8081 2606 ⊕ royaloakfritham.co.uk
Flack Manor Flack's Double Drop; Hop Back Summer Lightning; house beer (by Bowman); 3 changing beers (sourced locally; often Dark Revolution, Monkey Brewhouse, Steam Town) Ⓖ
A thatched cottage, modestly extended, with three rooms and an impressive fireplace, its large garden has an ice cream kiosk in summer and a marquee. The legendary ploughman's lunches and accompanying salads favour local ingredients, including home-made pork pies, and on some evenings a pizza or fish & chip van visits. Accommodation is in shepherd's huts in the adjacent field. A nearby black postbox served the Victorian gunpowder factory near Eyeworth pond.
Q❀❀❀◑♦❀♪

Gosport

Four-Ale Taproom Ⓛ
45 Stoke Road, PO12 1LS
☎ (023) 9258 4455 ● fouraletaproom.co.uk
4 changing beers (sourced regionally; often Exmoor, Newtown) Ⓖ
The first micropub in the Portsmouth area, which opened in 2018. The beers are in a gravity stillage along one wall of the bar, and the furniture consists of high stools and old casks with industrial tables. There are four cask ales normally from the south of England, real ciders, several craft beers plus bottles and cans to take away. House ales occasionally appear from Newtown. A cheese board is available on Sunday lunchtimes. Q ᘒ ♣ ● P �☐ 🖨 🌞 🛜

Junction Tavern ♈
1 Leesland Road, Camden Town, PO12 3ND
☎ (023) 9258 5140
3 changing beers (sourced nationally; often Goldmark, Parkway, Portobello) Ⓗ
A relatively small pub situated on the site of the Fareham to Gosport railway, which is now a cycle track. Old railway photographs adorn the walls, with pumpclips over the bar. The real ales normally include a dark beer, and the pub is one of the few outlets occasionally serving cask beer from the local Powder Monkey brewery. A beer festival takes place over the Easter weekend.
ᘒ 🕸 ♣ �☐ (E1) 🌞 🛜

Hammer Vale

Prince of Wales
Hammer Lane, GU27 1QH
☎ (01428) 652600 ● princeofwaleshaslemere.co.uk
Dark Star Hophead; Fuller's London Pride; Gale's HSB; 2 changing beers (sourced nationally; often Fuller's) Ⓗ
Not to be missed, this 1924 pub has many original features, including stained-glass windows, one for Amey's of Petersfield, who built this imposing roadhouse in anticipation of an A3 route which did not materialise. Well worth visiting in order to sample the Pride, HSB and other Fuller's group guests. With a large outside seating area and car park the pub is well sited for walkers and campers. Enthusiastic and friendly hosts Nick and Becky do excellent meals and bar snacks.
Q ᘒ 🕸 🕽 ⅁ Å P 🌞 🛜 ♫

Hardley

Vibrant Forest Brewery Taproom Ⓛ
Unit 3, The Purlieu Centre, Hardley Industrial Estate, SO45 3AE
☎ (023) 8200 2200 ● vibrantforest.co.uk
1 changing beer (sourced locally; often Vibrant Forest) Ⓖ
This taproom serves one gravity-fed ever-changing cask ale, apart from event days when the number can be increased. An additional 12 membrane keg lines serve a variety of beers including IPAs, DIPAs, dark beers and Pilsners, supplemented by canned and bottled beers and a variety of wines. The mezzanine, with its own bar and toilets, can be hired for parties and events. Street food is often available in the huge yard at weekends. Closed Monday to Wednesday, check website for details.
Q 🕸 🕽 ⅁ �☐ (9) 🌞 🛜 ♫

Havant

Old House at Home
2 South Street, PO9 1DA

☎ (023) 9248 3464 ● oldhouseathomehavant.co.uk
Fuller's London Pride; Gale's Seafarers Ale, HSB; 2 changing beers (sourced nationally; often Dark Star, Fuller's) Ⓗ
One of the few buildings to have survived the 1760 fire, it began life as five cottages built from timber recovered from the Spanish Armada. The building then became a bakery and part of the oven can still be seen in the lounge bar. Finally it was made into a pub and it still retains two bars. Its claim to fame is that it held the last dancing bear in England. To the rear is a large hidden garden. ᘒ 🕸 🕽 ᘏ ♣ �“ ᛟ 🛜

Hawkley

Hawkley Inn
Pococks Lane, GU33 6NE
☎ (01730) 827205 ● hawkleyinn.co.uk
Flower Pots Perridge Pale, Pots Bitter; 2 changing beers (sourced regionally; often Flower Pots, Triple fff) Ⓗ
Set high up in the South Downs, this free house is popular with walkers. It describes itself as a 'free hoose', from the large moose's head that adorns one wall. It is divided into several drinking areas which are largely bare-boarded with simple wooden tables and chairs, giving it a rustic feel. A small front veranda with bench seating and a large rear garden provide space for outside drinking. ᘒ 🕸 ᘏ 🕽 ● 🌞 🛜 ♫

Hill Head

Crofton ✓
48 Crofton Lane, PO14 3QF
☎ (01329) 609925 ● ourlocal.pub/pubs/crofton-fareham
St Austell Tribute; Sharp's Doom Bar; 3 changing beers (sourced nationally; often Flower Pots, Laine) Ⓗ
Estate pub in a quiet residential area, which underwent a major refurbishment in 2020, including a new kitchen. The premises comprise a large lounge bar intended for diners and a smaller public bar. There is a function room with skittle alley which gets booked up well in advance plus a large outdoor drinking area, which is popular during fine weather. Q ᘒ 🕸 🕽 ⅁ ♣ P ᘏ (21) 🌞 🛜 ♫

Hinton

Drop the Anchor Brewery
Building 9 East Close Farm, Lyndhurst Road, BH23 7EF
● droptheanchorbrewery.co.uk
Drop The Anchor Misty Mountain Hop, Black Dog Porter, Otakaro NZ Pale, Breaking Glass Hazelnut Latte Porter-Stout, It's My Shadow, The Phoenix IPA; 3 changing beers (sourced locally) Ⓖ
Located next to the brewery, this is one of a number of buildings on a Victorian farm. All the beers served are brewed on site and include a good range of styles, including some multi-award winners at festivals across the country. Regular events are held, sometimes in the adjacent small theatre, including beer festivals, live music, dances and plays. Local cider is also available along with freshly cooked pizza. Dog-friendly, with ample parking. Open on Friday and Saturday afternoons only. Q 🕸 🕽 ⅁ Å ● P 🌞 🛜 ♫

Holybourne

Queen's Head
20 London Road, GU34 4EG
☎ (01420) 513617

3 changing beers (sourced nationally; often Morland, Palmers, St Austell) Ⓗ
Traditional, friendly sprawling local on the edge of the village, with two beers from the Greene King list and a guest usually from the southern counties. The separate restaurant, available to drinkers, serves home-made food with generous portions: the home-made pies are not for the faint-hearted. Booking is requested if eating. The extensive garden with children's activities, is popular in the summer months when opening hours may be extended. Darts and pool are also played.
🗝😊🕽♣️P🖳(65) ❀

Hook

Crooked Billet

London Road, RG27 9EH
☎ (01256) 762118 ⊕ thecrookedbilletpub.co.uk
Sharp's Doom Bar; Timothy Taylor Landlord; 1 changing beer Ⓗ
The Crooked Billet is situated on London Road near Hook and has been a free house under the same ownership for 37 years. In summer you can enjoy the pleasant riverside garden or the air-conditioned bars, restaurant or snug. In winter, warm up around one of the traditional log fires. A selection of good food and real ales are always available. The landscaped riverside beer garden is used for live events and an annual beer festival. Q🗝😊🕽♿️P❀🛜

Horsebridge

John O'Gaunt Inn

Horsebridge Road, SO20 6PU (½ mile off A3057)
☎ (01794) 388644 ⊕ johnofgaunt.co.uk
Palmers IPA, Dorset Gold; 2 changing beers (sourced regionally; often Palmers) Ⓗ
A welcoming village local which is convenient for walkers and cyclists using the nearby Test Way trail. A free house, it serves regular and changing ales from Palmers brewery of Bridport and occasionally a guest ale. Families and dogs are welcome in the L-shaped bar area which has a log-burner and an open fire. An outdoor covered seating area is available to the rear. Locally sourced food is freshly prepared all day and bar snacks are available. Q🗝😊🕽♣️❀P❀🛜♪

Hythe

Dusty Barrel Ⓛ

Unit 5 Pylewell Road, SO45 6AP
⊕ thedustybarrel.co.uk
4 changing beers (sourced regionally; often Flower Pots, Steam Town, Vibrant Forest) Ⓗ
A busy two-floored micropub opening out to seating on the pedestrian precinct. Industrial rustic decor mixes with record sleeves on the upstairs wall. A piano and a record deck add to the charm of the pub and hint at the popular live music and entertainment sessions every Saturday evening. There is an ever-changing selection of four real ales, six membrane keg beers and four draught ciders, as well as Mexican street food served Wednesday to Saturday. Closed Mondays. Q😊♿️♣️🚆🖳(8,9)❀♪

Little London

Plough Inn

Silchester Road, RG26 5EP
☎ (01256) 850628
3 changing beers (sourced regionally; often Bowman, Flower Pots, Little London) Ⓖ
This old, cosy, traditional village local can rightly be called a gem. Enjoy changing real ales, join in lively conversation, sit in front of a log fire or relax in the peaceful, spacious beer garden. Dogs and families are welcome, and it is also popular with visitors to Pamber Forest and nearby Silchester Roman site. Baguettes are available at lunchtime. Local CAMRA Pub of the Year 2018. Q🗝😊❀P🖳(14)❀

Long Sutton

Four Horseshoes

The Street, RG29 1TA (signed from B3349) SU748470
☎ (01256) 862488
2 changing beers (sourced nationally; often Palmers) Ⓗ
A quintessential rural pub, simply decorated and set in the rolling open countryside of the Hampshire Downs. Formerly a Gale's tied house, it has been free of tie for many years, offering two low-strength guest beers, one always from Palmers brewery. There is a monthly quiz and two jazz nights a month in the spacious but cosy bar which has two real fires. Simple English dishes are served, with a popular roast on Sunday. Opening hours are limited. Q🗝😊🕽❀P❀🛜♪

Longparish

Cricketer's Inn

SP11 6PZ
☎ (01264) 720424 ⊕ thecricketersinnlongparish.co.uk
Otter Ale; Palmers Copper Ale; 2 changing beers Ⓗ
This is a rural village pub full of character, serving real ales from four handpumps. The large beer garden has some covered seating, a summerhouse, fire pits and an outdoor wood-fired pizza oven for Sunday evening use. Specialising in food, the pub also has its own smokehouse and serves home-smoked produce. Families and well-behaved dogs are welcome. The quaint village is popular with walkers and cyclists. Q🗝😊🕽❀P❀🛜

Plough Inn

SP11 6PB
☎ (01264) 720069 ⊕ ploughinn.org
4 changing beers (often Timothy Taylor) Ⓗ
This traditional village pub in the heart of the Test Valley dates from 1721 but was closed for seven years until the local community purchased and refurbished it extensively. Fresh, locally-sourced food is served daily and themed food events feature. Real fires make for cosy drinking. It has a pleasant outside beer garden, parking and is central for local walks and cycle paths. Dogs and families are welcome. Winner of the CAMRA National Pub Saving Award 2023. Q😊🕽♿️❀🛜

Lower Farringdon

Golden Pheasant Ⓛ

Gosport Road, GU34 3DJ
☎ (01420) 588255 ⊕ golden-pheasant.com
Bowman Swift One; Dark Star Hophead; Sharp's Doom Bar; 3 changing beers (sourced regionally) Ⓗ
The owners have run pubs in the area for many years, and 12 years ago they brought their expertise to this delightful privately-owned free house. Seven handpumps serve three permanent and up to three guest beers. The food is freshly cooked with vegetarian options and the fish & chips warrant special mention, due to the 'secret recipe' batter used. Accessible down the A32 four miles from Alton, this is a pub not to be missed. Q🗝😊🕽P❀🛜♪

Lower Wield

Yew Tree 🅛
SO24 9RX SU636398
☎ (01256) 389224 🌐 theyewtreelowerwield.co.uk
House beer (by Flower Pots); 2 changing beers (sourced locally; often Stonehenge, Triple fff) 🅗
This popular, though isolated, family-run pub is a rural gem, surrounded by picturesque rolling countryside, with an old yew tree at its door. A small one-bar, two-room pub, it is food-led with locally-sourced home-made fare. The outside space, some of it covered, is extensive and the pub caters for cyclists, ramblers, horse-riders and dogs. Live music events are held. Q🏵️🛏️⏰◑ⅅP🐾🤍🎵

Lymington

Monkey Brewhouse 🅛
167 Southampton Road, SO41 9HA
☎ (01590) 676754 🌐 monkeybrewhouse.co.uk
Monkey Brewhouse Tollhouse, Sea Wall; 1 changing beer (sourced locally; often Monkey Brewhouse) 🅗
A brewpub consisting of a small bar area, serving three real ales plus four keg beers all brewed on-site, beyond which is a larger, elegant lounge room with impressive fireplace and high rafters. To the side is a raised area that has vista windows onto the brewery. The brewery can also be viewed from a large outside patio area, which leads to a garden behind an 18th-century toll house. A range of gastro pub food is served.
🏵️⏰🍴◑ⅅ&P🖃(6)🤍🎵

Mapledurwell

Gamekeepers 🅛
Tunworth Road, RG25 2LU
☎ (01256) 322038 🌐 thegamekeepers.co.uk
Andwell Resolute Bitter; 2 changing beers 🅗
The Gamekeepers is a charming gastropub in a quaint thatched village. Run for the past 20 years by the same family, it features exposed beams and a flagstoned floor, hinting at the building's long history. Outside are a patio and garden. A single bar serves both the restaurant and a drinking area with settees and a real fire, and local ales are guaranteed. Locally-produced food is served daily.
Q⏰◑P🤍

Mattingley

Leather Bottle 🅛
Reading Road, RG27 8JU
☎ (0118) 932 6371
Brunning & Price Original; 4 changing beers (sourced locally) 🅗
The Leather Bottle is a Grade II-listed village pub dating from 1714 with period features which include mellow Hampshire brick. Inside you'll find relaxed surroundings and a single bar with a changing range of ales, often local. Food is a major offering – booking is advised – and can be enjoyed inside or out in the beautiful garden. Regular events includes charity dog walks, food and drink tastings, coffee mornings and walks. Dogs are welcome on a leash. The pub is popular with cyclists and walkers. Q🏵️⏰◑⅂P🐾🤍🎵

Milford on Sea

Wash House
27 High Street, SO41 0QF
☎ (01590) 644665 🌐 thewashhousebar.co.uk
House beer (by Piddle); 3 changing beers (sourced locally; often Fine Tuned, Hop Back, Piddle) 🅗

Formerly a launderette, now a delightful micropub which serves four ales by handpump, mainly from local breweries, and several real ciders. House beer The Wash House is brewed by Piddle brewery. The pub has several quirky features, including a washing machine door fitted into an old beer barrel and washing machine drums as lampshades. Food is available by ordering at the bar which is then supplied from local cafés or the chip shop. Q&🍴🖃(X1)🐾🎵

New Milton

Hourglass
8 Station Road, BH25 6JU
☎ (01425) 616074
4 changing beers (sourced nationally) 🅖
A lovely micropub situated on the main street in New Milton, just a short walk from the main line railway station between Bournemouth and Southampton. It serves a good selection of gravity-fed real ales and membrane keg beers, and six ciders including My'n'Ers Cider. No food is served but you are welcome to bring in orders from local takeaways; plates, cutlery and condiments are happily provided. On the first Thursday of the month the pub opens early at midday for 'Thirsty Thursday'. Q🚲🍴🖃(X1,X2)🐾🤍🎵

North Waltham

Fox 🅛 ✅
Popham Lane, RG25 2BE (between village and A30)
☎ (01256) 397288 🌐 thefox.org
Courage Best Bitter; Renegade Good Old Boy; Sharp's Doom Bar; 1 changing beer (sourced locally; often Hogs Back, Ringwood, Young's) 🅗
This lovely traditional country pub on the edge of the village, near junction 7 of the M3 overlooks extensive farmland. The pub is divided into two: a popular restaurant and a welcoming public bar with wood-burning stove. Food is served in all areas and features local seasonal produce. Outside there is an extensive beer garden and children's play area. Ushers signage is still visible at the rear. Q🏵️⏰◑⅂P🐾🤍🤍

North Warnborough

Mill House 🅛
Hook Road, RG29 1ET (from M3 jct 5 head towards Odiham and pub is on the right)
☎ (01256) 702953
Hogs Back TEA; house beer (by St Austell); 5 changing beers (sourced regionally; often Andwell, Longdog, Triple fff) 🅗
This traditional Grade II-isted building was one of eight mills of Odiham in the Domesday Book. Last used as a corn mill in 1895, it became a pub restaurant in the 1980s. It has a pleasant central upstairs bar area and oak-panelled dining areas downstairs , one of which has a view of the waterwheel. The extensive landscaped garden has outdoor seating overlooking the millpond on the Whitewater River. There is an old barn used for functions, and extensive parking. Q🏵️⏰◑P🖃(13)🐾🤍

Overton

Old House at Home
Station Road, RG25 3DU
☎ (01256) 770335 🌐 theoldhouseathome.com
Black Sheep Best Bitter; Dark Star Hophead; St Austell Tribute; 2 changing beers (often Brains, Exmoor) 🅗
The Old House at Home has a traditional local pub feel but is also home to a Thai restaurant with takeaway

service and a good vegetarian choice. It has five real ale pumps serving three regular and two changing beers. Outside is a conservatory, and beer garden with a play area and decking. The pub hosts a fun pub quiz on Sunday and participates in local crib, pool, darts and quiz leagues. Sports TV is a feature. ✆❀✿❍◐♣P🚃(76)✿❀

Red Lion 🅛
37 High Street, RG25 3HQ
☎ (01256) 212053 ⊕ theredlionoverton.co.uk
Bowman Swift One; Flower Pots Pots Bitter; Sharp's Doom Bar 🅗
This popular, traditional village pub regularly serves real ales from Hampshire. It is divided into three areas, including a restaurant, main bar and a snug with wood-burning stove. An extensive food menu is served Thursday to Saturday, as well as Sunday lunch. There is an attractive beer garden, partially-covered patio area and separate spacious function room with a skittle alley. Live music features on Friday. A famous gin distillery is located nearby. Q✆❀✿◐♣♣P🚃(76,86)✿❀♪

Park Gate

Gate 🅛
27-29 Middle Road, SO31 7GH
☎ (01489) 886677
Steam Town Barton; 2 changing beers (sourced regionally; often Steam Town) 🅗
A good-sized micropub, which opened in 2019 on the site of a former estate agent. The agent's map of the local area has been retained on one wall. Comfortable seating is provided for about 40 customers, with additional outside tables and chairs in the summer. In addition to the three cask ales, real cider and several craft keg beers are available. Occasional live music is available at weekends and a Brewers Club meets once a month. ✆❀✿(Swanwick)♣♣P🚃(X4)✿❀

Petersfield

Old Drum
16 Chapel Street, GU32 3DP
☎ (01730) 300208 ⊕ theolddrum.com
House beer (by Long Man); 2 changing beers (sourced nationally; often Long Man) 🅗
This town-centre pub has a single bar divided into several drinking areas. Although traditional, it has a modern feel. Decoration is simple, with bare-boarded floors and a mix of wooden chairs, stools and some comfortable armchairs. The main part of the bar is an extension to the original building, dating from the 1920s. Some of the internal walls are covered with postage stamps. To the rear is a small patio garden. ❀✿◐❀🚃

Townhouse 🅛
28 High Street, GU32 3JL
☎ (01730) 265630 ⊕ townhousepetersfield.co.uk
3 changing beers (sourced nationally; often Bowman, Flower Pots, Langham) 🅗
A popular bistro-style micropub in the town centre. It has a single bar and, although fairly open-plan, there are several distinct drinking areas. An upstairs room can be hired for private functions. The changing range of cask beers nearly always includes offerings from small, independant local breweries. Cans and keg beers from small breweries are also often available. To the rear is a modest patio garden. Themed beer festivals are occasionally held. ✆❀✿◐❀♣P🚃✿❀♪

Portchester

Cormorant ✅
181 Castle Street, PO16 9QX
☎ (023) 9237 9374 ⊕ cormorantpub.co.uk
Gale's Seafarers Ale, HSB; Sharp's Doom Bar; 2 changing beers (sourced nationally; often Flower Pots, Fuller's, Hop Back) 🅗
Close to the northern reaches of Portsmouth Harbour, which offers pleasant coastline walks, the Cormorant is a traditional pub whose walls are decorated with numerous seafaring pictures and artefacts. There are also several stuffed birds including a cormorant, puffin and kingfisher. A short walk down Castle Street lies Portchester Castle, reputed to be the best-preserved Roman fortress in Europe. The castle grounds and 12th-century St Mary's church are open to the public. ✆❀✿◐♣P🚃(3)✿❀♪

Portcullis Taphouse 🅛
6 New Parade, 38 West Street, PO16 9UY
☎ 07538 929204
3 changing beers (sourced nationally; often Newtown) 🅖
Situated in Portchester shopping precinct, the Portcullis Taphouse opened in 2021. On offer is a frequently changing range of cask beers, craft beers and ciders. A cheeseboard is a Sunday regular and on Thursday evening a vinyl night when customers' discs are played. Various mobile outdoor caterers provide food on special occasions and television sports are also shown. There are large free car parks to the north and south of the precinct. ♿❀♣●◐🚃✿

Portsmouth

Barley Mow 🅛 ✅
39 Castle Road, Southsea, PO5 3DE
☎ (023) 9282 3492 ⊕ barleymowsouthsea.com
Fuller's London Pride; Gale's HSB; 6 changing beers (sourced nationally) 🅗
A large friendly pub with a community focus. Eight real ales are served in both the quieter lounge bar and separate, livelier public bar. The pub regularly hosts an impressive array of events including live music, quizzes, raffles, pool, darts, golf teams, bar billiards, shove-ha'penny and chess league. Board games are also available. An award-winning patio garden is a real gem and suntrap on warmer days. Children are welcome until evening. ✆❀✿♣🚃(3)✿❀♪

Bridge Tavern
54 East Street, Old Portsmouth, PO1 2JJ
☎ (023) 9275 2992 ⊕ bridge-tavern-portsmouth.co.uk
Dark Star Hophead; Fuller's London Pride; Gale's Seafarers Ale, HSB; 1 changing beer (sourced nationally; often Fuller's, Dark Star) 🅗
Now somewhat hidden, this is a traditional pub in the heart of the Camber Docks – the home of Portsmouth's small fishing fleet. It is divided into several drinking areas on two levels. The name comes from the double swing bridge that used to cross the dock. One exterior wall has a large mural of the cartoon 'Portsmouth Point' by Thomas Rowlandson. There is an old ship's telegraph attached to one wall but it will cost you if you use it! ❀◐🚃(25)❀♪

Hole in the Wall 🅛
36 Great Southsea Street, Southsea, PO5 3BY
☎ (023) 9229 8085 ⊕ theholeinthewallpub.co.uk
Flower Pots Goodens Gold; 6 changing beers (sourced nationally) 🅗

The Hole is a true free house and recipient of multiple awards. It received one of the 50 CAMRA Golden Awards in 2021 for ongoing excellence in promoting the world of beer, cider and pub culture. The ever-changing selection of six nationally-sourced cask ales is accompanied by an interesting selection of cans to take away as well as a sweet tuckshop. Sadly it no longer does food. Thursday is quiz night. On Friday last admission is one hour before closing. Q ♠ ● ⇦ ⊟ (3) ☺ 🏵 ☂

Lawrence Arms ⑃ ●

63 Lawrence Road, Southsea, PO5 1NU
☎ 07522 495032
5 changing beers (sourced nationally) ℍ
Dating back to 1887 this street-corner pub's L-shaped bar faces a large lounge area. A friendly community pub, there are weekly meat raffles and quizzes, bar billiards and board games. The bar features a rotating selection of five ales plus a bottle shop and take home pints. There is also an ample selection of real ciders. Food includes toasties and Sunday roasts. A former local CAMRA Pub of the Year and current Cider Pub of the Year.
🏵 ⊛ ☖ ♣ ● ⊟ (18) 🏵 ☂ ♫

Lord Palmerston ●

84-90 Palmerston Road, Southsea, PO5 3PT
☎ (023) 9272 8000
Greene King IPA, Abbot; Sharp's Doom Bar; 3 changing beers (sourced nationally; often Irving, Langham) ℍ
A Wetherspoon pub is named after Henry John Temple, 3rd Viscount Palmerston who authorised the building of a series of fortifications around the city, known as Palmerston's Folly as they were never used in anger. The front part of the pub has a high ceiling – archways divide this section and another low-ceilinged drinking area. The pub is decorated with memorabilia relating to Lord Palmerston and local resident Sir Alec Rose, the second person to sail single-handed around the world.
🏵 ⊛ ◑ ☖ ● ⊟ ☂

Merchant House

9-11 Highland Road, Eastney, PO4 9DA
12 changing beers (sourced nationally) ℍ/Ⓚ
Converted from two shops, this street-corner pub has a modern theme, with bare walls and floor. There are three drinking areas on different levels: the bar counter is at street level, with a raised area to the right; the third area is accesed via a staircase at the rear. Beers are sourced from small independant breweries from all parts of the country. The four cask beers are complemented by a mix of eight keg and membrane keg offerings. A large screen displays what is currently available. ⊛ ◑ ⊟ (1,2)

Northcote ⑃

35 Francis Avenue, Southsea, PO4 0HL
☎ (023) 9278 9888
Irving Invincible; Timothy Taylor Landlord; 2 changing beers (sourced locally; often Irving, Langham) ℍ
A substantial two-bar pub, a few minutes' walk from Albert Road, built for the Pike Spicer brewery whose logo still adorns one of the walls. The public bar has a pool table and dartboard and leads to a large patio garden. The lounge is comfortably decorated and displays memorabilia of comedians from the early days of cinema such as Laurel and Hardy and the Marx Brothers, and local resident Arthur Conan Doyle's most famous creation, Sherlock Holmes. ⊛ ♣ ● ⊟ (2) ♫

Old Customs House

Vernon Building, Gunwharf Quays, Gunwharf, PO1 3TY
☎ (023) 9283 2333 ● theoldcustomshouse.com

Dark Star Hophead; Fuller's London Pride; Gale's Seafarers Ale, HSB; 2 changing beers (sourced nationally; often Dark Star, Fuller's) ℍ
Grade II-listed, the pub was the administrative offices of HMS Vernon before the construction of the Gunwharf Quays shopping complex. Now it is the only traditional pub in the area. The conversion to a pub is sympathetic, with many of the old rooms being retained as smaller drinking areas. Some of these are named after famous former residents of Portsmouth. It is unsurprisingly decorated with Naval memorabilia. It hosts occasional beer festivals and tap takeovers featuring local breweries. 🏵 ⊛ ◑ ☖ ☖ ⇌ (Harbour) ⊟ 🏵 ☂

Pembroke

20 Pembroke Road, Old Portsmouth, PO1 2NR
☎ (023) 9282 3961
Draught Bass; Fuller's London Pride; Greene King Abbot ℍ
A traditional pub with strong connections to the Royal Navy. It is on the route of Lord Nelson's last walk to join HMS Victory and sail to Trafalgar. It was formerly named the Little Blue Line and features in books by Royal Navy Captain and author Frederick Marryat. A short walk from the pub is the Royal Garrison Church, the oldest such church in Britain, dating back to 1212. Part of the church roof was destroyed by a firebomb in WWII.
♣ ⊟ (25) 🏵 ☂ ♫

Phoenix

13 Duncan Road, Southsea, PO5 2QU
☎ (023) 9278 1055
Gale's HSB; Timothy Taylor Landlord; 1 changing beer (sourced nationally; often Irving, Urban Island) ℍ
A genuine community local, this street-corner pub is a short distance from Albert Road and retains its two bars. The bare-boarded public bar is decorated with articles about the history of Portsmouth. The lounge walls are adorned with photographs of people who have performed at the nearby Kings Theatre, including three of The Goons. Next to the lounge is a small, quirky patio garden which in turn gives access to a comfortable snug, part of the former Dock End brewery. ⊛ ● ⊟ (2) 🏵 ☂

Rose in June ⑃ ●

102 Milton Road, Milton, PO3 6AR
☎ (023) 9282 4191 ● theroseinjune.co.uk
Gale's HSB; Goddards Wight Squirrel; Otter Amber; 8 changing beers (sourced nationally; often Arundel) ℍ
A substantial two-bar pub a short walk from Fratton Park. Popular with football fans, it can be busy on match days. Up to 11 cask ales are served, as well as real ciders. Both bars are traditionally decorated. The public bar has a pool table and darts, and there is comfortable seating in the lounge. The garden to the rear is probably the largest pub garden in the city and also has its own bar. Several beer festivals are held during the year.
Q 🏵 🏵 ⊛ ◑ ♣ ● ⊟ 🏵 ☂

Ship Anson ●

10 The Hard, Portsea, PO1 3DT
☎ (023) 9282 4152
Greene King IPA; Morland Old Speckled Hen; 4 changing beers (sourced nationally; often St Austell, Timothy Taylor, Wadworth) ℍ
Formerly two pubs, as can be seen by the different building styles and internal architecture, the King & Queen was merged with the Ship Anson in the 1980s. Situated on The Hard, it is convenient for visiting the Historic Dockyard, HMS Warrior and Gunwharf Quays. Unsurprisingly, the pub is packed with naval memorabilia. There is a small part-covered patio garden. 🏵 ⊛ ◑ ☖ ☖ ⇌ (Harbour) ⊟ 🏵 ☂

Sir Loin of Beef 🅛

152 Highland Road, Eastney, PO4 9NH
☎ (023) 9282 0115
Gale's HSB; Irving Frigate; 6 changing beers (sourced regionally; often Frome, Hop Back, Langham) 🅷
A popular street-corner local a short walk from Eastney seafront, Bransbury Park and the Eastney Engine Houses museum. The main bar is comfortably furnished with banquette and armchair seating and is divided into two areas. A recent refurbishment has added a separate bar to the rear, offering more seating. It has TV screens for sporting events and is available for functions.
🏠🍴(1,2)🌸

Still & West

2 Bath Square, Old Portsmouth, PO1 2JL
☎ (023) 9282 1567 🌐 stillandwest.co.uk
Fuller's London Pride; Gale's Seafarers Ale, HSB; 1 changing beer (sourced nationally; often Fuller's, Gale's) 🅷
Opened as the Whistling Still in 1733, the Still & West (since 1903) is situated on the edge of Portsmouth Harbour. The large seaside patio is an excellent place to watch the comings and goings of the busy harbour but beware of the wakes from large boats at high tide. Not surprisingly the pub's decor has a nautical theme. The upstairs rooms, also equipped for meetings, offer wonderful views of the harbour and can be hired for private functions. 🏠🌸🌜♿🍴(25)🌸🛜

Vaults

41-47 Albert Road, Southsea, PO5 2SF
☎ (023) 9286 4712 🌐 thevaults-southsea.co.uk
Fuller's London Pride, ESB; Gale's Seafarers Ale, HSB; 3 changing beers (sourced nationally; often Dark Star, Fuller's) 🅷
This substantial pub has a somewhat bohemian feel. The bars have different focuses with one serving cask beer and another, known as the Beer Vaults, dedicated to craft keg beer, including some local offerings. The labyrinthine interior includes a number of drinking areas on several floors, and a roof terrace. The floors are bare-boarded and seating is a mix of stools, banquette seating and traditional tables and chairs. The walls are adorned with shelves and local memorabilia. 🏠🌸🍴(2)🌸🛜♫

Poulner

London Tavern 🅛 ✅

Linford Road, BH24 1TY
☎ (01425) 473819 🌐 thelondontavern.com
Ringwood Fortyniner; Timothy Taylor Landlord; house beer (by Ringwood); 3 changing beers (sourced nationally; often Hop Back, Sixpenny) 🅷
Traditional brick-built country pub up a lane just off the A31 at Poulner Hill. Although geared up for food – serving local produce where possible – it still has the feel of a pub and drinkers are given a friendly welcome. There are two separate rooms and an outside covered drinking area. In winter a roaring log fire will keep you warm. Up to six beers are sold, with guest ales coming from local breweries. Quiz, music and event nights are held.
🏠🌸🍴♣🍴(Ringo)🌸🛜♫

Romsey

Old House at Home

62 Love Lane, SO51 8DE (near Waitrose car park)
☎ (01794) 513175 🌐 theoldhouseathomeromsey.co.uk
Fuller's London Pride; Gale's Seafarers Ale, HSB; 2 changing beers (sourced nationally; often Fuller's) 🅷

A Fuller's tied pub comprising an 18th-century thatched building and a 19th-century extension. Conveniently situated in the town centre close to the railway station and bus station, the pub has three inside areas comprising a bar area with booths and a wood-burner, a cosy restaurant area and a raised area. To the rear is a courtyard garden with heating and shelter where some major sporting events are shown on TV, and a secluded raised area. 🌸🍴≢P🍴🌸🛜♫

Selborne

Selborne Arms 🅛

High Street, GU34 3JR
☎ (01420) 511247 🌐 selbornearms.co.uk
Bowman Swift One; Courage Directors; 3 changing beers (sourced regionally; often Hogs Back, Langham, Triple fff) 🅷
Originally a traditional two-bar village pub now greatly extended, this welcoming local has real fires and a friendly atmosphere. Up to five cask beers are available, many from local microbreweries with more during the village's October Zig Zag Festival. Beer bats offering three thirds of cask beers for the price of a pint are a welcome feature. Extensive menus showcase local and home-made produce with vegetarian and gluten-free options. The safe play area in the garden is popular with children. Q🏠🌸🍴♣P🍴(38)🌸🛜

Shedfield

Wheatsheaf Inn 🅛

Botley Road, SO32 2JG
☎ (01329) 833024
Flower Pots Perridge Pale, Pots Bitter, Goodens Gold; 1 changing beer (sourced locally; often Flower Pots, Steam Town, Stonehenge) 🅖
Friendly, popular two-bar roadside pub dispensing mainly Flower Pots beer directly from casks behind the bar, plus a choice of two Westons ciders. It has been in the Guide continuously since 1998. The pub is split between two rooms, warmed by a double-sided wood-burning stove. Good home-cooked food is served at lunchtimes. Live blues, jazz or folk music features on most Saturday evenings and a meat draw every Sunday. The garden's flowers are delightful in summer.
Q🌸🍴♣P🍴(69)🌸🛜♫

Sherfield on Loddon

Four Horseshoes 🅛

Reading Road, RG27 0EX
☎ (01256) 882296 🌐 the4horseshoes.co.uk
Timothy Taylor Landlord; 1 changing beer (often Sherfield Village) 🅷
This family-run village pub is Grade II-listed and dates back to the 16th century. With traditional low beams, bench seating and wood-burners it has a single bar serving four areas, one with sports TV. At the front is a pleasant patio with an awning for outside entertaining. Family and dog-friendly, the pub has a skittle alley/function room. They hold regular jazz, quiz and food-themed evenings. Sherfield Village beer is regularly available. Q🏠🌸🍴♣P🍴(14)🌸

Sopley

Woolpack Inn

Ringwood Road, BH23 7AX
☎ (01425) 672252 🌐 thewoolpacksopley.co.uk
Flack Manor Flack's Double Drop; 1 changing beer (sourced nationally; often Exmoor, Sandbanks) 🅷

Mid-18th-century thatched pub lying between the Christchurch to Ringwood road and a spur of the River Avon. The main bar area has wooden beams, some low, especially the one that leads to a lower stone-floored room that has a wood-burner. To the side is a large conservatory leading to a patio area and riverside garden that is reached via a small footbridge. A wide range of fresh home-made seasonal food is served all day. ✿❀❍P❀❄

Southampton

Beards & Boards

33 Bedford Place, SO15 2DG
⊕ beardsandboards.co.uk
3 changing beers (sourced nationally; often Flower Pots, Steam Town, Vibrant Forest) Ⓗ
A welcoming and friendly one-roomed micropub, furnished in an industrial-urban decor with skateboards on the wall. The bar, benches and tables are made from reclaimed wood, a range of board games and a retro games console are available, and record sleeves on the wall reflect the background music played. The pub offers competitions, cider festivals and tap takeovers, alongside the changing selection of three quality national and local cask beers, 10 keg taps and four draught ciders. Closed Mondays. ✿よ♣➤❀

Bookshop Alehouse

21 Portswood Road, SO17 2ES
4 changing beers (sourced locally; often Eight Arch, Elusive, Vibrant Forest) Ⓗ
Formerly a bookshop, converted to a micropub in 2016, it has a front room still with a bookcase full of books, steps up to a small bar area and a separate room downstairs. Four handpumps provide beers from a variety of breweries, and there are four keg taps. Vegan-friendly beers are clearly marked. No food is available but you may bring some in from the nearby outlets. A portable ramp is available allowing wheelchair access. Closed Mondays. Qよ≥(St Denys)♣➤❀❄

Brewhouse & Kitchen ⊘

47 Highfield Lane, SO17 1QD
☎ (023) 8055 5566
Brewhouse & Kitchen Speedwell, Supermarine, Walk The Line; 1 changing beer (sourced locally; often Brewhouse & Kitchen (Southampton)) Ⓗ
Part of the ever growing Brewhouse & Kitchen chain, this venue opened in 2015. The old public bar houses the 2½ barrel (720 pint) plant where all the pub's real ales are brewed, of which three are regular and the fourth is a seasonal brew under the 'Project Cask' umbrella. It also has a large selection of around 20 or more craft keg beers. Good-quality food is served from noon every day. There is a large garden at the rear and tables at the front. ✿❀❍よ♣P➤(1,U2) ❀❄

Butcher's Hook

7 Manor Farm Road, SO18 1NN
☎ (023) 8178 2280 ⊕ butchershookpub.com
3 changing beers (sourced nationally) Ⓖ
A lovely little micropub opened in 2014. Previously a butcher's shop, the original tiling and butcher's rails have been left in situ. There is indoor seating for 25 people and a few outdoor benches. Two or three constantly-changing cask beers, a good selection of bottles and cans and several craft keg beers are served. It is a lively place, with midweek being quieter. Customers are welcome to bring their own takeaway food. Closed on Mondays, and occasionally for private events.
Q✿よ≥(Bitterne) ♣➤(20) ❀❄♪

Dancing Man ⓛ

Wool House, Town Quay, SO14 2AR
☎ (023) 8083 6666 ⊕ dancingmanbrewery.co.uk
Dancing Man Old Fashioned, Jesus Hairdo, Jack O'Diamonds; 2 changing beers (sourced nationally) Ⓗ
The iconic Grade I-listed Wool House on Town Quay, built in the 14th century, is the only freestanding medieval warehouse in Southampton. In 2014 plans were approved for the Dancing Man brewery to open the building as a tourist centre, microbrewery and restaurant, and it was formally opened in 2015. One-off and rare brews are regularly available. The brewery has recently more than doubled its brewing capacity to keep up with the high demand. ✿❀❍よ➤❀❄♪

Freemantle Arms ⓛ

31 Albany Road, SO15 3EF
☎ (023) 8077 2536 ⊕ thefreemantlearms.co.uk
Flower Pots Goodens Gold; house beer (by Ringwood); 3 changing beers (sourced regionally; often Bowman, Dorset, Goddards) Ⓗ
A mid 19th-century pub with a lot of Victorian character and up to five real ales on the bar. The one main bar has a conservatory and well-maintained garden at the rear. The pub is dog friendly and allows children until evening. The interior is decorated with local history photographs and old craftsmen's tools. Millbrook is the nearest railway station but the pub is only a five minute bus ride from Southampton Central. Q✿≥(Millbrook)♣➤❀♪

Guide Dog ⓛ

38 Earl's Road, SO14 6SF
☎ (023) 8063 8947
Dark Star American Pale Ale; Flower Pots Goodens Gold; Steam Town Stoke Pale; 7 changing beers (sourced nationally; often Steam Town) Ⓗ
Housed in a residential road off Bevois Valley, the pub consists of a front room and the 'Dog House' to the rear; the latter leads to a small outside smoking area. Six or seven beers are normally served from a variety of breweries, more when busy. It can get crowded at peak times especially when Southampton men's football team are playing at home. The pub has won a number of awards including local CAMRA Pub of the Year several times. Q➤(20,U6)❀❄♪

Hop Inn ⓛ

199 Woodmill Lane, SO18 2PH
☎ (023) 8055 7723
Gale's HSB; Steam Town Stoke Pale, Firebox; 1 changing beer (sourced nationally) Ⓗ
Situated near the picturesque River Itchen, this popular 1930s two-bar pub has two entrances. The homely lounge bar is split by a central fireplace and has pictures, china ornaments and themed wall plates. The public bar houses sports TVs, games and music. Traditional, mainly home-made, pub meals are very popular (not served Sun or Mon). Three cask ales showcase a strong commitment to LocAle. With folk music, quiz nights and live music, there is always something going on. ✿❀❍よ♣P➤(16,20) ❀❄♪

Key & Anchor

90 Millbrook Road East, SO15 1JQ
☎ (023) 8022 5674
Dartmoor Jail Ale; St Austell Proper Job; Wadworth 6X; 1 changing beer (sourced nationally; often Titanic) Ⓗ
A friendly street-corner local with four handpumps serving three regulars and one occasional guest. The building dates back to 1862 and sits on a quiet road. Bar stools, tables and comfortable seating surround the U-shaped bar. Exterior seating can be enjoyed at the front and in the garden. The eclectic jukebox welcomes all

tastes, and sits opposite the log fire. Darts, bingo, meat draws, quizzes and occasional bands fill this traditional pub's calendar. ✿≢(Central)♣☷☺🛜♫

Olaf's Tun 🍺

8 Portsmouth Road, SO19 9AA

☎ (023) 8044 7887 🌐 olafstun.co.uk

6 changing beers (sourced regionally; often Bowman, Flower Pots, Red Cat) Ⓗ

A friendly micropub comprising a long narrow room with six handpumps and eight kegs with a changing selection of beers from a wide range of breweries. There is also a good selection of wines. Home-made pizzas are available. Olaf's Tun can be found a short walk from the River Itchen near the eastern end of Woolston Bridge, and is well-served by public transport, especially buses from Southampton railway station. CAMRA Regional Pub of the Year 2022. Q✿✪◑&≢(Woolston)♣●☷☺🛜

Park Inn

37 Carlisle Road, SO16 4FN

☎ 07596 203702 🌐 theparkinn.co.uk

Wadworth Henry's IPA, 6X, Swordfish; 3 changing beers (sourced nationally; often Ossett, Theakston, Timothy Taylor) Ⓗ

A popular welcoming street-corner local, situated close to busy bus stops at Shirley precinct. The pub underwent a small refurbishment during 2022, removing the dartboard and providing extra seating. Three real ales are always available, increasing to five or six at weekends. A clean tidy pub that always puts the customer first, it is decorated with local photos and memorabilia. Quiz nights are Wednesday and Sunday and a meat draw is on Sunday lunchtimes. ✿♣☷☺🛜

Platform Tavern Ⓛ ✓

Town Quay, SO14 2NY

☎ (023) 8033 7232 🌐 platformtavern.com

Dark Star Hophead; Fuller's London Pride; 2 changing beers (sourced locally; often Vibrant Forest) Ⓗ

A popular historic pub, with a part of the old city walls visible, sitting close to the site of the city's old gun platform, hence the name. African masks and instruments decorate the walls while fabric-covered ceilings, a fire and deep armchairs add a cosy and warm feel to the two-roomed pub. The second room hosts the restaurant which, due to popularity, regularly spills into the main bar. The pub prides itself on regular live music. ✿◑♣●☷☺🛜♫

South Western Arms

38-40 Adelaide Road, SO17 2HW

☎ (023) 8122 0817

9 changing beers (sourced nationally) Ⓗ

Refurbished in 2018, this characterful Victorian-era pub retains some original features though most internal walls have long gone. Up to nine real ales from local and national breweries are served. A paved back garden has a large, partially-covered smoking area while the front car park has a popular pizza van from Thursday to Saturday. Games, in the form of a pool table, darts and table-football, are on the first floor and regular live music is hosted on the ground floor. ✿≢(St Denys) ♣P☷(20) ☺♫

Witch's Brew Ⓛ

220 Shirley Road, SO15 3FL

☎ 07403 871757

5 changing beers (sourced nationally; often Flower Pots, Steam Town, Wantsum) Ⓖ

A small, friendly micropub on Shirley Road. Up to five ales are available, all gravity dispensed. The pub has two rooms with the beer being served from a bar at the back

of the second room. A small outside drinking area at the front of the pub overlooks the road and a garden at the back has a smoking section. The garden is planted with flowers, using repurposed bathroom porcelain as flower pots. Closed Monday to Wednesday. Q✿♣●☷☷☺

Southwick

Golden Lion Ⓛ

High Street, PO17 6EB

☎ (023) 9221 0437 🌐 goldenlionsouthwick.co.uk

5 changing beers (sourced regionally; often Bowman, Langham, Palmers) Ⓗ

A sizeable pub divided into three rooms, one of which is for diners. Being close to the former HMS Dryad, its main claim to fame is being the unofficial officers' mess during WWII. The lounge bar was used by Eisenhower, Bradley, Montgomery, Prince Philip and Earl Mountbatten amongst others. Not surprisingly, the pub is decorated with military memorabilia. To the rear is the Southwick brewhouse. Although no longer an operational brewery, the brewing kit is still in place. Q✿☎✿◑♣●P☺🛜♫

Steep

Harrow ★ Ⓛ

Harrow Lane, GU32 2DA

☎ (01730) 262685 🌐 theharrowinnsteep.co.uk

2 changing beers (sourced locally; often Bowman, Flack Manor) Ⓖ

Although remote, this small pub is only just over a mile walk from Petersfield. It has two bars with serving hatches rather than normal counters. Beer is served direct from casks stillaged behind the serving areas. It has been in the same family since 1932, and is now run by two sisters who were born in the pub. The toilets are in a separate building across the road. The pub is cash only – no cards are accepted. Q✿◑●P☺

Tichborne

Tichborne Arms Ⓛ

SO24 0NA (1¼ miles S of B3047 Alresford Rd jct) **SU5719930412**

☎ (01962) 588346 🌐 tichbornearms.com

Triple fff Moondance; 3 changing beers (sourced locally; often Bowman, Flack Manor, Triple fff) Ⓗ

A picturesque, thatched, 1939-built pub owned by the Tichborne Estate. Inside are a large bar with wood-panelling and an open fire, and a handsomely furnished area which was formerly the patio. Outside are a covered patio, an attractive garden with children's play area, and views of trees and fields. Tichborne's Anglican church is notable for its pre-reformation Catholic chapel, one of only three in England. Food served all day from opening, except on Sunday, when service starts at lunchtime. Card payment only. ☎✿◑&P☺🛜

Titchfield

Wheatsheaf Ⓛ

1 East Street, PO14 4AD

☎ (01329) 842965

🌐 thewheatsheaf-titchfield.foodanddrinksites.co.uk

Flower Pots Pots Bitter; 3 changing beers (sourced regionally; often Flower Pots, Hop Back) Ⓗ

Situated in a conservation area, this 17th-century pub is owned by the licensee, bought with the help of crowdfunding. The premises comprise a main bar and small snug, with an outdoor area and bistro restaurant, although food is also served in the bar. Sunday lunches are popular and need to be booked well in advance. Two annual beer festivals are held in December or January and in July. No food on Monday, Tuesday lunchtimes or Sunday evenings. Q≿❀◑♿◕P🚌(X4)🐾♫

Totton

6 Barrels

31 Salisbury Road, SO40 3HX

☎ (023) 8178 3030 🌐 6barrels.co.uk

Steam Town Stoke Pale; 3 changing beers (sourced locally; often Hop Back, Parkway, Twisted) 🄷

A former shop and Thai restaurant in the centre of town, fitted out in rustic style with long tables and benches both inside and out. Four handpumps dispense Stoke Pale and up to three changing guests. Keg beers and a variety of cider and perries are also available, and a customer loyalty scheme is in operation. Live music is played on Saturday and occasional Friday evenings. A largescreen TV is brought in for major sporting events. It is easily accessed by public transport.
❀♿≈♣◕🚌(12,X7)🐾ᯤ♫

Twyford

Phoenix Inn 🄻

High Street, SO21 1RF

☎ (01962) 713322 🌐 thephoenixinn.co.uk

Flower Pots Pots Bitter, IPA; Morland Old Speckled Hen; St Austell Tribute; Timothy Taylor Landlord; 2 changing beers (sourced locally; often Flower Pots, Hop Back) 🄷

Despite being a Greene King pub, four out of the eight handpumps dispense local beers, mostly from Flower Pots and Hop Back. The bar serves a long split-level room with parquet floor, decorated with old local photos and barrel ends on the far wall. At the rear is a skittle alley that can be hired for catered events. Outside is a covered patio and beer garden with a marquee. The pub serves home-cooked traditional pub food. Closed Monday.
≿❀◑♣P🚌(69,E1)🐾ᯤ♫

Upham

Brushmakers Arms

2 Shoe Lane, SO32 1JJ (top of the village near the pond) SU5399620606

☎ (01489) 860231 🌐 thebrushmakersarms.com

Bowman Swift One; Flack Manor Flack's Double Drop; Flower Pots Goodens Gold; 1 changing beer (sourced regionally; often Hop Back, Steam Town, Stonehenge) 🄷

A cosy, friendly village pub, that was previously a school and a brush-makers, serving four local real ales. Inside are low-beamed ceilings, an open fire and various antique items, including brushes and a cabinet of vintage beer bottles. Outside seating is available at the front and in an old English garden, with potting shed, at the rear. Locally sourced food is served from an ever-changing menu. On Mondays and Tuesdays the pub is only open in the evening. Food is served Wednesday to Sunday.
Q❀◑♣◕🐾ᯤ♫

Vernham Dean

George Inn

Back Lane, SP11 0JY

☎ (01264) 737279 🌐 thegeorgeatvernhamdean.co.uk

Bowman Swift One; Flack Manor Flack's Double Drop; Stonehenge Pigswill; 1 changing beer 🄷

This traditional village pub dates back to the 17th century and features eyebrow windows. It is situated in a pretty village with numerous foot and cycling paths, including to nearby Fosbury Hillfort. There is outside seating to the front and an enclosed beer garden at the rear. The interior features low oak-beamed ceilings and fireplaces. Locally produced food is served and themed nights are regularly held. An annual beer festival is run in August.
Q≿❀◑P🐾ᯤ♫

Whitchurch

Prince Regent 🄻

104 London Road, RG28 7LT

☎ (01256) 892179

Hop Back Crop Circle, Summer Lightning 🄷

The Prince is a traditional friendly local, 'up the hill' in this rural town. It has a single bar and small rear drinking area overlooking the Test Valley. A jukebox, pool table and sports TV screens feature, with an emphasis on football. Occasional quizzes and live music, including karaoke are held. The pub may have extended evening opening hours at weekends. ♣P🚌(76)🐾♫

Whitchurch Sports & Social Club 🄻

Winchester Street, RG28 7RB (S of village centre)

☎ (01256) 892493 🌐 whitchurchsport.co.uk

Flowerpots Perridge Pale; 2 changing beers (sourced locally; often Flowerpots) 🄷

Tucked away near the Millennium Meadow, this large club features two bars (members' and public) serving real ales. It is home to Whitchurch FC, a squash club, darts and indoor and outdoor bowling clubs. The green can be viewed from the comfortable lounge bar. Regular events include quizzes, discos, live music and occasional private functions. It is open evenings and weekends, longer if the football is on (call to check times). CAMRA members welcome. ≿❀P🚌(76,86)ᯤ

Widley

George Inn

Portsdown Hill Road, PO6 1BE

☎ (023) 9222 1079 🌐 the-george-inn.co.uk

Flower Pots Goodens Gold; Fuller's London Pride; Gale's HSB; Timothy Taylor Landlord; 3 changing beers (sourced nationally; often Goddards, Irving, Langham) 🄷

Set on top of Portsdown Hill, the pub offers views over Portsmouth and the Isle of Wight. Part of the building is the former Widley fire station, and it used to be a tram stop on the Portsdown & Horndean Light Railway. The bar has an unusual wood-panelled counter and the transport theme is continued with an old bus stop sign fixed to a pillar. It is decorated with brewery memorabilia, much relating to the old Brickwoods brewery in Portsmouth. Q❀◐♣P🚌🐾ᯤ♫

Winchester

Black Boy 🄻

1 Wharf Hill, SO23 9NQ

☎ (01962) 861754 🌐 theblackboypub.com

Alfred's Saxon Bronze; Flower Pots Pots Bitter; Hop Back Summer Lightning; 1 changing beer (sourced locally; often Bowman, Hop Back, Flack Manor) 🄷

Lively, quirky free house on the outskirts of Winchester, near to the River Itchen, serving four local real ales. The central rustic wooden bar serves multiple wood-beamed rooms each decorated with various weird items, from stuffed animals to vintage meters to fire buckets. Outside is a large patio with plenty of covered seating. Food is limited to pizzas on Tuesday and Thursday evenings only. Next door is the Black Hole that has 10 en-suite double B&B rooms. ❀🛏◑♣🚌(4,WPR)🐾ᯤ♫

Fulflood Arms 🅛

28 Cheriton Road, SO22 5EF

☎ (01962) 842996 ∰ thefulfloodarms.co.uk

Morland Old Speckled Hen; St Austell Tribute; 5 changing beers (sourced locally; often Queen Inn, Flower Pots) Ⓗ

Classic 19th-century back-street corner local with the original dark-green tiled façade, frosted-glass windows and signage of its former Winchester brewery ownership. Inside is a smart capacious single bar with wood-burning stove and a library. The walls are adorned with scenes of old Winchester and a city map can be seen on the ceiling. Patios, both front and rear, are an attraction. Sports events are shown on TV. No food is served, but takeaways may be ordered. ❀≕♣🚲(3,4)🐾🛜

Hyde Tavern 🅛

57 Hyde Street, SO23 7DY

☎ (01962) 862592 ∰ hydetavern.co.uk

Flower Pots Pots Bitter; 3 changing beers (sourced regionally; often Flower Pots, Steam Town) Ⓗ/Ⓖ

An ancient Grade II-listed building with fine twin-gabled frontage. Step down from street level into the cosy, unspoilt low-beamed front bar and smaller back room, with narrow stairs leading to a hidden cellar room and the garden. The pub hosts regular folk and other live music upstairs and in the cellar. No food is served, but takeaways can be ordered in, with plates and cutlery provided for a small charge. Up to four beers are available, including one on gravity.
Q❀≕♣●🖥🚲(67) 🐾🛜♫

Queen Inn 🅛 ✅

28 Kingsgate Road, SO23 9PG

☎ (01962) 853898 ∰ thequeeninnwinchester.com

Flack Manor Flack's Double Drop; Flower Pots Goodens Gold; Queen Inn A Long Way From Pillowcases; 5 changing beers (sourced locally; often Siren, Queen Inn, Steam Town) Ⓗ/Ⓖ

A relaxed and affable pub, situated close to Winchester College and a pleasant walk from the city centre. A microbrewery can be viewed from the front bar and three of its beers are normally available. In addition, up to five real ales are sourced from other local breweries. The comprehensive food menu uses locally sourced ingredients, complemented by roast lunches on Sunday. Outside, the large garden to the rear and a sheltered front patio provide extra seating.
Q🛏❀◑P🚲(1,69) 🐾🛜

Wykeham Arms 🅛

75 Kingsgate Street, SO23 9PE

☎ (01962) 853834 ∰ wykehamarmswinchester.co.uk

Dark Star Hophead; Flower Pots Goodens Gold; Fuller's London Pride; Gale's Seafarers Ale, HSB; 1 changing beer (sourced regionally; often Fuller's) Ⓗ

Sensitively refurbished in 2022, the Wykeham is a multi-roomed, Grade II-listed, 18th-century pub, close to Winchester College, Kingsgate, and the cathedral. Seating in the main bar is at old school desks, and the memorabilia adorning all rooms has a notable Nelsonian bias. The wine list includes 30 wines available by the glass, and the food has won awards. Dogs are welcomed; intrusive mobile phones are not. Note the Victorian postbox on the wall opposite the main entrance. Q❀🛌◑🚲(1,69)🐾🛜

Wonston

Wonston Arms ♚ 🅛

Stoke Charity Road, SO21 3LS

☎ 07909 993388 ∰ thewonston.co.uk

4 changing beers (sourced locally; often Bowman, Flower Pots, Oakham) Ⓗ

This community-focused pub is a real gem in a quaint village 15 minute's walk from Sutton Scotney and the closest bus stop. With a quirky exterior resembling a beach, the interior is homely and cosy in contrast. The pub only serves drinks but has regular pop-up food vendors plus a popular curry night which must be pre-booked. Regular activities include live music, quizzes and other events. Cyclists, walkers and dogs are welcome. It was CAMRA National Pub of the Year 2018 and Local Pub of the Year 2018-2022. Q❀♣P🐾🛜♫

Breweries

Alfred's

Unit 6 Winnall Farm Industrial Estate, Easton Lane, Winchester, SO23 0HA

☎ (01962) 859999 ∰ alfredsbrewery.co.uk

Alfred's is a 10-barrel, state-of-the-art brewery located close to the centre of Winchester. Production of Saxon Bronze is complemented by returning favourites and experimental beers. 🍴◆

Saxon Bronze (ABV 3.8%) BITTER
Well-balanced, copper-coloured bitter, with minimal aroma. Malt dominates the taste with some hops in the finish.

Andwell SIBA

Andwell Lane, Andwell, RG27 9PA

☎ (01256) 761044 ∰ andwells.com

⊗ Brewing commenced in 2008 on a 10-barrel plant. The brewery relocated and expanded in 2011 to an idyllic riverside location with a new bespoke 20-barrel plant. Beer is distributed to Hampshire, Surrey, Wiltshire, Berkshire, Greater London and the Isle of Wight. More than 200 outlets are supplied. In 2020 Andwells new brewhouse shop, bar and café opened behind the brewery. ‼🍴◆

Resolute Bitter (ABV 3.8%) BITTER
An easy-drinking bitter. The malty aroma, leads into a similarly malty flavour with some bitterness and a sweetish finish.

Gold Muddler (ABV 3.9%) BLOND
Light golden standard bitter. Aroma of hops and malt; characteristics carried into flavour with solid bitterness and dry, biscuity finish.

King John (ABV 4.2%) BITTER
Malty bitter, low in hops with loads of caramel and toffee underlying sweetness, leading to some dryness in the finish.

Bat Country (NEW)

Unit D, Whinwhistle Road, East Wellow, SO51 6BH

☎ (01794) 331400 ∰ batcountrybrewco.com

Bat Country Brew Co is a small batch brewery founded in 2021 by two brothers. Located in Hampshire, it produces a variety of different beers in various formats.

The Dirt (ABV 4.2%) BITTER
Mosquito Pimpstick (ABV 5.6%) BITTER

Botley

Botley Mills, Mill Hill, Botley, SO30 2GB

☎ (01489) 784867 ☎ 07909 337212

∰ botleybrewery.com

⊗ Botley Brewery was established in 2010 and uses a five-barrel plant. A small bar next door, appropriately named the Hidden Tap, serves three of its ales and the occasional guest. ⬛♦LIVE☙

HPA (ABV 3.8%) PALE
Pommy Blonde (ABV 4.3%) BITTER
Amber bitter with malty, orange and grapefruit nose. Hops come through in taste leading to pronounced bitterness and dry finish.
English IPA (ABV 5.1%) PALE
An earthy rich and piney English IPA. Decent hoppiness with lasting, pronounced dryness, but a well-rounded malt character throughout.
Wildern (ABV 5.7%) RED

Bowman SIBA

Wallops Wood, Sheardley Lane, Droxford, SO32 3QY
☎ **(01489) 878110** ⊕ bowman-ales.com

⊗ Brewing started in 2006. A new 40-barrel plant came on line in 2013, this is now working alongside the original 20-barrel plant. In addition to the standard beers, a range of seasonal brews and monthly specials are produced. Bowman also brew the Suthwyk Ales range of beers. ‼♦LIVE

Swift One (ABV 3.8%) BLOND
Easy-drinking blonde, well-balanced, sweet maltiness and clean fresh hoppiness, leading to bittersweet finish and slightly dry, hoppy aftertaste.
Meon Valley Bitter (ABV 3.9%) BITTER
Complex, well-balanced traditional, copper-coloured bitter; sweet with initial maltiness in taste and aroma leading to a lingering bitterness.
Wallops Wood (ABV 4%) BITTER
Malt dominates this light brown session bitter. Some dried fruit flavours balanced by toffee notes and sweetness in the finish.

Contract brewed for Suthwyk Ales:
Old Dick (ABV 3.8%) BITTER
Pleasant, clean-tasting pale brown bitter. Easy-drinking and well-balanced. Brewed using ingredients grown on Bowman's farm.
Liberation (ABV 4.2%) BITTER
Skew Sunshine Ale (ABV 4.6%) GOLD
An amber-coloured beer, brewed using homegrown ingredients. Initial hoppiness leads to a fruity taste and finish.
Palmerston's Folly (ABV 5%) SPECIALITY

Brew Forest (NEW)

Units B1-B2, Setters Farm Workshops, Mount Pleasant Lane, Lymington, SO41 8LS ⊕ thebrewforest.com

Opened in 2022 by brother and sister team, David and Helen. The Brew Forest is a nanobrewery and taproom located in the New Forest. ☙

Brewhouse & Kitchen SIBA

⬛ **26 Guildhall Walk, Portsmouth, PO1 2DD**
☎ **(023) 9289 1340** ⊕ brewhouseandkitchen.com/venue/portsmouth

⊗ Part of the Brewhouse & Kitchen chain, producing its own range of beers. Carry outs and brewery experience days are offered. ‼⬛♦

Brewhouse & Kitchen SIBA

⬛ **47 Highfield Lane, Southampton, SO17 1QD**
☎ **(023) 8055 5566** ⊕ brewhouseandkitchen.com

⊗ Part of the Brewhouse & Kitchen chain. Opened in 2015 it offers its own range of eclectic beers; producing four core beers and a regularly changing Project Cask beer. ‼⬛♦☙

Brewhouse & Kitchen SIBA

⬛ **51 Southsea Terrace, Southsea, Portsmouth, PO5 3AU**
☎ **(023) 9281 8979**

Part of the Brewhouse & Kitchen chain, producing its own range of beers. Carry outs and brewery experience days are offered.

CrackleRock

The Old Cooperage, High Street, Botley, SO30 2EA
☎ **07733 232806** ⊕ cracklerock.co.uk

⊗ Cracklerock began brewing in 2014 at the Old Cooperage in the centre of Botley. Its tap moved to larger premises near the brewery in 2018. ‼⬛♦

Crackerjack (ABV 3.8%) BITTER
Verified (ABV 4%) PALE
Fire Cracker (ABV 4.2%) BITTER
Gold Rush (ABV 4.5%) GOLD
Dark Destroyer (ABV 4.9%) PORTER
Crafty Shag (ABV 5%) BITTER
Crackatoa IPA (ABV 6.2%) IPA

Crop (NEW)

⬛ **Greenwich, 39 Osborne Road, Portsmouth, PO5 3LR**
☎ **07432 478582** ⊕ cropbeer.co.uk

Crop Beer was founded in 2021 by brewer Donncha Burke. Initially contract brewing at both Trinity, Lichfield, and Dark Revolution, Salisbury, it took on the lease of the brewery at the Greenwich in Southsea, Portsmouth, in 2022.

Dancing Man

⬛ **Wool House, Town Quay, Southampton, SO14 2AR**
☎ **(023) 8083 6666** ⊕ dancingmanbrewery.co.uk

⊗ Having opened in 2011 before moving to the historic Wool House in 2015, Dancing Man has recently undergone a large increase in brewing capacity. The outside seating area has also been expanded. ‼⬛♦LIVE

Drop The Anchor

9 East Close Farm, Lyndhurst Road, Hinton, Christchurch, BH23 7EF ☎ **07806 789946**
⊕ droptheanchorbrewery.co.uk

⊗ Neil Hodgkinson began brewing in 2017 using a 2.5-barrel plant situated in the loft area of the Christchurch Emporium. This has now relocated to Victorian farm buildings in Hinton in the New Forest. Beer is available in a number of local pubs, and a small bar and shop is situated in the brewery (open Fri-Sun). All beers are unfined. ⬛♦LIVE☙

Misty Mountain Hop (ABV 3.8%) GOLD
Silent Stones (ABV 4.7%) PALE
Tucktonia (ABV 4.7%) PALE
Black Dog Porter (ABV 4.9%) PORTER
The Admiral (ABV 5.2%) BROWN
Otakaro NZ Pale (ABV 5.5%) BLOND
40 Past Midnight (ABV 6%) SPECIALITY
Breaking Glass Hazelnut Latte Porter-Stout (ABV 6%) SPECIALITY
It's My Shadow (ABV 6%) SPECIALITY
The Phoenix IPA (ABV 6%) IPA

Fallen Acorn

Unit 7, Clarence Wharf, Mumby Road, Gosport, PO12 1AJ ⊕ **fallenacornbrewing.co**

Fallen Acorn is a 20-barrel microbrewery in Gosport. It produces high quality beer from traditional styles and brewing techniques, to pushing modern boundaries and combining a range of brewing experience with a passion for innovation. Its flagship beer is Hole Hearted. ⏲ ➤ ◆ LIVE ✦

Pompey Royal (ABV 4.3%) BITTER
Well-balanced malty traditional bitter. Initial strong caramel flavours, with hints of chocolate leads towards a sweet and slightly bitter finish.
Awaken (ABV 4.5%) PALE
Hole Hearted (ABV 4.7%) GOLD
A golden ale with strong citrus hop aroma. This continues to dominate the flavour, leading to a long, bittersweet finish.

Flack Manor SIBA

8 Romsey Industrial Estate, Greatbridge Road, Romsey, SO51 0HR
☎ **(01794) 518520**
⊕ **flack-manor-brewery.myshopify.com**

⊗ Flack Manor started brewing in 2010, and continues as the sole upholder of Romsey's long brewing tradition. It's one of the few remaining breweries in the British Isles using the double-drop method. Its 20-barrel capacity was recently increased by the addition of a one-barrel pilot plant. All barley used is Maris Otter, and most beers contain only British hops. Flack's beers are supplied to many outlets within 50 miles of Romsey, and may also be found in JD Wetherspoon outlets. ➤ ◆ LIVE ✦

Flack's Double Drop (ABV 3.7%) BITTER
A classic amber session bitter. Hops, malt and some bitterness in the taste, with more hop and some malt in the finish.
Romsey Gold (ABV 4%) GOLD
Flack Catcher (ABV 4.4%) BITTER
A well-balanced, amber best bitter with some fruit aroma and throughout with good hop bitterness in the balanced taste and finish.

Flower Pots SIBA

Brandy Mount, Cheriton, SO24 0QQ
☎ **(01962) 771735** ⊕ **theflowerpots.co.uk**

⊗ Flower Pots began production in 2006, now making it Hampshire's oldest independent brewery. The 10-barrel brewery, and neighbouring pub of the same name, are in a pretty Hampshire village. It brews six core beers, plus a monthly special. In 2019 the brewery and pub were taken over by three local partners, whilst the two sibling pubs (Wheatsheaf and Albion) were retained by the original owners. ◆

Perridge Pale (ABV 3.6%) GOLD
Very pale, easy-drinking golden ale. Honey-scented with high hops, grapefruit and bitterness throughout. Crisp with some citrus notes.
Pots Bitter (ABV 3.8%) BITTER
Refreshing, easy-going bitter. Dry, earthy hop flavours balanced by robust maltiness. Bitter throughout with hoppy aroma and dry, bitter finish.
Buster's Best (ABV 4.2%) BITTER
Cheriton Porter (ABV 4.2%) PORTER
Dry porter packed with blackcurrant flavours. Distinctive roastiness and malty throughout, combining with pleasing bitterness leading to a bittersweet finish.
Goodens Gold (ABV 4.8%) GOLD

Complex, full-bodied, golden-coloured ale, bursting with hops and citrus fruit and a snatch of sweetness, leading to long, dry finish.
IPA (ABV 6%) IPA
Rich and full-bodied IPA with uncompromising hoppiness and strong grapefruit character, a robust maltiness and rich fruity finish.

Gilbert White's

Gilbert White's House, High Street, Selborne, GU34 3JH
☎ **(01420) 511275** ⊕ **gilbertwhiteshouse.org.uk/the-brewhouse**

⊗ One-barrel nanobrewery staffed by volunteers which opened commercially in 2020. Attached to the Gilbert White Museum producing bottled, cask-conditioned and keg beer, it's situated in the original brewhouse dating from 1765. One brew utilises an original recipe. Bottled beer is sold through the museum shop. The beer is available at its one tied pub, Jubilee Tap Room, Selborne village, and is produced on demand for the free trade, and increasingly for festivals and other events. ➤

Garden Kalendar (ABV 4.2%) BITTER

Growling Gibbon SIBA

The Incuhive Space, Hursley Park Road, Hursley, SO21 2JN ⊕ **growlinggibbon.com**

Growling Gibbon Brewery was established by brewer Ralph McFadyen in 2022. Located in the former stables of Hursley House, mainly focussing on brewing pale ales and IPAs using a one-barrel brew plant. Currently supplying local outlets, beer is available in KeyKeg or can. Draught beer can be purchased in growlers direct from the brewery. ⏲ ➤

Irving SIBA

Unit G1, Railway Triangle, Walton Road, Portsmouth, PO6 1TQ
☎ **(023) 9238 9988** ☎ **07946 906234**
⊕ **irvingbrewers.co.uk**

⊗ Established in 2007 by former Gale's brewer Malcolm Irving using a 15-barrel plant. Around 120 outlets are supplied in Hampshire, Sussex and Surrey with beers available further afield through beer swaps with other breweries. Speciality beers may be ordered for festivals. Off-sales available Thursday/Friday. ⏲ ➤ ◆

Frigate (ABV 3.8%) PALE
Satisfying session bitter. Hoppy, with a floral aroma and initial sweetness, leading to bitterness and a smooth, slightly dry finish.
Type 42 (ABV 4.2%) BITTER
Traditional brown bitter. Burnt toffee aroma leads to hedgerow fruitiness complementing crystal malt. Resinous hops grow into surprisingly dry finish.
Admiral Stout (ABV 4.3%) STOUT
Well-balanced oatmeal stout, with plenty of fruit and roast, together with pleasant hint of coffee and short bitter finish.
Invincible (ABV 4.6%) BITTER
Tawny-coloured strong bitter. Sweet and fruity with underlying maltiness throughout and gradually increasing dryness, contrasting with the sweet finish.
Iron Duke (ABV 5.3%) PALE
Refreshing, well-balanced English IPA. Marmalade nose, with strong bitterness and a robust sweetness throughout, which softens the lemony sherbet finish.

Little London

Unit 6B Ash Park Business Centre, Ash Lane, Little London, RG26 5FL
☎ (01256) 533044 ☎ 07785 225468
⊕ littlelondonbrewery.com

⊗ Brewing began in 2015 using a six-barrel plant. Three fermentation vessels ensure a production capability of 60 firkins per week, with capacity for expansion.

Doreen's Dark (ABV 3.2%) MILD
Blacksmith's Gold (ABV 3.5%) GOLD
Red Boy (ABV 3.7%) BITTER
Hoppy Hilda (ABV 3.8%) GOLD
Luvly (ABV 3.9%) BITTER
Pryde (ABV 4.2%) BITTER
Ash Park Special (ABV 4.9%) BITTER

London Road Brew House

🏠 67-75 London Road, Southampton, SO15 2AB
☎ (023) 8098 9401 ☎ 07597 147321
⊕ londonroadbrewhouse.com

⊗ Brewing commenced in 2017 in the London Road Brew House using a six-barrel plant. Now owned by the Tap It Brewery, all beer brewed on site is keg.

Longdog

Unit A1, Moniton Trading Estate, West Ham Lane, Basingstoke, RG22 6NQ
☎ (01256) 324286 ☎ 07579 801982
⊕ longdogbrewery.co.uk

⊗ Established in 2011, the Longdog Brewery is named after a type of Lurcher used for hare coursing – once a popular pastime in the North Hampshire downs.
‼🍺◆LIVE◈

Skinny Dog (ABV 1.5%) BITTER
Refreshing low alcohol bitter. Predominantly malty, fruity aroma continues into the taste combined with some dry bitterness. A short finish.

Bunny Chaser (ABV 3.6%) BITTER
Malt dominates this amber-coloured session bitter throughout. Some hops come through with growing bitterness and a fading background sweetness.

Golden Poacher (ABV 3.9%) BLOND
Light, refreshing, blond with lemony nose and honied taste. Lingering malty sweetness and some hops and residual bitterness in finish.

Basingstoke Pride (ABV 4.2%) BITTER
Malty and rather sweet session bitter. Decent level of English hops in the taste combined with some subtle fruitiness.

Red Runner (ABV 4.2%) BITTER
Satisfying mahogany-coloured red ale, with solid malt backbone. Hedgerow fruits and hops, with peppery tones and lasting dry hop bitterness.

Lovely Nancy (ABV 4.8%) PALE
Full-bodied, golden straw-coloured pale ale. Hints of honey, lemon and pineapple, with malty sweetness that diminishes into increasingly bitter finish.

Lamplight Porter (ABV 5%) PORTER
Splendid porter, smoky and drier than many, with strong roast flavours giving way to blackberry taste and slightly vinous finish.

IPA (ABV 6%) IPA
Classic English IPA; rich and earthy with hops pushed hard. Lemony notes, hints of spice lead to a bittersweet finish.

Makemake

Unit 1.2, Central Point, Kirpal Road, Portsmouth, PO3 6FH
☎ (023) 9273 5939
⊕ makemakebeer.myshopify.com

Makemake Brewing has been producing modern craft beers since 2019. Originally based in the Greenwich Brewpub, Southsea, the brewery moved to Central Point in 2022. The new premises house a state-of-the-art brewery plus taproom. No real ale. ◈

Maverick (NEW)

Ganders Business Park, Forge Road, Kingsley, GU35 9LU ⊕ maverickbrewingco.com

This small batch craft brewery and taproom opened in 2023 in a farm building in the village of Kingsley. The beers, mainly heavily-hopped pale ales and IPAs, are unfined and unfiltered. ◈

Monkey

🏠 Monkey Brewhouse, 167 Southampton Road, Lymington, SO41 9HA
☎ (01590) 676754 ☎ 07835 270153
⊕ monkeybrewhouse.co.uk

A five-barrel brewery housed in an oak-framed extension to the pub, brewing a wide range of both cask and keg beers.

Newtown

25 Victoria Street, Gosport, PO12 4TX
☎ (023) 9250 4294 ⊕ newtownbrewery.co.uk

Newtown is one of the smallest UK breweries with just a half-barrel plant. Full mash beers are produced on demand for local pubs and beer festivals. The number of pubs supplied increased during 2022.

Pig Beer

Hop House, Setley Ridge, Brockenhurst, SO42 7UF
☎ (01590) 607237 ☎ 07747 462139 ⊕ pigbeer.com

Pig Beer is an 18-barrel brewery operated by two brothers and their cousin. Currently producing bottled beers only, but expected to produce KeyKeg beers for local outlets if there is a demand.

Powder Monkey SIBA IFBB

Priddy's, Heritage Way, Gosport, PO12 4FL
⊕ powdermonkeybrewing.com

Powder Monkey, situated in a former gunpowder magazine, started brewing in 2021. There is a visitors centre on the premises, and a nearby pub which serves as a taproom. During 2022 the brewery acquired an extra nearby building, and consequently extra brewing capacity. The emphasis is on keg and canned beer, but occasionally cask beer is produced for nearby pubs and beer festivals. ‼🍺◆◈

Queen Inn

🏠 28 Kingsgate Road, Winchester, SO23 9PG
☎ (01962) 853898 ⊕ thequeeninnwinchester.com

⊗ The three-barrel brewery replaced earlier kit and was installed in 2022. Currently brewing twice a week, it produces three or four beers mainly for the pub, but occasionally other local pubs are supplied. New experimental one-off brews use different German hop varieties.

Red Cat

Unit 10, Sun Valley Business Park, Winnall Close, Winchester, SO23 0LB
☎ (01962) 863423 ⊕ redcatbrewing.co.uk

Red Cat Brewing Company was established in 2014 using an 11-barrel plant. It supplies Hampshire and bordering counties. A small bar and shop in the brewery sells a range of products. Brewing is currently suspended. ▰

Ringwood

Christchurch Road, Ringwood, BH24 3AP
☎ (01425) 471177 ⊕ ringwoodbrewery.co.uk

⊗ Ringwood was bought in 2007 by Marston's. Production has been increased to 50,000 barrels a year. Some 750 outlets are supplied. Ringwood beers are now available in Marston's pubs all over the country. Part of Carlsberg Marston's Brewing Co. ‼▰◆

Razorback (ABV 3.8%) BITTER
Copper-coloured session bitter dominated by malt with some toffee and berry fruit character, leading to a short, bittersweet finish.
Boondoggle (ABV 4.2%) BITTER
Golden-coloured light, easy-drinking session bitter. Quite malty with some peach and apricot nose and sweet tropical fruit palate.
Fortyniner (ABV 4.9%) BITTER
Caramel, biscuity aroma, with hints of damson, lead to a sweet taste, balanced with some malt, fruit and hop flavours.
Old Thumper (ABV 5.1%) BITTER
Powerful, sweet, copper-coloured bitter. A fruity aroma preludes a sweet, malty taste with fruit and caramel and a bittersweet aftertaste.

Brewed under the Bombardier brand name:
Bombardier (ABV 4.1%) BITTER
A heavy aroma of malt and raspberry jam. Traces of hops and bitterness are quickly submerged under a smooth, malty sweetness. A solid, rich finish.

Brewed under the Eagle Brewery name:
IPA (ABV 3.6%) PALE

Sherfield Village SIBA

Goddards Farm, Goddards Lane, Sherfield on Loddon, RG27 0EL ☎ 07906 060429
⊕ sherfieldvillagebrewery.co.uk

Production started in 2011 in a converted barn on a working dairy farm. Using a five-barrel plant, the brewery supplies local pubs and regional festivals. Extensive use is made of New World hops, particularly those from New Zealand. All beers are unfined. ◆LIVE

Southern Gold (ABV 4%) GOLD
Green Bullet (ABV 4.3%) GOLD
A strong lemony nose, with hops dominating the taste building to a strong aftertaste with a big astringent hit at the end.
Single Hop (ABV 4.3%) GOLD
Pioneer Stout (ABV 5%) STOUT

Southsea

Southsea Castle, Clarence Esplanade, Southsea, Portsmouth, PO5 3PA ☎ 07939 063970
⊕ southseabrewing.co.uk

⊗ Launched in 2016, Southsea Brewing is located in an old ammunition storage room within the walls of a coastal defence fort built by Henry VIII in 1544. All beers are unfined, unfiltered and unpasteurised, and bottled onsite. ▰LIVE

Low Tide (ABV 3.8%) PALE
Casemate IPA (ABV 5.4%) PALE

Staggeringly Good SIBA

Unit 10, St Georges Industrial Estate, Rodney Road, Southsea, PO4 8SS
☎ (023) 9229 7033 ⊕ staggeringlygood.com

This Dino-centric brewery began production in 2014 and is now a 20-barrel facility producing 140K hectolitres/annum with a core circulation of three regularly-brewed beers and a bevy of cutting edge, boundary pushing ales with a strong focus on heavily-hopped IPAs and extreme sours. All beers are real ales and available in KeyKeg and cans. With an onsite shop and taproom hosting festivals, DJ sets, live music and more. ‼▰◆LIVE◢

Steam Town SIBA

▤ **Steam Town Brewhouse, 1 Bishopstoke Road, Eastleigh, SO50 6AD**
☎ (023) 8235 9130 ⊕ steamtownbrewco.co.uk

☺Steam Town is a six-barrel microbrewery with its own craft beer bar and restaurant, established in 2017. Many other local pubs, clubs and micropubs within a 10-mile radius also sell its ales, as well as beer festivals and outlets further afield by arrangement. Steam Town beers are available in many formats: cask, keg, mini-cask/keg, bottles and cans. ‼▰◆

Stoke Pale (ABV 3.8%) GOLD
Light golden ale with hops dominating but complemented by some light pineapple notes and sweetness, with a short, dry, bitter finish.
Barton (ABV 4%) BITTER
Traditional light brown bitter with some toffee notes leading to malty sweetness balanced by bitterness and a lingering dry finish.
NZ Pale (ABV 4.2%) PALE
Reefer (ABV 4.2%) PALE
Modern pale ale, with an aroma of citrus fruits and grapefruit flavours leading to a smooth but predominantly bitter finish.
Firebox (ABV 4.6%) RED
Complex American red with distinctive aroma of redcurrants and jelly, leading to full-bodied malty sweetness and a refreshing hop bite.
Bishop's APA (ABV 4.8%) PALE
Steam Stout (ABV 5%) STOUT
West Coast IPA (ABV 5.4%) PALE

Tap It

Unit 6, Muira Industrial Estate, William Street, Southampton, SO14 5QH ☎ 07484 649425
⊕ tapitbrew.co.uk

The first brew by enthusiastic homebrewer Rob Colmer was in 2018. Tap It is an eight-barrel plant producing eight regular beers mainly in KeyKeg and bottles. Occasional cask-conditioned beers are available. There is an onsite taproom, and a bar in Southampton is planned. ‼▰◢

Triple fff SIBA

Magpie Works, Station Approach, Four Marks, GU34 5HN
☎ (01420) 561422 ⊕ triplefff.com

⊗ Established in 1997 close to a stop on the Watercress Line Heritage Steam Railway, the brewery and all the beers (except Alton's Pride) are named following a musical theme. The fff refers to fortissimo, meaning louder or stronger. Brewing on a 50-barrel plant since 2006, multiple CAMRA awards have been won. Two pubs are owned: the Railway Arms, Alton, and the Artillery Arms, Southsea. ‼☞◆LIVE

Alton's Pride (ABV 3.8%) BITTER
Full-bodied, brown session bitter. Initial maltiness fades as citrus notes and hoppiness take over, leading to lasting hoppy bitter finish.

Pressed Rat & Warthog (ABV 3.8%) MILD
Toffee aroma, hints of blackcurrant and chocolate lead to well-balanced flavour with roast, fruit and malt vying with hoppy bitterness.

Moondance (ABV 4.2%) PALE
An aromatic citrus hop nose, balanced by bitterness and sweetness in the mouth. Bitterness increases in finish as fruit declines.

Goldfinger (ABV 5%) SPECIALITY

Urban Island SIBA

Unit 28 Limberline Industrial Estate, Limberline Spur, Portsmouth, PO3 5DZ
☎ (023) 9266 8726 ⊕ urbanislandbrewing.uk

⊠ Urban Island began production in 2015 and now has a capacity of 12 barrels. The range is distributed throughout Hampshire and neighbouring counties. In addition to cask it also has a range of beer available in cans and KeyKeg. Canned beers can be ordered online and delivered nationwide. ‼☞◆

Urban Pale (ABV 3.8%) GOLD
Unfined yellow ale. Aroma of orange, pink grapefruit and tangerine, leading to a robust hoppy taste and softer bittersweet finish.

Mosaic (ABV 4%) GOLD

Great use of Mosaic hops. Dry and hoppy with pronounced citrus, tropical fruit and grapefruit throughout. Lingering, bitter finish. Unfined.

Ground Swell (ABV 4.5%) GOLD

DSB – Dolly's Special Beer (ABV 4.6%) BITTER
A well-balanced, refreshing, golden-coloured bitter. Unfined, with hints of strawberry and some bitterness in the finish.

Frequency & Vibration (ABV 4.8%) GOLD

Vibrant Forest

The Purlieu Centre, Units 3-6, Hardley Industrial Estate, Hardley, SO45 3NQ
☎ (023) 8200 2200 ☎ 07921 753109
⊕ vibrantforest.co.uk

⊠ In 2019 Vibrant Forest Brewery relocated to a four-unit brewery at Hardley and increased in size to a 12-barrel plant, with its own canning machine, plus taproom. A mezzanine floor has been added, with its own bar and two extra toilets, increasing the capacity of the taproom, which can be hired for functions. ‼☞◆✦

Summerlands (ABV 3.5%) PALE

PUPA (ABV 4.5%) PALE

Farmhouse (ABV 5%) SPECIALITY

Single Hop Pale Ale (ABV 5%) PALE

Kick-Start (ABV 5.7%) SPECIALITY

Metropolis (ABV 6%) IPA
Intense resinous hoppiness dominate this Black IPA. Complex with chocolate notes and tropical fruits lead to a dry, hoppy finish.

Kaleidoscope (ABV 6.5%) IPA

Umbral Abyss (ABV 8.8%) SPECIALITY

Old House at Home, Havant (Photo: Geoff Marsh)

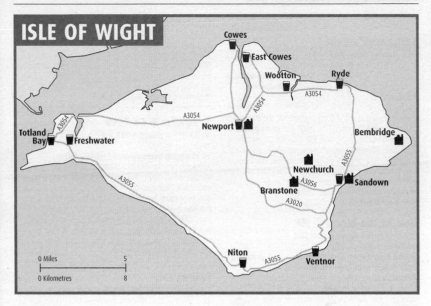

Cowes

Ale House
5A Shooters Hill, PO31 7BE
☎ (01983) 294027
4 changing beers (sourced nationally) Ⓖ
This cosy bar is conveniently situated in the main street of Cowes and is small, friendly and sometimes crowded. There is a choice of four real ales from stillage in a range that rotates regularly – expect to find the occasional mild or porter. A varying choice of cider is also on offer.
Q ☕ & ● ♣ (1) ❀ ⛁

Anchor Inn Ⓛ
1 High Street, PO31 7SA (opp Sainsbury's)
☎ (01983) 292823 ⊕ theanchorcowes.co.uk
Adnams Ghost Ship; Goddards Fuggle-Dee-Dum; 1 changing beer (sourced nationally) Ⓗ
Originally the Three Trumpeters back in 1704, this pub is close to the Marina, tempting visiting yachtsman for their first pint ashore. A conversion has integrated the stables and added a pleasant beer garden. A good selection of beer is on offer, with a local ale from Goddards and two others available. The varied menu is served in prodigious quantities. Live entertainment features regularly. Accommodation is in seven comfortable rooms.
☕ ❀ ⛵ ◑ ♣ (1) ❀ ⛁ ♪

Duke of York Ⓛ ✅
Mill Hill Road, PO31 7BT (towards floating bridge)
☎ (01983) 295171 ⊕ dukeofyorkcowes.co.uk
Timothy Taylor Landlord; 2 changing beers (sourced regionally; often Goddards, Yates') Ⓗ
Popular street-corner town pub with a reputation for interesting and appetising freshly prepared food. The charming interior features comfortable armchairs and memorabilia and signs celebrating Cowes and its association with yachting and the sea. There are more tables outside on the front terrace and a drinking area to the side. Well-priced accommodation is available for that cosy weekend away. Q ☕ ❀ ⛵ ◑ ▶ P ♣ (1) ❀ ⛁ ♪

Painters Arms ✅
51 Cross Street, PO31 7TA
☎ (01983) 300977 ⊕ thepaintersarms.co.uk

Timothy Taylor Landlord; 1 changing beer (sourced nationally) Ⓗ
This superb building dates from 1903. Join in with the friendly banter at the bar, dominated by sports TV, or find a table outside in the beer garde or in Francki Place, named after the Polish captain whose destroyer ORP Blyskawica defended Cowes during air raids in 1942. An earlier Painters Arms stood at the head of Temperance Terrace, a renowned Cowes alleyway community, now sadly a car park. ☕ ❀ P ♣ (1) ❀ ⛁ ♪

East Cowes

Ship & Castle Ⓛ
21 Castle Street, PO32 6RB
☎ (01983) 716230
3 changing beers (sourced regionally; often Adnams, Goddards, Island) Ⓗ
After several years this characterful town-centre drinking establishment returned to being a free house, with three well-kept real ales on offer – even in winter. It is not overly large and you are assured a warm welcome and reasonable prices. Frequent and lively music sessions are hosted. It is handy for the ferry terminal and near the floating bridge to Cowes. ☕ & ▲ ♣ ♣ (4,5) ❀ ♪

Freshwater

Red Lion Ⓛ
Church Place, PO40 9BP SZ346872
☎ (01983) 754925 ⊕ redlion-freshwater.co.uk
St Austell Proper Job; 3 changing beers (sourced nationally; often Butcombe, Renegade, Timothy Taylor) Ⓗ
Former three-bar coaching inn dating back to the 11th century, now converted to one large bar but still retaining much of its character. It is situated in the most picture-postcard area of Freshwater, in the church square by the Causeway, and enjoys views of the River Yar towards Yarmouth. The pub is noted for its fine food (diners are advised to book ahead). It may close early in winter. A guide for a walk to the Wheatsheaf in Yarmouth is available. Q ❀ ◑ ▶ P ♣ (7,12) ❀ ⛁

Newport

Bargeman's Rest 🗒
Little London Quay, PO30 5BS
☎ (01983) 525828 🌐 bargemansrest.com
Goddards Fuggle-Dee-Dum; Ringwood Razorback, Fortyniner; 3 changing beers (often Andwell, Marston's) ⓗ
This locally owned pub has previously been an animal feed store, and a sail and rigging loft for the barge fleet that once used the river. The huge bar room provides intimate drinking areas, and the nautical memorabilia, decor and ambience are what you would expect from a traditional, well-seasoned pub. The outdoor drinking area is only a few feet from the bustling River Medina. Beer and food are consistently good and the range varied. Live entertainment features most nights.
꩜🏠🌢🌀👶P🖤❀🎵

Man in the Moon 🗒 ✅
16-17, St James Street, PO30 5HB
☎ (01983) 530126
Greene King Abbot; Sharp's Doom Bar; 7 changing beers (often Goddards, Island) ⓗ
Opened in 2014, this impressive Wetherspoon conversion of the former Congregational Church maintains the character of the original while adding sympathetic extensions. The drinking/dining areas include an upstairs gallery and an outdoor area where dogs and children are welcome. Although a food-led pub, the beers are well kept, with a good selection of local brews featuring among the large rotating selection of ales. You may find the excellent Island Brewery RDA here and often a cider on handpump. ꩜🏠🌢🌀👶🖤🛜

Newport Ale House 🗒
24A Holyrood Street, PO30 5AZ
☎ 07708 018051
3 changing beers (sourced nationally) ⓖ
This listed building has previously traded as a hairdresser, undertakers and posting house and stables. It is the island's smallest pub, recalling the days when there were many such establishments in Newport. Hugely popular with all generations, it is a pub where conversation comes easy, and it can get very crowded and noisy. Live music is often hosted, including on a Sunday afternoon. The beer choice is always interesting and varied. No meals, but snacks are high quality. A former local CAMRA Pub of the Year. Q꩜🖤❀🛜🎵

Niton

No.7 🗒
High Street, PO38 2AZ
☎ (01983) 730280
Greene King Abbot; 2 changing beers (often Shepherd Neame, Yates') ⓗ
No.7 opened when the village inn closed for a short time, and has since become the hub of village life, also serving as a post office, newsagent, confectioner and tea room. Pizzas from the wood-fired oven are ever-popular. Darker beers and local specialities are regular visitors. A unique establishment with an excellent garden and patio. Closing time is dependent on custom.
Q꩜🌢🌀🖤(6)

Ryde

Castle Inn
164 High Street, PO33 2HT
☎ (01983) 613684 🌐 castleinnisleofwight.co.uk
Fuller's London Pride; Gale's HSB; 1 changing beer (often Fuller's) ⓗ

Thomas Vanner, who operated the Ryde to Newport stagecoach, opened this large public house in 1850. The fine building stands proud at the junction with the High Street, and owing to its impressive etched windows is Grade II listed, which may have saved it from demolition or conversion in the mid 1980s. It has enjoyed a long-standing reputation for its ales; HSB is a best seller.
꩜🌢≠(Esplanade) ♠🖤(9,4) ❀🛜

S. Fowler & Co 🗒 ✅
41-43 Union Street, PO33 2LF
☎ (01983) 812112
10 changing beers (sourced nationally) ⓗ
Although not the most charismatic pub in the Wetherspoon chain, this converted drapery store offers a constantly changing range of well-kept beers. Its name was suggested by the local CAMRA branch – not only is it the name of the former store, but also that of the first local CAMRA chairman and revered early campaigner. The family-friendly food area is upstairs. It is situated in the centre of town, with a bus stop conveniently outside.
Q꩜🌢👶≠(Esplanade) 🖤🛜

Solent Inn
7 Monkton Street, PO33 1JW
☎ (01983) 613761 🌐 solentinnryde.co.uk
Goddards Fuggle-Dee-Dum; St Austell Proper Job; 1 changing beer (sourced nationally) ⓗ
Excellent street-corner local with a warm, welcoming atmosphere. Parts of this handsome pub are ancient, going back to medieval times. It originally fronted the sea before the reclamation of land, hence the name. Meal times can change depending on the season. There is live music at the weekend.
Q꩜🌢🌀👶≠(Esplanade) ♠🖤❀🎵

Star Coffee & Ale House
40 High Street, PO33 2HT
☎ (01983) 722658 🌐 ryde.cafe
2 changing beers (sourced regionally) ⓗ
This handsome Victorian building dates back to 1873. Situated on the corner of Star Street and the High Street, it is a well-supported town pub with a friendly, welcoming atmosphere. After a complete refurbishment during lockdown it is now established, with new landlords and a bright outlook. There are always two beers on offer, and up to four available in the busy season. ꩜≠(St Johns Road)♠🖤❀🛜

Sandown

Boojum & Snark
105 High Street, PO36 8AF
☎ 07886 437688 🌐 boojumandsnark.co.uk
6 changing beers (often Boojum & Snark) Ⓚ
Opened during the pandemic, this brewpub and taproom is aimed at the real ale and craft beer enthusiast. Situated on the High Street in the centre of town, it serves an always changing range of their own beers from membrane kegs, with new brews always underway. A range of canned beer from neighbouring brewers is available. Regular cultural events are held and the walls function as an art gallery. 👶♠🖤🛜

REAL ALE BREWERIES
Boojum & Snark 🍺 Sandown (NEW)
Goddards 🍺 Branstone
Island Newport
Wight Knuckle 🍺 Bembridge
Yates' Newchurch

Castle Inn 🅛

12-14 Fitzroy Street, PO36 8HY (off High St)

☎ (01983) 403169

Gale's HSB; Goddards Fuggle-Dee-Dum; Banks's Hobgoblin Gold; 3 changing beers (sourced regionally; often Andwell, Hop Back, St Austell) 🅗

The Castle is an excellent town free house and locals' pub, and home to crib and darts teams. Six real ales are on offer including the best from local breweries. There is a children's room at the back and a patio for warm weather. The TV is only turned on for special events. Happy hour is popular, as is the Sunday quiz. Beer festivals are held twice a year, usually featuring local ales and cider. Q🕭🌣✿♣🛏🌼🤶🛜🎵

Culver Haven Inn 🅛

Culver Down, PO36 8QT (by the monument on Culver Down) SZ63258565

☎ (01983) 406107 ⊕ culverhaven.com

2 changing beers (sourced nationally; often Fuller's, Goddards, Ringwood) 🅗

Cosy restaurant and pub perched on Culver Down overlooking Sandown Bay and Bembridge Harbour. The view back down the hill is spectacular. Nearby is the Culver Battery, an impressive remnant of the Napoleonic Wars and built to protect Portsmouth (opened regularly by the National Trust). The pub has an excellent and varied menu. Closed during February. Q🕭🌣✿🤶🍴P🌼🤶🛜

Totland Bay

Highdown Inn ♥ 🅛

Highdown Lane, PO39 0HY (E of Alum Bay on Old Rd) SZ324858

☎ (01983) 752450 ⊕ highdowninn.com

5 changing beers (sourced regionally; often Banks's, Island, Ringwood) 🅗

Situated close by Faringford House, once home to Alfred Lord Tennyson, this hospitable pub is an ideal base for walkers and cyclists. A range of home-cooked food includes a seasonal variety of fresh local game, fish and vegetables and a children's menu. A large outside covered area is good for summer and winter. Unfortunately, no buses serve the pub in winter. B&B accommodation is in three comfortable rooms and there is a campsite close by. Q🕭🌣✿🍴Å P🛜

Waterfront 🅛

The Beach, PO39 0BQ

☎ (01983) 756969 ⊕ thewaterfront-iow.co.uk

Sharp's Doom Bar; 3 changing beers (sourced regionally; often Dorset, Island, St Austell) 🅗

Pleasant and popular pub/restaurant beside the sea, enjoying excellent Solent views to Portland and beyond. Beers are reasonably priced and the constantly changing range has increased in recent years, with a range of styles, including stouts and milds, and up to 12 waiting in the cellar. During the summer months there is a tented area outside, and the pub is accessible from the cliff path. Food includes a Sunday roast. Opening times are extended in the summer. Q🕭🌣✿🍴P🌼🤶🛜🎵

Ventnor

Spyglass Inn 🅛

The Esplanade, PO38 1JX

☎ (01983) 855338 ⊕ thespyglass.com

Ringwood Razorback, Fortyniner; 3 changing beers (sourced locally; often Andwell, Goddards, Yates') 🅗

A 19th-century ex-guesthouse at the western end of Ventnor Esplanade in a superb position overlooking the English Channel. The temptation has been avoided to knock all the rooms into one; instead, they have been incorporated into the overall layout. The inn has considerable character and boasts a large collection of seafaring memorabilia. Food is served and local seafood is a speciality. Entertainment features most evenings and Sunday lunchtime. Families are welcome. The beer range may reduce to four in winter. 🕭🌣✿🛏🍴P🌼🤶🛜🎵

Volunteer 🅛

30 Victoria Street, PO38 1ES

☎ (01983) 852537

5 changing beers (sourced regionally; often Goddards, Marston's, Yates') 🅗

Built in 1866, the Volunteer is a wonderful pub, one of the smallest on the island. This former winner of local CAMRA Pub of the Year has been tastefully refurbished. Up to five beers are available including a local brew. No fruit machines, no video games, no children – this is a pure adult drinking house and one of the few places where you can still play rings and enjoy a traditional games night. Closing time varies. Q♣🚃(3,6)🌼🎵

Wootton

Cedars

2 Station Road, PO33 4QU

☎ (01983) 882593 ⊕ cedarsisleofwight.co.uk

Fuller's London Pride; Gale's Seafarers Ale, HSB 🅗

This late Victorian 2-bar village local has a prominent position at the top of Wootton High Street. It is a large pub, though, curiously, it has one of the smallest front doors on the island. There is a children's room and a large garden with a play area. Smokers are spoilt as the outdoor smoking area is adapted from a beautiful Victorian outbuilding. The menu is extensive and the friendly bar staff ensure a good atmosphere. Close to the steam railway. Q🕭🌣✿🍴♣P🚃(4,9)🌼🛜

Breweries

Boojum & Snark (NEW)

🏭 **105 High Street, Sandown, PO36 8AF**

⊕ boojumandsnark.co.uk

Taking its name from the Lewis Carroll poem, this brewpub was set up in 2020 by life long friends, Julie and Tracy. Producing one-barrel per brew day, the beers are served via membrane keg with a small amount available in cans. **LIVE**

Goddards SIBA

Branstone Farm, Branstone, PO36 0LT

☎ (01983) 611011 ⊕ goddardsbrewery.com

⊗ Anthony Goddard established what is now the oldest active brewery on the Isle of Wight, in 1993. Originally occupying an 18th century barn, a new brewery was built in 2008, quadrupling its capacity. It has since been increased again following a move to Branstone Farm in 2023. Goddards' remain a locally-focused business distributing ales on the island, and easily-accessible southern English counties. Beers are also contract brewed for Crumbs Brewery, where breadcrumbs replace about a quarter of the malt usual in the brewing process. 🍴♦◆

Ale of Wight (ABV 3.7%) BITTER
Starboard (ABV 4%) GOLD
Wight Squirrel (ABV 4.3%) BITTER
Fuggle-Dee-Dum (ABV 4.8%) BITTER
Brown-coloured, strong ale with plenty of malt and hops.

Island SIBA

Dinglers Farm, Yarmouth Road, Newport, PO30 4LZ
☎ (01983) 821731 ⊕ islandbrewery.co.uk

⊠ Island Brewery is the realisation of Tom Minshull's ambition to brew real ales to complement the existing family-owned drinks distribution business. Brewing commenced in 2010 using a 12-barrel brewery. More than 100 outlets are supplied direct. ‼◆

Nipper Bitter (ABV 3.8%) GOLD
Wight Gold (ABV 4%) BITTER
Yachtsmans Ale (ABV 4.2%) BITTER
Wight Knight (ABV 4.5%) BITTER
Vectis Venom (ABV 4.8%) BITTER
Earls RDA (ABV 5%) STOUT

Wight Knuckle SIBA

🛏 **Pilot Boat Inn, Bembridge, PO35 5NN**
☎ (01983) 872077 ⊕ wightknucklebrewery.com

Wight Knuckle Brewery was founded in 2021 by two brothers and their father, and is based at the Pilot Boat, Bembridge. They wanted to bring modern, craft beers to the Isle of Wight so created the island's first microbrewery. It uses natural British ingredients and is brewed in a sustainable way. All beers are unfined, unfiltered, unpasteurised and vegan. The brewery also features a pizzeria. V

Yates' SIBA

Unit 4C, Langbridge Business Centre, Newchurch, PO36 0NP
☎ (01983) 867878 ⊕ yates-brewery.co.uk

Brewing started in 2000 on a five-barrel plant at the Inn at St Lawrence. In 2009 it moved to Newchurch and upgraded to 10-barrel plant. The brewery was moved on the same site in 2015 to sit alongside the wholesale unit at Newchurch. In 2022 the old kit was replaced with a newly-commissioned 15-barrel plant, including five fermenting vessels. ◆

Golden Bitter (ABV 4%) GOLD
Islander (ABV 4%) BITTER
Sea Dog (ABV 4%) GOLD
Beachcomber (ABV 4.3%) BLOND
Dark Side of the Wight (ABV 5%) SPECIALITY

Volunteer, Ventnor

Public transport information

Leave the car behind and travel to the pub by bus, train, tram or even ferry...

Using public transport is an excellent way to get to the pub, but many people use it irregularly, and systems can be slightly different from place to place. So, below are some useful websites and phone numbers where you can find all the information you might need.

Bus Services: The maximum fare in England will be held at £2.50 single until the end of 2024.

Combined travel information

The national **Traveline** system gives information on all rail and local bus services throughout England, Scotland and Wales. Calls are put through to a local call centre and if necessary your call will be switched through to a more relevant one. There are also services for mobiles, including a next-bus text service and smart-phone app. The website offers other services including timetables and a journey planner with mapping.

- 0871 200 22 33
  www.traveline.info

LONDON

In London use Traveline or **Transport for London (TfL)** travel services. TfL provides information and route planning for all of London's Underground and Overground, Docklands Light Railway, National Rail, buses, River Buses, Tramlink. Detailed ticketing information helps you find the most cost-effective ways to travel.

- 0343 222 1234
  www.tfl.gov.uk

Train travel

National Rail Enquiries covers the whole of Great Britain's rail network and provides service information, ticketing, online journey planning and other information.

- 03457 48 49 50
  www.nationalrail.co.uk

Coach travel

The two main UK coach companies are **National Express** and **Scottish Citylink**. Between them, they serve everywhere from Cornwall to the Highlands. Their websites offer timetables, journey planning, ticketing, route mapping, and other useful information. CAMRA members can benefit from 20% off travel with National Express*. See **camra.org.uk/benefits** for details.

- National Express: 08717 81 81 81
  www.nationalexpress.com

- Scottish Citylink: 0141 352 4444
  www.citylink.co.uk

Megabus

(A Stagecoach Company) operate various long-distance services between major cities and towns in England and Scotland, also Cardiff in Wales.

- 0900 160 0900 (Premium phone line).

Scottish ferries

Caledonian MacBrayne (CalMac) operate throughout Scotland's islands, stretching from Arran in the south to Lewis in the north.

- 0800 066 5000
  www.calmac.co.uk

Northern Ireland & islands

For travel outside mainland Britain but within the area of this Guide, information is available from the following companies:

NORTHERN IRELAND

- Translink: 028 9066 6630
  www.translink.co.uk

ISLE OF MAN

- Isle of Man Transport: 01624 662 525
  www.iombusandrail.im

ISLE OF WIGHT

- Southern Vectus Bus services covering all the Island: 0330 0539 182

JERSEY

- Liberty Bus: 01534 828 555
  www.libertybus.je

GUERNSEY

- Island Coachways: 01481 720 210
  www.buses.gg

Public transport symbols in the Guide

Pub entries in the Guide include helpful symbols to show if there are stations and/or bus routes close to a pub. There are symbols for railway stations (⇌); tram or light rail stations (Ⓡ); London Underground, Overground or DLR stations (⊖); and bus routes (🚌). See the 'Key to symbols' on the inside front cover for more details.

---

*Membership benefits are subject to change.

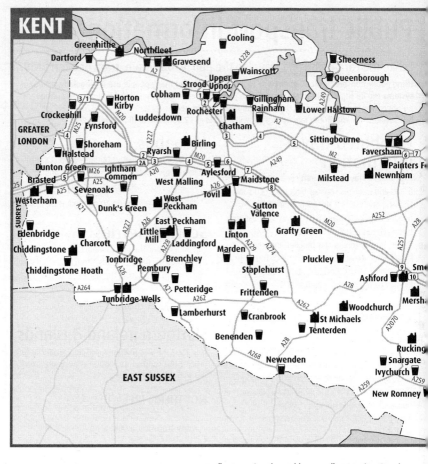

KENT

[Map of Kent showing locations including: Greenhithe, Dartford, Northfleet, Gravesend, Cooling, Wainscott, Sheerness, Queenborough, Horton Kirby, Cobham, Upper Upnor, Strood, Gillingham, Rainham, Lower Halstow, Crockenhill, Eynsford, Luddesdown, Rochester, Chatham, Sittingbourne, Faversham, Painters Fi, Shoreham, Birling, Ryarsh, Milstead, Newnham, Halstead, Dunton Green, Ightham Common, Aylesford, Maidstone, Brasted, West Malling, Tovil, Westerham, Sevenoaks, West Peckham, Sutton Valence, Edenbridge, Dunk's Green, East Peckham, Linton, Grafty Green, Chiddingstone, Charcott, Little Mill, Laddingford, Marden, Pluckley, Ashford, Sm, Chiddingstone Hoath, Tonbridge, Pembury, Brenchley, Staplehurst, Woodchurch, Mersh, Tunbridge Wells, Petteridge, Frittenden, St Michaels, Tenterden, Lamberhurst, Cranbrook, Benenden, Rucking, Newenden, Snargate, Ivychurch, New Romney. Labels: GREATER LONDON, SURREY, EAST SUSSEX]

Ashford

County Hotel ⊘

10 High Street, TN24 8TD (at lower end of High St)
☎ (01233) 646891
Greene King Abbot; Ruddles Best Bitter; Sharp's Doom Bar; 4 changing beers (sourced nationally) ⊞
This pub was built around 1710, as a doctor's home and medical practice, becoming a hotel in the 19th century and acquired by Wetherspoon in 1988. It now has a spacious bar with three separate seating areas and courtyard. Two real ciders are dispensed from polypins in the fridge. Food is available all day every day. Children are allowed in the dining area until 9pm. Summer and autumn national and international beer festivals are held. Q⏰♿◐🐕♿≉(International)●🚌🎵

Aylesford

Little Gem

19 High Street, ME20 7AX
☎ (01622) 715066
Goacher's Fine Light Ale ⒼD**, Gold Star Strong Ale** ⊞**; 2 changing beers (sourced locally; often Goacher's)** Ⓖ
One of the smallest pubs in Kent this Grade II-listed 12th-century building has now been restored by local brewer Goacher's following a 10-year period of closure. Beware the low doorway as you enter, as well as the step down. A large inglenook fireplace provides winter warmth. The

floor area is enhanced by a small mezzanine. Beer is supplied from a handpump or by gravity feed from cooled casks. Snacks, cider and other drinks are also available. Q⏰♿🐕♿🎵

Beltinge

Copper Pottle Ⓛ

84 Reculver Road, CT6 6ND
☎ 07710 001261 ⊕ copperpottle.co.uk
Ramsgate Gadds' No. 5 Best Bitter Ale; 3 changing beers (sourced regionally; often Kent, Mighty Oak, Tonbridge) Ⓖ
Originally a pet food shop, this friendly micropub, opened in 2015, has an attractive blue-tiled frontage. Drinks are dispensed from a temperature-controlled cellar via a small bar counter. An assortment of high and low narrow tables encourages conversation, and the walls are decorated with amusing posters and postcards. Every six weeks there is a charity fundraising event, which might be a quiz evening, food night or a barbecue. The south-facing garden is a good place to enjoy a beer, cider or wine. Open on bank holiday Mondays. Q⏰♿♣●🚌♿

Benenden

Bull

The Street, TN17 4DE
☎ (01580) 240054 ⊕ thebullatbenenden.co.uk

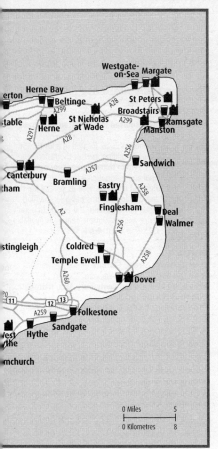

Brasted

Stanhope Arms L ✔

Church Road, TN16 1HZ
☎ (01959) 546829 ⊕ thestanhopearms.com
3 changing beers (sourced locally; often Bexley, Marston's, Westerham) Ⓗ
Situated next to the village church whose car park is available for customers, this family-run pub has been refurbished to a high standard. The open-plan bar contains a mixture of seating types and leads through to a separate restaurant. The large garden includes a patio and children's play area and the rural feel belies its position between the A25 and M25. Charrington's cider is sold alongside three to four, mostly local, real ales. Monthly jazz and blues jam sessions are held.
Q ⏰ ☕ 🕸 🍴 & ♣ 🚲 P 🚋 (1,401) ☻ 🛜

Brenchley

Halfway House L ✔

Horsmonden Road, TN12 7AX (½ mile SE of village)
☎ (01892) 722526 ⊕ halfwayhousebrenchley.co.uk
House beer (by Tonbridge); 5 changing beers (sourced locally; often Cellar Head, Goacher's, Only With Love) Ⓖ
The award-winning Halfway House is a much-loved, quirky and characterful family-run rural pub conveniently situated on a bus route serving Tunbridge Wells and Tenterden. The spacious gardens contain covered seating and a separate children's play area. Usually at least six local beers are served directly from the cask, of which two are house specials. Regular beer festivals are organised for bank holidays along with music nights. An extensive range of food is provided, with daily specials chalked on the blackboard. Q ⏰ ☕ 🕸 🍴 ♣ 🚲 P 🚋 (297) ☻ 🛜

Broadstairs

Magnet

37 Albion Street, CT10 1NE
☎ 07515 600527
3 changing beers (sourced regionally; often Canterbury Ales, Ramsgate, Shivering Sands) Ⓗ
Set back from the seafront, this alehouse features Kentish ales and ciders alongside others from further afield, including craft beer. A large beer bottle chandelier sets the scene. The beer and cider-loving owners are also passionate about live music and hold monthly jam sessions. Corner picture windows flood all areas with light and the wood stove creates winter warmth and cosiness. An eclectic range of tables and seating provide comfortable spaces for groups or couples.
🕸 ⇌ ♣ 🚆 🐾 ☻ 🎵

Royston 🏆

2 The Broadway, CT10 2AD
4 changing beers (often Kent, Pitchfork, Vocation) Ⓖ
An uber-stylish micropub and coffee shop near the station that opened in September 2021. A large double-glazed chill room displays 4 local and national ales including high-end brewers, and there is an extensive range of cider, canned craft beer, wine and spirits. The attention to detail is exemplary – providing a comfortable and relaxing ambiance. The toilet is boutique standard. Outside seating is available in good weather. Often open later than advertised if busy. Local CAMRA pub of the year 2023. 🕸 ⇌ ♣ 🚆 🐾 ☻

Harvey's Sussex Best Bitter; Larkins Traditional Ale; 1 changing beer (sourced locally; often Long Man) Ⓗ
Standing beside the large village green is this imposing 17th-century free house. The public bar is characterised by wooden floors, exposed oak beams and a large inglenook fireplace. A separate dining room serves locally grown produce, although meals may also be taken in the bar (no food Sun eve). Booking is advisable for the Friday fish & chips evening. An open mic night is held on alternate Tuesdays, and Sundays have late afternoon music sessions. Everything a village pub should be! Q ⏰ ☕ 🕸 🍴 ♣ 🚲 P 🚋 (297) ☻ 🛜 🎵

Bramling

Haywain L

Canterbury Road, CT3 1NB
☎ (01227) 720676 ⊕ thehaywainbramling.co.uk
Fuller's London Pride; Hopdaemon Incubus; 2 changing beers (sourced regionally; often Goacher's, Musket, Ramsgate) Ⓗ
Classic friendly country pub featuring hop bines, a cosy snug and a charity library where books are sold for 50p each. Traditional games include bat and trap. There is a Wednesday crib night. Guest beers are usually from Kent breweries, and an annual beer festival is hosted in May in a marquee in the attractive garden. Excellent home-cooked food is served, made using local produce. Booking for meals is essential. Closed on Mondays and Tuesdays. 🕸 🍴 ♣ 🚋 ☻ 🛜

Canterbury

Bell & Crown 𝕃
10-11 Palace Street, CT1 2DZ
☎ (01227) 784639
Long Man Best Bitter; 3 changing beers (sourced locally; often Canterbury Ales, Iron Pier, Tonbridge) Ⓗ
Traditional city-centre wood-panelled pub with an ever-changing range of local beers. The seating in front of the pub gives a superb view of Canterbury Cathedral, and is enjoyed by locals and visitors alike. The flint walls of the ancient King's School are opposite. Palace Street is part of the King's Mile and has many small independent shops. The classic jukebox means the pub is lively at weekends and the cosy atmosphere makes it a lunchtime favourite. ❀◐⇌(West)🚌🐾♫

Eight Bells
34 London Road, CT2 8LN
☎ (01227) 454794
Young's London Original, London Special Ⓗ
A small, traditional local dating from 1708 and rebuilt in 1902, retaining original embossed windows and outside toilets, and decorated with memorabilia. There is a quiz, usually on the first Wednesday of the month. Four darts teams play every week and their trophies are on display. The only food is a Sunday lunchtime roast, for which booking is advised. There is an attractive small walled garden and a comfortable heated smoking area.
❀◐⇌(West)♣🚌🐾📶♫

Foundry Brew Pub 𝕃
77 Stour Street, CT1 2NR (just off High St)
☎ (01227) 455899 🌐 thefoundrycanterbury.co.uk
Canterbury Brewers & Distillers Foundryman's Gold, Foundry Torpedo, Streetlight Porter Ⓗ
This brewpub is the home of Canterbury Brewers & Distillers. Double doors from the bar open into the attractive brewery and restaurant area, which is available for functions and brewery tours. Three ales are usually on tap, alongside a wide range of keg-conditioned beers, all brewed on the premises. The taster tray of five third-pints is popular. Vodka, rum and gin are also made here. Food is served every day. A former winner of Kent Tourism Pub of the Year. ❀◐◑♿⇌(East)🍎🚌📶

Monument
37 St Dunstan's Street, CT2 8BZ
☎ (01227) 451666 🌐 themonumentcanterbury.com
Dark Star Hophead; 2 changing beers (often Canterbury Ales, Cellar Head, Wantsum) Ⓗ
The pub was established in 1803 but the building is 400 years old. With St Dunstan's church just opposite, the street outside was the main route into Canterbury from London for over a millennium. The pub's name comes from a large wooden crucifix which once stood outside, a landmark for pilgrims to Canterbury. The pub has three bars, including a cosy snug. Piano music plays on Thursday evenings and Sunday lunchtimes, and there is a quiz every Monday. A tempting food menu is served.
❀◑⇌(West)🍎🚌📶♫

New Inn
19 Havelock Street, CT1 1NP (off ring rd near St Augustine's Abbey)
☎ (01227) 464584 🌐 newinncanterbury.co.uk
7 changing beers (often Oakham, Ramsgate, Thornbridge) Ⓗ
A Victorian back-street terraced pub a few minutes' walk from the cathedral, St Augustine's Abbey and the bus station. The welcoming main bar has a cosy wood-burner, a jukebox and a changing range of seven cask beers. The floor was hand-stencilled by the landlady. At the back is a long, bright conservatory with board games. Beer festivals are held on the Whitsun and August bank holiday weekends indoors and in the attractive garden. There is an Airbnb self-catering apartment upstairs. Local CAMRA Pub of the Year 2022. Q❀🛏♣🍎🚌🐾📶♫

Thomas Tallis Alehouse 𝕃
48 Northgate, CT1 1BE
🌐 thethomastallisalehouse.co.uk
3 changing beers (sourced locally; often Ramsgate, Tonbridge) Ⓖ
This ale house opened in 2016, located in a lovely 15th-century half-timbered building, part of the historic Hospital of St John. Two to four different Kent cask beers and many national and international beers are stocked – in KeyKeg, bottles and cans – as well as several Kentish ciders. One of the two front rooms has a log-burning stove, the rear snug has armchairs and a sofa. Generally a seat/table service applies. Outside seating is available on the street. Q❀⇌(West)♣🍎🚌🐾📶

Unicorn 𝕃 ✔
61 St Dunstan's Street, CT2 8BS
☎ (01227) 463187 🌐 unicorninn.com
3 changing beers (often Canterbury Ales, Ramsgate, St Austell) Ⓗ
A comfortable pub, near the historic Westgate, dating from 1604. It has an attractive suntrap garden. Bar billiards is played and a quiz is held every Sunday evening. Guest beers are often from one of several Kent

REAL ALE BREWERIES

Breakwater ✦ Dover
By The Mile Broadstairs (brewing suspended)
Canterbury Ales Chartham
Canterbury Brewers ▮ Canterbury
Curious Ashford
Docker West Hythe (NEW)
Farriers Arms ▮ Mersham
Fonthill ▮ Tunbridge Wells
Four Candles ▮ St Peters
Goacher's Tovil
Goody ✦ Herne
Hinks Ruckinge
Hop Fuzz West Hythe
Hopdaemon Newnham
Iron Pier ✦ Gravesend
Isla Vale Margate
Kent Birling
Larkins Chiddingstone
Mad Cat Faversham
McCanns ✦ St Michaels
Musket ✦ Linton
Nelson ✦ Chatham (brewing suspended)
No Frills Joe Greenhithe
Northdown ✦ Margate
Pig & Porter Tunbridge Wells
Ramsgate (Gadds') Broadstairs
Romney Marsh New Romney
Running Man Chatham
Shepherd Neame Faversham
Shivering Sands ✦ Manston
Stag Woodchurch
Swan on the Green ▮ West Peckham (brewing suspended)
Time & Tide ✦ Eastry
Tír Dhá Ghlas ▮ Dover
Tonbridge East Peckham
Wantsum ✦ St Nicholas at Wade
Westerham ✦ Westerham
Whitstable Grafty Green

microbreweries, and beer updates are posted on Facebook, Twitter and Instagram. Cider is from Kentish Pip, and there is a wide range of bottled beers. Food is good value, with a meal deal on selected days. Sporting events (not Sky) are televised unobtrusively.
ⓑ⊛◐⇌(West)♣●🛍🚲🎵

Charcott

Greyhound 🅻
off Camp Hill, TN11 8LG (½ mile N of B2027 at Chiddingstone Causeway)
☎ (01892) 870275 ⊕ thegreyhoundcharcott.co.uk
Larkins Traditional Ale; 3 changing beers (sourced locally; often Canterbury Ales, Fonthill, Titsey) 🅷
Situated in a pretty rural spot in a tiny hamlet and popular with walkers, the Greyhound is a welcoming, traditional pub serving four beers. Bright and airy, it is divided into several distinct drinking and dining areas with a large garden to the side and an alfresco covered space at the front. With a reputation for home-made dishes using their own farm meats and locally sourced produce, booking for Sunday lunch in particular is advised. Family and dog friendly.
ⓑ⊛◐⇌(Penshurst)●🚲(210)🌑🎵

Chiddingstone Hoath

Rock 🅻
Hoath Corner, Rywell Road, TN8 7BS (1½ miles S of Chiddingstone)
☎ (01892) 870296 ⊕ therockchiddingstone.com
Larkins Traditional Ale; 2 changing beers (sourced nationally; often Larkins, Otter, Ringwood) 🅷
Featuring brick flooring, an inviting inglenook fireplace, extensive wooden beams and the ancient game of ring the bull, the Rock oozes character. Despite its rural location, it attracts visitors in cars, on cycles, on foot and even on horseback. Cosy and informal, the desire is to remain a proper pub with proper grub, catering for a community dedicated to rural pursuits. The staple Larkins Traditional is brewed just a couple of miles down the road. Bring your dog – everyone else does!
Qⓑ⊛◐♣P🌑🛜

Cobham

Darnley Arms 🅻
40 The Street, DA12 3BZ
☎ (01474) 814218 ⊕ thedarnleyarms.com
Greene King IPA; Iron Pier Perry St. Pale, Bitter 🅷
This friendly local is situated in the centre of a charming small village. It features a large horseshoe-shaped bar with a separate small side room for meetings. The décor features local memorabilia including the coat of arms of the Darnley family who lived at nearby Cobham Hall. The wide menu offers traditional English food, with fish Fridays and a pie and a (locally brewed) pint offer every day. There is also a Thai night on Wednesday.
Qⓑ⊛🚐◐♣P🚲(416)🌑🛜

Coldred

Carpenters Arms 🅻
The Green, CT15 5AJ
☎ (01304) 830190
2 changing beers (sourced locally; often Kent, Ramsgate, Romney Marsh) 🅷/🅖

This 18th-century two-roomed inn overlooks the village green and duck pond. Its simple furniture and décor have remained largely unchanged for the last 50 years and it has been identified by CAMRA as having a nationally important historic pub interior. At least two real ales, including one from Kent, are served, alongside real ciders from a variety of cider makers. This community pub is the hub of the village and regular community events include vegetable competitions and a monthly book club. A beer festival is held in summer. Qⓑ⊛Å♣●P🌑🛜

Cooling

Horseshoe & Castle 🅻
Main Road, ME3 8DJ
☎ (01634) 221691 ⊕ horseshoeandcastle.com
Shepherd Neame Master Brew; 2 changing beers (sourced locally) 🅷
In the quiet village of Cooling, the pub is near the ruined castle once owned by Sir John Oldcastle, on whom Shakespeare's Falstaff was modelled. The graveyard was used to film Great Expectations and the area was know as Dickens' Country as he wrote many novels around this area. Quality accommodation is available as well as a separate restaurant, where seafood is a speciality. The choice of ales mainly come from Kent breweries. The owners have been here for 34 years.
Qⓑ⊛🚐◐♣●P🌑

Cranbrook

Larkins' Alehouse
7 High Street, TN17 3EB
☎ 07786 707476 ⊕ larkins-alehouse.co.uk
4 changing beers (sourced locally; often Cellar Head, Goacher's, Larkins) 🅖
A community-focused micropub in a former florist shop, putting the heart back into the town. It has a simply-furnished room, with servery at the rear. Beyond the cool room and toilet is the covered and heated courtyard garden. A chalkboard menu displays beers, ciders and other drinks. Homemade snacks and chutneys are available but customers are welcome to bring their own food or takeaways. Local CAMRA Pub of the Year and Cider Pub Of The Year 2019-2022.
Qⓑ⊛♣●🚲(5,297)🌑🛜

Crockenhill

Chequers ✅
Cray Road, BR8 8LP
☎ (01322) 662132 ⊕ chequerscrockenhill.co.uk
Courage Best Bitter; 3 changing beers (sourced regionally; often Fuller's, Westerham) 🅷
Friendly village local offering one permanent beer and three changing guest ales from a wide selection of breweries. Meals are served daily with seniors discounts at the beginning of the week. There is a quiz on Monday evenings and various other events on regular occasions. Several pictures of old Crockenhill indicate that the pub has been a hub of village life for many years. Opening hours are subject to demand so it may close earlier in the evening. ⓑ⊛◐♣P🚲(477)🌑🛜🎵

Dartford

Dartford Working Men's Club 🅻
Essex Road, DA1 2AU
☎ (01322) 223646 ⊕ dartfordwm.club

Courage Best Bitter; 7 changing beers (sourced nationally; often Adnams, Marble, Oakham) ⊞
A former CAMRA National Club of the Year, this CIU club serves eight real ales on handpump plus ciders on gravity. It hosts the BBC award-winning Dartford Folk Club every Tuesday night and has live music every Thursday and Saturday night and on the last Sunday afternoon of each month, with tribute acts on alternate Fridays. Quiz night is the first Wednesday of every month. CAMRA members are welcome as guests.
🚌🕮⚽◑≠♣🍴♿🕎🎵

Foresters

15/16 Great Queen Street, DA1 1TJ
☎ (01322) 223087
Adnams Ghost Ship; Harvey's Sussex Best Bitter; 1 changing beer (sourced nationally; often Exmoor, Robinsons, Timothy Taylor) ⊞
Traditional Victorian side-street local, just off East Hill, five minutes' walk from the town centre. Quiet at lunchtimes but often busy in the evenings with live sports on TV and darts, pool and crib teams. The U-shaped bar has a log-burning fire at one end. The graveyard opposite contains the unmarked pauper's grave of famed steam pioneer Richard Trevithick, its approximate location being indicated by a plaque on the north wall. 🚌⚽&≠♣P🕎♿

Long Dog 🗍

8 Market Street, DA1 1ET
☎ 07444 209938
5 changing beers (sourced nationally; often Iron Pier, Kent) Ⓖ
Dartford's first micropub, renamed following a change of management. The bar is decorated with a map and pictures of old Dartford. Seating includes modified beer casks. Five or six real ales are available, as well as Turners cider. Third-pint tasters are available in units of three, six or nine. There is live music on Saturday and a fortnightly quiz, with open mic nights planned for Thursdays. A free cheeseboard is offered from 2pm on Sundays. Customers accompanied by a dog receive a 10% discount. 🚌≠♣🕎🕎♿🎵

Malt Shovel ✅

3 Darenth Road, DA1 1LP
☎ (01322) 224381 🌐 maltshovelda1.co.uk
St Austell Tribute; Timothy Taylor Landlord; Young's London Original; 1 changing beer (sourced nationally; often Adnams, Fuller's) ⊞
Traditional country-style pub, dating from 1673, five minutes' walk from the town centre. It has two separate bars, a small tap room with a low ceiling, featuring an 1880s Dartford brewery mirror, and a larger saloon bar leading to a conservatory where lunchtime and evening meals are served Thursday to Saturday, and Sunday lunch. The large beer garden is accessed from the conservatory. There is a quiz on Monday evenings, crib on Tuesdays, and a monthly jazz night.
Q⚽◑≠♣🕎P🕎(B)🎵

Deal

Farrier 🗍 ✅

90 Manor Road, CT14 9DB
☎ (01304) 360080
Brains Rev James Original; 3 changing beers (sourced locally; often Canterbury Ales, Wantsum) ⊞
This family-owned, Grade II-listed traditional black-and-white beamed pub is one of the oldest pubs in Deal. With its community feel, and friendly welcome and atmosphere it is a relaxing place for a drink and a chat.

There is plenty of seating and three open fires. A variety of ales are on offer, mostly from Kent breweries. At the back is a pool/darts room with disabled toilets, and a large covered and heated patio. Monthly quiz nights and a Sunday meat raffle are held. 🚌⚽&🅰🕎🕎(81)♿🛜

Just Reproach 🗍

14 King Street, CT14 6HX
4 changing beers (sourced nationally; often Kent) Ⓖ
A welcoming micropub located in Deal town centre. Its high benches and table service make for a friendly, convivial atmosphere. It's back to basics, with no keg beer, fruit machines or music. Make sure your mobile phone is switched off! Up to five real ales, regularly featuring Kent breweries, are gravity-dispensed from the cool room. Ciders typically feature one from Kent. There's a wide selection of craft beers, alongside wines, gins and soft drinks. Events include cheese Sunday and quiz nights. Q🚌⚽≠♣🕎🕎♿

Ship Inn 🗍

141 Middle Street, CT14 6JZ
☎ (01304) 372222
Ramsgate Gadds' Hoppy Pale, Gadds' No. 7 Bitter Ale, Gadds' No. 5 Best Bitter Ale; Timothy Taylor Landlord; 1 changing beer (often Young's) ⊞
Located in Deal's historic conservation area, this unspoilt, traditional inn is a short walk from the town centre. Dark wooden floors and subdued lighting create a warm and comfortable atmosphere, complemented by the nautical decor. The wood-burning stove is welcome in winter. A wide variety of drinkers enjoy a good selection of beers dispensed from five handpumps, including beers from Ramsgate and Timothy Taylor. The small cosy rear bar overlooks a large patio garden, accessed by a staircase, with a covered smoking area. 🚌♣♣♿

Smugglers Record Shop 🗍

9 King Street, CT14 6HX
☎ 07850 474296 🌐 shop.smugglersrecords.com
5 changing beers (sourced nationally; often Bristol Beer Factory, Oakham, Time & Tide)
Independent and vibrant vinyl record shop and bar, situated just off Deal's seafront. A large selection of vinyl is for sale, and the background music is an eclectic mix featuring local bands, world, folk, psych and roots. Two cask ales are served on gravity, with a third on busier weekends. These usually feature ales from a local brewery, for example Time & Tide. Real cider is from Kentish Pip, and there's a great selection of craft beer, canned and bottled beers, cider and wines.
🚌⚽≠🕎🕎♿🛜🎵

Dover

Breakwater Brewery Taproom 🗍

St Martin's Yard, Lorne Road, CT16 2AA
☎ 07866 198075
Breakwater Dover Pale Ale, Blue Ensign, Cowjuice Milk Stout; 6 changing beers (sourced locally; often Breakwater) Ⓖ
The brewery tap is on the former site of the Harding's Wellington brewery, which closed in 1890. The bar is modern, well-lit and furnished with chunky wooden furniture, colourful table runners and a bar counter resembling a stone breakwater. There's a large patio at the front and a smaller one which overlooks the river. Cask ales from the brewery are served on gravity along with the pub's own house ciders. Stone-baked pizzas are available from the in-house pizzeria. Regular live music events are held. 🚌⚽◑&🕎🕎♿🎵

Eight Bells [L] ✔
19 Cannon Street, CT16 1BZ
☎ (01304) 205030
Greene King Abbot; Ruddles Best Bitter; Sharp's Doom Bar; 7 changing beers (often Wantsum) [H]
Popular and bustling Wetherspoon pub on the shopping precinct, opposite the historic St Mary's Church. Inside, there's one large room with a long bar, sofas and a raised restaurant area. At the front, an enclosed seating area looks out on to the precinct. Twelve handpumps dispense a range of regular and guest ales, usually with at least one beer from a Kent microbrewery. Two beer festivals are held each year and there are real ale offers on Monday. Handy for buses and trains.
Q🐴✿◐◑♿🚆(Priory)🚌📶

Hoptimist Taproom & Bar [L]
3 Bench Street, CT16 1JH
☎ 07515 367802 🌐 thehoptimisttaproomandbar.co.uk
6 changing beers (sourced locally; often Kent, Pig & Porter, Time & Tide)
Anyone looking for a comfortable environment for a pint of cask ale or real cider should try this modern taproom, near Dover's Market Square. There's a good selection of beer styles from Kent breweries with occasional guests from further afield. Real cider is from Biddenden and Kent Cider. There's also modern craft beer, premium keg beers and an ever-changing gin menu. On Sunday, a courtesy cheeseboard is provided. There's a selection of board games and occasional music and food events are held. 🐴✿🚆(Priory)♣🍎🚌(62,68)🐾♫

Louis Armstrong [L]
58 Maison Dieu Road, CT16 1RA
☎ (01304) 204759
4 changing beers (sourced locally; often Ramsgate, Romney Marsh, Canterbury Ales) [H]
This renowned music venue has held live events for over 50 years, including rock, folk, jazz and comedy. The large L-shaped bar and stage is surrounded by music posters, a large mirror and long bench seating. A good range of ales are sold, principally from Kent microbreweries, with an occasional cider from Kent. On Wednesday evenings good-value food is served. Fortnighty charity quizzes are held. To the rear there is a pleasant beer garden. It opens at 5.30pm on Sunday, if jazz is playing. ✿◑♣🍎🚌🐾📶♫

White Horse [L] ✔
St. James Street, CT16 1QF
☎ (01304) 213066 🌐 thewhitehorsedover.co.uk
Harvey's Sussex Best Bitter; Timothy Taylor Landlord; 1 changing beer (sourced locally; often Old Dairy, Wantsum) [H]
Possibly the oldest pub in Dover, its history can be traced back to 1574. The mix of simple but comfortable furniture, walls adorned with cross-channel swimmers' signatures and eclectic décor make for a pleasant and interesting pub to drink and eat in. Locals and tourists enjoy up to three real ales, from local and national breweries and real cider from Dudda's Tun. Home-cooked food is available and there's a bring your own food event on Wednesday. At the back, there's a terrace garden. 🐴✿◐◑🍎🐾

Dunk's Green

Kentish Rifleman [L]
Roughway Lane, TN11 9RU (jct with Dunk's Green Rd, 4 miles N of Tonbridge, off A227)
☎ (01732) 810727 🌐 thekentishrifleman.co.uk
Harvey's Sussex Best Bitter; 3 changing beers (sourced locally; often Greene King, Pig & Porter, Tonbridge) [H]
A characterful and welcoming 16th-century country pub serving mainly local real ales and Kentish Biddenden cider. Plenty of public footpaths around afford pleasant country walks and a bus running between Tonbridge and Borough Green stops outside the pub. Food features prominently (not served Sun or Mon eves) along with Tuesday pie and a pint nights and a monthly moules night. A small entrance bar area provides for drinkers, with outdoor seating to the front and a peaceful garden to the rear. Q🐴✿◐◑🍎P🚌(222)🐾📶

Dunton Green

Miners Arms [L] ✔
22 London Road, TN13 2UF
☎ (01732) 462214
3 changing beers (sourced locally; often Kent, Timothy Taylor, Tonbridge) [H]
Formerly built to cater for railway construction workers, the pub now serves as a valuable community asset serving up to three rotating, mostly Kentish, beers. The bar area has a log fire and leads through to a covered and heated terrace with sofas before opening out onto a large garden incorporating communal huts, seating and a children's section. A quiz night is held on alternate Tuesdays and live music or DJs often make the Miners a lively place to be at weekends. 🐴✿◐🚆♣🚌(1,8)🐾📶♫

Dymchurch

Hidden Treasure [L]
30 High Street, TN29 0NU
☎ (01303) 874049
2 changing beers (sourced locally) [H]
This is a friendly family-run micropub in the heart of Dymchurch, close to the historic Martello Tower, which is open to the public by appointment, and to the beach. Real ales, usually one from a Kentish brewer, are served through three handpumps with some extra beers occasionally dispensed from the fridge cabinet. Ciders on gravity are also dispensed from the fridge cabinet. There are several drinking areas, with a corridor connecting them to the bar area. Q🐴✿⛺🚆🍎🚌(102)🐾📶

Eastry

Five Bells ✔
The Cross, CT13 0HX
☎ (01304) 611188 🌐 thefivebellseastry.com
2 changing beers (sourced nationally; often Fuller's, Harvey's, Timothy Taylor) [H]
In the heart of the village, this local CAMRA Community Pub of the Year, provides a traditional and welcoming atmosphere, with its comfortable lounge bar and dining room. Two or three ales are served, with occasional Kentish ales. The old fire station, with historic memorabilia, serves as a sports/function room. Home-made food is served all day. The busy calendar features food events, live music, quiz nights and an Easter beer festival. The suntrap garden has a children's play area and pétanque pitch. 🐴✿🛏◐◑⛺♣P🚌(81)🐾📶♫

Edenbridge

Secret Cask ⓛ
91 High Street, TN8 5AU (at S end of High St near bridge)
☎ 07595 262247
4 changing beers (sourced locally; often Gun, Pig & Porter, Three Legs) ⓖ
Located close to the bridge over the river Eden, this shop conversion comprises two small, simply-furnished rooms and a counter behind which beers are served direct from the cask. The choice of four ales, selected from Kent and Sussex breweries, are displayed on a chalkboard alongside craft keg offerings and a range of real ciders from Biddenden. A no-frills, dog-friendly micropub where the focus is on jovial conversation or the playing of board games over an interesting choice of drinks.
Q⇌(Town) ♣●🖵🌼🎜

Eynsford

Five Bells
High Street, DA4 0AB
☎ (01322) 863135
Harvey's Sussex Best Bitter; 2 changing beers (sourced nationally; often Fuller's) Ⓗ
Traditional community pub in the heart of an attractive village. The public bar retains a homely atmosphere with wooden tables and a wood-burning fire in winter. It also has a comfortable separate saloon bar with a dartboard. There is a pleasant garden to the rear and a small car park. Dogs are welcome in the public bar. Food is not served here, so diners may wish to try its larger sister pub, the Malt Shovel, nearby. 🐾❀♣●🖵(421)🌼🎜

Faversham

Bear Inn
3 Market Place, ME13 7AG
☎ (01795) 532668 ● bearinnfaversham.co.uk
Shepherd Neame Master Brew; 1 changing beer (sourced locally; often Shepherd Neame) Ⓗ
16th-century pub located in Faversham's historic market square, popular with visitors and locals alike. The impressive historic pub interior with wood panelling has been identified by CAMRA as regionally important. There are three separate bar areas off the corridor which runs the length of the building. A general knowledge quiz is held on the last Monday of the month. A good place to try Shepherd Neame beers, they often serve a seasonal or guest beer. A couple of tables out the front of the pub are popular in summer. Q◖⇌♣🖵🎜

Elephant 🍷 ⓛ
31 The Mall, ME13 8JN
☎ (01795) 590157
5 changing beers (sourced regionally; often Canterbury Ales, Mighty Oak, Rother Valley) Ⓗ
Two-roomed traditional free house with separate function room out the back, there is much nautical memorabilia on the walls. The landlord takes pride in serving good real ale, occasionally including a beer matured in the cellar, and the pub has won CAMRA awards over many years. It plays host to local clubs and regular live music. A well-tended and attractive walled garden at the back, and a log fire within makes it a good pub to visit any time of the year. Local CAMRA Pub of the Year 2023. 🐾❀⇌♣●🖵🌼🎜

Furlongs Ale House
6A Preston Street, ME13 8NS
☎ 07747 776200
5 changing beers (sourced locally; often Canterbury Ales, Kent, Ramsgate) Ⓗ
An often busy micropub, with a heated and covered outside seating area at the rear. Beers are drawn by handpump from the cellar to the small bar, with many sourced from Kent microbreweries or from across the UK. The emphasis is on the hop. There is wooden bench-style seating and solid tables inside, and the bar is air-conditioned when required. Kentish gins, a selection of wines and ciders are also served. Snacks consist of various smoked nuts. Q🐾❀⇌●🖵🌼

Shipwrights Arms ⓛ
Hollowshore, ME13 7TU (over 1 mile N of Faversham at the confluence of Faversham and Oare creeks) TR017636
☎ (01795) 590088 ● theshipwrightsathollowshore.co.uk
Harvey's Sussex Best Bitter; Kent Prohibition; house beer (by Goacher's); 5 changing beers (sourced locally; often Goacher's, Kent) ⓖ
This 300-year-old free house by the sea wall has been run by the same family for 25 years. It is well worth the 45-minute walk from Faversham, or the slightly longer but picturesque sea wall path walk. A wooden-clad building with cosy interior reflecting its nautical heritage, with associated ornaments and pictures on display. There are comfortable seating options around the fireplaces. A large garden at the rear is open from spring to autumn, with outside seating at front in all seasons. Opening hours are extended in summer. In severe winter weather telephone to check opening times. Q🐾❀◖♣P🌼

Sun Inn
10 West Street, ME13 7JE
☎ (01795) 535098 ● sunfaversham.co.uk
Shepherd Neame Master Brew, Spitfire; 1 changing beer (often Shepherd Neame) Ⓗ
The 14th-century Sun Inn, in Faversham's conservation area, is brimming with intriguing original features, including inglenook fireplaces, oak beams and a lovely courtyard garden. Popular with diners in Faversham, food is available at breakfast, lunchtimes and evenings (no food Sun eve). Eight comfortable and characterful bedrooms provide stylish accommodation. The early opening times do not allow the sale of alcohol.
❀🛏◖⇌🖵

Finglesham

Crown Inn ⓛ
The Street, CT14 0NA
☎ (01304) 612555 ● crowninnatfinglesham.co.uk
House beer (by Dark Star); 2 changing beers (often Canterbury Ales, Romney Marsh) Ⓗ
You'll find a warm welcome and a friendly atmosphere at this traditional village pub. Three real ales are served, one usually from a Kent brewery. Home-made food is available breakfast, lunchtimes and evenings, including a Sunday roast. The restaurant opens onto the garden, with children's play area. A variety of events are held throughout the year with bat & trap played in summer. B&B accommodation is available in the modern lodges. The magnificent Kentish barn is available for functions and weddings. 🐾❀🛏◖♣P🖵(81)🌼🎜🎵

Folkestone

Bouverie Tap ⓛ
45 Bouverie Road West, CT20 2SZ

☎ (01303) 255977 🌐 thebouverietap.co.uk
3 changing beers (sourced locally) Ⓗ
This alehouse was extended into the adjacent shop and courtyard in 2020 and is decorated with interesting old posters. The pub offers three changing local ales and cider. Food is prepared from locally sourced ingredients and wholesome roasts are available on Sundays. Breakfasts are available on Saturday and Sunday from 8.30 and alcohol served from 9am for those who like the 'hair of the dog' with their breakfast! Dogs are welcome and well-behaved children up to 7pm.
🌜🏵🌑🕭≷(Central) ⬤🖵🐾🎝

East Cliff Tavern

13-15 East Cliff, CT19 6BU
☎ (01303) 251132
1 changing beer (sourced locally) Ⓗ
Friendly terraced back-street local, a pub since 1862, run by the same family for over 50 years. It can be approached via the footpath across the disused railway line, a short walk from the harbour. Usually offering two beers often from local breweries, with Biddenden or Kingswood cider on gravity behind the bar. Old photographs of Folkestone decorate the walls and community events include weekly raffles. Opening hours may vary, check if making a special visit.
Q🏵♣⬤🖵(91,102) 🐾🎝

Firkin Alehouse

21 Cheriton Place, CT20 2AY
☎ 07894 068432 🌐 firkinalehouse.co.uk
4 changing beers (sourced regionally) Ⓖ
This welcoming micropub offers up to four cask beers, usually one from a Kent microbrewery, and up to six ciders served by gravity from a temperature-controlled room. The display fridge offers a selection of bottled and canned foreign and British beers with a limited wine selection. Bar snacks include pickled eggs, pickled onions, and other basic fare. No music or pub games, but good company and conversation make the Firkin Alehouse a place to enjoy a good drink and relax.
Q🕭≷(Central) ⬤🖵🐾

Kipps' Alehouse

11-15 Old High Street, CT20 1RL
☎ (01303) 246766 🌐 kippsalehouse.co.uk
3 changing beers (sourced regionally; often Mad Cat) Ⓖ
This alehouse follows the general principles of the micropub movement and serves real ales directly from the cask, which usually include a Kentish ale, an award-winner and another unusual beer from around the country, all sourced from small independent microbreweries. Several ciders are on sale from boxes, and there are a variety of bottled craft beers and draught international lagers. Music is played on some Sunday afternoons. 🌜🏵🌑🕭♣⬤🖵🐾≷🎝

Frittenden

Bell & Jorrocks ✓

Biddenden Road, TN17 2EJ TQ815412
☎ (01580) 852415 🌐 thebellandjorrocks.co.uk
Goacher's Fine Light Ale; Harvey's Sussex Best Bitter; 1 changing beer (sourced nationally; often Goacher's) Ⓗ
A charming village pub that is the social centre of the local community. Previously called the Bell, it gained its current name when the pub opposite, the John Jorrocks, closed in 1969. Originally a coaching inn dating from the early 18th century, its stables house a beer festival in mid April with around 25 beers. It is a good base for

walking in the picturesque Low Weald countryside that surrounds the village. Excellent food is served and a pizza van calls on Sunday evenings. 🌜🏵🌑🕭▲♣🐾≷🎝

Gillingham

Frog & Toad

38 Burnt Oak Terrace, ME7 1DR
☎ (01634) 577030
3 changing beers (sourced nationally; often Wantsum) Ⓗ
This traditional back-street local is just 10 minutes' walk from the town centre. A three-times local pub of the year, there are up to three changing ales on handpump. There is a TV for sports events and occasional entertainment is hosted at weekends. The large patio garden at the rear has covered wooden tables and seating, along with an outdoor bar and stillage for when the pub runs beer festivals.
🌜🏵≷♣🖵🖵(176,177) 🐾≷🎝

Past & Present Ⓛ

15 Canterbury Street, ME7 5TP
☎ 07725 072293
4 changing beers (sourced nationally) Ⓖ
Multiple winner of local CAMRA Pub of the Year and Cider Pub of the Year, this two-level pub, with different styles of seating, is popular with all ages. Four changing ales and up to 12 ciders are served from a chiller room to your table. Filled rolls and bar snacks are available. A TV screen showing sports events and a dartboard, popular with regulars, are on the lower level. There is plenty of community spirit here, with regular events held.
Q🌜≷♣⬤🖵🖵(116,176) 🐾

Will Adams

73 Saxton Street, ME7 5EG (on corner with Lock St)
☎ (01634) 575902
3 changing beers (sourced nationally; often Adnams, Oakham) Ⓗ
Inside this pub you will find murals of the life and times of Will Adams who was the first English man to visit Japan. The pub offers up to three ales mostly from Oakham and Adnams and five ciders in boxes on the bar. Food is only available when Gillingham FC is playing at home. It does not open on Monday and Tuesday unless Gillingham FC is at home, when it will open at 5pm. It closes between 3 and 4.45 on match days.
🏵🌑≷♣🖵🐾≷

Gravesend

Compass Alehouse Ⓛ

7 Manor Road, DA12 1AA
☎ 07951 550949 🌐 thecompassalehouse.co.uk
4 changing beers (sourced nationally) Ⓖ
Micropub with a small front room with high bench seats and a smaller snug off a little courtyard to the rear. Four ever-changing real ales and three ciders are available, often from Kent producers. Convivial atmosphere and conversation is paramount but talking on mobile phones is discouraged and incurs a fine for charity. A water bowl is provided for dogs. Regular events include games nights on Tuesdays and two beer festivals. Local branch Pub of the Year 2022. Q🌜🏵🕭≷♣⬤🖵🐾

Jolly Drayman

1 Love Lane, Wellington Street, DA12 1JA (off Milton Road, E of town centre)
☎ (01474) 352355 🌐 jollydrayman.co.uk

Dark Star Hophead; Fuller's London Pride; St Austell Proper Job; 1 changing beer (sourced nationally; often Iron Pier) [H]
This cosy pub on the eastern edge of the town, also known as the Coke Oven, is part of the former Walker's brewery. It features quirky low ceilings and a relaxed atmosphere and has been extended to provide a more spacious bar and some extra seating. Daddlums (Kentish skittles) is played most Sunday evenings and men's and ladies darts teams are hosted. There is regular live music, quizzes and monthly open mic sessions. Food is limited to hot snacks at present. 🐎❀🛏♿🚆♣P🚌🐾📶♫

Three Daws 🏆 [L]
Town Pier, DA11 0BJ
☎ (01474) 566869 🌐 threedaws.co.uk
5 changing beers (sourced nationally; often Cellar Head, Iron Pier, Tonbridge) [H]
Historic riverside inn, offering views of the Thames and passing river traffic and boasting stories of ghosts, press gangs, smugglers, secret tunnels and more. The bar is upstairs, with a large function room below. Inside is divided into small rooms with photos and pictures of local or marine interest and very few right angles. Meals made using local ingredients are served until 9pm every day. Live music is played on Fridays, quizzes on Sundays and beer festivals are held in August and October.
🐎❀◐🚆♣🚌📶♫

Three Pillars [L]
25 Wrotham Road, DA11 0PA (on A227 opp Civic Centre)
☎ 07794 348529 🌐 threepillarsgravesend.co.uk
Changing beers (sourced nationally; often Cellar Head, Kent, Mighty Oak) [G]
Small cellar bar underneath the Masonic Hall, reached by steep steps to the right of the hall. Two carpeted front rooms lead to the brick-floored bar area. The ceilings are low throughout and there are photos of Gravesend pubs past and present. There is a quiz on the third Thursday of each month and live music on some Sundays. Six or more real ales and about 10 ciders are available. Patrons must not use the Masonic Hall car park. 🐎🚆🍎🚌🐾♫

Halstead

Rose & Crown [L]
Otford Lane, TN14 7EA
☎ (01959) 533120
Larkins Traditional Ale; Tonbridge Traditional Ale; 4 changing beers (sourced regionally; often Cellar Head, Fuller's, Titsey) [H]
Located close to the North Downs Way in good walking and cycling country this attractive Grade II-listed flint-built pub can be reached using a regular bus service from Orpington. Customers may choose from a sports-oriented public bar, cosy lounge or annex with tea room and restaurant. Popular home-cooked food includes an over 60s special offer on Tuesday and Wednesday lunchtimes. The garden incorporates a children's play area, patio and barbecue and a bar in summer when bat and trap is played. 🐎❀◐♿♣P🚌(R5,R10)🐾📶

Hastingleigh

Bowl Inn [L]
The Street, TN25 5HU TR095449
☎ (01233) 750354 🌐 thebowlonline.co.uk
2 changing beers (sourced locally) [H]
This lovingly restored listed village pub near the Wye National Nature Reserve displays vintage advertising material and retains many period features. The main bar welcomes families but the snug room is child free and used for village meetings. A beer festival is held August bank holiday Monday. Excellent sandwiches and baguettes are available on Saturdays. Five-time local CAMRA Pub of the Year winner, including in 2022.
Q🐎❀◐♣🍎📶

Herne

Butcher's Arms [L]
29A Herne Street, CT6 7HL (opp church)
☎ 07908 370685 🌐 micropub.co.uk
Ramsgate Gadds' No. 5 Best Bitter Ale; 3 changing beers (sourced regionally; often Ramsgate) [G]
Britain's first micropub, opened in 2005, is a real ale gem and the inspiration for others. Once a butcher's shop, it still has the original chopping tables. The compact drinking area ensures lively banter. The range of ales changes frequently and customers can also buy beer to take home. The Butcher's Arms has won many CAMRA awards and the landlord was voted one of CAMRA's top 40 campaigners. Opening hours are now limited to Tuesday to Friday evenings, but groups can be accommodated on Saturday lunchtimes by arrangement.
Q🍺🚌🐾

Herne Bay

Bouncing Barrel 🏆 [L]
20 Bank Street, CT6 5EA
☎ 07777 630685
4 changing beers (sourced regionally; often Musket, Northdown, Wantsum) [G]
A welcoming micropub with bench seating for 20 customers around old workshop tables. The beer range changes regularly and comes from a wide selection of microbreweries countrywide, often including beers from Kent. Local snacks are available. The venue is named after the bombs used in the Dambusters raid, which were tested off the coast nearby. The pub has a mural of a Lancaster flying past the Reculver Towers. Regular small beer festivals are held throughout the year.
Q🐎♿♣🍎🚌🐾

Parkerville
219 High Street, CT6 5AD
☎ 07939 106172
4 changing beers (sourced locally; often Long Man, Mighty Oak, Oakham) [G]
Lively micropub housed in a former music store. The spacious front seating area has a corner bar, and a small stage with a piano in the front window. The back bar has a TV screen for big events only. Beers are often from local microbreweries and there is a good selection of ciders, whiskies, rums, artisan gins and wines. Occasional live music is staged, and the pub celebrates its birthday every 13th July with music and food. Q🐎♿🍎🚌🐾♫

Horton Kirby

Bull [L]
Lombard Street, DA4 9DF
☎ (01322) 860341 🌐 thebullhortonkirby.com
Dark Star Hophead; Hardys & Hansons Bitter; 2 changing beers (sourced nationally; often Kent, Oakham) [H]
Friendly comfortable one-bar village local with a large garden affording views across the Darent Valley. The pub has two regular and two rotating guest ales, of which

one is often dark. Food includes pizzas on Tuesday nights. Booking is recommended for the Sunday roasts. There is an open mic night on the first Friday of each month and a quiz on the last Monday. Games include cribbage and board games. Parking in the vicinity can be difficult. ⏰♿♣🅿️🚃(414) ✿🛜🎵

Hythe

Potting Shed 🄻
160A High Street, CT21 5JR
☎ 07780 877226
3 changing beers (sourced regionally) ⊞
Hythe's only micro-alehouse, at the Folkestone end of Hythe High Street, serves an interesting range of ales from around the country. One local Kentish beer is usually served. A range of three chilled ciders is also available from boxes. Limited bar snacks are sold. Small, convivial and welcoming, where chatter and laughter abound, this is a good place to enjoy a drink and interesting conversation after visiting the High Street. ✿♦🚃✿🛜

Three Mariners 🄻
37 Windmill Street, CT21 6BH
☎ (01303) 260406
Young's London Original; 3 changing beers (sourced locally) ⊞
This traditional back-street corner pub is well worth a visit and is an ideal destination for a relaxing drink when visiting Hythe. Friendly staff and loyal customers are happy to have a chat while you enjoy a pint of the local or regional beers on offer. With no food available, the pub attracts customers due to the excellent quality and selection of its real ales and cider, which can be enjoyed in the bars or in the partly-heated outside area. ✿≈♣♦🚃✿🎵

Ightham Common

Old House ★ 🄻
Redwell Lane, TN15 9EE (½ mile SW of Ightham village, between A25 and A227) TQ590558
☎ (01732) 886077 🌐 oldhouse.pub
6 changing beers (sourced locally; often Goacher's, Larkins, Long Man) Ⓖ
Kentish red-brick, tile-hung cottage located in a narrow isolated country lane. The main bar features a Victorian wood-panelled counter, parquet flooring and an imposing inglenook fireplace. The pub has been identified by CAMRA as having a nationally important historic pub interior. Up to six changing beers are dispensed by gravity, often from wooden casks, including at least one bitter, a golden ale and a dark beer. Kentish ciders are always available. Local CAMRA Pub of the Year 2018-2021. It may close earlier in the evening if not busy. Q✿🅰♣♦🅿️✿🛜

Ivychurch

Bell Inn ✅
Ashford Road, TN29 0AL (signposted from the A2070 between Brenzett and Hamstreet) TR028275
☎ (01797) 344355 🌐 thebellinnivychurch.com
St Austell Tribute; Sharp's Doom Bar, Atlantic; 2 changing beers (sourced regionally) ⊞
A pretty, medieval 16th-century free house situated adjacent to St George's Church. A warm welcome awaits everyone who visits. Their real ales and beers have won many awards, and it is a four-time local CAMRA Pub of

the Year winner. During the colder months, a wood-burning stove adds to the comfortable atmosphere. The Bell Inn is well worth finding and is steeped in Marshland history as it was once the centre of operations of the Romney Marsh 'owler' wool smugglers. ⏰♿♣♦🅿️🚃(11B) ✿🛜🎵

Laddingford

Chequers
The Street, ME18 6BP TQ689481
☎ (01622) 871266 🌐 chequersladdingford.co.uk
Harvey's Sussex Best Bitter; 2 changing beers (sourced nationally) ⊞
An attractive oak-beamed pub dating from the 15th century, it is at the heart of village life. A variety of events are held throughout the year, including a beer festival at the end of April. A log fire burns in winter, and the pub frontage is a sea of flowers in summer. Good food is served and a wide selection of sausage dishes is available on Thursdays. The large garden has children's play equipment. Buses stop outside. Q⏰♿🕚♣🅿️🚃(23,25) ✿🛜🎵

Lamberhurst

Chequers 🄻
The Broadway, TN3 8DB
☎ (01892) 891850 🌐 chequerslamberhurst.com
Harvey's Sussex Best Bitter; 1 changing beer (sourced locally; often Burning Sky, Cellar Head, Westerham) ⊞
A friendly welcome can be expected in this atmospheric 15th-century pub, located in the centre of a quiet and pretty village. Plenty of seating is provided at traditional pub tables and chairs, comfy sofas and armchairs spread across a variety of rooms, with flagstone flooring and low wooden beams in the main bar. There is a good selection on the menu ranging from grazing to full dining. Usually two local beers are on handpump with an interesting range of mainly local craft keg. Q⏰♿🕚♣🅿️🚃(256) ✿🛜

Linton

Armoury 🏆
Loddington Farm, Loddington Lane, ME17 4AG
☎ (01622) 749931 🌐 musketbrewery.co.uk
6 changing beers (sourced locally; often Musket) Ⓖ
The Musket brewery moved to its new premises in 2018. The Armoury tap bar overlooks the brewhouse and has stillage for eight casks; four beers are usually available. Comfortable seating and tables are inside and a large grassed area opposite the entrance offers tables, umbrellas and cushioned casks, with shade under the many trees. A large tent/marquee has bench seating with heating and lighting. Pizzas are usually available and bookable monthly themed dining events like Burns' night are held Q⏰♿🕚&♦🅿️🚃✿🛜🎵

Little Mill

Man of Kent 🄻 ✅
226 Tonbridge Road, TN12 5LA (½ mile W of East Peckham)
☎ (01622) 871345 🌐 themanofkentpub.co.uk
Harvey's Sussex Best Bitter; Timothy Taylor Landlord; Tonbridge Coppernob; 1 changing beer (sourced regionally; often Gun) ⊞

A former coaching inn dating back to 1588 with an attractive tile-hung façade overlooking a sunny terrace with table seating and parasols. Further seating extends around by the streamside where customers may feed the expectant fish. An impressive double-sided wood-burning fireplace is guarded by carved wooden owls and separates a cosy bar from the saloon. Booking for meals (served lunchtimes and Fri and Sat eves) is strongly advised. The landlord proudly displays his membership of Timothy Taylor's Champion Club for excellent cellarmanship. Q❄☺✿◑◗▲P🚪(208)🌸🐾

Lower Halstow

Three Tuns L
The Street, ME9 7DY
☎ (01795) 842840 🌐 thethreetunsrestaurant.co.uk
4 changing beers (sourced locally; often Wantsum, Goacher's) Ⓗ
True village pub with friendly, bustling, cheerful atmosphere and lively chatter. The owners actively support real ale, offering mainly Kentish ales; third-pint flights are available for the indecisive; and several local ciders including Dudda's Tun. The pub has a good reputation for high-quality locally sourced food and has won many awards. A beer festival is held during the summer bank holiday. A log fire, sofa seating, brick walls and beams add character. Local CAMRA Pub of The Year 2022. ☺✿🛏◑◗&♣●P🚪🐾🎵

Luddesdown

Cock Inn L
Henley Street, DA13 0XB TQ664672
☎ (01474) 814208 🌐 cockluddesdowne.com
Adnams Southwold Bitter, Broadside; Goacher's Real Mild Ale, Fine Light Ale; Harvey's Sussex Best Bitter; Shepherd Neame Master Brew Ⓗ
Proudly traditional rural free house dating from 1713, it has been under the same ownership since 1984. Keen walkers can reach it by footpath from Sole Street station. It has two distinct bars, a large conservatory, a comfortable heated smoking area and separate function room where local clubs and societies meet. Traditional pub games are played including bar billiards and darts with several different types of board. Children are not allowed in the bars or garden. Q✿♣P🐾

Golden Lion L ✓
Luddesdown Road, DA13 0XE
☎ (01474) 815644 🌐 thegoldenlionpub.uk
Iron Pier Perry St. Pale, Bitter; Young's London Original; 1 changing beer (often Iron Pier) Ⓗ
Large rural pub with a comfortable bar area and a restaurant extension offering good-value meals. It hosts several groups including a custom car club and an investment group, and regular quiz evenings. Also featured are open mic nights and charity race nights. It boasts a log fire, a covered outside smoking area and a large car park. The pub is both family and dog-friendly and popular with walkers. Beer festivals are held on Whitsun Saturday and August Bank holiday Saturday. ☺✿◑◗♣P🚪🐾🛜

Maidstone

Cellars Alehouse
The Old Brewery, Buckland Road, ME16 0DZ (if front gates in Rocky Hill closed, use rear entry to old Style &

Winch brewery via alley alongside railway; access is by steps down from yard)
☎ (01622) 761045 🌐 thecellarsalehouse.co.uk
14 changing beers (sourced nationally; often Iron Pier, Kent, Tonbridge) Ⓖ
Step down into the former barley wine cellar of the old Style & Winch brewery, flagstone flooring and a collection of old pub signs await. Comfortable pub seating and oil lamps give a cosy atmosphere and pumpclips line the vaulted ceiling. Six cask and eight keg ales as well as 10 local and 10 fruited ciders are all perfectly kept in a temperature-controlled cool room. A selection of wines, spirits, canned and bottled beers is maintained. Bar snacks are available. Q☺≉(West) ♣●P🚪🐾

Flower Pot
96 Sandling Road, ME14 2RJ
☎ (01622) 757705 🌐 flowerpotpub.com
Goacher's Gold Star Strong Ale; 8 changing beers (sourced nationally; often Kent, Oakham, Thornbridge) Ⓗ
A street-corner alehouse with split-level bars. The upper bar has nine handpumps serving ales from microbreweries, and a log fire in the winter. The lower bar has a pool table and is used for Tuesday jam nights and music nights on some Saturdays. Up to four ciders and perries are usually available and a small selection of KeyKeg beers. An outdoor covered and heated seating area is open most of the year. Food is served Wednesdays to Saturdays with pizzas being particularly popular. ✿◑≉(East)♣●🍴🚪(101)🐾🛜🎵

Olde Thirsty Pig ✓
4A Knightrider Street, ME15 6LP
☎ 07762 279907 🌐 thethirstypig.co.uk
3 changing beers (sourced locally; often Musket, Tonbridge) Ⓗ
Reputedly the third-oldest building in the town, dating from around 1430, this pub has massive timber beams, sloping floors and nooks and crannies across its two storeys. Originally an Archbishop's Palace estate farmhouse, four handpumps now dispense ales, mainly from Kent microbreweries. Draught cider is stocked alongside many bottled beers, including some foreign ones. Two small meeting rooms are available for booking, and there is a heated and covered courtyard area. The bus station is a short walk away. ✿♣●🚪🐾

Rifle Volunteers
28 Wyatt Street, ME14 1EU
☎ (01622) 750540 🌐 theriflevolunteers.co.uk
Goacher's Real Mild Ale, Fine Light Ale, Gold Star Strong Ale; 1 changing beer (sourced locally; often Goacher's) Ⓗ
A Victorian stone-built single bar pub situated only a short walk away from Maidstone town centre. It is one of three Goacher's tied houses and retains some bar fittings from the turn of the last century. The absence of jukebox, piped music or gaming machines emphasise that is a place for conversation or a quiet drink. The courtyard garden is used mainly in summer. Light snacks are not advertised but can be made to order. A popular fun quiz open to all is held every other Tuesday. Q✿◑≉(East) ♣●🍴🚪🐾🛜

Society Rooms ✓
Brenchley House, Week Street, ME14 1RF
☎ (01622) 350910
Greene King Abbot; Ruddles Best Bitter; Sharp's Doom Bar; 4 changing beers (sourced nationally; often Southwark, Tonbridge, Wantsum) Ⓗ

Known locally as the Glass House, this large Wetherspoon pub is close to the main station and is a well-lit building with glass walls. A fireplace stands in the middle and there is an enclosed patio at the rear. Main sporting fixtures are shown on the large cinema screen (sound off). It hosts Meet the Brewer events in addition to twice-yearly ale festivals. At least six beer pumps and two for cider are kept. A quiz is held every Monday evening. Q🍺✿◑♿⇌(East)🚌(101)🐾📶

Walnut Tree
234 Tonbridge Road, ME16 8SR
☎ (01622) 727260
Goacher's Fine Light Ale; Harvey's Sussex Best Bitter; 1 changing beer (sourced nationally; often Musket, St Austell) 🄷
A cosy L-shaped local that is warmed by a central fire. The interior displays various sayings and quotes. Comfortable furnishings are used throughout. Regular live music is played on Friday evenings and popular comedy nights are held on the third Thursday of the month. A live band music quiz is held on the first Thursday. A jukebox is provided. The locally brewed Goacher's Fine Light Ale is a regular as is Harvey's Sussex Best Bitter. Private functions may be catered for on request. 🍺✿◑♣🍎P🚌(3,7)🐾♫

Marden

Marden Village Club
Albion Road, TN12 9DT
☎ (01622) 831427 🌐 mardenvillageclub.co.uk
Shepherd Neame Master Brew; 5 changing beers (sourced regionally; often Goacher's, Kent, Ramsgate) 🄷
At this Grade II-listed club and community hub six real ales are offered. Five change regularly and are generally from local Kent microbreweries. One dark beer is always available. Many of the club's members are involved in the snooker and darts teams; others simply enjoy the friendly ambience. Bingo and music evenings are held. Card-carrying CAMRA members are welcome but regular visitors will be required to join. CAMRA National Club of the Year 2022. ♿⇌♣🍎🚌(23)🐾📶♫

Margate

Fez
40 High Street, CT9 1DS
2 changing beers 🄶
This eclectically furnished micropub, opened in 2015, has a mixture of high and low tables along with some raised bench seating. Brewery and fairground memorabilia adorn the walls while musical instruments are fixed on the ceiling. The small bar counter at the rear has a temperature-controlled cellar room with cask ales and ciders on gravity dispense. A limited wine range along with a selection of soft drinks are available.
🍺⇌♣🚌🐾📶

Mechanical Elephant ✔
Marine Terrace, CT9 1XJ
☎ (01843) 234100
Greene King Abbot; Ruddles Best Bitter; Sharp's Doom Bar; 2 changing beers 🄷
Ideally located opposite the main beach, with a flower-bedecked summer balcony offering the famous sunset views. This Wetherspoon is a quiet daytime pub, while on Friday and Saturday evenings recorded music is played. Good-value food and a good selection of well-kept ales is on sale, including Kent and regional guest beers. The staff are friendly and helpful. Its name derives from a large roving mechanical elephant that gave rides along the sea front in the 1950s. 🍺◑♿⇌🚌📶

Two Halves
2 Marine Drive, CT9 1DH
☎ 07538 771904
5 changing beers 🄶
This friendly, welcoming micropub has an incredible location on Margate's seafront. No matter what the weather this micropub has a great aspect – customers can enjoy the sunsets out of the window or just watch the world go by. The landlord knows his ales and sources them from all around the country. Beer and cider is kept in great condition in a large stillage room. Look out for the old-fashioned postcards in the loo. Q⇌🍎🚌🐾

Milstead

Red Lion
Rawling Street, ME9 0RT
☎ (01795) 830279 🌐 theredlionmilstead.co.uk
Goacher's Fine Light Ale, Special/House Ale, Best Dark Ale 🄷
Traditional family-run country pub, set in the village of Milstead, three miles from Sittingbourne, with a well-kept range of permanent Goacher's ales. Various groups meet in the pub on an ad hoc basis. There is a large patio and garden, and a well-sized car park to side of pub. This welcoming pub's aim is to provide food of good quality at a reasonable price, including Sunday lunches.
Q🍺✿◑P🐾

New Romney

Smugglers' Alehouse 🄻
10 St Lawrence Court, High Street, TN28 8BU
☎ 07919 156336
3 changing beers (sourced locally) 🄷
A micropub located at the south end of the High Street where you can relax with a drink or join in with the varied conversations between customers and staff. Well-behaved dogs on leads are welcome. In addition to the ever-changing real ales and ciders on offer, there is a selection of wines and spirits. Tea and coffee is usually available upon request and various snacks (including pickled eggs) are also available. The pub accepts cash only. Q⛺🍎P🚌🐾

Newenden

White Hart 🄻
Rye Road, TN18 5PN (on the A28 in centre of village) TQ834273
☎ (01797) 252166 🌐 thewhitehartnewenden.co.uk
Harvey's Sussex Best Bitter; Rother Valley Level Best; 2 changing beers 🄷
This 16th-century characterful free house serves the local community with an ever-changing selection of fine cask ales. It is an ideal base from which to explore the area, whether it be a nostalgic steam train journey through beautiful countryside on the Kent and East Sussex Railway, a visit to one of the many National Trust properties on the doorstep or a drive down to the coast. Pub quizzes are held on the first Monday of the month, except on bank holidays.
🍺✿🛏◑♿⛺⇌(Northiam)♣🍎P🚌(2)🐾📶♫

Northfleet

Iron Pier Taproom Ⓛ

Units 6 & 7, May Industrial Estate, May Avenue, DA11 8RU

☎ (01474) 569460 🌐 ironpier.beer

Iron Pier Perry St. Pale, Bitter, Wealdway Ⓖ

Brewery taproom opened in 2018. The Iron Pier brewery is only the second to operate in the Gravesend area since Russell's was swallowed by Truman's in the 1930s. There is plenty of seating, with an excellent view of the brewery itself and a large TV for sports fans. Three regular Iron Pier beers are available, with others depending on production at the time. A selection of KeyKeg and bottled beers, gins, wines and soft drinks are also available. P🍴🚲 (483,489)♣

Painters Forstal

Alma

ME13 0DU

☎ (01795) 533835 🌐 almafaversham.co.uk

Shepherd Neame Master Brew; 1 changing beer (sourced regionally; often Shepherd Neame) Ⓗ

Popular country pub situated in the centre of the village. It is well regarded for its food, for which tables may be booked. There is a small car park and a large, well maintained garden. The pub has bat and trap and hosts occasional themed events. Up to three Shepherd Neame beers are available. Dogs on leads are allowed in the public bar. Q🛇🏵🕩♣P🚲 (660)

Pembury

King William IV

87 Hastings Road, TN2 4JS

☎ (01892) 458241 🌐 kingwilliampembury.com

Greene King IPA; St Austell Proper Job; 4 changing beers (sourced regionally; often Dark Star, Wadworth, Young's) Ⓗ

A thriving and friendly local pub, well-appointed with plenty of seating and large front and rear gardens which are popular on warm evenings. The landlady is a local and has worked hard to revive the establishment and improve the décor and ambience while being very supportive of community initiatives. There are two bar billiards teams and traditional pub games such as darts are played. Live music is performed, usually on Saturdays and jam nights on the second Thursday of the month. 🛇🏵♣●P🚲(6,297) ♣🛜♪

Petteridge

Hopbine Ⓛ

Petteridge Lane, TN12 7NE (1 mile E of Matfield)

☎ (01892) 722561 🌐 thehopbine.pub

Harvey's Sussex Best Bitter; house beer (by Cellar Head); 1 changing beer (sourced locally; often Tonbridge) Ⓗ

Tucked away in a tiny hamlet yet only a 10 minute stroll from a bus route along the Brenchley Road, the Hopbine offers a friendly welcome and a choice of three local beers and a cider from Turners. The cosy interior has a central open fire while an attractive, verdant garden tiers down to a children's play area. Food is served Wednesday to Sunday with pizza a speciality. A piece of history is retained with former King & Barnes brewery signage. Q🛇🏵🕩♣●P🚲(297)♣🛜

Pluckley

Rose & Crown ✅

Mundy Bois Road, Mundy Bois, TN27 0ST (between Pluckley, Egerton and Smarden) TQ908455

☎ (01233) 840048 🌐 theroseandcrownpluckley.co.uk

Harvey's Sussex Best Bitter; Whitstable Native Bitter; 1 changing beer (sourced nationally) Ⓗ

This tile-hung 17th-century pub combines the warmth of a traditional Kentish country free house with a first-class restaurant. Situated off the beaten track between the villages of Pluckley, Egerton and Smarden, it lies in farmland in the heart of the Weald of Kent and there are many good walks to be enjoyed nearby. The village bar is hop-entwined and has a welcoming fire; the saloon also features a log burner. The Guinness Book of Records named Pluckley the most haunted village in England, reputedly with 12 ghosts. 🛇🏵🕩🕭♣AP♣🛜♪

Queenborough

Admiral's Arm Ⓛ

West Street, ME11 5AD (in Trafalgar Court, 30yds left from crossroads of High St and Park Rd)

☎ (01795) 668598 🌐 admiralsarm.co.uk

4 changing beers (sourced nationally; often Lancaster, Ramsgate, Settle) Ⓗ/Ⓖ

A three room micropub which opened on Trafalgar Day in 2016. Four real ales are sold through handpumps, along with a large range of 12 or more ciders/perries on gravity dispense, all from a temperature-controlled room. Ale can also be served on gravity dispense from the cellar and there is an extensive range of gins and a good choice of pub snacks. The décor is mainly lifeboat and nautical themed. CAMRA Kent Pub of the Year 2019. Q🛇🏵🕩≈♣●P🚲(334) ♣🛜♪

Rainham

Mackland Arms Ⓛ

213 Station Road, ME8 7PS (5 mins' walk N of railway station)

☎ (01634) 232178 🌐 macklandarms.co.uk

Shepherd Neame Master Brew, Bishops Finger; 1 changing beer (sourced regionally; often Shepherd Neame) Ⓗ

On entering the L-shaped one-room bar with lower wall wood panelled, you are greeted by a bar with handpumps dispensing two Shepherd Neame beers. The front bar has a fireplace to the left with a display of books and a television showing mainly football updates. This leads to the rear drinking area with two dartboards then to a covered patio area for smokers and a large garden. The pub is less than 5 minutes' walk from Rainham station. 🛇🏵≈♣🚲(327)♣

Prince of Ales Ⓛ

121 High Street, ME8 8AN (near centre of Rainham, next door to Post Office)

☎ 07982 756412 🌐 princeofales.co.uk

4 changing beers (sourced nationally; often Kent, Tonbridge) Ⓖ

Situated on the main A2, next to the Post Office, this micropub is run by a dedicated team and is furnished with wooden tables and benches. Four ever-changing mostly Kentish ales are served direct from the cask from a chiller room which can be viewed from the bar area. Up to 10 ciders and a selection of bar snacks are available. There is a small outside seating area. An annual beer festival is held in March. Q🏵≈♣●🍴🚲(132)

Railway ✓

113 Station Road, ME8 7SF (opp railway station)
☎ (01634) 365396
Greene King Abbot; Sharp's Doom Bar; house beer (by Greene King); 4 changing beers (sourced nationally) Ⓗ

As its name suggests this Wetherspoon pub is ideally situated opposite Rainham railway station so you can enjoy a pint while keeping an eye on the live departures screen. It is open daily, serving a selection of real ales and ciders from 9am. Food is served all day and the pub plays host to a weekly quiz. There are quiet nooks and crannies to hide away, or you can enjoy your refreshments among the bustle of the regulars.
🛏🕮🌐◐🚲🚉(132) 🛜

Ramsgate

Artillery Arms

36 West Cliff Road, CT11 9JS
☎ (01843) 853202
Oakham Citra; Ramsgate Gadds' No. 5 Best Bitter Ale; 4 changing beers (often Ramsgate, Wantsum) Ⓗ

One of the most authentic of all the Ramsgate pubs, this is unashamedly a no-frills real ale boozer with a wide selection of beers on draught. The tables and seats vary from traditional bar stools through to aircraft seating, which gives the multi-level pub an interesting feel. It's packed full of character, from the stunning stained-glass windows to the mix of memorabilia adorning the walls. There is a military theme throughout. Popular open mic and food nights are held. ◐♣🍴🚲🌸♪

Hovelling Boat Inn

12 York Street, CT11 9DS
☎ 07968 800960
5 changing beers Ⓖ

A welcoming, dog-friendly micropub that serves a good range of cask ale and ciders /perries, brought to your table by the friendly and well-informed staff from a rear cellar room where they are kept in a temperature-controlled environment and dispensed on gravity. The chalkboard lists up to six beers that are available. Good chat and putting the world to rights is a common pastime in this superb micro. A pleasant outdoor pétanque area at the rear of the establishment offers somewhere to enjoy the warmer days. Q🛏🌐♣🍴🚲🌸

Montefiore Arms

1 Trinity Place, CT11 7HJ
☎ (01843) 593265
Ramsgate Gadds' Hoppy Pale, Gadds' No. 7 Bitter Ale; 3 changing beers (often Ramsgate) Ⓗ

This award-winning traditional snug back-street local enjoys a good reputation with real ale drinkers in the Thanet area. The pub's name and sign are unique, honouring the great Jewish financier and philanthropist Sir Moses Montefiore who lived locally for many years and was a benefactor to the town's poor. The pub showcases the beers of the Ramsgate brewery along with changing guest ales and Biddenden cider.
🌐♣🍴🚲(Loop) 🛜

Pub Ramsgate

87 High Street, CT11 9RJ
☎ (01843) 585404 🌐 instagram.com/thepubramsgatenew
3 changing beers (sourced nationally; often Iron Pier, Shivering Sands, Wantsum) Ⓗ

A modestly sized, industrial-styled and welcoming micropub offering a good selection of cask and craft beers alongside cider and the occasional Bavarian beer or two. It can be found on the way down the High Street

from Ramsgate station, but its unobtrusive frontage is well hidden. Take-outs are available. Springfest and Oktoberfest beer festivals are hosted when special draught Bavarian beers are sourced directly for the event. 🛏♣🍴🚲🐕🌸

Red Lion

1 King Street, CT11 8NN
☎ (01843) 586713
3 changing beers (often Ramsgate) Ⓗ

Busy pub in the heart of the town centre, probably the oldest surviving pub in the town. It has a mixed lunchtime clientele, but evening customers are predominantly younger people, especially when loud rock music is played. There is a raised area towards the rear with a pool table. Beers from the Ramsgate brewery (Gadds') are normally available on handpump along with beers from further afield. ♣🚲(38,39)🛜♪

Royal Victoria Pavilion ✓

Harbour Parade, CT11 8LS
☎ (01843) 854420
Greene King Abbot; Ruddles Best Bitter; Sharp's Doom Bar; 3 changing beers Ⓗ

This splendid pub opened as a Wetherspoon in 2017 in what was originally a dance hall and then casino. It has two floors with separate bars and is said to be the largest Wetherspoon in the country. The pub has a ground floor beach-front bar garden, along with first floor roof terrace. Although the pub opens at 8am alcohol is not served until 9am. Children are permitted until 9pm.
🛏🌐◐🍴🚲🛜

Rochester

12 Degrees Ⓛ

352 High Street, ME1 1DJ
☎ 07512 040453 🌐 rams-micropub-12degrees.business.site
6 changing beers (sourced locally) Ⓖ

Six gravity-fed beers and four bag-in-box ciders are served from seven glass doors behind a well crafted bar. Opposite are a row of tables and a piano, on the walls are prints, photos and postcards of Rochester as well as quirky signs. There is a basement with extra seating and tables, where you will find a dartboard. This area is also used for live music once or twice a month, there is also an open mic night held weekly. Q🚉(Chatham)♣🍴🚲♪

Coopers Arms 🍺

10 St Margarets Street, ME1 1TL (behind cathedral)
☎ (01634) 404298 🌐 thecoopersarms.co.uk
Timothy Taylor Landlord; Young's London Original, London Special; house beer (by Tonbridge); 4 changing beers (sourced regionally; often Canterbury Ales, Mad Cat, Tonbridge) Ⓗ

Situated behind both the cathedral and castle, a short stroll from the busy High Street, this charming building, previously the home of monks, dates from 1199 and first became a pub in 1543. The front bar is of particular interest with an impressive beamed ceiling and fireplace. A short passageway leads to a more modern rear bar and pleasant garden which is busy in summer. Lunchtime meals are available Thursday to Sunday and there is a fortnightly quiz night. 🌐◐🚉P🚲🌸 🛜

Man of Kent Ale House Ⓛ

6-8 John Street, ME1 1YN (200yds off A2 from bottom of Star Hill)
☎ 07989 881850
8 changing beers (sourced locally; often Canterbury Ales, Ramsgate, Tonbridge) Ⓗ

This wonderful traditional pub serves up to eight cask ales, all from Kent breweries, an extensive real cider range and a wide selection of German and Belgian beers, both on tap and in bottles. There is an enclosed garden with allows for pleasant drinking. Live music acts perform on Thursdays, and on Sundays there is a jam session. The exterior of the pub has outstanding tiled sign from the long-closed Kent brewery of Style & Winch. Dogs are welcomed. ✿≈♣🏠🍴🚪(155)💗♫

Who'd Ha' Thought It
9 Baker Street, ME1 3DN (off Maidstone Rd)
☎ (01634) 830144 ⊕ whodha.com
3 changing beers (sourced nationally; often Harvey's, Titan) Ⓗ
A friendly back-street local off Maidstone Road with a spacious wood-panelled bar that has two TVs showing sports. Three ever-changing cask ales are served, one usually from a Kent brewery. Various filled rolls are available at lunchtimes. To the rear is a snug area with books and games ideal for small groups. There is a log fire for the winter months. Outside there is a raised garden with a covered stillage area used for beer festivals. ➔✿♣P🚪(155)💗🛜♫

Ryarsh

Duke of Wellington
Birling Road, ME19 5LS
☎ (01732) 842318 ⊕ dukeofwellingtonryarsh.com
Harvey's Sussex Best Bitter; St Austell Proper Job; Timothy Taylor Landlord; 1 changing beer (sourced nationally) Ⓗ
A 16th-century pub with inglenook fireplaces in each of its two bars. To the left, the main bar leads through to the toilets. The restaurant to the right displays part of an original wattle and daub wall behind glass. A covered and heated patio and the garden are accessed through bifold doors and there are some tables at the front. Good food is available daily and there are popular Sunday roasts. A jazz evening is held on the first Thursday of the month. Ramblers are welcome. Q➔✿🕏P💗🛜♫

Sandgate

Earl of Clarendon
Brewers Hill, CT20 3DH (25yds up footpath off the A259 Esplanade between Seabrook and Sandgate)
☎ (01303) 248684 ⊕ the-earl-of-clarendon.business.site
3 changing beers Ⓗ
This ex-Mackeson, Whitbread and Shepherd Neame free house was originally built as a hotel and provided refreshment to troops as it is on a path between Shorncliffe Camp and the sea. Outdoor tables overlook the sea. The pub serves continuously changing beers from all over Britain, usually including at least one local beer. Third-pint glasses are available. Live music is played occasionally during the summer and tasty home-made food is served every day. Bar billiards is available, and football, cricket and snooker are shown on satellite TV. 🕏♣🚪💗♫

Sandwich

New Inn Ⓛ
2 Harnet Street, CT13 9ES
☎ (01304) 612335 ⊕ newinn-sandwich.co.uk
Adnams Ghost Ship; Sharp's Doom Bar; 1 changing beer (sourced locally; often Ramsgate) Ⓗ

Located in the centre of this medieval Cinque Port, this impressive-looking pub is an ideal respite from wandering around this historic market town. The wood panelling and carpeted bar give the pub a traditional and comfortable feel. At the front there is some on-street seating, allowing you to watch Sandwich life go by. Two regular ales are supported by a guest ale from the Ramsgate brewery. Home-cooked food is available all day, made from local fresh produce. Regular live music and food events are held. ➔✿🕏🍴🔥Å♣P🚪💗🛜♫

Red Cow Ⓛ
12 Moat Sole, CT13 9AU
☎ (01304) 613399
3 changing beers (often Exmoor, Harvey's, Ramsgate) Ⓗ
You cannot miss the large red cow on the front of this Grade II*-listed building, used by market traders in years gone by. It has a comfortable and traditional country pub ambience with its tiled floors and exposed beams. Up to three real ales are served, usually including one from the Ramsgate brewery. The menu offers traditional pub food, alongside pie and pint night, Friday fish special and a Sunday roast. There is a large, pleasant suntrap garden. Dogs are allowed in the restaurant. ➔✿🕏Å♣P🚪💗🛜♫

Sevenoaks

Anchor
32 London Road, TN13 1AS
☎ (01732) 454898
House beer (by Wantsum); 2 changing beers (sourced regionally; often Ramsgate) Ⓗ
The Anchor is a friendly town-centre pub run for over 40 years by effervescent landlords Barry and Phil. A Guide regular of over 20 years standing, great pride is taken over the quality and range of the cask ales with Wantsum Imperial always available alongside two independent regional brews, one of which is usually from Ramsgate brewery. Good-value meals are served at lunchtimes with roasts proving very popular. Darts and poker evenings feature and regular live music is performed on Wednesday evenings. 🕏♣🚪💗🛜♫

White Hart Ⓛ
Tonbridge Road, TN13 1SG (1 mile S of town centre on A225)
☎ (01732) 452022 ⊕ brunningandprice.co.uk/whitehart
Harvey's Sussex Best Bitter; house beer (by St Austell); 3 changing beers (sourced locally; often Lakedown, Pig & Porter, Wantsum) Ⓗ
Dating from the early 17th century, the White Hart was built alongside Kent's first turnpike road and adjacent to Knole Park. The stylish yet informal interior is characterised by a number of unique cosy spaces arranged around the central bar. Between four and six beers from small south-eastern brewers feature alongside changing real ciders. Dog walks are organised for the last Saturday of each month gathering at 10am for coffee and pastries and returning at 11.30 for a pint. Q➔✿🕏&♣P🚪(402)💗🛜

Sheerness

Flying Sheep Micropub
193 High Street, ME12 1UJ
☎ 07958 134282
4 changing beers (sourced regionally; often Iron Pier, Lancaster, Wantsum) Ⓗ

Micropub opened in 2018 – its aviation and local sheep theme reflect Sheppey's past involvement in aircraft manufacture and sheep farming. Seating is mainly at high tables and high stools but there are several comfortable airline seats. An interesting and ever-changing range of beers from near and far are sold. Themed nights are held on Wednesdays. Ciders are sold on gravity dispense direct from polypins in chiller room. ♿✿≽(Sheerness-on-Sea) ♣♥♐🖵(360) ❀🖤

Shoreham

Samuel Palmer 🅛

Church Street, TN14 7RY

☎ (01959) 525442 ⊕ thesamuelpalmer.com

Larkins Traditional Ale, Best; 2 changing beers (sourced regionally; often Lister's, Three Acre, Three Legs) 🅗

A beautiful 2022 renovation by the owners Mount Vineyard saw the pub renamed in tribute to the former village resident and landscape painter whose works adorn the walls. Wooden flooring and panelling, exposed brickwork, soft lighting and log burners flanking the bar elicit a warm and cosy feel. Walkers visiting this attractive area can enjoy an outside terrace with covered seating and heaters. A separate restaurant area operates from Thursday onwards while bar food is available throughout the week until 6pm. ➣✿◑ὖ≽P🖵(2)❀🖤

Sittingbourne

Donna's Ale House 🅛

20 West Street, ME10 1AB

5 changing beers (sourced locally; often Goody, Mad Cat, Wantsum) 🅗

Opened in 2017, this mircopub has contemporary decor inside with seating at high benches, tables and stools. Four handpumps dispense ales with emphasis on Kentish makers, and occasional offerings from out of county. A chalkboard gives a description of the beers on offer. Over 100 gins are also sold. A selection of snacks is available – typically cheese boards, pie and mash and chilli with nachos. This welcome town-centre addition to the real ale scene is proving to be popular with all. ➣◑≽♥🖵

Fountain of Ale

37 Station Street, ME10 3ED

☎ (01795) 488613

Shepherd Neame Master Brew; 3 changing beers (sourced regionally; often Kent, Wantsum) 🅗

Located opposite Sittingbourne railway station and now known as the Fountain of Ale, there has been a welcome reinvention of this historic pub, where the local CAMRA branch was founded 41 years ago. This characterful pub has a number of interesting features including a snug area. Four real ales are currently available, but this may increase over time. ➣✿≽♣♥🖵❀🛜♪

Paper Mill 🅛

2 Charlotte Street, ME10 2JN (N of Sittingbourne station, almost in Milton Regis; at the corner of Church St and Charlotte St)

☎ 07927 073584 ⊕ thepapermillmicropub.co.uk

3 changing beers (sourced regionally; often Goacher's, Salopian) 🅖

Popular one-room micropub located close to Sittingbourne town centre and railway station, it has bench seating around four large wood tables. Local beers feature alongside ales from national brewers such as Blue Monkey and Cloudwater. A range of real ciders are available. Chalkboards display the beer list, which

includes a number of interesting KeyKeg offerings. Occasional events such as Meet the Brewer and pub quizzes take place. Opening hours can be flexible with advance notice. Q➣♿≽♣♥🖵(334,347)❀

Smeeth

Dog House Pub 🅛

Evegate Business Park, Station Road, TN25 6SX (S of the A20 at Smeeth crossroads; at the rear of the Business Park)

☎ 07340 985064 ⊕ thedoghousepub.co.uk

3 changing beers (sourced locally) 🅖

This small pub/café on the Evegate Business Park offers an ever-changing selection of local ales and ciders, and homemade food. There is a small patio providing space for smokers, and alfresco drinking and dining in fine weather. Live music is performed most Friday and Saturday evenings and there are periodic live jam nights. Families and dogs are welcome in this old vets' dogs convalescing barn. ➣✿◑♥P❀🛜♪

Snargate

Red Lion ★ 🅛

TN29 9UQ (on B2080, 1 mile NW of Brenzett) TQ990285

☎ (01797) 344648

Goacher's Real Mild Ale; 3 changing beers (often Canterbury Ales, Goacher's, Rother Valley) 🅖

A regular Guide entry since 1981, this unspoilt 16th-century smugglers' pub has been in the same family for over 100 years. It passed to the next generation in 2016, but is still universally known as Doris's. Inside, the multi-room layout is decorated with posters from the 1940s and the Women's Land Army. Identified by CAMRA as having a nationally important historic pub interior, this superb pub is well worth a visit. Beer festivals are held in June near to the summer solstice, with a mini festival in October. Q✿♣♥P🖵(11B)❀

Staplehurst

Lord Raglan

Chart Hill Road, TN12 0DE (½ mile N of A229 at Cross-at-Hand) TQ786472

☎ (01622) 843747 ⊕ lord-raglan.co.uk

Goacher's Fine Light Ale; Harvey's Sussex Best Bitter; 1 changing beer (sourced locally) 🅗

An unspoilt free house retaining the atmosphere of a country pub from bygone days and owned by the same family for many years. The bar is hung with hops and warmed by two log fires and a stove. The large orchard garden catches the evening sun. Excellent food is served from a popular menu. Perry and local Double Vision cider are stocked. Well-behaved children and dogs are welcome. It is 15 minutes' walk from the Cross-at-Hand (No.5) bus stop on the A229. Q✿◑♥P❀

Strood

10:50 From Victoria 🅛

Rear of 37-39 North Street, ME2 4SJ (in a railway arch opp Asda car park)

☎ 07941 449137

6 changing beers (sourced regionally) 🅗/🅖

Situated next to the Asda car park and approached through a side gate beside it, the entrance path leads to a garden with bench seats and tables facing a stage area and beach huts. The bar area is wood-panelled

throughout with wall-mounted bench seats and tables with railway memorabilia and pictures on the wall. The serving hatch serves up to six beers and ciders with two chalkboard menus on the facing wall. Mobile phone use is not permitted in the bar area.
Q✿⓵♿≑♣♠P🚲(191) ❁🛇♪

Sutton Valence

Queen's Head
High Street, ME17 3AG
☎ (01622) 843225 🌐 thequeenshead-pub.co.uk
Goacher's Fine Light Ale; Timothy Taylor Landlord; Young's London Original; 1 changing beer (sourced nationally; often Musket) 🅷
A splendid village pub offering stunning views overlooking the Weald, with a hop-garlanded central bar and inglenook fireplace offering a blazing log fire in winter. A large dining area is on the right and two snug areas are to the left. An interesting raised garden is above small car park at rear and the old stables feature a full-size snooker table. Quiz night is alternate Mondays. Darts, dominoes and cribbage are played, and occasional live music and karaoke are featured.
🛏✿⓵P🚲(12) ❁🛇

Tankerton

Tankerton Arms 🄻
135 Tankerton Road, CT5 2AW
☎ 07897 741811
4 changing beers (sourced regionally; often Iron Pier, Kent, Westerham) 🄶
This friendly micropub, situated among Tankerton's small shops, has a firm policy of supporting Kent microbreweries and the range of four cask beers changes frequently. There are also some Keykeg beers and occasional beer swaps with regional breweries. The pleasant, airy room is lined with high wooden tables and stools, and is adorned with bunting and pictures of Thames sailing barges and the sea forts. There is a patio in front for outdoor drinking. Q🛏✿⓵♿♣♠🚲❁🛇

Temple Ewell

Fox
14 High Street, CT16 3DU
☎ (01304) 823598
3 changing beers (sourced nationally; often Courage, Marston's, Timothy Taylor) 🅷
A traditional village pub with a warm welcome for locals and visitors. Real ales, in a good range of styles and strengths, can be enjoyed in the main bar or in one of the smaller rooms. A variety of events, quiz nights, curry nights and occasional music evenings keep the place busy. A charity beer festival in June is organised by the local Rotary Club. There is an attractive streamside garden with a skittle alley. The pub is close to Kearsney Abbey gardens and to public transport.
🛏✿⓵≑(Kearsney) ♣P🚲❁🛇♪

Tenterden

This Ancient Boro' 🍺
3 East Cross, TN30 6AD
☎ (01580) 388815 🌐 thisancientboro.com
9 changing beers (sourced nationally) 🄶
A Whitbread pub which closed in 1968 and reopened as an alehouse and tapas bar in 2018. The pub is a hybrid of the original and a micropub, with no live music or gaming machines. An ever-changing variety of beers are available on gravity, dispensed from cooled casks on stillage behind the bar, together with various ciders served from a fridge. There is an interesting snack/tapas menu. Local CAMRA Pub of the Year in 2020 and 2023.
Q🛏⓵≑(Town) ♣♠🚲❁🛇

Tonbridge

Fuggles Beer Café 🄻 ✅
165 High Street, TN9 1BX (N end of High St near parish church)
☎ (01732) 666071 🌐 fugglesbeercafe.co.uk/about
Tonbridge Coppernob; 3 changing beers (sourced nationally; often 360 Degree, Downlands, Vocation) 🅷
As an important part of the Tonbridge pub scene, Fuggles attracts a wide range of customers with its continental café-style vibe. Three to four cask ales, chosen from a wide range of respected breweries, are supplemented by an extensive and interesting choice of craft keg. There is also an eclectic range of bottles and canned beers and two varying real ciders. Young and knowledgeable staff welcome you in a comfortable and casual atmosphere. Food includes toasties, cheese and charcuterie platters.
🛏⓵♿≑♣♠🚲❁🛇

Nelson Arms 🍺 🄻
19 Cromer Street, TN9 1UP
☎ (01732) 358284 🌐 thenelsonarms.com
8 changing beers (sourced nationally; often Kent, Ramsgate, Surrey Hills) 🅷
Winner of local CAMRA Pub of the Year and Cider Pub of the Year for the last two years, the Nelly continues to delight and surprise customers with their range of seven to nine ever-changing beers and around a dozen real ciders, alongside a large selection of craft keg beers. Monthly Saturday evening live music is performed, regular Sunday quizzes organised and occasional brewery showcase events are featured. Themed food nights are held during the week and the home-cooked Sunday lunches are highly recommended.
✿⓵≑♣♠🚲(211) ❁🛇♪

Tunbridge Wells

Fuggles Beer Café 🄻 ✅
28 Grosvenor Road, TN1 2AP (opp Tesco bus stop)
☎ (01892) 457739 🌐 fugglesbeercafe.co.uk/about
Tonbridge Coppernob; 3 changing beers (sourced nationally; often Gun, Oakham, Ramsgate) 🅷
A deceptively spacious town-centre establishment which combines the best elements of a British pub and a continental café-style bar. The constantly changing cask beers and cask ciders are supplemented by an impressive number of often quite exotic craft keg offerings and bottled beers. Frequent events showcase breweries from home and abroad, or different beer styles, making Fuggles a place to congregate for those seeking variety and interest in their beers. Toasties and charcuterie bar snacks are served. 🛏⓵♿≑♣♠🚲❁🛇

George 🄻
29 Mount Ephraim, TN4 8AA
☎ (01892) 539492 🌐 thegeorgepubtunbridgewells.co.uk
Fonthill Good Morning Captain, Creedence; Gun Zamzama IPA; Long Man Best Bitter; 3 changing beers (sourced locally; often 360 Degree, Only With Love, Pig & Porter) 🅷

After some previous incarnations the George's owners have returned the pub to its former coaching inn style – with improvements! The old stables have been converted into the home of Fonthill brewery and a cosy Tap Room is open Friday evenings and all day Saturday. A partly-covered secluded rear garden has also been created. Internally there are comfortable sofas, several large tables enabling groups to meet and converse, and two log burners active in winter. A selection of traditional board games is available. 🌳🏠🍴♿♣👜🚪🚆🐕🛜

Grove Tavern ✔

19 Berkeley Road, TN1 1YR

☎ (01892) 526549 🌐 grovetavern.co.uk

Harvey's Sussex Best Bitter; Timothy Taylor Landlord; 2 changing beers (sourced nationally; often Harvey's, Marston's) Ⓗ

Suitably placed within Tunbridge Wells' attractive old village area and only five minutes' walk from the rail station and numerous bus routes, this well-loved pub has benefitted from new visitors drawn by its appearance in the Guide for more than 20 years. On entry, customers may first be greeted by the friendly resident dog before receiving a similarly amiable welcome from the locals. A cosy pub where conversation over a few good beers is the order of the day. 🌳🍴♣👜🚪🐕🛜

Royal Oak Ⓛ

92 Prospect Road, TN2 4SY

☎ (01892) 542546 🌐 theroyaloaktw.co.uk

Harvey's Sussex Best Bitter; 5 changing beers (sourced regionally; often Cellar Head, Five Points, Iron Pier) Ⓗ

The Oak is a family-owned, spacious and well-kept free house a short walk from the town centre and railway station. With up to seven handpumps the focus is on providing a choice of ever-changing beers, mainly from Kent and Sussex, together with real ciders from Turners and Charrington's. Entertainment is promoted with live bands performing most Saturday evenings and during the Tunbridge Wells Fringe Festival. A chalkboard advertises forthcoming music, events and quizzes. A pizza van serves on Friday and Saturday evenings 5-9pm. 🌳🏠🍴♣👜P🚪(6,285)🏳️🛜♬

Sussex Arms Ⓛ

Sussex Mews, TN2 5TE (off the Pantiles)

☎ (01892) 549579 🌐 thesussextw.co.uk

Fonthill Good Morning Captain; Long Man Best Bitter; 2 changing beers (sourced nationally) Ⓗ

An historic pub hidden away behind the picturesque Pantiles area of town serving an interesting selection of ever-changing ales and cider to supplement a regular Tunbridge Wells-brewed Fonthill beer. The cosy main bar has an open fire and log burners at either end and TV screens show major sporting events. Both covered and uncovered outdoor seating is available for warmer days. Regular events, including live music and comedy, are held in the basement which can also be hired for private events. 🌳🏠🍴♣👜🚪🐕🛜♬

Upper Upnor

King's Arms

2 High Street, ME2 4XG

☎ (01634) 717490 🌐 kingsarmsupnor.co.uk

5 changing beers (sourced nationally) Ⓗ

Four real ales offer a choice of strong, blonde, brown and black beers. The pub has a good reputation for food, served lunchtimes and evenings either at the bar or in the restaurant. At least four ciders and a larger section of European bottled beers are also sold. There is a large garden with seating, some of it covered. The free village car park is next door. Just down the cobbled High Street from the pub is the Upnor Castle which looks over the River Medway to Chatham Dockyard. Q🌳🏠🍴♿♣👜P🚪(197)🏳️🛜

Wainscott

Crafty Fox

1 Hollywood Lane, ME3 8AG

☎ (01634) 921088

3 changing beers (sourced regionally; often Grainstore, Kent) Ⓗ/Ⓖ

A two-bar pub with a log-burning stove in the main bar, lit when it is cold. It is the quiet room of the former working men's club. Various board games are played and families are welcome. The back bar has a dartboard. There is a small seating area outside at the front of the pub. 🌳🏠♿♣👜🚪(191)🏳️

Walmer

Berry 🍷 Ⓛ

23 Canada Road, CT14 7EQ

☎ (01304) 362411 🌐 theberrywalmer.com

Harvey's Sussex Best Bitter; Oakham Citra; Thornbridge Jaipur IPA; 12 changing beers (often Ramsgate, Time & Tide) Ⓗ

A pleasant 15 minute walk along Deal's seafront brings you to this multi award-winning alehouse offering a warm welcome and friendly service. The bar has a light and airy feel and at the back there is a pleasant courtyard. There is great choice of quality ales and ciders, with up to 11 cask beers, seven KeyKeg ales (many from Time & Tide), and more than 12 ciders. Two beer festivals are hosted annually. Events include quiz nights, live music and pop-up food nights. 🌳🏠♣👜🚪🏳️♬

Freed Man Ⓛ

329 Dover Road, CT14 7NX

☎ (01304) 364457 🌐 thefreed-man.co.uk

4 changing beers Ⓗ

The unremarkable exterior hides a micropub providing everything for the discerning drinker. Up to four real ales, predominantly from local breweries, are served from a Victorian beer engine. Alongside these are real ciders, wines, selected spirits and authentic draught and bottled European lagers. The decor is cosy and warm with nautical memorabilia covering the reclaimed wood walls. Food can be brought in and the staff will provide plates and cutlery. Regular events include a Thursday ladies' night and monthly quiz night. Q🌳🔺🍴♣👜🚪🏳️🛜

West Malling

Bull Inn

1 High Street, ME19 6QH

☎ (01732) 842753 🌐 thebullwestmalling.com

Fuller's London Pride; Goacher's Gold Star Strong Ale; Young's London Original; 4 changing beers (sourced nationally; often Goacher's, Musket) Ⓗ

Some distance from the rest of the town's pubs, at the north end of the High Street close to the village green and the Hope statue, lies this traditional free house. There is a focus on local beers, and a lower-priced beer badged as Bull's Malling Special is often from Musket. The terraced garden features covered areas and heaters for colder months but is a surprising suntrap in summer. A quiz is held on Monday evenings. Q🌳🏠🍴🚪(72,151)🏳️🛜♬

Malling Jug
52 High Street, ME19 6LU (in a narrow alley opp Swan St between a funeral directors and a charity shop)
☎ (01732) 667832
Kent Session Pale; 6 changing beers (sourced nationally) G
Hidden down an alleyway off the High Street, this former residential property has been converted to a small, modern pub with its own courtyard garden at the rear. Current and forthcoming beers, mainly from microbreweries, are shown on a chalkboard and on clipboards located throughout the pub. A periodic table of beer styles helps you find your preferred style. Beers are served straight from the cask and may be ordered as pints, halves or three third-pint samplers on beer bats. Q❀🕮&🗲♣🌳🚪(72,151)🐾🎴

Westgate-on-Sea

Bake & Alehouse
21 St Mildred's Road, CT8 8RE
☎ 07913 368787 ⊕ bakeandalehouse.com
5 changing beers G
Welcoming micropub situated down the alleyway next to the Carlton Cinema, an oasis for the real ale drinker and a frequent local CAMRA pub of the Year winner. A selection of between six and eight real ales, sourced mainly from Kentish breweries, with other beers from all around the country, are served straight from the cask with love by John the landlord and his small select team. Locally produced pork pies are also available. Q◖🗲♣🌳🚪🐾

Whitstable

Handsome Sam L
3 Canterbury Road, CT5 4HJ
☎ 07947 984991
4 changing beers (sourced locally; often Four Candles, Pig & Porter, Tonbridge) G
Popular micropub just outside the town centre, 10 minutes' walk from the railway station. Named after the original owner's late cat, the high-ceilinged pub has original exposed beams and a cat motif is used throughout. Catman murals adorn the walls – the Catman artist lives locally. The beers are usually, but not always, from Kent breweries, and the draught cider is from Biddenden. Check the Facebook page for details of televised major sporting events and quiz nights. Q🕭🐕🗲🌳🚪🐾

Ship Centurion L ✅
111 High Street, CT5 1AY
☎ (01227) 264740
Adnams Southwold Bitter; 4 changing beers (sourced regionally; often Canterbury Ales, Goacher's, Ramsgate) H
A friendly and traditional town-centre pub. Colourful hanging baskets add to its charm in summer, and pictures of Whitstable are displayed in the bar. A Kentish beer is always served. Home-cooked bar food includes authentic German dishes. A roast is served on Sundays, booking advised. Live music plays on Thursday evenings (except in January). A good place to watch sport on Sky and BT. 🕭◖🗲♣🌳🚪🐾🎴♫

Twelve Taps
102 High Street, CT5 1AZ
☎ (01227) 770777 ⊕ thetwelvetaps.co.uk
12 changing beers (sourced regionally; often Kernel, Left Handed Giant, Verdant) K

A craft beer bar decorated in warm colours with wooden floors and a pleasant suntrap courtyard. Twelve KeyKeg beers are served – try a sample paddle of three beers to find your favourites. Many artisan gins, including the in-house Whitstable Gin, are also available, plus interesting soft drinks, snacks and cocktails. Look out for the drag bingo night on the last Tuesday of the month. Check Twitter for the winner of the dog of the day award. Open on bank holiday Mondays. 🕭🐾&🗲🚪🐾🎴

Breweries

Breakwater
St Martin's Yard, Lorne Road, Dover, CT16 2AA
☎ (01304) 410144 ☎ 07979 867045
✉ andrea@breakwater.brewery.co.uk

⊗ Brewery and taproom run on micropub lines behind Buckland Corn Mill in former industrial premises and on the site of the former Wellington Brewery. ♦LIVE ⚒

Dover Pale Ale (ABV 3.5%) BITTER
East Kent Gold (ABV 4.2%) GOLD
Red Ensign (ABV 4.2%) BITTER
Blue Ensign (ABV 4.3%) BITTER
Cowjuice Milk Stout (ABV 4.4%) STOUT
American Pale Ale (ABV 5%) PALE

By The Mile
Broadstairs, CT10 1SL ☎ 07900 954680
✉ jon@bythemilebrewery.co.uk

⊗ By the Mile began brewing in 2016 in domestic premises. Brewing is currently suspended.

Canterbury Ales SIBA
Canterbrew Ltd, Unit 7, Stour Valley Business Park, Ashford Road, Chartham, CT4 7HF
☎ (01227) 732541 ☎ 07944 657978
⊕ canterbury-ales.co.uk

⊗ Brewing commenced in 2010. An eight-barrel plant is used. ‼♦

The Wife of Bath's Ale (ABV 3.9%) GOLD
A golden beer with strong bitterness and grapefruit hop character, leading to a long, dry finish.
The Reeve's Ale (ABV 4.1%) BITTER
The Miller's Ale (ABV 4.5%) RED

Canterbury Brewers
⧉ **Foundry Brew Pub, 77 Stour Street, Canterbury, CT1 2NR**
☎ (01227) 455899
⊕ canterburybrewers-distillers.co.uk

⊗ Canterbury Brewers started in the Foundry Brewpub in the heart of Canterbury in 2011. The eight-barrel plant is purpose-built. Popular events are held there including the Kent Green Hop Festival (late September/early October). A wide range of spirits are now distilled in the brewpub, and three ciders are produced. ‼♦

Curious
Unit 1, Victoria Road, Ashford, TN23 7HQ
☎ (01580) 763033

Office: Level 2, Civic Centre, Tannery Lane, Ashford, TN23 1PL ⊕ curiousbrewery.com

⊗ Situated next to Ashford International Railway Station, this multi-million pound investment by former parent company Chapel Down, opened in 2019 prior to being taken over by Risk Capital Partners in 2021. It is a modern, state-of-the-art brewery, with a shop, tasting room (ground floor), bar and 120-seater restaurant (upstairs) featuring the Curious Brew core range, and special/seasonal brews. Products are widely available in keg, bottle and can (previously contract brewed). Fresh unpasteurised, filtered beer from the brewery is served from tanks above the bar. Tours and tastings offered. ‼🍴

Docker (NEW)

Unit 14, Riverside Craft Centre, West Hythe, Folkestone, CT21 4NB
☎ **(01303) 883220** 🌐 **dockerbrewery.com**

Brewing and baking commenced in 2016 inside a container on Folkestone Harbour Arm. A 10-barrel commercial plant is used, situated a stone's throw from Hop Fuzz Brewery (qv) and the Unit 1 pub. Its brewery tap is the Goods Shed, Canterbury. Docker's ethos is enviro-forward with local hops used for brewing. All ales are live, unfiltered and vegan. Cans are sold at retail outlets and online, kegs at pubs nationally. ‼🍴♦V

Farriers Arms

🍴 **The Forstal, Mersham, TN25 6NU**
☎ **(01233) 720444** 🌐 **thefarriersarms.com**

Brewing commenced in 2010 in this brewpub owned by a consortium of villagers. ‼♦

Floc (NEW)

Unit 7a, Wincheap Industrial Estate, Cotton Road, Canterbury, CT1 3RB 🌐 **flocbrewing.com**

Floc is a community-driven brewery producing unfiltered, vegan-friendly beer in keg and can. It began on a one-barrel brew plant in Margate before moving to its new home in Canterbury. Its taproom is open at weekends. V♦

Fonthill

🍴 **c/o George, 29 Mount Ephraim, Tunbridge Wells, TN4 8AA**
☎ **(01892) 539492**
🌐 **thegeorgepubtunbridgewells.co.uk**

⊗ Fonthill is a small-batch brewery located in the George pub. Beers are available in the pub as well as its two sister pubs in Tunbridge Wells.

Four Candles

🍴 **1 Sowell Street, St Peters, CT10 2AT** ☎ **07947 062063** 🌐 **thefourcandles.co.uk**

⊗ Based in the cellar of the micropub of the same name, Four Candles uses a 2.5-barrel plant and produces up to 10 nine-gallon casks with each brew. Never brewing the same ale twice, the brewery supplies the micropub, which is named after the well known Two Ronnies sketch. ‼

Goacher's

Unit 8, Tovil Green Business Park, Burial Ground Lane, Tovil, Maidstone, ME15 6TA
☎ **(01622) 682112** 🌐 **goachers.com**

A traditional brewery that uses only malt and Kentish hops for all its beers. Phil and Debbie Goacher have concentrated on brewing good, wholesome beers without gimmicks. Two tied houses and around 30 free

trade outlets in the mid-Kent area are supplied. Special is brewed for sale under house names. ‼♦

Real Mild Ale (ABV 3.4%) MILD
A rich, flavourful mild with moderate roast barley and a generous helping of chocolate malt.
Fine Light Ale (ABV 3.7%) BITTER
A pale, golden brown bitter with a strong, floral, hoppy aroma and aftertaste. A hoppy and moderately-malty session beer.
Special/House Ale (ABV 3.8%) BITTER
Best Dark Ale (ABV 4.1%) BITTER
Dark in colour but light and quaffable in body, this ale features hints of caramel and chocolate malt throughout.
Crown Imperial Stout (ABV 4.5%) STOUT
A good, well-balanced roasty stout, dark and bitter with just a hint of caramel and a lingering creamy head.
Gold Star Strong Ale (ABV 5.1%) BLOND
A strong pale ale brewed from 100% Maris Otter malt and East Kent Goldings hops.

Goody SIBA

Bleangate Brewery, Braggs Lane, Herne, CT6 7NP
☎ **(01227) 361555** 🌐 **goodyales.co.uk**

Goody Ales began brewing in 2012 using a 10-barrel plant. A wood-burning boiler is used to heat the water for the brews using wood from its copse, thereby minimising the use of non-renewable fuel. An onsite bar and shop, the Cathedral, is open (limited hours). 🍴♦LIVE🍺

Good Evening (ABV 3.4%) MILD
Genesis (ABV 3.5%) RED
Good Health (ABV 3.6%) BITTER
Good Life (ABV 3.9%) BLOND
Good Heavens (ABV 4.1%) BITTER
Good Sheppard (ABV 4.5%) BITTER
Goodness Gracious Me (ABV 4.8%) BITTER
Good Lord (ABV 5%) PORTER

Hinks

1 Dimon Villas, Hamstreet Road, Ruckinge, TN26 2NT
☎ **07518 569041** ✉ **hinkscraftbrewery@gmail.com**

🌀A nanobrewery established in 2018 that mainly retails mini kegs and bottle-conditioned ales. ♦LIVE

Hop Fuzz SIBA

Unit 8, Riverside Industrial Estate, West Hythe, CT21 4NB ☎ **07858 562878/ 07730 768881**
🌐 **hopfuzz.co.uk**

Two friends started brewing in 2011 alongside the Royal Military Canal. Now sandwiched between Docker and its former taproom, Unit 1 where beers from both brewers are always available. Its commercial plant is plumbed with a thermostatic cooling system for year-round consistency. Cask, kegs and bottles are delivered nationally. ♦

Fallout (ABV 3.6%) BLOND
English (ABV 4%) BITTER
American (ABV 4.2%) GOLD
Martello (ABV 4.5%) RED

Hopdaemon SIBA

Unit 1, Parsonage Farm, Seed Road, Newnham, ME9 0NA
☎ **(01795) 892078** 🌐 **hopdaemon.com**

Tonie Prins originally started brewing in Tyler Hill near Canterbury in 2000 and moved to a new site in

Newnham in 2005. The brewery currently supplies more than 100 outlets. ‼◆LIVE

Golden Braid (ABV 3.7%) BITTER
A refreshing golden session bitter with a good blend of bittering and aroma hops underpinned by pale malt.
Incubus (ABV 4%) BITTER
A well-balanced, copper-hued best bitter. Pale malt and a hint of crystal malt are blended with bitter and slightly floral hops to give a lingering hoppy finish.
Skrimshander IPA (ABV 4.5%) BITTER
Green Daemon (ABV 5%) SPECIALITY
Leviathan (ABV 6%) BITTER

Iron Pier SIBA

Units 6 & 7, May Industrial Estate, May Avenue, Northfleet, Gravesend, DA11 8RU ⊕ ironpier.beer

⊠ Iron Pier Brewery was established in 2017 using a 15-barrel plant. It takes its name from the oldest iron pier in existence residing on the River Thames at Gravesend. An onsite taproom offers the brewery's beers plus other local brews. ‼◆⬦

Perry St Pale (ABV 3.7%) GOLD
Joined at the Hop Pale Ale (ABV 3.8%) GOLD
Bitter (ABV 4%) BITTER
Wealdway (ABV 4.5%) GOLD
Cast Iron Stout (ABV 4.7%) STOUT
Rosherville Red (ABV 4.8%) RED

Isla Vale

Margate, CT9 5DJ
☎ (01843) 292451 ☎ 07980 174616
⊕ islavalealesmiths.co.uk

⊠ Isla Vale was established in 2014 from a residential address in Westbrook (Margate) and supplies local micropubs. A one-barrel plant is used to brew its core range as well as a specially commissioned beer for the Wheel Alehouse, Birchington. ◆

Kent SIBA

The Long Barn, Birling Place Farm, Stangate Road, Birling, ME19 5JN
☎ (01634) 780037 ⊕ kentbrewery.com

⊠ Kent Brewery was founded in 2010 by Toby Simmonds (ex-brewer from Dark Star) and Paul Herbert. A 10-barrel plant has been in operation at the Birling site since 2011. More than 300 outlets are supplied direct, mainly throughout Kent, Sussex and London. More than a dozen regular beers are produced plus a constantly changing list of specials. House beers are also brewed for The Craft Beer Co pubs. Casks are also sold thoughout the UK and abroad, particularly in Sweden and Finland. ◆LIVE

Session Pale (ABV 3.7%) PALE
Black Gold (ABV 4%) PALE
Pale (ABV 4%) PALE
Cobnut (ABV 4.1%) BITTER
Kent Golding Bitter (ABV 4.1%) BITTER
Zingiber (ABV 4.1%) SPECIALITY
Quiet American (ABV 4.2%) GOLD
Single Hop (ABV 4.5%) GOLD
Stout (ABV 4.5%) STOUT
Prohibition (ABV 4.8%) PALE
The New Black (ABV 4.8%) PALE
Tropic Ale (ABV 4.9%) PALE
Brewers Reserve (ABV 5%) GOLD

Koomor

c/o New Dartford Sports Bar, 13 Spital Street, Dartford, DA1 2DJ

Formed in 2020, the brewery now cuckoo brews at various locations, however, initial brews were conducted in the cellar of the Dartford Sports Bar. Koomor produce cask and bottled beers, currently only for the local area. The beers are all vegan and utilise whole hops from Kent, and may be cloudy. V

Bark (ABV 3.6%) MILD
Trunk (ABV 3.8%) BITTER
Branch (ABV 4.2%) GOLD
Earth (ABV 4.8%) PORTER
Petal (ABV 4.8%) PALE

Larkins SIBA

Larkins Farm, Hampkins Hill Road, Chiddingstone, TN8 7BB
☎ (01892) 870328 ⊕ larkinsbrewery.co.uk

⊠ Larkins brewery was founded by the Dockerty family in Rusthall, Kent, in 1986, on the site of the original Royal Tunbridge Wells Brewery. In 1988 the brewery relocated to Larkins Farm in Chiddingstone. All beers include hops grown on a four-acre site near the farm and are brewed with its own yeast strain. The brewery delivers direct to around 40-50 pubs and restaurants within a 20-mile radius. ‼◆

Traditional Ale (ABV 3.4%) BITTER
Pale (ABV 4.2%) PALE
Best (ABV 4.4%) BITTER
Full-bodied, slightly fruity and unusually bitter for its gravity.
Porter (ABV 5.4%) PORTER
Each taste and smell of this potent black beer reveals another facet of its character. An explosion of roasted malt, bitter and fruity flavours leaves a bittersweet aftertaste.

Mad Cat SIBA

Brogdale Farm, Brogdale Road, Faversham, ME13 8XZ
☎ (01795) 597743 ☎ 07960 263615
⊕ madcatbrewery.co.uk

⊠ Established in 2012 by Peter Meaney in a refurbished cold store using an eight-barrel plant. Beers are distributed to local pubs. Bottles and polypins are available from the brewery and Peter often attends local markets, festivals and events. ‼◆

Red Ale (ABV 3.9%) RED
Crispin Ale (ABV 4%) BLOND
Golden IPA (ABV 4.2%) PALE
Platinum Blonde (ABV 4.2%) BLOND
Emotional Blackmail (ABV 4.5%) SPECIALITY
Jet Black Stout (ABV 4.6%) STOUT

McCanns

Haffenden Farm, Bugglesden Road, St Michaels, TN30 6TG ☎ 07894 013271

Formerly known as Angels & Demons, brewing began in 2016 using a 20-barrel plant. Capacity increased to 30 barrels in 2023 when the brewery moved into the old oast at Hukins Hop Farm. The oast also has a 60-seat taproom brasserie and 120 seat patio. Onsite glamping is available. Hop, brewery and tasting tours are available all year. Two brands are brewed; the McCanns range of traditional ales, and the Angels & Demons range of craft keg beer. Keg, cask and cans are sold nationally. ‼⬦

Harry Hop (ABV 3.7%) BITTER
Hockley Soul (ABV 4.2%) STOUT

Brewed under the Angels & Demons brand name:
Bombay Social (ABV 3.8%) PALE
Racing Tiger (ABV 4.2%) SPECIALITY
Panama Jazz (ABV 4.8%) RED
I Spy Dragonfly (ABV 5%) GOLD
ADH Me (ABV 5.2%) PALE
Goldilocks is Dead (ABV 5.3%) GOLD
Black Taxi to the Moon (ABV 5.4%) SPECIALITY

MootBrew

Court Farm, Pilgrims Road, Upper Halling, Rochester, ME2 1HR ⊕ mootbrew.co.uk

An independent microbrewery in the heart of Kent. A brewery and onsite taproom are being built but at present beers are cuckoo-brewed in partnership with the London Beer Lab in Brixton.

Musket SIBA

Unit 7, Loddington Farm, Loddington Lane, Linton, ME17 4AG
☎ **(01622) 749931** ☎ **07967 127278**
⊕ musketbrewery.co.uk

Launched in 2013 with a five-barrel plant, this family-owned brewery is based at Loddington Farm, Linton, in the heart of the Kent countryside. Expanding to a 15-barrel plant with onsite taproom, it now supplies more than 300 pubs, micropubs and clubs throughout Kent and Medway. ♦✦

Trigger (ABV 3.6%) BLOND
Fife & Drum (ABV 3.8%) BLOND
Matchlock (ABV 3.8%) MILD
Ball Puller (ABV 4%) BITTER
Flintlock (ABV 4.2%) BITTER
Muzzleloader (ABV 4.5%) SPECIALITY

Nelson SIBA

Unit 2, Building 64, The Historic Dockyard, Chatham, ME4 4TE
☎ **(01634) 832828** ⊕ nelsonbrewery.co.uk

☺Nelson have been in the Historic Dockyard, Chatham since 1995. Nelson supplies over 350 outlets across the country, thanks in part, to a deal with a national courier. It also carries out brewery swaps. Home to the Gemstone Ales range, whose beers are supplied to its own pub, the Fisherman's Arms, Maidstone, as well as in the free trade. All ales can be supplied bottle-conditioned, in cans, kegs, polypins, and cask. Brewing is currently suspended. ‼️🍺♦LIVE✦

No Frills Joe

50 Wakefield Road, Greenhithe, DA9 9JE ☎ **07516 725577**

⊗ Unpasteurised, unfiltered, and unfined vegan beers are produced on a small five-barrel plant, and may be cloudy. The range is available in pubs nationwide. Up to eight different beers are available in cans. LIVE V

Joe Solo Pale Ale (ABV 5.5%) GOLD

Northdown SIBA IFBB

Unit J1C/A, Channel Road, Westwood Industrial Estate, Margate, CT9 4JS ☎ **07791 441219**
⊕ northdownbrewery.co.uk

⊗ Northdown began brewing in 2018 using a seven-barrel plant. It is run by Jonny and Katie Spanjar and takes its name from their original intention to run out of the Northdown area of Margate. The origins of a Northdown brewery date back to the 1600s. ‼️🍺♦LIVE✦

Bright Island (ABV 3.8%) BLOND
Dune Buggy (ABV 3.8%) PALE
Bitter Seas (ABV 4%) BITTER
Pale Ale Mary (ABV 4%) BITTER
Reginald Perrin (ABV 4%) BLOND
Tidal Pool (ABV 4.6%) PALE
Easterly (ABV 6%) IPA

Pig & Porter

9 Chapman Way, Tunbridge Wells, TN2 3EF
☎ **(01892) 615071** ⊕ pigandporter.co.uk

⊗ Originally brewing at several microbreweries in Sussex and Kent, brewing has taken place on its own plant in Tunbridge Wells since 2013, using a 10-barrel plant. ♦

Farmboy's Wages (ABV 3.8%) PALE
Blackbird (ABV 4%) STOUT
Skylarking (ABV 4%) PALE
Slave to the Money (ABV 4.1%) BITTER
Stone Free (ABV 4.3%) PALE
Got the Face On (ABV 4.5%) PALE
Jumping Frog (ABV 4.5%) GOLD
All These Vibes (ABV 5.3%) PALE

Ramsgate (Gadds') SIBA

1 Hornet Close, Pyson's Road Industrial Estate, Broadstairs, CT10 2YD
☎ **(01843) 868453** ⊕ ramsgatebrewery.co.uk

Ramsgate was established in 2002 at the back of a Ramsgate seafront pub. In 2006 the brewery moved to its current location, allowing for increased capacity and bottling. A 25-hectolitre brew plant is used. ‼️🍺♦

Gadds' Hoppy Pale (ABV 3.6%) BLOND
Gadds' No. 7 Bitter Ale (ABV 3.8%) BITTER
Gadds' Seasider (ABV 4.3%) BITTER
Gadds' No. 5 Best Bitter Ale (ABV 4.4%) BITTER
Gadds' SheSells SeaShells (ABV 4.7%) GOLD
Gadds' No. 3 Kent Pale Ale (ABV 5%) BLOND
Gadds' Faithful Dogbolter Porter (ABV 5.6%) PORTER
Gadds' Black Pearl (ABV 6.2%) STOUT

Romney Marsh

Unit 7, Jacks Park, Cinque Ports Road, New Romney, TN28 8AN
☎ **(01797) 362333** ⊕ romneymarshbrewery.com

⊗ Romney Marsh Brewery launched in 2015. The team consists of husband and wife, Matt Calais and Cathy Koester, plus Matt's dad, Brian Calais. The barley, wheat and oats used for the beers are sourced in Britain, and hops are worldwide. Beer is supplied to outlets throughout Kent and East Sussex, plus cases of bottled beers can also be ordered online for nationwide delivery. ‼️🍺LIVE

Romney Best Bitter (ABV 4%) BITTER
Romney Amber Ale (ABV 4.4%) PALE
Marsh Sunset (ABV 4.8%) RED
Romney APA (ABV 5%) PALE

Running Man

26 Greenway, Davis Estate, Chatham, ME5 9UX

Running Man was established in 2018 by Chris Mildren with assistance from a relative. It is a small batch producer with occasional bottling.

Shepherd Neame IFBB

17 Court Street, Faversham, ME13 7AX
☎ (01795) 532206 ⊕ shepherdneame.co.uk

⊗ Shepherd Neame traces its history back to at least 1698, making it the oldest continuous brewer in the country. The company has around 300 tied houses in the South-East, nearly all selling cask ale. More than 2,000 other outlets are also supplied by this independent family brewer. The cask beers are made with mostly Kentish hops, and water from the brewery's own artsian well. The Cask Club offers a new and different cask ale every month or so. ‼ ▉ ◆LIVE

Master Brew (ABV 3.7%) BITTER
A distinctive bitter, mid-brown in colour, with a hoppy aroma. Well-balanced, with a nicely aggressive bitter taste from its hops, it leaves a hoppy/bitter finish, tinged with sweetness.
Whitstable Bay Pale Ale (ABV 3.9%) PALE
Spitfire Gold (ABV 4.1%) GOLD
Spitfire (ABV 4.2%) BITTER
Malty caramel with bitter hops and caramelised fruit and citrus flavours. Spiciness builds and remains in the hoppy dry finish.
Bishops Finger (ABV 5%) BITTER

Shivering Sands

91 Maple Leaf Business Park, Manston, CT12 5GD
☎ 07805 061343
⊕ shivering-sands-brewery.business.site

⊗ Established in 2020. Situated in an industrial estate outside the airfield at Manston, near Ramsgate, it uses an eight-barrel plant, brewing once a week. Its onsite taproom is open on Saturdays and at other times by arrangement. ◆

Spring Tide (ABV 3.8%) PALE
Maunsell (ABV 4%) BITTER
Estuary Porter (ABV 4.1%) PORTER
Golden Sands (ABV 4.5%) PALE
Knock John (ABV 4.5%) BITTER
Ribersborg Stout (ABV 4.7%) STOUT

Stag

Little Engeham Farm, Bethersden Road, Woodchurch, TN26 3QY ☎ 07539 974068 ⊕ stagbrewery.co.uk

⊗ Operating since 2016 at Engeham Farm, also home to Kent's largest steam rally. All brews are dry-hopped and unfiltered before leaving the five-barrel commercial plant. Stag beer can be bought at the rally, in local pubs and minikegs online. ◆LIVE

Screaming Sika (ABV 5%) GOLD

Swan on the Green

▤ Swan on the Green, West Peckham, Maidstone, ME18 5JW
☎ (01622) 812271 ⊕ swan-on-the-green.co.uk

⊗ The brewery was established in 2000 in an old coal shed behind the Swan on the Green pub using a two-barrel plant. Brewing is currently suspended. ‼◆

Time & Tide

Statenborough Farm, Felderland Lane, Eastry, CT14 0BX ☎ 07739 868256
⊕ timeandtidebrewing.co.uk

Time & Tide Brewery was founded in 2013 and is situated on the outskirts of Eastry, Kent. Five regular beers are brewed as well as a range of seasonal ales, including those brewed with hops from the Deal Hop Farm community hop growing project. Its taproom, open during the summer, features a good range of its own beers as well as an extensive range of canned beer from other microbreweries. ‼ ▉ ◆LIVE V◆

Tír Dhá Ghlas

▤ Cullins Yard, 11 Cambridge Road, Dover, CT17 9BY
☎ (01304) 211666 ⊕ cullinsyard.co.uk

⊗ Brewing began in 2012 using a two-barrel plant. Beers are only available in the bar/restaurant and occasionally at the nearby Royal Cinque Ports Yacht Club.

Tonbridge SIBA

Unit 19, Branbridges Industrial Estate, East Peckham, TN12 5HF
☎ (01622) 871239 ⊕ tonbridgebrewery.co.uk

⊗ Tonbridge Brewery was launched in 2010 using a four-barrel plant, expanding to a 12-barrel one in 2013. It supplies pubs, clubs and restaurants throughout Kent, East Sussex and South-East London. While cask-conditioned beer remains its core focus, the brewery started bottling and canning, which has expanded its keg range. It continues using the live yeast which originated from Barclay Perkins of Southwark. While the range has expanded to include hops from Europe, North America and New Zealand, the majority are still sourced in Kent.

Golden Rule (ABV 3.5%) GOLD
Traditional Ale (ABV 3.6%) BITTER
Coppernob (ABV 3.8%) BITTER
Countryman (ABV 4%) BITTER
Rustic (ABV 4%) MILD
Blonde Ambition (ABV 4.2%) BLOND
Old Chestnut (ABV 4.4%) BITTER
American Pale (ABV 5%) PALE
Velvet Raven (ABV 5.2%) STOUT

Wantsum SIBA

Kent Barn, St Nicholas Court Farm, Court Road, St Nicholas at Wade, CT7 0PT
☎ (01227) 910135 ⊕ wantsumbrewery.co.uk

⊗ Wantsum Brewery, established by James Sandy in 2009, takes its name from the nearby Wantsum Channel. Located in St Nicholas at Wade just outside Canterbury. Wantsum brews a wide range of traditional and modern craft ale styles packaged in cask, keg, minikegs, polypins, bottles and cans, supplied to outlets throughout the south of England. An onsite taproom and shop showcases a wide selection of the beers. An online shop ships nationwide. ‼ ▉ ◆LIVE ◆

More's Head (ABV 3.7%) BITTER
Ruby golden brown beer with fruity American hops and rye.
1381 (ABV 3.8%) BLOND
Black Prince (ABV 3.9%) MILD
Imperium (ABV 4%) BITTER
Montgomery (ABV 4%) PALE
An amber-coloured, light, easy, summer session beer with American hops that are light and refreshing. Spicy finish. Simcoe, Columbus, Centennial hops.

One Hop (ABV 4.2%) GOLD
Dynamo (ABV 4.3%) GOLD
Turbulent Priest (ABV 4.4%) BROWN
Hurricane (ABV 4.5%) GOLD
Fortitude (ABV 4.6%) BITTER
Black Pig (ABV 4.8%) PORTER
Black porter with sweet aroma. The flavour is of sweet malt, roasty chocolate and fruit that fade in the finish.
Golgotha (ABV 5.5%) STOUT
Smooth, rich dry roasty stout with dark fruits and malt throughout.
Ravening Wolf (ABV 5.9%) SPECIALITY

Westerham SIBA

Beggars Lane, Westerham, TN16 1QP
☎ (01732) 864427 ⊕ westerhambrewery.co.uk

⊠ Having moved in 2017 to a new, purpose-built brewery, Westerham opened a taproom with 12 taps serving beer straight from the maturation tank. The brewery benefits from the supply of Greensand aquifer water from an onsite borehole. It also utilises original heritage yeasts from the former Black Eagle Brewery, thus maintaining a link to the Kent style of the past. More than 500 outlets are supplied in Kent, Surrey, Sussex and London. ‼☰♦LIVE♠

Grasshopper Kentish Bitter (ABV 3.8%) BITTER
Summer Perle (ABV 3.8%) GOLD
Spirit of Kent (ABV 4%) GOLD
British Bulldog (ABV 4.1%) BITTER
1965 – Special Bitter Ale (ABV 4.8%) BITTER

Audit Ale (ABV 6.2%) BITTER

Whitstable SIBA

Little Telpits Farm, Woodcock Lane, Grafty Green, ME17 2AY
☎ (01622) 851007 ⊕ whitstablebrewery.co.uk

Whitstable Brewery was founded in 2003. It currently provides all the beer for the Whitstable Oyster Company's three restaurants, its hotel and a brewery tap, as well as supplying pubs all over Kent, London and Surrey. ♦

Native Bitter (ABV 3.7%) BITTER
A classic copper-coloured Kentish session bitter with hoppy aroma and a long, dry bitter hop finish.
Renaissance Ruby Mild (ABV 3.7%) MILD
East India Pale Ale (ABV 4.1%) PALE
A well-hopped golden IPA with good grapefruit aroma hop character and lingering bitter finish.
Oyster Stout (ABV 4.5%) STOUT
Pearl of Kent (ABV 4.5%) BLOND
Winkle Picker (ABV 4.5%) BITTER
Kentish Reserve (ABV 5%) BITTER

XYLO

⬛ Unit 1, 2-14 High Street, Margate, CT9 1AT
☎ (01843) 229403 ⊕ xylobrew.com

Neil Wright and Ben Atkins set up the XYLO brewery and pub in 2019 using a four-barrel brew plant built in the pub cellar. Keg and canned beer only at the moment. ‼

Nelson Arms, Tonbridge

OXFORDSHIRE

Abingdon

Brewery Tap 🅛
40-42 Ock Street, OX14 5BZ
☎ (01235) 521655 ⊕ thebrewerytap.net
**Loose Cannon Gunners Gold; LoveBeer Bonnie Hops;
Renegade Good Old Boy; 2 changing beers (sourced
locally; often Oxford, White Horse, XT)** Ⓗ
Morland created a tap for its brewery in 1993 from three
Grade II-listed town houses. The brewery is no more but
the pub, run by the same family since it opened, has
thrived. It offers a diverse range of beers, all sourced
locally, and hosts two or three beer festivals each year
featuring ales from further afield. The pub has three
rooms, two of them away from the bar, and a courtyard
outside. Q🍸🐕🛇🍴◐&♣️P🔔🐾🛜♪

Broad Face 🍺 🅛
30-32 Bridge Street, OX14 3HR
☎ (01235) 538612 ⊕ broadfaceabingdon.co.uk

**Dark Star Hophead; 7 changing beers (sourced
nationally; often Loose Cannon, Morland, White
Horse)** Ⓗ
Deceptively large, two-roomed, Grade II-listed pub near
the river with a small outside seating area on Thames
Street. The building was erected in 1840 but there are
records of a pub on the site dating back to 1734, and
possibly before that under a different name. Mystery
surrounds the stories behind the pub's unique name,
which are written on the outside wall, but omit the most
likely explanation – that it was originally called the
Saracen's Head and the sign was over-painted. Local
CAMRA Towns and Villages Pub of the Year 2023.
Q🍸🐕🛇◐&🔔🛜♪

Narrows 🅛 ✅
25 High Street, OX14 5AA
☎ (01235) 467680
**Greene King Abbot; Ruddles Best Bitter; Sharp's
Doom Bar; 4 changing beers (sourced nationally)** Ⓗ
Wetherspoon conversion of the former post office in
2013. The pub is named after this part of the High Street,

which, during the 19th century, was called the Narrow. The long bar leads to the former sorting office and telephone exchange, providing more space for drinkers and diners. There are plenty of historic photos and a traditional red phone box. Abingdon's was the last manual telephone exchange in England when it closed in 1975. ⬥❀◑ᵭ⬥⚲

White Horse Ⓛ ✓

189 Ock Street, OX14 5DW
☎ (01235) 524490
Greene King IPA; Morland Original Bitter; 2 changing beers (sourced nationally; often Loose Cannon, Wadworth) Ⓗ
Originally owned by the Borough of Abingdon, the White Horse dates back to 1845 and had a number of tenants who were coal merchants and publicans before the Morland family ownership. In 1999 Greene King became the new owners and extended this Grade II-listed building to provide dining facilities. This traditional English pub has a beer garden in front and its own car park. ⬥❀◑ᵭ♣P⚲❀⚲♪

Adderbury

Bell Inn Ⓛ ✓

High Street, OX17 3LS (off A4260 in centre of village)
☎ (01295) 810338 ⊕ thebelladderbury.co.uk
Hook Norton Hooky, Off The Hook, Old Hooky; 2 changing beers (sourced locally; often Hook Norton) Ⓗ
A traditional English pub with a good range of Hook Norton ales. Expect a warm welcome from the landlord and the locals at this true community hub. Authentic Neapolitan pizzas are served Friday and Saturday evenings. Sport is often shown on TV. An enclosed patio beer garden overlooks the church. The pub is the spiritual home of Adderbury Morris Men, and hosts regular folk club and music events. Two en-suite B&B rooms (including a family room) are available. Closed Monday-Thursday afternoons and Tuesday-Thursday lunchtimes. Q⬥❀☒◑ᵭ⚲♣⚲(S4)❀⚲♪

Coach & Horses ✓

The Green, OX17 3ND
☎ (01295) 810422 ⊕ coachandhorsesadderbury.co.uk
Wadworth Henry's IPA, 6X, Swordfish Ⓗ
The long-serving tenants here were deservedly awarded the Wadworth Community Pub of the Year in 2014 and their charity work continues. Three handpumps dispense ales from the Wadworth portfolio. Set in a prime location in this attractive ironstone village, just off the A4260, it certainly offers value for money from the bar menu with good, honest pub grub, including Sunday roasts (booking advisable). There is an outside seating area overlooking the village green. Closed Monday lunchtimes and Tuesday-Thursday afternoons. Q⬥❀◑ᵭP⚲(S4)❀⚲♪

Ashbury

Rose & Crown Ⓛ ✓

3 High Street, SN6 8NA
☎ (01793) 378354 ⊕ roseandcrownatashbury.co.uk
Arkell's 3B; 1 changing beer (sourced locally; often Arkell's) Ⓗ
This welcoming 16th-century coaching inn nestles at the foot of the White Horse Downs, within a mile of The Ridgeway, in the centre of the scenic village of Ashbury. It offers a range of beers from Arkell's brewery, with 3B being especially popular. Food offerings include traditional pub fare and à la carte and is sourced from

local suppliers. Accommodation is available in seven sympathetically refurbished en-suite rooms. Not to be missed. Q⬥❀☒◑ᵭ⬥♣P⚲(47)❀⚲♪

Balscote

Butchers Arms ♛ ✓

Shutford Road, OX15 6JQ
☎ (01295) 730750 ⊕ thebutchersarmsbalscote.co.uk
Hook Norton Hooky; 3 changing beers (sourced nationally; often Hook Norton) Ⓖ
A friendly welcome awaits in this cosy parlour pub where Hook Norton beers and a monthly guest are served straight from the cask behind the bar. The building was once an abattoir and still has an ice-house in the garden. Home-made fish & chips is served on Friday evening and burgers on Saturday evening. There is a monthly quiz on a Wednesday (curries served), and occasional live music. A roaring fire in winter and a lovely beer garden make this a pub for all weathers. Local CAMRA County Pub of the Year 2023. Q⬥❀◑♣P❀♪

Bampton

Morris Clown Ⓛ

High Street, OX18 2JW
☎ (01993) 850217
2 changing beers (sourced locally; often Chadlington, North Cotswold, White Horse) Ⓗ
This simply furnished single-bar free house, run by the same family for two generations, has a log fire in the winter and some unusual murals on the wall, painted by one of the family and depicting other members of the family. The name change by former owners Courage (in 1975 from New Inn) proved controversial as morris dancing teams have a fool, not a clown; this led to a 25-year boycott by the town's dancers. Closed every lunchtime and weekday afternoons. Q⬥❀♣⬥P⚲(19)❀⚲

Banbury

Coach & Horses

Butchers Row, OX16 5JH

REAL ALE BREWERIES	
Amwell Springs ✦ Cholsey	
Barn Owl Gozzards Ford	
Bicester ▤ Bicester	
Brakspear ✦ Witney	
Chadlington Chadlington	
Church Hanbrewery ✦ North Leigh	
Craftsman Abingdon	
Earth Ale Frilford Heath	
Faringdon ▤ Faringdon	
Hook Norton Hook Norton	
Little Ox Freeland	
Loddon ✦ Dunsden	
Loose Cannon ✦ Abingdon	
LoveBeer Milton	
Oxford ✦ Horspath	
Parlour Garford	
South Oxfordshire (SOX) Ipsden	
Tap Social Movement ✦ Kidlington	
Thame Thame	
Turpin Hook Norton	
Virtue Milton-under-Wychwood (NEW)	
White Horse Stanford in the Vale	
Woodstock Woodstock	
Wriggly Monkey ✦ Bicester	
Wychwood ✦ Witney	

☎ (01295) 266993 ⊕ thecoachandhorsesbanbury.com
Hook Norton Hooky, Off The Hook, Old Hooky; 1 changing beer (sourced locally; often Hook Norton) 🅷
This popular town-centre pub provides an energetic vibe and a comfortable, relaxing space for refreshment and socialising. Three or four Hook Norton beers are available, along with ciders and made-to-order cocktails. The Coach hosts regular live music events, including Banbury Folk Club each Wednesday night. The locally sourced menu is changed regularly. Alfresco drinking and dining can be enjoyed in the a small enclosed beer garden to the rear of the pub. Closed Monday.
⊛◑♿♨⚂♫

Three Pigeons
3 Southam Road, OX16 2ED
☎ (01295) 275220 ⊕ thethreepigeons.com
Purity Pure Gold; Sharp's Doom Bar; 2 changing beers (sourced nationally) 🅷
Beautiful 17th-century thatched coaching inn on the main road through Banbury, close to the town centre. There are two regular beers, usually Doom Bar and a Purity Ale, which are always in good condition. You can enjoy them in the fabulous outside courtyard in summer, or in front of the feature fireplace with wood-burner in colder months. The pub has a reputation for interesting, high-quality food, and three luxury bedrooms make a good base for a relaxing break. Closed at lunchtime on Monday and Tuesday. Q✿⚘⊛◑♿P⊟☀🛜

White Horse 🅛
50-52 North Bar Street, OX16 0TH
☎ (01295) 277484 ⊕ whitehorsebanbury.com
Everards Tiger; Turpin Golden Citrus; 2 changing beers (sourced nationally) 🅷
Friendly and welcoming community pub that always has at least four handpumps in use, offering a range of styles, including a new guest ale that is announced every Wednesday, plus several ciders. Friday nights are busy, featuring local bands or a disco with DJ. Sunday attractions include popular lunches and an entertaining monthly quiz. The sheltered courtyard garden is a lovely space for a drink. Beer festivals take place on St George's Day and Easter. Closed Monday.
Q✿⚘◑♿♣⚂⊟☀🛜♫

Beckley

Abingdon Arms 🅛
High Street, OX3 9UU
☎ (01865) 655667 ⊕ theabingdonarms.co.uk
Little Ox Yabba Dabba Doo; Oxford Prospect; 2 changing beers (sourced locally; often Chadlington, Loose Cannon, Vale) 🅷
A lovely old pub with a fine garden affording great views across Otmoor. There is a small bar and separate dining area. The arms in question are of James Bertie (1653-1699) who was created 1st Earl of Abingdon in 1682. The Bertie family owned the village until 1919 when it was broken up and sold off in lots. The pub was put up for sale in 2016 and bought by a local community group after a community share offer. Closes at 8pm Sunday-Tuesday. Q✿⊛◑♣P☀🛜

Bicester

Angel ✅
102 Sheep Street, OX26 6LP
☎ (01869) 360410 ⊕ theangelbicester.co.uk
6 changing beers (sourced regionally; often Rebellion, Vale) 🅷

At the west end of Sheep Street, a five-minute walk from the centre of town, the Angel has a good range of local guest ales on its six handpumps. The welcoming bar area has a pleasant ambience, and a log fire adds comfort on chilly days. Outside there is a large seating area, a permanent marquee, an outdoor snug and a barn, which is home to the Pizza boys pop-up restaurant Wednesday to Friday 5-9pm. Closed Monday-Friday lunchtimes.
Q✿⊛♿⇌(North) P⊟❀🛜♫

Brightwell-cum-Sotwell

Red Lion 🅛
Brightwell Street, OX10 0RT (S off A4130)
☎ (01491) 837373 ⊕ redlionbcs.co.uk
Amwell Springs Stay Jammy; Loddon Hullabaloo; 2 changing beers (sourced nationally; often Loddon, Loose Cannon) 🅷
A popular Grade II-listed thatched inn dating from the 16th century in a quiet village. Its cosy bar features exposed beams and an inglenook fireplace with log-burner, and leads to a restaurant area. The beers are usually from local breweries and a good-quality seasonal menu is served (no food Sun eve or Mon and Tue). The rear courtyard garden is a summer suntrap, and a heated marquee provides comfortable dining and drinking all year round. The pub hosts weekly meat raffles and regular live music. Closed Monday, Tuesday lunchtimes and weekday afternoons.
⚘⊛◑♿♣⚂P(23,33)❀🛜♫

Burford

Angel Inn ✅
14 Witney Street, OX18 4SN
☎ (01993) 822714 ⊕ theangelatburford.co.uk
Hook Norton Hooky, Old Hooky; 2 changing beers (sourced locally; often Hook Norton) 🅷
A small, cosy and welcoming 16th-century inn just off the High Street, warmed by a real fire. Stools and comfortable seating in front of the bar area cater for those wanting to sample the four draught ales from Hook Norton brewery, or locally sourced bar meals. There is a cosy restaurant, and a lovely courtyard and walled garden with some covered seating outside. Families and dogs are welcome. Q✿⊛⚂◑♿⚂(233,853)❀🛜♫

Golden Pheasant
91 High Street, OX18 4QA
☎ (01993) 823223
Greene King IPA, Abbot; 3 changing beers (sourced nationally; often North Cotswold) 🅷
A traditional stone building on Burford's High Street, this 18th-century coaching inn offers a warm welcome. Inside the traditional pub and hotel, which boasts a roaring log fire, are five handpumps, with four Greene King and one guest ale on offer. Food can be enjoyed in the comfy bar or the restaurant. Outside there is a courtyard area, and there are 18 guest rooms available. The pub also has its own gin, produced locally.
Q✿⚘⊛◑♿⚂(233,853)❀🛜♫

Caulcott

Horse & Groom
Lower Heyford Road, OX25 4ND
☎ (01869) 343257 ⊕ horseandgroomcaulcott.co.uk
3 changing beers (sourced nationally; often Church End, Goff's, Vale) 🅷
A charming 16th-century coaching house, warm and cosy with a welcoming fire in the winter. A free house, it offers three changing ales. The French landlord's passion

for food is reflected in a changing menu based on local fresh seasonal produce. Booking is recommended, especially Thursday steak night and Sunday lunch. The Bastille Day beer festival weekend is well worth visiting. The garden is popular in summer. Local CAMRA Pub of the Year on several occasions. Closed Monday on Tuesday, afternoons (Wed-Sat) and Sunday evenings. Q♿✿◑P🅿️

Chadlington

Tite Inn

Mill End, OX7 3NY

☎ (01608) 676910 ⊕ thetiteinn.co.uk

Chadlington Oxford Blue; 2 changing beers (sourced locally; often Chadlington) Ⓗ

A warm welcome awaits at this cosy country pub nestled in the Evenlode valley. There is a choice of three or four beers from the nearby Chadlington brewery, and a good local and seasonal menu. Your beer can be enjoyed by the cosy fireplace in winter, and in the beautiful hillside beer garden in summer. Tite is old local dialect for spring – water runs under the pub and down the hill. Closed Monday and Tuesday, and from 7pm on Sunday. Q♿✿◑Å🅿️🚲(S3,X9)♣🔉♪

Charlbury

Rose & Crown

Market Street, OX7 3PL

☎ (01608) 810103 ⊕ roseandcrown.charlbury.com

Hop Kettle Cricklade Ordinary Bitter; Salopian Oracle; 6 changing beers (sourced nationally; often Oakham, XT) Ⓗ

An ever-popular wet sales pub that has now been in this Guide for a well-deserved 37 consecutive years. It has a traditional front bar, a back bar, ideal for gatherings and meetings, and an outside space to enjoy a pint in summer. Two regular and six ever-changing ales and six traditional ciders and perries add to the fantastic choice. Pop-up food is available most Saturdays, and there is regular live music. A former local and county CAMRA Pub of the Year. Opens at 2pm Monday to Thursday. ♿✿Å🚲🍴🚲(S3,X9)♣🔉♪

Checkendon

Black Horse Ⓛ

Burncote Lane, RG8 0TE (500yds along narrow lane NE from Checkendon-Stoke Row road) SU666841

☎ (01491) 680418

Rebellion IPA; Renegade Good Old Boy; 1 changing beer (sourced nationally) Ⓖ

Hidden in the Chilterns woods is this 350-year-old three-roomed pub, run by the same family since 1916. It welcomes an eclectic mix of locals, walkers, horse riders and cyclists. Filled rolls and chips at lunchtime are the only food available. Dogs are welcome, if they are small, quiet and on a lead. It has been identified by CAMRA as having a regionally important historic pub interior. Closed on Monday, Tuesday-Saturday afternoon, and Sunday from 8pm. Q♿✿Å♣P♣

Chinnor

Red Lion Ⓛ ✅

3 High Street, OX39 4DL

☎ (01844) 353468 ⊕ theredlionchinnor.co.uk

4 changing beers (sourced nationally) Ⓗ

Multi-roomed pub that is over 300 years old and was originally three cottages. Beyond the busy bar is a separate public bar, and a lounge area with an inglenook

fireplace and wood-burning stove. A varied range of ales is served, often from local and national microbreweries. Outside is a large covered paved area with ample seating. Regular events include quiz nights. Closed lunchtimes Monday to Friday. ♿✿P🚲(40)♣🔉♪

Chipping Norton

Chequers

Goddards Lane, OX7 5NP (next to theatre, on corner of Spring St)

☎ (01608) 644717 ⊕ chequerschippingnorton.co.uk

Dark Star American Pale Ale; Fuller's London Pride; Gale's HSB; 3 changing beers (sourced nationally) Ⓗ

A traditional English pub with an emphasis on real ale and local food. Up to six ales from Fuller's, Dark Star and Gale's, along with other guests, are available. The bar has three separate areas, all with flagstones, beams and log fires, and an airy restaurant and large function space to the rear. The feature fireplace warms the small main bar area in winter and is an excellent place to relax. Handy for the local theatre and cinema. Closed Monday. Q♿◑♣♠🍴♣🔉♪

Clifton

Duke at Clifton Ⓛ

Main Street, OX15 0PE

☎ (01869) 226334 ⊕ thecliftonduke.co.uk

Turpin Golden Citrus; 3 changing beers (sourced regionally; often North Cotswold, Tring, XT) Ⓗ

This 17th-century Grade II-listed thatched country inn nestles in a delightful village above the River Cherwell. Whatever the season, it is a perfect setting to sample award-winning ales, many of which are from local brewers. The pub is warmed by a roaring fire in the inglenook fireplace, and has a superb garden for fine weather. Food is served from a locally sourced menu. Accommodation is available in rooms, an Airstream caravan, Winnebago motorhome, shepherd huts and serviced campsite. Walkers, dogs and wellies welcome. Closed Monday, Tuesday to Thursday lunchtimes, and Sunday evenings. Q♿✿🚐◑Å♣P♣🔉

Deddington

Red Lion

Market Place, OX15 0SE

☎ (01869) 338777 ⊕ redliondeddington.co.uk

Fuller's London Pride; St Austell Tribute; 1 changing beer (sourced nationally) Ⓗ

Reopened in 2019 in an attractive marketplace location, this is now established as the premier village pub. The menu focuses on excellent home-cooked plant-based dishes and fish & chips. The nearby castle grounds and surrounding countryside, with extensive views across the River Cherwell valley, make it an attractive stop on a country walk or when exploring the surrounding local ironstone villages of Banburyshire. Closed Monday, Tuesday to Friday lunchtimes and Sunday from 7pm. ♿✿◑P🚲(S4)♣♪

Dunsden

Loddon Tap Yard Ⓛ

Dunsden Green Farm, Church Lane, RG4 9QD

☎ (0118) 948 1111 ⊕ loddonbrewery.com/tapyard

Loddon Hullabaloo; 2 changing beers (sourced locally; often Loddon) Ⓗ

A popular tap yard next to the main Loddon brewhouse, serving a selection of the brewery's ales on handpump. With both indoor and outdoor seating, including covered decking, it is the perfect place to enjoy a pint in the beautiful countryside. Street food is frequently available from vendors in the courtyard. The farm shop sells local produce, including cheese, vegetables, bread and meat as well as Loddon beers and local ciders, wines, spirits and liqueurs. Closed Monday except bank holidays, Sunday evenings, and winter evenings Tuesday to Thursday. ⏰❀◐&♣●P❑(800)❀🐾🎵

Fewcott

White Lion ✪
Fritwell Road, OX27 7NZ
☎ (01869) 573709 ⊕ thewhitelionfewcott.com
2 changing beers (sourced nationally; often St Austell) Ⓗ
A family-friendly rural free house that is the hub of the community. It is warm and cosy, with a welcoming fire in the winter, and a popular garden for summer; this is a place to enjoy good conversation and excellent beer. It serves two changing ales (one only midweek), which are often new or seasonal. Major sporting events are shown on TV. Food trucks provide food either Fridays or Saturdays. Open Wednesday to Sunday from the afternoon. ⏰❀🚲&♣🐾❀🎵

Henley-on-Thames

Bird in Hand
61 Greys Road, RG9 1SB
☎ (01491) 575775
Brakspear Gravity; Fuller's London Pride; 3 changing beers (sourced nationally; often Rebellion, Timothy Taylor, Tring)
Celebrating 29 consecutive years in the Guide, the Bird has flourished under the stewardship of the same family throughout. Three guest beers complement the two regulars. TVs show sporting events, and the pub is home to darts and cribbage teams and hosts regular quiz nights. The family room leads to a delightful garden boasting a pond and aviary. Dogs on leads are welcome. A frequent winner of local CAMRA Pub of the Year. Closed weekday afternoons and Sunday from 9pm. Q⏰❀🅰≋♣📶🐾❀🎵

Hook Norton

Malthouse Kitchen (Hook Norton Brewery Visitor Centre)
Brewery Lane, OX15 5NU (follow brown tourist signs to Hook Norton Brewery)
☎ (01608) 730384
Hook Norton Hooky Mild, Hooky, Off The Hook, Old Hooky; 3 changing beers (sourced locally; often Hook Norton) Ⓗ
The visitor centre, popular with locals and tourists, encompasses a well-stocked shop dispensing brewery merchandise, the licensed Malthouse Kitchen restaurant (open every day for breakfast and lunch) and a museum area. Highly recommended brewery tours are run by appointment every day of the week, themed evening events and open tap beer nights on the second Wednesday of the month. The 1899 Board Room can be hired for corporate events and conferences and the Steep is licensed for weddings. Shire horses and a steam engine are added attractions. Closed evenings. ⏰❀◐&♣P❑(488) 🐾❀📶

Pear Tree Inn Ⓛ ✪
Scotland End, OX15 5NU (follow brown tourist signs to Hook Norton Brewery)
☎ (01608) 737482 ⊕ peartreeinnhooknorton.co.uk

Hook Norton Hooky Mild, Hooky, Off The Hook, Old Hooky; 2 changing beers (sourced locally; often Hook Norton) Ⓗ
A welcoming rural local close to the Grade II-listed Victorian tower brewery, with its restaurant and shop. This wet sales-driven pub, under the excellent management of a longstanding village resident, serves the full range of Hooky beers, which may be enjoyed in the cosy bar or large family-friendly beer garden. Delivery is by horse-drawn dray on Friday lunchtime. Accommodation is available, making this ideal for staying over before or after an award-winning brewery tour. Q⏰❀🅿🛏◐&♣P❑(488)🐾❀📶🎵

Horley

Red Lion Ⓛ
Hornton Lane, OX15 6BQ
☎ (01295) 730427
Hook Norton Hooky; Turpin Golden Citrus; Wye Valley Butty Bach Ⓗ
Friendly pub that is the focal point of the village, offering a warm welcome to locals, visitors, walkers and well-behaved dogs. Its serves three handpumped ales all year round, and a fourth for special occasions. Aunt Sally, darts and dominoes are played here. The lovely and tranquil garden area is ideal for that summer evening tipple. The St George's Day annual beer festival is a must. Local CAMRA Pub of the Year 2022. Open Tuesday to Saturday evenings and Sunday lunchtimes and afternoons. ❀🅰♣🐾📶🎵

Letcombe Regis

Greyhound Inn Ⓛ
Main Street, OX12 9JL
☎ (01235) 771969 ⊕ thegreyhoundletcombe.co.uk
4 changing beers (sourced nationally; often Oakham, Salopian, Thornbridge) Ⓗ
Large, welcoming pub in the centre of the village, featuring a single bar with dining areas and an original inglenook fireplace. It serves four constantly changing handpumped beers. Locally sourced home-cooked food is available, and can be enjoyed in the garden during the summer months. The pub is within a couple of miles of the Ridgeway and provides a place of refreshment and rest for wayfarers, with accommodation in eight en-suite bedrooms. Parking is available at the side of the pub. Local CAMRA Pub of the Year 2022. Q⏰❀🅿🛏◐&🅰P🐾❀📶🎵

Lewknor

Leathern Bottle
1 High Street, OX49 5TW (N off B4009 near M40 jct 6)
☎ (01844) 351482 ⊕ theleathernbottle.co.uk
Brakspear Gravity; Courage Directors; Young's London Special Ⓗ
Featuring in all but one edition of the Guide, this traditional Grade II-listed country pub has been run by the same family since 1980. It serves good home-cooked pub food, and has a family-friendly garden. The venue offers a warm welcome to all, including walkers from the nearby Ridgeway; some of the best trails start and finish here. It is also a short walk from stops on the Oxford-London and airline coach routes. Closed Monday except bank holidays, Tuesday-Saturday afternoons and Sunday from 4.30pm. ⏰❀◐&♣P❑🐾❀📶

Long Wittenham

Plough ㄥ
24 High Street, OX14 4QH
☎ (01865) 407738 ⊕ theploughinnlw.co.uk
Butcombe Original; 2 changing beers (sourced nationally; often Amwell Springs, Loose Cannon) ⊞
A traditional Grade II-listed family-friendly pub built in the 17th century in this rural south Oxfordshire village. Its large garden stretches down to the River Thames and has ample outdoor seating and a children's play space. There are two bar areas and a separate restaurant. One regular and two changing beers are served, from breweries and microbreweries mainly in the south-east. The pub hosts many community events, notably Wittfest, a music festival each June/July that raises money for local charities. Closed Monday, and Sunday from 9pm.
🌣🕏🕼🖢🅰♣🚊(95,D1) 🐾🛜♪

Longcot

King & Queen ㄥ
Shrivenham Road, SN7 7TL
☎ (01793) 784348 ⊕ longcotkingandqueen.co.uk
Loose Cannon Gunners Gold; 3 changing beers (sourced locally; often Little Ox, Ramsbury, White Horse) ⊞
It is thought that the King & Queen was built around 200 years ago to cater for the navvies working on the Wilts & Berks Canal which passes nearby. It offers a good selection of beers from local breweries. The interior comprises an extensive open-plan drinking area and, to one side, a restaurant serving substantial meals. Outside is a tranquil beer garden. The pub provides one of the best views of White Horse Hill and the famous 3,000-year-old white horse. B&B accommodation is offered in seven rooms. Closed Monday lunchtimes.
Q🌣🕏🕼🖢🅰🚊(67) 🐾🛜♪

Milton

Plum Pudding ㄥ
44 High Street, OX14 4EJ
☎ (01235) 834443 ⊕ theplumpuddingmilton.co.uk
Loose Cannon Abingdon Bridge; LoveBeer OG; 1 changing beer (sourced nationally) ⊞
Plum Pudding refers to the Oxford Sandy and Black pig, one of the older and rarer British breeds. The pub serves three real ales plus up to four real ciders. It hosts regular live music, and beer festivals in April and October. Sitting in the pleasant walled garden, you would not suspect that you are only a couple of minutes from the busy A34. Six en-suite rooms are available. A former local CAMRA Pub of the Year and repeat local Cider Pub of the Year. Bank holiday hours may vary.
🌣🕏🕼🖢♣🚊🐾🛜♪

Northmoor

Red Lion ㄥ ✔
Standlake Road, OX29 5SX
☎ (01865) 300301 ⊕ theredlionnorthmoor.com
Loose Cannon Abingdon Bridge; Vale VPA; 2 changing beers (sourced locally; often Cotswold Lion, Little Ox, North Cotswold) ⊞
Traditional village inn with whitewashed stone walls, heavy oak beams, real fires and a large garden. The pub has gone from strength to strength since it was purchased by the local community from Greene King in 2014. The focus is on local produce with a changing menu of home-cooked food, some of which is grown in the pub's kitchen garden. The small bar serves a selection of three or four local beers (maybe two in winter). Closed Monday and Tuesday, and Wednesday to Friday afternoons. Q🌣🕏🕼🖢♣🅿🐾🛜♪

Oxford

Bear Inn ㄥ
6 Alfred Street, OX1 4EH
☎ (01865) 728164 ⊕ bearoxford.co.uk
Fuller's London Pride, ESB; Gale's HSB; 2 changing beers (sourced regionally; often Dark Star, Fuller's, Oxford) ⊞
The Bear's precise age is open to debate but it is definitely old; the present building dates back to 1606 and has been identified by CAMRA as having a regionally important historic pub interior. Tucked away behind the Town Hall, it is a tied house in more ways than one, renowned for its collection of tie remnants taken from customers. A small pub popular with students and visitors, it gets crowded at times, but there is more seating in a paved area to the rear. Closed Monday lunchtimes. Q🌣🕏🕼≈♣🚊🛜♪

Chequers ㄥ ✔
130A High Street, OX1 4DH (down narrow passageway off High St, 50yds from Carfax)
☎ (01865) 727463
Fuller's London Pride; St Austell Nicholson's Pale Ale; 4 changing beers (sourced nationally; often Hook Norton, St Austell, Timothy Taylor) ⊞
Grade II-listed pub down a passageway off the High Street. Much of the building dates back to the early 16th century when it was converted from a moneylender's tenement to a tavern, hence the name. Note the fine carvings and windows, and the ceiling in the lower bar. There is an upstairs bar with three handpumps. A cobbled courtyard provides space for alfresco drinking, dining and smoking. Q🌣🕏🕼≈♣🚊🐾🛜

Gardener's Arms ㄥ
39 Plantation Road, Walton Manor, OX2 6JE
☎ (01865) 559814 ⊕ thegardenersarms.com
2 changing beers (sourced regionally; often Little Ox, Loose Cannon, XT) ⊞
Established in the 1830s, this is a cosy pub down a narrow street off Woodstock Road. A popular and relaxing place to eat and drink, it serves some of the finest vegetarian and vegan food in the city. At the rear is a large and pleasant garden, as well as the outside toilets. The famous weekly quiz is on Sunday evening. Table service is in operation due to small bar area. Closed Monday and Tuesday lunchtimes and Monday to Friday afternoons. Q🌣🕏🕼♣🐾🛜

Jolly Farmers ㄥ
20 Paradise Street, OX1 1LD
⊕ jollyfarmers-oxford.co.uk
Otter Bitter; 1 changing beer (sourced locally; often Chadlington, LoveBeer, Oxford) ⊞
Oxford's oldest LGBTQ+ venue is a 17th-century building, though the first record of it being a pub is in 1829. There are two small, low-beamed rooms, a raised area to the rear with the bar, and a short flight of stairs that lead to a terrace and small garden. The pub welcomes everybody, so don't be put off by its branding. You can also order your own takeaway food and get it delivered.
Q🌣🕏≈♣🚊🐾🛜♪

Mason's Arms ㄥ ✔
2 Quarry School Place, Headington Quarry, OX3 8LH
☎ (01865) 764579 ⊕ themasonsarmshq.co.uk

Harvey's Sussex Best Bitter; Rebellion Smuggler; Vocation Bread & Butter; 2 changing beers (sourced nationally) Ⓗ
Family-run community pub hosting many games leagues, including bar billiards and Aunt Sally. The guest ales are varied and turn over quickly, and a wide range of bottled beers is also stocked. The venue is home to the Headington beer festival in September. A heated decking area and garden lead to the function room which hosts music and comedy nights. A regular local CAMRA City Pub of the Year. Closed Sunday evenings and Monday. Open from 5pm Tuesday to Friday and 3pm on Saturday. Q✿🅱️✿&♣️P🖵(H2) ✿🍴♫

Rose & Crown Ⓛ

14 North Parade Avenue, North Oxford, OX2 6LX (½ mile N of city centre, off Banbury Rd)
☎ (01865) 510551 ⊕ roseandcrownoxford.com
Adnams Southwold Bitter; Hook Norton Old Hooky; Oxford Trinity; 1 changing beer (sourced locally; often Little Ox, Loose Cannon, XT) Ⓗ
This characterful free house on a vibrant north Oxford street is a time capsule with two small rooms and many original features. A friendly community pub, it has been run by the same landlords for 40 years. There is no intrusive music and mobile phone use is not permitted. It has been identified by CAMRA as having a regionally important historic pub interior. Closed Monday to Thursday afternoons in August and September.
Q✿🅱️🍴◑♣️🖵🛜♫

Royal Blenheim 🍷 Ⓛ

13 St Ebbes Street, OX1 1PT
☎ (01865) 242355
Everards Tiger; Titanic Plum Porter; White Horse Bitter; Village Idiot; 6 changing beers (sourced nationally; often Dark Star, Titanic, White Horse) Ⓗ
Single-room Victorian pub next to Modern Art Oxford – the building is all that is left of Hanley & Co Ltd, City Brewery. It was built in 1889 for Hanley's on the site of two alehouses, in what was then a very rough part of the city. The pub is owned by Everards but leased to Titanic brewery, who run it in association with White Horse brewery. Ten handpumps dispense a range of White Horse and Titanic beers, one from Everards, plus guests. Local CAMRA City Pub of the Year 2023.
Q✿🅱️&≋♣️🍴🐾🛜

Teardrop Ⓛ

Unit 21, Covered Market, High Street, OX1 3DU (on Avenue 1 towards Market St)
☎ (01865) 244407 ⊕ teardropbar.co.uk
Church Hanbrewery Ale X IPA; 1 changing beer (sourced locally; often Church Hanbrewery, Little Ox, XT) Ⓖ
Opened by Church Hanbrewery, in a retail unit in the Grade II-listed covered market, this 'nanopub' is rather spartan. Beer is served directly from casks on stillage or on tap from the cellar. It sells its own, somewhat unusual, beers, and others from small breweries in the county, in one-third and two-third pint measures at relatively high prices. All the ales are available for takeaway in 750ml containers. It is only open when the market is. Q✿🅱️✿≋🖵

Tile Shop Ale House

10 Windmill Road, Headington, OX3 7BX
☎ 07838 809303 ⊕ alepub.co.uk
Tring Ridgeway; 1 changing beer (sourced locally; often Oxford, Tring) Ⓖ
Headington's first micropub forms part of a tile shop near the central crossroads of this eastern suburb. As you might expect, it is full of tiles. The pub serves two ales,

one regularly changing, straight from the cask. It also offers a real cider, local gin, and wine. Mobile phone use is discouraged and there is no music or Wi-Fi. There are some bar snacks or food can be brought in. Closes at 8pm every day (9pm Fri and Sat). ✿♣️🍴🖵✿

White Hart

12 St Andrew's Road, Headington, OX3 9DL (opp church in Old Headington village)
☎ (01865) 761737 ⊕ thewhitehartheadington.com
Everards Tiger; 4 changing beers (sourced nationally; often Everards, Holden's, White Horse) Ⓗ
Terraced stone-built pub offering a good selection of Everards ales and guests. The interior is divided into three, with two small bars, and there is a large garden. Note the framed extract from a play The Tragi-Comedy of Joan of Hedington, by Dr William King of Christ Church written in 1712 about the proprietor of a dishonourable alehouse; thankfully the pub now has a much better reputation. The food is traditional and home-made, with pies a speciality. Closes at 6pm on Sundays.
Q✿🅱️✿◑P🖵✿🛜

White Hart Ⓛ

126 Godstow Road, Wolvercote, OX2 8PQ
☎ (01865) 511978 ⊕ thewhitehartwolvercote.co.uk
3 changing beers (sourced locally; often Amwell Springs, Loose Cannon, XT) Ⓗ
A former bakery, this small open-plan local opposite the green at Lower Wolvercote was possibly also once a blacksmith's. Since 2014 it has been a community-run pub with a welcoming and family-friendly feel. It serves three or four regularly changing local ales. Food is available on Wednesday to Friday evenings and Sunday brunch is offered. The pub hosts regular music nights featuring jazz, sea-shanties and Irish folk. Closed Monday to Friday lunchtimes, Monday and Tuesday afternoons and Sunday from 8pm. 🅱️✿◑&♣️P🖵(6)✿🛜♫

White Horse

52 Broad Street, OX1 3BB
☎ (01865) 204801
Black Sheep Best Bitter; Timothy Taylor Landlord; 3 changing beers (sourced nationally; often Adnams, Dark Star, Loose Cannon) Ⓗ
Sandwiched between the two entrances to Blackwell's bookshop is this classic Grade II-listed city-centre inn. With a long and narrow bar and a small snug at the rear, it claims, justifiably, to be the smallest pub in Oxford. It is popular with students and tourists and featured regularly in Inspector Morse and later Lewis. Winston Churchill and Bill Clinton are reputed to have frequented the pub in their student days. Closed Monday lunchtimes.
Q✿🅱️◑≋🖵

White Rabbit Ⓛ

21 Friars Entry, OX1 2BY (alley between Magdalen St and Gloucester Green)
☎ (01865) 241177 ⊕ whiterabbitoxford.co.uk
5 changing beers (sourced locally; often Oxford, Siren, Vale) Ⓗ
Before being renamed the White Rabbit in 2012, this was the Gloucester Arms, which described itself as Oxford's premier rock pub. It has a small bar surrounded by three separate areas. Five local real ales are usually on offer, with one sometimes swapped for cider. Hand-made pizzas are a speciality, with gluten-free bases available. Outside is a covered paved space with heated seating. The pub has been identified by CAMRA as having a regionally important historic interior. ✿◑≋♣️🖵🛜

Playhatch

Flowing Spring

Henley Road, RG4 9RB (on A4155)
☎ (0118) 969 9878 ⊕ theflowingspringpub.co.uk
**Tring Colley's Dog, Ridgeway; 2 changing beers
(sourced nationally; often Hook Norton, Palmers,
Tring)** Ⓗ
Sociable 18th-century country pub on the edge of the
Chilterns. This free house features two regular plus two
varying beers. It serves home-made meals to suit all
dietary needs, with award-winning gluten-free, dairy-
free, vegetarian and vegan options. Events include
monthly unplugged nights, classic car and bike meets,
and summer concerts in the large garden. The pleasant
covered balcony and large riverside garden are ideal for
summer. Standalone motorhomes or campervans are
welcome when pre-booked. Closed Monday, Tuesday to
Friday afternoons and Sunday from 5pm.
ᕀᏸᏪ♣ⓓP❀♠≋♫

South Moreton

Crown Ⓛ

High Street, OX11 9AG (in centre of village)
☎ (01235) 810005 ⊕ thecrown-southmoreton.co.uk
**Loose Cannon Abingdon Bridge; house beer (by
Amwell Springs); 1 changing beer (sourced
nationally; often North Cotswold, White Horse, XT)** Ⓗ
Community pub that was previously owned by
Wadworth and closed for several years. The licensees
place emphasis on showcasing local ales, including
collaborating with Amwell Springs for a regular house
beer, Ye Olde Dash & Tipple. Freshly prepared food is
sourced locally to support businesses in the area and the
menu changes to reflect this. Local CAMRA Pub of the
Year and Cider Pub of the Year 2022. Closed Tuesday,
Monday and Wednesday lunchtimes, and Sunday from
5pm. QᕀᏸᏪⓓ Å♣♠P🖵(94S)❀≋♫

Steventon

North Star ★ Ⓛ

2 Stocks Lane, OX13 6SG (at end of The Causeway off
B4017)
**3 changing beers (sourced regionally; often Amwell
Springs, Butts, Loose Cannon)** Ⓖ
Identified by CAMRA as having a historic interior of
outstanding national importance, this Grade II-listed pub
is next to The Causeway, a listed ancient monument.
Popular with locals and visitors, it hosts many village
clubs and social events. Inside are two bars, one with
three settles around an open fireplace, and a separate
function room. Three beers are served by gravity and
presented through a stable door or hatch. Not to be
missed. Closed Monday, Tuesday to Friday lunchtimes
and afternoons. ᏸ❀♣P🖵(X2)❀≋

Stoke Lyne

Peyton Arms

School Lane, OX27 8SD
☎ 07546 066160
Hook Norton Hooky, Old Hooky Ⓖ
An unspoilt rural gem, with the bar at its heart and no
handpumps. Two Hook Norton ales are served directly
from the cask from a small room behind the bar. This is a
place for conversation around the small bar or by the fire,
and memorabilia surrounds you. The bar is for adults
only; children are welcome in the garden (no dogs
allowed). It has been identified by CAMRA as having a
regionally important historic pub interior. Closed Monday

to Wednesday and weekend evenings, it is open from
5pm Thursday and Friday, and from 2pm at weekends.
Q❀P

Sutton Courtenay

George ♇ Ⓛ ✅

4 Church Street, OX14 4NJ (on B4016)
☎ (01235) 848142 ⊕ georgesuttoncourtenay.co.uk
**Amwell Springs Rude Not To; Loose Cannon Abingdon
Bridge** Ⓗ
An imposing, Grade-II listed, 17th-century half-timbered
building with two main bar areas. A small meeting room
lies beyond the other bar. There is an attractive enclosed
garden at the rear with a large covered paved area. No
food is served, though items purchased at the small deli
counter in the entrance can be eaten in the pub (or taken
away) and there are occasional pop-up street food
vendors on some Fridays and Saturdays. Local CAMRA
Pub of the Year 2023. Closed Monday to Thursday
afternoons. Qᏸ❀P🖵(33)❀≋

Thame

Cross Keys Ⓛ ✅

East Street, OX9 3JS
☎ (01844) 218202 ⊕ crosskeysthame.co.uk
**XT Four; 7 changing beers (sourced nationally; often
Thame)** Ⓗ
A cosy, friendly and popular drinkers' local. It serves an
ever-changing range of ales and ciders and local
breweries often feature alongside unusual ales from
small and microbreweries from around the country. On
busy evenings, it is not uncommon for several beers to
be changed. It hosts many community events, such as
comedy nights, live music and local clubs. Former local
CAMRA Cider Pub of the Year. Closed Monday to Friday
afternoons. Q❀♣♠🖵≋

Falcon ✅

1 Thame Park Road, OX9 3JA
☎ (01844) 212118
**Hook Norton Hooky, Old Hooky; 1 changing beer
(sourced regionally; often Hook Norton)** Ⓗ
Hook Norton's only pub in Thame is a Victorian brick-built
establishment about half a mile out of the town centre. It
has a large L-shaped bar, and has some seating outside
at the front which is useful for cyclists using the nearby
Phoenix Trail, the disused railway between Thame and
Princes Risborough. Darts, dominoes and shove ha'penny
are played by the locals. Closed Monday, Tuesday to
Friday lunchtimes and Sunday from 7.30pm.
❀ⓓ♿♣P🖵≋

Wallingford

Cross Keys Ⓛ ✅

48 High Street, OX10 0DB
☎ (01491) 915888 ⊕ thecrosskeyswallingford.com
**House beer (by XT); 3 changing beers (sourced
nationally; often Draught Bass, Vale)** Ⓗ
A 17th-century pub in a Grade II-listed building retaining
many original features such as exposed low beams, large
fireplaces and internal cellar. The house beer is Keys
Amber. The large, fenced garden sits on probable Saxon-
age town ramparts. Pop-up food stalls offering varying
choices are present at the rear of the pub from
Wednesday to Sunday. It has wheelchair access into the
pub and the pop-up food area but there are no disabled
toilet facilities. Local CAMRA Cider Pub of the Year 2023.
Closed Monday to Thursday lunchtimes.
ᏸ❀ⓓ Å≈(Cholsey & Wallingford) ♣♠P🖵❀≋♫

Wantage

King's Arms Ⓨ L ✓
39 Wallingford Street, OX12 8AU (E of Market Square)
☎ (01235) 765465 ⊕ kingsarmswantage.co.uk
6 changing beers (sourced nationally) Ⓗ
A friendly, open-plan pub with panelling and polished wooden floors. It was given a new lease of when refurbished by owners Oak Taverns in 2020. Six handpumps adorn the bar, serving constantly changing beers, with six ciders also available. The large rear garden has a grassy slope, and tables and chairs for drinkers. Local CAMRA Pub of the Year and local CAMRA Cider Pub of the Year 2023. Closed Monday to Thursday lunchtimes. Q❀✿&♣●🖩❀🎵

Royal Oak L
Newbury Street, OX12 8DF (S of Market Square)
☎ (01235) 763129 ⊕ royaloakwantage.co.uk
Wadworth 6X; 8 changing beers (sourced nationally) Ⓖ
A multi award-winning street-corner pub that is a mecca for the discerning drinker. All beers are served by gravity, along with 30 or more ciders and perries. The walls display photographs of ships bearing the pub's name. The lounge features wrought-iron trelliswork covered in pump clips, while table football is available in the public bar. Awarded local CAMRA Pub of the Year many times, including 2021, and local Cider Pub of the Year 2022. Closed weekday lunchtimes and every afternoon.
Q❀♣●🖩❀🎵

Shoulder of Mutton L
38 Wallingford Street, OX12 8AX (E of Market Square)
☎ (01235) 767158
Butts Barbus Barbus; 5 changing beers (sourced nationally) Ⓗ
Friendly and popular Victorian corner pub a short walk from the town centre, serving five constantly changing beers on handpump to suit all tastes. The interior has recently been redesigned to allow greater space for customers. The pub hosts an open mic night on Tuesdays. It has featured in this Guide many times and is a former local, county and regional CAMRA Pub of the Year.
Q❀🚲●🖩❀🎵

Watlington

Spire & Spoke L
21 Hill Road, OX49 5AD (E off B4009)
☎ (01491) 614956 ⊕ theSpireandSpoke.co.uk
Timothy Taylor Landlord; 4 changing beers (sourced regionally; often Oxford, White Horse, XT) Ⓗ
The Spire & Spoke serves three or four guest beers sourced mainly from local breweries. It also offers coffee, home-made cakes and deli light bites all day, and pizzas are cooked in the wood-fired oven. The Ridgeway crosses the road nearby. The pub garden gives a good view of the White Mark chalk triangle on Watlington Hill, originally cut to look like a spire on the parish church. Alcoholic drinks are served from 11am. Closes at 9.30 Sunday to Thursday. ❀✿&♣AP🖩(11,137)❀🎵

West Hanney

Plough L
Church Street, OX12 0LN
☎ (01235) 868987 ⊕ theploughathanney.co.uk
4 changing beers (sourced nationally; often Butcombe, Loose Cannon, Timothy Taylor) Ⓗ
Friendly, picturesque 16th-century thatched pub that is the hub of the community. Sold in 2015 by Punch Taverns to a local community group, it has been refurbished and now serves four changing beers. It has a cosy, beamed and alcoved split-level bar with open fire, and a separate dining room serving traditional British food. Most of the local clubs meet here from time to time. In summer Aunt Sally is played in the local league. Closed Monday, and Sunday evenings.
❀✿&♣A♣P❀🎵

Wheatley

Cricketer's Arms L
38 Littleworth, OX33 1TR (walk W along Littleworth Rd from Wheatley)
☎ (01865) 872738 ⊕ the-cricketers.com
2 changing beers (sourced nationally; often Loddon, Loose Cannon, Woodforde's) Ⓗ
A typical village local that was smartened up when new management took over in 2020. It normally serves three ales in the summer, and now offers authentic Thai food. There is a fenced off garden with an Aunt Sally throw. Parking is limited but there is a free car park 100yds away. The pub is on National Cycle Route 57. On Monday to Thursday it is open evenings only.
Q❀✿●♣P🖩(46)❀🎵

Whitchurch Hill

Sun L
Hill Bottom, RG8 7PU
☎ (0118) 984 3909 ⊕ thesunwhitchurchhill.co.uk
Loddon Hoppit; Renegade Good Old Boy; 1 changing beer (sourced locally) Ⓗ
A traditional village local, rebuilt in 1910, the Sun was bought from Brakspear in 2013 by a local businessman and became a free house. It serves two regular local real ales and traditional good-value, home-cooked pub food lunchtime and evenings Wednesday to Sunday, including a roast on Sundays. A log fire warms the bar on cold winter days and benches at the front and on the rear patio are ideal for warmer weather. The pub hosts many events, such as quiz nights, classic car shows and informal chess games; details can be found on their Facebook page. Closes on Sunday and Monday from 8pm. ❀✿●♣P🖩(146)❀🎵

Whitchurch on Thames

Greyhound L ✓
High Street, RG8 7EL (on B471)
☎ (0118) 984 1485
⊕ thegreyhoundwhitchurchonthames.co.uk
XT Four; 2 changing beers (sourced nationally) Ⓗ
A former ferryman's cottage, the Greyhound has a main L-shaped bar with a low ceiling and plenty of beams and wood panelling, all decorated in a contemporary, minimalist style. A small meeting/function room has been opened up to the right of the entrance, which can be booked by groups. It has an attractive garden to the rear with plenty of seating. Pop-up hot food is available most evenings and at weekends. Closed Monday to Thursday lunchtimes.
Q❀✿●A≠(Pangbourne)♣●P🖩(143,146)❀🎵

Witney

Angel Inn L ✓
42 Market Square, OX28 6AL
☎ (01993) 703238
Brakspear Oxford Gold; Wychwood Hobgoblin Gold, Hobgoblin Ruby; house beer (by Marston's) Ⓗ
A Grade II-listed free house at one time owned by Joseph Early of the blanket manufacturing dynasty and a brewer.

It has a fine front bar with low beams and a bay window, with plenty of space for drinkers and diners to the rear. Outside is a small paved and walled courtyard. The beer range is mostly from Marston's – its Wychwood brewery is just around the corner, but the beer goes to Burton-on-Trent to be casked. One of the regular beers is sometimes replaced by a guest. ⊛◑♣🖾(S1,S2)❀🛜🎵

Drummer's Bar 🅛

8 Langdale Court, OX28 6FG (walk down passageway directly opp Blue Boar in town centre)
☎ (01608) 677717 ⊕ drummersbar.co.uk
2 changing beers (sourced locally; often Church Hanbrewery, Goff's, Little Ox) 🅗
Witney's first micropub was founded by a father and son team who started a nearby brewery, Oxbrew, which merged with Little Ox brewery. The pub has two handpulls from casks and six taps from kegs and serves an ever-changing selection of beers from small local breweries. All Little Ox beers are gluten-free unless stated otherwise. Closed Monday and Tuesday, Wednesday to Thursday lunchtimes and afternoons, and Sunday from 7pm. QP🖾(S1,S2)🛜🎵

Eagle Tavern 🅛 ✅

22 Corn Street, OX28 6BL
☎ (01993) 700121
Hook Norton Hooky, Hooky Gold, Old Hooky; 1 changing beer (sourced locally; often Hook Norton) 🅗
This Grade II-listed building has been an inn from the beginning of the 19th century, when it was the Coach & Horses. It has been owned by Hook Norton for over 20 years and serves a range of the brewery's ales, alongside malt whiskies, bourbons, gins, and rums. The interior has three seating areas and lots of dark wood. You can see the cellar through the window next to the bar. Closed Monday and Tuesday, every lunchtime except Saturday, and Wednesday and Thursday afternoons.
Q⊛♿♣🖾(S1,S2)❀🛜

Breweries

Amwell Springs SIBA

Westfield Farm House, Westfield Road, Cholsey, Wallingford, OX10 9LS ☎ 07812 396619
⊕ asbco.co.uk

Brewing began in 2017 on a 70-litre plant using water from a spring in the farmhouse grounds. Capacity expanded in 2019 to six barrels. Beers are available in local pubs. 🍺LIVE ◈

Chairman Dave (ABV 3.5%) BITTER
Stay Jammy (ABV 3.8%) BITTER
Rude Not To (ABV 4%) GOLD
Eazy Geez (ABV 4.5%) GOLD
Mad Gaz (ABV 5.2%) PALE

Barn Owl

Buildings Farm, Faringdon Road, Gozzards Ford, OX13 6QH ☎ 07724 551086

⊗ Located in an historic barn on a farm just outside Abingdon, brewing began in 2016 using a four-barrel plant. Beers can be found in local free trade outlets.

Old Scruttock's Bitter (ABV 3.9%) BITTER
Golden Gozzard (ABV 4%) GOLD
Gozzard's Guzzler (ABV 4.4%) BITTER
Gozzards Glory (ABV 4.5%) BITTER
Old Scruttock's Dirigible (ABV 5%) PORTER

Bicester

🍴 **Angel, 102 Sheep Street, Bicester, OX26 6LP**
☎ (01869) 360410 ⊕ theangelbicester.co.uk

Brewing commenced in 2017 in an outhouse behind the Angel, Bicester. Beers are brewed occasionally and supplied solely to the pub.

BMAN

Unit 50, Monument Business Park, Warpsgrove Lane, Chalgrove, OX44 7RW ⊕ bmanbrewery.co.uk

Established by food scientist Alex Berryman in a freight container in 2021. Production is currently limited to kegs and cans of American-style IPAs. Outlets include the Big Scary Monsters Social Club and the Library in Oxford.

Brakspear

Eagle Maltings, The Crofts, Witney, OX28 4DP
☎ (01993) 890800 ⊕ brakspear-beers.co.uk

Brakspear beers have been brewed in Oxfordshire since 1779. Beers continue to be traditionally-crafted at the Wychwood Brewery (qv) in the historic market town of Witney, using the original Victorian square fermenters, and the renowned double drop fermenting system. Part of Carlsberg Marston's Brewing Co. ‼🍺◆LIVE ◈

Gravity (ABV 3.4%) BITTER
Oxford Gold (ABV 4%) GOLD

Chadlington SIBA

Blaythorne Farm, Cross's Lane, Chadlington, OX7 3NE
☎ (01608) 676823 ☎ 07931 482807
⊕ chadlingtonbrewery.com

Based in the Cotswolds, brewing began with small-batch brews, but the brewhouse, which opened in 2019 is capable of supplying a growing range of customers. The brewery utilises renewables and pure spring water. Family-owned, it makes visitors very welcome, hosting events and holding Brew-your-Own days. Its beers can be frequently found at the Tite Inn in Chadlington, which acts as the brewery tap. 🍺

Golden Ale (ABV 4%) GOLD
Oxford Blonde (ABV 4%) BLOND
Oxford Blue (ABV 4.2%) GOLD

Church Hanbrewery

Unit F2, New Yatt Business Centre, New Yatt, North Leigh, OX29 6TJ
☎ (01993) 774986 ☎ 07907 272617

Office: **Tithe Barn South, Church Hanborough, OX29 8AB** ⊕ churchhanbrewery.com

⊗ Brewing commenced in 2016 on a small scale in the owner's kitchen. A year later, a 250-litre plant was installed in a small industrial unit in New Yatt near Witney. It was upgraded to 500-litres in 2021. Now producing mainly bottles and keg, plus some cask for the taproom next door and the Teardrop bar in Oxford's indoor market (one-off brews regularly seen in both). 🍺LIVE ◈

Ale X IPA (ABV 4.5%) PALE
Rauk (ABV 5%) SPECIALITY
Red Beetter (ABV 5%) SPECIALITY
Bluenette (ABV 5.5%) PORTER
Mat Black (ABV 5.5%) PALE

Craftsman

Abingdon, OX14 3TA ☎ 07743 041916
✉ justinlevans@btinternet.com

A 100-litre microbrewery in the owner's garage which started commercial production in 2021. It produces a wide range of styles for bottling, which are sold in local markets, country fairs and similar places, plus the occasional cask for local beer festivals.

Earth Ale

Bothy Vineyard, Oakley Park, Faringdon Road, Frilford Heath, OX13 6QW ☎ 07508 553546 ⊕ earthale.com

After brewing at various London breweries, Earth Ale settled down at the Chocolate Factory complex in 2019, then moved to the Vale of The White Horse in 2021, using a six-barrel plant. A wide range of beers is available in kegs, cans and bottles. **LIVE**

Elements

Unit 2, Upton Downs Farm, Upton, Burford, OX18 4LY ☎ 07984 308670 ⊕ elementsbrewery.co.uk

Began brewing in 2018 on a six-barrel plant, producing small-batch, hop-forward beers. No real ale. 🛒◆

Faringdon

🏠 Swan, 1 Park Road, Faringdon, SN7 7BP

Faringdon Brewery opened in 2010. After a period of closure, brewing restarted in 2019, stopped again when the brewer left in 2021 and restarted in 2023 with a new brewer. All beers are supplied to the brewery tap, the Swan, when available.

Hook Norton SIBA IFBB

Brewery Lane, Scotland End, Hook Norton, OX15 5NY ☎ (01608) 737210 ⊕ hooky.co.uk

⊗ One of the finest examples of a Victorian tower brewery, and the oldest independent brewery in Oxfordshire, Hook Norton has been brewing since 1849. The current premises were built in 1900 and still house much of the original machinery, including a 25hp steam engine. Shire horses make deliveries to local pubs. Family-owned, it combines its heritage with a modern approach. Various parts of the brewery are available for hire and customers can spend a day brewing their own beer. ‼🛒◆**LIVE**

Hooky Mild (ABV 2.8%) MILD
A chestnut brown, easy-drinking mild. A complex malt and hop aroma give way to a well-balanced taste, leading to a long, hoppy finish that is unusual for a mild.
Hooky (ABV 3.5%) BITTER
A classic, golden session bitter. Hoppy and fruity aroma followed by a malt and hops taste and a continuing hoppy finish.
Off The Hook (ABV 4.3%) GOLD
Old Hooky (ABV 4.6%) BITTER
A strong bitter, tawny in colour. A well-rounded fruity taste with a balanced bitter finish.

Little Ox SIBA

Unit 6, Wroslyn Road Industrial Estate, Freeland, OX29 8HZ
☎ (01993) 881941 ☎ 07730 496525

Office: 25 Castle Road, Wootton, OX20 1EQ
⊕ littleoxbrewery.co.uk

Little Ox began production in 2016 and uses its 17-hectolitre (10 barrel) plant to produce beer in cask, keg and can. It offers a small core range, a larger range of seasonal and occasional beers, and also brews an experimental beer every month (which includes a barrel-aged project released at the end of the year). It supplies more than 50 pubs, restaurants and off-licences and offer free local delivery around Oxfordshire. 🛒◆GF V

Hufflepuff (ABV 3.8%) GOLD
Wipeout (ABV 4.2%) GOLD
Ox Blood (ABV 4.3%) RED
Yabba Dabba Doo (ABV 4.8%) BITTER

Loddon SIBA

Dunsden Green Farm, Church Lane, Dunsden, RG4 9QD ☎ (0118) 948 1111 ⊕ loddonbrewery.com

☺This family-run brewery was established in 2002 in a brick-and-flint barn (originally a grain store). The custom-built, 17-barrel plant typically produces 120 barrels per week and supplies more than 700 outlets far and wide. To complement the existing taproom, an onsite farm shop opened in 2021. ‼🛒◆GF V✦

Hoppit (ABV 3.5%) BITTER
Pale session bitter with hops dominating the aroma. Malt and hops in the balanced taste followed by a bitter aftertaste.
Hullabaloo (ABV 4.2%) BITTER
Session bitter with fruit in the initial taste. This develops into a balance of hops and malt in the mouth followed by a bitter aftertaste.
Citra Quad (ABV 4.4%) GOLD
Ferryman's Gold (ABV 4.4%) GOLD
Premium golden ale with a strong hoppy character throughout, accompanied by fruit in the taste and aftertaste.
Hocus Pocus (ABV 4.6%) OLD
Ruby-coloured old ale with dark malt, fruit and caramel aroma, joined by sweetness in the taste. There is a malty, bitterness to the finish.
Dragonfly (ABV 5.2%) PALE

Loose Cannon SIBA

Unit 6, Suffolk Way, Abingdon, OX14 5JX ☎ (01235) 531141 ⊕ lcbeers.co.uk

Brewing began in 2010 using a 15-barrel plant, reviving Abingdon's brewing history after the Morland Brewery closed in 2000. Beers can be found in an increasing number of local pubs and within 50 miles of the brewery. Loose Cannon operates an attractive taproom. A membership scheme enables customers to buy beer at a 10% discount. ‼🛒◆✦

Gunners Gold (ABV 3.5%) GOLD
Abingdon Bridge (ABV 4.1%) BITTER
Detonator (ABV 4.4%) BITTER
Porter (ABV 5%) PORTER
India Pale Ale (ABV 5.4%) PALE

LoveBeer SIBA

95 High Street, Milton, OX14 4EJ ☎ 07434 595145 ⊕ lovebeerbrewery.com

Starting as a small-scale passion project in 2013, LoveBeer quickly outgrew its original 0.5-barrel plant and expanded to six barrels in 2017. The family-run brewery supplies pubs around Oxfordshire and Berkshire as well as beer festivals and farm shops. In addition to its core and seasonal range, LoveBeer brews bespoke beers for special occasions. 🛒◆**LIVE**

Doctor Roo (ABV 3.7%) BITTER
Molly's (ABV 4%) BITTER
Not on your Nelly (ABV 4%) GOLD
OG (ABV 4.1%) PALE
Skyfall (ABV 4.3%) GOLD
Bonnie Hops (ABV 4.6%) PALE

Lovibonds

Friar Park Stables, Badgemore, Henley-on-Thames, RG9 4NR
☎ (01491) 576596 ⊕ lovibonds.com

Founded by Jeff Rosenmeier, Lovibonds has been brewing American-style craft beer since 2005. Named after Joseph William Lovibond (inventor of the Tintometer to measure beer colour). Beers are unfiltered and unpasteurised. In 2017, a purpose-built brewery was established in Henley, with a steam-heated mash tun and copper. Beers are available at some local outlets and by Click & Collect (Saturdays). It has added to its limited release beers ('Hold Our Beer'); its intended to explore historic styles and develop new ideas.

Oxford

Unit 1, Coopers Yard, Manor Farm Road, Horspath, OX33 1SD
☎ (01865) 604620 ☎ 07710 883273
⊕ oxfordbrewery.co.uk

⊠ A family-owned and run brewery, it began brewing in 2009 and supplies outlets in the Oxford area. All beers are suitable for vegans. ‼🍺♦V🌾

Prospect (ABV 3.7%) BITTER
Trinity (ABV 4.2%) PALE
Vivid Dreams (ABV 4.2%) GOLD
Let the Dragon See the Wolf (ABV 4.5%) BITTER
Scholar (ABV 4.5%) BITTER
Matilda's Tears (ABV 5%) PALE

Parlour

Chadwick Farm, Garford, Nr Abingdon, OX13 5PD
☎ (01865) 392227 ☎ 07799 183119

Office: Ock Barn, Garford, OX13 5PD
✉ ben@milletsfarmcentre.com

Run by three brothers-in-law, this small brewery was set up in a converted milking parlour in 2020. It brews beer in 240L batches, which can be bottle-conditioned or kegged. LIVE

South Oxfordshire (SOX)

Unit 1, Icknield Farm, Icknield Road, Ipsden, OX10 6AS ☎ 07704 307182

Office: Windrush Innovation Centre, Howbery Business Park, Benson Lane, Wallingford, OX10 8BA
⊕ soxbrewery.co.uk

South Oxfordshire Brewery (SOX) began brewing cask ales in early 2022 at White Horse Brewery (qv). In late 2022 SOX purchased White Horse. A four-barrel plant is installed at its premises in Ipsden. 🍺

Pale Ale (ABV 3.5%) PALE
Mr Toad's (ABV 3.9%) BITTER
Midnight Belle (ABV 4%) BITTER

Tap Social Movement SIBA

Unit 16A, Station Field Industrial Estate, Rowles Way, Kidlington, OX5 1JD
☎ (01865) 236330

Office: 27 Curtis Industrial Estate, North Hinksey Lane, Botley, OX2 0LX ⊕ tapsocialmovement.com

The three founders (who have a criminal justice background) established the brewery in 2016 to provide training and work opportunities for those serving prison sentences. Brewing is conducted on its 6,000-litre plant. Beer is produced in kegs, cans and occasionally cask, the latter appearing as guest ales at White House, Oxford, and Lock 29, Banbury. The original Botley site is a popular tap. The former LAM brewery site in Kennington is now a bakery, coffee bar and takeaway outlet for its cans. A new Market Tap is due to open in Oxford's covered market. 🍺◆

Thame

East Street, Thame, OX9 3JS
☎ (01844) 218202
✉ thamebrewery@btinternet.com

⊠ The one-barrel brewery at the Cross Keys is no longer in use. The long-standing publican, Peter Lambert also works at XT (qv) and brews Thame beers there from time to time.

Turpin

Turpins Lodge, Lodge Farm, Tadmarton Heath Road, Hook Norton, OX15 5DQ
☎ (01608) 737033 ⊕ turpinslodge.co.uk/turpin-brewery

⊠ Brewing started in 2013, with brewing capacity extended in 2019. A number of local pubs are supplied regularly, as well as a few pubs further afield in Oxford, Rugby and Birmingham. ◆

Golden Citrus (ABV 4.2%) GOLD

Virtue (NEW) SIBA

The Old Forge, Alfred Groves Industrial Estate, Shipton Road, Milton-under-Wychwood, OX7 6JP ☎ 0330 223 6801 ⊕ virtuebrewing.co.uk

A new microbrewery established in 2022, producing craft beers in cans and kegs. All beers are unfined, unfiltered and are suitable for vegans. Beers can be ordered online with free delivery to the UK mainland. V

White Horse SIBA

3 Ware Road, White Horse Business Park, Stanford in the Vale, SN7 8NY
☎ (01367) 718700 ⊕ whitehorsebrewery.co.uk

☺White Horse was founded in 2004. In 2018 a new management team took over the running of the brewery. In 2022 White Horse Brewery was purchased by South Oxfordshire Brewery (qv) aka SOX. White Horse has major outlets in Oxfordshire, as well as supplying other outlets nationally. In addition to its regular beers, a range of seasonal monthly beers is brewed. A number of one-off beers are brewed under the Luna brand name. ‼🍺♦

WHB (White Horse Bitter) (ABV 3.7%) BITTER
Black Beauty (ABV 3.9%) MILD
Stable Genius (ABV 4%) BITTER
Village Idiot (ABV 4.1%) GOLD
The Dons' Dark Ale (ABV 4.3%) BITTER
Wayland Smithy (ABV 4.4%) BITTER

Woodstock

24 Shipton Road, Woodstock, OX20 1LL ☎ 07481 569419 ⊕ woodstockbrewery.co.uk

A nanobrewery which started in 2021 on 70-litre brewing kit. A range of bottle-conditioned beers are produced, which are sold online, at local pubs and shops and at local markets through the Thames Valley Farmers' Market cooperative. **LIVE**

Super Sports (ABV 3.2%) PALE
Gullwing Lager (ABV 4%) BLOND
Full Tilt (ABV 4.2%) BITTER
Charabanc (ABV 5.3%) BITTER
Ambassador (ABV 5.5%) IPA

Wriggly Monkey SIBA

B.131 Motor Transport Yard, Bicester Heritage Centre, Buckingham Road, Bicester, OX27 8AL
☎ (01869) 246599 ☎ 07590 749062
⊕ wrigglymonkeybrewery.com

Established in 2018 on a 1.25-barrel kit and later expanded to 10 barrels, the brewery and its taproom are based in an old motor transport workshop at an automotive centre on the old RAF Bicester site. It is named after the compartment of a chain-drive mechanism of the Fraser Nash car. The brewery also has an online shop offering mail delivery, 'click & collect', and free local delivery options. ‼ ⋤ LIVE ✦

Wychwood

Eagle Maltings, The Crofts, Witney, OX28 4DP
☎ (01993) 890800 ⊕ wychwood.co.uk

Wychwood brewery is located in the Cotswold market town of Witney. The brewers take inspiration from the myths and legends associated with the ancient medieval Wychwood forest. Part of Carlsberg Marston's Brewing Co. ‼ ⋤ ✦ LIVE ✦

Hobgoblin Ruby (ABV 4.5%) OLD

Brewed under the Young's brand name:
London Original (ABV 3.7%) BITTER
London Special (ABV 4.5%) BITTER

Broad Face, Abingdon (Photo: Bob Smith)

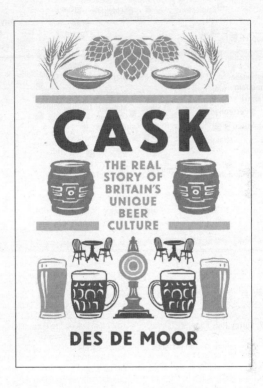

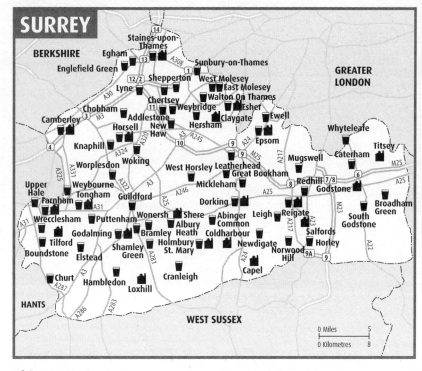

SURREY

BERKSHIRE

GREATER LONDON

Staines-upon-Thames
Egham
Englefield Green
Sunbury-on-Thames
Shepperton
West Molesey
Lyne
East Molesey
Chertsey
Walton On Thames
Chobham
Weybridge
Esher
Camberley
Addlestone
Claygate
Ewell
Horsell
Hersham
Knaphill
New Haw
Whyteleafe
Worplesdon
Woking
Epsom
Titsey
Upper Hale
Weybourne
West Horsley
Leatherhead
Mugswell
Caterham
Farnham
Tongham
Guildford
Great Bookham
Redhill
Wrecclesham
Puttenham
Mickleham
Godstone
Broadham Green
Godalming
Wonersh
Shere
Dorking
Abinger
Leigh
Reigate
South Godstone
Tilford
Bramley Heath
Albury
Common
Coldharbour
Salfords
Holmbury
Newdigate
Horley
Boundstone
Shamley
St. Mary
Norwood Hill
Elstead
Green
Churt
Hambledon
Cranleigh
Capel
Loxhill

HANTS

WEST SUSSEX

0 Miles 5
0 Kilometres 8

Abinger Common

Abinger Hatch 🅛
Abinger Lane, RH5 6HZ TQ11574596
☎ (01306) 730737 ⊕ theabingerhatch.co.uk
Firebird Heritage XX; Surrey Hills Ranmore, Shere Drop 🅷
This highly attractive 17th-century inn can be found opposite the church in this tiny village. The pub interior rambles over three levels, one with large flagstones on the floor. Throughout there are wooden beams and posts. Good food is a feature, with a varied menu on offer, and the kitchen is open all day. There may be barbecues on Saturdays in summer if the weather is fine.
Q ☺ ⊛ ◐ P ♞ (22) ♣ 🛜

Addlestone

RAOB Club
136 Church Road, KT15 1SQ
☎ (01932) 883335
Shepherd Neame Spitfire; 1 changing beer (sourced nationally; often Hook Norton) 🅷
A 10-minute walk from the town centre shops and restaurants is the Royal Antediluvian Order of Buffaloes, whose principal aims are friendship, charitable works, social activity and mutual support. This community social club also prides itself on its real ale. Inside is a TV showing sports, and a games room with pool and darts. There is live music some Saturday nights, and a monthly quiz. CAMRA members can be signed in as guests on production of their membership card.
☺ ⊛ ♿ ♣ P ♞ (461,557) ♣ 🛜 ♫

Albury Heath

William IV 🅛
Little London, GU5 9DG TQ06554673

☎ (01483) 202685 ⊕ thewilliamivpub.com
Gale's Seafarers Ale; Harvey's Sussex Best Bitter; Surrey Hills Shere Drop; 1 changing beer 🅷
The building has its origins in the 16th century and boasts beams, flagstones and a large fireplace where a welcoming wood fire burns brightly in winter. There are two traditional bars with a dining room up a few steps where excellent home-made meals are served. There is seating outside with half under a stylish canopy. The pub sits on a quiet lane adjoining extensive woodland and is popular with walkers. Q ⊛ ◐ P ♣

Boundstone

Bat & Ball 🅛
15 Bat & Ball Lane, GU10 4SA (off Sandrock Hill Rd via Upper Bourne Ln) SU833444
☎ (01252) 792108 ⊕ thebatandball.co.uk
Dark Star Hophead; Hop Back Summer Lightning; Triple fff Moondance; 3 changing beers (sourced regionally; often Triple fff, Young's) 🅷
A traditional country free house dating back 150 years, set in the Bourne Valley near Farnham. It has been run by the same family for two generations. The pub has several different rooms, with an open log fire, panelled walls and oak beams. The attractive garden has a children's play area and is popular with families on warmer days. There is an annual beer festival, a weekly quiz on Tuesday and live music once a month. An afternoon menu is served at weekends.
Q ☺ ⊛ ◐ ♿ ♣ P ♞ (16,17) ♣ 🛜 ♫

Bramley

Jolly Farmer 🅛
High Street, GU5 0HB
☎ (01483) 893355 ⊕ jollyfarmer.co.uk

Crafty Brewing Hop Tipple; house beer (by Crafty Brewing); 6 changing beers (sourced nationally; often Crafty Brewing, Firebird, Heritage) Ⓗ
Originally a stagecoach inn, this is now a privately owned free house serving eight real ales. It has a cosy, welcoming atmosphere, with dark wood beams and decor that celebrates the countryside and beer, featuring historic beer mats and pumpclips. The L-shaped bar offers a diverse range of real ales, keg beers, plus real ciders in summer. There is accommodation available in four en-suite rooms and a three-bedroom flat. Bramley is served by buses from Guildford and Horsham.
⊛🐸🛏️◖♣🌳♿️🅿️🚃😻🛜

Broadham Green

Haycutter Ⓛ
69 Tanhouse Road, RH8 9PE TQ39075134
☎ (01883) 776955
Brunning & Price Original; 4 changing beers Ⓗ
This uniquely named Brunning & Price pub serves food all day. The main bar area has been divided in two; the front part has been further divided and can be used for private dining. There is comfortable seating throughout, plus three real fires. Outside is a large patio, and a garden with a children's play area. The beer range changes frequently but always features at least one local ale. Monthly walks for dog owners start from the pub.
⊛😻◖♿️🅿️😻🛜

Camberley

Claude du Vall Ⓛ ✅
77-81 High Street, GU15 3RB
☎ (01276) 672910
Greene King Abbot; Ruddles Best Bitter; Sharp's Doom Bar; 3 changing beers (sourced nationally; often Dorking, Tillingbourne, Windsor & Eton) Ⓗ
The Claude du Vall is conveniently close to the station and bus stops, at the end of the High Street. The large, modern interior is divided into a number of different seating areas. The long bar offers three regular beers and three guests, maybe four on a busy weekend. Wetherspoon's reputation for good-value food and drinks attracts customers throughout the day. Muted TV screens generally show news programmes and occasional sports events. ⊛😻◖♿️🚃🅿️🛜

Caterham

King & Queen Ⓛ
34 High Street, CR3 5UA (on B2030)
☎ (01883) 345303 ⊕ kingandqueencaterham.co.uk
Dark Star Hophead; Fuller's London Pride, ESB; 1 changing beer Ⓗ
Dating back to the 1840s and converted from three former cottages, the pub retains three distinct areas. The front section is a public bar, the high-ceilinged middle section is a games room with a dartboard, and there is a small cosier section at the back. There are patios front and back and a covered smoking section at the rear. The pub is named after the joint monarchy of William and Mary and displays their portraits. ⊛😻♣🅿️🚃😻🛜

Chertsey

Olde Swan Hotel
27 Windsor Street, KT16 8AY
☎ (01932) 562129 ⊕ theoldeswanhotel.co.uk
Sharp's Doom Bar; Tring Side Pocket for a Toad; 2 changing beers (sourced nationally; often Dorking, Timothy Taylor) Ⓗ

Refurbished when acquired by Mclean Inns, without spoiling its historic charm, the Olde Swan has a mellow ambience with its shabby-chic decor. Four ales are usually on offer, as well as real cider. The menu features stonebaked pizza, home-made burgers, and sizzling steaks, with Mexican night on Friday. A covered patio at the rear is for alfresco drinking. Accommodation includes double, twin, and family rooms. the pub is handy for the M25/M3 and Thorpe Park. Local CAMRA Cider Pub of the Year 2023. ⊛😻🛏️◖🍴🌳🅿️🚃🛜♪

Chobham

Horse & Groom Ⓛ
30 High Street, GU24 8AA
☎ 07709 658066
⊕ horse-and-groom-micropub.business.site
3 changing beers (sourced locally) Ⓗ
The first micropub locally, the Horse & Groom was previously a hairdresser's; however, long before that it was part of the original Horse & Groom that closed in 1960. Describing itself as 'a village pub but smaller', it definitely has a local's pub feel, with social chat a key part of the atmosphere. Beers are sourced directly from local breweries and a local traditional cider is also available. Cheese plates are available, or you can bring your own food. Q⊛😻🌳🚃(39A,73)

White Hart Ⓛ
58 High Street, GU24 8AA
☎ (01276) 857580 ⊕ whitehart-chobham.co.uk
Brunning & Price Original; 4 changing beers (sourced locally) Ⓗ
A lovely rambling building next to the village church on the historic High Street. It serves five ales in a variety of strengths and styles, mostly from local breweries, with the distance from the pub displayed. There are two restaurant areas and a less formal space as you enter. Log fires keep the pub warm in winter and in the summer you can watch cricket from garden at the rear. Q⊛😻◖♿️🅿️🚃(39A,73)😻🛜

Churt

Crossways Inn Ⓛ
Churt Road, GU10 2JS
☎ (01428) 714323 ⊕ thecrosswaysinn.co.uk

REAL ALE BREWERIES	
Ascot ⚡	Camberley
Big Smoke ⚡	Esher
Brightwater	Claygate
By The Horns	Salfords
Crafty	Loxhill
Dorking ⚡	Capel
Farnham	Farnham (NEW)
Felday 🍺	Holmbury St Mary
Fuzzchat 🍺	Epsom
Godalming Beerworks 🍺 ⚡	Godalming
Godstone ⚡	Godstone
Hogs Back ⚡	Tongham
Leith Hill 🍺	Coldharbour
Pilgrim ⚡	Reigate
Surrey Hills ⚡	Dorking
Thames Side ⚡	Staines-upon-Thames
Thurstons	Horsell
Tilford 🍺	Tilford
Tillingbourne	Shere
Titsey	Titsey
Trailhead ⚡	Dorking

Hop Back Crop Circle H; **3 changing beers (sourced regionally)** G
Friendly two-bar pub with a homely ambience. It is at the centre of village life and popular with local groups as well as customers from farther afield, including ramblers and cyclists. Food may feature in future but currently drinkers are welcome to bring their own sandwiches or snacks. Three traditional ciders are usually available and may be from any independent cider maker. The pub is close to lovely countryside and walks. ❀♣🖤P🖵(19)❀

Cranleigh

Three Horseshoes L ✔

4 High Street, GU6 8AE (on B2128)
☎ (01483) 276978 ⊕ threehorseshoescranleigh.co.uk
Harvey's Sussex Best Bitter; 5 changing beers H
This two-bar 17th-century pub features an inglenook fireplace with a roaring wood fire in winter. The long-gone Brufords brewery used to stand behind the pub and some photos in the lounge bar show the building. Good home-made food is served daily (but not on Sun eve). The elaborate walled garden boasts a spectacular children's playhouse and the patio is covered against the weather. Five constantly changing guest beers are sold, mostly coming from local brewers. ➳❀🕽👌♣P🖵❀❀

Dorking

Cobbett's L

23 West Street, RH4 1BY (on A25 one-way system eastbound)
☎ (01306) 879877 ⊕ cobbettsdorking.co.uk
3 changing beers G
This excellent micropub and bottleshop is in an old part of town and was once a shop selling dolls' houses. Up to three constantly changing cask beers and three ciders plus six keg and around 200 different canned and bottled beers are available, sold by knowledgeable staff. The tiny pub is in a back room with its own heated patio garden and is a great place to go and chat. Local CAMRA Cider Pub of the Year 2023. Q➳❀🕽⇌(West)🖤🐾❀❀

Cricketers L ✔

81 South Street, RH4 2JU (on A25 one-way system westbound)
☎ (01306) 889938 ⊕ cricketersdorking.co.uk
Dark Star Hophead; Fuller's London Pride, ESB; 1 changing beer (often Fuller's) H
Comfortable, attractive pub with an L-shaped bar with old mirrors, photographs and adverts on the bare brick walls. The pub is well known for the quality of its beer. It holds beer festivals and events such as an onion competition. Terrestrial sport, especially rugby, may be shown and there are board games, darts and a monthly quiz. Well-behaved dogs are welcome. Food is available Wednesday to Friday lunchtimes. The pub is closed on Monday. ➳❀🕽♣🖵❀❀

East Molesey

Bell L ✔

4 Bell Road, KT8 0SS (off B369)
☎ (020) 8941 0400
Greene King IPA; Morland Old Speckled Hen; 4 changing beers (sourced nationally; often St Austell, Timothy Taylor, Twickenham) H
A quirky, welcoming back-street inn, close to the main shopping street. It claims to date from 1460, although the building itself is 16th century – it was later East Molesey's first post office. The 18th-century highwayman Claude Duvalier hid from the Bow Street Runners here.

Several separate drinking areas make it ideal for a quiet pint or larger gathering. The large garden has a children's play area. Various TV screens show sport, which can be avoided if preferred. Quiz night is Tuesday.
➳❀🕽♣P🖵(411)❀❀

Egham

Egham United Services Club L

111 Spring Rise, TW20 9PE (close to A30 Egham Hill)
☎ (01784) 435120 ⊕ eusc.club
Rebellion IPA; Surrey Hills Ranmore; 3 changing beers (sourced nationally; often Kent, Oakham, Titanic) H
Local CAMRA Club of the Year and a previous National Club of the Year finalist. A changing range of ales includes something dark, and there is usually a real cider available from the cellar. Three beer festivals a year showcase an eclectic range of ales, mostly from the newest micros around. The club is comfortably furnished with sports TV, and hosts live music some Saturday evenings. CAMRA members can be signed in as guests on production of their membership card.
➳❀👌♣🖤P🖵❀♪

Red Lion ✔

53 High Street, TW20 9EW
☎ (01784) 473276 ⊕ redlionegham.com
Greene King Abbot; Sharp's Doom Bar, Atlantic; 3 changing beers (sourced nationally; often Rebellion, Wadworth, Windsor & Eton) H
Smartly refurbished town centre local usually offering six ales from national and local breweries, plus a selection of bottled beers. An interesting food menu includes snacks, lunch and dinner. Sky and BT Sports TV are shown on several screens. There is a quiet non-TV dining area, and paved courtyard with tables and covered shelter, as well as a function room at the rear with space for up to 60 guests. ❀🕽⇌P🖵❀

Elstead

Elstead Royal British Legion Club

Staceys Farm, Thursley Road, GU8 6DG
☎ (01252) 702195
Sharp's Doom Bar; 1 changing beer (sourced nationally; often Adnams, Hop Back, Triple fff) H
Lovely timber-framed, Grade II-listed, 16th-century former farmhouse. The club has a strong pubby feel and CAMRA members are welcome. The main bar is comfortably furnished, and leading off it is a lounge with TV and pool table. The well-priced regular beer is supplemented by a changing guest ale, often from a smaller brewery and chosen from customer requests. There is also a dartboard and bowling green. Local CAMRA Club of the Year 2023. Q➳❀♣P🖵(46)❀❀♪

Englefield Green

Beehive L

34 Middle Hill, TW20 0JQ
☎ (01784) 431621 ⊕ beehiveegham.co.uk
Fuller's London Pride; 1 changing beer (sourced locally; often Dark Star) H
This cosy, well-kept Fuller's local is open plan with a light and airy feel. It offers a full range of hot drinks including quality coffees, and extensive daily food menu – Sunday roasts are particularly popular. Usually there are two ales available from the Fuller's stable. On cooler days there is a real log fire, and on warmer ones a sheltered patio garden, as well as seating out the front. Closes early on Sundays. ➳❀🕽P🖵(8,441)❀❀♪

Happy Man ✓
12 Harvest Road, TW20 0QS (off A30)
☎ (01784) 433265
4 changing beers (sourced nationally; often Exeter, Otter, Tring) Ⓗ
In Victorian times two houses were converted to a pub serving workers building nearby Royal Holloway College. Refurbished but virtually unchanged, this previous local CAMRA Pub of the Year is a popular haunt for students and locals. Up to four rotating ales, both local and national are available. Occasional beer festivals are held on the heated and covered rear patio. Pub games include darts, and there are quiz nights. Food is usually available every day. ❀◖♣🖵🐾

Epsom

Jolly Coopers 🍸 Ⓛ
84 Wheelers Lane, KT18 7SD (off B280 via Stamford Green Rd)
☎ (01372) 723222 ⊕ jollycoopers.co.uk
Surrey Hills Ranmore; 4 changing beers (sourced regionally; often Dark Star, Fuzzchat) Ⓗ
Close to Epsom Common, this pub is more than 200 years old. It is divided in two, with a carpeted bar area is to the left, and to the right a larger area with polished parquet flooring, used mainly for dining. The decor is modern, with painted walls. There is a large paved garden at the rear. The pub is busy at weekends and quieter during the week. Fuzzchat brewery is in an outbuilding at the back. A changing real cider is sold.
🐕❀◖♣👤🖵(E9,E10) 🐾🛜

Rifleman Ⓛ
5 East Street, KT17 1BB (on A24)
☎ (01372) 721244
Greene King London Glory; Surrey Hills Ranmore; house beer (by Hardys & Hansons); 2 changing beers (sourced locally; often Hogs Back, Twickenham, Windsor & Eton) Ⓗ
Small corner pub in the shadow of a bridge carrying the railway to and from London. It is decorated in a traditional style featuring two fireplaces and dark-green wood panelling, but also has some modern features such as bare brickwork and high tables at the front. There is a pleasant garden to the rear, an oasis of calm close to central Epsom. The name comes from the Surrey Rifle Volunteers who trained nearby. 🐕❀◖♦🚆🐾

Esher

Wheatsheaf Ⓛ
40 The Green, KT10 8AG
☎ (01372) 464014 ⊕ wheatsheafesher.co.uk
Surrey Hills Shere Drop; Young's Bitter Ⓗ
Imposing inn, about 200 years old, opposite Esher Green. This smart, popular local has a vibrant atmosphere and is comfortably furnished throughout in a modern style. Its spacious and modern interior comprises a large central bar and several seating areas. Drinkers and diners are equally welcome, with high-quality food available all day and occasional gourmet evenings held. The bar area has an open fire. A bicycle rack is provided at the rear. A former local CAMRA Pub of the Year. 🐕❀◖♿🖵🐾🛜

Ewell

Queen Adelaide
272 Kingston Road, KT19 0SH (on A240)
☎ (020) 8393 2666
4 changing beers (sourced nationally) Ⓗ
Large roadhouse pub, rebuilt in 1932, comfortably furnished with a mixture of seating and tables. Changing beers are from the Ember Inns list. There is a Cask Ale Club on Mondays and Thursdays when all real ales are reduced in price. Quiz night Wednesday, steak night Thursday and acoustic music performed on the last Thursday of the month as well as live bands twice a month. Children are welcome until 10pm.
🐕❀◖♿🚆(Stoneleigh) 👤🖵(406,E16) 🐾🛜♪

Farnham

Hop Blossom
50 Long Garden Walk, GU9 7HX (between Waitrose and Castle St) SU838469
☎ (01252) 710770 ⊕ hopblossom.co.uk
Dark Star Hophead; Fuller's London Pride; Gale's Seafarers Ale; 1 changing beer (sourced nationally; often Fuller's) Ⓗ
A traditional friendly pub with a warm welcome, tucked away in the centre of Farnham. The original wooden floor adds character and the furniture is comfortable. The subdued lighting adds to the ambience. In winter there is a log fire and the recently added antique grate adds individuality to the pub. This is a dog friendly hostelry.
🐕🚆🖵🐾🛜♪

Godalming

Richmond Arms ✓
149 High Street, GU7 1AF
☎ (01483) 921561 ⊕ therichmondarmsgodalming.co.uk
St Austell Tribute; Young's London Original; 1 changing beer (sourced regionally) Ⓗ
A traditional and unspoilt locals' pub at the southern end of Godalming's High Street, handy for buses and the train station. The main bar at the front of the pub has maroon half panelling and a fireplace at each end. The public bar at the rear has a separate entrance. Behind the pub there is a raised garden with plenty of seating.
🐕❀◖♿🚆♣🖵🐾🛜

Star Inn ✓
17 Church Street, GU7 1EL
☎ (01483) 417717 ⊕ starinngodalming.co.uk
St Austell Tribute Ⓗ**; 13 changing beers (sourced nationally; often Godalming Beerworks)** Ⓗ/Ⓖ
Dating from around 1830, the Star has a small public bar at the front and a main room to the side leading to a patio garden and separate lounge. Up to 14 real ales are stocked as well as 10 ciders and perries, plus mead. Beer festivals are held at Easter and Halloween. The pub is a regular winner of CAMRA cider awards and is home to Godalming Beerworks whose beers can be regularly found on the bar. 🐕❀◖♦🚆♣🖵🐾🛜♪

Great Bookham

Anchor ✓
161 Lower Road, KT23 4AH (off A246 via Eastwick Rd)
☎ (01372) 452429
Fuller's London Pride; Surrey Hills Ranmore; Young's London Original Ⓗ
Historic Grade II-listed inn dating from the 15th century. Low-beamed ceilings, wooden floors, exposed brickwork, and an inglenook with a real fire in winter give the pub a traditional and homely feel. A charity quiz night is held every Tuesday (book ahead) and a meat raffle every Sunday. There is a patio garden with a pond and heated smoking area at the front. Children are not allowed in the bar. Q❀◖♣🖵(479)🐾🛜

Guildford

King's Head

27 King's Road, GU1 4JW (on A320 Stoke Rd)
☎ (01483) 568957 ● kingsheadguildford.co.uk
Dark Star Hophead; Fuller's London Pride, ESB; Gale's HSB; 1 changing beer (sourced nationally; often Dark Star, Fuller's, Twickenham) Ⓗ
Built in 1860 as two cottages, which soon became a beer house, this pub is noted for its attractive hanging baskets. Its interior is deceptively spacious and now much enlarged. Service is from both sides of a central bar, with the full range of Fuller's beers available, including seasonals. Traditional pub food is served. TV sport is screened in most areas. Quiz night is Tuesday and acoustic music fortnightly on Thursdays.
🌫🏵🕮≉(London Road) ♣P🖵🏵🛜🎵

Royal Oak

15 Trinity Churchyard, GU1 3RR (behind Trinity Church)
☎ (01483) 457144 ● royaloakguildford.co.uk
Fuller's London Pride; Gale's HSB; 3 changing beers (sourced nationally; often Dark Star, Fuller's) Ⓗ
This former Gale's pub has been serving real ale since 1870. It was built as an extension to the rectory next door, with a hall upstairs and rooms at ground level. These rooms are now the bar area and show the building's heavily beamed structure. Outside there is a patio area on one side, while a couple of tables overlooking Trinity churchyard are on the other. Three brewery-supplied guest beers are available.
🌫🏵♣P🖵🏵🛜🎵

Hambledon

Merry Harriers Ⓛ ✔

Hambledon Road, GU8 4DR SU967391
☎ (01428) 682883 ● merryharriers.com
Surrey Hills Shere Drop; 3 changing beers (sourced locally; often Crafty Brewing, Dorking, Greyhound) Ⓗ
This impressive 16th-century country inn, popular with walkers and cyclists, takes you back in time. It stands on a quiet country lane, in the heart of picturesque Hambledon village, set against the backdrop of the Surrey Hills in a designated area of outstanding natural beauty. There is an inglenook fireplace in the bar and benches on the forecourt outside, with a garden to the rear, overlooking a field that is home to the pub's llamas.
🌫🏵🛏🕮♣P🏵🛜🎵

Hersham

Bricklayers Arms

6-8 Queens Road, KT12 5LS (off A317)
☎ (01932) 220936
Hogs Back Surrey Nirvana; Hop Back Crop Circle; Shepherd Neame Spitfire Ⓗ
This two-bar Victorian street side pub, just off the green, has built up a fine reputation, having been run by the same landlord for the past 40 years. It is divided into a spacious public bar with a real fire, and a comfortable saloon, where excellent food is served, including daily specials. Features include wonderful external floral displays and a secluded rear garden. Two letting rooms are available. Parking can be difficult.
Q🏵🛏🕮♣&(458,515) 🏵🛜

Royal George ✔

130 Hersham Road, KT12 5QJ (off A244)
☎ (01932) 220910 ● royalgeorgepub.co.uk
Big Smoke Solaris Session Pale Ale, Cosmic Dawn; 3 changing beers Ⓗ

The pub was built in 1964 and the name refers to a ship from the Napoleonic Wars. It has one L-shaped bar with upholstered banquette seating and chairs and a real fire, all contributing to a comfortable atmosphere. Food is served every day, with a range of special offers. There is a decked rear garden and an inviting front garden with benches. At least one changing beer is usually from a local brewery. Quiz night is Tuesday.
🌫🏵🕮&P🖵(555) 🏵🛜

Holmbury St Mary

Royal Oak Ⓛ

The Glade, Felday Road, RH5 6PF
☎ (01306) 898010 ● theroyaloakholmbury.co.uk
Harvey's Sussex Best Bitter; 3 changing beers (often Felday, Firebird, Surrey Hills) Ⓗ
In a beautiful setting by the picturesque church and village green, this 17th-century pub is a popular destination with walkers and cyclists. The Felday brewery is located at the pub. The cosy bar has a real fire and home-made meals are served here and in the rear dining room, which is to be found up some stairs. There are gardens at the front and rear plus an outside bar.
🌫🏵🕮P🖵(32) 🏵🛜

Horley

Jack Fairman Ⓛ ✔

30 Victoria Road, RH6 7PZ (main shopping street near Waitrose)
☎ (01293) 827910
Greene King Abbot; Ruddles Best Bitter; Sharp's Doom Bar; 4 changing beers Ⓗ
This distinctive Art Deco-style building in the town centre was formally a garage used by Jack Fairman, a local motor racing driver. After use as a tyre centre, it opened as a Wetherspoon pub, conveniently close to the station and bus stops. Of the three guest ales, one is normally LocAle, two are from national brewers, and one of them will usually be a dark beer. Food is available all day. News or sport is shown on three TV screens on silent with subtitles. Q🌫🏵🕮&≉🖵🛜

Horsell

Crown 🍷 Ⓛ

104 High Street, GU21 4ST
☎ (01483) 771719
Surrey Hills Shere Drop; Thurstons Horsell Gold; 4 changing beers (sourced regionally; often Thurstons) Ⓗ
Welcoming two-bar community local with six real ales in the saloon bar. Normally three beers are from Thurstons, who started brewing in pub and are now located next door. This wet pub with no food is a rarity for the area. The large garden has two pétanque pistes and is used for at least one beer festival a year. Regular motorcycle and scooter club meets are held in the summer. A former CAMRA Surrey Pub of the Year, and local Pub of the Year 2023. 🌫🏵♣P🖵(48)🏵🛜🎵

Knaphill

Garibaldi

134 High Street, GU21 2QH
☎ (01483) 473374 ● thegaribaldiknaphill.co.uk
2 changing beers (sourced regionally) Ⓗ
On the edge of Knaphill, this pub has a compact interior, exposed beams and wooden floors. Two or three changing cask ales are served, with regional breweries favoured. Monday is real ale club night, with beers sold

at reduced prices, and a beer festival is held at Easter. The pub hosts a Sunday evening quiz and raises a lot for local charities through a wide range of events, including an annual cycle ride. ♿🐕🏠◐🅿🚲(39A,48)🐾🛜♪

Leatherhead

Running Horse 🅛
38 Bridge Street, KT22 8BZ (off B2122)
☎ (01372) 372081 🌐 running-horse.co.uk
Shepherd Neame Spitfire; Surrey Hills Ranmore Ⓗ
Overlooking the River Mole, this Grade II*-listed two-room pub, dating from 1403, features a real log fire, home-made, locally sourced food, a courtyard seating area and a large beer garden. The public bar has a TV, pool table and dartboard, and the cosy lounge bar features low ceilings and exposed beams. Elizabeth I apparently spent the night here. Quiz night is Tuesday and live bands play monthly, with a charity music event on May Day. Children are allowed until 9pm.
Q♿🐕◐⇌♣🅿🐾🛜♪

Leigh

Plough at Leigh 🅛
Church Road, RH2 8NJ
☎ (01306) 611348 🌐 theploughatleigh.co.uk
Harvey's Sussex Best Bitter; Pilgrim Progress; 3 changing beers (sourced nationally) Ⓗ
Overlooking the village green is this local's pub, parts of which date from the 15th century. The weatherboarded exterior to the right contains a low-beamed lounge bar, leading to a cosy restaurant serving a good variety of home-cooked food; available all day. The friendly public bar offers darts and other bar games, along with the daily papers. Children are welcome here. Dogs are also welcome and have their own water bowl and biscuit jar.
♿🐕◐♣🅿(22,433)🐾🛜

Lyne

Royal Marine
Lyne Lane, KT16 0AN
☎ (01932) 873900 🌐 royalmarinelyne.co.uk
House beer (by Hardys & Hansons); 1 changing beer (sourced nationally; often Fuller's) Ⓗ
The name of this cosy rural pub commemorates Queen Victoria's review of her troops in 1853 on nearby Chobham Common. Royal Marine memorabilia, a collection of drinking jugs and other bric-a-brac are on display. Home-cooked food is served Monday to Friday, with sandwiches for a lighter meal, and roast lunches on Sunday. A second real ale is available when demand allows. There is an extensive garden at the rear. The pub is closed Monday lunchtime and Saturday.
Q♿🐕◐♣🅿🐾🛜

Mickleham

King William IV 🅛
4 Byttom Hill, RH5 6EL (off A24 southbound behind 51 Degrees North café)
☎ (01372) 372590 🌐 thekingwilliamiv.com
Hogs Back TEA; Surrey Hills Shere Drop; 1 changing beer (sourced locally; often Crafty Brewing, Dorking, Tillingbourne) Ⓗ
A quaint, welcoming country pub dating from 1790, nestled on a hillside. The cosy main bar has a log fire and there is a smaller bar to the front. An attractive outside terrace, with some tables under cover, enjoys stunning views over the Mole Valley. Good home-made food is served – book ahead for lunch, especially on summer

weekends. Steep steps can make access difficult. A public car park is on the A24 southbound. Opening hours vary with the seasons. Q♿🐕◐🅿(465)🐾🛜

Mugswell

Well House Inn 🅛 ✓
Chipstead Lane, CR5 3SQ (off A217) TQ25845526
☎ (01737) 830640 🌐 thewellhouseinn.co.uk
Fuller's London Pride; Surrey Hills Shere Drop; 2 changing beers (sourced locally; often Dorking, Surrey Hills) Ⓗ
A real country pub, some of which is Grade II-listed and dates from the 16th century – and is supposedly haunted by the ghost of Harry the Monk. The pub is named after St Margaret's Well in the garden, which is listed in the Domesday Book. The pub is largely given over to dining but has two bar areas, each with a real fire in winter, and has extensive outside seating. Dogs are welcome in the bars but not the restaurant. ♿🐕◐♣🅿🐾🛜

New Haw

White Hart
New Haw Road, KT15 2DS (by Wey Navigation at New Haw Lock)
☎ (01932) 842927 🌐 thewhitehartnewhaw.co.uk
House beer (by Ringwood); 2 changing beers (sourced nationally; often Bedlam, Salcombe) Ⓗ
Originally built in 1787 to serve bargemen on the Wey Navigation, the pub was rebuilt in 1861. It has more recently been refurbished in a contemporary style as a single-bar pub serving food and drink in pleasant surroundings. One house beer and two rotating guests are available. The large canalside garden won first place for a community garden in the local Green Fingers of Runnymede competition. There is a bouncy castle and children's play area outside, and a barbecue in good weather. ♿🐕🚃◐🅿(455,456)🛜♪

Newdigate

Surrey Oaks 🍺 🅛
Parkgate Road, Parkgate, RH5 5DZ (between Newdigate and Leigh) TQ20524363
☎ (01306) 631200 🌐 thesurreyoaks.com
Surrey Hills Ranmore, Shere Drop; 4 changing beers (sourced nationally) Ⓗ
This multi-award winning 16th-century free house serves a changing range of six cask beers (one a dark ale), 12 craft keg beers and 24 ciders. There are a number of distinct areas, with low beams, flagstones and an inglenook fireplace with log-burning stove. The lovely large garden includes a heated and covered area and a children's play area. The pub hosts popular beer festivals in May and August. Good food is sold daily, and breakfast at the weekend. Q♿🐕◐♣🅿(21,50)🐾🛜

Norwood Hill

Fox Revived 🅛
Norwood Hill, RH6 0ET
☎ (01293) 229270
Brunning & Price Original; 4 changing beers Ⓗ
This bright and airy pub on a country crossroads has an extensive restaurant area but is welcoming to drinkers, with four mainly local guest beers available. The bar area contains a small real fire and leather armchairs. The large garden offers views of the North Downs and Box Hill. The pub is so named because it was rebuilt after the original pub, the Fox Inn, burned down. Good food is available all day. ♿🐕◐♿🅿(22)🐾🛜

Puttenham

Good Intent
60-62 The Street, GU3 1AR
☎ (01483) 923434 ● goodintentputtenham.co.uk
Sharp's Doom Bar; Timothy Taylor Landlord; house beer (by Crafty Brewing) ⊞
Attractive, welcoming village pub. Classic red carpets and contrasting dark varnished woodwork and a massive inglenook fireplace contribute to a warm, comfortable ambience. The layout and bar are L-shaped, with the handpumps split between the long and short sides of the bar. Low partitions break up the floor space, creating separate areas. The North Downs Way passes the door and one of Surrey's few remaining hop growers is at the other end of the village. Q⌂❄◐ ♠P🅿🐾🛜♪

Redhill

Garibaldi ⃝
29 Mill Street, RH1 6PA
☎ (01737) 773094 ● thegaribaldiredhill.co.uk
5 changing beers (sourced nationally) ⊞
This not-for-profit and community-run pub has stood for over 150 years opposite Redhill Common. There is a single room, with a small side area that contains a dartboard. Two TV screens show televised sport at a discreet volume. A large number of social events are run by the pub, including at least two beer festivals. The large garden, with views across Redhill, is extremely well tended. The beer range changes frequently and usually includes at least two LocAles. ⌂❄♠🚌🐾🛜

Hatch ⃝
44 Hatchlands Road, RH1 6AT (on A25 W of town)
☎ (01737) 423342
Pilgrim Surrey, Progress; 3 changing beers ⊞
Dating from the 17th century, this comfortable and deceptively-spacious pub was once a workhouse with a hayloft for horses. It became Pilgrim brewery's first pub in 2022. The L-shaped bar offers up to five cask beers, plus up to 12 keg lines, mostly from their brewery. There are two more secluded rooms to the left and a cosy fire to the right. A local pizzeria takes over the kitchen from Wednesdays to Sundays. Q⌂❄◐♠🚌🐾🛜

Reigate

Bell Inn ⃝
21 Bell Street, RH2 7AD (on A217)
☎ (01737) 244438
6 changing beers ⊞
This town-centre pub is one of the oldest in Reigate. Packed with character, it has one long, narrow, low-ceilinged bar room, plus an external seating area to the rear. The beer menu changes regularly but usually includes one each from local breweries Surrey Hills, By the Horns and Titsey, plus three other regional beers. No food is served but drinkers are welcome to bring their own. Note the large old Ordnance Survey map on the ceiling. ⌂❄≋🚌🐾🛜

Hop Stop Bar
73 Bell Street, RH2 7AN (on A217 S of town centre)
☎ (01737) 221781 ● hopstopbeers.co.uk
Surrey Hills Shere Drop; 1 changing beer (sourced nationally) ⊞
Opened in 2019, this former restaurant is now a modern, continental-style bar. It usually serves two cask beers and has an additional nine lines that are used for an eclectic array of keg beers and cider, details of which are shown on an electronic board. There is also a chiller cabinet with an assortment of international bottles and cans, which are available to drink in-house or for take-away. Beers can also be ordered online for collection. ⌂≋🚌🐾🛜

Pilgrim Brewery Tap Room ⃝
11 West Street, RH2 9BL (off A25 towards Dorking)
☎ (01737) 222651 ● pilgrim.co.uk
6 changing beers ⃝
The oldest brewery in Surrey, founded in 1985, has been under the current ownership since 2017. The Tap Room is next door to the brewery itself, in what used to be the company office. Additional seating outside offers views of Reigate Priory Cricket Ground. There will usually be six cask and six keg beers available, all brewed on-site. No food is served but you can bring your own. Dominoes, shove ha'penny and board games are available. Q⌂❄≋♠P🅿🐾🛜

Shamley Green

Red Lion ✅
The Green, GU5 0UB
☎ (01483) 664161 ● redlionshamleygreen.com
Sharp's Doom Bar; Surrey Hills Shere Drop; 2 changing beers (sourced nationally; often Crafty Brewing, Firebird, Timothy Taylor)
Opposite the cricket green is this traditional village pub comprising a small bar with separate, well-regarded, restaurant (booking advisable) and function room. There is a secluded garden at the rear, and tables at the front facing the village green. No food is served on Sunday evenings, when the pub closes at 8pm. The guest beers are from the Punch lists, usually from a regional brewery. Dogs are welcome throughout the pub and garden. Well-served by buses at all times. Q⌂❄◐P🅿(53,63)🐾🛜

Shepperton

Barley Mow 🍺 ⃝
67 Watersplash Road, TW17 0EE (off B376 in Shepperton Green)
☎ (01932) 225326
Hogs Back TEA; Hop Back Summer Lightning; 3 changing beers (sourced regionally; often Lister's, Tillingbourne, Twickenham) ⊞
Friendly community local in Shepperton Green, to the west of the main village centre. Five handpumps serve two regular and three changing guests. Pump clips adorn the bar and beams, along with CAMRA certificates, including a 50th anniversary gold award. Entertainment includes jazz on Wednesday, a quiz night on Thursday, live rock or blues on Friday or Saturday night, and a charity raffle on Sundays. There is a heated patio at the rear. Local CAMRA Pub of the Year 2023. ❄♠P🅿(400,458) 🐾🛜♪

South Godstone

Fox & Hounds ⃝ ✅
Tilburstow Hill Road, RH9 8LY
☎ (01342) 893474 ● foxandhounds.org.uk
Fuller's London Pride; Greene King Abbot; 4 changing beers (sourced regionally) ⊞
This delightful building, parts of which date back to 1368, first became a pub in 1601. There are many original features including a large inglenook in the restaurant. The cosy, low-ceilinged bar area has high-backed settles and a fireplace. The garden features a children's play area with a wooden pirate ship. An ever-changing menu of home-cooked, locally-sourced food, plus specials, is available. ⌂❄◐♠P🐾🛜

Staines-upon-Thames

Thames Side Brewery

1 Hale Street, TW18 4UW (next to Travelodge near entrance to Two Rivers car parks)

☎ 07749 204242 ⊕ thamessidebrewery.co.uk

Thames Side White Swan Pale Ale, Egyptian Goose India Pale Ale, Black Swan Porter; 3 changing beers (sourced locally; often Five Points, Thames Side) H

The new home of the excellent Thames Side brewery, following the complete refit of a former restaurant that is still ongoing. Six real ales from the brewery's regular and occasional range are served, plus a full range of other drinks. Plenty of seating is available, with comfy sofas in one corner. Regular live music features, including open mic nights. Food is available when the kitchen is open, so check ahead. ⊛P🚱♿♪

Sunbury-on-Thames

Magpie L ✓

64 Thames Street, TW16 6AF

☎ (01932) 782024 ⊕ magpiesunbury.com

Greene King IPA; 1 changing beer (sourced regionally; often Mad Squirrel, Sambrook's) H

Refurbished rambling old riverside pub on two levels, with one regular and up to four changing real ales (usually from London and other local microbreweries) available in the downstairs bar. The outside drinking area overlooks the Thames. Food is available daily. The pub name relates to a member of the Grand Order of Water Rat's horse, and a blue plaque commemorates the founding of the entertainment industry charity here in 1889. ⊛🕭◑♣🚃(216)♿🛜

Tongham

Hogs Back Brewery Shop & Tap Room L ✓

Manor Farm, The Street, GU10 1DE

☎ (01252) 783000 ⊕ hogsback.co.uk

Hogs Back Surrey Nirvana, TEA; 2 changing beers (often Hogs Back) H/G

In rural Surrey, nestling under the Hogs Back ridge, the taproom is a converted kiln. Tables can be booked in advance for a deposit, though walk-ins are also welcome. Two regular beers are supplemented by seasonal specials and real Somerset cider in bottles. The Hanger Bar is used for harvesting in September and otherwise hosts special events such as live music and comedy nights, as well as showing major sporting fixtures. The on-site shop is open daily. ⊛🕭●P🚱♪

Upper Hale

Alfred Free House

9 Bishops Road, GU9 0JA

☎ (01252) 820385 ⊕ thealfredfreehouse.co.uk

6 changing beers (sourced nationally; often Ascot, Wantsum) H

This friendly local pub, tucked away down a residential road, features a bar area and a restaurant that can also be used for functions. The six regularly changing ales are sourced nationally, including at least one dark beer. Fresh home-made food, using locally sourced ingredients, is served Wednesday to Saturday evenings and Sunday lunchtime. The pub hosts events including charity quiz nights and a beer festival each Easter. The pub is closed on Monday. Q🕭⊛◑♿♣P🚃(5)♿♪

Walton on Thames

Walton Village

29 High Street, KT12 1DG

☎ (01932) 254431 ⊕ thewaltonvillage.com

Hogs Back TEA; 1 changing beer (sourced locally) H

Modern high street pub in a converted shop premises, featuring exposed brickwork and wood panels. The large front bar has a raised seating area and there is a room to the rear for private events. A wide range of food is served all day, prepared in an open-plan kitchen in the centre of the pub. It attracts a diverse clientele. A popular quiz night is held on Thursdays, and other attractions include a table tennis table and mini dog bar with water and treats. 🕭⊛◑●♣🚃♿🛜

West Horsley

Barley Mow L

181 The Street, KT24 6HR

☎ (01483) 282693 ⊕ barleymowhorsley.com

Hogs Back TEA; Surrey Hills Ranmore, Shere Drop H

A classic pub in the heart of the Surrey Hills, with some flagstone flooring. The large building incorporates the Malting House to the rear, which is available for functions. Thai food is available lunchtime and evening and traditional English dishes at lunchtimes (no food on Sun). The garden has a substantial open grassed area which is great for dogs and has seating dotted around. Will open on request at 11.30 for the bus from Guildford. 🕭⊛◑♣P🚃(478)♿🛜♪

West Molesey

Royal Oak ✓

317 Walton Road, KT8 2QG (on B369)

☎ (020) 8979 5452

Fuller's London Pride; St Austell Tribute; 2 changing beers (sourced nationally; often Sharp's, St Austell) H

Situated next to the church, this pub dates from about 1860 and is at the heart of the community. The comfortably furnished open-plan bar is divided into two areas, with a quiet lounge area to the left. Wood panelling completes the traditional pub feel, along with oak beams, horse brasses and plates. Families are welcome until evening and there is a secure garden to the rear. Live music plays every other Saturday and open mic nights are held on Mondays and Wednesdays. 🕭⊛♣P🚃(411,461)♿🛜

Weybourne

Running Stream ✓

66 Weybourne Road, GU9 9HE

☎ (01252) 323750

Greene King IPA; Hardys & Hansons Bitter; Timothy Taylor Dark Mild; 1 changing beer H

A good old-fashioned, friendly locals' pub. The handpumps dispense between three and six beers depending on demand, one of which will generally be a dark beer. Food is served at lunchtimes and consists of various home-cooked meals including vegetarian, vegan and gluten-free options (outside of these hours you should phone ahead). There is a pleasant garden at the rear. Regular events include vintage car rallies and quiz nights. Q⊛◑♣P🚃♿🛜

Weybridge

Old Crown

83 Thames Street, KT13 8LP (off A317)

☎ (01932) 842844 ⊕ theoldcrownweybridge.co.uk

Courage Best Bitter, Directors; Young's London Original; 1 changing beer (sourced nationally) Ⓗ
A Grade II-listed pub with a weatherboarded façade that dates to at least 1729. There are several areas to meet the varied needs of drinkers and diners. The two gardens are popular in summer and mooring for small boats is provided at the waterside, which is at the confluence of the River Wey and the Thames. The changing beers vary in source and can be from smaller brewers. Food is available every lunchtime and in the evening Thursday-Saturday. Q☽❀◑►🅿🖥☙🎐📶

Whyteleafe

Radius Arms

205 Godstone Road, CR3 0EL (on A22)
☎ 07514 916172
4 changing beers Ⓗ/Ⓖ
This friendly and welcoming micropub brings welcome choice to this part of Surrey with its ever-changing selection of beer and cider. There are at least four cask ales on offer: two pale ales, one bitter and one dark. Four KeyKegs and 12 ciders provide more choice. A pickled onion competition, a beermat-festooned ceiling and furniture recycled from the Olympic Park are some of the quirky features. There is also a small library. Closed on Mondays. Q❀❧🍴🖥🖥☙

Woking

Herbert Wells Ⓛ ✅

51-57 Chertsey Road, GU21 5AJ
☎ (01483) 722818
Greene King Abbot; Ruddles Best Bitter; Sharp's Doom Bar; 7 changing beers (sourced nationally) Ⓗ
A varied range of up to seven guest beers are served at this popular town-centre Wetherspoon, which is close to bus stops and the railway station. The large open-plan bar is decorated with HG Wells-inspired features including an invisible man sitting in the window and its own time machine. A wealth of information about local history covers the walls of both the main bar and the smaller side room. Children are accommodated when eating. Q☽◑&❧🍴🖥📶

Woking Railway Athletic Club

Goldsworth Road, GU21 6JT (behind offices at east end of Goldsworth Rd) TQ003585
☎ (01483) 598499
3 changing beers (sourced nationally) Ⓗ
Lively club tucked away near Victoria Arch, serving three or four beers. One side is sports-oriented, with darts, pool and Sky Sports; the other is quieter. Walls are decorated with old railway pictures. Show a CAMRA membership card or copy of this Guide for entry. This area is due to be redeveloped but the club is assured of a place in the new development. Local CAMRA Club of the Year 2019-2022. ☽❧♣🅿🖥📶

Wonersh

Grantley Arms

The Street, GU5 0PE
☎ (01483) 893351 ⊕ thegrantleyarms.co.uk
Surrey Hills Shere Drop; Young's London Original; 1 changing beer (often Hogs Back) Ⓗ
Half-timbered village pub dating to late 16th century with later extensions. A recent refurbishment exposed more of the frame of the building creating a bright and cheerful interior. The pub is food-led using locally sourced ingredients where possible, with meals served all day, but not all tables in the bar are bookable and

there is no pressure to eat. Buses stop outside, including evening and Sunday services from Cranleigh and Guildford. ☽❀◑&🅿🖥(53,63)☙📶

Worplesdon

Fox Inn Ⓛ

Fox Corner, GU3 3PP
☎ (07841 204004) ⊕ thefoxinnfoxcorner.com
6 changing beers (sourced nationally; often Ascot, Surrey Hills, Triple fff)
A convivial and welcoming free house consisting of three separate rooms. Each has subdued lighting and low beams and contains an eclectic collection of effects that make the rooms interesting without being cluttered. Beside the pub, which is set well back from the road, is a patio, and beyond that a substantial garden. Food is provided by a different pop-up stall each evening. ☽❀◑🅿🖥(28,91)☙📶🎵

Wrecclesham

Sandrock Ⓛ

Sandrock Hill Road, GU10 4NS SU830444
☎ (01252) 447289 ⊕ sandrockwrecclesham.co.uk
Bowman Swift One; Exmoor Gold; Hogs Back TEA; St Austell Proper Job; Timothy Taylor Landlord; Triple fff Moondance; 1 changing beer (sourced nationally; often Fuller's, Hop Back, Ringwood) Ⓗ
Traditional pub with a contemporary feel, offering seven regular cask ales, including Fuller's London Pride, plus a guest ale on handpump. Thai food is available in the separate restaurant Wednesday to Sunday evening and weekend lunchtimes. There is a patio garden terrace at the rear and a small car park. Live music plays once a month on a Saturday. Major sporting events are shown on terrestrial TV. Q☽❀◑&♣🅿🖥(16,17)☙📶🎵

Breweries

Ascot SIBA

Unit 4, Lawrence Way, Camberley, GU15 3DL
☎ (01276) 686696 ⊕ ascotbrewing.co.uk
⊠ Founded in 2007 and rebranded as Ascot Brewing Company in 2017. The brewery moved to new premises with an expanded 22,000-litre fermentation capacity in 2020. The new taphouse is on a mezzanine floor with a view over the brewery and is the venue for regular comedy nights and live events. A beer range is brewed under the brand name Disruption IS Brewing. 🚩♦LIVE🍴

Gold Cup (ABV 4%) GOLD
A lemony aroma leads to a dry, bitter taste, with more citrus flavours. Hoppy finish with a hint of sweetness.
Starting Gate (ABV 4%) BITTER
A pale brown session bitter with malt flavours present throughout. Dry with a lasting sharp and bitter finish.
Final Furlong (ABV 4.2%) BITTER
A well-balanced, copper-coloured bitter, with biscuity malt sweetness to the fore. Some citrus fruitiness and clean, hoppy aftertaste.
5/4 Favourite (ABV 4.6%) PALE
Grapefruit aroma, with Cascade hops providing a crisp bitterness in the taste, balanced with some biscuit in aroma and aftertaste.
Front Runner (ABV 4.8%) PALE
Anastasia's Stout (ABV 5%) STOUT
Burnt coffee aromas lead to a roast malt flavour in this black beer. Notably fruity throughout, with a bittersweet aftertaste.

Big Smoke SIBA

Unit D3, Sandown Industrial Estate, Esher, KT10 8BL
☎ (01372) 469606 ☎ 07859 884190
⊕ bigsmokebrew.co.uk

⊗ Brewing began at the Antelope, Surbiton, in 2014. In 2019 Big Smoke moved to a new purpose-built 30-hectolitre brewery in Esher with an onsite taproom. ♦❦

Solaris Session Pale Ale (ABV 3.8%) PALE
Unfined golden ale with bitter grapefruit flavour, some malt and a long dry bitter finish. Hoppy fruity nose.
Dark Wave Porter (ABV 5%) PORTER
Creamy, black porter with a dry roasty bitter character balanced by a caramelised sweetness.
Electric Eye Pale Ale (ABV 5%) PALE
Full bodied golden ale with fruity nose and flavours of grapefruit, lemon and stone fruits overlaid with sweet biscuit. Initially the hops are floral becoming more peppery in the dry, bitter finish.
Underworld (ABV 5%) SPECIALITY
Sweet smooth stout with hints of chocolate and coffee in the aroma and taste coupled with toasted nuts and vanilla.

Brightwater

9 Beaconsfield Road, Claygate, KT10 0PN
☎ (01372) 462334 ☎ 07802 316389
⊕ brightbrew.co.uk

⊗ Established in 2013 at Claygate in Surrey, Brightwater is a five-barrel brewery producing traditional beers. The range is available at its brewery tap, Platform 3, outside Claygate Station, and other Surrey and South London pubs.

Little Nipper (ABV 3.3%) BITTER
A rather thin, hoppy bitter with a hint of a citrus taste and a bitter, slightly dry finish.
Top Notch (ABV 3.6%) BITTER
Citrus notes dominant the aroma of this mid brown bitter. It has a reasonably well-balanced taste with some bitterness in the finish.
Ernest (ABV 3.7%) PALE
TPL (ABV 3.7%) BITTER
Village Green (ABV 3.8%) GOLD
Daisy Gold (ABV 4%) BITTER
Golden-coloured ale with a moderate tropical fruit hoppy character and some balancing malt leading to a bittersweet finish.
Wild Orchid (ABV 4%) SPECIALITY
All Citra (ABV 4.3%) GOLD
Lip Smacker (ABV 4.8%) BITTER
Coal Porter (ABV 4.9%) SPECIALITY

By The Horns SIBA

Unit 11, The IO Centre, Salbrook Road Industrial Estate, Salbrook Road, Salfords, RH1 5GJ
☎ (020) 3417 7338 ⊕ bythehorns.co.uk

⊗ By the Horns began brewing in 2011 with a 5.5-barrel plant but had outgrown its original site by 2020. A new site in Salfords, Surrey opened in 2021. Cask is a big part of the production, with the rest of its output in keg and cans. Its brewery tap is near to its old site inside the AFC Wimbledon Stadium. ⊟

Panowow (ABV 3.8%) BITTER
Stiff Upper Lip (ABV 3.8%) BITTER
Classic amber-coloured bitter, well-balanced with hops throughout with hints of citrus and honey. Dry bitter finish.
Hopadelic (ABV 4.3%) GOLD

Smooth golden ale with grapefruit, gooseberry, citrus and lemon rind notes overlaid with hops. Building bitterness in the lingering finish.
Lambeth Walk (ABV 5.1%) PORTER
Black-ruby full-bodied porter with black cherry, sultanas, coffee and a sweet treacle character. Developing, lingering dark bitter roast cocoa.

Crafty SIBA

Thatched House Farm, Dunsfold Road, Dunsfold, Loxhill, GU8 4BW
☎ (01483) 276300 ⊕ craftybrewing.co.uk

⊗ Established in 2014 behind the famous Dunsfold aerodrome, Crafty Brewing opened a new plant in 2019. It brews contemporary versions of traditional beer styles. The 'Crafty Cares' beers support various charities, including Surrey Search & Rescue. It supplies nearly 200 regional pubs, local shops and markets. All beers are available nationally to order online in mini-kegs, bottles, and cans. The brewery hosts regular open days (see website for details). ⊟♦

Loxhill Biscuit (ABV 3.6%) BITTER
Golden bitter which belies its strength. Initial biscuity aroma and taste with a dry bitter finish, from the Challenger hops.
One (ABV 3.9%) PALE
Golden-yellow beer with Chinook and Sorachi Ace hops. Tropical fruits aroma, leads to full dry fruity finish. Hints of coconut.
Blind Side (ABV 4%) BITTER
A traditional, light brown bitter. Predominantly malty throughout. Toffee and some roast character lead to a bittersweet finish.
Hop Tipple (ABV 4.2%) GOLD
Beautifully-balanced pale ale. Light and easy-drinking with resinous modern hops and a crisp finish coming from dry-hopping.

Dorking SIBA

Aldhurst Farm, Temple Lane, Capel, RH5 5HJ
☎ (01306) 877988 ⊕ dorkingbrewery.com

⊗ Dorking started brewing in 2008 at premises in west Dorking. In 2017 production moved to a new, larger site in Capel capable of producing 35,000 pints per week. Beers can be found in Surrey, Sussex, Hampshire and London. ‼⊟♦❦

Surrey XPA (ABV 3.8%) BITTER
Pilcrow Pale (ABV 4%) GOLD
Smokestack Lightnin' (ABV 4%) SPECIALITY
DB One (ABV 4.2%) BITTER
Hoppy best bitter with underlying orange fruit notes. Some balancing malt sweetness in the taste leads to a dry, bitter finish.
Black Noise (ABV 4.5%) PORTER
Rich, full-flavoured porter with blackberries dominating the aroma. Rounded bitterness with underlying hop character throughout with a biscuity finish.
Red India (ABV 5%) RED
Five Claw (ABV 5.1%) PALE

Farnham (NEW)

2 Pierrepont Home Farm, Farnham, GU10 3BS

⊗ Farnham Brewing Co (FBC) is a microbrewery nestling in the beautiful rural setting of the Surrey Hills Area of Outstanding Natural Beauty. Established by three local families, it brews a variety of ales from the traditional to modern IPAs and American pale ales. Visitors are welcome.

Felday

▤ Royal Oak, Village Green, Felday Glade, Holmbury
St Mary, RH5 6PF
☎ (01306) 730654 ⊕ feldaybrewery.co.uk

Brewing began in 2017 on a custom-made plant in a
small, purpose-built, building next to the Royal Oak pub
car park. Almost all of the beer is supplied to the pub
although it may occasionally be seen elsewhere. ♦

Fuzzchat

▤ Jolly Coopers, 84 Wheelers Lane, Epsom, KT18 7SD
☎ (01372) 723222 ⊕ fuzzchatbrewery.co.uk

⊗ Fuzzchat is Epsom's first brewery in more than 90
years. Housed behind the Jolly Coopers, it used to be an
old blacksmith's cottage, recently restored after being
derelict for several years. A Fuzzchat is anyone born on
Epsom Common. ‼♦

Godalming Beerworks

▤ Star Inn, 17 Church Street, Godalming, GU7 1EL
⊕ godalming.beer

⊗ A unique nanobrewery attached to a CAMRA award-
winning pub. ♦

Godstone SIBA

Flower Farm, Oxted Road, Godstone, RH9 8BP
☎ 07791 570731

Office: 3 Willow Way, Godstone, RH9 8NQ
⊕ thegodstonebrewers.com

⊗ The Godstone Brewers was established in 2015 using
a one-barrel plant but moved to larger premises on a
farm in Godstone. It now uses a 12-barrel plant to
produce core beers, and a five-barrel plant for a variety
of 'specials' and one-off's. Beers are named with local
themes. Local outlets are supplied, and a taproom has
been built. All beers are suitable for vegans. ‼ ▤ ♦LIVE V♦

Up, Up and Away (ABV 2.7%) GOLD
Trenchman's Hop (ABV 3.8%) BITTER
Redgate (ABV 4%) BITTER
Pondtail (ABV 4.1%) PALE
Junction 6 (ABV 4.2%) BLOND
Forever (ABV 4.3%) GOLD
Rusty's Ale (ABV 4.4%) BITTER
Tunnel Vision (ABV 4.6%) SPECIALITY
Buzz (ABV 4.7%) SPECIALITY
Bitter Entropy (ABV 5.3%) BITTER
Dubbel (ABV 5.5%) SPECIALITY
Polly's Potion (ABV 6.5%) PORTER

Hogs Back SIBA

Manor Farm, The Street, Tongham, GU10 1DE
☎ (01252) 783000 ⊕ hogsback.co.uk

⊗ Traditional, family-owned brewery boasting an
extensive range of award-winning ales, established
1992. It planted its own hop garden in 2014 (now has
6,500 plants). It's open for guided tours and the shop
sells all its beers, plus 300+ of the best UK and World
bottled beers, craft cans and cider. Newly opened
brewery tap (housed in a former hop kiln), offers live
music, comedy, quizzes and live sport, as well as hosting
an annual Hop Harvest festival in September. ‼ ▤ ♦LIVE ♦

Surrey Nirvana (ABV 4%) PALE
Refreshing session pale ale. Sweet, moderately full-
bodied leading to an initially sweet finish with hop
bitterness becoming more evident.
TEA (ABV 4.2%) BITTER

A tawny-coloured best bitter with toffee and malt
present in the nose. A well-rounded flavour with malt
and a fruity sweetness.

Leith Hill

▤ c/o Plough Inn, Coldharbour Lane, Coldharbour,
RH5 6HD
☎ (01306) 711793 ⊕ ploughinn.com

⊗ Leith Hill was established in 1996 at the Plough Inn
and was moved to converted storerooms at the rear in
2001, increasing capacity to 2.5 barrels in 2005. New
owners took over in 2016. ‼LIVE

Pilgrim SIBA

11 West Street, Reigate, RH2 9BL
☎ (01737) 222651 ⊕ pilgrim.co.uk

⊗ Pilgrim was the first microbrewery in Surrey, set up in
1982 in Woldingham before moving to its current
premises in Reigate in 1984. After being bought by new
owners in 2017 it enlarged to a 12-barrel brew length
and opened a taproom. Beers are available in many local
outlets. ‼ ▤ ♦ ♦

Quench (ABV 3.4%) BITTER
Surrey (ABV 3.7%) BITTER
Pineapple, grapefruit and spicy aromas. Biscuity
maltiness with a hint of vanilla balanced by a hoppy
bitterness and refreshing bittersweet finish.
Session IPA (ABV 3.9%) PALE
Progress (ABV 4%) BITTER
Well-rounded, tawny-coloured bitter. Predominantly
sweet and malty with an underlying fruitiness and hint of
toffee, balanced with a subdued bitterness.
Saracen (ABV 4.5%) STOUT

Surrey Hills SIBA

Denbies Wine Estate, London Road, Dorking, RH5 6AA
☎ (01306) 883603 ⊕ surreyhills.co.uk

⊗ Surrey Hills began brewing in 2005 near Shere,
moving to Dorking in 2011. Nearly 95% of production is
sold within 15 miles of the brewery. The beers have won
several local and national awards. ‼ ▤ ♦ ♦

Ranmore (ABV 3.8%) GOLD
Glorious, light, flavoursome session beer. An earthy
hoppy nose leads into a grapefruit and hoppy taste and a
clean, bitter finish.
Shere Drop (ABV 4.2%) PALE
Hoppy with some balancing malt. Pleasant citrus aroma,
noticeable fruitiness in taste, with some sweetness.
Gilt Complex (ABV 4.6%) GOLD
Initial citrus fruitiness quickly gives way to a piercing hit
of bitter hops fading slowly in a big dry finish.
Gilt Trip (ABV 4.6%) GOLD
Greensand IPA (ABV 4.6%) PALE
A strong-flavoured and easily-drinkable IPA, with intense
grapefruit and hops in the aroma and taste and soft
citrusy finish.
Collusion (ABV 5.2%) GOLD
Golden ale with changing hop mix. Has pale malt
backbone, with citrus and tropical flavours combined
with characteristics of marmalade.

Thames Ditton

Office: PO Box 1037A, Thames Ditton, KT1 9BS
☎ 07761 473621
✉ thamesdittonbrewery@gmail.com

Established in 2020, it produces two regular cask beers,
available in selected local outlets, one bottled lager, and

occasional, limited edition cask ale. All beers currently contract brewed elsewhere.

Henry's Alt (ABV 4.5%) BITTER
Screaming Queen (ABV 5%) IPA

Thames Side SIBA

1 Hale Street, Staines-upon-Thames, TW18 4SU
☎ 07703 518956 ⊕ thamessidebrewery.co.uk

⊠ Founded in 2015 by CAMRA member Andy Hayward using a four-barrel plant. In 2020 a one-barrel pilot brew kit for experimental and developmental brews was added. It moved to its current brewery and taproom on the banks of the River Thames in 2022. A full range of beers are named after birds found on or near the nearby river, while specials follow a musical theme. !!♦◆

Harrier Bitter (ABV 3.4%) BITTER
Heron Ale (ABV 3.7%) BITTER
Malty traditional English bitter, with a tangerine fruit flavour. Balanced with impressive dry finish and loads of flavour for strength.

White Swan Pale Ale (ABV 4.2%) PALE
New World pale ale. Grapefruit pith and grassy hops almost overpowering biscuit maltiness. Some sweetness in finish with crisp biscuitiness.

Egyptian Goose IPA (ABV 4.8%) PALE
English IPA with initial floral aroma leading to an earthy mango fruitiness as sweetness builds and a balanced bitter finish.

Wryneck Rye IPA (ABV 5.6%) IPA
Spicy rye IPA, with lychees and increasing lemony taste balanced by rye and New World hops. Short, dry, bitter finish.

Thurstons

The Courtyard, 102c High Street, Horsell, GU21 4ST
☎ (01483) 729555 ☎ 07789 936784
⊕ thurstonsbrewery.co.uk

⊠ Originally based in the Crown, Horsell, Thurstons moved next door in 2014 when the brewery upgraded to a 4.5-barrel plant. The brewery supplies pubs across Surrey. ♦LIVE

Small IPA (ABV 3%) PALE
Horsell Best (ABV 3.8%) BITTER
Traditional, well-balanced bitter, initially malty with strong caramel and redcurrant flavours throughout and balancing bitterness, becoming drier in finish.

Horsell Gold (ABV 3.8%) PALE
Light fruit and slightly nutty aroma, lead to some bitterness and malt, which soon fades into a light bitter finish.

Milk Stout (ABV 4.5%) STOUT
Smooth, sweet stout, with chocolatey and sweet malt flavour. Pleasant sharpness as lactose comes through leading to slightly dry finish.

Un-American Pale Ale (ABV 4.6%) PALE
Well-hopped, American-style pale using English grown hops. Grapefruit and pineapple grow into full-bodied sweetness and lingering bitterness.

Tilford

🍶 **Duke of Cambridge, Tilford Road, Farnham, GU10 2DD** ☎ 07710 500967
✉ mark@tilfordbrewery.beer

⊠ Tilford Brewery is a 2.5-barrel plant situated in an old coaching house adjacent to the Duke of Cambridge pub. It supplies its award-winning cask ales to pubs and clubs in Surrey and Hampshire plus beer festivals. !!🍻

Tillingbourne

Old Scotland Farm, Staple Lane, Shere, GU5 9TE
☎ (01483) 222228 ⊕ tillybeer.co.uk

⊠ Tillingbourne was established in 2011 on a farm site previously used by Surrey Hills Brewery using its old 17-barrel plant. Around 25 local outlets are supplied. !!🍻♦

The Source (ABV 3.3%) GOLD
Light and crisp golden ale with strong grapefruit flavours. Packed full of Citra hops and drinking well above its strength.

Black Troll (ABV 3.7%) PALE
A black IPA in which initial roast notes are eventually overpowered by citrus hop through to the finish.

Dormouse (ABV 3.8%) BITTER
Predominately sweet and malty, with strong toffee notes and a short fruity finish.

AONB (ABV 4%) GOLD
Golden ale in which Cascade hop dominates throughout. Some balancing malt in the aroma and taste.

Falls Gold (ABV 4.2%) GOLD
Whilst hops dominate, balancing malt is evident throughout. Hints of grapefruit in aroma and taste lead to a dry finish.

Whakahari (ABV 4.6%) PALE
Hop Troll (ABV 4.8%) PALE
Big hop flavours together with peach and apricot. Sweet, fruity taste leads to a floral bitter finish.

Summit (ABV 6%) IPA

Titsey SIBA

Botley Hill Farmhouse, Limpsfield Road, Titsey, CR6 9QH
☎ (01959) 528535 ⊕ titseybrewingco.com

⊠ A microbrewery established in 2017 on the Titsey Estate, it is in the process of moving to larger premises on the same estate. A borehole has been sunk and is doubling the size of the brewing plant. There will also be a taproom onsite. It supplies the associated Botley Hill Farmhouse and increasingly to other local outlets. Ales are named after historic owners of the Titsey Estate. Innes Lager and all the bottles are suitable for vegans. ♦LIVE V

Gresham Hopper (ABV 3.7%) GOLD
Leveson Buck (ABV 3.7%) PALE
Gower Wolf (ABV 4%) BITTER

Trailhead

Goldenlands Farm, Punchbowl Lane, Dorking, RH5 4DX ⊕ trailheadbrew.com

Established in 2021 in farm buildings just south of Dorking. Beers are mostly available in keg, but may occasionally appear in cask. The taproom is open daily. ◆

A glass of bitter beer or pale ale, taken with the principal meal of the day, does more good and less harm than any medicine the physician can prescribe. **Dr Carpenter, 1750**

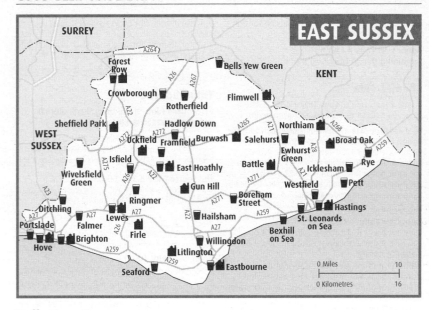

Bells Yew Green

Brecknock Arms ✅
Bayham Road, TN3 9BJ
☎ (01892) 750237
Harvey's IPA, Sussex Best Bitter; 1 changing beer
(sourced locally; often Harvey's) ⊞
Accessible by foot, rail, and road, the Brecknock is an
attractive, family-run country pub. The real ales and
traditional home-cooked food on offer, including their
renowned Sunday roasts, are complemented by the
friendly welcome and good service. The garden barn, in
the spacious rear area, has capacity for 60 people. Very
much a local community hub, it is quiet and cosy and
there is a TV and games room in a converted building in
the car park. Q➤❀◑&♿≠(Frant)♣P🛒❀🐾📶

Bexhill on Sea

Albatross Club (RAFA) 🄻
15 Marina Arcade, TN40 1JS (on seafront 200yds E of De
La Warr Pavilion)
☎ (01424) 212916 ⊕ bexhillrafa.co.uk
5 changing beers ⊞
Refurbished during lockdown this welcoming club is well
worth a visit. In 2016 it was CAMRA National Club of the
Year. Many local and national beers are served from the
five handpumps, with real cider also available. This
comfortable club holds two beer festivals a year. CAMRA
members are always welcome to be signed in, with a
minimum £1 donation to RAF charities. Food is only
served on Friday lunchtimes.
Q➤◑&♿≠(Bexhill)●🛒🐾📶♫

Brickmaker's Alehouse 🏆 🄻
27 Sea Road, TN40 1EE
☎ (01424) 602778 ⊕ brickmakersalehouse.co.uk
5 changing beers Ⓖ
Friendly, welcoming micropub based in a converted
wholefood deli in Bexhill town centre, close to the
railway station, bus routes and the seafront. Owned and
run by two cask ale and cider enthusiasts, drinkers can
always expect no fewer than five real ales and four real
ciders, sourced locally, regionally, and nationally,
dispensed by gravity from a temperature-controlled

display. Draught take-outs are available, and a good
selection of canned beers. Monthly live music sessions
are held. Local CAMRA Pub of the Year 2022 and 2023.
Q➤❀≠(Bexhill)♣●🛒🖥🐾📶♫

Traffers Bar 🄻
19 Egerton Road, TN39 3HJ
☎ (01424) 210240
Harvey's Sussex Best Bitter; 2 changing beers ⊞
Welcoming street-corner local situated close to the
seafront, Egerton Park, Bexhill Museum, and a few
minutes' walk from the town centre. Three cask ales
served – Harvey's Best and two from Sussex or Kent, with
occasional guests from further afield. Food, including
vegetarian and vegan options is available, with
occasional theme nights – booking is advisable,
especially on Sundays. There are popular weekly quiz
nights and monthly live music. A function room is
available. Local CAMRA LocAle Pub of the Year 2022.
Q➤❀◑≠(Collington)🛒(98,99)🐾📶♫

Boreham Street

Bull's Head 🄻
The Strait, BN27 4SG
☎ (01323) 831981 ⊕ bullsheadborehamstreet.com
Harvey's Sussex Best Bitter; house beer (by
Harvey's); 2 changing beers ⊞
The original Harvey's tied pub has been in the Guide for
many years because of its range of Harvey's beers. With
a large garden and car park, its campsite is a popular
holiday location. The internal décor is rustic, with
wooden flooring and furniture and timber-panelled
walls. The pub is a local hub for many events, and also
offers good wholesome food. The previous landlord
retired in late 2022, but continuity was ensured as
existing staff took over the licence.
Q➤❀◑ΑP🛒(98)🐾📶♫

Brighton

Basketmakers Arms 🄻
12 Gloucester Road, BN1 4AD
☎ (01273) 689006 ⊕ basket-makers-brighton.co.uk

Fuller's London Pride, ESB; 5 changing beers (sourced nationally; often Fuller's, Gale's) ⊞
A much-loved Brighton institution, this busy two-room street-corner pub, popular with young and old alike, is located on the edge of Brighton's famous bohemian North Laine. Eight handpumps serve a selection from the Fuller's range plus guests and a real cider. Locally sourced home-made food is available every day and includes Seafood Saturday and very popular traditional Sunday roasts. The walls are adorned with old metal signs and tobacco tins. Live jazz music plays on the first Sunday of every month. ⏰❀◑⇌●🗐❦🛜♪

Brighton Bierhaus 🅛

161 Edward Street, BN2 0JB
☎ (01273) 686386 ⊕ brightonbierhaus.pub
5 changing beers (sourced nationally; often Brighton Bier, Downlands) ⊞
This single-bar pub is centrally situated near the Royal Pavilion and Brighton Pier. It was the local CAMRA Pub of the Year 2019. It serves up to five changing beers and two ciders on handpump along with keg and bottled beers. Food may be ordered from various local carry-out establishments and occasionally there is food available from pop-up vendors in the bar. There is a free cheeseboard on Sundays. The muted television shows BT Sport. ⏰❀●🗐❦🛜

Evening Star 🅛

55-56 Surrey Street, BN1 3PB (200yds S of station)
☎ (01273) 328931 ⊕ eveningstarpub.co.uk
7 changing beers (sourced regionally; often Burning Sky, Downlands, Vibrant Forest) ⊞
A classic, friendly pub/alehouse, five minutes' walk from the station, majoring in good real ale and craft beers. It has a warm, cosy interior and tables outside. The original home of Dark Star brewery, formerly housed in the cellar, it is now an independent free house. Ten handpumps dispense seven real ales and three real ciders. A Sri Lankan-inspired pop-up kitchen serves food most evenings. ❀◑🅖⇌♣🗐❦🛜

Great Eastern 🅛 ✅

103 Trafalgar Street, BN1 4ER
☎ (01273) 677654
5 changing beers ⊞
A small and atmospheric single-bar pub located at the Northern edge of Brighton's vibrant North Laine area. This cosy, traditional pub is a short walk from Brighton station and close to the main St Peter's bus stops. Five, often local, guest beers are available. No food, no screens, and no machines. At weekends DJs play classic jazz, blues, soul and rock from a record deck at the end of the bar. ❀⇌🗐❦🛜♪

Haus on the Hill 🅛

58 Southover Street, Hanover, BN2 9UF
☎ (01273) 601419 ⊕ hausonthehill.pub
3 changing beers (sourced locally; often Brighton Bier, Downlands) ⊞
This pub, previously the Southover, is now operated by Brighton Bier. Being at the top of a steep hill it is probably best approached by bus. It has two function rooms upstairs and a covered patio for smokers. Conversation is the norm here and there is no TV or jukebox. Beers are from local breweries, often Brighton Bier, and including a dark beer plus a cider. A number of bottled beers and keg beers, both British and foreign, complete the range. Q⏰❀◑♣●🗐(18,23)❦🛜

Hole in the Wall

Queensbury Mews, BN1 2FE
☎ (01273) 763961 ⊕ theholeinthewall.net

5 changing beers (sourced nationally; often Hand, Oakham, Thornbridge) ⊞
Formerly the Queensbury Arms, this cosy two-bar traditional pub is tucked away behind the Metropole hotel. The walls display posters from old Brighton seaside shows. Tap takeovers and Meet the Brewer events are organised. Keg beers and a bag-in-box cider are served in addition to real ales, with the latter always including a dark beer. Toad can be played in the back bar. Local CAMRA Pub of the Year 2022. Q♣●🗐❦🛜

Lord Nelson Inn 🅛 ✅

36 Trafalgar Street, BN1 4ED
☎ (01273) 695872 ⊕ lordnelsonbrighton.co.uk
Harvey's Sussex Best Bitter; 4 changing beers (sourced locally; often Harvey's) ⊞
This flagship Harvey's pub is just down Trafalgar Street, not far from Brighton station. In 2016 it had a makeover, incorporating the shop next door. Still cosy and traditional, with food available every day, this is the place to sample Harvey's beer range including their craft ones. It is divided into separate drinking areas based on the original layout, with bare wood floors and the occasional rug. Being on a gently sloping road, the levels vary a bit. ❀◑⇌🗐❦🛜♪

Maris & Otter 🅛

114 Western Road, BN1 2AB
☎ (01273) 900845 ⊕ themarisandotter.co.uk
Harvey's Sussex Best Bitter; 4 changing beers (sourced locally; often Burning Sky, Harvey's) ⊞
Situated close to Brighton's main shopping district and on many bus routes, this two-room, single-bar Harvey's tied house has smart modern furnishings within exposed brick walls. There are plenty of tables inside and an on-street outside drinking area. A good range of pub food is served Monday to Saturday. There is a quiz on Wednesdays and open mic night on Thursdays. Background music is unobtrusive. ⏰❀◑🅖🗐🛜

Mitre Tavern 🅛 ✅

13 Baker Street, BN1 4JN
☎ (01273) 622759

REAL ALE BREWERIES

1648 🍺	East Hoathly
360° ✦	Sheffield Park
Battle ✦	Battle
Beak ✦	Lewes
Beer Me 🍺	Eastbourne
Brewing Brothers 🍺	Hastings
Brighton Bier	Brighton
BRZN	Brighton
Burning Sky	Firle
Cellar Head ✦	Flimwell
FILO	Hastings
Flying Trunk	Forest Row
Gun ✦	Gun Hill
Hand ✦	Brighton
Harvey's	Lewes
Laine 🍺	Brighton
Lakedown ✦	Burwash
Long Man ✦	Litlington
Loud Shirt ✦	Brighton
Moon 🍺	Brighton
Old Tree	Brighton
Rother Valley	Northiam
Three Acre	Uckfield
Three Legs ✦	Broad Oak
UnBarred ✦	Brighton
Watchmaker's Arms 🍺	Hove

Harvey's Sussex Best Bitter; 2 changing beers (sourced locally; often Harvey's) ⊞
This is a traditional back-street, beer-drinkers' pub on a corner location close to the London Road shopping area. The bar area has wood panelling, plenty of tables and a mix of seats, stools and pew benches. Three handpumps serve well-kept Harvey's beers. There are three TVs, however the sound volume is kept low. A food offering is planned. ❀≋♣🖵🏨♿🧀🛜

Prince Albert L
48 Trafalgar Street, BN1 4ED
☎ (01273) 730499 ⊕ princealbertbrighton.co.uk
5 changing beers (sourced locally; often Burning Sky, Long Man) ⊞
Vibrant multi-room pub close to Brighton station. There is a public bar, small saloon bar, two other large rooms without bar counters and an upstairs music room. Decoration and paintwork are 1970s-style and highly colourful. There is a small external courtyard at the rear, and several tables on the pavement outside the pub. Real cider and perry are prominently advertised, and there are five handpumps. No meals, but food can be brought in from the many local suppliers in North Laine. 🛏❀≋♣♿🧀🛜♪

Crowborough

Cooper's Arms L
Coopers Lane, TN6 1SN
☎ (01892) 654796
Harvey's Sussex Best Bitter; 3 changing beers (sourced nationally) ⊞
A welcoming drinkers' local and Guide regular for many years. Usually at least two changing beers are offered, often sourced locally, as well as the regular Harvey's Sussex Best Bitter. No food is available apart from bar snacks such as crisps and nuts. The pub's legendary beer festivals are currently suspended until the planned extension of the main bar is complete. Two wood-burning stoves keep the bar areas warm in winter while the pleasant garden is available for the warmer months. Contactless payment is preferred. Q🛏❀P🧀🛜

Wheatsheaf L ✓
Mount Pleasant, TN6 2NF
☎ (01892) 663756 ⊕ wheatsheafcrowborough.co.uk
Harvey's Sussex Best Bitter; 3 changing beers (sourced locally; often Harvey's) ⊞
White weatherboarded traditional pub, located away from the town centre, near the station. Dating from the 18th century, this Harvey's tied house features a central bar serving three separate seating areas each with photos showing the pub's history and a log fire in winter months. Lunches and evening meals are available Tuesday to Saturday (no food Sat eve). Access to the outside seating area with its colourful hanging baskets during the summer is from the middle bar area. Q🛏❀◐≋♣P🖵(228,229) 🧀🛜♪

Ditchling

White Horse L
16 West Street, BN6 8TS
☎ (01273) 842006 ⊕ whitehorseditchling.com
Harvey's Sussex Best Bitter; 4 changing beers (sourced locally) ⊞
This 12th-century inn lies below the parish church in the picturesque, historic village of Ditchling. Its cellar leads to a network of tunnels under the village, thought to have been used for smuggling in times past. With accommodation, the White Horse can cater for weddings,

birthday parties or be used as a stopover while walking the South Downs Way. Log fires in winter, excellent food and ever-changing quality guest beers are certain to fortify the traveller. Q🛏❀🏨◐🖵🖵(167,168)🧀🛜♪

East Hoathly

King's Head L
1 High Street, BN8 6DR
☎ (01825) 840238 ⊕ thekingshead.org
1648 Signature; Harvey's Sussex Best Bitter; 2 changing beers (sourced locally; often 1648) ⊞
This classic country pub has been the centre of the village community since it was established 250 years ago. A free house, it offers a selection of its own beers brewed in the 1648 brewery located in the converted stables next door. Harvey's Best Bitter plus a local real cider are also always available. Well-priced home cooked-food is served all week at lunchtime and in the evenings apart from on Mondays. Q🛏❀◐🅰♣P🖵(54)🧀🛜

Eastbourne

Crown L
22 Crown Street, Old Town, BN21 1PB
☎ (01323) 724654
Gun Scaramanga Extra Pale; Harvey's Sussex Best Bitter ⊞; **Young's London Special** ⊞/🅖; **2 changing beers** 🅖
This popular two-room boozer located in the Motcombe area of Eastbourne is a regular entry in the Guide, having featured for 10 consecutive years. It serves a range of beers from national and local brewers. Three or four beer festivals are held during the year, with the barrels racked in the back room. Steps lead up to a large garden, the site for occasional music concerts in summer. 🛏❀🖵🧀🛜♪

Farm
15 Friday Street, Langney, BN23 8AP
☎ (01323) 766049 ⊕ thefarmfridaystreet.co.uk
Harvey's Sussex Best Bitter; Timothy Taylor Landlord; 2 changing beers (often Long Man, Three Acre) ⊞
Originally a medieval farmhouse which was converted to a pub in the late 1970s, the Farm still retains its original charm with oak beams and ornate open fireplaces. It serves good food as well as usually four well-kept ever-changing ales. The restaurant is set over several levels with a large bar area shared by drinkers and diners. There is also a large garden with seating. Q🛏❀◐♿P🖵🧀🛜♪

Hurst Arms L ✓
76 Willingdon Road, Ocklynge, BN21 1TW
☎ (01323) 419440 ⊕ thehurstarms.com
Harvey's Sussex Best Bitter; 4 changing beers (sourced locally; often Harvey's) ⊞
Local award-winning pub serving a full range of well-kept Harvey's beers. The public bar has a pool table, darts, jukebox and TV, while the comfortable lounge is quieter. Outside are an undercover heated smoking area at the rear and a front garden with seating. Situated on local bus routes, it has limited car parking. Opening hours are extended on bank holiday Mondays. ❀♿♣P🖵🧀🛜

Lamb Inn L ✓
36 High Street, Old Town, BN21 1HH
☎ (01323) 720545 ⊕ thelambeastbourne.co.uk
Harvey's Sussex Best Bitter, Armada Ale; 1 changing beer (sourced locally; often Harvey's) ⊞
This cosy historic inn, dating from 1180, is in the heart of Eastbourne's Old Town next to the parish church. It has

three bars, including one showing occasional televised sport and another mainly for dining. There is also a first floor function room and B&B accommodation in four beautiful rooms. Period features include beamed ceilings and a glass-covered well. Live music, comedy nights and theatrical productions are regular events, Food includes vegetarian and vegan options. Tours of the large crypt and beer cellar are available on request.
Q ✿ 🛏 ◑ ⑃ ♣ P 🚃 ❀ 🎵

London & County 🄻 ✓

46 Terminus Road, BN21 3LX
☎ (01323) 746310

Greene King Abbot; Ruddles Best Bitter; Sharp's Doom Bar; 3 changing beers (sourced nationally) 🄷
Arranged on two floors, each with a bar, this Wetherspoon Lloyds No.1 bar occupies the former London & County Bank and is conveniently close to all local bus services and trains. Varying guest beers are on offer, including at least one LocAle. Food is served all day. Muted TV screens display news, and music is played in the evening, with a DJ on Friday/Saturday evenings, when a smart casual dress code applies. In 2023 it celebrated 10 consecutive years in the Guide.
✿ 🐕 ◑ ⑃ ♿ 🚃 ❀ 🎵

Ewhurst Green

White Dog Inn 🄻 ✓

Village Street, TN32 5TD
☎ (01580) 830264 ⊕ thewhitedogewhurst.co.uk

Harvey's Sussex Best Bitter; house beer (by Rother Valley); 2 changing beers 🄷
A recent local CAMRA country Pub of Year, which welcomes drinkers and diners alike. Exposed beams with hops and horse brasses give it the atmosphere of a traditional old English rural pub. The restaurant features painted murals of nearby Bodiam Castle and Great Dixter. Excellent food is served lunchtime and evenings, and all day in summer. The large garden offers views of the Rother Valley featuring Bodiam Castle.
Q ✿ 🐕 ❀ 🛏 ◑ ▲ ♣ ● P 🚃 (349) ❀ 🎵

Falmer

Swan Inn 🄻 ✓

Middle Street, BN1 9PD (just off A27 in N end of village)
☎ (01273) 681842

Palmers Tally Ho!; 5 changing beers (sourced regionally; often Downlands, Long Man, Palmers) 🄷
This is a traditional family-run free house in the village of Falmer near the universities. It has three bar areas and a barn with bar available for functions. Food is available but ring ahead to check for times. There are small outdoor seating areas at both sides of the pub. It gets busy when Brighton & Hove Albion play at home – opening hours vary on match days and it will open in the event of Monday evening games.
Q ✿ 🐕 ◑ ⑃ ⇌ ♣ P 🚃 (28,29) ❀ 🎵

Forest Row

Swan

1 Lewes Road, RH18 5ER
☎ (01342) 822318 ⊕ theswanatforestrow.com

Cellar Head India Pale Ale; Harvey's Sussex Best Bitter 🄷
A country pub with a large family-friendly garden, six bedrooms, a restaurant and a bar. The food menu focuses on seasonal, locally sourced produce, hand-prepared and updated regularly. Operated by Kent winery Hush Heath, they feature their wines and their

own keg IPA and lager brewed by Cellar Head. A local produce market is held in the car park on Wednesday mornings. ✿ ❀ 🛏 ◑ ▲ ❀

Framfield

Hare & Hounds 🄻

The Street, TN22 5NJ
☎ (01825) 890118 ⊕ hareandhounds.net

Harvey's Sussex Best Bitter; 1 changing beer (sourced locally) 🄷
Cosy and welcoming traditional village pub dating from 1428. The snug bar features an inglenook fireplace. Food is served lunchtime and evenings Tuesday to Saturday with traditional roasts on Sundays. Dogs are welcome. A children's play area in the garden ensures the pub offers something for all ages. Local real cider is sourced from Bignose & Beardy. Very much a community pub, it was voted local CAMRA Pub of the Year 2020- 2022.
Q ✿ 🐕 ◑ ⑃ ▲ ♣ ● P 🚃 ❀ 🎵

Hadlow Down

New Inn ★ 🄻

Main Road, TN22 4HJ (on the 272)

Harvey's IPA, Sussex Best Bitter; 1 changing beer (sourced locally; often Harvey's) 🄷
A traditional village pub with interior fittings such as ceramic spirit casks and a panelled counter dating from 1885 when the pub was rebuilt following a fire, it has been identified by CAMRA as having a nationally important historic pub interior. This is a no frills venue designed for good company and good conversation, there is no room here for machines or music! It is renowned locally for excellently-kept beer and a warm welcome. Bar food is available at weekends only.
Q ✿ ▲ ♣ P 🚃 (248) ❀ 🎵

Hailsham

George Hotel 🄻 ✓

3 George Street, BN27 1AD
☎ (01323) 445120

Greene King Abbot; Ruddles Best Bitter; Sharp's Doom Bar; 2 changing beers (sourced nationally) 🄷
A busy town-centre pub showing Wetherspoon's model at its best, popular with locals and visitors. Quiz nights are a regular feature on Monday evenings. At least five real ales, including one LocAle are offered; a real cider or perry always available, with up to three in warmer months, served from a dedicated cool room. Outside are a quiet enclosed rear patio and a terrace at the side. A two-times former local CAMRA Cider Pub of the Year, and runner-up in 2020. Q ✿ 🐕 ◑ ⑃ ♿ ● 🚃 ❀

Hastings

Albion 🄻

33 George Street, Old Town, TN34 3EA
☎ (01424) 439156 ⊕ albionhastings.com

Harvey's Sussex Best Bitter; 3 changing beers (sourced nationally; often Bedlam, Lakedown) 🄷
Heritage pub on the seafront with traditional hand-written signage. Once a Scottish & Newcastle outlet it has clan tartans incorporated into wooden panels in the rear bar. The bar top is covered with beautiful zincwork. The function room has a stage where live music is played every Tuesday and Saturday. Often quiet during the day, the pub gets busy in the evenings and weekends. The Pasty Shack, on the seafront side, sells award-winning pasties and pie and mash. ✿ 🐕 ◑ ♣ ● 🚃 ❀ ❀ 🎵

Dolphin L ✓

11-12 Rock-a-Nore Road, Old Town, TN34 3DW
☎ (01424) 434326 ⊕ thedolphinpub.co.uk
Dark Star Hophead; Harvey's Sussex Best Bitter; Young's London Special; 3 changing beers (sourced nationally) Ⓗ
The pub dates from the late 18th century and sits between the East Cliff and the Stade shingle beach, home to Britain's largest beach-launched fishing fleet. The terrace overlooks the famous net huts. It is adorned with memorabilia and old photographs of the local fishing community. The pub offers lunch every day, with fish & chips on a Monday evening and a full menu on Friday evening. A quiz is held on Thursdays. Third-pint taster paddles are available. Q ➣ ⊛ ⊕ ► 🖨 ⬤ 🐾 ☏ ♪

First In Last Out L

14-15 High Street, Old Town, TN34 3EY (near Stables Theatre)
☎ (01424) 425079 ⊕ thefilo.co.uk
FILO Crofters, Churches Pale Ale, Gold; 2 changing beers (sourced regionally) Ⓗ
The FILO is a family-run free house, serving and brewing award-winning beer since 1988. The pub is a traditional local with cosy booth seating and the convivial buzz of conversation. The brewery is located just two minutes' walk away, producing four regular ales using the full-mash process, plus their popular winter porter Cardinal. Alongside the beer, quality food, prepared from scratch, is served. Live music is a feature, with regular Sunday evening gigs – see the website for details.
Q ➣ ⊕ ♣ 🖨 🖨 ⬤ 🐾 ☏ ♪

Jenny Lind L ✓

69 High Street, Old Town, TN34 3EW
☎ (01424) 421392 ⊕ jennylindhastings.co.uk
Greene King Abbot; Long Man Best Bitter; 4 changing beers Ⓗ
Friendly and popular pub in the medieval Cinque Port of Hastings; nestled between independent shops in the old town, just a short walk from the beach. They often serve more than six real ales. Interesting and tasty Korean street food is available Wednesday to Sunday. The back bar is welcoming and cosy, and it has steeply terraced outdoor spaces. The pub is well known for its beer festivals (with 10 handpumps in operation) plus frequent and varied live music. The pub is named after the famous opera singer who may have stayed in the area.
Q ➣ ⊛ ⊕ ► ♣ ⬤ 🐾 ☏ ♪

Jolly Fisherman

3 East Beach Street, Old Town, TN34 3AR
☎ (01424) 428811 ⊕ jollyfishermanhastings.com
2 changing beers Ⓗ
This pub has a long history. The building known as the Jolly Fisherman dates from 1769 and was first licensed in 1834, serving fishermen and locals until it closed its doors in 1959. Reopening 57 years later as Hastings' first micropub, it is now popular with locals and tourists alike. The intimate single bar in traditional style creates a warm, friendly atmosphere. Three changing cask ales and six craft beers are usually available. Local CAMRA Cider Pub of the Year 2020. ➣ ♣ ⬤ 🐾 ☏

Hove

Foghorn L

55 Boundary Road, BN3 4EF
☎ (01273) 419362 ⊕ thefoghornmicro.com
5 changing beers (sourced regionally; often Brighton Bier, Burning Sky) Ⓖ
The Foghorn is situated on the busy corner of New Church Road and Boundary Road, but within is a quiet haven for drinkers. Opened in 2018, this enterprise has soon become a go-to venue with its wide-ranging selection of beers. The cooled stillage room sits just behind the bar and can be viewed through the glass partition. Furniture and décor is best described as minimalist. Toilets are very well maintained. Q ➣ ⅖ ≠ (Portslade) ⬤ 🖨 🐾 ☏

Neptune Inn L

10 Victoria Terrace, BN3 2WB (on Coast Rd E of King Alfred leisure complex)
☎ (01273) 736390 ⊕ theneptunelivemusicbar.co.uk
Greene King Abbot; Harvey's Sussex Best Bitter; Long Man Session IPA; 2 changing beers (sourced locally) Ⓗ
Friendly no frills single-bar Victorian pub close to the King Alfred centre and Hove seafront. A reclining figure of Neptune rests above the old Courage signage at the front. Five beers are available including two ever-changing guests plus occasionally a real cider during the summer months. Dogs are welcome. Live music features strongly with blues or rock every Friday and jazz Sundays – see the website for details. 🖨 (700) 🐾 ♪

Watchmaker's Arms ♀ L

84 Goldstone Villas, BN3 3RU
☎ (01273) 776307 ⊕ thewatchmakersarms.co.uk
5 changing beers (sourced regionally; often Brighton Bier, Downlands) Ⓖ
This micropub has a small well-used outside seating area, with two tables on the pavement outside the premises. Four cask beers are generally on sale, served from a cold room behind the bar – these rotate fortnightly. Details of the beers currently on sale can be found on the pub website. The cask beers are almost always from small breweries, with many from Sussex, Hampshire and Kent. Real cider is always available, mainly sourced from local producers.
Q ≠ ♣ ⬤ 🖨 (7,21) 🐾 ☏

Westbourne

90 Portland Road, BN3 5DN
☎ (01273) 823633 ⊕ thewestbournehove.co.uk
4 changing beers (sourced locally; often Burning Sky, Downlands, Franklins) Ⓗ
A large Victorian pub in a busy shopping area, popular with all ages. Recently altered to create a single bar area, four changing beers are mainly from Sussex micros. Real cider is available together with a selection of craft and bottled keg beers. Good quality food includes vegan and vegetarian dishes. Several bus routes stop just outside. Families and dogs are welcome, and there is a large covered outside drinking area and a rear patio garden.
➣ ⊛ ⊕ ► ≠ (Aldrington) ⬤ 🖨 🐾 ☏

Icklesham

Queen's Head L

Parsonage Lane, TN36 4BL (opp village hall)
☎ (01424) 814552 ⊕ queenshead.com
Greene King Abbot; Harvey's Sussex Best Bitter; 2 changing beers (sourced locally) Ⓗ
Built in 1632 as two dwellings, before becoming a pub in 1831, this delightful 17th-century inn marks its 40th consecutive year in the Guide in 2024. Open fires, excellent good-value home-made food, a beer garden, pétanque pisté and superb views over the Brede Valley all make it popular with locals, walkers on the nearby 1066 Country Walk and other visitors. Pub quizzes and live music feature regularly. ➣ ⊛ ⊕ ♣ ⬤ P 🖨 (100) 🐾 ☏ ♪

Isfield

Laughing Fish L ✓

Station Road, TN22 5XB (off A26 between Lewes and Uckfield)

☎ (01825) 750349 ⊕ laughingfishisfield.com

Long Man Best Bitter; 3 changing beers (sourced locally; often Greene King, Gun, Long Man) Ⓗ

Formerly the Half Moon, then the Station Hotel, this 1860s pub is next to the preserved Lavender Line. WWII brought the custom of Canadian troops, but not without incident. In the 1950s it was the HQ of the District Angling Club – the probable origin of the present name. It combines the Greene King portfolio with guest beers from Sussex breweries. Good pub food is served and entertainment includes a range of games including bar billiards and regular live music events.

👪❀🕭◑♿♣♠♣Ⓟ🖵 (29) ✿ 🎅 ᕤ

Lewes

Black Horse L

55 Western Road, BN7 1RS

☎ (01273) 473653 ⊕ theblackhorselewes.co.uk

Burning Sky Plateau; Greene King Abbot; Harvey's Sussex Best Bitter; 4 changing beers (sourced regionally; often Greene King) Ⓗ

A Greene King Local Heroes pub that allows the licensee to source and stock Sussex ales and produce. This traditional community pub in the western end of the town has feature bay windows and a large main bar with a real fire together with a quieter back bar. Four TVs show most sporting events. Home-made food includes vegan options. The pub's teams play a wide variety of games including toad-in-the-hole and crib.

👪❀🕭◑♿♣🖵 (28,29) ✿ 🎅 ᕤ

Brewers Arms L

91 High Street, BN7 1XN (near Lewes Castle)

☎ (01273) 475524 ⊕ thebrewersarmslewes.com

Harvey's Sussex Best Bitter; 4 changing beers (sourced regionally; often Burning Sky, Gun, Harvey's) Ⓗ

A two-bar pub with distinct offerings – the front bar being quiet and more food-oriented with the back bar offering darts and pool. There is an annual beer festival and the pub has a stoolball team. It is popular on match days with Lewes FC, Brighton & Hove Albion and away fans. Food, including traditional breakfasts, is served. The exterior features the former owners, Page and Overton's Croydon Ales. 🕭◑≈♣♠🖵 (28,29) ✿ ᕤ

Elephant & Castle L

White Hill, BN7 2DJ (off Fisher St, near old police station)

☎ (01273) 473797

Harvey's Sussex Best Bitter; 3 changing beers (sourced locally) Ⓗ

A spacious pub with three rooms that is able to show football, rugby, and other sports in different areas. On Thursdays a large selection of craft bottled and canned beer is available to consume on the premises at take-away prices. There is a large function room upstairs available for hire. The pub is home to many clubs including the Commercial Bonfire Society. The food is locally sourced. 🕭◑≈♣♠🖵 (127,132) ᕤ

Gardener's Arms L

46 Cliffe High Street, BN7 2AN

☎ (01273) 474808

Harvey's Sussex Best Bitter; 5 changing beers (sourced nationally; often Gun, Harvey's, Rother Valley) Ⓗ

A traditional, genuine free house near Harvey's brewery in Cliffe High Street. It is a one-roomed pub with a wooden floor and central bar. Five changing guest ales are dispensed, generally sourced from small breweries across the country. The pub is popular with Lewes and Brighton FC fans on match days. A real cider is always available. A dark beer festival is held in March. Dogs are especially welcome, but no children are allowed. Outside seating is at the front and side of premises.

≈♣❀🖵 (28,29) ✿ 🎅 ᕤ

John Harvey Tavern L ✓

1 Bear Yard, Cliffe High Street, BN7 2AN (opp Harveys Brewery)

☎ (01273) 479880 ⊕ johnharveytavern.co.uk

Harvey's IPA Ⓗ**, Sussex Best Bitter** Ⓖ**, Armada Ale** Ⓗ**; 3 changing beers (sourced locally; often Harvey's)** Ⓗ/Ⓖ

Housed in a former stable block of the Bear Inn, opposite Harvey's brewery and next to the River Ouse, the bar boasts wooden beams, a slate floor, log burner and two large wine vats providing cosy seating areas. Children are only allowed in the restaurant. There is a large function/dining room upstairs. The outside tables are a suntrap in summer and therefore very popular. There is a folk night on Tuesdays and occasionally music on Sundays.

Ⓠ👪🕭◑≈♣🖵 (28,29) ✿ 🎅 ᕤ 🎵

Lansdown Arms L

36 Lansdown Place, BN7 2JU

☎ (01273) 470711

Harvey's Sussex Best Bitter; Thornbridge Jaipur IPA; Timothy Taylor Landlord; 1 changing beer (sourced locally; often Gun, Long Man) Ⓗ

Close to the railway station at the foot of a steep hill, this smallish pub is popular with fans and visitors to both Lewes FC and Brighton & Hove Albion on match days. The dark and cosy pub was built in 1827, before the arrival of the railway in Lewes and was, at one time, a Whitbread house. It hosts popular live music most weekends, regularly featuring local bands, and has a free jukebox. Local artists' work is displayed on the walls.

👪◑≈🖵 ✿ 🎅 ᕤ 🎵

Lewes Arms ✓

1 Mount Place, BN7 1YH

☎ (01273) 473152 ⊕ lewesarms.co.uk

Dark Star Hophead; Fuller's London Pride; Gale's Seafarers Ale, HSB; Harvey's Sussex Best Bitter; 2 changing beers (sourced regionally; often Adnams, Butcombe) Ⓗ

This is a characteristic corner pub comprising three small rooms plus a central lobby with serving hatch. An upstairs function room contains a small theatre stage, and there is an outside terrace. Toad-in-the-hole is played here. Good food is served including excellent Sunday lunches. The pub is home to the world pea-throwing championship, dwyle flunking, spaniel racing and other unusual events. A three-day music festival is hosted in August and an annual pantomime in March. Real cider is occasionally available.

Ⓠ👪🕭◑≈♣🖵 (28,29) ✿ 🎅 ᕤ 🎵

Rights of Man L ✓

179 High Street, BN7 1YE

☎ (01273) 486894 ⊕ rightsofmanlewes.com

Harvey's IPA, Sussex Best Bitter; 2 changing beers (sourced locally; often Harvey's) Ⓗ

A small one-bar pub near the law courts. The front bar has two tall tables near the front windows – wonderful for having a pint and watching the world go by. Dark oak-panelled walls and etched glass screens form booths. The rear area has pictures of each local bonfire society on the wall and more seating. Good-quality food is served lunchtimes and evening. The artificial grass-covered roof terrace is a real suntrap in the summer. ✿◑≢⊒(28,29) ✿🐾♠

Swan Inn ✅
30A Southover High Street, BN7 1HU
☎ (01273) 480211 ⊕ theswaninnlewes.co.uk
Harvey's IPA, Sussex Best Bitter; 2 changing beers (sourced locally; often Harvey's) Ⓗ
The Swan is a traditional, old-fashioned two-bar public house. Its low ceilings, wonky walls and open fire epitomise the country pub of yesteryear. Visitors can expect a warm and friendly welcome. In the winter the fires are roaring, in the summer the vast, award-winning garden is an absolute delight. Food is served all day, with daily specials to reflect the season. The pub takes pride in being a true community gem which caters for all. ᏻ✿◑&♣P⊒✿

Pett

Royal Oak Ⓛ ✅
Pett Road, TN35 4HG
☎ (01424) 812515 ⊕ royaloakpett.com
Harvey's Sussex Best Bitter; 3 changing beers (sourced locally) Ⓗ
The Oak is a quintessential village inn housed in an attractive 18th-century Grade II-listed building. Warmed by two open fires and providing up to four real ales and excellent food – both often locally sourced – it is welcoming and popular with locals and visitors alike. Events include quizzes and occasional live music. In addition to the bar area there is a separate dining area. Outside there is an extensive garden area for outdoor eating and drinking, and a pétanque court. Q ᏻ✿◑●P⊒(347) ✿🐾♪

Portslade

Stanley Arms Ⓛ
47 Wolseley Road, BN41 1SS (on corner of Wolseley Rd and Stanley Rd)
☎ (01273) 701738 ⊕ thestanley.com
Harvey's Sussex Best Bitter; 5 changing beers (sourced regionally; often Downlands, Harvey's, Long Man) Ⓗ
A good, old-fashioned, back-street pub, this two-bar gem is the hub of the community. Six beers are served mainly but not exclusively from Sussex brewers and always include a dark beer. There is a quiz night every Wednesday, live music Friday and Saturday, open mic nights every other Thursday plus live TV sports. A colourful heated patio smoking area is a feature. Children are welcome until evening. Takeaway food can be delivered to the pub. Q ᏻ✿≢(Fishersgate) ♣⊒(2,46) ✿🐾♪

Ringmer

Anchor Inn Ⓛ
Lewes Road, BN8 5QE
☎ (01273) 812370 ⊕ anchorringmer.com
Harvey's Sussex Best Bitter; 3 changing beers (sourced locally; often Bedlam, Only With Love) Ⓗ
Situated opposite the village green in the centre of Ringmer, this family-run free house dates from 1742. Food is served lunchtimes and evenings during the week and all-day Saturday. The guest ales are usually from local Sussex breweries with real cider from Southdown Cider. Two large garden areas adjoin the building, with a separate small terrace garden. Bar games are popular

and include toad-in-the-hole, darts, and cribbage. A variety of board games are also provided. ᏻ✿◑♣●P⊒(28) ✿🐾♪

Rotherfield

King's Arms ♟ Ⓛ
High Street, TN6 3LJ
☎ (01892) 853441 ⊕ katn6.com
Harvey's Sussex Best Bitter; 3 changing beers (sourced locally) Ⓗ
This 17th-century pub in the centre of a busy village features two seating areas with the rear bar area being particularly spacious. Inglenook fireplaces in both areas are used in winter months. Very much a community pub, the beers and food served from their varied menu are usually sourced locally. There is a large outdoor terrace with plenty of seating from which to enjoy the views of the local countryside during warmer months. Q ᏻ✿◑&♣P⊒(252) 🐾✿♪

Rye

Waterworks Ⓛ
Tower Street, TN31 7AT
☎ (01797) 224110 ⊕ ryewaterworks.co.uk
8 changing beers (sourced locally) Ⓖ
Now with its own brewery and taproom nearby, this is the area's first micropub, housed in a 300-year-old building with a fascinating history, (ask for a leaflet). A friendly welcome is guaranteed along with extensive real ales and ciders, and award-winning Scotch eggs and pork pies. A gluten-free beer is always available. Many of the objects that adorn the pub – including the chair you might be sitting on – are actually for sale! Local CAMRA Cider Pub of the Year. Q ᏻ✿&≢♣●🐾✿

Ypres Castle Inn Ⓛ
Gun Garden, TN31 7HH (accessed from the A259 up a flight of steps; of down fewer steps from Church Square)
⊕ yprescastleinn.co.uk
House beer (by Rother Valley); 2 changing beers (sourced locally) Ⓗ
The Wipers is an attractive 17th-century weatherboarded pub adjacent to the even older 13th-century castle which houses Rye Museum. A log fire in the large bar gives a warm welcome in colder months, while the large beer garden gives superb views across Romney Marsh in warmer weather. Quality bar snacks are offered alongside local cheeses, cured meats and pork pies. The house beer from Rother Valley is Ypres Castle Bitter. Open on bank holiday Mondays. Card payment only. Q ᏻ✿≢●P✿✿

Salehurst

Salehurst Halt Ⓛ
Church Lane, TN32 5PH (follow Church Ln from the A21 Robertsbridge roundabout)
☎ (01580) 880620 ⊕ salehursthalt.co.uk
Harvey's Sussex Best Bitter; 2 changing beers (sourced locally) Ⓗ
Close to Robertsbridge, the Halt, a cosy family-run free house is worth seeking out. Three changing local ales are usually on offer alongside a local cider. This pub serves the community well and the menu is full of local produce – booking is advised. The bar top is unusually covered in two pence pieces encased in glass. It has a pleasant garden overlooking the hop fields of the Rother Valley and a small function room upstairs. Q ᏻ✿◑♣●🐾✿♪

Seaford

Old Boot Inn L

16 South Street, BN25 1PE
☎ (01323) 895454
Harvey's Sussex Best Bitter; 4 changing beers (sourced regionally; often 360 Degree, Gun, Harvey's) Ⓗ
This deceptively large pub, under the same ownership as the Gardener's Arms in Lewes, has entrances in both South Street and High Street. Wheelchair access is possible. There are plenty of tables and food is served, with a wide range of roasts on Sundays. Harvey's Best Bitter is always to be found on one of the six handpumps along with Old Ale in season. Four ever-changing guests and six bag-in-box ciders complete the range.
ਠ⊛◖◔❀♠❀⊗ ♪

Steamworks L

Cafe Unit, Seaford Station, Station Approach, BN25 2AR
☎ (01323) 895541
4 changing beers (sourced locally; often 360 Degree, Bedlam, Long Man) Ⓖ
Right on the station platform the Steamworks is a two-room buffet bar which provides a coffee service to the early morning commuters and then becomes a micropub with four interesting, normally local, beers dispensed using an unusual gravity system. The decor and furniture is distressed industrial sanded-down woodwork as if the Ragged Trousered Philanthropists had only recently left! Entrance is both from street and station platform. Real cider is from Silly Moo. Snack food, such as pasties, is available. Q⊛❀♠❀⊗ ♪

St. Leonards on Sea

Nag's Head

8-9 Gensing Road, TN38 0ER
☎ (01424) 445973
Harvey's Sussex Best Bitter; 3 changing beers (sourced locally; often Gun, Long Man) Ⓗ
This recently renovated pub is situated to the west of London Road, in a quiet residential area. The front entrance leads into the U-shaped bar, centrally located, on which five handpumps are sited, serving both national and local ales. Gun and Long Man breweries feature regularly. Entertainment includes live music evenings once or twice a month on Saturdays and on all Sundays, together with a quiz night on Wednesdays and a meat raffle on Sunday afternoons.
Q⊱⊛❀≠(Warrior Square) ❀⊗ ♪

Tower

251 London Road, Bohemia, TN37 6NB
☎ (01424) 721773
Dark Star Hophead; 5 changing beers (sourced nationally) Ⓗ
This lively community pub is popular with sports fans, showing all the main football, rugby, and cricket matches as well as other sports. It regularly hosts live music, arranges occasional visits to sporting events or breweries and holds a popular beer festival in February. The U-shaped bar, traditional decor, sofas and wood-burning stove create a convivial atmosphere. Six cask ales and up to seven ciders are on offer. It celebrated 10 consecutive years in the Guide in 2023.
⊱≠(Warrior Square) ♣❀◔❀⊗❀ ♪

Welcome L

56 Sedlescombe Road North, TN37 7DA
☎ (01424) 233334
3 changing beers (often Lakedown, Long Man) Ⓗ

This roadside pub, with its single large bar, has an enclosed garden and off-road parking. It was renamed and refurbished after coming under new ownership in 2017. With welcoming staff and a comfortable bright interior, the pub lives up to its new name. All real ales are Sussex-brewed, and a varied, appetising food menu is available all week, with brunch served from 11am on Friday and Saturday. Q⊱⊛◖P❀♠❀⊗❀ ♪

Westfield

New Inn L

Main Road, TN35 4QE
☎ (01424) 752800 ⊕ newinnwestfield.com
House beer (by Long Man); 2 changing beers (sourced locally) Ⓗ
Located in the centre of the village, this light and airy, family and dog friendly, community-focused pub is popular with locals and visitors alike. Inside, the L-shaped layout features a main restaurant with a drinking area beyond. A conservatory is to the side of the restaurant. To the rear there is a spacious outside seating area and a large car park. Fairly-priced food, using locally sourced ingredients, is of excellent quality – booking is advisable. Q⊱⊛◖&P❀♠❀⊗

Willingdon

Red Lion

99 Wish Hill, BN20 9HQ
☎ (01323) 502062 ⊕ theredlion-willingdon.co.uk
Hall & Woodhouse Badger Best Bitter, Tanglefoot; 1 changing beer (often Hall & Woodhouse) Ⓗ
A pleasant village pub, popular for food and drink, with plenty of seating, including a separate dining room. Two regular beers are served, with a seasonal beer from March to December, all from Hall & Woodhouse. Home-cooked food is served, the menu is rotated seasonally, and occasional events are held, such as a pie week. The pub is mentioned in George Orwell's novel Animal Farm, and displays an old local pub map showing original pub names. ⊱⊛◖P❀♠❀⊗

Wivelsfield Green

Cock Inn L

North Common Road, RH17 7RH (900yds E of B2112)
☎ (01444) 471668 ⊕ cockinn-wivelsfield.co.uk
Harvey's Sussex Best Bitter; 2 changing beers (sourced locally; often Harvey's) Ⓗ
A two-bar pub on the eastern edge of the village, popular with walkers, cyclists and locals alike. A more frequent bus service is available at the other end of the village on routes 40/40X. Two guest beers supplement the Harvey's. In summer real cider is available. There is a large garden/seating area to front and a smaller outdoor area to the side. The recently refurbished lounge bar has a timber-panelled bar counter. Look out for the cow bell!
Q⊱⊛◖♣P❀(167,168) ❀⊗ ♪

Breweries

1648

⊟ **Old Stables Brewery, Mill Lane, East Hoathly, BN8 6QB**
☎ (01825) 840830 ⊕ 1648brewing.co.uk

⊠ The 1648 brewery, set up in the old stable block at the King's Head pub in 2003, derives its name from the year of the deposition of King Charles I. One pub is owned and more than 40 outlets are supplied. ‼⚑◆LIVE

Hop Pocket (ABV 3.7%) GOLD
Triple Champion (ABV 4%) BITTER
Signature (ABV 4.4%) GOLD
Laughing Frog (ABV 5.2%) BITTER

360°

Unit 24b, Bluebell Business Estate, Sheffield Park, TN22 3HQ
☎ (01825) 722375 ⊕ 360degreebrewing.com

⊗ Under new management since 2020 but still brewing at Sheffield Park, adjacent to the famous Bluebell Railway. The brewery is committed to producing high quality cask-conditioned ales, and has increased its output of craft keg and cans. ‼️🍺◆✦

Double Act Pale (ABV 4.1%) GOLD
Bluebell Best (ABV 4.2%) BITTER
Session IPA (ABV 4.3%) PALE
Fastback Pale Ale (ABV 5%) PALE

Abyss SIBA

Unit 3, The Malthouse, Davey's Lane, Lewes, BN7 2BF
⊕ abyssbrewing.co.uk

⊗ Founded in Lewes in 2017, then moving to Framfield later that year, the brewery returned to Lewes at the old Southdown Brewery Malthouse in 2021. Cask beers are not normally produced but the onsite taproom (open Thu-Sat) offers a changing range of vegan-friendly keg beers from the eight-barrel brew plant. These can also be purchased to take away while a home delivery service is available (details online). Brewery tours (4-15 people) can be arranged by email. ‼️V✦

Battle

The Calf House, Beech Farm, North Trade Road, Battle, TN33 0HN
☎ (01424) 772838 ⊕ battlebrewery.co.uk

Battle Brewery is an eight-barrel brewery located in the heart of 1066 country in the historic town of Battle. Established in 2017, local pubs, cafés and shops are supplied. A brewtap/micropub was opened in 2021 at the top of Battle High Street selling beers direct from the cask, plus its bottled range. 🍺✦

Fyrds Gold (ABV 3.8%) GOLD
Conquest (ABV 4.1%) BITTER
One Hop Wonder (ABV 4.3%) PALE
Alan the Red (ABV 4.4%) RED
Black Arrow (ABV 4.5%) PORTER
Abbey Pale IPA (ABV 5%) PALE
Harolds EyePA (ABV 5.6%) PALE
Senlac Imperial Stout (ABV 10.5%) STOUT

Beak SIBA

Unit 14, Cliffe Industrial Estate, Lewes, BN8 6JL
☎ (01273) 473094 ☎ 07985 708122
⊕ beakbrewery.com

Originally a nomad brewery, with recipes tested on a nano kit, Beak now has its own 15-barrel brewery and taproom in Lewes. ✦

Beer Me

⊟ The Belgian Café, 11/23 Grand Parade, Eastbourne, BN21 3YN
☎ (01323) 729967 ⊕ beermebrewery.co.uk

⊗ Beer Me was launched in 2014 by the owners of the Belgian Café in Eastbourne, building on 10 years in the catering industry. It uses a 2.5-barrel plant and produces

continental-style beers which are served direct from the brewery. ‼️◆

Brewing Brothers

⊟ Imperial, 119 Queens Road, Hastings, TN34 1RL
☎ 07985 505810 ⊕ brewingbrothers.org

⊗ Brewing began in 2016 in the Imperial, Hastings. The brewery has a 2.5-barrel capacity with four fermenting vessels. A wide range of brother-themed beers have been brewed to date, including a collaboration with Half Man Half Burger. Up to eight beers on cask and keg can feature at any one time. A brewery tap in Ivy House Lane opened in 2022. ◆

Brighton Bier

Unit 10, Bell Tower Industrial Estate, Roedean Road, Brighton, BN2 5RU ☎ 07967 681203
⊕ brightonbier.com

Brighton Bier was established in 2012. It operates a 15-barrel brewery close to the centre of the city and also owns the Brighton Bierhaus pub. Beers are available throughout the UK and exported to Europe and Asia.

Thirty Three (ABV 3.3%) GOLD
Brighton Bier (ABV 4%) GOLD
West Pier (ABV 4%) GOLD
Underdog (ABV 4.2%) BITTER
IPA (ABV 5%) PALE
No Name Stout (ABV 5%) STOUT
Grand Porter (ABV 5.2%) PORTER

BritHop

Ringmer ☎ 07883 223127 ⊕ brithopbeer.com

Established in 2018. A penchant for the Britpop music scene of the 90s comes through in the beer names. Brewing is currently suspended.

BRZN

Unit 2, Cobblers Thumb, 10 New England Road, Brighton, BN1 4ZR ✉ buybrzn@gmail.com

BRZN was founded as a cuckoo brewery in 2019 but in 2020 moved into its own premises in the Preston Circus region of Brighton. Its range is brewed in small batches, without isinglass finings and in keg and cask. Seasonals and specials are always available. ◆

Burning Sky SIBA

Place Barn, The Street, Firle, BN8 6LP
☎ (01273) 858080 ⊕ burningskybeer.com

⊗ Burning Sky started brewing in 2013 using a 15-barrel plant, based on the Firle Estate in the South Downs. It is owned and run by Mark Tranter (ex-Dark Star head brewer). The brewery has its own yeast strains suited to the beer styles. It specialises in pale ales and Belgian-inspired farmhouse beers and has an extensive barrel-ageing programme. LIVE

Plateau (ABV 3.5%) GOLD
Aurora (ABV 5.6%) IPA

Cellar Head SIBA

The Barn, Pillory Corner, Flimwell, TN5 7QG ☎ 07391 557407 ⊕ cellarheadbrewing.com

⊗ Cellar Head Brewery is situated on the border between Sussex and Kent, in Flimwell. It has recently installed and commissioned a new, gas-fired, 20-barrel brewhouse with fermentation capacity in excess of

280HL. It uses predominately local hops and malts to produce a range of beers in cask and keg, varying in style and taste. The modern brewery building also houses a tap, shop and canning line, allowing for off-sales. Besides core beers, new and innovative small batch brews are often available. !! 🍴 ♦

Session Bitter (ABV 3.5%) BITTER
Amber Ale (ABV 4%) GOLD
Session Pale Ale (ABV 4.2%) PALE
Single Hop Pale (ABV 4.6%) SPECIALITY
India Pale Ale (ABV 5%) PALE

FILO

The Old Town Brewery, Torfield Cottage, 8 Old London Road, Hastings, TN34 3HA
☎ (01424) 420212 ⊕ filobrewing.co.uk

⊗ Owners of the First In Last Out (FILO) set up their own brewery in the back of the pub in 1985, to become Hastings first brewpub. The current owners took over in 1988, and in 2011 relocated the brewery to the nearby Grade II-listed stable at Torfield Cottage. The brewery continues to supply ales to the FILO pub, together with many other pubs within Hastings, and throughout Sussex and Kent. ♦

Crofters (ABV 3.8%) BITTER
Churches Pale Ale (ABV 4.2%) PALE
Old Town Tom (ABV 4.5%) SPECIALITY
Gold (ABV 4.8%) GOLD

Flying Trunk

The Cement Stores, Highgate Works, Tomtits Lane, Forest Row, RH18 5AT ☎ 07710 642848
✉ hello@flyingtrunkbrewery.co.uk

Brewing began in 2022 based in premises formerly used by High Weald Brewery.

Furnace Brook

Trolliloes Lane, Cowbeech, BN27 4QR
☎ (01435) 830835 ⊕ furnacebrooke.co.uk

Small-batch brewery producing hand-crafted bottled beers with local hops and no finings or sulphites.

Gun SIBA

Hawthbush Farm, Gun Hill, TN21 0JX
☎ (01323) 700200 ☎ 07900 683355
⊕ gunbrewery.co.uk

⊗ Gun Brewery is located on a beautiful 140-acre, organic, mixed farm in the Sussex Weald. After selling its first pint in 2015 and outgrowing the converted barn it started in, a brand new brewery and taproom was built on the farm, opening in 2022. Using its own spring water, a core range of beers is brewed with monthly specials as well as a barrel-ageing programme.
!! 🍴 LIVE ♦

Scaramanga Extra Pale (ABV 3.9%) PALE
Parabellum Milk Stout (ABV 4.1%) STOUT
Chummy Bluster Best Bitter (ABV 4.4%) BITTER
Project Babylon Pale Ale (ABV 4.6%) PALE
Zamzama IPA (ABV 6.5%) IPA

Hand SIBA

🯅 33 Upper St James's Street, Kemptown, Brighton, BN2 1JN ☎ 07508 814541

2nd Site: Unit 6a, Garcia Trading Estate, Canterbury Road, Worthing, BN13 1AL ☎ (01273) 286693

⊙ Brighton's tiny Hand in Hand Brewpub hides the smallest commercially operating tower brewery in the world, and is the smaller sibling of its production site in Worthing. It was founded in 1989. The Worthing site houses a taproom and shop. !! 🍴 ♦

Harvey's IFBB

Bridge Wharf Brewery, 6 Cliffe High Street, Lewes, BN7 2AH
☎ (01273) 480209 ⊕ harveys.org.uk

⊗ Established in 1790, this independent family brewery operates from the banks of the River Ouse in Lewes. A major development in 1985 doubled the brewhouse capacity to more than 38,000 barrels a year. There are plans to re-establish small brew lengths of special beers, including replicating old recipes. Harvey's supplies real ale to all its 45 pubs and about 550 free trade outlets in the South East. !! 🍴 ♦ LIVE

Dark Mild (ABV 3%) MILD
A dark copper-brown colour. Roast malt dominates the aroma and palate leading to a sweet, caramel finish.
IPA (ABV 3.5%) PALE
Sussex Wild Hop (ABV 3.7%) GOLD
Sussex Best Bitter (ABV 4%) BITTER
Full-bodied brown bitter. A hoppy aroma leads to a good malt and hop balance, and a dry aftertaste.
Old Ale (ABV 4.3%) OLD
Armada Ale (ABV 4.5%) BITTER
Hoppy amber best bitter. Well-balanced fruit and hops dominate throughout with a fruity palate.

Laine

🯅 North Laine Bar & Brewhouse, 27 Gloucester Place, Brighton, BN1 4AA
☎ (01273) 683666 ⊕ laine.co.uk

⊗ Laine launched its first brewery in 2012, in Brighton, using a five-barrel plant based within the North Laine pub. The brewing equipment and process can be viewed from the bar. A number of sister breweries in pubs in Acton, Hackney and Battersea in London were established between 2013-2015 but have since been closed. A new sister brewery in Wandsworth has recently opened. !! 🍴

Lakedown SIBA

Lakedown Farm, Swife Lane, Burwash, TN21 8UX
☎ (01435) 685001 ⊕ lakedownbrewing.com

Lakedown Brewing Co was established in 2020. Beers are available in can, bottle, keg and cask. 🍴 GF V ♦

American Pale Ale (ABV 4.2%) PALE
English Pale (ABV 4.2%) PALE
Best Bitter (ABV 4.4%) BITTER
American Red (ABV 4.8%) RED
IPA (ABV 5%) PALE

Larrikin

🯅 Urchin, 15-17 Belfast Street, Hove, BN3 3YS
☎ (01273) 241881 ✉ hello@urchinpub.co.uk

Following two years of homebrewing research, commercial brewing began in 2018 in the Urchin, Hove, a shellfish and craft beer pub. Beer is only available in the pub, mainly in keg, with cask-conditioned beer available infrequently.

Long Man SIBA

Church Farm, Litlington, BN26 5RA

☎ (01323) 871850 ⊕ longmanbrewery.com

⊠ Long Man began brewing in 2012 using a 20-barrel stainless steel plant. Hops and grain are sourced-locally alongside homegrown barley and locally-drawn water. A traditional strain of Sussex yeast is used. ‼🍺♦

Long Blonde (ABV 3.8%) BLOND
Best Bitter (ABV 4%) BITTER
Copper Hop (ABV 4.2%) BITTER
Old Man (ABV 4.3%) OLD
Sussex Pride (ABV 4.5%) BITTER
Rising Giant (ABV 4.8%) PALE

Lost + Found

12-13 Ship Street, Brighton, BN1 1AD
⊕ lostandfoundbrewery.com

Brewing began in 2016. No real ale.

Lost Pier

Office: 28 Fourth Avenue, Hove, BN3 2PJ
⊕ lostpier.com

Launched in 2017, the three founders transferred more than 50 years of joint experience in the wine industry to brewing. Cuckoo brewing at two local breweries, the beer is unpasteurised, unfiltered and vegan-friendly. The Assemblage series blends beer and wine. **V**

Loud Shirt SIBA

Unit 5, Bell Tower Industrial Estate, Roedean Road, Brighton, BN2 5RU
☎ (01273) 087077 ☎ 07979 087945
⊕ loudshirtbeer.co.uk

⊠ The brewery was established in 2016 using a 10-barrel plant in the Kemptown area of Brighton. The current owner, Elias, took over in 2021. The taproom is open in the summer (Thu-Sun, website for times). Most production goes into bottles and cans; however there are usually at least two cask beers available. Look out for its psychedelic van around town and at festivals. Beers are available at selected Sussex pubs and bottle shops and at Whitehawk football club. ‼🍺♦

Hazed & Confused (ABV 4.5%) PALE
El Dorado American Pale Ale (ABV 5.5%) PALE

Merakai

Unit 12, Squires Farm, Palehouse Common, Framfield, Uckfield, TN22 5RB ⊕ merkaibrewing.com

Merakai Brewing was established in 2020. It produces cans and one-litre bottles.

Moon

▤ **Independent, 95 Queens Park Road, Brighton, BN2 0GH**
☎ (01273) 602822 ⊕ theindepentent.pub

Nanobrewery situated in the Independent in Brighton, established in 2020. Beers are produced under the watchful eye of head brewer Martyn Haddock.

Old Tree

Old Tree, Yachtwerks, 28-29 Richmond Place, Brighton, BN2 9NA ☎ 07413 064346
⊕ oldtree.house

A co-operative based in Brighton producing a unique range of small-batch, probiotic and celebration drinks. It supplies its own zero-waste Silo restaurant. Brewing and gardening are combined, and a production process is used that contributes to land regeneration. **LIVE**

Only With Love

Little Goldsmiths Farm, Beechy Road, Uckfield, TN22 5JG
☎ (01825) 608410 ☎ 07786 830368
⊕ onlywithlove.co

⊠ Only with Love was founded in 2020 by Steve Keegan and Roger Warner. It produces kombucha and beer in the heart of Sussex with all products sustainably created, packaged and delivered.

People's Captain

39 Sackville Road, Hove, BN3 3WD
⊕ peoplescaptain.co.uk

People's Captain was an idea conceived by Greg Bateman, a professional rugby player. Along with friends Stewart Beale and Jason Reeves, the company was established to brew craft beer while also contributing to positive mental health. Every beer sold raises money via the People's Captain Foundation.

Rother Valley

Gate Court Farm, Station Road, Northiam, TN31 6QT
☎ (01797) 252922 ☎ 07798 877551
⊕ rothervalleybrewery.co.uk

⊠ Rother Valley Brewey was established in Northiam in 1993, overlooking the Rother Levels and the Kent & East Sussex Railway. Brewing on a 10-barrel plant, around 100 outlets are supplied direct. Established and new hop varieties are sourced locally. ♦

Black Ops (ABV 3.8%) PALE
Smild (ABV 3.8%) MILD
Valley Bitter (ABV 3.8%) BITTER
Level Best (ABV 4%) BITTER
Full-bodied, tawny, session bitter with a malt and fruit aroma, malty taste and a dry, hoppy finish.
Copper Ale (ABV 4.1%) BITTER
Hoppers Ale (ABV 4.4%) BITTER
Boadicea (ABV 4.5%) BLOND
Blues (ABV 5%) OLD
NIPA (ABV 5%) GOLD

Route21

145 Bridgemere Road, Eastbourne, BN22 8TY
✉ wordpress@route21brewing.co.uk

Established in 2020 Route 21 produces hoppy, hazy and juicy, unfiltered and unfined vegan craft beers. **V**

Three Acre SIBA

Dairy Yard, Little Goldsmiths Farm, Beechy Road, Uckfield, TN22 5JG ☎ 07450 315960
⊕ threeacrebrewery.co.uk

⊠ Founded in 2019 by three lifelong friends on a farm in rural Sussex, this award-winning brewery's main focus is on cask beers, combining traditional ales alongside a range of more modern styles. Many are also available bottle-conditioned or in cans. The beers are available in many local outlets and beyond, and there are plans to further enlarge the existing 10-barrel plant and increase production capacity. There is also a new mobile bar with four handpumps for outside events. **LIVE**

Session Pale (ABV 3.7%) PALE
Best Bitter (ABV 4%) BITTER
Hazy Pale (ABV 4.6%) PALE

Blood Orange Pale (ABV 4.9%) SPECIALITY
IPA (ABV 5%) GOLD

Three Legs

Unit 1, Burnt House Farm, Udimore Road, Broad Oak, TN31 6BX ☎ 07939 997622 ⊕ thethreelegs.co.uk

⊠ The Three Legs was started in 2014 by two friends who met studying winemaking and viticulture at university. It has grown from a nanobrewery to a 10-barrel plant in a converted farm barn. Beers can be found in most free-houses and bottle shops across the south east as well as its taproom. Beers are ever changing with the majority modern, hop-forward and unfined. !! ➡ LIVE ✦

Pale (ABV 3.7%) PALE
Session IPA (ABV 4.5%) GOLD

UnBarred SIBA

UnBarred Brewery & Taproom, Elder Place, Brighton, BN1 4GF ☎ 07850 070471 ⊕ unbarredbrewery.com

⊠ UnBarred was born and bred in Brighton and Hove, established in 2014 in the shed of founder and head brewer, Jordan. It now has a brewery and taproom in central Brighton. Beers are brewed with creativity and passion, with the brewery best known for its NEIPA's and stout styles. LIVE ✦

Watchmaker's Arms

🏠 **84 Goldstone Villas, Hove, BN3 3RU**

Hove's first micropub has its own 100-litre microbrewery, producing under the Beercraft Brighton brand name. Beer is primarily for the Watchmakers but is available in other local pubs.

Brewers Arms, Lewes (Photo: Matthew Black / Flickr CC BY-SA 2.0)

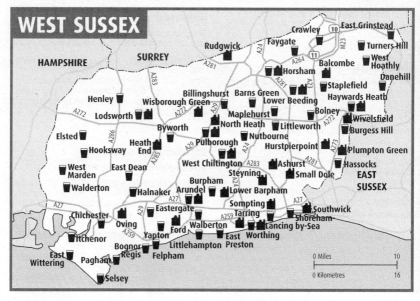

WEST SUSSEX

Arundel

King's Arms [L] ✓
36 Tarrant Street, BN18 9DN
☎ (01903) 885569
Fuller's London Pride; 4 changing beers (sourced regionally; often Firebird) Ⓗ
The King's Arms, built circa 1625, is the oldest pub in Arundel. Situated in a small but vibrant street off the High Street this is a lively drinkers' pub where conversation rules. Popular with locals and visitors alike it has two bars and a patio garden. No food is served but customers can bring their own. The pub is involved in many of the events that take place in the town.
Q ❄ ♣ � (85,700) ✿ 🖤 ➿

Red Lion ✓
45 High Street, BN18 9AG
☎ (01903) 882214 ∰ redlionarundel.com
Sharp's Doom Bar; Timothy Taylor Landlord; 2 changing beers (sourced nationally) Ⓗ
Reputed to be over 200 years old, this handsome red-brick building occupies a prominent position in the main street of this historic and characterful town, being well placed for the castle, cathedral, river, and Wildfowl Trust. Changing guest beers usually feature at least one local ale. Excellent food is served all day and there is a quieter restaurant area to the rear of the pub. Music plays every Saturday. ❄ ✿ ◑ ♣ 🖤 ➿ 🎵

Barns Green

Queen's Head [L]
Chapel Road, RH13 0PS
☎ (01403) 730436 ∰ thequeensheadbarnsgreen.co.uk
Dark Star Hophead; Harvey's Sussex Best Bitter; 1 changing beer (sourced regionally) Ⓗ
A cosy 17th-century village pub, with old timber beams and a large inglenook fireplace used in winter. It is mainly open plan, with three seating areas and a small separate room. A garden with a covered seating area is at the back. There is a quiz night on the second Tuesday of the month, an open mic night on the first Thursday of the month, and a charity coffee morning on the last Friday of the month. Q ❄ ✿ ◑ ♪ ▲ P ✿ ➿

Billingshurst

Billi Tap [L]
44 High Street, RH14 9NY
2 changing beers (often Brolly, Little Monster)
Opened in 2021, this welcoming high-street micropub is the brewery tap for both Brolly and Little Monster breweries, with two cask ales and seven keg lines. The beer range is ever changing and there is a local cider. Food is provided some days, particularly Saturdays, by food trucks that park behind the pub, and there is a Sunday cheeseboard. You are welcome to bring in takeaways from other local establishments to eat in the pub. Q ❄ ♣ 🖤 (100)✿

Bognor Regis

Dog & Duck
65 High Street, PO21 1RY
2 changing beers (often Goldmark, Langham) Ⓗ
Originally opened in 2018, this friendly micropub moved round the corner to its new, more spacious premises in 2021. Two changing cask ales are served, one usually a stronger beer. Two ciders are available alongside five craft keg taps, with tasters available from knowledgeable staff. Regular tap takeovers are held and the pub hosts an annual beer festival in March in a local hall. There is also a large range of interesting bottled and canned beers. Q ❄ ✇ ♣ 🖤 ✿ 🖤 🎵

Waverley
18 Marine Drive West, PO21 2QA (on seafront at W end of promenade)
☎ (01243) 955557 ∰ waverleypub.co.uk
4 changing beers (sourced locally; often Langham) Ⓗ
A pub with a perfect seafront location at the far western end of the promenade at Bognor Regis. The large bar area has an informal dining area off to the right as you enter. The bar has a mixture of comfortable sofas and tables to enable you to take advantage of the fabulous sea views. The decked terrace at the front of the pub is covered and can be enjoyed all year round. Local breweries are favoured, especially Langham.
✿ ◑ 🖤 (600) ➿

Bolney

Bolney Stage 🅛
London Road, RH17 5RL
☎ (01444) 881200
4 changing beers Ⓗ
On the old London to Brighton coaching route, this pub dates to the 16th century. The large bar area has three separate dining areas. The rooms feature huge inglenook fireplaces, ancient flagstones, open-timbered ceilings and crooked beams, together with comfy old furniture. A blackboard by the bar gives tasting notes on the four regularly changing beers, mainly from Sussex breweries. There is enclosed beer garden to the rear.
👪❀◑♿🅿🚆(273) ❀ 🐾 ☂

Burgess Hill

Quench Bar & Kitchen 🅛
2-4 Church Road, RH15 9AE
☎ (01444) 253332 🌐 quenchbar.co.uk
Harvey's Sussex Best Bitter; 2 changing beers (sourced regionally) Ⓗ
Located close to the railway station and bus stops, this bar occupies a location at the top end of the town's original shopping street. It comprises a bar area together with a comfortable lounge. In addition to cask beers there is a varied range of bottled beers, spirits, teas and espresso coffees. There are old clocks above the bar and a display case of old cameras in the lounge. A limited number of tables and chairs are provided outside.
◑🚆🚌☂♪

Burpham

George 🅛
Main Street, BN18 9RR (Turn N off A27 nr Arundel Station and follow the country lane through Wepham to Burpham)
☎ (01903) 883131 🌐 georgeatburpham.co.uk
Arundel Sussex Gold; Long Man Long Blonde; 1 changing beer (sourced locally) Ⓗ
This attractive village inn was saved from possible closure by local residents and following tasteful renovation, reopened in 2013. A small single bar, with four handpumps, offers local ales. The gastropub features an innovative menu. The car park behind the pub, shared with the recreation ground, affords great views across the Arun valley and is the starting point for a network of local walks. Walkers are welcome. Closed on Mondays and Tuesdays. Q👪❀◑🐾☂

Byworth

Black Horse Inn 🅛
The Street, GU28 0HL (head E from Petworth on the A283 for 1 mile then left into The Street) SU987211
☎ (01798) 342424 🌐 blackhorseatbyworth.co.uk
Hogs Back TEA; Young's London Original; 2 changing beers (sourced locally; often Crafty Brewing) Ⓗ
Friendly unspoilt Grade II-listed village pub dating from 1791. Inside, this untouched 16th century inn has the perfect olde worlde country look and feel. The front bar has a traditional atmosphere with its large fireplace and real fire in winter. It is separate from the restaurant and has an excellent selection of beer from local breweries, which changes regularly. Evening meals are served on during the week, from Easter until autumn. A Guide regular, and a previous local CAMRA Pub of the Year.
Q👪❀🏠◑♣🐾🅿🚆(1) ❀ 🐾 ☂

Chichester

Bell Inn
3 Broyle Road, PO19 6AT (on A286 just N of Northgate, 1100yds from station)
☎ (01243) 783388 🌐 thebellinnchichester.com
3 changing beers (sourced locally; often Langham, Long Man, Vibrant Forest) Ⓗ
Cosy and comfortable city local with a traditional ambience enhanced by exposed brickwork, wood panelling and beams. A rear patio garden with covered smoking area is heated in winter. The pub tends to be busiest when the Festival Theatre is open, pre- and post-show. The three beers are from mostly Sussex and Hampshire micros, complemented by a monthly changing food menu. There is a small parking area and a public car park opposite. Closed on Monday from January to March. Q❀👪❀◑🅿🚆(60)❀ 🐾 ☂ ♪

Chichester Inn 🅛
38 West Street, PO19 1RP (at Westgate roundabout)
☎ (01243) 783185 🌐 chichesterinn.co.uk
Harvey's Sussex Best Bitter; 3 changing beers (sourced regionally; often Langham, Vibrant Forest) Ⓗ
Pleasant two-bar pub with a real fire in the front bar surrounded by comfortable chairs, and a mix of seating and table types elsewhere. The larger public bar to the rear features regular live music on Wednesday, Friday and Saturday evenings. Outside is an attractive walled garden with a heated and covered smoking area. Four B&B rooms are available. Food includes Sunday lunches. There is a strong emphasis on LocAles.
❀🏠◑🚆♣🐾🅿🚆❀ 🐾 ☂ ♪

Eastgate
4 The Hornet, PO19 7JG (500yds E of Market Cross)
☎ (01243) 774877 🌐 eastgatechichester.co.uk
Dark Star Hophead; Fuller's London Pride; Gale's Seafarers Ale, HSB; 2 changing beers (sourced nationally; often Fuller's) Ⓗ

REAL ALE BREWERIES
Adur Steyning
Arundel 🍺 Ford
Balcombe 🍻 Balcombe
Bedlam Plumpton Green
Brew Studio Sompting
Brewery 288 Heath End
Brewhouse & Kitchen 🍻 Horsham
Brewhouse & Kitchen 🍻 Worthing
Brolly 🍺 Wisborough Green
Downlands Small Dole
Fauna 🍺 Arundel
Firebird 🍺 Rudgwick
Goldmark 🍺 Arundel
Greyhound West Chiltington
Gribble 🍻 Oving
Hairy Dog 🍺 Wivelsfield
Heathen 🍺 Haywards Heath
Hepworth North Heath
Horsham 🍺 Horsham
Hurst Hurstpierpoint
Kissingate 🍺 Lower Beeding
Langham Lodsworth
Lister's Lower Barpham
Pin-Up Southwick
Ridgeway Pulborough
Top-Notch Haywards Heath
Vine 🍻 Tarring (brewing suspended)
Wingtip Ashurst

Welcoming town centre pub with an open-plan bar and tables for diners. Good quality traditional pub meals are served daily. There is a heated patio garden to the rear, which is the venue for a beer festival in July. The pub attracts locals, holidaymakers and shoppers from the nearby market, with a warm welcome and traditional pub games such as darts, cribbage and pool. Music is turned up on Friday and Saturday late evenings, while live bands perform once a month.
ஃ⊛①♣됨(51,700) ☙ ❖ ♪

Crawley

Brewery Shades 🍺 ⅃
85 High Street, RH10 1BA
☎ (01293) 514255 ⊕ breweryshades.co.uk
Timothy Taylor Landlord; Vocation Life & Death; 6 changing beers (sourced regionally) ⊞
Possibly the oldest building on Crawley High Street, this wet-led pub was originally a gaol, dates to the 1400s and comes complete with two active ghosts. The licensee has a true passion for the trade, demonstrated by the inspired range of guest ales and ciders which are always in excellent condition. The haunted upstairs room is available for meetings. Good food is served during the day and evening – check the specials board.
ஃ⊛①⇌♣됨❖

Danehill

Coach & Horses ⅃
School Lane, RH17 7JF
☎ (01825) 740369 ⊕ coachandhorses.co
Harvey's Sussex Best Bitter; 1 changing beer (sourced locally; often 360 Degree, Cellar Head) ⊞
A traditional country pub dating from 1847 and retaining many original features. The public and saloon bars have real fires and simple farmhouse-style furniture. Locally produced Black Pig cider is always on the bar, and occasionally its perry too. The separate restaurant area serves locally sourced, high-quality food. The large garden is a delight in summer and includes a children's play area. Q⊛①♣❖됨(270)☙❖

East Dean

Star & Garter ⅃
PO18 0JG (village centre, E end of the village green)
☎ (01243) 811318 ⊕ thestarandgarter.co.uk
Arundel Sussex IPA; 2 changing beers (sourced regionally) ⊞
An 18th-century free house situated by the duckpond in this charming downland village. The large bar has an area for dining and it is renowned for good food, using local seasonal produce, with fresh local seafood a speciality (Sun lunchtime booking is essential). Beer is poured straight from the cask from a cold room behind the bar. There is a large walled garden to the rear which can host outdoor functions. Check the opening hours before traveling. ஃ⊛⋈①&P☙❖

East Grinstead

Engine Room ⅃
The Old Mill, 45 London Road, RH19 1AW
☎ (01342) 327145 ⊕ theengineroomeg.com
5 changing beers (sourced locally) ⅁
Up a path between the shops close to Whitehall bus stop in London Road, the pub is a downstairs labyrinth of small seating areas, good for small groups to hold conversations. Between five and seven ever-changing cask ales are served on gravity, plus four via membrane

keg and six or seven ciders. Beer festivals are held in March and October. Note that the pub's downstairs location limits accessibility. Q⇌♣됨됨❖♪

East Preston

SP Alehouse
23 Sea Road, BN16 1JN
☎ 07736 928347
House beer (by Langham); 1 changing beer (often Firebird) ⅁
This friendly micropub in East Preston opened in 2020. Nicely decorated, with plenty of wood in view plus pumpclips on the walls, it has a mixture of high- and low-level seating inside. It sells the house beer, plus cask ales from a cool room behind the bar, mainly sourced from local breweries. At least four good quality craft keg beers are available, plus cider, wines, gin, soft drinks, and a traditional mead. Bar snacks are available and there is a free cheeseboard on a Sunday. ♣❖됨(700)

East Wittering

Shore Inn ⅃
Shore Road, PO20 8DZ (50yds from the sea)
☎ (01243) 674454 ⊕ theshorepub.co.uk
Fuller's London Pride; Hop Back Summer Lightning; Langham Hip Hop; Palmers Dorset Gold; Sharp's Doom Bar ⊞
Friendly beachside pub popular with locals, particularly dog owners, and the many summer visitors. There are two main bars offering good-value beers, a children's area and a partly covered outside area for eating, drinking and smokers. The good-quality lunchtime menu can be enjoyed either in the bar or restaurant, and extremely inviting dishes are on offer at fair prices (see selection on blackboard). It has occasional live music – see the website for details.
Qஃ⊛①&♣P됨(52,53)☙♪

Eastergate

Wilkes' Head 🍺 ⅃ ✅
Church Lane, PO20 3UT (off A29 in old village, 350yds S of B2233 roundabout, 1¼ miles W of Barnham station) SU943053
☎ (01243) 543380
5 changing beers (sourced nationally; often Bedlam, Langham) ⊞
Small Grade II-listed red-brick pub built 1803 and named after 18th-century radical John Wilkes. There is a cosy lounge left of the central bar and, to the right, a larger room with inglenook fireplace, flagstones and low beams, plus a separate restaurant. At the rear is a permanent marquee with seating plus a heated smokers' shelter and a large garden. There are five well-chosen changing beers, and regular beer festivals are held. Local CAMRA Pub of the Year 2023.
Qஃ⊛①&♣P됨(66,85)☙❖

Elsted

Three Horseshoes
GU29 0JY (at E end of village)
☎ (01730) 825746 ⊕ 3hs.co.uk
Bowman Wallops Wood; Flower Pots Pots Bitter; Young's London Original; 2 changing beers (sourced locally; often Hop Back) ⅁
Old and cosy rural inn divided into small rooms, including one reserved for dining and one with a blazing wood-burning stove in winter. Outside, the large, pleasant garden enjoys superb views of the South Downs. In

summer there are four beers (mainly from local micros), and three in winter, all served by gravity from a stillage alongside the bar. Meals are substantial and of high quality. This is a popular and homely pub, which you will be reluctant to leave. Q❀⏻◑♣P❀

Faygate

Frog & Nightgown L
Wimlands Lane, RH12 4SS
☎ (01293) 852764 ⏏ thefrogandnightgown.co.uk
Harvey's Sussex Best Bitter; Surrey Hills Ranmore; 2 changing beers (sourced locally) Ⓗ
Vibrant, cosy pub that was comprehensively refurbished after changing hands in 2015. There are normally two real ales available. Regular events include quiz nights, classic car meets, live music, and open mic nights. A pizzeria restaurant was added to the rear of the pub in 2021, in addition to the tearoom annex. It is known as the fastest pub in West Sussex due to its motorsport connections. Q☎❀⏻P🅿❀♠

Felpham

George
102 Felpham Road, PO22 7PL (in the village, 120yds from Felpham Way traffic lights)
☎ (01243) 824177 ⏏ georgeinnfelpham.co.uk
Goldmark Dave, Liquid Gold, American Pale Ⓗ
A pleasant two-bar pub with a small locals' bar on the right with a TV. A larger bar to the left has a fire. This then leads into a small dining area on the right or to the back where there is a large conservatory. A pleasant enclosed garden is at the rear. A choice of three cask beers from Goldmark are offered.
Q☎❀⏻♣P🅿(600,700) ❀♠♫

Halnaker

Anglesey Arms ✅
Stane Street, PO18 0NQ (on A285)
☎ (01243) 699644 ⏏ theangleseyarms.com
Timothy Taylor Boltmaker Ⓗ/Ⓐ; **2 changing beers (sourced locally; often Long Man)** Ⓗ
Close to the Goodwood Estate, which owns the freehold, this family-run, listed, Georgian pub and dining room features a wood- and flagstone-floored public bar with a log fire which retains the atmosphere of the traditional village pub, plus a comfortable restaurant renowned for good food made with local produce. The quiet, two-and-a-half-acre rear garden includes tables in a spacious covered area. Dogs are welcome.
Q☎❀⏻♿P🅿(55,99) ❀♠♫

Hassocks

BN6 Craft Beer & Tap L
54 Keymer Road, BN6 8AR
☎ (01234) 567890 ⏏ thebn6tap.co.uk
3 changing beers (sourced locally; often 360 Degree, Goldmark, Hurst) Ⓖ
Micropub opened in former shop, specialising in Sussex-made drink products. This includes cask beer (served by gravity from a cool room), craft/keg, wines and gins. A cask beer from Hurst brewery is normally available. The long narrow bar leads to a small rear garden. The traditional Sussex pub game of toad-in-the-hole is a feature. A disabled access toilet is provided, and the bar has fully disabled access from the street. Q❀♿≈♣🅿❀♠

Haywards Heath

Lockhart Tavern L
41 The Broadway, RH16 3AS
☎ (01444) 440696 ⏏ thelockharttavern.co.uk
6 changing beers (sourced locally; often Gun) Ⓗ
This centrally located free house conversion of a retail premises is often busy. The pub consists of two distinct areas with drinkers being catered for at the front with high tables and matching seating, while towards the rear of the pub there is a wood-panelled dining area. There is a covered seated area outside. Good food is served lunchtime and evenings with regular menu changes. The pub stocks a wide choice of wines, spirits, keg, canned and bottled beers. Q❀❀⏻≈🅿❀♠

Henley

Duke of Cumberland L
GU27 3HQ (off A286, 2 miles N of Midhurst) SU894258
☎ (01428) 652280 ⏏ dukeofcumberland.com
Harvey's Sussex Best Bitter; Langham Hip Hop; Timothy Taylor Landlord; 1 changing beer (sourced locally; often Langham) Ⓖ
Stunning 15th-century inn nestling against the hillside in over three acres of terraced gardens with extensive views. The rustic front bar has scrubbed-top tables and benches, plus log fires at both ends, while to the rear is a dining extension that blends in perfectly with the original pub and offers much-needed additional space. Outside is a smokers' shelter with its own woodburner. A former local CAMRA Pub of the Year, this is a rural gem. It may close early on Sunday evenings in winter.
Q❀⏻♣P🅿(70) ❀♠

Hooksway

Royal Oak
PO18 9JZ SU815163
☎ (01243) 535257 ⏏ royaloakhooksway.co.uk
Arundel Castle, Sussex IPA; Langham Hip Hop; 1 changing beer (often Langham) Ⓗ
An idyllic and unspoilt country pub in walking country, situated on the South Downs Way; perfect for getting away from it all. Popular with hikers, horse riders and people with young families, there is a large garden with play area for children. In winter two lovely log fires greet you. On offer are three permanent real ales and a regular guest, mainly from local breweries. An extensive menu caters for all tastes, including a varied children's menu. Check opening times before visiting. Q❀⏻P❀♠♫

Horsham

Anchor Tap L
16 East Street, RH12 1HL
3 changing beers (sourced nationally) Ⓗ
Now free of tie, this popular pub continues to offer customers an eclectic choice of brews. The knowledgeable team behind the bar source interesting beers both local and from afar. There are three handpumps in use, plus a back bar dispensing 10 keg beers. The pub was originally the tap of the Anchor Hotel. In January 1975 a Horsham branch of CAMRA was formed here. ♠♿≈🅿❀♠

Black Jug
31 North Street, RH12 1RJ
☎ (01403) 253526 ⏏ blackjug-horsham.co.uk
Firebird Parody; Harvey's Sussex Best Bitter; 2 changing beers (sourced nationally) Ⓗ

A large bustling town-centre pub, the Jug is something of a Horsham institution. It has a welcoming interior with bookshelves, pictures, a fire and friendly efficient staff. Two regular ales are available, with rotating guests and a cider. There is an extensive range of whisky and gin. Excellent food is served all day and the pub is popular as a venue to meet and chat with no intrusive music. It is close to the railway station and Arts complex. Q⏵❄❀◑&♿≠♣⌂Ɽ⏰

King's Arms ⎣

64 Bishopric, RH12 1QN
☎ (01403) 451468 ⊕ kingsarmshorsham.com
Crafty Brewing Hop Tipple; Firebird Heritage XX; 3 changing beers (sourced locally) ⊞
This 18th-century coaching inn in the town centre was the King & Barnes brewery tap and is situated in the Bishopric, some 100 yards from the site of the former brewery. A comfortable two-bar pub, now operated by North and South Leisure Ltd, it has five handpumps serving mostly local ales and two keg lines. Food is served, including quality Sunday roasts. Live music plays every Friday and there are Monday music nights and an open mic on alternate Thursdays. ❀◑Ɽ⏰♪

Malt Shovel ⎣

15 Springfield Road, RH12 2PG
☎ (01403) 252302
Surrey Hills Shere Drop; 5 changing beers (sourced regionally) ⊞
Close to the town centre, the pub has six handpumps on year-round, plus two ciders and a mix of bottles and canned ales. It doesn't stock any regular ales but has a focus on local beers and usually offers at least one dark ale. There is live music every Saturday night, as well as regular open mic and jam events. The landlord and his friendly staff take great pride in the real ale. There is good parking for a town-centre pub. ❀◑&♣P Ɽ⏰⏰♪

Piries Bar

15 Piries Place, RH12 1NY (down narrow alley adjoining Carfax)
☎ (01403) 267846 ⊕ piriesbar.com
Long Man Long Blonde; Timothy Taylor Landlord ⊞
In a building dating from the 15th century with exposed original timber beams, the pub is tucked away down a narrow alley adjoining Horsham's Carfax. It comprises a small downstairs room, an upstairs lounge and a small modern extension in character with the building. Regular charity events are organised. Evenings here can be lively, with karaoke on Sundays, quiz nights on Tuesdays and occasional live music. With two cask ales always on the go, this bar is well worth a visit. ⏵◑≠Ɽ⏰⏰♪

Itchenor

Ship

The Street, PO20 7AH (on main street, 100yds from waterfront)
☎ (01243) 512284 ⊕ theshipinnitchenor.co.uk
Arundel Castle; St Austell Proper Job; 1 changing beer (sourced regionally; often Langham, Long Man) ⊞
Popular pub in the main street of an attractive village on the shore of picturesque Chichester harbour. The cosy bar decorated with yachting memorabilia adds to the pub's character and is complemented by a pleasant front patio and further outside seating and a bar at the back. The separate restaurant area offers a wide range, including local seafood. Accommodation is available in a two bedroom apartment and a three bedroom cottage. May be closed on Monday and Tuesday in winter. Q⏵❄⇌❀◑&♣P⏰⏰♪

Lancing

Stanley Ale House ⎣

5 Queensway, BN15 9AY (N of station)
☎ (01903) 366820 ⊕ thestanleyalehouse.com
Downlands Best; Langham Arapaho; 3 changing beers (sourced regionally) Ꮐ
This former launderette opened as a family-run micropub/ale house in 2014. Located 200 yards north of the railway station, near local shops, it offers several changing ales, plus ciders, wine and gin. The owners have listened to customers so now have both keg and cask beers. There is ample seating inside and outside. Bar snacks are available. There is a weekly quiz, regular music nights, takeaway night and other events. A variety of board games are available. Q⏵❀◑&≠♣Ɽ⏰⏰♪

Littlehampton

George Inn ✅

14-18 Surrey Street, BN17 5BG (5 mins' walk E from station, close to pedestrianised area)
☎ (01903) 739863
Greene King IPA, Abbot; Sharp's Doom Bar; 4 changing beers (sourced locally; often Marston's, Shepherd Neame, Wychwood) ⊞
This large town-centre pub is named after an old inn which was situated nearby. Adorning the walls inside the pub are pictures of old Littlehampton, which evoke memories of a past era. There is a variety of comfy seating in the two main areas, some of which is partitioned. Outside is a patio area for drinking. Handpumps serve ales from around the country including some from local breweries. The normal range of Wetherspoon food and drink is available. ⏵❀◑≠Ɽ⏰

New Inn ✅

5 Norfolk Road, BN17 5PL (N from Sea Rd)
☎ (01903) 713112 ⊕ newinnla.co.uk
Harvey's Sussex Best Bitter; 1 changing beer (sourced nationally; often Timothy Taylor) ⊞
The New Inn is a friendly community pub just a short walk from the beach, offering regularly changing ales. This traditional inn has two bar areas. The front bar has ample seating, a real fire and hosts weekly pub quizzes and regular charity events. The rear bar has a pool table and dartboard, and shows live sport. A free jukebox is a feature of Monday nights. There is a heated courtyard at the back. ⏵❀♣Ɽ⏰⏰

Littleworth

Windmill

Littleworth Lane, RH13 8EJ (from A24 or A272 follow signs to Partridge Green along B2135, pub is signposted)
☎ (01403) 710308 ⊕ windmilllittleworth.com
Harvey's Sussex Best Bitter; 2 changing beers (sourced regionally; often Dorking, Long Man) ⊞
Popular independently-owned country pub with friendly staff and locals. This 17th-century inn retains many original features including stone floors and low beams. There is an inglenook fire in the lounge and a wood burner in the bar where crib is played regularly. The ceiling is covered in old agricultural implements, and there is a range of second-hand books in the lobby. The inn has seven characterful bedrooms giving an opportunity for an overnight stay. Q⏵❄❀◑◑&♣P⏰Ɽ(17)⏰⏰

Lodsworth

Langham Brewery Tap

The Granary, Langham Lane, GU28 9BU (½ mile N of A272 at Halfway Bridge) SU92682260

☎ (01798) 860861 🌐 langhambrewery.co.uk

Langham Session Bitter, Hip Hop, Arapaho; house beer (by Langham) Ⓗ; 6 changing beers (sourced locally; often Langham) Ⓖ

A brewery tap, opened in 2021, converted from outbuildings of the 18th-century granary barn that houses the brewery itself. Fronting onto a courtyard behind the brewery there is indoor and outdoor seating and a bar with five handpumps plus six keg taps dispensing a selection of Langham beers. Additional beers (as available) can be fetched from the brewery's cold store across the yard, and take-outs of Langham's cask-conditioned, keg, bottled and canned beers can also be purchased. ☝🏠🍴&🅰♣🅿🐾🛜♪

Lower Beeding

Kissingate Brewery

Pole Barn, Church Lane Farm Estate, Church Lane, RH13 6LU

☎ (01403) 891335 🌐 kissingate.co.uk

Kissingate Sussex, Black Cherry Mild, Chennai, Pernickety Pale; 4 changing beers (sourced locally) Ⓖ

This is the taproom for the Kissingate brewery where you will find a selection of beers from the Kissingate range served on gravity, plus cider and perry from local producers such as Black Pig, Seacider and JB and a well-stocked bar. Events include Saturday festivals in May and October, and curry nights. There is a function area upstairs. 🏠&🅰🅿🚲🐾🛜♪

Maplehurst

White Horse Ⓛ

Park Lane, RH13 6LL

☎ (01403) 891208 🌐 whitehorsemaplehurst.co.uk

4 changing beers (often Downlands, Harvey's, Kissingate) Ⓗ

Under the same ownership for 38 years, this splendid and welcoming country pub has featured in the Guide 35 times, and is popular with locals, cyclists and walkers. The cosy interior, with its unusually wide wooden bar, boasts real fires and many interesting artefacts and bric-a-brac. Good honest fare is provided, with the emphasis on beer and conversation. Many local ales feature, with a good selection of dark brews. Local JB cider is also available. Q☝🐕🏠🍴♣🅿🐾🛜

Nutbourne

Rising Sun Ⓛ

The Street, RH20 2HE (on A283 from Storrington; turn right after bridge over River Chilt) TQ075188

☎ (01798) 812191 🌐 therisingsunnutbourne.co.uk

Fuller's London Pride; Harvey's Sussex Best Bitter; St Austell Tribute; 1 changing beer (sourced locally) Ⓗ

This unspoilt 16th-century village free house is a fine old stone building, with ironstone in its construction, it has retained its character. The front part is Victorian, with a listed outdoor privy. The bare-floored drinking area contrasts with the separate well-appointed restaurant. A traditional drinkers' pub, with enthusiastic staff, the landlord celebrated 40 years running it in 2023. Food is sourced locally when possible and there is live music from time to time. Q🏠🍴♣🅿🐾🛜♪

Pagham

Inglenook Ⓛ

255 Pagham Road, PO21 3QB SZ892986

☎ (01243) 262495 🌐 the-inglenook.com

Fuller's London Pride; Langham Best; 4 changing beers (sourced nationally; often Arbor, Moor Beer, Vibrant Forest) Ⓗ

A 16th-century Grade II-listed hotel, restaurant and free house. There is always a selection of excellent well-hopped real ales available from highly-regarded microbreweries, alongside local real ciders. The cosy bar areas have real fires and there is a large garden to the rear and a patio area at the front. Local CAMRA Pub of the Year 2015-2017. Q☝🐕🏠🍴🍴🅿🚲(600)🐾🛜

Lamb ✅

144 Pagham Road, PO21 4NJ (corner of Barton Close)

☎ (01243) 262168 🌐 thelambinnpagham.com

Fuller's London Pride; Greene King Abbot; Harvey's Sussex Best Bitter; Sharp's Doom Bar; 1 changing beer (sourced nationally; often Timothy Taylor) Ⓗ

This timber-beamed 17th-century inn has one large bar area which also contains small, cosy drinking alcoves. A large area to the side is reserved for dining. There are two gardens, one of which is for adults only. To the front there is a car park as well as a covered bus shelter. Nearby attractions are the beach at Pagham and Pagham Harbour Nature Reserve, popular with birdwatchers. ☝🏠🍴🅿🚲🐾🛜♪

Pulborough

White Horse

Mare Hill, RH20 2DY (on A283 on E outskirts of village)

☎ (01798) 872189 🌐 whitehorsepulborough.com

Dark Star Hophead; Fuller's London Pride; Gale's HSB Ⓗ

Popular drinker's pub situated half a mile east of town with a cosy rustic bar and a more formal restaurant. Food is served all sessions and staff offer a warm welcome to visitors. The pub was saved from closure in 1989 after a campaign by locals and CAMRA. There are glorious views across the Pulborough Brooks and the South Downs National Park. There is a menu of specially selected wines, sparkling wines and Champagne – a favourite is award-winning locally produced Nyetimber. For users of the car park opposite, beware crossing the busy A283. ☝🏠🍴🚲(1)🐾🛜

Selsey

Hopp Inn

153 High Street, PO20 0QB

☎ 07743 275093 🌐 theHoppInn.co.uk

3 changing beers (sourced nationally) Ⓖ

Formerly the Crab Pot, now under family ownership, this micropub serves real ales and ciders from the cool room beside the bar. Three or four cask ales are always on tap. Bar food and snacks are available. There are regular quizzes, and live music most Sunday afternoons. The mixture of high and low seating makes for a relaxed and friendly atmosphere; a warm welcome is assured for visitors and locals alike (especially cribbage players!). 🅰♣🐾🚲(51)🐾🛜♪

Shoreham-by-Sea

Duke of Wellington Ⓛ

368 Brighton Road, BN43 6RE (on A259)

☎ (01273) 441297 🌐 dukeofwellingtonbrewhouse.co.uk

Gun Zamzama IPA; 6 changing beers (sourced regionally; often Dark Star, Downlands, Titanic) Ⓗ
Welcoming free house with seven cask beers on offer from Sussex and beyond, which always include a dark beer. It has a single bar with bench seating and a log fire in winter. There is a regular quiz on Monday and live music on Friday, Saturday and Sunday. Open mic and folk nights are held every other Thursday. Regular quarterly beer festivals include a wassail. The patio garden is a suntrap in the summer months and heated in the winter. Takeaway food can be eaten in the pub.
🛇🏵♨♣🖢🚃(2,700)❀☂♫

Staplefield

Jolly Tanners Ⓛ
Handcross Road, RH17 6EF
☎ (01444) 400335
Harvey's Sussex Best Bitter; 5 changing beers (sourced locally) Ⓗ
On the north corner of the village green, this welcoming venue combines all the best elements of a village inn. The spacious bar is divided into two distinct areas, with two log fires adding to the cosy feel. There is an extensive range of guest beers, always including two dark ales, and real cider is also sold. A good range of tasty food is served at all sessions. This is a friendly place and still very much a locals' pub.
Q🛇🏵◑&♣P🚃(271)❀☂♫

Turners Hill

Crown
East Street, RH10 4PT
☎ (01342) 715218 ⊕ thecrownturnershill.co.uk
Harvey's Sussex Best Bitter; 2 changing beers (sourced regionally; often St Austell) Ⓗ
A tastefully decorated 16th-century farmhouse and 17th-century barn with Jacobean oak beams make up this pub, which converted to an inn in 1706. It holds a St George's Day celebration, a beer festival to coincide with the London to Brighton cycle ride, and a 30-ale festival in October. Leather settees surround a large open fire in the bar area, with another open fire in the restaurant, which serves traditional English dishes.
Q🛇🏵◑&♣P🚃(84,272)❀☂

Walberton

Holly Tree
The Street, BN18 0PH
☎ (01243) 553110 ⊕ hollytreewalberton.com
Harvey's Sussex Best Bitter; 3 changing beers (sourced locally; often 360 Degree, Goldmark, Langham) Ⓗ
Victorian village pub which reopened in 2013 after a lengthy closure. The owners have carried out a thorough refurbishment and extended the pub, transforming it into a popular dining venue. The decor is unusual, with several rooms having a mixture of furniture interacting with a range of wall decorations, mirrors, ornaments and pictures that invite exploration of the extended interior. The original two front bars have been retained, and in the right-hand one four handpumps dispense mainly local beers including usually one from Langham and one from Goldmark. Q🛇🏵◑&♣P🚃(66A,85)❀☂♫

Walderton

Barley Mow
Breakneck Lane, PO18 9ED SU790106
☎ (023) 9263 1321 ⊕ thebarleymow.pub

Harvey's Sussex Best Bitter; Otter Amber; 3 changing beers (sourced regionally; often Harvey's, Langham, Ringwood) Ⓗ
An attractive free house in the centre of this picturesque village, popular with walkers and visitors to the South Downs National Park. Much of this cosy traditional pub caters for diners, but drinkers are most welcome in the large bar area. There are log fires in winter and the pretty garden alongside the River Ems is popular in summer. There are usually five handpumps in use, featuring two bers from Harvey's. The skittle alley can double as a function room. Q🛇🏵◑&♣P🚃(54)❀☂

West Chiltington

Five Bells 🍺 Ⓛ
Smock Alley, RH20 2QX (approx 1 mile S of old village centre) TQ092171
☎ (01798) 812143
5 changing beers (sourced nationally; often Harvey's, Palmers) Ⓗ
This friendly village free house is a Guide regular. Dating from 1935, this former King & Barnes pub has been run by the same couple since 1983. The handpumps are on what is probably Sussex's longest copper-top counter. Local and regional ales served; one is usually a dark ale. There is a large copper-hooded open fire. Locally sourced home-cooked food is served in the bar and large conservatory (not Sun eve). Local CAMRA Pub of the Year 2023. Q🏵🚌◑P🚃(1,74)❀☂

West Hoathly

Cat Ⓛ
Queen's Square, North Lane, RH19 4PP
☎ (01342) 810369 ⊕ catinn.co.uk
Firebird Parody; Harvey's Sussex Best Bitter; 2 changing beers (often Harvey's, Long Man) Ⓗ
Set in a picturesque hilltop village in the heart of the Sussex countryside, this 16th-century free house is within reach of several attractions. It retains oak beams and two inglenook fireplaces. There is an outside terrace, where food and drink can be consumed in the summer months. Five local ales are on the bar and good-quality food is cooked to order, using mostly local suppliers. This cosy pub has four letting rooms.
Q🛇🏵🚌◑&AP🚃(84)❀☂

West Marden

Victoria Ⓛ
PO18 9EN (just W of B2146 in village centre)
☎ (023) 9263 1330 ⊕ victoriainnwestmarden.com
Harvey's Sussex Best Bitter; Langham Hip Hop; 1 changing beer (sourced locally; often Bowman, Hogs Back, Otter) Ⓗ
Comfortable old rural inn at the heart of its tiny downland community, now free of all ties after being purchased by an enthusiastic young couple during 2021. Many country pursuits, including walking, riding and shooting, are supported. Inside there are several intimate spaces in which to drink and dine, with a log-burning stove for cold evenings. The front garden has splendid views of the surrounding hills. Changing beers feature mainly local breweries alongside others from further afield. Q🛇🏵◑A♣P🚃(54)❀☂♫

Worthing

Brewhouse & Kitchen (Worthing) Ⓛ
14 Wykeham Road, BN11 4JD
☎ (01903) 948222

House beer (by Brewhouse & Kitchen (Worthing)) ℍ
The former Beechwood Hall Hotel was taken over by Brewhouse & Kitchen and opened in 2021. The original building has been refurbished and extended sympathetically. This is the first Brewhouse & Kitchen site which is also a hotel, so it is described as a BrewTel. It serves several ales and keg beers brewed in-house, alongside a good food menu. The large garden has outside seating areas including covered pods. Some ales and rooms pay tribute to the history of this building. ⬥❀✉◑♿⬥≷P🚌(9) ♣ 🛜

Egremont 🄻
32 Brighton Road, BN11 3ED (a short walk from seafront and town centre)
☎ (01903) 600064
Harvey's Sussex Best Bitter; 3 changing beers (sourced locally; often Goldmark, Harvey's, Only With Love) ℍ
An attractive late-Georgian gem with a quirky interior, exterior signage and stained-glass windows show it was originally owned by Kemp Town Brewery of Brighton. The pub was refurbished in 2015. Handpumps deliver four rotating ales plus two ciders; keg beers and over 50 gins are also available. The Egremont has a reputation for its home-made food, having won two awards. Sunday roasts are substantial and popular. There is live music on Friday and Saturday, and the landlord-hosted quiz every Wednesday is a treat. ⬥◑♣♥🚌♣🛜

Fox & Finch Alehouse 🄻
8 Littlehampton Road, BN13 1QE (on N side of A259, across from Thomas A Becket pub) ⊕ thefoxandfinch.co.uk
Fallen Acorn Pompey Royal; 1 changing beer (often Downlands) 🄶
Worthing's fifth micropub opened in 2019 and quickly became popular, offering a warm welcome to all. The premises are decorated in a homely traditional pub style with high and low tables and comfortable seating. A cold room behind the bar houses the ale served directly from the cask, while keg selection is from taps on the bar. There is a range of Belgian beers, fine wine and a small selection of spirits. Limited outside seating is available. A former local CAMRA Pub of the Year. ⬥♿♣🚌♣🛜

Green Man Ale & Cider House 🄻
17 South Street, Tarring, BN14 7LG (40yds N of West Worthing railway crossing)
☎ 07984 793877
5 changing beers (sourced regionally; often Downlands, Tring, Wantsum) 🄶
Worthing's third micropub opened in 2016 in a former café 40 yards north of West Worthing crossing. The temperature-controlled cool room is visible from the pub, which is furnished with high-level tables, benches and stools arranged to encourage interaction and chat. The pub is known for a friendly atmosphere and consistently well-kept ales, gravity-dispensed, which always include a dark ale. Several ciders and perries, as well as gins and wines are available. A former local CAMRA Pub of the Year and Cider Pub of the Year. Cash only.
Q≷(West Worthing) ♣♣🚌(7,10) ♣

Parsonage Bar & Restaurant 🄻
6-10 High Street, Tarring, BN14 7NN (at S end of Tarring High St – not to be confused with High St Worthing)
☎ (01903) 820140 ⊕ theparsonage.co.uk
Burning Sky Plateau; Harvey's Sussex Best Bitter; 1 changing beer (sourced locally; often Harvey's) ℍ
Situated in the heart of Tarring village, this lovely Grade II-listed 15th-century building was originally three cottages. It has been a quality restaurant since 1987 but

the bar now has several well-kept local ales, often with a dark ale in winter. Customers are welcome to drink without having a meal although the set menu, which includes a drink, is good value. The courtyard garden is great for the warmer weather. A former local CAMRA Pub of the Year. Q❀◑≷(West Worthing)🚌(6,16)♣🛜

Refreshment Rooms
Salvington Hill, High Salvington, BN13 3BE (top of Salvington Hill on corner of Furze Rd)
Harvey's Sussex Best Bitter; 1 changing beer (sourced locally) ℍ
Opened in March 2022 in former small general stores premises, this venue describes itself as a shop and micropub. The pleasantly decorated interior has comfortable seating at wooden tables. The local shop with cakes, tea and coffee opens early, with the bar opening later. Two local ales plus various keg, cider, bottled and canned beers, wine and spirits are available. Food vans visit some evenings, mainly at the end of week and weekends, with offerings such as pizza, tacos, mac and cheese, and burgers. There is outdoor seating and car parking. ◑P🚌(7)♣🛜

Toad in the Hole
1 Newland Road, BN11 1JR (just S of the railway bridge and Morrisons)
Hand Low 5, Bird, Chop ℍ
Built in the 1870s, formerly the Castle Alehouse, this pub was taken over by HandBrewCo and reopened in March 2022. It is a short walk from Worthing town centre and station and sells beers from the Hand brewery which is located in West Worthing. The Sussex pub game Toad is available for customers to play. Three cask ales plus a good selection of keg beers are available, with canned beer from Hand and Cloak & Dagger also sold. ≷♣🚌♣🛜♫

Yapton

Maypole 🄻
Maypole Lane, BN18 0DP (off B2132 ½ mile N of village; pedestrian access across railway from Lake Lane, 1¼ miles E of Barnham station) SU978042
☎ (01243) 551417
Bedlam Phoenix IPA; Lister's Best Bitter; 2 changing beers (sourced locally; often Downlands, Pitchfork) ℍ
Small, characterful 18th-century flint-built free house hidden away from the village centre, down a narrow lane ending in a pedestrian crossing over the railway. The cosy, often lively, lounge boasts a large inglenook with a wood-burning stove and a row of six handpumps dispensing up to four beers, usually from local breweries. There is also a traditional public bar with jukebox and darts. Dogs are welcome throughout the pub.
Q⬥❀♿♣P🚌♣🛜♫

Breweries

Adur
Brick Barn, Charlton Court, Mouse Lane, Steyning, BN44 3DG
☎ (01903) 867614

Office: 2 Sullington Way, BN43 6PJ
⊕ adurvalleycoop.com

⊠ Adur Brewery, nestled in the heart of the South Downs, was launched in 2008 on a 5.5-barrel plant, marking the return of brewing to the Adur Valley after an interval of nearly 100 years. The brewery was sold to the Adur Valley Co-Operative in 2012, including the Adur

Brewery name and recipes. A large part of the output is sold as bottle-conditioned beer. **!! ◆ LIVE**

Ropetackle Golden Ale (ABV 3.4%) GOLD
Hop Token: Amarillo (ABV 4%) BITTER
Hop Token: Summit (ABV 4%) BITTER
Velocity (ABV 4.4%) BITTER
Black William (ABV 5%) STOUT
Robbie's Red (ABV 5.2%) RED

Arundel

Unit C7, Ford Airfield Industrial Estate, Ford, Arundel, BN18 0HY
☎ (01903) 733111 ⊕ arundelbrewery.co.uk

⊗ Founded in 1992, Arundel Brewery is the historic town's first brewery in 70 years. It also brews for the Bison Crafthouse, Brighton. A taproom was opened in 2019 called the Brewhouse Project, which is based on the Lyminster Road on the outskirts of Arundel. **!! ☕ ◆ ♦**

Black Stallion (ABV 3.7%) MILD
A dark mild with well-defined chocolate and roast character. The aftertaste is not powerful but the initial flavours remain in the clean finish.
Castle (ABV 3.8%) BITTER
A pale tawny beer with fruit and malt noticeable in the aroma. The flavour has a good balance of malt, fruit and hops, with a dry, hoppy finish.
Sussex Gold (ABV 4.2%) GOLD
A golden-coloured best bitter with a strong floral hop aroma. The ale is clean-tasting and bitter for its strength, with a tangy citrus flavour. The initial hop and fruit die to a dry and bitter finish.
Sussex IPA (ABV 4.5%) PALE
Stronghold (ABV 4.7%) BITTER
A smooth, full-flavoured premium bitter. A good balance of malt, fruit and hops comes through in this rich, chestnut-coloured beer.
Wild Heaven (ABV 5.2%) PALE

Balcombe

🍺 **Half Moon, Haywards Heath Road, Balcombe, RH17 6PA**
☎ (01444) 811582 ✉ mail@halfmoonbalcombe.com

Balcombe is a microbrewery established in 2021 by 13 beer enthusiasts.

Bedlam

St Helena Farm, St Helena Lane, Plumpton Green, BN7 3DH
☎ (01273) 978015 ⊕ bedlambrewery.co.uk

Eco-friendly Bedlam Brewery operates from the heart of the South Downs on a farm with solar power. All spent grain is donated to cattle on the farm and hops are composted. More than 1,000 pubs and bars are supplied across London and the south of England. **!! LIVE**

Phoenix IPA (ABV 3.9%) PALE
Benchmark Sussex Best Bitter (ABV 4%) BITTER
Wilde East Coast Pale Ale (ABV 4.4%) PALE
Amagansett American Pale Ale (ABV 5%) PALE

Bestens

Unit 8b, Hooklands Farm, Lewes Road, Scaynes Hill, RH17 7NG
☎ (01403) 892556 ⊕ bestensbrewery.co.uk

The brewery opened in 2018 in Lower Beeding as a one-barrel plant, increasing to four-barrel capacity in 2020 and moving to Scaynes Hill in 2022. The brewery operates a taproom in Haywards Heath, as well as a mobile outlet in the town. Real ale is occasionally available. 🍺

Brew Studio

39 Meadowview Road, Sompting, BN15 0HU
☎ 07980 978350

⊗ Brew Studio started off as a 0.5-barrel nanobrewery in 2017 and has since upgraded to a 2.5-barrel plant. Around 20 outlets are supplied direct.

Brewery 288

Burton Park Road, Heath End, Duncton, Petworth, GU28 0JU

Brewery 288 is a microbrewery specialising in traditional real ales. All beers are bottle-conditioned. **LIVE**

Brewhouse & Kitchen SIBA

🍺 **38 East Street, Horsham, RH12 1HL**
⊕ brewhouseandkitchen.com/horsham

A 2.5-barrel plant producing cask and keg beers. 'Project Cask' beers are produced alongside the core range. Brewery experience days are available.

Brewhouse & Kitchen SIBA

🍺 **Wykeham Road, Worthing, BN11 4JD**
☎ (01903) 948222 ⊕ brewhouseandkitchen.com/venue/worthing

⊗ Part of the Brewhouse & Kitchen chain, producing its own range of beers. Carry outs and brewery experience days are offered. **!! ◆**

Brolly

No 5, Kiln Industries, Lowfold Farm, Fittleworth Road, Wisborough Green, RH14 0ES ☎ 07720 847017
⊕ brollybrewing.co.uk

Brolly was established in 2017 by keen homebrewer Brook Saunders. Beers are available in local pubs, at the onsite bar, and at the brewery tap, Billi Tap in Billingshurst. 🍺 ◆

Little Pearl (ABV 3.5%) STOUT
Aroha (ABV 3.8%) PALE
Lifeline (ABV 3.8%) MILD
Madre (ABV 4%) PALE
Choco-lots (ABV 4.1%) STOUT
Chub IPA (ABV 4.3%) PALE
Spanky McDanky (ABV 4.5%) PALE
C.O.W (ABV 4.8%) PALE
How Now (ABV 5%) BROWN
Natural Spring Water (ABV 5%) PALE
Jolly Brolly Brown Ale (ABV 5.2%) BROWN
Old Ale (ABV 5.4%) OLD

Cloak & Dagger SIBA

Unit 6a, Garcia Trading Estate, Canterbury Road, Worthing, BN13 1AL ☎ 07378 300570
⊕ cloakanddaggerbrewing.com

Cloak & Dagger was established by three friends from Brighton in 2017. Beers are available in can and keg. The brewery tap is Cloak Room, Kemptown. 🍺

Downlands SIBA

Unit Z (2a), Mackley Industrial Estate, Small Dole, BN5 9XE
☎ (01273) 495596 ⊕ downlandsbrewery.com

⊠ A 10-barrel brewery set up in 2012 distributing beers across the south east of England. ‼ ◆

Root Thirteen (ABV 3.6%) GOLD
Best (ABV 4.1%) BITTER
Bramber (ABV 4.5%) BITTER
Devils Dyke Porter (ABV 5%) PORTER
Devils Dyke Salted Caramel (ABV 5%) SPECIALITY

Endangered

Building OPQ Unit D&E, S.M Tidy Industrial Estate, Ditchling Common, Hassocks, BN6 8SG
✉ hello@endangeredbrewing.com

With a focus to brew an easy-to-navigate core range of premium session beers with lower ABV, hops and malts sourced from the UK. Can artwork features endangered species. Currently does not have its own brewhouse so is utilising spare capacity at other breweries.

Escapist (NEW)

Unit 4a, Hambrook Business Centre, Cheesemans Lane, Chichester, PO18 8XP
☎ (01243) 776599 ☎ 07545 905610
⊕ theescapistchichester.co.uk

The Escapist Craft Beer Bar in Crane Street, Chichester, opened a brewery at Hambrook in the Sussex countryside in 2022. As well as producing its own beers, it participates in collaborations with likeminded brewers.

Fauna

Norfolk Estate Office, London Road, Arundel, BN18 9AS ☎ 07742 144340 ⊕ faunabrewing.com

Combining three core values of conservation, environmentalism and good beer, Fauna Brewing was launched in 2021. The brewery work with three charity partners in aid of endangered species that benefit from each beer sale. ◢

Firebird SIBA

Old Rudgwick Brickworks, Lynwick Street, Rudgwick, RH12 3UW
☎ (01403) 823180 ⊕ firebirdbrewing.co.uk

⊠ Firebird began brewing in 2013 and has grown rapidly with new beers, new vessels, an extended warehouse and an expanded team. There is an upstairs bar onsite. ‼ ☰ ◆ LIVE ◢

Two Horses (ABV 3.8%) PALE
Heritage XX (ABV 4%) BITTER
Parody (ABV 4.5%) GOLD

Goldmark SIBA

Unit 23, The Vinery, Arundel Road, Poling, Arundel, BN18 9PY
☎ (01903) 297838 ☎ 07900 555415
⊕ goldmarks.co.uk

⊠ Ex-biochemist and homebrewer Mark Lehmann began commercial brewing in 2013 using an 12-barrel plant. The brewery specialises in pales and porters in cask. Seasonal brewery tours and takeway taproom Fridays and Saturdays. ‼ ☰ LIVE ◢

Session Pale (ABV 3.7%) PALE
Dave (ABV 3.8%) BITTER
Liquid Gold (ABV 4%) GOLD
Hop Idol (ABV 4.4%) PALE
Mosaic Pale (ABV 4.4%) PALE
American Pale (ABV 4.8%) PALE

Black Cherry (ABV 4.8%) PORTER
Sussex Warrior (ABV 4.8%) BITTER
Vertigo Craft Lager (ABV 4.8%) SPECIALITY
Pitch Shifter IPA (ABV 5%) PALE

Goodwood

The New Brewery, Stane Street, North Heath, RH20 1DJ ⊕ goodwood.com/estate/home-farm/goodwood-brewery

Beers are available in bottle and keg in restaurants and bars across the Goodwood estate and can be ordered online. The beer is brewed by Hepworth (qv) using ingredients grown on the estate.

Greyhound

Watershed, Smock Alley, West Chiltington, RH20 2QX
☎ (01798) 815822 ☎ 07973 625510
⊕ greyhoundbrewery.co.uk

⊠ Established in 2015 by husband-and-wife team Nick and Sarah Allen, Greyhound is a 7.5-barrel brewery. In 2017 the brewery took over production of Ballard's Brewery beers. Cask beer was discontinued in 2022, with the brewery now concentrating on bottles and cans. All beers are unfined, unfiltered, gluten free and vegan-friendly. ‼ ◆ LIVE GF V

Gribble

☷ **Gribble Inn, Oving, PO20 2BP**
☎ (01243) 786893 ⊕ gribbleinn.co.uk

⊠ Established in 1980 using a five-barrel plant, the Gribble Brewery is the longest-serving brewpub in the Sussex area, independently-owned and run by the licensees since 2005. A number of local outlets are supplied. ◆

Hairy Dog

Unit 38, More House Farm, Wivelsfield, Haywards Heath, RH17 7RE ⊕ hairydogbrewery.beer

⊠ Overlooking the South Downs National Park, the brewery's ethos is to use Sussex ingredients wherever possible and to pursue a policy of sustainability. An onsite taproom is open Friday. ◢

Gun Dog (ABV 0.4%) PALE
Hounded Best Bitter (ABV 4.1%) BITTER
Far Fetched Pale Ale (ABV 4.2%) PALE
Bloodhound Red IPA (ABV 5.5%) RED

Heathen

Hop Sun, Triangle Road, Haywards Heath, RH16 4HW
☎ (01444) 456217 ☎ 07825 429428
⊕ heathenbrewers.co.uk

Heathen opened its new brewery in 2021, moving from the more restricted premises at the Grape & Grain off-licence into a former barn. The new premises has an adjoining taproom, which is open Thursday-Saturday. Beers are unfiltered, unpasteurised and mostly vegan-friendly, served via air pressure from tanks or in casks. ‼ ◆ LIVE V ◢

Atemporal Rites (ABV 3.9%) PALE
Session IPA (ABV 4.7%) PALE
NEIPA (ABV 5.2%) GOLD

Hepworth SIBA

Stane Street, North Heath, RH20 1DJ
☎ (01403) 269696 ⊕ hepworthbrewery.co.uk

⊠ Hepworth's was established in 2001. 274 outlets are supplied. Originally situated in Horsham, a new brewery site in North Heath opened in 2016. Its organic status is ratified by the Soil Association. Beers are contract brewed for Hiver. ‼️🍺◆LIVE

Traditional Sussex Bitter (ABV 3.5%) BITTER
A fine, clean-tasting amber session beer. A bitter beer with a pleasant fruity and hoppy aroma that leads to a crisp, tangy taste. A long, dry finish.
Dark Horse (ABV 3.8%) BITTER
Summer Ale (ABV 3.8%) BITTER
Pullman First Class Ale (ABV 4.2%) BITTER
A sweet, nutty maltiness and fruitiness are balanced by hops and bitterness in this easy-drinking, pale brown best bitter. A subtle bitter aftertaste.
Prospect Organic (ABV 4.5%) GOLD
Classic Old Ale (ABV 4.8%) OLD
Iron Horse (ABV 4.8%) BITTER
There's a fruity, toffee aroma to this light brown, full-bodied bitter. A citrus flavour balanced by caramel and malt leads to a clean, dry finish.

Horsham

Unit 3, Blatchford Close, Horsham, RH13 5RG
✉️ horshambrewingco@mail.com

Horsham Brewery Company Ltd began brewing in 2021 to sell to local pubs. Set up by Rohan and Tim, it brews a wide variety of beers and opened a taproom in 2022. It produces cask and KeyKeg beers, with some beer also available in cans. All beers are named after places local to Horsham. A beer festival is held every September at the Drill Hall, Horsham. ◆

Causeway (ABV 3.8%) PALE
Victory (ABV 3.8%) PALE
Trafalgar (ABV 4%) IPA
HBC (ABV 4.2%) BITTER
Sun Oak (ABV 4.2%) RED
Normandy (ABV 4.7%) SPECIALITY
Bishopric (ABV 5.2%) STOUT
Carfax (ABV 6.2%) IPA

Hurst SIBA

Highfields Farm, Hurstpierpoint, BN6 9JT ☎ 07866 438953 🌐 hurstbrewery.co.uk

Hurst was founded in 2012, reviving a name dating back to 1862.

Founders Best Bitter (ABV 4.2%) BITTER
Keepers Gold (ABV 4.4%) SPECIALITY
Watchtower (ABV 5.5%) PORTER

Kiln

Chiddinglye Farm, West Hoathly, RH19 4QS ☎ 07800 556729

Office: 1st Floor, 30 Church Road, Burgess Hill, RH15 9AE 🌐 thekilnbrewery.co.uk

Kiln brewery was set up by two friends in 2014. Following a search for new premises, it has joined forces with Missing Link Brewery. Although Kiln's website is focusing on keg and canned beer, it is continuing to produce cask beers, but are no longer sticking with a core range.

Kissingate

Pole Barn, Church Lane Farm Estate, Church Lane, Lower Beeding, RH13 6LU
☎ (01403) 891335

Office: 2 Drury Close, Maidenbower, Crawley
🌐 kissingate.co.uk

⊠ Kissingate Brewery was founded in 2010 by husband-and-wife team Gary and Bunny Lucas. Current production capacity is eight barrels. The brewery building is a converted barn set in a wooded valley near the village of Mannings Heath. It has a taproom and minstrels gallery. The brewery is available to hire for private events. ‼️🍺◆LIVE ✦

Storyteller (ABV 3.5%) GOLD
Sussex (ABV 4%) BITTER
Black Cherry Mild (ABV 4.2%) SPECIALITY
Moon (ABV 4.5%) BITTER
Old Tale Porter (ABV 4.5%) PORTER
Chocolate & Vanilla Oatmeal Stout (ABV 4.8%) SPECIALITY
Chennai (ABV 5%) BITTER
Nooksack (ABV 5%) GOLD
Pernickety Pale (ABV 5%) BITTER
Smelter's Stout (ABV 5.1%) STOUT
Powder Blue (ABV 5.5%) PORTER
Stout Extreme Jamaica (ABV 6%) STOUT
Six Crows (ABV 6.6%) STOUT
Blackeyed Susan (ABV 7%) STRONG
Murder of Crows (ABV 10%) STOUT

Langham SIBA

Old Granary, Langham Lane, Lodsworth, GU28 9BU
☎ (01798) 860861 🌐 langhambrewery.co.uk

⊠ Langham Brewery was established in 2006 in an 18th century granary barn and is set in the heart of West Sussex with fine views of the rolling South Downs. It is owned by Lesley Foulkes and James Berrow who brew and run the business. The brewery is a 10-barrel, steam-heated plant and more than 200 outlets are supplied. ‼️🍺◆

Session Bitter (ABV 3.5%) BITTER
Saison (ABV 3.9%) SPECIALITY
Hip Hop (ABV 4%) GOLD
Golden ale packed full of hops. Crisp bitterness with hint of sweetness leading to an enticing dry and sharp finish.
Triple XXX (ABV 4.4%) MILD
Best (ABV 4.5%) BITTER
Arapaho (ABV 4.9%) PALE
Langham Special Draught (LSD) (ABV 5.2%) BITTER

Lister's SIBA

Michelgrove Lane, Lower Barpham, Ford Lane, Patching, BN13 3XW
☎ (01903) 885950 ☎ 07775 853412
🌐 listersbrewery.com

Brewing began in 2012 using a 0.25-barrel kit. The brewery relocated in 2014 and expanded to a five-barrel plant.

Best Bitter (ABV 3.9%) BITTER
Golden Ale (ABV 4.1%) GOLD
Limehouse Porter (ABV 4.1%) PORTER
American Pale Ale (ABV 4.2%) PALE
IPA (ABV 4.3%) PALE
Special (ABV 4.6%) BITTER

Little Monster

Office: Burton Warren, Burton Park Road, Petworth, GU28 0JS 🌐 littlemonsterbrew.com

Brewing began in 2018. Owner Brenden collaborates with other breweries to produce his beers.

Missing Link

The Old Dairy, Chiddinglye Farm, West Hoathly, RH19 4QS ⊕ missinglinkbrewing.com

Missing Link was established in 2017. A state-of-the-art brewery, it welcomes other users, branding itself as a collective of like-minded breweries. Contract brewing and canning are also carried out. No real ale.

Pin-Up

Unit 3, Block 3, Chalex Industrial Estate, Manor Hall Road, Southwick, BN42 4NH
☎ (01273) 411127 ☎ 07888 836892
⊕ pinupbrewingco.com

⊠ Pin-Up began brewing in 2011, initially having its beers contract brewed at an Essex brewery. In 2014 it obtained its own plant and began brewing in Southwick, and expanded from a five-barrel to a 10-barrel plant in 2015. Its first pub, the United Brethren, Chelmsford, opened in 2016. ♦LIVE

Honey Brown (ABV 4%) BITTER
Session IPA (ABV 4.1%) PALE
Summer Pale (ABV 4.1%) PALE
Red Head (ABV 4.2%) RED
Milk Stout (ABV 4.5%) STOUT

Ridgeway

Stane Street, North Heath, Pulborough, RH20 1DJ
☎ (01491) 873474

Office: Ridgeway Brewing Ltd, South Stoke, RG8 0JW
⊕ ridgewaybrewery.co.uk

Set up by ex-Brakspear head brewer Peter Scholey, Ridgeway specialises in bottle-conditioned beers, although cask beers are occasionally available at beer festivals and locally. A new brewery has been operational since 2016, located within Hepworth Brewery's new premises near Pulborough, sharing some facilities. LIVE

Sussex Small Batch

23 The Vinery, Poling, Arundel, BN18 9PY ☎ 07718 222425

Office: 48 Henty Road, Worthing, BN14 7HE
✉ ssbbrewery@outlook.com

⊠ Jim Brown started the Sussex Small Batch Brewery in 2018, focusing on producing quality stouts with a difference. Brewing takes place using spare capacity at Goldmark Brewery (qv). Cask stout is available from time to time in a few select pubs in Worthing, but most production is canned and available throughout the UK via Eebria. Collaboration brews are sometimes available.

Tiramisu Stout (ABV 5.5%) STOUT
Zucotto Stout (Chocolate & Raspberry) (ABV 5.5%) STOUT
Smoked Chilli Chocolate Stout (ABV 5.8%) STOUT

Top-Notch

Office: 60 Wickham Way, Haywards Heath, RH16 1UQ
☎ 07963 829368 ✉ topnotchbrewing@hotmail.com

A one-barrel brewery situated in a converted residential outbuilding. Beer styles change with each brew. LIVE

Vine

🖥 Vine, 27-29 High Street, Tarring, Worthing, BN14 7NN
☎ (01903) 201121 ✉ thevinepub@hotmail.com

⊠ Brewery established in 2018 in the barn at the rear of the Vine pub. Beer is sold exclusively at the pub. Brewing is currently suspended.

Wingtip

The Grain Shed, Ford Lane, Ashurst, BN44 3AT
☎ (0333) 224 4888 ⊕ wingtipbrewing.com

⊠ Established in 2015, Wingtip is influenced by the history of Shoreham Airport and its founders experience of aviation and travel. Beers are available in pubs and bars around Sussex and London.

Autopilot (ABV 3.9%) BLOND

The language of beer

Nose: the aroma. Gently swirl the beer to release the aroma. You will detect malt: grainy and biscuity, often likened to crackers or Ovaltine. When darker malts are used, the nose will have powerful hints of chocolate, coffee, nuts, vanilla, liquorice, molasses and such dried fruits as raisins and sultanas. Hops add superb aromas of resins, herbs, spices, fresh-mown grass and tart citrus fruit — lemon and orange are typical, with intense grapefruit notes from some American varieties. Sulphur may also be present when waters are 'Burtonised': i.e. gypsum and magnesium salts have been added to replicate the famous spring waters of Burton-on-Trent.

Palate: the appeal in the mouth. The tongue can detect sweetness, bitterness and saltiness as the beer passes over it. The rich flavours of malt will come to the fore but hop bitterness will also make a substantial impact. The tongue will also pick out the natural saltiness from the brewing water and fruit from darker malts, yeast and hops. Citrus notes often have a major impact on the palate.

Finish: the aftertaste, as the beer goes over the tongue and down the throat. The finish is often radically different to the nose. The aroma may be dominated by malt whereas hop flavours and bitterness can govern the finish. Darker malts will make their presence felt with roast, chocolate or coffee notes; fruit character may linger. Strong beers may end on a sweet or biscuity note but in mainstream bitters, bitterness and dryness come to the fore.

JOIN THE CAMRA STORY

People from all walks of life join CAMRA. They're brought together by a love of real ale, cider and perry, the traditions of the pub and a desire to protect them. Be part of the story and seek out your local branch. Keep real ale alive and share tasting notes. Volunteer at a festival or campaign to protect everything you love for the future. Discover the many ways to celebrate our shared passions.

Join as a member from only £30.50† today – as a thank you for being a hero in the CAMRA story, your membership gets you...

- A **welcome pack**, including membership card, to help you make the most of your membership

- Access to award-winning, quarterly *BEER* **magazine** and **What's Brewing** online news

- £30* worth of **CAMRA real ale** ** **vouchers**

- Access to the **Real Ale Discount Scheme**, where you receive discounts on pints at over 3,500 participating pubs nationwide

- **Learn & Discover** online resources to help you discover more about beer and brewing

- **Free or reduced entry** to CAMRA beer festivals

- The opportunity to **campaign for great real ale, cider and perry,** and to save pubs under threat from closure

- **Discounts on CAMRA books** including our best-selling *Good Beer Guide*

- Social activities in your local area and **exclusive member discounts online**

Whether you're a dedicated campaigner, a beer enthusiast looking to learn more about beer, or you just love beer and pubs, CAMRA membership is for you. Join us today!

Join the campaign at
camra.org.uk/join

CAMRA, 230 Hatfield Road, St Albans, Herts AL1 4LW.
Tel: 01727 798440 Email: camra@camra.org.uk

Rates and benefits are subject to change.
† Concessionary rates may be lower.
* Joint members receive £40 worth of vouchers.
** real ale, cider and perry, subject to terms and conditions.

Campaign
for
Real Ale

South West

CORNWALL

ISLES OF SCILLY

ST MARTIN'S

TRESCO

ST MARY'S

Isles of Scilly

ST AGNES

Trebarwith Stran

Rock

Padstow

St Ma

Edmonton

Bodmin

Newquay

A3059

A392

Quintrell Downs

A3075

Indian Queens

Pol

Perranporth

Zelah

A3058

St Austell

Trevaunance Cove

Towan Cross

Truro

Grampound

Bridge

A390

Vogue

Mevagissey

Redruth

Perranwell

Piece

Ponsanooth

Portscatho

Zennor

St Ives

Hayle

Penryn

Treen

Trewellard

Newbridge

Crowlas

Nancenoy

Falmouth

St Just

Penzance

Helston

Porthleven

Gunwalloe

Pednavounder

Cadgwith

Altarnun

Rising Sun Inn

PL15 7SN (off A30 at Five Lanes, then 2 miles NW beyond Altarnun village) SX215825

☎ (01566) 86636 🌐 therisingsuninn.co.uk

Firebrand Patchwork Rocket Pale; 3 changing beers (sourced nationally) 🅷

This 150-year-old pub, in a former farmhouse on the outskirts of Altarnun, is now a thriving community inn and tap for the nearby Firebrand brewery. The cosy, warm interior has beamed ceilings, an open fireplace, and antique guns and various pictures on the walls. The pub is spacious, with ample seating in the bar, two small annexes for pool and drinkers, and a separate restaurant. Outside is a large patio and grassed area for games. Food is cooked with locally sourced ingredients.
Q🕭🏵🌓&🅰♣♠P🐾🖥🎵

Blisland

Blisland Inn

The Green, PL30 4JF (off A30 E of Bodmin) SX100732
☎ (01208) 850739
House beer (by Tintagel) 🅷**; 4 changing beers (sourced nationally)** 🅷/🅶

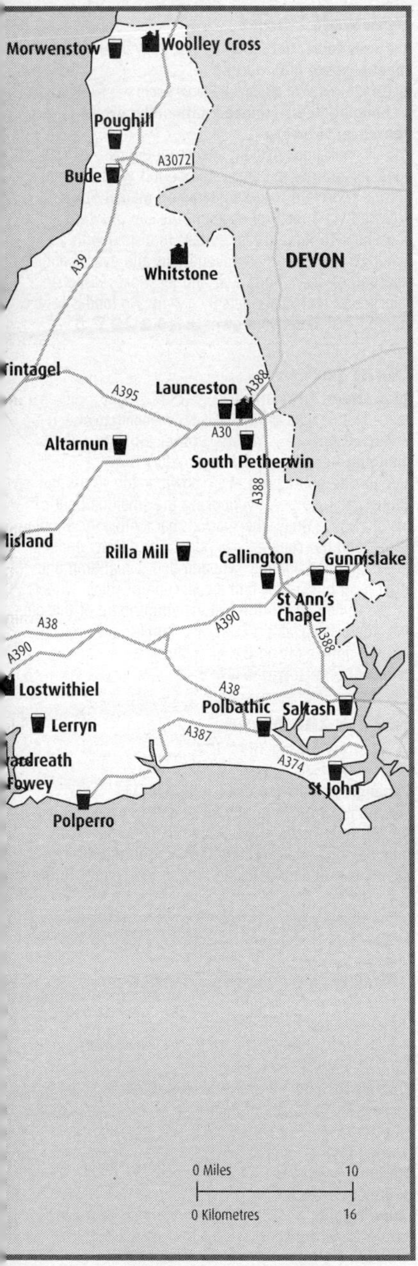
Morwenstow
Woolley Cross
Poughill
A3072
Bude
A39
Whitstone
DEVON
Tintagel
A395
Launceston
A388
A30
Altarnun
South Petherwin
A388
Blisland
Rilla Mill
Callington
Gunnislake
St Ann's Chapel
A390
A38
A390
A388
Lostwithiel
A38
Polbathic
Saltash
Lerryn
A387
Pardreath
A374
Fowey
St John
Polperro
0 Miles
10
0 Kilometres
16

Friendly rural community pub by the only village green in Cornwall. The Blisland, on the edge of Bodmin Moor, retains its reputation as a real ale destination and has served more than 3,000 different real ales over the years. It usually has at least five or six beers available, with several brewed locally, and frequently changing draught ciders including more unusual varieties. Freshly prepared meals use local produce. The decor is eclectic and includes barometers, Toby jugs and coffee mugs as well as an impressive collection of pumpclips and beermats. Popular with walkers and cyclists. A former CAMRA National Pub of the Year and winner of many other local CAMRA awards. Q

Bodmin

Hole in the Wall ✔

16 Crockwell Street, PL31 2DS (entrance from town car park)

☎ (01208) 72397 theholeinthewallbodmin.co.uk

Dartmoor Jail Ale; Draught Bass; Sharp's Atlantic; 3 changing beers (sourced nationally) H

Popular locals' pub built in the 18th century as a debtors' prison. The pub can be accessed direct from the public car park or through a secluded, leafy garden containing its own hop bine and stream, and presided over by a rather bleached stuffed lion. The single bar, which is subdivided by archways, contains a large and eclectic collection of antiques and military memorabilia. Upstairs is a separate function room. It has twice won local CAMRA Pub of the Year. Q (26,11)

Bridge

Bridge Inn

Bridge Row, TR16 4QW

☎ (01209) 842532

Dartmoor Legend; Sharp's Atlantic; 2 changing beers H

Former 18th-century hunting lodge, now a small, traditional granite Cornish Inn that is reputedly haunted. The atmosphere in the L-shaped bar is warm and friendly, with a local character. Traditional brown hues dominate, with partly wood-cladded walls, a carpeted floor, and a few local pictures on display. The riverside beer garden has a boules piste, while the nearby old Portreath tramroad offers a delightful coast-to-coast walk through Cornish mining history. Buses to Redruth and Truro stop outside during the day.
Q P (48,49)

Bude

Barrel at Bude

36 Lansdown Road, EX23 8BN

☎ (01288) 356113 thebarrelatbude.com

5 changing beers (sourced locally) H

This small micropub opened in 2017 in a former fancy dress shop in the centre of town. All the beers and ciders are sourced from within Cornwall and Scilly by the owner/proprietor without recourse to the wholesale trade. The philosophy is that the beers in place on opening on Thursday should all be consumed by the Sunday ('Drink the Barrel Dry' afternoon), ready for restocking for the following week. Cornish organic gins and local wines are also available. P ♫

Cadgwith

Cadgwith Cove Inn

TR12 7JX

☎ (01326) 290513 cadgwithcoveinn.com

Otter Bitter; Sharp's Doom Bar, Atlantic; 4 changing beers (sourced regionally) H

Three-roomed inn tucked away by the harbour and South-West Coastal Path in a compact fishing village on the Lizard Peninsula. Over 300 years old, the pub remains largely unspoilt since its smuggling days. Relics from the local seafaring past and photos of shipwrecks and local scenes adorn the half-panelled walls, while the bar also sports rope handles hanging from the beams (for when the pub lists). Expect some lively singing in the evenings, with itinerant musicians often performng.

Callington

Cornish Ancestor

6 Newport, PL17 7AS (just off A386)
☎ (01579) 208300
**3 changing beers (sourced regionally; often
Salcombe, Teignworthy, Tintagel)** G

A former pet shop, Cornwall's latest micropub serves three real ales by gravity dispense, and up to seven varying real ciders depending on demand. It is a quiet pub – conversation is the main entertainment with no distracting noisy machines. The bar area has a serving worktop, with a beer and cider menu chalkboard. The interestingly shaped interior is furnished throughout with functional barrels, wooden furniture and walls adorned with local pictures. No food, but local takeaways will deliver. Q🕏🕮&♣🍴🚋(12,79)🐾❅

Crowlas

Star Inn

TR20 8DX (on A30, 3 miles E of Penzance)
☎ (01736) 740375
**Penzance Mild, Crowlas Bitter, Potion No 9, Brisons
Bitter; 2 changing beers (sourced nationally)** H

This welcoming free house is the brewery tap for the Penzance Brewing Company, with an attractively priced and extensive range of excellent beers produced at the rear of the pub. There is a good-sized U-shaped bar, with a pool area, no noisy machines, and a cosy lounge space with comfortable seating, as well as an adjacent small meeting room. This is essentially a beer-drinkers' local where friendly conversation is the main entertainment. Don't miss it! 🕮♣P🚋(T1,17)🐾❅

Edmonton

Quarryman Inn

PL27 7JA (just off A39 near the Royal Cornwall showground)
☎ (01208) 816444 ⊕ thequarryman.co.uk
**Otter Bitter; Padstow May Day; 2 changing beers
(sourced locally)** H

A diversion to this characterful and convivial free house, where conversation and banter thrive, is well rewarded. Its quiet, comfortable interior divides into a small public bar with flagstoned flooring, and a larger carpeted lounge, with dining in both areas. Local art and sporting memorabilia feature among the somewhat eclectic decor. The pub is renowned for the quality of its local beers and food. The Padstow and Otter brews are supplemented by other locally made beers. Q🕏🕮🕪♠♣P🚋(11,95) 🐾❅

Falmouth

'front 🍷

Custom House Quay, TR11 3JT
**10 changing beers (sourced nationally; often
Tintagel, Treen's)** H

A warm welcome is guaranteed at this lively cellar-style bar on Custom House Quay. The bar front is decorated with old wooden cask sections, while a large range of ales are dispensed from the 10 handpumps in use. Beers are sourced mainly from Cornwall, catering for all styles and tastes. A popular quiz is held on Sunday evenings. No food is available but you may bring your own. A 10 per cent discount on real ales is offered before 6pm daily. 🕏🕮&≷(Town)♣🐾♪

Beerwolf Books

3-4 Bells Court, TR11 3AZ (up side alley off the shopping street opposite M&S clock)
☎ (01326) 618474 ⊕ beerwolfbooks.com
**6 changing beers (sourced nationally; often
Penzance, St Ives)** H

Pub or bookshop? Actually, it's both! Popular with all ages, this former maritime storage loft with pleasant outside courtyard is tucked away off Market Street. It is accessed via a flight of stairs, at the top of which is the bookshop. To the right is the bar, furnished with six handpulls dispensing an adventurous and ever-changing selection of beers from near and far. Boxes dispense a selection of real local ciders by gravity. No food is served but you may bring your own. 🕏🕮♣🍴🚋🐾❅♪

Chain Locker

Quay Street, TR11 3HH
☎ (01326) 311085 ⊕ thechainlockerfalmouth.co.uk
St Austell Anthem, Tribute, Proper Job, Hicks H**; 2
changing beers (sourced regionally)** H/G

Harbourside pub tucked away down a side street and through an archway, overlooking the small harbour of Custom House Quay. The spacious bar, with a rectangular near-island bar counter, has numerous distinct drinking areas. Subdued lighting, wooden floors, maritime and other local bric-a-brac and a collection of ships' wheels on the ceiling add to the historic atmosphere of this old pub. Food is available all day, and families are welcome. Alfresco drinking is on the quay outside.
🕏🕮🛏🕪&≷(Town)♣🚋🐾❅♪

Moth & the Moon

31 Killigrew Street, TR11 3PW
☎ (01326) 315300
4 changing beers (sourced regionally) H

This small town-centre pub has a dark yet modern, cosy interior. Downstairs, the bar room is open plan with an intimate snug. More seating upstairs surrounds a tiny glass-sided outdoor smoking area in the centre. To the

REAL ALE BREWERIES

Ales of Scilly St Mary's: Isles of Scilly
Atlantic ♦ Indian Queens
Black Flag ♦ Perranporth
Blue Anchor 🍺 Helston
Castle Lostwithiel
Cornish Crown Penzance
Driftwood Spars Trevaunance Cove
Dynamite Valley Ponsanooth
Firebrand ♦ Launceston
Forge Woolley Cross
Harbour Bodmin
Keltek Redruth
Krow Redruth
Lizard Pednavounder
Longhill Whitstone
Mine St Ives
Newquay Brewing Project ♦ Zelah
Padstow Padstow
Penzance 🍺 Crowlas
Seven Stars 🍺 Penryn
Sharp's Rock
Shoals ♦ Porthleven (NEW)
Skinner's (Goodh) ♦ Truro
St Austell ♦ St Austell
St Ives ♦ Hayle
Tintagel Tintagel
Treen's Ponsanooth
Tremethick Grampound
Verdant ♦ Penryn

rear of the pub is a large suntrap terrace, popular in summer. Up to four changing ales are generally available from local breweries. On Tuesdays there is a folk, acoustic and song session night, and an open mic night on Wednesdays. ⊛❀♣♥❄♪

Oddfellows Arms

Quay Hill, TR11 3HA
☎ (01326) 218611
Sharp's Atlantic; house beer (by Sharp's); 1 changing beer (sourced nationally) Ⓗ
This small, unpretentious and traditional single-bar community pub is tucked away up a hilly side street off the town centre. Popular with locals and visitors, it is decorated with old photographs, and has a convivial atmosphere in which to enjoy the three beers normally available. The front bar hosts the dartboard while a small back room has the pool table and real fire in winter. The pub holds jam nights and organises various outings for the locals throughout the year. ⧖(Town)♣♥❄♪

Seaview Inn

Wodehouse Terrace, TR11 3EP
☎ (01326) 311359 ⊕ seaviewinnfalmouth.co.uk
3 changing beers (sourced nationally) Ⓗ
This comfortable, traditional town pub has a large open-plan island bar and, as the name suggests, excellent views over Falmouth harbour and Carrick Roads with all their maritime activity. The locals are a friendly mix of all ages and the pub is child and dog-friendly. A games area hosting darts and pool is at the back of the pub, which also has an excellent Sunday lunchtime carvery. ➔⊛♨⟲♣♥❄

Seven Stars ★ ✓

The Moor, TR11 3QA
☎ (01326) 312111 ⊕ thesevenstarsfalmouth.com
Draught Bass; Sharp's Atlantic, Sea Fury; 3 changing beers (sourced locally; often Treen's) Ⓖ
This timeless, unspoilt town-centre pub has been in the same family for over 170 years and is not to be missed. It has had a sympathetic makeover and has been identified by CAMRA as having a nationally important historic pub interior. It has a lively narrow taproom with beers served on gravity, two quieter rooms at the rear, and an upstairs drinking area created from a former bottle store. The old bottle and jug hatch is still in evidence. Q➔⊛♥❄

Fowey

Galleon Inn

12 Fore Street, PL23 1AQ (in centre of town)
☎ (01726) 833014 ⊕ galleon-inn.co.uk
Firebrand Patchwork Rocket Pale; Sharp's Doom Bar; 3 changing beers (sourced regionally; often Bath Ales, Dartmoor, Sharp's) Ⓗ
This riverside pub in the town centre dates back 400 years. Now fully modernised, it is reached off Fore Street through a glass-covered corridor with a colourful marine life mural. The only free house in Fowey, it features mainly Cornish ales and offers delightful harbour views from the main bar and conservatory. Tables outside overlook the water and there is a heated, sheltered courtyard. A wide range of meals is available daily. Accommodation is available, with some rooms affording river views. ➔⊛♨⟲♿♣♥(24,25)❄♪

Gunnislake

Rising Sun Inn

Calstock Road, PL18 9BX (off A390) SX432711
☎ (01822) 832201

Dartmoor Legend, Jail Ale; 2 changing beers (sourced regionally) Ⓗ
Friendly, oak-beamed 17th-century inn with much charm and character, lying in a conservation area in a rural setting off the beaten track. It serves a good choice of up to four real ales, mainly from Cornish or other West Country breweries. Exposed stone walls and wooden beams allow an extensive display of chinaware, and a beautiful terraced garden affords views over the Tamar Valley. A true community pub hosting various local activties. Q➔⊛♨⟲➔♣♥♥Ⓟ(79,118)❀❄♪

Gunwalloe

Halzephron Inn

TR12 7QB (off A3083, Helston-Lizard road) SW657224
☎ (01326) 240406 ⊕ halzephron-inn.co.uk
Sharp's Doom Bar; 3 changing beers (sourced nationally) Ⓗ
This quiet, welcoming 500-year-old inn was once the haunt of smugglers, who used a shaft from the pub to a still-existing underground tunnel. The two traditional bars remain, the lounge doubling as a restaurant with adjacent snug, with another restaurant area in an extension to the rear. Accommodation is in two en-suite rooms. The pub name derives from the old Cornish 'als yffrin' meaning 'cliffs of hell', and timbers from many nearby shipwrecks were incorporated into its structure. Q➔⊛♨⟲♥Ⓟ(36,37)❀❄

Helston

Blue Anchor

50 Coinagehall Street, TR13 8EL
☎ (01326) 562821 ⊕ spingoales.com
Blue Anchor Flora Daze, Jubilee IPA, Spingo Middle, Spingo Special; 2 changing beers (sourced locally; often Blue Anchor) Ⓗ
A former monks' rest, this 15th-century brewpub is one of the oldest in Britain, changing little over the years and retaining much of its original character. Two separate small bars – one with an open fire – are found to the right of the central passageway, and two sitting rooms to the left, all with slate floors. To the rear are a skittle alley and partly-covered garden area with its own bar. Commemorative special brews may appear on special occasions. Q➔⊛♨⟲♣♥♥❄♪

Launceston

Bell Inn

1 Tower Street, PL15 8BQ (in town centre next to parish church tower)
☎ (01566) 779970 ⊕ bellinnlaunceston.co.uk
House beer (by Holsworthy Ales); 5 changing beers (sourced regionally) Ⓗ
Cosy 16th-century town pub, originally built to house stonemasons erecting the nearby church. Conversation rules in this locals' pub, with an ever-changing range of mostly local beers and two ciders, although the available selection may be reduced out of season. A separate family room, available for local groups to use, features interesting frescoes uncovered when previous owners stripped away decades of modernisation. Cribbage and pub games are played. Food is limited to pasties or pork pies. Q➔⊛♣♥Ⓟ(12,97)❀❄

Lerryn

Ship Inn ✓

Fore Street, PL22 0PT
☎ (01208) 872374 ⊕ theshipinnlerryn.co.uk

Sharp's Doom Bar, Atlantic, Sea Fury; 1 changing beer (sourced locally) Ⓗ
Beside the River Fowey stands this charming free house, a truly traditional village inn. Its quiet and convivial interior divides into distinct areas: a slate-floored bar at the front, where up to four quality ales are offered and an extensive menu served, and at the rear, the popular Willows restaurant, with its interesting home-cooked menu. A raised terrace conservatory extension affords river views. Comfortably furnished throughout, wooden partitions, old photographs and a vintage jukebox add character. Riverside parking is nearby.
Q ☞ ✿ ⌂ ◑ ♣ ❀ ☀ 🎜

Lostwithiel

Globe Inn

3 North Street, PL22 0EG (near railway station, on town side of river bridge)
☎ (01208) 872501 ⊕ globeinn.com
Otter Bitter; Tintagel Cornwall's Pride; 2 changing beers (sourced regionally) Ⓗ
In the narrow streets of this old stannary (tin-mining) town, close to the medieval bridge, stands this cosy 13th-century pub. Conversation thrives in the quiet ambience within, ideal to enjoy a pint. The atmospheric interior accommodates a single bar with several drinking and dining areas. Towards the rear is an intimate, stylish restaurant adjoining a sheltered suntrap patio. An extensive home-cooked menu features fish and game. The varying beer menu offers up to four ales. En-suite accommodation is available. Q ☞ ✿ ⌂ ◑ A ≠ ❀ ☀ 🎜

Mevagissey

Fountain Inn

3 Cliff Street, PL26 6QH
☎ (01726) 842320 ⊕ mevagissey.net/fountain.htm
St Austell Cornish Best Bitter, Hicks, Tribute Ⓗ
Friendly two-bar 15th-century inn near the harbour, with slate-flagged floors, exposed stone walls and low-beamed ceilings. The decor includes photographs and paintings of old Mevagissey. The back Smugglers Bar once housed a pilchard press – a glass plate in the floor covers the former fish-oil sump, which also served as a store for contraband. The menu offers a range of home-cooked dishes, using local produce wherever possible. Nearby buses connect with St Austell and the Lost Gardens of Heligan. Q ☞ ⌂ ◑ ♿ ♣ 🚌 (24) ❀ ☀

Morwenstow

Bush Inn

Crosstown, EX23 9SR (off A39, N of Kilkhampton)
SS208150
☎ (01288) 331242 ⊕ thebushinnmorwenstow.com
St Austell Tribute, Hicks; 1 changing beer (sourced locally; often Forge, Tintagel) Ⓗ
This ancient former chapel dates in parts back to 950AD. Unassuming externally, it is a gem internally and is simply furnished, with slate floors, granite walls and exposed beams in the two small bar rooms, one of which is subdivided into separate drinking areas. Conversation is the main entertainment, although there is occasional live music. A large garden offers outstanding views over the valley and seawards. The guest beer is Cornish or from a nearby Devon brewery such as Otter.
Q ☞ ✿ ⌂ ◑ ♣ ● P 🚌 (217) ❀ ☀ 🎜

Nancenoy

Trengilly Wartha Inn

Nancenoy, TR11 5RP (off B3291 near Constantine)
SW732283
☎ (01326) 340332 ⊕ trengilly.co.uk
3 changing beers (sourced nationally; often Brains, Penzance, Verdant) Ⓗ
This versatile inn lies in extensive grounds that include a lake, in an isolated steeply-wooded valley – the pub's name means 'settlement above the trees'. Originally a farmhouse, it has a variety of furniture and rooms, the wood-beamed bar displaying pictures by local artists. A conservatory extension doubles as a family room. The changing beers increase to three in summer, while a wide-ranging and imaginative food menu uses fresh local produce from named suppliers. Accommodation includes garden rooms and safari tents.
Q ☞ ✿ ⌂ ◑ ♣ P ● ☀ 🎜

Newbridge

Fountain Inn

Newbridge, TR20 8QH (on A3071)
1 changing beer (sourced locally; often Penzance) Ⓖ
Traditional cottage-style Cornish inn, the last pub in the parish of Sancreed, a quiet hamlet on the main Penzance to St Just road. A warm welcome is assured at the Fountain, which boasts beamed ceilings, exposed granite walls and a spectacular inglenook with log-burner. Sunday lunches (booking advised) are served, as well as food and snacks lunchtime and evenings Wednesday to Saturday. There are traditional music jam sessions on alternate Tuesdays, and the odd bingo or quiz night.
Q ☞ ✿ ⌂ ◑ P 🚌 (A17) ❀ ☀

Newquay

Great Western Hotel

Cliff Road, TR7 2NE
☎ (01637) 872010 ⊕ greatwesternnewquay.co.uk
St Austell Tribute, Proper Job; 2 changing beers (sourced locally; often St Austell) Ⓗ
Art Deco-style hotel with a modern, spacious, open-plan bar and dining area that can be segmented into more private function rooms. Large windows to the side and rear give spectacular views to the beach below and across to the harbour and coastline. There is an extensive garden area with similar views. The hotel, which offers comfortable accommodation, is family and dog-friendly and has a strong community focus. It is only minutes walk from the railway station.
☞ ✿ ⌂ ◑ ♿ ≠ ♣ P 🚌 ❀ ☀ 🎜

Red Lion ✅

North Quay Hill, TR7 1HE (NW side of town centre, overlooking the harbour)
☎ (01637) 872195
Sharp's Doom Bar, Atlantic, Sea Fury; 3 changing beers (sourced nationally; often Timothy Taylor) Ⓗ
Deceptively spacious open-plan pub with a flagstoned bar and log-burning stove, overlooking Newquay harbour and sandy beaches along the coast. The kitchen preparation area is clearly visible and offers a wide selection of freshly cooked lunch and evening meals from the standard Stonegate menu. Dogs are welcome in all areas except the restaurant. Locals and tourists are attracted to the live bands playing on Friday and Saturday evenings. The pub is a short walk from the town centre.
☞ ✿ ◑ ♿ ♣ P 🚌 ❀ ☀ 🎜

Padstow

Golden Lion Hotel

Lanadwell Street, PL28 8AN

☎ (01841) 532797 ⊕ goldenlionpadstow.com

Firebrand Patchwork Rocket Pale; Sharp's Doom Bar; Tintagel Castle Gold ⊞

Padstow's oldest pub is well over 400 years old and still used for stabling the famous Old 'Oss, which makes its energetic appearance every May Day during the famous 'Obby 'Oss celebrations. The busy, low-beamed public bar is partitioned to create a family dining area, while the quieter lounge is spacious and comfortable. There is also a seated patio outside. The pub is a little way from the bustling harbour area, but is often quite crowded during the summer season. ► ✿ ☎ ◑ ◵ ▲ ♞ (11,56) ✿ ☎

Penzance

Dock Inn

17 Quay Street, TR18 4BD

☎ (01736) 362833 ⊕ thedockinnpenzance.co.uk

Blue Anchor Spingo Middle; Penzance Potion No 9; Sharp's Doom Bar ⊞

Old one-time fishermen's pub near the dockside and close to the Isles of Scilly ferry pier. The pub extends through two old cottages with the bar in the upper level and a comfortable lounge/dining area in the lower, beyond which is a pool room. The decor includes a large picture mirror as well as a mix of nautical and mining pictures and bric-a-brac, and a stuffed bird in a cage. Meals are served Wednesday-Saturday evenings and Sunday lunchtimes. Q ► ✿ ☎ ◑ ◵ ♣ ♟ ♞ ✿ ☎ ♫

Farmer's Arms

38 Causewayhead, TR18 2ST

☎ (01736) 362627

Sharp's Sea Fury; Timothy Taylor Landlord; 1 changing beer ⊞

At the top of a pedestrianised shopping street, this quirky, traditional pub is not to be missed. The long, narrow bar area has a beamed ceiling and wooden floor, tables and old fixed bench seating, and wood panelling. On one wall at the rear is a collection of posters of famous films, but with a difference – they have been given Cornish themes! A music area hosts live bands on Friday evenings and an open mic on Sunday afternoons. ✿ ⇌ ♣ ♞ ☎

Perranwell

Royal Oak

TR3 7PX

☎ (01872) 863175 ⊕ theroyaloakperranwellstation.co.uk

4 changing beers (sourced regionally; often Exeter, Padstow, Penzance) ⊞

This small 18th-century cottage-style village pub prioritises both good beer and food. Most tables are set for dining, but drinkers are equally welcome, as the many regulars at the bar will testify. Bookings for meals are advisable, especially in the evening. The beers vary frequently and are mostly from Cornish or Devon breweries. The pub holds monthly quiz nights and fundraising events for local charities. Q ► ✿ ◑ ⇌ ♣ ♞ ♟ (36,46) ✿ ☎ ♫

Piece

Countryman Inn

TR16 6SG (on Four Lanes-Pool road) SW679398

☎ (01209) 215960 ⊕ countrymaninns.com

Courage Best Bitter ⊞**, Directors** ⊞**/**Ⓖ**; St Austell Tribute; Theakston Best Bitter; 1 changing beer (sourced locally; often Treen's)** ⊞

A traditional and friendly country pub and former miners' shop, run by the same landlord for over 35 years. Built in the 19th century, it is set amid the historic local mining landscape, close to walking and cycle trails. There are two bars, the larger with a granite fireplace and cast-iron range. The smaller bar room is more in a public bar style and is where families are welcome. There is entertainment most evenings and Sunday lunchtimes. ► ✿ ◑ ▲ ♣ ♟ (42) ✿ ☎ ♫

Polbathic

Halfway House

PL11 3EY (on A387 between Trerulefoot and Torpoint)

☎ (01503) 232986

St Austell Proper Job; house beer (by Salcombe); 1 changing beer (sourced regionally; often Firebrand) ⊞

A 16th-century former coaching inn, village local and community library. It is surprisingly large inside, with separate public and lounge bars, and further rooms beyond that used for dining. The smallish 'public' is the normal focus of the pub's daily life, hosting the pool table and dartboard and boasting an unusual stone fireplace above which is mounted an old wagon wheel. A large beer garden at the rear is on a steep hillside and reached via flights of steps. ► ✿ ☎ ◑ ◵ ♣ ♞ ♟ (72) ✿ ♫

Polmear

Ship Inn ⊘

Polmear Hill, PL24 2AR (on A3082)

☎ (01726) 812540

Sharp's Doom Bar; St Austell Proper Job; 2 changing beers (sourced regionally; often Dartmoor, Wadworth) ⊞

Cosy free house that is popular with locals and summer visitors. It is close to Par beach and the coastal footpath (boats used to tie up at the quay behind the pub). There are several drinking and dining areas, with wagon wheels forming an unusual partition. It is an ideal family pub, boasting a large garden and play area, with a function room upstairs and a big car park. Occasional beer festivals are held, as well as unusual competitions for charity. Q ► ✿ ◑ ◵ ▲ ♣ ♞ ♟ (25) ✿ ☎ ♫

Polperro

Blue Peter Inn

Quay Road, PL13 2QZ (far end of W side of harbour)

☎ (01503) 272743 ⊕ thebluepeterinn.com

Firebrand Patchwork Rocket Pale; Otter Bitter; St Austell Tribute; 4 changing beers (sourced regionally; often Dartmoor) ⊞

Named after the naval flag, this friendly inn is reached up a steep flight of steps near the quay, and is the only pub in the village with a sea view. In summer it offers up to four ales from Cornwall and Devon, with a varied menu of home-cooked dishes available all day. Featuring low beams, wooden floors, unusual souvenirs and work by local artists, the pub is popular with locals, fishermen and visitors. ► ✿ ◑ ▲ ♣ ✿ ☎ ♫

Crumplehorn Inn

The Old Mill, Crumplehorn, PL13 2RJ (on A387, top of town near coach park)

☎ (01503) 272348 ⊕ thecrumplehorninn.co.uk

St Austell Tribute, Proper Job; 4 changing beers (sourced locally; often Sharp's, Tintagel) Ⓗ
Once a mill and mentioned in the Domesday Book, this 14th-century inn at the entrance to the village still has a working waterwheel outside. The split-level bar has three comfortable areas with low-beamed ceilings and flagstone floors. A spacious outside patio by the millstream offers large parasols as sunshades. A varied menu includes locally sourced food. B&B or self-catering accommodation is available. It is a ½-mile walk from the pub down to the harbour. ♿☆✎◗▲P🚫(72,73)🐾🛜♫

Portscatho

Plume of Feathers
The Square, TR2 5HW
☎ (01872) 580321 ⊕ plumeoffeathers-roseland.com
St Austell Tribute, Proper Job; 2 changing beers (sourced nationally; often Banks's, St Austell, Timothy Taylor) Ⓗ
Built in 1756, the Plume is the second-oldest building in the village, and the hub of the local community. Inside is a traditional wood-beamed, slate-walled pub with cosy nooks and a separate restaurant. The pub is in the Cask Club for St Austell brewery's small batch beers. The selection of St Austell ales may be supplemented by a changing beer, for example Ringwood, Hobgoblin and Shepherd Neame. Food is home-cooked and locally sourced. The pub hosts events such as the August regatta. Q♿☆✎◗▲🚶🚫(50)🐾🛜

Poughill

Preston Gate Inn
Poughill Road, EX23 9ET (just outside Bude, on Sandymouth Bay road) SS224077
☎ (01288) 354017 ⊕ prestongateinn.co.uk
Firebrand Patchwork Rocket; Sharp's Atlantic, Sea Fury; 1 changing beer (sourced locally; often Tintagel) Ⓗ
This cosy 16th-century building, originally two cottages, has been a village pub since 1983. The spacious U-shaped room hosts a dartboard at one end of the bar, while the other, roomier, end has more seating and a roaring log fire in winter. Conversation rules here, and the pub supports darts and quiz teams. Meals include steak nights and fish & chip lunchtimes. The beer range may reduce in winter and the cider varies. The name Preston comes from the Cornish for priest. Q♿◗▲♣🚶P🚫(128,218)🐾🛜♫

Quintrell Downs

Two Clomes
East Road, TR8 4PD (on A392)
☎ (01637) 871163
Sharp's Doom Bar; 2 changing beers (sourced regionally; often Dartmoor, Sharp's) Ⓗ
Named after the two fireside ovens situated either side of the open fireplace – which is now fitted with a wood-burning stove – this 18th-century free house is popular for eating out. Various extensions to the original building have added a separate restaurant (booking is advisable, even in winter). Background music plays and there is a TV screen for sporting occasions. The pub is conveniently situated on a main route into Newquay and close to campsites. ♿☆◗♿▲≉♣P🚫(21,91)🐾🛜

Rilla Mill

Manor House Inn
PL17 7NT (N and E of Liskeard, off B3254)

☎ (01579) 362354 ⊕ manorhouserilla.co.uk
Dartmoor Legend, Jail Ale; 1 changing beer (sourced locally) Ⓗ
Comfortable community pub and restaurant in the Lynher Valley, on the edge of Bodmin Moor. There are three rooms, one of which has slated and carpeted flooring, the other two are restaurant areas. The changing beers are mainly from Cornish breweries and meals generally feature local produce. The 17th-century pub is allegedly haunted by three ghosts. Nearby are the open-air Sterts Theatre and a dairy that makes a variety of Cornish cheeses. Dartmoor's Jail Ale may alternate with Legend. Q♿☆◗♣P🚫(236)🐾🛜♫

St Ann's Chapel

Rifle Volunteer Inn
PL18 9HL (on A390)
☎ (01822) 851551 ⊕ riflevolunteer.com
St Austell Tribute; 2 changing beers (sourced regionally; often Dartmoor, Stannary) Ⓗ
Former mine captain's house, converted to a coaching inn during the mid-19th century. The main bar has been extended to accommodate a conservatory, popular with diners for the view over the garden. Meals are cooked using locally sourced ingredients. A separate public bar caters for more dedicated drinkers and has a pool table and dartboard. The changing beers are usually from local breweries. The pub offers panoramic views across the Tamar Valley and is in good walking country. Q♿☆◗♿♣P🚫(79)🐾🛜

St Ives

Pilchard Press Alehouse
Wharf Road, TR26 1LF (in alleyway between Talay Thai and Cornish Pasty Shop)
☎ (01736) 791665
6 changing beers (sourced locally; often Penzance, Treen's) Ⓗ/🧊
Opened in 2016, this tiny bar in an old stone-walled cellar is Cornwall's first micropub. Located up an alleyway off the harbourside near the Lifeboat Inn, it can be difficult to find, but is nevertheless worth seeking out. A friendly little pub with a wood-topped bar, it is furnished with bar stools and a few tables and chairs, offering space for around 20-25 customers. It offers up to six real ales, mainly from Cornish microbreweries, and ciders. Q♿▲≉🚶(T2,17)🐾♫

St John

St John Inn
PL11 3AW
☎ (01752) 829299 ⊕ stjohninn.co.uk
Draught Bass; 2 changing beers (sourced nationally; often Teignworthy, Woodforde's) Ⓗ
Reached down narrow country lanes, this 16th-century village pub and community shop is constructed from two former cottages. The pub is cosy, with an L-shaped bar room with beamed ceiling, floor of red tiles, wooden furniture and a warming open fire for winter. A cosy snug opposite the bar, a patio with seating at the front, and an attractive beer garden add to the appeal of this picturesque and welcoming pub. Live events are hosted in a semi-permanent marquee. Q♿☆▲♣🚶P🚫🐾♫

St Just

Star Inn ✔
1 Fore Street, TR19 7LL
☎ (01736) 788767

St Austell Cornish Best Bitter, Tribute, Proper Job; 3 changing beers (sourced regionally; often St Austell) ⓗ

No food, just excellent beer and friendly banter at this traditional pub. The atmospheric main bar is enhanced by its dark, quirky decor, open fire and mining and rowing artefacts. The wood-beamed ceiling is adorned with flags, mostly of the Celtic nations. A room opposite doubles as a meeting place for community groups, while an enclosed beer garden is at the rear. The pub is part of St Austell's select Cask Club, and offers the brewery's small batch beers when available. ♿❀&▲🅿❀🐾

St Mabyn

St Mabyn Inn

Churchtown, PL30 3BA

☎ (01208) 841266 ⊕ stmabyninn.com

Firebrand Bootleg Billy, Patchwork Rocket Pale; Sharp's Doom Bar; Tintagel Cornwall's Pride ⓗ

Next to the church stands this attractive 17th-century free house, the village local where conversation thrives. A charming traditional pub, it features a single bar with adjoining snug, games room, well-appointed restaurant and extensive beer garden. Open fires, wood furnishings including settles, stained-glass partitions and windows add character, complemented by an interesting collection of toby jugs, horse brasses and vintage advertising. With four quality ales, local cider, and ever-changing food choice (including Thai nights), this pub is worth seeking out. Q♿❀🕚&▲♣🅿🚆(96)❀🐾♪

St Mary's: Isles of Scilly

Atlantic

Hugh Street, TR21 0PL

☎ (01720) 422417 ⊕ atlanticinnscilly.co.uk

St Austell Cornish Best Bitter, Tribute, Proper Job, Hicks; 1 changing beer (sourced regionally) ⓗ

Don't be put off by the 'restaurant' sign outside – this is a busy pub and hotel. The spacious open-plan interior has distinct drinking areas, and a separate dining room offering a good range of food. Bar meals are also available. Food is an important part of the operation, but this is also a pub for beer and conversation. Children are welcome until 9pm. A small patio to the rear overlooks the harbour. Q♿❀🛏🕚▲🐾🗢

Saltash

Cockleshell

73 Fore Street, PL12 6AF

☎ 07776 343673

House beer (by Atlantic); 3 changing beers (often Harbour, Summerskills, Treen's) Ⓖ

This independently-owned micropub in the centre of Saltash was newly opened in the summer of 2020 in a converted retail unit. It has no TV, loud music or electronic gaming machines to distract from the convivial atmosphere. A selection of unusual real ales and ciders can be found here, plus a range of wines and gins. National brands are also on offer as well as five craft keg beers. Q🗢♣🚆(2,72)🐾❀

Two Bridges

13 Albert Road, PL12 4EB

☎ (01752) 242244 ⊕ the2bridges.co.uk

3 changing beers (sourced locally) ⓗ

On a steep hill above the River Tamar and adjacent to Saltash railway station, this small, attractive building is a real locals' pub, but still welcoming to visitors. It features wooden furniture and bench seats along the walls,

together with old local photos of the area. Three ever-changing beers are on offer, usually from local breweries. Up some steps at the rear is a pleasant, well-furnished garden with fine views of the two famous Tamar bridges that span the river. ♿❀🗢♣🚆(2,72)❀🗢♪

South Petherwin

Frog & Bucket

PL15 7LP (just off B3254)

☎ (01566) 776988 ⊕ frogandbucket.co.uk

3 changing beers (sourced nationally) ⓗ

Roomy purpose-built village pub, opened in 1989, despite local opposition, and now a friendly focus for community social life and welcoming to all ages. Up to three varying guest ales are on offer. Off the main bar are a separate lounge and a games room, and two other rooms, one of which can double as a restaurant or function room. The pub offers fine Dartmoor views and is a focus for vintage vehicles in summer. Q♿❀🕚&♣🅿🚆(236)❀🗢

Tintagel

Olde Malt House

Fore Street, PL34 0DA

☎ (01840) 770461 ⊕ malthousetintagel.com

Tintagel Castle Gold, Cornwall's Pride, Harbour Special ⓗ

This charming 14th-century inn retains many of its original features. Located in the heart of the historic village of Tintagel, the pub has a suntrap front courtyard offering country views and spectacular sunsets. It serves three real ales from the local brewery and also offers a varied food menu. There are three distinct drinking areas, each of which can seat up to 20 people. Accommodation is available at reasonable prices. Q❀🛏🕚▲🚆(95)❀

Towan Cross

Victory Inn

TR4 8BN

☎ (01209) 890359

Firebrand Patchwork Rocket Pale; St Austell Tribute; Tintagel Arthur's Ale; 1 changing beer (sourced locally) ⓗ

This welcoming family-run free house, where you may enjoy fine Cornish ales and locally sourced quality food, is worth a visit. Originally a 17th-century coaching inn, opened to quench the thirst of local miners, it now satisfies numerous locals and tourists. Set on the clifftop over Porthtowan, its quaint open-plan single bar interior separates into several drinking and dining areas, extending to a conservatory. The spacious beer garden features raised decking and extensive seating in a restful setting. Q♿❀🕚▲♣🅿🚆(304,315)❀🗢

Trebarwith Strand

Mill House Inn

Trebarwith Strand, PL34 0HD (off B3263, near Tintagel)

SX058865

☎ (01840) 770200 ⊕ themillhouseinn.co.uk

Tintagel Castle Gold, Harbour Special; 1 changing beer (sourced locally; often Sharp's, Tintagel) ⓗ

Converted 16th-century corn mill and waterwheel set beside a stream in a deep, wooded valley. This friendly inn has a stone-flagged bar area that is accessed up a flight of steps beside an adjacent drinking terrace. The restaurant extension offers an imaginative menu that changes daily. Though primarily a food and

accommodation establishment, the bar nevertheless functions as a pub for drinkers, with a mix of local beers mostly from nearby Tintagel Brewery.
Q☺🏠🍽◐♣P♥🐾📶♪

Treen (Zennor)

Gurnard's Head

TR26 3DE (on B3306, Land's End to St Ives coast road)
☎ (01736) 796928 ⊕ gurnardshead.co.uk
3 changing beers (sourced locally; often St Ives) Ⓗ
Situated on the spectacular St Just to St Ives coastal road and close to the South West Coast Path, this welcoming and strikingly coloured inn takes its name from the nearby headland. It has a large bar with a log fire, cosy snug and stylish restaurant, with wooden furnishings and local artworks adding to the ambience. Beers are always from Cornish microbreweries, while daily food choices reflect the availability of local produce. With accommodation available, this popular stopover for coast path and moorland walkers.
Q☺🏠🍽◐♣🐾P🐾📶

Tresco: Isles of Scilly

New Inn

Townshill, New Grimsby, TR24 0QQ
☎ (01720) 423006 ⊕ tresco.co.uk/staying-on-tresco/the-new-inn
3 changing beers (sourced locally; often St Austell, St Ives) Ⓗ
Excellent old pub near New Grimsby harbour. The 'Driftwood Bar' is the heart of the island community, and is adorned with wood from old wrecks and other marine relics. Extensions to the garden and a covered pavilion add to the pub's attractions. The varying beers are mostly from Cornish breweries, with a couple of St Austell brews generally present. Occasional bank holiday beer festivals are held. ☺🏠🍽◐♣🐾📶♪

Trevaunance Cove

Driftwood Spars ✅

Quay Road, TR5 0RT
☎ (01872) 552428 ⊕ driftwoodspars.co.uk
Driftwood Spars Blue Hills Bitter; 5 changing beers (sourced locally; often Driftwood Spars, Tintagel) Ⓗ
Friendly, vibrant community brewpub with accommodation. A former 17th-century mine warehouse and sail loft, it features three wood-beamed bars on different levels, with lead-light windows and granite fireplaces. The decor is mainly nautical and shipwreck-themed. Upstairs, the restaurant affords panoramic sea views, above that is a cliffside beer garden. The lower beer garden faces the Driftwood Spars brewery, whose beers are always present on the bar. There's regular live entertainment, including theatre, and the pub holds three annual beer festivals.
Q☺🏠🍽◐♣🐾P🐾(U1A,316)🐾📶♪

Trewellard

Trewellard Arms

Trewellard Road, TR19 7TA (on B3318/B3306 jct)
☎ (01736) 788634 ⊕ goodpubfoodlandsend.com
4 changing beers (sourced regionally; often Exeter, St Austell, Tintagel) Ⓗ
A warm welcome is assured at this family-run free house in what was formerly a mining counthouse, then a hotel. There is a cosy, beamed single bar, and restaurant with a secluded dining space. Log burners enhance the homely atmosphere. Taste of the West silver-award-winning

home-cooked food is served. The beer menu varies constantly with up to four regionally sourced ales and two ciders. Outside is a paved patio area where occasional beer festivals are held.
Q☺🏠🍽◐♣🐾P🐾📶♪

Truro

Old Ale House

7 Quay Street, TR1 2HD (near the bus station)
☎ (01872) 219462 ⊕ theoldalehousetruro.co.uk
6 changing beers (sourced nationally) Ⓗ
This friendly and lively city-centre pub is housed in a former milliner's shop. The lower main bar, which is mainly for the casual drop-in drinker, is atmospheric with beamed ceilings, subtle lighting, wooden flooring, various artefacts and plentiful seating. Up to six real ales and several ciders are offered, plus an impressive range of craft ales and 14 foreign beers. Upstairs is a quieter drinking area and function room. Customers may bring their own food. Live music features frequently.
Q☺🚻♣🐾🐾📶♪

Tywardreath

New Inn

Fore Street, PL24 2QP
☎ (01726) 813073 ⊕ thenewinncornwall.co.uk
Bath Ales Gem Ⓖ; Draught Bass; St Austell Tribute, Proper Job; Timothy Taylor Landlord; 1 changing beer (sourced nationally) Ⓗ
This classic village pub, built in the mid-18th century by mine owners, is a perfect example of a community local and the hub of village life. Groups meet here regularly, and fêtes are held in the extensive gardens. Although tied to a brewery, the landlord serves a guest beer and Draught Bass, which the pub is covenanted to sell in perpetuity. Good conversation and regular live music provide the entertainment. There is a separate restaurant area to the rear. Q☺🏠◐ 🐾P🐾(24)🐾📶

Vogue

Star Inn ✅

St Day Road, TR16 5NP (on Redruth to St Day road)
☎ (01209) 820242 ⊕ starinnvogue.biz
5 changing beers Ⓗ
This innovative community village inn hosts a library branch, hairdressing salon, boules court, campsite, meetings and social events, plus music, quizzes and karaoke. Lively, welcoming and family-friendly, the pub slakes the thirst of a diverse custom offering an ever-changing range of beers plus good-quality home-cooked food. The cosy, relaxed and characterful interior accommodates a single bar, quiet lounge and separate restaurant. Outside is sheltered seating, an extensive garden with reinforced marquee, and ample parking. Worth seeking out. Q☺🏠◐♿🐾♣🐾P🐾(40)🐾📶

Zennor

Tinner's Arms

TR26 3BY (off B3306 St Ives to St Just coast road)
☎ (01736) 796927 ⊕ tinnersarms.com
House beer (by Sharp's); 2 changing beers (sourced locally) Ⓗ
Popular with locals, walkers and tourists, this atmospheric, ancient granite pub is nestled next to the church, in an idyllic setting in a picturesque village with associations to local mermaid legends and DH Lawrence. The ambience of the single bar is enhanced by exposed wood, granite walls and rustic furnishings. There is also a

suntrap beer garden. The adjacent restaurant features local produce – booking is advised.

🥘⊗🛏◐●♣♠P🅿️😋📶📶♪♫

Breweries

Ales of Scilly

2b Porthmellon Industrial Estate, St Mary's, Isles of Scilly, TR21 0JY ☎ **07737 721599** ⊕ **alesofscilly.co.uk**

⊗ Opened in 2001, Ales of Scilly is the most south-westerly brewery in Britain. Several island pubs and restaurants are regularly supplied, plus the occasional mainland beer festival. Special one-off beers are produced during the year in celebration of significant island events. Most real ale output occurs during the busier holiday months (March-October), although some production is maintained during winter for local pubs. ‼🍺♦

Challenger (ABV 4.2%) BITTER
Amber best bitter with faint malt and hop nose. A refreshing, light beer with apricot flavours throughout and gentle malty bitterness.

Atlantic

Unit 5, Indian Queens Trading Estate, Warren Road, Indian Queens, TR9 6TL
☎ **(01726) 457506** ⊕ **atlanticbrewery.com**

⊗ Specialist microbrewery producing organic and vegan ales. All ales are unfiltered and finings-free. There are eleven core brews including four food-matched dining ales developed with Michelin-recognised chef Nathan Outlaw. Casks are supplied locally and to London, with bottle-conditioned beers available nationally. ♦LIVE V♦

Soul Citra (ABV 4%) PALE
A gold beer with citrus hop aroma. Smooth and creamy mouthfeel with dominant citrus hop flavours. Moderate bitterness and sweetness.

Azores (ABV 4.2%) GOLD
Unfined gold beer. Citrus and resinous hops dominate the aroma and taste with tropical fruits. Refreshing bitter and dry finish.

Earl Grey PA (ABV 4.5%) SPECIALITY
Cloudy amber organic speciality ale. Hop aroma leads to powerful citrus fruit flavours becoming intense. Fairly bitter and dry.

Elderflower Blonde (ABV 4.5%) SPECIALITY
Pale yellow, light, crisp floral beer with elderflower nose. Elderflower and gooseberry fruits with soft citrus and pine hops flavours.

Mandarina Cornovia (ABV 4.5%) SPECIALITY
Pale gold speciality beer with full mandarin citrus fruit flavour matched by firm biscuit malt and resin/earthy hop notes.

Masala Chai PA (ABV 4.5%) SPECIALITY
Sea Salt Stout (ABV 4.5%) SPECIALITY
Coffee stout. Roast malt, chocolate and toffee aroma. Complex smoky malt with underlying resinous hops and peanuts, saltiness and sweetness.

Simcotica (ABV 4.5%) GOLD
Blue (ABV 4.8%) PORTER
Smooth, rich porter with heavy roast malt aroma and taste. Smoky liquorice, bitter coffee and chocolate flavours with sweet fruit.

Honey Ale (ABV 4.8%) SPECIALITY
Fistral Pilsner (ABV 5.2%) SPECIALITY
Full-flavoured copper wheat beer. Sweet, stone-fruit flavours blend with biscuit malt and citrus hops. Malt finish with hops and dryness.

Black Flag

Unit 1D, New Road, Perranporth, TR6 0DL
☎ **(01872) 858004** ⊕ **blackflagbrewery.com**

⊗ Black Flag began brewing in 2013 and relocated to Perranporth in 2019. A new eight-barrel plant was installed in 2020 and the brewery began producing a wider range of beer styles using organic malts. All beers are unfined and unpasteurised, available in cans, bottles and kegs. Growlers of draught keg are sold or refilled in the taproom where wood-fired pizzas are a popular eat in or takeaway. ♦LIVE♦

Blue Anchor

🍺 **50 Coinagehall Street, Helston, TR13 8EL**
☎ **(01326) 562821** ⊕ **spingoales.com**

☺A 15th century, family-run, thatched brewpub. The oldest continuously brewing in the country. Home to the world famous Spingo ales, from the brewery at the rear of the Blue Anchor, using its own well water. It was built sometime in the 18th century. Beforehand, Spingo was brewed within the confines of the pub. The Spingo name derives from the word 'Stingo', used in the old English dictionary of 1625, to describe British strong beer. ‼♦LIVE

Flora Daze (ABV 4%) BITTER
Pale brown bitter with light flowery aroma, caramel and balanced malt, fruit and hops in the mouth. Lingering bitter finish.

Jubilee IPA (ABV 4.5%) PALE
Amber premium bitter with malty, fruity hop nose and taste, balanced by fresh hop bitterness. Gentle bitter finish with sweet malt.

Ben's Stout (ABV 4.8%) STOUT
Creamy dark stout with coffee roast aroma. Roast malt with liquorice and cherry flavours. Bittersweet finish with apples and cloves.

Spingo Middle (ABV 5%) BITTER
Heavy tawny ale with dominant malt and balancing peppery hop bitterness. Nuts, spices and dates flavours. Long, malty, earthy finish.

Spingo Special (ABV 6.6%) STRONG
Smooth, red, strong ale. Red wine aroma. Kaleidoscope of powerful sweet stone fruits, smoky malt and hop flavours. Vinous and earthy.

Bluntrock

Unit 8, Higher Pityme Industrial Estate, St Minver, Wadebridge, PL27 6NS

Office: 1a Eddystone Road, Wadebridge, PL27 7AL
⊕ **bluntrockbrewery.co.uk**

This nanobrewery commenced brewing as Lowlands Brewing in four converted shipping containers in 2021, using a one-barrel plant. It rebranded to Bluntrock in 2022. It will soon have an additional 10-barrel plant on a site nearby. Its tap has regular music and food events, details on website or social media. ♦GF V♦

Castle SIBA

Unit 9A, 7 Restormel Industrial Estate, Liddicoat Road, Lostwithiel, PL22 0HG ☎ **07880 349032**
⊕ **castlebrewery.co.uk**

⊗ The brewery was established in 2007 using a one-barrel plant. A new 200-litre plant was added in 2016. All brews are unfined and are suitable for vegetarians and vegans. The brewery carries out its own bottling, and some for other breweries. 🍺♦LIVE V

Golden Gauntlet (ABV 4%) GOLD

Light, golden bitter with gentle fruity nose. Heavy malt and bitter taste dominate the fruity hop, persisting into the finish.
Restormel Gold (ABV 4.1%) PALE
Cornish Best Bitter (ABV 4.2%) BITTER
Once a Knight (ABV 5%) BITTER

Cornish Crown

End Unit, Badger's Cross Farm, Badger's Cross, Penzance, TR20 8XE
☎ (01736) 449029 ☎ 07870 998986
⊕ cornishcrown.co.uk

⊠ This six-barrel brewery was launched in 2012 on a farm high above Mounts Bay by the brewer, and landlord, of the Crown Inn, Penzance, which acts as the brewery tap. Beer is available locally and as far as the Southampton Arms, London. !!LIVE

Causeway (ABV 4.1%) BITTER
Tawny bitter with a malty caramel nose. Initially malty with resinous, citrus hop bitterness emerging. Stone fruits. Long bitter finish.
Helter India Pale Ale (ABV 4.2%) PALE
Madagascan Vanilla Porter (ABV 5.2%) PORTER

Driftwood Spars SIBA

Driftwood Brewery, Trevaunance Cove, St Agnes, TR5 0RY
☎ (01872) 552591 ⊕ driftwoodsparsbrewery.com

⊠ Established in 2000, production on the custom-built, five-barrel plant expanded with the installation of additional fermentation and conditioning capacity. Annual production now stands at 1,500 barrels. A small batch beer range named Cove is produced, from which a portion of sales income is donated to local charities. !!▤◆LIVE

Spars (ABV 3.8%) BITTER
Refreshing bitter with a balance of sweet malt and grassy, earthy hops, hedgerow and stone fruit flavours. Rising bitter finish.
Blue Hills Bitter (ABV 4%) BITTER
Amber with caramel malt aroma. Refreshing balance of non-citrus hops, malt and apple fruit. Long bitter, dry finish.
Bolster's Blood (ABV 5%) PORTER
Dark brown porter. Coal-smoke and peaty malt flavour with dark chocolate and dried fruits. Bitterness and burnt malt persist.
Lou's Brew (ABV 5%) GOLD
Golden beer laden with orange and grapefruit flavours, spice notes and some malt. Tropical fruit aromas and long-lasting tangy bitterness.
Stippy Stappy (ABV 5.5%) IPA
Alfie's Revenge (ABV 6.5%) STRONG
Rich strong red ale with dominant malt aroma and flavour. Kaleidoscope of dried and stone fruit, sweetness and light bitterness.

Dynamite Valley

Units 5 & 6, Viaduct Works, Frog Hill, Ponsanooth, TR3 7JW
☎ (01872) 864532 ☎ 07990 887613
⊕ dynamitevalley.com

⊠ Dynamite Valley was set up in 2015 following a successful crowdfunding campaign and is located close to a historic gunpowder site near Falmouth. Beers are influenced by European and US beer styles. The brewery has expanded into bottling and canning. It has acquired the Rebel Brewery brand name and beers. ▤

Gold Rush (ABV 4%) BITTER
Smooth gold bitter with light malt nose. Malt dominates throughout with bitterness, honey, apricot and pear drops. Long malty, bitter finish.
Ambrys Cornish Amber Ale (ABV 4.3%) BITTER
Kennall Vale Pale (ABV 4.3%) PALE
Viaduct Pale Ale (ABV 4.4%) PALE
Gold, premium pale ale with honey and grapefruit aroma. Bitter citrus and pineapple hops and biscuit malt flavours with barley sugar.
TNT IPA (ABV 4.8%) PALE
Golden premium pale ale with malt and hop aroma. Heavy citrus hop bitterness with toffee apples, pear drops and malt balance.
Black Charge (ABV 5%) STOUT
Black oatmeal style sweet stout. Powerful flavours of roast coffee, dark chocolate, malt and molasses throughout. Bitter, dry, short finish.
Frog Hill Cornish IPA (ABV 6%) IPA

Firebrand SIBA

Unit 2, Southgate Technology Park, Pennygillam Industrial Estate, Launceston, PL15 7ED
☎ (01566) 86069 ⊕ firebrandbrewing.co.uk

⊠ Firebrand began brewing in 2008 and has steadily increased its range and production since then. The award-winning brewery currently uses a 12-barrel plant. Beers are available in pubs across Cornwall. The tap has regular music events, details on the website. !!▤◆LIVE ✦

Bootleg Billy (ABV 4%) PALE
Patchwork Rocket Pale (ABV 4.2%) PALE
A golden session pale ale with aroma of malt with mixed citrus and non-citrus hops. Assertive bitter hop dominance in the mouth balanced by sweet and faintly roast malt and gentle dryness, all running the long finish. Grapefruit, tropical and vine fruits are all present.
West Coast Session IPA (ABV 4.2%) PALE
An Howl (ABV 4.8%) PALE
Beast of Bodmin (ABV 5%) BITTER
Ruby red premium bitter with a light bite of bitter fruitiness. Strong malt with hints of molasses, vine and dried fruit softening to mellow toffee/caramel. Peppery hop bitterness. Prunes, pears and apricot fruit tang. Fairly short finish with bitterness fading last.

Forge

Wilderland, Woolley Cross, EX23 9PW
☎ (01288) 331669 ☎ 07837 487800
✉ forgebrewerybeer@gmail.com

⊠ This multi-award-winning brewery was set up near Bideford in Devon by Dave Lang, who commenced brewing in 2008 using a five-barrel plant. The brewery relocated to Cornwall in 2017. ◆LIVE

Discovery (ABV 3.8%) BITTER
Gold-coloured bitter bursting with hops from start to finish. Some subtle hints of fruit to the discerning palate too.
Blonde (ABV 4%) BLOND
Pale ale with light citrus aroma. Zesty citrus hop in the mouth balanced by a little malt. Bitter and dry.
Litehouse (ABV 4.3%) PALE
Pale ale with faint tropical fruit hop aroma. Light balance of sweet malt and hop bitterness fading into a short finish.
IPA (ABV 4.5%) PALE
Rev Hawker (ABV 4.6%) BITTER
Tamar Source (ABV 4.6%) BITTER
Premium bitter with malt and earthy hop aroma. Dominant crystal malt with bitterness and sweet stone fruit flavours. Bitterness rises.

Goodh SIBA

Unit 3, Moorland Road Business Park, Indian Queens, TR9 6GX
☎ (01726) 839970 ☎ 07834 407964
⊕ goodhbrew.com

Goodh Brewing has expanded rapidly since its birth as the new owner of Woodmans. It can now produce 5,000 litres per week and focuses on canned and kegged beers with numerous variations and names across a wide range of styles. The brewery also runs a tap in Truro, the Old Print Works. ☛

Harbour

Trekillick Farm, Kirland, Bodmin, PL30 5BB
☎ (01208) 832131 ☎ 07870 305063
⊕ harbourbrewing.com

⊠ Harbour is an innovative brewery founded on the outskirts of Bodmin in 2011. Brewed using local spring water, the regular beers are established in an increasing number of outlets. A new 30-barrel plant was installed in 2016, and more conditioning tanks in 2017. As well as producing cask and keg, bottling and canning is also done onsite. ♦

Light (ABV 3.7%) BLOND
Yellow beer with citrus hop aroma. Dominant zesty citrus hops with some pineapple and pear drops. Long hoppy finish.

Daymer Extra Pale (ABV 3.8%) PALE
Pale ale with citrus aroma. Lemon and lime dominate with grainy malt and earthy hop. Bitterness remains, sweetness fades, becoming dry.

Amber (ABV 4%) BITTER
Pale brown bitter with a floral hop aroma and malt. Biscuit malt throughout with apple, peach and plum, balanced by hops.

Cornish Bitter (ABV 4%) BITTER
Amber bitter with malty, hoppy nose. Biscuit malt and spicy hops dominate the flavour with sweet fruit and lasting bitterness.

New Zealand Gold (ABV 4.2%) GOLD
Golden ale with light hop nose. Strong pine needle hop flavour. Bitter, sweet and dry throughout.

Ellensberg (ABV 4.3%) PALE
Amber ale with powerful tropical and citrus aroma. Strong juicy mango and grapefruit flavour. Both sweet and bitter. Long finish.

Session IPA (ABV 4.3%) PALE
India Brown Ale (ABV 4.9%) BROWN
Smooth copper beer. Heavy body and balanced sweet malt and bitter hop flavour, with plums, prunes and some butterscotch.

IPA (ABV 5%) GOLD
Amber American IPA with powerful citrus hop aroma and taste. Marmalade, red grapefruit and orange flavours with assertive bitterness.

Panda Eyes (ABV 5%) SPECIALITY
Puffin Tears (ABV 5%) BITTER
Cascadia (ABV 5.2%) BITTER
Light No. 2 (ABV 5.2%) BITTER
Antipodean IPA (ABV 5.5%) IPA
Little Rock IPA (ABV 5.5%) IPA
Porter (ABV 5.5%) PORTER
Smooth, creamy, black porter with roast malt aroma. Malty, smoky and sweet followed by a bitter tang. Sweet finish.

Hellstown West Coast IPA (ABV 5.8%) IPA
Pale (ABV 6%) IPA
New World IPA with powerful citrus hop aroma. Intense citrus hop flavour with marmalade, orange and bitterness. Hoppy, slightly dry finish.

Howl (NEW)

Polmear Hill, Par, PL24 2AR
☎ (01726) 467254 ⊕ howlbrewery.co.uk

Howl is a new brewery located just 300m from Par Sands. Craft ales are dreamed up, tested and perfected in small batches and the menu changes every couple of weeks. Hops-flavoured water is also available. No live beer.

Ideal Day (NEW)

Crocadon Farm, St Mellion, PL12 6RL

Ideal Day, established in 2023 near Saltash, make beers focused on where their ingredients, especially their grain, comes from and how it was farmed. Its brewing inspiration comes from Belgian farmhouse traditions, classic British beers and modern innovation. It strives to create beers while supporting farmers who are saving our soils and ecosystems with regenerative agriculture. No real ale.

Keltek SIBA

Candela House, Cardrew Way, Redruth, TR15 1SS
☎ (01209) 313620 ⊕ keltekbrewery.co.uk

⊛ Keltek (Celtic in Cornish) began brewing award-winning ales in 1997, and was founded by Stuart Heath. It started as a 2.5-barrel plant in Stuart's disused stable block on the Roseland Peninsula. Several moves and expansions mean it is now based in Redruth, and can brew more than 250 barrels a week. In 2013 Keltek acquired four pubs in south-west Cornwall (the second brewery in Cornwall to own an estate of pubs). Two more were acquired in 2016. ☛♦

Even Keel (ABV 3.4%) BITTER
Pale brown session bitter. Refreshing malt and hop taste with apple, plum and pear drops. Gentle dry and bitter finish.

Lance (ABV 4%) PALE
Gold bitter with light fruity aroma. Grassy citrus hops, apples, malt and hints of elderflower and butterscotch. Long bitter finish.

Magik (ABV 4%) BITTER
Pale brown bitter with smoky malt and zesty hop aroma. Sweet, woody malt with spicy and orange marmalade hop flavours.

Phoenix (ABV 4.5%) BITTER
Golden best bitter. Powerful fruity hops with high bitterness but backed with solid malt which lingers well on the finish.

King (ABV 5.1%) BITTER
Copper-coloured premium bitter with malt and fruit aromas. Biscuit malt balanced by earthy hops and tropical and citrus fruit.

Pilot Gig (ABV 5.2%) PORTER
Reaper (ABV 6%) BITTER
Tawny winter bitter with full malt, molasses, resinous hops and vine fruit flavours. Toffee, liquorice, fruitcake hints. Lingering malt finish.

Beheaded (ABV 7.5%) STRONG
Tawny strong ale with balanced malt and hops. Sherry sweet with honey, toffee and fruit notes and a bittersweet finish.

Krow

Penventon Terrace, Redruth, TR15 3AD
✉ contact@krowbrewing.co.uk

Microbrewery established in Redruth. The head brewer gained experience brewing with several breweries in Cornwall, having initially started out as a homebrewer. It is currently producing small-batch brews and developing a core range.

Lacuna

Unit 19, Kernick Industrial Estate, Penryn, TR10 9EP
⊕ lacunabrewing.com

Owners Tristan and Ben's ethos for Lacuna Brewing is simple and sustainable, being committed to reaching zero carbon brewing as soon as possible. Three canned beers are available. Its taproom is open every Saturday. No real ale. ⚡

Lizard

The Old Nuclear Bunker, Pednavounder, Coverack, TR12 6SE
☎ (01326) 281135 ⊕ lizardales.co.uk

Launched in 2004 in St Keverne, Lizard Ales is now based at former RAF Treleaver, a massive disused nuclear bunker in the countryside near Coverack on the Lizard Peninsula. Specialising in bottle-conditioned ales, it mainly supplies local shops and pubs. ‼LIVE

Longhill

Longhill Cottage, Whitstone, EX22 6UG
☎ (01288) 341466

⊗ Longhill began brewing in 2011 using a 0.5-barrel plant, upgraded in 2012 to a four-barrel plant to meet demand. Paul and Sue brew one beer, available in the bar at the rear of the brewery.

Hurricane (ABV 4.8%) BITTER
Full-bodied, tawny, premium bitter with earthy malt aroma. Quite bitter with fruit and resinous hop flavours. Refreshing and persistent bitterness.

Lost (NEW)

Unit 12, Lanteague Studios, Scotland Road, Zelah, TR6 9JG
☎ (01637) 876873 ⊕ lostbrewing.co

Established by brothers Daniel and Jamie in 2018, Lost Brewing provides a small range of craft keg beers for its own bar – café by day, bar in the evenings. In 2023 their joint brewery with Newquay Brewing Project opened in Zelah. No real ale. ⚡

Mine

The Brewery, Consols, St Ives, TR26 2HW
☎ (01736) 793001 ☎ 07500 957962
⊕ minebrewing.com

☺A nanobrewery located in St Ives, Cornwall, brewing small-batch beers available in cask, bottle and keg. There are plans to install a new larger capacity kit. ♦LIVE V

Mild (ABV 3.1%) MILD
Consols (ABV 3.7%) BITTER
FeS2 (ABV 4%) PALE
Ransom (ABV 4.2%) PALE
Cousin Jack (ABV 4.6%) PALE
In Vein (ABV 4.6%) STOUT
Mines Best (ABV 4.6%) BITTER
Southwest Coast (ABV 5%) PALE
Adit (ABV 6%) IPA

Newquay Brewing Project

Unit 12, Lantague Studios, Scotland Road, Zelah, TR6 9JG ☎ 07720 399942
⊕ newquaybrewingproject.com

After travelling the world, owners Ash and Kez purchased the eight-barrel, former Fowey brewplant, to brew a range of beer styles similar to those they enjoyed while travelling. In 2023 they relocated and their joint brewery and taproom with Lost Brewing (qv) opened in Zelah. They are trying to be as carbon neutral and environmentally-friendly as possible, without compromising on flavour. A small but growing range of three beers are all vegan-friendly, unfined and unpasteurised and are available can-conditioned or in kegs. LIVE V⚡

Newquay Steam

New Inn, Newquay Road, Goonhavern, TR4 9QD

Newquay Steam Brewery commenced in 2020. Three beers, one cider, a rum and gin are currently produced under the name.

Padstow SIBA

The Brewery, Unit 4a, Trecerus Industrial Estate, Padstow, PL28 8RW
☎ (01841) 532169 ☎ 07834 924312
⊕ padstowbrewing.co.uk

⊗ Owners Des and Caron Archer established the brewery in 2013, using a 0.5-barrel plant, which has since been upgraded to 10 barrels. Besides the integral brewery shop, two licenced town-centre tasting rooms have been established. ‼☞♦LIVE V

Pale Ale (ABV 3.6%) PALE
Thin golden beer. Citrus hops dominate flavours with bitter grapefruit, sweet tropical fruits and a trace of malt. Lingering finish.
Padstow Local (ABV 4%) BITTER
Amber session bitter with a fruity aroma. Dominant apricot and bitter flavour with some biscuit malt. Long sweet, fruity finish.
Windjammer (ABV 4.3%) BROWN
American brown ale with dominant malt plus summer and citrus fruits. Distinct malt aroma. Bitter and sweet throughout. Dry finish.
IPA (ABV 4.8%) PALE
Refreshing pale ale. Fully-hopped on the nose and taste with grapefruit and orange bitterness. Sweet finish with citrus hops.
Padstow May Day (ABV 5%) PALE
Premium gold/yellow ale with mango and other tropical fruit leading aromatic citrus hops. Gentle malt sweetness and quite bitter.

Penzance

⊟ Star Inn, Crowlas, TR20 8DX
☎ (01736) 740375 ☎ 07763 956333
⊕ penzancebrewingcompany.com

⊗ Owner Peter Elvin began brewing in 2008 on a self-built, five-barrel plant in the old stable block of the Star Inn. Following expansion, full production now exceeds 1,400 barrels a year. Production now includes bottled core range beers. There are well over 25 selected outlets supplied now, including a local convenience store. ‼♦

Mild (ABV 3.6%) MILD
Smooth auburn mild. Coffee and chocolate dominate the taste with fruit notes. Fading sweet roast malt finish. A changed beer.
Crowlas Bitter (ABV 3.8%) BITTER
Refreshing copper session bitter with light malt aroma. Light biscuit maltiness and hops. Lingering finish of malty bitterness with dryness.
Potion No. 9 (ABV 4%) PALE

Refreshing pale ale. Grapefruit hops and tropical fruit flavours dominate with pine resin notes, biscuit malt and flashes of bubblegum.

Crows-an-Wra (ABV 4.3%) BLOND
Golden beer with citrus hoppy aroma. Grapefruit bitter hops dominate the long-lasting taste with a light hoppy, dry finish.

Brisons Bitter (ABV 4.5%) BITTER
Full-bodied, tawny bitter with malt aroma. Biscuit malt dominates the taste with robust sweetness, fruit esters and hop bitterness.

Trink (ABV 5.2%) BLOND
Blond ale with grapefruit nose. Punchy pine-resin hop flavours with grapefruit, marmalade and peaches. Dry, bittersweet and hoppy finish.

Zythos (ABV 5.3%) PALE

IPA (ABV 6%) IPA
Smooth golden genuine IPA with hoppy aroma. Powerful hop bitterness with light malt and tropical fruits, finishing bitter and dry.

Pipeline

Great Western Railway Yard, St Agnes, TR5 0PD
☎ 07973 178877 ⊕ pipelinebrewing.co.uk

Pipeline Brewing Co crafts small batches of vibrant, hoppy beers on the North Cornwall coast. Using fresh ingredients and Cornish water, it creates craft beers that showcase the best of New World hops. No live beer.
🍺V♦

St Austell SIBA IFBB

63 Trevarthian Road, St Austell, PL25 4BY ☎ 0345 241 1122 ⊕ staustellbrewery.co.uk

☺Founded in 1851, St Austell brewery remains fully independent and family-owned. Cask ale is available in all its pubs, and is widely available nationally. St Austell also brews limited edition cask beers throughout the year as well as a range of keg and bottled beers. A ten-barrel, small-batch plant is used to brew regular beers for its Cask Club (available in 40 selected outlets, and at its Hicks Bar), and to make a range of experimental bottle beers. In 2016 it purchased Bath Ales (qv). ‼🍺♦LIVE ♦

Cornish Best Bitter (ABV 3.4%) BITTER
Light, refreshing bitter with little aroma. Gentle biscuit malt and hops flavour with fruity bitterness. Malty, bitter, faintly dry finish.

Anthem (ABV 3.8%) GOLD
Smooth, refreshing, golden ale. Fruit aroma. Citrus fruits and peaches dominate the taste. Sweet malt detectable. Dry and bitter throughout.

Nicholson's Pale Ale (ABV 4%) PALE
Copper bitter. Hops dominate the taste with citrus and tropical fruits and malt. Dry bitterness rises in the finish.

Tribute (ABV 4.2%) BITTER
Amber bitter with malt and fruity hop aroma. Dominant hop bitterness balanced by sweet malt, ending refreshingly bitter and fruity.

Proper Job (ABV 4.5%) GOLD
Smooth premium golden ale with citrus hop aroma. Copious citrus fruits with bitterness, dryness and crisp hop bitter and grapefruit finish.

Hicks (ABV 5%) BITTER
Tawny premium bitter with malt nose. Powerful malt and vine fruit flavour with balancing bitterness. Long malty and floral finish.

St Ives SIBA

Unit 5, Marsh Lane Industrial Estate, Hayle Industrial Park, Hayle, TR27 5JR

☎ (01736) 793467 ☎ 07702 311595
⊕ stives-brewery.co.uk

⊠ Originally located in St Ives, it purchased a larger site in Hayle with a state-of-the-art, 25-barrel plant as the main brewery. The new site also incorporates a taproom, bar and café. The original two-story site in St Ives has been retained as a café and tourist attraction. The brewery has also established a St Ives town centre tasting room and shop. ‼🍺♦LIVE ♦

Boilers Golden Ale (ABV 4%) PALE
Gold colour with fruity, hoppy aroma. Strong, bitter citrus hop flavours balanced by sweet and nutty biscuit malt. Bitter, hoppy finish.

Hella Pale (ABV 4.2%) PALE

Porth Pilsner (ABV 4.4%) SPECIALITY

Meor IPA (ABV 4.8%) PALE

Slipway (ABV 5%) PALE

Alba IPA (ABV 5.2%) PALE

Back Road West (ABV 6.5%) IPA

Seven Stars SIBA

🍺 Seven Stars, 73 The Terrace, Penryn, TR10 8EL
☎ (01326) 531398 ⊕ sevenstarspenryn.co.uk/ micro-brewery

Brewing began in 2020 using a 2.5-barrel plant. The brewery is located in an outbuilding of the Seven Stars pub, adjacent to the beer garden. Beers appear in the pub under the Hidden Brewery brand name.

Sharp's

Pityme Business Centre, Rock, PL27 6NU
☎ (01208) 862121 ⊕ sharpsbrewery.co.uk

⊠ Sharp's was founded in 1994 and within 15 years had grown from producing 1,500 barrels a year, to 60,000. It was bought by Molson Coors in 2011. Heavy investment has brought the capacity up to 200,000 barrels a year. The company owns no pubs and delivers beer to more than 1,200 outlets across South England via temperature-controlled depots in Bristol and London. Part of Molson Coors PLC. 🍺♦LIVE

Doom Bar (ABV 4%) BITTER
Amber bitter with sweet taste, balanced biscuit malt and grassy hops. Stone fruits, lemon and raisins. Lingering malty, bitter finish.

Atlantic (ABV 4.2%) BITTER
Golden light bitter with citrus hop and fruit aroma. Malt, elderflower and caramel sweetness balanced by grapefruit and resinous hops.

Solar Wave (ABV 4.6%) PALE

Sea Fury (ABV 5%) BITTER
Smooth auburn premium bitter with malt and caramel aromas. Dominant sweet malt with berry, stone and dried fruits with spice hints.

Shoals (NEW)

The Shipyard, Porthleven, TR13 9JY ☎ 07817 241024
⊕ shoalsbrewery.com

⊠ Opened in early 2022, the brewery is located in an historic central Porthleven venue occupying the buildings of the old shipyard. The taproom is open to the public Thursday-Sunday. ♦

Harbinger Pale Ale (ABV 4.2%) PALE

Porter Leven (ABV 5.3%) SPECIALITY

Baulk Breaker (ABV 6.6%) IPA

Skinner's (Goodh)

Riverside, Newham Road, Truro, TR1 2DP

☎ **(01872) 271885** ⊕ **skinnersbrewery.com**

⊗ Award-winning brewery established in 1997. The previous ownership was forced into administration in 2022. Following the consequent sale the total brewery complex plus titles and recipes were purchased by local brewery, Goodh Brewing Co. The new owners operate Skinner's independently from their other brewery. They aim to produce the full range of Skinner's iconic beers, either as core range or seasonals, plus additional new brews. The brewery entered full production in June 2023 and opened to the public in July 2023. A major addition is a kitchen facility to the Tap Yard Bar. ‼️ ▤ ♦ ☙

Betty Stogs (ABV 4%) BITTER
Deep amber bitter with a gentle hop and malt aroma. Bitter resinous hops balanced by sweet malt flavours with traces of honey and fruit. Traces of grapefruit and pineapple. Sweet malt fades into the long bitter finish with rising dryness.

Chapel Rock (ABV 4%) PALE
Straw-coloured beer in the golden ale style with an intriguing aroma of fresh grass, toffee, Burton sulphur 'snatch' and peardrops. The taste starts with summer fruits, lime, lemon, orange and grapefruit with honey and peardrops. Balancing malt flavour is soon overtaken by bitterness and dryness in to the finish.

Hops 'n' Honey (ABV 4%) SPECIALITY
A gold speciality beer containing honey that is evident in the delicate aroma and earthy hop notes. Citrus and grassy hops combine with honey, apple, tropical fruit and sweet malt flavours. Pleasant bitterness which lingers in the dry finish.

Lushingtons (ABV 4.2%) BLOND
Refreshing fruity and easy-drinking blond summer beer with persistent head. Strong aroma of mango with spicy hops and faint oranges. Quite bitter on the tongue, becoming more so in the finish. Tropical fruits dominate the flavour with mango at the forefront plus pineapple and Seville oranges and a hint of grapefruit. Sharpness balanced by gentle sweetness. Long, fruity, bitter finish with rising dryness.

Cornish Knocker (ABV 4.5%) PALE
Smooth and refreshing golden pale ale with fragrant marmalade hops and malt on the nose. Citrus and floral hops blend with biscuit malt with hints of butterscotch toffee and plums to give a pleasing balance. Lasting bitterness in the finish.

Pennycomequick (ABV 4.5%) STOUT
A creamy smooth, dark brown, sweet stout with roast grain aroma. Heavy malt and bitter roast coffee, fig and cherry flavours in the mouth with hints of damson and burnt plum jam. Mellow, rich and deep. Roast, dry finish.

Porthleven (ABV 4.8%) PALE
Robust pale ale with crisp citrus hop and pine nose. Refreshing and smooth body with lemon peel and resinous hop in the mouth balanced by light malt, bitter grapefruit and sweet tropical and stone fruit tones. Bitterness and citrus hop in the long finish.

Tintagel SIBA

Condolden Farm, Tintagel, PL34 0HJ
☎ **(01840) 213371** ⊕ **tintagelbrewery.co.uk**

⊗ Established in 2009 in a redundant milking parlour on the highest farm in Cornwall, using a 7.5-barrel plant and water from its own spring. A purpose-built brewery, shop, restaurant and visitor centre opened in 2017. The brewery is powered by a wind turbine and uses only wet yeast and English malt and hops. ‼️ ▤ ♦

Castle Gold (ABV 3.8%) PALE

Refreshing pale ale with malt aroma. Citrus hop, tropical fruits, cherries, sweet malt and dry, bitter flavour. Hop bitter finish.

Cornwall's Pride (ABV 4%) BROWN
Pale brown bitter with malt aroma. Sweet, grainy malt with toffee and summer fruits. Late dried fruit and coffee hints.

Sir Lancelot (ABV 4.2%) PALE

Arthur's Ale (ABV 4.4%) BITTER
Ruby brown complex beer with balance of sweet toffee, malt and bitter, earthy hops. Hints of figs and vine fruits.

Pendragon (ABV 4.5%) PALE
Golden beer with citrus hop nose. Refreshing, strong grapefruit citrus and pine hop bitterness. Hints of toffee, honey and malt.

Harbour Special (ABV 4.8%) OLD
Tawny old ale with ripe fruity, malty aroma. Rich nutty malt, stone fruits and esters taste, finishing bitter and malty.

Merlins Muddle (ABV 5.2%) BITTER
Auburn, creamy premium bitter. Spicy hop bitterness balanced by smoky malt flavours and a complex mixture of fruits. Bitter finish.

Caliburn (ABV 5.8%) OLD
Dark old ale. Smoky, roast malt and Christmas pudding fruits with rich and complex flavours including treacle and earthy hops.

Treen's

Unit 3, Viaduct Works, Frog Hill, Ponsanooth, TR3 7JW
☎ **(01872) 719633** ☎ **07552 218788**
⊕ **treensbrewery.co.uk**

⊗ This family-run brewery was founded in 2016, initially using spare capacity at another local brewery. It now has its own premises using a 12-barrel plant. Bottling was introduced in 2018. An additional 12-barrel fermentation vessel was acquired in 2021. ♦

Essential (ABV 3.8%) PALE
Bitter golden pale ale with grassy, peppery hops and biscuit malt flavours. Citrus and stone fruit notes. Long, bitter finish.

Classic (ABV 4.3%) BITTER
Tawny bitter with malt aroma. Robust malt balanced by spicy hop bitterness. Coffee, molasses with light summer and stone fruits.

Local (ABV 4.3%) PALE
Amber pale ale with malty and hoppy aroma. Balanced malt and bitter hops with stone fruit, oranges and bitter finish.

Sunbeam (ABV 4.8%) PALE
Smooth gold pale ale. Refreshing citrus, spicy, bitter hop and malt flavours with fruit and caramel hints. Long, bitter finish.

Resolve (ABV 5.2%) STOUT
Dark brown, strong, sweet stout with dark chocolate aroma. Dominant smoky coffee, bitter chocolate, molasses flavours with malt and stone fruit.

Tremethick

Tremethick Brewery, Grampound, TR2 4QY ☎ **07726 427775** ⊕ **tremethick.co.uk**

⊗ Tremethick began brewing in 2015, and are now well-established as a small, village brewery with strong community support. Bottle sales dominate but casks are supplied to a few pubs and to all-important beer festivals. Monthly brewery open evenings are popular with locals. ‼️LIVE

Gwella (ABV 3.7%) BITTER

Amber bitter with bready malt and citrus hop aroma. Assertive malt is balanced by citrus hops with candied peel fruit.

Pale Ale (ABV 4.3%) PALE
Gold pale ale with light aroma. Dominant bitter grapefruit and apples, grassy hops and underlying malt. Long bitter citrus finish.

Dark Ale (ABV 4.6%) MILD
Complex dark brown ale. Nutty malt with kaleidoscope of fruit flavours. Quite sweet with hints of coffee-roast. Faintly bitter and hoppy.

Red IPA (ABV 4.8%) PALE
Auburn bitter with light grapefruit and malt aroma. Grapefruit and marmalade flavours masking malt and other fruits. Long bitter, dry finish.

Verdant

Unit 30, Parkengue, Kernick Road, Penryn, TR10 9EP
☎ **(01326) 619117** ⊕ **verdantbrewing.co**

Verdant was established in 2014 by keen homebrewers who love hop-forward beers. It moved to new premises in 2020 and upgraded from a 10-barrel to a new 20-barrel plant. The brewery started producing cask ale in 2020. 🛒🦯

Penpol (ABV 3.8%) PALE
Lamanva (ABV 4%) BITTER
Argal (ABV 4.4%) GOLD
Burnthouse (ABV 4.6%) PORTER

Old Ale House, Truro (Photo: Timara Easter)

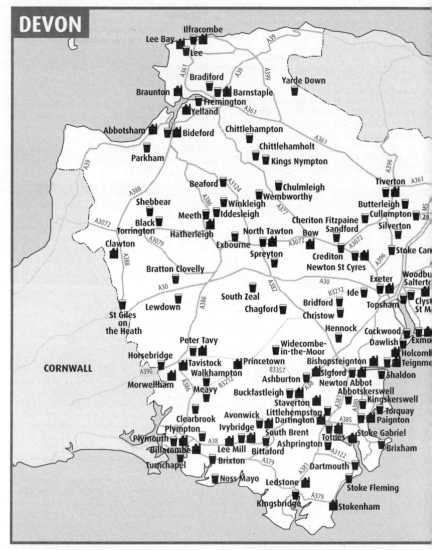

Abbotskerswell

Two Mile Oak Inn 🄻

Totnes Road, TQ12 6DF (on the A381 between Newton Abbot and Ipplepen)

☎ (01803) 812411 🌐 twomileoakinn.co.uk

Dartmoor Jail Ale; Otter Bitter; 1 changing beer 🄶
A two-bar olde-worlde pub that dates back to 1702, formerly a farmhouse then licensed in 1703. It is still sympathetic to its heritage, with wooden floor, oak beams and a cosy log fire. There is a separate restaurant area. Otter Bitter, Dartmoor Jail and a guest are served straight from casks behind the bar. The pleasant courtyard garden has views across Dartmoor.
Q ➳ ❀ ◑ ◐ ♿ ♠ P 🚃 (92,177) ❀ 🛜 ♫

Ashburton

Old Exeter Inn 🄻

26 West Street, TQ13 7DU (on main road through the centre of Ashburton, opp church)

☎ (01364) 652013 🌐 oldexeterinn.com

1 changing beer 🄶
Originally built in 1130 to house the workers building the nearby church, with additions in 17th century, this friendly local is the oldest pub in Ashburton. It has a wood-panelled L-shaped bar with a granite shelf behind for serving the gravity-fed ales. There are two seated areas either side of the entrance, with two rear seating areas and flagstoned corridor leading to the secluded walled garden at the back. Local cider and perry is sold.
Q ➳ ❀ ◑ ◐ ♠ 🚃 (X38,88) ❀ 🛜

Ashprington

Durant Arms

TQ9 7UP (exit Totnes on the A381; left turn signposted after 1 mile)

☎ (01803) 732240 🌐 durantarms.co.uk

Dartmoor Jail Ale; Noss Beer Works Church Ledge 🄷**; 2 changing beers** (sourced regionally; often Teignworthy, Otter) 🄷/🄶

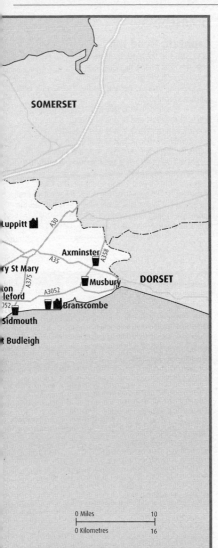

SOMERSET

Luppitt

Axminster

ry St Mary

Musbury   DORSET

kon
leford   Branscombe

Sidmouth

Budleigh

| 0 Miles | 10 |
| 0 Kilometres | 16 |

Orchards and Westons are served. The lounge is now the sports bar. The village is served by Country Bus 91 between Plymouth and Totnes. Closing times may be extended, depending on custom.
⚶🏵️🍺🚃♿🅰️♣️🚪P🍴(91)☀️🐾♪

Axminster

Axminster Inn 🅻 ✅
Silver Street, EX13 5AH
☎ (01297) 34947 🌐 axminsterinn.pub
Palmers Copper Ale, IPA, Dorset Gold, 200; 1 changing beer (sourced locally) Ⓗ
The Axminster Inn is a friendly traditional pub, lying just off the town centre, with a real log fire for the winter months and a lovely enclosed beer garden to enjoy in warmer weather. It's a Palmers house, offering a good range of their real ales. Live music is featured. Free Wi-Fi is available and there is a skittle alley and dartboard. The pub is dog friendly. Children are welcome up until 7pm.
⚶🏵️🌿♣️🚪P🍴🐾🛜♪

Barnstaple

Panniers 🅻 ✅
33-34 Boutport Street, EX31 1RX (opp Queen's Theatre)
☎ (01271) 329720
Sharp's Doom Bar; Ruddles Best Bitter; Greene King Abbot; 4 changing beers (sourced regionally) Ⓗ
Centrally located opposite the Queen's Theatre and close to the historic Pannier Market, this popular JD Wetherspoon pub maintains an ever-changing selection of real ales from local and West Country breweries, as well as those from further afield. Framed prints, hung throughout the comfortable premises, depict various items relating to the history of Barnstaple. To the rear, a pleasant courtyard garden drinking area is a suntrap in summer. ⚶🏵️🍺♿🚪🍴🛜

Reform Inn 🅻
Reform Street, Pilton, EX31 1PD
☎ (01271) 323164 🌐 reforminn.co.uk
Barum Original, Breakfast; 1 changing beer (sourced locally) Ⓗ
Well-established, popular community local and brewery tap for Barum brewery. From the main road, look above roof level for the pub sign to locate it. The skittle alley is the location for the annual Green Man beer festival in July and other regular beer festivals are held during the year. In the public bar, there is a pool table and darts board. Music events are held occasionally, look at website or Facebook for details. ♣️🍴🐾🛜

Beaford

Globe Inn 🏆 🅻
Exeter Road, EX19 8LR (on main road in centre of village)
☎ (01805) 603920 🌐 globeinnpub.co.uk
3 changing beers (sourced regionally) Ⓗ
Traditional and cosy country inn, with a passion for real ale and craft beers to suit all tastes. Three changing and mainly local ales are usually available, alongside a comprehensive drinks menu that includes more than 40, often legendary, bottled and bottle-conditioned beers from around the globe. Proud of its environmental credentials, the pub also offers a seasonal and attractively priced food menu, using the best ingredients from local producers. Local CAMRA Pub of the Year 2022 and 2023. Q⚶🏵️🛏️🍺♣️🚪🍴🐾🛜♪

A small, family-run 18th-century inn with wood-burning fires and slate floors, offering en-suite and B&B accommodation and a restaurant serving local produce. Local beers and some choices from further afield are on the bar, and there is an annual beer festival in September. The pub is close to the River Dart and only three miles from Totnes. It is on the South Devon National Cycle Route 28 and the Dart Valley scenic walking trail from Totnes. Q⚶🏵️🛏️🍺♦️P🍴(B2C)☀️🛜♪

Avonwick

Avon Inn 🅻
Avonwick, TQ10 9NB
☎ (01364) 73475 🌐 avon-inn.org.uk
Dartmoor Legend, Jail Ale; Draught Bass; 1 changing beer (sourced regionally) Ⓗ
The pub is situated at the crossroads in the centre of the village, and at the centre of the community with various events regularly taking place, advertised on its website. Up to 10 ciders from Ashridge, Countryman, Sandford

Bideford

Joiners Arms

EX39 2DR

☎ (01237) 472675

Sharp's Doom Bar; 2 changing beers (sourced regionally) ⊞

The Joiners Arms is a friendly old-style English pub with accommodation. Local ales, lagers and cider are all offered. Situated in the heart of the town next to the historic Pannier Market, the pub hosts a number of pub teams and is the focus of regular community events including popular music nights. There is live music every weekend, and a skittle alley and function room. ⊛♣P❁♥♪

Bittaford

Horse & Groom ⓛ

Exeter Road, PL21 0EL

☎ (01752) 892358

Dartmoor Jail Ale; 4 changing beers (sourced locally; often Exeter, South Hams, Summerskills) ⊞

A family-owned pub run by Dawn, son Pierre and husband Oliver, who is a real ale enthusiast. Good home-cooked food is served, and there are six pumps, with two dedicated to real cider and the others predominantly offering ales from local breweries in Devon and Cornwall. Third-pint tapas are available. There is a long bar and separate dining area. A beer festival, and a cider and sausage festival, are hosted during the year, supporting local charities. Local CAMRA Country Pub of The Year 2022. ➤❁Ⓤ▲♣♥P➡(X38,Gold)❁♪

Black Torrington

Black River Inn

Broad Street, EX21 5PT SS465056

☎ (01409) 231888 ⊕ blackriverinn.co.uk

3 changing beers (sourced regionally) ⊞

Village pub with a growing reputation for real ale and good food. Three regularly-changing real ales are kept, together with two local ciders. The tastefully decorated public bar with adjacent eating area leads through to the separate restaurant which can also be used as a function room. Outside, the attractive garden has views over the Torridge valley and surrounding countryside. Near to both the Tarka Trail and Ruby Way, the pub is particularly attractive to walkers and cyclists. Food on Tuesday and Wednesday is limited to bar snacks only. Q➤❁Ⓤ▲P❁♥♪

Bradiford

Windsor Arms ⓛ

55 Bradiford, EX31 4AD (on main road through village, approximately ½ mile N of Pilton)

☎ (01271) 343583

GT Ales Thirst of Many; 1 changing beer (sourced locally) ⊞

A community-oriented, friendly village local within easy walking distance of Barnstaple town centre. Two changing real ales are kept, both from local brewery GT Ales. Good, freshly-cooked and locally sourced food is served Friday to Sunday in the separate lounge bar. A function room, with skittle alley, pool table and dartboard is at the rear of the pub. ➤❁Ⓤ♣➡❁♥♪

Branscombe

Fountain Head Inn ⓛ

EX12 3BG (on the outskirts of the village on the road from the Donkey Sanctuary to Beer)

☎ (01297) 680359 ⊕ fountainheadinn.com

Branscombe Branoc, Golden Fiddle; 1 changing beer (sourced locally) ⊞

Set in a beautiful coastal valley, this walker-friendly old pub is at the west end of one of England's longest villages, approximately a mile and a quarter from Branscombe beach. Ancient features such as the inglenook fireplace, wood panelling and flagstone floors greet the customers while the bar offers Branscombe brewery ales and ciders. Good value home-cooked food is served from an ever-changing menu. The Forge restaurant has its own small log fire and bar but you can eat anywhere in the pub. A beer festival is held on the closest weekend to the summer solstice. Q➤❁Ⓤ♣♥P➡(899)❁♪

REAL ALE BREWERIES

Barnaby's Staverton
Barum 🍺 Barnstaple
Bays Paignton
Beer Engine 🍺 Newton St Cyres
Branscombe Branscombe
Bridgetown 🍺 Totnes
Checkstone 🍺 Exmouth
Clearwater Bideford
Combe ✦ Ilfracombe
Cottage Beer Project Tiverton
Country Life Abbotsham
Crossed Anchors 🍺 Exmouth
Dartmoor Princetown
Devil's Pleasure Sigford
Devon Earth Buckfastleigh
Exeter ✦ Exeter
Fat Belly Ilfracombe (brewing suspended)
Grampus 🍺 Lee Bay
GT Braunton
Hanlons Newton St Cyres
Hatherland Tiverton
Holsworthy Clawton
Isca Holcombe
Ivybridge ✦ Ivybridge
Morwell Morwellham
New Devon Exeter
New Lion ✦ Dartington
Noss Beer Works Lee Mill
Otter ✦ Honiton: Luppitt
Powderkeg Woodbury Salterton
Red Rock ✦ Bishopsteignton
Riviera Totnes: Stoke Gabriel
Roam ✦ Plymouth
Salcombe ✦ Ledstone
South Hams Stokenham
Stannary ✦ Tavistock
Summerskills Plymouth: Billacombe
Tally Ho! 🍺 Hatherleigh
Tavistock Peter Tavy (NEW)
Taw Valley ✦ North Tawton
Teignmouth Teignmouth
Teignworthy Newton Abbot
Topsham ✦ Exeter
Totnes 🍺 Totnes
TQ Beerworks ✦ South Brent
Turk's Head 🍺 Exeter
Utopian Bow
Yelland Manor ✦ Barnstaple: Yelland

Bratton Clovelly

Clovelly Inn ⓛ

Bratton Clovelly, EX20 4JZ (between A30 and A3079)
SX464919
☎ (01837) 871447 ⊕ clovellyinn.co.uk
Dartmoor Jail Ale; Sharp's Doom Bar; 1 changing beer (sourced regionally) Ⓗ
Dating back to the 18th century, this truly authentic rural Devon pub lies at the heart of the local community. The cosy main bar, with a large wood-burning stove, is complemented by two separate dining areas (advisable to book in evenings) and a games room. The bar features an oak fireplace lintel inscribed '1789'. Three real ales are kept, with a cider from local Sandford Orchards. Good home-cooked food is available daily.
ち❀《❶と▲♣❀Pⵗ(633) ❀♪

Bridford

Bridford Inn ⓛ

EX6 7HT
☎ (01647) 252250 ⊕ bridfordinn.co.uk
Dartmoor Jail Ale; 3 changing beers (sourced nationally) Ⓗ
This pub frequently appears in the Guide and was local CAMRA Pub of the Year in 2015 and 2018. There are four handpumps on the bar and a number of real ciders. Situated high above the valley floor, this 17th-century inn, which was converted from two cottages to a pub in the late 1960s, has stone walls, beamed ceilings, an inglenook fireplace and panoramic views of the surrounding hills from the its gardens. It also houses the village shop. ち❀《❶と♣❀Pⵗ(360)❀ 🛜♪

Brixham

Queen's Arms 🍷 ⓛ ✅

31 Station Hill, TQ5 8BN (from Brixham Library go up Church Hill East, then Station Hill)
☎ (01803) 852074 ⊕ thequeensarmsbrixham.co.uk
6 changing beers (sourced nationally; often Branscombe, Salcombe, Teignworthy) Ⓗ
A single-bar, end-of-terrace pub with a well-deserved reputation for the quality of its beers and multiple real ciders, winning it the local CAMRA Pub of the Year award three times. It has a welcoming atmosphere with a strong community ethos. Live music features on Wednesdays and at weekends, with a Friday meat draw and a Sunday quiz. In early December it hosts a charity beer festival with over 50 real ales and ciders.
ち❀♣❀Pⵗ(17) ♪

Vigilance ⓛ ✅

5 Bolton Street, TQ5 9DE
☎ (01803) 850489
Dartmoor Legend; Greene King IPA, Abbot; Sharp's Doom Bar; 4 changing beers (sourced nationally) Ⓗ
Town centre Wetherspoon pub named after the last sailing ketch built in Brixham's Upham shipyard in 1926, now fully restored and moored in the harbour. Local, mostly nautical, prints adorn the walls and an imposing old ship's figurehead looks down on customers from its wall mounting. Food is served all day. The pub holds various beer, cider, and wine festivals throughout the year. ち❀《❶と❀Pⵗ🛜

Brixton

Foxhound Inn ⓛ

Kingsbridge Road, PL8 2AH
☎ (01752) 880271 ⊕ foxhoundinn.co.uk

Dartmoor Jail Ale; house beer (by Summerskills); 3 changing beers (sourced nationally; often Caledonian, Courage, Summerskills) Ⓗ
An 18th-century former coaching house in a rural village just east of Plymouth, with two separate bars and a small restaurant. Traditional English meals are served daily, featuring locally sourced ingredients. Lookout for Red Coat, an ale crafted by the landlord, among the four guest ales. A monthly charity quiz night is held. The village is served by a frequent daytime bus service.
Qち❀《❶▲♣❀Pⵗ❀

Buckfastleigh

King's Arms

14-15 Fore Street, TQ11 0BT (in centre of town)
☎ (01364) 643432
Bridgetown Shark Island Stout; Teignworthy Gun Dog; 1 changing beer (sourced locally) Ⓗ
The pub was purchased from Admiral Taverns a few years ago. It is a free house with mainly local ales on sale, and has been fully refurbished. There is an entrance hallway with a small public sports bar at the front of the pub and a larger lounge bar with plenty of comfortable seating at the rear, also showing sports. The pub has a pleasant beer garden with plenty of seating, and a small function room. ち❀🖂♣ⵗ(X38,88)❀ 🛜♪

Butterleigh

Butterleigh Inn ⓛ

The Green, EX15 1PN (opp church) SS9746108212
☎ (01884) 855433 ⊕ butterleighinn.co.uk
3 changing beers (sourced regionally) Ⓗ
Situated in a small tranquil village, this proper country inn has been in the Good Beer Guide for over 35 years. Four handpumps serving three ales and one real cider. The beers rotate from regional breweries and are often seasonal specials, and the cider is sourced from at least three different cider producers. There is a garden with patio, and a separate modern dining room at the rear of the inn where wholesome home-made food is served.
Qち❀🖂《❶♣❀P❀🛜

Chagford

Globe Inn ⓛ ✅

9 High Street, TQ13 8AJ
☎ (01647) 433485 ⊕ theglobeinnchagford.co.uk
Dartmoor IPA, Jail Ale; Otter Bitter; 1 changing beer (often Exeter) Ⓗ
This Grade II-listed pub which was once a coaching inn and coopery overlooks the churchyard and is a focal point of this historic Dartmoor stannary town. The public bar retains its Victorian counter and bar-back thought to date from the 1930s. This, and the separate lounge bar and dining room, both have open log fires. Good food is served, and there is music, a cinema club and other events. A courtyard garden is at the rear and parking is nearby. The ciders are mainly Sam's.
ち❀🖂《❶❀ⵗ(173,178) ❀ 🛜♪

Cheriton Fitzpaine

Ring of Bells ⓛ

EX17 4JG
☎ (01363) 860111 ⊕ theringofbells.com
2 changing beers (sourced regionally) Ⓗ
This thatched Grade II-listed pub sits at one end of this picturesque village, by the parish church. Two changing beers are normally available at the single bar. Fine food, largely locally sourced, is available lunchtimes and

evenings but those seeking a snack, a quiet pint by the fire or a few drinks with friends in the garden are equally welcome. Binka the landlady has made this a pub for everyone, including their children and the dog.
ᗐ❀◑♣●P❀

Chittlehamholt

Exeter Inn ♈ ᒾ
EX37 9NS
☎ (01769) 540281 ⊕ exeterinn.co.uk
Otter Ale; St Austell Proper Job; GT Ales Thirst of Many ℍ
A traditional 16th-century coaching inn, on the old road from Barnstaple to Exeter, with four cosy eating areas and a pleasant south-facing patio. The food is locally sourced, home-cooked and varies with the seasons. The pub retains many of its original architectural features including a real fire which has a bread oven. Various past photographs of the village adorn the walls. There is a popular quiz night once a month and a holiday cottage is available, see the pub's website or Facebook for details.
Qᗐ❀◑ᒾ♣●P❀♪

Chittlehampton

Bell Inn ᒾ
The Square, **EX37 9QL** (opp St Hieritha's parish church)
SS636254
☎ (01769) 540368 ⊕ thebellatchittlehampton.co.uk
Butcombe Original; 1 changing beer (sourced regionally) ℍ
In the same family since 1975, popular with locals and visitors alike. This busy village local has been in the Guide continuously since 1997, having won several CAMRA awards in recent years including local CAMRA Pub of the Year. The bar area contains notable sporting memorabilia and there is a games room downstairs. The good-value food is home-cooked and is served both in the bar and adjoining restaurant. The gardens outside are extensive with great views, and are ideal for children.
ᗐ❀◑◑ᒾ♣●P➾(658,859) ❀♪

Christow

Teign House Inn ᒾ
Teign Valley Road, **EX6 7PL**
☎ (01647) 252286 ⊕ teignhouseinn.co.uk
Otter Bitter; 3 changing beers (sourced regionally; often Exeter, Powderkeg, South Hams) ℍ
A welcoming and atmospheric country pub with beams and log fires, situated on the edge of Dartmoor in the Teign Valley. The pub enjoys strong support from locals who enjoy the regular live music and monthly quiz. Great home-cooked pub food is served. The sizeable garden attracts locals and families alike, while the adjoining field has space for caravans, campers, and tents.
Qᗐ❀◑ᒾ♣●P➾(360) ❀♪

Chulmleigh

Old Court House
South Molton Street, **EX18 7BW**
☎ (01769) 580045 ⊕ oldcourthouseinn.co.uk
Dartmoor Dartmoor IPA; Butcombe Butcombe Original; 1 changing beer (sourced regionally) ℍ
Charles I stayed here in 1634 when he held court (hence the name) and this is commemorated with an original coat of arms in one of the bedrooms, while a replica hangs above the fireplace in the main bar. Today this friendly, cosy local features two regular real ales, usually joined by a guest beer in summer. Good home-cooked

food can be taken in the bar area, the separate dining room, or the pretty cobbled courtyard garden.
ᗐ❀◑◑ᒾ♣●➾(377) ❀♈

Clearbrook

Skylark Inn ᒾ
PL20 6JD
☎ (01822) 853258 ⊕ skylarkclearbrook.com
Dartmoor Jail Ale; St Austell Proper Job; Tavistock Master Ale; 1 changing beer (sourced regionally; often Butcombe, Otter) ℍ
Typical Dartmoor village pub, popular for its excellent food, serving up to four South West real ales, one of which is usually from Dartmoor. The beer range may vary, with beers from St Austell and Tavistock breweries making regular appearances. An annual beer festival is held over the August bank holiday weekend. Food is served daily and all day at weekends. Catch the Stagecoach 1 bus from Plymouth or Tavistock to Clearbrook Cross – the pub is approximately 20 minutes' walk. Qᗐ❀◑P❀

Clyst St Mary

Half Moon Inn
Frog Lane, **EX5 1BR**
☎ (01392) 873515 ⊕ thehalfmoonclyst.co.uk
Exeter Ferryman; 1 changing beer ℍ
Friendly village pub with a great atmosphere. Locally sourced food at reasonable prices is available lunchtime and evenings, with smaller portions available. Two or three real ales are on offer. The pub was completely refurbished in 2020 and is within walking distance of Exeter Chiefs Rugby Club and Westpoint Exhibition Centre. There are three en-suite B&B rooms available. Dogs are welcome in the bar area.
Qᗐ❀◑◑ᒾ➾(9) ❀♈

Cockwood

Ship Inn ᒾ ✓
Church Road, **EX8 8NU** (just off the A379, outside Starcross, close to Cockwood harbour)
☎ (01626) 890373 ⊕ shipinncockwood.co.uk
Dartmoor Jail Ale; St Austell Tribute, Proper Job; 2 changing beers (sourced nationally) ℍ
A busy family-run pub, close to the picturesque harbour at Cockwood, with a roaring log fire in winter and a large beer garden with views of the estuary to enjoy in warmer weather. Popular with drinkers and diners alike, it offers a choice of three regular ales and usually two rotating guests, and has an excellent food menu. Meals are prepared with local produce where possible including a varied choice of locally-caught fish. The bus stops 100 yards across the bridge. Qᗐ❀◑●P➾(2)❀♈

Crediton

Crediton Inn
28A Mill Street, **EX17 1EZ**
☎ (01363) 530451
4 changing beers (sourced nationally) ℍ
The framed indenture certificate dates this inn to 1878, with windows etched with the ancient town seal. It is a genuine free house serving two to four real ales. The skittle alley doubles as a function room. No food is served except packaged bar snacks. Well-behaved dogs are welcome. Opening times may vary, please phone to check. Children under 14 are not allowed.
❀≈♣●P➾(5) ❀♈

Duke of York L

74 High Street, EX17 3JX

☎ (01363) 775289

Dartmoor IPA; 2 changing beers (sourced regionally) Ⓗ

A one-bar, Grade II-listed pub at the top of the high street, a family-run free house since 2002, which has one regular beer and one or two changing beers on offer, depending on demand, mainly from different breweries. Amazon, Sky and BT Sports can be shown on three screens. Men's and women's darts teams play here, and there is a south-facing garden. The number 5 bus passes the door. 🏠♣🅿️😺🎵🛜

Cullompton

Pony & Trap L ✓

10 Exeter Hill, EX15 1DJ (on B3181 S of town)

☎ (01884) 34182

Bays Devon Dumpling; Dartmoor Jail Ale; Draught Bass; 5 changing beers (sourced regionally) Ⓗ

A traditional local with good atmosphere and mixed clientele. Many local darts and skittles teams are based here. It has a smart interior featuring a log-burner, making it cosy in winter; while flowers and ornaments give it a homely feel. Up to eight real ales are on offer, including a house beer, plus three real ciders. There is a garden and seating area. Pub games are played and a Sunday roast is available. Q🌟🔴♣🅿️😺🎵

Dartmouth

Cherub Inn ✓

13 Higher Street, TQ6 9RB

☎ (01803) 832571 ⊕ the-cherub.co.uk

5 changing beers (sourced locally; often Otter, St Austell) Ⓗ

Situated in the centre of Dartmouth, a nautical town famous for its Tudor buildings, the Cherub is one of the best and the oldest, a Grade II-listed 14th-century former merchant's house. Beams made from old ships' timbers feature in the bar which boasts six handpumps serving local and national cask ales. An intricate winding staircase leads to the cosy restaurant and facilities on the two upper floors. It may open later on Monday and Tuesday in winter. 🌟🔴🅰️(Kingswear)♣🅿️😺🛜

Dawlish

Brunswick Arms L

9-10 Brunswick Place, EX7 9PB

☎ (01626) 862181 ⊕ thebrunswickarms.co.uk

Otter Ale; Sharp's Doom Bar; 2 changing beers (sourced locally) Ⓗ

Family-orientated pub overlooking The Lawn and Brook. Its outside seating is a good spot to sit in the afternoon sun watching the famous black swans of Dawlish. Two guest ales are usually on offer, plus a changing real cider, and food is available. Skittles, pool and darts are played; children and dogs are welcome. Easily accessible by train and bus. Happy hour is 5-6 all week, but an hour earlier on Sunday. 🌟🔴🅰️🚆♣🅿️😺🛜🎵

Swan Inn

94 Old Town Street, EX7 9AT

☎ (01626) 863677

St Austell Tribute, Proper Job; 1 changing beer (sourced regionally) Ⓗ

A friendly locals' pub, reputedly the oldest in Dawlish, dating from 1642 and located in the old part of town. It has a large patio and garden and a covered heated smoking area. Real cider is always available and there is

an outside bar from May onwards during the summer months. Price promotions are available, with all for cask and keg beers at £3 per pint Monday, Wednesday 5-7pm and Friday 5-8pm. Dogs are welcome. Q🌟🏠♣🅿️🅿️😺🛜🎵

East Budleigh

Sir Walter Raleigh Inn L

22 High Street, EX9 7ED (off B3178 opp Hayes Ln)

☎ (01395) 442510

Teignworthy Gun Dog; 3 changing beers Ⓗ

This welcoming 16th-century free house is set in the middle of the delightful village of East Budleigh, the birthplace of Sir Walter Raleigh. A community-run pub, the building was originally two cottages that were converted into a Jacobean-style pub in the 18th century. Many of the original features still remain, with wooden beams throughout the two different areas, the Old Jug and Bottle hatch behind the bar, and a couple of quirky alcoves. Q🌟🔴◑🅰️♣🅿️(157)😺

Exbourne

Red Lion L ✓

High Street, EX20 3RY (200yds N of jct with A3072)

SS602018

☎ (01837) 851551 ⊕ theredlionexbourne.co.uk

Dartmoor IPA, Legend; 1 changing beer (sourced regionally) Ⓖ

This friendly village local has a well deserved reputation for the quality and consistency of its ales and has been local CAMRA Pub of the Year several times in recent years. Casks are set on stillage at the end of the L-shaped bar and feature Legend from Dartmoor and other locally brewed ales. The pub does not serve food but customers can bring their own snacks or get a takeaway delivered. There is always good conversation to be enjoyed here. Q🌟🏠🅿️🅿️😺🛜🎵

Exeter

Bowling Green L ✓

29-30 Blackboy Road, EX4 6ST

☎ (01392) 490300 ⊕ bowlinggreenpub.co.uk

3 changing beers (sourced locally) Ⓗ

Originally an 18th-century pub called the Ropemakers, the Bowling Green is a cosy local situated away from the main city centre close to Exeter City Football Club at St James Park. It has an extensive selection of reasonably-priced pub food including pizzas and gluten-free and vegetarian options. Four real ales are available, three are rotating and from local breweries. Live music is played every Saturday night and on Sunday afternoon followed by a quiz in the evening. Q🌟🔴◑🅰️🚆(St James Park) ♣🅿️😺🛜🎵

George's Meeting House L ✓

38 South Street, EX1 1ED (near bottom of South St)

☎ (01392) 454250

Greene King IPA, Abbot; Sharp's Doom Bar; 4 changing beers Ⓗ

This Wetherspoon pub opened in 2005 having been sympathetically converted from a Unitarian Chapel dating from 1760. Many of the original features remain unaltered; these include two upstairs galleries with seating, a pulpit and stained-glass windows. A range of national, regional and local real ales are served. Food is available throughout the day and evening. A newer extension, which is at the rear of the main building, leads to an outdoor seating area on two levels. Q🌟🔴◑🅰️🚆(Central)🅿️🛜

Hour Glass Inn L

21 Melbourne Street, EX2 4AU (300yds from Exeter quayside)
☎ (01392) 258722 ⊕ hourglassexeter.co.uk
Exeter Lighterman, Avocet, 'fraid Not, Ferryman, Darkness; 1 changing beer (sourced locally) ℍ
A traditional hostelry, established in 1848 and now operated by Exeter brewery. In a back-street hub, it is close to the quayside and about five minutes' walk from the main city centre. The dining room has been newly refurbished and dinner is available Thursday, Friday and Saturday evenings, with lunch on Friday, Saturday and Sunday. Snacks and light meals are available at all other times. ◑🖵🏠🐾🛜

Imperial L ✓

New North Road, EX4 4AH
☎ (01392) 434050
Greene King IPA, Abbot; 7 changing beers ℍ
This pub was built in 1810 as a private house, converted to a hotel and opened as a Wetherspoon pub in 1996. It features a range of beers from local and national breweries. There is an orangery, and a large beer garden. Located close to the university, there is a bus stop directly outside the premises. Regular beer festivals are held, featuring local, national and international breweries. Food is served all day. St David's railway station is nearby. Q🌳🐾◑🕭≉(St David's)🚶P🖵🛜

Royal Oak

79-81 Fore Street, Heavitree, EX1 2RN
☎ (01392) 969215 ⊕ royaloakpubheavitree.co.uk
Dartmoor Jail Ale; Otter Ale; St Austell Tribute; 1 changing beer (sourced regionally) ℍ
This historic 1800s thatched, multi-room pub is on the B3183 through Heavitree, close to two public car parks. A relaxing snug is on the right after entering via an original Dartmoor Prison door and tack from the last heavy horse from the prison is displayed above the welcoming fireplace. The public bar to the left leads to several roomy areas. Outside there are front and rear courtyard seated areas. Bar snacks are available. Q🌳🐾🖵🏠🛜

Sawyer's Arms L ✓

121 Cowick Street, EX4 1JD (opp St Thomas church)
☎ (01392) 269520
Greene King IPA, Abbot; Sharp's Doom Bar; 5 changing beers (sourced nationally) ℍ
This 1960s pub on the main street running past St Thomas Church replaced an earlier public house on the same road. It is now a Wetherspoon establishment, following all conventions of the well-established chain. Roomy with good sized bar, there are plenty of tables and seating both inside and outside. Beer festivals and Meet the Brewer events are held. Large televisions mostly show BBC News 24 on mute with subtitles. Q🌳🐾◑🕭≉(St Thomas)🖵🛜

Ship Inn ✓

1-3 Martins Lane, EX1 1EY
☎ (01392) 272040
Exeter Avocet; Greene King IPA, Abbot; Otter Ale; 2 changing beers (sourced regionally) ℍ
A historic city-centre pub situated along a narrow passageway between the High Street and Cathedral Green. It is one of the oldest pubs in Exeter and Sir Francis Drake used to visit. Four regular ales feature along with two guests, mostly local. The pub offers good-value food served all day including a children's menu. Live entertainment features on Wednesday, Friday and Saturday. 🌳◑🕭≉(Central)🚶🖵🏠🛜♪

Thatched House Inn 🍽 L ✓

Exwick Road, EX4 2BQ
☎ (01392) 272920 ⊕ thatchedhouse.net
Greene King Abbot; house beer (by Greene King); 6 changing beers (sourced locally; often Dartmoor, Hanlons, Salcombe) ℍ
This thatched building dates from the 1600s and is a community establishment next to Exwick playing fields, opposite the Exeter College Sports Hub. It is close to the river and convenient for dog walkers, cyclists and sightseers. Seven real ales and one real cider are usually available, together with great value home-cooked food featuring local ingredients and producers. On-street parking is available nearby and the pub is on the Stagecoach E2 bus route. 🌳🐾◑♣🚶🖵(E2)🏠🛜

Topsham Brewery Taproom

Haven Road, EX2 8GR
☎ (01392) 275196
3 changing beers 🄶
Historic stone building on the popular Exeter Quay, with an outside garden seating area and a view from the bar of the brewery next door. Often busy with families and dog walkers during the day, but can get livelier at night with regular music, and a pizza van at the front door. Hours are extended during summer, with earlier weekday opening, and it closes later on busy Sundays. 🐾≉(St Thomas) 🐾🏠

Exmouth

Bicton Inn L ✓

5 Bicton Street, EX8 2RU
☎ (01395) 272589 ⊕ bictoninn.co.uk
Dartmoor Jail Ale; Hanlons Citra IPA, Port Stout; 3 changing beers (sourced locally) ℍ
A friendly and popular back-street local, offering good beer and chat. It has won the local CAMRA Community Pub of the Year award four times and has previously been local Pub of the Year. Regular live music including a weekly folk night takes place, along with a monthly quiz. The pub hosts an annual beer festival, usually in late winter. Up to six real ales and two keg ciders are normally on offer, including several LocAles. 🌳≉♣🖵(57) 🏠🛜♪

First & Last Inn L

10 Church Street, EX8 1PE (off B3178 Rolle St)
☎ (01395) 263275
Dartmoor Jail Ale; Otter Ale; Teignworthy Neap Tide; 2 changing beers (sourced locally; often Checkstone) ℍ
Victorian pub near the town centre with a public car park opposite. A genuine free house, with three distinct areas and a courtyard patio with heated awnings. Checkstone brewery started here in 2016 and supplies the pub with changing ales from an increasing range. Changing real ciders are also available, sometimes including their own. Games include pool and darts, and there is a skittle alley. Televised sport is prominent and there is regular live music early on Sunday evenings. 🐾≉♣🚶🖵(57)🏠♪

Grapevine L

2 Victoria Road, EX8 1DL
☎ (01395) 222208 ⊕ thegrapevineexmouth.com
Crossed Anchors Bitter Exe, American Pale Ale; 3 changing beers (sourced locally; often Crossed Anchors) ℍ
Situated in the centre of Exmouth, the Grapevine is a stylish Victorian building, with several distinct seating areas. It is home to Crossed Anchors brewing and Ruby Diner burgers. There are six handpumps, 12 craft taps and bottle-conditioned Crossed Anchor beers. Two keg

ciders and two bag-in-a-box real ciders are rotated regularly. Bottled German and Belgian beers are also available. There is occasional live music on a Friday and live international rugby is shown on the big screen. ⏰🏠🍴🚐👥♿⛽🚌(57) ✿♪

GWRSA Railway Club 🅛

3-5 Royal Avenue, EX8 1EN
☎ (01395) 274010 ⊕ gwrsaexmouth.co.uk
Greene King Abbot; Hanlons Yellow Hammer; 2 changing beers Ⓗ
A community-focused club with several small outdoor seated areas and superb views of the Exe Estuary. This club has four real ales on handpump, two of which are changing beers usually from local breweries. Traditional games are played, weekly live music is usually on Saturday night and quiz nights every Thursday. Bar snacks are available. The club is open to the public and everyone is welcome. ⏰🏠🍴♿♣🚌🚐🛜♪

Holly Tree

161 Withycombe Village Road, EX8 3AN (leave A376 at Gipsy Lane lights, turn left at roundabout)
☎ (01395) 273740
St Austell Tribute, Proper Job; 3 changing beers (sourced nationally) Ⓗ
A popular pub about a mile from Exmouth town centre. Although owned by St Austell the guest beers are from national breweries. There are several rooms off the large open bar, one housing the pool table and dartboards. This vibrant pub supports four darts teams and two pool teams. Locals can often be found playing the card game euchre on a Sunday afternoon, only stopping for the meat draw. Children are welcome until 7pm. BT Sports is shown on the television. ⏰🏠♣🚐🚌(97)✿

Powder Monkey 🅛 ✅

2-2A The Parade, Town Centre, EX8 1RJ
☎ (01395) 280090
Bays Devon Dumpling; Dartmoor Jail Ale; Greene King Abbot; Ruddles Best Bitter; Sharp's Doom Bar; 4 changing beers Ⓗ
A Wetherspoon pub named after Nancy Perriam, whose sewing skills earned her a berth in the navy where she also acted as a powder monkey. Nancy lived in nearby Tower Street. Powder monkey was naval slang for boys and girls who filled shells and cartridges with gunpowder on board ships of war. The building was converted from local newspaper offices. The bar is adjacent to the central seating areas, with a number of rooms off it.
Q⏰🏠🍴♿🚐🚌(57) 🛜

Fremington

New Inn

Old School Lane, EX31 2NT
☎ (01271) 373859 ⊕ thenewinnfremington.com
2 changing beers (sourced locally; often GT Ales) Ⓗ
Friendly family-run village local with a warm welcome, usually featuring at least two ales from GT brewery. The pub has a growing and well-deserved reputation for its home-cooked food, particularly Indian and spiced cuisine. A separate snug and games room has pool, darts and extra large Jenga. There is live music every Saturday evening from about 9pm, with a quiz and karaoke on alternating Wednesday evenings. Dogs are made welcome, and the large car park is very useful.
Q⏰🏠🍴♣🚐🚌✿🛜♪

Hennock

Palk Arms 🅛

Church Road, TQ13 9QB (take B3344 from A38 to Chudleigh Knighton and follow Hennock signs)
☎ (01626) 836584 ⊕ theonlypalkarms.co.uk
Bays Devon Dumpling; Dartmoor Legend; Teignworthy Gun Dog; 3 changing beers (often Dartmoor, Otter, Teignworthy) Ⓗ
Set high up in the Teign Valley and reputed to be haunted this 16th-century free house is popular with walkers, cyclists, campers, and sightseers alike. It has a revamped dining area with stunning views over the countryside, and two log-burning stoves to keep patrons warm. The pub is close to the unique village library and is an ideal place from which to explore both Hennock's mining history and the beautiful surrounding area.
Q⏰🏠🍴♿♣🚐🚌🛜✿♪

Horsebridge

Royal Inn

PL19 8PJ (off the A384 Tavistock to Launceston road)
SX401748
☎ (01822) 870214 ⊕ royalinn.co.uk
St Austell Proper Job; 4 changing beers (sourced nationally; often Otter, Salcombe, Timothy Taylor) Ⓖ
Originally built as a nunnery in 1437 by French Benedictine monks and reported to have been visited by Charles I, the pub overlooks an old bridge on the River Tamar, connecting Devon to Cornwall. It features half-panelling, stone floors, log fires and traditional styling in the bar and lounge, with another larger room off the lounge. It has a terraced garden with sheltered seating and free Wi-Fi. All the beers are served on gravity; the locally sourced food is recommended.
Q🏠🍴🚐🚌(115)✿🛜

Iddesleigh

Duke of York

EX19 8BG (off B3217 next to church) SS570083
☎ (01837) 810253 ⊕ dukeofyorkdevon.co.uk
Bays Topsail; Otter Bitter; 1 changing beer (sourced nationally) Ⓖ
A 15th-century thatched village inn with old beams, inglenook fireplaces and an unfailingly friendly atmosphere. Real ales are dispensed on gravity, while cider comes from nearby Sam's. The pub is renowned for its generous portions of locally sourced, home-cooked food. Close to the Tarka Trail, River Torridge and Stafford Moor Fishery, there are seven en-suite rooms for visitors. A popular beer festival is held every August bank holiday weekend. Q⏰🏠🍴♿🍴♣🚐🛜

Ide

Poachers Inn 🅛

55 High Street, EX2 9RW (3 miles from M5 jct 31, via A30)
☎ (01392) 273847 ⊕ poachersinn.co.uk
Branscombe Branoc; Exeter Tomahawk; 3 changing beers (sourced locally) Ⓖ
Busy village pub with a friendly atmosphere, serving a varied menu of home-made locally sourced produce, including excellent-value fish & chips on Wednesday evenings to eat in or take away. Dogs are welcome in the comfortably furnished bar, with old sofas, chairs and a big log fire in winter. There is also a large beer garden overlooking the glorious Devon countryside. The landlord is a keen rugby fan and games are shown on the television in the bar. Q⏰🏠🍴🍴▲🚐🚌(360)✿🛜

Ilfracombe

Hip & Pistol L
8 St James Place, EX34 9BH
☎ (01271) 549651
Draught Bass; Greene King Abbot; 1 changing beer (sourced nationally) ⊞
This extensively modernised old Georgian house has a nautical theme, with the flooring a special feature. It shows the bay around Ilfracombe in pictorial form, with local landmarks and shipwrecks plotted, together with an impressive pub logo shown in an image of a compass. Outside there is a pleasant beer garden in front of the pub. There is always a good selection of real ales, ciders and food offerings available. Only 50 yards from Ilfracombe bus terminus. ☎❀◐⇄Å🖢🖪(21)❀🛜

Wellington Arms L
66-67 High Street, EX34 9QE
☎ (01271) 864720
Sharp's Doom Bar; Fuller's London Pride; Greene King Abbot; 2 changing beers (sourced nationally) ⊞
A friendly town local, originally two pubs and now a listed building. There are separate public and lounge bars and a games room, while the cosy lounge retains its original beams and large open fire. TVs and music sound systems enable multiple channels to be shown, making the pub particularly popular with sports enthusiasts. Up to five competitively-priced ales are usually available. Regular live music sessions, quiz nights and beer festivals are held. No under 18s allowed. ❀Å🖢P🖪❀🛜♫

Ivybridge

Imperial Inn
28 Western Road, PL21 9AN
☎ (01752) 651091 ⊕ theimperialivybridge.co.uk ·
Dartmoor Jail Ale; St Austell Tribute; 1 changing beer (sourced locally)
New licensees, Anna and Craig, took over in 2020 and offer a warm and welcoming pub that was recently tastefully refurbished. Dartmoor Jail Ale and St Austell Tribute are the regular live beers with one guest ale sourced from a Devon brewery, complementing the popular and varied food menu (no food Mon to Wed). There is a large garden and a real fire. There is no wheelchair access to the beer garden. ☎❀◐⇄P🖪❀🛜♫

Kings Nympton

Grove Inn L
EX37 9ST (in centre of village) SS683194
☎ (01769) 580406 ⊕ thegroveinn.co.uk
Exmoor Ale; Hanlons Yellow Hammer; 1 changing beer (sourced regionally) ⊞
This Grade II-listed 17th-century thatched inn has low beams, flagstone floors, an open fire in winter, and a pretty enclosed terrace to enjoy in summer. A recent local CAMRA Pub of the Year and Cider Pub of the Year, it usually has three real ales available, together with a good range of ciders. The pub also has a reputation for its excellent home-cooked food, which can be enjoyed in the dining area, adjacent to the bar. Q☎⇄◐♣P❀🛜

Kingsbridge

Hermitage Inn
8 Mill Street, TQ7 1ED
☎ (01548) 853234 ⊕ the-hermitage-inn.edan.io

2 changing beers (sourced locally; often Summerskills, Teignworthy) ⊞
Popular with the locals in this market town, this extremely friendly pub with log fires and a traditional interior has a pleasant enclosed beer garden to the rear. The pub boasts an eclectic range of local beers, normally two at any given time, with bar snacks and basket meals on Friday nights and lunchtimes during the summer. Regular live music proves very popular. Facebook is a key source of information if you are planning a visit. Q☎⇄❀◐♣🖢P🖪❀🛜♫

Kingskerswell

Park Inn
15 Coles Lane, TQ12 5BQ
☎ 07837 127750
3 changing beers (sourced regionally; often Greene King, Sharp's, Teignworthy) ⊞
This free house is a single-bar pub with a warm and welcoming atmosphere and busy social calendar. Twelve differing ales rotate across the three handpumps on the bar, mainly from South-West breweries such as Dartmoor, Exmoor, Hunters, Teignworthy and others. They are joined by real ciders. There is a car park to the left of the premises, together with an extensive garden split into discrete areas, much of which is canopied as it gets the sun all day. ☎❀⇄♣P🖪(174,888) ❀🛜♫

Lee

Grampus Inn L
Lee, EX34 8LR (at end of lane; keep left of post office) SS483463
☎ (01271) 862906 ⊕ thegrampusinn.co.uk
Grampus Bitter, Ale ⊞
With parts dating back to the 14th century, a cosy interior and an attractive garden with outdoor table tennis table, this dog-friendly pub is particularly popular with tourists, especially walkers. Three real ales from West Country breweries are kept, together with a real cider, usually from Sandford Orchards, and Westons Country Perry. Good, locally sourced home-made food is served. The landlord, an accomplished fiddle player, encourages local musicians in open session on Friday evenings. Q☎⇄❀◐⇄Å♣🖢P🖪❀🛜♫

Lewdown

Blue Lion Inn L
EX20 4DL
☎ (01566) 783238
Dartmoor IPA, Jail Ale; 1 changing beer (sourced regionally) ⊞
Family-owned and run roadside inn, set on the old, now bypassed A30 between Okehampton and Launceston. Originally a 17th-century farmhouse on the Lewtrenchard Estate, the property was extended in the early 1900s. Now home to numerous local groups, several pub teams are also supported. Although predominantly drinks-oriented, good-value food is also served Tuesday to Saturday in the evenings. Accommodation is offered in two well-appointed rooms. ☎⇄❀◐⇄♣🖢P🖪❀🛜♫

Littlehempston

Tally Ho L
TQ9 6LY SX813627
☎ (01803) 862316 ⊕ tallyhoinn.co.uk
Dartmoor Legend; 2 changing beers (sourced locally) ⊞

This 14th-century stone-built typical church house inn has been owned by the community since 2014. With just one long room, stone walls, pews and benches, two log burners make it very cosy. Outside is a covered yard and garden leading to its own car park. There are various events, with live music and a monthly Wednesday quiz night. The guest beers are usually sourced from local breweries and a frequently changing real cider is also offered. Q♨❀◑♿♣●P🚂🚌(X64,177)🐾📶♫

Meavy

Royal Oak Inn 🄻

PL20 6PJ (on the village green)

☎ (01822) 852944 🌐 royaloakinn.org.uk

Dartmoor Jail Ale; St Austell Proper Job; house beer (by Bath Ales); 1 changing beer (sourced regionally; often Dartmoor, Otter, Tavistock) 🄷

People come from miles around to enjoy the food and drink of this tucked-away, civilised but unpretentious 16th-century pub. In the summer, sit outside on one of the benches by the legendary tree and watch children play on the village green. In winter, relax in the public bar and enjoy the conversation, dogs and roaring fire. There is an interesting range of cider, with a festival in August and occasional live music.
Q♨❀◑▲♣●🚌(56)🐾📶♫

Meeth

Bull & Dragon 🄻

EX20 3EP (on A386)

☎ (01837) 811742 🌐 thebullanddragon-meeth.business.site

3 changing beers (sourced regionally) 🄷

This friendly traditional thatched pub has been an inn since circa 1490. It sits at the end of the Tarka trail cycling route, on the A386 between Torrington and Hatherleigh. There is a lounge area with a piano, regular quiz nights and a monthly singalong. Good local home-made food adds to the offering. A garden and car park are at the front of the pub. Local CAMRA Cider Pub of the Year 2023.
Q♨❀◑♿♣●P🚌🐾📶♫

Musbury

Hind 🄻

The Street, EX13 8AU

☎ (01297) 553553 🌐 thehindmusbury.co.uk

3 changing beers 🄷

The Hind is a free house situated on the crossroads of the A358, on The Street, in the village of Musbury, three miles south of Axminster. There is a public bar, and a lounge/restaurant, where good-value home-cooked food is available at lunchtimes and Thursday to Saturday in the evening; on Saturday mornings breakfast is available. There is a front courtyard with stunning views over the Axe Valley. A good-sized function room/skittle alley has recently opened. Q♨❀◑♣●P🚌(885)📶♫

Newton Abbot

Dartmouth Inn

63 East Street, TQ12 2JP

☎ (01626) 202309 🌐 the-dartmouth-inn.business.site

Dartmoor Legend, Jail Ale; 1 changing beer (sourced locally; often Exeter, Teignworthy) 🄷

Dating from 1684 and originally called the Great Dane where men would be hired for the Newfoundland fishing fleet. Something of a Tardis, its narrow frontage gives way to long, narrow split-level environment dominated by thick and solid stone walls which contrast with the soft furniture. The bar is immediately to the left when entering, with some sofa seats opposite, whilst down some steps there is another drinking area with an open fireplace. Q♨❀♿⇌♣P🚌🐾📶♫

Maltings Taphouse & Bottle Shop

Tuckers Maltings, Teign Road, TQ12 4AA (500yds from Newton Abbot railway station)

☎ (01626) 334734 🌐 themaltingstaphouse.co.uk

House beer (by Teignworthy); 2 changing beers (sourced nationally; often New Lion) 🄷

Located within an historic building close to Templer Way footpath, the large ground-floor bar is adorned with memorabilia from the days when malt was produced here. The wooden tables and benches add to the rustic charm. Upstairs are a function room and an outside terrace. Three handpumps dispense real ale, often from the neighbouring Teignworthy brewery. Keg beers, real ciders and a vast range of bottled beers are also available. Live music by local bands and artists features regularly. Q❀♿⇌●P🚌(12)🐾📶♫

Richard Hopkins ✔

34-42 Queen Street, TQ12 2EH

☎ (01626) 323930

Greene King Abbot; Sharp's Doom Bar; 7 changing beers (sourced nationally) 🄷

Originally Rockley's Department store and situated halfway between the railway station and the town centre. Unusually for a Wetherspoon pub it has an outside drinking area with a covered veranda by the entrance. One long bar with up to 10 handpumps serves local beers and ones from further afield. The pub is broken up in to separate areas with some raised, and is dominated by a large staircase at the far end.
♨❀◑♿⇌P🚌📶

Newton Poppleford

Cannon Inn

High Street, EX10 0DW

☎ (01395) 568266 🌐 pubindevon.com

2 changing beers (sourced nationally) 🄶

Cheery, welcoming, two-bar pub with tables for dining in the lounge bar and restaurant area. Real ales are served by gravity from stillage behind the bar. This is a friendly locals' pub busy with passing trade. Good-value home-cooked food, served lunchtimes and evenings, covers most traditional pub favourites, and is of a very tasty standard. Well-behaved dogs are allowed. There are two large gardens, and a skittle ally. The only pub in the village, and a community hub.
Q♨❀◑♿▲♣●P🚌(52,157)🐾📶♫

Newton St Cyres

Beer Engine 🄻

EX5 5AX (beside railway station, N of A377)

☎ (01392) 851282 🌐 thebeerengine.co.uk

Beer Engine Rail Ale, Piston Bitter; 3 changing beers 🄷

Victorian pub, built in 1850 on the Exeter to Barnstaple Tarka Line. A destination pub, home-cooked food made with locally sourced produce is served lunchtimes and evenings. Part of the downstairs area has been converted into a second bar to accommodate sports fans and to serve the large, covered area between the pub and the railway line. The pub brews its own ales and five are usually available. The downstairs bar allows views of the brewery. Q♨❀◑♿⇌●P🐾

North Tawton

Railway Inn L

Whiddon Down Road, EX20 2BE (1 mile S of town, just off A3124; next to former North Tawton railway station) SS666000

☎ (01837) 82789 ⊕ therailwaynorthtawton.co.uk

Teignworthy Reel Ale; 1 changing beer (sourced regionally) ℍ

Good value and a warm welcome always await you at this friendly Devon local. A longstanding Guide entry and frequent local CAMRA Pub of the Year finalist. Adjacent to the former North Tawton railway station, there are numerous old railway photos on the walls. Reel Ale from Teignworthy is normally joined by a guest ale from another West Country brewery, together with a real cider in summer. The dining room is popular in the evening (no food Thu), also Sunday lunchtimes. Assistance dogs only. Q❤️🐕🍴◑➕🅿️🚲🛜

Noss Mayo

Ship Inn L

PL8 1EW

☎ (01752) 872387 ⊕ nossmayo.com

Dartmoor Jail Ale; Noss Beer Works Church Ledge, Ebb Rock; St Austell Tribute; 1 changing beer (sourced regionally; often Bath Ales, Noss Beer Works) ℍ

Popular with ramblers and seafarers alike, this fine split-level pub is situated on an inlet of the Yealm estuary. Four ales and excellent food are available daily. A former local CAMRA Pub of the Year, it is an ideal start or finish point for a walk to sample the breathtaking river and sea views along the route of Lord Revelstoke's Drive. If sailing, ring ahead to ascertain the tide times and mooring availability. There is no bus service in the evening or on Sundays. Q❤️🐕🍴◑&🅿️🚲(94)🌸

Ottery St Mary

Volunteer Inn

Broad Street, EX11 1BZ

☎ (01404) 814060 ⊕ volunteerinnottery.co.uk

Otter Bitter; 3 changing beers (sourced regionally) Ⓖ

The pub has been part of Ottery St Mary's history since 1810, when it opened as a dwelling, hostelry and recruitment centre for the Napoleonic War. In the centre of the town, it is deservedly popular. The front bar is unashamedly traditional, while the rear bar is more modern. All real ales, mainly sourced from local breweries, are delivered by gravity. Food is served seven days a week, including a traditional Sunday roast, in the refurbished and extended restaurant. 🐕🍴◑&➕🅿️(4)🌸🛜🎵

Paignton

Henry's Bar L ✅

53 Torbay Road, TQ4 6AJ

☎ (01803) 551190 ⊕ henrysbarpaignton.co.uk

Sharp's Doom Bar; 2 changing beers (sourced nationally; often Dartmoor, Exmoor, Teignworthy) ℍ

Great town centre pub in the main street of Paignton serving local and national real ales and ciders. It boasts an impressive long bar, has five handpumps with two regular beers, two guests, and a traditional cider, plus various bottles and polyboxes. This is a real hub of the community and is involved in many local events. Home-cooked food is served daily with a renowned roast on Sunday. Dogs are welcome, and families until 10pm. 🐕🍴◑🚲➕🅿️🌸🛜

Paignton Conservative Club

34 Palace Avenue, TQ3 3HB

☎ (01803) 551065

Dartmoor Jail Ale; 2 changing beers (often Exmoor, Salcombe, Skinner's) ℍ

Established as a private members club in 1885, three hand-pumped real ales are usually served from local and national brewers and the club has a reputation for consistent quality. The stone-carved entrance to this old building leads to the bar before going downstairs to a spacious function room where many events such as bingo, cabaret and quiz nights take place. Upstairs is another function room and a snooker hall with two tables. Q🐕◑&🚲➕🅿️🚲🛜🎵

Talk of the Town L ✅

46-52 Torbay Road, TQ4 6AL

☎ (01803) 668070

Dartmoor Jail Ale; Greene King Abbot; Ruddles Best Bitter; Sharp's Doom Bar; 3 changing beers ℍ

A late Victorian property that was once two guesthouses, situated halfway between the railway station and the beach. It is now a Wetherspoon pub and opened in 2010. It is essentially one large room on two levels with adequate comfortable seating and dark wood panelling, with the usual displays of framed local history and people. It has a tabled pavement area at the front of the premises, together with a small decking area overlooking a park at the rear. Q🐕❤️◑&🚲🅿️🛜

Torbay Inn ✅

34 Fisher Street, TQ4 5ER (300yds from The Big Tree bus stop)

☎ (01803) 392729

Sharp's Sea Fury; St Austell Tribute; Wye Valley HPA; 1 changing beer (often St Austell) ℍ

Paignton's oldest inn dating back to the early 1600s when the sea was on its doorstep and fish market opposite, hence the address of Fisher Street. It retains an old-fashioned layout with separate lounge and public bars boasting four handpumps each, serving national and local real ales with a warm welcome. Time is called via a ship's bell recovered from a wreck by a local diver, and it's documented that the Roundhead General Fairfax stayed here prior to a civil war battle in Exeter. Q🐕❤️&➕🅿️🚲(12,120)🌸🛜🎵

Parkham

Bell Inn L ✅

Rectory Lane, EX39 5PL (½ mile S of the A39 at Horns Cross; on the opp corner to the village primary school) SS387212

☎ (01237) 451201 ⊕ thebellinnparkham.co.uk

3 changing beers (sourced regionally) ℍ

Sympathetically restored after a serious fire in 2017, this 13th-century thatched inn, with its cob walls, oak beams and woodburner fires, has retained all of its olde-worlde charm. Three and sometimes four changing real ales are available, with usually at least one of these coming from a local brewery. Good home-cooked food is served lunchtimes and evenings Wednesday to Saturday, either in the bar or the adjacent raised restaurant area, while the Sunday roast is also popular. Q🐕❤️🍴◑➕🅿️🚲(372)🌸🛜

Peter Tavy

Peter Tavy Inn

Lane Head, PL19 9NN

☎ (01822) 810348 ⊕ petertavyinn.com

Dartmoor IPA, Jail Ale; 3 changing beers (sourced regionally; often Tavistock) ⊞

In a quiet village on the edge of Dartmoor, the inn has a small central bar serving a varying range up to five local beers including Dartmoor and Tavistock ales. It also has two larger rooms traditionally decorated throughout, with slate, beams and log burners. A patio and hidden garden are added attractions. The pub is renowned for its food, but drinkers are made welcome. The inn is situated on the National Cycle Route 27, and is near a caravan and camping site. Q⌂❄◐▲♣P☐(46,95)❀☀

Plymouth

Artillery Arms ⓛ

6 Pound Street, Stonehouse, PL1 3RH (behind Stonehouse Barracks and Millbay Docks)

☎ (01752) 262515

Draught Bass; 1 changing beer (sourced locally; often Dartmoor, South Hams, Summerskills) ⊞

Cracking back-street local tucked away in the old quarter of Stonehouse, close to the magnificent Grade I-listed Royal William Yard, and reflecting the area's military connections. One guest beer from a South West brewery such as Dartmoor, South Hams or Summerskills, and at least one varying real cider or perry are normally available to supplement the Draught Bass. An out-of-season beach party takes place on the last weekend of February, and charity monkey racing also features.
❀●☐(34,34A) ❀☀♪

Bread & Roses ⓛ

62 Ebrington Street, PL4 9AF

☎ (01752) 659861 ⊕ breadandrosesplymouth.co.uk

Exeter Avocet; 2 changing beers (sourced regionally; often Hanlons, Salcombe, Summerskills) ⊞

This friendly, sympathetically restored late-Victorian pub is popular with university staff, but has a mixed clientele. Up to three live beers are available, which are organic or Fairtrade wherever possible, just like the snacks. The beers are selected from local and regional breweries, including small batch and speciality beers unusual for the area. The pub promotes artistic and musical creativity, and is a vibrant music hub for local talent.
●☐(23,24) ❀☀♪

Britannia Inn ⓛ ✓

2 Wolseley Road, Milehouse, PL2 3BH

☎ (01752) 607596

Dartmoor Jail Ale; Greene King Abbot; Ruddles Best Bitter; Sharp's Doom Bar; changing beers (sourced nationally; often Bays, Exmoor, Summerskills) ⊞

An Edwardian pub, built in the 1830s, and situated opposite the Plymouth Citybus depot, Central Park and the Life Centre, and a short walk from Home Park, the home of Plymouth Argyle FC. The pub itself was built by the grandfather of Captain Scott (of Antarctic fame). Since becoming a JD Wetherspoon in 1999, the pub has established a well-earned reputation for its live beers, with 10 handpumps dispensing beers from local and national breweries, as well as at least one real cider, with local ciders appearing regularly. Q⌂❄◐占●☐☀

Dolphin Hotel ⓛ ✓

14 The Barbican, PL1 2LS

☎ (01752) 660876

Dartmoor Jail Ale; Draught Bass; St Austell Tribute; Sharp's Doom Bar, Atlantic; Timothy Taylor Landlord; 2 changing beers (sourced regionally; often Otter, St Austell, Sharp's) ⊞

A Plymouth institution, this unpretentious hostelry is steeped in history. Up to eight ales are all dispensed by gravity from the cask. Full of character, this charming pub

has tiled floors, well-used wooden benches and a traditional open fire, all creating the perfect ambience. The walls are adorned with paintings by local artist, the late Beryl Cook, who painted many of the characters she encountered in the Dolphin. Local CAMRA City Pub of the Year 2022. ●☐(25)❀

Duchy of Cornwall ⓛ

14 Anstis Place, Stonehouse, PL1 5JT

☎ (01752) 954045

1 changing beer (sourced locally; often Dartmoor, Salcombe, Summerskills) ⊞

Michelle and Rob welcome you to this traditional back-street pub with modern decor. This vibrant establishment champions the local community and hosts regular live music along with pool and darts teams. There's a relaxed atmosphere, with one rotating cask ale, kept in excellent condition, available to enjoy. Beers are mainly sourced from Devon breweries such as Bays, Dartmoor, Salcombe and Plymouth-based Summerskills, although some national favourites also appear. ♣☐❀♪

Fawn Private Members Club ⓛ

39 Prospect Street, Greenbank, PL4 8NY

☎ (01752) 226385

Bays Topsail; Dartmoor Legend; 3 changing beers (sourced regionally; often Sharp's, St Austell, Teignworthy) ⊞

This mid-19th century establishment was originally the Fawn Inn/Hotel, prior to converting to a club. CAMRA members are welcome with a valid membership card; regular visitors will be required to join. Up to four guest ales from the local area are generally served, as well as a rotating range of local cider from Countryman. The club is popular for rugby and other televised sports, and supports multiple dart and euchre teams. Local CAMRA Club of the Year 2023. ╾♣●☐❀♪

Ferry House Inn ⓛ ✓

888 Wolseley Road, Saltash Passage, PL5 1LA

☎ (01752) 361063 ⊕ ferryhouseinn.com

Dartmoor Best, Legend, Jail Ale ⊞

A warm welcome awaits you and your dog from the landlord and locals at this picturesque pub on the River Tamar. Three regular West Country ales are served, as well as good home-cooked food. A decking area on the edge of the river gives spectacular views of both road bridge and Brunel's iconic 1859 railway bridge. Photos, some dating back to the turn of the 20th century, adorn the walls. Quiz night is Sunday.
⌂❄╾◐占●☐(13) ❀☀

Fisherman's Arms ⓛ

31 Lambhay Street, Barbican, PL1 2NN

☎ (01752) 268243 ⊕ fishermansarms.co.uk

House beer (by Summerskills); 2 changing beers (sourced regionally; often Dartmoor, Salcombe, South Hams) ⊞

Owner Donna turned this former St Austell establishment back into a pub serving great food back in 2014. The house beer is brewed by Summerskills and is supplemented by two ales sourced from Devon and Cornwall. The pub interior is cosy and the décor is regularly updated. Traditional pub grub at affordable prices is supplemented by specials. Close to the Royal Citadel and the Barbican, turn right on exiting the pub, and head down the stone steps to find yourself on Castle Street. ⌂◐♣●☐(25)❀☀♪

Fortescue Hotel ♈ ⓛ ✓

37 Mutley Plain, PL4 6JQ

☎ (01752) 660673

Bays Devon Dumpling; Dartmoor Legend; Exeter County Best; Salcombe Lifesaver; South Hams Eddystone; 5 changing beers (sourced nationally; often Exeter, Salcombe, Summerskills) Ⓗ
This multi award-winning and lively local is frequented by a broad section of the community, and conversation flourishes. Up to eight live beers are usually available on tap including four or five beers from the local area, and up to eight real ciders. Live evening entertainment takes place regularly, and a quiz takes place on Sunday evenings. The patio beer garden draws crowds in the summer and is heated in winter. Terrestrial TV sport is also shown. Local CAMRA City Pub of the Year 2023.
ᕲ❀≭♣♠♥❄♿❤♪

Indian Inn
82 Devonport Road, Stoke, PL3 4DF
☎ (01752) 556438
2 changing beers (sourced locally; often Summerskills) Ⓗ
A small family-run one-bar pub in the Stoke Village area of Plymouth. Two varying live beers are available, usually one from Plymouth brewer, Summerskills, alongside other Devon breweries. There is lots of Indigenous American decor featured in the pub. Darts matches take place most weekday evenings, and there is a real fire in winter with comfortable armchairs from which to enjoy it. The pub is dog friendly.
Q❀≭(Devonport)♣➤(34)❤

Lounge
7 Stopford Place, Devonport, PL1 4QT
☎ (01752) 561330
Draught Bass; 2 changing beers (sourced regionally; often Otter) Ⓗ
Located in a quiet residential area, this street-corner local is situated near to Devonport Park, and offers a warm welcome. The wood-panelled bar is comfortable and relaxing, although may be busy at times with Plymouth Albion RFC's ground nearby. 'One weaker, one stronger' than the regular Bass is the rule for guest ales, with lighter and darker brews also alternating. A secluded garden at the front offers a retreat for smokers. Food is available daily (no food Mon).
Qᕲ❀◑≭(Devonport)♣♥➤(32,34)❤♪

Minerva Inn Ⓛ
31 Looe Street, Barbican, PL4 0EA
☎ (01752) 223047 ⊕ minervainn.co.uk
St Austell Tribute; 3 changing beers (sourced locally; often Summerskills, St Austell) Ⓗ
Plymouth's oldest hostelry, dating from around 1540, and within easy walking distance of the city centre and the historic Barbican, attracts a varied clientele. It has a long and narrow bar, leading through to a cosy seating area at the rear. Two guest beers are supplemented during the spring and autumn beer festivals, where beer could, and does, come from all over the country. Live music is played on Thursday to Sunday evenings, and Sunday lunchtime. ᕲ❀♥➤❤♪

Prince Maurice Ⓛ
3 Church Hill, Eggbuckland, PL6 5RJ
☎ (01752) 771515
Dartmoor Jail Ale; St Austell Tribute, Proper Job, Hicks; South Hams Sherman; 2 changing beers (sourced locally; often Hanlons, Summerskills, Teignworthy) Ⓗ
There is very much a village feel about this four-times local CAMRA Pub of the Year, which sits between the church and village green. The six regular ales are supplemented by a changing guest ale. It is named after the Royalist General, the King's nephew, who had his headquarters nearby during the siege of Plymouth in the

Civil War. Two log fires keep you warm in winter, adding to the ambience. No food is served at weekends.
Qᕲ❀◑♣♥P➤(28A)♿❤♪

Providence Ⓛ
20 Providence Street, Greenbank, PL4 8JQ
☎ (01752) 946251
3 changing beers (sourced regionally; often Bridgetown, St Austell, Summerskills) Ⓗ
This welcoming hostelry, tucked away within the back-street labyrinth of Greenbank, is well worth seeking out. One of the smallest pubs in Plymouth, what it lacks in size it makes up for in atmosphere and character. The interior is smart but comfortable and the real fire in winter is wonderful. Three competitively priced live beers, from a range of breweries, are generally available as are two or three real ciders. There are no fruit machines here; the sound is generated by conversation.
Q≭♣♥➤❤♿

Roam Brewery Tap Ⓛ
New Victoria House, Western Park Road, Peverell, PL3 4NU
☎ (01752) 251059 ⊕ roambrewco.uk
Roam Hometown Pale Ⓖ, Tavy IPA Ⓗ; 2 changing beers (sourced locally; often Roam) Ⓗ/Ⓖ
Situated in the former New Victoria Brewery Company premises, the Taproom has a light and airy feel, with two large tinted windows allowing the sun to flood in. Two live beers from the range will usually be available, supplementing the six craft beers also on tap including guest beers. Third-pint tapas is also available. As well as the brewery itself, there is an on-site brewery shop and bakery open six days a week, and pizzas when the tap is open, Thursdays to Sunday. ᕲ❀◑♿P➤(61,62)❤

Vessel Beer Shop
184 Exeter Street, St Jude's, PL4 0NQ
☎ 07796 667449 ⊕ vesselbeer.co.uk
Changing beers (sourced nationally)
An independent bar and beer shop, located a few minutes' walk from Plymouth city centre and opposite the Friary retail park. It stocks over 300 different beers from some of the best breweries in Britain and around the world. Bottle- and can-conditioned live beers are sold with some craft beer on draught. Regular events include Meet the Brewer or Food Producers; and beer tastings and beer styles. See social media for up-to-date activities. ➤

Plympton

London Inn Ⓛ ✓
8 Church Road, Plympton St Maurice, PL7 1NH
☎ (01752) 343322 ⊕ londoninnpub.co.uk
Draught Bass; changing beers (sourced regionally; often Bays, Dartmoor, South Hams) Ⓗ
This friendly 16th-century pub, situated next to the church, is the epitome of a typical village inn. The pub serves up to eight live beers, supplemented by several real ciders. The cosy lounge bar is adorned with a large collection of Royal Naval memorabilia, while the public bar boasts a pool table, dartboard and TV's for sports enthusiasts. Regular beer festivals are held. The pub is allegedly haunted by Captain Hinds. Dogs are welcome.
Qᕲ❀♣♥P➤❤♿♪

Union Inn Ⓛ
17 Underwood Road, Underwood, PL7 1SY
☎ (01752) 336756 ⊕ unioninnplympton.com
4 changing beers (sourced regionally; often Exeter, Summerskills, Teignworthy) Ⓗ

A warm welcome is assured at this traditional, cosy, early 19th-century hostelry. The landlord of this family-run community pub is a beer hunter, sourcing changing brews to charm his regulars' palates, and to create a year-round beer festival. The four beers on offer are sourced regionally, but could be from almost anywhere. It is the same with the cider selection which is also sourced from far and wide in this former local CAMRA Cider Pub of the Year runner-up. Q🕏🟢♣🟡P🖵🌳🛇♪

St Giles on the Heath

Pint & Post 🔳

PL15 9SA (just off main road through village, on opp side of road to village shop)
☎ (01566) 779933
2 changing beers (sourced locally; often Dartmoor) 🅗
This thatched village local was once two cottages before becoming a pub and post office, hence the name. A friendly family-run pub close to the Cornish border, it offers good home-cooked food (including takeaways) and a regular Wednesday quiz night. Legend from Dartmoor is one of the two well-kept ales, joined by a locally sourced guest ale. See their Facebook page for extended opening hours. Dog are welcome throughout the pub. Q🕏🟢🟡♣🟡P🌳🛇♪

Sandford

Lamb Inn

The Square, EX17 4LW
☎ (01363) 773676 ⊕ lambinnsandford.co.uk
Powderkeg Speak Easy Transatlantic Pale Ale; 2 changing beers (sourced locally; often Dartmoor, Powderkeg, Teignworthy) 🅗
A busy 16th-century free house in in the village centre, with open fires, comfy sofas and a warm, welcoming atmosphere. It is well supported by locals and visitors alike. As well as regular and changing beers, they also offer Sanford Orchards ciders. There is a large tiered garden, seven B&B rooms, and a skittle alley also used as a cinema and for live music and events. The short, changing food menu features local and fresh produce and is popular so book ahead. Opening hours are extended in summer and during school holidays. Q🕏🟢🟡🟡♣🟡P🖵(369)🌳🛇♪

Shaldon

Ferry Boat Inn 🔳

The Strand, TQ14 0DL
☎ (01626) 872340
Sharp's Doom Bar; 1 changing beer (often Salcombe, Teignworthy) 🅗
Situated in an ideal location on the Teign estuary, near to the beach with its parked boats and the foot ferry to Teignmouth which is rumoured to be the oldest in the country. The pub has one long and narrow bar with beamed ceilings, wooden panelling and photographs of old Shaldon as well as a Victorian fireplace. A restaurant is upstairs. Across the road is a beer garden on the estuary where food is served in summer. 🕏🟢🟡♣P🖵(22)🌳🛇♪

Shebbear

Devil's Stone Inn 🔳

EX21 5RU (in village square, opp church) SS438094
☎ (01409) 281210
St Austell Tribute; Dartmoor Jail Ale; Otter Amber; 1 changing beer (sourced regionally) 🅗

A 17th-century former coaching inn at the heart of the village. This warm, cosy venue, allegedly haunted, has wood beams, flagstoned floors and open fireplaces. The single bar has four handpumps serving three regular ales and a guest. New owners took over in early 2021 and have been gradually increasing the food offering, which now includes evenings and Saturday breakfast, with ingredients locally sourced where possible. A large garden, games room and separate dining room complete the picture. In the church opposite you will find the Devil's Stone that is turned every year on 5th November to ward off evil spirits. Q🕏🟢🟡🟡♣P🖵(72)🌳🛇♪

Sidmouth

Anchor Inn ✅

Old Fore Street, EX10 8LP
☎ (01395) 514129 ⊕ theanchorinn-sidmouth.co.uk
Sharp's Doom Bar; St Austell Tribute, Proper Job; 1 changing beer (sourced locally) 🅗
Large welcoming pub, situated just off the Esplanade, with a good ambience and friendly, helpful staff. Popular with tourists and locals alike, it has seating outside and a garden at the rear. Three regular ales are usually on tap with a guest added in summer. Good-value home-cooked food is served. It is especially busy during Sidmouth Folk Week when the garden and car park are given over to events. Dogs are welcome outside but not inside. 🕏🟢🟡♣P🖵🛇♪

Silverton

Lamb Inn 🔳

Fore Street, EX5 4HZ
☎ (01392) 860272 ⊕ thelambinnsilverton.co.uk
Exeter Avocet; 2 changing beers (sourced locally) 🅖
Popular family-run pub located in the centre of Silverton, with stone floors, stripped timber, old pine furniture, and a large open real fire. Three ales are served by gravity from a temperature-controlled stillage behind the bar. There is a well-used function room, regular quiz nights and occasional live music. Good-value home-cooked food is served lunchtimes and evenings, plus a popular Sunday roast. Q🕏🟡🟡♣🟡🖵(55B)🌳🛇♪

South Zeal

King's Arms 🔳

EX20 2JP (centre of village) SX649936
☎ (01837) 840300 ⊕ thekingsarmssouthzeal.com
Dartmoor IPA, Legend; 1 changing beer (sourced regionally) 🅗
Thatched 14th-century village local, which is not only at the hub of the community, but also attracts many visitors exploring the area. Well-behaved dogs are particularly welcome here. The regular Dartmoor beers are accompanied by a changing guest ale and locally made cider during summer months. Good food is served lunchtimes and evenings every day. Regular live music sessions are held throughout the year and the pub plays a central role during the Dartmoor Folk Festival in August. Q🕏🟢🟡🟡♣P🖵🌳🛇♪

Spreyton

Tom Cobley Tavern 🔳

EX17 5AL (off A3124 in village) SX6986096761
☎ (01647) 231314 ⊕ tomcobleytavern.co.uk
Clearwater Eric's ESB; Utopian Bow 🅗; 6 changing beers (sourced regionally; often Parkway) 🅗/🅖
Local CAMRA Cider Pub of the Year in 2023. Built in the 16th century and named after a local folklore figure this

pub should be on everybody's bucket list. The bar area has a warming fire in the winter months and a small side room. At the rear is a separate restaurant and access to the garden. Four ales are served in winter, with up to 10 in summer and there is always a dark beer available. Seven or more real ciders complete the picture. A former National CAMRA Pub of the Year. Q✤⭑🌣🕭⬱◖❶♣❷P🌣☂

Stoke Canon

Stoke Canon Inn
High Street, EX5 4AR
☎ (01392) 840063 ⊕ stokecanoninn.com
St Austell Tribute; 3 changing beers (sourced nationally) Ⓗ
The Stoke Canon Inn is a community-owned and run pub, saved from extinction by a dedicated team of volunteers from the village. It offers a spacious beer garden for warmer weather, and a wood-burner for the winter months. Good-quality home-cooked food is served. Live events are featured – check website for details. Opening hours may vary. The pub was awarded the Queen's Award for Voluntary Service in 2020.
🌣✤🌣◖♣❷P🖿(55,355) 🐾☂♪

Stoke Fleming

Green Dragon
Church Road, TQ6 0PX (opp village church)
☎ (01803) 770238 ⊕ thegreendragon-pub.business.site
House beer (by Otter); 2 changing beers (sourced locally) Ⓗ
Conveniently positioned on both a crossroads and the South West Coast Path, with Blackpool Sands half a mile away, this quintessential village pub, a focus for the local community, features a large log-burning open fire. The background music is subdued and there are no gaming machines. Local legend suggests there is a tunnel underneath the floor to the nearby beach and, some say, a ghost. The extensive garden has benefited from a recent makeover and now has an outside bar.
🌣✤🌣◖P🖿(93) 🐾☂♪

Teignmouth

Blue Anchor Inn Ⓛ
Teign Street, TQ14 8EG
☎ (01626) 772741
6 changing beers (sourced regionally; often Exeter, Palmers, Teignmouth) Ⓗ
Grade II-listed and one of the best free houses for miles, with a constantly changing range including the dark beers favoured by the landlord. The landlady is responsible for the blaze of colour in the garden in the summer and the plethora of Christmas decorations. There is one simple bar area with hatch for serving the excellent side garden with covered area to the rear. Beer festivals are held at Easter and in late summer, and dogs are always welcome. 🌣🌣⭑♣🖿(2,22)🐾♪

Tiverton

White Ball Inn ✓
8 Bridge Street, EX16 5LY
☎ (01884) 251525
Bays Devon Dumpling; Greene King Abbot; Ruddles Best Bitter; Sharp's Doom Bar; 6 changing beers (sourced regionally) Ⓗ
Former coaching inn, situated just off the town centre, next to the Exe Bridge. Built around 1823, it became a Wetherspoon in 1998 and was restyled in 2019 to include upstairs toilets, a downstairs extension and

sliding and fold out doors to the large rear seating area and terrace. Look out for the glass-covered well in the floor. There is a pay and display car park at the rear. Up to 10 real ales are available. 🌣✤◖🌣⭑❷🖿☂

Topsham

Bridge Inn ★ Ⓛ
Bridge Hill, EX3 0QQ
☎ (01392) 873862
Branscombe Branoc; changing beers (sourced regionally) Ⓖ
An historic, cosy, 16th-century inn, beautifully positioned overlooking the river Clyst. Run by five generations of the same family since 1897, it was visited by the Queen in 1998. This pub is a delight for real ale fans with a continually varying range of beers dispensed by gravity direct from the cellar. There are two rooms in the unspoilt interior plus the malthouse which is used at busy times and for functions. Traditional lunches such as ploughmans and sandwiches are served.
Q✤◖⮌❷P🖿(57,T) 🐾♪

Exeter Inn Ⓛ
68 High Street, EX3 0DY
☎ (01392) 873131
St Austell Proper Job; 3 changing beers (sourced regionally) Ⓗ
A pub since at least 1860, some parts of this partially-thatched building date from the 17th century when it was a coaching inn and blacksmiths. The Exeter Inn is a friendly local serving up to four ales and two ciders. Three TVs show various sports, while the front area has a dartboard and more seating. There is a small, sheltered, garden and smoking area at the side. Dogs are welcome.
🌣✤⭑⮌♣❷🖿☂♪

Torquay

Hole in the Wall Ⓛ
6 Park Lane, TQ1 2AU
☎ (01803) 200755 ⊕ holeinthewalltorquay.co.uk
Butcombe Gold; Dartmoor Jail Ale; Timothy Taylor Landlord; 4 changing beers (sourced regionally) Ⓗ
Torquay's oldest inn, circa 1540, is an atmospheric pub popular with tourists and locals. It is tucked behind the harbour in one of the town's oldest areas. The interior has cobbled floors and low-beamed ceilings and the walls are adorned with placards and artefacts from Torbay's maritime history. It has a large restaurant serving a variety of foods for all tastes. This pub is a hotspot for real ale drinkers with local and national beers on throughout the year. 🌣✤◖⭑P🖿🐾☂♪

Totnes

Albert Inn Ⓛ
32 Bridgetown, TQ9 5AD (from Totnes centre cross river, pub is 100yds on left)
☎ (01803) 863214 ⊕ albertinntotnes.com
Bridgetown Albert Ale, Bridgetown Bitter, Cheeky Blonde, Shark Island Stout, Westcountry IPA; 2 changing beers (sourced locally) Ⓗ
A cracking old-school community pub which commemorates the physicist Albert Einstein. It's the only public house in the Bridgetown district of Totnes. Based in an old chapel of rest, it hosts regular beer and cider festivals. Noted for its traditional meals, the pub also holds themed culinary evenings and is a base for darts, quiz and hockey teams. It's the Bridgetown brewery tap and boasts a small, but delightful, beer garden to the rear. Q🌣✤🌣◖⭑♣▲❷P🖿🐾☂♪

Bay Horse Inn ⃞

8 Cistern Street, TQ9 5SP (at top of the main shopping street)

☎ (01803) 862088 ⊕ bayhorsetotnes.com

4 changing beers (sourced locally; often Bays, Otter, Salcombe) ⃞

This characterful and welcoming community hostelry is well worth finding. It holds occasional beer and cider festivals as well as regular folk sessions plus jazz and quiz nights. It is also home to the renowned local Purl and a Pint knitting club. The pub has a spacious and well-kept beer garden which hosts many diverse events. While there is no food available patrons are welcome to bring in their purchases from the local shops. Q✿☆쇼ৈ♿⬅♣●P🖵(92,164) 🐾❄🎶

Totnes Brewing Company

59 High Street, TQ9 5PB (at the top of the High St by the Market Square) ⊕ barrelhousetotnes.co.uk

Totnes Vixen, Citra, New Castle ⃞

Popular and quirky brewpub founded in 2014 which only brews for the pub. The beer range showcases local ales, with up to three of its own beers on the bar. It is a community-focused pub hosting numerous weekly events in the main bars, the beer garden and upstairs in the Barrel House Ballroom music venue. There is also a good range of key-keg ales and craft ales in can and bottle. Takeaway food maybe brought in. Q✿쇼A⬅●🖵🐾🛜🎶

Turnchapel

Boringdon Arms ⃞ ✅

13 Boringdon Terrace, PL9 9TQ

☎ (01752) 402053 ⊕ boringdon-arms.net

Dartmoor Jail Ale; Fuller's London Pride; 2 changing beers (sourced regionally; often Exmoor, Sharp's) ⃞

The Bori is a traditional and dog-friendly former Regional CAMRA Pub of the Year, with six letting rooms. It sits in a waterside village on the South West Coast Path, and benefits from a regular bus service from Plymouth or a short water taxi from the Barbican. Four live beers are usually available and are supplemented during four beer festivals held throughout the year. Good-value, home-cooked food is served daily. There are two secluded gardens to the rear. Q✿☆✉◑♣●🖵(2,2A)🐾🛜🎶

Walkhampton

Walkhampton Inn 🍷 ⃞

PL20 6JY

☎ (01822) 258697 ⊕ walkhamptoninn.co.uk

3 changing beers (sourced regionally; often Exeter, Firebrand, Salcombe) ⃞

Set in the centre of the village, this welcoming 17th-century local displays traditional features throughout the bar, dining areas and snug. Up to four ever-changing live beers are available, and up to nine real ciders. There are quiz, live music and open mic nights throughout the year, with annual live beer and cider festivals. The pleasant courtyard beer garden hosts summer events. This is a good, old-fashioned, dog-friendly country pub. Local CAMRA Rural and Cider Pub of the Year 2023. Q✿◑♣●P🖵(55,56)🐾🛜🎶

Wembworthy

Lymington Arms

Lama Cross, EX18 7SA (on a minor road, midway between Eggesford and Winkleigh)

☎ (01837) 83572 ⊕ lymingtonarms.co.uk

Teignworthy Reel Ale; 2 changing beers (sourced regionally) ⃞

A friendly, welcoming pub set in the mid-Devon countryside, with a large car park that is often home to a classic car club. It has attractive outdoor seating, a sunny bar/dining area and a characterful restaurant. Eggesford Station, where all Tarka Line trains stop, lies only two fairly easily walked or cycled miles away. The regular Teignworthy Reel Ale, is usually accompanied by at least one other West Country beer, while good locally sourced and home-cooked food is served. Q✿☆◑♿P🐾🎶

Widecombe-in-the-Moor

Rugglestone Inn ⃞

TQ13 7TF (¼ mile from the centre of the village)

☎ (01364) 621327 ⊕ rugglestoneinn.co.uk

House beer (by Teignworthy); 4 changing beers (sourced regionally) 🄶

Originally a cottage, this Grade II-listed building was converted to an inn back in 1823. It is surrounded by peaceful moorland and is just a few minutes' walk from the centre of the village. Inside, there is a cosy bar with a wood-burner and two further rooms, one of which has an open log fire. Outside is a large, sheltered garden with picnic tables and a car park just down the road. Ciders sold include the local Hunt's Cider. Q✿☆✉◑A♣●P🖵(271,672)🐾

Winkleigh

King's Arms ⃞

The Square, Fore Street, EX19 8HQ (in village square)

☎ (01837) 682681 ⊕ kingsarmswinkleigh.co.uk

Teignworthy Reel Ale; Hanlons Yellow Hammer; 3 changing beers (sourced locally) ⃞

Grade II-listed 16th-century thatched village pub. The single bar has low-beamed ceilings, a flagstone floor and a welcoming wood-burning fire for colder months. Good food from a varied menu can be enjoyed in a series of intimate dining rooms featuring naval memorabilia, books and an intriguing, glass-capped well. To the rear is a cosy private function room. Up to five, mainly Devon-sourced real ales are usually available, together with two ciders from nearby Sam's. Q✿☆◑A♣●🖵(315)🐾🛜🎶

Yarde Down

Poltimore Arms ⃞

EX36 3HA (2 miles E of Brayford on jct with unclassified road from South Molton to Simonsbath) SS725356

Exeter Lighterman ⃞; **1 changing beer (sourced regionally)** 🄶

Dating back to the 13th century, this old beamed coaching inn lies in a remote area of glorious Exmoor countryside. The ivy-clad pub is so remote it generates its own electricity, and water is drawn from a spring. The Poltimore Arms is an atmospheric and welcoming locals' pub, which retains many interesting and original features, including, it is said, a friendly ghost. Q✿☆A♣P🐾🛜

Breweries

Barnaby's SIBA

The Old Stable, Hole Farm, Staverton, TQ11 0LA

☎ (01803) 762730 ⊕ barnabysbrewhouse.com

Soil Association-certified organic brewery established in 2016. Occasional cask ale production. A planned doubling of the size of the premises will enable a four-fold increase in production. New beers have been added to the range. Barnaby's Brewhouse is one of the most sustainable breweries in Britain, aiming in the near future to be completely off grid. ♦V

Dark Dunkel (ABV 4.8%) SPECIALITY
Pilsner (ABV 4.8%) SPECIALITY
Red Helles (ABV 4.8%) SPECIALITY
English IPA (ABV 5.4%) PALE
Green Tomato Saison (ABV 6%) SPECIALITY

Barum SIBA

▤ Reform Inn, Pilton High Street, Pilton, Barnstaple, EX31 1PD
☎ (01271) 329994 ⊕ reforminn.co.uk/barum-brewery

⊠ Barum Brewery was established in 1996 by Tim Webster and is housed in a conversion attached to the Reform Inn, which is now run by Tim. The Reform continues to act as the brewery tap as well as serving other locally-sourced ales. Distribution is exclusively within Devon. ‼♦LIVE

Bays SIBA

Aspen Way, Paignton, TQ4 7QR
☎ (01803) 555004 ⊕ baysbrewery.co.uk

Bays Brewery is a multiple award-winning, family-run business based in Torbay on the Devon coast. Its passion is to brew premium ales using the finest local ingredients while also supporting the community and protecting the environment. It is committed to reduce its carbon footprint with 30kw of solar panels on the roof to help power the brew process. Spent grains are used by local farmers for cattle feed, spent hops are used on local allotments as fertilisers and yeast extracts are sent to an anaerobic digester in Plymouth to help power a dairy farm. ‼▬♦V

Topsail (ABV 4%) BITTER
A tawny session bitter with complex aroma. Malty, bitter taste leading to a long, dry and refreshing aftertaste.
Gold (ABV 4.3%) GOLD
Smooth, golden ale. Light aroma and taste of hops, malt and caramel. Lingering hoppy aftertaste.
Devon Dumpling (ABV 5.1%) BITTER
Strong ale, easily drinkable. Light aromas of hops and fruit continue through taste and lingering aftertaste.

Beer Engine SIBA

Newton St Cyres, EX5 5AX
☎ (01392) 851282 ⊕ thebeerengine.co.uk

⊠ The Beer Engine was established in 1983 and is the oldest working microbrewery in Devon. The brewery is visible in the downstairs bar in the pub through multiple viewing windows. Several outlets are supplied, as well as local beer festivals. ‼♦

Branscombe SIBA

Branscombe, EX12 3DP
☎ (01297) 680511 ⊕ branscombebrewery.co.uk

⊠ The brewery was set up in 1992 in cowsheds at the back of a National Trust-owned farm, overlooking the sea at Branscombe. The brewery owners converted the sheds, digging its own well. In 2008 a new 25-barrel plant was shoehorned in through the roof to increase capacity. ♦LIVE

Branoc (ABV 3.8%) BITTER

Amber session bitter. Hops and malt throughout with good bitterness in taste and aftertaste.
Golden Fiddle (ABV 4%) GOLD
Summa This (ABV 4.2%) BITTER
Strong bitterness throughout, touch of grapefruit and tangerine notes with malty biscuitiness.
Summa That (ABV 5%) GOLD

Bridgetown SIBA

▤ Albert Inn, Bridgetown Close, Totnes, TQ9 5AD
☎ (01803) 863214 (Pub) ☎ 07517 926040
⊕ albertinntotnes.com/bridgetown-brewery

⊠ Bridgetown started brewing in 2008 using a two-barrel plant in the outbuildings of the Albert Inn, Totnes. Beers are available in an increasing number of local outlets. ‼▬♦LIVE

Albert Ale (ABV 3.8%) BITTER
Pale bitter, malt dominating throughout. Roast and caramel in aroma, taste and aftertaste with a little bitterness on the tongue.
Bitter (ABV 4.2%) BITTER
A tawny-coloured bitter with malt on the nose. The taste is malt and slightly fruity with a bitter, malty, dry finish.
Cheeky Blonde (ABV 4.5%) GOLD
Shark Island Stout (ABV 4.5%) STOUT
Smooth stout with strong malt and roast throughout. Touches of liquorice and chocolate lead to a bitter finish.
Westcountry IPA (ABV 4.7%) PALE

Bulletproof

91 Mutley Plain, Plymouth, PL4 6JJ ☎ 07703 733570

Office: Highlands, 1 Queen's Road, Lipson, Plymouth, PL4 7PJ ⊕ bulletproofbrewing.co

⊠ Small-scale brewery established in an outbuilding in 2016. It uses a 50-litre pilot plant to refine recipes before upscaling, using spare capacity at larger breweries. All beers are unfiltered and unfined. ♦

Checkstone

▤ First & Last Inn, 10 Church Street, Exmouth, EX8 1PE
☎ (01395) 263275

Checkstone Brewery, named after the Checkstone reef outside the Exe Estuary, is a one-barrel plant inside the First & Last pub, Exmouth, established in 2016. Like the brewery, the beers are named after various sea features around Exmouth. ♦

Clearwater

Unit 1, Little Court, Manteo Way, Gammaton Road, Bideford, EX39 4FG
☎ (01237) 420492 ☎ 07891 562005
⊕ clearwaterbrewery.co.uk

⊠ Established in 1998, Clearwater is a 10-barrel brewery regularly supplying more than 250 outlets across the South West and nationally with its Devon's Own-labelled beers. Beers are also available at the brewery tap, the Champ, Appledore. ▬♦LIVE

Expedition Ale (ABV 3.7%) BROWN
Real Smiler (ABV 3.7%) GOLD
Eric's ESB (ABV 4.1%) BITTER
Mariners (ABV 4.2%) GOLD
Proper Ansome (ABV 4.2%) BITTER
A dark brown bitter, malty-flavoured, slightly sweet. In the style of a winter warmer.
Riff IPA (ABV 4.3%) PALE

Combe

Unit 4, Lundy View, Mullacott Cross Industrial Estate, Ilfracombe, EX34 8PY
☎ (01271) 267030 ☎ 07973 488409
⊕ combebrewingcompany.co.uk

⊗ Combe Brewing Co was established in early 2020, in a recently closed brewery. It produces bottle-conditioned ales to meet its small but growing client base. The owners, Richard and Michelle, have previous experience in the trade. A five-barrel plant is used. Bottle label artwork is designed by a local artist, Karen French. ‼ ॓ LIVE ✦

Harbour (ABV 3.7%) BITTER
Beach Blonde (ABV 4.1%) BLOND
Ruby Sunset (ABV 4.7%) RED
Dark and Stormy (ABV 5%) PORTER

Cottage Beer Project

Brockhole Cottage, Morebath, Tiverton, EX16 9BZ
☎ 07422 731152 ✉ dan@cottagebeerproject.co.uk

Nanobrewery opened in 2021 to brew bottle-conditioned beers in classic styles in 200-litre brew runs. Beers are sold online and at local retailers, cafés and events, primarily within Devon and Somerset. The core range is supported by seasonal and one-off beers, with occasional cask for special events. ✦ LIVE V

Country Life SIBA

The Big Sheep, Abbotsham, Bideford, EX39 5AP
☎ (01237) 420808 ☎ 07971 267790
⊕ countrylifebrewery.co.uk

⊗ Country Life is based at the Big Sheep tourist attraction. The brewery offers a beer show and free samples in the shop during the peak season (April-October). A 15.5-barrel plant was installed in 2005, making Country Life the biggest brewery in North Devon. Regular, seasonal and bottle-conditioned beers are available at approximately 100 outlets, the brewery shop, and online. ‼ ॓ ✦ LIVE

Old Appledore (ABV 3.7%) BITTER
Reef Break (ABV 4%) BITTER
Shore Break (ABV 4.4%) GOLD
Black Boar/Board Break (ABV 4.5%) PORTER
Complex, well-balanced aromas. Unusual, dry, bitter hop taste leading to softer aftertaste with unexpected roasted malt and caramel.
Golden Pig (ABV 4.7%) BITTER
Country Bumpkin (ABV 6%) OLD

Crossed Anchors

⬛ Grapevine, 2 Victoria Road, Exmouth, EX8 1DL
☎ (01395) 222208 ☎ 07843 577608
⊕ crossedanchors.co.uk

⊗ Crossed Anchors was established in 2015. In 2016 a six-barrel plant became operational in the old stables of the Grapevine in Exmouth town centre. In 2022 an additional two 2,100-litre conical fermenters were added. Beers are increasingly available across Devon and the South-west, as well as in the Grapevine. ‼ ॓ ✦ LIVE

Sweet Session O'Mine (ABV 3.8%) PALE
Pale ale with light citrus/tropical aroma and taste, smooth mouthfeel with bitter finish.
Bitter Exe (ABV 4%) BITTER
American Pale Ale (ABV 4.2%) PALE
Very light brown-coloured ale. As a lot of sweet malt and fruit on aroma. Sweet tropical fruits dominate the taste with slight bitter finish.

Big Red Ale (ABV 5.2%) RED

Dartmoor SIBA

The Brewery, Station Road, Princetown, PL20 6QX
☎ (01822) 890789 ⊕ dartmoorbrewery.co.uk

⊗ Formerly named Princetown, Dartmoor Brewery was established in 1994. It is the highest brewery in England (1,465ft above sea level). In 2005 it moved locally to a new, purpose-built building. In both 2012 and 2013 capacity was increased. In 2017 a further extension was built giving a brewing capacity of 540 barrels. The brewery is a traditional ale producer and all beer is brewed using English Malt. ‼ ॓ ✦

Best (ABV 3.7%) BITTER
IPA (ABV 4%) PALE
There is a flowery hop aroma and taste with a bitter aftertaste to this full-bodied, amber-coloured beer.
Dragon's Breath (ABV 4.4%) SPECIALITY
Sweet, winter warmer best bitter. Full-bodied, sweet, fruity with treacle hints. Malt, roast and caramel from start to finish.
Legend (ABV 4.4%) BITTER
Complex beer full of aromas and flavours. Malt and caramel dominate balanced in an aftertaste of bitter hops. Well-rounded.
Jail Ale (ABV 4.8%) BITTER
Stronger session ale with complex notes dominated by malty sweet bitterness. Well-rounded caramel and fruit with a pleasant aftertaste.

Devil's Pleasure

Higher Sigford Farm, Sigford, TQ12 6LD ☎ 07847 228249 ⊕ thedevilspleasure.com

Brewery founded in 2020 on the edge of Dartmoor National Park, near Newton Abbot. It specialises in brewing punchy, bold craft beers which are unfiltered and naturally hazy.

Devon Earth SIBA

Buckfastleigh ☎ 07927 397871

Office: 7 Fernham Terrace, Torquay Road, Paignton, TQ3 2AQ ✉ info@devonearthbrewery.co.uk

⊗ Devon Earth brewery is located on the banks of the River Dart on the edge of Dartmoor and is run on a part-time basis. The brewery is proud to support local charities and supplies local and national beer festivals and free houses. ✦ V

Devon Earth (ABV 4.2%) GOLD
Grounded (ABV 4.7%) BITTER
Lost in the Woods (ABV 5.2%) PORTER

Exeter SIBA

Unit 1, Cowley Bridge Road, Exeter, EX4 4NX
☎ (01392) 259059 ⊕ exeterbrewery.co.uk

⊗ Exeter began brewing in 2003 and is the largest brewery in the city, supplying more than 600 outlets in Devon, Cornwall, Dorset and Somerset. It moved to its present site in 2012, having outgrown its previous location. ‼ ॓ ✦ ✎

Lighterman (ABV 3.5%) BITTER
Tomahawk (ABV 3.5%) BITTER
Slight biscuit/malty aroma, biscuit and a tinge of orange and a slight toffee bitter finish.
Avocet (ABV 3.9%) BITTER

A refreshing light low ABV ale, slight citrus/fruit on nose which comes out more on taste. An easy-drinking, summer-style beer.

'fraid Not (ABV 4%) GOLD
Easy to drink, refreshing with a gentle lingering aftertaste.

Ferryman (ABV 4.2%) BITTER
A malty, slightly-spiced biscuit with a sweetness to the ale. An easy-drinking, session traditional bitter.

County Best (ABV 4.6%) BITTER

Darkness (ABV 5.1%) STOUT
Full-bodied stout. Roasted malt dominates the aroma. Complex taste with roast chocolate. Hints of liquorice in a bitter finish.

MC6 – Mash Concentration 6 (ABV 6%) BITTER
An old ale-style ale with a sweet taste with lots of malts and roasts blending together giving a lovely continuous aftertaste.

Fat Belly

Unit 8F, Commercial Point, Mullacott Cross Industrial Estate, Ilfracombe, EX34 8PL
☎ (01598) 753496 ☎ 07946 133332
⊕ fatbellybrewery.co.uk

⊠ Established in Lynbridge in 2016 at the Cottage Inn, using a three-barrel plant located at the rear of the pub. It relocated to its current premises in 2018, installing a new 10-barrel plant. As well as the pub it also supplies a growing number of outlets in the Exmoor area. Brewing is currently suspended. ♦ LIVE

Gilt & Flint

Haye Farm, Haye Lane, Musbury, EX13 8ST ☎ 07904 035640 ⊕ giltandflint.com

This brewery is based on the beautiful Haye Farm in an Area of Outstanding Natural Beauty in East Devon. Using age old traditional brewing techniques, it has created organic, modern, New World, bottle-conditioned beers, ciders and soft drinks. All of the agricultural by-product goes to feed the free-range livestock on the farm. LIVE

Grampus

🗏 **Grampus Inn, Lee Bay, EX34 8LR**
☎ (01271) 862906 ⊕ thegrampus-inn.co.uk

⊠ Grampus was established in 2014 at the back of the Grampus Inn by Bill Harvey, the pub owner and brewer. It is a small plant using traditional brewing methods, but combining unique and unusual ingredients. All beers are available in the local area. A small batch gin distillery was added in 2019. ♦ LIVE

GT

Unit 5, The Old Aerodrome, Chivenor Business Park, Barnstaple, EX31 4AY
☎ (01271) 267420 ☎ 07909 515170 ⊕ gtales.co.uk

⊠ Established in 2013, GT Ales is housed in a World War II aircraft hangar at Chivenor. An onsite brewery shop has been added to the five-barrel brewery. All five award-winning core ales are available in cask, bottle (limited availability) and can. Limited edition small-batch brews are regularly produced and own brand beers are also brewed for local customers. ‼ 🍺 ♦ LIVE

Thirst of Many (ABV 4.2%) BITTER
North Coast IPA (ABV 4.3%) PALE
Blonde Ambition (ABV 4.5%) BLOND
Dark Horse (ABV 4.5%) BITTER
Crimson Rye'd (ABV 4.8%) RED

Hanlons SIBA

Hill Farm, Half Moon Village, Newton St Cyres, EX5 5AE
☎ (01392) 851160 ⊕ hanlonsbrewery.com

⊠ Hanlons, one of Devon's largest brewers since 2013, supply a range of award-winning ales nationwide. The purpose-built brewery also has a shop, bar and restaurant. In 2019 it bought Prescott Ales of Cheltenham. ‼ 🍺 ♦

Firefly (ABV 3.7%) BITTER
Malty and fruity light bitter. Hints of orange in the taste.

Citra IPA (ABV 4%) PALE
An easy-drinking citrus/floral IPA.

Yellow Hammer (ABV 4.2%) PALE
Zesty fruit aroma, pineapples on taste with a nice sweetness counteracted by bitterness. Even though available all year, its got a summer ale style to it. Very refreshing.

Brewers Blend (ABV 4.5%) BITTER
Malty biscuit aroma, with a malty biscuit taste with lemons in the background. An easy-drinking bitter.

Port Stout (ABV 4.8%) SPECIALITY
Hints of caramel and port on aroma. Ruby port flavour with dried raisin taste with a slight hint of caramel and chocolate. All flavours carry through on aftertaste.

Stormstay (ABV 5%) BITTER
Tawny and full-bodied. Caramel with hints of malt on the nose. Triumvirate of malt, caramel, hops develop into lingering bitterness.

Brewed under the Prescott Ales name:
Hill Climb (ABV 3.8%) PALE
Pit Stop (ABV 4%) PALE
Chequered Flag (ABV 4.2%) BITTER
Podium Finish (ABV 4.8%) STOUT
Grand Prix (ABV 5%) BITTER

Contract brewed for Wickwar:
Falling Star (ABV 4.2%) GOLD
A golden premium beer made with Maris otter barley and a blend of three choice hops, giving a floral aroma and a light malty finish.

Hatherland

Hatherland Mill Farm, Lower Washfield, Tiverton, EX16 9PG
☎ (01398) 351165 ⊕ hatherland.co.uk

Owner and founder, Lawrence Bunning, decided to combine his love for beer with reutilising unused space on his family farm, setting up the brewery in the old dairy shed. Water is drawn from a bore hole. Passionate about the environment, solar energy is utilised from panels on the brewery roof and heat from the wood chip boiler. Brewing waste is used to feed the farm's prize-winning, rare-breed cattle. LIVE

Sand Martin (ABV 4.7%) PALE

Holsworthy

Unit 5, Circuit Business Park, Clawton, Holsworthy, EX22 6RR
☎ (01566) 783678 ☎ 07879 401073
⊕ holsworthyales.co.uk

⊠ Holsworthy Ales is a 5.5-barrel microbrewery situated in the heart of Devon's Ruby Country. Brewing began commercially in 2011. Its intention is to make its beers taste as clean and natural as possible, so no chemicals or finings are added to the soft Devon water used in many of its ales. ‼ 🍺 ♦ LIVE V

Mine's a Mild (ABV 3.5%) MILD

A rich malty taste, lightly hopped to give a good balance and finish.

Sunshine (ABV 4%) GOLD
A yellow golden ale with a good body and smooth in the mouth. Hops overwhelm all else, but there is a hint of fruit in the aroma and the taste is fresh and bitter. The hoppy aftertaste is enhanced by bitterness.

St George (ABV 4.1%) GOLD

Bang On (ABV 4.2%) BITTER

Muck 'n' Straw (ABV 4.4%) BITTER
A smooth copper-coloured best bitter. Traditionally hopped it is hops that dominate throughout with hints of malt in the aroma and taste and a slightly dry aftertaste. A well-balanced beer from lasting hoppiness on the nose to a more subtle aftertaste.

Tamar Black (ABV 4.8%) STOUT
A rich, smooth stout, dark in colour. Malt and roast are evident from nose to aftertaste, with hints of coffee and liquorice. A complex beer with fruit, hops and caramel all present. Full of flavour, rich and satisfying.

Hop on the Run (ABV 5%) PALE

Proper Lager (ABV 5%) SPECIALITY

Old Market Monk (ABV 6.1%) SPECIALITY

Isca SIBA

Court Farm, Holcombe Village, Dawlish, EX7 0JT
☎ 07773 444501 ✉ iscaales@yahoo.co.uk

⊠ Established in a disused milking parlour in 2009, Isca has developed a large range of ales. Seasonal and special brews are often available at beer festivals, including outside of the region. ♦LIVE

Citra (ABV 3.8%) BITTER

Dawlish Summer (ABV 3.8%) GOLD

Golden Ale (ABV 3.8%) GOLD

Dawlish Bitter (ABV 4.2%) BITTER

Glorious Devon (ABV 4.4%) BITTER

Gold (ABV 4.5%) GOLD

Holcombe White (ABV 4.5%) SPECIALITY

Dawlish Pale (ABV 5%) PALE

Black IPA (ABV 6%) IPA

Devon Pale (ABV 6.8%) IPA

Ivybridge

Unit 3, Glanvilles Mill, Ivybridge, PL21 9PS
☎ (01752) 894295 ☎ 07512 961085
⊕ ivybridgebrewing.co.uk

Established in 2018, Ivybridge Brewing Company is a social enterprise brewery that provides training and paid work for people from the local area with learning disabilities. It upgraded to a 2.5-barrel kit in 2021 and set up a taproom and shop where its trainees serve its four core beers on draught and bottle conditioned. It also supplies local outlets. All profits from beer sales are reinvested in the business to create more opportunities for trainees. ☕LIVE ✦

Many Hands

Dunkeswell Airfield, Dunkeswell, EX14 4LF
☎ (01404) 892100 ⊕ manyhandsbrew.com

Many Hands Brew Co began brewing in 2017, producing small-batch, bottled beers. Each bottle sold makes a contribution to local charities.

Morwell

Morwellham Quay, Morwellham, PL19 8JL
☎ (01822) 832766 ⊕ morwellham-quay.co.uk/morwellham_brewery

Established in 2017 at this Victorian tourist attraction by brewer George Lister. Using a 100-litre plant, three bottle-conditioned beers are brewed, which are available in the onsite shop and café, as well as a growing number of local outlets. It also supplies cask beers to the Ship Inn. ☕LIVE

Adit (ABV 4.2%) BITTER

Miner (ABV 4.4%) GOLD

Hop (ABV 4.8%) PALE

New Devon

Froginwell Vineyard and Cider Barn, Woodbury Salterton, Exeter, EX5 1EP
☎ (01395) 239900 ☎ 07976 981334
⊕ newdevonbrewing.co.uk

A collective of brewers and cider makers who have been inspired by the craft beer movement. Initially producing one beer, New Devon Ale, but others will make an appearance during the year. ♦

New Devon Ale (ABV 4.5%) PALE

New Lion SIBA

Unit 6E, Webbers Way, Shinners Bridge, Dartington, TQ9 6JY
☎ (01803) 226277 ⊕ newlionbrewery.co.uk

⊠ Community-owned brewery, established in 2013 and named after the Lion Brewery (renowned for Totnes Stout but closed in the 1920s). It is a modern, five-barrel brewhouse, producing a range of core ales, seasonals and dozens of one-off White Label beers annually; many in collaboration with local producers and businesses. It runs a popular membership scheme and taproom/bottle shop, which also acts as a live venue. ☕♦LIVE V✦

Pandit IPA (ABV 4.9%) PALE
In the style of an American IPA. Slightly sweet with a fruity hoppy taste.

Noss Beer Works SIBA

Unit 6, Ash Court, Pennant Way, Lee Mill, PL21 9GE
☎ 07977 479634 ⊕ nossbeerworks.co.uk

⊠ Noss Beer Works was formed in 2012 using a six-barrel plant. The beers are made from only the finest locally-sourced hops and malts. ‼♦LIVE

Black Rock (ABV 4%) PALE

Church Ledge (ABV 4%) BITTER
Bitter dominated by hops and fruit throughout. Hoppy and citrusy, slight caramel balances bitter dryness. Slight kick at the end.

Mew Stone (ABV 4.3%) BITTER
Malty biscuit aroma which follows on taste. Quaffable session bitter.

Ebb Rock (ABV 4.9%) BITTER

Otter SIBA

Mathayes, Luppitt, Honiton, EX14 4SA
☎ (01404) 891285 ⊕ otterbrewery.com

⊠ A family-run brewery set high up in the Blackdown Hills. Environmental responsibility lies at the heart of its ethos. Otter's eco cellar has been built underground and is naturally chilled. The beers are made from the brewery's own spring water and locally-sourced ingredients. ♦✦

Bitter (ABV 3.6%) BITTER
Well-balanced session bitter with a fruity nose. Biscuity overtones, hop, lemon and apricot with bitter taste and dry aftertaste.

Amber (ABV 4%) BITTER
Light, refreshing and mellow with hints of citrus hoppiness. Creamy and delicate with hops and fruit.
Bright (ABV 4.3%) GOLD
A light and refreshing golden ale with delicate malt, and fruit leading through hops to a lingering bitter aftertaste.
Ale (ABV 4.5%) BITTER
Malt dominates from nose to throat. Sweet fruit, toffee and caramel with a dry aftertaste, full of flavour.
Head (ABV 5.8%) BITTER
Smooth strong ale. Caramel malt throughout. Full-bodied with rich malty fruitiness and a chocolate hint, leaving a bitter aftertaste.

Powderkeg SIBA

10 Hogsbrook Units, Woodbury Salterton, EX5 1PY
☎ (01395) 488181 ⊕ powderkegbeer.co.uk

⊠ Powderkeg was established in 2015 brewing small batches of beer. It combines international beer styles with new ingredients sourced from around the world. GF V

Idler (ABV 3.9%) BITTER
Chestnut-coloured session ale, malty aroma with hints of raisins. Malty taste with a slight bitter finish.
Speak Easy Transatlantic Pale Ale (ABV 4.3%) BITTER

Red Rock SIBA

Higher Humber Farm, Bishopsteignton, TQ14 9TD
☎ (01626) 879738 ⊕ redrockbrewery.co.uk

⊠ Red Rock first started brewing in 2006 using a four-barrel plant and upgraded in 2011 to a 7.5-barrel one. It is based in a converted barn on a working farm using locally-sourced malt, fresh hops and the farm's own spring water. It has a bar and can accommodate private functions. ‼ 🍽 ♦ LIVE V ♠

Lighthouse IPA (ABV 3.9%) PALE
Red Rock (ABV 4.2%) BITTER
Break Water (ABV 4.6%) BITTER

Riviera

4 Yonder Meadow, Stoke Gabriel, Totnes, TQ9 6QE
☎ 07857 850110 ⊕ rivierabrewing.co.uk

⊛ Riviera started brewing commercially in 2015 using a one-barrel plant. European and New World hops are used in addition to various British varieties. ♦

RBC Best (ABV 3.8%) BITTER
RPA (Riviera Pale Ale) (ABV 3.9%) PALE
Devonian (ABV 4.1%) BITTER
Gold (ABV 4.2%) GOLD

Roam

New Victoria House, Weston Park Road, Plymouth, PL3 4NU
☎ (01752) 396052 ☎ 07971 411727
⊕ roambrewco.uk

⊠ Roam produce small-batch beers using a combination of traditional and modern brewing techniques and local ingredients. A six-barrel plant is used. ‼ 🍽 ♦ LIVE ♠

Tavy Gold (ABV 4%) BITTER
Hometown Pale (ABV 4.1%) PALE
A nice, fruity, hopped, American-style pale ale. Fruit aroma, tastes of grapefruit and mango with lasting finish on the palate.
Tavy Best Bitter (ABV 4.3%) BITTER

Malt dominates the nose and taste with caramel, roast and hops overpowering a subtle hint of fruit. A complex aftertaste.
Sound Bitter (ABV 4.5%) BITTER
A good drinkable best bitter, full-flavoured on body content.
Tavy IPA (ABV 4.8%) PALE
Gold ale dominated by hops and fruit from start to finish. Slight fruit/straw aroma. Citrus/hoppy dry taste. Dry/bitter finish.
Tavy Porter (ABV 5.2%) PORTER
Full-bodied porter. Malt, liquorice, chocolate nose. Slightly bitter fruity taste. Roasted coffee and touch of vanilla in the aftertaste.
Double Take (ABV 7.1%) STRONG
An American brown ale with lots of body, swimming in fruity hops. Sweet on taste, complex mix of malty/roast flavours. A beer to saviour.

Salcombe SIBA

Estuary View, Ledstone, TQ7 4BL
☎ (01548) 854888 ⊕ salcombebrewery.com

⊠ Salcombe Brewery was purpose built on the site of a decommissioned water reservoir, which utilises the natural ambient temperature of the underground facility for storing ales at perfect conditioning temperature. The brewery has close ties with both the RNLI and the Seahorse Trust. ‼ 🍽 ♦ ♠

Devon Amber (ABV 3.8%) BITTER
Salcombe Gold (ABV 4.2%) GOLD
Citrus aroma coming from the USA fruity hops. Tastes of apricot, peach and melon in with a mellow biscuit touch in the backgound. A very refreshing ale.
Shingle Bay (ABV 4.2%) BITTER
Seahorse (ABV 4.4%) BITTER
Toffee malt is evident throughout this complex yet subtle mix of everything you would expect from a best bitter.
Lifesaver (ABV 4.8%) BITTER
A refreshing ale, deep copper in colour, with a smack of citrus and orange peel and luscious malty flavour. A dry citrus finish with a taste of liquorice.
Island Street Porter (ABV 5.9%) PORTER
A really good porter. Creamy head, aroma of chocolate/coffee and cherries giving a black forest gateau taste. Flavours linger on tongue during aftertaste.

South Hams SIBA

Stokeley Barton, Stokenham, Kingsbridge, TQ7 2SE
☎ (01548) 581151 ⊕ southhamsbrewery.co.uk

⊠ South Hams has been brewing ales for 19 years in Start Bay, Devon. A family-run brewery, it supplies more than 350 outlets in Plymouth and South Devon with wholesalers distributing further afield. ‼ 🍽 ♦ LIVE

Devon Pride (ABV 3.8%) BITTER
A surprisingly full-bodied ale for a session beer. Fruity malty aroma, with a malty biscuit taste and mixed fruits.
Shippen (ABV 4%) BITTER
Gently-flavoured brew with caramel hop aroma. Hints of citrus nose, bittersweet flavour and stone fruit backbone with dry bitter aftertaste.
Stumble Bee (ABV 4.2%) SPECIALITY
Wild Blonde (ABV 4.4%) BLOND
Subtle notes of malt, roast and caramel, dominated by fruity hops. These persist to a refreshing hint of lemon.
Eddystone (ABV 4.8%) BITTER
Strong, amber, summery ale. Hoppy, caramel, slightly citrus nose. Dryer taste with light fruit and hops. Dry yet fruity finish.
Sherman (ABV 6.4%) IPA

A strong American pale ale, a thick-flavoured beer, very fruity and sweet on aroma/taste and aftertaste.

Stannary SIBA

Unit 6, Pixon Trading Centre, Tavistock, PL19 8DH
☎ (01822) 258130 ⊕ stannarybrewing.shop

Stannary began operating in 2016 using a 2.5-barrel plant, moving to larger premises with a six-barrel plant in 2018. The brewery tap is open on Friday-Saturday showcasing its many unfined and unfiltered craft beers with street food at weekends and occasional live entertainment. The shop is open Monday-Thursday. See website for openings. 🛒♦⚒

Summerskills SIBA

15 Pomphlett Farm Industrial Estate, Broxton Drive, Billacombe, Plymouth, PL9 7BG
☎ (01752) 481283 ⊕ summerskills.co.uk

⊗ Established in a vineyard in 1983 at Bigbury-on-Sea, Summerskills moved to its present site in 1985. It is the oldest brewery in Plymouth. Wholesalers and pub companies provide national distribution and the beers regularly appear in a growing selection of local outlets. 🛒♦LIVE

Start Point (ABV 3.7%) GOLD
Westward Ho! (ABV 4.1%) BITTER
Malt dominates a light nose. Gentle bitterness introduces its malty-fruit friends. Malt and bitterness remain, with bitterness dominating the conversation.
Tamar (ABV 4.3%) BITTER
A sweet malty taste, with a slight bitter finish. A refreshing easy-drinking traditional best bitter.
Stout (ABV 4.4%) STOUT
Strong coffee aroma, slight sweetness on the taste with coffee/chocolates on tongue. Bitter finish.
Devon Dew (ABV 4.5%) GOLD
Malty aroma but not too hoppy on the nose. A sweet lemon taste comes through followed by grapefruit. An easy drinkable golden bitter.
Devon Frost (ABV 4.5%) GOLD
A slight nutty roast on the nose and also on taste with grapefruit flavours on the tongue.
Menacing Dennis (ABV 4.5%) BITTER
Bolt Head (ABV 4.7%) BITTER
Fruit-hop nose has roast-malt hints. Bitter flavours with sweet malt, roast and hoppiness. Lingering bitter finish with background malt and fruit.
Whistle Belly Vengeance (ABV 4.7%) RED
Strong aroma of rich malts, tastes of dates and liquorice sweetness in this strong ale.
Dragon Pioneer (ABV 4.8%) PALE
A floral citrus aroma, grapefruit on taste with a floral tang and crispiness to it. Slightly herbal finish to a refreshing beer.
Plymouth Porter (ABV 5%) PORTER
Strong sweet chocolate aroma, tastes of chocolate and toffee. Aftertaste dies off quickly, a nice drinkable sweet porter.
Indiana's Bones (ABV 5.6%) OLD
Old ale with good body. Rich malty roasts aroma bursting with strong sweet flavours on the tongue. Slightly dryer finish.

Tally Ho!

🍴 **14, Market Street, Hatherleigh, EX20 3JN** ☎ 07779 339 089 ⊕ tallyhohatherleigh.co.uk

⊗ Having stood idle at the rear of the Tally Ho! pub for 14 years, the brewery was resurrected in 2015, and then sold in 2018. The current owner and brewer took over in 2020. As well as the pub, several local free houses and other establishments are supplied. ♦

Tavistock (NEW)

The Old Root House, Harragrove Farm, Peter Tavy, PL19 9JR ☎ 07564 869198 ⊕ tavistockbrewery.co.uk

Located in Dartmoor National Park, and overlooking Peter Tavy, Tavistock Brewery is a family run business which has been five years in the planning and design. After renovating a farm building previously used as an old dairy, brewing commenced in 2022. Three beers are brewed on the four-barrel plant and are currently available in a small but growing number of local pubs and bars.

Golden Ale (ABV 4.3%) GOLD
English Ale (ABV 4.5%) BITTER
Master Ale (ABV 4.9%) BITTER

Taw Valley

Westacott Farm, Westacott Lane, North Tawton, EX20 2BS ☎ 07900 002299 ⊕ tawvalleybrewery.com

Established in 2017 in a Grade-II listed, 17th century thatched barn. Beer is delivered in the brewery dray, a VW camper van. ♦LIVE⚒

Black Ops (ABV 3.9%) BITTER
Tawton Session Ale (ABV 4%) PALE
Devon Jester (ABV 4.2%) PALE
Kennard's Steam (ABV 4.3%) BITTER
Copper Best (ABV 4.4%) BITTER

Teignmouth SIBA

Warehouse 1, Old Quay Street, Teignmouth, TQ14 8ES
☎ (01626) 770846 ⊕ teignmouthbrewery.co.uk

The brewery opened in 2019. Currently a six-barrel brew length, brewing three regular beers (also available bottle-conditioned) and a number of seasonal beers. There is a continued focus on quality cask beers and these are distributed across the south Devon area. The brewery continues to diversify the style of beers it produces on a seasonal basis. ♦LIVE

Templer (ABV 4%) BITTER
Portside (ABV 4.3%) BITTER
Deckhand (ABV 4.5%) GOLD

Teignworthy

The Maltings, Teign Road, Newton Abbot, TQ12 4AA
☎ (01626) 332066 ⊕ teignworthybrewery.com

⊗ Teignworthy Brewery opened in 1994 within the historic Tucker's Maltings building and remains family run. Based on a tower system with open squares, the 20-barrel plant produces up to 50 barrels a week and supplies around 150 outlets in Devon and Somerset plus wholesalers further afield on a pre-arranged basis. It diversified in 2017 with the addition of the Black Dog gin distillery. ‼🛒♦LIVE

Neap Tide (ABV 3.8%) PALE
Reel Ale (ABV 4%) BITTER
Subtle aromas. The taste is also gentle with malt and fruit dominating the hops. The aftertaste is dry.
Thirsty Blonde (ABV 4.2%) BLOND
Gun Dog (ABV 4.3%) BITTER
Easy-drinking, session best bitter. Fruity throughout. Dry aftertaste lingers; sweetness and fruit over malt and caramel, progressing into hoppiness.

Topsham

The Warehouse, Haven Road, Exeter, EX2 8GR
☎ 07735 591557 ✉ topshambrewery@gmail.com

The brewery was established in 2018 and moved to its current location at the popular Exeter Quay in 2019. A new 1,200-ltire plant was commissioned in 2023. The taproom, with an outside drinking area, is next to the brewery, which is visible from the bar. There are frequent one-off brews, normally available as keg, with some appearing in cask along with the regular and seasonal beers at the brewery tap. ♦ ❧

Serenity (ABV 3.8%) BITTER
Ask Your Dad (ABV 4.3%) BITTER
Goat Walk (ABV 4.6%) PALE

Totnes

🏠 **The Barrel House, 59a High Street, Totnes, TQ9 5PB**
☎ 07974 828971 ⊕ barrelhousetotnes.co.uk/about-us

⊗ Brewing on a 300-litre kit, positioned behind the bar, since 2014, A family-run tap only brewing for consumption on the premises. Output has increased to six beers permanently on tap at the bar, plus a host of locally brewed and European craft ales (on tap, and in bottles and cans). Focus is on local, with all house taps coming from within Devon & Cornwall. ♦

TQ Beerworks SIBA

Unit 6, Kingswood Court, Long Meadow, South Brent, TQ10 9YS ⊕ tqbeerworks.com

TQ is a small, family-run brewery dedicated to bringing craft beer to Torbay and the surrounding area. It does not have a core range. All beers are unfined, unfiltered and vegan-friendly. LIVE V❧

Turk's Head

🏠 **202 High Street, Exeter, EX4 3EB**
☎ (01392) 706013 ⊕ turksheadexeter.com

A historic public house, refurbished by City Pub Group during 2020/2021, brewing a range of up to five live beers. The range is expected to increase. !! GF V

Utopian SIBA

Unit 4, Clannaborough Business Units, Bow, EX17 6DA
☎ (01392) 769765 ⊕ utopianbrewing.com

Utopian began brewing in 2019 producing craft lagers. 2022 saw a live beer range, branded OMK, plus a few cask ales. ♦

Whyte Bar

c/o 25 Paris Street, Exeter, EX1 2JB

Whyte Bar, pronounced Whyte Bear, was founded in 2018 as a cuckoo brewery by Andy Whyte and Joel Barnard. Brewing has taken place at local breweries, such as Many Hands and Topsham (qv). Its own bar, Cuckoo Bar, is now open. Real ale is planned for the near future, with either handpumps or half-pins on the bar. Currently all beers are served as KeyKeg from numerous taps behind the bar. ❧

Yelland Manor

Lower Yelland Farm, Yelland, Barnstaple, EX31 3EN
☎ 07770 267592 ✉ yellandmanor@gmail.com

⊗ Located on the Taw Estuary and close to the Tarka Trail, this five-barrel plant in a converted milking parlour, was established in 2013. It supplies a small number of local pubs and hotels, although the majority of sales are now made from the premises, either as takeaways or for consumption as part of a 'brewery experience'. Small functions are also catered for. !! 🚲 ♦ ❧

English Standard (ABV 4.1%) BITTER

Bicton Inn, Exmouth (Photo: Steve Murray)

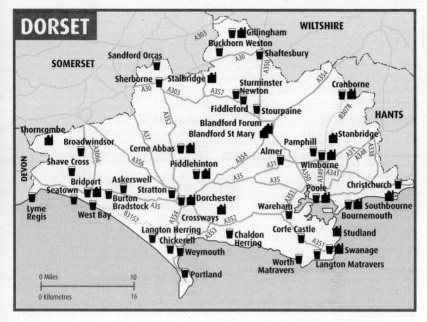

Almer

World's End 🛈

DT11 9EW (off B3075 nr jct with A31)
☎ (01929) 459036 ⊕ worldsendalmer.co.uk
House beer (by Lyme Regis); 3 changing beers (sourced regionally; often Lyme Regis) 🅗
A large thatched country pub with an interesting history, part of the nearby Charborough Estate. The pub has been here for nearly 600 years, though it was renovated after having burnt down some 30 years ago. It is split into two areas, with a single long low bar that is divided into sections, giving an overall cosy atmosphere, with diners using one end and drinkders the other. Up to four ales are available, and cider from Cranborne Chase.
⚄🕮🕪🍴👜🅟🌼

Askerswell

Spyway Inn

DT2 9EP
☎ (01308) 485250 ⊕ thespywayinn.com
3 changing beers (sourced locally; often Cerne Abbas, Exmoor, Otter) 🅖
Family-friendly 16th-century smuggler's inn perched on the lower slopes of Eggardon Hill on the outskirts of Askerswell. There's a snug main bar and further rooms for dining. The gravity-served real ales are sourced from local and West Country brewers, and local cider is also available. Mind your head when exiting into the large garden, which has plenty of seating, including six covered pods, and superb views across the countryside.
Q⚄🕮🚌🕪👜🅟🌼🛜♫

Bournemouth

Acorn

1492 Wimborne Road, BH11 9AD
☎ (01202) 575062
6 changing beers (sourced regionally; often Goddards, Hattie Brown's, Sixpenny) 🅗
This imposing 17th-century pub was originally a coaching inn and is rich in history. It was previously named Gullivers, due its connection with Isaac Guliver, a local smuggler. It is in the safe hands of a family who previously ran an award-winning pub nearby and offers a well-chosen selection of ales from the L-shaped bar which serves two distinct areas. The landlord plays music on Sunday afternoons and live music features occasionally. There is also shove-ha'penny and a dartboard. No children after 6pm. ⚄♣👜🅟🖵🌼

All Hail Ale

10 Queens Road, BH2 6BE
☎ 07786 045996
4 changing beers (sourced nationally) 🅗
A vibrant micropub and bottle shop, this former restaurant has been skilfully converted, with wooden flooring and polished-wood bar and tables. Five handpumps serve a range of ales from independent breweries nationwide, alongside a real cider. Ten keg pumps offer a varied and well-chosen selection of beers. Popular tap takeovers are held to showcase some of the major new craft ales; a large blackboard lists the beers available. ●👜🚌🐾🛜♫

Cricketers

41 Windham Road, BH1 4RN
☎ (01202) 985056
Fuller's London Pride; 2 changing beers (sourced nationally) 🅗
A splendid Victorian gem built in 1847, making it Bournemouth's oldest pub. It retains many original features and is rich in mahogany and stained glass. It is just a short stroll from Bournemouth rail/bus interchange, and is close to the Vitality Stadium, so it is popular with football supporters on match days. Lunches are available at weekends only, including roasts. Tuesday is quiz night, and pool, darts and other in-house games give this pub an excellent vibe. ⚄🕪♣👜🅟🖵(2)🌼🛜♫

Firkin Shed

279 Holdenhurst Road, BH8 8BZ
☎ (01202) 302340
4 changing beers (sourced regionally) 🅗

'The Shed' is a quirky, friendly, family-run micropub and a former CAMRA National Cider Pub of the Year. Tables and benches hug the walls of the main bar area and snug, which are decorated with flags, musical instruments, puppets and skulls. A shed is used as the bar, hosting a constantly changing range of cask and keg beers alongside an impressive cider range. The garden area is a great place to relax and enjoy the summer sunshine. ✿●🖳(2)❀

Goat & Tricycle ✓
27-29 West Hill Road, BH2 5PF
☎ (01202) 314220 ⊕ goatandtricycle.co.uk
Butcombe Adam Henson's Rare Breed, Original, Gold; Liberation Ale, Herm Island Gold, IPA; 5 changing beers (sourced regionally) Ⓗ
An award-winning traditional pub, popular with drinkers and diners. It was originally two adjoining pubs, the left of which is listed and has a fine tiled frontage. Eleven handpumps serve mostly Butcombe and Liberation Ales, as well as Stan's ciders. Good, freshly cooked food is served daily, except Sunday evenings, with gluten-free options available. A partly covered courtyard caters for smokers and alfresco drinkers. Sunday is quiz night. Under-18s are not admitted. ✿◑●🖳❀🛜

Micro Moose
326 Wimborne Road, BH9 2HH
⊕ micromoose.co.uk
5 changing beers (sourced regionally) Ⓗ
This friendly hostelry offers superb British ales with Canadian hospitality. The ales are served from handpumps and always in excellent condition. They are sourced from around the region and the selection changes quite frequently. Real cider is also available, plus a selection of Canadian bottled beer to tempt you while sitting in the Canadian-themed surroundings, with flags and moose-related items. Q&●🖳❀

Poole Hill Brewery Ⓛ
41-43 Poole Hill, BH2 5PW
☎ (01202) 557583 ⊕ poolehillbrewery.com
7 changing beers (sourced locally; often Southbourne Ales) Ⓗ
The bar is on the ground floor of a handsome listed Victorian building, with the Southbourne Ales brewery to the rear viewable through a glazed partition. A function room and small cinema are in the basement. Seven handpumps offer a selection from the eight different Southbourne beers that are regularly brewed, together with other beers brewed under the Tingay brand. Brewery tours take place several times a week. There is regular live music. &🖳♪

Silverback Alehouse
518 Wimborne Road, BH9 2EX
☎ (01202) 510988 ⊕ silverbackalehouse.co.uk
4 changing beers (sourced regionally; often Brew Shack, Gritchie, Plain) Ⓖ
This long, narrow micropub is a friendly and relaxed place to enjoy a drink. Just take a seat on a bench or at one of the high set tables and the staff will come and take your order. You have a choice from four regionally sourced ales or ciders, which are always in good order. For the hungry there are bar snacks, or you can bring your own food. Q&♣●🖳❀🛜

Bridport

Bull Hotel Ⓛ
34 East Street, DT6 3LF
☎ (01308) 422878 ⊕ thebullhotel.co.uk
Fuller's London Pride; Gale's HSB Ⓗ

This former 16th-century coaching inn, now belonging to Fuller's, features a large, golden bull on the frontage. A small hotel bar leads to a sunny courtyard and the Bull Hotel pizzeria (which was formerly the site of the first pizzeria of the Stable chain of restaurants). The Monmouth Bar, situated away from the main dining area, has a separate entrance from the street and tends to be open in the late afternoon and evenings. Q🍽✿🚪◑▣&●P🖳❀♪

Crown Inn Ⓛ
59 West Bay Road, DT6 4AX
☎ (01308) 422037
Palmers Copper Ale, IPA, Dorset Gold, 200, Tally Ho! Ⓗ
Spacious and unpretentious traditional pub on the A35 roundabout between Bridport and West Bay, popular with locals and holidaymakers. It serves the full range of beers from the historic Palmers brewery, which is less than half a mile away. Good home-made food is served every day, and takeaways are available. Free live music can be enjoyed on Saturday evenings and Sunday afternoons. Outside is a beer garden and a large car park. 🍽✿◑&♣●P🖳(X53) ❀🛜♪

Pursuit of Hoppiness
15 West Street, DT6 3QJ
☎ (01308) 427111 ⊕ hoppiness.co.uk
Brew Shack Bills Bitter; 5 changing beers (sourced nationally; often Bristol Beer Factory, Eight Arch, Vibrant Forest) Ⓗ
Near the town hall is this single-room micropub which accommodates up to two dozen people, with the same number seated outside. A fast-changing range of beers from local, regional and national breweries is supplemented by various bottled and canned beers in the fridge. Beers and ciders can be sampled before purchase and even canned to take away. Ciders are usually from West Milton. Payment by card only. Q🚪✿♣●P🖳❀🛜

Tiger Inn ✓
14-16 Barrack Street, DT6 3LY
☎ (01308) 427543 ⊕ tigerinnbridport.co.uk
5 changing beers (sourced regionally; often Exmoor, Hanlons, Sharp's) Ⓗ

A busy Victorian pub tucked away just off the town centre. The five changing real ales are predominately from the West Country. The main bar is decorated with dried hops and beer mats and boasts a large-screen TV showing mainly sporting events, plus a dartboard. To the rear is a smaller, quieter bar and a cocktail bar/function room. Outside are two well-maintained seating areas. Look for the rare Groves Brewery etched window.
ॐ❀🌙🍴🍺🚶🏠♿🚭🔊

Woodman Inn

61 South Street, DT6 3NZ
☎ (01308) 456455 🌐 thewoodman.pub
4 changing beers (sourced regionally; often Cerne Abbas, Copper Street, Exmoor) Ⓗ
A friendly pub with a focus on quality beers, wide-ranging in style, and up to 12 boxed real ciders. The real ales turn over very quickly (check out the pub's Facebook page). There is a stone-floored single bar with a fire, and a skittle alley to the rear. Tables at the front make the most of the sunny aspect, and to the rear is a quiet, pleasant garden. Regular events include folk nights, storytelling and wassailing. Local CAMRA Cider Pub of the Year 2023. ॐ❀🚶🅿🚭♿🔊

Broadwindsor

White Lion 🍽 Ⓛ ✅

The Square, DT8 3QD
☎ (01308) 867070 🌐 whitelionbroadwindsor.co.uk
Palmers Copper Ale, IPA, Tally Ho! Ⓗ
Set in a beautiful West Dorset village, this 17th-century inn was threatened with closure, but in 2022 was successfully taken over and renovated by the community on a tenancy agreement with local brewer Palmers. Food is available from a fish & chip van on Tuesday evenings and a pizza van on alternate Thursdays (plates and cutlery provided by the pub). Local CAMRA Pub of the Year 2023. Q❀ॐ♣🚶🍴(CB3)♿

Buckhorn Weston

Stapleton Arms

Church Hill, SP8 5HS (between A303 and A30)
ST75652462
☎ (01963) 370028 🌐 stapletonarms.co.uk
Flower Pots Pots Bitter; house beer (by St Austell); 1 changing beer (sourced locally; often Parkway, Plain, Quantock) Ⓗ
Impressive and friendly village pub set in lovely countryside on the northern fringes of the Blackmore Vale. Excellent food is served, as well as classic bar snacks such as hand-made sausage rolls. Children, dogs and muddy boots are most welcome, as is the roaring fire in winter. At the rear is a secluded garden and a large car park. Accommodation is in four individually designed bedrooms. Ramps are available to provide step-free access to the pub. Q❀ॐ🛏🍴🅿♿🚭🔊

Burton Bradstock

Anchor Inn

High Street, DT6 4QF
☎ (01308) 897228 🌐 anchorinn.pub
Dartmoor Jail Ale; Otter Bitter; 1 changing beer (sourced regionally; often Exmoor, St Austell, Timothy Taylor) Ⓗ
One of the few free houses in this part of rural Dorset, the Anchor is located in a pretty village with a beautiful beach nearby. Inside there are several dining areas and a separate public bar. Local seafood is the specialty. Up to four beers are selected from Dartmoor, Dorset, Exmoor,

Sharp's and St Austell breweries. The accommodation consists of three en-suite rooms.
Q❀ॐ🛏🍴🅿🚶🅿(X53)♿🚭🔊

Three Horseshoes Ⓛ ✅

Mill Street, DT6 4QZ
☎ (01308) 897259 🌐 threehorseshoesburtonbradstock.co.uk
Palmers Copper Ale, IPA, Dorset Gold, 200, Tally Ho!; 1 changing beer (sourced locally; often Palmers) Ⓗ
A 300-year-old thatched pub serving the full range of local Palmers beers and real cider. Good, home-cooked food is the main focus here and is served all day throughout April to September. There is a suntrap beer garden for the summer and log fires for the winter. The pub is popular with visitors to nearby Hive beach. The car park is opposite and the village shop is next door. Opening hours are more restricted in winter, and the pub is closed on Mondays. Q❀ॐ🍴🅿🚶🅿(X53)♿🚭🔊

Cerne Abbas

Cerne Abbas Brewery Tap

Chescombe Barn, Barton Meadows Farm, DT2 7JS
☎ (01300) 341999 🌐 cerneabbasbrewery.com
3 changing beers (sourced locally; often Cerne Abbas) Ⓖ
Cerne Abbas brewery was founded in 2014 on a farm in the Cerne Valley. Their beers are alway brewed with local ingredients and are served in the rustic-style taphouse, which is used for numerous local events (ticket holders only). You can also bring your own picnic. The beers have appeared at the House of Commons and on BBC1's Saturday Kitchen. It is just a short walk from the bus stop (service 5, weekdays only) in the village. ॐ❀🅿♿🔊

Chaldon Herring

Sailor's Return Ⓛ

DT2 8DN
☎ (01305) 854441 🌐 sailorsreturnpub.com
Cerne Abbas Ale; Otter Ale; Palmers Copper Ale; 1 changing beer (sourced regionally; often Cerne Abbas, Flack Manor, Palmers) Ⓗ
Historic thatched inn on the edge of a tranquil village, a few miles from the Jurassic Coast. The pub dates from the 1860s though the buildings are much older. There are several dining and drinking areas, with flagstone floors throughout. An original inn sign hangs in the main bar. Wednesday is pie night with roasts on Sunday. On Friday night food is served only in the restaurant area (booking advisable). Restricted opening hours in winter.
Q❀ॐ🍴🚶🅿♿🚭🔊

Chickerell

Lugger Inn Ⓛ

West Street, DT3 4DY
☎ (01305) 766611 🌐 theluggerinn.co.uk
2 changing beers (sourced regionally; often Exmoor, Piddle, St Austell) Ⓗ
Popular village pub that is over 200 years old, tucked away just off the picturesque coast road. The menu offers pub classics and child-friendly dishes. The pub hosts monthly quiz nights, themed evenings and live music most Sunday afternoons. The skittle alley doubles as a function room and there are 14 en-suite letting rooms, one on the ground floor with full wheelchair accessibility. There is outside seating in a sunny garden across a quiet road.
ॐ❀🛏🍴🚶🅿🅿(8,X53)♿🚭🔊

Christchurch

Saxon Bar ♈

5 The Saxon Centre, Fountain Way, BH23 1QN

☎ (01202) 488931

4 changing beers (sourced nationally) Ⓖ

A friendly, single-room micropub, close to the town centre with perimeter seating and high tables made from wood reclaimed from Bounemouth Pier. The pub offers a variety of well chosen ales, direct from the cask, and up to 10 real ciders all served direct to your table. Speciality bar snacks, local and international spirits, and four KeyKeg beers are also available. Winter hours may vary. Regional CAMRA Cider Pub of the Year and local Pub of the Year 2023. ❀≈●🖿🐾

Corfe Castle

Bankes Arms Hotel Ⓛ ●

23 East Street, BH20 5ED

☎ (01929) 288188 ⊕ bankesarmshotel.co.uk

Palmers IPA, 200; 2 changing beers (sourced regionally; often Ringwood) Ⓗ

Historic 16th-century Grade II-listed hotel, owned by the National Trust, that retains many of its original features including a town drinkers' bar. Regular beers from Palmers are served, alongside beers recreated by the Dead Brewers Society, brewed by Barnet. Occasional beer festivals are held in the summer. The restaurant to the rear serves excellent home-cooked food. A large picturesque garden overlooks Swanage Steam Railway and Corfe Castle station and enjoys fantastic views of the Purbeck hills.

Q🏵🗲🚲🌒🖐&≈(Swanage) ●P🖿(40,30) 🐾🛜

Corfe Castle Club

70 East Street, BH20 5EQ (off A351)

☎ (01929) 480591

Ringwood Razorback; Timothy Taylor Landlord; 1 changing beer (sourced nationally) Ⓗ

Friendly club in a Purbeck stone-built former school in the village centre. The main bar has upholstered bench seating and a TV for major sporting events, plus darts and Purbeck longboard shove-ha'penny. An upstairs room has a pool table and can be hired for meetings. Filled rolls are available all day. The spectacular garden boasts a boules court and views over the Purbeck hills. Visitors are welcome with a CAMRA membership card or copy of the Guide. Local CAMRA Club of the the Year 2023. Convenient for the castle or steam railway.

❀≈(Swanage) ♣P🖿(40,30) 🐾🛜

Fox Inn Ⓛ

8 West Street, BH20 5HD

☎ (01929) 480449 ⊕ thefoxinncorfecastle.com

Butcombe Adam Henson's Rare Breed; Hattie Brown's Moonlite; 2 changing beers Ⓗ

Delightful 16th-century inn nestled in the heart of historic Corfe Castle and retaining many original features and links to the stone industry for which the area is famous. The front door opens into a small traditional snug with steps down to the main bar area where good pub food is served. Towards the rear is an elongated garden complete with barbecue shack and fine views over the castle and surrounding Purbeck hills. The heritage Swanage steam railway is just a stone's throw away. Q🏵🐕🌒🖐&≈(Swanage)🖿(40,30)🐾

Cranborne

Sixpenny Tap Ⓛ

Holwell Farm, Holwell, BH21 5QP (1 mile from village centre on B3078)

☎ (01725) 762006 ⊕ sixpennybrewery.co.uk

Sixpenny 6d Best Bitter, 6d Gold, 6d IPA; 3 changing beers (sourced locally; often Sixpenny) Ⓗ

Housed in a converted Victorian stables and packed full of quirky miscellaneous items, the Sixpenny Tap has established itself at the heart of the local community. With the Sixpenny brewery located next door, their popular range of ales are served with pride and enthusiasm. The pub hosts many successful and colourful community and charity events in the extensive courtyard, and a warm welcome awaits everyone. This is a real countryside gem, set within picturesque farmland, and even has its own Tardis. Q🏵&♣●P🐾🛜

Dorchester

Blue Raddle

9 Church Street, DT1 1JN

☎ (01305) 267762 ⊕ blueraddle.co.uk

Cerne Abbas Blonde; St Austell Tribute; 3 changing beers (sourced regionally; often Bath Ales, Dartmoor, Palmers) Ⓗ

Very much a locals' pub, reflected in the quirky photos and paraphernalia that adorn the walls and bar, but strangers are made equally welcome. The bar dominates and is decorated with covers of Private Eye and old beer pumpclips. Seating is on soft furnished benches alongside wooden tables and chairs. Food is locally sourced and cooked by the publican's wife. The pub is closed Monday to Thursday and when the owners are on holiday, so best to phone in advance.

Q🌒≈(South) 🖿🐾🛜

Convivial Rabbit

1 Trinity House, Trinity Street, DT1 1TT (down the alley to the left of Pennywise)

☎ 07717 158853 ⊕ convivialrabbit.co.uk

6 changing beers (sourced nationally) Ⓖ

This popular micropub serves a changing selection of around six real ales of varying styles and strengths, sourced from micro and independent British breweries. Local ciders, lagers, wines, gins and tea and coffee are also available. Regular live music features, including Sunday folk nights. The pub is tucked away in an alley off Trinity Street, but easily accessed via South or West stations and is well worth seeking out. Closed Monday and Tuesday. Q🏵≈(South)♣●🖿🛜♪

Copper Street Brewery Tap Room Ⓛ

8 Copper Street, DT1 1GH

☎ 07395 664390

3 changing beers (often Copper Street) Ⓖ

The glass-fronted taproom is opposite Dorchester South railway station. The comfortably furnished bar, which serves three of the brewery's own beers as well as tea and coffee, can accommodate around 20 customers, with more seating outside. It is partitioned off from the brewery, which is visible through a viewing window. There is a wall-mounted bottle shop, stocking the brewery's full range of ales, and a TV for sporting events. Q🐕🏵&≈(South) 🖿(10) 🐾🛜

Tom Browns Ⓛ

47 High East Street, DT1 1HU

☎ (01305) 264020 ⊕ tombrownspub.co.uk

Copper Street Saxon Gold; Dorset Tom Brown's; 2 changing beers (sourced regionally; often Cerne Abbas, Copper Street, Plain) Ⓗ

Town-centre alehouse with wood-floored public bar, a real fire and basic furnishings. The pub is a keen supporter of local breweries and makes the perfect starting place for a walk along the River Frome via the secluded garden. It is lively on Saturday nights with the

sound of banter and live music, but is currently under threat of redevelopment. Well worth a visit.
♿☆♣♠🅗🖵🕿📶♪

Fiddleford

Fiddleford Inn
DT10 2BX (off A357 between Sturminster Newton and Blandford)
☎ (01258) 472886 ⊕ thefiddlefordinn.net
4 changing beers 🅗
Recently refurbished inn dating from around 1740 that retains some original features. The building hosted a brewery in the 18th and 19th centuries and has also been used as a malt house and an old coaching stop. The pub has a relaxing atmosphere, a well-stocked bar with real ales, and great food in the separate restaurant. It is ideal for country walks and for visiting the nearby Fiddleford Manor. Q♿☆🅗🖵🆒🕽P🐾♪

Gillingham

Phoenix
The Square, SP8 4AY
☎ (01747) 823277
St Austell Proper Job; Sharp's Doom Bar; 1 changing beer (sourced locally; often Hattie Brown's) 🅗
Originally a 15th-century coaching inn with its own brewery and stable, this pub was rebuilt and renamed the Phoenix following a fire in the 17th century. It has an open-plan layout with two areas and an open fire. In addition to the two Cornish regular beers there is always one from Dorset brewery Hattie Brown's. Real ciders are sometimes available in the summer. There is seating outside and two public car parks nearby.
♿☆🅰🚆🖵(X2)🐾📶

Langton Herring

Elm Tree Inn
Shop Lane, DT3 4HU
☎ (01305) 871257 ⊕ theelmtreeinn.co.uk
2 changing beers (sourced regionally; often Cerne Abbas, Dorset, Lyme Regis) 🅗
A 17th-century pub recently refurbished to a high standard. The dining area has a log fire, and dogs are welcome in the bar area and beer garden. It is popular with discerning diners, especially at weekends, so it is advisable to book ahead. The house beer is from Lyme Regis brewery. The pub is at the heart of the small coastal village of Langton Herring, a short walk from Chesil Beach and the Fleet, on the Jurassic Coast. Closed Monday and Tuesday. Q♿☆🅗🖵🐾📶♪

Langton Matravers

King's Arms
27 High Street, BH19 3HA
☎ (01929) 422979
Butcombe Original; 3 changing beers (sourced nationally; often Hattie Brown's, St Austell) 🅗
Dating back to 1743, this Grade II-listed, Purbeck stone-built pub features rooms off a central bar area with original flagstone floors. It is a family-friendly community pub that welcomes dogs and is popular with visitors. It serves fine pub food and hosts a village shop. The rear garden is a suntrap. The seaside town of Swanage is close by, as are many fine walks where you can explore the Purbecks and the South West Coast Path.
Q♿☆🅘🅰🖵(40)🐾📶

Lyme Regis

Harbour Inn
23 Marine Parade, DT7 3JF
☎ (01297) 442299 ⊕ harbourinnlymeregis.co.uk
Otter Ale; St Austell Tribute; 1 changing beer (often St Austell) 🅗
Standing opposite the harbour and the sandy beach, much of the outside seating is on the beach itself. There is further seating at the entrance on a raised veranda, which is a good place to watch the world go by. Inside is a bar area, largely used for dining, and behind this is the restaurant area. The food is highly regarded, with fish being a specialty. ♿☆🖵(X53,31)🐾

Lyme Regis Brewery Tap
Mill Lane, DT7 3PU
☎ (01297) 444354 ⊕ lymeregisbrewery.com
3 changing beers (sourced locally) 🅗
The taproom for the brewery can be found tucked away in the Town Mill courtyard off Coombe Street. Previously the premises were a malthouse and the town's first power station. There are three Lyme Bay cask ales available plus eight keg beers from the brewery. Seating is limited inside so be prepared to sit in the charming courtyard. No disabled access but there is a disabled toilet off the courtyard. ♿☆🖵🐾📶♪

Pamphill

Vine Inn ★
Vine Hill, BH21 4EE (off B3082)
☎ (01202) 882259
2 changing beers (sourced regionally; often Otter, Plain) 🅗/🅖
Identified by CAMRA as having a nationally important historic pub interior, this multi-award winning country pub is owned by the National Trust. It has been managed by the same family for 120 years – and by the current landlady for over 30 years. There are two cosy bars, an upstairs room, and a large patio and garden. Light snacks of ploughman's and toasties are served during lunchtimes. This is a real gem, and popular with walkers and cyclists. Opening times may vary in winter.
Q☆🅘♣P🐾

Piddlehinton

Thimble Inn 🄻 ✅
14 High Street, DT2 7TD
☎ (01300) 348270 ⊕ thimbleinn.co.uk
Palmers Copper Ale, IPA, Dorset Gold; 1 changing beer (sourced locally; often Palmers) 🅗
This thatched Palmers house sits alongside the River Piddle. Though set out mainly for dining, drinkers are made very welcome. The beers often include Palmers Tally Ho! There is a log-burner, flagstone flooring in the bar areas and low beams. A perspex-covered well is a feature; its water level rises with the water table. It has two riverside gardens and is a former winner of the local CAMRA Garden of the Year. ♿☆🅘♿🅰♣P🐾📶♪

Poole

Barking Cat Alehouse 🍷
182-184 Ashley Road, BH14 9BY
☎ (01202) 258465 ⊕ thebarkingcatalehouse.co.uk
8 changing beers (sourced nationally; often Bristol Beer Factory, Hattie Brown's, Siren) 🅗
Vibrant, multi award-winning pub with 12 keg and four cider lines complementing the range of cask ales. Beers are sourced from the best local and national breweries,

with something on offer to satisfy most tastes and styles. There are regular beer festivals and live music, while the back room can also be booked for functions. Patrons may order food from the Chinese restaurant next door.
㋡&≅(Bransome) ♣●🖥🍺(M1,15) ☀🌐🎵

Bermuda Triangle
10 Parr Street, BH14 0JY
☎ (01202) 748087 🌐 bermudatrianglepub.com
5 changing beers (sourced nationally; often Oakham, Palmers) Ⓗ
Established in 1870, this great local drinkers' pub is at the heart of Ashley Cross. The cosy interior has five distinct bar areas – find your way through the bookcase to find the hidden sixth. It is nautically themed, decorated to reflect the Bermuda Triangle story, and there are also American vehicle registration plates. The patio with fairy lights is very inviting and there is also a roof terrace. Brunch is served on Sundays.
☀≅(Parkstone) ●🖥(M1,M2) ☀🌐🎵

Brewhouse
68 High Street, BH15 1DA
☎ (01202) 685288
Frome Funky Monkey, The Usual; 1 changing beer (sourced nationally; often Frome) Ⓗ
This multi award-winning pub has been a long established feature of Poole High Street, and a reliable source of interesting ales from Frome brewery, as well as well-chosen ales from national microbreweries. Real cider is also available. Entering from the High Street, you find tables in the window and beyond the busy bar area there is an area for pool and darts. This no-frills, traditional community pub offers a warm welcome to locals, visitors and their dogs. ☀≅♣●🖥☀🌐

Butcher's Dog
37-39 Parr Street, BH14 0JX
☎ (01202) 739539 🌐 butchersdogdorset.com
2 changing beers (sourced regionally; often Brew Shack, Eight Arch, New Bristol) Ⓗ
Single-room bar decorated in a modern industrial style, with a cosy and welcoming feel. It has mixed-level seating from which to peruse the wall-mounted beer lists. The beer range fuses traditional and modern, offering up to two cask and 16 craft ales from microbreweries, plus a can fridge for on-site or takeaway consumption. There is street-front seating and a large, covered, keller-style rear garden. The pub is dog and bicycle-friendly. ☀●)≅(Parkstone)●🖥(M1)☀🌐

Poole Arms Ⓛ ✅
19 The Quay, BH15 1HJ
☎ (01202) 673450 🌐 poolearms.co.uk
Dorset Jurassic; Flack Manor Flack's Double Drop; St Austell Proper Job; 1 changing beer (sourced regionally) Ⓗ
Originating from 1635 and steeped in history, this distinctive green-tiled quayside pub is popular with locals and tourists. Wood-panelled walls adorned with photographs of old Poole dominate the cosy single room bar area serving up to five real ales. The extensive menu offers locally sourced, award-winning seafood. Quayside bench seating at the front provides a great space to watch the many activities taking place in the bustling harbour. Q☀●)🖥(8)

Portland

Cove House Inn ✅
Chesil Beach, DT5 1AW
☎ (01305) 820895 🌐 thecovehouseinn.co.uk

Ringwood Fortyniner; Sharp's Doom Bar; 1 changing beer (sourced locally; often Dorset) Ⓗ
An 18th-century public house next to the promenade at the southern end of the Chesil Beach. It is popular with locals and visitors, especially divers and sailors from the nearby National Sailing Academy. There are spectacular views of the Jurassic Coast, notably at sunset. In inclement weather you can sit by the fire and watch the storms batter the beach (the window shutters are not just for decoration). Locally caught seafood features on the menu. Q☀●)♣🖥(1)☀🎵

George Inn ✅
133 Reforne, DT5 2AP
☎ (01305) 820011
Greene King Abbot; 3 changing beers (sourced nationally; often Butcombe, St Austell, Timothy Taylor) Ⓗ
Housed in one of the oldest dwellings on Portland, the George has been a pub since 1805. It consists of three separate drinking areas and a large beer garden. Themed food evenings are occasionally held, and there are usually three guest ales on offer. The pub is close to some spectacular cliff walks and a restored 18th-century church. Dogs are welcome. ㋡☀●)🖥(1)☀🌐🎵

Sandford Orcas

Mitre Inn
DT9 4RU
☎ (01963) 220271 🌐 mitreinn.co.uk
3 changing beers (sourced nationally; often Apex, Church End, Fine Tuned) Ⓗ
A classic traditional free house and a community asset. Its cosy bar and separate restaurant have flagstone floors and open fires. Beers are from national, regional and local brewers. Two beer festivals are held each year. The elevated rear garden is accessed by steps. Good-quality traditional food is served; booking is essential for Sunday lunch. The pub is popular with passing ramblers and cyclists. It has two high-standard letting rooms. Well worth seeking out. Q㋡☀●)♣P🖥(39)☀🌐

Seatown

Anchor Inn Ⓛ ✅
DT6 6JU
☎ (01297) 489215 🌐 theanchorinnseatown.co.uk
Palmers IPA, Dorset Gold, 200; 1 changing beer (sourced locally; often Palmers) Ⓗ
A family- and dog-friendly traditional country pub on the Jurassic Coast. There are plenty of coastal walks nearby to build up an appetite for their fantastic food using locally sourced ingredients. Warm up by the open fires or enjoy the sea views towards West Bay or Golden Cap from the large terraces. Accommodation is available in three luxury rooms. Payment by card only.
Q㋡☀⊠)&▲●☀🌐

Shaftesbury

Mitre
23 High Street, SP7 8JE
☎ (01747) 853002 🌐 themitredorset.co.uk
Young's London Original, London Special; 1 changing beer (often St Austell) Ⓗ
Historic pub close to the town hall at the top of the famous Gold Hill, with grand views from the patio overlooking the beautiful Blackmore Vale. Popular with younger drinkers on Friday and Saturday evenings but catering for all with an extensive food menu. The pub often hosts charity quizzes and occasional live music

nights. Open daily for lunch, dinner and afternoon tea, the menu is a mixture of British classics and traditional meals. 🛏️⊛◖❶&🖵♫

Olde Two Brewers
24 St James Street, SP7 8HE
☎ (01747) 852210 ⊕ 2brewers.co.uk
Fuller's London Pride; Wadworth 6X; 1 changing beer (sourced nationally) Ⓗ
A traditional pub nestled at the foot of Gold Hill (the setting for the iconic Hovis advert). The original landlords, two brothers, chose to brew their own beer at the pub and then travel around at festival time selling on their ales. The garden has good views. The area was once bustling with businesses like tanneries and laundries, taking advantage of abundant water from the old pump house. 🛏️⊛◖❶🐾P🖵☺🐾♫

Shave Cross

Shave Cross Inn
Shave Cross, DT6 6HW
☎ (01308) 868358 ⊕ shavecrossinn.co.uk
Gyle 59 Shave X Pale, Vienna Session Lager, Capitalist Hippie-Flower Power, Shave X Gold, Shave X Beer; 2 changing beers (sourced locally; often Cerne Abbas, Exmoor, Gyle 59) Ⓗ
Nestled in the heart of Marshwood Vale, just under four miles from the beauty of the Jurassic Coast. This thatched, Grade II-listed flint stone-building has origins dating back to the 14th century, with flagstones worn away by 700 years of monks, pilgrims and cyclists. As well as Gyle 59 ales on draught, their bottle-conditioned beers are also available, together with Dorset Nectar cider. The pub is a Brit Stop site, with free overnight parking for campers and motor homes.
Q⊛🖼️◖❶▲♣🐾P☺🐾♠

Sherborne

Digby Tap
Cooks Lane, DT9 3NS
☎ (01935) 813148 ⊕ digbytap.co.uk
4 changing beers (sourced regionally; often Cerne Abbas, Otter, Teignworthy) Ⓗ
A lively, 16th-century free house close to the famous abbey and railway station. The owners of over 20 years have retained the character of the building, with its four separate drinking areas, flagged floors and cosy corners. The four changing beers are sold at extremely reasonable prices as are the lunchtime meals. This is a real drinkers' pub – an institution in the town and surrounding area. Q⊛◖❶♣🚌🖵(58,5)☺♫

Stourpaine

White Horse Inn ✅
Shaston Road, DT11 8TA
☎ (01258) 453535 ⊕ whitehorse-stourpaine.co.uk
Gritchie English Lore; Sharp's Doom Bar; house beer (by Flack Manor); 2 changing beers (sourced locally; often Cerne Abbas, Sixpenny) Ⓗ
Wonderful village free house, originally two adjoining cottages, the pub has multiple cosy spaces with beams and open fireplaces. The five handpumps offer national and regional ales and cider lovers can enjoy Cranborne Chase direct from the box. Close to the North Dorset Trailway, the pub offers walkers and cyclists a well-earned break; dogs are welcomed with their own firkin of water. The garden areas help make this an appealing destination all year round. Q🛏️⊛◖❶♣🐾P🖵(X3)☺🐾

Stratton

Saxon Arms
20 The Square, DT2 9WG
☎ (01305) 260020 ⊕ thesaxon-stratton.co.uk
Butcombe Original; Timothy Taylor Landlord; 1 changing beer (sourced regionally; often Butcombe, St Austell) Ⓗ
Next to the church and village hall, this popular pub is the hub of the village. It offers a good range of ales (local and national), ciders and lagers, and has a good reputation for food, which is sourced locally. There is a great outside seating area for the summer, and in winter a welcoming wood-burner warms the open-plan bar and restaurant. Q🛏️⊛◖❶&♣P☺🐾

Sturminster Newton

White Hart Alehouse
Market Cross, DT10 1AN
☎ (01258) 472558 ⊕ whitehartalehouse.co.uk
6 changing beers (sourced nationally; often Eight Arch, Gritchie) Ⓗ
Built in 1708, this thatched Grade II-listed public house sits in the heart of the town. The interior is open plan, but there are two defined areas; at one end is a large TV and at the other a large open fire. The pub offers up to six real ales and 10 craft beers, and good-quality pub food is available at reasonable prices. There is a secure beer garden at the rear, which was formerly their car park. Live music features occasionally.
🛏️⊛◖❶🖵(X4,X10)☺🐾♫

Swanage

Black Swan Ⓛ ✅
159 High Street, BH19 2NE
☎ (01929) 423846 ⊕ blackswanswanage.co.uk
Dorset Dorset Knob; 2 changing beers (sourced nationally) Ⓗ
A traditional Grade II-listed pub on the High Street, about half a mile from the seafront. There are two bars with stone floors and log fires. The pub serves three well-kept ales. It is renowned for its quality food and booking for tables is essential (phone reservations only). The suntrap garden catches the evening sunshine.
Q🛏️⊛◖❶�ê P🖵(40,50)☺🐾

Red Lion
63 High Street, BH19 2LY
☎ (01929) 423533 ⊕ redlionswanage.com
Sharp's Doom Bar; Timothy Taylor Landlord; 3 changing beers (sourced nationally; often Dorset, Oakham, Otter) Ⓖ
Traditional 17th-century inn at the heart of the historic town, serving up to five ales on gravity from the ground floor cellar behind the public bar. The large selection of real ciders and perries is a big draw, with the range displayed on blackboards in both bars. The lounge has a restaurant area where quality food is served, with curry and steak nights always popular. The large, partly-covered garden is busy throughout the year.
Q🛏️⊛🖼️◖❶�ê♣P🖵(40,50)☺🐾

Wareham

Horse & Groom Ⓛ ✅
St Johns Hill, BH20 4LZ
☎ (01929) 552222
5 changing beers (sourced regionally; often Butcombe, Hattie Brown's, Palmers) Ⓗ

Situated in the heart of Wareham is this cosy pub with a reputation for good food and service. In winter customers can enjoy a real fire, while the pleasant courtyard garden is welcoming in summer. Five real ales are offered plus real cider. The pub hosts charity quiz nights and their famed curry evenings. They are proud to be the local CAMRA Pub of the Year and Rural Pub of the Year. ▷❀◑▶⬤🖵(40,X54)❀🛜

King's Arms ✓
41 North Street, BH20 4AD
☎ (01929) 552503 ⊕ kingsarmswareham.co.uk
6 changing beers (sourced nationally; often Brains, Harvey's, Sharp's) Ⓗ
Traditional thatched pub with its roots in the 1500s – a survivor of the great fire of 1762. There is a cosy bar with real fire in winter plus a drinking corridor and dedicated dining area. The large beer garden is the venue for a varied range of music events in the summer and these move inside during the cooler months. Home-cooked food is available throughout the day, in addition to themed evening dining experiences and wine tasting.
Q▷❀◑▶≢⬤🖵(40,X54)❀🛜

West Bay

George Hotel ⓛ ✓
18 George Street, DT6 4EY
☎ (01308) 423191 ⊕ georgewestbay.com
Palmers Copper Ale, IPA, Dorset Gold, 200; 1 changing beer (sourced locally; often Palmers) Ⓗ
Large and welcoming pub by the picturesque harbour. It consists of a separate public bar, dedicated eating area and a riverside garden with its own bar in the summer. Local cider is on offer, plus at least four Palmers beers which are brewed nearby in their historic thatched brewery. Wholesome, reasonably-priced pub food is served, and there are six en-suite bedrooms. Open every day throughout the year. Q▷❀❀◑◀▶🗲♣⬤🖵(X53)❀🛜

Weymouth

Dolphin Hotel
67 Park Street, DT4 7DE
☎ (01305) 839273
Hop Back Crop Circle, Summer Lightning; 1 changing beer (sourced regionally; often Hop Back) Ⓗ
A Hop Back brewery pub only a few minutes' walk to the beach and close to both the railway station and local bus routes. The interior is light, airy and divided into three rooms, two lounge rooms, both with TVs showing either sports or 60s-80s music, and a function room at the rear with a pool table. Summer Lightning and Crop Circle are the regular beers with one other Hop Back guest beer usually Entire Stout (winter) or Taiphoon (summer).
▷🖾≢♣🖵(1)❀🛜♪

Globe Inn
24 East Street, DT4 8BN
☎ (01305) 786061
Butcombe Original; Dartmoor Jail Ale; St Austell Proper Job; Sharp's Sea Fury; 2 changing beers (sourced regionally; often Cerne Abbas, Fine Tuned, Quantock) Ⓗ
Free house with a friendly welcome, tucked away on a street corner just 30 yards from the iconic harbourside. The Globe is a short distance from the town centre, the beach and the esplanade, and in summer offers a distinct change from the packed waterside. There is a jukebox and a separate games room with pool table and dartboard. Guest ales are mainly from local or regional breweries. ▷♣🖵❀🛜

Wimborne

Green Man ✓
1 Victoria Road, BH21 1EN
☎ (01202) 881021 ⊕ greenmanwimborne.com
Wadworth Henry's IPA, 6X, Swordfish Ⓗ
A friendly, traditional 18th-century pub in the centre of town, with one bar and four separate drinking areas. It features award-winning floral displays, a wood-burner, ubiquitous brasses and the infamous Green Man in the entranceway floor. Games are available on the patio and there is regular live music. Food offerings include steak nights, fish Fridays and Sunday roasts.
▷❀◑▶P🖵(3,13)❀🛜♪

Oddfellows Arms ⓛ
Church Street, BH21 1JH
☎ (01202) 88966 ⊕ oddfellowsarmswimborne.co.uk
Badger Best Bitter, Fursty Ferret, Tanglefoot Ⓗ
A small and quirky one-bar local situated just off The Square, near the site of the former Oddfellows Hall. It has been a pub since the 1800s, and was previously a morgue. It may have been a pub before that, though this cannot be verified as property numbers were not then used. Quiz nights and occasional live music feature.
Q♣🖵(3,13)❀♪

Taphouse
11 West Borough, BH21 1LT
☎ (01202) 911200
7 changing beers (sourced locally; often Dark Star, Eight Arch, St Austell) Ⓗ
Quirky, busy bar situated near the centre of the historic market town. It is a happy gathering place, full of atmosphere, and serves a great range of beers, details of which are available on the blackboard opposite the bar. The friendly staff are helpful and always on hand. Conversation rules – this is a place to meet and make friends. Live music features on Sundays.
❀🖵(3,13)❀🛜♪

Worth Matravers

Square & Compass ★ ⓛ
BH19 3LF (off B3069)
☎ (01929) 439229 ⊕ squareandcompasspub.co.uk
Hattie Brown's HBA, Moonlite; 3 changing beers (sourced regionally) Ⓖ
A real gem, this multi-award winning pub has been identified by CAMRA as having a nationally important historic pub interior. It has been in the same family since 1907 and has appeared in every edition of the Guide. Two rooms either side of a serving hatch convey an impression that little has changed over the years. The sea-facing garden offers fantastic views across the Purbecks and fossils are displayed in the small adjacent museum. Pasties are available. Beer and cider festivals are held in October and November respectively.
Q▷❀♣⬤❀♪

Breweries

Barefaced SIBA

Unit 1, Holland Business Park, Blandford Forum, DT11 7TA
☎ (01258) 268088 ⊕ barefacedbrewing.co.uk

⊠ Barefaced Brewing was established in 2017 by two friends, Nick Horne and Tom Cooper, in one of their garden sheds in Wimborne. A move to Bournemouth was followed by a move to its new location in Blandford

Forum, which has allowed for expanded production and a taproom. ‼️ ☕ ♦ LIVE ✦

So You've Travelled (ABV 4.4%) GOLD
Heartbreak Stout (ABV 5.4%) STOUT
Flash IPA (ABV 5.9%) IPA

Boscombe

Bournemouth ☎ 07549 844099

Office: 17 Gloucester Road, Bournemouth, BH7 6DQ
⊕ bbco.beer

⊠ A nanobrewery launched commercially in 2022 using a three-barrel plant in a converted outhouse of a residential property. Brewer Jarrod Thompson began homebrewing in his native Nassua in New Hampshire more than twenty years ago. No real ale.

Brewers Folly

Ashton Farm House, Stanbridge, Wimborne, BH21 4JD
☎ 07463 554434 ⊕ brewersfolly.co.uk

⊠ Founded in 2017, it is now brewing on a five-barrel plant in Stanbridge with plans to move the brewery to Honeybrook Farm where it has recently opened a brewery tap, with meeting and function space. Direct deliveries throughout Dorset and much of Hampshire plus shipments further afield on request. ‼️ ☕ ♦

Session Pale Ale (ABV 4.2%) PALE
Summer Haze (ABV 4.6%) PALE
10w-40 (ABV 5%) STOUT
Chocolate Milk Porter (ABV 5%) PORTER
Azacca IPA (ABV 5.5%) IPA
Citra IPA (ABV 5.5%) IPA
Ekuanot IPA (ABV 5.5%) IPA
Kohatu IPA (ABV 5.5%) IPA
Mosaic IPA (ABV 5.5%) IPA
Sabro IPA (ABV 5.5%) IPA
Simco IPA (ABV 5.5%) IPA

Brewhouse & Kitchen SIBA

🍴 154 Commercial Road, Bournemouth, BH2 5LU
☎ (01202) 055221 ⊕ brewhouseandkitchen.com

⊠ Part of the Brewhouse & Kitchen chain, producing its own range of beers. Carry outs and brewery experience days are offered. ‼️ ☕

Brewhouse & Kitchen SIBA

🍴 17 Weymouth Avenue, Dorchester, DT1 1QY
☎ (01305) 265551 ⊕ brewhouseandkitchen.com

⊠ Part of the Brewhouse & Kitchen chain, producing its own range of beers. Carry outs and brewery experience days are offered. ‼️

Brewhouse & Kitchen SIBA

🍴 3 Dear Hay Lane, Poole, BH15 1NZ
☎ (01202) 771246 ⊕ brewhouseandkitchen.com/poole

⊠ Opened in 2015 this outlet is an excellent addition to the Brewhouse & Kitchen chain. Following the B&K style of a two-barrel brewery on open display; producing beers for the pub and off-sales with beer also offered out to the free trade. Two seasonal beers are brewed each quarter. Brewery experience days, meet the brewer and tapping parties are regular events. ‼️ ♦ LIVE

Brewhouse & Kitchen SIBA

🍴 147 Parkwood Road, Southbourne, Bournemouth, BH5 2BW
☎ (01202) 055209 ⊕ brewhouseandkitchen.com/southbourne

⊠ Part of the Brewhouse & Kitchen chain, breathing new life into the once derelict Malt & Hops pub in the heart of Southbourne. The brewery opened in 2016 and has a core range of nine ales. Tours and brewing days are offered, as well as a number of special events.

Cerne Abbas SIBA

Chescombe Barn, Barton Meadows Farm, Cerne Abbas, DT2 7JS
☎ (01300) 341999 ☎ 07506 303407
⊕ cerneabbasbrewery.com

⊠ Established in 2014 by Vic Irvine and Jodie Moore. Beers are made as naturally as possible using chalk-filtered water from their own spring. Many seasonal beers are produced, some with non-conventional ingredients. All beers are brewed with organic Maris Otter barley grown in the Cerne Valley. On the second Saturday in September, a community brew is produced using hops grown at the brewery and by people living nearby. ‼️ ☕ ♦ ✦

Ale (ABV 3.8%) BITTER
Gold/amber ale with gentle hop aroma. Refreshing balanced bitter sweet taste. Long, dry finish.
The Big Lubelski (ABV 3.9%) BLOND
Blonde (ABV 4.2%) BLOND
Hops to the fore in New World style, fairly light on palate with spicy bitterness balanced with sweetness fading to astringency.
Danny's Brew (ABV 4.4%) BITTER
Tiger Tom Ruby Mild (ABV 4.4%) MILD
Mellow, malty ruby brown ale with hints of chocolate in aroma, taste and aftertaste. Malt balanced by bitterness leading to a dry, slightly bitter aftertaste.
Leggless Jester (ABV 4.7%) GOLD
Mrs Vale's Ale (ABV 5.6%) OLD
Caramel and dried fruit have strong presence with warming enduring finish in this complex old ale. Presents as much stronger than the ABV suggests.
Gurt Stout (ABV 6.2%) STOUT
Gurt Coconuts Rum Stout (ABV 7.2%) SPECIALITY
A strong sweet stout with very prominent coconut elements in aroma, taste and aftertaste.

Copper Street

8 Copper Street, Brewery Square, Dorchester, DT1 1GH ☎ 07395 664390
⊕ copperstreetbrewery.co.uk

⊠ Brewery started in 2018, in the new Brewery Square development (ex Eldridge Pope), next to Dorchester South Station. New owners, Alistair and Tina Burrell are updating the premises, and keeping the business as it was. There is a bottle shop and brewery tap; plus a couple of beer festivals. Nine or ten beers are brewed throughout the year. ☕ ♦ ✦

Scramasax (ABV 4.1%) PALE
871 (ABV 4.3%) BITTER
Egbert's Stone (ABV 4.3%) BITTER
Shield Wall (ABV 4.3%) BITTER
Aethel Sword (ABV 4.5%) BITTER
Saxon Gold (ABV 4.7%) GOLD
Dark Ages (ABV 5.5%) PORTER

Dorset (DBC) SIBA

Unit 7, Hybris Business Park, Warmwell Road, Crossways, DT2 8BF
☎ (01305) 777515 ⊕ dbcales.com

⊠ Founded in 1996, Dorset Brewing Company started in Hope Square, Weymouth, which was once the home of the Devenish and Groves breweries. In 2010 it moved to purpose-built premises near Dorchester. Here spring water is used in its state-of-the-art brewing equipment. Beers are available in local pubs and selected outlets throughout the South West. !! ☛ ♦ ♦

Dorset Knob (ABV 3.9%) BITTER
Complex bitter ale with strong malt and fruit flavours despite its light gravity.
Jurassic (ABV 4.2%) BITTER
Clean-tasting, easy-drinking bitter. Well-balanced with lingering bitterness after moderate sweetness.
Origin (ABV 4.3%) GOLD
Durdle Door (ABV 5%) BITTER
A tawny hue and fruity aroma with a hint of pear drops and good malty undertone, joined by hops and a little roast malt in the taste. Lingering bittersweet finish.

Eight Arch SIBA

Unit 1, Stone Lane Industrial Estate, Wimborne, BH21 1HB
☎ (01202) 889254 ☎ 07554 445647
⊕ 8archbrewing.co.uk

⊠ Multi award-winning brewery commenced in 2015 with a five-barrel plant on a industrial estate on the outskirts of Wimborne and expanded to 10 barrels in 2021. In 2023 it moved to new premises across the road with twice the floor space, allowing for more brewery events. Its onsite taproom is open every Friday (not Jan) between 3-8pm, with street food available. The beers are distributed to local pubs and clubs as well as nationally. !! ☛ ♦ LIVE ♦

Session (ABV 3.8%) PALE
Square Logic (ABV 4.2%) PALE
Little Dragon (ABV 4.5%) SPECIALITY
Dainty (ABV 4.8%) PALE
Easy Life (ABV 5%) PALE
Corbel (ABV 5.5%) IPA
Strong golden ale with hops dominating yet balanced with bitterness.

Gyle 59 SIBA

The Brewery, Sadborow Estate Yard, Thorncombe, TA20 4PW
☎ (01297) 678990 ☎ 07508 691178 ⊕ gyle59.co.uk

⊠ Gyle 59 is a 10-barrel brewery that began commercial production in 2014. Bottling takes place onsite with bottles being available by mail order. !! ☛ ♦ LIVE

Take It Easy (ABV 2.5%) BITTER
Freedom Hiker (ABV 3.7%) BITTER
Lyme Regis Ammonite (ABV 3.7%) BITTER
Toujours (ABV 4%) SPECIALITY
Vienna Session Lager (ABV 4.2%) SPECIALITY
Halcyon Daze (ABV 5%) SPECIALITY
IPA (ABV 5.3%) PALE
Nettle IPA (ABV 5.3%) SPECIALITY
Dorset GIPA (ABV 5.4%) SPECIALITY
Starstruck (ABV 6.6%) SPECIALITY
The Favourite (ABV 6.6%) PORTER
Double IPA (ABV 7.3%) IPA

Brewed under the Capitalist Hippie brand name:
Flower Power (ABV 4.3%) BITTER

Far Out (ABV 5%) PALE
Summer of Love (ABV 6.6%) STRONG

Contract brewed for Lyme Regis
Rebel (ABV 4.2%) BITTER

Hall & Woodhouse (Badger) IFBB

Bournemouth Road, Blandford St Mary, Blandford Forum, DT11 9LS
☎ (01258) 452141 ⊕ hall-woodhouse.co.uk

⊠ Hall & Woodhouse has been brewing in the heart of the Dorset countryside since 1777. Owned and run by the seventh generation of the Woodhouse family, it brews with local spring water filtered through the Cretaceous chalk downs and drawn up 120ft from its wells.
A leading, independent UK brewer, its well-known range of Badger ales is award-winning, and it has an estate (around 200 pubs) across southern England. Its ales are available exclusively in Hall & Woodhouse public houses. !! ☛ ♦ ♦

Badger Best Bitter (ABV 3.7%) BITTER
Well-balanced bitter with malt caramel sweetness and hop fruitiness.
Fursty Ferret (ABV 4.1%) BITTER
Easy-drinking best bitter with sweet bitterness that lingers into a dry after taste with a hint of orange.
Tanglefoot (ABV 4.7%) GOLD
Relatively sweet-tasting and deceptive, given its strength. Pale malt provides caramel overtones and bittersweet finish.

Hattie Brown's

Whitecliff Farm, Whitecliff Road, Swanage, BH19 1RJ
☎ (01929) 439075 ⊕ hattiebrownsbrewery.co.uk

⊠ Hattie Browns began brewing in 2014 moving to its present location in 2015. Owned by Jean Young and Kevin Hunt, who formerly ran the Square and Compass, Worth Matravers.

HBA (ABV 3.8%) BITTER
Well-balanced session bitter with initial malt flavours followed by a balanced hop and sweet finish.
Moonlite (ABV 3.8%) PALE
Easy-drinking, session pale ale, richly-hopped with refreshing strong citrus flavours and long lingering finish.
Mustang Sally (ABV 4.3%) BITTER
Agglestone (ABV 4.5%) BITTER
Kirrin Island (ABV 4.5%) PALE
Premium, blonde-coloured pale ale with hop flavours dominating the malt biscuit base.
Spangle (ABV 4.6%) BITTER
Sirius (ABV 4.8%) PALE
Swanage Nut (ABV 4.8%) BROWN
Full Moon (ABV 5%) GOLD
Herkules (ABV 5%) PALE
Crow Black (ABV 5.1%) PORTER
Excellent strong mild with roast aromas, and rich malt and dried fruit pudding flavours, Lovely lingering aftertaste. Deceptively easy-drinking.
Dog on the Roof (ABV 6%) GOLD

Isle of Purbeck SIBA

▤ Bankes Arms, Manor Road, Studland, BH19 3AU
☎ (01929) 450227 ⊕ isleofpurbeckbrewery.com

Founded in 2003, and situated in the grounds of the Bankes Arms Inn, in the heart of the magical Isle of Purbeck. The pub and brewery overlook the sea at Studland and Old Harry Rocks on the Dorset section of the Jurassic World Heritage Coast. This 10-barrel plant produces five core beers, several seasonal beers and

Purbeck Pommes cider, available locally, and also nationwide via exchange swaps with other micros, and at beer festivals. ◆LIVE

Purbeck Best Bitter (ABV 3.6%) BITTER
A classic malty best bitter with rich malt aroma and taste and smooth, malty, bitter finish.
Equinox (ABV 4%) BLOND
Fossil Fuel (ABV 4.1%) BITTER
Amber bitter with complex aroma with a hint of pepper; rich malt dominates the taste, leading to a smooth dry finish.
Solar Power (ABV 4.3%) GOLD
Tawny mid-range ale brewed using Continental hops. Well-balanced flavours combine to provide a strong bitter taste but short, dry finish.
Studland Bay Wrecked (ABV 4.5%) BITTER
Deep red ale with slightly sweet aroma reflecting a mixture of caramel, malt and hops that lead to a dry, malty finish.
Full Steam Ahead (ABV 4.8%) BITTER
Mid-brown beer with hop/malt balance in the flavour and a long dry aftertaste

Knight Life

27 Feversham Avenue, Queenspark, Bournemouth, BH8 9NH ☎ 07722 564444 ⊕ knightlifebrewing.com

Established in 2018, Knight Life has a three-barrel system, with six three-barrel fermenters. Canning machine is in-house. It now has its own tap house, with 12 lines in the heart of busy Ashley Cross, in Poole.

Lyme Regis SIBA

Lyme Regis Brewery, Mill Lane, Lyme Regis, DT7 3PU ☎ (01297) 444354 ⊕ lymeregisbrewery.com/

⊠ Lyme Regis Brewery (formerly Town Mill Brewery) began brewing in 2010 and is situated in a part of the Town Mill that previously housed the Lyme Regis electricity generator. Historically also used as a brewer's malthouse, the building now houses its licenced taproom with a one-barrel pilot kit. All cask beers are currently brewed on contract by Gyle 59 Brewery to the original Town Mill Brewery recipes. 🍴◆LIVE ◆

Palmers SIBA IFBB

Old Brewery, West Bay Road, Bridport, DT6 4JA ☎ (01308) 422396 ⊕ palmersbrewery.com

⊠ Palmers is one of Britain's only thatched breweries and dates from 1794. It is situated in Bridport, the heart of the Jurassic Coast in south-west Dorset. The company continues to make substantial investment in its 54 tenanted pubs, all serving cask ale. An additional 400 outlets are supplied within the free trade. ‼🍴

Copper Ale (ABV 3.7%) BITTER
Beautifully-balanced, copper-coloured light bitter with a hoppy aroma.
IPA (ABV 4.2%) PALE
Hop aroma and bitterness stay in the background in this predominately malty best bitter, with some fruit on the aroma.
Dorset Gold (ABV 4.5%) GOLD

> Give my people plenty of beer, good beer and cheap beer, and you will have no revolution among them.
> **Queen Victoria**

More complex than many golden ales thanks to a pleasant banana and mango fruitiness on the aroma that carries on into the taste and aftertaste.
200 (ABV 5%) BITTER
This is a big beer with a touch of caramel sweetness adding to a complex hoppy, fruit taste that lasts from the aroma well into the aftertaste.
Tally Ho! (ABV 5.5%) OLD
A complex dark old ale. Roast malts and treacle toffee on the palate lead in to a long, lingering finish with more than a hint of coffee.

Piddle

Unit 24, Enterprise Park, Piddlehinton, Dorchester, DT2 7UA ☎ (01305) 849336 ☎ 07730 436343 ⊕ piddlebrewery.co.uk

⊠ Established in 2007, with new owners in 2014. The brewery produces a broad range of beers from its location in the Piddle Valley in Dorset. Some beer names reflect this unusual name. Beers are available in pubs and retail outlets across Dorset and beyond. ◆

Dorset Rogue (ABV 3.9%) BITTER
Piddle (ABV 4.1%) BITTER
Cocky (ABV 4.3%) PALE
Bent Copper (ABV 4.8%) BITTER
Slasher (ABV 5.1%) BLOND

Poole Hill SIBA

41-43 Poole Hill, Bournemouth, BH2 5PW ☎ 07469 172568 ⊕ poolehillbrewery.com

⊠ Award-winning Poole Hill Brewery was created by Jennifer Tingay, head brewer, CEO and creator of Southbourne Ales and Tingay's craft beer. Originally a cuckoo brewery, the 20-barrel brewery and taproom was created in a Victorian ironmongers and latterly a disused car showroom after attracting £280K from crowdfunding. The Southbourne Ales brand comprises traditional beer styles from light ale to oatmeal stout. The Tingay's brand features styles from APA, to floral to smoked to Doppelboch, and punchy low alcohol brews. ‼🍴◆LIVE ◆

Brewed under the Southbourne Ales brand name:
Paddlers (ABV 3.6%) BITTER
Easy-drinking bitter with subtle malt flavour and hints of hop bitterness in the aftertaste.
Sunbather (ABV 4%) BITTER
Dry red ale with some caramel sweetness and a lingering nutty after taste.
Headlander (ABV 4.2%) BITTER
Traditional best bitter with intense malt aroma and sweet flavour. Complex and moreish with hop bitterness in aftertaste.
Grockles (ABV 4.5%) GOLD
Refreshing, well-balanced golden ale with subtle sweet aromas and gentle hop finish.
Stroller (ABV 4.6%) STOUT
Strong mild crossed with old ale, complex flavours of hop malt and fruit but well-balanced.

Brewed under the Tingay's brand name:
Armed with Flowers (ABV 4.5%) SPECIALITY
Digies (ABV 5%) PALE

Remedy Oak SIBA

Horton Road, Wimborne, BH21 8ND ☎ (01202) 612509 ⊕ remedyoakbrewery.co.uk

The Remedy Oak Brewing Company was established commercially in 2020. It is based in a redeveloped barn in the grounds of the Remedy Oak Golf Club. Traditional styles as well as hop-forward craft beers are produced. An onsite taproom opened in 2021. ⬛◆

Sandbanks SIBA

Unit 6, 4-6 Abingdon Road, Nuffield Industrial Estate, Poole, BH17 0UG
☎ (01202) 671950 ⊕ sandbanksbrewery.net

⊗ Opened in 2018 on a local industrial estate using a five-barrel plant and a one-barrel plant for one-off brews. The beer is becoming increasingly availably in the local free trade with one-off and special beers available in the taproom. ⬛◆◆

Bitter (ABV 3.9%) BITTER
Refreshing session bitter with pleasant malt character.
Free Bird (ABV 4.2%) PALE
Golden Years (ABV 4.3%) GOLD
Back in Black (ABV 5%) STOUT
Easy-drinking stout with roast malt on tongue and hints of liquorice and coffee, lingering rich fruit aftertaste.
Wayward Son IPA (ABV 5%) PALE

Sixpenny SIBA

The Old Dairy, Holwell Farm, Cranborne, BH21 5QP
☎ (01725) 762006 ⊕ sixpennybrewery.co.uk

⊗ Founded in 2007, Sixpenny moved into its present home of renovated Victorian farm buildings near Cranborne, in 2016. This allowed for the expansion of the brewery bar and shop (Sixpenny Tap), in converted stables next door. Sixpenny has been brewing to its 20-barrel plant capacity for some while now to meet demand. Plans are afoot to increase the amount of bottled beer available all year round. ‼⬛◆◆

6d Best Bitter (ABV 3.8%) BITTER
6d Gold (ABV 4%) GOLD
6d IPA (ABV 5.2%) PALE

Small Paul's

Gillingham, SP8 4SS
☎ (01747) 823574 ✉ smallbrewer@btinternet.com

⊗ Launched in 2006, this half-barrel brewery is located in the owner's garage. Brewing is now reduced to about once a month and on demand. A small number of local pubs, clubs and beer festivals are supplied direct and beers can be brewed to order.

Stripey Cat

▤ Tiger Inn, 14-16 Barrack Street, Bridport, DT6 3LY
☎ (01308) 427543 ⊕ tigerinnbridport.co.uk/the-stripey-cat-craft-brewery

Brewing began in 2017 at the Tiger Inn, producing ales exclusively for the pub. Brewing is currently suspended.

Way Outback

146 Seabourne Road, Southbourne, BH5 2HZ
Offfice: 144 Seabourne Road, Southbourne, BH5 2HZ
⊕ thewayoutback.co.uk

Started in 2017 and born in a shed, Way Outback is based in Southbourne. Now located in a modern brewery run by owner and head brewer Richard Brown, and specialises in beers using high quality ingredients using 100% green energy and recycling grain and yeast. ◆

Wriggle Valley SIBA

Unit 4, The Sidings, Station Road, Stalbridge, DT10 2SS
☎ (01963) 363343 ☎ 07599 677139
⊕ wrigglevalleybrewery.co.uk

Wriggle Valley began brewing in 2014 using a three-barrel plant in a converted garage. It relocated to Stalbridge in 2017 to an industrial unit and changed hands in 2020. Beers are mainly supplied within a 20-mile radius of the brewery. A taproom was opened at the brewery in 2019. ⬛◆LIVE◆

Dorset Nomad (ABV 3.8%) BITTER
Golden Bear (ABV 4%) BLOND
Golden ale with fruit notes in the aroma and taste leading to a dry, slightly astringent finish.
Dorset Pilgrim (ABV 4.2%) BITTER
A traditional best bitter with some malt and fruit in the aroma developing hop and bitterness in the taste with a more bitter balanced finish.
Copper Hoppa (ABV 4.5%) BITTER
Light malt and hop aroma with a relatively sweet taste predominated by fruit and caramel which linger in a pleasant aftertaste along with slight bitterness coming forward.
Valley Gold (ABV 4.5%) GOLD
Golden ale with some fruit and hop in the aroma with bitterness and astringency developing with a light citrus note in the taste and through to a bitter aftertaste.

Kitchen of an inn

In the evening we reached a village where I had determined to pass the night. As we drove into the great gateway of the inn, I saw on one side the light of a rousing kitchen fire beaming through a window. I entered, and admired for the hundredth time that picture of convenience, neatness, and broad honest enjoyment, the kitchen of an English inn. It was of spacious dimension, hung around by copper and tin vessels, highly polished, and decorated here and there with a Christmas green. Hams, tongues, and flitches of bacon were suspended from the ceiling; a smoke-jack made its ceaseless clanking behind the fireplace, and a clock ticked in one corner. A well-scoured deal table extended along one side of the kitchen, with a cold round of beef, and other hearty viands upon it, over which two foaming tankards of ale seemed mounting guard. Travellers of inferior order were preparing to attack this stout repast, while others sat smoking or gossiping over their ale, on two high-backed oaken settles beside the fire.

Washington Irving, Travelling at Christmas, 1884

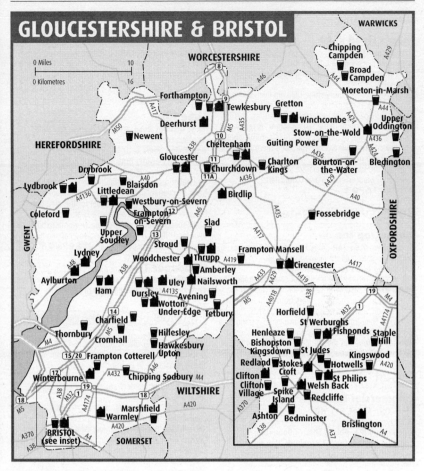

Amberley

Black Horse L

Littleworth, GL5 5AL (N end of Village)
☎ (01453) 872556 ⊕ theblackhorseamberley.co.uk
3 changing beers (sourced nationally; often Gloucester, Keep Brewing, Stroud) Ⓗ
A busy, friendly, family-run pub on the edge of Minchinhampton Common. On the right, an L-shaped public bar culminates in a conservatory with stunning views across the Nailsworth Valley to Selsley Common. To the left is the lounge/restaurant, leading to a tiny snug with comfy sofas and a window view. Bar and lounge both benefit from wood-burning stoves. The terraced gardens command views of the River Severn and the Forest of Dean, and have recently been equipped with six pods allowing outside use in inclement weather. ☺⊛◐&♣♠♥

Avening

Bell L

29 High Street, GL8 8NF (at the bottom of the High St on B4014)
☎ (01453) 836422 ⊕ thebellavening.co.uk
Timothy Taylor Landlord; 1 changing beer (often Butcombe) Ⓗ
This pleasant village local in the heart of the Cotswolds is a friendly, confidently run old inn with exposed stone

walls, two bay window seats and a roaring woodburner. The jovial, amicable regulars are always chatty; enjoying the offerings from the attractive open bar, which features up to four different ales at busy times. The refurbished, comfortable dining area serves a competitively priced menu in collaboration with a local Indian restaurant. This pub can be quietly addictive and quite difficult to leave. Q☺⊛◐♣♦📗♥

Blaisdon

Red Hart L

GL17 0AH (signed from A4136 E of Longhope or A48 N of Westbury-on-Severn)
☎ (01452) 831717 ⊕ redhartinn.co.uk
Otter Bitter; 3 changing beers (sourced nationally; often Bespoke, Kingstone, Wye Valley) Ⓗ
This wonderfully welcoming pub is renowned for its excellent food and well-kept ales. A lovely old building, with worn flagstones in the bar coupled with a cracking fireplace and a plethora of memorabilia, makes drinking a real pleasure. There are designated dining areas, but no separate restaurant, so everyone can enjoy the convivial atmosphere; at busy times be prepared to mix it with a rack of lamb, not to mention free-range children, as meals encroach into the bar area. A well-tendered garden is an ideal place for families to enjoy in the summer. ☺⊛◐&♣♠♥P🐾

327

Bledington

King's Head L ✓

The Green, OX7 6XQ (off B4450 on village green)
☎ (01608) 658365 ⊕ kingsheadinn.net
Hook Norton Hooky; 3 changing beers (sourced regionally) Ⓗ

A delightful, 16th-century stone-built inn overlooking the village green. The pub has original old beams and an open inglenook log fire with high back settles. This free house, with 12 comfortable letting rooms, is renowned for its wide range of ale and food. Bledington is about four miles from Stow-on-the-Wold, and there are good local walks to nearby villages, with Kingham station close by. The two guest beers are selected from local brewers in Gloucestershire and Oxfordshire.
Q ㊈ ⚇ ⌂ ◑ ♣ P ❀ 🥾 ⚲

Bourton-on-the-Water

Mousetrap Inn L

Lansdowne, GL54 2AR (300yds W of village centre)
☎ (01451) 820579 ⊕ themousetrapinn.co.uk
4 changing beers (sourced locally) Ⓗ

This recently refurbished traditional Cotswold stone free house, in the Lansdowne part of Bourton close to the centre, offers four changing beers from local breweries. With friendly service it welcomes locals, tourists, children and dogs. Nine letting rooms are available. A patio area in front of the pub with tables and hanging baskets provides a suntrap in the summer. Local CAMRA Pub of the Year 2022. Q ㊈ ⚇ ⌂ ◑ ♿ P 🚃 (801,855) ❀ ⚲

Bristol

Commercial Rooms L ✓

43-45 Corn Street, BS1 1HT
☎ (0117) 927 9681
Greene King IPA, Abbot; Sharp's Doom Bar; 9 changing beers (often Glastonbury, Hop Union, Twisted Oak) Ⓗ

This Grade II-listed building dating from 1810 was Bristol's first Wetherspoon pub. In a central location, it is a good start or end point for a pub tour of Bristol, with up to nine guest beers available. There is a quieter galleried room at the rear, but the Great Room does get busy at peak times. The interior features Greek revival-style decor, a stunning ceiling with dome, portraits, and memorabilia from its days as a businessmen's club. Wheelchair access is on request via the side entrance in Small Street. Q ㊈ ◑ ♿ ◕ 🚃 ⚲

Cornubia

142 Temple Street, BS1 6EN
⊕ thecornubia.co.uk
6 changing beers Ⓗ

Originally built in 1775, this cosy traditional pub, tucked away off Victoria Street, is a short walk from Temple Meads railway station. It is a long-term Guide entry with a good range of changing ales, usually including a dark ale, plus Cornubia house beer from Twisted Oak brewery. The attractive beer garden has an extended seating area to both the front and side of the pub, some of which is lit and covered. Bar snacks, including pies, sausage rolls and Scotch eggs are usually available.
❀ ≈ (Temple Meads) ◕ 🚃 ❀ ⚲

Gryphon

41 Colston Street, BS1 5AP
☎ 07894 239567
4 changing beers Ⓗ

The Gryphon is a shrine to dark beer and great rock and heavy metal music. Posters, guitars and pumpclips adorn the walls. Up to four rapidly changing brews are served, many dark and often strong. Triangular in shape due to its corner plot, it is situated just a few yards uphill from the Bristol Beacon concert hall. Live bands sometimes play upstairs, and beer festivals are held in February and September. Children and dogs are admitted at the licensee's discretion. Sunday opening time may vary.
🚃 ❀ ⚲ 🎵

Lime Kiln

17 St Georges Road, BS1 5UU (behind City Hall)
☎ 07903 068256
6 changing beers Ⓗ

Named after nearby Lime Kiln Dock, covered over in 1903, this unpretentious free house directly behind the City Hall dispenses a constantly changing range of six beers in a variety of styles, more during the periodic beer festivals. Beers are often unusual for the area but local breweries also feature and there is at least one traditional cider available. You are welcome to bring your own food. There is on-street metered parking and a public car park directly opposite. ㊈ ❀ ◕ P 🚃 ❀ ⚲

Llandoger Trow

King Street, BS1 4ER
☎ 07908 226603 ⊕ llandogertrow.co.uk

REAL ALE BREWERIES	
Arbor Bristol	
Ashley Down Bristol	
Ashton Cheltenham	
Basement Beer ✦ Bristol: Stokes Croft	
Bath Ales Bristol: Warmley	
Battledown ✦ Cheltenham	
Bespoke ✦ Littledean	
Brewhouse & Kitchen 🍺 Bristol: Clifton	
Brewhouse & Kitchen 🍺 Cheltenham	
Brewhouse & Kitchen 🍺 Gloucester	
Bristol Beer Factory ✦ Bristol: Ashton	
Clavell & Hind ✦ Birdlip	
Corinium ✦ Cirencester	
Cotswold Lion Cheltenham	
DEYA ✦ Cheltenham	
Donnington Stow-on-the-Wold	
Fierce & Noble ✦ Bristol: St Werburgh's	
Forest, The Lydney	
Fresh Standard ✦ Woodchester	
Gloucester ✦ Gloucester	
Goff's Winchcombe	
Good Chemistry ✦ Bristol: St Philips	
Hal's Dursley (brewing suspended)	
Hop Union ✦ Brislington	
Incredible Bristol: Brislington	
Inferno ✦ Tewkesbury	
Keep 🍺 Nailsworth	
King Street 🍺 Bristol: Welsh Back	
Left Handed Giant ✦ Bristol: St Philips	
Little Martha 🍺 Bristol: St Philips	
Lucifer Wotton-Under-Edge	
Lydbrook Valley 🍺 Lydbrook	
Moor ✦ Bristol	
New Bristol ✦ Bristol	
New Street Bristol	
Stroud ✦ Thrupp	
Tapestry ✦ Bristol: St Philips	
Tewkesbury Deerhurst (NEW)	
Three Engineers ✦ Winterbourne (brewing suspended)	
Tiley's 🍺 Ham	
Two Tinkers Aylburton	
Uley ✦ Uley	
Wiper and True ✦ Bristol	
Zerodegrees 🍺 Bristol	

5 changing beers (often Bristol Beer Factory, Theakston, Timothy Taylor) ⊞
Architecturally important and impressive historic inn in which Daniel Defoe reputedly met Alexander Selkirk, who became the inspiration for Robinson Crusoe. It is also said to be the inspiration for the Admiral Benbow pub in Stephenson's Treasure Island. Reopened in 2021 after a closure of more than two years, it has been reinvented as an alehouse while retaining distinct drinking areas. The opening of several rooms on the first floor has increased capacity considerably. Five changing cask ales are served alongside 28 keg lines from UK and overseas breweries. Card payments only. ❀●🖾🛜

Moor Beer

Days Road, BS2 0QS
☎ (0117) 941 4460 ⊕ moorbeer.co.uk
1 changing beer (sourced locally; often Moor Beer)
The brewery tap room is open from Wednesday to Saturday, when a cask beer is served straight from the barrel. Real ale in a can from Moor is also sold. Up to 15 keg beers are available, which may include lambic and sour beers from the likes of Cantillon, as well as Moor's own beers. Pop-up food from a range of suppliers sometimes feature. The tap room is open as an off-licence on Monday and Tuesday during the day.
❀≉(Temple Meads) 🚌(506) ❀

Old Fish Market

59-63 Baldwin Street, BS1 1QZ (200yds from city centre)
☎ (0117) 921 1515 ⊕ oldfishmarket.co.uk
Fuller's Oliver's Island, London Pride, ESB; 2 changing beers (sourced nationally; often Arbor, Siren) ⊞
There's something for everyone at this Fuller's outlet, which was refurbished in 2014 with decor, seating and lighting in the style of a relaxed lounge. There is a stadium-like atmosphere when major sporting events are shown on the big screen. Live jazz music features every Sunday evening. Between 20 and 30 gins are a great attraction for any fan of the spirit. Food includes a range of chowders, stone-baked pizzas and Sunday roasts. The pub is dog-friendly, with treats and water bowls provided. 🐕🍴♠🖾❀🛜♪

Seven Stars

1 Thomas Lane, BS1 6JG (just off Victoria St)
☎ (0117) 927 2845 ⊕ 7stars.co.uk
6 changing beers ⊞
This popular historic free house is tucked away in a lane 10 minutes' walk from the city centre and from Temple Meads station. It is very much a beer-focused pub with up to six beers of all styles and strengths and at least one real cider. Sunday afternoons feature quality live acoustic music. No food is served but you may bring in your own. There is an outdoor seating area and an informative plaque detailing how the pub featured in the 18th century anti-slavery campaign.
❀≉(Temple Meads) ♠🖾❀🛜♪

Shakespeare Tavern ⊘

68 Prince Street, BS1 4QD
☎ (0117) 929 7695
Greene King IPA, Abbot; 5 changing beers (sourced locally; often Bristol Beer Factory, Gloucester, Hanlons) ⊞
By Bristol's historic docks, close to the city centre and Queen's Square, this converted Georgian town house claims to have the longest continuous ale licence in Bristol. Seven handpumps offer two regular ales plus four or five changing guests of varying styles from breweries near and far. There is a regular Wednesday night pub quiz and monthly Friday night live music. A large

selection classic pub meals is on offer. There are benches on the front terrace for watching the world pass by.
Q🐕❀❀🍴●🖾❀🛜♪

Bristol: Bedminster

Bristol Beer Factory Tap Room

291 North Street, BS3 1JP
☎ (0117) 902 6317 ⊕ bristolbeerfactory.co.uk/taproom
Bristol Beer Factory Notorious, Fortitude; 3 changing beers (sourced locally; often Bristol Beer Factory) ⊞
A short walk from Ashton Gate stadium, and busy on match days, this popular and comfortable brewery taproom expanded into neighbouring premises in January 2023, creating a separate room known as the Studio. Both bars are furnished with an assortment of tables, benches, chairs, stools, and sofas. Five Bristol Beer Factory beers are sold alongside eight keg lines. Sporting events on big screen TVs are shown in the Studio, which has more of a sports bar feel with darts and table football. Brewery tours and beer tastings are held regularly. The shop offers cans, cases, merchandise and mini tins to take away. 🐕❀♠🍴🖾(24)❀🛜

Old Bookshop

65 North Street, BS3 1ES
☎ (0117) 373 8907 ⊕ theoldbookshopbristol.com
2 changing beers (often Left Handed Giant, Tiley's, Vocation) ⊞
Recently refurbished with a light, airy feel, this friendly, relaxing and eclectic café bar offers two guest cask ales from local breweries and from further afield, as well as large range of German and Belgian beers on draught and in bottles. Check the extensive printed beer menu to see what is available on the day – it changes frequently. The food served is entirely plant-based, with a curry of the week, and other street food-type Indian dishes.
❀🍴≉(Bedminster) ●🖾(24) ❀🛜

Tobacco Factory Café Bar

Raleigh Rd, BS3 1TF
☎ (0117) 902 0060 ⊕ tobaccofactory.com/cafe-bar
Bristol Beer Factory Notorious, Fortitude; 3 changing beers (sourced locally; often Arbor, Good Chemistry, Siren) ⊞
Built in 1912, the Tobacco Factory was part of the vast Imperial Tobacco estate across South Bristol. Saved from demolition in 1993, the café bar opened in 2001, and has been transformed into a thriving, vibrant venue offering good quality, locally produced vegetarian and vegan food and drink. The six handpumps feature mainly local breweries. The outside yard hosts a local market every Sunday morning, and the very popular Factoberfest beer festival in September. Card payment only.
🐕❀🍴♠●🖾(24) 🛜♪

Bristol: Bishopston

Annexe

Seymour Road, BS7 9EQ (behind Sportsman pub near county cricket ground)
☎ (0117) 949 3931
Dark Star Hophead; St Austell Tribute; Timothy Taylor Landlord; 4 changing beers ⊞
Spacious community pub close to Gloucestershire County Cricket Ground and not far from the Memorial Stadium which means it can be busy on match days. At one side is a conservatory which is family friendly until evening. The pub is sport-oriented with several TVs showing live sport, including one on the partially covered patio outside. Pizzas are served until late every evening and on Sundays roasts are available at lunchtime. The regularly

changing guest beers can include some interesting options. No dogs are allowed, even on the patio.
ᏖⱭ◑▯🖂🛜

Bristol: Clifton Village

Portcullis

3 Wellington Terrace, BS8 4LE (close to Clifton side of suspension bridge)
☎ (0117) 973 0270 🌐 theportcullisclifton.com
Bristol Beer Factory Fortitude; 2 changing beers (sourced nationally; often Exmoor, Fine Tuned, Gloucester) Ⓗ
A pub since 1821, the building is part of a Georgian terrace close to Clifton Suspension Bridge. There is a downstairs bar and an upstairs lounge that is also used for functions. The decor is cosy and includes many photos of film stars. As well as one regular beer there are two changing guests from local breweries and further afield, along with a large range of Belgian beers in bottles and on tap. The rear garden is accessed from upstairs.
Ɑ◑♣🖂(8,505) 🏵🛜

Bristol: Fishponds

Snuffy Jack's

800 Fishponds Road, BS16 3TE
☎ (0117) 965 1198 🌐 snuffyjacks.co.uk
4 changing beers Ⓖ
The name of this micropub relates to a former head miller at the nearby Snuff Mills. There are usually four changing gravity-fed real ales plus three craft keg lines and several ciders. Local breweries feature, plus some from further afield. Both dog and child friendly, the pub has a community focus with a quiz every second Wednesday, and a board game night on the last Sunday of the month. A new beer garden to the rear opened in 2022. It is conveniently located near to multiple bus routes with direct links to many areas. QᏖⱭ🖂🏵

Bristol: Henleaze

Westbury Park Ⓛ

Northumbria Drive, BS9 4HP
☎ (0117) 962 4235 🌐 westburyparkpub.co.uk
Butcombe Original; St Austell Tribute; Timothy Taylor Landlord; 2 changing beers (sourced locally; often Arbor, Purity, Wiper & True) Ⓗ
Featured as the Kebab & Calculator in the BBC series The Young Ones this circular pub is smartly decorated and furnished with dining tables and comfortable seating throughout the open-plan interior. Outside there are extensive seating areas and in front of the pub nine wooden booths with individual lighting and heating have been added. There are up to five cask ales on handpump, with one of them being substituted for real cider in the summer. Quality fresh, locally sourced food, from a regularly changing seasonal menu, is served.
ᏖⱭ◑♿♣P🖂🛜

Bristol: Horfield

Drapers Arms Ⓛ

447 Gloucester Road, BS7 8TZ
🌐 thedrapersarms.co.uk
7 changing beers Ⓖ
Bristol's first micropub, opened in 2015, prides itself on a changing selection of up to seven real ales on gravity, mostly from Bristol and the surrounding counties. 'Beer miles' are noted for each beer on the blackboard beer menu and at least one gluten-free and vegan beer is usually available. Wine and bar snacks are also served,

but no keg beer, bottled beer, lager or cider. This popular and friendly place follows the micropub tradition of focusing on good beer and conversation, with no music or TV. QⱭ🖂🏵

Bristol: Hotwells

Bag of Nails

141 St Georges Road, BS1 5UW (5 mins' walk from cathedral towards Hotwells)
☎ 07941 521777 🌐 catpub.co.uk
6 changing beers Ⓗ
Close to the floating harbour this small partially gas-lit terraced free house dates from the 1860s. It serves six changing cask ales from independent breweries both local and further afield. A dark ale is usually available, but no draught lager is served. The interior features terracotta colours, portholes in the floor, pub cats roaming free and eclectic music from a proper record player. Board games and an extensive Lego collection are available for customers. Tuesday is quiz night. 🖂

Grain Barge

Mardyke Wharf, Hotwell Road, BS8 4RU (moored by Hotwell Rd, opp Baltic Wharf Marina)
☎ (0117) 929 9347 🌐 grainbarge.com
Bristol Beer Factory Notorious, Fortitude, Independence; 1 changing beer (sourced locally; often Arbor, Good Chemistry, New Bristol) Ⓗ
This moored barge, built in 1936 and converted into a floating pub by Bristol Beer Factory in 2007, boasts great views of the SS Great Britain, the floating harbour and passing boats. There is seating with wooden tables at either end of the central bar, and an extended shelf by the window overlooking the water. Additional seating can be found in an outdoor area on the top deck and on the pavement outside. It hosts regular themed food nights, a quiz on Mondays, and live music some evenings. ᏖⱭ◑♣P🖂🏵🛜♪

Merchants Arms

5 Merchants Road, BS8 4PZ
☎ (0117) 927 3709 🌐 themerchantsarms.co.uk
Cheddar Ales Gorge Best; 3 changing beers (often Exmoor, St Austell, Twisted Oak) Ⓗ
A traditional pub, free of tie, close to the Cumberland Basin, selling mainly South-West cask-conditioned ales. Both rooms are furnished with dark-wood seating and there is a real log fire in the front room. A wide range of board games is available and occasional poetry nights take place. The pub is renowned for home-made Scotch eggs, hand-finished pork pies and real Cornish pasties. There is a small free car park 50 yards behind the pub.
QᏖ♣P🖂🏵🛜♪

Bristol: Kingsdown

Green Man

21 Alfred Place, BS2 8HD
☎ (0117) 925 8062
3 changing beers (sourced locally; often Bristol Beer Factory, Good Chemistry) Ⓗ
This small Grade II-listed pub, licensed since 1851, in a heritage-listed street with many fine Georgian buildings, offers a selection of cask beers from local breweries. Somerset cider is sold, as well as local keg beers and a large range of gins. The pub hosts regular live bands, and these events are popular, with standing room only. A selection of board games is available to play. There is a small patio to the rear for smokers. Ꮦ♣🖂(13)🏵🛜♪

Hare on the Hill

41 Thomas Street North, BS2 8LX

☎ (0117) 987 8462

4 changing beers (sourced locally; often Arbor, Bristol Beer Factory, Moor Beer) Ⓗ

A friendly and welcoming small street-corner local with an impressive traditional green-tiled frontage. The smartly refurbished wooden interior is decorated with an eclectic range of prints and paintings. Four handpumps offer a range of beers, usually including a dark ale, with local breweries well represented. The keg fonts include a Belgian-style beer and a wheat beer. The pub hosts an array of live entertainment including sea shanty singing, jazz, folk and open mic sessions. At other times music comes from a collection of vinyl records.

ふ❀≢(Montpelier) ●🖵❀🛜♪

Highbury Vaults

164 St Michael's Hill, BS2 8DE

☎ (0117) 973 3203 ● highburyvaults.co.uk

St Austell Tribute, Proper Job; Young's London Original; 2 changing beers (often Goff's, Teignworthy, Young's) Ⓗ

In the same hands for many years, this pub is popular with university and hospital staff. Dating from the mid-19th century, its interior is dark and dimly lit, with a small front snug bar, which was the original pub. Beyond is the main drinking area with a bar billiards table, and a large, heated patio and garden with impressive floral arrangements. Good-quality food is served every lunchtime and evening, except Sunday evening. Toilets are down steep stairs in the original vaults.

Q❀◑≢(Clifton Down) ♣🖵(72) ❀🛜

Hillgrove Porter Stores

53 Hillgrove Street North, BS2 8LT

☎ (0117) 924 9818

10 changing beers (sourced regionally) Ⓗ

A popular community pub serving a wide range of beers in a variety of styles from the 10 handpumps. The interior of the pub is horseshoe-shaped, with a variety of furniture, a large array of pumpclips on the walls, and stained-glass windows. To one side of the pub is a patio garden with a covered seating area. Japanese food is available in the evenings, with a reduced menu on Sundays and Mondays. There are occasional DJ sets.

ふ❀◗≢(Montpelier) ●🖵❀

Robin Hood

56 St Michael's Hill, BS2 8DX

☎ (0117) 983 1489

2 changing beers (sourced regionally; often Bristol Beer Factory, Moor Beer, Siren) Ⓗ

Originally a grocer's, but a licensed premises since 1841, this Grade II-listed pub combines traditional features, such as wood panelling and flooring and an original arched-window frontage, with contemporary murals by local artists, a dumbwaiter disguised as Dr Who's Tardis, and knitted caps on the handpumps. Popular with students and university staff, the pub serves two or three cask beers, usually from local breweries, plus nine craft keg beers. Quiz night is Wednesday and there are occasional comedy nights. ふ❀◗🖵(72)❀🛜♪

Bristol: Redcliffe

Golden Guinea

19 Guinea Street, BS1 6SX

● thegoldenguinea.co.uk

House beer (by St Austell); 3 changing beers (sourced locally; often Arbor, Bristol Beer Factory, New Bristol) Ⓗ

Cosy back-street local, close to the waterside, with wooden floors, contemporary flock wallpaper and urban art on the walls. Reclaimed furniture and French mirrors give the pub a modern but retro feel. There are three terraces and an eclectic music policy. A regular house beer from St Austell brewery is served, with guest beers usually from local breweries such as Arbor, Bristol Beer Factory and New Bristol. A range of local bottled and canned beers is also stocked. ❀🖵❀♪

King's Head ★

60 Victoria Street, BS1 6DE

4 changing beers (sourced locally; often Burnt Mill, Good Chemistry, Saltaire) Ⓗ

Close to Temple Meads station and Castle Park, this classic small pub, originally dating from around 1660, has been identified by CAMRA as having a nationally important historic pub interior; the magnificent mid-Victorian bar back is the second oldest known to CAMRA in the UK. A narrow area around the bar leads to the 'Tramcar Bar' at the rear. Now in the hands of Good Chemistry brewery, two of its beers and two guest cask ales from far and wide are served, and the aim is to always have a dark beer available.

Q❀≢(Temple Meads) 🖵❀🛜

Portwall Tavern

Portwall Lane, BS1 6NB

☎ (0117) 922 0442 ● portwalltavern.co.uk

3 changing beers (sourced regionally; often Exmoor, Gloucester, Twisted) Ⓗ

Opposite the magnificent St Mary Redcliffe church, this comfortable one-bar Victorian pub has survived the redevelopment of almost everything around it. The pub was refurbished in 2018 and inside there is a range of tall seating with polished wood tables and cosy padded booths, some delightfully ornate mirrors and a mix of tiled and wood flooring. Beers come from small to medium-sized regional breweries. A main meal menu is served lunchtimes Monday to Friday, with a pizza menu available weekday evenings. ❀◗≢(Temple Meads)🖵

Bristol: Redland

Good Measure Ⓛ

2B Chandos Road, BS6 6PE

☎ (0117) 903 9930

3 changing beers (sourced locally; often Arbor, Siren, Good Chemistry) Ⓗ

This small boutique bar is set in the heart of Redland. Three handpumps dispense Good Chemistry beers and a guest ale. A range of keykeg and keg beers, canned beers from Good Chemistry, bottled Belgian beers, artisan ciders and organic wines are also sold. Takeaways can be brought in but on Thursday evenings Mr Noodle is in residency. Quiz night is Monday. There is level access to the pub and an outside patio area at the side.

ふ❀≢(Clifton Down) 🖵❀🛜

Bristol: St Judes

Swan with Two Necks

12 Little Ann Street, BS2 9EB (off Wade St, near Old Market)

☎ (0117) 955 1837

3 changing beers (sourced locally; often Arbor, Moor Beer, Siren) Ⓗ

This small, single-bar venue, tucked away in a side street near Old Market, has again become a beer destination as it was back in the 1990s. Three regularly changing cask beers are served, mainly, but not always, from local breweries, plus a real cider. In addition 14 keg lines dispense a variety of beers, lagers and cider. Food is currently limited to simple snacks, and music is from the vinyl collection behind the bar. ⛄♣●🎀🟦🛜🎵

Wiper & True Old Market Taproom
Unit 11-15 City Business Park, Easton Road, BS5 0SP
☎ (0117) 941 2501
House beer (by Wiper & True); 1 changing beer (often Left Handed Giant, Thornbridge, Wiper & True) Ⓗ
A spacious new taproom opened in July 2022 in a modern industrial unit at the eastern end of Old Market. Walk past the Royal Mail depot and around the outside of the brewery to the entrance at the rear. Many beers are served, mainly from Wiper & True, with two on cask – usually Kaleidoscope and a guest beer. There is bench seating inside where you can view the impressive brewery. Food trucks serve food outside, where there is also plenty of seating, some under cover.
⛄🕸🌙♿≢(Lawrence Hill)🟦🌸🛜

Bristol: St Philips

Barley Mow
39 Barton Road, BS2 0LF (400yds from rear exit of Temple Meads station over footbridge)
☎ (0117) 930 4709
Bristol Beer Factory Notorious, Fortitude, Milk Stout; 5 changing beers (often Bristol Beer Factory, Siren, Tapestry) Ⓗ
Bristol Beer Factory's flagship outlet is only 10 minutes' walk from the rear exit of Temple Meads station. There are eight hand pumps offering four beers from the brewery plus constantly changing guests of varying styles, mostly from local breweries. There is also a good bottled and canned beer selection from around the world and an interesting craft keg offering. Occasional beer-related events are held, along with a regular Tuesday pub quiz. The small food menu includes vegan options. There is a walled rear beer garden, and benches at the front. Q⛄🕸🌙▶≢(Temple Meads)🟦(506)🌸🛜

Bristol: St Werburghs

Duke of York Ⓛ
2 Jubilee Road, BS2 9RS (S side of Mina Rd park)
☎ (0117) 279 5781
4 changing beers (sourced locally; often Arbor, Electric Bear, Moor Beer) Ⓗ
Tucked away in a side street, this popular local has an eclectic clientele and decor to match. The wooden floors, coloured fairy lights, and intriguing range of memorabilia and artefacts create a welcoming grotto-like atmosphere. Notable features include a rare refurbished skittle alley, carved wooden mirrors, a Grand Old Duke of York exterior mural painted by a local artist and a pleasant garden area. Four changing beers are served, mostly from breweries in Bristol and the surrounding area, with the range of styles including a dark ale. ⛄🕸≢(Stapleton Road)♣🟦🛜

Bristol: Spike Island

Orchard Inn
12 Hanover Place, BS1 6XT (off Cumberland Rd near the SS Great Britain)
☎ 07405 360994 ⊕ orchardinn.co.uk
Otter Bitter; St Austell Proper Job; 1 changing beer (sourced regionally; often Arbor, Bristol Beer Factory, Gloucester) Ⓖ
Nestled on a street corner in Spike Island, this friendly, traditional pub is close to the marina and just a short stroll or ferry ride from the city centre. Three ales are

available, either straight from the barrel behind the bar or fetched from the cellar, where they share space with up to 20 ciders and perries. Sport is occasionally shown on TV in a raised area that doubles up as stage space for live jazz or blues music. Locally sourced rolls, pasties and pork pies are usually available. ⛄🕸🌙🟦(506,M2)🌸🎵

Broad Campden

Bakers Arms Ⓛ
GL55 6UR (signed off B4081, at NW end of village)
☎ (01386) 840515 ⊕ bakersarmscampden.com
Prescott Hill Climb; Wye Valley HPA, Butty Bach; 1 changing beer (sourced locally) Ⓗ
Popular all year round with both locals and tourists alike, this fine old village local and genuine free house was first licensed as a public house in 1724. A photograph of the building in 1905 shows it as the village bakery and grain store. It boasts Cotswold stone walls, exposed beams and a fine inglenook. Excellent food is available in the bar and dining room extension and there is a large outside garden and children's play area. Local guest beers alongside regular ales are served from its handsome oak bar. Q⛄🕸🌙♣●P🌸🛜

Charfield

Plough Inn
68 Wotton Road, GL12 8SR
☎ (01453) 845297
4 changing beers Ⓗ
An attractive single-room micropub, it features two open fireplaces and a large covered outdoor seating area, heated in winter, which utilises the original off-sales hatch for service. It offers four real ales plus lagers and ciders. There is a piano in the bar and live music is a regular feature. One of the more unusual features is the large gnu head mounted above the fireplace, which gives its name to the occasional house beer. Q⛄🕸P🟦(60,85)🌸🛜🎵

Charlton Kings

Royal
54, Horsefair Street, GL53 8JH (in centre of village opp church)
☎ (01242) 228937 ⊕ royalpub.co.uk
4 changing beers (often Bath Ales, Dartmoor, Otter) Ⓗ
On the eastern fringes of town is this popular village restaurant/pub which underwent a major refurbishment a few years ago. The central bar has some comfy sofas, adjacent to which is a lounge area. Guest ales are typically from Hogs Back and Bath breweries. No food is served on Sunday evenings after 8pm. There is a large garden as well as patio areas. The pub hosts beer festivals with live music most bank holidays, plus regular live music, quizzes, and meet the brewer evenings. Q⛄🕸🌙♿P🟦(B,P/Q)🌸🛜🎵

Cheltenham

Beehive Inn Ⓛ ✅
1-3 Montpellier Villas, GL50 2XE
☎ (01242) 702270 ⊕ thebeehivemontpellier.com
6 changing beers (often Hop Back, Thornbridge, Timothy Taylor) Ⓗ
A bustling popular local in the residential Suffolks area of town, close to Montpellier, with up to six ales and a cider. A separate first-floor function room has a good range of food available including a popular bar menu. A beer festival is generally held annually and there are

regular live music evenings. The secluded courtyard garden to the rear is popular in the summer.
🌣🏠🕮♣🍴🐾📶♪

Cheltenham Motor Club 🅛

Upper Park Street, GL52 6SA (first right off Hales Rd from London Rd lights, 100yds on right; pedestrian access from A40 via Crown Passage opp Sandford Mill Rd junction)

☎ (01242) 522590 ⊕ cheltmc.com

6 changing beers (often Tiley's) Ⓗ

This friendly club is located just off London Road. It is the three-times winner of National Club of the Year, as well as multiple other awards. Six regularly changing ales from across the country, including a dark ale and a local ale, are joined on the bar by least one keg, generally from Deya, and at least one real cider plus a range of bottled Belgian beers. There is an annual beer festival plus meet the brewer or brewery takeover evenings. Local darts and pool teams play. Non-members are welcome for occasional visits for nominal fee. Card only no cash payments. Q🌣🏠♣🍴🚌🐾📶

Jolly Brewmaster 🅛

39 Painswick Road, GL50 2EZ (off A40 Suffolk Rd, between Suffolks and Tivoli, 200yds S along Painswick Rd)

☎ (01242) 772261

7 changing beers (often Arbor, Bespoke, Moor Beer) Ⓗ

This frequent local CAMRA Pub of the Year boasts 13 handpumps feature a changing range of ales sourced nationally, including up to six ciders. This busy and friendly community hub features original etched windows, a horseshoe bar and open fire. It is a traditional drinking pub; with no food menu, but hot bar snacks such as pasties and pies are generally available later in the week. The attractive courtyard garden is popular in summer, with regular Friday barbecues.
Q🌣🏠🍴🚌(10,94U)🐾📶

Kemble Brewery 🅛 ✓

27 Fairview Street, GL52 2JF (off Northern ring road, jct of Fairview Rd/St Johns Ave, turn left into Fairview St beside Machine Mart, pub is 100yards on right)

☎ (01242) 701053

Wye Valley HPA, Butty Bach; 4 changing beers Ⓗ

This small popular back-street local can be hard to find, but is well worth the effort. Originally a butchers shop in 1845, it became a pub in 1847 and was soon producing ciders, hence the name, but no brewing has taken place in recent times. The pub was fully refurbished 2016. Up to six ales are generally available, from near and far. There is a small attractive walled garden to the rear featuring a new servery for summer barbecues and pizzas. Q🌣🏠🕮♣🐾📶♪

Moon Under Water 🅛 ✓

16-28 Bath Road, GL53 7HA (from E end of High Street, take Bath Rd, pub is 100m on left)

☎ (01242) 583945

Greene King Abbot; Ruddles Best Bitter; Sharp's Doom Bar; 5 changing beers Ⓗ

A open-plan Wetherspoon Lloyds bar just off the east end of the pedestrianised high street. A decked area at the back overlooks the River Chelt and Sandford Park. Some five changing guest ales from local to countrywide supplement the regular beers, plus a selection of real ciders. The dance floor is only used Friday and Saturday evenings, with a generally quiet atmosphere at other times. There is an interactive quiz night on Monday. Children allowed until evening. 🌣🏠🕮♿🚌📶

Railway Inn

New Street, GL50 3QL (400yds W from The Wilson museum, past St James Square)

☎ (01242) 522925

Stroud Tom Long; 2 changing beers Ⓗ

A smart local, just west of the town centre, off the lower high street near Waitrose, which has recently gone free of tie. It has two main rooms – a large lounge with some comfy sofas at one end, and a small cosy bar to the road frontage. There is a garden with a terrace for smokers. Thai food and smokey barbecue cuisine are now the main food focus, available every day until evening. Q🌣🏠🕮P🐾

Sandford Park Alehouse 🍺 🅛

20 High Street, GL50 1DZ (E end of High St, past Strand on right)

☎ (01242) 690242 ⊕ sandfordparkalehouse.co.uk

Oakham Citra; Wye Valley Butty Bach; 7 changing beers Ⓗ

National Pub of the Year 2015 and a frequent local winner in recent years, this contemporary alehouse has a U-shaped main bar area complete with bar billiards, a cosy front snug with wood-burning stove and a large south-facing patio/garden. A function room/lounge is on the first floor. 10 handpumps feature constantly changing ales from microbreweries sourced nationally and locally, plus at least one cider and 16 speciality lagers and craft beers. Q🌣🏠🕮♣🚌🐾📶

Strand 🅛

40-42 High Street, GL50 1EE (at E end of High St just past pedestrian area)

☎ (01242) 373728 ⊕ thestrandcheltenham.co.uk

7 changing beers (sourced regionally; often Clavell & Hind) Ⓗ

A modern, wine bar-style pub, offering at least three ales mainly sourced from the region and often featuring a brewery of the month, plus at least one cider and several craft keg beers. Good-value food is served daily, including a gourmet burger night on Wednesday evening. An upstairs function room is available for hire, along with a cellar bar, home to live comedy and music nights. The large south-facing patio/garden provides a pleasant outdoor drinking area for those summer days.
🌣🏠🕮♿🚌🐾📶♪

Chipping Campden

Eight Bells 🅛

Church Street, GL55 6JG

☎ (01386) 840371 ⊕ eightbellsinn.co.uk

Hook Norton Hooky; North Cotswold Cotswold Best; Purity Pure UBU; Wye Valley HPA Ⓗ

The Eight Bells was originally built in the 14th century to house the stonemasons that built St James' church and was later used to store the peel of eight bells. The inn was rebuilt using most of the original stone and timbers during the 17th century. What exists today is an outstanding example of a traditional Cotswolds inn with cobbled courtyard. Four handpumps serve local and regional ales and two real ciders.
Q🌣🏠🛏🕮♿♣🚌(21)📶

Chipping Sodbury

Horseshoe

2 High Street, BS37 6AH

☎ (01454) 537557 ⊕ horseshoechippingsodbury.co.uk

7 changing beers (sourced regionally; often Palmers, Quantock, Uley) Ⓗ

One of the oldest buildings in the town, this hub of the community was formerly a stationery shop, then briefly a wine bar, and was converted into a pub in 2013. It serves seven beers, often unusual but mostly from the West Country, including dark or strong choices, as well as many different gins. There are three linked rooms with assorted furniture, a restaurant upstairs and a pleasant rear garden. Breakfast and lunchtime meals are served. ⏱❀❶♣❀🍽❀🎵

Churchdown

Old Elm Inn L
Church Road, GL3 2ER
☎ (01452) 530961 ⏺ theoldelminn.co.uk
Sharp's Atlantic; 4 changing beers (sourced locally; often Stroud) Ⓗ
Set in the heart of Churchdown village, this fabulous, spacious hostelry is deservedly popular. A great mix of modern and traditional fittings gives a warm ambience throughout. The pub has gained a great reputation for their food – the menu features good vegetarian options – and booking is highly advised. Serving five quality beers, mainly Locale, the pub hosts lively quiz and music nights, plus occasional food and drink tasting evenings; main sporting events are shown in the sports bar. Families are welcome and the garden has a children's play area. There are five well-appointed letting rooms. ⏱❀🛏❀🚶♿♣P🟥❀🎵

Cirencester

Drillman's Arms
34 Gloucester Road, GL7 2JY (on old A417, 200yds from A435 jct)
☎ (01285) 653892
House beer (by Marston's); 3 changing beers (sourced nationally) Ⓗ
A proper locals drinking haunt, this lively Georgian inn, perched beside a busy road, has a warm, convivial lounge with wood-burner, a pub games dominated public bar and a busy skittle alley. Run by the same family for over three decades, this lovely free house features low-beamed ceilings, horse brasses, brewery pictures and well-priced beer. Fresh flowers grace the frontage and the immaculate toilets. Sunday lunches are available, and the outside seating area is popular with the local dog walking fraternity. They host an annual summer bank holiday beer festival. ❀❶▲♣P❀🎵

Hop Kettle
4 The Woolmarket, GL7 2PR (in the Woolmarket between Dyer St and Waterloo) SP025020
⏺ hop-kettle.com
Hop Kettle Cricklade Ordinary Bitter / COB, North Wall; 3 changing beers (often Hop Kettle) Ⓗ
Local CAMRA Pub of the Year, this impressive micropub in a former Toy Shop in Cirencester's Woolmarket is operated by the local Hop Kettle Brewery and is a welcome addition to the real ale offering in the town. There are five handpumps, eight craft kegs and two cider taps. There is also a range of interesting local and brewery based gins and other spirits. It is furnished in modern comfortable fashion with a range of seating options. The kitchen is operated on a pop-up street-food basis, with a variety of menus and styles. ⏱❶♿🛏🎵

Marlborough Arms L
1 Sheep Street, GL7 1QW
☎ (01285) 651474

Goff's Jouster; North Cotswold Windrush Ale; 3 changing beers (sourced nationally; often Corinium) Ⓗ
A real ale haven, offering five beers sourced from regional and microbreweries, plus boxed ciders and perries, and a fridge with an interesting range of cans and bottles. This lively, wooden-floored pub lies opposite the old GWR station. It is a previous local CAMRA Pub of the Year winner. Brewery memorabilia adorns the walls, with pews and a deep-set fireplace adding character, while the ceiling is disappearing behind the encroaching pumpclip collection. There is a small sheltered rear patio. Occasional beer festivals are held. ❀♣❀❀🍽🎵

Twelve Bells L ✅
12 Lewis Lane, GL7 1EA (straight ahead at traffic lights off A435 roundabout)
☎ (01285) 652230 ⏺ twelvebellscirencester.com
Wye Valley Bitter; 2 changing beers Ⓗ
Named after the peal of 12 in the parish church, this Grade II-listed pub is close to the main shopping area of town. Comprising of three main drinking areas, the front room with bar is a popular spot for a beer and a chat while watching local darts teams; the middle and back rooms are primarily for dining but not exclusively. Outside is a sunny and colourful garden with a gazebo for the smoking fraternity. Car parking is limited but there is a large car park only 200 yards away and on-street in the evening. Q⏱❀❶🚶♿P🟥❀🎵

Coleford

Dog House Micro Pub
13-15 St. John Street, GL16 8AP
☎ 07442 787015 ⏺ thedoghousemicropub.co.uk
4 changing beers (sourced locally) Ⓗ/Ⓖ
Local CAMRA Pub of the Year, this friendly micropub offers a constantly-changing selection of beers from four handpumps, sourced nationally. Something dark is usually available throughout the year. A selection of real ciders are sold from boxes, and there is an impressive gin and rum range. A dog friendly environment, the pub may host regular charity pub quizzes, vinyl nights and showcase local musicians and bands, even fishing and knitting clubs. Do not be surprised to see tasty offerings from the conveniently-located chippy being consumed. No admittance or re-admittance after 10.30pm. Q⏱❀🟥❀🎵

Cromhall

Royal Oak L
Bibstone, GL12 8AD (on B4058, 3 miles E of J14 on M5)
☎ (01454) 430993 ⏺ royaloak-cromhall.co.uk
5 changing beers (sourced regionally; often Cotswold Lion, Uley) Ⓗ
Built in 1674 this spacious single bar pub is situated in the hamlet of Bibstone at the edge of Cromhall. The bar has up to five ales on handpump and a draught cider. It has two separate dining areas, both with impressive Jacobean inglenook fireplaces. The main bar area has a glass-covered well and a splendid stained-glass window behind the bar. There is disabled access. Families and dogs are welcome, but no dogs in the restaurant area. Q❀❶🚶♿P🟥❀🎵

Drybrook

Hearts of Oak L
The Cross, GL17 9EE (in centre of village)
☎ (01594) 730783

Wye Valley Bitter, Butty Bach; 1 changing beer (sourced locally) ⊞

A cracking family run pub that reopened in 2022 after a sympathetic refurbishment, following a two-year closure. The owners used to run a tied pub in the Cotswolds, so are enjoying the freedom to do what suits both themselves and their local clientele. Approached through the car park, it is a clean, comfortable, welcoming community hub with two log fires. Thursday evening is often quiz night, and there are regular music nights to delight and entertain most tastes. Food is served all day Tuesday to Saturday and Sunday lunchtimes, and snacks are usually available.
Q ☞ ❀ ◑ 🅰 ♣ P 🚃 ❀ ♪

Dursley

New Inn 🅛

82-84 Woodmancote, GL11 4AJ (on A4135 Tetbury road)
☎ (01453) 519288
5 changing beers (sourced regionally) ⊞
Known as a dog friendly establishment, where the owners' dogs often provide the greeting. This is a welcoming, comfortable pub that features a large L-shaped public bar with tiled floor and a wood-burning fire during cold weather, and also a smaller lounge. It serves an eclectic selection of regularly-changing guest beers usually, but not exclusively, from smaller breweries, often those requested by regulars. There is a garden at the rear, which is popular on sunny days.
☞ ❀ ♣ ● P 🚃 (61) ❀

Old Spot Inn 🅛

2 Hill Road, GL11 4JQ (by bus station and free car park)
☎ (01453) 542870 ⊕ oldspotinn.co.uk
Uley Old Ric; 7 changing beers (sourced nationally) ⊞
An excellent free house dating from 1776, serving up to eight ales, plus ciders and perrys. Named after the Gloucestershire Old Spot pig, a porcine theme blends with the extensive brewery memorabilia, low ceilings, wood-burning stove and welcoming staff to create a convivial atmosphere. There is an attractive garden and a heated outdoor covered area. Freshly prepared food is served at lunchtimes. On the Cotswold Way, it is popular with walkers, and hosts regular events in the evenings.
Q ☞ ❀ ◑ & ● 🚃 ❀ 🛜

Forthampton

Lower Lode Inn 🅛

GL19 4RE (follow sign to Forthampton from A438 Tewkesbury to Ledbury road) SO8788231809
☎ (01684) 293224 ⊕ lowerlodeinn.co.uk
Wye Valley Butty Bach; 1 changing beer (often Bespoke) ⊞
Blessed with views across the River Severn to Tewkesbury Abbey, this attractive 15th-century brick-built venue, with its three acres of lawns, is a popular stopover for boats and is a Camping and Caravan Club site. Food, advertised as simple and wholesome, is excellent quality and value for money. A beer festival is held in September. A small ferry operates from the Tewkesbury side from Easter to mid-September. Day fishing is available, plus en-suite accommodation. Opening times are reduced in winter so check ahead.
Q ☞ ❀ ◑ 🅰 ● P ❀ ♪

Fossebridge

Inn at Fossebridge ✅

GL54 3JS (A429)

☎ (01285) 720721 ⊕ innatfossebridge.co.uk
Butcombe Original; North Cotswold Windrush Ale; Wadworth 6X; 2 changing beers (sourced locally) ⊞
The Inn at Fossebridge is located in the pretty hamlet of Fossebridge, where the Fosse Way drops into the Cotswolds valley of the River Coln, an area of outstanding natural beauty. An attractive one-bar inn with old timbers, a fine flagstone floor and open fires, the premises also benefits from an outstanding four-acre garden with a lake and river. A selection of regional ales and guests from local breweries can be enjoyed in these cosy surroundings. Q ☞ ❀ 🅰 ◑ ● P ❀ 🛜

Frampton Cotterell

Rising Sun

43 Ryecroft Road, BS36 2HN
☎ (01454) 772330
Hop Union Maiden Voyage, Moose River; 3 changing beers (often Hop Union) ⊞
This village local is the brewery tap for the Hop Union brewery in Brislington. The log-burning stove, archways and slate pillars add to the ambience. Additional seating can be found up the stairs to the left, and there is a restaurant in the warm conservatory. Lunchtime snacks and more substantial evening meals are served from an extensive menu, with all food made in-house. The skittle alley can be booked for private functions.
Q ❀ ◑ ♣ P 🚃 (Y6) ❀ 🛜 ♪

Frampton Mansell

Crown Inn 🅛

GL6 8JG (off A419 Cirencester to Stroud road opp Jolly Nice café and farmshop)
☎ (01285) 760601 ⊕ thecrowninn-cotswolds.co.uk
Butcombe Original; Sharp's Doom Bar; Stroud OPA/Organic Pale Ale; Uley Bitter ⊞
This thriving, friendly village inn dates from 1633 when it was a cider house. Three simply but elegantly furnished rooms feature exposed stone walls and wooden beams, with a fire in each room. The left-hand room has a stone staircase – with a lighted candle on each step – winding around a 15th-century fireplace. This room opens into a lower room which was once the village slaughterhouse. The suntrap front garden offers fine views over the Golden Valley. Attached is a modern 12-bedroom hotel annex with car parking. ☞ ❀ 🅰 ◑ & ♣ P ❀ 🛜

Frampton-on-Severn

Three Horseshoes 🅛

The Green, GL2 7DY (off B4071)
☎ (01452) 742100 ⊕ threehorseshoespub.co.uk
Timothy Taylor Landlord; Uley Bitter; 1 changing beer ⊞
Situated at the southern end of England's longest village green, this lovely 19th-century two-bar rural community pub is a gem. Originally built by a farrier, both bars have coal fires, and dogs are welcome in the flagstoned public bar. Their food is home-cooked, especially their unique '3-Shu pie', which is freshly baked to order. A rear garden features a double boules court, which hosts annual championships. Blessed with some active, keen locals, regular community events – including lots of evening jamming sessions – are popular, with a noticeable bias towards traditional music. Q ☞ ❀ ◑ & 🅰 ● ❀ 🛜 ♪

Gloucester

Brewhouse & Kitchen (Gloucester Quays)

Unit R1 St Anne Walk, Gloucester Quays, GL1 5SH
☎ (01452) 222965
Brewhouse & Kitchen Shed Head, Stevedore, SS Banner ⊞

Situated by the side of the Gloucester to Sharpness Canal, this bar/restaurant brews its own range of beers on site and is a delight to visit. Outdoor seating by the canal is great for a fine day, and much of the seating indoors allows customers to watch the brewing in progress. Beer tasting events, Meet the Brewer and brewing days are all frequently available. Regular beers plus a seasonal cask, and a range of keg beers are all brewed here. Please chat to the friendly, well-informed staff, and learn more about their fine products. ⟟⟨⟩⟟⟟⟟⟟⟟

Drunken Duck

Bull Lane, GL1 2HG
☎ 07725 754852 ⊕ angiesbar.co.uk
2 changing beers (sourced nationally) ⊞

The city's smallest bar, tucked away just off Westgate Street. A friendly and welcoming venue where you can choose to join in with the conversation in the almost bijou bar, or tuck yourself away in the surprisingly spacious room upstairs, and dawdle on the retro games machines. Two regularly-changing ales are available, plus a plethora of spirits and mixers, making it popular with the weekend 'sing along' crowd. Maybe not the best place to visit for the shy and tongue-tied, the banter here is friendly, inclusive and usually fun; occasionally quite loud. Following a refurbishment in 2023, the pub was renamed from its former name of Angie's.
⟟⟟⟟⟟⟟

Fountain Inn ⌾ ⊘

53 Westgate Street, GL1 2NW (down an alley between nos 51 & 55)
☎ (01452) 522562 ⊕ thefountaininngloucester.com
Bristol Beer Factory Independence; Dartmoor Jail Ale; St Austell Tribute; Timothy Taylor Landlord; 2 changing beers ⊞

With a well deserved reputation for offering some cracking beers, coupled with a popular menu, and conveniently located for events at the Cathedral, this 17th century inn is on the site of an ale house known to have existed in 1216. A passage leads from Westgate Street into a courtyard that is garlanded with flowers in warmer months. The Cathedral bar has a panelled ceiling and carved stone fireplace, the Orange Room serves as an overflow area or a room for private functions. It is especially busy on rugby match days. ⟟⟨⟩⟟⟟⟟⟟

Linden Tree

73-75 Bristol Road, GL1 5SN (on A430, S of docks)
☎ (01452) 527869 ⊕ lindentreepub.co.uk
Wadworth 6X; Wye Valley Butty Bach; 2 changing beers (sourced nationally) ⊞

At the end of a Grade-II listed Georgian terrace, with a 'country' feel inside; this pub has an open log fire with unusual canopy, beamed ceilings and exposed stone walls. The front bar offers a variety of seating, and at the rear of the pub there is a skittle alley, function room and sports bar. There is a patio in front and the bus from the city centre stops nearby. Substantial home-made meals are served, excluding in the evening on weekends, with a Sunday carvery. Well-priced accommodation is available. The guest ales are from family brewers.
⟟⟟⟨⟩⟟⟟(12,60) ⟟

Pelican Inn ⟟ ⌾ ⊘

4 St Marys Street, GL1 2QR (WNW of cathedral)
☎ (01452) 582966 ⊕ pelicangloucester.co.uk
Wye Valley Bitter, The Hopfather, HPA, Butty Bach, Wholesome Stout; 3 changing beers (sourced nationally) ⊞

Voted both regional and local CAMRA Pub of the Year 2022, this wonderfully run two room establishment was rescued by Wye Valley brewery in 2012. Twice yearly beer festivals and a tap takeover are highlights of the year. The single bar is dominated by conversation and a large fire, with the beams rumoured to be from Drake's Golden Hind – originally named the Pelican. As well as regularly changing ciders and perries, a wide selection of cans showcases modern trends in small batch brewing prowess. The attractive patio area at the rear hosts a food wagon on rugby match days. ⟟⟟⟟⟟⟟⟟⟟⟟⟟⟟⟟⟟⟟

Turks Head Inn

7-9 St Aldate Street, GL1 1RP
☎ 07771 982356 ⊕ turksheadinn.co.uk
4 changing beers (sourced nationally) ⊞ /⟨G⟩

The city's first micropub, which relocated from Southgate Street to St Aldate Street in April 2022, has retained its fan base, selling four cask ales and a varied selection of ciders. This is the ideal pub for technophobes as mobile phones are not encouraged and there is no WiFi or social media in any form. The pub is blessed with both a horseshoe bar and a spare staircase; the upstairs rooms are a lovely spot to sit and put the world to rights. It is a cash-only hostelry, which does not permit children.
⟟⟟⟟⟟

Gretton

Royal Oak ⌾

Gretton Road, GL54 5EP (E end of the village, 1½ miles from Winchcombe)
☎ (01242) 604999 ⊕ royaloakgretton.co.uk
St Austell Tribute, Proper Job; Wye Valley HPA; 2 changing beers (sourced regionally) ⊞

A warm welcome is assured from the local owners of this popular Cotswold pub set in two acres of grounds. All the regular beers are from St Austell and Wye Valley. Food can be eaten in the L-shaped bar or in the conservatory with its outstanding views across the Vale of Evesham. The Royal Oak dates from about 1830 and the large garden includes a children's play area and a tennis court. The Gloucestershire Warwickshire heritage railway runs past the garden. ⟟⟟⟨⟩⟟⟟⟟P⟟⟟

Guiting Power

Farmers Arms

Winchcombe Road, GL54 5TZ
☎ (01451) 850358
Donnington BB, Cotswold Gold, SBA ⊞

A large Donnington tenanted pub set in a remote Cotswold village which is an ideal base for walking in classic countryside. It has a large beer garden and parking, with exposed beams and real fire inside. Classic pub grub is served. Now under new management, it is run by a local couple who aim to welcome all to the pub and offer the full range of Donnington Ales served from large sweeping bar. The skittle alley is regularly used for functions. ⟟⟟⟨⟩⟟P⟟

Ham

Salutation Inn ⌾

Ham Green, GL13 9QH (from Berkeley take the road signposted to Jenner Museum)

☎ (01453) 810284 🌐 the-sally-at-ham.com
Tiley's Special Bitter; 5 changing beers (sourced nationally; often Arbor, Bristol Beer Factory, Moor Beer) Ⓗ
Multi-award winning rural free house, popular with locals and visitors alike, offering up to six real ales and nine real ciders and perries plus an extensive bottled beer and cider menu. The on-site microbrewery Tiley's Ales produces a range of traditional ales. There are three bars – two of which share a central wood burner – and a skittles alley/function room. Locally made hot pies are served on Friday evenings and weekend lunchtimes; there are also folk nights and singalongs.
Q🍼❀◐♿♣●P🐾ᯤ♫

Hawkesbury Upton

Beaufort Arms Ⓛ
High Street, GL9 1AU (off A46, 6 miles N of M4 jct 18)
☎ (01454) 238217 🌐 beaufortarms.com
Bristol Beer Factory Independence; Butcombe Original; 3 changing beers (sourced regionally) Ⓗ
An attractive Grade II-listed Cotswold stone free house, built in 1602, close to the historic Somerset Monument. It features separate public and lounge bars, a dining room and skittle alley/function room, which houses a large collection of ancient brewery and local memorabilia. Up to five ales are served, plus a traditional cider on handpump. The pub has an attractive garden with a barbecue used for community activities. The friendly locals assure visitors a warm welcome.
Q🍼❀◐◑♿♣●P🚌🐾ᯤ

Hillesley

Fleece Inn Ⓛ
Chapel Lane, GL12 7RD (between Wotton-Under-Edge and Hawkesbury Upton)
☎ (01453) 520003 🌐 thefleeceinnhillesley.com
Wye Valley Butty Bach; 5 changing beers (often Arbor, Church End, Oakham) Ⓗ
An attractive 17th-century village pub set in the heart of Hillesley. It has a single bar with a wood-burning stove, a separate lounge/dining room and a snug area. The pub serves up to six real ales and also features guest craft keg and draft cider. Food is available at lunchtime and in the evening. There is a large attractive lawned garden with a safe play area for children and private car park. Dogs are welcome. Q🍼❀◐◑●P🚌🐾ᯤ♫

Kingswood

Lyons Den
121 Regent Street, BS15 8LJ
4 changing beers (often Bristol Beer Factory, Glastonbury, Tiny Rebel) Ⓖ
This micropub opened in 2019 in a former charity shop at the eastern end of the main shopping street. The bar area as you enter is simply furnished and there is a small snug space at the rear. The cask ales, keg beers and ciders for sale are displayed on a retro-style computer screen on the wall. Board games are available to play and there is low-volume background music. Look out for regular tap takeovers from local breweries and some from further afield. Dogs are made very welcome.
Q🍼♿●🚌🐾

Littledean

Littledean House Hotel
Broad Street, GL14 3JT (on A4151)
☎ (01594) 822106
Wye Valley Butty Bach; 2 changing beers (sourced nationally; often Fuller's, Timothy Taylor, Tiny Rebel) Ⓗ
Located at the western end of the village, this charming pub bar, set within the hotel, is a real treat. The convivial landlord takes great pride in his ales, and enjoys finding gems of memorabilia to grace the displays in the main drinking areas. The bar has been recently renovated to give a timeless, yet trendy aesthetic. The lovely log fire makes for a cosy spot on an autumnal evening; and in the summer you can enjoy the beer garden, with lovely views, which is hugely popular with locals and guests alike. 🍼❀🛏♿♣●Pᯤ

Lydbrook

Forge Hammer Ⓛ
Forge Row, GL17 9NP (B4234)
☎ (01594) 822106 🌐 theforgehammer.co.uk
Lydbrook Valley IPA, Viaduct Pale Ale; 1 changing beer Ⓗ
This cracking place close to the picturesque river Wye, but this landscape was once dominated by tin plating works and furnaces. The Lydbrook Valley Brewing Co was established by the landlord in 2018, brewing exclusively for the pub. The Spice Garden Indian restaurant is incorporated into the premises, which means that the main bar can get busy, especially when board games are out on the tables, and folk are having a quick pint before collecting their food. The covered smoking area is usually lively as well. 🍼❀◐◑⛺♣Pᯤ

Marshfield

Catherine Wheel
39 High Street, SN14 8LR (if using postcode in sat nav check it is not showing Colerne)
☎ (01225) 892220 🌐 thecatherinewheel.co.uk
Butcombe Haka; 2 changing beers (sourced locally; often Flying Monk) Ⓗ
The Catherine Wheel is an impressive example of provincial baroque architecture, much of it dating back to the 17th century, although some interior features look older. Simple, sympathetic decor complements the exposed stone walls and large open fireplaces. There is a large cosy bar area with rooms off and a courtyard-style garden with a covered area. Inside it feels like a traditional Cotswold pub, with good ale, good food and a warm and welcoming interior. Q🍼❀🛏◐◑P🚌🐾ᯤ♫

Moreton-in-Marsh

Bell Inn 🏆 Ⓛ ✔
High Street, GL56 0AF (A429)
☎ (01608) 651688 🌐 thebellinnmoreton.co.uk
Prescott Hill Climb; Purity Pure UBU; Timothy Taylor Landlord; 2 changing beers (sourced locally; often Hook Norton, North Cotswold) Ⓗ
An old coaching inn, dating from 18th century, with a real fire and good food. The interior has been pleasantly refurbished and comprises of a mainly open plan area, which has been sympathetically divided into more intimate snug sections. A large courtyard area is found through the old arched entrance with an enclosed garden at the rear. Famed for its links with Lord of the Rings author J. R. R. Tolkien, a map of Middle-earth adorns the walls. Local and national ales available.
Q🍼❀🛏◐◑♿⛺⇌P🚌(801) 🐾ᯤ♫

Newent

Cobblers L
7 Church Street, GL18 1PU
☎ 07891 815654
4 changing beers (often Jennings, Ringwood) Ⓗ
Cobblers, located in the in the centre of Newent, can claim to be Gloucestershire's first micropub. It is bigger than you might imagine, with the cosy front bar leading on to two further rooms at the back converted from what was once local council offices. There are usually four gravity fed ales on offer plus cider and a large selection of artisan gins. If you are hungry, you can order a meal from the local Indian restaurant, and it will be delivered to your table. Thursday nights are live music nights.
Q✿🍴

King's Arms
Ross Road, GL18 1BD (on B4221)
☎ (01531) 820035 ⊕ kings-arms-newent.business.site
4 changing beers (often Bespoke, Shepherd Neame, Titanic) Ⓗ
The pub has a comfortable refitted bar area with open fires, a large function room and skittle alley, and a big lower bar and dining room. There is also a spacious outdoor decked courtyard. Four regularly changing ales are served and the pub has a good reputation for home-cooked food, offering a wide menu including speciality pizzas, midweek deals and popular Sunday lunches. Local CAMRA Pub of the Year in 2020. Q�　🍴♣P

Slad

Woolpack L
Slad Road, GL6 7QA (On B4070)
☎ (01452) 813429 ⊕ thewoolpackslad.com
Stroud Budding; Uley Bitter, Pigs Ear; 1 changing beer (sourced regionally; often Butcombe, Clavell & Hind) Ⓗ
A popular 17th century inn, clinging to the side of the Slad Valley, boasting superb views. Cider with Rosie author Laurie Lee was a regular and was instrumental in saving the pub from closure. The pub has been lovingly restored and enhanced, with built-in dark wooden settles in the end rooms. A recent seamlessly-executed two-storey extension to the rear has enlarged the kitchen and added a new restaurant area to the right-hand end room, with a ceiling painting of the Slad Valley.
Q�　✿🍴▲♣🐾🎵

Staple Hill

Wooden Walls Micropub
30 Broad Street, BS16 5NU
☎ 07858 266596 ⊕ thewoodenwallsmicropub.com
5 changing beers Ⓖ
Micropub opened in 2018 in a former carpet shop on the main shopping street. The single room is pleasantly furnished, with wooden booths and walls. Drinks currently available are displayed on a large blackboard surrounding the serving hatch. Five cask ales are on offer alongside real ciders, several craft keg beers, gin and wine, but no lager. There are a few steps up to the toilets and paved rear garden. Board games are available to play. Q�　✿♣🍴🖥✿

Stroud

Ale House L
9 John Street, GL5 2HA (opp Cornhill Farmers' Market)
☎ (01453) 755447 ⊕ thealehousestroud.com

Burning Sky Plateau; Tiley's IPA; 6 changing beers (sourced nationally; often Fyne, Grey Trees, Kirkstall) Ⓗ
Built in 1837 for the Poor Law Guardians, this Grade-II listed building is a mecca for ale lovers. The bar occupies the double-height top-lit former boardroom, where an all-year-round beer festival showcases beers from Howling Hops, Mallinsons, Vocation and many more – plus a cider and perry. Opposite is a blazing log fire and adjoining are two smaller rooms. Live music is played at weekends, with jazz once a month on Thursday. Sunday is quiz night. Food consists of home-made curries, chilli and other dishes. A restored 1932 bar billiards table is a popular recent addition. ✿🍴👤♣🍴🖥✿🎵

Crown & Sceptre L
98 Horns Road, GL5 1EG
☎ (01453) 762588 ⊕ crownandsceptrestroud.com
Stroud Budding; Uley Bitter, Pigs Ear; 1 changing beer (sourced regionally; often Blue Anchor, Butcombe, North Cotswold) Ⓗ
Lively back-street local at the heart of its community. The walls display an eclectic mix of framed prints, posters and clocks. There is even some stained-glass. Local groups meet round a large table in a side room — including knit & natter on Tuesday. The pub also has its own motorcycle society. It is famed for its Up the Workers good-value set meal on Wednesday, and Sunday roasts. Sport is screened in the back bar. A terrace to the rear offers panoramic views across the valley to Rodborough Common. �　✿🍴♣🖥(8)✿🎵

Lord John ✔
15-17 Russell Street, GL5 3AB (walk up Station Rd from station and turn right onto Russell St; pub is 50yds up on right-hand side)
☎ (01453) 767610
Greene King Abbot; Ruddles Best Bitter; Sharp's Doom Bar; 3 changing beers (often Hook Norton, Hop Union, Theakston) Ⓗ
Behind a handsome red brick and Cotswold-stone façade, Wetherspoon's sympathetic conversion of the town's former post office has produced an L-shaped bar with a south-facing walled courtyard. The pub is dominated by the large greenhouse-style glazed skylight which used to light the sorting office. The bar counter runs down the right-hand side with booths and individual high tables opposite. The rear has been designed to resemble an old-fashioned railway carriage, complete with overhead luggage racks and a curved, boarded ceiling. �　✿🍴🖥(67,69)✿

Prince Albert L ✔
Rodborough Hill, GL5 3SS (corner of Walkley Hill)
☎ (01453) 755600 ⊕ theprincealbertstroud.co.uk
4 changing beers (sourced nationally; often Bristol Beer Factory, Church End, Thornbridge) Ⓗ
This lively, cosmopolitan, Cotswold-stone inn below Rodborough Common has been run by the same family for 27 years. Simultaneously bohemian, homely and welcoming – with a big reputation for live music – the single L-shaped bar is full of local art, music and film posters, and an idiosyncratic mix of furniture, fittings and memorabilia. Stairs lead up from the large covered courtyard to a walled garden with an elegant cruck-framed shelter. Food consists of pizzas and burgers. Live music on Sunday and Monday evenings is ticketed. Local CAMRA Pub of the Year. �　✿🍴♣🖥(40,69)✿🎵

Tetbury

Royal Oak L ✔
1 Cirencester Road, GL8 8EY (On B4067)

☎ (01666) 500021 ⊕ theroyaloaktetbury.co.uk
**2 changing beers (sourced regionally; often Hop
Kettle (Cricklade), Moor Beer, Otter)** Ⓗ
Clever design options have make this totally renovated
pub a joy to visit, utilising the existing features to merge
a traditional feel to a practical, modern layout,
deservedly winning awards in the process. Swathes of
wooden surfaces provide a welcoming feel, a small
fireplace at one end adding warmth. Six handpumps
include Severn Cider and a vegan ale from Moor – chosen
to match the vegan menu option. The 'one pot' menu
option is popular, with more dining space upstairs. Lively
music and beer festivals are hosted, and letting rooms
are available. ➷❀✿◑&♣♠P❀☂♫

Tewkesbury

Berkeley Arms ✪

8 Church Street, GL20 5PA (between Tewkesbury Cross
and Abbey on old A38)
☎ (01684) 290555
**Wadworth Henry's IPA, Horizon, 6X, Swordfish; 2
changing beers (often Goff's, Wadworth)** Ⓗ
A 15th-century half-timbered Grade II-listed pub, just off
Tewkesbury Cross. At the rear of this two-bar venue, a
barn, believed to be the oldest non-ecclesiastical
building in this historic town, is used as a meeting room
year round. Live music is performed on Friday and
Saturday evenings. Buses to Cheltenham and Gloucester
stop close by. Former winner of Wadworth's Best of the
Best award. ➷❀&▲♣♦➡(41)❀☂♫

Cross House Tavern ♥ Ⓛ

108 Church Street, GL20 5AB
☎ 07931 692227
**7 changing beers (often Clavell & Hind, Enville,
Salopian)** Ⓗ
Tewkesbury's first micropub was originally two houses in
the early 16th century. It was extended in the 17th
century, and extensively renovated throughout circa
1865. The Cross House Tavern's heritage has been
restored with a great deal of dedication. It has again
become a Victorian-style establishment serving real local
ales (including vegan beer), ciders, perries, wines and
snacks – many sourced from within 20 miles. The beer is
served from tapped casks much as it was when the
building was known as the Tolsey Inn and Coach House in
the early 20th century. Q▲♦➡❀☂

Nottingham Arms Ⓛ ✪

129 High Street, GL20 5JU (on A38 in town centre)
☎ (01684) 491514 ⊕ nottinghamarms-tewkesbury.co.uk
**Sharp's Doom Bar; 3 changing beers (often Enville,
Purity, Sharp's)** Ⓗ
A 14th-century town centre hostelry with two
welcoming rooms – a public bar at the front and the bar/
restaurant behind – with timber predominating. Framed
photographs of old Tewkesbury adorn the walls. Four
ales are generally served. They are getting noticed for
their excellent, well-priced food, served lunchtimes and
evenings. Knowledgeable staff will happily tell you about
the resident ghosts. Live music on most Friday and
Sunday evenings and Thursday is quiz night.
➷◑▲♣♦➡❀☂♫

Royal Hop Pole Ⓛ ✪

94 Church Street, GL20 5RS (in centre of town between
the Abbey and Cross)
☎ (01684) 278670
**Greene King IPA; Hook Norton Old Hooky; Hop Union
Old Higby; Ruddles County; 4 changing beers (sourced
locally)** Ⓗ

This well-known landmark is an amalgamation of historic
buildings from the 15th and 18th centuries. It has been
known as the Royal Hop Pole since being visited in 1891
by Princess Mary of Teck (later Queen Mary, Royal
Consort of George V). The Hop Pole is mentioned in
Dickens' Pickwick Papers. Purchased by JD Wetherspoon,
it reopened in 2008. There is wood panelling on almost
every wall of this spacious, multi-roomed drinking
establishment, with a large patio and garden area at the
rear. Q➷❀✿◑&▲P➡❀☂

Thornbury

Anchor Inn Ⓛ ✪

Gloucester Road, BS35 1JY
☎ (01454) 281375 ⊕ theanchorthornbury.co.uk
**Draught Bass; St Austell Proper Job; 5 changing beers
(often Butcombe, Frome, Timothy Taylor)** Ⓗ
Licensed since 1695, this friendly, traditional inn serves
two regular beers and five changing guests. Good home-
cooked food is available daily, including a Tuesday lunch
club. There are two large rooms, one of which has been
split to provide a function/meeting area and is also used
by local artists. The pub has its own darts, cribbage and
cricket teams, and hosts a quiz night on Sundays. The
attractive garden includes a boules piste and children's
play area. ➷❀◑♣P➡(60,T1)❀☂♫

Thrupp

Stroud Brewery Tap Ⓛ

Kingfisher Business Park, London Road, GL5 2BY (take
A419 from Stroud, turn right down Hope Mill Ln just
before the painted bus shelter, immediate right turn and
the brewery is on your left over the bridge at the end)
☎ (01453) 887122 ⊕ stroudbrewery.co.uk
**Stroud Tom Long, OPA/Organic Pale Ale, Budding; 1
changing beer (often Stroud)** Ⓗ
Occupying a new purpose-designed building beside the
Thames and Severn Canal, the brewery taproom opens
directly onto a terrace beside the towpath. To one side is
an open kitchen with an Italian wood-fired pizza oven.
Seating consists mostly of wooden benches beside long
tables – resembling at times a diminutive Bavarian beer
hall. These benches are augmented by squishy leather
sofas and large oak casks for vertical drinking. At the far
end – with small windows allowing glimpses of the
brewery – is a small stage with an upright piano.
➷❀◑&♦P➡(54A,69) ❀☂♫

Upper Oddington

Horse & Groom Ⓛ ✪

Upper Oddington, GL56 0XH (top of village, signed off
A436 E of Stow)
☎ (01451) 830584 ⊕ horseandgroom.uk.com
**Prescott Hill Climb; Wye Valley Butty Bach; 1 changing
beer (sourced locally)** Ⓗ
This privately owned 16th-century inn is run by friendly
licensees. The extended bar area for locals is linked by a
real open log fire in an inglenook setting to its own
sitting room. A weekly changing guest ale is usually from
a Gloucestershire brewer, and real cider is from
Dunkertons. There is a large car park and attractive
garden and patio area. The pub is situated in good
walking country close to Stow and has eight letting
bedrooms. Q➷❀✿◑P➡❀☂

Upper Soudley

White Horse Inn

Church Road, GL14 2UA (B4227)

☎ (01594) 825968

2 changing beers (sourced nationally) [H]

Still retaining the original layout with separate bar and lounge, this wonderful hostelry is an unspoilt Forest local. The pub sign still has the 'castle emblem' of the old West Country breweries, a rare survivor. Located in a pleasant wooded valley, covered with bluebells in the spring, the area is popular with walkers; Soudley Ponds and the Dean Heritage Museum are close by. Blessed with a much-loved skittle alley, the owners love the way it has become a proper community hub, a meeting point for many groups including archaeologists and morris dancers. 🐴❀♿♣P🚌(717)🐾

Westbury-on-Severn

Lyon Inn

The Village, GL14 1PA (A48)

☎ (01452) 760221 🌐 thelyoninn.com

3 changing beers [H]

Once known as the old Red Lion, earliest references go back as far as the 16th century, but the ancient looking timbers are an early 20th century addition. Conveniently situated on the main A48 route, this lovely hostelry offers a warm welcome. The new owners have revived the fortunes by sensitively opening up previously under-used areas to create some 'fine dining' spaces, while retaining the traditional ambience as much as they can. Three ales are usually available, often locally sourced, with an unusual array of memorabilia on the walls of the drinking and dining areas. Q🐴❀🛏◐P🚉

Winchcombe

Corner Cupboard

83 Gloucester Street, GL54 5LX (on B4632)

☎ (01242) 602303 🌐 cornercupboardwinchcombe.co.uk

Skinner's Betty Stogs; Timothy Taylor Landlord; Wye Valley Butty Bach; 1 changing beer (sourced locally) [H]

Situated on the outskirts of Winchcombe this traditional inn built circa 1550 has several bars and rooms allowing the customer to choose their own style and company. Good-value food is served in pleasant surroundings, with flagstoned floors, oak panelling and Cotswold stone walls. The bar is stocked with real ale including guest ales. There is a car park at the rear.
Q🐴❀◐♿♣P🚌🐾📶

Wotton-under-Edge

Falcon Steakhouse [L]

20 Church Street, GL12 7HB (at bottom of Long St shopping area)

☎ (01453) 521894 🌐 falconsteakhouse.com

3 changing beers (sourced locally) [H]

A free house built in 1659, the quirky layout of the interior features rooms on differing levels. The cosy single bar has a wood-burning fire and leads to a snug with a flagstoned floor. The dining room specialises in steaks from the family farm – which can also be purchased in the pub – and locally sourced ingredients. Competitively priced beers are selected by customer vote from brewers within a 25 mile radius. A popular haunt with walkers traversing the Cotswold Way.
Q🐴◐♣🍎🚌🐾📶

Breweries

Arbor SIBA

181 Easton Road, Easton, Bristol, BS5 0HQ
☎ (0117) 329 2711 🌐 arborales.co.uk

⊗ Founded in 2007, Arbor has a brew length of 20 barrels with 16 fermenting vessels. Willing to experiment, more than 300 beers have been produced. The current range reflects modern tastes and leans towards hoppy pale ales and IPAs plus some interesting red and dark ales. 🛒♦LIVE GF

Mosaic Gluten Free (ABV 4%) PALE
Hoppy aroma, flavours of soft tropical fruit with floral notes on a light malt background leaving a gentle bittersweet aftertaste.

Shangri La (ABV 4.2%) PALE
Yellow best bitter with hoppy aroma, light malt and tropical fruit on the palate and a clean, refreshing, bitter finish.

Blue Sky Drinking (ABV 4.4%) BITTER
Malty aroma and background flavour with hints of berry fruits and spice. Hop bitterness increases in the short, balanced finish.

C Bomb (ABV 4.7%) PALE
Distinctive New World hop aroma, citrus fruit and pine flavours bring bitterness to the palate continuing into the lingering aftertaste.

The Devil Made Me Brew It (ABV 5.5%) STOUT
A velvetty speciality beer in stout style. Floral and citrus hops in the aroma, coffee and slightly burnt toffee flavours – sweet but with a bitter finish.

Yakima Valley (ABV 7%) IPA
A strong, full-bodied IPA. Hoppy and very fruity. Sweetness which is well-balanced with bitterness, lasting into a soft bitter aftertaste.

Breakfast Stout (ABV 7.4%) STOUT
Rich, full-bodied stout with roasted malt, dark fruit, liquorice, coffee, chocolate and oatmeal flavours all evident in this complex brew.

Ashley Down

St Andrews, Bristol, BS6 5BY
☎ (0117) 983 6567 ☎ 07563 751200
✉ ashleydownbrewery@gmail.com

⊗ Ashley Down began brewing in 2011 using a 5.5-barrel plant in the owner's garage. It suffered a major fire in 2017. Production resumed in 2022, in the owners reinstated garage. A small range of beers are regularly brewed, that are interspersed with one-offs. ♦V

Ashton

Cheltenham, GL53 9LW ☎ 07796 445822
🌐 ashtonbrewery.co.uk

⊗ Nanobrewery established in Ashton Keynes, Wiltshire, in 2018. The brewery moved in 2020 to Cheltenham. A range of live beers are produced which are unfined cask and bottle-conditioned. LIVE V

Mosaic (ABV 4.4%) GOLD
Gold (ABV 4.5%) PALE
Shot In The Dark (ABV 4.6%) SPECIALITY
Hazy Blonde (ABV 4.8%) PALE

Basement Beer

32 Upper York Street, Stokes Croft, Bristol, BS2 8QN
☎ 07702 430808 🌐 basementbeer.co.uk

⊠ Basement expanded its brewing capacity in early 2023 and continues to brew a variety of innovative and progressive beers, supplying both the onsite tap and a number of Bristol pubs and bars. Several of the beers feature collaborations with local tea blenders and coffee roasters. ♠

Citra Single Hop Pale (ABV 3.9%) PALE
Galaxy Hopping (ABV 6.2%) IPA
Juicy, hop-forward IPA with grapefruit to the fore and pineapple and tropical fruit undertones before a balanced, bittersweet finish.

Bath Ales

Hare Brewery, Southway Drive, Warmley, Bristol, BS30 5LW
☎ (0117) 947 4797 ⊕ bathales.com

⊠ Established in 1995, Bath Ales was taken over by St Austell in 2016. Since 2018 Bath Ales' beers have been brewed in a new high-tech brewery, including cask, bottling and kegging lines. The Hare Brewery layout was fine tuned during 2020-2021 and more automation added. In 2022 a new canning line was installed. 🛒GF

Gem (ABV 4.1%) BITTER
Pale brown best bitter with sweet fruit and malt flavours and a hint of caramel. Little aroma but a balanced taste with a short bitter finish.

Battledown SIBA

Coxhorne Farm, London Road, Charlton Kings, Cheltenham, GL52 6UY ☎ 07734 834104
⊕ battledownbrewery.com

⊠ A family brewery since 2005, it brews a range of ales, lager and craft beers on its 13-hectolitre plant, installed in 2020. The brewery is supplied by spring water from the Cotswold hills, which are located behind the brewery. ‼🛒LIVE♠

Pale Ale (ABV 3.8%) PALE
Original (ABV 4.4%) BITTER
West Coast IPA (ABV 5.2%) PALE

Bespoke SIBA

Church Farm, Church Street, Littledean, GL14 3NL
☎ (01452) 929281 ☎ 07951 818668
⊕ bespokebrewery.co.uk

⊠ Brewing moved to premises at Littledean, with a farm tap. Both cask-conditioned and keg beers are produced using a 12-barrel plant. Beers are available from the farm tap and brewery shop. Special-labelled bottles are offered for celebratory occasions. ‼🛒♠♠

Saved by the Bell (ABV 3.8%) BITTER
Forest Gold (ABV 4%) GOLD
Beware The Bear (ABV 4.2%) BITTER
Going Off Half-Cocked (ABV 4.6%) PALE
Money for Old Rope (ABV 4.8%) STOUT
Over a Barrel (ABV 5%) OLD

Brewhouse & Kitchen SIBA

🍺 31-35 Cotham Hill, Clifton, Bristol, BS6 6JY
☎ (0117) 973 3793 ⊕ brewhouseandkitchen.com/bristol

⊠ This addition to the Brewhouse & Kitchen chain opened in 2015. A 2.5-barrel plant is used to produce five core ales and regular seasonal brews. Head Brewer Will Bradshaw, formerly of Gloucester Ales, joined in 2016. All beers are unfined. ‼♠

Brewhouse & Kitchen SIBA

🍺 Unit 7, The Brewery, St Margaret's Road, Cheltenham, GL50 4EQ
☎ (01242) 509946 ⊕ brewhouseandkitchen.com

⊠ This addition to the Brewhouse & Kitchen chain opened in 2016 using a three-barrel plant. ‼♠

Brewhouse & Kitchen SIBA

🍺 Unit R1, St Anne Walk, Gloucester Quay, Gloucester, GL1 5SH
☎ (01452) 222965 ⊕ brewhouseandkitchen.com

⊠ Opened in 2015 as part of the Brewhouse & Kitchen chain using a three-barrel plant. Based by the canal, it has a lovely outdoor area. ♠

Bristol Beer Factory

The Old Brewery, Durnford Street, Ashton, Bristol, BS3 2AW
☎ (0117) 902 6317

Office: 291 North Street, Ashton, Bristol, BS3 1JP
⊕ bristolbeerfactory.co.uk

⊠ A fiercely independent brewery at the heart of the Bristol beer scene since 2004. Based on North Street (the cultural hub of south Bristol), in a 200-year-old red brick building, with 180 years of brewing heritage (including Ashton Gate Brewing Co, which closed in 1933). More than 40 beers are produced annually. ‼🛒♠♠

Notorious (ABV 3.8%) BITTER
Fruity hop aroma, light malt on the palate overlaid with citrus and tropical fruits before a lingering, dry bitter aftertaste.
Fortitude (ABV 4%) BITTER
Amber ale with a light malty base overlaid with traditional English hop flavours before a clean and slightly dry finish.
Milk Stout (ABV 4.5%) STOUT
Roasted malt aroma, creamy flavours of chocolate dusted cappuccino with dark stone and dried vine fruit, increasingly bitter aftertaste
Independence (ABV 4.6%) BITTER
Initial hop aroma, well-balanced flavours blend the fruity citrus hops with a malty backbone leaving a clean bittersweet aftertaste.

Clavell & Hind SIBA

The Old Haulage Yard, Old Cirencester Road, Birdlip, Gloucester, GL4 8JL
☎ (01452) 238050 ⊕ clavellandhind.co.uk

Clavell & Hind is a 20-barrel brewery based in the Cotswold countryside. ‼♠♠

Coachman (ABV 3.8%) SPECIALITY
Blunderbuss (ABV 4.2%) GOLD
Rook Wood (ABV 4.4%) BITTER

Corinium

Unit 1a, The Old Kennels, Cirencester Park, Cirencester, GL7 1UR ☎ 07716 826467
⊕ coriniumales.co.uk

⊠ Established in 2012, Corinium Ales brew classic and contemporary award-winning ales on a 2.5-barrel plant located in small, historic old kennels in Cirencester Park, just outside the town centre. An onsite taproom showcases the range, which is also available at a growing number of local outlets, events and pubs. ‼🛒♠LIVE V♠

Firebird VI (ABV 4%) BITTER
Corinium Gold I (ABV 4.2%) GOLD
Mosaic (ABV 4.5%) PALE
Plautus V (ABV 4.5%) PALE
Bodicacia IV (ABV 4.7%) PALE
Centurion II (ABV 4.7%) STOUT
Ale Caesar III (ABV 5%) PALE

Cotswold Lion SIBA

Hartley Farm, Hartley Lane, Leckhampton Hill, Cheltenham, GL53 9QN
☎ (01242) 870164 ⊕ cotswoldlionbrewery.co.uk

⊗ Previously located in a grain store on a farm in the Cotswolds, Cotswold Lion brewery relocated in 2021. It produces a core range of five beers using a 10-barrel plant. ☛LIVE

Shepherd's Delight (ABV 3.6%) BITTER
Hogget (ABV 3.8%) BITTER
Best in Show (ABV 4.2%) BITTER
Malty, spicy, earthy aroma. Hedgerow fruits, caramel and bitter balance. Hops, caramel, pear esters develop on aftertaste. Light dry finish.
Golden Fleece (ABV 4.4%) PALE
Drover's Return (ABV 5%) BITTER

DEYA SIBA

Unit 27, Lansdown Industrial Estate, Gloucester Road, Cheltenham, GL51 8PL
☎ (01242) 269189 ⊕ deyabrewing.com

DEYA Brewing Company was established in 2016. It brews innovative, hop-forward beers, all of which are unfiltered, unfined and unpasteurised, and available in keg and cans, with occasional casks. In 2019 it expanded into a new 25,000 sq ft premises with a bespoke 40-hectolitre four-vessel brewhouse to significantly increase capacity. A taproom has also been opened. ☛V◆

Donnington IFBB

Upper Swell, Stow-on-the-Wold, GL54 1EP
☎ (01451) 830603 ⊕ donnington-brewery.com

Thomas Arkell bought a 13th century watermill in 1827 and began brewing onsite in 1865. The waterwheel is still in use. Thomas's descendant Claude owned and ran the brewery until his death in 2007, supplying 20 outlets direct. It has now passed to Claude's cousin, James Arkell, also of Arkells Brewery, Swindon (qv). ☛LIVE

BB (ABV 3.6%) BITTER
A pleasant, amber bitter with a slight hop aroma, a good balance of malt and hops in the mouth and a bitter aftertaste.
Cotswold Gold (ABV 4%) GOLD
Citrus malty/sweet caramel aroma. Bright with developing hops, fruit notes and malt. A dry hop bitter finish with some citrus.
SBA (ABV 4.4%) BITTER
Malt dominates over bitterness in the subtle flavour of this premium bitter, which has a hint of fruit and a dry malty finish.

Fierce & Noble

25 Mina Road, St Werburgh's, Bristol, BS2 9TA
☎ (0117) 955 6666 ⊕ fierceandnoble.com

Founded in 2017 to supply beer to the Grounded community café chain in Bristol, beers can now be found across Bristol and the South West. A range of IPAs and occasional specials are brewed on an eight-barrel plant. The onsite taproom and brewery shop regularly hold

events, and are open year round on Wednesday-Sunday.
‼☛◆♦

Session IPA (ABV 4.2%) PALE
American Pale Ale (ABV 5%) PALE
Abundant powerful hop flavours add pine and tropical fruit to the slightly sweet malt background, before a lingering bitter aftertaste

Forest, The

The Old Workshop, Lydney Park Estate, Lydney, GL15 6BU ☎ 07766 652837
⊕ theforestbrewery.co.uk

Originally named Brythonic Beer (a trading name it still retains), The Forest nanobrewery began in a Bristol suburb in 2015. The brewery relocated several times within Gloucestershire, finally settling in Lydney. Beers can be found at the Dog House micropub and the Forest Deli, both Coleford – mainly available bottle-conditioned, but the occasional cask beer also makes an appearance. LIVE

Hang Hill Hazy (ABV 4%) PALE
Black Spell Porter (ABV 5.7%) SPECIALITY
Forest Strong Bitter/ FSB (ABV 5.8%) BITTER

Fresh Standard SIBA

Unit 25, Merrets Mill Industrial Centre, Bath Road, Woodchester, GL5 5EX
☎ (01453) 802400 ⊕ thefreshstandard.co.uk

⊗ Founded in 2020 by experienced brewer Richard Taylor, in space rented from Artisan Ales. It initially brewed two core beers alongside one-off brews. In 2022 it relocated to its own premises, complete with taproom, when wife Charlotte joined the team. Beers can be purchased from the website. ☛◆V♦

Bright (ABV 3%) PALE
Horse Brass (ABV 4%) BITTER
Solution (ABV 4.8%) PALE
Red Mild (ABV 6%) MILD
Pothering (ABV 6.2%) IPA

Gloucester SIBA

Fox's Kiln, West Quay, The Docks, Gloucester, GL1 2LG
☎ (01452) 668043 ☎ 07503 152749
⊕ gloucesterbrewery.co.uk

⊗ Situated in the historic Gloucester Docks, brewing began in 2011 and has expanded into larger dockside premises to meet demand. Further expansion is planned. The original site is now its bar (named Tank). The full range of beers is regularly available in Gloucestershire and beyond. Beers are brewed in cask, keg and cans, most are unfined. A range of gins and vodkas is also distilled onsite. The brewery is committed to being carbon neutral. ‼☛LIVE♦

Session Pale (ABV 3.7%) PALE
Gloucester Gold (ABV 3.9%) GOLD
Priory Pale (ABV 3.9%) GOLD
Cascade (ABV 4.2%) BITTER
Session IPA (ABV 4.5%) PALE
Dockside Dark (ABV 5.2%) PORTER
New England IPA (ABV 5.2%) PALE

Goff's SIBA

9 Isbourne Way, Winchcombe, Cheltenham, GL54 5NS
☎ (01242) 603383 ⊕ goffsbrewery.com

⊗ Goff's is a family concern that has been brewing cask-conditioned ales since 1994. The ales are available regionally in more than 200 outlets and nationally through wholesalers. Three regular ales are supplemented by the seasonal 'Jester' range (12 beers). ▬◆

Lancer (ABV 3.8%) GOLD
Bright gold. Verbena, lemony-grass and light pear aroma. Light-bodied, easy-drinking, some citrus bitterness and long, drying finish.
Jouster (ABV 4%) BITTER
Earthy, pepper hop aroma. Relatively sweet, mild hop bitterness, some hedgerow fruits. Drying aftertaste but bitterness and fruit fade quickly.
Tournament (ABV 4%) BITTER
Earthy, spicy hops, sweet malt, hedgerow fruits aroma. Caramel/toffee, bitter English hops taste. Long finish with drying hops and fruit.
Fallen Knight (ABV 4.4%) BITTER
Cheltenham Gold (ABV 4.5%) GOLD
Bright gold, strong USA hop/citrus aroma. Balanced citrus hop, malt sweetness, with no dominating flavour. Citrus aftertaste, long, drying finish.
White Knight (ABV 4.7%) BLOND
Bright, light malt aroma with fruit, hop and earthy sweetness. Citrus hops and fruit lead to a bitter, drying finish.
Jester Brew 6 Mango IPA (ABV 5%) SPECIALITY
Hazy orange with a massive mango aroma. Malt, hops, citrus, yeast and sulphur add balance. A fruity, bitter, drying finish.

Good Chemistry SIBA

Unit 2, William Street, St Philips, Bristol, BS2 0RG
☎ (0117) 903 9930 ⊕ goodchemistrybrewing.co.uk

⊗ Good Chemistry was established in 2015 in a warehouse in St Philips, Bristol, by Bob Cary and Kelly Sidgwick, using a 10-barrel plant. As the name suggests, all brewery and beer logos have a scientific theme. The brewery has a taproom and canned beer shop. ▬LIVE V◆

Time Lapse (ABV 3.8%) BITTER
Aroma and flavours are balanced with a malty foundation supporting soft fruit and light citrus with a hoppy bitterness which grows into the finish.
Natural Selection (ABV 4%) PALE
Hops and pale malt aromas, initially sweet body is followed by hoppy bitterness which continues into the short, dry finish.
Kokomo Weekday (ABV 4.3%) PALE
Hazy golden-coloured ale with hop and sweet fruit aroma which continues onto the palate before a short bitter finish.

Hal's

22A, Woodmancote, Dursley, GL11 4AF ☎ 07765 890946

Hal's is a one-barrel microbrewery established in Dursley in 2016, occasionally producing a number of small-batch beers for the New Inn, Woodmancote, Dursley and beer festivals. Brewing is currently suspended. ◆

Hawkstone

College Farm, Stow Road, Lower Slaughter, Bourton on the Water, GL54 2HN
☎ (01451) 824488 ⊕ hawkstone.co

An independent producer of craft lager and speciality keg beers. The brewery was established in 2005 and expanded in 2010. More than 150 outlets are supplied, mainly in the Cotswolds and London. The brewery

changed ownership and name in 2022 (was Cotswold). ‼▬◆

Hop Union SIBA

20 Bonville Road, Brislington, BS4 5QH
☎ (0117) 957 2842 ⊕ hopunionbrewery.co.uk

⊗ Originally established as Great Western in 2008, the brewery relocated and rebranded to Hop Union in 2021. The move allowed for much-needed expansion and enables canning and kegging onsite. One pub, the Rising Sun, Frampton Cotterell, is owned, as well as a shop at the new brewery site. A taproom opened 2022. ‼▬◆◆

HPA (Hambrook Pale Ale) (ABV 4%) PALE
Hoppy yellow pale ale with zesty citrus flavours and hints of tropical fruit, leading to a moreish bittersweet finish.
Maiden Voyage (ABV 4%) BITTER
Traditional-style English bitter; malty backbone with just a hint of caramel supporting a soft bitterness and subtle fruit flavour that all continue into the well-balanced finish.
Bees Knees (ABV 4.2%) SPECIALITY
Golden-coloured beer, bitter with malt nose and flavour and some honey. Lasting astringent bitter aftertaste.
Old Higby (ABV 4.8%) OLD
Malty nose with dark berry hints, roasted flavour overlaid with fruity raisins and dry bitterness which continues into the finish.
Moose River (ABV 5%) PALE
Light citrus aroma, delicate hop taste with long lasting bitter finish.

Incredible SIBA

214/224 Unit 1, Broomhill Road, Brislington, Bristol, BS4 5RG ☎ 07780 977073
⊕ incrediblebrewingcompany.com

⊗ This microbrewery specialises in producing small batches of beer using a 2.5-barrel plant. It was established in 2014 by head brewer Stephen Hall with the aim of promoting experimental beers and traditional recipes. ‼◆LIVE

Milk Stout (ABV 4.4%) STOUT
Pale Ale (ABV 4.4%) PALE
Amber Ale (ABV 5.2%) BITTER
Black IPA (ABV 5.6%) IPA
Grapefruit IPA (ABV 5.6%) IPA
Indian Pale Ale (ABV 6.6%) IPA

Inferno

17 Station Street, Tewkesbury, GL20 5NJ
☎ (01684) 294873 ☎ 07854 949731
✉ infernobrewery@yahoo.com

⊗ Inferno began in 2018, after many years of home brewing, using a 2.5-barrel kit which was installed in 2019. Four regular ales and a number of well-received seasonal ales are brewed. The beers are available in local Gloucestershire pubs, clubs and at beer festivals. ◆◆

Spark (ABV 3.8%) PALE
Golden Embers (ABV 4.2%) PALE
Citrus hop aroma, mandarin, white pepper, earthy notes, minimal malt. Initial sweetness leads to a long, dry, bitter, citrus aftertaste.
Tinder Box (ABV 4.5%) PALE
Dark colour, hedgerow fruits, spice and a malty nose. Earthy, bittersweet autumn fruits with some caramel. Long, bitter dry finish.
Cinder Stout (ABV 4.8%) STOUT
Wheat Storm (ABV 5%) SPECIALITY

Fresh, zingy Belgian Wit. Yeasty banana, clove, coriander and pear esters. Wheat, biscuit, spicy banana with floral/wood from Camille herb.

Mental Martha (ABV 5.5%) SPECIALITY
Prometheus (ABV 5.8%) IPA
Triple-hopped, bright, spicy, earthy aroma with oyster mushroom notes and honey. Spicy hops, strong malt backbone. Long bitter finish.

Vulcan (ABV 6%) PORTER

Keep

🏠 Village Inn, The Cross, Nailsworth, GL6 0HH
☎ (01453) 835715 ☎ 07877 569586
✉ paul@dropinpubs.com

After a break of 96 years, brewing returned to Nailsworth in 2004, at the Village Inn. The pub and brewery were sold in 2016 to Paul Sugden and Adam Pavey, who changed the brewery name from Nailsworth to Keep Brewing. Brewing takes place on a six-barrel kit below the bar, with new recipes trialled on a 40-litre pilot plant.
♦LIVE

King Street

🏠 Riverside House, Welsh Back, Bristol, BS1 4RR
☎ (0117) 405 8948

Office: City Pub Group Plc, Essel House, 2nd Floor, 29 Foley Street, London, W1W 7TH
⊕ kingstreetbrewhouse.co.uk

⊠ The King Street Brew House is owned by The City Pub Group, which has several pubs and brewpubs around the country. The compact brewery is on the ground floor, with the fermenting vessels and conditioning tanks in the basement. The enthusiastic onsite brewer produces a wide range of beers, from regular favourites to one off/seasonal specials. Guest beers are also available. The City Pub Group's other pub in Bristol, the Prince Street Social, is also supplied. ‼♦LIVE

Left Handed Giant

Unit 3, Wadehurst Industrial Estate, St Philips Road, St Philips, Bristol, BS2 0JE

Second Site: LHG Brewpub, Compressor Building, Hawkins Lane, Finzels Reach, Bristol, BS1 6EU
⊕ lefthandedgiant.com

Left Handed Giant started in 2015 as a cuckoo brewery using spare capacity at other local breweries. The physical brewery with a taproom opened in 2017. Two years later it opened a brewpub in Bristol city centre. The original brewery site is mainly responsible for the new beers and collaborations (released on a regular basis). Typically these are single-batch brews. Beers are available nationally. A small amount of the output goes into cask. ‼♦✦

Little Martha

🏠 23 Oxford Street, St Phillips, Bristol, BS2 0QT
⊕ littlemarthabrewing.co.uk

This brewpub is located in a railway arch close to Bristol Temple Meads Station. Brewing commenced in late 2021 prior to the official bar opening at the end of the year. Two core beers are brewed, along with one-off specials.
🍺♦

Lost & Grounded SIBA

91 Whitby Road, Bristol, BS4 4AR
☎ (0117) 332 7690 ⊕ lostandgrounded.co.uk

Brewing began in 2016. The brewery has a focus on German and Belgian-style beers. No live beers. ‼🍺✦

Lucifer

9, Ellerncroft Road, Wotton-Under-Edge, GL12 7AX
☎ 07886 604690 ⊕ luciferbrewhouse.co.uk

Lucifer Brewhouse was established in 2019 using a one-barrel plant. It produces a growing number of small batch beers for pubs in the local area. Most of the cask-conditioned beers are also available bottle-conditioned.
♦LIVE

Mild Side (ABV 3.6%) MILD
Mocha Choc Stout (ABV 4.2%) STOUT
Fallen Angel Bitter (ABV 4.3%) BITTER
Wotton Hop Project (ABV 4.4%) GOLD
GL12 (ABV 4.7%) PALE

Lydbrook Valley

🏠 Forge Row, Lydbrook, GL17 9NP
☎ (01594) 860310 ✉ andy@theforgehammer.co.uk

Brewing commenced in 2018 in the Forge Hammer pub in Lydbrook. Alison and Andrew Jopson use full mash to produce beers for sale in the pub.

Mills

Jumpers Lane Yard, Berkeley, GL13 9BW ☎ 07848 922558 ⊕ millsbrewing.com

Mills was established in Berkeley in 2016 by husband-and-wife team Genevieve and Jonny Mills. Wort is produced in multiple locations, which is then fermented in wooden vessels at its premises in Berkeley using 100% wild yeasts and bacteria from the local surroundings. The lambic-style, bottle-conditioned beers are mostly available via its online store. LIVE

Moor SIBA

Days Road, Bristol, BS2 0QS
☎ (0117) 941 4460 ⊕ moorbeer.co.uk

⊠ Starting out in Somerset in 2007, Moor is an established part of the Bristol beer scene and exports around the world. The Bristol brewery features a taproom and shop. The Moor London Vaults, Bermondsey doubles as a Tap and for ageing beers. All beers are unfined, naturally hazy, vegan-friendly and naturally-conditioned with live yeast. Its canned beers were the first in the UK to be recognised as real ale by CAMRA. It was also one of 16 breweries given a CAMRA Gold award during its 50th Anniversary. ‼🍺♦LIVE V✦

Nano Cask (ABV 3.8%) BITTER
Hints of fruit in the aroma, bittersweet flavours of malt and hops which soon fade in the short finish.
Revival (ABV 3.8%) PALE
Cloudy orange colour with some peachy aroma, flavours of slightly resinous hops and a gentle bitterness in the short finish.
Resonance (ABV 4.1%) PALE
Light and refreshing bittersweet pale ale with generous citrus flavours and subtle pine notes overlaid on a light malt base.
Illumination (ABV 4.3%) BITTER
Pale golden colour with hoppy aroma, balanced flavours of pale malt, hoppy bitterness and sweet estery fruits with hints of background spice.
Distortion (ABV 4.7%) PALE
Stout (ABV 5%) STOUT

Roasted malt aroma, slightly smoky on the palate with liquorice, dark fruit, coffee and dark chocolate all lingering into the complex aftertaste.

PMA (ABV 5.3%) PALE
Aroma and flavours are both well-balanced with biscuity malt, hops and tropical fruit before a short bittersweet ending.

Hoppiness (ABV 6.5%) IPA
Hop-forward nose with hints of honey. Full-bodied, with tropical fruit flavours and bitterness which increases into the finish.

Old Freddy Walker (ABV 7.3%) STRONG
Roasted malt and dark fruit aromas, flavours balance roasted malt with liquorice treacle and blackberry before a slightly dry finish.

New Bristol SIBA

20a Wilson Street, Bristol, BS2 9HH ☎ 07837 976871
⊕ newbristolbrewery.co.uk

⊗ Having started out in 2013 with his brother Tom, Noel James, wife Maria and assistants now brew on a fifteen-barrel plant. Year-round beers are supplemented by regularly released brews based on progressive and modern themes, which include IPAs and stouts. All beers are unfined and unfiltered, with some oak barrel-aged, and many available in cans. The premises house a shop, taproom and kitchen, which opens Thursday-Sunday. ‼ ⋤ ♦ LIVE ♪

Cinder Toffee Stout (ABV 4%) SPECIALITY
Caramelised honey and roasted malt aromas, sweet flavours of honeycomb and chocolate, some hop bitterness in the slightly dry finish.

Wonderland IPA (ABV 4.1%) PALE
Tropical fruit aroma and juicy fruit hop burst of pinapple and mango flavours with some bitterness in the short finish.

Joy of Sesh (ABV 4.2%) BITTER
Powerfully-hopped, naturally hazy, unfined beer with citrus and tropical fruits on the palate and a long bitter finish.

Super Deluxe Stout (ABV 7%) SPECIALITY
Banana and vanilla aromas. The taste and mouthfeel is like vanilla ice cream, but this sweetness contrasts with an assertive bitterness.

New Street

Volunteer Tavern, 9 New Street, Old Market, Bristol, BS2 9DX
☎ (0117) 955 8498 ⊕ volunteertavern.co.uk

⊗ New Street Brewing is located in the building next door to the 17th century Volunteer Tavern. Currently one regular beer is brewed on site, with seasonal specials also available from time to time. ♦

Volly Pale (ABV 4%) PALE
Slightly hazy, powerfully American hopped pale ale. Fruity aroma, sharp pithy citrus flavour and bitterness that lingers in the aftertaste.

Stroud SIBA

Kingfisher Business Park, London Road, Thrupp, GL5 2BY
☎ (01453) 887122 ⊕ stroudbrewery.co.uk

⊗ Established in 2006, Stroud Brewery supports the local ecomony and its ales are available in 40-50 pubs, independent retailers and its brewery shop. All beers have full organic status and are available in cask or keg as well as in cans. Beers are no longer available in bottles. ‼ ⋤ ♦ ♪

Tom Long (ABV 3.8%) BITTER
OPA (Organic Pale Ale) (ABV 4%) PALE
Big Cat (ABV 4.5%) STOUT
Budding (ABV 4.5%) PALE

Tanners

Office: 118 High Street, Staple Hill, Bristol, BS16 5HH
⊕ tanners-ales.co.uk

Tanners was established in 2015 in the old stables at the rear of the White Hart Inn, Wiveliscombe. However, the stables have been demolished and the beer is now believed to be brewed under contract by Parkway of Somerton.

Tapestry

Unit B, Totterdown Bridge Industrial Estate, Albert Road, St Philips, Bristol, BS2 0XH
⊕ tapestrybrewery.com

Previously known as Cocksure, this 10-barrel brewery was established in 2016, and moved from the Severn Vale to Bristol in 2018. Tapestry is a social enterprise brewery that provides training and employment for people with learning disabilities. A small range of three beers is available. ♦ LIVE V ♪

Tewkesbury (NEW)

Unit 29, Highfield Business Park, Tewkesbury Road, Deerhurst, GL19 4BP ☎ 07415 118197
✉ info@tewksbrew.co.uk

⊗ Formed in 2020, cask brewing commenced in 2022. Plans have been put in place to bring in bottling and canning capability as well as several new beers, a shop and a taproom. ‼ ♦ LIVE V

Gold (ABV 4.5%) PALE
Pale (ABV 4.5%) BLOND
Dark Knight (ABV 5.7%) STOUT

Three Engineers SIBA

The Cow Byers, Winterbourne, BS36 1SD ☎ 07787 895182 ⊕ threeengineersbrewery.co.uk

⊗ Nanobrewery established near Bristol in 2017 by three engineers working in the aerospace industry who are passionate about beer. Eight cask beers are brewed, all named after aircraft with a connection to Bristol. The beers are supplied to a number of local pubs and micropubs and are available in the taproom at the brewery in Winterbourne Medieval Barn. Brewing is currently suspended. ⋤ ♪

Tiley's

⊟ **Salutation Inn, Ham, GL13 9QH**
☎ (01453) 810284 ⊕ sallyatham.com

⊗ This 2.5-barrel microbrewery was established in an outbuilding of the award-winning Salutation Inn in 2015. It concentrates on producing small batches of beer, predominantly in cask, some in KeyKeg. Some of the brewery's output is sold onsite at the Salutation Inn. The rest goes to more than 25 selected local pubs.

Ordinary Bitter (ABV 3.8%) BITTER
Ordinary Pale (ABV 3.8%) PALE
Special Bitter (ABV 4.3%) BITTER
Special Pale (ABV 4.5%) PALE
ESB (ABV 5.2%) BITTER
IPA (ABV 6.5%) IPA

Two Tinkers

Aylburton
☎ (01594) 840100 ☎ 07711 368397
⊕ twotinkers.co.uk

Nanobrewery producing five core beers in traditional British and Belgian styles, plus a number of seasonal specials. Can-conditioned, vegan-friendly beers are available at more than 10 local shops and markets. Kegged beer is also supplied to a local taproom. The brewery has a small hop yard. ♦LIVE V

Uley

The Old Brewery, 31 The Street, Uley, GL11 5TB
☎ (01453) 860120 ⊕ uleybrewery.com

⊠ Brewing at Uley began in 1833 as Price's brewery. After a long gap, the premises were restored and Uley Brewery opened in 1985. Now operating a 10-barrel plant, it uses its own spring water. Uley delivers to 40-50 outlets in the Cotswolds area. !!⊨♦♦

Pale (ABV 3.8%) PALE
Bitter (ABV 4%) BITTER
A copper-coloured beer with hops and fruit in the aroma and a malty, fruity taste, underscored by a hoppy bitterness. The finish is dry, with a balance of hops and malt.
Hussar (ABV 4.2%) GOLD
Old Ric (ABV 4.5%) BITTER
A full-flavoured, hoppy bitter with some fruitiness and a smooth, balanced finish. Distinctively copper-coloured, this is the house beer for the Old Spot Inn, Dursley.
Taverner (ABV 4.5%) BITTER
Old Spot Prize Strong Ale (ABV 5%) BITTER
A ruby ale with an initial strong malty sweetness that develops into a smooth dry malty finish. A beer that is deceptively easy to drink.
Pigs Ear (ABV 5%) PALE

A golden pale ale with an initial refreshing taste with a hint of fruitiness that develops into a light malty finish. A smooth, quaffable, strong ale.

Wickwar

Old Brewery, Station Road, Wickwar, GL12 8NB
☎ (01454) 292000 ⊕ wickwarpubco.co.uk

Wickwar was established as a 10-barrel brewery in 1990. In 2004 it expanded to 50 barrels. Moles Brewery and pubs were acquired in 2017, bringing its pub estate up to 20. This has now been rationalised to 16. Brewing ceased in 2020 to concentrate on its pubs estate, with all beers contract brewed by several breweries.

Wiper and True SIBA

Units 11-15, City Business Park, Easton Road, Bristol, BS5 0SP
☎ (0117) 941 2501 ⊕ wiperandtrue.com

Originally launched in 2012 by Michael Wiper as a nomad brewery, Wiper and True has operated since 2015 using its own 20-barrel plant. Producing an ever-changing range of seasonal specials along with several core beers. A proportion of its output goes into cask. The beers are available locally in Bristol and Bath, nationally and internationally. !!⊨♦LIVE♦

Zerodegrees SIBA

🍴 53 Colston Street, Bristol, BS1 5BA
☎ (01179) 252706 ⊕ zerodegrees.co.uk

⊠ A chain of four brewpubs, the first began brewing in 2000 in Blackheath, London. Each incorporates a computer-controlled, German plant producing unfiltered and unfined ales and lagers. All beers use natural ingredients, are suitable for vegetarians, and are served from tanks using air pressure (not CO2). !!♦

Royal Hop Pole, Tewkesbury (Photo: Dave_S / Flickr CC BY 2.0)

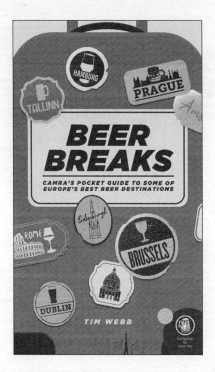

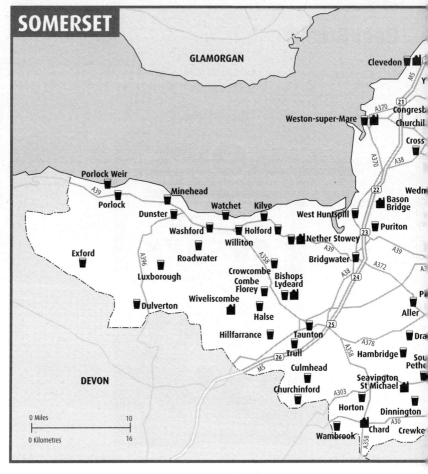

SOMERSET

GLAMORGAN

Clevedon

Congresb
Weston-super-Mare
Churchil
Cross
Bason
Bridge
Porlock Weir
Minehead
Wedn
Porlock
Watchet   Kilve
Dunster
West Huntspill
Puriton
Washford
Holford
Williton
Nether Stowey
Exford
Roadwater
Bridgwater
Luxborough
Crowcombe
Bishops
Combe
Lydeard
Florey
Dulverton
Wiveliscombe
Aller
Halse
Dra
Hillfarrance
Taunton
Trull
Hambridge
Sou
Pethe
Culmhead
Seavington
Churchinford
St Michael
Horton
Dinnington
Wambrook
Chard Crewke

DEVON

0 Miles   10
0 Kilometres   16

Aller

Old Pound Inn

1 High Street, TA10 0RA (centre of village)
☎ (01458) 250469 ⊕ oldpoundinn.com
Butcombe Original; Teignworthy Reel Ale; 1 changing beer (sourced regionally; often Exmoor, Otter) Ⓗ
This lovely 16th-century inn stands on the ground of the old village pound. A varying selection of three regional ales and a local cider is on handpump. There is a separate restaurant/function room, public lounge and a delightful snug. A wonderful open Dutch fire is a feature in the centre of the bar. Excellent food, including a Sunday carvery, is served in the bar or restaurant.
Ⓣ⊛🏠◖&♣♠💷☕(16) 🐾🍴♫

Bath

Bath Brew House ✔

14 James Street West, BA1 2BX
☎ (01225) 805609 ⊕ thebathbrewhouse.com
Bath Brew House Gladiator, Emperor; 3 changing beers (sourced regionally; often Bath Brew House) Ⓗ
A 2013 refurbishment turned what was the Midland Hotel into a City Pub Company brewpub. The on-site brewery, Bath Brew House, produces two regular beers – the malty Gladiator and the hoppy, citrussy Emperor – and up to four additional beers. The cider is produced locally. A large bar leads to a dining area and a good-

sized beer garden. The upstairs room hosts sports TV, quizzes, comedy and other events.
⊛◖&🦼(Spa) 💷🐾🍴♫

Bell

103 Walcot Street, BA1 5BW
☎ (01225) 460426 ⊕ thebellinnbath.co.uk
Bristol Beer Factory Independence; Butcombe Adam Henson's Rare Breed; Hop Back Summer Lightning; Otter Ale; St Austell Cornish Best Bitter; 1 changing beer (sourced regionally) Ⓗ
The Bell was purchased by 536 of its regulars, fans, and staff, following a community buy-out in 2013. It has five regular ales plus one or two ever-changing guests from local micros. Live music is a mainstay with bands playing Monday and Wednesday evenings and Sunday lunchtimes Open-mic nights on Thursday evenings are held in the separate Back Bar to the rear. Features include bar-billiards, board games and even a tiny launderette. At the rear is a walled garden with covered seating. Ⓣ⊛◖♣💷🐾🍴♫

Cross Keys ✔

Midford Road, Combe Down, BA2 5RZ
☎ (01225) 849180 ⊕ crosskeysbath.co.uk
Butcombe Original; 2 changing beers (sourced locally) Ⓗ
An historic inn, dating from 1718, on the southern outskirts of the city. It is close to the beautiful Midford

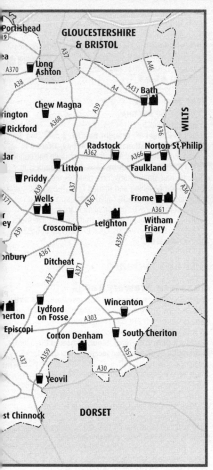

Dating back to between 1748 and 1750, the Huntsman was taken over by Fuller's in 2012 and fully refurbished. It is now a smart gastro-pub with a bar on the ground floor and an à la carte-style restaurant, with its own bar upstairs. Two guest beers are usually on offer, and live music is played on the second Friday of the month. This pub is popular on the days Bath rugby club plays at home. ᗡ⟨⟩≋(Spa)🚌🐾🛜📶♫

New Inn

23-24 Monmouth Place, BA1 2AY
☎ (01225) 442944 ⊕ newinnbath.co.uk
Uley Old Spot Prize Strong Ale; 3 changing beers (sourced regionally; often Butcombe, Exeter) Ⓗ
A small and friendly pub with a modern tiled bar area and further seating upstairs in a small room and a roof terrace. Originally owned by Wadworth brewery, it was reopened in 2016 after major internal and external refurbishment, and is now operated by Banwell House – the same group that operate Victoria Pub & Kitchen in Bath. Beers are usually sourced from local brewers. 🌼⟨⟩≋(Spa)🍴🚌🐾🛜♫

Old Green Tree ★

12 Green Street, BA1 2JZ
☎ (01225) 448259
Butcombe Original; house beer (by Blindmans); 3 changing beers (sourced locally) Ⓗ
A classic, unspoilt pub in a 300-year-old building. The three oak-panelled rooms include a superb northern-style drinking lobby. Although the pub can get crowded, there is often space in the comfortable back bar. Guest beers are generally sourced from local microbreweries, with a stout or porter usually on offer in the winter months. A local farmhouse cider is also available, along with a range of fine wines and malt whiskies. Sunday hours in winter may be longer. Q≋(Spa)🍴🚌

Pulteney Arms ⬤

37 Daniel Street, BA2 6ND (on corner of Daniel St and Sutton St)
☎ (01225) 463923 ⊕ thepulteneyarms.co.uk

valley and popular with walkers. Featuring two or three ales, with guests often from a selected local Brewery of the Month's range. Highly recommended, gastro-standard, home-made food is available all sessions. The main bar on the left still has many original features including an open fire. The restaurant is on the right and split across three levels. Parking is a bit restricted. ᗡ🌼⟨⟩♿🍴🚌(3,D2)🐾🛜

Crystal Palace

10-11 Abbey Green, BA1 1NW
☎ (01225) 482666 ⊕ crystalpalacepub.co.uk
Fuller's London Pride, ESB; 2 changing beers (often Butcombe, Wild Beer) Ⓗ
A handsome old building set on the pretty Abbey Green. It was refurbished by Fuller's in 2014, and is now an upmarket-feeling city centre pub. There are usually at least two Fuller's beers on plus one or two guests ales – some from local brewers, others from interesting breweries further away. Full table service is available in the lounge. There is a glass-covered sitting area at the rear of the pub. ᗡ🌼⟨⟩♿≋(Spa)🚌🐾🛜

Huntsman

1 Terrace Walk, BA1 1LJ
☎ (01225) 482900 ⊕ huntsmanbathpub.co.uk
Bath Ales Prophecy; Fuller's London Pride; Gale's HSB; 2 changing beers (sourced regionally) Ⓗ

REAL ALE BREWERIES

Abbey Bath
Apex Corton Denham
Bason Bridge Bason Bridge
Bath Brew House 🍺 Bath
Black Bear 🍺 🍂 Wiveliscombe (brewing suspended)
Blindmans Leighton
Butcombe Wrington
Cheddar 🍂 Cheddar
Clevedon 🍂 Clevedon
Electric Bear 🍂 Bath
Exmoor Wiveliscombe
Fine Tuned Somerton
Frome Frome
Golden River Bath (NEW)
Nuttycombe Wiveliscombe
Parkway Somerton
Pinkers Weston-Super-Mare
Portishead 🍺 Portishead
Quantock 🍂 Bishops Lydeard
Ralph's Ruin 🍺 Bath
Stowey Nether Stowey
Tapstone 🍂 Chard
Twisted Oak Wrington
Verse 🍺 🍂 Bath (brewing suspended)
Windy 🍺 Seavington St Michael
Wookey Wells

Bath Ales Gem; Timothy Taylor Landlord; Wye Valley HPA; 2 changing beers (sourced nationally; often Exmoor, Fuller's, Otter) ⊞
Tucked away near the end of Great Pulteney Street, this pub dates back to 1792. There are five gas light fittings (now sadly condemned) above the bar. The decor shows an emphasis on sport, particularly rugby. The cat symbol on the pub sign refers to the Pulteney coat of arms. The food menu is deservedly popular (no food on Sun eve). The guest beers are usually from a national brewery. Traditional style ciders are served. The pub is likely to be closed 3pm-5pm midweek during the winter and Monday-Tuesday year round; check before travelling.
🕏❀◑♪♣♠♿🐾🐽♞

Raven 🍷
6-7 Queen Street, BA1 1HE
☎ (01225) 425045 ⊕ theravenofbath.co.uk
Cheddar Ales Potholer; Exeter Darkness; Frome The Usual; house beer (by Blindmans); 4 changing beers (sourced regionally; often Branscombe, Lister's, New Bristol) ⊞
A busy 18th-century free house in the heart of Bath, extended in 2022 and now boasting three bars and five separate seating areas. Up to 10 ales are on offer, attracting guests from far and wide. The two 'house' beers are brewed exclusively by local brewery Blindmans. Real cider, sourced from local producers, is always available. Up to four mini beer festivals are held. Pieminister pies are served, including on Sunday evenings, which is a rarity for Bath. Local CAMRA Pub of the Year 2023. Q❀◑🌭⇌(Spa)♣🍴🖥🐽♞🎵

Ring o'Bells
10 Widcombe Parade, BA2 4JT
☎ (01225) 727599
4 changing beers (often Butcombe, Exeter, Timothy Taylor) ⊞
A friendly and lively Widcombe pub with a village pub feel yet only a stone's throw from the city centre. Rugby is often on one of several TV screens, making it especially popular on match days when the large upstairs function is brought into use. The main bar is a single long room with a range of wooden tables overlooking the street and along one wall facing the bar counter. Four changing ales are served, along with well-regarded food.
🕏❀◑⇌(Spa)🐽🖥🐽♞🎵

Royal Oak
Lower Bristol Road, Twerton, BA2 3BW (on A36 at intersection with road to Windsor Bridge)
☎ (01225) 481409 ⊕ theroyaloakbath.co.uk
Ralph's Ruin Ivory Tower, Sirius, Dark Side of the Ralph; 5 changing beers (often Bristol Beer Factory, Butts, Downton) ⊞
Eight real ales are usually served here, alongside an interesting range of ciders, perries and bottled British and Belgian beers. Two to four of the ales come from the pub's own brewery, Ralph's Ruin, and up to six guest beers from microbreweries near and far. There is live music on Wednesday evening and most weekends, and regular quiz nights. Outside is a small secluded garden and a small car park. Local CAMRA Pub of the Year 2020.
❀⇌(Oldfield Park)♦P🖥(5,15)🐽♪

Salamander
3 John Street, BA1 2JL
☎ (01225) 428889
Bath Ales Gem; St Austell Proper Job, Big Job; 2 changing beers (sourced locally; often Bath Ales, St Austell) ⊞
An 18th-century building, tucked away in a side street, that opened as a coffee bar in 1957 and got a pub licence

five years later. Taken over by St Austell in 2017, it looks and feels like a pub that's been there for a century or more, with wooden floorboards, wood panelling and subdued lighting adding to the ambience of the ground-floor bar, created from several small rooms. A popular restaurant upstairs uses local ales used in cooking.
◑⇌(Spa)♣🖥🐽♞

Star Inn ★ ✔
23 Vineyards, BA1 5NA
☎ (01225) 425072
Abbey Bellringer ⊞**; Draught Bass** Ⓖ**; 3 changing beers (sourced nationally; often Abbey, Titanic)** ⊞
A main outlet for Abbey Ales, this classic town pub dating from 1760 was fitted out by Gaskell and Chambers in 1928. Its four small rooms have benches around the walls, wood panelling and roaring fires. The smallest room has a single bench, called Death Row. Bass is served from the cask and complimentary snuff is available. Cheese night is every Thursday and live music features on Friday evenings. Local CAMRA Pub of the Year 2022. Q♣🖥🐽♞🎵

Bishops Lydeard

Quantock Brewery Tap ᴸ
Westridge Way, Broadgauge Business Park, TA4 3RU (follow signs to West Somerset Railway WSR, and the shop is on the left just before station)
☎ (01823) 433812 ⊕ quantockbrewery.co.uk
Quantock QPA, Wills Neck, Stout, Plastered Pheasant; 2 changing beers (sourced locally; often Quantock) ⊞
Quantock's tap room with up to six of the brewery's cask beers on handpump. There are also two Quantock KeyKeg beers always available plus a monthly small batch KeyKeg (subject to availability). One or two guest KeyKeg beers are available, typically from Northern Monk, Salopian, Thornbridge and Weird Beard. A brewery shop supplies takeaway bottles and other brewery gifts. There is an annual beer festival in July and regular live band, comedy and quiz nights. Street food is available Friday and most Saturday evenings.
🕏❀🚴⇌(Bishop's Lydeard)♦P🖥(28)🐽♞🎵

Bridgwater

West India House
101 Durleigh Road, TA6 7JE (top of Durleigh Rd hill)
☎ (01278) 452533 ⊕ westindiahouse.co.uk
Butcombe Original; Sharp's Doom Bar; 2 changing beers (sourced locally; often Cheddar Ales, St Austell, Twisted Oak) ⊞
Constructed in 1936, there has been a pub of the same name on the site for many years – the name derived from the days when Bridgwater was a bustling port. For a quiet drink in cosy surroundings there is the lounge bar complete with open log fire; for a more vibrant atmosphere try the saloon bar which has been extended and refurbished with modern decor and has three good ales from Butcombe, Sharp's and occasionally Cheddar Ales, Twisted Oak and St Austell. Q🕏❀◑♣♦P🖥🐽♪

Cheddar

Bath Arms
Bath Street, BS27 3AA
☎ (01934) 742425 ⊕ batharms.com
Cheddar Ales Gorge Best, Potholer; 1 changing beer (often Cheddar Ales) ⊞
Large friendly pub close to Cheddar village centre, set back from the road, with an impressive creeper-clad exterior giving way to a thriving L-shaped bar area, and a

separate dining room. There is outdoor seating where the old stagecoaches would have parked at an older inn called The George which stood on the roadside in front of the present pub. There is a pleasant garden and a car park to the rear. Freshly-cooked meals are served throughout the pub. ⏱🍴🛏🍷🍺♿🅰️🅿️🐕🌐📶

Cheddar Ales Tap Room
Unit 5, Winchester Farm, Draycott Road, BS27 3RP
☎ (01934) 744193 🌐 cheddarales.co.uk
Cheddar Ales Gorge Best, Potholer, Hardrock, Crown And Glory; 2 changing beers (often Cheddar Ales) 🎱
Taproom for Cheddar Ales brewery, situated just outside the world-famous village. The venue is a pleasant diversion from the tourist hotspot and serves up to six cask ales brewed on site. A takeaway service is also available. Cider, gins and wines are served, along with wood-fired pizzas at weekends, except during the winter months. There is indoor and outdoor seating, and occasional live music events take place on Saturdays. Check the website for opening times as they can be changeable. ⏱🐕🍷♿🅰️🅿️🐕🎵

Chew Magna

Queens
Silver Street, BS40 8RQ
☎ (01275) 627647 🌐 thequeenschewmagna.co.uk
Butcombe Original; 2 changing beers (sourced locally; often Bristol Beer Factory, Wiper & True, New Bristol Brewery) 🎱
Tucked away behind the parish church, this attractive and secluded pub was totally refurbished in 2021. The focus is on high quality food, but drinkers are made welcome. Butcombe Original and two changing local cask ales are served. There is a private dining room, a large outside area to the rear, and new luxury B&B accommodation. It is popular with local residents as well as diners from further afield. Cribbage nights are held weekly.
⏱🍴🛏🍷♿🅿️🐕📶

Churchill

Crown Inn 🅛
The Batch, Skinners Lane, BS25 5PP (off A38, 400yds S of A368 jct)
☎ (01934) 852995 🌐 crowninnchurchill.co.uk
Butcombe Original; Palmers IPA; St Austell Tribute; house beer (by St Austell); 2 changing beers (often Bristol Beer Factory, Exmoor, Otter) 🎱
Long-time Guide regular and winner of many CAMRA awards, this classic old pub is tucked away down a small lane close to the village centre. Several cosy rooms with stone-flagged floors are warmed by two log fires, and offer an assortment of seating. Excellent food is provided at lunchtimes made using local ingredients. Six ales from local and regional breweries are served on gravity. Outside drinking areas are to the front and rear. Families are welcome away from the bar itself.
Q⏱🐕🍷🅰️🍺🐕🚆(51)🐕📶🎵

Churchinford

York Inn ✅
Honiton Road, TA3 7RF
☎ (01823) 601333 🌐 yorkinn.co.uk
Dartmoor Jail Ale; Otter Bitter, Amber; 1 changing beer (sourced regionally) 🎱
The York Inn, situated in the Blackdown Hills, is a traditional hostelry dating back, in some parts, to the 16th century. It features an open fireplace and oak beams, at the same time offering contemporary facilities

and a good range of four cask ales and one real cider. Good traditional home-cooked food includes a specialist range of pies. ⏱🐕🍷♣🍺🅿️🐕📶🎵

Clevedon

Fallen Tree Micropub 🅛
43 Hill Road, BS21 7PD
☎ 07493 924386
4 changing beers (sourced locally; often Cheddar Ales, Frome, Twisted Oak) 🎱
Opened in 2018, and located in a shopping area up a hill from the Grade-I listed Clevedon Pier, this micropub was the first in the region. Between four and six ales are served straight from casks, usually from local breweries such as Cheddar Ales, Frome and Twisted Oak, but with occasional guests from further afield. Reasonably-priced local gins, Prosecco, wines and soft drinks are also sold. There is no music or fruit machines, just quiet conversation. Q⏱♿♣🍺🚆🐕

Royal Oak ✅
35 Copse Road, BS21 7QN (behind ice cream parlour near pier; footpath along alley leads to pub)
☎ (01275) 563879 🌐 theroyaloakclevedon.co.uk
Butcombe Original; Sharp's Doom Bar, Atlantic; Timothy Taylor Landlord; 1 changing beer (sourced regionally) 🎱
Lively, friendly, mid-terrace venue close to the seafront and connected to it via an alley. It has a large front window and an unexpectedly spacious interior with many rooms. This community hub is home to cribbage and cricket teams, with a quiz on Monday and acoustic music one Sunday a month. Live sport is screened. The winner of various awards, it hosts many events for the local community. Food is served at lunchtimes and includes daily specials and a range of salad options.
Q⏱🍷♣🚆🐕📶🎵

Combe Florey

Farmers Arms 🅛
TA4 3HZ (on A358 between Bishops Lydeard and Williton)
☎ (01823) 432267 🌐 farmersarmsatcombeflorey.co.uk
Exmoor Ale, Gold; Timothy Taylor Landlord 🎱
A thatched 14th-century Grade II-listed pub with cob walls, medieval chimney and fireplace and a restored staircase. The bar serves up to three cask ales and one real cider plus some unusual keg beers, bottled beers and a large selection of gin and malt whisky. The restaurant serves a very good quality menu using locally sourced produce with various special menus. There is a splendid garden and a large pizza oven used uring the summer months for various special occasions.
Q⏱🐕🍷♿🍺🅿️🐕📶🎵

Congresbury

Plough 🅛
High Street, BS49 5JA (off A370 at B3133 jct)
☎ (01934) 877402 🌐 the-plough-inn.net
Twisted Oak Fallen Tree; 5 changing beers (sourced locally; often Exmoor, St Austell, Twisted Oak) 🎱/🎱
Characterful village inn with flagstone floors and many original features, decorated with interesting local artefacts. Up to five guest ales, mainly from local breweries, are served from a row of old cask heads behind the bar and one handpump. Several real ciders are also stocked. The pub has a deserved reputation for the quality of its food, which is served lunchtimes and evenings, except Sunday evening, which is quiz night.

351

Real fires and a large garden make this a year-round destination. Mendip Morris Men meet here.
Q☻🏠🍴🚲❤🅿🚪(A3,X1) ❀🤟

Crewkerne

King William Inn

Barn Street, TA18 8BP (take A30 towards Chard; at fringe of town, the uphill Barn St is on the left)
☎ (01460) 279615 ⊕ kingwilliamcrewkerne.com
3 changing beers (sourced nationally; often Bristol Beer Factory, Oakham, Quantock) ⊞
A short walk from the town centre towards Chard takes you to this well-hidden traditional pub. There are three changing ales and two ciders and the array of pumpclips adorning the beams indicates the huge range of beers that have been served. New beers are advertised on Twitter. There is an early-evening happy hour every Monday and Wednesday. For music lovers there is an acoustic night on the last Wednesday of each month.
☻🍴♣❤🅿🚪❀🎵

Croscombe

George Inn

Long Street, BA5 3QH (on A371 between Wells and Shepton Mallet)
☎ (01749) 342306 ⊕ thegeorgeinn.co.uk
House beer (by Blindmans); 2 changing beers (often Cheddar Ales, St Austell) ⊞
Attractive 17th-century inn, refurbished by the owner, serving at least four guest ales from West Country independents and hosting two beer festivals a year. Blindmans King George and George and Dragon are exclusively brewed for pub. Four real ciders are available, with Hecks Kingston Black and Thatchers as regulars. There is a large main bar, snug with fireplace, a family room, separate dining room, and a skittle alley/meeting room to rear. Food is home-cooked using locally sourced ingredients in a modern theatre kitchen. The large garden has a covered terrace. B&B accommodation is in four en-suite rooms. Q☻🏠🍴🛏🚲🍴❤🅿🚪❀🤟🎵

Cross

New Inn

Old Coach Road, BS26 2EE (on A38/A361 jct)
☎ (01934) 732455 ⊕ newinncross.co.uk
Otter Bitter, Ale; 3 changing beers (often Bristol Beer Factory, Cheddar Ales, Twisted Oak) ⊞
A 17th-century roadside inn on the A38 in the Mendip Hills Area of Outstanding Natural Beauty, close to the historic medieval town of Axbridge. Three guest beers, often rare for the area, are usually available as well as two regular ales from Otter. The pub is popular for its extensive food menu, using quality local produce, served all day. Families and dogs are welcome. The large hillside garden with children's play facilities offers a fine view of the Mendip Hills and Somerset Levels. There is a small car park opposite. ☻🏠🍴🛏🅿🚪(48)❀🤟

White Hart

Old Coach Road, BS26 2EE
☎ (01934) 733108 ⊕ whitehartcross.co.uk
Bath Ales Gem; St Austell Tribute; 2 changing beers (often Dartmoor, St Austell) ⊞
A 17th-century inn, reopened in 2019 after refurbishment. It is reputed to be haunted by one of Hanging Judge Jeffreys' victims. Inside there is a games bar with pool and darts, and a door leading to a lounge-style area. Beers come from the St Austell stable, with an occasional guest from elsewhere. Lunches are served

plus evening meals on Fridays. The nearby bus stop is a Hail and Ride halt. There is a large car park opposite.
☻🍴🛏🛏🅿🚪(48) ❀🤟🎵

Crowcombe

Carew Arms 🅛

TA4 4AD (village is signed off A358)
☎ (01984) 618631 ⊕ thecarewarms.co.uk
Exmoor Ale, Gold; house beer (by Marstons); 1 changing beer (sourced regionally; often Nuttycombe, Quantock) ⊞
A 17th-century rural pub at the foot of the beautiful Quantock Hills. The flagstone public bar has a historic inglenook, and the large garden looking towards the Brendon Hills makes this popular with locals, walkers and dogs. The bar/restaurant serves locally sourced food with some restaurant tables set within the old stables area. The skittle alley doubles as a function room. There are up to four ales, including one changing guest ale, and two real ciders. B&B accommodation is in six rooms.
Q☻🏠🍴🛏🛏🅿🚪(28) ❀🤟🎵

Culmhead

Holman Clavel Inn

TA3 7EA (¼ mile off B3170)
☎ (01823) 421070 ⊕ theholmanclavelinn.co.uk
Hanlons Yellow Hammer; Otter Bitter, Amber; 1 changing beer (sourced regionally) ⊞
This is a real country pub set in the Blackdown Hills Area of Outstanding Natural Beauty, with four good ales straight from the barrel, Harry's cider, wine, food and company. No TV or machines but children, dogs, walkers, cyclists and muddy boots are welcome. Food is sourced from local farmers, suppliers and local businesses and gluten-free diners and vegetarians are catered for. Local musicians play Irish style sessions every first Thursday of the month. Q☻🏠🍴🛏🛏❤🅿❀🎵

Dinnington

Dinnington Docks Inn ✅

TA17 8SX (approx 3 miles E of Ilminster off B3168)
☎ (01460) 52397 ⊕ dinningtondocks.com
Butcombe Original; Hanlons Yellow Hammer; Teignworthy Gun Dog; 1 changing beer (sourced locally; often Bristol Beer Factory, Exmoor, Fine Tuned) ⊞
A quirky gem, this traditional Somerset country pub has beautiful views from its large garden. A pub that wears its heart on its sleeve, it supports the local community and offers a warm welcome to locals and visitors alike. It has a good selection of three permanent and one guest ales to suit all tastes, along with a good selection of wines and spirits and this, combined with its renowned hearty meal menu, makes this a must-visit pub.
Q☻🏠🍴♣❤🅿❀

Ditcheat

Manor House Inn

Wraxall Road, BA4 6RB
☎ (01749) 860276 ⊕ manorhouseinn.co.uk
Butcombe Original; 1 changing beer (sourced regionally; often Quantock) ⊞
A characterful 17th-century inn, built with impressive Ditcheat red brick, and featuring flagstone floors and roaring log fires. Set in a village famous for horse racing, it has a good reputation for food, drink and accommodation, with a warm welcome and a great atmosphere. It was originally owned by the Lord of the

Manor, Edmund Dawe, and was called the White Heart, but by 1861 had become known as the Manor House Inn.
Q☋❀⇌◑♣●P≋

Drayton

Drayton Crown

Church Street, TA10 0JY (in centre of village near the church)
☎ (01458) 250712 🌐 thedraytoncrown.co.uk
Butcombe Original; Timothy Taylor Landlord; 2 changing beers (sourced nationally; often Butcombe, Otter, Tapstone) Ⓗ
This pub has undergone a modern refurbishment but has retained character with flagstone floors and beams. Food is provided from a modern kitchen and there is a skittle alley/function room. It normally serves three or four ales from regional and national breweries and a cider. Outside there is lots of seating and a lawn area. There are four en-suite quality B&B rooms if you would like to stay.
☋❀⇌◑♿♣●P≋♫

Dulverton

Bridge Inn 𝕃

20 Bridge Street, TA22 9HJ
☎ (01398) 324130 🌐 thebridgeinndulverton.com
Exmoor Ale; St Austell Tribute; 2 changing beers (sourced regionally; often Bath Ales, St Austell) Ⓗ
A warm, welcoming pub dating from 1845. As the name implies it is close to a bridge crossing the River Barle upstream from its confluence with the River Exe. Situated in the delightful small town of Dulverton, the pub has a cosy single-room bar with a wood-burning stove and an extended restaurant area. There is always an interesting selection of national cask ales. Check the website for restricted opening hours in winter.
Q☋❀◑▲♣●P🚌🐾≋

Dunster

Luttrell Arms Hotel

36 High Street, TA24 6SG
☎ (01643) 821555 🌐 luttrellarms.co.uk
Exmoor Ale; Otter Amber; 1 changing beer (sourced locally; often Quantock) Ⓗ
This hotel with 28 unique bedrooms is on the site of three ancient houses dating back to 1443. The back bar with an open log fire features some of the oldest glass windows in Somerset and there is fine plasterwork on the lounge ceiling. You can dine in the fine restaurant or, if you prefer, order a bar snack. The view of Dunster Castle from the back garden is spectacular. Mini beer and cider festivals are held.
Q☋❀⇌◑▲♣●🚌(28,198) 🐾≋

Exford

White Horse Inn

TA24 7PY (on the B3224 W of Wheddon Cross)
☎ (01643) 831229 🌐 exmoor-whitehorse.co.uk
Exmoor Ale, Gold; 2 changing beers (sourced locally) Ⓗ
Set in the pretty village of Exford, within Exmoor National Park, this is an ideal base for walking, fishing and various country pursuits. The long bar features fine ales and a choice of 200 malt whiskies in the separate whisky bar. There are 28 en-suite rooms and a honeymoon suite. The outside tables are set on the bank of the River Exe. The food menu ranges from fine dining to bar snacks, featuring locally sourced produce.
Q☋❀⇌◑♿♣●P🐾≋

Faulkland

Tucker's Grave ★

BA3 5XF
☎ (01373) 834230 🌐 tuckersgraveinn.co.uk
Butcombe Original Ⓖ
A gem from a bygone age, identified by CAMRA as having a nationally important historic pub interior, this pub was built in circa 1700, and has changed little since. Tucker hanged himself nearby and is buried at the crossroads outside. There is no bar in the original inn, the beers and Thatchers cider are served from an alcove. Shove-ha'penny is played and there is a skittle alley. The old milking parlour behind the pub was converted into a modern function room and bar in 2021.
Q☋❀◗▲♣●P≋♫

Frome

Griffin

Milk Street, BA11 3DB
☎ (01373) 228283 🌐 griffinfrome.com
Frome Funky Monkey, Morello Bordello; 1 changing beer (often Frome) Ⓗ
Situated in the part of Frome known as Trinity, the Griffin was formerly the brewery tap for Milk Street (now Frome) brewery. Depending on the time of year, up to three Frome ales, or guests, as well as a range of craft beers are stocked. The single bar retains some original features such as etched windows and wooden floor. Food is available daily, with burgers and street food coming from locally sourced ingredients and suppliers.
☋❀◑P🚌(184) 🐾

Just Ales

10 Stony Street, BA11 1BU
☎ (01373) 462493 🌐 justalespart2.com
4 changing beers (sourced nationally; often Magpie, Slaughterhouse, Tollgate) Ⓗ
Frome's first micropub opened in 2018 serving up to four real ales on handpump as well as a large range of local ciders. Simply furnished and based in what was previously a small café, it is in the heart of Frome's vibrant St Catherine's district. Very dog friendly, the pub's hound is a constant and noticeable presence. Steep stairs lead to very basic toilet in the cellar. Cash only – cards are not accepted.Closed on Monday. Q●🚌🐾≋

Glastonbury

George & Pilgrims

1 High Street, BA6 9DP (near the Market Cross)
☎ (01458) 831146
Bristol Beer Factory Fortitude; Otter Bitter; 2 changing beers (sourced nationally; often Bristol Beer Factory, Quantock) Ⓗ
This three-storied Grade I-listed stone-built gatehouse inn boasts a panelled embattled frontage with mullion windows. Walking through the stout doorway there is a corridor leading to the rear patio and several tabled alcoves on the right. The Pilgrims Bar on the left oozes olde worlde charm including medieval artefacts. There are four well-kept real ales and a choice of ciders. It is worthwhile reading about the history of the inn over a pint. Q☋❀⇌◑▲●P🚌🐾≋♫

King Arthur 𝕃

31-33 Benedict Street, BA6 9NB
☎ (01458) 830338 🌐 thekingarthurglastonbury.com
3 changing beers (sourced locally; often Bristol Beer Factory, Parkway, St Austell) Ⓗ
Lively free house hidden just off the High Street, it concentrates on beer, a good range of ciders and music.

An interesting mix of people support the pub. There is a garden and music venue room with regular live music most nights. Parking is available in the street only or the town car parks. Bus routes are within easy walking distance. ✿❀Ⓓ&♨🅿♣🌐🛜♪

Halse

New Inn
TA4 3AF
☎ (01823) 432352 ● newinnhalse.com
Exmoor Ale; Quantock QPA; 1 changing beer Ⓗ
Nestling between the Quantock Hills and Exmoor National Park the New Inn is an 18th-century former coaching inn situated in the quaint village of Halse, five miles from Taunton and only 40 minutes' walk from the West Somerset Railway. Ales come from Quantock, Exmoor with one pump providing a changing local ale. Facilities include B&B rooms, a quiz, folk music and themed menu evenings. Local CAMRA Pub of the Year runner up in 2022. Q✿⊶❀Ⓓ&♣🅿🌐🛜♪

Hambridge

Lamb & Lion
The Green, TA10 0AT (on B3168 in village)
☎ (01460) 281774 ● lambandlionhambridge.co.uk
St Austell Tribute, Proper Job; 1 changing beer (often Quantock) Ⓗ
A splendidly refurbished 17th-century village inn with some parts dating from the 16th century. The pub has hamstone mullion windows and flagstone floors and a wealth of beams throughout. A fireplace sits at each end of the pub which has a bar area for drinkers and a restaurant area for diners. There is a splendid upstairs terrace with lovely views of the surrounding countryside. Unusually, there is a Port and Cheese room for private dining. ✿❀Ⓓ&♣🅿🛜♪

Hillfarrance

Anchor Inn 🗍
TA4 1AW
☎ (01823) 461334 ● theanchorinn.net
Exmoor Ale; Otter Ale; St Austell Tribute Ⓗ
Large 300-year-old family-run village free house that caters for drinkers in a cosy bar and diners in the large restaurant. A two-sided log burner separates the bar from a smaller dining area. There is also a large function room. Food, including a Sunday carvery, is locally produced and home-cooked . Accommodation is available in five en-suite rooms. Outside is a large car park and garden with a children's play area.
Q✿⊶❀Ⓓ♣🅿🌐🛜

Holford

Plough Inn 🗍 ✔
TA5 1RY
☎ (01278) 741624 ● theploughinnholford.co.uk
Sharp's Doom Bar; 1 changing beer (sourced locally; often Exmoor) Ⓗ
This 16th-century country inn is situated at the foot of the Quantock Hills. Walkers, bikers and dogs are made welcome by a large open fire in the colder months and pleasant garden in warmer times. The Plough won a local tourism award for the best dog-friendly business of the year in 2023. As well as the usual water and treats, it also supplies towels, blankets and a 'doggy menu' of both food and drinks – including 'bottom sniffer' beer!
✿❀Ⓓ⚥♣🅿🌐🛜

Horton

Five Dials Inn
Goose Lane, TA19 9QQ
☎ (01460) 55359 ● thefivedials.co.uk
Otter Bitter; Sharp's Doom Bar; 1 changing beer (often Otter) Ⓗ
Old coaching inn which has been given a contemporary facelift. It serves three real ales and traditional local ciders from Perry's and Burrow Hill including the famous Somerset Cider Brandy. There is a menu of fresh seasonal food with a daily changing specials board. The inn offers six guest rooms with en-suite showers and was awarded four stars by Enjoy England. There is also a self-contained studio apartment which includes kitchen and dining facilities. Open on bank holiday Mondays.
✿❀Ⓓ⚥♨🅿🌐🛜

Huish Episcopi

Rose & Crown ★ 🗍
TA10 9QT (on A372 in village)
☎ (01458) 250494 ● elisroseandcrown.co.uk
Teignworthy Reel Ale; 3 changing beers (sourced regionally; often Fine Tuned, Hop Back, Otter) Ⓗ
Thatched 17th-century inn known as Eli's after the former owner Eli Scott who took over the pub in 1920. The pub is still in the same family. The hub of the pub is the rare counterless flagstoned taproom which which usually serves four cask ales and leads out to four cosy parlours. Regular music features. A Brit Stop pub that offers free overnight stops for motorhome travellers.
Q✿❀⚥♣♨🅿🌐🛜♪

Kilve

Hood Arms 🗍
TA5 1EA (on A39)
☎ (01278) 741114 ● thehoodarms.co.uk
Exmoor Gold; St Austell Tribute; 1 changing beer (often Quantock) Ⓗ
Former 17th-century coaching inn set beside the main road, near a beach frequented by fossil hunters. It has oak beams and an open fireplace, a comfortable bar and separate restaurant. Outside is a walled garden where boules is played in the summer. There are nine en-suite rooms and it is an ideal base for walkers with easy access to the Quantock Hills and the Coleridge Way. It offers good food and wines and welcomes dogs.
Q✿⊶❀Ⓓ&⚥♣♨🅿🌐🛜♪

Litton

Litton
The Litton, BA3 4PW
☎ (01761) 241554 ● thelitton.co.uk
Cheddar Ales Potholer; house beer (by Hop Union); 2 changing beers (often Cheddar Ales, Bristol Beer Factory, Quantock) Ⓗ
A large 15th-century village pub where the emphasis is on comfort without ruining the character of the lovely building. The old part has a country pub feel, while the restaurant area is bright and breezy. There is a riverside terrace at the rear and a large patio garden at the front with steps up to the car park. Accessible parking is at the rear of the building, from where you can get to the pub and the upmarket accommodation. Guest beers are usually only served in the summer months.
✿❀Ⓓ&🅿ⅈ🌐🛜

Long Ashton

Angel Inn ✓

172 Long Ashton Road, BS41 9LT

☎ (01275) 392244 ⊕ theangelinn-longashton.co.uk

Draught Bass; Otter Bitter; St Austell Tribute; Sharp's Doom Bar; 1 changing beer (sourced nationally; often Timothy Taylor) ⊞

This late 15th-century free of tie roadside inn retains a real rural charm despite being less than a mile from Bristol. The Smoke Room acts as a snug, while diners can enjoy the Parlour with its lovely old fireplace, branched off the main bar area. The rear courtyard has traditionally been a haven for swallows in summertime. Quiz night is every third Wednesday of the month, and there is occasional live music. ★❀✿❀❀◑❀➡(X7,X9)❀❀♪

Lower Godney

Sheppey Inn

BA5 1RZ

☎ (01458) 831594 ⊕ thesheppey.co.uk

4 changing beers (sourced locally; often Frome, Pitchfork, Wookey Ale) ⊞

A quirky many-roomed pub with graphic arts, taxidermy, and surreal ornaments, set in the wilds of the Somerset levels, to the west of Wells. It has a good range of ever-changing real ales, plus six or more craft beers from home and overseas, and up to 12 ciders on gravity. Outside the barn-like interior is a lovely terrace overlooking the eponymous River Sheppey, where otters have been spotted. The food is highly recommended. Often closed on Mondays, ring to check. ★❀✿◑❀♣❀❀♪

Luxborough

Royal Oak Inn Ⓛ ✓

TA23 0SH (2½ miles from B3224 between Wheddon Cross and Raleghs Cross)

☎ (01984) 641498 ⊕ royaloakinnluxborough.co.uk

Butcombe Original; Exmoor Ale; 2 changing beers (sourced regionally; often Nuttycombe) ⊞

Set within Exmoor, this ancient village pub has an original flagstone floor in the main bar and a large inglenook fireplace and serves a range of four cask ales. A second bar has a pool table and a radiogram if you wish to play some vinyl. Three intimate dining areas serve freshly-cooked meals made using seasonal produce. Popular with ramblers and shooting parties, it is dog friendly. If you wish to sit outside there is a sunny river garden. Q★✿✿◑❀♣❀❀❀

Lydford on Fosse

Cross Keys Inn Ⓛ

TA11 7HA (next to the A37 between Yeovil and Shepton Mallet, at traffic lights in village)

☎ (01963) 240473 ⊕ crosskeysinn.info

Bristol Beer Factory Fortitude; Church End Goat's Milk; 2 changing beers (sourced regionally; often Fine Tuned, Hanlons, Hop Back) Ⓖ

A traditional 16th-century pub with flagstone floors, blue lias stonework and a wealth of beams. The open-plan bar has a fireplace at each end and a snug area. This is a community pub with many events organised such as live music, a beer festival, comedy nights and charitable events. Camping is available on site with 29 pitches, a shower block and toilets. There are up to five gravity poured ales available including the house beer. Q★✿❀✿◑❀♣❀❀➡(667)❀❀♪

Minehead

Kildare Lodge ✓

Townend Road, TA24 5RQ (2 mins from town centre)

☎ (01643) 702009 ⊕ kildarelodge.co.uk

St Austell Tribute; 3 changing beers (sourced regionally) ⊞

This cracking locals' pub is a Grade II-listed building in the Arts and Crafts style, close to Minehead town centre. It has a bar, two lounges and a dining room. Twelve en-suite rooms include a bridal suite with a four-poster bed. Two beer festivals are held every year with up to 20 beers available. The pub is in the local boules and quiz leagues. It is a great base for exploring Exmoor National Park, Dunster and the coast. Q★❀▲❀♣❀❀➡(28,198)❀

Old Ship Aground

Quay Street, TA24 5UL (beside Minehead harbour)

☎ (01643) 703516 ⊕ theoldshipaground.com

Hall & Woodhouse Badger Best Bitter, Fursty Ferret ⊞

Built in 1906 between the harbour and the lifeboat station, the pub has 12 letting rooms with fantastic views over the Bristol Channel. Exmoor National Park is only a 20 minute drive away and it is within walking distance of the town centre and the West Somerset Railway. The pub holds themed food nights through the week and there is a Sunday carvery. Beer festivals are held and there is live music on a Friday night. ★❀✿◑❀▲❀➡(28,198)❀❀❀

Quay Inn

Quay Street, TA24 5UJ

☎ (01643) 707323 ⊕ thequayinnminehead.co.uk

3 changing beers (sourced regionally; often Dartmoor, Exmoor, Nuttycombe) ⊞

A new addition to the Guide with a good range of three changing cask ales usually from local and regional breweries. Recently refurbished, it offers excellent views of the Bristol Channel. Good pub food is served at reasonable prices. There are regular live music evenings and open mic nights are held on the first and third Wednesday of the month. It featured on and won Channel 4's Four in a Bed competition in 2001. ★❀✿◑▲❀❀➡(28, 198)❀♪

Nailsea

Nailsea MicroPub

Unit 4, Ivy Court, 63A High Street, BS48 1AW

☎ 07496 428350

4 changing beers (sourced locally) Ⓖ

Nailsea's first micropub which opened in 2019, serves up to six ales straight from the cask, along with two real ciders. Beers of all styles can come from around the country, but more often they are sourced from local breweries. Bottles and cans of beers and ciders are sold along with gins, wines, alcohol-free beers and soft drinks. Reasonably-priced bar snacks are also available. There is no dedicated parking but there are ample public car parks nearby. Q❀♣❀➡❀

Nether Stowey

George Ⓛ

1 St Mary Street, TA5 1LJ

☎ (01278) 732248 ⊕ georgestowey.com

2 changing beers (often Bays, Dartmoor, Exmoor) ⊞

The George is the oldest pub in the village and can trace its history back to 1616, although original building dates back another century. It is a friendly multi-roomed pub with a real fire, dark wood interior and Tiffany lamps. Historical photographs of the village adorn the walls. A function room is available upstairs. No food is served but you are welcome to bring your own or the post office/ cafe across the road will deliver. Happy hours are every weekday afternoon. ⏰🏠🚫♿🅿🚌(14)🐾🛜♪

Norton St Philip

George ✅
High Street, BA2 7LH
☎ (01373) 834224
Butcombe Adam Henson's Rare Breed, Original, Haka Ⓗ
An historic Grade I-listed building dating from at least 1327, the George has a good claim to being the oldest pub in the country (according to English Heritage). The beamed bar features a distinctive fireplace. There are several other rooms used for drinking and dining, including a large dining room at the rear and a Dungeon bar, both accessed from the attractive cobbled courtyard. Steps lead from the car park to an enclosed garden which has views across the Mead to the church.
Q⏰🏠🚫🍴🅿🐾🛜

Pitney

Halfway House 🍺 🅛
Pitney Hill, TA10 9AB (on B3153 between Langport and Somerton)
☎ (01458) 252513 ⊕ thehalfwayhouse.co.uk
Hop Back Summer Lightning; Otter Bright; Teignworthy Reel Ale; 5 changing beers (sourced regionally; often Fine Tuned, Parkway, Quantock) Ⓖ
An outstanding pub serving between eight and 10 regional ales on gravity, alongside many bottled beers and four real ciders. The inside is traditional, with flagstone flooring, old solid wooden tables and benches, and three real fires. This basic but busy pub deserves its many accolades including being in the Guide for over 25 years and gaining the ultimate award of National Pub of the Year in 1996. It serves superb home-cooked food and a recent addition is accommodation provided in The Hut.
Q⏰🏠🚫🍴🐾🅿(54)🐾🛜

Porlock

Ship Inn 🅛 ✅
High Street, TA24 8QD
☎ (01643) 862507 ⊕ shipinnporlock.co.uk
Exmoor Ale, Beast; Otter Amber; St Austell Tribute, Proper Job; 3 changing beers (sourced regionally; often Quantock) Ⓗ
Known locally as the Top Ship, the bar is a gem with its flagstone floor, open fire and settle seating. It has changed little since featuring in R. D. Blackmore's novel Lorna Doone. The pub dates from the 13th century and sits at the bottom of the notorious Porlock Hill that takes you up to Exmoor. Up to eight ales and a local cider are available and good food can be enjoyed in its restaurant or in the delightful three-tiered garden in summer.
Q⏰🏠🚫🍴♿🅰♣🐾🅿(10,EXMO)🐾♪

Porlock Weir

Ship Inn 🅛
TA24 8PB (take the B3225 from Porlock)
☎ (01643) 863288 ⊕ shipinnporlockweir.co.uk
Exmoor Ale, Stag; St Austell Tribute, Proper Job; 2 changing beers (sourced regionally; often Otter) Ⓗ
The 400-year-old pub offers fantastic views of the Bristol Channel and South Wales coast. It is set next to the small harbour and pebbled beach. Located in Exmoor National Park, it is ideal for walkers on the South West Coast Path. It is busy in the summer and has a pay and display car

park opposite. A beer festival is held at the end of July with up to 50 ales available. Dog-friendly accommodation is available.
Q⏰🏠🍴♿🅰♣🐾🅿(10) 🐾🛜♪

Portishead

Ship
310 Down Road, BS20 8JT
☎ (01275) 848400
Draught Bass; Otter Bitter; Sharp's Doom Bar Ⓗ
A large hostelry with traditional opening hours on the coast road between Clevedon and Portishead. You can enjoy extensive views and spectacular sunsets over the Severn Estuary from the recently extended garden. The landlord has been at the pub that he built since 1973 and is a fount of local knowledge. Meals are served at lunchtimes only, but you can get pasties in the evening. There is a small library of books with a particularly good selection on local history. 🏠🍴♣🐾🅿(X4)🐾

Siren's Calling 🍺 🅛
315 Newfoundland Way, Portishead Marina, BS20 7PT
☎ (01275) 268278 ⊕ sirenscalling.co.uk
5 changing beers (often Bristol Beer Factory, Ilkley, Track) Ⓗ
A modern single-room waterside bar serving up to six cask ales and nine craft keg beers in a variety of styles. Beers from the north of England often feature, reflecting the landlord's heritage. Still ciders are also sold. The pub is simply furnished, with large front windows overlooking the many boats moored in the marina. Only basic bar snacks are served but customers are welcome to bring in fish & chips from next door. Regular beer festivals are held. ⏰🏠♿🐾🅿🐾🛜♪

Windmill Inn 🅛
58 Nore Road, BS20 6JZ (next to former municipal golf course above coastal path)
☎ (01275) 818483 ⊕ thewindmillinn.org
Butcombe Original; Fuller's London Pride; 1 changing beer (often Fuller's) Ⓗ
Large split-level pub with a spacious patio to the rear, plus an extension enjoying panoramic views. It is above the coastal path on the edge of town; the Severn Estuary and both Severn bridges can be seen on clear days. It started life as a windmill in the 1830s, became a pub in 1960, and was acquired by Fuller's in 2014. A varied menu is served all day with table bookings available. Dogs are allowed in the main bar area only.
Q⏰🏠🍴♿🅿(X4) 🐾🛜

Priddy

Hunters' Lodge
Old Bristol Road, BA5 3AR (at isolated crossroads 1 mile from A39, close to TV mast) ST549500
☎ (01749) 672275
Butcombe Original; Cheddar Ales Potholer Ⓖ
The landlord of this timeless classic roadside inn has been in charge for 53 years. Priddy is the highest village in Somerset, and is popular with cavers and walkers. The pub's three rooms include one with a flagged floor. All beer is served direct from casks behind the bar; local cider is also on offer. Simple home-cooked food is excellent and exceptional value. A folk musicians' drop-in session is held on Tuesday evening. The garden is pleasant and secluded. Mobile phones aren't welcome but dogs are. Cash payments only.
Q⏰🏠🍴♿♣🐾🅿(683) 🐾♪

Queen Victoria Inn ✅
Pelting Drove, BA5 3BA
☎ (01749) 676385 ⊕ thequeenvicpriddy.co.uk
Butcombe Adam Henson's Rare Breed, Original H
This creeper-clad inn, which has been a pub since 1851, has four rooms featuring low ceilings, flagged floors and two log fires. It is a wonderfully warm and relaxing haven on cold winter nights, and is particularly popular during the Priddy Folk Festival in July. Reasonably priced home-cooked food is a speciality. There is a lovely beer garden with six sheds named after royal palaces. Children are welcome and there is a play area by the car park. Q🏠🕮🌞🕩🄰P🐾🛜♪

Puriton

37 Club L
1 West Approach Road, Woolavington Road, TA7 8AD
(5 mins from M5 jct 23 of between Bridgwater and Wells)
☎ (01278) 685190 ⊕ 37club.co.uk
St Austell Anthem, Tribute, Proper Job; 3 changing beers (sourced regionally; often Nuttycombe, Quantock) H
On the site of the former Royal Ordnance Factory which was allocated the number 37. A large club offering a great many facilities to members and visitors. It has two bars and its multi-roomed layout incorporates a concert room, two skittle alleys, a dining room and a snooker room with five tables. Outside are a beer garden, fishing lake and football pitch. CAMRA members are welcome with a membership card. 🏠🌞🕩🄰♣P🖳(75)🐾♪

Radstock

Fromeway
Frome Road, BA3 3LG
☎ (01761) 432116 ⊕ fromeway.co.uk
Butcombe Original H**; 2 changing beers (sourced nationally; often Otter, Twisted)** H/🄰
This friendly free house has been run by the same family for six generations and is now in the capable hands of Emily, the youngest daughter of the present generation. There is great selection of weekly changing ales from all over the country. The food is traditional, with classics as well as more contemporary dishes, and booking is advised. The pub has an award-winning garden. Regular charity events, quiz nights, and walks take place from month to month. May be closed Monday and Tuesday. 🏠🌞🕮🕩P🖳(768,178)🐾🛜

Rickford

Plume of Feathers
Leg Lane, BS40 7AH (off A368, 2 miles from A38; approaching from Churchill, the left U-turn into Leg Ln is extremely tricky)
☎ (01761) 462682 ⊕ theplumeoffeathers.com
Bristol Beer Factory Fortitude; Sharp's Doom Bar H**; 1 changing beer (sourced locally; often Bristol Beer Factory)** G
This 17th-century building has been a pub since the 1800s. Its interior is divided into several areas, including a restaurant with a real fire. There is a garden to the rear and a stream running along the front, leading to a ford. Guest beers are often from Bristol Beer Factory. A popular charity duck race takes place in July. The pub provides a pleasant and convenient base from which to walk, fish and explore the Mendips. Car parking is limited. Q🏠🌞🕮🕩🄰♣P🖳(672)🐾🛜

Roadwater

Valiant Soldier L ✅
TA23 0QZ (off A39 at Washford)
☎ (01984) 640223 ⊕ thevaliantsoldier.co.uk
Dartmoor Jail Ale; Exmoor Ale H
The pub dates back to 1720 and is ideal for country walks and exploring nearby Exmoor, the coast and Dunster. This vibrant locals' pub has quiz, pool, darts and nine skittles teams to see it through the winter months. It is set by a small river where you can relax and watch the ducks and, if you are lucky, kingfishers. Good quality locally sourced food is served. It has been run by Mike the landlord for over 30 years. 🏠🌞🕮🕩♣🕭P🐾🛜♪

Somerton

Etsome Arms
6 West Street, TA11 7PS
☎ 07907 046213
6 changing beers (sourced locally; often Bristol Beer Factory, Fine Tuned, Parkway) G
This micropub, among the first in Somerset and a winner of local CAMRA awards, is well worth a visit. A cosy, friendly venue, it serves between four and six ales on gravity, depending on the time of week and season, with all changing regularly. Seating is comfortable sofas or traditional tables and chairs. Quality cold bar snacks are sourced locally and include a range of scotch eggs and pies. Children and dogs are welcome. 🏠🌞♣🕭🖳(54,77)🐾🛜

White Hart Inn
Market Place, TA11 7LX (centre of village)
☎ (01458) 272273 ⊕ whitehartsomerton.com
Cheddar Ales Potholer; 2 changing beers (sourced regionally; often Fine Tuned, Otter) H
The White Hart has been trading as an inn in Somerton's delightful market square since the 16th century. You cannot miss the large model of a white hart on the entrance porch. It is much larger inside than you might first envisage, with plenty of tables for dining or for coffee and cakes. A courtyard provides alfresco eating and drinking. A winner of numerous awards and recommended in multiple reviews by the national press. 🏠🌞🕮🕩🕭🕭🖳(54,77)🐾🛜♪

South Cheriton

White Horse
Cabbage Lane, BA8 0BL
☎ (01963) 370394 ⊕ moaningtoad.co.uk
Cheddar Ales Potholer; Dartmoor Jail Ale; Gritchie Moon Lore; 1 changing beer (sourced regionally) H
A characterful and genuine privately owned freehouse facing onto the A357, now the nearest pub to Templecombe and enjoying strong support from locals and visitors alike. A drinker's pub which welcomes diners on Thursday to Saturday evenings and Sunday lunchtimes. Warm, snug and eclectically decorated, it has an outside drinking area and garden. The former skittle alley is now a restaurant and function room. Well-behaved dogs and children are welcome. Q🏠🌞🕩P🖳(58)🐾🛜♪

South Petherton

Brewers Arms L
18-20 St James Street, TA13 5BW (½ mile off A303 in centre of village)
☎ (01460) 241887 ⊕ the-brewersarms.com

Otter Bitter; 3 changing beers (sourced nationally; often Bristol Beer Factory, Fine Tuned, Hop Back) ⌂
This pub is just half a mile from the A303 and has appeared in 25 consecutive editions of the Guide. During this time around 3,000 different ales have been served and documented. The Brewers is a hub of village life, a true community pub that keenly supports local events and charities. Beer festivals are held over both spring and summer bank holiday weekends. Regular live music and quiz nights feature. The adjoining Old Bakehouse provides excellent quality food.
Ġ❀☎⏰▲♣●🚃(81) ❀🐾♪

Taunton

Perkin Warbeck 🅛 ✅

22-23 East Street, TA1 3LP
☎ (01823) 335830
Greene King Abbot; Ruddles Best Bitter; Sharp's Doom Bar; 3 changing beers (sourced nationally; often Butcombe, Exmoor, Otter) ⌂
This Wetherspoon pub is named after the man who claimed to be the rightful heir to the throne of England in 1497. Recently refurbished, the pub has one of the longest bars in the county and at the rear is a splendid outside terrace. Somerset cricket memorabilia adorn the walls, as befits the fact that the pub is a stone's throw from the cricket ground. An excellent range of ales and ciders kept. Ġ❀⏰🖐●🚃☎

Ring of Bells 🅛

16-17 St James Street, TA1 1JS
☎ (01823) 259480 ● theringofbellstaunton.com
5 changing beers (sourced nationally; often Oakham, Otter, Quantock) ⌂
Being close to Somerset cricket ground, this pub is a favourite haunt of cricket fans. Wooden-floored, there are two bar areas with open fires, a downstairs eating area, upstairs restaurant and large outside courtyard. The five cask beers are from local, regional and national breweries and you may find some interesting keg beers. Excellent locally produced food is served and booking is recommended. Sporting events are shown on a TV in the bar area. Ġ❀⏰🚆🚃❀☎

Wyvern Social Club 🅛

Mountfields Road, TA1 3BJ (off South Rd, approx 1 mile from town centre)
☎ (01823) 284591 ● wyvernclub.co.uk
4 changing beers (sourced regionally; often Exmoor, St Austell) ⌂
For over 35 years this club has been a great venue to drink real ales and cider. A members-only club with a visitor licence, show a CAMRA membership card to be signed in as a guest. The club is the hub for rugby, cricket and squash clubs who use the attaching playing fields. It has bas been voted local CAMRA Club of the Year on many occasions over the last 20 years. The 99 bus route operates Saturday daytime only.
Ġ❀⏰♣●🚃(99) ☎♪

Trull

Winchester Arms

Church Road, TA3 7LG
☎ (01823) 284723 ● winchesterarmstrull.co.uk
4 changing beers (sourced regionally; often Dartmoor, Exmoor, Otter) ⌂
Thriving community free house on the outskirts of Taunton and near to the Blackdown Hills. A comfortable bar area, usually with a range of four cask ales, is separated from the long dining area by a fireplace. The

locally sourced home-cooked food is excellent. A streamside garden is perfect for families and dogs, and becomes the venue for entertainment and barbecues. Sunday nights are popular for quizzes, and there is occasional live music. The pub offers good-value accommodation. Q Ġ❀🛏⏰♣●🚃(97)❀☎♪

Wambrook

Cotley Inn

TA20 3EN (from A30 W out of Chard, take left fork by toll house and almost immediately left again; continue for just over 1 mile on narrow lane following signs for pub)
☎ (01460) 62348 ● cotleyinnwambrook.co.uk
Otter Bitter; 2 changing beers (sourced regionally; often Exeter, Teignworthy) Ｇ
A traditional country pub that is well worth finding. Inside the main entrance is a bar area with a welcoming wood-burning stove to greet you in the winter months. To the right of the bar is a challenging skittle alley and to the left you will find dining areas where you can sample the excellent food. Ales are served from gravity racking behind the bar. The pub is in a wonderful rural setting where sitting outside is a delight. Ġ❀⏰♣●P☎☎♪

Washford

White Horse Inn 🅛

Abbey Rd, TA23 0JZ (take road towards Cleeve Abbey off the A39)
☎ (01984) 640415 ● exmoorpubs.co.uk
3 changing beers (sourced regionally; often Sharp's, St Austell) ⌂
The pub dates from 1709 and is near to the ruins of Cleeve Abbey and close to the Torre cider farm. This riverside free house is an ideal base for visits to the coast, Exmoor National Park, the Quantock Hills and the West Somerset Steam Railway. A good range of locally sourced food is available. Various charity events are held including the famous bike pub run. B&B accommodation is available in the pub and in a separate lodge.
Q Ġ❀🛏⏰♣●P🚃(28) ❀☎

Watchet

Esplanade Club 🅛

5 The Esplanade, TA23 0AJ (opp the marina)
☎ 07876 353819 ● esplanadeclub.net
Sharp's Doom Bar; 4 changing beers (sourced regionally; often Exmoor, St Austell) ⌂
Built in the 1860s as a sail-making factory and now home to the Boat Owners Association. The club is an archive of local history and memorabilia, with unique murals and even its own Tardis. There are great views over the marina and Bristol Channel. The club is a busy music venue with live acts every weekend, open mic on the first Tuesday of the month and folk every fourth Wednesday. A five-time winner of the local CAMRA Club of the Year award and a Guide entry for 15 years.
Ġ❀▲🚆♣●🚃(28) ❀☎♪

Pebbles Tavern

24 Market Street, TA23 0AN (nr museum)
☎ (01984) 634903 ● pebblestavern.co.uk
3 changing beers (sourced nationally; often Nuttycombe, Timothy Taylor) ⌂/Ｇ
This small unique tavern has won numerous CAMRA awards for Cider Pub of the Year since 2014, and was the runner-up in the National competition in both 2015 and 2022. As well as the ales there can be up to 30 ciders, 60 gins, 24 rums and 64 whiskies. You are welcome to bring in food to eat from various shops in Watchet. Poetry

night is the first Tuesday of the month and regular music nights include folk, sea shanty, acoustic and jazz.
🕭🛇Å⇌♣♿🖪🖵(28) 🐾🛜♪

Star Inn 🅛

Mill Lane, TA23 0BZ
☎ (01984) 631367 ● starinnwatchet.co.uk
4 changing beers (sourced regionally; often Dartmoor, Exmoor, Nuttycombe) 🅗
This two-time local CAMRA Pub of the Year has been in the Guide for 20 consecutive years. It is renowned for friendly staff and its congenial atmosphere and is also the brewery tap for Nuttycombe brewery. The pub hosts dart, quiz and boules teams and holds music nights in the summer. Is home to the Sunday night Bad Boys club. Mick's beer tours have run over 100 trips from the pub.
🕭❀🛈♿Å⇌♣♿🐾🛜♪

Wedmore

New Inn 🅛

Combe Batch, BS28 4DU
☎ (01934) 712099
Butcombe Original; Timothy Taylor Landlord; 1 changing beer (sourced regionally; often Cheddar Ales, Exmoor, Fine Tuned) 🅗
This classic village inn is the centre for many local events including the famous annual turnip prize, spoof and penny chuffin. The public bar, lounge and dining areas are complemented by a beer garden to the rear. A chalkboard lists forthcoming ales, mainly from the West Country, with two dispensed from handpumps and two on gravity. Traditional, good-value home-cooked food is served. There is a skittle alley/function room and skittles and darts provide a hive of activity in winter.
Q🕭❀🛈♿Å♣♿🖵(67) 🐾🛜♪

Wells

Crown Inn

Town Hall Square, BA5 2RP
☎ (01749) 673457 ● crownatwells.co.uk/pub
Butcombe Original; Cheddar Ales Crown And Glory; Sharp's Doom Bar; 2 changing beers (sourced regionally) 🅗
Although a hotel and bistro, the separate bar is run as a pub, now with a recently extended range of well-kept ales. Enter the bar via the door on the left of the main entrance. The Crown is a lovely old building overlooking the main square and market place, while the cathedral is a few minutes walk away. William Penn, the Quaker, preached to a large crowd outside the building 1685.
🕭🛒🛈🖪🖵🐾🛜

Full Moon

42 Southover, BA5 1UH
☎ (01749) 678291
House beer (by Fine Tuned); 3 changing beers (sourced regionally; often Cheddar Ales, Pitchfork, St Austell) 🅗
A smart, friendly locals' free house just off the city centre. The interior of the pub comprises a public bar with sports TV and jukebox, and a quieter lounge area which is divided between the bar, a snug-like area and a section suitable for dining. Out at the back is the city's largest pub courtyard, and a beer garden beyond there. Wilkins cider is served. Families and dogs are welcome.
❀🛇Å♣♿🖵🐾🛜♪

West Chinnock

Muddled Man 🅛 ✓

Lower Street, TA18 7PT
☎ (01935) 881235 ● themuddledmaninn.co.uk
3 changing beers (often Bays, Hop Back, Otter) 🅗
A popular traditional free house in a picturesque village. The large beer garden with its exceptional flower boxes, troughs and baskets is a sight to be seen. A warm welcome is extended to visitors and locals alike. Good home-cooked food is served by the happy and jovial family team. The pub specialises in a variety of steaks and a Sunday lunch so popular it must be pre-booked. There as always a good range of three well-kept ales and a real cider.
Q🕭❀🛒🛈♿♣🐾🛜

West Huntspill

Crossways Inn 🅛

Withy Road, TA9 3RA (on the A38)
☎ (01278) 783756 ● thecrosswaysinn.com
8 changing beers (sourced nationally; often Bristol Beer Factory, Dartmoor) 🅗
This fabulous 17th-century characterful inn was the well-deserved winner of the local CAMRA Pub of the Year award for 2022, and for the last seven consecutive years. It has several charming bar areas, a dining room, two log fires during winter and an outside fireplace for smokers. A range of eight cask, three keg, 20 craft canned ales and a selection of real ciders ensure a wide range of drinks for all tastes. A beer festival is held on the last weekend in July. Good local pub food is served.
🕭❀🛒🛈♿Å♣🖵(21) 🐾🛜♪

Weston-super-Mare

Black Cat 🅛

135 High Street, BS23 1HN
☎ (01934) 620153
3 changing beers (often Cheddar Ales, Electric Bear) 🅖
A micropub that opened in 2018 in a former clothes shop at the Playhouse Theatre end of the High Street. Up to four cask ales of varying styles and strengths are served, chosen from local breweries, and a few from further afield, plus at least two real ciders and seven craft keg beers. Dogs are welcome, as are children until later in the evening. There is reasonable access for those of limited mobility. Look for the impressive black cat mural.
Q🕭♣♿🖪🖵🐾🛜

Brit Bar 🅛 ✓

118 High Street, BS23 1HP
☎ (01934) 632629
5 changing beers (often Bristol Beer Factory, New Bristol, Quantock) 🅗
Established town-centre pub bought by the current owners at auction after a period of closure. It has been given a bright, modern makeover while retaining the important traditional elements. Five changing beers are served, always including some dark brews. Bag-in-box real cider is usually sold too. Live music features at weekends in the covered courtyard, which is heated in cold weather, and families are welcome there too at all hours. The pub hosts its own version of the Brit Awards every February. 🕭❀⇌♿🖵🐾🛜♪

Criterion ✓

45 Upper Church Road, BS23 2DY
☎ 07983 851707
Courage Directors 🅗; **St Austell Tribute; 1 changing beer (often St Austell)** 🅖

Genuine free house and traditional community pub, just off the seafront in the Knightstone area. Believed to be one of the oldest pubs in town, it has interesting local photos on the walls. Pub games feature strongly, with darts, table skittles and a cribbage team. Bar snacks are available, and filled rolls at lunchtime. The pub is big on rugby and dogs. Occasional morris dancing features.
&♣🚃(1,4)🐾

Duke of Oxford 🅛

27 Oxford Street, BS23 1TF
☎ (01934) 417762 ⊕ dukeofoxford.co.uk
Exmoor Gold; 3 changing beers (sourced locally; often Quantock, Twisted Oak) 🅗
Reopened in 2016 after a long period of closure, this pub is just outside the main shopping area and near the seafront. It was refurbished as a café-style bar with accommodation, and has a grand piano; jazz music sometimes features. The beers are usually from local breweries and there is real cider. A small outdoor space is accessible via stairs. Note that the pub may close early during the off-season. 🚪🏵🛏🍴&➤♣🍺🚃🐾🎵♪

Fork N' Ale Taproom & Kitchen

18 Walliscote Road, BS23 1UG
☎ (01934) 627937 ⊕ forknale.com
5 changing beers (sourced locally) 🅗
Opened in 2019 this pub is conveniently located in the town centre near the seafront and railway station. It has a modern look and feel, with an interior of wood, metal and brick, as well as a few comfy sofas. There is a big focus on the beer, with between four and six on at any one time. The food menu consists of main courses and small plates. Toilets are upstairs so not ideal for those with limited mobility. ◐➤🚃🐾🎵♪

Regency

22-24 Lower Church Road, BS23 2AG
☎ (01934) 633406
Butcombe Original; St Austell Anthem, Tribute; Timothy Taylor Landlord; 1 changing beer (sourced nationally; often Dark Star) 🅗
Comfortable, friendly town-centre local serving a good range of regular beers plus one guest. It has pool, skittles and crib teams, and also offers a quiet refuge for conversation. There is a games room to the left as you enter, with TV and jukebox, separate from the main bar area; children are welcome here and it can be used for parties and functions. Outside are front and rear patios. Live music often features on Sundays. Filled rolls are available all day. 🚪🏵&♣🚃🐾♪

Williton

Mason's Arms 🅛

2 North Road, TA4 4SN
☎ (01984) 639200 ⊕ themasonsarms.com
3 changing beers (sourced regionally; often Dartmoor, Exmoor, St Austell) 🅗
This beautiful thatched 16th-century inn has oak beams throughout and offers five en-suite rooms in the adjoining annexe. The pub hosts quiz teams in the local league. It has a pleasant beer garden where locals and visitors alike sit and relax. It has a good reputation for its food and serving three quality cask ales. Rich's cider is always available. Close to the Quantock Hills and West Somerset Railway and a short drive from Exmoor National Park. Q🚪🏵🛏◐&🅰♣🍺🚃(28)🐾🎵

Wincanton

Nog Inn

South Street, BA9 9DL
☎ (01963) 32998 ⊕ thenoginn.com
Otter Amber; Sharp's Sea Fury; 2 changing beers (sourced regionally; often Otter, Plain) 🅗
This attractive listed pub with a striking Georgian façade, fronts a long, narrow, building with parts dating back to the 16th century. A secluded sunny garden with covered seating can be found at the far end of the property. The guest ales are often seasonal and an extensive range of continental beers is always available. Home-cooked pub classics use locally sourced and seasonal ingredients where possible. 🚪🏵🛏◐♣🚃(58,667)🐾🎵

Witham Friary

Seymour Arms ★

BA11 5HF
☎ (01749) 684280
Cheddar Ales Potholer 🅗
A hidden rural gem, this pub has probably changed very little over the last 50 or so years (apart from new loos!). Built in the 1860s as a hotel to serve the nearby Mid-Somerset GWR branch railway station, it was part of the Duke of Somerset's estate. Sadly, in the 1960s, Dr Beeching closed the station, and the hotel became a quiet country pub. One, locally sourced beer, and cider are served from a glass-panelled hatch in the central hallway. Q🚪🏵♣🍺🐾

Yatton

Butchers Arms 🅛

31 High Street, BS49 4JD
☎ (01934) 838754
St Austell Tribute; Twisted Oak Fallen Tree 🅗/🅖; 2 changing beers (sourced locally; often Twisted Oak) 🅗
On the main road through the village, this free-of-tie pub occupies a 14th-century building that retains many original features including a feature bay window. Mind your head as you go in – there are low ceilings throughout. Steps lead up to a rear restaurant area and toilets, with a beer garden beyond. The changing beers are often from Twisted Oak in Wrington but may include offerings from other local breweries. Wheelchair users can access the garden and the bar via portable ramps. 🚪🏵◐🅰🍺🐾🎵♪

Yeovil

Quicksilver Mail ✅

168 Hendford Hill, BA20 2RG (at jct of A30 and A37)
☎ (01935) 424721 ⊕ quicksilvermail.com
Butcombe Original; 2 changing beers (sourced nationally; often St Austell, Timothy Taylor) 🅗
Roadside pub with a unique name commemorating a high-speed mail coach. The pub has been run by the same landlord since 2002 and has been an almost constant fixture in the Guide. There is a large single bar and separate dining area serving excellent food and a well-priced range of wine. The pub is a well-known live music destination and holds comedy, bingo and quiz nights in the bar or function room.
🚪🏵🛏◐🅰♣🚃(6,96)🐾🎵♪

William Dampier ✅

97 Middle Street, BA20 1LN
☎ (01935) 412533

Greene King Abbot; Ruddles Best Bitter; Sharp's Doom Bar; 6 changing beers (sourced nationally) ⊞ The pub is named after William Dampier who was born in nearby East Coker and who was the first Englishman to explore parts of what is today Australia, and the first person to circumnavigate the world three times. As you enter there is a bar on the left, usually with a range of six cask ales. Being a Wetherspoon the ales turn over quickly. ⌂◑&●⛟≋

Breweries

Abbey SIBA

Abbey Brewery, Camden Row, Bath, BA1 5LB
☎ (01225) 444437 ⊕ abbeyales.co.uk

Founded in 1997 Abbey Ales was the first brewery in Bath for more than 50 years. It supplies more than 80 regular outlets within a 20-mile radius and its beers are more widely available in the South West via wholesalers. Three pubs are operated in Bath. ♦

Bath Best (ABV 4%) BITTER
Slight malt aroma, subtle caramel sweetness balanced with some hop bitterness and dark fruit on the palate, short dry aftertaste.
Bath Pale Ale (ABV 4.2%) PALE
Bellringer (ABV 4.2%) BITTER
Refreshing and clean-tasting with balanced flavours of pale fruit, English hops and biscuity malt, before a bittersweet, dry aftertaste.

Apex

Denham Cottage, 2 Queen's Court, Corton Denham, DT9 4LR ☎ 07817 806730 ⊕ apex.beer

Apex Beer is a nanobrewery based near Sherborne. Its mission is to brew beer to the highest standards using the latest technology. All beers are unfined, meaning they are slightly cloudy. Expansion is planned to supply direct to the public as well as to the trade. V

Bason Bridge SIBA

Unit 2, 129 Church Road, Bason Bridge, TA9 4RG
☎ 07983 839274 ⊕ bbbrewery.co.uk

⊠ Brewery founded in Somerset in 2018. Initially, two beers were brewed, but after the successful launch, many more are now available. All beer is brewed on its 20-barrel plant.

Bridge Copper Ale (ABV 3.8%) BITTER
Harding's Pale Ale (ABV 3.9%) PALE
Harding's Best Bitter (ABV 4%) BITTER
Bridge Double Hopped Pale Ale (ABV 4.2%) PALE
Amarillo Citra Pale Ale (ABV 4.3%) PALE
Bridge Best Bitter (ABV 4.4%) BITTER
Harding's IPA (ABV 4.8%) PALE
Bridge Stout (ABV 5%) STOUT
ESB (ABV 5.2%) GOLD
NEIPA (ABV 5.5%) IPA

Bath Brew House SIBA

City Pub Company, 14 James Street West, Bath, BA1 2BX
☎ (01225) 805609

Office: City Pub Group Plc. Essel House, 2nd Floor, 29 Foley Street, London, W1W 7TH
⊕ thebathbrewhouse.com

⊠ Previously known as the James Street Brewery, Bath Brew House opened in 2013. It is owned by the City Pub Company, which owns several other pubs and brewpubs around the country. The compact brewery is on the ground floor, with the fermenting vessels and conditioning tanks on the first floor. The onsite brewer produces a wide range of beers. The company's other pub, the Cork, Bath, is also supplied. ‼⛟♦

Black Bear

c/o Bear Inn, 8-10 North Street, Wiveliscombe, TA4 2JY
☎ (01984) 623537 ⊕ blackbearbrewery.co.uk

⊠ Established in 2013, Black Bear is situated at the Bear Inn, Wiveliscombe, where Head Brewer Jon Coward and Assistant Brewer Peter Saxby create Black Bear Bitter and Goldihops, and a selection of seasonal offerings for the small estate of four pubs. Brewing is currently suspended. ♦🍽

Blindmans SIBA

Talbot Farm, Leighton, Frome, BA11 4PN
☎ (01749) 880038 ⊕ blindmansbrewery.co.uk

Established in 2002 in a converted milking parlour and purchased by its current owners in 2004, this five-barrel brewery has its own water spring. In addition to its core range of ales, which are available locally and nationally, the brewery produces bespoke branded beers for pubs and other customers. ♦

Buff Amber (ABV 3.6%) BITTER
Funny Farm (ABV 4%) PALE
Golden Spring (ABV 4%) GOLD
Mine Beer (ABV 4.2%) BITTER
Icarus (ABV 4.5%) BITTER

Butcombe

Cox's Green, Wrington, BS40 5PA
☎ (01934) 863963 ⊕ butcombe.com

⊠ Originally established in 1978, Butcombe moved to a purpose-built brewery with a 150-barrel plant in 2005. The brewery was bought by the Jersey-based Liberation Group in 2015. Around 500 outlets are supplied direct and similar numbers via wholesalers and pub companies. Butcombe opened a new distribution centre with a bottling line in Bridgewater in 2018. The brewery has an estate of around 20 managed and 20 tenanted pubs. ‼⛟♦GF

Adam Henson's Rare Breed (ABV 3.8%) GOLD
Subtle aroma of unripe fruit with sulphurous hints. Malty flavour is masked by dry bitterness which continues into the finish.
Original (ABV 4%) BITTER
Sweet tasting bitter with malt dominating over a trace of dark fruit, both soon fade in the rapid ending.
Gold (ABV 4.4%) GOLD
Amber golden ale with light aroma of fruit and hops, leading to well-balanced flavours of malt, pale fruit and hops. Bitter aftertaste.

Contract brewed for Wickwar Brewery:
BOB (ABV 4%) BITTER
Amber-coloured, this has a distinctive blend of hop, malt and apple/pear citrus fruits. The slightly sweet taste turns into fine, dry bitterness, with a similar malty, lasting finish.

Cheddar SIBA

Winchester Farm, Draycott Road, Cheddar, BS27 3RP
☎ (01934) 744193 ⊕ cheddarales.co.uk

⊗ Established in 2006 in the heart of the Mendips, Cheddar Ales has expanded capacity to enable it to brew up to 100 barrels a week. Production is split approximately 75% cask-conditioned ale, 25% bottle-conditioned. Its bottling plant produces around 120,000 bottles annually and all bottled ales are gluten-free. Around 450 outlets are supplied including pubs, clubs and the off trade. A visitor centre and taproom opened in 2020. !! �▶ ◆ LIVE GF ✦

Bitter Bully (ABV 3.8%) BLOND
Light session bitter with flowery hops on the nose and a dry, bitter finish.
Gorge Best (ABV 4%) BITTER
Malty bitter with caramel and fruit notes followed by a short bittersweet aftertaste.
Piney Sleight (ABV 4%) GOLD
Potholer (ABV 4.3%) GOLD
Refreshing flavours combine soft fruit sweetness with hop bitterness on a light malt background before a clean, balanced finish.
Hardrock (ABV 4.4%) GOLD
Fruity hop aroma, balanced flavours of tropical fruit and bitterness on a pale malt background before a clean bitter ending.
Totty Pot (ABV 4.4%) PORTER
Roasted malts dominate this smooth, well-flavoured porter. Hints of coffee and rich fruits follow with a well-balanced bitterness.
Crown & Glory (ABV 4.6%) BITTER
Lightly-hopped aroma, background malt balanced with fruity hops in the crisp bittersweet flavour before a dry and bitter finish
Goat's Leap (ABV 5.5%) IPA
Light malt aroma with enticing toffee and red liquorice hints. Traditional hop flavours and fruity sweetness, clean bitter finish

Clevedon SIBA

Unit 1, Tweed Road Trading Estate, Clevedon, BS21 6RR ☎ 07907 583415
✉ cheers@clevedonbrewery.co.uk

A small brewery founded in 2016. Ownership changed in 2019. It is regarded as a local brewery by owners and patrons alike. Following a complete rebranding, most of the beers, including seasonal ones, are now named with a twist to the locality. It focuses on using British malts and hops for its core beers. !! �▶ ✦

Gold (ABV 3.8%) GOLD
BS21 (ABV 4.1%) BITTER
Best (ABV 4.4%) BITTER
Percy's Porter (ABV 4.4%) PORTER
Roasted malt with coffee and chocolate balanced with blackberry and liquorice notes on the palate before a short, dry finish.
IPA (ABV 5%) PALE
Blonde (ABV 5.2%) BLOND

Electric Bear SIBA

Unit 12, Maltings Trading Estate, Locksbrook Road, Bath, BA1 3JL
☎ (01225) 424088 ⊕ electricbearbrewing.com

Electric Bear began brewing in 2015 using a purpose-built, 18-barrel plant, expanding capacity in 2016, 2018, and 2020. Its taproom showcases a selection of the range, including exclusive one-offs. A wide range of beer is available in cans and kegs and all are unfiltered, unfined and unpasteurised. !! �▶ ◆ LIVE ✦

Glitch (ABV 4.6%) PALE

Exmoor SIBA

Golden Hill Brewery, Old Brewery Road, Wiveliscombe, TA4 2PW
☎ (01984) 623798 ⊕ exmoorales.co.uk

Somerset's largest independent brewery was founded in 1980 in the old Hancock's brewery, which closed in 1959. In 2015 it moved to new, larger premises within 100 yards of the original site, doubling capacity. More than 400 outlets in the South West are supplied, plus others nationwide via wholesalers and pub chains. In 2022 it launched the Pathfinder range of small batch craft beers. ◆

Ale (ABV 3.8%) BITTER
Mid-brown, medium-bodied session bitter. Mixture of malt and hops in the aroma and taste lead to a hoppy, bitter aftertaste.
Pale (ABV 4.2%) PALE
Gold (ABV 4.5%) BITTER
Golden best bitter with balance of malt and fruity hop on the nose and palate with sweetness following. Bitter finish.
Stag (ABV 4.8%) BITTER
A pale brown beer with a malty taste and aroma and a bitter finish.
Beast (ABV 6.6%) STRONG

Fine Tuned SIBA

Unit 16, Wessex Park, Bancombe Trading Estate, Bancombe Road, Somerton, TA11 6SB
☎ (01458) 897273 ☎ 07872 139945
⊕ finetunedbrewery.com

Established in Langport, Somerset in 2016, but relocated to its current site in 2017. ◆ LIVE

Pitch Perfect (ABV 3.8%) BITTER
Langport Bitter (ABV 4%) BITTER
Sunshine Reggae (ABV 4.2%) PALE
Free Style (ABV 4.5%) GOLD
Twist & Stout (ABV 4.5%) STOUT
Hop Culture (ABV 5%) GOLD

Frome SIBA

Unit L13, Marshall Way, Commerce Park, Frome, BA11 2FB
☎ (01373) 467766 ⊕ fromebrewingcompany.com

⊗ Formerly Milk Street Brewery, the business changed its name in 2018. The brewery was established in 1999 behind the Griffin pub, Frome, before moving to an industrial unit on the edge of town in 2016, and increasing its capacity to 60 barrels. Beer is supplied direct to local outlets and wholesalers are used to distribute further afield. !! ◆

Funky Monkey (ABV 4%) BITTER
Ra (ABV 4.1%) GOLD
The Usual (ABV 4.4%) BITTER
Rounded ale with malty biscuit, caramel and hedgerow fruit evident in aroma and taste, all lingering into the balanced ending.
Zig-Zag Stout (ABV 4.5%) STOUT
Gulp IPA (ABV 4.8%) BITTER
Beer (ABV 5%) BLOND
Galaxy Australian Pale Ale (ABV 5.2%) PALE

Gert Lush

Hurn Farm Buildings, Ashmore Drove, Wells, BA5 1NS
☎ 07476 662948 ⊕ gertlushbeer.co.uk

Gert Lush is a craft brewery situated near Wells on the Somerset Levels. All beers are brewed using organic malt, hops, carefully-cultured yeasts and spring water and are suitable for vegans. Most are also gluten-free. No real ale. **GF V**

Glastonbury

Park Corner Farm, Glastonbury, BA6 8JY
☎ **(01458) 830750** ⊕ **glastonburyales.com**

Established in 2002 as Glastonbury Ales on a five-barrel plant, it changed ownership and moved to Somerton, increasing capacity to a 20-barrel plant. Cider is also produced. In 2019 it relocated to Glastonbury. All cask-conditioned beers are brewed at Parkway Brewing Co Ltd.

Golden River (NEW)

160 Coronation Avenue, Bath, BA2 2JR

A nanobrewery with a 25-litre brew length established in 2022 and launched at Bath Beer Festival in early 2023. Beer is supplied in 20-litre bag in box.

Nuttycombe SIBA

Ford Road, Wiveliscombe, TA4 2RE
☎ **(01823) 802400** ⊕ **nuttycombebrewery.co.uk**

Cotleigh Brewery closed in 2021 and was purchaed by a well-respected and long-established local publican, Ross Nuttycombe, in 2022. Production of its own core range of beers commenced that year. At the end of 2022 it purchased the rights to brew the former Cotleigh beers, followed in 2023 by the rights to also brew the former RCH/Pitchfork brands, all to the original recipes. ♦

Cheers! (ABV 3.7%) BITTER
Just One More! (ABV 4%) BITTER
Doonicans (ABV 4.2%) PALE

Parkway

Unit 11, Wessex Park, Somerton Business Park, Somerton, TA11 6SB
☎ **(01458) 897240** ⊕ **parkwaybrewing.co.uk**

Parkway began its journey into brewing in 2018, having purchased the former Glastonbury Ales plant and equipment. Although located in the small market town of Somerton, Parkway is named after a road in North London's Camden Town. The brewery also contract brew for others under license. **LIVE**

Giggle & Titter (ABV 3.8%) BITTER
Cheeky Monkey (ABV 4%) BLOND
Norwegian Blue (ABV 4.2%) BITTER

Contract brewed for Glastonbury Brewery:
Mystery Tor (ABV 3.8%) BITTER
Golden bitter with floral hop and fruit on the nose and palate, sweetness giving way to bitter hop finish. Full-bodied.
Lady of the Lake (ABV 4.2%) BITTER
Full-bodied amber best bitter with hops balanced by fruity malt flavour and a hint of vanilla. Clean, bitter hop aftertaste.
Love Monkey (ABV 4.2%) GOLD
Black As Yer 'At (ABV 4.3%) STOUT
Hedge Monkey (ABV 4.6%) BITTER
Golden Chalice (ABV 4.8%) GOLD
Thriller Cappuccino Porter (ABV 5%) SPECIALITY

Contract brewed for Tanners Ales:

> There can't be a good living where there is not good drinking. **Benjamin Franklin**

Box of Frogs (ABV 4%) GOLD

Pinkers

148, Quantock Road, Weston-Super-Mare, BS23 4DP
☎ **07775 746300** ⊕ **pinkerscraftbrewery.co.uk**

Small-batch microbrewery brewing all grain craft beers using fresh ingredients from British suppliers.

Portishead

▤ Unit 3, The Precinct, Portishead, BS20 6AH
☎ **07526 636167** ⊕ **portisheadbrewing.com**

Brewing started in 2018 before relocating the following year into its permanent home in Portishead town centre. In 2020, it expanded into the adjacent unit. It continues to supply a small number of local businesses. Around ten beers are regularly brewed, ranging from lagers to stouts, available as draught keg and bottle-conditioned. The majority of the beer is sold through the brewpub and also online sales. Brewing equipment is visible from the brewpub. Guest beers and food available. ⬛ ♦ **LIVE**

Quantock SIBA

Westridge Way, Broadgauge Business Park, Bishops Lydeard, TA4 3RU
☎ **(01823) 433812** ⊕ **quantockbrewery.co.uk**

⊗ Quantock is a family-run brewery that started trading in Wellington in 2007 on an eight-barrel plant. It has since expanded and moved to its current location in 2015. The brewery supplies beer to outlets throughout the South West, and further afield via wholesalers. The taproom and shop are open five days and three evenings a week, with the former regularly playing host to live bands and comedy nights. An annual beer festival is held in July. ⬛ ♦ V♦

QPA (ABV 4%) PALE
Wills Neck (ABV 4.3%) GOLD
Stout (ABV 4.5%) STOUT
Plastered Pheasant (ABV 4.8%) PORTER
Titanium (ABV 5.1%) PALE

Ralph's Ruin

▤ Royal Oak, Lower Bristol Road, Bath, BA2 3BW
☎ **(01225) 481409** ⊕ **ralphsruin.co.uk**

Brewing commenced in 2017 using a two-barrel plant in the old kitchen of the Royal Oak. Beer is only available in the pub. ♦

Stowey

Old Cider House, 25 Castle Street, Nether Stowey, TA5 1LN
☎ **(01278) 732228** ⊕ **stoweybrewery.co.uk**

Somerset's smallest brewery was established in 2006, primarily to supply the owners' guesthouse and to provide beer to participants at events run from the accommodation. The small quantities of beer produced are also supplied to the George, Nether Stowey. ‼♦

Tapstone

11 Bartlett Park, Millfield, Chard, TA20 2BB
☎ **(01460) 929156** ⊕ **tapstone.co.uk**

⊗ Founded in 2015, the brewery was custom built around a brewing process that preserves delicate hop oils – making beers with a saturated hop flavour. It is growing its own hops two miles from the brewery. There

is a small onsite taproom. All beers are unfined and hazy.
‼ 🍺 V ✦

Twisted Oak SIBA

Yeowood Farm, Iwood Lane, Wrington, BS40 5NU
☎ (01934) 310515 ⊕ twistedoakbrewery.co.uk

⊗ Twisted Oak began brewing in 2012 using a five-barrel plant, crafting small batches of unique ales. It is situated in a former agricultural building on a working farm in the North Somerset countryside. Beer is available in several local outlets. ◆LIVE

Fallen Tree (ABV 3.8%) BITTER
Superb bittersweet session bitter. Aroma and flavour of hops and ripe fruit. Complex and satisfying bitter astringent finish.

Crack Gold (ABV 4%) BITTER
A balanced, golden-coloured ale, with some light malt, hop bitterness and slightly sweet orange undertones and a lingering bittersweet aftertaste.

Wild Wood (ABV 4%) BITTER
Little aroma. Very smooth with flavours of hops and fruit and a little malt. Minimal aftertaste.

Crack Hops (ABV 4.2%) PALE
Hops on the nose, pale malt with fruity orange and grapefruit hints on the palate leaving a balanced bittersweet aftertaste.

Old Barn (ABV 4.5%) RED
Fruity red ale. Well-balanced flavour with a very long bitter finish.

Spun Gold (ABV 4.5%) GOLD
Classic golden ale with a soft mouthfeel. Spicy notes to the fruity malt aroma and flavour. Hops in the aroma develop into a bitter finish.

Leveret (ABV 4.6%) BITTER
Amber best bitter with light citrus aroma. Initial pale malt flavours combine with hoppy bitterness that lingers in the aftertaste.

Solstice (ABV 4.7%) BITTER
Nicely-balanced ale with English hop bitterness and impressions of dark fruit overlaid on a rich and smooth malty background.

Sheriff Fatman (ABV 5%) GOLD
Amber-coloured ale with hops dominant on both the nose and the slightly citrus palate, also in the bitter finish.

Slippery Slope (ABV 5.3%) PORTER
Rich velvety porter with roasted malt, chocolate, coffee, vanilla, dark berries and gentle hop bitterness all combining on the palate.

Ghost Town (ABV 5.7%) STOUT

Verse

🏠 1a Piccadilly Place, London Road, Bath, BA1 6PL

Verse Brewing began production in 2021 and is based in the Chapter One pub. However, brewing is currently suspended. ✦

Windy

🏠 Volunteer Inn, New Road, Seavington St Michael, TA19 0QE
☎ (01460) 240126 ⊕ thevolly.co.uk

The brewery was established at the Volunteer Inn in 2011 using a four-barrel plant. The name stems from the time when alterations were carried out to the back of the pub and the workmen suffered extremes of varying weather conditions. All beers are named with a weather theme. ‼ ✦

Wookey

9 Sadler Street, Wells, BA5 2RR ☎ 07487 352280

Office: High Street, Wookey, BA5 1JZ
⊕ wookeyale.co.uk

Wookey Brewing was established in 2020 by Samuel and Simon to create a local beer for the famous village of Wookey Hole. It is their long term aim to produce the beer in a new brewery in the Wookey area. A number of trade outlets are supplied in the South West. 🍺✦

Arthur's Point (ABV 4%) BITTER
Light roast aroma, hop and dark chocolate bitterness with sweet plums on the palate, short liquorice and sherbert finish.

Halloween Rift (ABV 4%) PALE

Witch Way Home (ABV 4%) PALE
Hop-forward aroma, refreshing citrus and tropical fruit flavours on a light malt background before a lingering dry finish.

Autumn Gail (ABV 4.2%) BITTER
Sweetish malt nose, balanced flavours of hop bitterness with caramel and banana esters with some peppery spice in the aftertaste.

Deer Leap (ABV 4.4%) GOLD

Yonder SIBA

The Workshop, Rookery Farm, Binegar, Radstock, BA3 4UL
☎ (01749) 681378 ⊕ brewyonder.co.uk

A farmhouse-style brewery founded by Stuart Winstone and Jasper Tupman, formally of Wild Beer fame, in 2018. Yonder focuses on wild yeasts, foraged ingredients and barrel-ageing. All ingredients are sourced locally, within about 40 minutes of the brewery. ✦

Learned drinker

He was a learned man, of immense reading, but is much blamed for his unfaithfull quotations. His manner of studie was thus, he wore a long quilt cap, which came two or rather three inches at least over his eies, which served him as an umbrella to defend his eies from the light. About every three houres his man was to bring him a roll and a pot of ale to refocillate (refresh) his wasted spirits so he studied, and dranke, and munched some bread and this maintained him till night, and then he made a good supper.

An Oxford man, William Prynne (1600-69), as described by John Aubrey in Brief Lives, ed. John Buchanan-Brown, 2000

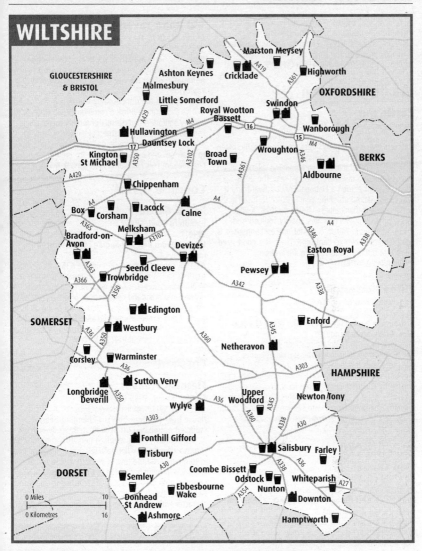

WILTSHIRE

Aldbourne

Crown ✓
The Square, SN8 2DU
☎ (01672) 540214 ⊕ thecrownaldbourne.co.uk
Sharp's Doom Bar; Timothy Taylor Landlord; 2 changing beers (sourced nationally) Ⓗ
A friendly pub that gets busy at weekends, the Crown has a Dalek outside and a Tardis waste bin just down the road, both references to the Dr Who episode shot in the village. Inside, the main bar has a welcoming fire in winter. There is another tiny bar to the right and a restaurant behind. There are five en-suite rooms, making it an excellent place to stay when visiting the nearby ancient sites and the Ridgeway.
⊛⇦ℐ◖ ⚐ ♣🚪(46,48) ❁ 🛜 ♫

Ashton Keynes

White Hart Ⓛ ✓
High Road, SN6 6NX
☎ (01285) 861247 ⊕ thewhitehartashtonkeynes.com

Ramsbury Gold; St Austell Tribute; 2 changing beers (sourced nationally) Ⓗ
A popular community pub in the Cotswold Water Park Area of Ashton Keynes. The interior has three distinct areas: a small bar with games and television, the main bar area and the restaurant. There is a function room at the back. There are four real ales with two of them constantly changing guests. The good-quality food uses locally sourced ingredients. Outside there is a secluded garden at the back and one of the four village crosses at the front. ⊛⊛◖♣P🚪(93A)❁🛜♫

Box

Quarrymans Arms Ⓛ ✓
Box Hill, SN13 8HN (.)
☎ (01225) 743569
Butcombe Original, Gold; 2 changing beers (sourced regionally; often Butcombe) Ⓗ
A Butcombe brewery pub in a hamlet off the A4 between Box and Corsham. With over 250 years of history and views over the Bybrook valley towards Bath, it is popular

with locals and visitors. A high-quality, varied menu is offered in the restaurant, bar and garden. There is a car park, but disabled access is limited, although assistance is happily provided. The steep walk up from the bus stop is well worth it. ❤️🏨🍴◗🅿🚌(X31)🐾🛜

Bradford-on-Avon

Castle Inn
Mount Pleasant, BA15 1SJ
☎ (01225) 309317 ⊕ thecastleinnboa.co.uk
Palmers IPA; 3 changing beers (sourced locally; often Frome, Otter, Three Daggers) Ⓗ
A popular, comfortable pub, commanding splendid views across the town towards Salisbury Plain. The 2008 refurbishment earned a National CAMRA award and it was local CAMRA Pub of the Year in 2017. It closed in the pandemic, but thankfully reopened in 2021. A wide range of hand-pulled real ales, mainly sourced from microbreweries in Wiltshire, Bristol, and east Somerset, is complemented by excellent food. There is a good-sized garden at the front and children are welcome.
❤️🏨🍴◗♿☗🅿🚌(D1)🐾🛜

Three Horseshoes
55 Frome Road, BA15 1LA
☎ (01225) 865876
3 changing beers (sourced locally; often Cheddar Ales, Plain, Stonehenge) Ⓗ
The Horseshoes is a nice old coaching inn at the edge of the town centre next to the rail station. It comes complete with the old wooden door where the horses went through to a yard. At the bar there are usually three constantly changing beers, often local. Live bands play on Friday, Saturday, and Sunday nights. At the back there is a small garden/terrace with seating. Parking is at the rear and a bit limited. 🏨≉♣🅿🚌(D1)🛜♫

Broad Town

Hop Chapel Ⓛ
29 Broad Town Road, SN4 7RB
☎ 07889 078648 ⊕ broadtownbrewery.co.uk
Broadtown Best Bitter, Fettler's Finest; 2 changing beers (often Broadtown) Ⓗ
Originally the site of the Broadtown microbrewery (the brewery has now scaled up and moved to Calne), the Hop Chapel is themed as a monastic style taproom, beautifully completed with ornate reclaimed wood, vintage glass panelling, stained-glass windows and a pipe organ. The iconic alpacas roam outside in the field. Events and music festivals are held throughout the year, under a tent set up in the garden. ❤️🏨♿🅿🐾♫

Chippenham

Flying Monk
6 Market Place, SN15 3HD
☎ (01249) 460662
North Cotswold Windrush Ale; 4 changing beers (sourced nationally; often North Cotswold, Tollgate) Ⓗ
Situated beside the historic Buttercross, the pub offers Belgian and craft beers and three draught ciders in addition to the cask ale. The main bar is open plan with a short flight of stairs up to a small lounge. There are periodic live music and other performances and a twice-monthly meat raffle. The annual Chippenham Folk Festival at the end of May has performances outside the pub. Not normally open on Sunday evenings.
≉●🚌🐾🛜♫

Old Road Tavern ✅
Old Road, SN15 1JA
☎ (01249) 247080
Bath Ales Gem; Marston's 61 Deep; Stonehenge Danish Dynamite; 3 changing beers (sourced nationally; often Harvey's, Hop Union, Timothy Taylor) Ⓗ
Well-kept ales are dispensed by welcoming staff at this 140-year old Grade II-listed community pub close to the railway station. A diverse mix of locals enjoys conversation. There is a large garden with plenty of seating and a cabin with heated seats. The pub is home to local folk music and is a venue for the annual Chippenham Folk Festival in May. ❤️🏨≉♣🚌🐾🛜♫

Coombe Bissett

Fox & Goose ♈ Ⓛ
Blandford Road, SP5 4LE
☎ (01722) 718437 ⊕ foxandgoose-coombebissett.co.uk
Sharp's Doom Bar; 2 changing beers (sourced nationally) Ⓗ
An 18th-century coaching inn on the A354, three miles south of Salisbury, this popular community pub has a local village clientele and a welcoming atmosphere. Divided into a bar and restaurant, it offers an extensive menu with changing specials. Outside there are pleasant gardens and a covered smoking area. Guest ales are from local and national breweries. Local CAMRA Rural Pub of the Year 2023. ❤️🏨◗🅿🚌(20,29)🐾🛜

Corsham

Flemish Weaver
63 High Street, SN13 0EZ
☎ (01249) 591959 ⊕ flemishweaver.co.uk
House beer (by Ramsbury); 3 changing beers (sourced nationally; often St Austell, Wadworth) Ⓗ
A 17th-century ale house which gets its name from the Flemish weavers who fled religious persecution and who in turn enhanced the town's woollen industry. This charming building is situated in the oldest part of Corsham near Corsham Court. Refurbished in 2022, the Flemish Weaver is an intriguing yet traditional pub full of character with many nooks and crannies. They rightly

REAL ALE BREWERIES

Arkell's Swindon
Broadtown 🔨 Calne
Dark Revolution 🔨 Salisbury
Downton 🔨 Downton
Drink Valley 🍺 Swindon
Flying Monk 🔨 Hullavington
Gritchie 🔨 Ashmore
Hop Back Downton
Hop Kettle 🔨 Cricklade / Swindon
Kettlesmith 🔨 Bradford-On-Avon
Plain 🔨 Sutton Veny
Ramsbury Aldbourne
Rude Giant Wylye (NEW)
Rusty Garage 🔨 Swindon
Shed Ales Pewsey (brewing suspended)
Stealth 🔨 Melksham
Stone Daisy 🔨 Fonthill Gifford
Stonehenge Netheravon
Three Daggers Edington
True Story 🔨 Westbury (NEW)
Twisted Westbury
Wadworth 🔨 Devizes
Wessex Longbridge Deverill
World's End 🍺 Pewsey

pride themselves on the quality of their food and beer. The garden area will be reinstated for 2024 following building work. 🐕🌓♣🖥😺🛜

Three Brewers
51 Priory Street, SN13 0AS
☎ (01249) 701733 ● threebrewerscorsham.co.uk
Draught Bass; 2 changing beers (sourced nationally) 🅷
Traditional, welcoming, community pub set in the heart of Corsham, serving a large wine and gin range, bar snacks, coffee and cake as well as real ale. The two good-sized rooms – a bar and a snug – have tables and seating. A games room with a skittle alley, pool table, darts and board games also serves as a meeting room. There is a beer garden at the rear. High-quality hot and cold snacks are sold at all times.
Q🐕😺♣P🖥(X31) 😺🛜♪

Corsley

Cross Keys Inn
Lye's Green, BA12 7PB
☎ (01373) 832406 ● crosskeyscorsley.co.uk
Butcombe Original; Fuller's London Pride; 1 changing beer (sourced locally; often Frome, Plain) 🅿
This rural gem has a large open fire and a warm welcoming atmosphere. In 2016 the pub was taken over by a village consortium. A good selection of guest ales, mainly sourced from local breweries, is available, along with excellent bar food and restaurant meals. The pub is in an excellent walking area on the Somerset border, close to Longleat House and its safari park.
🐕😺🌓🅰♣P😺🛜

Cricklade

Red Lion 🅻
74 High Street, SN6 6DD
☎ (01793) 750776 ● theredlioncricklade.co.uk
Hop Kettle Cricklade Ordinary Bitter, North Wall; St Austell Tribute, Proper Job; 5 changing beers (sourced nationally; often Hop Kettle, St Austell, Timothy Taylor) 🅷
A friendly, popular and comfortable pub which features part of the old Saxon town wall in the building. There is a large garden where beer festivals are held, and covered seating, next to the original Hop Kettle microbrewery. There are nine real ales on offer split between Hop Kettle, St Austell, and guests from elsewhere. Excellent food is served and there are five B&B rooms.
Q🐕😺🚐🌓●🖥😺🛜

Dauntsey Lock

Peterborough Arms 🅻
SN15 4HD
☎ (01249) 247833 ● peterborougharms.com
Flying Monk Habit; 1 changing beer (sourced regionally) 🅷
Saved by the Wilts & Berks Canal Trust and restored by their volunteers, the pub sits alongside the old canal. It offers real ales and good pub food and is home to both skittles and darts teams. There is a log-burner for the winter and a beer garden for summer. Note that the road down Lyneham Bank is likely to be closed well into 2024 but the road from the west (Chippenham and M4) is open. Former winner of a CAMRA Design Award.
Q🐕😺🌓🅶♣🅰♣●P😺🛜

Devizes

British Lion ✅
9 Estcourt Street, SN10 1LQ (on A361 opp Kwik Fit)
☎ (01380) 720665 ● britishliondevizes.co.uk
4 changing beers (sourced nationally; often Palmers, Plain, Stonehenge) 🅷
The British has been ever-present in the Guide for over 28 years. An unpretentious free house with wooden floors, cosy settles and an eclectic group of talkative regulars, it is an essential port of call in town. There are four handpumps and the beers change frequently throughout the week. Time it right and you can savour eight different real ales. The knowledgeable landlord is always pleased to offer his advice. Not to be missed.
😺●P🖥🖥(49) 🛜

Snuffbox
2-3 Snuff Street, SN10 1DU
● thesnuffbox.co.uk
Changing beers 🅺
Popular craft ale bar serving a choice of up to five bag in box real ciders, usually from SeaCider or Snailsbank. There is no cask ale but normally a choice of nine changing beers which are a mix of keg and membrane keg and cover a range of styles from pales to sours and stouts – often an imperial stout. There is a wide range of canned and bottled craft beers, gins and wine. ●🖥😺🛜

Southgate Inn
Potterne Road, SN10 5BY
☎ (01380) 722872
Hop Back GFB, Fuggle Stone, Crop Circle, Entire Stout, Summer Lightning; 1 changing beer 🅶
It is well worth the five-minute walk from the town centre for the welcome at this cosy, friendly pub with three separate bar areas, lots of nooks and crannies and a large courtyard. Still ciders and perry accompany the wide selection of ales from Hop Back which can vary and may include a guest from Downton. There is live music throughout the weekend, an acoustic jam session every Wednesday, and a Ukelele group on Friday afternoons. Well-behaved dogs are positively encouraged.
🐕😺♣●P🖥(2,210) 😺🛜♪

White Bear ✅
33 Monday Market Street, SN10 1DN
☎ (01380) 727588 ● whitebeardevizes.co.uk
Wadworth Henry's IPA; 5 changing beers (sourced nationally) 🅷
Recently refurbished throughout, this old coaching inn with original beams and open fires dates from the 1500s. It has six pumps serving real ales, of which up to two are Wadworth – usually IPA and a seasonal/varying offering, plus up to four other guest ales. A dark beer is usually available plus a still cider. Food is served all week and dogs are welcome. The pub does not have a car park, but there is plenty of parking nearby. 🚐🌓●🖥😺🛜

Donhead St Andrew

Forester 🅻
Lower Street, SP7 9EE ST917249
☎ (01747) 828068 ● theforesterdonheadstandrew.co.uk
Flack Manor Double Drop; 1 changing beer (sourced locally; often Gritchie) 🅷
This 17th-century thatched pub in the centre of this quiet village was built from stone from the nearby Wardour Castle. There are two beers from local breweries, usually Flack Manor and Gritchie. The pub is popular with walkers and offers a range of home-cooked and flexible meal options from lunchtime into the evening.
Q🐕😺🚐🌓●P😺🛜

Easton Royal

Bruce Arms ★ 🅛
Easton Road, SN9 5LR
☎ (01672) 810216 ⊕ brucearms.co.uk
Butcombe Original; St Austell Tribute; 2 changing beers (sourced regionally; often Ramsbury) Ⓗ
This mid-19th-century local has been identified by CAMRA as having a nationally important historic pub interior. There is a small cosy bar with furniture that probably goes back to the 1850s and a small lounge with easy chairs and piano. The four real ales include two changing guests, normally from local breweries. The pub exists in splendid isolation, so its campsite with full facilities is an asset that makes it a good venue for meetings and rallies. Food and opening times vary seasonally. Q➰🕭🌠👜Å♣P🐾❄️

Ebbesbourne Wake

Horseshoe
The Cross, SP5 5JF
☎ (01722) 780474 ⊕ thehorseshoe-inn.co.uk
Bowman Swift One; Gritchie English Lore; 2 changing beers (sourced locally; often Brew Shack) Ⓖ
Unspoilt 18th-century inn in a remote rural setting at the foot of an ox drove, run by the same family for 52 years and by the present landlord for 36. There are two small bars displaying an impressive collection of old farm implements and a pleasant garden. The original serving hatch just inside the front door is still in use. Good local food is available Wednesday to Sunday. Real cider is usually available. Local CAMRA Rural Pub of the Year 2019-2022. Q➰🕭🌠👜Å👜P🚫(29)🐾

Edington

Three Daggers
Westbury Road, BA13 4PG
☎ (01380) 830940 ⊕ threedaggers.co.uk
Three Daggers Daggers Blonde, Daggers Ale, Daggers Edge; 1 changing beer Ⓗ
Refurbished village pub with its own on-site brewery, offering a range of beers that can vary depending on the time of year. The pub has a main bar with three distinct drinking areas which lead into a seating area and a dining room. Two mirrors hide TV screens that are occasionally used for sporting events. At the rear there is a lovely garden. Excellent accommodation is available. Q➰🕭🌭🌠👜P🚫❄️

Enford

Swan 🅛 ✅
Long Street, SN9 6DD
☎ (01980) 670338 ⊕ theswanenford.co.uk
4 changing beers (sourced locally; often Plain, Stonehenge, Twisted) Ⓗ
16th-century Grade II-listed pub purchased by villagers for the community in 1998. It is one of only a handful of pubs in the country with the inn sign hanging on a gantry over the road. Old beams, an inglenook fireplace with a roaring wood fire in winter, sloping walls and quiet nooks and crannies add to its character. Flights of three third-pints help you sample a selection of mainly local ales. Their good food menu features changing specials. ➰🌠👜♣👜P🚫(X5) 🐾❄️

Farley

Hook & Glove
The Street, SP5 1AB

☎ (01722) 712247 ⊕ thehookandglove.co.uk
Greene King Abbot; 1 changing beer (sourced locally) Ⓗ
Five miles east of Salisbury, the pub lies in the Clarendon forest, which is excellent for walking. There is a snug bar and a larger bar/restaurant area – both have wood fires during the winter. The pub is well known for its food – meals are cooked fresh using locally sourced produce. Outside is a large fenced area which is safe for children. Well-behaved dogs on leads are welcome. Two pétanque terrains are available during the summer months and are free to book. Q➰🕭🌠👜👜P🐾❄️

Hamptworth

Cuckoo Inn
SP5 2DU
☎ (01794) 338461
Hop Back Summer Lightning; Palmers Dorset Gold; house beer (by Hop Back); 3 changing beers (sourced regionally) Ⓖ
Friendly real ale pub in the Wiltshire countryside. All ales are served straight from the cask. The main room is square, encouraging people to talk, and there are three further rooms to sit in. A bar operates in the large, dog-friendly garden during summer months. Food comprises pies, jackets, rolls, soups and other warming bites with a fish & chip van present on Fridays. Beer festivals with music are held in May and September. Q➰🕭🌠👜Å♣👜P🐾❄️🎵

Highworth

Rose & Crown
19 The Green, SN6 7DB
☎ (01793) 764699
Sharp's Doom Bar, Sea Fury; 3 changing beers (sourced nationally; often Timothy Taylor, Young's) Ⓗ
This is one of the oldest pubs in Highworth. Friendly staff help make it popular with locals. Inside features wooden beams decorated with hops, and old advertising signs on the walls. There are five handpumps serving three changing ales and two Sharp's regulars. The lunch menu is good quality and value. Occasional folk sessions are hosted on a Saturday evening. At the back there is a large garden with a boules pitch and a pirate ship for the kids. ➰🌠👜♣P🚫(7,77)🐾❄️🎵

Kington St Michael

Jolly Huntsman 🅛
SN14 6JB
☎ (01249) 750305 ⊕ jollyhuntsman.com
2 changing beers (sourced locally) Ⓗ
You can be sure of a friendly welcome at this free house on the high street in the centre of the village. The 18th-century building was formerly the White Horse brewery, and one of the wells used for brewing still exists. There is an open log fire in winter. As well as the ales, two regional draught ciders are often available. It has an excellent menu but check limited opening and food hours before traveling. Q➰🌭🌠👜P🚫🚌(X44)🐾❄️

Lacock

Bell Inn 🅛
The Wharf, SN15 2PJ
☎ (01249) 730308 ⊕ thebellatlacock.co.uk
House beer (by Hop Union); 3 changing beers (sourced regionally; often Hop Union, Palmers) Ⓗ
A popular free house outside Lacock village, to the south-east towards Bowden Hill. The friendly and welcoming

staff and a good and varied food menu complement the house and guest ales. The pub has extensive seating indoors and outdoors including a barn with dining tables and a comfortable drinking area around a wood-burner. Two beer festivals are held each year. It is an ideal finishing point for walks around Bewley Common and Bowden Hill. Q✿✿◑♣P🖟🛇🌐☎

Little Somerford

Somerford Arms ✔
The Hill, SN15 5JP
☎ (01666) 826535 🌐 somerfordarms.com
Ramsbury Farmer's Best; Sharp's Doom Bar; 2 changing beers (sourced locally) ⑭
At the foot of the Cotswolds, this is a warm and welcoming family-run free house with a large room and dining area. There is a small separate bar at the back and a conservatory and covered outdoor seating. Three or four ales are generally available and high-quality food with seasonal menus including vegan, gluten free and dairy-free options. It is advisable to book for meals via the website. Takeaway food is available Monday to Saturday. ✿✿◑&P🖟(91)🛇♪

Malmesbury

Whole Hog ⓛ
8 Market Cross, SN16 9AS
☎ (01666) 825845 🌐 wholehogmalmesbury.co.uk
Ramsbury Farmer's Best; Stonehenge Pigswill; Wadworth 6X; Young's London Original; 1 changing beer (sourced regionally) ⑭
Wood-panelled bar and dining establishment overlooking the historic market cross in the town centre. To the rear is the partially ruined 12th-century abbey where the monk Elmer attempted flight from the roof with wings he had made. Wholesome locally sourced food is served in the separate dining room while the bar is for drinking, conversation and observing everyday life in this busy hilltop town. A pub central to the community, it offers a relaxed and welcoming atmosphere for locals and visitors alike. Q✿✿◑♠🖟🛇

Marston Meysey

Old Spotted Cow
SN6 6LQ
☎ (01285) 810264 🌐 theoldspottedcow.com
3 changing beers (sourced regionally; often Butcombe, Prescott, St Austell) ⑭
With large gardens and a cosy interior with log fires and beamed ceilings, this traditional Cotswold-stone pub is popular with locals and visitors. In the bar there are three real ale handpumps. Food is only available on certain days – check the website. The Thames Path is nearby, making the pub attractive to hikers, and the source of the River Thames is less than 20 miles away. There is accommodation in an on-site Airbnb.
✿✿◑◑&♣P🛇🌐

Melksham

Hiding Place Micropub
15 High Street, SN12 6JY
☎ (01225) 899022 🌐 thehidingplace.co.uk
4 changing beers (sourced locally; often Stealth) ⑭
Two-storey micropub with tables downstairs in a bright and welcoming open-plan area, and comfortable sofas upstairs. It is run in conjunction with the nearby Stealth brewery whose beers are found on the bar, as well as guest beers from brewery swaps. Real cider is served by gravity from a chilled cellar directly behind the bar. There are also keg beers, wines, spirits and high quality small plate food. Payment is by card only. Q✿✿♠🖟🛇🌐

Market Tavern
18 Market Place, SN12 6EX
☎ (01225) 587396 🌐 themelkshammarkettavern.co.uk
House beer (by Stealth); 5 changing beers (sourced locally; often Frome, Ramsbury, Twisted) ⑭
Reopened in 2021 following a change of ownership and a major refurbishment in a traditional tavern style. The quality food, the array of frequently changing ales, and the friendly staff make it well worth a visit. The attractive building, with parts dating from the 18th century, has many booths, a quirky layout and decor, and three log-burners. Hops, hanging from the ceiling, are a major feature, along with comfortable chairs and seating. Outside there is a lovely courtyard. ✿✿◑&♣🖟🛇♪

Newton Tony

Malet Arms ⓛ
SP4 0HF
☎ (01980) 629279 🌐 maletarms.co.uk
4 changing beers (sourced locally) ⑭
Charming and historic pub, with a restaurant extension, in the conservation area of the village and with the river Bourne flowing past in winter. The window in the larger bar is reputed to come from a galleon. Run by the same family for 24 years, the landlord is as enthusiastic and proud of his high-quality food as he is of his ales. Four mainly local beers change weekly and Old Rosie cider is served. The pub welcomes walkers and dogs.
Q✿✿◑P🖟🛇

Nunton

Radnor Arms ⓛ
SP5 4HS
☎ (01722) 329722 🌐 theradnor.com
Exmoor Gold; 3 changing beers (sourced locally) ⑭
A popular, spacious pub dating from 1853 and named after the local landowner. The landlady and her staff offer a warm welcome to all, including families, children and dogs. Three dining areas adjoin the main bar and an extensive and regularly changing menu is provided to suit all tastes. The large open garden extends to the river and has a secure children's playground. The pub hosts an annual summer festival. Q✿✿◑&P🖟(44)🛇🌐

Odstock

Yew Tree Inn ✔
Whitsbury Road, SP5 4JE
☎ (01722) 329786 🌐 yewtreeinnodstock.com
Timothy Taylor Landlord; 2 changing beers (often Ringwood) ⑭
This black-and-white-timbered inn with thatched roof and heavily beamed interior is the quintessential English country pub. A genuinely warm welcome greets visitors. The cosy restaurant and bar share a large inglenook fire. The large garden provides a tranquil eating and drinking area in the summer and has a nice decked area with good displays of hanging baskets. Q✿✿◑P🖟(44)

Pewsey

Coopers Arms ⓛ
37-39 Ball Road, SN9 5BL
☎ (01672) 562495
5 changing beers (sourced nationally; often Ramsbury, St Austell, Stonehenge) ⑭

It is worth seeking out this down-to-earth thatched pub on the eastern edge of Pewsey. It has an historic interior with an open-plan bar and two side rooms. In the winter there is a warming fire. Five forever changing real ales are served, often sourced regionally. There is no regular food, but snacks are available plus the odd pop-up kitchen. Happy hour is every weekday night 5-7pm. Accommodation is available with holiday cottages in a separate block at the back. Q☰🕏⛺♿🌳♣♠P🚃(X5)🏵️🐕☀🎵

Royal Wootton Bassett

Five Bells 🍸 🅛 ✅

Wood Street, SN4 7BD

☎ (01793) 849422

7 changing beers (sourced nationally; often Bristol Beer Factory, Hop Kettle Swindon, St Austell) 🅷

Dating from before 1841, this busy and cosy traditional thatched local free house has a beamed ceiling and open fires. The landlord and landlady have been running it for nearly 25 years. The bar has seven handpumps for changing real ales and one for Old Rosie cider. Food is served every lunchtime and most evenings (not Sun or Mon). The pub has darts and crib teams. Ever-present in the Guide since 2002 and a regular local CAMRA Pub of the Year winner. 🏵️🕏♣P🚃(55,31)🐕☀

Salisbury

Deacons 🅛

118 Fisherton Street, SP2 7QT

☎ (01722) 322866 🌐 deaconssalisbury.com

2 changing beers (often Rude Giant) 🅷

A friendly, independently-owned free house, a stone's throw from Salisbury railway station and a short walk from the cathedral. A small front bar leads up a couple of stairs to a larger back room. Real ales always feature something from Rude Giant brewery, accompanied by up to two from elsewhere. The pub hosts occasional live music, quiz nights and beer festivals. A former local CAMRA Pub of the Year. 🚆♣🚃🐕☀

Duke of York 🍸 🅛

34 York Road, SP2 7AS

☎ 07881 812218

Hop Back GFB; 6 changing beers (sourced locally; often Downton, Stonehenge, Plain) 🅷

A popular free house sporting local beers and two changing traditional ciders. The focus is on the community with an informal Sunday night quiz, whisky club and thriving conversation. The pub is home to the Fisherton History Society and hosts other occasional events. Live music plays every other Saturday. The garden has plenty of tables and a covered area where barbecues are held on summer weekends. Local CAMRA Pub of the Year 2022 and 2023. 🏵️🚆♣♠🚃🐕☀

Haunch of Venison ★ 🅛

1 Minster Street, SP1 1TB

☎ (01722) 411313 🌐 haunchpub.co.uk

Butcombe Original; Stonehenge Danish Dynamite; Wye Valley HPA; 1 changing beer (sourced regionally) 🅷

A fine old Inn, identified by CAMRA as having a nationally important historic interior. The main bar, The Commons, has a rare pewter-topped bar. A tiny second bar features old spirits taps and floor tiles recovered long ago from a refurbishment of the cathedral. Upstairs, the House of Lords area contains the mummified hand of a card cheat. Upstairs again there are two separate dining rooms, one with a fireplace dating back to 1588. 🕏🕏🚆🐕☀

Rai d'Or 🅛

69 Brown Street, SP1 2AS

☎ (01722) 327137 🌐 raidor.co.uk

2 changing beers (sourced locally; often Downton) 🅷

Historic 13th-century city centre free house with a blue plaque commemorating a 14th-century landlady. The open fire, log-burner and low ceilings make for an appealing ambience. Excellent, reasonably priced Thai food is complemented by two ever-changing beers, usually one local. It can be busy at food times. Bar drinkers are always welcome but call ahead if you prefer a table for drinking or eating. A regular in the Guide since 2004. 🕏♣🍴🐕☀

Village Freehouse 🅛

33 Wilton Road, SP2 7EF

☎ (01722) 329707

Downton Quadhop; 2 changing beers (sourced nationally) 🅷

A fully refurbished, lively pub near the railway station. Microbrewery beers come from near and far. There is always at least one dark brew, stout, porter or mild available with customer requests welcome. Teams are fielded in the local crib, cricket and football leagues and two TVs show Sky Sports with the sound off much of the time. Filled rolls are available or you are welcome to bring your own food. Three-time local CAMRA Pub of the Year. 🚆🐕☀

Winchester Gate 🅛

113-117 Rampart Road, SP1 1JA

☎ (01722) 503362 🌐 thewinchestergate.com

4 changing beers (sourced regionally; often Stonehenge, Plain, Hattie Brown's) 🅷

Characterful free house, an inn since the 17th century, which once provided for travellers at the city's east tollgate. Four handpumps offer changing ales alongside two keg craft ales and real ciders from across the country. Beer and cider festivals are held, sometimes in association with a live music event. A small, partially covered garden offers a pleasant area to sit out, particularly during the summer. The pub is renowned for live music every Friday and Saturday, and frequently on Thursdays too. 🏵️♣🚃🐕☀🎵

Wyndham Arms 🅛

27 Estcourt Road, SP1 3AS

☎ (01722) 331026 🌐 hopback.co.uk/pubs/the-wyndham-arms

Hop Back GFB, Citra, Crop Circle, Summer Lightning; 1 changing beer (often Hop Back) 🅷

The birthplace of the Hop Back brewery, the pub is now celebrating 37 consecutive years in the Guide. A traditional ale house, it has a single bar serving Hop Back ales – normally with Taiphoon in summer and Entire Stout alternating with their monthly specials in winter – and a selection of bottled beers and wines. Two small rooms provide quiet spaces and more seating. This is a pub for conversation, good-natured banter and fine ales. A former local CAMRA Pub of the Year. 🕏♣🚃🐕

Seend Cleeve

Brewery Inn

SN12 6PX

☎ (01380) 828463

Butcombe Original; Otter Ale; 1 changing beer (sourced locally; often Plain, Ramsbury, Twisted) 🅷

A traditional rustic country pub close to the Kennet and Avon canal that manages to be exceptionally well run without taking itself too seriously. Welcoming to all, it hosts many events throughout the year, and remains a focus for the community. Inside there is a bar area plus a pool/TV room. The large outside areas contain heated dining pods, decked areas and a large, lawned beer garden. There are always two cask ales, with a third at weekends. Q☺☆❀◑♣P❀❖❄

Semley

Benett Arms
Village Green, SP7 9AS (1 mile E of A350) ST891270
☎ (01747) 830221 ⊕ thebenettarms-semley.co.uk
House beer (by Wriggle Valley); 5 changing beers (sourced locally; often Fine Tuned, Salcombe, Twisted) Ⓗ
A genuine free house sitting by the village green and pond in a quiet village in an area popular with walkers. It has two bars, and a marquee and tables on the green opposite. There are four beers and Laycock cider to choose from. Excellent home-cooked food is served every day. A warm welcome is offered to all, including families and dogs. Three letting rooms and a shepherd's hut are available. Q☺☆❀◑&P❀❄

Swindon

Beehive ✔
55 Prospect Hill, SN1 3JS
☎ (01793) 523187 ⊕ bee-hive.co.uk
House beer (by Greene King); 5 changing beers (sourced regionally; often Greene King, Hardys & Hansons) Ⓗ
This four-room pub retains its quirky charm and layout. It dates from 1871 and is built on a corner on a hill, giving a nearly triangular layout on five different levels. It is a popular live music venue, hosting performances on most Thursday and Friday nights. Pictures and other art are displayed and for sale. The long-standing landlord is proud of its community role, support for local charities and traditional feel. ♣➡❀❄♫

Drink Valley Ⓛ
Unit C Fleet Square, SN1 1RQ
☎ (01793) 692980 ⊕ thedrinkvalley.com
6 changing beers (sourced nationally; often Drink Valley) Ⓗ
Swindon's newest brewpub is, naturally, a free house. It has a smart, modern appearance with an airy, café-style layout inside. There are six handpumps with four serving Drink Valley beers, brewed on the brewery kit visible just behind the bar, and two for guest beers. There are also 12 keg taps for craft beers and ciders. Good-value Indian street food is available Thursday, Friday and Saturday. ☺☆◑&⇌➡(22) ❀❄

Glue Pot
5 Emlyn Square, SN1 5BP
☎ (01793) 497420 ⊕ hopback.co.uk/pubs/the-glue-pot
Downton New Forest Ale; Hop Back Citra, Crop Circle, Entire Stout, Summer Lightning; 2 changing beers (sourced regionally; often Downton, Hop Back) Ⓗ
The Glue Pot is an unspoilt corner pub, part of the historic GWR Railway Village. There are seven Hop Back or Downton real ales including some seasonal ones, and it stocks a wide range of real ciders. A selection of sandwiches, wraps and subs is always available. Monday is Book and Beer club night and there is a quiz on Wednesday evenings. Local CAMRA Cider Pub of the Year 2022. Q❀&⇌♣➡❀

Hop Inn Ⓛ
8 Devizes Road, Old Town, SN1 4BH
☎ (01793) 613005 ⊕ hopinnswindon.co.uk

House beer (by Ramsbury); 7 changing beers (sourced regionally; often Arbor) Ⓗ
Having begun the Devizes Road real ale boom, the Hop Inn moved two doors down from its original location to larger premises. This free house has eight handpumps serving seven forever changing guest ales, including at least one dark beer. Six box ciders are available. The interior is decorated in an eclectic style, including tables and chairs made from reclaimed wood. Local art works are often featured. Interesting, good-value food is available from the kitchen. ☺☆◑➡❀❖❄

Little Hop
7 Devizes Road, Old Town, SN1 4BJ
⊕ littlehop.co.uk
5 changing beers (sourced nationally; often Arbor) Ⓗ
Little sister to the nearby Hop Inn, the Little Hop was Swindon's first micropub and helped launch the real ale revival in Devizes Road. The small, brightly coloured modern pub has five handpumps stocking an ever-changing range of beers. In the corner of the pub there is a well-stocked bottle fridge featuring beers, often from the Bristol area. Local art is often featured on the walls. Q&●➡(9,11) ❀❄

Wyvern Tavern Ⓛ ✔
49-50 Bridge Street, SN1 1BL
☎ (01793) 484924
Butcombe Original; 3 changing beers (sourced nationally; often Arbor, Bristol Beer Factory) Ⓗ
A large town-centre chain pub with large and varied seating areas plus a long bar, all on one level. It has a better-than-average interest in and sale of real ales and features one regular and three changing guest beers. It can be lively, especially later in the week and at weekends. Essentially a sports bar, it has a number of TV screens showing various sports and news during the week. ☺☆◑&⇌♣●➡❀❖❄

Tisbury

Boot Inn Ⓛ
High Street, SP3 6PS
☎ (01747) 870363
3 changing beers (sourced locally) Ⓖ
Fine village free house built of Chilmark stone, licenced since 1768 and run by the same family since 1976. It has a relaxed, friendly atmosphere and offers a cordial welcome to all. Join in the conversation at the bar or find a quiet table at which to enjoy well-kept ales served from casks behind the bar. The beer range often increases at weekends and in summer. Excellent food is served and there is a spacious garden. Q☺☆◑⇌♣●P➡(25,26) ❀❄

Trowbridge

King's Arms
5 Castle Street, BA14 8AN
☎ (01225) 751310 ⊕ thekingsarmstrowbridge.co.uk
Butcombe Original; Sharp's Doom Bar; 2 changing beers (sourced regionally; often Dartmoor, St Austell) Ⓗ
Following an extensive 2010 refurbishment, this town-centre pub reopened as a smart, welcoming free house. A single drinking area served by a central bar has partitions creating a number of separate, snug-like areas. The patio behind the pub, with its listed tree, makes a pleasant spot for an alfresco drink. An interesting and varied food menu is offered. The beer range includes two guests, usually from the larger microbreweries in the West Country. Q☺☆◑▲⇌➡❄

Stallards

15-16 Stallard Street, BA14 9AJ
☎ (01225) 767855 ⊕ thestallards.co.uk
Plain Independence ⊞
Originally built in 1857, the Stallards has a modern, light, welcoming feel. A single bar serves three drinking areas. At weekends live bands play in the lower bar area, while there is comfortable seating next to the fire near the bar. There is a pool table at the back of the pub and a secluded patio area outside. The landlady's two friendly small dogs ensure an enthusiastic welcome.
🏮🏵️&✦🕭🚌🛜🎅♪

Upper Woodford

Bridge Inn

SP4 6NU
☎ (01722) 783203 ⊕ bridgeinn-woodfordvalley.co.uk
St Austell Proper Job; Sharp's Doom Bar; 2 changing beers (sourced nationally) ⊞
Family-run pub in the Woodford Valley with a large, award-winning garden alongside the River Avon. Food is served lunchtimes and evenings with a steak night special on Monday evenings. Two seasonal beers change when the clocks change in March and October. There are a number of footpaths in the area with picturesque views. Cycling along the valley is also very popular.
Q🏵️🕼&P🎅🛜

Wanborough

New Calley Arms ℂ

2 Ham Road, SN4 0DF
☎ (01793) 790615
Sharp's Doom Bar; 3 changing beers (sourced regionally; often Frome, Prescott, Ramsbury) ⊞
Traditional 19th-century pub in the beautiful village of Wanborough that is popular with locals and visitors. The pub has a light and airy feel, with an open fire and a log-burner in use when required. Four real ales are served, three of them changing guests sourced regionally. A proud, family-run business, it serves honest food with the finest ingredients. It is the venue for an annual beer festival which raises funds for the local church.
🚆🏵️🕼&✦P🚌(46A,48A)🎅🛜♪

Warminster

Bath Arms ✔

41 Market Place, BA12 9AZ
☎ (01985) 853920
Greene King Abbot; Ruddles Best Bitter; Sharp's Doom Bar; 2 changing beers (sourced regionally; often Twisted) ⊞
Refurbished and reopened by Wetherspoon in 2014, this Grade II-listed building is one of the town's three remaining 18th-century coaching inns. The beers include the usual Wetherspoon range plus a good selection of guests, many of them from breweries within 30 or so miles of the town. The upper floors of this large, comfortable pub operate as a hotel with 10 rooms. The train station is just five minutes' walk away.
🚆🏵️🏨🕼&✦🚌🛜

Fox & Hounds

6 Deverill Road, BA12 9QP
☎ (01985) 216711
St Austell Tribute; 2 changing beers (sourced locally) ⊞
A friendly two-bar local: the main bar has a pool table and sports TV at the rear, and a quiet snug bar is at the right-hand side of the entrance. There is a large skittle

alley and function room at the back. Guest real ales are usually from local and regional breweries. Ciders are from Rich's, Inch's and Thatchers, with several from Weymouth and sometimes a guest. A local CAMRA multiple award-winning pub including Pub of the Year 2023. Q🏵️&✦🍺P🚌🎅🛜

Westbury

Angel

3 Church Street, BA13 3BY
☎ (01373) 822648
Twisted Pirate; 3 changing beers (sourced locally; often Plain, St Austell, Twisted) ⊞
Recently reopened, this lovely old pub is tucked away in the centre of town. There are up to four beers, normally one from local brewer Twisted, and the others from the south and West Country. A couple of ciders from local suppliers are normally available. It sometimes hosts live music, and there is sport on the TV. There are two rooms offering accommodation. 🏮🏵️🏨✦🍺🚌(D1)🎅🛜♪

Whiteparish

Parish Lantern ℂ

Romsey Road, SP5 2SA
☎ (01794) 884392 ⊕ theparishlanternwhiteparish.co.uk
Hop Back Citra; St Austell Proper Job; Timothy Taylor Landlord; 1 changing beer (sourced locally) ⊞
A welcoming pub run by the same couple since 1991. The single bar has a central fireplace and areas for dining and darts. Guest beers are from Hop Back, Downton or other local breweries. There are family events on bank holidays and occasional beer festivals. Food is served lunchtimes and evenings, including regular themed nights. A spacious garden with play equipment for children leads to a camping area with space for five caravans. Q🚐🏵️🕼▲✦P🚌(X7)🎅🛜

Wroughton

Carters Rest ℂ

57 High Street, SN4 9JU
☎ 07816 134966
Goff's Cheltenham Gold; 6 changing beers (sourced regionally) ⊞
First mentioned in 1671, this popular real ale pub was extensively altered around 1912 to give it its current Victorian appearance. In 2017 a smart new interior was introduced, which retains the two-room feel, with a single shared bar. The current beer range is seven, with eight at the weekend. Ales are mainly from small independent breweries within a 50 mile radius, although occasionally they may be farther afield. Monday is darts night and Thursday poker. Q🚐🏵️&✦P🚌(9,49)🎅🛜

Breweries

Arkell's SIBA IFBB

Kingsdown, Swindon, SN2 7RU
☎ (01793) 823026 ⊕ arkells.com

⊠ 2023 marked the 180th anniversary of Arkell's Brewery, which was established in 1843 by John Arkell. The Arkell family still brew in the original Victorian brewhouse. The brewery owns nearly 100 pubs across Wiltshire, Gloucestershire, Oxfordshire, Berkshire and Hampshire. In 2018 a brewery shop and visitor centre opened onsite. Seasonal beers are brewed frequently, often linked to sporting/national events. ‼🏮♦

Wiltshire Gold (ABV 3.7%) GOLD
3B (ABV 4%) BITTER
A medium brown beer with a strong, sweetish malt/caramel flavour. The hops come through strongly in the aftertaste, which is lingering and dry.
Hoperation IPA (ABV 4.2%) PALE

Broadtown SIBA

Porte Marsh Industrial Estate, 3 Maundrel Road, Calne, SN11 9PU ☎ 07889 078648

Hop Chapel: The Old Coachhouse, 29 Broad Town Road, Broad Town, SN4 7RB
🌐 broadtownbrewery.co.uk

Opened in 2019, Broadtown began brewing in the old coach house of the 19th century Hart Brewery. 118 years on, the village has a brewery again. Broadtown have a range of five core ales and produce an ever-changing list of seasonal and one-off ales. In 2021 the Hop Chapel, a Trappist-themed taproom and beer garden, opened onsite. The brewery is home to three alpacas and a lime green double-decker bus. A second larger site in Calne came on stream in 2022. ♦ LIVE GF V 🌱

Spring Back (ABV 3.8%) GOLD
Fettler's Finest (ABV 4.7%) BITTER
Black Llama (ABV 4.8%) PORTER
Gricer's Choice (ABV 4.8%) PALE
Wide to Gauge (ABV 5.2%) PALE
Line of Sight (ABV 5.6%) IPA

Dark Revolution

Unit 3-5, Lancaster Road, Salisbury, SP4 6FB
☎ (01722) 326993 🌐 darkrevolution.co.uk

In the beautiful Wiltshire countryside, just north of Salisbury, Dark Revolution Brewery & Taproom is uniquely located in a tranquil setting, overlooking the historic airfield at Old Sarum. The 15-barrel brew plant has been producing beer since 2017. Homebrewers at heart, it's driven by innovation and curiosity. The new 50-litre test kit allows new techniques and flavour combinations trials. 🚩 ♦ LIVE 🌱

Orbital (ABV 3.5%) BLOND
So.LA (ABV 4.5%) PALE
A cloudy, light, naturally-carbonated, West Coast-style pale ale that surprises the nose and the palate with citrus hoppy freshness that fades to dry, citrus, floral finish.
Velveteen (ABV 4.8%) STOUT
A smooth, rich black stout, served unfined. Noticeable malt and roast in the taste with balanced bitterness through to the finish.

Downton

Unit 11, Batten Road, Downton Industrial Estate, Downton, SP5 3HU
☎ (01725) 513313 🌐 downtonbrewery.com

⊠ Downton was set up in 2003. The brewery has a 20-barrel brew length and produces around 1,500 barrels a year. Around 100 outlets are supplied direct. A range of regular beers is produced together with speciality and experimental beers. The brewery offers an off-site mobile bar service and has an online shop. A regular bar is open on Fridays and sales are available onsite. 🚩 LIVE 🌱

New Forest Ale (ABV 3.8%) BITTER
An amber-coloured bitter with subtle aromas leading to good hopping on the palate. Some fruit and predominate hoppiness in the aftertaste.
Quadhop (ABV 3.9%) GOLD

Pale golden session beer, initially hoppy on the palette with some fruit and a strong hoppiness in the aftertaste . Its all about the hops.
Elderquad (ABV 4%) SPECIALITY
Golden yellow bitter with a floral fruity aroma leading to a good well-hopped taste with hints of elderflower. Dryish finish with good fruit and hop balance.
Honey Blonde (ABV 4.3%) SPECIALITY
Straw-coloured golden ale, easy-drinking with initial bitterness giving way to slight sweetness and a lingering, balanced aftertaste.
Nelson's Delight (ABV 4.5%) SPECIALITY
Downton Dream (ABV 4.8%) PALE
A premium pale ale with obvious East European influences. Hoppy on aroma and taste with a particularly dry finish and a hint of lemon citrus notes.
Moonstruck (ABV 5.5%) BITTER
A dark ruby-coloured premium bitter with malt and caramel in the aroma and taste which also carries notes of dried fruit and plum. A dry finish with some bitterness and lingering taste.
Chimera IPA (ABV 6.8%) IPA
Golden yellow strong IPA with good balance of hops and fruit, slight sweetness and some malt notes, all through to the aftertaste.

Drink Valley

🍴 **Unit C, Fleet Square, Swindon, SN1 1RQ**
☎ (01793) 692980 🌐 thedrinkvalley.com

Drink Valley opened in 2021. It has an open, airy, café-style layout to the bar area, where the brewing equipment can be seen. It brews a core range of three ales, but seasonal beers are also regularly available. ♦

Flying Monk SIBA

Unit 1, Bradfield Farm, Hullavington, SN14 6EU
☎ (01666) 838415 🌐 flyingmonkbrewery.com

⊠ Named after Elmer, an 11th century monk at nearby Malmesbury Abbey who attempted flight from the abbey tower using self-made wings. Owned by the farm business at which it is located, allowing reduced waste by using brewery by-product as cattle feed. A stone-built barn next to the brewery has been attractively converted to a café tap, offering some of the brewery's cask and keg beers and incorporating the brewery shop. 🚩 ♦ 🌱

Wingman (ABV 3.7%) GOLD
Elmers (ABV 3.8%) PALE
A refreshing session beer with floral and citrus aromas, followed by an encouraging bitter finish.
Habit (ABV 4.2%) BITTER
An amber-coloured, traditional English best bitter with a contrast of sweet and bitter flavours from a Maris Otter mash and Kentish hops
Mighty Monk (ABV 4.3%) BLOND

Gritchie

Ashgrove Farm, Ashmore, SP5 5AW
☎ (01747) 828996 🌐 gritchiebrewingcompany.co.uk

⊠ Owned by film director Guy Ritchie, this brewery, in converted farm buildings on the Ashcombe Estate, started brewing in 2017. It uses its own borehole water and estate-grown barley. Both cask and KeyKeg beers are produced, with new beers regularly developed. It doubled capacity to 40-barrels in 2023 with dedicated fermenters for experimental brews. Beers are distributed locally with plans to expand nationally. The Lore of the Land, Fitzrovia, London, is the brewery tap. ♦ 🌱

Moon Lore (ABV 3.6%) GOLD

Summer Lore (ABV 3.6%) GOLD
English Lore (ABV 4%) BITTER
A copper-coloured bitter with some hint of fruit in the aroma. A sweet slightly bitter taste which diminishes quickly.

Hop Back

Units 22-24, Batten Road Industrial Estate, Downton, SP5 3HU
☎ (01725) 510986 ⊕ hopback.co.uk

⊗ Founded in 1987, Hop Back owns nine pubs and distributes nationally. The flagship beer, Summer Lightning, has won numerous CAMRA awards. Brewing regular and seasonal beers with a unique house yeast and sourcing its primary English Hops from grower-owned cooperatives. ‼ ⬛ ♦ LIVE

GFB (ABV 3.5%) BITTER
A light gold, refreshing, session bitter. The hoppy aroma leads to bitterness initially, lasting through to the finish with some fruit.

Citra (ABV 4%) BLOND
Pale yellow almost straw-coloured with lemon and grapefruit on the aroma and taste, rapidly developing a balanced hoppy aftertaste.

Fuggle Stone (ABV 4%) BITTER
Fresh-tasting, slightly sweet, malty session bitter with the sweetness and hops leading to a gentle dry aftertaste.

Crop Circle (ABV 4.2%) GOLD
A pale yellow best bitter with a fragrant hop aroma, complex hop, fruit and citrus flavours with a balanced hoppy, bitter/sweet aftertaste.

Taiphoon (ABV 4.2%) SPECIALITY
A clean-tasting, light, fruity beer with hops and fruit on the aroma, complex hop character and lemongrass notes in the taste, slight sweetness balanced with some astringency in the aftertaste.

Entire Stout (ABV 4.5%) STOUT
A smooth, rich, ruby-black stout with strong roast and malt aromas and flavours, with a long bitter sweet and malty aftertaste.

Summer Lightning (ABV 5%) BLOND
Strong golden ale with a hoppy aroma and slightly astringent bitterness in the taste, balanced with some fruit sweetness, in the dry aftertaste.

Hop Kettle SIBA

Swindon: Unit 4, Hawksworth Industrial Estate, Newcombe Drive, Swindon, SN2 1DZ
☎ (01793) 750776

Second Site: Red Lion, High Street, Cricklade, SN6 6DD

Third Site: Tap & Brew, 51 Devizes Road, Swindon, SN1 4BG ⊕ hop-kettle.com

Brewing began in a barn behind the Red Lion Inn, Cricklade, in 2012, using a one-barrel plant. Due to demand, a larger four-barrel plant followed, which supplies the pub and is also used for experimental brews. A new ten-barrel plant was installed in an old Royal Mail warehouse in Swindon in 2016. A new Tap & Brew pub followed in 2019 which also brews experimental beers for sale in that pub. ♦ ⬥

Cricklade Ordinary Bitter (COB) (ABV 3.8%) BITTER
Chameleon (ABV 4%) BITTER
Dog Star (ABV 4%) PALE
Lode Star (ABV 4.3%) PALE
North Wall (ABV 4.3%) BITTER
East Star (ABV 4.8%) GOLD
Rising Star (ABV 4.8%) GOLD
Red Star (ABV 5.2%) RED

ESB (ABV 5.3%) BITTER
Evening Star (ABV 5.5%) PORTER
Flapjack Maramalade (ABV 7.8%) SPECIALITY

Kettlesmith SIBA

Unit 16, Treenwood Industrial Estate, Bradford-On-Avon, BA15 2AU
☎ (01225) 864839 ⊕ kettlesmithbrewing.com

⊗ Kettlesmith is an independent microbrewery established in 2016. It brews modern interpretations of a wide variety of beer styles, drawing inspiration from the brewer's background in America and England, as well as a love of Belgian beer. ‼⬛♦LIVE ⬥

Streamline (ABV 1.2%) SPECIALITY
Outline (ABV 3.8%) BITTER
Faultline (ABV 4.1%) PALE
Plotline (ABV 4.4%) STOUT
Fogline (ABV 4.7%) SPECIALITY
Coastline (ABV 4.9%) SPECIALITY
Ridgeline (ABV 5%) RED
Timeline (ABV 5.4%) PALE
Skyline (ABV 5.6%) SPECIALITY

Plain

Unit 17b-c, Deverill Trading Estate, Sutton Veny, BA12 7BZ
☎ (01985) 841481 ⊕ plainales.co.uk

⊗ Plain Ales started production in 2008 on a 2.5-barrel plant in a garage, and expanded to a 10-barrel plant in 2010 to keep up with demand for its award-winning ales. 2018 saw the introduction of its Kult Brewing Co brand to brew edgier beers. Bottling now forms an important part of its sales. ‼♦⬥

Sheep Dip (ABV 3.8%) BITTER
Balanced session bitter with some hop bitterness and dark stone fruit flavours complementing the malty background, leaving a satisfying bittersweet aftertaste.

Innocence (ABV 4%) PALE
Hoppy aroma, sweet tropical fruit on the palate balanced with hop bitterness which both continue in the satisfying bittersweet finish.

Inspiration (ABV 4%) BITTER
Independence (ABV 4.5%) PALE
Refreshing hoppy pale ale with balanced bittersweet flavours of citrus and tropical fruits with subtle hints of pine and spice.

Ramsbury SIBA

Stockclose Farm, Aldbourne, SN8 2NN
☎ (01672) 541407 ⊕ ramsburybrewery.co.uk

⊗ The Ramsbury Brewing & Distilling Company started brewing in 2004 using a 10-barrel plant, situated high on the Marlborough Downs in Wiltshire. The brewery uses home-grown barley from the Ramsbury Estate. Expansion in 2014 saw an upgrade to a 30-barrel plant with a visitor centre and a well to provide the water. A distillery that uses grains grown on the estate became operational in 2015. ‼⬛♦LIVE

Farmer's Best (ABV 3.6%) BITTER
Deerstalker (ABV 4%) BITTER
Ramsbury Pale Ale (RPA) (ABV 4%) PALE
Gold (ABV 4.5%) GOLD
Red Ram (ABV 4.5%) SPECIALITY
Chalk Stream (ABV 5%) PALE
Belapur IPA (ABV 5.5%) IPA

Rude Giant (NEW)

Great Bathampton Farm, Wylye, BA12 0QD ☎ 07513 857480 ⊕ rudegiant.com

Brewing began in 2023 following the takeover of the site previously used by Blonde Brothers Ltd.

Rude Best (ABV 3.9%) BITTER
Rude Pale Ale (ABV 4.3%) PALE

Rusty Garage

Unit 115, Rivermead Business Centre, Westlea, Swindon, SN5 7EX ☎ 07889 928241
⊕ rustygaragecraftbrewery.com

Microbrewery established in Swindon in 2020, producing a range of small-batch beers available in canned and bottle formats, all named after a motoring theme. ◆

Shed Ales

Broadfields, Pewsey, SN9 5DT
☎ (01672) 564533 ☎ 07769 812643
⊕ shedales.com

Shed Ales was launched in 2012 operating from a one-barrel plant in a converted garden shed. The brewery currently produces three core ales and several bespoke beers, available at selected local outlets including the brewery-owned Shed Alehouse, a micropub in Pewsey. Brewing is currently suspended. ◆

Stealth

Unit 3, Intercity Industrial Estate, Melksham, SN12 8DE
☎ (01225) 707111 ☎ 07917 272482
⊕ stealthbrew.co

Business commenced in 2014 and has been under the current name since 2018. It moved to its present premises in 2021 where a taproom operates from time to time. Most beers are unfined and the range changes frequently. Sales in cask, keg, can and bag-in-box are to the trade as well as directly to the public. An associated company owns two micropubs. !!◆◆

Covert (ABV 3.9%) PALE
Doublecrosser (ABV 4%) PALE
Enigma (ABV 4.2%) STOUT
Tiptoe (ABV 4.2%) BITTER
Invisible (ABV 4.7%) PALE
Hibernation (ABV 5%) GOLD
Surreptitious (ABV 7.3%) IPA

Stone Daisy (NEW)

The Old Carpenters Workshop, Fonthill Gifford, SP3 5SN
☎ (01747) 356108 ☎ 07887 847057
✉ jon.carson@wiltshiredistilling.com

Stone Daisy Brewery takes its name from the medieval 'witch marks', in the shape of daisy wheels, carved into the stone of its buildings. Traditonal equipment and methodology, coupled with some modern techniques, produce beers available in cask, bottle and can. Beers can be found across Wiltshire and beyond. ◆

Cow Down (ABV 3.8%) PALE
Snail Creep Hanging (ABV 4.2%) BITTER
Park Bottom (ABV 4.5%) PALE

Stonehenge SIBA

The Old Mill, Mill Road, Netheravon, SP4 9QB
☎ (01980) 670631 ⊕ stonehengeales.co.uk

⊠ The brewery was founded in 1984 in what was originally a water-driven mill built in 1914. In 1993 the company was bought by Danish master brewer Stig Andersen and his wife Anna Marie, and now supplies more than 300 outlets. From 2013 a new borehole, accessing the Salisbury Plain aquifer, has been supplying the brewery's water. It is of such pristine quality that the brewery now bottle and sell it under the Stonehenge name. !!◆

Spire Ale (ABV 3.8%) BITTER
A pale golden-coloured session bitter with an initial bitterness giving way to a well-rounded bitter aftertaste with discernible fruit balance.

Pigswill (ABV 4%) BITTER
Medium-bodied malty bitter, some fruit and caramel on the aroma and taste, balanced bitter sweet finish with hops throughout.

Heel Stone (ABV 4.3%) BITTER
Complex and interesting aroma of resinous hops and stoned fruit, sweet malty taste with developing hops bitterness and fruity finish.

Great Bustard (ABV 4.8%) BITTER
Rich peppery aroma, full taste of malt, hops, with slight floral and peppery notes. Dry fruity finish with good bitterness.

Danish Dynamite (ABV 5%) GOLD
A sweet aromatic aroma, complex malty taste with bitterness and fruit, medium finish with a mix of hops and fruit.

Three Daggers SIBA

47 Westbury Road, Edington, Westbury, BA13 4PG
☎ (01380) 830940 ⊕ threedaggersbrewery.com

⊠ The brewery consists of a purpose-built, 2.5-barrel plant, in a building used as a farm shop beside the Three Daggers pub. In recent years it used spare capacity at Stonehenge Brewery but has now resumed brewing on it's own plant at Edington, for the pub, the shop and the local free trade. !!🍺

Daggers Blonde (ABV 3.6%) BLOND
Daggers Ale (ABV 4.1%) BITTER
Daggers Edge (ABV 4.7%) BITTER

True Story (NEW)

7 Curtis Centre, Kingdom Avenue, Northacre Industrial Park, Westbury, BA13 4EW
☎ (01225) 800153

Office: 3 Lyme Avenue, Warminster, BA12 8LN
⊕ truestorybrewing.com

Nanobrewery that commenced brewing in 2022. ◆

Twisted SIBA

Unit 8, Commerce Business Centre, Commerce Close, Westbury, BA13 4LS
☎ (01373) 864441 ⊕ twisted-brewing.com

⊠ Twisted began brewing in 2014. It is an independent brewery producing traditional ales with a modern twist.
◆LIVE

Heritage Mild (ABV 3.4%) SPECIALITY
Three & Sixpence (ABV 3.6%) PALE
With a fullness of body that belies its strength, this session pale combines the sweetness of tropical fruit with the bitterness of citrus all sitting on a light malt base with a hint of caramel. The sweetness becomes more pronounced as it lingers in the long finish.

Rider / Three Lions (ABV 4%) BITTER

The flavours of slightly understated American hops give impressions of mango and tangerine, and are layered onto a biscuit malt foundation. The dry hop bitterness increasingly asserts itself in the short but moreish ending.

Pirate (ABV 4.2%) BITTER
Traditional lightly hopped english bitter. Slight floral notes on the nose, malt on the palate is combined with some spice and ripe fruit with an earthy hop bitterness which soon fades in the short aftertaste.

Urban Legend (ABV 4.3%) GOLD
A refreshing and balanced golden ale. Light malt and citrus hop in the aroma are replicated on the palate, with the soft citrus notes complementing the malty background and dry bitterness which continue into the aftertaste.

Finnegan's No. 1 (ABV 4.4%) SPECIALITY
Distinctive aroma and flavour of coffee with dark roast malt and some hop bitterness in the background. Coffee is also evident in the dry aftertaste.

Canteen Cowboy (ABV 4.5%) GOLD
A blend of American hops give this premium golden ale the aroma of a fresh fruit salad. The sweetish malt supports the cocktail of fresh fruit flavours on the palate, whilst the hop bitterness increases towards the finish.

Gaucho / Fly Half (ABV 4.6%) BITTER
The malty, slightly roasted and fruity aroma acts as a precursor to the full bodied and satisfying taste of a solid malty backbone and background hop bitterness, overlaid with the flavour of forest fruits before a long lasting and well balanced bittersweet aftertaste.

ViBiSh (NEW)

95 Basepoint Business Centre, Rivermead Industrial Estate, Rivermead Drive, Westlea, SN5 7EX
⊕ **vibishbrewing.co.uk**

Established by three friends in 2023 to brew craft beers that they enjoy drinking themselves. Cask beer may be occasionally available. ◆

Wadworth SIBA IFBB

Folly Road Brewhouse, Folly Road, Devizes, SN10 2HT
☎ **(01380) 723361** ⊕ **wadworth.co.uk**

⊠ Established in 1875 by Henry Alfred Wadworth, this impressive, family-owned brewery has a modern brewhouse and a microbrewery, which enables it to create unique, small-batch beers. Its traditional horse-drawn drays deliver beer daily around Devizes. Wadworth has more than 150 pubs in the South-West of England. in 2023 the brewery relocated to a new site in Folly Road. ‼ ⊨ ◆LIVE ◆

Henry's IPA (ABV 3.6%) BITTER
Horizon (ABV 4%) BITTER
6X (ABV 4.1%) BITTER
Copper-coloured ale with a malty and fruity nose, and some balancing hop character. The flavour is similar, with some bitterness and a lingering malty, but bitter finish.
Swordfish (ABV 5%) SPECIALITY

Wessex

Rye Hill Farm, Longbridge Deverill, BA12 7DE
☎ **(01985) 844532** ⊠ **wessexbrewery@gmail.com**

⊠ This four-barrel brewery, hidden away on a farm industrial complex in the West Wiltshire Area of Outstanding Natural Beauty, was established in 2021. The brewery sources its malt from the nearby Warminster Maltings. Around 2010, two new fermenters were installed. A handful of regular outlets are supplied, with wider availability via selected wholesalers. The brewery is able to brew beer for other concerns when capacity permits. ◆

Stourton Pale Ale (ABV 3.5%) PALE
Kilmington Best (ABV 4.2%) BITTER
Deverill's Advocate (ABV 4.5%) GOLD
Warminster Warrior (ABV 4.5%) BITTER

World's End

⊟ **Crown Inn, 60 Wilcot Road, Pewsey, SN9 5EL**
☎ **(01672) 562653** ⊕ **thecrowninnpewsey.com**

⊠ World's End Ales was established in 2009 on a one-barrel plant at the rear of the Crown Inn, Pewsey. World's End is the 18th century name for the area in which the brewery is located. Three regular beers are available, plus seasonal specials. ‼ ◆

Rai d'Or, Salisbury (Photo: Jim Linwood / Flickr CC BY 2.0)

West Midlands

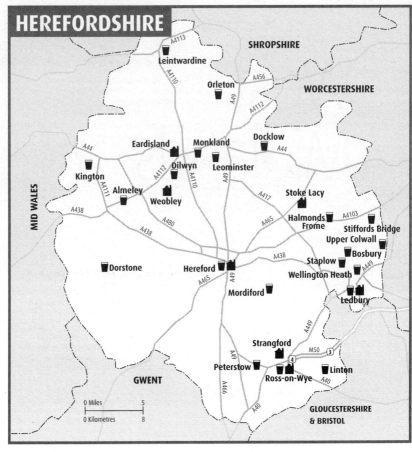

HEREFORDSHIRE

SHROPSHIRE

Leintwardine

Orleton

WORCESTERSHIRE

Eardisland Monkland Docklow

Dilwyn Leominster

Kington

Almeley Weobley

Stoke Lacy

MID WALES

Halmonds Frome

Stiffords Bridge

Upper Colwall Bosbury

Dorstone

Staplow

Hereford

Wellington Heath

Mordiford Ledbury

Strangford

GWENT

Peterstow Ross-on-Wye Linton

0 Miles   5
0 Kilometres   8

GLOUCESTERSHIRE & BRISTOL

Almeley

Bells Inn 🅛

HR3 6LF (in village)
☎ (01544) 327216 ⊕ thebellsinnalmeley.com
Goff's Lancer; Three Tuns XXX; 1 changing beer (sourced locally; often Hobsons, Milestone) Ⓗ
A genuine welcome is guaranteed at this enthusiastically run, traditional country inn set in the heart of its rural community, which incorporates an award-winning farm shop and delicatessen. The low-ceilinged bar has an alcove housing the dartboard. Home-prepared lunches are served plus fish & chips every Friday evening (booking required). The guest beer is typically from a local brewery. A former local CAMRA Pub of the Year runner-up. 🅱❀🌢♣♠🅿🅿❀🎵

Bosbury

Bell Inn 🅛 ✔

HR8 1PX (on B4220, in village)
☎ (01531) 640285
Ludlow Ludlow Best; Wye Valley Butty Bach; 1 changing beer (often Three Tuns) Ⓗ
A friendly and welcoming two-bar black-and-white half-timbered inn at the heart of its community, set in a terrace opposite the imposing village church, the bells of which lend the place its name. A restaurant area serving food (not Tue or Sun eve) contrasts with a basic yet comfortable public bar, replete with grand fireplace,

alcoves, books and newspapers. A large garden features at the rear. Plenty of on-street parking is available.
Q🅱❀🌢♣♠🅿🚍(417) ❀🌢

Dilwyn

Crown Inn 🅛

HR4 8HL
☎ (01544) 318063 ⊕ thecrowninndilwyn.co.uk
Wye Valley HPA, Butty Bach; 2 changing beers (often Hobsons, Three Tuns) Ⓗ
Herefordshire's first community-owned pub was originally a black-and-white coaching inn, before the lovely village was bypassed. The 17th-century building has been refronted and much altered, although many beams remain visible in the two bars. Meals and bar snacks are available with roasts on Sunday and senior citizens lunch on Wednesday. The pub fields several pub

REAL ALE BREWERIES

Corn 🍺 Ross-on-Wye (NEW)
Hereford 🍺 Hereford
Ledbury Ledbury
Motley Hog 🍺 Ross-on-Wye
Simpsons 🍺 Eardisland
Weobley Weobley
Wobbly ✦ Hereford
Woofy's Strangford (NEW)
Wye Valley Stoke Lacy

game teams. An acoustic music session is held every third Thursday in the month (participation welcomed). The garden includes a children's play area.
Q ♿ ❄ ⬤ ♣ ▶ P 🐕 ♪

Docklow

King's Head

HR6 0RX (on A44)
☎ (01568) 760960 ⊕ kingsheaddocklow.co.uk
Ludlow Gold; Wye Valley HPA, Butty Bach; 2 changing beers (often Wye Valley) Ⓗ
A 17th-century roadside pub in beautiful surroundings. Its single bar, with dining areas to each side, features old, exposed beams, and is decorated in a modern style. Outside is a large part-covered patio, and lawns with seating pods and picnic tables, plus a children's play area – all with views over open countryside. Steak night is on Tuesday, quiz last Wednesday of the month, curry night on Thursday, and roast on Sunday.
♿ ❄ ⬤ ♿ ♣ P 🐕 🐕 ♪

Dorstone

Pandy Inn Ⓛ

HR3 6AN (signed off B4348)
☎ (01981) 550273 ⊕ thepandyinn.co.uk
Three Tuns XXX; Wye Valley Butty Bach; 1 changing beer Ⓗ
Opposite the little village green, the Pandy boasts a history dating back to the 12th century. Although now opened out inside, discrete areas provide for a more intimate feel, alongside timber framing, exposed stone walls and a huge fireplace. The pub caters equally for drinkers and diners, with an interesting range of dishes, including vegetarian, and opens on weekday lunchtimes for groups by prior arrangement. Gwatkins cider is on handpump. There is a monthly quiz and curry night (booking advisable). Winter hours apply early October to early April. Q ♿ ❄ ⬤ ♣ ⬤ P 🐕 🐕 🐕 ♪

Halmonds Frome

Major's Arms Ⓛ

WR6 5AX (just over 1 mile N of A4103 at Bishops Frome)
SO675481
☎ (01531) 640261
Purity Pure Gold; Wye Valley HPA; 1 changing beer (often Ledbury) Ⓗ
An isolated hillside pub that used to be a cider mill. The high-ceilinged main bar has stone walls and a large wood-burner, always alight in the winter. An archway leads through to another drinking area. Outside is an extensive terrace on two levels from which there are superb views, particularly sunsets, over west Herefordshire and into Wales. Complimentary bar snacks are often provided, and there is occasionally live music.
♿ ❄ Å ♣ P 🐕 🐕 ♪

Hereford

Barrels Ⓛ ✅

69 St Owen Street, HR1 2JQ
☎ (01432) 274968
Wye Valley Bitter, The Hopfather, HPA, Butty Bach, Wholesome Stout; 1 changing beer (sourced locally; often Wye Valley) Ⓗ
A local CAMRA Pub of the Year seven times, the Barrels is a community pub of the highest order; a must-visit Hereford institution with a welcome for all. There is no food, no gimmicks, just bags of character across five rooms. A fantastic covered courtyard to the rear hosts a

charity beer and music festival each October. Events include jazz evenings on the first Monday of the month, and comedy on some Wednesday evenings. Television is available throughout for major events, but otherwise in one bar only. ♿ ❄ ≈ ♣ ⬤ 🚃 🐕 🐕 ♪

Beer in Hand

136 Eign Street, HR4 0AP
☎ 07543 327548
5 changing beers Ⓖ
Herefordshire's first micropub, this minimalist, single-bar establishment was converted from a launderette in 2013. In recent years it has won local CAMRA Pub of the Year and Cider Pub of the Year. With an impressive chilled racking system, it typically sells up to five ales on cask, six keg beers, and eight, mainly local, ciders and perries. Snacks are always available and artisan pizzas are made on-site Thursday evening. Quiz night is the first Wednesday and folk night the third Thursday of the month. Q ♿ ❄ ♿ ♣ ⬤ 🚃 🐕

Orange Tree

16 King Street, HR4 9BX
☎ (01432) 264684
Black Country Bradley's Finest Golden, Pig on the Wall, Fireside; 6 changing beers Ⓗ
Dating from the 17th century, this small, single-bar pub is a recent addition to the Black Country Inns estate. Grade II-listed for the original front part of the building, it has been slightly enlarged and thoroughly refurbished in a more cosy and traditional style than previously. Significantly increasing the choice of ales in the city, details of up to 10 ales plus two ciders are displayed on large screens. Snacks such as pork pies and cobs are served. ♿ ❄ Å ♣ ⬤ 🚃 (33) 🐕 🐕

Vaga Tavern Ⓛ ✅

Vaga Street, HR2 7AT
☎ (01432) 509927
Wye Valley Bitter, Butty Bach; 1 changing beer Ⓗ
A friendly community pub in Hunderton, which is near the River Wye and accessible from the city centre via a pleasant riverside walk and cycleway. Acquired by Wye Valley brewery, it consists of two spacious rooms and a skittle alley, with a large garden to the rear including a children's play area. Activities include regular live music, skittles and darts matches, and events for the whole family. Filled rolls are normally available.
♿ ❄ ♣ 🚃 (75) 🐕 ♪

Kington

Olde Tavern ★ Ⓛ

22 Victoria Road, HR5 3BX
☎ (01544) 231417
4 changing beers (often Hobsons, Ludlow, Three Tuns) Ⓗ
A living, breathing Victorian timewarp, once called the Railway Tavern (the railway closed in the 1950s) and before that the Tavern in the Fields. In the lobby there is an original serving hatch. To the left is a small bar with original timber work, bench and alcove seating, and numerous curios; to the right is the old smoke room with its fine flagstone floor and bench seating. This local favourite serves traditional pub grub Wednesday to Sunday, with Wednesday curry night, Thursday steak night and Sunday lunches. Q ♿ ❄ ⬤ Å ♣ 🚃 🐕

Ledbury

Feathers Hotel

25 High Street, HR8 1DS

☎ (01531) 635266 ⊕ feathersledbury.co.uk
3 changing beers (often Ledbury) Ⓗ
An elegant black-and-white Elizabethan coaching inn, one of the flagship hotels for the county, the Feathers has recently benefited from a major refurbishment. Features inside this fine Grade II*-listed building include a function room that was once the town theatre, and hand-painted murals in the upstairs corridors. The smart, plush, quiet bar is complemented by a restaurant and separate coffee shop and eatery (open daytimes). The toilets are fully accessible. Payment is by card only.
Q ᐳ ✿ ⌛ ⁐ ◑ 𝄞 & P ✿ ♥ 🎵

Prince of Wales Ⓛ ✓

Church Lane, HR8 1DL
☎ (01531) 632250 ⊕ powledbury.com
Hobsons Town Crier; Ledbury Dark, Pale Ale; Otter Amber; 2 changing beers (often New Bristol, Siren) Ⓗ
Tucked away down a picturesque cobbled alley leading to the church, this 16th-century timber-framed pub has two bars plus an alcove where folk jam sessions are held on Wednesday evening. A multi-award winner, it is a genuine community pub – always bustling with locals and visitors. Draught cider is available as well as one rotating craft beer and an extensive range of foreign beers in bottles and cans. The bar meals are good value, and booking is advisable for Sunday roasts.
ᐳ ✿ ◑ ♣ ♥ 🎡 ✿ 🎵

Talbot Hotel Ⓛ ✓

14 New Street, HR8 2DX
☎ (01531) 632963 ⊕ talbotledbury.co.uk
Wadworth Horizon, 6X; Wye Valley Butty Bach Ⓗ
An outstanding black-and-white half-timbered hotel and bar dating back to the 1590s, with direct links to the English Civil War. Various comfortably furnished seating areas, with discreet nooks and corners, surround a central bar-servery facing a splendid fireplace. The restaurant, with its superb wood-panelling, offers affordable good food using locally sourced ingredients, while conventional bar snacks are also available in the bar. ᐳ ✿ ⌛ ◑ ⁐ 🎡 ✿ 🎵

Leintwardine

Sun Inn ★ Ⓛ

Rosemary Lane, SY7 0LP (off A4113, in village)
☎ (01547) 540705
Hobsons Mild, Best; Ludlow Stairway; Wye Valley Butty Bach Ⓗ
A national treasure and one of the last parlour pubs, the Sun was saved in 2009 following a CAMRA-led campaign. The redbrick-tiled public bar features bench furniture and a simple fireplace. Another room is the untouched parlour from where landlady of 74 years, Flossie Lane, once held court. To the rear is a stylish pavilion-style extension overlooking the garden; venue for the August bank holiday Sunday beer festival. Light lunches are served daily. Fish & chips from next door may be eaten in the garden. Q ᐳ ✿ ◑ & ▲ ♣ 🎡 ✿ 🎵

Leominster

Chequers Ⓛ ✓

63 Etnam Street, HR6 8AE
☎ (01568) 612473
Wye Valley Bitter, HPA, The Hopfather, Butty Bach, Wholesome Stout; 1 changing beer (often Wye Valley) Ⓗ
Probably the oldest pub in the town, with a fine timber-framed façade and interesting protruding gables. A wonderful front bar was at one time two bars, but still

has much charm, with a tiled floor, original fireplace, timbers and cosy window alcoves. To the rear is a more conventional lounge bar, a games room and a patio with a feature oak-timbered shelter. Snack food is available. Children over 13 are admitted. A quiz is held monthly on a Wednesday, and jazz on the first Fridays in summer.
Q ✿ ⁐ ♣ ♥ P 🎡 ✿ 🎵

Linton

Alma Inn Ⓛ

HR9 7RY (off B4221, W of M50 jct 3) SO659255
☎ (01989) 720355 ⊕ almainnlinton.co.uk
Butcombe Butcombe Original; Ludlow Gold; 3 changing beers (often Bristol Beer Factory, Hop Shed) Ⓗ
Hidden behind a plain façade is an understated but multi-award winning pub of outstanding calibre. The convivial front bar, with wood-burner and original timber furniture, contrasts with the rear pool room and a separate wood-panelled dining room. Hearty, freshly prepared pub classics are offered, with seasonal specials, light bites and bar snacks. Events include the nationally renowned Linton Music Festival in July, hosted in the extensive gardens, along with a beer festival. A quiz is held every last Sunday of the month. A former local CAMRA Pub of the Year. Q ᐳ ✿ ◑ ♣ P ✿ 🎵

Monkland

Monkland Arms Ⓛ

HR6 9DE (on A44, W end of village)
☎ (01568) 720510 ⊕ themonklandarms.co.uk
Hobsons Best; Wye Valley Butty Bach; 2 changing beers (sourced locally; often Bewdley, Ludlow) Ⓗ
A single bar serves the main drinking area, with dining areas to the side and back that drinkers are more than welcome to occupy. The beer garden to the rear, with covered seating, has views across open country. Home-cooked locally sourced food is served, including traditional Sunday lunches. Up to seven local draught ciders are available, and a range of four real ales. There is a quiz on the last Wednesday of the month and live music on some Saturdays and Sundays.
ᐳ ✿ ◑ ♣ ♥ P 🚌 (502) ✿ 🎵

Mordiford

Moon Inn ✓

HR1 4LW (on B4224, in village)
☎ (01432) 873067 ⊕ mooninnmordiford.co.uk
Ludlow Gold; Otter Bitter; St Austell Proper Job; Timothy Taylor Landlord Ⓗ
This comfortable half-timbered two-bar village inn started life as a farmhouse over 400 years ago. Popular with locals and with families visiting from Hereford, it benefits from its proximity to the Mordiford Loop – a well-known local walk – as well as the rivers Lugg and Wye. Traditional, locally sourced pub food is served, with a pie and pud night on Wednesday. There is a children's play area in the garden, plus a camping and caravan site to the rear. ᐳ ✿ ◑ ▲ ♣ P 🚌 (453) ✿ 🎵

Orleton

Boot Inn Ⓛ

SY8 4HN (off B4361, in village)
☎ (01568) 780228 ⊕ bootinnorleton.co.uk
Hobsons Best, Twisted Spire; Ludlow Ludlow Blonde; 1 changing beer Ⓗ
The Boot reopened under community ownership in 2019, following a period of closure. A major refurbishment of

this distinguished Grade II-listed, 16th-century, half-timbered masterpiece has been achieved to good effect. It has been sympathetically opened out while maintaining a separate dining room, snug and original inglenook fireplace. High-quality seasonal food is served – booking is advised (and essential at weekends). There is occasional live music. ⏰🏠🍽🅿🚃(490)♫

Peterstow

Yew Tree Inn

HR9 6JZ (on A49, in village)
☎ (01989) 562815 ⏏ rosscider.com
Hobsons Best; Wye Valley Bitter; 2 changing beers (often Lancaster, Townhouse) Ⓗ
The Yew Tree was taken over in 2014 by the Ross-on-Wye Cider & Perry Company. The four ales and two draught ciders are complemented by a large range of bottled cider and perry. Guest beers are often from distant microbreweries. A cider shop is open 12-6pm. A games night is held on Tuesday, and music on Friday. Meals consist of pop-up events advertised locally and on Facebook. A camping/caravan site is available with a toilet and shower block. Hereford to Ross bus service 32 stops in the village. Q⏰🏠🍽🅿🚃(32)🐕📶♫

Ross-on-Wye

Tap House Ⓛ

1 Millpond Street, HR9 7AP
☎ 07510 156708
6 changing beers (sourced nationally; often Motley Hog) Ⓗ
Opened in 2018, this micropub occupies what was, until 1965, the brewery tap for Alton Court brewery. It serves six real ales, mainly from its own Motley Hog brewery, and also from small breweries further afield, and has transformed the choice of real ale in Ross. Three local ciders and seven keg beers are also served. The simply-furnished room and snug are augmented by seating on the pavement at the front. Meals consist mainly of wraps and burgers with some interesting fillings. A former local CAMRA Pub of the Year. Q🍽🚃🐕

Staplow

Oak Inn Ⓛ

Bromyard Road, HR8 1NP (on B4214)
☎ (01531) 640954 ⏏ theoakinnstaplow.co.uk
Bathams Best Bitter; Ledbury Pale Ale; 2 changing beers (often Bathams, Three Tuns, Wye Valley) Ⓗ
A stylishly renovated and well-run roadside country inn offering exceptional food, good beer and quality accommodation. A contemporary public area neatly divides into three – a reception bar area with modern sofas and low tables, a snug, and a main dining area featuring an open kitchen. At the rear is a further room with scrubbed tables. Booking is essential for food and accommodation. Q⏰🏠🛏🅿🚃(417)🐕📶

Stiffords Bridge

Red Lion Inn Ⓛ

WR13 5NN (on A4103)
☎ (01886) 880318 ⏏ redlioncradley.co.uk
Wye Valley Butty Bach; 5 changing beers (often Ledbury) Ⓗ
This multi-roomed roadside pub is as popular with out-of-town diners as it is with locals and drinkers. A survivor of multiple floods, it is characterised by modern flagstone floors, wood panelling, bare brick walls, cosy window alcoves and a large fireplace with a wood-

burner. There are pleasant and extensive gardens to the rear where events are hosted. Traditional locally sourced food dominates the menu. The guest beers are from breweries far and near, many unusual for the area, supplemented by a craft keg beer and two real ciders. ⏰🏠🍽🚃🅿🐕📶♫

Upper Colwall

Chase Inn Ⓛ

Chase Road, WR13 6DJ (off B4218, turning at upper hairpin bend signed British Camp) SO766431
☎ (01684) 540276 ⏏ thechaseinnmalvern.co.uk
Holden's Golden Glow; 2 changing beers (often Purity, Three Tuns) Ⓗ
Small and cosy two-bar free house hidden away in a quiet wooded backwater on the western slopes of the Malvern Hills. With a genteel atmosphere, it is popular with walkers and locals alike. It comprises a small lounge for dining (booking advisable at weekends) and a long, narrow public bar, both adorned with many artefacts and curios. A delightful manicured rear beer garden commands panoramic views across Herefordshire to the Welsh Hills. A quiz is held on the first Monday of the month. Q⏰🏠🐕🅿🚃(675)🐕📶

Wellington Heath

Farmers Arms Ⓛ

Horse Road, HR8 1LS (in village, E of B4214)
☎ (01531) 634776 ⏏ farmersarmswellingtonheath.co.uk
Ledbury Bitter; Wye Valley Butty Bach; 2 changing beers (often Gloucester, Ledbury, Salopian) Ⓗ
Follow the signs carefully to find this pub in its dispersed rural community. The bar and main dining area are in the original mid 19th-century building, and on either side are more modern extensions housing a games room with pool table and a restaurant. The food ranges from burgers and pub classics to steaks and speciality dishes. Up to four local draught ciders are available in summer. A popular Beer & Beast festival is held in July. ⏰🏠🍽🚃🅿🚃(675)🐕📶♫

Breweries

Corn (NEW)

🍺 Corn Exchange (Kings Head Hotel), 8 High Street, Ross-on-Wye, HR9 5HL

Small brewery in the Corn Exchange, part of the Kings Head Hotel, in Ross-on-Wye. Brewing mainly for the pub, its ales can also be found in the local free trade.

Hereford

🍺 88 St Owen Street, Hereford, HR1 2QD
☎ (01432) 342125 ✉ jfkenyon@aol.com

Although there has been a small brewery on this site since 1992, Hereford began life as the Spinning Dog Brewery in 2000, changing its name in 2010. After a period as primarily a brewpub, in 2017 it began to expand its distribution to pubs in Herefordshire and Pembrokeshire. ‼◆LIVE

Owd Bull (ABV 3.9%) BITTER
Hereford Dark (ABV 4%) MILD
HLA (Herefordshire Light Ale) (ABV 4%) PALE
Celtic Gold (ABV 4.5%) GOLD
Mutley's Revenge (ABV 4.8%) BITTER
Mutts Nuts (ABV 5%) BITTER

Ledbury SIBA

Gazerdine House, Hereford Road, Ledbury, HR8 2PZ
☎ (01531) 671184 ☎ 07957 428070
⊕ ledburyrealales.co.uk

⊛Established in 2012, Ledbury Real Ales uses hops grown in Herefordshire and Worcestershire with other materials sourced locally, where possible. The beers are sold mainly within a 15-mile radius of the brewery. ‼◆

Bitter (ABV 3.8%) BITTER
Dark (ABV 3.9%) MILD
Gold (ABV 4%) GOLD
Ledbury Pale Ale (ABV 4%) PALE

Motley Hog

▤ Tap House, 1 Millpond Street, Ross-on-Wye,
HR9 7AP ☎ 07510 156708
✉ motleyhogbrewery@gmail.com

Gaining HMRC registration early in 2021, Motley Hog is a 300-litre brewery based at the Tap House, Ross-on-Wye. The aim is to bring small scale, commercial brewing back to the town for the first time since 1956, with two core ales, and various specials during the year.

Odyssey

Brockhampton Brewery, Oast House Barn, Bromyard,
WR6 5SH
☎ (01885) 483496 ☎ 07918 553152
⊕ odysseybrewco.com

⊠ This six-barrel brewery was established in 2014 by Alison and Mitchell Evans, who previously owned the Beer in Hand, Hereford. The original building, a restored barn on a National Trust estate, has been retained. A wide range of beers is brewed, predominantly served in keg and can and occasionally bottled for special release.

Simpsons

▤ White Swan, Eardisland, HR6 9BD
☎ (01544) 388635 ⊕ thewhiteswaneardisland.com

Tim Simpson acquired the White Swan in 2011 and set up the brewery at the rear of the pub in 2013. All beers are brewed for consumption in the White Swan. ◆

Weobley

Jules Restaurant, Portland Street, Weobley, HR4 8SB
☎ (01544) 318206 ☎ 07493 269189
⊕ theweobleybrewing.co

Commercial brewing began in 2019 at this nanobrewery, which is part of Jules restaurant in the village of Weobley and is run by chef and head brewer Tom Evans. Four beers are regularly brewed along with two occasional beers, available from the brewery, restaurant and other local outlets and pubs. The bulk of the production is bottled, cask is a rare bonus.

Wobbly

Unit 22c, Beech Business Park, Tillington Road,
Hereford, HR4 9QJ
☎ (01432) 355496 ⊕ wobblybrewing.co

Wobbly began brewing in 2013 in a small business park in Hereford and is closely linked with its sister canning company, BPS. The brewery has a refurbished taproom, open every day, selling its cask-conditioned beers, cider and street food, plus an onsite shop. A new canning line has greatly increased capacity. Core beers are now available in several pubs throughout Herefordshire. Wobbly are now brewing its signature series of craft ales on draught. ‼▤◆LIVE ✦

Wabbit (ABV 4%) PALE
Gold (ABV 4.2%) GOLD
American Amber Ale (ABV 4.5%) BITTER
Crow (ABV 4.5%) STOUT
Welder (ABV 4.8%) BITTER
IPA No. 3 (ABV 6%) IPA

Woofy's (NEW)

Strangford, HR9 6QT ⊕ woofysbrewery.com

Established in 2020 and based near Ross-on-Wye, the brewery produces handcrafted beers inspired by the owner's boxer dog, Sir Woofy Woofington.

Wye Valley SIBA IFBB

Stoke Lacy, HR7 4HG
☎ (01885) 490505 ☎ 07970 597937
⊕ wyevalleybrewery.co.uk

Founded in 1985 in the back of a village pub, this award-winning brewery is now producing around 250,000 pints per week and delivers direct to more than 1,200 pubs, including eight of its own. Its products are also available through selected wholesale and retail stockists. ‼▤◆LIVE

Bitter (ABV 3.7%) BITTER
A beer whose aroma gives little hint of the bitter hoppiness that follows right through to the aftertaste.
The Hopfather (ABV 3.9%) BITTER
HPA (ABV 4%) PALE
A pale, hoppy, malty brew with a hint of sweetness before a dry finish.
Butty Bach (ABV 4.5%) BITTER
Wholesome Stout (ABV 4.6%) STOUT
A smooth and satisfying stout with a bitter edge to its roast flavours. The finish combines roast grain and malt.

The importance of the pub

Perhaps the workman spends, night after night, more than he should on beer. Let us remember, if he needs excuse, that his employers have found him no better place and no better amusement than to sit in a tavern, drink beer (generally in moderation), and talk and smoke tobacco. Why not? A respectable tavern is a very harmless place; the society which meets there is the society of the workman; it's his life; without it he might as well have been a factory hand of the good old time – such as hands were 40 years ago; and then he should have but two journeys a day – one from bed to mill, and the other from mill to bed.

Walter Besant, As We Are and As We May Be, 1903

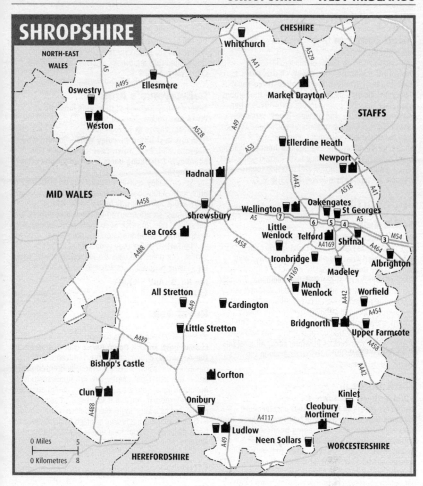

Albrighton

Harp Hotel Ⓛ

40 High Street, WV7 3JF
☎ (01902) 375047
Black Country Bradley's Finest Golden, Pig on the Wall, Fireside; 7 changing beers (sourced nationally) Ⓗ
Refurbished in 2021 this traditional village local now has a single U-shaped room served by a central bar. There is a large outdoor area with plenty of tables and a covered smoking area. Three regular beers and often monthly specials from Black Country Ales are available along with changing beers from around the UK. Quizzes are held on the first Tuesday of the month and a darts team plays on Monday. Children are welcome until 7pm.
ⓈⓀ&≠♣🖵(891) ✿ 🌐

All Stretton

Yew Tree Inn Ⓛ

Shrewsbury Road, SY6 6HG
☎ (01694) 328953 🌐 yewtree-allstretton.co.uk
Wye Valley Butty Bach, HPA; 2 changing beers (sourced locally) Ⓗ
A Grade II-listed, three-roomed local situated in a pretty village surrounded by the Shropshire Hills, only 10 miles from the historic market town of Shrewsbury. The premises consists of a public bar and a separate lounge, each with its own character, but with an overall atmosphere of comfort, permanence and tradition. There are low beams, log fires and masses of photographs, paintings and other ornaments adorning the walls. There is a large pleasant outdoor area by the main door and a dining room. Dogs are welcome in the bar. Accommodation is in four en-suite rooms.
QⓈ≠🛏♦P🖵(435) ✿

REAL ALE BREWERIES

All Nations 🍺 Telford
Clun 🍺 Clun
Corvedale 🍺 Corfton (brewing suspended)
Finney's Wellington
Hobsons ⚡ Cleobury Mortimer
Joule's Market Drayton
Ludlow ⚡ Ludlow
Plan B Newport
Rowton 🍺 Wellington
Salopian Hadnall
Severn Valley Bridgnorth (brewing suspended)
St Annes Lea Cross
Stonehouse ⚡ Weston
Three Tuns 🍺 Bishop's Castle

Bishop's Castle

Three Tuns Inn L

Salop Street, SY9 5BW

☎ (01588) 638797 ⊕ thethreetunsinn.co.uk

Three Tuns Rantipole, XXX, Stout, Cleric's Cure; 1 changing beer (sourced locally; often Three Tuns) ⊞

A truly historic pub, this is linked to one of the famous four brewpubs still brewing in the early 1970s when CAMRA was founded. The brewery is now separately owned but supplies the majority of pub's beer. It has been extended into four rooms – on one side is the lounge, on the other, the ever-popular front bar leading to the central snug and extended oak-framed generously glazed dining room. Function and meeting rooms are available for hire. Q✿⊁✿⏶Å♣➡(553)✿❖🏵♪

Bridgnorth

Bell & Talbot L

2 Salop Street, High Town, WV16 4QU

☎ (01746) 763233 ⊕ bellandtalbotbridgnorth.co.uk

Hobsons Town Crier; Ludlow Gold, Stairway; Wye Valley Butty Bach, HPA ⊞

Affectionally known as the Bell, this traditional, friendly pub has a small snug and L-shaped bar. A conservatory leads to the partially covered courtyard outside. Dogs are welcome, as are well-behaved owners. Sky Sports screens show football, rugby, and other sports. The bar, adorned with many traditional features, has two open fires to warm your cockles in winter time. All local bus routes call at Sainsbury's, 200 yards away in Old Smithfield. ✿✿≷♣➡✿❖♪

Black Horse L

4 Bridge Street, Low Town, WV15 6AF

☎ (01746) 762415 ⊕ theblackhorsebridgnorth.co.uk

Bathams Best Bitter; Hobsons Town Crier; Three Tuns XXX; Wye Valley HPA; 1 changing beer (sourced regionally; often Enville) ⊞

First licensed in 1810, this Low Town free house is popular with all ages. It has three rooms: a front bar with a rustic feel but modern atmosphere, a panelled lounge bar, and a conservatory to the side. There are two external drinking areas. Two rooms have TVs which show a variety of live sport to an enthusiastic audience. There is often live entertainment on Saturday night. En-suite B&B accommodation is available. Most bus routes stop nearby. ✿✿⏸✿➡✿❖♪

Fosters Arms L

56 Mill Street, Low Town, WV15 5AG

☎ (01746) 765175

Banks's Amber Ale; Hobsons Town Crier; Wye Valley HPA; 1 changing beer (sourced nationally) ⊞

This popular Low Town pub has been in the same family since 1988. The busy front bar hosts regular pub games as well as showing major sporting events. A side corridor leads to a comfortable lounge on the left and then to the pool room. Beyond is a long garden, also accessed from Doctor's Lane alongside, which leads down to the riverbank, Severn Park and the Edgar Davis Ground, home of Bridgnorth Rugby. Most bus routes stop outside. ✿✿⏸≷♣➡✿❖

Golden Lion 🍷 L

83 High Street, High Town, WV16 4DS

☎ (01746) 762016 ⊕ goldenlionbridgnorth.co.uk

Holden's Black Country Mild, Black Country Bitter, Golden Glow, Special; 1 changing beer (sourced locally) ⊞

A 17th-century coaching inn with a central serving area. To the right of the front door is the public bar with sports TV; there's also a small lounge to the left and another at the rear. There is access from both the rear lounge and the bar to the smoking and outside drinking areas, as well as the car park. Vehicle access is from St Leonards Close. Filled rolls are usually available at lunchtime. Q✿⏸✿⏸≷♣➡✿❖

Railwayman's Arms L

Severn Valley Railway Station, Hollybush Road, WV16 5DT (follow signs for SVR)

☎ (01746) 760920 ⊕ svr.co.uk

Bathams Best Bitter; Bewdley Worcestershire Way; Hobsons Mild, Best, Town Crier; house beer (by Bewdley); 2 changing beers (sourced locally; often Bewdley) ⊞

The Severn Valley Railway's popular pub on Platform 1 of Bridgnorth Station has been licensed continuously since 1861 and is full of railway memorabilia. Of the 10 handpumps, six are reserved for regular ales, three for guests and one for cider. Soak up the atmosphere of a steam railway while sitting outside with a pint. It opens at 11am when the railway is operating, including Sunday, but hours and days are reduced in winter when the railway is closed. Q✿✿⏸⏸≷♣➡(9,436)✿❖

Cardington

Royal Oak

SY6 7JZ

☎ (01694) 771266 ⊕ at-the-oak.com

Ludlow Best; Sharp's Doom Bar; 2 changing beers ⊞

The Royal Oak, dating back to the 15th century, is reputedly Shropshire's oldest continually licensed pub, and is the archetypal country inn. The single room is multi-functional with a bar, lounge and dining area, and has a relaxed ambience. It is low-beamed and dominated by a large inglenook fireplace which provides a home for various interesting artefacts. A good choice of beers includes a mix of local and regional brews and a draught cider. Q✿⏸✿Å♣➡(540)✿❖

Clun

White Horse Inn L ✅

The Square, SY7 8JA

☎ (01588) 640305 ⊕ whi-clun.co.uk

Clun Loophole, Pale Ale, Citadel; Hobsons Best; Wye Valley Butty Bach; 2 changing beers (often Salopian) ⊞

16th-century inn and posthouse standing in the old market square of a timeless town, described by AE Housman as one of the quietest places under the sun. Inside is an L-shaped bar with low beams and adjoining dining room, which has been extended into the properties on either side, serving excellent, reasonably priced food. The pub is linked to the Clun brewery and stocks its products. Rotating real ciders are available. There is a secluded garden outside. Jam nights are held once a month. ✿✿⏸✿⏸Å♣➡➡✿❖♪

Ellerdine Heath

Royal Oak L ✅

Hazles Road, TF6 6RL (1 miles from A442, signposted Ellerdine Heath) SJ603226

☎ (01939) 250300

Hobsons Best; Wye Valley HPA, Butty Bach; 3 changing beers (sourced locally; often Rowton, Salopian) ⊞

A long-standing Guide entry, known locally as the Tiddly, at the heart of the local rural community. Features include a real fire, three regular beers, three guests and real cider. Substantial cobs and snacks are always available. There is a smoking shed and large car park outside. Dominoes is played every Monday, and poker on the last Tuesday of the month. Bike night is hosted on Wednesday March to October. Disabled access is at the rear. This gem welcomes locals, visitors, famiies and dogs alike. Winter hours may vary. Q♿☕🅓♿♣♠♿P🐾🐶🛜

Ellesmere

White Hart L

Birch Road, SY12 0ET
☎ (01691) 624653
House beer (by Plan B); 2 changing beers (sourced locally) H

A Grade II-listed building of the early Jacobean period, with a wealth of exposed timber, but also some later alterations. Back in the Guide after a change of management, the interior comprises a public bar and lounge. The drinking area to the rear has a tented gazebo. The pub was once owned by the Border brewery of Wrexham. Three guest beers include offerings from local breweries. It is convenient for the Llangollen Canal as the marina is close by. 🏠♿P🚃🐶🛜♪

Kinlet

Eagle & Serpent L

DY12 3BE
☎ (01299) 841227
Hobsons Mild, Town Crier; Wye Valley HPA H

This beamed 17th-century pub in a rural village has a roomy bar and a large dining area to the rear. Other separate drinking areas surround a log fire. There are four handpulls, dispensing at least three cask ales from local breweries. Bar snacks, lunchtime and evening menus are available. A welcoming family-run pub, it is popular with walkers and cyclists. The hourly Bridgnorth to Kidderminster bus stops outside. On the Geopark Way Trail and close to the Wyre Forest.
🐾🏠🅓♿♣P🚃(125) 🐶🛜

Little Stretton

Green Dragon

Ludlow Road, SY6 6RE
☎ (01694) 722925 ⊕ greendragonlittlestretton.co.uk
Ludlow Gold; Ruddles Best Bitter; Wye Valley HPA, Butty Bach; 1 changing beer H

Set in a picturesque location in the Shropshire Hills Area of Outstanding Natural Beauty, with an abundance of walks in the district. The L-shaped bar has a comfortable and welcoming feel, and the pleasant dining areas are well used. A collection of wonderfully shaped clay pipes on the bar wall may well be of interest. The beer is mostly from local breweries, as is the cider.
🐾🏠🅓♿P🚃(435) 🐶🛜

Little Wenlock

Huntsman of Little Wenlock

Wellington Road, TF6 5BH
☎ (01952) 503300 ⊕ thehuntsmanoflittlewenlock.co.uk
Wye Valley Bitter; house beer (by Ruddles); 4 changing beers (sourced locally; often Hobsons, Rowton, Three Tuns) H

Nestling below the prominent Wrekin hill, this village pub is well used by locals, walkers and visitors to this scenic area near Telford, and is the focus of village life. Food is served all day in the restaurant and the cosy bar with its warming fire. The varied menu features Sunday roasts, and a separate nibbles menu is available in the

bar. B&B rooms, a holiday cottage, and motor caravan hook ups are available. Dogs allowed in the bar only.
Q♿☕🅓♿♣♠P🐾🐶🛜

Ludlow

Blood Bay

13 High Street, SY8 1BS
Uley Bitter, Pale; 1 changing beer H

A conserved Victorian property, refurbished to look exactly as it would have in the 1800s. It has a public bar, a tiny snug and a back bar but no outside area. Up to three beers are served. Under-16s are not permitted, nor is smoking anywhere in the vicinity of the pub (including e-cigs). Use of mobile phones is also prohibited on the premises. Dogs on leads are welcome on the ground floor only. Toilets are located on the first floor.
Q🚃🐶🚃🐶

Charlton Arms

Ludford Bridge, SY8 1PJ (just over the Ludford Bridge)
☎ (01584) 872813 ⊕ thecharltonarms.co.uk
Hobsons Best; Ludlow Gold, Stairway; Wye Valley Butty Bach; 1 changing beer (often Hobsons) H

This fine building overlooks the River Teme, and is situated on the historic Ludford Bridge up toward Ludlow's last remaining fortified gate and the town centre. It has an attractive bar and a spacious lounge leading to a separate dining room with a terrace. The impressive function suite and roof bar offer fine views across the river towards the town. Accommodation is in 10 en-suite rooms. Dogs are allowed in the bar.
Q♿☕🅓♿♣♠P🚃🐶🛜♪

Church Inn

The Buttercross, SY8 1AW
☎ (01584) 874034 ⊕ thechurchinn.com
Hobsons Best; Ludlow Gold; Wye Valley HPA, Butty Bach H

Popular 14th-century town centre pub which has undergone a comprehensive refurbishment. The ground-floor drinking area has a contemporary feel with a range of seating. Local beers and gins are served. There is also an upstairs seating area with spectacular views of the Church of St Laurence, from which the pub takes its name. Accommodation is available. Traditional and gastro-style meals are served. 🐾🏠🅓♿🚃🐶🛜

Ludlow Brewing Co L

Station Drive, SY8 2PQ
☎ (01584) 873291 ⊕ theludlowbrewingcompany.co.uk
Ludlow Best, Blonde, Gold, Black Knight, Stairway; 1 changing beer (sourced locally; often Ludlow) H

The brewery tap and visitor centre for the Ludlow Brewing Company. An imaginative conversion of a former goods shed, hence the alternative name of the Railway Shed. Built on two levels, there are mash tuns on the upper level, along with comfortable seating and tables, and an outside balcony. The ground floor, where dogs are welcome, boasts hand-crafted timber tables and benches, as well as the bar and shop. Brewery visits are available by arrangement. There are occasional beer festivals and events including music.
Q♿🏠🅓♿🚃♿P🚃🐶🛜

Queens L

113 Lower Galdeford, SY8 1RU (just off town centre, opp Co-op)
☎ (01584) 879177 ⊕ thequeensludlow.com
Hobsons Best; Ludlow Gold; Wye Valley Butty Bach; 1 changing beer (sourced locally; often Hobsons, Ludlow) H

Named after Queen Victoria, this is a popular pub and café bar with a decent range of local ales. Look out for the guest beer offered at a competitive price. The light and airy L-shaped bar has three distinct areas, with dining down a short flight of steps. Bar meals are available, with local produce a proud boast. The large enclosed patio garden has views toward Ludford. The monthly quiz is always well attended. ❀🖾🕪&≉♣🖵🌢☎🎵

Much Wenlock

George & Dragon 🄻 ✔
2 High Street, TF13 6AA
☎ (01952) 727009 🌐 thebestpubintheworld.com
Wye Valley HPA; 4 changing beers (sourced nationally; often Hobsons) 🅗
A lively, friendly pub popular with both locals and visitors to this beautiful, historic small town. Whilst the front bar is rather small, there is additional seating to the rear. Original features include beams, with hanging whisky jars, and there are welcoming fires. There is a varied food offering, mostly home-made. The variety of changing beers has now increased. Dogs are welcome in the front bar only. Q🏵❀❀🕪▲♣🖵(18,436)☎🎵

Neen Sollars

Live & Let Live 🄻
DY14 9AB (1 mile off A456 to the W of Mamble)
SO668720
☎ (01299) 832391
Hobsons Best; Wye Valley HPA; 1 changing beer (sourced locally; often Bewdley, Ludlow, Three Tuns) 🅗
A rural gem, parts of which date from the 13th century. Awash with elaborate reclaimed woodwork, the main bar leads to a number of rooms, including the smaller original bar and a large dining area. Locally sourced home-cooked food includes seasonal specials. A range of malt whiskys and gins complements the local ales. There are extensive views towards Clee Hill and Ludlow from the elevated beer garden. A holiday let is available and motorhomes may be parked overnight.
Q🏵❀🖾🕪♣P☎🌢

Newport

Railway Tavern
62 Upper Bar, TF10 7EJ
☎ (01952) 811177
Black Country Bradley's Finest Golden, Chain Ale, Pig on the Wall, Fireside; 6 changing beers (sourced nationally) 🅗
A comfortable Black Country Ales pub refurbished to a high standard in 2019. It has 12 handpumps with four regular and six changing beers, plus two ciders. There is a friendly atmosphere and an enthusiastic landlord. There are two real fires, with a sunny upstairs terrace for outside drinking. Snacks are available. An alcove houses a dartboard and two teams are supported. Bingo is played weekly, quiz night and folk sessions are held monthly. Families, and dogs, are welcome until early evening. 🏵❀&🖨🖵(5)☎🌢🎵

Onibury

Apple Tree
SY7 9AW (up a short side road from the A49 level crossing)
☎ (01584) 856633 🌐 appletreeonibury.co.uk
Wye Valley HPA; Ludlow Gold, Stairway 🅗

A welcoming village inn with a quirky appearance. The pub was the Griffin Inn in 1877, but spent a considerable period as a retail outlet. Now a pub again, the emphasis is on good beer and friendly conversation. There are three rooms, with the main bar at the front and a small garden. Car parking is available in the nearby village hall car park. Q❀🕪♣P🖵(435)☎🌢

Oswestry

Bailey Head 🍺 🄻
Bailey Head, SY11 1PZ (in market square opp Guildhall)
☎ (01691) 570418 🌐 baileyhead.co.uk
Stonehouse Station Bitter; 5 changing beers (sourced nationally) 🅗
Award-winning free house located in the market square near the old castle. The pub offers one permanent and five constantly changing real ales, vegan-friendly options included, a minimum of three KeyKeg beers, four draught real ciders and a perry. Beers are sourced locally, regionally and nationally, usually from microbreweries, and served in thirds if requested. Food can be ordered in. Events include tap takeovers, Meet the Brewer and music or quiz nights. Dogs are especially welcome. The market car park is nearby. 🖨&♣●🖵☎🌢☎

Shifnal

Anvil Inn 🄻
22 Aston Road, TF11 8DU
☎ (01952) 462686
Black Country Bradley's Finest Golden, Pig on the Wall, Fireside; 5 changing beers (sourced regionally) 🅗
Popular family-run Black Country Ales pub with a real fire and 10 handpulls, supporting many local pastimes including darts and domino teams, curry evenings and coach trips to other pubs. Substantial fresh bar snacks are always available. A garden area at the rear sports a large gazebo. Beer festivals are held three times a year and feature foot-long hot dogs. Dogs are welcome. Free car parking is 150 yards away, while the train station is 100 yards on foot. Q❀&≉♣●P🖵☎🌢☎

King's Yard
2 Cheapside, Bradford Street, TF11 8BN
☎ 07957 250734
Wye Valley HPA, Butty Bach; 2 changing beers (sourced regionally) 🅗
A popular micropub situated in a retail unit close to the railway station. There are four handpulls, two dedicated to Wye Valley beers, one for dark and one for a guest, usually sourced locally. Eight craft beers are also sold on tap, while numerous bottles and cans are available from refrigerators. There are seating areas upstairs and downstairs. Hot food is served weekday lunchtimes. Free council parking is located nearby. Q🏵&≉♣●P🖵☎

Plough Inn 🄻
26 Broadway, TF11 8AZ
☎ (01952) 463118 🌐 theploughinnshifnal.co.uk
Hobsons Best; Three Tuns Best; Timothy Taylor Landlord; 6 changing beers (sourced regionally) 🅗
Traditional free house dating back to the 17th century, run by the same family since 2012. A cosy, quarry tiled interior leads to an extensive function room. A large suntrap beer garden at the rear is incredibly popular in warm weather and also boasts a covered heated area. Up to eight cask ales and two ciders are available, and home-cooked pub food, including pies, is a firm favourite. Dogs are allowed in the garden.
Q🏵❀🕪≉♣●🖵☎🌢☎

Shrewsbury

Abbey L ✓

83 Monkmoor Road, Monkmoor, SY2 5AZ
☎ (01743) 236788
Sharp's Doom Bar; 6 changing beers ⊞
A large pub with several alcoves, plus a beer garden with heated and covered areas. The publican, an ale enthusiast, offers beers from a range of breweries in varied styles, and a number of sparkling and still ciders, not all real. Craft keg is available and food is served every day. There are regular community events including quizzes and occasional live music and beer events (festivals and Meet The Brewer).
荏霂◑&♣●P➡(1) 🕏 ♪

Anchor ✓

137 Frankwell, Frankwell, SY3 8JX
☎ (01743) 537169
Timothy Taylor Landlord; Wye Valley HPA, Butty Bach ⊞
Once owned by Wem brewery, also by Wrekin brewery of Wellington, the Anchor is a traditional one-roomed pub conveniently located opposite Theatre Severn. A small but secluded smoking area is available to the rear, and because of the limited disabled access a ramp can be provided on request. A real cider is often available from the cellar if requested. 荏霂◑≷♣●➡❀♪

Cross Foxes

27 Longden Coleham, SY3 7DE (close to River Severn in suburb of Longden Coleham)
☎ (01743) 355050
Draught Bass; Salopian Shropshire Gold; Three Tuns XXX ⊞
The pub has been a free house since its purchase from Mitchells & Butlers in the late 1980s, and run by the same family since 1985. It has one large L-shaped room, with the bar and major drinking area on the large stroke, the smaller stroke occupied by darts and another drinking area. The main part has an efficient wood-burner and the walls are adorned with sports trophies and a fine Bass mirror. Q&♣➡🕏

Loggerheads ★ L ✓

1 Church Street, SY1 1UG
☎ (01743) 362398
Brakspear Oxford Gold; Marston's EPA, Pedigree; 2 changing beers (sourced nationally) ⊞
This 18th-century Grade II-listed pub in the town centre has been identified by CAMRA as having a nationally important historic pub interior. It has a small bar and three other rooms: the Lounge; the Poet's Room (which features portraits of Shropshire poets); and the Gentlemen's Room (so-called because until 1975 it was gents only). The Gentlemen's and Poet's are served from a hatch. The pub hosts regular folk and acoustic music events with a cheap night on Tuesday. Q≷●➡❀♪

Montgomery's Tower L ✓

Lower Claremont Bank, SY1 1RT
☎ (01743) 239080
Greene King IPA; Salopian Shropshire Gold; 4 changing beers (often Sharp's, Slater's) ⊞
Close to the Quarry Park and handy for Theatre Severn, this Lloyds No.1 offers a choice of two bars. To the left is a large, open area rich in natural light, with a smoking area to the rear. The bar to the right provides quieter surroundings and subdued lighting, except on Friday and Saturday when there is a DJ. The walls display prints illustrating local history and famous Salopians.
荏霂◑&≷●➡🕏♪

Nag's Head L ✓

22 Wyle Cop, SY1 1XB
☎ (01743) 362455
Hobsons Best; Timothy Taylor Landlord; Wye Valley HPA; 2 changing beers (often Titanic) ⊞
Situated on the historic Wyle Cop, the main architectural features of this popular Grade II-listed, timber-framed building are best appreciated externally. To the front there is notable upper-storey jettying, and in the pleasant beer garden to the rear there are the timber remnants of a 14th-century hall house. The old-style interior has remained unaltered for many years. The pub is said to be haunted and features on the Shrewsbury Ghost Trail. 霂≷♣➡❀

Prince of Wales L

30 Bynner Street, Belle Vue, SY3 7NZ
☎ (01743) 343301 ● theprince.pub
Hobsons Mild, Twisted Spire; Salopian Golden Thread; St Austell Tribute; 2 changing beers (sourced locally) ⊞
Welcoming two-roomed community pub with heated smoking shelter and large suntrap deck, adjoining a bowling green overlooked by a 19th-century maltings. Darts, dominoes and bowls teams abound. Beer festivals are held in February and May. Shrewsbury Town FC memorabilia adorn the building, with some of the seating from the old Gay Meadow ground skirting the bowling green. Westons Rosie's Pig is served on handpull. In 2019 the pub deservedly reached the last 16 of the CAMRA National Pub of the Year competition.
Q荏❀&♣●P➡❀♪

Salopian Bar L ✓

Smithfield Road, SY1 1PW
☎ (01743) 351505
Oakham Citra; Salopian Oracle; 3 changing beers (often Oakham, Salopian) ⊞
A multi-room pub, expanded and refurbished following flooding in 2020, now with an added separate lounge building. The bar's management strives to vary the beer, cider and perry range to satisfy demand for variety. Regular cider and perry is available, and a good and increasing range of bottled beers, including gluten-free, can also be bought. Largescreen TVs show coverage of major sports events. It is popular with all age groups, and there is regular live music on Friday evening.
&≷●➡❀🕏♪

Tap & Can

13 Castle Gates, SY1 2AB
☎ 07837 490495
4 changing beers ⊞
Opened in 2019, this single-room bar close to the town railway station has its counter at the far end. Four handpumps offer a changing range of real ales, plus KeyKeg and craft keg beers. Cans are served from vast fridges near the bar, available to drink in or take away. The rear wall of the Gents is the exposed castle foundations and is over 900 years old. Dogs are welcome. ◗≷➡❀

Three Fishes L

4 Fish Street, SY1 1UR
☎ (01743) 344793
4 changing beers (sourced regionally; often Salopian) ⊞
15th-century building standing in the shadow of two churches, St Alkmund's and St Julian's, within the maze of streets and passageways in the town's medieval quarter. Freshly prepared food is available at lunchtimes and early evenings Monday to Saturday, and Tuesday to Friday afternoons. The pub offers a range of up to five

local and national ales, usually including some dark beers, and real ciders and perries. It is a friendly pub with no TV screens and good conversation. Q◑▩≢♣♠▢❀🐾🛜

Woodman ⓛ

32 Coton Hill, SY1 2DZ
☎ (01743) 351007
Salopian Shropshire Gold; Ossett White Rat; Wye Valley Butty Bach; 2 changing beers (sourced regionally) Ⓗ

Part-brick and part half-timbered black and white corner pub, originally built in the 1800s, destroyed by fire in 1923, and rebuilt in 1925. The building is reputedly haunted by the ex-landlady who died in the fire. The wonderful oak-panelled lounge has two real log fires and traditional settles, and the separate bar has the original stone-tiled flooring, wooden seating, fire, and listed leaded windows. The courtyard has a heated smoking area and seating. The bar specialises in pale, hoppy beers. Q🌣❀≢♣♠▢❀🛜♫

Telford: Ironbridge

Coracle Micropub & Beer Shop

27 High Street, TF8 7AD
☎ (01952) 432664
Changing beers (sourced nationally; often Glasshouse, Salopian, Verdant) Ⓗ/Ⓐ

A welcoming gem of a pub, only a few yards from the historic Ironbridge. The building was formerly a printer's, jeweller's, and butcher's, in true micropub tradition. The name reflects the local production and operation of coracles on the River Severn. There is always one Salopian beer plus three other changing beers. Around 120 bottled and canned beers are also available. Locally made bar snacks are available, but customers can also bring in their own food. Children welcome until 7pm. Q🌣Å♣♠▢(8,18)❀🛜

Telford: Madeley

All Nations ⓛ

20 Coalport Road, TF7 5DP (signed off Legges Way, opp Blists Hill Museum)
☎ (01952) 585747 ⊕ allnationsinn.co.uk
House beer (by All Nations); 2 changing beers (sourced regionally; often Hobsons, Ludlow) Ⓗ

One of the last four historic brewhouses remaining in the country at the start of the 1970s, near Blists Hill Museum and the World Heritage Area. Now a CAMRA Golden Award Winner, the pub is famed for its friendly clientele, substantial fresh baps (black pudding and cheese a speciality), and All Nations beer plus two guests. A small, cosy, dog-friendly interior has a wood-burner for winter. Outside there are many drinking areas. Camping is available in the field at rear of the pub. Evening opening times may vary. Q🌣❀⋈Å♠P❀🛜♫

Telford: Oakengates

Crown Inn ⓛ ✅

Market Street, TF2 6EA
☎ (01952) 610888 ⊕ crown.oakengates.net
Hobsons Twisted Spire, Best; 10 changing beers (sourced nationally; often Big Hand, Burton Bridge, Rudgate) Ⓗ

Cosy, traditional three-room town pub with real fires in front and rear bars. Offers real cider, mild and stout/porter. There are 14 cooled handpulls with more for beer festivals in May and October. A regular comedy club, live music, quiz and games nights are hosted (details on Facebook). There is level access via the courtyard at the

rear from bus station and car park. Quality bar snacks and extensive range of overseas bottled beers are available. CAMRA Golden Award winner.
Q🌣❀&♣≢♠P▢🐾🛜♫

Old Fighting Cocks ⓛ

48 Market Street, TF2 6DU
☎ (01952) 615607
Oakham Citra; Everards Old Original; Rowton Meteorite, Ironbridge Gold, Area 51; 4 changing beers (sourced nationally) Ⓗ

Popular family-run Rowton brewery pub with 12 handpulls, three for Rowton's own beers, plus Everards Old Original, Oakham Citra, and four changing beers and three ciders. Contains many period features and log burners in most of its four cosy, welcoming rooms. A function room is available, and there is a large outside area with covered section. Bar snacks available and dogs are welcome. It's close to other real ale pubs, and to good public transport links and car parks.
Q❀&≢♣♠▢🐾🛜

Station Hotel ⓛ

42 Market Street, TF2 6DU
☎ (01952) 612949
8 changing beers (sourced nationally; often Abbeydale, Bathams, Pictish) Ⓗ

With an ever-changing selection of beer dispensed from nine handpulls, three festivals held on May and August bank holidays, plus one in December, this pub, on the Oakengates triangle, has been in the Guide for a number of years. There is a welcoming fire in the front bar, and along with two further rooms, is fully accessible with a refurbished toilet. Home-made rolls and pies are available. A heated smoking patio is at the rear. Pub opening times may vary. Q❀&≢♣▢🐾🛜

Telford: St Georges

St Georges Sports & Social Club ⓛ

Church Road, St Georges, TF2 9LU
☎ (01952) 612911 ⊕ stgeorgesclub.co.uk
Three Tuns XXX; 7 changing beers (sourced regionally; often Ludlow, Salopian, Wye Valley) Ⓗ

A friendly, welcoming, private members club which frequently wins the local CAMRA Club of the Year award. Eight handpulls dispense mostly regional beers in a spacious lounge bar which shows live sport on largescreens and has views of the sports fields. The club features a large function room which is available for hire, with bespoke bar and on-site catering services available. Card-carrying CAMRA members and people with this Guide are welcome at all times. 🌣❀&♣P▢🛜♫

Telford: Wellington

Pheasant Inn ▼ ⓛ

54 Market Street, TF1 1DT
☎ (01952) 260683
Everards Tiger; Rowton Ironbridge Gold, Area 51; 8 changing beers (sourced nationally; often Bristol Beer Factory, Mallinsons, Oakham) Ⓗ

Rowton's brewery tap is one of their three family-run traditional pubs and was local CAMRA Pub of the Year 2022. Nine handpulls are on display, three for Rowton's ales, four for changing beers (at least one is a dark beer), plus two changing ciders. There is a large beer garden with covered area. Home-made food is served Tuesday to Saturday lunchtimes; bar snacks are available any time. Public car parks nearby. Disabled access is via the rear door; dogs are welcome. Q🌣❀◑&≢♠▢🐾🛜

Wrekin Inn 🄻

26 Wrekin Road, TF1 1RH (located just off ring road by the leisure centre on the edge of town)
⊕ rowtonbrewery.com
Rowton Ironbridge Gold, Area 51; house beer (by Rowton); 3 changing beers (sourced nationally) ⊞
A recently refurbished traditional real ale pub run by Rowton brewery. There are two comfortable bar areas with log-burners and a pool room. Three Rowton beers on handpull, plus three guests and a dark beer are offered, and an extensive craft range from the fridge. Regular live music features at weekends, but it is quiet at other times. It has good public transport links and is less than half a mile from the brewery and its tap house, the Pheasant Inn. Q🛏️🕮👶🌳♿≠♣♠🖿🚆❄🛜🎵

Upper Farmcote

Lion O'Morfe 🄻

Upper Farmcote, WV15 5PS (½ mile from A458 signpost Claverley) SO770919
☎ (01746) 389935
Hobsons Town Crier; Wye Valley HPA; 2 changing beers (sourced locally; often Enville, Ludlow, Three Tuns) ⊞
A former Georgian farmhouse that became a pub in the early 1850s. A popular locals' pub which is also frequently visited by walkers and cyclists, the pub has justifiably won several recent local CAMRA awards. There are several rooms: bar, snug, lounge and conservatory, and also a beer garden. There are usually five local ales and a local cider on handpump to accompany the substantial meals which are served every lunchtime (not Mon in winter) and Wednesday to Saturday evenings. Q🛏️🕮👶🎍👤♣♠🖿❄

Weston

Stonehouse Brewery 🄻

Stonehouse, Weston Road, SY10 9ES (just off A483 Oswestry bypass)
☎ (01691) 676457 ⊕ stonehousebrewery.co.uk
Stonehouse Wrangler, Station Bitter, Cambrian Gold; 1 changing beer (often Stonehouse) ⊞
The family-run Stonehouse Brewery Visitor Centre bar is part of the brewery and next to the preserved Cambrian Railway. The rustic-styled Centre sells only Stonehouse products – at least four cask beers, their own keg beers, Sweeney Mountain Cider and distilled on-site Henstone spirits. Bottles, gift packs and fill your own facilities are available. Brewery tours are by appointment. Food is served Wednesday to Sunday in summer, and Thursday to Sunday in winter. Q🛏️🕮👶🎍♿♣♠🖿🚆❄🛜

Whitchurch

Black Bear 🄻

High Street, SY13 1AZ
☎ (01948) 663800
Salopian Shropshire Gold; Stonehouse Station Bitter; house beer (by Big Hand); 2 changing beers ⊞
A welcome return to the Guide for this tastefully renovated black and white pub. It lies opposite the historic St Alkmund's church at the top of High Street. The ornate bar has six handpulls serving an ever-changing range of guest beers from both local and lesser-known national microbreweries, with pumpclips adorning the walls, ceiling and bar area. Cider is served on gravity. There are two separate dining areas and an upstairs meeting room. Q🕮🎍♣🖿🚆🎵

Worfield

Dog & Davenport Arms 🄻

Main Street, WV15 5LF (from A454 towards village, then turn towards church and the pub is opp the school)
☎ (01746) 716020
Hobsons Town Crier; Wye Valley HPA; 1 changing beer (sourced locally) ⊞
Known locally as the Dog, this 19th-century inn was formerly called the Greyhound. It was first licensed in 1800, when owned by the Earl of Dartmouth. It has a separate bar with a low ceiling and a lounge with wood-burners leading to the restaurant. Local ales are served as well as home-made food. Outside there are two patio areas offering a variety of seating. The hourly Wolverhampton-Bridgnorth bus stops ½ mile away in Wyken. Q🛏️🕮🎍👶♿♣🖿(114)❄🛜

Breweries

All Nations

🍺 **20 Coalport Road, Madeley, Telford, TF7 5SU**
☎ **(01952) 585747** ✉ allnationsinn@btinternet.com

☺One of the famous four last brewpubs, it was established in 1832 and run by just two families for the first 151 years. Although, the present owner, Jim Birthwhistle, sadly passed away, Andy Brough continues to brew as he has done for the last ten years. The brewery is a ten-barrel plant.

Bitter (ABV 3.9%) BITTER

Clun SIBA

🍺 **White Horse Inn, The Square, Clun, SY7 8JA**
☎ **(01588) 640523** ✉ clunbrewery@gmail.com

☺Established in 2007 behind the White Horse, Clun, as a microbrewery. A 2.5-barrel plant was installed in 2010, and brewing has increased steadily since then, with beers supplied to the trade across the West Midlands and the Welsh Marches. Cask, bottle-conditioned and bright beer is available for sale to the public. Ad-hoc brewery tours are available (enquire at bar). ◆LIVE

Loophole (ABV 3.5%) BITTER
Pale Ale (ABV 4.1%) BITTER
Solar (ABV 4.3%) SPECIALITY
Green Man (ABV 4.4%) BITTER
Citadel (ABV 5.9%) BITTER

Corvedale

🍺 **Corvedale, Corfton, Craven Arms, SY7 9DF**
☎ **(01584) 861239** ⊕ corvedalebrewery.co.uk

☺Brewing started in 1999 behind the pub. The brewery and pub were sold, and brewing was suspended. ‼◆LIVE

Finney's

51 Wrockwardine Road, Wellington, TF1 3DA
☎ **(01952) 412224** ✉ finney@blueyonder.co.uk

A half-barrel capacity microbrewery supplying local pubs in Wellington and Oakengates as well as Shropshire beer festivals on an occasional basis since 2010. The brewery produces a small but steadily expanding range of hand-crafted ales in a range of styles, upon request from the pubs they appear in. Most made with traditional hop varieties. Beers produced commercially include an award-winning strong dark bitter and a pale bitter often produced for Christmas.

Hobsons SIBA

Newhouse Farm, Tenbury Road, Cleobury Mortimer, DY14 8RD
☎ (01299) 270837 ⊕ hobsons-brewery.co.uk

Established in 1993 in a former sawmill, Hobsons relocated to a farm site with more space in 1995. A second brew kit, bottling plant and a warehouse have been added along with significant expansion to the first brewery. Beers are supplied within a 50-mile radius. The brewery utilises environmental sustainable technologies where possible. A visitor centre was added in 2014, which also now operates as a taproom. !! ⬛LIVE ⚫

Mild (ABV 3.2%) MILD
A classic mild. Complex layers of taste come from roasted malts that predominate and give lots of flavour.
Twisted Spire (ABV 3.6%) GOLD
Best (ABV 3.8%) BITTER
A pale brown to amber, medium-bodied beer with strong hop character throughout. It is consequently bitter, but with malt discernible in the taste.
Old Prickly (ABV 4.2%) PALE
Town Crier (ABV 4.5%) GOLD

Joule's

The Brewery, Great Hales Street, Market Drayton, TF9 1JP
☎ (01630) 654400 ⊕ joulesbrewery.co.uk

Re-established in 2010, following a break of 40 years. Joule's is situated in Market Drayton, and has access to pure mineral water drawn from the same aquifer as the original brewery. It runs a collection of over 40 taphouses across its heartland of Shropshire, Staffordshire and Cheshire. !! ⚫

Pure Blonde (ABV 3.8%) BLOND
Pale Ale (ABV 4.1%) PALE
Slumbering Monk (ABV 4.5%) BITTER

Ludlow SIBA

The Railway Shed, Station Drive, Ludlow, SY8 2PQ
☎ (01584) 873291
⊕ theludlowbrewingcompany.co.uk

☺Established in 2006, the brewery occupies a converted railway sidings shed. Beers are produced using a 20-barrel plant and a microplant called the Derailed Brewing Co for one-off beers. The premises also function as a taproom (which now has regularly-changing beer from the micro plant including some experimental keg beers), visitor centre and event area. !! ⬛ ⚫

Best (ABV 3.7%) BITTER
Blonde (ABV 4%) BLOND
Gold (ABV 4.2%) GOLD
Black Knight (ABV 4.5%) STOUT
Red Dawn (ABV 4.5%) RED
Stairway (ABV 5%) GOLD

Plan B

Audley Avenue Enterprise Park, Audley Avenue, Newport, TF10 7DW
☎ (01952) 810091 ⊕ newbrew.co.uk

☺Plan B is a family-run brewery set up in 2016 using a 10-barrel plant. Cask-conditioned ale is available within a 30-mile radius of the brewery. It has its own bottling plant and all beers are available from the shop or online. !! ⬛LIVE

New Alchemy (ABV 3.9%) BITTER
New Session IPA (ABV 4%) PALE

American Pale Ale (ABV 4.1%) IPA
New Tun (ABV 4.2%) IPA
Boscobel Bitter (ABV 4.3%) BITTER
Newport Pale Ale (ABV 4.4%) PALE

Rowton SIBA

🍺 **Pheasant, 56 Market Street, Wellington, TF1 1DT**
☎ 07854 885870 ⊕ rowtonbrewery.co.uk

Rowton Brewery is an independent, family-run brewery established in 2008. Originally based at the family farm in the village of Rowton, a second brewing site was established in 2017 behind the Pheasant Inn in Wellington, with Wellington now the sole brewing location. The brew length of the brewery is six barrels. ⬦

St Annes

St Annes Church, Shorthill, Lea Cross, SY5 8JE
☎ (01743) 860296 ☎ 07530 556951

Office: 38 Hafren Road, Shrewsbury, SY3 8NQ
⊕ shropshirebeers.co.uk

⊠ Brewing began in 2017. This independent brewery is in the quirky location of a restored and occasionally functioning church. Recipes are Scandinavian-influenced but traditional British real ales. A broad range of beer styles is produced. !!⬦

Three Erics (ABV 3.7%) BITTER
Golden Dart (ABV 3.8%) GOLD
Lea Cross Dark (ABV 3.9%) MILD
Tumbledown Dick (ABV 4.2%) BITTER
Round the Wrekin (ABV 4.7%) BITTER
Iron & Fire (ABV 7.5%) STOUT

Salopian SIBA

The Old Station Yard, Station Road, Hadnall, SY4 3DD
☎ (01743) 248414 ⊕ salopianbrewery.co.uk

☺The brewery was established in 1995 in an old dairy on the outskirts of Shrewsbury but moved in 2014 to its new location in an industrial unit in the village of Hadnall, where it now produces more than 150 barrels a week of its multi award-winning ales, for distribution throughout the midlands, and further afield. To capitalise on the small pack market, the brewery has invested in its own canning line. !! ⬛ ⚫LIVE

Shropshire Gold (ABV 3.8%) GOLD
Oracle (ABV 4%) GOLD
Citrus aromas lead to an impressive dry and increasing citrusy taste.
Darwins Origin (ABV 4.3%) BITTER
Pale brown in which hops and fruit are dominant. Hops top the aftertaste with a pleasing lingering bitterness. Well-balanced with a moreish demand.
Hop Twister (ABV 4.5%) GOLD
Lemon Dream (ABV 4.5%) SPECIALITY
Golden Thread (ABV 5%) GOLD
Kashmir (ABV 5.5%) BITTER
Automaton (ABV 7%) STRONG
Gold with pine forest aromas and peaches! Syrup with a kick. Dry hints and exotic astringency as hops give a dry finish but sweet balance.

Severn Valley

The Stables, Hollow Ash Lane, Bridgnorth, WV15 6ET
☎ 07402 636482 ✉ beer@severnvalleyales.co.uk

The trading name of Bridgnorth Brewery Ltd, Severn Valley Ales started brewing in 2019 producing a range of beers in different packaging formats. The main outlet is

Bridgnorth Rugby Club, but beers can be found in other pubs in Bridgnorth. Brewing is currently suspended.

Stonehouse SIBA

Stonehouse, Weston, SY10 9ES
☎ **(01691) 676457** ⊕ **stonehousebrewery.co.uk**

Stonehouse is a family-run brewery, distillery and cider maker. Established in 2007, it operates a 22-barrel plant. It is next to the Cambrian Heritage Railways line and includes a shop, bar and restaurant. Direct delivery is within 30 miles of the brewery. !! ◉ ✦

Wrangler (ABV 3.8%) IPA
Station Bitter (ABV 3.9%) BITTER
Cambrian Gold (ABV 4.2%) GOLD

Three Tuns SIBA

⊟ Salop Street, Bishop's Castle, SY9 5BN ☎ 07973 301099

Office:16 Market Square, Bishops Castle, SY9 5BW
⊕ **threetunsbrewery.co.uk**

Brewing on this site started in the 16th century and was licensed in 1642. A small-scale tower brewery from the late 19th century survives. Three Tuns was one of only four pub breweries still running in the 1970s. Today its beers can be found throughout the Midlands at selected free houses. !! ◉ ✦ LIVE

Mild (ABV 3.4%) MILD
Rantipole (ABV 3.7%) BITTER
Best (ABV 3.8%) BITTER
Solstice (ABV 3.9%) PALE
XXX (ABV 4.3%) BITTER
A pale, sweetish bitter with a light hop aftertaste that has a honey finish.
Stout (ABV 4.4%) STOUT
Dark brown to black. Mixed dried fruit aroma with yeast. Bitter start, fruity with roast. Balanced finish with fruit and sweetness among the hops.
Cleric's Cure (ABV 5%) IPA
Old Scrooge (ABV 6.5%) BARLEY

Three Fishes, Shrewsbury (Photo: Nigel Parker)

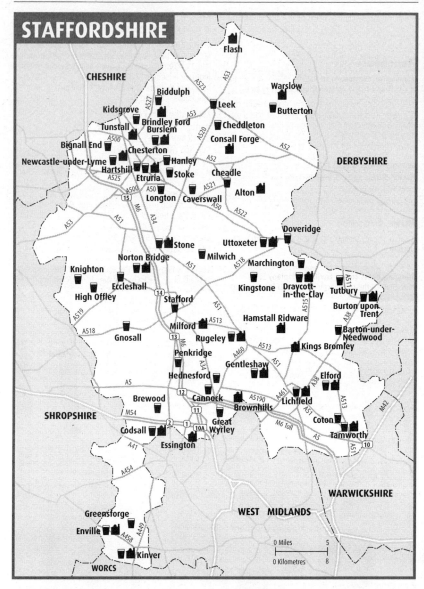

STAFFORDSHIRE

CHESHIRE

Flash
Biddulph
Warslow
Kidsgrove
Leek
Butterton
Tunstall
Brindley Ford
Burslem
Cheddleton
Bignall End
Chesterton
Consall Forge
Newcastle-under-Lyme
Hartshill
Hanley
DERBYSHIRE
Etruria
Stoke
Cheadle
Longton
Caverswall
Alton
Stone
Doveridge
Norton Bridge
Uttoxeter
Milwich
Marchington
Knighton
Eccleshall
Kingstone
Draycott-in-the-Clay
Tutbury
High Offley
Stafford
Burton upon Trent
Gnosall
Milford
Hamstall Ridware
Barton-under-Needwood
Penkridge
Rugeley
Kings Bromley
Hednesford
Gentleshaw
Elford
Brewood
Cannock
Lichfield
SHROPSHIRE
Brownhills
Coton
Codsall
Great Wyrley
Tamworth
Essington
WARWICKSHIRE
WEST MIDLANDS
Greensforge
Enville
Kinver
WORCS

0 Miles 5
0 Kilometres 8

Barton-under-Needwood

Royal Oak

74 The Green, DE13 8JD (½ mile S of B5016 via Wales Lane)
☎ (01283) 713852
Marston's Pedigree; 2 changing beers (sourced nationally) H /G

Bustling community local on the southern edge of the village, home to many traditional pub game teams and a base for several local sports teams. While parts of the building date back to the 16th century, the pub has only existed since the mid-1800s. Public bar and lounge customers are served from a central sunken bar below the level of the rest of the ground floor. A separate conservatory offers access to the garden. Beers are on handpump, or by gravity direct from the cask on request.
Q ⧖ ❀ ♣ P ⊟ (12) ❁ ☎

Biddulph

Crafty Flanker

35 High Street, ST8 6AW
☎ 07973 764298
5 changing beers (often Front Row) H

A welcome new entry to the Guide. This tiny micropub is owned and run by the small independent, locally based Front Row brewery, with all house beers having rugby-themed names. A showcase for Front Row beers, a range of six cask ales are sold, with four more on keg taps, some unusual lagers plus a range of real cider. No national branded beers or lagers are ever sold here! A large range of locally produced specialist gins are stocked. Major sporting events are shown in the small back room. An even smaller upstairs function room is available to hire. Q ◑ ⊟ ♫

Bignall End

Swan ✓

58 Chapel Street, ST7 8QD (just off B5500 near Audley)
☎ (01782) 720622 ⊕ dorbiere.co.uk/the-swan
Draught Bass; Oakham Citra; 6 changing beers (sourced nationally) ⊞

This popular pub sits at the heart of the community and a warm welcome from both staff and customers awaits you. There is a bar area, a comfortable lounge and a large pleasant beer garden. The eight real ales are sourced from many different breweries, and a range of ciders and perries is also available. Bingo, major live sports and charity events are regular occurrences, and beer and cider festivals are held throughout the year. A real gem in the area. ☎☺♣♠🍴(4,1a)☺📶

Brewood

Swan 🍷 ⓛ ✓

15 Market Place, ST19 9BS
☎ (01902) 850330
Burton Bridge Stairway to Heaven; Holden's Black Country Bitter; Three Tuns XXX; Wye Valley HPA; 2 changing beers (often Enville, Salopian) ⊞

Busy characterful old coaching inn, with low-beamed ceilings and seasonal log fires. Its village centre location makes it convenient for the Shropshire Union Canal and the Staffordshire Way. Cosy snugs, displaying early prints of the district, flank the central bar which, unusually for the area, stocks nearly 80 malt whiskies and 20 gins from around the world. There is a traditional skittle alley upstairs which doubles as a function room and hosts a fun quiz on Sunday evenings. Major Freeview sporting events are shown. Q☎☺♣P🍴(877,878)☺📶

Burton upon Trent

Beeropolis

81 High Street, DE14 1LD (on W side of northern end of High St)
4 changing beers (sourced regionally) ⊞

Refreshed and renamed in 2021, this micropub is on the ground floor of a Grade II-listed end-terrace building. The comfortable single room features upholstered bench seating around the periphery, with a raised area under the shop-style windows. There is a small bar counter to the side towards the rear, with the stillage room behind. The Gents incorporates an unusual keg urinal! Beers and other drinks are listed on a TV screen near the bar. No pub car park, but public car parks are nearby.
Q☎☺♠🍴☺

Coopers Tavern ★

43 Cross Street, DE14 1EG (off Station St)
☎ (01283) 567246
Draught Bass; Joule's Pale Ale Ⓖ, Slumbering Monk ⊞; 6 changing beers (sourced regionally) ⊞/Ⓖ

Classic 19th-century ale house, once the Bass Brewery tap but currently part of the Joule's estate. Following a sympathetic refurbishment and expansion in 2017, the pub incorporates five linked rooms. The intimate inner tap room has retained its barrel tables and bench seating, with the beer served from a small counter by the cask stillage. Fruit wines, plus up to six ciders/perries (choice varies) are also available. Impromptu folk music regularly features on Tuesday evening, and live music most Sunday afternoons.
☎☺≠(Burton on Trent) ♠🍴☺📶♫

Devonshire Arms 🍷

86 Station Street, DE14 1BT (on corner of jct with Milton St)

☎ (01283) 480022
Burton Bridge Bridge Bitter, Stairway to Heaven; Draught Bass; Gates Burton Reservoir; Titanic Plum Porter; 3 changing beers (sourced regionally) ⊞

Popular old pub, now a free house, dating from the 19th century and Grade II listed. Brewery memorabilia is displayed in the refurbished public bar at the front; to the rear is a larger, more comfortable, split-level lounge featuring an 1853 map of Burton, old local photographs and unusual arched wooden ceilings. An extended rear patio is adorned with flower borders and hanging baskets. The Tuesday food evening has a theme, such as fish, pies or steak. Football fans are welcome, including away supporters. ☎☺🍴≠(Burton on Trent)♣P🍴☺📶

Dog Inn

5 Lichfield Street, DE14 3QZ (opp Burton College; near jct with High St/New St)
☎ (01283) 517060
Black Country Pig on the Wall, Fireside; house beer (by Black Country); 7 changing beers (sourced regionally) ⊞

An attractive half-timbered terrace pub near the town centre, dating back to the early 19th century. Radically revitalised by Black Country Ales in 2015, an impressive selection of cask ales (and other draught drinks) is offered. Internally, a large, comfortable, square single room surrounds a central bar and features a wood-framed ceiling and wood panelling on the walls, plus three real fires and numerous framed old photographs of Burton. Available beers and other drinks are listed on a wall-mounted screen near the bar. ☎♣🍴☺📶♫

Elms Inn ✓

36 Stapenhill Road, Stapenhill, DE15 9AE (on A444)
☎ (01283) 535505 ⊕ dorbiere.co.uk/the-elms
Draught Bass; Timothy Taylor Landlord; 2 changing beers (sourced nationally; often Marston's) ⊞

REAL ALE BREWERIES

Beowulf Brownhills
Blythe Hamstall Ridware
Brewhouse & Kitchen 🍴 Lichfield
Burton Bridge Burton upon Trent
Consall Forge Consall Forge
Crown Brewhouse 🍴 Elford (brewing suspended)
Enville Enville
Firs 🍴 Codsall
Flash Flash
Fountain Essington (NEW)
Front Row Brindley Ford
Gates Burton Burton upon Trent
Gentlewood Gentleshaw
Inadequate 🍴 Stoke-on-Trent: Etruria
Izaak Walton 🍴 Norton Bridge
Kinver Kinver
Lymestone Stone
Marston's Burton upon Trent
Peakstones Rock Alton
Quartz Kings Bromley
Roebuck Draycott-in-the-Clay
Shugborough Milford (brewing suspended)
Six Towns 🍴 Tunstall (brewing suspended)
Tamworth 🍴 Tamworth
Titanic Stoke-on-Trent: Burslem
Tower 🍴 Burton upon Trent
Trinity 🍴 Lichfield
Uttoxeter 🍴 Uttoxeter
Vine Inn 🍴 Rugeley
Weal Chesterton
Wilsons of Warslow 🍴 Warslow (NEW)

Lively local on the opposite bank of the River Trent from the town centre. Built as a private house in the late 19th century, this is one of Burton's original parlour pubs. Sensitively renovated, the small public bar, snug and a side room at the front of the pub are largely unchanged. In contrast, the lounge to the rear has been extended and refurbished in a modern style. Food is normally limited to light snacks, but themed food evenings are sometimes held. There is occasional live entertainment. ☼❀♣🖳(18)❀🤎♿🛜♪

Roebuck Inn ✔

101 Station Street, DE14 1BT (on corner of jct with Mosley St)
☎ (01283) 511213 ⊕ roe-buck-inn.co.uk
Draught Bass; Greene King Abbot; Marston's Pedigree; Theakston Old Peculier; 2 changing beers (sourced regionally) Ⓗ
Friendly Victorian corner-terrace pub near the railway station, once the Ind Coope Brewery tap, opposite the former brewery. The original classic Draught Burton Ale was launched here in 1976. Inside, there is a long narrow single room with dark wood panelling and the bar counter down one side. A small patio at the rear is available for outdoor drinking, plus a few tables and chairs outside at the front in summer. Live music is played early Sunday evening.
❀🚲≷(Burton on Trent) ♣🖳🤎🛜♪

Weighbridge Inn

Grain Warehouse Yard, Derby Street, DE14 2JJ (off S end of Derby St, A5121, one-way section)
☎ 07758 546922
Muirhouse Tick Tock Ⓗ**; 3 changing beers (sourced regionally)** Ⓗ/Ⓖ
Two-room micropub created in a late-Victorian former coal yard office in 2015 and now operated by the Muirhouse brewery. It is close to the railway station and en route to Burton Albion's Pirelli Stadium, nearly a mile distant. The bar counter is in the main room, with the available beers and other offerings listed on a blackboard. A cosy smaller room is located through a doorway at the far end; both rooms feature fireplaces. Meals are limited to pre-booked Sunday lunches. Children are welcome until early evening.
☼❀◗≷(Burton on Trent) ♣🤎🖳🤎

Butterton

Black Lion Inn Ⓛ

ST13 7SP (in centre of village next to the church)
☎ (01538) 304232 ⊕ blacklioninn.co.uk
Draught Bass; 2 changing beers (often Storm, Wincle) Ⓗ
A charming pub with plenty of olde-worlde charm set in the heart of the village next to the church, within the Peak District National Park and close to the Manifold trail. There is a single bar, a separate restaurant, and a good-sized car park. The old range is warming on cold winter days. The husband and wife team source their guest beers from local independents. The beers are diverse for a country pub and something unusual for the area can frequently be found. Q❀🚲◗👜▲♣P🤎

Cannock

Arcade ▼

49 Mill Street, WS11 0DR (opp Morrisons car park)
☎ (01543) 462920 ⊕ thearcadecannock.co.uk
3 changing beers (sourced locally; often Green Duck, Hobsons, Salopian) Ⓗ

This gem of a pub on the outskirts of the town centre has a post-industrial feel with exposed brickwork in the bar. The back room is a comfortable lounge with period furniture and local historic photography, leading to an outside area with wooden decking. The pub currently serves up to three real ales, with bar snacks also available. A weekly quiz night is hosted on Wednesday, open-mic evening once a month on Sunday and local street food every Friday. ☼❀👜♣🤎🛜♪

Linford Arms ✔

79 High Green, WS11 1BN
☎ (01543) 469360
Greene King Abbot; Ruddles Best Bitter; Sharp's Doom Bar; 5 changing beers (sourced nationally; often Adnams, Backyard, Salopian) Ⓗ
Established town-centre Wetherspoon pub serving up to eight real ales and ciders. The pub name originates from the builders' merchant that formerly occupied the premises. The seating area is on two floors with quieter alcoves, and a separate snug. Food is served all day. Two ale festivals are held each year and local breweries feature regularly. There are good bus and rail links. Not to be missed if you are visiting Cannock. ☼❀◗👜🖳🤎🛜

Merchant ✔

9-11 Market Place, Cannock Chase, WS11 1BS
☎ (01543) 500293
Butcombe Original; Purity Pure UBU; Titanic Plum Porter Ⓗ
Built in 1889, this is one of Cannock's oldest buildings built and still operating as a pub. This open-plan one-floor public house has modern furniture and fixtures, and local photographs complement the decor. There are two real ales consistently on, and food is served all day. Sport TVs can be found throughout the venue and the pub actively encourages families. ☼◗👜≷P🖳🤎🛜

Newhall Arms

81 High Green, WS11 1BN
☎ 07852 573042
Wye Valley HPA; 5 changing beers (often Green Duck, Shiny, Wye Valley) Ⓗ
Opened in 2016, Cannock's first micropub is family owned and a must-visit pub with great beers and fantastic staff. Serving local and national cask ales, alongside craft kegs and cans, you're guaranteed to find a beer to make you want another. No-nonsense snacks and fresh cheese and onion cobs go hand-in-hand with the drinks to make this a true gem. Q❀👜♣P🖳🤎🛜

Caverswall

Auctioneers Arms Ⓛ

The Green, ST11 9EQ
☎ (01782) 461127 ⊕ auctioneersarms.co.uk
Draught Bass; 3 changing beers (often Titanic) Ⓗ
The Knocks, as it is affectionately known to locals, reopened its doors in 2018. It is now a thriving pub, owned and run by the community, right at the heart of village life. Cakes and light snacks are served all day with a fuller menu offered some lunchtimes and in the early evening. Other meals, including a pie special night, are growing in popularity. Regular quizzes and live music events help support this great little local boozer, with four real ales sold in good condition.
Q☼❀◗♣P🤎🛜♪

Cheadle

Bakers Arms

21 High Street, ST10 1AA (100yds from Leek Rd roundabout)
☎ (01538) 756237
Draught Bass; 5 changing beers (often Dancing Duck, Mobberley) Ⓗ
A welcome return to the Guide this year for this lovely little boozer. Named after its former use as a local bakery, the Bakers Arms opened in 2017. Three separate areas and a superbly set out rear yard contrive to make the most of the small space. A real fire, comfortable seating and suntrap outdoor seating make visiting the Bakers a pleasure. Jenga, Wednesday crib and weekend evening live music are popular with locals and visitors.
Q✿❀♣P🖵(32,32X)❀🤶💬🎵

Bird in Hand Ⓛ

117 Tape Street, ST10 1ER
☎ (01538) 421126
Burton Bridge Bridge Bitter; Dancing Duck #Wet February; 2 changing beers (often Brunswick, Burton Bridge) Ⓗ
A well-deserved entry into the Guide, this small, traditional, terraced street-corner pub occupies a main road position just outside the town centre. Two rooms have lovely coal fires. A large screen shows major sporting events, another room houses a dartboard, and a pool table is found in the ante-room. The cosy snug is quieter and also has a real fire. There is a patio outside for smokers. The licensees always give a warm welcome, as do the bar staff. Q♣🖵(32,32X)❀

Cheddleton

Black Lion 🏆 Ⓛ

12 Hollow Lane, ST13 7HP (turn off A520 into Hollow Ln opp Red Lion; pub is 100yds up the hill next to church)
☎ (01538) 360620
Draught Bass; Timothy Taylor Landlord; 4 changing beers (often Salopian, Wincle) Ⓗ
The Black Lion is a comfortable village pub, with real fires in the winter. It is close to the Flint Mill Museum and the Cauldon Canal, and beside the Grade II-listed St Edward's Church, which has a Wardle family connection and Arts and Crafts features. Recently refurbished in a modern rustic style, outside there is a patio area to the front and an enclosed beer garden at the rear. An excellent range of well-kept beers is offered from this former local CAMRA Pub of the Year. Q🛏✿❀◑≈♣P🖵(16)❀🎵

Codsall

Firs Club Ⓛ

Station Road, WV8 1BX (entrance from shared Co-op car park off Station Rd)
☎ (01902) 844674 🌐 thefirscodsall.com
5 changing beers (sourced locally) Ⓗ
Frequent local award winner and CAMRA Regional Club of the Year 2022. It contains a bar area, quiet lounge and separate sports lounge with a pool table. Five changing ales usually including a mild, are mainly local, and occasionally feature a beer from the in-house brewery. A beer festival is held in November. The Firs Suite, a dedicated function area, is available to hire for weddings and other events. A pedestrian entrance in Wood Road is handy for the bus stop. Q🛏✿❀≈♣P🖵(5,10B)🎵

Love & Liquor

1-3 Church Road, WV8 1EA
☎ (01902) 843277

5 changing beers (sourced nationally; often Abbeydale, Salopian, Wye Valley) Ⓗ
This converted shop in the centre of Codsall is always popular and a mainstay of the local real ale scene. An upstairs room with bench seating has a large TV showing sport. Downstairs is a bar area with comfortable seating, a wood-burning stove and another TV. Pavement tables provide an outdoor drinking area. Five changing ales, usually including a stout or porter, are served.
✿≈🖵(5,10B)🤶🎵

Coton

Fox Inn ✓

Lichfield Road, B79 7SH
☎ (01827) 318951 🌐 classicinns.co.uk/thefoxinntamworth
Sharp's Doom Bar; 3 changing beers Ⓗ
Imposing white-painted three-storey roundabout pub; the column-style pub sign hints at its previous Ember Inn incarnation. Note also the anonymous brick wall across the road which is actually a flood defence against the neighbouring river Tame. Not as large inside as one might expect, the pub has a wealth of outdoor seating; choose between the paved beer terrace to the front or the large grassy garden to the rear. Generally three guest beers are on the bar, often featuring national big-name ales. 🛏✿◑♣P🖵🛜

Doveridge

Cavendish Arms ✓

Derby Road, DE6 5JR
☎ (01889) 358586 🌐 cavendisharms.com
Marston's Pedigree; 2 changing beers (often Uttoxeter, Wye Valley) Ⓗ
Large corner Grade II-listed building slightly away from the village high street, on the old route of the A50. Having changed hands in 2021, there is a good choice of well-kept ales plus a gin bar. With friendly service, the food menu includes gluten-free options. Regular functions are held and there is a large garden area, welcoming for families and larger parties. On Sunday, the only food served is from the roast menu.
Q🛏✿❀♣P🖵(1)🤶🎵

Draycott-in-the-Clay

Roebuck

Toby's Hill, DE6 5BT (Toby's Hill/A515 junction, 600yds N of village)
☎ (01283) 821135 🌐 theroebuckdraycott.co.uk
Roebuck Blonde, Hopzester, Bitter, Porter, IPA; 1 changing beer (sourced locally; often Roebuck) Ⓗ
Welcoming early 19th-century family-owned free house, close to the A50/A515 junction and Staffordshire/ Derbyshire boundary. The pub showcases beers from the associated Roebuck brewery, which is in a splendid English oak-framed building to the rear of the large car park. Traditional home-cooked food is served in the restaurant and cosy bar (no meals Sun eve). The Klondike Mill Steam Preservation Centre is nearby and the National Trust's Sudbury Hall and Museum of Childhood are within easy reach, as is the national football centre at St George's Park. 🛏✿◑P🖵🤶🛜

Eccleshall

Ecclian

27 High Street, ST21 6BW
🌐 ecclian.com

Draught Bass; Thornbridge Jaipur IPA; 2 changing beers (sourced nationally; often Lymestone, Three Tuns) [H]
A new family-friendly, comfortable and welcoming pub run along traditional lines. The beer range varies, and over 100 whiskies and 10 brandies are stocked. Tea and coffee are also available. Food includes fresh rolls and a range of bar snacks, but customers are welcome to bring their own takeaway food from local establishments. Bingo sessions are held one Wednesday a month, and there is a popular weekly horse racing naps competition, as well as occasional live music. A pavement seating area is outside. Q🐴✿♿🐾📶♫

Kings Arms Hotel ✔
17 Stafford Street, ST21 6BL
☎ (01785) 850294 🌐 kingsarmseccleshall.com
Marston's Pedigree; house beer (by Wainwright); 4 changing beers (sourced nationally; often Acorn, Izaak Walton, St Austell) [H]
A former coaching inn and local inland revenue office once known as the Unicorn, restored and refurbished in 2017, and now a friendly free house. Parts of the original building are visible. Various rooms are served by a central bar. It has an interesting selection of beers, both local and national, often including those from the nearby Izaak Walton brewery. This excellent, well run pub, warm and cosy in winter, is one not to be missed. B&B accommodation is available, and there is a covered beer garden. 🐴✿🛏◑♿♣P🚌🐾📶

Elford

Crown Inn L
The Square, B79 9DB (600yds E of A513) SK189106
☎ (01827) 383602
2 changing beers (sourced nationally; often Backyard, Burton Bridge) [H]
A well-hidden village pub, known locally for its food and ale offerings. A number of small rooms around the central servery include an intimate bar room and a quirky little space which was formerly the above-ground cellar. Solid fuel heating gives a rosy glow in winter. Food is served Wednesday to Saturday evenings – often themed – and Sunday lunchtime. Two or three ales are on sale, featuring Bass when it is available. 🐴◑♣P🐾📶

Enville

Cat Inn 🏆 L
Bridgnorth Road, DY7 5HA (on A458)
☎ (01384) 872209 🌐 thecatinn.com
Enville Simpkiss, Ale, Ginger Beer; Olde Swan Original; 4 changing beers (sourced nationally; often Enville, Wye Valley) [H]
This idyllic country pub serves as the tap house for Enville, and a warm welcome is guaranteed. The interior is reminiscent of a country cottage and has multiple rooms in which to dine and imbibe, with several having their own real fires. Home-made food is served. The majority of the cask offering is staple and seasonal Enville beers, but you will also find a small number of guest beers and up to two real ciders. Q🐴✿◑🍎P🐾📶

Gentleshaw

Olde Windmill
Windmill Lane, WS15 4NF SK051118
☎ (01543) 682468 🌐 redcatpubcompany.com
Draught Bass; 3 changing beers (sourced nationally; often Beowulf, Bristol Beer Factory, Castle Rock) [H]
A welcoming 400-year-old country pub. The friendly staff are sharply attired, and serve equally sharp food and drink offerings. Free of tie, the guest ales are usually interesting beers from microbreweries. The cosy bar is dog friendly, while the wood-panelled lounge offers freshly cooked meals including interesting specials. Both rooms feature old beams and open fires. There are plenty of walkable routes nearby and it was a recent local CAMRA Pub of the Season winner. 🐴✿◑♿P🐾

Gnosall

George & the Dragon
46 High Street, ST20 0EX
☎ 07779 327551 🌐 georgeandthedragongnosall.com
Holden's Black Country Mild, Golden Glow; Leatherbritches Dovedale; Parkway Cheeky Monkey; 1 changing beer (sourced regionally) [H]
This lovely little pub opened in 2015 and has won local CAMRA Cider Pub of the Year and Pub of the Year awards. The building dates from 1736 and has seen many changes of use, including house, shop and off licence. It has two rooms served by one bar. With no TVs, no music and no games machines it has a good old-fashioned appeal. Tasty home-made snacks are available at the bar, but they sell out fast. Only cash is accepted.
Q🐴♣🍎🚌(5) 🐾

Great Wyrley

Andys' Ale House L
Unit 8 Quinton Court, WS6 6DZ (in the Quinton Court Precinct)
☎ 07311 661688
5 changing beers (often Bristol Beer Factory, Green Duck, Sarah Hughes) [H]
A welcoming one-room micropub with a traditional feel and friendly staff, located in the Quinton Court Shopping Centre. This pub has no music or TVs, just good conversation. A monthly quiz is held on the first Monday of the month, there is a monthly poker night, and pub games are played. Bar snacks are available including cobs and pork pies.
🐴♿🚆(Landywood) ♣🍎P🚌(x51) 🐾📶

Swan
162 Walsall Road, WS6 6NQ
☎ 07745 299085
2 changing beers (sourced locally) [H]
This public house located on the high street is a one-room bar with open fire. The walls of the pub display local history and football memorabilia pictures providing a homely feel, with the bar staff giving you a warm welcome. There is a separate function room which can be used for additional seating if necessary and a monthly pub quiz is held. 🐴✿♣P🚌(X51)🐾📶♫

Greensforge

Navigation
Greensforge Lane, DY6 0AH
☎ (01384) 273721
Enville Ale; Three Tuns XXX; 2 changing beers (often Hobsons, Holden's, Olde Swan) [H]
Modern, food-oriented, open-plan pub with an unspoiled interior which is deservedly popular with locals and walkers. There is a spacious outdoor area where drinkers can enjoy their beer and take in the relaxing pastoral views. The pub is located on the Staffordshire & Worcestershire Canal towpath which connects Stourton and Hinksford. There is a large car park directly opposite the pub. Q🐴✿◑P🐾📶

Hednesford

Cross Keys Hotel Ⓛ

42 Hill Street, WS12 2DN
☎ (01543) 879534
Draught Bass; Salopian Oracle; Wye Valley HPA, Butty
Bach; 4 changing beers (sourced nationally; often
Beowulf, Ludlow, Oakham) Ⓗ

A former coaching inn dating back to 1746 with sporting
and historic photographs decorating the walls of this
traditionally styled pub. A separate bar and lounge serves
up to eight real ales. This is the closest pub to the home
ground of local football team Hednesford Town FC. It is
rumoured that the infamous highwayman Dick Turpin
stopped here on his famous ride to York.
✿⌂✦P🖵(3,60) 🛜

High Offley

Anchor Inn ★

Peggs Lane, Old Lea, ST20 0NG (from A519 at
Woodseaves turn W on High Offley Road by chapel, then
left on Peggs Ln) SJ775256
☎ (01785) 284569
Wadworth 6X Ⓗ

On the banks of the Shropshire Union Canal, by bridge 42,
the pub has changed little since the 19th century and is
recognised by CAMRA as having a nationally important
historic interior. There are two rooms, each with a coal
fire. Beer is brought up from the cellar. A gorgeous
garden, with seating, is between the pub and the
towpath. The pub is normally open Friday to Sunday, but
may open weekday evenings in summer – check before
visiting. It is well worth searching out.
Q🕭✿♿🌢♣✦P✿

Kidsgrove

Blue Bell

25 Hardingswood, ST7 1EG (off A50 near Tesco, by canal
bridge)
☎ (01782) 774052 ● bluebellinnkidsgrove.com
Whim Arbor Light; 5 changing beers (sourced
nationally) Ⓗ

Traditional canalside pub offering six real ales and a good
range of ciders, plus a warm welcome from the hosts. It
has two separate areas off the main bar and a smaller
room at the back. The well-kept beer range features
different styles, always including one dark ale. There is a
beer garden to the rear. The pub holds an annual beer
festival as well as seasonal and charity events. It is
popular with locals, walkers and canal users.
Q🕭✿🌢♿≠✦P🖵(3,4A) ✿🛜

Kingstone

Shrewsbury Arms Ⓛ

Uttoxeter Road, ST14 8QH
☎ (01889) 500181 ● shrewsburyarmskingstone.co.uk
Dancing Duck Ay up; Marston's Pedigree; Uttoxeter
Bartley Bitter; 2 changing beers (sourced regionally;
often Dancing Duck, Uttoxeter) Ⓗ

A delightful community-run country inn and the perfect
place to enjoy excellent fine ales and traditional home-
cooked food. Situated in the centre of the small village of
Kingstone, a warm and friendly atmosphere awaits in
both bar and restaurant. Several permanent and
changing handpulled ales from independent brewers
adorn the bar. Facilities include a beer garden and large
outside seating area, and the pub is family-friendly, with
dogs also allowed. Q🕭✿🌢♿♣✦P✿🛜

Kinver

Cross Inn Ⓛ

Church Hill, DY7 6HZ
☎ (01384) 881698
Black Country Bradley's Finest Golden, Pig on the
Wall, Fireside; 4 changing beers (sourced nationally;
often Fixed Wheel, Oakham, Salopian) Ⓗ

A popular destination Black Country Ales outlet with a
real fire, serving up to six guest beers. Tasty and
tempting food is served at the weekend including hot
pork sandwiches. A small number of flatscreen
televisions show football fixtures on match days. There is
a large adjacent car park and Stourbridge buses stop
nearby, but there is no service after 6pm or on Sunday.
🕭♿♣✦P🖵(228) ✿🛜♪

Knighton

Haberdashers Arms

Newport Road, ST20 0QH (between Adbaston and
Knighton) SJ753275
☎ (01785) 280650
Wye Valley Butty Bach; 1 changing beer (sourced
locally; often Rowton) Ⓗ

This country pub dates from the 1840s, and the licensee
of 25 years offers a warm welcome. The four compact
rooms are all served from a central bar. The pub hosts a
range of events in its large garden, including the annual
Potato Club Show and music festivals – see the pub's
Facebook page for details. The collection of oil lamps is
not just for decoration, on Lamp Nights electric lights are
switched off and the lamps are lit, creating a relaxed
atmosphere. Q🕭✿🌢🌢♣✦P✿🛜♪

Leek

Benks

39 Stockwell Street, ST13 6DH
☎ (01538) 382783
Draught Bass; 2 changing beers (often Mobberley) Ⓗ
Friendly, unassuming, street-corner free house run by
the same family for over 50 years. The very much hands-
on landlady owner is passionate about beer quality and
attention to detail. The 100-year-old mechanical till
complements four antique handpumps, serving regular
Bass plus rotating guests from both local and national
breweries. It is well patronised by league sports teams,
having several dartboards and two pool tables. There is
occasional live music plus a great jukebox. A suntrap rear
yard contains an original well which is illuminated on
request. Small functions are catered for. ✿♣🖵✿🛜♪

Blue Mugge Ⓛ

17 Osbourne Street, ST13 6LJ (off A53 Buxton Rd)
☎ (01538) 384450 ● bluemugge.co.uk
Draught Bass; 4 changing beers (sourced nationally;
often Coach House) Ⓗ

Just outside the town centre, this unassuming terraced
street-corner local is now an established Guide entry.
Owned and run by the same family for over 40 years, the
building has several distinctly separate themed rooms, a
result of three adjoining properties being knocked into
one. The unique layout has bar service from a central
octagonal pillar, with the beer pumps and taps behind
the staff. Two handpulls are believed to be 120 years old.
Constantly changing guest ales are listed on a
blackboard. Good-value food is available lunchtimes. The
bus station is nearby. Q🕭✿🌢🖵✿🛜♪

Cobblers Ⓛ

1-5 Russell Street, ST13 5JF
☎ (01538) 381190

Draught Bass; Greene King Abbot; 4 changing beers (often Manning Brewers, Salopian, Wincle) [H]
Opening in October 2015, The Cobblers is a welcome addition to the list of great places Leek has to offer for real ale drinkers. This small, intimate pub has six handpulls serving four rotating guests, plus the permanent Bass, with regular beers from local breweries Wincle and Salopian. The small snug area to the rear is available to hire for private functions. **Q👪🚌🐾**

Fountain Inn [L]

14 Fountain Street, ST13 6JR
☎ (01538) 382060 🌐 caldmoretaverns.co.uk
Draught Bass; Exmoor Gold; Wye Valley Butty Bach; 5 changing beers (sourced nationally; often Exmoor, Front Row, Wincle) [H]
A magnificent bank of 10 handpulls greets the eye on entering this smart town-centre local, a former CAMRA Regional Pub of the Year. Eight real ales change regularly and always include a darker, stronger brew. Real ciders are also on sale. Live music on Sunday plus a beer raffle help make this friendly community pub a real gem. Four smart rooms upstairs offer accommodation, with plenty of places to eat nearby. **Q👪❀🛏♣⚽🚌🐾📶♫**

Roebuck [L]

18 Derby Street, ST13 5AB (on main shopping street)
☎ (01538) 385602
Everards Tiger; Titanic Steerage, Iceberg, White Star, Plum Porter, Captain Smith's Strong Ale; 4 changing beers (sourced regionally; often Magic Rock, Salopian, Tiny Rebel) [H]
Located in the town centre, this Titanic Brewery-owned former coaching inn dates back to 1626 and has a distinctive black-and-white wooden-framed frontage. It is a well-deserved entry to the Guide, offering up to 13 ales at busier times, mainly from the Titanic range, plus four guest ales, real cider and a range of craft beers. Award-winning food is served all day, including breakfast. Regular live music and outdoor events take place in the large rear beer garden. The bus station is nearby. **Q👪❀◐◗P🚌🐾📶♫**

Lichfield

Beerbohm

19 Tamworth Street, WS13 6JP
☎ (01543) 898252 🌐 beerbohm.bar
4 changing beers (sourced nationally) [H]
A cosy Belgian-accented café-bar, featuring continental draught and bottled beers alongside the four real ales. A large, comfortable upstairs room offers views of the busy pedestrian street below, while the downstairs bar room is decorated with beer enamels, gilded mirrors and globular chandeliers. Draught beers can be canned for takeout. There is occasional live music. Simple snacks are served, but you can bring your own food, with plates and cutlery provided. The unisex toilets are upstairs.
Q👪🚆(City) 🚌🐾📶

Bitter-Suite [L]

55 Upper St John Street, WS14 9DT
☎ 07852 179340 🌐 bittersuite.co.uk
5 changing beers (sourced nationally) [G]
Close to the city rail station, this pub has three comfortable rooms but no bar counter, so service is to your table. The five real ales and five ciders are complemented by gins, wines and bottled beers. Simple snacks are offered, or you can bring your own food. There is a large beer terrace to the rear, with occasional live music. Children are welcome during the day. Monday is quiz night, which finishes with a fish & chip supper.
Q👪❀🚆(City) 🚌🐾

Horse & Jockey [L]

8-10 Sandford Street, WS13 6QA
☎ (01543) 410033
Holden's Golden Glow; Marston's Pedigree; Wye Valley HPA, Butty Bach; 4 changing beers (sourced nationally) [H]
A compulsory stop on any tour of Lichfield's vibrant real ale scene, this is the city's longest-serving Guide entry, with a secure future now that the hosts own the freehold. The regular ales are joined by four guests, usually from smaller breweries. Various comfortable areas surround the central bar, and there is a large suntrap beer terrace to the rear and side. Sports screenings are popular. Freshly-made rolls and a pork pie/cheeseboard selection are always available. A 21-plus age policy is applied. **❀◐🚆(City)♣🚌🐾**

Pig

20 Tamworth Street, WS13 6JJ
☎ (01543) 756156 🌐 thepiglichfield.co.uk
3 changing beers (sourced nationally) [H]
Derby Brewing Company's first pub outside Derbyshire, with the central bar featuring a varying selection of Derby ales. A number of craft keg beers are also offered. The spacious interior features modern, fairly muted decor, with painted wooden panels and bare brickwork chimney breasts. The suntrap beer terrace to the rear has plenty of seating. There is limited parking to the rear.
👪❀🚆(City) ♣P🚌📶

Marchington

Dog & Partridge

Church Lane, ST14 8LJ (250yds along Church Ln from High St)
☎ (01283) 820394 🌐 dogandpartridgemarchington.co.uk
Draught Bass; 3 changing beers (sourced locally; often Abbeydale, Gates Burton, Uttoxeter) [H]
A gem of a village inn with Bass always available, plus a selection of local guest ales on several handpumps. Formerly a restaurant, the pub is split into four main indoor areas with open fires. Food is served lunchtimes and evenings. A pleasant beer garden to the rear is popular in the summer months. The pub is renowned locally for its weekly live music sessions and regular beer festivals. Parking is available to the side of the pub and close by at the church. Children are welcome.
Q👪❀◐◗⛺P🚌(402) 🐾📶♫

Milwich

Green Man ✔

Sandon Lane, ST18 0EG (on B5027 in centre of village)
☎ (01889) 505310 🌐 greenmanmilwich.com
Draught Bass; Ruddles Best Bitter; 3 changing beers (sourced nationally; often Greene King) [H]
More or less a permanent fixture in the Guide, appearing for 30 consecutive years to-date, this is a true community pub with an open fire and lots of craic. It has a wooden-floored bar area with a smaller eating and drinking area to the rear. A huge lush green garden hosts a free music festival in the summer. There is a jukebox and TV, though both are rarely used. **Q👪❀◗♣P🐾📶♫**

Newcastle-under-Lyme

Boat & Horses

2 Stubbs Gate, ST5 1LU (opp Morrisons, 500yds from bus station)
☎ (01782) 911528

Draught Bass; Facer's North Star Porter; Salopian Oracle; Thornbridge Jaipur IPA; 2 changing beers (sourced nationally) ⊞
This friendly and pleasant pub on the edge of the town centre (less than a five minute walk from the bus station) offers six real ales (four permanent and two guests) alongside four or more real ciders and a selection of craft beers in cans and bottles. The elongated open-plan layout has a feel of three separate areas; the main bar area plus two slightly raised areas at each end. ⛵❀❀♨✿♪

Bridge Street Ale House ㏐

31 Bridge Street, ST5 2RY
☎ (01782) 499394 ⊕ bridgestreetalehouse.co.uk
5 changing beers (sourced nationally; often Beartown, Facer's) ⊞/Ⓖ
The first micropub in the area, the capable hands of Grum and his hospitable staff make this is a special place for regulars and newcomers alike. The pub oozes charm and appeal, enhanced by the quirky decor. Five changing guest beers are on handpull from various breweries, with more occasionally available straight from the barrel. Nine real ciders and an extensive range of speciality rums add to the individuality of this fantastic pub. A Newcastle real ale institution. Q❀♣●♨✿♪

Cask Bar

1-2 Andrew Place, ST5 1DL
☎ (01782) 870560
Sarah Hughes Dark Ruby Mild; 4 changing beers (sourced nationally) ⊞
Award-winning microbar which opened in 2017, located just outside of Newcastle-under-Lyme town centre. One room houses a variety of different seating, from ordinary tables and chairs to higher 'posing'-style tables. Sarah Hughes Dark Ruby Mild is the permanent cask beer along with four changing guests, a rotating craft keg selection, and one of the best gin selections in the area. Meals are served Wednesday to Sunday (times vary).
Q⛵◑●♨✿☎

Crossways (Bottlecraft)

Nelson Place, ST5 1RP (at end of the Ironmarket by Fountain Roundabout, opp Queens Gardens)
☎ (01782) 405280 ⊕ bottlecraft.beer
5 changing beers (sourced nationally) ⊞
The Crossways is a welcome addition to the fantastic ale scene in Newcastle-under-Lyme from the team at Bottlecraft in Hanley. A warm welcome is assured from the friendly and enthusiastic bar staff. It offers a range of unusual and interesting traditional and craft beers across five cask and 12 keg taps, plus bottles and cans, all in a classic pub environment. Beers are served in pint, two-thirds and one-third measures. A pool table is available. ●♨✿☎♪

Hopinn

102 Albert Street, ST5 1JR
☎ (01782) 711121 ⊕ hopinn.net
Black Sheep Best Bitter; Draught Bass; Oakham Citra; 5 changing beers (sourced nationally; often Mallinsons, Northern Monk, Oakham) ⊞
Comfortable, friendly pub on the edge of Newcastle-under-Lyme offering an outstanding range of eight cask ales from both local and national breweries, supplemented by up to five KeyKeg beers. There are three comfortably furnished rooms. The staff are friendly and attentive, and there is a true community feel to the pub, which came third in the local CAMRA Pub of the Year competition in 2022. Sports events are screened, and newspapers provided. ⛵♣●♨✿

Mellards

Mellard's Warehouse, Market Lane, ST5 1AA
☎ (01782) 610497
3 changing beers (sourced nationally) ⊞
Smart modern bar which is housed in an old warehouse building. The pub is split level with the bar on the ground floor containing high tables and chairs, while settees and armchairs can be found on the upper level. The bar prides itself on the four handpulls, including a draught cider, plus a great range of keg beers. A large selection of bottled beers and cans is also available. The large outside seating area is to the front of the bar. ❀●♨✿☎

Norton Bridge

Railway Inn

Station Road, ST15 0NT
☎ (01785) 761395 ⊕ izaakwaltonbrewhouse.com
Izaak Walton Grayling, Rainbow Trout, Redeye Bass, Zonker I.P.A.; house beer (by Izaak Walton); 1 changing beer (sourced locally) ⊞
The Railway is the Izaak Walton brewery tap and shop. The brewery is on-site and the six handpumps dispense beers from the Brewhouse range. The bar has been fully refurbished to a good standard. Tea and coffee are always available together with home-made cake and a wide range of bar snacks. A fish & chip shop attends the car park on the first Wednesday of each month. Takeaways are available ranging from a single bottle to three or six packs, as are boxes of draught beers. Q⛵❀♿♣●P✿☎

Penkridge

Horse & Jockey

24 Market Street, ST19 5DH
☎ (01785) 716299
Black Country Bradley's Finest Golden, Pig on the Wall, Fireside; 7 changing beers (sourced nationally; often Holden's, Salopian, Titanic) ⊞
A warm, friendly pub completely renovated to a high standard by Black Country Ales in late 2021. There is a single bar which rambles around several distinct drinking areas. Rolls from renowned Jasper's of Penkridge and bar snacks are available. Two of the 12 handpumps are reserved for cider but these might not always be real. It opened in 1754 when the licensee was John Cope. ⛵❀♿≈♣●♨✿☎♪

Rugeley

Rusty Barrel

Fernwood Shopping Centre, Green Lane, WS15 2GS
⊕ rustybarrel.co.uk
4 changing beers (sourced locally; often Backyard, Beowulf, Blythe) ⊞
The pub takes its name from the owner's love of classic VW vehicles. This one-room micropub has simple painted brick walls. The ceiling is adorned with pumpclips showing the vast array of beers that have been sold. There are four handpumps offering different choices of beers and at least five real ciders. The atmosphere is friendly and the bar staff will make you feel welcome. Q⛵♿♣P♨(826,828) ✿

Vine Inn

Sheep Fair Close, WS15 2AT
☎ (01889) 574443
Vine Inn EPA, Vanilla Porter, Grapefruit IPA; 1 changing beer (sourced locally; often Vine Inn) ⊞
An old-styled pub on a quiet street owned by the same family for two generations. The pub retains a traditional

multi-room layout with a spacious bar to the front incorporating an open fire and quarry tiles, a small snug behind the bar, plus a room to the rear. There is also a large function room upstairs which can hold live music events. The pub has its own brewery on site with regular food events and quiz nights. Q✿点♣✿⛱♪

Stafford

bod
57-59 Bodmin Avenue, ST17 0EF
☎ (01785) 661506 ⊕ bodcafebars.co.uk/stafford
Titanic Steerage, Iceberg, Plum Porter; 3 changing beers (often Titanic) Ⓗ
The first of Titanic brewery's bod chain of café bars opened in 2018, named after its location Bodmin Avenue and advertising breakfast, brunch, lunch, dinner, snacks or even a well-deserved pint after a hard day's graft. Four Titanic beers are on draught. It opens for hot and soft drinks from 8.30am, and alcoholic drinks from noon. It occupies a former Co-op shop; ironically the new Co-op shop opposite occupies the site of a former pub. Gluten-free and vegan options are available on the menu.
Q☜⊕点&⛱✿⛱

Shrewsbury Arms
75 Eastgate Street, ST16 2NG
☎ (01785) 248240
Black Country Bradley's Finest Golden, Chain Ale, Pig on the Wall, Fireside; 6 changing beers (sourced nationally) Ⓗ
Part of the Black Country Ales chain and fully refurbished in 2016, this pub concentrates on offering a wide range of beers from local and nationwide breweries to complement their own range. Three ciders are also available, but may not always meet CAMRA's definition of real cider. There are three open fires in cold weather and a conservatory that is bookable for private functions. Light snacks are always available. It is said the spirits in bottles aren't the only ones around!
Q☜✿≉♣⛱✿⛱♪

Stoke-on-Trent: Burslem

Bull's Head ▾ ⒧
14 St John's Square, ST6 3AJ
☎ (01782) 834153
Titanic Steerage, Iceberg, White Star, Plum Porter; 6 changing beers (sourced nationally) Ⓗ
The Titanic brewery tap offers 10 real ales, 10 ciders and perries served from the cellar, and a selection of draught and bottled Belgian beers. It has a large central bar where bar billiards, a skittle table and jukebox can be found. Customers can also opt for the intimacy of the snug. A beer garden to the rear has many covered tables. The pub is close to Port Vale FC, opening early for home supporters on match days, and is involved with community events in the area. Q☜✿♣⛱⛱(3)✿⛱

Bursley Ale House
Wedgwood Place, ST6 4ED
☎ (01782) 911393
4 changing beers (often Abbeydale, Blue Monkey, Charnwood) Ⓗ
Smallish pub on two floors, formerly run along the lines of a microbar; the cellar is on the ground floor to the right of the door, behind glass-fronted doors. Up to four changing ales are served from handpump off the bar and can be sourced from any brewery in the country. A large beer garden is at the front of the pub.
✿≉(Longport) ♣⛱(3,98)

Johny's Micro Pub ⒧
9 St John's Square, ST6 3AH
4 changing beers (sourced nationally) Ⓗ
This comfortable micropub on St John's Square opened in 2016. On the ground floor, its small square room with chairs and tables ensures that conversation is never far away. The four, well-kept, real ales change regularly and can be from anywhere in the country. There are several real ciders in the fridge, alongside a good selection of bottles and cans. The toilets are on the first floor, as is the Harold Harper suite which is available for meetings and small parties. Q≉(Longport)♣⛱(3,98)✿

Stoke-on-Trent: Etruria

Holy Inadequate ⒧
67 Etruria Old Road, ST1 5PE
☎ 07771 358238
Inadequate Roundhouse Stout, Tickety Boo; Joule's Pale Ale; 6 changing beers (sourced nationally; often Inadequate) Ⓗ
A regular winner of the local CAMRA Pub of the Year, this fantastic pub showcases a huge range of beers from across the UK, plus beers from its on-site Inadequate brewery. Bottled beers are also available. Three seating areas with log-burners, plus a large beer garden, provide plenty of space, and the traditional decor in the main bar gives a cosy feel. Friendly and welcoming to everyone, this is a perfect place to spend time drinking excellent beer. Q✿✿♣⛱(4)✿⛱

Stoke-on-Trent: Hanley

Bottlecraft
33 Piccadilly, ST1 1EN (next to the Regent Theatre)
☎ (01782) 911819 ⊕ bottlecraft.beer
2 changing beers (sourced nationally)
Modern and friendly craft bar and bottle shop in the heart of Hanley, nestled next to the Regent Theatre. With two cask beers and 10 rotating craft ales plus a vast range of bottled and canned beers from around the world, there is something to suit all tastes. Knowledgeable staff are always happy to help you choose. A small cosy seating area is downstairs plus a large upstairs area, and outdoor tables to enjoy the sunshine. There are regular beer tasting events and poetry/spoken word nights. Take-out is available.
Q☜点♣⛱✿⛱

Coachmakers Arms ★
65 Lichfield Street, ST1 3EA (opp Hanley bus station)
☎ 07876 144818 ⊕ coachmakersarms.co.uk
Draught Bass; 4 changing beers (sourced nationally) Ⓗ
The Coachmakers is the first pub you will encounter on leaving the bus station. It is one of the few remaining pubs of its type left in the city, comprised of four small rooms, with a dividing passage and serving hatch. The passage has been recognised by CAMRA as historically important. An extremely friendly atmosphere always pervades, driven by the main source of entertainment, conversation. As for the beers, Bass is king, accompanied by three ever-changing and quality ales, plus up to five real ciders. It is also handy when visiting the Victoria Hall. Q☜♣⛱P⛱✿

Unicorn Inn ✅
40 Piccadilly, ST1 1EG
Draught Bass; Fuller's London Pride; 2 changing beers Ⓗ
Situated in Hanley opposite the Regent Theatre, the Unicorn is a fine example of the idea of what a traditional

pub should be. The one room, with a snug section at the far end, is comfortably furnished, and with the brass and ceramic menagerie adorning the walls and ceiling, it creates a feeling of bygone years. Bass and London Pride are the mainstay beers on the bar accompanied by Old Rosie and two ever-rotating ales. Bar snacks are always available plus theatre interval drinks can be pre-ordered. 🚍🛜

Victoria Lounge Bar 🗓

5 Adventure Place, ST1 3AF (next to Hanley bus station, opp Victoria Hall entrance)

☎ (01782) 273530 🌐 thevictorialoungebar.co.uk

Draught Bass; Ossett White Rat; Salopian Oracle; 3 changing beers (sourced nationally) 🖽

To have been created and run by the same family for 39 years says a lot about the standards that have been set and maintained by this extremely popular hostelry. The large split-level room is furnished to a high quality, with the presence of chesterfield settees adding to the cosy atmosphere. Six handpulls are available with Bass, Oracle and White Rat plus three ever-rotating ales. It is situated close to the Victoria Hall and bus station. Q🌜◑🖧🚍🛜

Woodman 🗓

3 Goodson Street, ST1 2AT

☎ (01782) 213996

House beer (by Facer's); 7 changing beers (sourced nationally) 🖽

Situated in Hanley town centre, and part of the respected Caldmore Taverns chain, the Woodman has a large split-level bar that features a snug to the rear. It has garnered quite a reputation for the outstanding range and quality of its beers. The 10 handpulls on display are testament to this, with seven ever-rotating ales served alongside the unique resident Woodman Pale and two handpulled ciders. Q♣👜🚍🛜

Stoke-on-Trent: Hartshill

Artisan Tap

552 Hartshill Road, ST4 6AF

☎ (01782) 618378

4 changing beers (sourced nationally) 🖽

Part of the 'Hartshill Mile' since 2017, this popular pub is a converted workshop with real character, bigger than it looks from the outside. The large main bar has a stage for its many live music events, and a separate quieter lounge area to the rear has gorgeous decor and comfortable seating. A generous outdoor area for sunny evenings completes the picture. A great range of four rotating ales from across the UK is offered plus bottled beers and up to three real ciders. Dogs are welcome. Q🏵♣👜🚍(11)🛜🛜🎵

Greyhound 🗓

67 George Street, ST5 1JT

☎ (01782) 635814

Titanic Iceberg, White Star, Plum Porter, Captain Smith's Strong Ale; 5 changing beers (sourced nationally; often Titanic) 🖽

A warm welcome awaits at this dog-friendly pub on the outskirts of Newcastle-under-Lyme. The second pub in the Titanic fleet, the Greyhound boasts nine handpumps showcasing Titanic ales as well as a fantastic, ever-changing range of beers from across the UK. A great selection of bottled beers as well as country wines and real cider make this an excellent choice for a quality drink. Tasty bar snacks are available. There is occasional live music, and open mic nights, plus a regular pub quiz on Sunday night. Q🌜👜🏵🚍(11)🛜🛜🎵

Sanctuary 🗓

493-495 Hartshill Road, ST4 6AA

☎ (01782) 437523 🌐 sanctuaryhartshill.co.uk

4 changing beers (sourced locally) 🖽

A true sanctuary in every sense, this wonderfully cosy pub features four constantly rotating real ales, up to four varied real ciders and a choice of bottled beers plus wines and gins. Ales are sourced from both local brewers and from further afield. Decorated in a cosy and eclectic style, including quirky features such as leather car seats and a rocking chair, this one-room pub feels like a home from home where all are made welcome. There are monthly open mic nights. Q🌜♣👜🚍(11)🏵🛜

Stoke-on-Trent: Longton

Congress Inn 🗓

14 Sutherland Road, ST3 1HJ (near Longton Police Station)

☎ (01782) 763667 🌐 congressinnlongton.co.uk

Adnams Broadside; 6 changing beers (sourced nationally; often Castle Rock, Townhouse) 🖽

A convivial, multi award-winning, two-roomed pub, just outside the centre of Longton, dedicated to the dispense of good-quality real ale from a host of microbreweries. The left-hand room contains the bar where the three permanent beers are joined by up to six guest beers. The right-hand room houses the dartboard, and is used for meetings and the annual beer festival, held every May. It's hard for the real ale fan to go wrong in a place like this – four ciders and a good selection of beer in bottles are also available. 🚆(Longton)♣👜🚍🎵

Stoke-on-Trent: Stoke

Glebe 🗓

35 Glebe Street, ST4 1HG

☎ (01782) 860670

Joule's Pure Blonde, Pale Ale, Slumbering Monk; 1 changing beer (sourced nationally; often Joule's) 🖽

Situated between the railway station and Stoke town centre, this superb Joule's establishment has one of the most stunning interiors in the area with its stained-glass windows, tiled flooring, and wood-panelled walls. The addition of candles on all tables creates the perfect environment for both drinking and dining. The three Joule's mainstay beers are always accompanied by a seasonal beer, and alongside the quality kitchen menu, a tasty and extensive cheese board is offered. ◑🚆(Stoke-on-Trent) 🚍🏵🎵

London Road Ale House 🗓

241 London Road, ST4 5AA

☎ (01782) 698070

6 changing beers (sourced nationally) 🖽

Situated a short walk from Stoke town centre this one-room, but spacious, micropub has a lot to offer visitors. Being a true free house allows it to aquire beers from small independent brewers as well as popular requests, and the six perpetually changing quality beers are enhanced by a range of both cans and bottled beers. Home-made Thai food is available for dine in, or to take away. A friendly welcome is always extended to customers old and new. Q◑♣👜🚍(21)🏵

Wheatsheaf 🗓 ✅

84-92 Church Street, ST4 1BU

☎ (01782) 747462

Greene King Abbot; Ruddles Best Bitter; Sharp's Doom Bar; 5 changing beers (sourced nationally) 🖽

Situated in the centre of Stoke town centre this small and cosy Wetherspoon pub is extremely popular and has acquired a reputation for the quality and condition of the beers it sells. All amenities are available on one well laid out floor with a decently stocked bar that is typical of the pub chain. Of the 10 handpulls available about five are dedicated to both local, and well researched national beers, with Titanic a favourite. The food is of course from the Wetherspoon menu. Q ⑤ ◑ ♿ ≠ (Stoke-on-Trent) 🚃 🛜

Stone

Borehole ♈

Unit 5 Mount Road Industrial Estate, Mount Road, ST15 8LL
☎ (01785) 813581 ⊕ lymestonebrewery.net
Lymestone Stone Cutter, Stone Faced, Foundation Stone, Ein Stein, Stone the Crows; 1 changing beer (sourced nationally) ⊞

The Lymestone brewery tap, a few metres from the brewery itself, it is effectively two rooms with a log-burner in between, and a lovely enclosed suntrap garden to the rear. Snacks are available at all times and dogs are especially welcome. Children are welcome until evening. The full range of Lymestone beers are served, along with their seasonal beer, and maybe a regional guest ale too. Real cider is available. Open mic night is on Wednesday, and there is occasional live entertainment – check their Facebook page. Q ⑤ ❀ ≠ ♣ ♠ P ❀ 🛜 ♫

Royal Exchange

26 Radford Street, ST15 8DA (on corner of Northesk St and Radford St)
☎ (01785) 812685
Everards Tiger; Titanic Steerage, Iceberg, White Star, Plum Porter; 2 changing beers (sourced nationally) ⊞

A comfortable, welcoming Titanic pub with several regular beers plus one national and one seasonal guest beer. There are two distinct bay-windowed front bar areas to the left and right of the entrance, one with a solid fuel fire. The interior extends behind the bar to a lounge area. Children and dogs are welcome. Curry night is on Monday, and booking is advised. There are no TVs or musak here, just good craic, and some live entertainment from time to time – visit their Facebook page for details. Q ⑤ ❀ ≠ ♣ 🚃 ❀ 🛜 ♫

Swan Inn

18 Stafford Street, ST15 8QW (on A520 near Trent and Mersey Canal)
☎ (01785) 815570
House beer (by Coach House); 8 changing beers (sourced nationally) ⊞

A truly independent free house, close to the Trent and Mersey Canal, with nine handpulls, eight of which vary almost daily. It has two rooms with open fires at each end and a pleasant outside walled, partially-covered area to the rear. The Swan is strictly 18+, with free live music Thursday, Friday and Saturday evenings. There is a cask beer loyalty card (buy 10 pints, get one free), and it regularly wins CAMRA accolades including several local Pub of the Year awards. ❀ ♿ ♠ 🚃 (101) ❀ 🛜 ♫

Tamworth

Old Bank House

9 Ladybank, B79 7NB
☎ 07907 097935
5 changing beers ⊞

Opened as a pub in 2021, this attractive Victorian building was formerly home to Sir Robert Peel's Tamworth Savings Bank. It dates from 1845 and bears a blue plaque marking its history. A small bar area serves four comfortable rooms. A pleasant beer terrace is to the rear, and in fine weather there's also seating to the front. There are generally five varied and interesting ales. Monday is a drink-up day with lower ale prices. ❀ ♠ 🚃 ❀ 🛜 ♫

Sir Robert Peel ⓛ

13-15 Lower Gungate, B79 7BA
☎ (01827) 300910
5 changing beers (often Church End) ⊞

Featuring in every issue of the Guide since 2005, the Peel was recognised in CAMRA's national 50th anniversary Golden Awards. It is named after the former prime minister, known for his role in the creation of the police force and the Tamworth pig. Five changing ales are complemented by a good selection of foreign bottled beers. There is occasional live music. A large and peaceful beer garden is to the rear, with ancient stone walls, overlooked by the historic St Editha's Church. ❀ ≠ 🚃 ❀

Tamworth Tap ♈ ⓛ ✔

29 Market Street, B79 7LR
☎ (01827) 319872 ⊕ tamworthbrewing.co.uk
8 changing beers (sourced nationally) ⊞

CAMRA's National Pub of the Year for 2022 occupies an elegant building which is also home to Tamworth brewery. The cosy upstairs rooms have Tudor features, the historic courtyard beer terrace to the rear offers striking views of Tamworth Castle, and there is café-style seating to the front. Eight handpulls usually feature one Tamworth ale, the rest from near and far. Various snacks are offered, plus a wide range of ciders, gins, wines and bottled beers. Regular live music features. ❀ ≠ ♠ 🚃 ❀ 🛜 ♫

Tutbury

Cask & Pottle

2 High Street, DE13 9LP (close to mini-roundabout at centre of village)
☎ 07595 423614 ⊕ caskandpottle.co.uk
4 changing beers (sourced regionally) Ⓖ

East Staffordshire's first micropub, opened in 2013 in a former sweet shop. The small, bright, single room on the ground floor of a Victorian terrace features pine benches and tables, but no bar counter. One wall is decorated with an aphorism, a mural, and a table of ale measures (a pottle is an archaic name for a half-gallon measure). A window at the rear offers a view of the stillage. Three ciders and a perry are usually available from various sources. Q ⑤ ♿ ♠ 🚃 ❀

Cross Keys

39 Burton Street, DE13 9NR (E side of village, 300yds from A511)
☎ (01283) 813677
Burton Bridge Draught Burton Ale; 3 changing beers (sourced regionally) ⊞

Privately owned 19th-century free house, overlooking the Dove valley and providing a fine view of Tutbury Castle from the extended patio. The two split-level rooms – public bar and lounge – have a homely feel and are served from a similarly split-level bar. A separate large dining room to the rear serves evening meals Wednesday to Saturday, and Sunday lunches (pre-booking advised). This is the only pub in the area which has offered Draught Burton Ale from its launch by Ind Coope in 1976 through its 2015 reincarnation by Burton Bridge. ⑤ ❀ ◑ ♿ P 🚃 ❀ 🛜 ♫

Uttoxeter

Night Inn ⛾ Ⓛ

Lion Building, 8 Market Place, ST14 8HP
☎ 07426 191886 ⊕ nightinn.co.uk
4 changing beers (sourced locally; often Uttoxeter) Ⓗ
Established in 2020 by the Uttoxeter Brewing Company, the Night Inn is a modern bar with an upstairs area that can be booked for occasions. Three of the brewery's ales are served on a rotating basis, plus a guest. There are regular events including music and comedy nights.
Q🕏🕏&≉P🚪🚌🌣🛜♫

Breweries

Beowulf

Forest of Merica, Chasewater Country Park, Pool Lane, Brownhills, WS8 7NL
☎ (01543) 454067 ☎ 07789 491801
⊕ beowulfbrewco.co.uk

Beowulf Brewery is noted for its long history of award-winning ale. Both dark and light ales are brewed. Its ever-expanding range of beers appear thoughout the Midlands area in independent real ale and micro pubs. It also produces bottled-conditioned beers which can be purchased from the brewery. !!◆LIVE

Beorma (ABV 3.9%) BITTER
A perfectly-balanced session ale with a malty hint of fruit giving way to a lingering bitterness. Background spice excites the palate.
Mango Sypian (ABV 4.3%) SPECIALITY
Chasewater Bitter (ABV 4.4%) BITTER
Golden bitter, hoppy throughout with citrus and hints of malt. Long mouth-watering, bitter finish.
Black & Blueberry (ABV 4.5%) SPECIALITY
Boomer (ABV 4.5%) BITTER
Pale brown with lots of caramel aroma. Bitter start with a sweet malty background which develops to a mouth-watering finish with dry lips.
Chase Buster (ABV 4.5%) BLOND
Dark Raven (ABV 4.5%) MILD
So dark with apple and bonfire in the aroma, so sweet and smooth like liquid toffee apples with a sudden bitter finish.
Swordsman (ABV 4.5%) BITTER
Pale gold, light fruity aroma, tangy hoppy flavour. Faintly hoppy finish.
Folded Cross (ABV 4.6%) BITTER
Malt and caramel aromas and tastes with hints of fruity biscuits are nudged aside by the robust hops which give lingering bitter edges.
Hurricane (ABV 4.6%) BITTER
Wuffa (ABV 4.6%) GOLD
Chocolate Porter (ABV 4.7%) PORTER
Dragon Smoke Stout (ABV 4.7%) STOUT
Black with a light brown creamy head. Tobacco, chocolate, liquorice and mixed fruity hints on the aroma. Bitterness fights through the sweet and roast flavours and eventually dominates. Hints of a good port emerge.
Finn's Hall Porter (ABV 4.7%) PORTER
Dark chocolate aroma, after dinner mints, coffee and fresh tobacco. Good bitterness with woodland hints of Autumn. Long late bitterness with lip-drying moreishness.
Heroes Bitter (ABV 4.7%) BITTER
Gold colour, malt aroma, hoppy taste but sweetish finish.
Mercian Shine (ABV 5%) BITTER
Amber to pale gold with a good bitter and hoppy start and a hint of nutmeg. Plenty of caramel and hops with

background malt leading to a good bitter finish with caramel and hops lingering in the aftertaste.
Clout (ABV 6%) BITTER
Nordic Noir (ABV 6%) MILD
Dark brown with full liquorice aroma. Rich liquorice tastes with subtle tastes of chocolate and cinnamon. Gently moreish.
IPA (ABV 7.2%) STRONG
Killer Stout (ABV 7.3%) STOUT

Blythe SIBA

Blythe House Farm, Lichfield Road, Hamstall Ridware, WS15 3QQ
☎ (01889) 504461 ☎ 07483 248723
⊕ blythebrewery.co.uk

⊗ Blythe began brewing in 2003 using a 2.5-barrel plant in a converted barn. Only organic ingredients are used wherever possible. Following a buyout by two brothers in 2017, the brewery increased its range of beers. 15 outlets are supplied direct with others supplied by wholesalers throughout the region. !!◆LIVE

Bagot's Bitter (ABV 3.8%) BITTER
Amber in colour with a fruit start and sweetness which develops to a smooth, bitter finish. A lightly-hopped, easy-drinking beer.
Ridware Pale (ABV 4.3%) BITTER
Bright and golden with a bitter floral hop aroma and citrus taste. Good hop-sharp, bitter and refreshing. Long, lingering bite with ripples of citrus across the tongue.
Summer Breeze (ABV 4.3%) BITTER
Staffie (ABV 4.4%) BITTER
Hoppy and grassy aroma with hints of sweetness from this amber beer. A touch of malt at the start is soon overwhelmed by hops. A full hoppy, mouth-watering finish.
Palmers Poison (ABV 4.5%) BITTER
Refreshing darkish beer. Tawny but light headed. Coffee truffle aroma, pleasingly sweet to start but with a good hop mouthfeel.
Gold Rush (ABV 4.6%) BITTER
Dark Horse (ABV 4.7%) STOUT
Knobbled Horse (ABV 4.7%) SPECIALITY
Dark Ruby (ABV 5%) MILD
Johnsons (ABV 5.2%) PORTER
Black with a thick head. Refreshingly hoppy and full-bodied with lingering bitterness of chocolate, dates, coal smoke and liquorice.

Brewhouse & Kitchen SIBA

🯅 **1 Bird Street, Lichfield, WS13 6PW**
☎ (01543) 224740 ⊕ brewhouseandkitchen.com/lichfield

⊗ Established in 2016, the 2.5-barrel brewery kit located on the ground floor area of the pub allows customers to see the whole brewing process. Frequent specials and one-off's are brewed alongside a core range, mainly for consumption in the pub. !!🯅◆

Burton Bridge SIBA

24 Bridge Street, Burton upon Trent, DE14 1SY
☎ (01283) 510573 ⊕ burtonbridgebrewery.co.uk

☺The brewery was established in 1982 by Bruce Wilkinson and Geoff Mumford and owns three pubs in the local area, including its award-winning brewery tap. More than 300 outlets are supplied directly, along with being distributed nationally. It now also brews Heritage branded beers following the closure of the plant at the National Brewing Centre. !!🯅◆LIVE

Golden Delicious (ABV 3.8%) BITTER
A Burton classic with sulphurous aroma and well-balanced hops and fruit. An apple fruitiness, sharp and refreshing start leads to a lingering mouth-watering bitter finish with a hint of astringency. Light, crisp and refreshing.

Sovereign Gold (ABV 4%) BITTER
Sweet caramel aroma with a grassy hop start with malt overtones. Fresh and fruity with a bitterness that emerges and continues to develop.

XL Bitter (ABV 4%) BITTER
Another Burton classic with sulphurous aroma. Golden with fruit and hops and a characteristic lingering aftertaste hinting of toffee apple sweetness.

XL Mild (ABV 4%) MILD
Black treacle initial taste after liquorice aroma. Sweet finish with a touch of bitterness.

Bridge Bitter (ABV 4.2%) BITTER
Gentle aroma of malt and fruit. Good, balanced start finishing with a robust hop mouthfeel.

Burton Porter (ABV 4.5%) PORTER
Chocolate aromas and sweet smooth taste of smoky roasted grain and coffee.

Damson Porter (ABV 4.5%) SPECIALITY
Faint roast, caramel and dark fruit nose. Cough mixture and Blackjack beginning. Uncomplicated profile with a fractious mix of bitter fruitiness and yeasty maltiness.

Draught Burton Ale (ABV 4.8%) BITTER
Fruity orange aroma leads to hoppy start, hop and fruit body then fruity aftertaste. Dry finish with fruity hints.

Bramble Stout / Top Dog Stout (ABV 5%)
SPECIALITY
Smoky aroma with a fruit hint from black liquid. Roast start with briar dry fruit emerging, then a sharp black fruit taste emerges to balance the burnt effect. Sweetish, dry blackberry finish with prolonged mouth watering.

Stairway to Heaven (ABV 5%) BITTER
Golden bitter. A perfectly-balanced beer. The fruity and hoppy start leads to a hoppy body with a mouth watering finish.

Festival Ale (ABV 5.5%) BITTER
Caramel aroma with plenty of hop taste balanced by a full-bodied malty sweetness.

Thomas Sykes (ABV 10%) BARLEY
Kid in a sweetshop aroma. Rich, fruity, spirited tastes – warming and dangerously drinkable.

Consall Forge

3 Railway Cottages, Consall Forge, ST9 0AJ

A one-barrel brewery set in the heart of the Staffordshire Moorlands adjacent to the Churnet Valley Railway. The Black Lion at Consall Forge is a regular outlet.

Dark Ruby Mild (ABV 5.2%) MILD
Equilibrium (ABV 6%) STOUT

Crown Brewhouse

The Square, Elford, B79 9DB
☎ (01827) 383602 ✉ bluecatsup@hotmail.com

A one-barrel plant, established in 2017, housed in a former store room attached to the Crown pub. Beers are brewed almost exclusively for the pub, but can be found at local beer festivals and events. Brewing is suspended.

Enville SIBA

Coxgreen, Hollies Lane, Enville, DY7 5LG
☎ (01384) 873728 ⊕ envilleales.com

⊗ Enville Brewery is sited on a picturesque Victorian, Grade II-listed farm complex, using natural well water, traditional steam brewing and a reed and willow-

effluent plant. Enville Ale is infused with honey and is from a 19th century recipe for beekeeper's ale passed down from the former proprietor's great-great aunt. All beer is distributed in cask to a large, locally-based free trade. 🚆◆

Simpkiss (ABV 4%) BITTER
Caramel smooth start, caramel body with sweet malt and hop bite. Fruity hop finish, easing finish and satisfying.

American Pale Ale (ABV 4.2%) PALE
White (ABV 4.2%) SPECIALITY
Yellow with a malt, hops and fruit aroma. Hoppy but sweet finish.

Ale (ABV 4.5%) SPECIALITY
Sweet malty aroma and taste, honey becomes apparent before bitterness finally dominates.

Old Porter (ABV 4.5%) PORTER
Black with a creamy head and sulphurous aroma. Sweet and fruity start with touches of spice. Good balance between sweet and bitter, but hops dominate the finish.

Ginger Beer (ABV 4.6%) SPECIALITY
Golden bright with gently gingered tangs. A drinkable beer with no acute flavours but a satisfying aftertaste of sweet hoppiness.

Firs

Station Road, Codsall, WV8 1BX
☎ (01902) 844674 ⊕ thefirscodsall.com

Beers are brewed onsite in the CAMRA award-winning Firs, and are exclusive to the club.

Flash

Moss Top Farm, Moss Top Lane, Flash, Quarnford, SK17 0TA ☎ 07967 592345 ⊕ flashbrewery.uk

The brewery is located high in the Peak District and was founded by two friends who brew on a part-time basis. All natural ingredients are used including spring water and seaweed finings (making the beer vegan-friendly). Three bottle-conditioned beers are produced and are sold at Leek Market (only sales outlet). LIVE V

Fountain (NEW)

Unit 10, Essington Light Industrial Estate, Bognop Road, Essington, WV11 2BH

Formerly Morton Brewery, the plant was purchased in 2023 by the owner of the Fountain Inn, Gornal, to supply ales to sell in the pub. The brewplant remains housed in its former site.

Freedom SIBA

1 Park Lodge House, Bagots Park, Abbots Bromley, WS15 3ES
☎ (01283) 840721 ⊕ freedombrewery.com

Freedom specialises in producing hand-crafted English lagers, all brewed in accordance with the German Reinheitsgebot purity law. No real ale. ‼🚆

Front Row SIBA

Unit A3, The Old School, Outclough Road, Brindley Ford, ST8 7QD ☎ 07861 718673
⊕ frontrowbrewing.co.uk

After starting operations in Congleton in 2012 on a 2.5-barrel plant, Front Row expanded to an eight-barrel plant in 2014. It moved to its current location at the end of 2018 to allow for further increase in capacity. There is a brewery tap in nearby Biddulph. ‼◆

Number 8 (ABV 3.7%) MILD

Crouch (ABV 3.8%) BITTER
LOHAG (Land of Hops and Glory) (ABV 3.8%) GOLD
Touch (ABV 4%) BITTER
Sin Bin (ABV 4.2%) GOLD
Try (ABV 4.2%) BITTER
Half-Time (ABV 4.5%) SPECIALITY
Pause (ABV 4.5%) STOUT
Red Roses (ABV 4.5%) STOUT
Pride (ABV 4.6%) BITTER
Blindside (ABV 4.7%) GOLD
Crafty Flanker (ABV 4.7%) GOLD
Rucked (ABV 5.2%) OLD
Converted (ABV 5.4%) PORTER
Oblensky (ABV 7.3%) PORTER

Gates Burton

Reservoir Road, Burton upon Trent, DE14 2BP
☎ (01283) 532567 ☎ 07957 930772
🌐 gatesburtonbrewery.co.uk

◎The Gates Burton Brewery was established in 2011 using a one-barrel plant. Now expanded to a three-barrel plant, representing cottage brewing at its finest. All beer is available in cask in the free trade. ‼♦

Reservoir (ABV 4.6%) BITTER
Light brown beer with a white head provides a malt and hop aroma. Caramel starts before a spicy hop and malt middle leads to a mouthwatering bitter finish.
Gates Burton Ale (GBA) (ABV 4.8%) BITTER
Damn (ABV 5%) BITTER
Reservoir Gold (ABV 7.5%) BARLEY

Gentlewood

Fir Tree Cottage, Tithe Barn, Gentlewood, WS15 4LR
☎ 07544 146900
✉ gentlewoodbrewery@hotmail.com

Gentlewood began in 2018 and is co-owned and run by Darren Williams and Ben Colthorpe. It is a Staffordshire-based brewery specialising in traditional cask ales using British hops and grain. Frequent seasonal brews complement the core range. ♦

Heritage (ABV 4.2%) BITTER

Inadequate

🏠 Holy Inadequate, 67 Etruria Old Road, Stoke-On-Trent, ST1 5PE
☎ (01782) 915170 ☎ 07771 358238
✉ paulcope.cope@gmail.com

◎This one-barrel plant commenced brewing behind the Holy Inadequate in 2018 and mainly supplies the pub with an ever-changing range of beers (up to four at any one time). Other local pubs are sometimes supplied, along with local beer festivals.

Kickabo

Unit 7B, Harvey Works, Lingard Street, Stoke On Trent, ST6 1ED 🌐 kickabobrewery.com

A small, three-barrel brewery set up in Burslem in the Potteries in 2020. Its aim is to recreate beers that will feature styles from across the world. Currently available in keg or cans. ♦

Kinver SIBA

Unit 1, Britch Farm, Rocky Wall, Kinver, DY7 5NW
☎ 07715 842676 🌐 kinverbrewery.co.uk

◎Established in 2004, Kinver brewery produces a wide range of different beer styles including one-off specials.

The brewery relocated in 2012 to a new 10-barrel plant on the edge of Kinver due to increased demand. An ever-increasing number of pubs, mainly in the midlands, and beer festivals are supplied with the award-winning ales. ‼♦LIVE

Light Railway (ABV 3.8%) BLOND
Straw-coloured session beer. A fruity and malty start quickly gives way to well-hopped bitterness and lingering hoppy aftertaste.
Cavegirl Bitter (ABV 4%) BLOND
Edge (ABV 4.2%) BITTER
Amber with a malty aroma. Sweet fruity start with a hint of citrus marmalade in the spicy edged malt; lasting hoppy finish that is satisfyingly bitter.
Noble (ABV 4.5%) GOLD
Fruity hop aroma. Very fruity start then the grassy hops give a sharp bitter finish with malt support.
Maybug (ABV 4.8%) BLOND
Half Centurion (ABV 5%) BITTER
A golden best bitter; malty before the American Chinook hop takes command to give a balanced hoppy finish and provide the great aftertaste.ô
Black Ram Stout (ABV 5.2%) STOUT
Witchfinder General (ABV 5.5%) PORTER
Khyber (ABV 5.8%) BITTER
Golden strong bitter with a Centennial hop bite that overwhelms the fleeting malty sweetness and drives through to the long dry finish.

Lymestone SIBA

The Brewery, Mount Road, Stone, ST15 8LL
☎ (01785) 817796 ☎ 07891 782652
🌐 lymestonebrewery.net

◎Lymestone commenced brewing in 2008. Based in the old Bents Brewery, it uses a 10-barrel plant. A family-run business, daughter Sarah joined the brew team as one of the UK's youngest brewsters. The brewery delivers in a 50-mile radius, works with national wholesalers and has its own pub adjacent to the brewery. ‼🚚♦

Stone Cutter (ABV 3.7%) BITTER
Hoppy and grassy aroma, clean, sharp and refreshing. A hint of caramel start then intense bitterness emerges with a good bitter aftertaste and touch of mouthwatering astringency.
Stone Faced (ABV 4%) BITTER
Foundation Stone (ABV 4.5%) BITTER
An IPA-style beer with pale and crystal malts. Faint biscuit and chewy, juicy fruits burst on to the palate then the spicy hops pepper the taste buds to leave a dry bitter finish.
Ein Stein (ABV 5%) GOLD
Stone the Crows (ABV 5.4%) STOUT
A rich dark beer from chocolate malts. Fruit, roasts and hops abound to leave a deep lingering bitterness from the hop mix.
Abdominal Stoneman (ABV 7%) STRONG

Marston's

Shobnall Road, Burton upon Trent, DE14 2BW
☎ (01283) 531131 🌐 marstons.co.uk

◎Brewing in Burton since 1834, it houses the only working Burton Union fermenters. Developed in the 19th century, they are used to cleanse the new style of pale ale yeast. Only Pedigree is fermented in them, but the yeast is used in other beers. A nanobrewery within the visitors centre (DE14) is used for small-batch brews. Contract brewing includes Draught Bass brewed for AB Inbev. A joint venture with Carlsberg in 2020 led to the company being renamed Carlsberg Marston's Brewing Company. ‼🚚♦LIVE

EPA (ABV 3.6%) PALE
61 Deep (ABV 3.8%) GOLD
Light, golden to amber ale with intense tropical fruit and citrus aromas. Sweet tropical start with hints of spice. Hoppy bitterness overcomes the fruit and leaves a pleasant mouthwatering feel.
Pedigree (ABV 4.5%) BITTER
Pale brown to amber with a sweet hoppy aroma and hint of sulphur. Malt with a dash of hop flavours give a satisfying tasty finish.
Old Empire (ABV 5.7%) IPA
Sulphur dominates the gentle malt aroma. Malty and sweet to start but developing bitterness with fruit and a touch of sweetness. A balanced aftertaste of hops and fruit leads to a lingering bitterness.

Brewed for A-B InBev
Draught Bass (ABV 4.4%) BITTER
Hints of caramel aroma and taste, lightly hopped for a short bitter finish.

Brewed under the Courage brand name:
Best Bitter (ABV 4%) BITTER
Directors (ABV 4.8%) BITTER

Brewed under the Jennings Brewery brand:
Cumberland Ale (ABV 4%) BITTER

Molson Coors (Burton)

137 High Street, Burton upon Trent, DE14 1JZ
☎ (01283) 511000 ⊕ molsoncoorsbrewers.com

Molson Coors is the result of a merger between Molson of Canada and Coors of Colorado, US. Coors established itself in Europe in 2002 by buying part of the former Bass brewing empire, when Interbrew (now A-B InBev) was instructed by the British Government to divest itself of some of its interests in Bass. Coors owns several cask ale brands. It brews 110,000 barrels of cask beer a year (under licensing arrangements with other brewers) and also provides a further 50,000 barrels of cask beer for other breweries. In 2011 Molson Coors bought Sharp's brewery in Cornwall (qv). No cask ale is produced in Burton or Tadcaster.

Peakstones Rock SIBA

Peakstones Farm, Cheadle Road, Alton, ST10 4DH
☎ 07891 350908

Office: 1 Tape Street, Cheadle, ST10 1BB
⊕ peakstonesrock.co.uk

⊠ Peakstones Rock are a family-run brewery established in 2005 with a five-barrel plant located on a farm in the Peak District National Park. The brewery was expanded to 10-barrel capacity in 2009. It supplies an expanding free trade market in the North Midlands and surrounding areas. ‼ ♦ LIVE

Nemesis (ABV 3.8%) BITTER
Biscuity aroma with some hop background. Sweet start, sweetish body then hops emerge to give a fruity middle. Bitterness develops slowly to a tongue-tingling finish.
Pugin's Gold (ABV 4%) GOLD
Chained Oak (ABV 4.2%) BITTER
Alton Abbey (ABV 4.5%) BITTER
Black Hole (ABV 4.8%) OLD
Grassy aroma with malt background. Hops hit the mouth and intensify. Bitterness lingers with some mouth-watering astringency.
Oblivion (ABV 5.5%) BITTER

Quartz SIBA

Archers, Alrewas Road, Kings Bromley, DE13 7HW
☎ (01543) 473965 ⊕ quartzbrewing.co.uk

☺Quartz is a small craft brewery which was established in 2005 by Scott and Julia Barnett. Around 50 outlets are supplied direct. ‼ ➤ ♦

Blonde (ABV 3.8%) BLOND
Little aroma, gentle hop and background malt. Sweet with unsophisticated sweetshop tastes.
Crystal (ABV 4.2%) BITTER
Sweet aroma with some fruit and yeasty Marmite hints. Hoppiness begins but dwindles to a bittersweet finish.
Extra Blonde (ABV 4.4%) BITTER
Sweet malty aroma with a touch of fruit. Sweet start, smooth with a hint of hops in the sugary finish.
Heart (ABV 4.6%) BITTER
Pale brown with some aroma of fruit and malt. Gentle tastes of fruit and hops eventually appear to leave a bitter finish.
Cracker (ABV 5%) BITTER

Roebuck SIBA

Roebuck, Tobys Hill, Draycott-in-the-Clay, DE6 5BT
☎ 07903 396885 ⊕ roebuckdraycott.co.uk

☺Brewing began in 2017 using a six-barrel plant, in a purpose-built, English oak-framed, new building behind the Roebuck Inn. Master Brewer Steve Topliss was Carlsberg Tetley's last head brewer in Burton. Enquiries welcomed for brewery visits and tasting tutorials, with good food at the family-owned adjacent pub. ‼

Blonde (ABV 3.7%) BLOND
Hopzester (ABV 4.2%) BITTER
Bitter (ABV 4.5%) BITTER
IPA (ABV 5.2%) PALE

Shugborough

Shugborough Estate, Milford, ST17 0XB
☎ (01782) 823447 ⊕ shugborough.org.uk

Brewing in the original brewhouse at Shugborough (home of the Earls of Lichfield) restarted in 1990, but a lack of expertise led to the brewery being a static museum piece until Titanic Brewery of Stoke-on-Trent (qv) began helping in 1996. Brewing is currently suspended. ‼

Six Towns

🍺 **Wheatsheaf, 234 High Street, Tunstall, ST6 5TT**
☎ (01782) 922628 ⊕ sixtownsbrewery.com

Previously known as Sunset Taverns, Six Towns is a small, independent brewery at the rear of the Wheatsheaf pub in the Potteries. Brewing is currently suspended.

Staffordshire

12 Churnet Court, Cheddleton, ST13 7EF
☎ (01538) 361919 ☎ 07971 808370
⊕ staffordshirebrewery.co.uk

Brewing started in 2002. The brewery was renamed from Leek Brewery in 2013 at which time cask production ceased, being replaced by filtered, pasteurised bottled beers only. A small pilot plant is sometimes used to contract brew for Wicked Hathern (qv) when time permits. ‼

Contract brewed for Wicked Hathern Brewery:
Albion Special (ABV 4%) BITTER
Hawthorn Gold (ABV 4.6%) GOLD

Tamworth

29 Market Street, Tamworth, B79 7LR

☎ (01827) 319872 ☎ 07712 893353
🌐 tamworthbrewing.co.uk

Owner/brewer George Greenaway brought brewing back to Tamworth town centre after a gap of 70 years. Brewing started in 2017 in a former shop, which dates back to Tudor times and also serves as a tap. In 2020 brewing moved into the adjacent building, which records indicate was a brewhouse in the 1750s. The move allowed production on its five-barrel plant to double, and included the provision of an off-licence. Local outlets and festivals are supplied. ‼🛒♦◆

Hopmaster (ABV 4.2%) GOLD
Big Game (ABV 4.5%) BITTER
Amber-hued with a malty aroma. Generous malt taste with spicy sides. Hints of pepper and lemon lurk under the hop bitterness which emerges with a mouth-watering bite.
Ethelfleda (ABV 4.5%) BITTER
Full malt aroma from this golden beer. Sweet and grassy mix to start, developing to a bitter finish.
Hoppy Poppy (ABV 4.6%) GOLD
Our Aethel (ABV 4.8%) STOUT
Whopper (ABV 6.5%) IPA

Titanic SIBA

Callender Place, Burslem, Stoke-on-Trent, ST6 1JL
☎ (01782) 823447 🌐 titanicbrewery.co.uk

Ⓢ One of the earliest microbreweries, founded in 1985. Now owned by two local beer loving brothers, it has grown from a small, seven-barrel brewery, to producing over four million pints of its award-winning ales per year. With an expanding fleet of tied pubs and the Bod chain of café bars, it also supplies free trade customers in the Midlands, North West and further afield. Captain Smith, captain of the Titanic was born in Stoke on Trent, hence the name. ‼♦LIVE

Mild (ABV 3.5%) MILD
Fresh fruity hop aroma leads to a caramel start then a rush of bitter hoppiness ending with a lingering dry finish.
Steerage (ABV 3.8%) BITTER
Pale yellow bitter. Flavours start with hops and fruit but become zesty and refreshing in this light session beer with a long, dry finish.
Lifeboat (ABV 4%) BITTER
Dark brown with fruit, malt and caramel aromas. Sweet start, malty and caramel middle with hoppiness developing into a fruity and dry lingering finish.
Anchor Bitter (ABV 4.1%) BITTER
Amber beer with a spicy hint to the fruity start that says go to the rush of hops for the dry bitter finish.
Iceberg (ABV 4.1%) SPECIALITY
Yellow, gold sparkling wheat beer with a flowery start leading to a great hop crescendo.
Cherry Dark (ABV 4.4%) SPECIALITY
Cappuccino Stout (ABV 4.5%) SPECIALITY
Black with a vanilla and strong coffee nose leading to a sweet taste again with strong coffee. Aftertaste is sweet.
Chocolate and Vanilla Stout (ABV 4.5%) SPECIALITY
Chocoholic paradise with real coffee and vanilla support. Cocoa, sherry and almonds lend depth to this creamy, drinkable 'Heaven in a glass' stout.
Stout (ABV 4.5%) STOUT
Roasty, toasty with tobacco, autumn bonfires, chocolate and hints of liquorice; perfectly balanced with a bitter, dry finish reminiscent of real coffee.
White Star (ABV 4.5%) BITTER
Hints of cinnamon apple pie are found before the hops take over to give a bitter edge to this well-balanced, refreshing, fruity beer.

Plum Porter (ABV 4.9%) SPECIALITY
Dark brown with a powerful fruity aroma. A sweet plum fruitiness gives way to a gentle bitter finish.
Captain Smith's Strong Ale (ABV 5.2%) BITTER
Red brown and full-bodied, lots of malt and roast with a hint of honey but a strong bittersweet finish.

Tower

Old Water Tower, Walsitch Maltings, Glensyl Way, Burton upon Trent, DE14 1PZ
☎ (01283) 562888 ☎ 07771 926323
🌐 towerbrewery.co.uk

Ⓢ Tower was established in 2001 by John Mills in a converted derelict water tower, originally built for Thomas Salt's Brewery in the 1870s. The conversion was given a Burton Civic Society award for the restoration of an industrial building. The premises incorporate a public bar, open Friday evenings only, plus an outside bar on a patio in summer. Tower has around 20 regular outlets. ‼🛒♦◆

Bitter (ABV 4.2%) BITTER
Gold-coloured with a malty, caramel and hoppy aroma. A full hop and fruit taste with the fruit lingering. A bitter and astringent finish.
Gone for a Burton (ABV 4.6%) BITTER
Imperial IPA (ABV 5%) PALE

Trinity

Unit 4, The Shires, Essington Close, Lichfield, WS14 9AZ ☎ 07886 809835 🌐 trinitybrewco.com

Set up in 2021, the name refers both to the three spires of Lichfield's cathedral and the three owners. An eight-barrel brew kit is used, along with a pilot plant for trial brews. A wide range of styles is produced, mainly for can and keg, but cask output is growing. Barrel-aged beers are planned. There is an onsite taproom, generally open at weekends. Beers are widely available in the local free trade. ◆

Uttoxeter SIBA

26b Carter Street, Uttoxeter, ST14 8EU ☎ 07789 476817 🌐 uttoxeterbrewingcompany.com

Established in 2016, The Uttoxeter Brewing Company is a microbrewery producing hand-crafted real ales. A combination of passion, knowledge and hard work produces ales demonstrating distinctive aromas and delicious flavours, exploiting the famous Burton-Upon-Trent hard water. 🛒◆

Bunting's Blonde (ABV 3.7%) BLOND
Dark Horse Mild (ABV 3.7%) MILD
Ground Breaker (ABV 4%) GOLD
? (ABV 4.5%) PALE
Admiral Gardner (ABV 4.5%) GOLD
Bartley Bitter (ABV 4.5%) BROWN
Dr Johnson's Contrafibularity (ABV 4.5%) PALE
Earthmover (ABV 4.5%) GOLD
Final Furlong (ABV 4.5%) BITTER
Sargeant's Special Ale (ABV 4.6%) PALE
Chinook (ABV 4.7%) PALE
Earthmover Gold (ABV 4.7%) PALE
Full Gallop (ABV 4.7%) BROWN
Paddock Porter (ABV 4.8%) PORTER
Uxonian (ABV 4.9%) BITTER
American IPA (ABV 5.2%) PALE
Yogi Beer (ABV 6.1%) IPA

Vine Inn

Vine Inn & Brewery, Sheep Fair, Rugeley, WS15 2AT

☎ (01889) 574443 ✉ chris@thevinebrewery.com

⊗ The Vine Brewery is based in Rugeley, within the Vine Inn public house, parts of which date back to the 16th century. The brewery's beers can be found in a number of pubs in the Cannock Chase area.

Izaak Walton

🍺 Railway Inn, Station Road, Norton Bridge, ST15 0NT
☎ 07496 097883 ✉ steve@iwbrewhouse.co.uk

Originally on a small trading estate, the brewery relocated to a new building to the rear of the Railway public house. Beers are on an angling/fly fishing theme as Izaak Walton, who wrote 'the Compleat Angler', resided in the vicinity during the 17th century. ‼

Grayling (ABV 3.9%) PALE
Rainbow Trout (ABV 4.2%) GOLD
Petrifying Piranha (ABV 4.3%) PORTER
Redeye Bass (ABV 4.4%) BITTER
Gudgeon (ABV 4.5%) BITTER
Zonker IPA (ABV 4.6%) IPA
King Carp (ABV 4.8%) PALE
Gentle gold beer. Gentle hoppy taste but deceptively strong.
Bombay Duck (ABV 5%) BITTER
Woolly Bugger (ABV 5.1%) SPECIALITY
Pike (ABV 6%) MILD

Weal

Unit 6, Newpark Business Park, London Road, Chesterton, ST5 7HT
☎ (01782) 565635 ⊕ wealales.co.uk

Weal Ales was established in 2014 by Paul and Andrea Wealleans and was sold to new owners in 2023. It uses a six-barrel plant and bottles many of its beers, supplying independent outlets and events both locally and nationally.

This is the Modern Weal (ABV 3.8%) PALE
Wagon Weal (ABV 4.1%) BITTER
Wealy Hopper (ABV 4.2%) PALE
Weller Weal (ABV 4.6%) PALE
Noir (ABV 4.8%) PORTER
Centwealial Milk Stout (ABV 4.9%) STOUT
Weally Wonka (ABV 5.4%) PALE
Ginger Weal (ABV 5.5%) SPECIALITY
Lemon & Ginger Weal (ABV 5.5%) SPECIALITY

Wilsons of Warslow (NEW)

🍺 Greyhound Inn, Leek Road, Warslow, SK17 0JN
☎ (01298) 84782 ⊕ thegreyhoundinnwarslow.com

Started brewing commercially at the beginning of 2023 on a two-barrel plant alongside the Greyhound Inn in Warslow with beers finding their way into the trade throughout the Staffordshire Moorlands and the Peak District.

Tamworth Tap, Tamworth (Photo: Robert Hamnett-Day)

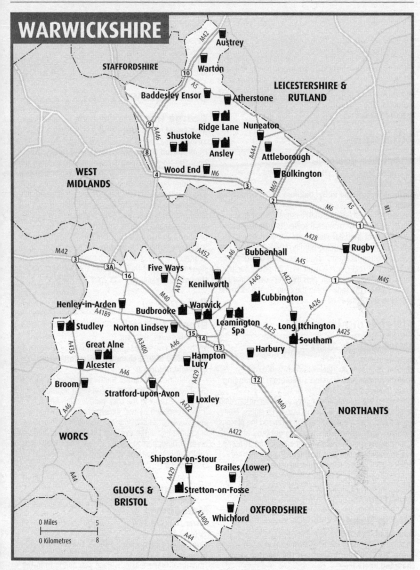

WARWICKSHIRE

Austrey
STAFFORDSHIRE
Warton
10
A5
Baddesley Ensor
Atherstone
LEICESTERSHIRE & RUTLAND
9 A46
Ridge Lane
Nuneaton
8
Shustoke
Ansley
Attleborough
WEST MIDLANDS
Wood End
M6
4
3
Bulkington
M69
2
M6
A5
M1
A428
M42
A452
A46
Bubbenhall
Rugby
3
A45
M45
3A
Five Ways
A45
A423
1
16
Kenilworth
Cubbington
A426
M40
A4177
A445
Henley-in-Arden
Warwick
A4189
Budbrooke
Long Itchington
A435
Studley
Norton Lindsey
Leamington Spa
A425
Southam
Great Alne
15
14
Harbury
Alcester
A3400
13
Hampton Lucy
Broom
A46
A429
12
Stratford-upon-Avon
Loxley
M40
A422
NORTHANTS
WORCS
A422
A44
Shipston-on-Stour
Brailes (Lower)
GLOUCS & BRISTOL
A429
Stretton-on-Fosse
Whichford
OXFORDSHIRE
A3400
A44

0 Miles 5
0 Kilometres 8

Alcester

Royal Oak

44 High Street, B49 5AB

☎ (01789) 565211

Brains Rev James Original; St Austell Tribute; Wye Valley Bitter; 1 changing beer (sourced nationally; often Fuller's) Ⓗ

Friendly 18th-century Grade II-listed building, with an open-plan layout including snug areas and a log fire, plus a small rear garden with seating. The landlord and her loyal staff have a passion for real ales and ciders and provide a varied selection for customers. Regular live music sessions are held on Thursday and often themed food events on Friday evening, plus a good Sunday lunch is served. ☕🕮⑪🚱♿🚪🏠🐕❄🎵

Turks Head

4 High Street, B49 5AD

☎ (01789) 765948 ● theturkshead.net

Purity Jimbo; 3 changing beers (sourced nationally; often St Austell, Salopian, Wye Valley) Ⓗ

A busy, centrally located town pub, with exposed beams and roaring log fires, that is well worth a visit. The landlords, who have been here for 20 years, are dedicated to real ale. They source their beers from local breweries, as well as from Shropshire, Yorkshire and South Wales. Good food is a daily feature and there is a separate dining room as well as a quiet garden. The pub provides street bars for the annual town festivals. CAMRA Warwickshire Pub of the Year 2022. Q☕🕮⑪⑪♿🚪🚌🏠🐕❄🚲🛜

Ansley

Lord Nelson Inn 🍸 Ⓛ

Birmingham Road, CV10 9PQ

☎ (024) 7639 2305 ● thelordnelsoninnansley.co.uk

Sperrin Ansley Mild, Head Hunter, Band of Brothers, Third Party, Thick as Thieves; 3 changing beers Ⓗ

This nautically themed pub has been run by the same family since 1974, incorporating a brewery at the rear of the building since 2012. Nine handpulls dispense their own Sperrin brews, plus guests from microbreweries. An extensive food menu is served, with meal nights and tribute nights hosted, plus a monthly quiz held in the Victory restaurant. The suntrap courtyard garden is the venue for a beer festival and barbecue in August. This is the pub's 30th consecutive entry in the Guide. ዄ⊛❈◑₾P⊟❀ᚎ♪

Atherstone

Angel Ale House 🅛
24 Church Street, CV9 1HA
☎ 07525 183056
Leatherbritches Mad Ruby; Oakham Citra; 3 changing beers 🅗
This attractive pub on the market square, next to the church with its rare octagonal tower, is a frequent local CAMRA Pub of the Year winner. Its interior features an inglenook fireplace with log-burning stove. There are five real ales, often local and always including a dark beer, plus up to 10 real ciders. Customers can select music from a large vinyl selection, plus there are occasional live bands. Park on the square or in the council car park to the rear. ❈≈₾P⊟(48,65)❀

Attleborough

Attleborough Arms
Highfield Road, CV11 4PL
☎ (024) 7638 3231 ⊕ attleborougharmspub.co.uk
Banks's Amber Ale; Marston's Pedigree; 3 changing beers (sourced nationally) 🅗
Large open-plan pub selling a good and often interesting range of various beers from the Marston's stable. Many value-for-money meal deals are on offer and the place is popular with lunchtime diners. It can get busy at times, particularly when Nuneaton Town are playing at home. Live bands are screened and local bands are supported. Buffets can be catered for on special occasions, and there is a large outdoor seating area. ❈◑⅖♣P⊟❀ᚎ♪

Austrey

Bird in Hand 🏆
Main Road, CV9 3EB
☎ (01827) 830260 ⊕ birdinhandaustrey.co.uk
Marston's Pedigree; house beer (by Marston's); 4 changing beers 🅗
This attractive thatched and timber-framed pub dates from the 15th century and is the focal point of this small rural village. Note the ancient octagonal wayside cross by the front entrance. There is a small bar room, a snug to the rear and a large lounge featuring a number of intimate areas. The sizeable garden to the rear features a large pop-up marquee, available for functions. Up to four guest ales offer interesting choices, usually including a dark beer. Q⊛❈◑⅖♣P⊟❀ᚎ

Baddesley Ensor

Red Lion
The Common, CV9 2BT (from the Grendon roundabout on A5 go S up Boot Hill) SP273983
☎ (01827) 718186
Greene King Abbot; Marston's Pedigree; 3 changing beers 🅗
Welcoming and traditional village pub whose character hasn't changed in many decades. The interior is spacious but intimate, with no food featured, just ale and

conversation. The comfy seating and log fire are enhanced by a music-free environment. Four guest ales are served, from major national and small local breweries. The sparkler is willingly removed on request. Off-road parking is available opposite. Please note that lunchtime opening is at weekends only. Q♣❀P⊟❀ᚎ

Brailes (Lower)

George Inn 🅛
High Street, OX15 5HN
☎ (01608) 685788 ⊕ thegeorgeatbrailes.co.uk
Hook Norton Hooky Mild, Hooky, Old Hooky; house beer (by Hook Norton); 1 changing beer (often Hook Norton) 🅗
This stone-built coaching inn has six handpumps serving a good selection of Hook Norton ales. An open fire in the flagstone-floored bar provides winter warmth and the large garden has an Aunt Sally pitch, children's playground, and covered smoking area. There is a pool table and a restaurant, plus live music plays early Saturday evening. The inn takes its name from the nearby St George church, which was, apparently, built by stonemasons after they had built the pub as a place to stay while working on it. ዄ⊛⊟◑♣P⊟❀ᚎ♪

Broom

Broom Tavern 🅛
32 High Street, B50 4HL
☎ (01789) 778199 ⊕ broomtavern.co.uk
Wye Valley HPA; 2 changing beers (often North Cotswold, Purity) 🅗
A lovely brick and timber multi-room building with a great amount of character. It has been tastefully made over while keeping the cosy snug and log fire in winter. It was reopened by two experienced chefs who now produce great food using local ingredients, served at lunchtime and in the evening. Local beers are frequently on offer here, plus at least one real cider. There is a choice of beer gardens, and dogs are welcome. Q⊛◑♣P❀

Bubbenhall

Malt Shovel 🅛
Lower End, CV8 3BW
☎ (024) 7630 1141
Church End Fallen Angel; Fuller's London Pride; Greene King Abbot; Sharp's Doom Bar 🅗
Traditional Grade II-listed village pub dating from the 17th century. Its main bar is the hub of the community, enjoyed by regulars who always extend a friendly welcome. The large lounge area to the front is more food-oriented, serving highly recommended home-cooked food, with regular pie nights and fish nights a

REAL ALE BREWERIES	
Church End	Ridge Lane
Church Farm ✦	Budbrooke
Fizzy Moon 🍺	Leamington Spa
Fosse Way	Southam
Freestyle 🍺	Shustoke
North Cotswold	Stretton-on-Fosse
Old Pie Factory	Warwick
Purity	Great Alne
Slaughterhouse	Warwick
Sperrin 🍺	Ansley
Warwickshire	Leamington Spa: Cubbington
Weatheroak	Studley
Windmill Hill	Leamington Spa

feature. The pub is handy for the nearby Ryton Pools Country Park and National Agricultural Centre.
Q❄✿❶P🖵(24) ✿

Bulkington

Weavers Arms

12 Long Street, CV12 9JZ
☎ (024) 7631 4415 ⊕ weaversarms.co.uk
Draught Bass; 2 changing beers (often Black Sheep, Timothy Taylor) Ⓗ

Family-owned, two-roomed traditional village pub converted from weavers' cottages. It has a wood-panelled games room, log-burning fireplace and slate floor. A large, well-kept beer garden accommodates barbecues in the summer. The pub is worth visiting for the quality of its Bass and friendly banter from the landlord. Children are welcome and private functions catered for. The Pork Pie Club, Weavers Walkers and Hillbilly Golf Society all hold regular meetings here.
❄✿♣🖵(56) ✿🗲

Five Ways

Case is Altered Ⓛ

Case Lane, Five Ways, Haseley, CV35 7JD (off Five Ways Rd near A4141/A4177 jct) SP225701
☎ (01926) 484206 ⊕ caseisaltered.com
Old Pie Factory Pie In The Sky; Wye Valley Butty Bach; 2 changing beers (sourced locally) Ⓗ

A classic unspoilt country pub with a bar and separate snug. It has been identified by CAMRA as having a historic pub interior of regional importance. The current landlady has been here for more than 30 years, after taking over from her grandmother. The traditional bar billiards table still takes old sixpences, which can be bought from the bar. Memorabilia includes a Victorian print of a former Leamington brewer in the bar, a clock from another old local brewer, and a propeller from a WWI fighter plane on the ceiling. Monday is cribbage night. Q✿⬢♣P

Great Alne

Mother Huffcap Ⓛ

Spernall Lane, B49 6HY
☎ (01789) 638005 ⊕ motherhuffcap.co.uk
Purity Jimbo; house beer (by Purity); 2 changing beers (often Timothy Taylor, Wye Valley) Ⓗ

An early 18th-century, Grade II-listed building houses this country pub, which reopened in 2021 under new owners to serve the local community after being closed for nearly three years. The Purity beers, and Hogan's cider in summer, are produced less than three miles from this free house. Locally sourced food is prepared on-site, to be eaten in or taken away. The menu includes gluten-free, vegetarian and vegan options. Bus X19 passes the door. There is a good-sized car park and garden.
❄✿❶⬢♠P🖵(X19) ✿🗲♪

Hampton Lucy

Boars Head Ⓛ ✅

Church Street, CV35 8BE
☎ (01789) 840533 ⊕ theboarsheadhamptonlucy.com
Timothy Taylor Landlord; house beer (by Greene King); 3 changing beers (sourced locally; often Church End, North Cotswold, Slaughterhouse) Ⓗ

Friendly, popular village pub originally built in the 17th century as a cider house. Situated on a Sustrans route and close to the River Avon, it is frequented by cyclists, walkers and visitors to nearby Charlecote Park. Five real

ales are normally served, with at least two LocAles. The menu offers fresh, locally sourced home-made food. The walled rear garden is popular in good weather, and an annual themed beer festival is held in late May.
❄✿❶P✿🗲♪

Harbury

Crown Inn

Crown Street, CV33 9HE
☎ (01926) 614995 ⊕ crowninnharbury.co.uk
Butcombe Original; St Austell Proper Job; 1 changing beer Ⓗ

A Grade II-listed limestone pub that was built in this picturesque village in 1785. Inside is a cosy bar, a comfortable lounge area at the rear, and a separate restaurant. There is a covered drinking area outside. The bar normally features two regular beers and one changing guest. The pub plays host to a crib team and holds occasional music nights and quizzes.
Q❄✿❶⬢♠P🖵(200) ✿🗲♪

Henley-in-Arden

Three Tuns 🏆

103 High Street, B95 5AT
☎ (01564) 792723
Church End Goat's Milk; Fuller's London Pride; Sharp's Doom Bar; Wye Valley Butty Bach; 1 changing beer (sourced locally; often Church End) Ⓗ

A small, unpretentious 16th-century drinkers' pub with a single bar serving two rooms. Popular with locals, many of whom frequent the establishment to play darts and cribbage, the pub is usually busy and the atmosphere is always friendly. Five real ales are served in consistently good condition. No hot food is served, though pub snacks are usually available, alongside home-made sausage rolls and cobs. Parking is on the main street outside the pub. Q❄⬢⬡♠🖵(X20)✿🗲

Kenilworth

Ale Rooms & Gin Bar Ⓛ

7 Smalley Place, CV8 1QG (opp clock tower)
☎ (01926) 513087
6 changing beers (sourced regionally; often Church End, Silhill) Ⓗ

A light, airy and welcoming contemporary bar in a pleasant spot opposite the clock tower. Up to six changing real ales are on offer, and a large selection of gins. Live music is hosted every Friday, and an interesting collection of album covers adorns the walls. Upstairs is a chill-out lounge available for private hire and community use. There is a seating area in front of the pub for customer use. ❄⬡⬢🖵(11,X17)✿🗲

Old Bakery 🏆 Ⓛ

12 High Street, CV8 1LZ (near A429/A452 jct)
☎ (01926) 864111 ⊕ theoldbakerykenilworth.co.uk
Wye Valley HPA; 3 changing beers (sourced regionally) Ⓗ

Small pub in a former bakery in the old town. Beams, bare floorboards, rustic furniture, subtle lighting and pictures generate a cosy feel to the main bar and separate snug. This independent, family-run free house offers frequently changing guest ales. A mix of locals and visitors, plus guests occupying the 14 en-suite rooms, ensures that conversation flows. There is limited disabled parking and access at the rear of the premises. Local CAMRA Pub of the Year 2023. Q❄✿🛏⬡P🖵(11)✿🗲

Leamington Spa

Benjamin Satchwell ✔

112/114 The Parade, CV32 4AQ (almost opp town hall)
☎ (01926) 883733
Greene King Abbot; Ruddles Best Bitter; Sharp's Doom Bar; 4 changing beers (often Hook Norton, Marston's, Silhill) [H]
Named after a renowned local benefactor who discovered Leamington's second spring in 1784, this pub bears all the hallmarks of the Wetherspoon style. Converted from two shops, it is large, stretching back to Bedford Street. The building's split levels have been used well to create comfortable seating areas. The upper level hosts an impressively long bar. Wall panels depict local history and personalities. 🐎◐♿🚆🍎🚌📶

New Inn

197 Leam Terrace, CV31 1DW
☎ (01926) 422861 🌐 thenewinnleamington.co.uk
Eagle IPA; Sharp's Doom Bar, Atlantic, Sea Fury; 2 changing beers (often Byatt's) [H]
A traditional pub in a wide Victorian terrace on the outskirts of town. The original pub has been extended into the property next door. A central door opens directly onto the bar, with a seating area to the left and a games area to the right leading to an extension at the rear. Quality home-cooked food is served. A quiz is hosted every other Wednesday. Outside is a good-sized walled garden. 🐎❀◐♿♣🚌(63,64)🐾📶♫

Woodland Tavern [L]

3 Regent Street, CV32 5HW
☎ (01926) 425868
Slaughterhouse Saddleback Best Bitter; Timothy Taylor Landlord; 2 changing beers [H]
Traditional Victorian street-corner pub located close to the centre of Leamington Spa and enjoyed by locals and visitors alike. It features a public bar and separate lounge that doubles as a function room. The unique, partially covered courtyard features murals depicting local references and jokes. There is also a further function room housed off the courtyard. On the side of the building is a large colourful mural showing a dray and horses delivering ale to the pub. Real cider is from Napton Cidery. ❀♿🚆♣🍎🚌🐾📶♫

Long Itchington

Harvester

6 Church Road, CV47 9PE (off A423 at village pond, then first left)
☎ (01926) 812698 🌐 theharvesterinn.co.uk
3 changing beers (often Church End, Purity) [H]
White-fronted pub near the village pond, on the corner of the square. Inside is a main bar, a small drinking area and a restaurant specialising in good-value steaks. The ale range changes frequently, usually supporting smaller breweries. Real cider and a Belgian fruit beer are also on the bar. The pub hosts a beer festival each May bank holiday. A large walled courtyard garden to the rear has a wood-fired pizza oven. **Q**🐎❀◐♿⛺🍎🚌(64)🐾📶♫

Loxley

Fox Inn

Goldicote Road, CV35 9JS
☎ (01789) 840933 🌐 foxloxley.co.uk
2 changing beers (sourced regionally; often Church End, North Cotswold) [H]
This friendly pub in the heart of the village was bought in 2020 by the community and is wholly owned by 223 shareholders from Loxley and the surrounding towns and villages, plus supporters from around the world. Traditional pub food is provided. Sibling cider is brewed locally from apples grown in the village. It is popular with walkers and cyclists (National Cycle Route 41 runs nearby) and route 7 bus from Banbury to Stratford stops outside. 🐎❀◐♿🍎**P**🚌(7)🐾📶

Norton Lindsey

New Inn 🏆 [L] ✔

Main Street, CV35 8JA
☎ (01926) 258411 🌐 thenewinn.pub
Greene King IPA; Timothy Taylor Landlord; 2 changing beers (sourced locally; often Church End, M&B, Slaughterhouse) [H]
Warwickshire's first community-owned pub opened in 2017 after fundraising saved it from closure – it was purchased by a collective of more than 200 people. Located on a street corner in the heart of the village, the pub features a wooden floor and an open-plan interior that gives a light and airy feel. Food is locally sourced, with many specials on offer. Circular walks start and end here. **Q**🐎❀◐**P**🐾📶

Nuneaton

Anker Inn

Weddington Road, CV10 0AN
☎ (024) 7632 9193
Ossett White Rat; Sharp's Doom Bar; Theakston Old Peculier; 2 changing beers [H]
Situated on a main route into Nuneaton, this community-focused pub is known for the quality of its Theakston Old Peculiar. Various sports teams are based here and other activities include quizzes, jam sessions and live music. The pub hosts several charity events throughout the year including a music festival in August. Convenient for nearby Old Edwardians Rugby Football Club.
🐎❀◐🚆♣**P**🚌🐾📶♫

Felix Holt [L] ✔

3 Stratford Street, CV11 5BS
☎ (024) 7634 7785
Greene King Abbot; Ruddles Best Bitter; Sharp's Doom Bar; 4 changing beers (often Byatt's, Oakham) [H]
Large Wetherspoon outlet in the town centre. The pub takes its name from a novel by George Eliot, and the literary theme is reflected in the decor consisting of books and pictures of local history. Look out for the comical metal sculptures on the walls. A good range of guest beers includes local ales. There are tables and chairs outside for alfresco drinking and eating.
Q🐎◐♿🚆🚌📶

Lord Hop [L]

38 Queens Road, CV11 5JX
☎ (024) 7798 1869 🌐 lordhopnuneaton.co.uk
4 changing beers [H]
Town-centre micropub on two floors, the large upper floor boasting settees, a small library and selection of board games. Four or more real ales are served from handpull, with up to eight ciders or perries from the chiller. Wine, gins, bottled lager and soft drinks are also sold. Snacks are available, or bring your own takeaway. CAMRA magazines are provided for reading. No under-18s are permitted, and assistance dogs only. Regular local CAMRA Pub of the Year contender. **Q**🚆**P**🚌📶

Ridge Lane

Church End Brewery Tap 🄻

Ridge Lane, CV10 0RD (2 miles SW of Atherstone)
☎ (01827) 713080 ⊕ churchendbrewery.co.uk
Church End Goat's Milk, Gravediggers Ale, What the Fox's Hat, Fallen Angel; 4 changing beers 🄷
This brewery tap is hidden from the road, with access opposite Tom Piper Close. The brewery is visible from the bar area. Eight handpulls serve the bar and vestry, with a mild always on tap. Ciders are dispensed direct from the barrel. Under-18s are allowed inside the vestry until 6pm, and are welcome in the garden meadow. The pub hosts a monthly quiz night. Brewery tours are available by prior arrangement. Open Thursday to Sunday, plus Wednesday evenings in summer. Q🌳🞉🞉♿AP🖳🞉🞉🎜

Rugby

Merchants Inn 🄻

5-6 Little Church Street, CV21 3AW
☎ (01788) 571119
Nethergate Venture; Oakham Bishops Farewell; Purity Mad Goose 🄷**; 6 changing beers (sourced nationally)** 🄷/🄶
Popular town-centre pub with flagstone floors and an open fire. The interior is a museum of brewery memorabilia, with a large room to the rear that doubles as a function room. Rugby and cricket are popular on the TV. Activities are held throughout the year and include Belgian and German nights, beer festivals and gin and cider weekends. Locally produced snacks include pork pies and sausage rolls. Local CAMRA Pub of the Year for the last two years. 🌳🞉🞉♿♣♠P🖳🞉🞉🎜

Raglan Arms

50 Dunchurch Road, CV22 6AD (on A426 near to gyratory and town centre)
☎ (01788) 575881
Black Country Bradley's Finest Golden, Pig on the Wall, Fireside; 9 changing beers (sourced nationally) 🄷
A friendly pub with a warm welcome. There is a bar with darts and skittles, a lounge and a cosy snug which doubles as a meeting room. The regular ales are complemented by seasonal Black Country Ales brews, plus up to four guest beers from regional and local breweries. Bar snacks are available and there is occasional live music. Well-behaved dogs are welcome. Quiz nights are held monthly on a Thursday. 🌳🞉♣♠P🖳🞉🞉

Rugby Tap 🄻

4 St Matthews Street, CV21 3BY (close to town centre, adjacent to A426 gyratory)
☎ 07540 490377 ⊕ rugbytap.com
8 changing beers (sourced regionally; often Byatt's, Church End, Phipps NBC) 🄶
Micropub featuring a long room with a large selection of gravity-served draught ales and ciders racked at the far end. The atmosphere promotes conversation and there is no electronic entertainment. The pub serves up to six LocAles, beers from Oakham, two draught craft beers from New Bristol brewery, an Oslo pilsner and a selection of canned and bottled craft beers. There is outside seating at the front, with a view of the famous Rugby School. Q🌳🞉🖳🞉

Seven Stars 🄻

40 Albert Square, CV21 2SH
☎ (01788) 535478 ⊕ sevenstarsrugby.co.uk
Byatt's Platinum Blonde; Everards Tiger; 7 changing beers (sourced nationally) 🄷

Traditional multi-roomed community pub with a focus on quality beer and cider. Its 14 handpumps dispense an ever-changing selection of light and dark ales, plus four ciders, which are augmented by six craft beers. Food highlights include pie and a pint on Wednesday evening and Sunday lunchtime. Home-made Scotch eggs, filled rolls and locally produced pork pies are also available. Rugby is popular on the bar's TV. A former local CAMRA Pub of the Year. No children after 7pm.
Q🌳🞉🞉🞉⮙♠♣🖳🞉🞉🎜

Squirrel Inn 🄻

33 Church Street, CV21 3PU
☎ (01788) 578527
4 changing beers (sourced nationally; often Dow Bridge, Marston's, Parkway Brewing) 🄷
A warm welcome is guaranteed at this historic free house, Rugby's jewel in the town. A real fire and pictures of old Rugby contribute to the intimate ambience. Ales from Dow Bridge, Parkway Brewing and Phipps breweries are frequently served alongside Marston's beers and two ciders. Live music is a regular attraction, with various genres performed on Saturday evening and an open mic night on Wednesday. National CAMRA Golden Award winner. ♣♠🖳🞉🞉🎜

Town & County 🄻

12 Henry Street, CV21 2QA
☎ 07487 413960
Church End Gravediggers Ale; 2 changing beers (sourced nationally; often Church End, Otter, Wye Valley) 🄷
Small town-centre club that has been trading since 1933 and is making its sixth appearance in this Guide. Its four handpumps include two dispensing changing guest ales from breweries near and far. The club hosts dominoes and skittles teams, and holds regular events including monthly quizzes, occasional live music and coach trips. CAMRA members are welcome and guests may be signed in. Q🌳♣🖳🞉

Victoria Inn 🄻

1 Lower Hillmorton Road, CV21 3ST
☎ (01788) 544374
Oakham Citra; 4 changing beers (sourced nationally; often Abbeydale, Oakham, Titanic) 🄷
A beautiful Victorian corner pub just outside the town centre – a true gem and the last of its kind in Rugby. Built in a wedge shape, the multi-roomed local features a traditional bar, larger refurbished lounge and two relatively new snugs converted from the kitchen and store room. Filled rolls are available at the weekend. The pub shows sport on TV and hosts quiz nights on Thursday and Sunday. 🌳🞉♣🖳🞉🞉🎜

Shipston-on-Stour

Black Horse Inn 🄻

Station Road, CV36 4BT
☎ (01608) 238489 ⊕ blackhorseshipston.co.uk
Prescott Hill Climb; Wye Valley Butty Bach; 1 changing beer (sourced regionally; often North Cotswold) 🄷
Stone-built with a thatched roof, this is the oldest pub in town – it has held a licence since 1540. There are two bars, each with an open fire for winter warmth. Three handpumps serve two regular ales plus one changing. There is plenty of garden space, with a covered smoking area and a stage for live music in summer. A Thai restaurant provides delicious authentic dishes (takeaway available) and a cider festival is usually held on the August bank holiday. Q🌳🞉🞉♣P🖳🞉🞉🎜

Thirst Edition 🏆

46 Church Street, CV36 4AS
☎ (01608) 664974 🌐 thirstedition.co.uk
North Cotswold Shagweaver [H]; 3 changing beers (sourced regionally; often Acorn, Allsopp's, Hop Back) [G]
A micropub in this small market town serving up to 250 different cask ales each year, though there are duplicates often sourced from local breweries such as North Cotswold. A dozen still ciders and many gins are also available. It hosts live music on two Fridays each month, and since opening in 2018, the pub has raised over £10,000 for local causes from its popular Thursday night quiz. The 50 bus from Stratford stops nearby. Local CAMRA Pub of the Year 2023. Q♣🍎🚌(50)🐾📶♫

Shustoke

Griffin Inn [L]

Church Road, B46 2LB (on B4116 on sharp bend)
☎ (01675) 481205
Theakston Old Peculier; Wye Valley Butty Bach; 8 changing beers (sourced nationally; often Oakham) [H]
Family-owned rural pub which has championed real ale for over four decades. The spacious but intimate interior features a stone bar, inglenook fireplaces and beams decorated with ancient beer mats. No music interrupts the hum of conversation. There is always one real cider, and up to four in summer. Children are welcome on the beer terrace, in the conservatory, and on the extensive meadow-style garden. Home-cooked lunches are served (no food Sun). Q🐴❀◐⛺🍎P🐾📶

Stratford-upon-Avon

Stratford Alehouse [L]

12B Greenhill Street, CV37 6LF
☎ 07746 807966 🌐 thestratfordalehouse.com
4 changing beers (sourced nationally; often Byatt's, North Cotswold, XT) [G]
A family-run, one-bar micropub offering a wide range of gravity cask and keg ales, ciders, wines and gins. A friendly welcome is provided in a relaxing environment for chatting, relaxing, making new friends or reading the papers. More than 1,600 different beers from over 400 breweries have been served since the pub opened in 2013. Packet snacks are available, as are free doggy treats. Occasional TV sport is shown and there may be live or vinyl music events.
🚆(Stratford Upon Avon) 🍎🚌🐾♫

Studley

Weatheroak Tap House [L]

21A High Street, B80 7HN
☎ (01527) 854433 🌐 weatheroakbrewery.co.uk
Weatheroak Bees Knees, Victoria Works, Keystone Hops; 3 changing beers (sourced locally; often Beowulf, Enville, Weatheroak) [H]
Popular and welcoming micropub with two small, cosy rooms. It is the outlet for the nearby Weatheroak brewery, whose off-sales are available, alongside their own stout in winter months; also guest beers from other small breweries, plus a range of gins. Typical bar snacks such as Scotch eggs are sold in the summer. Takeaway food can be brought in; there is a chip shop next door. The pub prides itself on supporting local community events. Q🐴♣🍎P🚌(X19,247)🐾📶

Warton

Office [L]

Church Road, B79 0JN
☎ (01827) 894001
Draught Bass; 2 changing beers (often Church End) [H]
Formerly the Boot, this community-focused pub caters for a wide audience, particularly as it is now the last one in the village. The large bar area is dominated by sports TV, and there is a raised side area and a comfy upstairs room with a free pool table. There are open fires both upstairs and downstairs. At the back of the pub is a suntrap beer terrace on two levels. Regular live music and quizzes are hosted. 🐴❀♣P🐾📶

Warwick

Cape of Good Hope [L]

66 Lower Cape, CV34 5DP (off Cape Rd)
☎ (01926) 498138 🌐 thecapeofgoodhopepub.com
Church Farm Harry's Heifer; Hook Norton Hooky; Wye Valley Butty Bach; 3 changing beers [H]
Historic alehouse on the Grand Union Canal, dating from 1798 and welcoming to canal users and locals. The original building on the waterside is now the front bar, with a modern extension to the rear. Internal decorations feature canal memorabilia, including interesting maps. Three permanent real ales are offered, along with three locally sourced guest beers. The friendly staff are knowledgeable, and proud to serve local ales and food. There is outdoor waterside seating next to a double lock that can get busy. 🐴❀◐◑⛺♣P🚌(G1)🐾📶♫

Eagle

The Holloway, CV34 4SJ
☎ (01926) 493673
3 changing beers (sourced regionally; often Byatt's, North Cotswold, Vocation) [H]
The Eagle is Warwick's smallest pub, located in an old cellar tucked away on the famous Holloway, just off the square. This quirky little pub, frequented by locals and visitors alike, has three changing cask beers and two craft taps. The seating is cosy and friendly, with some seating on the pavement outside. There is often themed music playing, and games nights are hosted.
Q🐴❀🚆🐾📶♫

Four Penny Pub

27/29 Crompton Street, CV34 6HJ (near Racecourse, between A429 and A4189)
☎ (01926) 491360 🌐 4pennyhotel.co.uk
6 changing beers [H]
The pub is in a Georgian building dating from around 1800 and lies a short distance from the town centre, close to the racecourse and castle. Its name derives from the price of a cup of coffee and tot of rum that was charged to workers building the nearby Grand Union Canal in the early 1800s. The single, split-level room has a contemporary feel and a relaxed atmosphere, enhanced by the absence of machines. There is an outside seating area. Accommodation is in 14 en-suite rooms. Q🐴🛏◐◑⛺🍎P🚌🐾📶♫

Old Post Office [L]

12 West Street, CV34 6AN
☎ 07765 896155
North Cotswold Shagweaver; Phipps NBC India Pale Ale [H]; 2 changing beers [H]/[G]
Warwick's first micropub was converted from an old post office and opened in 2014. It is a traditional, yet quirky establishment, with an interesting interior featuring eclectic curios adorning the walls. Popular with real ale enthusiasts and local residents, the pub has four handpull

cask ales, four craft keg beer taps and up to eight real ciders. A former local CAMRA Pub of the Year, and runner-up on many occasions. ॐ⚲◆🖵☕

Wild Boar 🅛

27 Lakin Road, CV34 5BU
☎ (01926) 499968 ⊕ wildboarwarwick.co.uk
Slaughterhouse Saddleback Best Bitter; 9 changing beers (often Everards, Slaughterhouse) 🄷
This taphouse for Slaughterhouse brewery is an award-winning Project William community pub near the railway station. The end-of-terrace Victorian building has a bar, snug and separate beer hall, which was formerly a skittle alley. Regular beers include Slaughterhouse, Everards and guest ales. Outside is an attractive patio hop garden – the hops are used for Slaughterhouse's annual brew, the Hop Head. Q ॐ🕭🕪≒♣🖵(X17)☕🎵

Whichford

Norman Knight 🅛

CV36 5PE (2 miles E of A3400 at Long Compton, facing village green)
☎ (01608) 684621 ⊕ thenormanknight.co.uk
Hook Norton Hooky; Prescott Hill Climb; house beer (by Goff's); 2 changing beers (sourced regionally; often Goff's, Purity, XT) 🄷
A friendly pub in the centre of this picturesque village, popular with locals and visitors. Its attractive decor and stone-flagged floor contribute to a cosy and comfortable ambience. High-quality food features locally sourced ingredients where possible. It holds monthly music nights, and in summer hosts classic car meetings on the third Thursday of the month. Muddy boots and muddy paws are always welcome. Accommodation is available in high-spec glamping pods behind the garden. Motorhomes are welcome and electric car charging is available. Q ॐ🕭🖾🕪Å♣🖵P🖵☕🎵

Wood End

Warwickshire Lad ✅

Broad Lane, B94 5DP
☎ (01564) 742346 ⊕ thewarwickshirelad.co.uk
Silhill Hop Star; Wye Valley HPA; house beer (by Silhill); 1 changing beer (often Silhill) 🄷
Country pub and restaurant offering excellent freshly-prepared food using local produce. Four well-kept ales are usually available, and Silhill brewery, which now has a brewing lab in the garden, used for experimental beers and brewing experience days, features strongly. The pub is welcoming to children and well-behaved dogs on leads, and there is a pub garden with outside decking area. Q ॐ🕭🕪≒P☕🎵

Breweries

BRUBL (NEW)

Unit 3, Railway Arch, Victoria Business Centre, Neilston Street, Leamington Spa, CV31 2AZ
⊕ brubl.beer

Experimental microbrewery and taproom in Leamington Spa. ♂

Church End SIBA

Ridge Lane, Nuneaton, CV10 0RD
☎ (01827) 713080 ⊕ churchendbrewery.co.uk

⊠ The brewery started in 1994 in an old coffin shop in Shustoke. It moved to its present site in 2001 and has expanded over the years. It currently operates a 24-barrel, purpose-built plant. Many one-off specials and old recipe beers are produced. Its award-winning beers are available throughout the Midlands. ‼🍴◆LIVE

Brewers Truth (ABV 3.6%) PALE
Goat's Milk (ABV 3.8%) PALE
Gravediggers Ale (ABV 3.8%) MILD
What the Fox's Hat (ABV 4.2%) BITTER
A beer with a malty aroma, and a hoppy and malty taste with some caramel flavour.
Vicar's Ruin (ABV 4.4%) PALE
A straw-coloured best bitter with an initially hoppy, bitter flavour, softening to a delicate malt finish.
Stout Coffin (ABV 4.6%) STOUT
Fallen Angel (ABV 5%) PALE

Church Farm SIBA

Church Farm, Budbrooke, CV35 8QL
☎ (01926) 411569 ⊕ churchfarmbrewery.co.uk

Over a decade ago the farm's dairy herd departed and the milking equipment was repurposed for brewing. Four years later production moved to a 20-barrel plant as sales expanded. Water for brewing comes from an onsite well. More than 150 regular outlets are supplied. Its mobile bar is a regular at Warwickshire events. Brewery tap yard open Friday and Saturdays (winter excepted). ‼LIVE ♂

Pale Ale (ABV 3.8%) PALE
Session IPA (ABV 3.8%) PALE
Brown's Porter (ABV 4.2%) PORTER
Harry's Heifer (ABV 4.2%) BITTER
IPA (ABV 5%) PALE

Fizzy Moon

🏠 Fizzy Moon, 35 Regent Street, Leamington Spa, CV32 5EE
☎ (01926) 888715 ⊕ fizzymoonbrewhouse.com

Fizzy Moon is a bar and microbrewery in the heart of Leamington Spa, brewing a range of small batch beers, exclusively for consumption in the bar. All beers are unfined and so naturally hazy.

Fosse Way SIBA

Elms Farm, Plough Lane, Bishops Itchington, Southam, CV47 2QG ☎ 07956 179999
⊕ fossebrew.co.uk

⊠ In 2022 the brewery was relocated and expanded and a full time partner taken on (former owner of Red Moon brewery). Most production is bottled and sold in Warwickshire markets. Some Red Moon brands, plus ciders, have been added to the range. ◆LIVE

Aurora (ABV 3.6%) PALE
Sentinel (ABV 4.5%) BITTER
Dark Side (ABV 4.8%) PORTER

Freestyle

🏠 Church Road, Shustoke, B46 2LB
☎ (01675) 481205 ⊕ griffininnshustoke.co.uk

Griffin Inn started brewing in 2008 in the old coffin shop adjacent to the pub. In 2017 the brewery was updated to a modern, more efficient 2.5-barrel plant. At this time the name was changed to Freestyle though the business is still owned by the Pugh family who run the Griffin. Beers are available for the free trade as well as selling through the pub. ‼◆

Dark (ABV 3.8%) MILD
Pale Ale (ABV 3.8%) BITTER

Shawbury Blonde (ABV 4.2%) BLOND
Bullion (ABV 4.4%) GOLD
Yeti IPA (ABV 4.5%) PALE
Black Magic Woman (ABV 4.8%) PORTER
Muzungu (ABV 5.5%) BITTER
Red Rye PA (ABV 5.5%) RED

North Cotswold SIBA

Unit 3, Ditchford Farm, Stretton-on-Fosse, GL56 9RD
☎ (01608) 663947 ⊕ northcotswoldbrewery.co.uk

☺North Cotswold started in 1999 as a family run 2.5-barrel plant, which has since been upgraded to 10-barrel capacity. Beers are also produced under the Shakespeare brand name, available in cask and bottles. 🍷◆LIVE

Windrush Ale (ABV 3.6%) BITTER
Jumping Jack Flash (ABV 3.8%) GOLD
Moreton Mild (ABV 3.8%) MILD
Cotswold Best (ABV 4%) BITTER
Green Man IPA (ABV 4%) PALE
Shagweaver (ABV 4.5%) BITTER
Hung, Drawn 'n' Portered (ABV 5%) PORTER
Freedom IDA7 (ABV 5.2%) IPA

Brewed under the Shakespeare Brewery brand name:
Bard's Best (ABV 4.2%) BITTER
Falstaff's Folly (ABV 4.2%) BITTER

Old Pie Factory

4 Montague Road, Warwick, CV34 5LW ☎ 07816 413026 ⊕ oldpiefactorybrewery.co.uk

☺Brewing began in 2011 using a 5.5-barrel plant and is a joint venture between Underwood Wines, Stratford upon Avon, and the Case is Altered, Five Ways.

Bitter (ABV 3.9%) BITTER
Pie In The Sky (ABV 4.1%) PALE
Humble Pie (ABV 4.2%) BITTER
I.Pie.A. (ABV 4.5%) PALE
American Pie (ABV 5.5%) IPA

Purity SIBA

The Brewery, Upper Spernal Farm, Spernal Lane, Great Alne, B49 6JF
☎ (01789) 488007 ⊕ puritybrewing.com

☺Brewing began in 2005 in a plant housed in converted barns. The brewery prides itself on its eco-friendly credentials. It supplies its award-winning beers into the free trade within a 70-mile radius (plus London), delivering to more than 500 outlets. 🍷🍷◆GF V

Bunny Hop (ABV 3.5%) PALE
Pure Gold (ABV 3.8%) GOLD
Mad Goose (ABV 4.2%) BITTER
Pure UBU (ABV 4.5%) BITTER

Slaughterhouse SIBA

Bridge Street, Warwick, CV34 5PD
☎ (01926) 490986 ☎ 07951 842690

Second site: Wild Boar, 27 Larkin Road, Warwick, CV34 5BU ⊕ slaughterhousebrewery.com

☺Production began in 2003 on a four-barrel plant in a former slaughterhouse. Around 30 outlets are supplied, mostly within five miles of the brewery. The brewery premises are licensed for off-sales direct to the public. In 2010 Slaughterhouse opened its first pub, the Wild Boar in Warwick, adding a two-barrel brew plant that brews specials for the pub. 🍷🍷

Saddleback Best Bitter (ABV 3.8%) BITTER
Extra Stout Snout (ABV 4.4%) STOUT
Boar D'eau (ABV 4.5%) GOLD
Wild Boar (ABV 5.2%) BITTER

Sperrin

🍴 Lord Nelson Inn, Birmingham Road, Ansley, CV10 9PQ
☎ (024) 7639 2305 ☎ 07917 772208
⊕ sperrinbrewery.co.uk

Sperrin began brewing in 2012 on a six-barrel plant. The pub always has five of its beers available and two or three at its sister pub, the Blue Boar, Mancetter. 🍷🍷◆LIVE

Ansley Mild (ABV 3.5%) MILD
Head Hunter (ABV 3.8%) BITTER
Band of Brothers (ABV 4.2%) GOLD
Third Party (ABV 4.8%) RED
Thick as Thieves (ABV 6.8%) STOUT

Warwickshire

Bakehouse Brewery, Queen Street, Cubbington, Leamington Spa, CV32 7NA
☎ (01926) 450747 ⊕ warwickshirebeer.co.uk

A six-barrel brewery in a former village bakery which has been in operation since 1998. More unusual craft beers are available under the Bakehouse Brewery brand name. The brewery came under the 52 Degree Brewing umbrella in 2023. 🍷◆LIVE

SPA (Spa Pale Ale) (ABV 3.8%) PALE
Darling Buds (ABV 4%) PALE
Duck Soup (ABV 4.2%) BITTER
Lady Godiva (ABV 4.2%) GOLD
Yer Bard (ABV 4.3%) BITTER

Brewed under the Bakehouse brand name:
Liquid Bread (ABV 4.5%) GOLD

Weatheroak

Unit 7, Victoria Works, Birmingham Road, Studley, B80 7AP
☎ (01527) 854433 ☎ 07771 860645

Office: Weatheroak Tap House, 21a High Street, Studley, B80 7HN ⊕ weatheroakbrewery.co.uk

⊗ The brewery was set up in 1997 at Weatheroak Hill. It is now in a spacious factory unit in Studley. Weatheroak supplies 20 outlets. Off-sales available for all beers at the Tap House on the High Street in Studley. 18 and 36 pint polypins are available with notice. 🍷◆

Bees Knees (ABV 3.7%) BITTER
This straw-coloured quaffing ale has lots of hoppy notes on the tongue and nose, and a fleetingly sweet aftertaste.
Victoria Works (ABV 4.3%) PALE
Redwood (ABV 4.4%) BITTER

Windmill Hill SIBA

14 Victoria Business Centre, Neilston Street, Leamington Spa, CV31 2AZ ⊕ whbrewery.co.uk

Windmill Hill is an independent microbrewery using a three-barrel plant brewing small-batch beers. Around 30 outlets are supplied direct. Beers are available in cask and keg formats as well as small package.

Table Beer (ABV 2.9%) BITTER
Amber Post (ABV 4.2%) BITTER
The Chesterton (ABV 4.2%) BITTER
Grindstone (ABV 4.5%) GOLD

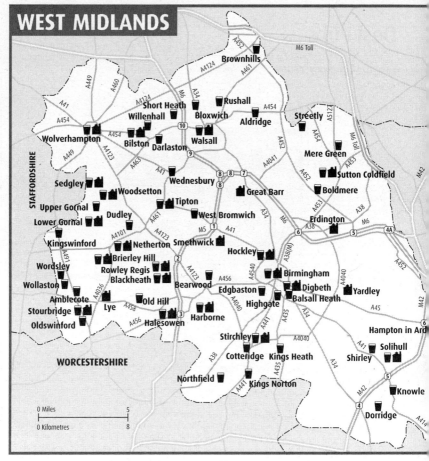

WEST MIDLANDS

Aldridge

Turtle's Head 🅛

14 Croft Parade, WS9 8LY

☎ (01922) 325635 ⊕ theturtleshead.co.uk

4 changing beers (sourced regionally) 🅗

Opened in 2015, this micropub in the centre of Aldridge, within a shopping parade, offers a warm welcome. It has four handpulls serving a range of ever-changing ales, mainly from local and regional breweries. Bar snacks include freshly-made cobs, scratchings and complimentary cheese and pâté on Sunday. Customers may bring their own food if they are drinking. Closed on Monday except for bank holidays. Discounts are available on Tuesday. 🌫️❀🖑🖂🐾🛜

Amblecote

Red Lion

147 Brettell Lane, DY8 4BA

☎ (01384) 671743 ⊕ theredlionamblecote.co.uk

Holden's Golden Glow; Salopian Oracle, Lemon Dream; 3 changing beers (sourced nationally; often Salopian) 🅗

This smart and inviting pub, exuding class, is partly owned by the Furious Pub Company and was smartly refurbished in 2021. It is popular with a wide customer mix and can get busy on Friday and Saturday nights. Full meals and a selection of freshly-made cobs and pies are

served all day. A selection of real ales with two changing guests from small breweries both local and national is on the bar. A dress code operates on Thursday to Sunday evenings. Q🌫️◑🖑🖂🛜♪

Robin Hood 🅛

196 Collis Street, DY8 4EQ (on A4102 one way street off Brettell Ln A461)

☎ 07436 793462

Bathams Best Bitter; Enville Ginger Beer; St Austell Proper Job; Three Tuns XXX; Wye Valley HPA; 3 changing beers (sourced nationally) 🅗

A traditional Black Country local with fine ales and always a warm welcome; 2015 saw the pub celebrate 160 years as a licenced house. The front rooms house a wonderful beer bottle collection including international and historic brews. The pub serves freshly-made cobs and pork pies, and features some national guest ales, but the LocAle scheme is emphasised with more local beers on permanent sale. The rear outside area now has a permanent marquee. Q🌫️❀🛏️◑🕭🖑P🖂(6,16)🛜

Swan 🍺 🅛

10 Brettell Lane, DY8 4BN (on A461, ½ mile after A491)

☎ (01384) 591600

Enville Ale; Holden's Golden Glow; Salopian Oracle; Wye Valley HPA; 4 changing beers 🅗

This free house has been totally refurbished by the owners of the Red Lion down the road. There is now only one room served by a central bar. The difficult entry with

Black Country Bradley's Finest Golden, Pig on the Wall, Fireside; 9 changing beers (sourced nationally; often Black Country) Ⓗ
A former HSBC bank, this single-room, open-plan pub began trading in 2014 following a thorough refurbishment, and is now decorated in the established Black Country Ales theme to a high standard. It serves up to 12 real ales and three still ciders. The beer cellar is on the same floor and can be viewed through a glass inspection panel. Standard bar snacks, including crusty cobs, are available. Q ১ ⊛ ① ᵭ ♣ ● 🖫 ✿ 🛜

Bilston

Cafe Metro

46 Church Street, WV14 0AH (opp St Leonards Church and town hall)
☎ (01902) 498888 ⊕ cafe-metro.co.uk
Wye Valley Butty Bach; 4 changing beers (sourced nationally; often Blue Monkey, Oakham, Thornbridge) Ⓗ
A tucked-away micropub accessed via the same side street off Church Street as the Metro station; it does not front onto Church Street. The Backroom@Cafe Metro's main room has a friendly atmosphere with good seating. A separate servery features a massive range of British and international beers in bottles and cans. Large cobs, bar snacks and pork pies are always available. Occasional beer festivals and live music are hosted. A small outside seating area is to the right of the front door.
Q ᭰ ♿ (Central) ● P 🖫 🛜 ♪

Birmingham: Balsall Heath

Old Moseley Arms Ⓛ

53 Tindal Street, B12 9QU (400yds off Moseley Rd)
☎ (0121) 440 1954 ⊕ oldmoseleyarms.co.uk
Bathams Best Bitter; Church End Goat's Milk; Enville Ale; Wye Valley HPA, Butty Bach Ⓗ
This is one of Birmingham's hidden gems, run by Sukhi for over 25 years. The left bar has an 80-inch screen for sport, the right bar has a jukebox. Upstairs is for functions, and there are comfy sofas in the recently extended garden/smoking area. A superb tandoori menu is served in the evening and all day Sunday. The pub gets busy when international and T20 cricket matches are played at Edgbaston, 10 minute's walk away.
১ ⊛ 🖫 (50) 🛜 ♪

Birmingham: City Centre

Briar Rose ⊘

25 Bennetts Hill, B2 5RE
☎ (0121) 634 8100
Greene King Abbot; Ruddles Best Bitter; Sharp's Doom Bar; 4 changing beers (sourced nationally) Ⓗ
This large, city-centre Wetherspoon has a number of eating and drinking areas. The main bar can get busy, especially after work and at weekends. Food and drink are the usual Wetherspoon fayre but guest beers can be interesting. Decorated in a 1930s Art Deco style, wall decorations show a number of prints and photographs of well-known Birmingham people and landmarks. The pub is named after paintings by Edward Burne-Jones, who was born over the road. Accommodation is available upstairs. ১ ⊨ ① ⇌ (New Street) ♿ (Grand Central) 🖫 🛜

Bull Ⓛ

1 Price Street, B4 6JU (off St. Chads Queensway)
☎ (0121) 333 6757 ⊕ thebullbirmingham.co.uk

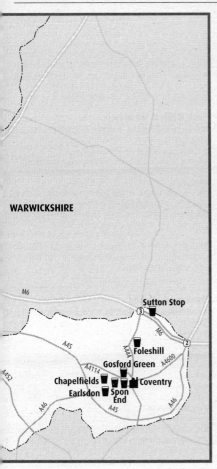

WARWICKSHIRE

M6

Sutton Stop
③

M6

②

A45   A4114   Foleshill
Gosford Green   A4600
Chapelfields   A4114   Coventry
Earlsdon   Spon   A46
End
A46   A45

the old serving hatch has gone allowing customers to walk straight to the bar. The original metal bar separator in the lounge is now used as a garden feature. The derelict buildings to the rear have gone and a tidy smoking area has been created. Only cobs and snacks are available. Local CAMRA Pub of the Year 2023.
⊛ ① 🖫 (6) ✿ 🛜 ♪

Bearwood

Bear Tavern ⊘

500 Bearwood Road, B66 4BX
☎ (0121) 429 1184
Greene King IPA, Abbot; 4 changing beers (sourced nationally; often Oakham) Ⓗ
Busy open-plan community local dominated by a central bar, with sports screens scattered throughout – live matches are often shown. Attentive staff serve an interesting range of nationally sourced real ales and up to two bag-in-box real ciders. A large wooden-floored function room is available to hire upstairs. Affordable classic pub food is served, and a diverse clientele spanning all age groups is attracted here.
১ ⊛ ① ᭰ ♣ ● 🖫 🛜 ♪

Midland

526-528 Bearwood Road, B66 4BE
☎ (0121) 429 6958

Church End Gravediggers Ale; Hook Norton Old Hooky; Oakham Citra; 2 changing beers (sourced nationally; often Backyard, Burning Soul, Green Duck) ⊞
A quirky country-style pub in the centre of Birmingham, near Aston University. This friendly-staffed popular back-street local is one of the oldest pubs in Birmingham and has a snug, comfortable and homely feel. Two distinct drinking areas surround a U-shaped bar with a smaller back room offering more privacy. A collection of 300 jugs adorns the ceiling, along with a number of old pictures and memorabilia. A small garden area is at the rear. Traditional, hearty pub food is served and guest beers change regularly. There are 11 en-suite bedrooms available. ❀❦✠⦿&≈(Snow Hill)Ɽ(St Chads)🚪❀🐾 ⧖

Colmore

116 Colmore Row, B3 3BD
☎ (0121) 238 1041 ⊕ colmoretap.co.uk
Thornbridge Astryd, Brother Rabbit, Lord Marples, Jaipur IPA; 5 changing beers (sourced nationally; often Saltaire) ⊞
This Thornbridge pub is a worthy winner of a CAMRA design award in the conversion to pub category. It retains extensive wood panelling and high quality fixtures and fittings from its previous days as a bank. Four regular Thornbridge beers are served plus five guests, as well as 20 gins along with a comprehensive pizza menu, including gluten-free. There is a pool table downstairs. It can get busy with office workers after work.
⦿⦿&≈(New Street) Ɽ(Town Hall) ♣🚪❀⧖

Craven Arms ⎣

Upper Gough Street, B1 1JG (in sidestreet near the Mailbox)
☎ (0121) 643 2852
Black Country Bradley's Finest Golden, Pig on the Wall, Fireside; 6 changing beers (sourced nationally; often Fixed Wheel, Mallinsons, Salopian) ⊞
This early 19th-century former Holder's outlet, restored and refurbished in 2022 by Black Country Ales, sports an attractive blue-tiled exterior and a cosy one room interior. Handpulls take prominence on the bar and, in addition to three permanent Black Country beers, six changing guest casks come from breweries across Birmingham and the West Midlands. Three changing craft keg lines and cider are also served. Cobs, pork pies and sausage rolls are available at most times and a real fire may await when cold.
⦿≈(New Street) Ɽ(Town Hall) ❀⧖♪

Head of Steam

Somerset House, 36 Temple Street, B2 5DP
☎ (0121) 643 6824
Camerons Road Crew; 9 changing beers (sourced regionally; often Blue Monkey) ⊞
The Birmingham branch of the Camerons' chain features a large and spacious interior, split across three levels, decorated in a steampunk style. An island bar occupies the centre of the middle level, and there is plenty of seating and booths for people to enjoy a wide variety of food and drinks. Ten handpulls showcase Camerons' own beers and offerings from local breweries. Keg lines include international beers such as Delirium and La Chouffe and a wide range of beers from around the world in bottles and cans are sold.
⦿&≈(New Street) Ɽ(Corporation Street) ♣🚪⧖

Old Contemptibles ⎣ ✅

176 Edmund Street, B3 2HB (100yds from Snow Hill Station)
☎ (0121) 200 3310
St Austell Nicholson's Pale Ale; Sharp's Doom Bar; 6 changing beers (sourced nationally) ⊞

A Nicholsons pub, popular with office workers in central Birmingham, handily located close to Snow Hill Station. A large, single wood-panelled room is divided into distinct drinking areas, with a cosy snug at the rear. A changing range of beers are served from seven handpulls on the bar. The pub name derives from the British Expeditionary Force who fought in France in the First World War. Hearty food is available. ⦿⦿≈(Snow Hill)Ɽ(Bull Street)🚪❀

Post Office Vaults ⎣

84 New Street, B2 4BA (entrances on both New St and Pinfold St)
☎ (0121) 643 7354 ⊕ postofficevaults.co.uk
Hobsons Mild; house beer (by Kinver); 4 changing beers (sourced nationally; often Abbeydale, Oakham) ⊞
A two-minute walk from the Stephenson Street entrance to New Street station and close to Victoria Square, this subterranean bar offers a range of eight traditional beers in excellent condition. It always stocks at least 350 different bottled beers from all over the world – one of the largest ranges in the country – and serves 14 ciders and perries. The extremely knowledgeable staff will make your visit a pleasure.
Q≈(New Street) Ɽ(Town Hall) ♣❀🚪❀⧖

Prince of Wales

84 Cambridge Street, B1 2NP (behind ICC/NIA and Rep Theatre)
☎ (0121) 413 4180

Black Country Bradley's Finest Golden, Chain Ale, Pig on the Wall; 4 changing beers (sourced nationally) H A well-loved pub that continues to thrive after a sympathetic refurbishment by Black Country Ales in 2022. This single-room pub is a welcome oasis for the community, close to Centenary Square, the ICC, NIA and the Rep Theatre. Expect the usual Black Country beers plus up to four guests. Freshly-made cobs and pasties are on offer. Quiz night is fortnightly on Tuesday. An interesting display of old views of Birmingham adorns the walls. ♿(Library)🚐🐾🛜

Wellington L

37 Bennetts Hill, B2 5SN (5 mins from New Street and Snow Hill stations)

☎ (0121) 200 3115 🌐 thewellingtonrealale.co.uk

Black Country Bradley's Finest Golden, Pig on the Wall, Fireside; Oakham Citra; Purity Mad Goose; Wye Valley HPA; 9 changing beers (sourced nationally; often Fixed Wheel, Froth Blowers, Titanic) H A Guide regular, this Black Country Ales local has been run by the same landlord for 18 years. There are 27 handpulls over two floors, dispensing seven regular beers and nine guests. A broad range of whiskies, rums and gins are available from the impressive back fitting. The suntrap roof terrace is a hidden oasis in the urban landscape. Regular quizzes, folk nights and cheese nights are held. Food is not served – feel free to bring your own and plates will be provided.
Q❀&≥(Snow Hill) ♿(Grand Central) ♣🚌🚐🛜

Birmingham: Cotteridge

Red Beer'd L

1891 Pershore Road, B30 3DJ
2 changing beers (often Fownes) H
Set over two floors, this micropub in a converted shop is conveniently located for Kings Norton railway station. Serving from two cask handpulls and up to 10 keg taps, beers are often from local breweries such as Fownes, Halton Turner, and Leviathan. They also serve up to four ciders or perries from Hogan's and Oliver's. Comfier seating is available on the ground floor, while upstairs there are chairs and barrels plus the toilet. Dogs are welcome and encouraged. Third and half pints are available. Card payment only. Drinkers can bring food from outside. ಶ≥(Kings Norton)🍴🚐🐾🛜

Birmingham: Digbeth

Spotted Dog L

104 Warwick Street, B12 0NH
☎ (0121) 772 3822
Castle Rock Harvest Pale; Holden's Black Country Mild; 2 changing beers (sourced nationally) H
A multi-roomed traditional pub, family-owned and with the same landlord since the 1980s. Rugby and Irish sports are shown on largescreen TVs. Outside is an extensive covered garden and smoking area with heaters, a large real fireplace, a barbecue, a projection screen and eclectic adornments. Traditional Irish music night is on alternate Mondays, jazz night on Tuesday, and the pub is the home of Na Madrai golf society and the Digbeth O'lympics. There is a competitively priced cask mild on the bar. Busy when Birmingham City play at home.
ಶ❀&≥(Bordesley) 🍴🚐🛜♪

Birmingham: Edgbaston

Physician

Harborne Road, B15 3DH
☎ (0121) 272 5900

Timothy Taylor Boltmaker; Titanic Plum Porter; 2 changing beers (sourced nationally) H ·
An upmarket pub located in the large historic former BMI building that used to house the vast Sampson Gangee Library for the History of Medicine. It has been sympathetically converted to a multi-room pub with an emphasis on good food. The main bar has high tables and chairs with easy chair seating around an open fireplace. The subsequent rooms are laid out for food with dining tables and chairs. A range of ales are available along with wines, gins and spirits. The extensive food menu changes daily.
Q ಶ❀🅿️🕯️&≥(Five Ways) 🅿🐾🛜

Birmingham: Harborne

Hop Garden

19 Metchley Lane, B17 0HT (100yds from High Street, at back of M&S)
☎ (0121) 427 7904
5 changing beers (sourced nationally) H
Small and cosy, just off the main High Street, the pub is serious about craft beer – even to the point of not stocking many mainstream products. It serves five real ales from small and local breweries, up to 10 craft beers and up to 10 ciders. There is also an interesting selection of bottled and canned beers. The decor is original and eclectic. There is ample heated seating in the Garden Shed at the rear, as well as outside seating in the garden, with occasional music and pop-up food events held. Dogs are especially welcome. Q ಶ❀🕯️&♣🍴🚐🐾🛜♪

White Horse L

2 York Street, B17 0HG
☎ (0121) 608 7641 🌐 whitehorseharborne.com
Church End Gravediggers Ale; Greene King Abbot; Ostlers Terry's Gold; 3 changing beers (sourced regionally; often Holden's, Thornbridge, Wye Valley) H
Small, friendly, traditional community pub just off Harborne High Street. Beers from Ostlers brewery, based at the back of the pub, are served as well as guests on up to six handpulls. A two-room pub, the smaller room has four rotating craft beers on KeyKeg (occasionally keg) from Ostlers and other small breweries. Check what is available in real time via the beer board on their website. There is also a gig guide showing upcoming artists for Saturday night live music. There are TVs throughout the pub showing sport. Q ಶ❀&🍴🚐🐾🛜♪

Birmingham: Highgate

Lamp Tavern L

157 Barford Street, B5 6AH (550yds from A441 Pershore Rd near bottom of Hurst St)
☎ (0121) 688 1220
3 changing beers (sourced nationally; often AJs, Froth Blowers, Hobsons) H
A hidden gem of a pub, almost the last of its kind, on the edge of Digbeth, run by the same landlord for 29 years. The pub has a homely feel, despite its industrial location, with a small single bar. It closes early if there are no customers, so ring ahead if intending a later visit. The function room at the back holds about 35 people. Rugby is shown if on terrestrial TV, and there is a folk club on Friday evening. The bar is cash only; nearest cash points are on Digbeth High Street. &🚐🐾♪

Birmingham: Hockley

1000 Trades

16 Frederick Street, B1 3HE

☎ (0121) 233 6291 ⊕ 1000trades.org.uk
4 changing beers (sourced nationally) Ⓗ
Sporting bare boards and brickwork, this bar has two distinct areas. The front bar area offers a small number of tables around an open fire, while the raised rear section has booth-style seating for eating and drinking. Up to four cask beers are served along with four keg lines for craft beers. The food is upmarket and from guest chefs and pop-ups. Sunday lunches are popular and booking is advised. A variety of events are hosted including open mic, theatre and themed music nights. The pin badge wall downstairs honours this 19th-century building's history.
🛇🕭❁◑🕭⅊(Jewellery Quarter) ⍾(Jewellery Quarter) ❀🛜♪

Burning Soul Brewery Ⓛ
Unit 1 Mott Street Industrial Estate, B19 3HE
☎ 07826 813377 ⊕ burningsoulbrewing.com
13 changing beers (sourced locally; often Burning Soul)
A brewery and taproom just off Great Hampton Street in Hockley. One cask handpull and 11 KeyKeg lines all dispense live beer. Situated on an industrial estate, the decor is functional but comfortable, and there is outdoor decking for the warmer months. A good range of canned beer is available. Opening hours can vary, so check social media for details. Card payment is preferred.
Q❁≉(Jewellery Quarter) ⍾(St Paul's) ♣P🖪

Rock & Roll Brewhouse Ⓛ
19 Hall Street, B18 6BS
☎ 07969 759649
Rock & Roll Voodoo Mild; 2 changing beers (sourced locally; often Rock & Roll) Ⓗ
A quirky brewery taproom on the first floor above the brewery, in the heart of the Jewellery Quarter, it is well worth checking out. Three real ales are available, all brewed on-site and vegan. There is a focus on a love of music, with memorabilia adorning the walls, books available to read and live music at the weekends. When live music isn't being performed a set list of vinyls are played, often themed around music news that week. Check social media for details. It can get busy when bands are playing.
≉(Jewellery Quarter) ⍾(St Paul's) ❀🍺♪

Birmingham: Kings Heath

Hop & Scotch 🍸 Ⓛ
9 Institute Road, B14 7EG
☎ (0121) 679 8807 ⊕ hopscotchbrum.com
4 changing beers (sourced locally; often Green Duck, Kinver, Malvern Hills) Ⓗ
Friendly and welcoming microbar with four handpulls featuring ales from local and more distant breweries, including Green Duck and Kinver, together with an interesting range of KeyKeg beers from local breweries, some of which are vegan-friendly. Bottled and canned ales are also sold. Hogan's cider is usually available. The bar attracts a wide age range and can get busy in the evening. Dogs are welcome, with treats offered. Opening hours vary – see the website for up-to-date times.
🛇◑❀🖪❁🛜♪

Kings Heath Cricket & Sports Club
Charlton House, 247 Alcester Road South, B14 6DT
☎ (0121) 444 1913 ⊕ kingsheathsportsclub.com
Wye Valley HPA, Butty Bach; 1 changing beer (sourced nationally) Ⓗ
A welcoming two-roomed sports club, just south of Kings Heath. Upon entering, the right-hand room is a small, cosy lounge, while the left-hand room is a large sports

bar complete with two large TV screens, a dartboard and several snooker tables. There is parking to the front of the building, as well as a large Pay & Display car park to the rear. Poker night is on Monday, with darts Tuesday, and curry night Wednesday. CAMRA members are asked to sign the visitors guest book. Q🛇❁◑🕭⅊♣P🖪🛜♪

Red Lion ★
229 Vicarage Road, B14 7LY
☎ (0121) 444 2803
Purity Pure UBU; St Austell Tribute; 2 changing beers (often Salopian, Timothy Taylor) Ⓗ
A Grade II-listed imposing Neo-Gothic designed pub built in 1908. It has an open plan design decorated in the Ember Inns style that incorporates original features. It was refurbished in 2023. There is a large garden at the front and plenty of parking spaces to the rear. The focus is on food, but three or four cask beers are available at all times. Regular quizzes are held Sunday and Thursday and poker on a Monday night. Ale prices are reduced on Monday and Thursday. 🛇❁◑⅊P🖪🛜♪

Birmingham: Kings Norton

Navigation ✓
1 Wharf Road, B30 3LS
☎ (0121) 451 1090
Greene King Abbot; Ruddles Best Bitter; Sharp's Doom Bar; 3 changing beers (sourced nationally) Ⓗ
Reopened as a Wetherspoon in 2021, following three years of closure, the original premises have been sympathetically refurbished and extended. It has a single large, open-plan room with plenty of seating and a long bar across the back. More secluded areas are at the edges. Exposed timbers and brickwork and an open fireplace feature, and there are a large number of old photos and information on Kings Norton Green, the surrounding area, and historic local people. There is a large outdoor paved drinking area to the front and rear. 🛇❁◑⅊P🖪🛜

Birmingham: Northfield

Black Horse Ⓛ ✓
Bristol Road South, B31 2QT (Opp Sainsbury's)
☎ (0121) 477 1800
Greene King Abbot; Ruddles Best Bitter; Sharp's Doom Bar; 4 changing beers (sourced nationally; often Purity, Silhill) Ⓗ
A Grade II-listed brewer's Tudor pub, it has been identified by CAMRA as having a nationally important historic pub interior after being refurbished and reopened by Wetherspoon in 2010. Built in 1929 to the Bateman & Bateman design, this midland roadhouse replaced an earlier, smaller pub that had been on the site. It is a multi-room pub with extravagant half-timbered exterior, baronial hall with tie-beam roof, and barrel-vaulted lobby. There is a large car park to the side and a bowling green to the rear. A function room is available upstairs. Q🛇❁◑⅊≉(Northfield)P🖪🛜

Birmingham: Stirchley

Birmingham Brewing Company Taproom
Unit 15 Stirchley Trading Estate, Hazelwell Road, B30 2PF
☎ (0121) 724 0399 ⊕ birminghambrewingcompany.co.uk
Birmingham Pale Brummie, Bitter Brummie; house beer (by Birmingham); 3 changing beers (often Birmingham) Ⓗ

Craft beer brewery and tap on Stirchley Trading Estate. The tap is open Thursday to Sunday, serving up to four cask beers and four kegs, including one low/no alcohol option. Locally made ciders are also served, as well as wines, spirits and soft drinks. Food is available at weekends from a changing lineup of street food vendors. A large outdoor seating area is available during summer months. ⌂⊛◑⇒(Bournville)●➡❀♫

Wildcat Tap
1381-1383 Pershore Road, B30 2JR
☎ (0121) 213 2623 ⊕ stirchleywildcat.co.uk
4 changing beers (sourced nationally) Ⓗ
Located on the Pershore Road, this independent bar is spacious for a micropub, with adequate seating, although it does get busy at weekends with a mixed age group clientele. The beer range of cask and keg is adventurous and interesting, with up to four cask beers on handpump and eight craft keg lines, complemented by a selection of bottled craft beers, gin, whisky and soft drinks. A vast array of tabletop games are available to play. Convenient for buses 27, 45, and 47 and close to Bournville railway station. ⌂❧⇒(Bournville)♣●➡❀☂

Blackheath

Britannia ⊘
124 Halesowen Street, B65 0ES
☎ (0121) 559 0010
Greene King Abbot; Ruddles Best Bitter Ⓗ**; Sharp's Doom Bar** Ⓗ**/**Ⓖ**; 6 changing beers (sourced nationally)** Ⓗ
An L-shaped Wetherspoon outlet at the very heart of Blackheath. The garden at the rear provides a pleasant space away from the main A4099. The exposed brick façade is often decorated with hanging baskets in the warmer seasons. Six changing beers are accompanied by three permanent beers. Pictures placed throughout the pub depict local monuments and historic characters. Food is served all day, every day. A small car park for customers can be accessed via Cross Street.
⌂⊛◑❧⇒(Rowley Regis)♣●➡❀☂

Cyder & Cobb
167 Halesowen Street, B65 0ES (exit Market Place island onto Halesowen St and pub is on right)
☎ 07849 402244
Ludlow Blonde; Wye Valley HPA; 3 changing beers (sourced nationally; often Oakham, Salopian, Thornbridge) Ⓗ
An intimate and well-appointed micropub that opened in 2021. The interior contains six wooden tables and benches. A standing bar serves up to four beers with guests sourced nationally, and a selection of real ciders. A variety of small breweries are usually featured. Easy-listening music is played, and it is a very pleasant way to spend a few hours. A selection of cobs and pies is available. ⌂❧⇒(Rowley Regis)♣●➡❀☂♫

Bloxwich

Bloxwich Showman ⊘
156 High Street, WS3 3JT
☎ (01922) 495366
Greene King Abbot; Ruddles Best Bitter; Sharp's Doom Bar; 3 changing beers (sourced nationally) Ⓗ
Busy Wetherspoon pub, located on High Street, an impressive conversion of a former cinema. Themed around Pat Collins, well known in the early 1900s for his funfairs and presidency of the Showman's Guild, he was a local councillor, mayor of Walsall and MP for the area. Easily accessible by public transport the airy, split-level

pub serves up to six real ales including the Wetherspoon regulars. Food is served all day and children are welcome until evening. ⌂◑❧⇒➡(32)☂

Boldmere

Bishop Vesey Ⓛ
63 Boldmere Road, B73 5XA
☎ (0121) 355 5077
Greene King Abbot; Oakham Citra; Ruddles Best Bitter; Sharp's Doom Bar; 8 changing beers (sourced nationally; often Backyard, Oakham) Ⓗ
Busy and popular Wetherspoon named after the town's Tudor benefactor, recognised with a carved wooden pulpit by the entrance. A continuous Guide entry for over two decades, it offers a good mix of guest beers, many from local microbreweries, and the usual food offering. As well as extensive seating areas upstairs and down, there is a spacious rooftop garden, and a smaller beer garden downstairs to the rear.
⌂⊛◑❧⇒(Wylde Green)♣➡☂

Boldmere Tap
363 Boldmere Road, B73 5HE
☎ (0121) 386 2218
Joule's Pure Blonde, Pale Ale, Slumbering Monk; 1 changing beer Ⓗ
Taken over by Joule's in 2014, this street-corner local has been refurbished to the brewery's trademark high standard. There is lots of reclaimed wood, including some intricate carved panels, plus a number of elegant stained glass areas. The main room splits into a number of intimate areas, and there is a large room to the side which in turn leads to a small function room. Seasonal ales from Joule's feature on the bar.
⌂◑⇒(Chester Road)♣P➡❀

Brierley Hill

Pens Ale
High Street, DY5 4RP (adjacent to Pensnett Fish Bar)
☎ 07496 419811
Holden's Golden Glow; 3 changing beers (sourced nationally) Ⓗ
The sister bar to the popular Tivi Ale micropub in Tividale, Pens Ale opened in 2021. It is a smart, plush, modern open-plan bar sporting up to four real ales sourced nationally and locally, as well as other refreshments, and has a wide customer mix. Quiz nights are held monthly on Tuesday, and a range of traditional bar snacks is served. ⌂●❀

Rose & Crown Ⓛ
161 Bank Street, DY5 3DD (B4179)
☎ (01384) 936166
Holden's Black Country Bitter, Golden Glow, Special; 1 changing beer (often Holden's) Ⓗ
This traditional pub was originally two terraced properties. One end of the bar is dominated by a dartboard. A conservatory provides extra space and is used as a function room, opening onto a small garden with tables and benches. There is a bus stop outside, or a five minute walk takes you to Brierley Hill High Street, which is served by several bus routes. Holden's seasonal beers are rotated. Q⌂⊛♣P➡❀☂

Vine
10 Delph Road, DY5 2TN
☎ (01384) 78293
Bathams Mild Ale, Best Bitter Ⓗ
An unspoilt brewery tap with an ornately decorated façade proclaiming the Shakespearian quotation

'Blessing of your heart, you brew good ale'. An elongated pub with a labyrinthine feel, the front bar is staunchly traditional, while the larger rear room has its own servery, leather seating and a dartboard. The homely lounge was partly converted from former brewery offices. Local specialties, such as faggots and home-made pies, are served weekdays, with generously filled rolls and pork pies at all times.
Q ⛺ ✿ ◑ ♣ P ₪ (8) ✿ ᗡ

Brownhills

Jiggers Whistle ⍅
5-7 Brownhills High Street, WS8 6ED
☎ 07854 356976
House beer (by Green Duck); 3 changing beers (sourced regionally) ⅲ
Opened in 2017, this micropub has one room split into three inter-connected drinking areas. It offers a wide range of cask and craft beers and some real ciders. As well as beers from regional breweries, its own beers are produced locally by both Backyard and Green Duck breweries. Bar snacks are available at weekends. The owners offer customers a warm and friendly welcome, are keen to support local events and groups, including a darts team. Closed on Tuesday. Q ⛺ ♣ ✿ P ₪ ✿ ᗡ

Coventry: Chapelfields

Hearsall Inn ⍅
45 Craven Street, CV5 8DS (1 mile W of city centre, off Allesley Old Rd)
☎ (024) 7671 5729 ⊕ hearsallinn.com
Church End Goat's Milk; Draught Bass; 2 changing beers (sourced locally; often Byatt's, Church End) ⅲ
Built in the 1850s to serve the historic watchmaking district, this free house is celebrating 25 years of being in the same family's ownership. It has separate bar and lounge areas and a paved patio at the front with a wall-mounted defibrillator. The pub is home to a darts team and hosts traditional Irish music on Tuesday night as well as local community meetings. Four handpumps dispense local and regional beers. Freshly made batches are available throughout the day. ⛺ ✿ ♣ ₪ ✿ ᗡ

Coventry: City Centre

Gatehouse Tavern ⍅
44-46 Hill Street, CV1 4AN (close to Belgrade Theatre and Spon St, near jct 8 of ring road)
☎ (024) 7663 0140
6 changing beers (sourced locally; often Byatt's, Church End) ⅲ
A unique pub, rebuilt by the landlord from the shell of the former Leigh Mills gatehouse. A long term entry in the Guide, it is dedicated to high quality real ale, good value food and televised sports of all kinds; the latter evidenced by the depiction of the emblems of the rugby Six Nations in a stained-glass window. The beer garden is the largest in the city centre and is popular during the summer months. ⛺ ✿ ◑ ✿ ₪ ✿ ᗡ ♪

Golden Cross ⍅ ✅
8 Hay Lane, CV1 5RF (near the old cathedral ruins)
☎ (024) 7655 1855 ⊕ thegoldencrosscoventry.co.uk
Bath Ales Gem; Titanic Plum Porter; Wye Valley HPA; 1 changing beer (sourced locally; often Bath Ales, Byatt's, Church End) ⅲ
Located in the shadow of Coventry's famous bombed out cathedral, this medieval pub is one of two claimants to being the oldest pub in the city. Subject to corporate vandalism by a former brewery owner in the 1970s, it

has since been nicely restored to near its former glory. An upstairs room hosts bands on Friday and serves diners at other times. An open mic night is hosted on Tuesday evenings. Gluten-free food is served. Q ✿ ◑ ◑ ₪ ✿ ♪

Hops d'Amour ☩ ⍅
67 Corporation Street, CV1 1GX
☎ (024) 7767 2100 ⊕ hops-damour.business.site
6 changing beers (sourced regionally) ⅲ
Situated in the former Singer's Sewing Centre, this family-owned micropub offers six cask and four craft keg beers plus boxed ciders, from both local brewers and others not normally seen in the area. Bottled and canned beers are also available to drink in or to take away. In keeping with the micropub ethos, conversation takes the place of electronic entertainment and gaming machines. Local CAMRA Pub of the Year and Cider Pub of the Year 2023. Q ✿ ₪

Old Windmill ⍅ ✅
22-23 Spon Street, CV1 3BA
☎ (024) 7625 1717 ⊕ theoldwindmillcoventry.co.uk
Theakston Old Peculier; 5 changing beers (sourced nationally; often North Cotswold, Timothy Taylor) ⅲ
A popular timber-framed pub in historic Spon Street and one of two claimants to being the city's oldest. It is split into several small rooms with the Victorian brewhouse being of particular interest. The pub is able to source a wide range of interesting beers. Locally produced pork pies, pasties and a range of cheeses are available and recommended. Beer festivals are held at least once a year. The outdoor seating area at the rear is open Friday to Sunday only. ✿ ♣ ✿ ₪ ✿ ᗡ

Town Wall Tavern ✅
Bond Street, CV1 4AH (behind Belgrade Theatre)
☎ (024) 7622 0963
Brains Rev James Original; Draught Bass; Theakston Best Bitter, Old Peculier; Wye Valley HPA; 3 changing beers (sourced nationally; often North Cotswold) ⅲ
Traditional city-centre pub dating from the 1820s, popular with theatre-goers from the nearby Belgrade Theatre. Three distinct drinking areas, including the legendary Donkey Box, are served from a central bar. Up to six real ales are available including at least one dark beer, and good-quality food is served. Look out for the Atkinsons window in the lounge bar which also features photographs of old Coventry. Televised sport is shown in the public bar only. ◑ ₪ ✿ ♪

Coventry: Earlsdon

City Arms ⍅ ✅
1 Earlsdon Street, CV5 6EP (on roundabout at centre of Earlsdon)
☎ (024) 7671 8170
Greene King Abbot; Ruddles Best Bitter; Sharp's Doom Bar; 7 changing beers (sourced nationally; often Byatt's, Grainstore, Purity) ⅲ
A large 1930s mock-Tudor Wetherspoon pub located on the roundabout in the heart of the bustling suburb of Earlsdon. Regular beers are augmented by up to seven changing guest ales. There are information boards dotted around inside the pub describing the history of the local area. On-site parking is limited but there are good bus links to the city centre, universities and Coventry railway station. A mixture of locals and visitors means it can get busy at weekends. ⛺ ✿ ◑ ↔ P ₪ (5,11) ✿

Royal Oak ✅
22 Earlsdon Street, CV5 6EJ (100yds from Earlsdon roundabout)
☎ (024) 7667 6658 ⊕ royaloakearlsdon.co.uk

Draught Bass; Froth Blowers Piffle Snonker; Greene King IPA; Timothy Taylor Landlord; 1 changing beer (sourced locally; often Church End) ⒣
A welcome return to the Guide for this popular traditional pub in the heart of Earlsdon, serving locals and visitors alike. The lounge and bar areas are supplemented by a back room and an attractive walled patio garden. The attentive bar staff offer a table service which is especially useful when the pub is busy. Bar snacks are available and more substantial meals can be ordered from the restaurant next door and consumed in the patio garden. Q❀🚃(5,11) ❀

Coventry: Foleshill

Byatt's Brewhouse Bar 🅛

Unit 7-8 Lythalls Lane Industrial Estate, Lythalls Lane, CV6 6FL

☎ (024) 7663 7996 🌐 byattsbrewery.co.uk
6 changing beers (sourced locally; often Byatt's) ⒣
Established in 2016, this pleasant brewhouse bar on a small industrial estate showcases up to six rotating real ales and craft beers from Byatt's range. Drinkers can enjoy the ground floor taproom or head upstairs to the mezzanine and admire the commissioned artwork. Bottle-conditioned beers are also available for takeaway. Opening hours are limited, but the bar and adjacent brewery space usually opens for Saturday home football fixtures at the nearby Coventry Building Society Arena. 🕭க்P🚃❀❀🎵

Coventry: Gosford Green

Twisted Barrel Brewery & Tap House 🅛

Unit 11 FarGo Village, Far Gosford Street, CV1 5ED
☎ (024) 7610 1701 🌐 twistedbarrelale.co.uk
Twisted Barrel Beast Of A Midlands Mild, Detroit Sour City, God's Twisted Sister, Sine Qua Non; 19 changing beers (sourced nationally) ⒣/🅟
Situated in FarGo Village, home to artisanal businesses, independent food outlets and cultural events, this vegan tap house has 16 keg and two cask lines offering a wide variety of their own beers plus guests from local and national breweries. A small hot vegan food offering is available at busy times. Beers can be enjoyed overlooking the brewery or outside in the large seating area. Regular events include the popular homebrew club, quiz nights and themed evenings. 🕭❀க்🚃❀❀

Coventry: Spon End

Broomfield Tavern 🅛

14-16 Broomfield Place, CV5 6GY (adjacent to the rugby ground but hidden from the main road)
☎ (024) 7663 0969
Church End Fallen Angel; Froth Blowers Piffle Snonker; 5 changing beers (sourced nationally) ⒣
A genuine free house and thriving community local. Despite going through a prolonged period of renovation, the pub remains cosy and welcoming and continues to offer a large variety of good quality real ales and real ciders. Some ales are now served from oak casks. It can get busy during the early evenings and before and after rugby games at the adjacent Butts Park Arena. Filled batches are often available on rugby match days. The pub is dog-friendly. Q❀🚃❀🎵

Coventry: Sutton Stop

Greyhound Inn

Sutton Stop, Hawkesbury Junction, CV6 6DF (off Grange Rd at jct of Coventry and Oxford canals)
☎ (024) 7636 3046 🌐 thegreyhoundlongford.co.uk
Draught Bass; Greene King Abbot; 3 changing beers (sourced nationally) ⒣
An award-winning pub dating from the 1830s. Located at Hawkesbury Junction where the Coventry and Oxford canals meet, the canalside patio is an idyllic setting for narrowboat watching. In the winter drinkers can enjoy a real fire in the cosy bar area. At the rear there is a separate bar and garden for summer events. A wide range of food is served in the bar and restaurant, with booking recommended for the latter. The pub endeavours to stock one locally-brewed ale. Q🕭❀⏻க்P🚃(22)❀❀

Darlaston

Swan ✓

16 Victoria Road, WS10 8AA
☎ (0121) 729 9194 🌐 swandarlaston.com
2 changing beers (sourced nationally; often Exmoor, Purity, Wye Valley) ⒣
Near the town hall, the Swan is a cosy and friendly local pub which boasts historic features such as original etched windows and a snug. At the rear, a garden with bench tables and two covered smoking areas can be found. The two changing ales come from national and regional breweries. Acoustic jam sessions are held every Wednesday, a quiz on Monday and Karaoke on Friday. Darts and dominoes are played, and there is no sports TV. Q🕭❀♣P🚃(310)❀❀🎵

Dorridge

Knowle & Dorridge Cricket Club ✓

Station Road, B93 8ET (corner of Station Rd and Grove Rd)
☎ (01564) 774338 🌐 knowleanddorridgecc.co.uk
3 changing beers (sourced nationally; often Abbeydale, Salopian) ⒣
This established cricket club is located in an upmarket residential area. Visitors are welcome to try the ever-changing range of up to three cask conditioned ales, always in excellent condition and often from interesting breweries. There are no entry restrictions, but club members are able to purchase drinks at a reduced price. There is outside seating to watch top-class cricket in the Birmingham league. Bar snacks and filled rolls are usually available. Local CAMRA Club of the Year three years in succession. 🕭❀⏻க்➤♠P🚃(S2,S3)❀❀

Dudley

Full Moon ✓

58-60 High Street, DY1 1PS
☎ (01384) 212294
Greene King Abbot; Ruddles Best Bitter; 5 changing beers (sourced nationally; often Titanic) ⒣
The Full Moon is a large centrally located Wetherspoon pub offering good-value food and drink. It opened in 1996 having originally been a large town-centre department store and then a pizza restaurant. The atmosphere is friendly and comfortable, and historic local photographs and facts adorn the walls. It is close to the main Dudley bus station where buses from all over the region terminate. Food is served all day. 🕭⏻க்♣❀🚃❀

Malt Shovel

46 Tower Street, DY1 1NB (off the Broadway A459; opp Dudley College Evolve Campus)
☎ (01384) 252735
Holden's Golden Glow; 4 changing beers (sourced nationally; often Oakham) ⊞
Originally known as the Lord Wellington in the 19th century, this exciting and trendy town-centre establishment is now part of the Red Pub Co portfolio. As such, there is a popular balance of both locally-produced cask beers and modern, national breweries on the bar. Yorkshire breweries are often showcased. The mixture of seating styles includes classic benches, which contrast nicely with the high stools. There is a small number of gaming and betting machines. ☺◖ℙ🖳✿🛜♫

Halesowen

Swan 🅛

282 Long Lane, B62 9JY
☎ (0121) 559 5207
Black Country Bradley's Finest Golden, Pig on the Wall, Fireside; 9 changing beers ⊞
A former local CAMRA Pub of the Year, this popular, comfortable pub was saved from the bulldozers in 2014 by local campaigners and Black Country Ales. The central bar serves two main drinking areas. Twelve ales and five real ciders are available, as well as a fine selection of gins. Regular beer festivals are held. A staircase leads to the toilets and gives access to the garden and smoking area to the rear. There is limited parking but adequate street parking can be found nearby.
Q✿♿♣👜ℙ🖳(14,X8) 🛜♫

Hampton in Arden

White Lion ✅

10 High Street, B92 0AA
☎ (01675) 442833 ⊕ thewhitelioninn.com
Otter Ale; St Austell Proper Job; Theakston Best Bitter; Wye Valley HPA; 1 changing beer (sourced nationally) ⊞
A charming 17th-century timber-framed building with Grade II listed status, the White Lion has been licensed since 1838. It features an L-shaped lounge and dining area which is light, airy and open plan, and a separate public bar, both with lovely real fires. Quality British pub food with a French accent is served. The quantity and quality of real ales is always of the highest level. The pub looks to rotate two of its regular beers every five to six months. This traditional country pub is well worth a visit.
☺✿🏠◖♿≠(Hampton-in-Arden) ℙ🖳(82) ✿🛜

Kingswinford

Bridge Inn

110 Moss Grove, DY6 9HH (A491)
☎ (01384) 293880
Black Country Bradley's Finest Golden, Chain Ale, Pig on the Wall, Fireside; 5 changing beers (sourced nationally; often Black Country) ⊞
Open-plan Black Country Ales pub that is deservedly popular with a wide mix of customers. It offers a broad range of up to nine cask beers along with ciders, some of which may be real. Cobs, pork pies, sausage rolls and samosas (sourced locally) are available daily. The accent is very much on a homely feel with a lot of community atmosphere, and is well worth a visit.
Q☺✿♿♣👜ℙ🖳✿🛜

Knowle

Ale Rooms

1592 High Street, B93 0LF
☎ (01564) 400040 ⊕ alerooms.co.uk
7 changing beers (sourced nationally; often Church End, Silhill) ⊞
This micropub on the High Street, in a converted shop that was formerly a funeral director's, is a welcome addition to the Knowle pub scene. The pub stocks at least one real ale from the local Silhill brewery, along with one from Church End, guest ales, real cider, wines and spirits, including speciality gins. There is free Wi-Fi and the usual pub snacks are available. A former local CAMRA Pub of the Year and West Midlands pub of the year in 2019.
👄🖳(S3) ✿🛜♫

Lower Gornal

Fountain Inn

8 Temple Street, DY3 2PE (on B4157, 5 mins from Gornal Wood bus station)
☎ (01384) 596317
Church End Fallen Angel; Greene King Abbot; Hobsons Town Crier; Wye Valley HPA, Butty Bach; 5 changing beers (sourced nationally) ⊞
This venue is a destination for both quality real ales and pub food. To the rear, the courtyard with bench tables has been refurbished to a high standard. Up to 10 real ales are served, and those conditioning in the cellar are listed on a board opposite the main bar. There is an elevated, separate restaurant to the rear of the pub.
☺✿◖♣🖳(17,27) ✿♫

Mere Green

Ale Hub

4 Hill Village Road, B75 5BA
⊕ alehub.co.uk
Wye Valley Butty Bach; 3 changing beers (sourced nationally) ⊞
A former solicitor's office which gained a new life in 2021 when it reopened as a micropub, part of a small chain of bars of the same name. As well as the central area, there is a smaller room to the rear. The three guest ales are generally from smaller breweries, and craft beers, wines, and a range of gins are available. The toilets are on the first floor. There is a monthly bingo evening, plus a weekly quiz night on Monday.
☺≠(Butlers Lane) 🖳✿🛜

Mare Pool ✅

294 Lichfield Road, B74 2UG (behind shops on E side of Lichfield Rd)
☎ (0121) 323 1070
Greene King IPA, Abbot; Sharp's Doom Bar; 4 changing beers ⊞
This is a busy Wetherspoon pub whose name refers to the many pools that used to surround Sutton Coldfield. The watery theme is reflected in the decor, with hundreds of hanging glass droplets. The comfortable interior is complemented by café-style seating outside at the front, plus an enclosed beer terrace to the side. Free parking is time-limited.
Q☺✿◖♿≠(Four Oaks) 👄ℙ🖳🛜

Netherton

Old Swan ★ 🅛

89 Halesowen Road, DY2 9PY (in Netherton centre on A459 Dudley-Old Hill road)
☎ (01384) 253075

Olde Swan Original, Dark Swan, Entire, Netherton Pale Ale (N.P.A.), Bumble Hole Bitter; 1 changing beer (sourced locally; often Olde Swan) Ⓗ
Attracting customers from near and far, the home of the Olde Swan Brewery is one of the last four remaining English home-brew pubs still brewing when CAMRAwas formed in 1974. Recognised by CAMRA as nationally important, the labyrinthine interior features an ornate Swan ceiling and standalone burner in the bar. The pub also has a cosy snug and a two-roomed lounge where food is available, plus other nooks and crannies to imbibe in. Q❀❀⑊☙♣P🖵❀🛜

Old Hill

Wheelie Thirsty Ⓛ

215 Halesowen Road, B64 6HE
☎ 07876 808468
Fixed Wheel Wheelie Pale, Chain Reaction Pale Ale, Blackheath Stout, No Brakes IPA; 4 changing beers (often Fixed Wheel)
Located on the the high street, this is the second outlet for Fixed Wheel brewery. With a wide cross section of customers, it is popular with out-of-town visitors, but remains a real community pub. A range of up to four ciders, a guest cask ale and an enterprising variety of keg craft beers are also served. Events such as quiz and pizza nights take place monthly, with music hosted in the afternoon every second Sunday.
❀❀⑊♣P🖵(19,X10) ❀🛜♫

Oldswinford

Seven Stars Ⓛ

Brook Road, DY8 1NQ (on B4186, opp roadway to front entrance of Stourbridge Junction station)
☎ (01384) 441566
Black Country Bradley's Finest Golden, Chain Ale, Pig on the Wall, Fireside; 9 changing beers Ⓗ
A magnificent Edwardian Grade II-listed building; look out for the ornate tiling and timber bar on the interior. Inside this huge pub there are two bars with three rooms – lounge, bar and snug – plus a function room. Outside is a spacious courtyard and a smoking area to one side. Letting rooms are available. A total of 25 handpulls across the two bars feature both Black Country beers and guest ales. Three of the pulls are used for cider. Black Country grub is served.
❀❀✚⑊♣♦≠(Stourbridge Junction) ♣♦P🖵(142,7) ❀🛜♫

Rowley Regis

Britannia Pub & Brewery

Rowley Village, B65 9AT
☎ (0121) 559 3415
House beer (by Britt); 3 changing beers (sourced regionally; often Church End, Holden's, Salopian) Ⓗ
Following a high-specification refurbishment, this multi-roomed pub reopened in 2017 offering a welcome combination of real ales, real ciders and hearty food. The bay windows in the shabby chic lounge provide natural lighting and there are multiple real fires throughout the building. The lounge, bar and the conservatory are all spacious and each room has a unique feel. Blues and rock bands regularly perform in the conservatory area.
Q❀❀❀⑊♣♦P🖵(X8,14A) ❀🛜♫

Rushall

Manor Arms ★

Park Road, off Daw End Lane, WS4 1LG (Off B4154 At Canal Bridge)
☎ (01922) 642333
Banks's Amber Ale, Sunbeam; Bombardier; Wainwright; 1 changing beer (sourced nationally) Ⓗ
A canalside pub, founded around 1105 and rebuilt in the 17th century, it is thought to have held a licence for ale since 1248. The pub retains exposed beams and open fires in both bars. Handpulls are situated along the wall, resulting in it being known locally as the pub with no bar. Situated next to a country park and nature reserve, it is a little off the beaten track but well worth a visit.
Q❀❀❀P🖵(997) ❀

Sedgley

Beacon Hotel ★ Ⓛ

129 Bilston Street, DY3 1JE (A463)
☎ (01902) 883380 ⊕ sarahhughesbrewery.co.uk
Sarah Hughes Pale Amber, Sedgley Surprise, Dark Ruby Mild; 2 changing beers (sourced nationally) Ⓗ
A unique destination pub, the brewery tap for Sarah Hughes also offers progressive guest beers. This Grade II-listed pub is brimming with character, and deservedly popular – queues have been known to assemble ahead of opening time. The biggest selling beer by some margin is the award-winning Sarah Hughes Dark Ruby Mild. The large garden has children's play facilities at the rear and is used to host various annual events such as Black Country Day. Q❀❀❀P🖵

Clifton ✔

Bull Ring, DY3 1RX (A459)
☎ (01902) 677448
Greene King Abbot; Ruddles Best Bitter; Sharp's Doom Bar; changing beers (sourced nationally; often Beowulf, Oakham, Salopian) Ⓗ
Multi-level Wetherspoon outlet at the heart of Sedgley. Popular with drinkers and diners of all ages, it gets exceptionally busy during peak weekend hours. The building opened as a cinema in 1937 before becoming a bingo hall in the 1970s. A taxi rank is located immediately outside the premises and a Pay & Display car park can be accessed via Townsend Avenue.
Q❀❀⑊☙♦P🖵🛜

Mount Pleasant

144 High Street, DY3 1RH (A459)
☎ 07950 195652
10 changing beers (sourced nationally; often Enville, Oakham, Wye Valley) Ⓗ
Known locally as the Stump, this popular free house serves a selection of nine beers. It has a mock-Tudor frontage and a Tardis-like interior. The front bar is the first room off a long corridor. The lounge areas have an intimate feel, with two rooms on different levels housing various nooks and crannies, both with a real coal stove. The pub is on the main No.1 bus route, or a five-minute walk from the centre of Sedgley. Q❀♣P🖵(1)❀

Shirley

Shaking Hand

Unit 24 Parkgate, Stratford Road, B90 3GG
☎ (0121) 733 1176 ⊕ theshakinghand.co.uk
4 changing beers (sourced nationally) Ⓗ
A friendly, light and airy – though small – single-room pub in the Shirley Parkgate shopping centre near Asda. Four regularly-changing guest ales, including a dark ale, are served, from local and national independent

breweries. Five craft beers, also including a dark, complete the offering. The pub has all of the feel of a micropub but has embraced some of the needs of the modern clientele such as sports television and background music. A changing range of canned craft beer is also available. There is always a warm welcome and excellent quality beer. ⏰ㅕP🖥🐱📶

Short Heath

Duke of Cambridge ⓛ

82 Coltham Road, WV12 5QD
☎ (01922) 712038
Black Country Bradley's Finest Golden, Pig on the Wall, Fireside; 9 changing beers (sourced nationally; often Blue Monkey, Green Duck, Salopian) Ⓗ
A homely, welcoming pub converted from 17th-century cottages. The public bar has a stove and original wooden beams, and an array of handpulls dispense beers from Black Country Ales, alongside many changing beers and a few ciders. The quieter lounge has been tastefully refurbished and has its own bar. A rear room caters for darts and pool, and is used for functions and beer festivals. Traditional bar snacks, cobs and pork pies are available. A beer garden is at the rear.
⏰❀♣🖥(41,69)🐱♪

Solihull

Fieldhouse

10 Knightcote Drive, B91 3JU
☎ (0121) 703 9209
St Austell Tribute, Proper Job; Timothy Taylor Landlord; 3 changing beers (sourced nationally; often Black Sheep, Titanic, Purity) Ⓗ
Part of the Ember Inns chain, this large, modern pub is tastefully decorated and comfortably furnished. It features three large fires – one real, two coal-effect – and pleasant patio areas. Six ales are usually served, with two guest ales from across the country. Often busy, the pub attracts a wide range of ages. Regular quiz nights are on Sunday and Tuesday, and on Monday and Thursday all cask ales are discounted. The pub hosts monthly tribute acts and occasional Meet the Brewer events, as well as sponsoring a local football team, the Fieldhouse.
⏰❀◑ㅕP🖥(A9,5)📶

Pup & Duckling ♟

1 Hatchford Brook Road, B92 9AG
☎ (0121) 247 8358 ⊕ pupandduckling.co.uk
8 changing beers (sourced nationally; often Shiny, Leatherbritches, Byatts) Ⓗ
A family-run three-room micropub, serving up to eight real ales and two craft beers. The main, front room has a bar and a bottle store, and the middle and extended back rooms provide extra seating, as does the garden area. Bar snacks are available and customers can bring their own food from takeaways close by. Local breweries are often featured, but the landlord also has a knack of obtaining interesting beers from national independents. Regular beer updates can be found online, and a Thursday quiz raises money for local charities.
Q❀🖥(73,957)🐱📶

Stourbridge

Duke William ⓛ

25 Coventry Street, DY8 1EP (corner of Coventry St and Duke St)
☎ (01384) 440202 ⊕ craddocksbrewery.com
Craddock's Saxon Gold, Crazy Sheep, Monarch's Way, Troll; 4 changing beers (sourced nationally) Ⓗ

Locally listed Edwardian town-centre pub and home of Craddock's brewery. The pub consists of a main bar and adjacent snug with real fires, and an upstairs function room. Four Craddock's beers and four guests are available, as well as varied ciders. Traditional pie and mash is served on Thursday and Friday evenings, Saturday afternoons and Sunday lunchtimes. Cold snacks are also available most times. There are regular events, and brewery tours can be arranged. A summer beer and cider festival, with over 15 ales and ciders, is held.
Q❀◑ㅕ≷(Town)🍴🖥🐱📶♪

Hop Vault

9 Market Street, DY8 1AB
☎ 07858 312883 ⊕ thehopvault.com
3 changing beers (sourced nationally) Ⓗ
This recently opened specialist bottle shop sells cans and bottles from all over the country and Europe, some of which are bottle-conditioned. A tasting room is now open offering 12 keg taps and three cask beers, plus cans and bottles from the cold store. Extensions to the bar area are planned. The premises used to be a bank vault and more recently the hi-fi shop Music Matters.
≷(Town) P🖥

Red House Boutique ⓛ

21-26 Foster Street East, DY8 1EL
☎ (01384) 936430
Enville Ale; Holden's Golden Glow; 6 changing beers (sourced nationally) Ⓗ
Large, single-bar free house near to Stourbridge Interchange. Originally part of the Hogshead chain, this refurbished pub has returned to being an alehouse. Beers from Enville, Fixed Wheel and Three Tuns are usually be on the bar but may change from those listed. A range of KeyKeg beer is also on sale. Gourmet snacks can be enjoyed at all times including Scotch eggs and flavoured scratchings. The fridges behind the bar are widely stocked with bottles from around the world.
❀ㅕ≷(Town)🍴🖥🐱📶♪

Royal Exchange ⓛ

75 Enville Street, DY8 1XW (on A458, just off ring road)
☎ (01384) 396726
Bathams Mild Ale, Best Bitter Ⓗ
This pub has a busy traditional bar to the front and a newly extended small, cosy lounge to the rear, accessed through a side passage. The bar is decorated with a small collection of whisky bottles and boxes, pewter tankards and foreign bank notes. Beer is served in handled glasses on request. The large beer garden to the rear contains a heated smoking area. Bathams XXX is available in winter only. A public car park is directly opposite.
Q❀♣P🖥(8,242)

Waggon & Horses ⓛ

31 Worcester Street, DY8 1AT
☎ (01384) 395398
Enville Ale, Ginger Beer; Ludlow Gold; house beer (by Purple Moose); 3 changing beers Ⓗ
A 2015 refurbishment has created a comfortable, welcoming alehouse. There is a small cask ale bar to the front with a narrow passageway leading to a larger rear bar that has several craft keg taps. To the side is a cider bar with a small serving hatchway, offering two or more real ciders. A heated seating area exists at the rear. Parking can be difficult in the narrow surrounding streets.
⏰❀ㅕ≷(Town)🍴🖥(7,125)🐱📶

Streetly

Brew House

49 Boundary Road, B74 2JR

☎ (0121) 353 3358
4 changing beers ⓗ
A popular micropub, unsurprisingly busy as the local area is dominated by chain pubs that focus mainly on food. Opened in 2018, it sits at the end of a parade of small shops. Up to four ales are offered with an emphasis on novelty, witnessed by the growing array of pumpclips on display. Craft beers, ciders and spirits are also offered. There are occasional sports screenings and live music. Car parking is available at the front in the area shared by the shops. ⓢ❀♿🅿🚐♠♿🎵

Sutton Coldfield

Station ✅

44 Station Street, B73 6AT (near Sutton Coldfield station southbound platform)
☎ (0121) 362 4961
Sharp's Doom Bar; Timothy Taylor Landlord; 6 changing beers (sourced nationally) ⓗ
Eight varied ales feature at this attractive rail-themed pub; with different choices in front and back bars it is best to check the boards. Right next to the station, the pub is ideal for commuters, with a view of the departures board from the bar. Straightforward comfort food is available throughout the day. Quizzes, live music and comedy nights are among the entertainment. In summertime, the multi-level beer terrace to the rear hosts DJs and live music. ⓢ❀◖◗♿🚆🚐♠♿🎵

Tipton

Fountain

51 Owen Street, DY4 8HE
☎ (0121) 522 3606
Greene King Abbot; Wye Valley HPA; 2 changing beers (sourced nationally; often Salopian) ⓗ
A canalside pub in the heart of the Black Country, enjoyed by boaters and locals alike. In the mid-19th century it was a training base for Tipton-born British heavyweight prize fighter William Perry, better known as the Tipton Slasher. His statue stands in Coronation Gardens opposite. Food is served Monday to Thursday lunchtime. Cobs and pork pies are also available throughout the day. Greene King Abbot Ale and Wye Valley HPA are served, plus two changing guest ales which are usually pale beers. Q☕ⓢ❀◖🚆🅿🚐♠♿

Rising Sun ⓛ

116 Horseley Road, DY4 7NH (off B4517)
☎ (0121) 557 1940
Black Country Bradley's Finest Golden, Pig on the Wall, Fireside; 7 changing beers (sourced nationally) ⓗ
A former CAMRA National Pub of the Year which reopened in 2013 following refurbishment by Black Country Ales. This imposing Victorian hostelry has two distinct rooms warmed by open fires, and a large yard at the rear with patio heaters and an outbuilding. There are seven changing guest beers plus the three Black Country Ales core beers, and up to five traditional ciders. Cobs are served. Great Bridge, a 10-minute walk away, has frequent bus services to Dudley, West Bromwich and Birmingham. ❀♣♿🚐(22)♠♿🎵

Upper Gornal

Jolly Crispin

25 Clarence Street, DY3 1UL (on A459)
☎ 07789 352147
Abbeydale Absolution; Fownes Crispin's Ommer; Oakham Citra, Bishops Farewell; 5 changing beers

(sourced nationally; often Blue Bee, Neepsend, Saltaire) ⓗ
A popular free house which was brought under the Red Pub Company umbrella in 2021. The house beer is brewed by Fownes, and the changing beers are sourced from a wide array of breweries. The spacious lounge encourages drinking and conversation. There is also a smaller bar and an outbuilding with flatscreen TVs showing sport. Various crusty cobs are available daily; with hot pork cobs with stuffing and roast potatoes served on Fridays and Saturdays. Regular tap takeovers and beer festivals are held. ⓢ❀♣👜🅿🚐(1)♠♿🎵

Walsall

Black Country Arms ⓛ

High Street, WS1 1QW (in market, opp Asda)
☎ (01922) 640588 ⊕ blackcountryarms.co.uk
Black Country Bradley's Finest Golden, Pig on the Wall, Fireside; 13 changing beers (sourced nationally; often Mallinsons, Salopian, Titanic) ⓗ
A short walk from the train and bus station, this pub has an impressive selection of constantly changing real ales and sometimes a real cider. It is open plan with comfortable seating and quieter areas. The staff offer a warm welcome to all, even during busier periods. Pub meals are available during the day from Tuesday to Saturday. Entertainment is held regularly on Saturday night and there are sports TVs spread around the pub. Dogs are welcome in all areas. ❀◖🚆♣👜🅿🚐♠♿🎵

Fountain Inn ⓛ

49 Lower Forster Street, WS1 1XB (off A4148 ring road)
☎ (01922) 633307
Backyard Blonde, Gold; 6 changing beers (sourced regionally; often Backyard, Fixed Wheel, Green Duck) ⓗ
The brewery tap for Backyard Brewhouse with up to eight beers on handpull. The two rooms are served by a central bar in this family-run pub which has a friendly atmosphere and welcoming staff. Bar snacks include pork pies and filled rolls. Vinyl nights take place once a month, live tribute acts are on most Saturdays and a weekly pizza night on Thursday is popular. The heated outdoor terrace provides shelter for smokers and alfresco drinkers. Q☕ⓢ❀🚆♣👜🚐♠🎵

Lyndon House Hotel ⓛ

9-10 Upper Rushall Street, WS1 2HA (below St Matthew's Church)
☎ (01922) 612511
Dark Star Hophead; Holden's Golden Glow; Timothy Taylor Landlord; 1 changing beer (often Green Duck, Holden's) ⓗ
The comfortable bar has a coal-effect fire, an island counter, cosy corners and plenty of exposed wood and brick giving it a traditional feel. With the dining room and outdoor terraces, it is unexpectedly spacious. Four cask beers are available on the bar including a changing beer, often from local breweries Green Duck or Holden's. Meals are served lunchtimes and evenings, except on Sunday when there is a lunchtime carvery; lunchtime hot club sandwiches are good value. Karaoke provides entertainment on Sunday evening.
Q☕ⓢ❀◖◗♿🅿🚐(51,77) ♿

Pretty Bricks 🍸 ⓛ

5 John Street, WS2 8AF (near magistrates court, off B4210)
☎ (01922) 612553
Black Country Bradley's Finest Golden, Pig on the Wall, Fireside; 6 changing beers (sourced nationally) ⓗ

On the edge of town, this is a real back-street gem dating from 1845. This small, friendly and cosy pub has a front bar with a wood fire, lounge, upstairs function room and small blue-brick courtyard. Originally called the New Inn, its current name derives from the coloured glazed brick frontage. Cobs and pork pies provide sustenance alongside the extensive range of ales from nearby and further afield. A folk night is held every second Thursday of the month. Q⊛♣⇥♠♦🛒🌑🐱🎵

St Matthew's Hall ⊘

Lichfield Street, WS1 1SX (adjacent to town hall)
☎ (01922) 700820
Greene King Abbot; Ruddles Best Bitter; Sharp's Doom Bar; 4 changing beers (sourced nationally) ⊞
A stunning Grade II-listed Wetherspoon pub in the centre of Walsall, easily accessible by public transport and with plenty of parking nearby. Originally built as Walsall's first permanent subscribers' library, the interior features library shelves, dining and comfy seating areas, and an airy conservatory, while outside is a large beer garden. Beer festivals feature throughout the year and entertainment is hosted every Friday and Saturday evening until late. A changing selection of ales supplements the three regular beers and food is served all day. Children are welcome until evening.
🛏⊛🕙&⇥♠♦🛒🌑🎵

Victoria L

23 Lower Rushall Street, WS1 2AA
☎ (01922) 635866
Backyard Bitter; Banks's Sunbeam; Church End Gravediggers Ale; Wye Valley Butty Bach; 3 changing beers (sourced regionally; often AJs, Fixed Wheel, Salopian) ⊞
Popular two-roomed pub, dating from 1845, close to the town centre, with a pleasant garden and smoking facilities at the rear, where there is a large Pay & Display car park. Steaks are available on Wednesday and traditional lunches on Sunday. Open mic and quiz nights are held regularly. Friday night Blues, Sunday evening live entertainment and retro games nights are on a monthly cycle. A pool table is located upstairs. Local beers are available and sometimes a real cider.
🛏⊛🕙⇥♠♦🛒🌑🎵

Walsall Arms

17 Bank Street, WS1 2EP (behind the Royal Hotel, off A34)
☎ 07837 302075
Wye Valley Bitter, HPA, Butty Bach; 3 changing beers (sourced regionally; often Salopian) ⊞
A refurbished back-street pub with a large comfy carpeted bar area and a small bar accessed via the passageway. It is just a short walk from Walsall town centre, behind the Royal Hotel. The pub features an open fire, old Walsall photographs and has two TV screens. A patio painted in Italianate fashion is at the rear. Traditional Sunday lunches are available, with themed food every Thursday evening (pre-orders only). Live music is played most Saturdays and karaoke is hosted on Friday and Sunday evenings. ⊛🕙&♠🛒(51,377)🌑🎵

Walsall Cricket Club

Gorway Road, WS1 3BE (off A34, by university campus)
☎ (01922) 622094 ⊕ walsall.play-cricket.com
Wye Valley HPA; 1 changing beer (sourced regionally; often Backyard, Castle Rock) ⊞
On a fine summer's day the sound of leather on willow welcomes you at this green oasis on the outskirts of town. The club room has had a major renovation and now provides luxurious comfort and a panoramic view of the field. It contains local cricket memorabilia and two

large TV screens. There is occasional entertainment and the venue is popular for function hire. CAMRA members may visit by showing a valid membership card. Sunday hours are reduced in winter. 🛏⊛&♠🛒(51)🌑🎵

Wheatsheaf L

4 Birmingham Road, WS1 2NA
Wye Valley HPA, Butty Bach; 2 changing beers (sourced locally; often Enville, Fownes, Green Duck) ⊞
Friendly, open-plan community local with live music most weekends. Four real ales are served including two changing beers from local brewers. Games night is held every Tuesday evening. Live music is very much a feature of the pub with rehearsal evenings on Wednesday, open mic on Thursday, bands every Friday and Saturday, and jazz on Sunday afternoon. 🛏⇥♠🛒(51)🌑🎵🎶

Wednesbury

Bellwether ⊘

3-4 Walsall Street, WS10 9BZ
☎ (0121) 502 6404
Greene King Abbot; Oakham JHB; Ruddles Best Bitter; 7 changing beers (sourced nationally) ⊞
Just off the marketplace and main shopping area, this pub has a large L-shaped room on a split level. Open-plan seating is to the front of the bar with more intimate bench seating found at the rear. The pub is decorated with images of historic events and characters associated with the town. The large garden area at the rear offers a tranquil oasis for contemplation. Ten handpulls serve the usual Wetherspoon regulars plus seven changing beers. Food is served all day. Q🛏⊛🕙&♣♠♦🛒🌑

Olde Leathern Bottel ⊘

40 Vicarage Road, WS10 9DW (just off A461; bus 311 from Walsall is 5 mins' walk)
☎ (0121) 505 0230
4 changing beers (sourced nationally; often Adnams, Hook Norton, Wye Valley) ⊞
The front areas of the pub are set in cottages dating from 1510, while a later extension contains a comfy lounge. The small snug is often used as a function room. The four rooms have many old photos, with the bar displaying one of the pub from 1887 and a map of Wednesbury from 1846. Live solo artists perform on Saturday night and there is a regular quiz on Sunday. The four changing beers are sourced from around the country.
🛏⊛🕙♣🛒(11) 🌑🎵🎶

West Bromwich

Three Horseshoes L

86 Witton Lane, B71 2AQ
☎ (0121) 502 1693
Black Country Bradley's Finest Golden, Pig on the Wall, Fireside; 4 changing beers (sourced nationally) ⊞
A refurbished one-roomed pub, taken on by Black Country Ales in 2016, with 10 handpulls installed. The spacious interior is furnished in a traditional style and there is a large beer garden for enjoying fine weather. The staff of this expansive hostelry offer a warm welcome and create a friendly atmosphere. Beers are from Black County Ales, as well as regional and national breweries. TVs show live sport, and fresh cobs and pork pies are available all day. 🛏⊛&♣♠♦🛒(79,49)🌑🎵🎶

Willenhall

Robin Hood 🗓

54 The Crescent, WV13 2QR (200yds from A462/B4464 jct)
☎ (01902) 635070

Black Country Bradley's Finest Golden, Pig on the Wall ℍ, Fireside ℍ/G; 6 changing beers (sourced nationally) ℍ

A traditional-style public house with welcoming staff and a friendly clientele. The L-shaped interior has a warming real fire during the winter months. There are up to nine real ales on the bar and sometimes real ciders. A variety of cobs, hot pies and pork pies are available throughout the day. Quizzes are held on Thursday and a local archery club meets on adjacent land on Saturday.
❀♣💰P🚆(529) ☻ 📶

Wollaston

Foresters Arms 🗓 ✅

Bridgnorth Road, DY8 3PL (on A458 towards Bridgnorth)
☎ (01384) 394476 ● foresterswollaston.co.uk

Enville Ale; Holden's Golden Glow; Ludlow Gold; Wye Valley HPA; 1 changing beer ℍ

Located on the ridge, ideal for ramblers, this warm, cosy and friendly traditional pub is situated on the outskirts of Wollaston next to open fields. The L-shaped room provides a convenient area where diners can sample good-value quality food. Quizzes are usually held on the first and third Sunday of each month with regular themed evenings also held. There is a heated and covered smoking area plus a large, furnished marquee in summer which is available for hire.
🚶❀◑🕏P🚆(8,242) ☻ 📶

Wolverhampton

Combermere Arms

90 Chapel Ash, WV3 0TY (on A41, Tettenhall Rd)
☎ (01902) 421880

Timothy Taylor Landlord; 5 changing beers (sourced nationally) ℍ

A Grade II-listed building with original sash windows. Situated a short walk or bus ride from the city centre, the pub comprises three charming rooms with cosy fireplaces replete with classic adverts. Pie, sausage and cheese tasting festivals are held annually and there is occasional live entertainment. The rear has a courtyard and beer garden. The renowned tree in the Gents is still growing despite being trimmed. Hurst View cider is usually available. Q🚶❀💰P🚆☻ 🎵

Great Western 🗓

Sun Street, WV10 0DG (pedestrian access from city centre via railway station car park and Corn Hill)
☎ (01902) 351090

Bathams Best Bitter; Holden's Black Country Mild, Black Country Bitter, Golden Glow, Special; 2 changing beers (sourced regionally; often Holden's) ℍ

A Grade II-listed, former CAMRA National Pub of the Year situated near the former low-level railway station, sympathetically refurbished in 2021. It attracts a varied clientele, including a rock climbing club and railway groups. Railway memorabilia are displayed and cosy real fires blaze in the winter. Meals are served at lunchtimes and until early evening (not Sun), and cobs and pork pies are available every day. Holden's merchandise is available (by pre-ordering only) at the same price as the brewery's shop. Q🚶❀◑⇌Q(St George's)♣💰🚆☻ 📶

Hail to the Ale 🗓

2 Pendeford Avenue, Claregate, WV6 9EF (at Claregate Island bus stop)
☎ 07846 562910 ● mortonbrewery.co.uk/httahome.htm

6 changing beers (sourced locally; often Newbridge) ℍ

A welcoming one-room micropub, the first in the West Midlands, with a focus on beer and conversation. It has an outside seating area. Six handpulls serve Newbridge beers plus guests, usually from local microbreweries. Also available from the cellar are three ciders or perries. Locally-sourced pies, cheese, sausage rolls and Scotch eggs are available along with 10 fruit wines. Check the website for bank holiday hours, events and holiday closures. Q🚶❀♣💰P🚆(5,6)☻ 🎵

Hogshead ✅

186 Stafford Street, WV1 1NA
☎ (01902) 717955

10 changing beers (sourced nationally) ℍ

A large 19th-century traditional city-centre building with an attractive terracotta brick exterior. A stained-glass window above the entrance displays the original name, the Vine. The large single room is divided into separate areas, with TVs showing sport throughout the pub. It serves a range of 10 cask ales with more available through membrane KeyKeg dispense. There are regular brewery tap takeovers, and a large number of ciders, mostly from Lilley's. It is popular with all age groups. 🚶❀◑🕏⇌Q(St George's)🚌📶🎵

Keg & Comfort 🍷 🗓

474 Stafford Road, Oxley, WV10 6AN
☎ 07952 631032 ● kegandcomfort.co.uk

4 changing beers (sourced locally) ℍ

The city's second micropub opened in 2018 in a former bank. The contemporary-styled main room has a striking bar, custom-built using coloured bottles, seating for around 40, and old barrels as tables for people who prefer to stand. A small side room houses a large sofa and games cupboard. Attention to detail helps to provide a welcoming atmosphere. Four changing ales, one dark, five ciders or perries and a selection of fruit wines are served. Local CAMRA Cider Pub of the Year 2019 and 2020. Q🚶🕏♣💰P🚆(3,4)☻ 🎵

Lych Gate Tavern 🗓

44 Queen Square, WV1 1TX (off Queen Square opp Barclays Bank by St Peter's Church)
☎ (01902) 399516

Black Country Bradley's Finest Golden, Pig on the Wall, Fireside; 6 changing beers (sourced nationally) ℍ

A warm and friendly, traditional city-centre pub housed in one of the oldest buildings in Wolverhampton. The Georgian frontage dates from 1726 and the timber-framed rear is circa 1500. Featuring 10 handpumps, the bar area is located down a short flight of stairs, with a function room upstairs. All floors have lift access. A rear courtyard provides outdoor seating. Cobs are served but customers may bring their own food, with plates and cutlery provided. Q🚶❀🕏⇌Q(St George's)♣💰🚆☻ 📶

Penn Bowling & Social Club

10 Manor Road, Penn, WV4 5PY
☎ (01902) 342516 ● pennbowlingclub.com

4 changing beers (sourced nationally; often Enville, Green Duck, Newbridge) ℍ

The hub of this family-friendly community club is a large room which overlooks the floodlit crown bowling green, featuring a largescreen TV for sports. A smaller quiet room, the Red Room, is accessed from the main bar. A large function room is used for regular events and entertainment. The patio area is ideal for watching bowls matches during the season. A children's adventure playground and seating area are outside. Cobs and bar snacks are available. ♿🏵❄♣P🚆(16)♠🐕🔊

Posada

48 Lichfield Street, WV1 1DG

Wye Valley HPA; 3 changing beers (sourced nationally; often Bath Ales, Ossett, Robinsons) 🅗
Dating from 1886, this Victorian Grade II-listed city-centre pub has a ceramic exterior and interior tiled walls, original bar fittings – including rare snob screens – and is little-altered since a remodelling in 1900 by local architect Fred T. Beck. It attracts a varied clientele and is quiet during the day but busy in the evening and weekends, especially when Wolverhampton Wanderers are at home. There is a courtyard to the rear with a smoking area. Lunchtime meals are served by an arrangement with the next door café. Cobs are also served. Closed Sundays. ♿🏵◑🚆≹🅀(St George's)🐕🔊

Royal Oak 🅛 ✅

70 Compton Road, WV3 9PH

☎ (01902) 422845 ⊕ theoakchapelash.com

Banks's Mild, Amber Ale, Sunbeam; Marston's Old Empire; Wainwright Amber 🅗
A friendly hostelry, just a short walk or bus ride from the city centre, serving a wide range of real ales from the Marston's portfolio. This lively pub hosts open mic on Tuesday and live bands on Friday, and on Sunday afternoons in summer. Part of the community, it raises money for local and national charities. Pub and local history maps are displayed, including a list of former licensees. The pub is the headquarters of the Old Wulfrunians Hockey Club. Cobs and scotch eggs are served. Covered, heated outdoor seating is available.
♿🏵♿♣P🚆(10,9) 🐕🔊

Starting Gate 🅛

134 Birches Barn Road, Penn Fields, WV3 7BG

☎ 07834 673888

5 changing beers (sourced regionally; often Ludlow, Sarah Hughes, Wye Valley) 🅗
Opened in 2018, this small outlet occupies a former bank branch and retains the original counter and wings. The impressive rear door to the garden, which offers covered seating, also reflects its previous use. The small bar area leads to a cosy lounge, with another lounge upstairs reached by an open spiral staircase. The paintings, silks and other memorabilia signal the owner's brother's interest in horse racing, hence the name of the pub. It is warm and welcoming, with friendly local regulars.
Q🏵♿🍴🚆(2) 🐕🔊

Stile Inn 🅛 ✅

3 Harrow Street, Whitmore Reans, WV1 4PB (off Newhampton Rd East/Fawdry St)

☎ (01902) 425336

Banks's Amber Ale, Mild, Sunbeam; 1 changing beer (sourced regionally) 🅗
An excellent late-Victorian street-corner pub built in 1900, featuring a public bar, smoke room and snug. It is a true community local with an emphasis on sports – darts and dominoes feature inside, crown green bowls on the unusual L-shaped green outside, and it is busy with Wolverhampton Wanderers fans on match days. Excellent-value food, including Polish dishes, is served. Friday is disco night and Saturday is karaoke. Sky and BT Sports are shown in all rooms. ♿🏵◑♣🚆(5,6)🐕🔊

Summer House

290 Newhampton Road West, Whitmore Reans, WV6 0RS

☎ (01902) 745213

St Austell Proper Job; 3 changing beers (often Enville, Oakham, Wye Valley) 🅗
A friendly community pub dating back to the 1860s. The bar features a roaring real fire in winter and is decorated with football memorabilia. The central servery links a comfortable lounge, showing local history on the walls, and a dining area where a substantial Indian menu is available. There is a large garden for barbecues and outside drinking, and a covered, heated area for smokers. Q🏵◑◐♿🚆(6)🐕🔊

Swan 🅛

Bridgnorth Road, Compton, WV6 8AE (at Compton Square bus stop, A454)

☎ (01902) 754736 ⊕ swanpubwolverhampton.co.uk

Banks's Mild, Amber Ale, Sunbeam; Marston's Old Empire; Wainwright; 1 changing beer (sourced nationally) 🅗
Built around 1780, this Grade II-listed former coaching inn is popular with locals, boaters, ramblers and cyclists alike, as it is close to the Staffordshire and Worcestershire Canal and Smestow Valley Nature Reserve. The bar is the place for lively banter. There is also a games room and a quieter snug. Quizzes are held on Tuesday, a darts team plays on Wednesday and folk group on Thursday. The pub hosts an annual charity dog show and the weekly local pigeon flyers' club. Q♿🏵♣P🚆(10,62)🐕🔊🔊

Woodsetton

Park Inn 🅛

George Street, DY1 4LW (on A457, 200yds from A4123)

☎ (01902) 661279

Holden's Black Country Mild, Black Country Bitter, Golden Glow, Special; 2 changing beers (often Holden's) 🅗
Busy brewery tap that has been owned by the Holden family for more than a century. The bar has a chalkboard advertising guest beers (up to three), and a large flatscreen TV showing BT Sport, though this is not intrusive. There is also a raised dining area, a games room with a pool table, and a conservatory, which is used for Dudley Winter Ales Fayre planning meetings. Pub grub is served all week, except Sunday.
♿🏵♣P🚆(81,229) 🐕🔊

Wordsley

Bird in Hand 🏆

57 John Street, DY8 5YS

☎ (01384) 865809

Enville Ale; Hobsons Town Crier; Holden's Golden Glow; 3 changing beers (sourced nationally) 🅗
A Red Pub Company pub and the current local CAMRA Pub of the Year. This traditional back-street corner local has a wide customer mix and serves an enterprising range of up to three guest beers, including some rarely seen. The pub exudes an air of friendliness and homeliness. Rooms include a bar with live TV sports, a quiet lounge and an outside covered seating area with heating. It is close to the Stourbridge Canal, with moorings a few minutes' walk away.
Q♿🏵◑♣🚆🚆🔊

New Inn 🅛

117 High Street, DY8 5QR (A491)

☎ (01384) 295614

Bathams Mild Ale, Best Bitter 🅗
Acquired by Daniel Batham Ltd in 2008, this L-shaped bar serves a single room with a small annexe at one end, plus a patio area and pleasant garden outside. A variety

of cobs are available. Children are welcome in the garden but not allowed in the pub. Bathams Mild Ale, only available in a limited number of pubs across the Bathams estate, is sold. ⏱🏠♿🅿🐕☺🛜

Breweries

AJ's

Unit 11, Ashmore Industrial Estate, Longacre Street, Walsall, WS2 8QG ☎ 07860 585911 ✉ ajs-ales@hotmail.com

⊗ Set up by experienced brewer Andy Dukes and his wife Charlotte, AJ's Ales was established in 2015 and uses a four-barrel plant with three fermenting vessels and a cool room. It brews three times a week, mainly supplying local pubs and further afield through local wholesalers. ♦

Blackjack Mild (ABV 3.6%) MILD
Stuck on Blondes (ABV 3.9%) BLOND
Best Bitter (ABV 4%) BITTER
Dukey's Delight (ABV 4.1%) GOLD
SPA (ABV 4.2%) PALE
Gold (ABV 4.3%) GOLD
Stuck in the Mud (ABV 4.3%) STOUT
Ruby (ABV 4.4%) BITTER
IPA (ABV 4.6%) PALE
Stuck in the Doghouse (ABV 4.7%) GOLD

Angel SIBA

62A Furlong Lane, Halesowen, B63 2TA ☎ 07986 382919 ⊕ angelales.co.uk

Angel Ales began commercial brewing in 2011. The brewery building has been a chapel of rest, a coffin makers' workshop and a pattern makers' before becoming a brewhouse. Beers are produced using organic ingredients where possible. ‼♦LIVE

Ale (ABV 4.1%) PALE
Krakow (ABV 4.5%) SPECIALITY
Ginger Stout (ABV 4.8%) SPECIALITY

Attic SIBA

29b Mary Vale Road, Stirchley, Birmingham, B30 2DA ☎ 07470 643758 ⊕ atticbrew.com

Since its launch in 2018 this brewery, set in an industrial estate close to Bournville Railway Station, has increased its kit size, range of beers and its fanbase. Its main production is KeyKeg, but it also serves cask on the premises and in a number of Birmingham micropubs. The beer range encompasses a number of styles and strengths and includes collaborations. Beers are available in a number of Birmingham pubs. ✏

Backyard SIBA

Unit 8a, Gatehouse Trading Estate, Lichfield Road, Brownhills, Walsall, WS8 6JZ ☎ (01543) 360145 ⊕ tbb.uk.com

☺Backyard began brewing in 2008 and expanded in 2012 to a 12-barrel plant brewing up to 50 barrels a week. It now brews beers under the Backyard, Grasshopper and Warwickshire names and is owned by 52 Degrees Brewing. Beers can be found in free houses throughout the Midlands. ‼🍴♦

Bitter (ABV 3.8%) BLOND
The Hoard (ABV 3.9%) GOLD
Blonde (ABV 4.1%) BLOND

Americana (ABV 4.3%) PALE
Gold (ABV 4.5%) GOLD
IPA (ABV 5%) PALE
Antipodean (ABV 5.6%) IPA

Banks's

Park Brewery, Wolverhampton, WV1 4NY ☎ (01902) 711811 ⊕ bankssbeer.co.uk

Banks's was founded as maltsters in 1840, starting brewing in 1874, and moving to Park Brewery in 1875. It became the principal brewery of Wolverhampton and Dudley Breweries (W&DB), founded in 1890. In 2007 the Marston's name was adopted following takeover by W&DB in 1999. A joint venture with Carlsberg in 2020 led to the company being renamed Carlsberg Marston's Brewing Company. Alongside the traditional Banks's beers it also produces Wainwrights, Lancaster Bomber and Bombardier Gold, as well as contract brewing. Part of Carlsberg Marston's Brewing Co. ‼🍴

Mild (ABV 3.5%) MILD
An amber-coloured, well-balanced, refreshing session beer.
Amber Ale (ABV 3.8%) BITTER
A pale brown bitter with a pleasant balance of hops and malt. Hops continue from the taste through to a bittersweet aftertaste.
Sunbeam (ABV 4.2%) BLOND

Brewed for Marston's:
Wainwright Amber (ABV 4%) BITTER
Wainwright Golden (ABV 4.1%) GOLD

Brewed for Wychwood Brewery:
Hobgoblin Gold (ABV 4.2%) GOLD

Brewed under the Bombardier brand name:
Bombardier Gold (ABV 4.1%) GOLD

Brewed under the Mansfield brand name:
Cask Ale (ABV 3.9%) BITTER

Bathams IFBB

Delph Brewery, Delph Road, Brierley Hill, DY5 2TN ☎ (01384) 77229 ⊕ bathams.com

☺A classic, Black Country, small brewery established in 1877. Tim and Matthew Batham represent the fifth generation to run the company. The Vine, one of the Black Country's most famous pubs, is also the brewery tap. The company has 12 tied houses and supplies around 30 other outlets. Batham's Best Bitter is sometimes delivered in 54-gallon hogsheads to meet demand. ♦

Mild Ale (ABV 3.5%) MILD
A fruity, dark brown mild with malty sweetness and a roast malt finish.
Best Bitter (ABV 4.3%) BITTER
A pale yellow, fruity, sweetish bitter, with a dry, hoppy finish. A good, light, refreshing beer.

Birmingham SIBA

Unit 17, Stirchley Trading Estate, Hazelwell Road, Birmingham, B30 2PF ☎ (0121) 724 0399 ☎ 07717 704929 ⊕ birminghambrewingcompany.co.uk

Birmingham Brewing Co was established in 2016 and is based in a small unit on a trading estate in Stirchley. Its growing range of vegan and gluten-free beers are available in the trade in cask or keg, and also in cans direct from the brewery or many local bottle shops. ‼♦GF V

Pale Brummie (ABV 4%) PALE
Bitter Brummie (ABV 4.1%) BITTER

Black Country IFBB

🏭 Rear of Old Bulls Head, 1 Redhall Road, Lower Gornal, DY3 2NU
☎ (01384) 401820

Office: 69 Third Avenue, Pensnett Trading Estate, Kingswinford, DY6 7FD ⊕ blackcountryales.co.uk

☺A compact brewery located at the back of the Bull's Head in Lower Gornal, which recommenced brewing in 2004. In 2012 much of the old equipment was replaced with a new kit, which can brew up to 15 barrels at a time and is currently doing so three times a week. Beers can be found in its own tied estate as well as certain free houses nationwide. ‼♦

Bradley's Finest Golden (ABV 4.2%) GOLD
Chain Ale (ABV 4.2%) GOLD
Pig on the Wall (ABV 4.3%) MILD
A ruby brown coloured beer with an aroma of dried fruit and a hint of banana, a malt and fruit initial taste leading to a subtle finish with a hint of astringency.
Fireside (ABV 5%) BITTER

Brewhouse & Kitchen SIBA

🏭 8 Birmingham Road, Sutton Coldfield, B72 1QD
☎ (01217) 966838 ⊕ brewhouseandkitchen.com/sutton-coldfield

☺Sutton Coldfield's first modern brewery commenced production in 2016. The 2.5-barrel plant produces traditional cask and craft keg beers using hops from Hereford and the New World for in-house consumption, for other pubs as guest ales and beer festivals on request. ‼♦

Britt

18 Rowley Village, Rowley Regis, B65 9AT
☎ (0121) 559 3415

Formerly the Pig Iron Brewery, brewing moved to the current site behind the Britannia pub in Rowley Village and is now called the Britt Brewery. The bulk of the production is sold in the pub, with some Pig Iron branded beers sold further afield.

Brew Brittania (ABV 4.2%) BITTER
Britt Pop (ABV 4.9%) BITTER

Brewed under the Pig Iron brand name:
Blonde (ABV 3.8%) PALE
EPA (ABV 4.2%) PALE
IPA (ABV 4.2%) PALE
Unbeweavable (ABV 4.2%) BITTER
APA (ABV 4.5%) PALE

Burning Soul

Unit 1, 51 Mott Street, Hockley, Birmingham, B19 3HE
☎ (0121) 439 1490 ☎ 07793 026624
⊕ burningsoulbrewing.com

Established in 2016, the name Burning Soul reflects a passion for beer and brewing. It is a five-barrel, full-mash brewery with a taproom. The brewery's varied range of live beer in KeyKeg, can or cask is sold onsite and in a growing number of free trade outlets in the Midlands. The range includes sours, saisons and hoppy pale ales alongside dark beers of all styles. ‼▬♦

Byatt's SIBA

Unit 7-8, Lythalls Lane Industrial Estate, Lythalls Lane, Coventry, CV6 6FL
☎ (024) 7663 7996 ⊕ byattsbrewery.co.uk

☺Since being established in 2011 and expanding in 2016, Byatt's has gained many fans with its extensive beer list brewed throughout the year, together with an increasing range of seasonal beers. A brewhouse bar with six handpumps also serves ciders on draught or gravity. Tours and tasting sessions can be booked and private hire is available. Coventry Building Society Arena is nearby. ‼▬♦LIVE ✦

XK Dark (ABV 3.5%) MILD
Coventry Bitter (ABV 3.8%) BITTER
Easy-drinking session bitter. Has an earthy taste from the bitter hops used. The aftertaste retains the strong bitterness.
Platinum Blonde (ABV 3.9%) BLOND
A blond beer having hints of citrus and sulphur, with a mild lemony after taste tempered by fruit sweetness.
Phoenix Gold (ABV 4.2%) GOLD
A refreshing golden ale with an earthy taste. Leading to a crisp citrus hop notes in the aftertaste.
All Day Foreign Extra Stout (ABV 4.9%) STOUT
Regal Blond (ABV 5.2%) GOLD

Craddock's

Duke William, 25 Coventry Street, Stourbridge, DY8 1EP
☎ (01384) 440202 ⊕ craddocksbrewery.com

⊠ Although currently contract brewed elsewhere, Craddock's beers are exclusively available in its chain of five pubs in Stourbridge, Worcester, Droitwich and Birmingham. Ten beers form the core range, availability varies. Brewing is currently suspended. ♦LIVE

Cult Of Oak

Unit 15, Central Park Industrial Estate, Netherton, DY2 9NW ☎ 07530 193543

Cult of Oak was set up by Beer Sommelier Roberto Ross in 2019. Specialising in barrel-aged strong ales of varying styles, most of the beers are brewed collaboratively and are canned or bottled with some going into the trade or festivals in cask. Beers are available at Roberto's Bar, Birmingham.

Davenports SIBA

Unit 5, Empire House, 11 New Street, Smethwick, B66 2AJ
☎ (0121) 565 5622
✉ info@davenportsbrewery.co.uk

☺Davenports brewery occupies part of a distribution warehouse in an industrial unit in Smethwick on the outskirts of Birmingham. The 7.5-barrel plant produces a selection of beers under the Davenports name with some occasional beers branded as being from the former Highgate brewery of Walsall and Dares brewery of Birmingham. Beers can be found in the growing estate of tied houses as well as the free trade. ♦

Mild (ABV 3.5%) MILD
Gold (ABV 3.9%) PALE
Original Bitter (ABV 4.2%) BITTER
IPA (ABV 4.4%) PALE

Dhillon's SIBA

14a Hales Industrial Estate, Rowleys Green Lane, Coventry, CV6 6AL
☎ (024) 7666 7413 ⊕ dhillonsbrewery.com

Established in 2014 as Lion Heart and relaunched as Dhillon's in 2015 with a new range of beers. The main focus is on craft bottled and canned beers but cask ales are also brewed. The brewery tap is open Friday evenings and before rugby and football matches at the nearby Coventry Building Society Arena. ‼♦⬥

Bright Eyes GPA (ABV 3.8%) PALE
Fair Lady (ABV 4.5%) PALE
The Ambler Gambler (ABV 4.5%) GOLD
Red Rebel IPA (ABV 6.2%) IPA

Fixed Wheel

Unit 9, Long Lane Trading Estate, Long Lane, Blackheath, B62 9LD ☎ 07766 162794
⊕ fixedwheelbrewery.co.uk

⊠ Set up in 2014 by cycling and brewing enthusiasts Scott Povey and Sharon Bryant, this full mash brewery is situated on a trading estate on the Blackheath/Halesowen border. It brews several times a week using an eight-barrel plant. Beside the core range, there are regular single hop and specials brewed. The award-winning ales are available throughout the Midlands and further afield. A canning plant was purchased in 2021. See social media for taproom opening times. ‼☒♦LIVE⬥

Through & Off (ABV 3.8%) PALE
Wheelie Pale (ABV 4.1%) PALE
Chain Reaction Pale Ale (ABV 4.2%) PALE
Blackheath Stout (ABV 5%) STOUT
No Brakes IPA (ABV 5.9%) IPA

Fownes SIBA

Unit 2, Two Woods Estate, Talbots Lane, Brierley Hill, DY5 2YX ☎ 07790 766844

Office: 42 The Ridgeway, Sedgley, DY3 3UR
⊕ fownesbrewing.co.uk

☺The brewery was established in 2012 by James and Tom Fownes in premises to the rear of the Jolly Crispin, Upper Gornal. A later expansion saw the brewery moved to a new larger site in Brierley Hill. Frequent specials along a 'Dwarfen Ales' theme are brewed in addition to the core range. Fownes opened its first pub, the Royal Oak, Burton, in 2020. ‼♦LIVE

Elephant Riders (ABV 4%) BITTER
Gunhild (ABV 4%) SPECIALITY
Bright with creamy lingering head. Smooth mouthfeel. Pleasant earthy aroma with hints of blackcurrants and honey. Pear drops and caramel with some malt and blackcurrant flavour. Dry malty aftertaste.
Crispin's Ommer (ABV 4.1%) BITTER
Royal Oak Bitter (ABV 4.2%) BITTER
Frost Hammer (ABV 4.6%) PALE
Blonde and bright with a clingy head. Pine resin, nutmeg, malt, lemon and floral aroma. Dry mouthfeel with coffee, sweet malt and grapefruit flavours. Grapefruit and hoppy aftertaste
Firebeard's Old Favourite No. 5 Ruby Ale (ABV 5%) MILD
Creamy head, rich red colour. Malty, fresh earth, rhubarb and some coffee in the aroma. Smooth mouthfeel. Dark chocolate and plum dominate the flavour with hints of malt and coffee. A pleasant dryness in the aftertaste, with hints of coffee, plum and cocoa.
King Korvak's Saga (ABV 5.4%) PORTER

Pear drop and cocoa aroma with hints of coffee. Coffee, toasted malt, blackcurrant and slight cocoa taste, with rich malty tones in the aftertaste.

Froth Blowers

Unit P35, Hastingwood Industrial Park, Wood Lane, Erdington, B24 9QR ☎ 07966 935906
⊕ frothblowersbrewing.com

⊠ Froth Blowers began brewing in 2013, the name derived from the Ancient Order of Froth Blowers, an organisation dedicated to 'Lubrication in Moderation'! The brewery has the capacity to brew 20 barrels at a site only metres away from its original one, with most of the beers consumed within 30 miles of the brewery. In addition to the core range, half a dozen seasonal beers are brewed. Certain beers are available in five-litre minikegs. ♦

Piffle Snonker (ABV 3.8%) BLOND
Straw-coloured. Aroma is almost jammy with a little malt and hop. Taste is well-balanced with a slightly hoppier aftertaste.
Bar-King Mad (ABV 4.2%) BITTER
Wellingtonian (ABV 4.3%) PALE
John Bull's Best (ABV 4.4%) BITTER
Gollop With Zest (ABV 4.5%) GOLD
Hornswoggle (ABV 5%) BLOND

Glasshouse

Unit 6b, Waterside Business Park, Stirchley, B30 3DR
⊕ glasshousebeer.co.uk

Located at the far end of a business park the brewery is now easily accessed via the canal towpath. Beers are available in a variety of styles, tastes and strengths, mostly keg and KeyKeg but occasionally in cask form, either at the tap or in a number of Birmingham outlets. Its brewery tap is open Friday and Saturday (please check before travelling). ⬥

Green Duck SIBA

Unit 13, Gainsborough Trading Estate, Rufford Road, Stourbridge, DY9 7ND
☎ (01384) 377666 ⊕ greenduckbrewery.co.uk

☺Green Duck began brewing in 2012 and relocated to its present site in Stourbridge in 2013. Experimental beers are brewed alongside a core range. The brewery has an onsite taproom, the Badelynge Bar, where the brewing equipment is visible through a glass partition. Demand for small package beers saw the brewery invest in a canning plant together with Twisted Barrel Brewery in 2020. ‼♦⬥

ZPA (Zesty Pale Ale) (ABV 3.8%) PALE
Session IPA (ABV 4%) PALE
Pale gold with a tropical aroma derived from mosaic hops. Very refreshing with a dry pine and resin aftertaste.
Blonde (ABV 4.2%) SPECIALITY
Gold with a sharp fruity aroma. Lots of passionfruit in the taste. Aftertaste is balanced with fruit sweetness and hops.
American Pale (ABV 4.5%) PALE

Halton Turner

40 Trent Street, 1 Rea Court, Digbeth, Birmingham, B5 5NL ☎ 07821 447329 ⊕ haltonturnerbrew.co

Established in 2018, Halton Turner started on a small plant in Hall Green, Birmingham, but moved to a larger plant in Digbeth in 2021. Brewing a wide range of beers in cask and KeyKeg, the beers are mainly found in the local area. Frequent events and festivals are hosted at the brewery taproom. ◆

Babyface (ABV 3.8%) PALE
Serenade (ABV 4%) PALE
Primo (ABV 4.5%) BITTER
Blindspot (ABV 5%) STOUT

Holden's SIBA IFBB

George Street, Woodsetton, Dudley, DY1 4LW
☎ (01902) 880051 ⊕ holdensbrewery.co.uk

☺A family brewery spanning four generations, Holden's began life as a brewpub in 1915. Continued expansion means it now has 19 tied pubs in its estate. ‼️🍺◆

Black Country Mild (ABV 3.7%) MILD
A good, red/brown mild; a refreshing, light blend of roast malt, hops and fruit, dominated by malt throughout.
Black Country Bitter (ABV 3.9%) BITTER
A medium-bodied, golden ale; a light, well-balanced bitter with a subtle, dry, hoppy finish.
Golden Glow (ABV 4.4%) BITTER
Special (ABV 5.1%) BITTER
A sweet, malty, full-bodied amber ale with hops to balance in the taste and in the good, bittersweet finish.

Sarah Hughes

🏠 Beacon Hotel, 129 Bilston Street, Sedgley, DY3 1JE
☎ (01902) 883381 ⊕ sarahhughesbrewery.co.uk

⊗ Nationally-renowned, Victorian tower brewery behind the Beacon Hotel, which has been brewing since 1987. It attracts visitors from near and far. The brewery is famous for its Dark Ruby Mild, which has a cult following. The beers are served in the Beacon Hotel as well as a growing number of free trade outlets. ‼️◆

Pale Amber (ABV 4%) BITTER
Sedgley Surprise (ABV 5%) BITTER
A bittersweet, medium-bodied, hoppy ale with some malt.
Dark Ruby Mild (ABV 6%) MILD
A dark ruby strong ale with a good balance of fruit and hops, leading to a pleasant, lingering hops and malt finish.

Indian SIBA

119b Baltimore Trading Estate, Baltimore Road, Great Barr, B42 1DD
☎ (0121) 296 9000 ⊕ indianbrewery.com

Six-barrel brewery, established in 2005 as the Tunnel Brewery at the Lord Nelson Inn. It relocated to the picturesque stable block at Red House Farm in 2011. In 2015 Tunnel's owners went their separate ways, with Mike Walsh retaining the brewery and renaming it the Indian Brewery. Later that year it was sold to new owners and relocated to the outskirts of Birmingham. Beers are normally only found in its own two pubs. ‼️

Indian Summer (ABV 4%) GOLD
IPA (ABV 4.9%) PALE
Bombay Honey (ABV 5%) SPECIALITY
Peacock (ABV 5%) BITTER

Infinity

Sladepool Farm Road, Birmingham ☎ 07915 948058
⊕ Infinitybrewing.uk

Infinity Brewing Company was established in 2020 and is a one-barrel nanobrewery producing small batch craft

beer. These small runs allow it to trial different recipes and flavours.

Leviathan

Unit 4, 17 Reddicap Trading Estate, Sutton Coldfield, B75 7BU ☎ 07983 256979 ⊕ leviathanbrewing.co.uk

Established in 2018 by Chris Hodgetts, Leviathan is a microbrewer of unique, small-batch craft beers. There is now a taproom (Thu-Sun; times on website and social media). There are plans to start bottling again and home deliveries are available (see website). 🍺◆

Mashionistas

Coventry, CV5 6AF ☎ 07960 196204
⊕ mashionistas.com

Mashionistas was formed in 2018 by Flo, Jon and Simon with several years of home brewing experience between them. They brew on a one-barrel plant in a garage in their spare time. Only producing small batches gives them the flexibility to experiment using a wide variety of different ingredients. Since its inception many well-received KegKeg beers have been produced. All output is vegan-friendly. V

New Invention

Unit 2, Pinfold Industrial Estate, Walsall, WS3 3JS
☎ 07955 629538 ⊕ newinventionbrewery.co.uk

Opened in 2020, the brewery produces a wide range of beer styles, mainly in keg and can for its own taproom, and distribution into the local free trade. ◆

Newbridge

Unit 3, Tudor House, Moseley Road, Bilston, WV14 6JD
☎ 07970 456052 ⊕ newbridgebrewery.co.uk

First established in 2014, the five-barrel plant incorporates six original Grundy cellar tanks. Occasional specials are brewed to complement the regular beers. The beers are permanently available at the Hail to the Ale micropub in Wolverhampton and can also be found in other pubs and clubs around the city.

Little Fox (ABV 4.2%) BITTER
Solaris (ABV 4.5%) BITTER
Indian Empire (ABV 5%) BITTER

Olde Swan

🏠 Olde Swan, 89 Halesowen Road, Netherton, DY2 9PY
☎ (01384) 253075

☺A famous brewpub best known as Ma Pardoe's after the matriarch who ruled it for years. The pub has been licensed since 1835 and the present brewery and pub were built in 1863. Brewing continued until 1988 and restarted in 2001. More than 30 outlets are supplied through distributors. ‼️◆

Original (ABV 3.5%) MILD
Straw-coloured light mild, smooth but tangy, and sweetly refreshing with a faint hoppiness.
Dark Swan (ABV 4.2%) MILD
Smooth, sweet dark mild with late roast malt in the finish.
Entire (ABV 4.4%) BITTER
Faintly hoppy, amber premium bitter with sweetness persistent throughout.
NPA (Netherton Pale Ale) (ABV 4.8%) PALE
Bumble Hole Bitter (ABV 5.2%) BITTER

Sweet, smooth amber ale with hints of astringency in the finish.

Ostlers

🍺 White Horse, 2 York Street, Harborne, B17 0HG
☎ (0121) 427 8004 ⊕ whitehorseharborne.com

Started up at the rear of the White Horse pub in Harborne, the brewery was in occasional production for a few years. It now has a 4.5-barrel plant, brewing a small range of core beers alongside frequent specials and seasonal beers, many available in KeyKeg as well as cask. The beer is mainly found in the White Horse pub but can be found in other free houses in the Birmingham area. ♦

Printworks SIBA

🍺 Windsor Castle Inn, 7 Stourbridge, Lye, DY9 7BS
☎ (01384) 897809 ⊕ printworksbrewery.co.uk

Ⓟ Printworks started full production in 2019 with Emily Sadler at the helm. Based at the Windsor Castle, Lye, which is the main outlet for the beers. Beers are mostly named after typefaces to reflect a family printing heritage. Core beers and various specials are produced. Equipment is visible through a window in the seating area. ‼♦

Red Moon

25 Holder Road, Yardley, Birmingham, B25 8AP
☎ 07825 771388

Office: 39 Kimberley Road, Solihull, B92 8PU
⊕ redmoonbrewery.co.uk

Red Moon Brewery was started in 2015 by two friends. Beer names are inspired by their own life events. The bulk of production is bottled, however some cask beer finds its way into the local free trade. Currently only brewing occasionally for specific events. ♦

Back Yard BBQ (ABV 4.5%) BITTER
Poison's Pleasure (ABV 4.5%) RED
Screaming Dwarf (ABV 4.5%) GOLD

Rock & Roll

19 Hall Street, Jewellery Quarter, Birmingham,
B18 6BS ☎ 07922 554181
✉ rnrbrewhouse@outlook.com

⊠ The Rock & Roll brewery started as Birmingham's only rooftop pub brewery, set up by experienced brewer Mark Shepherd. In 2014 Brewster Lynn Crossland joined and now does all of the brewing. In 2016 the brewery moved and expanded to a six-barrel plant. In 2020 it moved to its current location in the Jewellery Quarter. Specials and experimental beers are regularly available. A brewhouse bar is open at weekends. All beers are suitable for vegans. ‼♦V

Brew Springsteen (ABV 4.2%) PALE
Thirst Aid Kit (ABV 4.2%) PALE
Mash City Rocker (ABV 4.5%) PALE
Voodoo Mild (ABV 5%) MILD

Silhill

Oak Farm, Hampton Lane, Catherine-de-Barnes,
Solihull, B92 0JB
☎ (0845) 519 5101 ☎ 07977 444564

Office: PO Box 15739, Solihull, B93 3FW
⊕ silhillbrewery.co.uk

⊠ Established in 2010, Silhill is a small, independent brewery based in premises just outside Solihull town centre using a 10-barrel plant. Bottling operations commenced in 2015. Beers are available in Solihull, Birmingham and Stratford-upon-Avon. ‼LIVE

Gold Star (ABV 3.9%) SPECIALITY
Blonde Star (ABV 4.1%) BLOND
Hop Star (ABV 4.2%) PALE
Pure Star (ABV 4.3%) BITTER
Super Star (ABV 5.1%) GOLD

Sommar

Unit 3B, Canalside, Utilita Arena, Birmingham, B1 2AA

Office: 41 St Marks Crescent, Ladywood, Birmingham,
B1 2PY ⊕ sommar.co.uk

⊠ Started in 2019 this microbrewery brews a wide range of beers of various strengths and styles for its taproom and several others around the region. Beers are keg and KeyKeg. The taproom has up to 18 taps in use, including guest beers from smaller breweries and collaborations. It now has three outlets in the Birmingham area. Located on the canalside near Utilia Arena, brewery masterclass tours are available (see website). ♦

Toll End

🍺 Waggon & Horses, 131 Toll End Road, Tipton,
DY4 0ET
☎ (0121) 502 6453 ☎ 07903 725574

The four-barrel brewery opened in 2004. With the exception of Phoebe's Ale, named after the brewer's daughter, all brews commemorate local landmarks, events and people. Nearly all of the brewery's output is sold in the Waggon & Horses. ‼LIVE

Triumph

39 Hawthorn Lane, Tile Hill, Coventry, CV4 9LB
☎ 07903 131512 ✉ triumphbrewing@aol.com

Triumph is a nanobrewery offering brew days to the public who want to try homebrewing with professional standard equipment. Occasional collaboration brews are done with other brewers.

Twisted Barrel

Unit 11, Fargo Village, Far Gosford Street, Coventry,
CV1 5ED
☎ (024) 7610 1701 ⊕ twistedbarrelale.co.uk

⊠ Founded in 2013 in a garage, the brewery moved in 2015 to Fargo Village, home to artisanal businesses and arts and music events. It has since relocated to larger premises on the same site. With a capacity of 5,200 litres, and an onsite bar, the brewery hosts a vibrant homebrew club, and holds a a variety of events on a regular basis. Beers are distributed throughout the UK. A canning machine purchased in 2021 has given greater flexibility. ‼📅♦LIVE V♦

Detroit Sour City (ABV 4.5%) SPECIALITY
God's Twisted Sister (ABV 4.5%) STOUT
A well-balanced, easy-drinking stout with hints of malt, coffee and fruit undertones finishing with a bitter aftertaste.
Sine Qua Non (ABV 4.5%) PALE
A hazy pale, unfined vegan ale with hints of grapefruit and apricot which linger on the aftertaste.
Kazan (ABV 5.5%) IPA

Two Towers SIBA

29 Shadwell Street, Birmingham, B4 6HB
☎ (0121) 439 3738 ☎ 07795 247059
⊕ twotowersbrewery.co.uk

⊠ Originally established in 2010 on a site in the Jewellery Quarter, Birmingham, the 10-barrel brewery is now located behind its brewery tap, the Gunmakers Arms, and is visible from the beer garden. Frequent specials and bespoke beers supplement the core range. The beers can be found in cask at the Gunmakers, and it has a range of beers in bottles that are widely available in restaurants and other local outlets. ‼ 🍺 ♦ LIVE

Baskerville Bitter (ABV 3.8%) BITTER
Hockley Gold (ABV 4.1%) GOLD
Complete Muppetry (ABV 4.3%) BITTER
Chamberlain Pale Ale (ABV 4.5%) PALE
Peaky Blinders Mild (ABV 4.5%) MILD
Jewellery Porter (ABV 5%) STOUT

Underground Medicine

Upper Eastern Green Lane, Coventry, CV5 7DN
☎ 07921 120932

A Coventry nanobrewery producing a wide range of craft beers in keg and KeyKeg.

Victoria, Walsall (Photo: Elliott Brown / Flickr CC BY-SA 2.0)

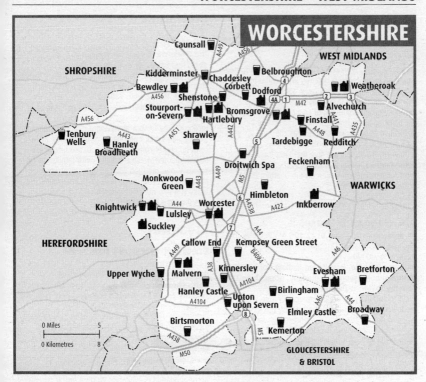

WORCESTERSHIRE

WEST MIDLANDS

SHROPSHIRE

Caunsall
Kidderminster
Belbroughton
Bewdley Chaddesley
Corbett
Shenstone Dodford
Stourport- Weatheroak
on-Severn Bromsgrove Alvechurch
Hartlebury Finstall
Tenbury Shrawley Tardebigge Redditch
Wells Hanley
Broadheath Droitwich Spa Feckenham
Monkwood WARWICKS
Green
Knightwick Himbleton
Worcester Inkberrow
Lulsley
Suckley
HEREFORDSHIRE Callow End Kempsey Green Street
Upper Wyche Kinnersley Evesham Bretforton
Malvern Birlingham
Hanley Castle Broadway
Upton Elmley Castle
upon Severn
Birtsmorton Kemerton

0 Miles 5
0 Kilometres 8

GLOUCESTERSHIRE
& BRISTOL

Alvechurch

Weighbridge 🏆 🅛

Scarfield Wharf, Scarfield Hill, B48 7SQ (follow signs to
marina from village) SP022721

☎ (0121) 445 5111 🌐 the-weighbridge.co.uk

**House beer (by Woodcote); 4 changing beers
(sourced locally)** 🅗

This cosy canalside pub has won many CAMRA awards. It
was once the old Weighbridge office for offloading coal
barges to horse and cart for local deliveries. It has two
small lounges, a public bar and a pleasant garden. A
covered area outside can be used for functions. Regular
beer Bridge 61 is a specially brewed pale ale by
Woodcote brewery, and four changing beers are locally
sourced, one of which is a mild, as well as a real cider
and a craft ale. Spring and autumn beer festivals are
held. Q🕸🐕🕪⇄🚲P🛜

Belbroughton

Holly Bush Inn

Stourbridge Road, DY9 9UG (on A491 Stourbridge Rd)

☎ (01562) 730207

**Hobsons Mild, Town Crier; Holden's Black Country
Bitter; 2 changing beers (sourced regionally; often
Hobsons, Three Tuns, Woodcote)** 🅗

Set back from the A491, this traditional inn with an open
fire was originally built in the 1700s. Beers from the
Hobsons range are served along with guest ales and real
Westons cider. The characterful interior comprises a
lounge/dining area, a central bar, and a small raised
restaurant. A traditional pub menu includes good-value
specials and fish options. Dogs are welcome. A winner of
CAMRA awards including local Pub of the Year.
Q🕸🐕🕪&♣🚲P🖥(318) 🐾

Bewdley

Bewdley Brewery Tap

Bewdley Craft Centre, Lax Lane, DY12 2DZ (Lax Ln is off
Severn Side S, the Tap is at back of brewery)

☎ (01299) 405148 🌐 bewdleybrewery.co.uk

**Bewdley Worcestershire Way, Baldwin IPA, Jubilee,
Worcestershire Sway, William Mucklow's Dark Mild; 1
changing beer (sourced locally; often Bewdley)** 🅗

Bewdley brewery produces a range of six regular cask
ales and a greater number of bottled beers, some for the
Severn Valley Railway. The spacious taproom, at the rear
of a former school building, is adorned with railway and
brewery memorabilia, and always has a friendly
welcome and a lively pub atmosphere. Six of the
brewery's cask ales are served through half-pint pulls,
giving each pint a perfectly clear dispense, and the full
range of bottled beers is available. Closed on Monday
except bank holidays. 🕸&P🖥🐾🛜

Black Boy 🅛

50 Wyre Hill, DY12 2UE (up Sandy Bank from Cleobury
Rd at Welch Gate)

☎ (01299) 400088 🌐 theblackboybewdley.co.uk

**Bewdley Worcestershire Way; Wye Valley Butty Bach;
3 changing beers (sourced locally; often Fownes,
Hobsons, Three Tuns)** 🅗

Perched above the town, this friendly inn is worth the
climb. The attractive half-timbered building is the oldest
pub in Bewdley, with a beamed interior and open fire in
winter. Up to five beers are served, plus a real cider or
two. Cobs and pork pies are available, and hot meals
three days a week. Attractions include bar skittles,
bagatelle, board games and shove-ha'penny. A folk
session is hosted on the second Wednesday of each
month and a quiz on Sunday. Closed on Monday.
Q🕸🐕🕪🅐♣🚲🖥(8,292) 🐾🛜♪

Great Western L

Kidderminster Road, DY12 1BY (near SVR station – walk past signal box and under viaduct)
☎ (01299) 488828
Bewdley 2857, Worcestershire Way; 3 changing beers (sourced locally; often Ludlow, Wye Valley) ⊞
Conveniently located a short way from the Severn Valley Railway station, the pub's traditional interior has a railway theme reminiscent of an earlier age. Overlooking the bar is an upper level from which to admire the glazed decorative tiling. Pub snacks such as cobs and tasty local pork pies are in keeping with the traditional pub ambience. On the bar are five real ales, including the house beer 2857, from Bewdley, named after a GWR locomotive sometimes seen on the nearby railway viaduct. ⏱❀≋♣P�❀🐾 🛜

Old Waggon & Horses L

91 Kidderminster Road, DY12 1DG (on Bewdley to Kidderminster road at Catchem's End)
☎ (01299) 403170
Bathams Mild Ale, Best Bitter; Ludlow Gold; 1 changing beer (sourced regionally; often Three Tuns, Timothy Taylor, Wye Valley) ⊞
Popular and friendly locals' and visitors' pub with a central bar serving three distinct areas. The small wooden-floored snug has a dartboard; the larger room has a wood-burner and roll-down screen for sporting events, but at most times conversation prevails. Guest ales come from local and regional breweries. Lunch and evening meals are available from Wednesday to Saturday, with just a lunchtime carvery on Sunday (two sittings). There are monthly pie nights and tapas nights. The attractive terraced flower garden is on many levels. Q⏱❀≋◑≋♣Pⴰ❀🐾 🛜♪

Birlingham

Swan Inn

Church Street, WR10 3AQ
☎ (01386) 750485 ⊕ theswaninn.co.uk
Goff's Cheltenham Gold; 1 changing beer (often Purity, Three Tuns) ⊞
A pretty thatched free house tucked away at the edge of this quiet village. Although the emphasis is on dining there is a small, separate, black-and-white beamed bar. The conservatory overlooking the fine garden is for dining, with fresh fish specials featuring on the menu. The log cabin-style covered seating in the garden is ideal for outdoor drinking. Q❀◑Pⴰ (382)❀ 🛜

Birtsmorton

Farmers Arms

Birts Street, WR13 6AP (off B4208) SO790363
☎ (01684) 833308 ⊕ farmersarmsbirtsmorton.co.uk
Hook Norton Hooky, Old Hooky; Wye Valley Butty Bach; 2 changing beers (sourced locally; often Hobsons) ⊞
Grade II-listed black-and-white village pub dating from 1480, found in a quiet spot down a country lane. The large bar area has a splendid inglenook fireplace while the cosy lounge has old settles and low beams. There is level access to the bar. Good-value, home-made, traditional food is on offer daily. Beer from a small local independent brewery is often available. The safe, spacious garden, complete with swings, provides fine views of the Malvern Hills. A caravan site is nearby. Q⏱❀◑♣ⴰ❀🐾 🛜

Bretforton

Fleece Inn ★ L

The Cross, WR11 7JE (near church)
☎ (01386) 831173 ⊕ thefleeceinn.co.uk
Purity Mad Goose; Uley Pigs Ear; Wye Valley Bitter; 3 changing beers (sourced nationally; often North Cotswold, Purity, Wye Valley) ⊞
A 15th-century timber-framed village pub owned by the National Trust on the edge of the Cotswolds. It is recognised by CAMRA as having a nationally important historic pub interior and has a world-famous 17th-century pewter collection. The pub also has its own orchard garden which is popular with families in the summer, and the food comes highly recommended. Morris dancers and music feature all year round. This really is a pub not to be missed. Q⏱❀◑◑&♣ⴰPⴰ❀ 🛜♪

Broadway

Crown & Trumpet Inn L ✅

14 Church Street, WR12 7AE
☎ (01386) 853202 ⊕ crownandtrumpet.co.uk
Goff's Cheltenham Gold; North Cotswold Shagweaver; Timothy Taylor Landlord; 1 changing beer (sourced locally; often North Cotswold) ⊞
Picturesque 17th-century Cotswold-stone inn situated just off the village green. This hostelry has lots of character, with oak beams, a log fire and Flowers brewery memorabilia. Classic and local dishes are served alongside local and guest ales, plus several ciders and perries. Entertainment is hosted on Friday and Saturday. Accommodation is available. Worth a visit if you are on the Cotswold Way or touring Shakespeare's Country. Q❀◑♣❀❀ 🛜♪

Bromsgrove

Golden Cross Hotel L ✅

20 High Street, B61 8HH (S end of High St)
☎ (01527) 870005
Greene King Abbot; Ruddles Best Bitter; Sharp's Doom Bar; 9 changing beers (sourced regionally) ⊞
A busy town-centre Wetherspoon pub in a former hotel and coachhouse. It is split-level and has 12 booths with stained-glass surrounds and an open fire. Daily themed food deals and manager's specials are always on offer. Three regular core beers are served, plus nine varied guests, many from local breweries. The licensee asks for suggestions on beer choices and reacts to feedback. During seasonal festivals cask ales from across the UK are promoted. ⏱❀◑&♣ⴰPⴰ 🛜

REAL ALE BREWERIES

Ambridge Inkberrow (brewing suspended)
Bewdley ◆ Bewdley
BOA (Brothers of Ale) ◆ Stourport-on-Severn
Boat Lane ◆ Evesham
Brew61 Bromsgrove
Friday Beer Malvern (brewing suspended)
Hartlebury Hartlebury
Hop Shed ◆ Suckley
Lakehouse Malvern
Little Beer Evesham (NEW)
Sociable ◆ Worcester
Spilsbury & Jones ◆ Worcester (NEW)
Teme Valley 🍺 ◆ Knightwick
Weatheroak Hill 🍺 Weatheroak
Woodcote Bromsgrove: Dodford
Worcester Worcester

Hop Pole

78 Birmingham Road, B61 0DF (200yds from town centre)

☎ 07522 847127

Wye Valley HPA, Butty Bach; 3 changing beers (sourced regionally; often Attic, Woodcote, Wychwood) ⊞

A community-style pub with a great atmosphere. It features bands covering various music styles every Friday and Saturday night. The bar area gives good views of the stage and there is comfortable seating at the front. An upstairs games room has a league pool table. The smoking area is in the beer garden to the rear. ☺🦮♿♣🖥♥🐾🛜♫

Ladybird Inn 🄻

2 Finstall Road, B60 2DZ (on B4184 on corner of roundabout near station) SO969695

☎ (01527) 878014 ⊕ ladybirdinn.co.uk

Bathams Best Bitter, Sharp's Doom Bar, Sea Fury; Wye Valley HPA, Butty Bach ⊞

This popular local is situated near the town's railway station. Decor is light and airy, with a large busy bar to the front, and a lounge with a polished wooden floor to the rear. A meeting room is available on the first floor and a function room suitable for parties is situated on the ground floor. Filled rolls and other substantial snacks are available throughout the day. ☺🦮♿≍♣P🖥♥🐾🛜♫

Little Ale House

21 Worcester Road, B61 7DL (corner of Station St)

☎ 07791 698641

6 changing beers (often Hobsons, Woodcote) Ⓖ

Micropub with a cosy atmosphere, with raised seating and tables mounted on large wooden barrels; streetside seating is also available. Up to six ales are dispensed by gravity from local independents such as Hobsons, Wye Valley and Woodcote. A range of ciders and perries is also stocked and take-away containers are available. Dogs are welcome. A council car park is nearby and the town's bus station is a five-minute walk away. Q☺♣♥🖥🐾🛜

Callow End

Old Bush 🄻

Upton Road, WR2 4TE (small lane off B4424) SO835497

☎ (01905) 830792 ⊕ old-bush.com

Butcombe Original; Hobsons Twisted Spire; Wye Valley Butty Bach; 1 changing beer (sourced locally) ⊞

Village local with a black-and-white exterior, situated in a quiet road. The cosy, beamed interior has a log-burner in the lounge area, and all walls are adorned with an eclectic mix of artefacts and pictures. One guest beer, sourced locally, is usually available. There are separate dining areas for the very good home-made food, and customers may also eat in the bar. The large and attractively laid out garden has country views, benches, a children's play area and a large aviary with many colourful birds. ☺🦮🌳◑▲♣P🖥♥🐾🛜

Caunsall

Anchor Inn 🄻

Caunsall, DY11 5YL (off A449 Kidderminster to Wolverhampton road)

☎ (01562) 850254 ⊕ theanchorinncaunsall.co.uk

Hobsons Best, Town Crier; Wye Valley HPA, Butty Bach; 1 changing beer (sourced locally; often Hobsons) ⊞

Friendly village inn renowned for its excellent real ales, traditional cider, and well-filled cobs and pork pies. The

central doorway leads into the bar with its 1920s furniture and horse-racing memorabilia. Outside, the garden is a suntrap in summer. Easily reached from the nearby canal, this gem of as pub is well worth stopping off for. It is popular, and can get busy, especially at lunchtimes and weekends. A winner of many local CAMRA awards, most recently Silver Pub of the Year 2023. Q☺🦮♣♥P🖥(9A,9C)🐾🛜

Chaddesley Corbett

Swan 🄻

High Street, DY10 4SD SO892737

☎ (01562) 777302 ⊕ theswanchaddesleycorbett.co.uk

Bathams Mild Ale, Best Bitter ⊞

Dating from 1606, this traditional inn sits at the heart of the village, featuring a public bar, side room with a real fire, and an impressive warm and welcoming lounge with a raised area for entertainment. Cobs and pies are available at lunchtime. Quiz, jazz, and open mic nights are held regularly. There is a large enclosed garden with a children's play area overlooking beautiful countryside. The pub is popular with walkers and cyclists. Bathams XXX is available in December. Regular events are held such as the Chaddesley Corbett Classic Car & Bike Show. Q☺🌳▲♣P🖥(52)🐾🛜♫

Droitwich Spa

Hop Pole 🄻

40 Friar Street, WR9 8ED (100yds from Norbury Theatre)

☎ (01905) 770155

Wye Valley HPA, Butty Bach, Wholesome Stout; house beer (by Woodcote); 1 changing beer ⊞

Popular 18th-century pub located in the old part of Droitwich between the Norbury Theatre and the fire station. There is a separate pool room adjoining the bar and a recently refurbished patio area at the rear. Four locally sourced beers are usually available, plus occasional guests. Good-value food is served at lunchtimes, and pub games plus live music on some weekends ensure a convivial atmosphere. ☺🌳◑≍♣♥P🖥♥🐾🛜♫

Talbot

19 High Street, WR9 8EJ

☎ (01905) 773871

Craddock's Crazy Sheep, Monarch's Way, Saxon Gold; 2 changing beers (sourced locally; often Fixed Wheel, Hobsons) ⊞

A friendly traditional inn at the top of High Street, with a front bar, large rear room, beer garden and sun terrace. Eight handpulls serve Craddock's beer range, plus changing ales, with the brewery's loyalty card scheme in use. The food menu is based on traditional pub dishes, but check food times in advance as they can vary. A raised garden patio and separate function room are available. Occasional themed nights, live music and monthly quiz are held. Q☺🌳◑≍♣♥P🖥(144)🐾🛜

Elmley Castle

Queen Elizabeth 🄻

Main Street, WR10 3HS

☎ (01386) 710251 ⊕ elmleycastle.com

Wye Valley Bitter; 3 changing beers (sourced nationally; often Goff's, Hop Shed, North Cotswold) ⊞

Named after Elizabeth I, who visited the village in August 1575, this old pub has a fresh, modern feel inside. It is a community pub, owned by 26 local residents who rescued it from closure. The bar has a flagstone floor, timber beams and a roaring fire. The comfortable lounge and separate dining room also act as a café during the day. It is a good place to start and end a walk up Bredon Hill. Two annual beer festivals are held on May and August bank holidays. Q➲ॐ❀◑▮P🛏❀🐾🛜

Evesham

Red Lion ◨

6 Market Place, WR11 4RE
☎ (01386) 429123 🌐 redlionevesham.co.uk

Butcombe Original; North Cotswold Moreton Mild; 2 changing beers (sourced regionally) 🅗

Community local tucked away in the corner of Market Place, with a main bar, seating area at front and side and smaller snug with its own bar and inglenook fireplace. Regular live music sessions are held throughout the week. There is no TV or food, although you are welcome to order from nearby food outlets. Four handpumps serve two regular and two changing real ales, and one real cider. Winner of a local CAMRA special award in 2023. Q➲ॐ❀≈♣◑▮🛏❀🛜♪

Trumpet Inn 🏆 ◨ ✅

13 Merstow Green, WR11 4BD (off Merstow Green car park)
☎ (01386) 442816

Hook Norton Hooky, Off The Hook, Old Hooky; 1 changing beer (often Hook Norton) 🅗

Friendly and welcoming traditional pub – probably the most westerly outlet of the Hook Norton tied estate – tucked away at the southern end of the High Street opposite the Merstow Green car park. It has a large grassed garden at the rear with further seating at the front. Home-made food is served daily, with many weekly specials and Sunday roasts. Regular darts matches are held and live sports are on TV. Local CAMRA Pub of the Year 2023. ➲ॐ❀◑▲≈♣🛏❀🛜♪

Feckenham

Rose & Crown ✅

High Street, B96 6HS
☎ (01527) 892188 🌐 roseandcrownfeckenham.co.uk

Banks's Amber Ale; Brakspear Oxford Gold; 1 changing beer (sourced locally; often Woodcote) 🅗

A welcoming family-run Grade II-listed pub in a pretty village. A traditional bar offers up to four real ales, plus at least one real cider. A wide menu of pub classics is served in the cosy lounge, with wooden settles for seating. There is a large enclosed beer garden at the rear. An annual beer festival is held over the August bank holiday. Parking is limited but there is a free car park 200 yards away. Q➲ॐ❀◑♿♣◑❀🛜♪

Finstall

Cross Inn ◨

34 Alcester Road, B60 1EW (on B4184 Finstall corner)
☎ (01527) 577328

Black Country Bradley's Finest Golden, Pig on the Wall, Fireside; 4 changing beers (sourced nationally) 🅗

Black Country Ales pub that features their portfolio beer range, as well as guest beers and ciders. Nine handpumps dispense beers (including a dedicated dark ale) and ciders, which are displayed on electronic screens. Cobs, pork pies and local Scotch eggs are available. The pub hosts charity and other events, and crib and dominoes are played. The small garden area has a heated shelter. Local CAMRA Pub of the Year 2021 and 2022, and County Pub of the Year 2019 and 2022. ➲ॐ❀◑♿♣◑P🛏(52,52A)❀🛜

Hanley Broadheath

Fox Inn ◨

WR15 8QS (on B4204 E of Tenbury Wells) SO671652
☎ (01886) 853189

Bathams Best Bitter; Brakspear Oxford Gold; 1 changing beer 🅗

A large 16th-century black-and-white timbered free house. The bar is decorated with hops and has a large fireplace with a wood-burning stove. The panelled dining area is separated from the bar by wooden beams. The games room has a pool table, TV and darts. Home-made food, including Sunday lunch, is available, with bar snacks at any time. Q➲ॐ❀◑▲♣◑P🛏(309)❀🛜♪

Hanley Castle

Three Kings ★ ◨

Church End, WR8 0BL (signed off B4211) SO838420
☎ (01684) 592686

Butcombe Original; 4 changing beers (often Beowulf, Hop Shed) 🅗

This unspoilt 15th-century country pub on the village green near the church has been identified by CAMRA as having a nationally important historic pub interior. Run by the same family since 1911, it remains a rare example of a place for conversation over a beer. There is a small snug with a large inglenook, serving hatch and settle wall. Nell's Lounge has another inglenook and plenty of beams. The three guest ales are often from local breweries and include a stout or porter. Live music features on Sunday evening, with regular lunchtime sing-arounds on Fridays. Cash only. Q➲ॐ❀♣◑P🛏(332)❀♪

Hartlebury

Tap House ◨

Station Road, DY11 7YJ (backs onto Hartlebury Station platform)
☎ (01299) 253275 🌐 thetaphousehartlebury.co.uk

Hartlebury Hooker, Off the Rails, Rambo Mango, APA; 2 changing beers (sourced nationally; often Hobsons, Woodcote, Wye Valley) 🅗

A modern conversion of the former railway station, next to the platform at Hartlebury station. The lounge bar has comfortable bench seating and a large fireplace with a wood-burner. Outside, tables and covered seating on the terrace overlook the valley. Home-cooked food is available all day including light lunches, baguettes, full meals and a specials board. Six or seven real ales are from national and local breweries including four from the adjacent Hartlebury brewery. Usually closes mid-evening; food finishes at 8pm. ➲❀◑♿≈P❀🛜

Himbleton

Galton Arms ◨

Harrow Lane, WR9 7LQ
☎ (01905) 391672 🌐 thegaltonarms.co.uk

Banks's Amber Ale; Bathams Best Bitter; Wye Valley HPA; 1 changing beer (sourced locally) 🅗

This friendly and welcoming rural pub on the edge of the village is popular with locals and visitors alike. It is one of very few outlets for Bathams in the area. The unspoilt interior has original beams that divide the space, and is warmed by open fires. Good-value food is served in one of two separate dining areas. Sports TV is shown in the bar area. The beer garden is suitable for children. Q➲ॐ❀◑♿P🛏(356)❀

Kemerton

Crown ℒ
High Street, GL20 7HP
☎ (01386) 725020 🌐 thecrownkemerton.co.uk
Wye Valley HPA, Butty Bach; 1 changing beer (often Goff's) Ⓗ
A delightful old pub in the centre of an idyllic Cotswold village, run by two locals who are passionate about providing a first-class experience. Situated at the foot of the famous Bredon Hill, it is ideal for walkers, and a traditional log fire greets customers in the cosy bar. There is a courtyard behind and a separate dining room serving meals prepared with local produce. B&B accommodation is available for those wishing to stay longer.
✿🛏️◑🚗🚌(540) 🐾♪

Kempsey Green Street

Huntsman Inn ℒ
Green Street, WR5 3QB (from A38 at Kempsey via Post Office Ln) SO868490
☎ (01905) 820336
Bathams Best Bitter; Greene King IPA; Morland Original Bitter Ⓗ
A 300-year-old former farmhouse that is now a cosy and friendly local with exposed beams throughout. A small main bar with a real fire to the front, with a larger bar down steps to the rear. A separate restaurant serves reasonably priced home-cooked food, but the pub is closed at lunchtimes during the week. There is also a skittle alley with its own bar, an attractive garden and a large car park. Dogs are welcome in the bar and lounge.
🌞✿◑♣P🐾

Kidderminster

Bear & Wolf 🏆 ℒ
11-17 Worcester Street, DY10 1EA
☎ (01562) 227150
House beer (by Fixed Wheel); 5 changing beers (sourced nationally; often Fownes, Moor Beer, Vocation) Ⓗ
Modern town-centre pub opened in 2019, specialising in real ales and ciders. It is deceptively spacious, with a mix of sofas, tables and high stools. Quiet background music encourages conversation and on weekends live music is featured. There are six real ales from local and regional breweries, always including a dark ale, plus some unusual beers and a variety of canned craft beers. Cobs are usually available. Local CAMRA Gold Pub of the Year 2022 and 2023. ♿➤🚗🐾🛜♪

King & Castle ℒ
Comberton Hil, DY10 1QX (next to main line station and part of Severn Valley Railway terminus)
☎ (01562) 747505
Bathams Best Bitter; Bewdley Worcestershire Way; 6 changing beers (sourced regionally; often Backyard, Salopian, Three Tuns) Ⓗ
Atmospheric recreation of a GWR terminus station bar and waiting room of the Severn Valley Railway. Handpumps dispense up to eight beers from local and regional breweries. Pub meals, cobs and snacks are available from the bar until evening, and in the restaurant when trains run. Bottled beers from Bewdley are served on the trains, and pubs along the line attract visitors using the railway. Local CAMRA Gold Pub of the Year 2019 and Bronze in 2020. May close Mondays and Tuesdays except when trains run – call ahead to check.
Q🕰️✿◑♿➤♣P🚗🐾🛜

Weavers Real Ale House ℒ
98 Comberton Hill, DY10 1QH (300yds down hill from railway station)
☎ (01562) 229413
Britt Blonde, Working Mon's Dark; Three Tuns XXX; 5 changing beers (sourced nationally; often Bristol Beer Factory, Fownes, Three Tuns) Ⓗ
One-room conversational pub serving eight interesting and changing real ales and up to four real ciders on handpump, sometimes including a perry, along with craft beers on tap. At least one dark ale is always on, and cobs are available. The pub is close to the railway station and convenient for a pint and a chat on the way into town. An award-winning local CAMRA Pub of the Year and Cider Pub of the Year, and National Pub of the Year Finalist.
Q🕰️♿➤🚗🐾🛜

Kinnersley

Royal Oak
WR8 9JR
☎ (01905) 371482 🌐 theroyaloakkinnersley.co.uk
4 changing beers (often Butcombe, Cotswold Lion, Wye Valley) Ⓗ
A rural pub at the centre of a quiet village, with a front bar and separate restaurant areas behind. Patio benches are out the front for warmer weather. The changing beers are often from local craft breweries. Live music features on the last weekend of each month. Children and dogs are welcome. It is close to the National Trust's Croome Park. B&B accommodation is offered in the converted stable block. Q🕰️✿🛏️◑♿🏕️♣P🚗🐾🛜♪

Knightwick

Talbot ℒ
WR6 5PH (on B4197, 400yds from A44 jct)
☎ (01886) 821235 🌐 the-talbot.co.uk
Teme Valley T'Other, This, That Ⓗ **; 2 changing beers (often Teme Valley)**
A 14th-century coaching inn off the main road. There is a large lounge bar, divided into two by a huge fireplace, a separate taproom and an attractive conservatory. A small wood-panelled restaurant serves an imaginative menu using local ingredients. There is a beer garden to the side and another at the front leading down to the river. A food trailer operates in the summer. Teme Valley brewery is behind the pub. Beer festivals feature in April, June and early October (for green-hopped beers). Dogs and walkers are welcomed.
Q🕰️✿🛏️◑♿♣P(420) 🐾🛜♪

Lulsley

Fox & Hounds ℒ
WR6 5QT
☎ (01886) 821228 🌐 foxandhoundslulsley.com
Ledbury Gold; Wye Valley HPA; 2 changing beers (often Goff's, Three Tuns) Ⓖ
A large pub in a rural village, with two bars from the original Victorian building, warmed by an open fire. The building has been extended with a large dining room and conservatory on the side featuring a baby grand. There is level access to the bar through the front door. At the back is an extensive garden and children's play area, with the river Teme and the Worcestershire Way beyond. Local beers and local produce are on the menu. A beer festival is held on the spring bank holiday.
Q🕰️✿◑♣P🐾🛜

Malvern

Great Malvern Hotel L
Graham Road, WR14 2HN (near crossroads with Church St)
☎ (01684) 563411 🌐 great-malvern-hotel.com
St Austell Proper Job; Timothy Taylor Landlord; 2 changing beers Ⓗ
Comfortable hotel public bar, a short walk from the Malvern Theatres complex, making it ideal for pre- and post-performance refreshment. It offers some interesting and local ales, and meals are served in the bar and in the nook dining area. There is a separate comfortable lounge with lots of sofas. The Great Shakes cellar bar features sports TV and is available for hire. Parking is limited on-site, but there is plenty of public parking nearby. Front access is via a flight of steps; smaller steps are to the side. ♿✿🛏◖◗⇌(Great Malvern)P🖪🐾🛜

Nag's Head L
19-21 Bank Street, WR14 2JG (near Graham Rd by Link Top common)
☎ (01684) 574373 🌐 nagsheadmalvern.co.uk
Banks's Amber Ale; Hook Norton Old Hooky; Wainwright; 8 changing beers (often Otter) Ⓗ
A free house with a wide selection of permanent beers and guests, plus two draught ciders. Nooks and crannies filled with mismatched furniture and foliage provide a homely environmental and the pub is busy throughout the week. Several fires burn brightly in winter. Quality food is served in the bar and separate restaurant, which has level access (but the bar does not). There is a large, covered, heated outdoor area to the front and quiet garden at the rear. The car park is small but there is ample on-street parking. Dogs are welcome (and numerous). Q✿◖◗♣🖤P🖪(44)🐾🛜♫

Weavers
14 Church Street, WR14 2AY
5 changing beers Ⓗ
Modern craft and draught ale bar in former shop, with five handpumps for real ales and two for still cider. Snacks are available but no food is served – customers can order from the Fig across the road or bring in their own hot food. A few tables are outside on the street, and there is a patio garden to the rear. The room upstairs has comfy sofas, a dartboard and board games. There is level access to the bar and ground floor. No car park, but there is plenty of parking nearby.
✿♿⇌(Great Malvern) ♣🖤🖪🐾

Monkwood Green

Fox L
WR2 6NX (S edge of Monkwood Nature Reserve, 1½ miles from A443) SO803601
☎ (01886) 889123
Wye Valley Butty Bach; 1 changing beer Ⓗ
Single-bar village local set on the common with seating around the fireplace. The Fox is the centre of many events, including skittles and indoor air rifle shooting, and has traditional pub games. Dogs are welcome, and it is ideally placed for walks in the Monk Wood nature reserve, which is renowned for butterflies and moths. Music nights are hosted on the last Friday of the month. It is a rare outlet for Barker's cider and perry.
Q✿🛏✿▲♣🖤P🖪(308)🐾♫

Redditch

Black Tap
Church Green East, B98 8BP (near top of Church Green East, opp fountain)

☎ (01527) 585969 🌐 blacktapredditch.co.uk
Backyard Blonde; 3 changing beers (sourced locally; often Oakham, Purity) Ⓗ
A converted office building and former brewpub, conveniently located near the town centre. The main bar has a roaring fire, which adds to the friendly atmosphere. A varied and interesting selection of beers is usually available along with cider. A small side room can also be booked, and live music usually features at weekends. A Pay & Display car park is close by. ♿✿🛏♣🖤P🖪🐾🛜♫

Shenstone

Plough L
DY10 4DL (off A450/A448 in village) SO865735
☎ (01562) 777340
Bathams Mild Ale, Best Bitter Ⓗ
This traditional pub has been at the heart of the village since 1840. The long single bar serves both the public bar and the lounge, which has a real fire and memorabilia of the Parachute Regiment and the Falklands War. Bathams Mild and Bitter are served all year while the stronger XXX is available in December. Snacks include cobs and pork pies. A large enclosed courtyard serves as an overflow, and there is a small patio to the front. Q✿🛏♿♣P🐾🛜

Shrawley

New Inn L
New Inn Lane, WR6 6TE (B4196 between Stourport and Worcester)
☎ (01299) 822701
Wye Valley HPA, Butty Bach; 1 changing beer (sourced nationally; often Greene King, Hobsons) Ⓗ
An independent community pub in the Worcestershire countryside, with a lounge bar, log-burner and a separate restaurant area. Being close to Shrawley Woods, it is well placed for a pint after a walk; dogs are welcome. Light snacks are served at lunchtimes, and a full menu is available in the evenings. On Sunday, traditional lunches are served until evening. The spacious garden has plenty of seating and an attractive illuminated garden. Wye Valley and other beers are available. Closed on Monday, except bank holidays.
Q✿✿◖◗▲♣P🖪(294,296) 🐾🛜

Stourport-on-Severn

Black Star L ✓
Mitton Street, DY13 8YP (just off top end of High St next to canal)
☎ (01299) 488838 🌐 theblackstar.co.uk
Wye Valley The Hopfather, HPA, Butty Bach, Wholesome Stout; 5 changing beers (sourced regionally; often Fixed Wheel, Hobsons, Three Tuns) Ⓗ
Situated next to the canal, there are moorings just through the bridge towards the basins. An attractive beer garden with a shelter, tables and raised flowerbeds overlooks the canal. The changing range of beers is from Wye Valley and other local breweries. Food is served all week, except Monday and Sunday evenings, and the menu includes steaks, fish, burgers, vegetarian and vegan options, sandwiches, baguettes and a variety of home-cooked meals. Local CAMRA Gold Pub of the Year 2020 and Bronze in 2023. ♿✿◖◗🖪🐾🛜♫

BOA Tap Room
Baldwin Road, DY13 9AX
☎ (01299) 488100 🌐 brothersofale.co.uk
BOA Peace Out, Lock N Load, The 7, 2 Step, Bone Idle, Loud Mouth; 1 changing beer (often BOA) Ⓗ

The BOA taproom and brewery is housed in a high-vaulted room, beneath an impressive old timber-trussed roof. Suspended above the tables and seating is an interesting chandelier made from old oil drums. The bar features eight handpumps, including a real cider, and six craft taps, all serving the brewery's range of interesting beers. Outside is a seating area to enjoy beer in the sunshine and during warm evenings. It is open Friday to Sunday and on bank holidays. ♿🍺🚪(3)🌞🐕🛜♪

Hollybush 🅛

Mitton Street, DY13 9AA (a short walk from main street down Gilgal)
☎ (01299) 827435
Black Country Bradley's Finest Golden, Pig on the Wall, Fireside; Sharp's Doom Bar; 4 changing beers (sourced regionally; often Burton Bridge, Mallinsons, Salopian) 🅷
A welcoming pub serving up to nine real ales from independent breweries in a relaxed and friendly atmosphere. A single bar serves a split-level lounge with many ancient timbers, a snug and an upstairs function room with a dartboard. The flower-filled beer garden at the back, accessed from upstairs, is a tranquil suntrap in summer. Good-value cobs, pork pies and Scotch eggs are available at any time of the day. Regular weekly events include live music, quizzes and TV sports.
Q🐕🌞🐱♣🚪🐕🛜♪

Tardebigge

Alestones

Unit 23 Tardebigge Court, B97 6QW
☎ (01527) 275254 🌐 alestones.co.uk
4 changing beers (sourced locally) 🅷
A well-maintained micropub sitting in a courtyard alongside several small independent shops and businesses. There are usually four beers available, including a golden ale, dark beer and a best bitter as well as real cider and perry. Though extended to the rear and side, the pub still retains its cosy convivial atmosphere, but now with room to stretch your legs. Local musicians are hosted once a month on Sunday. Pub snacks are usually available. Q🐕🌞♣🚪P🚪(52,52A)♪

Tenbury Wells

Market Tavern

Market Square, WR15 8BL
☎ (01584) 810982
Black Country Bradley's Finest Golden, Pig on the Wall, Fireside; 6 changing beers 🅷
Situated next to the historic Grade II-listed market hall, the Market Tavern has recently reopened after extensive refurbishment by Black Country Ales. As well as real ales from their own microbrewery in Lower Gornal, the pub offers a selection of six guest ales and two guest ciders. Fresh cobs, pork pies and Scotch eggs are available daily.
Q🍺♣🚪🐕

Upper Wyche

Wyche Inn 🅛

Wyche Road, WR14 4EQ (on B4218, follow signs from Malvern to Colwall)
☎ (01684) 575396 🌐 thewycheinn.co.uk
Wye Valley HPA; 3 changing beers (sourced regionally; often Ledbury) 🅷
Situated above Great Malvern, this free house is the highest pub in Worcestershire, with panoramic views towards the Cotswolds from the bar and patio. It has two bars on different levels, with a dedicated dining area in

one, offering home-cooked food. The regular real ales are paired with others from small and microbreweries. Green-hop beers are available throughout October. B&B accommodation, self-contained flats and a cottage are all available, making it ideally situated for hill walkers and those who wish to stay over.
Q🌞🛏🍴🐕♣P🚪(675)🌞🐕🛜♪

Upton upon Severn

Olde Anchor Inn 🅛 ✅

5 High Street, WR8 0HQ
☎ (01684) 593735 🌐 anchorupton.co.uk
Hobsons Best; St Austell Tribute; Sharp's Doom Bar; Wye Valley Butty Bach; 2 changing beers 🅷
An traditional old black & white oak-beamed pub dating from 1601 and mentioned in Cromwell's dispatches. It has low ceilings and many small rooms and alcoves, plus a patio garden. The bar, featuring a large fireplace and range, is separate from the restaurant area. Sandwiches and a full food menu are available. An additional wood-panelled function room is available for meetings and parties. Events are hosted throughout the year including quizzes. Q🌞🍴🚪🚪🐕🛜♪

Weatheroak

Coach & Horses 🅛

Weatheroak Hill, B48 7EA (Alvechurch to Wythall road) SP057740
☎ (01564) 823386 🌐 coachandhorsesinn.uk
Holden's Golden Glow; Hook Norton Old Hooky; Weatheroak Hill Slow Lane, IPA, Cofton Common; 5 changing beers (sourced nationally; often Hobsons, St Austell) 🅷
Traditional rural coaching inn with an idyllic beer garden. The bar remains untouched, with a log fire, tiled floor and old church pews, while a modern lounge offers comfy sofas and a restaurant. Four beers are usually stocked from the on-site brewery housed in the former stables, alongside a wider selection from regional independents. Freshly made rolls are always available. Sunday evening opening hours may vary in winter. The pub is adjacent to Icknield Street, the old Roman road.
🐕🌞🍴🐕♣P🐕🛜

Worcester

Ale Hub Micropub 🅛

Unit 1B, Abbotsbury Court, WR5 3TY
🌐 alehub.co.uk
Wye Valley Butty Bach; 3 changing beers (sourced locally; often Bewdley, Dancing Duck, Salopian) 🅷
Opened in 2021, this micropub is in a converted shop premises, close to the Tesco superstore, in the residential district of St Peter's to the south of the city, accessible by bus. It offers four changing, and often unusual, handpulled ales, alongside cocktails and craft keg. It has is a warm friendly atmosphere, with weekly bingo and quiz nights. There is level access to the bar. Dogs are welcome. Q🐕🚪(32)🐕

Bull Baiters Inn

43-49 St Johns, WR2 5AG
☎ (01905) 427601 🌐 bullbaiters.com
6 changing beers (sourced locally) 🅷
A small bar housed in a medieval building with an interesting history, previously a hall house. A high beamed ceiling and a large stone fireplace give an olde-worlde ambience conducive to conversation. A small room upstairs provides additional seating, and features an original painted wall and a mummified cat. The ever-

changing beers, up to six, are usually sourced locally and are complemented by eight ciders and perries. Simple snacks are available. Q🏠🌳🍴🍽🍺🐕🛜

Dragon Inn 🍸

51 The Tything, WR1 1JT (on A449, 300yds N of Foregate St Station)

☎ (01905) 25845 ⊕ thedragoninnworcester.co.uk

Church End Goat's Milk, Gravediggers Ale, What the Fox's Hat, Fallen Angel; 4 changing beers (often Church End) Ⓗ

A Georgian building on the edge of the city centre run by Church End brewery. The room at the front has a cosy fire, while the bar is towards the back. The old passageway to the side has seating and is decorated with odds and ends. The yard behind features another covered area, with a log-burner for colder months, and more seating beyond. There is easy level access through the gates at the rear. Bar snacks such as Scotch eggs are always available.

Q🏠🌳♿➴(Foregate Street) 🌳🍴🍽🛜♪

Imperial Tavern Ⓛ

35 St Nicholas Street, WR1 1UW

☎ (01905) 619472

Black Country Bradley's Finest Golden, Pig on the Wall, Fireside; 6 changing beers (often Oakham, Salopian) Ⓗ

This smart city pub is run by the Black Country brewery. It serves three real ales from the brewery alongside up to six from small breweries around the country and up to six real ciders. Three drinking areas are joined by the bar running front to back. Pictures of old Worcester pubs and street scenes decorate the walls. Cobs are available at lunchtime. There is level access to the bar.

Q🍽♿➴(Foregate Street) 🌳🍴🍽🐕🛜♪

Plough Ⓛ

23 Fish Street, WR1 2HN (on Deansway)

☎ (01905) 21381

Hobsons Best; 4 changing beers (sourced regionally; often Salopian) Ⓗ

A Grade II-listed pub near the cathedral. A short flight of steps leads to a tiny bar with rooms leading off to either side. The beers usually come from breweries in Worcestershire and the surrounding counties, but occasionally from small breweries further afield. Draught cider and perry is from Barbourne in the city. There is also an ever-changing range of whiskies for the connoisseur. Outside is a small patio area. Filled rolls are available at weekends and when the cricket is on.

Q🍽🌳♿➴(Foregate Street) 🌳🍴🍽♪

Breweries

Ambridge

Unit 2A, Priory Piece Business Park, Priory Farm Lane, Inkberrow, WR7 4HT ☎ 07498 628238
⊕ ambridgebrewery.co.uk

⊛Ambridge commenced brewing in 2013, initially for the family run pub, and expansion was achieved by acquiring the Wyre Piddle brewery. As well as the main beer range a number of seasonal and specials are brewed throughout the year. Occasional small run bottling is also carried out. Brewing is currently suspended. ‼♦LIVE

Bewdley SIBA

Unit 7, Bewdley Craft Centre, Lax Lane, Bewdley, DY12 2DZ

☎ (01299) 405148 ⊕ bewdleybrewery.co.uk

⊗ Bewdley began brewing in 2008 on a six-barrel plant in an old school. This was upgraded to a 10-barrel plant in 2014. Beers are brewed with a railway theme for the nearby Severn Valley Railway. The brewery has an onsite tap and shop. Element gin is also produced. 🍺♦LIVE♦

Worcestershire Way (ABV 3.6%) GOLD
Refreshing golden ale with a citrus, faintly orange peel aroma, leads to a balanced hop, malt and grapefruit taste and a lingering hoppy finish.
Baldwin IPA (ABV 4.2%) GOLD
Jubilee (ABV 4.3%) BITTER
Pale colour, fruit and citrus aroma, sweet malt with underlying citrus taste.
Red Hill (ABV 4.4%) BITTER
Worcestershire Sway/ 2857 (ABV 5%) BITTER
Complex, amber-coloured bitter, sometimes badged as 2857. Fragrant malty aroma, well-balanced, slightly sweet malt and hops taste with hints of toffee and marmalade, malt with citrus and meadow grass finish.
William Mucklow's Dark Mild (ABV 6%) MILD
Dark in colour, malty, sweetish fruity flavour with slight liquorice finish.

BOA (Brothers of Ale)

Unit 3, Anglo Buildings, Baldwin Road, Stourport-on-Severn, DY13 9AX
☎ (01299) 488100 ☎ 07725 724934
⊕ brothersofale.co.uk

What started as a hobby soon became a passion and BOA Brewery was established in 2018, before opening its doors in 2019. It is situated in the heart of Stourport-on-Severn and produces New World-style hoppy beers. ♦

Peace Out (ABV 3.6%) BITTER
Lock n Load (ABV 4.2%) GOLD
The 7 (ABV 4.2%) BITTER
2 Step (ABV 4.4%) PALE
Re-wind (ABV 4.7%) GOLD
VVD Oatmeal Stout (ABV 4.7%) STOUT
Bone Idle (ABV 4.8%) GOLD
Loud Mouth (ABV 5.2%) GOLD

Boat Lane

Unit 3, Streamside Business Park, Boat Lane, Offenham, Evesham, WR11 8RS
☎ (01386) 719558. ⊕ boatlanebrewery.co.uk

A microbrewery established in 2017 by Ian Hazeldene in a small village near Evesham. An ever-changing range of beers are brewed, with up to eight available in the brewery bar at weekends. ♦

Brew61 SIBA

Greenfields Farm, Upton Warren, Bromsgrove, B61 7EZ
☎ (01527) 879472 ⊕ brew61.co.uk

Tim Dunkley started brewing as a hobby, opening a small 'pub' for friends and family on the farm. As his brewing prowess grew the equipment he used grew, and he needed more space. A purpose-built brewery with newer larger equipment, enabled him to supply a growing demand locally. Bottles and kegged ales are sold direct from the farm. 🍺

Greenfields Gold (ABV 3.8%) PALE
Grazing Girls (ABV 4.5%) GOLD
Hop On (ABV 4.5%) GOLD

Friday Beer

Unit 4, Link Business Centre, Link Way, Malvern, WR14 1UQ
☎ (01684) 572648 ⊕ thefridaybeer.com

Founded in 2011, the Friday Beer Co primarily produces bottle-conditioned ales. The range of bottles now sells across the region and to a growing number of outlets, from Birmingham to London, and south of the M4 corridor (including local restaurants and venues). Beer is rarely available in cask form. Brewing is currently suspended. ‼ ☴ LIVE

Hartlebury

Station Park, Station Road, Hartlebury, DY11 7YJ
☎ (01299) 253617 ☎ 07831 570117
✉ hartleburybrewingco@icloud.com

Formerly the site of Attwoods Brewery, the Hartlebury Brewing Co was established in 2019 by David Higgs, the owner of the Tap House pub adjacent to Hartlebury Railway Station. It supplies the Tap House and local free trade.

Bitter Strikes Back (ABV 3.8%) BITTER
Hooker (ABV 4%) PALE
Pale ale, malt and hops predominate on the nose, background berry fruits, then notes of grapefruit, hops, pear and melon in the taste. Finish is grapefruit fading into bitterness and finally malt.
Off the Rails (ABV 4.2%) GOLD
Golden ale, fruity aroma with a hint of honey sweetness, flavours of grapefruit, hint of nectarine and some toffee leading to a spicy aftertaste of grapefruit and a long bitter finish.
Rambo Mango (ABV 4.3%) SPECIALITY
Yellow speciality beer with mango, aromas of yeast, biscuit and a hint of mango, fruity bitter taste of hops, grapefruit, mango in the background followed by a long hoppy, then bitter finish.
APA (ABV 4.5%) PALE
Smooth yellow ale, malt and hops predominate on the nose with some background berry fruits, grapefruit, hops and pear followed by grapefruit fading into bitterness and malt in the aftertaste.

Hop Shed SIBA

Old Chicken Shed, Stocks Farm, Suckley, WR6 5EQ
☎ (01886) 884110 ☎ 07484 688026
⊕ hopshed.co.uk

Originally named Unity Brew House, brewing began in 2016, using a 10-barrel plant. It is the only brewery in the UK located on a commercial hop farm. Based in an old chicken shed, the beers are named after breeds of chicken. An onsite bar is open Friday-Saturday. ◆

Wybar (ABV 3.6%) BITTER
Sebright Golden Ale (ABV 3.8%) GOLD
Pekin (ABV 4%) PALE
Sultan (ABV 4.2%) GOLD
Frizzle British IPA (ABV 4.5%) GOLD

Lakehouse

Lake House, Peachfield Road, Malvern, WR14 3LE
☎ 07532 440634 ⊕ lakehousebrewery.com

☺Lakehouse was established in 2016 and is situated at the foot of the idyllic Malvern Hills, within the grounds of a country house and fishing lake, from which it takes its name. Beers can be found in pubs, bottle shops, restaurants, supermarkets and online retail outlets. ‼ LIVE

Little Beer (NEW)

Cornmill Road, Evesham, WR11 2LL
⊕ littlebeerbrewingcompany.co.uk

The Little Beer Brewing Co is a small batch nanobrewery that believes in returning to the basics of brewing. Keeping it simple by repeating recipes helps it to produce quality beer.

Sociable SIBA

6 – 8 Britannia Road, Worcester, WR1 3BQ ☎ 07957 583984 ⊕ thesociablebeercompany.com

☺A small craft brewery just outside Worcester city centre, established in 2017. An onsite taproom is open on Fridays. A small range of core beers is brewed, mainly for sale in the local area. ◆

Shindig (ABV 3.6%) BITTER
Bash (ABV 4%) BITTER
Wingding (ABV 4.2%) GOLD

Spilsbury & Jones (NEW)

Orleton Court Farm, Worcester, WR6 6SU ☎ 07966 294032 ⊕ spilsburyandjones.co.uk

Launched in 2018, this brewery produces beer in small batches from hops grown within a few hundred yards of the brewery. ◆

Teme Valley SIBA

🏠 **Talbot, Bromyard Road, Knightwick, WR6 5PH**
☎ (01886) 821235 ☎ 07792 394151
⊕ temevalleybrewery.co.uk

☺Teme Valley was established in 1997 to brew beer for the Talbot, Knightwick. Only hops grown in Herefordshire and Worcestershire are used in brewing, including Green Hop specials during the season. Beers are supplied throughout the West Midlands and Marches. All beers are now gluten-free. ‼ ◆ LIVE GF ◆

T'Other (ABV 3.5%) PALE
This (ABV 3.7%) BITTER
That (ABV 4.1%) BITTER
Talbot Blonde (ABV 4.4%) BLOND
Wotever Next? (ABV 5%) BITTER
Roasted malt and toffee aromas lead to a complex taste of stone fruits, dark malt, hops and melon. The finish is at first of slightly smoky malt and fruits fading into lingering dry hops.

Weatheroak Hill

🏠 **Coach and Horses, Weatheroak Hill, Alvechurch, B48 7EA**
☎ (01564) 823386 ☎ 07496 289924
✉ weatheroakhillbrewery@gmail.com

Established in 2008, Weatheroak Hill Brewery has been supplying the Coach & Horses with quality beers brewed onsite on its six-barrel brewery for over a decade, travelling a mere 50 meters from grain to glass. The free trade and CAMRA festivals are also supplied, and customers can order online for pick up and delivery. ‼ ◆

IPA (Icknield Pale Ale) (ABV 3.8%) PALE
Impossible IPA (ABV 4.1%) PALE
Slow Lane (ABV 4.4%) PALE
Cofton Common (ABV 4.9%) SPECIALITY

Wintrip

7 Copenhagen Street, Worcester, WR1 2HB

☎ (01905) 612808 ☎ 07964 196194
⊕ wintripbrew.co

Wintrip began brewing in 2014 as Three Shires Brewery on a hand-built plant in Worcester before moving to new premises at the Oil Basin Brewhouse. Local outlets are supplied. Beers may be brewed under contract at other breweries.

Butchers Beastly Best (ABV 4%) BITTER
Salt Mine Stout (ABV 4.6%) SPECIALITY

Woodcote SIBA

Woodland Road, Dodford, Bromsgrove, B61 9BT
☎ 07779 166174 ⊕ woodcotebrewery.co.uk

⊗ Opened in 2015 as Woodcote Manor in former dairy outbuildings attached to the brewer's house, the name was shortened to Woodcote in 2020. The original one-barrel plant has now expanded to seven barrels at new premises nearby, with a new mash tun and copper. The regular beers are distributed to a number of local pubs.
♦ LIVE

SSS (ABV 3.8%) GOLD
XPA (ABV 3.9%) BLOND

Half Cut (ABV 4.2%) PALE
Weavers Exclusive (ABV 4.4%) GOLD
Squires Gold (ABV 4.5%) BITTER
Oatmeal Stout (ABV 4.7%) STOUT
Dark in colour, roasted malt, chocolate and coffee tones are evident in the aroma and flavour, leading to a satisfying slightly bitter finish.
IPA (ABV 5%) GOLD
Golden, well-balanced and hoppy, grapefruit aromas are followed by a pronounced hop and slightly spicy taste, with a lingering bitter finish.

Worcester

Arch 49, Cherry Tree Walk, Worcester, WR1 3AU
☎ 07906 432049 ⊕ worcesterbrewingco.co.uk

A small brewery in the heart of Worcester and home to Sabrina Ales. A range of beers is brewed in rotation using traditional British hops, named with a loose association to the English Civil War.

Holy Ground (ABV 4.2%) BITTER
Powick Porter (ABV 4.5%) PORTER
1651 (ABV 5.1%) BITTER
Sabrina's Dark Ruby Ale (ABV 5.5%) BITTER

Plough, Shenstone (Photo: Andy Checketts Consultancy)

East Midlands

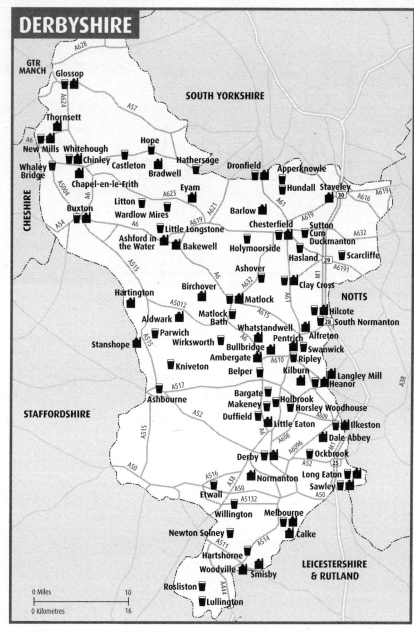

DERBYSHIRE

Map labels:
GTR MANCH · Glossop · Thornsett · New Mills · Whitehough · Chinley · Whaley Bridge · Castleton · Chapel-en-le-Frith · Hope · Hathersage · Bradwell · Dronfield · Apperknowle · Hundall · Staveley · Buxton · Eyam · Litton · Wardlow Mires · Little Longstone · Barlow · Chesterfield · Sutton Cum Duckmanton · Scarcliffe · Ashford in the Water · Bakewell · Holymoorside · Hasland · Ashover · Birchover · Clay Cross · Hartington · Matlock · NOTTS · Aldwark · Matlock Bath · Hilcote · Parwich · Whatstandwell · South Normanton · Stanshope · Wirksworth · Pentrich · Alfreton · Kniveton · Bullbridge · Swanwick · Ambergate · Ripley · Belper · Kilburn · Langley Mill · Heanor · Ashbourne · Bargate · Makeney · Holbrook · Horsley Woodhouse · Duffield · Little Eaton · Ilkeston · Dale Abbey · Derby · Ockbrook · Normanton · Long Eaton · Sawley · Etwall · Willington · Melbourne · Newton Solney · Calke · Hartshorne · Woodville · Smisby · Roshliston · Lullington

SOUTH YORKSHIRE · CHESHIRE · STAFFORDSHIRE · LEICESTERSHIRE & RUTLAND

0 Miles 10
0 Kilometres 16

Apperknowle

Traveller's Rest 🄻

High Street, S18 4BD SK384782

☎ (01246) 460169

Acorn Barnsley Bitter; Bradfield Farmers Blonde; Timothy Taylor Landlord; 3 changing beers (sourced nationally; often Fuggle Bunny, Rudgate, Titanic) Ⓗ
The Travs, also referred to locally as the Corner Pin, is a traditional country pub with several different seating areas around a corner bar. Up to six quality real ales are sold, together with numerous fruit-based ciders and perries. The outdoor roadside seating area affords sweeping views across the Drone Valley. Good-quality

food is on offer including the ever-popular cheese and pork pie platters, which can also be ordered to take away. Q🕸🛏🌮🕭♣🅿🚲(15)🐾🛜

Ashbourne

Smith's Tavern 🍷

36 St John Street, DE6 1GH

☎ (01335) 300809

Banks's Sunbeam; Brakspear Gravity; Marston's Pedigree; Ringwood Fortyniner; 1 changing beer (sourced locally) Ⓗ
Small, highly traditional town-centre pub, with as many as seven real ales on. The landlord selects the widest

possible choice from Marston's portfolio of beers, and is also allowed one free choice guest ale, served at weekends, typically from a local brewery. Locally-sourced pork pies are usually available. There is a good selection of around 25 malt whiskies, and tutored tastings are offered throughout year. A frequent winner of local CAMRA Pub of the Year, six times in last nine years, including 2022. Q☞♣☺♥

Ashover

Old Poets' Corner 🄻

Butts Road, S45 0EW (downhill from church)
☎ (01246) 590888
Everards Tiger; Titanic Iceberg, Plum Porter, Captain Smith's Strong Ale; 6 changing beers (sourced regionally; often Castle Rock, Everards, Thornbridge) 🄷
This award-winning village pub has a warm welcoming atmosphere with open fires on cold days. Recently taken over by Titanic brewery, it offers 10 hand-pulled ales, including many from the Titanic range, along with changing guest ales, traditional ciders, draught and bottled Belgian beers and country wines. Winner of CAMRA national Cider Pub of the Year 2006 and local CAMRA Pub of the Year four times including 2015. Dogs are welcome. Q☺🏠◄◑&♣●P➕(63,64)☺♥♪

Bargate

White Hart

Sandbed Lane, DE56 0JA
☎ (01773) 827397
Oakham Citra; Timothy Taylor Boltmaker; 4 changing beers (sourced nationally) 🄷
The White Hart is a cosy two-roomed pub in the heart of Bargate, just outside the town of Belper. With a reputation for friendly staff, good beer and a welcoming atmosphere, it is popular with locals and has an excellent selection of changing cask and keg ales. Walkers are always welcome and bar snacks are usually available. A large beer garden is situated to the rear. Frequent local CAMRA Pub of the Year, winning the East Midlands Award in 2018. Q☞☺♣●P➕(71)☺♥

Belper

Angels Micro Pub 🏆

Market Place, DE56 1FZ (top right side of Market Place)
☎ 07527 163316
Oakham Citra; Thornbridge Jaipur IPA; Titanic Plum Porter; 5 changing beers (sourced nationally) 🄶
A quirky, friendly and popular micropub offering at least eight cask ales, the selection gradually decreasing by Sunday when the majority has been consumed! Tap takeovers or beer style events are a frequent feature. Ten real ciders plus bar snacks are also available. Live artists play most Sunday afternoons. Local CAMRA Mild Trail Winner 2019, CAMRA Cider Pub of the Year 2020 and local CAMRA Pub of the Year 2023.
☞☺&◄●P➕☺♥♪

Arkwright's Real Ale Bar

6 Campbell Street, DE56 1AP
☎ (01773) 823117
Marston's Pedigree 🄷/🄶; 6 changing beers (sourced nationally) 🄷
Situated below the Strutt Club in the centre of Belper and named after Sir Richard Arkwright, an important 18th-century mill owner, Arkwright's is a modern, friendly, one-roomed real ale bar. Popular with local drinkers, constantly changing cask ales and home-made bar

snacks are always available. A no under-14s rule ensures a quiet and relaxing environment for adults, often with live acoustic music at weekends. ☺&◄♣●🚌☺♥♪

Railway ✅

25 King Street, DE56 1PW
☎ (01773) 689987 ● railwaybelper.co.uk
Lincoln Green Marion, Archer, Hood, Tuck; 4 changing beers (sourced nationally; often Lincoln Green) 🄷
A large town-centre pub, refurbished to a good standard by Lincoln Green brewery, offering eight cask and six keg

REAL ALE BREWERIES

14 Lock ▣ Bullbridge (NEW)
3Ps Woodville
Aldwark Artisan Aldwark
Alter Ego ✦ Alfreton
Ashover Clay Cross
Bad Bunny Ambergate
Bang The Elephant Langley Mill
Bentley Brook ✦ Matlock
Big Stone Chinley (brewing suspended)
Birch Cottage Sawley
Birchover ▣ Birchover
Black Hole Little Eaton
Bottle Brook Kilburn
Brampton Chesterfield
Brunswick ▣ Derby
Buxton ✦ Buxton
Chapel-en-le-Frith Chapel-en-le-Frith
Collyfobble ▣ Barlow
Dancing Duck Derby
Derby Derby
Dovedale Stanshope
Draycott Dale Abbey
Drone Valley ✦ Dronfield
Eyam Eyam
Falstaff ▣ Derby: Normanton
Furnace ▣ Derby
Globe ▣ Glossop
Hartshorns Derby
Hollow Tree Whatstandwell
Instant Karma ▣ Clay Cross
Intrepid Bradwell
Leadmill Heanor
Leatherbritches Smisby
Little Derby
Marlpool ▣ Heanor
Matlock Wolds Farm Matlock
Moody Fox Hilcote
Moot ▣ Matlock
Morgan Brewmasters ▣ ✦ Melbourne
Muirhouse Ilkeston
Old Sawley ▣ Long Eaton
Peak Ashford in the Water
Pentrich Pentrich
Popeye ▣ Heanor (NEW)
RBA Derby
Red Dog Ilkeston (NEW)
Resting Devil ▣ Chesterfield
Rock Mill New Mills (brewing suspended)
Shiny ✦ Little Eaton
Silver Staveley
Temper ▣ Dronfield
Thorley & Sons Ilkeston
Thornbridge Bakewell
Thornsett ✦ Thornsett
Tollgate ✦ Calke
Torrside New Mills
Townes ▣ Staveley
Urban Chicken Ilkeston
Whim Hartington

ales, with a loyalty card scheme on cask ales. It has a large beer garden to the rear. Bar meals are available until early evening and occasional live music on Saturdays is popular. This is a welcome addition to the award-winning main shopping street of Belper, providing a pub walk link between Bridge Street and Market Place pubs. ☞❀⌖◑&≈❀P⊞❀🛜♪

Buxton

Ale Stop 🗓

Chapel Street, SK17 6HX
☎ 07801 364619
4 changing beers (sourced nationally) 🅗
The first micropub in the High Peak, a two-room converted shop off Buxton Market Square. Beer is the main event here, with four changing ales from microbreweries up and down the country, as well as two boxed ciders. The objective is to bring to Buxton beers that are rarely, if ever, seen in the town. The enthusiastic staff ensure a warm and friendly welcome. An eclectic choice of background music on vinyl is played. A log-burning stove is a welcome addition for the winter. ☞&◑❀❀🛜♪

Buxton Brewery Cellar Bar 🗓

George Street, SK17 6AT
☎ (01298) 214085
4 changing beers (sourced locally; often Buxton) 🅗
Owned and run by Buxton brewery, the bar is next door but one to the Tap House. The single room is divided into two seating areas and the décor is simple, with an original brick vaulted ceiling. Four cask beers from the brewery are served from handpumps on the bar. There is also a selection of Buxton KeyKeg, canned and bottled beers, as well as cider from Hogan's. An outdoor seating area is at the front. ❀❀≈❀⊞❀

Buxton Tap House 🗓

11-16 The Old Court House, George Street, SK17 6AT
☎ (01298) 214085
4 changing beers (sourced locally; often Buxton) 🅗
The Tap House is in Buxton's café quarter at the rear of the crescent. The tap for Buxton brewery, it has four handpumps serving a regularly changing range of the brewery's cask beers, and up to 16 fonts serve a variety of KeyKeg beers in different styles and strengths. The beers available are listed on the beer blackboard. A varied food menu is also available. The cellar is shared by the nearby Cellar Bar. ☞❀&≈❀⊞❀🛜

Cheshire Cheese 🗓

37-39 High Street, SK17 6HA
☎ (01298) 212453
Everards Tiger; Titanic Steerage, Iceberg, White Star, Plum Porter, Captain Smith's Strong Ale; 4 changing beers 🅗
A double-fronted building of considerable age, which was refurbished before reopening under the management of Titanic in 2013. The pub is essentially open-plan but is split into several distinct areas. Low ceilings with original beams add to the cosy atmosphere and there are two open fires. The bar boasts an array of 10 handpumps serving a range of Titanic beers and guests. Home-made food is available. Entertainment is provided on Saturday evenings and there is a quiz on Sundays. Q☞❀◑&⌖P⊞❀🛜♪

RedWillow Buxton 🗓

1 Cavendish Circus, SK17 6AT
☎ (01298) 807582
RedWillow Wreckless; 2 changing beers (sourced locally; often RedWillow) 🅗

Opened in late 2017 and located in a former bank in the centre of Buxton, this is RedWillow brewery's second bar. Original features have been retained such as etched windows and the mahogany and glass office, with the addition of a new bar and smaller mezzanine area. Three of the brewery's cask ales are served from handpumps on the bar and craft keg beers from various breweries are available. Cider is from Hogan's. Pizzas are served daily and there is live music weekly. ☞◑&≈❀⊞❀🛜

Castleton

Olde Nag's Head 🗓

1 Cross Street, S33 8WH
☎ (01433) 620248 ⊕ yeoldenagshead.co.uk
Abbeydale Moonshine; Sharp's Doom Bar; 4 changing beers (sourced locally; often Abbeydale, Bradfield, Intrepid) 🅗
The bar area of this busy family run 17th-century coaching inn has a feature fireplace, exposed stone walls and carved wooden chairs and is adjacent to the stylish restaurant. The impressive array of handpumps dispense what is possibly the largest range of cask beers in the Hope Valley, mainly sourced from local breweries. There is a quiz on Friday nights and live music every Saturday night. ☞❀◑ ▲P⊞(173,272)❀🛜♪

Chesterfield

Anchor 🗓

Factory Street, Brampton, S40 2FW
☎ (01246) 460070
Timothy Taylor Landlord; 4 changing beers (often Ashover, Empire, Thornbridge) 🅗
A lively pub with music and weekly quiz nights, it has five handpull beers on the bar. Landlord is their permanent offering, with the four on rotation usually Ashover, Abbeydale, Thornbridge or Empire brews. Craft beer offerings are also usually available. Food is served in the evening during the week, and from lunchtime at weekends. A dartboard and pool table are available, as well as good outside seating for warmer days. ❀◑♣⊞♪

Beer Parlour 🗓

1 King Street North, Whittington Moor, S41 9BA
☎ 07870 693411 ⊕ the-beer-parlour.co.uk
8 changing beers (sourced nationally; often Abbeydale) 🅗
The Beer Parlour is a cosy, popular drinking establishment which is slightly tucked away off the main road and close to the home stadium of Chesterfield FC. Up to eight changing real ales are available via handpump to drink in or take out, and there is an extensive selection of fonts dispensing continental ales and ciders. Bottled continental and local beers and box cider and perries also available to drink in or take away. Q&⊞❀

Chesterfield Alehouse 🗓

37 West Bars, S40 1AG
6 changing beers 🅗
A popular micropub with good, friendly staff and an excellent selection of beers and locally-produced ciders. Six lines of cask ales, eight KeyKeg taps and extensive bottle range give plenty to choose from. Regular tap takeovers feature breweries not often seen in the area. Local CAMRA Cider Pub of the Year 2023. A seating area upstairs can be booked, and free-to-air sports are often shown in the upstairs room. Q&♣❀⊞❀🛜

Chesterfield Arms ♟ Ⓛ

40 Newbold Road, S41 7PH
☎ (01246) 236634 ⊕ chesterfieldarms.co.uk
Draught Bass; Everards Tiger; Timothy Taylor Landlord; Resting Devil Twisted Pale; 6 changing beers (sourced nationally; often Abbeydale, Oakham, Thornbridge) Ⓗ

A multi-award winning real ale pub in Chesterfield serving homemade pizzas alongside real ales, craft beers, ciders and everything else in between. 2022 has seen the introduction of its own brewery, the Resting Devil and their house brew, Twisted Pale is a permanent addition to the bar's roster of up to 10 cask ales. A weekly quiz is held on Wednesday, as well as regular live music and beer festivals. The conservatory doors open up on warm summer evenings. Local CAMRA Pub of the Year 2022 and 2023. Q ✆ ⛲ ⓓ ♿ ☐ (1,1A) ● ⚲ 🎵

Glassworks Ⓛ

388 Sheffield Road, Whittington Moor, S41 8LF
☎ (01246) 768688 ⊕ theglassworkschesterfield.co.uk
Brampton Golden Bud; 6 changing beers (sourced nationally; often Brampton) Ⓗ

The third of Chesterfield-based Brampton brewery's pubs was acquired in 2019 and is situated opposite the home of Chesterfield FC. The bar has up to eight handpulls, one for the regular ale, one for a rotating popular cider with the remaining being for a wide range of Brampton ales plus ever-changing guests. The main bar area has two sports TV screens and there is a snug to the rear. Historical photos adorning the walls. Q ⛲ ♣ ☐ ● ⚲ 🎵

Market Pub Ⓛ

95 New Square, S40 1AH
☎ (01246) 273641 ⊕ themarketpub.co.uk
8 changing beers (sourced nationally) Ⓗ

Premium gastro-pub located in the Chesterfield market square. Typically eight changing cask ales are on offer alongside quality home-cooked food made with local produce served lunchtime and early evening. Regular events held include murder mysteries, gourmet food nights, wine, whiskey and spirit tastings and general knowledge and music quizzes. Several small beer festivals are held throughout the year. Check Facebook and their website for further details. Payment by card is not accepted. ⛲ⓓ ⛺ ♣ ☐ 🎵

Rose & Crown Ⓛ ✓

104 Old Road, Brampton, S40 2QT (1¼ miles from Chesterfield town centre on the jct of Old Rd and Old Hall Rd)
☎ (01246) 563750 ⊕ roseandcrownbrampton.co.uk
Brampton Golden Bud, Best; Everards Tiger; 7 changing beers (sourced nationally; often Brampton) Ⓗ

A Project William pub by Everards, this award-winning pub is a tied house to Brampton brewery situated at the top end of the Brampton Mile. There are monthly live jazz sessions, regular real ale festivals and live music evenings throughout the year. The drinks selection includes bottled Belgian beers, seven changing beers on handpump, keg fonts and up to 10 ciders and perries. There is a compact snug, and memorabilia from the old Brampton brewery festoons the walls.
Q ✆ ⛲ⓓ ♣ ☐ (170) ● ⚲

Spread Eagle

7 Beetwell Street, S40 1SH
☎ (01246) 234971 ⊕ thespreadeagle.co.uk
4 changing beers (sourced nationally; often Ashover, Thornbridge, Timothy Taylor) Ⓗ

This historic Grade II-listed public house has been carefully refurbished inside and out. Four beers are

normally available, typically including Jaipur, Landlord, Ashover Citra and Peak Ales Best. This cosy and traditional pub also hosts six luxury en-suite bedrooms and has a private car park in the town centre. There is a well-appointed patio area to the rear. On Saturdays and Sundays breakfast is offered, as well as food lunchtime through to evening (not Mon-Tue). Q ✆ ⓓ ♿ ☐ ● ⚲

Tap House

318 Chatsworth Road, Brampton, S40 2BY
☎ (01246) 234731
Draught Bass; 8 changing beers (sourced nationally) Ⓗ

Traditional friendly pub with a central bar, etched windows and tiled flooring. It serves a wide choice of up to nine changing local and national beers, normally including Draught Bass. Music can be heard in the main bar monthly, see their Facebook page or flyers for dates and details. A quiet room is available to the rear of the pub, which also has a covered outdoor area. Hot and cold snacks are available along with hot roast cobs on Sunday. Local CAMRA Spring Pub of the Season 2023. ⛲☐ ● ⚲

Tramway Tavern Ⓛ ✓

192 Chatsworth Road, Brampton, S40 2AT
☎ (01246) 200111 ⊕ tramwaytavern.co.uk
Brampton Golden Bud, Best; Everards Tiger; 5 changing beers (often Brampton) Ⓗ

This is the second tied house for the Brampton brewery, and is their tap, only two minutes' walk from the brewery itself. Eight handpulls on the bar feature up to four Brampton ales, one Everards and three guests. A selection of world beers are also available, along with traditional ciders and perries. An area is dedicated to pictures and history of the old Chesterfield tram service that once passed by. An outdoor courtyard to the rear contains the Tramshed function room. Q ⛲ ♣ ☐ ● ⚲

Clay Cross

Rykneld Turnpyke Ⓛ

4 John Street, S45 9NQ
☎ (01246) 250366
4 changing beers Ⓗ

Formerly Egstow Working Men's Club, the Rykneld Turnpyke (named after Rykneld Street, the old road between Chesterfield and Derby) is the brewery tap of the Instant Karma brewing company (not currently brewing). It features a large bar with up to four cask ales, craft keg and a variety of bottles and ciders. There is a large open room divided into different areas, with comfortable seating and two log burners. It has a cosy and welcoming feel and is dog friendly. A former local CAMRA Pub of the Year on several occasions.
♣ ● ☐ (54) ⚲

Derby

Alexandra Hotel Ⓛ

203 Siddals Road, DE1 2QE
☎ (01332) 293993 ⊕ alexandrahotelderby.co.uk
Castle Rock Harvest Pale; 7 changing beers (sourced nationally) Ⓗ

A Castle Rock pub serving the brewery's own beers and up to five guest ales, with a good range of styles. There is also a wide selection of UK and continental bottled and canned beers of varying styles. Themed food nights are held monthly. The lounge is adorned with breweriana and the bar with railway memorabilia. A class 37 railway locomotive cab resides in the car park. The birthplace of Derby CAMRA in 1974. Q ✆ ⛲ ✉ ♿ ≠ ♣ ☐ ● ⚲

Brunswick Inn L

1 Railway Terrace, DE1 2RU

☎ (01332) 290677 ⊕ brunswickderby.co.uk

Brunswick White Feather, Triple Hop, The Usual; Everards Beacon Hill, Tiger; Timothy Taylor Landlord; 8 changing beers (sourced nationally) ⊞

Built in 1841, this is the oldest purpose-built railway inn in the UK. The flatiron-shaped pub is part of the North Midland Railway Village and was restored from a derelict condition and reopened in 1987 – evidenced by the press-cuttings in the main bar. The Brunswick microbrewery was added in 1991 and is visible at one end of the pub. The large pub features four separate rooms, flagstoned floors and an upstairs function area. Gets busy on match days. Truly unmissable.

Q ☽ ❀ ◑ ᵭ ≉ ♣ ♠ ➡ P ❀ ⟨ ♪

Creaky Floorboard L

179 Kedleston Road, DE22 1FT

☎ 07974 749517

House beer (by Derby); 3 changing beers (sourced locally) ⊞

This micropub is deceptively spacious with two interior rooms and a courtyard garden. Established in 2018, from a former doctors' surgery, the interior layout still resembles a terraced house. The bar in the right-hand room, with a real fire, offers good real ale, normally including a LocAle. Pork pies, cobs and four pint takeaways are available. Books, cards and board games are offered and an open mic night is hosted every Tuesday. Limited parking at front. Q ❀ ♠ ➡ ❀

Exeter Arms L ✓

13 Exeter Place, DE1 2EU

☎ (01332) 605323 ⊕ exeterarms.co.uk

Dancing Duck Ay up; Marston's Pedigree; 4 changing beers (sourced nationally) ⊞

This quirky, multi-roomed pub was formed from a number of different buildings and the interior boasts numerous sections, including a raised area, as a result. The site has been a licensed premises for over 100 years. Offering six handpumps, including the best selection of Dancing Duck ales in any Derby pub, complemented by contemporary, cutting-edge food, this gem of a pub also boasts a secluded courtyard garden and memorabilia from the punk rock band Anti-Pasti. ☽ ❀ ◑ ➡ ❀ ⟨

Falstaff ▾ L

74 Silverhill Road, Normanton, DE23 6UJ

☎ (01332) 342902 ⊕ falstaffbrewery.co.uk

Falstaff Fistful of Hops, Phoenix, Smiling Assassin; 1 changing beer (sourced locally) ⊞

Originally a coaching inn before the Normanton neighbourhood was built up, it is now the Falstaff brewery tap and the only real ale house in the area. This three-roomed corner pub sits awkwardly among traditional terraced housing. The rear lounge is a shrine to Offilers brewery, with a large display of memorabilia. Other collectables can be viewed in the games room and second bar room. Local CAMRA Pub of the Year 2023.

Q ☽ ❀ ♣ ➡ (4,7) ❀

Flowerpot L

23-25 King Street, Cathedral Quarter, DE1 3DZ

☎ (01332) 204955 ⊕ flowerpotderby.com

Marston's Pedigree; Oakham Bishops Farewell; Sharp's Doom Bar; Whim Hartington IPA ⊞; 5 changing beers (sourced nationally) ⊞/�servG

Dating from around 1800 but much expanded from its original premises into the neighbouring car tyre centre, this vibrant pub reaches back from the roadside frontage and divides into several interlinking rooms. One room provides the stage for regular live bands; another has a

glass cellar wall revealing stillaged casks. The popular Gurkha curry nights take place every Tuesday and Wednesday evening. An attractive outside seating area provides a summer entertainment area.

☽ ❀ ◑ ᵭ ♣ ♠ ➡ ❀ ⟨ ♪

Furnace Inn L

9 Duke Street, DE1 3BX

☎ (01332) 385981

Furnace Fun Sponge; Shiny 4 Wood; 6 changing beers (sourced nationally) ⊞

A former Hardys & Hansons pub that reopened in 2012, it has been transformed into a real ale mecca. It is now the tap for the Furnace brewery and features up to eight real ales and three ciders/perries complemented by a variety of UK craft beer. There are two distinct open-plan rooms, with a central bar and a large rear garden. Poker, quiz and cheese nights feature weekly with regular beer festivals held throughout the year. ☽ ❀ ◑ ᵭ ♣ ♠ P ❀ ⟨

Golden Eagle L

55 Agard Street, DE1 1DZ

☎ (01332) 230600

Titanic Plum Porter; 3 changing beers (sourced nationally) ⊞

Now a stand-alone corner building in an area of student accommodation, a large mural on the outside pays homage to Derby's history. Inside, the long single room has a wooden floor throughout. It is comfortable and welcoming, with a table next to the bar for newspapers and local interest books. A walled paved area at the back provides a pleasant alternative drinking spot. An upstairs function room is also available. ☽ ❀ ♣ P ➡ ❀ ⟨ ♪

Hole in the Wall L

24 Uttoxeter Road, Mickleover, DE3 0ZQ

☎ (01332) 501301 ⊕ holeinthewall-dbc.co.uk

Derby Business As Usual, Dashingly Dark; 4 changing beers (sourced regionally) ⊞

Opened in 2020, this is a former NatWest bank building on the corner with Station Road in the centre of Mickleover. The pub has a large pleasant single room with the bar at the back to one side. It is operated by the Derby Brewing Co, whose beers are prominent among the six hand-pulled beers on offer. There is an excellent selection of bar snacks. ♠ P ➡ ❀

Hoptimist L

91 Sitwell Street, Spondon, DE21 7FH

4 changing beers (sourced nationally) ⊞

Spondon's first micropub was converted from a hardware store in the centre of the village and opened in 2021. Entrance is into the front room, which hosts the bar and provides a selection of comfortable high and low seating. The back room, set slightly lower, provides more seating in a bright atmosphere. The bar features a changing range of beers, normally including some local ales. ᵭ ➡

Little Chester Ale House L

4 Chester Green Road, Chester Green, DE1 3SF

☎ 07830 367125

Draught Bass; Hartshorns Ignite; 2 changing beers (sourced nationally) ⊞

The first micropub in Derby is located on the corner of Chester Green. The layout has been reworked since first opening, with the bar moving to the back of the pub and every inch of space being put to good use. This is Hartshorn's brewery tap but it also features other guest ales. There is a sheltered garden area to the rear, and vibrant, fresh quirky decoration throughout.

Q ☽ ♣ ➡ ❀ ⟨

No. 189 Ⓛ

189 Blenheim Drive, Allestree, DE22 2GN

Little Brewing Company Epiphany Pale Ale; Shiny Affinity; 4 changing beers (sourced regionally) Ⓗ

Opened in 2018 in the large Allestree estate, this former launderette and then beauticians has proved popular. The single-room micropub offers a choice of six real ales, with three craft ale taps also on the bar. Furnishings include a mix of high and low seating, while outside there is a large covered seating area at the front. There is a good bus service to the centre of Derby.
Q ⎈ ❀ ✿ P � ◉ 🛈

Peacock Inn Ⓛ

87 Nottingham Road, DE1 3QS

☎ (01332) 370713

Hartshorns Ignite; Marston's Pedigree; Whim Flower Power; 2 changing beers (sourced nationally) Ⓗ

This attractive 18th-century stone-built roadside pub used to be a staging post on the main coach road out of Derby, which ran alongside the old Derby Canal. The front and back rooms are set on different levels but served by a central bar. The decoration consist of wooden floors, stove burners, photos of old Derby and Derby County memorabilia. There is a large patio area at the rear of the pub. Q ⎈ ❀ ✿ & ● ✿ 🎵

Smithfield Ⓛ

Meadow Road, DE1 2BH

☎ (01332) 986601 ⊕ smithfieldderby.co.uk

Draught Bass; 9 changing beers (sourced nationally) Ⓗ

Situated near the town centre on the banks of the River Derwent with views towards Derby and Bass' Recreation Ground, and a short walk from the main bus station, this pub is the winner of numerous CAMRA awards. The bar boasts an eclectic range of ever-changing interesting beers, usually including two darks and supported by Draught Bass. There is a nice, subtle collection of breweriana on view. A separate quiet room with a real fire overlooks the patio, itself against the river. The pub has regular live music and hosts many beer-related activities. ⎈ ❀ ♣ ● P ➟ ✿ 🛈 🎵

Standing Order ✓

28-32 Iron Gate, Cathedral Quarter, DE1 3GL

☎ (01332) 207591

Draught Bass; Greene King Abbot; Marston's Pedigree; Ruddles Best Bitter; Sharp's Doom Bar; 12 changing beers (sourced nationally) Ⓗ

This large recently-refurbished city-centre Wetherspoons pub is located between the Market Place and the Cathedral. A long horseshoe bar sits in a huge and splendid ex-banking hall featuring high level paintings. At the side are a number of partitioned bays with banquette seating. There are also quieter and more private areas away from the main hall to one side and at the back. At the rear, a large patio has further seating. Q ⎈ ◐ ◑ & ● ➟ 🛈

White Swan Ⓛ ✓

Shepherd Street, Littleover, DE23 6GA

☎ (01332) 766481 ⊕ thewhiteswanlittleover.co.uk

Greene King Abbot; Little Brewing Company Epiphany Pale Ale; Marston's Pedigree; Morland Old Speckled Hen; 2 changing beers (sourced regionally) Ⓗ

Popular community pub situated in a hollow opposite the parish church in what was once Littleover village. Formerly a Festival Ale House and still keeping a choice range of guest ales, it is now owned by Greene King. Six beers are usually served; three national brands and three local beers. The pub is a long-standing holder of the cask marque accreditation. It has a good food reputation with

no booking policy. There is a big screen TV in the bar for sports fans, and wonderful hanging baskets in season.
⎈ ❀ ◐ ◑ ♣ ● P ➟ ✿ 🛈 🎵

Woodlark

76-80 Bridge Street, West End, DE1 3LA

☎ (01332) 292747

Dancing Duck Ay up; Draught Bass; 1 changing beer (sourced locally) Ⓗ

The Woodlark advertises its function with casks hanging on the outside wall. It is frequented by locals and students from the nearby student accommodation, and is often busy on football days. The pub consists of a large single room split by half-partitioning walls. The traditional wooden bar sits to the right on entry. There is a quiet patio area at the back of the pub which once backed onto a railway viaduct. ◑ ♣ ➟ 🛈

Dronfield

Coach & Horses Ⓛ ✓

Sheffield Road, S18 2GD

☎ (01246) 413269 ⊕ mycoachandhorses.co.uk

Thornbridge Lord Marples, Jaipur IPA; 4 changing beers (sourced locally; often Thornbridge) Ⓗ

Located next to the grounds of Sheffield FC (the world's oldest football club) this welcoming pub is operated by Thornbridge brewery and showcases both a good range of their beers and occasional guest ales across a wide range of styles and dispense. A shop selling a range of both canned and bottled beers along with Thornbridge merchandise was opened in 2022. There is a large outdoor drinking area including a heated covered section. The pub also hosts a quiz night
❀ ♣ P ➟ (43) ✿ 🛈 🎵

Dronfield Arms Ⓛ

Chesterfield Road, S18 2XE

☎ 07923 808332

Abbeydale Moonshine; Temper Relacite; 2 changing beers (sourced locally; often Temper) Ⓗ

The Arms became Dronfield's first brewpub in 2015. The kit is on display through a glass panel in the floor and is currently operated by Temper brewery which first brewed in late 2021. The pub features a long bar with up to four real ales, two ever changing, and a large, comfortable seating area. Also on the bar are several keg fonts including KeyKeg. There is an outside drinking area to the rear above a car park. Dogs and children welcome. Quiz nights are held. ⇌ ♣ P ➟ (44,43) ✿ 🛈 🎵

Duffield

Town Street Tap Ⓛ

17 Town Street, DE56 4EH

☎ 07925 461706 ⊕ thetownstreettap.co.uk

6 changing beers (sourced nationally) Ⓖ

Situated on the main road in Duffield, this is a micropub for Tollgate brewery, based on the Calke Estate near Ticknall. Six changing real ales are offered by table service, two from Tollgate and at least one is a dark beer. Four-pint take-out containers are also available. It has a nicely decorated interior with the modern style high tables. Occasional street food nights are hosted. Walkers with boots are welcome. The rear pub entrance and toilets have level access. Q ⇌ ♣ ● P ➟ ✿

Etwall

Spread Eagle

28 Main Street, DE65 6LP

☎ (01283) 735224

Draught Bass; Oakham Citra; Thornbridge Jaipur IPA; Timothy Taylor Landlord; 2 changing beers (sourced regionally) ⊞
This large 18th-century village pub near the church in the middle of Etwall was originally several different buildings. As a result there are three distinct areas inside, all served by a single horseshoe bar. Each area has screens showing sporting events but the volume is usually muted. There are outdoor tables in front of the pub for use in good weather. ❀♣🅿🚃🛜

Glossop

Bar 2 🄻
9 High Street East, SK13 8DA
☎ 07597 704447
Bradfield Farmers Blonde; 4 changing beers (sourced locally; often Bradfield, Stockport) ⊞
Originally named Tweed 2, this micropub opened in 2018. Up to six handpulled beers are on offer and craft keg lagers are also available, together with a good selection of wine and gins. This shop conversion is smart, comfortable and is a good size for a micropub. Discrete background music is quiet enough to allow drinkers to play traditional pub games, or to simply chat. There is also a retro video games table. Real ale is discounted on Monday and Wednesday. 🛏❀🕭⛲♣🚃❀🛜

Smithy Fold ⬤
Unit 11 Howard Town Shopping Park, Victoria Street, SK13 8HS
☎ (01457) 890070
Greene King Abbot; Ruddles Best Bitter; 5 changing beers (sourced nationally; often Coach House, Phoenix, Sharp's) ⊞
This popular Wetherspoon pub is situated in the town centre on the ground floor of an old cotton mill. There remain some original features and interesting artwork showing the history of the mill and some notable figures from the town. Breakfast is served each day until noon. Beers usually consist of three national brands with the remainder from regional and local breweries. 🛏❀🕭◖⛲🚃🛜

Hartshorne

Admiral Rodney Inn ⬤
65 Main Street, DE11 7ES (On A514)
☎ (01283) 227771
Draught Bass; Greene King Abbot; 3 changing beers (sourced regionally; often Thornbridge) ⊞
Traditional village local dating back to the early 19th century, but rebuilt and extended in the late 20th century to provide an open-plan L-shaped drinking space while retaining the original oak beams in the former snug. There is also a secluded raised area tucked away behind the bar. Two regular ales and up to three guests are usually available. Hot food, often 'pop-up', is available Wednesday to Friday evenings. The grounds include a cricket pitch, home of Hartshorne Cricket Club. 🛏❀◖⛲♣🍴🚃(2)❀🎵

Hasland

Hasland Working Mens Club
Hampton Street, S41 0LH
☎ (01246) 273660
6 changing beers ⊞
Hasland Club is a community resource, committed to providing a safe environment for members. The club also welcomes non-members and CAMRA members. There are no regular cask ales, but up to six different ales

across a range of styles are often available. Tap takeovers featuring local and national breweries and live music at weekends are regular events. The club also organises charity and community events. Sports TV is shown. 🛏⛲♣🚃(54)❀🛜🎵

Hathersage

Scotsman's Pack ⬤
School Lane, S32 1BZ
☎ (01433) 650253 🌐 scotsmanspackcountryinn.co.uk
Marston's Pedigree; 4 changing beers ⊞
Comfortable village pub converted from a former farmhouse in the 1920s, with three lounge areas served by a central bar. Welcoming to visitors and often busy with meal service during the day, but still popular with locals later in the evening. Robin Hood's companion Little John is reputably buried in the nearby churchyard and the pub displays artefacts alluding to the legendary outlaw. Q🛏❀🛏◖➤🚃(272)❀🎵

Heanor

Redemption Ale House 🄻
Ray Street, DE75 7GE
☎ 07887 568576
7 changing beers ⊞
A large open-plan micropub, on two floors. Formerly a butcher's shop; old framed photographs illustrate the pub's previous life. Up to seven regularly changing beers and 12 real ciders are served. Beer festivals are held throughout the year. The pub has an upstairs area which offers a variety of board games. A large collection of pumpclips adorn the walls. There is an attractive courtyard drinking area. Q❀🍴🚃❀🛜

Hilcote

Hilcote Arms
DE55 5HT
☎ (01773) 862696
4 changing beers ⊞
The Hilcote Arms reopened in 2017, having been closed since 2014. Extensive refurbishment has seen the introduction of four handpulls, a log burner, and new interiors throughout. Local ales are featured on the bar. Dog friendly, with children allowed until evening. Public transport is frequent from the stop one mile's walk away at East Midlands Designer Outlet shopping centre. Q🛏◖❀

Holbrook

Dead Poets Inn 🄻
38 Chapel Street, DE56 0TQ
☎ (01332) 780301
Draught Bass; Everards Old Original; Oakham Citra; 5 changing beers (sourced regionally; often Brunswick, Everards) ⊞
This beautiful olde-worlde village pub was built in 1800 and was initially called the Cross Keys. It is now owned by Everards brewery and leased by the Brunswick brewery based in Derby, with discounted ales from both breweries featuring regularly on the bar. A main flagstoned bar area with low ceilings, high-backed pews and a large open fire is flanked by a cosy snug. A newer, airy conservatory extension sits at the back, which leads to an outside drinking area. Q🛏❀◖♣🚃(71)❀🛜🎵

Holymoorside

Lamb Inn

16 Loads Road, S42 7EU

☎ (01246) 566167

Peak Ales Swift Nick, Bakewell Best Bitter, Chatsworth Gold; 3 changing beers Ⓗ

This quaint, traditional country pub is now owned by Peak Ales and serves their own cask ales alongside other regional breweries. Warm up next to the log fire on winter days or enjoy drinks alfresco on the pretty walled terrace. This locals' pub is unspoilt by progress, with a mixed clientele where all are welcome, including dogs and walkers - although not their muddy boots. Outside there is a paved drinking area ideal for warm summer evenings. Q❀♣P🚪(170)🐾

Hope

Old Hall Hotel ✅

Market Place, S33 6RH

☎ (01433) 620160 ⊕ oldhallhotelhope.co.uk

Theakston Best Bitter, Lightfoot, Old Peculier; 3 changing beers (sourced nationally) Ⓗ

Set in the heart of the village of Hope, this large and atmospheric 16th-century building has been an inn since 1730. It is popular for its locally sourced food and has five letting rooms together with extra facilities in the adjoining tearooms. Home of the Hope Valley Beer and Cider Festival, which is held on three bank holiday weekends a year, it also boasts a large collection of malt whiskies. Q❧🛏❀🍴◑ ⚲P🚪🐾🛜

Horsley Woodhouse

Old Oak Inn

176 Main Street, DE7 6AW

☎ (01332) 881299

8 changing beers (sourced regionally; often Bottle Brook, Leadmill) Ⓖ

As the tap house for the Leadmill and Bottlebrook Breweries, the Old Oak features a variety of their ales plus guests, all currently served on gravity from the RuRAD (Rural Real Ale Drinkers) bar. A traditional homely and welcoming village pub boasting four rooms of differing character, some having open fires, with a WiFi-free conversational atmosphere. At weekends there are additional beers available – making it effectively a mini beer festival. Local CAMRA Pub of The Year 2016. Q❧♿♣●P🚪🐾♪

Hundall

Miners Arms 🏆 Ⓛ

Hundall Lane, S18 4BS

☎ (01246) 414505

Drone Valley Dronny Bottom Bitter; Pictish Alchemists Ale; 3 changing beers (sourced nationally; often Church End, Titanic, Welbeck Abbey) Ⓗ

A traditional open-plan village inn that has won numerous CAMRA awards at both local and county levels. It offers a wide range of beers and fruit-based ciders with regular ales from Pictish and the nearby Drone Valley brewery. Three ever-changing guest beers are served, using lined oversize pint glasses. Limited range of bar snacks is available all day. A largescreen TV shows good range of sports channels. Dog-friendly, there is an excellent beer garden to the rear.
❧❀♣●P🖥🚪(15)🐾🛜♪

Ilkeston

Burnt Pig Ⓛ

53 Market Street, DE7 5RB

☎ 07812 158219

5 changing beers Ⓗ/Ⓖ

A well established, friendly and popular micropub, a regular entry in this Guide. Extending across three rooms, it has a collection of historical pub memorabilia. Five frequently changing cask ales are available, and there is a good selection of real ciders and continental bottled beers. Bar snacks include a selection of excellent cheeses and pork pies to eat in or take away, and their famous pork scratchings. There are good bus connections.
Q♣●🚪🐾

Dew Drop Inn Ⓛ

24 Station Street, DE7 5TE

☎ (0115) 932 9684

Oakham Bishops Farewell, Green Devil; 6 changing beers (sourced nationally; often Acorn, Blue Monkey, Castle Rock) Ⓗ

A traditional pub, with a bar and lounge on either side of the serving area, and a separate snug, it has been identified by CAMRA as having a nationally important historic pub interior. A regular entry in this Guide, it serves up to eight real ales, all to to an excellent standard. Two ciders are also available. Roaring fires heat the pub during winter months. Its close proximity to Ilkeston railway station makes this popular pub a convenient port of call on a visit to Ilkeston.
Q❧❀◑≈♣●🚪(27) 🐾

Kniveton

Red Lion at Kniveton

Main Street, DE6 1JH

☎ (01335) 345554

Marston's Pedigree; 2 changing beers Ⓗ

This attractive stone pub on the main road through the village changed hands in 2020 and is now run by local couple who also own a cider company. It serves a good well-kept range of beers from local breweries including Dovedale and Aldwark, and there is a great emphasis on ciders, including their own brand. The staff are friendly and welcoming, and a good range of excellent food served at most times. Local CAMRA Cider Pub of the Year 2022 and 2023. ❧❀🛏◑●P🐾🛜

Little Longstone

Packhorse Inn

Main Street, DE45 1NN

☎ (01629) 640471 ⊕ packhorselongstone.co.uk

Black Sheep Best Bitter; Thornbridge Brother Rabbit, Lord Marples, Jaipur IPA; 2 changing beers (often Thornbridge) Ⓗ

A small pub that began life as two miner's cottages, and has been welcoming drinkers since 1787. Situated just a short stroll from stunning views of Monsal Head, dogs and walkers are welcome. Fresh local produce is a passion, an ethos also extended to the beers, which always include a choice from the nearby Thornbridge brewery. There is a pleasant beer garden, and food is available all day at weekends. ❧❀◑Å♣🚪(173)🐾🛜

Litton

Red Lion Ⓛ ✅

Church Lane, SK17 8QU

☎ (01298) 871458 ⊕ theredlionlitton.co.uk

Abbeydale Absolution; Peak Ales Bakewell Best Bitter; 2 changing beers (sourced locally; often Acorn, Bradfield, Moorhouse's) ⊞
Nestling on the green and the only pub in the village, the Red Lion is a welcome refuge for locals and visitors alike. There is a large fireplace serving several rooms off a central passageway. Fresh food is served all day, every day. Not to be missed, the annual Wakes Week is at the end of June with events including a well dressing on the village green. ≿⊛⇔◑♣P🖵(65,173)🌑🐾

Long Eaton

Corner Room ⅃

Howitt Street, NG10 1ED
☎ (0115) 972 2197 ⊕ cornerroomlongeaton.co.uk
4 changing beers ⊞
A revived former Wetherspoon pub, with a large, open-plan interior furnished in a warm, contemporary style, with a number of seating areas. There is an interesting and attractive pitched rooflight featuring stained glass designs depicting Long Eaton's industrial past. Up to four cask beers are served, usually from local breweries. There is an extensive choice of meals available throughout the day. ≿◑&🖵(15,Sky)🌑🐾

Rowells Drinking Emporium ⅃

22 High Street, NG10 1LL
☎ 07809 627286
6 changing beers ⌷
New, spacious micropub opened in the former iconic Long Eaton draper's shop of the same name. The pub retains many of the original features and has been refurbished to a high standard, creating a relaxed and cosy atmosphere. Up to six real ales are dispensed by gravity; casks can be seen in the temperature-controlled cool room next to the bar. One or two real ciders, as well as tea and coffee, are available. Q&🖶🖵(15,Sky)🌑🐾🎵

York Chambers ⅃

40 Market Place, NG10 1LT
☎ (0115) 946 0999
6 changing beers ⌷
A popular and friendly micropub housed in a 1903 Midland Counties Bank. Grade II listed, the building is an interesting and unusual Art Nouveau design, and has a most impressive façade. The interior is little changed, retaining the original entrance lobby, light oak-panelled walls and chimney breast. Six regularly changing beers are dispensed by gravity. Real ciders, tea and coffee are also available. It is close to a number of bus routes. Q&🖶🖵(Sky,Igo) 🌑🐾

Lullington

Colvile Arms

Main Street, DE12 8EG (centre of village)
☎ 07510 870980 ⊕ thecolvilearms.com
Draught Bass; Marston's Pedigree; 2 changing beers (sourced regionally) ⊞
This popular 18th-century free house is at the heart of an attractive hamlet at the southern tip of the county. The public bar incorporates an adjoining hallway and features high-backed settles with wood paneling. The bar and a comfortable lounge are situated on opposite sides of a central serving area. A snug/function room overlooks the beer garden and lawn. Pop-up food vans visit every day except the last Sunday of the month which is quiz night. Q≿⊛♣P🌑🐾

Makeney

Holly Bush ★ ⊘

Holly Bush Lane, DE56 0RX
☎ (01332) 841729 ⊕ hollybushinnmakeney.co.uk
Marston's Pedigree ⌷; Thornbridge Jaipur IPA; Timothy Taylor Landlord; Whim Hartington IPA; house beer (by Thornbridge); 3 changing beers (sourced nationally) ⊞
The Holly Bush was once a farmhouse and brewery on the Strutt Estate, it stood on the Derby Turnpike before the new road (now the A6) opened in 1818. Dick Turpin reputedly drank in this late 17th-century grade II-listed pub with stone-flagged hideaways and welcoming fires in winter. It has been identified by CAMRA as having a nationally important historic pub interior. Eight cask and five keg ales are usually available with even more at the regular beer festivals. Walkers, families and dogs are welcome. Q≿⊛◑&♣P🖵🌑🐾

Matlock

bod Matlock

22 Dale Road, DE4 3LT
☎ (01629) 580382 ⊕ bodcafebars.co.uk/matlock
Everards Tiger; Titanic Steerage, Iceberg, Plum Porter; 2 changing beers (often Titanic) ⊞
A smart, sympathetic conversion of what was most recently a furniture shop, it comprises of a main room with two smaller rooms off. There are some original features including exposed brickwork. Built in the 1920s specifically for Boots the Chemist, a mural of the original frontage can be seen on the Garden Room wall. It's primarily a café bar which serves alcohol from 11am. There are up to six real ales, with 10 craft beers and Titanic gins on the bar. Q≿◑&🖵🌑🐾

Farmacy ⅃

76 Smedley Street, DE4 3JJ (jct of Bank Rd and Smedley St)
☎ (01629) 583350
5 changing beers (often Aldwark Artisan Ales) ⊞
Up the hill from the town centre and behind County Hall on Smedley Street, this cosy, split-level micropub is the tap for Aldwark Artisan Ales. They have five handpulls – one dispensing real cider – and usually feature several of their own beers. A range of pork pies and other snacks are available and they serve a range of gins and wines. Themed nights include music and quiz nights. Dogs are welcome. ≿⇌🖵🌑🐾

Newsroom ⅃

75-77 Smedley Street East, DE4 3FQ
☎ (01629) 583625
4 changing beers ⊞
This smart conversion from a newsagent to a micropub is an L-shaped room with some exposed brickwork and renovated sash windows. There are four real ales from interesting local and sometimes national microbreweries. Six craft ales normally include a stout and a lager, and at least one will be KeyKeg. There is a good range of gins and wines, and upwards of 60 different bottled and canned beers to drink or take away. &⇌🖵🌑

Twenty Ten ⅃

16 Dale Road, DE4 3LT
☎ (01629) 259793 ⊕ twentytenmatlock.co.uk
4 changing beers (sourced regionally) ⊞
A stone's throw from the local train and bus station, this bar nestles among the antique shops of Dale Road. It serves four real ales, with LocAles regularly on the handpulls. These are complemented by 16 draught craft

beers, of which at least eight are KeyKeg. Food is served at lunchtime followed by light bites menu until evening. Live music is performed on Friday and Saturday evenings. ඏ❀◖⇌🖳❀🛜♫

Matlock Bath

Fishpond 🅛

204 South Parade, DE4 3NR

☎ (01629) 55006 ⊕ thefishpondmatlockbath.co.uk

6 changing beers Ⓗ

At the south end of this historic spa town, and set into the limestone cliff-face, the Fishpond serves a wide range of real ales and ciders, with a strong focus on LocAle. Quality food is available seven days a week with the in-house bakery providing artisan breads, pastries and stone-baked pizzas. The new terraced gardens, bar and waterfall feature to the rear provide ideal surroundings for alfresco dining or for simply enjoying real ale in the sunshine. ඏ❀◖ఓ⇌P🛇🖳❀🛜♫

Melbourne

Spirit Vaults 🅛

53 Church Street, DE73 8EJ

☎ (01332) 300542 ⊕ thespiritvaults.co.uk

House beer (by Morgan Brewmasters); 3 changing beers (sourced locally) Ⓗ

Formally the Blue Bell, the multi-roomed Spirit Vaults dates from the 19th century. The pub is well located for visitors to the Hall and Norman parish church (12th century) which can be seen from the outdoor heated drinking area. It is also popular with walkers. The pub was extensively refurbished in 2020 when the in-house brewhouse, Morgan Brewmaster, was installed. House-brewed cask beers are complemented by a good range of guests, craft and Belgian beers.
❀🛏◖♣🖳(2,9)❀🛜

New Mills

Beer Shed

47B Market Street, SK22 4AA

☎ (01663) 742005

3 changing beers (sourced locally; often Black Iris, Bridge Beers, Torrside) Ⓗ

The Beer Shed is a micropub situated in a former video hire shop in the centre of New Mills close to all transport links. With a long narrow main room, an additional room downstairs and an outside gazebo in the rear yard this bar packs a lot into a small space. Three cask and six KeyKeg beers are on offer plus at least one lager (from Rothaus) and a real cider. Occasional comedy nights and monthly Mikkeller Running Club events are held.
❀⇌(Central)♣🖳❀

Chalkers Pool & Snooker Club

Redmoor Mill, Buxton Road, SK22 3JT

☎ (01663) 742336 ⊕ chalkerssnooker.co.uk/index.html

Wainwright; 1 changing beer (sourced locally; often Storm) Ⓗ

This recently refurbished snooker club is open to all, but payment is required to play snooker and pool. Though it is a sports-oriented venue with a largescreen TV showing football and other events next to the bar, the lounge area is off to one side and the sports events do not greatly impinge on those wanting a quiet drink. There is also a nicely appointed outside area with comfortable seating under cover. ❀⇌(Newtown)P🖳(199,61)

Mason's Arms

57 High Street, SK22 4BR

☎ 07745 575472

Wainwright; 4 changing beers (sourced locally; often Stockport, Storm) Ⓗ

The only pub in the conservation area of New Mills it is situated close to the Sett River Valley and Torrs Millennium Bridge. Extensively refurbished after takeover from Robinsons, the pub offers a good selection of good-value cask ales predominantly from local micros. It is a lively friendly pub with a strong sports orientation and regular live music at weekends featuring local bands. There is a small drinking area outside. A minimum charge applies for card payments.
❀⇌(Central)♣P🖳❀🛜♫

Newton Solney

Brickmakers Arms

9-11 Main Street, DE15 0SJ (on B5008, opp jct with Trent Ln)

☎ 07525 220103 ⊕ brickmakersarms.pub

Burton Bridge Sovereign Gold, Bridge Bitter, Stairway to Heaven, Top Dog Stout; 1 changing beer (sourced regionally) Ⓗ

This cosy local at the end of an 18th-century terrace of cottages was converted into a pub in the early 19th century for workers at a nearby brickworks. It features a narrow central bar leading at one end to a room served through a hatch, and at the other to an impressive oak-panelled room. The street entrance hallway houses a small bring-and-take library, beyond which is a small function/meeting room. Q ඏ❀♣♣P🖳(V3)❀🛜♫

Ockbrook

Royal Oak 🅛

55 Green Lane, DE72 3SE

☎ (01332) 662378 ⊕ royaloakockbrook.com

Draught Bass; 4 changing beers (sourced nationally) Ⓗ

An attractive 18th-century pub with a number of small rooms. Run by the Wilson family since 1953, they have brought about many improvements while retaining the original character and features. Excellent home-cooked food is served every day. A large function room allows the pub to host community and public events including live music and open mic nights. Outside there are two pleasant gardens, one with an enclosed play area for children. Has received a National CAMRA Golden Award.
Q ඏ❀◖ఓ♣♣P🖳❀🛜♫

Parwich

Parwich Royal British Legion Club

Dam Lane, DE6 1QJ

☎ (01335) 390501

Dancing Duck Ay up; 2 changing beers Ⓗ

Sitting in the heart of the picturesque village, not far from the local pub, this comfortable and welcoming club is open to all visitors. The impressive outdoor area is popular in the warmer months. At least three real ales are usually available, one tapped direct from the cellar room, usually from local breweries such as Dancing Duck, Wincle or Distant Hills. Local CAMRA Club of the Year 2022 and 2023, and regional winner in 2022. ඏ❀ఓ♣♣

Ripley

Red Lion ✅

Market Place, DE5 3BR

☎ (01773) 512875
Greene King Abbot; Ruddles Best Bitter; Sharp's Doom Bar; 7 changing beers (sourced nationally; often Thornbridge) ⊞

A former Home Brewery pub, built in the 1960s and easily identified by the large red lion rampant on the pub frontage. Facing the Victorian Ripley Town Hall and Market Place at the centre of this busy market town, it is close to the main bus stops. A typical Wetherspoon outlet, the pub serves a large selection of guest beers and the food menu is available all day. ⓺✿◐◖ᵹ◆P⊟☞❄

Talbot

1 Butterley Hill, DE5 3LT
☎ 07494 767374
9 changing beers (sourced nationally) ⊞

A traditional Victorian flatiron-shaped pub, the Talbot is a welcoming and popular community pub, a short walk from the town centre. It has a real fire in winter and an excellent selection of up to nine changing real ales pulled from casks stored on an original stone stillage, plus up to six real ciders. Local CAMRA Pub of the Year 2022. Q⣿ᵹ◆P⊟❄☞♫

Rosliston

Bull's Head

Burton Road, DE12 8JU (NW edge of village)
☎ (01283) 762642 ⊕ bullsheadrosliston.co.uk
Draught Bass; Marston's Pedigree; 2 changing beers (sourced regionally) ⊞

Late 19th-century brick-built free house with a comfortable public bar and smart, cosy lounge, both featuring open fires and beamed ceilings. There is also a large function room in a converted stable block. A collection of china bulls is displayed behind the bar, and intricate encased models of a Burton union brewing system can be found in both the public bar and the function room. Bingo is played on alternate Wednesday evenings; open mic night is Thursday.
⣿✿◖A♣◆P⊟(22) ❄☞♫

Sawley

Sawley Junction ⃝L

176 Tamworth Road, NG10 3JU
☎ 07966 757407
6 changing beers (sourced regionally) ⃝G

Renovated to a high standard, this micropub has the feel of a traditional station bar and tea shop (the pub takes nearby Long Eaton railway station's former name). It has up to six gravity-dispensed beers on offer as well as a number of real ciders. Bar snacks and hot drinks are available throughout the day. A popular local, its proximity to the railway station also makes it handy for commuters. Open on bank holiday Mondays.
Q⣿✖(Long Eaton) ◆P⊟(Sky,15) ❄

Scarcliffe

Horse & Groom ⃝L

Mansfield Road, S44 6SU (on the B6417 between Clowne and Stoney Houghton)
☎ (01246) 823152
Black Sheep Best Bitter; Greene King Abbot; Welbeck Abbey Red Feather, Atlas; 3 changing beers (sourced nationally; often Abbeydale, Oakham, Ossett) ⊞

A coaching inn from the 1800s which has been owned by the same family for 26 years. It has a tap room, main bar and spacious family- and dog-friendly conservatory to the rear which also leads to a large beer garden. There are up to four regular beers, often including Welbeck

Abbey and up to three changing national ales. There are two bus stops just outside the pub, one serving the Chesterfield and Langwith route, the other Mansfield and Sheffield. Q⣿✿◆P⊟(53,1)❄♫

South Normanton

Clock Inn

107 Market Street, DE55 2AA
☎ (01773) 811396 ⊕ theclockinn.co.uk
Burton Bridge XL Bitter; 2 changing beers ⊞

This multi-room pub has a lounge and public bar area with a central bar serving both rooms. Up to three beers are available at weekends, with fewer offered during the week. There is a nice lawn and garden to the rear with outdoor seating and a covered smoking area. Sky Sports and BT Sports are available in both rooms on large projection screens. Dogs are welcome in the public bar side only. Q⣿✿◆P⊟(9.1)❄☞

Market Tavern ⃝L

41 High Street, DE55 2BP
5 changing beers (often Blue Monkey, Marble, Thornbridge) ⊞

A welcome addition to the local real ale scene this two-roomed micropub has been caringly renovated from a closed former charity shop. Located on the High Street just off the Market Place, this pub offers up to five ever-changing real ales, usually sourced from local breweries, and up to six traditional ciders. Dogs and children are welcome at all times. A range of craft cans is available to drink in or take away. Cask Marque accredited
Q⣿♣◆P⊟(9.1) ❄☞

Sutton cum Duckmanton

Arkwright Arms ⃝L

Chesterfield Road, S44 5JG (A632 between Chesterfield and Bolsover)
☎ 07803 006926 ⊕ arkwrightarms.co.uk
House beer (by Whim); 5 changing beers (sourced locally; often Ashover, Thornbridge, Whim) ⊞

There is always a warm welcome at this mock-Tudor fronted free house, with three cosy rooms all with open fires and comfortable furniture. The impressive wood-panelled bar boasts an excellent range of guest ales, many from local breweries. Regular beer festivals are held at Easter and on bank holidays. Good food is served from lunchtime to early evening (not Mon and Tue). Winner of numerous CAMRA awards at both local and regional level. Local CAMRA Pub of the Year 2022.
⣿✿◖A♣P⊟❄

Swanwick

Steampacket Inn

Derby Road, DE55 1AB
☎ (01773) 607771
Draught Bass; 5 changing beers (sourced nationally; often Blue Monkey, Derby, Nottingham) ⊞

A friendly Pub People Company pub situated in the centre of Swanwick, the Steampacket boasts an excellent and constantly changing range of well-kept real ales and ciders, many of them from local microbreweries. A popular and lively pub at the weekends with regular live music and a beer festival in winter and summer. Quiz night is on Tuesdays and it has a welcoming fire in winter, wth outdoor tables in summer.
⣿ᵹ♣◆P⊟❄☞♫

Wardlow Mires

Three Stags' Heads ★ 🅛

Mires Lane, SK17 8RW (jct A623/B6465)
☎ (01298) 872268
Abbeydale Deception; house beer (by Abbeydale); 1 changing beer (sourced regionally; often Eyam, Intrepid) 🅗
A quaint 300-year-old pub with two small rooms, stone-flagged floors and low ceilings. Unspoilt, it is one of the few pubs in the area identified by CAMRA as having a nationally important historic pub interior. An ancient range warms the bar and the house dogs, one of which gave the name to the house beer – Black Lurcher. Traditional cider is only available in summer.
Q✿⏰Å♠P🖵(173) ✿

Whaley Bridge

Goyt Inn ✅

8 Bridge Street, SK23 7LR
☎ (01663) 732710
5 changing beers (sourced nationally; often Timothy Taylor) 🅗
Tucked away in the centre of Whaley Bridge and close to the historic Whaley Bridge Canal Basin at the end of the Peak Forest Canal, which once was the northern end of the Cromford and High Peak Railway. This end-of-terrace pub is a true local and fulfils its role well. It is characterful, dog-friendly and welcoming with a changing range of real ales. There is also a small but attractive patio/beer garden at the rear.
Q✿≉♣🖵(199,61) ✿

Whaley Nook

20 Old Road, SK23 7HR (turn up Old Rd opp Co-op, bar is on the left)
Abbeydale Deception; 3 changing beers (sourced locally; often Abbeydale, Eyam, Thornbridge) 🅗
Two-room pub with a small cosy front bar with another small room at the rear. There is also a little French café-style seating outside on the pavement. Four handpumps offer one regular beer and three changing beers from local breweries, plus six craft beers and a real cider on fonts. A loyalty card system operates during the week. An interesting selection of gins from far and wide are available and works by local artists are displayed for sale.
Q✿≉♠🖵(199,61)

Whitehough

Old Hall Inn 🅛

SK23 6EJ (nr Chinley, 750yds off B6062)
☎ (01663) 750529 ⊕ old-hall-inn.co.uk
Abbeydale Deception; Wainwright; 6 changing beers (sourced locally; often Marble, Ossett, Thornbridge) 🅗
The 16th-century Whitehough Hall forms part of this superb country inn which has previously won CAMRA Regional Pub of the Year, the Great British Pub award for best cask pub in the region for several years and is a regular entry within this Guide. Eight ales, including six regularly changing beers from quality local micros, complement those available at the adjacent Paper Mill Inn (under the same ownership). A popular menu features dishes using local produce. A popular beer festival is held in September.
✿✿🛏⏰Å♠P🖵(190) ✿🤍

Willington

Dragon 🅛 ✅

13 The Green, DE65 6BP

☎ (01283) 704795 ⊕ thedragonatwillington.co.uk
Draught Bass; Marston's Pedigree; Sharp's Doom Bar; 3 changing beers (sourced locally) 🅗
This pub's origins can be traced back to the construction of the Trent and Mersey Canal. The rear garden overlooks the canal while the front garden has a fenced childrens' play area. The pub has been expanded into the adjacent cottage to give an additional dining area but retains its a low ceiling olde-worlde feel. The Bridgeside restaurant doubles as a function room.
✿✿🛏⏰♿≉♠P🖵(V3) ✿🤍🎵

Wirksworth

Feather Star 🍷 🅛

Market Place, DE4 4ET
☎ 07931 424117 ⊕ thefeatherstar.co.uk
5 changing beers 🅗
There are five regularly changing beers on handpumps, sourced locally and regionally, and the tap wall offers up to 13 crafts beers and lagers, plus five real ciders. The owners have joined forces with Umami, a restaurant in the same building, to provide hot bar snacks and their takeaway food can be eaten in the bar. A Feather Star is the name for a Crinoid fossil found locally in the limestone around Wirksworth.
Q✿≉(Ecclesbourne Valley) P🖵(6.1) ✿🎵

Breweries

14 Lock (NEW)

🍺 Canal Inn, 30 Bullbridge Hill, Bullbridge, DE56 2EW
☎ (01629) 534888 ⊕ thecanalatbullbridge.co.uk/14-lock-brewery
Brewing commenced in 2022. The brewery is located in the cellar of the Canal Inn at Bullbridge and supplies the four outlets of the Moorwood Hotel Group.

3P's

Burton Road, Swadlincote, Woodville, DE11 7JE
☎ 07590 285975 ⊕ 3psbrewery.co.uk

Innovative nanobrewery with a 600-litre Elite stainless steel two-vessel system, founded in 2020 by an enthusiastic homebrewer. Using only the freshest natural ingredients, all beers are vegetarian and vegan-friendly (apart from the milk stout). 3P's brew beers with innovative twists throughout the year, alongside its core range. The name comes from Pits, Pots and Pipes for which Woodville was once renowned. Micropubs in Burton, Swadlincote and Derby are supplied. V

Bob ā Oleā (ABV 4.5%) BITTER
Knocker Upper (ABV 4.8%) BLOND
Big Butty (ABV 5%) BITTER
Tubthumper (ABV 5.3%) PALE

Aldwark Artisan

Lydgate Farm, Aldwark, Matlock, DE4 4HW
☎ (01629) 540720 ☎ 07834 353807
⊕ aabrewery.co.uk

⊗ This 10-barrel plant is housed in an old milking shed on a rural working farm, producing its first brew in 2017. Water comes from the farm's own bore hole, filtered through the strong limestone hills of the peak district. It has created the 'AAA' range of craft ales.

Nostrum Gold (ABV 3.8%) GOLD
Elixir Gold (ABV 3.9%) GOLD
Baabarian Gold (ABV 4%) PALE

Roan (ABV 4%) BITTER
Nostrum Amber (ABV 4.2%) BITTER
Eight Million (ABV 4.5%) GOLD
Hare of the Hill (ABV 4.6%) BLOND
Aldwark Pale (ABV 4.8%) PALE
Frankenstein (ABV 5.4%) PORTER

Alter Ego SIBA

Unit B2, Salcombe Road, Meadow Lane Industrial
Estate, Alfreton, DE55 7RG
☎ (01773) 475126 ☎ 07989 655828
✉ matt@alteregobrewing.co

Alter Ego upgraded in 2022 to a six-barrel brewery
located in Alfreton producing full-flavoured, small-batch
beers in cask and keg. The brewery tap is the Tip Inn
micropub, Loscoe. ♦

Echo Chamber (ABV 3.8%) PALE
Mr Brown (ABV 4.2%) BITTER
Blonde Protagonist (ABV 4.3%) BLOND
S'more Fire (ABV 5.2%) STOUT
Incognito (ABV 5.8%) IPA

Aristotle

c/o Unit 4, Silver House Griffen Close, Staveley,
Chesterfield, S43 3LJ
☎ (01246) 470074 ☎ 07496 757619
✉ richard@silverbrewhouse.com

⊗ A splinter brewery company set up from within Silver
Brewhouse to produce alternative beers on the same kit
for cask, keg, bottles and can. ♦

Ashover SIBA

Unit 1, Derby Road Business Park, Clay Cross, S45 9AG
☎ (01246) 251859 ⊕ ashoverbrewery.com

⊗ Brewing began in 2007 on a 3.5-barrel plant in the
garage of the cottage next to the Old Poets' Corner,
Ashover. It moved to a 10-barrel brewery in the
neighbouring village of Clay Cross in 2015. The brewery
serves local freehouses across Derbyshire and further
afield, including many festivals and have won many
CAMRA awards. !!LIVE

Light Rale (ABV 3.7%) BITTER
Light in colour and taste, with initial sweet and malt
flavours, leading to a bitter finish and aftertaste.
Font (ABV 3.8%) GOLD
Poets Tipple (ABV 4%) BITTER
Complex, tawny-coloured beer that drinks above its
strength. Predominantly malty in flavour, with increasing
bitterness towards the end.
Littlemoor Citra (ABV 4.1%) PALE
The Fabrick (ABV 4.4%) GOLD
Rainbows End (ABV 4.5%) GOLD
Slightly smooth, bitter golden beer with an initial
sweetness. Grapefruit and lemon hop flavours come
through strongly as the beer gets increasingly dry
towards the finish, ending with a bitter, dry aftertaste.
Red Lion (ABV 4.6%) RED
Coffin Lane Stout (ABV 5%) STOUT
Excellent example of the style, with a chocolate and
coffee flavour, balanced by a little sweetness. Finish is
long and quite dry.
Butts Pale Ale (ABV 5.5%) PALE
Pale and strong, yet easy to drink golden bitter.
Combination of bitter and sweet flavours mingle with an
alcoholic kick, leading to a warming yet bitter finish and
aftertaste.
Milk Stout (ABV 6%) STOUT

Bad Bunny

Ambergate, DE56 2EW ☎ 07519 605362
⊕ badbunnybrewery.co.uk

Founded by husband-and-wife team Mike and Clare
Chettle, brewing commenced in 2019. They now run a
1000-litre plant at their home in Bullbridge, Derbyshire,
supplying local pubs with fresh, unfiltered casks, as well
as occasional can and bottle releases. 🍴♦LIVE

Johnny Utah (ABV 4.5%) IPA

Bang The Elephant

Unit 14, Bailey Brook Industrial Estate, Amber Drive,
Langley Mill, NG16 4BE ☎ 07539 652055
✉ bangtheelephantbrewing@hotmail.com

⊗ Bang The Elephant is a neo-victorian, steam punk-
inspired, six-barrel brewery, creating small batch beers
for the cask, keg and bottle market.

Gigglemug (ABV 4%) BITTER
Podsnappery (ABV 4%) GOLD
Half Rats (ABV 4.4%) PALE
Elephant In The Room (ABV 4.5%) PALE
Penny Dreadful (ABV 4.5%) STOUT
Sons of Liberty APA (ABV 5%) PALE
What Makes Larry Happy (ABV 5.2%) IPA
Bricky (ABV 5.6%) IPA
Odissi (ABV 6%) IPA

Bentley Brook

Unit 3, Lumsdale Mill, Lumsdale, Matlock, DE4 5EX
☎ 07483 831640

Office: 1 Hilltop Terrace, The Cliff, Matlock, DE4 5FY
⊕ bentleybrook.co.uk

⊗ Formed in 2018, this 2.5-barrel brewery is located in
the heart of Lumsdale Valley and named after the local
brook. It offers unfined, small batch beers available to
purchase in the local area and at the brewery. LIVE ♦

Big Stone SIBA

Ashen Clough, Maynestone Road, Chinley, SK23 6AH
☎ 07867 652062 ⊕ bigstonebeer.co.uk

This small operation started brewing on a 2.5-barrel kit in
2019. It is based in large out-buildings connected to a
private house, on the outskirts of Chinley, in the heart of
the Peak District. Beers are available in bottles from local
outlets. Casks are supplied to a limited number of local
pubs. An onsite spring provides all the water used in
production. The brewery has suspended production
during 2023 with plans to restart commercial brewing in
2024. ♦LIVE

Birch Cottage

Birch Cottage, Wilne Road, Sawley, NG10 3AP
☎ 07966 757407
✉ birchcottagebrewery@outlook.com

Birch Cottage is a nanobrewery established in 2018
brewing small batch beers. Its brewery tap, Sawley
Junction, opened in 2018.

Footsteps (ABV 3.9%) GOLD
Inner Smile (ABV 4%) GOLD
Bit 'O' 52 (ABV 4.3%) BITTER
Sawley Stout (ABV 4.3%) STOUT
BCB (Birch Cottage Bitter) (ABV 4.4%) BITTER
Windmill Stout (ABV 4.5%) STOUT
No Code (ABV 5.3%) GOLD
Big Hard Sun (ABV 5.8%) IPA

Birchover

⊟ Red Lion, Main Street, Birchover, DE4 2BN
☎ (01629) 650363 ⊕ red-lion-birchover.co.uk

⊠ Brewing started at the Red Lion pub in the picturesque Peak District village of Birchover in 2016, and upgraded to a five-barrel plant by enthusiastic pub/brewery owner in 2017. Core range beers are named after local Stanton Moor landmarks and are to be found alongside seasonal specials on the pub bar. ♦LIVE

Black Hole SIBA

Unit 3a, Old Hall Mill Business Park, Alfreton Road, Little Eaton, DE21 5EJ
☎ (01283) 619943 ☎ 07812 812953
⊕ blackholebrewery.co.uk

⊠ Established 2007 with a 10-barrel plant in the former Ind Coope bottling stores, Burton-on-Trent, it moved to its current location in 2017. Fermenting capacity (36 barrels) enables production of up to four brews per week. Some are marketed under Little Eaton Brewery and Mr Grundy's Brewery. Around 400 outlets are supplied direct, and many more via wholesalers. Since 2014, the brewery has been owned by GHH Llp, which also owned the now closed Mr Grundy's Brewery. ‼♦

Bitter (ABV 3.8%) BITTER
Amber glow and malt and spicy hop aroma. Fresh, lively session beer hopped to give a clean crisp finish of hoppy dryness and touch of astringency.
Cosmic (ABV 4.2%) BITTER
Almost golden with an initial malt aroma. The complex balance of malt and English hops give lingering tastes of nuts, fruit and dry hoppy bitterness.
Supernova (ABV 4.8%) GOLD
Pure gold. Like marmalade made from Seville oranges and grapefruit the aroma mimics the sweet start but gives into the hops which deliver a dry, lingering bitter finish.
IPA (ABV 5.2%) PALE
Milky Way (ABV 6%) SPECIALITY
Honey and banana nose advises the sweet taste but not the sweet, dry spicy finish from this wheat beer.

Brewed for Small Beer, Lincoln:
Lincoln Imperial Ale (ABV 3.8%) BITTER

Brewed under the Little Eaton brand name:
Bates' Pale Ale (ABV 3.8%) PALE
Bagnall Bros Bitter (ABV 4.2%) BITTER
Delver's Drop IPA (ABV 4.8%) SPECIALITY
Old Mill Stout (ABV 5%) SPECIALITY

Brewed under the Mr Grundy's brand name:
Passchendaele (ABV 3.9%) PALE
Big Willie (ABV 4.3%) GOLD
Sniper (ABV 4.6%) BITTER
Lord Kitchener (ABV 5.5%) IPA

Bottle Brook

Church Street, Kilburn, Belper, DE56 0LU
☎ (01332) 880051 ☎ 07971 189915

⊠ A sister brewery to Leadmill (qv), Bottle Brook was established in 2005 using a 2.5-barrel plant on a tower gravity system. New World hops are predominantly used. The core range of beers is supplemented by one-off brews.

Columbus (ABV 4%) GOLD
Heanor Pale Ale (ABV 4.2%) PALE
Roadrunner (ABV 4.8%) GOLD
Mellow Yellow (ABV 5.7%) GOLD
Rapture (ABV 5.9%) GOLD

Sand in the Wind (ABV 6.1%) GOLD

Brampton SIBA

Units 4 & 5, Chatsworth Business Park, Chatsworth Road, Chesterfield, S40 2AR
☎ (01246) 221680 ⊕ bramptonbrewery.co.uk

☺The original Brampton Brewery closed in 1955. In 2007 a new brewery was established, and brewing commenced on an eight-barrel plant. Three tied houses are situated close to the brewery. ‼⊟♦LIVE

Golden Bud (ABV 3.8%) GOLD
Crisp and refreshing golden bitter with a pleasant balance of citrus, sweetness and bitter flavours. Light and easy to drink.
1302 (ABV 4%) PALE
Griffin (ABV 4.1%) PALE
Best (ABV 4.2%) BITTER
Classic, drinkable bitter with a predominantly malty taste, balanced by caramel sweetness and a developing bitterness in the aftertaste.
Impy Dark (ABV 4.3%) OLD
Strong, roasted coffee aroma and a rich flavour of vine fruit and chocolate combine to make this a tasty mild ale.
Jerusalem (ABV 4.6%) BITTER
Tudor Rose (ABV 4.6%) PALE
Wasp Nest (ABV 5%) BITTER
Strong and complex with malt and hop flavours and a caramel sweetness.
Speciale (ABV 5.8%) IPA

Brunswick SIBA

⊟ 1 Railway Terrace, Derby, DE1 2RU
☎ (01332) 410055 ☎ 07534 401352
⊕ brunswickbrewingcompany.co.uk

⊠ Derby's oldest brewery. It is a 10-barrel tower plant built as an extension to the Brunswick Inn in 1991. Bought by Everards in 2002, the brewery is now run separately, yet in conjunction with the pub. It supplies the Brunswick Inn, Dead Poets Inn, Everards, wholesalers, and the free trade within 100 miles. Brunswick also swaps with other breweries. Beers are also produced under the Engine Shed Project brand name. ‼♦LIVE

White Feather (ABV 3.6%) PALE
Triple Hop (ABV 4%) BLOND
The Usual (ABV 4.2%) BITTER
Railway Porter (ABV 4.3%) PORTER
Rocket (ABV 4.7%) PALE
Black Sabbath (ABV 6%) OLD

Brewed under the Engine Shed Project brand name:
Ubiquitous (ABV 6%) IPA

Buxton SIBA

Units 4A & B, Staden Business Park, Staden Lane, Buxton, SK17 9RZ
☎ (01298) 24420 ⊕ buxtonbrewery.co.uk

☺Set up in 2009 as a five-barrel plant, Buxton now uses a 20-barrel plant. Its brewery tap is in Buxton. The tasting room at the brewery has views of the countryside. A wide range of small-batch beers is brewed year round. Cask beers are available nationally. Live beer is available in KeyKeg and cans using its own canning machine. Stronger beers are available in bottles. ⊟♦LIVE⊘

Little Tor (ABV 3%) BITTER
Moor Top (ABV 3.6%) PALE
Low Tor (ABV 3.8%) RED

Right to Roam (ABV 3.8%) BITTER
HDA #1 - Ernest (ABV 4%) BITTER
Gatekeeper (ABV 4.1%) PORTER
SPA (ABV 4.1%) PALE
Best Bitter (ABV 4.2%) BITTER
Blonde (ABV 4.6%) BLOND
Monsal Mild (ABV 4.8%) MILD
Mantel (ABV 5.4%) IPA
Mild (ABV 6%) MILD

Chapel-en-le-Frith SIBA

5 Market Place, Chapel-en-le-Frith, SK23 0EW
☎ 07951 524003 ⊕ chapelcraftbrewing.co.uk

☺Opened in 2016, this small brewery is located at the rear of Chapel-en-le-Frith post office. The brewing kit consists of a single 200-litre capacity integrated system supplemented by a 20-litre trial kit. Bottles and five-litre mini casks are available from the post office. Cask ales are available from a limited number of local outlets. 🍺

Siena (ABV 4.1%) GOLD
Savinjski (ABV 4.2%) GOLD
Rye The Hell Not (ABV 4.3%) RED
Isambard (ABV 4.4%) PALE
Busted Monkey (ABV 4.6%) BROWN
Craken Edge (ABV 4.6%) BITTER
Leningrad (ABV 5%) RED
Elysium Amber Ale (ABV 5.4%) BITTER
Acadian (ABV 5.6%) IPA
Hoppy as Funk (ABV 5.8%) IPA
Sinamarian Black IPA (ABV 6%) IPA
USA (ABV 8%) IPA

Collyfobble

🍺 Peacock, Hackney Lane, Barlow, S18 7TD
☎ (0114) 289 0340 ⊕ collyfobblebrewery.com

☺This impressive looking, gleaming 4.5-barrel plant is housed in the grounds of the Peacock at Barlow and can be viewed through the large glass panels built into the design. There is also a tasting room available to hire. The ales are brewed mainly for the Peacock although they are available wholesale and may be found at the neighouring Tickled Trout Inn and other local hostelries. ‼

Dancing Duck SIBA

1 John Cooper Buildings, Payne Street, Derby, DE22 3AZ
☎ (01332) 205582 ☎ 07581 122122
⊕ dancingduckbrewery.com

⊠ Dancing Duck was established in 2010 by Rachel Mathews using a 10-barrel brew plant. Its name comes from the local greeting 'ay up me duck'. Brewery tap is the Exeter Arms, Derby. ‼🍺♦

Quack Addict (ABV 3.8%) BITTER
Ay up (ABV 3.9%) PALE
Brown Clough (ABV 4%) BITTER
Waitangi (ABV 4%) PALE
Ginger Ninja (ABV 4.1%) SPECIALITY
Nice Weather (ABV 4.1%) BITTER
Back Sack & Quack (ABV 4.2%) MILD
Donald *UCK! (ABV 4.2%) GOLD
Release The Quacken (ABV 4.2%) GOLD
Sapphire (ABV 4.2%) GOLD
22 (ABV 4.3%) BITTER
DCUK (ABV 4.3%) PALE
Beaky Blinders (ABV 4.5%) GOLD
Dark Drake (ABV 4.5%) STOUT
Waddle it be? (ABV 4.5%) PALE

Gold (ABV 4.7%) GOLD
Indian Porter (ABV 5%) PORTER
Quack Me Amadeus (ABV 5%) SPECIALITY
Abduction (ABV 5.5%) IPA
Imperial Drake (ABV 6.5%) STOUT

Derby SIBA

Masons Place Business Park, Nottingham Road, Derby, DE21 6AQ
☎ (01332) 365366 ☎ 07887 556788
⊕ derbybrewing.co.uk

A family-run microbrewery, established in 2004 in the old Masons paintworks varnish shed by Trevor Harris, founder and former brewer at the Brunswick Inn, Derby (qv). The business has grown over the years and five venues are now owned across Derbyshire and Staffordshire with more in the pipeline. More than 400 outlets are supplied including major retailers. In addition to the core range there are at least two new beers each month. ‼🍺♦

Hop Till You Drop (ABV 3.9%) BLOND
Business As Usual (ABV 4.4%) BITTER
Penny's Porter (ABV 4.6%) PORTER
Dashingly Dark (ABV 4.8%) STOUT
Mercia IPA (ABV 5%) PALE
Quintessential (ABV 5.8%) GOLD

Dovedale

Damgate Farm, Stanshope, DE6 2AD ☎ 07714 105035 ✉ info@dovedalebrewing.co.uk

⊠ A small, independent craft brewery with a six-barrel (1,000-litre) capacity, specialising in small-batch brewing, enabling it to produce a large range of different and limited edition beers. By concentrating on online sales locally and nationally, it has found new markets as well as consolidating its position as a premium local craft beer producer. Beer is available in cask, KeyKeg, bottle and minikeg. ♦LIVE

Echo Beach (ABV 3.8%) GOLD
Pale (ABV 3.8%) BLOND
Stout (ABV 4.6%) SPECIALITY
IPA (ABV 5.6%) IPA
Blonde (ABV 5.9%) BLOND

Draycott

Ladywood Lodge Farm, Spondon Road, Dale Abbey, DE7 4PS ☎ 07834 728540
✉ draycottbrewingcompany@yahoo.co.uk

⊠ Microbrewery established in 2014, supplying local pubs and beer festivals. It relocated to new premises in 2015, which saw beer range and capacity increase. A tap house in Draycott village is also operated.

Top of the Hops (ABV 3.8%) PALE
Lamb & Flag (ABV 4%) PORTER
Butcher's Bitter (ABV 4.2%) BITTER
California Steam Beer (ABV 4.2%) RED
Piano Man Blues (ABV 4.2%) RED
Lord Have Mercy (ABV 4.5%) SPECIALITY
Obsidian (ABV 4.5%) SPECIALITY
Tap House Tipple (ABV 4.5%) PALE
Minnesota North Star American Red Ale (ABV 4.7%) RED
Irish Red Ale (ABV 5%) RED

Drone Valley SIBA

Unstone Industrial Complex, Main Road, Unstone, Dronfield, S18 4AB ☎ 07794 277091
⊕ dronevalleybrewery.com

Community-owned, five-barrel brewery that began brewing commercially in 2016. All the brewing is carried out by volunteers under the supervision of qualified, experienced brewers. Profits go to local good causes. New owner members are always welcome. The brewery is open every Saturday and holds open days throughout the year. !! ☰ ♦ LIVE ✦

Dronny Bottom Bitter (ABV 3.7%) BITTER
Gosforth Gold (ABV 4%) GOLD
Dronfield Best (ABV 4.3%) BITTER
Coal Aston Porter (ABV 4.5%) PORTER
Fanshaw Blonde (ABV 4.8%) PALE
Stubley Stout (ABV 5%) STOUT
IPA (ABV 5.2%) GOLD
Candelriggs (ABV 5.8%) MILD
Carr Lane Black Label (ABV 6%) BITTER

Eyam

Unit 4, Eyam Hall Craft Centre, Main Road, Eyam, Hope Valley, S32 5QW ☎ 07976 432682
⊕ eyamrealalecompany.com

Brewing began in 2017 using a 1.5-barrel plant producing keg and bottle-conditioned beers. Most output goes to its shop and events but 10 local outlets are also supplied. ☰ LIVE

Falstaff

▤ 24 Society Place, Normanton, Derby, DE23 6UH
☎ (01332) 342902 ☎ 07947 242710
⊕ falstaffbrewery.co.uk

Attached to the Falstaff freehouse, the brewery dates from 1999 but was refurbished and reopened in 2003 under new management as a 3.5-barrel plant. Updated again in 2017, it now operates as a six-barrel plant producing a core range of six beers plus specials. More than 30 outlets are supplied. ♦

3 Faze (ABV 3.8%) GOLD
Fist Full of Hops (ABV 4.5%) GOLD
Phoenix (ABV 4.7%) BITTER
A smooth, tawny ale with fruit and hop, joined by plenty of malt in the mouth. A subtle sweetness produces a drinkable ale.
Smiling Assassin (ABV 5.2%) BITTER
Darkside (ABV 6%) MILD
Good Bad & Drunk (ABV 6.2%) BITTER

Furnace

▤ 9 Duke Street, Derby, DE1 3BX
☎ (01332) 385981
✉ furnaceinn@shinybrewing.com

Six-barrel brewhouse in the beer garden of the Furnace Inn on Duke Street. Supply is mainly for the pub, but beers can be seen at beer festivals and specialist pubs across the UK.

Globe

▤ 144 High Street West, Glossop, SK13 8HJ
☎ (01457) 852417 ⊕ globepub.co.uk

Globe was established in 2006 by Ron Brookes on a 2.5-barrel plant, in an old stable behind the Globe pub. His grandson Toby is now the main brewer. The beers are

mainly for the pub but special one-off brews are produced for beer festivals. ♦

Hartshorns

Unit 4, Tomlinsons Industrial Estate, Alfreton Road, Derby, DE21 4ED ☎ 07830 367125
✉ hartshornsbrewery@gmail.com

Hartshorns began brewing in 2012 using a six-barrel plant installed by brothers Darren and Lindsey Hartshorn. The brewery owns three pubs, the Little Chester Ale House, Peacock in Derby, and Belper House, Belper.

Barley Pop (ABV 3.8%) BITTER
Ignite (ABV 3.9%) GOLD
Full Nelson (ABV 4.6%) PALE
Fusion (ABV 4.6%) GOLD
Shakademus (ABV 5.4%) GOLD
Psychotropic (ABV 5.8%) GOLD
Apocalypse (ABV 6.2%) GOLD

Hollow Tree

3 Glen Road, Whatstandwell, Matlock,, DE4 5EH
☎ 07920 843754 ⊕ hollowtreebrewing.co.uk

Nanobrewery with five core beers. Brewing began in 2019. There are also limited and seasonal releases which use ingredients sourced and foraged from the local area. ♦ LIVE

Instant Karma

▤ 4 John Street, Clay Cross, S45 9NQ
☎ (01246) 250366 ⊕ instantkarmabrewery.co.uk

Instant Karma began brewing in 2012 using a five-barrel plant with a brew length of 15 barrels per week. The brewery is part of the Rykneld Turnpyke brewpub.

Intrepid SIBA

Unit 12, Vincent Works, Stretfield Road, Bradwell, S33 9HG ☎ 07936 174364 ⊕ intrepidbrewing.co

Based in the Hope Valley in the Peak District, Intrepid commenced brewing in 2014 using an eight-barrel plant located in an old smelting mill. It's a small-batch brewery, producing beers in cask, keg and bottle.

Leadmill

Unit 3, Heanor Small Business Centre, Adams Close, Heanor, DE75 7SW ☎ 07971 189915
✉ leadmill@fsmail.net

Set up in Selston in 1999, Leadmill moved to Denby in 2001 and again in 2010 to Heanor. A sister brewery to Bottle Brook (qv), the brewery tap is at the Old Oak, Horsley Woodhouse. ♦

Langley Best (ABV 3.6%) BITTER
Mash Tun Bitter (ABV 3.6%) BITTER
Old Oak Bitter (ABV 3.7%) BITTER
Dream Weaver (ABV 4.3%) GOLD
Linebacker (ABV 4.6%) BLOND
B52 (ABV 5.2%) BITTER
American Girl (ABV 5.6%) IPA
Rajah Brooke (ABV 5.6%) BLOND
Mellow Yellow (ABV 5.7%) BITTER
Slumdog (ABV 5.9%) GOLD

Leatherbritches

Brewery Yard, Tap House, Annwell Lane, Smisby, LE65 2TA ☎ 07976 279253
⊕ leatherbritchesbrewery.co.uk

⊚The brewery, founded in 1993 in Fenny Bentley, has relocated and expanded over the years. It moved to its current address in 2011, where it effectively took over the existing Tap House Brewery (established 2010) but continued to brew the latter's beers. Since 2015, however, Tap House beers have become rebadged Leatherbritches products. !! ◆ LIVE

Goldings (ABV 3.6%) BITTER
Bounder (ABV 3.8%) GOLD
Lemongrass & Ginger (ABV 3.8%) SPECIALITY
Ashbourne Ale (ABV 4%) PALE
Cad (ABV 4%) BITTER
Dr Johnson (ABV 4%) BITTER
Scoundrel (ABV 4.1%) PORTER
Mad Ruby (ABV 4.4%) BITTER
Raspberry Belter (ABV 4.4%) SPECIALITY
Ashbourne IPA (ABV 4.7%) PALE
Hairy Helmet (ABV 4.7%) GOLD
Spitting Feathers (ABV 4.8%) BITTER
Bespoke (ABV 5%) BITTER
Game Over (ABV 5%) BITTER
Porter (ABV 5.5%) PORTER
Scary Hairy Export (ABV 7.2%) IPA

Little SIBA

Unit 9, Robinson Industrial Estate, Shaftesbury Street, Derby, DE23 8NL
☎ (01332) 987100 ⊕ littlebrewing.co.uk

Established in 2015 as Littleover Brewery, in 2020 it changed hands and in 2022 rebranded as Little Brewing Company. Using an eight-barrel kit, the team brew three times a week. The award-winning core range is vegan and gluten free. ☛ ◆ GF V

Loop (ABV 3.7%) PALE
Here Comes the Sun (ABV 3.9%) PALE
King George's Bitter (ABV 4%) BITTER
Epiphany Pale Ale (ABV 4.1%) PALE
The Panther Oatmeal Stout (ABV 4.2%) STOUT
Hush (ABV 4.4%) PALE
Taj Session IPA (ABV 4.6%) PALE
Rambler (ABV 5.6%) IPA

Contract brewed for Boot Beer Ltd:
Clod Hopper (ABV 3.9%) GOLD
Bitter (ABV 4.3%) BITTER

Marlpool

⊟ 5 Breach Road, Marlpool, Heanor, DE75 7NJ
☎ (01773) 711285 ☎ 07963 511855
⊕ marlpoolbrewing.co.uk

Marlpool was founded in 2010 by brothers Andy and Chris McAuley. The two-barrel brewery is situated behind the Marlpool Ale House. The brewery yard doubles up as a beer garden and the majority of the beer is sold through the Ale House and served unfined. The remainder is sold to reputable outlets. !! ◆ LIVE

Matlock Wolds Farm SIBA

South Barn, Cavendish Road, Farm Lane, Matlock, DE4 3GZ
☎ (01629) 697989 ☎ 07852 263263
⊕ woldsfarm.co.uk

⊠ Since starting in 2014 this family-run brewery has expanded several times. A five-barrel plant is currently used in a converted barn on the owner's 17th century farm. The full range of cask and bottle-conditioned ales are vegetarian and vegan-friendly. Seasonal beers are available, including in KeyKeg. ◆ LIVE V

Simcoe (ABV 3.8%) GOLD

High Tor (ABV 4%) PALE
To the Bitter End (ABV 4.2%) BITTER
Riber Gold (ABV 4.3%) GOLD
100cc (ABV 4.9%) BITTER
Classic Porter (ABV 4.9%) PORTER

Moody Fox

Hilcote Country Club, Hilcote Lane, Hilcote, DE55 5HR
☎ 07702 253235 ✉ moodyfoxbrewery@gmail.com

Established in 2016, Moody Fox is a microbrewery specialising in traditional ales using the finest hops and barley from around the world. One micropub is owned, the Garrison, Mansfield.

Cub (ABV 3.8%) BITTER
Pale Tale (ABV 5.4%) PALE

Moot

⊟ c/o Red Lion Inn, Matlock Green, Matlock, DE4 3BT
☎ 07886 630985 ⊕ moot-ales.co.uk

⊚Moot Ales was established in 2018 and all its beers are available in the Red Lion pub to which it is attached. It has expanded its core range to allow most beer styles to be sampled: blonde, traditional best bitter, golden ale, IPA and a porter/stout. All beers are available in bottles. In addition, a craft keg beer is produced. LIVE

Morgan Brewmasters

⊟ Spirit Vaults, 53 Church Street, Melbourne, DE73 8EJ
☎ (01332) 300542 ☎ 07946 851828
✉ info@thespiritvaults.pub

⊚Fully refurbished in 2020, this brewery is incorporated into the Spirit Vaults, Melbourne (formerly the Blue Bell Inn, brewery tap for Shardlow brewery), and can be viewed from within the pub. It brews new recipes with a modern twist, plus the ever popular Reverend. !! ◆

Vaults Gold (ABV 4.2%) GOLD
Reverend (ABV 4.5%) BITTER
Vaults Dark (ABV 5%) STOUT

Muirhouse

Unit 1, Enterprise Court, Manners Avenue, Manners Industrial Estate, Ilkeston, DE7 8EW ☎ 07916 590525
⊕ muirhousebrewery.co.uk

Muirhouse was established in 2009 in a domestic garage in Long Eaton. It expanded in 2011 to its present location in Ilkeston and the plant was upgraded in 2016 to 7.5 barrels. !! ◆

Ruby Jewel (ABV 3.8%) RED
Shunters Pole (ABV 3.8%) BLOND
Shopping for Hops (ABV 3.9%) PALE
Fully Fitted Freight (ABV 4%) GOLD
Summit Hoppy (ABV 4%) PALE
Tick Tock (ABV 4%) BITTER
Blueberry Porter (ABV 4.1%) PORTER
Magnum Mild (ABV 4.5%) MILD
Pirate's Gold (ABV 4.5%) GOLD
Hat Trick IPA (ABV 5.2%) PALE
Stumbling Around (ABV 5.2%) RED

Old Sawley SIBA

⊟ White Lion, 352a Tamworth Road, Long Eaton, NG10 3AT
☎ (0115) 837 0250 ☎ 07722 311209
⊕ oldsawley.com

⊠ A 10-barrel microbrewery installed at the rear of the White Lion in Sawley. The White Lion stocks a full range of brews and the brewery is supplying Midland beer festivals, local pubs and pubs across the East Midlands. ♯♯♦LIVE

Oxbow (ABV 3.9%) BITTER
Little Jack (ABV 4.3%) PALE
Plummeth the Hour (ABV 4.5%) SPECIALITY
Tollbridge Porter (ABV 4.5%) PORTER

Peak SIBA

3-6 Park Farm Industrial Units, Longstone Lane, Ashford in the Water, DE45 1NH
☎ (01246) 583737 ⊕ peakales.co.uk

☺Peak Ales opened 2005 in a former derelict farm building on the Chatsworth Estate, aided by a DEFRA Rural Enterprise Scheme grant and support from trustees of Chatsworth Settlement. Main production moved to a new facility at Ashford in the Water in 2014 to increase capacity. On the original site there is a distillery and a shop for sales of its beer, merchandise and Chatsworth Gin. ♯♯🍴♦

Swift Nick (ABV 3.8%) BITTER
Easy-drinking, copper-coloured bitter with balanced malt and hops and a gentle hoppy bitter finish.
Bakewell Best Bitter (ABV 4.2%) BITTER
Ful-bodied tawny bitter with a hoppy bitterness against a malty background, leading to a hoppy dry aftertaste.
Chatsworth Gold (ABV 4.6%) SPECIALITY
Speciality beer made with honey, which gives a pleasant sweetness leading to a hop and malt finish.
Black Stag (ABV 4.8%) STOUT
DPA (Derbyshire Pale Ale) (ABV 5%) PALE
IPA (ABV 6%) IPA

Pentrich SIBA

Unit B, Asher Lane Business Park, Asher Lane, Pentrich, DE5 3RB
☎ (01773) 741700 ⊕ pentrichbrewing.com

⊠ Two former home brewers began producing beer in their garage in Pentrich before moving to share the plant at The Beehive Inn, Ripley in 2014. In 2016 they moved into their own premises using secondhand equipment. In 2019 they purchased a made-to-order, 16-barrel plant. Every brew produced is a special brew (no regular beers). Local free trade outlets are supplied while a wholesaler distributes more widely. ♦

Popeye (NEW)

🍴 Hop Wright Inn, 8 Ray Street, Heanor, DE75 7GE
✉ wrightsbunch@gmail.com

Onsite brewery for the Hop Wright Inn micropub.

RBA

8 Oswestry Close, Oakwood, Derby, DE21 2RT
☎ 07943 367765 ✉ rbabrewery@gmail.com

In 2015 two friends, Richard Burton and Colin Fryer, began homebrewing in a shed in a back garden. Five years later they decided to sell commercially, and production increased accordingly. The 0.25-barrel plant brews once a week with occasional brews being bottled. Further increase in production is planned.

Red Dog (NEW)

Unit 6, Gallows Industrial Park, off Furnace Road, Ilkeston, DE7 5EP ☎ 07460 480457
⊕ reddogales.com

10-barrel microbrewery located on the Nottinghamshire and Derbyshire border producing a modern take on traditional cask ales.

Rolling Home (ABV 3.8%) PALE
Bonny Best (ABV 4.4%) BITTER
Pit Black (ABV 4.5%) STOUT
Unit 6 (ABV 4.9%) IPA

Resting Devil

🍴 Chesterfield Arms, 40 Newbold Street, Chesterfield, S41 7PH

Established in 2022 at the Chesterfield Arms, producing cask ales for the pub and occasionally for beer festivals. Bottled beers are also available.

Rock Mill

Office: 81-83 Bridge Street, New Mills, SK22 4DN
☎ (01663) 743999 ☎ 07971 747050
✉ rbpine@hotmail.co.uk

⊠ Rock Mill is a microbrewery established by Ray Barton, a former homebrewer, in 2016. Brewing is currently suspended while new premises are sought. 🍴♦

Shiny

Unit 10, Old Hall Mill Business Centre, Little Eaton, Derby, DE21 5EJ
☎ (01332) 902809 ⊕ shinybrewing.com

Brewing commenced in 2012 using a six-barrel plant sited in the beer garden of the Furnace Inn, Derby. After initially brewing solely for the pub, 2014 saw an increase in scale and output, with beers distributed across most of the country. A second 12-barrel brew plant was added in 2015 to increase capacity and host a visitor centre, taproom and shop. 🍴♦LIVE 🍴

New World (ABV 3.7%) BITTER
Happy People (ABV 4.1%) PALE
Wrench (ABV 4.4%) STOUT
4 Wood (ABV 4.5%) BITTER
Affinity (ABV 4.6%) GOLD
Disco Balls (ABV 5.3%) PALE

Shottle Farm

Office: School House Farm, Lodge Lane, Shottle, DE56 2DS
☎ (01773) 550056 ☎ 07877 723075
⊕ shottlefarmbrewery.co.uk

Located in the hills above Belper, the Grade II-listed farm is part of the Chatsworth Estate. Established in 2011 with a 10-barrel plant, beers are now contract brewed elsewhere. Shottle Farm has an onsite bar (limited opening hours), the Bull Shed, which is the only outlet for its beers. ♦LIVE

Silver SIBA

Units 3 & 4, Silver House, Adelphi Way, Staveley, S43 3LJ
☎ (01246) 470074 ☎ 07496 757619
✉ richard@silverbrewhouse.com

⊠ Silver Brewhouse is a 12-barrel brewery producing hop-forward and traditional ales. It also brews under the brand names Industrial Ales and Funky Hop Donkey including a range of single hopped ales under the Arkwright Pal label. 🍴♦LIVE

West Coast Pale Ale (ABV 3.7%) PALE
Baby Ghost IPA (ABV 3.9%) GOLD
Independence APA (ABV 4.1%) PALE
Eyup Cocka! (ABV 4.3%) GOLD
Anubis Porter (ABV 5.2%) PORTER
Grey Ghost IPA (ABV 5.9%) IPA

Brewed under the Industrial Ales brand name:
Brickworks Bitter (ABV 4%) BITTER
Stephensons Pale (ABV 4%) PALE
Arkwrights Pale (ABV 4.1%) PALE
Coal Face Stout (ABV 4.5%) STOUT
Iron Ore IPA (ABV 5%) PALE

Taddington

Blackwell Hall, Blackwell, Buxton, SK17 9TQ
☎ (01298) 85734 ✉ richard@moravka-lager.co.uk

Taddington started brewing in 2007, and brews one Czech-style, unpasteurised lager in two different strengths.

Temper

🍴 Dronfield Arms (Basement), 91 Chesterfield Road, Dronfield, S18 2XE ☎ 07725 639648

Office: 18 Egerton Road, Dronfield, S18 2LG
⊕ temperbrewing.com

⊗ Situated in the basement of the Dronfield Arms, this 5.5-barrel plant is run by Chris Wigg who started brewing there in 2021. The beers are mainly brewed for the upstairs Arms bar, in both cask and KeyKeg, and are also available wholesale.

Thorley & Sons

Ilkeston, DE7 5JB ☎ 07899 067723
✉ dylan.thorley1@yahoo.co.uk

Thorley & Sons began brewing commercially in 2016 on a 1.5-barrel plant located in an old coach house at the rear of brewer Dylan Thorley's house.

Pale & Interesting (ABV 4.5%) PALE

Thornbridge SIBA

Riverside Business Park, Buxton Road, Bakewell, DE45 1GS
☎ (01629) 815999 ⊕ thornbridgebrewery.co.uk

☺The first Thornbridge craft beers were produced in 2005 using a 10-barrel brewery, housed in the grounds of Thornbridge Hall. The beers have gained considerable success with over 300 consumer and industry awards won. A 30-barrel brewery opened in Bakewell in 2009. The original site continues to develop new, seasonal and speciality beers. 200 outlets are supplied direct. 12 pubs are managed and owned. 🍴🍴♦LIVE V

Wild Swan (ABV 3.5%) BLOND
Extremely pale yet flavoursome and refreshing beer. Plenty of lemon citrus hop flavour, becoming increasingly dry and bitter in the finish and aftertaste.
Astryd (ABV 3.8%) GOLD
Brother Rabbit (ABV 4%) BITTER
Lord Marples (ABV 4%) BITTER
Smooth, traditional, easy-drinking bitter. Caramel, malt and coffee flavours fall away to leave a long, bitter finish.
The Wednesday (ABV 4%) BLOND
Ashford (ABV 4.2%) BITTER
AM:PM (ABV 4.5%) GOLD

Market Porter (ABV 4.5%) PORTER
Kipling (ABV 5.2%) GOLD
Golden pale bitter with aromas of grapefruit and passion fruit. Intense fruit flavours continue throughout, leading to a long bitter aftertaste.
Jaipur IPA (ABV 5.9%) IPA
Flavoursome IPA packed with citrus hoppiness nicely counterbalanced by malt and underlying sweetness and robust fruit flavours.
Cocoa Wonderland (ABV 6.8%) SPECIALITY
Saint Petersburg Imperial Russian Stout (ABV 7.4%) STOUT
Good example of an Imperial stout. Smooth and easy to drink with raisins, bitter chocolate and hops throughout, leading to a lingering coffee and chocolate aftertaste.

Contract brewed for Kelham Island Brewery:
Pale Rider (ABV 5.2%) PALE

Thornsett

Thornsett Fields Farm, Briargrove Road, Thornsett, Birch Vale, SK22 1AX ☎ 07803 477812
⊕ thornsettbrewery.co.uk

☺Located on Thornsett Fields Farm in Thornsett, High Peak, the brewery uses a one-barrel plant with three fermenters. The brewery is off-grid, and is as sustainable and eco-friendly as possible, relying on renewable energy sources. Alongside the brewery is an organic hop yard with eight different hop varieties. Its onsite taproom has open days with local food traders. 🍴♦

Blue Ron's Ale (ABV 3.4%) BLOND
Home Sweet Home (ABV 3.6%) MILD
Best Bitter (ABV 4%) BITTER
He's Behind You (ABV 4.2%) PALE
Beep Beep Corner (ABV 5%) STOUT
New Mills Madness (ABV 5%) PALE

Tollgate SIBA

Unit 1, Southwood House Farm, Staunton Lane, Calke, LE65 1RG
☎ (01283) 229194 ⊕ tollgatebrewery.co.uk

⊗ This six-barrel brewery was founded in 2005 on the site of the former Brunt & Bucknall Brewery in nearby Woodville, but relocated to new premises on the National Trust's Calke Park estate in 2012. Around 20 outlets are supplied direct, mainly in the North Midlands, with most cask production directed to the brewery's three micropubs: Queens Road Tap, Leicester, Tap at No.76, Ashby-de-la-Zouch, and Town Street Tap, Duffield, plus the onsite Tap, the Milking Parlour. 🍴🍴♦LIVE V♦

Hackney Blonde (ABV 3.9%) SPECIALITY
Duffield Amber (ABV 4.4%) BITTER
Ashby Pale (ABV 4.5%) PALE
Old Rasputin (ABV 4.5%) STOUT
Red Star IPA (ABV 4.5%) PALE
Billy's Best Bitter (ABV 4.6%) BITTER

Torrside

New Mills Marina, Hibbert Street, New Mills, SK22 3JJ
☎ (01663) 745219 ☎ 07539 149175
⊕ torrside.co.uk

☺Established by three friends in 2015, Torrside brews a wide range of beers on a 10-barrel plant, under the tagline Hops, Smoke, Monsters. A changing line-up of largely hop-driven, smoked and strong beers are sold to pubs, bars and bottle shops within a 50-mile radius. All beers are unfined. Brewery tap events usually take place one weekend each month (March-September) and there's also a smoked beer festival held in September.

The Shrub Club, Torr Vale Mill, permanently serves five Torrside beers (KeyKeg). ‼️ 🍴 LIVE

Candlewick (ABV 4%) STOUT
Yellow Peak (ABV 4.2%) PALE
Franconia (ABV 5.2%) SPECIALITY
I'm Spartacus (ABV 6.8%) IPA

Townes

🏠 Speedwell Inn, Lowgates, Staveley, Chesterfield, S43 3TT
☎ (01246) 472252

Townes Brewery was started by Alan Wood in 1994 at an old ice cream factory and moved to its present site, the Speedwell Inn at Staveley, in 1997. The brewery and pub were taken over by Lawrie and Nicoleta Evans on Alan's retirement in 2013. They continue to use Alan's recipes at the five-barrel brewery. Townes beers are rarely found outside the pub, other than occasional swaps and at beer festivals.

Urban Chicken SIBA

Ilkeston, DE7 5EH ☎ 07976 913395
⊕ urbanchickenale.co.uk

Upgraded in 2022 to a 2.5-barrel brewery, producing small-batch beer for local pubs, restaurants, bottle shops and beer festivals. It was registered as a commercial brewery in 2016. Beers are produced in cask and can and are unfined.

Hop a Doodle Brew (ABV 4.2%) PALE
Pit Pony Stout (ABV 4.9%) STOUT
Benno Bitter (ABV 5.4%) BITTER
Subliminal Vision (ABV 6.3%) IPA
The Day is My Enemy (ABV 6.7%) IPA

Whim

Whim Farm, Hartington, SK17 0AX
☎ (01298) 84991 ⊕ whimales.co.uk

Whim Ales began brewing in 1993 in an outstanding location at Whim Farm near Hartington in the Derbyshire Dales, Peak District. It produces cask ales using the finest ingredients, Derbyshire hill water and its own yeast. The beers are available in 50-70 outlets and the brewery's tied house, Wilkes Head, Leek. ♦

Marynka (ABV 3.3%) GOLD
Arbor Light (ABV 3.6%) GOLD
Hartington Bitter (ABV 4%) PALE
Earl Grey Bitter (ABV 4.2%) BITTER
Hartington IPA (ABV 4.5%) PALE
Flower Power (ABV 5.3%) GOLD

Brunswick Inn, Derby (Photo: Stuart McMahon)

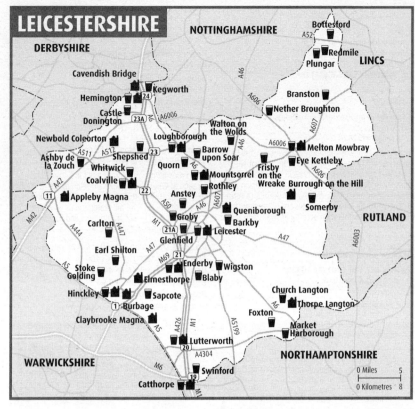

LEICESTERSHIRE

Anstey

Mash & Press L

46A Albion Street, LE7 7DE

☎ 07960 776843 ⊕ ansteyale.co.uk

House beer (by MonsteX Brewery); 4 changing beers (sourced locally; often MonsteX Brewery) Ⓗ

Established in 2015, the Mash & Press is a collaboration between Anstey Ale brewery and Charnwood Cider, and serves as tap house for both. Located in a two-storey former bakery, the upstairs bar has up to four changing cask ales on handpull, as well as up to four keg lines and eight real ciders, along with local wines, and a wide range of gins and other spirits. Outside is a newly refurbished beer garden with plenty of seating. The pub and its garden are dog friendly. ☎❀●🚃🐾🐕🛜

Ashby De La Zouch

Tap at No.76

76 Market Street, LE65 1AP

⊕ tollgatebrewery.co.uk

Tollgate Ashby Pale; 4 changing beers (often Tollgate) Ⓗ

This micropub on the high street was originally a medieval farmhouse and is one of the oldest buildings in town. Now a Tollgate brewery house, it offers a warm and friendly welcome. It serves five real ales, and third-pint tasting trays are available for those wishing to try the whole range of available beers. A large selection of bottle-conditioned Tollgate beers is available to take away. Snacks include pork pies. Q&🚃🐾

Barkby

Malt Shovel

27 Main Street, LE7 3QG

☎ (0116) 269 2558 ⊕ maltshovelbarkby.co.uk

Thwaites Original, Gold, Amber; 1 changing beer (often Thwaites) Ⓗ

This family-friendly village pub serves good-value home-cooked food in the bar and restaurant, while offering drinkers a warm welcome. Guest beers are supplied by Thwaites, and often come from other English breweries in the north-west. A beer festival is held on the first weekend in August. There is a large garden area for the summer months, leading down to the Barkby Brook. ☎❀🍴&P🚃🐾🛜

Barrow upon Soar

Navigation

87 Mill Lane, LE12 8LQ

☎ (01509) 412842

Greene King Abbot; 2 changing beers (sourced nationally; often Adnams, Marston's, Moorhouse's) Ⓗ

A warm and friendly pub that welcomes dogs and muddy boots, and children until 9pm. The open-plan main bar has distinct seating areas and a warming log-burner. There is a small snug at the front. Note the bar top incorporating old penny coins. The canalside patio is popular in summer, and moorings are available for passing pleasure boats. There is a function room available for hire. ☎❀🍴▶♿≈(Barrow-upon-Soar) ♣🚃(2) 🐾🛜♪

Blaby

Bakers Arms
The Green, LE8 4FQ
☎ (0116) 278 7253 ● thebakersarms.com
Everards Tiger, Old Original; 1 changing beer (often Everards) Ⓗ
Built in 1485 and first licensed in the mid 19th century, the Bakers Arms is a hidden gem in a back street near the village centre. There are three separate rooms formed from the cottages that were converted into the pub. The oven from the on-site bakery has been restored and is used for occasional bread-making courses. Good food is served and local cider is available in the summer. ⬔🕏🕮🍺🚌(84,85)🌸

Bottesford

Bull Ⓛ
Market Street, NG13 0BW
☎ (01949) 842288
Castle Rock Harvest Pale; Fuller's London Pride; Theakston Best Bitter Ⓗ
Set on the main road through this busy Leicestershire village, well served by train and bus, the Bull has a large bar area with a real fire and a separate lounge for quieter drinking, plus a function room. Three cask ales are served, including one LocAle. Outside is a seating area and a good-sized car park. Memorabilia in the lounge and a plaque outside commemorate Stan Laurel and Oliver Hardy's visits in the 1950s, when Laurel's sister was the landlady. 🕏🕮🅿🚌🛜♪

Branston

Wheel Inn 🍷 Ⓛ
Main Street, NG32 1RU
☎ (01476) 248165 ● thewheelinnbranston.co.uk
3 changing beers Ⓗ
This attractive stone-built 18th-century village pub houses a cosy bar with seating plus a larger restaurant with rustic tables and a real fire. The attractive outdoor area is quiet and relaxing in the summer months, with traditional outbuildings used for beer festivals and live music. The Wheel boasts an extensive food menu, using locally sourced ingredients where possible, including produce from the Belvoir Estate. Q🕏🕮🅿🛜♪

Carlton

Gate Hangs Well Ⓛ
39 Barton Road, CV13 0DB
☎ (01455) 290806 ● thegatehangswell.com
Church End What the Fox's Hat; Draught Bass; Sharp's Doom Bar; 1 changing beer Ⓗ
Village pub set in a beautiful rural location, with an L-shaped bar and a conservatory with views across open fields. A new restaurant/café has been added in a recent refurbishment. Beers include one from the local Church End brewery, Bass, Doom Bar and one guest. Popular quiz nights are held on the last Tuesday of every month, and there are also live music events. Q🕏🕮🅿🚌(153)🌸♪

Castle Donington

Flag
32 Borough Street, DE74 2LA
☎ 07841 374441
5 changing beers Ⓖ
A thriving micropub in the heart of a busy street. It serves real ales straight from the casks, visible from a

temperature-controlled cool-room cellar. It also has a range of ciders and an extensive selection of quality wines by the glass. Seating is available outside when the weather permits. Skylink bus services make it accessible from Derby, Nottingham, Loughborough and Leicester. Q🕏🍺🚌🛜🛜

Catthorpe

Cherry Tree Ⓛ
Main Street, LE17 6DB (on main road through village ½ mile from A5)
☎ (0116) 482 7042 ● cherrytreecatthorpe.co.uk
3 changing beers (sourced locally; often Dow Bridge, Langton, Phipps NBC) Ⓗ
Welcoming, two-roomed village local with a modern twist, which has been sympathetically renovated by the new owners. Ales from Catthorpe's Dow Bridge brewery take pride of place on the bar alongside English red and white wines, local gins and whiskies. Locally sourced home-cooked food includes vegetarian, vegan and children's options. The south-facing terrace and garden overlook the Avon Valley. Local CAMRA Country Pub of the Year 2022. Q🕏🕮🅿🌸🛜♪

Church Langton

Langton Arms Ⓛ
Main Street, LE16 7SY
☎ (01858) 545396 ● thelangtonarms.com
4 changing beers (sourced nationally; often Charnwood, Langton) Ⓗ
Reopened by Little Britain Pub Co in 2018 after a two-year closure, the Langton Arms has been extended and refurbished and serves amazing local beers and great seasonal food that is cooked on site. The pub manages to combine the feeling of a local country pub with a high-quality restaurant. With a garden suitable for summer and winter, this pub is worth visiting any time of the year. 🕮🅿(44)🌸🛜

Coalville

Rock Café & Bar
97 Meadow Lane, LE67 4DQ
☎ 07710 532970 ● rockales.beer

REAL ALE BREWERIES
Buswells 🍴 Burbage
Charnwood Loughborough
Dow Bridge Catthorpe
Elmesthorpe Elmesthorpe
Emperor's Newbold Coleorton
Everards Leicester
Golden Duck Appleby Magna
Great Central Leicester
Hemlock Hemington
Langton Thorpe Langton
Mill Hill Enderby (NEW)
MonsteX 🍴 Loughborough
Moonface ✦ Loughborough
Mount St Bernard Coalville
New Buildings Hinckley
Parish Burrough on the Hill
Pig Pub 🍴 Claybrooke Magna
Q Queniborough
Round Corner ✦ Melton Mowbray
Soar 🍴 Mountsorrel (NEW)
Treehouse Cavendish Bridge
Zero Six Lutterworth

House beer (by Shiny); 6 changing beers (sourced nationally) ⓗ

Previously a convenience store in a leafy suburb, this is a welcome addition to Coalville's beer scene. Deservedly popular, with the largest selection of real ales in the area plus a craft 'beer wall', the Rock also has an extensive selection of gins and wines. The café serves a wide range of dishes, sourced and prepared locally, and at competitive prices. Cobs are available at the bar for those with a hearty appetite. Q❀➤❀◑₲♣♿⚲🚆(29)❀🐾✿

Earl Shilton

Shilton Vaults
3 The Hollow, LE9 7NA
☎ 07715 106876
Draught Bass; 4 changing beers ⓗ

Previously a bank, this welcoming pub with friendly staff opened in 2018. There are three rooms – the main bar, a central room and the original vault – as well as a small outdoor space. The air-conditioned ground floor cellar has racking for 12 casks, and three or four real ales are available, alongside craft lagers, eight traditional ciders and speciality gins. Toilets are upstairs. Sister pub to the Pestle & Mortar in Hinckley. Q❀🚲♣♿⚲✿

Enderby

Everards Meadows 🛴
Cooper Way, LE19 2AN
☎ (0116) 201 4100 ⊕ everardsmeadows.co.uk
Everards Beacon Hill, Sunchaser, Tiger, Old Original; house beer (by Everards); 2 changing beers ⓗ

The new home of Everards brewery incorporates the Beer Hall, a large pub and restaurant. The full range of Everards regular beers is available, plus short-run specials, and three unique brews served from copper tanks behind the bar. The site of the old brewery opposite is now a large shopping area. Extensive grounds with walks connect up with the canal towpath and the Great Central Way footpath. ➤❀◑₲♿⚲🚆(50,X84)❀✿

New Inn
51 High Street, LE19 4AG
☎ (0116) 286 3126
Everards Tiger; 2 changing beers (often Everards) ⓗ

Friendly thatched village local dating from 1549, tucked away at the top of the High Street. Everards' first tied house, the pub is well known locally for the quality of its beer and is frequented by the brewery's staff. Three rooms are served by a central bar, with long alley skittles and a function room in a covered walkway to the rear. Outside there is a patio area. Lunches are served Wednesday to Saturday. Q➤❀◑♣⚲🚆(50)❀✿

Eye Kettleby

Eye Kettleby Lakes Clubhouse 🛴
Eye Kettleby Lakes, LE14 2TD
☎ (01664) 565900 ⊕ eyekettlebylakes.com
Langton Inclined Plane Bitter; Sharp's Doom Bar; 1 changing beer (sourced nationally) ⓗ

The Eye Kettleby Lakes clubhouse is the hub of the holiday park and home to a bar and tearoom. The clubhouse offers a relaxing environment for guests to enjoy a drink from a fully stocked bar with local ales and over 30 different gins. The bar is open till late from Tuesday to Sunday in spring and summer, and in the evening from Wednesday to Saturday during autumn and winter. Visitors are advised to contact reception for exact opening times. Q➤❀🚲◑₲♿⚲P❀✿♪

Foxton

Bridge 61 🛴 ✅
Bottom Lock, LE16 7RA
☎ (0116) 279 2285 ⊕ foxtonboats.co.uk
Adnams Southwold Bitter; 1 changing beer (sourced locally; often Langton) ⓗ

The smaller of the two pubs situated at the bottom of the famous flight of 10 Foxton locks. The two-roomed interior comprises a snug with a serving-hatch bar and a larger room with wide doors that open out onto the waterfront. The garden has barbecue facilities and is an ideal spot for watching the boats pass by. The guest beer is from the nearby Langton brewery. Food is served all day. Weekend hours may be extended during the summer months. Q➤❀◑₲♿⚲🚆(44)❀

Frisby on the Wreake

Bell Frisby 🛴
2 Main Street, LE14 2NJ
☎ (01664) 43496 ⊕ thebellfrisby.com
Charnwood Vixen; 2 changing beers (sourced locally) ⓗ

The Bell has reopened as a community-owned pub. It has three real ales, one regular and two locally sourced changing ales. The interior consists of three rooms with traditional wooden beams, and is clean and bright with simple decor. There's a conservatory to the rear used as a community hub and an overflow for pub diners (there is a limited menu). The outside tables and chairs are used as a non-smoking area. Q➤❀◑♣P🚆❀✿

Glenfield

Forge Inn 🛴
Main Street, LE3 8DG
☎ (0116) 287 1702 ⊕ theforgeinn.co.uk
Everards Tiger, Old Original; 2 changing beers (sourced nationally) ⓗ

A village pub on the edge of Leicester with a welcoming atmosphere. Two regular and two guest beers are available, with a changing cider, usually from a local producer. Modern British food is available in the restaurant and snacks in the bar. Quiz night is Sunday. A charity music festival is held in May. The pub has launched a bring back jugs campaign which continues to be well received. Q➤❀◑₲♿♣⚲🚆(40,13)✿

Groby

Stamford Arms 🛴
2 Leicester Road, LE6 0DJ
☎ (0116) 287 5616 ⊕ stamfordarms.co.uk
Everards Beacon Hill, Tiger, Old Original; 4 changing beers (sourced nationally) ⓗ

At the heart of the community since 1921, the Stamford Arms is a fantastic pub that also sells food. It has seven cask ales, craft beer, cider and an extensive gin selection. The extensive food offering is traditional with daily specials and a pizza oven. Covered outdoor dining pods are available, seating up to four people. A recent local CAMRA Country Pub of the Year. ➤❀◑₲♣⚲P🚆❀✿♪

Hemington

Jolly Sailor
21 Main Street, DE74 2RB
☎ (01332) 812665
Draught Bass; 4 changing beers (sourced regionally) ⓗ

This 17th-century building is thought to have originally been a weaver's cottage. A pub since the 19th century, it is now the only one in the village. It retains many original features including old timbers, open fires and a beamed ceiling – convenient for hanging the collection of beer mugs. There is a large seating area outside. Well filled rolls are available. Q❄️✿&P❀☀️🧡🛜

Hinckley

Elbow Room

26 Station Road, LE10 1AW

☎ 07900 191388

6 changing beers (sourced nationally) G

This family-run micropub, decorated in an industrial style, offers a warm welcome and a great atmosphere. The ales and ciders are served by gravity directly from the cellar which is behind sliding glass doors. The beers are supported by a range of high-quality wines, world craft beers and lagers, whiskies, vodkas and over 40 gins, as well as a range of soft drinks. Pork pies and Scotch eggs are sold. There is no TV, jukebox or gaming machine as conversation is king. Children are welcome until evening. Q❄️✿&♣●🖥🧡🛜

New Plough Inn ♟ ✅

Leicester Road, LE10 1LS

☎ (01455) 615037 🌐 thenewploughinn.co.uk

Courage Directors; Marston's Pedigree; Tetley Bitter; 5 changing beers (sourced nationally) H

Opened at the beginning of the last century, it was called the New Plough because a pub called the Plough was already in existence in Hinckley. This welcoming and friendly local pub features old settles, a skittles alley, over 50 gins, and rugby memorabilia that reflects sponsorship of the local team. The landlady is a longstanding CAMRA member and the pub has raised over £150,000 for charity via the monthly quiz. Local CAMRA Pub of the Year in 2022 and 2023. ❄️✿♣🖥🧡🛜

Pestle & Mortar 🅛

81 Castle Street, LE10 1DA

☎ 07715 106876 🌐 thepestlehinckley.co.uk

Draught Bass; 8 changing beers (sourced nationally) H

Opened in 2015, Hinckley's first micropub is a frequent winner of both the local CAMRA Pub of the Year and Cider Pub of the Year awards, and is a former winner of East Midlands Cider Pub of the Year. Up to 22 changing traditional ciders are on offer, and handpumps deliver up to eight changing real ales from casks behind the bar. Cobs are available. This comfortable, quirky micropub, with a friendly atmosphere, satisfies a wide range of drinking tastes. Q❄️⇌♣●🖥(8)🧡🛜

Queen's Head

Upper Bond Street, LE10 1RJ

☎ 07951 063484

Draught Bass; 3 changing beers H

A warm welcome awaits at this multi award-winning family-run Victorian free house serving Bass alongside three ever-changing real ales. The original building dates back to 1809 and has been sympathetically refurbished. It features open fires, a Victorian range, and a new snug, helping to create a cosy atmosphere. A large pleasant beer garden to the rear is a suntrap during the summer months. A four-time local CAMRA Pub of the Year. ✿&♣🖥(158,148)

Kegworth

Red Lion

24 High Street, DE74 2DA

☎ (01509) 672466 🌐 redlionkegworth.co.uk

Charnwood Salvation, Vixen; Courage Directors; Marston's Pedigree; 3 changing beers (sourced nationally; often Dancing Duck) H

Refurbished Georgian building on the historic A6 route, with six rooms including a restaurant and the new lodge. It serves seven cask beers, along with a large selection of gins, whiskies and wines. Sunday lunch is popular. Outside is a beer garden with ample seating, and a large car park. Q❄️✿⇌🌙◑&♣P🖥🧡🛜♪

Leicester

Ale Stone

660 Aylestone Road, Aylestone, LE2 8PR

Leatherbritches Ashbourne Ale; 2 changing beers (sourced locally) H

Micropub in a converted shop unit, featuring a nicely furnished interior with wooden benches and dados all round. A large barrel with a millstone top forms a table in the centre. Up to three real ales, plus two ciders, are stillaged in a temperature-controlled glass-fronted cellar, which is visible from the bar. Ham and cheese cobs are available. Q❄️✿●🖥🧡🛜

Ale Wagon 🅛

27 Rutland Street, LE1 1RE

☎ (0116) 262 3330 🌐 thealewagon.co.uk

Hoskins Brothers Hob Bitter, IPA, 3 C's, Old Navigation; 4 changing beers (sourced regionally; often MonsteX Brewery) H

City-centre pub whose 1930s interior features an original oak staircase. It has two rooms with tiled and parquet floors and a central bar. On the walls are photos of the former Queen's Hotel, which was across the road from this pub in the 1930s, and the former Hoskins brewery. The pub still serves Hoskins family recipe beers. A function room is available to hire. Handy for the nearby Curve Theatre. ⇌●🖥

Babelas

77 Queens Road, Clarendon Park, LE2 1TT

☎ (0116) 270 7744

Oakham Citra; Timothy Taylor Landlord; 1 changing beer H

Converted wine merchant's shop in an area favoured by academics and urban professionals. The bar is spread over two floors, with quirky internationally sourced antiques throughout. The large front windows open up to create a continental ambience on warmer days. It is often busy at weekends, but always civilised. ❄️♣🖥(44,83)🛜

Black Horse

65 Narrow Lane, Aylestone, LE2 8NA

☎ (0116) 283 7225

Everards Tiger; 3 changing beers (often Titanic, Everards) H

Welcoming traditional Victorian pub with a distinctive bar servery, set in a village conservation area on the edge of the city. Up to eight real ales are available, as well as a changing range of four real ciders, and home-cooked food. Quiz night is Sunday and comedy features regularly. Beer festivals and community events are regularly hosted. There is a large beer garden, and a skittle alley and function room are available for hire. Coaches are welcome by prior arrangement. Q❄️✿🌙◑♣●🖥🧡🛜♪

Blue Boar ⓛ

16 Millstone Lane, LE1 5JN

☎ (0116) 319 6230 ⊕ blueboarleicester.co.uk

Beowulf Finn's Hall Porter; house beer (by Shiny) Ⓗ; **7 changing beers** Ⓗ/Ⓖ

This single-room micropub, named after the Blue Boar Inn where Richard III stayed before the Battle of Bosworth Field. The cellar is visible through a glass partition behind the bar. Guest beers are from microbreweries around the country, including many rare brews. Local pork pies and well-filled cobs are sold. Board games and reading material may be found on the shelves, and there are displays of old maps of Leicester on the walls. Q❄ ☞ ≉ ♣ ➊ 🍴 🦮 ⚘ 🛜 ♫

Globe

43 Silver Street, LE1 5EU

☎ (0116) 253 9492 ⊕ theglobeleicester.com

Everards Tiger, Old Original; 4 changing beers (often Everards) Ⓗ

A snug near the entrance and an island servery surrounded by small rooms are features of this historic pub, which serves a good range of beer and cider alongside real ale. An upstairs function room has its own servery. There is a good collection of local photos and bric-a-brac throughout. Restored gas lights are used on special occasions. ☞ ◐ ♿ ≉ ➊ 🦮 ⚘ 🛜

High Cross ✔

103-105 High Street, LE1 4JB (400yds from Clock Tower on corner of High St)

☎ (0116) 251 9218

Greene King Abbot; Ruddles Best Bitter; Sharp's Doom Bar; 6 changing beers (sourced nationally) Ⓗ

This Wetherspoon conversion of a former shop is named after the cross marking the centre of medieval Leicester (it has been resited in Jubilee Square nearby). The room is a large L-shaped area with some changes of level to split it into different areas. The range of guest beers often includes ones from local breweries. There are twice-yearly beer festivals as part of national company events. There is an attractive non-smoking yard at the back. ☞ ❄ ◐ ♿ ➊ 🦮 🛜

King's Head

36 King Street, LE1 6RL

☎ (0116) 254 8240

Black Country Bradley's Finest Golden, Chain Ale, Pig on the Wall, Fireside; 7 changing beers Ⓗ

A traditional one-room city-centre local owned by Black Country Ales. Twelve handpulls serve seven regularly changing guest ales and a cider. A range of bottles is also stocked. Meals are not served but filled cobs are often available. Live sport is shown on TV. Its open fire and covered roof terrace make it popular throughout the year with real ale and cider enthusiasts, as well as visitors to the local football and rugby grounds on match days. ❄ ≉ ➊ 🦮 ⚘ 🛜

Old Horse ✔

198 London Road, LE2 1NE

☎ (0116) 254 8384 ⊕ oldhorseleicester.co.uk

Everards Sunchaser, Tiger, Old Original; 3 changing beers (sourced nationally; often Everards) Ⓗ

Traditional 19th-century coaching inn, handy for dog walkers, students and sports supporters. It has four guest beers that change monthly, and a cider bar serving eight handpulled options. Tasty, good-value food is served, including a Sunday carvery. Behind the building is the largest pub garden in Leicester, complete with children's play equipment. Regular quiz nights, karaoke and special events take place. A frequent local CAMRA Cider Pub of the Year. ☞ ❄ ◐ ♿ ♣ ➊ P 🦮 ⚘ 🛜 ♫

Real Ale Classroom ⓛ

22 Allandale Road, Stoneygate, LE2 2DA

☎ (0116) 319 6998 ⊕ therealaleclassroom.com

4 changing beers (often Pentrich, Polly's, Two by Two) Ⓖ

Classroom-themed micropub run by former teachers in a converted suburban shop. The furniture includes reclaimed desks with original graffiti and the beers are written up on a blackboard. Cask, KeyKeg ales and ciders are served from a home-made chiller cabinet behind the high bar. Seating around large tables in both rooms encourages conversation between regulars and visitors, and a log-burner warms the rear room. Crisps, nuts and scratchings are available and the pub sells take-away cans. Q ☞ ❄ ♣ ➊ 🍴 🦮 ⚘ 🛜 ♫

Salmon

19 Butt Close Lane, LE1 4QA (from Clock Tower walk down Churchgate, Butt Close Ln is second left)

☎ (0116) 253 2301

Black Country Bradley's Finest Golden, Chain Ale, Pig on the Wall, Fireside; 7 changing beers (sourced nationally) Ⓗ

A small corner local whose single U-shaped room is decorated in bright traditional style. A Black Country Ales pub since 2016, it has a friendly, welcoming atmosphere and a strong sports following. The 12 handpumps serve beers from Black Country Ales alongside two real ciders and guest breweries. Cobs, pork pies and Scotch eggs are available throughout the day. Bus stations are nearby. Q ☞ ❄ ♿ ♣ ➊ 🦮 ⚘ 🛜 ♫

Two-Tailed Lion

22 Millstone Lane, LE1 5JN

☎ (0116) 224 4769 ⊕ thetwotailedlion.com

3 changing beers Ⓗ

A modern, beer-orientated pub, which was originally a Victorian dwelling, featuring three handpumps and six keg taps with a regular rotation of beers in a wide variety of styles. There is also a well-stocked bottle and can fridge. Unobtrusive music is played in the bar. As well as the small downstairs bar with a range of comfortable seating there are two upstairs rooms that can be hired. The food offering is samosas. ☞ 🦮 ⚘ 🛜

Loughborough

Moonface Brewery & Tap

13 Moira Street, LE11 1AU (Moira St is accessed from Barrow St)

☎ (01509) 700171

4 changing beers (sourced nationally; often Moonface) Ⓖ

Popular micropub offering a constantly changing range of three to five real ales served direct from casks stillaged behind the counter. Two changing KeyKeg brews are also served, and there is a range of bottled Belgian beers. The in-house Moonface microbrewery is visible in a room directly behind the bar. Live music, craft evenings and fish & chips evenings feature. Local CAMRA Micro and Cider Pub of the Year 2023. Q ❄ ♿ ➊ 🦮 (2,127) ⚘ 🛜

Needle & Pin

15 The Rushes, LE11 5BE

☎ 07973 754236

4 changing beers (sourced nationally) Ⓗ

Loughborough's first genuine micropub, created from an old electronics shop in 2016, continues to serve an impressive, ever-changing range of handpulled and gravity-fed real ales, plus a choice of several ciders and perries. More than 80 types of foreign and craft bottled beers are also available. There is more extensive seating available upstairs. Pizzas can be ordered from a local supplier and delivered to your table. Card payment only. Q☕🍴🍺🚌♿♪

Organ Grinder 🍸

4 Woodgate, LE11 2TY

☎ (01509) 264008

Blue Monkey BG Sips, Primate Best Bitter, Guerrilla; 5 changing beers (sourced locally; often Blue Monkey) Ⓗ

Close to the town centre, this popular Blue Monkey brewery pub offers eight cask ales. The stable bar at the back reflects the pub's past life as a coaching inn. A choice of four real ciders sometimes includes a perry, and there are also Belgian bottled beers. Bar snacks include sausage rolls and an interesting range of pork pies. Live music most weekends. Local CAMRA Pub of the Year 2023. 🛏🏵🍴🚽🚌♿🛜♪

Wheeltapper

60 Wood Gate, LE11 2TZ

☎ (01509) 230829 🌐 wheeltapper.co.uk

5 changing beers (sourced regionally; often Nene Valley, Shiny, Shipstone's) Ⓗ

Ground-floor pub in a modern building whose decor has a railway theme, including reproduction posters and a board displaying photos of the the Great Central Heritage Railway, which is nearby. Furniture is basic. Five handpulls dispense the wide range of real ales, with regularly changing craft beers and real ciders also available. The pub is wheelchair accessible and dog friendly. 🏵♿🚆(Central)♣🐕🚌♿🛜

White Hart

27 Churchgate, LE11 1UD

☎ (01509) 236976 🌐 benpimlico.com/whitehart/home

Charnwood Salvation, Vixen; Timothy Taylor Landlord; 3 changing beers (sourced locally; often Leatherbritches) Ⓗ

Large, single-roomed pub close to the Market Place. The secluded patio and beer garden to rear are popular in sunny weather. Regularly changing guest beers are from local breweries such as Leatherbritches and Charnwood. Bar snacks and tapas are available until early evening. Live music features on Friday and Saturday evenings or occasional weekends. There is a 21 and over policy. 🛏🏵🍴♣🚌♿🛜♪

Lutterworth

Fox

34 Rugby Road, LE17 4BN (½ mile on main road from M1; 400yds from Whittle roundabout)

☎ (01455) 553877 🌐 fox-lutterworth.co.uk

Draught Bass; Sharp's Doom Bar; 2 changing beers (sourced nationally; often Purity, Timothy Taylor, Wadworth) Ⓗ

Welcoming 18th-century establishment at the southern end of Lutterworth, described as the town's village pub. An L-shaped, open-plan interior with a wooden floored bar and carpeted dining area is warmed by two open fires. Meals are served lunchtime and evenings, including excellent Sunday roasts. Thai food is available in the evenings in the adjacent Sawasdee restaurant. Outside is a large landscaped award-winning garden and drinking area. Quizzes are held on Tuesday evenings. 🏵🍴🐕🚌(58,X45)♿🛜♪

Real Ale Classroom

4 Station Road, LE17 4AP

☎ 07824 515334 🌐 therealaleclassroom.com

4 changing beers (sourced nationally) Ⓖ

A spacious micropub with a schoolroom theme owned by former teachers. It offers a constantly changing line-up of four cask and four craft keg ales, plus a wide range of bottled and canned beers and five ciders. The back room has a log-burner for winter and the fantastic beer garden can be enjoyed in the summer months. Friendly staff are knowledgeable about the drinks on offer, including excellent gin and spirits from local distillers. Pub snacks are locally sourced. Q🏵♣🐕🚌(X84,58)♿🛜♪

Unicorn

29 Church Street, LE17 4AE (town centre, near church)

☎ (01455) 552486 🌐 unicornlutterworth.co.uk

Draught Bass; Greene King IPA; 2 changing beers (sourced nationally; often Timothy Taylor) Ⓗ

Traditional street-corner local with a black-and-white frontage, built in 1919 on the site of an 18th-century coach house in the town centre near the church. The large public bar, with its open fire, shows TV sports. The small comfortable lounge, divided by a central fireplace, has photographs of old Lutterworth and doubles as a family-friendly area with the adjacent games room. Darts, dominoes and skittles teams are hosted. 🛏♣🚌(8,X44)♿🛜

Market Harborough

Admiral Nelson

49 Nelson Street, LE16 9AX

☎ (01858) 433173

Bombardier; 3 changing beers Ⓗ

A friendly and welcoming locals' pub in a quiet street west of the centre of this historic market town. There is a lounge with TV (often showing rugby) and a bar with darts, pool, jukebox and another TV. The pub has an outside courtyard with a heated and covered smoking area with seating. Food is also available, and there is a function room. 🏵🍴♣P🚌♿🛜♪

Beerhouse

76 St Mary's Road, LE16 7DX (directly behind St Marys chippy)

☎ (01858) 465317

6 changing beers (sourced nationally) Ⓟ

Market Harborough's first micropub is in a converted furniture shop. The focus is very much on beer – no food, gaming machines or loud music. There are 20 taps for draught products – the first eight for cask ales, the rest for KeyKegs and ciders. Monday night is quiz night, with occasional comedy nights and live music. A book club, vinyl nights and cider festival are also hosted. 🛏🏵♿🚆🐕P🚌♿🛜♪

Melton Mowbray

Charlie's Bar

7 King Street, LE13 1XA

☎ 07852 232937

2 changing beers (sourced nationally) Ⓚ

Located in a 14th-century former manor house, this is one of Melton Mowbray's oldest buildings, with a timber frame dating back to 1301. In the 1500s it was known as the manor of John Mowbray. A more contemporary use of the building was as Manchester and Son Clothiers, and their signage still appears to the front of the pub. It sellis a wide range of beer styles and cider from new and innovative breweries and producers. 🏵🚆🍴🚌(5,19)♿

Half Moon ✓

6 Nottingham Street, LE13 1NW

☎ (01664) 562120

Castle Rock Harvest Pale; Draught Bass; 1 changing beer (sourced nationally) 🅗
A long and narrow two-roomed building, next door to Ye Olde Pork Pie Shoppe in the middle of an old row of half-timbered buildings. The front bar starts on street level but then climbs to a higher level and the serving area. A small lounge is to the rear of this, leading to a courtyard to the rear and side of the building where there is a covered smoking area with tables and chairs.
🌣🏵♿🅿🖪🌣🛜♪

Kettleby Cross 🅛 ✅
Wilton Road, LE13 0UJ
☎ (01664) 485310
Greene King IPA, Abbot; Sharp's Doom Bar; 6 changing beers (sourced nationally) 🅗
The Kettleby Cross is a JD Wetherspoon new-build, opened in 2007 as a flagship eco-pub, complete with a prominent wind turbine on the roof. The pub stands close to the bridge over the nearby River Eye and is named after the cross that once directed travellers in the direction of Ab Kettleby. The interior consists of a large single room on two levels. As with most Wetherspoon pubs, it is usually busy with a good atmosphere.
🌣🕮♿♿🖪🛜

Mountsorrel

Sorrel Fox
75 Leicester Road, LE12 7AJ
☎ (0116) 230 3777
Charnwood Salvation, Vixen; 2 changing beers (sourced locally; often Charnwood) 🅗
Charnwood brewery's first micropub, a cosy, single-roomed bar. It serves the brewery's popular cask ales and craft beers, as well as an imported Austrian lager, plus bottled ciders, quality wines, a selection of gins and a couple of rums. Freshly made sausage rolls and a selection of bar snacks are available, with added cobs at the weekend. It is close to the A6, with a stop for buses to Leicester, Loughborough and Shepshed nearby.
Q♣🖪(127)🌣🛜

Swan Inn
10 Loughborough Road, LE12 7AT
☎ (0116) 230 2340
Black Sheep Best Bitter; Castle Rock Harvest Pale; Grainstore Ten Fifty; 2 changing beers (often Soar) 🅗
A traditional 17th-century, Grade II-listed coaching inn, entered via a narrow arch into a courtyard. The split-level interior has open fires, stone floors and low ceilings, and includes a small dining area. Good-quality, interesting food is cooked to order, the menu changing weekly and featuring regular themes. Outside is a long secluded riverside garden. The attached Soar microbrewery is visible in an adjacent building. Local CAMRA Pub of the Year 2022. Q🌣🏵🕮●🖪🌣♪

Nether Broughton

Anchor
Main Road, LE14 3HB
☎ (01664) 822461
Ringwood Razorback; 1 changing beer 🅗
A cosy village roadside pub on the A606 that reopened in 2015. The main bar has a real fire and a dartboard, and a separate dining area offers a quieter space. The pub has a large carpark, and pleasant outside seating. Traditional pub food is served regularly, with occasional themed nights. The pub hosts regular charity events, and welcomes families and dogs. 🌣🏵🕮♣🖪🌣♪

Plungar

Anchor 🅛
Granby Lane, NG13 0JJ
☎ (01949) 860589
3 changing beers 🅗
This brick building in the heart of this small Leicestershire village dates from 1774, having previously served as the local courtroom. The pub houses a large bar, cosy lounge and a separate pool room. Outside is an attractive beer garden and seating area. Up to three cask ales are served, featuring at least one local beer. There is a generous car park, making the pub popular with horse riders and cyclists. Local CAMRA Pub of the Year 2022.
Q🌣🏵♿♣🅿🖪(23)🌣🛜

Quorn

Royal Oak
2 High Street, LE12 8DT
☎ (01509) 415816 🌐 theroyaloakquorn.co.uk
Charnwood Vixen; St Austell Tribute; Timothy Taylor Landlord; 1 changing beer 🅗
Traditional 160-year-old inn in the centre of the village, formerly three terraced cottages. The internal walls were removed to open up the building, retaining many original features including beamed ceilings, tiled floors and an open log fire. Draught cider is occasionally available as the guest brew. A sheltered covered courtyard is to the side. Q🌣🏵🏵🚲Å●🖪🌣🛜

Redmile

Windmill ✅
4 Main Street, NG13 0GA
☎ (01949) 842281 🌐 thewindmillinnredmile.co.uk
2 changing beers (sourced locally; often Castle Rock, Shipstone's) 🅗
A privately owned and run restaurant and bar in Redmile, a mile down the hill from Belvoir Castle. It has two rooms: a lounge, and a stone-floored bar complete with log fire. Outside is a generous terrace. It enjoys a cult status among fans of television show Auf Wiedersehen Pet, in which the Windmill appeared as the Barley Mow, and photos taken during filming are on display.
Q🌣🕮Å🅿🖪🌣🛜

Rothley

Blue Bell Inn
59 Town Green Street, LE7 7NW
☎ (0116) 230 2201 🌐 thebluebellrothley.com
3 changing beers 🅗
This former Ansells local has full restaurant facilities. A raised entrance with a shady patio leads into the small front bar area divided into two parts, which is home to a dartboard and where weekend karaoke is held. At the back, in the former skittle alley, is the large restaurant, with an open kitchen and impressive exposed roof timbers. The 126-127 Leicester-Loughborough bus stops at the end of Town Green Street.
🌣🏵🕮♿♣🖪(126,127)🌣🛜♪

Woodman's Stroke
1 Church Street, LE7 7PD
☎ (0116) 230 2785 🌐 thewoodies.co.uk
Charnwood Vixen; Woodforde's Wherry; Bass; 1 changing beer 🅗
The Woodies is a quintessentially English village pub, with thatched roof, exposed ceiling joists and stone floors. Out the back is a paved terrace with heated parasols, beyond which is a pétanque piste in the large

garden rolling down to Rothley brook. It has one guest and three regular beers, as well as a fine selection of wines. Good food is available weekday lunchtimes only. The large amount of rugby, cricket and golf memorabilia on display reflects the enthusiasm for sport. Q ⏵ ❀Ⓚℙ🖵 (126,127) ♣ ☜

Sapcote

Sapcote Club

19-21 Hinckley Road, LE9 4FS
☎ (01455) 272300 ⊕ sapcoteclub.co.uk
3 changing beers (sourced nationally) Ⓗ
This club offers a warm and friendly welcome to three different rooms, all with private bars, featuring regular games nights and entertainment throughout. It was refurbished in 2020 with re-upholstered benches, new floor tiling at the bar and repainted walls. Sky and BT Sports are shown in the main bar and the lounge. Local CAMRA Club of the Year 2022 and 2023. ⏵ Ġ ♣ ℙ

Shepshed

Black Swan

21 Loughborough Road, LE12 9DL
☎ (01509) 458929
Draught Bass; Greene King Abbot; Timothy Taylor Landlord; 2 changing beers (sourced nationally) Ⓗ
Multi-roomed pub in a prominent position close to the town centre, serving two guest beers alongside the regulars. The main room has two drinking areas, both with comfortable seating. A further small room can be used by families, and is available for hire for functions. Shepshed Dynamo football ground is nearby.
Q ⏵ ❀ ♣ ℙ🖵🖵 ♣ ☜

Hall Croft Tap

20-22 Hall Croft, LE12 9AN
☎ (01509) 729920 ⊕ charnwoodbrewery.co.uk/micropubs
Charnwood Salvation, Vixen; 2 changing beers (sourced locally; often Charnwood) Ⓟ
Charnwood brewery's second micropub features a central courtyard with a bar/lounge on one side and a large snug on the other, where families with children are welcome until 7pm at the weekend only. Snacks including pork pies are available. A flight of steps leads up from the courtyard to a large garden with seating at the rear of the pub. Wheelchair access is possible in the pub and courtyard, but not the garden.
⏵ ❀ Ġ🖵 (126,127)

Somerby

Stilton Cheese ♥ Ⓛ

High Street, LE14 2QB
☎ (01664) 454394 ⊕ stiltoncheeseinn.co.uk
Grainstore Ten Fifty; Marston's Pedigree; 3 changing beers (sourced nationally) Ⓗ
Welcoming family-run pub built in local ironstone in the late 16th century. It has a cosy bar with adjoining room featuring an eclectic mix of copper pots and pans, horse brasses, pictures of hunting scenes and a stuffed pike and badger. At least four real ales are always available, often from local breweries. Local CAMRA Pub of the Year 2019, 2020 and 2022. Q ⏵ ❀Ⓚⅅ ♣ ℙ🖵 ☜

Stoke Golding

George & Dragon Ⓛ

Station Road, CV13 6EZ
☎ (01455) 213268

Church End Goat's Milk, Gravediggers Ale, What the Fox's Hat, Stout Coffin, Fallen Angel; 2 changing beers (sourced locally; often Church End) Ⓗ
Renowned village local serving eight real ales from Church End brewery and a real cider. Good, home-cooked lunches feature local produce and bar snacks made on the premises are always available. The second Tuesday of each month is steak night, and lunch is served on the last Sunday. Close to the historic Bosworth Battlefield, the pub supports a number of clubs and societies. A popular destination for walkers, cyclists and boaters from the nearby Ashby Canal. Q ⏵ ❀ⓀⒶ♣ ♠ ℙ🖵 ♣ ☜

Swinford

Chequers ✔

High Street, LE17 6BL (near church)
☎ (01788) 860318 ⊕ chequersswinford.co.uk
Adnams Southwold Bitter; 2 changing beers (sourced nationally; often St Austell, Timothy Taylor) Ⓗ
A warm welcome is assured at this family-run community local, whose landlord has been in place for more than 36 years. The menu caters for all and includes vegetarian and children's options. The large garden and play area are popular with families in good weather. A marquee provides the venue for the annual music festival and is available for private hire. Pub games include table skittles. The 18th-century Stamford Hall, with a caravan park and museum, is less than a mile away. ⏵ ❀Ⓘ Ⓐ ♣ ℙ ♣ ☜ ♫

Walton on the Wolds

Anchor

2 Loughborough Road, LE12 8HT
☎ (01509) 880018
Charnwood Salvation; Draught Bass; Timothy Taylor Landlord; 1 changing beer (sourced regionally) Ⓗ
The Anchor is in the centre of a small village within easy reach of Leicester and Nottingham via the A46. It is a popular venue for locals as well as the many walkers, with or without their dogs, who stop for a well-earned rest. Outside is an elevated seating area to the front and a garden and large car park to the rear.
Q ⏵ ❀ 🖴Ⓘ ℙ🖵🖵 (27) ♣

Whitwick

Three Horseshoes ★

11 Leicester Road, LE67 5GN
☎ 07736 677855 ⊕ thethreehorseshoes-whitwick.co.uk
Draught Bass; Marston's Pedigree; 1 changing beer (sourced nationally) Ⓗ
Nicknamed Polly's after a former landlady, the Three Horseshoes was originally two separate buildings but now has two rooms. To the left is a long bar with a quarry-tiled floor and open fires, wooden bench seating and pre-war fittings; to the right is a similarly furnished small snug. It has been identified by CAMRA as having a nationally important historic pub interior. Q ⏵ ❀ ♣ 🖵

Wigston

Tap & Barrel

58 Leicester Road, LE18 1DR
☎ 07734 480280
5 changing beers Ⓖ
The unpretentious ambience in this pub is enhanced by bare timber floorboards, exposed ceiling joists braced with traditional timber herringbone strutting, a freestanding log-burning stove and ornamental turned spindles in the balustrade to the open staircase leading

to an extra seating area. The bar is built of rustic timber, with a thick slab of waney edge beech as the counter. Beer is dispensed behind the bar from casks kept in a perspex-fronted cooler cabinet with only taps poking through. 🛏♿♣♠P🚪🐾🛜♫

Breweries

Buswells

🏠 Lime Kilns Pub, Watling Street, Burbage, LE10 3ED
☎ (01455) 631158 ⊕ limekilnsinn.co.uk

Brewing started at the Lime Kilns pub, Burbage, in 2016 as a small batch brewery. It expanded to a two-barrel plant in 2017, providing up to 14 ales for the pub and other outlets, on demand. Bespoke brews are provided for events including several local beer festivals.

Charnwood SIBA

22 Jubilee Drive, Loughborough, LE11 5XS
☎ (01509) 218666 ⊕ charnwoodbrewery.co.uk

⊛Family-run, 10-barrel brewery, established in 2014. It offers core beers and up to three monthly specials across a wide range of styles. All beers are widely available locally, including at its two micropubs, the Sorrel Fox, Mountsorrel, and Hall Croft Tap, Shepshed. Planning permission has been granted for a third pub in Barrow upon Soar. Online ordering is available for local deliveries. ‼🚚♦

Salvation (ABV 3.8%) GOLD
Vixen (ABV 4%) BITTER
Blue Fox (ABV 4.2%) GOLD
APA (American Pale Ale) (ABV 4.8%) PALE
Old School (ABV 5%) OLD

Dow Bridge

2-3 Rugby Road, Catthorpe, LE17 6DA
☎ (01788) 869121 ☎ 07790 633525
⊕ dowbridgebrewery.co.uk

Dow Bridge commenced brewing in 2001 and takes its name from a local bridge where Watling Street spans the River Avon. The brewery uses English whole hops and malt with no adjuncts or additives. Seasonal and bottle-conditioned beers are also available. 🚚♦LIVE

Bonum Mild (ABV 3.5%) MILD
Complex dark brown, full-flavoured mild, with strong malt and roast flavours to the fore and continuing into the aftertaste, leading to a long, satisfying finish.
Acris (ABV 3.8%) BITTER
Centurion (ABV 4%) BITTER
Legion (ABV 4.1%) GOLD
Ratae'd (ABV 4.3%) BITTER
Tawny-coloured, full-bodied beer with bitter hop flavours against a grainy background, leading to a long, bitter and dry aftertaste.
DB Dark (ABV 4.4%) MILD
Gladiator (ABV 4.5%) BITTER
Fosse Ale (ABV 4.8%) BITTER
Praetorian Porter (ABV 5%) PORTER
Onslaught (ABV 5.2%) BITTER

Elmesthorpe

Church Farm, Station Road, Elmesthorpe, LE9 7SG
☎ 07754 321283 ⊕ elmesthorpebrewery.com

Elmesthorpe was established in 2017 by a beer enthusiast and pub landlord. The brewery has gone from strength to strength and now supplies many pubs and taprooms in Leicestershire, Nottinghamshire, Warwickshire, Derbyshire and Staffordshire.

Tight Bar Steward (ABV 3.7%) MILD
CAPA (ABV 3.8%) BITTER
Aylmers Ale (ABV 4.1%) BITTER
Barons Best Bitter (ABV 4.3%) BITTER
Hansom Ale (ABV 4.4%) GOLD
Lord Cullens Ruby (ABV 4.5%) BITTER
Debbie Does (ABV 4.9%) GOLD
Ale O'Clock (ABV 5.2%) BITTER
Taking the Biscuit (ABV 5.3%) BITTER

Emperor's

Newbold Farm,, 2 Worthington Lane, Newbold Coleorton, Coalville, LE67 8PH
⊕ emperorsbrewery.co.uk

Former homebrewer now brewing imperial stouts and porters commercially.

Everards SIBA

Cooper Way, Everards Meadows, Leicester, LE19 2AN
☎ (0116) 201 4100 ⊕ everards.co.uk

⊛Everards was established in 1849 by William Everard and remains an independent, fifth generation family company. It has an estate of 153 pubs throughout the East Midlands and beyond. In 2021, a new state-of-the-art brewery was opened, comprising a main brewery, small-batch brewery, beer hall, shop and offices. All beers are brewed in-house again. Limited edition beers, small batch beers, and brewery tours are also available. ‼🚚♦

Beacon Hill (ABV 3.8%) BITTER
Light, refreshing, well-balanced pale amber bitter in the Burton style.
Sunchaser (ABV 4%) GOLD
Tiger (ABV 4.2%) BITTER
A mid-brown, well-balanced best bitter crafted for broad appeal, benefiting from a long, bittersweet finish.
Old Original (ABV 5.2%) BITTER
Full-bodied, mid-brown strong bitter with a pleasant rich, grainy mouthfeel. Well-balanced flavours, with malt slightly to the fore, merging into a long, satisfying finish.

Golden Duck

Unit 2, Redhill Farm, Top Street, Appleby Magna, DE12 7AH ☎ 07846 295179
⊕ goldenduckbrewery.com

Golden Duck began brewing in 2012 using a five-barrel plant. It is run by the father, son and daughter team of Andrew, Harry and Hayley Lunn. Beers have a cricket-related theme and are always available in Mushroom Hall, Albert Village and Cellar Bar, Sir John Moore Hall, Appleby Magna (Fri eve only). ♦LIVE

Hayles' Ale (ABV 3.8%) BITTER
Tinners Tipple (ABV 4.1%) GOLD
Extra Pale (ABV 4.2%) PALE
LFB (Lunns First Brew) (ABV 4.3%) GOLD
Lunnys No. 8 (ABV 4.8%) BITTER
Nosey Parker (ABV 5%) GOLD
For England (ABV 5.1%) GOLD
Reverend Green (ABV 5.5%) IPA

Great Central

Unit B, Marlow Road Industrial Estate, Leicester, LE3 2BQ ☎ 07584 435332 ⊕ gcbrewery.co.uk

⊗ After a hiatus of some three years brewing restarted in 2019 on a two-barrel plant, primarily to supply the brewery tap, the Wheeltapper in Loughborough. Beers are named with a railway theme. ◆

Hemlock

37 Main Street, Hemington, DE74 2RB ☎ 07791 057994 ✉ hembrew@yahoo.com

Established in 2015 in Leicestershire on the borders of Derbyshire and Nottinghamshire, this two-barrel plant is located in the outbuildings of a 17th century thatched cottage. Beers are available across Derbyshire, Nottinghamshire, Leicestershire and Staffordshire. It produces a growing number of pale ales and several seasonal beers. ‼◆LIVE

Lemonhead (ABV 3.8%) GOLD
Harvest Moon (ABV 4.1%) GOLD
Twisterella (ABV 4.1%) PALE
Bossanova (ABV 4.3%) BLOND
Hoptimystic (ABV 4.3%) BITTER
Village Idiot (ABV 4.3%) BITTER
California Dreaming (ABV 4.5%) PALE

Langton SIBA

Grange Farm, Welham Road, Thorpe Langton, LE16 7TU
☎ (01858) 540116 ☎ 07840 532826
⊕ langtonbrewery.co.uk

Established in 1999 in outbuildings behind the Bell Inn, East Langton, the brewery relocated in 2005 to a converted barn at Thorpe Langton, where a four-barrel plant was installed. Further expansion in 2010 and 2016 significantly increased capacity. ‼◆LIVE

Rainbow Bridge (ABV 3.8%) GOLD
Caudle Bitter (ABV 3.9%) BITTER
Copper-coloured session bitter that is close to pale ale in style. Flavours are relatively well-balanced throughout with hops slightly to the fore.
Union Wharf (ABV 4%) BITTER
Inclined Plane Bitter (ABV 4.2%) BLOND
Thomas Lift (ABV 4.4%) BITTER
Bullseye (ABV 4.8%) STOUT

Mill Hill (NEW)

Unit 3, King Street, Enderby, LE19 4NT ☎ 07411 644245 ⊕ millhillbrew.co.uk

An independent, family-owned-and-run microbrewery, established in 2022. Brewing vibrant and refreshing beers supporting local suppliers, a wide selection of the beers can be found in the Mill Hill Cask & Coffee micropub, Enderby.

A Man is Not a Camel (ABV 3.7%) PALE
Clives Vibe (ABV 4.2%) PALE
Wanna Croggeh (ABV 5.2%) IPA

MonsteX

Falcon Business Park, Meadow Lane, Loughborough, LE11 1HL ☎ 07960 776843 ⊕ monstex.co.uk

⊗ MonsteX (formally Anstey Ale Brewery) set up in 2015 by Christina and Stuart Slessor to make a single beer for Christina's Father's club. The business has grown and expanded brewing capacity to cope with increasing demand, moving to larger premises in Loughborough in 2023 with a new 5.5-barrel plant. Since brewing commenced, the range of beers and styles have increased and the Monstex brand introduced to cater for the craft beer market. Although the brewery has grown, it still holds true to its ethos of remaining family-run, brewing quality beers for the free trade. ‼◆LIVE ◆

Lakeside (ABV 3.9%) BITTER
Neddy's (ABV 3.9%) PALE
Packhorse Bridge (ABV 4%) BITTER
Fluthered (ABV 4.5%) SPECIALITY
Darkroom (ABV 4.7%) STOUT
Nook IPA (ABV 5%) PALE

Moonface

13 Moira Street, Loughborough, LE11 1AU
☎ (01509) 700171 ⊕ moonfacebrewery.co.uk

⊠ Moonface Brewery has been running since 2018, brewing in six-firkin batches. Two Moonface beer types are on the bar in the taproom at any time, one often served from a wooden cask. ◆

X No. 1 (ABV 3.6%) MILD
Best Bitter (ABV 4.2%) BITTER
Citra (ABV 4.5%) PALE
Mid Atlantic Pale (ABV 4.7%) PALE
London Porter (ABV 5.6%) PORTER

Mount St Bernard SIBA

Oaks Road, Coalville, LE67 5UL
☎ (01530) 832298 ☎ 07453 760874
⊕ mountsaintbernard.org/tynt-meadow

This Cistercian monastery has been brewing its Trappist beer since 2017. It is the first ever recorded such beer to be brewed in England. Currently its only brew is the bottle-conditioned Tynt Meadow, which is available at the monastery and through outlets around the country. ‼☰LIVE

New Buildings SIBA

Unit 3, Southways Industrial Estate, Coventry Road, Hinckley, LE10 0NJ
☎ (01455) 635239 ☎ 07795 954392

Office: 24 Leicester Road, Hinckley, LE10 1LS
⊕ newbuildingsbrewery.com

⊙New Buildings Brewery brew using the David Porter 5.5-barrel system and also have an 18-gallon system. The smaller system is used for trialling new recipes and specials. The eight regular beers are sold predominantly in the Midlands to freehouses and some 35 Wetherspoon pubs.

Lighthouse Pale Ale (ABV 3.9%) PALE
Windmill Best Bitter (ABV 4.1%) BITTER
Farmhouse (ABV 4.2%) GOLD
Treehouse Marmalade IPA (ABV 4.2%) GOLD
Courthouse Porter (ABV 4.5%) PORTER
Cruckhouse (ABV 4.5%) RED
Manorhouse (ABV 4.5%) RED
Summerhouse Pale Ale (ABV 5.5%) PALE

Parish

6 Main Street, Burrough on the Hill, LE14 2JQ
☎ (0116) 430 0020 ☎ 07715 369410
⊕ parishbrewery.co.uk

Parish began brewing in 1983 and now operates on a 20-barrel plant, with capacity to brew a further 12 barrels. The brewery is located in a 400-year-old building next to the Stag & Hounds, supplying real ale in cask to many pubs across Leicestershire and Derbyshire. Beer is always available at the Melton & District Indoor Bowls Club. One-off brews are produced for beer festivals both locally and across surrounding counties. ‼◆LIVE

Proper Charlie (ABV 3.9%) GOLD
PSB (ABV 3.9%) BITTER

A refreshing pale session ale. Distinctive floral aroma with mild hints of pine. Sharp hop bitterness balanced with crisp malt flavours in the taste giving way to a lovely lingering floral finish.

Pig Pub

🍽 Pig In Muck, Manor Road, Claybrooke Magna, LE17 5AY
☎ (01455) 202859 ⊕ piginmuck.com/brewery

Brewing began in 2013 using a two-barrel plant, upgraded to a five-barrel plant built by head brewer Kev Featherstone. 🚩♦LIVE

Q Brewery

Queniborough, LE7 3DL ☎ 07762 300240
⊕ qbrewery.co.uk

A microbrewery situated in a converted building behind the house of head brewer Tim Lowe. It was established in 2014 and uses a 0.5-barrel brew kit. Beers can also be brewed on demand.

St Mary's Mild (ABV 3.5%) MILD
Ridgemere (ABV 3.8%) BITTER
4Q (ABV 4%) BITTER
Hop (ABV 4.2%) GOLD
Invincibull (ABV 4.4%) STOUT
IPA (ABV 5%) PALE
1630 (ABV 5.5%) BITTER
Rupert's Revenge (ABV 7.3%) STRONG

Round Corner

Melton Mowbray Market, Scalford Road (Gate 2), Melton Mowbray, LE13 1JY
☎ (01664) 569855 ⊕ roundcornerbrewing.com

Round Corner Brewing was launched in 2018. The state of-the-art brewery and its taproom are in the old sheep shed in the historic Melton Mowbray market. Multi award-winning, it produces a range of keg beers covering a variety of styles. In 2022 it restarted brewing real ale with one brew planned each month. Following

the installation of a canning line in 2020 the brewery is able to sell its beers directly from its online shop. ‼♦

Soar (NEW)

🍽 Swan Inn, 10 Loughborough Road, Mountsorrel, LE12 7AT
☎ (0116) 230 2340 ⊕ theswaninn.online

A small onsite brewery supplying the Swan Inn and local beer festivals.

Steamin' Billy

Office: 5 The Oval, Oadby, LE2 5JB
☎ (0116) 271 2616 ⊕ steamin-billy.co.uk

☺Pub Company that has a range of beers contract brewed for its pubs.

Tipsy Fisherman (ABV 3.6%) BITTER
Bitter (ABV 4.3%) GOLD
1485 (ABV 5%) BITTER
Skydiver (ABV 5%) BITTER

Treehouse

Cavendish Bridge, Shardlow, DE72 2HL

Treehouse Brewery was established in 2022 and is based in Cavendish Bridge.

Zero Six

16a High Street, Lutterworth, LE17 4AD
⊕ zerosixbrew.co.uk

Zero Six Brew Co Ltd launched in 2021. It focuses on small batch beers in bottle, keg and cask. The brewery shares premises with the Cork & Hop, a tasting venue and bottle shop dedicated to local and hard to find award-winning beers across the UK and Europe. LIVE

Hakuna Ma Strata (ABV 4.5%) SPECIALITY
Vanilla Stout (ABV 4.5%) STOUT

Half Moon, Melton Mowbray (Photo: It's No Game / Flickr CC BY 2.0)

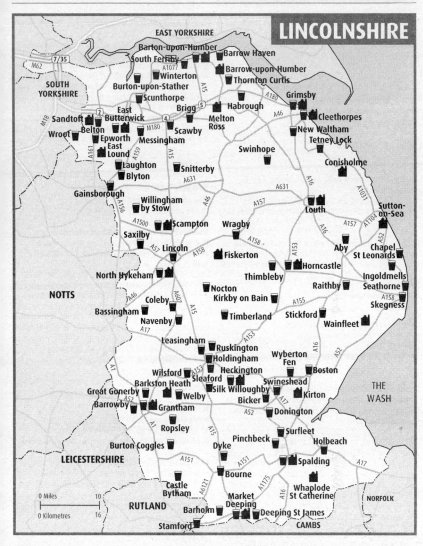

LINCOLNSHIRE

Aby

Railway Tavern ♟

Main Road, LN13 0DR (off A16 via South Thoresby)

☎ (01507) 480676 ⊕ railwaytavern-aby.co.uk

2 changing beers (sourced nationally) Ⓗ

A rural inn that was closed when the licensees took it on over 19 years ago; since then it has grown to the successful pub it is now, serving the community and raising money for charity. It has won numerous awards including local CAMRA Country Pub of the Year four times. It offers a wide range of real ales and a food menu based on produce from the area. Two holiday cottages are available for short breaks or week-long bookings. Q❀🍴🚲⏰🅿♣❀

Barholm

Five Horseshoes ♟ 🄻

PE9 4RA

☎ (01778) 560238

Adnams Southwold Bitter; Draught Bass; Oakham JHB; 3 changing beers (often Church End, Hopshackle, Ossett) Ⓗ

A classic 18th-century country pub, built from local Barnack stone. It is comprised of two bars, two cosy side rooms and a pool room. A wood fire burns throughout the winter. Three permanent and three changing real ales are on offer. Pizzas are available on Friday and street food on Saturday evenings, while barbecues and live music events in the large garden are a feature of the summer months. Well known for its support of local charities. Local CAMRA Rural Pub of the Year 2023. Q❀🍴🚲⏰🅿❀🛜♪

Barrow Haven

Haven Inn

Ferry Road, DN19 7EX (approx ½ mile E of Barrow-upon-Humber)

☎ (01469) 530247

Timothy Taylor Landlord; 2 changing beers (sourced nationally; often Theakston) Ⓗ

Built in 1730 as a coaching inn in the quiet North Lincolnshire countryside for travellers using the former ferry, the Haven has been renowned for hospitality, good food and drink and comfortable lodgings ever since. Full of character, a warm welcome awaits, with a bar, lounge and large comfortable conservatory. A perfect place for walkers on the Humber bank to call in for a well-kept pint. ⌂☆✦⏀Ⅱ◑&≠P✿

Barrowby

White Swan ✔
Main Street, NG32 1BH
☎ (01476) 562375
Castle Rock Harvest Pale; Sharp's Doom Bar; 2 changing beers Ⓗ
Popular village pub run by the same landlord for over 30 years. Offering two regular and two changing guest ales, it also provides locally sourced traditional home-made food Wednesday to Saturday. There is a comfortable lounge, separate bar area and a further area where the local darts, cribbage and pool teams play. Outside there is a heated smoking area and a secluded garden. The first Sunday of the month is quiz night. Located just off the A1 and A52 this pub is a must-visit.
Q⌂☆⏀Ⅱ◑&♣P⏠✿ি♪

Barton-upon-Humber

Sloop Inn
81 Waterside Road, DN18 5BA (follow Humber Bridge viewing signs)
☎ (01652) 637287
Pennine Millie George; Shadow Bridge Dragon Slayer; Theakston Best Bitter; Timothy Taylor Boltmaker; 1 changing beer (sourced regionally; often Shadow Bridge Brewery) Ⓗ
This welcoming 19th-century multi-roomed pub, popular with both locals and walkers, has recently been refurbished throughout to a high standard, but original features such as the Delft fireplace tiles and stained-glass windows remain. Traditional pub food is served. Four regular real ales are normally available, plus a changing guest beer. The Far Ings Nature Reserve, Waters' Edge Visitor Centre, Ropewalk, Ropery Hall and the Humber Bridge are all nearby attractions. ⌂☆⏀Ⅱ◑&▲≠(Barton-upon-Humber) ♣P⏠⏮(350,250) ✿

White Swan Ⓛ
66 Fleetgate, DN18 5QD (follow signs for railway station)
☎ (01652) 661222
House beer (by Westgate); 4 changing beers (sourced regionally; often Great Newsome, Horncastle Ales, Yorkshire Heart) Ⓗ
Multi award-winning 17th-century coaching inn opposite the bus/train interchange. The Swan offers a warm welcome to all, hosting community groups, traditional pub games and a monthly vinyl night. Four ever-changing cask ales are complemented by a rotating craft keg beer. An annual beer festival is held in the characterful, renovated coaching outbuildings. Popular weekend brunches are available. Winner of several local CAMRA awards. Q⌂☆✦&≠(Barton-upon-Humber) ♣P⏠(250,350) ✿ি♪

Bassingham

Bugle Horn Inn
19 Lincoln Road, LN5 9HQ
☎ (01522) 789773 ⊕ bassinghambuglehorn.co.uk

Greene King London Glory; 2 changing beers (sourced nationally) Ⓗ
Built in the 17th century as an inn, the Bugle Horn is a traditional locals' pub retaining many of its original features, including beamed ceilings and open fires. The lounge bar has an open fire and the bar has two sports TV screens. Food is available in a separate dining room, with steak nights on a Wednesday and Thursday, and Sunday lunch. At least two constantly-changing beers are available. The pub hosts two darts teams as well as football and cricket teams. A regular quiz takes place on the last Friday of the month. ⌂☆⏀Ⅱ◑♣P⏠(47)✿

Belton

Crown Inn Ⓛ
Church Lane, DN9 1PA (turn off A161 at All Saints' church and follow the road behind)
☎ (01427) 872834
Bradfield Farmers Blonde; Great Newsome Frothingham Best; Oakham Citra; Wainwright; 2 changing beers (sourced regionally; often Banks's, Tetley) Ⓗ
Situated behind All Saints' church, this pub can be difficult to find, but well worth the effort. For many years it has been a haven for the discerning drinker. Winner of many CAMRA awards, at least four, and often six, cask ales are available. Light beers and pale ales are especially popular. The Crown does not offer meals, but bases its appeal on its consistently good-quality real ales. Beer festivals are held in the summer months.
⌂☆▲♣P⏠(399) ✿ি♪

Bicker

Red Lion
Donington Road, PE20 3EF
☎ (01775) 821200 ⊕ redlionbicker.co.uk
Morland Old Speckled Hen; Timothy Taylor Landlord; 1 changing beer Ⓗ
A typical country inn with low beams and tiled floor, in a pleasant setting. Extensively and tastefully redecorated in 2015, it reopened after two years closure. This

welcoming multi-roomed pub has a small bar and is a popular dining venue with an extensive, varied menu. The pub is known to date from at least 1665, the year of the Great Plague of London. 🏠🛏️🍴◑♿🅿️🚆(59)🛜♪

Blyton

Black Horse
93 High Street, DN21 3JX
☎ (01427) 628277 ⊕ blackhorseblyton.com
Batemans XB, Gold, XXXB; 1 changing beer Ⓗ
Recently refurbished, the Black Horse Inn is one of two pubs in the village and is sited at the northern end. The interior is divided into five distinct areas; three for dining and two drinking areas. All dining areas are dog-friendly and one features depictions of owners' dogs. Beers from Batemans are supplemented by three changing offerings, sometimes from local brewers. Self-contained accommodation is available and there is generous parking and outside drinking space.
Q🏠🛏️🍴◑♿🅰️♣🅿️🐾🛜

Boston

Carpenters Arms
20 Witham Street, PE21 6PU
☎ (01205) 362840 ⊕ carpentersarmsboston.com
Batemans XB, Gold, XXXB; 1 changing beer (often Batemans) Ⓗ
This multi-roomed low-ceilinged traditional local is hidden in the maze of side streets off the medieval Wormgate and overlooked by the magnificent Boston Stump. Despite being close to the town centre, you may need to ask for directions more than once to find it! There is a patio area outside for sunny days. The kitchen and letting rooms are currently undergoing refurbishment, but food and accommodation will be available shortly.
🏠🛏️≈♣🚆🐾🛜♪

Eagle
144 West Street, PE21 8RE
☎ (01205) 361116
Castle Rock Harvest Pale, Preservation, Screech Owl; 5 changing beers (often Castle Rock) Ⓗ
Part of the Castle Rock chain, the Eagle is known as the real ale pub of Boston. This two-roomed, friendly hostelry has an L-shaped bar with a large TV screen for big sports events. The smaller lounge has a cosy feel. The pub stocks a wide range of guest ales, and at least one cider. A function room upstairs is home to Boston Folk Club. Friday is quiz night – allegedly the hardest in town.
Q🏠♿♣🍴🚆🐾🛜♪

Goodbarns Yard ✅
8 Wormgate, PE21 6NP
☎ (01205) 355717 ⊕ goodbarnsyard.co.uk
Adnams Ghost Ship; Timothy Taylor Landlord; 1 changing beer (sourced nationally) Ⓗ
The 700-year old pub is situated in a cobbled medieval street which runs parallel to the River Witham, northwards away from the Boston Stump. Popular for meals, its restaurant is usually busy. Old signs and pictures of Boston adorn the walls. A large garden with tables and covered patio areas overlooks the river. In winter, an open fire welcomes you into the pub.
🏠🛏️◑≈

Bourne

Anchor
44 Eastgate, PE10 9JY
☎ (01778) 422347

House beer (by Dancing Duck); 4 changing beers (sourced regionally; often Nene Valley, St Austell, Thornbridge) Ⓗ
Traditional two-roomed locals' pub with an attractive patio by the banks of a tributary of the River Glen. Strong on sports, with darts played, BT Sports on the TV and several sporting trophies on display. It raises funds for the local Air Ambulance service. The house beer, Bourne Particular, is supplied by Dancing Duck as is Roundheart, brewed for sister pub the Hand & Heart in Nottingham. It won a local CAMRA Gold Award in 2017. There is a small car park. 🏠🛏️♿♣🐾🅿️🛜♪

Brigg

Black Bull
3 Wrawby Street, DN20 8JH
☎ (01652) 653995 ⊕ blackbull-brigg.craftunionpubs.com
Sharp's Doom Bar; 1 changing beer (sourced regionally; often Adnams, Theakston, Timothy Taylor) Ⓗ
Busy, friendly, town-centre pub with reasonably-priced beers, now owned by the Craft Union pub chain. There are three rooms and a courtyard beer garden with cabins. The pub is sports oriented, with large TVs and its own football club. Themed days, fundraising events for charities, darts tournaments and regular live music are organised. If you want to watch sport with a well-kept ale in hand, this pub does that for you.
🛏️♿≈♣🅿️🚆(4) 🐾🛜

Yarborough Hunt 🅛
49 Bridge Street, DN20 8NS (across bridge from marketplace)
☎ (01652) 658333
Lincolnshire Craft Best Bitter, Lincoln Gold, Bomber County; 3 changing beers (sourced regionally; often Acorn, Castle Rock, Wadworth) Ⓗ
Former Sargeant's brewery tap, originally built in the 1700s, this is a traditional pub which retains its original features. Simply furnished, with open fires, it has been extended to give five rooms. This is the main outlet for Lincolnshire Craft Beers and also has an extensive range of up to 14 craft beers and ciders. No food is available but cold food can be brought in and consumed on the premises. An outdoor courtyard has separate cabins. Dog are welcome, daily newspapers are provided and there is free Wi-Fi. Q🏠🛏️♿≈♣🐾🚆(4,X4)🐾🛜

Burton Coggles

Cholmeley Arms
Village Street, NG33 4JP
☎ (01476) 550225 ⊕ thecholmeleyarms.co.uk
3 changing beers Ⓗ
An award-winning country pub with three handpulls set in an acre of grounds in the centre of a pretty village between Stamford and Grantham. With four en-suite ground floor rooms available in an annex it is an ideal stopping off point for those traveling or the perfect place to stay if you're exploring the local area. Run by the same licensees since 2009, they have bought this lovely old pub back to life, with a combination of a friendly team and a welcoming atmosphere. Q🏠🛏️🍴◑🅿️🐾

Burton-upon-Stather

Ferry House Inn 🅛 ✅
Stather Road, DN15 9DJ (follow campsite signs through village, down hill at church)
☎ (01724) 721783 ⊕ ferryhousepub.co.uk

2 changing beers (sourced regionally; often Batemans, Docks, Wold Top) ⓗ

Popular, friendly village pub on the banks of the River Trent which has been in the same family for over 60 years. Two guest beers and real cider are sold, and the pub has its own microbrewery – check ahead for available beers. Good value home-cooked, locally sourced food is available from Friday to Sunday. There is a large outdoor seating area and children's play area. A popular meeting place for local heritage groups, it hosts annual beer festival on the first weekend in September as well as occasional live music. Traditional pub games are played. Q❀☞❀◖▮⅙▲♣❀P🖳(60)❀🛜

Castle Bytham

Castle Inn 🅛

High Sreet, NG33 4RZ
☎ (01780) 411223 🌐 castleinnbytham.co.uk
Hop Back Summer Lightning; 3 changing beers ⓗ
This beautiful 17th-century gem is one of the original public houses in this historic village. The décor consists of old oak beams, period furnishings and walls hung with antique prints and artefacts. The owners and staff are warm and welcoming, making everyone's visit memorable. Summer Lightening is permanently on, with regularly-changing guest ales sourced regionally and nationally. An excellent menu of home-made food cooked on a wood-fired stove in the bar is available lunchtime and evenings. Q❀☞❀◖♣❀❀♫

Chapel St Leonards

Admiral Benbow

The Promenade, PE24 5BQ
☎ (01754) 871847 🌐 admiralbenbowbeachbar.co.uk
Black Sheep Best Bitter; 2 changing beers ⓗ
Beach bar located on the promenade with an outside seating area on the Hispaniola boat deck. Opening times and facilities are dependent on the weather and are limited in winter – but if the flag is flying they are open. Bar snacks are sold, with picnic trays and plastic glasses available to take out your favourite ale onto the beach. Dogs on leads are welcome, with blankets and dog treats available. ☞❀🐾🛜

Cleethorpes

Message in a Bottle

91-97 Cambridge Street, DN35 8HD
☎ (01472) 453131 🌐 miabcleethorpes.net
1 changing beer ⓗ
Pub and bottle shop that offers something different. The original seating area – fondly known as 'The Cage' – is outside but now boasts heat lamps. Indoor seating is available inside the shop. The pub offers two cask ales but is only open at weekends; the bottle shop is open most days. Pop-up food events are held throughout the year and can get busy, though passers-by will usually find a seat, and a warm welcome is ensured. ☞⅙⇌🖳(4)❀♫

No.1 Pub

Railway Station Approach, DN35 8AX
☎ (01472) 696221
Draught Bass; house beer (by Batemans); 6 changing beers (sourced regionally) ⓗ
A large railway bar on Cleethorpes station. This popular local has a main bar with a smaller real ale-themed back room overlooking the station platform. The walls are adorned with local railway memorabilia. There is outside

seating at the front for warmer weather. The pub is known for its home-cooked meals. Live music features most weekends and the pub also has a yearly music festival. ▮⇌♣❀P🖳❀🛜♫

No.2 Refreshment Room

Station Approach, DN35 8AX
☎ 07905 375587
Hancocks HB; Rudgate Ruby Mild; Sharp's Atlantic, Sea Fury; 2 changing beers (sourced nationally) ⓗ
Local CAMRA award-winning pub, set on the railway station. Known locally as 'Under the clock', this small one-roomed bar has been a regular feature in the guide. Quality ales are served in a convivial atmosphere. There is always an excellent selection, usually including one dark beer, as well as a range of ciders. ❀⇌❀🖳🛜

Willy's

17 High Cliff, DN35 8RQ
☎ (01472) 602145
Willy's Original; 2 changing beers (sourced nationally) ⓗ
A seafront bar with views over the Humber Estuary to the Yorkshire coast. Limited outdoor seating is available. There is a microbrewery on the site which brews Willy's Original Bitter. The pub mainly operates from a downstairs bar – an upstairs bar is used for functions. Good-quality locally sourced home-made food is served. A mixed age range sees a gentler quieter crowd in the afternoon, with the pub getting busier in the evenings. ☞❀◖⇌❀🖳❀

Coleby

Tempest Arms

Hill Rise, LN5 0AG
☎ (01522) 810258 🌐 thetempestarms.co.uk
Batemans XXXB; Timothy Taylor Landlord; 2 changing beers (sourced nationally; often Thornbridge, York) ⓗ
Perched on the edge of an escarpment south of Lincoln, the pub is close to the Viking Way long-distance path. At its heart is a three-sided bar. Picture windows along one side provide panoramic views towards the Trent. Outside is a patio and a beer garden. In winter, two log burners add to the cosy feel. Meals from an extensive menu can be enjoyed in the bar or the restaurant. Monthly quiz and open mic nights are held. ☞❀◖P🖳(1)❀🛜

Deeping St James

Thirsty Giraffe 🅛

65 Manor Way, PE6 8PX (in a small shopping parade)
☎ 07756 066503 🌐 thirstygiraffe.co.uk
6 changing beers (sourced regionally; often Bowler's, Church End, Hopshackle) ⓖ
Created from a former bistro, this is the first micropub in the Deepings. Expect interesting beers and lively banter. All the ales are served from the cellar and the range usually includes a dark beer and something from local breweries Hopshackle or Bowler's. A large selection of bag-in-box ciders, including fruit ciders, is stocked as well as a small range of continental lagers. Food may be ordered from the adjacent takeaways, with plates and cutlery provided. The nearest bus stop is a 10 minute walk. Q❀P🖳(102)❀

Donington

Black Bull

7 Market Place, PE11 4ST
☎ (01775) 822228 🌐 theblackbulldonington.co.uk

Batemans XB; Sharp's Doom Bar; 2 changing beers (often Batemans) Ⓗ
Busy local just off the A52. Five handpumps feature three regular beers and occasionally two varying guest beers from small brewers as well as large regionals. The comfortable bar has low, beamed ceilings, wooden settles and a cosy fire in winter. Due to the return in 2020 of the remains of Captain Matthew Flinders, navigator and cartographer, born 1774, to his birthplace, Donington, the pub has an exclusive beer named in his honour, brewed by Batemans. ⓈⓀⓄⓅⓏⓈⓋ

Dyke

Wishing Well Inn ⊘
21 Main Road, PE10 0AF
☎ (01778) 422970 ⊕ thewishingwellinn.co.uk
Greene King Abbot; Timothy Taylor Landlord; 1 changing beer (often Black Sheep) Ⓗ
A comfortable hostelry which retains a pub atmosphere in the bar, despite its popularity for meals. The Wishing Well is housed in what was once a row of three shops. The well that gives the pub its name can be seen in the restaurant. A large campsite is attached. The village takes its name from the nearby Roman Car Dyke, which runs along the western edge of the Fens. ⓈⓀⓄⓅⓏⓈⓋ

East Butterwick

Dog & Gun Ⓛ
High Street, DN17 3AJ (off A18 at Keadby Bridge, E Bank)
☎ (01724) 782324 ⊕ doggunpub.com
3 changing beers (sourced locally; often Dark Tribe) Ⓗ
Village community pub set on the banks of the River Trent. Under new ownership since 2016, the pub ambience has been retained along with the on-site Dark Tribe microbrewery. The three rooms are supplemented by an outdoor drinking area and picnic-style bench seating on the riverbank. Dark Tribe beers are always available, including occasional seasonals. Quiz night is Tuesday. The pub has a regular clientele and is popular with walkers, cyclists, motor enthusiasts and lovers of the traditional English pub. ⓈⓀⓄⓅⓏ(12)ⓈⓋ

Epworth

Old School Inn
10 Battle Green, DN9 1JT (from A161 turn left at lights on to Station Rd and head first left)
☎ (01427) 875835 ⊕ theoldschoolinnepworth.co.uk
Timothy Taylor Landlord; 2 changing beers (sourced nationally; often Adnams, Bradfield) Ⓗ
This converted school house which opened as pub in the 1980s is popular with beer and food enthusiasts alike. Now family-run, the Old School Inn always offers at least two cask ales. It also has an extensive food menu and has the capacity to stage a number of events. Quiz night is Wednesday. Real cider is sometimes available. QⓈⓀⓄⓅⒶⓅ(399)ⓈⓋ

Gainsborough

Blues Club
Northolme, North Street, DN21 2QW
☎ (01427) 613688
Horncastle Ales Angel of Light; 2 changing beers Ⓗ
The club has a bar area with several TVs showing sport, a quieter lounge and a large function room which hosts regular live entertainment (admission charges may apply). Two or three changing real ales are usually

available and details of forthcoming beers can be emailed to customers on request. CAMRA guests are always welcome on production of a membership card. ⓈⓀ(Central)ⓀⓅⓈⓋ

Eight Jolly Brewers Ⓛ
Ship Court, DN21 2DW
5 changing beers Ⓗ
Gainsborough's flagship real ale haven, featured in the Guide since 1995, is housed in a 300-year-old Grade II-listed building. Six or more ever-changing beers are always on sale, many from northern micros but new breweries from all areas feature. Real cider and continental bottled beers are also available. Opening hours may vary. Live music is making a return this year. QⓈⓀ(Central)ⓀⓅ(200)

Elm Cottage Ⓛ
138 Church Street, DN21 2JU
☎ 07554 537038 ⊕ the-elmcottage.co.uk
Jennings Cumberland Ale; Wainwright; 1 changing beer (sourced nationally) Ⓗ
The pub is situated close to Gainsborough Trinity's football ground and the Blues Club and gets busy on home match days. There are usually at least four beers, some from the Marstons portfolio, but microbrewery beers are frequently available. The pub is popular with local amateur sports teams. Weekly live music is featured. A previous winner of several local CAMRA awards. QⓈⓀⓄ(Central)ⓀⓅⓈⓋ♪

Sweyn Forkbeard Ⓨ ⊘
22-24 Silver Street, DN21 2DP
☎ (01427) 675000
Greene King Abbot; Ruddles Best Bitter; Sharp's Doom Bar; 4 changing beers Ⓗ
This town-centre Wetherspoon establishment, the local CAMRA Pub of the Year 2019, is one of the must-do pubs in town. Three or four rotating guest beers often feature some oddities for this part of the country. Customers can ask for their favourite beer and it often appears. The pub is named after the Danish King of England in 1013, whose son Canute is reputed to have stopped the Aegir. Cheap, good food is available until close. ⓈⓄⓀ(Central)ⓀⓅⓈ

Grantham

Chequers Ⓛ
25 Market Place, NG31 6LR
☎ (01476) 570149
3 changing beers (sourced nationally; often Brewsters) Ⓗ
A cosmopolitan and contemporary bar that features beers from local breweries Brewsters and Zest. Other beers include offerings from Bakers Dozen, Kelham Island and Framework, supplemented further with changing guest beers. Located on a paved side street between the High Street and the Market Square, known locally as Butchers Row, it has a relaxing atmosphere during the day and comes alive on the evenings and weekends. QⓈⓀⓄⓅⓈⓋ

Grantham Railway Club Ⓛ
Huntingtower Road, NG31 7AU
☎ (01476) 564860
2 changing beers Ⓗ
A community-run club, voted local CAMRA Club of The Year since 2020, which supports Grantham's three local brewers. This former British Rail Staff Association club plays host to numerous cribbage, darts and domino teams as well as supporting various social and community organisations. There is live music every

Saturday night, with a spacious back room available to hire. CAMRA members are welcome. Please call during opening hours or find them on social media for up-to-date entertainment information. 🐴❀♿🚆♣P🐾📶♫

Lord Harrowby 🏆 [L]
65 Dudley Road, NG31 9AB
☎ (01476) 563515
Brewsters Hophead; 4 changing beers (sourced nationally) [H]
A friendly back-street community pub, one of the few in Grantham, it's an example of how pubs used to be. It has a traditional Victorian-style bar, snug, lounge and a real fire. Darts, pool and crib are all played in local leagues. A great enclosed area at the back plays host to at least two beer festivals and live music. A LocAle is always on offer, while the landlady and her son, CAMRA members and real ale enthusiasts, source four changing guest beers. Afternoon meals are served from Thursday to Sunday (booking advised for Sundays). Q❀◐◑🚆♣🍎🐾📶♫

Great Gonerby

Recruiting Sergeant
10 High Street, NG31 8JP
☎ (01476) 562238
Everards Tiger; 2 changing beers (sourced nationally) [H]
A popular village pub just outside Grantham. With a warming log burner in the main bar, home-cooked food, a separate restaurant and function room at the rear of the pub and sponsoring its own local football team this pub really is a great community local. The large decked seating area outside is an asset all year round. Live music plays on the last Saturday of each month and an open mic night is on the second Thursday.
Q🐴❀◐◑♿♣P🚌🐾📶♫

Grimsby

Barge
Victoria Street, DN31 1NH
☎ (01472) 340911 🌐 thebargegrimsby.co.uk
Navigation New Dawn Pale; house beer (by Eagle) [H]
As the name implies, this is an old converted grain barge that is berthed in the town centre near all bus routes. It has a slight list to starboard, but do not worry, it has had this for over 20 years. Usually quieter during the day, but still attracting a mixed crowd, it is livelier in the evening once the jukebox is turned on. Monday has a quiz night with a free supper. An outdoor seating area is to the front. 🐴❀🚆(Town)🚌

Docks Beers
The Church, King Edward Street, DN31 3JD
☎ (01472) 289795 🌐 docksbeers.com
4 changing beers (often Axholme, Docks) [H]
Housed in an old church, Docks brewery taproom sells three cask ales and a craft beer selection. Axholme beers are served, often featuring collaborations with other breweries. It has recently increased capacity and you can sit and watch the brewery staff at work making and selling ale. An entertainment event venue is to be found upstairs, known as Docks Academy. The Mockingbird food cabin is outside in an old shipping container and is a permanent fixture. 🐴♿🚆(Docks)P🚌🐾♫

Rutland Arms
26 Rutland Street, DN31 3AF
☎ (01472) 357362
Old Mill Traditional Bitter; 3 changing beers [H]
Close to both the bus and train stations this pub tends to be a favourite with local and away football supporters. Recently refurbished, it has one single long room with a pool table and dartboard at one end. Four handpumps dispense a selection of real ale. Formerly an Old Mill pub the pub generally still serves one Old Mill beer. A TV shows live sporting events.
Q🐴❀🚆(New Clee) ♣🍎P🚌📶♫

Yarborough Hotel 🏆 ✔
29 Bethlehem Street, DN31 1JN
☎ (01472) 268283
Greene King Abbot; Ruddles Best Bitter; Sharp's Doom Bar; 12 changing beers (sourced nationally) [H]
Large open-plan pub serving 12 real ales from both national brands and breweries in the Lincolnshire area. Like many in the Wetherspoon chain it can be get busy at times. After a troubled past where it was under threat of demolition, the pub has been restored as a grand hotel next door to Grimsby Town railway station and is now thriving again. Q🐴❀🛏◐◑♿🚆(Town)🍎🚌

Habrough

Station Inn
Station Road, DN40 3AP
☎ (01469) 572896
3 changing beers (sourced regionally; often Bradfield, Theakston, Timothy Taylor) [H]
Originally a hotel, built in 1848 for the Great Grimsby and Sheffield Junction Railway, this pub has a good community spirit. Live bands are featured once a month on Saturday and this, together with karaoke, theme nights and traditional pub games, make for a lively environment. Three handpumps feature changing beers from regional brewers. There is one large room with access to the bar and a smaller area for pool and bar games. 🐴❀🚆♣🍎P🐾♫

Heckington

8 Sail Brewery Bar
Heckington Mill, Hale Road, NG34 9JW
☎ (01529) 469308 🌐 8sailbrewery.co.uk
8 Sail Ploughmans Lunch, Windmill Bitter, Fenman, Froglet, Rolling Stone, King John's Jewels; 3 changing beers (sourced locally; often 8 Sail) [H]
Situated in part of the Heckington Windmill complex, this single-room brewery bar features a restored Victorian bar, and church pew and Britannia bar seating. Three changing 8 Sail Brewery beers are usually available, alongside an occasional guest. A selection of German bottled beer and local cider is also stocked. Beer festivals are held in July on the Heckington Show weekend. It may close earlier on weekends in winter.
Q🐴❀♿🚆♣🍎P🚌🐾📶♫

Holbeach

Crown Hotel
5 West End, PE12 7LW
☎ (01406) 423941 🌐 the-crown.co.uk
Sharp's Doom Bar; 2 changing beers (sourced locally; often Austendyke, Tydd Steam) [H]
A traditional local pub which has served the town for over 300 years. It retains its beamed ceiling and other woodwork, and a brick-fronted bar. Home-cooked meals are served at lunchtime when the pub has a relaxed atmosphere. Younger and noisier customers fill up the place in the evenings. There is a beer garden to the side, and a pool table and dartboard are located in the upstairs room. 🐴❀🛏◐◑♣P🚌🐾📶♫

Holdingham

Jolly Scotchman ✓
18 Lincoln Road, NG34 8NP
☎ (01529) 304864
Greene King IPA, Abbot; 2 changing beers (sourced locally; often 8 Sail) ⊞
Located at the northern end of Sleaford, near the A17 Holdingham roundabout, the pub boasts a modern open-plan interior with a mix of seating styles. A multicoloured tile floor surrounds the wooden bar front. The restaurant area is of garden room format, with large picture windows. A food-orientated pub, being part of the Flaming Grill chain, there are plenty of meal offers. It can get busy at certain times, so advance booking is advisable. ⑅❀◑♿P☂♪

Horncastle

King's Head
16 Bull Ring, LN9 5HU
☎ (01507) 523360
Batemans XB, Gold, XXXB; 1 changing beer (sourced regionally) ⊞
A comfortable, cosy and friendly pub which, unusually for this locality, has a thatched roof, hence its local name the Thatch. Three beers from Batemans are generally available plus a guest. Reputedly the pub inspired an OO gauge Hornby model, an example of which is displayed behind the bar. Summertime sees the pub resplendent with hanging baskets and it has been the winner of Bateman's Floral Display competition. Try spotting the pub cat, Rufus. ⑅❀◐●🍴♨❀☂♪

Old Nick's Tavern
8 North Street, LN9 5DX
☎ (01507) 526862
4 changing beers (sourced locally; often Horncastle Ales) ⊞
Built in 1752 as a coaching inn, this original building is now a town-centre pub with its own microbrewery, the home of Horncastle Ales. The head brewster is the the landlord's daughter. There are five handpumps, four of which usually showcase beers from the Horncastle brewery. The pub has been refurbished and the decor incorporates the old pub sign and historic photos of the pub. Regular live bands play. There is currently no food served. ⑅❀♣♨❀☂♪

Ingoldmells

Countryman 🄻
Chapel Road, PE25 1ND
☎ (01754) 872268
House beer (by 8 Sail) ⊞
The privately-owned Countryman appears to be a modern building but it incorporates the early 19th century Leila Cottage. A notorious smuggler, James Waite, used to reside here when Ingoldmells was a wild and lonely place, but he certainly would not recognise the current holiday coast, with Skegness, Butlins and Fantasy Island nearby. The pub is on northern bus routes from Skegness. Beers were previously supplied by its own on-site brewery, but this has now closed and the house beers are brewed by 8-Sail brewery in Heckington. ⑅❀◑♿♠P🚐

Kirkby on Bain

Ebrington Arms
Main Street, LN10 6YT
☎ (01526) 354560 ⊕ ebringtonarms.com

Batemans XB; Timothy Taylor Landlord; 2 changing beers ⊞
Attractive country pub close to the River Bain and dating from 1610. World War II airmen used to slot coins into the ceiling beams to pay for beer when they returned from missions over Germany. Sadly, many of these coins are still in situ and make a unique memorial to those who lost their lives. The popular restaurant offers good food made with local produce (booking advised). One guest beer is offered in winter, increasing to two in summer. Q⑅❀◐♿♠P(65)❀☂♪

Laughton

Ingram Arms
10 Blyton Road, DN21 3PR
☎ (01427) 628465
Dark Tribe Terrier; 2 changing beers ⊞
A first entry to this Guide in this village pub which is noted for its food. The pub is a member of the Lincolnshire Bell Target League who meet on Tuesday evenings. Beers from Dark Tribe, a nearby brewery in West Stockwith, are available, with one or two varying real ales. The pub website gives regular updates on meal options. Q⑅❀◐♿AP🚐❀☂♪

Leasingham

Duke of Wellington
19 Lincoln Road, NG34 8JS
☎ (01529) 419000 ⊕ thedukeofwellington-leasingham.com
Marston's Pedigree; Wainwright; 2 changing beers (often Ringwood, Woodforde's) ⊞
A community-owned pub in every sense, with games days and nights, quizzes in daytime and evenings, food-themed nights, as well as open mic once a month. The two guest ales are often Wherry, Boondoggle or Bass. Originally a thatched pub named the Sun, the pub was renamed when it was bought by a local officer following the Battle of Waterloo. The pub has a cosy, comfortable, lounge and a spacious garden with plenty of outdoor seating. Q⑅❀◐♣P🚐❀☂♪

Lincoln

Adam & Eve Tavern
25 Lindum Road, LN2 1NT
☎ (01522) 537108 ⊕ adamandevelincoln.co.uk
Morland Old Speckled Hen; Castle Rock Harvest Pale; Timothy Taylor Landlord; 1 changing beer (sourced nationally) ⊞
An imposing, Grade II-listed building dating back to 1701. The pub stands opposite Pottergate Arch, a gateway of the medieval wall that surrounded Lincoln Cathedral. The interior is spacious, although the ceilings are low. It comprises a main bar with several nooks, a side room and a separate area for pool and darts. A beer garden is built into the hillside. Live music features regularly and there is a weekly quiz. Two screens show sporting events. ⑅❀◐♣P🚐❀☂♪

BeerHeadZ
4 Eastgate, LN2 1QA
☎ (01522) 255430 ⊕ beerheadz.biz
3 changing beers (sourced nationally) ⊞
A bright colourful pub with an industrial feel situated in the uphill city area. It serves up to four cask ales, craft keg beers, two ciders and a range of bottled and canned beers. Oversized glasses are used. Customers are welcome to bring in their own food or order in from outside suppliers. Regular events include quizzes and tap takeovers. Dogs are welcome. ●��🚐❀☂♪

Birdcage ✔

54 Baggholme Road, LN2 5BQ
☎ (01522) 274478 ⊕ birdcagelincoln.com

Sharp's Doom Bar; 3 changing beers (sourced nationally; often Ferry Ales, Milestone, Zest) Ⓗ

A single-roomed, street-corner pub refurbished in a clean, modern style with a mix of traditional tables and chairs. The enclosed patio area is a suntrap. Three changing beers complement the regular ale and the selection of boxed ciders. There are frequent music nights, with open mic, karaoke and bands, plus comedy and spoken-word events. Fortnightly Sunday lunches can be booked, and there is regular pop-up food. A dog-friendly pub, welcoming bar staff and locals will greet all who enter. ❀🦽🐾🛜♪

Cardinal's Hat

268 High Street, LN2 1HW
☎ (01522) 527084

Timothy Taylor Landlord; Ossett White Rat; Adnams Mosaic; house beer (by Lincolnshire Craft); 4 changing beers (sourced nationally) Ⓗ

Said to be named after Cardinal Wolsey, Bishop of Lincoln from 1514 to 1515, this pub is housed in a building formerly used by St John's Ambulance. The area the pub resides in was restored in 2015, but the Grade II-listed building dates back to the 15th century, and its current form shows off some of its original features. Multi-roomed, it is ideal for a quiet drink for a few, or larger groups enjoying the extensive drinks menu, bar snacks, charcuterie boards and cheeses. ♿❀🜨&⇌(Central) ⬤🛜♪

Golden Eagle

21 High Street, LN5 8BD
☎ (01522) 521058

Castle Rock Harvest Pale; Pheasantry Best Bitter; 7 changing beers (sourced nationally; often Castle Rock, Pheasantry, Welbeck Abbey) Ⓗ

A popular local at the southern end of High Street, it is close to Lincoln City's football ground and gets busy on match days. The building dates from the 1700s. Up to nine real ales are served from two bars. The pub is dog-friendly and the cosy front lounge has a log burner. The large garden has covered and heated seating. Two beer festivals are held annually and, in summer, the barbecue may be fired up. ♿♣⬤P🦽❀🛜♪

Joiners Arms ✔

4 Victoria Street, LN1 1HU
☎ 07871 887459

4 changing beers (sourced nationally) Ⓗ

Nestled among the Victorian terraces, this traditional back-street boozer has two open fires. Three steps lead to the bar. The back room has a pool table, dartboard and a retro Space Invaders machine. The quirky beer garden features funky sculptures which extend to the steampunk-inspired bike racks located in the car park. Four handpumps serve an ever-changing selection of ales. Tuesday is quiz night with an open mic night every other Saturday and a monthly air rifle target shooting night. Four-legged friends are warmly welcomed. ❀♣🐾🛜♪

Morning Star ✔

11 Greetwell Gate, LN2 4AW
☎ (01522) 514269 ⊕ morningstarlincoln.co.uk

Timothy Taylor Boltmaker; Sharp's Doom Bar; Wainwright; 3 changing beers (sourced nationally) Ⓗ

This well-decorated traditional pub is a short walk from the cathedral and castle and extends a warm welcome to all that enter. In the summer months enjoy the suntrap beer garden, or warm yourself by the open fire in the main bar in winter. There is a small library so you can enjoy a good book while you have a quiet drink in the snug to the rear of the bar. Q❀P🦽🐾🛜

Ritz ⃓ ✔

143-147 High Street, LN5 7PJ
☎ (01522) 512103

Sharp's Doom Bar; Ruddles Best Bitter; Greene King Abbot; 5 changing beers (sourced nationally) Ⓗ

With its distinctive Art Deco design and neon-style external lighting, the Ritz is a landmark corner building on Lincoln's Lower High Street. It opened as a cinema in 1937 and during the 1980s and 90s live entertainment was staged, in addition to films being shown. After closure in 1996, the building was acquired by JD Wetherspoon and the foyer and stalls area opened as a pub two years later. Meet the Brewer evenings are held. Q♿❀🜨&⇌(Central) 🦽🛜

Strugglers Inn ♟ ⃓ ✔

83 Westgate, LN1 3BG
☎ (01522) 535023

Greene King Abbot; Timothy Taylor Landlord; 7 changing beers (sourced nationally; often Brewsters, Pheasantry, Welbeck Abbey) Ⓗ

The award-winning Struggs stands in the shadow of Lincoln Castle and is popular with locals and visitors alike. The walls of the two rooms are festooned with old photographs and the ceilings are covered with pumpclips. Enter right for the cosy snug. The sunken garden is a suntrap with splendid floral displays. The numerous guest beers offer a range of styles and strengths, and local brews always feature. There is live music most weekends and the Practice Christmas in September is always great fun. Q❀♣🐾🦽❀♪

Tiny Tavern

107 High Street, LN5 7PY
☎ 07761 123697

5 changing beers (sourced nationally) Ⓗ

What better way is there to preserve two Grade II-listed 17th-century cottages than to turn them into a small pub? A cosy interior includes a window seat, fireplace, counter, dartboard and access to an unexpected garden area at the rear. Ring the bell on the right door to be admitted, and leave by the other! The beers are from all over the country; real cider is sometimes available. ❀⇌(Central) ♣🐾🦽

Louth

Brown Cow ✔

133 Newmarket, LN11 9EG (top of Newmarket on Church St jct)
☎ (01507) 605146

Black Sheep Best Bitter; Castle Rock Harvest Pale; Fuller's London Pride; 1 changing beer Ⓗ

A friendly freehouse run by long-standing owners with a great atmosphere and, most importantly, great beer. This pub is a popular community meeting place and is a must when visiting Louth. A free quiz is held on the first Sunday of the month. The kitchen serves traditional, home-cooked food, made with locally sourced products. ♿❀🜨&▲🦽❀🛜♪

Cobbles Bar

New Street, LN11 9PU (off Cornmarket)

Black Sheep Best Bitter; 1 changing beer Ⓗ

Traditional pub-style bar based in the centre of town, with friendly staff at all times. This small but accommodating venue has multiple personalities, from a bustling coffee shop serving light lunches to a busy pre-club local with a DJ and live music at weekends. It has a good beer trade, with two contrasting cask ales, as well as a huge selection of exotic spirits. Disabled access is right through the front doors. ⊕⅃&⬚🛜

Consortium Micropub 🅛

13C Cornmarket, LN11 9PY

☎ (01507) 600754 ⊕ theconsortiumlouth.co.uk

Consortium Black Frog, Best Bitter, Thanks Pa, Obliging Blonde, ZigZag 🅗

The micropub is in a small courtyard next to the Masons Arms Hotel, 50 yards from the Market Place. The pub has its own microbrewery and distillery located on a nearby industrial estate. The brewery produces a massive range of diverse real ales and gins. Usually there are six ales on the bar as well as a well-stocked gin shelf, and bottled ales, ciders and lagers are also sold on a stall in the nearby market. Q ♿ ♿ ⅃ ♣ ♠ P ⬚ (51) 🐾 🛜

Gas Lamp Lounge 🅛

13 Thames Street, LN11 7AD (bottom of Thames St by factories)

☎ (01507) 607661 ⊕ sales12018.wixsite.com/ firehousebrewery

1 changing beer 🅗

A unique pub, this is one of only 22 pubs in the UK still lit by gas lamps. There is no music or games machines, just good pub traditions. Four regular beers from the upstairs brewery are served, plus a guest beer. Benches are set along the canalside, ideal for enjoying a drink during the summer and inside there is a roaring log burner to sit beside in the winter months. Dogs are welcome. Q ♿ ⅃ ♣ ♠ P ⬚ 🐾 🛜 ♫

Olde Whyte Swanne ✓

45 Eastgate, LN11 9NP

☎ (01507) 824141 ⊕ whyteswannelouth.co.uk

Draught Bass; Timothy Taylor Landlord; 2 changing beers 🅗

The oldest pub in a pretty market town, established in the early 1600s. Upon entering this Grade II-listed building you are met by traditional low-beamed ceilings and a real fire. Beyond this is another modern room which is used for dining and meetings. The bar offers a good variety of beers and cider on handpump. Q ♿ 🏠 ⊕ ⅃ ⬚ 🐾 🛜

White Horse Inn

Kenwick Road, LN11 8EG

☎ (01507) 603331

Brains Rev James Original; Fuller's London Pride; 3 changing beers (often Marston's) 🅗

This friendly local pub in the historic town of Louth has a great atmosphere and is a welcoming place for the whole family. Popular with locals, it serves hearty home-cooked meals, real ales and wines. A quiz is on Thursday evenings. This dog-friendly pub has and outdoor seating area and a large car park. Opening hours may vary in the winter – please call for details. Q ♿ 🏠 ⊕ ⅃ ♠ P ⬚ 🐾 🛜

Woolpack 🅛

Riverhead Road, LN11 0DA

☎ (01507) 606568 ⊕ woolpacklouth.com

Batemans XB, Gold, XXXB; 1 changing beer 🅗

The Woolpack is situated close to the theatre and is popular with drinkers and diners alike. It usually offer four or five real ales on handpull. The Grade II-listed building is located next to the canal and has disabled access and baby changing facilities. There is an outside beer garden and ample parking. Dogs are welcome. ♿ 🏠 ⊕ ⅃ P ⬚ 🐾 🛜

Market Deeping

Vine Inn 🅛

19 Church Street, PE6 8AN

☎ (01778) 348741

Butcombe Original; Sharp's Doom Bar; 3 changing beers (often Abbeydale, Blue Monkey, Skinner's) 🅗

Formerly a Charles Wells pub, now a free house, this small, friendly local features oak beams and stone floors, with many 20th-century prints on the walls. There is a large patio at the rear. Five handpumps dispense an ever-changing range of interesting ales from near and far. Boxed real cider is available. Free nibbles are provided Sunday lunchtime and early evenings during the week. The television is only used for major sporting events. The pub celebrated 10 years in this Guide in 2022. 🏠 ♠ P ⬚ (101) 🐾 🛜 ♫

Messingham

Pooley's

46 High Street, DN17 3NT

☎ 07860 799178

5 changing beers (sourced regionally; often Batemans, Salopian, Thornbridge)

Popular village local decorated in rustic style, open in the evenings from Wednesday to Sunday. It has a bar at one end which serves three distinct drinking areas which all have wooden or flagstone floors and real fires. Conversation is encouraged. Vintage pictures and signs displayed throughout. Five changing real ales are normally available plus an extensive range of wines and spirits, including 22 different gins. Always welcoming, this pub is the winner of several local CAMRA awards. Q ⅃ ⬚ (100,103) 🐾 🛜

Navenby

Lion & Royal

57 High Street, LN5 0DZ

☎ (01522) 810368

Greene King IPA, Abbot; 3 changing beers (sourced nationally; often Parkway, Welbeck Abbey) 🅗

Formerly the Lion, the name was changed after a visit by the Prince of Wales in 1870. Guy Gibson of 617 Squadron fame spent his wedding night in this imposing, Grade II-listed building. The bar has a flagged floor and an impressive fireplace. There is an enclosed beer garden and a large car park. The pub is on the Lincoln to Grantham bus route. There is a weekly quiz and regular live music. Bar food is served. 🏠 🏠 ⊕ ⅃ ♣ P ⬚ (1) 🐾 🛜 ♫

New Waltham

Farmhouse ✓

Station Road, DN36 4PH

☎ (01472) 827472 ⊕ thefarmhousegrimsby.co.uk

St Austell Tribute; Sharp's Doom Bar; 3 changing beers 🅗

Reopened in late 2022 after a refurbishment, this attractive looking pub is set back from the road by the beer garden. Catering for all ages, and welcoming to groups, it is open plan but with several secluded areas, although none are too far from the main buzz of the pub. There is a warming fire located at each end. A comprehensive food menu is available all day and live music plays at weekends. 🏠 🏠 ⊕ ⅃ ♣ P ⬚ (8) ♫

Nocton

Ripon Arms 🅛

Main Street, LN4 2BH
☎ 07989 449353

3 changing beers (sourced nationally) 🅗

A community-run pub known locally as the pub within the Hub. A friendly reception awaits with a wide selection of drinks available. The wooden access ramp off the car park provides additional access to the bar lounge and the outside seating area. An annual Beerfest and an Oktoberfest are part of the events calendar. A monthly quiz night is held the first Saturday of the month, and there is occasional live music. Families and dog are welcomed, and there are traditional pub games available. ᠿ❀☙♣●P🖵(31,IC5)❀☞

North Hykeham

Centurion

Newark Road, LN6 8LB
☎ (01522) 509814

Bombardier Gold; Sharp's Doom Bar; 2 changing beers (sourced nationally; often Adnams, Oakham, St Austell) 🅗

Centurion was named to reflect the rich Roman history of the area. Built over 50 years ago in the late 60's, the pub is a community hub popular with diners and drinkers alike. Booking is advised if you want to guarantee a table. Whether dining, drinking or both, a warm welcome awaits you, especially in the colder months when the fire is lit. Ideally located next to a large supermarket so you can enjoy a pre or post shopping pint! ᠿ❀◑♿P🖵☞

Pinchbeck

Ship

Northgate, PE11 3SE
☎ (01775) 711746

Adnams Ghost Ship; Black Sheep Best Bitter; Greene King Abbot; 2 changing beers (often Hopshackle, Welland) 🅗

Thatched pub on the banks of the River Glen by the railway bridge at the western end of Knight Street. The pub has been given a sympathetic update and is smart, neat and tidy but retains a warm and cosy appeal. Food is farm to fork, locally sourced, fresh quality produce. Events are held throughout the year, ranging from beer, wine and spirit tasting evenings to an annual garden party with car shows and live music. ᠿ❀◑P🖵❀☞♫

Raithby

Red Lion

Raithby Road, PE23 4DS
☎ (01790) 753727

Batemans XB; 2 changing beers (often Ferry Ales, Batemans) 🅗

Cosy village pub built around 1650, with beamed low ceilings in the many small rooms that surround the bar. Pictures of outdoor pursuits, and old photographs adorn the walls. The pub sits in an attractive quiet village in the Wolds that is excellent for walking and cycling. The various small rooms are now very popular dining areas. The pub is closed on bank holidays. Qᠿ❀◑♿♣P🖵❀☞

Ropsley

Green Man

24 High Street, NG33 4BE
☎ (01476) 585897 ● green-man-ropsley.co.uk

Wainwright; 3 changing beers (sourced nationally; often Caledonian, Grainstore, Theakston) 🅗

This 17th-century village pub has an impeccable reputation for its beer quality and its innovative food which uses exotic meats, locally sourced game and seafood. Themed food and drink matching evenings are held regularly, and it is also renowned for an extensive bottled beer range. The relaxed tearoom area is frequented by walkers and cyclists. A pleasant tranquil beer garden with a covered area provides outdoor seating in all weathers. Local CAMRA Pub of the Year 2020 and 2021. ᠿ❀◑♣❀☞

Ruskington

Shoulder of Mutton

11 Church Street., NG34 9DU
☎ (01526) 832220

Sharp's Doom Bar; Theakston Best Bitter; 2 changing beers (sourced regionally) 🅗

A popular and thriving pub in the heart of the village attracting customers of all ages. It is one of the oldest buildings in the village and was once a butcher's shop, hence the name. A few old meat hooks can still be seen in the wooden ceiling in the bar. Changes have been made in recent years but have not spoiled the essential character. Standing guard outside is Knight and Day, a sculpture from Lincoln's 2017 Knight's Trail. ❀⇌♣P🖵(31) ❀☞

Saxilby

Anglers ✪

65 High Street, LN1 2HA
☎ (01522) 702200 ● anglerspublichouse.com

Theakston Best Bitter; 3 changing beers (sourced nationally; often Brewsters, Pheasantry, Welbeck Abbey) 🅗

Built about 1850 as the Railway Hotel, the name changed to the Anglers in 1895. Now a family-run community local, it is home to various sports and pub games teams. Old pictures of the village decorate the lounge bar. An outside area, partly covered, includes a boules court, and hosts street food occasionally. Close to the station, bus stops and moorings on the Fossdyke, the country's oldesr canal. Guest beers often include local ales. Q❀▲⇌♣P🖵❀☞

Scampton

Dambusters Inn 🅛

23 High Street, LN1 2SD
☎ (01522) 731333 ● dambustersinn.co.uk

8 changing beers (sourced nationally; often Ashover, Bradfield, Pheasantry) 🅗

This thriving village pub/restaurant is packed with memorabilia and prints relating to the famous bombing raid. Murals add to the wartime feel. The front extension has a roof terrace and bifold doors at the rear open onto a patio. The eight handpumps offer an ever-changing selection of ales, many from local breweries. An annual beer festival is held around the anniversary of the Dambusters mission. Local CAMRA Pub of the Year on numerous occasions. Q❀◑●P🖵(103)❀☞

Scawby

Sutton Arms

10 West Street, DN20 9AN (on main road through village)
☎ (01652) 652430 ● suttonarmsscawby.co.uk

Sharp's Doom Bar; house beer (by Milestone); 1 changing beer (sourced regionally; often Milestone) Ⓗ
Attractive, well-appointed village local with a strong emphasis on food. It has a spacious interior with large lounge for dining, a separate dining room and a smaller snug bar facing the road. There is also a large outdoor gazebo set aside for meals. Food is served lunchtime and evenings throughout the week. Two permanent real ales are stocked with Sutton Best Bitter being a house beer. A rotating guest ale from Milestone is also available. The snug bar is dog-friendly. 🐕🏠🍽️🕹️&P🅿️🍴🎵

Scunthorpe

Blue Bell ✓
1-7 Oswald Road, DN15 7PU (at town-centre crossroads)
☎ (01724) 863921
Greene King Abbot; Ruddles Best Bitter; 6 changing beers (sourced regionally; often Acorn, Bradfield, Milestone) Ⓗ
Large open-plan town-centre Wetherspoon set across on two levels, it was extended and refurbished in 2019. The beer garden is at ground level, with a large open area on first floor accessed by stairs and a lift. Food is served all day. Wetherspoon's beer festivals are supported and special days such as Burns Night, St George's Day and St Patrick's Day are recognised with real ales. A large council-run car park is available at the rear of the pub. 🐕🏠🍽️🕹️&≠🅿️🖥️🅿️🎵🍴

Honest Lawyer
70 Oswald Road, DN15 7PG
☎ (01724) 276652 🌐 honestlawyerbar.co.uk
Sharp's Sea Fury; 2 changing beers (sourced nationally; often Greene King, Milestone) Ⓗ
Legal-themed pub with long, narrow bar, close to the town centre and railway station, it was refurbished in 2021. There is a small, heated outdoor drinking area at front of pub. Three real ales usually available. Regular open mic nights are held as well as local live music and comedy nights. Other events include psychic nights and an annual flag day at the end of the football season. An upstairs restaurant is currently closed. 🏠&≠🅿️🎵🍴

Malt Shovel
219 Ashby High Street, DN16 2JP (in Ashby Broadway shopping area)
☎ (01724) 843318
Ossett White Rat; 5 changing beers (sourced regionally; often Abbeydale, Acorn, Oakham) Ⓗ
This self-styled country pub in the town comprises a main open plan-bar area and a conservatory extension, all on one level. Carpeted throughout, it has tables and a mix of chair and bench seating. The front beer garden has benches and umbrellas. Food is always popular and booking is recommended. One permanent real ale is joined by up to five rotating guests, plus ciders drawn straight from the cellar. Quiz night is Thursday and live music plays most Saturdays. A new sports bar is next door. 🐕🏠🍽️🕹️&🖥️🅿️🎵

Seathorne

Seathorne Arms
Seathorne Crescent, PE25 1RP
☎ (01754) 767797
2 changing beers (often Batemans, Greene King) Ⓗ
Set back from Roman Bank, 15 minutes' walk from Butlin's, the pub has a large outside seating area and a spacious single-room interior with partioned areas for

eating, pub games, drinking and watching TV. Trade is seasonal, due to the local caravan sites, and the pub is closed in January, with closing times varying in February and March. The landlord operates a constantly rotating two beer selection. During lockdown the pub refurbished the seating and extended the outside area. 🐕🏠🍽️🕹️&🚲🖥️🍴🎵🍴

Silk Willoughby

Horseshoes
London Road, NG34 8NZ
☎ (01529) 414092 🌐 horseshoessilkwilloughby.co.uk
Sharp's Doom Bar; Timothy Taylor Landlord; 2 changing beers (sourced locally; often Batemans) Ⓗ
Situated in a quiet village just south of Sleaford, this is a welcoming, recently refurbished free house. As well as the regular beers, there is always one Batemans beer available. The landlord holds regular quiz nights with proceeds going to local charities. Live music includes regular acoustic music events and occasional bands; see the Facebook page for details. There is an attractive outdoor area with seating, and large car park. 🐕🏠🕹️🅿️🍴🎵♫

Skegness

Vine Hotel
Vine Road, PE25 3DB (off Drummond Rd)
☎ (01754) 763018 🌐 thevinehotel.com
Batemans XB, XXXB; 1 changing beer (often Batemans) Ⓗ
A delightful building, one of the oldest in Skegness, dating from the 18th century and set in two acres of pleasant grounds. Inside are comfortable wood-panelled bars in which to enjoy a quiet pint or two after experiencing some of the noisier attractions and bustle of Skegness. Within striking distance of the Gibraltar Point National Nature Reserve, walking trails, beach and golf links, the inn has reputed Tennyson connections. 🐕🏠🍽️🕹️&🖥️🅿️🍴🎵

Sleaford

Carre Arms Hotel
Mareham Lane, NG34 7JP
☎ (01529) 303156 🌐 carrearmshotel.co.uk
Black Sheep Best Bitter; 3 changing beers (often Draught Bass, Marston's) Ⓗ
A privately run hotel previously owned by Bass, located adjacent to the Bass Sleaford maltings complex which is now awaiting a regeneration scheme. There is a comfortable bar area with two rooms, offering three regularly-changing real ales from both larger regional breweries and local breweries. A cider is often available on handpump. An extensive food menu is offered, served in the bar area or restaurant. There is a pleasant covered courtyard, ideal on inclement days. Jazz piano is played in the bar Friday and Saturday evenings. Q🐕🏠🍽️🕹️&≠🅿️🍴🎵♫

White Horse
Boston Road, NG34 7HD
☎ (01529) 968003
Milestone Cromwell Best; 1 changing beer (often Batemans, Horncastle Ales) Ⓗ
Located on the junction of Carre Street and Boston Road, the pub serves the housing area along the Boston Road. One of the few remaining traditional locals' pubs in Sleaford, with wet sales only. The interior has been opened out into a single L-shaped room, but which still retains a cosy feel, with photos of old Sleaford adorning

the walls. Do not be fooled by the clock above the fiireplace – it displays an anticlockwise face. Sports predominate, with both darts and pool teams. ⬆️❀⬅️♣P🏠🛜♪

Snitterby

Royal Oak

High Street, DN21 4TP (1½ miles from A15)
☎ (01673) 818273 🌐 royaloaksnitterby.co.uk
JW Lees Bitter; Rooster's Buckeye; Stancill Barnsley Bitter Ⓗ; 4 changing beers (sourced regionally; often Ferry Ales) Ⓗ/Ⓖ
Traditional family-run village pub with wooden floors and log fires, offering good beer, company and conversation. At least five real ales including three regular beers and a real cider are on offer, including two from local breweries. Outside there is a landscaped seating area beside a small stream, shaded by a weeping ash. The snug room shows live sports on TV. Opening hours may vary, and are updated on the pub website. Q⬆️❀👓♣👍P🏠

South Ferriby

Nelthorpe Arms

School Lane, DN18 6HW (off A1077 Scunthorpe to Barton road)
☎ (01652) 633260 🌐 nelthorpe-arms.business.site
Shadow Bridge Brewery Battle Standard, Dragon Slayer; 1 changing beer (sourced locally; often Shadow Bridge Brewery) Ⓗ
An attractive local just off the main road through the village. The two-sided bar serves a spacious area with darts and pool and a separate restaurant. There is also a cosy room with a log burner – called the Wilson Snug – at one end. Two beers from the local Shadow Bridge brewery are stocked – Dragon Slayer is a permanent fixture while the other is rotated with a core beer or seasonal offering. Food is available from Tuesday to Sunday. Accommodation is in six well-appointed rooms. ⬆️❀🛏🚪👓♣👍P🚆(350) 🐾🛜♪

Spalding

Prior's Oven Ⓛ

1 Sheep Market, PE11 1BH
☎ 07866 045778
3 changing beers (sourced locally; often Digfield, Tydd Steam, Austendyke) Ⓖ
The first micropub to be opened in Lincolnshire, the building was part of the Priory of Spalding and is believed almost 800 years old. Because of its shape it has always been known as the Oven or the Prior's Oven and has been used as Spalding Monastic Prison. Its more recent use was as a bakery and it became a pub in 2013. The ground floor bar has a vaulted ceiling. Beers can be served in third-pint measures. Q⬅️👍🚪🐾

Red Lion Hotel ✪

Market Place, PE11 1SU
☎ (01775) 722869 🌐 redlionhotel-spalding.co.uk
Draught Bass; Woodforde's Wherry; 1 changing beer (sourced nationally) Ⓗ
The Red Lion is a carefully refurbished 18th-century family-run hotel. The cosy, comfortable and welcoming bar overlooks the marketplace. It is popular owing to its consistently well-kept range of cask ales, which the bar staff take great pride in serving in top condition. It is a rare outlet for Bass in the locality. On fine sunny days the experience is enhanced with tables and chairs outside beneath attractive floral displays. ⬆️🛏👓🚪❀🐾🛜♪

Stamford

Jolly Brewer Ⓛ

1 Foundry Road, PE9 2PP
☎ (01780) 755141
Grainstore Ten Fifty; Oakham JHB; 2 changing beers (sourced nationally; often Adnams, Blue Monkey, Fuller's) Ⓗ
A traditional pub built of local stone, dating back to 1830 and twice local CAMRA Pub of the Year. The Brewer boasts a roomy split-level drinking area with open fires in the winter, and a separate dining area. The car park and large patio hosts a pétanque court, while pub games, including the World Pushpenny Championships, are a feature. Four handpumps dispense local and national ales, and a range of malt whiskies is available. Q❀👓◑❀♣👍P🚆(9,202) 🐾

King's Head

19 Maiden Lane, PE9 2AZ
☎ (01780) 753510 🌐 kingsheadstamford.co.uk
Black Sheep Best Bitter; 3 changing beers (sourced locally; often Bakers Dozen, Drum and Monkey, Nene Valley) Ⓗ
A 19th-century family-run free house of small stature, but with a big reputation for excellent food and beer. This one-roomed, stone-built pub features a wooden-beamed ceiling and has a quaint suntrap garden to the rear, with cover and heating for inclement weather. The pub serves four constantly-changing ales from the length and breadth of the country with a further eight craft taps offering all manner of beer styles. Popular with diners at lunchtime. It was voted local CAMRA Town Pub of the Year in 2022. Q❀👓◑❀🚆

Tobie Norris

12 Saint Pauls Street, PE9 2BE
☎ (01780) 753800 🌐 kneadpubs.co.uk/our-pubs/the-tobie-norris
Hopshackle Special Bitter; Oakham Citra Ⓗ; 3 changing beers (sourced regionally; often Abbeydale, Nene Valley) Ⓗ/Ⓖ
This ancient stone building, parts of which date back to 1280, was bought by Tobie Norris in 1617 and used as a bell foundry. Formerly a RAFA club, a major refurbishment gained it CAMRA's Conversion to Pub Use Award in 2007. It now has many small rooms with real fires, stone floors and low beams. Five handpumps serve beers from local and country-wide breweries, with other ales sometimes available directly from the cask. A former local CAMRA Pub of the Year. Card payments only. Q⬆️❀👓◑❀♣🚆(202,203) 🐾🛜

Stickford

Red Lion Inn Ⓛ

Church Road, PE22 8EP
☎ (01205) 480395
House beer (by St Austell); 2 changing beers (often Black Hole, Brains, Greene King) Ⓗ
The pub name Red Lion, one of the most common in England, is frequently found hereabouts because it was an heraldic emblem of the 14th century John of Gaunt, Earl of Lancaster and Lord of the Manor at nearby Bolingbroke Castle. The pub has one larger open-plan room, with a small separate dining and function room. The owners are keen on live music, with regular events shown on their Facebook page. ⬆️❀◑🅰👍P🚆(113) 🐾🛜♪

Surfleet

Crown Inn

6 Gosberton Road, PE11 4AB

☎ (01775) 680830

Sharp's Sea Fury; 1 changing beer Ⓗ

This little gem of a pub, tastefully refurbished, has comfortable setees and couches in the bar/lounge area near to its large open fire. The adjacent mezzanine floor with its intimate area adds to the ambience as does the grand piano in the restaurant. Lana the ghost is reputed to be a constant companion – she was run over by the London stagecoach. Apparently the first morris dancing was held outside in 1796. The guest beer changes on a weekly basis. All meals need to be prebooked.
ॐ❍ধ়PᾺ令

Swineshead

Green Dragon

Market Place, PE20 3LJ

☎ (01205) 821381

Batemans XB; Theakston Traditional Mild; 3 changing beers (sourced regionally) Ⓗ

Originally called the Green Dragon, its fortunes gradually declined until new owners brought it back to life with a new name. A change of ownership has now seen the pub revert to its original name, and it is now a vibrant and thriving village local, successfully blending old and new to recreate a genuine community pub with an emphasis on beer and traditional pub games. Pizza and bar snacks to eat in or take away are available Thursday to Saturday. ॐ❀ৗ♣Ὰ(K59)❀令

Swinhope

Clickem Inn

Binbrook Road, LN8 6BS (2 miles N of Binbrook on B1203)

☎ (01472) 398253 ⊕ clickem-inn.co.uk

Batemans XXXB; Timothy Taylor Landlord; house beer (by Pheasantry); 3 changing beers (sourced regionally; often Horncastle Ales, Rudgate) Ⓗ

Set in the picturesque Lincolnshire Wolds, this is a popular stopping place for walkers and cyclists. The name originates from the counting of sheep passing through a nearby clicking gate. Renowned for its home-cooked food which is served in the bar and conservatory, the choice of drinks includes six real ales and a traditional cider. The house beer is Terry's Tipple. There is pool, darts and a jukebox. Monday is quiz night. A covered, unheated area is provided for smokers.
Qॐ❀ৗᾺ♣❀❀令

Tetney Lock

Crown & Anchor

Lock Road, DN36 5UW

☎ (01472) 388291

Sharp's Doom Bar; 2 changing beers (sourced nationally) Ⓗ

Overlooking the historic but now defunct Louth Navigation canal, this is a convenient watering hole for lovers of outdoor pursuits. Dogs are welcome in the public bar —the landlord keeps a jar of dog biscuits on the bar for them. There is a pleasant garden at the rear, while at the front is a patio overlooking the canal. Traditional Sunday lunches are served. Guest beers are available in the summer months. Qॐ❀ৗPᾺ令

Thimbleby

Durham Ox

Main Road, LN9 5RB

☎ (01507) 527152 ⊕ durhamoxpubthimbleby.co.uk

Adnams Ghost Ship; Batemans XB; 1 changing beer (sourced regionally) Ⓗ

This fine country inn is over 200 years old and reopened in 2013. A welcoming pub with beamed ceilings, cowshed bar and RAF corner, it also has a large field at the rear for caravans and camper vans. There is an extensive menu serving local produce. The pub is named after a huge 18th-century ox which toured the country and which, at its largest, weighed 270 stone.
ॐ❀ৗᾺ♣PᾺ❀♪

Thornton Curtis

Thornton Hunt Inn

17 Main Street, DN39 6XW (on A1077 between Wooton and Barton)

☎ (01469) 531252 ⊕ thornton-inn.co.uk

Timothy Taylor Golden Best, Landlord; 1 changing beer (sourced regionally; often Black Sheep, Shadow Bridge Brewery) Ⓗ

This village local is housed in a Grade II-listed building dating back to the 18th century. The main bar serves an open-plan drinking and dining area decorated in attractive country inn style with wooden ceiling beams, decorative plates and brasses, vintage signs and hunting prints. It is popular for the lunchtime and evening meals. Two Timothy Taylor beers are featured permanently plus a changing guest ale. The pub is a member of the Timothy Taylor Champion Club denoting beer excellence.
ॐ❀❀ৗᾺ令

Timberland

Penny Farthing

4 Station Road, LN4 3SA

☎ (01526) 378881 ⊕ thepennyfarthinginn.co.uk

Timothy Taylor Landlord; 1 changing beer (sourced nationally; often Milestone) Ⓗ

A country pub in the heart of the village. It has a large open-plan layout with various spaces for dining and a comfortable seating area. At least two beers are available. Food is sourced locally and specials are on offer from Tuesday to Friday. The Wednesday steak nights and Sunday lunches are always popular. A regular quiz takes place on Tuesday and occasional comedy and music evenings are held. Families and dogs are welcome. Five en-suite bedrooms are available. Qॐ❀❀ৗ♣PᾺ令

Welby

Crown & Anchor

Main Street, NG32 3LP

☎ (01400) 230021 ⊕ crownandanchorwelby.co.uk

Fuller's London Pride; Oakham JHB; 1 changing beer (sourced nationally) Ⓗ

Dating back 300 years, this lovely pub is full of character and offers a warm friendly welcome. The wood-fronted bar in the main room has a log burner creating a cosy yet light and spacious feel. Old wooden beamed ceilings in the overflow bar area show the age and history of this pub. The bar serves two regular real ales and one changing. Food is served daily, including a traditional Sunday roast. Dogs are more than welcome.
ॐ❀❀ৗᾺ♣PᾺ♪

Willingham by Stow

Half Moon 🄻
23 High Street, DN21 5JZ
☎ (01427) 788340
Batemans Gold, XB; Sharp's Doom Bar; 1 changing beer 🄷
Traditional style village pub in a building dating back to 1850. It has a public bar, lounge bar, an open fire and a beer garden. Three regular and one changing beer are usually available. Food is available from Thursday to Sunday and the fish & chips are popular with locals and visitors. Entertainment nights and themed charity nights are held on a relatively regular basis. Opening times may vary, phone ahead to check. Q☕❀◑&♣●🖥🌣

Wilsford

Plough Inn
Main Street, NG32 3NS
☎ (01400) 664037 ⊕ theploughinnwilsford.co.uk
Black Sheep Best Bitter; Timothy Taylor Landlord; 1 changing beer (sourced nationally) 🄷
Traditional old two-bar village pub next to the church, with a wood-beamed ceiling, open fires and friendly service. There is a small walled back garden, and good local walks nearby. Three well-kept real ales and a nice range of wines pair well with the high-quality food served from the kitchen. Booking for food is essential to avoid disappointment. Children are welcome. ❀◑♣P

Winterton

George Hogg 🄻 ✔
25 Market Street, DN15 9PT
☎ (01724) 732270 ⊕ thegeorgehogg.co.uk
Draught Bass; 3 changing beers (sourced regionally; often Batemans) 🄷
This popular Grade II-listed marketplace village pub is a local CAMRA award winner. It has large lounge/dining room, public bar and upstairs restaurant, both with real fires. Good value, locally sourced bar and restaurant meals are available Wednesday to Sunday. It is a popular meeting place for local football teams and supporters club. An annual beer festival is held in May. Traditional pub games are played. Q☕❀◑♣P🖥(350)🌣🛜

Wragby

Ivy
Market Place, LN8 5QU
☎ (01673) 858768
4 changing beers (sourced nationally; often Oakham, Ringwood, St Austell) 🄷
A 17th-century, village-centre pub, nine miles east of Lincoln. Tables fill the alcoves and edges of the wooden beamed and paneled bar, with two separate rooms off the main bar. A wood-burning stove gives a homely feel. Sport is screened in the main bar area and there is a popular quiz on Sunday evening. Sandwiches and toasties are served throughout the day. Upstairs are six en-suite bedrooms. There is free parking opposite. Q❀🛏♣🖥(50,56)🌣🛜

Wroot

Cross Keys
High Street, DN9 2BT (on the main street in centre of village)
☎ (01302) 770231
Black Sheep Best Bitter; Kirkstall Leeds Pale; Theakston Best Bitter; 2 changing beers (sourced regionally; often Pheasantry, Welbeck Abbey, Westgate) 🄷
A genuine community pub situated in one of Lincolnshire's more remote locations. The Cross Keys serves a local population of fewer than 500 and is a focal point of many local activities. A regular in this Guide for several years. At least two cask ales (up to four at weekends) are always available. A winner of local CAMRA awards under the present and previous licensees, this pub is always worth a visit. No longer accessible by public transport. ☕❀◑▲♣P🌣🛜

Wyberton Fen

Hammer & Pincers ✔
Swineshead Road, PE21 7JE
☎ (01205) 361323 ⊕ hammerandpincers-boston.co.uk
Adnams Ghost Ship; Fuller's London Pride; Sharp's Doom Bar; Woodforde's Wherry 🄷
A lively family-run community pub on the outskirts of Boston, situated close to the Downtown Shopping Centre and supermarket. The pub has two rooms and a conservatory area, with a 1970s feel to the main public bar. It is popular for its reasonably priced meals, including breakfast, and a typical pub-style menu later in the day. An outside seating area to the front is decorated with flower baskets in the summer. ☕❀◑&♣P🖥🌣🛜

Breweries

8 Sail SIBA
Heckington Windmill, Hale Road, Heckington, NG34 9JW
☎ (01529) 469308 ⊕ 8sailbrewery.co.uk

☺Established in 2010, 8 Sail Brewery operates on a six-barrel brew plant. It nestles in the shadow of Heckington Windmill, Britain's only eight-sailed windmill, from where it takes its name. The Mill helps to mill malted grain for the brewery. The shop stocks bottle-conditioned beers alongside local ciders. The front of the brewery has been converted into a Victorian-style bar, which has beer on handpump daily. The large outside area is weather dependent (hours may vary). 🚩♦LIVE🍴

Millwright Mild (ABV 3.5%) MILD
Ploughman's Lunch (ABV 3.8%) PALE
Windmill Bitter (ABV 3.8%) BITTER
Froglet (ABV 4%) PALE
Fenman Bitter (ABV 4.1%) BITTER
Rolling Stone (ABV 4.3%) PALE
King John's Jewels (ABV 4.5%) GOLD
Windy Miller (ABV 4.6%) STOUT
Fen Slodger (ABV 5%) BITTER
Mayflower (ABV 5%) PALE
Victorian Porter (ABV 5%) PORTER
Old Colony (ABV 5.3%) PALE
Black Widow (ABV 5.5%) MILD
John Barleycorn (ABV 5.5%) PALE

Brewed for Leila Cottage:
Leila's Lazy Days (ABV 3.6%) PALE
Ace Ale (ABV 3.8%) BITTER
Leila's One Off (ABV 5.1%) OLD

Austendyke
The Beeches, Austendyke Road, Weston Hills, Spalding, PE12 6BZ ☎ 07866 045778

Austendyke Ales began brewing in 2012 using a seven-barrel plant. The brewery is operated on a part-time basis by brewer Charlie Rawlings and business partner Nathan

Marshall, who handles sales. The brewery owns and runs micropub the Prior's Oven, Spalding.

Long Lane (ABV 4%) BITTER
Sheep Market (ABV 4%) GOLD
Bakestraw Bitter (ABV 4.1%) PALE
Bake House (ABV 4.5%) BITTER
Holbeach High Street (ABV 4.5%) BITTER
Hogsgate (ABV 5%) BITTER

Bacchus

🛏 Bacchus Hotel, 17 High Street, Sutton-on-Sea, LN12 2EY
☎ (01507) 441204 ⊕ bacchushotel.co.uk

Bacchus began brewing in 2010 and now has a two-barrel plant supplying the Bacchus Hotel. ‼LIVE

Batemans SIBA IFBB

Salem Bridge Brewery, Mill Lane, Wainfleet, PE24 4JE
☎ (01754) 880317 ⊕ bateman.co.uk

☺Bateman's Brewery is one of Britain's few remaining independent, family-owned and managed brewers. Established in 1874, it has been brewing award-winning beers for four generations. Justifiably proud of its heritage it is, nevertheless, forward-looking and progressive. All of its tied and managed houses serve cask-conditioned beer. See website for seasonal and speciality beers. ‼🍺♦🕊

XB (ABV 3.7%) BITTER
A well-rounded, smooth, malty beer with a blackcurrant fruity background. Hops flourish initially before giving way to a bittersweet dryness that enhances the mellow malty ending.

Gold (Also known as Yella Belly Gold) (ABV 3.9%) GOLD

Salem Porter (ABV 4.8%) PORTER
A black and complex mix of chocolate, liquorice and cough elixir.

XXXB (ABV 4.8%) BITTER
A brilliant blend of malt, hops and fruit on the nose with a bitter bite over the top of a faintly banana maltiness that stays the course. A russet-tan brown classic.

Blue Bell

🛏 Cranesgate South, Whaplode St Catherine, PE12 6SN
☎ (01406) 540300 ☎ 07788 136663
⊕ thebluebell.net

☺Founded in 1998 behind the Blue Bell pub. The brewery is owned by the pub after previously operating as a separate business. Beers are only available at the pub and to private customers. ‼♦LIVE

Brewster's SIBA

Unit 5, Burnside, Turnpike Close, Grantham, NG31 7XU
☎ (01476) 566000 ⊕ brewstersbrewery.com

⊗ Brewster is the old English term for a female brewer, and award-winning Sara Barton is a modern example. Originally established in the Vale of Belvoir in 1998, it moved to Grantham in 2006. Brewster's produces a range of traditional and innovative beers with two regularly-changing ranges. ‼🍺♦

Hophead (ABV 3.6%) BITTER
Marquis (ABV 3.8%) BITTER
A well-balanced and refreshing session bitter with maltiness and a dry, hoppy finish.
Aromantica (ABV 4.2%) BITTER

Hop A Doodle Doo (ABV 4.3%) BITTER
Decadence (ABV 4.4%) GOLD
Aromatic Porter (ABV 4.5%) PORTER
Dragon Street Porter (ABV 4.9%) PORTER
American Pale Ale (ABV 5%) PALE
Rundle Beck Bitter (ABV 5.5%) BITTER
Virago IPA (ABV 5.8%) IPA
IPA (ABV 6%) IPA

Consortium

Unit 10, Fairfield Industrial Estate, Louth, LN11 0YG
☎ (01507) 600754 ⊕ theconsortiumlouth.co.uk

☺The Consortium Brewing Co was set up in 2016 to serve the Consortium micropub and tasting lounge. It was situated in the Cornmarket of Louth, down a small passageway close to the Masons Arms. A large, diverse range of ale and gin styles is now brewed on the Fairfield Industrial Estate. It has produced more than 100 different ales since production started and bottles them for sale on the market (Wed, Fri, Sat), within 20 metres of the pub. ‼♦🕊

Dark Tribe

🛏 Dog & Gun, High Street, East Butterwick, DN17 3AJ
☎ (01724) 782324 ⊕ darktribe.co.uk

☺Situated on the banks of the River Trent in the Dog & Gun pub, this 2.5-barrel brewing plant produces beers for the pub and local outlets. The award-winning brewery has been established since 1996. A range of one-off beers is produced throughout the year. ‼♦

Docks SIBA

The Church, King Edward Street, Grimsby, DN31 3JD
☎ (01472) 289795 ⊕ docksbeers.com

Brewing began in 2018 using a 15-barrel plant in a converted Edwardian Church in Grimsby. The brewery was originally named Axholme Brewing Co, with beers brewed under that name. ‼🕊

Brewed under the Axholme Brewing Co name:
Magnitude (ABV 3.9%) PALE
Hard Graft (ABV 4%) PALE
Cleethorpes Pale Ale (ABV 4.2%) SPECIALITY
Lightning Pale Ale (ABV 4.3%) PALE
Graveyard Shift (ABV 4.5%) STOUT
Never Say Die (ABV 6%) IPA
Special Reserve (ABV 7.2%) STRONG

Don Valley

The Old Airfield, Belton Road, Sandtoft, DN8 5SX
☎ (01709) 580254 ☎ 07951 212722
⊕ donvalleybrewery.co.uk

☺The brewery, established in 2016, changed ownership in 2018. It moved in 2019 to a new site in Sandtoft in Lincolnshire with new brewing equipment, doubling the capacity. A canning line was installed in 2020. ♦🕊

Bit o' That (ABV 4%) BITTER
Atomic Blonde (ABV 4.3%) BLOND
Gongoozler (ABV 4.5%) STOUT
Go Your Own Way (ABV 5%) GOLD

Ferry Ales SIBA

Ferry Hill Farm, Ferry Road, Fiskerton, LN3 4HU
☎ (0800) 999 3226 ☎ 07790 241999
⊕ ferryalesbrewery.co.uk

Ferry Ales Brewery (FAB) began brewing in 2016 using a five-barrel plant. It is situated just outside Fiskerton,

Lincolnshire. Beers can be found in the Lincoln area and beyond. A range of between 12-15 beers are available in cask, keg, bottle and can. 🍺

Just Jane (ABV 3.8%) BITTER
49 SQN (ABV 4.9%) BITTER
Smokey Joe (ABV 4.9%) PORTER

Firehouse

🍺 Gas Lamp Lounge, 13 Thames Street, Louth, LN11 7AD
☎ (01507) 608202 ☎ 07961 772905
⊕ firehouse-brewery.co.uk

☺Owned by Jason Allen and Louise Darbon, Firehouse Brewery was founded in 2014 and started production in the village of Manby on part of the site of the former RAF station. In 2016 a 2.5-barrel plant was purchased from Fulstow Brewery and relocated to the Thames Street Brewery in Louth. Beers are available in the free trade and from the bar located at the brewery, the Gas Lamp Lounge. ♦

Mainwarings Mild (ABV 3.6%) MILD
Marsh Mild (ABV 3.8%) MILD
FGB (ABV 3.9%) BITTER
Northway IPA (ABV 4.2%) PALE
Woodman Pale Ale (ABV 4.4%) BLOND
Pride of Fulstow (ABV 4.5%) PALE
Wobbly Weasel (ABV 4.9%) BITTER
Lincolnshire Country Bitter (ABV 5.1%) BITTER

Fuddy Duck

Unit 12, Kirton Business Park, Willington Road, Kirton, PE20 1NN ☎ 07881 818875
⊕ thefuddyduckbrewery.co.uk

Small brewery based in Kirton near Boston, where brewing commenced in 2016.

Pale Ale (ABV 4%) PALE
American Red Ale (ABV 4.5%) RED
Blonde Ale (ABV 4.5%) SPECIALITY
Dark Porter (ABV 4.5%) PORTER
German Ale Altbier (ABV 4.5%) SPECIALITY
Biere De Garde (ABV 6.5%) SPECIALITY

Greg's

🍺 Dambusters Inn, 23 High Street, Scampton, LN1 2SD
☎ (01522) 730123 ⊕ dambustersinn.co.uk

☺Established in 2013, the microbrewery is situated on the premises of the Dambusters Inn. A number of house ales are produced by publican Greg Algar. ♦

Hopshackle

Unit F, Bentley Business Park, Blenheim Way, Northfields Industrial Estate, Market Deeping, PE6 8LD ☎ 07894 317980
⊕ hopshacklebrewery.co.uk

☺Hopshackle was established in 2006 using a five-barrel plant. A 10-barrel plant was installed in 2015. More than 20 outlets are supplied direct. Bottled beer is available online. ‼♦LIVE

Simmarillo (ABV 3.8%) GOLD
PE6 (ABV 4%) GOLD
King Street (ABV 4.2%) PALE
Special Bitter (ABV 4.3%) BITTER
Historic Porter (ABV 4.8%) PORTER
Hopnosis (ABV 5.2%) GOLD

Horncastle

🍺 Old Nicks Tavern, 8 North Street, Horncastle, LN9 5DX
☎ (01507) 526862 ⊕ horncastleales.co.uk

Brewing began in 2014 using a 3.75-barrel plant. The brewery is situated at the rear of Old Nicks Tavern with beer available in the pub plus other Lincolnshire outlets. It has its own bottling plant and a beer in box scheme is also available for pre-ordering. ‼🍺

Midnight Tempter (ABV 3.6%) MILD
Damned Deceiver (ABV 3.8%) BITTER
Wicked Blonde (ABV 3.9%) BLOND
Angel of Light (ABV 4%) BITTER
Lilith's Lust (ABV 4.1%) BITTER
Satan's Fury (ABV 4.1%) PALE
Dragon's Flame (ABV 4.3%) BITTER
Sacrificed Soul (ABV 4.3%) BITTER
Lucifer's Desire (ABV 4.8%) GOLD

Lincolnshire Craft SIBA

Race Lane, Melton Ross, DN38 6AA
☎ (01652) 680001 ⊕ lincolnshirecraftbeers.com

Lincolnshire Craft Beers is the company formed by Mark Smith who bought the Tom Wood Brewery in 2017. It continues to brew the Tom Wood range of beers on the 60-barrel Melton Ross plant. ♦

Best Bitter (ABV 3.7%) BITTER
A good citrus, passion fruit hop dominates the nose and taste, with background malt. A lingering hoppy and bitter finish.
Melton Mild (ABV 3.7%) MILD
Lincoln Gold (ABV 4%) GOLD
Bomber County (ABV 4.8%) BITTER
An earthy malt aroma but with a complex underlying mix of coffee, hops, caramel and apple fruit. The beer starts bitter and intensifies to the end.
Imp Stout (ABV 4.8%) STOUT

Little Big Dog

Barrow-upon-Humber, DN19 7SH
⊕ littlebigdogbeer.co.uk

Commercial home-based brewery, first brewed in 2020. Beers are available in cask, keg and can.

Pantiles (ABV 3.8%) BITTER
Make it Real Pale (ABV 4.2%) GOLD
Watchmaker (ABV 4.2%) PALE
Fog on the Humber (ABV 4.8%) GOLD

Melbourn

All Saints Brewery, All Saints Street, Stamford, PE9 2PA
☎ (01780) 752186

A famous Stamford brewery that opened in 1825 and closed in 1974. It re-opened in 1994 and is owned by Samuel Smith of Tadcaster (qv). No real ale. ‼

Newby Wyke SIBA

Unit 24, Limesquare Business Park, Alma Park Road, Grantham, NG31 9SN
☎ (01476) 565682 ⊕ newbywyke.co.uk

⊗ The brewery is named after a Hull trawler skippered by brewer Rob March's grandfather. It started life in 1998 as a 2.5-barrel plant in a converted garage then moved to premises behind the Willoughby Arms, Little Bytham. In 2009 it moved back to Grantham. ‼♦

Banquo (ABV 3.8%) BLOND
Summer Session Bitter (ABV 3.8%) BITTER
Orsino (ABV 4%) BLOND
Comet (ABV 4.1%) BITTER
Kingston Topaz (ABV 4.2%) GOLD
Black Beerd (ABV 4.3%) STOUT
Bear Island (ABV 4.6%) BLOND
White Squall (ABV 4.8%) BLOND
Blonde-hued with a hoppy aroma. Generous amounts of hop are well-supported by a solid malty undercurrent. An increasingly bittersweet tang makes itself known towards the finish.
HMS Quorn (ABV 5%) GOLD
White Sea (ABV 5.2%) BITTER
The Deep (ABV 5.4%) STOUT
Chesapeake (ABV 5.5%) BITTER
HMS Queen Elizabeth (ABV 6%) BLOND
Yamoto (ABV 6%) BLOND

Pig Barn

Low Hall Road, East Lound, DN9 2LU
☎ (01427) 754339

Located in a converted piggery, this is one of the smallest breweries in the UK. Brewing commenced in 2019, with the first cask beers being launched commercially in 2020. Beers are available both cask and bottle-conditioned and can be found in pubs and at festivals around the Isle of Axholme, Lincolnshire. LIVE

Hoppy Red Ale (ABV 4.3%) RED
The Duke's Return (ABV 4.3%) PALE
Corolean Pale Ale (ABV 4.4%) PALE
Fool's Gold (ABV 4.4%) GOLD
Haxey IPA (ABV 4.7%) GOLD
Ken's Best Bitter (ABV 4.8%) BITTER

Poachers

Newark Road, North Hykeham, LN6 9SP
☎ (01522) 807404 ☎ 07954 131972
⏚ poachersbrewery.co.uk

⊛The brewery was founded in 2001 in buildings on the former RAF Swinderby site. In 2006 the plant was relocated to outbuildings at the rear of the brewer's home. Regular outlets in Lincolnshire and surrounding counties are supplied direct; outlets further afield, via beer swaps with other breweries. An onsite bar is open to the public on a Friday evening and for groups at other times by prior arrangement. ‼♜♦♪

Trembling Rabbit Mild (ABV 3.4%) MILD
Shy Talk Bitter (ABV 3.7%) BITTER
Rock Ape (ABV 3.8%) BITTER
Poachers Pride (ABV 4%) BITTER
Tedi Boy (ABV 4%) PALE
Bog Trotter (ABV 4.2%) BITTER
Lincoln Best (ABV 4.2%) BITTER
Billy Boy (ABV 4.4%) BITTER
Imp Ale (ABV 4.4%) BITTER
Black Crow Stout (ABV 4.5%) STOUT
Hykeham Gold (ABV 4.5%) SPECIALITY
Monkey Hanger (ABV 4.5%) BITTER
Jock's Trap (ABV 5%) BITTER
Trout Tickler (ABV 5.5%) BITTER

Shadow Bridge

Unit 1, Humber Bridge Garden Centre, Far Ings Road, Barton-upon-Humber, DN18 5RF
☎ (01652) 660083

Brewery located in the shadow of the Humber Bridge, hence the name, which opened in 2022. The three core beers plus seasonals are available in cask and bottle both in the taproom and shop. Spent grains are used by the neighbouring farm for its livestock. ☒♦♪

Battle Standard (ABV 3.8%) BITTER
Dragon Slayer (ABV 4.1%) GOLD
Wizard's Ruin (ABV 4.3%) STOUT

Welland

Cradge Bank, Spalding, PE11 3AN ☎ 07732 033702
⏚ wellandbrewery.co.uk

Welland Brewery commenced in 2018 and was set up by Tom Bradshaw and Dave Jackson, assisted by the owner and brewer of nearby Austendyke Ales, Charlie Rawlings. A taphouse is planned.

Shipshape Blonde (ABV 3.7%) GOLD
Sneaky St.Oat (ABV 3.9%) STOUT
Fen Tiger (ABV 4%) GOLD
Flatland Bitter (ABV 4%) BITTER
Pale RyeNo (ABV 4.1%) SPECIALITY
YFM (ABV 4.2%) GOLD
Jack Rawlshaw (ABV 4.4%) BITTER
Black Cow (ABV 4.7%) STOUT
Rusty Giraffe (ABV 5%) BITTER
Mad Cow (ABV 5.4%) STOUT
Lincoln Red (ABV 6.2%) RED
Red Tsar (ABV 10%) STOUT

Wickham House

Church Lane, Conisholme, Louth, LN11 7LX ☎ 07817 467303 ✉ bearplumb64@gmail.com

⊛Wickham House was formed in 2018 as a small, artisan brewery concentrating on traditional ales produced in small batches. It has started producing bottled-conditioned beers (Blonde and Bitter range). Plans are underway to get licenced, with a small B&B attached. It has also increased capacity to 200-litres.

Blonde Jester (ABV 4%) BLOND
Kings Island Bitter (ABV 5.2%) BITTER

Willy's

⛿ **17 High Cliff Road, Cleethorpes, DN35 8RQ**
☎ (01472) 602145

The brewery opened in 1989 to provide beer mainly for its in-house pub in Cleethorpes, although some beer is sold in the free trade. It has a five-barrel plant with maximum capacity of 15 barrels a week. The brewery can be viewed at any time from pub or street. ‼♦

Zest SIBA

Heath Lane, Barkston Heath, Grantham, NG32 2DE
☎ (01476) 572135 ⏚ zest-brewery.com

⊛In 2020 Zest was rebranded from Oldershaw Brewery, which had been brewing since 1997. Owned and run by brewster Kathy Britton, Zest produces a core range of beers in both traditional and contemporary styles, as well as seasonal ales. Bespoke bottled and cask beers can be created to order and a mobile bar service (Bar Zest) is also available. ‼☒♦

Heavenly Blonde (ABV 3.8%) BLOND
Newton's Drop (ABV 4.1%) BITTER
Balanced malt and hops but with a strong bitter, lingering taste in this mid-brown beer.
Mosaic Blonde (ABV 4.3%) BLOND
Atomic IPA (ABV 4.5%) BLOND
Blonde Volupta (ABV 5%) GOLD

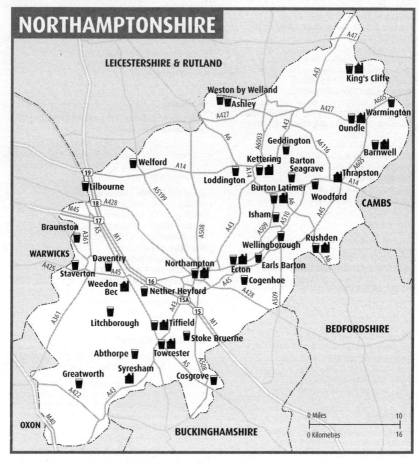

NORTHAMPTONSHIRE

Abthorpe

New Inn 🄻
Silver Street, NN12 8QR (off Main St, left at church)
☎ (01327) 857306 ⊕ newinnabthorpe.uk
Hook Norton Hooky, Off The Hook, Old Hooky; 1 changing beer (often Hook Norton) Ⓗ
A tranquil country hostelry tucked away, close to the village green and church. It is a quintessentially English village pub built of local mellow sandstone, complete with an inglenook fireplace with seating and low ceilings. Welcoming to visitors and locals alike, it serves good food, with meats sourced from the owner's farm, plus ales that are still brewed in the traditional way by Hook Norton, whose seasonal beers feature as guests. Fresh fish from Billingsgate Market is a speciality.
🅃🕸🄸🌓🍴♣🅿🐾🛜♫

Ashley

George 🄻
21 Main Street, LE16 8HF (off B664)
☎ (01858) 565900 ⊕ thegeorgeatashley.com
Sharp's Doom Bar; Timothy Taylor Boltmaker; 1 changing beer (sourced locally; often Grainstore, Langton, Oakham) Ⓗ
Following a campaign by residents, this traditional 17th-century ironstone village pub has been saved from being converted into houses. It stands proud above a patch of grass at the roadside. Inside has been opened out,

though there are still two separate areas for dining and drinking. Home-cooked food varies, with Tuesday night pie (winter) or fish & chips (summer) and Wednesday steak nights. The Coach House to the rear has been redecorated to a high standard and offers six individual rooms. 🅃🕸🄰🄸🌓🍴♣🅿🐾🛜

Barnwell

Montagu Arms 🄻
PE8 5PH
☎ (01832) 273726
Adnams Ghost Ship; Digfield Fools Nook, Barnwell Bitter; 1 changing beer (sourced locally) Ⓗ
Overlooking the local river and bridge, this 16th-century stone-built inn has a public bar at the front, with original exposed beams on the ceiling and walls, a large restaurant to the rear and a new drinking area to the side. There is a large play and camping area at the rear. The car park is also behind the pub and accessed via the village hall entrance. There is disabled access from the rear but only to the restaurant. 🅀🕸🄸🌓🅿🚌🐾

Barton Seagrave

Stirrup Cup 🄻 ✅
Woodland Avenue, NN15 6QR (off A14 jct 10)
☎ (01536) 722841 ⊕ thestirrupcupbartonseagrave.co.uk

Banks's Amber Ale; Courage Directors; 2 changing beers (sourced regionally; often Nene Valley, Potbelly) [H]
A popular, welcoming community-focused estate pub that is about to celebrate 60 years in business. The traditional sports bar features darts, pool and skittles, along with large sports TVs. The coffee lounge offers breakfast, lunches and afternoon teas until early evening Monday-Friday. There is an emphasis on beer choice, with guests often from Potbelly. Regular events involve a quiz (Wed) and jazz (Thu) plus live bands once a month. It is ideally situated for a break off the A14.
🐴✿◐♿♣P🚌🐾📶♫

Braunston

Admiral Nelson

Dark Lane, NN11 7HJ (bottom of Dark Ln, on W side of village) SP548649
☎ (01788) 891900 🌐 admiralnelsonbraunston.co.uk
Everards Tiger, Old Original; 3 changing beers (sourced nationally; often Brunswick, Everards) [H]
Built circa 1730, this family-run pub pre-dates the adjacent Grand Union Canal. Dining areas are at both ends of the building, with several settees in front of the L-shaped bar. There is lots of outside seating next to the lock and on the lawn beside the canal. The menu offers a choice of traditional home-cooked food using locally sourced ingredients mixed with a few more exotic options. Braunston Marina is nearby. Q🐴✿◐P🚌🐾📶

Burton Latimer

Dukes Arms [L] ✔

123 High Street, NN15 5RL (off A14 jct 10)
☎ (01536) 390874
3 changing beers (sourced nationally; often Avalanche, Potbelly, Roman Way) [H]
A community pub with four handpumps (one cider) after many years of being keg only. It supports local micros when pumps allow. The central U-shaped bar serves the opened-out rooms, which feature comfortable leather seating and more traditional seating in the small bay windows. The walls are adorned with vinyl LPs, and there is a collection of books that can be read. No parking, but a free car park is just across the road.
🐴✿♣🍎🚌🐾📶

Cogenhoe

Royal Oak ✔

Whiston Road, NN7 1NJ (on High St towards E end of village)
☎ (01604) 890922 🌐 theroyaloakcogenhoe.co.uk
St Austell Tribute; 3 changing beers (sourced regionally; often Timothy Taylor) [H]
This traditional country pub which features a central bar around two opened-out rooms is a welcome addition the Guide. It has a modern, contemporary look, with a wooden floor leading to the rear restaurant. Outside is an extensive covered patio and garden with large TVs for sporting events. The four ales feature changing beers from Timothy Taylor and one from a local brewery, often Roman Way. Forthcoming beers are listed on a chalk board. Q🐴✿◐♿⛺P🚌(43)🐾📶♫

Cosgrove

Barley Mow ✔

7 The Stocks, MK19 7JD
☎ (01908) 562957 🌐 thebarleymowcosgrove.co.uk
Everards Beacon Hill, Sunchaser, Tiger; 1 changing beer (sourced regionally; often Titanic) [H]
A beautiful countryside pub backing onto the Grand Union Canal by Bridge 65. Located in a lovely 17th-century building, the main bar and adjoining segregated areas provide a charming environment, especially when the log fire is blazing. Outside is a patio leading onto a lovely garden. The home-cooked food is suitable for all dietary requirements. Events are staged throughout the year and may include murder mystery evenings and a monthly quiz. Q🐴✿◐♿⛺P🚌(90,90A)🐾📶♫

Daventry

Early Doors [L]

3 Prince William Walk, NN11 4AB
☎ 07976 247312 🌐 earlydoorsdaventry.com
House beer (by Potbelly); 4 changing beers (sourced locally; often Towcester Mill, Vale, XT) [G]
The first Northamptonshire micropub is run by a father-and-daughter team who took over from the founders. Tucked away down a narrow alley, this is a warm and welcoming oasis in the heart of Daventry, with a real community feel. The bar is simply decorated and is made from reclaimed doors and weathered scaffolding planks. A traditional range of brown, strong, session and dark beers are always available, and all on gravity.
Q♿🍎P🚌🐾

Earls Barton

Saxon Tavern [L]

25B The Square, NN6 0NA
☎ 07956 462352
Phipps NBC India Pale Ale; 3 changing beers (sourced regionally; often Grainstore, Potbelly, Roman Way) [H]
A large, comfortable and relaxed single-roomed micropub with welcoming hosts. It stands in the centre of a village between the famous Barkers Shoes and Earls Barton's historic Saxon Tower, in premises that had previously been the local headquarters of the Magic Circle. Up to six casks with cooling jackets are stillaged behind the bar. It has an extensive range of gins and rums, and box ciders from the fridge. Q✿♣🍎P🚌🐾♫

Ecton

Three Horseshoes [L]

23 High Street, NN6 0QA (off A4500)
☎ (01604) 407446
Benjamin Franklin Dougal's Thumper; St Austell Proper Job; house beer (by Benjamin Franklin); 1 changing beer (sourced locally) [H]

REAL ALE BREWERIES

Avalanche Burton Latimer
Benjamin Franklin 🛢 Ecton
Digfield Barnwell
Great Oakley Tiffield
King's Cliffe King's Cliffe
Maule Northampton
Nene Valley ◆ Oundle
Phipps NBC ◆ Northampton
Potbelly Kettering
Rockingham King's Cliffe
Roman Way ◆ Weedon Bec
Silverstone Syresham
Three Hills ◆ Thrapston
Towcester Mill ◆ Towcester
Weldon Rushden

A white-washed ironstone pub that has been extended over many years, although the original pub is said to date from 1757. The name is from the forge that was originally on the site, where Benjamin Franklin's uncle Thomas was the last of the family to work. The Franklin name is being used for the brewery that was established three years ago in outbuildings. The traditional multi-room layout has been retained, with a separate bar and games area featuring Northants skittles and darts. ♿🛏♣🅿🚃👃🛜🎵

Geddington

Star Inn 🅛

2 Bridge Street, NN14 1AD (from A43 turn onto West St and follow to village square)
☎ (01536) 745990 🌐 thegeddingtonstar.co.uk
Greene King Abbot; 3 changing beers (sourced locally; often Digfield, Nene Valley) 🅷
Attractive 17th-century pub situated directly opposite what is considered to be the finest of the surviving Eleanor Crosses. The main entrance contains the former off-sales window, with doors leading to a traditional bar and lounge bar. A restaurant leads off the lounge bar, with a further raised area towards the rear. Three guests beers are from local breweries. Good-quality pub food is served. ♿🛏🌓👤♿🚃(15)👃🛜🎵

Greatworth

Greatworth Inn

Chapel Road, OX17 2DT (off B4525)
☎ (01295) 521426 🌐 thegreatworthinn.co.uk
Fuller's London Pride; St Austell Tribute; Wadworth 6X; 1 changing beer (sourced regionally; often Dancing Duck) 🅷
A 16th-century stone-built pub in the centre of an attractive village. Following the return of its owners to the village it is back to its former glory and is now a free house. Numerous improvements have been made and it has retained its cosy, traditional atmosphere. The bar area features an inglenook fireplace and log-burning stove; there is also a dining area. A soapbox derby is held in June and a music/beer festival in August. An outside bar is open in the summer. Closed Sunday-Tuesday. ♿🛏🌓👤♣🅿👃🛜🎵

Isham

Lilacs 🅛

39 Church Street, NN14 1HD (off A509, at church)
☎ (01536) 722348 🌐 thelilacsisham.co.uk
Greene King IPA; 3 changing beers (sourced locally; often Oakham, Potbelly, Roman Way) 🅷
A welcoming, community-owned village pub – whose name is derived from a local breed of rabbit – that has been owned by local residents since 2019. It has a small lounge, the former snug with a dartboard, and a large room at the rear, which is often set out for meals. Food is available lunchtimes and evenings, except Sunday when a carvery is provided. Regular quiz nights and live music nights are held. Guest beers are from local breweries, including Roman Way and Oakham. Q♿🛏🌓👤♿♣🚃(X4)👃🛜

Kettering

Alexandra Arms 🅛

39 Victoria Street, NN16 0BU
☎ (01536) 522730

Hop Back Summer Lightning; Marston's Pedigree; Wychwood Hobgoblin Gold; 11 changing beers (sourced nationally; often Potbelly) 🅷
Traditional street-corner local in the town centre. The landlord searches out new beers all the time, which are served through 14 handpumps. You will always find a beer from an unknown brewery here, along with others from around the county, and often one from nearby Potbelly. Two opened-out rooms contain a settee, and walls are covered in breweriana and pumpclips. The rear bar has a TV and Northants skittles. A patio to the rear is a real suntrap. Q👃♣🚃👃

Earl of Dalkeith ✅

13-15 Dalkeith Place, NN16 0BS
☎ (01536) 312589
Greene King Abbot; Ruddles Best Bitter; Sharp's Doom Bar; 2 changing beers (sourced nationally) 🅷
Formerly a furniture shop, this Wetherspoon pub opened in 1996 and is named after the Earl of Dalkeith, the title given to the eldest son of the Duke of Buccleuch. The pub is on two levels downstairs, with a bar down the side, while an upstairs area has a gallery and is surrounded by bookcases. Historic photographs of local buildings adorn the walls. Two beer festivals are held every year. Q♿🛏🌓👤🚃👃🛜

Kettering Midland Band Social Club 🅛

2 Hallwood Road, NN16 9RG
☎ (01536) 512929 🌐 midlandbandsocialclub.co.uk
St Austell Tribute; Sharp's Doom Bar; house beer (by Potbelly); 5 changing beers (sourced regionally; often Titanic) 🅷
A popular club, tucked away close to Rockingham Road Pleasure Park. In addition to the long public bar, it has a small, sunken lounge area, a separate games area, and a large concert room. The five guest ales are from established micros and will always contain a dark beer. An active social diary sees regular entertainment and trips. Local CAMRA Club of the Year 2023. ♿🛏🌓♣🅿🚃👃🛜🎵

King's Cliffe

Cross Keys 🅛

2 West Street, PE8 6XA
☎ (01780) 470030 🌐 thecrosskeysinnkingscliffe.co.uk
Digfield Barnwell Bitter; house beer (by King's Cliffe); 1 changing beer (sourced locally; often Grainstore) 🅷
Independently owned, family-run free house in the heart of the village. The main bar has a TV, dartboard and jukebox, with photos of old King's Cliffe adorning the walls. There is a small snug at the front with a bar, which is used as dining room. At the rear is a lounge room, with a rare Northants Hood skittles table, leading onto a large restaurant. All rooms have open fireplaces; two are stone inglenooks. There is a car park to the rear. The pub received a local CAMRA Gold Award in 2023. 🌓🛏🌓♣🅿🛜

Lilbourne

Head of Steam

10 Station Road, CV23 0SX (1 mile from A5; just off Rugby Rd)
☎ 07933 100850
St Austell Tribute; Wye Valley Butty Bach 🅷
Converted from a house in 2013, this thriving, railway-themed, community free house regularly wins the local CAMRA Country Pub of the Year. Friendly conversation dominates in this welcoming pub, creating a comfortable

atmosphere. The large garden, with an outside bar throughout the summer, makes this a great summer venue. Sunday lunches are served, and there are steak and cheese nights once a month on a Thursday. Q♿☼🕙🌰🍴P♪🐾🛜♪

Litchborough

Old Red Lion 🅛

4 Banbury Road, NN12 8JF (opp church)
☎ (01327) 830064 🌐 oldredlionlitchborough.co.uk
Great Oakley Wot's Occurring; house beer (by Sharp's); 1 changing beer (sourced regionally) 🅗
A traditional four-roomed stone-built village pub that is well worth seeking out, popular with walkers and cyclists on the Knightly Way. The original bar remains relatively unchanged and features flagstone flooring and seats inside a large, inviting inglenook. The rear snug is a comfy casual room with double doors leading to a courtyard. One guest beer is available. Q♿☼🌰P♪🛜

Loddington

Hare at Loddington

5 Main Street, NN14 1LA (on village loop)
☎ (01536) 710337
Wainwright Amber; 2 changing beers (sourced regionally; often Church End, King's Cliffe, Phipps NBC) 🅗
The Hare is a listed building set in a conservation area in a picturesque village. It stands back in the middle of Main Street and has a pleasant front garden. Inside are four areas, with two set out for dining. There is an emphasis on home-cooked food using local producers, and vegetarian and vegan options are offered. Food is available every day. The guest beers are from national and local breweries, with real cider available. Closed on Mondays. Q♿☼🕙🌰♣P🖵(35)🐾

Nether Heyford

Foresters Arms 🅛

22 The Green, NN7 3LE
☎ (01327) 340729
2 changing beers (sourced locally) 🅗
The father-and-daughter owners have made many improvements since buying this attractive ironstone pub in 2012, not least the introduction of an enlightened choice of two rotating beers, one of which is always sourced locally. Real cider is available on gravity dispense. Opposite the village green, the pub remains the hub of village life, and though predominantly wet-led, simple bar meals and snacks are often available. The pool and skittles table is situated in the back room and there is a pleasant beer garden. On Thursday and Friday evenings a mobile pizza van sets up shop in the pub forecourt. ☼🕙♣🖵(D3)🐾🛜♪

Northampton

Albion Brewery Bar 🅛

54 Kingswell Street, NN1 1PR
☎ (01604) 946606 🌐 phipps-nbc.co.uk
Phipps NBC Diamond Ale, Red Star, Cobbler's Ale, India Pale Ale, Ratliffe's Celebrated Stout, Bison Brown; 1 changing beer (sourced locally) 🅗
Phipps NBC went back to its roots in 2014, returning to this Victorian brewery in the heart of Northampton. The brewery bar subsequently opened and features an added oak and glass partition between the bar and brewery, enabling the brewing process to be viewed. Almost all of the bar fittings are reclaimed, with many coming from

closed Phipps NBC pubs. Eight handpumps serve six ales from the brewery, plus a rotating guest, with the final pump reserved for a Northamptonshire cider. Q♿🕙🌰♣🚃♿🖵(7,X6)🐾🛜♪

Black Prince 🅛

15 Abington Square, NN1 4AE
☎ (01604) 631752
8 changing beers (sourced nationally; often Phipps NBC, Digfield, Jennings) 🅗
The former home of J Church brewery and sister to the Olde England (which is 10 minutes' walk away on the Kettering Road), this pub and music venue has a large function room and surprisingly spacious beer garden. Its horseshoe-shaped bar serves up to eight beers and six ciders. Olde England-labelled beers are contract brewed by Potbelly in Kettering. In 2022 it was voted Best Local Live Venue by the the Northamptonshire Music Awards. ☼🌰🖵🛜♪

Cordwainer 🅛 ✅

The Ridings, NN1 2AQ (near to jct with Fish St)
☎ (01604) 609000
Fuller's London Pride; Greene King Abbot; Oakham JHB; Phipps NBC Gold Star; Ruddles Best Bitter; Sharp's Doom Bar; 7 changing beers (often Theakston) 🅗
Large, popular Wetherspoon town-centre pub which has recently been refurbished and now has a first-floor terrace and a ground-floor garden area. There is a large bar on each floor with two sets of handpumps. A wide choice of 12 real ales and occasionally real cider is available. Food is served throughout the day, with specials each day. It hosts up to four annual beer festivals. ☼🕙🌰♣🖵🛜

Kingsley Park Working Men's Club 🅛

120 Kingsley Park Terrace, NN2 7HJ
☎ (01604) 715514
Greene King IPA; Timothy Taylor Landlord; 3 changing beers (sourced nationally; often Brains, Wychwood) 🅗
Long-established and thriving working men's club, founded in 1892 in a nearby street and now on a main road in a residential area. There are always five handpumps in use, serving two regular and three changing beers, overseen by an award-winning steward. A former local CAMRA Club of the Year. The club welcomes CAMRA members. Q♿🌰♣🛜♪

Lamplighter 🅛

66 Overstone Road, NN1 3JS
☎ (01604) 631125 🌐 thelamplighter.co.uk
3 changing beers (sourced locally; often Nene Valley) 🅗
Popular, traditional street-corner pub, just off the town centre. This superb community local has an open fire in the bar and a heated courtyard. There are three or four rotating beers from established micros, including LocAles. Home-cooked food is served and children are welcome during meal times. The pub hosts regular DJ nights, live music and a quiz every Wednesday night. Food and drinks are sourced from local businesses. ☼🌰🕙🌰♣🖵🛜♪

Malt Shovel Tavern 🅛

121 Bridge Street, NN1 1QF
☎ (01604) 234212 🌐 maltshoveltavern.com
Nethergate Melford Mild; Oakham Bishops Farewell, JHB; Phipps NBC India Pale Ale; 4 changing beers (sourced regionally; often Milestone) 🅗
The former NBC brewery tap is a popular, award-winning pub near the town centre, opposite the Carlsberg

brewery. Inside is a fantastic exhibition of breweriana. The pub serves real cider, local ales, and Belgian draught and bottled beers. At least one dark beer is always on offer. Hot snacks are available from the bar counter. Live blues bands play on the first Wednesday of every month. The pub has a strong rugby following.

ﾺ⌖⚙☕≈♣♿🚍(3,11)🐾☀♫

Olde Cobbler 🅛

Acre Lane, NN2 8BN
☎ (01604) 844016 🌐 oldecobbler.co.uk
Phipps NBC India Pale Ale; 4 changing beers (sourced locally; often Greene King, Phipps NBC, Potbelly) Ⓗ
A family pub and restaurant in the residential area of Kingsthorpe. It has three distinct areas – bar, restaurant and function room – alongside a good-sized garden which is an ideal space for families and friends to meet. Four ales are always available, with the emphasis on LocAle. A varied menu features British night (Mon), curry night (Wed) and steak night (Fri). Breakfast is served on Saturday and Sunday. ﾺ⚙🕪♿🅿🚍(14)🐾☀♫

Pomfret Arms 🅛

10 Cotton End, NN4 8BS
☎ (01604) 555119 🌐 pomfretarms.co.uk
Great Oakley Wot's Occurring, Tiffield Thunderbolt, Delapre Dark; Phipps NBC India Pale Ale Ⓗ**; 2 changing beers (sourced locally; often Great Oakley, Phipps NBC)** Ⓗ/Ⓖ
Town pub on the south-west side of the River Nene in Cotton End. Its small central bar has six handpumps serving the front opened-out room and rear bar. The lovely beer garden contains a building which formerly housed the brewery, plus a function room. Great Oakley beers are regularly available, and some beers are served by gravity dispense. Food is served Friday to Sunday.
ﾺ⚙🕪♿●🚍🐾☀♫

Road to Morocco 🍷 🅛

Bridgwater Drive, NN3 3AG (can be walked from Abington Park E)
☎ (01604) 632899
Greene King IPA; Phipps NBC India Pale Ale; St Austell Tribute; Theakston Old Peculier; 1 changing beer (sourced nationally) Ⓗ
A popular 1960's brick-built estate pub with two connected but distinctly different rooms. The bar is quite lively, especially when live sports are shown on TV, and pool and darts are played here. The homely lounge is quieter, though it has two large TV screens showing sports. Five handpumps usually serve real ale, with one saved for the popular Old Peculier. Quiz nights are held every Tuesday. Local CAMRA Town Pub of the Year 2023.
Qﾺ⚙☕♿♣●🅿🚍(5)🐾☀

Oundle

Ship Inn 🅛

18 West Street, PE8 4EF
☎ (01832) 273918 🌐 theshipinnoundle.co.uk
Brewsters Hophead; St Austell Tribute; 1 changing beer Ⓗ
This Grade II-listed, 16th-century pub is welcoming and full of character, with low-beamed ceilings and a cosy open fire. It has two bars, with many small rooms adjoining. The pub is said to be haunted by a former landlord who met his demise by throwing himself out of a bedroom window. Wednesday is steak night, with generous discounts applied. Accommodation is in two stone annexes and a small cottage to the rear.
Q⚙🛏🕪♿▲♣🅿🚍(X4)🐾☀♫

Tap & Kitchen

Oundle Wharf, Station Road, PE8 4DE
☎ (01832) 275069 🌐 tapandkitchen.com
Nene Valley Australian Pale, Release the Chimps, Egyptian Cream; 5 changing beers (sourced locally) Ⓗ
The main outlet for Nene Valley brewery, this pub has spacious eating and drinking areas and waterside seating at the front. Built in a revamped wharfside warehouse, the Industrial Revolution ethos has been retained, with chrome and wood, cogs and rails. An extensive menu of home-cooked and locally sourced food is available. Live music plays on occasion. Up to eight Nene Valley real ales are available, plus a selection of craft beers and ciders. ﾺ🕪●🅿🚍🌐🐾☀♫

Rushden

Rushden Historical Transport Society 🅛

Station Approach, NN10 0AW (on ring road)
☎ (01933) 211815 🌐 rhts.co.uk
Phipps NBC India Pale Ale; 5 changing beers (sourced regionally; often Marston's, Woodforde's) Ⓗ
This award-winning club occupies the former Midland Railway station. The former ladies' waiting room is now the bar, with gas lighting and walls adorned with enamel advertising panels, railway photos and many CAMRA awards. On the platform, carriages provide a meeting room, Northants skittles, and a buffet for the numerous open days held during the year when steam and diesel train rides are provided. A beer festival is held in September. Show a copy of the Guide to sign in.
Qﾺ⚙☕♿♣●🅿🚍🐾

Staverton

Countryman ✅

Daventry Road, NN11 6JH (on A425)
☎ (01327) 311815 🌐 thecountrymanstaverton.co.uk
Wainwright Amber; 2 changing beers (sourced locally; often Church End, Hook Norton) Ⓗ
A delightful and popular 17th-century ironstone coaching inn that is now the last survivor of the three pubs that once served this lovely village close to Daventry. The long, wooden-beamed bar serves four areas, and an open hearth fire between the rooms provides some seclusion. The new tenants offer a good choice of ales, and there is often a locally brewed beer on offer.
Qﾺ⚙🕪♿🅿🚍(66)🐾☀

Stoke Bruerne

Boat Inn ✅

Bridge Road, NN12 7SB
☎ (01604) 862428 🌐 boatinn.co.uk
Banks's Amber Ale; Marston's 61 Deep, Old Empire; Ringwood Razorback; Wainwright Amber; 1 changing beer (sourced nationally) Ⓗ
Situated on the banks of the Grand Union Canal, the Boat Inn has been owned and operated by the Woodward family since 1877. The delightful tap bar's interconnecting rooms have canal views, open fires, original stone floors and window seats, while an adjoining room has Northants skittles. It is popular with diners – a large extension houses the lounge, restaurant and bistro. Additional beers are sold in summer. A canal boat is available for parties to hire. Breakfast is served.
ﾺ⚙🕪♿♣●🐾☀♫

Tiffield

George at Tiffield 🄻
21 High Street North, NN12 8AD (in centre of village)
☎ (01327) 350587 🌐 thegeorgeattiffield.co.uk
Great Oakley Wot's Occurring; 1 changing beer (often Great Oakley) 🄷
A 16th-century building with Victorian additions. This true community pub takes part in many village activities. It has a cosy bar, games room with Northants skittles, and a back room restaurant that can be booked for small functions. The tap for Great Oakley brewery, which is just outside the village, it features two of their beers. The garden has recently been extended and updated with lovely gazebos. ⛺❀◑♿▲♣P🚌🐾ᯤ♫

Towcester

Towcester Mill Brewery Tap 🄻
Chantry Lane, NN12 6YY
☎ (01327) 437060 🌐 towcestermillbrewery.co.uk
Towcester Mill Mill Race, Steam Ale, Black Fire, Saxon Shield; 2 changing beers (sourced locally) 🄷
Popular and welcoming brewery tap in a Grade II-listed mill dating from 1794, straddling the old mill race, and adjacent to Bury Mount where the town's fort once stood. The bar retains many original features, including beams, stonework, and a wooden floor, with a second room to cope with demand. Two upstairs rooms are now in use. Outside is a large garden alongside the mill. Two guest ales from other local breweries and six ciders are available. Q⛺❀♿●P🚌🐾ᯤ♫

Warmington

Red Lion
Peterborough Road, PE8 6TN
☎ (01832) 280362 🌐 theredlionwarmington.com
Dark Star Hophead; Timothy Taylor Landlord 🄷
Built of local stone around the turn of the 18th century, this popular family-run village pub has a small, olde-worlde bar and an inglenook fireplace with an adjacent restaurant. The bar serving area stretches across to a separate lounge dining room. Home-cooked food is available every day except Monday and Tuesday. Guests are advised to book a table, especially on Sundays, as food is popular and there may be changes to the opening times. A large beer garden has Roman-influenced seating. Q❀◑P🚌(24,X4)🐾

Welford

Wharf Inn 🏆 🄻 ✔
A5199, NN6 6JQ (on A5199 by canal basin)
☎ (01858) 575075 🌐 wharfinnwelford.co.uk
Grainstore Ten Fifty; Marston's Pedigree; Oakham Bishops Farewell; 3 changing beers (sourced regionally) 🄷
Friendly pub, dating from 1814, at the end of the Welford arm of the Grand Union Canal. Inside, the main room is segregated by an open fireplace between two rooms. A snug to the back of the bar is occasionally used. Guest beers are often sourced locally. Good-value food is served. The pub is popular with walkers and a leaflet with suggested routes is available. Two beer and cider festivals are held on May and August Bank Holidays. Local CAMRA Rural Pub of the Year 2023.
Q⛺❀⛟◑♿●P🚌(60)🐾ᯤ♫

Wellingborough

Coach & Horses 🄻
17 Oxford Street, NN8 4HY (800yds from Market Square)
☎ (01933) 441848
🌐 thecoachandhorseswellingborough.co.uk
9 changing beers (sourced regionally; often Hop Back, Oakham, Salopian) 🄷
A regular CAMRA award winner and long-standing Guide entry, this popular town-centre local has a constantly changing choice of nine real ales and seven ciders. The central bar serves three drinking areas adorned with breweriana. Traditional home-cooked food is served (not Sun eve, Mon and Tue), with a wide choice of pies being a feature. Regular live music and quiz nights are featured. Q⛺❀◑♿♣●🚌🐾ᯤ♫

Little Ale House 🄻
14A High Street, NN8 4JU
☎ 07870 392011
5 changing beers (sourced locally; often Oakham, Potbelly) 🄷/🄶
A wonderfully friendly one-roomed micropub whose small size encourages social interaction between customers and the landlady. Five rotating real ales are served on handpump, including a mild, porter or stout. In addition, four draught ciders are offered, and a good selection of gins, single malt whiskies, wines and soft drinks are stocked. A rear garden is now open and there are pavement tables. Close to Jacksons Lane municipal car park. Local CAMRA Town Pub of the Year 2022.
Q⛺❀♣●P🚌🐾ᯤ

Little R'Ale House 🄻
Midland Road, NN8 1NQ (on station platform)
☎ 07366 966505 🌐 thelittleralehouse-bar.business.site
4 changing beers (sourced locally; often Nene Valley, Potbelly) 🄶
A charming micropub on the station platform, occupying the former munitions building and filled with memorabilia. Up to four ales are served straight from the barrel, as well as two ciders and an interesting range of bottled beers and craft cans. The outside patio area allows outdoor summer drinking. Occasional music events and comedy nights are held. The pub is dog friendly and popular with locals and commuters alike. Opening times may vary according to season and train timetables. Q⛺❀⇌●P🚌🐾ᯤ♫

Weston by Welland

Wheel & Compass
Valley Road, LE16 8HZ (off B664)
☎ (01858) 565864 🌐 thewheelandcompass.co.uk
Banks's Amber Ale; Greene King Abbot; Marston's Pedigree; 2 changing beers (sourced nationally) 🄷
A rural pub in the picturesque Welland Valley which has been refurbished by opening up the entrance lobby and incorporating part of the former dining area with flagstone floors, a wood burner and sofas. An outside drinking area offers good views across the Welland Valley and is an ideal playground for children. This is an ideal stopping off place for walkers of the Jurassic Way which runs close by. Good-value food is served, with lunchtime specials. ⛺❀◑♿●P🐾ᯤ

Woodford

Dukes 🄻
83 High Street, NN14 4HE (off A510)
☎ (01832) 732224

Greene King Abbot; Sharp's Doom Bar; 4 changing beers (sourced nationally; often Digfield, Elgood's, Hop Back) Ⓗ

A popular community-focused pub overlooking the village green, renamed in honour of the Duke of Wellington who was a frequent visitor to the area. Inside are multiple rooms, including a lounge restaurant and upstairs games room. Excellent reasonably-priced home-cooked food is available. Regular music nights are held, along with a May bank holiday beer festival and August bank holiday music festival. Local CAMRA Rural Pub of the Year 2022. Q ⌖ ⬤ ⬤ ♣ ⬤ P ⊟ (16X) ❀ 🛜 ♪

Breweries

Avalanche

5 Goodwood Close, Burton Latimer, NN15 5WP
⊕ avalanchebrew.co.uk

Avalanche Brewery is a nanobrewery formed by two former homebrewers, aiming to put a modern twist on classic styles. Most cask beers produced are one-off beers to allow creativity to thrive. Beers are unfined and unfiltered. Output is primarily cask and keg alongside short canning runs.

Pulsar (ABV 3.6%) PALE
Notts Pale (ABV 3.8%) PALE

Boot Town

c/o Bosworths Garden Centre, 110 Finedon Road, Burton Latimer, NN15 5QA ☎ 07958 331340
⊕ boottownbrewery.co.uk

One-barrel microbrewery, established in 2017, based at the old Copper Kettle Homebrew Shop, producing an ever-changing range of beers with a modern craft theme, with output into mainly kegs and cans. 🍴

Carlsberg-Tetley

Jacobson House, 140 Bridge Street, Northampton, NN1 1PZ
☎ (01604) 668866 ⊕ carlsberg.co.uk

International lager brewery, which while brewing no real ales is a major distributor of cask beer. The Tetley-owned real ales are mostly brewed by Camerons Brewery of Hartlepool. A joint venture with Carlsberg in 2020 led to the company being renamed Carlsberg Marston's Brewing Company.

Digfield SIBA

Lilford Lodge Farm, Barnwell, PE8 5SA
☎ (01832) 273954 ⊕ digfield-ales.co.uk

⊗ Digfield Ales started brewing in 2005. In 2012 it moved to a larger premises near Barnwell, where a reed bed was installed and the brewhouse was equipped with a new 15-barrel plant. More than 40 free houses are supplied. ♦

Fools Nook (ABV 3.8%) GOLD
The floral aroma, dominated by lavender and honey, belies the hoppy bitterness that comes through in the taste of this golden ale. A fruity balance lasts.
Chiffchaff (ABV 3.9%) GOLD
An amber-gold pale ale with a distinct hoppy aroma.
Barnwell Bitter (ABV 4%) BITTER
A fruity aroma introduces a beer in which sharp bitterness is balanced by dry, biscuity malt.
Old Crow Porter (ABV 4.3%) PORTER

A rich, full-bodied porter with a balanced, roasted malt finish.
March Hare (ABV 4.4%) BLOND
A straw-coloured premium ale with a subtle fruit flavour.
Shacklebush (ABV 4.5%) BITTER
This amber brew begins with a balance of malt and hop on the nose which develops on the palate, complemented by a mounting bitterness. Good, dry, finish with lingering malt notes.
Mad Monk (ABV 4.8%) BITTER
Fruity beer with bitter, earthy hops in evidence.

Benjamin Franklin

🏠 **Three Horseshoes, 23 High Street, Ecton, NN6 0QA**
☎ (01604) 407446
✉ sales@benjaminfranklinbrewery.co.uk

The Benjamin Franklin is a microbrewery at the Three Horseshoes, Ecton village. Its name is directly associated with the family of one of the founding fathers of the USA.

Great Oakley SIBA

Ark Farm, High Street South, Tiffield, NN12 8AB
☎ (01327) 351759 ⊕ greatoakleybrewery.co.uk

⊗ Award-winning brewery established in 2005 in Great Oakley, relocating to Tiffield in 2012. It is run by Guy Jenkins who took over in 2017. More than 60 outlets are supplied, including brewery tap, the George, Tiffield.
♦LIVE

Welland Valley Mild (ABV 3.6%) MILD
Egret (ABV 3.8%) GOLD
Wagtail (ABV 3.9%) GOLD
Wot's Occurring (ABV 3.9%) BITTER
Tiffield Thunderbolt (ABV 4.2%) PALE
Gobble (ABV 4.5%) BLOND
Delapre Dark (ABV 4.6%) OLD
Abbey Stout (ABV 5%) STOUT
Tailshaker (ABV 5%) GOLD

King's Cliffe

Unit 10, Kingsmead, Station Road, King's Cliffe, PE8 6YH ☎ 07843 288088 ⊕ kcbales.co.uk

⊗ In 2014, exactly 100 years after the last brewery in King's Cliffe ceased brewing, village resident Jeremy O'Neill set up this venture. It currently produces five barrels a week. 🍴♦

5C (ABV 3.8%) GOLD
A light bitter with balanced taste of malt and hops and a refreshing bitter finish.
No. 10 (ABV 4%) PALE
Amber beer with a clean malty taste and a long bitter finish.
66 Degrees (ABV 4.6%) BITTER
Amber beer with a floral aroma, a balanced taste of malt and hops, and a long bitter finish.
B5 (ABV 4.6%) PALE
P51 (ABV 5.1%) PORTER
A rich dark porter with a smooth roast and chocolate taste and a malt, fruit and bitter chocolate finish.

Maule SIBA

Rothersthorpe Trading Estate, Northampton, NN4 8JH
⊕ maulebrewing.com

Brewing began in 2014 on a self-built plant. Production is mainly unfiltered keg and bottle-conditioned beers, but cask-conditioned ales are occasionally produced for festivals. The beers are available from various local stockists, including its tap in Northampton, as well as featuring on the London craft beer scene. LIVE

Nene Valley

Oundle Wharf, Station Road, Oundle, PE8 4DE
☎ (01832) 272776 ⊕ nenevalleybrewery.com

⊗ Nene Valley Brewery was established in 2011. A bespoke 15-barrel plant was installed in former Water Board premises in 2012. Further expansion in 2016 has doubled the floorspace. A taproom (Tap & Kitchen), opened on the same site in 2014. !! ☵ ◆LIVE ◈

Simple Pleasures Ale (ABV 3.6%) GOLD
A light, clean and refreshing beer with a pleasing citrus hop aroma and flavour.
Blonde Session Ale (ABV 3.8%) GOLD
Grain and fruit aroma with a bitter fruit flavour with some burnt malt which predominates in the aftertaste
Manhattan Project (ABV 4%) BITTER
Grapefruit and New World hops aroma is followed by grapefruit and tropical fruits flavour, and a dry bitter aftertaste
Bitter (ABV 4.1%) BITTER
Floral hop and malt aroma introduces a full, clean biscuit malt taste balanced by bitterness and some fruit, ending with a long malt and bitter finish
Woodcock's Relish (ABV 4.3%) BITTER
Australian Pale (ABV 4.4%) BITTER
Release the Chimps (ABV 4.4%) PALE
Rich malty aroma with grapefruit notes, dry bitter hoppy and grapefruity flavour and a lingering slightly astringent aftertaste.
Egyptian Cream (ABV 4.5%) STOUT
Pulping on your Stereo (ABV 4.5%) SPECIALITY
Hop Stash: Simcoe (ABV 5%) PALE
Big Bang Theory (ABV 5.3%) PALE
Well-balanced pale ale with a huge hop aroma giving way to malty sweetness and a gentle bitter finish.
A Beer Named LEEROY (ABV 5.5%) IPA
Supersonic (ABV 6%) SPECIALITY
A pale wheat beer brewed with gin & tonic botanicals including lemons, juniper and cardamom.
Bible Black (ABV 6.5%) PORTER
An inviting aroma of malt and fruit leads to a rich tasting beer where blackberry dominates but is balanced by malt, hops and some bitterness. The lingering finish is bitter sweet, with fruit assertive.
Fenland Farmhouse Saison (ABV 7.2%) SPECIALITY
Mid-Week Bender (ABV 7.4%) STRONG

Phipps NBC SIBA

Albion Brewery, 54 Kingswell Street, Northampton, NN1 1PR
☎ (01604) 946606 ☎ 07717 078402
⊕ phipps-nbc.co.uk

Founded initially in Towcester in 1801, Phipps had been brewing in Northampton since 1817. Following a takeover by Watney Mann in 1960 the brewery closed in 1974. The company name, trademark and recipes were acquired and Phipps beers reappeared in 2008. The founding Phipps family re-joined the company in 2014 allowing the historic Albion Brewery and its associated bar to be restored and Phipps brewing to return to the town after a 40-year absence. !! ◆LIVE ◈

Thrupenny Bitter (ABV 3.6%) BITTER
Red Star (ABV 3.8%) BITTER
Honey malt aroma, a flavour of rye, some sweetness and hints of dark cherry and a dry bitter aftertaste.
Steam Roller (ABV 3.8%) BITTER

Biscuity aroma with some sweetness followed by earthy, spiced bitterness with hints of plum which continue in the dry aftertaste.
Midsummer Meadow (ABV 3.9%) BITTER
Cobbler's Ale (ABV 4%) BITTER
IPA (ABV 4.3%) GOLD
Ratliffe's Celebrated Stout (ABV 4.3%) STOUT
Becket's Ale (ABV 4.5%) BITTER
Bison Brown (ABV 4.6%) MILD
Black Star (ABV 4.8%) BITTER
Roasted malt aromas with liquorice notes followed by a bitter coffee chocolate flavour and a dry bitter coffee aftertaste.
Last Orders (ABV 4.8%) BITTER
Kinky Boots (ABV 4.9%) SPECIALITY
Gold Star (ABV 5.2%) PALE

Potbelly SIBA

31-44 Sydney Street, Kettering, NN16 0HY
☎ (01536) 410818 ☎ 07834 867825
⊕ potbelly-brewery.co.uk

Potbelly started brewing in 2005 on a 10-barrel plant and supplies around 200 outlets. A new craft brand called A Bloke Down the Pub was launched in 2021. Beers are also contract brewed for the Olde England Ales estate under the Olde England name. !! ☵ ◆LIVE

Best (ABV 3.8%) BITTER
Sweet malty aroma with a delicately spiced raisiny dried fruit flavour and a light bitter aftertaste.
Lager Brau (ABV 3.9%) SPECIALITY
A Piggin' IPA (ABV 4%) PALE
Hop Trotter (ABV 4.1%) GOLD
Piggin' Saint (ABV 4.2%) PALE
Beijing Black (ABV 4.4%) MILD
Pigs Do Fly (ABV 4.4%) GOLD
Hedonism (ABV 4.5%) BITTER
Slightly sweet aroma with citrus notes followed by a sharp hoppy flavour with hints of grapefruit and a bitter aftertaste.
Black Sun (ABV 5%) STRONG
SOAB (ABV 5%) BITTER
Crazy Daze (ABV 5.5%) BITTER
Slightly sweetish aroma followed by a sharp bitter flavour with hints of dried fruit, and a lingering bitter aftertaste.

Brewed under the A Bloke Down the Pub brand name:
Clever Colin (ABV 4%) GOLD
Handy Andy (ABV 4.2%) GOLD
Dangerous Darren (ABV 4.3%) BROWN
Gorgeous Gary (ABV 4.5%) GOLD
Majestic Mark (ABV 5.1%) GOLD
Philanthropist Phil (ABV 5.2%) BITTER
Incredible Ian (ABV 5.6%) BLOND

Contract brewed for the Olde England Ales estate:
Black Prince (ABV 6%) PORTER

Rockingham SIBA

1 Kingsmead, Station Road, King's Cliffe, PE8 6YH
☎ (01832) 280722

Office: 25 Wansford Road, Elton, PE8 6RZ
⊕ rockinghamales.co.uk

⊗ Rockingham is a small brewery established in 1997 that operated from a converted farm building near Blatherwycke, Northamptonshire, with a two-barrel plant producing a prolific range of beers, although it has recently moved to a new site at King's Cliffe. It supplies half a dozen outlets. ◆

Forest Gold (ABV 3.9%) BLOND
Hop Devil (ABV 3.9%) GOLD
White Rabbit (ABV 4%) GOLD
Fruits of the Forest (ABV 4.3%) BITTER
After Dark Stout (ABV 5%) STOUT

Roman Way

Building 79, The Old Depot, Bridge Street, Weedon Bec, NN7 4PS ⊕ romanwaybrewery.co.uk

Roman Way Brewery was established in 2019. It has built up an interesting and extensive list of beers which is now in double figures. Its shop and taproom are usually open to the public on Friday and Saturday with pop up food and regular events. 🛒◆

Barbarian Best (ABV 3.8%) BITTER
Carpe Diem (ABV 3.9%) PALE
Tribune (ABV 3.9%) PALE
Senate Gold (ABV 4.1%) GOLD
Hints of orange throughout. Dry earthy aroma, a bitter flavour with orchard fruits and a lingering bitter aftertaste.
Claudius IPA (ABV 4.7%) GOLD
Boudicca (ABV 5.5%) IPA
Pantheon (ABV 6%) PALE

Silverstone SIBA

Kingshill Farm, Syresham, NN13 5TH ☎ 07835 279400 ⊕ silverstonebrewery.co.uk

Established in 2008 Silverstone Brewery is a traditional tower brewery located near the celebrated motor racing circuit. The brewery has won multiple awards for it's beers which are supplied in bottles, cask and KeyKeg. ‼◆

Ignition (ABV 3.4%) BLOND
Pitstop (ABV 3.9%) BITTER
Polestar (ABV 4.1%) STOUT
Chequered Flag (ABV 4.3%) BITTER
Octane (ABV 4.8%) BITTER
Classic IPA (ABV 5.6%) IPA

Three Hills

3 & 5 Cosy Nook, Thrapston, NN14 4PS

Second Site (Outpost): Arch 7, Almond Road, Bermondsey, London, SE16 3LR ☎ (020) 8050 4984 ⊕ threehillsbrewing.com

Named after the ancient communal tombs on the outskirts of the village of Woodford, Three Hills is a small-batch brewery established 2016. Initially producing only in bottle, can and KeyKeg, it now produces occasional cask beers. Three Hills purchased the Affinity brewery site/kit in 2020 and brews in London under the Outpost name. Production is now undertaken at a new site in Cosy Nook, Thrapston. In 2022 it opened the Way Station

Tap Room in the warehouse adjacent to the production site. ◆

Towcester Mill SIBA

The Mill, Chantry Lane, Towcester, NN12 6AD
☎ (01327) 437060 ⊕ towcestermillbrewery.co.uk

⊠ A five-barrel brewery situated at the Grade-II listed Old Mill in Towcester. There is a taproom and beer garden onsite together with off-sale facilities. ‼🛒◆

Crooked Hooker (ABV 3.8%) BITTER
Golden/amber colour with a honeyed fruit aroma, a slighlty earthy taste with some fruit and a bitter finish.
Mill Race (ABV 3.9%) BLOND
Slightly citrus aroma followed by a dry citrus taste with hints of grapefruit with a long bitter aftertaste
Bell Ringer (ABV 4.4%) PALE
Sweetish malty aroma followed by a bitter flavour with zesty orange marmalade notes and an earth and spicy aftertaste.
Steam Ale (ABV 4.5%) BITTER
Sweetish aroma with fruit and citrus, complex well-balanced flavours with passionfruit and citrus notes persisting in the lingering aftertaste.
Black Fire (ABV 5.2%) STOUT
Treacle and vanilla aftertaste with roast malt notes, a dry bitter dark chololate flavour and a dark pruney aftertaste.
Roman Road (ABV 5.2%) PALE
Tropical fruit aroma followed by a good balance of malt and hops with pineapple notes and a long bitter aftertaste.

Weldon

Bencroft Grange, Bedford Road, Rushden, NN10 0SE
☎ (01536) 601016

Office: 12 Chapel Road,, Weldon, NN17 3HP
⊕ weldonbrewery.co.uk

Weldon Brewery originally started brewing in 2014 on a two-barrel plant at the Shoulder of Mutton, after which the brewery was originally named. In 2016 the brewery acquired the premises and 3.5-barrel kit of the former Copper Kettle brewery in Rushden and became the main production facility, with the brewery being renamed Weldon. ◆

Diab-Lo (ABV 3.7%) PALE
Essanell (ABV 3.8%) MILD
Dragline (ABV 3.9%) GOLD
Stahlstadt (ABV 4%) BLOND
Galvy Stout (ABV 4.2%) STOUT
Windmill (ABV 4.2%) BITTER
Mad Max (ABV 4.4%) PALE
Paradisium (ABV 4.4%) PALE
Roman Mosaics (ABV 4.6%) PALE

The discreet barman

Over the mahogany, jar followed jorum, gargle, tincture and medium, tailor, scoop, snifter and ball of malt, in a breathless pint-to-pint. Discreet barman, Mr Sugrue thought, turning outside the door and walking in the direction of Stephen's Green. Never give anything away – part of the training. Is Mr so-and-so there, I'll go and see, strict instructions never to say yes in case it might be the wife. Curious now the way the tinge of wickedness hung around the pub, a relic of course of Victorianism, nothing to worry about as long as a man kept himself in hand.
Jack White, The Devil You Know

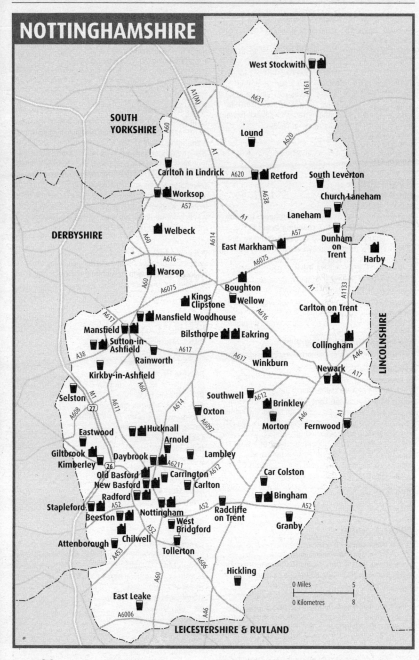

NOTTINGHAMSHIRE

ENGLAND

West Stockwith

SOUTH YORKSHIRE

Lound

Carlton in Lindrick

Retford

South Leverton

Worksop

Church Laneham

Welbeck

Laneham

DERBYSHIRE

East Markham

Dunham on Trent

Harby

Warsop

Boughton

Wellow

Carlton on Trent

Kings Clipstone

Mansfield Woodhouse

Mansfield

Bilsthorpe Eakring

Collingham

Sutton-in-Ashfield

Rainworth

Winkburn

Newark

Kirkby-in-Ashfield

LINCOLNSHIRE

Selston

Southwell

Oxton

Brinkley

Morton

Fernwood

Eastwood

Hucknall

Arnold

Lambley

Giltbrook

Kimberley

Daybrook

Car Colston

Old Basford

New Basford

Carrington

Carlton

Bingham

Radford

Stapleford

Nottingham

Radcliffe on Trent

Beeston

West Bridgford

Granby

Attenborough

Chilwell

Tollerton

Hickling

East Leake

| 0 Miles | 5 |
| 0 Kilometres | 8 |

LEICESTERSHIRE & RUTLAND

Arnold

Robin Hood & Little John Ⓛ ✅

1 Church Street, NG5 8FD (on corner of Cross St)
☎ (0115) 920 1054 ⊕ therobinhoodandlittlejohn.co.uk
Lincoln Green Marion, Archer, Hood, Tuck; 16 changing beers (often Everards) Ⓗ
Former Home Brewery pub now operated by Lincoln Green under the Everards Project William scheme. Dating back to 1726, it was once a coaching inn. The bar features Home Ales memorabilia, while the lounge has details of the pub's history and the local area, and there is a piano. The rear courtyard has outdoor seating and a covered skittle alley. There are 10 real ale pumps in each bar showcasing Lincoln Green beers, plus guests from microbreweries, and a real cider wall with four taps dispensing real ciders. ❀☻♿♣🚜🚌🚲📶♪

Attenborough

Bird Hide Ⓛ

139 Attenborough Lane, NG9 6AA
☎ 07305 089387 ⊕ thebirdhide.uk

507

House beer (by Old Sawley); 5 changing beers (sourced regionally; often Blue Monkey, Castle Rock, Lenton Lane) Ⓖ
Small village micropub opened in 2021, selling six cask ales – mainly from local breweries – ciders, and Apothecary Mead from Sherwood Forest. It is a friendly, comfortable place to gather, with a perfect suntrap outdoor seating area. A bike rack is provided for visiting cyclists. Snacks include five flavours of pork scratching – hand-weighed on old-fashioned scales – several flavours of nuts and an interesting range of crisps.
🛏️🏵️&⚓🚲🅿️🚃🐾🛜♪

Beeston

Crown Inn ★ 🅛
Church Street, NG9 1FY
☎ (0115) 967 8623
Blue Monkey BG Sips; Brewsters Hophead; Dancing Duck 22; Everards Tiger; 7 changing beers Ⓗ
A 19th-century Grade II-listed alehouse, acquired and sympathetically refurbished by Everards. Eleven cask ales, craft beers and real ciders are offered from this former East Midlands Pub of the Year. Five distinct drinking areas include a snug and a three seat 'confessional', once used as a hideaway by the local vicar. An outside bar offers further cask ales and craft beers during the summer. Although busy, the pub retains its community feel, with a cosy atmosphere throughout. Substantial snacks are available.
Q🛏️🏵️&⚓🚃(Centre)♣🐾🅿️🚃🐾🛜♪

Star Inn 🅛
22 Middle Street, NG9 1FX
☎ (0115) 854 5320 ⊕ starbeeston.co.uk
House beer (by Lenton Lane); 9 changing beers Ⓗ
This former Shipstone's pub, still with branded windows, has been restored to its former glory. It offers 10 cask ales alongside a wide selection of whiskies, gins, rums and wines. Decor is tasteful and minimal with three separate rooms, complemented by a permanent marquee, a sports/games room and a spacious garden and patio outside. Families are welcome during the day. Meals are available, alongside a popular and extensive range of bar snacks.
🛏️🏵️🍴🍺&⚓🚃(Centre)♣🐾🅿️🚃🐾🛜♪

Victoria Hotel 🅛
85 Dovecote Lane, NG9 1JG
☎ (0115) 925 4049 ⊕ vichotelbeeston.co.uk
Black Sheep Best Bitter; Brains Rev James Original; Castle Rock Harvest Pale; Full Mash Séance; 7 changing beers (sourced regionally) Ⓗ
Located alongside the platform of Beeston railway station, this restored Victorian masterpiece has mass appeal. Eleven real ales are joined by real ciders/perries, an extensive whisky and wine menu, and a renowned food menu. Taster trays of three third-pints are also offered. Two distinct bars are complemented by a dining room, and outside is a covered, smoke-free seating area. VicFest is hosted in July and beer festivals feature throughout the year. Q🏵️🍺&⚓🚃(Centre)🐾🅿️🚃🐾🛜♪

Bingham

Horse & Plough 🅛
Long Acre, NG13 8AF
☎ (01949) 839313
Castle Rock Harvest Pale, Preservation; 7 changing beers Ⓗ
A former Methodist chapel in the heart of a busy market town, this small pub has a traditional interior with a

flagstone floor. A terrace was added in 2019 and a pool room in 2022. Up to nine cask ales and four ciders are served. Four times local CAMRA Pub of the Year, the Horse & Plough always offers a wide range of styles and strengths of real ale and cider, showcasing smaller producers alongside Castle Rock and other established favourites. 🏵️&⚓🐾🚃🐾🛜♪

Wheatsheaf
Long Acre, NG13 8BG
☎ (01949) 837430 ⊕ thewheatsheafbingham.co.uk
6 changing beers Ⓗ
The Wheatsheaf reverted to its traditional name when it reopened 2016 under new ownership. Ten handpumps offer a range of changing cask ales and ciders. Food is served lunchtimes and evenings in the bar and the separate restaurant. The pub has a real fire in the bar, a fantastic outdoor terrace and hosts live music every week. A former local and regional CAMRA Cider Pub of the Year. 🛏️🏵️🍴🍺&⚓🐾🅿️🚃🐾🛜♪

Car Colston

Royal Oak ✅
The Green, NG13 8JE
☎ (01949) 20247 ⊕ royaloakcarcolston.co.uk

REAL ALE BREWERIES	
Aither Mansfield Woodhouse (NEW)	
Angel 🍴 Nottingham	
Beermats 🌾 Winkburn	
Beeston Hop Nottingham: Beeston	
Black Iris 🌾 Nottingham: New Basford	
Black Market 🍴 Warsop	
Blue Monkey Nottingham: Giltbrook	
Brewhouse & Kitchen 🍴 Nottingham	
Castle Rock 🌾 Nottingham	
Cat Asylum 🌾 Collingham	
Dukeries 🌾 Worksop	
FireRock Sutton in Ashfield	
Flipside Nottingham	
Full Mash Stapleford	
Good Stuff 🍴 Daybrook	
Grafton Worksop	
Harby 🍴 Harby	
Harrison's Retford	
Idle 🍴 West Stockwith	
Jacaranda Brinkley (NEW)	
Kings Clipstone Kings Clipstone	
Lenton Lane Nottingham	
Lincoln Green Nottingham: Hucknall	
Linear Bingham	
Liquid Light 🌾 Nottingham	
Lord Randalls Newark	
Magpie 🌾 Nottingham	
Maypole Eakring	
Milestone 🌾 Newark	
Navigation Nottingham	
Neon Raptor 🌾 Nottingham	
Newark Newark	
Nottingham 🌾 Nottingham: Radford	
Pheasantry East Markham	
Prior's Well 🍴 Mansfield	
Reality Nottingham: Chilwell	
Reckless Dweeb Bilsthorpe	
Rufford Abbey Boughton (brewing suspended)	
Scruffy Dog 🍴 Sutton-In-Ashfield	
Shipstone's Nottingham: Old Basford	
Tom Herrick's Carlton on Trent	
Vaguely Bingham	
Welbeck Abbey Welbeck	

Bombardier; Wainwright; 2 changing beers ⊞
This country inn – a former hosiery factory – is situated on one of England's largest village greens. The pub has a cosy bar with comfortable seating and a real fire, a separate, generously-sized restaurant, and a separate function room. Four beers, all from the Marston's range but often featuring less-heralded varieties, are available in the bar. Food is served lunchtimes and evenings. There is a skittle alley to the rear, plus a beer garden and camping facilities. ⽒❀⏃❶♿♣♠P♥❄🎜

Carlton in Lindrick

Grey Horses Inn 🅛
The Cross, S81 9EW (in centre of old village) SK592845
☎ (01909) 730252
6 changing beers (sourced locally; often Chantry, Welbeck Abbey) ⊞
The Grey Horses is situated in the heart of the village within the conservation area. It has a front bar accessible from the street, a large lounge area where excellent food is served and a large beer garden. The pub serves six real ales: two or three usually from Welbeck Abbey and three or four guest beers from local breweries. A former winner of local CAMRA Pub of the Season, there is always a welcoming atmosphere.
Q⽒❀⏃♿♣P♠(21,22)♥❄🎜

Church Laneham

Ferryboat Inn
Church Laneham, DN22 0NQ (opp River Trent, close to church) SK814765
☎ (01777) 228350
Greene King Abbot; Pheasantry Dancing Dragonfly; 2 changing beers (sourced locally) ⊞
Friendly Trent-side pub with open-plan bar area with TV, separate dining room, a conservatory and outside seating. Abbot Ale and Dancing Dragonfly are the regular real ales, plus two guest beers, usually from local breweries. There is an extensive, reasonably priced menu. Due to the nearby caravan park the pub can get busy. It is not unusual for the river to flood opposite the pub. Q⽒❀⏃♿♣♠❶♠P♠(P190)♥❄🎜

Daybrook

Abdication 🅛
89 Mansfield Road, NG5 6BH (opp gates of former Home Brewery) ⊕ theabdication.co.uk
4 changing beers ⊞
This modern, friendly micropub is based in the Home Ales Brewery Coronation Buildings (built in 1936/37), opposite the former brewery. The four ever-changing cask ales, four craft lines and three ciders are sourced from microbreweries, small producers or the on-site nanobrewery Good Stuff brewing, and include a mix of styles. An archway splits the single room, giving an appearance of a much larger area. Dogs are very welcome. It is closed during the first two weeks of January. Q⽒♿♣♠❶♥❄🎜

Dunham on Trent

White Swan
Main Street, NG22 0TY (on A5, as you enter from Markham Moor) SK813745
☎ (01777) 228307
Pheasantry Pale Ale; 2 changing beers (sourced locally) ⊞
An attractive village pub at the side of the A57 and close to the River Trent. The pub has a separate bar, a

reasonably-sized dining room and a function room. Pheasantry PA is the regular beer and there are two changing guest real ales, usually from local breweries. Outside there is ample seating and a large children's play area. The pub has its own fishing lake and camping and caravan park. ⽒❀🚐⏃❶♿♣P🚲♥❄🎜

East Leake

Round RobINN 🅛
54 Main Street, LE12 6PG
☎ (0150) 985 2988
6 changing beers (sourced locally) 🅖
Micropub opened 2015, serving six local beers on gravity, cooled on racks behind the bar. A range of ciders and continental bottled beers is also available. Seating is a mixture of chairs, cushioned benches and high stools. The single room accommodates up to 45 patrons, and a small outdoor area to the front offers alfresco drinking. Food is restricted to light bar snacks.
Q⽒♿♣♠🚲(1)♥🎜

Eastwood

Gamekeeper's 🅛
136 Nottingham Road, NG16 3GD
5 changing beers ⊞
Opened in 2017, this micropub in the centre of Eastwood serves up to five local ales. The bar is at the back, with a seating area at the front and an alcove space to the left. There is also an extensive garden/patio area at the rear of the pub. Pub snacks are normally available.
Q⽒❀♿♣❶♥❄

Tap & Growler 🅛
209 Nottingham Road, Hill Top, NG16 3GS
⊕ tapandgrowler.co.uk
Acorn Barnsley Bitter; Oakham Bishops Farewell ⊞; 8 changing beers (sourced locally) ⊞/🅖
Micropub selling up to 10 real ales, five on handpump, with up to a further five on gravity. Local ciders are also avaiable, and nine craft beer taps are on the back wall of the bar. Whilst the name is partially derived from the US word for a take-out container (growler), when the building was being renovated a ceramic lion was found and is now proudly on display as The Growler. A patio garden to the rear seats around 50.
Q⽒❀♿♣♠❶🚲♥❄🎜

Fernwood

Brews Brothers Micropub & Coffee House
Rubys Avenue, NG24 3RQ
☎ (01636) 705475
4 changing beers ⊞
Now in its second year in the Guide, Brews Brothers is a modern micropub on the recently built Fernwood Estate, on the outskirts of Newark and just off the A1. It offers a range of three cask ales – often from independent breweries – ciders, and interesting craft ales on tap. It is also a coffee shop for the local community and serves popular food, specialising in home-made pies. There is a regular quiz night and live music. Q⽒❀⏃♿♣P🚲♥❄🎜

Granby

Marquis of Granby
Dragon Street, NG13 9PN
☎ (01949) 859517
Brewsters Hophead, Marquis; 4 changing beers ⊞

Believed to be the original Marquis of Granby, dating back to 1760 or earlier, this small two-roomed pub is the brewery tap for Brewster's. Alongside the Brewster's range, the guest beers usually come from microbreweries. Yorkstone floors complement the yew bar tops and wood-beamed rooms, and the lounge has a welcoming open fire in winter. No food is served but regular visits from Great Street Food vans are popular. The pub also houses a small village store. Local CAMRA Pub of the Year 2022. Q❧🍴&♣♦P₽🐾🛜

Hickling

Plough Inn
Main Street, LE14 3AH
☎ (01664) 822225 ⊕ ploughinnhickling.com
5 changing beers ⊞
The Plough at Hickling is an attractive village pub with a large beer garden situated opposite the Hickling basin of the Grantham Canal in the heart of the Vale of Belvoir. It offers a wide range of lunchtime and evening food, and serves up to five cask ales, plus up to five craft beers and real cider. An annual beer festival and beer-related events such as food & beer matching evenings are held. Children and dogs are welcome.
Q❧🍴🍽&♣♦P₽🐾🛜

Hucknall

Byron's Rest 🅛
8 Baker Street, NG15 7AS
Titanic Plum Porter; 4 changing beers (often Black Iris, Magpie, Shipstone's) ⊞
This micropub was converted from a sewing shop in 2018. A narrow establishment with a snug just off the entrance, it extends considerably to the rear where the bar is located, and has comfortable bench seating, creating a convivial atmosphere. It serves five real ales and up to 15 real ciders, most of which are sourced locally. Outside at the back, the covered secret garden provides a tranquil oasis. Local CAMRA LocAle Pub of the Year. Q🍴🍽≉₽♣♦₽🐾♫

Kimberley

Roots Emporium
17 Nottingham Road, NG16 2NB
☎ 07864 572037
6 changing beers ⊞
Formerly a bespoke furniture and gift shop, this micropub is furnished and built from much of the stock of the former business. It was originally quite small, but a rear garden and former garage have increased the available space. The patio at the front extends the drinking area further. Walls and cabinets are adorned with interesting memorabilia, including items relating to the former Kimberley brewery. Beers are generally from microbreweries with local beer available.
Q❧🍴&♦₽(R1,34)🐾

Kirkby-in-Ashfield

Dandy Cock Ale House ✅
184a Victoria Road, NG17 8AT
☎ 07854 054060 ⊕ thedandycock.co.uk
4 changing beers (sourced locally; often Dancing Duck, Little Critters) ⊞
Micropub offering an every-changing range of four real ales and up to six real ciders on tap. There are two small rooms, with views into the cellar behind the bar. A range of wines and spirits is also available, with a choice of over 200 different gins. Acoustic nights are occasionally

hosted. There is on-street parking and a bus stop directly outside the front door. Very dog friendly.
Q❧&≉♦🐾🐾♫

Dog House
84-86 Station Street, NG17 7AP
☎ 07414 743988
3 changing beers (often Blue Monkey, Purple Moose) ⊞
Two-roomed town-centre micropub serving up to three hand pulled beers and five real ciders. A small selection of bottled beers is also available, alongside a few selected spirits and lagers. The pub is directly beside the town's main bus stops and a 10-minute walk from the train station. It is dog friendly and children are welcome until evening. A quiz night is held on Sunday.
Q🍴&≉₽🐾🛜

Regent ✅
Kingsway, NG17 7BQ
☎ (01623) 687630
Courage Directors; Greene King Abbot; Ruddles Best Bitter; Shepherd Neame Spitfire; Wychwood Hobgoblin Ruby; 4 changing beers ⊞
Converted from the former Regency cinema by JD Wetherspoon, this pub on the corner of Kingsway has a large open-plan format with a smaller separate dining area to the front. The pub has a big emphasis on cask ales, offering up to 10 choices at any one time. The usual range of Wetherspoon meals are served all day every day. Families are welcome. ❧🍴&≉♦₽🛜

Lambley

Woodlark Inn 🅛
Church Street, NG4 4QB
☎ (0115) 931 2535 ⊕ woodlarkinn.co.uk
Theakston Best Bitter; Timothy Taylor Landlord; 3 changing beers ⊞
Located in the quaint-sounding Upper Dumbles area of Lambley village, this traditional pub dates back to the 19th century and is popular with locals and visitors from afar. Five cask ales are served from the bare red-brick bar with exposed beams, and the lounge/restaurant is popular for its excellent home-cooked food. The landlord holds three well-attended weekend beer festivals each year. Q❧🍴🍴♣♦P₽(46,47)🐾🛜

Laneham

Bees Knees 🅛
Main Street, DN22 0NA (centre of village) SK803762
☎ (01777) 228090
Don Valley Atomic Blonde; Ossett Silver King; Pheasantry Dancing Dragonfly; 3 changing beers (sourced nationally) ⊞
A quirky country pub, converted from a former shop, with three small rooms and some outside seating. Well supported by locals, it serves three regular real ales, three rotating guest beers including a stout or porter, over 180 gins, and excellent food (booking recommended). Quiz night is Wednesdays and jazz plays on the first Sunday of the month. A former local CAMRA Pub of the Season. Q❧🍴🍴&▲♦P₽🐾🛜♫

Lound

Bluebell Inn
Town Street, DN22 8RN (on main street through village) SK691864
☎ (01777) 818457 ⊕ bluebellinnlound.co.uk

3 changing beers (sourced locally; often Abbeydale, Bradfield, Welbeck Abbey) H
A traditional village pub with a lounge bar where food is served and a taproom with a pool table. Three changing real ales, usually from local breweries, are served. The pub has gained a good reputation for the quality of the food and the beers. Outside is a large car park and a partly covered seating area. Quiz night is Wednesday. Accommodation is available in three rooms.
Q ও ✿ ♨ ◑ ৬ ♣ P ➡ ❀ 🎵

Mansfield

Bold Forester ✓
Botany Avenue, NG18 5NF
☎ (01623) 623970
Greene King IPA, Abbot; Hardys & Hansons Olde Trip; Morland Old Speckled Hen; 8 changing beers (often Little Critters, Pheasantry, Prior's Well) H
Hungry Horse-branded pub and restaurant offering up to 12 real ales, usually six from Greene King and six guest beers. Food is served daily. The open-plan interior has largescreen TVs showing most major sports. The beer garden is popular with families in the summer. Situated on the main road into Mansfield, it has a large car park and regular bus services passing the door.
ও ✿ ◑ ৬ ⇌ ♣ P ➡ ❀ 🎵

Brown Cow
31 Ratcliffe Gate, NG18 2JA
☎ (01623) 645854 ⊕ browncow-mansfield.co.uk
Everards Tiger; 9 changing beers H
Owned by Everards brewery and run as a Project William business. A range of up to 12 real ales is offered alongside ciders, craft keg beers and international bottled beers. There are two separate bar areas and a function room upstairs, plus a popular courtyard beer garden. The pub is a short walk from the town centre. Recently awarded best pub on the M&A CAMRA Ale Trail 2023. Q ও ✿ ◑ ⇌ ♣ ● P ➡ ❀ 🎵

Railway Inn
9 Station Street, NG18 1EF
☎ (01623) 623086
4 changing beers (often Dukeries, Full Mash, Pheasantry) H
Close to the town centre bus and train stations, this community pub serves popular home-cooked meals, with daily special and offers available. As well as the main bar area there are two separate rooms for diners or those looking for a quieter space. Up to four real ales and up to two real ciders are offered. The walled rear garden is popular in the summer. Q ও ✿ ◑ ⇌ ● ➡ ❀ 🎵

Mansfield Woodhouse

Greyhound Inn
82 High Street, NG19 8BD
☎ (01623) 464403
Adnams Broadside; Caledonian Deuchars IPA; 3 changing beers (often Robinsons, Timothy Taylor) H
Run single-handedly by the same landlady for over 25 years, the Greyhound was recognised with a special achievement award in 2017. Five beers and one cider are available in a traditional pub environment – no food, just bar snacks and lively conversation in two separate rooms. Weekly activities include open the box, play your cards right, quiz nights and card bingo. Pool, darts and dominoes are played in the public bar. Dogs are welcome in the taproom. ✿ ♣ P ➡ ❀

Morton

Full Moon Inn ✓
Main Street, NG25 0UT
☎ (01636) 830251 ⊕ thefullmoonmorton.co.uk
Acorn Barnsley Bitter; Navigation New Dawn Pale; Timothy Taylor Landlord; 2 changing beers H
Welcoming village pub serving up to four real ales, with at least one from a regional or local brewery. Low ceilings with natural oak beams and brickwork, and two open log fires, give the pub a modern yet rustic and cosy feel. Food is served daily in the restaurant area and includes a popular Sunday lunch. There is a large car park, a play area for children and an outside drinking area.
Q ও ✿ ◑ ৬ ♣ P ❀ ❖ 🎵

Newark

Just Beer Micropub 🏆
32A Castle Gate, NG24 1BG (in Swan & Salmon Yard, off Castle Gate)
☎ (01636) 312047 ⊕ justbeermicropub.biz
4 changing beers (sourced nationally) H
Friendly micropub offering a varied range of cask ale, craft beer on tap, and cider and perry. Snacks include local pork pies, cheeseboards and pork scratchings. Traditional pub games are played. Several beer festivals are held throughout the year and there is a popular quiz night once a week. Twice regional CAMRA Pub of the Year and local Pub of the Year 2023. Since opening in 2010 they have served over 5,000 different cask ales. Q ৬ ▲ ⇌ (Castle) ♣ ● 🖥 ❀ ❖

Organ Grinder
21 Portland Street, NG24 4XF
☎ (01636) 671768
Blue Monkey BG Sips, Primate Best Bitter, Infinity IPA, Guerrilla, Ape Ale, Infinity Plus 1; 1 changing beer (sourced regionally) H
Opened in 2014, this no-nonsense, beer-drinking pub offers real ales from Blue Monkey and often a guest alongside real cider, a range of bottled beers and an extensive range of spirits. The Monkey Room has a dartboard and a large TV screen, and books, games and a piano are available for customer use. Bar snacks are served. It hosts a popular quiz every other Wednesday. A covered smoking area is to the rear. Local CAMRA Cider Pub of the Year 2023. ✿ ⇌ (Castle) ♣ ● ➡ ❀ ❖ 🎵

Prince Rupert 🅛
46 Stodman Street, NG24 1AW
☎ (01636) 918121
Brains Rev James Original; Oakham Citra; 4 changing beers (sourced nationally) H
Reopened in 2010, this historic pub dates back to around 1452. It is multi-roomed on two separate levels, with exposed beams evident in several snug rooms and various interesting artefacts and brewery memorabilia decorating the walls and ceilings. There is a small but pleasant patio garden. Up to four ales are available and an extensive lunchtime and evening menu is served. A former local CAMRA Pub of the Year, it has featured in the guide for 13 consecutive years.
Q ও ✿ ◑ ⇌ (Castle) ➡ ❀ ❖ 🎵

Nottingham: Carlton

Brickyard ✓
Standhill Road, NG4 1JL
☎ (0115) 987 8707
Lincoln Green Archer, Hood; 3 changing beers H
This former social club was renovated by Lincoln Green and reopened in 2018. The pub contains a number of

items of Hardys & Hansons memorabilia, complete with a scale model of the former brewery cleverly built into a table. Although fairly small overall, a snug is located at the back of the pub to the right of the bar. Mainly Lincoln Green beers are served, with occasional guests. Craft keg beers also sold. 🏠🚗😺🎐♪

Old Volunteer 🅛

35 Burton Road, NG4 3DQ
☎ (0115) 987 2299
10 changing beers (often Flipside) 🅗
Refurbished by Flipside brewery in 2014, the brewery tap showcases four of their beers alongside guests and a real cider. The interior is separated into distinct areas using unusual bare wood dividing beams, with a raised corner and varied floor materials. Outside is a patio area with parasols, leading to the main entrance. Food choices include speciality burgers. Snacks are on offer at all times. Beer festivals are held in a car park marquee.
🏠🕪♿≠(Carlton)🌭P🚗😺🎐♪

Nottingham: Carrington

Doctor's Orders 🅛

351 Mansfield Road, NG5 2DA
☎ (0115) 960 7985 🌐 doctorsordersmicropub.co.uk
5 changing beers (sourced locally) 🅗
Small beer emporium with an intimate atmosphere. A square front lounge leads to a corridor flanked on one side by a narrow raised benched seating area with a small bar-cum-serving area at the rear. Beer and cider are served to your table from handpumps at the back of the bar. The pub maintains its philosophy of providing a range of microbrewery beers in a comfortable, friendly environment. Q🏃🏠😺♣🌭P🚗😺🎐

Nottingham: Central

BeerHeadZ

Cabman's Shelter, 1A Queens Road, NG2 3AS
(adjoining Nottingham station)
☎ 07542 773753 🌐 beerheadz.biz
5 changing beers 🅗
Small but sympathetically restored Edwardian cabman's shelter, adjacent to the main railway station entrance. The single room has a central bar and retains period features including bench chests, wooden panelling, windows and coat hooks. There is a long table-shelf with high stools opposite the bar. Five real ales change regularly and are seldom repeated, and there are several draught ciders. A large choice of bottles and cans is also available to enjoy in or take out. 🏠≠🍴🌭🍺🚗😺

Fox & Grapes 🅛

21 Southwell Road, NG1 1DL
☎ (0115) 841 8970
Castle Rock Harvest Pale, Preservation, Elsie Mo, Screech Owl; 4 changing beers 🅗
Impressive renovation of an Edwardian-fronted Victorian pub by Castle Rock brewery in 2017. The former two-room layout has been opened up into a single L-shaped room with raised areas on either side of the front door. A high ceiling and large windows give a light, airy feel. Nicknamed Pretty Windows from the fancy Edwardian window frames (which were sadly lost in a 1970s refit). The pub serves eight real ales, ciders, seven keg beers, locally produced coffee and gin, and artisan food.
🏃🏠😺♿🚌(Lace Market)🌭🚗😺🎐♪

Good Fellow George

11-15 Alfreton Road, Canning Circus, NG7 3JE
🌐 thegoodfellowgeorge.co.uk

4 changing beers 🅗
Conversion of a former bank, in a curved mid-20th century building overlooking the busy Canning Circus junction. The bar frontage is adorned with two pence pieces, commemorating the building's former use. Four handpumps and 15 craft taps supply the beer. Seating is mainly varnished tables and chairs with upholstered settles at fixed window tables. To the rear, there is a small mezzanine level and covered outdoor smoking area with wooden benches. High-quality cheese and charcuterie platters are an excellent-value and popular feature. 🏃♿♣🌭🚗😺🎐♪

Kean's Head 🅛

46 St Mary's Gate, Lace Market, NG1 1QA
☎ (0115) 947 4052
Castle Rock Harvest Pale; 5 changing beers 🅗
This cosy one-room pub, named after the 19th-century actor Edmund Kean, is owned by Castle Rock brewery and stands opposite the imposing medieval St Mary's Church in the city's historic Lace Market district. It has a diverse clientele and serves exciting Indian street food, freshly prepared in-house. The guest beers always provide a varied choice of styles. There is a wide selection of craft beers, along with three handpumps dispensing real cider and an impressive selection of gins and whiskies. 🏃🕪♿≠🚌(Lace Market)🌭🚗😺🎐

King William IV 🅛

6 Eyre Street, Sneinton, NG2 4RG
☎ (0115) 958 9864 🌐 new.thekingbilly.co.uk
Black Iris Snake Eyes; Oakham Citra, Bishops Farewell; 5 changing beers 🅗
Known widely as the King Billy, this Victorian gem on the edge of the city centre is close to the Motorpoint Arena. A family-run free house that oozes charm and character, it is a haven for real ale drinkers, with a choice of up to eight microbrewery ales from near and far, as well as real cider. Folk music is popular on Thursday nights. The pub sign won a national award in 2015.
Q🏃🏠🕪♣🚌(43,44) 😺🎐♪

Organ Grinder 🅛

21 Alfreton Road, Canning Circus, NG7 3JE
☎ (0115) 970 0630
Blue Monkey BG Sips, Primate Best Bitter, Infinity IPA, Guerrilla, Infinity Plus 1; 3 changing beers (sourced locally) 🅗
Previously the Red Lion, this single-roomed, multi-level pub has modern decor, but retains a traditional pub feel and boasts a piano and a wood-burning fire. To the rear are a few steps leading up to a heated and partially covered yard. Further up is an attractive decked area and the first-floor function room. A range of Blue Monkey beers is offered, as well as a few guest beers.
🏃🏠🕪♣🌭🚗😺🎐♪

Partizan Tavern

13-15 Manvers Street, NG2 4PB
☎ 07974 361645
4 changing beers (sourced regionally) 🅗
This micropub, opened in 2021, has added to the growing beer scene in the Sneinton Market area. The name comes from the Serbian football club that the landlord visits regularly; a collection of Partizan Belgrade FC programmes are hung on the walls. It serves four varying real ales, four real ciders/perries and four craft beers, along with a large selection of bottles and cans. The L-shaped single room with two large windows overlooks the street. Cobs are available Friday to Sunday.
🏃♣🌭🚗😺🎐

Sir John Borlase Warren Ⓛ ✓

1 Ilkeston Road, Canning Circus, NG7 3GD

☎ (0115) 988 1889

Everards Tiger; 11 changing beers (often Lincoln Green) Ⓗ

An Everards Project William pub run by Lincoln Green brewery, situated in the centre of Canning Circus. The lower bar area can be hired for private parties and there is a small snug at the far end of the bar. Outside is a secluded, enclosed pub garden and a large rooftop patio, which is a quiet haven in the centre of a busy area. The pub showcases 12 real ales, featuring Lincoln Green and guests from breweries near and far.

🌊🐾◑Ҩ(Nottingham Trent University) ♣🍴🖵🗑🛜🎵

Vat & Fiddle Ⓛ

Queens Bridge Road, NG2 1NB

☎ (0115) 985 0611

Castle Rock Harvest Pale, Session, Preservation, Oatmeal Stout, Elsie Mo, Screech Owl; 6 changing beers Ⓗ

This 1937 Art Deco gem, two minutes from Nottingham rail and tram station, is the brewery tap for the adjoining Castle Rock brewery. At least seven of the 13 handpumps serve cask beers from the Castle Rock range, with guest beers representing LocAles and others from further afield. There are over 10 real ciders. The outside area to the rear, overlooking the brewery yard, features an impressive mural depicting Nottingham events over the years. Hot food is served all week.

🌊🐾◑♿🚆🍴🖵🗑🛜🎵

Nottingham: New Basford

Lion Inn Ⓛ

44 Mosley Street, NG7 7FQ

☎ (0115) 970 3506 ⊕ thelionatbasford.co.uk

Draught Bass; 9 changing beers Ⓗ

A large traditional free house with a horseshoe central bar and rustic bare-brick decor. The focus is on an ever-changing range of cask ales and traditional ciders from near and far. Outside they have extensive heated covered decking areas and a large seated garden. Live music features every weekend with widely differing styles being played. The pub welcomes four-legged friends and is a past winner of the Rover Dog Friendly Pub of the Year.

🌊🐾◑♿Ҩ(Shipstone Street) ♣🍴🖵🗑🛜🎵

Nottingham: Radford

Plough Inn Ⓛ

17 St Peter's Street, NG7 3EN

☎ 07815 073447

Nottingham Rock Ale Bitter, Rock Ale Mild, Legend, Extra Pale Ale; 4 changing beers Ⓗ

This traditional two-roomed public house is the brewery tap for the adjoining Nottingham brewery and features a number of their ales with some changing guests. It has a wide-ranging clientele, including students from the extensive accommodation nearby. The cosy interior has two wood-burning stoves. They host a popular quiz night once a week and have a couple of live music evenings a month. Q🌊🐾◑♣🍴P🖵🗑🛜🎵

Oxton

Old Green Dragon Ⓛ ✓

Blind Lane, NG25 0SS

☎ (0115) 965 2243

6 changing beers Ⓗ

Tastefully refurbished over 10 years ago, this local CAMRA Village Pub of the Year is now a classic traditional village pub which incorporates a contemporary eating venue. There is an ever-changing selection of six real ales from breweries both near and far, as well as at least two real ciders. Outside is an enclosed rear garden and a seated patio area to the front. The pub car park has three electric car-charging points. 🌊🐾◑♿♣🍴P🗑🛜🎵

Radcliffe on Trent

Chestnut Ⓛ ✓

Main Road, NG12 2BE

☎ (0115) 933 1994

Black Sheep Best Bitter; Brewsters Hophead; Timothy Taylor Boltmaker; 4 changing beers (sourced regionally) Ⓗ

Popular cask beer-led village pub. Originally the Cliffe Inn, following a major refurbishment in 2006 it became the Horse Chestnut, and in 2015 simply the Chestnut. Seven real ales are served, including ever-changing guests, which always include a locally brewed ale. Quality home-made food, ranging from stonebaked pizzas through to classic British dishes, is served in a relaxed, casual atmosphere. 🌊🐾◑♿🚆(Radcliffe-on-Trent) P🖵🗑🛜🎵

Yard of Ale

1 Walkers Yard, NG12 2FF (off Main Rd, between Costa and public car park)

☎ (0115) 933 4888 ⊕ yard-of-ale.business.site

7 changing beers Ⓗ

Small, friendly micropub in a former café and chocolate shop in the centre of the village. The premises are narrow, with access from the side, with steps up to a small room with basic seating and tables. A smaller second room to the left offers further space. Up to seven ever-changing guest ales are available which always include at least one locally brewed beer and a dark ale. Q🚆(Radcliffe-on-Trent) P🖵🗑

Rainworth

Inkpot

Kirklington Road, NG21 0JY

☎ (01623) 230500

4 changing beers (often Batemans, Bradfield, Leatherbritches) Ⓗ

This micropub, converted from a former betting shop, usually serves a range of up to four real ales and 11 real ciders. It is named after the octagonal building that used to stand nearby, now demolished, which was the toll house for the road to Mansfield. A former local CAMRA Cider Pub of the Year and Pub of the Season. Q🌊🍴🖵(28,141) 🗑🎵

Retford

Beer Under the Clock Ϙ

3 Town Hall Yard, DN22 6DU (off Market Square, through arch at side of the town hall, opp Butter Market) SK705811

☎ 07985 102192 ⊕ beerundertheclock.com

5 changing beers (sourced nationally) Ⓗ

This small, friendly pub – formerly known as BeerHeadZ – serves five rotating beers – including a dark beer and a bitter- three ciders, a range of bottled and canned beers and a limited range of wines and spirits. The beers, often one-offs from near and far, are kept in excellent condition and served in oversized glasses. Local CAMRA Pub of the Year in 2022 and 2023. Q🐾♿🍴P🖵🗑🛜🎵

Black Boy Inn L
14 Moorgate, DN22 6RH
☎ (01777) 7099
3 changing beers (sourced locally; often Little Critters, Pheasantry) Ⓗ
A traditional pub just off the town centre with a good regular trade. Recently refurbished, this open-plan pub has a dartboard, live sport on TV, a comfortable smoking area and outside seating. Up to three changing real ales are normally available, all sourced from local breweries and reasonably priced. Visitors are always made welcome in this cosy hostelry. Q☺☕♣P🛏❀🐾🔊

Brew Shed
104-106 Carolgate, DN22 6AS (on Carolgate bridge opp Masonic Hall) SK706807
☎ (01777) 948485 ⊕ harrisonsbrewery.com/the-brew-shed
Harrison's Vacant Gesture, Best Bitter, Coconut Shy P.A., Proof of Concept; 2 changing beers (sourced locally; often Harrison's) Ⓗ
The Brew Shed is the tap for Harrison's brewery. The pub consists of an open-plan room at street level and a smaller downstairs room that leads onto the large canalside patio. Five or six Harrison's beers are on offer, plus the occasional guest beer, a variety of kegs, and a good selection of gins, spirits, wines and ciders. A former Nottinghamshire CAMRA Pub of the Year and East Midlands runner-up. Q☺☕◐&♣P🛏❀🔊

Idle Valley Tap L
Carolgate, DN22 6EF (at S end of main shopping area)
☎ (01777) 948586
Welbeck Idle Valley Pale, Idle Valley Red; house beer (by Welbeck Abbey); 6 changing beers (sourced nationally; often Abbeydale, Ilkley, Welbeck Abbey) Ⓗ
A welcoming pub, initially the tap for the Idle Valley brewery, but since the brewery closure beers are sourced elsewhere. Up to eight real ales are available, plus keg and bottled ales. There is a midweek teatime 50p discount on real ales. The one-room pub has a pool table and dartboard and the outside space has been utilised to a maximum with seating that attracts large numbers in fine weather. Former local CAMRA award winner. ☕❀&P🛏❀🔊♫

Selston

Horse & Jockey
Church Lane, NG16 6FB
☎ (01773) 781012
6 changing beers Ⓗ/Ⓖ
A drinkers' gem dating from 1664, with wooden bench seating, large open fires and flagstone floors. Up to six real ales are available, two served under gravity from stone trestles. A real cider or perry is also always available. A quiz is held on Sunday evening and a folk night every Wednesday. Look out for Selstock Beer and Music Festival in July. A winner of many CAMRA awards. Q☺☕&♣🍴P🛏❀

South Leverton

Plough Inn
Town Street, DN22 0BT (opp village hall) SK785810
☎ (01427) 880323
2 changing beers (sourced locally; often Beermats, Milestone) Ⓗ
You could drive through the village and not see this pub, but then you would miss out on a little gem. The small, two-roomed local is an old-fashioned, traditional pub where everybody is made welcome. Some of the seating

appears to be old church pews, and there is a large amount of seating outside. Two rotating guest beers are available, usually from local breweries.
Q☺☕♣P🛏❀🐾🔊

Southwell

Final Whistle
Station Road, NG25 0ET
☎ (01636) 814953
Brewsters Hophead; Draught Bass; Everards Tiger; Salopian Oracle; 6 changing beers (sourced nationally; often Oakham) Ⓗ
Located at the end of the Southwell Trail, a disused railway line now a traffic-free trail, this comfortable, multi-roomed pub has a railway theme and is teeming with memorabilia. The courtyard garden is laid out like a mock station, with a separate bar and function room called The Locomotion. Ten handpumps always offer Bass, a stout or porter, and a range of real ales, with real cider also available. Quiz nights are Sunday and Tuesday, folk club is on a Thursday. A variety of quality bar snacks are available. Q☺☕&♣🍴P🛏(28,100)❀🔊♫

Old Coach House 🍴 L
69 Easthorpe, NG25 0HY
☎ (01636) 819526
Oakham JHB; 6 changing beers (sourced nationally) Ⓗ
Traditional, cosy, open-plan pub with five different drinking areas, oak beams and a large range fire. Six regularly changing real ales are on handpump from both local and national breweries, often including Oakham JHB and Timothy Taylor Landlord. Live music features regularly on Saturday night, and an open mic session is held on the last Sunday of the month. Outside to the rear is a well-kept patio garden. Local CAMRA Pub of the Year 2020 and 2023. Q☺☕&▲♣🛏❀🔊♫

Stapleford

Horse & Jockey 🏆 L
20 Nottingham Road, NG9 8AA
☎ (0115) 875 9655 ⊕ horseandjockeystapleford.co.uk
Full Mash Horse & Jockey; 12 changing beers Ⓗ
This pub offers 13 ales, including a house beer from local Full Mash brewery, plus 12 ever-changing ales, one craft beer and four real ciders. The main bar has open-plan seating, and there is a further seating area up a couple of steps, which can serve as a function room. The food includes bar snacks (filled cobs, pork pies and sausage rolls), pies (available all day) and pizzas on Thursdays. The pub also has accommodation. Twice National CAMRA Pub of the Year finalist. Q☺☕❀🛏◐&♣P🛏❀🔊♫

Sutton-in-Ashfield

Duke of Sussex
Alfreton Road, NG17 1JN
☎ (01623) 511469 ⊕ duke-of-sussex.co.uk
6 changing beers (often Oakham, Pentrich, Welbeck Abbey) Ⓗ
Large open-plan pub serving up to six real ales from a central bar connecting the bar and restaurant. It is owned by the local Pub People Company of South Normanton. Food is served daily and offers are always available. Live music and quiz nights are hosted and most live football matches are shown. Q☺◐&P🛏(9.1)❀🔊♫

FireRock
24 Outram Street, NG17 4FS
☎ 07875 331898

3 changing beers (often Adnams, FireRock, Oakham) ⊞

Opened in 2018, this large open-plan bar is the tap for FireRock Brewing. Up to three real ales are on offer alongside a wide range of KeyKeg beers, bottles and cans. A good range of (often rare) spirits is also available. Regular live music is hosted on the stage and there is a smaller snug space with a nautical decor. FireRock brewery is on site in a room to the back. ⬧&P➰❀♪

Picture House ●

Forest Street, NG17 1DA

☎ (01623) 554627

Greene King Abbot; Ruddles Best Bitter; 6 changing beers ⊞

A popular Wetherspoon pub near the bus station. Art Deco in style, and open plan with a high ceiling, it was originally built as the King's cinema in 1932, then closed and reopened in 1967 as the Star Bingo and Social Club. The bingo hall survived into the 1990s, and was used as the Picture House Night Club. The pub features up to eight real ales and real ciders. ⬧❶&●➰❀

Scruffy Dog

Station Road, NG17 5HF

☎ (01623) 550826 ⊕ thescruffydog.co.uk

8 changing beers (often Scruffy Dog) ⊞

Comfy sofas and a real fire on colder days welcome visitors to this dog-friendly pub. Refurbished by the current owners, it has its own on-site Scruffy Dog microbrewery – the brew plant is visible from the end of the main seating area. Up to eight changing real ales are usually available from the brewery, plus a couple of guest ales. Q⬧❀&●P➰❀☎

Tollerton

Air Hostess

Stanstead Avenue, NG12 4EA (corner of Burnside Grove)

☎ (0115) 648 0439 ⊕ theairhostesstollerton.co.uk

Timothy Taylor Landlord; 5 changing beers (sourced regionally) ⊞

The Air Hostess is a community-owned pub that was remodelled following its purchase from a local brewery. It offers up to six real ales – one regular and five from a mix of local and regional independent breweries – and home-cooked food is available daily. The pub is comfortably furnished, and its beer garden is popular in the summer, with a pizza kitchen at weekends. The pub hosts and promotes many community events and stages a summer beer festival. Q⬧❀❶&●P➰❀☎♪

Wellow

Olde Red Lion ℟

Eakring Road, NG22 0EG (opp the maypole on the village green) SK669660

☎ (01623) 861000

Maypole Olde Lion Ale; house beer (by Maypole); 2 changing beers (sourced regionally; often Bombardier, Castle Rock) ⊞

Situated on the village green, with its maypole, this 400-year-old village pub participates in a large event on May Day. The traditional wood-beamed interior includes a restaurant, lounge and bar areas. Photographs and maps depicting the history of the village are on the walls. Three real ales are available – Olde Lion Ale and two rotating guest beers. Rufford Park, Sherwood Forest and Clumber Park are all nearby. Q⬧❀❶●P➰❀☎

West Bridgford

Poppy & Pint ℟

Pierrepont Road, NG2 5DX

☎ (0115) 981 9995

Castle Rock Harvest Pale, Preservation, Screech Owl; 8 changing beers ⊞

Former British Legion Club converted in 2011. It has a large main bar with a raised area and a family area with a café bar (children welcome until evening). An upstairs function room hosts a folk club and the beer garden overlooks a former bowling green. Twelve handpumps dispense Castle Rock beers, plus guests, often from new breweries. There are usually two real ciders and excellent food is served. ⬧❀❶&●P➰❀☎♪

Stratford Haven ℟

2 Stratford Road, NG2 6BA

☎ (0115) 982 5981

Castle Rock Harvest Pale, Preservation, Elsie Mo, Screech Owl; 5 changing beers ⊞

A former pet shop, the 'Strat' has a single central bar with extended seating at the back and a secluded snug to the right. Up to nine cask ales plus a cider are available on handpump at any one time, and include at least four from owner Castle Rock's portfolio. Guest ales are predominantly from local and national microbreweries. Pizza night is on Wednesdays and traditional roasts are served on Sunday. Q⬧❀❶&●➰❀☎♪

West Stockwith

White Hart ℟

Main Street, DN10 4EY SK790947

☎ (01427) 892672 ⊕ idlewhitehart.co.uk

House beer (by Idle); 1 changing beer (sourced locally) ⊞

A popular country pub close to the River Trent, Chesterfield Canal and West Stockwith Marina. A single bar serves the bar, lounge and dining areas. The range of four or five changing real ales are usually from the Idle brewery, which is housed in outbuildings at the side of the pub. The area is especially busy during the summer with canal and river traffic. ⬧❀❶&●P➰(97)❀♪

Worksop

Liquorice Gardens ℟ ●

1A Newcastle Street, S80 2AS (just off town centre)

☎ (01909) 512220

Greene King Abbot; Ruddles Best Bitter; Sharp's Doom Bar; 4 changing beers (sourced nationally; often Little Critters, Milestone, Pheasantry) ⊞

This friendly Wetherspoon pub, just outside the town centre, has gained a good reputation for its real ales. There are usually seven on at all times, often including a dark beer, plus a vast selection of ciders and craft beers. Several beer festivals are held each year. The pub is popular with oldies at lunchtime and a younger crowd in the evenings. ⬧❀❶&⇌●➰❀

Mallard

Station Approach, S81 7AG (on railway station Platform 1)

☎ 07973 521824

4 changing beers (sourced nationally) ⊞

Formerly the station buffet, this small, cosy pub offers a warm welcome. The four changing real ales usually include a dark beer and a bitter, and there are two ciders, a selection of foreign bottled beers, country fruit wines and specialist gins. There is a downstairs room for special occasions. Four beer festivals are hosted each year. The recipient of many local CAMRA awards. Q❀⇌❀●P➰❀

Breweries

Aither (NEW) SIBA

12 Mill Way, Old Mill Lane Industrial Estate, Mansfield Woodhouse, NG19 9BG ☎ 07703 828594
✉ slawrence@aitherbrewery.co.uk

Taking its name from Greek mythology, and meaning 'from the heavens', Aither Brewery was established in 2022 by Scott Lawrence and Ashleigh Hunt, brewing traditional English ales. Scott spent ten years at Batemans previously. Beers are available in Mansfield and the wider Nottinghamshire area initially.

Equinox (ABV 3.8%) PALE
Artimus (ABV 4%) PALE
Sirius (ABV 4.2%) BLOND

Angel

Angel, 7 Stoney Street, Nottingham, NG1 1LG
☎ (0115) 948 3343
✉ angelmicrobrewery@gmail.com

Situated inside one of Nottingham's oldest, haunted, and cave-filled pubs. The Angel Microbrewery uses a 2.5-barrel plant, nestled in the bar of the 400-year-old pub. Beers are available at the Angel, and the Golden Fleece in Nottingham.

Beermats SIBA

New Yard, Winkburn, NG22 8PQ
☎ (01636) 639004 ⊕ beermatsbeer.co.uk

Beermats was founded in 2017 by three friends while drinking in a pub. The brewery is located on the Winkburn Estate in old dairy buildings. Beers are named around the theme of the humble beermat. ⏛🍺◆LIVE◆

Charismatic (ABV 3.8%) BITTER
Pragmatic (ABV 3.8%) BITTER
Format (ABV 3.9%) PALE
Team Mates (ABV 3.9%) PALE
Soul Mate (ABV 4.2%) GOLD
Diplomat (ABV 4.6%) STOUT
Ultimate (ABV 4.9%) RED

Beeston Hop

Enfield Street, Beeston, NG9 1DN
✉ john@beestonhop.co.uk

⊗ A nanobrewery launched in 2015 producing mainly bottle-conditioned beers, it moved to Beeston in 2023. Cask beers are occasionally produced for festivals using capacity at other breweries. The beers are unfined, unfiltered and unpasteurised. LIVE

Black Iris SIBA

Unit 1, Shipstone Street, New Basford, Nottingham, NG7 6GJ
☎ (0115) 979 1936 ⊕ blackirisbottleshop.co.uk

Black Iris began brewing in 2011 using a six-barrel plant behind the Flowerpot pub in Derby. It expanded to a brand new 10-barrel plant in 2014 and relocated to premises in Nottingham. Beers are distributed nationally through wholesalers and by direct order to the local free trade. Innovation and collaboration ensure that new beers are consistently being added to the range. 🍺◆

Snake Eyes (ABV 3.8%) PALE
Golden-coloured ale with intense hoppy aroma and taste with lingering bitter finish

Bleeding Heart (ABV 4.5%) BITTER
Red rye malty ale balanced with roast and hops and a bitter finish.
Endless Summer (ABV 4.5%) BITTER
Golden in colour with a tropical citrus fruit presence throughout, from aroma to aftertaste with a gentle bitter finish.
Stab in the Dark (ABV 5%) STOUT
Black stout with New Zealand hops, roast malt and coffee flavours, moderate bitter finish.

Black Market

The Workman's, 43 High Street, Warsop, NG20 0AE
☎ 07824 363373 ⊕ blackmarketbrewery.co.uk

Beers first appeared from Black Market in 2016. The 2.5-barrel plant is situated in the basement of the Workman's/Black Market Venue in Warsop. There are three regular beers brewed. Nearly all the brews are consumed onsite, though a few go to pubs and beer festivals in the locality.

Blue Monkey SIBA

10 Pentrich Road, Giltbrook Industrial Park, Giltbrook, Nottingham, NG16 2UZ
☎ (0115) 938 5899 ⊕ bluemonkeybrewery.com

Blue Monkey was established in 2008 as a 10-barrel plant, but moved in 2010 to a bigger site to meet increasing demand. It now brews around 15,000 pints a week to supply more than 1,000 local outlets, and selected national distributors. The brewery has four pubs all called the Organ Grinder (Nottingham, Arnold, Loughborough and Newark). ⏛🍺

Marmoset (ABV 3.6%) BITTER
BG Sips (ABV 4%) PALE
Pale golden hoppy beer, brewed mainly with Brewers Gold hops. Very fruity and bitter.
Primate Best Bitter (ABV 4%) BITTER
Infinity IPA (ABV 4.6%) PALE
Golden ale packed with Citra hops.
Chocolate Amaretto (ABV 4.9%) SPECIALITY
This Guerrilla is flavoured with chocolate and amaretto. Sweetness is the dominant characteristic and overtakes the usual malt and roast.
Chocolate Guerilla (ABV 4.9%) STOUT
Chocolate Orange (ABV 4.9%) SPECIALITY
Guerrilla (ABV 4.9%) STOUT
A creamy stout, full of roast malt flavour and a slightly sweet finish.
Ape Ale (ABV 5.4%) PALE
Intensely-hopped strong golden ale with dry bitter finish.
Infinity Plus 1 (ABV 5.6%) BITTER
Pithy grapefruit, citrus zest, hop forward with pronounced bitterness that lingers on the aftertaste. Biscuity with a hint of caramel.

Brewhouse & Kitchen SIBA

Trent Bridge, Nottingham, NG2 2GS
☎ (0115) 986 7960 ⊕ brewhouseandkitchen.com/venue/nottingham

Part of the Brewhouse & Kitchen chain, producing its own range of beers. Carry outs and brewery experience days are offered. ⏛

Castle Rock SIBA

Queensbridge Road, Nottingham, NG2 1NB
☎ (0115) 985 1615 ⊕ castlerockbrewery.co.uk

Castle Rock, established in 1998, quickly developed a reputation for producing high quality, consistent cask beers, which continues to this day, with five from the core range winning awards at national level. Throughout the year, Castle Rock brew an eclectic range of special and one-off beers in cask, keg and can, from the traditional to the more experimental and modern styles. ‼ ➠ ♦LIVE ♦

Our House (ABV 3.6%) BLOND
Black Gold (ABV 3.8%) MILD
A dark ruby mild. Full-bodied and fairly bitter.
Harvest Pale (ABV 3.8%) PALE
Pale yellow beer, full of hop aroma and flavour. Refreshing with a mellowing aftertaste.
Session (ABV 4%) PALE
Preservation (ABV 4.4%) BITTER
A traditional, copper-coloured English best bitter with malt predominant. Fairly bitter with a residual sweetness.
Oatmeal Stout (ABV 4.6%) STOUT
Elsie Mo (ABV 4.7%) BITTER
A strong golden ale with floral hops evident in the aroma. Citrus hops are mellowed by a slight sweetness.
Screech Owl (ABV 5.5%) BITTER
A classic golden IPA with an intensely hoppy aroma and bitter taste with a little balancing sweetness.

Cat Asylum

12 Besthorpe Road, Collingham, NG23 7NP
☎ (01636) 892229 ☎ 07773 502653
✉ henry.bealby@lineone.net

☺Established in 2017, Cat Asylum is a microbrewery specialising in historic recipes from Britain and around the world. ‼ ➠ ♦

Wee Moggie (ABV 3.8%) BLOND
Columbus Pale (ABV 4.9%) BLOND
Simcoe Pale Ale (ABV 5.1%) BLOND
The Big Smoke Stout (ABV 5.8%) PORTER
Newark IPA (ABV 6.1%) IPA

Dukeries

18 Newcastle Avenue, Worksop, S80 1ET
☎ (01909) 731171 ☎ 07500 119299
⊕ dukeriesbrewery.co.uk

☺Founded in 2012 the brewery is located in the Dukeries Tap premises in the heart of Worksop. Beer brewed is available at the tap only, which is open on Friday and Saturday. ♦ ♦

FireRock

20-24 Outram Street, Sutton in Ashfield, NG17 4FS
☎ 07875 331898 ⊕ firerockbrewing.com

☺FireRock Brewing Co is an independent microbrewery and craft beer bar specialising in hop-forward craft beers.

Flipside

c/o Magpie Brewery, Unit 4, Ashling Court, Iremonger Road, Nottingham, NG2 3JA
☎ (0115) 987 7500 ☎ 07958 752334

Office: Old Volunteer, 35 Burton Road, Carlton, NG4 3DQ ⊕ flipsidebrewery.co.uk

⊗ Andrew and Maggie Dunkin established an initial six-barrel brewery in an industrial unit in Colwick in 2010, expanding to 12 barrels in 2013 in a larger adjacent unit. The brewery opened its own tap, the Old Volunteer, Carlton, in 2014. In 2016 it relocated again to share the plant at Caythorpe Brewery. With the closure of that brewery it now shares with Magpie Brewery. ♦LIVE V

Sterling Pale (ABV 3.9%) PALE
Golden ale with a citrus aroma and hoppy taste, leading to a bitter and peppery finish.
Dark Denomination (ABV 4%) MILD
BIt CO1n (ABV 4.1%) GOLD
Copper Penny (ABV 4.2%) BITTER
Golden Sovereign (ABV 4.2%) GOLD
Franc in Stein (ABV 4.3%) GOLD
Golden ale with a floral hop aroma, leading to a hoppy and bitter finish
Random Toss (ABV 4.4%) GOLD
Kopek Stout (ABV 4.5%) STOUT
Full-bodied dark stout with a coffee aroma and assertive roast flavours throughout and a balanced bitterness
Flipping Best (ABV 4.6%) BITTER
Brown-coloured, malty, strong bitter with lasting malt, bitterness and subtle hop flavours.
Dusty Penny (ABV 5%) PORTER
Clippings IPA (ABV 6.5%) IPA
Russian Rouble (ABV 7.3%) STOUT
Strong dark stout with balanced malt, roast and fruit flavours.

Full Mash

17 Lower Park Street, Stapleford, NG9 8EW
☎ (0115) 949 9262 ⊕ fullmash.co.uk

☺Brewing commenced in 2003 and has grown steadily since, with a gradual expansion in outlets and capacity. ♦

Horse & Jockey (ABV 3.8%) GOLD
Easy-drinking golden ale with moderate hoppy aroma and finish.
Whistlin' Dixie (ABV 3.9%) BITTER
A nicely-balanced, refreshing and easy-drinking session bitter, yellow/straw in colour.
Séance (ABV 4%) GOLD
Predominantly hoppy golden beer, with a refreshing bitter finish.
Illuminati (ABV 4.2%) BITTER
Gently-hopped golden ale with initial hops and bitterness giving way to a short bitter finish.
Wheat Ear (ABV 4.2%) SPECIALITY
A yellow wheat-based beer with a citrus aroma, bitter hop flavour and a bittersweet aftertaste.
Warlord (ABV 4.4%) BITTER
Amber-coloured beer with an initial malt taste leading to a dry bitter finish.
Apparition (ABV 4.5%) BITTER
A pale hoppy bitter brewed with Brewers Gold hops.
Northern Lights (ABV 4.7%) STOUT
A smooth black stout with bitter, roasted coffee notes.
Manhattan (ABV 5.2%) PALE
Bhisti (ABV 6.2%) IPA
This IPA has a sweet, caramel aroma, flavoursome bitter taste, but lightly-hopped.

Good Stuff

▤ Abdication, 89 Mansfield Road, Daybrook, NG5 6BH
⊕ theabdication.co.uk

Good Stuff Brewing at the Abdication, is a nanobrewery located inside the Abdication micropub. Capacity is 0.5-barrels so occasional beers can only be found at the pub and local beer festivals.

Grafton

Walters Yard, Unit 4, Claylands Industrial Estate, Worksop, S81 7DW
☎ (01909) 307710 ☎ 07542 012610

Office: 8 Oak Close, Crabtree Park Estate, Worksop, S80 1BH ⊕ graftonfineales.co.uk

⊚Founded in 2007 as Grafton Brewing Company, behind the Packet Inn on Bescoby Street in Retford. Relocated to the present premises in Worksop in 2014, where the plant was increased in size from five to 15 barrels to meet demand. The brewery tap is its microbar, the Malt House, Potter Street, Worksop. ‼♦

Pasha Pasha (ABV 4%) GOLD
Raspberry Redemption (ABV 4%) SPECIALITY
Golden ale with a raspberry aroma and taste, leading to a sweet and slightly bitter finish.
Vanilla Heights (ABV 4%) SPECIALITY
Copper Jack (ABV 4.5%) BITTER
Garside Gold (ABV 4.5%) GOLD
Priorswell Pale (ABV 4.5%) PALE
Apricot Jungle (ABV 4.8%) SPECIALITY
Bananalicious (ABV 4.8%) SPECIALITY
Caramel Stout (ABV 4.8%) STOUT
Tango with a Mango (ABV 4.8%) SPECIALITY
Black Abbots (ABV 5%) STOUT
Coco Loco (ABV 5%) SPECIALITY
Dark-coloured, smooth-drinking ale, infused with coconut, gentle bitterness
Don Jon (ABV 5%) PALE

Harby

目 Bottle & Glass, 5 High Street, Harby, NG23 7EB
☎ (01522) 703438
⊕ wigandmitre-lincoln.blogspot.co.uk

Harby Brewstore is a four-barrel malt extract brewery established in 2015 and located at the Bottle & Glass in Harby. Most output goes to the three pubs in the small Wig & Mitre pub group; the Wig & Mitre, Lincoln, Caunton Beck, Caunton and the Bottle & Glass itself.

Harrison's

Unit 1, 108 Carolgate, Retford, DN22 6AS ☎ 07850 228383 ⊕ harrisonsbrewery.com

⊚A three-barrel brewery built completely from scratch by brewer Christopher Harrison-Hawkes. The first brew was in 2018. Shortly afterwards four beers were available at its own pub, the Brew Shed (which stands metres from the brewery). In 2019 the pub moved next door to larger premises. 2019 saw the production of bottle-conditioned beers, and in 2020 real ale in a can, produced and packaged onsite. ‼♦LIVE

Vacant Gesture (ABV 3.8%) BLOND
Idaho 7 (ABV 3.9%) PALE
Best Bitter (ABV 4%) BITTER
Pale Ale (ABV 4%) PALE
Ruby Mild (ABV 4%) MILD
5 Pints All English Bitter (ABV 4.1%) BITTER
Sabro (ABV 4.1%) PALE
Proof of Concept (ABV 4.3%) PALE
Stout (ABV 4.3%) STOUT
American Brown Ale (ABV 4.9%) BROWN
Harrison's Plum Porter (ABV 5.6%) PORTER
Porter (ABV 5.6%) PORTER
Planet Amarillo (ABV 6.9%) IPA

Tom Herrick's

The Stable House, Main Street, Carlton on Trent, NG23 6NW ☎ 07877 542331
⊕ tomherricksbrewery.co.uk

Tom Herrick installed his bespoke, 2.5-barrel, stainless steel brewery at the front of his premises during 2014, and began small scale commercial brewing in 2015. The brewery is only operated on a part-time basis with output going to festivals and local pubs.

Bomber Command (ABV 3.9%) BITTER
Black Lace (ABV 4.2%) STOUT
1721 Plum Porter (ABV 5%) SPECIALITY
Broadsword (ABV 5%) BITTER
East India (ABV 5.4%) IPA

Idle

目 White Hart Inn, Main Street, West Stockwith, DN10 4EY
☎ (01427) 892672 ☎ 07831 618436
⊕ idlewhitehart.co.uk

⊚Following the retirement of previous owners, Kevin Thacker purchased the pub and brewery. He runs the brewery with daughters Olivia and Katie running the pub. Numerous refinements and improvements have been made to both. Some brewing recipes are retained and seasonal specials are likely to be introduced. ‼♦

Jacaranda (NEW)

Brinkley

Office: 7 St John Street, Mansfield, NG18 1QH
✉ jacarandabc@outlook.com

Brewing began in 2022 producing various beer styles in both cask and bottle. The core beers are named after assorted bird species. ♦

Warbler (ABV 4%) RED
Jackdaw (ABV 4.2%) PALE
Wagtail (ABV 4.2%) PALE
Goldfinch (ABV 4.5%) GOLD

Kings Clipstone

Keepers Bothy, Kings Clipstone, NG21 9BT
☎ (01623) 823589 ☎ 07790 190020
⊕ kingsclipstonebrewery.co.uk

Located close to the heart of Sherwood Forest, Kings Clipstone began brewing in 2012 using a five-barrel plant. The owners, David and Daryl Maguire, produce a range of core beers plus one-off brews and seasonals. Beers are available to freehouses, festivals and wholesale markets. ♦

Palace Pale (ABV 3.6%) GOLD
Hop On (ABV 3.8%) PALE
Amazing Gazing (ABV 4%) BITTER
Isabella (ABV 4.1%) BLOND
Tabaknakas (ABV 4.1%) GOLD
Hopical (ABV 4.2%) GOLD
Moonbeam (ABV 4.2%) BITTER
Sire (ABV 4.2%) BITTER
Monarch Ale (ABV 4.3%) BITTER
King John's EPA (ABV 4.4%) BITTER
Royal Stag Stout (ABV 4.5%) STOUT
Squires Desire (ABV 4.8%) BITTER
Queen Bee (ABV 5.1%) BITTER

Lenton Lane

Unit 5G, The Midway, Lenton Industrial Estate, Nottingham, NG7 2TS ☎ 0333 003 5008
⊕ lentonlane.co.uk

⊗ Lenton Lane began brewing in 2014 under the name Frontier, after taking over the brewing plant at the Flower Pot pub, Derby. Lenton Lane changed its name in 2016 and relocated to a purpose-built brewery in Nottingham using a 10-barrel plant. The brewery produces a range of Single Malt & Single Hop beers (SM&SH), along with various other regular beers. 🍴♦LIVE V

Newbird (ABV 3.7%) PALE
Pale Moonlight (ABV 3.7%) PALE
36 Degrees North (ABV 3.9%) BITTER
Nice fairly hoppy bitter with malty overtones. Balanced and refreshing.
Gold Rush (ABV 4.2%) GOLD
Outpost (ABV 4.5%) BITTER
Twist & Stout (ABV 5%) STOUT
200 Not Out (ABV 6%) IPA

Lincoln Green SIBA

Unit 5, Enterprise Park, Wigwam Lane, Hucknall, Nottingham, NG15 7SZ
☎ (0115) 963 4233 ☎ 07748 111457
⊕ lincolngreenbrewing.co.uk

☺Established in 2012 Lincoln Green Brewing Co operates a 10-barrel plant. The brewery takes its name from the colour of dyed woollen cloth associated with the legend of Robin Hood. Beers are named with a respectful nod towards the Nottinghamshire legend. A range of craft beers is available in keg and can. Bottled beers are available online, in supermarkets and at the brewery shop and includes occasional limited edition, special bottle-aged and bottle-conditioned beers. A rotating occasional range of beers is also available, see website for details. Unique beers using different yeast strains and unusual ingredients are also offered under the Blackshale Project range. ▉♦LIVE

Marion (ABV 3.8%) PALE
Subtly-hopped golden ale with citrus aroma and a dry bitter finish.
Archer (ABV 4%) PALE
Citrus golden ale with American hops and a moderately bitter finish.
Hood (ABV 4.2%) BITTER
Tawny-coloured ale with balanced hops and bitterness.
Tuck (ABV 4.7%) PORTER
Full-bodied and rich dark ale with roast and malt flavours throughout.

Linear

Bingham, NG13 8EU ⊕ linear.beer

Small-scale, 50-litre brewery, started production in 2016 and is located at the owner's home. Primarily produces a range of bottle-conditioned beers, on occasion it supplies casks for selected local stockists. Also collaborates with other nanobreweries for local beer festivals and events. LIVE

Liquid Light SIBA

Unit 9, Robin Hood Industrial Estate, Alfred Street South, Nottingham, NG3 1GE
⊕ liquidlightbrewco.com

A strong ethos of community and inclusiveness at its core, with beers influenced by rock and psychedelic music. Moving to its own premises in 2021, with a taproom open weekends, featuring many visual and music-oriented events throughout the year. A popular inclusion at tap takeovers and craft beer festivals across the country. Vegan food, hot and cold, available all year round. ♦♦

Day Tripper (ABV 4.3%) PALE
A hazy session pale, fruity and hoppy

Lord Randalls

Holme View Farm, High Street, Laxton, Newark, NG22 0NX ☎ 07712 078346 ✉ randallig@aol.com

The five-barrel brewery equipment was purchased in 2018 from the defunct Market Harborough Brewery. Brewing commenced 2020. The proprietors are the Randall family and the head brewer is Dean Penny.

Huntsman Best Bitter (ABV 4%) BITTER
Laxton Original (ABV 4%)
Tally-Ho Light Ale (ABV 4%) PALE
Landlords De-Light (ABV 4.9%) GOLD

Magpie SIBA

Unit 4, Ashling Court, Iremonger Road, Nottingham, NG2 3JA
☎ (0115) 874 5467 ☎ 07419 991310
⊕ magpiebrewery.com

☺Launched in 2006 using a six-barrel plant, the brewery upgraded to 17.5-barrels in 2017. Only British hops and malt are used in the core range, with the Wanderlust range taking more worldly influences and ingredients. A 2.5-barrel plant is used for small batch brews and trials. Beers also appear under the Mardy Bum brand name. Its shop and taproom opened in 2019 at the brewery (see website for details). ▉♦♦

Hoppily Ever After (ABV 3.8%) BLOND
Golden bitter, gently-hopped with biscuit malt flavours and a bitter finish.
Flipside Sterling Pale (ABV 3.9%) PALE
Best (ABV 4.2%) BITTER
A malty traditional pale brown best bitter, with balancing hops giving a bitter finish.
Cherry Raven (ABV 4.4%) SPECIALITY
Raven Stout flavoured with cherry. Sweet, fruity aroma, malty with a hint of vanilla. The cherry isn't overpowering.
Raven Stout (ABV 4.4%) STOUT
Dark stout with roast coffee aroma and taste leading to a dry bitter finish.
Thieving Rogue (ABV 4.5%) GOLD
A hoppy golden ale with a long-lasting, bitter finish.
Flipside Flipping Best (ABV 4.6%) BITTER
Jay IPA (ABV 5.2%) PALE

Maypole

North Laithes Farm, Wellow Road, Eakring, NG22 0AN
☎ 07971 277598 ⊕ maypolebrewery.co.uk

☺The brewery opened in 1995 in a converted 18th-century farm building. After changing hands in 2001 it was bought by the former head brewer, Rob Neil, in 2005. ♦

Midge (ABV 3.5%) PALE
Little Weed (ABV 3.8%) GOLD
Mayfly Bitter (ABV 3.8%) BITTER
Celebration (ABV 4%) BITTER
Gate Hopper (ABV 4%) GOLD
Mayfair (ABV 4.1%) SPECIALITY
Hop Fusion (ABV 4.2%) GOLD
Maybee (ABV 4.3%) SPECIALITY
Major Oak (ABV 4.4%) BITTER
Wellow Gold (ABV 4.6%) BLOND
Platinum Blonde (ABV 5%) BLOND

Milestone SIBA

Great North Road, Cromwell, Newark, NG23 6JE
☎ (01636) 822255 ⊕ milestonebrewery.co.uk

☺The brewery was established in 2005. Milestone currently brew on a 12-barrel plant and more than 150 outlet are supplied. ‼▉♦LIVE ✿

Best Bitter (ABV 3.7%) BITTER

Lion's Pride (ABV 3.8%) BITTER
New World Pale (ABV 3.9%) PALE
Shine On (ABV 4%) BITTER
Azacca Gold (ABV 4.2%) BLOND
Loxley Ale (ABV 4.2%) GOLD
Black Pearl (ABV 4.3%) STOUT
Maid Marian (ABV 4.3%) GOLD
Cromwell Best (ABV 4.4%) BITTER
Crusader (ABV 4.4%) BLOND
Rich Ruby (ABV 4.5%) RED
Honey Porter (ABV 4.9%) PORTER
Little John (ABV 5%) BITTER
Fletcher's Ale (ABV 5.2%) GOLD
Colonial Pale Ale (ABV 5.5%) PALE
Raspberry Wheat Beer (ABV 5.6%) SPECIALITY

Navigation SIBA

Trent Navigation Inn, 17 Meadow Lane, Nottingham,
NG2 3HS
☎ (0115) 986 9877 ⊕ navigationbrewery.com

⊚Located in Nottingham, just a stone's throw from the
iconic Trent bridge, the brewery combines historic
Victorian premises, cutting edge technology and a team
of brewing experts. ‼️🍺

Patriot (ABV 3.8%) BITTER
Tawny-coloured, malty bitter.
New Dawn Pale (ABV 3.9%) PALE
Golden-coloured ale with initial fruit and hops and a
bitter finish.
Sailing on the 7 C's (ABV 4%) RED
Tropical Pale (ABV 4%) GOLD
Eclipse (ABV 4.1%) STOUT
Dark roast stout aroma and aftertaste with bitterness and
some sweetness.
Rebel (ABV 4.2%) GOLD
A hazy golden ale, strongly-hopped and fruity with a
lingering bitter finish.
Hazy Pale (ABV 4.5%) BLOND
American IPA (ABV 5.2%) GOLD
A west-coast IPA, hop-forward with grapefruit and melon
and a citrus finish.
Saviour (ABV 5.5%) PALE
Golden in colour with assertive hop aroma and citrus fruit
taste throughout with a balanced bitterness.

Neon Raptor

Unit 14, Avenue A, Sneinton Market, Nottingham,
NG1 1DT ☎ 07367 358661
⊕ neonraptorbrewingco.com

Neon Raptor is a small independent brewery producing
modern and traditional beer styles from a central
Nottingham site, in the heart of the city's creative
quarter, since 2018. Beers are available in cask, keg and
cans and can be found in the taproom at the brewery or
in bars, pubs and shops locally and across the country.
🍺♦V🍴

Newark

77 William Street, Newark, NG24 1QU ☎ 07804
609917 ⊕ newarkbrewery.co.uk

Established in 2012 on the site of a former maltings,
Newark Brewery uses an eight-barrel plant.

Newark Best (ABV 3.8%) BITTER
NPA (Newark Pale Ale) (ABV 3.8%) PALE
BLH4 (ABV 4%) PALE
Norwegian Blue (ABV 4%) GOLD
Pure Gold (ABV 4.5%) GOLD
Summer Gold (ABV 4.5%) GOLD

Winter Gold (ABV 4.5%) BITTER
Phoenix (ABV 4.8%) BITTER
5.5 (ABV 5.5%) BITTER

Nottingham SIBA

Plough Inn, 17 St Peter's Street, Radford,
Nottingham, NG7 3EN
☎ (0115) 942 2649 ☎ 07815 073447
⊕ nottinghambrewery.co.uk

Re-established in 2000 after post-war closure by
Whitbread of the original Nottingham Brewery in the
1950s. Investment by a new majority shareholder will
mean a site move for the brewery in 2023-2024 to allow
space for expansion. Plans for kegging and canning are
proposed, but the core ethos of the brewery remains the
same; traditional cask ales, serving the local market. ‼️🍴

Rock Bitter (ABV 3.8%) BITTER
A pale and bitter, thirst-quenching hoppy beer with a dry
finish.
Rock Mild (ABV 3.8%) MILD
A reddish-black malty mild with some refreshing
bitterness in the finish.
Trent Bridge Inn Ale (ABV 3.8%) BITTER
A gold-coloured, hoppy session ale with a long bitter
finish.
Legend (ABV 4%) BITTER
A fruity and malty pale brown bitter with a touch of
sweetness and bitterness.
Extra Pale Ale (ABV 4.2%) PALE
A hoppy and fruity golden ale with a hint of sweetness
and a long-lasting bitter finish.
Cock & Hoop (ABV 4.3%) BITTER
Dreadnought (ABV 4.5%) BITTER
Well-balanced best bitter. Blend of malt and hops give a
rounded fruity finish.
Bullion (ABV 4.7%) GOLD
A refreshing premium golden ale. Brewed with a single
malt variety, it is triple-hopped and exceptionally bitter.
Foundry Mild (ABV 4.7%) MILD
Supreme (ABV 5.2%) GOLD
A strong amber fruity ale. A touch of malt in the taste is
followed by a sweet and slightly hoppy finish.

Pheasantry SIBA

High Brecks Farm, Lincoln Road, East Markham,
NG22 0SN
☎ (01777) 872728 ☎ 07948 976749
⊕ pheasantrybrewery.co.uk

⊚Pheasantry began brewing in 2012 using a 10-barrel
plant from Canada. The brewery is situated in a listed
barn on a Nottinghamshire farm and incorporates a
wedding and events venue. It supplies more than 200
pubs, restaurants, venues and bottle shops across
Nottinghamshire, Lincolnshire, Derbyshire and South
Yorkshire. In addition to the core range a different artisan
beer is brewed every 2-3 weeks. The bottling line,
installed in 2018, has capacity for contract bottling. 🍺

Best Bitter (ABV 3.8%) BITTER
Pale Ale (ABV 4%) PALE
Ringneck Amber Ale (ABV 4.1%) BITTER
Amber-coloured best bitter, initial malt and caramel
leading to a brief bitter dry finish.
Black Pheasant Dark Ale (ABV 4.2%) PORTER
Lincoln Tank Ale (ABV 4.2%) BITTER
Excitra (ABV 4.5%) GOLD
Dancing Dragonfly (ABV 5%) BLOND

Prior's Well SIBA

🏠 Littleworth, Mansfield, NG18 1AH

☎ (01623) 632393 ⊕ priorswellbrewery.co.uk

Originally established in a National Trust building on the Clumber Park Estate, but brewing ceased there in 2014. The brewery was subsequently sold and the five-barrel plant modernised and relocated to a site in Mansfield Woodhouse in 2016 with an onsite bar. In 2019 it transferred operations to its new brewpub on the ground floor of the former Mansfield Brewery. ‼

Citra (ABV 3.9%) GOLD
Baby Wolf (ABV 4%) GOLD
Incensed (ABV 4%) BITTER
Silver Chalice (ABV 4.2%) GOLD
Kumquat May (ABV 4.3%) SPECIALITY
Mosiac (ABV 4.4%) BLOND
Blade (ABV 4.7%) BITTER
Priory Gold (ABV 4.7%) GOLD
Prior's Pale (ABV 4.8%) PALE
Resurrected (ABV 4.8%) BITTER
Wolfcatcher (ABV 4.8%) PALE
Dirty Habit (ABV 5.8%) IPA

Reality

127 High Road, Chilwell, Beeston, Nottingham,
NG9 4AT ☎ 07801 539523
✉ alandenismonaghan@hotmail.com

⊗ Since starting in 2010, the brewery has built up a loyal following of pubs locally, while supplying beer festivals across the country, functions and individual customers. ♦

Virtuale Reality (ABV 3.8%) PALE
No Escape (ABV 4.2%) PALE
Bitter Reality (ABV 4.3%) BITTER
Stark Reality (ABV 4.5%) SPECIALITY
Reality Czech (ABV 4.6%) SPECIALITY

Reckless Dweeb

Forest Link, Bilsthorpe, NG22 8PR ☎ 07969 779763
⊕ recklessdweeb.com

Established in 2020 and upgraded in 2022 to a 200-litre plant, Reckless Dweeb Brew Co is a nanobrewery nestled in a quiet village in the heart of Nottinghamshire. ♦

Son of My Brother (ABV 5.1%) GOLD
Did You See That Ludicrous Display Last Night? (ABV 8.2%) IPA

Rufford Abbey

Meden Road, Boughton, NG22 9ZD

Originally known as Headstocks, the brewery was established in 2017 to produce Prussia Lager in collaboration with a partner brewery in Kaliningrad on the Lithuania/Poland border. In 2018 cask-conditioned beer was added to the range. Brewing is currently suspended.

Scruffy Dog

🍺 94 Station Road, Sutton-In-Ashfield, NG17 5HF
☎ (01623) 550826 ⊕ thescruffydog.co.uk

Microbrewery at the Scruffy Dog pub in Sutton-in-Ashfield.

Shipstone's SIBA

Little Star Brewery, Fox & Crown, 33 Church Street,
Old Basford, Nottingham, NG6 0GA
☎ (0115) 837 4200 ⊕ shipstones.com

☺ Established in 1996 as Fiddlers Ales, becoming Alcazar Brewery on change of ownership in 1999. A full-mash,

10-barrel brewery, it is located behind the Fox & Crown. It changed hands in 2016, the name changed again, and a new portfolio of beers was established, but was short-lived. It soon reverted back to Alcazar. In late 2016 Shipstone's took over brewing, producing its range of beers that had previously been contract brewed. Beers are also brewed under the Hollow Stone Brewing Co brand name. ‼♦

Original (ABV 3.8%) BITTER
Pale brown, malty, traditional bitter, well-balanced in both hops and bitterness without either becoming overpowering.
Nut Brown (ABV 4%) BITTER
Gold Star (ABV 4.2%) GOLD
Golden in colour with a delicate citrus hop and slight dry bitter finish.
IPA (ABV 5.5%) IPA
Hop bitterness with a citrus aroma and malty aftertaste.

Brewed under the Hollow Stone Brewing Co brand name:
Oligo Nunk (ABV 4%) GOLD
Pale Ale (ABV 4.2%) PALE
Bitter hop flavour with a fresh citrus finish.
Waitomo (ABV 4.5%) PALE
Aruru (ABV 4.7%) BITTER
Sorbeto (ABV 5%) SPECIALITY

Source House

20 Acacia Way, Edwalton, Nottingham, NG12 4DA
☎ 07834 722481 ⊕ sourcehouse.co.uk

Established in 2021. Source House brew beers using only British malt and hops, experimenting with local and homegrown ingredients.

Vaguely

15 Lune Way, Bingham, NG13 8YX ☎ 07969 137248
⊕ vaguelybrewing.co.uk

⊗ Vaguely Brewing launched as a commercial nanobrewery in 2019 following four years of homebrewing and recipe development. It produces vaguely traditional beers that are naturally-conditioned, unfiltered and unfined. **LIVE V**

Bitter (ABV 4.2%) BITTER
Hazy (ABV 4.5%) PALE
Porter (ABV 4.7%) STOUT
Pale Ale (ABV 6%) IPA

Welbeck Abbey SIBA

Brewery Yard, Welbeck, S80 3LT
☎ (01909) 512539 ☎ 07921 066274
⊕ welbeckabbeybrewery.co.uk

Starting in 2011, General Manager Claire Monk has grown the brewery to focus on supplying just over 17,000 pints of quality beer into local pubs, bottled beer shops and restaurants. Produce from the brewery, bakehouse and dairy can all be found under one roof in the Welbeck Farm Shop. Welbeck is one of the historic Nottinghamshire estates. Beer is also brewed for Stocks Brewing Co, Doncaster. ‼

Georgiana (ABV 3.7%) BLOND
Red Feather (ABV 3.9%) RED
Skylight (ABV 4.1%) PALE
Atlas (ABV 5%) IPA

Brewed for Stocks Brewing Co:
St Leger Gold (ABV 4.1%) BLOND
Select (ABV 4.3%) BITTER
Old Horizontal (ABV 5.3%) OLD

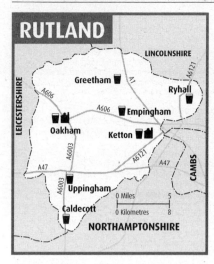

RUTLAND

LINCOLNSHIRE

LEICESTERSHIRE

Greetham

Ryhall

A606

A606 Empingham

Oakham

Ketton

A6003

A47

A6121

A47

CAMBS

A6003

Uppingham

0 Miles 5

Caldecott

0 Kilometres 8

NORTHAMPTONSHIRE

Caldecott

Plough Inn
16 Main Street, LE16 8RS
☎ (01536) 770284
Grainstore Rutland Osprey; Langton Inclined Plane Bitter; 2 changing beers ⓗ
Attractive sandstone-built pub on the village green. The traditional, open-plan interior incorporates a bar area, restaurant and a relaxing snug. The restaurant is popular and booking is essential. There is a large garden to the rear and it also has a front terrace area. Beers are sourced from local breweries including Grainstore and Langton. Q❄☕⑪♿Å♠P🚌❀

Empingham

Empingham Cricket & Social Club
Exton Road, LE15 8QB
☎ (07813 177293) ⊕ empinghamcsc.org
Magpie Best; 2 changing beers (often Greg's, Stockport) ⓗ
The club is run by volunteers and has limited hours, but these are regularly extended by sporting and other functions such as live music events, so please check Facebook and the club website for details. The Club is used by many local organisations and has a community focus. It is noted for the quality and variety of the ales served, all from microbreweries, and an annual beer festival is held to coincide with the final matches of the Six Nations rugby in March. Q❄☕♿P🚌❀ᵜ

Greetham

Plough
23 Main Street, LE15 7NJ
☎ (01572) 813613 ⊕ theploughgreetham.co.uk
Timothy Taylor Boltmaker, Knowle Spring, Landlord; 1 changing beer ⓗ
A former Mann's pub, with a decent beer range. The new owners have made many changes, including a new ice cream parlour and tea room in the garden; both are open from Easter. Good-value pub food is served daily using local suppliers and food from their own pub allotment. This community-focused pub has undergone extensive work to enlarge the outdoor seating area. Live music plays at weekends and regular quiz nights are held. Former local CAMRA Pub of the Year.
Q❄☕⑪Å♠♠P🚌❀ᜒ♪

Ketton

Railway
Church Street, PE9 3TA
☎ (01780) 721050
Grainstore Ten Fifty; 2 changing beers (often Bakers Dozen, Oakham) ⓗ
A traditional village local situated in the shadow of the impressive church, serving good beer and wine in a welcoming and friendly atmosphere. The Grade II-listed building is several hundred years old, with much character and more than a little charm. Food is not normally served but functions can be catered for. A fourth beer can be added at busy times. Local and regional CAMRA Pub of the Year winner. Q❄☕♠P🚌❀

Oakham

Grainstore Brewery Tap 🍷
Station Approach, LE15 6EA
☎ (01572) 770065 ⊕ grainstorebrewery.com
Grainstore Cooking, Rutland Osprey, Triple B, Ten Fifty; 6 changing beers (often Grainstore) ⓗ
A pub and brewery in a cleverly converted small warehouse, retaining some original features. It is adjacent to Oakham station. Brewery tours are available but must be booked in advance. Ten handpumps offer a wide range of beers, always including a mild. Home-made food is served, with breakfasts at weekends. Live bands feature regularly, and beer and cider festivals are held, with the main one being over August bank holiday. Walkers and their dogs are welcome. A regular local CAMRA award winner. ❄⑪♿⇌♠♠P🚌❀ᜒ♪

Ryhall

Green Dragon
The Square, PE9 4HH
☎ (01780) 751999 ⊕ thegreendragonryhall.co.uk
Greene King IPA; 3 changing beers (often Church End, Grainstore, Nene Valley) ⓗ
Former Melbourns stone-built pub in the heart of the village. The main building was built in the 17th century and is Grade II listed. Its low ceilings, and nooks and crannies give the Green Dragon pub a nice cozy feel. Under new management, superb home cooked meals are served using locally sourced ingredients. A former local CAMRA Pub of the Year. Q❄☕⑪♠🚌(202)❀ᜒ♪

Uppingham

Crown Inn ⓛ
19 High Street East, LE15 9PY
☎ (01572) 822302 ⊕ crownuppingham.co.uk
Everards Beacon Hill, Sunchaser, Tiger; 2 changing beers ⓗ
The Crown was originally a coaching inn, dating back to 1704 when two separate dwellings were altered to make one building. Under new management, it offers two Everards ales and occasional guest beers. Tapas-style food is served in the bar and restaurant, and live music often plays at weekends and bank holidays. The pub participates in the Uppingham Town Beer Festival. En-suite accommodation is available. ❀🛏⑪♿♠P🚌❀ᜒ♪

REAL ALE BREWERIES

Bakers Dozen Ketton
Grainstore ♠ Oakham

Breweries

Bakers Dozen SIBA

Unit 5, Ketton Business Estate, Pit Lane, Ketton, PE9 3SZ
☎ (01780) 238180 ⊕ bakersdozenbrewing.co.uk

☺Baker's Dozen is a two-person microbrewery with brewing taking place on a five-barrel plant installed in 2015. The beers favour hoppy styles with some occasional brews unfined. ♦

Acoustic Landlady (ABV 3.4%) PALE
Jentacular (ABV 3.5%) GOLD
Magic Potion (ABV 3.8%) GOLD
Sinc Stream (ABV 4%) BITTER
Stamford Pale (ABV 4%) PALE
Cuthberts Fee (ABV 4.1%) BLOND
Bull Run (ABV 4.3%) BITTER
Straight Outta Ketton (ABV 4.5%) PALE
Electric Landlady (ABV 5%) GOLD
12 Second Panda (ABV 6%) IPA

Grainstore SIBA

Station Approach, Oakham, LE15 6RE
☎ (01572) 770065 ⊕ grainstorebrewery.com

☺Grainstore, the smallest county's largest brewery, has been in production since 1995, founded by Tony Davis and Mike Davies. After 45 years in the industry Tony decided to retire, handing thre reins to his son, William, and Peter Atkinson. More than 200 outlets are supplied. Beers are also brewed under the Stoney Ford brand name. ‼♦⬥

Rutland Bitter (ABV 3.4%) BITTER
Rutland Panther (ABV 3.4%) MILD
This superb reddish-black mild punches above its weight with malt and roast flavours combining to deliver a brew that can match the average stout for intensity of flavour.
Cooking (ABV 3.6%) BITTER
Tawny-coloured beer with malt and hops on the nose and a pleasant grainy mouthfeel. Hops and fruit flavours combine to give a bitterness that continues into a long finish.
Red Kite (ABV 3.8%) BITTER
Rutland Osprey (ABV 4%) GOLD
Triple B (ABV 4.2%) BITTER
Initially hops dominate over malt in both the aroma and taste, but fruit is there too. All three linger in varying degrees in the sweetish aftertaste of this brown brew.
Zahara (ABV 4.2%) GOLD
Ten Fifty (ABV 5%) BITTER
Pungent banana and malt notes on the nose. On the palate, rich malt and fruit is joined by subtle hop on a bittersweet base. Dry malt aftertaste with some fruit.
Rutland Beast (ABV 5.3%) OLD
Nip (ABV 7.3%) BARLEY

Brewed under the Stoney Ford brand name:
Sheepmarket Supernova (ABV 3.8%) GOLD
PE9 Paradise Pale (ABV 4%) PALE
All Saints Almighty (ABV 4.2%) BITTER

Cracking the code

A brief outline of beer styles from other countries.

Abbey Beer: a commercial Belgian beer based – sometimes loosely – on the ales brewed by Trappist monasteries in that country.

Alt: German word meaning Old, a reference to the fact that the style predates modern lager. The beer is copper coloured and originates in Dusseldorf.

Bock: German name for a strong lager beer from Bavaria, often aged for as long as a year. Labels often have a goat as a symbol as Bock means billygoat in the Bavarian dialect. Spelt Bok in the Netherlands where the style can be ale rather than lager.

Brune or Bruin: Belgian/Dutch term for a brown beer.

Dubbel and Tripel (Double and Triple): strong ales associated with the Belgian Trappist tradition. The terms originated at the Westmalle monastery near Antwerp. Dubbel is a strong brown ale, Tripel a stronger golden one. Quadrupel is an even stronger beer – but not four times stronger than a Dubbel.

Dunkel: a German dark lager.

Gruit: medieval-style beer from Belgium and the Netherlands that use a mixture of herbs and spices in place of hops.

Hefe/Hefe Weisse: Hefe is German for yeast and any beer 'mit Hefe' means it's unfiltered. Weisse is the German for wheat and a Hefe Weisse beer is an unfiltered wheat beer.

Helles: a German pale lager, lower in strength than a Pils or Pilsner.

Kölsch: golden ale from Cologne, protected by a government ordinance.

Lambic: Belgian beer style made by 'spontaneous fermentation', using wild yeasts in the atmosphere and stored in wood for long periods. A blended beer using young and old lambics is called gueuze.

Pils/Pilsner/Pilsener: golden lager that was first brewed in the Bohemian city of Pilsen, now in the Czech Republic.

Trappist: ale brewed by Trappist monks in Belgium and the Netherlands. Monastic beers carry a symbol of authenticity from the International Trappist Association that confirms that monks are in control of the brewing process, though they may employ lay workers.

United Kingdom of Beer

Adrian Tierney-Jones

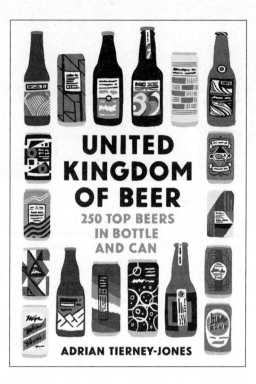

There is a thirst for good beer on these islands, a thirst for beer that satisfies the soul, quenches the thirst and leaves the drinker glowing with satisfaction. You might be in the mood for a muscular Best Bitter, or a brooding, midnight-black Imperial Stout as you cosy up with a loved one on a cold winter's night, or perhaps you fancy a crisp and briskly amiable lager while hanging out with friends on a sunny afternoon.

Whatever avenue your desire takes you down, whatever the occasion, be assured that there is a beer for you and acclaimed beer writer Adrian Tierney-Jones will help you make the right choice with his selection of 250 of the very best beers in bottle and can from around these islands.

RRP: £17.99   ISBN: 978-1-85249-378-3

For this and other books on beer and pubs, visit CAMRA's online bookshop at **shop1.camra.org.uk** or call 01727 867201.

Discounts are available for CAMRA members.

Yorkshire

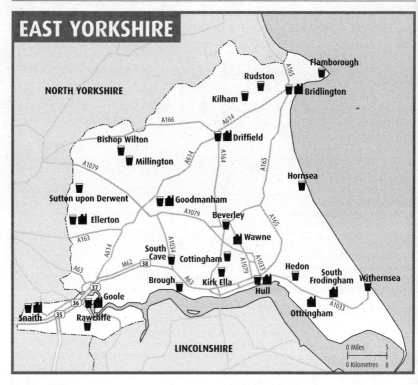

EAST YORKSHIRE

Map locations: Flamborough, Rudston, Bridlington, Kilham, NORTH YORKSHIRE, Driffield, Bishop Wilton, Millington, Hornsea, Sutton upon Derwent, Goodmanham, Ellerton, Beverley, Wawne, South Cave, Cottingham, Hedon, South Frodingham, Withernsea, Brough, Kirk Ella, Hull, Goole, Ottringham, Snaith, Rawcliffe, LINCOLNSHIRE

0 Miles 5 / 0 Kilometres 8

Beverley

Chequers Micropub ⃝

15 Swaby's Yard, Dyer Lane, HU17 9BZ (off Saturday Market)

☎ 07964 227906

5 changing beers (sourced regionally; often Brass Castle, Great Newsome, North Riding (Brewery)) ⊞

Yorkshire's first self-styled micropub, converted from a baker's shop, it opened in 2013 and is located in a secluded yard off Saturday Market close to the bus station. Local breweries are well represented on the bar plus micros from across the UK. Several ciders/perries are sold as are three craft keg beers. With no television or loud music, Chequers is a place for quiet conversation. A selection of board games are available for customers. There is a seating area in the courtyard to the front. Q❄❀≈♣🖩😺

Dog & Duck ⃝

33 Ladygate, HU17 8BH (off Saturday Market adjacent to Browns store)

☎ (01482) 862419 ⊕ bedandbreakfastbeverley.com

Black Sheep Best Bitter; Great Newsome Sleck Dust; Timothy Taylor Landlord; 2 changing beers (sourced regionally; often Wold Top, Yorkshire Heart) ⊞

The pub was built in the 1930s and has been run by the same family since 1972. It is comprised of three distinct areas: a bar with a period brick fireplace and bentwood seating, a front lounge with an open fire and a rear snug. The good-value, home-cooked lunches are popular. Guest accommodation is provided in six purpose-built self-contained rooms to the rear with self-contained parking. Close to Beverley bus station. The pub retains some original terrrazzo flooring in the rear lobby. 🛏🍽◐≈♣🖩😺🛜

Green Dragon ✓

51 Saturday Market, HU17 8AA

☎ (01482) 889801 ⊕ thegreendragonbeverley.co.uk

Abbeydale Moonshine; Black Sheep Best Bitter; Sharp's Doom Bar; Wainwright; 6 changing beers (sourced nationally; often Adnams, Purity, Timothy Taylor) ⊞

Narrow-fronted 17th-century inn accessed down a side passageway and a further rear entrance off Lairgate. The Green Dragon was refurbished in 2018 and updated to increase its appeal to families and diners. It serves breakfast from 10am and other meals all day. Sports fans are catered for with several largescreen televisions, including outdoors. There is a wide range of beer styles available from up to 10 handpumps and further KeyKegs. Quiz night is every Tuesday. 🛏❀◐&≈🖩😺🛜

Monks Walk ⃝

19 Highgate, HU17 0DN

☎ (01482) 880871 ⊕ monkswalkinn.com

5 changing beers (sourced regionally; often Great Newsome, Wold Top, Yorkshire Heart) ⊞/Ⓖ

Dating back to the 13th century, the building was built as a merchant's warehouse. There is a small front bar and a longer rear bar with a wood/coal fire at the end. Access to the bars is via a passageway with a small pool room on the opposite side. Conversation is encouraged at this genuine free house. The sheltered beer garden and separate courtyard have splendid views of the minster. Five handpumps typically dispense pale, bitter, dark and strong ales. Q🛏❀&≈♣🖩😺🛜♫

Royal Standard ✓

30 North Bar Within, HU17 8DL

☎ 07947 247492

Sharp's Doom Bar; Tetley Tetley Bitter; Wainwright; 1 changing beer (sourced nationally; often Black Sheep) Ⓗ
Small, traditional pub located just inside North Bar close to St Mary's Church. It is believed to have been built in the 17th century, though the black and white exterior dates from the early 1900s. Inside are two separate drinking areas with a shared bar. The small front bar has bench seating while the rear lounge bar is more comfortable. Outside there is plenty of space for the summer months. Up to four handpulls dispense regional and national beers. The pub supports various local charities. ⓈⓉⒼ♿🅿🐾🍴🛜

Bishop Wilton

Fleece ⓁⓁ
47 Main Street, YO42 1RU
☎ (01759) 368251 🌐 thefleeceinn.info
Black Sheep Best Bitter; Theakston Best Bitter; Wold Top Bitter; 1 changing beer (sourced locally) Ⓗ
This watering hole is popular with walkers exploring the dry valleys of the Yorkshire Wolds. The pub has an open-plan layout around a horseshoe-shaped bar, with a cosy games corner well away from the dining tables. Guest beers often come from local microbreweries. Opening times may vary, please phone in advance to avoid disappointment. ❄🚃🍺🎵

Bridlington

Marine Bar ⓁⓁ ✅
North Marine Drive, YO15 2LS (1 mile NE of centre)
☎ (01262) 675347 🌐 expanse.co.uk/marinebar
Theakston Best Bitter; Timothy Taylor Landlord; Wold Top Anglers Reward; 2 changing beers (sourced regionally; often Acorn, Bradfield, Pennine) Ⓗ
Large open-plan bar, part of the Expanse Hotel. Superb views of the North Bay from the recently added roof garden make the perfect backdrop when enjoying the home-cooked food served here daily. Several canvases of local sunrises and scenic features are displayed in the bar. Attracting a good mix of regulars, a warm welcome awaits the influx of summer visitors. Ample parking is available along the promenade. A land train operates along the promenade during the summer. Ⓖ❄🚃🍴♿🅿🚌(14)🐾🛜🎵

Old Ship Inn 🍷
90 St John Street, YO16 7JS
☎ (01262) 401906
Bridgehouse Porter; 3 changing beers (sourced nationally; often Acorn, Rudgate, Yorkshire Heart) Ⓗ
Dating from 1860, this multi-roomed pub comprises of the main bar with leather-backed bench seating and a pool table, a large comfortable lounge room which doubles as a function room plus a smaller room to the rear. There is an extensive collection of Frank Meadow Sutcliffe photographs of Whitby and a smaller number featuring Bridlington. The handpull beers are usually sourced from regional Yorkshire breweries with occasional national beers available. Local CAMRA Pub of the Year 2023. Ⓖ❄🚃🍴♿🅿(124,5A)🐾🛜🎵

Telegraph ⓁⓁ
110 Quay Road, YO16 4JB (10 mins from station)
☎ 07411 281651
3 changing beers (sourced nationally; often Pennine, Wold Top) Ⓗ
A popular local, family-run, community-focused pub situated a short walk from the railway station and en route to Bridlington old town. The welcoming one-room

interior is divided into three distinct areas; one hosts the pool table and a television for sports coverage, the main bar area has plentiful seating, and the final area features a comfortable lounge. There is also an extensive, well-furnished, walled beer garden featuring a chimnea, to the right-hand side and rear of the pub. ❄🚃♿🅿🍴🐾🛜🎵

Three B's Micropub ⓁⓁ
2 Marshall Avenue, YO15 2DS
☎ (01262) 604235 🌐 threebspubbrid.co.uk
Acorn Barnsley Bitter; 3 changing beers (sourced regionally; often Blue Bee, Half Moon, North Riding (Brewery)) Ⓗ
Opened in 2020 this micropub, run by dedicated CAMRA members is set over two floors and bills itself as Bridlington's real ale destination. The four real ales are generally sourced from small Yorkshire microbreweries, and will usually feature a dark beer backed by at least one beer of a high gravity. Regional Cider Pub of the Year 2023 with a range of 10 or more ciders, some sourced from Yorkshire. Homemade sausage rolls as well as pie & peas are available. QⒼ❄♿🚃🍴♿🅿🐾🛜🎵

Brough

Centurion Arms ⓁⓁ
39 Skillings Lane, HU15 1BA
4 changing beers (sourced regionally; often Great Newsome, Half Moon, Wold Top) Ⓗ
A converted shop unit, located among a number of small businesses supporting the local community. This is unlike any other pub in the village, with an ever-changing range of real ale and cider; evidenced from the extensive collection of pump badges which add to the eclectic variety of paraphernalia decorating the pub. Social interaction and conversation is encouraged between regulars and strangers. Locally produced artwork is also on show. A quiz is on Wednesday evenings. Dog snacks are provided. Ⓖ❄♿🚃🍴♿🅿(158)🐾🎵

Cottingham

Hugh Fitz-Baldric ⓁⓁ
144 Hallgate, HU16 4BB
🌐 the-hugh-fitz-baldric-of-cottingham.business.site
5 changing beers (sourced nationally; often Timothy Taylor) Ⓗ
Converted from a shop on the main street of the largest village in England, the pub consists of one room with quiet corners. It is named after a local Cottingham man from the 1400s who became the first Sheriff of Yorkshire.

REAL ALE BREWERIES
Aitcheson's Wawne
All Hallows 🍺 Goodmanham
Atom Hull
Belschnickel Hull
Bone Machine ✦ Hull
Bricknell Hull
Bridbrewer 🍺 Bridlington
Bridlington 🍺 Bridlington
Crafty Little Ottringham
Great Newsome South Frodingham
Half Moon ✦ Ellerton
Old Mill Snaith
Raven Hill Driffield
Spotlight Goole (brewing suspended)
Vittles Hull
Woolybutt Brew Shed Hull
Yorkshire Brewhouse Hull

It is furnished with repurposed items and a log burner adds cosiness in winter. Altogether this makes for a peaceful place to enjoy the range of real ales, gins and other drinks reflecting changing trends. Children are welcome until 8pm. Dogs allowed in the beer garden. A former local CAMRA Pub of the Year. Q ☼ ✿ ♿ ⇌ 🚍

Driffield

Butchers Dog 🅛

57 Market Place, YO25 6AW (Entrance is via the arch way)

☎ (01377) 252229 ● thebutchersdog.co.uk

6 changing beers (sourced locally; often Half Moon, Ossett) Ⓗ

The Butchers Dog was a micropub which has moved within Driffield to the Market Place, taking over a pub formerly known as Middle Pub. Upon entering from the arched passageway there is a long thin bar-room that extends through to an independent bistro known as Ox (open Thu-Sun). Thursday is music afternoon. Beers can be sampled on a three drink paddle. A range of social and community events take place on a regular basis. Q ☼ ✿ ◑ ⇌ ● 🚍 ♫

Ellerton

Boot & Shoe

Main Street, YO42 4PB

☎ (01757) 288346

House beer (by Dark Horse) Ⓗ

A welcoming country village inn dating from the 17th century. The building, unusually, wraps around a very large tree. A cosy bar features exposed brick, a side bar is served via a hatch and there are two further rooms. All have real fireplaces, low ceilings and even lower doorways (watch your head). To the rear is a pleasant sunny patio and a large grassy beer garden. Charity events are sometimes held. Q ♣ P ✿

Flamborough

Viking Hotel

North Marine Road, YO15 1BA

☎ (01262) 851455

Rudgate Viking; 3 changing beers (sourced regionally; often Acorn, Wensleydale) Ⓗ

A pleasant walk from Flamborough's North Landing and the nearby Haven Caravan Park, this seemingly isolated pub is divided into three separate areas. Good food and well-kept beer matched with a cheerful welcome greet all comers. Delightful views across fields take in the two lighthouses and can offer glimpses of the local wildlife. Real fires feature during the winter months. The pub can get busy during holiday seasons. Q ☼ ✿ ◑ ⇆ Å ♣ P 🚍 ✿ ♫

Goodmanham

Goodmanham Arms 🅛

Main Street, YO43 3JA

☎ (01430) 873849

All Hallows No Notion Porter, Ragged Robyn; Hambleton Stallion Amber; Ossett Yorkshire Blonde; Theakston Best Bitter; 3 changing beers (sourced locally; often All Hallows, Hambleton) Ⓗ

A characteristic village local with the All Hallows Brewery attached, it is close to the Wolds Way footpath. Log fires warm both of the cosy bars which are candlelit during dark winter nights. An extension, decorated with vintage artefacts on a motoring theme, provides additional space. Hearty meals are freshly cooked and served

lunchtimes and on Monday and Wednesday evenings. Dogs are welcome except when food is being served. Local CAMRA village Pub of the Year many times. Q ☼ ✿ ◑ ⏰ 🚍 ♫

Goole

Tom Pudding

20 Pasture Road, DN14 6EZ (2 mins walk from station)

☎ 07563 830828

4 changing beers (sourced regionally; often Great Newsome, Hambleton, Wold Top) Ⓗ

Opened in 2017 by two CAMRA members with an enthusiasm for real ale, this micropub was formerly a newsagents. There is interesting internal brickwork and exposed wooden beamed ceiling. The pub can accommodate up to 50 people and is often sought out by travelling football fans on their way to Hull and Doncaster as it is only two minutes' walk from railway station. Four ales, frequently from Hambleton or Wold Top, include a gluten-free beer, and there are up to four real ciders from producers such as Dudda's Tun. ⇆ ♣ ● 🚍 (155,X55) ✿ ♫

Hedon

Hed'On Inn

7 Watmaughs Arcade, St Augustine Gate, HU12 8EZ

☎ (01964) 601100

Black Sheep Best Bitter; 4 changing beers (sourced nationally; often Black Sheep, Iron Pier, Top Rope) Ⓗ

A micropub, converted from a disused carpet shop, adjacent to a car park at the end of a shopping arcade in the centre of this historic market town. The premises are tastefully decorated with recycled fittings. There is one regular and four changing beers, covering the full spectrum of beer styles, together with real ciders, bottled beers and a range of spirits and wines. A quiz is held on Wednesday night. ♿ ● P 🚍

Hornsea

Stackhouse Bar

8B Newbegin, HU18 1AG

☎ (01964) 534407

4 changing beers (sourced nationally) Ⓗ

Established in 2014, this micropub converted from a shop can be found opposite the church by the traffic lights. The single room is fitted out with repurposed furniture providing an intimate atmosphere for drinking and conversation and attracting a mixed clientele. An interesting choice of cask ales are complemented by an extensive range of craft beers and real ciders. There is a separate function room. ☼ Å ● 🚍 ✿ ❁ ♫

Hull

Admiral of the Humber 🅛 ✔

1 Anlaby Road, HU1 2NT

☎ (01482) 381850

Batemans XXXB; Greene King Abbot; Ruddles Best Bitter; Sharp's Doom Bar; 6 changing beers (sourced nationally; often Great Newsome) Ⓗ

A Wetherspoon hotel that was a former paint and wallpaper shop. It is now a large single room, mostly on one level, that is ideally suited to those finding steps or stairs a problem. There is a large open-air roof top garden for smokers and non-smokers alike (closes 10pm). A designated area is set aside for diners during the day; children are welcome until 9pm. The pub is close to the Bonus Arena. The pub is away fan-friendly for visiting sports teams. Q ☼ ✿ ◑ ⏰ ♿ ⇌ 🚍 ☎

Alexandra Hotel L

69 Hessle Road, HU3 2AB

☎ (01482) 327455

7 changing beers (sourced locally; often Mallinsons, Rudgate, Yorkshire Heart)

Known as the Alex, new ownership in 2019 transformed this Grade II-listed Victorian pub into a real ale gem with up to seven cask ales, including at least one stout and several real ciders. Good conversation features highly along with motor sport-themed memorabilia. There is a fine bar back and (now electric) gas light fittings inside and terracotta tiling outside. The pub supports local charities and can organise local picks up and drops for a donation. It is home to the Parrot brewery. ❀⊠◭♿♣●P⊡🚪❀♫

Furley & Co L

18-20 Princes Dock Street, HU1 2LP (opp dockside entrance to Princes Quay shopping centre)

☎ (01482) 229649 ⊕ furleyshull.co.uk

4 changing beers (sourced regionally; often Brass Castle, Dock Beers, North Riding (Brewery)) ⊞

Welcoming family-friendly bar overlooking the waterfront of the former Princes Dock. Historically the premises were warehousing and offices for a local shipping company, Furley & Company, circa 1750. The décor is modern with a colourful collage of musical and film posters on one wall. Four cask ales from regional breweries are available as well as a large selection of craft ales and ciders. The pub has a varied food menu that caters for all tastes. ❀❀◑♿≈🚪🐾❀

George Hotel

Land of Green Ginger, HU1 2EA

☎ (01482) 226373

Theakston Old Peculier; Timothy Taylor Landlord; 3 changing beers (sourced regionally; often Ossett, Saltaire, Wye Valley) ⊞

Totally refurbished in 2020, located in the heart of the old town on Hull's most famous street. The downstairs real ale bar, with wood-panelled walls and ceiling beams retains some period fittings. Splendid, glazed leaded windows have been retained. Also of note is reputedly the smallest pub window in England dating from its former coaching inn days. Upstairs a second bar has TVs for sporting events. ♣🚪

Hop & Vine ♥ L

24 Albion Street, HU1 3TG (250yds from Hull New Theatre and Central Library)

☎ 07507 719259

4 changing beers (sourced nationally; often Brass Castle, Great Newsome, Salopian) ⊞

An atmospheric basement bar free house serving three to four changing guest beers, largely from independent Yorkshire breweries. A selection of six nationally sourced still ciders and perries are stocked along with a large list of bottled continental beers and a good selection of international whiskies, including from Yorkshire's own distillery. Oversized lined glasses are used for real ales. A variety of pub games are available to customers, including nine men's morris and shove-ha'penny; there is a monthly Sunday games night. ❀❀Å≈♣●🛢🚪🐾❀

Minerva Hotel L

Nelson Street, HU1 1XE

☎ (01482) 210025 ⊕ minerva-hull.co.uk

Tetley Tetley Bitter; 5 changing beers (sourced regionally; often Bone Machine, Timothy Taylor, Yorkshire Brewhouse) ⊞

Overlooking the Humber estuary and Victoria Pier, this famous pub, built in 1829, is a great place to watch the ships go by. Photos and memorabilia are a reminder of the area's maritime past. The central bar serves various rooms including a tiny three-seat snug. The former brew house was converted to provide an additional drinking area and is available for functions. Connected to The Deep visitor attraction by a footbridge at the mouth of the River Hull. ❀❀◑♿🚪(16)❀

Old Bull & Bush

56 Green Lane, HU2 0HH

☎ (01482) 327661

2 changing beers (sourced nationally; often Great Newsome, Morland) ⊞

Traditional back-street local situated in an industrial area west of the River Hull. Two competitively-priced guest ales come from both local and national breweries. There is a television and a pool table in the main bar. The small back room is quieter and popular on weekend lunchtimes. The licensee has owned the pub for over 25 years and the Grade II-listed building has many original features. ♣

Pave L

16-20 Princes Avenue, HU5 3QA

☎ (01482) 333181 ⊕ pavebar.co.uk

3 changing beers (sourced regionally; often Brass Castle, Rooster's, Scarborough) ⊞

The original pavement café in this popular area of the city, this continental-style bar attracts a diverse range of customers. There are four guest ales, usually regional or local, and a varied range of European draught and bottled beers. A changing cider is sold. Close to the Hull City Stadium it is away fan-friendly. Live music plays on Sunday afternoon. ❀❀♿●🚪❀♫

Scale & Feather

21 Scale Lane, HU1 1LF

☎ 07808 832295

4 changing beers (sourced nationally; often Marble, North Riding (Brewery), Thornbridge) ⊞

Located in the heart of Hull's old town, this traditional pub with a modern interior is well known for its continually-changing cask ales and ciders. A firm favourite with locals due to its inviting atmosphere and regular quiz nights and food events. It is a large single-roomed pub with an upstairs function room and a small smoking area out back. ❀●🚪❀❀

St John's Hotel

10 Queens Road, HU5 2PY

☎ (01482) 341013 ⊕ stjohnshull.com

Banks's Sunbeam; Marston's Old Empire; Wainwright; 2 changing beers (sourced nationally; often Brakspear, Ringwood) ⊞

Unspoilt Grade II-listed community local, it has been identified by CAMRA as having a nationally important historic pub interior and was once a regular haunt of the late poet laureate, Philip Larkin. Built in 1865 and remodelled by Hull brewery in 1904-5, it comprises three unique, characterful rooms. Both the front, L-shaped, public bar and rear lounge, with original bench seating, encourage friendly conversation. Another larger room houses a pool table and is used for occasional beer festivals. Live music occurs every Tuesday. Two separate garden areas, one paved, are popular in summer. Q❀❀♿♣P🚪❀❀♫

Station Inn L

202 Beverley Road, HU5 1AA

4 changing beers (sourced regionally; often Great Newsome, Milestone, Rudgate) ⊞

The pub was built in the late 19th century to serve Stepney station on the Hull to Withernsea railway. It has a 20th-century mock-Tudor façade and was recently refurbished to a high standard. The public bar has an open fire and the back room is used occasionally for live entertainment. The pub serves up to four changing real ales and two real ciders. ♿❀♣🍴🚌🐾♪

Vintage 🏳

28 Silver Street, HU1 1JG

☎ (01482) 325104 🌐 vintagebarhull.business.site

3 changing beers (sourced regionally; often Mill Valley, Ossett) 🅷

In the heart of Hull's old town, this pub conversion of a former jeweller's shop opened in 2017. Small, friendly and comfortable, with a gallery wall featuring local artists, the pub's relaxed atmosphere is enjoyed by a mixed clientele. There is an acoustic night every Wednesday and live music some Friday evenings and every Sunday afternoon. As well as the real ales on offer there is a wide range of other drinks available. Q♿👌🖥❀🛜♪

White Hart ★ 🏳

109 Alfred Gelder Street, HU1 1EP

☎ 07538 470546 🌐 whiteharthullpub.co.uk

5 changing beers (sourced regionally; often Great Newsome, North Riding (Brewery), Rudgate) 🅷

Located on the edge of Hull's old town, this Grade II-listed pub features a half-timbered frontage. Identified by CAMRA as having a nationally important historic pub interior, it has a rare example of a ceramic bar made by Burmantofts of Leeds, who also made many other features such as the original bar back which dates from 1904. There is a pool table in the rear bar and sports are shown on large screens in both bars. Outside there is a sheltered beer garden. ♿❀◐♣🍴P🖥❀🛜♪

Kilham

Old Star Inn

Church Street, YO25 4RG

☎ (01262) 420619

Theakston Best Bitter; 2 changing beers (sourced regionally; often Great Newsome, Ossett) 🅷

Located in the centre of the village, opposite the imposing church, this delightful, beamed-ceiling pub contains three distinct areas off the bar. In winter two of these areas have real fires, giving it a homely and welcoming atmosphere. A corridor gives access to the sizeable beer garden. Locally sourced, high-quality food is served all day. Locals, walkers, bikers and cyclists are all made equally welcome. The local Raven Hill brewery shares some familial links. Q♿❀◐▲♣P❀🛜♪

Kirk Ella

Beech Tree

South Ella Way, HU10 7LS

☎ (01482) 654350

Dark Star Hophead; Fuller's London Pride; 6 changing beers (sourced nationally; often Black Sheep, Thornbridge, Timothy Taylor) 🅷

Open-plan pub on the western outskirts of Hull, owned by a pub company committed to cask ale. Up to eight real ales are available, including at least one dark beer; try-before-you-buy is encouraged. Food is served every day with brunch at weekends. Wednesday is quiz night. Families with children are welcome and a real fire makes for a hospitable winter feel. Buses stop close to the pub until early evening, and a later-running route is only a 10-minute walk away. ♿❀◐👌P🖥(154)🛜

Millington

Gait

Main Street, YO42 1TX

☎ (01759) 302045 🌐 thegaitinn.co.uk

Black Sheep Best Bitter; Theakston Best Bitter; 3 changing beers (sourced locally; often C'84, Half Moon, Wold Top) 🅷

Delightful Yorkshire Wolds pub, that provides a warm welcome (seasonally by means of a wood-burning stove) to both locals and the many walkers enjoying the attractions of Millington Woods and Pastures. An idiosyncratic bar is filled with a range of ornaments and local pictures. Sit at kitchen-type tables to enjoy hearty, home-made food served from an extensive menu. Two regular cask beers are served, with at least one guest cask beer, typically all from Yorkshire, and there is an annual beer festival with up to 35 beers. ♿❀🛏◐♣P❀🛜♪

Rawcliffe

Jemmy Hirst at the Rose & Crown

26 Riverside, DN14 8RN (from village green turn N on Chapel Ln)

☎ (01405) 837902

Timothy Taylor Landlord; 5 changing beers (sourced locally; often Bradfield, Little Critters, Ossett) 🅷

A traditional award-winning free house in the heart of the village. The pub is famed for a warm welcome and is a community hub, hosting a wide variety of events, clubs and live music. Landlady Jill has invested in modernising the cellar and introducing more ales and drinks while still maintaining the much-loved traditional interior. Overlooking the River Aire, the pub has an open fire and welcomes both dogs and families. A must for fans of a proper local pub. Q♿❀≈♣P🖥(401,88)❀

Rudston

Bosville Arms 🏳

Main Street, YO25 4UB (located on the B1253 at edge of village)

☎ (01262) 371426 🌐 bosvillearms.co.uk

3 changing beers (often Wold Top) 🅷

Purchased by the local community following a local campaign to save the pub in 2020 it was subsequently refurbished and reopened in mid 2021. This now welcoming establishment, which features a central bar, provides several areas for fine dining to complement their cask beers. Seasonal ingredients are locally sourced wherever possible. Outside there is a car park, a beer garden and a separate accommodation block. Q♿❀🛏◐▲P❀♪

Snaith

Plough Inn ✅

Shearburn Terrace, DN14 9JJ

☎ (01405) 480106 🌐 speakeasycompany.uk

Don Valley Atomic Blonde, Gongoozler, Go Your Own Way; 7 changing beers (sourced nationally; often Nailmaker, Rudgate, Settle) 🅷

The Plough Inn is a Grade II-listed, traditional pub. It has two main rooms, both served by one central bar. The public bar has a large fireplace with log burner, while the lounge is cosier with chesterfield sofas and armchairs. The large, paved beer garden has a raised sun terrace and stables that contain a pool stable and dartboard. Home-cooked food is available daily, including Sunday dinners. Various events and live music nights are hosted throughout the year. ♿❀🛏◐👌≈♣P🖥(401)❀♪

South Cave

Bear Inn

61 Market Place, HU15 2AS
☎ (01430) 422482
4 changing beers (sourced nationally; often Bradfield, Timothy Taylor, Wold Top) Ⓗ

The Bear Inn is situated in the South Cave conservation area, less than a mile from the A63/M62. This 150-year-old pub serves food and has a regularly changing selection of cask beers. It has a recently remodelled main bar, a conservatory and a beer garden. The pub holds quizzes, has live music and shows live sports on TV. It is listed as an Asset of Community Value, giving it protection from development.
ᔔ❀◑ᕹ⬥P🍽(x4)❀🛜♪

Sutton Upon Derwent

St Vincent Arms Ⓛ

Main Street, YO41 4BN
☎ (01904) 608349 ⏚ stvincentarms.co.uk
Fuller's London Pride; Kirkstall Three Swords; Theakston Old Peculier; Timothy Taylor Golden Best, Landlord; 1 changing beer (sourced nationally) Ⓗ

This pretty white-painted village free house is now in its third generation of family ownership. The pub offers an excellent range of beers, with five regulars and one changing guest ale, usually from a local independent brewer. The cosy bar to the right, featuring a large Fuller, Smith & Turner mirror, is popular with locals. Another small bar to the left, with a serving hatch, leads to the dining rooms. This pub offers great service with excellent food beyond the usual pub fare. Q ᔔ❀◑P

Withernsea

Captain Williams

6 The Promenade, HU19 2DP
☎ (01964) 270084
Timothy Taylor Boltmaker, Knowle Spring; Titanic Plum Porter; 1 changing beer (sourced regionally) Ⓗ

Formerly known as the Marine Bar, the pub was built as a private dwelling in 1893 and is named after the original builder and owner Captain William Newman. The interior has been fully refurbished including adding a nautical feature wall. Relax in the comfortable lounge area with panoramic views of the North Sea. Accommodation is provided courtesy of five en-suite letting rooms and three chalets. Food is served Thursday to Sunday – booking is recommended for Sunday lunches. Live acts perform monthly at weekends. ᔔ❀⇹◑ᕹP🍽❀♪

Old Boat Shed Ⓛ

2 Seaside Road, HU19 2DL
☎ 07812 446689
4 changing beers (sourced regionally; often Black Sheep, Great Newsome, Wold Top) Ⓗ

This small pub is housed in a building originally built in 1881 to house the Withernsea lifeboat station before it was decommissioned in 1913. Four cask ales and three real ciders are served in this community-focused bar where conversation is actively encouraged in preference to loud music or television. Beers and ciders can be sampled using a beer bat holding three third-pints. There is a comfortable raised seating veranda to the front. Children and dogs welcome. There is occasional live music. Q ᔔ❀ᕹ♣◑🚌(76,129)❀♪

Breweries

Aitcheson's

Windham Farm, Ferry Road, Wawne, HU7 5XY
☎ 07456 063670

Office: 2 Wheelhouse Court, Hull, HU6 5BF
⏚ aitchesons.co.uk

⊕Formerly the East Yorkshire Beer Co, Aitcheson's is a small batch brewery. It was established by Steve and Avril Aitcheson in a 17th century refurbished former boatshed on the banks of the River Hull, in 2020. Beers are available in multiple formats. Brewing experience days are popular and bookable in advance. ♦

Endike Black (ABV 3.8%) MILD
Hoppy Blonde (ABV 4%) BLOND
King Billy Bitter (ABV 4.2%) BITTER
Earl de Grey IPA (ABV 4.5%) PALE
Full Measure Porter (ABV 4.5%) PORTER
Oddfellows Red (ABV 4.7%) RED

All Hallows

🏠 **Main Street, Goodmanham, YO43 3JA**
☎ (01430) 873849 ⏚ thegoodmanhamarms.co.uk

⊕Abbie Logozzi, landlady of the Goodmanham Arms, started brewing in 2012 in outbuildings behind the pub. The ex-Goodmanham Brewery buildings were purchased and a five-barrel plant installed. The brewery name comes from the adjacent 12th century All Hallows Church. Local legendary characters are used in the naming of some of the beers. Brews are supplied to the pub and some free trade. 🛒♦

Atom SIBA

Unit 4-5, Food & Tech Park, Malmo Road, Sutton Fields Industrial Estate, Hull, HU7 0YF
☎ (01482) 820572 ⏚ atombeers.com

⊠ Atom Brewing Co was founded in 2014 by Allan Rice and Sarah Thackray. Most of its production goes into can and keg, but cask ales are produced in rotation or on demand, around a core range. Atom's ethos is science and education based, so working with local colleges, it runs regular brewing schools and classes. All beers are unfined and unfiltered (so naturally hazy). ‼♦

Schrodingers Cat (ABV 3.5%) BITTER
Quantum State (ABV 4.2%) PALE
Dark Matter (ABV 4.5%) SPECIALITY

Belschnickel SIBA

146 Ella Street, Hull, HU5 3AU
☎ (01482) 348747 ⏚ belschnickel.co.uk

Launched in 2022, Belschnickel Brewery work on a small scale with a 50-litre brewhouse to produce a small core range of canned beers and bottle-conditioned speciality beers brewed for ageing. All the brewing, canning and packaging is completed in-house. All beers are unfiltered and unpasteurised. Its branding and labels are produced in collaboration with a local artist. LIVE

Bone Machine

20 Pier Street, Hull, HU1 1ZA ☎ 07931 313438
✉ beer@bonemachinebrewing.com

⊠ Finnish brothers Marko and Kimmo worked at a number of breweries around Yorkshire before setting up their own – Bone Machine in Pocklington, during 2017.

They relocated to Hull's popular Humber Street area, along Pier Street, in 2019 with a five-barrel brewing plant that produces beers in keg and can, plus cask (also in wooden barrel) on demand. ◆

Back Bone (ABV 3.7%) BITTER
Cloud Piercer (ABV 4.7%) BITTER
Dream Machine (ABV 5.2%) BITTER

Bricknell

Bricknell Avenue, Hull, HU5 4ET ☎ 07729 722953
⊕ bricknellbrewery.co.uk

Bricknell's range comprises 16 bottle-conditioned, vegan-friendly ales, two of which are seasonal. Some hops are grown on-site, some sourced locally. Everything is hands-on, from brewing, to hand-bottling and labelling, to delivery. Brewing takes place twice a week, and includes many ales from 19th century recipes. The brewery sells to local pubs, bars and restaurants as well as directly to the public and to local beer festivals. ◆LIVE V

Anchor Pale Ale (ABV 4.1%) PALE
Cascade Pale (ABV 4.8%) PALE
Bosphorous 1875 Ruby Ale (ABV 5.4%) MILD
Double Anchor IPA (ABV 5.6%) IPA
Lodona 1862 (ABV 5.8%) IPA

Bridbrewer

⊟ 2A Chapel Street / 5 King Street, Bridlington, YO15 2DN
☎ (01262) 674300 ☎ 07727 107435
⊕ bridbrewerandtaproom.co.uk

⊙After two years developing his recipes as a home brewer Stuart Fisher launched his unfined beers commercially in 2020 from his brewpub located in central Bridlington. A 50-litre Braumeister kit is used. Most beers are vegan-friendly and include golden IPAs, bitters and various stouts and porters; all available to drink in or takeaway from the bar. ‼️⊟◆LIVE V

Bridlington

⊟ 10 Prospect Street, Bridlington, YO15 2AL
☎ (01262) 674418

The brewery, founded in 2014 in the grounds of the Telegraph Inn, Bridlington, later moved to the rear of the Pack Horse, supplying the pub. It relocated again in 2019 to the rear of the Moon Tap pub. The beers regularly change and are available in the Moon Tap and Pack Horse.

Crafty Little

Carr House Farm, Ottringham, HU12 0AL ☎ 07774 189916

Office: 109 Alfred Gelder Street, Hull, HU1 1EP
⊕ thecraftylittlebrewery.co.uk

⊙This family-run business, based in East Yorkshire, was founded in 2017. After a short hiatus, the Crafty Little Brewery has now returned to brewing having found a suitable new home in the East Yorkshire village of Ottringham.

Apex Predator (ABV 3.8%) GOLD
ChamAleon (ABV 4%) BITTER
A6 D3 (ABV 4.5%) GOLD
Red Tale (ABV 4.5%) MILD
Silk Stout (ABV 4.5%) STOUT
Black Ryeno (ABV 4.6%) SPECIALITY
Perky Porter (ABV 4.8%) PORTER
Wolf Bite APA (ABV 4.8%) PALE

Snake Charmer (ABV 5.5%) SPECIALITY

Great Newsome SIBA

Great Newsome Farm, South Frodingham, Winestead, HU12 0NR
☎ (01964) 612201 ⊕ greatnewsomebrewery.co.uk

⊙Nestled in the Holderness countryside, Great Newsome began brewing in 2007 in renovated farm buildings. A range of beers is now brewed using barley from the farm and brewing can be seen from a viewing area. Expansion into other farm buildings in 2018, and again in 2019, increased brewing capacity to 20-barrels. Contract brewing is carried out on behalf of other local breweries. Beer is distributed throughout the UK and overseas. ‼️⊟◆

Sleck Dust (ABV 3.8%) BLOND
Pricky Back Otchan (ABV 4.2%) BITTER
Frothingham Best (ABV 4.3%) BITTER
Holderness Dark (ABV 4.3%) MILD
Jem's Stout (ABV 4.3%) STOUT
Liquorice Lads Stout (ABV 4.3%) SPECIALITY

Half Moon

Forge House, Main Street, Ellerton, York, YO42 4PB
☎ (01757) 288977 ☎ 07741 400508
⊕ halfmoonbrewery.co.uk

Established in 2013 by Tony and Jackie Rogers, the brewery is situated in a former blacksmith's forge with a capacity of 5.5-barrels. Brewing takes place two-three times a week. ◆LIVE ⚒

Dark Masquerade (ABV 3.6%) MILD
Old Forge Bitter (ABV 3.8%) BITTER
F'Hops Sake (ABV 3.9%) BITTER

Old Mill SIBA

Mill Street, Snaith, DN14 9HU
☎ (01405) 861813 ⊕ oldmillbrewery.co.uk

⊙Opened in 1983 in a 200-year-old former malt kiln and corn mill, the brew-length is 60 barrels. The brewery is building a tied estate, now standing at 16 houses. Beers can be found nationwide through wholesalers and around 80 free trade outlets are supplied direct. The RT Brew Co range is produced for HB Clark (qv). ‼️◆

Bullion IPA (ABV 3.7%) GOLD
Jack's Batch 34 (ABV 3.8%) BITTER
Traditional Bitter (ABV 3.8%) BITTER
La Bolsa Coffee Porter (ABV 4.5%) SPECIALITY

Pumphouse

Unit 10D, Twydale Business Park, Skerne Road, Driffield, YO25 6JX ☎ 07811 180195
✉ david@pumphousebrewing.co.uk

Launched in 2019, Pumphouse Brewing are a craft brewery producing small batch, one-off beers available in keg and bottle. The constantly-changing range is unfined and unfiltered. ⚒

Raven Hill

Raven Hill Farm, Driffield, YO25 4EG ☎ 07979 674573
⊕ ravenhillbrewery.com

Raven Hill Brewery started trading in 2018. Based on a Yorkshire farm near Kilham, it brews five regular beers of varied styles and produces regular seasonal beers in small batch quantities. ◆

Summit (ABV 3.6%) PALE

Chalk Stream (ABV 4%) GOLD
Brook (ABV 4.3%) GOLD
Ridge Way (ABV 5.5%) STOUT
Elevation (ABV 6.2%)

Spotlight

The Goddards, Goole Road, Goole, West Cowick, DN14 9DJ ☎ 07713 477069 ⊕ spotlightbrewing.co.uk

☺Spotlight is a social enterprise that is passionate about good beer. All beers are brewed, packaged and delivered by people with learning disabilities. The beer names reference medical conditions. Brewing is currently suspended. ‼️🍺♦

Vittles

Hull Trinity Market, Trinity House Lane, Hull, HU1 2JH ☎ 07598 098632 ⊕ vittlesandcompany.co.uk

Vittles & Co started brewing in 2018 at the Trinity Market, Hull. The site can produce just 50 litres at a time. The brewery name comes from the fact that the owner loves to pair beer and food, hence the old name for food, vittles. 🍺

Woolybutt Brew Shed

31 Alexandra Road, Hull, HU5 2NS ☎ 07966 511242
✉ woolybuttbrewshed@hotmail.com

☺Woolybutt Brew Shed is a two-barrel brewery. Rob Sutherland moved to commercial brewing after years of homebrewing experience.

English Pale Ale (ABV 4.4%)

Yorkshire Brewhouse

Matrich House, Goulton Street, Hull, HU3 4DD
☎ (01482) 755199 ⊕ yorkshirebrewhouse.com

☺Founded in 2017 by friends Jon Constable and Simon Cooke as a weekend family venture. The brewery started with a 200-litre capacity and has now expanded to 2,500 litre per batch. It supplies cask, bag in box and bottle-conditioned ale to East Yorkshire outlets, and online. Most of the beers are given names that mirror Yorkshire dialect or have a local connection. **LIVE**

1904 (ABV 3.8%) BITTER
Reet (ABV 3.8%) BITTER
EYPA (ABV 3.9%) PALE
Tenfoot (ABV 3.9%)
Ey Up (ABV 4%) BITTER
Faithful (ABV 4.5%) STOUT
Flippin Eck (ABV 4.6%) OLD
Red Robin (ABV 4.6%) STOUT
Well Chuffed (ABV 4.9%) PALE

Three B's Micropub, Bridlington (Photo: Stewart Campbell)

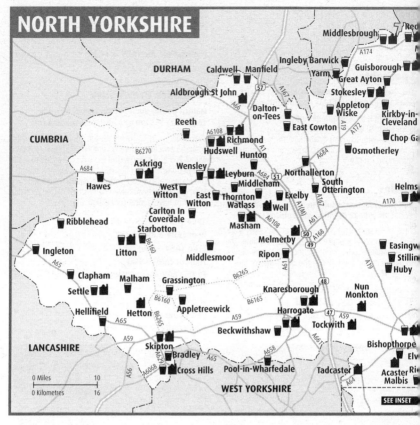

NORTH YORKSHIRE

Appleton Wiske

Lord Nelson

High Street, DL6 2AD
☎ (01609) 881351 ⊕ lordnelsoninn.org.uk
Theakston Best Bitter; 1 changing beer (sourced nationally) Ⓗ

A true local's pub facing the beautiful village green in the centre of the picturesque award-winning village of Appleton Wiske near Northallerton. The pub is divided into two rooms, one set out for meals and the other a welcoming bar for drinkers. Takeout food is available Friday and Saturday evening, with a sit-in Sunday lunch. Two beers are always on – a traditional house bitter and a rotating local lighter beer. Themed dining is available on Thursdays during the year, check the website for details. ⊛◑P✿

Appletreewick

Craven Arms Ⓛ

BD23 6DA
☎ (01756) 720270 ⊕ craven-cruckbarn.co.uk
Dark Horse Craven Bitter, Hetton Pale Ale, Night Jar; Theakston Old Peculier; Wharfedale Wharfedale Blonde; 2 changing beers (sourced regionally) Ⓗ

Dating from 1548, this multi-roomed free house has stone-flagged floors, oak beams and gas lighting. The bar features an original Yorkshire range while the cosy taproom has an open fire and ring the bull. A snug behind the bar leads to the cruck barn, built in the 21st century using ancient techniques. This can be hired for functions and hosts occasional events including music

and a beer festival in October. Two additional guest beers are added in summer. Accommodation is in three shepherd's huts. Payment is by card only.
Q⊛⊛⇔◑⚒&♣⊛P☐(74A)✿♥♪

Askrigg

Crown Inn Ⓛ ✅

Main Street, DL8 3HQ
☎ (01969) 650387 ⊕ crowninnaskrigg.co.uk
Theakston Best Bitter; Wensleydale Semer Water; 2 changing beers (sourced locally; often Theakston, Wensleydale) Ⓗ

A three-roomed family-run pub, at the top of the main street of the village, which attracts a good mix of locals and visitors, and is particularly popular for its bar meals sourced from local suppliers. The interior has been partly opened out but retains much of its traditional character, with an impressive range in the cosy snug, and open fires to warm cold walkers seeking shelter from the fells. Check the website for winter opening hours.
⊛◑⚒♣⊛P☐✿♥

King's Arms Ⓛ

Main Street, DL8 3HQ
☎ (01969) 650113 ⊕ kingsarmsaskrigg.com
Black Sheep Best Bitter; Theakston Best Bitter; 3 changing beers (sourced locally; often Yorkshire Dales) Ⓗ

A historic Grade II-listed Dales free house of great character which starred as the Drover's Arms in the original All Creatures Great and Small. A huge open fireplace and a painting of the Askrigg Friendly Society

Unspoilt, family-run rural gem, resting among a hamlet of cottages, run by an accomplished fine artist who is also celebrating 43 years of continuous service to the licensed trade. It comprises the small Big Bar and an even smaller Small Bar, which, uniquely, sandwich a sweet shop. Pleasant outdoor drinking facilities overlook the Murk Esk. Sandwiches, pies, beer cake and traditional sweets are always available. Hours change during winter. A must visit pub! Q✠✿♿&♣♠🐾

Beckwithshaw

Smiths Arms 🔆 ✅
Church Row, HG3 1QW
☎ (01423) 504871
Black Sheep Best Bitter; Greene King IPA; Timothy Taylor Landlord; 2 changing beers (often Daleside, Rooster's, Saltaire) Ⓗ
A Chef & Brewer food-led venue in an 18th-century building that, as the name suggests, was formerly a blacksmith's forge. Set in a quiet hamlet to the south-west of Harrogate, the pub comprises an L-shaped bar area and a separate restaurant. An excellent menu with many seasonal dishes is offered throughout the day in both the restaurant and bar. The five handpumps serve three permanent beers and two changing ales, sourced locally. Boxed ciders are also available, usually Lilley's. Card payments only. ✠✿◑&P♿♥

Bishopthorpe

Bishopthorpe Sports & Social Club 🔆
12 Main Street, YO23 2RB
☎ (01904) 707185 ⊕ bishopthorpeclub.co.uk
Black Sheep Best Bitter; 2 changing beers (sourced regionally) Ⓗ
Local CAMRA Club of the Year 2023, this is a popular destination in the village. Close to the river, you can arrive by boat and enjoy Black Sheep Bitter and two rotating guests, usually LocAles. The annual St Patrick's beer festival encourages non-members to enjoy an extended range of real ales and ciders and to raise money for the support of local community sports teams. ✠&♣P♿♥🎵

Marcia Inn 🔆 ✅
29 Main Street, YO23 2RA
☎ (01904) 706185 ⊕ marciainnbishopthorpe.co.uk
Kirkstall Leeds Pale; Timothy Taylor Landlord; 2 changing beers (sourced locally; often Half Moon, Rooster's, Rudgate) Ⓗ
This popular village community local's landlord is so passionate about real ale that he has recently installed an on-site brewery the Bishy Brewhouse. Four handpumps serve mainly LocAle. There is an annual beer and cider festival in the large rear garden which also has a children's play area and covered seating. A good range of award-winning food is served in a relaxed and friendly atmosphere. Pub games, a Wednesday quiz night and support for local clubs and teams make for a relaxed and friendly atmosphere. Q✠✿◑&♣P♿(11)♥🎵

Bradley

Slaters Arms 🔆 ✅
Crag Lane, BD20 9DE (SE corner of village on back road to Kildwick)
☎ (01535) 632179
Ossett Blonde; Timothy Taylor Golden Best, Boltmaker; 1 changing beer (sourced locally) Ⓗ
Two-roomed local, half a mile from the canal. The large outdoor area has extensive views of the Aire Valley. The

add character to the stone-flagged bar. There are separate dining rooms plus a vaulted games room to the rear and a small outdoor courtyard. Three house beers are from the Yorkshire Dales brewery, a few hundred yards away. If you want to eat at busy times reserving a table is recommended. ✠✿◑▲♬(156)♿♥🎵

Beal

Jenny Wren
Main Street, DN14 0SS
☎ (01977) 328404
Ossett White Rat; Timothy Taylor Boltmaker; 1 changing beer (sourced regionally) Ⓗ
Quirky but traditional pub serving Timothy Taylor Boltmaker, Ossett White Rat and up to two guest ales. The pub has been refurbished to a high standard, but an interesting front bar room has been preserved in original condition for over 50 years. Although it has a central serving area, the pub is split into various drinking and dining areas, with three rooms of varying size, from a small snug to a large main bar, and there are real open fires. There is level access to the building. Q◑P♬(476)🎵

Beck Hole

Birch Hall Inn ★ 🔆
YO22 5LE (approx 1 mile N of Goathland)
☎ (01947) 896245 ⊕ beckhole.info
Black Sheep Best Bitter; 2 changing beers (sourced regionally) Ⓗ

main lounge, with horse brasses and wooden beams, has an open fireplace and real fire. The separate cosy back room is adorned with sporting photos, mainly of the local cricket teams which are based at the pub. Well-behaved children are permitted during the day or if eating. A quiz is on the last Wednesday of the month. A Timothy Taylor Champion Club member.
රු෯◑♣Ⴒ戸(71,78A) ⍟↺

Burn

Wheatsheaf ℒ
Main Road, YO8 8LJ
☎ (01757) 270614 ● wheatsheafburn.co.uk
5 changing beers (often Ossett, Timothy Taylor) ⊞
Traditional country pub serving a varied range of guest beers, mainly from Yorkshire breweries, and popular for its excellent, reasonably-priced food. There is a collection of artefacts from bygone days and memorabilia of the 578 and 431 Squadrons stationed at Burn in World War II. The Wheatsheaf stages regular beer festivals, quiz nights, live music, barbecues and many other activities. Dogs are welcome. Q⛵෯◑ᵹ♣Ⴒ戸(476,405)⍟🐾♪

Caldwell

Brownlow Arms
DL11 7QH
☎ (01325) 718471 ● brownlowarms.co.uk
Timothy Taylor Landlord; 2 changing beers (sourced nationally) ⊞
The Brownlow Arms, set in the quiet village of Caldwell, could be described as the perfect country inn. It boasts a fine dining restaurant as well as two cosy bars with open log fires where you are guaranteed to find some welcoming locals. Serving three cask ales which always include Timothy Taylor Landlord alongside an ever-changing selection, often from the Yorkshire Dales, requests are always welcome! They serve a huge choice of home-cooked food to accompany your ale.
Q⛵෯◑ᵹⴅ🐾🛜

Carlton In Coverdale

Foresters Arms ℒ
DL8 4BB
☎ (01969) 640272 ● forestersarmscoverdale.com
Theakston Best Bitter; Wensleydale Gamekeeper; 3 changing beers (sourced locally; often Black Sheep, Timothy Taylor) ⊞
Worth seeking out, this 250-year-old free house is named after the Foresters friendly society, a mutual aid body for local people in this picturesque area. It is on the Dales cycle route and convenient for the Forbidden Corner fantasy maze (advanced booking essential). In community ownership since 2011, the pub's low-beamed ceilings and open fire contribute to its character, with wooden settles fashioned from pews from the former village church. Q⛵ﲾ◑ᵹ♣Ⴒ🐾🛜♪

Chop Gate

Buck Inn
TS9 7JL (on the B1257, between Stokesley and Helmsley)
☎ (01642) 778334 ● the-buck-inn.co.uk
3 changing beers (sourced regionally) ⊞
Set amid a walkers' paradise, and close to the route of Wainwright's Coast-to-Coast walk, this picturesque family-run village pub offers a truly Yorkshire pub with a Teutonic twist. Three handpulls and seven especially imported draught lagers, brewed under the 500-year-old German Purity Laws, are served, together with real

home-made food, again half Yorkshire/half German. There are six en-suite bedrooms, some designated dog-friendly, while free camping is offered to those campers who also choose to dine here. Opening hours vary in winter. Q⛵ﲾﲾ◑Ⴒ戸(M4)⍟🛜

Clapham

Lake House ℒ
Church Avenue, LA2 8EQ
☎ (015242) 51144
House beer (by Elland); 1 changing beer (often Elland, Settle, Wishbone) ⊞
In the heart of a major tourist village, the old manor house, dating back to circa 1620, houses a bunkhouse and a café and bar with bare floorboards, bench seats and some books. A huge fireplace (dated 1701) holds a wood-burning stove. Do not overlook the bottled beers and ciders. The café and the bar are in separate but connected rooms. It is next to the National Park car park. ﲾﲾ◑ⴅ♣Ⴒ(581)⍟🛜♪

REAL ALE BREWERIES

3 Non Beards 🍺 ✦	York
Ainsty ✦	Acaster Malbis
Another Beer ✦	Elvington
Black Sheep ✦	Masham
Brass Castle	Malton
Brew York ✦	York
Captain Cook	Stokesley
Copper Dragon	Skipton
Craven ✦	Cross Hills
Crooked ✦	Church Fenton
Cropton	Cropton
Daleside	Harrogate
Dark Horse	Hetton
Great British Breworks	Kirkbymoorside
Guisborough ✦	Guisborough
Hambleton	Melmerby
Harrogate ✦	Harrogate
Helmsley ✦	Helmsley
Ice Cream Factory	York
Jolly Sailor 🍺 ✦	Selby
Lady Luck ✦	Whitby
LAMB	Litton
Little Black Dog	Carlton
Live	Hudswell (brewing suspended)
Malton	Malton
Mithril	Aldbrough St John
North Riding (Brewery)	Snainton
North Riding (Brewpub) 🍺	Scarborough
Pennine	Well
Play ✦	Middlesbrough
Redscar 🍺	Redcar
Richmond ✦	Richmond
Rooster's ✦	Harrogate
Rudgate	York: Tockwith
Samuel Smith	Tadcaster
Scarborough	Scarborough
Selby Middlebrough	Selby
Settle	Settle
Theakston ✦	Masham
Turning Point ✦	Knaresborough
Twisted Wheel	Cropton
Wensleydale ✦	Leyburn
Whitby ✦	Whitby
Wold Top	Wold Newton
Yorkshire Dales ✦	Askrigg
Yorkshire Heart	Nun Monkton

Cloughton

Bryherstones Country Inn

Newlands Road, YO13 0AR (½ mile up Newlands Rd off A171 at Cloughton)
☎ (01723) 870744 ⊕ bryherstonescountryinn.co.uk
Timothy Taylor Landlord; 1 changing beer (sourced regionally) ⓗ
A stone-built pub nestling between the North York Moors and the coast, just outside the village of Cloughton. Back in the hands of the Shipley family since 2009, it has been restored to its former glory. Its many rooms, full of interesting features and ornaments, include a separate games room. As well as being a designated Timothy Taylor Champion Club establishment they offer an extensive locally sourced food menu (booking is advised). Children and dogs are welcome; there is a play area in the spacious beer garden.
Q❀⏰⏸️🅰️♣️🅿️🚃(115) 🐾🛜

Hayburn Wyke Hotel Ⓛ

Newlands Road, YO13 0AU (off the Ravenscar road, 1½ miles N of jct with the A171)
☎ (01723) 870202 ⊕ hayburnwykeinn.co.uk
Black Sheep Special Ale; Theakston Old Peculier; 2 changing beers (sourced regionally; often Wold Top) ⓗ
An 18th-century coaching inn in woodland next to the disused Scarborough to Whitby railway, and only minutes away from the Cleveland Way coastal path and rocky beach. It is popular with cyclists and walkers. Home-made food is served lunchtimes and evenings (no food Mon eve), with the Sunday carvery a local favourite. En-suite accommodation is available. Outside is a well-provisioned children's play space and a sizeable heated smoking area. It operates reduced hours in winter.
Q❀⏰⏸️🅰️♣️🅿️🚃(115) 🐾🛜🎵

Cross Hills

Craven Brew Co Tap Room Ⓛ

Midland Mills, Station Road, BD20 7DT (in industrial estate on right, over railway bridge from Cross Hills)
☎ (01535) 637451 ⊕ cravenbrew.co.uk
Craven Session Pale Ale, Black Angus Porter; 4 changing beers (sourced locally; often Craven, Kirkstall) ⓗ
This is the tap room in the industrial unit that houses Craven Brew Co. The emphasis in the bar is on good company, friendly chatter and the appreciation of good beer. The main area features patio doors, while there is a cosy snug behind the bar and an upstairs room with bar billiards. In fine weather customers spill out into the yard outside. Five reasonably-priced ales are available, with at least four supplied by Craven Brew Co, one of which is usually dark. It hosts occasional music evenings and events. Q❀⏰⏸️🅿️🚃(66)🐾🛜

Gallagher's Ale House Ⓛ

1-3 East Keltus, BD20 8TD (in village centre)
☎ 07375 789498
5 changing beers (sourced nationally) ⓗ
This popular micropub is located in what used to be Gallagher's bookmakers shop. The five changing ales usually include a dark beer, a pale bitter and a strong or speciality beer. The cellar can be viewed through a window to the left of the bar. No electronic music or TV disturbs the conversation. Parking is available adjacent to the Co-op store round the corner.
Q♣️🅿️🚃(M4,66) 🐾🛜🎵

Dalton-on-Tees

Chequers Inn ⏹️

The Green, DL2 2NT
☎ (01325) 721213 ⊕ thechequersinndalton.co.uk
Bombardier; Ringwood Boondoggle; 1 changing beer (sourced nationally) ⓗ
Traditional inn dating back to the 1840s, comprising a bar, lounge and restaurant, with a warm welcome guaranteed. With friendly and welcoming staff, it combines the atmosphere of a traditional pub with a contemporary restaurant. Up to three beers are Marston's mainstays, but well kept. Food is available every day, with traditional Sunday lunches served. Overnight accommodation comprises five rooms overlooking the green and its pump. The pub is handy for Croft Circuit.
Q❀⏰⏸️🏨⏸️♣️🅿️🚃(X27) 🐾🛜

Danby

Duke of Wellington Ⓛ

West Lane, YO21 2LY (300yds N of railway station)
☎ (01287) 660351 ⊕ dukeofwellingtondanby.co.uk
Copper Dragon Scotts 1816; Daleside Bitter; 1 changing beer (sourced regionally) ⓗ
This 18th-century inn is set in idyllic countryside, close to the Moors National Park Centre and the local traditional baker's shop. The inn was used as a recruiting post during the Napoleonic Wars. A cast-iron plaque of the first Duke of Wellington, unearthed during restorations, hangs above the fireplace. All beers are from Yorkshire. At lunchtime, sandwiches can be brought into the pub. During the evening, the kitchen offers traditional British home-cooked meals at their very best, using local produce. Q❀⏰⏸️🏨≈♣️🅿️🚃🐾

Drax

Drax Sports & Social Club Ⓛ

Main Road, YO8 8PJ
☎ (01757) 618041 ⊕ draxsandsclub.co.uk
2 changing beers (sourced regionally) ⓗ
Nestled in the shadow of the giant Drax power station this club is full of energy and enthusiasm. A lively bar area is supplemented by a huge function room which is often the venue for beer festivals and similar events. The club takes a little effort to get to but there are some buses from nearby Selby. A well-deserved local CAMRA Club of the Year in both 2018 and 2020. ❀🅰️♣️🅿️

Easingwold

George Hotel Ⓛ

Market Place, YO61 3AD
☎ (01347) 821698 ⊕ the-george-hotel.co.uk
Black Sheep Best Bitter; 7 changing beers (sourced regionally) ⓗ
An old coaching inn which had a Georgian make over and a much more recent spruce-up. With eight beer lines and a focus on local ales this is not one to miss if in the Easingwold area. The coming soon board only adds to the temptation. A recently opened-up side room adds to the bay winow seats from which it is a joy to watch the activity in the bustling market square. Q❀⏰🏨⏸️♣️🅿️🚃🛜

East Cowton

Beeswing ⏹️

Main Street, DL7 0BD
☎ (01325) 378349 ⊕ thebeeswing.weebly.com
3 changing beers (sourced nationally) ⓗ

Traditional country village pub with two bars, a pool room and a highly rated restaurant. Named after a locally bred champion racehorse, there are numerous racing references. Three ever-changing beers come from breweries countrywide and one craft ale is served. Real fires create a relaxing atmosphere. The staff are welcoming and the pub caters to the local community with regular music and quizzes. Q ☜ ⌖ ◑ ◖ ◐ ♣ P ☻ ☂ ≋

East Witton

Cover Bridge Inn L

DL8 4SQ (½ mile N of village on A6108 to Middleham)
☎ (01969) 623250 ⊕ thecoverbridgeinn.co.uk
Black Sheep Best Bitter; Theakston Old Peculier; Timothy Taylor Landlord; 5 changing beers (sourced regionally; often Rudgate, Wensleydale) ⊞
A splendidly traditional Dales inn. The River Cover runs along the foot of the attractive garden and play area, near its confluence with the River Ure. Fathom out the door latch and you will be able to enjoy the warm welcome in the unspoiled public bar, or sit in the tiny lounge. There is a choice of local beers and guests, and the ham and eggs option on the food menu has a strong following. Middleham Castle and Jervaulx Abbey are both within a mile. Q ☜ ⌖ ⇌ ◑ ◖ Å ♣ P ☷ (159) ☻ ☂ ♫

Egton Bridge

Horseshoe Hotel

YO21 1XE
☎ (01947) 895245 ⊕ thehorseshoehotel.co.uk
Theakston Best Bitter; 3 changing beers (sourced regionally) ⊞
Secluded unspoilt 18th-century gem nestled in a horseshoe-shaped hollow. Located in beautiful countryside, it can be accessed by road, from the railway station or by walking over the stepping stones across the River Esk. Old-fashioned settles and a large fire furnish the bar, while picnic tables make outdoor drinking a pleasure. Four handpumps feature some interesting beers. A farm shop has recently been added, while an outdoor bar, with two extra handpulls, opens during summer. Accommodation is in six en-suite bedrooms. Q ☜ ⌖ ⇌ ◑ ◖ ≈ (Egton) ♣ P ☷ (95) ☻ ☂

Exelby

Exelby Green Dragon L

High Row, DL8 2HA
☎ (01677) 427715 ⊕ exelbygreendragon.co.uk
Black Sheep Best Bitter; Timothy Taylor Landlord; 2 changing beers (sourced regionally; often Ossett, Rudgate, Wensleydale) ⊞
The knocked-through interior of this community-owned pub provides a number of separate areas, and features two wood-burning stoves. A spacious separate restaurant opens on to the decked terraced beer garden. The slightly altered new name distinguishes the pub from the Green Dragon in nearby Bedale. Numerous village activities include the book club, gardening club, a weekly coffee morning and the monthly women's group known as the Dragons. A popular beer and cider festival is held on the August bank holiday weekend. Opening times vary according to season. ☜ ⌖ ⇌ ◑ ◖ Å ♣ P ☻ ☂ ≋

Filey

Cobblers Arms

2 Union Street, YO14 9DZ
☎ (01723) 512511

Wainwright; **4 changing beers (sourced regionally; often Great Newsome, Isaac Poad)** ⊞
A micropub in the centre of Filey that started out as a private residence before becoming a cobblers shop, from which the pub takes its name. The front bar area encourages conversation and there is a second smaller snug to the rear which is available for meetings free of charge. The bar offers four changing guest ales and real cider. There is a regular quiz on a Tuesday night and occasional live music. Dogs and families are welcome. Q ☜ ⌖ ◖ ◑ ▮ ☷ (12,13) ☻ ☂ ≋ ♫

Star Inn ✓

23 Mitford Street, YO14 9DX
☎ (01723) 512031 ⊕ thestarfiley.co.uk
Black Sheep Special Ale; Bradfield Farmers Blonde; Theakston Best Bitter; 3 changing beers (sourced nationally) ⊞
Located just off Filey town centre, the Star has a large main room incorporating a pool table to the left-hand side, and a separate restaurant/function room to the rear. Three regular beers and three rotating guests are offered. Freshly cooked meals are served lunchtimes and evenings (except Mon). Live entertainment features occasionally, and pub teams participate in a local pool league. Smokers are catered for outside at both the front and rear. ☜ ⌖ ◑ ◖ ≈ ♣ ☷ (12,13) ☂ ♫

Grassington

Foresters Arms L ✓

20 Main Street, BD23 5AA
☎ (01756) 752349 ⊕ forestersarmsgrassington.co.uk
Black Sheep Best Bitter, Riggwelter; Tetley Tetley Bitter; Timothy Taylor Landlord; 2 changing beers (sourced locally; often Timothy Taylor, Wensleydale) ⊞
Located just off the cobbled town square, the Foresters is a lively inn, popular with locals and visitors alike, which has been run by the same family for decades. The main bar and pool/TV area are to the left and further seating to the right leads to a separate dining room. Accommodation is available in seven en-suite rooms and fishing permits for the local River Wharfe can be bought at the pub. A quiz is held on Mondays. Secure cycle storage is available for staying guests. ☜ ⌖ ⇌ ◑ ◖ ♣ ☷ (72,72B) ☻ ☂ ひ ♫

Great Ayton

Royal Oak Hotel L ✓

123 High Street, TS9 6BW (in centre of village opp High Green)
☎ (01642) 722361 ⊕ royaloakgreatayton.co.uk
Theakston Old Peculier; Timothy Taylor Landlord; Wainwright; 1 changing beer (sourced regionally) ⊞
A warm welcome is assured at this extensive family-run, 18th-century Grade II-listed building and former coaching house, which sits at the heart of the community and village life. Always busy, the pub is as equally famed for its four beers as for its food, with breakfast, lunch and dinner served, and various offers promoted throughout the week. A separate bar, a function room, an enclosed courtyard and four en-suite bedrooms are also available. Q ☜ ⌖ ◑ ◖ ☷ (28,81)

Tannery

The Arcade, High Street, TS9 6BW (continue for 50yds through the archway next to baker's shop)
☎ (01642) 909030 ⊕ thetanneryayton.co.uk
4 changing beers (sourced regionally) ⊞

Set back from the High Street within a courtyard, this former hairdresser's has been tastefully refurbished and is now the village's micropub. Opened in 2018 by experienced licensees, it has always attracted a discerning clientele. Four rotating guest beers generally include a stout, while craft ales and an extensive gin menu are also served by knowledgeable staff. Third-pint bats are available. Free cheese and biscuit evenings are hosted, with any donations going to charity. Q&⌑(28,81) ✿

Grosmont

Crossing Club
Co-operative Building, Front Street, YO22 5QE (opp NYMR car park; ring front door bell for entry)
☎ 07766 197744
4 changing beers (sourced regionally) Ⓗ

Set amid beautiful scenery in the Esk Valley, this former local CAMRA Club of the Year is located opposite the NYMR/Esk Valley railway stations in what was the village Co-op's delivery bay. Converted by dedicated villagers 25 years ago, a warm welcome always awaits CAMRA members. Over 1,600 different beers have been served during the Club's history. Railway enthusiasts will note both the steam and diesel memorabilia adorning the walls. It is open summer evenings; hours may vary during winter. Stairs need to be negotiated both to the bar and to the toilets. Q ⇌ ♣ ⛿ ✿

Guisborough

Monk ⒧
27 Church Street, TS14 6HG (at E end of Westgate)
☎ (01287) 205058
Timothy Taylor Landlord; 3 changing beers (sourced regionally) Ⓗ

This contemporary venue is an upmarket addition to the town's social life and attracts a discerning clientele. It sits opposite Gisborough Priory, which was razed to the ground by King Henry VIII in 1540. Legend has it that a 12th-century Black Monk made use of a tunnel, discovered during recent renovations, for his nefarious night-time activities. The tunnel's access steps are on view. Four beers, with several from the local brewery, are served. Better-value tasting paddles are available.
&⌑(5,X93) ✿ 🛜 ♫

Harrogate

Blues Café Bar ⒧
4 Montpellier Parade, HG1 2TJ
☎ (01423) 566881 ⊕ bluesbar.co.uk
4 changing beers (often Isaac Poad, Ossett, Rooster's) Ⓗ

A small single-room café bar, modelled on an Amsterdam café bar, which has been going for over 30 years. Located in the town centre, it overlooks the lovely Montpellier Gardens. Noted for live music seven days a week, with three sessions on a Sunday, it is popular with music lovers and can get busy. Upstairs is the Gin Bar and Yorkshire Tapas restaurant, a room with seating in large booths where customers can watch the band on a TV screen while dining or drinking. Four handpumps dispense beers mostly from local breweries, often including a dark beer. ⓓ⇌⛿🛜↻♫

Devonshire Tap House ⒧
10 Devonshire Place, HG1 4AA
☎ (01423) 568702
Timothy Taylor Boltmaker; 6 changing beers (often Ilkley, Kirkstall, Turning Point) Ⓗ

A cosy old pub, rescued, restored and renovated in 2014, then refurbished and reopened again by new independent operators in 2019. It retains its original semi-circular counter and stained-glass canopy, and has wood flooring throughout and a mix of wooden benches, tables and chairs. Four handpumps on each side of the bar dispense a largely changing selection of beers from Yorkshire and northern breweries, also sometimes including a cask cider. There are 12 keg lines and a beer fridge. The food offering is pizzas, including gluten-free and vegan options. ☕✿ⓓ⇌⛿✿🛜

Disappearing Chin
38 Beulah Street, HG1 1QH (opp bus station)
☎ 07539 942344
3 changing beers Ⓗ

Compact bar in a shop unit opposite the bus station accessible from both Station Parade and Beulah Street. A long, narrow bar with a cool, botanical vibe, there are plenty of bar stools, and a large sofa at one end. In the warmer months, café-style tables and chairs are placed outside on pedestrianised Beulah Street. Three handpumps serve changing cask ales, always including a dark beer, there are eight craft keg fonts, and a large fridge at the front of the bar has a selection of cans and bottles. Card payments only. ☕&⇌⛿✿🛜♫

Harrogate Tap 🍺 ⒧
Station Parade, HG1 1TE
☎ (01423) 501644 ⊕ harrogatetap.co.uk
11 changing beers (often Brew York, Harrogate, Rooster's) Ⓗ

Overlooking Harrogate station, this is an impressive transformation of a neglected railway building of similar style to the Tapped Brew Company's bars at York and Sheffield stations. Comprising a long bar room and a separate snug, the décor features dark wood panelling, a tiled floor and tasteful Victorian-style fittings. A diverse range of cask ales is available on two banks of six handpumps, always including a gluten-free beer. The ales are complemented by boxed ciders such as Broadoak or Pulp, as well as craft kegs and bottled world beers. Local CAMRA Pub of the Year 2023. ☕&⇌⛿✿

Little Ale House
7 Cheltenham Crescent, HG1 1DH
⊕ alehouseharrogate.co.uk
5 changing beers Ⓗ

Harrogate's first micropub, comprising one main room with the counter at the back, a downstairs cellar room, and front and rear outside seating. As with many micropubs, the beers are kept cool in a glass cabinet to one side. Five handpumps dispense cask ales, always including a dark, and there are also boxed ciders from a range of producers, occasionally including a real cider such as Thornborough. KeyKeg beer, whiskies and small-batch gins are also available. The yard to the rear has bench seating, with service from a window in summer. Card payments only. Q✿⇌⛿✿

Major Tom's Social ⒧
The Ginnel, HG1 2RB
☎ (01423) 566984 ⊕ majortomssocial.co.uk
Turning Point Wavelength; 3 changing beers (often Harrogate, North, Rooster's) Ⓗ

Café bar housed in a former antiques emporium above a vintage shop in a busy area of Harrogate town centre, providing real ale, craft keg, pizza, music and art. Simply furnished, with wooden tables and chairs, the décor is in a mix of styles to suit its eclectic customers, and includes artwork for sale. Four handpumps dispense a variety of ales, usually from a range of smaller breweries, often including the local Rooster's and Turning Point, and a real cider such as Dudda's Tun is usually available. Local CAMRA Cider Pub of the Year 2023. Card payments preferred. ⮞◑≈●🅿🐾🛜♪

Oatlands 🅛

1 Coronation Grove, HG2 8BY
☎ (01423) 871534 ⊕ theoatlands.co.uk
Kirkstall Leeds Pale; Rooster's Yankee; Tetley Tetley Bitter 🅗

Social club in a relatively dry area a little over a mile south of Harrogate town centre serving three cask ales, two of which are sourced from local breweries, including nearby Rooster's. The club, which was established in 1899, comprises two large rooms; to the right-hand side is the main bar with plenty of comfortable seating, a pool table and dartboard, and to the left is a concert room where entertainment events and parties are held. Local CAMRA Club of the Year 2023.
⮞✿✿≈(Hornbeam Park) ♣🅿🖥🐾🛜♪

Old Bell 🅛 ✅

6 Royal Parade, HG1 2SZ
☎ (01423) 507930
Timothy Taylor Boltmaker; 6 changing beers (sourced locally; often Ilkley, Kirkstall, Northern Monk) 🅗

A Market Town Taverns establishment, the Old Bell opened in 1999 on the site of the Blue Bell Inn which closed in 1815 and was later demolished. President Bill Clinton visited the inn during a visit to Harrogate in 2001. Later the same year the pub expanded into the former Farrah's toffee shop, where there is a collection of Farrah's memorabilia. The interior was refurbished in 2017, with new leather armchairs and updated decor. Eight handpumps serve beers from mostly local breweries, always including a dark. Cask cider from producers such as Westons is also usually available.
⮞◑≈🖥🐾🛜♪

Starling 🅛

47 Oxford Street, HG1 1PW
☎ (01423) 531310 ⊕ murmurationbars.co.uk
Timothy Taylor Boltmaker; 5 changing beers (sourced locally; often Kirkstall, Rooster's, Vocation) 🅗

A relaxed café bar with a contemporary feel, enlarged in 2022 with a tasteful extension of the ground floor. The long front-facing bar counter is constructed from reclaimed wood and holds six handpulls with a well-chosen range of mostly Yorkshire ales offering a good mix of styles and strengths, usually including a dark beer; boxed ciders, often Westons, are also available. The beers are displayed on a TV screen behind the bar and on screens upstairs, with a live feed to the website. There are two additional large rooms upstairs. Stone-baked pizzas are a favourite here. Card payments preferred.
⮞✿◑≈🖥🐾🛜♪

Tap on Tower Street 🅛 ✅

Tower Street, HG1 1HS
☎ (01423) 565600 ⊕ thetapontowerstreet.co.uk
Ilkley Mary Jane; 6 changing beers (often Rooster's, Timothy Taylor) 🅗

Street corner pub close to West Park Stray which was completely refurbished in modern style by new operators in 2017, although the three-room layout of the original pub was retained. Food is available all day, mainly in the form of hot and cold snacks rather than formal cooked meals. Takeaway bottles and cans are available from fridges in the public bar, and the rear room has a selection of over 300 board games. There are four handpumps in each of the front bars serving a good mix of Yorkshire ales; one pump is devoted to cider, often Old Rosie. ⮞✿◑≈🖥🐾🛜

Winter Gardens 🅛 ✅

4 Royal Baths, HG1 2WH
☎ (01423) 877010
Ruddles Best Bitter; Daleside Blonde; Sharp's Doom Bar; Greene King Abbot; Theakston Old Peculier; 5 changing beers 🅗

Tasteful conversion of the main hall of the vast Victorian Royal Baths complex retaining many original features, with Harrogate Turkish Baths next door. On entering from the Parliament Street entrance, there is a lounge area with stone-arched side alcoves. A sweeping bifurcated stone staircase carries you down to the spacious high-ceilinged bar area below. The pub serves the usual Wetherspoon core range of beers, plus locally sourced guests, dispensed across three sets of handpumps. Boxed ciders are available, usually Westons or Gwynt y Ddraig. Step-free access is from the lower entrance, in The Ginnel. ⮞✿◑♿🖥🐾🛜

Hawes

Board Inn 🅛 ✅

Market Place, DL8 3RD
☎ (01969) 667223 ⊕ theboardinn.co.uk
Black Sheep Best Bitter; Theakston Best Bitter; Timothy Taylor Landlord; 1 changing beer (sourced locally) 🅗

A comfortable but traditional one-bar pub located in the heart of this busy Dales centre, popular with walkers and other visitors. There is a warming coal fire in winter and an outdoor seating area at the front. Home-cooked food is served all day during the summer but not during winter afternoons. The guest beer may not be available in winter. There are five en-suite letting rooms.
⮞🛏◑♣🖥🐾🛜

White Hart Inn 🅛

Main Street, DL8 3QL (on westbound side of one-way system)
☎ (01969) 667214 ⊕ whiteharthawes.co.uk
Black Sheep Best Bitter; Theakston Old Peculier; 4 changing beers (sourced locally; often Pennine, Wensleydale, Yorkshire Dales) 🅗

Comfortable 16th-century coaching inn on the town's short one-way system. A large dining room is popular with visitors and a smaller bar features an attractive stone hearth and mock-wood panelling, which works remarkably well. Guest beers are often from the local Yorkshire Dales, Wensleydale and Pennine breweries. Food is served daily and includes beef and lamb from the family farm. ⮞🛏◑♿♣🖥🐾🛜♪

Hellifield

Black Horse Hotel 🅛

Main Road, BD23 4HT
☎ 07425 868011
3 changing beers 🅗

Large rambling village pub, a popular venue for dining and drinking. The spacious main lounge has comfy settees and coffee tables surrounded by more conventional seating. Note the collection of musical instruments. There is also a tap room, accessed off the main A65, and a small dining room suitable for meetings and family gatherings. Paved areas either side of the building offer ample outdoor seating. Three changing real ales are available (four in summer), often from local breweries. ⮞✿🛏◑♿♣🅿🖥(580)🐾🛜♪

Helmsley

Helmsley Brewing Co

18 Bridge Street, YO62 5DX
☎ (01439) 771014 ⏣ helmsleybrewingco.co.uk
Helmsley Yorkshire Legend, Striding the Riding, Howardian Gold; 4 changing beers (sourced locally; often Helmsley) Ⓗ
The brewery tap for the Helmsley Brewing Company is close to the market square in the picturesque centre of Helmsley, the only market town in the North York Moors National Park, and the perfect base for enjoying the wider area. Three regular and four changing beers from their own range are available. Brewery tours and an on-site shop complete the full beer experience. There is a large covered beer garden. 🍴🛜♪

Huby

Mended Drum Ⓛ

Tollerton Road, YO61 1HT
☎ (01347) 810264 ⏣ themendeddrum.com
Goose Eye Bitter; 4 changing beers (sourced locally; often Bone Machine, Brass Castle, Northern Monk) Ⓗ
The lively centre of this rural community, with a Terry Pratchett connection, was the local CAMRA Pub of the Year in 2019. Welcoming familes, dogs and cyclists, this large, open-plan pub is bigger than it looks. Its knowledgeable landlord serves an interesting range of changing local beers and ciders. There are two beer festivals a year and a quiz night on the second Thursday of the month. A quality menu of modern street food is served, with vegetarian, vegan and gluten-free options. 🛬🕸🌙🚼♿♣🅿🚪(40)🐾🛜♪

Hudswell

George & Dragon Ⓛ

DL11 6BL
☎ (01748) 518373 ⏣ georgeanddragonhudswell.co.uk
Rudgate Ruby Mild; Wensleydale Falconer; 5 changing beers (sourced locally) Ⓗ
At the heart of the village, this homely multi-roomed country inn was CAMRA National Pub of the Year for 2016, a runner-up in 2020, and has been Champion Pub of Yorkshire several times. A pleasant walk from Richmond (if you do not mind the 300+ steps!) brings you to the pub's large beer terrace with fantastic panoramic views over the Swale valley. Rescued by the community, it boasts its own library, shop, allotments and other community facilities as well as food and drink. Food on Mondays and Tuesdays is limited to sandwiches, with roasts on Sundays. Q🛬🕸🌙🔊♣♿♣🅿🚪(30)🐾🛜♪

Hunton

Countryman's Inn 🍷 Ⓛ

South View, DL8 1PY
☎ (01677) 450554 ⏣ countrymansinn.co.uk
3 changing beers (sourced locally; often Pennine, Wensleydale) Ⓗ
Welcoming community-owned free house which escaped closure after a lively campaign by villagers and is now thriving. Separate drinking areas offer comfortable seating around a central bar. Guest beers are usually LocAles, often including Wensleydale and Pennine beers. Coffee mornings are held on Mondays and Thursdays, and regular quiz nights contribute to local charities. Every September the village hosts the Hunton Steam Gathering. Q🛬🕸🌙🔊♣🅿🚪(155)🐾🛜♪

Ingleby Barwick

Beckfields ⊘

Beckfields Avenue, TS17 0QA (W off the A1045, along Ingleby Way, then first left along Beckfields Ave)
☎ (01642) 766263
4 changing beers (sourced nationally) Ⓗ
If your passion is for well-known and stronger best and premium beers, then this popular and uniquely named community pub will serve you well. The pub is situated at the heart of one of the six villages that make up what is reputedly Europe's largest private housing estate. Under the stewardship of a licensee with many years' service to the trade, four handpulls operate on a rotating guest basis. An extensive pub grub menu is also served. 🛬🕸🌙🔊♿♣🅿🚪(15)🐾🛜

Ingleton

Old Post Office

8 High Street, LA6 3AA
☎ (01524) 805544 ⏣ theoldpostofficebar.co.uk
House beer (by Lancaster); 2 changing beers (sourced regionally; often Lancaster) Ⓗ
The Old Post Office microbar was the village post office for almost a century and is located at the top end of the village shops. Originally licensed in 2015, it has now been converted into a quirky and cosy bar whose decor is best described as an eclectic mix of opulence and industrial. The OPO serves real cask beer, bottled ales, artisan gins, whiskey and other premium spirits. They also offer a large range of handcrafted bar snacks. A small back room may host folk evenings in future. 🕸🐾♪

Kirk Smeaton

Shoulder of Mutton

Main Street, WF8 3JY (follow signs from A1)
☎ (01977) 620348
Black Sheep Best Bitter; 1 changing beer (sourced regionally; often Bradfield, Stancill) Ⓗ
Convenient for the Went Valley and Brockadale Nature Reserve, this welcoming, traditional village pub is popular with walkers and the local community. The beer is sourced direct from the brewery and the quality is superb. It is an award-winning free house and comprises a large lounge with open fires and a cosy, dark-panelled snug. The spacious beer garden has a covered and heated shelter for smokers. There is ample parking. Quiz night is Tuesday. Q🛬🕸♣🅿🚪(409)🐾🛜

Kirkby-in-Cleveland

Black Swan

Busby Lane, TS9 7AW (800yds W of B1257) NZ539060
☎ (01642) 712512 ⏣ theblackswankirkby.co.uk
Bradfield Farmers Blonde; Sharp's Doom Bar; Timothy Taylor Landlord; Wainwright; 1 changing beer (sourced regionally) Ⓗ
Nestling at the foot of the Cleveland Hills, at the crossroads of this ancient village, this warm and cosy free house is under the stewardship of a licensee of over 25 years standing, and where a genuine welcome is always afforded from the friendly staff. It comprises a bar, an adjacent pool room, a lounge/restaurant, a conservatory and a patio seating area. Four regular beers and a guest are available. Good-value meals are served, including daily specials. 🛬🕸🌙🔊♿🅿🚪(89)🐾🛜

Knaresborough

Blind Jack's L

19 Market Place, HG5 8AL
Black Sheep Best Bitter; 5 changing beers (sourced nationally) H

An entry in the Guide for over 30 years, this is a Georgian listed building with bare-brick walls and wooden floorboards, comprising two small rooms on the ground floor and two similar rooms up a steep staircase. It provides a focal point both for locals and the many visitors who appreciate the excellent selection of ales, the cosy ambience and lively banter. The diverse beer range includes at least one dark and one gluten-free choice, as well as a range of craft kegs. A trompe l'oeil painting on the exterior features the pub's namesake, Blind Jack Metcalf. Q ➔ ♠ 💀 🎵

Cross Keys L ✔

17 Cheapside, HG5 8AX
☎ (01423) 863562
Ossett Butterley, Yorkshire Blonde, White Rat, Silver King; 2 changing beers (sourced locally; often Ossett, Rudgate) H

A former Tetley's house, refurbished by Ossett brewery in its trademark style, with stone-flagged floors, bare-brick walls and stained glass. This traditional pub serves up to six cask ales, mostly from the Ossett stable, with occasional beers from other breweries. There are also at least two boxed ciders, mostly Lilley's, and usually a real cider such as Seacider. Thursday is quiz night and a live band plays monthly on Saturday nights. A DJ plays motown, soul and funk records on the first Sunday of every month. ➔ ♠ 💀 ● ♠ 🎵

Half Moon L ✔

1 Abbey Road, HG5 8HY
☎ (01423) 313461 ● thehalfmoonfreehouse.com
Rooster's YPA (Yorkshire Pale Ale); 3 changing beers (sourced locally; often Kirkstall, Sunbeam, Turning Point) H

Popular riverside free house, next to Low Bridge, where friendly staff always give a warm welcome. The original bare brick walls, real fire and wood-burning stove all contribute to its cosy atmosphere. There is a small, attractive, enclosed outdoor space, with tables and chairs and some benches under heated awnings; dogs are welcome in the outside area. Four handpumps dispense a varying range of beers, mostly from Yorkshire breweries. A grazing menu of meat and cheese boards complements the beers, served every day; you can order pizzas on weekday evenings. Coffee and home-made cakes are also available. ➔ ♠ ● ➔ ➔ (8) ☂ 🎵

Lastingham

Blacksmith's Arms

Anserdale Lane, YO62 6TN
☎ (01751) 417247 ● blacksmithsarmslastingham.co.uk
Saltaire Blonde; Theakston Best Bitter, Old Peculier; 1 changing beer (sourced regionally; often Daleside, Rudgate) H

Pretty stone inn in a conservation village opposite St Mary's church which is famous for its 11th century crypt. The interior comprises a cosy bar with York range lit in winter, a snug, and two dining rooms. Excellent-quality food including local game dishes is served alongside interesting guest beers and a changing guest cider, often Thistly Cross. A secluded beer garden is to the rear which includes a pizza oven. This remote pub is popular with locals, walkers and shooting parties. Dogs are permitted outside only. Q ➔ ♠ 💀 ●

Leavening

Jolly Farmers L

Main Street, YO17 9SA
☎ (01653) 658276 ● jollyfarmersinn.co.uk
Ossett Yorkshire Blonde; Timothy Taylor Landlord; 2 changing beers (sourced regionally; often Great Newsome, Half Moon) H

Seventeenth-century pub on the edge of the Yorkshire Wolds between York and Malton, it is a popular stopping off point for ramblers as well as locals. With its intriguing series of rooms featuring low ceilings and tiled flagged floors, the pub is homely and welcoming, serving locally sourced food and a range of local and regional ales. The pub hosts annual beer and gin festivals. The outside drinking area boasts table football and a cask of drinking water for dogs, complete with handpump! Q ➔ ♠ ● ♠ ● P 💀 ☂ 🎵

Leyburn

King's Head L

Grove Square, DL8 5AE
☎ (01969) 622694
Theakston Best Bitter; Timothy Taylor Landlord; Wensleydale Semer Water; 1 changing beer (sourced locally; often Wensleydale) H

Set off the main market place, at the junction of the moor road and the Richmond road, this friendly locals' pub is a rare example of a wet-led house in this tourist area, offering a selection of well-kept cask ales at attractive prices. An enthusiastic provider of sports TV, especially football, which is well-supported, and supplier of regular live music. The interior has been knocked through, but the bar, lounge and games room have the feel of separate areas. It has a pool table, two dartboards, fruit machines, open fires and the only jukebox in town. ➔ ♠ 💀 ☂ 🎵

Litton

Queen's Arms L

BD23 5QJ (in Littondale approx 5 miles from B6160)
☎ (01756) 770096 ● queensarmslitton.co.uk
Timothy Taylor Boltmaker; 2 changing beers (sourced locally; often LAMB) H

This building was transformed into a pub in 1843, with open fires, mullioned windows, oak-beamed ceilings and a stone-flagged bar area. Outside there is a garden with tables and chairs, which provide stunning views of the surrounding valley. The emphasis is on the locally sourced food – booking is recommended. The dining room is available for private functions. The two or three changing beers will include LAMB beers (the brewery is behind the pub but is not a connected business). ➔ ♠ 💀 ● ♠ ♠ 💀 ☂

Malham

Lister Arms L ✔

Gordale Scar Road, BD23 4DB
☎ (01729) 830444 ● listerarms.co.uk
Thwaites Original, IPA, Gold; 3 changing beers (sourced locally; often Dark Horse, Settle, Thwaites) H

Substantial stone-built Grade II listed inn dating from 1723 or earlier, overlooking the green. The tiled entrance hall opens to the stone-flagged main bar, with separate areas to left and right and a dining room/restaurant beyond. The large secluded garden at the rear has ample comfortable seating. Food is served all day, with breakfast and brunch on offer in the morning, and the main menu thereafter. Home-made cakes and cream teas are also available. Malham can get busy on weekends and school holidays. ♿🛏🕮🌳◑ ▲P🚲🐾☀

Malton

Blue Ball

14 Newbiggin, YO17 7JF
☎ (01653) 690692 🌐 theblueballinnmalton.co.uk
Tetley Bitter; Timothy Taylor Landlord; 1 changing beer (sourced locally) ⊞
This Grade II-listed establishment dating from the 16th century has been identified by CAMRA as having a nationally important historic pub interior. It was named the Blue Ball in 1823. The low front elevation hides a maze-like interior, with the frontward cosy bar, compact servery and linking corridor retaining most of the historical flavour. A smoking area is at the rear. Home-cooked food is served daily (except Wed).
Q♿🛏🌳◑&♿♣🚲🐾☀♪

Brass Castle Brewery Tap House ℓ

10 Yorkersgate, YO17 7AB
☎ (01653) 698683 🌐 brasscastle.co.uk
2 changing beers (sourced locally; often Brass Castle) ⊞
Formerly a town-centre temperance hotel, this recent addition to Malton's beer scene is a short walk from the railway station. The single-roomed bar is tastefully designed in a rustic style, with one wall partially adorned with barrel staves. Two regularly changing cask ales are offered together with six craft keg ales, alongside an extensive range of bottled beers. Snacks may be purchased at the bar. There is a smoking/drinking area to the rear of the premises and an upstairs seating area.
Q♿🛏&♿♣🐾☀

Manfield

Crown Inn 🍷 ℓ

Vicars Lane, DL2 2RF (500yds from B6275)
☎ (01325) 374243 🌐 thecrowninnmanfield.co.uk
Village White Boar ⊞/ℙ**; Draught Bass; 5 changing beers (sourced nationally)** ⊞
This 18th-century inn in a quiet village has won local CAMRA Country Pub of the Year 17 times, and was previously Yorkshire Pub of the Year. It has two bars with a real log fire in main bar, a games room and an extensive beer garden. A mix of locals and visitors create a friendly atmosphere. Up to six guest beers from microbreweries and up to five ciders or perries are available. Q♿🛏🌳◑♣P🚲(29)🐾☀

Marske-by-the-Sea

Clarendon ℓ

88-90 High Street, TS11 7BA
☎ (01642) 490005
Black Sheep Best Bitter; Camerons Strongarm; Copper Dragon Golden Pippin; Theakston Best Bitter, Old Peculier; 1 changing beer (sourced regionally) ⊞
The Middle House, as it is also known, is a popular one-room locals' pub, where little has changed since the 1960s. Six beers are served from the mahogany island bar, a rarity on Teesside. The walls are adorned with interesting photographs of yesteryear. There is no TV, no pool table, no children nor teenagers, just regulars indulging in convivial conversation. There is no catering either, but tea and coffee are always available. A recent local CAMRA award winner.
Q🐾≉(Marske) P🚲(X3,X4) ☀

Smugglers Den ℓ

7 Redcar Road, TS11 6AA (next to St Mark's Church)
☎ 07802 469727
4 changing beers (sourced locally) ⊞
Located in the centre of town, this converted quaint, and recently refurbished two-storey cottage is still a rather quirky, but equally stylish and friendly microbar. Now in its fifth year of operation, four rotating LocAle guest beers are served in the downstairs bar, where a log burner keeps everybody warm. Two additional rooms upstairs are also available, one housing a pool table. Live music takes place on Friday and Saturday evenings. Opens Thursday to Sunday. ≉(Marske)♣🚲(X3,X4)🐾♪

Masham

Bay Horse ℓ ✓

5 Silver Street, HG4 4DX
☎ (01765) 688158 🌐 bayhorseatmasham.co.uk
Black Sheep Best Bitter; Theakston Best Bitter, Old Peculier; Timothy Taylor Landlord; 1 changing beer (sourced locally; often Ossett, Pennine, Wensleydale) ⊞
Friendly pub just off the Market Place welcoming tourists and locals alike. As well as the front bar there is a dining area up a short flight of steps, a rear garden and five en-suite letting rooms. A selection of home-cooked food is served using fresh local produce; meal times may vary in winter. Up to six cask ales are served from both Masham and local Yorkshire breweries. Cask ends and pipework form a feature in the main front bar. ♿🛏🌳◑🚲🐾☀♪

Bruce Arms ℓ ✓

3 Little Market Place, HG4 4DY
☎ (01765) 689372
Black Sheep Best Bitter; Theakston Best Bitter, Lightfoot, Old Peculier; 1 changing beer ⊞
A traditional pub tucked away in a side street off the market place. This is a whitewashed building with an interior of partly exposed stone, ceiling beams and wood, with bench seating throughout. It has one room that appears to have been created out of three smaller ones. There is a large TV in one room and a darts board, there is also a pleasant rear garden. The pub has two letting rooms. 🛏◑♣🚲🐾☀♪

White Bear ℓ ✓

Wellgarth, HG4 4EN
☎ (01765) 689319 🌐 whitebearmasham.co.uk
Theakston Best Bitter, Lightfoot, Old Peculier ⊞
Theakston's only pub, an award-winning venue and a great favourite with the locals as well as directors and staff from the brewery. A large dining area to the left and a cosy taproom to the right offer exclusively Theakston's beers. Unusually for the Yorkshire Dales, this building was a victim of wartime bombing, following which it was derelict for many years before it was rescued and renovated to a high standard. A popular beer festival is hosted in June featuring over 30 real ales.
♿🛏🌳◑&♣P🐾☀♪

Middleham

Black Bull Inn ℓ

Market Place, DL8 4NX
☎ (01969) 624792 🌐 theblackbullinn.co.uk
Theakston Best Bitter; Wensleydale Semer Water; 2 changing beers (sourced locally; often Yorkshire Dales) ⊞
Friendly family-owned pub with a good selection of real ales situated in a major racehorse-training centre. It has three rooms, the largest more for dining than drinking,

with televisions in each bar. It serves good-quality food and there is a log-burner in the main bar. A good centre for Dales walking, it hosts regular events and offers tailor-made cycling packages for all the Tour de Yorkshire enthusiasts. ⏰🍴🅿(159)🐾🅿♿🎵

Richard III Hotel L
Market Place, DL8 4NP
☎ (01969) 623240 ⊕ richard111hotel.co.uk
Black Sheep Best Bitter; Theakston Best Bitter; Old Peculier; Wensleydale Semer Water; 1 changing beer (sourced locally) Ⓗ
Family-run pub located in a principal horse racing training hub. Next to Middleham Castle, it opens daily for breakfast and is a good start or end point for a variety of walks. Inside is a modest bar with a big adjoining lounge and snug to rear, and then a dining room. Tiled throughout, there are real fires in bar and snug, and a log-burner in the adjoining bar area. With tables on the cobbles at the front, breakfast can be had watching and listening to the racehorses trot by. Reduced menus on Wednesdays. Regular live music is played. Accommodation is in seven rooms.
⏰🍴🕚🅿(159,859) 🐾 🎵

Middlesbrough

Chapel @ Whitehouse Street
Whitehouse Street, TS5 4BY (adjacent to St Cuthbert's Church, near Newport bridge)
☎ (01642) 214441 ⊕ whitehousestreet.co.uk
6 changing beers (sourced nationally) Ⓗ
A former Primitive Methodist Mission Hall, dating to about 1890, located at the west end of the town. It has been sympathetically renovated throughout, retaining many original features from its former use. The refurbishment has created a bright, airy, friendly atmosphere. Six beers, ranging from lighter ales to darker beers and stouts are dispensed on a rotating guest basis. Three third-pint glasses are served on bespoke miniature pews. Real cider is also available, as well as bar nibbles. Live music, beer/cider festivals and Food Fridays feature. Q⏰🕚♿🅰♣🌸🅿🕹🐾📶🎵

Infant Hercules L
84 Grange Road, TS1 2LS (just S of Cleveland Centre and N of university campus)
☎ 07980 321626
4 changing beers Ⓗ
A warm welcome is always guaranteed at this successful micropub, located in the town's original solicitors' quarter and handy for the Law Courts and the Riverside Stadium. This CAMRA award-winning pub is named after Gladstone's description of the town in 1862, after he had witnessed the expansion of the town's ship-building and steel furnaces. Third-pint tasting bats are available. The pub continues to act as the preferred venue for past members of Teesside University Real Ale Society (TURAS). ⏰🌸♿🚆🐾📶

Isaac Wilson L
61 Wilson Street, TS1 1SF (at N end of town, close to railway station)
☎ (01642) 247708
Camerons Strongarm; Sharp's Atlantic; 3 changing beers (sourced nationally) Ⓗ
Popular pub named after a 19th-century railway industry magnate and company director of the world's first railway, the Stockton and Darlington. The Isaac, a former Wetherspoon's conversion of the old Law Courts, has recently gained new owners and continues to follow, more or less, the chain's formula. Two regular beers and three local guests, together with good-value food, are served. The single room interior has walls adorned with photographs of old Middlesbrough. Third-pint glasses are available. ⏰🕚♿🚆🅿📶

Middlesmoor

Crown Hotel L
Main Street, HG3 5ST
☎ (01423) 755204
Black Sheep Best Bitter; Dark Horse Hetton Pale Ale; Theakston Best Bitter; 1 changing beer (sourced locally) Ⓗ
Unspoilt former shooting lodge, now a family-run hotel, high in Nidderdale, with glorious views down the dale. The availability of accommodation, home-cooked food and log fires make it popular with walkers and sportsmen. The pub is decorated in the traditional no-nonsense fashion for the Dales and comprises three rooms with the servery in the main room and comfortable seating and eating areas to the sides, including a family room. There is a selection of walking sticks available for purchase in the bar.
⏰🌸🍴🕚🅰♣🅿🐾📶🔄

Northallerton

Fleece L
89 High Street, DL7 8PP
☎ (01609) 770891
6 changing beers (often Ossett, Pennine, Wensleydale) Ⓗ
With its earliest parts dating from the 15th century this Grade II-listed medieval sandstone and half-timbered building stands next to the Town Hall. It is the oldest pub in Northallerton and has several separate drinking spaces, with dining areas opening out to the rear. The six handpumps feature regularly changing beers, usually from Yorkshire breweries, and the pricing is competitive. ⏰🌸🕚🅿🐾

Oddfellows Arms L
251 High Street, DL7 8DJ (off main part of High St, behind parish church)
☎ (01609) 259107
3 changing beers (sourced regionally; often Ossett, Wensleydale) Ⓗ
Hidden behind the parish church, by the cemetery gates, the Oddies does not appear to be on the High Street, despite its address. A thriving back-street community pub, it handles a mainly local trade and is popular with darts players, T|V football fans and church bell-ringers. Refurbished in a simple but traditional style with an open-plan interior, there is a games room upstairs and a secluded beer garden to the rear. ⏰🌸♣🍴🐾📶🎵

Origin
2 Friarage Street, DL6 1DP (just off High St near hospital)
☎ (01609) 775900 ⊕ originsocial.co.uk
Ossett White Rat; 3 changing beers (sourced regionally; often Timothy Taylor, Wensleydale) Ⓗ
Just off the High Street, in the premises of the former Tithe Bar, this smart bar opened in late 2021 marketed as a 'small plates restaurant bar'. The focus is on food, served both in the downstairs bar and the upstairs restaurant. It serves four well-kept ales on handpump, usually including a blonde and a golden or pale ale, as well as a range of interesting craft keg beers and wine from an extensive wine list. ⏰🕚♿🅿📶

Stumble Inn L

4 Garthway Arcade, DL7 8NS (in pedestrian arcade off High St next to Grovers shop)
☎ 07817 568042
5 changing beers (sourced regionally) ⊞
This friendly and cosy micropub is just off the town's High Street, down a small shopping arcade opposite the town hall. It serves a selection of local ales, craft beers and up to 20 ciders, and staff are keen to offer tasting advice and guidance. With no music, gaming machines, WiFi, children or sports TV, there is just good old-fashioned chat plus a quiz on the last Sunday each month and seasonal beer and cider festivals. The drinks choice always includes a dark beer. Q●❑❀

Old Malton

Royal Oak Pub & Kitchen

47 Town Street, YO17 7HB (400yds off A64 Malton bypass)
☎ (01653) 696968 ⊕ theroyaloakoldmalton.co.uk
Leeds Pale; 2 changing beers (sourced regionally) ⊞
Historic Grade II-listed inn in a picturesque village off the A64 close to Eden Camp military museum. At the front of the pub is a cosy snug, to the rear is a larger room with original beams complete with brasses and a log fire, leading to an extensive beer garden with a large covered smoking area. Three handpumps serve beers mainly from Yorkshire. Traditional home-cooked meals are available. Children and dogs are welcome. The bus stops outside. ❄❀◑♿♣●❑❑(840)❀❀

Osmotherley

Golden Lion L

6 West End, DL6 3AA
☎ (01609) 883526 ⊕ goldenlionosmotherley.co.uk
Timothy Taylor Landlord; 2 changing beers (sourced locally; often Helmsley, Wold Top) ⊞
Set in the centre of a picturesque village on the edge of the North York Moors National Park and at the start of the long-distance Lyke Wake Walk, this old inn is popular with hikers, casual visitors and locals. Much of the focus is on high-quality food but drinkers are always made welcome. Two changing beers are from local or Yorkshire breweries, and the view from the outside drinking tables makes them a popular place to enjoy them on fine days. Dogs are welcome with well-behaved owners.
Q❄◑▲❑(80,89) ❀❀

Pickering

Sun Inn ♜ L

136 Westgate, YO18 8BB (on A170, 400yds W of traffic lights in town centre)
☎ (01751) 473661 ⊕ thesuninn-pickering.co.uk
Tetley Bitter; 5 changing beers (sourced regionally) ⊞
Friendly local CAMRA Rural Pub of the Year winner, close to the steam railway. Six real ales are offered, often from Yorkshire micros, and several traditional ciders. A cosy bar with a real fire leads to a separate room, ideal for families and special events, where local artists display their work. The large beer garden is used for the annual beer festival in September. Regular events include fortnightly acoustic music, charity quizzes and monthly vinyl nights. Dogs on leads, children and walkers are welcome. ❄❀♿≠♣●❑❑(128,840)❀♫

Pocklington

Market Tap

11-13 Market Place, YO42 2AS
☎ (01759) 307783
9 changing beers (often Brew York) ⊞
Situated overlooking the market place, this 19th-century building and former newsagent provides a light, spacious and modern feel over two floors. An extensive range of up to nine cask beers and nine craft keg beers are on offer including five cask regulars from Brew York. Off-sales of wines, beers and ciders are available too. Food is served on Saturday and Sunday lunchtimes, and evenings Wednesday to Sunday. ❄◑♿❑❑❀❀

Pool-in-Wharfedale

Hunters Inn L

Harrogate Road, LS21 2PS
Abbeydale Moonshine; Black Sheep Best Bitter; Morland Old Speckled Hen; Ossett Yorkshire Blonde; White Rat; 3 changing beers (often Bradfield, Copper Dragon, Goose Eye) ⊞
A single-storey building on the main Harrogate to Bradford road with views across lower Wharfedale. The large single-room interior incorporates a raised area with a warming real fire during the colder months, while the windowed front wall gives views across to the southern ridge of Wharfedale. The long bar houses an array of handpumps dispensing a varied selection of ales sourced mainly from Yorkshire breweries. There is a pool table and video jukebox at one end. Children are welcome during the day. ❄❀♣❑(X52,A2)❀❀↺♫

Redcar

Rita's Pantry L

1 Esplanade, TS10 3AA (opp Beacon)
☎ 07730 445483
3 changing beers (sourced nationally) ⊞
A former amusement arcade is now the town's first micropub. Situated on the seafront, from where the petrified forest can be seen at low tide, a warm welcome is extended to CAMRA members, locals and visitors alike. Three interesting rotating beers are served and third-pint glasses are available. The amiable licensee hosts various social events, including a music quiz on Sunday. The pub is popular on social media.
❀◑♿▲≠(Central) ❑(X3,X4) ❀❀♫

Reeth

Buck Hotel L ✓

DL11 6SW
☎ (01748) 884545 ⊕ thebuckreeth.co.uk
Bradfield Farmers Blonde; Theakston Best Bitter; 3 changing beers (often Allendale, Pennine) ⊞
Originally an 18th-century coaching inn, the pub is sited prominently at the top of the green, and is therefore also known as 'the top house'. It retains many original features with beamed ceilings, an open fire and an ice house. Tables on the patio at the front offer stunning views over the dale, while the beer garden (closed in winter) is a suntrap. In high season meals service may be extended, and all meals are on a first-come first-served basis. ❄❀♿◑♿▲♣❑(30)❀❀♫

Ribblehead

Station Inn

Low Sleights Road, LA6 3AS (on B6255 nr B6479 jct)
☎ (015242) 41274 ⊕ thestationinnribblehead.com

Black Sheep Best Bitter, Riggwelter; house beer (by Tirril); 2 changing beers (sourced locally; often Settle) ⊞
Built in 1874 at the same time as the nearby viaduct, this pub is a welcome refuge in a bleak spot in the midst of superb walking country and is much used by hikers. It was refurbished in 2017 to provide a rustic look throughout, with a cheery range in the snug. Frequented by a surprisingly large number of locals, there is a good train service, but buses are rare. A bunk barn is available next door – the wild camping behind the pub is no more.
⍭✿⌂⏴◗⇌♣P🖵(830)❀❞🎜

Riccall

Greyhound ⊘
82 Main Street, YO19 6TE
☎ (01757) 248650 ⊕ greyhoundriccall.com
Black Sheep Best Bitter; Ossett Yorkshire Blonde; Timothy Taylor Landlord; 3 changing beers ⊞
Four miles north of Selby you'll find a welcoming pub in the heart of the historic village of Riccall. This family-run village pub dates back to the late 1800s and has up to six cask beers on the bar. Popular with locals and visitors alike, many of whom who enjoy River Ouse walks and the Trans Pennine cycle trail. The large beer garden can get busy on warmer days. Timothy Taylor's Champion Club member. Regular live music. ⍭✿Å♣P🖵❀❞🎜

Richmond

Buck Inn ⊘
29 Newbiggin, DL10 4DX
☎ (01748) 517300 ⊕ thebuckrichmond.co.uk
Timothy Taylor Landlord; 2 changing beers (often Black Sheep, Ossett) ⊞
Rambling old free house of character situated on a cobbled street off the town centre. There is a small snug at the front, comfortably furnished eating areas and a main bar to the rear which features dartboard, pool table and sports TV. Beyond this is the suntrap beer garden with its spectacular views over the River Swale and the Norman castle. Meal times vary according to the season, so check beforehand. Q⍭✿⌂⏴◗♣🖵❀❞🎜

No 29 Alehouse & Gin Bar ╚
29 Frenchgate, DL10 4HZ
☎ (01748) 850491
⊕ number-29-alehouse-gin-bar.business.site
3 changing beers (sourced locally; often Mithril, Rudgate, Wensleydale) ⊞
Real ale, craft beer, gin, wine and tapas bar located just off the foot of Richmond's market place on the road down to the former station complex. The single, small bar has simple decor with a wooden floor. Food such as cured meat and cheese sharing boards, ploughman's and various delicious tapas dishes are available. Beers are usually local or regional, often from Mithril, Rudgate and Wensleydale breweries. May close early if quiet. ◗🖵❀

Ripon

One Eyed Rat ╚
51 Allhallowgate, HG4 1LQ
☎ (01765) 607704
Ossett White Rat; Saltaire Blonde; 4 changing beers (often Bosun's, Ilkley, Pennine) ⊞
An entry in this Guide for many years, the One Eyed Rat was refurbished and reopened under new management in 2020. A Grade II-listed building set within a terrace of 200-year-old houses, its narrow frontage leads to a warm and welcoming hostelry. The pub has a long,

narrow interior with traditional seating and an open fire, and there is a large garden at the rear, including a sizeable covered area. A varied selection of cask ales is available, usually including a dark beer, and often a real cider from Orchards of Husthwaite. Q⍭✿⌂◗🖵❀❞↻

Royal Oak ⊘
36 Kirkgate, HG4 1PB
☎ (01765) 602284 ⊕ royaloakripon.co.uk
Timothy Taylor Golden Best, Boltmaker, Landlord, Landlord Dark; 2 changing beers (often Ossett, Saltaire, Timothy Taylor) ⊞
This venue is in what was an 18th-century coaching inn, now beautifully renovated in the modern idiom, in the centre of historic Ripon between the cathedral and the Market Square. Timothy Taylor's most northerly tied house, the Royal Oak serves a top-quality range of the brewery's beers alongside a pale beer from another Yorkshire brewery. The pub is separated into relaxed dining areas with log-burning stoves and comfortable seating, and offers a first-class locally sourced menu. You can stay in one of the six stylish and comfortable bedrooms, and a hearty English breakfast is included. ⍭✿⌂⏴◗🖵❀❞

Water Rat ╚ ⊘
24 Bondgate Green, HG4 1QW
☎ (01765) 602251 ⊕ thewaterrat.co.uk
Rudgate Jorvik Blonde; Theakston Best Bitter; 2 changing beers (often Ilkley, Rudgate) ⊞
Located by the side of the River Skell with a fine view of Ripon Cathedral and the river from its large windows and riverside terrace, this is Ripon's only riverside pub, in fact so close to the river that it has been flooded in the past. An emphasis on affordable home-cooked traditional English pub food means it tends to get busy at times. There is a small drinking area near the bar, and a snug at the front. Four cask ales are served and a popular Northern Soul event is held monthly. ⍭✿◗🖵❀❞🎜

Robin Hood's Bay

Bay Hotel ╚
The Dock, YO22 4SJ (at the end of a very steep road, down towards the bay from top car park)
☎ (01947) 880278 ⊕ bayhotel.info
Adnams Ghost Ship; Theakston Best Bitter, Lightfoot; Wainwright ⊞
This magnificent Grade II-listed 1822 building is the finish line for Wainwright's Coast-to-Coast 192-mile walk from St Bees. The bottom bar, named in his honour, provides access to the Dock patio, situated at the seawater's edge and which provides superb panoramic views. With a licensee of 25 years' service, a friendly welcome awaits regulars, visitors, their children and their dogs. An extensive good-value home-cooked menu is available. Access to this part of the village is not easy for the less mobile. ⍭✿⌂◗🖵(X93)❀

Rosedale Abbey

Coach House Inn
YO18 8SD
☎ (01751) 417208 ⊕ coachhouseinn.co.uk
Black Sheep Best Bitter; 4 changing beers (sourced locally; often Ryedale, Wold Top, Yorkshire Heart) ⊞
Country inn and restaurant located in the beautiful moorland village of Rosedale Abbey in the heart of the North York Moors National Park. There is a great choice of real ales ranging from dark to amber and blonde/IPA, and the overall quality is very good. The bar staff are friendly and helpful. Q⍭✿◗♿Å♣P🖵❀❞🎜

Saltburn-by-the-Sea

Saltburn Cricket, Bowls & Tennis Club Ⓛ

Marske Mill Lane, TS12 1HJ (next to leisure centre)
☎ (01287) 622761 ● saltburn.play-cricket.com
3 changing beers (sourced nationally) Ⓗ

Visitors are made welcome at this thriving members club and local CAMRA multi-award winner, including Club of the Year 2023. Located north of the town, within walking distance of transport links, the club is well supported by the local community and is now celebrating 27 years of continuous Guide recognition. Three beers are served, often not even lasting the evening. An enthusiastic steward hosts a variety of events. The balcony, ideal for lazy summer afternoons, overlooks the cricket field. Please check winter opening hours.
క≒(Saltburn) ♣P🖵(X3,X4) ☀

Scarborough

Cellars

35-37 Valley Road, YO11 2LY
☎ (01723) 367158
Bradfield Farmers Blonde; Camerons Strongarm; Daleside Monkey Wrench; 1 changing beer (sourced nationally; often Rooster's) Ⓗ

A frequent Guide entry, this family-run pub was converted from the cellars of a Victorian town house. Four handpumps dispense guest beers from nationwide micros. Locally sourced home-cooked food is served, with Sunday lunches always popular. Quiz night is Tuesday, open mic night is Wednesday, local acoustic acts play on Thursday, and Saturday is live music night. The patio out front is popular in summer. Children and dogs are welcome and accommodation is available.
క➏✺ⓘ❶க♣P☀🗢♫

Craft Bar

7 Northway, YO11 1JH
☎ 07460 311059 ● thecraftbar.co.uk
4 changing beers (sourced nationally) Ⓗ

A welcome addition to the Scarborough beer scene, the bar is located opposite the Stephen Joseph Theatre and adjacent to Scarborough railway station. A single-room shop conversation with a mix of contemporary and vintage furnishings. Four cask ales, 13 craft keg taps and a wide selection of ciders together with a range of wines and spirits are available. An extensive choice of bottles and cans can be drunk onsite or taken away. Regular live music is played at weekends and there is a quiz night on Wednesday. ➏≒❶🖵☀🗢♫

North Riding Brew Pub Ⓛ

161-163 North Marine Road, YO12 7HU
☎ (01723) 370004 ● northridingbrewpub.com
6 changing beers (sourced nationally; often North Riding (Brewery), North Riding (Brewpub)) Ⓗ

Scarborough's only brewpub, serving at least six continually changing beers from local breweries and microbreweries around the UK. It always has one or more North Riding (Brewery) beer together with some brewed on the premises. These are complemented by up to six craft keg beers from around the world, and an extensive range of craft bottled beers. There is a public bar, complete with pool table, and a quiet comfortable lounge, refurbished in 2022, both with real fires. Quiz night is Thursday. Q➏✺♣❶🖵(843,X94)☀🗢

Scarborough Borough Council Employees Welfare Club Ⓛ

Dean Road, YO12 7QS

☎ (01723) 364593
3 changing beers (sourced regionally; often Great Newsome, Mallinsons, North Riding (Brewery)) Ⓗ

Close to the town centre, this club, dating from 1935, comprises a large bar area with an adjacent snooker room. The three cask ales often feature one from Mallinsons, reflecting the preference of the steward, and a dark beer. Club teams participate in local snooker, darts and domino leagues. The club welcomes guests and is popular with cricket-goers especially during Scarborough CC-hosted Yorkshire county games. An outdoor drinking/smoking area is available. Customers can bring in and consume their own food. ➏✺≒♣🖵(11,333)☀

Scholars Bar

6 Somerset Terrace, YO11 2PA
☎ (01723) 372826
Hambleton Nightmare Porter; Ossett Yorkshire Blonde, White Rat; Theakston Old Peculier; 2 changing beers (sourced regionally; often Rat, Thornbridge, Timothy Taylor) Ⓗ

A warm, friendly atmosphere prevails at this busy town-centre pub at the rear of the main shopping centre. The large front bar is dominated by TV screens showing major sporting events, and there is a smaller games area to the left rear of the bar. Two rotating guest beers, usually from Yorkshire microbreweries, are offered, with Theakston Old Peculier served from a wooden cask, plus real ciders and perry from Mr. Whitehead's. The Thursday night quiz is popular. ≒♣❶🖵(10)☀🗢

Stumble Inn

59 Westborough, YO11 1TS (200yds SW of railway station)
6 changing beers (sourced nationally; often Kelchner, Potbelly, Whitby) Ⓗ

The first micropub in Scarborough, this was a welcome addition to the local real ale scene, quickly gaining a positive reputation for its beer and cider. Located a short walk from the railway station, the former solicitors' office is a small, single-roomed venue offering six rotating guest ales, with local breweries always represented. Numerous ciders and perries are also stocked. An ideal place for a cosy chat and chill out. There is an external seating area, popular in summer. Dogs are welcome. ✺க❶🖵☀

Tap & Spile ❷

94 Falsgrave Road, YO12 5AZ
☎ (01723) 507666
Black Sheep Best Bitter; Camerons Strongarm; Theakston Old Peculier; Timothy Taylor Landlord; 1 changing beer (sourced nationally) Ⓗ

Sympathetically restored Grade II-listed public house, not far from the town centre, serving five cask ales. There are two main rooms plus a small snug where local memorabilia is displayed. This thriving local has a friendly atmosphere and is a venue for live music with Sunday afternoons particularly popular when Sunday lunches are also available. TV sports are shown in one bar. A beer garden is situated at the rear. Dogs are welcome in the tap room. ➏✺ⓘ❶≒♣P🖵☀🗢♫

Valley Bar Ⓛ

51 Valley Road, YO11 2LX
☎ (01723) 372593 ● valleybar.co.uk
5 changing beers (sourced nationally; often Pennine, Rooster's, Scarborough) Ⓗ

The bar, recently relocated adjacent to the original cellar bar, is a large room divided into several drinking areas. There is also a pool room and a separate function room. Of note is the remarkable decor utilising antique furniture. Five guest beers are offered, usually including

one or more from Scarborough brewery. Real ciders and perries are also sold, together with a selection of Belgian bottled beers. Accommodation is available.
Q ⏾ ⌖ ✿ 🛏 ♣ ♠ 🚃 ♿ 🍴 ☂ 🎵

Selby

Doghouse 🅛
8 Park Street, YO8 4PW
☎ 07495 026173 ⊕ littleblackdogbeer.com/
thedoghouseselby
5 changing beers (often Little Black Dog) ⊞
Selby's first craft beer café featuring five cask beers from their own brewery based at Carlton, together with four ciders and a large range of craft keg beers. The upstairs room is a meeting place for many local groups, regular live music and occasional guest food suppliers. You can be sure of a warm welcome at this family-run bar.
✿ ≈ ● 🎵

Settle

Golden Lion 🅛 ✔
Duke Street, BD24 9DU
☎ (01729) 822203 ⊕ goldenlionsettle.co.uk
Thwaites Mild, Original, IPA, Gold, Amber; 1 changing beer (sourced locally; often Settle) ⊞
Built in around 1670, this Thwaites-managed former coaching inn has two comfortable high-ceilinged rooms for drinking. The main bar has wood panelling, a grand staircase and a huge fireplace. The Lion's Den is accessed from the bar or via a low door off the street. The separate dining area is bright and colourful. Outside seating is in the sheltered yard. Breakfast is served from opening, with alcoholic drinks available from 10am. The external door is locked at 10.30pm (earlier in winter) except for residents. ⏾ ✿ 🛏 🍴 ◐ Å ≈ ♣ ♠ P 🚃 ♿ ☂ 🎵

Talbot Arms 🅛 ✔
High Street, BD24 9EX
☎ (01729) 823924 ⊕ talbotsettle.co.uk
Theakston Best Bitter; house beer (by Settle); 3 changing beers (sourced regionally; often Pennine, Wensleydale, Wishbone) ⊞
Just off the square, this family-run free house, claiming to be the oldest pub in town, offers a welcoming and friendly atmosphere. In winter a stove glows in the large stone feature fireplace to the left. A pleasant, terraced beer garden is at the rear. The guest beers are usually from Cumbria, Lancashire or Yorkshire. A 'bingo' quiz is held on the first and third Monday of month. Good-value food is served seven days a week, with booking advisable at weekends and school holidays. There is limited parking behind the pub (through the arch).
⏾ ✿ ◐ Å ≈ ♣ P 🚃 ♿ ☂ 🎵

Skipton

Beer Engine ♟ 🅛
1 Albert Street, BD23 1JD
☎ 07930 810763
6 changing beers (sourced nationally) ⊞
A well-established micropub in a tiny street between the town centre and the canal. Six handpumps dispense varying beers, always including one blonde or pale ale and one dark beer, plus a character beer. Extended in 2022, the bar now includes craft keg fonts. The cask beers are stored in refrigerated cabinets behind the bar while the keg products are in stored in a separate cupboard. The ambience is friendly and welcoming. Well-behaved dogs are welcome. Local CAMRA Pub of the Year 2023. Q ⏾ ≈ 🚃 ♿ ☂

Boat House 🅛
19 Coach Street, BD23 1LH
☎ (01756) 701660
Wishbone Tiller Pin; 4 changing beers (sourced regionally) ⊞
Tucked out of the way, this pub is accessed through an arch from Coach Street or via the canalside path. The bar is light and airy with picture windows looking onto the canal basin and the decor has a canal theme. A cobbled outdoor drinking area offers the opportunity to enjoy a beer while watching the boats go by. An old-style stove keeps the bar warm in winter. One dark cask ale and craft keg beers are usually available. ⏾ ✿ ♿ ≈ 🚃 ♿ ☂ 🎵

South Otterington

Otterington Shorthorn 🅛
DL7 9HP
☎ (01609) 773816 ⊕ otteringtonshorthorn.co.uk
Daleside Bitter; 2 changing beers (sourced locally; often Ossett, Rudgate) ⊞
An old free house situated on the A167 crossroads, featuring a comfortable interior which has been opened out into a carpeted lounge bar with an eating area in a separate room off the bar. Guest ales are usually sourced from small Yorkshire breweries and often include a dark beer. No accommodation, but the pub has its own holiday let to the rear. Takeaway meals are available.
Q ⏾ ◐ Å ♣ 🚃 ♿ 🎵

Staithes

Cod & Lobster Inn
High Street, TS13 5BH (at end of the High St, just before the sea)
☎ (01947) 840330 ⊕ codandlobster.co.uk
Black Sheep Best Bitter; Helmsley Howardian Gold; Timothy Taylor Boltmaker; York Guzzler ⊞
Superbly positioned at the seawater's edge in this picturesque sleepy fishing village, the pub comprises a large open-plan room where four beers are served. Good-value traditional meals are served. On sunny days a pleasant patio, overlooking the chilly sea, becomes popular. However, during high tides, combined with north-easterly winds, you are advised to use the roadside door or risk getting wet. Access to this part of the village is not ideal for the less mobile. ⏾ ✿ ◐

Starbotton

Fox & Hounds 🅛
BD23 5HY
☎ (01756) 760269 ⊕ foxandhoundsstarbotton.co.uk
Timothy Taylor Landlord; Wharfedale Blonde; 2 changing beers (often Dark Horse, Wensleydale, Yorkshire Dales) ⊞
A family-run, whitewashed 17th-century inn, divided into two cosy rooms, with flagstone floors and a large stone fireplace enhancing the atmosphere. In fine weather the sheltered patio at the front provides extra seating and is good for basking in the Yorkshire sunshine. A locally brewed golden ale and dark beer are served alongside the regular beers. Lunch is available daily and evening meals are served Wednesday to Sunday. The daytime community-run bus stops outside.
⏾ ✿ 🛏 ◐ ♣ P 🚌 (72B,874) ♿

Stillington

White Bear 🅛
Main Street, YO61 1JU

☎ (01347) 810338 ⊕ thewhitebearinn-york.co.uk
Leeds Pale; house beer (by Rudgate); 3 changing beers (sourced regionally) ⊞
The beating heart of the real ale scene in Stillington and beyond. Look out for the numerous polar bears scattered around, but none of them bites. The three changing beers add variety to the two excellent regulars and the rare example of an autovac system is put to good use. A sensible rejig of opening sees the pub closed on Monday and Tuesday, but the other days are as busy as ever and well worth the wait. ♿🏠🍺◐♣🅿🚃(40)🐾�🔊↺

Stokesley

Green Man 🅛 ✅
63 High Street, TS9 5BQ (near police station, towards West Green)
☎ 07500 045598
Timothy Taylor Landlord; 2 changing beers (sourced regionally) ⊞
A warm welcome is assured at Stokesley's first micropub, which has become the go-to place for locals and visitors alike. With its back-to-basics approach, striving to adhere to the established micropub norms, the bar, seating and tables have all been constructed from beech trees by a local family friend. No TV, no music, no jukebox, no one-armed-bandit and no food, just pleasant conversation with the engaging owners. Three handpulls, real cider and several Belgian bottled beers help the conversation flow. Q🍺🚃(29,81)

White Swan 🅛 ✅
1 West End, TS9 5BL (at W end of town, 150yds beyond shops)
☎ (01642) 714985 ⊕ whiteswanstokesley.co.uk
Captain Cook Sunset, Slipway, Endeavour; 5 changing beers (sourced locally) ⊞
Home of the Captain Cook brewery, this friendly 18th-century pub is at the west end of the pretty market town. Eight handpulls serve six beers from the Captain Cook portfolio of 10 beers, together with two interesting guests, while two real ciders are also always available. Beer festivals are held at Easter and in October. Open mic night is Tuesday, quiz night is Wednesday, while music night is Thursday. The sheltered outdoor drinking area overlooks the brewery. Over-18s only. 🌟♣🍺🚃(89,28)🐾🔊♪

Thornton Watlass

Buck Inn 🅛 ✅
Village Green, HG4 4AH
☎ (01677) 422461 ⊕ buckwatlass.co.uk
Black Sheep Best Bitter; Theakston Best Bitter; Timothy Taylor Landlord; Wensleydale Falconer; 1 changing beer (often Pennine) ⊞
Overlooking the village green, this traditional country inn, with five letting rooms, features a cosy bar room with a real fire, a lounge/dining room and a large function room known as the Long Room. The building has been refurbished throughout by the owners, while retaining a village pub atmosphere. Excellent meals are available and four regular Marston beers are served, with a changing ale added in summer. Live trad jazz music is hosted on Sunday lunchtimes once a month. The Bedale to Masham bus stops nearby on Tuesdays, Wednesdays and Fridays. 🌟🏠◐🅿🚃(144)🐾🔊♪

Wensley

Three Horseshoes 🅛
DL8 4HJ (on A684)

☎ (01969) 622327
Black Sheep Best Bitter; house beer (by Wensleydale); 2 changing beers (sourced nationally; often Wensleydale) ⊞
Traditional old country pub on the A684, with its small bar and dining room both featuring low beams and real fires. Outside there is a terraced beer garden offering glorious views across Wensleydale, forming a real suntrap on fine days. Wholesome and reasonably priced lunchtime and evening meals are served daily, except Mondays, and the pub also offers takeaways. Guest beers in busier months are usually from Wensleydale brewery. Q♿🌟◐♣🅿🚃(156)🐾🔊♪

West Heslerton

Dawnay Arms 🅛
Church Street, YO17 8RQ
☎ (01944) 728507 ⊕ dawnayarms.co.uk
Theakston Best Bitter; 3 changing beers (sourced regionally; often Great Newsome, Half Moon, Wold Top) ⊞
This village local located just off the A64 has a main bar divided into drinking, eating and games areas, together with a separate restaurant. One regular beer is offered in addition to three guests from Yorkshire microbreweries. High-quality, locally sourced, home-cooked meals are available, with booking recommended for Sundays. Teams participate in local pool, darts and dominoes leagues. At the rear is a spacious beer garden and a partially-covered smoking/drinking area. Two en-suite rooms are available. ♿🌟🏠◐♿▲♣🅿🚃(843)🐾🔊

West Witton

Fox & Hounds 🅛
Main Street, DL8 4LP (on A684)
☎ (01969) 623650 ⊕ foxwitton.com
Black Sheep Best Bitter; Theakston Best Bitter; 3 changing beers (sourced locally; often Wensleydale, Yorkshire Dales) ⊞
This welcoming, Grade II-listed family-run free house is full of character. A real community local, it has a down-to-earth bar and games room popular with locals and visitors alike. Good-value meals are served and the dining room boasts an inglenook fireplace with quaint stone oven. Once a rest house for 15th-century Jervaulx Abbey monks, it has a pleasant patio at the rear; beware the tight entry to the car park. Known to locals as the Fox to distinguish it from the Fox and Hounds in West Burton further up the dale. ♿🌟🏠◐▲♣🅿🚃🐾🔊

Whitby

Arch & Abbey
2-4 Skinner Street, YO21 3AJ (at S end of Skinner St, towards St Hilda's Terrace)
4 changing beers (sourced regionally) ⊞
This well established and popular micropub, situated close to the noted Botham's bakery, is operated by enthusiastic licensees who strive to adhere to the original micropub ethos. This successful crowd-funded start-up is located in what was once an old-fashioned ladies' dress shop that would not look out of place in a heritage museum. Four interesting beers, six or more mixed ciders, and a huge range of spirits, all distilled in Yorkshire, are served. Children are allowed until evening. Q♿🚶🚃(X93,840)🐾🔊

Black Horse 🅛 ✅
91 Church Street, YO22 4BH (on E side of swing bridge on the way to Abbey steps, close to market place)

☎ (01947) 602906 ⊕ the-black-horse.com
3 changing beers (sourced nationally) ℍ
This busy little multi-roomed gem, dating from the 1600s, offers a warm welcome. The frontage, with its frosted glass, together with one of Europe's oldest public serving bars, was built in the 1880s and remains largely unchanged. Beers from the Punch list are served from five handpumps. Snuff, tapas, olives, Yorkshire cheeses and hot drinks are always available, while hot lunches are also served during the winter months. Accommodation is in four bedrooms.
Q ☎ 🛏 ◖ & ♣ 🖪 (X93,840) ✿ 🛜 ♪

Little Angel ℒ ✔

18 Flowergate, YO21 3BA (200yds W of swing bridge, 200yds N of railway and bus stations)
☎ (01947) 820475 ⊕ littleangelwhitby.co.uk
9 changing beers ℍ
Now the home of Lady Luck brewery, locals and visitors alike are afforded a genuine friendly welcome at this popular pub, where, it is rumoured, the remains of the Castle form part of the structure. Largescreen sports TVs, live music, an outdoor beer terrace, and even a horse mount for those requiring this facility, complement the nine beers served to three separate rooms from a three-sided central bar. Local CAMRA Best Whitby Pub for three years running. ☎ ❀ ◖ ♣ 🖪 (X93,840) ✿ 🛜 ♪

Quirky Den

11 Grape Lane, YO22 4BA (E side of swing bridge)
☎ 07792 715152
Theakston Old Peculier; 2 changing beers (sourced regionally) ℍ
Opened in 2018, this is a rather special gem of a micropub, with so much packed into such a small place. A genuine welcome is assured from the enthusiastic and knowledgable owners. The pub is noted for serving Theakston Old Peculier from wooden sherry casks. Third-pint bats are available. It closes each year in January, once the pub has been drunk dry, and reopens in time for the Easter break. If you visit just one pub in Whitby, make sure it is this one. ⇌ 🖪 (X93,840) ✿

Station Inn ℒ ✔

New Quay Road, YO21 1DH (opp bus and NYMR/EVR stations)
☎ (01947) 600498 ⊕ stationinnwhitby.co.uk
Black Sheep Best Bitter; Ossett Yorkshire Blonde, Silver King; Theakston Old Peculier; Timothy Taylor Boltmaker; Whitby Jet Black; 2 changing beers (sourced regionally) ℍ
Next to the harbour and marina, this popular multi-roomed pub, now owned by the Bermondsey Pub Company, is under the proud stewardship of an enthusiastic licensee who ensures that the eight beers, including two guests, always encompass an eclectic range of varying beer styles. Situated opposite the bus station and NYMR/Esk Valley Railway station, this pub has become the discerning travellers' waiting room. Live music features three evenings a week. There are four letting bedrooms. 🛏 ⇌ 🖪 (X93,840) ✿ 🛜 ♪

Waiting Room ℒ

2 Whitby Station, Langborne Road, YO21 1YN (by the main entrance to the NYMR/EVR station)
5 changing beers (sourced nationally) ℍ
Located on the platform that the NYMR steam trains use, the friendly staff at Whitby's first micropub strive to adhere to the original micropub values, with no keg beers/lagers, no spirits, no jukebox and no television. Five handpumps and 10 real and fruit ciders help to promote a pleasant atmosphere and lots of convivial conversation. The six-yard-square pub gets busy at times,

so please do not be disappointed if there isn't any room. A local CAMRA Cider Pub of the Year winner.
Q & ⇌ ● 🖪 (X93,840) ✿ 🛜

Whitby Brewery Tap ℒ

East Cliff, YO22 4JR (at the top of the 199 steps)
☎ (01947) 228871 ⊕ whitby-brewery.com
Whitby Abbey Blonde, Whaler, Saltwick Nab, Smugglers Gold, Jet Black, IPA ℍ
Away from the hustle and bustle of the town, perched on the cliff edge in the shadow of the abbey, the brewery now includes a small bar that serves up to five of the brewery's seven beers, together with a bottle shop. Drinkers imbibe close to the liquor tank, mash tun and copper, or sit in the courtyard when the weather isn't too inclement. Tours are available (please book ahead), that always include tastings of the beers.
Q ☎ ❀ ◖ & Å ⇌ P 🖪 (840,X93) ✿

Yarm

New Inn 🍷 ℒ

119 High Street, TS15 9BB (enter via Brandlings Court ginnel at N end of High St)
4 changing beers (sourced locally) ℍ
This former chocolate boutique, and now local CAMRA Pub of the Year 2023, is Yarm's first micropub, where a contemporary atmosphere prevails, enhanced by light background music. Besides four guest beers and real cider, cans of craft ale and Belgian bottled beers are also served. Third-pint glasses are available. Conversation is a must where rubbing shoulders with fellow drinkers becomes inevitable. Top quality snacks, sourced from a local award-winning farm shop, sweets and doggie treats are also served. Q ● 🖪 (7,17) ✿

York

Ackhorne ℒ

9 St Martins Lane, YO1 6LN
☎ (01904) 671421
Ainsty Cool Citra; Rudgate Jorvik Blonde, Ruby Mild; house beer (by Half Moon); 2 changing beers (sourced locally; often Brew York, Rooster's, Yorkshire Heart) ℍ
Situated near the city centre in an alley at the bottom of Micklegate, this dog-friendly pub regularly serves a selection of six real ales. There is a raised outside terrace for summer drinking and two quiz nights to keep pub-goers entertained. Simply put, this is a traditional pub with a large open interior and a pleasant, friendly atmosphere. ☎ ❀ ◖ ♣ ● 🖪 ♪

Blue Bell ★ ℒ ✔

53 Fossgate, YO1 9TF
☎ (01904) 654904 ⊕ bluebellyork.com
Bradfield Farmers Blonde; Rudgate Ruby Mild; Timothy Taylor Landlord; Wold Top Bitter; house beer (by Brass Castle); 2 changing beers (sourced locally; often Half Moon, Rooster's) ℍ
This historic Grade II*-listed pub, last decorated in 1903, with a vibrant front bar and cosy rear room, has been identified by CAMRA as having a nationally important historic pub interior. Their very own Master Cellarman keeps excellent permanent ales alongside regularly rotating guest ales, complemented by a good range of craft, cider, wine and spirits. The strict house rules include a no groups policy and produce an atmosphere that is friendly and promotes rich conversation for locals and visitors alike. This gem of a place was local CAMRA pub of the year in 2022. Q & ♣ 🖪 ✿ 🛜

Fox

168 Holgate Road, Holgate, YO24 4DQ
☎ (01904) 787722
Ossett Yorkshire Blonde, White Rat, Silver King, Excelsius; Tetley Bitter; 3 changing beers (sourced regionally; often Fernandes, Ossett, Rat) Ⓗ
Located in the Holgate district of York, the Fox is a pub with a great atmosphere whose history is linked to the golden age of rail. It was sympathetically restored by Ossett brewery in 2014. Beer festivals in the spring and summer always prove popular, and the pub provides outdoor catering on a regular basis throughout the year. It has the largest beer garden in York, with a serving hatch open on busy days. See social media for up-to-date events. ὄ🏵♿🅿🚃(1,5)🏵🅯🛜♪

Golden Ball ★ Ⓛ

2 Cromwell Road, YO1 6DU
☎ (01904) 849040 ⊕ goldenballyork.co.uk
Acorn Barnsley Bitter; Ainsty Assassin; Timothy Taylor Golden Best; 3 changing beers (sourced regionally; often Salopian, Stubbee, Whitby) Ⓗ
A fine Victorian street-corner community run local with an impressive glazed brick exterior that was extensively refurbished by John Smith's in 1929. Grade II-listed, it has four very different rooms – a main bar, back room, comfortable lounge and snug. Outside is a large south-facing beer garden. Seven handpumps serve three permanent ales plus three changing guests. Local produce is on sale in the bar as well as Scotch eggs, pork pies and nuts. Q🕭🏵♿🌂♣🏵♪

Maltings Ⓛ

Tanners Moat, YO1 6HU
☎ (01904) 655387 ⊕ maltings.co.uk
Black Sheep Best Bitter; York Guzzler; 5 changing beers (sourced nationally; often Rooster's) Ⓗ
The Maltings has been a must for beer-lovers for 30 years, continuously improving to stay ahead of the competition. The beer range and quality, in both cask and keg, is excellent, covering all styles and strengths, along with a good selection of real cider. The food options are fairly typical for a pub, but the quality, quantity and value are outstanding. An extension added a few years ago provides more space and an outdoor area whilst maintaining the pub's unique character. Q🏵◑🌂♣🚃♪

Market Cat

6 Jubbergate, YO1 8RT
☎ (01904) 637023 ⊕ marketcatyork.co.uk
Thornbridge Lord Marples, Jaipur IPA; 6 changing beers (often Hawkshead, Tapped (Sheffield), Thornbridge) Ⓗ
In the heart of York, adjoining the Shambles market, this pub is operated by Thornbridge and Pivovar. With traditional pub decor on the ground floor, the first and second floors feature large windows with fine views of the market below and the skyline towards York Minster. A real pizza oven is a feature of the upper floors. A changing range of real ales is served from eight handpumps, with a mixture of beers from Thornbridge, Tapped and other independent breweries. ὄ◑🌂🚃🏵🛜

Minster Inn ✪

24 Marygate, YO30 7BH
☎ (01904) 849240 ⊕ minsterinn.com
Ilkley Blonde; Ossett White Rat; Timothy Taylor Boltmaker; 2 changing beers (sourced regionally) Ⓗ
This traditional Edwardian pub serves a wide range of popular stone-baked pizzas along with other fare. The pub has a front bar, two side rooms and a heated covered area towards the rear with table service for drinks and food. It is advisable to book a table for late afternoon, evening and weekend visits! It is within close walking distance of the Museum gardens, the Yorkshire Museum, Ouse riverside and the city centre. Q🕭🏵♿◑🚃🏵

Phoenix ▾

75 George Street, YO1 9PT
☎ (01904) 656401 ⊕ phoenixinnyork.co.uk
Timothy Taylor Landlord; 4 changing beers (sourced regionally; often Saltaire, Wold Top) Ⓗ
Independently-run true free house next to Fishergate within the city walls. Friendly and welcoming, the excellent choice of cask beers usually includes a dark beer. There is a real log fire in the front room on colder days. It is renowned locally for live music on most nights, mainly jazz and blues. The small, enclosed beer garden has a fine view of the city wall. There is a bar billiards table in the back room. A true gem and not to be missed. Local CAMRA Pub of the Year 2023. Q🏵♣🚃🏵🛜♪

Rook & Gaskill Ⓛ

12 Lawrence Street, YO10 3WP
☎ (01904) 671548 ⊕ rookandgaskillyork.co.uk
6 changing beers (sourced nationally; often Brass Castle, Castle Rock, Turning Point) Ⓗ
This thriving pub is home to locals, students and beer devotees. A wide range of reasonably-priced ales is served, including from on-site brewery 3 Non Beards and other LocAles. Six cask lines, 20 KeyKeg taps and three real ciders cater for all tastes, and there is a good range of food cooked to order. A Thursday night quiz and other events are hosted at this former local CAMRA Pub of the Year. 🏵◑♣🚃🏵🛜

Slip Inn Ⓛ

Clementhorpe, YO23 1AN
☎ (01904) 621793 ⊕ theslipinnyork.co.uk
Leeds Pale; Rudgate Ruby Mild; Timothy Taylor Boltmaker; 5 changing beers (sourced nationally; often Brass Castle, Marble, Turning Point) Ⓗ
Legendary back-street free house in former shipbuilding neighbourhood, lovingly restored and improved. It attracts loyal clientele of serious beer lovers with its large and interesting beer range. Occasional festivals and music events are held in the rear beer garden. An attractive stained glass door and local history displays provide interest. Darts, dominoes, cards and other games are available, and dogs and families are welcome. A former local CAMRA Pub of the Year. ὄ🏵♣🚃(11)🏵♪

Swan ★ Ⓛ

16 Bishopgate Street, YO23 1JH
☎ (01904) 634968 ⊕ theswanyork.co.uk
Half Moon Dark Masquerade; Tetley Bitter; Timothy Taylor Landlord; house beer (by Half Moon); 4 changing beers (sourced nationally; often Half Moon, Revolutions, Stubbee) Ⓗ
On entering this historic Grade II-listed pub you'll be greeted by an ever-changing upcoming beers board. Good things may come to those who wait, but don't worry as the eight beers on tap, including their own house blonde, offer a range of tastes and styles for everyone. The pub is a haven for locals while welcoming newcomers in search of good beer. You can take a seat in the front or back room, stand in the traditional West Riding-style drinking lobby or in the partially-covered beer garden. 🏵♣🚃(11,26)🏵

Volunteer Arms Ⓛ

5 Watson Street, YO24 4BH
☎ (01904) 541945 ⊕ volunteerarmsyork.co.uk

Bradfield Farmers Blonde; Brass Castle Bad Kitty; Leeds Yorkshire Gold; Rooster's Buckeye; Timothy Taylor Landlord; 2 changing beers (sourced nationally) ⌂

Hidden up a back street near the iron bridge over the main rail line is this gem of a street-corner pub rescued from closure and punching well above its weight. Popular with locals and discerning beer drinkers, five permanent Yorkshire ales and two changing, often interesting guests from all over are on offer, alongside four interesting keg beers from Farmers and Turning Point, and two changing craft keg beers. Quiz night is every Sunday. ☕✤♿≒●🍴(1,5)👹☎

Waggon & Horses 🅛

19 Lawrence Street, YO10 3BP
☎ (01904) 637478 ⊕ waggonandhorsesyork.com
Batemans XB, XXXB; Oakham Citra; 4 changing beers (sourced nationally; often Ossett, Rooster's) ⌂
Run by a young but well-established couple, this multi-roomed pub offers B&B accommodation. Seven cask ales are on sale, with the option to enjoy them in rooms with a TV or in quieter surroundings. There is a pleasant beer garden and outside drinking area where you can enjoy the LocAle beers on offer. Bar billiards and a large collection of board games provide entertainment. ☕✤🛏🛋♣🍴👹☎

York Tap

Railway Station, Station Road, YO24 1AB
☎ (01904) 659009 ⊕ yorktap.com
Timothy Taylor Golden Best, Boltmaker, Knowle Spring, Landlord; 18 changing beers (sourced nationally; often Anarchy, Tapped (Sheffield), Thornbridge) ⌂
Award-winning conversion of the Victorian tea rooms on York station which opened as a pub in 2010. The ornate ceiling, Art Deco stained-glass windows, terrazzo floors and stained-glass ceiling domes create an impressive backdrop to the central bar with 20 handpumps. On sale are 18 cask beers plus two ciders or perries, as well as a large range of keg and bottled beer. All styles and strengths are represented. No meals are served, though pies are available at the bar. 👹♿≒●🍴👹

Breweries

3 Non Beards

🍴 Rook & Gaskill, 12 Lawrence Street, York, YO10 3WP ☎ 07980 994210 ⊕ 3nonbeards.co.uk

😀Launched in 2019 as a partnership of three friends, this one-barrel brewery is in the basement of the award-winning Rook & Gaskill. Advised by innovative local brewers, the beer range can be found in the pub and at beer festivals. Around 30 brews per year means an eclectic variety of mainly one-offs, and frequent single hop beers. ♦🤏

Ainsty SIBA

Manor Farm, Intake Lane, Acaster Malbis, York, YO23 3UJ
☎ (01904) 703233 ☎ 07983 604989
⊕ ainstyales.co.uk

😀Based in the ancient York & Ainsty Wapentake in York, this award-winning, brewery and taproom opened in 2016 with a 10-barrel kit, supplying venues mainly in Yorkshire, but also throughout the UK via wholesalers and online. The taproom is open on Friday plus Saturdays (May-Oct) with street food and live music. ‼🍴♦🤏

Northern Lights (ABV 3.6%) GOLD
Flummoxed Farmer (ABV 4%) BLOND
Bantam Best (ABV 4.2%) BITTER
Cool Citra (ABV 4.4%) PALE
Assassin (ABV 4.9%) STOUT

Another Beer

Unit 3, Handley Park, Elvington Industrial Estate, York Road, Elvington, YO41 4AR ☎ 07403 264242
⊕ anotherbeer.co.uk

Launched in 2019 by James Fawcett, Another Beer moved from York city centre into the former Hop Studio in Elvington in 2022. Additional space and increased brewing capacity has seen an expansion into cask production. Beers are available in York as well as having distribution across Yorkshire, Manchester and the Midlands. 🤏

Bayonet

Office: Cotswold Street, Brompton, DL6 2BX
⊕ bayonetbrewing.co.uk

Established in 2021 by Serviceman Alex Postles, the brewery is a part-time operation with long-term aims to expand into premises in Northallerton. Focusing on innovative, modern craft beers the brewery has established itself in the local area and is rapidly spreading further afield. The core range is supported by a rotating array of specialist IPAs, pale ales and stouts. ♦V

Delta Lima Six (ABV 4%) PALE

Black Sheep SIBA

Wellgarth, Masham, Ripon, HG4 4EN
☎ (01765) 689227 ⊕ blacksheepbrewery.co.uk

😀Established in 1992 by Paul Theakston, a member of Masham's famous brewing family, the brewery operation was sold to Breal Group in 2023. It is situated in the former Wellgarth Maltings and uses the traditional Yorkshire Square fermenting system. The company supplies the free trade across Yorkshire and the North, with national supply through pubcos and wholesale channels. It acquired York Brewery and its pub estate in 2018. ‼🍴♦🤏

Best Bitter (ABV 3.8%) BITTER
Respire (ABV 4%) PALE
Special Ale (ABV 4.4%) BITTER
Riggwelter (ABV 5.9%) BITTER

Brass Castle SIBA

10A Yorkersgate, Malton, YO17 7AB
☎ (01653) 698683 ⊕ brasscastle.co.uk

😀Having begun life modestly in 2011 on a one-barrel kit in the owner's garage, the brewery, now based in the centre of Malton, expanded its capacity in 2023 from a 12 to 25-barrel state-of-the-art plant. All beers produced are vegan-friendly and brewed to a gluten-free recipe (canned beers certified gluten free). Traditional and modern interpretations of beer styles, with the occasional flair for the outlandish and use of unconventional ingredients. The adjacent brewery tap (open Tues–Sun) showcases up to ten draft beers, with many more available for off-sales. ‼🍴♦GF V

Session Mini IPA (ABV 3.6%) PALE
Northern Blonde (ABV 3.9%) BLOND
Hoptical Illusion (ABV 4.3%) PALE
Misfit (ABV 4.3%) GOLD
Bluebell IPA (ABV 4.5%) IPA
Fruit Lupe (ABV 4.8%) PALE

Bad Kitty (ABV 5.5%) SPECIALITY
Sunshine (ABV 5.7%) IPA

Brew York SIBA

Unit 6, Enterprise Complex, Walmgate, York, YO1 9TT
☎ (01904) 848448

Second Site: Handley Park, Outgang Lane, Osbaldwick, YO19 5UP ⊕ brewyork.co.uk

☺Established in 2016, Brew York was born out of two friends' passion for beer and brewing. The original brewery is located within York's historic city walls, a 15-minute walk from the station. A unique taproom and beer hall (including kitchen) with riverside beer garden sits alongside the original 10-barrel brewery which now specialises in barrel-aged and mixed fermentation beers. A new state-of-the-art, twin 30-barrel brewery has been built to the east of the city for larger scale production. ‼️🍴♦️🍂

Calmer Chameleon (ABV 3.7%) PALE
Minstermen Pride (ABV 3.7%) PALE
Haze of Thunder (ABV 4.2%) PALE
Tonkoko (ABV 4.3%) SPECIALITY

Captain Cook

Rear of White Swan, 1 West End, Stokesley, TS9 5BL
☎ (01642) 714985 ⊕ whiteswanstokesley.co.uk

☺Having celebrated its 20th anniversary in 2019, the Captain Cook Brewery is located behind the 18th century White Swan pub. The brewery, which supplies the pub, uses a four-barrel plant. ‼️♦️

Navigator (ABV 4%) GOLD
Sunset (ABV 4%) GOLD
Slipway (ABV 4.2%) BLOND
Endeavour (ABV 4.3%) BROWN
Skippy (ABV 4.3%) GOLD
Black Porter (ABV 4.4%) PORTER
APA (ABV 4.7%) PALE
Schooner (ABV 4.7%) STOUT
IPA (ABV 5.1%) PALE

Cold Bath

🏠 46 Kings Road, Harrogate, HG1 5JW ☎ 0330 880 7009 ⊕ coldbathbrewing.com

Launched in 2018, Cold Bath's onsite brewery can be viewed on the mezzanine level above the bar. All beers are available in the pub and wider free trade.

Copper Dragon

Snaygill Industrial Estate, Keighley Road, Skipton, BD23 2QR
☎ (01756) 243243 ⊕ copperdragon.co.uk

☺Copper Dragon brew in Skipton using a 15-barrel plant. As well as the core range of Copper Dragon beers, Recoil Craft beers are also brewed, with both brands also featuring special editions.

Best Bitter (ABV 3.8%) BITTER
Golden Pippin (ABV 3.9%) BLOND
Golden session beer, fruity and hoppy in aroma and taste. Citrus comes comes through in the aftertaste which is increasingly bitter.
Black Gold (ABV 4%) MILD
Silver Myst (ABV 4%) SPECIALITY
Scotts 1816 (ABV 4.1%) BITTER

Brewed under the Recoil brand name:
Antidote (ABV 3.8%) BLOND

Craven SIBA

Units 9-10, Midland Mills, Station Road, Cross Hills, BD20 7DT
☎ (01535) 637451 ⊕ cravenbrew.co.uk

☺A cask-led and focused brewery established in Cross Hills in 2022. The 16-barrel plant brews twice weekly producing five core beers together with specials. The adjacent taproom is open daily. ‼️♦️

Session Pale Ale (ABV 3.7%) PALE
Balanced, yellow, premium bitter. Citrusy hops on the nose with underlying orange sweetness that leads to a short, sweet finish.
Best Yorkshire Bitter (ABV 3.8%) BITTER
Light brown session bitter. Malt led in taste, balanced with a roasty nuttiness and citrus overtones. Finish is increasingly bitter.
Extra Fine Ale (ABV 4.2%) BITTER
Hop-led, yellow session bitter, with initial malt sweetness overtaken by a tropical fruitiness leading to a long bitter finish.
Black Angus Porter (ABV 4.5%) PORTER
Sweet malts and roast on the nose. Followed by tastes of bitter chocolate, liquorice and dark cherries. Finish is long and bitter with balancing fruity sweetness.
Craven Pale Ale (ABV 4.8%) BITTER
Golden-coloured bitter with malty base overlaid with grassy hoppiness. Citrus fruit comes through and leads to a long increasing bitter finish. A big beer for its strength.

Crooked

Units 12-15, The Garages, Leeds East Airport, Church Fenton, LS24 9SE ☎ 07890 526505
⊕ crookedbrewing.co.uk

☺After teaching homebrewing, Steve, Andy, Hudson and Mark started brewing in 2017 on the old RAF airfield at Church Fenton. Beers are increasingly available in a number of city centre pubs and bars in York and Leeds and many brews are canned for wider distribution. The brewery tap, Crooked Tap, opened in 2019 at Acomb Green, York, with another opening in Driffield in 2023. ♦️🍂

Spokes (ABV 4%) BITTER
Standard Bitter (ABV 4.2%) BITTER
The Lash (ABV 4.4%) PALE
XX (ABV 4.6%) PALE
Rufus (ABV 4.8%) PORTER

Cropton

Rear of New Inn, Main Street, Cropton, YO18 8HH
☎ (01751) 469800

☺Established in 1984, the brewery was built behind the New Inn in 1994. After various incarnations the brewery returned to Lee family ownership in 2023. Beers are available throughout Yorkshire and nationally through wholesalers. ‼️♦️LIVE

Yorkshire Pale (ABV 3.8%) PALE
Yorkshire Classic (ABV 4%) BITTER
Yorkshire Golden (ABV 4.2%) GOLD
Yorkshire Moors (ABV 4.6%) BITTER

Daleside SIBA

Camwal Road, Starbeck, Harrogate, HG1 4PT
☎ (01423) 880022 ⊕ dalesidebrewery.com

☺Daleside Brewery was established in the mid-1980s, and moved to its current site in 1992. Beers are sold to local, regional and national customers and export markets include Denmark, Sweden and Australia. 🚚♦️

Bitter (ABV 3.7%) BITTER
Blonde (ABV 3.9%) BLOND
Old Leg Over (ABV 4.1%) BITTER
Monkey Wrench (ABV 5.3%) BITTER

Dark Horse SIBA

Coonlands Laithe, Hetton, Nr. Skipton, BD23 6LY
☎ (01756) 730555 ⊕ darkhorsebrewery.co.uk

☺Dark Horse began brewing in 2008. The brewery is based in an old hay barn within the Yorkshire Dales National Park. Around 50 outlets are supplied direct.

Craven Bitter (ABV 3.8%) BITTER
Well-balanced bitter with biscuity malt and fruit on the nose continuing into the taste. Bitterness increases in the finish.
Blonde Beauty (ABV 3.9%) GOLD
Hetton Pale Ale (ABV 4.2%) PALE
Earthy bitterness on the palate overlaying a malty base and a spicy citrus character.
Night Jar (ABV 4.2%) BITTER
A malty, fruity bitter in aroma and taste. Caramel and dark fruits lace the finish

Elvington

Station Yard, York Road, Elvington, YO41 4EL
☎ (01904) 607167 ⊕ pivovarorders.co.uk/
elvington-brewery

Part of the Pivovar Group that was established in 2021 to brew Mittel Pils lager for its pubs. No real ale. ♦

Great British Breworks

34 Dove Way, Kirkby Mills Industrial Estate,
Kirkbymoorside, YO62 6QR
☎ (01751) 433111 ☎ 07876 827475

Office: c/o Black Swan Hotel, 18 Birdgate, Pickering,
YO18 7AL ⊕ blackswan-pickering.co.uk/breworks

☺Brewing started on a permanent basis in the yard of the Black Swan, Pickering, in 2016, on a 2.5-barrel plant. In 2021, the brewery expanded by taking over the 12-barrel brewing plant in Kirkbymoorside previously used by Turning Point Brewery. The Black Swan serves as the brewery tap. ♦

Great Scot (ABV 3.8%) BITTER
Lightheaded (ABV 4%) PALE
Pathfinder (ABV 4.5%) BLOND
Coal Porter (ABV 4.6%) PORTER

Guisborough

14 South Buck Way, Guisborough, TS14 7FJ ☎ 07703
002858 ✉ info@guisboroughbrewery.co.uk

⊠ Established in 2020 using a five-barrel plant. The extensive core range consists of thirteen beers, brewed on a rotational basis, so not all of the beers are available all of the time. Events are held regularly and visitors, by arrangement, are made welcome. The brewery is open on Fridays and Saturdays for on and off sales. ‼▤♦

Dark Habit (ABV 3.7%) MILD
Delight (ABV 3.7%) BITTER
Alchemy (ABV 3.8%) BITTER
Realm (ABV 3.9%) GOLD
Phoenix (ABV 4%) RED
Daze (ABV 4.3%) IPA
Elevator (ABV 4.5%) IPA
Nut Kin (ABV 4.5%) PORTER
BOBA (ABV 5%) BROWN
Dangerous Brian (ABV 5%) SPECIALITY

Vypa (ABV 5.5%) IPA

Hambleton SIBA

Melmerby Green Road, Melmerby, HG4 5NB
☎ (01765) 640108 ⊕ hambletonbrewery.co.uk

☺Established 1991 by Nick Stafford in a barn at the bottom of his in-laws' garden. Now it's run by Nick's daughter Rachel and son-in-law Ben. Since 2007 it's operated from purpose-built premises near Ripon (100 barrels a week capacity). A core range of eight beers, plus cask ale is contract brewed for Village Brewer, Black Dog and Wharfe Beer Yorkshire. A bottling line handles brands for others. A canning line was added 2022 (unfiltered beers sold locally and via website). ‼▤♦

Session Pale (ABV 3.6%) PALE
Bootleggers Pale Ale (ABV 3.8%) PALE
Thoroughbred IPA (ABV 4%) PALE
Pink Grapefruit (ABV 4.1%) SPECIALITY
Stallion Amber (ABV 4.2%) BITTER
Stud Blonde (ABV 4.3%) GOLD
Black Forest (ABV 5%) SPECIALITY
Nightmare Porter (ABV 5%) STOUT

Contract brewed for Black Dog Brewery:
Whitby Abbey Ale (ABV 3.8%) BITTER
Schooner (ABV 4.2%) PALE
Rhatas (ABV 4.6%) BITTER

Contract brewed for Village Brewer:
White Boar (ABV 3.8%) BITTER
Bull (ABV 4%) GOLD

Contract brewed for Wharfe:
Verbeia (ABV 3.6%) BITTER
Tether Blond (ABV 3.8%) GOLD

Harrogate SIBA

Unit 7, Hookstone Centre, Hookstone Chase,
Harrogate, HG2 7HW ☎ 07593 259425
⊕ harrogatebrewery.co.uk

☺Established in 2013, the brewery also uses the names Spa Town Ales, and It's Quicker By Ale on its logo and pumpclips. The brewery has a capacity of 10 barrels, and brews several times each week. ▤♦

Harrogate Pale (ABV 4.2%) GOLD
Cold Bath Gold (ABV 4.4%) BLOND
Pinewoods Pale Ale (ABV 4.4%) GOLD
Plum Porter (ABV 4.8%) SPECIALITY
Vanilla Porter (ABV 4.8%) SPECIALITY
Beeching Axe (ABV 5.2%) BITTER
Kursaal Stout (ABV 6.7%) STOUT

Helmsley SIBA

18 Bridge Street, Helmsley, YO62 5DX
☎ (01439) 771014 ☎ 07525 434268
⊕ helmsleybrewingco.co.uk

☺Located within the North York Moors National Park, brewing began in 2014. The brewery has a viewing gallery, tasting room and tap. Local pubs are supplied. ‼▤LIVE♦

Yorkshire Legend (ABV 3.8%) BITTER
Striding the Riding (ABV 4%) BITTER
Howardian Gold (ABV 4.2%) GOLD
Honey (ABV 4.5%) SPECIALITY
H!PA (ABV 5.5%) IPA

Ice Cream Factory

21 Fetter Lane, York, YO1 9TA ☎ 07880 547393
⊕ theicecreamfactory.com

Nano-brewery located in the old Capaldi's ice cream factory, established in 2017.

Isaac Poad SIBA

Office: Hay House, Baxby Manor, Husthwaite, YO61 4PW
☎ (01423) 358114 ⊕ isaacpoadbrewing.co.uk

☺Established in 2016 by a local grain merchant, which formerly supplied malting barley to local maltsters, the brewery continues despite the subsequent demise of the parent company. Pending construction of its own brew plant, production is actually carried out at another local brewery. ♦

No. 86 Golden Ale (ABV 3.6%) GOLD
1863 Best Bitter (ABV 3.8%) BITTER
No.91 Craft Ale (ABV 3.9%) GOLD
All Four Yorkshire Red Ale (ABV 4.2%) RED
No.84 India Pale Ale (ABV 4.5%) PALE
Piccadilly Porter (ABV 4.8%) PORTER

Jolly Sailor SIBA

▤ **Olympia Hotel Tap House, 77 Barlby Road, Selby, YO8 5AB**
☎ (01757) 707564 ☎ 07923 635755
⊕ jollysailorbrewery.uk

☺The Jolly Sailor Brewery is an independent family-run microbrewery established in 2013 in the grounds of the Olympia Hotel Tap House in Selby, on the nearby River Ouse and close to the 11th century abbey. Beers are brewed on a six-barrel plant and available at the brewery's Jolly Sailor Inn, Cawood, and extensively in the free trade. ‼▤♦☙

Selby Bitter (ABV 3.8%) BITTER
Selby Blonde (ABV 3.8%) BLOND
Selby Pale (ABV 3.9%) PALE
Selby Mild (ABV 4%) MILD
Milk Stout (ABV 4.5%) STOUT
Dark Nights Porter (ABV 5%) PORTER

Lady Luck

▤ **Little Angel, 18 Flowergate, Whitby, YO21 3BA**
☎ (01947) 820475 ☎ 07920 282506

☺Lady Luck is a 0.5-barrel brewery situated at the back of the Little Angel, Whitby. Brewing began in 2018 and takes place four times a week. Beers, some infused with spirits, are distributed across North Yorkshire as well as at beer festivals. ♦LIVE

Kraken (ABV 3.9%) IPA
Pirate's Treasure (ABV 4%) GOLD
Shipwreck Blonde (ABV 4.2%) BLOND
Black Cat (ABV 4.5%) PORTER

LAMB

Queens Arms, Litton, BD23 5QJ ☎ 07900 013245
⊕ lambbrewing.com

☺The LAMB Brewing Company brews on a 600-litre plant behind the Queen's Arms in Litton. Independently-owned, the beer is served in the pub, as well as a few other outlets in the local area. Cask, boxed and pouched beers are available.

X Mild (ABV 3.2%) MILD
X Mild (Dark) (ABV 3.2%) MILD
Ruby brown mild with a malty aroma. Fruit background to caramel and sweet nuttiness in the taste. Finish of cocoa.
Bitter (ABV 3.7%) BITTER

Brown session bitter with malt and hops in the aroma. Fruit and a subtle nuttiness in the taste, lead to a lingering bitter finish.
Pale (ABV 3.9%) GOLD

Little Black Dog

Carlton Brewery, Duddings Farm, Carlton, DN14 9LU
☎ 07495 026173 ⊕ littleblackdogbeer.com

Established in 2015, Little Black Dog is a small batch, family-run brewery. All beer is unfined, unpasteurised and unfiltered. The brewery tap is the Doghouse, Selby. ▤♦

Yorkshire Bitter (ABV 3.8%) BITTER
Big Red American Amber (ABV 4.5%) RED
Oatmeal Stout (ABV 4.5%) STOUT

Live

Hudswell ✉ livebrewco@gmail.com

Four-barrel microbrewery set up by the team behind the 2016 National Pub of the Year, the George & Dragon, Hudswell. It specialises in small-scale one-off brews utilising traditional techniques and locally foraged ingredients. Brewing is currently suspended.

Malton

5 Navigation Wharf, Off Yorkersgate, Malton, YO17 7AA ☎ 07946 776613 ⊕ maltonbrewery.com

Microbrewery situated on the banks of the Derwent, operating since 2018. Owner Howard Kinder had previously launched Horsetown Beers in 2016. The brewery produces Yorkshire Pudding beer in bottles. LIVE

Mithril

Aldbrough St John, DL11 7TL
☎ (01325) 374817 ☎ 07889 167128
✉ mithril58@btinternet.com

☺Mithril started brewing in 2010 in old stables opposite the brewer's house on a 2.5-barrel plant. Owner Pete Fenwick, a well-known craft brewer, brews twice a week to supply the local areas of Darlington, Richmond and Teesdale. A new beer is usually brewed every two weeks. ♦

Dere Street (ABV 3.8%) BITTER
Flower Power (ABV 3.9%) SPECIALITY
A66 (ABV 4%) GOLD
Kingdom of Ovingtonia (ABV 4%) BROWN

Molson Coors (Tadcaster)

Tower Brewery, Wetherby Road, Tadcaster, LS24 9JR
⊕ molsoncoorsbrewers.com

Molson Coors is the result of a merger between Molson of Canada and Coors of Colorado, US. Coors established itself in Europe in 2002 by buying part of the former Bass brewing empire, when Interbrew (now A-B InBev) was instructed by the British Government to divest itself of some of its interests in Bass. Coors owns several cask ale brands. It brews 110,000 barrels of cask beer a year (under licensing arrangements with other brewers) and also provides a further 50,000 barrels of cask beer for other breweries. In 2011 Molson Coors bought Sharp's brewery in Cornwall (qv). No cask ale is produced in Burton or Tadcaster.

North Riding (Brewery)

Unit 6, Barker's Lane, Snainton, YO13 9BD

☎ (01723) 864845 ⊕ northridingbrewery.com

🍺Having outgrown the brewpub in Scarborough, Stuart Neilson established a 10-barrel brewery in East Ayton on the outskirts of Scarborough in 2015. In early 2019 operations moved to a much larger premises in Snainton, enabling further expansion of brewing capacity. Concentrating on hop-forward beers, distribution is throughout the North of England and the Midlands. ♦LIVE

Mosaic Pale Ale (ABV 4.3%) PALE
Citra Pale Ale (ABV 4.5%) PALE

North Riding (Brewpub)

⛴ North Marine Road, Scarborough, YO12 7HU
☎ (01723) 370004 ⊕ northridingbrewpub.com

🍺Brewing commenced in 2011 using a two-barrel plant situated in the cellar of the pub, which is now brewing to capacity with three fermenting vessels. ♦

Pennine SIBA

Well Hall Farm, Well, Bedale, DL8 2PX
☎ (01677) 470111 ⊕ pennine-brewing.co.uk

🍺Located in the village of Well near Masham, the brewery has been in production on this site since 2013 using an 18-barrel plant complete with lauter tun. Beer is supplied to pubs throughout the North of England as well as to beer festivals and local outdoor events. ‼♦

Amber Necker (ABV 3.9%) BITTER
Hair of the Dog (ABV 3.9%) BITTER
Heartland (ABV 3.9%) BITTER
Millie George (ABV 4.1%) PALE
Scapegoat (ABV 4.2%) GOLD
IPA (ABV 4.4%) PALE

Play

8 Cannon Park Way, Middlesbrough, TS1 5JU
☎ (01642) 244769 ⊕ playbrewco.com

Launched in 2019, Play Brew is a brewery, taproom and event space. The 20-hectolitre plant produces unfiltered beers available in keg, cans and occasionally in cask, distributed throughout the north. ♦✦

Redscar SIBA

⛴ Cleveland Hotel, 9-11 High Street West, Redcar, TS10 1SQ
☎ (01642) 513727 ☎ 07828 855146
⊕ redscar-brewery.co.uk

🍺Redscar first brewed in 2008. In 2014 it increased its capacity to a five-barrel plant. The brewery supplies the hotel, local pubs and beer festivals. ‼♦

Blonde (ABV 3.8%) BLOND
Poison (ABV 4%) BITTER
Beach (ABV 5%) BITTER

Richmond SIBA

Station Brewery, Station Yard, Richmond, DL10 4LD
☎ (01748) 828266 ⊕ richmondbrewing.co.uk

🍺Richmond opened in 2008 in the renovated Victorian station complex beside the River Swale. Production is split 50/50 between cask-conditioned and bottled beers. The former are available in the local area at the Castle Tavern, Richmond, as well as direct from the brewery. ‼🍺♦LIVE✦

Homefront (ABV 3.5%) MILD
SwAle (ABV 3.7%) MILD

Gundog Bitter (ABV 3.8%) BITTER
Station Ale (ABV 4%) BITTER
Greyfriars Stout (ABV 4.2%) STOUT
Red Rufus (ABV 4.2%) RED
Dale Strider (ABV 4.5%) GOLD
Stump Cross Ale (ABV 4.7%) OLD
Pale Ale (ABV 5%) PALE
1071 (ABV 7.1%) IPA

Rooster's SIBA

Unit H5, Fifth Avenue, Hornbeam Park, Harrogate, HG2 8QT
☎ (01423) 865959 ⊕ roosters.co.uk

🍺Roosters is an independent, family-owned brewery and taproom which celebrated its 30th anniversary in 2023. Weekly production capacity is 200 barrels, which includes one-off experimental beers, brewed as part of the brewery's Outlaw Project. 🛒♦✦

Buckeye (ABV 3.5%) GOLD
Highway 51 (ABV 3.7%) PALE
Capability Brown (ABV 4%) BITTER
YPA (Yorkshire Pale Ale) (ABV 4.1%) PALE
London Thunder (ABV 4.2%) PORTER
Yankee (ABV 4.3%) PALE
Hops and gentle fruitiness make this is an easy-drinking, well-balanced, light gold beer, some grapefruit present, finishing dry.
TwentyFourSeven (ABV 4.7%) PALE
Thousand Yard Stare (ABV 5.4%) PALE
Baby-Faced Assassin (ABV 6.1%) IPA
Strength In Numbers (ABV 7%) IPA

Rudgate SIBA

2 Centre Park, Marston Moor Business Park, Tockwith, York, YO26 7QF
☎ (01423) 358382 ⊕ rudgatebrewery.co.uk

🍺Rudgate Brewery is in its 32nd year in 2024. It is situated in the heart of Yorkshire, in the Vale of York, on the old RAF Marston Moor airfield. The old Roman road of Rudgate runs through the airfield and led the Vikings into Jorvik (York), which is what inspires many of the beer names. It brews six core cask beers and two seasonals each month. ♦

Jorvik Blonde (ABV 3.8%) BLOND
Viking (ABV 3.8%) BITTER
An initially warming and malty, full-bodied beer, with hops and fruit lingering into the aftertaste.
Battleaxe (ABV 4.2%) BITTER
A well-hopped bitter with slightly sweet initial taste and light bitterness. Complex fruit character gives a memorable aftertaste.
Ruby Mild (ABV 4.4%) MILD
Nutty, rich ruby ale, stronger than usual for a mild.
Valkyrie APA (ABV 5%) PALE
York Chocolate Stout (ABV 5%) STOUT

Salt Steel

Office: 24 St Cuthberts Way, Darlington, DL1 1GB
⊕ saltsteelbrewing.com

Established in 2020 and forged from the industrial landscapes of Teeside and Cheshire, Salt Steel Brewing have been collaborating with other brewers in the North East.

Scarborough SIBA

Unit 21b, Stadium Works, Barry's Lane, Scarborough, YO12 4HA
☎ (01723) 367506 ⊕ scarboroughbrewery.co.uk

⊙Scarborough is a family-run brewery established in 2010, now using a 10-barrel plant. Beers can be found in the family-owned Valley Bar and Rivelyn Hotel as well as being the sole suppliers to Merchant Bar, Scarborough. ♦

Trident (ABV 3.8%) PALE
Citra (ABV 4.2%) GOLD
Sealord (ABV 4.3%) GOLD
Stout (ABV 4.6%) STOUT
Hello Darkness (ABV 5%) PORTER

Selby Middlebrough SIBA

131 Millgate, Selby, YO8 3LL
☎ (01757) 702826 ✉ martinsykesuk@yahoo.com

Small batch brewery launched in 2022. Beers are produced primarily for its brewery tap, Howden Arms, Howden, East Yorkshire.

Settle SIBA

Unit 2B, The Sidings, Settle, BD24 9RP
☎ (01729) 824936 ⊕ settlebrewery.co.uk

⊙Settle Brewery is located in an industrial unit adjacent to Settle Railway Station. Brewing started in 2013 using a 12-barrel plant. It supplies more than 40 outlets across Cumbria, North and West Yorkshire and Lancashire. The beers are also available through wholesalers. Beers are occasionally branded as Nine Standards. !!♦

Jericho Blonde (ABV 3.6%) BLOND
Ribblehead Bitter (ABV 3.8%) BITTER
Hoffman Gold (ABV 4.1%) GOLD
Attermire Pale (ABV 4.3%) PALE
Epic IPA (ABV 4.4%) PALE
Ernie's Milk Stout (ABV 4.5%) STOUT
A ruby red beer with fruity roasted malt and caramel aromas. Roast malt, vine fruits and dark chocolate lead to a long bitter finish.
Old Smithy Porter (ABV 4.7%) PORTER
Roasty porter with coffee and dark fruits. Hints of liquorice and plums in the aroma. The finish is bitter and roasty.

Samuel Smith

The Old Brewery, High Street, Tadcaster, LS24 9SB
☎ (01937) 832225 ⊕ samuelsmithsbrewery.co.uk

⊙Fiercely-independent, family-owned company. Tradition, quality and value are important, resulting in brewing without any artificial additives. The majority of products are vegan-friendly, with the exception of Old Brewery Bitter and Yorkshire Stingo. All real ale is supplied in traditional wooden casks. LIVE V

Old Brewery Bitter (ABV 4%) BITTER

John Smith

The Brewery, Tadcaster, LS24 9SA
☎ (01937) 832091 ⊕ heineken.com

The brewery was built in 1879 by a relative of Samuel Smith (qv). John Smith's became part of the Courage group in 1970 before being taken over by S&N and now Heineken UK. John Smith's cask Magnet has been discontinued. No real ale

Theakston SIBA

The Brewery, Masham, HG4 4YD
☎ (01765) 680000 ⊕ theakstons.co.uk

⊙An independent, family business, established in 1827 by Robert Theakston. From 1984, for 19 years the brewery was in non-family hands. Following a successful buy back in 2003, the company returned to family control, managed by Simon Theakston and his three brothers (great-great grandsons of the founder). Significant investment in the brewery since then has provided additional capacity and flexibility to meet growing demand and variety of beers brewed. !!♦❧

Best Bitter (ABV 3.8%) BITTER
Easy-drinking amber ale with a good malty fruity taste with some bitterness.
Black Bull Bitter (ABV 3.9%) BITTER
Lightfoot (ABV 4.1%) PALE
XB (ABV 4.5%) BITTER
Malt forward sweet beer rounded out by some fruitiness, light brown in colour.
Old Peculier (ABV 5.6%) OLD
A complex, full-bodied, dark brown strong ale. Malty and roasty with hints of treacle, coffee and liquorice, finishing sweet and fruity.

Turning Point SIBA

Unit 3, Grimbald Park, Wetherby Road, Knaresborough, HG5 8LJ
☎ (01423) 869967 ⊕ turningpointbrewco.com

⊗ Two friends, Cameron Brown and Aron McMahon, began brewing in Kirkbymoorside in 2017, before relocating to the former Roosters brewery in Knaresborough in 2019. All beers are unfined and unfiltered. The Falcon, Micklegate, York, is the brewery tap. ♦❧

Wavelength (ABV 4.5%) GOLD
Lucid Dream (ABV 5%) SPECIALITY
Disco King (ABV 5.1%) PALE

Twisted Wheel

Rear of New Inn, Cropton Lane, Cropton, YO18 8HH
☎ 07463 895811 ⊕ twistedwheelbrewco.co.uk

⊙Twisted Wheel began brewing in 2020 using a 10-barrel brew plant. In 2020 it moved from Standish to Warrington and subsequently, in 2023, across the Pennines to Cropton, North Yorkshire. An extensive range of beer is available in cask, can and keg. ♦V

Wensleydale SIBA

Unit 4, Badger Court, Harmby Road, Leyburn, DL8 5BF
☎ (01969) 622463 ☎ 07765 596666
⊕ wensleydalebrewery.co.uk

⊙Wensleydale was set up in 2003 and moved to larger premises in Leyburn in 2018 utilising a 12-barrel plant. Around 400 outlets are supplied direct in Yorkshire, Co Durham, Teeside, Tyneside and Cumbria. There is an onsite shop and special events bar. A regular different special is brewed every week. !!☲♦❧

Falconer (ABV 3.9%) BITTER
Semer Water (ABV 4.1%) PALE
Gamekeeper (ABV 4.3%) BITTER
Well-balanced hoppy bitter, malty start with some fruitiness. All flavours linger until the hop bitterness dominates the finish.
Black Dub (ABV 4.4%) STOUT
Malty and roast start with caramel sweetness along with hints of fruit and coffee. The finish sees all flavours persisting with the roast bitterness still in charge.

Whitby SIBA

East Cliff, Whitby, YO22 4JR

☎ (01947) 228871 ☎ 07516 116377
🌐 whitby-brewery.com

Whitby Brewery was established in 2012 under the Conquest name. It expanded in 2016 to a new site in the shadow of Whitby Abbey, with a 20-barrel capacity. Music events are hosted occasionally at weekends. Due to local demand, most of the beer is only distributed in the Whitby area. ‼ ☞ ⚭

Abbey Blonde (ABV 3.8%) BLOND
Whitby Whaler (ABV 4%) PALE
Saltwick Nab (ABV 4.2%) RED
Smugglers Gold (ABV 4.2%) BITTER
Jet Black (ABV 4.5%) PORTER
IPA (ABV 5.2%) BITTER

Wold Top SIBA

Hunmanby Grange, Wold Newton, Driffield, YO25 3HS
☎ (01723) 892222 🌐 woldtopbrewery.co.uk

☺Family-owned, farm-based brewery Wold Top has been creating exceptional beer on the Yorkshire Coast since 2003. Using sustainably home-grown malting barley, chalk-filtered water, and powered by renewable energy, the brewery's range includes bitters, pale ales, golden ales, porters and IPAs, of which five are gluten-free. All beers are produced and packaged in-house and onsite using a modern 40-barrel brew kit. It also has the facility to contract package for other breweries too. ‼ ☞ ◆ GF

Bitter (ABV 3.7%) BITTER
Anglers Reward (ABV 4%) PALE
Wolds Way (ABV 4%) PALE
Headland Red (ABV 4.3%) BITTER
Against The Grain (ABV 4.5%) BLOND
Gold (ABV 4.8%) GOLD
Marmalade Porter (ABV 5%) SPECIALITY
Scarborough Fair IPA (ABV 6%) IPA

Yorkshire Dales

Abbey Works, Askrigg, DL8 4LP

☎ (01969) 622027 ☎ 07818 035592
🌐 yorkshiredalesbrewery.com

☺Situated in the heart of the Yorkshire Dales, brewing started in a converted milking parlour in 2005. In 2016 the brewery moved to larger premises. More than 150 pubs are supplied throughout the north of England. A taproom and bottle shop opened at the brewery in 2017. ‼ ☞ ◆ LIVE ⚭

Butter Tubs (ABV 3.7%) GOLD
Askrigg Bitter (ABV 3.8%) BITTER
Aysgarth Falls (ABV 3.8%) GOLD
Citrus hops and accompanying fruity aromas fill the mouth with their bittersweet flavours, leaving behind a long hoppy bitter finish.
Bainbridge Blonde (ABV 3.8%) BLOND
Buckden Pike (ABV 3.9%) BLOND
Drovers Arms (ABV 3.9%) MILD
Nappa Scar (ABV 4%) GOLD
Muker Silver (ABV 4.1%) BLOND
Askrigg Ale (ABV 4.3%) PALE
Garsdale Smokebox (ABV 5.6%) SPECIALITY

Yorkshire Heart SIBA

The Vineyard, Pool Lane, Nun Monkton, YO26 8EL
☎ (01423) 330716 ☎ 07838 030067
🌐 yorkshireheart.com

☺From 2011 Yorkshire Heart has been brewing at Nun Monkton near York, adjacent to the Yorkshire Heart vineyard and winery, run by the same family. The brewery uses a 12-barrel plant producing cask, which can be found in pubs around Yorkshire. ‼ ☞ ◆

Hearty Bitter (ABV 3.7%) BITTER
Rhubarbeer (ABV 3.7%) SPECIALITY
Blonde (ABV 3.9%) BLOND
Silverheart IPA (ABV 4%) PALE
Blackheart Stout (ABV 4.8%) STOUT
Platinum EPA (ABV 5%) PALE
Ghost Porter (ABV 5.4%) PORTER

Slip Inn, York (Photo: Stuart McMahon)

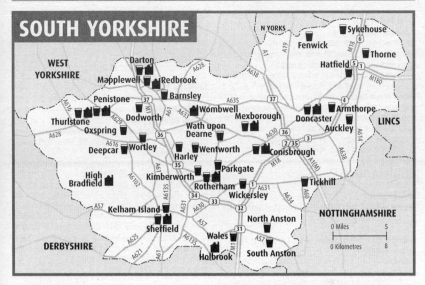

Armthorpe

Horse & Groom

Nutwell Lane, DN3 3JU (at edge of village on road to Cantley)

☎ (01302) 831658

Pheasantry Best Bitter; 1 changing beer (sourced nationally; often Oakham, Otter) Ⓗ

The second-oldest building in the village, this traditional pub used to be a coach house. Welcoming, with a cosy bar and spacious lounge with dining area, it also has a large beer garden with seating. Traditional home-made pub food is served. There is a music quiz on Tuesday, a general quiz on Sunday and a disco/music quiz on the first Saturday of the month. A darts team and golf society are based at the pub. Live music sometimes features.

ॐ✿◑♣P☷(81,82) ✿♪

Wheatsheaf

Church Street, DN3 3AE

☎ (01302) 835868

4 changing beers (sourced nationally; often Purity, Timothy Taylor, York) Ⓗ

A roadside pub serving excellent beers and a variety of good-quality food. Donna and Colin make you feel welcome, and there is plenty of entertainment here, including darts, dominoes, and pool. There are up to four changing real ales, and food is served Tuesday to Saturday, lunchtimes and evenings, with a popular carvery on Sundays. There is a good-sized outside drinking area at the front.

Q ॐ✿◑ఈ♣P☷(81,82) ✿♠♪

Auckley

Eagle & Child ✓

24 Main Street, DN9 3HS

☎ (01302) 770406 ⊕ eagleandchildauckley.co.uk

Acorn Barnsley Bitter; Black Sheep Best Bitter; Timothy Taylor Landlord; 2 changing beers (sourced regionally; often Abbeydale, Milestone) Ⓗ

A much-loved pub, on the main road in village, and winner of numerous CAMRA awards. Dating from early 19th century, it has real character. There are two bars, one with a TV, the other quieter, with tables for bar meals. The separate restaurant is decorated with photographs of local historic interest, and home-cooked meals have a deserved reputation. There is an outside seating area and a beer garden.

Q ॐ✿◑▲♣P☷(57f) ✿♠

Barnsley

George & Dragon Ⓛ

41-43 Summer Lane, S70 2NW

☎ (01226) 219316

4 changing beers (sourced locally) Ⓗ

Reopened in 2020 following a thorough refurbishment which included the reinstatement of real ale. The four constantly-changing cask ales are all from local breweries and always include a dark beer. Quality keg and canned beers are also available. The main bar is dominated by the splendid counter and bar back and comfy bench seating, and the room is tastefully decorated and adorned with attractive prints. There is a sizeable outdoor drinking area. Occasional live music is planned. Q ॐ✿≉P☷(43,44)♪

Heaven & Ale ♈ Ⓛ

66 Agnes Road, S70 1NH

☎ 07981 703786

4 changing beers (sourced nationally) Ⓗ

This former old Co-op store has had a wonderful conversion into a multi-roomed pub, with three rooms on the ground floor and a function room upstairs. An outside drinking area to the front is popular. The four real ales are from small micro and regional breweries from the whole of the UK but a couple are often local to the area. A former local and regional CAMRA Pub of the Year award winner. Q ॐ✿☷(43,44)✿

Jolly Tap on the Arcade Ⓛ

31 The Arcade, S70 2QP

⊕ jollyboysbrewery.co.uk

Jolly Boys Blonde; 4 changing beers (sourced locally; often Hilltop, Jolly Boys, Outhouse (Barnsley)) Ⓗ

Barnsley's first micropub was opened in 2017 by Two Roses brewery. This tiny one-up one-down pub is now owned by the Jolly Boys brewery. The bar serves up to five real ales alongside a choice of craft beers, all sourced locally. The pub is situated in the lovely Victorian Arcade and was a cake shop before becoming the micropub. The staff are welcoming and knowledgeable on the cask and craft beers on offer. Q≉♠✿♠✿♪

Old No 7 🅛

7 Market Hill, S70 2PX
☎ (01226) 244735 ● oldno7barnsley.co.uk
Acorn Barnsley Bitter, Blonde, Old Moor Porter; 5 changing beers (sourced regionally) 🅗
This town-centre ale house offers a range of up to eight real ales from Acorn and other microbreweries and a choice of real ciders and perry, alongside a wide range of craft and continental beers. This is the 12th consecutive year in the Guide for this popular venue. The downstairs bar is available for functions and meetings and opens on match days and busy Friday and Saturday evenings. Regular live music plays. ⇌♣🖫❀🏠🔊

Conisbrough

Hilltop 🅛

Sheffield Road, DN12 2AY (on main A630 Rotherham side of Conisbrough)
☎ (01709) 868811
Hilltop Classic Bitter, Golden Ale; 2 changing beers (often Hilltop) 🅗
A traditional free house in a 200-year-old building, serving four ales from their own brewery. On the Rotherham side of the village, standing alone on the main A630, it offers a relaxed, friendly atmosphere with a public bar and a lounge/dining area serving locally sourced food. Quiz night is Thursday. A former local CAMRA award-winner. Closed Tuesday to Thursday in winter. ⛱❀🕙♣P🖫(X78)❀🏠

Terminus

2 New Hill, DN12 3HA (10 mins walk downhill from town centre)
☎ 07397 853206
4 changing beers (sourced locally) 🅗
This micropub, sited near a former trolleybus terminus, gives a warm and friendly welcome to all. With four, usually local, rotating cask ales, its décor reflects local history and it has a large photo wall picturing eight local men who all joined up on the same day to serve in WW1. Dogs have their own treat jar on bar. Children are welcome until early evening. It is close to the Castle and bus stop, and half an hour's walk from the railway station. Q⛱❀🕙♣🖫(X78,221)❀🏠

Darton

Anvil Arms 🅛 ✅

28 Church Street, S75 5HG
☎ (01226) 805225
6 changing beers (sourced locally; often Nailmaker) 🅗
Formally the Old Co-Op Ale House, this micropub is now owned by Nailmaker brewery, serving six real ales and three ciders on handpull, with a 12-tap beer wall. Sympathetic updates to the pub during lockdown have given it new seating and outdoor drinking areas to the front and side of the building, while keeping the features people have come to love like the stone brick walls and log fire. This venue has definitely cemented itself on the Mapplewell and Darton real ale corridor. Q&⇌♣🖫❀

Darton Tap 🅛

70 Church Street, S75 5HQ
☎ (01226) 383444 ● dartontap.co.uk
Ossett White Rat; house beer (by Nailmaker); 2 changing beers (sourced locally) 🅗
Formerly a micropub, this venue has now extended in to the premises next door. Situated in the increasingly popular Darton and Mapplewell real ale corridor, this stylish pub has four cask lines, several draft lines and a

large spirits selection. Drinkers can enjoy a beer in a modern and comfortable environment, close to transport links. Dogs are welcome with doggie treats and foot towels available for them. Strictly over-18s only. &⇌P🖫🏠

Dodworth

Dodworth Tap

Station Road, S75 3JA
Ossett White Rat; house beer (by Nailmaker); 2 changing beers (sourced regionally; often Nailmaker, Timothy Taylor) 🅗
Close to Dodworth railway station, this pub was brought back from the brink in 2020 by the people who run the Darton Tap. They have lovingly restored the pub to its former glory, and a huge open fire place lost until the recent renovations, is now a feature. The refurbishment of the upper parts of the pub to create a function room were completed in early 2021. The pub now serves up to four real ales including a house beer, an extensive spirit collection and a good selection of craft beers. The huge beer garden has also been revamped. ⛱❀&⇌♣P🖫(21A,22)❀🏠

Doncaster

Doncaster Brewery Tap 🍺 🅛

7 Young Street, DN1 3EL
☎ (01302) 376436 ● doncasterbrewery.co.uk
Doncaster Sand House; 5 changing beers (sourced locally; often Doncaster) 🅗
Convenient for the town centre. Doncaster Brewery Tap was opened in 2014. The brewery, launched in 2012,

was relocated here, and provides up to six beers, all served in lined glasses. Guest beers are often available as are six traditional ciders and perries. The new Dystopia bar is open, offering craft beers. There's always something going on at the Tap, from quiz nights on Tuesday to spoken word night on Thursday. Ukulele sessions are held on Saturdays. Winner of several CAMRA awards. Q♿⇌♣●▯🚌(15,81)🐾📶♫

Draughtsman Alehouse

Station Court, DN1 1PE (on platform 3b of Doncaster station)

☎ 07999 874660 🌐 thedraughtsmanalehouse.co.uk

3 changing beers (sourced regionally; often Allendale, Northern Monkey, Thornbridge) 🄷

Located on platform 3b of Doncaster station, this venue was highly commended in CAMRA's pub design awards. The former Victorian buffet bar stood empty for 18 years, before restoration, showing off many of its original features. The original Victorian tiles have been brought back to life and mounted plan drawings of historic steam locomotives adorn the walls. The real ales come from regional brewers with occasional collaborations and tap takeovers. Locally made pies and other pub snacks are also available. Q♿⇌🚌📶

Hallcross

33-34 Hall Gate, DN1 3NL

🌐 hallcrossdoncaster.co.uk

Welbeck Abbey St Leger Gold, Select, Old Horizontal; 3 changing beers (sourced nationally; often Acorn, Elland, Rudgate) 🄷

Situated in a prominent location at the top of one of Doncaster's main streets, this pub has made a welcome return to the local real ale scene. The front bar plays background music and shows sport (muted except for major events). There is a separate soundproofed function room for live music at weekends. A courtyard at the rear also includes an undercover snug. The Hallcross is the home of the resurrected Stocks beers, previously brewed on the premises and now being brewed by Welbeck Abbey. Three guest ales are sourced from smaller breweries. ❀♿⇌🚌(21,25)🐾📶♫

Leopard ✔

2 West Street, DN1 3AA (5 mins' walk from railway station)

☎ (01302) 739460

6 changing beers (sourced regionally; often Acorn, Stancill, Titanic) 🄷

This street-corner pub, close to the town centre and railway station, has been a regular CAMRA award winner over the years. It has a superb tiled frontage, recalling its days as a Warwick & Richardson's house. There are two rooms downstairs, and a large one upstairs that regularly hosts live music at weekends. The pub is now run by Doncaster Culture and Leisure Trust, and often one of the six real ales on offer is from their own 1086 brewery. ❀◐♿⇌♣●P🚌(71,72)🐾📶♫

Little Plough ★ 🄻

8 West Laith Gate, DN1 1SF (close to Frenchgate shopping centre)

☎ (01302) 738310

Acorn Barnsley Bitter; Bradfield Farmers Blonde; 2 changing beers (sourced regionally) 🄷

A friendly haven for anyone wishing to escape the hustle and bustle of the town centre. Up to four cask ales are served on handpump in the front bar, with local breweries well supported. There is a quiet lounge/ function room to the rear and pictures of traditional agricultural scenes adorn the walls. The interior is little changed since 1934, a fact proved by plans that can be seen in the corridor. It been identified by CAMRA as having a nationally important historic pub interior. Q❀⇌♣🚌🐾📶

Queen (Crafthouse & Kitchen)

1 Sunny Bar, DN1 1LY (on the corner of Sunny Bar and Market Place)

☎ (01302) 562908

5 changing beers (sourced regionally) 🄷

An old established market place pub, which is an excellent venue to sample different beer styles. Up to five changing real ales are always available, along with a variety of craft keg beers and ciders. Close to the historic Corn Exchange and market, this is a welcome addition to the city's real ale scene. Live music plays at weekends. ❀♿⇌●🚌(15)🐾📶♫

Fenwick

Baxter Arms

Fenwick Lane, DN6 0HA (between Askern and Moss)

☎ (01302) 702671

Theakston Best Bitter; 2 changing beers (often Black Sheep, Bradfield, Stancill) 🄷

This award-winning free house, is truly a rural gem. The pub has been run by the same family for 34 years, and there is always a warm welcome. Three real ales from independent breweries are always available, and reasonably-priced fresh food sourced locally is served all day. Outside there is a lawned drinking area with garden picnic tables. There is ample car parking. Quiz night is Wednesday. A former local CAMRA award winner. Q🏠❀◐Ⓐ♣P🐾📶

Harley

Horseshoe 🄻

9 Harley Road, S62 7UD (off A6135 on B6090, 1 mile from Wentworth)

☎ (01226) 742204 🌐 thehorseshoeharley.co.uk

Neepsend Blonde; 2 changing beers (often Acorn, Greene King, Little Critters) 🄷

This cosy village local has been in the same family for many years. A community hub for well over a century it is home to sports teams. The real ales change frequently and often come from local breweries. Food available Monday, Friday and Saturday evenings with a carvery on Sunday afternoons. It gets busy when the pool team are at home and when the village gala is held in July. There is some seating in front of the pub, with a small outside area to the rear. Handy for the nearby Wentworth estate, Needles Eye and Elsecar Heritage Centre. ❀◐♣P🚌(44)🐾♫

Hatfield

Jack Hawley at the Grange 🄻

Manor Road, DN7 6SB

☎ 07769 927603

Timothy Taylor Boltmaker; 4 changing beers (sourced regionally; often Don Valley, Pheasantry, Welbeck Abbey) 🄷

This micropub is the project of a real ale enthusiast who was previously landlord of the Black Swan in Asselby. Access is via a staircase to the first floor. There is a long, narrow lounge, with mixed seating. One wall diplays four guitars and the other has the story of Jack Hawley, a local character from the 19th century, who was renowned for his hospitality. Local CAMRA Autumn Pub of the Season Year 2019. Q❀♣●P🚌(84,87A)♫

Kimberworth

Steptoe's Café Bar ⃝

192 High Street, S61 2DT

☎ (01709) 431637

4 changing beers (sourced regionally; often Bradfield, Chantry, Gorilla) ⃣

Café bar and micropub in a former hair salon. After a few false starts due to the pandemic it reopened in May 2021. Real ales on the four handpumps come from microbreweries near and far and can often be rare. Luxury coffees and teas, wines, spirits and cakes are also on offer. Cosy and welcoming, the interesting décor includes a display of old bus blinds, reclaimed furniture and other eclectic objects. Some snacks are available. QP⊟

Mapplewell

Talbot Inn ⃝ ⃝

Towngate, S75 6AS

☎ (01226) 385629 ⊕ thetalbotmapplewell.co.uk

Nailmaker Anvil Porter; 3 changing beers (sourced locally) ⃣

The first and original tap for Nailmaker brewery, this pub spearheaded the real ale revival in the area. With four rotating beers from the brewery and occasional guests, there are also tap takeovers from the likes of Magic Rock and North brewing. This pub is extremely popular with locals for everything from a quick pint and a meal to the ever popular speed quiz. There is a restaurant upstairs and food is alsoserved at all tables daily. During 2021 the pub has had a extensive sympathetic refurbishment from top to bottom and including the exterior.

Q⊛⃝⃝♣P⊟(1,X10) ⏻ ⧗

Wentworth Arms ⃝ ⃝

Greenside, S75 6AU

☎ (01226) 390702 ⊕ wentwortharms.co.uk

4 changing beers (sourced regionally; often Nailmaker) ⃣

Sister pub to the Talbot, this popular, relaxed place is know for its excellent and ever-changing array of real ale and craft beers. The pub has a well-cared for beer garden with lovely festoon lighting. During 2020, refurbishment work to the upstairs area created a new bar called the loft which can host private events or be used as a great place to chill and relax with a beer with friends. This pub has firmly positioned itself in the real ale triangle of Mapplewell, Darton and Baurgh Green.

⊛⃝♿P⊟(1,X10) ⏻ ⧗

Mexborough

Gorilla Beer Hall & Taproom

Canalside Industrial Estate, Cliff Street, S64 9HU (on dual carriageway across road from bus interchange)

☎ 07933 078364 ⊕ gorillabrewing.co.uk

Gorilla Silverback Blonde, Vanilla Gorilla; 3 changing beers (sourced nationally; often Gorilla) ⃣

The Gorilla Beer Hall is located on the canalside with outside seating overlooking the canal and moorings available for visiting boats and barges. It is adjacent to the main road through Mexborough and ideally situated for local bus and rail services. There are five handpumps in each bar serving beers brewed in the adjacent brewery. A dark beer and the award-winning Ape-X IPA usually feature. Weekends sometimes see ticket-only live music, but at these times the upstairs taproom is opened for a quieter environment. Gift sets are available to take away. Street food is available.

⊛⃝⃝♿⇌P⊟⏻⧗♪

Imperial Brewery Tap ⃝

Cliff Street, S64 9HU (opp bus station)

☎ (01709) 584000

Imperial Classical Bitter, Platinum Blonde; 4 changing beers (sourced locally; often Imperial) ⃣

A friendly brewery tap with lots to offer, especially for music-lovers. It has a main entertainment bar, a separate lounge area plus a games/function room. The six handpumps serve two permanent Imperial beers, with four rotating from Imperial, local or national breweries. Entertainment includes a battle of the bands on Tuesday, karaoke on Wednesday, an award-winning acoustic night on Thursday and a wide range of live music on Friday, Saturday and Sunday. ⊛⃝♿⇌♣⊟(220,221)⏻♪

North Anston

Little Mester ⃝ ⃝

Nursery Road, S25 4BZ

☎ (01909) 562484 ⊕ greeneking-pubs.co.uk/pubs/ south-yorkshire/little-mester

Greene King IPA; 4 changing beers (sourced locally; often Abbeydale, Stancill, Welbeck Abbey) ⃣

This large estate pub, built in the 1960s, was reopened following refurbishment in 2016 and now focuses on real ale. Up to four guest beers are sourced from far and wide though local breweries often feature strongly. There is a 10% discount for card carrying CAMRA members and a Cask Ale Club with a free pint offered for every seven purchased. It can be lively at the weekend, when a DJ and live entertainment feature. Handy for visiting the nearby Butterfly Farm and walks around Anston Stones.

⊛⃝⃝♿P⊟⏻♪

Oxspring

Smithy Arms ⃝

Bower Hill, S36 8YA

☎ 07712 929011

3 changing beers (often Abbeydale, Acorn, Chantry) ⃣

This popular micropub was opened in 2017 in the extended garage of the owner's house. Named the Smithy Arms, it is located on the site of a former blacksmith's. Opening four days a week, the pub serves three changing real ales, usually from local breweries. There is a wood-burning fire for cosy winter nights and a small beer garden to the rear. Quiz night is Thursday.

Q⊛⃝♿P⊟⏻

Parkgate

Little Haven Micro Bar ⃝

96 Broad Street, S62 6EN

☎ (01709) 710134

⊕ the-little-haven-micro-bar.business.site

3 changing beers (sourced locally; often Chantry, Little Critters) ⃣

Friendly, welcoming micropub, opened in 2018 in a former post office and hair salon. Four handpumps are joined by four craft taps, with local microbreweries often favoured. Nibbles and board games are available and musicians play on Tuesday and Saturday evenings. The decor is music themed. The former kitchen has been converted to a snug at the rear of the bar, and there is limited outside seating. Food may be brought in from nearby takeaways. A welcome break from Parkgate retail park and 15 minutes' walk from the tram/train stop there. Q⊛♣⊟⏻⧗♪

Penistone

Penistone Tap & Brewhouse
14 Market Street, S36 6BZ
☎ 07894 532456
2 changing beers (sourced regionally) Ⓗ
Opened in 2021, this micropub is under the same ownership as Woodland Brewing (formerly Whitefaced) and is a hugely welcome addition to the Penistone beer scene. The bar at the front has a handful of tables, and there are further tables in the old brewery area at the rear and a couple more outside. Two changing beers are served on handpump and six on keg. Q⇌☷⌂🖥🛜

Rotherham

Bluecoat Ⓛ ✔
The Crofts, S60 2DJ (behind town hall, off Moorgate Rd A618)
☎ (01709) 539500
Greene King Abbot; Ruddles Best Bitter; Sharp's Doom Bar; Welbeck Abbey Atlas; 6 changing beers (sourced regionally) Ⓗ
A former charity school, opened in 1776 by the Ffeofees of Rotherham, it became a pub named Ffeofees in 1981, then a Wetherspoon. Pictures of old Rotherham adorn the walls and a blue plaque on the façade commemorates its history. Up to 10 handpulled beers include seven changing guests, with local and national microbreweries favoured. Regular Meet the Brewer nights are held. A Guide regular and winner of numerous local CAMRA awards. ➺❀⓸Ⓓ⌂≷(Central)♣🅿🖥🛜

Bridge Inn Ⓛ
1 Greasbrough Road, S60 1RB (alongside Chantry Bridge, between bus and rail stations)
☎ (01709) 836818
Old Mill Traditional Bitter, Blonde Bombshell; 2 changing beers (sourced regionally; often Old Mill) Ⓗ
The birthplace of Rotherham CAMRA, making a welcome return to the Guide. It reverted to the original name after a spell as Nellie Denes. It is an Old Mill tied house, built in 1930 using stone from the original Bridge Inn, which dated back to the 1700s. The pub was recently redecorated in a Goth style and features some unusual furniture. Four real ales from Old Mill brewery are usually on the bar. There is live music every Saturday evening and most Fridays. ⌂≷(Central)♣🖥♫

Cutlers Arms 🏆 Ⓛ
29 Westgate, S60 1BQ
☎ (01709) 382581 🌐 cutlersarms.co.uk
Chantry New York Pale, Iron and Steel Bitter, Diamond Black Stout; 3 changing beers (sourced locally; often Chantry) Ⓗ
Dating from 1825 and rebuilt for Stones brewery of Sheffield in 1907 to the design of R. Wigfull with an impressive façade, it was saved from demolition in 2004, following a Grade II listing. Restored to Edwardian splendour by Chantry brewery, it reopened in 2014. It retains the original art nouveau windows, tiling and a curved bar counter with dividing screen. It has been identified by CAMRA as having a nationally important historic pub interior. The full range of Chantry beers, two real ciders and quality craft beers are available. It can be busy with live music at weekends. ❀◗≷(Central)●🖥❀🛜♫

Dragon's Tap Ⓛ
477 Herringthorpe Valley Road, Broom, S65 3AD
☎ 07864 680301

Chantry New York Pale; 5 changing beers (sourced regionally; often Elland, North Riding (Brewery), Oakham) Ⓗ
Micropub opened in 2018 in a former DIY shop, it is simply but tastefully decorated with modern art prints. Six changing beers are sourced from local and national microbreweries, with four craft keg beers available and bottled beers. No food is served, other than snacks, but you can bring in meals from nearby takeaways. Outside tables are at the front of the pub. There's a general knowledge quiz on Wednesday evening and live acoustic music on the third Sunday of the month in the upstairs room. Q❀☷●🅿🖥(X1,X10)❀♫

New York Tavern Ⓛ
84 Westgate, S60 1BD (jct of Coke Ln)
☎ (01709) 371155 🌐 newyorktavern.co.uk
Chantry New York Pale, Iron and Steel Bitter, Diamond Black Stout; 3 changing beers (sourced locally; often Chantry) Ⓗ
Wedge-shaped house that became a pub in 1856, it was refurbished and reopened by Chantry brewery in 2013 as a real ale-led pub. Previously the Prince Of Wales Feathers, it was renamed after a pub demolished when the nearby ring road was built, but retains the same manager as when it was the Feathers. At least six Chantry beers and two real ciders or perries are available, at competitive prices. Snuff and bar snacks are sold. It is handy for New York Stadium with Rotherham United memorabilia on display. ≷(Central)●🖥🛜♫

Stag Ⓛ ✔
111 Wickersley Road, Broom, S60 4JN (on A6021)
☎ (01709) 838929
Sharpp's Doom Bar; 4 changing beers (sourced regionally; often Acorn, Bradfield, Brains) Ⓗ
Former coaching inn on a busy roundabout east of the town, rebuilt in the 1920s. It was refurbished in 2017, creating one large room and a conservatory leading to extensive gardens on two levels. Up to four changing beers from local and national breweries are served. Food is not normally available. TV sport is popular, with several TV screens, including outside. There is karaoke and music quiz Thursday evenings with live music or DJ some weekend evenings. A cask loyalty scheme is operated. ➺❀♣🅿🖥(X1,X10)❀🛜♫

Sheffield: Central

Bath Hotel ★ ✔
66-68 Victoria Street, S3 7QL
☎ (0114) 249 5151
Abbeydale Deception; Acorn Barnsley Bitter; Thornbridge Jaipur IPA; 2 changing beers (sourced regionally; often Abbeydale, Bradfield, Thornbridge) Ⓗ
A careful restoration of the 1930s interior gave this two-roomed pub a conservation award, and it has been identified by CAMRA as having a nationally important historic pub interior. The bar lies between the tiled lounge, a small corridor drinking area and the cosy well-upholstered snug. Three regular beers and three guests are usually available. There is often live music and a weekly quiz on Thursdays. Food is light snacks only. Q🖥(University of Sheffield)♣🖥❀

Dog & Partridge Ⓛ ✔
56 Trippet Lane, S1 4EL
☎ 07354 471376 🌐 thedogsheffield.co.uk
Stancill Barnsley Bitter; Timothy Taylor Landlord; 2 changing beers (sourced regionally; often Abbeydale, Blue Bee) Ⓗ

Behind an impressive Gilmour's Brewery frontage, lies a comfortable multi-roomed pub served by a central bar. To the right of the entrance is a spacious taproom with dartboard, and on the left a smaller seating area. Behind the servery is a cosy snug with a hatch for service, and at the rear the lounge often features live music. The four changing beers are usually sourced from local breweries. A popular quiz is held Tuesday evenings.
🏻✿Q(City Hall) ♣🚇🚌✿🛜

Head of Steam 🅛

103-107 Norfolk Street, S1 2JE
☎ (0114) 272 2128
Camerons Strongarm; 6 changing beers (sourced regionally; often Abbeydale, Camerons) Ⓗ
A pub for some 20 years, this former bank was acquired by Camerons Brewery in 2015 and after extensive refurbishment reopened as part of the Head of Steam chain. Behind the imposing frontage the large single room is served by a central island bar, with a separate seating area at the rear leading on to an outside drinking area in Tudor Square. In addition to the brewer's own beers, the handpumps usually despense beers from independents in Yorkshire and the North East.
✿🕪&�465Q(Cathedral) ●🚌✿🛜♪

Old Queen's Head 🅛 ✔

40 Pond Hill, S1 2BG
☎ 07983 559073 🌐 theoldqueenshead.co.uk
Thwaites IPA, Gold; 3 changing beers (sourced locally; often Acorn, Blue Bee, Thwaites) Ⓗ
Dating from the Tudor period when it was originally the hunting lodge for the nearby Sheffield Castle, the pub is the oldest surviving domestic building in Sheffield, but now adjoins the transport interchange. The central bar serves a U-shaped lounge and is adjacent to a superb beamed dining room in the oldest part of the building. It is the meeting place for history groups, and is included in popular ghost tours. The food menu consists of the usual pub fare. 🏻✿🕪&�465Q(Fitzalan Square)♣🚌✿🛜

Red Deer 🅛 ✔

18 Pitt Street, S1 4DD
☎ (0114) 263 4000 🌐 thereddeersheffield.co.uk
Abbeydale Moonshine; 6 changing beers (sourced regionally) Ⓗ
A genuine, traditional local in the heart of the city. The small frontage of the original three-roomed pub hides an open-plan interior extended to the rear with a gallery seating area. As well as the impressive range of up to eight cask beers, there is also a selection of continental bottled beers. Meals are served lunchtimes and evenings daily. A popular quiz is held on Tuesday night, and an upstairs function room is available for bookings.
Q✿🕪Q(West Street) 🚌✿🛜♪

Rutland Arms 🅛

86 Brown Street, S1 2BS
☎ (0114) 272 9003 🌐 rutlandarmssheffield.co.uk
Blue Bee Reet Pale; 6 changing beers (sourced regionally; often Abbeydale, Blue Bee, Cloudwater) Ⓗ
Occupying a corner site in the Cultural Industries Quarter and near Sheffield's main railway station, the pub has operated as a freehouse since 2009. The comfortable interior provides ample seating either side of the central entrance, and the walls are covered in the pumpclips and font badges of the huge number of guest beers that have featured over the years. The beers are mostly from local and regional microbreweries. Food is served throughout the day. 🏻✿🕪�465Q(Sheffield Station)●🚌✿🛜

Sheffield Tap ★ 🅛

Platform 1b, Sheffield Station, Sheaf Street, S1 2BP
☎ (0114) 273 7558 🌐 sheffieldtap.com
Thornbridge Jaipur IPA; 9 changing beers (sourced nationally; often Tapped (Sheffield)) Ⓗ
This was originally the first class refreshment room for Sheffield Midland Station, built in 1904. After years of neglect, the main bar area was the subject of an award-winning restoration retaining many original features, and opened in 2009. There are usually three beers from the on-site Tapped brewery, opened in 2013 in the impresive former dining room and which can be viewed behind the glass screen. Further seating has been provided in the entrance corridor and to the right of the bar. Q🏻✿&�465Q(Sheffield Station)●🚌✿🛜

Triple Point Brewery 🅛

178 Shoreham Street, S1 4SQ
☎ (0114) 229 4769 🌐 triplepointbrewing.co.uk
Triple Point Gold; 3 changing beers (often Triple Point) Ⓗ
Impressive conversion of an indutrial warehouse-type building formerly used as a carpet showroom. Opened in 2019 in the premises originally operated by the former Sentinel brewery, the brewhouse is visible from the extensive seating area. The bar has four handpumps offering a selection of the core range and seasonal beers. The food offering is from Twisted Burger. There is an extensive beer garden to the front of the building.
✿&�465Q(Granville Rd) P🚌🛜

Sheffield: Deepcar

King & Miller

4-6 Manchester Road, S36 2RD
☎ (0114) 299 9644
Bradfield Farmers Blonde, Farmers Stout; house beer (by Bradfield); 2 changing beers (often Bradfield) Ⓗ
A two-roomed village local; the large taproom has a separate pool area at the rear. It features a Victorian fireplace with real fire and upholstered fixed seating. There are some fine etched Tennant Brothers windows with colourful stained-glass leaded crests. It opened as Bradfield brewery's second tied house in late 2018 after a sympathetic refurbishment. Up to six cask beers from the Bradfield range are available. ✿🕪🚌✿

Sheffield: East

Chantry Inn 🅛

400 Handsworth Road, Handsworth, S13 9BZ
☎ (0114) 288 9117
Chantry New York Pale, Iron and Steel Bitter, Diamond Black Stout; 2 changing beers (sourced regionally; often Chantry) Ⓗ
Housed in a former ecclesiastical building dating from the 13th century, in the churchyard of St Mary's Church, this is believed to be one of only four UK pubs set in consecrated ground. Becoming a pub in 1804 as the Cross Keys the name was changed to Chantry Inn in 2019 when it was taken over by the Chantry brewery of Rotherham. The three rooms – taproom, lounge and snug at the rear are served from a central bar. ✿●🚌✿🛜

Sheffield: Kelham Island

Crow Inn 🅛

35 Scotland Street, S3 7BS
☎ (0114) 201 0096
Abbeydale Heathen; 4 changing beers (sourced nationally; often Abbeydale, Arbor) Ⓗ

The former Old Crown Inn, after several years as just a hotel, reopened in 2019 as a freehouse under its new name, the Crow Inn. The old pub layout is still discernible with two comfotably furnished seating areas either side of the entrance corridor which leads to the bar area. With five handpumps and 11 keg lines, a wide range of cask and craft beers is available, together with a large spirit range including 40 malt whiskies. There are also seven hotel rooms. ✿🛏🚭♿🇶(Cathedral)🍴🚃☼📶

Fat Cat 🅛

23 Alma Street, S3 8SA

☎ (0114) 249 4801 ⊕ thefatcat.co.uk

Timothy Taylor Landlord; 8 changing beers (sourced nationally) 🔠

Opened in 1981 this is the pub that started the real ale revolution in the area. Beers from around the country are served alongside those from the adjacent Kelham Island brewery. Vegetarian and gluten-free dishes feature on the menu. The walls are covered with many awards presented to the pub and brewery. An anniversary beer festival is held in August.

Q🛏✿🌓♿🇶(Shalesmoor)🍴P🚃☼

Harlequin

108 Nursery Street, S3 8GG

☎ 07794 156916 ⊕ theharlequinpub.wordpress.com

5 changing beers (sourced regionally; often Jolly Boys, North Riding (Brewery), RedWillow) 🔠

The Harlequin takes its name from another former Ward's pub just round the corner, now demolished. The large open-plan interior features a central bar with seating on two levels. There are two regular beers from Jolly Boys, as well as guests from far and wide with the emphasis on microbreweries. A large range of real ciders is also available. Wednesday is quiz night and there is live music at weekends.

🛏✿🌓🇶(Castle Square)🍴🍴🚃☼🎵

Kelham Island Tavern 🍷 🅛

62 Russell Street, S3 8RW

☎ (0114) 272 2482

Abbeydale Moonshine; Acorn Barnsley Bitter; Blue Bee American 5 Hop; 9 changing beers (sourced nationally; often Abbeydale, Blue Bee, North Riding (Brewery)) 🔠

Former CAMRA National Pub of the Year and a regular regional and local winner, this small gem was rescued from dereliction in 2002. Thirteen handpumps dispense an impressive range of beers, always including a mild, a porter and a stout. At the rear of the L-shaped front bar area a consevatory has been added and in the warmer months you can relax in the pub's multi award-winning beer garden. Regular folk music features.

Q🛏✿🇶(Shalesmoor) 🍴🚃☼🎵

Shakespeare's Ale & Cider House 🅛

146-148 Gibraltar Street, S3 8UB

☎ (0114) 275 5959

Abbeydale Deception; RedWillow Feckless; 5 changing beers (sourced nationally; often Bad Seed, Blue Bee, North Riding (Brewery)) 🔠

Originally built in 1821, it reopened as a freehouse in 2011 following a refurbishment including the incorporation into the pub of the archway to the rear yard. The central bar serves three rooms including the extension and there is a further room across the corridor. The eight handpumps have featured over 6,000 different beers over the last 10 years, and up to 100 whiskies are also available. There is regular live music, and beer festivals are held twice a year.

Q✿🇶(Shalesmoor) 🍴🚃☼📶🎵

Wellington 🅛

1 Henry Street, S3 7EQ

☎ (0114) 249 2295

Neepsend Blonde; 4 changing beers (sourced regionally; often Neepsend, Rooster's) 🔠

A traditional two-roomed local opened as a free house in 1993. Now part of the small Sheaf Inns group of pubs it is the brewery tap for the nearby Neepsend brewery. Sympathetically refurbished, the rooms are comfortably decorated and welcoming. The handpumps feature at least three Neepsend beers and up to three changing guests mainly from micros,. An extensive range of malt whiskies is also on offer. Q✿🇶(Shalesmoor)🍴🚃☼

Sheffield: North

Blake Hotel 🅛

53 Blake Street, Upperthorpe, S6 3JQ

☎ (0114) 233 9336

Neepsend Blonde; 5 changing beers (sourced regionally; often Blue Bee, Neepsend) 🔠

This extensively restored community pub is located at the top of a steep hill (pedestrian handrails provided). It retains many Victorian features, including etched windows and mirrors. To the rear is a large decked garden. The pub has one of the largest whisky selections in Sheffield and a growing range of other spirits. There are no electronic games, TV or jukebox. The Blake reopened in 2010 after being closed for seven years. Q✿🇶(Langsett) 🍴🍴🚃(31) ☼

Gardeners Rest 🅛 ✅

105 Neepsend Lane, Neepsend, S3 8AT

☎ (0114) 272 4978

5 changing beers (sourced nationally; often Chin Chin, Helmsley, White Rose) 🔠

Taken over by the Gardeners Rest Community Society in 2017 after a share issue, this friendly pub provides guest beers from independent breweries sourced nationwide. There is live music at weekends and regular beer festivals. The cosy Dram Shop includes a bar billiards table and to the rear is a conservatory leading to an eclectically decorated beer garden overlooking the River Don. Q✿♿🇶(Infirmary Road)🍴🍴🚃☼🎵

New Barrack Tavern 🅛

601 Penistone Road, Hillsborough, S6 2GA

☎ (0114) 232 4225 ⊕ newbarracktavern.com

Bradfield Farmers Bitter; Castle Rock Harvest Pale; Screech Owl; 6 changing beers (often Castle Rock) 🔠

Friendly multi-roomed pub with an original 1936 floor plan, including a Gilmours branded doorstep and distinctive colourful exterior tiles. The snug has a local sports theme while the lounge features live bands and a monthly comedy club on the first Sunday. The seperate function room has three handpumps. In 2018 a new bottle/cider room was converted from a kitchen. Outside is an award-winning heated and covered patio garden. CAMRA Yorkshire Cider Pub of the Year 2019.

Q🛏✿🇶(Bamforth Street) 🍴🍴🚃☼📶🎵

Raven

35 Palm Street, S6 2XF

☎ (0114) 234 5905 ⊕ theraveninn.uk

6 changing beers (often Loxley) 🔠

Part of a back-street terrace, the Palm Tree, a former Tetley pub was taken over by the owners of Loxley brewery, reopening as the Raven in 2019. Six handpumps, including four Loxley beers, and nine craft keg taps lubricate this traditional friendly community pub. Events include live music, open mic nights and karaoke. 🛏✿🇶(Bamforth Street)🚃☼🎵

Wisewood Inn ⓛ
539 Loxley Road, Loxley, S6 6RR
☎ (0114) 233 4310 ⊕ wisewoodinn.co.uk
6 changing beers (often Bradfield, Loxley, Stancill) Ⓗ
The main bar has three rooms, including a pool room. Below is the cellar bar, which is available for hire. A large garden to the rear overlooks the Loxley Valley. In addition to Loxley beers, the five handpumps invariably include local beers and there are also eight keg taps. The extensive food menu includes continental sausages, pizzas and tapas. Adjacent to the cellar bar is Loxley brewery, which commenced production in 2018. It is a sister pub to the Raven in nearly Walkley.
ॐ❀◖♣P🚃🐾🎵

Sheffield: South

Beer Engine ⓛ
17 Cemetery Road, S11 8FJ
☎ (0114) 272 1356 ⊕ beerenginesheffield.com
Neepsend Blonde; 5 changing beers (sourced nationally; often Arbor, Manchester, Neepsend) Ⓗ
This traditional-style multi-roomed pub, cosy, with a great atmosphere, reopened in 2015 following a sympathetic refurbishment. A generous choice of high-quality drinks are provided for its wide-ranging clientele. The six changing cask beers come from an interesting mix of microbreweries from Sheffield and across the country. Excellent, mainly tapas-style food is served each evening. The large beer garden has a heated covered area. ❀◖🍽🚃🐾🎵

Brothers Arms ⓛ
106 Well Road, Heeley, S8 9TZ
☎ (0114) 258 3544
Abbeydale Deception; 7 changing beers (sourced nationally) Ⓗ
A classic, traditional local. Although the interior is open-plan, it is designed so the various areas of seating and the games area all feel individual and cosy. The pub's name reflects its association with locally well-known parody ukulele band The Everly Pregnant Brothers and live music is hosted every Thursday evening. The bar features eight real ales with six changing guests, together with a real cider. A quiz is held on Tuesdays.
ॐ❀♣🍽P🚃🐾🎵

Sheaf View ⓛ
25 Gleadless Road, Heeley, S2 3AA
☎ (0114) 249 6455
Neepsend Blonde; 7 changing beers (sourced regionally; often Neepsend, Pictish, Saltaire) Ⓗ
A 19th-century pub near Heeley City Farm, the Sheaf experienced a chequered history before becoming a real ale oasis since reopening as a freehouse in 2000. The walls and shelves are adorned with assorted breweriana and provide an ideal background for good drinking and conversation. A wide range of international beers, together with malt whiskies and a real cider, complement the eight reasonably-priced real ales. It is a busy pub, especially on Sheffield United match days.
Q❀♣🍽P🚃🐾

Sheffield: West

Beer House ⓛ
623 Ecclesall Road, Sharrow, S11 8PT
⊕ the-beer-house-172.mytoggle.io
6 changing beers (sourced nationally; often Abbeydale, Blue Bee, Neepsend) Ⓗ
Sheffield's first micropub opened in a small former shop unit in late 2014. The front of two rooms has level access

from the street and contains the bar with its bank of six handpumps displaying an ever-changing range of beers mainly from microbreweries, with local breweries well represented. The raised back room is focused around the fireplace. Outdoor seating is available to the front and in the rear beer garden. There is a quiz on Wednesday evenings. Q☕❀♣🍽🚃🐾🎵

Ecclesall Ale Club ⓛ
429 Ecclesall Road, Sharrow, S11 8PG
☎ (0114) 453 6818 ⊕ thebrewfoundation.co.uk/tap-house
5 changing beers (sourced regionally; often Bad Seed, Brew Foundation, Don Valley) Ⓗ
A busy one-roomed micropub in the heart of the bustling Ecclesall Road social scene, but only a stone's throw from the tranquil Botanical Gardens. Comfortably furnished with a cosy atmosphere, in contrast to the spartan decor of many micropubs. It is owned by the Brew Foundation. In addition to the five cask ales there is an extensive range of craft keg beers, bottles and cans from independent brewers. Q☕❀♣🍽🚃🐾

Hallamshire House ⓛ ✅
49 Commonside, S10 1GF
☎ (0114) 263 1062
Thornbridge Brother Rabbit, Jaipur IPA; house beer (by Thornbridge); 5 changing beers (sourced locally; often Thornbridge) Ⓗ
Operated by Thornbridge brewery, and known locally as the Tardis, the pub has two small comfy rooms at the front and, through the bar area, a large lounge and a snooker room with full-sized table. There is a courtyard drinking area downstairs with ample seating and soft furniture in the covered area. Quiz night is on Monday and on some Saturdays there is live music or a DJ.
Q☕❀♣♣🚃🎵

Itchy Pig Ale House ⓛ
495 Glossop Road, Broomhill, S10 2QE
☎ (0114) 327 0780 ⊕ theitchypig.co.uk
5 changing beers (sourced regionally; often Abbeydale) Ⓗ
A cosy, friendly micropub with a relaxed atmosphere and continental feel. The whitewashed walls are decorated with porcine-themed art work, hop sacks and dried hops.There is craftsman-standard carpentry including a bar made from Victorian era doors with a glass-covered bar top formed from two pence coins set in resin. A wide range of pork scratchings is available. Q♣🍽🚃(120)🐾

Rising Sun ⓛ ✅
471 Fulwood Road, Nether Green, S10 3QA
☎ (0114) 230 3855 ⊕ risingsunsheffield.co.uk
Abbeydale Daily Bread, Moonshine, Absolution; 7 changing beers (sourced regionally; often Blue Bee, Revolutions, Welbeck Abbey) Ⓗ
This pub is a large suburban roadhouse operated by local brewer Abbeydale. There are two comfortably furnished rooms with a log-burning fire between the main bar and the glass-roofed extension, which also has glass panels in the end wall. A range of four Abbeydale real ales are always served, with three or four guest real ales mainly from micros. Quizzes are on Sunday evenings. The Sunfest beer festival is held in July.
Q☕❀◖♣♣🍽P🚃(120,83A)🐾🎵

University Arms ⓛ
197 Brook Hill, Broomhall, S3 7HG
☎ (0114) 222 8969 ⊕ withus.com/universityarms
Welbeck Abbey Red Feather Ⓗ**; house beer (by Acorn)** Ⓗ/Ⓖ**; 6 changing beers (sourced regionally; often Abbeydale, Blue Bee, Thornbridge)** Ⓗ

Owned by the University of Sheffield, this former staff club has an open-plan lounge with a bar at one end adjacent to a small alcove seating area, and a conservatory leading to the large garden. There is additional seating upstairs with seperate rooms for snooker and darts. The guest beers are mostly sourced locally. Entertainment includes a quiz on Tuesday and open mic night on Wednesdays, during term time. Q☆🕏🕏🕏ᗒ🖳(University of Sheffield) ♣●🖳❀🛜🎵

South Anston

Loyal Trooper 🅻 ✅

34 Sheffield Road, S25 5DT (off A57, 3 miles off M1 jct 31 towards Worksop)
☎ (01909) 562203 🌐 loyaltrooperpub.co.uk
Abbeydale Moonshine; Bradfield Farmers Blonde; 2 changing beers (often Black Sheep, Bombardier, Timothy Taylor) Ⓗ
Friendly oak-beamed village local, parts of which date back to 1690. A range of real ales and good, wholesome, locally sourced food are sold at reasonable prices. Guest beers often come from local breweries. It was redecorated recently, but the layout is unchanged since the 1960s. The interior comprises a public bar, snug, lounge and a function room upstairs used by many local groups, including a thriving folk club. Close to St James's Church, it is on the Five Churches walk, handy for Anston Stones Wood and the nearby Butterfly Farm.
Q☆🕏🕏&♣🖳(19) 🛜🎵

Sykehouse

Old George Inn

Broad Lane, DN14 9AU (on main road, in centre of village)
☎ (01405) 785635 🌐 oldgeorgeinnsykehouse.co.uk
3 changing beers (often Sharp's, Timothy Taylor) Ⓗ
A large, characterful 200-year-old building featuring a log-burning stove and flagstone floors. There is a spacious, open-plan bar area with recently refurbished furniture and fittings, and another seating area and function room off the main bar area. Rustic oak beams abound, hinting at the building's past. A separate games room has a pool table. Outside is a camping field, patio area and garden. There is ample parking. Breakfast, lunch and evening meals are served daily, with booking advisable on Sundays. 🕏☆❀🕏&🅰♣🖳(84B)❀🛜🎵

Thorne

Windmill

19 Queen Street, DN8 5AA
☎ (01405) 812866
Little Critters White Wolf; 4 changing beers (sourced regionally; often Abbeydale, Banks's, Timothy Taylor) Ⓗ
Friendly community pub close to the town centre on a street parallel with the main road; good-natured conversation with staff and clientele is assured. Up to four well-kept real ales come from small independent breweries. The pub has a smart lounge with a conservatory area linked by an archway to another room with a pool table. There are ample outside drinking facilities and a garden with play equipment. Sunday is quiz night. 🕏☆≈(North)♣🖳(87,88A)❀🛜

Thurlstone

Crystal Palace 🅻

Towngate, S36 9RH (near war memorial on the A628)
☎ (01226) 766331

House beer (by Kibble); 2 changing beers (sourced locally; often Kibble) Ⓗ
Large stone-built pub on a back road. It has an uncomplicated interior with pool table at one end. Since 2021 it has been serving Kibble brewery beers, which are brewed in a former stable block in the car park. The owner/brewer is a former miner, which explains the Kibble name. A kibble is a big bucket used in pit shafts and the owner reckoned the mash tun looks like one. Beers are often named after coal seams. The pubs offers three permanent beers along with seasonal brews. ☆♣🖳❀🎵

Huntsman 🅻

136 Manchester Road, S36 9QW (on main A628 through village)
☎ (01226) 764892 🌐 thehuntsmanthurlstone.co.uk
Black Sheep Best Bitter; Timothy Taylor Landlord; 4 changing beers (sourced nationally) Ⓗ
A genuinely friendly local, drinking and talking pub make up this pub's lifeblood. Throw in old-fashioned pub games, LocAle and a dog-friendly ethos; and it shouldn't just be passed by. The choice of six real ales has contributed to the Huntsman being in the Guide for 13 consecutive years. The location of this village local on a major trans-Pennine route provides an interesting mix of regulars and passing trade. Food is served Tuesday evening and Sunday lunch only. There is no jukebox or TVs, but Wednesday evening is live music night.
Q🕏☆🕏♣🖳❀🛜🎵

Tickhill

Scarbrough Arms 🅻

Sunderland Street, DN11 9QJ (on A631 near Buttercross)
☎ (01302) 742977
Greene King Abbot; John Smith's Bitter; Timothy Taylor Landlord; 2 changing beers (sourced locally; often Chantry, Pheasantry, Welbeck Abbey) Ⓗ
A regular in the Guide since 1990, this stone-built pub dates back to the 16th century. There is a taproom at the rear which features darts and sports TV, while a spacious lounge can be found at the front. Between the two is a Barrel Room snug with barrel-shaped furniture. Outside are a large attractive beer garden and a covered smoking area. Quizes are held on Monday and Thursday evenings. Beer festivals feature in the summer.
Q🕏☆♣●🖳(22,205) ❀🛜

Wales

Duke of Leeds 🅻

16 Church Street, S26 5LQ (turn off A618 into School Rd, opp parish church)
☎ (0114) 698 5124
Abbeydale Moonshine; Theakston Best Bitter; 2 changing beers (sourced regionally; often Theakston, Timothy Taylor, Welbeck Abbey) Ⓗ
A 300-year-old former coaching inn, extensively refurbished and reopened under new ownership in 2015. The bar area leads to three other areas where drinks and meals may be consumed. Outdoor drinking areas afford views of the village and the upstairs function room holds 60 people. Changing beers are sourced both locally and from further afield. Food is freshly cooked to order. On the Five Churches Walk, it is popular with walkers and locals alike. It has won several local CAMRA awards.
🕏☆🕏🅰♣🖳(21)❀🎵

Wath upon Dearne

Church House L ✅

Montgomery Square, S63 7RZ

☎ (01709) 879518

Greene King Abbot; Ruddles Best Bitter; Sharp's Doom Bar; 3 changing beers (sourced regionally; often Acorn, Elland) H

Large pub with an impressive frontage, set in a town-centre pedestrianised square, it has a large outside area to the front. It was built in circa 1810 and consecrated by the nearby church in 1912, becoming a pub in the 1980s and a Wetherspoon in 2000. A wide variety of real ales from both national and local breweries are served. Handy for exploring the RSPB Old Moor Wetlands Centre and for Manvers Commercial Park, it has excellent access to bus services across the square. ⑤❀◑⑤&P₽令

Wath Tap L

49 High Street, S63 7QB

☎ (01709) 872150 ⊕ wathtap.co.uk

6 changing beers (sourced regionally; often Chin Chin, Elland, North Riding (Brewery)) H

A warm welcome is guaranteed at Rotherham's first micropub, opened in a former butcher's shop in 2016. Six changing real ales, mostly from local breweries, and five real ciders are served. These are listed on chalkboards by the bar. Food may be brought in from the surrounding takeaways. Seats at the front of the pub are protected from the rain by the original shop canopy. The pub was extended to the rear to create a separate room. Jam sessions are sometimes held and board games are available. Q&♣♠₽❀令♪

Wentworth

George & Dragon L

85 Main Street, S62 7TN (set back from the road on B6090)

☎ (01226) 742440 ⊕ georgeanddragonwentworth.com

Theakston Old Peculier; Timothy Taylor Landlord; 5 changing beers (sourced locally; often Bradfield, Chantry, Geeves) H

A village free house, licensed since 1804, offering seven changing real ales from local and regional brewers. It has a front patio and a large garden with a children's adventure playground at the rear. A craft shop and the Hoober Room, available for hire, also feature. Home-cooked food is served from an extensive menu, and a pop-up pie shop opens at weekends. A Guide regular and winner of numerous local CAMRA awards it is handy for historic Wentworth Woodhouse, Needle's Eye and Hoober Stand. Q⑤❀◑P₽(44,136)❀令♪

Wickersley

Three Horseshoes L ✅

133 Bawtry Road, S66 2BW (on A631)

☎ (01709) 739240

Black Sheep Best Bitter; Fuller's London Pride; Timothy Taylor Landlord; 2 changing beers (sourced locally; often Bradfield, Pennine, Welbeck Abbey) H

Popular pub, standing back from the busy A631 in the heart of this lively village. Reopened in 2016, following extensive refurbishment, it has been opened out into a large room with a central bar. The guest beers usually come from local or regional brewers. There is large upstairs function room and outside seating at the front and in the rear garden. Historic pictures of the area adorn the walls. Good-value food is available. It gets lively on weekend evenings. ⑤❀◑♣P₽♪

Wortley

Wortley Men's Club L ✅

Reading Room Lane, S35 7DB (in the centre of the village at the back of the Wortley Arms)

☎ (0114) 288.2066 ⊕ wortleymensclub.co.uk

Timothy Taylor Landlord; 2 changing beers (sourced nationally) H

A multiple CAMRA award-winning club including local, regional, and National Club of the Year. This is the 12th consecutive year the club has been in the Guide. Show your CAMRA membership card or a copy of this Guide on entry. The club is situated in the pretty rural village of Wortley near to Wortley Hall and gardens. The lovely building has exposed timber frames, ornate ceilings, wooden panelling and a real fire. Guest ales are sourced from local and national breweries. The club runs an annual beer festival in July. Q❀&♣♠P₽(23,23A)♪

Breweries

1086

Old Brewhouse, Cusworth Hall, Cusworth Lane, Doncaster, DN5 7TU

☎ (01302) 639880

Office: Doncaster Culture & Leisure Trust, The Dome, Doncaster Lakeside, Bawtry Road, Doncaster, DN4 7PD ⊕ 1086brewery.co.uk

☺1086 was established in 2018, in the original brewhouse of Cusworth Hall, an 18th century, Grade I, country house in Cusworth, near Doncaster. The brewery shares space with its popular brewery tap, the Old Brewhouse. Beers are also occasionally available at the Leopard, Doncaster. ♠

Abbeydale SIBA

Unit 8, Aizlewood Road, Sheffield, S8 0YX

☎ (0114) 281 2712 ⊕ abbeydalebrewery.co.uk

☺Established in 1996, Abbeydale, one of the largest and longest standing Sheffield breweries, produces more than 220 barrels a week (over 75% cask). At least one new beer is produced weekly, often including the popular Dr Morton's range (tribute to the owners). Small batch, mixed fermentation and barrel-aged brews are created under its Funk Dungeon project. Innovation, investment and expansion have enabled growth, including a substantial online offering. One pub is owned, the Rising Sun, Nether Green. ♦GF V

Daily Bread (ABV 3.8%) BITTER
Deception (ABV 4.1%) PALE
Heathen (ABV 4.1%) PALE
Moonshine (ABV 4.3%) PALE
Absolution (ABV 5.3%) PALE
Black Mass (ABV 6.66%) PORTER

Acorn SIBA

Unit 3, Aldham Industrial Estate, Mitchell Road, Wombwell, Barnsley, S73 8HA

☎ (01226) 270734 ⊕ acorn-brewery.co.uk

☺Acorn was set up in 2003 with a 10-barrel plant, expanding to 20 barrels when the brewery moved to larger premises. It currently has a 160 barrel a week capacity. All beers are produced using the Barnsley Bitter yeast strain, dating back to the 1850s. ‼☰♦LIVE

Yorkshire Pride (ABV 3.7%) BITTER

Golden-coloured session beer with pleasing fruit notes. A mouth-watering blend of malt and hops create a fruity taste which leads to a clean, bitter finish.

Barnsley Bitter (ABV 3.8%) BITTER
This brown bitter has a smooth, malty bitterness throughout with notes of chocolate and caramel. Fruity bitter finish.

Blonde (ABV 4%) PALE
A clean-tasting, golden-coloured hoppy beer with a refreshing bitter and fruity aftertaste.

Barnsley Gold (ABV 4.3%) GOLD
This golden ale has fruit in the aroma with a hoppy and fruitiness flavour throughout. A well-hopped, clean, dry finish.

Malthouse (ABV 4.4%) BITTER

Old Moor Porter (ABV 4.4%) PORTER
A rich-tasting porter, smooth throughout with a hint of chocolate and a hint of liquorice. A moreish porter.

Gorlovka Imperial Stout (ABV 6%) STOUT
This black stout is rich and smooth and full of chocolate and liquorice flavours with a fruity creamy finish.

Blue Bee

Unit 29-30, Hoyland Road Industrial Estate, Sheffield, S3 8AB ☎ 07375 659349 ⊕ bluebeebrewery.co.uk

Established in 2010, this 10-barrel, independently-owned brewery supplies throughout the East Midlands and Yorkshire. The beers are often found further afield. Blue Bee produce regular innovative specials and occasional collaborations. Most beers emphasise New World hops. A session pale, an IPA and a stout are always available. ◆

Hillfoot Best Bitter (ABV 4%) BITTER
Reet Pale (ABV 4%) PALE
American 5 Hop (ABV 4.3%) PALE
Triple Hop (ABV 4.3%) PALE

Both Barrels

56A Main Street, Mexborough, S64 9DU ☎ 07753 746618 ✉ anthony@bothbarrelsbrewing.com

Small-batch craft brewery specializing in a wide variety of beers and lagers, founded in 2021. Beers are available in all formats. No filtering or pasteurization of any products.

Bradfield SIBA

Watt House Farm, High Bradfield, Sheffield, S6 6LG ☎ (0114) 285 1118 ⊕ bradfieldbrewery.com

☺Based on a working farm in the Peak District National Park, Bradfield is one of the larger Sheffield breweries. Utilising pure Millstone Grit spring water, this family-run business was established in 2005. Direct delivery covers both the Midlands and the North. Beer is supplied further afield and there is a local home-delivery service. Monthly specials are available. Four pubs are owned: the King & Miller, Deepcar; the Nag's Head, Loxley; the Wharncliffe Arms, Wharncliffe Side; and the White Hart, Bradwell. 🛒◆

Farmers Bitter (ABV 3.9%) BITTER
Farmers Blonde (ABV 4%) BLOND
Farmers Brown Cow (ABV 4.2%) BITTER
Farmers Steel Cow (ABV 4.5%) BITTER
Farmers Stout (ABV 4.5%) STOUT
Farmers 5K (ABV 5%) PALE
Farmers Pale Ale (ABV 5%) PALE
Farmers Sixer (ABV 6%) GOLD

Brew Foundation

Office: 18 Jarrow Road, Sheffield, S11 8YB ☎ (0114) 282 3098 ☎ 07545 618894 ⊕ thebrewfoundation.co.uk

Family-run brewery. Following the passing of founder James, the beers are currently being contract brewed at Wincle Brewery. The beer is available in Beer Foundation outlets in Sheffield and occasionally distributed both east and west of the Pennines.

brewSocial SIBA

Princess Street, Sheffield, S4 7UU

Launched in 2022 brewSocial is a social enterprise dedicated to supporting and training people who are disadvantaged in the labour market. Located in a railway arch in Attercliffe and utilising the brewkit that was formerly in use at Little Ale Cart and then Neepsend. Brewery tap, theSocial, on Snig Hill is a regular outlet.

Chantry SIBA

Unit 1-2, Callum Court, Gateway Industrial Estate, Parkgate, Rotherham, S62 6NR ☎ (01709) 711866 ⊕ chantrybrewery.co.uk

☺Brewing returned to Rotherham with the opening of Chantry in 2012, using the latest brewing technology in a 20-barrel plant (built by Sheffield-based Moeschle UK). As well as the tap at the Brewery (open Frid/Sat; events most weeks), three other pubs are owned: Cutlers Arms & New York Tavern in Rotherham and Chantry Inn, Handsworth, Sheffield. Delivery is nationwide, with free local delivery. ‼🛒◆🍺

New York Pale (ABV 3.9%) PALE
Iron & Steel Bitter (ABV 4%) BITTER
Steelos (ABV 4.1%) PALE
Full Moon (ABV 4.2%) PALE
Diamond Black Stout (ABV 4.5%) STOUT
Kaldo (ABV 5.5%) BLOND
Mighty Millers (ABV 5.5%) BLOND
Special Reserve (ABV 6.3%) OLD

Dead Parrot

44 Garden Street, Sheffield, S1 4BJ

Established in Sheffield city centre in 2018 by the Simmonite brothers. Expansion in recent years has seen increased production using a 15-barrel plant followed by the opening of a brewery tap, Perch, in 2022. In 2021 Jamie Allsopp approached Dead Parrot with the aim of recreating some original 19th century recipes from Allsopps of Burton.

Doncaster

7 Young Street, Doncaster, DN1 3EL ☎ 07921 970941 ⊕ doncasterbrewery.co.uk

☺Established in 2012 and initially based at an industrial unit in Kirk Sandall, Doncaster, the brewery moved to new premises, in the city centre, in 2014 using a 15-barrel plant, and opened a micropub taproom. The brewer frequently trials new recipes for beers. ◆LIVE🍺

Sand House (ABV 3.8%) BLOND
Handsome Pat (ABV 4%) SPECIALITY
Cheswold (ABV 4.2%) BITTER
Rebellious Monk (ABV 4.5%) STOUT
First Aviation (ABV 5%) PALE

Emmanuales

70 Cromwell Street, Sheffield, S6 3RN ☎ 07881 995604 ⊕ emmanuales.co.uk

Emmanuales has been brewing beers of biblical proportions since 2014 AD, spreading the good news one beer at a time. Drawing upon the heritage of the Christian faith, they are not out to force religion down people's throats – just beer! Following a sabbatical in 2018 resumption of brewing was further delayed by the pandemic but full production resumed in 2021. Production now mostly available in can but some bottle, keg and cask is packaged. LIVE

Exit 33

Unit 1, Petre Drive, Sheffield, S4 7PZ ☎ (0114) 270 9991 ✉ office@exit33.beer

☺This eight-barrel brewery was founded in Sheffield in 2008 as Brew Company but rebranded as Exit 33 in 2014. In 2022 it began producing beers under the HQ Beers name. Social enterprise schemes are supported from the sales through the Harlequin, Sheffield. The plant and equipment is available for use by cuckoo breweries. Brewing is currently suspended. ♦

Fuggle Bunny SIBA

Unit 1, Meadowbrook Park Industrial Estate, Station Road, Holbrook, Sheffield, S20 3PJ ☎ (0114) 248 4541 ☎ 07813 763347 ⊕ fugglebunny.co.uk

⊠ Fuggle Bunny was established in 2014 and is an independent, family-run brewery. The plant, originally obtained from Flipside Brewery, has since been expanded. The core range is supplemented by occasional seasonal and special brews. Beers are delivered direct within a 40-mile radius of the brewery and are available nationally through wholesalers. Its first pub opened in Worksop in 2017. ‼☞

Chapter 5 Oh Crumbs (ABV 3.8%) BITTER
Chapter 9 La La Land (ABV 3.9%) PALE
Chapter 2 Cotton Tail (ABV 4%) GOLD
Chapter 6 Hazy Summer Daze (ABV 4.2%) GOLD
Chapter 8 Jammy Dodger (ABV 4.5%) BITTER
Chapter 1 New Beginnings (ABV 4.9%) BITTER
Chapter 3 Orchard Gold (ABV 5%) GOLD
Chapter 7 Russian Rare-Bit (ABV 5%) STOUT
Chapter 4 24 Carrot (ABV 6%) BITTER

Gorilla SIBA

Unit 3, Glasshouse Lane, Cliff Street, Mexborough, S64 9HU ☎ 07747 484368 ⊕ gorillabrewing.co.uk

Co-founders Jason White and Phil Paling launched Gorilla Brewing in 2020, utilising a 6-barrel kit, next to the Sheffield and South Yorkshire Navigation canal. Two pubs are operated, Rockingham Tap, Swinton and Track & Sleeper on Knaresborough Station. ♦

Silverback Blonde (ABV 3.8%) PALE
Monkey Magic (ABV 4.5%) SPECIALITY
Orang-A-Tang (ABV 4.5%) SPECIALITY
Kong (ABV 6%) IPA
Vanilla Gorilla (ABV 6%) SPECIALITY

Grizzly Grains

Unit 6, Sheaf Gardens, Duchess Road, Sheffield, S2 4BB ☎ 07807 242545 ✉ sambrewsbeers@gmail.com

Having purchased the equipment from Crosspool Alemakers in 2019, Sam Bennett commenced brewing in the Walkley area of Sheffield in 2020 before moving to an industrial unit in 2021. Sam produces a range of mostly one-off beers, including bottle-conditioned ales. ♦LIVE

Heist

107 Neepsend Lane, Sheffield, S3 8AT ⊕ heistbrewco.com

Established by Dan Hunt and Adam France in 2017 as a craft bar and bottle shop, Heist began brewing operations in Clowne, Derbyshire in 2018. The development of the new brewery and taproom site in Neepsend, Sheffield launched in 2021, showcasing 30 fresh beers on tap, alongside a strong community-focussed environment, welcoming to all the family. ‼☞♦

Hilltop

▤ Sheffield Road, Conisbrough, DN12 2AY ☎ (01709) 868811 ☎ 07947 146746 ⊕ thehilltophotel.co.uk

☺Established in 2016, Hilltop Brewery is a 3.5-barrel plant situated in the outbuildings of the Hilltop, Conisbrough. Beers are available in the hotel and other local outlets. ‼♦LIVE

Imperial

▤ Arcadia Hall, Cliff Street, Mexborough, S64 9HU ☎ (01709) 584000 ☎ 07428 422703 ✉ impbrewery@gmail.com

☺Brewing began in 2010 using a six-barrel tower brewery system located in the basement of the Imperial Club, Mexborough. Beer is available in the club as well as local outlets. ‼♦LIVE

Jolly Boys

Unit 16a, Redbrook Business Park, off Wilthorpe Road, Redbrook, S75 1JN ☎ 07808 085214 ⊕ jollyboysbrewery.co.uk

☺Jolly Boys started brewing in 2016 using spare capacity at a local brewery before moving to its own site the same year. The Jolly Tap on the Arcade, Barnsley, has now been joined by a second pub that opened in 2023, the Mallard at Moorthorpe railway station. ‼♦☞

Yorkshire Bitter (ABV 3.8%) BITTER
Blonde (ABV 4%) BLOND
Jolly Cascade Blonde (ABV 4%) BLOND
La Joll'a Blonde (ABV 4%) BLOND
Golden Best (ABV 4.5%) GOLD
Yorkshire Pale Ale (ABV 4.8%) PALE
Jolly Collier Porter (ABV 5%) PORTER
Jolly IPA (ABV 5.8%) IPA

Kibble

▤ Rear of Crystal Palace, 11 Towngate, Thurlstone, S36 9RH ☎ 07952 790245

☺Brewing began in 2021 in the former stable block of the Crystal Palace pub. The owner (an ex miner) on seeing the mash tun exclaimed it looked like a kibble (a big bucket used in pit shafts to move men and machinery) and the brewery name was born. A 2.5-barrel kit is used to produce mining-themed beers mostly named after local coal seams. The beers are rarely found outside the pub. ♦

Little Critters SIBA

80 Parkwood Road, Sheffield, S3 8AG
☎ (0114) 276 3171

Office: Horizon House, 2 Whiting Street, Sheffield,
S8 9QR ⊕ littlecrittersbrewery.com

A small batch, family-owned microbrewery. It opened in
2016, and operates on a 10-barrel brewing plant. Pubs
are supplied throughout Yorkshire, the East Midlands and
nationally. Brewery improvements took place in 2020
and the core range expanded. It also supplies beer in
cans through a number of bottle shops and via its online
shop. ♦LIVE

Little Hopper (ABV 3.6%) GOLD
Blonde Bear (ABV 4.2%) BLOND
Shire Horse (ABV 4.3%) BITTER
Raspberry Blonde (ABV 4.5%) BLOND
Sleepy Badger (ABV 4.5%) SPECIALITY
Malty Python (ABV 4.8%) BITTER
White Wolf (ABV 5%) PALE
Coco Nutter (ABV 6%) STOUT
Nutty Ambassador (ABV 6%) STOUT
Sultanas of Swing (ABV 6%) SPECIALITY
C Monster (ABV 6.5%) IPA

Little Mesters

352 Meadowhead, Sheffield, S8 7UJ ☎ 07859 889547
⊕ littlemestersbrewing.co.uk

Microbrewery and taproom established in 2020
producing beers in cask, keg and can. ♦

Lost Industry

14a Nutwood Trading Estate, Sheffield, S6 1NJ
☎ (0114) 231 6393
✉ beer@lostindustrybrewing.com

Lost Industry is a craft beer brewery run by a family of
beer enthusiasts, established 2015. Pushing boundaries
and brewing a wide range of creative beers, it is
becoming well known, in particular, for its sours. No core
range although favourites may be repeated. In little
more than two years over 100 distinct beers have been
brewed in a wide range of styles. A barrel-ageing
programme began 2018. Spare brewing capacity is
utilised by Steel City (qv).

Loxley

⬛ 539 Loxley Road, Sheffield, S6 6RR
☎ (0114) 233 4310 ⊕ loxleybrewery.co.uk

Established in 2018, Loxley use a five-barrel plant located
at the Wisewood Inn, partner-pub to the Raven in nearby
Walkley. Six regular cask beers complement an ever-
changing variety of specials. The beers are increasingly
available locally, with over 30 pubs supplied. Live beers
are bottled onsite and all brews (except milk stout) are
vegan-friendly. A growing range of keg beer, including
cans, is also available. Branded merchandise is on sale at
both pubs. LIVE V

Fearn (ABV 3.8%) PALE
Halliday (ABV 4%) BITTER
Revill (ABV 4%) BLOND
Lomas (ABV 4.4%) PALE
Gunson (ABV 4.8%) PALE
Black Dog (ABV 5%) STOUT

Mitchell's Hop House

354 Meadowhead, Sheffield, S8 7UJ
☎ (0114) 274 5587 ⊕ mitchellswine.co.uk

Brewing began in 2016 in a converted space at the back
of Mitchell's Wine Merchants. Beers are available from
the brewery shop and a growing number of local pubs
and beer retailers. All production is now bottled. ☛

Nailmaker

Unit 9, Darton Business Park, Barnsley Road, Darton,
S75 5NH
☎ (01226) 380893 ☎ 07973 824790
⊕ nailmakerbrewing.co

☺Nailmaker Brewery is located in an old carpet mill by
the river Dearne, using an eight-barrel plant. Nailmaking
was one of the largest local occupations in the early 19th
century. The extensive list of draught cask ales are
supplemented by bottles, cans, pouches and beer-in-a-
box. It has an onsite taproom, a tap in Darton (Anvil
Arms) and owns the Talbot Inn and Wentworth
Arms, Mapplewell. 2021 saw the addition of brewery
and distillery tours, and events in the visitor centre.
‼☛♦♠

Yorkshire Bitter (ABV 3.6%) BITTER
Wapentake (ABV 3.8%) GOLD
Auckland (ABV 4%) BITTER
Cascade (ABV 4%) PALE
Chinook (ABV 4%) PALE
Jester Pale Ale (ABV 4%) PALE
Mango Magic Pale Ale (ABV 4%) PALE
Mosaic (ABV 4%) PALE
Paleton Pale Ale (ABV 4%) PALE
Citra Grapefruit Pale Ale (ABV 4.1%) PALE
Citra Pale Ale (ABV 4.1%) PALE
Anvil Porter (ABV 4.4%) PORTER
Plum Porter (ABV 4.4%) PORTER
Wentworth (ABV 4.8%) BITTER
Clout Stout (ABV 5%) STOUT
Chocolate Safari Stout (ABV 5.5%) STOUT
Triple Chocolate Stout (ABV 5.5%) STOUT
Imperial Stout (ABV 8.8%) STOUT

Neepsend

Unit 13, 92 Burton Road, Sheffield, S3 8DA
☎ (0114) 276 3406 ⊕ neepsendbrewco.com

☺Established in 2015 by James Birkett and Gavin Martin,
after taking over Little Ale Cart Brewery, and moving to
new premises in Sheffield's Valley of Beer. A 10-barrel
plant is used, supplying beers locally, including to the
company's own pubs, Sheaf View, the Blake Hotel and
the Wellington. Despite only having one core beer, the
brewery produces an ever-changing range of hop-
forward seasonal ales. There is an onsite taproom that
opens occasionally. ♦♠

Blonde (ABV 4%) BITTER

On the Edge

Sheffield ☎ 07854 983197 ⊕ ontheedgebrew.com

On the Edge started brewing commercially in 2012 using
a 0.5-barrel plant in the brewer's home. Brewing takes
place once a week. Three local pubs are supplied as well
as beer festivals. There is no regular beer list as new
brews are constantly being tried.

St Mars of the Desert

90 Stevenson Road, Attercliffe, Sheffield, S9 3XG
☎ 07365 222101 ⊕ beerofsmod.co.uk

A family-run brewery, recognised as one of the 'top ten
new breweries in the world' by Rate Beer in 2020. Dann,
Martha and Scarlet brew a range of beers inspired by

many regional brewing cultures (American IPAs, or lagers inspired by Franconia and the Czech Republic, for example). The taproom is open most weekends between March and December for drinks and cans to take away. The brewery also ships cans to many independent retailers nationwide. 🍴◆

Stancill SIBA

Unit 2, Oakham Drive, off Rutland Road, Sheffield, S3 9QX

☎ (0114) 275 2788 ☎ 07809 427716

☺Stancill began brewing in 2014 and is named after the first head brewer and co-owner. It is situated on the doorstep of the late Stones' Cannon Brewery, taking advantage of the soft Yorkshire water. ‼

Barnsley Bitter (ABV 3.8%) BITTER
Blonde (ABV 3.9%) BLOND
India (ABV 4%) BITTER
No.7 (ABV 4.3%) BITTER
Stainless (ABV 4.3%) BITTER
Porter (ABV 4.4%) PORTER
Black Gold (ABV 5%) STOUT

Steel City

c/o Lost Industry Brewing, 14a Nutwood Trading Estate, Sheffield, S6 1NJ

⊗ Steel City was established in 2009 and operates as a cuckoo brewery, brewing on an occasional basis and when inspired. Brewing currently takes place at Lost Industry Brewing (qv). Much of the Steel City output is collaborations with other like-minded brewers, having a little fun producing interesting and experimental beers. ◆

Tapped

🍴 Sheffield: Sheffield Tap, Platform 1b, Sheffield Station, Sheaf Street, Sheffield, S1 2BP
☎ (0114) 273 7558

Leeds: 51 Boar Street, Leeds, LS1 5EL ☎ 0113 244 1953 ⊕ tappedbrewco.com

Brewing began in 2013 after the old station Edwardian dining rooms were converted into a four-barrel, onsite brewery with a viewing gallery at the Sheffield Tap pub. The beer is mostly sold onsite and via the company's specialist beer wholesale business, Pivovar, to its other outlets and occasionally into the free trade. A further onsite brewery was opened at the Leeds Tap in 2014 which supplies that pub. Part of the Pivovar group that also includes the Elvington brewery.

Toolmakers SIBA

6-8 Botsford Street, Sheffield, S3 9PF ☎ 07956 235332 ⊕ toolmakersbrewery.com

Toolmakers is a family-run brewery established in 2013 in an old tool-making factory, with the names of the beers reflecting this history. The regular brews are supplemented by a varying range of different styles and strengths and are available in the adjoining Forest pub which is owned. The function room at the brewery also doubles as the taproom. ‼◆

Lynch Pin (ABV 4%) BITTER
Razmataz (ABV 4.2%) BLOND
Flange Noir (ABV 5.2%) STOUT

Triple Point SIBA

178 Shoreham Street, Sheffield, S1 4SQ

☎ (0114) 229 4769 ☎ 07828 131423
⊕ triplepointbrewing.co.uk

Father and son operated modern brewery and bar conversion. The brewery is clearly visible from the drinking area which operates as the taproom for the brewery. ‼◆

Gold (ABV 4%) GOLD
Cryo (ABV 4.2%) IPA
Porter (ABV 4.4%) PORTER
Debut (ABV 5.5%) IPA

True North

47 Eldon Street, Sheffield, S1 4GY
☎ (0114) 272 0569

Office: 127-129 Devonshire Street, Sheffield, S3 7SB
⊕ truenorthbrewco.uk

True North began brewing in 2012 using spare capacity at Welbeck Abbey Brewery (qv). It opened its own plant in Sheffield in 2016. Dean Hollingworth is head brewer, supplying 11 pubs owned by the company plus other independent outlets.

Best Bitter (ABV 3.8%) BITTER
Blonde (ABV 4%) GOLD
Polaris (ABV 4.3%) BITTER

Ward & Houldsworth

Office: 62 Drakehouse Lane West, Beighton, Sheffield, S20 1FX ☎ 07912 028880 ⊕ ifinfused.com

Former Kelham Island brewer Paul Ward together with Darren Houldsworth established the company in 2019. Beers are contract brewed at Pheasantry (qv) and distributed from storage in Sheffield.

White Rose

Premises R/O, 7 Doncaster Road, Mexborough, S64 0HL
☎ (0114) 246 6334

Office: 119 Chapel Road, Burncross, Chapeltown, Sheffield, S35 1QL
✉ whiterose.brewery@btinternet.com

☺Established in 2007 by Gary Sheriff, former head brewer at Wentworth Brewery. Formerly sharing premises with Little Ale Cart, White Rose then brewed in Mexborough, sharing premises with Imperial Brewery (qv). In 2018 it moved to its own premises using a new seven-barrel plant. ‼◆

Original Blonde (ABV 4%) BLOND
Stairlift to Heaven (ABV 4.2%) BLOND
Raven (ABV 4.9%) STOUT

Woodland

14 Market Street, Penistone, S36 6BZ ☎ 07894 532456

Established in 2017 producing bottled and keg beers, the brewery moved into cask production in 2019, winning CAMRA awards the same year. Originally brewing from his residence, owner/brewer David Hampshaw soon relocated the two-barrel brewery into a taphouse in Penistone town centre. The brewery has been expanded to a five-barrel system, allowing for an increased range, a greater focus on cask ale, and wider distribution. Cans were introduced in 2020. The brewery is named after the highly-prized, local, whitefaced woodland sheep. ◆LIVE◆

Painted Tiles (ABV 4%) PALE
First Flight (ABV 6%) PALE

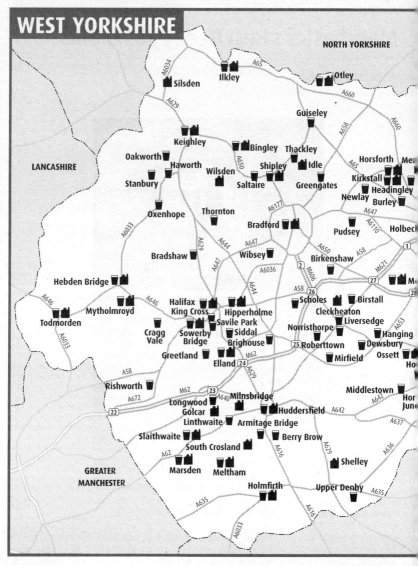

WEST YORKSHIRE

Ackworth

Boot & Shoe

Wakefield Road, WF7 7DF (on A638)

☎ (01977) 610218 🌐 bootandshoe.webs.com

Ossett Yorkshire Blonde, White Rat; 4 changing beers (sourced regionally) Ⓗ

A busy village pub dating back to the late 16th century, it is one of seven real ale outlets in the village. Extensively refurbished in 2021, it has retained its original features including the open fire range. There is a wood-fired pizza oven and Sunday roasts are served. Quiz night is on Thursday and live music on Saturday nights. Live sporting events are shown on Sky and BT Sport. The village cricket field is behind the pub. ❀🕭♣♿P🖵🐾🛜♫

Masons Arms Ⓛ

Bell Lane, WF7 7JD (on Bell Ln, a turning off A628 by a defunct railway bridge)

☎ 07966 501827

Bradfield Farmers Bitter, Farmers Blonde, Farmers Stout; 1 changing beer (sourced locally) Ⓗ

A Grade II-listed former coaching house dating from 1682 built of locally quarried stone. A unique display of old photographs portray the local social and industrial heritage. A central bar serves the main room, pool room and smaller lounge. There is a new courtyard beer garden to the rear with food served outside in summer. Live music on Saturday evenings and Sundays afternoons and the Thursday quiz night are all well attended. 🕭❀♿♣P🖵🛜♫

Armitage Bridge

Armitage Bridge Monkey Club Ⓛ

Dean Brook Road, HD4 7PB

☎ 07980 897105

2 changing beers (sourced locally; often Empire) Ⓗ

Refurbished and air-conditioned, this thriving and friendly little club in the hamlet of Armitage Bridge

where basket meals are served in summer. A takeaway service at other times is from Buffet Carte. The pub has gone from strength to strength under the current licensee and her partner. Q ☞ 🕮 🏵 🕮 & ♿ ➹ ♣ P 🚲 🐾 ♪

Bingley

Chip N Ern 🅛

73 Main Street, BD16 2JA
☎ (01274) 985501
7 changing beers (sourced locally; often Bingley, Darkland, Nailmaker) 🅷

A micropub on Bingley's Main Street and a popular destination on the local real ale scene. The wood-panelled ground floor bar has a distinctive and eclectic range of decorations. The seven cask ales include a varying range from local and regional breweries. Additional seating is available in the more modern-styled upstairs room with its own bar selling bottles and cans. It is close to the railway station and handy for exploring the famous Five Rise Locks on the adjacent Leeds-Liverpool Canal. ☞ & ➹ 🚲 🐾 ⚲ ♪

Birkenshaw

Halfway House 🅛

1 Whitehall Road East, BD11 2EQ (A58/A651 jct)
☎ (01274) 680614 🌐 thehalfwayhousepub.co.uk
Ossett Yorkshire Blonde, White Rat; Tetley Bitter; 3 changing beers (sourced regionally; often Black Sheep, Copper Dragon, Leeds) 🅷

A busy, traditional ex-Tetley local pub with a homely lounge. Pool is played on Tuesdays, with a music quiz on Thursdays and live music on Saturday evenings. Three tied and three free of tie beers are mostly from Yorkshire breweries and usually include darker styles. Food is home-made pizzas and burgers. Ales are sold at a discount Monday to Wednesday. Buses 254 and 255 pass the pub, wth 283 and 283A under 10 minutes' walk away. ☞ 🏵 🕮 ♣ P 🚲 (254,255) 🐾 ⚲ ♪

Birstall

Black Bull 🅛 ✅

5 Kirkgate, WF17 9PB (off A652 near jct of A643)
☎ (01274) 865609
Black Sheep Best Bitter; Ossett White Rat; 2 changing beers (sourced nationally; often Bradfield, Kirkstall, Moorhouse's) 🅷

A stone-built 17th-century community pub, important through the centuries. The upper room, used as a local magistrate's court in times gone by, is still preserved and is used for functions. On the ground floor is a snug, main bar area and a side room. The comfortable, traditional surroundings are warmed by an open fire in the winter, while behind the pub is a car park and a tidy beer garden. Traditional board games are available. ☞ 🏵 ♣ P 🚲 (200,283) 🐾 ↻ ♪

Bradford

Boar & Fable

30 North Parade, BD1 3HZ
🌐 boarandfable.com
3 changing beers (sourced locally; often Vocation, Wilde Child, Wishbone) 🅷

Opened in 2020, this small, stylish and comfortable bar gets its name from the legend of a ferocious boar that lived in the woods where Bradford now stands. It comprises a ground floor room with additional seating in a basement area. Three handpulls serve a varying range of usually locally sourced real ales. Nine keg taps offer an

---

serves up to three changing guest beers and one regular house beer from Empire. A regular local CAMRA Club of the Year, with the same manager for the last 15 years, it is a great place to relax with a pint on an evening and well worth seeking out. There is a pool room upstairs. No affiliation and no membership are required. ☞ 🏵 & ♣ 🚲 🐾 ⚲ ↻ ♪

Berry Brow

Railway

2 School Lane, HD4 7LT
☎ 07828 141807
6 changing beers (sourced locally; often Abbeydale, Castle Rock, Moorhouse's) 🅷

A popular and welcoming village local with six cask ales. Abbeydale, Castle Rock, Moorhouse's and Ossett feature prominently on the beer roster. Sports fans are well catered for with both Sky and BT Sports channels. There is a cosy snug with a real fire in winter, and a beer garden

additional selection of beers often including a dark beer and a sour. An extensive selection of bottled and canned beers is stocked. ⏱≷(Forster Square)�🐾📶♪

Corn Dolly L

110 Bolton Road, BD1 4DE

☎ (01274) 720219 ⊕ corndolly.pub

Abbeydale Moonshine; Moorhouse's White Witch; Timothy Taylor Boltmaker; 5 changing beers (sourced regionally; often Bridgehouse, Durham, Pictish) Ⓗ

Award-winning traditional freehouse run by the same family since 1989. Previously called the Wharfe, due to its location near to the former Bradford canal, it first opened its doors in 1834. An open-plan layout incorporates a games area to one end. Good-value food is served weekday lunchtimes. It has a friendly atmosphere and is popular before Bradford City matches. A collection of pumpclips adorn the beams. Close to the city centre and Forster Square railway station.

🏵◑&≷(Forster Square) ♣🅿🚌(640,641) ↻

Exchange Craft Beer House L

14 Market Street, BD1 1LH

☎ (01274) 306078

6 changing beers (sourced regionally; often Moor Beer, Nightjar, Wilde Child) Ⓗ

This establishment is located under the Victorian splendour that is the Wool Exchange building. Despite being a cellar bar, the pub has a light and airy feel. It is open plan, with a large seating area and bar under a brick barrel ceiling with a smaller raised seating area near the entrance. Six handpulls usually feature at least one real ale from owner, Nightjar brewery, plus others from smaller regional breweries, or further afield, in a variety of styles from light to dark.

⏱≷(Forster Square) ♣🚌🐾📶♪

Fighting Cock L

21-23 Preston Street, BD7 1JE (close to Grattans, off Thornton Rd)

☎ (01274) 726907

Theakston Old Peculier; Timothy Taylor Boltmaker, Landlord; 5 changing beers (sourced nationally; often Moorhouse's, Oakham, Pictish) Ⓗ

Drinkers' paradise in an industrial area, this multi-award winning traditionally-styled freehouse is 20 minutes' walk from the city centre and close to bus routes along Thornton Road and Legrams Lane. Up to eight real ales usually include at least one dark beer. A variety of ciders from Biddenden and other guest producers are often available, and foreign bottled beers are also offered. Good-value lunches are served Monday to Saturday. A large beer garden is opposite the pub. 🏵◑●🚌🐾📶↻♪

Jacob's Well L

5 Kent Street, BD1 5RL (by Jacobs Well roundabout at end of Hall Ings)

☎ (01274) 395628 ⊕ jacobs-well.co.uk

Abbeydale Deception; Half Moon Dark Masquerade; Sunbeam Bright Day; 3 changing beers (sourced regionally; often Bingley, Craven, Stubbee) Ⓗ

Traditionally-styled real ale and cider freehouse, dating from 1811, formerly known as Jacob's Beer House. It has an open-plan layout with a rustic feel, and a snug to the side of the bar. Nine handpulls offer a varying range of six real ales from local and regional independents and up to three real ciders from local producers. Numerous boxed ciders and perries are also available. The hand-made pies include some interesting fillings. Sit outside and watch the city bustle while supping good ale.

🏵◑≷(Interchange) ●🚌🐾📶↻♪

REAL ALE BREWERIES

Anthology ♦ Leeds
Barker Bridge Bradford (NEW)
Barker's South Crosland
Beer Ink ♦ Huddersfield
BEEspoke 🍺 Shipley
Bingley ♦ Wilsden
Bini Ilkley
Bone Idle Idle
Bosun's ♦ Wetherby
Bridgehouse Keighley
Briscoe's Otley (brewing suspended)
Chevin Otley
Chin Chin South Kirkby
Cobbydale 🍺 Silsden
Cooper Hill Leeds
Darkland ♦ Halifax
DMC Wakefield
Eagles Crag ♦ Todmorden
Elland Elland
Empire Slaithwaite
Fernandes 🍺 ♦ Wakefield
Frisky Bear ♦ Leeds: Morley
Goose Eye ♦ Bingley
Halifax Steam 🍺 Hipperholme
Henry Smith 🍺 Pontefract
Hogs Head 🍺 Sowerby Bridge
Horbury 🍺 Horbury
Horsforth ♦ Leeds: Horsforth
Ilkley Ilkley
Kirkstall ♦ Leeds: Kirkstall
Legitimate Industries Leeds
Little Valley Hebden Bridge
Lord's ♦ Golcar
Luddite 🍺 Horbury Junction

Magic Rock ♦ Huddersfield
Mallinsons Huddersfield
Marlowe Otley
Meanwood ♦ Leeds
Mill Valley ♦ Cleckheaton
Milltown Milnsbridge
Morton Collins 🍺 Sandal
Nightjar Mytholmroyd
Nook 🍺 Holmfirth
North ♦ Leeds
Northern Monk ♦ Leeds
Ossett ♦ Ossett
Piglove ♦ Leeds
Quirky ♦ Leeds: Garforth
Rat 🍺 Huddersfield
Ridgeside ♦ Leeds: Meanwood
Riverhead 🍺 Huddersfield: Marsden
Salt ♦ Shipley
Saltaire ♦ Shipley
Shadow ♦ Otley
Small World Shelley
Stod Fold Halifax
Stubbee ♦ Bradford
Sunbeam Leeds
Tarn 51 🍺 Altofts
Three Fiends Meltham
Tigertops Wakefield
Timothy Taylor Keighley
Truth Hurts ♦ Leeds: Morley
Vocation Hebden Bridge
Wetherby ♦ Wetherby
Wharfedale 🍺 Ilkley
Wilde Child ♦ Leeds
Wishbone ♦ Keighley
Zapato ♦ Marsden

Record Café
45-47 North Parade, BD1 3JH
☎ (01274) 723143 🌐 therecordcafe.co.uk
4 changing beers (sourced regionally; often Northern Monk, Revolutions, Track) 🄷
Multi-award winning modern café-style bar located in the city's independent quarter selling ale, vinyl and ham! Four handpulls serve constantly changing real ales sourced regionally in varying styles and including a dark beer. Real cider and perry are offered. Nine craft keg beers, many from independent brewers, are on tap. Food is offered in a charcuterie style specialising in hams and cheeses from Spain. In the upstairs mezzanine area it is possible to purchase vinyl records. Payment by card only.
🐎❀◗♿⇌(Forster Square) 🍎🚌🐾ᯤ↺

Sparrow 🄻
32 North Parade, BD1 3HZ
☎ (01274) 270772
Kirkstall Bitter, Pale Ale, Three Swords, Dissolution IPA, Black Band Porter; 1 changing beer (sourced regionally; often Kirkstall) 🄷
This simply furnished café-style pub was refurbished in 2018 by Kirkstall brewery. The interior has a traditional feel comprising painted walls with pictures and mirrors, many having a breweriana theme, and dark wood panelling. There is additional seating in the basement. Six handpulls serve Kirkstall brewery beers and occasional guest ales. Nine taps behind the bar serve kegged beers and a cider. The pub can get busy when Bradford City FC are playing at home.
🐎❀⇌(Forster Square) 🚌🐾ᯤ♫

Bradshaw

Golden Fleece 🄻 ✔
1 Bradshaw Lane, HX2 9UZ
☎ 07522 190990 🌐 goldenfleecebradshaw.co.uk
Saltaire Blonde; 4 changing beers (sourced nationally) 🄷
You are assured of a warm welcome at this traditional village pub. There is a comfortable lounge and a separate area for pool. A quiz night is held every Wednesday and entertainment every Saturday with a themed disco. Sports fans are catered for with Sky TV showing premium events. The pub has a large beer garden where you can enjoy excellent views across nearby countryside.
🐎❀♿▲♣P🚌ᯤ↺♫

Brighouse

Crafty Fox 🄻
44 Commercial Street, HD6 1AQ
☎ 07847 205425 🌐 craftyfox.bar
6 changing beers (sourced nationally; often Church End, Salopian, Vocation) 🄷
A family-run bar on the main shopping street, with a back door opening into Brighouse bus station. The industrial-style interior has wood-panelled walls, pallet tables and stools. The upstairs room has similar decor and is available for private functions and meetings. Blind beer tastings are organised once a month, and live acts and a quiz are hosted weekly. Open Wednesday to Sunday. 🐎⇌🚌🐾ᯤ↺♫

Market Tavern 🄻
2 Ship Street, HD6 1JX
☎ (01484) 769852
6 changing beers (sourced nationally; often Abbeydale, Neepsend, Salopian) 🄷
Micropub in a single-storey former pork pie factory next to the canalside open-air market. It has comfortable seating in the bar, a small snug by the entrance and a sheltered outside drinking area. At least one dark beer and two changing real ciders are on sale at all times. Snacks are available for customers and their dogs. Open Wednesday to Sunday and bank holiday Mondays.
Q🐎❀♿⇌🍎🚌🐾ᯤ

Castleford

Doghouse 🄻
16 Carlton Street, WF10 1AY (bottom end of main shopping street)
☎ (01977) 559793
6 changing beers (sourced locally) 🄷
A family-owned quirky craft ale bar located within the historic Roman settlement town of Castleford, with rotating and permanent ales available. The interior walls are adorned with song lyrics from years gone by and hand-painted art throughout. A cosy establishment with a small outside seating area to the rear. The bar hosts regularweekly music and quiz nights. Families and dogs are welcome. Q🐎❀♿⇌♣🍎P🚌🐾ᯤ♫

Junction 🄻
Carlton Street, WF10 1EE (enter Castleford on A655, pub is on corner with Carlton St at top of town centre)
☎ (01977) 277750 🌐 thejunctionpubcastleford.com
5 changing beers (sourced locally) 🄷
This rejuvenated pub specialises in beers from the landlord's own wooden casks. Up to six changing guest ales are available in the wood from enterprising local brewers. The large L-shaped bar is kept warm with open fires and a stove-heated snug can be used for functions. Folk afternoons are held on the last Sunday of the month. Dogs aee welcome. Handily situated for both the bus and railway stations. Q🐎⇌♣🚌🐾ᯤ↺

Cragg Vale

Robin Hood 🄻
Cragg Road, HX7 5SQ (on B6138 1½ miles S of Mytholmroyd)
☎ (01422) 885899
Timothy Taylor Boltmaker, Landlord; 3 changing beers (sourced regionally; often Abbeydale, Goose Eye, Small World) 🄷
Friendly, welcoming traditional split-level free house in a beautiful wooded valley and situated on the longest continuous hill climb in England, which is popular with competitive cyclists. There are also excellent walks nearby. On entering, the cosy bar – with a real fire in winter – is to the right and the larger dining room is to the left. Food is served Thursday to Sunday. Two Timothy Taylor beers are complemented by up to three guests from regional breweries. Q🐎❀◗▲🚌(900,901)🐾ᯤ↺

Crigglestone

Station Pub
Bretton Lane, WF4 3ER (take A636 Denby Dale Rd out of city for 3½ miles, then left on to Blacker Ln, ½ miles right on to Cliff Rd; pub signed from A636)
☎ (01924) 728519
Bradfield Farmers Blonde; Tetley Bitter 🄷
A family-run pub for 20 years, serving well-kept beer and home-cooked food. There is a large beer garden and children's play area. A function room is available for hire. Quiz night is Sunday with darts and dominoes played on Monday. There are Sky and BT Sports screens for the sporting enthusiasts. 🐎❀◗♿P🚌(96,435)🐾↺♫

Dewsbury

Shepherd's Boy ⓛ ✅
157 Huddersfield Road, WF13 2RP (on A644 ½ mile W of town)
☎ (01924) 454116
Ossett Butterley, Yorkshire Blonde, White Rat, Silver King; 2 changing beers (sourced regionally; often Nailmaker, Titanic, Vocation) Ⓗ
Located about half a mile from the town centre, this fine Ossett brewery reconstruction of a former Webster's pub features four distinct, comfortable drinking areas, with a trademark brick arch separating the front from the rear of the pub. The hidden beer garden behind and below the pub provides shade on summer days. Monday is poker night, Thursday is quiz night with food. Home-made snacks are sometimes available. Guest ales sometimes feature a strong or a dark ale.
✿♣P☷(202,203)🌂🗢🔄♫

West Riding Refreshment Rooms ♛ ⓛ
Dewsbury Railway Station, Wellington Road, WF13 1HF
☎ (01924) 459193
Timothy Taylor Landlord; 7 changing beers (sourced nationally; often Black Sheep, Vocation) Ⓗ
A multi-award winning pub in a Grade II-listed station building, which has been in the Guide for 29 years. A diverse range of real ales of differing styles and strengths is offered, with another pump often used for real cider. Lunches and Saturday breakfasts are served. At other times, pizzas and other bar snacks are available. Live music plays in the beer garden in summer. The first pub in the Beerhouses Group, all of which are renowned real ale pubs. ✿🍴◖≉♣🍴P☷🌂🗢🔄♫

Elland

Drop Inn ⓛ ✅
12 Elland Lane, HX5 9DU (off the link rd from the A629 to the town centre)
☎ (01422) 387484 ⊕ ossett-brewery.co.uk/pubs
Ossett Silver King, White Rat, Yorkshire Blonde; 2 changing beers (sourced nationally; often Acorn, Fuller's, Rat) Ⓗ
Stone flags and floorboards and a brick arch between rooms exhibit the Ossett Brewery pub style. French renaissance pictures add to the decor along with cigar containers, stone jars and tankards. A stove occupies a large cottage fireplace in the side room. French windows lead to a beer garden. A quiz is held every Thursday. Five beers in total are served, with two guest beers from other Ossett Group breweries and regional microbreweries. A dark beer is usually available.
🌂✿◖♣☷(501,503)🌂🗢

Elland Craft & Tap ⓛ
102 Southgate, HX5 0EP
☎ (01422) 370630 ⊕ craftandtap.co.uk
House beer (by Elland); 5 changing beers (sourced regionally; often Elland, Millstone, Wensleydale) Ⓗ
A community hub next to the market square, renowned for its friendly, convivial atmosphere, it has no music, screens or machines. A converted bank with taproom and bar and a lower lounge area, it is popular with locals, visitors and CAMRA members. There is always one bitter and one dark beer on handpull, plus the house ale from the local Elland brewery. It has floral displays in summer and a private room upstairs for hire. Quiz night is Wednesday. Q🌂✿◖P☷(501,503)🌂🗢

Greengates

Cracker Barrel
832 Harrogate Road, BD10 0RA
Tetley Bitter; 4 changing beers (sourced regionally; often Daleside, Sunbeam) Ⓗ
Refurbished in 2020, this small, friendly family-run micropub with a cosy feel comprises a single room with the bar positioned to the right-hand side. Tetley Cask Bitter is the regular real ale. The other four handpulls serve an ever-varying range of real ales, often including a dark beer, from regional breweries. Families and dogs are welcome. There is a small beer garden to the rear and outside seating to the front, next to the busy main road. 🌂✿🍴🗢🔄

Guiseley

Coopers ⓛ ✅
4-6 Otley Road, LS20 8AH
☎ (01943) 878835
Ilkley Blonde; Timothy Taylor Landlord; 6 changing beers (sourced locally; often Brass Castle, Kirkstall, Vocation) Ⓗ
Modern-style bar converted from a former Co-op store, with a main bar area, separate dining area and upstairs function room. Eight cask beers are generally from Yorkshire or northern breweries, with dedicated dark beer and gluten-free handpumps and large selection of other beers on tap and in bottles and cans. A diverse range of meals is available. Events are held in the large upstairs function room and this area also serves as extra dining space. Children allowed until early evening.
Q🌂✿◖🍴◖≉🍴🗢🗢♫

Guiseley Factory Workers Club ⓛ
6 Town Street, LS20 9DT
☎ (01943) 874793 ⊕ guiseleyfactoryworkersclub.co.uk
Black Sheep Best Bitter; 2 changing beers (sourced locally; often Acorn, Craven, Pennine) Ⓗ
Multi-award winning, three-roomed club founded over 100 years ago by the Yeadon and Guiseley Factory Workers Union. The bar serves both the lounge and the concert room and has changing guest ales sourced both locally and nationally. There is a snooker room with TV lounge and a large beer garden with lawn and stone-flagged patio. Occasional concerts are held at weekends. The club hosts many local clubs and organisations. CAMRA members welcome with this Guide or a membership card. ✿≉♣🍴P☷(27,34)🌂🗢♫

Halifax: Greetland

Greetland Social Club ⓛ
222 Rochdale Road, HX4 8JE
☎ (01422) 372966
2 changing beers (sourced regionally; often Elland, Goose Eye, Vocation) Ⓗ
A community-based social club open seven days a week with welcoming atmosphere, always offering two rotating real ales from local and regional breweries. Members receive beer discounts, with the club open to the public. It consists of a lounge, games room with two snooker tables and function room that hosts regular music, open mic, comedy and charity events. There is an outside drinking shelter and buses stop outside the door. Local CAMRA Club of the Year 2023. ✿♣☷🌂🗢🔄♫

Halifax: King Cross

Wainhouse Tavern L ✓

Upper Washer Lane, Pye Nest, HX2 7DR (take Edwards Rd off Pye Nest Rd)

☎ (01422) 339998

House beer (by Rudgate); 5 changing beers (sourced regionally; often Mallinsons, Rooster's, Rudgate) ⊞

Formerly home to the industrialist JE Wainhouse, famous for his elegant tower nearby, this pub became the Royal Hotel in the 1960s and acquired freehold status in 2014 as the Wainhouse Tavern. It boasts interesting architectural and decorative features and comprises a comfortable lower lounge bar at the front and a larger bar behind with pub games area and plenty of seating at tables. A good selection of beers is available, with home-cooked meals served most evenings and at weekends.
Q ප ★ ◑ ♣ P �'t (579,586) ♠ 🕏 ♫

Halifax: Savile Park

Big Six L

10 Horsfall Street, HX1 3HG (adjacent to Spring Edge Park at the top of Free School Ln)

☎ 07878 854447

Old Mill Traditional Bitter; 4 changing beers (sourced regionally; often Acorn, Elland, Phoenix) ⊞

A hidden gem in a row of terraces, with several cosy fireplaces and original features, this welcoming pub majors on good beer, real cider and conversation. Identified by CAMRA as having a regionally important historic pub interior, it has a through corridor separating the bar and games room from the two lounges. The pub's name derives from a mineral water company that operated here a century ago, whose memorabilia adorn the walls. A generously-sized garden is situated behind the pub. Q ✿ ♣ ● ➟ (577) ♠ ↺

Halifax: Siddal

Cross Keys ♇ L

3 Whitegate, HX3 9AE

☎ (01422) 300348 ⊕ crosskeyshalifax.co.uk

8 changing beers (sourced regionally; often Elland, Goose Eye, Wensleydale) ⊞

This 17th-century tavern has a real traditional feel. A snug beside the bar opens up to a much larger room with a central inglenook fireplace which is particularly cosy in winter. A smaller room behind the bar is ideal for small groups and for meetings. Live music is often featured on Sunday afternoons. Walkers and cyclists are always welcome. There is a large covered, heated area often used for events including the annual beer and music festival on the second weekend of August. Local CAMRA Pub of the Year 2023. Q ✿ ♣ P ➟ (541,542) ♠ 🕏 ♫

Halifax: Town Centre

Dukes L

16-18 Market Arcade, HX1 1NX

☎ 07305 100054 ⊕ dukeshalifax.bigcartel.com

3 changing beers (sourced nationally; often Anthology, Atom, Northern Monk) ⊞

Located within a Victorian arcade, an attractive frontage leads on to a bright, colourful, cheerful interior with an extensive splash of pink and turquoise. There is bench seating in the arcade while inside the furniture is rather minimalist. The colour scheme continues into the upstairs room which features tables with stool seating. Three cask ales are served from handpumps, with another two handpumps serving cider. There are also a dozen keg taps. Card payments only. ✿ ◑ ➟ ♣ ● ➟ 🕏

København L

6 Westgate Arcade, HX1 1DJ

⊕ kobenhavn.beer

6 changing beers (sourced nationally; often Arbor, Marble, Vocation) ⊞

A spacious, minimalist, Scandinavian-style bar that opened in Westgate Arcade in central Halifax in 2019. It has three tiered seating areas plus a covered outdoor drinking area in the arcade itself. Six beers are served on handpump, always including a dark brew, and there are also 24 keg lines in a wide range of styles. A private function room is available upstairs. ප ✿ ᵴ ➟ 🖫 🍴 ♠ 🕏 ↺

Meandering Bear L

21-23 Union Street, HX1 1PR

☎ 07807 136520 ⊕ meanderingbear.co.uk

5 changing beers (sourced nationally; often Lakes, Neptune, Torrside) ⊞

This modern and tastefully decorated bar is located close to Halifax Piece Hall and Westgate Arcade in the town centre. Its name is derived from a large bear that escaped from Halifax Zoo in 1913. The classy interior incorporates comfortable seating and is split level, with the bar on a higher level. Five beers are provided on handpull, one usually dark, and there are seven keg lines. Locally sourced/made bar food is available. Occasional beer festivals and Meet the Brewer nights are held. ◑ ➟ 🖫 ♠ 🕏

Three Pigeons ★ L ✓

1 Sun Fold, HX1 2LX

☎ (01422) 347001

Ossett Butterley, Yorkshire Blonde, White Rat, Silver King; 4 changing beers (sourced regionally) ⊞

A striking octagonal drinking lobby forms the hub from which five distinctive rooms radiate in this Art Deco pub, built in 1932 by Websters brewery. Sensitively refurbished and maintained by Ossett brewery, this venue attracts a variety of local groups and societies along with football and rugby enthusiasts. Four Ossett beers are always available. Four guest beers also feature, which usually include a stout or a porter.
Q ✿ ➟ ♣ P ➟ ♠ 🕏 ↺

Victorian Craft Beer Café L

18-22 Powell Street, HX1 1LN

⊕ victorian.beer

9 changing beers (sourced nationally; often Squawk, Track, Vocation) ⊞

An award-winning pub, opened in 2014, situated behind the Victoria Theatre. The main seating area has wooden floors and a tiled bar; to the left abundant cosy seating can be found in multiple rooms. It offers nine rotating ales from a wide range of breweries alongside 18 keg lines, a choice of Belgian and world beers and two draught ciders. Many beer-themed events and tap takeovers are held, including the celebrated annual dark beer festival, Back in Black.
Q ප ᵴ ➟ (Halifax) 🖫 ♠ 🕏 ↺ ♫

Hanging Heaton

Hanging Heaton Cricket Club

Bennett Lane, WF17 6DB

☎ (01924) 461804 ⊕ hangingheatoncc.co.uk

Bradfield Farmers Blonde, Farmers Pale Ale; 2 changing beers (sourced regionally; often Acorn, JW Lees) ⊞

A long-established, welcoming community club, local and regional CAMRA Club of the Year 2022. Smart and comfortable with fine views across the cricket pitch where the successful cricket team plays in the local

league. Snooker is taken seriously, the snooker tables being well used and bringing home prizes, with occasional visits by sporting celebrities. The handpumps have increased from one to four under the enthusiastic steward. Well-chosen guest beers are mainly from Yorkshire. Opening hours vary in winter.
🚽❀◑&♣P🚌(202)🌸🛜↺♪

Haworth

Fleece Inn L ✓
67 Main Street, BD22 8DA
☎ (01535) 642172 ⊕ fleeceinnhaworth.co.uk
Timothy Taylor Golden Best, Boltmaker, Knowle Spring, Landlord, Landlord Dark; 1 changing beer (often Timothy Taylor) ⊞
A stone-built coaching inn on Haworth's famous cobbled Main Street, with spectacular views over the Worth Valley and close to the KWVR historic heritage railway. A cosy room to the right and a lower-level dining area offer quiet alternatives to the busy bar. Locally sourced food and accommodation are offered, and breakfast is available to all. The beer garden is three storeys up from the bar, on the roof. A Timothy Taylor tied house, popular with tourists and locals alike. 🚽❀🛏◑&👶🚶♣🚌🌸🛜

Heath

King's Arms ★ L ✓
Heath Common, WF1 5SL (at edge of Heath Village on Heath Common, off A655 Wakefield-Normanton road)
☎ (01924) 377527 ⊕ thekingsarmsheath.co.uk
Ossett Yorkshire Blonde, White Rat, Silver King; 4 changing beers ⊞
The King's Arms, acquired by Clark's brewery in 1989, is now leased to Ossett brewery. Built in the early 1700s and converted into a public house in 1841, it consists of three oak-panelled rooms with gas lighting, plus a conservatory and gardens to the rear. In the summer months you can sit outside and relax peacefully amid the acres of common grassland surrounding the area. A quiz is on Tuesdays. Food is served lunchtimes and evenings Wednesday to Saturday, with Sunday lunches.
Q🚽❀◑&P🚌(188)🌸🛜

Hebden Bridge

Fox & Goose L ✓
7 Heptonstall Road, HX7 6AZ (at traffic lights on jct of A646 and Heptonstall Rd)
☎ (01422) 648052 ⊕ foxandgoose.org
Pictish Brewers Gold; 5 changing beers (sourced nationally; often Eagles Crag, Torrside, Wishbone) ⊞
West Yorkshire's first community co-operative pub extends a warm welcome to locals and visitors alike. A single bar serves three different flagstone-floored rooms and an upstairs covered, heated beer garden. The main bar is warmed by a real fire in winter while the room to the left often hosts live music. The room to the right has a dartboard. At least one vegan beer and one dark beer are usually available. Local CAMRA Pub of the Year 2019 and 2022 and local CAMRA Cider Pub of the Year 2023.
Q❀👶♣🚌🚋(590,592)🌸🛜♪

Old Gate Bar & Restaurant L
1-5 Old Gate, HX7 8JP
☎ (01422) 843993 ⊕ oldgatehebden.co.uk
Timothy Taylor Landlord; Vocation Bread & Butter; 6 changing beers (sourced nationally; often Marble, Rooster's, Thornbridge) ⊞
This smart, modern and popular bar serves quality food all day in the bar and upstairs restaurant. A striking

copper-topped bar serves two regular and six rotating real ales, one always a dark. Disabled access to each level of the split-level bar area is via separate doors off the patio fronting the pub. The large windows provide good views for people-watching from armchairs, benches and sofas. Regular and frequent bus services pass along the road outside. 🚽❀◑&👶🚶♣🚌🌸🛜↺

Hipperholme

Travellers Inn L ✓
53 Tanhouse Hill, HX3 8HN (off A58)
☎ (01422) 202494
Ossett Butterley, Yorkshire Blonde, White Rat, Silver King, Excelsius; 3 changing beers (sourced regionally; often Bingley, Rat, Stubbee) ⊞
Opposite the former railway station, this traditional, 18th-century, stone-built local has taken in adjoining cottages to create a series of distinct spaces. Well-behaved children and dogs on leads are welcome until early evening. A covered yard with heating is provided for smokers. Three guest beers are from Ossett group breweries and other regional microbreweries, always including a dark brew. Popular with walkers, Shibden Hall is close by. 🚽❀♣🚌(255,549)🌸🛜↺

Holmfirth

Nook (Rose & Crown) L ✓
7 Victoria Square, HD9 2DN (down alley behind Barclays Bank)
☎ (01484) 682373 ⊕ thenookbrewhouse.co.uk
Nook Baby Blond, Best, Blond, Oat Stout; 3 changing beers (often Nook) ⊞
The Nook, properly the Rose & Crown, dates from 1754, and is a well-known real ale pub in the heart of the village. Owned and run by the Roberts family for two generations, it has been dispensing beers from its own adjacent brewhouse since 2009, alongside occasional guest beers and Pure North ciders. Home-cooked food is served daily. There is a popular folk evening every Sunday, and real ale festivals both on the weekend before Easter and on the August bank holiday. The log fire is particularly warming on cold winter nights.
🚽❀🛏◑♣🚌🌸🛜↺♪

Horbury

Boons Horbury L ✓
6 Queen Street, WF4 6LP (in town centre off B6128 Horbury-Ossett road, opp Co-op)
☎ (01924) 280442
Timothy Taylor Landlord; 6 changing beers (sourced nationally) ⊞
Popular community pub located in the centre of town just off the High Street attracting people of all ages. The interior has a traditional layout around a central bar with Rugby League memorabilia on the walls. A sizeable outdoor drinking area is well used in summer. A guest cider is served and there is a beer festival on the first weekend in June. ❀♣🚌🌸🛜

Cricketers Arms L
22 Cluntergate, WF4 5AG (Cluntergate is a right fork off the High St at its lower end)
☎ (01924) 267032
Timothy Taylor Landlord; 6 changing beers (sourced regionally) ⊞
On the edge of the town centre this former Melbourne/ Tetley's house is now a genuine free house. The winner of many awards, including local CAMRA Pub Of The Year 2018 and 2019. A Monday poker night, Wednesday quiz

night and Friday meat raffle are held, with open mic on the second Sunday of each month and live music on the last Sunday. A range of craft, keg and gluten-free beers are stocked. Q ☺ ♿ ❀ ♣ ⬤ P ☕ ⌚ 🛜 ♫

Horbury Junction

Calder Vale Hotel Ⓛ

Millfield Road, WF4 5EB (from A642 follow signage through housing estate to Horbury Junction industrial area; or walk from canalside via tubular bridge)
☎ (01924) 277658
6 changing beers (sourced locally; often Luddite) Ⓗ
Established in 1874, this lovingly-restored Victorian Commercial Hotel is steeped in local industrial history. Reopened in 2019, it is home to the Luddite brewery, and has already been voted local CAMRA Pub of the Season and Yorkshire's dog-friendliest pub. It boasts Yorkshire Stone floors and log-burning fires. There is a delightful garden and nearby canal walks. Street food weekends are held and there is occasional entertainment in an upstairs room.
Q ☺ ☕◑ & ♣ ⬤ P ☕ ⌚ ♫

Horsforth

Granville's Beer & Gin House Ⓛ

24 Long Row, LS18 5AA
☎ (0113) 258 2661 🌐 granvilleshouse.co.uk
5 changing beers (sourced locally; often Vocation, Wilde Child) Ⓗ
Formerly a shop unit, now a single-room, long and relatively narrow pub with the bar separating front and rear areas, the latter giving access to further covered seating outside. There are also a couple of tables out the front. The decor is eclectic; doors decorate one wall, panelling another, bare brick yet another, while the floor is part tiled, part parquet. The inner front door handle is a repurposed pump handle. Children are permitted until early evening. Closed on Mondays during the winter months. ☺ ❀ ⇌ ⬤ ⌚ 🛜

Huddersfield

County Beerhouse

4 Princess Street, HD1 2TT
☎ (01484) 959722
Timothy Taylor Landlord; 5 changing beers (sourced regionally; often Little Critters, Vocation) Ⓗ
The County is now run by Beerhouses. Freshly refurbished in a contemporary style with an Art Deco twist, but retaining the original bar and coving partitions. Magnet windows and a John Smith's exterior lamp are retained as a nod to previous ownership. Six handpumps dispense beers sourced from Yorkshire, mainly from micros, and there are five craft keg lines. There is a rear function room. Handy for a drink after an event in Huddersfield Town Hall. ☺ ☕◑ ⇌ ⬤ ⌚ 🛜 ↻ ♫

Grove Ⓛ

2 Spring Grove Street, HD1 4BP
☎ (01484) 318325 🌐 thegrove.pub
Kirkstall Pale Ale; Oakham Citra, Green Devil; Thornbridge Jaipur IPA; 7 changing beers (sourced regionally; often Mallinsons, Marble, Vocation) Ⓗ
The Grove has a style of its own, expressed through its eye-catching artwork, snacks and live music. A veritable drinker's paradise with 11 handpulled ales taking in the full range of styles and strengths. Featured breweries always include Kirkstall, Mallinsons, Marble, Brass Castle, Oakham, Vocation and Thornbridge. Two craft ciders are available, and there is a superb menu of over 20 craft

kegs, 100+ bottled and canned beers and a comprehensive spirits range. The Grove is a must for visitors to Huddersfield. Q ☺ ❀ ⬤ & ⇌ ♣ ⬤ 🖻 ⌚ 🛜 ♫

Head of Steam Ⓛ

St George's Square, HD1 1JF (in station buildings, on right when exiting station)
☎ (01484) 454533
Camerons Strongarm, Road Crew; Thornbridge Jaipur IPA; Timothy Taylor Dark Mild; Vocation Bread & Butter; 9 changing beers Ⓗ
One of the famous pair of real-ale bookends at the railway station, and a favourite calling point on the Transpennine Real Ale Trail. The outlet is a large, four-roomed pub, and each room has its own character. One bar is dedicated to cask and one to keg. The pub's beer range is outstanding, with up to 14 real ales, complemented by real ciders/perries and an extensive British and world bottle range. Pies, mash and peas are served. ☺ ◑ & ⇌ ♣ ⬤ 🖻 ⌚ 🛜 ♫

King's Head

St George's Square, HD1 1JF (in station buildings, on left when exiting station)
Bradfield Farmers Blonde; Magic Rock Ringmaster; Timothy Taylor Landlord; 6 changing beers (sourced regionally; often Abbeydale, Oakham, Pictish) Ⓗ
A friendly welcome always awaits you in this award-winning pub. Situated in the Grade I-listed railway station and winner of a railway heritage award, it has been carefully restored with features including a beautiful tiled floor, wood panelling and wood-burning stoves. It serves four permanent and six rotating beers from breweries near and far. A mild, a dark beer, and one real cider are always available. Live music is played on Sunday afternoon. Hot food is served on match days.
◑ ⇌ ⬤ 🖻 ⌚ ↻ ♫

Rat & Ratchet Ⓛ ✓

40 Chapel Hill, HD1 3EB (on A616, just off ring road)
☎ (01484) 542400
Ossett Butterley, Yorkshire Blonde, White Rat, Silver King; Rat King Rat; 5 changing beers (sourced regionally; often Fernandes, Riverhead, Small World) Ⓗ
Multi award-winning pub owned by Ossett, with the on-site Rat microbrewery. The large open-plan main area still retains the feel of separate rooms. Nine handpumps offer beers from a range of breweries including the firm's own, with two permanent dark ales available. A generous range of ciders and perries are stocked. The pub hosts live music on the second and fourth Thursday of the month, and there is a quiz on Wednesday. Local CAMRA Pub of the Year 2022. There is a car park at the rear. ☺ ❀ ♣ ⬤ P 🖻 ⌚ 🛜 ↻ ♫

Sportsman ★ Ⓛ

1 St John's Road, HD1 5AY
☎ (01484) 421929
Timothy Taylor Boltmaker; 7 changing beers (sourced regionally; often Brass Castle, Thornbridge, Vocation) Ⓗ
This 1930s pub, with a 1950s refit by Hammonds (note the windows), is a previous winner of the CAMRA English Heritage Conservation Pub Design award. The superb curved central bar has a parquet floor and an interesting wooden entrance. Eight ales are arranged in strength order, with a dark beer always available. There is an excellent real cider offering, with two on handpump and two from boxes. Regular Meet the Brewer/Cider producer nights are hosted, and two rooms are regularly used for meetings, such as poker, poetry and music clubs. ☺ ❀ ⇌ ⬤ 🖻 ⌚ 🛜 ↻ ♫

Ilkley

Bar T'at L ✓
7 Cunliffe Road, LS29 9DZ
☎ (01943) 608888
Ilkley Mary Jane; Kirkstall Three Swords; Timothy Taylor Boltmaker, Landlord; 4 changing beers (sourced nationally; often Anspach & Hobday, Black Sheep, Bristol Beer Factory) ⊞
Popular and comfortable side-street pub converted from a former china shop. It is now in the Market Town Taverns group. It has a music-free bar area, additional seating in a basement room and outdoor seating. The pub is renowned for the quality of its beer and food, with the guest real ales featuring a good, often eclectic, variety of beer styles, many from Yorkshire breweries. A wide range of foreign beers is also offered. A home-cooked food menu is served every day.
Q ⏱ ❀ ◑ ≠ 🖵 ❀ 🕸

Flying Duck L ✓
16 Church Street, LS29 9DS (on A65)
☎ (01943) 609587 ⊕ theflyingduck.co.uk
Dark Horse Hetton Pale Ale; Wharfedale Black, Blonde, Best; 4 changing beers (sourced regionally; often Helmsley, Rooster's, Wharfedale) ⊞
Beautifully refurbished Grade II-listed traditional-style pub close to the town centre. Originally constructed as a farmhouse in 1709, it is reputed to be Ilkley's oldest pub building. It retains many original features including York stone and oak flooring, beamed ceilings, internal stonework and mullioned windows. Up to eight real ales, including four regulars from the in-house Wharfedale brewery, and two real ciders are available. Open on bank holiday Mondays. ⏱ ❀ ◑ ≠ 🖵 ❀ 🕸 ↺ ♪

Keighley

Brown Cow L
5 Cross Leeds Street, BD21 2LQ
☎ (01535) 382423
Timothy Taylor Boltmaker; 6 changing beers ⊞
A short walk from the town centre, this family-run free house is about quality, choice and the comfort of customers. Up to five guest beers come mainly from local micros, featuring at least one session beer, a strong one and a dark one. A quiz takes place on the second and last Wednesday of the month. The Brown Cow is a regular meeting place for community groups and a regular winner of CAMRA awards. A no bad language policy is in place. ⏱ ❀ ♣ ♠ ● 🖵 ❀ 🕸

Taylor's on the Green L ✓
Church Street, BD21 5HT
☎ (01535) 603053 ⊕ taylorsonthegreen.co.uk
Timothy Taylor Dark Mild, Golden Best, Boltmaker, Knowle Spring, Landlord, Landlord Dark ⊞
The interior of this Timothy Taylor's managed house is light and airy courtesy of a large atrium. The walls are decorated with photos of Taylor's long history and brewing process. A long bar boasts the full range of Taylor's cask ales, and a special cask may occasionally replace one of the six regular beers. Wood flooring leads you through a choice of seating areas offering booths, high stools, armchairs, sofas or bespoke wooden tables and chairs, and on to a part-heated outdoor area. Freshly-prepared food is offered daily, as are cakes and coffees. There is a brewery shop. ⏱ ❀ ◑ ♿ ≠ 🖵 ❀

Leeds: Burley

Cardigan Arms ★ L
364 Kirkstall Road, LS4 2HQ

☎ (0113) 226 3154 ⊕ cardiganarms.co.uk
Kirkstall Bitter, Pale Ale, Three Swords, Dissolution IPA, Black Band Porter; 1 changing beer (sourced locally; often Anthology, Kirkstall, Vocation) ⊞
The Cardigan Arms has always been a jewel in the Leeds pub crown, but local brewery Kirkstall have lovingly brought it back to former glory. There are four rooms, a drinking lobby and an upstairs quiz/function room. Whether you seek a traditional tap room, ornate woodwork, etched glass or bell pushes, the Cardigan has it all. Built in 1893 to an elaborate Italianate style and named after the Earl of Cardigan who was a major landowner in the area.
⏱ ❀ ◑ ♿ ≠ (Burley Park) ♠ 🖵 ❀ 🕸 ♪

Dave's Pies & Ale L
350 Kirkstall Road, LS4 2HQ
☎ (0113) 278 4555
Daleside Blonde; 2 changing beers (often Ilkley, Stancill, Wilde Child) ⊞
This small venue has a cosy and traditional feel despite only opening in 2021. One wall is covered with old mirrors from brewers and distillers. The traditional-looking bar hosts three handpulls with beers usually from Yorkshire breweries. Two ciders are available, one of which is usually fruit flavoured. A fridge offers a small but interesting range of beers from local breweries including alcohol-free ones. A variety of pork pies, served with peas, is also available. ⏱ ❀ ≠ (Burley Park) ● 🖵 ❀ 🕸

Kirkstall Brewery Tap & Kitchen L
100 Kirkstall Road, LS3 1HJ
☎ (0113) 898 0280 ⊕ kirkstallbrewerytap.co.uk
Kirkstall Pale Ale, Three Swords, Black Band Porter; 4 changing beers (sourced locally; often Kirkstall) ⊞
Traditional one-room pub set inside the thoroughly modern Kirkstall brewery, look out for the big K on the outside! Unsurprisingly, the full range of Kirkstall beers can be found on the bar. The single room is decorated with all manner of brewery and pub memorabilia collected over several years – from relatively common enamel advertisements and mirrors from long-lost breweries to pub signs and partition screens. The food available is mostly pizza, salads and sides.
⏱ ❀ ◑ ♿ ♿ ● 🖵 ❀ 🕸

Leeds: City Centre

Bankers Cat
29 Boar Lane, LS1 5DA
☎ (0113) 440 7998 ⊕ bankerscat.co.uk
Thornbridge Astryd, Lord Marples, Jaipur IPA; 5 changing beers (often Buxton, Thornbridge) ⊞
High-quality pub conversion by Thornbridge brewery and pub group Pivovar. A sumptuous yet traditional feel is created by the use of mahogany and leather in the seating area, which wraps itself nearly all the way round the bar. Booth seating is to the left and a more intimate snug-style area is to the right. For much of the 20th century the building was a bank, though when built in circa 1873 it was the Saracens Head Inn. ♿ ≠ 🖵

Duck & Drake L ✓
43 Kirkgate, LS2 7DR
☎ (0113) 245 5432 ⊕ duckndrake.co.uk
Bridgehouse Blonde; Rooster's Yankee; Theakston Old Peculier; Timothy Taylor Landlord; 10 changing beers (sourced locally; often Daleside, Elland, Saltaire) ⊞
Fine example of a two-roomed Victorian corner pub retaining some original features. The central bar with 15 handpumps sits in between and serves both rooms. There is usually at least one dark beer available. Live

music plays most nights. The Gents toilets feature traditional porcelain units from J Duckett and Son Ltd of Burnley. The beer garden out the back is well looked after and is a pleasant place place to enjoy a pint on a sunny afternoon in Leeds. ✿◑≈🍴🖥♿🛜♨🎵

Friends of Ham Ⓛ

4-8 New Station Street, LS1 5DL
☎ (0113) 242 0275 ⊕ friendsofham.co.uk
Anthology Pale Ale; Kirkstall Pale Ale; 2 changing beers (sourced locally) Ⓗ
Modern bar and charcuterie which features a wide range of interesting beers for all tastes on its modern-style scaffolded bar. A large blackboard provides information on the beers available both on cask and keg plus normally two ciders. A three or six sampling tray of third-pints is available. Around the central bar is a modern shabby-chic interior with diners and drinkers sharing the same space. The downstairs area hosts events such as beer tastings. ◑≈🍴🖥♿🛜

Head of Steam Ⓛ

13 Mill Hill, LS1 5DQ
☎ (0113) 243 6618
Camerons Strongarm; Timothy Taylor Boltmaker; 5 changing beers (sourced locally; often Camerons, Ilkley, Wilde Child) Ⓗ
This is a good-looking three-storey stone and brick pub with a curved frontage. Inside, on the octagonal island bar, beers from all around the world are available including a good range of cask ales and Belgian beers. Although essentially one opened-out room there are different areas – a few tables close to the bar, an alcove which can be used for live music, a raised area to the rear and an upstairs balcony area. ≈🖥♿🎵

Hop Ⓛ ✅

Granary Wharf,, Dark Neville Street, LS1 4BR
☎ (0113) 243 9854 ⊕ thehopleeds.co.uk
Ossett Butterley, Yorkshire Blonde, White Rat, Silver King, Voodoo, Excelsius; 2 changing beers (often Brew York, Tiny Rebel, Wilde Child) Ⓗ
Sited in two of a network of brick arches built in the 1860s to span the river and support the new station, the Hop is a lively pub on two levels with plenty of exposed brick and some music-inspired murals. Downstairs there is plenty of comfy seating in each arch and ample space around the bar, but it can get busy and noisy when there is a full band on, which is most Saturday evenings. More seating is upstairs. ✿◑≈🍴🖥♿🛜♨🎵

Lamb & Flag Ⓛ

1 Church Row, LS2 7HD
☎ (0113) 243 1255 ⊕ lambandflagleeds.co.uk
Kirkstall Leeds Pale, Yorkshire Gold, Leeds Best, Midnight Bell; 4 changing beers (sourced locally; often Brass Castle, Kirkstall, Ridgeside) Ⓗ
Nineteenth-century brick-built pub on a corner site which was previously called the Thirteen Bells after the bells of the nearby Leeds Parish Church (now Leeds Minster). After a long term closure, it was tastefully restored by Leeds brewery and reopened under the current name. There are two floors with various different areas, with exposed brickwork, timber and large windows. Upstairs is a balcony with seating that overlooks Leeds Minster and a covered and winter-heated courtyard. Award-winning food is available. ♿✿◑&≈🖥♿🛜

North Bar Ⓛ

24 New Briggate, LS1 6NU
☎ (0113) 242 4540 ⊕ northbar.com/northbar
2 changing beers (sourced locally; often North) Ⓗ

Small pioneering beer bar which opened way back in 1997 and has always had a relaxed, friendly atmosphere. Alongside the cask ales on the bar is a range of keg beers, many of which are from North brewery, offering a wide variety of styles and ABVs. Packed fridges provide an interesting selection of UK and international packaged beers. One of the cask beers is a pale from the brewery with the second sometimes from a guest brewery. ◑≈🍴🖥🛜

Scarbrough Hotel ✅

Bishopgate Street, LS1 5DY
☎ (0113) 243 4590
Black Sheep Best Bitter; St Austell Nicholson's Pale Ale, Tribute; Tetley Bitter; 3 changing beers (sourced nationally; often Oakham, Timothy Taylor, Titanic) Ⓗ
Often misspelled, the Scarbrough is named after its first owner, Henry Scarbrough, rather than the seaside town. The building, with its impressive tiled frontage, dates from 1765, becoming a pub in 1826. There is a long bar opposite the entrance with seating areas to either side and it provides a convenient spot to wait for a train from Leeds station. One of the few places still serving Tetley Bitter in central Leeds, the selection of guest ales is sourced from around the country. ✿◑&≈🖥🛜🎵

Tapped Leeds Ⓛ

51 Boar Lane, LS1 5EL
☎ (0113) 244 1953 ⊕ tappedleeds.co.uk
8 changing beers (often Kirkstall, Tapped (Leeds), Tapped (Sheffield)) Ⓖ
The bar consists of a single large room with fixtures and fittings blending retro and modern designs, large windows opening onto the street and small seating area outside. Alongside a wide variety of beers on draught is a good list of bottled and canned beers and ciders. A couple of the beers available are brewed on-site. Freshly-baked pizzas are served until two hours before closing. Under-18s are welcome until evening. No football colours are allowed and the dress code Friday and Saturday nights prohibits shorts and tracksuit bottoms. ♿✿◑&≈🖥🛜

Templar Ⓛ ✅

2 Templar Street, LS2 7NU
☎ (0113) 243 0318
Greene King IPA; Kirkstall Three Swords; Tetley Bitter; 5 changing beers (sourced locally; often Acorn, Bradfield) Ⓗ
Grade II-listed, with fine wood panelling from 1928 and splendid exterior with green and cream Burmantofts tiling, this is a traditional city-centre local's pub. The bowing courtier logo can be seen in the leaded window panes from when it was a Melbourne brewery pub. The cask beers are mainly from Yorkshire with a couple from the Greene King stable. The landlord and many staff have all served the pub for over 30 years. League darts and dominoes are played. ✿≈♣🍴🖥♿🛜♨

Three's a Crowd Ⓛ

76-78 North Street, LS2 7PN
☎ (0113) 295 6060 ⊕ threes-a-crowd.co.uk
House beer (by Rooster's); 3 changing beers (sourced locally; often Kirkstall) Ⓗ
A modern bare-boarded pub divided into three areas serving a good selection of local food and beer. The main room makes the most of its corner location with windows stretching virtually from floor to ceiling to give an open and airy feel. To the right is a smaller room with comfortable seating and behind the bar is a raised area used by diners. Food options include all-day nibbles. Outside is a small pavement drinking area. Table service is available for diners. ♿✿◑♿🛜

Town Hall Tavern L ✓

17 Westgate, LS1 2RA

☎ (0113) 244 0765

Timothy Taylor Dark Mild, Golden Best, Boltmaker, Knowle Spring, Landlord, Landlord Dark ⊞

Small traditional inter-war brick-built pub which dates from from 1926. The pub consists of a single room with open alcoves to the left and right of the door. Along the left-hand wall is the bar with its range of Timothy Taylor beers. The decor includes photographs of Leeds in times past on the walls. The pub has a a good reputation for its food and tables for dining can get booked up early on busy days. ◑➤♿❄

Wapentake L

92 Kirkgate, LS2 7DJ

☎ (0113) 243 6248

3 changing beers (sourced locally; often Kirkstall, Nailmaker) ⊞

Sited on one of the oldest streets in Leeds, Wapentake takes its name from an old word to describe an administrative area, a little piece of Yorkshire if you will. Opening in the morning primarily for the coffee, cake and brunch crowd, before drinkers arrive later. It is bare-boarded throughout its two floors with plenty of mix-and-match furniture. A place for individuality and relaxation a world away from the hustle and bustle of the city. ⬛❄◑➤♿❄♪

Whitelock's Ale House ★ L

Turk's Head Yard, LS1 6HB (off Briggate)

☎ (0113) 245 3950 ⊕ whitelocksleeds.com

Five Points XPA, Railway Porter; Kirkstall Pale Ale; Theakston Old Peculier; Timothy Taylor Landlord; 4 changing beers (often Ridgeside, Thornbridge, Vocation) ⊞

Described by John Betjeman as the very heart of Leeds, Whitelock's dates from 1715 and occupies a medieval burgage plot. The interior is largely unchanged since 1895 and is a feast of mirrors, polished metal and woodwork, stained glass, iron pillars and faience tiling. The outside yard is shared with the Turk's Head bar and has over 20 tables most of which are covered and have heaters. Food is served every day with lunch and dinner menus featuring locally sourced ingredients. ❄◑➤♿❄

Leeds: Headingley

Arcadia Ale House L ✓

34 Arndale Centre, Otley Road, LS6 2UE (corner of Alma Rd)

☎ (0113) 274 5599

Timothy Taylor Boltmaker; 7 changing beers (sourced locally; often Kirkstall, Ridgeside) ⊞

With two ground-floor rooms and an upstairs mezzanine level, this is an award-winning urban bar in the main Headingley shopping area. There is a mural of local landmarks above the bar. Alongside the real ale handpumps is an extensive range of canned, bottled and draught beers. There are always several vegan beer options. Also available is a wide selection of gins, some locally produced. Those under 18, large groups and fancy dress are not permitted. Dogs are positively encouraged. Q❄◑♿➤♿❄

Leeds: Holbeck

Grove Inn L

Back Row, LS11 5PL

☎ (0113) 244 2085 ⊕ thegroveinnleeds.co.uk

Daleside Blonde; 5 changing beers (often Ilkley, Purity, Saltaire) ⊞

Established in 1832 the Grove was remodelled in 1928-29 by its then-owners John Smith's of Tadcaster. A traditional four-room corridor pub with tiled entranceway leading to two small rooms on the right and taproom on the left. The rear Concert Room is an interwar addition and retains some original perimeter seating. Music is a strong feature and it can be heard in some form on most nights – a folk club started in the early 1960s and is still going strong. ❄◑➤♣➤♿❄♪

Leeds: Kirkstall

Kirkstall Bridge Inn L

12 Bridge Road, LS5 3BW

☎ (0113) 278 4044 ⊕ kirkstallbridge.co.uk

Kirkstall Pale Ale, Three Swords, Dissolution IPA, Black Band Porter; 3 changing beers (sourced locally; often Brew York, Five Points, Vocation) ⊞

Stone-built roadside pub next to the river Aire. Inside, the walls are decorated with pub memorabilia, chiefly mirrors. The main bar, at road level, has eight handpumps predominantly serving Kirkstall brewery beers. There are 10 keg lines which also include Kirkstall beers. An easy-to-miss snug is behind the bar. Down some steep stone stairs and level with the beer garden entrance is a second bar, where dogs are welcome. The disabled toilet is also at this lower level. ⬛❄◑➤(Headingley) P➤♿❄

West End House ✓

26 Abbey Road, LS5 3HS

☎ (0113) 246 4945

3 changing beers (sourced nationally; often Black Sheep, Purity, Timothy Taylor) ⊞

Stone-built busy local community pub and a beer house since at least 1867. It is located on the A65 adjacent to Kirkstall Leisure Centre, close to Kirkstall Abbey and half a mile from Headingley railway station. Normally three cask ales are available, with one of them from Timothy Taylor. Good-quality traditional British pub food is served. There is a small beer garden and smoking area outside, with partial level access from the rear entrance. There are regular quiz nights. ⬛❄◑➤(Headingley)➤♿❄↺

Leeds: Newlay

Abbey Inn L

99 Pollard Lane, LS13 1EQ (vehicle access from B6157 only)

☎ (0113) 258 1248

Kirkstall Three Swords, Black Band Porter; 5 changing beers (sourced locally; often Kirkstall, Ossett) ⊞

A stone-built former farmhouse, dating from 1714, which nestles between the River Aire and Leeds-Liverpool Canal. A celebrated community pub, the Abbey showcases a selection of predominantly local ales including a pump dedicated to a dark beer. The Abbey bustles with friendly locals throughout the week and events include a folk night and quizzes. Accessible by road from Pollard Lane, on foot over Pollard Bridge or along the canal from the Kirkstall Forge Station. Closed on Mondays during the winter months. ⬛❄◑➤(Kirkstall Forge) ♣P➤❄↺♪

Linthwaite

Sair L ✓

139 Lane Top, HD7 5SG (top of Hoyle Ing, off A62)

☎ (01484) 842370

5 changing beers (sourced locally; often Linfit, Theakston, Vocation) 🍺
Overlooking the Colne Valley, the Sair is a multi-roomed stone-built pub of great character. Four rooms, each with a real fire, are served from a central bar. Up to five different beers are available. At the heart of the local community, the pub gives a warm welcome to locals, visitors and their dogs. Pizza is served Thursday to Saturday evenings. A former National CAMRA Pub of the Year. Q❀❀▶♣🖵❀🖰🛜🖰♪

Liversedge

Black Bull 🅛 ✅
37 Halifax Road, WF15 6JR (on A649, close to A62)
☎ (01924) 403779
Ossett Butterley, Yorkshire Blonde, White Rat, Silver King, Excelsius; 3 changing beers (sourced nationally; often Goose Eye, Ossett, Rat) 🍺
Ossett brewery's first pub, the five rooms each have unique styles, all providing comfort and atmosphere. A dark ale is always on offer, plus guest beers from the group and wide-ranging independents. A regular Guide entry, the Black Bull is a popular, sociable community local with a warm welcome. Quiz night is Tuesday, darts and dominoes in local league on Mondays, and acoustic sessions on Sunday teatimes monthly. A fine, sheltered beer garden sits by a stream. The 229 bus route is a short walk away. Q❀❀❀♣♣P🖵(200,229)❀🛜🖰♪

Longwood

Dusty Miller Inn 🅛 ✅
2 Gilead Road, HD3 4XH
☎ 07946 589645 ⊕ dustymillerlongwood.com
Milltown Platinum Blonde, Black Jack Porter; Timothy Taylor Landlord; 3 changing beers (often Brunswick, Milltown, Newby Wyke)
Local historic photographs and stone floors dominate at this pub which is one of the two Milltown brewery taps. The cosy interior is open plan but has three distinct areas. Six real ales are served, showcasing the Milltown brews. Alongside are two changing guests, always including a dark beer, plus a permanent real cider. Locally made pies from Brosters Farm at Lindley Moor are served. There are great views up the Colne Valley from the outside benches. Q❀❀♣♣🖵(356)❀🛜🖰

Marsden

Riverhead Brewery Tap 🍺 🅛 ✅
2 Peel Street, HD7 6BR
☎ (01484) 844324 ⊕ theriverheadmarsden.co.uk
Ossett Silver King, Excelsius; Riverhead March Haigh, Redbrook Premium; 6 changing beers (often Riverhead) 🍺
At the centre of village life, the Riverhead is a modern brewpub owned by Ossett brewery. The microbrewery is visible from the main bar – beer doesn't get more LocAle than this. Ten beers are served: six Riverhead beers, two from Ossett as well as guests. A dark beer is usually available. The upstairs room has comfy seating and outside there is a riverside terrace for alfresco drinking. A popular venue with locals, visitors and their dogs. ❀❀❀♣♣P🖵(185) ❀🛜🖰

Meltham

Travellers Rest 🍺 ✅
Slaithwaite Road, HD9 5NH
☎ (01484) 851320 ⊕ travellersrestmeltham.co.uk

Milltown Platinum Blonde; Timothy Taylor Landlord; 6 changing beers (sourced regionally; often Milltown) 🍺
Located at the edge of the Pennine Moors and offering stunning views, this pub serves as one of the two Milltown brewery taps. It has modern decor following a refurbishment in 2017, and the pub is arranged on two levels. Eight handpumps feature beers from Milltown and other breweries, as well as a real cider. Always providing a friendly welcome, this local CAMRA Rural Pub of the Year 2023 is well worth the effort to visit. ❀❀❀❀♣♣P🖵(335,324) ❀🛜🖰♪

Middlestown

Little Bull 🅛
72 New Road, WF4 4NR (on A642 at crossroads in centre of village)
☎ (01924) 726142 ⊕ thelittlebull.co.uk
Abbeydale Deception; Timothy Taylor Landlord; 3 changing beers (sourced regionally) 🍺
This free house has been established since 1814. All food is locally sourced and home-cooked. A single bar services a number of smaller rooms with an open fire in colder weather. There is a Gin Bar on the last Saturday of the month and a beer festival is held on the last weekend in July. Meals served Monday to Friday and Sunday lunchtimes, with evening meals on Wednesday and Thursday. Monday is fish night and Wednesday is pie night. The National Coal Mining Museum is nearby. Q❀❀❀♣♣P🖵(232,128) ❀🛜🖰

Mirfield

Flowerpot 🅛 ✅
65 Calder Road, WF14 8NN (over river, 400yds S of railway station)
☎ (01924) 496939
Ossett Butterley, Yorkshire Blonde, White Rat, Silver King, Voodoo, Excelsius; 3 changing beers (sourced nationally; often Fernandes, Ossett, Rat) 🍺
A pub dating from 1807, tastefully restored by Ossett brewery and decorated in a charming rustic style with an impressive tile flowerpot as the centrepiece. There are four separate drinking areas and real fires. A terrace and a fine riverside beer garden are great for warm summer days. Nine ales are offered from Ossett's five breweries and independents, usually including a mild or stout, plus a cider. The pub is withing easy walking distance of the town centre, with access to the Brighouse to Mirfield canal walk. Q❀❀❀♣♣P🖵(261)❀🛜🖰

Knowl Club 🅛 ✅
17 Knowl Road, WF14 8DQ
☎ (01924) 493301
Black Sheep Respire; Saltaire Blonde; 2 changing beers (sourced regionally) 🍺
Having celebrated its 125th anniversary in 2013, the former Mirfield Liberal Club is ideal for a quiet pint and is open to both members and the public, holding club and public house licences. There is a single bar occupying a long, well-furnished room offering up to four beers, plus a private function room and pool table downstairs and a well-furnished snooker room upstairs. A small car park at the rear is accessed down an adjacent narrow alley. ❀❀❀♣P🖵(203,205) ❀🛜🖰

Navigation Tavern
6 Station Road, WF14 8NL (next to Mirfield railway station)
☎ (01924) 492476 ⊕ navigationtavern.co.uk

Magic Rock Hat Trick, Ringmaster, High Wire; Theakston Best Bitter, Lightfoot, Old Peculier; 2 changing beers (sourced regionally; often Small World) ⊞
Recently refurbished, this family-run free house is a rare outlet for Theakston XB and attracts a wide range of age groups and drinkers. Proud of its Donegal history, it often hosts live music and the large, sheltered canalside beer garden is used for charity events and occasional concerts. Winter comfort is aided by a large wood-burning fire. Light breakfast served until noon in the week, and hotpots after noon with full English at weekends. Free moorings for patrons. ❧☎♿≠P🖨(205,203)🛜ひ♫

Morley

Oscar's Bar ㄥ
2A Queen Street, LS27 9DG
3 changing beers (sourced locally) ⊞
Small friendly bar and café serving cask beers from mainly local breweries and a good range of draught, canned and bottled beers. Oscar's was the first of the new bars to spring up in the in the Morley Bottoms area, which has now become a bit a of local hotspot for beer drinkers. To the right of the bar is the entrance to a small additional seating area called The Nook. At the front is a small pavement seating area. ✿≠♠🖨🐾🛜

Mytholmroyd

Barbary's ㄥ
15-17 Bridge End, HX7 5DR
4 changing beers (sourced nationally; often Pomona Island, Squawk, Track) ⊞
Formerly a shop, this single-storey two-roomed micropub with modern decor is situated in the centre of Mytholmroyd. Four cask beers from national microbreweries are served on handpump, as well as eight craft keg beers. It hosts live music and DJ sets. There is an attractive covered paved area at the side with views over the River Calder, perfect for those sunny afternoons and evenings. ❧✿≠🖨🐾🛜♫

Norristhorpe

Rising Sun ㄥ
254 Norristhorpe Lane, WF15 7AN (½ mile off A62)
☎ (01924) 400190
Abbeydale Moonshine; Acorn Barnsley Bitter; Saltaire Blonde; Timothy Taylor Landlord; 2 changing beers (sourced locally; often Black Sheep, Nook) ⊞
This village local has a light and spacious bar area and cosy lounge areas with exposed brickwork and real fires. Beers are mainly from Yorkshire with guests from regional and national sources. Every Tuesday evening there is a popular quiz with prizes, and occasional live music is advertised on Facebook. There is a large well-maintained beer garden with ample seating and extensive views over the valley towards Mirfield and Emley Moor. A marquee can be hired for summer events. Q❧✿P🖨(261)🐾🛜ひ♫

North Featherstone

Bradley Arms ㄥ
96 Willow Lane, WF7 6BJ (on B6128 Castleford-Featherstone road, opp St Wilfrid's High School)
☎ (01977) 704256 ⊕ thebradleyarms.co.uk
House beer (by Acorn); 2 changing beers (sourced regionally) ⊞
Traditional multi-roomed pub with a large outdoor drinking area. The pub is rich in local history with links to the Featherstone Massacre of 1893. Cunninghame Graham gave his first speech on Worker's Rights here; note the inscription over the fireplace in the Tap Room. Weekly live music evenings are held, there is a quiz night on Wednesday and occasional pop-up food events. Q❧✿♣P🖨🐾🛜♫

Oakworth

Oakworth Social Club ㄥ
Chapel Lane, BD22 7HY
☎ (01535) 643931
Goose Eye Chinook Blonde; Timothy Taylor Golden Best; 1 changing beer (sourced locally; often Saltaire) ⊞
Friendly and welcoming, this imposing Victorian building on the main thoroughfare was originally built as the Liberal Club in the late 19th century. Now a social club with a thriving membership, it has a comfortable front lounge and a back bar with traditional games and a TV. Upstairs, a third room caters for functions and meetings. Quiz night is Monday, and regular live music events are staged (see Facebook). A former CAMRA Yorkshire Club of the Year runner-up, and local CAMRA Club of the Year 2022. ❧✿♿▲≠♣P🖨(K7)🐾🛜ひ♫

Snooty Fox ㄥ
Colne Road, BD22 7PB (on B6143 next to church)
☎ (01535) 642689
Goose Eye Spring Wells; Tetley Tetley Bitter ⊞
Set in a converted single-storey school, the main bar of the Snooty Fox has a largescreen TV for sport and a concert stage for regular live music at weekends. A smaller public bar houses the pool table. There is a beer garden to the rear with covered smoking area. Its layout and proximity to the parish church make it popular as a function venue for christenings, weddings and other family occasions. ❧✿▲P🖨(K7)🐾🛜♫

Ossett

Bier Huis ㄥ
17 Towngate, WF5 9BL (in shopping parade which backs on to bus station)
☎ (01924) 565121 ⊕ bierhuis.co.uk
3 changing beers (sourced locally) ⊞
A specialist beer shop stocking over 500 bottled beers from many Yorkshire breweries and also an extensive selection of foreign bottled beers with emphasis on Belgian and German beers. Bottled beers can be drunk on site, along with three changing draught beers and an extensive selection of draught ciders. A former local CAMRA Cider Pub of the Year. Q❧♿♠P🖨🐾🛜

George Hotel ⊘
64 Bank Street, WF5 8NW (edge of town centre, follow signs for adjacent police station)
☎ (01924) 265313
Ossett Yorkshire Blonde, White Rat; Tetley Bitter ⊞
A traditional town-centre pub with outdoor seating and wheelchair access. Food is available from Dan's Van in the car park. The George is dog friendly and welcomes children until 7.30pm. Live music and karaoke nights are a regular feature. Sky Sports is available for sports enthusiasts. Q❧✿♿♣P🖨🐾♫

Prop'ur Baa
3 New Street, WF5 8BH
☎ (01924) 265530
Abbeydale Moonshine; 4 changing beers ⊞
Family-owned micropub near the Town Hall that was established in 2019. A single bar with five handpumps

serves real ales from mainly Yorkshire breweries, alongside an extensive selection of gins. An atmospheric, dog-friendly pub, it hosts occasional acoustic live music sessions. There is complimentary tapas on Fridays and a cheeseboard on Sundays. A quiz night is on Wednesday with the proceeds going to local charities of the winner's choice. Q🖳🌸🐾🛜♪

Otley

Black Horse 🅻

2 Westgate, LS21 3AS

☎ (01943) 466590 ⊕ blackhorseotley.co.uk

Kirkstall Pale Ale, Three Swords, Dissolution IPA, Black Band Porter; 3 changing beers (sourced locally; often Anthology, Kirkstall) Ⓗ

The Black Horse is an impressive corner building dating from the start of the 20th century, with a Victorian-style interior. The imposing entrance on the corner of the building takes you into the main bar area with its wooden floor and array of brewery mirrors on the walls. To the left of the bar is the taproom and to the right of bar an opening leads to additional seating areas. There is also a large covered outside seating area. Q🛇🌸🍴🕪🖳🐾🛜♪

Junction Inn 🅻 ✅

44 Bondgate, LS21 1AD

Ossett Yorkshire Blonde; Theakston Old Peculier; Timothy Taylor Boltmaker, Knowle Spring, Landlord; 3 changing beers Ⓗ

A solid-looking stone-built pub on a prominent street-corner site on the approach from Leeds. To the front, roadside tables allow for outdoor drinking, while a beer garden is to the rear. Inside, the pub consists of a single room with a central fireplace and comfortable fixed seating which runs around the walls. Decoration in the half-panelled room includes a collection of pictures of old Otley. To the rear of the building is a covered and heating outside seating area. Children are permitted until evening. 🛇🌸♣🖳🐾🔄♪

Old Cock 🍷 🅻

11-13 Crossgate, LS21 1AA

☎ (01943) 464424

Daleside Blonde; Theakston Best Bitter; Timothy Taylor Landlord; 6 changing beers (sourced locally; often Acorn, Brass Castle, Rooster's) Ⓗ

Award-winning genuine free house which has been cleverly converted from a former café in such a way that you would think it has been a pub for many years. There are two low-ceilinged rooms downstairs with stone-flagged floors and a further room upstairs. Nine handpumps offer a changing range with the guest ales mostly from local breweries. At least one dark beer is regularly available, usually a mild, as well as a stout or porter. There is a small outdoor drinking area. No admittance to under-18s. Q🌸🔵🖳🐾🛜🔄

Oxenhope

Bay Horse 🅻 ✅

20 Uppertown, BD22 9LN (on A6033)

☎ (01535) 642921

Abbeydale Heathen; Rudgate Jorvik Blonde; Timothy Taylor Landlord; 4 changing beers (sourced regionally; often Moorhouse's) Ⓗ

A friendly village local that welcomes families and dogs. It has a pleasant single-bar setup with a real fire, a cosy room to the rear and a separate seating area up a flight of steps. The guest beers come from local breweries such as Bowland and Goose Eye. The pub is one of the main

stopping points for the annual village charity straw race. Regular live music is a feature.
🛇🌸♣≠🅿🖳(B3,K14)🐾🛜♪

Dog & Gun Inn 🅻 ✅

Denholme Road, BD22 9SN

☎ (01535) 643159 ⊕ dogandgunoxenhope.co.uk

Timothy Taylor Golden Best, Boltmaker, Knowle Spring, Landlord, Landlord Dark Ⓗ

This Timothy Taylor tied house is one of the highest 17th-century coaching inns in West Yorkshire. This traditional stone building has been sympathetically extended over the years. The emphasis is on food, but locals also support the pub for its real ale, warming open fire and good service. The pub hosts numerous charity events throughout the year. Private parties can be booked in the separate restaurant areas. In the Wells Restaurant to the right of the bar you can see the original well through a glass floor panel. 🛇🍴🕪🦽🅿🖳(K14,K15)🛜

Pontefract

Old Grocers 🅻

25 Beastfair, WF8 1AL

5 changing beers (sourced locally) Ⓗ

Pontefract's first micropub with seating for around 60 people over 2 floors and a small outdoor area. There is a regularly changing selection of cask beers, mainly from Yorkshire breweries. A quiz night is held every Wednesday and there are regular acoustic music sessions at weekends. A folk club meets on the last Sunday of the month. Q🌸≠(Tanshelf)♣🐾🛜🔄♪

Pudsey

Fleece 🅻

100 Fartown, LS28 8LU

☎ (0113) 236 2748

Copper Dragon Golden Pippin; Tetley Bitter; Timothy Taylor Landlord; Wainwright; 1 changing beer (sourced locally; often Timothy Taylor) Ⓗ

A community local in the Fartown area of Pudsey but surprisingly close to open countryside. To the left is the public bar, known locally as the Snug, simply decorated and with a loyal customer base. The lounge on the right extends the full depth of the pub and has plenty of comfy settles around the edge. Both areas are decorated with a few items of interest to movie buffs. To the rear is the neat and tidy beer garden. 🌸♣🅿🖳(4F,205)🛜♪

Rishworth

Booth Wood Inn 🅻

Oldham Road, HX6 4QU (on A672 towards M62 jct 22)
SE034170

☎ (01422) 825600 ⊕ boothwoodinn.co.uk

Bradfield Farmers Blonde; Elland Nettlethrasher; Joseph Holt Bitter; 1 changing beer (sourced nationally; often Bradfield, Pennine, Salopian) Ⓗ

A destination food pub serving meals every day with a good-value retro menu, all prepared on site. It retains a friendly, traditional country pub atmosphere with three main rooms, all interlinked with stone flooring around the bar. Four real ales are served via handpump. Acoustic music night is usually on Fridays. There is an outdoor space, part of which offers covered seating. The pub is close to the moors and just a short drive from junction 22 of the M62. Q🛇🌸🕪🦽🅿🛜🔄♪

Roberttown

New Inn 🛏 ✓
Roberttown Lane, WF15 7NP
☎ (01924) 500483 ⊕ newinnroberttown.co.uk
Abbeydale Moonshine; Bradfield Farmers Blonde; Timothy Taylor Landlord; 3 changing beers (sourced regionally; often Jolly Boys, Nailmaker, Wilde Child) Ⓗ

Centrally located in Roberttown, this welcoming free house at the heart of the local community comprises a taproom, the main lounge area, a pool room and a useful side room suitable for functions. Outside is a sunny seating area and a covered smoking shelter. There is a popular quiz with supper on Wednesdays, occasional live music at weekends, a charitable knit & natter night on Mondays and free pub grub on Friday teatimes. The 229 bus is a short walk away. ➢❀♣P🖵(260,261)🌢 🛜 🎵♫

Saltaire

Cap & Collar 🛏
4 Queens Road, BD18 4SJ
⊕ tinyurl.com/capncollar
3 changing beers (sourced nationally; often Bristol Beer Factory, Thornbridge, Wishbone)

Popular modern micropub with an open-plan café-style layout accommodating up to 35 customers. A beer garden and smoking area is at the rear. There is an additional outside seating area to the front. Up to four real ales are often from local breweries but can also be from further afield. Real cider is served on draught and there is a good selection of bottle-conditioned ales. A homebrew club and a book club meet here. There is a monthly games night. Q➢❀☼≋●🖵🌢🛜

SALT Bar & Kitchen 🛏 ✓
199 Bingley Road, BD18 4DH
☎ (01274) 582111
Ossett Butterley, Yorkshire Blonde, White Rat, Silver King; 5 changing beers (sourced regionally; often Abbeydale, Rat, Wilde Child) Ⓗ

A large pub built within an old tramshed, originally constructed in 1904, and rebranded by Ossett brewery in 2019. It has a large open-plan main room with horseshoe bar, dining room offset to one side and an upper mezzanine dining area. There is also access to the adjacent SALT Beer Factory. Real ales are mainly from Ossett brewery and associated brands with some guests. The large outdoor seating area is popular in good weather. Excellent meals include freshly made wood-fired pizzas. The pub can get busy at weekends. ➢❀🕼⑃点≋P🖵🌢♫

Salt Cellar 🍷 🛏 ✓
192 Saltaire Road, BD18 3JF (on A657)
☎ (01274) 955051
6 changing beers (sourced regionally; often Bingley, Half Moon, Oaks) Ⓗ

Traditional pub on the edge of the World Heritage Site of Saltaire village with a friendly, cosy feel. It comprises a two-roomed house with Victorian character, with comfortable seating, stained-glass partitions and bookshelves. Numerous pictures of old Saltaire adorn the walls. Six handpulls offer a varying range of real ales from local and regional breweries with a mixture of styles including usually at least one dark beer. Bands play on Saturday nights and there is a Thursday night quiz. ➢❀点≋P🖵🌢🛜♫♫

Sandal

Star ✓
Standbridge Lane, WF2 7DY (near Asda on the A6186 which links A61 and A636)
☎ (01924) 229674
5 changing beers (sourced regionally; often Morton Collins) Ⓗ

A cosy pub dating from 1821, with a streamside beer garden, the Star is leased by the Morton Collins brewery, which recently moved to the premises. It serves one or two of their beers plus four or five guests, mainly from local breweries. It is a welcoming pub with an open-plan layout and open fires in winter. A quiz night is held on Tuesday, and an annual beer festival. There is a function room for hire. Q➢❀🕼点♣P🖵(110)🌢🛜

Scholes

Stafford Arms 🛏 ✓
192 Scholes Lane, BD19 6LS (A649)
☎ (01274) 861387
Bradfield Farmers Blonde; Timothy Taylor Landlord; 4 changing beers (sourced regionally; often Acorn, Kirkstall, Moorhouse's) Ⓗ

An attractive pub on the edge of Scholes village, popular with locals and walkers and offering a warm, friendly welcome to all. It features an open-plan, comfortable layout with a large central fireplace and traditional decor, with a large beer garden with ample seating to the front and rear. It can be used for functions. Quiz night is Thursday, with open mic on Wednesday and live bands on Sundays. ➢❀♣P🖵(254,259)🌢🛜♫

Shipley

Crafty Kernel
16 Kirkgate, BD18 3QN
☎ 07932 239195
4 changing beers (sourced regionally; often Abbeydale, Brass Castle, Craven) Ⓗ

This pub with a modern, clean feel opened in March 2022 in a former shop close to the Market Square and bus interchange. An open-plan ground floor room contains the bar, with further seating in an upstairs room. Four handpulls serve a varying range of real ale, across a variety of styles, usually from regional brewers and often including a gluten-free option. A variety of craft keg beers are offered and there is an extensive wine selection. ➢🕼点≋🖵🌢🛜

Fox 🛏
41 Briggate, BD17 7BP
☎ (01274) 594826 ⊕ thefoxshipley.co.uk
BEEspoke Plan Bee, Shipley Stout; 4 changing beers (sourced regionally; often Bingley, Durham, Small World) Ⓗ

A small, independent, single-roomed, café-style bar that is friendly and welcoming. It is simply but smartly furnished with seating made from recycled church pews. Six handpulled ales include regulars from the in-house BEEspoke microbrewery and constantly varying guests beers. Real ciders, often including one from a local producer, are available as are a wide range of international bottled beers. Handy when waiting for trains as the station is close by. There is often live music on a Saturday night when the bar can become busy. ➢❀点≋●🖵🌢🛜♫

Hullabaloo
37-41 Westgate, BD18 3QX
☎ 07974 910838

4 changing beers (sourced regionally; often Brass Castle, Northern Monk, Wilde Child) Ⓗ
Popular, modern-style bar close to Shipley town centre and the bus interchange. Generally open-plan but with four distinct areas in a variety of styles over split levels. Four handpumps serve a variety of real ales, usually from regional brewers and often differing from other pubs in the area. An additional handpump serves cider. Artisan craft beers and a cider are also available on six keg taps. There is a weekly quiz on a Wednesday night. Children are welcome. ⚲♿◐�⇥🚃🐾🛜♪

Sir Norman Rae Ⓛ ✓
Victoria House, Market Place, BD18 3QB
☎ (01274) 535290
Greene King Abbot; Ruddles Best Bitter; Sharp's Doom Bar; 7 changing beers (sourced nationally; often Goose Eye, Phoenix, Saltaire) Ⓗ
A typical conversion by Wetherspoon from a former Co-op department store, this large, open-plan pub is a popular feature of the town centre. Ten real ale handpumps dispense three regular beers, sourced from large national breweries, and seven guests which are often from local breweries but can be from further afield. The good-value food is from the usual Wetherspoon menu. Nicknamed the Waiting Room due to its proximity to Shipley bus interchange. The railway station is also nearby. ⚲◐ძ⇥🚃🛜

Slaithwaite

Commercial Ⓛ
1 Carr Lane, HD7 5AN (village centre, off A62)
☎ (01484) 846258
Empire Moonrakers Mild; house beer (by Empire); **7 changing beers** (often Goose Eye, Wensleydale) Ⓗ
This popular free house has enjoyed deserved success. Nine handpumps serve a variety of beer styles – the keenly priced house beers are supplied by Empire brewery and include a permanent mild. The open-plan interior retains the feel of separate drinking areas, one featuring a real fire. Walkers and their dogs are welcome and the pub is a popular stop on the Transpennine Real Ale Trail. There is a pool room upstairs. Local CAMRA Mild Pub of the Year 2022. ❀⇥🚃🐾↺

Sowerby Bridge

Hogs Head Brew House & Bar Ⓛ
1 Stanley Street, HX6 2AH
☎ (01422) 836585 ⊕ thehogsheadbrewhouse.com
Hogs Head 6 To 8 Weeks, White Hog, Hoppy Valley, Old Schnozzler; 4 changing beers (sourced regionally; often Goose Eye, Phoenix, Vocation) Ⓗ
Close to the centre of Sowerby Bridge, the venue is an 18th-century former malthouse which has been extensively renovated. The former brewery is at the back of the building and can be viewed from the bar area. Four core Hogs Head beers are available as well as guest ales. There is plenty of seating in the huge, sprawling bar area, with additional, accessible seating provided upstairs at weekends, and an extensive, covered outdoor area across from the pub. Q⚲❀ძ⇥🚃🐾🛜↺

Stanbury

Friendly Ⓛ
54 Main Street, BD22 0HB (in village centre)
☎ (01535) 645528
House beer (by Settle); **2 changing beers** (sourced nationally; often Craven, Goose Eye, Small World) Ⓗ

Popular village local befitting its name which also attracts those walking the Pennine Way or visiting on an afternoon stroll. The pub is small and retains a traditional layout with two small lounges either side of a central bar plus a separate games room. There are south-facing benches outside the front door, and a small beer garden beyond the car park with impressive views across the valley to Oldfield. Stanbury is only two miles from Haworth but a million miles from its tourist hustle and bustle. Tea and coffee are available on request. ⚲❀🅰♣🅿🚃🐾🛜

Wuthering Heights Inn Ⓛ
Main Street, BD22 0HB (in village centre)
☎ (01535) 643332 ⊕ thewutheringheights.co.uk
Moorhouse's White Witch; Theakston Best Bitter; 2 changing beers (sourced regionally) Ⓗ
Set in a farming village, this popular, friendly inn dates from 1763. Warmed by log-burners, the traditional main bar displays photographs showing the history of the Stanbury. The cosy dining room has a BrüÑnte theme, and there is a third room that can be booked for parties and meetings. The rear garden has spectacular views down the Worth Valley and a separate camping area (no caravans). There is a quiz every Thursday. Well-behaved dogs and children are welcome. ⚲♿🚐◐🅰♣🅿🚃🐾🛜

Thackley

Ainsbury
7 Thackley Road, BD10 0RS (on jct of Thackley Rd, Ainsbury Ave and Crag Hill Rd)
☎ 07743 222138
3 changing beers (sourced regionally; often Ilkley, Sunbeam, Wensleydale) Ⓗ
A warm, friendly welcome is assured in this popular micropub. Formerly a corner shop and located within a residential area, a small downstairs room houses the bar and limited seating. Stone-flagged floors and much woodwork are present, creating a clean, comfortable environment. A slightly larger room upstairs provides more seating with tables. Space can be at a premium at busy times. Three handpulls serving a varying range of real ales. Q⚲🐖🚃🐾↺

Black Rat Ⓛ
530 Leeds Road, BD10 8JH
☎ 07525 006906
4 changing beers (sourced locally; often Kirkstall, Rudgate, Small World) Ⓗ
Previously a florist shop, this tiny micropub with capacity for approximately 15 people changed ownership in September 2022, but has maintained the standards for which it was known. A friendly welcome is assured. As there is no music, TV or games machines, conversation and banter is key. A varying selection of four real ales, primarily from Yorkshire breweries, is offered, with one line dedicated to dark beers. It can get busy, especially first thing after a working day. Q♿🐖🚃🐾❀

Thornton

Watchmaker Ⓛ ✓
South Square, BD13 3LD (off Thornton Rd)
⊕ thewatchmaker.co.uk
Ossett Yorkshire Blonde; Timothy Taylor Landlord; 2 changing beers (sourced regionally; often Goose Eye, Kirkstall, Stubbee) Ⓗ
Small and friendly micropub, reopened in 2019 as the Watchmaker following a change of management. It has two small rooms on the ground floor with the bar to the front. Its appearance is cosy and traditional with plenty of

timber on display and an old range in the rear room. Four handpulls serve two regular cask ales plus varying guests, usually including a dark beer. A courtyard provides additional outdoor seating and access to the toilets which are separate from the pub. Q☰♿🚆(67,607) 🐾🐕🛜

Todmorden

Alehouse
52 Patmos, Burnley Road, OL14 5EY
☎ 07407 747956
Eagles Crag Pale Eagle; 4 changing beers (sourced regionally) Ⓗ
A welcoming micropub with a community feel, located in a row of shops set back from the road; the River Calder is culverted under the partially-covered patio area. The wooden bar is at the rear of the single room, which features exposed brickwork and offers various seating options. Works by local artists, usually for sale, adorn the walls. Four changing ales usually include a dark option on the right-hand pump. Eagles Crag K++ (a dry-hopped version of Golden Eagle) is offered on KeyKeg.
🏵☰🍴🚆🐕🛜♪

Pub
5-9 Water Street, OL14 5AB
☎ 07711 994240
8 changing beers (sourced nationally) Ⓗ
Todmorden's first micropub relocated in June 2022 to a former café, resulting in more space and all rooms being located on the ground floor. The central bar recreates the look of the original and now offers additional handpumps and 10 taps for craft beer. There is a mix of seating options in the other rooms, including bespoke bench seating from the former premises. In good weather, pavement tables offer views of the parish church and impressive Victorian town hall.
Q🏵♿☰🚆🐕🛜

Upper Denby

George Inn Ⓛ ✅
114 Denby Lane, HD8 8UE
☎ (01484) 861347 🌐 thegeorgeinn-upperdenby.co.uk
Tetley Bitter; Timothy Taylor Landlord; 2 changing beers (sourced locally; often Acorn, Nailmaker, Small World) Ⓗ
This family-run village pub and free house is a regular winner of the local CAMRA Rural Pub of the Year and was Welcome to Yorkshire's Favourite Pub 2021. The pub is split into two separate areas – a comfortable lounge and a taproom. It is well known for its home-made pie and peas and its walks. Cyclists, walkers and dogs are welcome, and families until evening.
Q🏵🅟🍴🔸♣🚆🐕🛜

Wakefield

Black Rock 🍷 ✅
19 Cross Square, WF1 1PQ (between the Bull Ring and top of Westgate)
☎ (01924) 375550
Oakham Citra; Tetley Bitter; 4 changing beers (sourced regionally) Ⓗ
A famous, largely unspoilt old Melbourne house opened in 1842. An arched, tiled façade leads into this compact city-centre local with a warm welcome and comfy interior including photographs of old Wakefield. The Rock stands as one of the few proper pubs left in the middle of the clubs and bars of Westgate and is popular with drinkers of all ages looking for a real pint. Drinkers are

encouraged to suggest beers to try, with four regularly changing guest ales on offer. There is a free function room for private use. Q☰(Westgate)🚆🔄

Harry's Bar Ⓛ
107B Westgate, WF1 1EL (turn right from Westgate station, cross the road at traffic lights and the pub is at the back of the car park on the right)
☎ (01924) 373773
Wensleydale Gamekeeper; house beer (by Chin Chin); 6 changing beers Ⓗ
This small, one-roomed pub is set in an alleyway just off Westgate. A real fire and a bare-brick and wood interior plus vintage sporting pictures enhance this small, cosy pub. It serves a selection of bottled Belgian beers. An extensive decking area has been added to the side of the building. There is a fantastic view of Wakefield's famous 99-arched viaduct, which makes you wish steam trains were a regular feature. Q🏵♿☰(Westgate)🍴🅟🚆🛜🔄

Luis Bar at Fernandes Wakefield Ⓛ
5 Avison Yard, Kirkgate, WF1 1UA (turn right 100yds S of George St/Kirkgate jct)
☎ (01924) 386348 🌐 luisbar.co.uk
7 changing beers (sourced locally; often Fernandes, Ossett) Ⓗ
Formerly an Ossett managed pub and microbrewery, in 2021 it was transformed into the current venue. The brewers are now the landlady's husband, Howard, and his friend, Gerald 'Pecker' Wood. The pub has a large selection of real ales, craft beers and cocktails and hosts regular live music events.
Q☰☰(Kirkgate) ♣🍴🚆🐕🛜🔄♪

Wakefield Labour Club Ⓛ
18 Vicarage Street, WF1 1QX (at top of Kirkgate)
☎ (01924) 215626 🌐 theredshed.org.uk
5 changing beers (sourced regionally) Ⓗ
The Red Shed is a repurposed army hut that has been extensively refurbished inside and out. Home to many union, community and charity groups, there are 2 rooms, one of which can be hired for functions. There is an extensive collection of Union plates and badges adoring the walls. Quiz night is every Wednesday, with regular music events and open mic nights on the last Saturday of the month. Dogs and well-behaved visitors are welcome. Q☰♿☰(Kirkgate) ♣🅟🚆🐕♪

Wibsey

Dog & Gun Ⓛ
142/144 St Enoch's Road, BD6 3BU
☎ (01274) 677727 🌐 dogandgunwibsey.co.uk
Tetley Bitter; 3 changing beers (sourced regionally; often Empire, Ilkley, Stubbee) Ⓗ
Warm and welcoming traditional local on the outskirts of Bradford, set back from the road with a large car park. Inside, it has three distinct areas with different feels. The bar serves the smart lounge, with a smaller room to the side and another lounge to the rear. One regular real ale and three guest beers are always offered. Real ciders are often available. A weekly quiz is held on Wednesday and a competition night on Sundays. ☰🏵♣🍴🅟🚆🐕🛜🔄♪

Hooper Micropub Ⓛ
209 High Street, BD6 1JU
🌐 thehoopermicropub.co.uk
5 changing beers (sourced nationally; often Acorn, Marble, Salopian) Ⓗ
Cosy, friendly, split-level micropub in the urban village of Wibsey, popular with locals. The bar is situated on the upper level and there is comfortable seating in the lower part. Five handpulls offer a varying selection of beers that

are primarily sourced from the Yorkshire region but also occasionally from further afield. Photographs of old Wibsey provide a simple relief from the otherwise minimalist décor. Closing times may vary depending upon demand. Q ᗐ ᛄ ♣ 🖳 🛋 🕏 🎵

Breweries

Amity SIBA

🍴 15-16 Festoon Rooms, Sunny Bank Mills, Farsley, Leeds, LS28 5UJ ⊕ amitybrew.co

Launching in 2020 with its online shop, Amity Brew Co was founded by Russ Clarke (ex-BrewDog, Buxton, North Brewing Co, and Beer Hawk team member). Originally cuckoo brewing, its brewpub opened later the same year sporting a 10-hectolitre brew kit, producing modern interpretations of classic beer styles, as well as more experimental brews. No real ale. ‼ 🛒 ◆

Anthology

Unit 6, Armley Link, Armley Road, Leeds, LS12 2QN ⊕ anthologybrewing.co.uk

Established in 2018, Anthology is a small-batch, 2.5-barrel, Leeds-based brewery. Liam Kane brews an ever-evolving range of beers focussed on bold flavours. Beers are available in outlets around the city, and some further afield. There are occasional taproom events throughout the warmer months (see social media). It also likes to work with artistic/charitable organisations. ◆

Barker Bridge (NEW)

Manor Farm, Station Road, Cullingworth, Bradford, BD13 5HN ☎ 07378 398982 ⊕ deepcliff.co.uk

Barker Bridge Brewery was founded in 2022 by Matthew Barker at the site of the former Old Spot Brewery.

Arch Blonde (ABV 4%) BLOND
3B's (ABV 4.2%) GOLD

Barker's

14 Midway, South Crosland, Huddersfield, HD4 7DA ☎ 07876 540211 ✉ barkersbrewing@gmail.com

James Barker started as a homebrewer seven years ago, producing beers for friends. With invaluable help and guidance from Summer Wine Brewery and Neil at Milltown, he made the leap from homebrewer to commercial production in 2019. He continues to use his handbuilt, 60-litre brewplant, bottling a core range of seven beers. V

Beer Ink

Plover Road Garage, Plover Road, Lindley, Huddersfield, HD3 3PJ
☎ (01484) 643368 ☎ 07885 676711
⊕ beer-ink.co.uk

The Beer Ink Brewery is based in Lindley and opened in 2015 using an eight-barrel plant. It specialises in barrel-aged beers and regularly collaborates with other forward-looking breweries. Its onsite taproom and facilities were expanded and improved in 2020. ◆V◆

Et al (ABV 3.8%) PALE
Vellum (ABV 4%) PALE
Typo (ABV 4.4%) PALE
Lampblack (ABV 4.6%) STOUT
Scrawler (ABV 5%) IPA

BEEspoke

🍴 Fox, 41 Briggate, Shipley, BD17 7BP
☎ (01274) 594826 ⊕ thefoxshipley.co.uk

☺Brewing began in 2015 in the cellar of the Fox pub using a one-barrel plant. Beers are available in cask and keg from the pub and at local beer festivals. Shiny Cowbird Spirit Company is a sister business. ◆

Bingley SIBA

Unit 2, Old Mill Yard, Shay Lane, Wilsden, BD15 0DR
☎ (01535) 274285 ⊕ bingleybrewery.co.uk

Bingley is a small, family-run brewery that opened in 2014 using a six-barrel plant. It is located in a rural setting in the village of Wilsden, part of Bingley Rural Ward. Beers are distributed coast to coast and as far south as Derby. ‼ ◆

Endeavour (ABV 3.7%) BLOND
Goldy Locks Blonde (ABV 4%) BLOND
Azacca (ABV 4.1%) GOLD
Aire Gold (ABV 4.2%) GOLD
Session IPA (ABV 4.2%) GOLD
Steady State (ABV 4.2%) BITTER
Centennial (ABV 4.4%) GOLD
Tri State (ABV 4.5%) PALE
1848 Stout (ABV 4.8%) STOUT
Jamestown APA (ABV 5.4%) PALE

Bini

1b Railway Road, Ilkley, LS29 8HQ ⊕ binibrew.co

Nanobrewery located on the edge of Ilkley Moor producing hazy beers. Launched in 2020.

Bone Idle

28 The Green, Idle, BD10 9PX ☎ 07525 751574

Established in 2018 in a converted barn situated in the heart of Idle village. The brewery offers the public the opportunity to try brewing. All beers produced are sold exclusively in the Idle Draper pub next door. A mezzanine floor has a mini cinema/function room.

Bosun's SIBA

Unit 15, Sandbeck Park, Sandbeck Lane, Wetherby, LS22 7TW
☎ (01937) 227337 ⊕ bosunsbrewery.com

☺The first brew was produced in 2013 by a father and son who had both served in the armed forces. The brewery relocated from Horbury to Huddersfield in 2018 and subsequently to Wetherby in 2021 under new ownership. The regular beers are produced on a 10-barrel plant with some nautical-themed names. Canned beers are available from the online shop. ‼ 🛒 ◆ ◆

Tell No Tales (ABV 3.8%) BITTER
Bosun's Blonde (ABV 3.9%) BLOND
Maiden Voyage (ABV 3.9%) BITTER
Down The Hatch (ABV 4%) BITTER
King Neptune (ABV 4.3%) BITTER
Bosun's IPA (ABV 5.6%) IPA
Tempest (ABV 5.6%) IPA

Bridgehouse SIBA

Airedale Heifer, Bradford Road, Sandbeds, Keighley, BD20 5LY
☎ (01535) 601222

Office: Unit 1, Aireworth Mills, Aireworth Road, Keighley, BD21 4DH ⊕ bridgehousebrewery.co.uk

◉Bridgehouse began brewing in 2010. The brewery purchased the recipes and branding of Old Bear Brewery in 2014 and moved into its premises in Keighley. In 2015 the brewery relocated to its present address behind the Airedale Heifer pub in Sandbeds. Bridgehouse operate a bespoke 15-barrel brewery. Twelve pubs are operated. ‼◆

Tequila Blonde (ABV 3.8%) SPECIALITY
Initially sweet with hints of lime, finishing with a slight tingling aftertaste.
Blonde (ABV 4%) GOLD
A strong fruity aroma with a sharp burst of grapefruit on the tongue and a touch of sweetness in the background. Bitter finish.
Aired Ale (ABV 4.1%) BITTER
Brown beer with malty aroma. Malt, hops and fruit in equal balance with lingering fruitiness in a long bitter finish.
Porter (ABV 4.5%) PORTER
Black beer with red hints. Aromas of malt and liquorice lead to coffee, chocolate and wine fruit flavours which carry through to a bitter finish.
Holy Cow (ABV 5.6%) BITTER
Strong ale with juicy malt and full hop flavour, citrus overtones. Light hop aroma and a bitter finish.

Briggs Signature

c/o Unit 1, Waterhouse Mill, 65-71 Lockwood Road, Huddersfield, HD1 3QU ☎ 07427 668004 ⊕ briggssignatureales.weebly.com

⊗ Briggs Signature Ales started brewing in 2014 using spare capacity at Mallinsons (qv). Nick Briggs, also a member of the Mallinsons brewing team, produces a number of modern, hop-forward beers. ☛LIVE

Northern Soul (ABV 3.8%) BITTER
Rock & Roll (ABV 4%) BITTER
Hip Hop (ABV 4.2%) GOLD
Techno (ABV 4.2%) BITTER
Blues (ABV 4.6%) GOLD
Metal (ABV 5%) PORTER

Briscoe's

16 Ash Grove, Otley, LS21 3EL
☎ (01943) 466515 ✉ briscoe.brewery@talktalk.net

◉The brewery was launched in 1998 by microbiologist and chemist Dr Paul Briscoe, in the cellar of his house, with a one-barrel brew length. He is produces several beers on an irregular basis to meet demand. The beers are available in local Otley pubs. Brewing is currently suspended.

Chevin

Office: 1 Mount Pisgah, Otley, LS21 3DX
✉ chevinotley@gmail.com

Brewed in the shadow of the Chevin, in the famous pub town of Otley, Chevin Brew Co specialises in small batch brews (available in cask, keg and bottle). It is proud to use local ingredients, and works with local artists for the labels. It shares a small one-barrel brewery with sister brewery, Marlowe Beer Project.

Chin Chin

Unit 53F, Lidgate Crescent, Langthwaite Grange Industrial Estate, South Kirkby, WF9 3NS ☎ 07896 253650 ✉ david@chinchinbrewing.co.uk

◉David Currie founded the brewery in 2016 with his brother Andrew, before taking sole control. Initially

utilising a one-barrel plant in domestic premises, in 2018 there was expansion to a five-barrel plant, and relocation to its current location. An expanding range of small batch beers is supplied across Yorkshire, and to festivals nationwide. ‼

Clark's

Office: 136 Westgate, Wakefield, WF2 9SW
☎ (01924) 373328 ☎ 07801 922473 ⊕ hbclark.co.uk

◉Beers are contract brewed elsewhere. ◆

Classic Blonde (ABV 3.9%) BLOND
Merrie City Atlantic Hop (ABV 4%) BITTER
Merrie City Cascadian (ABV 4%) PALE
Merrie City Crystal Gold (ABV 4.2%) GOLD

Cobbydale

🛏 Red Lion, 47 Kirkgate, Silsden, BD20 0AQ
☎ (01535) 930884 ☎ 07965 569885
⊕ cobbydalebrewery.co.uk

◉Brewing began in 2017 at the Red Lion, Silsden. Originally only brewing one beer, others are now brewed on an occasional basis.

Cooper Hill

Highcliffe Industrial Estate, Bruntcliffe Lane, Morley, Leeds, LS27 9LR
☎ (0800) 783 2989 ⊕ cooperhillbrewery.co.uk

Cooper Hill commenced brewing in 2018 on equipment from the former Trinity Brewery, now relocated to Morley.

Best Bitter (ABV 3.8%) BITTER
Blonde (ABV 3.8%) PALE
Golden Ale (ABV 4.2%) GOLD

Darkland

Unit 4C, Ladyship Business Park, Mill Lane, Halifax, HX3 6TA
☎ (01422) 320100 ⊕ darklandbrewery.co.uk

◉Founded in 2018, Darkland is a microbrewery hidden away in a corner of an industrial estate. Beers can be ordered online in can, bottle and bag in the box. The beers can be sampled at the brewery tap on the last Saturday of the month. ◆♪

Tower Blonde (ABV 3.8%) BLOND
A straw-coloured blond ale with a malty body and a crisp bitter aftertaste.
Wolfenbrau (ABV 4%) BITTER
A malty, traditional bitter with a subtle roast flavour. There is a strong bitter aftertaste filling the mouth with a depth of flavour.
Immerse (ABV 4.4%) PALE
Fruity, golden-coloured pale ale. Malty with a lingering subtle well-rounded and lasting aftertaste.
Monterey Pale Ale (ABV 4.5%) PALE
Cat's Eyes (ABV 4.8%) STOUT
A black, velvety, well-balanced oatmeal stout. Plenty of roast and nutty flavours develop on the palate. The long aftertaste retains complexity and is surprisingly refreshing.
Unmasked Porter (ABV 5%) PORTER

DMC

Unit 2a, Cliffe Hill Works, Balne Lane, Wakefield, WF2 0DF ⊕ dmcbrewery.com

DMC Brewery, founded by husband and wife team Gez and Ele, produce the finest alcoholic ginger beer, made using fresh, natural ingredients, avoiding the use of synthetics, so the beers are gluten-free and mostly vegan. Four signature flavours, available for nationwide delivery, plus small batch, seasonal brews are produced. ♦GF V

Eagles Crag

Unit 21, Robinwood Mill, Todmorden, OL14 8JA
☎ (01706) 810394 ⊕ eaglescragbrewery.com

☺Eagles Crag is named after, and overlooked by, a prominent landmark, famous in local folklore. Its eight-barrel plant is situated in a former textile mill. Commercial brewing began in 2017 and the two founders both have over 35 years of brewing experience. Expansion has led to a range of styles – including an occasional Imperial Stout aged in whisky casks. Beers can be fined as vegan on request. Eagles Crag supply more than 200 outlets in Lancashire, Yorkshire and Manchester. 🍺♦V⚲

The Eagle's Feather (ABV 3.8%) BITTER
Traditional Yorkshire bitter. Malty and fruity with a dry bitter finish.
Pale Eagle (ABV 4%) GOLD
Easy-drinking, very well-balanced pale ale. Light citrus notes offset by a touch of sweetness giving a smooth, bitter finish.
The Eagle's Strike (ABV 4%) PALE
The Eagle's Jester (ABV 4.3%) PALE
Eagle of Kindness (ABV 4.4%) PALE
Pale ale with a golden blonde hue. Its hoppy character is balanced with notes of malt, packing a lot of flavour into a rounded body
Black Eagle (ABV 4.6%) STOUT
Luscious black creamy stout. Dry roast flavours develop in the mouth. The aftertaste is bitter and crisp.
The Eagle Has Landed (ABV 4.6%) BITTER
An amber best bitter with a good balance of fruit and malt. Moderate bitterness with a lingering malty finish.
Golden Eagle (ABV 4.7%) GOLD
A fruity, full-flavoured golden ale. Hoppy bitterness dominates the full mouthfeel and lasting finish.
Eagle of Darkness (ABV 5%) PORTER
Refreshing dark brown porter. A subtle blend of chocolate malt and raisin-like fruit develops into a mellow sweet aftertaste.
Bald Eagle (ABV 6.9%) IPA

Elland SIBA

Units 3-5, Heathfield Industrial Estate, Heathfield Street, Elland, HX5 9AE
☎ (01422) 377677 ⊕ ellandbrewery.co.uk

☺Orginally formed in 2002 as Eastwood & Sanders the company was renamed Elland in 2006 to reinforce its links with the town. The brewery has a capacity of 50 barrels (200 firkins) a week with further expansion and seasonal beers planned. ‼♦LIVE

Blonde (ABV 4%) BLOND
Creamy yellow, hoppy ale with hints of citrus fruits. Pleasantly strong bitter aftertaste.
South Sea Pale (ABV 4.1%) BITTER
Nettlethrasher (ABV 4.4%) BITTER
Smooth, amber-coloured beer. A rounded nose with some fragrant hops notes followed by a mellow nutty and fruity taste and a dry finish.
1872 Porter (ABV 6.5%) PORTER
Creamy, full-flavoured porter. Rich liquorice flavours with a hint of chocolate from roast malt. A soft but satisfying aftertaste of bittersweet roast and malt.

Empire SIBA

The Old Boiler House, Unit 33, Upper Mills, Slaithwaite, Huddersfield, HD7 5HA
☎ (01484) 847343 ☎ 07966 592276
⊕ empirebrewing.com

☺Empire Brewing was set up in 2006 in a mill on the bank of the scenic Huddersfield Narrow Canal, close to the centre of Slaithwaite. In 2011 the brewery upgraded from a five-barrel to a 12-barrel plant. Beers are supplied to local free houses and through independent specialist beer agencies and wholesalers. ‼♦LIVE

Chocolate & Cherry Mild (ABV 3.8%) MILD
Golden Warrior (ABV 3.8%) GOLD
Moonrakers Mild (ABV 3.8%) MILD
Strikes Back (ABV 4%) GOLD
Charlie Don't Surf (ABV 4.2%) BLOND
West Coast Pale (ABV 4.3%) PALE
White Lion (ABV 4.3%) BLOND

Farmers

Office: 98 Main Street, Haworth, BD22 8DP
☎ (01748) 886297 ⊕ farmersarmsmuker.co.uk/brewery

☺Formerly known as Haworth Steam, the five-barrel brewery has been in the Gascoigne family for more than 30 years. Beers are supplied exclusively to the two family-owned establishments. Beers are also sold under the Whitechapel brand name. 🍺

Fernandes

🍴 Luis Bar, 5 Avison Yard, Kirkgate, Wakefield, WF1 1UA ☎ 07949 833138 ⊕ luisbar.co.uk

☺Opened in 1997 and housed in a 19th century malthouse, Fernandes Brewery was sold to the Ossett Group in 2007. In 2021 it was extensively refurbished and reopened independent of Ossett, as Luis Bar @ Fernandes Brewery. ‼♦⚲

Frank's Head

19 Dymoke Road, Methley, LS26 9FG ☎ 07949 846438 ⊕ franksheadbrewery.co.uk

Established in 2020 in Methley producing small batch, hop-forward beers for canned distribution.

Frisky Bear

Unit 1, Vantage Point, Howley Park Road East, Morley, Leeds, LS27 0SU ☎ 07590 540210
⊕ friskybear.com

☺Established in 2016, Frisky Bear was originally based in Oscar's Bar in Morley Bottoms. An upgrade from one barrel to six barrel in 2019 saw a relocation to an industrial unit across town. The beers are available, unfined, in cask, keg and can, on a regularly rotating brewing schedule. ♦LIVE⚲

Grizzly Bear (ABV 4.5%) PALE

Goose Eye SIBA

Unit 5, Castlefield Industrial Estate, Crossflatts, Bingley, BD16 2AF
☎ (01274) 512743 ⊕ goose-eye-brewery.co.uk

☺Goose Eye is a family-run brewery established in 1991, supplying numerous regular outlets, mainly in Yorkshire and Lancashire. Goose Eye moved in 2017 to a custom-built brewery which has enabled it to increase production with a 20-barrel brew of regular beers and monthly specials. The well-appointed brewery bar is open every Friday and Saturday. ♦❖

Spring Wells (ABV 3.6%) PALE
Aromas of light malts and hops on the nose in this yellow session bitter. Pink grapefruit and strong hoppiness are balanced by a background of maltiness. Finish is long and increasingly bitter.
Bitter (ABV 3.9%) BITTER
Traditional Yorkshire brown session bitter, well-balanced malt and hops with a pleasingly bitter finish.
Black Moor (ABV 3.9%) MILD
Black-coloured mild with rich maltiness and roastiness that runs from aroma to finish. Vine fruits and dark chocolate create a balance finish.
Chinook Blonde (ABV 4.2%) BLOND
Assertive grapefruit hoppiness in the aroma and tropical flavours.
Golden Goose (ABV 4.5%) BLOND
Over & Stout (ABV 5.2%) STOUT
A full-bodied stout with roast and malt flavours mingling with hops, dark fruit and liquorice on the palate. Look also for tart fruit on the nose and a growing bitter finish.
Pommies Revenge (ABV 5.2%) BITTER
Golden strong bitter combining grassy hops, a cocktail of fruit flavours, a peppery hint and a hoppy, bitter finish.

Halifax Steam

🍺 **Conclave, Southedge Works, Brighouse Road, Hipperholme, HX3 8EF** ☎ 07506 022504
⊕ halifax-steam.co.uk

☺Brewing since 1999, the five-barrel plant supplies only the brewery tap, the Cock o' the North. It is now reputedly the oldest brewery in Calderdale. A range of permanent beers and different rotating beers are brewed throughout the year. ♦

Henry Smith

🍺 **Robin Hood, 4 Wakefield Road, Pontefract, WF8 4HN** ☎ 07547 573378

☺Set up behind the Robin Hood pub in Pontefract by Dean Smith in 2019 with the help of Revolutions Brewery (where Head Brewer, Paul Windmill, learned to brew). The plant is the former James & Kirkman kit with a few tweaks.

Hogs Head

🍺 **1 Stanley Street, Sowerby Bridge, HX6 2AH**
☎ (01422) 836585 ⊕ hogsheadbrewhouse.co.uk

☺The Hogs Head Brewery opened in a huge 18th century former malthouse at the end of 2015. The sixteen-barrel brewhouse has increased from eight-barrels since 2018. The handsome copper and stainless steel brewing vats of the original brewery are on display at the back of the bar area with the newer brewing vessels located in a building adjacent to the pub. Almost all the production is sold on the premises with occasional casks being provided to beer festivals. ♦

Horbury

🍺 **The Brewhouse, Cherry Tree Inn, 19 Church Street, Horbury, WF4 6LT** ☎ 07970 299292

☺Following the closure of Bob's Brewing Co, Horbury Ales took over the plant in 2016 and transferred production to the rear of the brewery tap, Cherry Tree Inn. Beers are available locally, regionally and nationally.

Now Then (ABV 3.8%) PALE
5 Hops (ABV 4.1%) PALE

First Light (ABV 4.1%) PALE
Tiramisu (ABV 4.3%) PORTER

Horsforth SIBA

143 New Road Side, Horsforth, Leeds, LS18 5NX
☎ 07854 078330 ⊕ horsforthbrewery.co.uk

☺Brewing began on a part-time basis in 2017 in the owner's garage, and then moved on to a small unit. 2020 saw relocation to larger premises, which incorporate a shop and taproom (accessed via an opening on the main street). In addition to the flagship beer, an ever-changing range of specials is produced. 🍺♦❖

My Horse Came Fourth (ABV 3.5%) SPECIALITY
Pale (ABV 4.5%) PALE
Schwarz Rose (ABV 5%) SPECIALITY
Mosaic (ABV 5.1%) PALE
Weise Rose (ABV 5.4%) SPECIALITY
Aubretia (ABV 5.5%) IPA
Night Ryder (ABV 5.5%) RED
Rubis (ABV 6.2%) SPECIALITY

Ilkley SIBA

40 Ashlands Road, Ilkley, LS29 8JT
☎ (01943) 604604 ⊕ ilkleybrewery.co.uk

☺Ilkley Brewery was founded in 2009 and has expanded rapidly since. Ilkley beers can be found throughout the UK and are now exported into Europe. The brewery is a frequent sponsor of local beer festivals and also holds regular onsite social events and brewery tours. ‼♦LIVE GF

Mary Jane (ABV 3.4%) PALE
Joshua Jane (ABV 3.7%) BITTER
Mild Mary (ABV 3.8%) MILD
Promise (ABV 3.8%) GOLD
Blonde (ABV 3.9%) GOLD
Pale (ABV 4.2%) PALE
Alpha Beta (ABV 4.5%) IPA
Lotus IPA (ABV 5.5%) IPA

Kirkstall SIBA

100 Kirkstall Road, Leeds, LS3 1HJ
☎ (0113) 898 0280

Second site: Midland Mills, Station Road, Cross Hills, BD20 7DT ⊕ kirkstallbrewery.com

☺Established in 2011 a few yards from the original Kirkstall Brewery beside the Leeds-Liverpool canal. In 2017 it moved to a new state-of-the-art brewery incorporating a 60-barrel plant, malting unit and canning line. Nearby Kirkstall Abbey and lost local industries are the inspiration for beer names. A secondary site, the former Naylor's brewery in Cross Hills, was purchased and began operation in 2022. In 2023 Kirkstall began brewing the former Leeds Brewery beers. The Kirkstall Bridge Inn is the Brewery Tap. ‼♦❖

Bitter (ABV 3.6%) BITTER
Pale Ale (ABV 4%) GOLD
A refreshing gold-coloured bitter beer with citric hop flavours, zesty bitterness especially in the finish which is lingering.
Three Swords (ABV 4.5%) GOLD
Good quantities of hops and juicy fruit define this yellow beer, a bitter taste and a tenacious pithy bitter finish.
Dissolution IPA (ABV 5%) PALE
Hops define this gold beer from the aroma, through the orange fruity taste and finishing dryly with yet more hops.
Black Band Porter (ABV 5.5%) STOUT

Dark smooth and rich with roasty smokiness, dried fruit and soft caramel balance the bitterness.

Brewed under the Leeds Brewery name:
Pale (ABV 3.8%) PALE
Hops and fruit, sometimes lemony, mix with a sweet maltiness through to the bitter hoppy finish, light gold colour.
Yorkshire Gold (ABV 4%) GOLD
Plenty of zesty citrus flavours supported by hops leading to a long-lasting bitter finish, a refreshing beer.
Best (ABV 4.3%) BITTER
A pleasing mix of malt and hops makes this smooth, copper-coloured, bittersweet beer, very drinkable.
Midnight Bell (ABV 4.8%) MILD
A full-bodied strong mild, deep ruby brown in colour. Malty and sweet with chocolate being present throughout.

Legitimate Industries SIBA

10 Weaver Street, Leeds, LS4 2AU
⊕ legitimateworldwide.com

Founded in 2016, the 30-barrel plant mainly brews keg beer for the company's Red's True Barbecue restaurant chain. However, under new ownership a wider portfolio of non-permanent beers are being produced, with canned output substantially increasing too (aided by the installation of a 200-litre pilot kit). A limited amount of cask beer is sometimes available in the local free-trade.

Little Valley SIBA

Unit 3, Turkey Lodge Farm, New Road, Cragg Vale, Hebden Bridge, HX7 5TT
☎ (01422) 883888 ⊕ littlevalleybrewery.co.uk

Ⓖ Little Valley began brewing in 2005 on a 10-barrel plant. All beers are organic and vegan, and Radical Roots is licensed by the Fairtrade Foundation. Around 300 outlets are supplied. 🍴♦LIVE V

Withens Pale (ABV 3.9%) PALE
Creamy, light gold-coloured, refreshing ale. Fruity hop aroma, flavoured with hints of lemon and grapefruit. Clean, bitter aftertaste
Radical Roots (ABV 4%) SPECIALITY
Full-bodied speciality ale. Ginger predominates in the aroma and taste. It has a pleasantly powerful, fiery and spicy finish.
Cragg Bitter (ABV 4.2%) BITTER
Tawny best bitter with a creamy mouth feel. Malt and fruit aromas move through to the palate which is followed by a bitter finish.
Dark Vale (ABV 4.5%) SPECIALITY
Dark brown speciality beer. Dark roast and fruit blend successfully with flavours of vanilla to create a smooth mellow porter.
Hebden's Wheat (ABV 4.5%) SPECIALITY
A pale yellow, creamy wheat beer with a good balance of bitterness and fruit, a hint of sweetness but with a lasting, dry finish.
Stoodley Stout (ABV 4.8%) STOUT
Very dark brown creamy stout with a rich roast aroma and luscious fruity, chocolate, roast flavours. Well-balanced with a clean bitter finish.
Tod's Blonde (ABV 5%) BLOND
Bright yellow, smooth golden beer with a citrus hop start and a dry finish. Fruity, with a hint of spice. Similar in style to a Belgian blonde beer
Moor Ale (ABV 5.5%) SPECIALITY
Tawny in colour with a full-bodied taste. It has a strong malty nose and palate with hints of heather and peat-smoked malt. Well-balanced with a bitter finish.
Python IPA (ABV 6%) IPA

Amber-coloured creamy beer with a complex bitter fruit palate subtly balanced by a malty sweetness, leading to a strongly lingering bitter after taste.

Lord's SIBA

Unit 15, Heath House Mill, Heath House Lane, Golcar, HD7 4JW ⊕ lordsbrewing.com

Established in 2015, Lord's Brewing Co is the brain child of three brothers-in-law, Ben, John and Tim. A picturesque 19th century mill houses the eight-barrel plant, large taproom and gift/bottle shop. 🍴♦⬥

Hodl Ultra Pale (ABV 3.8%) PALE
To The Moon (ABV 3.9%) PALE
Expedition Blonde (ABV 4%) BLOND
Ape Mafia American IPA (ABV 4.2%) IPA
Chosen Man (ABV 4.4%)
Malamute (ABV 4.5%)
Silver Spur (ABV 4.6%)
The Bandon Car Porter (ABV 4.8%) PORTER

Luddite

🏠 Calder Vale Hotel, Millfield Road, Horbury Junction, Wakefield, WF4 5EB
☎ (01924) 277658

Brewing began in 2019 at the Calder Vale pub in Horbury Junction. The pub was shut for five years until being reopened by a group of three former Horbury school friends, Ian Sizer, Tim Murphy and Gary Portman. The six-barrel plant brews, on average, once per week.

Magic Rock SIBA

Units 1-4, Willow Park Business Centre, Willow Lane, Huddersfield, HD1 5EB
☎ (01484) 649823 ⊕ magicrockbrewing.com

Magic Rock began brewing in 2011. The brewery is located about half a mile walk from Huddersfield town centre on an industrial estate. The 50-hectolitre brewhouse site also houses a taproom and distribution centre. In 2022 Magic Rock was purchased by Odyssey Inns Ltd along with the Magic Rock Tap at Holmfirth. The brewery specialises in barrel-aged ales, vegan beers and gluten-free beers. ‼♦LIVE GF V⬥

Hat Trick (ABV 3.7%) BITTER
Ringmaster (ABV 3.9%) GOLD
Inhaler (ABV 4.5%) GOLD
Common Grounds (ABV 5.4%) PORTER
High Wire (ABV 5.5%) IPA
Dark Arts (ABV 6%) STOUT

Mallinsons

Unit 1, Waterhouse Mill, 65-71 Lockwood Road, Huddersfield, HD1 3QU
☎ (01484) 654301 ☎ 07850 446571
⊕ drinkmallinsons.co.uk

Ⓖ Mallinsons was originally set up in 2008 on a six-barrel plant by CAMRA members Tara Mallinson and Elaine Yendall. The company moved to its current premises in 2012 with a 15-barrel plant and brewery shop. It specialises in hop-forward and single hop beers and has a permanent presence in numerous Huddersfield pubs. It holds an annual Mallytoberfest in October. ‼🍴♦LIVE

Wappy Nick (ABV 3.9%) BLOND
The aroma is lemony. Fruity citrus flavours develop on the palate giving way to smooth soft bitter aftertaste.

Marlowe

Office: 1 Mount Pisgah, Otley, LS21 3DX

One-barrel, small-batch brewery based in Otley, West Yorkshire. Sister brewery to Chevin Brew Co and brewing at same premises. Most of beer produced goes into bottles. The interesting beer range has included a fruited saison and an imperial stout.

Meanwood

1 Sandfield View, Leeds, LS6 4EU
⊕ themeanwoodbrewery.com

⊕The Meanwood Brewery was started by brothers Baz and Graeme Phillips in 2017. It focuses on brewing beer styles from around the world in keg and cask. 2021 saw expanded production and installation of an eight-barrel brew kit and canning line. The Terminus Taproom & Bottle Shop opened in 2018. ■◆

Herald (ABV 3.9%) PALE
As Above, So Below (ABV 4.5%) PALE
Black Goddess (ABV 4.9%) PORTER
Arecibo Message (ABV 5.7%) PALE

Mill Valley SIBA

Unit 10, Woodroyd Mills, South Parade, Cleckheaton, BD19 3NW
☎ (01274) 032017 ☎ 07565 229560
⊕ millvalleybrewery.co.uk

⊕Launched in 2016 on a three-barrel plant in Cleckheaton, after relocating to Liversedge in 2019 the brewery returned to Cleckheaton in 2022. More than 40 outlets are supplied as well as numerous beer festivals, a taproom is open Thursday-Sunday (check for times). Regular events are hosted. ‼◆●

Luddite Ale (ABV 3.8%) GOLD
Panther Ale (ABV 4%) GOLD
Yorkshire Bitter (ABV 4%) BITTER
Mill Blonde (ABV 4.2%) BLOND
Yorkshire Rose (ABV 4.2%) PALE
Black Panther (ABV 4.6%) STOUT
XTRA Fudge Stout (ABV 4.6%) SPECIALITY

Milltown SIBA

The Brewery, The Old Railway Goods Yard, Scar Lane, Milnsbridge, HD3 4PE ☎ 07946 589645
⊕ milltownbrewing.co.uk

⊕Milltown began brewing in 2011 using a four-barrel plant. Two pubs are owned, the Dusty Miller at Longwood, which acts as the official Brewery Tap, and the Traveller's Rest, Meltham. ‼◆LIVE

Spud's (ABV 3.8%) BITTER
Weaver's Bitter (ABV 3.8%) BITTER
American Pale Ale (ABV 3.9%) PALE
Platinum Blonde (ABV 4%) BLOND
Tigers Tail (ABV 4.1%) GOLD
Black Jack Porter (ABV 4.5%) PORTER

Morton Collins

■ Star, Standbridge Lane, Sandal, WF2 7DY
☎ (01226) 728746 ☎ 07812 111960

Office: 49 Willow Garth, Durkar, Wakefield, WF4 3BX
✉ ged.morton@aol.com

⊕Set up in 2016 by Ged Morton and Sam Collins using a 100-litre plant in Ged's garage. The brewery produces to demand but can brew every day if required. It took over the lease of the Star, Sandal, in 2016. Several of the

beers are named after the nearby Nature Reserve at Wintersett. The brewery kit was upgraded to 200 litres per brew in 2017.

Nightjar

2 Richmond House, Caldene Business Park, Mytholmroyd, HX7 5QL ☎ 07778 620800
⊕ nightjarbrew.co.uk

⊕Nightjar Brew Co was initially established in 2011 and was rebranded in 2018. Located in Mytholmroyd, this 10-barrel brewery has occasional open brewery nights, and supplies hundreds of free trade outlets across the UK. It combines a core range with around 15 new beers a year, in both cask and keg. Nightjar beers are always available in its two brewery taps: Nightjar, Hebden Bridge, and the Exchange Craft Beer House, Bradford. ◆

At One With Citra (ABV 3.9%) GOLD
Naturally-cloudy, pale yellow, single-hopped ale. Citrus flavours dominate the aroma and taste. This is followed by a mellow aftertaste.
Chosen (ABV 3.9%) BITTER
Come As You Are (ABV 4%) PALE
Hermit Crab of Hope (ABV 4%) PALE
Release the Pressure (ABV 4.1%) GOLD
Lost In Ikea (ABV 4.2%) PALE
Cosmonaut (ABV 4.4%) STOUT
Dark creamy stout with roasted malt dominating the aroma and taste. A liquorice flavour develops in the dry and bitter aftertaste.
To the Winchester (ABV 4.4%) BITTER
Zed's Dead (ABV 4.5%) PALE
Not All Heroes Wear Capes (ABV 5.5%) IPA
You Had Me at Hazy (ABV 5.9%) IPA
Don't Over Think Your Socks (ABV 6.2%) IPA
Supernova (ABV 6.9%) SPECIALITY
A dark, rich, creamy, full-bodied stout with a smooth chocolatey finish.
Emotional Support Hamster (ABV 7%) IPA

Nook SIBA

■ Riverside, 7b Victoria Square, Holmfirth, HD9 2DN
☎ (01484) 682373 ⊕ thenookbrewhouse.co.uk

⊕The Nook Brewhouse is built on the foundations of a previous brewhouse dating back to 1754, next to the River Ribble. Three brewery taps are supplied, two being restaurants with dishes matched to the beer, plus one onsite that rotates the 22 different ales. ‼◆LIVE

North SIBA

Springwell, Buslingthorpe Lane, Leeds, LS7 2DF
☎ (0113) 345 3290

Office: Regents Court, 39A Harrogate Road, Leeds, LS7 3PD ⊕ northbrewing.com

⊕Having opened in 2015, the brewery initially supplied the North Bar group of bars in and around Leeds. Expansion to 15-barrels on the original site quickly followed as the number of other outlets supplied increased. Due to substantially increased canned production, including national availability in supermarkets, further expansion was required, with the current premises opening in 2021. ‼◆●

Vanishing Point (ABV 3.8%) PALE
Seasons Reverse (ABV 4.3%) BITTER
Shadow Play (ABV 4.8%) PORTER

Northern Monk SIBA

Unit 7, Sydenham Road, Leeds, LS11 9RU

☎ (0113) 243 6430

Second site: The Old Flax Store, Marshalls Mill, Holbeck, Leeds, LS11 9YJ
⊕ northernmonkbrewco.com

◉After using spare capacity at other breweries in 2013, a 10-barrel plant was established in 2014 in a Grade II-listed mill. In 2017 a much larger second site with canning line was opened. 2019 saw further expansion into the adjacent former Leeds Brewery site, with a new 50-hectolitre brewkit installed in 2021. The mill hosts a taproom and events space. Most production is keg but cask-conditioned beer is available. ‼◆

Eternal (ABV 4.1%) PALE

Ossett SIBA

Kings Yard, Low Mill Road, Ossett, WF5 8ND
☎ (01924) 261333 ⊕ ossett-brewery.co.uk

◉Ossett is an independent brewery established in 1998, located in the heart of Yorkshire. Ossett Pub Company was formed in 2003 and now consists of more than 30 sites across Yorkshire. ‼🍴◆◆

Butterley (ABV 3.8%) PALE
Yorkshire Blonde (ABV 3.9%) BLOND
Sweet beer with peachy fruity flavours and gentle bitter finish.
White Rat (ABV 4%) GOLD
Inviting citrus hops and fruit aromas last throughout. Sweet adds body and balance. The hop bitterness rises in the slightly drier finish.
Silver King (ABV 4.3%) PALE
Voodoo (ABV 5%) SPECIALITY
Excelsius (ABV 5.2%) PALE

Piglove

Unit 6, Cross Green Lane, Leeds, LS9 8LJ ☎ 07718 630467 ⊕ piglovebrewing.com

Piglove is a small craft brewery based in Leeds. Inspired by the heritage of craft brewing in the UK and influenced by its co-founders' Venezuelan roots, its beers are bold, fragrant, unusual and exotic. Beers are organic and vegetarian. ◆

Omina (ABV 4.5%) IPA
Phantasticum Hop Healer (ABV 6.5%) SPECIALITY

Quirky

Unit 3, Ash Lane, Garforth, Leeds, LS25 2HG
☎ (0113) 286 2072 ⊕ quirkyales.com

◉Established in 2015, Quirky Ales brews two or three times a week on its 2.5-barrel plant. Simon Mustill and Richard Scott acquired the brewery in 2019 with Simon taking sole ownership in 2023. Aaron Getliffe is the full-time brewer. Its onsite taproom is open every weekend from Thursday evening, with occasional live music. Most of its beers are also available in bottles, which can be bought in the taproom and at delicatessens and farm shops. Brewing schools are frequently held, and available on request. 🍴◆

Porter (ABV 3.5%) PORTER
Blonde Ale (ABV 3.8%) BLOND
Two Islands (ABV 3.8%) GOLD
Bitter (ABV 4%) BITTER
Ruby (ABV 4%) BITTER
1 Hop Wonder (ABV 4.1%) GOLD
ITA (ABV 4.8%) BITTER
Hip Hop (ABV 5.5%) IPA
Classic (ABV 5.7%) MILD

Radiant

Office: 50 Eaton Hill, Leeds, LS16 6SE
⊕ radiantbrewing.co.uk

The brewery, brainchild of Stuart Hutchinson and Richard Littlewood, was launched in 2021. Stuart started out as a home brewer before taking the leap into commercial brewing, Radiant were currently utilising spare capacity at Darkland Brewery in Boothtown, near Halifax, while looking for an appropriate site in North Leeds. Brewing is currently suspended.

Rat

🍴 Rat & Ratchet, 40 Chapel Hill, Huddersfield, HD1 3EB
☎ (01484) 542400 ✉ ratandratchet@ossett-brewery.co.uk

◉The Rat & Ratchet was originally established as a brewpub in 1994. Brewing ceased and it was purchased by Ossett Brewery (qv) in 2004. Brewing restarted in 2011 with a capacity of 30 barrels per week. A wide range of occasional brews with rat-themed names supplement the regular beers. ◆

Ridgeside SIBA

Unit 24, Penraevon 2 Industrial Estate, Meanwood, Leeds, LS7 2AW ☎ 07595 380568
⊕ ridgesidebrewery.co.uk

◉Ridgeside began brewing in 2010 using a four-barrel plant. Regular outlets are supplied around Leeds and beers can be found across West and North Yorkshire. Cask beers are unfiltered and unfined. ◆◆

Plato (ABV 4%) PALE
Objects in Space (ABV 4.8%) PALE
Equator (ABV 5.6%) IPA
Milky Joe (ABV 5.6%) SPECIALITY

Riverhead

🍴 2 Peel Street, Marsden, Huddersfield, HD7 6BR
☎ (01484) 841270 (pub) ⊕ ossett-brewery.co.uk

◉Riverhead is a brewpub that opened in 1995, with an upstairs dining room. Ossett Brewing (qv) purchased the site in 2006 but runs it as a separate brewery. Many different beers are produced on a rotating basis. ‼◆

Salt

199 Bingley Road, Shipley, BD18 4DH
☎ (01274) 533848

Second Site: Unit 35.9 Cobalt, White Hart Triangle Estate, White Hart Avenue, Thamesmead, London, SE28 0GU ⊕ saltbeerfactory.co.uk

Housed in a Grade II-listed Edwardian tramshed, Salt is a state-of-the-art, 200-hectolitre brew plant and one of the Ossett group of independently-run breweries. The site includes a taproom and live music space. Two bars, branded as Craft Asylum, are operated. It bought the Hop Stuff brewery in Thamesmead when it was put up for sale by Molson Coors in 2021. ‼◆◆

Saltaire SIBA

Unit 7, County Works, Dockfield Road, Shipley, BD17 7AR
☎ (01274) 594959 ⊕ saltairebrewery.com

◉Saltaire Brewery opened in a converted gasworks by the River Aire in 2006 and has established itself as a leading independent brewer of cask ales. There is a stated emphasis on providing quality of product, whilst maintaining a steadfast commitment to an expanding range of cask and KeyKeg beers. Supplies pubs and retail outlets throughout the UK and worldwide. 🍺♦◆

South Island (ABV 3.5%) PALE
Titus (ABV 3.9%) BITTER
Blonde (ABV 4%) BITTER
Thirst-quenching and quaffable, this straw-coloured beer is slightly sweet and well-rounded with fruit, malt and hops in the taste and a fruity hoppy finish.
Citra (ABV 4.2%) PALE
Best (ABV 4.4%) BITTER
Amarillo (ABV 4.5%) PALE
Cascade (ABV 4.8%) PALE
Triple Choc (ABV 4.8%) SPECIALITY
A creamy, dark brown, roast, chocolate stout with a dry bitter finish and a rich chocolate aroma.
Unity (ABV 6%) IPA

Shadow

98 Boroughgate, Otley, LS21 1AE ☎ 07792 690536 ⊕ shadowbrewing.co.uk

Set up in 2019, originally in the owner's garage, Shadow Brewing moved in 2021 and now has its own taproom. A range of cask beers is produced on its one-barrel kit and via contract brewing with larger breweries. ◆

Small World SIBA

Unit 10, Barncliffe Business Park, Near Bank, Shelley, HD8 8LU
☎ (01484) 602805 ⊕ smallworldbeers.com

☺The brewery is situated in the former Barncliffe Mill near the picturesque village of Shelley. The beers are brewed on a 20-barrel Moeschle plant using spring water from an on-site bore hole. SALSA Plus Beer approved.
‼♦

Barncliffe Bitter (ABV 3.7%) BITTER
A traditional Yorkshire bitter. Malty and fruity with a long bitter farewell.
Long Moor Pale (ABV 3.9%) PALE
It's Never One (ABV 4%) GOLD
Port Nelson (ABV 4%) PALE
Spike's Gold (ABV 4.4%) GOLD
Thunderbridge Stout (ABV 5.2%) STOUT
Twin Falls (ABV 5.2%) PALE

Stod Fold

Stod Fold, Ogden, Halifax, HX2 8XL ☎ 07789 998775 ⊕ stodfoldbrewing.com

☺The 10-barrel Stod Fold Brewery is located on the edge of the moors in a renovated farm building. It supplies around 50 free trade outlets each year, mainly in Yorkshire, and occasionally does beer swaps with other brewing companies. Beers can always be sampled at the Stod Fold Brewery Tap, Dean Clough Mills, Halifax.
♦

Gold (ABV 3.8%) PALE
Refreshing, light, malty, fruity session ale with a smooth hoppy aftertaste.
Blonde+ (ABV 4.3%) BLOND
A fruity beer with a lingering dry finish. The main hop changes monthly and the fruit favour can therefore be citrusy or tropical.
Dark Porter (ABV 4.8%) PORTER
Easy-drinking, well-balanced, dark brown porter. Smooth and mellow with roast to the fore.
Dr Harris (ABV 5.7%) IPA

An amber-coloured traditional IPA with earthy/floral English hop flavours.

Stubbee SIBA

22 Harry Streetill, Dudley Hill, Bradford, BD4 9PH
☎ (01274) 933444 ⊕ stubbee.co

⊗ Launched as Salamander Brewery in 2000 the 40-barrel brewery was purchased by the McKenna Group and renamed Stubbee in 2021. Founder, Daniel Gent, remains head brewer and its cask ales retain the Salamander imagery on the pump clips. ‼♦◆

Blondie (ABV 4%) BITTER
Mudpuppy (ABV 4.2%) BITTER
A well-balanced, copper-coloured best bitter with a fruity, hoppy nose and a bitter finish.
Golden Salamander (ABV 4.3%) GOLD
Citrus hops characterise the aroma and taste of this golden premium bitter, which has malt undertones throughout. The aftertaste is dry, hoppy and bitter.
Spectre Stout (ABV 4.5%) STOUT
Rich roast malts dominate the smooth coffee and chocolate flavour. Nicely-balanced. A dry, roast, bitter finish develops over time.
Bright Black Porter (ABV 4.8%) PORTER

Sunbeam

52 Fernbank Road, Leeds, LS13 1BU ☎ 07772 002437
⊕ sunbeamales.co.uk

☺Sunbeam Ales was established in a house in Leeds in 2009, with commercial brewing beginning in 2011. Since moving, capacity has increased to a two-barrel plant based in a garage. The core range of ales (available in West and North Yorkshire at present) is brewed on rotation up to twice weekly, with occasional brews every six weeks or so. ♦

Bottoms Up (ABV 3.7%) PALE
Polka Hop (ABV 3.8%) PALE
Sun Beamer (ABV 3.8%) PALE
Bright Day (ABV 4.2%) PALE
Rain Stops Play (ABV 4.5%) BITTER

Tarn 51

🍴 Robin Hood, 10 Church Road, Altofts, Normanton, WF6 2NJ
☎ (01924) 892911 ✉ realale@tarn51brewing.co.uk

Tarn 51 uses a three-barrel plant situated at the Robin Hood in Altofts. Expansion is planned. Five other outlets are supplied.

Tartarus

Office: New Road Site, Horsforth, LS18 4NR
✉ tartarus.brewing@gmail.com

Nanobrewery based in Horsforth, Leeds, launched commercially in 2020. Producing small-batch, craft beers on a 100-litre kit.

Timothy Taylor SIBA IFBB

Knowle Spring Brewery, Keighley, BD21 1AW
☎ (01535) 603139 ⊕ timothy-taylor.co.uk

☺An independent, family-owned company established in 1858, it has occupied the Knowle Spring site since 1863. Pennine spring water is used to brew its award-winning ales on both the established main plant and a 10-barrel plant used to develop new beers, including occasional specials. 19 pubs are operated. ♦

Dark Mild (ABV 3.5%) MILD
Malt and caramel dominate throughout in this sweetish beer with background hop and fruit notes.

Golden Best (ABV 3.5%) MILD
Refreshing amber-coloured, traditional Pennine mild. A delicate fruit hoppy aroma leads to a fruity taste with underlying hops and malt. Fruity finish.

Boltmaker (ABV 4%) BITTER
Tawny bitter combining, hops fruit and biscuity malt. Lingering, increasingly bitter aftertaste. Formerly & sometimes still sold as Best Bitter. .

Knowle Spring (ABV 4.2%) BLOND
Tropical fruitiness on the nose leads to a bitter sweetness that carries through into the finish.

Landlord (ABV 4.3%) BITTER
Moreish bitter combining citrus peel aromas, malt and grassy hops with marmalade sweetness and a long bitter finish.

Landlord Dark (ABV 4.3%) OLD
A black beer with red highlights topped by a coffee-coloured head. Burnt caramel on the nose, Dark fruits with caramel in the taste leading to a light bitter finish

Three Fiends

Brookfield Farm, 148 Mill Moor Road, Holmfirth, Meltham, HD9 5LN ☎ 07810 370430
⊕ threefiends.co.uk

The brewery was set up by three friends in 2015 and is based in one of the outbuildings at Brookfield Farm. The original two-barrel kit was upgraded to an eight-barrel plant in 2019. Beers are available around Huddersfield and at CAMRA beer festivals. The Fourth Fiend, Meltham, is the brewery tap.

Stelfox (ABV 4%) IPA
Bad Uncle Barry (ABV 4.2%) PALE
Bandito (ABV 4.5%) PALE
Fudge Unit (ABV 4.8%) STOUT
Super Sharp Shooter (ABV 5.2%) IPA
Dark Side (ABV 5.3%) PALE
Punch Drunk (ABV 5.5%) PALE
Voodoo (ABV 6%) SPECIALITY
Panic Attack Espresso Stout (ABV 6.8%) SPECIALITY
Stelfoxed (ABV 7.5%) IPA

Tigertops SIBA

22 Oakes Street, Flanshaw, Wakefield, WF2 9LN ☎ (01229) 716238 ☎ 07951 812986
✉ tigertopsbrewery@hotmail.com

☺Tigertops was established in 1995 by Stuart Johnson and his wife Lynda who, as well as owning the brewery, ran the Foxfield brewpub in Cumbria (qv). After retiring, the brewery is now run on their behalf by Barry Smith, supplying five regular outlets. ♦

Cass 2CV (ABV 4.6%) BITTER

Truth Hurts

c/o MSS City Mills, Peel Street, Morley, Leeds, LS27 8QL
☎ (0113) 238 0382 ☎ 07950 567341
⊕ truthhurts.co.uk

☺Established in 2016 as Blue Square Brewery and rebranded as Truth Hurts in 2019. It produces one-off brews from its four-barrel plant in a split-level building that is part of a mill complex. ▨♦

Vocation SIBA

Unit 8, Craggs Country Business Park, New Road, Cragg Vale, Hebden Bridge, HX7 5TT

☎ (01422) 410810 ⊕ vocationbrewery.com

☺Vocation began brewing in 2015 and is located high above Hebden Bridge. Brewing capacity continues to increase at pace as it expands UK and Worldwide markets with a wide range of beer styles. This includes barrel-aged and a single hop series, as well as collaboration brews. Vocation have bars in Halifax, Hebden Bridge, Manchester and Sheffield. ▨♦

Bread & Butter (ABV 3.9%) GOLD
A feast of floral hops with citrus aroma and taste. Robust bitter aftertaste.

Heart & Soul (ABV 4.4%) GOLD
A golden ale with a strong citrus aroma. Hops dominate taste and aftertaste.

Pride & Joy (ABV 4.8%) PALE
Flavoursome IPA packed with citrus hoppiness. A hint of sweetness gives way to a mellow aftertaste.

Life & Death (ABV 5.5%) IPA
Naughty & Nice (ABV 5.9%) STOUT
A rich and smooth velvety stout. A combination of chocolate and roasted barley develops on the palate. The finish is bittersweet.

Wetherby

Beer Station, York Road Industrial Estate, York Road, Wetherby, LS22 7SU
☎ (01937) 584637 ☎ 07725 850654
⊕ wetherbybrewco.com

☺Wetherby Brew Co was established in 2017, and is a short walk from the town centre. It is independently-owned and operated from a three-barrel plant. ▨♦❧

Wharfedale SIBA

🯄 Back Barn, 16 Church Street, Ilkley, LS29 9DS
☎ (01943) 609587 ⊕ wharfedalebrewery.com

☺Wharfedale began brewing in 2012 using spare capacity at Five Towns brewery in Wakefield. Brewing moved to Ilkley in 2013 using a 2.5-barrel plant located at the rear of the Flying Duck pub, creating Wharfedale's first brewpub.

Wilde Child

Unit 5, Armley Road, Leeds, LS12 2DR
☎ (0113) 244 6549 ☎ 07908 419028
⊕ wildechildbrewing.co.uk

Established as one of the smallest breweries in Leeds in 2016, Keir McAllister-Wilde took his operation from a one-barrel plant in a garage to a 10-barrel operation in a 2,000sq ft unit, within two years. There are a large number of different ales in Wilde Child's portfolio. As well as distributing nationwide, beers are being sent to Holland, Spain and Finland. ❧

Opaque Reality (ABV 5.9%) SPECIALITY

Wishbone

2A Worth Bridge Industrial Estate, Chesham Street, Keighley, BD21 4NS
☎ (01535) 600412 ☎ 07867 419445
⊕ wishbonebrewery.co.uk

Established in 2015 and run by a husband and wife team with many years experience in the brewing industry. Beers are brewed on a modern 10-barrel plant. Beers are available around Yorkshire and Lancashire, as well as further afield via wholesalers. ❧

Blonde (ABV 3.6%) BLOND

Hoppy golden ale with a strong citrus character. A bitter hoppy and slightly astringent finish.

Eezee (ABV 3.8%)
Two Lapels (ABV 4%)
Flux (ABV 4.1%) PALE
Drover (ABV 4.2%) BITTER
Tiller Pin (ABV 4.2%) GOLD
Yellow session bitter. Citrus and hops on the nose. Hops and citrus dominate the flavour leading to a long citrus finish.

Tiny Pixie (ABV 4.2%)
Abyss (ABV 4.3%) STOUT
Caramel and coffee bean aroma in a stout of chocolate and liquorice leading into a malty finish.

Gumption (ABV 4.5%) BITTER
Well-balanced amber best bitter. Look for hints of dried fruit, biscuit and nuts, underpinned by dry hoppiness, leading to a bitter finish.

Zapato

Unit 1a, Holme Mills, West Slaithwaite Road, Marsden, Huddersfield, HD7 6LS
☎ (01484) 841201 ☎ 07788 513432
⊕ zapatobrewery.co.uk

Small company, established in 2016, that nomad brewed in the Leeds and Manchester areas prior to establishing a permanent home in Marsden. It produces innovative beers based on traditional European styles. Collaboration brews are a staple part of its output. 🍽 ♦

Pale (ABV 3.5%) GOLD
A light-bodied, refreshing golden ale. It has a hoppy aroma. Flavours of citrus fruits develop on the palate and the beer slips down easily.

Bothy (ABV 4.5%) BITTER
Tent (ABV 4.5%) PALE

Grove Inn, Leeds: Holbeck (Photo: Dermot Kennedy)

North West

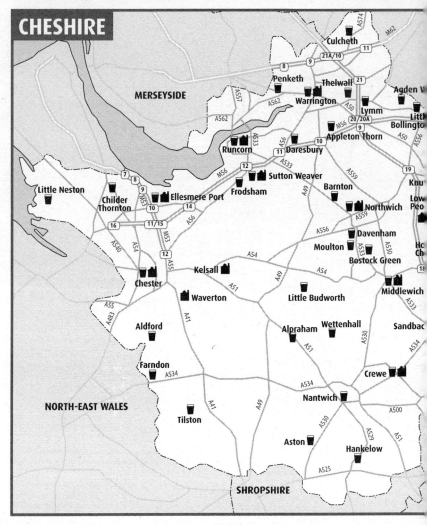

CHESHIRE

MERSEYSIDE

Culcheth
Penketh
Thelwall
Agden W
Warrington
Lymm
Littl
Bollingto
Appleton Thorn
Runcorn
Daresbury
Sutton Weaver
Frodsham
Barnton
Knu
Low
Peo
Childer Thornton
Ellesmere Port
Northwich
Little Neston
Davenham
Ho
Ch
Moulton
Bostock Green
Kelsall
Chester
Middlewich
Waverton
Little Budworth
Aldford
Wettenhall
Sandbac
Alpraham
Farndon
Crewe
Tilston
Nantwich
NORTH-EAST WALES
Aston
Hankelow

SHROPSHIRE

Agden Wharf

Barn Owl

Warrington Lane, WA13 0SW (on Bridgewater Canal, off A56)

☎ (01925) 752020 ● thebarnowlinn.co.uk

Moorhouse's White Witch; Wainwright; 2 changing beers (sourced locally; often Tatton) ⊞

This canalside pub is a good stop off if you are walking the towpath. Wooden carvings of a bear and a barn owl greet you at the front, while the interior is bright and airy, with a heated conservatory offering pleasant views over the Cheshire countryside. It serves good-value food, including specials for the over 60s. The outdoor pods on the canalside patio have become a permanent feature. ➠❀◑♿P♣🐕🛜

Aldford

Grosvenor Arms 🅛

Chester Road, CH3 6HJ (on B5130)

☎ (01244) 620228 ● grosvenorarms-aldford.co.uk

Timothy Taylor Landlord; Weetwood Eastgate; house beer (by Brightside); 4 changing beers (sourced nationally) ⊞

A spacious, stylish and unashamedly upmarket pub. Full of character, it is multi-roomed with a pleasant garden room leading to an outside terrace and garden backing on to the village green. Inside the decor is modern-traditional with lots of bare wood, bookcases, pictures and chalkboards. Four changing beers, which occasionally include a mild, complement the house beer brewed by Brightside, plus Weetwood and Timothy Taylor. High-quality food from an imaginative menu is popular and served all day. Q➠❀◑♿P🚆(5)🐕🛜

Alpraham

Travellers Rest ★ 🅛

Chester Road, CW6 9JA (A51, on N outskirts of village)

☎ (01829) 260523

Weetwood Best Bitter, Eastgate ⊞

This gem of a pub has been owned and run by the same family for over 110 years. There are four rooms, although only two are generally used, and entering them is like stepping back in time to the 1930s. It has been identified

Greater Manchester / Disley / Poynton / Wilmslow / Abberley / Bollington / Macclesfield / Gawsworth / Wincle / Congleton / Staffordshire / Derbyshire

0 Miles 5
0 Kilometres 8

---

by CAMRA as having a regionally important historic pub interior. The staff are friendly and unpretentious, and prices are very keen for the regular beers. This is a must for those seeking a traditional English pub.
Q🌳🟢♣P�🌸

Alsager

Lodge Inn 🏆

88 Crewe Road, ST7 2JA (jct Crewe Rd B5077 and Station Rd, opp Church Rd) ● thelodgeinnalsager.co.uk
Oakham Citra; house beer (by Marston's); 6 changing beers (sourced nationally) ℍ
A homely and dog-friendly two-roomed pub that has free dog biscuits and a real fire in the left-hand room. Popular with locals and visitors alike, it offers a warm welcome and a wonderful atmosphere. It houses Sunday sessions of the Alsager Music Festival in a large beer garden. Large cold pork pies are available. The pub is well served by local transport and there is a public car park at the rear. Its website features a digital beer board that shows current beers on sale. Local CAMRA Pub of the Year 2023. Q🌳🟢🌸●P🚗🌸🎵

Appleton Thorn

Appleton Thorn Village Hall

Stretton Road, WA4 4RT
☎ (01925) 261187 ● appletonthornvillagehall.co.uk
7 changing beers (sourced nationally; often 4Ts, Facer's, Merlin) ℍ
At the hub of the community and a CAMRA National Club of the Year more than once, the Hall has a sizeable function room and quieter lounge area. Real ales are mainly from independent breweries, and can be served in third-pint paddles. There is also a choice of real ciders and perries as well as up to five craft beers. Show a CAMRA card for admission – a small fee may be payable. Closed Monday to Wednesday.
Q🌳🟢🌸♣●P🚗🚆(Cat8,Cat7)🌸🎵

Aston

Bhurtpore 🅛

Wrenbury Road, CW5 8DQ (on Wrenbury Rd, just off the A530)
☎ (01270) 780917 ● bhurtpore.co.uk
10 changing beers (sourced nationally) ℍ
Winner of numerous CAMRA awards and now in its 31st year of consecutive entry in the Guide. There are up to 10 regularly changing real ales from mainly local breweries, and local Wrenbury cider. There are separate rooms for dining, where good-quality food is served (curries are a speciality). Dogs are welcome in the in the bar area. A large garden with bench seating with canopy cover is an added attraction. A regular meeting place for vintage motorcycle and car clubs. Q🌳🟢🌸🍴👭🌸▲●P🚆(72)🌸🎵

Barnton

Barnton Cricket Club 🅛

Broomsedge, Townfield Lane, CW8 4QL (200yds from A533, down a narrow drive to the left of Barnton Community Primary School)
☎ (01606) 77702 ● barntoncc.co.uk
Sharp's Doom Bar; 3 changing beers (sourced nationally) ℍ
A sport-based club arranged into two distinct rooms: the large lounge accommodates family parties and overlooks the patio and cricket pitch, while the smaller member's bar has TVs (sound muted) showing Sky or BT Sports. Cricket predominates in summer but at other times it's a good place to watch the big match of choice. Crown green bowls, squash, darts and dominoes are all played here, and there are quiz and bingo nights and occasional music events. Show your CAMRA membership card for admission. 🌳🌸🍴👭🌸♣P🚗(Cat9,N4)🌸🎵

Bollington

Poachers Inn 🅛

95 Ingersley Road, SK10 5RE
☎ (01625) 572086 ● thepoachers.org
Beartown Glacier; Storm Desert Storm; 3 changing beers (sourced locally) ℍ
Family-run community free house that is a flagship for real ale, with beers from local breweries and guest beers from ever-changing microbreweries, one of which is always a dark beer. The fresh, home-made food features locally sourced ingredients. A secluded beer garden is a suntrap. The pub is used as a meeting point for local groups and is popular with walkers. Quiz nights are held in aid of local charities on the second and last Sunday of each month. Dogs welcome. 🌳🌸🍴●P🚗🌸🎵

Vale Inn 🄻

29-31 Adlington Road, SK10 5JT
☎ (01625) 575147 ● valeinn.co.uk
Bollington White Nancy, Long Hop, Best, Oat Mill Stout, Eastern Nights 🄷
The Vale is a terraced 1860s pub with an open-plan single room and a cosy corner featuring a real fire. The detached garden overlooks the cricket ground and has its own bar in summer. The pub was refurbished in 2012 with new wooden flooring and modern decor but has lost none of its charm. Excellent home-cooked food is served, and Bollington beers are available to take away (pre-order advisable). The pub is close to the Macclesfield Canal and Middlewood Way.
🌜🏮🌓🄳♣🅟🖵🐾🛜

Bostock Green

Hayhurst Arms 🄻

London Road, CW10 9JP (off A533 Bostock Rd)
☎ (01606) 541810
House beer (by Brightside, Weetwood); 4 changing beers (sourced locally) 🄷
Built in 1845, this was previously the Bostock Green Social Club before being purchased by local upmarket pubco Brunning & Price. There is a relaxed atmosphere in the pub, and a board at the entrance proudly proclaims the bar as being the centre of operations. Dining is popular throughout (a private dining room is available for free hire by groups), but drinkers are equally welcome anywhere. Q🌜🏮🌓🕭♣🅟🐾🛜

Chester

Architect 🄻

54 Nicholas Street, CH1 2NX
☎ (01244) 353070
Weetwood Cheshire Cat; house beer (by Brightside); changing beers 🄷
Converted former regency home of architect and designer Thomas Harrison. Restored and opened in 2012 it lies in landscaped grounds close to the city walls and Roodee racecourse. The rambling original interior of the listed Georgian building has several rooms of varying sizes and intimacy while the sympathetic extension houses the bar and lower level dining area. Outside is a large patio and sloping lawns, which are particularly popular in horse-racing season. Up to seven ales are available, several local. Q🌜🏮🌓🕭🅟🖵🐾🛜

Bluestone

117 Christleton Road, CH3 5UQ (on main A41 route out of Chester)
☎ (01244) 738149 ● bluestonebar.co.uk
3 changing beers (sourced nationally) 🄷
Micropub styling itself as a craft beer and wine bar located in a parade of shops in the Boughton area of Chester. The single bar area has a mix of wooden top tables with either high stools or low level upholstered bench seats. Three changing cask ales are complemented by 10 cask beers, four real ciders and a wide selection of canned and bottled beers. Children are welcome until 7pm. A limited number of outside pavement seats are available. 🌜🍴🖵🐾🛜

Brewery Tap 🄻

52-54 Lower Bridge Street, CH1 1RU
☎ (01244) 340999 ● spittingfeathers.co.uk/the-brewery-tap
Spitting Feathers Thirstquencher, Special Ale; 5 changing beers (sourced nationally) 🄷

Stunning Jacobean great hall with high barrel-vaulted ceiling. Its features include an ornate sandstone fireplace, tapestries and stone floors that create a terrific ambience. A fitting winner of CAMRA's Heritage Conservation and Conversion to Pub Use award. Inventive, freshly prepared food is locally sourced. Seven ales are available, with several of Spitting Feathers' own beers complemented by a range of guests which are often from other local microbreweries. Reached by a flight of stone steps from street level. Q🏮🍴♣🖵🐾🛜

Cavern of the Curious Gnome

61 Bridge Street Row East, CH1 1NW
● thecavernofthecuriousgnome.co.uk
Ossett White Rat; 3 changing beers (sourced nationally; often Vocation) 🄷
Belgian-themed bar located on Chester's famous Rows. Enter via Paysan wine bar, then climb the steps up to this bar, where a colourful, large, papier-mache gnome gazes down on proceedings. Red-and-white spotted toadstool seats plus tables with bench seating catch the eye, with more quirkiness to be found among the decor. Four handpumps serve changing cask ales from all over the UK. Belgian offerings include lambics, gueuzes and Trappist ales plus Duvel served on draught. 🏮🌓🖵🐾🛜

Cellar 🍷

19-21 City Road, CH1 3AE
☎ (01244) 318950 ● thecellarchester.co.uk
Timothy Taylor Landlord; 5 changing beers (sourced nationally; often Marble) 🄷
Friendly street-level bar whose name relates to the function room in the cellar below. Deservedly renowned for its excellent selection of cask ales. A regular beer such as Timothy Taylor Landlord is complemented by five guest beers and three real ciders. There is also an extensive range of keg and bottled beers from around the world. Sport features on three large TV screens. The food offering consists of pizzas and meat and cheese platters.
🌓≋♣🖵🐾🛜

Cornerhouse

4-8 City Road, CH1 3AE
☎ (01244) 347518 ● cornerhousechester.com
Salopian Oracle; 3 changing beers (sourced nationally) 🄷
Situated in Chester's thriving Canal Quarter, this attractive, candlelit, mock-Tudor building features lots of

REAL ALE BREWERIES

4Ts Warrington
Beartown Congleton
Bollington Bollington
Brewhouse & Kitchen 🍴 Chester
Chapter ♦ Sutton Weaver
Coach House Warrington
Four Priests Middlewich
Happy Valley 🍴 Macclesfield
Hush ♦ Northwich
Merlin Arclid
Mobberley Lower Peover
Neighbourhood Poynton
Norton Runcorn
Oaks Ellesmere Port
Pied Bull 🍴 Chester
RedWillow Macclesfield
Spitting Feathers Waverton
Storm Macclesfield
Tatton Knutsford
Tom's Tap ♦ Crewe
Weetwood ♦ Kelsall
Wincle ♦ Wincle

bare brick and wood flooring. It offers one regular beer and three changing ales – usually one dark – plus an extensive bottled beer selection. Live music is hosted Thursday to Saturday with a quiz on Sunday. There is a a free-to-hire function room upstairs. Outside seating is at the front of the pub. Food is of the platter variety (meats and cheeses) plus snacks. ✿◑≒♣☐✿☎♪

Deva Tap
121 Brook Street, CH1 3DU (at city end of Hoole Bridge, close to railway station)
☎ (01244) 314440 ⊕ thedevatap.co.uk
Ossett White Rat; 2 changing beers (sourced regionally; often Thornbridge) ⊞
Originally built as a cacao house, this architecturally interesting building, by the end of the bridge and close to the station, is now a popular venue, with three distinct areas and outside seating in a small courtyard. The White Rat and two guest beers, often local, are supplemented by a wide variety of keg and bottled beers. Food is simple, including vegetarian and gourmet burgers. There are various meal deals throughout the week.
᠔✿◑&≒♥☐☐✿☎♪

Olde Cottage ✔
34-36 Brook Street, CH1 3DZ
☎ (01244) 324065 ⊕ oldecottagechester.co.uk
Otter Bitter; Wye Valley HPA; 2 changing beers (sourced nationally; often Brimstage, Butcombe) ⊞
Welcoming and traditional community local on the popular eating and drinking Brook Street, between the city centre and railway station. To the left is the games room with pool, darts and a bagatelle table (rarely seen outside Chester). The main bar has another dartboard, small TV and a real fire for the colder weather. Two regular beers are supplemented by two guests, one of which is free of tie. Various loyalty and discount schemes are offered. ✿≒♣☐✿☎

Telford's Warehouse Ⓛ
Canal Basin, Tower Wharf, CH1 4EZ (just off the city walls)
☎ (01244) 390090 ⊕ telfordswarehousechester.com
Salopian Oracle; Weetwood Cheshire Cat; 2 changing beers (sourced nationally) ⊞
Converted warehouse with a large glass frontage overlooking the Shropshire Union Canal basin. Some walls retain original features and are adorned with interesting industrial artefacts. Up to six changing beers are available, usually from microbreweries The pub is a popular live music venue, charging admission on some evenings after 9pm. Good-quality food is served, and the upstairs restaurant can also be hired for private functions. Outside seating is popular in good weather.
᠔✿◑♥P☐(1A)✿☎♪

Childer Thornton

Halfway House
New Chester Road, CH66 1QN (A41 close to M53 jct 5)
☎ (0151) 339 2202
4 changing beers (sourced nationally; often Weetwood) ⊞
Friendl,y traditional former coaching inn dating from the 1770s, based at the midpoint between Chester and New Ferry. Note the old prints of the pub and surrounds on the walls. The building retains much of its original character, with several drinking areas offering smart, comfortable seating. The community feel is evident, with darts and domino teams plus a golf society. The pub can be busy when sporting events are on TV. Quiz night is Thursday.
✿&♣P☐(1,X1)✿☎♪

Congleton

BarleyHops
29 High Street, CW12 1BG
☎ (01260) 295247
4 changing beers (sourced regionally) ⊞
This popular beer café relocated in 2021 to a former shop in the centre of town and has quickly re-established its place in the Guide. There is a single room downstairs with further seating available upstairs. Four rotating beers always offer something interesting and usually include a dark beer. The cask offering is complemented by real cider and a range of keg lines. Regular music evenings and other events are held, and there is a cocktail bar upstairs at weekends. ᠔♣♥☐✿☎♪

Beartown Tap Ⓛ
18 Willow Street, CW12 1RL
☎ (01260) 270775
Beartown Kodiak, Skinful, Lit; 4 changing beers (sourced locally; often Abbeydale, Beartown, Purple Moose) ⊞
Now independently owned, this continues to be the flagship pub for the nearby Beartown brewery and has won multiple CAMRA awards. Six Beartown beers are usually on offer plus a guest ale or cider. There is something happening most nights at this community local, whether it's street food, a quiz night, pub games or live music. Conversation thrives downstairs, with a log-burner for the winter, and there is an upstairs area with dartboard and outdoor terrace for the summer.
᠔✿◑♣☐(92)✿♪

Lord Mountbatten Ⓛ
70 Mill Street, CW12 1AG (off Mountbatten Way)
☎ 07811 199902 ⊕ lordmountbatten.freehostia.com
5 changing beers (sourced regionally) ⊞
This Congleton pub has the widest range of constantly changing beers from microbreweries, which are dispensed through five handpumps. New breweries always get a welcome here. The focus is clearly on the beer offering, with rugby and football TV viewing also popular. The owner manages and runs the pub and is always available to share his detailed knowledge of the existing and new local brewers. Pool and backgammon are played. ✿♣P☐✿

Queen's Head Ⓛ
Park Lane, CW12 3DE
☎ (01260) 272546
Draught Bass; Greene King Abbot; house beer (by Beartown); 2 changing beers (sourced regionally) ⊞
Independent free house opposite the railway station and by bridge 75 on the Macclesfield Canal. The pub faced closure a few years ago, but its popularity won the day and new owners took it on after a local campaign to save it. It has taken more of a focus on food recently and offers good-quality meals. Guest beers are generally from local and regional breweries. There is plenty of seating outside. ᠔✿◑≒P☐(94)✿☎♪

Crewe

Borough Arms Ⓛ
33 Earle Street, CW1 2BG (on Earle St rail bridge, entrance up steps in adjoining Thomas St)
10 changing beers (sourced nationally; often Fyne, Oakham, Thornbridge) ⊞
This multi award-wining freehold pub was established in 1867. It offers Oakham Inferno and nine changing handpulled real ales, with at least one dark ale, two ciders, and 19 free flow fonts. Hundreds of pumpclips adorn the ceilings and walls. Upstairs there are three

distinct seating areas. Stairs lead down to more seating and a wood-burner. From here a door takes you into a partly covered garden and smoking area, with 18 benches. Accessed by stone steps from Thomas Street. Q☺♿♣♠PꝚ(8) 🛜

Crewe Dog 🅛
Unit L, Market Hall, 27 Earle Street, CW1 2BL (inside Crewe Market Hall, jct Hill St and Earle St)
🌐 salty-dog.co.uk/the-crewe-dog
Tatton Tatton Blonde; 3 changing beers (sourced regionally; often Tatton) 🅗
The Crewe Dog is within the recently refurbished Crewe Market Hall and shares its location with various food and other retail outlets. Four handpumps dispense two beers from Tatton brewery plus two regional guests. An extensive range of craft beers are also available on draught. A Real Ale Club gives discounts for customers on Wednesdays. The many events include quiz nights on Thursday and occasional live music. The facilities and most of the seating is shared with the other outlets in the hall. ☺◐♿♣♠♥🗗Ꝓ(8)🐾🛜♪

Earl of Chester 🅛
104 Wistaston Road, CW2 7RE (jct Flag Ln and Wistaston Rd)
☎ (01270) 488244
Merlin Merlin's Gold; 2 changing beers (sourced locally; often Merlin) 🅗
Small, friendly, traditional two-roomed pub that sells reasonably priced beers. The name derives from the Cheshire Yeomanry, originally created in response to the growing fears of invasion from Napoleonic France. There are bar and lounge areas, with seating off to one side, plus a separate pool room that may be used for small functions. TVs in all the rooms show mainly major sporting events. There are regular quiz and bingo nights, with profits going to local charities. ☺❀♣Ꝓ(8)🐾🛜

Hops 🅛
Prince Albert Street, CW1 2DF (opp Lifestyle Centre at S end of Prince Albert St)
☎ (01270) 211100 🌐 hopsbelgianbar.co.uk
5 changing beers (sourced nationally; often Mobberley, Thornbridge, Townhouse) 🅗
A family-run bar with a friendly welcome for its wide range of clientele (and their dogs). Styled after a Belgian café-bar, it offers a fabulous range of bottled Belgian beers to complement the real and craft ales and cider offerings. The European-style sun terrace in front of the property is always popular. Inside is a large single room with the bar on the ground floor, with further seating available in the upstairs area. Q☺♿♿♣♠♥🗗🐾🛜

Culcheth

Liberty's Gin Bar 🅛
31-33 Common Lane, WA3 4EW
☎ (01925) 767029
3 changing beers (sourced locally; often Merlin) 🅗
Located in the main shopping area of Culcheth, this modern bar has a first-floor function room with a capacity of up to 200. Sports channels feature strongly on the TV screens in the main bar. Locally sourced guest beers are often from Merlin, including the house beer, Liberty Ale. As the name suggests, this bar also has a strong emphasis on gin, with over 200 to choose from. ☺❀♿♥🗗🛜♪

Daresbury

Ring o' Bells 🅛 ✅
Chester Rd, WA4 4AJ (just off A56 in centre of village)
☎ (01925) 740256
5 changing beers (sourced locally; often Phoenix, Titanic, Weetwood) 🅗
Another year in the Guide for this 19th-century pub. The half-timbered building was once the village courthouse and still retains many of its original features. Although food oriented, this LocAle serving Chef & Brewer pub has five handpumps that dispense beers mainly from the Weetwood range. Lewis Carroll (who was born nearby and whose father was the curate of the church opposite) memorabilia features prominently. There is a large beer garden to the rear. Well-behaved dogs are welcome. ☺❀◐♿♿Ꝓ(X30)🐾🛜

Davenham

Davenham Cricket Club 🅛
Butchers Stile, Hartford Road, CW9 8JF (down narrow, signed driveway near brick postbox)
☎ (01606) 48922 🌐 davenham.play-cricket.com
4 changing beers (sourced regionally; often Mobberley, RedWillow, Salopian) 🅗
Hidden away in an idyllic setting on the edge of the village is this friendly, welcoming community club. The outdoor seating terrace is an ideal place to enjoy the cricket and soak up the sun. Ever-changing local and regional real ales are dispensed from four handpumps. Two beer festivals are held each year. A largescreen TV shows sporting events. During the cricket season the opening hours are extended. Show your CAMRA card for admission. ☺❀♿Ꝓ(37)🐾🛜

Disley

Malt Disley
22 Market Street, SK12 2AA
☎ (01663) 308020 🌐 maltdisley.com
Ossett White Rat; 3 changing beers (sourced locally; often RedWillow, Titanic, Torrside) 🅗
Vibrant and friendly micropub housed in a shop in the village centre. The surprisingly spacious interior includes a downstairs games room. Up to four cask beers are available, mostly from local microbreweries. Ten KeyKeg beers (including three continental beers plus a cider), and a range of British and continental bottled beers are also on offer. A former local CAMRA Pub of the Year, and Cheshire Pub of the Year 2021. ☺🚲♣Ꝓ(199)🐾🛜♪

Ellesmere Port

Bondies Bar 🅛
2 Chester Road, Whitby, CH65 6RU
☎ (0151) 345 8560
House beer (by Coach House); 3 changing beers (sourced locally; often Oaks) 🅗
Ellesmere Port's first micropub, just outside the town centre, is named after a former landlord of the Sportsman's Arms which stood nearby. Bondies opened in 2021 and serves a good variety of drinks. The smart wood-panelled downstairs bar has simple wooden chairs and stools and upstairs is a lounge with comfortable leather sofas and a variety of games. There are a few outside seats at the front and back. ☺❀♣♠PꝚ🐾

Farndon

Hare 🅛
High Street, CH3 6PU

☎ (01829) 470072 ⊕ hareatfarndon.co.uk
Big Hand Super Tidy; Weetwood Best Bitter; 3 changing beers (sourced regionally; often Purple Moose, Tatton, Three Tuns) Ⓗ
Formerly the Greyhound, this smart village pub was relaunched in 2020. The pub comprises various cosy areas, all with comfortable seating and polished traditional furniture. Potted plants add greenery and a gallery of prints, pictures and photographs, many of a local nature, adorn the walls. The two regular beers are complemented by three guests, often including a darker beer during winter months. Good-quality food from an imaginative menu is available throughout the day.
🛆🌑◖P🖵(C56) 🌸 🛜

Frodsham

Helter Skelter Ⓛ
31 Church Street, WA6 6PN
☎ (01928) 733361 ⊕ thehelterskelter.co.uk
Ossett White Rat; Salopian Oracle, Darwins Origin; Weetwood Best Bitter; 4 changing beers (sourced nationally; often Peerless, Thornbridge) Ⓗ
Located close to the station, off Main Street, this small and lively single-room bar is a multiple winner of local CAMRA Pub of the Year awards. There are four regular cask ales and a further four changing guest ales from local and national breweries. Dark beers feature regularly. Other beers include rotating craft kegs, imported bottled beers and a rotating guest cider. Food is served in the bar and the upstairs Grill@31 restaurant.
◖🛪🖵🌸🛜♪

Gawsworth

Harrington Arms ★ Ⓛ
Church Lane, SK11 9RJ (off A536)
☎ (01260) 223325
Robinsons Wizard, Dizzy Blonde, Unicorn; 1 changing beer (sourced locally; often Robinsons) Ⓗ
A rural Cheshire gem, this Grade II-listed building has been identified by CAMRA as having a nationally important historic pub interior. There is a small bar area with separate rooms off it, all with character, including open fires and wood-burners. Beers are from the Stockport-based Robinsons brewery, to enjoy by themselves or to accompany the lunchtime and evening menus. In summer there is an outdoor area looking out on the adjacent farm. Q🛆🌑◖🛪🖵(38)🌸🛜

Hankelow

White Lion Ⓛ
Audlem Road, CW3 0JA (jct Audlem Rd A529 and Longhill Ln, opp green and pond)
☎ (01270) 432606 ⊕ thewhitelionhankelow.co.uk
Salopian Shropshire Gold; 4 changing beers (sourced regionally) Ⓗ
This community-owned pub reopened in March 2022 following a full refurbishment that includes a new accommodation suite. It offers four real ales from local breweries. The interior is surprisingly spacious, with several cosy nooks and crannies. Bare timber and well-worn floor tiles are the main features and the walls are wood panelled throughout. An upstairs function room overlooks the village green and there is a large paved and sheltered outside seating area with pergolas and plants. The pub is dog friendly.
Q🛆🌑🖂◖🛆P🖵(73) 🌸 🛜 ♪

Holmes Chapel

Beer Emporium Bottle Bank Ⓛ
24-26 London Road, CW4 7AL
☎ (01477) 534380 ⊕ beeremporiumbottlebank.co.uk
3 changing beers (often Merlin, Mobberley) Ⓗ
This bar/off-licence gets its name from its previous life as a NatWest Bank, as evidenced by the strong room at the rear, which is now used for customers' spirit bottles. A former local CAMRA Pub of the Year, this modern bar has up to four regularly changing cask ales and eight keg lines, with thirds available. Various regular events take place, including visits from a caterer providing wood-fired pizzas and 'cheesy Sundays', with complimentary cheese from 3pm. 🛆🌑🛆🛪🖂●🖵(42,316)🌸🛜♪

Victoria Club Ⓛ
Victoria Ave, CW4 7BE
☎ (01477) 535858
Merlin Merlin's Gold; Sharp's Doom Bar Ⓗ**; 1 changing beer (sourced locally; often Merlin)** Ⓟ
Welcoming local community sports club which welcomes non-members. Members benefit from discounts on drinks prices. Local CAMRA Club of the Year three years running to 2021. Beers are often sourced from the local Merlin brewery, but not exclusively. It's possible to enjoy a pint here while playing pub games such as pool and darts or watching some local cricket or national televised sports. 🛆🌑🛆🛪♣P🖵🌸🛜♪

Knutsford

Rose & Crown Ⓛ ✅
62 King Street, WA16 6DT
☎ (01565) 652366 ⊕ knutsfordroseandcrown.co.uk
RedWillow Weightless; Wainwright; Weetwood Cheshire Cat Ⓗ
Built in 1647, this old inn has a wonderful historic charm, with a black and white exterior with leaded stained-glass, graced with hanging baskets. Inside are exposed beams and a beautiful old fireplace. The open-plan ground-floor bar and restaurant are divided into discrete areas and there are two sharing tables near the bar. There is a good-sized rear outdoor seating area, and letting rooms are available. Two of the hand-pumped cask beers are from Cheshire. It can be busy, especially at weekends. 🌸🖂◖🛪P🖵(88,89)🌸🛜♪

Little Bollington

Swan with Two Nicks Ⓛ ✅
Park Lane, WA14 4TJ (signposted off A56)
☎ (0161) 928 2915 ⊕ swanwithtwonicks.co.uk
Timothy Taylor Landlord; 2 changing beers (sourced locally; often Coach, Dunham Massey) Ⓗ
A food-oriented pub with a spacious restaurant at the rear. Meals are served all day. Drinkers are welcome in a cosy front room with horse brasses and old pictures. The pub tends to be quiet after the end of food service, and may close early on Sundays in winter. It is close to the Bridgewater Canal, and a 10-minute walk from Dunham Massey (National Trust) where a footpath at Bollin Gate leads to a footbridge across the river. 🛆🌑◖P🖵(X5)🌸

Little Budworth

Egerton Arms Ⓛ
Pinfold Lane, CW6 9BS (on edge of village near Oulton Park and Budworth Common) SJ594654
☎ (01829) 760767 ⊕ egerton-arms.co.uk
Weetwood Best Bitter, Cheshire Cat; 4 changing beers (sourced regionally; often Bank Top, Salopian) Ⓗ

A change of ownership in 2021 has resurrected this friendly, vibrant country pub on the edge of the village. A wood-burner helps to create a cosy atmosphere in winter, while in summer outdoor seating and a beer garden gives the opportunity to watch cricket. Regular quizzes, musical events and beer festivals contribute to the ambience. It has a widescreen TV for sports events in the small side bar. ✿❀◗▲♣P❀🗲♪

Little Neston

Harp 🄻 ✅
19 Quayside, CH64 0TB (turn left at bottom of Marshlands Rd, pub is 300yds on left overlooking marshes)
☎ (0151) 336 6980
Joseph Holt Bitter; Peerless Triple Blond; Timothy Taylor Landlord; 2 changing beers (sourced nationally) 🄷
A former coal miners' inn converted from two cottages, the Harp has a public bar with a real fire in winter and a basic lounge. Set in a glorious location on the Deeside to Neston part of the national cycle network, the pub overlooks the Dee Marshes and North Wales, with a large garden and a drinking area abutting the edge of the marshes. Lunchtime food only, except a popular curry evening every Tuesday (booking advisable).
Q✿❀◗P🖵(22,487) ❀

Lymm

Brewery Tap 🄻
18 Bridgewater Street, WA13 0AB
☎ (01925) 755451 🌐 lymmbrewing.co.uk
Dunham Massey Dunham Dark; Lymm Bitter, Bridgewater Blonde; 4 changing beers (sourced locally; often Dunham Massey, Lymm) 🄷
A former red-brick post office in the centre of Lymm village near the Bridgewater Canal. Fully refurbished in 2022, it has cosy seating areas and a wood-burning fire. A dark beer is usually available among four changing beers, plus three regular ales. There is live music at the weekend and a twice-monthly open mic night. Local pies are available at all times. ✿❀◗❀🐾🗲♪

Macclesfield

Castle 🍺 ★ 🄻 ✅
25-27 Church Street, SK11 6LB (walk up cobbled street from Waters Green car park, on left as road bends right)
☎ (01625) 462646
3 changing beers (often RedWillow, Storm, Wincle) 🄷
This 18th-century listed pub, identified by CAMRA as having a nationally important historic pub interior, was sympathetically restored in 2021 and reopened. It is tucked away on a cobbled street near the station. The pub is small from the outside but has plenty of seating inside, with four separate rooms, two of which are served from a handsome bar area. The beer range from the three handpulls is often local and always includes a good mix of styles. There is an imaginative food menu.
✿❀◗≠♣🖵🗲♪

Happy Valley Tap & Pizza 🄻
73 Oxford Road, SK11 8JG
☎ (01625) 403988 🌐 73andpizza.co.uk
4 changing beers (sourced locally; often Happy Valley) 🄷
Happy Valley brewery's taproom features a wide range of ever-changing cask ales, mainly from the host brewery, as well as many others in keg and bottle. The multi-room pub boasts a suntrap rear garden, and is renowned for its home-made pizzas, which can be eaten in or ordered for takeaway. Regular live music events are featured. ✿❀◗🖵❀

Jack in the Box 🄻
Picturedrome, 102-104 Chestergate, SK11 6DU
Blackjack Irk Street Pale Ale, Jack In The Box Blonde, Pub Ale: Best Bitter; 4 changing beers (sourced locally; often Blackjack) 🄷
Blackjack's brewery bar is housed in the Picturedrome, which was originally the town's oldest cinema, dating from 1911. The bar overlooks a popular seating/dining area surrounded by stalls serving varied styles of street food. You can also take your drink down to the dining area. The house beers are provided by Blackjack brewery, and there is also a good range of guests from independent breweries and a wide selection of craft keg and real cider from boxes. ✿❀◗≛≠♣🖵(88,130)❀🗲

RedWillow 🄻
32A Park Green, SK11 7NA
☎ (01625) 830718
RedWillow Headless, Wreckless; 2 changing beers (often RedWillow) 🄷
This popular bar is the tap for the nearby RedWillow brewery. The tastefully converted former shop has kept its original period front, along with interesting modern decor. Beers on offer are displayed above the bar, with regular and special brews from the brewery on handpull and keg, plus a changing range of guest keg beers, always including at least one dark beer and one cider (usually on handpull). Food is provided by local kitchen takeovers. There is some pavement seating outside.
✿❀◗≛≠♣🖵❀🗲

Wharf 🄻
107 Brook Street, SK11 7AW
☎ (01625) 261879 🌐 thewharfmacc.co.uk
5 changing beers (sourced nationally; often Abbeydale) 🄷
A traditional end-of-terrace pub, a short walk from the town centre and close to the Macclesfield Canal, with an attractive canal boat theme. This multi award-winning free house has four handpulls serving local and regional beers, always including a gluten free beer. There are three different seating areas surrounding a central bar and a sheltered garden area at the rear. There is also a games area. Live music often features at weekends.
✿❀≛♣🖵(58) ❀🗲♪

Middlewich

White Bear Hotel 🄻
Wheelock Street, CW10 9AG (on lower end of Wheelock St, just off St Michael's Way A54)
☎ (01606) 837666 🌐 thewhitebearmiddlewich.co.uk
4 changing beers (sourced locally) 🄷
This 17th-century coaching inn was comprehensively restored in 2011 by the current owner. Its local real ales always include a dark ale and an IPA, and the pub is also renowned for its excellent food. With a large open-plan room off the bar, a separate restaurant, an alfresco patio and an upstairs function room, it appeals to a wide range of customers. A Guide regular for many years.
✿❀🛏◗♣P🖵(37,42) ❀🗲♪

Mobberley

Church Inn 🄻 ✅
Church Lane, WA16 7RD (opp the church, signposted from local roads)
☎ (01565) 873178 🌐 churchinnmobberley.co.uk

Dunham Massey Big Tree; Weetwood Jester IPA; house beer (by Dunham Massey, Weetwood); 2 changing beers (sourced regionally) ⏢
This Grade II-listed 300-year-old dining pub, sister of the nearby Bull's Head, retains vestiges of the old multi-room layout. The pub stands opposite the village church where Mallory of Everest is commemorated in stained glass (his father was vicar), and a house beer is named in his honour. There is a fire-lit cricket-themed bar, a characterful boot room and two dining rooms, with a private dining room upstairs and beer garden to rear. Information on local walks is available.
🌟🕭🚶♿P🚌(88) 🐾🐕📶

Moulton

Lion 🅛
74 Main Road, CW9 8PB
☎ (01606) 606049
Wainwright; 2 changing beers (sourced locally; often Merlin, Ossett, Tatton) ⏢
This former local CAMRA Pub of the Year is at the heart of the community. Drinking is the focus here and the pub is a rare local outlet for real cider. Stonebaked pizzas are available daily in the early evening, and there is a popular smartphone quiz held on a Thursday evening, as well as occasional music quizzes and karaoke evenings. Key sporting events are shown on the TV.
🌟🕭🚶🍴♣🍽🚌🐾📶♪

Nantwich

Black Lion 🅛
29 Welsh Row, CW5 5ED (on Welsh Row, opp Cheshire Cat)
☎ (01270) 628711 ⊕ blacklionnantwich.co.uk
Weetwood Best Bitter, Cheshire Cat, Old Dog; 3 changing beers (sourced regionally; often Coach House, Tatton) ⏢
A Grade II-listed black and white pub dating from 1664. It consists of a through bar and lounge with a real fire during colder months. There is an upstairs dining room with extra seating. The outside area includes covered and open seating, with an enclosed area, the Hop Room, linking it to the pub. Children are welcome until 5pm, but only the over-12s are allowed after that watershed. Well-behaved dogs are also welcome.
Q🌟🕭≒♣🍽🚌(84) 🐾📶♪

Wickstead Arms 🅛 ✔
5 Mill Street, CW5 5ST (jct of Mill St and Barker St)
☎ (01270) 610196 ⊕ wicksteadpubnantwich.co.uk
5 changing beers (sourced nationally) ⏢
A busy back-street local, a short stroll from Nantwich town centre, with a sports TV bar and a quieter lounge. The latter features an attractive large poster with a map of Battle of Nantwich (fought 25 January 1644), as well as old pictures of Nantwich. Five handpumps serve a range of changing beers – mostly LocAle – from the Punch Taverns list. The pub is dog friendly, with free treats. 🌟🕭♿≒🚌(84,85)🐾📶

Northwich

Salty Dog 🅛
21-23 High Street, CW9 5BY (in pedestrianised town centre) ⊕ salty-dog.co.uk
Tatton Gold; 3 changing beers (sourced locally; often Hush Brewing Co., Merlin, Tatton) ⏢
Housed in one of the town's black and white timbered buildings is this pub and award-winning independent music venue. The co-owner is a drummer in punk bands

and hosts weekly gigs featuring top names as well as new talent. In addition to music, spoken word and comedy nights feature regularly. Alongside the real ales there is an extensive range of bottled and canned British and European beers. 🌟🕭♿♣🚌🐾📶♪

Penketh

Ferry Tavern 🏆
Station Road, WA5 2UJ (from car park on Station Rd cross railway and canal) SJ5634986649
☎ (01925) 791117 ⊕ theferrytavern.com
Wainwright; house beer (by Ossett); 4 changing beers (sourced nationally; often Marble, RedWillow, Thornbridge) ⏢
In a scenic location next to the River Mersey, cross the the railway and canal from the car park to get here. It is popular with cyclists as it is close to the Trans Pennine Trail. The atmospheric interior has low-beamed ceilings and a balcony area which can be sectioned off for private functions. Outside is a large seating area in the extensive beer garden which overlooks the river and is popular in summer. Q🌟🕭🍴P🐾📶♪

Poynton

Cask Tavern
42 Park Lane, SK12 1RE
☎ (01625) 875157 ⊕ casktavern.co.uk
Bollington White Nancy, Long Hop, Best, Oat Mill Stout, Eastern Nights ⏢
Located in the centre of Poynton, this is one of three Bollington brewery taps in Cheshire showcasing their range of beers. It also offers a locally produced Moravka craft lager. The single-roomed pub has comfortable seating areas, including two outside spaces. A regular clientele has developed and a warm welcome is assured to all visitors. Toilets are upstairs. Card payments only.
🌟🕭♣🍽P🚌(391,392) 🐾📶

Runcorn

Ferry Boat ✔
10 Church Street, WA7 1LR
☎ (01928) 583380
Greene King Abbot; Ruddles Best Bitter; Sharp's Doom Bar ⏢; 2 changing beers (sourced nationally) ⏢ /Ⓖ
Large, busy Wetherspoon pub opposite Runcorn Old Town bus station. The three standard Wetherspoon beers are complemented on most days by two or three others. The pub name derives from the river crossing that used to operate between the towns of Runcorn and Widnes (on the opposite bank of the River Mersey) before the building of the Manchester Ship Canal in the 1890s. The Brindley theatre is 200 yards away. 🌟🕭🕭♿≒P🚌📶

Norton Arms
125-127 Main Street, WA7 2AD
☎ (01928) 567642 ⊕ thenortonarms.co.uk
Greene King IPA; 3 changing beers (sourced nationally; often Hardys & Hansons) ⏢
This is the 10th year in the Guide for this Grade II-listed two-roomed, oak beamed pub in the centre of Halton Village. Although sports TV dominates, except on Sundays when the sound is turned down in the lounge, this is still a nice find. Among its attractions are open mic nights, live music, quiz nights and a bowling green. It can get busy at weekends. A former local CAMRA Pub of the Year. 🌟🕭🕭♿♣P🚌🐾📶♪

Sandbach

Beer Emporium ⅃
8 Welles Street, CW11 1GT (off Hightown roundabout, down one-way street)
☎ (01270) 760113 🌐 thebeeremporium.com
5 changing beers ⊞
The large window at the front of this welcoming micropub casts plenty of light on those sitting at the tables, and a small room at the rear provides extra seating. Five handpumps, normally including a dark or malty ale, are supplemented by four keg lines. Oakham and Ossett ales are often featured, plus local Merlin and Four Priests offerings. The knowledgeable staff will advise on the extensive range of worldwide bottled and canned beers on the shelves lining the walls.
Q🎝🖴🖵(37,38)🌸🛜

Sutton Weaver

Chapter Brewing Tap ⅌ ⅃
Unit 2A, Clifton Road, WA7 3EH
☎ 07908 004742 🌐 chapterbrewing.co.uk
2 changing beers (sourced locally; often Chapter) ⊞
This taproom and shop is the home of Chapter's award-winning beers. Two cask ales are offered and up to nine keg beers from the brewery's portfolio, alongside real cider, a lager line and an occasional guest beer. Traditional bar snacks and occasional street food is available. Opening times are limited so it is advisable to check before visiting. The premises is on a small industrial estate and parking may sometimes be difficult.
🍴&P🖵🖴(2,X30)🌸

Thelwall

Little Manor ⅃
Bell Lane, WA4 2SX
☎ (01925) 212070
Brunning & Price Original; Hawkshead Windermere Pale; Lancaster Blonde; house beer (by Brightside); 5 changing beers (sourced regionally; often 4Ts, Coach House, Timothy Taylor) ⊞
Run by upmarket operators Brunning & Price, this previous local CAMRA Pub of the Year offers excellent food and real ale for the grateful visitor. Despite being close to an 8-lane viaduct carrying the busy M6 over the River Mersey and Manchester Ship Canal, the Little Manor is an oasis of peace in the heart of the historic village centre. Outside is a beer garden and large covered patio, perfect for alfresco dining and drinking.
Q🎝🌸🕙&♣P🖵🌸🛜♪

Tilston

Carden Arms ⅃
Mount View, Church Road, SY14 7HB
☎ (01829) 250900 🌐 cardenarms.co.uk
Coach House Gunpowder Premium Mild; Salopian Shropshire Gold; Weetwood Eastgate; 2 changing beers (sourced locally; often Big Hand, Spitting Feathers) ⊞
Impressive rural free house at the crossroads in the village. The interior has rug-covered wood and tiled floors, real fires, traditional furniture and attractive framed pictures on the plain white walls. In addition to the three regular beers are up to two guests, often from local microbreweries. High-quality food is served in the bar area and the stylish dining room. Upstairs, two adjoining Georgian rooms can be booked for groups. Accommodation is available in five bedrooms.
Q🛏🕙&♣P🖵(41)🌸🛜

Warrington

Albion ⅃
94 Battersby Lane, WA2 7EG (200yds N of A57/A49 jct)
☎ (01925) 231820
4 changing beers (sourced locally) ⊞
Victorian, Grade II-listed, former Greenall Whitley pub on the edge of town. Inside, it has a separate games room, bar and lounge with open fires. Outside is a courtyard surrounded by the original stables. The pub plays host to various community-focused activities throughout the year. Live music plays on Thursdays. Four cask ales are available, including Cheshire breweries. Local CAMRA Community Pub of the Year 2022.
🎝🌸≷(Central)♣🖵(17,25)🌸♪

Costello's Bar ⅃
36 Time Square, WA1 2NT
☎ (01925) 954846 🌐 costellosbar.co.uk/timesquare
8 changing beers (sourced locally; often Dunham Massey, Lymm) ⊞
This smart, new, eco-friendly build from Dunham Massey opened in 2022, next to the cinema in Time Square. It has an impressive specialist ventilation system which makes sure the bar is always full of fresh, clean air. An array of 10 handpumps serves up to eight changing cask ales from the Dunham Massey and Lymm brewing portfolios.
🎝🌸&≷(Central)🖵🌸🛜

Hop Emporium ⅃
Unit 11 Warrington New Market, Time Square, Academy Way, WA1 2NT
House beer (by Beartown); 3 changing beers (sourced regionally; often Beartown, Tiny Rebel) ⊞
This new bar in Warrington Market opened in 2020 and goes from strength to strength. Three rotating guest beers, usually including one dark beer, are offered, alongside a house beer from Beartown brewery. There is plenty of seating and food options from the Cookhouse in the market area. The bar gets busy on a Saturday when there is live music. A popular tap takeover is held on alternate months. 🎝🌸🕙&≷(Central)🖵🌸🛜

Lower Angel ⅃
27 Buttermarket Street, WA1 2LY (in pedestrianised town centre)
☎ 07375 881706
Liverpool Brewing Company Dark Mode; house beer (by Liverpool Brewing Company); 7 changing beers (sourced locally) ⊞
Taken over by Liverpool Brewing Company in 2022, this former Peter Walker pub still retains some of it previous ownership history, including stained-glass windows from the former Walkers brewery. The pub has a traditional vault, lounge, sheltered beer garden to the rear and outdoor seating in front. The seven rotating guest beers are mainly from LBC's extensive range and usually include a stout or porter. 🌸≷(Central)🖵🌸🛜♪

Tavern ⅃
25 Church Street, WA1 2SS
☎ 07747 668817
8 changing beers (sourced regionally; often 4Ts, Abbeydale, Mallinsons) ⊞
The Tavern is the brewery tap for 4Ts. The single-roomed pub offers a changing range of 4T beers, as well as other beers from around the country, and has tap takeovers once a month. It is very popular for watching sports on the multiple TVs, especially Rugby League. There is an outdoor drinking area in the yard to the rear, with heaters if required. The pub has featured in the Guide for 25 years. 🌸≷(Central)♣🖵🌸🛜

Wettenhall

Little Man
Winsford Road, CW7 4DL
Butcombe Original; Wainwright Amber; Wye Valley HPA; 1 changing beer (sourced nationally) ⊞
This open-plan pub is popular with the local farming and equestrian community, and has a friendly feel as you walk up the steps and through the front door. Step-free access is via a ramp to the side door. Renovated by the new tenants in early 2022, it is a comfortable place to enjoy a quiet pint. The pub's name is unique in the country. It can, allegedly, trace its history back to 1673 when it was the Little John Ale House. Q ⏰ ✿ ⚓ ♣ P ● ♿ ☞

Wilmslow

Coach & Four ⌊ ⊘
69-71 Alderley Road, SK9 1PA
☎ (01625) 525046 ● thecoachandfour.co.uk
Hydes 1863, Original, Lowry; 2 changing beers (sourced locally; often Hydes) ⊞
Large, comfortable old coaching house close to the centre of Wilmslow, catering to a wide mix of clientele. The single room is divided into secluded alcoves, and there is a restaurant. Food is served all day either in the restaurant or the bar area. Five Hydes beers are available, including some from the Ralf+Alf sub-brand. Outside is a covered and heated patio for smokers. Quiz nights, music and comedy are held, as well as charity and community events. There is also lodge-style accommodation. ⏰ ✿ ⚓ ◑ ♿ ⇋ ♣ P ♞ (130,88) ♿ ☞ ♪

Wincle

Wincle Brewery Shop ⌊
Tolls Farm Barn, Dane Bridge, SK11 0QE
☎ (01260) 227777 ● winclebeer.co.uk
3 changing beers (sourced locally; often Wincle) ⊞
With a breathtaking view across the Dane valley from the small beer garden, this brewery shop is well worth a visit. Three cask beers from the adjacent brewery are on handpump and a good selection of bottles from Wincle. There are also soft drinks and a few spirits, including gin from the nearby Forest Gin distillery. There are very few seats inside, but a log-burning stove keeps the lucky few warm in winter. Cakes are offered at weekends. Q ⏰ ✿ ♞ ♿ ☞

Breweries

4Ts SIBA
Unit 20, Manor Industrial Estate, Lower Wash Lane, Latchford, Warrington, WA4 1PL
☎ (01925) 417820 ☎ 07917 730184
● 4tsbrewery.co.uk

Brewing continues on the 12-barrel brew length kit. A core range of beers is regularly produced with many one-off specials. Occasional brews of Tipsy Angel beers are produced. The beers can be found in the Tavern, Church Street. A taproom is planned. !! ♦

SPA (ABV 3.8%) PALE
APA (ABV 4%) GOLD
WSB (ABV 4.2%) BITTER
IPA (ABV 4.6%) PALE
English Stout (ABV 5%) STOUT

Brewed under the Tipsy Angel Brewery name:
George Shaw Premium (ABV 4.3%) BITTER

Beartown SIBA
Bromley House, Spindle Street, Congleton, CW12 1QN
☎ (01260) 299964 ● beartownbrewery.co.uk

⊛Beartown began brewing in 1994 and uses a 25-barrel plant. The brewery underwent a significant refurbishment in 2022. It supplies more than 250 outlets. It also brews under the Manning Brewery name. !! ▤ ♦

Glacier (ABV 3.6%) BLOND
Best Bitter (ABV 3.7%) BITTER
Bluebeary (ABV 4%) SPECIALITY
Strong blueberry aromas and taste dominate the flavours, usually leaving a dry, hoppy bitter finish.
Kodiak (ABV 4%) PALE
Hops and fruit dominate the taste of this crisp yellow bitter and these follow through to the dryish aftertaste. Biscuity malt also comes through on the aroma and taste.
Arribear (ABV 4.2%) PALE
Skinful (ABV 4.2%) BITTER
Traditional bitter, malt and hops build together with some fruit. The bitterness lasts well in the finish.
Peach Melbear (ABV 4.4%) SPECIALITY
Strong peach aroma leads to a dry bitter beer with some of the expected fruity sweetness.
Kahuna (ABV 4.5%) SPECIALITY
Passion fruit aromas dominate this well-balanced very fruity beer. Some pleasant hops complement the sweetness and last well in the finish.
Lit (ABV 4.5%) BLOND
Creme Bearlee (ABV 4.8%) SPECIALITY
Chocolate and vanilla aromas with malty, caramel and roasty flavours combine with a sweet body to be followed by a dry finish.
Polar Eclipse (ABV 4.8%) STOUT
Classic black, dry and bitter stout, with roast flavours to the fore. Good hop on the nose follow through the taste into a long dry finish.
Quantock (ABV 5%) MILD

Brewed under the Manning Brewery name:
Woah Man (ABV 3.8%) PALE
Man Up! (ABV 4%) BITTER
Cave Man (ABV 4.2%) BITTER

Bollington SIBA
Adlington Road, Bollington, SK10 5JT
☎ (01625) 575380 ● bollingtonbrewing.co.uk

⊗ Bollington began brewing in 2008 with the Vale Inn, Bollington, as the brewery tap. The Park Tavern, and the Fountain both in Macclesfield, and the Cask Tavern, Poynton, are also owned. Around 40 outlets are supplied direct. !! ♦

Chinook & Grapefruit (ABV 3.6%) GOLD
Ginger Brew (ABV 3.6%) SPECIALITY
White Nancy (ABV 3.6%) BLOND
Fruity hoppy aroma, smooth sweet body, with hops providing balance as the bitterness continues with the fruit into a lasting finish.
Long Hop (ABV 3.9%) BLOND
A hoppy yellow beer with fruit and some sweetness for balance.
Bollington Best (ABV 4.2%) BITTER
A well-balanced bitter beer with plenty of hop bitterness which dominates the fruity sweet malt flavours, completed with a long mouthfeel and a lasting, rising bitter finish.
Dinner Ale (ABV 4.3%) BITTER
Oat Mill Stout (ABV 5%) STOUT
Smooth, easy-drinking stout with a fruity sweet taste that develops into a roast bitter finish with some hop, which intensifies on drinking.

Eastern Nights (ABV 5.6%) IPA
Peachy fruity aromas lead on to a sweet fruity middle which gives way to hoppy bitterness. A mouthful of complex flavours including alcohol make for an interesting beer.

Brewhouse & Kitchen SIBA

▋ Forest House, Love Street, Chester, CH1 1QY
☎ (01244) 404990 ⊕ brewhouseandkitchen.com/chester

☺Part of the national Brewhouse & Kitchen family, this brewpub is situated in a splendid building previously owned by JD Wetherspoon. As with all Brewhouse & Kitchen establishments it offers brewery experience days and beer masterclasses. ‼▛

Burtonwood

Bold Lane, Burtonwood, Warrington, WA5 4TH
☎ (01925) 220022 ⊕ thomashardybrewery.co.uk

Thomas Hardy's only brewery was acquired by Molson Coors in 2015. Currently producing no real ale, and operating solely as a contract brewer.

Chapter SIBA

Unit 2a, Sutton Quays Business Park, Clifton Road, Sutton Weaver, WA7 3EH ☎ 07908 004742
⊕ chapterbrewing.co.uk

Multi-award-winning Chapter Brewing was established in 2016 using an 11-barrel brew plant. It produces diverse 'fictional beers' inspired by literature in a range of styles. ▛♦⬧

Fossil Dinner (ABV 3.5%) GOLD
The Hay is Waiting (ABV 3.6%) BLOND
Gentle cloudy beer with malt and fruit aromas. Hops are tasted throughout gradually overtaking the sweet light-bodied centre.
Bread & Circuses (ABV 3.8%) PALE
Greatcoat (ABV 3.8%) PALE
Taller Than a House (ABV 3.9%) PALE
Runnen (ABV 4%) PALE
Blindfold Off (ABV 4.2%) BITTER
Unconsenting Soul (ABV 4.2%) GOLD
This fruity and hoppy bitter beer has plenty of impact on the palate, with sweetness drying out in the finish.
Hinges (ABV 4.3%) PALE
Practicable and Useful (ABV 4.3%) BLOND
Pemberley (ABV 4.4%) STOUT
Tilted Pieces (ABV 4.4%) PALE
Kandata (ABV 4.7%) PALE
Teeter (ABV 5.1%) PALE
That Old Rope (ABV 5.4%) PALE
Dead Man's Fist (ABV 5.5%) SPECIALITY
A complex, smoky beer with a sweet centre balancing roast flavours leading to a long peppery finish.
As Lazarus (ABV 7.2%) IPA

Coach House SIBA

Wharf Street, Howley, Warrington, WA1 2DQ
☎ (01925) 232800 ⊕ coachhousebrewery.co.uk

Established in 1991 following the closure of the Greenall Whitley Brewery earlier that year, Coach House Brewing Company is the oldest cask ale producer in Cheshire. It celebrated its 30th anniversary in 2021. With a weekly fermentation capacity of 240 barrels, it produces a core range of permanent beers, seasonal and special occasion brews, as well as an extensive range of fruit and spice beers. ♦

Coachman's Best Bitter (ABV 3.7%) BITTER
A well-hopped, malty bitter, moderately fruity with a hint of sweetness and a peppery nose.
Gunpowder Premium Mild (ABV 3.8%) MILD
Aromas of roast malts and caramel attract you to a pleasant sweet and toasty-tasting mild with a gentle finish.
Blonde (ABV 4.1%) BLOND
Cheshire Gold (ABV 4.1%) PALE
Cheshire Oak (ABV 4.1%) BITTER
Dick Turpin Best Bitter (ABV 4.2%) BITTER
Malty, hoppy pale brown beer with some initial sweetish flavours leading to a short, bitter aftertaste. Sold under other names as a pub house beer.
Blueberry Classic Bitter (ABV 5%) SPECIALITY
A sweet beer with fruity esters and tasting predominately of blueberries, finishing dry.
Post Horn Premium Pale Ale (ABV 5%) BLOND

Four Priests

2 Finney's Lane, Middlewich, CW10 9DR
⊕ fourpriests.co.uk

Start-up brewery established in 2022 and run by homebrewer-turned-professional Andy Thomason. The name originates from the carvings on the Saxon crosses in nearby Sandbach, where Andy lives. Much of the kit is from the closed GoodAll's brewery. Andy has been documenting the brewery's setup from the very start on the brewery's YouTube channel.

Moston Dragon (ABV 4%) BITTER
Cross Stout (ABV 4.2%) STOUT
Murghy Straight (ABV 4.2%) GOLD

Happy Valley

▋ 73 Oxford Road, Macclesfield, SK11 8JG
☎ (01625) 618360 ☎ 07768 107660
⊕ happyvalleybrewery.co.uk

⊗ Happy Valley was established in 2010 using a 2.5-barrel plant located in Bollington. In 2018 the brewery was sold and relocated to Macclesfield, and is based at the Happy Valley Tap & Pizza aka 73 & Pizza pub. ♦

Hush

Unit 4, Navigation Road, Northwich, CW8 1BE
☎ 07973 797500 ⊕ hushbrewing.co

☺Established in 2021 Hush has now relocated to its new premises in Northwich Town Centre. The five-barrel plant produces traditional and craft beers. Core beers, themed around the area, are distributed locally to selected free trade outfits festivals. An extended core range is planned and new beers being developed. Planning problems delayed completion and creation of the brewery tap, but a number of successful events have taken place. Tap development continues, further events are planned plus more extensive opening hours. ⬧

Coffee Session Stout (ABV 3.5%) STOUT
My Grain is Earl (ABV 3.7%) PALE
Northwich Pale Ale (ABV 4%) PALE
We Built This Citra on Rock Salts Home (ABV 4%) PALE
Weaver Las Vegas (ABV 4.3%) PALE
Beds Beneath Bitter (ABV 4.8%) BITTER

Merlin

3 Spring Bank Farm, Congleton Road, Arclid, CW11 2UD
☎ (01477) 500893 ☎ 07812 352590
⊕ merlinbrewing.co.uk

⊕Merlin started in 2010 and uses an eight-barrel plant in a modern farm unit. Beers are named on a Merlin theme, usually supplied to outlets within a 30-mile radius. The brewery is environmentally-friendly, using power from solar panels and a wind turbine, and spent water soaks away naturally through reed beds. ‼◆LIVE

Merlin's Gold (ABV 3.8%) PALE
Excalibur (ABV 3.9%) BLOND
Sweet throughout with a hoppy bitterness which takes control of the finish. Malt and fruit flavours add to the mix.
Spellbound (ABV 4%) BITTER
Avalon (ABV 4.1%) PALE
The Wizard (ABV 4.2%) PALE
Sweet fruity start with building bitterness and malt in the background. Finishes bitter with a long-lasting full mouthfeel.
Castle Black (ABV 4.4%) STOUT
Dark Magic (ABV 4.8%) MILD
Sweet malty start with plenty of roast malt flavours. Lightly hopped with the roast bitterness lingering.
Mythic IPA (ABV 5.5%) IPA
Dragonslayer (ABV 5.6%) OLD

Mobberley SIBA

Meadowside Barn, Hulme Lane, Lower Peover, WA16 9QH
☎ (01565) 873601 ⊕ mobberleybrewhouse.co.uk

Mobberley Brewhouse (MBH) started brewing as Mobberley Fine Ales in 2011 changing the name in 2015. Continued expansion has meant that it relocated to its third site in 2022. Approximately 50% of output is cask, the remainder being kegged or canned. It operates two pubs under the Project 53 name, and provides contract brewing and packaging for other breweries. ◆

Bunji (ABV 3.8%) PALE
Cheshire Pale (ABV 3.9%) PALE
1924 (ABV 4.5%) BITTER
Fruity malt aromas and taste lead on to a smooth hoppy bitter beer.
IPA (ABV 5.2%) PALE

Neighbourhood

Royal British Legion Club, St George's Road West, Poynton, SK12 1JY ☎ 07944 618869
✉ sales@neighbourhoodbrewco.com

⊕Neighbourhood Brew Co was founded in 2022. It began as a partnership between Dre Scuglia and Jake Astbury, but in early 2023 Dre left, and Corinne Goode became joint owner. Around 30 pubs, clubs and bars are supplied in the Stockport, Altrincham, Macclesfield and east Cheshire areas. ⭬◆

Telegram (ABV 3.8%) BITTER
Slow Sundays (ABV 4%) GOLD

Norton

Norton Priory, Tudor Road, Manor Park, Runcorn, WA7 1SX
☎ (01928) 577199 ☎ 07775 761114
⊕ nortonbrewing.com

Situated within the grounds of Norton Priory, the brewery was created as a social enterprise by Halton Borough Council to provide employment opportunities for people with learning disabilities, autism and other disabilities. It opened in 2011 with a 2.5-barrel plant. Beers in bottles, mini-kegs and casks are available for collection from the brewery only. ⭬

Oaks SIBA

Unit 6, Stanney Mill Industrial Estate, Dutton Green, Ellesmere Port, CH2 4SA ☎ 07526 437098
⊕ theoaksbrewing.co

Founded as Cheshire Brew Brothers in 2013 and taken into new ownership in 2017. The beers can be found in free and tied trade across North-West England and West Yorkshire. An ever-changing range of beers is produced to satisfy customer demand. ◆LIVE

Chester Gold (ABV 3.5%) GOLD
A fruity, hoppy bitter with a pleasant sweet finish.

Pied Bull

⯄ Pied Bull Hotel, 57 Northgate Street, Chester, CH1 2HQ
☎ (01244) 325829 ⊕ piedbull.co.uk

⊕Pied Bull began brewing in 2011 using a one-barrel plant. Beer is mainly for in-house consumption but local beer festivals are supplied and occasional brewery swaps occur. ◆

RedWillow SIBA

The Lodge, Sutton Garrison, Byrons Lane, Macclesfield, SK11 7JW
☎ (01625) 502315 ⊕ redwillowbrewery.com

⊕Established in 2010 by homebrewer Toby McKenzie and his wife Caroline. In 2015 brewing moved to a larger, purpose-built unit on the same site. The award-winning beers are distributed nationwide and are available from the brewery's own RedWillow bars in Macclesfield and Buxton. ◆

Headless (ABV 3.9%) PALE
Nicely-balanced with some malty sweetness. Fruit and hops show in the drinking with hop bitterness lasting to the end.
Feckless (ABV 4.1%) BITTER
Well-balanced best bitter, malt and hop in the taste with some fruit and roast flavours.
Weightless (ABV 4.2%) PALE
Well-rounded pale ale with a promise of fruit and hop at the start, full-bodied, bittersweet fruity middle and lasting finish.
Wreckless (ABV 4.8%) PALE
Hoppy fruity sweet pale ale that finishes on the drier side.
Heritage Porter (ABV 5.3%) PORTER
Sleepless (ABV 5.4%) RED
Breakfast Stout (ABV 5.6%) STOUT
A dark beer with strong aromas of chocolate, coffee and hazelnut alongside expected malt and roast. Composed to give a long smooth mouthfeel.
Smokeless (ABV 5.7%) SPECIALITY
Shameless (ABV 5.9%) IPA
Fruit and hops throughout with full-bodied sweetness and a long finish.
Restless (ABV 8.5%) SPECIALITY

Spitting Feathers SIBA

Common Farm, Waverton, CH3 7QT
☎ (01244) 332052 ☎ 07974 348325
⊕ spittingfeathers.co.uk

⊕Established in 2005, the brewery is located in a sandstone building set around a cobbled yard. Around 200 local outlets are supplied. Monthly Brewbarn sessions throughout the year include a brewery tour but tickets must be purchased in advance. ‼◆GF V

Session Beer (ABV 3.6%) PALE

Sweet malts have a consistent presence in this hoppy bitter beer.

Thirstquencher (ABV 3.9%) BLOND
A hoppy blond with citrus notes and some sweetness to balance.

Brainstorm (ABV 4%) GOLD

Special Ale (ABV 4.2%) BITTER

Old Wavertonian (ABV 4.4%) STOUT
Creamy and smooth stout. Full-flavoured with coffee notes in aroma and taste. Roast and nut flavours throughout, leading to a hoppy, bitter finish.

Rush Hour (ABV 4.5%) PALE
Sweet fruity start is quickly overtaken by hop bitterness which rises in the finish.

Empire IPA (ABV 5.2%) PALE

Storm SIBA

2 Waterside, Macclesfield, SK11 7HJ
☎ (01625) 431234 ⊕ stormbrewing.co.uk

☺Storm Brewing was founded in 1998. In 2001 it moved to its current location, an old riverside pub building. Now run by a brother and sister team, many local pubs are supplied, plus further afield. ◆LIVE

Beauforts Ale (ABV 3.8%) BITTER

Desert Storm (ABV 3.9%) BITTER

Bosley Cloud (ABV 4.1%) BLOND

Ale Force (ABV 4.2%) BITTER
Amber, smooth-tasting, complex beer that balances malt, hop and fruit on the taste, leading to a roasty, slightly sweet aftertaste.

Dexter (ABV 4.2%) GOLD

Downpour (ABV 4.3%) PALE

PGA (ABV 4.4%) SPECIALITY
Light, crisp, lager-style beer with a balance of malt, hops and fruit. Moderately bitter and slight dry aftertaste.

Hurricane Hubert (ABV 4.5%) BITTER

Silk of Amnesia (ABV 4.7%) BITTER
Smooth premium, easy-drinking bitter. Fruit and hops dominate throughout. Not too sweet, with a good lasting finish.

Isobar IPA (ABV 4.8%) PALE
Fruity (peach and apricot) aromas and taste in this sweet bodied beer that finishes with plenty of hops.

Red Mist (ABV 4.8%) BITTER

Tatton SIBA

Unit 7, Longridge Trading Estate, Knutsford, WA16 8PR
☎ (01565) 750747 ☎ 07738 150898
⊕ tattonbrewery.co.uk

☺Tatton is a family-owned business based in the heart of Cheshire. Brewing commenced in 2010 using a steam-fired, custom-built, 15-barrel brewhouse. It supplies pubs throughout Cheshire and the north-west. ‼☕◆

Session (ABV 3.7%) BITTER

XPA (ABV 3.7%) PALE

Blonde (ABV 4%) BLOND

Best (ABV 4.2%) BITTER

Black (ABV 4.5%) PORTER

Gold (ABV 4.5%) BITTER
Malt aromas lead to a well-balanced sweet and bitter beer, with hops lasting in the finish.

Tom's Tap

4-6 Thomas Street, Crewe, CW1 2BD ☎ 07931 573425
⊕ tomstapandbrewhouse.wordpress.com

Tom's Tap & Brewhouse consists of three units; brewery equipment in the first, live music and special events in

the middle, and a taproom in the third (open Thu-Sun). Cask ale is now delivered to many outlets far and wide but only keg beers are available in its own outlet. ‼◆

Weekend Project (NEW)

Meadowside Barn, Hulme Lane, Lower Peover, WA16 9QH
☎ (01565) 873601 ⊕ weekendproject.beer

Opened in 2013 by one of the directors of Mobberley Brewhouse (qv) it operates as a nomad brewery utilising both MBH kit and other breweries' plant as required. It is focussed on stronger, full-flavoured craft ales, usually in keg format.

Weetwood SIBA

The Brewery, Common Lane, Kelsall, CW6 0PY
☎ (01829) 752377 ⊕ weetwoodales.co.uk

☺Weetwood Ales, originally starting out in a barn back in 1992, now operates out of a modern 30-barrel plant close to Kelsall. Beers are available across the north-west and North Wales. Its onsite shop was remodelled into a taproom. It distils its own spirits from grain on a purpose-built sustainable site. ‼☕◆

Southern Cross (ABV 3.6%) PALE
Well-balanced pale ale with a lasting hoppy bitter finish.

Best Bitter (ABV 3.8%) BITTER
A traditional gentle bitter with a malty sweetness and a dash of fruit. The hop presence increases slightly to provide a drier finish.

Mad Hatter (ABV 3.9%) RED
A typical red beer, malty aromas lead to a fruity sweet middle backed up with a bitter finish.

Cheshire Cat (ABV 4%) BLOND
Gentle hoppy blond beer with dominating sweetness.

Eastgate (ABV 4.2%) BITTER
Well-balanced and refreshing clean amber beer. Citrus fruit flavours predominate in the taste and there is a short, dry aftertaste.

Oregon Pale (ABV 4.3%) BITTER
Malty, fruity and hoppy mouthfeel with a sweet centre and a lasting finish of hop bitterness.

Old Dog (ABV 4.5%) BITTER
Well-balanced amber beer. Malt, roast and fruit flavours are balanced by bitterness and sweetness.

Jester IPA (ABV 4.8%) PALE

Wincle SIBA

Tolls Farm Barn, Dane Bridge, Wincle, SK11 0QE
☎ (01260) 227777 ⊕ winclebeer.co.uk

☺Wincle Beer Co was set up in 2008, a 15-barrel plant is used. The beers are brewed using water from its own borehole. Its shop is housed in a converted stable next to the brewery. A monthly tap night is held on the evening of the first Friday. Check website for other events. ‼☕◆◆

Straight Furrow (ABV 3.7%) BITTER

Waller (ABV 3.8%) BLOND

Hen Cloud (ABV 3.9%) BLOND

Sir Philip (ABV 4.2%) BITTER
Malty aromas with some caramel. Hops come forward in the taste providing a dry finish.

Wibbly Wallaby (ABV 4.4%) BITTER

Life Of Riley (ABV 4.8%) BITTER

Burke's Special (ABV 5%) BITTER

Contract brewed for Brew Foundation:

Little Bitter That (ABV 3.8%) BITTER

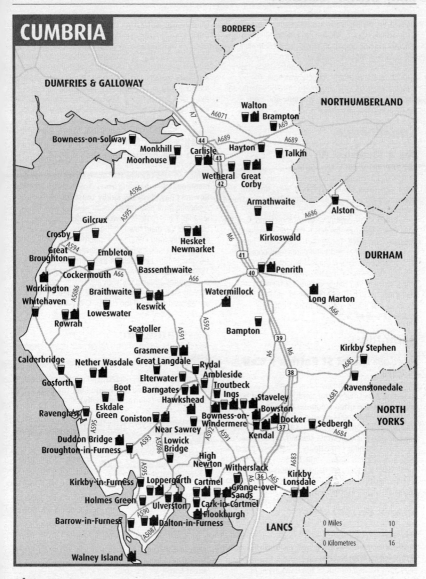

CUMBRIA

ENGLAND

Alston

Cumberland Inn L

Townfoot, CA9 3HX

☎ (01434) 381875 ⊕ cumberlandalston.co.uk
Firebrick Pagan Queen; 2 changing beers Ⓗ
This 19th-century inn overlooks the South Tyne river.
Close to the Coast-to-Coast cycle route and Pennine Way,
it is an ideal base to explore the highest market town in
England. The Cumberland has won many local CAMRA
awards, including cider awards, and always has a wide
selection of beers, ciders and perries to choose from.
Guest beers are dispensed from four handpumps. It was
refurbished over winter 2022 to provide a second bar.
Q❀☙✑❀⓿❀P🖵❀❄

Ambleside

Golden Rule

Smithy Brow, LA22 9AS

☎ (015394) 32257 ⊕ goldenrule-ambleside.co.uk
**Robinsons Wizard, Dizzy Blonde, Cumbria Way,
Cascade IPA; 3 changing beers (sourced regionally;
often Robinsons)** Ⓗ
The name epitomises the pub: it is a golden rule that
Lakeland visitors beat a path to the door, despite the
struggle up the hill, and a time-honoured tradition that
the pub will feature in the Guide. Although a basic old
inn, the pub has a cosy feel. It serves a good range of
well-kept Robinsons ales, which occasionally include its
Old Tom. The separate snug room is handy for families on
wet days and a rear courtyard has outdoor tables.
Q❀☙❀✦♣🖵❀❄

Royal Oak L ✔

Lake Road, LA22 9BU

☎ (015394) 33382
**Greene King IPA, Abbot; 6 changing beers (sourced
locally; often Kirkby Lonsdale, Theakston, Timothy
Taylor)** Ⓗ

Right in the centre of town and definitely best-in-class for a national chain, this popular Greene King pub features at least one local brewer on the bar alongside the usual offerings. The staff are welcomingly efficient and the small outside patio with jumbrellas is busy throughout the year with people watchers. The reasonably-priced food is from a centralised menu and always looks tasty. Dogs are welcome and even encouraged. ☺️🕸️🌐♿♣🚲🐾🛜♪

Armathwaite

Fox & Pheasant ✅
CA4 9PY

☎ (016974) 72162 ⊕ foxandpheasantarmathwaite.co.uk

Robinsons Dizzy Blonde, Cumbria Way, Unicorn; 1 changing beer (sourced nationally; often Hawkshead, Robinsons) Ⓗ

Atmospheric 17th-century coaching inn overlooking the River Eden. The main bar has a flagstone floor and an inglenook fire place. The former stables have been converted into a bar and eating area, and booking is recommended if dining. Original wooden beams, exposed stonework and stable stalls all add to the ambience, and you can be assured of friendly, welcoming service. The guest beer is usually a Robinsons seasonal, but others are now more frequently seen. ☺️🕸️🛏️🕙⬅♣🍴🅿️🐾🛜

Bampton

Mardale Inn at St Patrick's Well Ⓛ
CA10 2RQ

☎ (01931) 719202 ⊕ themardaleinn.com

Cumbrian Ales Loweswater Gold; 1 changing beer (sourced locally; often Cumbrian Ales) Ⓗ

A typical whitewashed Lakeland pub overlooking the Bampton valley and situated in a small hamlet close to Haweswater, it is well worth seeking out. It is now a successful Community Free House offering good local ale, food, and welcome to everyone. Recently refurbished to a high standard, there are flagstone floors and open fires. Lakeland pictures and photos include features about the nearby red squirrels. Four cosy en-suite rooms are ideal for walkers and cyclists. The Gents facility is an amusing conundrum. Q☺️🕸️🛏️🕙♿♣🅿️🐾🛜

Barngates

Drunken Duck Inn Ⓛ
LA22 0NG (signed off the B5286 Hawkshead to Ambleside road)

☎ (015394) 36347 ⊕ drunkenduckinn.co.uk

Barngates Cat Nap, Cracker, Tag Lag; 3 changing beers (sourced locally; often Barngates) Ⓗ

High above Ambleside, this traditional Lakeland dwelling reflects the simplicity, beauty and longevity of its natural environment. Water from the fells is drawn for their beers, brewed on-site by Barngates brewery. The bar has six handpumps and serves all of the Barngates beers in rotation. The outside seating area at the front offers dramatic views of the fells to the north-east. Dogs are allowed, except in the dining room.
Q☺️🕸️🕙♿🅿️🐾🛜

Barrow-in-Furness

Duke of Edinburgh Ⓛ ✅
Abbey Road, LA14 5QR

☎ (01229) 821039 ⊕ dukeofedinburghhotel.co.uk

Lancaster Amber, Blonde, Red; 5 changing beers (sourced regionally) Ⓗ

On the edge of the town centre near the station, the Duke is not as noisy as similar bars in the town. It has an airy feel with modern, comfortable furniture and a fine open fire. Paintings by local artists are displayed around the walls. Good-quality, reasonably priced bar meals are available; there is also a separate restaurant. Beers are mainly from Lancaster brewery, with guest ales plus three craft keg ales, and bottled beers from around the world. ☺️🛏️🕙♿⬅🅿️🚲🐾🛜

King's Arms Hawcoat Ⓛ
Quarry Brow, Hawcoat, LA14 4HY

☎ (01229) 828137

Cumbrian Ales Loweswater Gold; Kirkby Lonsdale Monumental; 4 changing beers (sourced locally; often Bowness Bay, Keswick, Kirkby Lonsdale) Ⓗ

A popular local pub, conveniently situated near the number 1 bus route in Hawcoat Village which runs between the main town centre and the hospital. It sells ales mainly from Cumbrian microbreweries, with a beer menu on a chalkboard listing forthcoming attractions. The pub, which has been on these premises since the 1860s, has been extensively extended and renovated, and features an open bar with adjacent separate rooms. Friendly staff give a warm welcome. Well-behaved dogs are allowed in one of the rooms. Q☺️♿♣🐾🛜

Bassenthwaite

Sun Inn
CA12 4QP

☎ (017687) 76439 ⊕ suninnbassenthwaite.co.uk

Jennings Cumberland Ale; house beer (by Banks's); 1 changing beer (sourced nationally) Ⓗ

REAL ALE BREWERIES

Barngates Barngates
Bowness Bay ◆ Kendal
Brack'N'Brew 🍺 Watermillock
Carlisle Carlisle
Coastline Walney Island (NEW)
Coniston 🍺 Coniston
Cumbrian Hawkshead
Eden River Penrith
Ennerdale ◆ Rowrah
Fell Flookburgh
Gan Yam ◆ Kendal
Grasmere Grasmere
Great Corby Great Corby
Handsome Bowston
Hawkshead ◆ Staveley
Healey's 🍺 Loppergarth
Hesket Newmarket Hesket Newmarket
Keswick ◆ Keswick
Kirkby Lonsdale ◆ Kirkby Lonsdale
Lakes ◆ Kendal
Langdale Docker
Logan Beck Duddon Bridge
Old Friends 🍺 Ulverston
Old Vicarage ◆ Walton
Shaws of Grange Grange-over-Sands
Strands 🍺 Nether Wasdale
Tirril Long Marton
Townhouse Dalton-in-Furness
Tractor Shed ◆ Workington
Ulverston 🍺 Ulverston
Unsworth's Yard ◆ Cartmel
Westmorland Kendal
Wild Boar 🍺 Bowness-on-Windermere
Windermere 🍺 Ings

Traditional 16th century pub located in the picturesque village of Bassenthwaite. There are original oak beams and an open fire which add to the quaint ambiance. Two regular beers and a seasonal guest ale, plus a wide range of malt whiskies and gins are available. The pub offers formal and informal dining, with food being locally sourced wherever possible. This community-focused pub offers a warm welcome to visitors and locals alike. Q✿❄➍❂⬤P✿❂

Boot

Woolpack Inn 🅛

CA19 1TH (¾ mile E of Boot village on approach to Hardknott Pass)
☎ (019467) 23230 ⬤ woolpack.co.uk
6 changing beers (sourced nationally; often Fyne, Tractor Shed, Windermere) 🅗

A family-run pub, the Woolpack's friendly atmosphere makes it is popular with tourists, walkers, families and locals. There is a refurbished traditional bar and restaurant, vodka bar, wood-burning stoves, a range of real ales, ciders and wine, and its Hardknott Café boasts a wood-fired pizza oven. The pub participates in the annual Boot Beer Festival held in June, when over 100 beers are sold by four pubs. Q✿❄➍❂⬤➍➤(Dalegarth for Boot)♣⬤P➍❂❂♫

Bowness-on-Solway

King's Arms

CA7 5AF
☎ (016973) 51426 ⬤ kingsarmsbowness.co.uk
2 changing beers (sourced nationally; often Jennings, Marston's) 🅗

Situated in the centre of the village, the King's Arms is a popular stopping-off point for visitors walking the Hadrian's Wall route. A true community pub, it has a library, band practice every other Sunday and a regular quiz on Thursday nights, and hosts pool, darts and domino teams. Set on the Solway coast in an Area of Outstanding Natural Beauty it is popular with bird-watchers and cyclists as well as walkers. Snacks are available thoughout the day in summer. Q✿❄➍❂♣P❂❂

Braithwaite

Coledale Inn

CA12 5TN (at top of village, off Whinlatter Pass)
☎ (017687) 78272 ⬤ coledale-inn.co.uk
3 changing beers (sourced locally; often Tirril, Tractor Shed) 🅗

The Coledale Inn was built in 1824 as a woollen mill, later becoming a pencil mill. This late Georgian building became a hotel in the 1970s, prior to which it had been a country club with accommodation. It has been in the hands of the same family for about 40 years. The hotel has two bars, 20 en-suite rooms and great views across Braithwaite to Skiddaw. Q✿❄➍❂⬤➍♣P➍(X5,77A)❂❂

Brampton

Howard Arms ✔

Front Street, CA8 1NG
☎ (016977) 42758 ⬤ howardarms.co.uk
Thwaites IPA, Gold, Amber; house beer (by Thwaites) 🅗

A modernised 18th-century country inn situated in the town centre; Charles Dickens is reputed to have slept here. There is a separate games room upstairs and

meeting and function rooms are available. Four handpumps dispense beers from the Thwaites range including one badged as Howard Arms. Breakfasts are served daily and the main menu shows a commitment to local produce and homemade cooking. ✿❄➍❂➍♣P➍(685)❂❂♫

Broughton-in-Furness

Manor Arms 🍷 🅛

The Square, LA20 6HY
☎ (01229) 716286 ⬤ manorarmsthesqaure.co.uk
Great Corby Blonde; Townhouse Charter; 5 changing beers (sourced regionally) 🅗

An outstanding free house owned by the Varty family for more than 30 years. Set in an attractive Georgian square, it has been the recipient of many CAMRA awards. Real ale dominates, always including a dark beer, and the bar also serves traditional cider and perry, making every day a mini beer festival. Two fires keep the pub warm and the bar staff are always friendly. Q✿❄➍❂♣➍❂❂

Calderbridge

Stanley Arms Hotel

CA20 1DN (on the A595)
☎ (01946) 841235 ⬤ stanleyarmshotel.com
Wychwood Hobgoblin Gold; 2 changing beers (sourced nationally; often Hawkshead, Tractor Shed) 🅗

This small village hotel is situated just inside the Lake District National Park. The pub has 14 en-suite rooms and offers a conference facility, popular restaurant, two bars and probably the best river-fronted beer garden in Cumbria. A minimum of two, but more often four ales are available, usually Wychwood Hobgoblin Gold and Ennerdale Blonde. Hearty meals, freshly-cooked with locally sourced foods wherever possible, are available every day. Q✿❄➍❂➍♣P❂❂

Cark-in-Cartmel

Engine Inn 🅛 ✔

LA11 7NZ
☎ (015395) 58341 ⬤ theengineinncartmel.co.uk
Lancaster Blonde; Timothy Taylor Landlord; 2 changing beers (sourced nationally) 🅗

A 17th-century inn, refurbished in 2010, making an excellent end to the walk from Grange described in CAMRA's Lake District Pub Walks book. Beers are selected to provide a range of styles. There is an open bar area with a cosy fire, separate rooms away from the bar and a riverside beer garden. Five en-suite rooms are available. Opening hours and food services times are reduced in winter. ❄➍❂➍➤(Cark & Cartmel)♣❂❂♫

Carlisle

301 Miles From London

Carlisle Citadel Station, Court Square, CA1 1QZ
☎ (01228) 593301
6 changing beers 🅗

Situated within Carlisle railway station on platform four, this railway pub and café is well placed for the Settle to Carlisle terminus. The location has served a number of purposes, including being the station buffet in the 1950s, and the pub features much of the fabric of the old building and other railway heritage, including the original stone fireplaces. It is named 301 Miles From London because Carlisle folklore claims that this is the distance from the capital, although it is actually thought to be 299 miles. ➍❂➤⬤➍❂♫

King's Head 🗓

Fisher Street, CA3 8RF
🌐 kingsheadcarlisle.co.uk
Cumbrian Ales Esthwaite Bitter; 3 changing beers (sourced regionally) 🅷
An excellent city centre pub, and winner of many CAMRA awards, it serves a range of guest ales from four handpumps. Pictures of old Carlisle adorn the internal walls and outside is an explanation as to why the city isn't in the Domesday Book. Good-value meals are served at lunchtime. The covered outdoor courtyard has a largescreen TV and regularly features live music. No children or dogs allowed. 🏵🕽🛒🚐🐾🏧🎵

Milbourne Arms

150 Milbourne Street, CA2 5XB
☎ (01228) 541194
2 changing beers (sourced locally) 🅷
Cosy and friendly single-room pub arranged around a central bar. This is a former State Management pub which, when built in 1853, served the thriving surrounding textile industry. Hand looms, spinning wheels, bobbins and shuttles from Linton Tweeds which would have been used in the nearby mills are to be found throughout the pub, along with archive photos of the industry. It is just 12 minutes' walk from Carlisle train station and is on local bus routes. 🐶🕽🛒🚐🏧🎵

Spinners Arms 🗓

Cummersdale, CA2 6BD
☎ (01228) 532928 🌐 thespinnersarms.org.uk
Carlisle Spun Gold, Flaxen, Magic Number; 1 changing beer (sourced locally; often Carlisle) 🅷
Cosy family-friendly hostelry, an original Redfern pub with unique and original features. It is situated less than half a mile from Carlisle's south-western boundary, close to the Cumbrian Way and National Cycle Route 7, which run alongside the picturesque River Caldew. There is regular live music, with Irish music sessions every first and third Wednesday. Children are welcome until evening and well-behaved dogs are permitted. The pub is the brewery tap for Carlisle Brewing Co, showcasing their beer on three pumps. 🐶🏵🛒♣🚐(75)🏧🎵

Sportsman Inn ✅

Heads Lane, CA3 8AQ
☎ (01228) 533799
Timothy Taylor Landlord; Wainwright; 1 changing beer 🅷
The oldest recorded pub in Carlisle, dating from 1747, there is a copy of a 15th century map of the area on display in the pub which suggests there was a building on the site at that time. It has a single, large room. The Sportsman was formerly a State Management pub – a plaque above the bar states it was part of the scheme between August 1916 and May 1973. 🐶🏵🕽🛒♣🚐🏧

Woodrow Wilson 🗓 ✅

48 Botchergate, CA1 1QS
☎ (01228) 819942
Great Corby Blonde; Greene King Abbot; Ruddles Best Bitter; Sharp's Doom Bar; Wainwright; 7 changing beers (sourced nationally; often Great Corby, Theakston, Thornbridge) 🅷
One of two almost adjacent Wetherspoons, this pub is in a refurbished Co-op building named after the former US president, whose mother was born in Carlisle. Up to 14 handpumps offer the largest range of real ales to be found in Carlisle. Food is available all day. At the rear there is a spacious outdoor seating area, heated patio and smokers' area. Children are welcome in some areas until evening. 🐶🏵🕽🛒🚐♿P🚐🏧

Cartmel

Royal Oak Inn 🗓

The Square, LA11 6QB
☎ (015395) 36692
Fell Ghyll, Crag; 3 changing beers (sourced nationally; often Fell) 🅷
A traditional village inn, located in the village square, within five minutes' walk of the famous priory and racecourse. A firm favourite with locals and tourists alike, the meals, decor and atmosphere are all excellent. A welcoming log fire and oak beams, some so low as to carry headroom warnings, give a rustic appeal. The extensive enclosed riverside garden at the rear is an attraction for families. Q🐶🏵🕽🛒🚐(530,532) 🏧🎵

Unsworth Yard Brewery 🗓

4 Unsworth's Yard, LA11 6PG
☎ 07810 461313 🌐 unsworthsyard.co.uk/brewery
Unsworth's Yard Crusader Gold; 3 changing beers (sourced locally; often Bowness Bay, Unsworth's Yard) 🅷
This tasting room sits at the front of a five-barrel brewery, with up to three of the brewery's beers available at all times. The room, which is available for functions by appointment, opens out on to a courtyard with extensive outdoor seating. High-quality bread and cheese shops, as well as a shop specialising in fine wines, surround the rest of the courtyard, giving this area an almost continental ambience. 🏵🚐♿🚐(532,530)🎵

Cockermouth

Cock & Bull

7 South Street, CA13 9RT (centre of town opp Sainsbury's)
☎ (01900) 827999 🌐 thenewcockandbull.co.uk
Coniston Bluebird Bitter; Great Corby Blonde, Fox Brown Ale; 2 changing beers (sourced regionally) 🅷
A community pub in the centre of town. It does not serve food, apart from bar snacks, but has a constantly changing range of real ales on two of the handpumps, mainly from smaller Cumbrian breweries. The venue is on three levels, with the main area having bar stools and two seating areas, with a TV showing sports in the front corner. The top level has pool table and dartboard. Below this, off the main bar, is a small, quieter room. 🐶🏵🚐🏧🎵

Swan Inn 🗓

52-56 Kirkgate, CA13 9PH
☎ (01900) 822425 🌐 swaninncockermouth.com
Banks's Amber Ale; Marston's 61 Deep; Wainwright, Amber; Wychwood Hobgoblin Gold; 1 changing beer (sourced nationally) 🅷
A true community pub, a short walk from the centre of the town and well supported by locals. This 17th-century inn has flagged floors, exposed beams, a real fire and quiet nooks and crannies. There are six handpumps with all of the beers served from the Marston's portfolio. A largescreen TV at the back of the pub is used for showing sports. It hosts a monthly whisky club and folk music sessions. Q🐶♣🚐🏧🎵

Coniston

Black Bull Inn & Hotel 🗓

LA21 8DU
☎ (015394) 41668 🌐 blackbullconiston.co.uk
Coniston Oliver's Light Ale, Bluebird Bitter, Bluebird Premium XB, Old Man Ale, Special Oatmeal Stout, No

9 Barley Wine; 3 changing beers (sourced locally; often Coniston) Ⓗ
Coniston Brewing Company's on-site taphouse is this 16th-century coaching inn, also serving good food in traditional comfortable surroundings. A full menu is served from noon. Six regular beers are supplemented by other beers from the brewery on a rotation basis – try a tasting paddle. The spacious bar and lounge are frequented by tourists in this popular, spectacular location near Coniston Old Man. The outside seating area is perfect in summer. Dogs are not allowed in the restaurant. ⏱☸🏨◖Ⓓ⅃♣Ⓟ🚃(X12,505)🐾🐱🛜

Crosby

Stag Inn ✅
Lowside, CA15 6SH
☎ (01900) 812549 ⊕ staginncrosby.com
Greene King IPA; Timothy Taylor Landlord Ⓗ
Popular with locals and visitors alike, the Stag is a welcoming pub located in a quiet village that has commanding views over the Solway Firth to the Scottish hills. There is a large central bar with two serving points, plus a dining area and some quiet corners. An extensive menu to suit all tastes is offered, with much of the produce sourced locally, but there are lots of tables for drinkers only. Q⏱☸◖Ⓓ♣Ⓟ🚃(300)🐾🛜

Dalton-in-Furness

Clarence
33 Ulverston Road, LA15 8EF
☎ 07974 467615
2 changing beers (sourced nationally; often Bowness Bay) Ⓗ
You will receive a warm welcome from all in this recently refurbished, friendly and community-focused pub. They are enthusiastic about cask ales; aiming to showcase local breweries. The pub has regular music sessions, and enthusiastic teams who compete in the local darts and pool leagues. Check their Facebook for details of special and charity events. ≥(Dalton)♣Ⓟ(6,X6)🐾🛜🎵

Elterwater

Britannia Inn ⓛ ✅
LA22 9HP
☎ (015394) 37210 ⊕ britinn.co.uk
Langdale Elterwater Gold; house beer (by Coniston); 3 changing beers (sourced locally; often Eden River, Langdale, Barngates) Ⓗ
A brilliant, friendly and deservedly popular pub, its small rooms soon fill up, and the benches in front play host to walkers and their dogs most days of the year. Beers, mostly local, are always in great condition, and include some from sister business Langdale brewery. Food is available all day, with dining-room bookings advised (by telephone) for the evening meal. For those who can walk no further, there are nine bedrooms at the pub, or the 516 bus stops just outside.
⏱☸🏨◖Ⓓ⅃Ⓐ♣Ⓟ🚃(516) 🐾🛜

Embleton

Embleton Spa
CA13 9YA (just off A66 in Embleton village)
☎ (017687) 76606 ⊕ embletonspa.co.uk
Cumbrian Ales Loweswater Gold; 1 changing beer (sourced locally) Ⓗ
Originally an 18th-century Lakeland farmhouse, this luxury hotel with swimming pool and leisure facilities, is set in a lovely location. Two well-kept changing ales are

served in the modern bar, which has a wood-burning stove. The large south-facing outdoor drinking area affords views of the local fells. An extensive menu is available, using local produce where possible and changing seasonally. ⏱☸🏨◖Ⓓ⅃Ⓟ🚃(X4,X5)🐾🛜

Eskdale Green

Bower House Inn
CA19 1TD (short walk from Irton Road station La'al Ratty)
☎ (019467) 23244 ⊕ bowerhouseinn.com
2 changing beers (sourced nationally; often Cumbrian Ales, Hawkshead, Timothy Taylor) Ⓗ
Nestled between Mitredale and Muncaster Fell, the Bower House Inn is a charming coaching inn dating back to 1751. Close to Scafell Pike and Wastwater, England's deepest lake, it is ideally situated to take full advantage of these stunning surroundings. The house beer, Bower House Ale, is brewed by Great Corby brewery and there are four other changing ales.
Q⏱☸🏨◖Ⓓ⅃Ⓐ≥(Irton Road)♣🐶🐾🛜

Gilcrux

Mason's Arms
CA7 2QX
☎ (016973) 23267
Courage Best Bitter; Theakston Best Bitter; 1 changing beer (sourced locally) Ⓗ
Friendly two-bar local pub with a television in one bar. The building, with reclaimed ships' timbers in its structure, dates back to 1865 and was originally a boot and shoe makers. It boasts a large fireplace with wood-burning stove, exposed beams and a fish tank built into a wall. Outside is a beer garden. Closed on Mondays except bank holidays. Q⏱☸◖Ⓓ⅃♣Ⓟ🐾🛜

Gosforth

Gosforth Hall Inn
Wasdale Road, CA20 1AZ (from A595 follow signpost to Wasdale; adjacent to St Mary's church)
☎ (019467) 25322 ⊕ gosforthhall.co.uk
4 changing beers (sourced nationally) Ⓗ
Gosforth Hall is a mid-17th century Grade II-listed building set in attractive surroundings at the edge of this West Lakeland village, close to Wasdale. The lounge reputedly has the widest-spanning sandstone hearth in England. In winter there are real fires in both bar and lounge. The menu is changed every two days but always features a selection of the landlord's home made pies. Q⏱☸🏨◖Ⓓ⅃♣Ⓟ🐾🛜

Grange-over-Sands

Keg & Kitchen ⓛ
Main Street, LA11 6AB
☎ (015395) 83003 ⊕ kegandkitchen.co.uk
Unsworth's Yard Sir Edgar Harrington's Last Wolf; Wainwright; 2 changing beers (sourced locally; often Bowness Bay, Unsworth's Yard) Ⓗ
Situated in the centre of Grange opposite the Post Office, the main bar and entrance of this family-run pub are on the middle floor. The upstairs has been converted to a games area containing a pool table. The lower area, called the Gin Pig, can be accessed from the pub or from a separate entrance and hosts open mic and cinema nights. It is also available for hire.
⏱☸◖⅃Ⓐ≥♣🚃🐾🛜🎵

Grasmere

Tweedies Bar & Lodge L

Red Bank Road, LA22 9SW

☎ (015394) 35300 ⊕ tweediesgrasmere.com

Cumbrian Ales Loweswater Gold; Coniston Old Man Ale; 10 changing beers (sourced nationally; often Coniston, Thornbridge, Track) H

The long-standing bar manager, Alex, is a self-confessed beer enthusiast, as demonstrated by the expertly curated and ever-changing list. Fortunately the selection of beers can be researched daily on the website; as well as the stars waiting in the wings. Few customers will manage to sample every beer on offer, whether cask or craft keg, but it's a fun challenge. Regular live music creates impromptu party evenings.

ॐ❀⇔◖❺⚅⬝P☰(555,599) ❀ 중 ♫

Great Broughton

Punch Bowl Inn

19 Main Street, CA13 0YJ

☎ (01900) 267070 ⊕ thepunchbowl.org

3 changing beers (sourced nationally) H

This small community pub, originally a 17th-century coaching inn, is run by a committee of local volunteers. It always has two locally sourced, often Cumbrian, beers which constantly change. Although it has limited opening hours, they are more than compensated for by the quality and variety of the real ales served. A guest beer weekend is held in February. CAMRA Cumbria Pub of the Year 2022. Q⑤♣P❀ 중

Great Corby

Queen Inn L

The Green, CA4 8LR

☎ (01228) 832032 ⊕ thequeeninn-greatcorby.co.uk

Great Corby Corby Ale, Blonde; 1 changing beer (sourced locally) H

Refurbished village pub over two storeys with two restaurant areas. Operating more like a restaurant than a pub, booking is essential if you wish to eat. There is a separate room for Sky sports, a conference room available and a private dining room. It serves a range of ales from the next door Great Corby Brewhouse, and occasionally hosts live music. Q⑤❀◖❺P❀ 중

Great Langdale

Old Dungeon Ghyll Hotel L

LA22 9JY

☎ (015394) 37272 ⊕ odg.co.uk

Cumbrian Ales Loweswater Gold; 5 changing beers (sourced locally; often Barngates, Fell, Cumbrian Ales) H

It may be a basic hostelry but the beer always hits the spot! The Hikers' Bar is attached to the Old Dungeon Ghyll Hotel at the narrow end of the Langdale Valley. It is in a stunningly beautiful location beneath the surrounding fells and is naturally popular with walkers. Local ales are featured on the bar alongside a basic food offering. Tables in the garden give the best views. The bus from Ambleside is an added bonus for the less-active visitor. Q⑤❀⇔◖❺⚅P☰(516) ❀ 중 ♫

Hayton

Stone Inn

CA8 9HR

☎ (01228) 670896 ⊕ stoneinnhayton.co.uk

2 changing beers (sourced locally) H

A traditional family-run pub situated in the village of Hayton, community-focused and home to the local leek club. There is an upstairs dining room which can be hired for small gatherings. A fine pair of 1904 Christ Church boat club oars adorn one wall; ask to see the CAMRA mirror. There is usually a choice of two real ales at weekends, occasionally from a local brewery. ॐ◖♣P❀ 중

Hesket Newmarket

Old Crown L ✔

CA7 8JG

☎ (016974) 78288 ⊕ theoldcrownpub.co.uk

Hesket Newmarket Haystacks, Black Sail, Helvellyn Gold, Doris' 90th Birthday Ale, Brim Fell IPA; 4 changing beers (sourced locally) H

Sitting in the heart of this lovely fellside village, the Old Crown is a showcase for the Hesket Newmarket brewery, which is immediately behind the pub. It is well known as the first co-operatively owned pub in the country and is popular with locals and visitors alike, with Prince (now King) Charles and Sir Chris Bonnington among its supporters. Opening hours are subject to change, please check the pub website before travelling.

Q⑤❀◖♣❀❀ 중

High Newton

Heft L

Newton in Cartmel, LA11 6JH (turn off High Newton bypass into hamlet; pub is in the centre, near X6 bus stop) SD402829

☎ (015395) 30017 ⊕ hefthighnewton.co.uk

4 changing beers (sourced locally; often Farm Yard, Fell, Lakes) H

This village local with a large restaurant area is worth a detour off the A590 High Newton bypass or a stop off the X6 bus from Kendal to Barrow-in-Furness. The three regular local ales are complemented by a varied selection of beers, both local and from further afield, across a range of styles. Excellent locally produced food is also served. Disabled access to the pub is via a door at the rear, which also leads to the restaurant area. Q⑤❀⇔◖❺⚅P☰(X6) ❀ 중

Holmes Green

Black Dog Inn L

Broughton Road, LA15 8JP (1½ miles from Dalton-in-Furness Tudor Square on Broughton Rd towards Askam) SD233761

☎ (01229) 316234 ⊕ blackdoginndalton.co.uk

Cumbrian Ales Esthwaite Bitter, Langdale, Loweswater Gold; 5 changing beers (sourced nationally; often Abbeydale, Cumbrian Ales, Oakham) H

This former coaching inn, with two real fires, quarry tiled floor and rustic beams, was recently refurbished but retains plenty of character, and a warm welcome awaits from the landlord and locals alike. With five real ales on offer, there is also live music monthly. The Dog Fest music festival is usually held on the Sunday of the August bank holiday weekend. Outside there is a decked seating area. ॐ❀⇔⚅♣P❀ 중 ♫

Ings

Watermill Inn L

LA8 9PY

☎ (01539) 821309 ⊕ watermillinn.co.uk

Windermere Collie Wobbles, A Bit'er Ruff, Windermere Blonde; 8 changing beers (sourced locally; often Windermere) ⊞
A converted watermill that has Windermere brewery as its beating heart, this village pub with rooms is a long-established gateway to the Lakes. The many beers have dog-themed names and, unsurprisingly, guests with four legs are as welcome as those with two and the menus cater for both, as do the bedrooms. There is a nearby campsite and the Lakes 555 bus stops outside – handy if you're sampling the renowned Shih Tzu Faced at 7% ABV. Q✿☆⇄🍴◑♿♣♠P🚍🐾🐕🛈🎜

Kendal

Factory Tap 🅛
5 Aynam Road, LA9 7DE
☎ (015394) 82541 ⊕ thefactorytap.co.uk
Fyne Jarl; 9 changing beers (sourced nationally; often Brass Castle, Fell, Gan Yam) ⊞
The name might conjure images of a brewery in an industrial unit, but this is a friendly, welcoming, pub-like place, with mostly local beers on numerous handpumps and keg taps. The changing beers are carefully chosen. Pizzas are available every Tuesday and Friday, with street food on the last Saturday of the month; see social media for details of this and tap takeovers. Your short walk from the town centre will be well rewarded, but be careful of the traffic. ☆✿◑♿P🚍🐾🛈🎜

Fell Bar 🅛
3 Lowther Street, LA9 4DH
☎ 07904 488014 ⊕ fellbrewery.co.uk
Fell Ghyll; 11 changing beers (sourced regionally; often Fyne, Gan Yam, Fell) ⊞
Fell brewery now has three tap bars and a pub to showcase its interesting range of hand-crafted cask and keg beers – this is the original trailblazer bar and always does it well. Ticked away down down Lowther Street, this four-storey house by the Town Hall has a bar at street level, music and events on the first floor and Jim's Pizza on the top. Underground is the extensive cellar and small toilets. The staff are enthusiastic and knowledgeable. ☆◑⇄♣♠🐾🛈🎜

Indie Craft Beer 🅛
32 Finkle Street, LA9 4AB
☎ (01539) 721450 ⊕ indiecraftbeer.co.uk
Lakes Pale Ale; 12 changing beers (sourced nationally; often Cloudwater, Northern Monk, Arbor) ⊞
Kendal's first craft keg bar has expanded into cask ales from local brewers. The owner personally tastes and selects every beer, so can answer all questions about live keg. Ranging over three floors, the micropub gives a nod to Manchester with its music and decor. Outside tables in the pedestrianised street are great for watching the world go by on sunny days. There may be a youthful vibe, but all beer lovers are welcome.
✿⇄♠🚍(555,X6) 🐾🛈🎜

New Union 🅛
159 Stricklandgate, LA9 4RF
☎ (01539) 726019 ⊕ thenewunion.co.uk
Fyne Jarl; 4 changing beers (sourced regionally; often Kirkby Lonsdale, Thornbridge, Bowness Bay) ⊞
Formerly a 'jack shop', the New Union was established as an inn in 1823. A crash course in drink on every visit, the award-winning Union holds regular tastings of beers, ciders and whiskies along with occasional Meet the Brewer events. The website has a useful calendar listing everything on offer, including live music, quizzes and much more. The four handpumps serve northern beers

and the two keg lines ring the changes. Cider and perry have their own menu, but draught is usually on the board. National Cider Pub of the Year 2019.
☆✿⇄♣♠P🚍(555) 🐾🛈🎜

Keswick

Dog & Gun ✅
2 Lake Road, CA12 5BT
☎ (017687) 73463
Cumbrian Ales Loweswater Gold; Greene King Abbot; Theakston Old Peculier; 5 changing beers (sourced nationally) ⊞
Open plan, olde-worlde pub in the centre of Keswick attracting visitors and locals alike – it can be very busy. There are eight handpumps, mostly serving Cumbrian beers, housed on a long bar. Slate and wooden floors, wooden beams and an open fireplace add to the character of the pub, which is renowned for its goulash. It regularly supports charities. ☆◑♣♠🚍🐾🛈🎜

Fox Tap 🅛
Brewery Lane, CA12 5BY
☎ (017687) 80700 ⊕ keswickbrewery.co.uk
Keswick Gold, Fox Pale; 5 changing beers (sourced locally) ⊞
Situated just outside the town centre, there has been a brewery on the site since 1875. The Fox serves all the Keswick brewery beers with six cask ales and four keg beers typically on offer, and staff will guide drinkers through the beers if required. Brewery tours are available, usually on Saturdays, and need to be pre-booked. There is an outside seating area and monthly social events are held. Dogs are welcome. Q✿♿P🎜

Wainwright 🅛
Lake Road, CA12 5BZ
☎ (017687) 44927 ⊕ thewainwright.pub
Fell Tinderbox IPA; 6 changing beers (sourced nationally; often Marston's) ⊞
With a distinctive black-and-white frontage and oak flooring within, this walkers' pub comprises two drinking areas served by an L-shaped bar. The interior is mountain themed with Wainwright memorabilia, and has a cosy ambience. The pub has a good reputation for food in terms of quality, quantity and price. Both beer and food are mostly Cumbrian sourced, and there is a map on display showing where the beers are from. A gluten-free beer is always on offer. Q☆✿◑♣♠🚍🐾🛈🎜

Kirkby Lonsdale

Orange Tree 🅛 ✅
9 Fairbank, LA6 2BD (turn left past the churchyard, pub is on your right)
☎ (015242) 71716 ⊕ theorangetreehotel.co.uk
Kirkby Lonsdale Singletrack, Monumental; 3 changing beers (sourced locally; often Kirkby Lonsdale, Bowness Bay, Handsome) ⊞
Formerly the Fleece, this warmly welcoming pub is near the church, in a peaceful part of this bustling little town. Six handpumps on the bar have Kirkby Lonsdale beers and usually one local guest. A still cider is also available. There's accommodation in six en-suite rooms and a strong food offering. The owner's love of Rugby Union is reflected in the Orange Tree name, borrowed from a pub near Twickenham, and in the framed pictures on the walls. ☆⇄◑♣♠(567)🐾🛈

Royal Barn 🅛 ✅
New Road, LA6 2AB
☎ (015242) 71918

Kirkby Lonsdale Tiffin Gold, Stanley's, Ruskin's, Singletrack, Monumental, Jubilee; 4 changing beers (sourced locally; often Kirkby Lonsdale) ⊞
The tap-house for Kirkby Lonsdale brewery may look like a plain barn from the outside, but once inside you'll discover a buzzing hive of beer activity. The bar showcases 12 handpumps and eight keg lines alongside a handful of ciders, often including Hogan's. An underground kitchen produces fresh pizzas, and coffee is roasted on site, ensuring that all tastes are catered for. Occasional live music and other events are listed on social media. The brewery's slogan is: We put the Ale in Lonsdale! ७◑●PᕅಈᏊᏕ♫

Kirkby Stephen

La'l Nook 🇱

1 Croft Street, CA17 4QJ
☎ 07506 075625
5 changing beers (sourced locally; often Langdale, Keswick, Tirril) ⊞
A rare treat awaits you in this tucked away micropub, open Friday to Sunday only. Stylish furnishings – slate grey with a hint of blue – and a comfy window seat make the one-room bar more nook than cranny. The short counter skillfully covers five cooled casks of weekly-changing local beers, with space for cider and live keg. Locals and visitors cosy up to relax, chat and catch-up. The unisex toilet facility is up steep steps and regulated by a novel entry and exit system. Q◔◥Pᕅ(S5)ಈ

Taggy Man 🇱

4 Market Street, CA17 4QS
☎ (017683) 72531 ⊕ taggyman.co.uk
House beer (by Kirkby Lonsdale); 3 changing beers (sourced locally; often Black Sheep, Cross Bay, Keswick) ⊞
Don't worry, the Taggy Man won't catch you on his nightly rounds to call curfew, as you'll be safe and toasty in this cosy, welcoming pub. Regulars and visitors mix and enjoy the well-kept local ales and tasty pies. It is always heartening to find a down-to-earth, traditional free house that ticks all the boxes, especially in a small market town. Kirkby Stephen has lots to offer and a long history to explore. ७ಈ◑७♣APᕅ(S5)ಈᏊ♫

Kirkby-in-Furness

Ship Inn 🇱

Askew Gate Brow, LA17 7TE
☎ 07733 276451
Townhouse Meg's Mild; 3 changing beers (sourced locally; often Cross Bay, Townhouse, Ulverston) ⊞
This 300 year-old family-run village inn is situated on the Cumbria Cycle Way. Only a two minute walk from the station, and a short stroll from crossroads on the main A595, there are magnificent views from the outside terrace over the Duddon Estuary. There is a warm, friendly atmosphere, enhanced by the log burner and a good choice of local ales which always includes a mild. Simple home-cooked food, including home-made pies, is served in the evening at weekends. Home-pickled eggs may also be available. ७ಈ◑७♣PಈᏊ♫

Kirkoswald

Fetherston Arms

The Square, CA10 1DQ
☎ (01768) 898284 ⊕ fetherston-arms.co.uk
Theakston Best Bitter; 3 changing beers (often Allendale, Hesket Newmarket) ⊞

The Fethers is situated in the centre of this historic village. Extensive alterations, and the friendly enthusiasm of the owners have helped convert this into a truly outstanding pub with a deservedly excellent reputation for its food. Three changing real ales are available from breweries such as Allendale and Hesket Newmarket. Although the village is not on a bus route it is 20 minutes' stroll from Lazonby station on the Carlisle to Settle line. Opening hours may change in winter. Q७ಈ◑●ಈᏊ

Loppergarth

Wellington Inn 🇱

Main Street, LA12 0JL (1 mile from A590 between Lindal and Pennington)
☎ (01229) 582388
Healey's Blonde; 4 changing beers (sourced locally; often Healey's) ⊞
Superb village local with its own microbrewery – a custom-made stainless steel plant which is viewable from the snug. Four handpumps dispense Healey's beers. These include an award-winning blonde and a golden bitter. A traditional darker best bitter, and a superb mild are occasionally available. Wood-burning stoves make the pub cosy, with games, books and good conversation all on offer. There is a quiz on alternate Saturdays. Well-behaved dogs on leads are welcome. ७ಈ♣ಈᏊ

Loweswater

Kirkstile Inn

CA13 0RU (off B5289, 7 miles S from Cockermouth)
NY140210
☎ (01900) 85219 ⊕ kirkstile.com
Cumbrian Ales Esthwaite Bitter, Langdale, Loweswater Gold; 3 changing beers (sourced regionally; often Cumbrian Ales) ⊞
A 16th-century Lakeland coaching inn, scenically located below Melbreak, Crummock Water and Loweswater. Originally the home of Loweswater Brewery, it is now the brewery tap for Cumbrian Ales. Expect low-beamed ceilings, solid wood tables, chairs and settles in three bar areas. There is an open fire for chilly days. Substantial bar meals are available from 12 noon and there is also a restaurant. The pub holds an annual beer festival in April. The outdoor seated drinking area has stunning views. Dog friendly up to 6pm. Q७ಈ◑७●PᕅಈᏊ

Lowick Bridge

Red Lion Inn 🇱

LA12 8EF (just off the A5084 on the Ulverston to Torver road)
☎ (01229) 885366 ⊕ redlion-lowick.co.uk
Bank Top Flat Cap; Great Corby Corby Ale; 1 changing beer (sourced locally) ⊞
This former Hartley's ale house, just off the road from Greenodd to Coniston, was purchased by the present owners from Robinsons in 2014 and is well worth finding. It is now a charming, comfortable country inn, popular with both locals and visitors to the Lakes. Friendly and welcoming, the pub is an ideal base to explore the hidden corners of the southern Lakes and the Furness and Cartmel peninsulas. Q७ಈ◑Pᕅ(X12)ᏊᏕ♫

Monkhill

Drovers Rest 🍷

CA5 6DB
☎ (01228) 576141

4 changing beers Ⓗ

A traditional country pub, close to the popular Hadrian's Wall Path, with a strong community focus. Although opened-up, the interior still has the feel of three distinct rooms. The bar area is cosy and welcoming, with a roaring fire in winter. Some interesting historical State Management Scheme documents adorn the walls. The Drovers is an oasis for lots of different and sometimes obscure (for the area) real ales. Winner of multiple CAMRA awards including at regional level.
ᕦ❀◑Å♣P🖵(93) ☙

Moorhouse

Royal Oak

CA5 6EZ

☎ (01228) 576475

Cumbrian Ales Loweswater Gold; house beer (by Timothy Taylor); 1 changing beer Ⓗ

This small country pub on the outskirts of Carlisle is over 250 years old, so be prepared to duck as you go through some of the doors. Log-burning stoves help provide a rustic atmosphere. A traditional home-cooked menu is available along with real ale from local breweries. Check its Facebook page for regular updates on beers and events. ❀☙❖🛜

Near Sawrey

Tower Bank Arms Ⓛ

LA22 0LF (on B5285 2 miles S of Hawkshead)

☎ (015394) 36334 ⊕ towerbankarms.co.uk

Barngates Tag Lag; Cumbrian Ales Loweswater Gold; Hawkshead Bitter; 3 changing beers (sourced locally) Ⓗ

A 17th century Lakeland inn next to the National Trust's Hill Top, Beatrix Potter's home. Its slate floors, oak beams and cast-iron range create a lovely atmosphere. Five handpumps serve local beer, with cider and perry dispensed by gravity. Booking is essential for evening meals. Families and dogs are welcomed. Accommodation is available in four en-suite rooms. There is a seasonal bus service connecting to the Windermere ferry and Hawkshead. Note that it is closed Mondays in winter. Q ᕦ❀⇌◑Å♣P🖵☙🛜

Nether Wasdale

Strands Inn Ⓛ

CA20 1ET

☎ (019467) 26237 ⊕ strands-brewery.co.uk

Strands Brown Bitter, Errmmm...; 6 changing beers (sourced locally) Ⓗ

The home of Strands brewery and gin distillery, this inn has an extensive food and beer menu of which they are justifiably proud. A range of around 40 beers are brewed on-site, of which six are available on the main bar all year round. Visit during the annual festival of beers in May to try the entire range. Children are welcome as well as dogs. The owners also run the Screes Inn opposite which serves up to six more beers during summer months. Q ᕦ❀⇌◑Å♣P☙🛜

Penrith

Dog Beck ✔

21-22 Southend Road, CA11 8JH

☎ (01768) 840491

Greene King Abbot; Sharp's Doom Bar; changing beers Ⓗ

Named after the historic Dog Beck that ran nearby, this Wetherspoon pub is situated conveniently between the main car park and the centre of Penrith. It has the usual large range of real ales, and food is served all day every day. The bar and downstairs area is a single open-plan room on different levels. There is a large upstairs outside courtyard area in which meals can be taken alfresco on warm summer days. Q ᕦ❀◑Å⇌≷(North Lakes)🖵🛜

Fell Bar Ⓛ

52 King Street, CA11 7AY

☎ (01768) 866860

6 changing beers Ⓗ

A small and intimate pub spread across three floors, in the centre of Penrith, which was only turned into a pub in 2012. It is the brewery tap for Fell brewery but serves a range of other cask ales and craft beers as detailed on the blackboard near the bar. The Fell holds regular quiz, comedy and music nights, which are advertised on the well-kept Facebook page. Local CAMRA Pub of the Year 2020-22. ᕦ≷(North Lakes)🖵☙🛜♪

Royal Ⓛ

Wilson Row, CA11 7PZ

3 changing beers Ⓗ

Traditional pub on the edge of the town centre with tiled walls and lots of mellow wood. It has three separate areas served by one bar. Two handpumps offer beers from all over the UK, including LocAles. It is home to darts, dominoes and pool teams, and there is full sports TV coverage. Live music sessions with a broad appeal are held on Sunday afternoons outside the football season.
ᕦ⇌◑Å≷(North Lakes) ♣☙🛜♪

Ravenglass

Inn at Ravenglass

Main Street, CA18 1SQ (N end of village, overlooking the Irish Sea)

☎ (01229) 717230

Fyne Jarl; 3 changing beers (sourced regionally; often Ennerdale Craft, Fell) Ⓗ

A 17th century inn, which has recently changed management, sitting beside the estuary with its wonderful views. In Roman and Viking times this was one of the five main ports in the country. With a good choice of four real ales and high-quality dining, this pub has a lot to recommend it. Close to Ravenglass stations for both the mainline and Ravenglass and Eskdale railways. Q ᕦ❀⇌◑Å≷♣P🖵(6)☙🛜

Pennington Hotel

Main Street, CA18 1SD

☎ (01229) 717222 ⊕ muncaster.co.uk/penningtonhotel

2 changing beers (often Ennerdale Craft, Fell) Ⓗ

This friendly hotel has a long history as a village pub. It is part of the Muncaster Castle estate (which has been owned by the same family for 400 years), the entrance to which is half a mile away. The hotel is situated right on the ancient Main Street, yards from the beautiful Ravenglass Estuary. The hotel has been tastefully modernised while keeping many old features. Quality food is well presented and locally sourced wherepossible. Two permanently changing, usually local, ales are available all year round.
Q ᕦ❀⇌◑Å≷P☙🛜

Ravenstonedale

Black Swan Hotel Ⓛ ✔

CA17 4NG

☎ (015396) 23204 ⊕ blackswanhotel.com

Black Sheep Best Bitter; Timothy Taylor Landlord; 2 changing beers (sourced locally; often Allendale, Kirkby Lonsdale, Coniston) ⊞
A family-owned hotel with a well-respected bar, the Swan prides itself on attention to detail when ensuring the comfort of guests. Two regular house ales are complemented by a couple of changing beers from around the area. The lovely garden by the stream completes the picture at this tranquil spot. A Western Dales return bus from Kendal passes the road end on Wednesdays – ideal for those wanting to stop off for a leisurely lunch. Q ⚲ ❀ ⇦ ◑ & P ⟐ (55) ♣ 🛜

Rowrah

Ennerdale Brewery Tap 𝕃
Chapel Row, CA26 3XS
☎ (01946) 862977 ⊕ ennerdalebrewery.co.uk
Ennerdale Craft Blonde, Pale, Darkest, Wild; 2 changing beers (sourced locally) ⊞
This brewery tap is a café by day and a bistro pub in the evening. It offers a warm, friendly setting with four regular ales and four seasonal ales available. There are also speciality beers on offer. The brewery is on site and tours are available if booked in advance via the website. Public transport is extremely limited, but the Tap is on the Coast to Coast cycle route. ⚲ ◑ & P 🛜 ♫

Rydal

Badger Bar (Glen Rothay Hotel) 𝕃
LA22 9LR
☎ (015394) 34500 ⊕ theglenrothay.co.uk
Barngates Goodhew's Dry Stout; 3 changing beers (sourced locally; often Great Corby, Bowness Bay, Fell) ⊞
A quaint old inn that meets visitor expectations of a typical Lakes hostelry. The bar has a handful of interesting local ales and the oldest room is especially popular with walkers and their dogs who dry out by the blazing fire. In summer the garden and car park will be busy so take the 555 or open-top 599 bus. In the evening try feeding the badgers, otherwise watch them on the webcam. Q ⚲ ❀ ⇦ ◑ ▲ ♣ P ⟐ (555,599) ♣ 🛜

Seatoller

Glaramara Hotel
CA12 5XQ
☎ (017687) 77222 ⊕ glaramara.co.uk
Cumbrian Ales Loweswater Gold; Tirril Borrowdale Bitter ⊞
Formerly a hostel, this hotel is in a striking location in the jaws of Borrowdale Valley, set in over five acres of grounds. The location of this upmarket 33-bedroomed hotel makes it an ideal base for fell walking and the nearby mountains, including Scafell Pike, Great Gable, Haystacks and Glaramara. Guests rub shoulders with local farmers in the attractive public bar which has two handpumps. ⚲ ❀ ⇦ ◑ & P ⟐ ♣ 🛜

Sedbergh

Dalesman 𝕃
Main Street, LA10 5BN
☎ (015396) 21183 ⊕ thedalesman.co.uk
5 changing beers (sourced locally; often Barngates, Cross Bay, Handsome) ⊞
A small market town free house with comfortable rooms that makes a great base for the Dalesway Walk and Cumbria Cycleway. The bar stocks an interesting selection of ales from Cumbria and Yorkshire, complemented by

local food served in in the two dining rooms. The front seating has been extended, with a spacious courtyard at the rear. Up to five cask beers are sourced from within a 30-mile radius and include Nine Standards from Settle and Barngates from Ambleside. ⚲ ❀ ⇦ ◑ ▲ P ⟐ 🛜

Thirsty Rambler 𝕃
14-16 Main Street, LA10 5BN
☎ 07874 838816 ⊕ thethirstyrambler.co.uk
5 changing beers (sourced locally; often Fell, Wensleydale, Settle)
A light and airy micropub designed for thirsty ramblers and their well-behaved dogs. Conversation and mingling are encouraged, helped along by the excellent local ales served in top-rate condition from three handpumps and two keg lines. Sedbergh intersects the Lakeland Fells and Yorkshire Dales, so there is always an interesting mix of customers who relish a good pint and a good natter. The enthusiastic young owners are knowledgeable and friendly, and run a tight ship. ● ⇦ ♣ ♫

Staveley

Beer Hall 𝕃 ✅
Hawkshead Brewery, Mill Yard, LA8 9LR
☎ (01539) 825260 ⊕ hawksheadbrewery.co.uk
Hawkshead Bitter, Red; 12 changing beers (sourced locally; often Hawkshead) ⊞
There's invariably a warm welcome from the personable and efficient staff at the bar counter. This is the flagship tap for Hawkshead brewery, attracting young families as well as the more serious walkers and drinkers. A new pool table upstairs is a focus for younger customers. The beers are from their competent and well-made cask range and more adventurous keg selection. A good stopping place for refreshment for those heading to the Lakes by bus or train. Q ⚲ ❀ & ▲ ⇌ ♣ P ⟐ (555) ♣ 🛜

Talkin

Blacksmiths Arms 𝕃
CA8 1LE
☎ (016977) 42111 ⊕ blacksmithstalkin.co.uk
Black Sheep Best Bitter; Hawkshead Windermere Pale, Bitter; 1 changing beer ⊞
Since taking over in 1997, the present owners have made this probably the most popular pub in the vicinity. The winning formula includes four real ales, a superbly-stocked bar, friendly efficient staff, no television and meticulous attention to detail. With a golf course and country park within two miles and plenty of other outdoor activities locally, it attracts visitors from far outside North Cumbria to this Area of Outstanding Natural Beauty. Q ⚲ ❀ ⇦ ◑ & ♣ P 🛜

Troutbeck

Mortal Man 𝕃
LA23 1PL
☎ (015394) 33193 ⊕ themortalman.co.uk
House beer (by Marston's); 4 changing beers (sourced nationally; often Tirril, Wainwright, Cumbrian Ales) ⊞
An ale house has stood here since 1689. Originally called the White House, and much-changed since those days, the hotel's current name comes from a poem on the inn sign. The low-ceilinged bar has smaller rooms off it and access to the hotel dining room. Half a dozen handpumps with mostly local beers are supplemented by a similar number of boxed ciders. The garden is a special feature and has views down the Troutbeck valley towards Windermere. Q ⚲ ❀ ⇦ ◑ ▲ P ⟐ ♣ 🛜

Ulverston

Avanti Capitola L
10-12 King Street, LA12 7DZ
☎ (01229) 588212
Lancaster Blonde; 2 changing beers (sourced locally) H
Smart, friendly and comfortable wine bar in the centre of the town serving up to three local real ales in addition to its selection of wines, cocktails and spirits. Cheese and meat platters can be pre-ordered. Coffee and home-made scones are available on Thursday (market day) in the morning. Q&≈₽(X6,6)♪

Devonshire Arms L
Braddyll Terrace, Victoria Road, LA12 0DH (next to railway bridge in town centre)
☎ (01229) 582537
3 changing beers (sourced regionally; often Cross Bay, Logan Beck) H
Conveniently situated between the bus and train stations, the Dev is a real locals' pub with a welcoming atmosphere. Four TVs provide comprehensive sports coverage, and there are two dartboards and a pool table. Five constantly changing cask ales are all dispensed on handpump. The outside seating area is popular in summer. A meat raffle is held on Sunday evening. The pub has received numerous awards from CAMRA over the years. ♿❀&A≈♣P♬❀🐾

Gather L
7 Market Street, LA12 7AY
☎ (01229) 318393 ⊕ gatherbeers.co.uk
2 changing beers (sourced nationally) H
A micropub and bottle shop owned by a CAMRA member. It was recently refurbished to give more seating downstairs, with additional seating upstairs, making for a pleasant and relaxing atmosphere. It has two handpumps plus eight KeyKeg beers, with an extensive range of interesting local, national and international bottled and canned beers and ciders. Tap takeovers and other events are occasionally held. Pizzas available. ≈●🐾❀🐾♪

Mill L ✓
Mill Street, LA12 7EB
☎ (01229) 581384 ⊕ mill-at-ulverston.co.uk
Lancaster Amber, Blonde, Black, Red; 6 changing beers (sourced nationally) H
The Mill has an interesting and characterful layout, centred around a restored original, but now static, waterwheel. The Cask Bar is on the ground floor. On Friday and Saturday both the Loft Bar on the second floor, serving evening cocktails, and the first-floor Terrace Bar with a separate outdoor patio area and largescreen TV, are open. Deservedly popular for quality food; booking is essential for the restaurant. There are picnic tables outside to the front. ♿❀🄌&≈₽(6,X6)❀🐾♪

Old Friends L
49 Soutergate, LA12 7ES
☎ (01229) 208195 ⊕ oldfriendsulverston.co.uk
Old Friends Best Friends, New Acquaintance, Old Pals Porter; 3 changing beers (sourced nationally) H
A 17th-century Grade II-listed locals' pub 200 yards uphill from the town centre. It has a cosy snug with an open fire in front of the bar. Another room with a TV is separated from it by a passageway with a hatch to the bar. Beers are mostly local, with three brewed in the pub's own brewery. A popular quiz night is held every Tuesday. There is a wonderful beer garden with heating in winter. Monday opening hours are extended on bank holidays. ♿❀♣₽❀🐾♪

Swan Inn L
Swan Street, LA12 7JX
☎ (01229) 582519
8 changing beers (sourced nationally) H
On the edge of the town centre, overlooking the A590, there's an open-plan feel here, despite having three distinct drinking areas. Premier League football and major sports events are screened, live music features occasionally, and a jukebox allows for all genres of music. A Sunday night quiz rounds off the entertainment. The beer garden is popular, especially in summer. Children are allowed until evening. ❀&₽(6,X6)❀🐾♪

Walton

Old Vicarage Bar & Brewery
CA8 2DH
☎ (01697) 543002 ⊕ oldvicaragebrewery.co.uk
3 changing beers (sourced locally) H
The smallest of microbreweries (300 litre capacity) but large enough to service the Old Vicarage bar and provide bottled beer for local and visiting customers. The bar is a cosy place to relax and try the beer. It is TV- and music-free, dog friendly and welcoming to walkers, cyclists, locals and visitors alike. Situated only 400 yards from the Hadrian's Wall Path. Q❀🄌❀🐾

Wetheral

Wheatsheaf Inn L ✓
CA4 8HD
☎ (01228) 560686 ⊕ wheatsheafwetheral.co.uk
Great Corby Corby Ale; 2 changing beers H
This early 19th-century pub, just a few minutes walk from the village green and railway station, is deservedly popular with locals and visitors alike. Along with Corby Ale from the local Great Corby Brewhouse there are two ever-changing ales sourced from local breweries. Good-value bar meals are served Wednesday to Sunday, with booking advisable at weekends. The regular Tuesday quiz nights are very well supported. ♿❀🄌≈♣P₽(75)❀🐾

Whitehaven

Candlestick ✓
21-22 Tangier Street, CA28 7UX
☎ (01946) 599032
4 changing beers (sourced nationally; often Cross Bay, Cumbrian Ales, Tractor Shed) H
An unusual refurbishment has given this historic pub an evening café bar/cocktail bar feel, while still catering for sports enthusiasts and regulars. The only free house in the town with Cask Marque accreditation, the Candlestick serves at least three, but usually four, ever-changing real ales and is the best chance of getting a stout or porter in Whitehaven. This bar is popular with locals and tourists alike, and has a knowledgeable ale-drinking staff. May close early on Sunday night if quiet. Q♿&≈₽❀🐾

Witherslack

Derby Arms Hotel L
LA11 6RH
☎ (015395) 52207 ⊕ derbyarms-witherslack.business.site
Bowness Bay Swan Blonde; 4 changing beers (sourced locally; often Fell, Keswick, Kirkby Lonsdale) H
Possibly the best pub you've never visited, although it is easily accessible from Kendal by bus or car. The central bar serves five traditionally-furnished rooms with a wide range of local ales in tip-top condition and good home-

cooked food. Most rooms have a fire and the games room has a pool table. Walkers and cyclists mix with regulars and diners to ensure a welcoming atmosphere with a lively buzz. Dogs like to visit too.

🕭🏯🛏🕪🕭💧♣️P🖵(X6) 🌢🛜🎵

Breweries

Barngates

Barngates, Ambleside, LA22 0NG
☎ (01539) 436347 ⊕ barngatesbrewery.co.uk

☺Barngates was established in 1997 to supply only the Drunken Duck Inn. It became a limited company in 1999. Expansion over the years, plus a new purpose-built, 10-barrel plant in 2008, means it now supplies more than 150 outlets throughout Cumbria, Lancashire and Yorkshire. ‼

Pale (ABV 3.3%) PALE
A well-balanced, fruity, hoppy pale ale with plenty of flavour for its strength.
Cat Nap (ABV 3.6%) PALE
Pale beer, unapologetically bitter, with a dry, astringent finish.
Cracker (ABV 3.9%) BITTER
A full-bodied hoppy beer with some balancing sweetness and fruit. There is plenty of taste in this cleverly constructed, copper-coloured beer.
Brathay Gold (ABV 4%) PALE
Attractive rich aroma of fruit, malt and hops is followed by plenty of fruit and bittering hops ending in a long bitter finish.
Goodhew's Dry Stout (ABV 4.3%) STOUT
The inviting roast aroma leads to an easy-drinking, full-bodied and well-balanced roasty stout.
Tag Lag (ABV 4.4%) BITTER
This traditional bitter is full on: fruit, noble hops, malt balance, good body with a crisp clean finish of hop bitterness.
Red Bull Terrier (ABV 4.8%) RED
An assertive roasty red beer with full mouthfeel. Initial sweetness and luscious fruit, give way to a lingering bitter finish.

Bowness Bay SIBA

Unit 10, Castle Mills, Aynam Road, Kendal, LA9 7DE
☎ (01539) 726800 ☎ 07823 347763
⊕ bownessbaybrewing.co.uk

☺Bowness Bay Brewing moved to Kendal in 2015 and increased capacity from five to 16 barrels. Now expanded to a 2,500-litre, automated, four-vessel brewing system, capable of brewing up to six times a day. The original five-barrel plant is used for small experimental brews. In 2020 grant funding allowed further expansion into keg beers. Onsite taphouse, the Barrel House, showcases the core range and seasonal specials. A live music space, the Venue, hosting beer festivals, weddings and private parties, opened 2021. Beers are also produced under the Appleby Brewery name. ‼♦☙

Lakeland Blonde (ABV 3.7%) BLOND
Swift Best (ABV 3.8%) BITTER
Hoppy bitter balanced by some malty sweetness and a little fruit.
Swan Blonde (ABV 4%) BLOND
Sweet, fruity, mild beer with gentle bittering hops.
Fell Walker (ABV 4.1%) BLOND
A sweet fruity beer with gentle hop bittering and a drying finish.

Raven Red (ABV 4.2%) BITTER
Sweet malty bitter with fruit and roast aromas, gentle hop bitterness and a dry finish.
Swan Gold (ABV 4.2%) BLOND
Fell Runner (ABV 4.6%) GOLD
Swan Black (ABV 4.6%) STOUT
Stout-like beer with a fruity, raisiny middle, grainy mouthfeel and roast bitter finish.
Tern IPA (ABV 5%) PALE
Well-balanced with some sweet malt and fruit to balance the lingering hoppy finish.
Steamer IPA (ABV 5.7%) IPA

Brack'N'Brew

🍴 **Brackenrigg Inn, Watermillock, CA11 0LP**
☎ (01768) 486206 ⊕ brackenrigginn.co.uk

☺Brewing started in 2015, set up in the old stable block at the rear of the Brackenrigg Inn, on the shores of Ullswater in the Lake District. A four-barrel plant is used to produce cask and bottled beers, which are sold across Cumbria and the north of England.

Alfred's Golden Ale (ABV 3.2%) BITTER
Boathouse Blonde (ABV 3.8%) BLOND
Rambling Bookkeeper Bitter (ABV 4.1%) RED
The Steamer Stout (ABV 4.4%) MILD
Aira Force IPA (ABV 5.9%) IPA

Carlisle SIBA

Unit 2, 12a Kingstown Broadway, Kingstown Industrial Estate, Carlisle, CA3 0HA
☎ (01228) 594959 ☎ 07979 728780
⊕ carlislerealale.com

☺Carlisle Brewing Company is a family-run brewery established in 2013. Initially using a 2.5-barrel plant in a shed behind the owner's freehouse, by 2015 it had expanded to a 10-barrel plant in an industrial unit. Beer is available in the Spinners Arms and other local outlets. ‼♦

Cumbrian Bitter (ABV 3.7%) BITTER
Bell (ABV 3.8%) PALE
Citadel (ABV 3.8%) PALE
Spun Gold (ABV 4.2%) BITTER
Sweet malty, fruity bitter with a lasting dry finish.
Flaxen (ABV 4.5%) BITTER
Magic Number (ABV 4.5%) BITTER

Coastline (NEW)

Far South End Cottage, Walney Island, LA14 3YQ

Family-owned 2.5-barrel microbrewery in an old barn conversion located on the south end of Walney Island, Cumbria. Brewing began in 2023. A number of local outlets are supplied.

Breakwater Blonde (ABV 3.8%) BLOND
Cranesbill IPA (ABV 4.6%) PALE
Cormorant Stout (ABV 5.8%) STOUT

Coniston

🍴 **Coppermines Road, Coniston, LA21 8HL**
☎ (01539) 441133 ⊕ conistonbrewery.com

☺The 10-barrel plant commenced brewing in 1995. The brewery is situated behind the Black Bull Inn, Coniston, and currently brews 40 barrels a week. Bluebird, XB and Old Man are bottle-conditioned and are brewed using Ridgeway Brewery. It supplies over 100 outlets with cask beers across the North West, and bottled beers are available in Asda, Sainsburys and Booths, as well as online. Bottled Gold and bottled Freebird (0.5% ABV) are gluten free. ‼ ⛟ LIVE GF

Oliver's Light Ale (ABV 3.4%) BLOND
A fruity, hoppy, gently bittered straw-coloured beer with plenty of flavour for its strength.

Bluebird Bitter (ABV 3.6%) PALE
A yellow-gold, predominantly hoppy and fruity beer, well-balanced with some sweetness and a rising bitter finish.

Bluebird Premium XB (ABV 4.2%) PALE
Well-balanced, hoppy and fruity bitter. Bittersweet in the mouth with dryness building.

Old Man Ale (ABV 4.2%) RED

Special Oatmeal Stout (ABV 4.5%) STOUT
A well-balanced, easy-drinking stout, fruity with a balanced ratio of malt to hop bitterness. A good starting point for novice stout drinkers.

Coniston K7 (ABV 4.7%) PALE
Balanced, fruity, hoppy bitter, plenty of body and a long hoppy bitter finish.

Thurstein Pilsner (ABV 4.8%) SPECIALITY
True to style; mild but unusually sweet, with a hoppy fruitiness.

Infinity IPA (ABV 6%) IPA
High impact IPA. Fruity aromas persist in the powerful but well-balanced hoppiness and sweetness with nothing being lost in the finish.

No 9 Barley Wine (ABV 8.5%) BARLEY
Hops and alcohol dominate with appropriate sweetness and fruit on the tongue. A full-bodied and beautifully balanced beer.

Crooked River (NEW)

c/o 2 Blooming Heather, Dearham, CA15 7EF
☎ 07888 141697 ⊕ crooked-river.co.uk

Initially starting brewing on a small scale in the autumn of 2022, most of this company's production is now cuckoo-brewed at Tractor Shed. Most of the output is live beer in keg or can, but occasionally a cask beer may be produced.

Cumbrian SIBA

Old Hall Brewery, Hawkshead, LA22 0QF
☎ (01539) 436436 ⊕ cumbrianales.com

☺First established in 2003, the brewery is located in an idyllic position in a renovated barn on the shores of Esthwaite Water. The success of Loweswater Gold has meant the brewery is thriving. ‼♦

Esthwaite Bitter (ABV 3.8%) PALE
Robust, refreshing bitter with plenty of hops, lasting well into the finish.

Langdale (ABV 4%) GOLD
Fresh grapefruit aromas with hoppy, fruity flavours and crisp, long hop finish, make for a well-balanced beer.

Grasmoor Dark Ale (ABV 4.3%) MILD
Dark fruity beer with complex character and roast nutty tones leading to a short, refreshing finish.

Loweswater Gold (ABV 4.3%) BLOND
A dominant fruity body develops into a light bitter finish. A beer that belies its strength.

Eden River SIBA

Hawksdale House, Hartness Road, Penrith, CA11 9BD
☎ (01768) 210565 ⊕ edenriverbrewco.uk

Originally named Eden Brewery, the name changed to Eden River in 2018. Set up in 2011, the brewery is run by Jason Hill, assisted by Linda and Chris. The five-barrel

plant was located at historic Brougham Hall but moved in 2017 to premises on a Penrith industrial estate. ‼♦LIVE

Fuggles (ABV 3.8%) PALE
Initially sweet, a gently-hopped pale beer with a bitter finish.

Beacon (ABV 4%) BITTER

Aurum (ABV 4.2%) BLOND
Gentle fruity and honey aromas to start, leading to a well-balanced sweet beer with a lasting hoppy finish.

Red Men (ABV 4.3%) RED

Emperor (ABV 4.6%) PALE
Fascinatingly fruity beer with balanced malt and hops and a hint of butterscotch combining to a rich bitter finish.

Ennerdale SIBA

Chapel Row, Rowrah, CA26 3XS
☎ (01946) 862977 ⊕ ennerdalebrewery.co.uk

☺This family-owned brewery began brewing in 2010 as a 10-barrel brewery in a converted barn. In 2016 the brewery moved to larger premises with plans for expansion. It distributes throughout Cumbria and the North of England. The brewery tap is open daily. ‼⛟♦⚲

Blonde (ABV 3.8%) BLOND
A sweet, fruity, light-coloured beer with gentle bitterness.

Darkest (ABV 4.2%) BROWN
Roast malty aromas and flavours combine with sweet fruitiness. The finish is of lasting dry roast malts.

Wild (ABV 4.2%) MILD
Fruity and hoppy beer with some balancing malt remaining in the long bitter finish.

Fell

Unit 27, Moor Lane Business Park, Flookburgh, LA11 7NG
☎ (01539) 558980 ☎ 07967 503689
⊕ fellbrewery.co.uk

☺Fell Brewery was founded in 2012 by homebrewer Tim Bloomer and friend Andrew Carter, brewing beers inspired by their travels in the US and Belgium. Production capacity is 15 barrels. It has five retail outlets situated in Cartmel, Chorlton (near Manchester), and Penrith, with two, one an events space, in Kendal. The brewery is powered by solar panels. ♦

Dark Mild (ABV 3.4%) MILD

Foss (ABV 3.4%) PALE

Ghyll (ABV 3.4%) GOLD
Inviting citrus aromas follow through nicely in this hoppy bitter beer with fruit and sweetness present for balance.

Ligh Mild (ABV 3.4%) MILD

Tinderbox IPA (ABV 6.3%) IPA
A complex beer with an immediate and lasting hit of bitterness. Moderate sweetness balances the resiny and citrus hop flavours until overtaken by a drying finish.

Gan Yam

3 Benson View Works, Shap Road Industrial Estate, Kendal, LA9 6NZ ⊕ ganyambrewco.uk

☺Initially a commercial home-based brewery based in north London when founded in 2018, it relocated to Kendal in early 2021. An onsite taproom is held most months. ♦⚲

PAL (ABV 3.9%) PALE
ALF (ABV 4.1%) BLOND
SIP (ABV 4.3%) PALE
KEN (ABV 5%) SPECIALITY

AYE (ABV 6%) IPA
TAR (ABV 7%) PORTER

Grasmere

Lake View Country House, Lake View Drive, Grasmere, LA22 9TD
☎ (01539) 435572 ☎ 07840 059561
⊕ grasmerepub.com

Brewing began in 2017 in old farm buildings at Lake View Country House. Beers are available at its nearby brewery tap and restaurant, the Good Sport. Cider is also produced.

Helles Lager (ABV 3.8%) SPECIALITY
Pale Ale (ABV 4%) BLOND
Sweet beer with a hint of bitterness and a drying finish.
Bitter (ABV 4.1%) BITTER
IPA (ABV 5.5%) IPA

Great Corby SIBA

The Green, Great Corby, CA4 8LR
☎ (01228) 560899 ⊕ greatcorbybrewhouse.com

⊕The brewery started in 2009 and has been locally-owned since 2020. The large sandstone, former honey factory now houses the brewing area and offices. The former brewing site at the Forge, across the village green, is now used for cask washing. Additional beers are brewed from springtime onwards. ‼◆

Tizzie Whizie (ABV 3.5%) PALE
Corby Ale (ABV 3.8%) BITTER
A fruity session beer with sweetness leading to gentle bitterness in the aftertaste.
Blonde (ABV 4%) BLOND
Some fruit in the aroma and then a sweet fruity and lightly-bittered taste which continues for a short time.
Lakeland Summit (ABV 4%) BLOND
Aroma and taste are dominated by fruity hops. Bitterness and some sweetness creep into the finish to create balance.
Stout (ABV 4.5%) STOUT
A good roasty start with some caramel and gentle hops, a sweet body to balance and finishing a little drier with all flavours lasting well.
Fox Brown Ale (ABV 4.6%) BROWN
Malty aromas follow into the taste and dominate with some hop bitterness and fruit. Gentle bitterness helps balance the malty sweetness.

Handsome SIBA

Bowstone Bridge Garage, Bowston, LA8 9HD ☎ 0344 848 0888 ⊕ handsomebrew.co.uk

⊕Founded in 2016 in the Lake District following it's previous existence as Houston Brewery in Scotland. Handsome is situated on the River Kent in an old MOT garage, formerly the blacksmith's for James Cropper's paper mills. In 2021, it opened a bar next to the River Kent in Kendal and another in Leeds.

Blonde (ABV 3.6%) BLOND
Light amber with a citrus twist that delicately cuts through its subtle sweetness and velvety-smooth finish.
Top Knot (ABV 3.7%) PALE
A pale hoppy fruity beer with some sweetness continuing through to the gentle finish. A touch of malt adds depth.
Hound (ABV 4%) PALE
Stranger (ABV 4.2%) BITTER
Blacksmith (ABV 4.6%) STOUT
Bar Steward (ABV 4.8%) BITTER

Hawkshead SIBA

Mill Yard, Staveley, LA8 9LR
☎ (01539) 822644 ⊕ hawksheadbrewery.co.uk

☺Established in 2002, it outgrew its original barn and moved to Staveley in 2006 to a purpose-built, 20-barrel brewery. Shortly afterwards a taproom was added. In 2018, production of the core range of beers was transferred to a brand new brewery in Flookburgh (which also brewed the Sadlers Peaky Blinders range), with the Staveley plant continuing to produce small batch beers. Following a business review, the Sadlers range has been discontinued and the operations at Flookburgh have been transferred to Staveley. ‼☲◆LIVE⌁

Iti (ABV 3.4%) GOLD
Mill Yard Mild (ABV 3.4%) MILD
Roast malt aromas start the theme and develop in the taste, with accompanying sweetness in this traditional mild.
Windermere Pale (ABV 3.4%) BLOND
Bitter (ABV 3.7%) BITTER
Mosaic Pale (ABV 4%) PALE
Hops give orange and peach aromas to the beer. Sweetness, fruit and hops on the palate develop into a hit of hop bitterness to finish.
Red (ABV 4.2%) RED
Lakeland Gold (ABV 4.4%) BLOND
A beer with plenty of hop bitterness throughout, just enough sweetness and an impactful, dry, lasting bitter finish.
Dry Stone Stout (ABV 4.5%) STOUT
This black stout progresses from a slightly sweet, fruity start to a mouth filling balance of lasting dry roast and hop bitterness.
Prime Porter (ABV 4.9%) PORTER
Complex, dark brown beer with plenty of malt, fruit and roast taste. Satisfying full body with a clean finish.
Brune (ABV 5.6%) BROWN

Healey's

⊟ **Wellington Inn, Main Street, Loppergarth, LA12 0JL**
☎ (01229) 582388

Healey's began brewing in the Wellington Inn in 2012 using a custom-made, 2.5-barrel, stainless steel plant. The brewery can be viewed through full-length windows in the pub. A range of different cask beer styles are brewed and are available at a variety of local pubs in the area including in the Wellington itself. Electrical power is provided by solar panels.

Hesket Newmarket SIBA

Old Crown Barn, Back Green, Hesket Newmarket, CA7 8JG
☎ (01697) 478066 ⊕ hesketbrewery.co.uk

⊕Founded in 1988, and bought by a co-operative in 1999 to preserve a community amenity. Cask beers are generally named after Cumbrian fells. Newer look beer styles have been introduced in recent years with traditional beers undergoing a rejuvenation. More than 10 cask ales are supplied across Cumbria with supply also available in bottles and cans. ‼◆

Skiddaw (ABV 3.6%) BITTER
Haystacks (ABV 3.7%) BLOND
Light, easy-drinking, thirst-quenching blond beer; pleasant for its strength.
Black Sail (ABV 4%) STOUT
A sweet stout with roast flavours.
Helvellyn Gold (ABV 4%) BLOND
Doris' 90th Birthday Ale (ABV 4.3%) BITTER

Scafell Blonde (ABV 4.3%) PALE
A hoppy, sweet, fruity, pale-coloured bitter.
Brim Fell IPA (ABV 4.5%) PALE
Catbells (ABV 5%) PALE
An ale with a nice balance of fruity sweetness and bitterness, almost syrupy but with an unexpectedly dry finish.
Smoked Porter (ABV 5.4%) SPECIALITY
Old Carrock Strong Ale (ABV 6%) OLD
Reddy brown strong ale, vine-fruity in flavour with slightly astringent finish.
West Coast Red (ABV 6.3%) RED
Double IPA (ABV 7.4%) IPA

Keswick SIBA

The Old Brewery, Brewery Lane, Keswick, CA12 5BY
☎ (01768) 780700 ⊕ keswickbrewery.co.uk

Keswick, owned by Sue Jefferson, began brewing in 2006 using a 10-barrel plant on the site of a brewery that closed in 1897. The brewery is set up to be environmentally-friendly using sheeps wool insulation in the vessels and reducing its environmental impact. Outlets include the Fox bar at the brewery, the Dog & Gun, Keswick, and many other pubs across Cumbria.
‼🛒♦⬦

Black Star (ABV 3.5%) BITTER
Gold (ABV 3.6%) PALE
Predominantly hoppy bitter with malts, sweetness and fruit and a dry bitter finish.
Bitter (ABV 3.7%) BITTER
Gentle bitter with hints of roasted malt and a sweetness which fades.
Thirst Rescue (ABV 3.8%) BITTER
Bitter beer with some fruitiness, full-bodied and a lasting bitter finish.
Fox Dark (ABV 4%) MILD
Fox Pale (ABV 4%) PALE
Thirst Run (ABV 4.2%) PALE
A well-balanced golden beer that maintains its fruitiness from start to finish.
Thirst Quencher (ABV 4.3%) BLOND
Light-bodied, fresh hoppy beer with fruit in the middle and a balancing sweetness.
Pale Ale (ABV 4.4%) PALE
KSB (Keswick Special Bitter) (ABV 4.8%) BITTER
Dark Horse (ABV 6%) BROWN
Malty sweet and fruity robust dark brown ale with gentle hop bittering and a lasting finish of the same but a touch drier.
K4 (ABV 6%) IPA
Thirst Celebration (ABV 7%) STRONG

Kirkby Lonsdale SIBA

Unit 2F, Old Station Yard, Kirkby Lonsdale, LA6 2HP
☎ (01524) 272221

Second site: Royal Barn, New Road, Kirkby Lonsdale, LA6 2AB ⊕ klbrewery.com

☺Kirkby Lonsdale is a family-run business established in 2009 on a six-barrel plant. In 2016 a further six-barrel plant was installed in its new brewery tap, the Royal Barn, Kirkby Lonsdale. ‼♦⬦

Crafty Mild (ABV 3.6%) MILD
A typical mild with powerful malty aromas and some caramel, which follows through in the taste and finish.
Tiffin Gold (ABV 3.6%) BLOND
A full-flavoured, grapefruity, hoppy and bitter beer with a dry finish.
Stanley's (ABV 3.8%) PALE
Hops dominate this sweet and fruity, well-balanced beer.

Ruskin's (ABV 3.9%) PALE
A tawny bitter with a distinctive aroma of fruit and malt. The clean, hoppy flavour is well-balanced with fruity sweetness leading to a sustained bittersweet finish.
Singletrack (ABV 4%) GOLD
Crisp citrus hops predominate in a well-balanced beer with a pleasant bitter finish.
Pennine Ambler (ABV 4.1%) BITTER
Radical (ABV 4.2%) RED
Malty beer with a caramel sweetness that is balanced by a bitter finish.
Monumental (ABV 4.5%) BLOND
Distinctly hoppy, a fruity, sweet, pale-coloured, full-bodied bitter.
Jubilee (ABV 5.5%) STOUT
Rich, well-balanced stout with malt. A long aftertaste retains this complexity and is surprisingly refreshing.
Imperial Dragon (ABV 8.2%) IPA

Lakes SIBA

Mintsfeet Road South, Kendal, LA9 6ND
☎ (01539) 324005 ⊕ lakesbrewco.com

Brewery opened in 2021 by former employees of Hawkshead brewery. ⬦

Pale Ale (ABV 3.5%) GOLD
A powerful aroma of citrus hops follows through to bitterness which builds upon drinking. There is balancing sweetness and fruit to create a cleverly-constructed beer for its strength.

Langdale

Cross Houses Farm, Docker, LA8 0DE ☎ 07876 838051
⊕ langdalebrewing.co.uk

☺Langdale Brewing was formed in 2018 by Steve Mitchell formerly of Eden Brewery, and Paul Fry of the Britannia Inn, Elterwater. The brewery USP is producing a range of cask ales using water harvested from a Langdale spring.

Bowfell Bitter (ABV 3.5%) BITTER
Elterwater Gold (ABV 3.8%) GOLD
Pikes Pale (ABV 3.9%) PALE
Bowfell Blonde (ABV 4.2%) BLOND
Bowfell Amber (ABV 4.3%) BITTER
Weiss Ghyll (ABV 4.5%) SPECIALITY

Logan Beck

The Barn at Beckfoot Farm, Duddon Bridge, LA20 6EU
☎ 07926 179749 ✉ loganbeckbrewing@gmail.com

The brewery has expanded from a 0.75-barrel to a 5.5-barrel plant (formerly Chadwicks). Cans and bottles are planned. Beer availability is limited but there are frequent seasonal specials and 'cupboard' brews. Regular beers use mainly locally-sourced ingredients.

Phoenix Pale (ABV 3.5%) PALE
Dusky Dark (ABV 3.7%) MILD
Gentle mild with some roast malt and sweetness with enough bitterness to give balance.
Proper (ABV 4%) BITTER
Sweet malty start with some roast pleasant hops and a lasting bitter finish.
Unbound Blonde (ABV 4.1%) BLOND
Navigator (ABV 4.3%) PALE
Proper XB (ABV 4.4%) PALE

Old Friends

🍺 **The Old Friends Inn, 49 Southergate, Ulverston, LA12 7ES**

☎ (01229) 208195 ☎ 07563 521575
⊕ oldfriendsulverston.co.uk

⊛Brewing began in 2019 in a room to the rear of the Old Friends pub in Ulverston. Beers are currently only available at the pub.

Old Vicarage

Old Vicarage, Walton, CA8 2DH
☎ (01697) 543002 ⊕ oldvicaragebrewery.co.uk

A microbrewery, bar and B&B accommodation in North Cumbria. Brewing experience days are offered. ⌗

OVB (ABV 4%) BITTER
Coachman (ABV 4.6%) BLOND
SB Special (ABV 5%) BLOND

Shaws of Grange

12 Station Yard, Grange-over-Sands, LA11 6DW
☎ (01539) 555349 ☎ 07951 009607
⊕ shawsofgrange.co.uk

This 0.5-barrel brewery began producing beers for sale in 2019. A range of four beers has been developed for sale in cask and by hand bottling. Virtually all the production has been sold in bottles since 2020, although the brewery will supply a cask on demand.

Strands

▤ **Strands Inn, Nether Wasdale, CA20 1ET**
☎ (01946) 726237 ⊕ strandshotel.com

⊛Strands Brewery is a ten-barrel plant with a 5,000-litre fermentation capacity. Six of the beers are available on the bar of the Strands Inn at all times or in the Screes, across the road. ‼◆LIVE

Tirril SIBA

Red House, Long Marton, CA16 6BN
☎ (01768) 361846 ⊕ tirrilbrewery.uk

⊛Established in 1999, Tirril Brewery has twice outgrown its premises. It delivers to more than 170 outlets, 100 of which regularly stock the beer. Contract brewing is also carried out for Bitter End Brewery. ‼◆

Original Bitter (ABV 3.8%) BITTER
Medium-bodied amber beer with caramel flavours and fruity aromas.
Ullswater Blonde (ABV 3.8%) BLOND
Grasmere Gold (ABV 3.9%) PALE
Kirkstone Gold (ABV 3.9%) GOLD
Old Faithful (ABV 4%) BITTER
Initially bitter, gold-coloured ale with an astringent finish.
1823 (ABV 4.1%) BROWN
Academy Ale (ABV 4.2%) BITTER
Borrowdale Bitter (ABV 4.2%) BITTER
Castlerigg Blonde (ABV 4.2%) GOLD
Hardknott Ale (ABV 4.2%) BITTER
Windermere IPA (ABV 4.3%) PALE
Red Barn Ale (ABV 4.4%) RED

Townhouse

35 Chapel Street, Dalton-in-Furness, LA15 8BY
☎ 07812 035143

Office: 52 Steel Street, Askam-in-Furness, LA16 7BP
✉ townhousebrewery@gmail.com

⊛Townhouse was setup in 2002 in Audley, Staffordshire with a 2.5-barrel plant that expanded to five barrels in 2004. In 2006 two further fermenting vessels were added producing the bulk of its beer for the Potteries. In 2021 the brewery relocated to Dalton-in-Furness, Cumbria. All cask beers have been vegan since 2005. Canning is planned. Charter is brewed exclusively for the award-winning Manor Arms in Broughton-in-Furness. V

Charter (ABV 3.5%) BLOND
Meg's Mild (ABV 3.9%) MILD
Flowerdew (ABV 4%) BITTER
Golden with a wonderful floral aroma. Fabulous flavour of flowery hops delivering a crisp hoppy bite and presenting a lingering taste of flowery citrus waves.
Furness IPA (ABV 4.9%) PALE

Tractor Shed SIBA

Tractor Shed, Calva Brow, Workington, CA14 1DB
☎ (01900) 68860 ⊕ tractor-shed.co.uk

⊛Renamed from Mitchell Krause in 2014 and having previously had its beers brewed under contract, brewing started in an old tractor shed on the family farm in 2013. After initially focusing on bottled and kegged continental-style beers, the first cask-conditioned beer was produced in 2014. The brewery contract brews for various other brewing companies. ‼⌗

Mowdy Pale Ale (ABV 3.9%) BITTER
An interesting, well-balanced beer with persistent fruitiness, sweet and hoppy centre giving way nicely to hop in the finish.
Clocker Stout (ABV 4%) STOUT
Tasty, easy-drinking start with malt and roast, a fruity centre some hop joining in at the end.

Ulverston

Lightburn Road, Ulverston, LA12 0AU
☎ (01229) 586870 ☎ 07840 192022
⊕ ulverstonbrewingcompany.co.uk

⊛The brewery occupies the octagonal bull ring of the old livestock market. There is a bar that overlooks the brew plant, which opens by prior arrangement and during some local festivals. Some beers have a Laurel and Hardy theme (Stan Laurel was born in Ulverston). ‼☲◆⌗

Flying Elephants (ABV 3.7%) PALE
Well-balanced pale session beer with malt, hops and some fruit and a lasting finish.
Celebration Ale (ABV 3.9%) PALE
Yellow fruity bitter with hints of tangerine and a notably sustained dry finish.
Harvest Moon (ABV 3.9%) BLOND
A well-balanced, pale, hoppy bitter.
Laughing Gravy (ABV 4%) BITTER
Malt and hops in the aroma with pleasing balance of sweet malt and hops in the taste. Some fruitiness adds flavour and the finish is long and clean.
Lonesome Pine (ABV 4.2%) BLOND
A fresh and fruity blond beer; honeyed, lemony and resiny with an increasingly bitter finish.
Fra Diavolo (ABV 4.3%) MILD

Unsworth's Yard SIBA

4 Unsworth's Yard, Ford Road, Cartmel, LA11 6PG
☎ 07810 461313 ⊕ unsworthsyard.co.uk

⊛Unsworth's Yard opened in 2011, brewing on a five-barrel plant. The brewery produces beers named after historic figures and legends associated with the Cartmel area. Beers are available in Cartmel pubs and other local outlets as well as the brewery's taproom. ‼☲⌗

Cartmel Thoroughbred (ABV 3.5%) GOLD

Cartmel Pale (ABV 3.7%) PALE
Peninsula Best (ABV 3.8%) BITTER
Crusader Gold (ABV 4.1%) GOLD
Eel River IPA (ABV 4.3%) PALE
Sir Edgar Harrington's Last Wolf (ABV 4.5%) BROWN
Well-balanced, rich fruity, tawny ale with gentle bitterness.
The Flookburgh Cockler (ABV 5.5%) PORTER

Westmorland

Kendal ☎ 07554 562662
✉ westmorlandbrewery@gmail.com

Westmorland began brewing in 2016 using a one-barrel plant.

Wild Boar

☱ Wild Boar, Crook Road, Bowness-on-Windermere, LA23 3NF

☎ (0845) 850 4604 ⊕ englishlakes.co.uk/ the-wild-boar

⊗ Brewing began in 2013 at the Wild Boar in Crook, a large, traditional Lakeland luxury hotel. The hotel is part of the English Lakes Hotels group and supplies its beers to hotels within the group. A new head brewer took over in 2023 and updated brewing equipment was installed to aid expansion of production. ♦

Windermere SIBA

☱ Watermill Inn, Ings, LA8 9PY
☎ (01539) 821309 ⊕ lakelandpub.co.uk

☺Originally known as Watermill, the brewery was established in 2006 in a purpose-built extension to the Watermill Inn. The beers have a doggy theme (dogs are allowed in the main bar). Windermere Brewing was originally a separate brand but all beers are now brewed under the name. ‼♦

King's Head, Carlisle (Photo: Stuart McMahon)

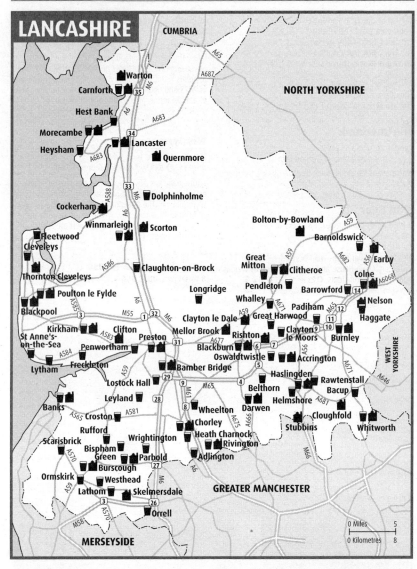

LANCASHIRE

CUMBRIA

NORTH YORKSHIRE

Warton
Carnforth 35
Hest Bank
Morecambe
Heysham
Lancaster
Quernmore
Dolphinholme
Cockerham
Winmarleigh
Scorton
Fleetwood
Cleveleys
Bolton-by-Bowland
Barnoldswick
Thornton Cleveleys
Claughton-on-Brock
Great Mitton
Clitheroe
Earby
Colne
Poulton le Fylde
Longridge
Pendleton
Barrowford
Nelson
Blackpool
Whalley
Padiham
Haggate
Kirkham
Clifton
Clayton le Dale
Great Harwood
Burnley
St Anne's-on-the-Sea
Preston
Mellor Brook
Rishton
Clayton le Moors
WEST YORKSHIRE
Penwortham
Blackburn
Oswaldtwistle
Accrington
Lytham
Freckleton
Bamber Bridge
Lostock Hall
Haslingden
Rawtenstall
Bacup
Leyland
Belthorn
Helmshore
Banks
Wheelton
Darwen
Cloughfold
Croston
Chorley
Stubbins
Whitworth
Rufford
Heath Charnock
Scarisbrick
Wrightington
Rivington
Bispham Green
Parbold
Adlington
Burscough
Ormskirk
Westhead
GREATER MANCHESTER
Lathom
Skelmersdale
Orrell
MERSEYSIDE

0 Miles 5
0 Kilometres 8

Accrington

Arden Inn

81 Abbey Street, BB5 1EH
☎ 07518 563663 ⊕ ardeninn.co.uk
4 changing beers (sourced nationally; often Bradfield, Timothy Taylor) Ⓗ
A traditional corner pub standing at the gateway to Accrington's historic town centre. Though essentially open-plan there are a number of separate drinking areas. It has is a pool table and dartboard, a pleasant atmosphere and everything you would expect from a town-centre pub. Live bands feature Fridays and Saturdays and live vocalists on Sundays. Buses to the Rossendale Valley and Manchester stop close by.
➔➡(464,X41) ♩

Canine Club Ⓛ

45-47 Abbey Street, BB5 1EN
☎ (01254) 233999

Tetley Bitter; 3 changing beers (sourced nationally; often Moorhouse's, Reedley Hallows) Ⓗ
An award-winning social club on a busy street in an area of the town centre known for its many independent retailers. The central bar serves a comfortable lounge to the front, and games room to the rear where snooker, pool and darts are played. There is a large upstairs function room. This traditional club is always busy but is welcoming to all. Alongside the Tetley Bitter there is a changing beer range featuring local breweries such as Reedley Hallows and Moorhouse's. Buses to the Rossendale Valley and Manchester stop close by.
➔♣➡(464,X41) 🛜 ♩

Grants Ⓛ

1 Manchester Road, BB5 2BQ
☎ (01254) 393938 ⊕ grantsbar.co.uk
Big Clock Pals 1916, Bitter and Twisted; 4 changing beers (sourced locally) Ⓗ

A large, imposing building close to the college on the southern edge of the town centre. The pub is home to the impressive Big Clock brewery, which can be viewed from the main drinking area. A number of Big Clock ales are available and third-pint tasting paddles are available to sample the range. A range of home-made pizzas and pasta dishes is available, with many vegetarian options. The wood-fired pizza oven provides a proper Italian twist. Q❀◗⇌●P🚌(464,X41)

Adlington

Old Post Office 𝕃

161 Chorley Road, PR6 9LP

☎(01204) 228969 🌐 escapebrewery.co.uk

4 changing beers (sourced locally; often Escape) 🄷

The Old Post Office opened in 2021 as a partnership between Bolton's Escape brewery and MV Pub Group. It is the brewery's tap bar, located in the old post office building near the Ridgway Arms (now Tesco). There are four handpumps serving Escape brewery cask ales and the occasional guest, with additional keg lines for craft ales from smaller North-West breweries such as Rivington, Chain House and Twisted Wheel, as well as quality lagers and ciders. Q❀⇌P🚌(125)🐾📶

Spinners Arms 𝕃

23 Church Street, PR7 4EX

☎(01257) 483331

Acorn Barnsley Bitter; 6 changing beers (sourced regionally; often Abbeydale, Oakham, Salopian) 🄷

Known as the Bottom Spinners to differentiate it from the other Spinners Arms in the village this pub celebrated 20 consecutive years in the guide in 2022. Built in 1838, it is welcoming and friendly, with no pool table or gaming machines inside, just an open log fire. A single bar serves three seating areas and there is a pleasant outdoor drinking area to the front. One regular cask ale and up to six alternating guest ales are served, often from local breweries. The bar menu offers home-cooked food, with Sunday specials. ❀◖⇌P🚌(8A)🐾📶

Bacup

Crown Inn 𝕃

19 Greave Road, OL13 9HQ (off Todmorden Rd)

☎(01706) 873982

Pictish Brewers Gold; 3 changing beers 🄷

Cosy, traditional country pub, just off the road out to Todmorden, with a large L-shaped bar and stone-flagged floors throughout. It was built in 1865 and once owned by Baxter's of Glentop brewery. A welcoming coal fire warms the atmosphere in the cooler months. There are always three beers available, usually sourced locally. Food is available most evenings. Quiz nights are held on Wednesday and Sunday. On the second floor is a function room accommodating up to 35 guests. There is a large patio beer garden to the front of the pub. ❀◗♿♣P🚌(465,7)🐾

Bamber Bridge

Beer Box 𝕃

Unit 3 143 Station Road, PR5 6LA

☎(01772) 339619

5 changing beers (sourced locally) 🄷

Bamber Bridge's second micropub opened in September 2018 on the main road running through the northern end of the town, and is in premises previously operated by North West Domestic Services. There is one relatively large room with plenty of seating indoors and some standing room, with an outside seating area as well to the front. Up to five real ales are available, mainly from local breweries and including one dark beer. Q♿⇌●🚌(125)🐾📶♫

Banks

Ralph's Wife's

Hoole Lane, PR9 8BD

☎(01704) 214678

Fell Crag; 1 changing beer (sourced locally) 🄷

A coffee shop and bar with two changing real ales, it has the usual friendly, welcoming attributes of micropubs. There is some seating outside. Tea and coffee, including a range of speciality teas, are also served. Previous events have included tapas nights and cheese and wine pairing. Now the only real ale outlet in Banks since the closure of the New Fleetwood in 2020, this is a welcome addition to the real ale scene in Southport and West Lancashire. QP🚌🐾📶

Barnoldswick

Barlick Tap Ale House 𝕃

8 Newtown, BB18 5UQ

☎07739 088846

REAL ALE BREWERIES

12 Steps 🛢 Darwen
4 Mice 🛢 Bolton-by-Bowland
Accidental Morecambe
Avid Quernmore
BB18 🛢 Earby
Beer Shack 🛢 Clitheroe
Ben's ◆ Chorley
Big Clock 🛢 Accrington
Bowland Clitheroe
Brewhouse Kirkham
Brewsmith Stubbins
Chain House ◆ Preston
Clay Brow Skelmersdale
Cross Bay ◆ Morecambe
Farm Yard ◆ Cockerham
Folly Clayton le Dale
Fuzzy Duck Poulton-le-Fylde
Hop Vine 🛢 Burscough
Hopstar Darwen
Hopworks ◆ Bamber Bridge (NEW)
Jimbrew ◆ Clifton (NEW)
Lancaster Lancaster
Mighty Medicine ◆ Whitworth
Moorhouse's Burnley
Northern Whisper Cloughfold
Old School ◆ Warton
Oscars Nelson
Parker Banks
Patten 🛢 Winmarleigh (brewing suspended)
Peregrine Rishton
Priest Town Preston
Problem Child 🛢 Parbold
Q Brew Carnforth
Reedley Hallows Burnley
Rivington ◆ Rivington
Rock Solid Blackpool
Rossendale 🛢 Haslingden
Shed Beer Thornton Cleveleys (NEW)
Snowhill Scorton
Three B's 🛢 Blackburn
Three Peaks Nelson
Thwaites Mellor Brook
Unbound Colne
West Coast Rock 🛢 Blackpool

5 changing beers (sourced nationally) ⓗ
A friendly one-roomed micropub, the first to be opened in the town, lying just off the main square. A choice of four constantly changing cask beers is available, one of which will be a dark beer. The fifth handpull is draft cider. Also on tap are three changing craft beers and a foreign lager. There is a large selection of bottled beers, many from Belgium, and craft cans. Dogs are welcome. Q🍴🚪(M1)🐾

Barrowford

Banker's Draft
143 Gisburn Road, BB9 6HQ
☎ 07739 870880
4 changing beers (sourced nationally) ⓗ
This imposing detached former bank is now a small and friendly micropub specialising in real ale and conversation with no loud music or TVs. The five handpumps dispense continually rotating cask ales from national small brewers, offering a great variety of beer styles from hoppy blondes and traditional bitters to dark beers. There is also a good selection of wines and bottled craft lagers and wheat beers, with at least one real cider normally on draft. Q🐂🍴●P🚪(2)🐾

Old Bridge Inn
146 Gisburn Road, BB9 6AT
☎ (01282) 695208
2 changing beers (sourced regionally) ⓗ
A far-flung former Robinsons pub which is now operating as a freehouse. It is close to the old pack horse bridge in Higherford, hence its name. Arranged across two areas there is a comfortable lounge and a games area with pool table. There is easy level access from the pavement and a small patio with benches to the side of the pub. Limited parking is available. 🐾P

Belthorn

Dog Inn 🄻
61 Belthorn Road, BB1 2NN
☎ (01254) 433188 ⊕ thedoginnatbelthorn.net
Reedley Hallows Filly Close Blonde; 2 changing beers (sourced locally; often Bowland, Reedley Hallows) ⓗ
This is the first community-owned pub in East Lancashire and is run as a community benefit society. It has flagged floors on several levels and a real fire. Set in in hill country, with great views across the moors and out to the coast, it is somewhere both dogs and walkers are welcome. Full meals are available lunchtime and evenings, with a coffee shop menu in between. Beers are mainly from local breweries. 🐾🅞🍴●P🚪🐾🛜♫

Bispham Green

Eagle & Child
Maltkiln Lane, L40 3SG
☎ (01257) 462297 ⊕ eagleandchildbispham.co.uk
Moorhouse's White Witch; 7 changing beers (sourced regionally) ⓗ
An 18th-century pub with eight handpumps, seven showcasing real ales. Moorhouse's White Witch, Wainwrights and Bowland brewery beers are usually available alongside a variety of guest ales. This busy country pub has won Good Pub Guide awards, and is noted for its food, with its meat sourced from the Ainscough family farm. The huge front and back beer gardens, with a wildlife area and great views, host a beer festival on the first May bank holiday. Quiz night is every Monday. 🐂🅞🍴●P🚪(337)🐾🛜

Blackburn

Black Bull 🄻
Brokenstone Road, BB3 0LL (corner of Brokenstone Rd and Heys Ln) SD666247
☎ (01254) 581381 ⊕ threebsbrewery.co.uk
Three B's Stoker's Slake, Bobbin's Bitter, Oatmeal Stout, Black Bull, Weavers Brew, Knocker Up; 2 changing beers (sourced locally; often Three B's) ⓗ
In the heart of rural Lancashire, this is an independent award-winning family-run pub with brewery and beer shop attached. It was built on a farmhouse in the 18th century, purchased by Robert Bell from Thwaites and transformed now to a place for those who appreciate fine beer and friendly conversation. There are eight handpumps serving a fine selection of Three B's ales including the exclusive Black Bull bitter. The three-beer wedges are popular. No jukebox, fruit-machines or food served – just a friendly relaxing atmosphere. Q🐂🐾🅞🍴P🐾

Drummer's Arms 🄻
65 King William Street, BB1 7DT
☎ (01254) 941075
Three B's Stoker's Slake; 4 changing beers (sourced locally; often Big Clock, Deeply Vale, Hopstar) ⓗ
A classic single-roomed bar sitting opposite the Town Hall on the pedestrianised shopping area. The walls are adorned with breweriana and old pub signs. There is regular live music and open mic sessions on the first Sunday of the month. At other times expect a range of unobtrusive background music. The bar always offers a range of beer styles from stouts through to hoppy bitters, with Stoker's Slake mild a regular. There is a pleasant terrace at front featuring upcycled drum tables and attractive bespoke garden planters. It may open an hour earlier if Blackburn Rovers have a home game. 🐾🥤🍴🚪♫

Blackpool

Blackpool Cricket Club
Barlow Crescent, West Park Drive, FY3 9EQ (follow signs to Stanley Park)
☎ (01253) 393347 ⊕ blackpoolcricket.co.uk
5 changing beers (sourced regionally; often Elland, Moorhouse's) ⓗ
On the western edge of the multi-award winning Stanley Park, around 20 minutes' walk from the town centre, this club, housed in the impressive pavilion, is a vibrant, local, social centre. A range of five changing beers is available to the visitor. A many-time local CAMRA Club of the Year. Quizzes and entertainment nights are regularly held, and upstairs functions rooms are available for social events. Several TVs show various sports events. There is free entry to the club and to all cricket games except Lancashire's. 🐂🅞🍴🅟P🚪(18)🛜♫

Cask
9 Layton Road, FY3 8EA
☎ (01253) 396321
4 changing beers (sourced nationally) ⓗ
Situated a mile or so from Blackpool town centre, en-route to Poulton-le-Fylde, six bus routes pass close by. Four ever-changing cask beers are always available, normally including a dark beer. This compact micro has a pleasant suntrap drinking area to the front and a walled area at the rear. The Cask is very much dog friendly. Layton Cemetery opposite contains the grave of the last known survivor of the Charge of the Light Brigade. Q🐂🐾🅞●🚪🐾🛜

Cask & Tap

82 Topping Street, FY1 3AD
🌐 caskandtap.co.uk
8 changing beers (sourced nationally) Ⓗ
A friendly welcome is always guaranteed at this quirky micropub, tucked just off Blackpool's main central square, a little over five minutes' stroll from the Tower. An ever-changing range of up to eight real ales from near and far is available, normally including a dark beer, plus a selection of craft beers and real ciders and perries. The decor is interesting with some of the lighting being made from recycled electrical test gear and even an old handpull. Dogs are welcomed with well-behaved owners. Q&≠(North)🚃(North Pier)●🖨🚲

JD Drinkwater's Alehouse

75 Highfield Road, FY4 2JE
4 changing beers (sourced nationally; often Bowness Bay, Cross Bay, Lancaster) Ⓗ
One of a number of micropubs opened locally during Covid restrictions, this is a great asset to the local real ale scene and an instant success. The landlord has previously been the licencee of several local pubs and it is named after his father JD. Situated on a busy South Shore thoroughfare, it is frequented by locals and visitors alike. The four ever-changing beers come from near and far. Note the unusual bar along with its many quirky features. ♿&≠(Pleasure Beach)♣🖨🚲

No.10 Ale House & Thai Kitchen

258 Whitegate Drive, FY3 9JW
☎ (01253) 694913 🌐 no10alehouseandthai.co.uk
4 changing beers (sourced nationally; often Pennine) Ⓗ
Blackpool's first micropub, which opened in 2018. A great place for watching sports, with several TVs, it is popular with home fans when Blackpool FC are playing at nearby Bloomfield Road. The kitchen serves restaurant-quality Thai food most evenings. An ever-changing range of beers is available, normally including a dark beer. There is sunny outdoor bench-style seating available. Local bus stops are close by. 🚲🖨🚲

Burnley

Boot Inn ✅

18 St James' Street, BB11 1NG
☎ (01282) 463720
Greene King Abbot; Ruddles Best Bitter; 6 changing beers (sourced nationally; often Reedley Hallows) Ⓗ
This large former Thwaites house, right in the middle of Burnley shopping area and close to the bus station, serves the usual Wetherspoon fare. It was rebuilt in the Edwardian Baroque Style in 1911 to the design of Blackpool architect H Thompson, replacing a former inn of the same name which had originally been a farmhouse, and is now Grade II-listed. There are several distinct drinking areas with a garden and smoking area to the rear. ♿🚲◑≠(Central)🖨🛜

Bridge Bier Huis Ⓛ

2 Bank Parade, BB11 1UH
☎ (01282) 411304 🌐 thebridgebierhuis.co.uk
Moorhouse's Premier; 4 changing beers (sourced regionally) Ⓗ
An award-winning freehouse serving home-made food, with a large open-plan bar area and a small snug to one side. Closed Monday and Tuesday unless Burnley FC are at home. It offers two Moorhouse beers and three from smaller nationally sourced breweries plus one cider or perry. Over 50 foreign bottled beers complement the seven beers on tap. Quiz night is Wednesday and

occasional live music events are held on Sundays. The owners celebrated 20 years in charge in June 2023. Q◑≠(Central)●🖨🚲♫

New Brew-m Ⓛ

11 St James Row, BB11 1DR
☎ 07902 961426
Reedley Hallows Pendleside; 5 changing beers (sourced nationally) Ⓗ
Smart micropub in the centre of town, hidden behind Barclays bank. It is run as the brewery tap for Reedley Hallows brewery but also serves guest beers sourced by brewer and owner Pete Goldsbrough. There are a limited number of bottled beers and ciders together with a small wine and spirit selection and packet snacks. The pub does not open on a Tuesday or Wednesday unless Burnley FC are playing at home. Q≠(Manchester Road) 🖨🚲🛜

Burscough

Thirsty Duck Ⓛ

Unit 9 & 10 Burscough Wharf, L40 5RZ
☎ (01704) 894600 🌐 thirstyduck.co.uk
Hawkshead Bitter; 4 changing beers Ⓗ
This new bar and bottle shop in the Burscough Wharf complex makes a welcome addition to the thriving real ale scene in Burscough. The tastefully decorated modern bar has five cask lines, 10 keg lines and real cider as well as a full range of wine and spirits. The bottle shop, called the Beer Haul, is just over the courtyard from the bar and is open whenever the bar is. For access please either ring the bell or speak to the staff in the Thirsty Duck. Q🚲&≠(Bridge) ♣●P🖨🚲🛜

Carnforth

Royal Station

Market Street, LA5 9BT
☎ (01524) 733636 🌐 royalstation.co.uk
4 changing beers Ⓗ
A traditional Victorian station hotel which has now benefited from a facelift. A grand entrance and a foyer lead to a tapas bar, while round the back is the larger and more basic Junction Bar, revamped in 2016, where the games, real ale and live music on Friday and Saturday can be found. In 1900, it became the Royal Station Hotel in recognition of the fact that the Duke of York, later to become George V, availed himself of the hotel's hospitality during a shooting trip. A microbrewery is planned. 🚲◑≠♣🖨🚲🛜♫

Snug

Unit 6, Carnforth Gateway Building, LA5 9TR (at the north end of the former mainline platform)
☎ 07927 396861 🌐 thesnugmicropub.blogspot.co.uk
5 changing beers Ⓗ
The Snug is the area's first micropub and embraces the ethos. The only drinks are ale, cider, wine, a few soft drinks and at least 10 good-quality gins. The only food is a few light snacks. The only sounds are conversation and the roar of the passing trains. Decor is similarly stripped-back comprising just painted walls, bare floorboards and chunky tall tables. The eye is naturally drawn to a beautiful glazed wooden cabinet, where all the drinks are stored. Paid parking is on the station car park. Q🚲&≠♣🖨🚲🚲

Chorley

Ale Station Ⓛ ✅

60 Chapel Street, PR7 1BS

☎ (01257) 368003
Abbeydale Deception; Joseph Holt Bitter; 7 changing beers (sourced locally; often Hawkshead, Pictish, Rock the Boat) ⊞
Independently run by the same family since 2016, this bar is conveniently situated adjacent to the bus station and just across the road from the railway station. Although a town-centre pub, it has a loyal band of local regulars. Up to nine changing real ales are served, mainly sourced from northern microbreweries. The landlord champions traditional English bitter; two examples of this style are always served. A digital display board provides train times. Pictures of old Chorley adorn the walls. Q≉♦🅟♥🛜

Ben's Tap
2 Market Place, PR7 1DA
☎ (01257) 367890 ⊕ bensbrewery.co.uk
6 changing beers (sourced locally; often Ben's, Twisted Wheel) ⊞
The brewery tap for Ben's brewery opened in March 2022 in a former café premises. The interior has a rustic feel with recycled wooden pallets lining the walls. Six cask ales are served from Ben's own range; draft beers are available in third-pint measures upwards. There is a range of craft ales, a real cider or two plus an excellent selection of bottles and cans at good prices, which may be drunk on the premises or taken away. No food is served, but you are welcome to bring your own. ⏰≉♦🅟♥🛜

Bob Inn
24 Market Place, PR7 1DA
☎ 07767 238410
3 changing beers (sourced nationally; often Three B's) ⊞
A tiny bar housed in a market stall, this is the smallest pub in the local area. Outside seating is available as well as seating in the market food hall. Conversation and banter are an important part of the experience. Three ever-changing cask beers are served, sourced from smaller breweries nationally, and usually including a dark beer. There is no food served, but you are welcome to bring your own. Q⏰🅖♿≉🅟♥

Flat Iron 🅛 ✅
21 Cleveland Street, PR7 1BH
⊕ flatironchorley.co.uk
Ossett White Rat; 3 changing beers (sourced locally; often Blackedge, Titanic) ⊞
This is a smart town-centre pub and part of the growing real ale scene in Chorley. It featured in the very first CAMRA Guide in 1974 when it was described as a 'true drinker's pub' and served beers from Tetley Walker in Warrington. These days, expect to find up to four cask ales with one regular beer – White Rat – plus three changing beers sourced within a 50 mile radius. Real cider is on handpump and beer tasting paddles are also available. Multiple TVs around the pub show televised sport. ⏰🅖≉♦🅟♥🛜♪

Malt 'n' Hops 🅛
50-52 Friday Street, PR6 0AA
☎ (01257) 260074
Bank Top Dark Mild; Ossett White Rat; 7 changing beers (sourced nationally; often Blackedge, Moorhouse's, Wily Fox) ⊞
Converted from an old shop in 1989, the pub is located close to the town's railway and bus stations. It features a bright yet traditional single L-shaped bar on two levels and a pleasant beer garden. A genuine free house it serves a regular mild, with up to nine guest ales usually sourced from Lancashire and Yorkshire micros including

Rat, Wily Fox, Ossett, Elland, Lancaster, Fernandes, Goose Eye and Blackedge. Good-value filled rolls and pork pies are usually available. CAMRA Lancashire Pub of the Year 2017. ⏰🅖≉🅟♥🛜♪

Mason's Arms 🅛
98 Harpers Lane, PR6 0HU
☎ (01257) 367038
4 changing beers (sourced locally; often Blackedge, Marble, Pictish) ⊞
A tastefully modernised multi-room pub a mile from the town centre. The taproom has four changing ales available at any one time, sourced mainly from north-east micros, but beers from further afield are also sold. The taproom and two distinct lounges complete with wood-burning stoves give distinctly different drinking areas with a partly covered beer garden to the rear. Pizzas are served Wednesday to Sunday evenings. Light and airy, this is a cosy pub with a reputation for good beer. ⏰🅖🅟(24,125)♥🛜♪

Riley's Taproom & Wine Bar 🅛
Victoria Buildings, 4 Cleveland Street, PR7 1BH
☎ 07889 496720
2 changing beers (sourced regionally; often Cloudwater, Rivington) ⊞
Riley's opened in December 2021, based in premises previously used as a greengrocer's. They specialise in craft ales and fine wines and there is a comfortable atmosphere with plenty of seating inside. Ten keg lines serve a range of craft beers sourced from mainly local breweries. Real cider is dispensed through membrane keg and there are two handpumps for cask ale enthusiasts. A full beer menu is provided on a large screen behind the bar. Cold platters are available at all times, subject to availability. ♿≉♦🅟🛜

Shepherds' Hall Ale House & Victoria Rooms 🅛
67 Chapel Street, PR7 1BS
☎ (01257) 270619
Vocation Bread & Butter; 8 changing beers (sourced nationally; often Oakham, Timothy Taylor, Vocation) ⊞
This friendly and welcoming bar next door to the bus station was the first micropub in Chorley, opening in 2014. It was refurbished in 2020 and significantly extended into adjoining premises in 2021. Up to nine beers are now served from microbreweries all over the country including regular beers from Vocation. You should find a wide range of beer styles, always including a dark beer. Third-pint beer paddles are available. Two real ciders, four craft keg lines often featuring Rivington beers, and a variety of other drinks mean there is something to suit all tastes. Q⏰≉♣♦🅟♥🛜♪

Claughton-on-Brock

Clockwork
Unit 5, Beacon Retail Park, Westfield Road, PR3 0EN
☎ (01772) 953622 ⊕ clockworkbars.co.uk
3 changing beers (often Avid)
Opened 2020 in a new retail unit amid extensive housing developments this has been a lifeline in an area where most of the old pubs have shut. A fairly typical micropub, it has a large front window and decor in industrial chic and muted colours. Local producers are favoured in all departments, and it is a welcoming place for a pint or even a coffee. Poker and comedy nights are held. 🅟🅟(40,41)🛜

Clayton le Moors

Old England Forever L ✓

13 Church Street, BB5 5HT

☎ (01254) 383332

Bank Top Bad to the Bone, Dark Mild, Flat Cap, Port O Call; 2 changing beers (sourced locally; often Bank Top) Ⓗ

Comfortable and welcoming Edwardian terraced pub close to Mercer Park and All Saints Church serving a large range of Bank Top beers. A single-roomed establishment with defined bar and lounge areas, it sits just off Barnes Square and is easily reached from the towpath of the Leeds Liverpool canal. Note the section of glass flooring in front of the bar through which the cellar can be viewed. The pub is wheelchair friendly and has fully accessible toilets. Q❀&♣♠🖪(6,7)♪

Cleveleys

Jolly Tars ✓

154-158 Victoria Road West, FY5 3NE

☎ (01253) 856042

Brains Rev James Original; Greene King Abbot; Ruddles Best Bitter; Sharp's Doom Bar; 6 changing beers (sourced nationally; often Coach House, Moorhouse's) Ⓗ

Named after a nine-strong, highly popular family of concert party entertainers who visited Cleveleys on a regular basis between the wars, their open-air shows attracted large audiences during summer months. This lively, friendly and welcoming pub attracts visitors and locals alike. It has a great reputation and can get quite busy, although you can enjoy a quiet drink in one the the secluded booths. Six ever-changing guest beers are always available. The drinking area at the front is popular in summer. ⛵❀◑&🖪🖪🛜

Shipwreck Brewhouse L

53 Victoria Road West, FY5 1AJ

☎ (01253) 540597 ⊕ theshipwreckbrewhouse.co.uk

5 changing beers (sourced locally) Ⓗ

Looking small from the outside, this micropub and café in the heart of Cleveleys' main street, is a real Tardis with two indoor seating areas, covered and heated outdoor areas to the front and rear and meeting rooms. There is an emphasis on Lancashire ales, of which five are normally available, including a dark beer. A menu of local snacks and pub food is offered. The modern, seaside-themed decor includes photographs of historic local shipwrecks and well-known landmarks. ❀◑&🖪♠🖪❀

Clitheroe

Ale House

12-14 Market Place, BB7 2DA

☎ 07530 045365 ⊕ thealehouseclitheroe.co.uk

5 changing beers (sourced nationally; often Deeply Vale, Lakeland Brewhouse, Wishbone) Ⓗ

A quirky, popular pub right in the centre of town. There is a slightly unfinished feel here but the beer range is excellent, varied and constantly changing. Dark beers, including a strong one, often feature. The bar area is quite snug but the other areas are fairly spacious. Most of the walls are covered in a riot of beer memorabilia. There are spectacular views of Pendle Hill from the upstairs windows. ▲≠🖪❀♪

Beer Shack ✓

22-24 King Street, BB7 2EP

☎ (01200) 426368 ⊕ thebeershack.uk

4 changing beers (sourced locally; often Carnival, Moorhouse's, Pentrich) Ⓗ

First opened in 2021, this new bar has now added four handpulls. Beers come mainly from well-known microbreweries and larger ones such as Lancaster. There is nearly always a dark cask beer available. Robb and Sam, the licensees, have now begun brewing on the premises. Food is limited in choice but is well thought out. The large outdoor area at the rear is a real suntrap. Convenient for both the railway and bus stations. ≠🖪❀🛜

New Inn L

20 Parson Lane, BB7 2JN

Coach House Gunpowder Premium Mild, Farriers Best Bitter, Blueberry Classic Bitter; Moorhouse's Premier, Pride of Pendle, Blonde Witch; 5 changing beers (sourced regionally; often Prospect, Saltaire) Ⓗ

The bar at the New Inn is a welcome sight, with at least 10 beers on offer. The bar itself is central with a number of smaller rooms clustered around it. In addition to the regular beers from Coach House and Moorhouse's you may also find the likes of Saltaire, Ilkley, Prospect or Wharfedale breweries represented. The pub dates from the early 1800s and faces Clitheroe Castle. It is just a short walk from the bus and railway stations. Q❀▲≠🖪❀♪

Colne

Admiral Lord Rodney L

Mill Green, BB8 0TA

☎ (01282) 219759 ⊕ thelordrodney.co.uk

9 changing beers (sourced regionally; often Goose Eye, Ilkley, Reedley Hallows) Ⓗ

A much-loved community pub in Colne's old South Valley area, the old industrial heart of the town. The stone-flagged floor includes mosaics and there are beautiful tiles up the inner staircase. Set across three rooms, the pub has become the meeting place for a number of clubs. There is regular live entertainment in the evening, plus local history and art displays. There has been a recent refurbishment with open fires and flagged floors, plus a much-improved outdoor seating area and a separate smokers' area. Q⛵❀◑♣♠🛜♪

Boyce's Barrel

7 New Market Street, BB8 9BJ

5 changing beers (sourced nationally) Ⓗ

Colne's first micropub offers an ever-changing range of real ales and real cider. A dark ale is always available. Expect plenty of banter and occasional live music. The pub is tastefully styled, with tall, polished wooden sleeper tables. It is reminiscent of a rail staging post. Q&≠♠🖪🖪❀♪

Croston

Wheatsheaf ✓

Town Road, PR26 9RA

☎ (01772) 600370 ⊕ wheatsheaf-croston.com

Goose Eye Chinook Blonde; 4 changing beers (sourced nationally; often Bowland, Titanic) Ⓗ

On the main road and overlooking the village green, this tastefully refurbished pub has a contemporary feel. It has a distinct area for dining as well as a comfortable drinking area with sofas and chairs, and a large patio area to the front. There's a wide choice of beers, generally sourced locally with one regular and four ever-changing ales, invariably including one dark beer. Food is served lunchtimes and evenings during the week and all day, including breakfast, at weekends. ⛵❀◑&≠🅿(112,337)❀🛜♪

Darwen

Bird in th'hand ⃞

225 Duckworth Street, BB3 1AU
☎ 07926 115292
4 changing beers (sourced regionally; often 12 Steps, Blackedge) ⊞
Home to 12 Steps brewery, named after the number down to the cellar, this is a brewpub and bottle shop with four handpumps, 10 craft lines and three for ciders. There are shelves full of Belgian, international and UK bottled beers and craft ciders which can be consumed on or off the premises. The three rooms include one with a log-burner. There is a front pavement terrace and a covered back yard. Toilets are upstairs. The name comes from the pub which stood here over 100 years ago.
✿≠🚃(1) ✿ ♪

Loom & Shuttle ⃞

165 Duckworth Street, BB3 1AT
☎ (01942) 259071
4 changing beers (sourced regionally) ⊞
A single-roomed bar with beer garden at the rear, this is the first pub venture for Mayflower brewery of Wigan. It is a sustainability-conscious cocktail, cask and craft ale bar with a large hand-picked selection of world beer, gins, rums and whiskys. A number of Mayflower traditional cask ales are served alongside guest beers. Situated on the busy A666, regular buses connecting Blackburn with Darwen and Bolton pass the door.
➳≠P🚃🐾✿

Number 39 Hopstar Brewery Tap ⃞

39-41 Bridge Street, BB3 2AA
☎ 07531 425352
Hopstar; 1 changing beer (sourced regionally; often Milestone) ⊞
Multi award-winning continental-style bar in the centre of Darwen offering both beer and cider. Five handpumps dispense beers from the Hopstar range, which usually includes a dark beer, and occasionally a guest ale. New brews are tried out here first but never last long due to popular demand. A large variety of bottled continental and world beers are available along with two or three ciders or perries. Live music Thursday and Saturday evenings. ➳✿≠🚃🐾✿🛜

Dolphinholme

Fleece

Bay Horse, LA2 9AQ
☎ (01524) 791233 🌐 fleeceinn.co.uk
Black Sheep Best Bitter; 3 changing beers (often Bowland, Farm Yard) ⊞
At first sight this former farmhouse is in the middle of nowhere, but as the nearby village and the country beyond have no pubs, it is the default local for quite a lot of people. It also welcomes visitors from elsewhere, with high-quality dining and luxury accommodation. The main entrance gives onto an old-fashioned hall with loads of old prints. The main bar, oak-beamed and with pews and usually a roaring fire is to the right, the dining room, opened 2004, to the left. There are two rooms off the bar, one designated a family room. ➳✿≠🛏🌭👍♣P🛜

Fleetwood

Steamer

Queens Terrace, FY7 6BT
☎ (01253) 681001
🌐 thesteamerfleetwood.foodanddrinksites.co.uk

Reedley Hallows Pendleside; 5 changing beers (sourced nationally; often Bowness Bay, Cross Bay, Kirkby Lonsdale) ⊞
Fleetwood's oldest surviving pub, the Steamer is situated across from the famous market. It offers a varying selection of up to six real ales in a traditional pub setting. The decor includes pictures and photographs of the local area, and of historic fishing vessels that reflect the pub's close association with the fishing industry and history of the town. Good food is available daily from noon with regular theme nights. Live entertainment features at weekends. Fleetwood Museum is nearby and is worth a visit to find out about local history.
➳✿🍴👍&🚃(Victoria St) ♣🚃✿🛜♪

Thomas Drummond ✅

London Street, FY7 6JE
☎ (01253) 775020
Greene King Abbot; Ruddles Best Bitter; Sharp's Doom Bar; 7 changing beers (often Marston's, Phoenix) ⊞
This former Sunday school takes its name from a local man who built most of the workers' cottages and churches of the town in the mid 18th century. This spacious, yet cosy pub guarantees a warm and friendly welcome. A good range of ales from light to dark and medium to strong come mainly from northern breweries, including seven ever-changing guest beers. A pleasant small beer garden can be found to the rear.
➳✿🍴&🚃(London St) 🚃🛜

Freckleton

Tap n' Drum

68-74 Lytham Road, PR4 1XA
☎ (01772) 634924
4 changing beers (sourced regionally; often Bowland, Farm Yard, Lancaster) ⊞
Situated a short walk from the centre of Freckleton, this micropub opened its doors at the end of 2019. A range of four ales, mostly from local brewers, await the thirsty drinker along with a selection of craft beers. A pleasant outdoor area is available to the front. Although there is a TV for live sporting events and live music is played on many weekends, this is mostly unobtrusive and the pub is an ideal spot for conversation. Buses between Preston and the Fylde Coast stop outside. ✿&♣🚃✿🛜♪

Great Harwood

1B Tap ⃞

1B Glebe Street, BB6 7AA
5 changing beers (sourced regionally) ⊞
On a side street opposite the post office, close to the historic Towngate square and preservation area, you will find this welcoming two-roomed bar housed in a historic former Co-operative Society building. The main room, featuring plenty of beer and brewery related items and old photos of Great Harwood, sells a changing and skillfully selected range of cask beers which always includes a stout or porter. Lancashire and Yorkshire breweries predominate. A side room offers additional seating. Note the collection of beer festival glasses on display in the bar. There is a small, covered outdoor area to the front in summer. Q🚃(6,7)🛜♪

Great Mitton

Aspinall Arms

Mitton Road, BB7 9PQ
☎ (01254) 826555

Brunning & Price Original; 5 changing beers (sourced regionally; often Acorn, Moorhouse's, Timothy Taylor) H
This large pub between Whalley and Clitheroe is predominantly focused on dining, but also sets much store by its cask beer. A mixture of smaller rooms and a larger open-plan area are arranged around a central bar. The six handpulls sell beers from the likes of Dent, Ossett, Phoenix and Goose Eye. The food here is great so it is wise to book in advance. The massive garden is right next to the River Ribble and is unbeatable in good weather. The 13th-century All Hallows church is close by. ⑤❀⊕◑▲P冖(5)❀🗇

Haggate

Hare & Hounds ✅
1 Halifax Road, BB10 3QH
☎ (01282) 424612
4 changing beers (sourced regionally) H
A traditional country pub in the Briercliffe area of Burnley. There are superb open views over the Pennine moorland from the rear patio area. Food is served Wednesday to Sunday and there are separate rooms to the front of the pub with a large restaurant/function room to the rear. Live music events are hosted at weekends. The bus from Burnley terminates 200 yards before the pub. ⑤❀⊕◑♣P冖(5)❀🗇♪

Haslingden

Griffin Inn 🅛
86 Hud Rake, BB4 5AF
☎ (01706) 214021 ⊕ rossendalebrewery.co.uk
Rossendale Floral Dance, Glen Top Bitter, Rossendale Ale, Halo Pale, Pitch Porter, Sunshine; 1 changing beer H
Situated on Hud Rake this is a traditional community pub and also the home of the Rossendale brewery situated on the lower floor below the pub. The large bar area has a separate area for pub games, and the expansive lounge has picture windows overlooking the local hills and valleys. On the hill facing the front sits the Halo panopticon. The pub is easily accessible, but there is a steep uphill walk from main road bus stops.
Q&♣🖝冖(464,X41) ❀🗇♪

Heath Charnock

Bay Horse 🅛 ✅
Babylon Lane, PR6 9ER
☎ (01257) 485849
Wily Fox Blonde Vixen, Crafty Fox; 2 changing beers (often Moorhouse's, Timothy Taylor) H
Dating from the 1750s, this attractive, stone-built pub overlooks open countryside and the Rivington Hills. Built as a coaching inn and later extended to include the old smithy, this multi-roomed pub has exposed stonework and beams and several open fires. To the rear is a bowling green and outdoor seating. Up to four cask ales are served on handpump, invariably including beers from Wily Fox brewery alongside traditional beers often from Timothy Taylor and Moorhouse's. Excellent home-cooked food with a modern twist is served daily. Walkers and dogs are welcome. ⑤❀⊨◑&♣P冖(8,8a)❀🗇

Yew Tree 🅛
Dill Hall Brow, PR6 9HA
☎ (01257) 480344 ⊕ yewtreeinnanglezarke.co.uk
Blackedge Pike; house beer (by Blackedge); 2 changing beers (sourced locally; often Blackedge, Bowland, Northern Monkey) H

Attractive, isolated stone-built pub with flagged floors and great views over open countryside. The pub is essentially open-plan but walls and partitions divide it into separate cosy areas. It has long had a reputation for quality food with a full range of meals available made from locally sourced produce wherever possible. Closing times can vary. Dogs are welcome in the bar area but not the restaurant. It showcases ales from the nearby Blackedge brewery and a guest or two from other independent local breweries. Q⑤❀⊕◑&▲P❀🗇♪

Helmshore

Robin Hood Inn 🅛 ✅
280 Holcombe Road, BB4 4NP
☎ (01706) 404200
Hydes Original; 4 changing beers H
Traditional stone-built village pub which, although opened up, still retains the impression of having three separate rooms with two open fires. The original Glen Top brewery windows are a feature. Beers from the seasonal ranges of Hydes and Beer Studio dominate the guest beers. Quiz nights are held on Thursdays. A small beer garden overlooking Helmshore Textile Museum and lodge can be reached by steps to the side of the pub. Q⑤❀&♣冖(11)❀

Hest Bank

Crossing 🍸
6 Coastal Road, LA2 6HN
☎ 07584 660075
5 changing beers H
A former café which opened as a micropub in 2018. A stone, possibly Victorian, building with a timber extension and a plate-glass window from café days. It has a U-shaped layout, with a bar counter near the entrance in one arm, a wood-burning stove in the middle, and a back room holding the games, bound copies of Railway magazine and photos of Hest Bank station which closed in 1969. The name refers to the fact that the pub is close to both one of the last level crossings on the West Coast Main Line and the ancient route over the sands. Q♣冖(5,55A)❀🗇

Heysham

Bookmakers ✅
364 Heysham Road, LA3 2BJ
☎ 07785 257648
5 changing beers H
This micropub, opened in 2019 in a former betting shop situated amongst other shops in a suburban neighbourhood, is a welcome addition to the real ale scene in the area. The single wedge-shaped room is decorated in industrial chic with a few comfy chairs and bar stools, and an arrangement of standing and seated areas. The pub attracts large numbers of locals. &♣冖❀

Kirkham

Kirkham Bierhaus
36 Poulton Street, PR4 2AH
☎ (01772) 417792 ⊕ kirkhambierhaus.co.uk
6 changing beers (sourced regionally; often Brightside) H
Based in the former Santander bank, this pub, which opened in February 2022, is already a popular favourite with locals. It has a bright interior and there is always a good conversational vibe in the air. A range of regularly changing beers, mostly from local brewers, is offered along with a range of German draft and bottled beers

and UK craft cans. A suntrap garden is to the rear. A small selection of food is served, with regular themed evenings. ⊛◑&⊟❀

Tap & Vent Brewhouse L
26 Poulton Street, PR4 2AB
☎ (01772) 382019 ⊕ tapandventbrewhouse.co.uk
5 changing beers (sourced regionally; often Brewhouse, Fuzzy Duck) Ⓗ
Looking like a traditional looking shop from the outside, this modern pub is located right in the centre of Kirkham, just up from the Market Square and bus stops. This is the tap for the Brewhouse brewery, located next door but one, although their beers do not dominate choice, and a good range of guest ales, continental lagers and bottled beers is also available. A quieter snug is hidden behind the bar and there is a sunny pavement area to the front.
Q⭢⊛◑&♣⊟❀🕏

Lancaster

Cornerhouse
34 New Street, LA1 1HU
☎ (01524) 845939 ⊕ cornerhouselancaster.co.uk
6 changing beers (sourced locally; often Bowness Bay, Kirkby Lonsdale) Ⓗ
Comprehensively refitted in 2018, this conversion of one end of an old department store is a modern interpretation of gin-palace style. Most of the space is restaurant, but there is a large bar offering the choice of communal drinking at a long marble-topped table or more discreet areas around the walls. There is also plenty of standing room. Cocktails are a speciality, with an amazing selection of spirits and mixers. Live music is played Thursday to Sunday. Outside tables are sheltered from the worst of the weather. ⊛&⇌♣⊟❀🕏♫

Jailor's Barrel ✓
64 Market Street, LA1 1HP
☎ (01524) 840316 ⊕ jailorsbarrel.co.uk
Hydes Original, Lowry; 4 changing beers (often Hydes) Ⓗ
Converted from retail premises in 2007, it has retained the façade with its huge curved windows. The interior was refurbished in 2016 in contemporary style with the bar now dominating the modestly-sized room. A quiet upstairs room is also open to the public, and can be reserved. There is a collection of bottled beers, some quite rare, strong and expensive! Cask ale is disounted on Monday. Q◑⇌♣⊟(BS)❀🕏♫

Three Mariners
Bridge Lane, LA1 1EE (nr Parksafe car park entrance)
☎ (01524) 388957 ⊕ thethreemarinerslancaster.co.uk
Oakham Citra; Robinsons Wizard, Dizzy Blonde; 7 changing beers Ⓗ
Commonly claimed to be the oldest pub in Lancaster, the Three Mariners certainly looks old, inside as well as out, but it's suffered some rebuilding and it had a comprehensive revamp in 2004. The cellar is excavated at first-floor level. The pub is now a popular watering hole with a loyal local clientele. Home-cooked, reasonably-priced food is available. Live music includes Irish folk on Tuesday with folk on the first Friday of the month and bluegrass on the third Friday. There is limited parking. Q⊛◑&♣⊟❀🕏♫

Tite & Locke
Lancster Railway Station, Meeting House Lane, LA1 5NW (on platform 3)
☎ (01524) 66737
Lancaster Amber, Blonde, IPA, Black, Red; 1 changing beer (often Lancaster) Ⓗ

A large part of the old station buildings now lies empty, but here a few rooms have been joined together and given a new use, decorated in a modern style without wallpaper or carpets. Curiously, although on the outside the station is built of the local gritstone, inside it can be seen to be mostly brickwork. It has four rooms, one with the bar, the others called first-, second- and third-class lounges. The first can be hired for functions, the beer store is visible from the third. ⊛⇌P⊟❀

White Cross L ✓
Quarry Road, LA1 4XT (behind town hall, on canal towpath)
☎ (01524) 33999 ⊕ thewhitecross.co.uk
Timothy Taylor Landlord; Wye Valley HPA; 8 changing beers (sourced regionally; often Allendale, Elland, Titanic) Ⓗ
A modern (1988) renovation of an old canalside warehouse with an open-plan interior and a light, airy feel. French windows open on to extensive canalside seating. There is a Tuesday quiz, and a beer and pie festival each April. It sits in the corner of an extensive complex of Victorian textile mills, now converted to other uses. The wide open spaces and general style makes it look like a circuit pub, but in fact much of the custom comes either from the residential areas up the hill or from the nearby workplaces. ⊛◑&♣P⊟🕏

Wobbly Cobbler
49 Scotforth Road, LA1 4SA
⊕ thewobblycobbler.co.uk
4 changing beers (often Avid, Farm Yard, Old School) Ⓗ
Micropub opened in 2020 in a former florist's, now an established community local. The large windows from the shop have been retained, and inside, dark grey walls and unpainted woodwork predominate. There are only minimal eats, except when street food is available on Saturdays, but the drink selection is quite varied. It has extensive sheltered outside seating and cccasional live music. Q⊛♣⊟♫

Lathom

Ship Inn
4 Wheat Lane, L40 4BX (take School Ln from Burscough, turn right after hump-backed bridge) SD452116
☎ (01704) 893117 ⊕ shipatlathom.co.uk
House beer (by Moorhouse's); changing beers (sourced regionally; often Black Sheep, Sharp's) Ⓗ
A traditional country pub set in an idyllic canalside location. The cosy central bar features a real fire and separates the two dining areas which serve food ranging from pub classics through to interesting and changing specials. There is a dog-friendly 'boot room' complete with log burner. The pub is popular all year but especially in summer, with its large beer garden. A highlight is the September Beer, Pie and Sausage festival featuring over 40 handpulled ales.
⭢⊛◑&⇌(Hoscar) P⊟(337,3A) ❀🕏

Leyland

Golden Tap Ale House L
1 Chapel Brow, PR25 3NH
☎ (01772) 431859
6 changing beers (sourced nationally) Ⓗ
Located in a former shop, this cosy one-roomed micropub opened its doors to the public in 2016. Up to six changing cask ales are served, sourced from microbreweries far and wide, usually including two dark beers and at least one from the local region. No food is

served other than a few snacks, but the pub is right in the heart of the town's fast-food and takeaway area. ☆✦♣♠✿(111) ☻❀

Market Ale House 🅛
33 Hough Lane, PR25 2SB
☎ (01772) 623363
6 changing beers (sourced nationally) 🅷
Opened in 2013 this was the area's first micropub. It is located at the entrance to the former Leyland Motors North Works, which now serves as the town's market hall. With an extension into the adjoining premises added in 2021 and an upstairs lounge, there is plenty of seating. Six changing real ales come from local and national breweries. Changing ciders, wine and a few spirits are also served. There's no TV but there is live acoustic music from 4.30pm on Sundays. There is an outside drinking area to the front with ample tables and seating. ✿✦♣♠✿(109,111)☻❀♪

Longridge

Applejacks 🅛
83 Berry Lane, PR3 3WH
☎ (01772) 782083
Reedley Hallows New Zealand Pale; 3 changing beers (sourced locally; often Bowland, Bradfield, Reedley Hallows) 🅷
This friendly family-run microbar in a former greengrocer's shop is situated on the main shopping street. The shop has been tastefully converted and includes an upstairs function room 'Apples and Pears' catering for up to 30 people and with its own bar. Free of tie, there are four rotating cask ales on handpump, often sourced from smaller independent local breweries, such as Reedley Hallows and Bowland. A blonde ale is usually featured. Breaking with the micropub trend, Applejacks is open seven days a week. Q✿✦♠(1)❀

Lostock Hall

Lostock Ale 🅛
7 Hope Terrace, PR5 5RU
6 changing beers (sourced locally; often Blackedge, Wily Fox) 🅷
Located within the pedestrianised Tardy Gate shopping area, this micropub opened in 2020 in former gift shop premises. Quickly becoming popular, it was the local CAMRA branch's Pub of the Season for spring 2022. Six changing cask ales often include beers from local breweries such as Pennine and Wily Fox, while there are also eight keg lines in place. This community-focused pub has a relaxed friendly atmosphere, and with the acquisition of the adjoining charity shop premises in late 2021, its floor space has more than doubled in size. ✿✦♠(109,111) ☻❀♪

Lytham

Craft House Beer Café
5 Clifton Street, FY8 5EP
☎ (01253) 730512
4 changing beers (sourced regionally) 🅷
This cosy micropub, now in its seventh year, guarantees a warm welcome. It has fast developed into a popular destination for real ale drinkers, and can get very busy. Four ever-changing beers are served, sourced from far and wide and always including a dark beer. These are supplemented by a selection of British and world craft beers in bottle and can. This small bar is dog-friendly and offers pavement seating, weather permitting. A small food menu is served daily. Q✿◑✦♠☻❀

Railway Hotel ✅
Station Road, FY8 5DH (next to fire station on B5259)
☎ (01253) 797250
Greene King Abbot; Ruddles Best Bitter; Sharp's Doom Bar; 4 changing beers (sourced nationally; often Coach House, Moorhouse's, Phoenix) 🅷
This two-story property was purpose-built next to Lytham's first railway station in 1847, and was originally named the Railway Hotel. Memorabilia depicting the era is displayed. A former Catterall & Swarbrick and then Bass house, Wetherspoon brought it in 2012 and revised its original name. The bright interior is split across different levels. The distinct themed areas include golf, railways and Lytham's halcyon days. Pleasant outdoor drinking areas exist to front and rear, with wheelchair access at the side. ☆✿◑♿✦♠❀

Taps ✅
12 Henry Street, FY8 5LE
☎ (01253) 736226
Greene King IPA; Robinsons Dizzy Blonde; 6 changing beers (sourced nationally; often Acorn, Moorhouse's) 🅷
Several times winner of the local CAMRA Pub of the Year Award, and national CAMRA Pub of the Year runner-up in 2011. Originally ostler's cottages and dating back to 1839, the pub has been in the Guide for 30 consecutive years during which time it has had only two landlords. A range of rapidly changing beers are available, always including a mild. The pub has an outside drinking area which is heated. There is a quiz every Monday night. Though this can be a busy pub service is usually prompt. ☆✿◑♿✦♣♠❀

Morecambe

Eric Bartholomew ✅
10-18 Euston Road, LA4 5DD
☎ (01524) 405860
Greene King Abbot; Ruddles Best Bitter; Sharp's Doom Bar; 5 changing beers (often Cross Bay) 🅷
Opened in 2004, this Wetherspoon pub near the seafront is dedicated to Eric Morecambe (born Eric Bartholomew). The open-plan pub functions on two levels, with an upstairs lounge and dinner area, while the long bar downstairs services an area with pictures of 19th-century Morecambe and some artwork with a Morecambe and Wise theme. There is some outside seating at front for smokers but outdoor drinking is not allowed. Close to shops and a public car park. Q✿◑♿✦♠❀

Little Bare
23 Princes Crescent, LA4 6BY
☎ 07817 892370
5 changing beers 🅷
An intimate micropub which opened in 2017 in a former off-licence, retaining the shop window. It features grey paint, bare floorboards and lit candles after dark and follows the micropub formula of no food, no music and no machines. Quiz night is Tuesday. There's a second room down a corridor with extra seating. A small suntrap beer garden lies to the rear of the premises and is accessed through the back room. ✿✦(Bare Lane) ♣♠(100,5) ☻

Torrisholme Taps ✅
312 Lancaster Road, LA4 6LY
☎ 07786 073626
5 changing beers 🅷
Micropub opened in 2021 amongst shops in an old village, now a suburb. Located in a former bridal shop it has a picture window, and is light and spacious for a

micro, with a wide range of beverages. Pies are on sale. There is a bike rack at the front but nearly all the customers walk here. Q🖳(1,1A)❀

Ormskirk

Cricketers 🅛
24 Chapel Street, L39 4QF
☎ (01695) 571123 ⊕ thecricketers-ormskirk.co.uk
7 changing beers (sourced regionally; often Salopian, Wainwright) 🄷
Situated close to Ormskirk town centre, the pub prides itself on both quality food and cask ales. It features six cask ales sourced from local and regional breweries and is a former CAMRA award winner. An extensive food menu is served all day in its restaurant or bar area. Cricket memorabilia around its walls reflects the pub's close relationship with Ormskirk Cricket Club.
🌃❀◑&≉P🖳(375,385) 🛜

Kicking Donkey
Narrow Moss Lane, L40 8HY
☎ (01695) 227273 ⊕ thekickingdonkey.co.uk
Lancaster Blonde; 3 changing beers (sourced regionally) 🄷
Elegant country pub which has recently been refurbished. Three handpulls offer a rotating selection of local ales, usually including one pale, one amber and one dark beer. Lancaster Blonde is a semi-regular due to its popularity. Opens bank holiday Mondays. They are a collection point for the Ormskirk Food Bank – food donations handed in at the bar result in entry to a prize draw. 🌃◑P🖳

Tap Room No. 12 🅛
12 Burscough Street, L39 2ER
☎ (01695) 581928
4 changing beers (sourced regionally) 🄷
This former shop has had a custom conversion into a Belgian-style single-room bar with wooden panels. It features four changing cask ales sourced regionally and aims to offer a porter or stout, an amber bitter and two pale beers of different strength, alongside an extensive range of foreign bottled beers and authentic foreign lagers on draft. There is a quiz every Wednesday and live music Friday and Saturday with background music during the rest of the week. ≉♣🖳❀🛜♪

Orrell

Delph Tavern
Tontine, WN5 8UJ
☎ (01695) 622239
5 changing beers 🄷
Free house, popular with locals and visitors, serving five ever-changing ales with an emphasis on local breweries. Bar snacks are provided on a Friday evening. Live sports are shown on a number of unobtrusive screens while a vault area offers pool and darts. The outside area has tables and chairs to relax and enjoy the good weather and offers a small play area for children. Weekly quiz nights are popular. 🌃❀◑&♣P🖳(352)❀🛜

Oswaldtwistle

Vault 🅛
343 Union Road, BB5 3HS
☎ (01254) 872279
Moorhouse's White Witch; 4 changing beers (sourced regionally) 🄷
A popular single-roomed bar on the busy main road through Oswaldtwistle. It is easy to reach by public

transport as buses from Accrington and Blackburn pass the door every few minutes. There is high bench seating around the walls and a standing area at the bar. The six handpumps dispense four changing beers and two ciders. Keen Rugby League supporters, the Vault sponsor one of the junior teams at Accrington Wildcats. Note the framed team photo in the bar. Q❀🖳(6,7)❀

Padiham

Boyce's Barrel
9 Burnley Road, BB12 8NA
☎ 07736 900111
4 changing beers (sourced nationally; often Craven, Rudgate) 🄷
A single-roomed micropub on the main road through town with a collection of advertising signs adorning the walls. It is the sister pub of Boyce's in Colne and run by the same management team. The pub is closed Monday to Wednesday. There is a small selection of wines, spirits and bottled beers together with bag-in-box cider. Food is limited to bar snacks. Buses to and from Burnley pass the door. Q❀🖳(M2,152)

Parbold

Wayfarer 🅛
1-3 Alder Lane, WN8 7NL
☎ (01257) 464600 ⊕ wayfarerparbold.co.uk
Problem Child (varies); 5 changing beers 🄷
A country pub with a focus on dining offering six handpulls and a range of craft keg beers. It has low-beamed ceilings with cosy nooks and crannies. Landlord and brewer Jonny Birkett is happy to show you around his on-site microbrewery, Problem Child brewing. Popular with walkers as it is close to the Leeds-Liverpool Canal and Parbold Hill, suggested walking routes can be found on the website. The countryside beer garden has very pleasant views.
Q🌃❀◑&≉❀P🖳(313,337) ❀🛜♪

Windmill Hotel
3 Mill Lane, WN8 7NW
☎ (01257) 462935 ⊕ thewindmillparbold.co.uk
Tetley Bitter; 4 changing beers (sourced nationally; often Wainwright) 🄷
Located close to the village centre next to an old windmill and adjacent to the Leeds-Liverpool Canal. Access is via stone steps. The main part of the building dates back to 1794 when it was used as a grain store. The interior is clean and welcoming with three real ales on the pumps. A warm welcome is given to drinkers, diners, bargees and walkers. The separate snug to the right of the doorway features delightful carved animals in the wooden panels and is the dog-friendly dining area. Please note this pub has no disabled access or WC.
Q🌃❀◑≉P🖳❀♪

Pendleton

Swan with Two Necks 🍷 🅛
Main Street, BB7 1PT
☎ (01200) 423112 ⊕ swanwithtwonecks.co.uk
5 changing beers (sourced regionally; often Goose Eye, Phoenix) 🄷
A plethora of awards acknowledge that this has been one of the best pubs in the area for the past decade. It has been run by the same owners for over 30 years. The five handpulls offer an ever-changing range that may feature beers from Blackedge, Fernandes, Rat and Goose Eye. Real cider is available. It is rumoured that the beer is so good because the landlord talks to it. Food is of high

quality yet reasonably priced. There are real fires during winter months and a large beer garden with amazing views. Q❀🅭�'♣P

Penwortham

Tap & Vine

69 Liverpool Road, PR1 9XD

☎ (01772) 751116 🌐 tapandvine.co.uk

4 changing beers (sourced locally) 🅗

Penwortham's first micropub, this is an upmarket wine bar-type establishment housed in a former art and crafts shop. It has limited seating, and can get quite busy at times. To the rear is a small secluded room with a wood-burning stove, and there is also a covered outdoor seating area for use in the warmer weather. Four changing beers are always available, often including some from lesser-known microbreweries. The food consists of snacks, pies and serving platters. Q🕭♣🖳🌣🛜♫

Poulton le Fylde

Old Town Hall

5 Church Street, FY6 7AP

☎ (01253) 892257

Moorhouse's Pride of Pendle; 6 changing beers (sourced locally; often Bowland, Reedley Hallows, Titanic) 🅗

Located in the heart of Poulton, facing the churchyard, the building started life in 1869 as a pub called the Bay Horse; it was later used as council offices until 1988 when it returned to its original use. The now open-plan layout retains some of its heritage features. Up to six ales are available. Live music is hosted every Saturday. Live sports play on many TVs, and a dedicated area is provided for horse-racing enthusiasts. 🕭🌣🛬(Poulton-le-Fylde)♣🖳🌣🛜♫

Poulton Elk ✅

22 Hardhorn Road, FY6 7SR

☎ (01253) 899667

Greene King Abbot; Ruddles Best Bitter; Sharp's Doom Bar; 7 changing beers (sourced nationally; often Bank Top, Bradfield, Moorhouse's) 🅗

On the site of the telephone exchange and formerly the Edge nightclub it was converted into a Wetherspoon pub in 2013. It is named after a locally-found 13,000-year-old elk skeleton that contained a sharpened flint, the earliest evidence of man in the area. There are two outdoor drinking areas, a front terrace and a larger area to the rear. It can be busy at weekends but swift service is normally the order of the day. 🕭❀🅭🌣🛬(Poulton-le-Fylde)🖳🛜

Thatched House ✅

30 Ball Street, FY6 7BG

☎ (01253) 891063

Bank Top Flat Cap; Bradfield Farmers Blonde; Timothy Taylor Landlord; 6 changing beers (sourced regionally; often Saltaire) 🅗

Past winner of local CAMRA Pub of the Year and serving a range of nine guest ales, of which six vary. This unmissable mock-Tudor pub is located in the corner of St Chad's churchyard. Pictures of sports and local history decorate many walls and there are two open fires and a log-burning stove. Often busy at weekends, outdoor drinking and smoking are in a small yard between the pub and former brew house, and on a roof terrace. Q❀🌣🛬(Poulton-le-Fylde)🖳🌣🛜

Preston

Black Horse 🍷 ★ ✅

166 Friargate, PR1 2EJ

☎ (01772) 204855

Robinsons Dizzy Blonde, Old Tom; 6 changing beers (sourced nationally) 🅗

Victorian Grade II-listed pub, close to the historic open market. With its tiled bar, walls and mosaic floor it has been identified by CAMRA as having a nationally important historic pub interior. Two front rooms are adorned with Robinsons memorabilia and photos of old Preston; the famous 'hall of mirrors' seating area is to the rear. Robinsons beers are available with an additional four ever-changing guest beers coming from far and wide. The pub is away-supporter football friendly. Awarded the 2019/20 George Lee Memorial Trophy and local CAMRA Pub of the Year 2023. Q🕭🌣≉♣🖳🌣🛜♫

Crafty Beggars Ale House

284 Garstang Road, Fulwood, PR2 9RX

☎ (01772) 954447 🌐 craftybeggars.co.uk

4 changing beers (sourced nationally) 🅗

Appearing in the Guide for a second year, this large micro with capacity for roughly 50 people opened in July 2020. It provides a traditional small pub atmosphere, selling four cask ales on handpump sourced mainly from the north-west area, craft ales, fine wines and boxes of real cider in the fridge. There are five changing keg lines, of which some may be KeyKeg. Carry-outs are also available. Homemade pizzas, paninis, breads and pies are served Monday to Saturday teatimes, and Crafty Cask Club is on Tuesdays. ❀🅭🌣🖳(125,23)🌣♫

Guild Ale House 🅛

56 Lancaster Road, PR1 1DD

☎ 07932 517444

7 changing beers (sourced regionally) 🅗

Preston's first micropub opened in 2016 just a few doors away from Preston's Guild Hall complex. The main room has high and low level seating and the high ceilings give a light and airy feel. A small lounge is tucked away to the rear and there is a comfortable lounge upstairs. Seven changing beers are mainly local or from Yorkshire, and there is at least one dark beer. A range of continental beers is available in keg and bottle. There is no jukebox, TV, or food, but live acoustic music plays on Sunday afternoons. A two-times local CAMRA Pub of the Year. Q🕭❀🌣≉♣●🖳🌣🛜♫

Moorbrook

370 North Road, PR1 1RU

☎ (01772) 823302 🌐 themoorbrook.co.uk

8 changing beers (sourced nationally) 🅗

This place is where the local CAMRA branch was formed in 1973. It has a traditional-style wood-panelled bar with two rooms off the main bar area, and an enclosed beer garden to the side and rear. Food features authentic wood-fired pizzas and home-made shortcrust pies. The eight guest beers come from all over the country, providing a wide choice of regional beer types while retaining a strong emphasis on microbreweries from the area. The venue gets busy on Preston North End match days. A former local CAMRA Pub of the Year. 🕭🌣🅭🌣🖳🌣🛜♫

New Continental

South Meadow Lane, PR1 8JP

☎ (01772) 499425 🌐 newcontinental.net

House beer (by Marble); 6 changing beers (sourced nationally) 🅗

An out-of-town pub by the River Ribble, Miller Park, and the large railway bridge. It has a main bar area, a lounge with a real fire in winter, plus a conservatory overlooking a sizeable beer garden. Live music and theatre are hosted regularly in the Boatyard events space, which has also been used for beer festivals. Eight handpumps serve a cider plus up to seven microbrewery beers, including the house ale from Marble and a dark brew. A beer menu is produced and updated each day. Freshly-cooked meals are available Wednesday to Sunday.

Q ☺ ☼ ⊛ ◐ & ≠ ◆ P ⬚ (119) ☻ ☎ ♫

Old Vic 🄻

79 Fishergate, PR1 2UH
☎ (01772) 828519
🌐 theoldvic-preston.foodanddrinksites.co.uk

Wainwright Amber; 6 changing beers (sourced regionally) ⊞
Situated opposite the railway station and on bus routes into the city, this popular pub provides travellers with a TV screen showing live updates of train departures. It gets busy at weekends, with a quiz on Sunday evening. The rear of the building has recently been extended, with pool players and darts enthusiasts now having a separate area. A large sun terrace caters for outdoor drinking. Seven handpumps offer a good range of beers with Yorkshire breweries including Ossett and Rat being particularly popular. The car park is only available on a Sunday and in the evenings. ⊛ ◐ ≠ ♣ P ⬚ (2,3) ☎

Orchard

Earl Street, PR1 2JA (on Preston covered market)
☎ 07756 583621 🌐 the-orchard-bar.business.site

3 changing beers (sourced nationally) ⊞
The Orchard was opened in 2018, a sister-pub to the Guild Ale House. Located within the Grade II-listed covered market the decor/framework is of wood recycled from the old market trestle boards plus lots of modern glass. No food but there is plenty on the neighbouring market, which can be ordered and taken in. Three cask ales and 10 craft ales are always available alongside real cider. Local CAMRA Pub of the Season spring 2023. Q ☺ ☼ ⊛ ≠ ♣ ◆ ⬚ ☎ ♫

Plug & Taps

32 Lune Street, PR1 2NN

4 changing beers ⊞
This craft beer and real ale focused bar features 10 keg lines and four handpumps, as well as a large can and bottle fridge. Expect to find changing beers from anywhere in the country or internationally, with a permanent Rivington brewery line. There are also occasional tap takeovers from various breweries. There is a large function room upstairs with a jukebox, air con in the main bar and an outside seating area for use in summer or in warm weather. Football away fan-friendly venue. ☺ ≠ ♣ ⬚ ☻ ☎

Tap End

450 Blackpool Road, Ashton-on-Ribble, PR2 1HX
☎ 07947 246022

4 changing beers (sourced locally) ⊞
Opened in 2021 in a former card and gift shop, this is a high-end micropub specializing in cask and craft ales generally sourced from local microbreweries. It has a fairly low-key atmosphere conducive to conversation; dark wood and metal with subdued lighting enhance this. Four handpumps dispense cask ales with a variety of styles on offer. Keg lines, bottles and cans provide alternatives. Changes to all beers are immediately uploaded to the Untapped and Real Ale Finder apps and beer menus are available providing full descriptions of current and future beers for your perusal. Q & ⬚ ☻ ☎

Twelve Tellers ⊘

14-15 Church Street, PR1 3BQ
☎ (01772) 550910

Greene King Abbot; Ruddles Best Bitter; Sharp's Doom Bar; 7 changing beers (sourced nationally) ⊞
Conversion of a former Trustees Savings Bank into a large, mostly open-plan pub with some small rooms and alcoves. It retains some features of its former life including its ornate ceiling and bank vaults, and has two extensively wood-panelled former boardrooms available for functions. There are 10 cask ales served on handpump. The large rear patio offers smoking and non-smoking areas. The ladies toilets have retained original copper-work. Expect bouncers on the door on weekend evenings when more formal dress is expected. ☼ ⊛ ◐ & ⬚ ☎

Vinyl Tap

28 Adelphi Street, PR1 7BE
☎ (01772) 555995

Oakham Citra; house beer (by Kirkby Lonsdale); 3 changing beers (sourced nationally) ⊞
Single-room bar adjacent to the university that opened in 2018 with up to five real ale pumps on the bar. People can select from an ever-growing 'pick and chose' vinyl selection or bring their own to be played while enjoying a drink and a bite to eat (authentic German hotdogs are available). Fridays and Saturdays feature live music with a rock and roots theme. There is a quiz every Tuesday and open mic on Wednesdays. Local CAMRA Pub of the Season spring 2022. ◐ ≠ ⬚ ☎ ♫

Winckley Street Ale House

8B Winckley Street, PR1 2AA
☎ (01772) 962017 🌐 winckleyale.co.uk

4 changing beers (sourced regionally) ⊞
In 2018 this premises initially opened as the Otter's Pocket and was a single-room bar and restaurant occupying the whole ground floor of a former shop. In 2020 the pub closed, before undergoing renovation, and has since reopened as the Winckley Street Ale House, offering a wider menu and great range of beers with up to four regularly changing cask ales as well as a range of 10 keg lines, with a strong focus on local/regional breweries. Popular with away football fans. Payment by cash or card. ☼ ⊛ ◐ & ≠ ⬚ ☻ ☎

Rawtenstall

Casked Ale House & Ginporium 🄻

14-16 Bury Road, BB4 6AA

House beer (by Reedley Hallows); 5 changing beers (sourced regionally; often Brewsmith, Irwell Works, Nightjar) ⊞
A large open-plan single-room bar with varied seating and imaginative lighting. On the edge of Rawtenstall town centre, just along from Fitzpatrick's famous temperance bar, it is a short walk from the bus station and the northern teminus of the East Lancashire heritage railway, which itself has a bar selling real ales. Up to six, mainly local, cask beers are available on handpump plus several modern keg beers. Many of the beers are sourced from breweries around the Rossendale Valley. ≠ ◆ ⬚ (464,X43) ☻ ♫

Hop Micro Pub 🄻

70 Bank Street, BB4 8EG
☎ 07753 775150 🌐 hopmicropubs.com

Deeply Vale Hop; 5 changing beers ⊞
Situated at the top end of Rawtenstall's cobbled Bank Street, close to the market, Hop is a pleasant and congenial venue with the atmosphere of the traditional

local pub. In addition to the bar there is a pleasant first floor lounge and a heated outside drinking area. With six handpulled cask ales, including the permanent Hop from Deeply Vale, as well as keg craft beers and ciders available, there is always a fantastic choice. A short walk from the bus station and from the northern terminus of the East Lancashire heritage railway. ✿≠✦P🖭✿

Rivington

Rivington Brewery Co. Tap 🕒

Home Farm, Horobin Lane, PR6 9HE
☎ 07859 248779 ⊕ rivingtonbrewing.co.uk
Rivington Beach House; 11 changing beers (sourced locally; often Rivington) Ⓗ

Opened in 2019 and housed in a converted stable block at the farm by the brewery, the bar showcases their extensive range of ales with up to three on handpump and 15 on keg. Cider and guest craft ales are also available. Walkers and their dogs are welcome, with outdoor seating providing beautiful views across the reservoir towards Winter Hill. The bar is lofty with bare stone walls and a large stone-topped bar counter. It was recently extended into the adjoining stable block providing a family-friendly dog-free zone. Local CAMRA Pub of the Season summer 2022. ⭆✿✿🍴◑ ▲P✿

Rufford

Hesketh Arms

81 Liverpool Road, L40 1SB (on A59 at jct with B5246)
☎ (01704) 821002
Moorhouse's White Witch, Pride of Pendle; 7 changing beers (sourced regionally; often Cross Bay, Phoenix, Reedley Hallows) Ⓗ

A spacious former Greenall's inn on the A59, the Hesketh is now a free house serving up to six ales mostly from local microbreweries. Set in the charming village of Rufford, it is near to the National Trust property of Rufford Old Hall, the delightful St Mary's Marina, and the popular Mere Sands nature reserve. A large split-level pub with several dining areas serving good-quality food throughout the day, monthly live entertainment and a Tuesday quiz attract a mixed clientele. Q⭆✿◑Ᏸ≠P🖭(2A,347) ♪

St Anne's-on-the-Sea

Fifteens of St Anne's 🍷 ✅

42 St Annes Road West, FY8 1RF
☎ (01253) 725852 ⊕ fifteensstannes.com
Bank Top Flat Cap; Joseph Holt Bitter; 8 changing beers (sourced nationally; often Castle Rock, Ossett, Titanic) Ⓗ

This popular and lively, multi-award winning community pub has been a fixture in the Guide since it opened. Set in an impressive former bank building, you can even sit in the old vault! Real ale is a matter of pride and passion here, though there is also live music every Saturday and a unique quiz every Sunday. Sport is available on a number of TVs at other times. A recent regional CAMRA Pub of the Year and local CAMRA Pub of the Year 2023. ⭆≠♣♦🖭✿♪

Hop Shoppe

2-2A Wood Street, FY8 1QS
☎ 07593 222535 ⊕ thehopshoppe.co.uk
4 changing beers (sourced nationally; often Beartown, Marble, Pentrich) Ⓗ

Opened in 2021, the Hop Shoppe has fast become a fixture in St Anne's. From the start the owner has made a point of a 'declaration of independents', actively

supporting small, independent UK suppliers. The atmosphere is open and welcoming, calm and relaxing; light and airy by day, chilled and intimate in the evening. There are 16 rotating craft beers, always including a sour, and an extensive choice of cans to drink in or take away. Q⭆✿◑Ᏸ≠♣🖭✿ ♀

Keg 'n' Cask

17 St Andrew's Road South, FY8 1SX
☎ 07913 791476
5 changing beers (sourced locally; often Copper Dragon, Lancaster, Reedley Hallows) Ⓗ

This multi-roomed micropub based in the town's first post office, just off the Crescent and handy for local amenities, has been a popular place for a drink since it opened in 2020. Its muted decor and soft background music, with no TVs or jukebox, make for a relaxing and calm atmosphere where conversation flows. A pavement drinking area provides an excellent spot for people watching. Five constantly changing beers provide an interesting range of mostly local beers, usually including one dark beer. ✿Ᏸ≠🖭✿

Pier Inn

8 St Anne's Road West, FY8 1RF
☎ (01253) 224156
Joseph Holt Two Hoots; house beer (by Joseph Holt); 4 changing beers (sourced nationally) Ⓗ

Bright and comfortable micropub at the western edge of St Anne's Square close to all local amenities and the pier, a large photo of which dominates one wall. The diamond pattern in the ceiling is a representation of a feature of many local houses built by the St Anne's Land Company under William Porritt. Six beers including four ever-changing guests are available, with one always being a dark beer. A small suntrap pavement seating area is available to the front. QᏰ≠🖭✿ ♀ ♪

Victoria ✅

Church Road, FY8 3NE
☎ (01253) 721041
Greene King IPA; Timothy Taylor Landlord; 4 changing beers (sourced nationally; often Hawkshead, Kirkby Lonsdale, Moorhouse's) Ⓗ

This traditional community pub is thriving again, having been rescued from redevelopment several years ago. Originally multi-roomed, it retains a number of discrete areas which gives it an intimate character which belies its size; with a separate vault housing a large screen for sports, and another for the full-sized snooker table. Family and dog-friendly, the Victoria hosts many social groups, a darts team and has a quiz on Thursday nights. A large, sun-filled outdoor drinking area is to the front of the pub. ⭆✿◑Ᏸ≠♣🖭(11,68)✿ ♀

Scarisbrick

Heatons Bridge Inn ✅

2 Heatons Bridge Road, L40 8JG (on B5242 road by Leeds-Liverpool Canal)
☎ (01704) 840549
2 changing beers (sourced regionally; often Moorhouse's, Tetley) Ⓗ

Great canalside pub dating from 1837, when it served as offices for the Leeds and Liverpool freight services. It is a traditional pub, with separate areas and home-cooked food. Pillbox beer is often served in reference to the WWII defensive structure outside. Twice-yearly military vehicle displays and annual classic bus services are hosted, with themed beers for the occasion. The pub is popular with families, walkers and cyclists, who enjoy the excellent rural setting and garden with eating area. ⭆✿◑Ᏸ♣▲🖭(375) ✿ ♀

Westhead

Prince Albert

109 Wigan Road, L40 6HY
☎ (01695) 573656
Moorhouse's Pendle Witches Brew; Tetley Bitter; 3 changing beers ⊞

A country community local on the main road between Ormskirk and Skelmersdale. With its warm atmosphere it is well worth the walk or the bus journey from the real ale desert of Skelmersdale. The freshly-cooked food and real ale are good value for money, and there are always some interesting guest ales from north-west breweries. The small central bar serves three distinct areas with real fires in the winter. The pub has a good selection of pub games such as darts and dominoes. The 310, 375 and 385 buses all stop outside. Q ❀ ⊞ ◑ ♣ P ➡ ☞

Whalley

Dog Inn ℒ

55 King Street, BB7 9SP
☎ (01254) 823009 ⊕ dog-innwhalley.co.uk
6 changing beers (sourced regionally) ⊞

Deservedly popular and usually crowded, especially at weekends, the Dog has been run by the same family since the early 1990s. Six handpumps serve a range of beers, changed continually, from breweries such as Acorn, Hetton, Moorhouse's, Peerless and Wishbone. Food is served at lunchtimes and is always excellent. This traditional, historic pub is close to the ruins of Whalley Abbey and is handy for exploring the picturesque Ribble Valley. With trains to Bolton and Manchester and buses to virtually everywhere in East Lancashire, Whalley is extremely well served by public transport. ❀ ❀ ◑ ⇌ ➡ ☞ ☞

Wheelton

Red Lion ℒ

Blackburn Road, PR6 8EU (in centre of village opp clock tower)
☎ (01254) 659890 ⊕ theredlionatwheelton.co.uk
Hawkshead Lakeland Gold; Timothy Taylor Landlord; 6 changing beers (sourced nationally; often Fyne, Oakham, Red Rose) ⊞

Built around 1826, this former Matthew Brown house retains many original features including a large stone lion at roof level above the door. It has a comfortable lounge with an open fire and a second room up a few steps. Close to the West Pennine Moors, many local walks pass by. Dogs are welcome and food is served every day. Eight handpumps showcase two regular beers and six changing real ales from larger independents, usually including a stout and a strong ale. Local CAMRA Pub of the Year 2022. Q ❀ ❀ ◑ P ⊟ ➡ (24) ❀ ☞ ♪

Whitworth

Whitworth Vale & Healey Band Club ℒ

498 Market Street, OL12 8QW
☎ (01706) 852484
Wainwright; 3 changing beers (sourced regionally) ⊞

Popular social club, notable for being the home of the award-winning local brass band of the same name. The club is part of a terrace on the main road through the town, with the regular 464 bus service passing by the door. It feels spacious, despite the low ceiling, and there is an outside seating area. A previous winner of local and regional CAMRA Club of the Year awards. ❀ ⊟ ➡ (464) ❀ ☞ ♪

Winmarleigh

Patten Arms

Park Lane, PR3 0JU (on B5272 3 miles N of Garstang)
☎ (01524) 791484 ⊕ thepattenarms.co.uk
Wainwright; 3 changing beers (sourced nationally) ⊞

Genuine, isolated free house situated on a B-road away from any villages, yet enjoying regular local custom. This Grade II-listed building possibly dates back to 1860. With a single bar has a country pub feel, with high-backed bench seats, cream-painted walls and open fires. There is a separate restaurant, and terraced seating overlooking a bowling green. Since 2019 there has been a tiny brewery in the cellar but, at time of writing, this is currently mothballed. ❀ ◑ ▲ ♣ P ❀ ☞ ♪

Wrightington

White Lion

117 Mossy Lea Road, WN6 9RE
☎ (01257) 425977 ⊕ thewhitelionwrightington.co.uk
Banks's Amber Ale; Jennings Cumberland Ale; 6 changing beers ⊞

This popular country pub has a great offering for diners and drinkers, with eight handpumps and a good range of food. The pub runs a Monday Club with drinks offers and a quiz on Tuesdays. It is highly community-orientated, running the village scarecrow festival, and offering themed evenings throughout the year. Families are welcome – there is a large beach hut-themed garden area outside and board games for entertainment inside. Q ❀ ❀ ◑ ❀ P ❀ (111) ❀

Breweries

12 Steps

🍺 Bird in th'hand, 225 Duckworth Street, Darwen, BB3 1AU ☎ 07926 115292

Started brewing in 2021 on a 2.5-barrel plant in the cellar of the Bird in th'hand. The name comes from the number of steps down to the cellar of the building.

4 Mice

🍺 Coach & Horses, Main Street, Bolton-by-Bowland, BB7 4NW
☎ (01200) 447331
⊕ coachandhorsesribblevalley.co.uk

⊛ A four-barrel brewery in a gastro-pub, situated in the Trough of Bowland.

Accidental

Old Market Court, Morecambe, LA4 5HS ☎ 07930 592749 ⊕ accidentalbrewery.com

Initially a brewpub located on the edge of Lancaster city centre in an 18th century converted stable block, which opened in 2018. In 2021 it opened a new brewery in Morecambe where all production was moved to with the original site remaining as a brewery tap. Occasional cask ale is produced.

Avid SIBA

Red Moss Farm, Quernmore, LA2 0QW ☎ 07976 275762 ⊕ avidbrewing.co.uk

Avid was established in 2015 by two experienced homebrewers. The 7.5-barrel microbrewery is based in picturesque Quernmore, near Lancaster. Water is used from a local borehole.

Golden Ale (ABV 3.9%) GOLD
American Pale (ABV 4%) PALE
New Zealand Pale (ABV 4%) PALE
Milk Stout (ABV 4.5%) STOUT
IPA (ABV 5%) PALE
TropicAle (ABV 5%) PALE
Irish Coffee Stout (ABV 6%) SPECIALITY
Pint Of (ABV 6.4%) IPA
Whoopass (ABV 7%) IPA

BB18

BB18 Brewing Tap, 31-33 Victoria Road, Earby, BB18 6UN ☎ 07908 591343
⊕ bb18-brewery-tap.business.site

☺This brewpub opened 2020. A five-barrel plant is used.

Beer Shack

Beer Shack, 22-24 King Street, Clitheroe, BB7 2EP
☎ (01200) 426368 ⊕ thebeershack.uk

This brewery first brewed in 2022 and is based above the Beer Shack.

Ben's

Unit 17, Yarrow Business Centre, Yarrow Road, Chorley, PR6 0LP
☎ (01257) 367480 ⊕ bensbrewery.co.uk

☺Established in 2021, the brewery is situated in part of an office furniture suppliers showroom. The taproom is only open for special events. ♦

Arawak (ABV 3.8%) PALE
Wellington (ABV 3.8%) GOLD
Beyond The Pale (ABV 4%) PALE
She Is My Country Still (ABV 4%) PALE
The Light Brigade (ABV 4%) PALE
Alright Treacle (ABV 4.5%) SPECIALITY
Blighty (ABV 4.5%) PALE
The Duke (ABV 4.5%) BITTER
Mean Old Bastard (ABV 5.7%) STOUT
Proper Grafter (ABV 5.7%) STOUT

Big Clock

Grants, 1 Manchester Road, Accrington, BB5 2BQ
☎ (01254) 393938 ☎ 07766 163497
⊕ thebigclockbrewery.co.uk

☺Brewing commenced at the iconic Grants Pub and Brewhouse, just off Accrington town centre, in 2014. The specially-commissioned brewery can be viewed from the bar area. A new, smaller brewery has been installed. This is to run along side the existing larger six-barrel plant, for production of smaller, speciality beers for a new canning line. Beer is supplied to around a dozen outlets across East Lancashire.

Bowland SIBA

Holmes Mill, Greenacre Street, Clitheroe, BB7 1EB
☎ (01200) 443592 ⊕ bowlandbrewery.com

☺Founded in 2003, this family-run business uses a 30-barrel plant, together with a nanobrewery for experimental brews, and serves 250+ outlets. The site features a beer shop and beer hall with 42 handpumps featuring beers from Lancashire and beyond. ‼🍺♦LIVE

Pheasant Plucker (ABV 3.7%) BITTER
Gold (ABV 3.8%) PALE
Well-balanced, pale, hoppy ale with delicate citrus hop notes and a long, dry, bitter finish.
Boxer Blonde (ABV 4%) BLOND

Bumble (ABV 4%) SPECIALITY
Hen Harrier (ABV 4%) PALE
Gentle aromas of malt, hops and fruit start this satisfying fruity bitter which has a lasting, rich finish.
Buster IPA (ABV 4.5%) BITTER
Deer Stalker (ABV 4.5%) STOUT

Brewhouse

The Old Bank, 30 Poulton Street, Kirkham, PR4 2AB
☎ 07738 275438 ✉ info@lythambrewery.co.uk

☺Well-established, family-run brewery that began in 2007 as Lytham Brewery. In 2021 it moved to Kirkham were the brewery is situated in the Old Bank restaurant where brewing restarted in 2022. Rebranding took place in 2023. ♦

Brewsmith SIBA

Unit 11, Cuba Industrial Estate, Stubbins, Ramsbottom, Bury, BL0 0NE
☎ (01706) 829390 ⊕ brewsmithbeer.co.uk

Brewsmith is a 10-barrel microbrewery established in 2014 by the Smith family – James, Jennifer and Ted. It produces a range of cask and bottle-conditioned ales in traditional British beer styles. ‼♦LIVE

Mosaic (ABV 3.5%) PALE
Bitter (ABV 3.9%) PALE
Gold (ABV 4.2%) PALE
New Zealand Pale (ABV 4.2%) PALE
Pale (ABV 4.2%) PALE
APA (ABV 5%) PALE
Oatmeal Stout (ABV 5.2%) STOUT

Budweiser (Samlesbury)

Cuerdale Lane, Samlesbury, Preston, PR5 0XD

No real ale.

Chain House

139-142 Market Street West, Preston, PR1 2HB
☎ 07707 511578

Office: 20 Brookdale, New Longton, PR4 4XL
⊕ chainhousebrewing.com

Brewing began in 2017. Popularity grew and beers occasionally appear in a handful of pubs in the Preston area. Producing predominantly keg and canned beers, there have been successful collaborations with breweries such as Rivington and Farm Yard Ales. The brewery relocated to the heart of Preston in 2022 and includes a taproom. Chain House cask ale has been trialled at the tap. ♦

Clay Brow

256 Carfield, Skelmersdale, WN8 9DW ☎ 07769 581500 ✉ claybrownano@gmail.com

Nanobrewery that started production in 2017.

Eclipse (ABV 5.4%) STOUT
Mr P's (ABV 5.7%) SPECIALITY
Mrs P's (ABV 6%) IPA

Corless

c/o Station Road, Scorton, PR3 1AN ☎ 07983 563917

Began brewing as a cuckoo brewer in 2018 using spare capacity, mostly at Avid.

Cross Bay

Unit 1, Newgate, White Lund Industrial Estate,
Morecambe, LA3 3PT
☎ (01524) 39481 ⊕ crossbaybrewery.co.uk

Cross Bay commenced brewing in 2011 on a 28-barrel
brew plant. An onsite taproom opened in 2018. The
beers are widely available across north-west England.
‼🍴♦🖐

Halo (ABV 3.6%) BLOND
A crisp and hoppy, pale bitter.
Vesper (ABV 3.8%) PALE
RIPA (ABV 4%) RED
Omega (ABV 4.2%) PALE
Sunset (ABV 4.2%) BLOND
Sweet bitter with a rising bitter finish.
Zenith (ABV 5%) BLOND
Fruity sweetness followed by some hop bitterness with a
little dryness in the finish.
Guell (ABV 5.1%) BITTER

Farm Yard SIBA

Gulf Lane, Cockerham, LA2 0ER
☎ (01253) 799988 ⊕ farmyardbrew.co.uk

The brewery, set up in 2017 on a remote farm, has
continued to expand and diversify with home deliveries,
event weekends and even dedicated buses running at
certain times, from local urban centres. The brewery
underwent a rebranding in early 2022. A vibrant taproom
is open every weekend and features regular live bands
and street food. ‼🍴♦🖐

Holmes Stead (ABV 3.4%) BITTER
TVO 54 (ABV 3.7%) BLOND
Haybob (ABV 3.9%) GOLD
Sheaf (ABV 4.1%) BLOND
Hoof (ABV 4.3%) SPECIALITY
Chaff (ABV 4.7%) BLOND
Gulf (ABV 5.8%) IPA

Folly

Clayton le Dale, BB1 9JF ☎ 07709 306467
⊕ follybrewery.com

Commercial home-based brewery set up in 2020 by a
former Thwaites employee. A one-barrel plant is used. ♦

Impello (ABV 4%) SPECIALITY
Lux (ABV 4.5%) PALE
Vestigia (ABV 4.5%) SPECIALITY

Fuzzy Duck SIBA

18 Wood Street, Poulton Industrial Estate, Poulton-le-
Fylde, FY6 8JY ☎ 07904 343729
⊕ fuzzyduckbrewery.co.uk

Fuzzy Duck was established in 2006. It relocated to
Poulton-le-Fylde later that year, expanding capacity to an
eight-barrel plant. The brewery delivers over a wide area
of North-West England. A range of single-hopped beers is
also available. Most beers are available bottle-
conditioned. ‼♦LIVE

Golden Cascade (ABV 3.8%) PALE
Mucky Duck (ABV 4%) STOUT
Pheasant Plucker (ABV 4.2%) BITTER
Cunning Stunt (ABV 4.3%) BITTER
Ruby Duck (ABV 5.3%) OLD

Hop Vine

🏠 Hop Vine, Liverpool Road North, Burscough,
L40 4BY
☎ (01704) 893799 ☎ 07920 002783
✉ mikejulie6465@gmail.com

Hop Vine began brewing in 2017 using the four-barrel
plant of the defunct Burscough Brewery. It is situated in
old stable buildings in the courtyard to the rear of the
Hop Vine. Beer is usually only supplied to the pub and
the Legh Arms, Mere Brow. 🍴♦

Hopstar SIBA

Unit 9, Rinus Business Park, Grimshaw Street,
Darwen, BB3 2QX ☎ 07933 590159
⊕ hopstarbrewery.co.uk

Hopstar first brewed in 2004 on a 2.5-barrel plant and
expanded in 2010 to a new unit with a six-barrel plant.
More than 100 outlets are supplied around Lancashire
and the Greater Manchester area. The brewery tap is
Number 39 in Darwen. ‼♦LIVE

Chilli Beer (ABV 3.8%) SPECIALITY
Dark Knight (ABV 3.9%) MILD
Off t'Mill (ABV 3.9%) PALE
Smokey Joe's Black Beer (ABV 3.9%) STOUT
Lancashire Gold (ABV 4%) BLOND
Lush (ABV 4%) BITTER
JC (ABV 4.1%) BITTER

Hopworks (NEW)

Unit 335, Ranglet Road, Walton Summit Centre,
Bamber Bridge, PR5 8AR ⊕ hopworksbrewing.com

Operating with a 10-barrel plant and nine fermenting
vessels, this brewery started production in 2023. The
onsite taproom is open every day. 🖐

Jimbrew (NEW)

Provinder House, Clifton Fields, Lytham Road, Clifton,
PR4 0XG ☎ 07739 859300 ⊕ jimbrew.co.uk

Brewing commenced in 2022. All beers are unfiltered,
unfined and gluten-free. No real ale is currently produced
but it may be during the currency of this Guide. GF 🖐

Lancaster SIBA

Lancaster Leisure Park, Wyresdale Road, Lancaster,
LA1 3LA
☎ (01524) 848537 ⊕ lancasterbrewery.co.uk

Lancaster began brewing in 2005. The brewery moved
to new premises in 2010 and installed a larger 60-barrel
brewing plant. ‼🍴♦

Amber (ABV 3.6%) BITTER
Amber malt flavours lead to an increasingly astringent
bitter finish.
Blonde (ABV 4%) BLOND
Well-balanced pale bitter with fruity body and hops
lasting well into the finish.
IPA (ABV 4.2%) PALE
Black (ABV 4.5%) STOUT
A satisfying and robust, roast bitter beer with hints of
sweet fruitiness.
Red (ABV 4.8%) RED
A characterful beer with plenty of fruits, roast malt and
hops, well balanced with a lasting finish.

Mighty Medicine

Unit 4, Daniel Street, Whitworth, OL12 8BX

☎ (01706) 558980 ⊕ mightymedicine.com

Established in 2016, this brewery is committed to using the finest ingredients to produce an eclectic range of beers. A taproom is attached to the brewery. 🍺✦

Stunning Blonde (ABV 3.9%) BLOND
Greedy Boy (ABV 4%) BITTER
Madchester Cream (ABV 4.2%) PALE
Magic Malt (ABV 4.5%) RED

Moorhouse's SIBA

The Brewery, 250 Accrington Road, Burnley,
BB11 5EN
☎ (01282) 422864 ⊕ moorhouses.co.uk

Established in 1865 as a soft drinks manufacturer, the brewery started producing cask-conditioned ale in 1978. A new brewhouse and visitor centre opened in 2012. Three pubs are owned. ‼✦

Black Cat (ABV 3.4%) MILD
A dark mild-style beer with delicate chocolate and coffee roast flavours and a crisp, bitter finish.
Premier (ABV 3.7%) BITTER
A clean and satisfying bitter aftertaste rounds off this well-balanced hoppy, amber session bitter.
White Witch (ABV 4%) BLOND
Delicate citrus aroma. Sweet fruity taste balanced with gentle bitterness. Increased bitterness in crisp citrus finish.
Pride of Pendle (ABV 4.1%) BITTER
Well-balanced amber best bitter with a fresh initial hoppiness and a mellow, malt-driven body.
Straw Dog (ABV 4.2%) GOLD
Blonde Witch (ABV 4.4%) BLOND
Pronounced sweet taste with gentle pithy bitterness and touch of citrus fruit. Dry finish. Slight fruity hop aroma.
Pendle Witches Brew (ABV 5.1%) BITTER
Well-balanced, full-bodied, malty beer with a long, complex finish.

Northern Whisper

Hill End Mill, Hill End Lane, Cloughfold, BB4 7RN
☎ (01706) 230082
⊕ northernwhisperbrewingco.co.uk

First brewing in 2017, the brewery has expanded over time to own two pubs. ✦

Soft Mick (ABV 3.8%) PALE
Oppenchops (ABV 4%) GOLD
Yammerhouse (ABV 4.5%) PALE
Beltie (ABV 4.8%) STOUT
Chinwag (ABV 5.6%) IPA

Old School SIBA

Holly Bank Barn, Crag Road, Warton, LA5 9PL
☎ (01524) 740888 ⊕ oldschoolbrewery.co.uk

☺A 12-barrel brewery, founded in 2012, located in a renovated 400-year-old former school outbuilding overlooking the picturesque village of Warton. Beer is mainly sold to free houses within a 40-mile radius. ‼✦✦

Junior (ABV 3.6%) PALE
Hopscotch (ABV 3.7%) GOLD
Initially hoppy, astringency builds in this satisfying beer, ending with a bitter finish.
Textbook (ABV 3.9%) BLOND
Pale beer with malt and hops in the taste, creamy texture and a dry bitter finish.
Detention (ABV 4.1%) PALE
Light amber hoppy bitter with lingering aftertaste.
Headmaster (ABV 4.5%) BITTER

Oscars

Unit 1, Riverside Works, Brunswick Street, Nelson,
BB9 0HZ
☎ (01282) 616192 ⊕ oscarsbrewery.co.uk

☺Originally based in Preston, the brewery was taken over in 2017 by the Lancashire Beer Co, a pub supplies wholesaler in Nelson. In 2018 the brewery name was changed to Oscars and a new range of beers introduced. Production moved to purpose-built premises in Nelson at the parent company in 2019.

Notorious D.O.G. (ABV 3.8%) PALE
Top Dog (ABV 3.8%) PALE
Dog Father (ABV 3.9%) BITTER
Gun Dog (ABV 4%) BLOND
Space Dog (ABV 4.2%) PALE

Parker

Unit 3, Gravel Lane, Banks, PR9 8BY
☎ (01704) 620718 ☎ 07949 797889
✉ theparkerbrewery@gmail.com

☺Parker was established in 2014 using a 25-litre kit, but quickly expanded to a five-barrel plant. In 2018 the brewery opened its own micropub, the Beer Den, Southport. In 2021 a second micropub was opened, Beer Den 2, Crossens. ‼LIVE

Centurion Pale Ale (ABV 3.9%) PALE
Barbarian Bitter (ABV 4.1%) BITTER
Saxon Red Ale (ABV 4.5%) RED
Viking Blonde (ABV 4.7%) BLOND
Dark Spartan Stout (ABV 5%) STOUT
Well-balanced stout with a burnt smoky roast aroma, roast strong on tasting with a little sweetness, ending with mellow flavours and some bitterness to finish.

Patten

🏠 Patten Arms, Park Lane, Winmarleigh, PR3 0JU
☎ (01524) 791484
✉ thepattenarmswinmarleigh@gmail.com

Brewing started in 2019 using a small plant in the cellar of the Patten Arms. Five different beers are brewed on rotation and only on sale at the pub. Brewing is currently suspended.

Peregrine

B9 Riverside Industrial Estate, Hermitage Street,
Rishton, BB1 4NF ☎ 07757 404231
⊕ peregrinebrewingltd.com

Brewing began in 2020 using a 1.5-barrel plant. ✦

What What? (ABV 3.6%) BLOND
Flight of the Falcon (ABV 3.7%) GOLD
Atomic (ABV 3.9%) BLOND
Próst! (ABV 4%) PALE
Brut IPA (ABV 4.5%) PALE
Hayabusa (ABV 4.5%) PALE
Red Aiofe (ABV 4.5%) RED
Mutiny (ABV 4.8%) PORTER
Serendipity (ABV 4.8%) PALE

Priest Town

139 Ribbleton Avenue, Preston, PR2 6YS
⊕ priesttownbrewing.com

Priest Town is a craft microbrewery in Preston, operational since 2017. It uses a 2.5-barrel plant. Almost all production is in small pack form. It runs a bottle shop on Preston Market where it's beers are regularly available. 🍺

Problem Child

🏠 Wayfarer Inn, 1 Alder Lane, Parbold, WN8 7NL
☎ (01257) 464600 ☎ 07588 736926
🌐 problemchildbrewing.co.uk

Problem Child began brewing in 2013 using a five-barrel plant at the Wayfarer Inn, Parbold, where two beers from the range are always available. ‼

Q Brew

58 Lower North Road, Carnforth, LA5 9LJ
☎ (01524) 903105 🌐 qbrew.co.uk

⊛ Q Brew started brewing in 2019 and is Carnforth's first microbrewery.

Reedley Hallows SIBA

Unit B3, Farrington Close, Farrington Road Industrial Estate, Burnley, BB11 5SH ☎ 07749 414513
🌐 reedleyhallows.co.uk

⊛ Brewing started on this four-barrel plant in 2012. Having moved to larger premises, the brewery now has nine fermenters to cope with demand. ‼

Beer O'Clock (ABV 3.8%) BLOND
Old Laund Bitter (ABV 3.8%) BITTER
Filly Close Blonde (ABV 3.9%) BLOND
Pendleside (ABV 4%) GOLD
Gentle malt and hops in the aroma lead to a fruity and peppery bitterness which continues to a dry finish.
Monkholme Premium (ABV 4.2%) BLOND
New Laund Dark (ABV 4.4%) STOUT
Griffin IPA (ABV 4.5%) PALE
Fruity, hoppy bitter with sweet fruity flavours and a light bitter finish.
New Zealand Pale (ABV 4.5%) PALE
Nook of Pendle (ABV 5%) BITTER

Rivington

Home Farm, Horrobin Lane, Rivington, PR6 9HE
☎ 07859 248779 🌐 rivingtonbrewing.co.uk

⊛ Established in 2015 using a three-barrel plant, the brewery moved to its current address in 2020. A 12-barrel plant is now used. A number of local outlets are supplied direct from the brewery. Approximately 20 per cent of production is supplied in cask form, but all beers are unpasteurised, unfiltered and unfined. Experimental brews and collaborations are regularly available.
‼🍺♦LIVE🍂

Beach House (ABV 3.8%) GOLD
Clouded Eyes (ABV 4.2%) PALE
Moving South (ABV 4.2%) PALE
Walking in Circles (ABV 4.2%) PALE

Rock Solid

Office: Forest Gate, Blackpool, FY3 9AW ☎ 07963
860080 ✉ rocksolidbrewingcompany@gmail.com

⊛ This brewery, based at the owner's home, started brewing in 2017 using a one-barrel plant. ♦

Rossendale

🏠 Griffin Inn, 84 Hud Rake, Haslingden, BB4 5AF
☎ (01706) 214021 🌐 rossendalebrewery.co.uk

⊛ The brewery acquired the brew plant previously used by Porter Brewing Co in 2007 and is based in the cellar of

the Griffin Inn in Haslingden. The Sportsman in Hyde and many other local outlets are also supplied. 🍺

Shed Beer (NEW)

Thornton Cleveleys

⊛ Home-based commercial brewer, with beers first appearing in 2019. The beers have become more widely available after a micropub was opened in Fleetwood in 2022.

Mild (ABV 3.6%) MILD
Citra (ABV 4%) GOLD

Snaggletooth

c/o Rear of 11 Pole Lane, Darwen, BB3 3LD ☎ 07810
365701 🌐 snaggletoothbrewing.com

Snaggletooth was established in 2012 by three beer geeks with a passion for crafting ales. A 2.5-barrel plant is used at the Hopstar Brewery (qv) in Darwen, Lancashire. Beers are available throughout East Lancashire and Manchester ♦

Allotropic (ABV 3.8%) PALE
BeEr (ABV 3.9%) PALE
I Ain't Afraid of Noh Ghost (ABV 3.9%) GOLD
Three Amigos (ABV 3.9%) GOLD
Déjà Brewed (ABV 4%) PALE
Rolling Maul (ABV 4.1%) PALE
'Cos I'm a Lobster (ABV 4.2%) RED
Avonaco (ABV 4.3%) PALE

Snowhill

Snowhill Cottage, Snow Hill Lane, Scorton, PR3 1BA
☎ (01524) 791352

⊛ Snowhill was established in 2015. A one-man operation, which occasionally brews on a 1.5-barrel plant. Pubs are mostly supplied within a 20-mile radius of the brewery. An environmentally-friendly set-up sees the spent grain feeding local cattle and waste water treated through a small reed bed. ♦

Pale (ABV 3.7%) GOLD
Copycat (ABV 3.8%) BITTER
Blonded (ABV 3.9%) BLOND
Gold (ABV 3.9%) GOLD
Best Bitter (ABV 4.2%) PALE
Black Magic IPA (ABV 4.2%) PALE
Porter (ABV 4.8%) PORTER
Winter Porter (ABV 4.8%) PORTER

Three B's

🏠 Black Bull, Brokenstone Road, Blackburn, BB3 0LL
☎ (01254) 581381 🌐 threebsbrewery.co.uk

Robert Bell acquired the Black Bull in 2011 and the brewpub now supplies 50 outlets. ‼♦LIVE

Stoker's Slake (ABV 3.6%) MILD
Lightly-roasted coffee flavours are in the aroma and the initial taste. A well-rounded, dark brown mild with dried fruit flavours in the long finish.
Bee's Knees (ABV 3.7%) PALE
Honey Bee (ABV 3.7%) SPECIALITY
Bobbin's Bitter (ABV 3.8%) BITTER
Bee Blonde (ABV 4%) BLOND
Black Bull (ABV 4%) BITTER
Ju-bee-lation (ABV 4.1%) PALE
Black Bull Lager (ABV 4.5%) SPECIALITY
Doff Cocker (ABV 4.5%) BLOND
Knocker Up (ABV 4.8%) PORTER

A smooth, rich, creamy porter. The roast flavour is foremost without dominating and is balanced by fruit and hop notes.

Old Bee (ABV 5.8%) OLD

Three Peaks

Unit 6, Holt Court, Pendle Street, Nelson, BB9 7EB
☎ 07790 539867 ⊕ threepeaksbrewery.co.uk

⊛Named after the three Yorkshire Dales mountains and established in 2006, owners Chris and Jennifer Holt moved the five-barrel plant to new modern premises while retaining the services of previous owner/brewer, Colin Ashwell. Its philosophy is to produce quality ales using premium ingredients to celebrate the great outdoors. Beers are currently supplied to outlets in the Dales, West Yorkshire and East Lancashire. ‼◆

Fell Walker (ABV 3.6%) PALE
Pen-y-Ghent Bitter (ABV 3.8%) BITTER
The malty character of this mid-brown session bitter is balanced by fruit in the aroma and taste. The finish is malty and hoppy.
Ingleborough Gold (ABV 4%) GOLD
Whernside Pale Ale (ABV 4.2%) PALE
Blea Moor Porter (ABV 4.5%) PORTER
Dark brown porter has a predominantly roast malt character, with a background of dark fruit and a woody note.
Plum Porter (ABV 4.5%) SPECIALITY
Malham Tarn Stout (ABV 5%) STOUT

Thwaites IFBB

Myerscough Road, Mellor Brook, BB2 7LB
☎ (01254) 686868 ⊕ thwaites.co.uk

⊛Founded in 1807, Thwaites moved from Blackburn in 2018 to a rural site five miles away in the Ribble Valley.

A 20-barrel plant brews exclusively for the company's 215 tenanted pubs, 13 managed Inns of Character, eight hotels and two lodges. 10 cask seasonals are produced and landlords who join the 1807 Cask Beer Club and stock the core range can select from a monthly list of guest cask beers from other breweries, plus Marston's Wainwright. ◆

Mild (ABV 3.3%) MILD
Refreshing dark mild with gentle fruit and roast in the nose, a sweet centre and a dry clean finish.
Original (ABV 3.6%) BITTER
TBC (Thwaites Best Cask) (ABV 3.8%) BITTER
IPA (ABV 4%) PALE
Gold (ABV 4.1%) GOLD
Amber (ABV 4.4%) BITTER

Unbound SIBA

Lenches Road, Colne, BB8 8EU ☎ 07886 062825
⊕ unboundbrew.co.uk

Brewing commenced early 2021. ◆

Nocturnal (ABV 6.5%) STOUT

West Coast Rock

🍺 1877 The Brew Room, 137-139 Church Street, Blackpool, FY1 3NX
☎ (01253) 319165 ⊕ thebrewroom1887.co.uk

⊛Historic Blackpool pub, which reopened as a specialist beer outlet in 2017 and first brewed in 2018 using a six-barrel plant. Many of the beers have a Blackpool Football Club theme, the club being founded in the pub in 1887. ‼◆

White Cross, Lancaster (Photo: Stuart McMahon)

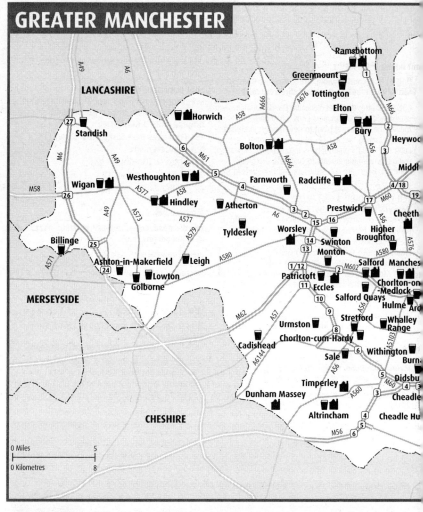

GREATER MANCHESTER

Altrincham

Costello's Bar Ⓛ

18 Goose Green, WA14 1DW (alleyway from Stamford New Rd/opp Regent Rd, adjacent to new hospital)
☎ (0161) 929 0903 ⊕ costellosbar.co.uk
Dunham Massey Dunham Dark, Big Tree Bitter; 5 changing beers (sourced locally; often Dunham Massey) Ⓗ
Sitting on one side of Altrincham's historic Goose Green, in a pedestrianised area of mainly cafés, bars and restaurants, Costello's serves as the Dunham Massey brewery tap. Seven handpumps showcase the brewery's range, along with occasional guests from other breweries. The bar has a modern feel and was recently extended, providing better facilities and more drinking space. Outside is a covered and heated seating area on Goose Green itself. ❧➌ⓖ♿ℯ♪♣🐾🛜

Pi Ⓛ

18 Shaws Road, WA14 1QU
☎ (0161) 929 9098 ⊕ pibar.co.uk
Brightside Odin Blonde; 2 changing beers (sourced regionally; often Mobberley, RedWillow, Storm) Ⓗ

Unassuming bar opposite the popular Altrincham Market Hall, alongside various eateries and takeaways. Three handpumps serve the relatively compact ground-floor bar area which is supplemented by additional space upstairs. Outside seating is provided in a small beer garden to the rear, with chairs and tables also placed on the Shaws Road frontage when the weather is warmer. A variety of table top games are available.
❧➌ⓖ♿ℯ♪♣🐾🛜

Rustic

41 Stamford New Road, WA14 1EB
☎ (0161) 928 9190 ⊕ rusticalty.com
Brightside Odin Blonde; 3 changing beers (sourced nationally; often Marble) Ⓗ
Following a few changes of name and owners, Rustic has been running in its current guise for the last few years. Four handpumps dispense local and national beers, and a number of keg beers and cocktails are also served. A long, narrow area to the left has booth seating, and upstairs is a large room available for functions. Comedy nights are held on the first Thursday of the month. US diner-style food is always available. ❧🍴ⓖ♿ℯ♪♣🐾🛜

WEST YORKSHIRE

imford · A58 · Littleborough

Rochdale · M62 · 22

21 · A640

A672

ton · A627(M) · A672

20 · A663

Chadderton

Oldham · A62 · Dobcross

A669 · Uppermill

Lydgate · Greenfield

22 · A627 · A670 · A635 · Mossley

Hollinwood

oylsden · Ashton-under-Lyne

ts · 23 · Stalybridge

A635 · M60 · Dukinfield

orton · 24 · 1 · M67 · 3 · Hyde

Denton · A628

Broadbottom

ton Chapel · A560 · 25 · DERBYSHIRE

27 · 26 · A626 · Romiley

tockport · Marple · Marple Bridge

A6 · Hazel Grove

hall · A6

Ancoats

Cask

2 New Union Street, Cotton Field Wharf, M4 6FQ (over a bridge from Redhill St)
☎ (0161) 392 0809
4 changing beers (sourced regionally; often Mobberley, Pictish, Squawk) Ⓗ
The sister pub to Cask on Liverpool Road is a single-room bar on the ground floor of a newly built complex, adjacent to the Rochdale Canal and within the New Islington marina area. It serves a changing range of four handpulled ales from local and regional breweries (fewer in summer), plus a cider on handpump and 20 keg beers, including many German beers. Local CAMRA Pub of the Year 2021. ♿☂(New Islington)♣●❀⛅

Ashton-in-Makerfield

Twisted Vine Ale House Ⓛ

15 Wigan Road, WN4 9AR
7 changing beers (sourced regionally) Ⓗ
This former local CAMRA Pub of the Year and Cider Pub of the Year opened in 2018. The bar offers seven cask pumps, three keg taps, boxed ciders and a selection of

gins, spirits and wines, alongside craft bottles and cans ready to drink in or take away. There is usually a large selection of beers available from Hophurst brewery in Hindley. Live music plays on the first Thursday of the month and weekly on Sundays. Over-18s only. 🚌❀♫

Ashton-under-Lyne

Ash Tree ✔

9-11 Wellington Road, OL6 6DA
☎ (0161) 339 9670
Greene King Abbot; Moorhouse's Blonde Witch; Ruddles Best Bitter; Sharp's Doom Bar; 4 changing beers (sourced nationally) Ⓗ
Popular Wetherspoon pub facing the Victorian Market Hall, in the town centre. It was extended into the former snooker hall next door in 2019 and its upper-floor veranda brightens the interior and overlooks a spacious beer garden with covered booths that is well-used in fine weather. Families are welcome, particularly in the lower dining area. Situated close to the new bus/tram interchange and also the train station.
♿☸❅◐🔌♿🚆🅿🚌⛅

Dog & Pheasant

528 Oldham Road, OL7 9PQ
☎ (0161) 330 4894
Banks's Amber Ale; Marston's Pedigree; 2 changing beers (sourced regionally; often Banks's, Wainwright) Ⓗ
Close to the border with Oldham on the northern edge of town, this friendly local near the Medlock Valley Country Park has been a frequent entry in this Guide since 1992. The large U-shaped bar serves three areas, plus another room at the front. The beer range is supplemented by two guest beers from the Marston's portfolio. A menu of good-value food includes vegetarian options. Quiz nights are on Thursday evenings and open mic night is on Monday. Q☸◐♿🅿🚌(409)♫

Half Way House Ⓛ

123 Whiteacre Road, OL6 9PJ
☎ (0161) 343 1344
3 changing beers (sourced locally; often Bridge Beers, Joseph Holt) Ⓗ
This large, popular open-plan locals' pub was first licensed in 1860. A good-sized beer garden at the rear is popular during pleasant weather. There is also an upstairs function room with capacity for 50 people. Up to three cask beers are available, all at reasonable prices. Live entertainment takes place on Friday and Saturday, plus karaoke on Sunday. Live Premier League football from Sky and BT Sports is shown on TV.
♿☸🚆🅿🚌(38,39) ⛅♫

Tapsters Ⓛ

31 Old Street, OL6 6LA (100yds from SE corner of Market Hall)
☎ (0161) 465 0205
3 changing beers (sourced locally; often Bridge Beers, Millstone) Ⓗ
Previously a high-street shop in the town centre, Tapsters is close to the indoor market and the bus and rail stations. Opened in 2018, it has been fitted out to a high standard, creating a welcoming, comfortable, spacious place. There is a small courtyard beer garden to the rear. Up to three mainly local beers, normally of differing styles, feature at any time. Functions for up to 20 people are catered for. Background music plays and the TV is muted when on. ☸🚆🅿🚌⛅♫

Atherton

Atherton Arms
6 Tyldesley Road, M46 9DD
☎ (01942) 875996
Joseph Holt Bitter, Two Hoots Ⓗ
Traditional public house with a great atmosphere and facilities, including a full-sized snooker table and function room. It is known for its superb beer garden, which has TV screens and heaters. The beer is competitively priced and promotions change on a monthly basis. The pub offers a wide range of events, with live entertainment at the weekends and most sports shown throughout the week. ➲❀&♣️P🚃(V2)🛜♪

Taphouse
119 Market Street, M46 0DF
☎ (01942) 367519
5 changing beers (sourced locally) Ⓗ
Micropub on the main street in the centre of Atherton. Inside this comfortable, friendly one-room bar there are four tables with extra seating at the sides. Upstairs are two comfortable lounge areas, one of which is air-conditioned. There is a pleasant beer garden to the rear. Beers are generally sourced from small regional microbrewers and are competitively priced. A real-time beer list is available online. ➲❀&🚃(V2)♥🛜

Bamford

Hare & Hounds
865 Bury Road, OL11 4AA
☎ (01706) 369189
Wainwright; 2 changing beers Ⓗ
A traditional stone-built pub on the main Rochdale to Bury road. L-shaped inside with upper and lower bars, it has a real fire in the lower bar/dining area. Although a Thwaites tied house, the landlord is keen to maintain a rotating guest beer policy within the options available from the Thwaites range. To the rear of the pub is a beer garden with views across fields. ➲❀◑♣️P🚃♥🛜

Billinge

Masons Arms
99 Carr Mill Road, WN5 7TY
☎ (01744) 603572
5 changing beers (sourced regionally) Ⓗ
Friendly, traditional, community-based pub on the edge of open countryside, run by members of the same family for over 200 years. The warm and welcoming bar allows the opportunity to chat without loud music, and is adorned with rugby memorabilia. There is also a quiet side lounge area. All areas are dog and child friendly. Outside is an extensive landscaped beer garden overlooking the countryside, and an interesting smoking shelter. ❀&♣️P🚃(137)♥🛜♪

Bolton

Bank Top Brewery Tap Ⓛ
68-70 Belmont Road, Astley Bridge, BL1 7AN
☎ (01204) 302837 ⊕ banktopbrewery.com
Bank Top Dark Mild, Flat Cap, Pavilion Pale Ale, Palomino Rising; 5 changing beers (sourced locally; often Bank Top) Ⓗ
The original taphouse for the multi award-winning Bank Top brewery, which is based less than a mile away. This street-corner community local has two rooms and a large outdoor area with smoking shelter. There are nine handpumps showcasing ales from Bank Top, including regulars Flat Cap, Pavilion Pale and Dark Mild, plus others from the brewery stable, the current seasonal or special, and a guest beer. A real cider is sometimes among the ciders on offer. ➲❀&♣️🚃(1,534)♥🛜

Bunbury's
397 Chorley Old Road, BL1 6AH
☎ 07952 344838 ⊕ bunburys.co.uk
3 changing beers (sourced locally; often Blackedge, Marble, Siren) Ⓗ
One of a growing number of micropubs based in former retail outlets, this cosy bottleshop with a bar serves a range of the more unusual beers and beer styles. This

includes three constantly changing ales on handpump from local breweries such as Torrside, Siren, Marble and Blackedge, plus those from similar breweries further afield. They also stock a wide range of often rare bottled beers from around the world, as well as a choice of interesting modern keg beers. Q☺♣♠🍴🖰(125)🏆♿🛜

Great Ale at the Vaults L

Vaults Below Market Place, BL1 2AL
☎ (01204) 773548
House beer (by Deeply Vale); 2 changing beers (sourced locally; often Durham) 🅷
Atmospheric bar situated in the centre of the refurbished vaults of the former Market Hall, whose upper floors contain shops and a cinema. Handpumps dispense two guest beers – one pale, one dark – plus house beer Grey T'Ale, specially brewed by nearby Deeply Vale. Tasting paddles of cask ale are available. Cold bar food is offered, while in the wider Vaults area there is a choice of alternative food outlets. Q☺🕽🕭&♿P🖰🛜♪

King's Head L

52/54 Junction Road, Deane, BL3 4NA
☎ 07947 532741
Bank Top Dark Mild, Flat Cap; 1 changing beer (sourced regionally; often Moorhouse's, Timothy Taylor) 🅷
Located near Deane Parish Church in the Deane Village conservation area, this pub is in a late 18th-century Grade II-listed building, which was extended in the mid 19th century. It has three rooms, one with a cast iron range and the other two with low, wooden ceiling beams. Crown Green bowls and a children's play area are available. The pub is set back from the road, with a two-tier car park that is partially surrounded by woodland. Q☺🏠&♣P🖰(520,573)🏆🛜♪

Northern Monkey Bar L

Nelson Square, BL1 1AQ
☎ 07825 814631 ⏺ northernmonkeybrew.co.uk
4 changing beers (sourced locally; often Northern Monkey) 🅷
This pub was set up and renovated from what was previously a restaurant, though originally it was the dining room of the Pack Horse Hotel which dominated this side of Nelson Square before being converted to student accommodation. The four real ales include Northern Monkey beers and sometimes a couple of guests. At least one dark ale is normally available. Eight fonts serve modern keg beers from Northern Monkey and elsewhere. Basic pub food is offered during opening hours. ☺🕽≢♣🖰🏆🛜♪

One for the Road

Stalls F14 to F15, Ashburner Street Lifestyle Hall, BL1 1TJ
☎ 07725 338773
House beer (by Stockport); 2 changing beers (sourced locally; often Deeply Vale) 🅷
This microbar is located in the Lifestyle Hall of Bolton's award-winning indoor market, and has a choice of three beers from a wide range of smaller breweries. Sharing the same large seating area at the front of the bar is a choice of takeaway food stalls, with dishes from Malaysia to Cameroon alongside the more standard sandwiches and pasties. Opening days and hours are restricted to those of the main market. A former local CAMRA Pub of the Year. Q☺&≢P🖰🛜

Bramhall

Mounting Stone

8 Woodford Road, SK7 1JJ (at jct Bramhall Ln South)

☎ (0161) 439 7563 ⏺ themountingstone.co.uk
Bollington Long Hop, Best; 4 changing beers (sourced locally) 🅷
The sister pub to Cheadle Hulme's Chiverton Tap, this is a cosy, friendly micropub right in the village centre. The former blacksmith's operates over two floors – ground and basement – with a small beer garden to the rear. The name derives from a local large stone that allowed riders to mount their horses. Alongside the Bollington ales are up to four beers, often from microbrewers – one usually a dark brew – and eight keg beers. The pub has an on-site one-barrel brewery named Made of Stone. Q☺🏠&≢♣🖰🏆🛜

Broadbottom

Harewood Arms L ✅

2 Market Street, SK14 6AX
☎ (01457) 762500 ⏺ theharewoodarms.co.uk
Green Mill Gold, Northern Lights; 4 changing beers (sourced locally; often Green Mill) 🅷
A large pub for all the community in this quiet village on the edge of the Peak District. Home to the Green Mill brewery, it serves several Green Mill ales plus occasional seasonal and guest beers. Partially open-plan, with various seating areas and two real fires, the pub also has a beer garden to the rear. Approximately five minutes' walk from Broadbottom railway station. ☺🏠&🕽≢♣🖰(341)🏆🛜

Burnage

Reasons to be Cheerful

228 Fog Lane, M20 6EL (jct of Elmsmere Rd, near Burnage station and Parrs Wood Rd)
☎ (0161) 425 9678 ⏺ reasonsbeercafe.co.uk
3 changing beers (sourced locally)
Modern beer café in a former shop premises near Burnage railway station. The small, inconspicuous frontage hides a long but welcoming interior, including an alcove providing seating and a view of the street. The L-shaped bar has three handpulls, while eight craft beer taps adorn the back bar, and there is also a display rack and fridge for off-sales. A secluded rear room can accommodate up to 20 people. Occasional quizzes and wine tastings are a feature. Card payment only. Q☺🏠≢♣🖰🏆🛜

Bury

Art Picture House L ✅

36 Haymarket Street, BL9 0AY (opp Metro/bus station interchange)
☎ (0161) 705 4040
Brightside Odin Blonde; Greene King Abbot; Moorhouse's Blonde Witch; Ruddles Best Bitter; changing beers 🅷
A Wetherspoon pub in a beautifully restored former 1920s cinema, opposite the bus/tram interchange. The large seating area is on two levels with several private booths facing the back bar. Eight handpumps dispense regular and ever-changing beers. It can get busy at lunchtimes on market days (Wed and Fri). Food is available all day every day. The pub makes a handy stop for the first or last pint of the day. ☺🕽&≢(Bolton Street)🖰🛜

Broad Street Social L

9 Broad Street, BL9 0DA
☎ (0161) 204 7387 ⏺ broadstreetsocial.co.uk
Brewsmith Bitter, Pale, Oatmeal Stout; 1 changing beer (often Brewsmith, Marble) 🅷

This welcoming bar is the Brewsmith Brewing Co tap. It usually has its own beers on handpump, plus one or two guest real ales, all of high quality and served well. The interior is small but well laid out. There are no TVs or gaming machines so conversation is the order of the day, with quiet background music. A stamp card discount scheme operates Wednesday, Thursday and Sunday, with a free pint for every six stamps. Q ॐ ≢ (Bolton Street) ▯▯❀♪

Trackside Bar 🕒 ⊘
Bolton Street Station, BL9 0EY (platform 2 on ELR)
☎ (0161) 764 6461 ⊕ eastlancsrailway.org.uk/plan-your-day-out/food-drink/the-trackside.aspx
Changing beers ⊞
Owned by the East Lancashire Heritage Railway, the pub is situated on Platform Two of Bury Bolton Street station. It boasts eight handpumps of constantly changing ales, plus real ciders. The beer is always in good order and there is usually at least one dark ale on. Refurbished in 2022, there is an outside seating area on the platform where you can watch the steam trains. Local CAMRA Pub of the Year and Cider Pub of the Year 2022.
ॐ❀◑৬★▲≢(Bolton Street) ▯●P▯❀♥♪

Cadishead

Grocers
152A Liverpool Road, M44 5DD (close to Moss Ln)
☎ 07950 522468
3 changing beers (sourced regionally; often Blackedge, Brewsmith, Coach House) ⊞/ⓖ
This micropub is a frequent local CAMRA Pub of the Year winner and was regional Cider Pub of the Year 2022. There is no bar in the single room, beers are brought to you by the proprietor from a separate air-chilled room, served on handpull and by gravity. Three ciders or perries are also served. The lack of TV, music or other electronic entertainment means that conversation rules. There is a yard to the rear for outside drinking. May close early if quiet. Q ॐ❀৬●▯(67,100)❀

Castleton

Old Post Office Ale House 🕒
858 Manchester Road, OL11 2SP
☎ (01706) 645464
House beer (by Pictish); 4 changing beers (sourced locally; often Beartown, Outstanding) ⊞
First-time visitors, and their dogs, are guaranteed a warm welcome from the locals at this family-run ale house. It is a real community hub, with five handpulled beers, always including Old Postie 3.8% ale from Pictish (Rochdale brewery), two full juice ciders, Czech and German lagers on draught plus cocktails, craft cans and bottles. You can request your favourite music, or play pool, or enjoy the beer garden overlooking the Rochdale Canal in fine weather. A card scheme is in operation.
Q❀≢●▯(17) ❀♥

Chadderton

Crown Inn 🕒
72 Walsh Street, OL9 9LR (off Middleton Rd via Peel St)
☎ (0161) 915 1557
4 changing beers (sourced locally; often Leatherbritches, Millstone) ⊞
Popular family-run local free house, within reasonable walking distance of Chadderton town centre and the Freehold tram stop. It offers up to four changing real ales on handpump, often locally from Millstone, with ales from Leatherbritches being available on a frequent basis.

Football, darts and other live sports are shown on TV. There is live music at weekends and an inviting beer garden at the back.
ॐ❀৬♬(Freehold) ♣▯(415,159) ♥♪

Rose of Lancaster ⊘
7 Haigh Lane, OL1 2TQ
☎ (0161) 624 3031 ⊕ roseoflancaster.co.uk
JW Lees Manchester Pale Ale, Bitter; 3 changing beers (sourced locally; often JW Lees) ⊞
This attractive roadside pub by the Rochdale Canal boasts a conservatory restaurant, lounge bar and a separate vault showing sporting events. Service is swift and cheerful, and discerning management ensures a pleasant visit. Drinkers and diners mix comfortably in the busy lounge. The covered patio, with views of the canal, is popular in fine weather. Handy bus and train links make for easy travel to this well-run and popular pub. Seasonal and Lees Boilerhouse beers are always available.
❀◑৬≢(Mills Hill) ♣P▯(59) ❀♥♪

Cheadle

Wobbly Stamp
130 Stockport Road, SK8 2DP (jct Park Rd)
☎ (0161) 523 0188
House beer (by Stancill); 3 changing beers (sourced regionally) ⊞
Opened in 2020 in a former post office by two local businessmen. The deceptively long main room has plenty of seating, with two booths towards the back of the pub. The interior is a mix of rough-planed timber, plasterboard and bare brick all variously adorned with local artwork, breweriana and mirrors. Outside drinking areas are at the front and side of the building with views over a local park. Three rotating guests always include a dark beer. Q ॐ❀৬●▯(11,370)❀♥♪

Cheadle Hulme

Chiverton Tap
8 Mellor Road, SK8 5AU (off Station Rd)
☎ (0161) 485 4149 ⊕ thechivertontap.co.uk
Bollington Long Hop, Best; 4 changing beers (sourced locally) ⊞
Friendly micropub in what was once Arthur Chiverton's draper's shop. Note the mosaic in the doorway of the double-fronted former shop. Alongside the Bollington beers are four cask lines and eight keg taps with an ever-changing selection, all from UK micros. In addition, there is an extensive range of bottles and cans. In 2019 it added a first-floor room and an outside area at the rear with tables. Local CAMRA Pub of the Year 2022.
Q ॐ❀৬≢●▯❀♥

Cross Keys ⊘
10 Adswood Road, SK8 5QA (to E of jct Ladybridge Rd)
☎ (0161) 485 1386
Hydes Dark Ruby, Original, Lowry ⊞
Dating from the inter-war period, this pub has been altered over the years. Now it is a series of inter-connecting areas at the front, each having their own distinctive character, traditional decor, comfortable seating and open fires. A separate large vault-cum-games room is situated at the back. A decent sized outdoor area is a real suntrap in summer. A large upstairs function room is available. There's entertainment with live DJs every Friday and sometimes live music once a month. Darts and crib are played on Tuesdays.
❀♣P▯❀♥

Chorlton-cum-Hardy

Beer House ♥ ℓ
57 Manchester Road, M21 9PW
☎ (0161) 881 9206
Marble Pint, Manchester Bitter; 4 changing beers (sourced regionally; often Pomona Island, RedWillow, Vocation) ℍ
Ever-popular micropub whose knowledgeable staff provide a warm welcome. The focus is on quality beer, with regulars Marble Bitter and Pint plus a changing selection of guests. Top-quality craft beers are served from the keg, along with excellent canned and bottled brews. Traditional games supplement games console favourites from the 1980s. No food is served but bar snacks are available. Quiz on Mondays. Local CAMRA Pub of the Year 2023. ♿✿❀ℛ(Chorlton)♣🚆(86)🌺🛜

Fell Bar Chorlton
518 Wilbraham Road, M21 9AW
☎ (0161) 881 7724
4 changing beers (often Fell) ℍ
Small but popular bar in a row of takeaways and restaurants. One of the taps for Fell brewery, the cask offering is usually all Fell and often includes a dark beer, with occasional guests. The keg offering does have more variety, with 11 taps from the likes of Verdant and Kernel and sometimes local collabs. Hogan's cider is available. Green tiles and wood throughout bring a bit of tradition to this modern bar. The interesting background music is never too intrusive. ℛ(Chorlton)♣❀🚆

Font ℓ
115-117 Manchester Road, M21 9PG
☎ (0161) 871 2022 🌐 thefontbar.wordpress.com
4 changing beers (sourced nationally; often Mallinsons, RedWillow, Track) ℍ
Featuring up to four varying real ales on the bar, one usually from RedWillow or Mallinsons, alongside eight keg regularly changing keg lines. Hogan's cider is available on draught, plus bottled beers and ciders. The bar is known for its good-value cocktails. The open kitchen serves breakfast as well as a full menu daily, which changes every few months. A popular quiz is held every Tuesday. Closed Mondays except for comedy night on first Monday of month. Home to Chorlton Homebrewers. ♿✿◑▶ℛ(Chorlton)❀🚆(86)🌺🛜

Chorlton-on-Medlock

Sandbar
120-122 Grosvenor Street, M1 7HL (jct A34/B5117, off Oxford Rd) 🌐 sandbarmanchester.co.uk
Facer's Clwyd Gold; Phoenix Arizona; 4 changing beers (sourced regionally; often Blackjack) ℍ
Originally two 18th-century town houses, this is now one of the longest-established bars on the university area beer scene. Quirky and bohemian, it is popular with students and university staff alike. There are regular exhibitions of photographs and paintings, and displays of old curios. The cask beers are usually local and are accompanied by modern British and European bottled, canned and kegged beers, plus a changing guest cider. Home-made vegetarian and vegan pizzas are available most days. Payment by card only.
✿◑▶≉(Oxford Road)❀🚆🌺🛜

Denton

Crown Point Tavern ℓ
16 Market Street, M34 2XW (in pedestrianised Denton Civic Square)

Stockport Crown Best Bitter; 5 changing beers (sourced locally) ℍ
Micropub with six real ales, including a dark beer, typically sourced from Greater Manchester. A blackboard lists useful information such as style and taste, and flights of three third-pints are available. There is cider in a box from Lilleys, plus bottled craft beers, also mostly from Greater Manchester producers. Live music features every weekend on either Friday or Saturday. Outside seating is available at the front. A 10% discount is offered to senior citizens on weekdays. ♿♿♣🚆🌺🛜♫

Didsbury

Fletcher Moss ✅
1 William Street, M20 6RQ (off Wilmslow Rd, via Albert Hill St)
☎ (0161) 438 0073
Hydes Dark Ruby, Hopster, Original, Lowry; 2 changing beers (sourced regionally) ℍ
This gem of a pub is named after the alderman who donated the nearby botanical gardens to the city. The buzz of conversation is audible before opening the door, and though now a drinks-only operation, this has not detracted from its popularity. Look for the assortment of porcelain teapots; this is part of the late landlady's 100-piece collection now under the care of her husband who took on the role of manager. Q✿♿ℛ(Village)🚆🛜♫

Gateway ✅
882 Wilmslow Road, M20 5PG (jct Kingsway and Manchester Rd)
☎ (0161) 438 1700
Greene King Abbot; Ruddles Best Bitter; house beer (by Brightside); 5 changing beers (sourced nationally) ℍ
This comfortable and popular 1930s roadhouse is conveniently located opposite the public transport interchange for bus, tram and rail. It stands out due to its welcoming atmosphere, enthusiastic staff and excellent beer. This large Wetherspoon pub's central island bar is surrounded by distinct seating areas, ensuring that you can always have a quiet drink somewhere, however busy it gets. Extensive outside seating is available. Note the imagery detailing the high-frequency 142 bus service that terminates at the Parrs Wood leisure complex.
Q♿✿◑≉(East)ℛ(East Didsbury)🅿🚆🛜

Royal Oak
729 Wilmslow Road, M20 6WF (jct Old Oak St)
☎ (0161) 434 4788
Banks's Amber Ale, Sunbeam; Marston's 61 Deep, Pedigree; Wainwright Amber; 1 changing beer (often Ringwood) ℍ
Built around 1850 this multi-roomed pub is akin to the community centre of the village. The large central horseshoe-shaped bar displays an impressive collection of old porcelain spirit vats. The pub is famous for its award-winning cheese and pâté lunches (served Mon-Sun) which many have tried to copy but none have been able to surpass for choice or value. The pub is especially busy when Man City football club are playing at home. A changing monthly guest beer is served.
✿◑▶ℛ(Village)🚆🌺🛜

Dobcross

Dobcross Band & Social Club ℓ
Platt Lane, OL3 5AD
☎ (01457) 873741 🌐 dobcross.club

JW Lees Bitter; Joseph Holt Bitter; 2 changing beers (sourced locally; often Bowland, Millstone, Phoenix) ⊞
Now over 100 years old, this club's building was rebuilt in 1967 and enjoys superb views from the bowling green at the front. It hosts three brass bands, and has a full-size snooker table in the games room. A function room stages concerts as well as rehearsal space. The John Holden lounge (named after the long-serving steward) seats around 25 in comfortable surroundings. A repeat winner of local CAMRA Club of the Year, it made the last four of the National competition in 2022.
ﻝﻉﻀ♣P🚪(356) ✿🛜♪

Swan Inn (Top House)
The Square, OL3 5AA
☎ (01457) 238690 ⊕ swaninndobcross.com
Banks's Sunbeam; Courage Directors; Jennings Cumberland Ale; Marston's Pedigree; Wainwright ⊞
Built in 1765 for the Wrigley family of chewing gum fame, the Swan is a traditional stone pub overlooking the attractive village square. The ground floor has been well renovated with flag floors throughout and consists of three rooms, each with an open fire. Good home-cooked food is served with weekly specials. Annual events such as the Whit Friday Brass Band Contest and August Rushcart Festival are popular. Quiz night is Thursday.
Q♿ﻉﻀ◑🚪(X356) ✿🛜♪

Droylsden

Silly Country Bar & Bottle Shop 🍺 🅛
121 Market Street, M43 7AR
4 changing beers (sourced locally; often Bridge Beers, Millstone) ⊞
Open-plan bar and bottle shop with an outside drinking area. Four cask-conditioned beers are served from local and regional breweries. One cider and one perry are also available (usually one boxed and one on handpump) plus an enterprising selection of bottled/canned beers. Customers can bring their own food. Treats for dogs are available behind the bar. Metrolink stop is Droylsden (Blue Line). Q♿ﻉﻀﻀ♣●🚪✿🛜

Dukinfield

Angel 🅛
197 King Street, SK16 4TH
☎ 07399 662974
Sharp's Doom Bar; 2 changing beers (sourced locally; often Bridge Beers, Millstone) ⊞
Friendly, family-run community pub on the main road close to the centre of Dukinfield. There is a pleasant, well-furnished lounge, where entertainment and quizzes take place, and a taproom with pub games. TV sports are shown throughout the pub. Comedy club nights take place regularly in the upstairs function room with the Dukinfunny Club. The function room, with its own bar, is available to hire. ♿ﻉ◑♣P🚪(330)✿🛜

Elton

Elton Liberal Club 🅛
New George Street, BL8 1NW
☎ (0161) 764 1776 ⊕ eltonliberalclub.co.uk
2 changing beers (often Brewsmith, Brightside) ⊞
A friendly social club where you can enjoy a warm welcome and a drink in a safe environment. They have an arrangement whereby non-members are signed in for £1 per visit. It sports two handpulls, with beer sourced locally, and there are three snooker tables. There is a large outdoor seating area by the bowling green, which

is a lovely suntrap. The club has various leisure activities and entertainment most weekends.
Q♿ﻉﻀ♣P🚪(480) ✿🛜♪

Farnworth

King's Arms Hotel 🅛
2 Mossfield Road, BL4 0AB
☎ (01204) 577357
Cross Bay Zenith; 4 changing beers (sourced locally; often Blackedge, Ossett, Small World) ⊞
A popular local with a modern, friendly feel that offers something for everyone. The pub usually serves beers from various well-regarded breweries such as Ossett, Blackedge, Small World, Titanic, Navigation and Bank Top. There is always a dark beer among the selection. There is a pool table, a free jukebox, unobtrusive TV, a quiet corner, and a comfortable beer garden/smoking area. It also provides accommodation, room only.
Q♿ﻀ♣🚪(129,36) 🛜

Golborne

Queen Anne
14 Bridge Street, WA3 3PZ
☎ (01942) 726922 ⊕ queenanne-golborne.co.uk
2 changing beers (sourced regionally) ⊞
Tucked away on Bridge Street, just off the East Lancs Road, the Queen Anne is handy for Haydock Park racecourse and caters for pre-race parties. Home-cooked food is served in the bar and separate dining area with early-bird specials available on weekdays, plus Sunday roasts. There is plenty of parking space and the well-kept beer garden is a real suntrap in the summer.
Q♿ﻉ◑P🚪(10) 🛜

Gorton

Vale Cottage
Kirk Street, M18 8UE (off Hyde Rd, E of jct Chapman St)
☎ (0161) 223 4568 ⊕ thevalecottage.co.uk
Timothy Taylor Landlord; 2 changing beers (sourced nationally) ⊞
Hidden away off busy Hyde Road and sited in the Gore Brook conservation area, the Vale Cottage feels like a country local transplanted to the inner city. The low-beamed ceilings, wood-burning stove and multiple drinking areas all add to the cosy, out-of-town feel. The atmosphere is relaxed and friendly with conversation to the fore. Events include a music quiz, a folk night on selected Sundays, a general knowledge quiz on Tuesday night, and steak night on the last Thursday of each month. Q♿ﻉ◑ﻀ⇌(Ryder Brow)P🚪🛜♪

Greenfield

Railway Inn ✅
11 Shaw Hall Bank Road, OL3 7JZ (opp station)
☎ 07376 440324
Millstone Tiger Rut; 5 changing beers (often Acorn, Brains, Ossett) ⊞
Unspoilt pub comprising a central bar, lounge, games area and taproom which boasts a log fire and old photos of Saddleworth. The Railway is a popular venue for live music on Thursday, Friday and Sunday, and has six real ales available. It is also a stop-off on the Trans-Pennine Real Ale Trail. The pub is in a picturesque area and affords beautiful views across Chew Valley from the upgraded beer garden. It is a great base for outdoor pursuits.
♿ﻉÅ⇌♣P🚪(180,350) ✿🛜♪

Wellington Inn Ⓛ

29 Chew Valley Road, OL3 7AF (near Tesco)
**Millstone Citra, Tiger Rut; Ossett Butterley;
Wainwright Amber; 1 changing beer (sourced locally;
often Ossett)** Ⓗ

A family-run end-of-terrace village free house with a
friendly feel. The stone-built pub comprises a small bar
area, a main room popular with diners, and a side room
with TV, dartboard, cribbage and dominoes. Home-
cooked food comes from The Stockpot, with daily
specials available on Wednesdays, Fridays and Sundays.
Pies and puddings are popular, along with Friday fish
dishes. Some pavement seating fronts the pub.
ᵴ🌢👤🜨♣🚌(180,350) 🐾🛜

Greenmount

Greenmount Cricket Club

Brandlesholme Road, BL8 4DX
☎ (01204) 883667 🌐 greenmountcricketclub.com
**Brewsmith Bitter; 2 changing beers (often Bowland,
Moorhouse's)** Ⓗ

Friendly and welcoming club, open all year round. In
summer you can sit outside on a warm weekend
watching cricket and supping fine ales. It regularly offers
three cask lines from changing breweries, with
Brewsmith featuring permanently. A catering service
operates from Thursday to Sunday. The club has had a
major refurb of the lounge bar area, with new toilets that
include a separate accessible facility. Well-behaved dogs
welcome. ᵴ🌢🌢🅿🚌(474)🐾🛜

Hazel Grove

Grove Alehouse

145 London Road, SK7 4HH (opp Hope St)
☎ 07594 123174
**5 changing beers (sourced regionally; often
Titanic)** Ⓗ

Micropub with an airy feel, set in former butcher's shop
premises. The bar is made from reclaimed wood and sits
at the rear corner of an L-shaped drinking area, with a
good mix of bench seating, bar stools, and tables and
chairs, all cleverly shoe-horned into the small interior.
Five handpumped beers include a dark ale, usually a beer
from Titanic, the rest are mostly sourced from local
brewers. Bring-your-own cheese tastings are held on the
second Sunday of the month. Q ᵴ🌢🜨♣🚌🛜♪

Heaton Chapel

Heaton Hops

7 School Lane, SK4 5DE (jct Manchester Rd)
🌐 heatonhops.co.uk
**3 changing beers (sourced regionally; often Timothy
Taylor)** Ⓗ

Since opening in 2015, this cosy, intimate and popular
micropub has won many local awards. As well as the
main bar area, there is a small room downstairs and a
reasonable amount of seating outside by the pavement.
Three cask ales are available, in addition to the eight keg
taps (some of which can be taken away in special
flagons). A large range of bottle-conditioned beers are
also on sale. Heaton Chapel railway station and 192 bus
stop are a short walk away. ᵴ🌢🜨🚌

Heaton Moor

Beer Shop

13 Kingsleigh Road, SK4 3QF (jct Mauldeth Rd)
3 changing beers (sourced regionally) Ⓗ

Despite the name, this is very much a pub, although
there is also a range of bottles and cans to take away.
Since taking over in 2020, the new owner has made this
a welcome oasis in an area of few pubs. Old film posters,
mixed furniture and 60s-influenced fabrics create a
bohemian feel. The three cask beers, usually from local
brewers, always include a dark offering and are
supplemented by an imported lager and two live real
ales on keg. Q ᵴ🌢🅿🚌(25,197)🐾🛜

Higher Broughton

Star Inn

2 Back Hope Street, M7 2FR (from jct of Knoll St and
Great Clowes St head N 60yds then left)
☎ (0161) 792 4184 🌐 staronthecliff.co.uk
**2 changing beers (sourced regionally; often
Brightside, Taylors)** Ⓗ

The first urban community-owned pub in the UK, this
small back-street local is quite a surprise. Enter through a
narrow porch into a small vault/bar area, then to the left
is the main seating area with padded seats around two
bay windows, a jukebox and a TV. A further room has a
pool table and dartboard. Outside is a partially covered
patio, and an outbuilding that contains the accessible
toilets. 🌢🚌(97,98)🐾

Hindley

Hare & Hounds Ⓛ

31 Ladies Lane, WN2 2QA
☎ 07305 640675
5 changing beers Ⓗ

This small but traditional pub is located between Hindley
railway station and the town centre. There is a large,
comfortable lounge, a distinct bar/vault area and a
charming beer garden to the rear, renovated to a high
standard in 2020. The lounge displays pictures from
bygone Hindley and has a largescreen TV for sports. The
pub is home to darts and dominoes teams playing in the
local leagues. Beers are from Wigan Brewhouse along
with other breweries both local and further afield.
ᵴ🌢🜨🚌(7) 🐾🛜

Hollinwood

Railway Hotel Ⓛ

13 Railway Road, OL9 7LG
☎ 07712 681176
**Joseph Holt Bitter; Timothy Taylor Landlord; 3
changing beers** Ⓗ

A popular free house in a convenient location opposite
Hollinwood tram stop and adjacent to the main A62
Oldham-Manchester road, served by 83 and 84 buses.
The pub has five handpumps, with two regular ales from
Holts and Taylors (it is a Timothy Taylor Champion Club
member) and three constantly changing ales. It has one
large room with a front bar area and rear dining area.
Food is served daily, except Sunday. Live music is played
at weekends. ᵴ🌢🌢👤🅿🐾🛜♪

Horwich

B33R@33

33 Lee Lane, BL6 7AX
☎ 07596 029443 🌐 b33r33.com
2 changing beers (sourced locally) Ⓗ

A bar created in the centre of Horwich by four local beer
enthusiasts. It has a bright, airy, contemporary feel with
background music complementing convivial chat. Two
cask ales from some of the best local breweries are
available alongside keg fonts dispensing beers from

independent breweries, including one from nearby Rivington brewery. A range of real ciders are served from handpump, keg font, bag-in-box and bottle.
🏠❀●🖫(125) ❀🕏

Bank Top Brewery Ale House 🗓 ⊘

36 Church Street, BL6 6AD
☎ (01204) 693793 ⊕ banktopbrewery.com
Bank Top Bad to the Bone, Dark Mild, Flat Cap, Pavilion Pale Ale; 5 changing beers (sourced locally; often Bank Top) 🗓
Immaculate pub showcasing Bolton's award-winning Bank Top brewery. It is situated in a conservation area opposite Horwich Parish Church and alongside cottages associated with the area's history of textiles and bleaching. Choose from eight Bank Top cask beers, including Dark Mild, a former Champion Mild of Britain, plus one changing guest. Frequent buses stop outside the door, making it a good place to start your visit to the town, or finish a walk in the nearby countryside.
🏠❀♣●🖫(125) ❀♫

Brewery Bar 🍷 🗓

Moreton Mill, Hampson Street, BL6 7JH (just behind Old Original Bay Horse)
☎ (01204) 692976 ⊕ thebrewerybar.co.uk
Blackedge Hop, Black, Pike; 4 changing beers (sourced locally; often Blackedge) 🗓
This bar is on the first floor above the award-winning Blackedge brewery, which is visible through glass windows at the entrance. Converted from industrial premises and retaining some original features, it has bench tables with comfortable upholstered seating. Choose from seven cask beers plus an extensive keg offering, all brewed on the premises, supplemented with occasional guests. There is usually at least one real cider available. Note the toilets are on the ground floor and there is no lift. 🏠❀🕼♣●🖫(125,516)❀🕏♫

Crown 🗓

1 Chorley New Road, BL6 7QJ
☎ (01204) 693109
Joseph Holt Mild, IPA, Bitter, Two Hoots; 4 changing beers (sourced locally; often Bank Top, Blackedge) 🗓
A historic landmark pub close to the beautiful countryside around Lever Park and Rivington. It serves a range of Joseph Holt's beers and up to four guest ales from local breweries. The multi-room layout provides home to many community activities including darts, pool and chess. Elsewhere are quiet drinking areas and a large sports TV. Home-cooked food is served every day. Winner of a CAMRA 50th anniversary Golden Award in recognition of its long-term contribution to cask ale.
🏠❀🕼♣P🖫(125,575) ❀🕏♫

Hulme

Salutation

12 Higher Chatham Street, M15 6ED
☎ (0161) 247 6465 ⊕ thesalutationpub.com
Bollington White Nancy, Long Hop, Best, Oat Mill Stout, Eastern Nights 🗓
A gem of a pub tucked away off the busy Oxford Road, between Manchester Metropolitan University Students Union and the new School of Digital Arts. In 2011 MMU purchased the pub from Punch Taverns and in 2013 the Student Union took control of running it. It is popular with staff and locals, as well as students. The pub is a Bollington brewery tap, with five beers on handpump. Food is available every day.
🏠❀🕼🕿⇌(Oxford Road) ♣🖫🕏♫

Hyde

Cheshire Ring Hotel 🗓

72-74 Manchester Road, SK14 2BJ
☎ 07917 055629
6 changing beers (often Beartown) 🗓
One of the oldest pubs in Hyde, this cash-only free house can have up to six guest beers from micros near and far (including Beartown), in addition to ciders, perries and continental brews. A selection of bottled beers is also stocked. Home-made curries are served on Thursday evenings, and Sunday is quiz night. The opening hours vary with the season and it may close early on Mondays and Tuesdays. 🏠❀⇌(Central)🖫(201,202)❀

Jack's Bar

3 Hamnett Street, SK14 2EX
☎ 07962 367676
3 changing beers (sourced locally; often Bradfield, Thornbridge) 🗓
Smart, cosy and friendly micropub just off Hyde Market Place and close to the bus station. Formerly named Tweed Tap, it was tastefully refurbished before reopening under new management in 2021. It is surprisingly spacious and is decked out in old dark wood to give a rustic feel. It serves three ever-changing beers, often from fairly local breweries and usually including a stout or porter. Three third flights are also available. Closed Tuesdays and Wednesdays. Q🕼⇌(Central)🖫

Joshua Bradley ⊘

Stockport Road, SK14 5EZ
☎ (0161) 406 6776 ⊕ thejoshuabradley.co.uk
Hydes Original; 4 changing beers (often Hydes) 🗓
Named after a former mayor of Hyde, this pub opened following an extensive renovation of the former Bamford Hall. It is set in its own grounds. Though primarily a large, open-plan, high-quality restaurant, there is a room – the snug – set aside purely for drinkers, to the right of the long bar. 🏠❀🕼🕼P🖫(330)🕏♫

Sportsman Inn 🗓

57 Mottram Road, SK14 2NN (next to exit from Morrisons car park)
☎ (0161) 368 5000 ⊕ elcubalibre.co.uk
Rossendale Floral Dance, Glen Top Bitter, Halo Pale, Pitch Porter, Sunshine; house beer (by Rossendale) 🗓
This former regional CAMRA award winner is popular with locals and retains its character. It offers a full range of Rossendale brewery ales. The upstairs restaurant serves Cuban tapas and vegetarian options. Wednesday is curry night, and on Sundays there is a traditional roast from noon until it has gone. The choice of food varies with day and time. The rear patio includes a covered and heated smoking area. It is on the main road, close to Hyde United football ground.
🏠❀🕼⇌(Newton for Hyde) ♣P🖫❀🕏

Leigh

Bobbin 🍷

38A Leigh Road, WN7 1QR
☎ (01942) 581242 ⊕ thebobbinleigh.co.uk
4 changing beers (sourced locally) 🗓
On the northern edge of the town centre, this one-room micropub offers a warm welcome and has comfortable seating. The bar is decorated with pumpclips and there are pictures for sale for charity. Prices are competitive, and a dark beer and real cider are always available. Beers are sourced from regional microbreweries, with current and forthcoming selections displayed on their website. Open from 1pm on Sundays when Leigh RLFC are playing at home. Q🕼🖫❀🕏♫

Thomas Burke Ⓛ ✓

20A Leigh Road, WN7 1QR
☎ (01942) 685640
Greene King Abbot; Moorhouse's Blonde Witch; changing beers Ⓗ
Popular with all ages, this Wetherspoon pub is named after a renowned Leigh tenor, known as the Lancashire Caruso. The pub divides into three areas: the main long bar, a raised dining area and, in what was once a cinema foyer, lounge-style seating. There is also a small courtyard at the back for outside drinking. A changing range of beers is sourced from breweries near and far, including the house beer, Leigh Leopards Blond Ale.
Q❄️🚫◑🛗🚃(V1)🛜

White Lion Ⓛ

6A Leigh Road, WN7 1QL
☎ 07960 435454
4 changing beers (sourced locally; often Wigan Brewhouse) Ⓗ
Opposite Leigh's historic parish church, just a few minutes' walk from the town centre, the White Lion is a friendly, welcoming pub. You can choose whether to enjoy the comfort of the main bar, the quiet of the snug, or bar games in the vault. Four handpumps dispense a selection of real ales from local and regional micros, principally Ossett and Wigan Brewhouse. Over-18s only.
Q🚫♿️♣🚃(V1,582)🛜♪

Littleborough

Hare on the Hill

132 Hare Hill Road, OL15 9HG (588 bus stops nearby)
☎ (01706) 375220 ⊕ beerbreadpork.pub
Vocation Bread & Butter Ⓗ; **4 changing beers (often Pictish, Saltaire, Tiny Rebel)** Ⓐ
Although relatively new, the Hare has quickly established itself as a warm and welcoming little pub, just outside the village centre. Four cask ales are available, one regular and three changing, and there is usually at least one real cider and one KeyKeg pump on. Reasonably priced food is available every day. The beer garden has cosy chalets, which are bookable, for inclement weather.
Q🚫❄️◑🅰🚶♣🚏🅿🚃(518)☀️🛜

Red Lion Ⓛ

6 Halifax Road, OL15 0HB
☎ (01706) 378195
House beer (by Robinsons); 2 changing beers (often Bowland) Ⓗ
Just outside the village centre, between the railway and canal, is this detached, old stone pub. There are four distinct rooms, each different in character: the main room is large and homely; the adjacent snug has comfortable high-backed chairs; and the other two rooms are for games and TV sport. Up to four guest beers supplement the two house beers. Q♿️🚶♣🚏🚃☀️🛜♪

White House Ⓛ

Blackstone Edge, Halifax Road, OL15 0LG
☎ (01706) 378456 ⊕ thewhitehousepub.co.uk
Timothy Taylor Landlord; Theakston Best Bitter; 2 changing beers (often Goose Eye, Phoenix) Ⓗ
Dating from 1671, this old coaching house was originally called the Coach & Horses. Situated 1,300 feet above sea level, where the Pennine Way crosses the road, it commands stunning views. Family run for over 30 years, it offers a warm and friendly welcome. Four handpumps serve two regular and two changing beers. Good food at a reasonable price is served daily from an extensive menu. A bus stop on the Rochdale to Halifax route is outside. Q🚫❄️◑♿️🅰🚏🚃(X58)🛜

Lowton

Travellers Rest ✓

443 Newton Road, WA3 1NZ
☎ (01925) 293222 ⊕ travellersrestlowton.com
2 changing beers (sourced regionally) Ⓗ
Traditionally country pub and restaurant, dating back to the 19th century, between Lowton and Newton-le-Willows, popular with locals, walkers and cyclists. There are a number of seating areas and a separate restaurant, with a bar area to the right for drinkers. Outside is a large garden and car park. A private room is available to hire for special occasions. Haydock Park racecourse is only a mile away. Q🚫❄️◑♿️🅿🚃(34)☀️🛜

Lydgate

White Hart Inn Ⓛ

51 Stockport Road, OL4 4JJ
☎ (01457) 872566 ⊕ thewhitehart.co.uk
JW Lees Bitter; Millstone Tiger Rut; Timothy Taylor Golden Best; 2 changing beers (often JW Lees) Ⓗ
Dating back to 1788, this stone building was once a police station. it was previously owned by the Gartside brewery but is now a free house, serving ales from mainly local breweries. There are log-burning stoves in the bar area and brasserie, and quality food is served daily from an award-winning kitchen. The pub hosts occasional special events. Accommodation man function rooms are available, and there are outstanding views of the surrounding countryside.
Q🚫❄️🛏◑♿️🅿🚃(84,184)🛜

Manchester

Britons Protection ★

50 Great Bridgewater Street, M1 5LE
☎ (0161) 236 5895
8 changing beers (sourced locally) Ⓗ
This Grade II-listed, 210-year-old multi-roomed ale and whisky house has been recognised by CAMRA as having a regionally important historic pub interior. It serves eight changing beers and some 360 different whiskies. The name comes from its history as an army recruitment venue, and murals depict the Peterloo massacre. The pub is famous for its ornate ceilings; other notable architectural features include a terrazzo-tiled corridor floor, original 1930s urinals, and the serving hatch through which people in the two rear rooms receive their beer from the front bar.
🚫❄️◑🚆(Deansgate)🚇(Deansgate-Castlefield)🚃☀️🛜

Bundobust Brewery

61-69 Oxford Road, M1 6EJ
☎ (0161) 511 8601 ⊕ bundobust.com
2 changing beers (sourced regionally) Ⓗ
Bundobust opened a brewery and tap in 2021 and serves Indian vegetarian street food, as well as beer and cider. Under an atrium roof, the bar has a modern industrial design with views of the open brewery. It seats up to 150 people and is a welcoming and accessible venue. They serve two guest cask beers on handpull and the 16 keg lines serve eight Bundobust beers, seven guest beers and a house cider produced by Hogan's.
🚫◑♿️🚆(Oxford Road)🚇(St Peters Square)☀️🛜

Café Beermoth

40A Spring Gardens, M2 1EN (entrance is on Brown St)
☎ (0161) 835 2049 ⊕ beermoth.co.uk
7 changing beers (sourced nationally) Ⓗ
Modern pub with a Belgian theme and a laid-back, enjoyable vibe, located in the heart of the city, not far from Market Street. The huge space houses the bar and a

smaller mezzanine floor. It has an extensive beer selection, with seven cask handpumps, 10 keg lines, and a large variety of bottled ales, including many popular imports from Germany and Belgium. Tap takeovers and beer samplings are among the events that visitors can look forward to. There are some seats outside.
ᵫ&ᴚ(Market Street) ●❀❀❄♫

Cask

29 Liverpool Road, M3 4NQ
☎ (0161) 819 2527
4 changing beers (sourced regionally; often Mallinsons, Pictish) Ⓗ
Entering the pub via the listed saloon-style doors, the first view is of the four handpumps, which feature a good range of styles and strengths. The rustic furniture gives this front room a traditional feel, while further in are bench seated booths and access to the courtyard garden. A further look will reveal an impressive selection of specialist beers, both local and imported. Real cider is also available in bottles. Customers can bring their own food, if they dispose of rubbish responsibly.
❀❄(Deansgate) ᴚ(Deansgate-Castlefield) ●�❀❄

City Arms ✔

46-48 Kennedy Street, M2 4BQ (near town hall, next door to Waterhouse pub)
☎ (0161) 236 4610
8 changing beers (sourced regionally; often Manchester, Titanic) Ⓗ
A small pub, nearly 200 years old, with two standard rooms and numerous original features. The bar and a few chairs are in the area overlooking the street, which is fairly basic. To the back is a cosier area where you can relax in good company. Eight handpulls give a wide variety of beer types in great shape; Titanic Plum Porter is a popular and reliable choice. The bar is frequently packed. ❀◐❄(Oxford Road)ᴚ(St Peters Square)♣🚌❀

Gas Lamp

50A Bridge Street, M3 3BW
☎ (0161) 478 1224 🌐 thegaslampmanchester.co.uk
4 changing beers (sourced nationally; often Pomona Island) Ⓗ
Opened in 2010 and housed in the basement of the former Manchester and Salford Children's Mission. The pub has an impressive frontage, with the small, easily missable doorway leading down to the subterranean bar. The main bar area has Victorian glazed-brick walls and wooden flooring. A narrow passageway leads to a cosy back room with photos of the building's history. One or two of the four cask beers are usually from the pub's own brewery, Pomona Island, in Salford. Payment by card only.
ᵫ❄(Salford Central) ᴚ(St Peters Square) ●🚌❀❄

Hare & Hounds ★

46 Shudehill, M4 4AA (opp Shudehill bus station)
☎ (0161) 832 4737
Joseph Holt Bitter; 2 changing beers (sourced regionally; often Robinsons) Ⓗ
Busy, Grade II-listed pub opposite Shudehill transport interchange. It has been identified by CAMRA as having a nationally important historic pub interior because of its prserved interior dating from 1925, though the pub is from the early 1800s. Take time to admire the mottled tile frontage before entering. The central bar serves all three rooms: front vault, central vault and lounge bar. Since its last listing it has enjoyed sympathetic redecoration, which includes a new selection of photographs of old Manchester.
❄(Victoria) ᴚ(Shudehill) 🚌❀❄ ♫

Lower Turks Head

36 Shudehill, M4 1EZ (opp Shudehill bus and metrolink interchange)
☎ (0161) 834 2910
Joseph Holt Mild, IPA, Bitter, Two Hoots; 1 changing beer (sourced locally; often Joseph Holt) Ⓗ
After being closed and lying empty for over 20 years, this pub reopened in 2013 and was acquired by Joseph Holt in 2021. There are several drinking areas on the split-level ground floor, as well as an upstairs lounge that leads to a roof terrace. An interesting feature is the raised drinking pews opposite the bar. The pub sits in a terrace opposite Shudehill tram shop and offers a full range of Holts beers, including specials, kept in excellent condition. Q♿ᵫ❀🚋❄(Victoria)ᴚ(Shudehill)🚌🚗❄

Marble Arch Inn ★

73 Rochdale Road, Collyhurst, M4 4HY (corner Gould St)
☎ (0161) 832 5914 🌐 marblebeers.com
Marble Manchester Bitter, Pint; 4 changing beers (sourced nationally; often Marble) Ⓗ
The Marble Arch was the birthplace of the city's iconic Marble brewery, now moved to Salford, and is an impressive Grade-II listed building. A striking pillared entrance porch leads to an equally impressive interior, with a famously sloping mosaic floor approaching an ornate bar. A good range of cask beer is served, and keg lines dispense both Marble and guest beers. There is a small range of carefully selected artisanal real and live ciders. At the rear is a dining area and a yard with well-designed kiosk shelters.
Q♿❀◐♦❄(Victoria) ᴚ(Shudehill) ●🚌❀❄

Molly House 🏆

26 Richmond Street, M1 3NB (jct Sackville St)
☎ (0161) 237 9329 🌐 themollyhouse.com
3 changing beers (sourced regionally; often Cloudwater, Mallinsons, RedWillow) Ⓗ
Tucked away just behind the main Canal Street section of the gay village, Molly House has the look of a traditional pub at first glance. Set on two floors, the ground floor has four handpumps, always with a range of choice from local breweries such as RedWillow, Cloudwater, Blackedge and Malllinsons. The adjacent kitchen serves tapas. There are more handpumps in the more glamorous first-floor room, though not all may be available. Local CAMRA Pub of the Year 2023.
Q♿❀◐♦&❄(Piccadilly) ᴚ(Piccadilly Gardens) ♣🚌🏠❄❄♫

Peveril of the Peak ★

127 Great Bridgewater Street, M1 5JQ (jct of Great Bridgewater St and Chepstow St)
☎ (0161) 236 6364
Millstone Tiger Rut; Timothy Taylor Landlord; Titanic Plum Porter; 1 changing beer (often Brightside) Ⓗ
This impressive Grade II-listed building stands alone with an outside drinking area created by a road diversion. The bar is an island between a pool room, snug and traditional bar. Dark wood and stained glass predominate. The four handpumps serve regular beers as displayed on a board by the snug. This is a rare venue for table football, played with great enthusiasm.
Q❀❄(Oxford Road) ᴚ(St Peters Square) ♣🚌❀♫

Piccadilly Tap

8 Gateway House, Piccadilly Station Approach, M1 2GH (up station approach, off London Rd)
☎ (0161) 393 4168 🌐 piccadillytap.com
5 changing beers (sourced nationally) Ⓗ
Opened in 2015 in a former shop unit on Manchester Piccadilly station approach, this bar has established itself

as a popular meeting point. The ground floor features a largely standing-room area with high and low tables; upstairs is a seating area with outdoor terrace, pool table and toilets. It features five real ales on the bar and a number of craft ales are dispensed from taps at the back. Fresh pizza is available from noon each day. Handy for trains. ♿🚲🕑≠(Piccadilly)🚃(Piccadilly)♣🚗🏠❀🛜

Port Street Beer House
39-41 Port Street, M1 2EQ (opp Brewer St)
☎ (0161) 237 9949 ● portstreetbeerhouse.co.uk
7 changing beers (sourced nationally; often DEYA, Track, Triple Point) Ⓗ
Vibrant pub split over two floors of a former shop in the Northern Quarter. The bar is on the ground floor, with outdoor pavement seating and an outdoor yard, and there is an additional upstairs room. An accessible toilet is on the ground floor. Seven handpumps and a number of keg lines provide an interesting range of beers, and the pub holds group beer tastings and regular tap takeovers. Its associated festival, IndyManBeerCon, made an important contribution to the growth of the city's beer scene.
♿🕑❀≠(Piccadilly) 🚃(Piccadilly Gardens) ♣🏠🚗❀🛜

Smithfield Market Tavern
37 Swan Street, M4 5JZ (corner of Coop St and Swan St)
● the-smithfield-market-tavern.business.site
6 changing beers (sourced nationally; often Blackjack) Ⓗ
Refurbished in 2020, the Smithfield is a lively, modern take on a traditional pub. It is the flagship venue for Blackjack brewery and serves six cask ales – four from Blackjack plus two guests – as well as 10 keg beers, a cider and an interesting selection of bottled brews. A traditional bar billiards table, dartboard and a small selection of board games provide entertainment. Local CAMRA Pub of the Year 2022.
♿🕑❀≠(Victoria) 🚃(Shudehill) ♣🏠🚗❀🛜

Society
101 Barbirolli Square, M2 3BD (down steps at back of Barbirolli Square) ● societymanchester.com
Vocation Bread & Butter, Heart & Soul; 2 changing beers (sourced locally) Ⓗ
In 2021 Vocation brewery from Hebden Bridge launched a bar in a shared kitchen and dining area called Society, in the back of Barbirolli Square. As you walk through the front doors the Vocation bar is directly in front of you. They boast the largest selection of beer taps in Manchester, with four handpumps on the bar and a wall of keg taps behind it. Five vendors offer street food. It has ramp or lift access.
♿🕑◑👍≠(Deansgate) 🚃(St Peters Square) ❀🛜

Track Brewery Tap
Unit 18, Piccadilly Trading Estate, M1 2NP
☎ (0161) 536 3975
Track Sonoma; 2 changing beers (sourced locally) Ⓗ
After a number of venues, the Tap joined the brewery in its new, US-inspired, all-in-one facility in the Piccadilly Trading Estate in 2021. There are 20 keg and three cask lines serving the freshest Track beer, plus some occasional guests. There is seating space for 80 in the open-plan layout, and a dedicated area for a food residency. Closed on Mondays.
❀◑👍≠(Piccadilly) 🚃(New Islington) ❀

Marple

Samuel Oldknow
22 Market Street, SK6 7AD
☎ (0161) 425 9530 ● samueloldknow.co.uk

6 changing beers (sourced regionally; often Brightside, Chadkirk, Strange Times) Ⓗ
Named after a local mill owner who was responsible for much of the development of Marple and Mellor some 200 years ago. This is a welcoming and slightly quirky two-level bar in a converted shop. Six vintage-style handpulls dispense changing real ales, plus real ciders from Biddenden. The regular beers are from local breweries: Brightside, Chadkirk and Strange Times. There is always a dark beer. A range of canned and bottled beers is also available to take away. Food consists of snacks and locally made pies. Q♿🕑🍴🏠🚗❀🛜🎵

Traders
111-113 Stockport Road, SK6 6AF
3 changing beers (sourced nationally) Ⓗ
Originally a shop conversion, this micropub expanded into the next-door premises in 2019, and a further expansion is planned. The industrial chic interior is brightened up by colourful wall paintings, posters and plants. Three handpumps serve regularly changing ales, and 12 keg lines serve a mix of beers. Pie and mash is served at meal times. Live music often features on Tuesday evening and some weekends, a quiz on a Wednesday, and occasional international sports games.
♿🕑◑▶≠(Rose Hill Marple) 🚗❀🎵

Marple Bridge

Northumberland Arms
64 Compstall Road, SK6 5HD
● thenorthumberlandarms.com
Robinsons Unicorn; Track Sonoma; 1 changing beer (sourced locally) Ⓗ
Former Robinsons house that reopened in 2017 as a pub owned and run by the community. It retains the feel of an unchanged, well-used local. The traditional exterior is enhanced by a pleasant beer garden. A small bar area serves three rooms, one of which is used for pub games. One beer is often a mild or a dark beer. Used by various groups for meetings and activities, the pub fulfils its role as a community venue. Frequent buses stop outside.
♿🕑♣🚗🛒(383,384) ❀🛜

Middleton

Ring o' Bells
St. Leonards Square, M24 6DJ
☎ (0161) 654 9245
JW Lees Manchester Pale Ale, Bitter; 2 changing beers (sourced locally; often JW Lees) Ⓗ
A pub since 1831, the Ringers has an elevated location opposite the medieval parish church, and enjoys stunning views across to Oldham and beyond. Lees seasonal and Boilerhouse beers are served. Occasional live music and quizzes add to the pub's community focus. A fabulous beer garden to the rear is a hidden bonus. It hosts an annual Maypole event on May bank holiday Monday, with a unique Pace Egg play on Easter Monday.
🕑♣🚗🛒(17) ❀🛜🎵

Tandle Hill Tavern
14 Thornham Lane, M24 2SD (1 mile on unmetalled lane from either A664 or A627)
☎ (0161) 376 4492
JW Lees Bitter, Stout; house beer (by JW Lees); 1 changing beer (sourced locally; often JW Lees) Ⓗ
Nestled amidst farms, this neat little pub is well worth the one-mile walk along a potholed road from Royton or Middleton direction. It has a bar and lounge area and a quiet side room. A rear beer garden and benches provide outdoor seating. The house beer is dry hopped Lees

Bitter, and Lees Boilerhouse beers feature. It is popular with walkers, and dogs are welcome. Phone ahead to check opening times in bad weather or in winter. No food is served. Q❀P❀

Monton

Monton Tap
165 Monton Road, M30 9GS
☎ 07413 487560
3 changing beers (sourced locally; often Brightside, Marble, Strange Times) Ⓗ
A converted shop premises in an up-and-coming area. Opened in 2018, the Monton Tap is has quickly become a popular venue, with three handpumps and an ever-changing variety of ales, often locally sourced. There is a good range of KeyKeg and bottles. This small pub also champions local gins and rums. ❀🖾❀🛜

Mossley

Church Inn Ⓛ
82 Stockport Road, OL5 0RF
☎ 07739 396818
Bowland Boxer Blonde, Hen Harrier; 2 changing beers (often Bowland) Ⓗ
This traditional corner local on the main road became a free house in 2017 under the ownership of the licensee. The bar, within the comfortable lounge, also serves a separate small games room where the pool table is popular. Saturday is karaoke night and on Tuesdays bluegrass music takes centre stage. The veranda at the rear provides a commanding view down the Tame valley. 🌃❀♣P🖾(356)❀🛜♪

Commercial Hotel Ⓛ
58 Manchester Road, OL5 0AA
☎ 07919 153879
Millstone Tiger Rut, Stout; Wainwright; 1 changing beer (often Marston's) Ⓗ
The Commercial opened in 1831 and was enlarged in 1859. It was the first pub in Bottom Mossley and initially catered for coach travellers and later for those arriving by rail. Nowadays it is more likely to be a stopping point for rail ale trail enthusiasts. The refurbished open-plan interior has a central bar. The Commie can be boisterous, particularly at weekends when you are likely to encounter a disco or karaoke. 🌃❀➡🖾(343,350)❀🛜♪

Gillery Ⓛ
1-3 Old Brow, OL5 0AD (Stamford Rd, immediately above the railway station)
☎ (01457) 237007 🌐 thegilleryinthebank.co.uk
Millstone Tiger Rut, True Grit; 1 changing beer (sourced locally; often Millstone) Ⓗ
This café-bar was converted from the last remaining bank in Mossley and opened in 2019. The stone building towers over Stamford Road immediately behind the railway station. Three handpumps dispense beers from the town's Millstone brewery. The pub welcomes all, including runners, walkers, and cyclists. Food is available until 9pm. Live music features most weekends, often from local musicians. There is also work from local artists on display. 🌃❀◑➡🖾❀🛜♪

Rising Sun Ⓛ
235 Stockport Road, OL5 0RQ
☎ (01457) 238236 🌐 risingsunmossley.co.uk
Millstone Tiger Rut, Stout, True Grit; 4 changing beers (sourced locally; often Saltaire, Thornbridge) Ⓗ
A former Wilsons pub but a free house for many years, the present owner added a small brewery in 2016 to

augment the range of regular beers (usually from nearby Millstone) and guest beers. Open-plan with log burning fires, there are fine views across the Tame valley towards the Pennines beyond. Several large TVs show mainly City and United matches, and with bands playing some nights there is frequently a boisterous atmosphere in the pub. 🌃❀P🖾(353)❀🛜♪

Oldham

Ashton Arms Ⓛ
28-30 Clegg Street, OL1 1PL (opp Odeon cinema complex)
☎ (0161) 630 9709
6 changing beers (sourced locally; often Millstone, Ossett, Pictish) Ⓗ
Traditional, well-run town-centre pub on two levels. An excellent range of four to six handpulled beers is available, sourced mainly from local microbreweries and always in good form. The pub also offers a range of Belgian and German beers, and often a real cider on handpump. Good value home-cooked food is served daily. Live sport is often on the TVs. Payment is cash only. Now in its 20th consecutive year in this Guide
Q❀◑🖾(Central)❀🖾🛜

Cob & Coal Tap Ⓛ
Units 12-14, Tommyfield Market, Albion Street, OL1 3BG
☎ (0161) 624 0446
6 changing beers (often Pictish, Thirst Class, Wishbone) Ⓗ
A warm, friendly welcome is assured at this cosy, bijou micropub, which has become a firm favourite with Oldham's real ale and cider drinkers. It boasts six changing real ales on handpump, all very carefully looked after and always in top condition. Real cider is also available on gravity. A variety of food is available from adjacent market stalls, and there is extra seating outside. A former CAMRA regional Pub of the Year and local Cider Pub of the Year. Q🖾(Central)❀🖾❀🛜

Fox & Pine 🍷
18 Greaves Street, OL1 1AD (halfway along Greaves St between Union St and Yorkshire St)
☎ (0161) 628 2475
Draught Bass; 10 changing beers (sourced regionally; often Durham, Mallinsons, Pictish) Ⓗ
A real gem in Oldham's real ale portfolio. A busy downstairs bar area has 10 handpumps serving a comprehensive range of styles, including three changing dark beers. Real cider and foreign beers are also on the bar. Upstairs there are extra rooms hosting many social and community groups. Fresh home-cooked food is available Thursday to Sunday. The pub is dog friendly. Local CAMRA Pub of the Year 2022 and 2023. It is a 5-minute walk from Oldham bus station.
Q❀◑♿🖾(Central)❀🖾❀🛜

Patricroft

Stanley Arms ★
295 Liverpool Road, M30 0QN (corner Eliza Ann St)
☎ 07833 092341
Joseph Holt Mild, Bitter Ⓗ
A small 1920s street-corner local – no more than 20 feet wide – with etched windows. Entering through the side door, turn right into a corridor with the bar and vault on your right and two comfy rooms to the left. The room at the end has an interesting cast iron range. Busiest times are late afternoon and early evening. With a wealth of fixtures and fittings from its heyday including etched

glass, art-nouveau style tilework and glazed timber, it was awarded Grade II-listed status in 2014 and has been recognised by CAMRA as having a nationally important historic pub interior. ✿♿≉♣🚃(67,100)

Prestwich

Keg, Cask & Bottle
Unit 7 Longfield Centre, M25 1AY
🌐 kegcaskbottle.co.uk
Marble Pint; 1 changing beer (often Brewsmith) Ⓗ
Located within the pedestrianised Longfield shopping precinct, this small microbar/off sales establishment has two handpulls serving rotating local cask ales, usually light and dark styles, from breweries such as Marble, Brewsmith, Track, Squawk and Brightside. In addition, there is a good selection of nationally and internationally sourced bottle and canned beers. It is convenient for the metrolink tram stop, and has acquired the unit next door to expand its space and selection. Q♿🚃(98)✿🌐

Royal Oak
23-25 Whittaker Lane, M25 1HA
☎ (0161) 773 8691
Hydes Original, Lowry; 1 changing beer (often Hydes) Ⓗ
Superb traditional local pub on a quiet street close to Heaton Park tram stop and convenient for buses. Three handpulls serve Hydes ales, which are kept in excellent condition by the management, who have run this friendly pub for 23 years. A comfortable through lounge area fronts the bar and to the rear is a large games room with bar where darts and other traditional pub games are played. The pleasant beer garden is ideal for sitting outside on warm days.
Q♿✿♿🚃(Heaton Park) ♣P🚃✿🌐♪

Radcliffe

New Inn
387 Ainsworth Road, M26 4HF
☎ (0161) 723 0583
Ossett White Rat; Sharp's Doom Bar; 1 changing beer Ⓗ
A traditional, friendly, red-brick pub, free of tie, with three real ales on offer. Refurbished in 2019, it has a clean and pleasant decor with comfortable seating. There is a large beer garden to the rear with BBQs in summer. Various activities take place, with free pool, karaoke, a quiz night, a weekly raffle, and live music on Saturday nights, giving it a real community feel. There is limited car parking on the unmade lane behind.
♿✿♿♣P🚃(98,471) ✿🌐♪

Ramsbottom

Casked
2-4 Prince Street, BL0 9FN
House beer (by Reedley Hallows); 4 changing beers (sourced locally; often Brewsmith, Red Rose) Ⓗ
A welcome addition to the vibrant real ale scene of Ramsbottom. Five handpumps serve ales sourced predominantly from local breweries such as Brewsmith, Deeply Vale and Reedley Hallows. Two changng real ciders are on gravity, and there are 15 keg lines. This single-floor open-plan pub is extremely dog friendly. In fact, if you take your hound in, its picture may appear on the pub's Facebook page. ✿♿≉●🚃✿🌐

Irwell Works Brewery Tap Ⓛ
Irwell Street, BL0 9YQ
☎ (01706) 825019 🌐 irwellworksbrewery.co.uk

Irwell Works Lightweights & Gentlemen, Breadcrumbs, Copper Plate, Costa Del Salford, Marshmallow Unicorn, Mad Dogs & Englishmen; 8 changing beers (often Irwell Works) Ⓗ
Located in the heart of Ramsbottom, above the brewery itself, the Tap is snug, friendly and full of character. Eight handpumps usually offer the full range of Irwell Works beers, which are traditional in style and brewed with English hops and barley. Snack food is available Friday to Sunday from noon. The pub is a worthwhile stop on the East Lancashire Railways Rail Ale Tours.
✿◗≉♣🚃🚃(472,474) ✿🌐♪

Ramsbottom Royal British Legion
Central Street, BL0 9AF
☎ (01706) 822483 🌐 branches.britishlegion.org.uk/branches/ramsbottom
Fyne Jarl; Ossett White Rat Ⓗ
This is a small, quiet social club just off the main street near the crossroads in the centre of town. Non-members are always welcome (no entry fee), but regulars would be expected to join the club. Two handpumps are on the bar with Fyne Ales Jarl and Ossett White Rat as permanent beers. The main bar is on the ground floor with a function room upstairs. ♿≉♣🚃(472,474)🌐♪

Rochdale

Baum Ⓛ
35 Toad Lane, OL12 0NU
☎ (01706) 352186 🌐 thebaum.co.uk
6 changing beers (sourced nationally; often Pictish, Vocation) Ⓗ
The Baum is situated in the Toad Lane conservation area, and its attractive, traditional appearance and tasteful decor reflect that. It serves six changing cask ales, plus usually a guest cider. The beers are kept well and served by knowledgeable staff. The food from the inventive menu is of a high standard but at reasonable prices. A former CAMRA National Pub of the Year.
Q♿✿◗◗🚃(Town Centre) ●🚃✿🌐

Bombay Brew
1 Drake Street, OL16 1LW
☎ (01706) 869502
House beer (by Vocation); 2 changing beers (sourced locally; often Pictish) Ⓗ
Formerly an old manor and coaching house, Bombay Brew has brought a whole new experience to Rochdale's real ale scene. Here you can drink well kept-real ale and enjoy innovative Indian-influenced food. There are three handpumps, one serving the house beer by Vocation, another with a guest ale, and the third usually with a cider on. Close to the bus and tram interchange.
♿◗≉🚃(Town Centre) 🚃✿🌐

D'Ale House
18 Drake Street, OL16 1NT
Brightside Odin Blonde; house beer (by Pictish); 4 changing beers (often Brightside, Pictish) Ⓗ
Close to the tram and bus interchange, this micropub opened in 2021 and has become a welcome addition to Rochdale's beer scene. Five handpumps are on the bar, serving a selection of local ales and some from slightly further afield. There are also two German beer fonts and eight keg taps. The bar is on an elevated platform towards the rear of the pub, with two lower seating areas either side. Q≉🚃(Town Centre)🚃✿🌐

Flying Horse Hotel Ⓛ
37 Packer Street, OL16 1NJ
☎ (01706) 646412 🌐 theflyinghorsehotel.co.uk

JW Lees Bitter; 9 changing beers (sourced locally; often Phoenix, Pictish, Serious) Ⓗ
Known locally as the Flyer, this is a three-time winner of CAMRA Greater Manchester Pub of the Year and has appeared in this Guide for 18 consecutive years. Dating from 1691 but rebuilt in 1926 into its present form, it stands opposite Rochdale's magnificent gothic Town Hall. Ten well-kept, quality cask ales, with nine constantly changing, are sold alongside two real ciders. It also offers an extensive menu of high-standard, good-value food.
ᘔ⇄◐⇌♢(Town Centre) ●P⊟❀ᯤ♫

Oxford

662 Whitworth Road, OL12 0TB
☎ (01706) 345709 ⊕ theoxfordrochdale.com
Wainwright; 2 changing beers (sourced nationally; often Serious) Ⓗ
A traditional, family-run, stone-built pub located on the A671 Rochdale to Burnley road. It has an enviable reputation for its food and service, and always has at least two well-kept real ales on, with capacity for more in busy seasons. The layout is open-plan, formed into two dining areas with the bar between. The main dining area is largely separated from the bar area.
Qᘔ✿◐♿P⊟(486) ᯤ

Romiley

Jake's Ale House

27 Compstall Road, SK6 4BT
☎ 07927 076941
5 changing beers (sourced locally) Ⓗ
In only a few years this micropub, in a former shop, has become a popular part of the Romiley pub scene. The double-front provides the small, relaxed bar area with a light and airy feel. There is also a small room to the rear. In addition to the five real ales, it serves craft beers on font and boxed ciders from Lilleys. It is close to the railway station, bus routes, and the Peak Forest Canal is a short walk away. Qᘔ⇌♣⊟❀

Sale

JP Joule Ⓛ

2A Northenden Road, M33 3BR
☎ (0161) 962 9889
Greene King Abbot; Ruddles Best Bitter; Sharp's Doom Bar; house beer (by Brightside); 6 changing beers (sourced nationally; often Beartown, Exmoor, Thornbridge) Ⓗ
Popular Wetherspoon pub on the main road in Sale. Two floors are connected by a grand staircase. The main bar is downstairs and there are more handpumps in the upstairs bar, as well as several keg lines serving lagers, cider (not real) and Guinness. An extensive food menu is available until 11pm. Live music and quiz nights are a regular feature and the pub hosts beer festivals several times a year. ᘔ✿◐♿♢⊟❀ᯤ

Salford

Eagle Inn

18-19 Collier Street, M3 7DW (off Queen St)
☎ (0161) 819 5002 ⊕ eagleinn.co.uk
Joseph Holt Bitter, Two Hoots; 1 changing beer (sourced locally) Ⓗ
Located close to Victoria Station and a five-minute walk from Manchester Cathedral. A hidden gem, this Grade II-listed award-winning pub and music venue, also known as the Lamp Oil, has three rooms off a central corridor, and has extended into the cottage next door to accommodate regular music performances. Outdoor seating is available in the surrounding roads. It serves two regular Holt's beers and usually one from Bootleg, with an Old Rosie cider on handpull.
Qᘔ✿♿⇌(Central) ♢(Victoria) ♣⊟❀ᯤ♫

King's Arms

11 Bloom Street, M3 6AN (corner of William St)
☎ (0161) 832 3605 ⊕ kingsarmssalford.com
House beer (by Strange Times); 4 changing beers (often Beartown, Stockport) Ⓗ
There is always something happening at the King's. Live music, plays and comedy nights are hosted upstairs, with a quiz night on Wednesday and needlecraft on a Monday evening. Downstairs, in a racetrack-shaped room, an entry corridor passes the snug to the left while the main lounge and bar is to the right, with a bench stretching three-quarters of the way around the wall. Another corridor leads out to the garden. Q✿◐⇌(Central)⊟♫

New Oxford 🏆 Ⓛ

11 Bexley Square, M3 6DB (off A6 Chapel St, close to Magistrates Court)
☎ (0161) 832 7082 ⊕ thenewoxford.com
House beer (by Phoenix); 16 changing beers (sourced regionally; often Empire, Moorhouse's, Phoenix) Ⓗ
A two-roomed corner-house dating from the 1830s. The central bar boasts 20 handpumps and over 20 fonts. The cask ales are sourced regionally, in a variety of styles, usually including at least one dark beer. The other three handpumps are for cider or perry. There is a large board listing a vast number of Belgian beers. An outdoor area has been fenced off in Bexley Square for drinking. A winner of many CAMRA awards.
ᘔ✿♿⇌(Central) ●⊟❀ᯤ

Salford Quays

Dockyard

Dockhouse, Media City, M50 2EQ (to right of Media City UK Metrolink stop)
☎ (0161) 713 3810 ⊕ dockyard.pub/media-city
House beer (by Strange Times); 3 changing beers (sourced nationally; often Marston's, Sharp's, Strange Times) Ⓗ
Large, warehouse-style premises in Media City, often used by personalities from the nearby BBC and ITV studios. A house beer and three other changing beers are complemented by local and international craft offerings. It features an open-plan kitchen and see-through cellar either side of the bar. The outside seating areas include greenhouses; plastic glasses only. Card payment only.
◐♿♢(Mediacityuk) ♣⊟(50,53) ❀ᯤ

Stalybridge

Bridge Beers Ⓛ

55 Melbourne Street, SK15 2JJ
☎ 07948 617145 ⊕ bridgebeers.co.uk
4 changing beers (sourced locally; often Bridge Beers) Ⓖ
A combined micropub and bottle shop on the main pedestrianised shopping street. There is a small entrance area leading into the bar, which sits in front of a row of stillaged casks of which four are generally available. The bottle display is opposite. Upstairs is a comfortable Victorian styled lounge featuring an eclectic mix of local heritage. The four constantly changing beers are mainly from Bridge Beers brewery and are dispensed by gravity. Occasionally locally sourced guest ales are also available.
Qᘔ⇌♣⊟❀

Cracking Pint

41 Melbourne Street, SK15 2JJ
☎ 07512 753544
3 changing beers (sourced locally; often Phoenix, RedWillow, Vocation) Ⓗ

Spacious microbar opened in 2017 by a local CAMRA member and located next to the canal in the main pedestrianised shopping street. It usually serves three changing real ales, sourced mainly from local breweries and some from further afield. There is also a good selection of bottled beers, many from Germany. This is a bar where conversation dominates in the absence of piped music, TV screens or fruit machines. Dogs and their well-behaved owners are welcome, as are children until 6pm. Q 🕏 ⬯ ⇄ 🖳 😷 🕏

Society Rooms ⊘

49-51 Grosvenor Street, SK15 2JN
☎ (0161) 338 9740
Greene King Abbot; Ruddles Best Bitter; Sharp's Doom Bar; 7 changing beers (sourced nationally; often Moorhouse's, Phoenix) Ⓗ

Popular split-level Wetherspoon in the town centre, named after the former Co-op store it now occupies. It was extended into adjacent premises in 2018, also adding a spacious beer garden, making it one of the largest Wetherspoons in the UK. Enthusiastic management and a strong focus on cask beers make this a favourite with local drinkers, with 10 real ales and two ciders usually available. Two beer festivals a year are held. A short walk from the bus terminus. Q 🕏 🕸 ◑ 🕭 ⇄ 🖳 🕏

Station Buffet Bar

Platform 4 Stalybridge Railway Station, Rassbottom Street, SK15 1RF (accessed from station platform 4)
☎ (0161) 303 0007
6 changing beers (sourced regionally; often Millstone, Timothy Taylor, Thornbridge) Ⓗ

One of the very few remaining Victorian station buffet bars and well worth missing a train for. This well-loved gem has 10 handpumps, with a minimum of five dispensing a variety of local and regionally sourced beers, plus at least one real cider or perry. A good range of bottled beers is also available. Sunday is quiz night, with Spanish classes on Mondays and folk music on Tuesdays. As part of the Transpennine Real Ale Trail, it can get busy on Saturdays. Q 🕸 ◑ 🕭 ⇄ ● 🖳 P 🖳 😷 🕏

Standish

Albion Ale House Ⓛ ⊘

12 High Street, WN6 0HL
☎ (01257) 367897 ⊕ albionalehouse.co.uk
8 changing beers Ⓗ

The first micropub in Standish, located in a former shop right on the High Street, it is now well established, with a loyal clientele, and won local CAMRA Community Pub of the Year 2022. Five cask conditioned ales are on offer, sometimes more, always including one dark beer. Snacks are usually available. There is occasional live music and beer festivals are held. Q 🕏 🕸 🕭 🖳 😷 🕏 ♪

Standish Unity Club Ⓛ

Cross Street, WN6 0HQ
☎ (01257) 424007 ⊕ standishunityclub.com
Sharp's Doom Bar; 4 changing beers (sourced regionally) Ⓗ

In the centre of Standish but tucked away so a little tricky to find, this popular club offers five real ales including one dark beer – often Titanic Plum Porter. The club is split into two sides: a large function room and a bar area

including the games room, and a quieter drinking area. A frequent winner of local CAMRA Club of the Year and runner-up for Regional Club of the Year. Q 🕏 🕭 ♣ P 🖳 🕏 ♪

Stockport

Angel Inn

20 Market Place, SK1 1EY (opp Market Hall)
☎ (0161) 429 0251
House beer (by Listers); 5 changing beers (sourced regionally) Ⓗ

After a 67-year closure, the Angel reopened in 2018. It has since gone from strength to strength and is now a regular in this Guide. While the interior is largely open-plan, it is nicely broken up, with a particularly attractive snug to the rear. In addition, there is a large outdoor drinking area at the back which is well-used in the summer. Live music features some evenings and Sunday afternoons when the pub can get busy. 🕏 🕸 🕭 ⇄ 🖳 😷 🕏

Arden Arms ★ ⊘

23 Millgate, SK1 2LX (jct Corporation St)
☎ (0161) 480 2185
Robinsons Dizzy Blonde, Unicorn, Trooper Ⓗ**, Old Tom; 1 changing beer (often Robinsons)** Ⓖ

Grade II listed and identified by CAMRA as having a nationally important historic pub interior, this multi-room pub is just down the hill from Stockport's Market Place. Note the superb curved, glazed bar, the grandfather clock, and particularly the snug, which can only be accessed through the bar area itself (one of only four such in the UK). The building alone warrants a visit, and the food is also recommended. The large, attractive courtyard hosts live music on winter Saturday nights. A true gem. 🕏 🕸 ◑ 🖳 (383,384) 😷 🕏 ♪

Bakers Vaults

Market Place, SK1 1ES (jct Vernon St)
Robinsons Dizzy Blonde, Unicorn, Trooper, Old Tom; Titanic Plum Porter; 3 changing beers (sourced nationally) Ⓗ

Located opposite the town's historic market hall, this lively and vibrant pub has a spacious interior with a comfortable arrangement of seating to the front of and behind the centrally sited bar. High ceilings and arched windows accentuate the gin-palace style in which the pub was built. It is one of the few Robinsons brewery houses to serve guest beers from other brewers. Live music features on Sunday afternoons. A former local CAMRA Pub of the Year. 🕏 🕸 ◑ ⇄ 🖳 😷 🕏 ♪

Blossoms

2 Buxton Road, Heaviley, SK2 6NU (jct Bramhall Ln)
☎ (0161) 222 4150
Robinsons Dizzy Blonde, Unicorn Ⓗ**, Old Tom** Ⓖ

Landmark street-corner local whose three rooms radiate off a traditional drinking lobby, served by the central bar. Many old features remain, particularly in the rear Smoke Room. The full Robinsons range is often available and includes a seasonal beer. Popular quizzes are held on a Thursday night, and the upstairs function room hosts live music at the weekend. An outside drinking area has been created from a cobbled section of street and the former toilets are now a smoking area. Q 🕸 ◑ ♣ P 🖳 😷 🕏 ♪

Magnet

51 Wellington Road North, Heaton Norris, SK4 1HJ (jct Duke St)
☎ (0161) 429 6287 ⊕ themagnetfreehouse.co.uk
Salopian Oracle; 13 changing beers (sourced nationally; often RedWillow, Track) Ⓗ

Popular, family-run pub that has been a free house for more than a dozen years. It offers 14 cask ales, alongside 12 craft keg beers; the digital display menu boards show the available selection. Occasional specials are served from the in-house Mount Crescent microbrewery. On entry, the left side is a bustling vault leading to a lower pool room. The right side leads to a series of other rooms. Outside is a two-storey beer terrace. A pizza vendor operates on Friday evenings. ♿🕭🍴≒♣P🖵🌰☀

Olde Vic

1 Chatham Street, Edgeley, SK3 9ED (jct Shaw Heath)
🌐 yeoldevic.pub
6 changing beers (sourced nationally) Ⓗ
Now owned by its regulars, Ye Olde Vic has undergone a continuous programme of improvements over the past four years, which has been done without compromising its unique atmosphere. There is bric-a-brac at every turn, while the ceiling and wall displays of pumpclips are testimony to the array of guest beers sold over the years – as well as a reminder of numerous defunct beers and breweries. The ever-changing guest ales come from small breweries around the UK. The beer garden at the back is a summer suntrap. Q🌞≒♣🖵🌰☀♫

Petersgate Tap 🏆

19A St Petersgate, SK1 1EB (jct Etchells St)
☎ 07925 078426 🌐 petersgatetap.com
6 changing beers (sourced regionally)
This family-run bar on two floors is a dark beer specialist and is local CAMRA Pub of the Year 2023 and Cider Pub of the Year for the last five years. Downstairs, recycled oak-topped tables and a mix of seating is arrayed beneath interesting wall posters and breweriana. Upstairs there is a well-stocked bottle shop with an additional drinking area that hosts live music, various events, and regular tastings. Food from local takeaways can be eaten inside. Well worth a visit. 🕭🌞♿≒●🖵🌰☀♫

Swan with Two Necks ★

36 Princes Street, SK1 1RY (jct Hatton St)
☎ (0161) 480 2185
Robinsons Dizzy Blonde, Unicorn, Old Tom; 1 changing beer (often Robinsons) Ⓗ
This pub was rebuilt in the 1920s and the interior has remained pretty much unchanged since then. Of particular note are the classic, light-oak panelled drinking lobby, and the top-lit middle room with mock-Tudor fireplace. Further back is a small lounge-cum-diner. A pie & mash menu is available at lunchtimes. The rear outside area was stylishly reworked a few years ago and now is a lovely spot to have a pint in the warmer months. It is close to the Red Rock complex.
Q🕭🌞🕭≒♣🖵(325,330)🌰☀

Stretford

Longford Tap 🅛

Unit 107 Stretford Mall, M32 9BA
☎ (0161) 865 7007
Marble Manchester Bitter; 3 changing beers (sourced regionally; often Blackjack, Dunham Massey, Runaway) Ⓗ
A former retail unit on the outside of Stretford Mall. The entire front opens to outside space, where smoking is permitted, while the interior is decorated with historical photographs of Stretford. Four handpumps serve local real ales, with five keg lines serving more of the same. Guinness, lagers and cider (not real) are also available. Alternate weekends play live music, karaoke and quiz nights. Local charity and community groups are actively supported. Customers can order freshly made pizza, to be delivered directly to their tables. 🕭🌞♿🖵🌰☀

Swinton

Park Inn

135-137 Worsley Road, M27 5SP (on A572 on corner of Shaftesbury Rd, 200yds from A580)
☎ (0161) 793 1568
Joseph Holt Mild, Bitter Ⓗ
A good, traditional and friendly community local that has been a Joseph Holt's pub since 1878. There is a vault to the left as you enter and a large lounge to the right, with a snug tucked away behind the central bar. Karaoke, disco and guest singers are often a weekend feature in the main room, while the other two rooms are reasonably quiet. Disabled access is via the car park to the rear. Q🌞♿🖵(2,73)🌰☀

White Horse Hotel ✓

384 Worsley Road, M27 0FH (opp Lime Ave)
☎ (0161) 794 2404
Greene King IPA; 5 changing beers (sourced nationally; often Big Bog, Brightside) Ⓗ
Swinton's oldest pub, dating back to the mid 1700s. Once a Boddington's house, the old building has been refurbished inside, with several distinct areas around a single bar. Live music/DJs features on Friday nights and there are regular quiz nights. Popular food is served until well into the evening and there is a special menu for coeliacs. 🕭🌞🕭♿♣P🖵🌰☀

Wobbly Stool

233 Manchester Road, M27 4TT
☎ 07764 621471
3 changing beers (sourced locally; often Beartown, Brightside) Ⓗ
Opened in 2019, this popular little bar has three handpumps and an ever-changing array of ales which are usually sourced locally. There is also a fine selection of craft beers on KeyKeg, bottled Belgian beers and cider from Westons. Bar games are available. Quiz night is Wednesday and there is a fortnightly open mic session during the summer. A few tables are placed at the front. 🌞♣🖵🌰☀

Tottington

Dungeon Inn ✓

9 Turton Road, BL8 4AW
☎ 07706 737753
Thwaites IPA, Gold; 2 changing beers Ⓗ
A traditional, family-friendly Thwaites pub built in 1904 that has been identified by CAMRA as having a nationally important historic pub interior. The quiet front lounge has a real open fire on cold winter days and there is a separate pool room off the main sitting area; also a beer garden at a lower level to the rear. Four handpulls serve regular and seasonal or guest beers. Sports are shown on TV. Live music features on certain Saturdays. Dogs are welcome. Q🕭🌞♣🖵(480,469)🌰☀♫

Tyldesley

Union Arms

83 Castle Street, M29 8EW
☎ (01942) 870645 🌐 unionarmstyldesley.co.uk
Thwaites IPA, Gold; 1 changing beer (sourced regionally; often Wigan Brewhouse) Ⓗ
This family-friendly pub is part of the local community. It is divided into several separate connected rooms, and there is also a large outside patio area. On the left side is the vault and on the right a lounge used at mealtimes. The guest beer is from Wigan Brewhouse (California is the most regular). Fresh home-cooked food is served until evening, and Sunday lunches are available. Most

sporting events are shown on TV. Once a month they host a lunch for dementia sufferers and carers, featuring music and dance. ♉❀◑♣⊟🐾

Urmston

Barking Dog

9A Higher Road, M41 9AB

☎ (0161) 215 0858 🌐 the-barking-dog.co.uk

House beer (by Banks's); 3 changing beers (sourced nationally; often Dunham Massey, Tatton) Ⓗ

Converted from a post office, this popular local venue has an L-shaped main room, with the bar covering half the length on one side. Handpumps on the bar dispense local or regionally sourced beers, alongside locally produced keg, gins and a good non-alcoholic range. Through a small corridor, the origins of the building are evident, with a strong room and, further on, the quiet snug, which is available for meetings. A weekly quiz is held, and a 2-4-1 deal on meals on Tuesday. ♉❀◑♿⇌♣⊟🐾ᯤ

Flixton Conservative Club

Abbotsfield, 193 Flixton Road, M41 5DF

☎ (0161) 748 2846 🌐 flixtonconservativeclub.co.uk

5 changing beers (sourced regionally; often Bank Top, Dunham Massey, Pictish) Ⓗ

A multi CAMRA award-winning club with five handpumps offering an ever-changing range of ales from mainly local breweries. A well-maintained, comfortable venue, the facilities including a bowling green, snooker tables, darts room and Sky/BT TV showing major sports events. It is a meeting place for guitar and cycle clubs, and also hosts regular events, including pensioners' afternoons, live music, quiz nights, bingo, race nights and charity fundraisers. Visitors are welcomed but must apply for membership if using on a regular basis.
♉❀⇌(Chassen Road) ♣P⊟(255,256) ᯤ

Lord Nelson

49 Stretford Road, M41 9LG

☎ 07827 850255

Joseph Holt Mild, Bitter; 1 changing beer (sourced locally; often Joseph Holt) Ⓗ

This imposing building, unlike any other in the area, was a courthouse and hotel when it first opened in 1805. Once inside, there are two cosy rooms on each side, a three-sided peninsular bar, a middle room with bright lighting, and vault containing a dartboard. Traditional bench seating surrounds the stools and tables. Outside is a small beer garden. This is very much a drinker's pub; the only food is crisps and nuts. Quiz night is Tuesday and there is a disco on Saturday. ❀⇌♣P⊟🐾ᯤ♫

Prairie Schooner Taphouse 𝕃

33 Flixton Road, M41 5AW

🌐 prairie-schooner-taphouse.co.uk

4 changing beers (sourced locally; often Brewsmith, Brightside, Track) Ⓗ

This relatively large micropub opened in 2014 and has become a favourite with real ale drinkers, both local and from further afield. The four ever-changing, mainly locally sourced cask ales are supplemented by eight craft beers on tap and by an extensive range of bottled and canned beers from the UK, USA and the continent. Hogan's and bottled ciders are also available. Two quiz nights are held each week (music and general knowledge), with a monthly board games night, plus occasional live music or DJ. Q♉❀♿⇌♣●⊟(255)🐾ᯤ

Westhoughton

Beer School 𝕃

88 Market Street, BL5 3AZ

☎ (01942) 396280 🌐 thebeerschool.co.uk

4 changing beers (sourced locally) Ⓗ

This micropub, decked out like a school, has developed into a lively and popular part of the local community. Four handpumps serve beers of varied style and strength, often from local suppliers. Up to four bag-in-box real ciders are available, mainly from leading real cider producers. Drinks can be sampled before ordering. Note that the toilets are upstairs. Local CAMRA Pub of the Year and Cider Pub of the Year 2022.
❀⇌♣●⊟(7,521)🐾ᯤ♫

Brewery Tap 𝕃

55 Market Street, BL5 3AG

🌐 blackedgebrewerytap.co.uk

7 changing beers (sourced locally; often Blackedge) Ⓗ

Opened in 2019, this is the second outlet for the award-winning local Blackedge brewery. It has the friendly, community feel of a micropub. The timber and brick decor is complemented by the subdued and artistic lighting to give a homely atmosphere. Seven handpumps serve the core range of Blackedge beers, supplemented by their seasonal and one-off beers. There are also 10 modern keg fonts with beers from Blackedge and sometimes one from Rivington. Note that the toilets are upstairs. ♉⇌●⊟(7,521)🐾ᯤ♫

Whalley Range

Hillary Step 𝕃

199 Upper Chorlton Road, M16 0BH

☎ (0161) 881 1978 🌐 hillarystep.co.uk

5 changing beers (sourced regionally; often Pomona Island, RedWillow, Squawk) Ⓗ

Modern bar in a small strip of shops and bars a short walk north of Chorlton. Five handpumps serve beers mostly from local and regional breweries such as RedWillow, Squawk, Pomona Island and Thornbridge, usually including a dark ale in winter. The eight keg fonts regularly feature Northern Monk and local breweries. Customers can use table service or order at bar. The outside drinking area is now permanently covered, with sides for winter protection, and opens up in summer. Nuts and nibbles are available.
♉❀Ṗ(Firswood) ♣⊟(86) 🐾ᯤ

Wigan

Anvil 𝕃

Dorning Street, WN1 1ND

☎ (01942) 239444

6 changing beers (sourced nationally; often Phoenix, Wainwright, Wigan Brewhouse) Ⓗ

Popular town-centre pub, close to the bus station, with seven handpumps offering various guest beers, two boxed ciders, six draught continental ales and a range of bottled beers. Several TV screens show sports action and the small snug has the wall of fame displaying numerous award certificates. There is a garden at the rear. Over-18s only. ❀⇌(Wallgate)⊟(All)

Crooke Hall Inn 𝕃

92 Crooke Road, WN6 8LR

☎ (01942) 236088

4 changing beers (often Moorhouse's, Wigan Brewhouse) Ⓗ

Large, multi-roomed canalside pub in picturesque Crooke village, just outside Wigan. Popular with locals and

visitors alike, dogs and children are welcome until 9pm. Home-made food features locally sourced ingredients where possible. There is a separate cellar bar, ideal for functions, and a large beer garden. The pub is very much the hub of the village and is a five-times winner of the local CAMRA Community Pub of the Year.
ȧ❀ɕ▶P☐(635,635) ❀❖ɻ

Doc's Alehouse ⅃

85 Mesnes Street, WN1 1QJ
☎ 07907 736618 ⊕ docs-alehouse.co.uk
5 changing beers (often Fyne, Twisted Wheel, Wily Fox) ⊞
Doc's AleHouse, formerly Doc's Symposium, is Wigan's first micropub. A warm welcome awaits you from the owners, who have been here since 2020. You will find five cask ales, European beers, ciders and bottled beers behind the bar. It is on the edge of Wigan town centre, a short walk from the bus and train stations, with outdoor seating overlooking Mesnes Park.
Q❀ɕ&≈(Wallgate) P☐❀❖

John Bull Chophouse

2 Coopers Row, Market Place, WN1 1PQ
⊕ johnbullchophousewigan.co.uk
House beer (by Thwaites); 10 changing beers ⊞
A vibrant and lively pub in a building over 300 years old, which was previously cottages, stables and a slaughterhouse. This popular town-centre venue has been run by the same family for over 40 years. There are six handpumps serving Thwaites beers. This quirky pub is spread over two floors, with the toilets upstairs, and has seating outside. It is reputed to have the best pub jukebox in the north-west. ❀≈(Wallgate)☐❖ɻ

Raven ⅃ ✓

5 Wallgate, WN1 1LD
☎ (01942) 239764 ⊕ theravenwigan.com
4 changing beers (sourced regionally) ⊞
This early 1900s Commercial Hotel was virtually derelict before a tasteful renovation in 2012 that retained and restored many original features, including tiles, panelling and windows. The retro decor is typical of this small local pub chain. It serves a varying range of real ales and cider on handpumps. There are cosy real coal fires in winter and two unobtrusive TVs. Good home-made pub food is offered at reasonable prices. Loyalty cards are in operation, and Wednesday cask critics night offers discount on real ale. ȧ❀ɕ&≈(Wallgate)☐❀❖ɻ

Real Crafty ♀ ⅃

9 Upper Dicconson Street, WN1 2AD
☎ (01942) 200364 ⊕ realcraftywigan.co.uk
Ossett White Rat; 4 changing beers ⊞
A real ale and craft beer emporium in Wigan town centre, five minutes' walk from the bus station and 10 minutes from both train stations. Five real ales are dispensed via handpull, alongside craft beer, cider and perry served from 30 keg fonts. The Beer Atlas offers a collection of beers in bottles and cans from around the world. Draught beers can be canned with the on-site canning machine for takeaway. A popular weekly quiz is hosted on Tuesday. Winner of CAMRA Regional Pub of the Year in 2022. ȧ❀&≈(Wallgate)♣●P☐❀❖ɻ

Sherrington's ⅃

57 Kenyon Road, WN1 2DU
☎ 07500 171114 ⊕ sherringtonsbar.com
Wily Fox Crafty Fox; 5 changing beers (sourced regionally) ⊞
An industrial-themed bar with six real ales on handpump, always including three from the Wily Fox stable, and three varying guests. There are also 10 craft/

lager/continental beer taps offering Peroni, Moretti and a Wily Fox brew, along with seven varying guests. A selection of UK and continental bottled beers is also stocked, and there is an upper-floor gin bar. Tea, coffee and hot chocolate are available. A former local CAMRA Pub of the Year. ȧ❀&●☐❀❖❖ɻ

Swan & Railway ⅃ ✓

80 Wallgate, WN1 1BA
☎ (01942) 375817 ⊕ swanandrailwayhotelwigan.co.uk
Bank Top Dark Mild; Draught Bass; 5 changing beers (sourced nationally) ⊞
Winner of a Historic England Conservation Award in 2021, the pub was built in 1898 by WEV Crompton. This beautiful classic period inn features an impressive stained-glass window, and a collection of historical photos of the old town, the railway and Rugby League. It has seven handpumps celebrating Draught Bass and also featuring local breweries such as Hophurst, Prospect, Wily Fox and Wigan Brewhouse. Directly opposite Wigan North Western railway station.
❀⇒ɕ▶≈(North Western) ♣☐❀❖ɻ

Tap 'n' Barrel ✓

16 Jaxon's Court, WN1 1LR
☎ (01942) 386966 ⊕ tapnbarrelwigan.co.uk
Hawkshead Windermere Pale; 2 changing beers (sourced regionally) ⊞
This former local CAMRA Cider Pub of the Year is located in Wigan's Victorian Quarter, conveniently adjacent to the bus station. The staff are friendly, welcoming and happy to provide advice on the selection of drinks available. The bar is split over three areas, the main bar, an upstairs seating area and a pleasant, heated undercover back room where live music plays on Sunday afternoons. There are six handpulls on the bar, usually serving three cask ales and three boxed ciders, alongside one or two draft craft beers. Q ȧ≈(Wallgate)☐❀❖ɻ

Wigan Central ⅃

Arch No. 1 & 2, Queen Street, WN3 4DY
☎ (01942) 246425 ⊕ wigancentral.bar
House beer (by Bank Top); 6 changing beers (sourced nationally) ⊞
This award-winning two-roomed pub has a railway-themed interior with a live feed displaying arrival and departure times from both Wigan railway stations. It sources real ales from all over, alongside a wide range of continental bottled beers. Live music plays on Sunday. Bar snacks are available. It is a four-times winner of the local CAMRA Pub of the Year and Cider Pub of the Year, and is also a former Greater Manchester Pub of the Year and runner-up National Pub of the Year.
Q&≈(North Western) ●☐❀❖ɻ

Withington

Victoria ✓

438 Wilmslow Road, M20 3BW (jct Davenport Ave)
☎ (0161) 434 2600
Hydes 1863, Dark Ruby, Hopster, Original, Lowry; 2 changing beers (sourced nationally) ⊞
This friendly Hydes community pub attracts a convivial cross-section of Withington life. It is usually busy all day, but especially in the evenings. Its late 19th-century exterior features etched windows that hide a large interior refurbished and opened out some years ago to create distinct drinking areas, each with its own atmosphere. A beer patio at the rear provides a useful escape from the bustle. Attractions include a poker school, twice-weekly quizzes, TV sport, and weekend live entertainment. ȧ❀♣☐❀❖ɻ

Breweries

Bank Top SIBA

The Pavilion, Ashworth Lane, Bolton, BL1 8RA
☎ (01204) 595800 ⊕ banktopbrewery.com

☺Bank Top was established in 1995. Since 2002, the brewery has occupied a Grade II-listed tennis pavilion housing an 11-barrel plant. Bank Top Brewery Estates was formed in 2010 and now owns three pubs, Bank Top Brewery Tap, Bank Top Ale House and Olde England Forever. ‼♦

Draymans Draught (ABV 3.6%) PALE
Bad to the Bone (ABV 4%) BITTER
Smooth, sweet malty drink with a light caramel background and hops with gentle bitterness that last.
Dark Mild (ABV 4%) MILD
Coffee roast aroma. Smooth mouthfeel, with roasted malt prominent throughout and some fruit. Moderate bitterness in aftertaste.
Flat Cap (ABV 4%) BITTER
Amber-coloured beer with a malty aroma. Balanced and lasting flavour of malt, fruit and bitter hops.
Pavilion Pale Ale (ABV 4.5%) PALE
A yellow beer with a citrus and hop aroma. Big fruity flavour with a peppery hoppiness; dry, bitter, yet fruity finish.
Nineteen Ninety Five (ABV 4.8%) PALE
Palomino Rising (ABV 5%) PALE
Port O' Call (ABV 5%) SPECIALITY
Dark brown beer with a malty, fruity aroma. Malt, roast and dark fruits in the bittersweet taste and finish.

Beer Nouveau

75 North Western Street, Ardwick, Manchester, M12 6DY ⊕ beernouveau.co.uk

☺Beer Nouveau has been producing heritage and experimental beers since 2015. Barrel-ageing and beers from the wood are a strong focus, and always feature at its weekend taproom. A passion for sustainability sees one-off brew runs using hops or fruit grown in Manchester, and the brewery tap caters from a 'waste food' social enterprise. The tap encompasses a beer garden in its urban orchard and frequently hosts special events. ‼⍟♦LIVE ✦

Peterloo Porter (ABV 4%) PORTER
Sunny Lowry (ABV 4.1%) BITTER

Big Trip (NEW)

Unit 5, City Court, Poland Street, Manchester, M4 6AL
☎ 07931 557943 ✉ jonny@bigtripbrewery.com

Brewing commenced in Ancoats in 2022, producing a variety of cask and keg beers, mainly hop-forward, hazy, unfiltered and unpasteurised. The keg range features low carbonation (1.2 volumes). New, limited run specials most months. Currently brewing three times per week.

Microdose (ABV 3.5%) PALE
Beautiful Things (ABV 4.2%) PALE
Desperately Seeking Dopamine (ABV 5.7%) IPA

Blackedge SIBA

Moreton Mill, Hampson Street, Horwich, BL6 7JH
☎ (01204) 692976 ☎ 07795 654895
⊕ blackedgebrewery.co.uk

☺Blackedge Brewery brews at a 10-barrel plant visible through a viewing window on the ground floor beneath the Brewery Bar – one of its two outlets. Its CAMRA and

SIBA award-winning beers are available throughout NW England and beyond. A strong core range is supplemented by seasonal brews in both cask and unfiltered keg formats. Most are also now freshly-canned and bottled onsite. ‼⍟♦LIVE ✦

Session (ABV 3.5%) GOLD
Refreshing citrus hops, with a full-bodied citrus hop aroma. Clean, dry finish with lingering bitter hops.
Zinc (ABV 3.5%) GOLD
Hop (ABV 3.8%) PALE
Assertively hoppy bitter beer. Citrus flavours with a lasting dry finish.
Brewers Gold (ABV 3.9%) BLOND
Dark Mild (ABV 3.9%) MILD
Pleasant chocolate and malt aroma leads to a full-bodied beer with dark fruits, sustained malt presence and roasty finish.
Black (ABV 4%) STOUT
Well-rounded and creamy dark beer with roast malt and balanced sweetness. Dry, bitter roast finish.
Cascade (ABV 4%) BLOND
Pike (ABV 4%) PALE
Smooth, copper-coloured beer with bitter hops and balanced sweetness, leading to a dry bitter finish.
West Coast (ABV 4.1%) GOLD
Citrus hop aroma and flavour. Sweet fruitiness balances lasting bitter hops.
Platinum (ABV 4.4%) BLOND
Blonde (ABV 4.5%) BLOND
Dark Rum (ABV 4.6%) SPECIALITY
Rich roast aroma and strong dry roast flavour. Accompanying taste of dried fruit and drawn-out, sweet finish.
IPA (ABV 4.7%) GOLD
Intense bitter hops with a long, drying finish.
Black Port (ABV 4.9%) SPECIALITY
Black beer with malty, fruity aroma. Rich, with chocolate and dark fruits to taste with a slightly drier finish.
Kiwi (ABV 5%) GOLD
Citrus hops and fruit in the aromas develop in the taste. Sweetness supports the flavours as the bitterness builds in the finish.

Blackjack SIBA

34-36 Irk Street, Manchester, M4 4JT
☎ (0161) 819 2767

Office: The Smithfield Market Tavern, 37 Swan Street, Manchester, M4 5JZ ⊕ blackjack-beers.com

☺Blackjack began in a railway arch in Manchester's Green Quarter in 2012. A new modern brew plant was installed in 2021, enabling the brewery to develop a new and improved range of traditional and modern vegan beers. Beers are widely available across the North of England and nationally as well as in its own Smithfield Tavern, three Jack In The Box food market bars and the brewery taproom (open weekends March-August – check social media). ‼♦✦

Irk Street Pale Ale (ABV 3.8%) GOLD
A burst of fruity, citrus, hoppy aromas draws one into a sweet fruity, hoppy beer. Bitterness grows on drinking lessening the impact of the fruity sweetness.
Jack In The Box Blonde (ABV 4%) BLOND
Pub Ale: Best Bitter (ABV 4.2%) BITTER
A complex mix of malty sweetness characterises this beer, which finishes with a lasting hop bitterness.
Salvation! Session IPA (ABV 4.5%) GOLD
Citrus hops to the fore starting with the aromas. The bitterness develops on drinking and there is some fruity sweetness to balance.
Early-Days Northern Porter (ABV 4.6%) PORTER

Bridge

Unit 6, Northend Road Industrial Estate, Northend Road, Stalybridge, SK15 3AZ ☎ 07948 617145
⊕ bridgebeers.co.uk/brewery

Bridge Beers commenced production in 2021 using a 2.5-barrel plant. Cask-conditioned and bottled ales are supplied to the brewery tap, located in the nearby town centre, as well as to other local outlets. 🍺

Citra (ABV 4%) PALE
El Dorado (ABV 4%) PALE
Galaxy (ABV 4%) PALE
4Bs (ABV 4.2%) BITTER
Mumbai (ABV 4.2%) GOLD
Dark Ruby Mild (ABV 4.5%) MILD
Dark Matter (ABV 4.7%) MILD

Brightside SIBA

Unit 10, Dale Industrial Estate, Radcliffe, M26 1AD
☎ (0161) 725 9644 ⊕ brightsidebrewing.co.uk

⊠ Brightside is a 20-barrel, family-run brewery producing real ales, craft beers and lager. A broad range of styles is produced, from traditional ales to more heavily-hopped beers with unusual yeasts. It has a brewery shop onsite for collections, and a web shop for local and national deliveries. Brightside prides itself on working as sustainably as possible, by limiting energy expenditure, recycling and reusing waste. As of 2022, all Brightside beers are gluten free. Vegan options are also widely available. 🍺♦GF V

Odin Blonde (ABV 3.8%) PALE
Fruity hop aromas. Moderate bitterness follows and persists into the finish. Some malt sweetness is evident.
B-Side Gold (ABV 4.2%) GOLD
Academy Ale IPA (ABV 4.5%) PALE
The Mancunian (ABV 4.5%) PALE
Full-bodied, sweet fruity beer with moderate bitter hops.
Maverick IPA (ABV 4.8%) PALE

Brewed for Brunning & Price Pub Co:
Traditional (North) (ABV 3.8%) BITTER

Bundobust SIBA

61-95 Oxford Street, Manchester, M1 6EJ
⊕ bundobust.com

Bundobust Brewery was established in 2020 but brews were not commercially available until 2021. Beer is exclusively for the Bundobust restaurant chain. No real ale.

Burton Road

Office: 65 Kingsfield Drive, Manchester, M12 6JL
✉ contact@burtonroadbrewing.co.uk

Manchester brewery producing cask, keg, cans and bottles focusing on pales and IPA. While most beer is contract brewed at Mobberley Brewhouse (qv), a small brew plant (30-litres) is also located within Withington Public Hall.

Mosaic Pale (ABV 4.2%) PALE
Pale Ale (ABV 4.8%) PALE

Chadkirk

Lancashire House, Green Lane, Romiley, SK6 3LJ
☎ 07966 125257 ⊕ chadkirkbrew.co.uk

Brewing commenced in 2020 at an industrial unit in Romiley. The brewery focuses on a core range of hop-forward beers using a rotating selection of American hops.

Easy (ABV 3.6%) PALE
US Triple Hop (ABV 4%) PALE
Zappa (ABV 4%) PALE
Motueka (ABV 4.2%) PALE
CCC (ABV 4.3%) PALE
Haze (ABV 4.3%) PALE
Citra (ABV 4.7%) PALE
Stout (ABV 5%) STOUT
APA (ABV 5.2%) PALE

Cloudwater SIBA

Units 7-8, Piccadilly Trading Estate, Manchester, M1 2NP
☎ (0161) 661 5943 ⊕ cloudwaterbrew.co

Cloudwater specialises in producing modern takes on classic styles, with a leaning towards hazy, hop-forward beers. It also releases a series of wild, spontaneous and aged beers from its barrel project, with a strong focus on seasonality of both styles and ingredients. The brewery tap is adjacent. 🍴♦

Deeply Vale

Unit 25, Peel Industrial Estate, Chamberhall Street, Bury, BL9 0LU ☎ 07749 856043
⊕ deeplyvalebrewery.com

☺Deeply Vale is a family-run business established in 2012. The brewery's name immortalises the Deeply Vale area near Bury, famed for legendary 1970s music festivals. The range of traditional beers with a modern twist produced from the six-barrel plant are distributed largely across North West England and West Yorkshire. ♦

DV US (ABV 3.8%) GOLD
Equilibrium (ABV 3.8%) GOLD
Crisp and refreshing bitter with a pale malt flavour and clean bitter hops. Dry finish with lingering hops.
Hop (ABV 3.8%) BITTER
Maverick (ABV 3.8%) PALE
White Wolf (ABV 3.8%) PALE
Citra Storm (ABV 4%) PALE
Optimum (ABV 4.2%) BITTER
DV8 (ABV 4.8%) STOUT
Supple fruity sweetness accompanying luscious coffee roast. Clean, gentle malt finish, with lingering sweetness. Coffee and raisin aroma.
Freebird (ABV 5.2%) PALE

Dunham Massey

100 Oldfield Lane, Dunham Massey, WA14 4PE
☎ (0161) 929 0663 ⊕ dunhammasseybrewing.co.uk

☺Opened in 2007, Dunham Massey brews traditional North-Western ales using only English ingredients. Around 30 outlets are supplied direct, along with the brewery tap, Costello's Bar, Altrincham. A sister brewery, Lymm (qv), opened in 2013 with Costello's Bar in Stockton Heath tied to both breweries. 🍺♦LIVE

Castle Hill (ABV 3.5%) PALE
Walker's Bitter (ABV 3.5%) BITTER
Little Bollington Bitter (ABV 3.7%) BITTER
Straw-coloured light ale with malt and citrus fruit taste and a dry, bitter finish.
Chocolate Cherry Mild (ABV 3.8%) SPECIALITY
Dunham Dark (ABV 3.8%) MILD
Dark brown beer with malty aroma. Fairly sweet, with malt, some roast, hop and fruit in the taste and finish.
Big Tree Bitter (ABV 3.9%) BITTER
Obelisk (ABV 3.9%) BLOND

Alty Ale (ABV 4%) BLOND
Dunham Milk Stout (ABV 4%) STOUT
Landlady (ABV 4%) PALE
Dunham Stout (ABV 4.2%) STOUT
Dunham XPA (ABV 4.2%) PALE
Stamford Bitter (ABV 4.2%) BITTER
Deer Beer (ABV 4.5%) BITTER
Cheshire IPA (ABV 4.7%) PALE
Dunham Porter (ABV 5.2%) PORTER
East India Pale Ale (ABV 6%) IPA
Dunham Gold (ABV 7.2%) STRONG

Escape

Unit P, Dodd Lane Industrial Estate, Chorley Road, Westhoughton, BL5 3NA
☎ (01204) 228969 ⊕ escapebrewery.co.uk

Small brewery launched in Bolton in 2019 by three friends. Brews a range of regular and occasional beers on a 2.5-barrel kit previously owned by Porter Brewing Co. Has a microbar in Adlington, The Old Post Office, selling Escape and guest beers.

If the Caravan's A Rockin' (ABV 3.8%) BLOND
Breakout Session (ABV 3.9%) PALE
Avoid Detection (ABV 4.2%) PALE
The Shackles Are Off (ABV 4.2%) GOLD
Tom, Dick and Harry (ABV 4.5%) PALE
Clocked Off (ABV 4.9%) PALE
Virgil Hilts (ABV 5%) BITTER

First Chop

B2 Barton Hall Business Park, Hardy Street, Eccles, M30 7NB ☎ 07970 241398 ⊕ firstchop.co.uk

Brewing began at Outstanding Brewery (qv) in Bury in 2012 before transferring to Salford in 2013. The brewery relocated again to Eccles in 2017 with increased capacity. It specialises in producing gluten-free beers. **GF**

AVA (ABV 3.5%) BLOND
POD (ABV 4.2%) SPECIALITY
IPA (ABV 5%) PALE
SYL (ABV 6.2%) IPA

Four Kings

Unit 15g, Newton Moor Industrial Estate, Lodge Street, Hyde, SK14 4LD ☎ 07951 699428
⊕ fourkingsbrewery.com

⊛ Four Kings, a six-barrel brewery opened in Hyde by friends with a mutual love of beer and has been brewing since 2016. Its onsite bar opens ad-hoc and is available for private functions. Beers can typically be found in pubs across Tameside, High Peak and at beer festivals in Greater Manchester and Yorkshire. Production remains occasional in the wake of the pandemic. P-Noot also brew here as a cuckoo. !! ☙ ♦ LIVE ✿

4Tune (ABV 4%) BITTER
4Ever (ABV 4.5%) PALE
4Most (ABV 5.5%) PORTER

Gasworks

☗ **5 Jack Rosenthal Street, Manchester, M3 4LY**
☎ (0161) 236 3689 ⊕ gasworksbrewbar.co.uk

Gasworks is a six-barrel brewpub from the team behind Dockyard, opened in 2016. It supplies Salford Quays and Dockyard, Spinningfields.

Green Arches (NEW)

☗ **Unit 11, Red Bank, Manchester, M4 4HF**

Situated in the Green Quarter, Green Arches is a bar and brewery founded in 2023 by Sam and Lee, who both formerly brewed at Beatnik Republic. A range of beer styles is brewed and available in keg.

Green Mill

☗ **Harewood Arms, 2 Market Street, Broadbottom, SK14 6AX** ☎ 07967 656887 ⊕ greenmillbrewery.com

⊛ Green Mill started brewing in 2007 on a 2.5-barrel plant and moved in 2010 to the Cask & Feather, Rochdale. The brewery relocated again in 2013 to the Harewood Arms, Broadbottom. A number of occasional beers are brewed. Around 40 outlets are supplied. ♦

Gold (ABV 3.6%) GOLD
Northern Lights (ABV 4.5%) BITTER
Big Chief (ABV 5.5%) BITTER

Heineken Royal Trafford

Royal Brewery, 201 Denmark Road, Manchester, M15 6LD

No real ale.

Hideaway

57 Farm Lane, Worsley, M28 2PG ☎ 07887 732725
⊕ hideawaybrewing.co.uk

Nanobrewery which started brewing in 2020. Each production run is currently limited to 25 litres.

Joseph Holt SIBA IFBB

The Brewery, Empire Street, Cheetham, Manchester, M3 1JD
☎ (0161) 834 3285 ⊕ joseph-holt.com

⊛ Founded in 1849, Joseph Holt is one of the UK's, leading, independent, family breweries. Now in its sixth generation, the business operates 123 pubs across Manchester and the North West and supplies ales to many pubs and clubs nationally. ☙

Mild (ABV 3.2%) MILD
A dark brown/red beer with a fruity, malty nose. Roast, malt, fruit and hops in the taste, with strong bitterness for a mild, and a dry malt and hops finish.
IPA (ABV 3.8%) BITTER
Golden bitter with biscuity malt, hops and restrained lemony notes. Dry, bitter finish.
Bitter (ABV 4%) BITTER
Pale brown beer with malt and hops in the aroma. Bitter taste with balanced malty flavour. Increased bitter finish.
Chorlton Pale Ale (ABV 4%) PALE
Two Hoots (ABV 4.2%) BITTER
Easy-drinking beer, smooth texture, well-balanced malty sweetness and gentle hops lead to a lasting bitter finish.

Brewed under the Bootleg brand name:
Chorlton Pale Ale (ABV 4%) PALE

Hophurst SIBA

Unit 8, Hindley Business Centre, Platt Lane, Hindley, WN2 3PA
☎ (01942) 522333 ☎ 07938 949944
⊕ hophurstbrewery.co.uk

⊛ Hophurst Brewery was started in 2014 by Stuart Hurst. Stuart's passion for producing craft ales, combined with 20 years of supporting businesses and re-skilling unemployed people, created a unique social enterprise brewery. It employs people over the age of 50 and guides them through its training programme. Twisted

Vine Ale House is its award-winning microbar in Ashton-in Makerfield town centre. ♪♦

Flaxen (ABV 3.7%) PALE
Campfire (ABV 3.9%) MILD
Light-bodied beer with bitter roasted malt.
Twisted Vine (ABV 4.1%) PALE
Cosmati (ABV 4.2%) BLOND
Debonair (ABV 4.9%) STOUT
Porteresque (ABV 5.5%) STOUT
Complex dark beer, with roast and fruit in aroma. Strong roast flavour with a developing sweet fruitiness. Lasting roast finish.

Howfen

Westhoughton, BL5 2BN ⊕ howfenbrew.co

Howfen began brewing in 2018 and is situated in the owner's garage. It is named after the dialect word for Westhoughton.

Hydes SIBA IFBB

The Beer Studio, 30 Kansas Avenue, Salford, M50 2GL
☎ (0161) 226 1317 ⊕ hydesbrewery.com

⊛Hydes Brewery has now been in the Manchester area for over 160 years. In 2012 it left the historic Queen's Brewery in Hulme and began brewing on a smaller, brand new site in Salford's MediaCity. The five core beers are supplemented by 18 seasonals (Ralf + Alf brand). The Beer Studio brand has been dropped. The new kegging line now produces Hydes' own lager, 'Dock 4', a nod to the old Ship Canal docks, alongside the Copper Kettle brands. ♦

1863 (ABV 3.5%) BITTER
Lightly-hopped, pale brown session beer with some hops, malt and fruit in the taste and a short, dry finish.
Dark Ruby (ABV 3.5%) MILD
Dark brown/red in colour, with a fruit and malt nose. Taste includes biscuity malt and green fruits, with a satisfying aftertaste.
Hopster (ABV 3.8%) BLOND
Original (ABV 3.8%) BITTER
Pale brown beer with a malty nose, malt and an earthy hoppiness in the taste, and a good bitterness through to the finish.
Lowry (ABV 4.7%) GOLD
Malt, hops and fruit compete for dominance in this strong beer. Fruit and bitter prominent in finish.

Irwell Works

Irwell Street, Ramsbottom, BL0 9YQ
☎ (01706) 825019 ⊕ irwellworksbrewery.co.uk

⊛Irwell Works has been brewing since 2010 in a building that once housed the Irwell Works steam, tin, copper and iron works. The brewery has a six-barrel plant, and brews nine regular beers, plus a range of seasonal beers. Its taproom is situated on the first floor. ♪♦⌀

Lightweights & Gentlemen (ABV 3.2%) GOLD
Light, refreshing, very pale ale with some fruitiness and a hoppy, bitter finish.
Breadcrumbs (ABV 3.6%) PALE
Tin Plate (ABV 3.6%) MILD
Copper Plate (ABV 3.8%) BITTER
Traditional northern bitter. Copper-coloured with satisfying blend of malt and hops and good bitterness.
Costa Del Salford (ABV 4.1%) GOLD
Steam Plate (ABV 4.3%) BITTER
Malty bitter beer with increasing bitter finish.
Iron Plate (ABV 4.4%) STOUT

Roast malt in the aroma is joined by hop and a toasty bitterness in the taste and finish.
Marshmallow Unicorn (ABV 4.4%) STOUT
Sweet stout with a balanced bitter roast and dry bitter finish.
Mad Dogs & Englishmen (ABV 5.5%) IPA
Full-bodied, bittersweet beer. Pronounced peppery and earthy hops. Hops develop to pine and citrus in aftertaste with prolonged bitterness.

JW Lees IFBB

Greengate Brewery, Middleton Junction, Manchester, M24 2AX
☎ (0161) 643 2487 ⊕ jwlees.co.uk

⊛Family-owned since its foundation by John Lees in 1828, the brewery has a tied estate of around 150 pubs, mostly in North Manchester, Cheshire, Lancashire and North Wales. The vast majority serve cask beer. The current head brewer is a family member. An in-house microbrewery, Boilerhouse, also produces a wide range of cask beers. ♪♦

Dark (ABV 3.5%) MILD
Formerly GB Mild, this is a dark brown beer with a malt and caramel aroma. Creamy mouthfeel, with malt, caramel and fruit flavours and a malty finish.
Manchester Pale Ale (ABV 3.7%) PALE
Golden beer, moderately-hopped and with gentle bitterness.
Bitter (ABV 4%) BITTER
Smooth copper-coloured beer with caramel malt in aroma and flavour. Dry bittersweet aftertaste.
Dragon's Fire (ABV 4%) BITTER
Stout (ABV 4.2%) STOUT
Founder's (ABV 4.5%) BITTER
Moonraker (ABV 6.5%) STRONG
A reddish-brown beer with a strong, malty, fruity aroma. The flavour is rich and sweet, with roast malt, and the finish is fruity yet dry. Available only in a handful of outlets.

Brewed under the Boilerhouse brand name:
Craft Pale (ABV 4.2%) PALE

Libatory

Altrincham ☎ 07957 227540

Office: Unit 3, Peel House, 30 The Downs, Altrincham, WA14 2PX ⊕ libatory.co.uk

A home-based nanobrewery, established in 2022. A 150-litre plant is used. Mostly available in cans but can do cask or keg by request. LIVE

Made of Stone

▤ 8 Woodford Road, Bramhall, SK7 2JJ

Nanobrewery situated at the back of the Mounting Stone micropub in Bramhall. Brewing began in 2018 on a one-barrel plant at the rear of the pub. The brewery specialises in twice monthly, one-off brews and collaborations with local brewers. Beers are usually supplied to the pub and the Chiverton Tap, Cheadle Hulme.

Manchester Union

96d North Western Street, Manchester, M12 6JL
⊕ manchesterunionbrewery.com

Manchester Union is a Central European-style, lager brewery co-founded by former Six O'clock brewer Ian Johnson. It uses a decoction technique in the mash and German lager malts. The beers under go several weeks conditioning in tanks. Beers are unfiltered and unpasteurised and available across Greater Manchester. ◆

Marble SIBA

Unit 7, Boston Court, Salford, M50 2GN
⊕ marblebeers.com

Originally founded at the Marble Arch pub in 1997, Marble Beers moved to a 15-barrel plant in Salford and opened an onsite taproom. Vegetarian beers are available in both its core and speciality ranges. It supplies its own Marble Arch and more than 70 other outlets. !!◆◆

Hindmarsh (ABV 3.7%) PALE
Pint (ABV 3.9%) GOLD
Fresh hop aroma of grapefruit. Clean citrus hop flavour with pale malt base.óDry bitter aftertaste and lasting hop.
Manchester Bitter (ABV 4.2%) BITTER
Biscuity aroma with floral hops. Balanced bitter hop and malt in taste. Full fruity palate. Dry bitter finish.
North South (ABV 4.2%) PALE
Prominent citrus aroma. Bitter citrus hop flavour balanced with moderate sweetness. Bitterness dominates after the initial taste, with drying mouthfeel.
Lagonda (ABV 5%) GOLD
Golden yellow beer with a spicy, fruity nose. Powerful citrus and bitter hops backed up by a pale malt base, with a dry fruitiness continuing into the bitter aftertaste.
Alf (ABV 5.4%) PALE
Extra Special Marble (ABV 5.5%) BITTER
Stout (ABV 5.7%) STOUT
Rich aroma of coffee and chocolate. Complex, bittersweet, roasted flavour with fruit and caramel. Smooth mouthfeel, with a drying finish.
Earl Grey IPA (ABV 6.8%) SPECIALITY
Sweet citrus aroma. Full-bodied, creamy mouthfeel. Bold Bergamot flavour balanced with sweetness and pronounced bitterness. Lasting hoppy taste.

Millstone SIBA

Unit 4, Vale Mill, Micklehurst Road, Mossley, OL5 9JL
☎ (01457) 835835 ⊕ millstonebrewery.co.uk

Established in 2003 by Nick Boughton and Jon Hunt, the brewery is located in an 18th century textile mill and uses an eight-barrel plant. More than 30 regular outlets are supplied. ☲◆

Citra (ABV 4%) BLOND
Tiger Rut (ABV 4%) PALE
Light fruity beer with hop aroma and gentle bitterness.
Trinnacle (ABV 4.2%) GOLD
Stout (ABV 4.5%) STOUT
True Grit (ABV 5%) GOLD

Northern Monkey

68 Chorley Street, Bolton, BL1 4AL ☎ 07825 814631
⊕ northernmonkeybrew.co.uk

Established in 2016 and relocated in 2021, Northern Monkey Brew Co is a six-barrel brewery with an onsite taproom. The original brewpub remains a town centre outlet. It brews a variety of ales, maintaining a traditional edge but with a modern twist. ◆◆

The Last Drop (ABV 3.6%) PALE
Winter Hill (ABV 3.8%) GOLD
Reenys Beans (ABV 4%) SPECIALITY
Sheephouse (ABV 4.2%) PALE
Dirty Harry (ABV 4.5%) BITTER
Funky Monkey (ABV 5.5%) IPA

Underdog (ABV 6%) MILD
Malt, hops, fruit and caramel aromas entice the palate. A smooth sweet beer with roast and fruit along with some gentle hop in the lingering finish.

P-Noot

Unit 15G, Newton Moor Industrial Estate, Lodge Street, Hyde, SK14 4LD ☎ 07931 986794

Office: 373 Stockport Road, Denton, M34 6EP
⊕ p-nootbrewco.com

☺Commenced brewing 2021 in the cellar of the Lowes Arms, moving brewing to Four Kings Brewery which has a six-barrel plant, also in Hyde, late 2022, as a cuckoo. The cask beers are primarily for the Lowes Arms in Denton, and are based on traditional recipes with a modern twist. The main output however, is a wide range of innovative craft keg ales, brewed for wider distribution. ◆

APEX EGA (ABV 3.8%) GOLD
Into the Light (ABV 4%) PALE
Stark BA (ABV 4.1%) PALE
Force 8 SB (ABV 4.3%) BITTER

Phoenix SIBA

Green Lane, Heywood, OL10 2EP
☎ (01706) 367 359
✉ cheers@phoenixbrewery.co.uk

☺Established in Ellesmere Port in 1982, Oak Brewery moved to the old Phoenix Brewery in Heywood and adopted the name in 1991. It now supplies more than 400 outlets plus wholesalers. Restoration of the old brewery, built in 1897, is ongoing. ◆

Hopsack (ABV 3.8%) BLOND
Navvy (ABV 3.8%) BITTER
Amber beer with a citrus fruit and malt nose. Good balance of citrus fruit, malt and hops with bitterness coming through in the aftertaste.
Monkeytown Mild (ABV 3.9%) MILD
Light roast aroma. Mild creamy roast flavour with sweet malt and some astringency. Lasting dry bitter finish.
Arizona (ABV 4.1%) GOLD
Yellow in colour with a fruity and hoppy aroma. A refreshing beer with citrus, hops and good bitterness, and a shortish dry aftertaste.
Spotland Gold (ABV 4.1%) GOLD
Pale Moonlight (ABV 4.2%) PALE
Black Bee (ABV 4.5%) SPECIALITY
White Monk (ABV 4.5%) GOLD
Yellow beer with a citrus fruit aroma, plenty of fruit, hops and bitterness in the taste, and a hoppy, bitter finish.
Thirsty Moon (ABV 4.6%) BITTER
Tawny beer with a fresh citrus aroma. Hoppy, fruity and malty with a dry, hoppy finish.
West Coast IPA (ABV 4.6%) PALE
Golden in colour with a hoppy, fruity nose. Strong hoppy and fruity taste and aftertaste with good bitterness throughout.
Double Gold (ABV 5%) PALE
Wobbly Bob (ABV 6%) BITTER
A red/brown beer with malty, fruity aroma and creamy mouthfeel. Strongly malty and fruity in flavour, with hops and a hint of herbs. Both sweetness and bitterness are evident throughout.

Brewed for Brunning & Price Pub Co:
Original (ABV 3.8%) BITTER
Smooth-textured beer with sweet maltiness balanced by hop bitterness rising in the finish.

Pictish

Unit 9, Canalside Industrial Estate, Woodbine Street East, Rochdale, OL16 5LB
☎ (01706) 522227 ⊕ pictish-brewing.co.uk

⊛The brewery was established in 2000 and supplies free trade outlets in the North-West and West Yorkshire. Famed for the consistency and clarity of its brews and its ever-changing single hop series of beers. ♦

Brewers Gold (ABV 3.8%) BITTER
Session pale ale with moderate levels of sweetness, malty character and hops.
Talisman IPA (ABV 4.2%) PALE
Strong hoppy aroma; hops and fruit in the taste. Some initial sweetness, but with hoppy bitterness throughout.
Alchemists Ale (ABV 4.3%) BITTER
A bitter beer with resiny hops. Malt aromas to start some sweetness ending with hoppy bitterness.

Pomona Island

Unit 33, Waybridge Enterprise Centre, Daniel Adamson Road, Salford, M50 1DS
☎ (0161) 637 2140 ☎ 07972 445474
⊕ pomonaislandbrew.co.uk

Brewery set up in 2017, close to Salford's Media City. Part owned by the people behind the Gas Lamp in Manchester city centre. Head brewer James Dyer is formerly of Tempest Brew Co (qv). ⬛◆

Pale (ABV 3.8%) PALE
Pungent fruity hop aroma. Sweet fruity taste with some bitterness. Gentle and balanced. Lasting delicate bitter finish.
Stout (ABV 4.5%) STOUT
APA (ABV 5.3%) PALE
Hoppy beer with fruit and moderate bitterness, leading to a rising bitter finish. Brewed with variable hops.

Red Rose SIBA

The Old Brewery, Back Square Street, Ramsbottom, BL0 9FZ
☎ (01706) 827582

Office: 2 Hameldon View, Great Harwood, BB6 7BL
⊕ redrosebrewery.co.uk

Brewing began in 2020.

Treacle Miner's Tipple (ABV 3.6%) MILD
Too Wet To Wo (ABV 3.8%) BITTER
Harlequin (ABV 4%) PALE
Rat Trap (ABV 4.3%) BLOND
Paddy O'Hacker's (ABV 4.6%) STOUT
Likeley More Bar Tat (ABV 6.1%) IPA

Rising Sun

⬛ **Rising Sun, 235 Stockport Road, Mossley, OL5 0RQ**
☎ (01457) 238236 ⊕ risingsunmossley.co.uk

⊛Brewing since 2016 using a two-barrel plant at the side of the Rising Sun. The beers are produced occasionally and are only available for sale in the pub. Beers of differing styles and strengths are available throughout the year.

Robinsons SIBA IFBB

Unicorn Brewery, Lower Hillgate, Stockport, SK1 1JJ
☎ (0161) 612 4061 ⊕ robinsonsbrewery.com

⊛The sixth generation of the Robinson family now run the brewery, founded in 1838. Following a significant reduction in the tied estate in recent years, there is now gradual expansion. The core range, bi-monthly seasonals, and other one-off beers are brewed, notably the Trooper range, in conjunction with Iron Maiden's Bruce Dickinson. In 2022 Robinsons announced plans to relocate brewing from the town centre site to the botting plant in nearby Bredbury. This move should be complete some time in 2024. ⬛◆

Citra Pale (ABV 3.4%) BLOND
Cumbria Way (ABV 4.1%) BITTER
Pale brown with a malty aroma, this beer has a balance of malt, some hops and a little fruit, with sweetness and bitterness throughout.
Cwrw'r Ddraig Aur (ABV 4.1%) GOLD
Unicorn (ABV 4.2%) BITTER
Amber beer with a fruity aroma. Malt, hops and fruit in the taste with a bitter, malty finish.
Cascade IPA (ABV 4.8%) PALE
Pale brown beer with malt and fruit on the nose. Full hoppy taste with malt and fruit, leading to a hoppy, bitter finish.
Trooper (ABV 4.8%) BITTER
Balanced amber beer with sweet malts and hops in aroma and taste.
Old Tom (ABV 8.5%) STRONG
A full-bodied, dark beer with malt, fruit and chocolate on the aroma. A complex range of flavours includes dark chocolate, full maltiness, port and fruits and lead to a long, bittersweet aftertaste.

Runaway

9-11 Astley Street, Stockport, SK4 1AW
☎ (0161) 832 2628 ☎ 07505 237078
⊕ therunawaybrewery.com

Runaway is located in a renovated and converted sheet metal fabrication unit close to Stockport's bus and rail stations. It began brewing in 2014 producing KeyKeg and bottle-conditioned beers. However, when production was moved to Stockport, cask-conditioned ales were added to the range in response to local demand. All core range beers are unfiltered and unpasteurised, with many available locally including in its own taproom. ⬛◆LIVE◆

Saddleworth

⬛ **Church Inn, Church Lane, Uppermill, Oldham, OL3 6LW**
☎ (01457) 820902 ⊕ churchinnsaddleworth.co.uk

⊛Set in an idyllic location near St Chad's Church, Saddleworth started brewing in 1997 in a 120-year old brewhouse at the Church Inn, in a valley overlooking Saddleworth Moor. Brewing is currently suspended.

Serious SIBA

Unit C5, Fieldhouse Industrial Estate, Fieldhouse Road, Rochdale, OL12 0AA ☎ 07840 301797
⊕ seriousbrewing.co.uk

Established in 2015 and run by husband and wife team Ken and Jenny Lynch. The beers are brewed using a six-barrel plant. The focus is on producing high quality beers drawing influences from traditional British ales, US craft beers and artisanal Belgian beers. Many outlets are supplied direct and the beers are available nationwide via wholesalers. A taproom opened at the brewery in 2019. ◆LIVE◆

Prime (ABV 4.2%) PALE
Evergreen (ABV 4.5%) BITTER

Hoppy aroma. Taste of fruit and bitter hops, with lasting bitterness. Crisp and bitter throughout. Background of sweet malt.
Moonlight (ABV 4.5%) STOUT
Medium-bodied dry stout with roast character that develops into a crisp bitter finish.
Redsmith (ABV 4.5%) BITTER
Goldrush (ABV 5.6%) SPECIALITY

Seven Bro7hers

Unit 63, Waybridge Enterprise Centre, Daniel Adamson Road, Salford, M50 1DS
☎ **(0161) 228 2404** ⊕ **sevenbro7hers.com**

Brewing began in 2014 using a 10-barrel plant. A new brewhouse and fermentation tanks doubled brewing capacity in 2017, and allowed for the brewing of speciality and one-off beers, plus a taproom. The Seven Bro7hers Beerhouse in Ancoats opened in 2016, and a new Beerhouse opened in 2019 in the Middlewood Locks area near Salford Central Station. Further venues have opened in Halifax, Liverpool and at Manchester Airport. !!▼◆

Session (ABV 3.8%) PALE
Fruity hop taste of tropical fruit well-balanced with bitter and pale malt. Citrus hop aroma. Refreshing bitter finish.

Squawk

Unit 4, Tonge Street, Ardwick, Manchester, M12 6LY
☎ **07590 387559** ⊕ **squawkbrewingco.com**

Squawk initially cuckoo-brewed in Huddersfield in 2013, with the first beers from the current Manchester railway-arch site appearing in 2014. In 2019, the brewery expanded to a 32-barrel capacity with additional fermenters and conditioning tanks. Some gluten-free beers are now available. The beers are packaged in cask, keg and can and are widely available in the North of England as well as being distributed nationally. ◆GF

Pavo (ABV 3.8%) GOLD
Light hoppy beer with balanced fruity aroma and taste. Dry bitter finish.
Crex (ABV 4.5%) PALE
Fruity and hoppy aroma. Sweet fruit balanced with bitter hops in the flavour, rising to a lasting dry bitter finish..
Corvus (ABV 7.4%) STOUT
Roast malt aroma and strong, lasting dark chocolate taste with touch of fruit.

State of Kind

Unit 4, Hemfield Court, Wigan, WN2 2ER ☎ **07765 808889** ⊕ **stateofkindbrew.co**

Launched in 2021, initially as a nomad brewery. State of Kind now has its own brewery and taproom. ◆

Steelfish

c/o 75 North Western Street, Manchester, M12 6DY
✉ **steelfishbrewing@gmail.com**

Steelfish started brewing in 2020 as a cuckoo brewer based at Beer Nouveau (qv).

Stockport

Unit 16, The Gate Centre, Bredbury Parkway, Stockport, SK6 2SN
☎ **(0161) 637 0306**
✉ **stockportbrewingcompany@gmail.com**

☺Stockport Brewing Company is the longest-running, award-winning microbrewery in Stockport. It began

trading in 2014 using an eight-barrel plant under the iconic Stockport Viaduct, before moving in 2017 to a larger, more modern facility at Bredbury. Beers are widely available in local outlets and throughout the UK via a trading agreement with other breweries. The beer range now includes single-hopped and fruit-infused cask ales. !!◆

Waimea (ABV 3.8%) PALE
Stockport Pale (ABV 3.9%) MILD
Cascade (ABV 4%) BLOND
Centaurus (ABV 4%) GOLD
South Island Pale (ABV 4.1%) PALE
Crown Best Bitter (ABV 4.2%) BITTER
Ginger Tinge (ABV 4.2%) SPECIALITY ·
Jester (ABV 4.2%) GOLD
Dark Oatmeal Stout (ABV 4.5%) STOUT
Excellent smooth, thick-bodied stout, plenty of roast, some fruit and sweetness to balance with a lasting finish of roast bitterness.
Stock Porter (ABV 4.8%) PORTER
Malty flavour and aroma with some treacle toffee. Coffee and chocolate roast notes and hint of dark fruit.

Strange Times SIBA

Units 1 & 2, Foundry, Ordsall Lane, Salford, M5 3LW
☎ **(0161) 873 8090** ⊕ **strangetimesbrewing.com**

Founded in 2020, a 24-barrel and a four-barrel kit are used with a focus on sustainability. A core range of four beers are available in 9g and 18g casks, and 30l & 50l kegs, alongside a core cold-filtered lager, and a range of seasonal and one-off specials. A canning line was installed in 2023. Apart from a speciality honey beer, all beers are vegan; most beers are unfiltered. ◆V

Neo Kosmo (ABV 4.1%) BLOND
Coyote (ABV 4.5%) BLOND
Mad King Sweeney (ABV 4.6%) RED
Memento Mori (ABV 5.5%) IPA

Stubborn Mule

Unit 1, Skelton Road, Timperley, WA14 1SJ ☎ **07730 515251** ⊕ **stubbornmulebrewery.com**

☺Brewing began in 2015. In 2022 the brewery moved to larger premises allowing it to increase production capacity. Brewer Ed Bright continues to brew its core beers with occasional one-off specials. The additional space allows for more frequent brew taps with more seating. See website for details. !!◆LIVE◆

Mandarin Candidate (ABV 3.4%) SPECIALITY
Li'l Napoleon (ABV 3.9%) GOLD
Absolute Banker (ABV 4.7%) BITTER
Pils, Thrills & Bellyaches (ABV 4.8%) SPECIALITY
Donkey Punch (ABV 5.5%) SPECIALITY
Pre-Prohibition Cream Ale (ABV 5.5%) GOLD
Single Hop IPA (ABV 5.7%) IPA
Chocolate Stout (ABV 5.8%) STOUT
WA15 Magnum IPA (ABV 7.2%) IPA

Sureshot

5 Sheffield Street, Manchester, M1 2ND
⊕ **sureshotbrew.com**

Started brewing in early 2022 in premises vacated by Track the previous year. ▼◆

Temperance Street (NEW)

75 North Western Street, Manchester, M12 6DY
☎ **07595 493462**

Community-focused brewery and taproom in the centre of Manchester. As well as producing its own beer, it makes its brewkit available to customers to trial their own recipes on a larger scale. ◆

Thirst Class

Unit 16, Station Road Industrial Estate, Reddish, Stockport, SK5 6ND
☎ (0161) 431 3998 ⊕ thirstclassale.co.uk

⊛Thirst Class opened in 2014 in the centre of Stockport using a purpose-built, two-barrel plant. In 2016 the brewery relocated to larger premises and installed a 10-barrel plant. Brewing is currently suspended. ☕◆LIVE V

Tin Head

Unit 22f, Bradley Fold Trading Estate, Radcliffe Moor Road, Radcliffe, Bury, BL2 6RT ☎ 07980 262766 ⊕ tinheadbrewery.co.uk

⊛Established in 2017, run by a father and son who are passionate about beers. The 60-seater taproom is dog-friendly, and the rear section offers music from solo artists. Generally eight craft keg beers are dispensed on font taps at the bar, together with gins. Beers are brewed as per real ale but dispensed as chilled keg. ‼◆

Track SIBA

Units 17 & 18, Piccadilly Trading Estate, Manchester, M1 2ND
☎ (0161) 536 3975 ⊕ trackbrewing.co

Track Brewing Co was established in 2014. Originally based in a railway arch underneath Manchester's Piccadilly Railway Station, it has recently expanded operations to a new site in central Manchester. It produces a wide range of beers styles as well as growing its barrel-ageing program. The new location has an onsite taproom and beer garden. ‼◆

Sonoma (ABV 3.8%) GOLD
An unfined, well-balanced sweet, fruity beer with moderate bitterness and plenty of citrus hops.

Ventile

Unit 4, Spur Mill, Broadstone Hall Road South, Stockport, SK5 7BY ⊕ ventilebrew.co

Ventile Brew Co began brewing in 2021 and is a modern, small-batch microbrewery.

Wakey Wakey

100 Brotherod Hall Road, Rochdale, OL12 7ED
✉ wakeywakeybrewingcompany@gmail.com

⊛The brewery gets its name from founder Anthony Jones, a beer lover who started homebrewing in 2018. Having improved his brewing equipment and gaining the required licenses, Anthony started selling his cask ales to pubs in Oldham and Rochdale in 2022.

Bunk (ABV 3.8%) BITTER
Bright & Early (ABV 4%) PALE
Fever Dream (ABV 5%) PALE

Wander Beyond SIBA

98 North Western Street, Manchester, M12 6JL
☎ (0161) 661 3676 ⊕ wanderbeyondbrewing.com

Wander Beyond launched in 2017 in a railway arch under Piccadilly Station. The range of beer available can vary, each beer is brewed for only a short period so the range is constantly changing. Styles and ingredients are unusual and sometimes unique. ☕◆

Peak (ABV 3.8%) PALE

Wigan Brewhouse

The Old Brewery, Brewery Yard, off Wallgate, Wigan, WN1 1JU
☎ (01942) 234976 ☎ 07764 936410
⊕ wiganbrewhouse.co.uk

⊛Wigan Brewhouse commenced brewing in 2018 after local businessman Martin Blythe leased the now-defunct AllGates Brewery premises, including the acquisition of beers formerly brewed by AllGates. Beers are also brewed to its own recipes, developed by head brewer Jonathan Provost with Martin's input. ‼◆

Pretoria (ABV 3.6%) BLOND
California (ABV 3.9%) BLOND
A pale yellow beer with a restrained hoppy and fruity aroma. It is clean and fresh-tasting, with hops and fruit in the mouth and a bitter hoppy finish.
Casino (ABV 3.9%) BITTER
Wigan Junction (ABV 3.9%) BITTER
Sweet malty beer with caramel in the nose and gentle hops providing a bitter finish.
Dry Bones (ABV 4%) BLOND
Slider (ABV 4%) BITTER
Tempo (ABV 4.1%) GOLD
Blue Sky Tea (ABV 4.2%) SPECIALITY
Kicker IPA (ABV 4.2%) PALE
Allnighter (ABV 4.3%) PALE
Station Road Stout (ABV 4.5%) MILD
Dark brown beer with a malty, fruity aroma. Creamy and malty in taste, with blackberry fruits and a satisfying aftertaste.

Wily Fox SIBA

1 Kellet Close, Wigan, WN5 0LP
☎ (01942) 215525 ⊕ wilyfoxbrewery.co.uk

A bespoke 20-barrel brewery, set up in 2016. Head brewer Dave Goodwin previously worked for Thwaites and Samuel Smith. ‼

Blonde Vixen (ABV 3.8%) BLOND
Light-bodied fruity beer.
Prohibition APA (ABV 3.9%) PALE
Hoppy beer with citrus character throughout.
Crafty Fox (ABV 4%) BITTER
Well-balanced bitter and malty sweetness, with fruity hops. Creamy mouthfeel, and bitter finish.
The Fox Hat (ABV 4.2%) GOLD
Fruity aroma. Citrus hop taste and bitter hoppy aftertaste.
Karma Citra (ABV 4.3%) GOLD
Citrus fruit in aroma and taste with balanced bitterness, and a dry finish.
Dark Flagon (ABV 4.4%) SPECIALITY

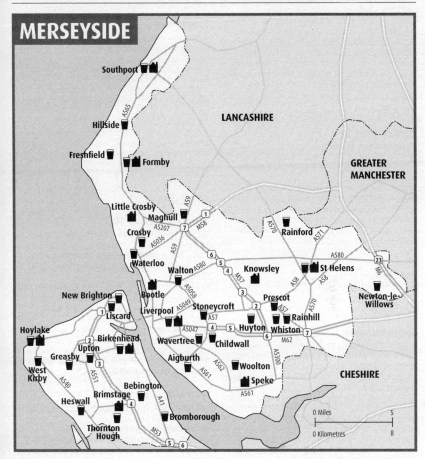

MERSEYSIDE

Southport · Hillside · Freshfield · Formby · Little Crosby · Maghull · Crosby · Waterloo · Walton · New Brighton · Bootle · Liscard · Liverpool · Stoneycroft · Hoylake · Birkenhead · Upton · Greasby · Wavertree · Childwall · West Kirby · Aigburth · Woolton · Heswall · Bebington · Speke · Brimstage · Bromborough · Thornton Hough

LANCASHIRE · Rainford · GREATER MANCHESTER · Knowsley · St Helens · Prescot · Rainhill · Newton-le-Willows · Huyton · Whiston · CHESHIRE

0 Miles 5
0 Kilometres 8

Bebington

Rose & Crown 🅛 ✅

57 The Village, CH63 7PL

☎ (0151) 644 5829 ⊕ roseandcrownbebington.co.uk

Thwaites Original, IPA, Gold, Amber; house beer (by Thwaites); 2 changing beers (sourced locally; often Big Bog, Brimstage, Neptune) 🅷

This old coaching inn, built in 1732, is a thriving, vibrant and friendly community local. It has a lounge, small bar and games room, with traditional decor and old photos of the area. Thwaites brews the house beer, Rose Gold, and some of the changing beers, with frequent guests from other mainly local breweries. Live music features. Nearby Port Sunlight village was founded by Lever in 1888 to house his soap factory workers and is the home of the Lady Lever Art Gallery.

Q ☆ ← (Port Sunlight) ♣ P ♞ (410,464) ❀ 🛜 ♫

Traveller's Rest ✅

169 Mount Road, CH63 8PJ

☎ (0151) 608 2988 ⊕ thetravsbebington.co.uk

Ossett White Rat; Timothy Taylor Landlord; 4 changing beers (sourced nationally; often Big Bog, Fuller's, Oaks) 🅷

Reputedly over 300 years old, this cosy former coaching inn is by the edge of Storeton Woods. It has a country pub feel and is decorated throughout with brasses and bric-a-brac. The main area has a central bar and there are two side rooms. The guest ales are sometimes from local microbreweries, and there is one changing real cider.

Quiz night is on Monday and live music plays on Saturday. No evening meals Monday and Tuesday.

Q ☆ ◖ 🕭 ♞ (464,487) ❀ 🛜 ♫

Birkenhead

Gallaghers Traditional Pub 🅛

20 Chester Street, CH41 5DQ

☎ (0151) 649 9095 ⊕ gallagherswirral.com/traditional-pub

6 changing beers (sourced nationally; often Brimstage, Rat, Salopian) 🅷

Multiple award-winning free house close to the Mersey ferries, rescued after closure and refurbished in 2010. It is decorated with a fascinating range of military memorabilia and a collection of shipping images. Meals are served daily except Monday evening and Sunday lunchtime. Live music every Sunday evening. The outside area at the rear has a retractable roof. The mural on the side wall of the pub commemorates the sinking of HMS Birkenhead and the Birkenhead Drill, 'women and children first.' ❀ ◖ ← (Hamilton Square) ♣ ♞ 🕭 ❀ ♫

Bromborough

Bow-Legged Beagle 🅛

11 Allport Lane, CH62 7HH

4 changing beers (sourced regionally; often Beartown, Brimstage, Neptune) 🅷

This friendly and comfortable pub is the third of the local Bow-Legged Beagle chain of micropubs. The selection of cask ales usually includes a session pale and a stronger IPA, plus a bitter or amber brew and a stout or porter. Its location in the main street, near the ancient market cross in the centre of Bromborough, makes it convenient for buses and it is a 10-minute walk from Bromborough Rake station. Winner of a local CAMRA Cellarmanship Award in 2022. Q ⑤ ⏛ 🚍 ❀

Crosby

Corner Post ℒ
25 Bridge Road, L23 6SA
☎ 07587 177453
5 changing beers (sourced locally; often Peerless, Rock the Boat) Ⓗ
Crosby's second micropub, located in a former post office, is easily spotted by the postbox outside. As well as real ales and cider, bottled continental beers, wine and soft drinks are available. Interesting pictures, depicting the history of the local area, adorn the walls. Well-behaved dogs are welcome. The pub is close to 53 bus route and a short walk from Blundellsands & Crosby railway station. It is also near Another Place, the Antony Gormley iron statue artwork on Crosby beach.
Q ≥ (Blundellsands & Crosby) ♣ ♠ 🚍 (53) ❀

Formby

Sparrowhawk
Southport Old Road, L37 0AB (adjacent to Formby bypass opp Woodvale Airfield)
☎ (01704) 882350
Salopian Oracle; Titanic Plum Porter; 3 changing beers (sourced regionally) Ⓗ
Large, open-plan Brunning & Price pub on the original road from Southport to Formby. It was built as the Dower House to the nearby Formby Hall and is situated in five acres of woodlands and gardens. The emphasis is on food but the pub always sells up to six real ales in excellent condition. The bus stop at Woodpile traffic lights is less than five minutes' walk away.
Q ⑤ 🕯 ⏛ ♿ ♣ P 🚍 (47,49) ❀ 🛜

Tin Shed ℒ
60 Brows Lane, L37 4ED
☎ (01704) 808220
5 changing beers (sourced locally; often Parker) Ⓗ
A micropub that opened in 2021 on Formby's main street, a 10-minute walk from the train station. There is ample seating inside, and the owners are starting a collection of pumpclips to show all the real ales that have been on sale since its opening. The pub is also keen to support local breweries. Q ⑤ ♿ ≥ ♣ ♠ 🚍 ❀ 🛜

Freshfield

Beer Station
3 Victoria Buildings, L37 7DB (opp Freshfield railway station)
☎ (01704) 807450
3 changing beers (sourced locally; often Neptune, Rock the Boat) Ⓗ
Freshfield's first micropub has a strong emphasis on all things local. Beers are sourced to promote the local brewers – with the exception of one beer a month from outside the region. The few spirits available also have their provenance checked. A fridge with bottled beers adds to the variety. Food comes in the form of local pies and nuts. The walls are decorated with work by local artists. Dogs on a lead are welcome.
Q ⑤ ♿ ≥ ♣ ♠ 🚍 (F1,F2) ❀ 🛜

Freshfield ℒ ⊘
1 Massams Lane, L37 7BD (from station turn inland into Victoria Rd and then left into Gores Ln)
☎ (01704) 874871
Greene King IPA, Abbot; Oakham Citra; 4 changing beers (sourced regionally) Ⓗ
A community pub at its heart with three distinct areas: a dining room serving quality food, a bar with numerous handpumps, and 'the flags', where well-behaved dogs are allowed. Sport is shown on three large TVs, and a real fire adds warmth in winter. The pub occasionally has real cider for festivals. This is a place to meet, talk and be with friends old or new. A former CAMRA National Pub of the Year finalist and multi award winner.
⑤ 🕯 ⏛ ♿ ≥ ♣ P 🚍 (F1,F2) ❀ 🛜

Greasby

Coach & Horses ⊘
Greasby Road, CH49 3NG
☎ (0151) 677 4509
Brains Rev James Original; Butcombe Original; 2 changing beers (sourced nationally; often Black Sheep) Ⓗ
In a whitewashed building dating back nearly 300 years is this charming street-corner pub. Tastefully redecorated in 2021, it has retained its character, and has the atmosphere of a traditional country local. The compact central bar serves several discrete areas including two small cosy rooms with real warming fires for the winter. Outside is a small garden to the side. Live music usually plays on Sunday and there is a folk/acoustic jam session every Monday. Q ⑤ 🕯 ♠ P 🚍 (437) ❀ ♫

Irby Mill ℒ ⊘
Mill Lane, CH49 3NT (on roundabout between Greasby and Irby)
☎ (0151) 678 0198 🌐 irbymill.co.uk
Brains Rev James Original; Ossett Yorkshire Blonde; Timothy Taylor Landlord; 4 changing beers (sourced nationally) Ⓗ
Originally a miller's house and later a café, the Irby Mill opened as a pub in 1980, with thick sandstone walls, low beams and a real fire. It comprises a small L-shaped, stone-floored bar and a lounge that is used mainly by diners. The pub has an excellent reputation for its locally sourced home-made food, with a menu to suit most

REAL ALE BREWERIES

Ad Hop Liverpool (brewing suspended)
Beer Station 🍺 Formby
Big Bog ⬧ Speke
Black Lodge ⬧ Liverpool
Brimstage Brimstage
Brooks Hoylake
Cains ⬧ Liverpool (brewing suspended)
Carnival ⬧ Liverpool
Glen Affric Birkenhead
Handyman 🍺 Liverpool
Hex Southport (NEW)
Howzat 🍺 St Helens
Liverpool Brewing ⬧ Liverpool
Love Lane 🍺 Liverpool
Melwood Knowsley (brewing suspended)
Neptune Liverpool
Peerless ⬧ Birkenhead
Rock the Boat Little Crosby
Southport Southport
Stamps Bootle
Top Rope ⬧ Liverpool
Tyton Liverpool (brewing suspended)

tastes. Nearby Royden Park and Thurstaston Common provide the pub with many passing hikers to supplement the strong local following. Q✿❀🕪◑🅿🚍(22)🐾🔊

Heswall

Beer Lab ℒ
53 Telegraph Road, CH60 0AD
☎ (0151) 342 5475 🌐 thebeerlab.co.uk
Peerless Triple Blond; 3 changing beers (sourced locally; often Black Lodge, Chapter, Neptune) Ⓗ
Heswall's first micropub opened in 2018 in a former cycle shop, an easy five minutes' walk from the main shopping area and the bus station. The relaxed, minimalist single-room bar is bright and airy, making the most of the available space. Eight real ciders are always on the bar, together with Belgian bottled beers. Beer is served in pint, one-third and two-third measures only. Local CAMRA Cider Pub of the Year 2020-22.
Q✿❀🍴🚍(22,472) 🐾🔊

Jug & Bottle ℒ
13 Mount Avenue, CH60 4RH
☎ (0151) 342 5535 🌐 the-jugandbottle.co.uk
Brains Rev James Original; Brimstage Trapper's Hat Bitter; Timothy Taylor Boltmaker; 3 changing beers (sourced regionally; often Beartown, Brimstage) Ⓗ
Built in the 1870s as a private house, before being converted to offices and then a pub, the Jug & Bottle has been in its present incarnation since 1993. Hidden behind the village hall and library, it is a short distance from the main shopping street. The pub has a strong emphasis on food. The open fires and different cosy areas inside create a warm and friendly atmosphere, while the decking outside gives fine views towards the the River Dee and north Wales.
Q✿❀🕪◑🅿🚍(22,471) 🔊

Hillside

Pines
3 Hillside Road, PR8 4QB
☎ 07454 453090
2 changing beers (sourced regionally) Ⓗ
An attractively decorated bar in what was once a hairdresser's in an area the previously had no pubs or bars but now has two award-winning outlets. Two handpumps offer a varied choice of beers, served alongside a selection of bottled ales. Sandwiches are delivered daily. An outside seating area at the front is popular in the warmer months. The bar can be either quiet and relaxing or noisy, depending on the time of day. Dog are welcome, with treats available.
✿❀🚍🅿(47) 🐾🔊♪

Hoylake

Black Toad ℒ
32 Market Street, CH47 2AF
☎ 07835 360691 🌐 theblacktoad.co.uk
4 changing beers (sourced regionally; often Chapter, Neptune, Peerless) Ⓗ
Micropub that opened in 2019 in a shop unit on the main shopping street. Its narrow main room and bar is attractively decorated with simple furniture. The owners ensure a balanced selection of cask beers at all times. In 2020 the pub expanded into the next-door shop to create a new lounge area. At the rear is a pleasant beer garden. Fresh pizza is served Thursday to Sunday evenings. Local CAMRA Pub of the Year runner-up in 2023. Q✿❀◑🚍(38,407)🐾🔊

Huyton

Barker's Brewery ℒ ✅
Archway Road, L36 9UJ
☎ (0151) 482 4500
Greene King Abbot; Ruddles Best Bitter; Sharp's Doom Bar; 4 changing beers Ⓗ
A large, airy Wetherspoon on the site of the old Huyton brewery, which was founded in 1825 and managed by the Barker family over four generations until 1925. The pub has a traditional feel and offers a good selection of ales, with at least one local and one dark beer available. The main dining area leads onto the beer garden at the rear. Alcohol is served from 9am. Children are not allowed on the premises after 9.30pm.
Q✿❀🕪◑ᕤ🅿🚍(10) 🔊

Liscard

Lazy Landlord Ale House ℒ
56 Mill Lane, CH44 5UG
☎ 07583 135616
Oakham Citra; 4 changing beers (sourced nationally; often Brimstage, Joseph Holt, Ossett) Ⓗ
Wirral's first micropub, opened in 2014 in converted shop premises. It is run by the Henry brothers, who are cask ale enthusiasts. Two small cosy rooms, decorated with breweriana, local art works and a small library, are served from the front bar. The pub hosts meetings of local societies and is mostly frequented by a mature, discerning clientele of regulars. A former local CAMRA Pub of the Year. Q✿❀♣🚍(410,432)🐾🔊

Liverpool: Aigburth

Little Taproom on Aigburth Road ℒ
278 Aigburth Road, L17 9PJ
🌐 aigburthtap.co.uk
5 changing beers (sourced locally; often Chapter, Neptune) Ⓗ
Friendly two-roomed micropub that opened in 2020 near Sefton Park, on a main road with excellent bus and Merseyrail services close by. The front bar has a number of handpulls serving beer and cider. Bottled and canned ales are stocked, and the range of spirits includes their own Sefton Park gin. Entertainment includes board games and a book club – there is no TV, jukebox or background music. Q♣🚍(82)🔊

Liverpool: Childwall

Childwall Fiveways ℒ ✅
179 Queens Drive, L15 6XS
☎ (0151) 738 2100
Greene King Abbot; Ruddles Best Bitter; 6 changing beers (sourced nationally; often Robinsons) Ⓗ
A former Higson's tied house, this large single-roomed pub opened as a Wetherspoon in 2010. Located in a leafy suburb, it has good motorway and public transport links. The refurbished interior is decorated with wood panelling, and outside there is a beer garden. It is a popular establishment and can get busy, especially at weekends. The site was used as a water tank during WWII. ✿❀🕪◑ᕤ🍴🅿🚍(79,81)🔊

Liverpool: City Centre

Augustus John ℒ
Peach Street, L3 5TX (off Brownlow Hill)
☎ (0151) 794 5507 🌐 the-augustus-john.business.site
5 changing beers (sourced nationally; often Peerless, Rock the Boat) Ⓗ

Run by the University of Liverpool, the Augustus John is an open-plan pub popular with students, lecturers and locals. The cask ales always include a range of styes, plus there are two ciders on handpump and many more in the cellar. Pizza is served at all times. A jukebox provides entertainment. Closed over Christmas and New Year. Card payment only. Local CAMRA Cider Pub of the Year.
❀◑&♣●🚃(79) 🛜

Baltic Fleet 🅛

33A Wapping, L1 8DQ
☎ (0151) 709 3116 ⊕ balticfleet.co.uk
Brimstage Trapper's Hat Bitter; 3 changing beers (sourced locally) Ⓗ
Grade II-listed building near the Albert Dock. It has a distinctive flatiron shape and the interior is decorated on a nautical theme. The existence of tunnels in the cellar has led to speculation that the pub's history may involve smuggling. Originally it had many doors to allow customers to escape when press gangs entered. It has an extensive outside drinking area. It can can get busy when events are on at the nearby M&S Bank Arena.
❀≈(James Street)●🚃🐱🛜♫

Belvedere 🅛

8 Sugnall Street, L7 7EB (off Falkner St)
4 changing beers (sourced regionally; often Ossett) Ⓗ
Tucked away in the Georgian area of the city, close to the famous Philharmonic Hall, and frequented by its orchestra members, this small two-roomed pub is a free house serving four rotating beers from mainly local microbreweries. Redeemed in 2006 from closure for housing development, the Grade II-listed building retains original fixtures and interesting etched glass features. It is a pub with a mixed local clientele, where various small cultural groups meet and good conversation thrives.
Q❀🚃(80A,86) 🐱🛜♫

Bridewell 🍸 🅛

1 Campbell Square, L1 5FB
☎ (0151) 707 2372 ⊕ thebridewellpub.co.uk
Kirkstall Three Swords; 3 changing beers (sourced nationally; often Conwy, Ossett) Ⓗ
An imposing, Grade II-listed building that dates from the mid-19th century when it was a police bridewell, or jail. The cells are used as seating areas and provide an unusual focus for the downstairs bar. There is an outdoor patio at the front. The pub is situated close to the Liverpool One shopping area, the Albert Dock and the riverfront. Local CAMRA Pub of the Year 2022 and 2023.
🛏❀≈(Central) 🚃🛜

Captain Alexander 🅛 ✅

15 James Street, L2 7NX
☎ (0151) 227 4197
Greene King Abbot; Ruddles Best Bitter; Sharp's Doom Bar; 4 changing beers (sourced nationally; often Big Bog, Peerless) Ⓗ
Close to the Pier Head and Albert Dock, this Wetherspoon pub features one bar, as well as a first-floor outdoor terrace. It opened in 2019 and is named after Alexander Allan, founder of the Allan Line Steamship Company, which had an office next door. The Allan Line pioneered trading with Canada and became world's largest privately owned shipping company in the early 19th century. 🛏◑&≈(James Street)●🚃🛜

Denbigh Castle

10 Hackins Hey, L2 2AW (off Dale St)
☎ (0151) 236 8558 ⊕ thedenbighcastle.co.uk
Kirkstall Bitter; 3 changing beers (sourced nationally) Ⓗ

Open-plan pub that has had many different identities before being refurbished and relaunched in 2020 as the Denbigh Castle, the original name from over 200 years ago. It is a sister pub to the Bridewell. The beer choice includes cask, craft beers and German lagers. The ground-floor bar is complemented by rooms up and down stairs for functons and events. Liverpool city tourism Pub of the Year 2021. ≈(Moorfields)●🚃🛜

Dispensary

87 Renshaw Street, L1 2SP
☎ 07472 291403 ⊕ dockleafbar.co.uk/thedispensary
Oakham Citra; Ossett White Rat; Titanic Plum Porter; 4 changing beers (often Liverpool Brewing Company, Ossett) Ⓗ
This lively city pub is a haven for real ale drinkers of all ages. The attractive bar area has Victorian features, and there is a raised wood panelled area to the rear. It was originally the Grapes – the old sign is behind the bar. It can be busy when live football matches are shown on the big TV screens. There is a food stall outside.
❀◑≈(Central) 🚃(86) 🛜

Doctor Duncan's 🅛 ✅

St Johns Lane, L1 1HF
☎ (0151) 709 5100 ⊕ doctorduncansliverpool.com
4 changing beers (sourced nationally; often Salopian) Ⓗ
This former Cains brewery flagship pub has an impressive Victorian interior consisting of four distinctively different drinking areas; the green tiled room is particularly handsome. The pub's name commemorates Doctor Duncan, the first chief medical officer of Liverpool and a ruthless campaigner against poor living conditions in Victorian times, and medical memorabilia can be found throughout. Beers are from the resurrected Cains brewery which is housed in a Mikhail group sister pub.
❀◑≈(Lime Street) ♣🚃🐱🛜

Excelsior 🅛 ✅

121-123 Dale Street, L2 2JH (close to Birkenhead Tunnel entrance)
☎ (0151) 352 9544 ⊕ excelsiorliverpool.co.uk
Timothy Taylor Landlord; 4 changing beers (sourced regionally; often Liverpool Brewing Company, Ossett, Salopian) Ⓗ
Named after a sailing ship this large corner pub is adjacent to what were Higsons brewery offices. A tastefully decorated and comfortable pub, it appeals to both a business and leisure clientele. The main room has a three-sided bar with a series of distinct seating areas. A large room off the main bar area includes a raised seating area which can be hired for meetings or other functions. Largescreen TVs show sports events, particularly football, but are generally silent otherwise.
◑≈(Moorfields) 🚃🛜♫

Fly in the Loaf ✅

13 Hardman Street, L1 9AS
☎ (0151) 708 0817 ⊕ markettowntaverns.co.uk
Okell's Bitter; Ossett White Rat; 4 changing beers (sourced nationally; often Kirkstall) Ⓗ
A former bakery, the name comes from the slogan 'no flies in the loaf'. Owned by Isle of Man brewer Okells, it serves their beers alongside a changing range of guests from around the country, many from microbreweries, and a good selection of foreign beers. The spacious interior has a light, airy frontage with contrasting wood-panelled areas towards the rear. There is a small, attractive on-street drinking area at the front and a function room upstairs. &≈(Central)🚃(86)🛜

Globe

17 Cases Street, L1 1HW (opp Central station)
☎ (0151) 707 0067 ⊕ theglobe.pub
Marston's EPA; Sharp's Doom Bar; Timothy Taylor Landlord; Wainwright; 2 changing beers (sourced nationally) H

Standing opposite Central station, this small, traditional pub is a former local CAMRA Best Community Pub. The Globe attracts people from all over the city – a buzz of lively conversation prevails, and visitors are equally welcomed. In the small back room a brass plaque commemorates the inaugural meeting of CAMRA Merseyside and 40th year celebrations were held here in 2014. The sloping floor in the bar area is legendary.
➤(Liverpool Central) ♿

Grapes L

60 Roscoe Street, L1 9DW
☎ (0151) 708 6870
8 changing beers (often Chapter, Neptune) H

This corner local dates back to 1804 and has the original Mellors signage outside. It is known as the 'Little Grapes', but following a major refurbishment several years back, an extension has made the pub larger. Stairs now lead to a partly sheltered patio area atop the extension. Most of the nine handpumps serve beers from local and smaller regional breweries, and one now regularly serves a real cider. An extensive selection of rums is kept. Live jazz every Sunday. ❀➤(Central)♦♿(82)🛜♪

Head of Steam

85-89 Hanover Street, L1 3DZ
☎ (0151) 708 6096 ⊕ theheadofsteam.co.uk
Camerons Strongarm; 6 changing beers (sourced locally; often Camerons, Neptune, Tiny Rebel) H

This large pub – previously the Abbey – opened in 2017 (it is not connected to the Head of Steam that was previously on Lime Street). It has lots of seating but can get busy, especially on evenings when major sporting events are shown live on TV. It stocks a large selection of foreign bottled and keg beers, such as Chimay. A private function area is available for bookings. Handy for Liverpool One shops. ◖➤(Central)♦♿(82,86)🛜♪

Lime Kiln L ✓

Fleet Street, L1 4NR
☎ (0151) 702 6810
Greene King Abbot; Ruddles Best Bitter; Sharp's Doom Bar; 8 changing beers (sourced nationally; often Big Bog, Peerless) H

On first impressions, the decor and layout may appear not to offer much for the real ale drinker, but cask ale is well catered for and available on the downstairs bar. Situated in the Concert Square area, the pub is a peaceful haven during the day, but after 8pm becomes a music and disco venue for the younger crowd. There is a drinking terrace outside. A Victorian warehouse occupied the site, which was home to manufacturing chemists, from the early 1900s into the 1950s.
🐾◖♿➤(Central)♦♿(82,86)🛜

Lion Tavern ★ L

67 Moorfields, L2 2BP
⊕ theliontavernliverpool.co.uk
Peerless Triple Blond; Wily Fox Crafty Fox; 3 changing beers (sourced nationally) H

Named after the locomotive that worked the Liverpool to Manchester Railway (and is on display at the Liverpool musuem). The Lion features mosaic floors, a tiled corridor, plus intricately etched and stained glass. Refurbished in 2017, it retains Grade II-listed status and has been identified by CAMRA as having a nationally important historic pub interior. Up to eight beers are from

the SIBA list, usually including local micros, are served. Cider is regularly available, and local gins are kept. There is a discount (Mon-Fri) for card-carrying union members. A former local CAMRA Pub of the Year.
◖➤(Moorfields) ♦♿❀🛜

Pen Factory

13 Hope Street, L1 9BQ
☎ (0151) 709 7887 ⊕ pen-factory.co.uk
Titanic Plum Porter; 4 changing beers (sourced nationally; often Ossett, Salopian, Titanic) H

The Pen Factory was opened in 2015 by the innovator of the original Everyman Bistro, entrepreneur Paddy Byrne. This large, open-plan, bistro-style establishment with a wood-burning stove and a small garden is a convivial place to drink and eat. At least five handpumps serve real ales and ciders. The food is excellent – not your average pub fare. It can be busy before or after productions at the nearby Everyman theatre or Philharmonic Hall.
❀◖♿➤(Central) ♦♿(86) ❀🛜♪

Peter Kavanagh's ★ ✓

2-6 Egerton Street, L8 7LY (off Catharine St)
☎ (0151) 709 3443
Greene King Abbot; 4 changing beers (sourced nationally; often Castle Rock) H

A Grade II-listed stuccoed pub in the Georgian quarter which has been identified by CAMRA as having a nationally important historic pub interior. The snugs display murals by Eric Robinson and there are fine stained-glass windows with wooden shutters. The benches have carved armrests thought to be caricatures of Peter Kavanagh, the licensee for 53 years until 1950. These features were not adversely affected when the pub was expanded, firstly in 1964 into next door, then in 1977 into next door but one. A former local CAMRA Pub of the Year. Q♿(80,86)❀🛜♪

Red Lion ✓

36 Slater Street, L1 4BX
⊕ redlionpubliverpool.com
Ossett White Rat; 4 changing beers (sourced nationally; often Ossett, Salopian) H

This traditional pub was converted from a terraced house in 2022 by the same owner as the Green Man in Lark Lane and the Vines (aka Big House) on Lime Street. Hanging knick-knacks, low lighting, bare walls and wooden panels all help create the atmosphere, and there is an interior courtyard and a games room. It is located in a busy late-night drinking area that is popular with clubbers, but by day it provides refuge from the city bustle. ❀◖➤(Central)♣♿♪

Roscoe Head

24 Roscoe Street, L1 2SX
☎ (0151) 709 4365 ⊕ roscoehead.co.uk
Timothy Taylor Landlord; Tetley Bitter; 4 changing beers (sourced locally) H

One of the 'famous five' pubs that have appeared in every edition of this Guide, the freehold of Roscoe Head was sold to the tenant in 2020 following a five-year campaign against the previous owners. This is a cosy four-roomed pub where conversation and the appreciation of real ale rules. Six handpumps serve beers from national and local breweries. Run by members of the same family for over 30 years, the name commemorates William Roscoe, a leading campaigner against the slave trade. Q◖➤(Central)♣♿(80,86)🛜

Ship & Mitre L

133 Dale Street, L2 2JH (by Birkenhead tunnel)
☎ (0151) 236 0859 ⊕ theshipandmitre.com

Flagship Lupa, Silhouette; 6 changing beers (sourced nationally; often Big Bog, Liverpool Brewing Company) Ⓗ

This 1930s Art Deco pub is partly hidden by the Queensway Tunnel entrance. Its name derives from two previous incarnations, the Flagship and the Mitre. It retains the original Art Deco bar and function room upstairs, but dowstairs had had a nautical themed makeover. Fifteen handpulls serve an ever-changing array of beers – including an impressive range of world beers – and real cider, with the friendly and knowledgeable staff always willing to make a recommendation. The pub brews its own Flagship beers using the plant at Stamps brewery.
⓪≢(Moorfields) ♣♠🍴🐾♿🛜

Vernon Arms Ⓛ

69 Dale Street, L2 2HJ
☎ (0151) 236 6132

Brains Rev James Original; house beer (by Stamps); 3 changing beers Ⓗ

Situated close to the business district, the Vernon retains the feel of a street-corner local. The single room bar serves three drinking areas including a back room with frosted glass windows advertising the Liverpool Brewing Company, which once again serves the pub. The main bar has wood panelling, several large columns and a small snug area. Real cider on handpull is unusual for the city centre. ⓪≢(Moorfields)♠🚆🛜♪

Liverpool: Stoneycroft

Cask Ⓛ

438 Queens Drive, West Derby, L13 0AR (near jct Queens Drive and Derby Ln)
☎ 07562 713967

5 changing beers (sourced nationally) Ⓗ

Comfortable, immaculate, one-roomed micropub that opened in 2015. There are usually four beers on Tuesday and Wednesday, five on a Thursday and up to seven from Friday. Special beers in wooden pins are sometimes available. Cider and perry is dispensed direct from taps at the rear of bar. Bottled beers are stocked. Some roadside parking is available. A former local CAMRA Pub of the Year. ♣♠🚆(60,81)♪

Liverpool: Walton

Raven Ⓛ ✅

72-74 Walton Vale, L9 2BU
☎ (0151) 524 1255

Fuller's London Pride; Greene King Abbot; Ruddles Best Bitter; Sharp's Doom Bar; 5 changing beers Ⓗ

An open-plan Wetherspoon pub that is popular with locals, particularly at weekends. It is themed on Edgar Allan Poe's The Raven – local pavement artist James William Carling created illustrations for the famous poem in the late 19th century. He later went to America and is buried in Walton Cemetery. Aintree, the home of the world-famous Grand National, is less than a mile away. Children are welcome until 9pm.
🚭⓪♿≢(Orrell Park) ♠🚆🛜

Liverpool: Wavertree

Willow Bank Ⓛ ✅

329 Smithdown Road, L15 3JA
☎ (0151) 733 5782

Greene King IPA, Abbot; Tetley Bitter; house beer (by Greene King); 4 changing beers (sourced nationally; often Big Bog, Ossett) Ⓗ

Vibrant, traditional, multi-room pub with the original public bar dating from the time it was a Walkers house. Up to eight changing guest beers are on offer – real ale night is a Tuesday – and there are occasional beer festivals. They also offer Westons Rosie cider. Good-value food is served, including Sunday lunches. Sports TV is shown on large screens from the popular roadside patio. Activities such as the quiz attract students, but the pub is also popular with shoppers and locals.
🚭🐾⓪♿🅿🚆(86)🛜

Liverpool: Woolton

Gardeners Arms Ⓛ

101 Vale Road, L25 7RW
☎ (0151) 428 0775

3 changing beers (sourced regionally; often Big Bog) Ⓗ

Friendly community pub situated the over the hill from Woolton village and separated from Menlove Avenue by blocks of flats. Their guests beers regularly include a local Big Bog brew. A quiz is held on Tuesday evenings. Woolton is famous as the home of the Beatles, and their original name, the Quarrymen, comes from Woolton quarry. You can visit St Peter's church, where they first met, and Eleanor Rigby's grave. 🚭🚆(76)🐾🛜♪

Maghull

Frank Hornby Ⓛ ✅

38 Eastway, L31 6BR
☎ (0151) 520 4010

5 changing beers (often Brightside, Elland, Saltaire) Ⓗ

A Wetherspoon establishment named after local man Frank Hornby, inventor of the Hornby train set. Samples of his work are on display in the pub, including Meccano and Dinky Toys. Situated in a surburban street, the bar is spacious and light, with a decked area outside at the front. A changing selection of guest ales is available, some from local breweries. Children are permitted until 10pm. Q🚭🐾⓪♿🅿🚆(133,310)🛜

Maghull Cask Café Ⓛ

43 Liverpool Road South, L31 7BN
☎ (0151) 526 3877

5 changing beers (sourced locally; often Neptune, Oakham) Ⓗ

This micropub is a hidden gem. Opened in 2018, it now serves a good range of changing cask ales, continental bottles and gins. Beers are from regional brewers such as Oakham, Titanic and Salopian. Friendly, knowledgeable staff help to create a great atmosphere where conversation prevails. The Liverpool-Leeds canal runs through Maghull and makes the pub makes the ideal base for a nice walk towards Burscough.
Q♿♠🚆(300,310) 🐾🛜

New Brighton

James Atherton

117-119 Victoria Road, CH45 2JD
☎ (0151) 638 8022

Brimstage Trapper's Hat Bitter; Ossett White Rat; 1 changing beer (sourced regionally; often Hawkshead) Ⓗ

Situated on the main shopping street, close to the seafront attractions and the Floral Pavilion Theatre, this pub was refurbished and reopened in 2019 as part of the regeneration of the Victoria Quarter of New Brighton and renamed after one of the founders of the town. The single-room pub is split into three areas served from one bar. Bright and airy with a lively atmosphere, it has comfortable seating and is decorated with local photographs. ⛄🕸️🍷👤♿🚆🖥️📶🎵

Magazine Hotel 🅛 ✓

7 Magazine Brow, CH45 1HP (above Egremont Promenade)

☎ (0151) 630 3169 ⊕ the-magazine-hotel.co.uk

Brimstage Trapper's Hat Bitter; Draught Bass; 3 changing beers (sourced regionally; often Beartown, Big Bog, Brimstage) Ⓗ

This unspoilt multi-roomed pub, dating from 1759, was restored after a fire in 2010 without losing its unique character. Three rooms lead off the main central bar area with its open fireplace. Renowned for its Draught Bass, other beers are often from local microbreweries. Overlooking Egremont Promenade, the pub has fine views over the River Mersey to Liverpool. Local CAMRA Pub of the Year 2020-2022 and regional Pub of the Year 2022. Q⛄🕸️🍷👤♣♿P🖥️(106,107)🕸️📶🎵♫

Stanley's Cask ✓

212 Rake Lane, CH45 1JP

☎ (0151) 691 1093

Ossett White Rat; 4 changing beers (sourced nationally; often Purple Moose, Robinsons, Theakston) Ⓗ

This ever-popular friendly local continues to thrive, due in no small part to the landlady who has a track record of serving good beer. The guest ales on offer often include seasonal beers from regional breweries, and usually a beer from a local brewery. It hosts various sports teams, quiz nights and regular popular live music including rock, blues and folk. Local CAMRA Community Pub 2022. 🕸️♿♣🖥️(410,433)🕸️📶🎵

Newton-le-Willows

Firkin

65 High Street, WA12 9SL

☎ (01925) 225700 ⊕ thefirkin.co.uk

8 changing beers (sourced locally) Ⓗ

A former shop, this small, friendly establishment dispenses a selection of eight real ales, including at least one dark, all of which are sourced from micro/SIBA breweries. Small seating areas are to the front and the rear, with pictures of old Newton on the walls. Free from background noise, this is somewhere to engage in conversation with like-minded people, and to make new friends. Closed Monday to Wednesday; over-18s only. Q🚆♿🖥️(22,34)🕸️📶

Prescot

Bard 🅛

57 High Street, L34 6HF

5 changing beers (sourced locally) Ⓗ

A Shakespeare-inspired micropub in Prescot featuring quality real ales, craft beers, ciders, wine and artisan spirits. There is normally a selection of cask and keg beers from local breweries and interesting beers from further afield. A selection of board games are available for customers to enjoy. The pub is normally closed on Tuesday but does open if Prescot Cables FC have a home match. A quiz night takes place on a Wednesday. Q⛄♿♣♿🖥️(10)🕸️📶

Watch Maker 🅛 ✓

60 Eccleston Street, L34 5QL

☎ (0151) 432 7030

7 changing beers (often Peerless) Ⓗ

A Wetherspoon freehouse with a friendly welcome. Alongside the standard national ales there is a focus on local breweries, earning the pub LocAle accreditation. Prescot was one of the main centres for watchmaking during the 18th and 19th centuries, and the pub is decorated with elements of watchmaking memorabilia. It has a small outside area to the front of the building and often organises coach trips and other social activities. ⛄👤♿🚆🖥️(10)📶

Rainford

Star Inn 🅛

Church Road, WA11 8PX

☎ (01744) 882639 ⊕ starinnrainford.co.uk

7 changing beers (sourced locally; often Coach House) Ⓗ

Standing near the edge of Rainford village, the Star has a cosy, comfortable bar at the front of the building serving beers sourced from local breweries, with a large selection of wine and a range of spirits available. Meals are served every day except Monday and Tuesday in the restaurant to the rear. ⛄🕸️👤P🖥️

Rainhill

Skew Bridge Alehouse 🅛

5 Dane Court, L35 4LU

☎ (0151) 792 7906 ⊕ skewbridge.co.uk

6 changing beers (sourced nationally) Ⓗ

This micropub in the centre of Rainhill offers a selection of six high-quality cask ales, four real ciders and two craft lagers. Locally sourced ales are complemented by beers from all over the UK. A good range of gins and single malt whiskies are also stocked. With no TV or music to distract customers, conversation is very much encouraged. A wide selection of board games is available for use. Q⛄🕸️♿🚆♣♿P🖥️(10A,61)🕸️📶

St Helens

Cricketers Arms 🅛

64 Peter Street, WA10 2EB

☎ (01744) 361846

13 changing beers (sourced locally) Ⓗ

A former CAMRA National Pub of the Year, this family-run community establishment has 13 handpulls, real ciders and a range of spirits. An outside bar increases the number of handpulls on the first weekend of the month (Apr-Oct). Freshly prepared stonebaked pizzas and cheese boards are available. In 2020 the on-site Howzat brewery started producing their own house beers for this pub and others within the local area. ⛄🕸️👤♿P🖥️(10)🕸️📶

George 🅛

George Street, WA10 1BU

2 changing beers (sourced locally; often Wigan Brewhouse) Ⓗ

A short walk from the main train and bus stations is this small, friendly town-centre local. It primarily serves beers from Wigan Brewhouse, with a range of international beers also available, as well as a selection of gins and other spirits. A small beer garden is to the rear of the pub. The pub is popular on St Helens RLFC match days. ⛄🕸️🚆(Central)♣P🕸️

Turk's Head 🍷 🅛

49 Morley Street, WA10 2DQ

☎ (01744) 751289

14 changing beers Ⓗ

Attractive Tudor-style 1870s pub near the town centre. Real ales and ciders are on 14 handpulls, and there is a large whisky and gin bar. The upstairs Tower Lounge serves cocktails plus craft and continental beers, and hosts live music on Saturday evening. Quality home-made food is available every day. There is a large beer garden to the side and rear with an outside bar, and the adjacent Cowley Grill serves food from Wednesday to Sunday. Local CAMRA Pub of the Year.
🐴❀◐🍎🚌(32)🐾📶♫

Southport

Barrel House [L]

42 Liverpool Road, Birkdale, PR8 4AY
☎ (01704) 566601
2 changing beers (often Parker, Salopian, Southport) [H]
A former newsagents until 2014, when the opening of a large supermarket nearby prompted the owner to change his business, this micropub is an Aladdin's cave of wonderful bottled beers, wines, loose leaf teas and speciality coffees. It also sells two real ales on handpumps, usually featuring local breweries such as Southport and Parker. And you can still buy a daily newspaper here! Q🐴❀♿⇌(Birkdale)♣🚌(49)🐾📶

Fleetwood Hesketh Sports & Social Club [L]

Fylde Road, PR9 9XH
☎ (01704) 227968 🌐 fleetwoodhesketh.com
3 changing beers (often Southport) [H]
Excellent local club in the north end of town. It was founded in 1925 when the land was gifted by the Fleetwood Hesketh family to be used as a recreation ground. Shortly after, two ex-army huts were acquired and erected by volunteers, earning the club the nickname 'The Hut'. The club has its own cricket team and features many other sports such as indoor bowls. CAMRA Regional Club of the Year 2022.
🐴♿♣P🚌(44)📶♫

Guest House ✔

16 Union Street, PR9 0QE
☎ (01704) 537660 🌐 guesthouse-southport.blogspot.com
Ruddles Best Bitter; Theakston Best Bitter; house beer (by Caledonian); 4 changing beers (often Bank Top, Phoenix, Southport) [H]
Close to the station and Lord Street, this listed building has an impressive frontage and interior with three separate wood-panelled drinking areas. There are 11 handpumps, one of which serves beer from a local microbrewery. A wide range of malt whiskies is also available. This quiet, traditional pub attracts a mixed clientele. It hosts a quiz night on Thursday and acoustic folk club nights on the first and third Monday of each month. It has outside seating at the front and a courtyard area to the rear. Q❀◐⇌🚌📶

Masons Arms

4 Anchor Street, PR9 0UT
☎ (01704) 534123
Robinsons Dizzy Blonde; Titanic Plum Porter; 2 changing beers (sourced nationally) [H]
Small pub tucked away behind the town's former main post office and close to the railway station. The only Robinsons pub in Southport, it has new tenants who are keen on their real ale. Its roaring log fire makes it an ideal winter haunt. The interior has been revamped with wood-panelled walls ⇌🚌🐾

Sir Henry Segrave [L] ✔

93-97 Lord Street, PR8 1RH (on A565, S end of Lord St)
☎ (01704) 530217
Greene King Abbot; Phoenix Wobbly Bob; Ruddles Best Bitter; Sharp's Doom Bar; Wainwright; 6 changing beers (sourced regionally; often Peerless, Robinsons, Saltaire) [H]
Named after a former land speed world-record holder, who used to race on Southport flats, this is a spacious Wetherspoon pub with an attractive 19th-century exterior. The manager is a strong supporter of real ale and runs regular beer festival trips, as well as occasional Meet the Brewer evenings. The 12 handpumps offer the best all-round choice of microbrewery beers in Southport – regular orders are placed with Phoenix, Saltaire, Titanic and Hawkshead. There is outside seating on Lord Street.
Q🐴❀◐♿⇌🚌📶

Tap & Bottles

19A Cambridge Walk, PR8 1EN
☎ (01704) 544322
4 changing beers [H]
A micropub in the arcade between Chapel Street and Lord Street, next to the Atkinson Centre. It serves four real ales from a wide variety of producers, with a preference for north-west breweries. A huge range of bottles and cans is also offered, not all of them real ale. In the former next door unit is a cosy seating area with benches and tables. A limited beer tapas menu is served all day. Q🐴❀♿⇌♣🍎🚌🐾📶

Thornton Hough

Red Fox 🏆 [L]

Neston Road, CH64 7TL
☎ (0151) 353 2920 🌐 brunningandprice.co.uk/redfox
Brightside Odin Blonde; house beer (by Brightside); 7 changing beers (sourced locally; often Brimstage, Neptune, Weetwood) [H]
An impressive sandstone building dating from the 1860s, set in extensive grounds. Refurbished in 2014, it is now a smart gastro-pub. The front bar area retains a pub feel, with the restaurant areas to either side. At the rear is a terrace and large garden. Changing beers are usually from local microbreweries and the house beer by Brightside is Brunning & Price Original Bitter. Up to 10 ciders are also available. Local CAMRA Pub of the Year 2023. Q🐴❀◐♿🍎P🚌(487)🐾📶

Upton

Bow-Legged Beagle [L]

19 Arrowe Park Road, CH49 0UB
☎ 07739 032624
4 changing beers (sourced regionally; often Brimstage, Neptune, Ossett) [H]
A micropub opened in 2018 in a former bank on a busy row of shops near the centre of the village. The light, airy, one-room bar has a friendly ambience, with wood-panelled walls, a wood floor and basic furnishings. Some of the old bank safes have been retained at the back of the pub. This is the second of three Bow-Legged Beagle micropubs in Wirral. Q🐴🚌(16,437)🐾📶

Waterloo

Four Ashes [L]

23 Crosby Road North, L22 0LD
6 changing beers (often Neptune, Rock the Boat, Wily Fox) [H]
A family-run micropub owned by the Ashe family – hence the name. On the site of a former restaurant, it is a

great addition to the vibrant real ale scene in and around Waterloo station. Beers are ordered directly from local microbreweries or through a wholesaler, resulting in a varied and interesting selection, and almost always including at least one dark beer. Beers conditioning in the cellar are displayed on the wall. Q&≉♣●日员(53,47)☀

Old Tap

40 Crosby Road North, L22 4QQ
4 changing beers (sourced nationally; often Neptune) 🅷

Opened in 2022, this bar was converted from a former clothes shop. A lovely tiled entrance leads to a narrow, high-ceilinged bar area with a timber floor. Up to four cask beers are available, with a range of keg products from the UK and Europe. A variety of canned and bottled beers are also offered. It is conveniently located for frequent buses to and from the nearby Waterloo Merseyrail station. Not wheelchair accessible. ᏰᏜ◑≉●员(63,47)☀❀

Trap & Hatch

135 South Road, L22 0LT
☎ (0151) 928 5837
3 changing beers (sourced regionally) 🅷

A micropub on a busy suburban street, with a stylish and modern interior, low lighting and long tables. The bar has three handpulls and the pub goes out of its way to source interesting beers that are not often seen in this area. Real cider is also served, and there is a good range of bottled beers. Music is non intrusive so as to not distract from good conversation. There is also live music on Saturday evenings. ❀Ꮝ≉●员(47,53)☀❀♪

Waterpudlian 🅛

99 South Road, L22 0LR (diagonally opp Waterloo station)
☎ (0151) 280 0035
5 changing beers (sourced locally; often Brimstage, Oakham, Salopian) 🅷

Previously Stamps Too, this former local CAMRA Pub of the Year was the area's first accredited LocAle pub. The friendly, open-plan bar, where lively banter often prevails, is the haunt of both real ale enthusiasts and live music fans. Five handpumps serve mainly local beers, from Liverpool, Brimstage, and Southport breweries in particular, with occasional beers from further afield. A sixth handpump dispenses real cider. Bands and local musicians feature Thursday to Sunday. &≉●员(53,133)☀❀♪

West Kirby

West Kirby Tap 🅛

Grange Road, CH48 4DY
☎ (0151) 625 0350 ⊕ westkirbytap.co.uk
Spitting Feathers Session Beer, Thirstquencher; 7 changing beers (sourced regionally; often Black Lodge, Neptune, Spitting Feathers) 🅷

A smart, modern open-plan bar with plain wooden panelling, bare brick walls and a log-burning stove. Owned by Spitting Feathers brewery, it serves a wide range of beers, mainly from microbreweries, and one real cider. Food includes platters of cheese, fish, cold meats and vegan snacks; serving times vary so check with the pub first. Live music plays on Saturday night, during which the pub is usually very busy. Close to the shops and a short walk to the beach for those trekking to Hilbre Island, tides permitting. ᏰᏜ◑≉●员(38,407)☀❀♪

White Lion 🅛 ✅

51 Grange Road, CH48 4EE
☎ (0151) 625 9037 ⊕ whitelionwestkirby.co.uk
Brains Rev James Original; 5 changing beers (sourced locally; often Theakston) 🅷

A 200-year-old sandstone building close to the centre of West Kirby. The pub is a little quirky and laid out over several different levels with lots of cosy nooks to sit in, along with a real fire to keep you warm in winter. During warmer months you can enjoy the lovely beer garden to the rear. There is a quiz on Monday night. Food serving hours vary so check in advance. ᏰᏜ◑≉員♦❀♪

Whiston

Beer EnGin 🅛

9 Greenes Road, L35 3RE
☎ 07496 616132
6 changing beers 🅷

Set in a row of shops, this cosy, single-room microbar is a delight as soon as you walk in. It serves six real ales, plus craft beers, wines and a selection of unusual gins. A warm welcome is assured for all, including dogs. Check opening hours before visiting on bank holidays. Local CAMRA Pub of the Year 2022. Q᜶Ꮝ≉●P员(61)☀

Breweries

Ad Hop

18 Severs Street, Liverpool, L6 5HJ ☎ 07957 165501

Ad Hop started life in 2014 at the Clove Hitch pub, moving a couple of times before ending up in much larger premises in 2017 where a 5.5-barrel plant was added to its existing 2.5-barrel one. Brewing is currently suspended. ♦LIVE

Azvex

Unit 16, King Edward Rise, Gibraltar Row, Liverpool, L3 7HJ ⊕ azvexbrewing.com

Azvex Brewing Co is a Liverpool-based brewery producing modern progressive beer. No real ale. ♦

Beer Station

🍺 3 Victoria Buildings, Victoria Road, Formby, L37 7DB
☎ (01704) 807450

☺A small half-barrel plant set up in 2019 at the rear of the Beer Station micropub, opposite Freshfield station. The beers are railway-themed and generally only available in the Beer Station, but are occasionally seen elsewhere.

Big Bog SIBA

74 Venture Point West, Evans Road, Speke, L24 9PB
☎ (0151) 558 0290 ☎ 07867 792466
⊕ bigbog.co.uk

Big Bog started life in Waunfawr, Wales in 2011, sharing its site with the Snowdonia Parc brewpub. Due to growth and expansion in 2016, the brewery moved to its present location in Speke, Liverpool, into a custom-built plant with a 10-barrel brew length. The brewery has its own licenced taproom (open Fri). 🍺♦♦

Bog Standard Bitter (ABV 3.6%) BITTER
Mire (ABV 3.8%) BITTER
Pride of England (ABV 3.8%) BITTER
Blonde Bach (ABV 3.9%) GOLD
Hinkypunk (ABV 4.1%) GOLD

Full-flavoured golden ale, fruity (citrus) hoppy aromas, dry hoppy beer, slightly sweet with a little pepperyness and a satisfying bitter finish

Stog (ABV 4.1%) STOUT
Jack O Lantern (ABV 4.2%) BROWN
Welsh Pale Ale (ABV 4.2%) BITTER
Jester (ABV 4.3%) GOLD
Morast (ABV 4.3%) SPECIALITY
Billabong (ABV 4.4%) GOLD
Blueberry Hill Porter (ABV 4.5%) SPECIALITY
Swampy (ABV 4.7%) RED
Will O the Wisp (ABV 4.7%) GOLD
Peat Bog Porter (ABV 4.9%) SPECIALITY
Bayou (ABV 5%) PALE
Quagmire (ABV 6%) BROWN

Brewed under the Strawberry Fields Brewery brand name:
Lucy (ABV 4.5%) BITTER
A pale amber beer only a light earthy hop and caramel aroma, sweet malty flavours with bitter fruity (citrus) hop flavours and a light peppery hop finish.
Marmalade Skies (ABV 4.5%) STOUT
An oatmeal stout with rich roasted malt and caramel aromas with orange notes. Raisin and orange flavours with dry hop bitterness. A light hop pine finish.

Black Lodge

Kings Dock Street, Baltic Triangle, Liverpool, L1 8JU
☎ 07565 299879 ⊕ blacklodgebrewing.co.uk

Brewery producing experimental and speciality beers. Moved to current brewery in 2019 with ex-Mad Hatter brewery kit. Frequently brews specials and collaboration beers. Its cask beers are increasingly available in local pubs but only keg and tin from the taproom. ♦✦

Crash on the Hill (ABV 3.9%) PALE

Brimstage SIBA

Home Farm, Brimstage, CH63 6HY
☎ (0151) 342 1181 ⊕ brimstagebrewery.com

Neil Young began brewing in 2006 using a 10-barrel plant in the heart of the Wirral countryside. Wirral's first brewery since the closure of the Birkenhead Brewery in the late 1960s. Since Neil passed away in 2018, his two sons now own the brewery. Outlets are supplied across the Wirral, Merseyside, Cheshire and North Wales. ‼♦

Sandpiper Light Ale (ABV 3.6%) GOLD
Trapper's Hat Bitter (ABV 3.8%) BITTER
A nicely-balanced beer, strong malt aromas, sweet hoppy malt flavours and a smooth bitter finish.
Rhode Island Red (ABV 4%) RED
Red, smooth and well-balanced malty beer with a good dry aftertaste. Some fruitiness in the taste.
Elder Pale (ABV 4.1%) SPECIALITY
Scarecrow Bitter (ABV 4.2%) BITTER
This best bitter has a good balance of flavours, some bitterness and sweetness along with a little fruit, these flavours develop in the finish with increased hops.
Oyster Catcher Stout (ABV 4.4%) STOUT
Shed Day Session IPA (ABV 4.4%) PALE
IPA (ABV 6%) PALE

Brooks

17 Birkenhead Road, Hoylake, CH47 5AE
⊕ brooks-brewhouse.co.uk

Brewing started in 2017 at this nanobrewery, which predominately produces bottle-conditioned beers. **LIVE**

Cains

39 Stanhope Street, Cains Brewery Village, Liverpool, L8 5RE ⊕ cainsbrewery.co.uk

Cains is a 10-hectolitre microbrewery brewing a mix of keg and cask. Many of the beers are brewed to original Cains recipes, with a few new offerings from the three-man brew team. Brewing is currently suspended. ‼✦

Carnival

Unit 3, King Edward Industrial Estate, Gibraltar Row, Liverpool, L3 7HJ ⊕ carnivalbrewing.me

Brewery and taproom incorporated in 2017 and opened in 2019 by keen homebrewers Dominic Hope-Smith and Adrian Burke. Specialist styles are brewed and range from light through golden to dark beers. The brewery has a core range but also releases ad-hoc specials or collaborates with other local, national and international breweries to release further specials. Beer is available online, at a few outlets in Liverpool, and at beer festivals. Brewery tasting tours (Fri and Sat) can be booked on the website. ‼☰♦✦

Carmen (ABV 4%) GOLD
A light hazy straw with fruity peach/mango hop flavours, refreshing fruity citrus flavours balanced by sweetness and a dry fruity bitter bitter hop finish
A Lovely Pint of Best Beside the Fire (ABV 4.4%) BITTER

Flagship

Office: Ship & Mitre, 133 Dale Street, Liverpool, L2 2JH
☎ (0151) 236 0859 ⊕ theshipandmitre.com/brewery

☺Launched in 2016, the Ship & Mitre Brewing Co rebranded as Flagship Beer in 2017, and primarily supplies the iconic city centre pub, the Ship & Mitre, with some sales locally and nationally. Beers are brewed using spare capacity at other breweries. Brewing is currently suspended. ♦

Glen Affric

Unit 2 & 3, Lightbox, Knox Street, Birkenhead, CH41 5JG ☎ 07742 020275

Office: 53 Wood Street, Ashton-under-Lyne, OL6 7NB ⊕ glenaffricbrewery.com

⊠ Established in 2016, a small-batch brewery which began producing cask-conditioned beers in 2023 alongside its extensive keg range. Its tank farm allows for a flexible brew length. The brewery contract brews for other breweries. ‼☰

Handyman

⊟ 461 Smithdown Road, Liverpool, L15 3JL
☎ (0151) 722 7422
⊕ handyman-bar-and-brewery.myshopify.com

Handyman Brewery is based within the Handyman Supermarket. For years this was a hardware store but has now been refurbished into the Handyman Pub, which opened in 2017. Its 400-litre brew kit is situated on a mezzanine floor above the bar. ♦

Hex (NEW)

66a Eastbourne Road, Birkdale, Southport, PR8 4DU
⊕ hexbrewing.co.uk

Hex Brewery opened 2022. Brews classic-style, vegan beers for cask and bottle. **LIVE V**

Howzat

⚑ **Cricketers Arms, Peter Street, St Helens, WA10 2EB**
☎ **(01744) 758021**

A brewery in the grounds of the Cricketer's Arms – a former CAMRA National Pub of the Year.

Liverpool Brewing SIBA

39 Brasenose Road, Liverpool, L20 8HL
☎ **(0151) 933 9660**
⊕ **liverpoolbrewingcompany.com**

☺Liverpool Brewing Company was established in 2018. A 20-hectolitre Vince Johnson brewkit with a fermenting volume of 200-hectolitres is used with extensive cold storage capacity to produce a range of traditional and new-wave beers. In 2022 it opened two venues, one of which is Sanctuary on Lime Street, Liverpool. ‼🍴♦

Little IPA (ABV 3.6%) PALE
Dark Mode (ABV 3.7%) MILD
Cascade (ABV 3.8%) GOLD
A medium-bodied pale golden beer with honeyed flowery citrus hop aromas, dry bitter citrus hops flavours with a dry fruity bitter finish with some light pine.
Liverpool Pale Ale (ABV 4%) BLOND
Light fruity hop aromas, sweet bitter flavours with a light malty finish.
24 Carat Gold (ABV 4.1%) GOLD
A medium-bodied straw beer with hoppy citrus fruity (clementine) aromas, sweet fruity slightly-oneyed flavours and dry hop bitterness, dry fruity hop finish.
Bier Head (ABV 4.1%) BITTER
Light amber beer with malt/roast and hop aromas with light apple notes, bitter hop and roasted malt flavours with a light peppery hop finish.
Syren's Call (ABV 4.2%) BITTER
Tropical Pale (ABV 4.2%) PALE
Pudding Lane (ABV 4.4%) SPECIALITY
Liverpool Stout (ABV 4.7%) STOUT
A dark rich smooth stout with aromas of caramel, vanilla and light fruit, biscuity caramel, vanilla flavours with bitter coffee on tasting, lasting dry bitter roast and a light fruity finish.

Love Lane

⚑ **62-64 Bridgewater Street, Liverpool, L1 0AY**
☎ **(0151) 317 8215** ⊕ **lovelanebeer.com**

Established in 2017 in the Baltic Triangle area of Liverpool, the 30-barrel plant can be seen from the Love Lane Bar & Kitchen pub. Craft beers are produced under this name, some cask-conditioned beers are badged as Higsons. A small, one-barrel plant is used for a beer academy for guest brewers. These beers are then sold in the brewery tap on Tuesdays, cask and keg. ‼♦

Brewed under the Higsons brand name:
Pale (ABV 3.8%) BITTER
Best Bitter (ABV 4.2%) BLOND

Melwood

The Kennels, Knowsley Park, Knowsley, L34 4AQ
☎ **07545 265283** ⊕ **melwoodbeer.co.uk**

☺Melwood began brewing in 2013 using a five-barrel plant in an old dairy. In 2016 the brewery moved to bigger premises in nearby old kennels on the Earl of Derby's Knowsley Estate. In 2019 it rebranded to add a small range of core beers, a series of modern beers, one-off specials and began experimenting with new styles and yeasts. Brewing is currently suspended. ♦

Neptune SIBA

Unit A, Arnos House, Wakefield Road, Liverpool, L30 6TZ
☎ **(0151) 222 3908** ⊕ **neptunebrewery.com**

☺Neptune began brewing in 2015 and was originally based in Maghull but expansion in 2023 led to a move to the outskirts of Liverpool. The beers are unfined and unfiltered and mostly named on a theme deriving from fish, the sea and mythological creatures, in keeping with the name. 2023 also saw the opening of a licenced premises in Maghull.

Forecast (ABV 3.9%) BITTER
Ezili (ABV 4%) PALE
Sea of Dreams (ABV 4.2%) PALE
Shifting Sands (ABV 4.3%) PALE
Mosaic (ABV 4.5%) PALE
A light golden premium beer with fruit grapefruit and mango aromas, light malty sweetness, fruity flavours with dry hop bitterness and a light fruity finish.
Wooden Ships (ABV 4.7%) PALE
Abyss (ABV 5%) STOUT
Rich roasted fruity aroma, sweet fruity oatmeal stout with a dry roast finish.

Peerless SIBA

The Brewery, 8 Pool Street, Birkenhead, CH41 3NL
☎ **(0151) 647 7688** ⊕ **peerlessbrewing.co.uk**

Peerless began brewing in 2009 and is under the directorship of Steve Briscoe. Beers are sold through festivals, local pubs and the free trade. ‼♦◆

Pale (ABV 3.8%) PALE
Triple Blond (ABV 4%) BLOND
Skyline (ABV 4.2%) BITTER
Langton Spin (ABV 4.4%) GOLD
Oatmeal Stout (ABV 5%) STOUT
Knee-Buckler IPA (ABV 5.2%) PALE
Full Whack (ABV 6%) IPA

Rock the Boat SIBA

6 Little Crosby Village, Little Crosby, L23 4TS
☎ **(0151) 924 7936** ☎ **07727 959356**
⊕ **rocktheboatbrewery.co.uk**

Rock the Boat began brewing in 2015 in a converted 16th century wheelwright's workshop and old blacksmiths. All draught beers are cask-conditioned, bottled versions are bottle-conditioned, as the brewery does not use cold conditioning tanks. Beer names relate to local themes, often reflecting the brewer's musical tastes and local landmarks. The beers are increasingly available in central and north Lancashire. Specials are brewed for Market Town Taverns pubs in Liverpool and a green hop beer is produced each year. LIVE

Liverpool Light (ABV 3.4%) BLOND
Light hoppy aromas on this refreshing straw bitter with a delicate hop flavour and a dry bitter finish.
(Sittin' on) The Dock (ABV 3.5%) MILD
Rich chocolate malt aromas, with caramel roast flavours and light sweetness with a mellow caramel roast finish.
Bootle Bull (ABV 3.8%) BITTER
Yellow Submarine Special (ABV 3.9%) GOLD
Waterloo Sunset (ABV 4.2%) BITTER
Smooth, medium-bodied, copper beer with rich malt fruity (orange) aromas, sweet malt and caramel flavours fruity with light hop bitterness and a fruit and malt finish.
Fab Four Liverpool IPA (ABV 4.4%) BLOND
A medium-bodied straw beer with fruity hop aromas, sweet fruity flavours and dry hop bitterness, finishing with light hop bitterness.

Southport SIBA

Unit 3, Enterprise Business Park, Russell Road,
Southport, PR9 7RF ☎ 07748 387652
⊕ southportbrewery.co.uk

☺Southport Brewery was established in 2004 on a five-barrel plant. Outlets are supplied in Southport, North-West England and nationally. ♦

IPA (ABV 3.6%) PALE
Sandgrounder Bitter (ABV 3.8%) PALE
Dark Night (ABV 3.9%) MILD
Full-bodied mild with fruity malt aromas dominating, lasting roast bitterness and hop, lots of flavour for the strength.
Golden Sands (ABV 4%) GOLD

Stamps

St Mary's Complex, Waverley Street, Bootle, L20 4AP
☎ 07913 025319 ⊕ stampsbrewery.co.uk

☺Brewing began in 2012, with beers named after famous world postage stamps. The brewery moved to its current site in 2017. The beers can be found regularly in Stamps Bar, Crosby, the Lock & Quay, Bootle, and the Caledonia, and the Vernon Arms, Liverpool. Beers may appear with the Republic of Liverpool brand name. There are plans to build a new brewery and pub as part of a local regeneration project alongside the Leeds-Liverpool canal in Bootle. !! ⇥

Blond Moment (ABV 3.6%) GOLD
Flying Cloud (ABV 3.7%) BITTER
Ahtanum (ABV 3.9%) GOLD
First Class (ABV 3.9%) PALE
Mail Train (ABV 4.2%) BITTER
Inverted Jenny (ABV 4.6%) BITTER
Rum Porter (ABV 4.6%) PORTER

Cascade (ABV 5%) PALE
Penny Black (ABV 5.5%) PORTER

Team Toxic

✉ gazza@theteamtoxic.co.uk

Team Toxic, led by Gazza Prescott, is a commissioner of beers producing a range of sometimes eccentric, one-off brews as well as some core brands. Some beers appear under Gazza's own Mission Creep label. No isinglass is used in any of the beers, some of which are made in collaboration with other breweries. Gazza likes bitter, hoppy pale ales and experimenting with beer styles and ingredients often influenced by his travels. Brewing is currently suspended.

Top Rope SIBA

Unit 6, Lipton Close, Liverpool, L20 8PU ☎ 07581 483075 ⊕ topropebrewing.com

☺Top Rope commenced brewing on a small scale on Merseyside in 2016, and expanded in 2018 moving to Sandycroft industrial estate, Deeside, North Wales. Further expansion led to a return to its current location in Bootle, Liverpool in early 2021 that coincided with the opening of the taproom. Output is mainly keg, but the supply ratio is approximately 45% cask beers (often named on a wrestling theme). !! ⬦

Tyton

c/o Ship & Mitre, 133 Dale Street, Liverpool, L2 2JH
☎ 07487 598787 ✉ tytonbrewing@gmail.com

Brewer now works at Ship & Mitre, Liverpool and occasionally brews Tyton beer using brew kit used by Flagship. Brewing is suspended.

Cricketers Arms, St Helens (Photo: Stuart McMahon)

North East

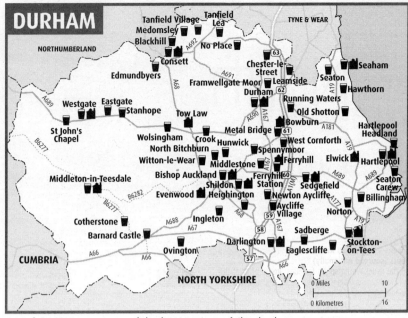

DURHAM

Co Durham incorporates part of the former county of Cleveland

Aycliffe Village

County
13 The Green, DL5 6LX
☎ (01325) 312273 ⊕ thecountyaycliffevillage.com
3 changing beers (sourced nationally) Ⓗ
Attractive, cream-coloured country free house overlooking the green in the picturesque village of Aycliffe. It was originally three 17th-century cottages but is now open plan with the bar and three dining areas unified by bright modern decor, complemented by older beams and log fireplaces. The current owners took over in 2020 and offer three guests and three craft beers alongside good food. There is accommodation in seven rooms. Q ⊛ ⇔ ⬧ P ☂

Barnard Castle

Old Well Inn Ⓛ ⦿
21 The Bank, DL12 8PH
☎ (01833) 690130 ⊕ theoldwellinn.co.uk
Timothy Taylor Golden Best, Landlord; house beer (by Mithril); 3 changing beers (sourced locally) Ⓗ
The boundary of this award-winning 17th-century town-centre inn incorporates part of the medieval castle wall. The pub has a cosy front bar and a comfortable lounge, a separate restaurant and an airy conservatory, plus an enclosed beer garden. At least five well-kept beers are available, including two guests from local micros and house beer Cummings & Goings from Mithril. Excellent food is served daily, including tasty authentic curries and Chinese. Accommodation is in seven en-suite rooms. Q ⊛ ⊛ ⇔ ⬧ ⬤ & ⬜ (75,76) ❀ ☂ ♪

Billingham

Billingham Catholic Club Ⓛ
37 Wolviston Road, TS23 2RU (on E side of old A19, just S of Roseberry Rd roundabout, next to bus stop)
☎ (01642) 901143 ⊕ catholicclub.co.uk
3 changing beers (sourced regionally) Ⓗ

Now in its 15th year of continuous Guide recognition, this Victorian mansion and former school is a friendly club, where actively supporting the local community comes high on the agenda. Dedicated volunteers ensure that the club's reputation for serving 150 different beers annually continues. Three beers are normally served, with eight others available throughout the popular bank holiday beer and music festivals. A previous local CAMRA Community Award winner and 2023 Club of the Year winner. ❀ & ♣ P ⬜ (35,36) ❀ ♪

Crafty Cock Ⓛ
113 Station Road, TS23 2RL (at the N end of Station Rd, close to the level crossing)
☎ (01642) 881478
3 changing beers (sourced locally) Ⓗ
This small, cosy bar was converted from a former restaurant and affords a warm welcome, with friendly and knowledgeable bar staff. It serves three beers, including offerings from local breweries, as well as an extensive gin menu. Third-pint tasting paddles are available. Mexican food is served Thursday to Saturday evenings, and Sunday lunches are also served, with a takeaway and a local delivery service available. The bar is renowned locally for its varied live bands. Quiz night is alternate Wednesdays. ◁ & P ⬜ (36,X10) ♪

Bishop Auckland

Bay Horse
38-40 Fore Bondgate, DL14 7PE (50yds N of the bus station)
☎ (01388) 609765 ⊕ dorbiere.co.uk/the-bay-horse
Maxim Double Maxim; Timothy Taylor Landlord; 1 changing beer (sourced nationally; often Anarchy, Wadworth) Ⓗ
There has been a pub on this site since 1530, and this lively, open-plan bar is a quiet relief from shopping during the week. With live music on Friday, speed quizzing on Thursday, and karaoke on Saturday, it becomes joyfully boisterous at the weekend, and is

popular for televised sport. It retains its roots as a long-established, proper pub, with pub games teams, and an open fire when needed. 🐕👶♿🚃🍴🛢🚪📶♪

Pollards 🅛

104 Etherley Lane, DL14 6TU (400yds W of the railway station)
☎ (01388) 603539
5 changing beers (sourced nationally; often Allendale, Consett, Marston's) Ⓗ
This comfortable and busy establishment is a great combination of traditional pub and pleasant diner, and is a 10-minute stroll from the town centre. Two of the four original areas, including the bar, boast open fires or log-burners, and there is a spacious restaurant to the rear where the famous Sunday carvery can be enjoyed. Five well-kept ales are augmented by good conversation.
Q🐕👶❄️◑👶🚃♣🅿🐕

Stanley Jefferson ✅

5 Market Place, DL14 7NJ
☎ (01388) 452830
Greene King Abbot; Ruddles Best Bitter; 6 changing beers (sourced nationally) Ⓗ
All the usual Wetherspoon facilities are on offer at this interesting conversion of former solicitors' offices. Several separate but linked drinking areas and a glass-roofed bar area provide the opportunity for privacy or company. Close to the Bishop of Durham's palace and park, the pub takes its name from local celebrity Stanley Jefferson —better known as Stan Laurel. There is a large walled garden to the rear and a small pavement patio to the front. Quiz night is Wednesday. 🐕❄️◑👶🚃

Blackhill

Scotch Arms 🅛 ✅

48 Derwent Street, DH8 8LZ
☎ (01207) 593709
3 changing beers (sourced nationally; often Big Lamp, Moorhouse's, Mordue) Ⓗ
A traditional community hostelry off the main street in Blackhill with a large L-shaped bar. The interior was freshened up to celebrate the licensee's 10-year anniversary in 2018. Up to three cask ales are on offer, always including local beers. This welcoming pub is home to pool and darts teams, a local football team, and is popular for sports TV. Charity nights and other live events often feature. Toasted sandwiches are available. 🐕◑♣🚃🐕📶♪

Chester-le-Street

Butchers Arms

Middle Chare, DH3 3QD (off Front St on left from Market Place)
☎ (0191) 388 3605
Marston's Pedigree; 3 changing beers (sourced nationally; often Ringwood, Wainwright, Wychwood) Ⓗ
A cosy pub acknowledged for the quality and quantity of its beers, selling at least four cask ales from the Marston's range. The pub is also noted for its food, with home-cooking a speciality. Sunday lunches are popular and good value. Teas and coffees are also served. Dogs are welcome and it is convenient for the railway station and all buses through the town. Quiz night is Tuesday.
Q🐕❄️◑👶🚃🚪(21,50) 🐕

Masonic Centre 🅛 ✅

Station Road, DH3 3DU
☎ (0191) 388 4905

Black Sheep Best Bitter; 4 changing beers (sourced nationally; often Cheviot, Marston's, Oakham) Ⓗ
Guests are more than welcome at the Masonic Centre just off Front Street in the heart of the town. As well as up to five changing real ales, you will also find one of the biggest selections of single malt whisky in the area. Sunday lunches and Friday fish suppers are popular. Local CAMRA Club of the Year 2020 and 2022.
🐕◑👶🚃🚪(21) 🐕📶

Wicket Gate 🅛 ✅

193 Front Street, DH3 3AX
☎ (0191) 387 2960
Greene King Abbot; Ruddles Best Bitter; 5 changing beers (sourced nationally) Ⓗ
This modern JD Wetherspoon pub reopened in 2020 after major refurbishment including a roof terrace. The name acknowledges the strong connection the town has with cricket, and various items of cricket memorabilia decorate the walls. the pub is close to the town club and the county club ground at the Riverside. It is roomy inside, with a single long bar championing local beers.
🐕❄️◑👶🚃♣🚪(21) 📶

Consett

Company Row 🅛 ✅

Victoria Road, DH8 5BQ
☎ (01207) 585600
Greene King Abbot; Ruddles Best Bitter; Sharp's Doom Bar; 3 changing beers (sourced nationally) Ⓗ
Modern pub named after the rows of houses built by the Derwent Iron Company for its workers; most of the buildings were demolished in the mid-1920s. This spacious and well-decorated Wetherspoon establishment is a real asset to Consett town centre. An excellent beer selection, including local ales, and good food make this social pub popular with a wide clientele of all ages.
🐕❄️◑👶♣🚪📶

Grey Horse 🍺 🅛 ✅

115 Sherburn Terrace, DH8 6NE (A692, then right along Sherburn Terrace)
☎ (01207) 502585 ⊕ consettaleworks.co.uk/the-grey-horse
Consett Steeltown, White Hot, Red Dust; 6 changing beers (sourced nationally) Ⓗ
Traditional pub dating back to 1848. The interior comprises a lounge and L-shaped bar, with a wood-beamed ceiling. Consett Ale Works brewery is located at the rear. Beer festivals are held twice a year, with a quiz

REAL ALE BREWERIES

Cameron s Hartlepool
Caps Off 🔨 Bishop Auckland
Castle Eden Seaham
Consett 🍺 Consett
Crafty Monkey Elwick
Crafty Pint 🍺 Darlington
Dark Sky Middleton-in-Teesdale (NEW)
Dionysiac Darlington
Durham 🔨 Bowburn
George Samuel 🔨 Shildon
Hill Island Durham
Hopper House Brew Farm 🔨 Sedgefield
Mad Scientist 🍺 Darlington
McColl's 🔨 Evenwood
North Pier Tow Law
Three Brothers 🔨 Stockton on Tees
Village Brewer Brew 22 🍺 Darlington
Weard'ALE 🍺 Westgate
Yard of Ale 🍺 Ferryhill

each Wednesday and open mic on Sunday. The coast-to-coast cycle route is close by. There is some bench seating outside at the front of the pub. A repeat local CAMRA Town Pub of the Year, including 2023. Q🕸♣🍴🍺🐾🛜♫

Cotherstone

Red Lion ⎣

Main Street, DL12 9QE
☎ 07871 650236 ⊕ theredlionhotel.blogspot.com
Yorkshire Dales Butter Tubs, Aysgarth Falls Ⓗ
An 18th-century Grade II-listed coaching inn, built in stone and set in an idyllic village. Simply furnished, this homely local with two open fires has changed little since the 1960s. There is no TV, jukebox or one-armed bandit, just good beer and conversation. Up to five real ciders are offered, including local cider producer Kemps. The venue is used by various local clubs, and the small garden is a suntrap. Children, dogs and clean boots are welcome. A former local CAMRA Community Pub of the Year.
🌳🕸♣🍴🖃(95) 🐾🛜

Crook

Horse Shoe ⎣ ✓

4 Church Street, DL15 9BG
☎ (01388) 744980
Greene King Abbot; Maxim Double Maxim; Ruddles Best Bitter; 5 changing beers (sourced nationally) Ⓗ
A busy and tastefully refurbished pub with four interlinked drinking areas making up the main part, and a pleasant sheltered patio to the side. There is the usual Wetherspoon acknowledgement of previous use, in this case a butcher's, in the metal bar top. Local history is reflected in the decor, with a surprise at the top of the stairs in the shape of old mining equipment.
🌳🕸◖🖃(X1,X46) 🛜

Darlington

Britannia ⎣ ✓

1 Archer Street, DL3 6LR (next to ring road W of town centre)
☎ (01325) 463787
Camerons Strongarm; 5 changing beers (sourced nationally) Ⓗ
Warm, friendly and popular local CAMRA award-winning inn – a bastion of cask beer since 1859. The pub retains much of the appearance and layout of the private house it once was. A comfortable traditional pub with a modestly enlarged bar and small parlour sitting either side of a central corridor. Listed for its historic associations, it was the birthplace of teetotal 19th-century publisher JM Dent. Four guest ales along with two regular ales (Camerons Strongarm and house beer Brit 163) are available. ♣P🐾🛜♫

Crafty Merlins Bottle Shop & Micropub

6 Bucktons Yard, DL3 7QL
☎ 07428 769106
3 changing beers (sourced nationally) Ⓗ
This one-man operation opened during the pandemic as a bottle shop for ordering online. The micropub has one room downstairs and one upstairs, as well as outside drinking in the yard. Up to three handpulls serve real ales, with an equal number of keg beers. The bar has a homely atmosphere with conversation very much to the fore, and could become the quirky real ale star of Darlington. Q🕸🐾🛜

Darlington Snooker Club ⎣

1 Corporation Road, DL3 6AE (corner of Northgate)
☎ (01325) 241388
4 changing beers (sourced nationally) Ⓗ
First-floor, family-run and family-oriented private snooker club which celebrated its centenary in 2015. A cosy, comfortable TV lounge is available for those not playing on one of the 10 top-quality snooker tables. Twice yearly the club plays host to a professional celebrity. Four guest beers are stocked from micros countrywide, and two beer festivals are held annually. Frequently voted CAMRA Regional Club of the Year, and a finalist for National Club in 2014, it welcomes CAMRA members on production of a membership card or copy of this Guide. Society of Preservation of Beers from the Wood North-East Club of the Year. 🌳◖≢

Half Moon ⎣

130 Northgate, DL1 1QS
☎ 07804 305175
7 changing beers (sourced nationally) Ⓗ
Old-school local pub just across the ring road from the town centre. It reopened in 2013 as a real ale pub following a long period of closure. It offers seven changing cask ales, including ones from micros unusual for the area, and occasional brews from their own Crafty Pint nanobrewery, as well as two ever-changing real ciders. It has a relaxed friendly atmosphere and welcomes dogs. There is a library section for borrowing and exchanging books. 🌳♣🐾🛜

House of Hop ⎣

4B Houndgate, DL1 5RL
4 changing beers (sourced nationally) Ⓗ
Smart, contemporary bar in the town centre's Imperial Quarter, with links to the local Three Brothers brewery. There are four ever-changing real ales, usually from across the North East and beyond. You can also find one of the widest ranges of craft keg beers in the town, plus ciders and cocktails. The pub also regularly features live music. Q🐾🛜♫

Number Twenty 2 ⎣ ✓

22 Coniscliffe Road, DL3 7RG
☎ (01325) 354590
Village White Boar, Bull, Old Raby; 7 changing beers (sourced nationally) Ⓗ
Town-centre ale house with a passion for cask beer and winner of many CAMRA awards. Ales are dispensed from up to 16 handpumps, including two real ciders and a stout or porter, along with 10 draught European beers. Huge curved windows, stained-glass panels and a high ceiling give the interior an airy, spacious feel. It is home to Village Brewer beers (including Zetland Pale), commissioned from Hambleton by the licensee. To the rear is the in-house nano distillery and microbrewery producing ale, gin and vodka. Sandwiches and snacks are available at lunchtime. Q🌳♿🛜

Old Yard Tapas Bar ⎣

98 Bondgate, DL3 7JY
☎ (01325) 467385 ⊕ tapasbar.co.uk
Bradfield Farmers Blonde; Fuller's London Pride; Timothy Taylor Landlord; 2 changing beers (sourced nationally) Ⓗ
An award-winning and interesting mix of a bar and Mediterranean taverna offering real ales alongside a fascinating blend of international wines and spirits in a friendly setting. Five guest beers from local micros and breweries countrywide are stocked, with an extra two sometimes available in a further room. Although this is a thriving restaurant, you are more than welcome to pop in for a beer and tapas. The pavement café very is

popular in good weather. Food is served lunchtime and evening Sunday to Friday and all day Saturday.
Q❄️🍴🍷🍺👶♿️🐾🐾📶

ORB Micropub ⓛ

28 Coniscliffe Road, DL3 7RG
☎ 07903 237246
6 changing beers (sourced nationally) Ⓗ

Darlington's first micropub, in a former beauty salon, provides the highest quality local real ales, craft beers and a large range of single malt whiskies. The friendly, knowledgeable staff serve six local real ales, 10 craft ales and two real ciders. With no TV or loud music, this is somewhere to relax and engage in conversation. ORB stands for Orchard Road Brewery. A former local CAMRA Pub of the Year. Q🐾

Quakerhouse Ⓨⓛ

2 Mechanics Yard, DL3 7QF (off High Row)
🌐 quakerhouse.co.uk
9 changing beers (sourced nationally) Ⓗ

Friendly and welcoming gem of a pub located in one of the town's historic Yards. A lively bar with nine handpulled guest beers from local and regional breweries and two changing real ciders. It is a popular live music venue, catering for all tastes, and entry is free. There is a music quiz on the first Tuesday of every month, when the pub opens late. Home to Mad Scientist microbrewery and Egor. Multiple winner of local CAMRA Town Pub of the Year and North-East Pub of the Year.
🍴♿️♣️🐾🐾📶🎵

Durham

Colpitts Hotel

Colpitts Terrace, DH1 4EG
☎ (0191) 386 9913
Samuel Smith Old Brewery Bitter Ⓗ

A refurbishment has given this late-Victorian, Grade II-listed pub a smart makeover, but it remains little changed from when it was first built. As with all Samuel Smith's pubs, the noise comes from the chatter of conversation rather than from music or TV. The unusual A-shaped building comprises a cosy snug, a pool room, and the main bar area partially divided by a fireplace. If you want to take a step back in time, this is the pub for you. Q❄️🍺♣️🍴

Dun Cow ⓛ ✅

37 Old Elvet, DH1 3HN
☎ (0191) 386 9219
Castle Eden Ale; Timothy Taylor Landlord; 1 changing beer (sourced nationally; often Castle Eden, Moorhouse's) Ⓗ

A Grade II-listed pub, parts of which date back to the 15th century. In 995AD Lindisfarne monks searching for a resting place for the body of St Cuthbert came across a milkmaid looking for her lost cow. She directed them to Dun Holm (Durham), and the pub is named after the historic animal. There is a small front snug with a larger lounge to the rear. An occasional guest beer is available. Q❄️♣️🍴(6,X12) 🐾📶

Half Moon Inn ✅

86 New Elvet, DH1 3AQ
☎ (0191) 374 1918 🌐 thehalfmooninndurham.co.uk
Draught Bass; Sharp's Doom Bar; 2 changing beers (sourced nationally; often St Austell, Timothy Taylor, Wainwright) Ⓗ

Popular city-centre pub, reputedly named after the crescent-shaped bar that runs through it. The decor throughout is traditional, featuring photos of the pub at the beginning of the 20th century. This friendly venue

with a relaxed atmosphere offers a good selection of ales. The large beer garden overlooks the river.
❄️♿️🍴(6) 🐾📶

Head of Steam ⓛ

3 Reform Place, DH1 4RZ (through archway from North Rd)
☎ (0191) 383 2173 🌐 theheadofsteam.co.uk
5 changing beers (sourced nationally; often Camerons, Leeds) Ⓗ

Vibrant pub with a continental feel, attracting beer lovers of all ages. As well as five real ales, it offers an extensive choice of draught and bottled beers from around the world. Tasting events are often held featuring a wide choice of ales and ciders. Excellent, good-value food is available and families are welcome during the day.
❄️🍴🍷♿️🚆🐾📶

Holy Grale

57 Crossgate, DH1 4PR
☎ (0191) 386 3851
Allendale Pennine Pale; 1 changing beer (sourced nationally) Ⓗ

A former board game café, this craft beer bar was opened in 2019 by the previous Landlord of the Old Elm Tree, just up the hill. A friendly open-plan venue with several keg taps and two handpulls, all serving an ever-changing range of good beer, alongside large fridges showcasing a range of bottles and cans. A vaulted basement is used for occasional live music.
❄️🚆🍴🐾🎵

Old Elm Tree Ⓨⓛ

12 Crossgate, DH1 4PS
☎ (0191) 386 4621
Timothy Taylor Landlord; 4 changing beers (sourced nationally; often Abbeydale, Consett, Cullercoats) Ⓗ

One of Durham's oldest inns, dating back to at least 1600. The interior comprises an L-shaped bar and a top room linked by stairs, and outside is a good-sized patio with heaters. The pub boasts a friendly atmosphere, attracting a mix of locals, students and visitors to the city. The pub hosts a Wednesday quiz (arrive early) and acoustic nights. Local CAMRA City Pub of the Year 2023.
❄️🐾🚆P🐾🐾🎵

Station House ⓛ

North Road, DH1 4SE
🌐 stationhousedurham.co.uk
4 changing beers (sourced nationally; often Fyne, Yorkshire Dales) Ⓗ/Ⓖ

An independent pub opened in 2015 by a couple who are passionate about real ale. It is friendly, with a back-to-basics approach and an emphasis on conversation, and serves a changing range of beer and cider. Handpumps have been installed, with gravity remaining an option. A dark beer is always available. A runner up in the national CAMRA Pub of the Year awards in 2022. Closed Mondays. Q❄️♿️🚆🐾🐾📶

Victoria Inn ★ ⓛ

86 Hallgarth Street, DH1 3AS
☎ (0191) 386 5269 🌐 victoriainn-durhamcity.co.uk
Big Lamp Bitter; 4 changing beers (sourced regionally; often Durham, Fyne) Ⓗ

This warm and welcoming Grade II-listed pub has remained almost unchanged since it was built in 1899, and has been in the same family for 40 years. It has a traditional, friendly atmosphere and the quaint decor, coal fires, cosy snug and genuine Victorian cash drawer help create an olde-world feel. No meals are served but toasties are available. The pub is popular with locals, students and visitors alike, and is a frequent local CAMRA

City Pub of the Year winner. The four star accommodation is in six en-suite rooms.
Q ☺ ⇆ ♣ ⊟ (6,PR2) ☙ 🛜

Waiting Room 🅛

Northbound Platform, Durham Railway Station, DH1 4RB
☎ (0191) 386 7773
Firebrick Pagan Queen; 1 changing beer (sourced locally; often Durham, Hadrian Border, Yard of Ale) ⛬
This attractive venue on Durham railway station's northbound platform is an interesting relaunch of the original 1872 Ladies' Waiting Room, out of use for many years other than as a storage facility. In keeping with the building's Grade II-listed status, the design is traditional, with Chesterfield-style seating, original floorboards and fireplaces, wood panelling and a dark-wood bar. Three handpumps showcase local beers. Q ❀ ᳘ ⇌ P ⊟ (40) ☙ 🛜

Woodman Inn

23 Gilesgate, DH1 1QW
☎ (0191) 697 5369 🌐 thewoodmaninndurham.co.uk
Timothy Taylor Landlord; 1 changing beer (sourced nationally; often Adnams, Maxim, Titanic) ⛬
Traditional pub just outside the city centre and very much a locals' favourite. It reopened in 2022 after a major refurbishment. It boasts arguably the city's best pub garden, which is a real suntrap in the summer. This pub is family- and dog-friendly and well worth a visit.
☺ ❀ ᳘ ♣ ⊟ ☙ 🛜 🎵

Eaglescliffe

Cleveland Bay

718 Yarm Road, TS16 0JE (jct of A67 and A135, N of Tees bridge)
☎ (01642) 780275 🌐 clevelandbay.co.uk
Timothy Taylor Landlord; Wainwright; 2 changing beers ⛬
This three-roomed locals' pub, now with extensive outdoor drinking facilities, has been under the proud stewardship of an enthusiastic licensee, with an enviable reputation for serving fine premium bitters for over 20 years. Third-pint glasses and tasting notes are available for the four handpumps. Their Blues at the Bay music evenings feature bands of national and international repute covering various genres. A free lunch is served on Sundays. A former local CAMRA Community Pub of the Year. Q ❀ ᳘ ♣ P ⊟ (7,17) ☙ 🛜 🎵

Eastgate

Cross Keys 🅛

A689, DL13 2HW (on the main road)
☎ (01388) 517234 🌐 crosskeyseastgate.co.uk
2 changing beers (sourced locally; often Allendale) ⛬
A proper family-run Weardale pub, popular with holidaymakers and locals, adjacent to the A689. The ancient 17th-century building has a pleasant interior with a lively, welcoming bar and a restaurant providing relaxed dining. Allendale brewery beers feature regularly, and there is a pleasant beer garden to the rear. Comfortable B&B accommodation is available for those wishing to explore the beautiful surrounding countryside.
Q ☺ ❀ ⇆ ◑ ⅄ ♣ P ⊟ (101) ☙

Edmundbyers

Derwent Arms

DH8 9NL (2 ½ miles W of A68)
☎ (01207) 255545 🌐 derwent-arms.co.uk

3 changing beers (sourced nationally; often Black Sheep, Cullercoats, Timothy Taylor) ⛬
Set in a lovely rural location close to Derwent reservoir. The three comfortable rooms are smartly furnished with roaring log fires in the winter months. Three handpumps dispense a wide range of local ales, and a full menu is offered all day featuring home-cooked food using local ingredients with a changing specials board. The pub is ideal for walkers. Accommodation is available for extending your stay to explore the area. Quiz night is Thursday. Q ☺ ❀ ⇆ ◑ ᳘ P ⊟ (773) ☙ 🛜

Ferryhill Station

Surtees Arms 🍺 🅛

Chilton Lane, DL17 0DH
☎ (01740) 655933 🌐 yardofalebrewery.com
Yard of Ale One Foot In The Yard; 4 changing beers (sourced locally; often Yard of Ale) ⛬
Traditional pub serving local and national ales and ciders as well as beers from the on-site Yard of Ale brewery. Annual beer festivals are held in the summer and at Halloween. Live music and charity nights are regular events. Lunches are served on Sunday only. A large function room is available. Local CAMRA Country Pub of the Year 2023 and a former regional Pub of the Year.
Q ☺ ❀ ◑ ⊟ ☙ 🛜 🎵

Framwellgate Moor

Fram Ferment 🅛

29B Front Street, DH1 5EE
🌐 framferment.co.uk
3 changing beers (sourced nationally; often Cullercoats, Durham, Fyne) ℗
A former NHS clinic converted to a bottle shop and taproom in 2019. Large fridges full of bottles and cans of both beer and cider line one wall. A large oak bar, believed to have previously been a Methodist pulpit, sits in front of a tiled tap wall, through which both the cask and keg beers are served. Seating options include a monks bench, cinema seats and pub stools, along with a couple of tables outside the front window.
☺ ❀ ᳘ ⇌ (Durham) ◐ ⊟ ☙ 🛜

Hartlepool

Anchor Tap Room & Bottle Shop 🅛

Stockton Street, TS24 7QS (on A689, in front of Camerons brewery)
☎ (01429) 868686 🌐 cameronsbrewery.com
Camerons Strongarm; 1 changing beer ⛬
When Camerons brewery discovered that it owned the adjacent derelict pub, its future was secured after it was converted into the brewery's visitor centre. Now in its 20th successful year, it has reverted to its original 1865 name and rebranded as a tap and bottle shop. Strongarm and the brewery's specials are always available, together with an array of limited edition and continental bottled beers. Located close to Stranton All Saints' Church, which is possibly of Saxon origin. ❀ ᳘ ⇌ P ⊟ (1,36) ☙

Hops & Cheese

9-11 Tower Street, TS24 7HH (100yds S of bus interchange/railway station)
☎ 07704 660417
3 changing beers ⛬
Run by an enthusiastic licensee, this unique, modern and original outlet represents a breath of fresh air. It combines beers and cider with top-class cheeses and charcuterie, served with all the trimmings, and available to take away if required. Comedy club, jazz and open mic

sessions, cheese/wine nights and vinyl nights are becoming more popular, and some events are pre-bookable/ticket only, making the pub occasionally off-limits to the passing visitor. ⏰❶Ⅰ♿≒🚆(1,36)🌸

Rat Race Ale House

Station Approach, Hartlepool Railway Station, TS24 7ED (on Platform 1)

☎ 07903 479378 ⊕ ratracealehouse.co.uk

4 changing beers (sourced nationally) Ⅱ

The second micropub in the country, now celebrating 14 years of continuous Guide recognition. It adheres to the original micropub norms: no lager; no spirits/alcopops; no TV/jukebox; no one-arm-bandit; even no bar! Since opening in 2009 more than 2,000 beers, sourced from over 500 different breweries, have been served direct to your table by the landlord himself. A porter or a stout is always available as well as two real ciders. A winner of multiple local CAMRA awards. Q♿≒♣●🚊(1,36)

Hartlepool Headland

Fisherman's Arms 🄻 ✅

Southgate, TS24 0JJ (on headland close to Fish Quay in Old Hartlepool)

☎ 07847 208599 ⊕ thefishhartlepool.co.uk

3 changing beers Ⅱ

The Fish, a local CAMRA multi-award winner, is a friendly, one-room locals' pub, recognised by the local council for its charitable support to the community. Now free of tie, it serves three changing beers. The pub's theme is 'keeping music alive', and it hosts well-supported open mic nights, with regular live music also featuring. A popular quiz is held on Sunday. There is no jukebox, TV, or one-armed-bandit. Two beer festivals, also with live music, are held annually. Winter opening hours may vary. Q🚽🚊(7)🌸🎵

Hawthorn

Stapylton Arms 🄻

Village Green, SR7 8SD

☎ (0191) 527 0778

3 changing beers (sourced regionally; often Allendale, Consett, Maxim) Ⅱ

Delightfully welcoming, locally owned village pub serving excellent food. It has two comfortable well-appointed rooms – one a bar and the other a lounge/restaurant. Three well-kept cask ales showcase the best of North-East breweries. The Monday quiz is well attended. This hidden-away pub is in an ideal location for walkers exploring the nearby Hawthorn Dene. Q⏰❶Ⅰ🅿🚊(22,23) 🌸🛜

Heighington

Bay Horse Inn ✅

28 West Green, DL5 6PE (5 mins from the A1 at jct 58 with A68)

☎ (01325) 312312 ⊕ bayhorseheighington.co.uk

Pennine Millie George; Timothy Taylor Landlord; 1 changing beer (sourced nationally) Ⅱ

Picturesque 300-year-old pub overlooking the award-winning village's large green. Its traditional interior with exposed beams and stone walls is partitioned into distinct drinking and dining areas, with a large restaurant extending from the lounge. Drinkers in the bar area can enjoy the good beer range in the evening. The pub steps away from traditional pub fare to offer a butcher's counter of meaty delights, cut and cooked to personal preference. ⏰❶Ⅰ♿🅿🚊

Hunwick

Joiners Arms

13 South View, DL15 0JW

☎ (01388) 417878 ⊕ thejoinersarmshunwick.co.uk

3 changing beers (sourced nationally; often Timothy Taylor) Ⅱ

Family-run village local with a welcoming bar, restaurant, tiny snug and covered yard/pool room. The bar is the place for proper conversation, along with three handpumps featuring a changing selection. Quality locally sourced food is served Wednesday to Saturday evenings, and daily at lunchtimes in the restaurant. There are picnic tables to the front. ⏰❶♣🅿🚊(108,109) 🛜

Ingleton

Black Horse 🄻

Front Street, DL2 3HS

☎ (01325) 730374

4 changing beers (sourced locally) Ⅱ

Free house and restaurant set back from the road in a picturesque village. This is a popular community hostelry with a relaxed atmosphere, and a friendly bar runs into the dining area. Four guest ales come from local micros within a 30-mile radius. Excellent Italian food is served in the restaurant Wednesday to Sunday. The pub hosts the local darts team and a weekly Sunday night quiz. It has a large car park. Q⏰❶♿♣🅿🚊(84)🌸🛜

Leamside

Three Horseshoes 🄻

Pit House Lane, DH4 6QQ (about ½ mile N of A690, just outside West Rainton)

☎ (0191) 584 2394 ⊕ threehorseshoesleamside.co.uk

Timothy Taylor Landlord; 5 changing beers (sourced nationally) Ⅱ

A country pub with an excellent restaurant, the Back Room (booking advisable). The traditional bar has open fires in winter and a large TV for sport. Five real ales are served. The pub is home to a local cycling club and hosts a quiz on Sunday evening. Local CAMRA Country Pub of the Year runner-up in 2023, and a former winner. Q⏰❶Ⅰ♿🅿🌸🛜

Medomsley

Royal Oak 🄻

7 Manor Road, DH8 6QN

☎ (01207) 560336

Hadrian Border Tyneside Blonde; Mordue Workie; 1 changing beer (sourced nationally; often Consett, Hadrian Border) Ⅱ

Traditional country-style pub with a warm, welcoming feel. It has a large bar with a selection of seating including soft sofas and leather chairs, and plenty of dining space. The pub serves a rotation of quality beers as well as good food. There is a large, attractive rear garden and ample parking to the front. Q⏰❶Ⅰ♿🅿🚊🌸🛜

Metal Bridge

Old Mill 🄻

Thinford Road, DH6 5NX (off A1M jct 61, follow signs on A177)

☎ (01740) 652928 ⊕ oldmilldurham.co.uk

4 changing beers (sourced nationally; often Bowland, Durham, Rudgate) Ⅱ

Originally an 1813 paper mill , the pub offers good-quality food and well-kept ales. Four handpumps serve a diverse range, with local breweries supplying at least one of the beers. The food menu is extensive, with daily specials written on a board above the bar. Larger groups are welcome in the conservatory. Accommodation is of a high standard, with all rooms en-suite.
Q ✤ ❀ ★ ◑ ⬧ & P ⊟ (56) ☗

Middlestone

Ship Inn L

Low Road, DL14 8AB (between Coundon and Kirk Merrington)
☎ (01388) 810904
4 changing beers (sourced nationally; often Caps Off, Consett, Maxim) Ⓗ
Regular drinkers come from far and wide to the Ship. It has a bar divided into three distinct areas with an open fire, and a large function room upstairs which is the location for occasional beer festivals. The rooftop patio has spectacular views. Various pieces of Vaux memorabilia are on display – one of the many subjects of conversation. A former local CAMRA Country Pub of the Year. Q ✤ ❀ ◑ & ♣ P ⊟ (56) ☀

Middleton-in-Teesdale

Teesdale Hotel L ✓

Market Place, DL12 0QG
☎ (01833) 640264 ⊕ teesdalehotel.co.uk
Black Sheep Best Bitter; 2 changing beers (sourced nationally) Ⓗ
A former coaching inn updated to provide excellent accommodation. This is a popular village local as well as a resting place for Pennine walkers (Middleton in Teesdale is often referred to as 'the capital of Upper Teesdale', with High Force and Cauldron Snout nearby). Up to two guest beers, often from local micros, are served. Meals can be enjoyed in the main bar or the comfortable restaurant. A farmers' market is held on the last Sunday of the month. Q ✤ ❀ ◑ Å P ⊟ ⊟ (95,96) ☀

Newton Aycliffe

Turbinia L

Parsons Centre, Sid Chaplin Drive, DL5 7PA (off Burnhill Way, next to Methodist church)
☎ (01325) 313034 ⊕ turbiniapub.co.uk
4 changing beers (sourced nationally; often Mithril, Three Brothers) Ⓗ
Named after the famous Tyneside ship, this friendly free house comprises a large lounge and function room with traditional pub decor, featuring a pictorial history of the Turbinia, and a woodchip fire. This local favourite serves an ever-changing variety of beers sourced locally and nationally, as well as craft gins. It hosts its own beer and cider festivals. Darts, dominoes and pool are played in the main bar during the week, and live music at the weekend. A former local CAMRA Pub of the Season. Dogs are welcome. ❀ ❀ & ♣ P ⊟ (7) ☀ ☗ ♪

No Place

Beamish Mary Inn L

DH9 0QH (follow signs to No Place off A693 from Chester-le-Street to Stanley)
☎ (0191) 392 0543 ⊕ beamish-mary-inn.co.uk
4 changing beers (sourced nationally; often Big Lamp, Consett, Great North Eastern) Ⓗ
Characterful pub renowned for its warm welcome, generously portioned pub grub and ample selection of

well-kept real ales. The location is handy for visitors to the famous open-air Beamish Museum nearby. Consett Ale Works and Great North Eastern beers are usually included among the range of LocAles on offer. Accommodation is available, including twin, double and family rooms. A former CAMRA National Pub of the Year. ❀ ❀ ❀ ◑ ⬧ & P ⊟ (8,8A) ☀ ☗

North Bitchburn

Red Lion

North Bitchburn Terrace, DL15 8AL (½ mile up the hill from A689 in Howden le Wear)
☎ (01388) 767071
3 changing beers (sourced nationally; often Black Sheep, Great North Eastern, Timothy Taylor) Ⓗ
High above the Wear Valley, the exterior of this old building belies its clean-cut, spacious interior. A local village pub, it is famous for top-quality ale, and the guest beers change regularly. A bright and comfortable bar area has a pool table, and there is a patio area to the rear of the building with views over the rooftops.
Q ✤ ❀ ♣ P ⊟ (1B,X1)

Norton

Highland Laddie ✓

59 High Street, TS20 1AQ
☎ (01642) 539570
Greene King Abbot; Ruddles Best Bitter; Sharp's Doom Bar; 7 changing beers Ⓗ
Named after the Scottish drovers who herded livestock to cattle markets as far south as London. During the Wetherspoon's conversion, the pub was significantly extended and now comprises two large open-plan areas, with the original snug retained. It boasts an excellent choice of seven guests, as well as the chain's contracted beers. There is also a patio for those wishing to brave the north-easterlies. Served by both local and express regional bus links. ❀ ❀ ◑ & ⬧ ⊟ (X7,X10) ☗

Old Shotton

Royal George

The Village, SR8 2ND
☎ (0191) 586 6500 ⊕ royalgeorgeoldshotton.co.uk
Timothy Taylor Landlord; 2 changing beers (sourced nationally; often Great North Eastern, Harviestoun, Rooster's) Ⓗ
Pub and restaurant situated on the old village green, reopened after a major refurbishment of a virtually derelict establishment in 2014 when the bar was reinstated. There is a separate larger lounge and restaurant area, as well as two bookable private dining rooms. Traditional pub grub and bar snacks are available. It is dog friendly, with complimentary treats available at the bar. Q ✤ ❀ ◑ P ⊟ (24) ☀ ☗

Ovington

Four Alls L

The Green, DL11 7BP (2 miles S of Winston & A67)
☎ (01833) 627302 ⊕ thefouralls-ovington.co.uk
Mithril Kingdom of Ovingtonia; 2 changing beers (sourced locally) Ⓗ
Friendly, stone-built 18th-century inn opposite the village green in what is known as the 'maypole village'. A Victorian sign denotes the four alls: 'I govern all (queen), I fight for all (soldier), I pray for all (parson), I pay for all (farmer).' The single-roomed interior has an 'upstairs' snug serving excellent, good-value food. Real ales include a dark and a light from local Mithril Ales, and

special house beer Kingdom of Ovingtonia. The rear beer garden is perfect on sunny days. A former local CAMRA Country Pub of the Year. Q ♿ ❀ ⏶⬤ ⅃ & ♣ P ✿ 🛜

Running Waters

Three Horse Shoes L

Sherburn House, DH1 2SR

☎ (0191) 372 0286 ⊕ threehorseshoesdurham.co.uk

2 changing beers (sourced nationally; often Consett, Durham, Yard of Ale) Ⓗ

Country inn nicely situated a few miles from Durham city, offering good food and drink plus comfortable accommodation. Two cask ales are served, usually at least one sourced locally, with alcohol available from noon. The interior was extensively refurbished in 2016, while the rear beer garden provides excellent views over open countryside. Q ♿ ❀ ⏶ ⅃⬤ & P 🛜

Sadberge

Buck Inn L

Middleton Road, DL2 1RR

☎ (01325) 335710

Maxim Samson; Mithril A66 Ⓗ

Friendly, traditional English pub overlooking the village green. Named after George Buck, a benevolent 18th-century landowner. It has two bars, one mainly for dining, and there are outdoor benches and tables in front. It is a supporter of local micros and always has one beer from Mithril. A variety of good food is served at lunchtimes and evenings (look out for their parmos). They have a monthly quiz and regular live music and race nights. The village sits atop a hill and is in a popular walking area. ♿ ❀ ⏶⬤ & P ➟ (20) 🛜

St John's Chapel

Blue Bell Inn L ✅

Hood Street, DL13 1QJ

☎ (01388) 537256 ⊕ thebluebellinn.pub

2 changing beers (sourced regionally; often Allendale, Consett, Firebrick) Ⓗ

Originally a pair of terraced cottages, the Blue Bell is a friendly and cosy pub with a bar across the front of the building leading to a small pool room, and a garden to the rear. Situated on the A689, it serves the local community and those who holiday in Upper Weardale. It is popular for pub games and also lends out books. Q ♿ ❀ ♣ ⅃ ➟ (101) ✿ 🛜

Seaham

Coalhouse L

39 Church Street, SR7 7EJ

☎ (0191) 581 6235

4 changing beers (sourced locally; often Cullercoats, Great North Eastern, Yard of Ale) Ⓗ

A former bookmakers' and now a much-valued part of Seaham's licensed trade. The pub was refurbished in 2018 using 100-year-old timbers salvaged from the town's demolished Co-op building. The decor celebrates the area's coal mining heritage, notably an impressive mural depicting Seaham pits. Four changing cask beers are offered along with five keg taps. ❀ ≠ ♣ ➟ (65,60) ✿ ♬

Hat & Feathers L ✅

57-59 Church Street, SR7 7HF

☎ (0191) 513 3040

Greene King Abbot; Sharp's Doom Bar; 4 changing beers (sourced nationally; often Maxim) Ⓗ

This Wetherspoon pub gets its name from the Doggarts store that occupied the site from the 1920s to the 1980s and had a department selling hats and feathers. Upstairs are old photographs depicting the headgear of the best-dressed ladies of the time. Other interesting pictures show the past history of Seaham. The furnishings are a mix of modern and traditional styles, including comfortable settees. Outside is a plaque displaying a history of the building. ♿ ❀ ⏶⬤ & ♣ ➟ 🛜

Seaton

Dun Cow L

The Village, SR7 0NA

☎ (0191) 513 1133

4 changing beers (sourced nationally; often Maxim, Jennings, Wainwright) Ⓗ

Friendly and unspoilt inn on the village green, featuring a public bar and lounge areas. This is a pub for good conversation or a game of darts; the TV is only used for special events. The changing guest beer selection usually comprises two light and two dark ales. No meals are served but toasties are always available. The pub hosts regular busker and acoustic music nights. A former local CAMRA Country Pub of the Year. ♿ ❀ & ♣ P ➟ (71) ✿ 🛜 ♬

Seaton Carew

9 Anchors

2 The Front, TS25 1BS (on sea front at jct with Station Ln)

☎ (01429) 598969

2 changing beers (sourced regionally) Ⓗ

This former flower shop, converted into a micropub in 2017, is now the pub of choice for the discerning drinker in this resort town. It is named after the rescue of nine crewmen from the Danish schooner Doris that sank off the coast in 1930. The friendly locals, sandstone walls, furniture made from driftwood and a bar constructed from a Welsh dresser all add to the ambience. Quiz night is Wednesday, while acoustic night is Thursday. There are views of the petrified forest at low tide. Q & ➟ (1) ✿ 🛜 ♬

Sedgefield

Dun Cow

43 Front Street, TS21 3AT

☎ (01740) 620894

Black Sheep Best Bitter; Timothy Taylor Knowle Spring; 1 changing beer (sourced nationally) Ⓗ

Run by the same landlord for over 40 years, this large and comfortable 18th-century inn has a county-wide reputation for good food using locally sourced produce. Prime minister Tony Blair and US president George W Bush famously had lunch here in 2003. There are three bars, including a farmers' bar-cum-snug, and restaurant. Three real ales are always available. Q ♿ ❀ ⏶⬤ P ➟ (X12) ✿ 🛜

Pickled Parson L

1 The Square, TS21 2AB

☎ (01740) 213131 ⊕ thepickledparson.co.uk

3 changing beers (sourced locally) Ⓗ

Formerly the Crosshill Hotel, it reopened in 2017 after a major refurbishment. It is named after the legendary village rector who died suddenly and whose wife had him preserved in salt so that she could fool his tenants into thinking he was still alive and so collect their rent. It offers food and drink, including cask ales, coffee, cakes and late meals. There are tables outside overlooking the village green. ♿ ❀ ⏶⬤ P ➟ (X12) ✿ 🛜

Shildon

Canteen Bar & Kitchen 🅛
Norland House, Byerley Road, DL4 1HE
⊕ canteen-bar-kitchen.co.uk
George Samuel Locomotion No 1, Leaves on the Line,
Harvey; 1 changing beer (sourced nationally; often
George Samuel) 🅗
An ambitious conversion of the former canteen of the
famous Shildon Wagon Works. The bar and brewery
share a single space, and an entrance with other
businesses in the building. There is a spacious drinking
area with picnic-style tables, where you can sit within
feet of the brewing vessels. The railway heritage is
reflected in the decor. Open for breakfast.
Q◐🕭♿≉P🍴(X1) ♪

Spennymoor

Frog & Ferret
Coulson Street, DL16 7RS
☎ (0191) 389 7246
6 changing beers (sourced nationally; often
Camerons, Consett, Hadrian Border) 🅗
Friendly family-run free house offering up to six
constantly changing real ales, sourced from far and wide,
with local and northern microbreweries well
represented. The comfortably furnished lounge has a bar
with brick, stone and wood cladding and a solid fuel
burner. Sports TV is featured and children are welcome
until 9pm. Live music is hosted each Saturday night and
monthly on Thursday and Sunday. 🍴❀◐🕭♣❀🛜♪

Grand Electric Hall 🅛 ✓
Cheapside, DL16 6DJ
☎ (01388) 825470
Greene King Abbot; Ruddles Best Bitter; Sharp's
Doom Bar; 3 changing beers (sourced nationally;
often Daleside, Maxim) 🅗
Formerly a cinema and bingo hall in the centre of town,
this bright and airy Wetherspoon conversion features
film-themed decor and fittings. It has a spacious main
area with a high ceiling and a smaller room on a lower
level. The large patio drinking area to the front is a
suntrap in summer. Alcoholic drinks are served from
9am. 🍴❀◐♿🖶(6,X21)🛜

Little Tap 🅛
King Street, DL16 6QQ
☎ (01388) 304001
5 changing beers (sourced regionally; often Daleside,
Durham) 🅗
Clever remodelling of a former sandwich shop as a smart
little bar. The plush carpet makes it unusually
comfortable for a micropub. The 'cellar' is very close to
the pumps – beer is housed in cleverly converted fridges
directly beneath the bar. Outside is a small yard in which
to take advantage of any sunshine. Handily located next
door to a Chinese takeaway. Q❀♿🖶❀

Stanhope

Grey Bull
17 West Terrace, DL13 2PB
☎ 07885 676575
3 changing beers (sourced nationally) 🅗
A community-focused hostelry with a warm welcome, at
the foot of Crawleyside Bank at the west end of town. It
has a busy bar area across the front and a lounge to the
rear with pool table, served by a central bar that
dispenses three cask beers. Tables to the front are
popular in fine weather. Convenient for the coast-to-
coast cycle route. Q❀🚆♣🖶(101)❀🛜

Stockton-on-Tees

Golden Smog 🍺
1 Hambletonian Yard, TS18 1DS (in a ginnel between
the High St and West Row)
☎ (01642) 385022
5 changing beers 🅗
The town's original micropub, this local CAMRA Pub of
the Year 2023, and a previous Regional Pub of the Year,
is named after the environmental conditions that used to
prevail on Teesside. Five beers, real ciders and a range of
craft beers are served alongside an impressive selection
of Belgian/German beers, all served in their own
matching glasses. Third-pints, served on bespoke Smog
tasting tables, are also available. An extensive selection
of free bar snacks are served on Sunday. The pub
supports various charitable causes. Q👄🖶❀

Hope & Union 🅛
9-10 Silver Court, TS18 1SL (E of High St, through a
ginnel off Silver St)
☎ (01642) 385022
4 changing beers 🅗
A bright, modern pub, tucked away in a quiet square in
the town's cultural quarter. 'Hope' was Robert
Stephenson's second locomotive and 'Union' was a
horse-drawn coach, both operated by world's first
passenger railway, the Stockton and Darlington. This
contemporary pub serves four interesting beers and a
large selection of craft ales, gins and whiskies. The cellar
is on open display, as is the kitchen, from where locally
sourced, freshly cooked and good-value dishes are
served all day, every day. ◑🖶

Kopper Keg
27 Dovecot Street, TS18 1LH (just off High St in centre of
town)
☎ 07984 624872
2 changing beers (sourced nationally) 🅗
A single-room micro run by an enthusiastic licensee, with
two handpulls and a wide range of craft beers, bottles
and cans. The real ale is always fresh (cask rarely lasts
more than a couple of days). Refectory-style tables add
to the environment, while two large screens, one at
either end, feature sport and music. The bar's Facebook
page keeps drinkers updated on which beers are
available. ♿🅰≉(Stockton)♣🖶❀🛜

Thomas Sheraton 🅛 ✓
4 Bridge Road, TS18 3BW (at S end of High St)
☎ (01642) 606134
Greene King IPA, Abbot; Sharp's Doom Bar; 4
changing beers 🅗
This Grade II-listed Victorian building, now in its 16th year
in the Guide, is a fine Wetherspoon's conversion of the
law courts and named after one of the country's great
Georgian cabinet makers, born in the town in 1751. The
large, airy interior comprises several separate drinking
and dining areas, together with a pleasant balcony and
an upstairs outdoor terrace. The guest beers, usually
local, are served alongside the chain's contracted beers,
together with a range of real ciders.
Q🍴❀◐♿≉(Thornaby) ♣👄🖶🛜

Tipsy Turtle 🅛
5 Regency West Mall, West Row, TS18 1EF (100yds W
of High St through any of the wynds)
☎ (01642) 670171
4 changing beers 🅗
Popular micropub in a mall containing several other
licensed outlets, and now established on the town's
micropub circuit. Four handpulls include at least one
serving a rarer beer style, while a wide selection of craft

beers, a dozen or more real and fruit ciders, and an interesting selection of bottled continental beers are also available. When busy, drinkers overflow into the mall, while at weekends the pub expands into the adjacent premises. Q♿🐕♿≷(Stockton)♣🚪😋🛜♪

Wasp's Nest 🅛
Wasps Nest Yard, 1 Calvert's Square, TS18 1TB (E of High St, through a ginnel off Silver St)
☎ 07789 277364
3 changing beers 🅗
Tucked away in a quiet square in the town's cultural quarter, between the Grade II-listed Georgian Theatre and the River Tees, the Wasps is firmly established in the town's social life. It is a modern, contemporary and lively pub, where three handpulls serve a selection of locally sourced beers, together with an extensive range of craft beers. Third-pint bats are also available. The pub's claim to fame is that it has the town's only outdoor patio drinking area. Q🌼♿🚪😋

Tanfield Lea

Tanfield Lea Working Men's Club
West Street, DH9 9NA
☎ (01207) 238783
2 changing beers (sourced nationally) 🅗
The village has no pub, reflecting its strong Methodist history, but guests are most welcome in this CIU-affiliated club, which has become something of a flagship for real ale in the area after a diet of keg beer for many years. TV sport is shown in the bar and there is a quiet, comfortable lounge. Traditional club activities such as bingo take place and there is usually a live act on Sunday. Three-time former local CAMRA Club of the Year. ♿♿♣P🚪≷♪

Tanfield Village

Peacock
Front Street, DH9 9PX
☎ (01207) 232720
Black Sheep Best Bitter; 1 changing beer (sourced nationally; often Purity, Timothy Taylor) 🅗
A warm welcome is guaranteed in this friendly, traditional, two-bar pub in a pretty village. The Peacock is popular with locals and visitors alike, including bell-ringers from the church opposite. Black Sheep is always available, alongside a changing guest beer. Lovely home-cooked meals are served Wednesday to Saturday evenings and Sunday lunchtime – the portions are generous and great value for money. There is a small beer garden and ample parking. Q♿🌼🍴♣P🚪(V8)♪

West Cornforth

Square & Compass
7 The Green, DL17 9JQ (off Coxhoe to W Cornforth road)
2 changing beers (sourced nationally; often Sharp's, Wadworth) 🅗
A proper drinking pub and friendly local on the village green in the old part of Doggy (the village's local nickname). It has sold real ale for more than 40 years. The pub is home to chess, darts and dominoes clubs and hosts a well-attended Thursday night quiz. There are good views towards the Wear Valley and Durham city. Q♿♣P🚪(56)😋♪

Westgate

Hare & Hounds 🅛
24 Front Street, DL13 1RX

☎ (01388) 517212
Weard'ALE Gold, Dark Nights; 2 changing beers (sourced nationally) 🅗
On the banks of the Wear, on the A689. The spacious stone-flagged bar is partially fitted out with items salvaged from the former village chapel, and is a great place to catch up on local news. The restaurant's patio overlooks the river; here the beer is being brewed beneath your feet. Food, including the famous Sunday carvery, is locally sourced. Q♿🐕♿♣♿P🚪(101)

Witton-le-Wear

Dun Cow
19 High Street, DL14 0AY
☎ (01388) 488294
2 changing beers (sourced nationally; often Timothy Taylor) 🅗
A welcoming local set back from the road through the village, with a single L-shaped room warmed by open fires at both ends. Dating from 1799, the bar is guarded by a sleeping fox. There are benches to the left of the bar, and seating outside offering pleasant views over the Wear valley. The decor includes the unique Weardale Hare. Q🌼♿♣P

Victoria 🅛
School Street, DL14 0AS
☎ (01388) 488058 🌐 thevicwlw.co.uk
3 changing beers (sourced regionally; often Allendale, Great North Eastern, Maxim) 🅗
Traditional village pub with a central bar serving two distinct drinking areas, the larger of which is split-level. The bright interior has clean lines and pleasant decor. The pub has great views over Wear Valley from the patio to the rear, and of the church to the front. There is a wood-fired pizza oven in the garden. It is close to the preserved Wear Valley Railway. B&B accommodation is available. 🌼🛏️♦P😋≷

Wolsingham

Black Lion 🅛
21 Meadhope Street, DL13 3EN (50yds N of Market Place)
☎ (01388) 527772
3 changing beers (sourced nationally) 🅗
Hidden away only a minute from the Market Place, this welcoming, comfortable gem is a great spot to relax. There is an open fire in the single, open-plan room, with a pool table to the rear and a TV showing sport to the front. Local charities benefit from the efforts of the pub. Opening hours may be longer in summer but it is best to check in advance if travelling. Q🌼♿♣🚪(101)😋≷

Breweries

Camerons
Lion Brewery, Stranton, Hartlepool, TS24 7QS
☎ (01429) 852000 🌐 cameronsbrewery.com

☺Camerons was founded in 1865, and is a family-owned business. Brewing is done by various team members, from office staff to brewery staff. A range of cask ales in association with the RNLI is produced throughout the year. A number of limited-run ales are produced through its Tooth & Claw pilot brewery. It also has a pub estate of more than 70 pubs, including the Head of Steam pubs. ‼🚚♦

Sanctuary Pale Ale (ABV 3.8%) BITTER

Hoppy bitter with a sweet body and a drying finish.
Strongarm (ABV 4%) BITTER
Traditional sweet malty bitter with fruity aromas and caramel sweetness lasting into the finish.
Old Sea Dog (ABV 4.3%) BROWN
Boathouse Premium Blonde Beer (ABV 4.4%) BLOND
Road Crew (ABV 4.5%) PALE

Brewed for Carlsberg Marston's Brewing Co:
Tetley Bitter (ABV 3.7%) BITTER
Malty sweetness and fruit with well balanced hops, a smooth body and a lasting bitter finish.
Tetley Gold (ABV 4.1%) GOLD

Caps Off

Unit 4, Henson Close, South Church Industrial Estate, Bishop Auckland, DL14 6QA ☎ 07900 551754 ⊕ capsoff.co.uk

Established in 2020, the brewery moved to larger premises in 2022 with new equipment and an onsite taproom. A wide range of styles is brewed. ♦

Have It! Best Bitter (ABV 4.1%) BITTER
A well-balanced, traditional bitter with crystal malt sweetness and a rising bitter finish.
Pale (ABV 4.3%) PALE
IPA (ABV 5%) PALE
Brown Ale (ABV 7.4%) STRONG

Castle Eden

8 East Cliff Road, Spectrum Business Park, Seaham, SR7 7PS
☎ (0191) 581 5711 ☎ 07768 044484 ⊕ cebl.co.uk

Using the name of the former Castle Eden Brewery (having acquired the intellectual rights and recipes), a new 20-barrel commercial plant was installed in 2015 along with a bottling/kegging plant. Besides its own brand production, the brewery also contract bottles for several local and national companies. ☒♦

Blond (ABV 3.9%) BLOND
English Pale Ale (ABV 4%) PALE
Ale (ABV 4.2%) BITTER
Faint malty and fruity aromas are precursors to a sweet malty gently bittered beer with some hop presence, finishing dry.
Red (ABV 4.4%) RED
Black (ABV 4.6%) STOUT

Consett SIBA

⧉ Grey Horse Inn, 115 Sherburn Terrace, Consett, DH8 6NE
☎ (01207) 591540 ⊕ consettaleworks.co.uk

Established in 2005 in the stables of a former coaching inn at the rear of the Grey Horse (Consett's oldest pub). The name, beers and branding commemorates the former steelworks in the town which closed in 1980. Beers are also available throughout the North East. ‼♦

Pale Ale (ABV 3.8%) PALE
Steeltown (ABV 3.8%) BITTER
A well-balanced bitter with caramel and maltiness at the start. Some fruit is evident in the sweet body and the hops linger in the finish.
Steel River (ABV 4%) GOLD
Steelworkers Blonde (ABV 4%) BLOND
White Hot (ABV 4%) GOLD
A sweet fruity beer with citrus hops lasting well into the finish.
Men of Steel (ABV 4.2%) BITTER
Consett Stout (ABV 4.3%) STOUT

Complex beer. roasty and sweet with some interesting fruitiness. The hop combines with the roast malts for a satisfying and lasting finish.
The Company (ABV 4.4%) GOLD
Porter (ABV 4.5%) PORTER
Sweet malts and caramel dominate throughout, with some fruit and a lasting finish.
Red Dust (ABV 4.5%) RED
Sweet, fruit and malt lead to a creamy, full-bodied, balanced red ale with caramel flavours and a lasting finish.
Foreman's IPA (ABV 4.8%) PALE

Crafty Monkey SIBA

Benknowle Farm, Elwick, Hartlepool, TS27 3HF
⊕ shop.craftymonkey.beer

Brewing commenced in 2018 using a five-barrel plant in converted farm buildings. Beers are available throughout County Durham, Teesside and North Yorkshire. The brewery has a pop-up bar for events.

Telegraph Session IPA (ABV 3.8%) PALE
Moneypenny EPA (ABV 4%) PALE
New Era (ABV 4.3%) BITTER
Ruby Ruby Ruby Ruby (ABV 4.5%) RED
Malty and hoppy red beer, sweet centre and smooth texture with a somewhat drier finish.
Reward IPA (ABV 4.7%) PALE
Cemetery Gates (ABV 4.8%) PORTER
Black Celebration (ABV 5%) STOUT

Crafty Pint

⧉ Half Moon, 130 Northgate, Darlington, DL1 1QS
☎ (01325) 469965 ☎ 07804 305175

Established in 2013 in the cellar of the Half Moon in Darlington. Originally a 10-gallon brew length, it was upgraded to a one-barrel plant in 2015. One-off beers are produced solely for the pub. ♦

Dark Sky (NEW)

Barclays Bank House, Market Place, Middleton-in-Teesdale, DL12 0QG ⊕ dskyb.co.uk

Brewing commenced in premises formerly occupied by Barclays Bank in Middleton-in-Teesdale, in an Area of Outstanding Natural Beauty in the North Pennines. Beers are brewed in small batches and the names are inspired by the local surroundings. Beers are available at the Teesdale Hotel in Middleton-in-Teesdale and other local outlets.

Dionysiac

19 Oaklands Terrace, Darlington, DL3 6AX ☎ 07557 502083 ✉ dionysiacbrewing@gmail.com

Starting in 2021, this nanobrewery takes its name from Dionysus, the Greek god of drunken madness. Producing small batches of high quality, artisanal bottled beers, the beer names reflect local history.

Donzoko

Office: Brougham Terrace, Hartlepool, TS24 8EY
☎ 07463 863647 ⊕ donzoko.org

Donzoko Brewing Company, founded by Reece Hugill in 2017, takes its inspiration and influences from Germany and translates this beer tradition, combined with techniques from modern UK and US craft brewing, into its beers. It is a cuckoo brewery that has teamed up with Gipsy Hill (qv) to produce its flagship lager in London.

Other beers are brewed at various breweries in the North East. No real ale.

Durham SIBA

Unit 6a, Bowburn North Industrial Estate, Bowburn, DH6 5PF
☎ **(0191) 377 1991** ⏛ **durhambrewery.com**

☺County Durham's oldest brewery, established in 1994. A core range of bottle, cask, mini-cask and keg beers is available all year round with two to three special brews appearing monthly. ‼ ▰LIVE ✦

Magus (ABV 3.8%) BLOND
Pale malt gives this brew its straw colour but the hops define its character, with a fruity aroma, a clean, bitter mouthfeel, and a lingering dry, citrus-like finish.
White Gold (ABV 4%) PALE
Hop and fruit on the nose builds in the mouth with added bitterness and sweet malts. Hop bitterness gains ground and lasts as the sweet malt and fruit diminish.
Dark Angel (ABV 4.3%) STOUT
This worthy stout is characterised by an abundance of different malty roast aromas and flavours. Balanced with gentle hops, sweetness and a touch of fruit.
Alabaster (ABV 7.2%) IPA

George Samuel

Unit 3, Norland House Business Centre, Shildon, DL4 1HE ☎ **07840 892751**

Named after the brewer's two sons, the brewery originally set up as a two-barrel plant in 2014 at the Duke of Wellington pub, Welbury, near Northallerton. It moved to Spennymoor and closed in 2018. The brewery reopened as an eight-barrel plant in 2020 in Shildon (the 'Cradle of the Railways'), in a unit which formerly housed the offices of Shildon Wagon Works. ✦

Locomotion No. 1 (ABV 4%) BLOND
Citrus hops and fruity aromas are complemented by a moderate sweetness with rising and lasting dry bitterness at the end.
Leaves on the Line (ABV 4.2%) BITTER
Travelling Light (ABV 4.5%) BLOND
Well-hopped blond beer with a sweet body, some fruit and citrus hops remain in the crisp dry finish.
Harvey (ABV 5.2%) PORTER
A smooth malty beer with some fruity sweetness and a dry roast finish.
Terminus (ABV 5.5%) IPA
Fruity, hoppy beer with sweetness in the body lasting into the finish. A well-balanced English IPA.

Hill Island

Unit 7, Fowlers Yard, Back Silver Street, Durham, DH1 3RA ☎ **07740 932584**
✉ **hillisland73@gmail.com**

☺Established in 2002, Hill Island is a literal translation of Dunholme, from which Durham is derived. It is part of Fowler's Yard Craft Workshops on the banks of the River Wear and can be reached by steps down from Silver Street. Nearly all production is sold through the pop-up bar, which operates at the brewery most Saturdays (see Facebook for details) including weekends coinciding with Durham events such as the Durham Fire & Ice Festival, and the Durham Miner's Gala. ‼ ▰◆

Peninsula Pint (ABV 3.7%) BLOND
Bitter (ABV 3.9%) BITTER
Stout for the Count (ABV 4%) STOUT
Fruit and roast malt aromas precede this straight-forward stout with lasting roast bitterness.

Neptune's (ABV 4.2%) BITTER
Cathedral Ale (ABV 4.3%) BITTER
THAIPA (ABV 4.3%) SPECIALITY

Hopper House Brew Farm

Racecourse Road, Sedgefield, TS21 2HL ☎ **07947 874278** ⏛ **hopperhousebrewfarm.co.uk**

Brewing commenced in 2019 on a one-barrel plant situated in a working dairy farm on the outskirts of Sedgefield. There is a taproom in an old milking parlour. Currently it only has a licence for the last weekend in the month and is open Friday (3-11pm) and Saturday (12-11pm). ✦

McColl's

Unit 4, Randolph Industrial Estate, Evenwood, DL14 9SJ
☎ **(01388) 417250** ⏛ **mccollsbrewery.co.uk**

Brewing commenced in 2017 using a 20-barrel plant. Outlets are supplied across the North-East and further afield. A taproom is open fortnightly. ✦

Petite Blonde (ABV 4.1%) BLOND
Lady Marmalade (ABV 4.4%) BITTER
North South (ABV 4.6%) PORTER
Suma IPA (ABV 5%) PALE

Mad Scientist

⏛ **Quakerhouse, 2-3 Mechanics Yard, Darlington, DL3 7QF**
☎ **(01325) 245052**

Brewing commenced in 2017 on a half-barrel plant situated in the cellar of the Quakerhouse.

North Pier SIBA

Unit 3a, Tow Law Industrial Estate, Tow Law, DL13 4BB ⏛ **northpierbrew.co.uk**

Brewing commenced in 2020 with beers available in County Durham and Wearside.

Rokerite (ABV 4%) PALE
Pale (ABV 4.2%) PALE
Cold Brew (ABV 4.7%) PORTER
Bounty Hunter (ABV 4.8%) STOUT

Steam Machine SIBA

Unit 14, The IES Centre, Horndale Avenue, Newton Aycliffe, DL5 6DS ☎ **07415 759945**
⏛ **steammachinebrew.com**

Founded by a husband and wife team with a homebrewing background of more than 10 years. Since opening in 2015 production has expanded. Beers are available mainly in keg but KeyKegs are occasionally supplied to beer festivals.

Three Brothers SIBA

Unit 4, Clayton Court, Bowesfield Crescent, Stockton on Tees, TS18 3QX
☎ **(01642) 678084** ⏛ **threebrothersbrewing.co.uk**

The vision of Kit Dodd who, after brewing for five years with another local brewery, and working with his brother David and brother-in-law Chris, established the brewery in 2016. It is situated on an industrial estate within the southern outskirts of Stockton-On-Tees. With backgrounds in chemical and mechanical engineering, the family use these skills to create their own recipes and ensure quality is maintained at the highest level. Beers

are traditional with some American-inspired beers.
🍴 🍽 ♦ LIVE ✔

The Bitter Ex (ABV 3.7%) BITTER
Trilogy (ABV 3.9%) BLOND
Pale, hoppy, citrus-flavoured blond with a bitter aftertaste.
Northern Pale Ale (ABV 4%) PALE
Au (ABV 4.2%) PALE
Session IPA (ABV 4.5%) PALE
Ruby Revolution (ABV 4.6%) RED
S'more Porter (ABV 4.8%) PORTER

Village Brewer Brew 22

🍺 22 Coniscliffe Road, Darlington, DL3 7RG
☎ (01325) 354590 ⊕ villagebrewer.co.uk

☺One-barrel microbrewery, established in 2013, which has been brewing on a regular basis since 2015. The plant is also used to produce the malt wash for the distilling of gin and vodka onsite. The beer strength and style varies from brew to brew.

Weard'ALE

🍺 Hare & Hounds, 24 Front Street, Westgate, DL13 1RX
☎ (01388) 517212

Brewing commenced in the Hare & Hounds in 2010. The beers are only sold on the premises.

Yard of Ale

🍺 Surtees Arms, Chilton Lane, Ferryhill, DL17 0DH
☎ (01740) 655933 ☎ 07540 733513
⊕ thesurteesarms.co.uk

☺Established in 2008, the 2.5-barrel microbrewery supplies ales to the Surtees Arms, beer festivals and to a growing number of pubs. It produces a core range of both cask and keg beers, with monthly specials.
🍴 🍽 ♦ LIVE

Gold (ABV 3.6%) GOLD
Yard Dog Brown Ale (ABV 4%) BROWN
Best By Yards (ABV 4.3%) BITTER
One Foot in the Yard (ABV 4.5%) BITTER
Gentle hoppy bitter with malty sweetness, finishing marginally more bitter than the other balancing flavours.

Station House, Durham (Photo: Stuart McMahon)

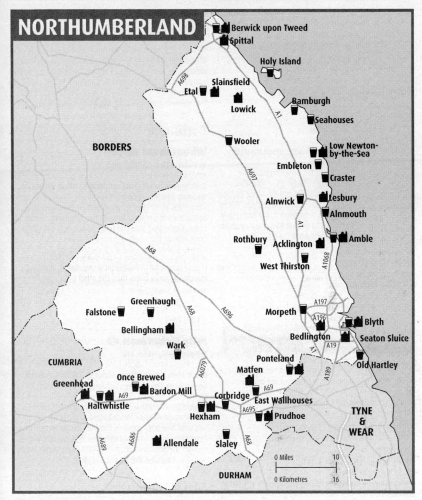

NORTHUMBERLAND

Berwick upon Tweed
Spittal
Holy Island
Slainsfield
Etal
Lowick
Bamburgh
Seahouses
Wooler
Low Newton-by-the-Sea
Embleton
Craster
Alnwick
Lesbury
Alnmouth
Rothbury
Acklington
Amble
West Thirston
Greenhaugh
Falstone
Morpeth
Blyth
Bellingham
Bedlington
Seaton Sluice
Wark
Ponteland
Old Hartley
Greenhead
Once Brewed
Matfen
Haltwhistle
Bardon Mill
Corbridge
East Wallhouses
Hexham
Prudhoe
TYNE & WEAR
Allendale
Slaley
DURHAM

BORDERS

CUMBRIA

0 Miles 10
0 Kilometres 16

Alnmouth

Red Lion Inn 🅛 ✔
22 Northumberland Street, NE66 2RJ
☎ (01665) 830584 ● redlionalnmouth.com
4 changing beers (sourced regionally) Ⓗ
A charming traditional 18th-century coaching inn with a cosy lounge bar featuring attractive woodwork. The decked area at the bottom of the garden enjoys panoramic views across the Aln Estuary. Guest beers usually include one local and two interesting brews from further afield. An annual beer festival is held in October, and there is occasional open air live music in the summer. The pub opens early for breakfast. Excellent individually designed en-suite B&B accommodation is available. Well-behaved dogs are welcome in the bar and beer garden. Q🌣♿🛏️◑🅟🚌(X18)🐾🛜🎵

Alnwick

Ale Gate 🅛
25 Bondgate Without, NE66 1PR
☎ 07979 101332
6 changing beers (sourced locally) Ⓗ
Sited in a former shop unit, latterly an insurance office, Alnwick's first micropub opened in early 2019. It has a

single open main room to the front, and a raised area to the rear. Six handpumps on the traditionally-styled dark wooden bar offer a regularly changing range of beers from local breweries. 🚌🐾

Harry's Bar
20 Narrowgate, NE66 1JG
☎ 07821 505028
Timothy Taylor Landlord; 3 changing beers (sourced regionally) Ⓗ
Located on historic Narrowgate in the heart of Alnwick, this vibrant micropub opened in 2021 following conversion from a former haberdashery shop. The door opens into a cosy main bar with stone-flagged flooring and ample seating. There is also window seating where you can gaze at passers-by as you enjoy one of the four real ales on offer from the small corner servery. There is another small seating area down steps at the rear of the premises. 🚌

Tanners Arms 🅛
2-4 Hotspur Place, NE66 1QF
☎ (01665) 602553
6 changing beers (sourced nationally) Ⓗ
Ivy-covered stone-built pub just off Bondgate Without, a short distance from Alnwick Garden. The rustic single

room has a flagstone floor and tree beer shelf. A large fireplace provides added warmth in winter. Acoustic music nights feature regularly, with open mic on the last Friday of the month. The varied real ales frequently come from north-east and Scottish Borders microbreweries. ⛲&♣🖨🐾🛜♪

Amble

Masons Arms 🅛
Woodbine Street, NE65 0NH
☎ (01665) 711234 🌐 masonsarmsamble.co.uk
3 changing beers (sourced locally; often Hadrian Border, Rigg & Furrow) 🅗
This large, multi-roomed pub is on a corner at the southern edge of the coastal village of Amble. Five handpumps adorn the bar and dispense a range of local brewery beers, including some from the Hadrian Border brewery. A function room is available for hire and regular quizzes are held. Boat trips to Coquet Island are available from the nearby harbour. 🏵🚍♣🖨(X18,X20)🐾

Bamburgh

Castle Inn
Front Street, NE69 7BW
☎ (01668) 214616 🌐 castleinnbamburgh.co.uk
Born Blonde, Amber 🅗
A U-shaped bar with wood panelling throughout and adorned with old photos, some of which are of the fishing trade. Both sides of the bar look like they were originally much smaller; note the cornices on the left-hand side. There are two fires; the one to the right is a traditional style range. An extension to the back provides an airy restaurant, beyond which is a large terrace and garden. ⛲🏵🕦🖨(418,X18)🐾🛜

Berwick upon Tweed

Atelier
41-43 Bridge Street, TD15 1ES
☎ (01289) 298180
3 changing beers (sourced regionally; often Hadrian Border) 🅗
Welcoming café bar with a shabby-chic interior. Three real ales are available, usually from Hadrian Border or other local breweries, and other kegged craft beers. The food on offer is all locally sourced and a real highlight. The specialities are hot shortcrust pies (with a variety of interesting fillings) and an excellent, locally sourced meat and cheese platter. ⛲≠(Berwick-upon-Tweed)🖨🐾🛜

Curfew 🅛
46A Bridge Street, TD15 1AQ
☎ 07842 912268
4 changing beers (sourced nationally) 🅗
Established for more than six years, Berwick's first micropub is located up a small lane which opens out into a large courtyard off Bridge Street. It has a small bar area with a bottle fridge to one side, offering interesting local keg beers and foreign bottles. The courtyard makes a pleasant outdoor drinking area in summer. Excellent pork pies are available. A regular CAMRA award winner. Q⛲🏵≠(Berwick-upon-Tweed) ♣🐾🐾

Blyth

Lounge
5-7 Simpson Street, NE24 1AX
☎ 07732 533976

Metalhead Hammer Best Bitter; house beer (by Metalhead); 3 changing beers (sourced nationally; often Metalhead) 🅗
Friendly micropub in the centre of Blyth. The tap for the Metalhead brewery, it also offers a range of over 20 ciders. Live music plays in the bijou, L-shaped bar at the weekends. Toasted sandwiches and snacks are available. Handily placed for bus services in to Blyth town centre. A five-minute walk from the bus station. &🖨🐾♪

Corbridge

Wheatsheaf Hotel 🅛
St Helens Street, NE45 5HE
☎ 07895 518071
2 changing beers (sourced locally; often Allendale, Hadrian Border, Timothy Taylor) 🅗
Reopened in 2018 after an extended closure and comprehensive refurbishment, this imposing, Grade II-listed, stone-built pub and hotel stands near the centre of Corbridge at the heart of Hadrian's Wall country. A Roman statue is housed on the exterior of the barn. There is a small bar area to the left of the door where the two handpumps are sited. To the right is an informal seating area, with a large restaurant to the rear. ⛲🏵🛏🕦&♣🖨🐾🛜

Craster

Jolly Fisherman ✅
9 Haven Hill, NE66 3TR
☎ (01665) 576461 🌐 thejollyfishermancraster.co.uk
Black Sheep Best Bitter; Timothy Taylor Landlord; house beer (by Laine); 1 changing beer (sourced regionally) 🅗
A superb coastal pub, located above the sea, with excellent views over the adjacent harbour and its own sea wall and beer garden. The pub has an excellent reputation for its crab sandwiches. It is popular with tourists as well as locals as the East Coast walk passes right by. ⛲🏵🕦&♣🖨(418,X18)🐾🛜

East Wallhouses

Robin Hood Inn 🅛
Military Road, NE18 0LL
☎ (01434) 672549 🌐 robinhoodinnhadrianswall.com

REAL ALE BREWERIES	
Allendale	Allendale
Alnwick	Lesbury
Backlash	Prudhoe
Bear Claw 🥢	Spittal
Brewis 🥢	Amble
Chasing Everest	Blyth (brewing suspended)
Cheviot 🥢	Slainsfield
First & Last 🥢	Bellingham
Flying Gang 🥢	Ponteland
Grounding Angels	Hexham (brewing suspended)
Hetton Law	Lowick (brewing suspended)
Hexhamshire	Hexham
High House Barn	Matfen
King Aelle 🍺	Seaton Sluice
Metalhead	Bedlington
Monkey House 🥢	Berwick upon Tweed (NEW)
Muckle	Haltwhistle
Rigg & Furrow 🥢	Acklington
Ship Inn 🍺	Low Newton-by-the-Sea
Twice Brewed 🍺	Bardon Mill
Wrytree	Greenhead

Hadrian Border Tyneside Blonde; Great North Eastern Rivet Catcher H
Located on the Military Road, 12 miles west of Newcastle, this stone-built pub offers good, locally produced beers and food. There is onsite wild camping and glamping at reasonable prices, as well as twin and double rooms. There is a large restaurant area to the rear of the pub and a bar area to the front. It provides a handy stopover on the Hadrian's Wall Path, for which it serves as an official checkpoint. ☎❀✉❀◑ ♠P❀❀♥

Embleton

Greys Inn L

Stanley Terrace, NE66 3UZ
☎ (01665) 576983
4 changing beers (sourced locally; often Alnwick) H
Pleasant, traditional inn in a lovely seaside hamlet, just a short walk from some of the best beaches in the country and Dunstanburgh Castle across the bay. It has three open fires and is home to a ladies' darts team, clay pigeon club and golf club. Note the rare McLennan & Urquhart's Edinburgh Ales mirror on the chimney breast. Winter hours may vary. ☎❀◑♣🚋(418,X18)❀♫

Etal

Black Bull L

TD12 4TL
☎ (01890) 820200 ⊕ theblackbulletal.co.uk
House beer (by Cheviot); 2 changing beers (sourced locally; often Cheviot) H
Northumberland's only thatched pub was fully renovated and reopened in 2018 in an attractive modern style, following a prolonged closure. Comfortable, modern furniture features throughout the spacious, open-plan interior. Three handpumps serve real ales exclusively from Cheviot brewery, with a special dark bitter made for the pub. There is a function room and large outdoor seating area. ☎❀◑♿P🚋(267)❀

Falstone

Blackcock Inn

NE48 1AA
☎ (01434) 240200 ⊕ theblackcockinnatfalstone.com
3 changing beers (sourced nationally) H
A 16th-century coaching inn in the beautiful village of Falstone, one mile from Kielder Water, in the middle of the Northumberland Dark Sky Park. There is an observatory at Keilder for stargazers (booking advised), and there are plenty of trails for hikers and mountain bike riders around the reservoir. The number of beers available in the pub varies with the seasons. ☎❀✉◑♿P❀♥

Greenhaugh

Holly Bush Inn L ✅

NE48 1PW
☎ (01434) 240391 ⊕ hollybushinn.net
Hadrian Border Grainger Ale; Twice Brewed Sycamore Gap; 3 changing beers (sourced locally; often Hexhamshire) H
Independently owned pub, over 300 years old and set in the heart of the Northumberland National Park and the Dark Sky Park, making it ideal for those with an interest in real ale and real stars. No TV and no mobile reception make for a peaceful drinking experience. The pub hosts informal jam sessions – bring your instrument if you like. A 10% happy hour discount applies Monday to Thursday 4-6pm. Q☎❀✉◑♿P❀♥

Haltwhistle

Haltwhistle Comrades Club L

2 Central Place, NE49 0DF
☎ (01434) 320666
3 changing beers (sourced nationally) H
Private club at the top of the main street, with comfortable surroundings. CAMRA members are welcome (bring your card). The club hosts several groups, including pigeon fancying, wildlife, gardening and angling. It is popular with tourists as a Hadrian's Wall heritage site is nearby. The club hosts an egg jarping (knocking/boxing) competition every Easter Sunday, which CAMRA members replicate on trips. The bar is graced with several photographs of yesteryear, including military and sport themes. ☎♿≷♣🚋❀

Hexham

County Hotel L ✅

Priestpopple, NE46 1PS
☎ (01434) 608444 ⊕ countyhotelhexham.co.uk
Hadrian Border Tyneside Blonde; Timothy Taylor Landlord; 1 changing beer (sourced nationally) H
The plush public bar in the famous town-centre County Hotel now subsumes the former and much smaller Argyles Bar which was down a side street. The new extended space is bright and comfortable. It is popular for food, with an extensive and varied menu supplemented with specials. It is handy for the bus station. Alcoholic drinks are served from 11am. ☎✉◑♿🚋❀

Heart of Northumberland L

5 Market Street, NE46 3NS
☎ (01434) 608013 ⊕ thehearthexham.com
Timothy Taylor Landlord; 4 changing beers (sourced locally) H
Five handpumps, four selling local ales, adorn the bar in this food-led independent free house. The single large room is divided almost in two near the end of the bar, with wooden floors throughout. A blazing fire in the large open fireplace warms things nicely in the back room. Excellent food is served with an emphasis on locally sourced produce and Northumbrian tradition. ☎❀◑♣🚋❀♫

Platform Bar L

Platform 2 Hexham Railway Station, Station Road, NE46 1ET
☎ (01434) 604997
6 changing beers (sourced locally) H
This single-room micropub opened in 2019 in the former waiting room on the westbound platform of Hexham station. It has perimeter seating with freestanding tables, and railway memorabilia on the walls. Alcohol is served from 10am, with tea, coffee and light snacks available earlier. It may stay open later than advertised depending on demand. The toilets are at the other end of the platform. Q≷🚋(684,AD122)❀

Tannery L ✅

22 Gilesgate, NE46 3QD
☎ (01434) 605537
2 changing beers (sourced nationally) H
Calling itself 'Hexham's living room', the Tannery is split into two distinct bars: to the left is a gin and cider bar with traditional pub games; to the right a large public bar serving six real ales. There is a beer terrace to the rear of the pub. Typical pub food is served and live music includes monthly folk sessions. Quiz night is Monday. ☎❀◑♿≷♣🚋❀

Victorian Tap ✔

Battle Hill, NE46 1BH
☎ (01434) 602039 ⊕ victoriantap.co.uk
3 changing beers (sourced nationally) Ⓗ
Busy, compact, street-corner local that still manages to carry a range of changing ales, despite the restrictive list of the owning pubco. The pub is divided into two drinking areas – a bar and a lounge both served from a central bar. It is a handy watering hole for visitors to the nearby Hexham Abbey. There is an outside drinking area in the back yard. Q❀❀◑⇌🖵❀

Holy Island

Crown & Anchor Hotel Ⓛ

Market Place, TD15 2RX (check tidetable for causeway crossing times)
☎ (01289) 389215 ⊕ holyislandcrown.co.uk
3 changing beers (sourced locally; often Cheviot, Rigg & Furrow) Ⓗ
Exposed floorboards and wooden tables and benches provide comfortable seating in the cosy bar – note the Gothic carving of a local monk in the corner. There is a comfortable sitting room to the rear. The large beer garden provides scenic views to Lindisfarne Castle and the ruined priory to the rear of the pub.
❀🏠◑🖵(477) ❀🛜

Low Newton-by-the-Sea

Ship Inn Ⓛ

Newton Square, NE66 3EL
☎ (01665) 576262 ⊕ shipinnnewton.co.uk
Ship Inn Sea Coal, Sea Wheat; 4 changing beers (sourced nationally; often Hadrian Border) Ⓗ
This small pub nestles in the corner of three sides of a square of former fishermen's cottages, a few yards from the beach. It attracts drinkers seeking ales from the in-house microbrewery, diners enjoying an excellent menu featuring fresh local ingredients, and walkers exploring the local scenery. A public car park is close by at the top of the hill. Opening times may vary in winter; phone ahead if travelling. Q❀❀❀◑❀♫

Morpeth

Black Bull Ⓛ

47 Bridge Street, NE61 1PE
☎ (01670) 512089
Anarchy Blonde Star; 2 changing beers (sourced nationally) Ⓗ
Recently renovated town-centre pub that looks deceptively small from the outside. Six handpulls serve two regular beers from the Heineken list, Anarchy Brew Co's Blonde Star, and up to three guests, often locally sourced. There is a dedicated fridge for craft beers, including some bottle-conditioned from the Anarchy Brew Co range. Food is served daily, usually made with local ingredients. ❀❀◑♿⇌🖵❀🛜♫

Joiners Arms Ⓛ

3 Wansbeck Street, NE61 1XZ
☎ (01670) 513540
Black Sheep Best Bitter; Draught Bass; 2 changing beers (sourced nationally; often Anarchy) Ⓗ
This popular former Sir John Fitzgerald outlet is located just over the footbridge from the town centre. It has a public bar to the front and lounge to the rear overlooking the river Wansbeck. There is now a beer garden by the river, next to the ornamental cannon. Swearing is prohibited. ❀⇌🖵❀

Office Ⓛ

Chantry Place, NE61 1PJ
☎ 07957 721066
Rigg & Furrow Run Hop Run; 5 changing beers (sourced locally) Ⓗ
The Office is a micropub that has no music or games machines. It features eight handpulls and three craft keg beers, all of local origin, as well as three real ciders dispensed on gravity from the glass-fronted fridge opposite the bar. No food is served. Dogs are welcome. Local CAMRA Pub of the Year 2022. Q⇌●🖵❀

Pleased to Meet You Ⓛ

Bridge Street, NE61 1NB
☎ (01670) 33397
House beer (by Almasty); 3 changing beers (sourced nationally) Ⓗ
Reopened in late 2021 after a lengthy closure and extensive redevelopment. The layout offers several discrete drinking areas on various levels, with the bar towards the rear. The walls have been taken back to bare brick and the various areas have been tastefully furnished. Work continues on the hotel accommodation. It also incorporates Emily's tearoom, which is open from 8am. ◑⇌🖵❀

Tap & Spile Ⓛ

23 Manchester Street, NE61 1BH
☎ (01670) 513894
Greene King Abbot; Hadrian Border Tyneside Blonde; Timothy Taylor Landlord; 5 changing beers (sourced nationally) Ⓗ
All are welcome at this popular locals' pub near the town's bus station. Seven handpulls offer a good choice of ales, with brews from Northumbrian breweries often available. The bar area at the front is usually busy, though there is a cosy lounge to the rear which is accessible from either side of the room. A traditional folk group plays on Sunday lunchtimes. Q❀♣◑●🖵❀🛜♫

Old Hartley

Delaval Arms Ⓛ

NE26 4RL
☎ (0191) 237 0489 ⊕ delavalarms.com
6 changing beers (sourced locally; often King Aelle) Ⓗ
Multi-roomed Grade II-listed building dating from 1748, with a listed WWI water storage tower (part of Roberts Battery) behind the beer garden. It is the first pub in Northumberland for those following the coastal route. Good-quality, affordable meals complement the beer from the on-site King Aelle brewery. To the left as you enter is a room served through a hatch from the bar and to the right a room where children are welcome. Q❀❀◑●P🖵(308,309) ❀🛜

Once Brewed

Twice Brewed Inn Ⓛ ✔

Miltary Road, Bardon Mill, NE47 7AN (on B6318)
☎ (01434) 344534 ⊕ twicebrewedinn.co.uk
6 changing beers (sourced nationally; often Twice Brewed) Ⓗ
An excellent, remote inn on the Military Road, near to Hadrian's Wall, Steel Rigg and Vindolanda, attracting walkers and tourists. It has a fully refurbished bar area and offers a wide range of bottled beers from around the world. It has full wheelchair access and welcomes dogs. B&B accommodation is offered in 18 en-suite bedrooms. The Twice Brewed Brew House started producing its own beers in 2017, using water from its own well. Q❀❀🏠◑♿▲P🖵❀🛜

Ponteland

Pont Tap 🄻

10 West Road, NE20 9SU

☎ 07446 098501

4 changing beers (sourced nationally) 🄷

The Pont Tap opened in 2020 in what was previously an interior design shop. It serves a good range of mostly local cask and craft keg beers, together with wine and spirits. The friendly welcome and comfortable surroundings make this a must visit if you are in the area. Q🚌

Prudhoe

Wor Local 🄻

Front Street, NE42 5HJ

☎ (01661) 598150

4 changing beers (sourced nationally) 🄷

Located on Prudhoe's Front Street, Wor Local (or Our Local if you're not a Geordie) is a micropub with room for around 40 customers. The layout of the bar, with its comfy seats and carpet, encourages conversation. Three beers are offered from the north-east and Cumbria in a variety of styles, and real ciders are always available. Snacks include pork pies, cheeses, crisps and nuts. There are lots of traditional pub and board games for customers' use. 🍎🚌🐾

Rothbury

Narrow Nick 🄻

High Street, NE65 7TB

☎ 07707 703182

4 changing beers (sourced locally) 🄷

Opened in 2016, this micropub was previously a clothes shop. The front windows feature Art Deco-style stained glass. The single room has the bar at one side sporting six handpumps offering a range of local brewery beers. A large range of gins is also kept. Wooden bar-back fittings have recently been added. Winter opening times may vary. Q🚌🐾

Seahouses

Olde Ship Inn 🄻

7-9 Main Street, NE68 7RD

☎ (01665) 720200 🌐 theoldeship.co.uk

Black Sheep Best Bitter; Hadrian Border Farne Island Pale Ale; Ruddles County; Theakston Best Bitter; 2 changing beers (sourced nationally; often Hadrian Border, Firebrick) 🄷

This former farmhouse, built in 1745, was converted to the licensed trade in 1812 and has been identified by CAMRA as having a regionally important historic pub interior. The pub has three quality bars adorned with a veritable treasure trove of 19th and 20th century maritime memorabilia. It offers an interesting menu of fish, seafood and snacks. Accommodation is also available, making it a great base for exploring the beautiful Northumberland coast.
Q🛏❀🍴◐♿♣P🚌(418,X18)

Slaley

Rose & Crown 🄻

Main Street, NE47 0AA

☎ (01434) 673996 🌐 roseandcrownslaley.co.uk

4 changing beers (sourced locally) 🄷

The Rose & Crown is a Grade II-listed building dating back to 1675 which has been providing a warm welcome to locals and visitors ever since. There are log fires in winter and a sheltered garden with long views in the summer. They offer a wide menu selection as well as a great choice of beers, wines and spirits. Summer hours may vary. 🛏❀🍴◐♿♣P🐾📶

Wark

Battlesteads Hotel 🄻 ✔

NE48 3LS

☎ (01434) 230209 🌐 battlesteads.com

4 changing beers (sourced nationally) 🄷

Well-appointed 1747 former farmhouse with a restaurant, large conservatory and a lovely walled garden to rear. The four handpulls provide an excellent choice of local ales, and there is also a good wine list and a range of organic soft drinks. Ingredients for the excellent food menu are sourced from within a 25-mile radius. High-quality accommodation includes ground floor rooms with disabled access. The pub is handy for PlusBus via Hexham Rail Station.
🛏❀🍴◐♿▲P🚌(680)🐾📶

West Thirston

Northumberland Arms 🄻 ✔

The Peth, NE65 9EE

☎ (01670) 787370 🌐 northumberlandarms-felton.co.uk

Rigg & Furrow Run Hop Run; Sharp's Doom Bar; 4 changing beers (sourced nationally; often Allendale) 🄷

This fine stone pub was originally a coaching inn in the 1820s for Hugh Percy, 3rd Duke of Northumberland. The building has been lovingly restored in an eclectic style while remaining warm, comfortable and welcoming. Bare stone walls and real fires add to the ambience. A large function room caters for groups of up to 30. The beer range is predominantly from local breweries.
🛏❀🍴◐P🚌(X15)📶

Wooler

Black Bull 🄻

High Street, NE71 6BY

☎ (01668) 281309

Hadrian Border Tyneside Blonde, Secret Kingdom; 1 changing beer (sourced nationally; often Hadrian Border) 🄷

The Black Bull Hotel is a 17th-century, stone-built inn on Wooler's main street, retaining much of its original character. It serves good, home-made food in the dining room or in the bar area every day at lunchtime and also in the evenings from Monday to Saturday. Wooler is situated in one of the most picturesque parts of Northumberland, with sandy beaches 30 minutes away, and is a good base for walkers, golfers and cyclists.
🍴◐🚌🐾

Tankerville Arms Hotel

Cottage Road, NE71 6AD

☎ (01668) 281581 🌐 tankervillehotel.co.uk

2 changing beers (sourced locally; often Hadrian Border) 🄷

A 17th-century coaching inn-style hotel at the northern end of Wooler. Bar and restaurant meals are served all day, with roasts available on Sundays. It holds a Civil Marriage License, allowing more spontaneous romantic couples to be married here. Self-catering cottages are available adjacent to the hotel, as well as 17 rooms in the main building. 🍴◐🐾📶

Breweries

Allendale SIBA

Allen Mill, Allendale, NE47 9EA
☎ (01434) 618686 ⊕ allendalebrewery.com

Established in 2006, the brewery is a 20-barrel plant in a historic lead smelting mill in the heart of the North Pennines Area of Outstanding Natural Beauty. Many of the beers reflect the heritage and identity of the local area. !! ₩ ♦

Wagtail Best Bitter (ABV 3.8%) BITTER
Amber bitter with spicy aromas and a long, bitter finish.
Golden Plover (ABV 4%) BLOND
Light, refreshing, easy-drinking blonde beer with a clean finish.
Pennine Pale (ABV 4%) PALE
Fruity citrus aromas and a sweet full mouth are enveloped by a lasting hop bitterness, some malty texture and a satisfying dryness.
Hop on (ABV 4.7%) GOLD
Adder Lager (ABV 5%) SPECIALITY
Anvil (ABV 5.5%) IPA
Wolf (ABV 5.5%) RED
Full-bodied red ale with bitterness in the taste giving way to a fruity finish.
Wanderlust (ABV 6.5%) IPA
Dirty Deeds (ABV 6.6%) IPA

Alnwick SIBA

Unit E-F, Hawkhill Business Park, Lesbury, NE66 3PG
☎ (01665) 830617 ☎ 07788 433499
⊕ alnwickbrewery.co.uk

Brewing started in the 1860s in the centre of Alnwick. The brewery was acquired in 1978 by Scottish brewer Dryboroughs, who closed it in 1986, but relaunched in 2003 with the assistance of the Duchess of Northumberland. Beers are also brewed under the Holy Island name.

Backlash

7A Earls Court, Prudhoe, NE42 6QG
☎ (01661) 830934 ⊕ backlashbrewery.co.uk

Brewing commenced in 2018, initially on a small scale for marketing purposes. Beers are only produced in bespoke batches via pre-order for events and special occasions, and available in bottle, cask or keg.

Bear Claw

Unit 3, Meantime Workshops, North Greenwich Road, Spittal, TD15 1RG ☎ 07919 276715
⊕ bearclawbrewery.com

Bear Claw began brewing in 2012 using a two-barrel plant, producing a variety of cask-conditioned ales and many bottle-conditioned beers, including some continental styles. All the beers are now fermented in oak, ex-wine barrels and conditioned for a minimum of one month, with some being barrel-aged. LIVE ♦

Brewis

Unit 4, Coquet Enterprise Park, Amble, NE65 0PE
☎ (01665) 714818 ⊕ brewisbeer.co.uk

Brewis Beer Co is a family-run nanobrewery featuring a bottle shop and taproom. ₩ ♦

Building Bridges (ABV 4.5%) PALE
Helm (ABV 4.7%) PORTER

Just Like Heaven (ABV 5.7%) IPA
Turning Tides (ABV 5.8%) IPA
Ebb & Flow (ABV 6.5%) IPA

Chasing Everest

15 Ponteland Square, Blyth, NE24 4SH
⊕ chasingeverestbrew.com

Founded in 2018 by Zak Everest, focusing on small batch brews. Many of the beers are dry-hopped, giving bold, hoppy flavours. Brewing is currently suspended.

Cheviot

Slainsfield, Cornhill on Tweed, TD12 4TP ☎ 07778 478943 ⊕ cheviotbrewery.co.uk

Brewing commenced in 2018 in converted hunt kennels on the historic Ford & Etal estate. It is a 7.5-barrel plant producing ales named after local landmarks and historical figures. Bottles are supplied to local businesses while the full range is distributed from Edinburgh to Newcastle and beyond to over 200 outlets. !! ₩ ♦

Sea Stack (ABV 3.7%) PALE
Upland Ale (ABV 3.8%) BITTER
ETale (ABV 4%) BITTER
Harbour Wall (ABV 4.2%) PALE
Black Hag (ABV 4.4%) STOUT
Trig Point (ABV 4.5%) PALE
Menhir (ABV 5.1%) STOUT

First & Last SIBA

Old Ambulance Station, Foundry Yard, Bellingham, NE48 2DA ☎ 07757 286357
⊕ firstandlastbrewery.co.uk

First & Last was established in 2016 by Red Kelly, a founder member of Stu Brew in Newcastle upon Tyne. Upgrading to a five-barrel plant in 2018, it relocated eight miles up the road to Bellingham in 2022 with further expansion to a 10-barrel plant plus the addition of a shop and taproom. Outlets in Northumberland and the Scottish Borders are supplied. ₩ ♦ ♦

Drove Road (ABV 3.7%) BITTER
Mad Jack Ha' (ABV 3.8%) PALE
Red Rowan (ABV 4%) BITTER
Equinox (ABV 4.1%) PALE
Reiver (ABV 4.2%) BITTER
Stell (ABV 4.3%) STOUT

Flying Gang

Unit 3, Meadowfield Industrial Estate, Ponteland, NE20 9SD ☎ 07789 958782
⊕ flyinggangbrewing.com

Brewing commenced in 2021 in an industrial unit in Ponteland, also incorporating a taproom which opens at weekends. The brewery is also involved in the running of the Left Luggage micropub in Monkseaton. ♦

Grounding Angels

6 Rear Battle Hill, Hexham, NE46 1BB ☎ 07508 175512 ⊕ grounding-angels.com

Brewing started in 2018 by Jamie Robson, using his family's experience of owning global drinks brand Fentimans. Golden Promise malt is used as a base for all of the beers, which are distributed nationwide. Brewing is currently suspended.

Hetton Law

Hetton Law Farm, Lowick, Berwick upon Tweed, TD15 2UL
☎ (01289) 388558 ☎ 07889 457140
⊕ hettonlawbrewery.co.uk

Brewing began in 2015 using a 2.5-barrel plant. Run by retired dentists Judith and Nicholas Grasse, it uses local spring water and locally grown malt. Due to the size of the brewery, availability on draught and in bottles is effectively limited to the local area. Brewing is currently suspended. ♦

Hexhamshire SIBA

Dipton Mill Road, Hexham, NE46 1YA
☎ (01434) 606577 ⊕ hexhamshire.co.uk

Hexhamshire is Northumberland's oldest brewery and is run by the same family since it was founded in 1993. The family also run the brewery tap, the Dipton Mill. Outlets are supplied direct and via the SIBA Beerflex scheme.

Devil's Elbow (ABV 3.6%) BITTER
Amber brew full of hops and fruit, leading to a bitter finish.

Shire Bitter (ABV 3.8%) BITTER
A good balance of hops with fruity overtones, this amber beer makes an easy-drinking session bitter.

Blackhall English Stout (ABV 4%) STOUT

Devil's Water (ABV 4.1%) BITTER
Copper-coloured best bitter, well-balanced with a slightly fruity, hoppy finish.

Whapweasel (ABV 4.8%) BITTER
An interesting smooth, hoppy beer with a fruity flavour. Amber in colour, the bitter finish brings out the fruit and hops.

High House Barn

High House Barn, High House Farm, Matfen, NE20 0RG
☎ (01661) 725527 ⊕ highhousebarn.co.uk

Formerly High House Farm Brewery (qv), the brewery re-opened under a new name and management in 2022 in the same premises.

King Aelle

🏠 Delaval Arms, Old Hartley, Seaton Sluice, NE26 4RL
☎ (0191) 237 0489

Brewing commenced in 2021 on a 2.5-barrel plant which was originally based at the Hop & Cleaver, Newcastle upon Tyne. It is now situated in an outbuilding at the Delaval Arms, Old Hartley. Beers are available in both cask and five litre mini casks.

Metalhead SIBA

Unit 9, Bowes Court, Barrington Industrial Estate, Bedlington, NE22 7DW ☎ 07923 253890
⊕ metalhead-brewery.co.uk

☺Metalhead Brewery began life in 2019 following a career change and a love of real ale and music. Beers are available in its micropub, the Lounge, Blyth. LIVE

Hammer Best Bitter (ABV 3.8%) BITTER
Old Knacker (ABV 3.8%) BITTER
Best Mate (ABV 4.2%) BITTER
Simply Red (ABV 4.6%) BITTER
Axl Gold (ABV 4.8%) GOLD
Archer (ABV 5.1%) BITTER

Monkey House (NEW)

Unit 1, Windmill Way, West Ramparts Business Park, Berwick upon Tweed, TD15 1UN ☎ 07718 489485
⊕ monkeyhousecider.co.uk

Run by Phil Elliot, a master brewer having had over 30 years experience in brewing and distilling. Primarily a cider producer, a range of beers is also brewed. ♦

Double Citra (ABV 4%) GOLD
Tommy the Miller (ABV 4%) BITTER
Irish Stout (ABV 4.8%) STOUT

Muckle SIBA

3 Bellister Close, Park Village, Haltwhistle, NE49 0HA
☎ 07711 980086 ⊕ mucklebrewing.co.uk

Established in 2016, Muckle Brewing is a tiny brewery in rural Northumberland, close to Hadrian's Wall. Beers are influenced by the local landscape.

Whin Sill Blonde (ABV 3.5%) BITTER
Tickle (ABV 4%) GOLD
Chuckle (ABV 4.2%) GOLD
Buster (ABV 4.5%) BITTER
Kings Crag (ABV 5.4%) PALE

Rigg & Furrow

Acklington Park Farm, Acklington, Morpeth, NE65 9AA ⊕ riggandfurrow.co.uk

Brewing commenced in 2017 in a former milking parlour. A taproom is open on selected dates (see website for details). ♦

Best (ABV 4%) BITTER
Run Hop Run (ABV 4.2%) PALE
Land Bier (ABV 4.8%) SPECIALITY
Farmhouse IPA (ABV 5.6%) IPA

Ship Inn

🏠 Ship Inn, Newton Square, Low Newton-by-the-Sea, NE66 3EL
☎ (01665) 576262 ⊕ shipinnnewton.co.uk

☺Brewing commenced in 2008 on a 2.5-barrel plant. Sixteen beers are brewed in constant rotation but are only available on the premises. A special beer is brewed for every 100 brews. Some beers are now available in cans but again only available from the Ship Inn. ♦LIVE

Twice Brewed SIBA

🏠 Twice Brewed Brewhouse, Bardon Mill, Hexham, NE47 7AN
☎ (01434) 344534 ⊕ twicebrewed.co.uk

☺Originally set up 2017, the Twice Brewed Brewery has since doubled its production capacity. Beers are available from the bar and adjoining Twice Brewed Inn, plus other local pubs. ‼🍺♦

Best Bitter (ABV 3.8%) BITTER
Sycamore Gap (ABV 4.1%) PALE
Ale Caesar (ABV 4.4%) BITTER
Steel Rig (ABV 4.9%) PORTER
Vindolana (ABV 5.3%) PALE

Wrytree

Unit 1, Wrytree Park, Greenhead, CA8 7JA

Brewing commenced in 2015.

Gold (ABV 3.9%) GOLD
Copper (ABV 4%) BITTER

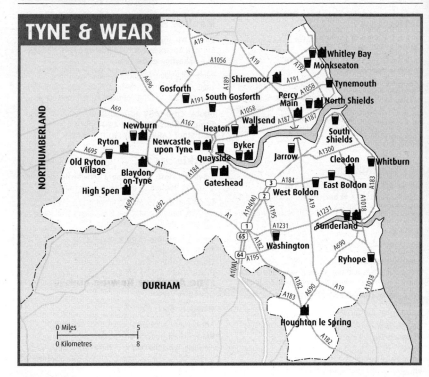

TYNE & WEAR

East Boldon

Grey Horse 🅛 ⦿
Front Street, NE36 0SJ
☎ (0191) 519 1796
6 changing beers (sourced nationally) 🅷
Distinctively fronted building which has a single open-plan room with a number of separate seating areas. There are six handpulls with five changing beers and one cider or perry. There is seating outside the front of the pub and a beer garden and car park at the rear. A largescreen TV in the bar shows regular sporting events. There is a function room upstairs which can be hired. Food is served daily from an extensive menu.
👪🏵🌙🛇🚻🅿🚍🐾🛜

Mid Boldon Club 🅛
Front Street, NE36 0SH
☎ 07799 311358
4 changing beers (sourced nationally) 🅷
A private members club that celebrated its centenary in 2012. The single room is on three levels, with one bar that has four handpulls. The changing cask beers are from local and independent breweries. There is a snooker table and live music once a month on a Thursday. Guests are welcome, just sign in. There is a bell at the side door to gain admittance. Local CAMRA Club of the Year 2023. 🆀👪♣🚍🐾🛜♪

Gateshead

Microbus 🍺
2 High Level Parade, NE8 2AJ
⊕ microbus.pub
6 changing beers (sourced nationally) 🅷
A campervan-themed micropub in a railway arch, directly opposite the entrance to High Level Bridge. This quirky pub is adorned with paraphernalia reflecting the owners' enthusiasm for these vehicles. Six handpulls and 10 taps

dispense a wide selection of beers mainly from northern breweries. There is a bus stop directly outside the pub with services provided by Go North East with a real time departure display inside the pub so you know when your next bus is coming. 👪🏵⇌(Newcastle)🚍♦🚍🐾🛜

REAL ALE BREWERIES

Almasty ✦ Shiremoor
Anarchy ✦ Newcastle upon Tyne
Big Lamp Newburn
Black Storm ✦ Percy Main
Blockyard Sunderland (NEW)
Brewlab Sunderland
Brinkburn Street ✦ Newcastle upon Tyne: Byker
Cullercoats Wallsend
Darwin North Shields
Dog & Rabbit 🍺 Whitley Bay
Firebrick Blaydon-on-Tyne
Flash House ✦ North Shields
Full Circle ✦ Newcastle upon Tyne
Great North Eastern ✦ Gateshead
Hadrian Border Newburn
Lazy Lizard 🍺 Cleadon (NEW)
Maxim ✦ Houghton le Spring
Northern Alchemy ✦ Newcastle upon Tyne: Byker
Out There Newcastle upon Tyne
Stu Brew Newcastle upon Tyne
Tavernale 🍺 Newcastle upon Tyne (brewing suspended)
Thirsty Moose Ryton (NEW)
Three Kings North Shields
TOPS (The Olde Potting Shed) High Spen
Two by Two Byker
Tyne Bank ✦ Newcastle upon Tyne
Vaux ✦ Sunderland
Whitley Bay Whitley Bay
Wylam ✦ Newcastle upon Tyne

Old Fox 🅛

10-14 Carlisle Street, Felling, NE10 0HQ
☎ (0191) 447 1980
5 changing beers (sourced nationally) Ⓗ
Only a short walk from Felling Metro station is this traditional single-room community pub with a roaring fire in the winter months. Ales are drawn both from national and local breweries. Snacks and Sunday lunches are available. There is live music over the weekend, and the dartboard is in frequent use. A friendly and welcoming pub with a beer garden at the rear.
🖕😺✳(Heworth) ◖(Felling) ♣🖥🐾🛜♫

Schooner 🅛

South Shore Road, NE8 3AF (just down from the jct between Saltmeadows Rd & Neilson Rd; vehicular access only from E end of South Shore Rd)
☎ (0191) 477 7404 ⊕ theschooner.co.uk
Ossett White Rat; 5 changing beers (sourced nationally) Ⓗ
On the banks of the Tyne, the Schooner currently has six handpumps for cask ales and one for cask cider. The selection changes regularly to showcase the best local and national ales and ciders. Great-value home-cooked food is served throughout the week, with traditional roasts on Sunday. Live music plays every Sunday afternoon, some Saturday nights, and on many other occasions. 🖕😺🕕🌜♣🖥(93,94)🐾🛜♫

Wheat Sheaf 🅛

26 Carlisle Street, Felling, NE10 0HQ
☎ (0191) 857 8404
Big Lamp Sunny Daze, Bitter, Prince Bishop Ale; 2 changing beers (sourced nationally) Ⓗ
Welcoming street-corner pub owned by Big Lamp brewery and patronised by a loyal band of regulars who often travel quite a distance to drink here. The pub features some original details, mismatched furniture, and real coal fires when needed. The outdoor toilets have original Victorian urinals. There is a fortnightly Monday night quiz, traditional folk music featuring keen local musicians on Tuesday night, and dominoes on Wednesday night. An original CAMRA clock keeps time behind the bar. Snacks are available.
🖕😺✳(Heworth) ◖(Felling) ♣🖥(27,93)🐾🛜♫

Jarrow

Gin & Ale House 🅛 ✅

Walter Street, NE32 3PQ (behind town hall)
☎ (0191) 489 7222
Ossett White Rat; Sharp's Doom Bar; Timothy Taylor Landlord; 2 changing beers (sourced nationally) Ⓗ
Dating from 1885, this well-appointed conversion of the old Crusader has a single room with wood panelling, local vintage photographs and pub memorabilia. There are five real ales available from local and national breweries – note the beer list on the blackboard to the right when you walk in. There is an early evening quiz every Sunday and Thursday is Buskers night. At the back of the pub is a large beer garden. 😺🕭🖥🛜♫

Monkseaton

Crafty Cold Well

Cauldwell Lane, NE25 8LN
4 changing beers (sourced nationally) Ⓗ
The owner this pub is dedicated to bringing something different to the local real ale scene. The four changing handpulls always include a dark beer, and there is always a changing real cider. The front room is accessed from street level with steps to the back room and servery

(please ask at bar for ramp for disabled access to the back room). Opening times may vary so check before visiting. 🖕😺🖥(57,57A)🛜

Newburn

Keelman 🅛

Grange Road, NE15 8NL
☎ (0191) 267 1689 ⊕ biglampbrewers.co.uk
Big Lamp Sunny Daze, Bitter, Summerhill Stout, Prince Bishop Ale, Keelman Brown; 1 changing beer (sourced nationally) Ⓗ
This tastefully converted Grade II-listed former pumping station is now home to the Big Lamp brewery – the Keelman is the brewery tap. A conservatory restaurant serves excellent food, and quality accommodation is provided in the adjacent Keelman's Lodge and Salmon Cottage. It is attractively situated by the Tyne Riverside Country Park, Coast-to-Coast cycleway and Hadrian's Wall National Trail. 🖕😺🛏🕕🕭🖥(22,71)🛜

Tyne Amateur Rowing Club 🅛

Water Row, NE15 8NL
⊕ tynerowingclub.org
4 changing beers (sourced nationally; often Hadrian Border, Firebrick) Ⓗ
Modern rowing club building with balcony overlooking the River Tyne and bridge at Newburn, about seven miles west of Newcastle city centre. Originally founded in 1852, it is one of the oldest sporting clubs in the country. There is a large car park adjacent and the National cycle route 72 passes along the front of the building. There is a function space available for hire.
🖕🕭🖥(22,62)🐾🛜

Newcastle upon Tyne: Byker

Brinkburn Street Brewery Bar & Kitchen 🅛

Unit 1B, Ford Street, Ouseburn, NE6 1NW
☎ (0191) 338 9039 ⊕ brinkburnbrewery.co.uk
8 changing beers (sourced locally) Ⓗ
The main attraction here is the range and quality of beers available. Most ales are brewed on-site, alongside a couple of guests, often from Steam Machine. Food is also a major feature, with a kitchen that uses locally sourced ingredients and serves traditional local dishes. The upstairs hall is used as a venue for occasional beer festivals and other events. The quirky bar features a collection of armoury and objets d'art. 🕕◖(Byker)♣

Free Trade Inn 🅛

St Lawrence Road, NE6 1AP
☎ (0191) 265 5764
Fyne Ales Jarl; house beer (by Almasty); 5 changing beers (sourced nationally) Ⓗ
Unique former Scottish & Newcastle pub with wonderful views of the Tyne bridges and Newcastle and Gateshead quaysides. Up to nine beers and five ciders are available on the bar. Interesting ales come from far and wide, with regular tap takeovers and an extensive range of foreign bottled beers. The jukebox is a classic – and free – and the beer garden is excellent. The pub hosts regular pop-up food vendors. A former local CAMRA Pub of the Year and Cider Pub of the Year.
Ⓠ🖕😺◖(Byker)♣🐕🖥(QA,QB)🐾🛜

Newcastle upon Tyne: City Centre

Beer Street 🅛

Arch 10, Forth Street, NE1 3NZ
3 changing beers (sourced nationally) 🅗
Sited in a railway arch, this micropub, with seating for 50 people, opened in 2018. There is a main bar area with five handpumps. Stairs at the rear give access to a mezzanine floor above, with pump badges from former beers adorning the staircase. Interesting artwork covers the walls, apparently inspired by the famous Hogarth paintings Beer Street and Gin Lane. Two large display fridges house a large bottle and can range to drink in or take away. ≥(Newcastle)🅡(Central Station)●●

Bridge Hotel 🅛

Castle Square, NE1 1RQ
☎ (0191) 232 6400
Sharp's Doom Bar; 8 changing beers (sourced nationally) 🅗
Large ex-Fitzgerald's pub situated next to Stephenson's spectacular High Level Bridge. The rear windows and patio have views of the city walls, River Tyne and Gateshead Quays. The main bar area, with many stained-glass windows, is divided into a number of seating areas, with a raised section at the rear. Guest beers come from far and wide. What is claimed to be the oldest folk club in the country is among live music events held in the upstairs function room.
※◑≥(Newcastle) 🅡(Central Station) 🛜 ♪

Crow's Nest 🅛 ⊘

Percy Street, NE1 7RY
☎ (0191) 261 2607
8 changing beers (sourced nationally) 🅗
Not far from the main bus and Metro interchanges, this large pub was tastefully refurbished a few years ago. The largely open-plan main bar has some more secluded seating areas, and there is small raised seating area to the rear. There is an outdoor drinking area with limited seating in front of the pub. ⏱※◑&🅡(Haymarket)🚌🛜

Fitzgeralds 🅛

60 Grey Street, NE1 6AF
☎ (0191) 230 1350
Anarchy Blonde Star; 5 changing beers (sourced nationally) 🅗
A large, open-plan pub that is much bigger inside than it appears from the outside. The bar is at the back of the pub and has six handpulls serving local and national beers, usually including a dark beer. There is plenty of seating and a large area in front of the bar is kept clear for standing. ≥🅡(Monument)🚌(53,Q3)🛜

Head of Steam

2 Neville Street, NE1 5EN
☎ (0191) 230 4236 ● theheadofsteam.co.uk
6 changing beers (sourced nationally; often Camerons) 🅗
Opposite the central railway station, this pub is unusual in having the main bar upstairs, where you will find six cask ales and a good selection of continental draught beers. Downstairs is one of the most popular live and recorded music venues in the city centre. There is no draught beer on sale in the downstairs venue, but it has an extensive range of cans and bottles.
≥(Newcastle) 🅡(Central Station) 🛜

Lady Greys 🅛 ⊘

20 Shakespeare Street, NE1 6AQ
☎ (0191) 232 3606 ● ladygreys.co.uk

House beer (by Ridgeside); 7 changing beers (sourced nationally) 🅗
Close to the historic Theatre Royal and busy shopping areas, it is good to see this pub, formerly the Adelphi, adding itself to the city-centre real ale scene. Beers are often from local brewers Hadrian Border, Allendale and others, with guests from all over the country. Refurbishment has added four more handpumps.
◑≥(Newcastle) 🅡(Monument) ●🛜

Mean-Eyed Cat 🅛

1 St Thomas Street, NE1 4LE
☎ (0191) 222 0952
Ossett White Rat; house beer (by Almasty); 4 changing beers (sourced nationally) 🅗
Situated in a former newsagent's in the street opposite Haymarket bus station, this one-room micropub opened in 2018 with six handpumps. It serves beers from local, national and international suppliers, alongside a range of eight craft keg beers. A good selection of up to six ciders is available – traditional still and served from the cellar. Mexican spirits are also on offer. There are street food pop-ups on occasion. 🅡(Haymarket)●🚌●

Mile Castle ⊘

Westgate Road, NE1 5XU
☎ (0191) 211 1160
Greene King Abbot; Ruddles Best Bitter; Sharp's Doom Bar; 7 changing beers (sourced nationally) 🅗
This highly regarded Wetherspoon pub boasts 20 handpulls across three floors. The name refers to the Roman forts that were built a mile apart – there is one reputed to be close by. Meals are served all day and evening throughout the pub, including a redecorated boothed area on the second floor created specifically for diners. Transport links are excellent, with rail and Metro stations nearby. Buses stop outside the front door. ⏱◑&≥(Newcastle) 🅡(Central Station) 🚌🛜

Newcastle Tap

Ground Floor, Baron House, 4 Neville Street, NE1 5EN
☎ (0191) 261 6636 ● tapnewcastle.com
6 changing beers (sourced nationally) 🅗
An open-plan single-room pub on the ground floor of a former office block next to the Head of Steam and opposite the Central Station and Royal Station Hotel. The beer casks and kegs are displayed behind glass on a mezzanine above the bar. Cask beers are dispensed by handpumps on the bar, with a tap wall behind the bar for the craft keg beers. Pizzas are served all day. Closing times may vary. ◑≥(Newcastle)🅡(Central Station)●🚌

Split Chimp 🅛

Arch 7, Westgate Road, NE1 1SA
● splitchimp.pub
6 changing beers (sourced nationally) 🅗
Newcastle's first micropub opened in 2015 in a refurbished railway arch behind Central Station opposite the site of the former Federation brewery. It relocated to this larger arch on Westgate Road in 2016. More spacious than some micropubs and split over two levels, it has six handpumps serving a wide selection of real ales, with one dedicated to the house beer, Clever Chimp 2, from Three Kings brewery. A selection of real ciders is also available, as well as foreign bottled beers. Winter opening hours may vary.
⏱≥(Newcastle) 🅡(Central Station) ♣●●🛜

Three Bulls Heads 🅛 ⊘

57 Percy Street, NE1 7RN
☎ (0191) 260 2984
Draught Bass; Timothy Taylor Landlord; 4 changing beers (sourced locally) 🅗

This two-storey pub offers three cask-conditioned real ales from handpulls on the ground floor bar. Food is served on both levels, with upstairs generally being quieter. It gets busy at weekends but there are lots of seating areas to accommodate everyone. The bar staff are friendly, and knowledgeable about the real ale. No children allowed at any time.
⓵&≠(Newcastle) ♞(Haymarket) 🛜

Tilleys Bar 🄻

105 Westgate Road, NE1 4AG
☎ (0191) 232 0692
Anarchy Blonde Star; Camerons Strongarm; 2 changing beers (sourced locally) 🄷
Popular with visitors from the nearby theatres and close to Central Station, this pub has seven handpumps adorning its L-shaped main bar, with a beer from Camerons and six rotating local brews. An overwhelming collection of over 180 bottled beers from all over the world is dominated by American and Belgian brands. Families are welcome until 7pm.
🕸≠(Newcastle) ♞(Central Station)♣🚌🐾🛜

Town Mouse Ale House 🍸 🄻

Basement, 11 St Mary's Place, NE1 7PG
🌐 townmousealehouse.co.uk
6 changing beers (sourced nationally) 🄷
This well-designed micropub is in the basement of what was a coffee shop and has space for around 50 people. The bar area is to the front, with more seating to the rear. A large blackboard gives details of the six cask beers and larger range of keg and bottled beers. Local CAMRA Pub of the Year 2023. 🕸♞(Haymarket)♣🐾🐾

Wobbly Duck

4 Eldon Square, NE1 7JG
5 changing beers (sourced nationally; often Almasty) 🄷
Micropub that opened in 2021 in a basement down a few stairs in a row of Georgian terraced houses in Eldon Square, near the shopping centre. A thorough refurbishment has given the interior a rustic feel. There are tables outside the front, as well as an enclosed paved outdoor drinking area, the Wobbly Garden, at the rear, with outdoor heaters. A sister pub to the Old Fox in Felling and Beer Street in Newcastle.
🕸≠(Newcastle) ♞(Monument) 🐾

Newcastle upon Tyne: Gosforth

County 🄻 ✅

High Street, NE3 1HB
☎ (0191) 285 6919
Draught Bass; Great North Eastern Rivet Catcher; Greene King IPA; Morland Old Speckled Hen; Timothy Taylor Landlord; 7 changing beers (sourced regionally) 🄷
A pub with a large L-shaped bar and stained-glass windows on the main road frontage. It attracts a variety of visitors, from office workers to students, and can get busy, especially at weekends. A separate quiet room at the back offers respite from the hustle and bustle of the main bar, and also doubles as a small meeting or function room. Several guest beers are available.
🕸🐾P🚌🐾🛜

Newcastle upon Tyne: Heaton

Chillingham 🄻

Chillingham Road, NE6 5XN
☎ (0191) 265 3992
6 changing beers (sourced nationally) 🄷

Close to Chillingham Road Metro station, this large two-roomed pub comprises a comfortable lounge and a bar with sports shown on TVs. It offers an excellent choice of local microbrewery beers, plus bottled beers, whiskies and a wine of the month. It hosts regular quiz nights, and the food menu is popular with locals and visitors alike. There is a function room upstairs.
🕸⓵♞(Chillingham Road) ♣🚌(62,63) 🛜

Heaton Tap 🄻

41A Warton Terrace, NE6 5LS
4 changing beers (sourced locally) 🄷
Micropub and bottle shop just off Chillingham Road in Heaton. The shop is in the front room and has a good range of premium bottled beers. A newly refurbished lounge area is to the rear, and there is an outside drinking area at the front of the pub. Four real ales are served, often including some from the wood as well as local ales.

Newcastle upon Tyne: Quayside

Crown Posada 🄻

31 Side, NE1 3JE
☎ (0191) 232 1269 🌐 crownposada.co.uk
6 changing beers (sourced nationally) 🄷
Recognised by CAMRA as having a regionally important historic pub interior, this pub has been sympathetically refurbished over the years by the owners and is an oasis of calm near the bustling Quayside district. The narrow street frontage shows two impressive stained-glass windows, behind which lies a small snug, the bar counter and a longer seating area. There's an interesting coffered ceiling, locally relevant photographs and cartoons of long-gone customers and staff on the walls. Local small brewers are enthusiastically supported, with three regular local ales.
≠(Newcastle) ♞(Central Station) 🚌(53,QA) 🛜

Newcastle upon Tyne: South Gosforth

Millstone 🄻

Haddricks Mill Road, NE3 1QL
☎ (0191) 285 3429
Allendale Pennine Pale; Anarchy Blonde Star; 2 changing beers (sourced nationally) 🄷
A modern, stylish pub, with beers sourced from local microbreweries as well as national favourites. Draught Bass has been a favourite of the regulars for many years. The pub reopened in 2021 following a major refurbishment which included further opening out and more free-standing furniture of various heights. Live music plays on Thursday evening.
🐕🕸⓵♞(South Gosforth) P🚌(55,X7) 🐾🛜

Victory ✅

43 Killingworth Road, NE3 1SY
☎ (0191) 285 1254 🌐 victorysouthgosforth.co.uk
Timothy Taylor Landlord; Wainwright Amber; house beer (by Wainwright); 3 changing beers (sourced nationally) 🄷
Established on this site since 1861, the pub takes its name from Nelson's flagship and once served the local mining community. It is essentially a single-roomed pub and there are two lounge areas each side of the entrance with some seating near the bar. A rear lounge overlooks the Ouseburn. 🕸⓵&♞(South Gosforth)P🚌🐾🛜♫

North Shields

Enigma Tap
60 Bedford Street, NE29 0AR
☎ 07792 822063
4 changing beers (sourced nationally) Ⓗ
Micropub in a former shop unit just off the main Northumberland Square. There is a seating area near the front entrance and a narrower raised area towards the rear incorporating the photograph-covered bar and craft beer tap board. Outside is a small patio in the back yard.
ᗯ🕮☸♣●🚪🐾🌸

Seven Stars Ⓛ
7 Albion Road, NE30 2RJ
☎ (0191) 257 3982
House beer (by Three Kings); 4 changing beers (sourced nationally) Ⓗ
Recently refurbished single-roomed pub that serves up to five real ales including a house beer from Three Kings brewery and four others. Seven craft beers from local breweries and other brewers around the country are also available. A small courtyard to the rear provides outdoor drinking. Bar snacks include Scotch eggs, pork pies and cheese boards. Regular quiz nights feature.
Q🕮&🚪🐾🌸

Old Ryton Village

Olde Cross Ⓛ
Burnmoor Lane, NE40 3QP
☎ (0191) 447 3460 ● yeoldecross.co.uk
Fyne Jarl; 4 changing beers (sourced locally) Ⓗ
This community-owned inn in the Tyne Valley is an attractive Edwardian half-timbered local in a lovely setting by the village green and the cross it is named after. The original Cross Inn dates from the mid-19th century and was partly rebuilt in 1909. The pub is a centre for the local community, hosting entertainment and activities. Two community events – the hirings, which take place in spring and autumn, and the annual carols at Christmas – are held on the village green. Winner of a CAMRA Pub Saving Award in 2020.
ᗯ&♣🚪(R1,R3) 🌸🎧

Ryhope

Guide Post Ⓛ ✅
Ryhope Street South, SR2 0RN
☎ (0191) 523 5735
Maxim Double Maxim; 2 changing beers (sourced nationally) Ⓗ
Friendly, popular and comfortable street-corner local run by an enthusiastic landlord who is passionate about his ale. There are three handpulls, with Maxim Double Maxim always on, plus two changing guest beers. There are sports TVs, a pool table, and regular weekend entertainment such as live music, with dominoes on Sunday. There is a pleasant enclosed garden at the back.
ᗯ🕮♣🚪🌸🎵

South Shields

Cask Lounge Ⓛ
Charlotte Terrace, NE33 1QQ
☎ 07513 906703
5 changing beers (sourced nationally) Ⓗ
South Shields' first micropub, in a former housing office opposite the town hall. It is run by an experienced couple who value the principle of the micropub, encouraging conversation, with no TVs or gambling machines. There are six handpulls dispensing regular changing real ales.

The pub's two rooms have comfortable seating, soft carpeting and background music. An ever-growing collection of pumpclips adorns the bar area. 🕮&🚪🐾🌸

Marine 🍴 Ⓛ
230 Ocean Road, NE33 2JQ
☎ (0191) 455 0280 ● the-marine.co.uk
Allendale Golden Plover; Draught Bass; 6 changing beers (sourced nationally) Ⓗ
Dating from 1868, this family-run free house is opposite Marine Park, near the seafront. Up to six changing and two regular cask ales are available. Left of the bar are raised areas for customers to sit in social groups. There is a games area to the right and a function room upstairs. Non-intrusive background music is played and pub food is served daily. Local CAMRA Pub of the Year 2023.
ᗯ🕮&🚪♣●P🚪(E1,516) 🌸🎶

Steamboat Ⓛ ✅
Mill Dam, NE33 1EQ (follow signs for Customs House)
☎ (0191) 454 0134
7 changing beers (sourced nationally) Ⓗ
The only pub in the north-east to be awarded a Golden Award as part of CAMRA's 50th celebrations, the Steamboat is full of character. Located opposite the Custom House, the split-level bar and small lounge are decorated in a nautical theme. Note the certificates adorning the walls. There are nine handpulls serving real ale and two boxed ciders. Popular beer festivals are held, as well as regular music nights. The pub is about 10 minutes' walk from public transport interchange.
🚪●🚪🌸🎶♪

Wouldhave Ⓛ ✅
16 Mile End Road, NE33 1TA
☎ (0191) 427 6014
Greene King Abbot; Ruddles Best Bitter; Sharp's Doom Bar; 9 changing beers (sourced nationally) Ⓗ
Named after local boat builder William Wouldhave, co-inventor of the self righting lifeboat, this town-centre pub had a major refit in 2021, extending the customer area and creating a new garden. The pub offers well-priced bar meals all day and a selection of real ales from 12 handpumps, with three regular beers and a rotation of guest ales. There are monthly tap takeovers and twice-yearly beer festivals. It is close to the town centre public transport interchange. Q🚪ᗯ🕮🕪&🚪(10,E1)🌸

Sunderland: City Centre

Chesters Ⓛ ✅
Chester Road, SR4 7DR
☎ (0191) 565 9952
6 changing beers (sourced nationally) Ⓗ
This popular pub just outside the city centre has a smart and comfortable interior. There is a large main bar area and a more intimate area at the back. Real ale and a cider are available from up to six handpulls, with at least one local ale. Meals are served all day. Outside is a large beer garden and pay car park (ask for a voucher before paying). A function room with private bar is available upstairs. ᗯ🕮🕪&🚪(Millfield)●P🚪🌸

Dun Cow ★ Ⓛ
High Street West, SR1 3HA
☎ (0191) 567 2262 ● pubculture.com/duncow
Allendale Pennine Pale; 5 changing beers (sourced nationally) Ⓗ
A Grade II-listed architectural gem of a building, next door to the Sunderland Empire, which has been recognised by CAMRA as having nationally important historic pub interior. It won two CAMRA/Historic England Awards for best restoration and conservation after a

refurbishment in 2014, and underwent a major external and internal makeover during 2021. A plaque outside shows the pubs' history. Real ale features on up to eight handpulls. There is a function room upstairs. Q&≈Q(Park Lane) P♠Ⓟ🌢 ♪

Fitzgeralds L

12-14 Green Terrace, SR1 3PZ

☎ (0191) 567 0852

Titanic Plum Porter; 8 changing beers (sourced nationally) Ⓗ

A Grade II-listed pub that has been in the Guide since 1983. It serves two regular beers complemented by up to seven guests. The pub comprises a large main bar with numerous seating areas and a smaller, nautically-themed Chart Room. Meals are served daily until early evening. Now owned by the Ladhur Group, the pub has retained its old name, and is also known as Fitzys. ꝏ🌢Ⓘ≈Q(Park Lane) 🖫🌢

Ivy House L

7A Worcester Terrace, SR2 7AW

☎ (0191) 567 3399 ⊕ ivyhousesunderland.co.uk

6 changing beers (sourced nationally) Ⓗ

Tucked away close to Park Lane public transport interchange, the Ivy House is well worth seeking out. Six changing guest ales feature, plus an extensive range of international bottled beers. Home-made pizzas and burgers are prepared in an open kitchen. There are themed meal nights and a Wednesday night quiz. Live music features on the second Saturday and last Sunday of the month. Recipient of a CAMRA Lockdown Hero Award in 2021. 🌢Ⓘ≈Q(Park Lane)P🖫🌢

Peacock L

287 High Street West, SR1 3ES

☎ (0191) 514 3494

Maxim Double Maxim; Timothy Taylor Landlord; 2 changing beers (sourced nationally) Ⓗ

Large and distinctive V-shaped city-centre pub that is a Grade II-listed building. Inside is a long bar to the left and smaller lounges to the right. The pub offers up to four real ales and meals are served until early evening. There is an event space on the first floor and recording studios on the second floor. Outside is a pleasant seating area with a Sunderland Historic Buildings blue plaque on the wall. 🌢Ⓘ&≈Q🖫🌢🛜♪

Ship Isis L

26 Silksworth Row, SR1 3QJ

☎ (0191) 567 3720

7 changing beers (sourced nationally) Ⓗ

Dating from 1885, the Ship Isis was restored to its original splendour in 2011. The bar has seven handpulls offering up to five cask beers and two ciders. A range of bottled and canned beers is also available. There is also a quieter snug, and upstairs is a function room. Throughout the pub the walls are adorned with old photographs. Food is available and Monday is quiz night. 🌢Ⓘ&≈Q(Millfield) ♠🌢🛜♪

Sunderland: North

Avenue L

Zetland Street, SR6 0EQ (just off Roker Ave)

☎ (0191) 567 7412

6 changing beers (sourced nationally) Ⓗ

A 15-minute walk from the Stadium of Light, this local pub is just off Roker Avenue. There are up to six changing real ale handpulls, serving local and national beers. Several real ciders are also available. On Thursday nights there is a popular quiz and a domino handicap on Sundays. There is a function room, which is also an

overflow if the main bar is busy, and a smart garden to the rear. Local CAMRA Cider Pub of the Year 2023. 🌢&♣♠P🖫(E1) 🌢🛜

Harbour View

Harbour View, SR6 0NU

☎ (0191) 567 1402

6 changing beers (sourced nationally) Ⓗ

A modern local pub opposite Roker Harbour and close to the beach, with six handpulls serving regularly changing real ales. It is a true home for real ale lovers and a relaxing place, with additional seating outside to enjoy the sun. An excellent selection of background music is played, while every Thursday evening the pub holds a popular speakeasy. A function room is available upstairs. 🌢P🖫(E1,18) 🌢♪

Lighthouse L

7 Sea Road, Fulwell, SR6 9BP

☎ 07817 884157

Maxim Double Maxim; 2 changing beers (sourced nationally) Ⓗ

Sunderland's first micropub is in the centre of Fulwell. The former café has been transformed into a small but comfortable bar. There is an outdoor drinking area at the rear and a small room upstairs. Three handpulls offer largely local beers, often from Maxim brewery. There is no TV, no gaming machines and no music, just conversation. There are frequent buses nearby to Sunderland and South Shields. Seaburn Metro is 10 minutes' walk. Q🌢Q(Seaburn)🖫🌢

Tynemouth

Tynemouth Lodge Hotel L

Tynemouth Road, NE30 4AA

☎ (0191) 257 7565 ⊕ tynemouthlodgehotel.co.uk

Black Sheep Best Bitter; Hadrian Border Tyneside Blonde; Marston's Pedigree; Wainwright Amber; 1 changing beer (sourced locally; often Hadrian Border) Ⓗ

An externally tiled 1799 free house, next to a former house of correction, that has featured in every issue of the Guide since 1983. The comfortable pub has a U-shaped lounge with the bar on one side and a serving hatch on the other. Once renowned for its Draught Bass, recent supply difficulties mean it is rarely available. The pub makes an ideal stopping-off point for those completing the Coast-to-Coast cycle route. Q🌢QP🖫(1) 🛜

Tynemouth Social Club L

15/16 Front Street, NE30 4DX

☎ (0191) 257 7542

2 changing beers (sourced nationally) Ⓗ

Formerly a Co-op, this well-established social club at the heart of Tynemouth has a full pub licence and welcomes visitors. After several attempts to sell real ale, the club now has a rotating guest beer policy which has stimulated demand. The ale is well kept by the bar/cellarman and the club is well worth a visit. Local CAMRA Club of the Year 2019 and 2022. 🖫🖫🛜

Washington

Courtyard L

Biddick Lane, NE38 8AB

☎ (0191) 417 0445 ⊕ thecourtyardbar.co.uk

8 changing beers (sourced nationally) Ⓗ

A long-time regular in the Guide, this light and airy café/bar is located in the Washington Arts Centre offers a warm welcome to drinkers and food lovers alike. Eight handpulls serve changing real ales from local, regional and national breweries. An extensive range of food is served in the afternoon and early evening. Outdoor seating is available in the spacious courtyard. Two popular beer festivals are held over the Easter and August bank holidays. ➷❀◑❶♿P🏠❀🛜

Sir William De Wessyngton 🅛 ✅

2-3 Victoria Road, NE37 2SY
☎ (0191) 418 0100
Greene King Abbot; Ruddles Best Bitter; Sharp's Doom Bar; 4 changing beers (sourced nationally) Ⓗ
A large, open-plan pub in a former ice-cream parlour and snooker hall, named after a Norman knight and lord of the manor whose descendants emigrated to the United States. As well as the three regular real ales, it offers at least four guest ales – some from local microbreweries. Good-value food is available all day. Twice-yearly beer festivals are held. The pub received a CAMRA Lockdown Hero Recognition Award in 2021. Q➷❀◑❶♿P🏠🛜

Steps 🅛

47 Spout Lane, NE38 7HP
☎ (0191) 415 0733
5 changing beers (sourced nationally) Ⓗ
Known as the Spout Lane Inn when it opened in 1894, this popular community pub was renamed the Steps in 1976. The small, comfortable and friendly lounge bar is divided into two drinking areas, with pictures of old Washington decorating the walls. Five changing beers are available, often selected by the regulars, with some from local microbreweries. Quizzes are held Tuesday and Thursday nights. Free hire is available for special events. Opening hours vary. Q❀♣P🏠🛜♫

West Boldon

Black Horse 🅛

Rectory Bank, NE36 0QQ (off A184)
☎ (0191) 536 1814
2 changing beers (sourced nationally) Ⓗ
Iconic coaching inn-style pub that can trace its history back to at least the early 1700s. The interior is split between a bar/lounge and restaurant. The walls are decorated with bric-a-brac and photos taken by the owner; note the hats suspended from the ceiling. Two handpulls serve changing local ales, normally light session ales. Meals can be taken in the bar or in the partially covered area outside. ❀◑♿P🏠❀

Whitburn

Blue's Micro Pub 🅛

Percy Terrace, SR6 7EW
4 changing beers (sourced nationally) Ⓗ
In the centre of Whitburn village, this micropub offers four cask ale handpulls and four real ciders. The room above is a bottle shop and there is an outdoor seating area. A cask club is held on Wednesday, Thursday is Pie and a Pint night, and there is free cheeseboard every Sunday. This small, friendly pub encourages conversation, with no TVs or gaming machines. Card payments only. Local CAMRA Cider Pub of the Year 2023. Q❀●🏠❀

Whitley Bay

Dog & Rabbit 🅛

36 Park View, NE26 2TH
☎ 07944 552716 🌐 dogandrabbitbrewery.co.uk
6 changing beers (sourced nationally) Ⓗ

This micropub, converted from a women's clothing shop, is a welcome addition to the number of pubs in the area. The corner bar's six handpumps serve mostly local beers. The owner's microbrewery has been installed in the pub, brewing Dog & Rabbit beers. With no music, Wi-Fi or sports TV, conversation is encouraged among visitors. Local CAMRA Pub of the Year 2020. Q➷🏠(Monkseaton) 🏠❀

Rockcliffe Arms

Algernon Place, NE26 2DT
☎ (0191) 253 1299
4 changing beers (sourced nationally; often Whitley Bay) Ⓗ
Outstanding back-street former Fitzgerald's pub, a few minutes' walk from the Metro station, now run by the Whitley Bay Brewing Co. This one-room establishment has distinct bar and lounge areas with a snug in between. There are four constantly changing beers, details of which are explained on notices above the dividing arch. Regular dart and domino matches are held in the snug. It is popular with locals and real ale drinkers. ❀🏠♣🏠(1)

Split Chimp 🅛

Unit 1, Ground Floor, Spanish City Dome, Marine Avenue, NE26 1BG
🌐 splitchimp.pub
House beer (by Three Kings); 3 changing beers (sourced nationally) Ⓗ
Micropub that opened in 2019 in one of the units of the recently refurbished Spanish City, overlooking the promenade along the North Sea coast. Its single room has a long bar counter facing the entrance, with seating around the periphery. The house beer from Three Kings is supplemented by a changing range of four beers from near and far. Winter opening hours vary – check before you visit. ➷❀●🏠❀

Breweries

Almasty

Unit 11, Algernon Industrial Estate, New York Road, Shiremoor, NE27 0NB
☎ (0191) 253 1639

Second site: Unit A2A, Benfield Business Park, Benfield, NE6 4NQ 🌐 almasty.co.uk

⊗ Opened in 2014, Almasty brews on two sites, both on 10-barrel kits. The original site runs the mixed/natural fermentation and barrel-ageing programme, the new site produces unfined, unfiltered beers with a continuously changing output. Beers include heavily-hopped pale ales, IPAs and rich stouts. A taproom and shop located at Benfield Business Park is open during summer weekends. Pumpclips are made from screen-printed, hand-sawn logs. Beers are supplied nationwide. ‼🍴◆⬧

Alpha Delta SIBA

18 Riversdale Court, Newburn, Newcastle upon Tyne, NE15 8SG 🌐 alphadeltabrewing.com

Alpha Delta Brewing launched in 2019 in the Newburn district of Newcastle. Producing modern-style, high gravity beers in keg and can, the beers are unfined, unfiltered and unpasteurized. Collaborations with various breweries across Europe take place.

Anarchy SIBA

Unit A1, Benfield Business Park, Newcastle upon Tyne, NE6 4NQ ⊕ anarchybrewco.com

A 20-barrel brewery, started in 2012 in Morpeth, and moved to Newcastle upon Tyne in 2018. Its focus is on session beers, plus an eclectic mix of one-offs and collaborations with a host of breweries from the UK and across the globe. !!LIVE ✦

Blonde Star (ABV 4.1%) BLOND
A sweet, gently-bittered, fruity beer.
Citra Star (ABV 4.1%) GOLD
Skin Deep (ABV 4.2%) PALE
Cult Leader (ABV 5.5%) PALE

Big Lamp

Grange Road, Newburn, Newcastle upon Tyne, NE15 8NL
☎ (0191) 267 1689 ⊕ biglampbrewers.co.uk

⊕The North East of England's oldest microbrewery. After relocating to a former water pumping station in 1997, it expanded to a 55-barrel plant. The brewery tap, Keelman, is next door with accommodation available. !!✦LIVE

Sunny Daze (ABV 3.6%) GOLD
Golden, hoppy session bitter with a clean taste and finish.
Bitter (ABV 3.9%) BITTER
A clean-tasting bitter, full of hops and malt. A hint of fruit with a good, hoppy finish.
Lamplight Bitter (ABV 4.2%) BITTER
Summerhill Stout (ABV 4.4%) STOUT
A rich, tasty stout, dark in colour with a lasting rich roast character. Malty mouthfeel with a lingering finish.
Prince Bishop Ale (ABV 4.8%) GOLD
A refreshing, easy-drinking bitter. Golden in colour, full of fruit and hops. Strong bitterness with a spicy, dry finish.
Keelman Brown (ABV 5.7%) OLD

Black Storm

31 Coble Dene, Royal Quays, Percy Main, NE29 6DW
☎ 07852 432467 ⊕ blackstormbrewery.com

Beers were originally contract brewed by Hadrian Border Brewery (qv) but the former Blackhill brewery was purchased in 2019 with brewing commencing shortly afterwards. In 2022, the brewery moved to the Royal Quays Outlet on North Tyneside. ✦

Blonde (ABV 4%) BLOND
Pilsner (ABV 4.1%) PALE
Gold (ABV 4.3%) GOLD
Porter (ABV 5.2%) PORTER
IPA (ABV 5.5%) IPA

Blockyard (NEW) SIBA

Queen Victoria Hotel, Harbour View, Sunderland, SR6 0PQ
☎ (0191) 300 2999 ⊕ blockyardbrew.co.uk

Established in 2022 at the rear of the Queen's Head Hotel, Roker. The 2.5-barrel plant was previously at One More Than Two Brewery, South Shields.

Blue

Unit G21, The Avenues, Eleventh Avenue, North Team Valley Trading Estate, Gateshead, NE11 0NJ
☎ (0191) 491 0221 ⊕ bluebrewing.co.uk

Nomad brewery using spare capacity at other breweries. Established in 2019 it acquired the rights to the Mordue

brand. Beerology branded beers are produced for the eponymous bar in Newcastle.

Brewed under the Mordue Brewery brand name:
5 Bridges (ABV 3.6%) BITTER
Blonde (ABV 4%) BLOND
Howay in a Manger (ABV 4.3%) BITTER
Workie (ABV 4.5%) BITTER
Radgie (ABV 4.8%) BITTER
IPA (ABV 5.1%) PALE

Brewlab

1 West Quay Court, Sunderland Entrerprise Park, Sunderland, SR5 2TE ⊕ brewlab.co.uk

Brewlab was founded 1986 in London by Dr Keith Thomas. It moved to Sunderland in 1991 and again in 2010 to a purpose-built facility. Brewlab provide training courses, analysis services and project support to the brewing industry. Its laboratory works with breweries throughout the UK looking after analysis requests. Brewlab Brews creates speciality beers often inspired by students. Some of the beers produced are based on analysis of historical recipes. The brews are served at local outlets and onsite.

Brinkburn Street SIBA

3 Hume Street, Byker, Newcastle Upon Tyne, NE6 1LN
☎ (0191) 338 9039 ⊕ brinkburnbrewery.co.uk

Brewing began in 2015, much influenced by West Coast US beer styles. Citrus flavours and highly-hopped bitterness is a feature of many of its beers. The brewery relocated to a new site in 2018. ✦

Fools Gold (ABV 3.8%) GOLD
The Pursuit of Hoppiness (ABV 3.9%) PALE
Byker Brown Ale (ABV 4.8%) BROWN

Cullercoats SIBA

Westfield Court, Unit 19, Maurice Road Industrial Estate, Wallsend, NE28 6BY ☎ 07837 637615
⊕ cullercoatsbrewery.co.uk

⊕Established in 2011, brewing takes place twice a week. The brewery champions English hops. ♦

Shuggy Boat Blonde (ABV 3.8%) BLOND
Lovely Nelly (ABV 3.9%) BITTER
Polly Donkin Oatmeal Stout (ABV 4.2%) STOUT
Fruity sweet and roast aromas precede a full-bodied stout with a roast sweet caramel centre and a lingering satisfying finish.
Jack the Devil (ABV 4.5%) BITTER
Light brown bitter with a sweet fruit start. Bittering hops last well in the finish.
Grace Darling Gold (ABV 5%) BITTER

Darwin

14 Prospect Terrace, North Shields, NE30 1DX
☎ 07900 921276 ⊕ darwinbrewery.com

⊕Established in 1994, Darwin was based in purpose-built premises in Sunderland which were shared with Brewlab. In 2022, the brewery was purchased by Three Kings Brewery and moved to North Shields. Darwin and Three Kings operate independently, producing separate ranges of beers and Gav Sutherland remains Head Brewer of Darwin. Darwin's core beers and seasonal offerings are available around the North East. !!♦LIVE

Expedition (ABV 3.8%) PALE
Evolution (ABV 4%) BITTER
Beagle Blonde (ABV 4.1%) BLOND

Chocolate and Vanilla Stout (ABV 5%) STOUT
Rolling Hitch (ABV 5.2%) PALE

Dog & Rabbit

▤ 36 Park View, Whitley Bay, NE26 2TH ☎ 07944 552716 ⊕ dogandrabbitbrewery.co.uk

The Dog & Rabbit brewery was established in 2015 and relocated to its current premises as a small one-barrel micro- brew pub in 2016. **LIVE**

Firebrick SIBA

Units 10 & 11, Blaydon Business Centre, Cowen Road, Blaydon-on-Tyne, NE21 5TW
☎ (0191) 447 6543 ⊕ firebrickbrewery.com

Firebrick began brewing on a 2.5-barrel plant in 2013, expanding to a 15-barrel plant in 2014. Beers are mostly available in pubs within the Tyne & Wear area and a few outlets further afield. ♦

Blaydon Brick (ABV 3.8%) BITTER
Coalface (ABV 3.9%) MILD
Elder Statesman (ABV 3.9%) BITTER
Tyne 9 (ABV 3.9%) SPECIALITY
Pagan Queen (ABV 4%) BLOND
Little Belgium (ABV 4.2%) SPECIALITY
Trade Star (ABV 4.2%) BITTER
Copper-coloured fruity bitter. Well-balanced with sweet malts some fruitiness and a long hoppy bitter finish.
Stella Spark (ABV 4.4%) PALE
Well-balanced sweet fruity and hoppy beer with a lasting finish.
Toon Broon (ABV 4.6%) BITTER
Tasty sweet, malty and fruity beer with some roast crystal caramels and hop bitterness emerging nicely in the finish.
Cushie Butterfield (ABV 5%) STOUT
Creamy stout with hints of blackcurrant and chocolate. Complex balance of sweet malts, roast and hop bitterness with a clean finish.
Wey-Aye P.A. (ABV 5.8%) IPA
Well balanced IPA with citrus hops, fruit and sweetness. The hops prevail in the finish.

Flash House

Unit 1A, Northumberland Street, North Shields, NE30 1DS ☎ 07481 901875
⊕ flashhousebrewing.co.uk

Flash House was set up by Jack O'Keefe in 2016, after a life-long appreciation of ale. It aims to bring the best beer styles the world has to offer to the North East, and continues to produce new guest and seasonal ales rather than maintaining a core range in cask. The brewery and taproom are situated a short walk from North Shields town centre and the revamped North Shields Fish Quay. ‼♦⚖

Full Circle SIBA

Hoults Yard, Walker Road, Newcastle upon Tyne, NE6 2HL
☎ (0191) 481 4114 ⊕ fullcirclebrew.co.uk

Brewing began in 2019 in Hoult's Yard in Byker, another addition to the real ale scene in this area. It also incorporates a taproom, plus the Pip Stop bottled beer shop. ▤⚖

Repeater (ABV 4.2%) PALE
Hoop (ABV 5.5%) IPA
Looper (ABV 6.4%) IPA

Great North Eastern SIBA

Contract House (Unit E), Wellington Road, Dunston, Gateshead, NE11 9HS
☎ (0191) 447 4462 ⊕ gnebco.com

Brewing began in 2016 on a 10-barrel plant. In 2017 the brewery expanded into the adjacent premises and a taproom and shop was opened, with an events space for live entertainment. Beers are supplied direct throughout the North-East, and nationally via wholesalers. ▤♦⚖

Claspers Citra Blonde (ABV 3.8%) BLOND
Styrian Blonde (ABV 3.8%) BLOND
Gold (ABV 4%) GOLD
Rivet Catcher (ABV 4%) BITTER
Session bitter with sweet malts and hops continuing through to a lasting, dry, bitter finish.
Taiheke Sun (ABV 4.2%) PALE
Delta APA (ABV 4.5%) PALE
Foxtrot Premium Ale (ABV 4.5%) BITTER
GNE Stout (ABV 4.6%) STOUT
Graphite (ABV 4.6%) BROWN
Hopnicity (ABV 5%) PALE

Hadrian Border SIBA

Unit 5, The Preserving Works, Newburn Industrial Estate, Shelley Road, Newburn, NE15 9RT
☎ (0191) 264 9000 ⊕ hadrian-border-brewery.co.uk

Based in Newburn near Newcastle-upon-Tyne, using a 40-barrel plant, the brewery can produce up to 200 barrels per week. Beer is delivered directly to the area between Edinburgh, North Yorkshire, Carlisle and the East Coast, and is also available nationally through wholesalers. A three-barrel plant is used for experimental craft brews. One pub is run – the Station East, Gateshead. ‼♦**LIVE**

Tyneside Blonde (ABV 3.9%) BLOND
Refreshing blonde ale with zesty notes and a clean, fruity finish.
Farne Island Pale Ale (ABV 4%) BITTER
A copper-coloured bitter with a refreshing malt/hop balance.
Northern Pale (ABV 4.1%) PALE
Secret Kingdom (ABV 4.3%) BITTER
Grainger Ale (ABV 4.6%) PALE
Northern IPA (ABV 5.2%) PALE
Ouseburn Porter (ABV 5.2%) PORTER
Traditional robust porter, made with Chocolate and Black Malt. Distinct bitter coffee finish

Lazy Lizard (NEW)

▤ The Stables, 38 Front Street, Cleadon, SR6 7PG
☎ (0191) 447 8460

Brewing commenced in 2022 at The Stables micropub in Cleadon, based within Cleadon Conservation Area. Run by three friends, its beers are available as part of the micropub's rotating guest beer policy.

Maxim SIBA

1 Gadwall Road, Rainton Bridge South, Houghton le Spring, DH4 5NL
☎ (0191) 584 8844 ⊕ maximbrewery.co.uk

☺Rising from the ashes of Sunderland brewer Vaux, Maxim was set up with a 20-barrel plant in Houghton-le-Spring in 2007. More than 100 outlets are supplied direct and two pubs are owned. A weekday phone and collect service is available for bottled beers and a brewery open night is held first Friday of the month. ▤♦⚖

Lambtons (ABV 3.8%) GOLD

Samson (ABV 4%) BITTER
Ward's Best Bitter (ABV 4%) BITTER
Swedish Blonde (ABV 4.2%) PALE
Sweet malt and fruit with moderate hop bitterness which lasts to provide a long dry finish.
Double Maxim (ABV 4.7%) BROWN
A roasty classic brown ale. Hops play their part giving a gentle bitterness to the dominant fruit, which reduces on drinking. A complex beer with an inviting smell of butterscotch.
Raspberry Porter (ABV 5%) SPECIALITY
Maximus (ABV 6%) OLD
Fruit and sweetness dominate this beer throughout along with crystal malts, hops and alcohol, combining to create a lasting full rich mouthfeel.

Northern Alchemy

The Old Coal Yard, Elizabeth Street, Byker, Newcastle upon Tyne, NE6 1JS ☎ 07834 386333 ⊕ wearenorthernalchemy.com

Brewing began in 2014. The brewery was situated in a converted shipping container, known as the Lab, just behind the Cumberland Arms. In 2017 it moved to larger premises in a former coal depot. All beers are unfined and unfiltered. Beers are always available in the Cumberland Arms, and from the taproom every weekend. ♦✦

US Session Pale (ABV 4.1%) PALE

Out There

Unit 4, Foundry Lane Industrial Estate, Newcastle upon Tyne, NE6 1LH ☎ 07946 579534 ⊕ outtherebrewing.com

Out There was established in 2012 by Steve Pickthall. Branding and beer names are themed around the 1950s space race.

Space is the Place (ABV 3.5%) BITTER
Laika (ABV 4.8%) SPECIALITY
Celestial Love (ABV 5.1%) BITTER

Stu Brew

Newcastle University, Merz Court, Newcastle upon Tyne, NE1 7RU ⊕ stubrew.com

Stu Brew is Europe's first student-run microbrewery based at Newcastle University. The brewery produces a wide range of beers including many seasonal and one-off beers whilst enabling students to run research projects on a range of brewing issues including reducing environmental impact and waste.

Lab Session (ABV 4.3%) PALE
Exam Room Tears (ABV 5%) SPECIALITY

Tavernale

▤ Bridge Tavern, 7 Akenside Hill, Newcastle upon Tyne, NE1 3UF
☎ (0191) 232 1122 ⊕ thebridgetavern.com

A two-barrel plant supplying beers to the Bridge Tavern only. All beers brewed are one-offs. Brewing is currently suspended. ♦

Thirsty Moose (NEW) SIBA

Unit 5c, Galaxy Business Park, Newburn Bridge Road, Ryton, NE21 4SQ ☎ 07862 087087 ⊕ thirstymoosebrewingco.com

Brewing commenced in 2022 by two partners with Canadian heritage and a passion for brewing.

Three Kings SIBA

14 Prospect Terrace, North Shields, NE30 1DX ☎ 07580 004565 ⊕ threekingsbrewery.co.uk

Three Kings started in 2012 using a 2.5-barrel plant, and has steadily upgraded it to its current 25-barrel capacity. Two house beers are brewed for local pubs. As well as the regular beers it typically brews two one-off beers each month. ♦

Shieldsman (ABV 3.8%) BITTER
Billy Mill Ale (ABV 4%) BITTER
Dark Side of the Toon (ABV 4.1%) STOUT
Dark roast malts and a sweet creamy body last through to a drier finish of roast bitter.
Ring of Fire (ABV 4.5%) PALE
Silver Darling (ABV 5.6%) IPA

TOPS (The Olde Potting Shed)

Collingdon Buildings, Collingdon Road, High Spen, NE39 2EQ

TOPS began brewing in 2013 using a five-barrel plant with a small test kit for experimental beers. Pubs are supplied direct within a 30-mile radius of the brewery.

Blondie (ABV 3.8%) BLOND

Two by Two

Unit 8, Morley's Yard, Byker, NE6 1PQ ☎ 07723 959168

Office: 14 Albany Gardens, Whitley Bay, NE26 2DY ⊕ @TwoByTwoBrewing

Brewing began in 2014 using a five-barrel plant in Wallsend on Tyneside. At the end of 2018 an additional five-barrel plant was installed, increasing capacity to 10 barrels. In 2022, the brewery moved to Byker, thus becoming another addition to this already burgeoning area for microbreweries. LIVE

Session IPA (ABV 4%) GOLD
Citrus hops are to the fore in this cloudy and notably hoppy golden ale which is cleverly balanced with fruity sweetness. The hoppy bitter theme persists long after the drinking ends.
Leap Frog (ABV 4.1%) PALE
Foxtrot Pale (ABV 4.5%) PALE
Snake Eyes Pale (ABV 4.6%) GOLD
Significant citrus and fruit aromas lead to a sweet, hoppy, full-bodied golden ale. Full advantage is made of the hops in the lasting hoppy, fruity finish.
Dragonfly (ABV 5.5%) IPA
Sitting Duck (ABV 5.7%) STOUT
American Pale Ale (ABV 5.8%) IPA
South Paw IPA (ABV 6.2%) IPA

Tyne Bank

375 Walker Road, Newcastle upon Tyne, NE6 2AB ☎ (0191) 265 2828 ⊕ tynebankbrewery.co.uk

⊠ Major changes have happened at the brewery with new ownership in 2023 and a focus on producing quality real ales and craft beers together with hosting events in its industrial taproom. The beer range has been reviewed with refreshed versions. A new range is now becoming available. ✦

Monument Bitter (ABV 4.1%) BITTER

Vaux

Unit 2, Monk Street, Sunderland, SR6 0DB ☎ (0191) 580 5770 ⊕ vaux.beer

Opened in 2020, Vaux is a five-barrel microbrewery resurrecting the old Vaux Brewery name (a major regional brewer, which closed in 1999). A taproom is open Friday, Saturday and Sunday. Further expansion of the brewery is planned. ▪◆

Black Wave (ABV 5%) STOUT

Whitley Bay

2-4 South Parade, Whitley Bay, NE26 2RG ☎ 07392 823480 ⊕ whitleybaybrew.com

☺Brewing commenced in 2016 on a five-barrel plant and was relocated to much larger premises in the centre of Whitley Bay in 2018. The brewery was expanded in 2022 in order to supply a local wholesaler as well as its direct sales to approximately 30 pubs.

137 Steps (ABV 3.9%) BLOND
Slow Joe (ABV 3.9%) BLOND
Warrior (ABV 3.9%) PALE
Remembrance (ABV 4%) PORTER

Kangaroo (ABV 4.2%) PALE
Spanish City Blonde (ABV 4.2%) BLOND
Dark Knight (ABV 4.3%) BROWN
Ghost Ships (ABV 4.3%) PALE
Texas Cleggy (ABV 5%) BITTER
Equinox (ABV 6.2%) IPA

Wylam

Palace of Arts, Exhibition Park, Newcastle upon Tyne, NE2 4PZ ⊕ wylambrewery.co.uk

☺Wylam commenced brewing in 2000 on a 4.5-barrel plant. In 2016 the brewery moved to Newcastle upon Tyne, and a new 30-barrel kit was installed at the Palace of the Arts, in the city's Exhibition Park. It hosts regular events and concerts in the main hall and has a separate taproom area (Fri-Sun). ◆◆

Gold (ABV 4%) GOLD
Fresh clean flavour, full of hops. This golden ale has a hint of citrus in the finish.
FLEEK (ABV 4.2%) PALE

Peacock, Sunderland: City Centre (Photo: Ken Paul)

NORTHERN
ISLES

SHETLAND

HIGHLANDS
&
WESTERN ISLES

ABERDEEN
& GRAMPIAN

TAYSIDE

LOCH LOMOND,
STIRLING
& THE
TROSSACHS

FIFE

ARGYLL &
THE ISLES

GREATER
GLASGOW &
CLYDE

EDINBURGH & LOTHIANS

AYRSHIRE
& ARRAN

BORDERS

DUMFRIES &
GALLOWAY

NORTHUMBERLAND

TYNE &
WEAR

NORTHERN
IRELAND

CUMBRIA

DURHAM

ISLE OF
MAN

NORTH
YORKSHIRE

LANCASHIRE

EAST
YORKS

WEST
YORKS

MERSEYSIDE

GREATER
MANCHESTER

SOUTH
YORKS

LINCOLNSHIRE

NW
WALES

NE
WALES

CHESHIRE

DERBYSHIRE

NOTTINGHAM-
SHIRE

SHROPSHIRE

STAFFORD-
SHIRE

LEICESTERSHIRE

NORFOLK

MID
WALES

HEREFORD-
SHIRE

WEST
MIDLANDS

WORCESTER-
SHIRE

WARWICK-
SHIRE

NORTHAMPTON-
SHIRE

RUTLAND

CAMBRIDGE-
SHIRE

SUFFOLK

WEST
WALES

GWENT

GLOUCS &
BRISTOL

OXFORD-
SHIRE

BUCKINGHAM-
SHIRE

BEDFORD-
SHIRE

HERTFORD-
SHIRE

ESSEX

GLAMORGAN

WILLSHIRE

BERKSHIRE

GREATER
LONDON

CHANNEL
ISLANDS

SOMERSET

HAMPSHIRE

SURREY

KENT

WEST
SUSSEX

EAST
SUSSEX

DEVON

DORSET

CORNWALL

ISLE OF
WIGHT

Wales

Wales

GLAMORGAN

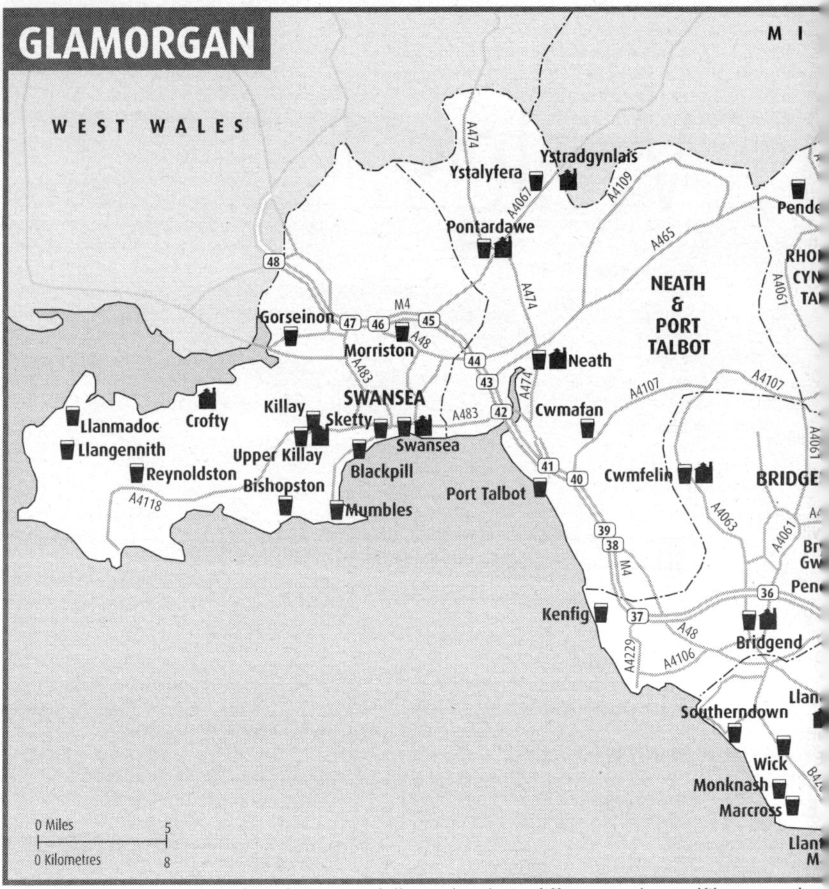
GLAMORGAN
WEST WALES
MI
Ystradgynlais
Ystalyfera
A474
A4067
A4109
Pontardawe
A465
Pende
NEATH
&
PORT
TALBOT
RHO
CYN
TA
A4061
48
M4
Gorseinon
47
46
45
A48
Morriston
A483
44
Neath
43
A474
SWANSEA
Killay
Sketty
A483
42
Cwmafan
A4107
A4107
Llanmadoc
Crofty
Llangennith
Upper Killay
Swansea
Reynoldston
Blackpill
41
Bishopston
40
Cwmfelin
BRIDGE
A4061
A4118
Port Talbot
Mumbles
A4063
39
38
A4061
M4
36
Kenfig
37
A48
Bridgend
A4229
A4106
Southerndown
Wick
Monknash
Marcross
0 Miles
5
0 Kilometres
8

Authority areas covered: Bridgend UA, Caerphilly UA (part), Cardiff UA, Merthyr Tydfil UA, Neath & Port Talbot UA, Rhondda, Cynon & Taff UA, Swansea UA, Vale of Glamorgan UA

Aberdare

Ieuan ap Iago ✓

6 High Street, CF44 7AA

☎ (01685) 880080

Greene King Abbot; Sharp's Doom Bar; 4 changing beers (sourced nationally; often Adnams, Marston's, Wychwood) Ⓗ

Busy Wetherspoon in the town centre, well placed for local amenities and public transport. It is named in honour of Ieuan ap Iago (Evan James), writer of the lyrics to the Welsh national anthem Hen Wlad Fy Nhadau. A wide range of ales and ciders are mostly sourced nationally. It also offers an extensive food service. Dare Valley Country Park is not far away, offering camping pitches by prior booking. ☕❀◐♿⛺≉●P🚌ᯤ

National Tap 🄻

Cross Street, CF44 7EG

☎ (01685) 267310 🌐 greytreesbrewery.com

Grey Trees Diggers Gold, Drummer Boy, Mosaic Pale Ale, Afghan Pale; 3 changing beers (sourced regionally; often Grey Trees, Purple Moose, Salopian) Ⓗ

Small, comfortable and welcoming micropub with an impressive reputation, located in the centre of Aberdare. It is the local outlet for nearby Grey Trees brewery and stocks a wide range of their beers, with guests regularly featuring past and current award-winning brewers. There is a subtle military theme to the memorabilia around the bar. Q❀⛺≉●🚌🐾ᯤ

Whitcombe Inn

Whitcombe Street, CF44 7DA

☎ (01685) 875106

Wye Valley Butty Bach; 2 changing beers (sourced nationally; often Sharp's, Wychwood) Ⓗ

Traditional and welcoming street-corner local, close to the main shopping area and the market. The single main bar has a pool room at the back. Sports TV often plays, but is rarely obtrusive except on rugby international match days. Children are welcome until 9pm. Occasional live music features. The pub is about a mile from the Dare Valley Country Park, with great walks and also pitches for campers and touring vans. ⛺≉♣🚌🐾ᯤ♫

Aberthin

Hare & Hounds

Aberthin Road, CF71 7LG

☎ (01446) 774892 🌐 hareandhoundsaberthin.com

Wye Valley HPA; 2 changing beers (sourced regionally; often Glamorgan, Grey Trees, Vale of Glamorgan) Ⓗ

Characterful village pub whose cosy public bar with thick stone walls, wooden beams and log fire is the focal point

4 changing beers (sourced regionally; often Grey Trees, Vale of Glamorgan, Well Drawn) G

Formerly a shop, converted in 2017, this is a single room with no bar – customers are served at their tables with blackboards showing what's on offer. As well as up to four predominantly Welsh cask ales on gravity, there is a craft keg beer. Most of the cider is fruit flavoured. The enthusiastic licensee is a keen fan of the Jam and named the pub after one of their songs. The memorabilia even extends into a series of tiles in the toilet.
Q❤♿⬇(Docks) ⬛(304,96) ♣🌵📶♫

Sir Samuel Romilly L ✔

8 Romilly Buildings, Broad Street, CF62 7AU

☎ (01446) 724900

Greene King Abbot; Ruddles Best Bitter; Sharp's Doom Bar; 2 changing beers H

This spacious Wetherspoon pub is named after a landowner and legal reformer of the 1800s. It opened in 2009 in a building that was previously a market hall, theatre and bank, the vault of which remains and is used as a seating area. A large mural above the side entrance depicts life in old Barry, with many more pictures of the town inside. A larger range of beers is available during sporting events. Q❤🅿♿◑🚲⬛(96,304)📶

Bishopston

Joiners Arms L

50 Bishopston Road, SA3 3EJ

☎ (01792) 232658 ⊕ thejoiners.info

Marston's Pedigree; Wadworth 6X; 2 changing beers (sourced nationally) H

Situated in the heart of the village, this 1860s stone-built free house remains popular with locals and visitors. The four cask handpumps are located in the rear lounge area where locals gather. The rustic-style dining area serves award-winning high-quality food, with some ingredients grown by the chef. A full menu is also available in the bar. The guest ales are mainly sourced locally and the cider is often from Llanblethian Orchards. Outside, the beer garden has its own bar shack and occasionally hosts live music. There is limited parking.
Q❤🅿♿◑♣🅿⬛(321)🌵📶♫

Barry

Barry West End Club L

54 St Nicholas Road, CF62 6QY

☎ (01446) 735739 ⊕ barrywestendclub.webs.com

Sharp's Doom Bar; Wye Valley HPA; 2 changing beers (often Wainwright) H

Multiple local CAMRA Club of the Year overlooking the old harbour and housed in a large, multi-floored red-brick building. Visitors are welcome and CAMRA members are treated as honorary club members. Home to cricket, football, snooker and skittles teams as well as chess, scuba diving and fishing clubs among others, there is always something going on here. Two beer festivals a year, live music on weekends, pub grub and a friendly atmosphere makes this club an essential visit.
Q❤🅿♿◑🚲🅿⬛(96,304)📶♫

Butterfly Collector

50A Holton Road, CF63 4HE

☎ 07542 673794

of the two-room bar. Good-value food is served some lunchtimes and most evenings (except Mon and Sun eve) and there are occasional music events, usually around public holidays. Major sporting events are shown on large screens. There is a small car park and outdoor seating at the front. ♿❀❶P🍽(14)❀🎵

Blackpill

Woodman ✔

120 Mumbles Road, SA3 5AS (near turn off for B4436, opp Blackpill Lido)
☎ (01792) 402700

Greene King IPA, Abbot; 2 changing beers (sourced nationally; often Greene King) Ⓗ
Historic pub and restaurant dating back to 1819 and attractively furnished. The deceptively spacious establishment, with its various nooks and alcoves, is situated on the main seafront road and the entrance to the beautiful Clyne Gardens. Popular with both families and diners, the pub also welcomes drinkers. An ever-changing range of ales is offered, often including one from a local brewery. There are three outside seating areas including a beer garden. ♿❀❶&P🍽(2,3)❀🎵

Bridgend

Coach

37 Cowbridge Road, CF31 3DH
Coach Bridgend Pale Ale Ⓗ**; 3 changing beers (often Coach, New Bristol, Thornbridge)** Ⓗ/Ⓖ
An incredible commitment to real ale and independent producers has been the basis for the running of this pub since the current owners took it on. Basically furnished but comfortable, there is an art wall for local artists to display their work. Events include open mic nights, outings and two beer festivals per year. The owners began brewing in 2018 – the brewery is visible from inside the pub. Two Coach cask beers are usually on sale and several craft beers. Q♿❀❖♣🍽(303,X2)❀🎵

Wyndham Arms ✔

Dunraven Place, CF31 1JE
☎ (01656) 673571

Greene King Abbot, IPA Ⓗ**; Sharp's Doom Bar** Ⓗ/Ⓖ**; 2 changing beers** Ⓗ
Named after a centuries-old local family, this pub dates from 1792. It is split into three distinct sections, with a variety of seating options including dining areas. A conference room is available for hire. The pub opens at 7am to serve breakfast and non-alcoholic drinks and the bar opens at 9am. Beers from Welsh breweries dominate. There are 25 en-suite bedrooms available. Q♿🛏❶&🍽❀

Brynnau Gwynion

Mountain Hare

Brynna Road, CF35 6PG
☎ (01656) 860453

3 changing beers (sourced nationally; often Glamorgan, Wye Valley) Ⓗ
This typical Welsh village inn has featured in the Guide for many years. It has been owned by the same family for over 40 years and has a traditional public bar, games room and a lovely old stone-walled lounge. The licensee began brewing on-site in 2014 and occasionally showcases his own beers. Sport is often on the TV in this rugby-lovers' pub. Staff and locals are most welcoming to visitors. Q♿❀❶&♣P🍽(64,404)❀🎵

Caerphilly

Malcolm Uphill ✔

89-91 Cardiff Road, CF83 1FQ
☎ (029) 2076 0720

Greene King Abbot; Ruddles Best Bitter; Sharp's Doom Bar; 2 changing beers (sourced nationally) Ⓗ
Comfortable and convenient Wetherspoon pub, well placed between the town centre shops and the main bus and rail transport hub. Usually one or two guest beers are offered, particularly at weekends, and up to two ciders. Meals are served during opening hours. The pub can be busy at weekends. It hosts a quiz on Sundays, when it tends to be a bit quieter. Ring the main entrance doorbell if the separate accessible entrance is needed. ♿❶&♿🍽❀

Cardiff: Birchgrove

Aneurin Bevan ✔

Caerphilly Road, CF14 4AD
☎ (029) 2054 4280

Greene King Abbot; Ruddles Best Bitter; 5 changing beers (sourced nationally) Ⓗ
A JD Wetherspoon pub that is smaller and more intimate than many, set in the middle of a busy road junction, to the north of Gabalfa flyover. It offers the usual Wetherspoon range of good-value food, plus a constantly changing wide range of ales. Live subtitled news (on silent) is on throughout the day. Recent additions include extra outside dining space. ♿❀❶&♣P🍽❀

Cardiff: Canton

Chapter Arts Centre

Market Road, Canton, CF5 1QE
☎ (029) 2030 4400 🌐 chapter.org

Banks's Amber Ale; Brakspear Oxford Gold; Marston's 61 Deep; 1 changing beer (sourced nationally) Ⓗ
A lively and eclectic arts centre/cinema complex in a converted Victorian high school, just off a busy main road. The guest beers, when available, are sourced from across the UK, and usually include small independents supplemented by a local ale. A number of fridges contain a fair range of bottled beers from continental producers, with the emphasis on Germany. ♿❀❶&🚊(Ninian Park) P🍽(16,17)❀🎵

Cardiff: Cathays

Cathays Beer House

109 Crwys Road, CF24 4NF

4 changing beers (sourced nationally; often Bristol Beer Factory, Liverpool Brewing Company) Ⓖ
Converted from a former post office, this single-room pub, with a small terrace to the front, is a welcome addition to this part of Cardiff, and worked hard throughout the various lockdowns to provide a takeaway service to the local community. The decor may be basic but the atmosphere is friendly and welcoming. It serves up to four ales on gravity, and a small selection of boxed ciders. Former local CAMRA Cider Pub of the Year. Q♿❀&♿🍽(8,9)❀❀

Cardiff: Cathays Park

Pen & Wig ✔

1 Park Grove, CF10 3BJ
☎ (029) 2037 1217

8 changing beers (sourced nationally; often Bristol Beer Factory, Grey Trees, Mumbles) Ⓗ

Large converted Victorian terraced residence, just off the city centre and near the national museum and university. The clientele is typically professional and white-collar during the day, and students in the evening. The beer range is from local, regional and national breweries. The pub hosts monthly Meet the Brewer and brewery takeovers. There is a large garden which includes a covered section, and a smoker's area. Prices are at the higher end for the area. ✿❀◑&⇌(Cathays)●🚆😺🛜

Cardiff: City Centre

Central Bar ✓
39 Windsor Place, CF10 3BW
☎ (029) 2078 0260
Greene King Abbot; Ruddles Best Bitter; Sharp's Doom Bar; 5 changing beers (sourced nationally) 🅷
Popular Wetherspoon pub just off Queen Street near its eastern end. This former nightclub has an upper storey used as an additional bar, open most times. There is an outdoor drinking area at the rear. The bar usually stocks the full range of available guest beers, with up to five available at any one time, as well as a number of real ciders/perries. ⛄✿❀&⇌(Queen Street)●🛜

Flute & Tankard 🍺
4 Windsor Place, CF10 3BX
☎ (029) 2039 8315 ● thefluteandtankard.com
5 changing beers (sourced nationally; often Grey Trees, Thornbridge, Wantsum) 🅷
A one-bar pub just off Queen Street at the quieter, eastern end of the city centre. Under current management, the Flute has become the city centre's leading real ale pub in terms of the range and quality of its beers. Musical performances, often jazz, and other events take place in an upstairs room. Note that , to avoid restrictions, the pub does not open on Principality Stadium rugby international days.
Q⇌(Queen Street) ●🎵

Gatekeeper ✓
9-10 Westgate Street, CF10 1DD
☎ (029) 2064 6020
Greene King Abbot; Ruddles Best Bitter; Sharp's Doom Bar; 5 changing beers 🅷
Former theatre, then auction rooms, and now a JD Wethersppon pub. As well as the usual listed beers, a choice of guests is available, often from local breweries. Additionally, there is a choice of real ciders/perries. One downstairs bar services two lower drinking areas, while another bar (not always open) services the balcony public area. A lift connects all areas.
✿❀◑&⇌(Central) ●🚆🛜

Head of Steam Cardiff
18-19 Church Street, CF10 1BG
☎ (029) 2037 2582
Camerons Strongarm; 5 changing beers (sourced nationally; often Castle Rock, Hydes) 🅷
The Cardiff Head of Steam branch is a few minutes' walk from the central railway station. Now established as part of the city's 'pub mile', it offers a good selection of cask and craft ales, with a range of Belgian/German beers providing further choice. A central island bar has seating spread around it, booths down one side, and a mix of tables down the other. Upstairs seating is also available.
◑&⇌(Central) ●😺🛜

Owain Glyndwr ✓
10 St John Street, CF10 1GL
☎ (029) 2022 1980
4 changing beers (sourced nationally; often Bristol Beer Factory, Gower, Mumbles) 🅷

A pub near the castle with a rounded exterior, which, following refurbishment, has seen the cask ale offering increase. Five handpumps now dispense beers from mainly Welsh micros such as Boss. There is a large bar and plenty of seating along with an outdoor seating area at the front of the pub. A function room is available upstairs. Several TVs show the latest sporting action. It gets particularly busy when Wales are playing in the Principality Stadium. ✿❀◑&⇌(Central)🚆😺🛜

Queen's Vaults ✓
29 Westgate Street, CF10 1EH
☎ (029) 2022 7966
Felinfoel Dragon Welsh IPA, Double Dragon; Sharp's Doom Bar; 2 changing beers (sourced nationally) 🅷
Large single-room pub opposite the Principality Stadium. The focus is on sports fans and there are a number of TVs in all areas of the pub. Consequently, it can get busy and noisy during matches. The guest beers can be sourced from anywhere in the UK. There is a fine selection of perries and ciders. As a John Bassett pub, it is known for reasonably-priced food and drinks.
◑&⇌(Central) ♣●🚆🛜

Tiny Rebel
26 Westgate Street, CF10 1DD
☎ (029) 2039 9557 ● tinyrebel.co.uk
5 changing beers (sourced regionally; often Tiny Rebel) 🅷
Landmark pub only a short drop-kick from the Principality Stadium. A variety of rooms are spread over two floors, all decorated in the brewery's trademark quirky style. Keg beers are from Tiny Rebel and other craft breweries. A smaller selection of cask ales from across the UK is usually available. Normally at least two boxed ciders are on handpump, and there is an eclectic food menu. Monthly quizzes, open mic and yoga events are held. Payment is by card only. ✿❀◑&⇌(Central)♣●🚆🛜

Zerodegrees
27 Westgate Street, CF10 1DD
☎ (029) 2022 9494 ● zerodegrees.co.uk
Zerodegrees Candy Factory, Our Mango, Downtown, The Bohemian; 4 changing beers (sourced locally; often Zerodegrees Cardiff) 🅰
A welcoming and friendly brewpub in a listed former bus garage with an interesting 1930s frontage. The brewery forms a backdrop to the well-stocked bar and beer storage tanks that rise to one side. Decor is contemporary and there are two upstairs areas for diners, one with a small patio. A wide variety of pizzas is available, plus an eclectic selection of dishes, from pasta and risotto to sausage and mash. Q✿❀◑&⇌(Central)🚆🛜

Cardiff: Grangetown

Grange
134 Penarth Road, CF11 6NJ
☎ (029) 2025 0669
Wye Valley Butty Bach; 3 changing beers (sourced regionally) 🅷
An example of how to rescue a pub which had been left to rot by its previous operators. This street-corner suburban pub plays an important community role in an area where most of the pubs have vanished in recent years. it has two rooms and a large rear garden area with a covered section. The refurbishment accommodates the remaining original architectural features including Art Deco-style doors and bench seating around the walls. A former local CAMRA Pub of the Year.
Q⛄✿❀◑⇌(Grangetown) ♣●🚆

Cardiff: Gwaelod Y Garth

Gwaelod Y Garth Inn

Main Road, CF15 9HH ST116839

☎ (029) 2081 0408 ⊕ gwaelodygarthinn.co.uk

6 changing beers (sourced nationally; often Thornbridge) Ⓗ

A characterful stone-built village local on the edge of Cardiff, on the lower slopes of the Garth mountain. Frequented by locals, walkers, and cyclists, it is the focal point of the village. The pub sports eight handpumps offering a range of real ales along with two traditional ciders. There is a separate games room next to the bar along with a high quality restaurant upstairs. The publican hosts a quiz with a difference on Thursday nights. Former local CAMRA Pub of the Year.
Q ℧ ❀ 🚲 ◑ & ♣ 🖵 (26B) ❀ 🖤 ⚲

Cardiff: LLandaf

Heathcock

58-60 Bridge Street, CF5 2EN

☎ (029) 2115 2290 ⊕ heathcockcardiff.com

3 changing beers (sourced regionally) Ⓗ

Situated at a junction on the main road, the pub has seen its fortunes revived under new management. The central bar serves an adjoining public bar, lounge, and the pleasant outdoor area at the rear of the premises, with an additional dining area in a former skittles alley. The bar is cosy and traditional with a small fireplace and a mix of furniture. The lounge is spacious and doubles as a dining room, albeit with a TV. ❀ ◑ ◐ 🖵 (25,122) ❀ ⚲

Cardiff: Pontcanna

Conway

58 Conway Road, CF11 9NW

☎ (029) 2022 4373

Greene King IPA; Vale of Glamorgan VOG South Island; 3 changing beers (sourced regionally; often Grey Trees, Woodforde's) Ⓗ

Set in the leafy urban village of Pontcanna, a mile or so from the city centre, the Conway has contemporary decor and an upmarket feel. A small front bar (where dogs are welcome) is linked by a corridor to a larger back bar where dining predominates. High-quality food featuring locally sourced produce is served. At least three guest beers are kept, generally sourced from established Welsh brewers. ℧ ◑ ◐ & ♣ 🖵 (25,122) ❀ ⚲

Cardiff: Roath

Andrew Buchan

29 Albany Road, CF24 3LH

☎ (029) 2115 5539

Rhymney Export Light, Bitter, Export; 1 changing beer (sourced locally; often Rhymney) Ⓗ

A great community pub in an area just to the north-east of the city centre. It is owned by Rhymney brewery and serves a good range of their beers, with occasional guests from elsewhere. Rhymney Dark is often available. A good range of ciders, usually from respected local producer Llanblethian Orchards, is also stocked. Real ale takeaways and filled rolls are served. BT Sport is played (silently), there are open mic nights on Mondays, occasional live bands and a jukebox.
❀ & ⇌ (Cathays) ♠ 🖵 (57,58) ❀ ⚲

Cowbridge

1 Town Hall Square

1 Town Hall Square, CF71 7DD

☎ (01446) 775217 ⊕ 1townhallsquare.com

Coach Bridgend Pale Ale Ⓗ**; 2 changing beers (sourced nationally; often Coach, Thornbridge, Tiny Rebel)** Ⓗ /Ⓖ

A fairly recent addition to the local beer scene, aimed squarely at the beer enthusiast. There is a small bar with a seating area off it, while a further two rooms are upstairs. The decor is traditional, with exposed stonework, tiled and wooden floors, and low beams. The entrance courtyard is a pleasant suntrap on a sunny day. Food is not served but customers are welcome to bring their own. The Coach brewpub in Bridgend is under the same ownership. ❀ ♠ 🖵 (X2,321) ❀ ⚲ 🎵

Vale of Glamorgan Inn

51 High Street, CF71 7AE

☎ (01446) 772252

Wye Valley HPA, Butty Bach; 1 changing beer (sourced nationally; often Draught Bass, Glamorgan) Ⓗ

Popular single-roomed pub in the centre of town where conversation is the usual entertainment. The wooden-floored bar has a warming range fire and to the rear is a flagstone-floored area with another stove. Photographs and pictures of local interest adorn the walls. Outside is an attractive enclosed beer garden with a separate covered and heated smoking area. The now well-established annual beer festival coincides with the town's food and drink festival in May. Good-value home-made food is served lunchtime Monday to Saturday.
Q ℧ ❀ ◑ 🖵 (X2,321) ❀ ⚲

Cross Inn

Cross Inn Hotel

Main Road, CF72 8AZ

☎ (01443) 223431

Wye Valley HPA; 2 changing beers (sourced nationally; often Fuller's, Sharp's) Ⓗ

A welcoming, traditional pub that attracts a strong following from locals and visitors alike. The large single room is divided into a bar area and a comfortable lounge in which home-cooked meals are served. Curry night is Wednesday, and Sunday lunches are popular. There is a large car park at the rear, and a comfortable outdoor drinking area including covered booths. A former local CAMRA Pub of the Year. Q ❀ ◑ & ♣ P 🖵 (124) ❀ ⚲

Cwmafan

Brit Ⓛ

London Row, SA12 9AH (from Port Talbot, take B4286 to Cwmavon, turn right after about a mile signed Maesteg, pub 200yds on right)

☎ (01639) 680247 ⊕ thebrit.wales

2 changing beers (sourced regionally) Ⓗ

This cosy, dog-friendly pub serves three rotating ales, many of which are sourced locally, plus a real cider. Renovated in 2014, the Brit now includes three bunk rooms plus a double en-suite, ideal for the Afan Valley mountain bikers. The pub hosts summer and winter beer festivals and is also noted for its good food. In January and February the pub may occasionally be closed on Mondays. A former local CAMRA Pub of the Year.
Q ℧ ❀ 🚲 ◑ & ♥ P 🖵 ❀ ⚲

Cwmfelin

Cross Inn

Maesteg Road, CF34 9LB

☎ (01656) 732476 ⊕ cerddinbrewery.co.uk

Cerddin Solar, Cascade; 3 changing beers (often Cerddin) H
Multiple local CAMRA Pub of the Year winner and home to the Cerddin brewery, this is a must-visit pub. Alongside the five cask beers, a good range of bottle-conditioned beers is also available. The traditional two-roomed Valleys inn offers a warm welcome, with friendly locals and knowledgeable staff. The Tuesday night quiz raises money for the local food bank. There is a patio area directly outside the brewery. Twice winner of CAMRA Regional Pub of the Year.
Q❀★❀(Garth)♣️⬛️(71)🐾🐾🎵

Deri

Old Club
93 Bailey Street, CF81 9HX
☎ (01443) 839333
1 changing beer (often Grey Trees) H
Friendly village free house, enjoying a new lease of life under fresh ownership. A genuine community hub where locals come to relax and enjoy the award-winning Grey Trees beers. The sports TV is not unduly intrusive, usually on only by request. The pub is a bus or taxi ride from Bargoed, or Sustrans Route 469 offers a pleasant alternative on dry days. Cwm Darran Country Park is nearby. ▲♣🖫(1)🎵

East Aberthaw

Blue Anchor
CF62 3DD
☎ (01446) 750329 ⊕ blueanchoraberthaw.com
Theakston Old Peculier; Wadworth 6X; Wye Valley HPA; 2 changing beers (often Glamorgan, Harbwr) H
Dating from 1380, this attractive thatched pub has been in the same family for over 75 years. Its thick stone walls house a labyrinth of rooms, with stone floors, wooden beams and open fires adding to the character and making the pub a tourist attraction for ale and food lovers alike. Up to five ales and award-winning food are served in the bar and the restaurant. The guest beer and cider are often locally produced. Q❀★❀⬛️P🖫(304)🐾

Gilfach Fargoed

Gilfach Workmens Club
87/89 Park Place, CF81 8LX
☎ (01443) 830210
2 changing beers (sourced nationally; often Glamorgan, Oakham) H
The long-established members' club is a friendly destination, where visitors are welcome. The front bar has comfortable lounge seating, and a sports TV which is usually on silently. There is also a large function room and a skittle alley. The only outlet for guest beers in the upper Rhymney Valley, the Workies has two constantly changing ales from a variety of local and national sources. ≉●🖫

Glan-y-Llyn

Fagins Craft Beer House & Art Café L
9 Cardiff Road, CF15 7QD
☎ (029) 2081 1800
2 changing beers (sourced regionally; often Grey Trees, Twt Lol) H
Cosy pub with a warm, friendly atmosphere and top-quality beers. The front bar hides a much larger mixed use area at the rear. Beers on tap often include local brewers Grey Trees and nearby Twt Lol, with Thornbridge Jaipur appearing from time to time. A selection of local

and national craft keg beers and bottled ciders is also available, along with real cider on handpull. Good-value meals are served in the bar and rear dining area. A popular destination for dog walkers. Q❀♿️⬛️(26,132)🐾🐾🎵

Gorseinon

Mardy Inn ✓
117 High Street, SA4 4BR
☎ (01792) 890600
Greene King IPA, Abbot; Sharp's Doom Bar; 2 changing beers (sourced nationally) H
This Wetherspoon pub was formerly a traditional high-street pub. Following a major refurbishment, it is now modern in style. It has a large single bar with several TVs for news and sport, with an adjoining airy extension looking over the furnished patio area. Many interesting pictures of old Gorseinon adorn the walls. The former Mardy Hotel has been a local landmark for more than a century, built in 1900-1 for the fast-developing town.
❀★❀♿️P🖫🐾

Groeswen

White Cross Inn
CF15 7UT (overlooking Groeswen Chapel)
☎ (029) 2085 1332 ⊕ thewhitecrossinn.co.uk
4 changing beers (sourced nationally) H
Delightful rustic free house in a rural setting overlooking Caerphilly, offering excellent choice and value. Four constantly changing beers are served, each pump dedicated to a particular style, including a dark. Three bottled ciders from local producer Williams Brothers are available. Home-made ham and cheese rolls are often served. The pub features an eclectic social calendar, appealing to many different tastes, including live music. Access is unsuitable for large vehicles.
Q❀★❀♣●P🐾🎵

Hendreforgan

Griffin Inn L
CF39 8YL (from Tonyrefail on A4093, turn down lane after Gilfach Goch village sign)
☎ (01443) 675144
Glamorgan Cwrw Gorslas/Bluestone Bitter, Jemimas Pitchfork H
Known locally as the Bog, this friendly pub has been in the same family for more than 60 years. Though out of the way, the pub is comfortable and full of warmth and character, with roaring fires in winter. The immaculate decor features oak furniture, gleaming brassware and memorabilia everywhere you look. Only cash is accepted at the bar (no cards), and an original Victorian till is in use. Under-18s are not allowed inside the pub.
Q❀★P🖫(150,172)🐾

Kenfig

Prince of Wales
CF33 4PR
☎ (01656) 740356 ⊕ princeofwalesinn.co.uk
Draught Bass; Gower Gold; Worthington's Bitter; 1 changing beer (sourced regionally) G
A heritage award-winning inn dating from the 15th century and steeped in local history. Visitors can expect three quality ales on gravity, good locally sourced food and a warm welcome. Family-friendly and popular with dog walkers, the pub is comfortable and cosy. Outside there is a stunning view over Kenfig Nature Reserve. The Draught Bass is renowned throughout the area and

outsells all the pub's lagers combined. Guest beers and cider are occasionally available. Closed on Mondays in winter. Q ♿ ❀ ⏰ ▶ P 🐾 🗢

Killay

Village Bar Café ✓

5-6 Swan Court, The Precinct, SA2 7BA
☎ (01792) 203311
Sharp's Doom Bar; 2 changing beers (often Grey Trees, Tenby) Ⓗ
Situated in a small shopping precinct in Killay on the gateway to Gower, the Village has changed its focus from a traditional pub to a café bar. It retains a single, split-level bar, offering three real ales. There is a quiz on Sunday and a charity quiz on Tuesday evenings. Light meals (toasties, sandwiches) are on offer during the afternoon. A popular Thai food evening is available on Wednesdays. ♿ ⏰ ♣ P 🖾 🐾 🗢 ♪

Llangennith

King's Head

SA3 1HX
☎ (01792) 386212 ⊕ kingsheadgower.co.uk
4 changing beers (sourced regionally; often Evan Evans) Ⓗ
Previously a row of three 17th-century stone-built cottages, this large pub has two separate bars and a variety of seating rooms, plus outside seating front and rear. Ales from local breweries are available (up to four in summer, fewer in winter). A variety of home-made food is served throughout the day. Situated at the western end of the Gower Peninsular, set back a short distance from the sandy stretches of Llangennith beach. ♿ ❀ 🛏 ⏰ ▲ ♣ ♠ P 🖾 (116) 🐾 🗢

Llanharry

Fox & Hounds

Llanharan Road, CF72 9LL
☎ (01443) 222124 ⊕ foxandhoundsllanharry.co.uk
3 changing beers (sourced nationally; often Glamorgan, Grey Trees, Thornbridge) Ⓗ
This large pub has an open-plan lounge with an open fire and settees at one end and more traditional pub furniture at the other. Good-value meals are served in both the bar and a separate restaurant section. The rear garden has lots of seating and a children's play area. A large car park is alongside, and the pub is well served by local buses. ♿ ❀ ⏰ ▶ ♿ P 🖾 (64,404) 🐾 🗢 ♪

Llanmadoc

Britannia Inn

SA3 1DB
☎ (01792) 386624 ⊕ britanniagower.com
Gower Gold; Sharp's Doom Bar; 1 changing beer (sourced nationally; often Wye Valley) Ⓗ
Timbers from ships wrecked on the nearby coast were used in the construction of this pretty and popular 17th-century pub in a quiet corner of Gower. There is a cosy bar at the entrance serving good food and beer, while the rear area has been converted into a fine dining restaurant. There is a beer terrace at the front, while a large beer garden at the rear enjoys stunning views over the nearby estuary and North Gower Marshes, and has a children's play area. ♿ ❀ ⏰ ▶ ▲ ♣ P 🖾 (116) 🐾 🗢

Llanmaes

Blacksmith's Arms

Tyle House Close, CF61 2XR
☎ (01446) 795996
Timothy Taylor Landlord; Wye Valley HPA; 1 changing beer Ⓗ
A popular village pub consisting of a large open-plan split-level room separated into three distinct areas: a dedicated restaurant (available as a private function room), a more relaxed dining area and a drinking space with a log fire. A large patio at the front of the pub is a suntrap in summer. Live music plays on the last Friday of each month. Q ♿ ❀ ⏰ ▶ ▲ ♣ P 🐾 🗢 ♪

Llantrisant

Wheatsheaf Hotel

High Street, CF72 8BQ
☎ (01443) 229367
2 changing beers (often Grey Trees) Ⓗ
Increasingly popular since a recent refurbishment, the Wheatsheaf has an eclectic range of furniture and fittings in its three rooms off the bar area, and a warm welcome for all. Darts, cards and quiz on Tuesdays, and music at least once a month are all popular. The beers often include local options. Buses stop nearby, and free car parks are a short walk away. Q ♣ 🖾 (100,404)

Llantwit Major

Old Swan Inn

Church Street, CF61 1SB
☎ (01446) 792230
4 changing beers (sourced locally; often Bluestone, Tomos & Lilford, Vale of Glamorgan) Ⓗ
The town's oldest pub is near the historic St Illtyd's Church and opposite the town hall. It has a popular front bar and a modern restaurant at the back, both of which serve excellent food and an ever-changing range of up to four ales, often sourced from local brewers. A craft beer line has recently been installed. Beer festivals are held in spring and summer, featuring local live bands. A weekly quiz is held on Tuesday evening and steak night on Wednesday. The town car park is nearby. Q ♿ ❀ ⏰ ▶ ♣ P 🖾 (303,304) 🐾 🗢 ♪

White Hart Inn

Wine Street, CF61 1RZ
☎ (01446) 796956 ⊕ oldwhitehart.uk
3 changing beers (often Glamorgan, Tomos & Lilford, Wadworth) Ⓗ
Dating back to the 15th century, this Grade II-listed pub is in the picturesque town square. The cosy public bar has a large log-burner, two TVs and three ales on sale. There is a separate restaurant offering a range of traditional food. A large beer garden at the back hosts popular music events and occasional small beer festivals. Seating outside at the front catches the afternoon sun. ♿ ❀ 🛏 ⏰ ▶ ▲ ≈ ♣ 🖾 (303,304) 🐾 🗢 ♪

Marcross

Horseshoe Inn

CF61 1ZG
☎ (01656) 890568 ⊕ theshoesmarcross.co.uk
Wye Valley Butty Bach; 2 changing beers (often Gower, Tomos & Lilford, Tudor) Ⓗ
The Shoes is a beautiful 19th-century pub in the hamlet of Marcross, offering a cosy interior with a large log burner. There are usually three ales on offer, one a Welsh brew. An extensive menu of good pub fare is served

lunchtime and evening. In summer the beer garden is delightful. With its friendly staff, the pub is popular with students from the local international college. It is an ideal starting point for spectacular coastal walks, taking in the nearby Nash Point cliffs and lighthouse.
Q👶❀◐◑♣P🚌(303)

Monknash

Plough & Harrow 🏆

CF71 7QQ

☎ (01656) 890209 🌐 ploughandharrowmonknash.co.uk

Draught Bass [G]; Glamorgan Jemimas Pitchfork [H]; 2 changing beers (often Wye Valley) [H]/[G]

Renowned 14th-century pub, originally a monastic farmhouse, retaining many original features and with an eclectic furnishing style that is always a surprise to newcomers. Up to four real ales are available on handpump or gravity, with local breweries well supported. There is also a selection of ciders and perries from local producers. Good pub meals are cooked from scratch using locally sourced ingredients. The large beer garden hosts festivals and live music in summer. Four holiday apartments are available.
Q👶❀🛏◐◑⛺P🚌(303) 🐾♫

Morriston

Red Lion Inn ✔

49 Sway Road, SA6 6JA (near central Morriston Cross opp fire station)

☎ (01792) 761870

Greene King Abbot; Ruddles Best Bitter; 6 changing beers (sourced nationally; often Draught Bass, Mumbles, Sharp's) [H]

This deceptively spacious Wetherspoon pub has a large, comfortable, open-plan room with an open log fire in the front and high bar stools at the back. On the walls are a number of pictures depicting the long-gone industrial history of the area. There is a community board advertising trips to breweries and other various local events. Guest ales often include at least one from a local brewery. 👶❀◐◑♿🍎P🚌📶

Mumbles

Beaufort Arms [L]

1 Castle Road, Norton, SA3 5TF (on a corner of a busy jct of minor roads, near A4067 'Mumbles Road' and seafront footpath)

☎ (01792) 514246

Draught Bass; Glamorgan Jemimas Pitchfork; Sharp's Atlantic; 1 changing beer (sourced locally; often Mantle, Mumbles) [H]

Charming 18th-century village local with a welcoming atmosphere. It was closed by its previous pub group owners but then bought privately in 2017 by a couple who have since tastefully renovated it. The pub has become popular by increasing its range of good beers. It has a traditional main bar with TV and dartboard and also a small, comfortable lounge. Both rooms have real fires, and there is a small beer garden at the rear. A quiz is held on Tuesdays. 👶❀♣🚌(2A,3A)🐾📶

Park Inn

23 Park Street, SA3 4DA

☎ (01792) 366738

4 changing beers (sourced regionally; often Evan Evans) [H]

The convivial atmosphere in this small establishment located in a village side street attracts discerning drinkers of all ages. Four handpumps (sometimes three in quieter winter months) dispense an ever-changing range of beers, with particular emphasis on independent breweries from Wales and the west of England. It has been redecorated in a relaxing wooden theme, with framed beer adverts scattered around the walls. A popular quiz is held on Thursday, with occasional music at weekends. Q👶❀♣🚌(2A,3A)🐾📶♫

Pilot Inn [L]

726 Mumbles Road, SA3 4EL

☎ 07897 895511

Draught Bass; 6 changing beers (sourced nationally; often Pilot Brewery) [H]

A friendly, welcoming local on the seafront at Mumbles, home to the Pilot Brewery. Seven ales are always available, usually including up to three rotating beers brewed on site. A wide range of bottled ciders is available and hot drinks are also served. This historic pub, built in 1849, is next to the coastal path and is popular with lifeboatmen, locals, real ale fans, walkers and cyclists. Dogs are welcome. A former Welsh and local CAMRA Pub of the Year. Q👶♣🍎P🚌🐾📶

Ty Cwrw

650 Mumbles Road, SA3 4EA (on the main seafront road, next to Carlton Hotel)

☎ 07488 298344

4 changing beers (sourced nationally; often Grey Trees, Tenby, Tomos Watkin) [H]

Small and friendly, independently owned pub – the name Ty Cwrw is Welsh for beer house. They have four real ales and six craft keg beers, all sourced from a variety of Welsh breweries and listed on a large blackboard. Although the frontage appears to be narrow from the outside, there is a second room behind the front room and the long wooden bar. Both rooms have a light, modern decor and feature artwork from local artists.
👶❀♣🍎P🚌🐾📶

Victoria Inn

21 Westbourne Place, SA3 4DB (in a small side street off Mumbles Rd; turn right at Davies Bakery, opp Boots, turn left opp coffee shop onto Gloucester Pl)

☎ 07388 160331

Bristol Beer Factory Independence; Draught Bass; Oakham Citra [H]; 2 changing beers (sourced nationally; often Courage, Glamorgan) [H]/[G]

Traditional and popular corner local in the heart of Mumbles, dating from the 1860s. Decorated in a traditional dark, comfortable style, it retains some original features of historic interest including a well in the bar area – the source of water in the days when the pub brewed its own beer. Live music plays most Sunday evenings and a quiz is held on Wednesday evenings.
👶❀♣🚌🐾📶♫

Neath

Borough Arms [L]

2 New Henry Street, SA11 1PH (off Briton Ferry road, near Stockhams Corner roundabout)

☎ (01639) 644902

4 changing beers (sourced regionally; often Glamorgan, Grey Trees) [H]

The emphasis in this welcoming, homely local is very much on ales and conversation. The new landlord and brewer occasionally has his own ales on tap, but there is always a good choice from regional breweries. The pub holds an annual GlastonBorough festival in May, featuring live music, plus a beer festival over the August bank holiday weekend. There is live acoustic music every Wednesday. Well worth the 10-minute walk from the town centre. Q❀🚆🚌📶♫

David Protheroe L ✓

7 Windsor Road, SA11 1LS (opp railway station)
☎ (01639) 622130
Greene King Abbot; Ruddles Best Bitter; Sharp's Doom Bar; 5 changing beers (sourced nationally; often Brains, Evan Evans) Ⓗ

A former police station and courthouse, the David Protheroe is named after the first policeman to be stationed in Neath. This Wetherspoon pub is ideally situated in the centre of town, directly opposite the railway station and a short walk from the bus terminus. The chain's familiar food and drinks are available, with three permanent and up to five changing guest beers, often including a locally brewed ale, plus real ciders. ⚫🕏⚫🖢🖢🞕🞕🞕

Penarth

Golden Lion

69 Glebe Street, CF64 1EF
☎ (029) 2070 1574 ⊕ jwbpubs.com/goldenlion
Felinfoel Double Dragon; 3 changing beers (often Glamorgan, Grey Trees, Vale of Glamorgan) Ⓗ

A traditional street-corner pub serving the local community, offering three or four beers predominantly from Welsh breweries, along with good-value food. The pub can sometimes be loud and lively with its popular jukebox and numerous sports televisions. The small beer garden is popular in warmer weather, with artificial grass and wall paintings depicting Penarth. This long-time Guide entry is well worth a visit. ⚫🕏⚫🞕(Dingle Road) ♣🞕(89A,94) 🞕

Windsor

95 Windsor Road, CF64 1JE
☎ (029) 2070 8675
3 changing beers (sourced nationally; often Courage, Marston's, Young's) Ⓗ

Following a change in emphasis from dining to a more traditional pub, the Windsor offers a comfortable environment with a variety of seating to accommodate groups of different sizes. It has a pool table and hosts entertainment through the week – live bands, quizzes and comedy nights. When not lively with events, it is usually quiet and a perfect place for a good conversation over the superbly kept ales chosen well from the range of Marston's beers. Q⚫🕏🞕(Dingle Road) 🞕(92,94) ⚫🞕♪

Pencoed

Little Penybont Arms

11 Penybont Road, CF35 5PY
☎ 07734 767937
2 changing beers (often Salopian) Ⓖ

Cosy micropub offering a couple of changing beers on gravity, several ciders and a large selection of single malt whiskies and gins. The Steak and Stamp restaurant two doors down, is under the same ownership and drinks from the pub are also available there. The pub itself sells excellent bar snacks including pork pies, nuts and home-made pork scratchings. Since opening, the pub has built up a strong local following. There is a quiz and pizza night on Wednesdays. Craft keg beer is also available. Q⚫🕏⚫◑🞕♣⚫🞕(64,404) ⚫🞕

Penderyn

Red Lion

Church Road, CF44 9JR
☎ (01685) 811914 ⊕ redlionpenderyn.com
Draught Bass; Gower Best Bitter Ⓖ

This old drovers' inn on the edge of the Brecon Beacons National Park is now a thriving gastro-pub. Though the focus is primarily on food, it still offers a limited number of real ales and keg beers. Log fires burn during the cold months, inviting walkers and hikers from nearby Moel Penderyn. High-quality food is served but booking is advised as it can be busy at times. ⚫◑🞕⚫P⚫🞕

Pontardawe

Pontardawe Inn L

123 Herbert Street, SA8 4ED (off A4067 into town, pub is off A474 flyover)
☎ (01792) 447562 ⊕ pontardaweinnpub.co.uk
3 changing beers (sourced nationally; often Marston's) Ⓗ

Former Welsh longhouse later converted to a drover's pub, situated alongside the River Tawe and local cycle path. A side room and stable below were added in 1850 by the Royal Mail as a sorting depot. The central bar serves two regular and up to five changing ales, which includes a locally produced ale, alongside a range of real ciders. Food is served daily in this multi award-winning pub. Seasonal beer and music festivals are held, with live music also featuring at weekends. ⚫🕏⚫◑🞕♣⚫P🞕⚫🞕♪

Pontsticill

Red Cow

Main Road, CF48 2UN (in centre of village)
☎ (01685) 387775
Wye Valley HPA; house beer (by Grey Trees); 1 changing beer (sourced regionally) Ⓗ

Welcoming, tranquil pub in the middle of Pontsticill with views of the Brecon Beacons. The bar is open plan and comfortably furnished, with a log fire in the cosy snug. The atmosphere is warm, friendly and inviting, and popular with summer visitors to the area. The guest beer is often from the Wye Valley or Grey Trees range. Popular meals are served – check ahead for times. Dogs are welcome, and there is a garden and large car park. Q⚫🕏⚫◑P⚫🞕

Pontypridd

Bunch of Grapes 🍺 L ✓

Ynysangharad Road, CF37 4DA (off A4054)
☎ (01443) 402934 ⊕ bunchofgrapes.pub
Cwrw Otley O1; 8 changing beers (sourced nationally; often Cwrw Otley, Grey Trees, Salopian) Ⓗ

Located just off the town centre, this busy and well-loved gem of a pub boasts many awards for beer and food. The recently opened Cwrw Otley microbrewery adds to the attractions, with its beers served alongside several guest beers. A variety of styles is served, plus a range of craft beers and ciders. The restaurant is highly acclaimed, with a menu featuring locally sourced ingredients. Special food and drink events occur throughout the year. Q⚫🕏⚫◑🞕🞕P🞕⚫🞕♪

Llanover Arms L

Bridge Street, CF37 4PE (opp N entrance to Ynysangharad Park, off A470)
☎ (01443) 403215
2 changing beers (sourced nationally; often Salopian) Ⓗ

This historic and popular free house has been owned by the same family for over a century. It was built around 1794 to serve boatmen on the Glamorgan Canal. It has three rooms linked by a passageway, each with its own distinct character and atmosphere. The pub is near the famous old town bridge and Ynysangharad Park with the restored National Lido of Wales. The Taff Trail passes close by. Q❀≈♣⊑

Patriot Bar 🅛

25B Taff Street, CF37 4UA
☎ (01443) 407915
Rhymney Bevans Bitter, Golden Ale, Bitter, Export; 1 changing beer (often Rhymney) Ⓗ
A converted shop unit that is now a Rhymney brewery tied house, near the bus station and a short walk from Pontypridd railway station. Known locally as the Wonky Bar, recalling its former skewed entrance, it is a lively pub with no frills, and enjoys a loyal following. Beers are well kept in the unusual upstairs cellar, prices are keen and turnover is brisk. ≈⊑❀☂

Tumble Inn ✅

4-9 Broadway, CF37 1BA
☎ (01443) 484390
Greene King Abbot; Ruddles Best Bitter; Sharp's Doom Bar; 3 changing beers (sourced regionally; often Boss, Glamorgan, Rhymney) Ⓗ
Previously the town's main post office, this roomy Wetherspoon pub is near the town centre opposite the impressive railway station, and on several main bus routes. The open-plan space is mainly on one level with two smaller raised tiers, served by a single bar. A pleasant outdoor patio overlooks the River Taff and is divided into smoking and non-smoking areas.
♿❀◑♿≈●⊑☂

Port Talbot

Lord Caradoc 🅛 ✅

69-73 Station Road, SA13 1NW (5 mins' walk from Port Talbot Parkway railway station)
☎ (01639) 896007
Greene King Abbot; Ruddles Best Bitter; Sharp's Doom Bar; 5 changing beers (sourced nationally; often Glamorgan, Rhymney, Tomos Watkin) Ⓗ
On the main shopping street, this Wetherspoon pub has a relaxed atmosphere, with a spacious, open-plan layout and a family-friendly area. The choice of beers is open to suggestion from customers, and a wide range is always available. A local ale is frequently on offer and up to three real ciders are also available. The walls are adorned with historic photographs of the town including famous people from the area. The pub has been recognised by Wetherspoon for its high standard of catering.
♿❀◑♿≈(Parkway)●P⊑☂

Porth

Rheola

Rheola Road, CF39 0LF
☎ (01443) 682633
Rhymney Bitter, Export; 3 changing beers (sourced locally; often Rhymney) Ⓗ
Friendly local pub offering a range of Rhymney beers, which are invariably well kept and good value for money. The bar features a pool table, dartboard and jukebox, and is often quite lively, whereas the comfortable lounge generally provides a quiet space and tends only to get busy at weekends. Activities include a quiz, whist, and a variety of live artists and bands at the weekend. The pub stands at the confluence of the two Rhondda rivers, and is well served by bus and rail.
❀≈♣P⊑(120,132) ☂

Quakers Yard

Glantaff Inn

Cardiff Road, CF46 5AH
☎ (01443) 441 1101 ⊕ glantaffinn.com
Rhymney Export; 1 changing beer (sourced nationally; often Greene King, Rhymney, Wye Valley) Ⓗ
Pleasant and friendly pub overlooking the River Taff, popular with locals as well as walkers and cyclists from the nearby Taff Trail. Good meals are served daily from opening until late evening. Live entertainment often features at weekends. Bunkhouse accommodation for up to six guests was added a few years ago.
❀⇔◑♿♣⊑❀☂♪♫

Reynoldston

King Arthur Hotel 🅛

Higher Green, SA3 1AD (on village green)
☎ (01792) 390775 ⊕ kingarthurhotel.co.uk
Gower Gold; Sharp's Doom Bar; 2 changing beers (sourced nationally; often Glamorgan, Tenby, Tomos Watkin) Ⓗ
A popular traditional family-owned hotel and an acclaimed wedding venue, situated at the foot of Cefn Bryn hill in beautiful Gower, overlooking the village green. Covered outdoor seating is available by the pub entrance, as well as a large seating area on the green itself. The cosy, atmospheric main and rear bars are open all day to drinkers and diners – there is also a separate restaurant. Home-cooked main meals and bar snacks made with local produce are available all day, as well as breakfasts for non-residents. ♿❀⇔◑♿P⊑☂♪

St Athan

Roost

Rock Road, CF62 4PG
☎ (01446) 753715 ⊕ theroostonrockroad.com
Wye Valley HPA; 1 changing beer (often Glamorgan, Wye Valley) Ⓗ
A major refurbishment of this pub – formerly the Four Bells – has created a more modern interior style but with some original features remaining such as the floorboards which now form the bar front. Comfy sofas and chairs surround the log burner, and there are tall tables and stools in the drinking area. Outside is a patio and grassy area where outdoor events such as barbecues can be held in the summer. Food from a varied menu is of a high standard. Accommodation in five rooms.
Q♿❀⇔◑P⊑(304) ☂

Sketty

Vivian Arms

106 Gower Road, SA2 9BT (at Sketty Cross, jct of A4118 and A4216)
☎ (01792) 516194 ⊕ vivianarmspubswansea.co.uk
Brains Rev James Original, SA; Marston's Pedigree; 2 changing beers Ⓗ
Situated on the main crossroads in Sketty, the Vivs is a spacious pub which offers reasonably-priced meals daily, including a popular Sunday lunch. It has a mixture of seating areas, and plenty of TV screens throughout the pub to show live sport. There is a small meeting room with seating for about 18. There is live music on Fridays and an open mic on the first Monday of the month, plus a general knowledge quiz on Sundays and music quiz on Wednesdays. ♿❀◑♣⊑❀☂♪

Southerndown

Three Golden Cups

CF32 0RW
☎ (01656) 880432 ⊕ thethreegoldencups.co.uk
Sharp's Doom Bar; 1 changing beer (sourced locally; often Glamorgan, Gower) Ⓗ
One of the few pubs on the Glamorgan Heritage Coast from which you can see the sea. The restaurant/lounge has a stone and wooden decor and is named after the Maria Jose, a ship wrecked nearby in 1914. Music evenings are held regularly and summer barbecues are popular. The campsite is adjacent to the pub – generally the camping season starts in March.
🛏️🅰️⒪🚶🅰️♣🅿️🚊(303) 🐾

Swansea

Bank Statement ✅

57-58 Wind Street, SA1 1EP
☎ (01792) 455477
Sharp's Doom Bar; 5 changing beers (sourced nationally; often Exmoor, Fuller's, Jennings) Ⓗ
A former Midland Bank, sympathetically transformed by Wetherspoon while retaining the original ornate interior. Trading as a Lloyds No. 1 Bar, the pub is at the heart of the city's popular bar quarter and has a large ground floor with plenty of seating. Additional seating is available on the upstairs terrace. It is popular with all ages, and is busy throughout the week. Sport is shown on its many screens. The bottled beer selection includes some real ales. 🛏️⒪🚶⇄🌭🚊📶

Brunswick Arms

3 Duke Street, SA1 4HS (between St Helens Rd and Walter Rd)
☎ (01792) 465676 ⊕ brunswickswansea.com
Butcombe Original; Courage Directors; Wye Valley Butty Bach Ⓗ**; 2 changing beers (sourced nationally)** Ⓗ/Ⓖ
A side-street pub with the air of a country inn in the city. Wooden beams and comfortable seating create a traditional, relaxing atmosphere. A local artist's work is displayed and is for sale. There are usually up to five beers available – one of the changing beers is gravity dispensed, often from a local microbrewery. A popular general knowledge quiz is held on Mondays, and a music quiz on Thursdays. ⒪🚶🌭🚊(200)📶

No Sign Bar ♟

56 Wind Street, SA1 1EG
☎ (01792) 465300 ⊕ nosignwinebar.com
Gower Gold; 3 changing beers (sourced nationally; often Butcombe, Mumbles, Tiny Rebel) Ⓗ
Historic narrow bar established in 1690, formerly known as Mundays Wine Bar and reputedly a regular haunt of Dylan Thomas. Architectural signs from various periods of the pub's past remain, some dividing the interior into separate bar areas. Quality food and wine are available, with up to five real ciders on sale. Live music features in the bar on Friday, Saturdays and often Sunday evenings. Bands also play in the Vault basement late evening.
🛏️🅰️⒪🚶⇄🌭📶♫

Potters Wheel

85-86 The Kingsway, SA1 5JE
☎ (01792) 465113
Ruddles Best Bitter; Sharp's Doom Bar; 4 changing beers (sourced nationally) Ⓗ
City-centre Wetherspoon pub with a long, sprawling bar area which has various seating arrangements, attracting a wide mix of customers. An interesting selection of guest beers is available, with a noticeable commitment

to local breweries. Real cider is always available. Photographs on the walls feature many local dignitaries associated with the area's industrial past, particularly the ceramics and pottery industries. Look for the CAMRA board and a beer suggestion box. The Quadrant bus station is nearby. 🛏️⒪🚶🌭🚊📶

Queen's Hotel

Gloucester Place, SA1 1TY (near Waterfront Museum)
☎ (01792) 521531
Theakston Best Bitter, Old Peculier; 2 changing beers (sourced nationally; often Bristol Beer Factory, Fuller's, Glamorgan) Ⓗ
This vibrant free house is near the Dylan Thomas Theatre, City Museum, National Waterfront Museum and marina. The walls display photographs depicting Swansea's rich maritime heritage. The pub enjoys strong local support and home-cooked lunches are popular. Evening entertainment includes a Sunday quiz, bingo on Wednesday and live music on Saturday. This is a rare local outlet for Theakston Old Peculier, in addition to a seasonal guest beer, often from a local microbrewery. Former local CAMRA Pub of the Year. ⒪♣🚊🌭📶♫

Uplands Tavern ✅

42 Uplands Crescent, Uplands, SA2 0PG
☎ (01792) 458242
Greene King IPA, Abbot; 2 changing beers (sourced locally) Ⓗ
Situated in the heart of Swansea's student quarter, the Tav attracts regulars from all walks of life and has a reputation for the quality and variety of its live music at weekends and Monday open mic nights. A large, single room pub and former haunt of Dylan Thomas, who is commemorated in a separate snug area. Shufl board (shuffleboard, with a concave playing surface) is a popular game here. There is a large heated outdoor drinking area. Quiz night on Tuesday. 🅰️🚶♣🚊🌭📶♫

Trefforest

Otley Brewpub & Kitchen Ⓛ

7 Forest Road, CF37 1SY
☎ (01443) 402033 ⊕ otleybrewpubandkitchen.com
Mabby Blue, Red; 1 changing beer (sourced regionally; often Bristol Beer Factory, Mabby) Ⓗ
Friendly brewpub, close to the university, serving a selection of beers from its own in-house microbrewery plus a guest. A changing range of craft beers is also offered. The spacious open-plan layout is well furnished. Staff are welcoming and informative. A modern menu is offered, with tasty street food and vegetarian options. It is popular with students as it is an easy stroll from the nearby campus. Close to the train station and bus route 100 to Pontypridd. 🛏️🅰️⒪⇄♣🌭🚊(90,100)🐾📶

Rickards Arms Ⓛ

61 Park Street, CF37 1SN
☎ (01443) 402305
⊕ therickardsarms-pontypridd.foodndrink.uk
Grey Trees Diggers Gold, Mosaic Pale Ale; Wye Valley Butty Bach; 1 changing beer (sourced locally; often Twt Lol) Ⓗ
Traditional, family-owned pub, close to the train station and the university and well served by buses. Beers are always well kept and good quality. Classic pub meals are served at reasonable prices. The beer garden is popular with students and locals alike, but note that access is via the upper floor. The pub opens early until late seven days a week. 🅰️⒪⇄♣🚊(90,100)🐾📶

Tyla Garw

Boar's Head

Coedcae Lane, CF72 9EZ (600yds from A473 over level crossing)

☎ (01443) 225400

2 changing beers (sourced nationally) Ⓗ

A pub that has a bar area with high wooden settles and a more contemporary layout to the rear. At least one beer is usually from local brewery Glamorgan Brewing. There are two dining areas offering a classic pub menu, and a coffee shop which doubles as a lounge bar in the evening. An enclosed patio area provides space for both diners and drinkers. Q✿✇❀◑≢(Pontyclun)P✿

Upper Church Village

Farmers Arms

St Illtyd Road, CF38 1EB

☎ (01443) 205766

Wye Valley HPA; 2 changing beers (sourced nationally) Ⓗ

Comfortable village local, popular with all ages. The beer range varies – it includes seasonal ales and some that are unusual for the area. There is a popular quiz every Tuesday, with a variety of events on other nights including bands and solo singers, and, on occasion, drinks tasting evenings and Q&A sessions with sporting personalities. Summer visitors can take advantage of the split-level beer garden. ❀P🚌(90,100)✿

Upper Killay

Railway Inn Ⓛ

553 Gower Road, SA2 7DS

☎ (01792) 203946

Draught Bass; Mumbles Lifesaver Strong Bitter; Wye Valley Butty Bach; 2 changing beers (often Glamorgan, Mumbles, Swansea) Ⓗ

Classic locals' pub set in woodlands in the Clyne Valley. The adjacent former railway line forms part of Route 4 of the National Cycle Network. There are two small rooms at the front, one being the main snug/bar, with a larger lounge at the rear. In winter the fire in the lounge provides welcome warmth and cheer. The local Swansea Brewing Company has moved alongside the pub and should be available regularly. An outside area hosts barbecues and music events, plus a quiz on Thursdays. Q✿♣●P🚌✿

Wick

Lamb & Flag Inn

Church Street, CF71 7QE

☎ (01656) 890278

2 changing beers (sourced regionally; often Glamorgan, Gower, St Austell) Ⓗ

An attractive pub that has barely changed over the years, with lots of stone, tile and wood. Inside is a traditional bar and comfortable lounge/dining room offering up to three beers. Good-value food using local ingredients is available. A pleasant small garden area is at the side of the pub. Q✿✇◑♣🚌(303)

Star Inn

Ewenny Road, CF71 7QA

☎ (01656) 890080 ⊕ thestarinnwick.co.uk

Wye Valley HPA; 2 changing beers (often Glamorgan) Ⓗ

Originally three farm cottages, the interior comprises a traditional bar with pew seating and a lounge/diner with flagstone flooring – both warmed by log-burning fires –

and an upstairs pool/function room. The friendly landlady, staff and locals make this a pleasant place to visit. Good food is available – the meat is supplied by an award-winning farm butcher a short distance away. Dogs are welcome in the bar. A former local CAMRA Pub of the Year. Q✿✇❀◑♣P🚌(303)✿⬤ 🛜

Ystalyfera

Wern Fawr Ⓛ

47 Wern Road, SA9 2LX (on main road through Ystalyfera)

☎ (01639) 843625

9 Lives Amber, Dark, Gold; 1 changing beer (sourced nationally) Ⓗ

Entering this quirky pub is like stepping back in time. Run by the same family for three generations, the two-roomed inn is full of industrial heritage from the local area. It has a cosy lounge and a friendly locals bar with an old-fashioned stove that keeps the room as warm as toast in the wintertime. The beers are brewed locally by 9Lives Brewing, plus one changing guest ale. Q♣🚌(X6,121) ✿

Breweries

9 Lives

Unit 303, Ystradgynlais Workshops, Trawsffordd Road, Ystradgynlais, SA9 1BS ☎ 07743 559736 ⊕ 9livesbrewing.co.uk

✇9 Lives Brewing was established in 2017 by Robert Scott (former brewer at the now defunct Bryncelyn Brewery), using the same six-barrel capacity equipment. A number of beers are replications of former Bryncelyn beers (renamed) and three new beers have been added. ‼◆LIVE

Amber (ABV 4%) PALE

Pale amber with a hoppy aroma. A refreshing hoppy, fruity flavour with balancing bitterness; a similar lasting finish. A beer full of flavour for its gravity.

Dark (ABV 4%) MILD

Dark brown with an inviting aroma of malt, roast and fruit. A gentle bitterness mixes roast with malt, hops and fruit, giving a complex, satisfying and lasting finish.

Gold (ABV 4.5%) BITTER

An inviting aroma of hops, fruit and malt, and a golden colour. The tasty mix of hops, fruit, bitterness and background malt ends with a long, hoppy, bitter aftertaste. Full-bodied and drinkable.

Bang-On

Unit 3, George Street, Bridgend Industrial Estate, Bridgend, CF31 3TS

☎ (01656) 760790 ⊕ bangonbrewery.beer

Established in 2016, this five-barrel plant produces a variety of unique beers. An onsite taproom offers tours and brew day experiences. Limited edition beers are also available. A bespoke service is offered with personalised labels (minimum of six bottles). ‼▤◆

DAD (ABV 3.9%) PALE
Tidy (ABV 4%)
Cariad (ABV 4.1%) BITTER
Bohemian Pilsner (ABV 4.2%)
Thirst Aid (ABV 4.4%) PALE
Fuster Cluck (ABV 9.5%) STRONG

Beer Riff

⊟ Pilot House Wharf, Swansea, SA1 1UN ☎ 07897 895511 ⊕ beerriffbrewing.com

⊗ An offshoot of Pilot Brewery Mumbles. The four-barrel brewery produces keg and canned beers that are unfiltered and unfined. It offers a variety of styles including one-offs. The integral bar offers great views over Swansea Marina.

Borough Arms

⊟ 2 New Henry Street, Neath, SA11 2PH
☎ (01639) 644902 ⊕ boroughbreweryneath.com

☺The Borough Arms and Borough Brewery were purchased in 2019. The new landlord was a former brewer with the now defunct Kite Brewery (absorbed by Glamorgan Brewery). Beers are brewed occasionally at the rear of the pub for consumption in-house only.

Boss

176 Neath Road, Landore, Swansea, SA1 2JT
☎ (01792) 381695 ⊕ bossbrewing.co.uk

⊗ The brewery opened in 2015 by Roy Allkin and Sarah John, using a 10-barrel plant. It relocated in 2017 to larger premises opposite the Liberty Stadium which now includes an onsite taproom that can be booked in advance. It went into administration late 2022 and was quicky rescued by a local businessman. A few beers were later produced under the Copperopolis name but it is not known whether the Boss identity will continue. There is a connection with the now ceased Wild Weather brewery.
‼◆LIVE⊘

Blonde (ABV 4%) BLOND
Black (ABV 5%) STOUT
Brave (ABV 5.5%) IPA
Boom (ABV 6%) PALE

Brains SIBA IFBB

Dragon Brewery, Pacific Road, Cardiff, CF24 5HJ
☎ (029) 2040 2060 ⊕ sabrain.com

☺In 2021, SA Brain put its freehold and leasehold pubs on the market. Most of these went to Carlsberg Marston's Brewing Co on a 25 year lease. The proceeds from the subsequent deals provided a foundation for the modern state-of-the-art facility, Dragon Brewery, to continue to brew in Cardiff. These beers are served in its former pubs, and widely in the free trade across the UK. ◆

Dark (ABV 3.5%) MILD
A tasty, classic dark brown mild, a mix of malt, roast, caramel with a background of hops. Bittersweet, mellow and with a lasting finish of malt and roast.
Bitter (ABV 3.7%) BITTER
Amber-coloured with a gentle aroma of malt and hops. Malt, hops and bitterness combine in an easy-drinking beer with a bitter finish.
SA (ABV 4.2%) BITTER
A mellow, full-bodied beer. Gentle malt and hop aroma leads to a malty, hop and fruit mix with a balancing bitterness.
SA Gold (ABV 4.2%) GOLD
A golden beer with a hoppy aroma. Well-balanced with a zesty hop, malt, fruit and balancing bitterness; a similar satisfying finish.
Rev James Original (ABV 4.5%) BITTER
A faint malt and fruit aroma with malt and fruit flavours in the taste, initially bittersweet. Bitterness balances the flavour and makes this an easy-drinking beer.

Contract brewed for Molson Coors

M&B Brew XI (ABV 3.6%) BITTER
Hancocks HB (ABV 3.7%) BITTER
Worthington's Bitter (ABV 3.7%) BITTER

Brew Monster SIBA

Unit 1, Lon Y Twyn, Caerphilly, CF83 1NW ☎ 07772 869856 ⊕ brewmonster.co.uk

⊗ Brew Monster launched in 2017. The beer range is available in all formats and tends to be brewed in rotation, albeit intermittently. Brewing relocated from Cwmbran to Caerphilly in 2021. The brewery is housed alongside a new taproom which opened in 2022. The move brought about a change to the core range which saw new beers introduced alongside older favourites. One-off beers are regularly produced (mainly keg). A brewery tap is in Cardiff city centre. ◆

Brewhouse & Kitchen SIBA

⊟ Sophia Close, Pontcanna, Cardiff, CF11 9HW
⊕ brewhouseandkitchen.com/cardiff

☺Former lodge, now extended with open and covered outside areas. Brewery experience days offered. In the absence of an onsite brewer, beers are brought in from other outlets in the chain. Brewing is currently suspended. ‼

Cerddin

⊟ Cross Inn, Maesteg Road, Maesteg, Cwmfelin, CF34 9LB
☎ (01656) 732476 ☎ 07949 652237
⊕ cerddinbrewery.co.uk

Brewpub established in 2010 using a 2.5-barrel plant in a converted garage adjacent to the pub, now enlarged to a four-barrel plant. Beer is usually only available in the pub. Seasonal beers brewed. ‼◆LIVE

Coach

⊟ 37 Cowbridge Road, Bridgend, CF31 3DH

Office: 2 Oldfield Road, Bocam Park,, Bridgend, CF35 5LJ

The Coach Brewing Co is a brewpub based at the award-winning free house The Coach. Launched in 2018, the brewery is visible in the pub for all to see. Occasional seasonal additions are brewed. Beers are also available in keg.

Cold Black Label SIBA

5 Squire Drive, Brynmenyn Industrial Estate, Bridgend, CF32 9TX
☎ (01656) 728081 ⊕ coldblacklabel.co.uk

Cold Black Label was initially founded in 2004, concentrating on its eponymous lager brand, and expanded into cask-conditioned beers 10 years later. In 2018, Cold Black Label and Brecon Brewing merged, with Buster Grant taking over all brewing, and 14 new beers were created. In 2019, Lithic Brewing joined the group, with these gluten-free beers mainly available in keg and can, with the occasional release of casks. ⬛GF

Glyder Fawr (ABV 4.2%) GOLD
Singing Sword (ABV 4.2%) SPECIALITY
Harlech Castle (ABV 4.4%) BITTER
Uncle Phil's Ale (ABV 4.4%) SPECIALITY
Bwlch Passage (ABV 4.5%) SPECIALITY
Chirk Castle (ABV 4.6%) GOLD
Miners Ale (ABV 4.6%) STOUT
Sand Storm (ABV 4.6%) GOLD

Guardian Ale (ABV 4.7%) GOLD
Crib Goch (ABV 5%) IPA
Nutty Ale (ABV 5%) BROWN
Pirate Bay (ABV 5%) PALE
Red Beast (ABV 6%) IPA
Miners Imperial Ale (ABV 7.5%) STOUT

Brewed under the Brecon Brewing name:
Copper Beacons (ABV 4.1%) BITTER
Gold Beacons (ABV 4.2%) GOLD
Orange Beacons (ABV 4.3%) SPECIALITY
Cribyn (ABV 4.5%) GOLD
Corn Du (ABV 5%) PALE
Red Beacons (ABV 5%) IPA
WRU IPA (ABV 5%) IPA
Pen y Fan (ABV 5.2%) IPA
Mind Bleach (ABV 10%) IPA
Mind Peroxide (ABV 10%) IPA

Brewed under the Lithic name:
Session IPA (ABV 4%) BITTER
Pale Ale (ABV 4.7%) PALE
Porter (ABV 4.8%) PORTER
Chocolate Vanilla Stout (ABV 5%) SPECIALITY

Crafty Devil

Unit 3, The Stone Yard, Ninian Park Road, Cardiff,
CF11 6HE ☎ 07555 779169
⊕ craftydevilbrewing.co.uk

⊠ Brewery has been in current location since 2017. It does not currently brew cask ale regularly, but produces bottled, canned and keg beer, which it supplies to markets and a number of other outlets in the local area. It currently operates two micro bars, one in Cardiff and one in Penarth. ‼︎▩

Dog's Window SIBA

8 Nant-Yr-Adar, Llangewydd Court, Bridgend,
CF31 4TY ☎ 07929 292930
⊕ dogswindowbrewery.com

Dog's Window is a small-batch brewery which started production in 2018, producing a range of craft beers to its own recipes. It has a core range of eight beers with an ever-changing list of limited editions (the Experimental Series). The mainstay of production is bottled beers, with the occasional keg and cask, which are brewed off-site by the proprietor. It can sell bottles direct to the public via appointment through the website. ▩♦LIVE

Fairy Glen

5 The Corn Store, Heol Ty Gwyn, Maesteg, CF34 0BG
☎ 07968 847878

Office: 60 Oaklands Avenue, Bridgend, CF31 4ST

A 10-barrel brewery commenced in 2018, producing keg beer for special events (not for pubs etc).

Flowerhorn

The Bridge Studios, 454 Western Avenue, Cardiff,
CF5 3BL ⊕ flowerhorn.co.uk

Established in 2019 by two friends, Andrew and Arran. Brewing was initially on a nomad basis (bottle and keg only). In 2020 it moved to its own site in Cardiff with a bespoke five-barrel plant. A canning line is planned. Beers are occasionally available cask-conditioned for festivals. A new project, Flowerhorn Dog Bakery, is in progress (making pale ale dog biscuits using the spent grain), with a portion of the profits donated to the Rescue Hotel, Cardiff. Its taproom is open on Friday and Saturday. ✦

Frank & Otis

Unit 7, River Bridge Business Centre, Cardiff,
CF15 7QR ☎ 07968 094270
⊕ frankandotisbrewing.co

Business started in 2019 with all beers contract brewed. In 2021 it opened a one-barrel brewery for smaller runs at Taff's Well near Cardiff. In 2022 production moved to Cardiff with bottling replaced by canning and an expansion into kegs. ▩

Freetime

19 St Lukes Court, Clarke Way, Winch Wen, Swansea,
SA1 7ER ☎ 07291 253227 ⊕ hello@freetimebeer.co

Small-batch brewery producing unfined beers.

Glamorgan SIBA

Unit B, Llantrisant Business Park, Llantrisant, CF72 8LF
☎ (01443) 406080

Office: Unit J, Llantrisant Business Park, Llantrisant,
CF72 8LF ⊕ glamorganbrewingco.com

☺This family-owned and run brewery moved to its present site in 2013. Production capability has increased year-on-year. A range of year round and seasonal beers are produced with additional special brews to mark notable events. Shop is open daily. Direct deliveries are made throughout Wales, and further afield by selected wholesalers and breweries. Major supermarkets are also supplied. In 2023 Glamorgan was awarded sole beer supplier to the Welsh Rugby Union and Principality Stadium, Cardiff. ▩♦

Cwrw Gorslas/ Bluestone Bitter (ABV 4%) BITTER
Welsh Pale Ale (ABV 4.1%) PALE
Jemimas Pitchfork (ABV 4.4%) BITTER
Thunderbird (ABV 4.5%) BITTER

Gower SIBA

Unit 25, Crofty Industrial Estate, Penclawdd, Crofty,
Swansea, SA4 3RS
☎ (01792) 850681 ⊕ gowerbrewery.com

⊠ Established in 2011 on a five-barrel brew plant at the Greyhound Inn, Llanrhidian, it moved to a new 20-barrel brewery in Crofty, Gower, in 2015. Seasonal and speciality ales are brewed alongside established beers. An onsite taproom was added in 2021 featuring events (details online). ‼︎▩♦⚬

Brew 1 (ABV 3.8%) BITTER
Best Bitter (ABV 4.5%) BITTER
Gold (ABV 4.5%) GOLD
Rumour (ABV 5%) RED
Shipwreck (ABV 5.1%) PALE
Power (ABV 5.5%) BITTER

Grey Trees

Unit 17-20, Robertstown Business Park, Aberdare,
CF44 8EZ
☎ (01685) 267077 ⊕ greytreesbrewing.com

National award-winning, family-owned brewery in the Welsh heartlands. From humble beginnings, the brewery recently moved to a new home in Robertstown, Aberdare. A brewery shop is planned and should be open during the currency of this Guide. The brewery operates its own microbar, the National Tap, Aberdare. Beers are supplied to the free trade in South Wales and beyond. ▩♦LIVE

Caradog (ABV 3.9%) BITTER

Black Road Stout (ABV 4%) STOUT
Diggers Gold (ABV 4%) GOLD
Drummer Boy (ABV 4.2%) BITTER
Mosaic Pale Ale (ABV 4.2%) PALE
Valley Porter (ABV 4.6%) PORTER
JPR Pale (ABV 4.7%) PALE
Afghan Pale (ABV 5.4%) PALE

Little Goat

Ynysmeudwy, Pontardawe, SA8 4PP ☎ 07590
520457 ⊕ littlegoatbrewery.co.uk

A 2.5-barrel brewery in an outbuilding of the owner's
private house. The main output goes into bottles but as
pub trade picks up, there will be greater concentration on
the range of cask beers. All beers are suitable for vegans,
being unfined and unfiltered. The brewery runs stalls at
local markets for bottled beer sales. Distribution is to
local areas as wholesalers are not used. LIVE V

Siencyn (ABV 4%) RED
Scapegoat (ABV 4.3%) BITTER
Golden Goat (ABV 4.4%) GOLD
Jumping Jack (ABV 4.9%) BITTER
Yankee Doodle Nanny (ABV 6.5%) SPECIALITY
Satan's Little Helper (ABV 6.6%) STOUT

Mabby

🍺 Mabby Brew Pub & Kitchen, Forest Road, Trefforest,
CF37 1SY
☎ (01443) 402033

Brewpub in the cellar of the Otley Arms supplying the
pub and few other outlets. The name is derived from a
partnership between brewer Matt Otley and his wife
Gabby. The beers have no names as such and each recipe
is referred to as a colour, with that colour being reflected
on the pumpclip. The beers are available in five-litre
casks.

Mad Dog SIBA

17-19 Castle Street, Cardiff, CF10 1BS ☎ 07864
923231 ⊕ maddogbrew.co.uk

The brewery has relocated to the centre of Cardiff,
opposite the Castle in a street corner plot. Its premises
include a taproom. A new brewer has been appointed.
Cask-conditioned beers are starting to form a basis of the
portfolio and a cask is usually to be found on the bar for
gravity dispense. ♦

Mountain Hare

🍺 Mountain Hare Inn, Brynna Road, Brynnau
Gwynion, CF35 6PG
☎ (01656) 860453 ⊕ mountainhare.co.uk

☺Paul Jones, licensee of the Mountain Hare, finally
realised his ambition of installing a brewery in his family-
owned pub when in 2013 a 1.5-barrel, custom-built
brewing plant was installed. Brewing is currently
suspended.

Mumbles SIBA

Unit 14, Worcester Court, Swansea Enterprise Park,
Swansea, SA7 9FD
☎ (01792) 792612 ☎ 07757 109938
⊕ mumblesbrewery.co.uk

⊗ Mumbles Brewery was established in 2011 and began
brewing in 2013 in the district of Mumbles. In 2015, the
brewery had a new permanent location, with a 10 barrel
plant installation. Director/brewer Rob Turner supplies

numerous pubs in South Wales and the Bristol area.
Seasonal and one-off beers are available. 🚲♦

Hop Kick (ABV 4%) PALE
Mile (ABV 4%) PALE
Malt Bitter (ABV 4.1%) BITTER
Murmelt (ABV 4.2%) SPECIALITY
Gold (ABV 4.3%) PALE
Beyond The Pale (ABV 4.4%) SPECIALITY
Oystermouth Stout (ABV 4.4%) STOUT
Lifesaver Strong Bitter (ABV 4.9%) BITTER
India Pale Ale (ABV 5.3%) PALE
Albina New World Pale (ABV 5.7%) IPA
Chocolate Vanilla Porter (ABV 6.2%) PORTER

Otley (NEW) SIBA

Ynysangharad Road, Pontypridd, CF37 4DA

A new venture, new premises and new plant. This
brewery is built on part of the car park at the Bunch of
Grapes pub. Both are run by Nick Otley, who was
involved in the previous Otley brewery, but this time,
brewing is intended to be just for the pub. Some beers
will be based on the old recipes. There is currently no
core range of beer.

Pilot Brewery

🍺 726 Mumbles Road, Mumbles, Swansea, SA3 4EL
☎ 07897 895511 ⊕ thepilotbrewery.co.uk

☺The Pilot Brewery began production on its 2.5-barrel
plant in 2013. It is located at the rear of The Pilot Inn on
the Mumbles sea front. The output is mainly for the Pilot
Inn but can also be supplied to festivals and other select
outlets. The proprietors have also set up Beer Riff
brewery.

Pipes

183A Kings Road, Cardiff, CF11 9DF ☎ 07776 382244
⊕ pipesbeer.co.uk

Pipes create examples of some of the unique and least
known beer styles from around the globe with no
preservatives or additives used in production. The main
output is bottled and keg beers although the occasional
cask beer is produced. 🚲♦

Swansea

🍺 Railway Inn, 533 Gower Road, Upper Killay,
Swansea, SA2 7DS
☎ (01792) 203946

☺Opened in 1996, with beers brewed at the Joiners
Arms, Bishopston. During the recent building and
commissioning of a brand new facility at the Railway Inn,
the owner and brewer Rory Gowland sadly passed away
and brewing was suspended. This has now
recommenced, brewing to the original recipes, and the
old favourites are back on tap at the Railway. ‼♦

Tomos & Lilford SIBA

Unit 11b, Vale Business Park, Llandow, Cowbridge,
CF71 7PF
☎ (01446) 677757 ☎ 07747 858514

Office: 117 Boverton Road, Llantwit Major, CF61 1YA
✉ info@tomosandlilford.com

⊗ Tomos & Lilford was launched in 2013 by
homebrewers Rolant Tomos, and brothers Rob and James
Lilford. The brewery supplies pubs and clubs across the
Vale of Glamorgan and further afield. 🚲♦

Summerhouse (ABV 3.6%) BITTER

Gwenith Du (ABV 4%) SPECIALITY
Nash Point (ABV 4%) BITTER
Vale Pale Ale (ABV 4.3%) PALE
Southerndown Gold (ABV 4.6%) GOLD
Big Boot (ABV 4.8%) BROWN

Twin Taff

8 Jenkins Place, Twynrodyn, Merthyr Tydfil, CF47 0ND
☎ 07564 187945 ✉ twintaffbrewery@outlook.com

☺Twin Taff was established in 2018 by twin brothers Darryl and Daniel Williams. It is Merthyr Tydfil's first town centre microbrewery. Brewing is currently suspended.

Twt Lol SIBA

Unit B27, Trefforest Industrial Estate, Pontypridd, CF37 5YB ☎ 07966 467295 ⊕ twtlol.com

Established in 2015 using a 10-barrel plant, the brewery has a capacity of 80 firkins a week, with the potential to expand to 160. All of its branding is produced in both Welsh and English. The brewery is now open on the first weekend of each month. Check website or social media for details. ‼ ▆ ♦ ⬥

Bwgan Brain (Scarecrow) (ABV 3.5%) BITTER
Buwch Goch Gota (Little Red Cow) (ABV 3.7%) RED
Glog (ABV 4%) BITTER
Twti Ffrwti (ABV 4%) GOLD
Cwrw'r Afr Serchog (Horny Goat Ale) (ABV 4.2%) GOLD
Cymryd y Pyst (ABV 4.4%) BITTER
Lol! (ABV 4.4%) GOLD
Glo in the Dark (ABV 4.5%) PORTER
Blŵbri (ABV 4.6%) SPECIALITY
Pewin Ynfytyn (Crazy Peacock) (ABV 4.8%) PALE
Pyncio Pioden IPA (Pretty Fly For a Magpie) (ABV 5%) PALE
Dreigiau'r Diafol (Diablo Dragons) (ABV 5.5%) IPA

Vale of Glamorgan SIBA

Unit 42, Atlantic Business Park, Barry, CF64 5AB
☎ (01446) 730757 ⊕ vogbrewery.co.uk

☺Established in 2005, expanding to a 10-barrel plant in 2023, the brewery has passed down to the third generation of ownership. It has two brands: Vale of Glamorgan – its heritage brand using only British hops, and VOG – using mostly US hops. Seasonals and collab brews with other brewers are also produced. Beers are frequently sold UK-wide through wholesale, breweries and festivals. It has a bottle and taproom (restricted opening). ♦ LIVE ⬥

Dancing in the Streets (ABV 4.1%) PALE
Maverick (ABV 4.2%) PALE
Paradigm Shift (ABV 4.2%) BITTER

Brewed under the VOG brand name:
Hotel Barrifornia (ABV 4%) PALE
South Island (ABV 4.2%) PALE

Tomos Watkin SIBA

Unit 3, Alberto Road, Century Park, Valley Way, Swansea Enterprise Park, Swansea, SA6 8RP
☎ (01792) 797280 ⊕ tomoswatkin.com

☺Brewing began in 1995, originally in Llandeilo behind the Castle Hotel. The brewery moved to Swansea in 2000 and was taken over by Hurns Mineral Water Company in 2002. More than 60% of production is bottled beer (not bottle-conditioned). ‼ ▆ ♦ ⬥

Delilah (ABV 4%) GOLD
Swansea Jack (ABV 4%) GOLD
Old Style Bitter (OSB) (ABV 4.5%) BITTER
Amber-coloured with an inviting aroma of hops and malt. Full-bodied; hops, fruit, malt and bitterness combine to give a balanced flavour continuing into the finish.
IPA (ABV 4.8%) PALE
Pecker Wrecker (ABV 5%) BITTER

Well Drawn

Unit 5, Greenway Workshops, Bedwas House Industrial Estate, Caerphilly, CF83 8HW
☎ (029) 2280 2240 ⊕ welldrawnbrewing.co.uk

This six-barrel brewery, established in 2017 in a small industrial unit on the outskirts of Caerphilly, is currently under second generation ownership. It has five core ales plus other seasonal casks alongside small-batch keg beers under the Philly Brew Co brand. They also produce a small number of bottle-conditioned ales in house. Most of its beer is supplied to the local free trade market or swapped with other UK breweries. ‼ ♦ LIVE

New Wave (ABV 4%) IPA
Bedwas Bitter (ABV 4.2%) BITTER
Caerphilly Pale (ABV 4.2%) PALE
WD Gold (ABV 4.4%) GOLD
Pontcanna Pale (ABV 4.6%) SPECIALITY

Zepto

Graig Fawr Lodge, Blackbrook Road, Caerphilly, CF83 1NF ☎ 07951 505524 ⊕ zeptobrew.co.uk

Established in 2016, Zepto is a 100-litre brewery set up by CAMRA member Chris Sweet. Although production is mainly bottled, cask-conditioned beers are occasionally brewed.

Zerodegrees SIBA

▤ 27 Westgate Street, Cardiff, CF10 1DD
☎ (029) 2022 9494 ⊕ zerodegrees.co.uk/cardiff

A state-of-the-art, computer-controlled German plant, producing unfiltered and unfined ales and lagers, served from tanks using air pressure that propels beer (without coming into contact with it) to the bar. Five regular brews, including a wheat beer and a fruit beer, are available. Additional beers are produced either occasionally or for the season. Part of a chain of four brewpubs.

Join CAMRA

The Campaign for Real Ale has been fighting for more than 50 years to save Britain's proud heritage of cask-conditioned ales, independent breweries, and pubs that offer a good choice of beer. You can help that fight by joining the campaign: see **www.camra.org.uk**

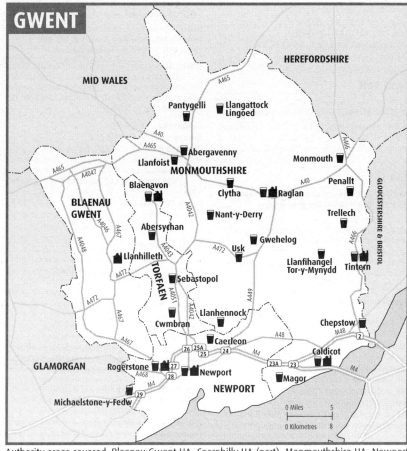

GWENT

Authority areas covered: Blaenau Gwent UA, Caerphilly UA (part), Monmouthshire UA, Newport UA, Torfaen UA

Abergavenny

Grofield ⓛ
Baker Street, NP7 5BB
☎ (01873) 858939 ⏺ grofield.com
Sharp's Doom Bar; house beer (by Tomos & Lilford); 1 changing beer (sourced nationally; often Wye Valley) Ⓗ

Just off the main pedestrianised area and next to the cinema, this family-run free house is run by a hugely experienced licensee. To the rear is a well-maintained garden, which on sunny days provides a green oasis in the middle of town. Popular pub meals are served Wednesday to Sunday; booking is advised. A well-attended pub quiz is held every Sunday evening, and men's and women's darts teams participate in the local league. ঌ❀⛬⬧♣🍴

Station Hotel
37 Brecon Road, NP7 5UH
☎ (01873) 854759
Draught Bass; Wye Valley HPA, Butty Bach Ⓗ

A short walk from the town centre, the Station remains a traditional, unspoilt pub, although both the station and the Abergavenny to Brecon railway it refers to are long gone. This solid building of local stone has been identified by CAMRA as having a nationally important historic pub interior: much of the original Victorian

interior remains, with its separate bar and lounge plus a small outside drinking area. The pub hosts a Wednesday night quiz and often features music on Fridays with a band or open mic evening. P🍴(X4)❀♪

Abersychan

Rising Sun ⓛ
Cwmavon Road, NP4 8PP
☎ (01495) 773256
Wye Valley Butty Bach; 2 changing beers (sourced locally; often Tomos & Lilford, Tudor, Untapped Brewing Co) Ⓗ

Charming roadside pub whose characterful public bar houses a restored inglenook fireplace with a log-burning stove. The cosy split-level lounge features another log stove and has pictures of the area on the walls. Beyond the lounge is spacious dining room where functions can be held. The guest ales are usually Welsh and change weekly. Outside is a pleasant garden and play area. The pub is a good base for local walks through Lasgarn Wood. Q ঌ❀⛬⬧♣P🍴(30)❀♪

Blaenavon

Lion Hotel
41 Broad Street, NP4 9NH

☎ (01495) 792516 ⊕ thelionhotelblaenavon.co.uk
**Glamorgan Jemimas Pitchfork; 1 changing beer
(sourced regionally; often Tomos & Lilford, Tudor)** Ⓗ
This comfortable hotel provides a handy base from which
to explore the local industrial World Heritage sites. It has
built a deserved reputation for excellent food, which can
be enjoyed in the restaurant or the traditional public bar.
Two handpumps dispense locally sourced ales which
may change according to customer preferences. Look out
for the plaque outside which describes a tumultuous
chapter in the town's past.
ﻌ❀⌂◑≉(High Level) P➡(X24,30) ≈

Caerleon

Bell Inn ✪
Bulmore Road, NP18 1QQ
☎ (01633) 420613 ⊕ thebellcaerleon.co.uk
**Timothy Taylor Landlord; Wye Valley HPA, Butty
Bach** Ⓗ
A low-beamed, 17th-century pub set in a pleasant
residential area near a former Roman burial ground. It
has an impressive stone façade behind which can be
found a fireside bar with adjoining snug. The restaurant is
very popular with diners savouring the excellent cuisine
on offer. Prints of old buildings and others of local
interest are dotted around the walls. The real ale range is
stable and reflects the choice of the regular drinkers.
ﻌ❀◑♣♠P➡(27,60) ❀ ≈ ♪

White Hart
28 High Street, NP18 1AE
☎ (01633) 430999
Greene King Abbot Ⓗ
A village favourite where the pleasant front and rear
sections are linked by a stand-up drinking area alongside
an impressive central bar that is open on three sides. The
decor features well-maintained polished wood panelling,
with the rear games room housing an attractive trophy
cabinet set in the wall. The bicentennial family tree of
the former Courage brewery, whose beers this pub
used to sell, is of interest. Abbot Ale is the beer of choice
for the locals. ﻌ❀♣➡(27,60)❀≈♪

Caldicot

Hive Mind Brewery Taproom Ⓛ
Unit 5F, Castleway Industrial Estate, NP26 5PR (in
corner of private car park at end of Castleway)
☎ 01402 953998 ⊕ wyevalleymeadery.co.uk
2 changing beers (often Hive Mind) Ⓖ
A well-designed and attractive taproom that belies its
unfashionable location on a light industrial estate unit on
the outskirts of town. It serves a successful range of real
ales brewed in the unit, plus the mead made with local
honey, with which the enterprise began. Expect two of
the house beers at any given time, with a choice of craft
beers. A shortcut footpath runs from the bus stop on
Caldicot bypass. ❀♠≉P➡(X74)❀♪

Chepstow

Queen's Head ♥ Ⓛ
12 Moor Street, NP16 5DD
☎ 07793 889613 ⊕ queensheadchepstow.co.uk
**8 changing beers (sourced regionally; often Gower,
Grey Trees, Untapped Brewing Co)** Ⓗ
The area's first micropub was a full-sized pub years ago
before a spell as business premises. Since launching in
the smaller form, it has increased in size to open up
much-needed additional drinking space. The bar counter
is a welcoming sight with an array of handpumps serving

real ales of various styles and strengths. Natural ciders
and perries are also sold. A multiple award winner and
local CAMRA Pub of the Year. Q≉●♠➡(73,X74)❀♪

Three Tuns Inn Ⓛ
32 Bridge Street, NP16 5EY
☎ (01291) 645797
**Kingstone Llandogo Trow; Wye Valley Butty Bach; 3
changing beers (sourced regionally; often Butcombe,
Kingstone, Untapped Brewing Co)** Ⓗ
At the lower end of an attractive old street, close to the
River Wye, this traditional pub sits in the shadow of
stunning Chepstow Castle. It offers drinkers up to five
cask ales, while diners can enjoy locally sourced produce
at lunchtimes. A two-level main bar area provides
comfortable seating, and there is a small room that leads
to a splendid garden. Live music sessions are hosted on
many Saturday evenings and Sunday afternoons, often in
the garden during fine weather. ﻌ❀⌂◑≉P➡❀≈♪

Clytha

Clytha Arms Ⓛ
Groesonen Road, NP7 9BW (on B4598 old road
between Abergavenny and Raglan)
☎ (01873) 840206 ⊕ clytha-arms.com
**Untapped Brewing Co Whoosh; 4 changing beers
(sourced nationally; often Uley)** Ⓗ
Featured in this Guide for over 30 consecutive years
under the expert leadership of the same licensees, this
popular country pub has become a pilgrimage for many.
Real ale drinkers have always been treated to an ever-
changing variety of beers from around the UK, with new
local breweries also well supported. Ciders and perries
are also available. The dining area serves good-quality
food – booking is recommended.
Qﻌ❀⌂◑▲♣♠P➡(83)❀♪

Cwmbran

Bush Inn Ⓛ
Graig Road, Upper Cwmbran, NP44 5AN
☎ (01633) 483764 ⊕ thebushuppercwmbran.co.uk
**3 changing beers (sourced regionally; often
Glamorgan)** Ⓗ
Cosy mountainside pub that was once four cottages
before becoming the popular community hub it is today.
Two distinct sections, both with fireplaces, cater for
drinkers through the day and also for diners in the
evening (pizzas Tue and Fri, curries Wed, steaks Thu).
Pictures of the locality during its industrialised days are
on display. Regional ales often appear among the beers
served from the three handpumps. There are good views
of Cwmbran in fine weather. ﻌ❀◑♣♠P➡(1,8)❀≈♪

John Fielding Ⓛ ✪
1 Caradoc Road, Southville, NP44 1PP
☎ (01633) 833760
**Greene King Abbot; Ruddles Best Bitter; Sharp's
Doom Bar; 2 changing beers** Ⓗ

Centrally located Wetherspoon pub close to transport links. The chain's formula of serving good-value food and drinks make this a busy place from morning to night. It is a welcome outlet for real ale in the town, and the two changing guest ales accompanying the regular beers are often supplied by local breweries. Seasonal real ale festivals inject further variety during the year. The pub is named after a local hero from Rorke's Drift in the Zulu Wars, and it maintains links with today's service veterans. Q✿❺✿◑ᶀ⇌✦♣P🖵(X3,X24)🛜

Queen Inn

Upper Cwmbran Road, Upper Cwmbran, NP44 5AX
☎ (01633) 484252
2 changing beers (sourced regionally) Ⓗ
Attractive pub with a rural backdrop and a bubbling mountain stream at the front. It was formerly three dwellings and this is reflected in the interior layout of restaurant, public bar and lounge. There are extensive outdoor facilities including a children's play area. The popular menu is entirely plant-based with ingredients sourced from local producers. Where possible the ales are also vegan and supplied from a local brewery.
✿❺◑♣♠P🖵(1,8) 🐾 ♪

Gwehelog

Hall Inn Ⓛ

Old Raglan Road, NP15 1RB
☎ (01291) 672381 ⊕ thehallinn.co.uk
Glamorgan Cwrw Gorslas/Bluestone Bitter; Wye Valley Butty Bach Ⓗ
Attractive roadside inn with a spacious rear garden and patio alongside a paddock with chickens and livestock. This is a traditional rural pub with thick stone walls, low beams and open fireplaces. Pictures mainly of horse-related scenes are dotted around, while two deer heads peer down from either side of a set of antlers on one wall. A separate restaurant area delivers good home-cooked food. The beer range reflects the locals' choice here. ✿❺◑♣P🖵(60)🛜

Llanfihangel Tor-y-Mynydd

Star on the Hill

NP15 1DT (near Llansoy)
☎ (01291) 650256
Kingstone Gold; Wye Valley Butty Bach; 1 changing beer (sourced regionally; often Wye Valley) Ⓗ
The public bar is comfortably furnished with sofas and a large wood-burning stove, and has a Great Britain theme with Union Jack memorabilia. Between this and the restaurant is a cosy snug with sofa seating. A separate entrance leads to the restaurant where home-cooked food is made to order. It has three more fireplaces and extends into a large conservatory. Wheelchair access is at the back through the conservatory. Well worth seeking out. Q✿❺✿◑ᶀ♠♣P✿

Llanfoist

Bridge Inn

Merthyr Road, NP7 9LH
☎ (01873) 854831 ⊕ bridgellanfoist.com
Evan Evans Cwrw; Glamorgan Jemimas Pitchfork; Wye Valley Butty Bach Ⓗ
Situated on the edge of the Brecon Beacons National Park is this attractive pub, named after the adjacent stone bridge across the River Usk. Inside, there is a split-level bar, with a wood-burning stove on the lower level. The TV screens are only switched on for major sporting events and, like the occasional live music, are never

allowed to drown the conversation. The garden is popular, with views across Abergavenny's Castle Meadows and the hills beyond. B&B accommodation is available. ✿❺✿◑♣P🖵(X4)🐾🛜♪

Llangattock Lingoed

Hunter's Moon Inn

NP7 8RR (2 miles off B4521 Abergavenny-Ross old road at Llanvetherine at road bridge at end of village) SO361201
☎ (01873) 821499 ⊕ hunters-moon-inn.co.uk
Wye Valley HPA Ⓗ/Ⓖ**, Butty Bach** Ⓗ**; 1 changing beer (sourced regionally)** Ⓗ/Ⓖ
Archetypal village pub in a small hamlet, next to the medieval church and Offa's Dyke Path. It is a free house, in which three generations of the family all play key roles in creating a great place to eat and drink. Inside, flagstone floors, thick beams and low ceilings reflect the building's antiquity. Outside, the large well-maintained gardens offer visitors views over the church and surrounding unspoilt countryside. Q✿❺✿◑♣P✿🛜

Llanhennock

Wheatsheaf

NP18 1LT (turn right 1 mile along Usk Rd heading N from Caerleon, then bear left at fork) ST353927
☎ (01633) 420468
Fuller's London Pride; 2 changing beers (sourced regionally; often Fuller's, Timothy Taylor, Wye Valley) Ⓗ
A fixture in the Guide for over 30 years, this excellent pub sits in delightful rural surroundings that offer extensive views. Its open fire and secluded garden make this an ideal year-round destination. Inside, the public bar is crammed with historic photographs and memorabilia, and usually serves a local beer. The game of boules is played in the car park. Q✿❺✿▲♣P✿🛜

Magor

Wheatsheaf Ⓛ ✅

The Square, NP26 3HN
☎ (01633) 880608
4 changing beers (sourced regionally) Ⓗ
Attractive, large pub set in a pleasant location off the village square. The interior has exposed stonework and wooden beams giving it an air of reassuring longevity. Traditional pub games are played in the Tap Room bar while two other sections divided by a fireplace have settles and a small library of reading material (including several copies of this guide). There is also a spacious restaurant. The beer range changes regularly and often includes locally brewed ales alongside guest beers from national and regional breweries.
✿❺◑ᶀ♣P🖵(62,X74) 🐾🛜♪

Michaelstone-y-Fedw

Cefn Mably Arms

CF3 6XS (turn N off A48 at Castleton, then follow road for just over a mile)
☎ (01633) 680347 ⊕ cefnmablyarms.com
Wye Valley HPA, Butty Bach; 1 changing beer (sourced nationally; often Wadworth) Ⓗ
A remote but busy country inn with an emphasis on an excellent range of freshly prepared meals. Its layout reflects the culinary focus; the interior is divided into three dining areas. Two regular beers and a guest (which may be dropped in the winter) are served alongside fine wines. Outside are attractive functional spaces to both

front and rear. A celebrated ancient oak tree dominates the large car park. There is no nearby public transport. Q❄️☺️🎵⏸️P🐾🍴📶

Monmouth

Punch House

4 Agincourt Square, NP25 3BT

☎ (01600) 713855 🌐 thepunchhousemonmouth.co.uk

Sharp's Doom Bar; Wychwood Hobgoblin Gold; Wye Valley Butty Bach Ⓗ

A Grade II-listed former coaching inn with a distinctive white exterior that stands out when approached from Monnow Street. The traditional interior displays interesting artefacts including the door of the old town gaol. Food is very much to the fore, including breakfast/brunch, but drinkers are well catered for. Letting rooms are available, and live entertainment features on Friday evenings. Children are welcome until 9pm in this family-friendly pub. ☺️🏠🎵⏸️👤🚘🍴(60)🐾📶🎵

Nant-y-Derry

Foxhunter Inn

NP7 9DN (either over the railway line after passing through Penperlleni or just before the railway bridge if travelling from E)

☎ (01873) 881101 🌐 foxhunterinn.com

Shepherd Neame Spitfire; Tomos & Lilford Nash Point; Wye Valley Butty Bach; 1 changing beer (sourced regionally; often Whitstable) Ⓗ

A fine old building that once used to serve as the tea rooms for rural Nant-y-Derry station, which was opposite. Since it reopened a few years ago, it continues to be both a popular bar and well-regarded restaurant. In warmer weather the garden seating area includes a marquee and heated wooden pods. Occasional entertainment is also a feature. Accommodation is available in two adjoining cottages. ❄️☺️🏠🎵⏸️👤P🐾

Newport

Alexandra

32 Commercial Street, NP20 1SS

☎ (01633) 376721

Rhymney Export; 2 changing beers (sourced locally; often Rhymney) Ⓗ

Named after Newport's Alexandra Dock, this popular pub is a recent conversion of a former bank and has created the first Rhymney outlet in the city centre. Modern styling and traditional character combine to make this a vibrant addition to Newport's pub scene. Alcoves and a raised rear level with high-table seating provide space for socialising throughout the day. Several TV screens play contemporary music and also show popular sporting events. ☺️👤🚆🚘📶🎵

Cellar Door

5 Clytha Park Road, NP20 4NZ

☎ 07930 857897 🌐 cellardoor.netlify.app

3 changing beers (sourced nationally) Ⓗ

Previously a small shop, the main area of this micropub also has a comfortable snug and an outside drinking area at the rear. Alongside handpulls for up to three real ales and two real ciders, three fonts dispense craft brews. A chilled cabinet provides further choice including local Anglo-Oregon beers. As a respite from TV and gaming machines, regularly changing modern artwork provides a background for conversation. There is live music on Sunday evenings. Q☺️🚆👤🍴🚘🐾🎵

Godfrey Morgan Ⓛ ✅

158 Chepstow Road, Maindee, NP19 8EG

☎ (01633) 221928

Brains SA; Greene King Abbot; Ruddles Best Bitter; Sharp's Doom Bar; 2 changing beers (sourced nationally; often Rhymney) Ⓗ

Named after the 1st Viscount Tredegar, survivor of the ill-fated Charge of the Light Brigade, this popular split-level Wetherspoon pub was once a cinema and displays pictures of film stars with local connections. Alongside the usual national ale range, the pub offers one or two more interesting options – it is a real ale oasis in what has become a good beer desert. There is a small car park at the rear - some or all of the charge is refundable with your first purchase. Q❄️☺️🎵⏸️👤P🚘(8,73)📶

John Wallace Linton Ⓛ ✅

19-21 Cambrian Road, NP20 4AD (off Queensway)

☎ (01633) 251752

Greene King Abbot; Ruddles Best Bitter; Sharp's Doom Bar; 3 changing beers (often Brains) Ⓗ

JD Wetherspoon's first Welsh outlet remains as popular as ever. Attracting both regular customers and passing trade, it is well placed for Newport's entertainment quarter and handy for public transport services. A corner of the pub is devoted to the exploits of local WWII naval hero, John Wallace 'Tubby' Linton. The chain's familiar food and drinks packages are available, as well as interesting guest ales. Seasonal beer and cider festivals are held. ❄️☺️🎵⏸️👤P🚘📶

Pen & Wig Ⓛ

22-24 Stow Hill, NP20 1JD

☎ (01633) 666818 🌐 jwbpubs.com/penandwig

Draught Bass; Glamorgan Jemimas Pitchfork; 5 changing beers (sourced regionally; often Brecon, Quantock, Tudor) Ⓗ

Bustling city centre pub attracting a varied clientele. Part of the attraction is the good choice of ales that always includes a dark option and the resident Bass. The internal layout offers several linked sections, each with TV screens so you are unlikely to miss key sporting moments. The food offering is substantial and popular, including a Sunday carvery. A spacious function room caters for various groups while the large decked patio at the rear gets busy in fine weather. ☺️⏸️🚆🍴P🚘(151)🐾🎵

Red Lion ✅

47 Stow Hill, NP20 1JH (on jct with Charles St)

☎ (01633) 961438

Wye Valley Butty Bach; 1 changing beer (sourced nationally; often Fuller's) Ⓗ

Popular, traditional pub a short uphill walk from the city centre. It is popular with sports fans, and the TV screens show various games, especially Rugby Union, with sporting memorabilia displayed around the walls. One section of the open-plan bar is given over to a games section with pool and the rarely seen shove ha'penny. National ale brands are usually on the handpumps. ☺️🚆🍴🚘(1,151)🎵

St Julian Inn

Caerleon Road, NP18 1QA

☎ (01633) 243548 🌐 stjulian.co.uk

Bath Ales Gem; Fuller's London Pride; 1 changing beer (sourced nationally; often Ludlow, Quantock, Wye Valley) Ⓗ

Over 30 consecutive appearances in this Guide bear testimony to the consistently high quality of the ales sold in this well-run roadside pub. Enjoying a location overlooking a bend in the River Usk, it offers views towards pleasant countryside and historic Caerleon. A public bar, wood-panelled lounge, games area and riverside balcony surround a central bar. There is also a downstairs skittles alley/function room. Guest ales favour those of a light and hoppy style.

ॐ✿◑♣P🖵(27,60) ✿ 🛜 ♫

Tiny Rebel

22-23 High Street, NP20 1FX
☎ (01633) 973934 ⊕ tinyrebel.co.uk
Tiny Rebel Cwtch; 3 changing beers (sourced nationally; often Tiny Rebel) ℍ

Next to Newport's Victorian indoor market is the flagship outlet for Tiny Rebel's innovative beers. The modern bar is attractively decorated with the contemporary artwork associated with Tiny Rebel brewery. The wide range of beers of all genres and formats offers great choice. Food is popular, with a fast-food-done-well style that you can watch being prepared through a window at the back of the bar. Downstairs, the Cwtch provides a quieter space when the main room is busy. ✿◑&⇌♣🖵✿ 🛜

Weird Dad Brewery Tap

23 Caerleon Road, NP19 7BU
☎ (01633) 244238 ⊕ weirddad.co.uk
3 changing beers (sourced regionally; often Weird Dad) ℍ

A short stroll from the city centre and Rodney Parade stadium, this brewery-tap-cum micropub has its own nanobrewery. The first of two small linked rooms contains a small bar dispensing cask and other live beers via handpull or gravity, alongside chillers offering interesting alternatives. There are stools by the window and tables and chairs in the next room. Opening hours are limited, with 8pm closing. 🖵(27,73)✿🛜

Pantygelli

Crown Inn ⓛ

Old Hereford Road, NP7 7HR
☎ (01873) 853314 ⊕ thecrownatpantygelli.com
Rhymney Hobby Horse; Wye Valley Bitter; 1 changing beer (sourced regionally; often Evan Evans, Glamorgan, Tomos Watkin) ℍ

A former local CAMRA Pub of the Year, this pub has an outstanding reputation for superbly-kept beer and excellent food. The pub is near Abergavenny, in beautiful rolling countryside between the Sugar Loaf and Skirrid mountains, and is popular with lovers of the outdoors. The views from the lovely patio makes it a great place to sit and enjoy the views with a pint or two. ॐ✿◑♣P

Penallt

Boat Inn

Lone Lane, NP25 4AJ
☎ (01600) 712615 ⊕ theboatpenallt.co.uk
Wye Valley HPA, Butty Bach; 1 changing beer (sourced regionally; often Kingstone) ℍ

This cosy two-roomed pub, nestling in its richly scenic Wye Valley setting, is best reached via a footpath alongside the neighbouring old railway bridge from Redbrook. Two Wye Valley ales and a varying guest are accompanied by several draught ciders. The extensive outdoor seating is ideal in fine weather. A good range of home-prepared dishes grace a tempting menu, particularly popular with walkers taking a break from the nearby Wye Valley and Offa's Dyke long-distance paths. Closed Tuesdays in winter. ॐ✿◑♣P🖵(69)✿♫

Raglan

Beaufort Arms

High Street, NP15 2DY
☎ (01291) 690412 ⊕ beaufortraglan.co.uk
Untapped Brewing Co Whoosh; Wye Valley Butty Bach ℍ

A family-owned former coaching inn, popular as both a pub and for its good-quality accommodation. Two regular ales, one each from Wye Valley and the village's Untapped brewery, are served in a cosy and creatively decorated bar, beyond which lies a large, comfortable lounge. Home-cooked meals often give a Mediterranean twist to traditional and modern Welsh dishes, bringing a taste of Spain to this peaceful corner of Wales. ✿◑◑P🖵(60,83) ✿ 🛜

Rogerstone

Tiny Rebel Brewery Bar

Cassington Road, Wern Industrial Estate, NP10 9FQ
(off Chartist Drive for vehicles)
☎ (01633) 547378 ⊕ tinyrebel.co.uk
Tiny Rebel Cwtch; 3 changing beers (sourced locally; often Tiny Rebel) ℍ

Modern, barn-type place, with an upstairs balcony offering views of the brewery through windows. Much focus is on promoting the Tiny Rebel brand, with merchandising including t-shirts and cans. An impressive array of handpulls line the bar, though with some duplication. A huge screen and quality sound system means that the pub can be noisy during sporting events. The veranda with its comfortable seating is a suntrap in summer. ॐ✿◑&♣P🖵(151)✿🛜♫

Sebastopol

Sebastopol Social Club ⓛ

Wern Road, NP4 5DU (on corner of Wern Rd and Austin Rd)
☎ (01495) 763808
Glamorgan Welsh Pale Ale; 2 changing beers (sourced regionally) ℍ

Social club where real ale lovers have enjoyed a large range of keenly priced beers and ciders, including guests rare for the area, over the years. CAMRA members are welcome on production of a membership card. Attractions include live entertainment, indoor sports and large TV screens. As well as the main room, there is a cosy lounge, large upstairs function room, and downstairs pool room. ॐ✿&♣P🖵(X3,X24)✿🛜♫

Tintern

Wye Valley Hotel

Monmouth Road, NP16 6SQ
☎ (01291) 689441 ⊕ thewyevalleyhotel.co.uk
Wye Valley Bitter; 1 changing beer (sourced locally; often Kingstone) ℍ

A distinctively shaped traditional and ever-popular hotel offering the modern touches needed to appeal both to locals and to visitors who have travelled far to enjoy the superb local scenery. At least one Wye Valley ale is always available, often alongside one from the nearby Kingstone brewery. There is also an impressive display of special and commemorative bottled beers. Home-cooked food is served in the bar and in the silver-service restaurant. ॐ✿◑◑&ΔP🖵(69)✿🛜

WALES

Trellech

Lion Inn

Church Street, NP25 4PA
☎ (01600) 860322 ⊕ lioninn.co.uk
Wye Valley Butty Bach; 3 changing beers (often Kingstone) ⌂

Traditional country inn located in a history-steeped village that is well worth exploring. The pub offers a charming bar centred around a fireplace on one side and, at a slightly higher level, a cosy lounge-cum-dining room with good food from an interesting menu. Ales are sourced from breweries local to the South Wales and the West Country. Beer and cider festivals and other events are held throughout the year.

Q♿❀₰◑🐕♿P🚃(65) ♣🐾♠♫

Usk

New Court Inn

62 Maryport Street, NP15 1AD
☎ (01291) 671319 ⊕ thenewcourtinn.co.uk
Draught Bass; Glamorgan Welsh Pale Ale; Wye Valley Butty Bach ⌂

Pleasant, relaxing back-street venue where customers can enjoy good food and fine ales. The long interior of linked sections contains an eclectic range of furniture. At the front is a comfortable drinking area in which to savour the popular regular ales, occasional guest beers and ciders, while the rear area is given over to dining. A suntrap garden at the back offers alfresco dining and drinking in fine weather. Comfortable accommodation is popular with visitors to the area.

Q♿❀₰◑🐕♿🚃(60,63) ♣🐾♠♫

Breweries

Anglo Oregon

Newport, NP19 4RR ☎ 07854 194966 ⊕ aobc.co.uk

Founded in the Forest of Dean in 2015, the brewery relocated to the owner's garage, in Nash, Newport, in 2017. It produces 330ml bottled ales, brewing 300 litres once a month (enough for 900 bottles). It regularly produces special, commemorative ales, often to do with local history. It occasionally produces 19-litre corny kegs for a couple of local pubs. It has a license for off-sales from the brewery.

Budweiser (Magor)

Magor Brewery, Magor, NP26 3DA

No real ale.

Hive Mind

Unit 5F, Severn Bridge Industrial Estate, Caldicot, NP26 5PR ☎ 07402 983998

Office: 19 River View, School Hill, Chepstow, NP16 5AX ⊕ hivemindbrewery.co.uk

Hive Mind is the beer brewing part of Wye Valley Meadery. Began brewing in 2021 offering beers infused with honey from its own hives. Bottles and casks available, the intiial range of cask beers consists of a golden ale, an IPA and a smoked porter. ‼🚃◆

The Pollinator (ABV 3.8%) PALE
Golden Hour (ABV 4.5%) GOLD
Honey Citra IPA (ABV 5.7%) IPA
Big Smoke (ABV 7%) PORTER

Kingstone

Tintern, NP16 7NX
☎ (01291) 680111 ⊕ kingstonebrewery.co.uk

Kingstone Brewery is located in the Wye Valley close to Tintern Abbey. Brewing began on a four-barrel plant in 2005. ‼🚃LIVE

Tewdric's Tipple (ABV 3.8%) BITTER
Challenger (ABV 4%) BITTER
Gold (ABV 4%) GOLD
Llandogo Trow (ABV 4.2%) BITTER
No. 1 Premium Stout (ABV 4.4%) STOUT
Classic (ABV 4.5%) BITTER
1503 (ABV 4.8%) BITTER
Abbey Ale (ABV 5.1%) BITTER
Humpty's Fuddle IPA (ABV 5.8%) IPA

Lines

🕮 37a Bridge Street, Usk, NP15 1BQ
⊕ linesbrewco.com

Lines opened as a brewpub in 2020 on the high street in the centre of Usk. The brewery, led by the former Celt Experience head brewer, occupies the ground floor through which you pass to access the rustic upper bar area serving beer and pizza. No real ale. ◆

Rhymney

Gilchrist Thomas Industrial Estate, Blaenavon, NP4 9RL
☎ (01495) 790456 ☎ 07831 350635
⊕ rhymneybreweryltd.com

☺An ideal venue to include when visiting the adjacent Pontypool & Blaenavon Preserved Railway, it is situated in the heart of a Unesco World Heritage Site, close to the National Mining Museum and the Blaenavon Iron Works, the first place in the world to make commercial steel. Established in 2005, the brewery is going from strength to strength. Its unashamedly traditional range of beers is available in its 11 tied houses, and in free houses throughout South Wales. ‼🚃◆LIVE

Hobby Horse (ABV 3.8%) BITTER
Dark (ABV 4%) MILD
Bevans Bitter (ABV 4.2%) BITTER
Golden Ale (ABV 4.2%) GOLD
General Picton (ABV 4.3%) BITTER
Export Light (ABV 4.4%) BITTER
Bitter (ABV 4.5%) BITTER
King's Ale (ABV 4.7%) BITTER
Export (ABV 5%) BITTER

Tiny Rebel

Wern Industrial Estate, Rogerstone, NP10 9FQ

Office: Sunnybank, St Brides, Wentlooge, Newport, NP10 8SQ ⊕ tinyrebel.co.uk

☺Tiny Rebel was founded in Newport, Wales, in 2012 by brothers-in-law Brad & Gazz. Many one-offs and seasonal beers are brewed to supplement the more established range. There is an increasing incidence of unfined beers. ‼🚃◆◆

Peloton Pale (ABV 4.2%) PALE
Cwtch (ABV 4.6%) RED

Tudor

Unit A, Llanhilleth Industrial Estate, Llanhilleth, NP13 2RX
☎ (01495) 214808 ☎ 07498 734896
⊕ tudorbrewery.co.uk

⊚Tudor began brewing in 2007 in Abergavenny and moved it to Llanilleth in 2012. Several local pubs are supplied, in addition to others further afield. There is a bar and function room in the office suite above the brewery, for which it has acquired a full license. It brews 700 litres at a time, five times a week. LIVE ⏺

Blorenge (ABV 3.8%) PALE
Black Mountain Stout (ABV 4%) STOUT
IPA (ABV 4%) PALE
Skirrid (ABV 4.2%) MILD
Super Hero (ABV 4.5%) PALE
Sugarloaf (ABV 4.7%) BITTER
Black Rock (ABV 5.6%) PORTER

Untapped

Unit 6, Little Castle Farm Business Park, Raglan, NP15 2BX
☎ **(01291) 690074**

Office: Unit 2, Wye Vale Way, Stretton Sugwas, Hereford, HR4 7BS ⊕ **untappedbrew.com**

Untapped has been at its premises since 2013. All beers except Triple S (a milk stout) are vegan-friendly. Two beer ranges are produced; a core and a premium. Beers are available in cask and bottle conditioned. ‼ ☒ ◆ LIVE V

Border Bitter (ABV 3.8%) BITTER
Sundown (ABV 4%) GOLD
Monnow (ABV 4.2%) BITTER
Whoosh (ABV 4.2%) PALE
Diolch (ABV 4.4%) PALE
UPA (ABV 4.5%) PALE

Triple S (ABV 4.9%) STOUT

Weird Dad

🖩 **The Filling Station, 23-23a Caerleon Road, Newport, NP19 7BU** ⊕ **weirddad.co.uk**

⊠ Consolidating its status as Newport's first microbrewery, Weird Dad maintains the formula with its unchanged core beer range and occasional specials. The 120-litre brew length Brewtools setup creates a variety of beer styles with all product being live beer. About a third of this is cask-conditioned, and the majority is dispensed at its onsite taproom and bottleshop. ‼ ☒ ◆ ⏺

Zulu Alpha

51b Symondscliffe Way, Caldicot, NP26 5PW ☎ **07578 196275/ 07899 794294**
✉ **info@zulualphabrewing.co.uk**

Brewing since 2018, Zulu Alpha uses a seven-barrel plant and has six fermenters. It has a taproom (open Fri-Sat) and an online shop. ⏺

New Horizon (ABV 4%) SPECIALITY
Caldi-kolsch (ABV 4.6%) SPECIALITY
Coco Loco (ABV 4.6%) SPECIALITY
Poco Loco (ABV 4.6%) PORTER
Voyager (ABV 4.8%) PALE
Citra IPA (ABV 5%) IPA
Freedom (ABV 5%) IPA
Evolution (ABV 5.2%) PALE

Punch House, Monmouth (Photo: Elliott Brown / Flickr CC BY-SA 2.0)

MID-WALES

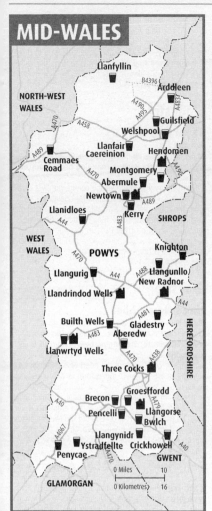

Authority area covered: Powys UA

Aberedw

Seven Stars Inn
LD2 3UW (next to church)
☎ (01982) 560762
Wye Valley HPA, Butty Bach ⊞
A community buy-out saved this historic village pub, close to an ancient church, scenic river gorge and castle mound. The large main bar has low beams, exposed stonework and a wood-burning stove. Two tables are outside at the rear and a bench seat outside at the front. Bar closing times are flexible so it is best to check ahead before visiting. Q♿🏠🍴🕐👦AP🐾🎵

Abermule

Abermule Inn
SY15 6ND
☎ (01686) 639110
2 changing beers (sourced locally) ⊞
Known locally as the 'Hotel', this pub has had a makeover in the last few years. It now has a separate smart restaurant and a spacious public bar with TV and sofas at one end. It is also now a free house and offers

two ales. There is a patio area for outside drinking, and a small caravan park is to the rear of the pub.
♿🏠🕐👦🅿🚆(71,X75) 🛜

Arddleen

Horseshoe Inn
Arddleen, Llanymynech, SY22 6PU
☎ (01938) 590690 🌐 horseshoeinnarddleen.co.uk
Stonehouse Station Bitter; Three Tuns XXX ⊞
A traditional country pub that dates from the 18th century. The open lounge/bar area has two separate seating areas and three ales are on offer. The large fireplace is decorated with horse brasses and there are some interesting old photos of the area. There is a separate dining room, and a function room is available, as well as a number of pleasant outside drinking areas. Open all day from noon in summer but check winter opening times. Q♿🏠🍴🕐👦🅿🚆(X71)🐾🛜🎵

Brecon

Brecon Tap
6 Bulwark, LD3 7LB
☎ (01874) 622888
4 changing beers (sourced regionally) ⊞
In a prime town-centre location, this contemporary bar has a light and airy feel, with comfortable seating throughout and walls lined with bottle-filled shelves. Three or four varying guest ales are offered, often from Welsh breweries, sometimes from further afield. There is also an interesting range of international and UK craft ales, plus simple food – good-value pies, sandwiches and the like. Bottled beers, wines, craft spirits and local artisan produce are available for off-sales.
Q♿🕐🍴🚆(X43) 🐾🛜

Hop in Beer & Gin House
37 The Watton, LD3 7EG
☎ (01874) 622092 🌐 hopinbeerandgin.co.uk
2 changing beers (sourced regionally; often Grey Trees) ⊞
Established in 2020 in difficult circumstances, the Hop In has quickly built an excellent reputation. Although compact, it has drinking areas on the ground floor and first floor, plus a small courtyard at the rear. The beer offering consists of two regularly changing real ales, five craft ales on tap and a wide range of bottled and canned beer. An equally impressive range of around 40 gins is available, which the knowledgeable staff are happy to advise on. Food is tapas, and excellent – booking is essential. Q♿🏠🕐🍴🚆(X43)🐾

Builth Wells

Fountain Inn ✅
7-9 Broad Street, LD2 3DT
☎ (01982) 553888
Wye Valley Butty Bach; 2 changing beers (often Salopian, Tiny Rebel) ⊞
Town-centre pub that is popular with locals. Decorated in a modern style, it retains a traditional feel, with plenty of

stonework, wood, floorboards and a welcoming wood-burner. The pub serves up to four real ales, which change regularly, plus a real cider. Sports TVs show major events and there is pool and darts in the bar. Next door is a café area and an upstairs terrace with a view of the River Wye. ◑🍺🍴🅿🚪

Bwlch

New Inn

Brecon Road, LD3 7RQ (on A40 between Brecon and Crickhowell)

☎ (01874) 730215 ∰ beaconsbackpackers.co.uk

Wye Valley Butty Bach; 2 changing beers (sourced regionally; often Grey Trees, Oakham, Salopian) 🅗

Lively and cosy village pub, popular with both locals and visitors. A comfortable dining area sits to the side of the bar, with armchairs around a huge fireplace. Two interesting guest beers supplement the regular ale, and excellent home-cooked food is available evenings and lunchtime at weekends – the pies are deservedly popular. Bunkhouse accommodation is available, making this an excellent base for exploring the surrounding Brecon Beacons and Black Mountains. Former local CAMRA Pub of the Year and a former South Wales regional winner. Q🕯🛏◑🍴🍺🅿🚪(X43)🐕🛜

Cemmaes Road

Dovey Valley Hotel ★

SY20 8JZ

☎ (01650) 511335 ∰ doveyvalleyhotel.com

2 changing beers (sourced locally; often Conwy, Evan Evans, Monty's) 🅗

Saved from the threat of closure in 2013, this unspoiled gem is now run as a dog-friendly pub and guest house serving a range of mainly Welsh ales. Identified by CAMRA as having a nationally important historic pub interior, it features original fittings, slate flooring, an open fire and includes a photo of the now defunct Cemmaes Road signal box opposite. The pub serves quality ales, plus food from Thursday to Sunday, and has a large beer garden and covered seating area. Q🕯🛏◑🍴🅿🚪(T12)🐕🛜

Crickhowell

Bear Hotel

High Street, NP8 1BW (in town centre)

☎ (01873) 810408 ∰ bearhotel.co.uk

Brains Rev James Original; Timothy Taylor Landlord; 2 changing beers (sourced regionally; often Glamorgan, Gower, Grey Trees) 🅗

Originally a 15th-century coaching inn, this is now an award-winning hotel and Guide regular. Its grand, multi-roomed bar features exposed beams, wood panelling, fine settles and an eclectic selection of furnishings and decorations. The two bar rooms have exposed fireplaces, as does one of the side rooms. Four ales are usually served, with guests often from independent Welsh breweries. Food is excellent and the varied menu features much local produce. An excellent base for exploring the surrounding Black Mountains and Brecon Beacons National Park. Q🕯🛏◑🍴🅗🍺🅿🚪(X43)🐕

Treebeards Bar

54 High Street, NP8 1BH

☎ (01873) 268668

Untapped Brewing Co Whoosh; 2 changing beers (often Grey Trees, Untapped Brewing Co) 🅖

Micropub in the heart of town, occupying part of what was once the Corn Exchange pub before it was converted

into award-winning smaller units. Established in recent years, it has built a good reputation and has brought variety to the local drinking scene. The comfortable bar has a friendly, cosy atmosphere and offers up to three real ales served straight from the cask, together with a selection of craft ales, mainly from Welsh independent breweries. 🛏🍴🚪(X43)🎵

Gladestry

Royal Oak Inn

HR5 3NR

☎ (01544) 370586 ∰ theroyaloakgladestry.co.uk

Wye Valley Butty Bach; 2 changing beers (sourced regionally) 🅗

A 17th-century pub in the village centre, run by a couple with an excellent local reputation for quality ale and food. The three real ales available include two changing beers from Hobsons, Three Tuns or Ludlow breweries. The pub is on Offa's Dyke Path, in the wilds of Radnorshire, and welcomes walkers and dogs on a lead. Open most lunchtimes and evenings. Q🕯🛏◑🍴🐕🅿🛜

Groesffordd

Three Horseshoes

LD3 7SN (just off B4558 in centre of village)

☎ (01874) 665672 ∰ threehorseshoesgroesffordd.co.uk

St Austell Tribute; 2 changing beers (sourced regionally) 🅗

Busy village-centre pub in the heart of the Brecon Beacons, boasting superb views from its outdoor seating areas. It is only a 10-minute walk from the Brynich lock on the Monmouthshire and Brecon Canal and is a popular stop for boaters and other visitors. The emphasis is very much on food, which is excellent, but the ales are always varied and interesting. Brynich caravan site and the Brecon YHA are also nearby. 🕯🍴◑🍴🍺🅿🐕🛜🎵

Guilsfield

Oak Inn

SY21 9NH

☎ (01938) 554741

Sharp's Doom Bar; Wye Valley HPA 🅗

This listed and much-altered 17th-century farmhouse has been refreshed and reopened by new landlords following a short closure. The bar is adorned with old photos of the pub and surrounding area and feels very cosy with its low, timbered ceiling. There is an extensive outdoor drinking area and covered smoking shelter. It also has a large car park and a children's playground. The restaurant has also been reopened and serves authentic Indian food. Q🕯🍴◑🍴🍺🅿🚪(X71,76)🐕🛜

Kerry

Kerry Lamb

SY16 4NP

☎ (01686) 670226 ∰ thekerrylambpowys.co.uk

Wye Valley Butty Bach; 1 changing beer (sourced regionally; often Timothy Taylor, Wye Valley) 🅗

Prominent red-bricked pub on the edge of the village, named after the Kerry Hill sheep. Locally owned, it seamlessly flits between its role as a community pub and restaurant with something to suit all tastes. It consists of a large lounge/bar, games room and a dining room. The St Michael and All Angels Church backs onto the rear creating a picturesque scene in the beer garden during warmer weather. 🛏◑🍴🍺🅿🚪(81)🐕🛜

Knighton

Watsons Ale House

24 High Street, LD7 1AT (near clock tower; up pedestrian street, on left next to chippy)
☎ (01547) 740017
3 changing beers Ⓗ
Popular micropub that was previously a tea room and a butcher's shop (spot the hooks and cold room door). They make and sell Watsons Real Powys Farmhouse Cider, and sell Skyborry cider and perry, which is also produced in the town. There are occasional pizza nights, or you can order food from the chippy next door – takeaway or delivered. Walkers and dogs are welcome.
Q❀◑≉⇘🖵(46) ☙ ⚘

Llanfair Caereinion

Goat Hotel

High Street, SY21 0QS (off A485)
☎ (01938) 810428 ⊕ thegoathotel.co.uk
3 changing beers (sourced locally; often Stonehouse) Ⓗ
Excellent 300-year-old beamed coaching inn whose welcoming atmosphere attracts both locals and tourists. The plush lounge, dominated by an impressive inglenook and open fire, has comfortable large armchairs and sofas. There is a dining room serving home-cooked food and a games room is situated at the rear. The choice of real ale usually contains a Shropshire beer. Beware the low-beamed entrance to the Gents.
Q❀❀⊯◑≉♣P🖵(87) ☙ ⚘

Llanfyllin

Cain Valley Hotel

High Street, SY22 5AQ
☎ (01691) 648366 ⊕ cainvalleyhotel.co.uk
2 changing beers (sourced locally) Ⓗ
Hotel built in the 17th century and originally called the Wynnstay Arms. The main part of the building is dominated by a staircase from the same period, and there are various nooks and crannies and wooden beams throughout. The public bar is on the right on entering; on the opposite side is a cosy lounge bar.
❀❀⊯◑ᵭ♣P🖵⚘ ⚘

Llangunllo

Greyhound Ⓛ

LD7 1SP (off A488 on B4356, in village centre)
☎ (01547) 550400
2 changing beers (sourced nationally; often Swan Brewery) Ⓗ
A traditional 16th-century village pub set in picturesque countryside, the first stop on the Glyndwr Way long distance footpath. The owners are CAMRA members who take good care of their beers, which are usually from a variety of local and regional breweries. They also stock Weston's Family Reserve cider. There are regular open mic music sessions on the first Saturday of each month.
Q❀❀Å≉♣🅿☙ ♫

Llangurig

Black Lion Hotel

SY18 6SG
☎ (01686) 440223
Three Tuns Best; 1 changing beer (sourced locally; often Three Tuns) Ⓗ
Built originally as a shooting lodge, the Black Lion was first licensed in 1633 and rebuilt as a hotel in the late

19th century. It is wooden-beamed with low ceilings and is split into two bars and a conservatory. The first bar acts as the games area, with a pool table and table skittles. The second lounge/dining area has wall seating, a stone fireplace and settles. There is also a side room with comfortable armchairs.
Q❀❀⊯◑ᵭ♣P🖵(X75,525) ☙ ⚘

Llangynidr

Red Lion

Duffryn Road, NP8 1NT (off B4558)
☎ (01874) 730223
Wye Valley The Hopfather; 2 changing beers (sourced regionally) Ⓗ
Popular village local, away from the main road, offering a warm welcome to walkers, boaters, families and dogs – the Monmouthshire and Brecon canal is a short walk away. The beer range changes regularly and good-value home-cooked food is served in the bar. A separate games area, outside seating and children's play area make this a pub for all. Regular quiz nights and live music also feature. ❀❀⊯◑≉♣P🖵☙ ⚘ ♫

Llanidloes

Angel Hotel

High Street, SY18 6BY (off A470)
☎ (01686) 414635 ⊕ angelinnllanidloes.co.uk
Greene King Abbot; 2 changing beers (often Three Tuns, Wye Valley) Ⓗ
Attractive and friendly edge-of-town pub with two comfortable bars. The larger of the two rooms has a large stone fireplace and old photographs on the walls. The smaller room has an interesting bar inlaid with old pennies. The restaurant can seat up to 40 people. The building was built in 1748 and the local Chartists held meetings here between 1838 and 1839. Outside seating is available at the front of the pub.
Q❀◑ᵭ🖵(X75,525) ⚘

Llanwrtyd Wells

Neuadd Arms Hotel Ⓛ

The Square, LD5 4RB
☎ (01591) 610236 ⊕ neuaddarmshotel.co.uk
6 changing beers (sourced regionally; often Felinfoel, Monty's, Purple Moose) Ⓗ
Large Victorian hotel serving as the tap for the Heart of Wales brewery. As well as its own beers, it serves a good range of real ciders. The Bells Bar features a large fireplace and an eclectic mix of furniture. The bells, formerly used to summon servants, remain on one wall, along with the winners' boards from some of the town's famous and unusual competitions. The lounge bar is a little more formal. The hotel takes part in the town's annual events, including a major beer festival over two weekends in November. Q❀⊯◑≉♣☙P☙

Montgomery

Dragon Hotel

Market Square, SY15 6PA
☎ (01686) 668359 ⊕ dragonhotel.com
4 changing beers (sourced regionally; often Monty's) Ⓗ
Dating from the mid 1600's, this former coaching inn has a distinctive Tudor black-and-white half-timbered frontage. It was once the principal coaching inn of the Powis estates, which was sold into private ownership in 1975. The bar is now to the rear of the hotel, giving more space for the clientele. There are patio areas to the front

and rear for outside drinking. The hotel also boasts an indoor swimming pool and a large function room. Q✿❄️⛵️◐🍴♿️🚲P🚆(T12,81) 🐾📶

Newtown

Brew Hub

13 High Street, SY16 2NX (on the High St between Iceland and Lloyd's bank)
☎ (01686) 610491
3 changing beers (sourced nationally) Ⓗ
Newtown's first café-bar has seen many uses over previous years, including a hairdresser's, a health food shop and a patisserie. It serves one ale on handpull, and the eight craft taps include two ciders. There are also bag in box ales, plus an excellent selection of spirits. The bar has table seating in its front half and wall benches and stools to the rear, plus an outdoor covered area. Bar snacks are planned for the future. Q✿❄️🍴🚆📶

Sportsman Ⓛ

17 Severn Street, SY16 2AQ (off A483)
☎ (01686) 623978
Salopian Oracle; Three Tuns Three Tuns Best, XXX; Wye Valley HPA, Butty Bach; 1 changing beer (sourced nationally) Ⓗ
Formerly Monty's Tap House, this pub is now a free house and has always a Wye Valley and a Salopian beer on tap. The pub is divided into three areas; a snug with comfortable wall seating, a main bar with a wood-burning stove, and a rear tiled games area with pool table, TV and darts. There is also a patio at the rear for outside drinking. Former local CAMRA Pub of the Year and former Welsh Cider Pub of the Year. Q✿♿️🍴🚆📶

Pencelli

Royal Oak ⏺

LD3 7LX
☎ (01874) 665396 ⊕ theroyaloakpencelli.com
Brains Rev James Original; 3 changing beers (sourced regionally; often Grey Trees, Tudor) Ⓗ
Comfortable and friendly family-run pub in a quiet village alongside the Monmouthshire and Brecon canal. Its extended opening hours are welcome in this part of the Brecon Beacons. The regular ale is supplemented with up to three others, usually from independent Welsh breweries. The pretty garden right next to the canal is a delight on a sunny day. The pub is popular with walkers, cyclists and boaters, with moorings available next to the garden. Q✿❄️◐♿️🅰️♣️🍴P🚆(X43)🐾📶♪

Penycae

Ancient Briton

Brecon Road, SA9 1YY (on A4067 Swansea to Brecon road, N of Abercrave)
☎ (01639) 730273
6 changing beers (sourced nationally; often Glamorgan, Grey Trees, Pitchfork) Ⓗ
Warm and family-friendly pub with a good atmosphere, situated on the A4067 Swansea to Brecon road, in the Brecon Beacons National Park. It has been local CAMRA Pub of the Year on numerous occasions for its range of ales and ciders. Plenty of car parking is available on site, and there is a campsite attached, making it ideal for campers and walkers. It is close to the famous Dan yr Ogof show caves and Craig y Nos castle.
✿❄️◐♿️🅰️♣️🍴P🚆(T6) 🐾📶

Welshpool

Old Bakehouse

14 Church Street, SY21 7DP
☎ (01938) 558860
4 changing beers (sourced locally; often Clun, Salopian, Stonehouse) Ⓗ
A micropub that opened in 2021 on the site of an old bakehouse, serving local real ales, cider, wines and a small selection of local spirits. No TVs, fruit machines or jukebox means good old-fashioned conversation rules. The relaxed environment makes it a great place to unwind on your own or with friends. There is an upstairs area with tables, armchairs, board games and books. It also has an outside enclosed drinking area. Takeaway containers are available. Q✿❄️♿️❄️♣️🍴🚆🐾

Ystradfellte

New Inn

CF44 9JE
☎ (01639) 721014 ⊕ waterfallways.co.uk
2 changing beers (sourced locally; often Glamorgan, Grey Trees) Ⓗ
A 16th-century village pub in the middle of Waterfall Country, a popular Brecon Beacons walking area. With two log fires, a covered outdoor terrace and beer garden at the front, there is a welcome whatever the weather. Two local ales are kept on tap, usually Grey Trees and others from Welsh independents. There is a strong focus on local produce, including spirits from nearby Penderyn Distillery. Real home-cooked food is served – the Boozy Cow Pie is very popular. Booking recommended. Q✿❄️◐🅰️🍴P🐾

Breweries

Antur (NEW)

Workshop & Offices, Near Mill Stores, Three Cocks, LD3 0SL ☎ 07825 154141 ✉ info@anturbrew.com

Showcasing the local landmarks within the Brecon Beacons National Park, Antur Brew Co opened in 2022. 'Antur' being the Welsh word for 'Adventure' embodies the brewery ethos. Heavily influenced by German and American styles, its small-batch 500-litre output is bottled onsite. ‼️🍺◆

Heart of Wales

🍺 Stables Yard, Zion Street, Llanwrtyd Wells, LD5 4RD ☎ (01591) 610236 ⊕ heartofwalesbrewery.co.uk

☺The brewery was set up with a six-barrel plant in 2006 in old stables at the rear of the Neuadd Arms Hotel. Beers are brewed using water from the brewery's own borehole. Seasonal brews celebrate local events such as the World Bogsnorkelling Championships. Cambrian Heart Ale was commissioned by and is brewed for the Cambrian Mountains Initiative, inspired by the former Prince of Wales, which aims to promote and support rural producers and communities in the region. ‼️🍺◆LIVE

Hwgga SIBA

6 Park Crescent, Llandrindod Wells, LD1 6AB ☎ 07767 358932 ⊕ hwggabrew.com

The brewery name is a pseudo Welsh version of the Danish term for cosy and welcoming (hygge). Output can be casked, kegged or bottled and a selection can always be sampled at the onsite taproom. Seasonal beers may also be available. The brewery delivers within a 30 mile radius of Llandrindod Wells. ‼️🍽️♦️♦️

Elan Valley Pale (ABV 4.1%) PALE
Lover's Leap (ABV 4.5%) BITTER
Shaky Bridge (ABV 5%) IPA

Left Bank SIBA

Ty Newydd Farm, Llangorse, LD3 7UA ☎ 07815 849523 🌐 leftbankbrewery.co.uk

After a spell brewing in various London locations, brewing has now relocated to what are the former premises of the Lithic brewery. Production is in bottle and cask form.

Hopla (ABV 4.2%) BITTER
Ty Coch (ABV 4.2%) RED

Lucky 7

Hay On Wye, HR3 5AW
☎ (01497) 822778 ☎ 07815 853353
🌐 lucky7beer.co.uk

A four-barrel brewery offering unfined beers suitable for vegans, but no real ale. V

Monty's SIBA

Unit 1, Castle Works, Hendomen, SY16 6HA
☎ (01686) 668933 🌐 montysbrewery.co.uk

Montgomeryshire's longest operating brewery began in 2009 and brews at Hendomen just outside Montgomery. The brewery produces four main cask beers with a large

number of seasonal and bottle-conditioned, gluten-free, and low-alcohol beers. ♦️LIVE GF

Old Jailhouse (ABV 3.9%) BITTER
MPA (ABV 4%) PALE
Sunshine (ABV 4.2%) GOLD
Mischief (ABV 5%) GOLD

Radnorshire

Timberworks, Brookside Farm, Mutton Dingle, New Radnor, LD8 2SU
☎ (01544) 350456 ☎ 07789 909748
🌐 radnorhillsholidaycottages.com

😊Set up in 2012 in a barn on the grounds of a farm offering holiday cottage accommodation, Radnorshire uses its own spring water. Drinkers staying at the cottages are supplied as well as a few local pubs. ‼️🍽️

Whimble Gold (ABV 3.8%) GOLD
Four Stones (ABV 4%) BITTER
Smatcher Tawny (ABV 4.2%) BITTER
Water-Break-Its-Neck (ABV 5.7%) PALE

Wilderness

Unit 54, Mochdre Industrial Estate, Newtown, SY16 4LE
☎ (01686) 961501 🌐 wildernessbrew,co.uk

The five-barrel brewery focuses on seasonal, barrel-aged and mixed fermentation beers. Belgian and farmhouse-style beers make up the majority of the range. As such, there are no regular beers.

All hands to the pumps

British beer is unique and so are the methods used for serving it. The best-known English system, the beer engine operated by a handpump on the pub bar, arrived early in the 19th century. It coincided with and was prompted by the decline of the publican brewer and the rise of commercial companies that began to dominate the supply of beer to public houses. In order to sell more beer, commercial brewers and publicans looked for faster and less labour-intensive methods of serving beer.

In 'The Brewing Industry in England, 1700-1830', Peter Mathias records that 'most beer had to be stored in butts in the publicans' cellars for the technical reason that it needed an even and fairly low temperature, even where convenience and restricted space behind the bar did not enforce it. This meant, equally inevitably, continuous journeying to and from the cellars by the potboys to fill up jugs from the spigots: a waste of time for the customer and of labour and trade for the publican. Drawing up beer from the cellar at the pull of a handle at the bar at once increased the speed of sale and cut the wage bill.'

The first attempt at a system for raising beer from cellar to bar was patented by Joseph Bramah in 1797. But his system – using heavy boxes of sand that pressed down on storage vessels holding the beer – was so elaborate that it was never used. But his idea encouraged others to develop simpler systems. Mathias writes: 'One of the few technical devices of importance to come into the public house since the publican stopped brewing his own beer was the beer engine. It was, from the first, a simple manually operated pump, incorporating no advances in hydraulic knowledge or engineering skill, similar in design to many pumps used at sea, yet perfectly adapted to its function in the public house.'

By 1801, John Chadwell of Blackfriars, London, was registered as a 'beer-engine maker' and soon afterwards Thomas Rowntree in the same area described himself as a 'maker of a double-acting beer-machine'. By the 1820s, beer engine services had become standard throughout most of urban England and Gaskell & Chambers in the Midlands had become the leading manufacturer, employing more than 700 people in their Birmingham works alone.

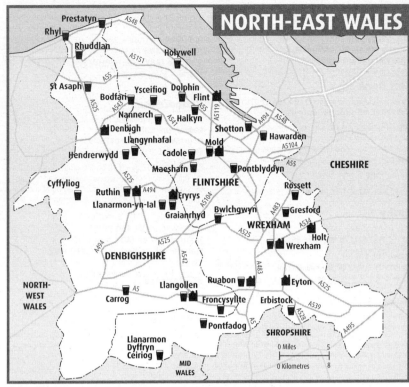

NORTH-EAST WALES

Authority areas covered: Denbighshire UA, Flintshire UA, Wrexham UA

Bodfari

Dinorben Arms 🅛

B5429, LL16 4DA (off A541, down B5429, 350yds on right) SJ092701

☎ (01745) 775090

Timothy Taylor Boltmaker; 6 changing beers (sourced locally; often Brunning & Price, Purple Moose) 🅗
Reputedly established in 1640, the building was derelict for eight years before it was acquired by Brunning & Price and transformed into and impressive gastro-pub. Its elevated position by the 16th-century church and tower offers fine views across the Vale of Clwyd. The spacious interior has several dining areas in typical B&P style, serving food all day. It also offers a good selection of real ales including three regular beers and four guests, usually from local micros. ★❀◐🕭🅟🖵(14)❀🛜

Bwlchgwyn

King's Head Inn 🅛

24 Ruthin Road, LL11 5UT (on A525)

☎ (01978) 753089

2 changing beers (sourced locally; often Big Hand) 🅗
Reopened after an impressive refurbishment, this small and friendly free house is on the main road through one of Wales' highest villages. The bar faces a well-furnished room with a wood-burner and large TV. To the side is another comfortable room with banquette seating and TV. The pub offers hearty and good-value bar meals, including breakfast on Friday and Saturday, but does not open early during the week. Bus services are limited. ★❀◐🅟🖵(X51)❀

Cadole

Colomendy Arms

Village Road, CH7 5LL (off A494 Mold-Ruthin road)

☎ (01352) 810217

5 changing beers 🅗
A wonderful free house just off the Mold to Ruthin Road, run by the same family for over 30 years and featuring in the Guide for most of that time. The recent tasteful addition of the print room and alpine lodge at the rear of the car park has added extra space without detracting from the character of the pub. The five ever-changing beers offer the best selection of real ales for miles. Popular with walkers from nearby Loggerheads Country Park. Q❀♣🅟🖵❀

Carrog

Grouse Inn

B5437, LL21 9AT (on B5437, off A5 at Llidiart Y Parc)

☎ (01490) 430272 ⊕ thegrouseinncarrog.co.uk

JW Lees Bitter, Founder's; 1 changing beer (often JW Lees) 🅗
Originally a farm and brewhouse, this friendly family-run inn has a single bar serving several rooms. It was tastefully refurbished in 2020 and has lost none of its fabulous character. Generous portions of home-cooked food are served in most areas of the pub, and there is a large outside covered patio that offers splendid views of the Dee Valley, Berwyn Mountains and 1660 Carrog Bridge. Carrog station on the Llangollen to Corwen railway is a short walk away. Q★❀◐🅰≒♣🅟🖵(T3,55)❀🛜

Cyffyliog

Red Lion Hotel 🅛

Cyffyliog, LL15 2DN (4 miles W of Ruthin, off B5105 at Llanfwrog)
☎ (01824) 710375 ⊕ redlionhotel.wixsite.com
Marston's 61 Deep, Pedigree; house beer (by Facer's); 1 changing beer (sourced locally) 🅗
Family-run village inn with parts dating back to the 17th century. The focal point is the welcoming lounge with a bar and an open fire. There is a cosy adjacent dining area with a further dining/function room. The public bar has a pool table and TV; don't miss the Gents toilet which is bedecked in numerous different wall tiles from a bombed Liverpool factory. Wednesday quiz nights and Thursday curry nights are popular. The pub also doubles up as the village shop. Q🖤🕪🅰🐾🌑❄♪

Dolphin

Glan yr Afon Inn 🅛

Milwr, CH8 8HE
☎ (01352) 710052 ⊕ glanyrafoninn.com
Facer's Dave's Hoppy Beer, Landslide 🅗
You can expect a warm welcome at this popular pub. Originally opened in the 16th century, it stands in an elevated position with a view of the Dee Estuary and Wirral peninsula. The inn serves food in the summer and provides accommodation. A central bar serves four separate seating areas and the dining room, while the games room has its own bar. Walkers and dogs are welcome and there is a real fire to keep you warm on cold days. 🖤🌑🛏🕪🚳🐾P🖵❄

Erbistock

Boat

LL13 0DL (follow signs from the A528, approx 1 mile W of Overton)
☎ (01978) 280205 ⊕ theboataterbistock.co.uk
Stonehouse Station Bitter; Timothy Taylor Landlord; 3 changing beers (sourced regionally; often Big Hand, Salopian, Weetwood) 🅗
The Boat dates back to the 13th century and has a wonderful picturesque location. The building takes advantage of its southerly outlook with outdoor seating offering exceptional views of the idyllic banks of the River Dee. The pub is mainly laid out for dining but there is also plenty of space for drinkers. The split-level bar, with handpumps on both sides, serves up to four cask beers, often from local breweries. Q🌑🕪🚳🅰P🌑

Froncysyllte

Aqueduct Inn

Holyhead Road, LL20 7PY (on A5)
☎ (01691) 777118
2 changing beers (sourced locally; often Izaak Walton, Weetwood) 🅗
A welcoming free house on the busy A5. The small central bar room leads to a games room with TV on the right and a comfortable lounge with a wood-burning stove to the left. Outside, a veranda offers panoramic views of the Pontcysyllte Aqueduct on the Llangollen Canal. Not to be missed is the mural that covers one gable end of the pub. Up to four changing ales are available. Food is served daily, with a traditional roast on Sunday. 🖤🌑🛏🕪🐾P🖵(64)🌑❄

Graianrhyd

Rose & Crown

Llanarmon Road, CH7 4QW (on B5430 off A5104)
☎ (01824) 780727 ⊕ theroseandcrownpub.co.uk
Wye Valley HPA; 2 changing beers 🅗
A traditional early 19th-century pub with a strong local following. The long bar serves two rooms, the main one of which has an open fire, copper-topped tables and a vast array of pumpclips. Guest beers are usually from local breweries. The pub is popular with tourists, walkers, fell runners and cyclists. Finishers in the local Dash in the Dark run refuel here on the chip baps, as do those taking part in the Three Taverns choir walking tour in May. Q🖤🌑🅰🐾P🖵(2)🌑

Gresford

Griffin Inn

Church Green, LL12 8RG
☎ (01978) 855280
2 changing beers (sourced nationally; often Timothy Taylor) 🅗
Friendly community pub with an irregular, open-plan layout adorned with many interesting pictures. Lively conversation at the bar does not impinge on the quieter corners. The landlady has been running the pub since 1973. It is sited where pilgrims came to drink in the Middle Ages, opposite All Saints Church whose bells are one of the Seven Wonders of Wales. There is a lawned area to the side with seating. Bus No.1 (Chester to Wrexham) stops in the village less than half a mile away. Q🖤🌑🐾P🖵(1)❄

Pant-yr-Ochain 🅛

Old Wrexham Road, LL12 8TY (off A5156, E from A483 follow signs to The Flash)
☎ (01978) 853525
Purple Moose Cwrw Eryri/Snowdonia Ale; Timothy Taylor Landlord; Titanic Plum Porter; Weetwood Eastgate; house beer (by Brightside); 4 changing beers (sourced regionally) 🅗
Impressive 16th-century dower house that retains many historic features, situated beside a small lake within extensive gardens. The central bar, dominated by a large double-fronted bar, leads to a variety of seating areas including a garden room, a small snug behind the period inglenook fireplace, and the patio and lawn outside. Though hugely popular, the pub retains a quiet feel. Food is served all day and five regular beers are supplemented by four guests and often a draught cider. Q🖤🌑🕪🚳🐾P🌑❄

Halkyn

Blue Bell Inn 🅛

Rhosesmor Road, CH8 8DL (on B5123)
☎ (01352) 780309

JW Lees Bitter; 3 changing beers (sourced locally; often Facer's) H
A traditional rural pub on Halkyn Mountain, the Blue Bell is a good base for exploring the local countryside and offers free guided walks around the area. Built in 1700 and named after a local privateers boat, the pub has a strong community focus, hosting regular events and societies. The beer range usually includes north Wales breweries, often Facer's, and also there is a wide selection of real ciders. ზ❀🅰♣♠P🖳❀☃

Hawarden

Glynne Arms 🅛
3 Glynne Way, CH5 3NS
☎ (01244) 569988 ⊕ theglynnearms.co.uk
Facer's This Splendid Ale; 3 changing beers (sourced locally; often Big Bog, Big Hand, Weetwood) H
A 200-year-old coaching inn at the heart of the village, serving locally sourced beers and good-quality food. The semi-circular bar serves both the bar area and adjacent dining room while there is also a separate restaurant with a real fire. The decor is sympathetic to the age of the building, with several references to the village's most famous resident, William Gladstone. Popular with walkers visiting the nearby castle and park.
ზ❀🕸🅗🅖≠♣♠P🖳(4,11)❀☃♫

Hendrerwydd

White Horse Inn 🅛
LL16 4LL (signed from B5429, near Llandyrnog)
☎ (01824) 790218 ⊕ whitehorserestaurant.co.uk
2 changing beers H
Rambling, oak-beamed, 16th-century inn that has been tastefully refurbished. Entrance is into the lounge with dining areas off two sides. There is a snug bar to the right with roaring fire in the winter, and a pool room behind the bar. Two ever-changing guest beers are sourced from local breweries. The restaurant is popular and highly rated for its locally sourced food. Dogs are allowed in the snug. Q ზ❀🕸🅖≤🅰P🖳(76)❀

Holywell

Market Cross ✅
9-11 High Street, CH8 7LA (on main walkway)
☎ (01352) 717800
Greene King Abbot; Purple Moose Ochr Dywyll y Mws/Dark Side of the Moose; Sharp's Doom Bar; 3 changing beers (often Big Bog, Purple Moose)
Converted in 2011 from a large retail outlet, this small Wetherspoon pub is located in the centre of Holywell High Street and named after the obelisk that stood outside. There are many pictures of old Holywell and the Greenfield valley displayed on the walls. The regular beers are complemented by three guest ales that often include local breweries, plus a real cider.
Q ზ🕸🅖♠🖳(X11,11)☃

Llanarmon Dyffryn Ceiriog

Hand at Llanarmon
LL20 7LD (end of B4500 from Chirk)
☎ (01691) 600666 ⊕ thehandhotel.co.uk
Stonehouse Station Bitter; Weetwood Cheshire Cat; 1 changing beer (sourced locally) H
Cosy free house in a scenic location at the head of the stunning Ceiriog Valley. Look for the giant carved wooden hand outside. Inside, the dog-friendly bar has an open fire, and hunting and local prints decorate the walls. The two real ales are usually from local brewers.

Food and accommodation are also of a high standard, and it has recently opened a spa. Walkers, cyclists and tourists are all welcome. Book at busy times.
Q ზ❀🛏🅖🅗◐🅖♠P🖳(64)❀☃

Llanarmon-yn-Ial

Raven Inn 🅛
Ffordd-Rhew-Ial, CH7 4QE (signed 500yds W of B5430)
☎ (01824) 780833 ⊕ raveninn.co.uk
Purple Moose Cwrw Eryri/Snowdonia Ale; 2 changing beers (sourced locally) H
Run with the help of volunteers for over a decade, this delightful old pub goes from strength to strength with all profits used to benefit the community. There is a friendly and inviting ambience from the moment you enter. The bar serves two carpeted areas and a tiled area to one side. The three guest beers served are from local breweries. Excellent locally sourced home-cooked food is served Thursday to Sunday. There are three self-catering rooms. Q ზ❀🛏🅖◐🅖♣♠P🖳(2)❀☃♫

Llangollen

Corn Mill
Dee Lane, LL20 8PN (on town side, W of River Dee bridge)
☎ (01978) 869555
Facer's Dave's Hoppy Beer; house beer (by Brightside); 3 changing beers (sourced nationally) H
A beautifully converted flour mill incorporating the water wheel, with a series of open-plan rooms spread over three levels, with bars on the first two floors. The large outside decking area has unparalleled views across the River Dee to the restored heritage steam railway station. The restaurant takes precedence here, with the drinking area in the ground-floor bar and outside. Five pumps dispense three regularly changing beers, and high-quality food is served throughout the day.
Q ზ❀🕸🅖🅗≤🅰≠♠🖳(5,T3)❀☃

Sun Inn 🅛
49 Regent Street, LL20 8HN (400yds E of town centre on A5)
☎ (01978) 860079
Elland 1872 Porter; Ossett White Rat; 4 changing beers (sourced nationally) H
A free house whose large front lounge features two open fires and a stage for live music. A smaller snug at the rear has mirrored panels and a large TV screen. This room is accessed via an enclosed partly covered rear seating terrace. The pub has a late licence with music Wednesdays to Saturdays – last entry is at 11pm. The pub is quieter in the early evening but can get busy later on, especially at weekends. 🕸🅰≠♣♠🖳(5,T3)❀☃♫

Sun Trevor
Sun Bank, LL20 8EG
☎ (01978) 860651 ⊕ suntrevor.co.uk
2 changing beers (sourced locally; often Stonehouse, Weetwood) H
An 18th-century pub overlooking the Llangollen Canal. The bar and lounge area features a large inglenook fireplace festooned with brasses and photos. There is a large separate dining area. Two changing beers are usually from local breweries. Food is served until evening. Outside seating is available, including some under a small marquee. Quiz night is on Wednesday. The pub is popular with walkers, cyclists and narrowboaters. Access is from the canal and bus stop opposite.
Q ზ❀🕸🅖🅰P🖳(5,T3)❀☃

Llangynhafal

Golden Lion Inn

LL16 4LN (at village crossroads)
☎ (01824) 790451 ⊕ thegoldenlioninnllangynhafal.com
2 changing beers (sourced locally; often Brakspear, Marston's) Ⓗ

Traditional and welcoming 18th-century village inn at the foothills of the Clwydian hills. The bar serves two distinct areas: the bar with a pool table and the lounge leading down to a dining area. The enthusiastic landlord has been at the helm for 13 years and takes particular pride in his beers and whiskies. The guest beer is often from a local brewery. There is a campsite at the rear. A regular of the Route 76 bus beer festival.

Q☆🍺🞄👕P🖫(76) ✿ 🛜

Maeshafn

Miners Arms Ⓛ

Village Road, CH7 5LR (off A494 in village centre)
☎ (01352) 810464 ⊕ miners-arms-maeshafn.com
Bowland Hen Harrier; Facer's Flintshire Bitter; Timothy Taylor Boltmaker Ⓗ

Dating from 1820, this pub in the hamlet of Maeshafn was linked to the development of lead mining in the area. Surrounded by scenic countryside, it is now popular with hikers. A refurbishment a few years ago saw the central bar area split from dining area by a double sided wood-burning stove, which creates a warm atmosphere throughout. There is also a pleasant seating outside area at the front of the pub. Food and snacks are available.

☆🕸🞄P🖫(2) ✿ 🛜

Mold

Glasfryn Ⓛ

Raikes Lane, CH7 6LR (off A5119 ½ mile N of Mold)
☎ (01352) 750500 ⊕ glasfryn-mold.co.uk
Purple Moose Cwrw Eryri/Snowdonia Ale; house beer (by Phoenix); 7 changing beers

Close to Theatre Clwyd and set in its own grounds opposite the civic centre, this large upmarket pub and restaurant was once the residence for circuit judges attending the nearby court. Operated by Brunning & Price, the interior is decorated in their usual style, with the emphasis on food which is served all day in three dining areas. There are extensive views over the surrounding countryside from the large beer garden.

Q☆🕸🌓👆P🖫(28) ✿ 🛜 🍷

Mold Alehouse 🍷 Ⓛ

Unit 2 Earl Chambers, Earl Road, CH7 1AL
☎ (01352) 218188
4 changing beers (sourced nationally; often Cwrw Ial, Facer's, Hafod) Ⓗ

Since opening in 2016 this micropub has won many CAMRA awards including Wales Pub of the Year 2022. It has gained a strong following based on good beer and conversation. It is centrally situated in a Grade II-listed building opposite the town hall. The four cask ales include a dark beer and there are also five keykeg lines and four ciders. Although no food is served, there is a café in the same building accessed by the same entrance. Q🞄🖫✿🛜

Nannerch

Cross Foxes Ⓛ

Village Road, CH7 5RD
☎ (01352) 741464 ⊕ cross-foxes.co.uk
2 changing beers (sourced locally; often Big Hand) Ⓗ

This delightful village pub near the church was built in 1780 and originally doubled up as a butcher's – the meat hooks are still present over the bar. The entrance leads into the main bar with its large fireplace. Off this are another small bar, a lounge and a function room. Three pumps serve changing beers, usually from local brewers including Big Hand. Beer festivals are held in March and October. ☆🌓♣P🖫🛜 🎵

Pontblyddyn

Bridge Inn

Wrexham Road, CH7 4HN (on A541, 3 miles S of Mold)
☎ (01352) 770087
2 changing beers Ⓗ

Fine old building situated at a crossroads, with the River Alyn at rear of the pub. The unspoilt interior has a warm and cosy front bar with a real fire, a room leading off to the right, and a separate restaurant to the left. There is also a courtyard area at the front and an extensive riverside beer garden and children's play area at rear.

Q☆🕸🌓👆P🖫✿🛜

Pontfadog

Swan Inn

Llanarmon Road, LL20 7AR (on B4500 next to post office)
☎ (01691) 718273 ⊕ theswaninnpontfadog.com
Stonehouse Cambrian Gold; 1 changing beer (sourced locally; often Stonehouse) Ⓗ

Welcoming village free house in the scenic Ceiriog valley. The cosy red-tiled bar, where the locals tend to congregate, features a central fireplace which separates the TV and darts area from the servery. The separate dining room leads to an outside space that is currently for residents only. Home-cooked food is available throughout the pub. Accommodation is available in the three bedrooms upstairs. Call ahead, especially in winter, as opening hours may change.

Q☆🕸🍺🌓♣P🖫(64) ✿ 🛜

Prestatyn

Archies Ⓛ

151 High Street, LL19 9AS
☎ (01745) 855333 ⊕ archiesbar.co.uk
Facer's Flintshire Bitter; 2 changing beers Ⓗ

Halfway up the High Street is this town-centre café-bar with a modern interior and a decking area at the front entrance where you can watch the world go by on sunny days. Food is available all day Saturday, and at Sunday lunchtime in the summer months. The bar opens at midday Tuesday to Thursday during the summer.

☆🌓👆🚆🖫(11,36) ✿ 🛜 🎵

Bar 236 Ⓛ

236 High Street, LL19 9BP
☎ (01745) 850084 ⊕ bar236.co.uk
3 changing beers (sourced locally) Ⓗ

This café-bar at the top of the High Street has been established for more than a decade. Its L-shaped room has a minimalist but pleasant feel, with a wood- boarded floor and blue-tiled bar front. Glass fronted on two sides, it offers open views inside and outside. TV sport is well catered for and there is live music at weekends, when it can be quite noisy. ☆🚆✿🛜 🎵

Rhuddlan

Castle Inn

Castle Street, LL18 5AE

Theakston Best Bitter; 1 changing beer (sourced nationally) Ⓗ
Friendly pub opposite the 13th-century ruins of Rhuddlan Castle. It has two large rooms separated by the central bar and a sizeable covered outdoor seating to the rear. Two cask ales are served, with Theakston's being a regular. The pub is popular with locals, and also attracts many tourists visiting the castle. There is a small car park opposite for use by patrons. ✿♣P🚫✿

Rhyl

Dove at Rhyl Ⓛ
2 St Margarets Buildings, St Margarets Drive, LL18 2HT (on A525, ½ mile from centre)
☎ 07908 957116
3 changing beers (sourced locally; often Dovecote) Ⓗ
Situated on the outskirts of town, this welcome addition to the pub landscape of Rhyl is the first in a small chain of pubs operated by Dovecote brewery under the Dove umbrella. The interior is bright and airy, featuring a mural of Rhyl High Street, and the atmosphere is relaxed and friendly. The cask beer range includes at least one from Dovecote plus two guests from local microbreweries. Closed Mondays except bank holidays.
Q ⍾✿●🚫(51) ✿♪

Esplanade Club
86 Rhyl Coast Road, LL18 3PP (on A548, 1 mile E of centre, on left next to Spar local)
☎ (01745) 338344
2 changing beers Ⓗ
Friendly and welcoming club in the Tynewydd area, on the main coast road. It serves up to two real ales from local and national brewers. Attractions include a three-quarter-sized snooker table. The club welcomes families and pets, and attracts visitors to the many holiday parks on its doorstep. A former local CAMRA Club of the Year.
⍾&🚫(11,35) ✿🛜

Rossett

Golden Lion Ⓥ
Chester Road, LL12 0HN
☎ (01244) 555300 ⊕ thegoldenlionrossett.co.uk
Theakston Best Bitter; Timothy Taylor Landlord; 1 changing beer (often Hydes) Ⓗ
Situated midway between Chester and Wrexham, this extensive whitewashed building has plenty of nooks and crannies, attractive bric-a-brac for wall decoration and smart, traditional furniture. The pub is popular with diners, with an array of dishes to suit all tastes, but the bar area remains the domain of the humble drinker. Cask ales are discounted on Mondays. An extensive outside garden features a large Nordic tipi. The pub claims to have a resident ghost known as Old Jeffrey.
⍾✿❶P🚫✿

Ruabon

Bridge End Inn Ⓛ
5 Bridge Street, LL14 6DA
☎ (01978) 810881
7 changing beers (sourced nationally; often Ossett, Rat, Salopian) Ⓗ
Welcoming, traditional, community-focused local, close to Ruabon railway station, with three low-ceilinged rooms and a covered outdoor drinking area. The deservedly won numerous awards since its revitalisation by the owners, including CAMRA National Pub of the Year. The changing range of up to seven cask ales may include a brew from the on-site McGivern brewery plus a

porter or a stout. There is usually a real cider. Families and well-behaved dogs are welcome in the lounge.
Q⍾✿⚑≉♣●P⍰🚫✿🛜♪

Ruthin

Castle Hotel Ⓥ
St Peters Square, LL15 1AA
☎ (01824) 708950
Greene King Abbot; Ruddles Best Bitter; Sharp's Doom Bar; 3 changing beers (often Big Hand, Conwy, Purple Moose) Ⓗ
JD Wetherspoon hotel in the historic market town of Ruthin. It has 17 guest bedrooms, and the interior is divided into different historic themes: Owain Glyndwr, the Myddelton family and Ruthin Castle. A feature is the Barrel Room, which mentions a long defunct brewery on the premises. The car park is for residents only. The town itself has many attractions such as the Old Gaol, Craft Centre and many fascinating buildings. The bar is guide dog-friendly. ⍾✿⚑❶&●P🚫(55,76)✿🛜

St Asaph

New Inn Ⓥ
Lower Denbigh Road, LL17 0EF
☎ 07874 055314
JW Lees Bitter; 2 changing beers (often JW Lees) Ⓗ
The interior of this pub consists of a main lounge bar area, a pool room with dartboard, and a separate back bar with a real open fire and another dartboard. There is also a raised outdoor area at the rear with a large landscaped garden below. The pub backs onto the River Elwy, with easy access for dog walkers. Two changing JW Lees beers are served, along with their bitter. There is a large car park. Q⍾✿♣P🚫(51)✿

Shotton

Central Hotel Ⓥ
2-4 Chester Road West, CH5 1BX
☎ (01244) 845510
Greene King Abbot; Ruddles County; Sharp's Doom Bar; 2 changing beers (sourced nationally) Ⓗ
A local landmark, built in the early 1920s beside the railway station. It had a major refurbishment in 2008 and reverted to its original name. The interior is in typical Wetherspoon mock-Edwardian style, with a single large bar partially separated into three similarly furnished areas. Two changing guest beers are served alongside three standard national beers. At the front is an open seating area between the pub and the street. There are monthly events including Meet the Brewer evenings.
⍾✿❶&≉P🚫🛜

Wrexham

Acton Park
Chester Road, LL11 2SN (on A5152, ¾ mile N of town centre)
☎ (01978) 314336
3 changing beers (sourced nationally; often Dark Star, Sharp's, Timothy Taylor) Ⓗ
Large open-plan estate pub, well furnished with tables and chairs. A cosier family dining area with soft seating is located towards the rear. A U-shaped bar serves all areas and there are a couple of real fires to keep you warm in winter. Toilets are on the first floor but there is an accessible WC on the ground floor. Up to three changing beers are available. On Mondays and Thursdays all beers are reduced in price. Real cider is available in summer.
⍾✿❶&●P🚫(1)🛜

Elihu Yale ✓

44-46 Regent Street, LL11 1RR
☎ (01978) 366646
Greene King Abbot; Ruddles Best Bitter; Sharp's Doom Bar; 5 changing beers (sourced nationally) 🅷
Named after the founder of Yale University who is buried in the town, this is now the only Wetherspoon outlet in Wrexham. Formerly a cinema, the pub is close to both rail and bus stations. One beer is usually from a north Wales brewery and there are two ciders. It consists of one room divided into several sections, with the quieter area near the front. Families are welcome until 10pm.
Q ⑤ ◁ ◐ & ♿ (Central) ● 🖪 🎅 ☂

Magic Dragon Brewery Tap 🍷 🅻 ✓

13 Charles Street, LL13 8BT
☎ (01978) 365156
Magic Dragon Ice Dragon, Eyton Gold; 5 changing beers (sourced regionally; often Salopian, Magic Dragon) 🅷
This single-roomed pub is the tap for Wrexham-based Magic brewery. Standing on the edge of what was known as the Beast Market, the building started off as the Elephant & Castle before becoming other businesses and finally returning to its roots as a pub. Six handpumps dispense at least four Magic Dragon beers including one or more dark ales. Live music plays every weekend, alternating between Friday and Saturday nights.
Q ♿ (Central) ● 🖪 🎅 ☂ ♪

Royal Oak

35 High Street, LL13 8HY
☎ (01978) 364111
Joule's Pure Blonde, Pale Ale, Slumbering Monk 🅷
Often known locally as the Polish Embassy, this Grade II-listed pub has a long, narrow interior with a real fire, lots of wood panels and many stained glass mirrors. Look out for the antelope head. The small roof garden is open from April to September. Food is not served but you are welcome to bring your own. Pub games are popular here. Q ♿ & ♿ (Central) ♣ ● 🖪 🎅 ☂

Ysceifiog

Fox ★

Ysceifiog Village Road, CH8 8NJ (signed from B5121)
☎ (01352) 720241 ● foxinnysceifiog.co.uk
Brains Bitter; Cwrw Llyn Porth Neigwl; 1 changing beer 🅷
Built around 1730, the Fox is a rare gem in a peaceful village location. It has been identified by CAMRA as having a nationally important historic pub interior, and features four small rooms, two of them for dining. Of particular interest is the bar with its unique sliding door and settles. The beer range usually includes a beer from Cwrw Llyn. Booking is recommended for the popular Sunday lunches. Outside is a children's playground.
Q ⑤ ⭐ ◐ ♣ P 🎅 ☂

Breweries

Beech Avenue

Lodge Farm, Borras Road, Holt, LL13 9TE ☎ 07917 841304 ● beechavenuebrewery.co.uk

Brewing commenced using a 30-litre kitchen plant. In 2020 the brewery upscaled and relocated to eco-friendly converted farm buildings. Speciality fruit or dry-hopped beers are available at various times in addition to a range of four cask-conditioned ales.

Gold (ABV 4%) GOLD
Pale (ABV 4.5%) PALE

Big Hand SIBA

Unit A1, Abbey Close, Redwither Business Park, Wrexham, LL13 9XG
☎ (01978) 660709 ● bighandbrewing.co.uk

☺Big Hand began brewing in 2013 and continues to operate from its ten-barrel plant on the outskirts of Wrexham despite the sad loss of brewery founder Dave Shaw in 2022. It offers a broad-ranging selection of beers, including several experimental ales, that are widely available throughout North Wales and West Cheshire ♦

Seren (ABV 3.7%) PALE
Pale, full-flavoured and hoppy with a fruity aroma and taste
Ostara (ABV 3.9%) BITTER
Solaris (ABV 3.9%) PALE
Sirrus (ABV 4%) PALE
Super Tidy (ABV 4%) PALE
A pale brown bitter beer with some citrus notes in the taste and peppery hops in the finish.
Bastion (ABV 4.2%) BITTER
A dry, malty best bitter, mahogany in colour with a full mouthfeel. Biscuity flavours and faint roast notes feature throughout
Little Black S (ABV 4.2%)
Appaloosa (ABV 4.5%) PALE
A full-bodied pale ale, some initial sweetness with strong New World hop flavours in the taste and spicy finish.
Spectre (ABV 4.5%) STOUT
A smooth, dry and satisfying stout with a good roast aroma. The taste is hoppy and bitter with hints of liquorice.
Havok (ABV 5%) PALE
A powerfully-hopped American IPA with strong and tangy citrus fruit bitterness throughout
Bad Gorilla (ABV 6%) MILD

Denbigh (Dinbych)

Crown Workshop, Crown Lane, Denbigh, LL16 3SY
☎ 07850 687701 ● bragdybinbych.co.uk

Brewing commenced in 2012 at the rear of the Hope & Anchor pub re-locating to the current premises in 2015. It now brews occasionally mainly to produce one-offs for special events and seasonal fairs etc. ♦LIVE

Facer's

A8-9, Ashmount Enterprise Park, Aber Road, Flint, CH6 5YL ☎ 07713 566370 ● facersbrewery.com

Set up in 2003 by now retired Dave Facer, it's now operated by long-time employee Toby Dunn. It is the oldest brewery in Flintshire. Sales average some 30

There is not a brewer who doesn't doctor his beer with something or other. Really something is in it. Four glasses made a Brooklyn man shoot down Dr Duggan in cold blood. Beer made a New York husband put a hole through his wife with a 22-calibre defender. Murder is in it. Who drinks lager beer is too apt to swallow the murder with it.
Elisha Chenery MD, 1889

barrels per week to around 100 outlets in North Wales and North West England. !! ♦

Mountain Mild (ABV 3.3%) MILD
A fruity dark mild, not too sweet, with underlying roast malt flavours and a full mouthfeel for its low ABV.

Clwyd Gold (ABV 3.5%) BITTER
Clean-tasting session bitter, mid-brown in colour with a full mouthfeel. The malty flavours are accompanied by increasing hoppiness in the bitter finish.

Flintshire Bitter (ABV 3.7%) BITTER
Well-balanced session bitter with a full mouthfeel. Some fruitiness in aroma and taste with increasing hoppy bitterness in the dry finish.

Abbey Blonde (ABV 4%) BITTER

Abbey Original (ABV 4%) BITTER
A sweetish golden beer with a good hop and fruit aroma, juicy taste and a dry, hoppy finish.

Abbey Red (ABV 4%) BITTER
A darker version of Abbey Original, copper-coloured with a sweet, malty taste and a bittersweet aftertaste.

North Star Porter (ABV 4%) PORTER
Dark, smooth, porter-style beer with good roast notes and hints of coffee and chocolate. Some initial sweetness and caramel flavours followed by a hoppy bitter aftertaste.

Game Changer (ABV 4.1%) BITTER

Sunny Bitter (ABV 4.2%) BITTER
An amber beer with a dry taste. The hop aroma continues into the taste where some faint fruit notes are also present. Lasting dry finish.

DHB (Dave's Hoppy Beer) (ABV 4.3%) BITTER
A dry-hopped version of This Splendid Ale with some sweet flavours also coming through in the mainly hoppy, bitter taste.

This Splendid Ale (ABV 4.3%) BITTER
Refreshing tangy best bitter, yellow in colour with a sharp hoppy, bitter taste. Good citrus fruit undertones with hints of grapefruit throughout.

Welsh Premium Lager (ABV 4.5%)

Landslide (ABV 4.9%) BITTER
Full-flavoured, complex premium bitter with tangy orange marmalade fruitiness in aroma and taste. Long-lasting hoppy flavours throughout.

Hafod

Old Gas Works, Gas Lane, Mold, CH7 1UR
☎ (01352) 750765 ☎ 07901 386638

Office: Gorwel, Hafod Road, Pantglas Gwernaffield, Mold, CH7 5ES ⊕ welshbeer.com

☺Hafod began brewing in 2011 on a small scale and upgraded to a new plant in the current premises in 2014, concentrating on beers in bottle and cask. The standard range is accompanied by regular seasonal and special brews throughout the year. The brewery shop operates on a click-and-collect basis and there are occasional open days. !! ☰ ♦

'Let's have filleted steak and a bottle of Bass for dinner tonight. It will be simply exquisite. I shall love it.'
'But my dear Nella,' he exclaimed, 'steak and beer at Felix's! It's impossible! Moreover, young women still under twenty-three cannot be permitted to drink Bass.'
Arnold Bennett,
The Grand Babylon Hotel, 1902

Sunrise (ABV 3.8%) GOLD
A pale and refreshing golden ale with citrus fruit bitterness evident throughout and a mouthwatering astringent finish.

Moel Famau Ale (ABV 4.1%) PORTER
A dark ale giving a dry, roasty taste with underlying sweet malt flavours.

Landmark (ABV 4.6%) BITTER
Copper-coloured and malty with a juicy mouthfeel. Fruit and faint roast flavours also feature in the taste.

Iâl

Pant Du Road, Eryrys, CH7 4DD ☎ 07956 440402
⊕ cwrwial.co.uk

Cwrw Iâl Community Brewery is run as a social enterprise with profits used for local community projects. The 10-barrel plant brews a core range as well as regular specials, in cask, keg and can. Additionally a second range is brewed under Crank branding.

Pocket Rocket (ABV 4%) PALE
Yellow in colour with citrus fruit prominent in the aroma and sharp, hoppy taste.

Kia Kaha! (ABV 4.3%) PALE
A dry, bitter beer, gold in colour with a fruity aroma leading to a good hoppy taste and finish.

Limestone Cowboy (ABV 4.5%) BITTER
A copper-coloured best bitter, malty with faint roast notes and fruit flavours. Hops dominate in the dry bitter finish.

Pothole Porter (ABV 5.1%) PORTER
A rich and fruity porter with a smooth mouthfeel and good roast notes in aroma and taste.

Llangollen

▤ Abbey Grange Hotel, Horseshoe Pass Road, Llantysilio, Llangollen, LL20 8DD
☎ (01978) 861916 ⊕ llangollenbrewery.com

Brewing began in 2010 on a 2.5-barrel plant. The brewery was updated and upgraded in 2014 to a 10-barrel plant. !! ☰LIVE

McGivern

▤ Bridge End Inn, 5 Bridge Street, Ruabon, LL14 6DA
☎ (01978) 810881 ☎ 07891 676614
⊕ mcgivernales.co.uk

☺The brewery was established in 2008 and was originally based at the brewer's home in Wrexham, but moved in 2011 to the award-winning Bridge End Inn, Ruabon using a 2.5-barrel plant. Production is continuing on an occasional basis. ♦

Magic Dragon

Plassey Brewery, Eyton, LL13 0SP
☎ (01978) 781675 ⊕ magicdragonbrewing.co.uk

Originally named Plassey, and later New Plassey, another new owner, brewer and personnel took over in 2017. Some beer replicates the old Plassey range but others are new recipes.

Burning Dragon (ABV 3.6%) PALE

Old Magic (ABV 3.6%) MILD
A dry dark mild with some roast and sweet flavours in the mainly fruity taste. Increasing hoppiness in the finish.

Border Bitter (ABV 3.8%) BITTER
A well-balanced session bitter with a fruity aroma, smooth malty taste, and a satisfying hoppy finish.

Eyton Gold (ABV 4%) GOLD

A full-flavoured golden ale with a dry, hoppy taste and a long-lasting bitter finish.

Green One (ABV 4.2%) GOLD
Golden brown and packed full of citrus hop flavours in the aroma, sharp taste, and peppery hops in the finish.

Obsidian (ABV 4.2%) STOUT

Hoppy Jester (ABV 4.5%) PALE

Polly's

Holland Farm, Blackbrook, Mold, CH7 6LU
☎ (01244) 940621 ⊕ pollysbrew.co

Pollys Brew Co was established in 2016, originally as Black Brook inside the stable of an old horse called Polly and have continuously expanded to what is currently a 23-hectolitre plant. It concentrates on KeyKeg and canned beer widely distributed throughout the UK and further afield. The beer range changes constantly.

Reaction

47 Erw Goch, Ruthin, LL15 1RS
✉ reactionbrewery@gmail.com

Brewing returned to Ruthin after many years when keen home brewer and CAMRA member Clwyd Roberts made his cask and KeyKeg beers available commercially in 2019. One-off beers are produced on a monthly basis with most of the output going to Mold Alehouse which acts as the brewery tap.

Sandstone

Unit 5a, Wrexham Enterprise Park, Preston Road, off Ash Road, North Wrexham Industrial Estate, Wrexham, LL13 9JT
☎ (01978) 664805 ☎ 07415 409625
⊕ sandstonebrewery.co.uk

☺Sandstone Brewery was established as a four-barrel plant in 2008. The brewery was taken over by the current owners in 2013. The beers are available at around 50 outlets in North-West England and North Wales. ‼🍴♦

Sandstone Edge (ABV 3.8%) BITTER
A satisfying session ale, this pale, dry, bitter beer has a full mouthfeel and a lingering hoppy finish that belies its modest strength.

Celtic Pride (ABV 4%) BITTER

Morillo (ABV 4.2%) BITTER

Twisted Dragon (ABV 5.8%) BITTER

Abyss (ABV 6.5%) STOUT

Wrexham Lager

42 St Georges Crescent, Wrexham, LL13 8DB
☎ (01978) 266222 ⊕ wrexhamlager.co.uk

Lager was first brewed in Wrexham in 1882 and returned to the town in 2011 with a 50-hectolitre brewery following the closure of the original brewery in 2000. The brewery produces a range of bottled and keg beers, some of which will be available in Tesco and Aldi supermarkets.

Come on in, the water's lovely

The importance of water to the brewing process is often overlooked. Most people know that barley malt and hops are the main ingredients used in beer making and that yeast turns malt sugars into alcohol. But 93% of even the strongest beer is made up of water – and the quality of the water is essential to the taste and character of the finished product.

Brewers call the water they use in the brewing process 'liquor' to distinguish it from cleaning water. Brewing liquor, whether it comes from natural wells or the public supply, will be filtered and cleaned to ensure its absolute purity. Care will be taken, however, to ensure that vital salts and irons are not removed during the filtering process, as they are essential to the production of cask beer.

The benchmark for brewing liquor is Burton upon Trent in the English Midlands. The natural spring waters of the Trent Valley have rich deposits of calcium and magnesium sulphates – also known as gypsum and Epsom salts. Salt is a flavour-enhancer and the sulphates in Burton liquor bring out the finest flavours from malts and hops. Since the 19th century, ale brewers throughout Britain and other countries have added salts to 'Burtonise' their liquor.

It's fascinating to compare the levels of salts in the water of three famous brewing locations: Burton, London and Pilsen. Pilsen is the home of the first golden lager beer, Pilsner. Brewers of genuine lager beers want comparatively soft brewing liquor to balance the toasted malt and gentle, spicy hop nature of their beers. Pilsen water has total salts of 30 parts per million, with minute amounts of calcium and magnesium.

London, once celebrated as a dark beer region, famous for mild, porter and stout, has 463 total salts per million, with high levels of sodium and carbonate. (Dublin, another dark beer city, has similar water to London's). Burton liquor has an astonishing level of total salts of 1,226 per million. If this figure is further broken down, Burton liquor is rich in magnesium, calcium, other sulphates and carbonate.

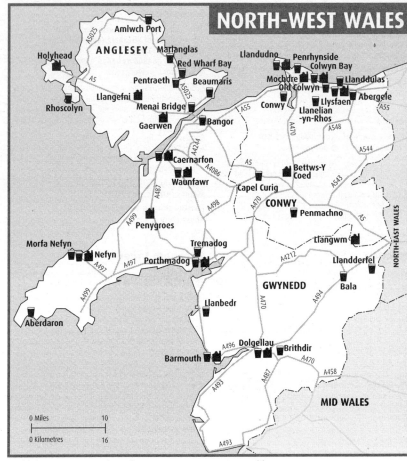

NORTH-WEST WALES

Authority areas covered: Anglesey UA, Conwy UA, Gwynedd UA

Aberdaron

Ty Newydd
LL53 8BE
☎ (01758) 760207 ● gwesty-tynewydd.co.uk
4 changing beers (sourced locally; often Purple Moose) Ⓗ
The hotel is at the centre of a picturesque and historic village at the end of the Llyn Peninsula. Beers are generally from local breweries and can accompany food chosen from the lunch and evening menus. Afternoon teas are available. An outside terrace gives stunning beach and sea views, and 11 en-suite bedrooms are available. The Wales coastal footpath passes through the village. Bus services run from Pwllheli. Q❄️🏠◑🅰️🛂🚃📶

Abergele

Hoptimist 🅛
32 Market Street, LL22 7AA
☎ 07538 336718
3 changing beers (sourced regionally) Ⓗ
An innovative conversion of a former building society, Abergele's first micropub opened in 2018. Originally a joint venture between Cwrw Ial and Dovecote breweries, it was taken over by a local family in 2021. Information regarding the beers and ciders is clearly displayed on a large blackboard on the back wall. A bank of taps offers a selection of cask ales, keg beers and ciders, with third-pints available on request. The large rear courtyard offers views into the small cellar.
Q❄️🅿️🎵⇌(Abergele & Pensarn) 🚃🐾♪

Amlwch Port

Adelphi Vaults 🏆
Quay Street, LL68 9HD
☎ (01407) 831754 ● adelphivaults.com
Wye Valley Butty Bach; 3 changing beers (sourced locally; often Purple Moose) Ⓗ
Built in the 1800s, this nautically themed two-room pub is near the old port and several museums dedicated to the old copper industry. The pub has four changing beers which are mainly Welsh. The small beer garden at the rear is a suntrap in summer. Situated on the Anglesey coastal path, it is popular both with locals and tourists.
Q❄️🅿️🎵◑♣️🐾📶♪

Bala

STORI 🅛
101 High Street, LL23 7AE (on A494 in town centre opposite Old Bulls Head and Co-op)
☎ (01678) 520501 ● storibeers.wales
2 changing beers (sourced locally) Ⓖ

A bottle shop with a taproom located in this popular town close to the lake and other attractions. The shop sells a wide range of beers and beer-related merchandise, with the emphasis on local products, and to the rear is the taproom. Cask and craft keg beers are available to either take away or enjoy in the cosy tasting room. The opening hours constantly vary so check before travelling. Q✦🍴🚃(T3)🌸

Bangor

Black Bull Inn (Tarw Du) ✓

107 High Street, LL57 1NS

☎ (01248) 387900

Greene King Abbot; Ruddles Best Bitter; 5 changing beers ℍ

A JD Wetherspoon pub in a converted church and presbytery at the top of the High Street. It has a long bar and spacious seating areas on two levels. A large outside patio overlooks upper Bangor and the university while a lower level beer garden provides excellent outside drinking spots. It is popular with students and busy during term time. ౽❀🕙&≠●🚃(5)🎫

Globe

Albert Street, LL57 2EY

☎ (01248) 362095

4 changing beers (sourced nationally; often Ossett, St Austell) ℍ

Traditional back-street pub in Upper Bangor, popular with locals and students. It is decorated with Welsh sporting photos and membrobilia, and is often busy when sporting events are shown on the multiple large TV screens. Four handpumps serve a rotating range of both national and local beers. Breakfast, lunch and evening pub meals are served. A mix of ticketed gigs are hosted on a regular basis, during which access can be restricted. 🕙≠♣🎫🎵

Patricks

59 Holyhead Road, LL57 2HE

☎ (01248) 353062 ⊕ patricksbar.com

3 changing beers (sourced regionally; often Big Bog, Facer's) ℍ

Lively Irish-themed bar in upper Bangor, popular both with locals and students. The bar has numerous TVs showing sporting events. On the bar are three handpumps with a regularly changing range of beers, including from north Wales breweries. The pub is on the bus route to Menai Straits, and close to the railway station. Opening hours are extended for sports and late-night drinking. ≠🚃🎫🎵

Barmouth

Myrddins Bar

Staffordshire House, Church Street, LL42 1EH

☎ (01341) 388060 ⊕ myrddinsbrewery.com

6 changing beers (often Myrddins) ℙ

Established in 2014, the taphouse for Myrddins brewery is on the main road through the town, close to the beach and coastal path. Six real ales on the bar usually include two of their own, plus four locally brewed beers and five real ciders on tap. There is also a good range of Welsh bottled beers, along with many gins distilled on-site. The single room is cosy, with ample seating. ౽🕙≠●🚃❀

Royal Hotel

King Edward Street, LL42 1AB

☎ (01341) 406214

4 changing beers ℍ

A pub located underneath the main hotel, accessed from the main road. It is on two levels, with the main bar next to the pub entrance; the lower level is mainly for playing pool. An eclectic mix of items are displayed around the walls and on the ceiling. Three handpulls in each bar serve three ales, usually sourced from local breweries. There is a small beer garden at the rear. ౽🏠🕙▶🚶≠♣🚃❀🎫🎵

Beaumaris

Castle Court Hotel ✓

Castle Square, LL58 8DA

☎ (01248) 810078 ⊕ castlecourtbeaumaris.co.uk

2 changing beers (sourced regionally) ℍ

Situated in the centre of this historic town, overlooking the castle, the former White Lion has been renovated by the current owners. It has a small beer garden at the rear, but in spring and summer the Castle Square provides an outdoor seating area. Two changing guest beers from small independent breweries are served. Lunchtime meals are only available during the school holidays. ౽❀🏠▲🚃❀🎵

Brithdir

Cross Foxes

LL40 2SG (jct of A470 and A487)

☎ (01341) 421001 ⊕ crossfoxes.co.uk

3 changing beers (sourced locally) ℍ /ᴳ

A refurbished Grade II-listed building near the foot of Cader Idris mountain, four miles from the historic town of Dolgellau. Its beers are usually from local breweries. Breakfast is served and meals are available all day. The pub is popular with walkers, tourists and residents, and dogs are welcome in the bar area. Q౽❀🏠🕙▶▲🚃(T2)❀🎫

Caernarfon

Anglesey Arms Hotel

Slate Quay, LL55 2PB

☎ (01286) 672158

3 changing beers (sourced locally)

An historic pub in a superb location with amazing views across the Menai Straits to Anglesey. Built up against the town walls and next to Caernarfon Castle, the pub attracts a mix of locals and tourists. Two rooms with a bar running between them which usually serves at least three ales. There is much outdoor seating beside the seawall, where you can take in the birdlife and breathtaking sunsets. The Welsh Highland Railway station is a short walk away. ౽🏠🕙▶≠P🚃(5)❀🎵

Black Boy Inn ✅
Northgate Street, LL55 1RW
☎ (01286) 673604 ⊕ black-boy-inn.com
5 changing beers (sourced regionally) Ⓗ
Characterful pub set within the town walls between the marina and castle. The historic town, a World Heritage Site, is well worth a visit, ending with a welcome pint at the Black Boy. The public bar and small lounge are warmed by roaring fires. A good range of food is served alongside a selection of guest beers. The restaurant has a Visit Wales Bronze award. There is a drinking area outside on the traffic-free street. A former local CAMRA Pub of the Year. Accommodation is in 47 en-suite rooms.
🛏😋🚑🌐🅓&🚶≉♿P🗐(5) 🌧 ⎯

Tafarn Y Porth ✅
7-9 Eastgate Street, LL55 1AG (just off Bangor Rd near post office)
☎ (01286) 662920
Greene King Abbot; 5 changing beers (sourced nationally) Ⓗ
Wetherspoon pub in a converted supermarket adjacent to the the historic town walls and close to the castle. It has a large open-plan interior and a spacious, partly covered courtyard outside with plenty of seating. The real ale range often includes local Welsh brews. The pub is conveniently located for the Welsh Highland Railway, which takes you to the heart of Snowdonia and down to the coast. Q🛏😋🌐🅓&🅰≉♣♿🗐(5)🌧

Capel Curig

Plas y Brenin Ⓛ
LL24 0ET
☎ (01690) 720214 ⊕ pyb.co.uk
3 changing beers (sourced locally) Ⓗ
Outdoor centre in an attractive rural area, formerly the Capel Curig Inn, which dated from 1798. Three handpumps dispense local beers. The raised bar overlooks two lakes, Llynnau Mymbyr, with spectacular views of Yr Wyddfa/Snowdon from an outdoor drinking area. The furnishing is basic but modern, with wooden floors, tables and chairs. Hearty and reasonably-priced food is served in the large dining area.
Q🛏😋🚑🅓&🅰♣P♿ 🌧

Colwyn Bay

Bay Hop
17 Penrhyn Road, LL29 8LG
⊕ thebayhop.co.uk
4 changing beers (sourced regionally) Ⓗ
Multi award-winning micropub and bottle shop with a welcoming, friendly atmosphere. Furnishings include wooden settles and chairs around larger tables, and tall barrel tables for those who prefer to stand. An extensive range of bottles and cans are on offer for drinking in or taking out. Pizzas from Jonny Doughs are available to be delivered on Monday evening. A former CAMRA North Wales Pub of the Year, and local Pub of the Year on several occasions. 🛏😋≉♣🗐(12,13)♿ 🌧

Black Cloak Taproom Ⓛ
71 Abergele Road, LL29 7RU
☎ (01492) 330274
4 changing beers (sourced regionally) Ⓗ
Brewpub that was opened in 2018 by two former employees of the Heavy Industry brewery, who are now brewing their own beer on site using a two-barrel plant. Ales are available on cask, keg and direct from a brite tank, and served in thirds, halves, two-thirds and pint measures. Guest beers are from quality breweries

throughout the UK, and bottled beers are also available. The taproom has comfortable seating and a convivial atmosphere. 🛏😋≉🗐(12,13)♿ 🌧

Pen-y-Bryn Ⓛ
Pen-y-Bryn Road, LL29 6DD
☎ (01492) 533360
Timothy Taylor Boltmaker; house beer (by Brunning & Price); 3 changing beers (sourced regionally) Ⓗ
Large, open-plan pub with bookcases, old furniture, walls decorated with old photographs and memorabilia from the local area, and real fires during the winter. Panoramic views over the Bay of Colwyn and the Great Orme can be admired from the terrace and garden. Food is served throughout the day and the menu changes daily. A boardroom-style function room for celebrations and meetings has been created in the cellar, opening out onto the garden. Q🛏😋🅓&P🗐(23)♿ 🌧

Conwy

Albion Ale House 🍺 ★ Ⓛ
Upper Gate Street, LL32 8RF
☎ (01492) 582484
8 changing beers (sourced locally) Ⓗ
Multi-room pub that has been superbly refurbished by the current owners – each room retains original 1920s features and several have interesting fireplaces. There is no music or TV, just pleasant conversation. The pub is managed by three local brewers – Conwy, Purple Moose and Snowdon Craft – showcasing their beers as well as guest ales. Paddles for three or six third-pints are offered. CAMRA awards include local and Welsh Pub of the Year. Q🛏😋≉♣🗐(5,19)♿ 🌧

Bank of Conwy
1 Lancaster Square, LL32 8HT
☎ (01492) 573741 ⊕ thebankofconwy.wales
3 changing beers (sourced regionally) Ⓗ
Craft beer bar opened in a Grade II-listed former bank. It uses many of the fittings from the original building, including the manager's office. The counter is now the bar and the vault still has the original fortified door. An extensive selection of beers is on offer in cask, keg and bottled forms. This is also a large selection of wines and gins. Food is available daily until early evening, with breakfasts at weekends. Sausages are available for dogs. Wednesday night is music night. 🛏🅓≉🗐♿ 🌧

Mulberry
Conwy Marina, Morfa Drive, LL32 8GU
☎ (01492) 583350
Robinsons Dizzy Blonde, Unicorn; house beer (by Robinsons); 1 changing beer Ⓗ
A nautically themed Robinsons pub on the marina, with a front patio overlooking the marina and the Conwy estuary across to Deganwy. The spacious ground-floor area features a rowing boat in the ceiling, with an open stairwell leading to a first-floor bar and restaurant. The patio also hosts a barbecue, plus a pirate ship that is a children's play area. 🛏😋🅓&P🗐(27)♿ 🌧

Dolgellau

Torrent Walk Hotel Ⓛ
Smithfield Street, LL40 1AA
☎ (01341) 422858 ⊕ torrent-walk-hotel.business.site
4 changing beers (sourced nationally)
An 18th-century hotel in the narrow streets of the historic town centre. It retains most of its multi-roomed interior and old fireplaces, though the bar fittings date from circa 1970. Note the Coffee Room etched panel in

the door from the lobby to the room on the right. A regularly changing range of four ales is served, mostly from Welsh breweries. An ideal base for walking in the Cadar Idris area. A former local CAMRA Pub of the Year. ⮂◗♣♨⊟♠

Llanbedr

Ty Mawr Hotel
LL45 2HH
☎ (01341) 241440 ⊕ tymawrhotel.com
4 changing beers �H
Small country hotel set in its own grounds. The modern lounge bar has a slate-flagged floor and cosy wood-burning stove. Unusual flying memorabilia reflect connections with the local airfield. French windows open out on a veranda and landscaped terrace with seating. A beer festival is held in a marquee on the lawn each summer. The hotel is popular with locals and walkers, and welcomes dogs and children. Bar meals are served lunchtime and evenings. Q⮂◗A⮂♣⊟♠

Llandderfel

Bryntirion Inn ⓛ
B4401, LL23 7RA (on B4401, 4 miles E of Bala)
☎ (01678) 530205 ⊕ bryntirioninn.co.uk
Purple Moose Cwrw Eryri/Snowdonia Ale; 1 changing beer (sourced locally) �H
Dating back to 1695, this former hunting lodge and coaching inn overlooks the Dee Valley. A cosy and comfortable bar area with a log fire is open all day. There are a number of other rooms to accommodate diners and families, including a large function room for special events. There is also a small covered and heated courtyard at the rear. The guest beer varies from local or national brewers. Two en-suite guest rooms are available upstairs. Q⮂⊛⮂◗♣P⊟(T3)♠♥

Llanddulas

Valentine
9 Mill Street, LL22 8ES
JW Lees Bitter; 2 changing beers (sourced nationally) �H
At the centre of this semi-rural seaside village stands this traditional village inn, dating from the 18th-century and built on the site of an old clay cottage. On entering, a well-furnished, comfortable lounge is on the left, and straight ahead is a separate public bar with TV – both with open fires in winter. Brewery memorabilia and many old framed photographs relating to the Valentine decorate the walls. An attractive walled garden and outdoor drinking area is at the rear of the pub. ⮂⊛◗A⊟(12,13)♠♥

Llandudno

Albert ⓛ
56 Madoc Street, LL30 2TW
☎ (01492) 877188
Conwy Clogwyn Gold; Timothy Taylor Landlord; 2 changing beers (sourced regionally) �H
Popular pub-restaurant just off the town centre and close to the railway station, featuring modern decor with interesting photographs and pictures on display. It serves several handpulled beers from local and independent breweries, plus a range of meals throughout the day. The beers on offer are clearly displayed on blackboards above and beside the L-shaped bar. Third-pint glasses are available. There is a heated and covered veranda seating area to the front. ⮂⊛◗♿⊟(5,12)♠♥

Cottage Loaf ⓛ
Market Street, LL30 2SR
☎ (01492) 870762 ⊕ the-cottageloaf.co.uk
Conwy Welsh Pride; Timothy Taylor Landlord; 2 changing beers (sourced regionally; often Purple Moose) �H
The building was previously a bakery, hence the name. Its interior features stone-flagged floors, an impressive fireplace and a raised timber-floored area. Much of the wood used came from the Flying Foam, a schooner shipwrecked at Llandudno's West Shore. The Loaf is a popular meeting place for people of all ages with excellent home-cooked food served all day every day. There is a conservatory-style restaurant area with enclosed outdoor terrace. ⮂⊛◗⮂⊟(5,12)♥

Snowdon
11 Tudno Street, LL30 2HB
☎ (01492) 872166 ⊕ thesnowdon.co.uk
Draught Bass; house beer (by Coach House); 4 changing beers (sourced regionally) �H
The Snowdon is one of the oldest pubs in Llandudno, featuring a large main drinking area with an attractive Snowdon mirror above the fireplace. The range of ales includes house beer Coach House Blue Sky. The raised pavement garden drinking area gives a fine view of the Great Orme, and the goats if you are lucky. It has won the Llandudno in Bloom award for its floral display several times in recent years. ⮂⊛◗⊟(5,12)♥♥

Tapps ⓛ
35 Madoc Street, LL30 2TL
☎ (01492) 870956
Conwy Welsh Pride; 4 changing beers (sourced regionally) �H
Llandudno's first micropub opened in 2017 in a former cake shop, featuring an open-plan bar at the front and a small snug to the rear. Welsh beer is to the fore and there is a large bottled beer selection to drink in or take away. Third-pint glasses are available. One of the tables is a chess board which transforms into a backgammon or card table – other board games are provided and there are books which can be borrowed. ⮂⊛⮂♣⊟(5,12)♥♥

Llanelian-yn-Rhos

White Lion Inn ⓛ ✅
LL29 8YA
☎ (01492) 515807 ⊕ whitelioninn.co.uk
Theakston Best Bitter; 2 changing beers (sourced regionally) �H
A regular in the Guide for over 30 years, this 16th-century inn, in the hills above Old Colwyn, next to St Elian's Church, greets you with a warm welcome. Gracing the entrance are two stone white lions, leading into the bar area with slate-flagged flooring and large comfortable chairs around log fires. Decorative stained glass is mounted above the bar in the tiny snug. The restaurant serves home-cooked food. There is jazz on Tuesday nights and quiz night is Thursday. Q⮂⊛◗♣P♥♥

Llysfaen

MASH ⓛ
Unit 2 Ty Mawr Enterprise Park, off Tan Y Graig Road, LL29 8UE
☎ (01492) 514305 ⊕ conwybrewery.co.uk
Conwy Rampart; 3 changing beers (sourced locally) �H
Micropub and Conwy brewery tap that has become a community hub since opening in 2018. It serves a range

of ales, lager, wines and spirits, with coffee, tea and soft drinks also available. Recent refurbishment has provided further indoor drinking space, complete with a largescreen TV, which is available for functions. Following the public footpath fingerpost at the front corner of the brewery leads to views over the bay of Colwyn towards the Great Orme. Third-pint glasses are available. ♿✿P🎁☀️🐾🛜♪

Marianglas

Parciau Arms
LL73 8NY
☎ (01248) 853766
3 changing beers (often Conwy) Ⓗ
Set on a sizeable plot on the edge of the village adjacent to a camping site, this free house has up to four ales, often from Conwy brewery. Its stained-glass windows and wood-panelled interior, along with nautical themed pictures and memorabilia, give it character. In summer the lawned beer garden is popular, while an open fire provides warmth in winter when the opening hours are reduced. ♿✿🅰️P🐾

Menai Bridge

Liverpool Arms ✅
St George's Pier, **LL59 5EY**
☎ (01248) 712453 ⊕ thelivvy.pub
Facer's Flintshire Bitter Ⓗ/Ⓖ; **3 changing beers** Ⓗ
A nautically themed pub frequented by locals, students in term time, and the local sailing fraternity. The Livvy has up to four cask ales on offer, along with good-quality pub food. A short walk takes you beneath the famous Grade I-listed Menai suspension bridge, and the pub is close to the quay for local seasonal tourist boats. The Welsh coastal path is also close by. ♿◑♿🚃🛜

Morfa Nefyn

Ty Coch Inn
Porthdinllaen, **LL53 6DB** (access on foot only)
☎ (01758) 720498 ⊕ tycoch.co.uk
2 changing beers (sourced regionally) Ⓗ
Opened as a pub in 1842 to serve local fishermen, Ty Coch enjoys an iconic position on the beach at beautiful Porth Dinllaen. It has been rated as one of the top beach bars in the world, and the views from the beach tables certainly justifying that claim. It can only be reached on foot, either along the beach (except at high tide) or by walking across the golf course. Always check low-season opening times. ♿◑🐾

Nefyn

Bragdy Llyn
Ffordd Dewi Sant, **LL53 6EG**
☎ (01758) 721981 ⊕ cwrwllyn.cymru
Cwrw Llyn Brenin Enlli, Cwrw Glyndwr, Seithenyn; 1 changing beer (sourced locally) Ⓗ
A friendly bar located within the modern Cwrw Llyn brewery on the edge of the village, near the coast and picturesque village of Porthdinllaen. A range of the brewery's ales are always available. The brewery can be seen through the large windows. Tours are available on request and include tasters of the core range of ales. ♿P

Old Colwyn

Crafty Fox Ⓛ
355 Abergele Road, **LL29 9PL**
☎ 07733 531766

Coach House Farriers Best Bitter, Post Horn Premium Pale Ale; 2 changing beers (sourced regionally) Ⓗ
Old Colwyn's first micropub opened in 2018 in two former retail units. The main entrance leads into the bar, in a former tattoo parlour, fearturing tables upcycled from cast iron Singer sewing machine bases and oak drop-leaf table tops. The lounge, furnished with a mixture of leather sofas and stools, is in a former butcher's shop. Photographs on the bar wall contrast the present street scene with that of a century ago. Q♿♣♿🚃(12,13)🐾🛜

Red Lion
385 Abergele Road, **LL29 9PL**
☎ 07720 206584
4 changing beers (sourced nationally) Ⓗ
Popular, centrally located free house serving up to four guest ales from breweries around the UK. It has an L-shaped lounge featuring a real coal fire, with antique brewery mirrors, local photographs and other memorabilia. There is also a separate public bar with a pool table, dartboard and several television screens. To the rear is a Victorian-style covered, enclosed and heated smoking conservatory. Note the classic-style pub sign outside. Q✿♣🚃(12,13)🐾🛜♪

Penmachno

Eagles Ⓛ
LL24 0UG
☎ (01690) 760177 ⊕ eaglespenmachno.co.uk
Greene King IPA; 2 changing beers (sourced locally) Ⓗ
Traditional pub set in a peaceful village in a secluded valley at the heart of Snowdonia, four miles from Betws-y-coed. A wood-burning stove in the bar ensures a warm welcome during the winter months. There is always at least one local ale on offer. The pub prides itself on being at the centre of community activities; local musicians perform on the first Wednesday of each month. The secluded rear garden provides delightful views up the valley. Q♿✿🅰️◑♣🚃(19)🐾🛜

Penrhynside

Penrhyn Arms
Pendre Road, **LL30 3BY** (off B5115)
☎ (01492) 549060 ⊕ penrhynarms.com
Banks's Amber Ale; 4 changing beers (sourced regionally) Ⓗ
Welcoming free house that serves guest ales, concentrating on new breweries and new beers, plus local ciders and perries. Its spacious single room pub has an L-shaped central bar, two real fires, and seating around large tables. Food highlights include Wednesday curry night, Thursday pie night, Sunday lunch, and wood-fired pizzas every night. The rear conservatory leads up to a raised landscaped garden terrace with extensive views of the coastline. There is live jazz on Mondays and occasional music on Saturdays. ♿✿◑♿🚃(14,15)🐾♪

Pentraeth

Panton Arms
The Square, **LL75 8AZ**
☎ (01248) 450959
Purple Moose Cwrw Glaslyn/Glaslyn Ale; 2 changing beers Ⓗ
A spacious 18th-century coaching inn with a long lounge bar and separate tap room. Popular with locals and tourists alike, the pub is in a great location for walks in the nearby forest. It has a large beer garden and a

frequent bus service making it convenient for linear coastal walks. Purple Moose Glaslyn is available all year round. Q➳✿❍❶◖⚑⌂◗🐾🌳🛜

Porthmadog

Australia

31-35 High Street, LL49 9LR
☎ (01766) 515957
Purple Moose Cwrw Eryri/Snowdonia Ale, Cwrw Ysgawen/Elderflower Ale, Ochr Dywyll y Mws/Dark Side of the Moose; 3 changing beers (sourced locally; often Purple Moose) Ⓗ

A pub since 1864, the Australia was taken over by Purple Moose Brewing in 2017 and serves as its taphouse. Most of the core real ale range is available, as well as seasonal and special occasion beers. Two rooms are served by a long wooden bar with six handpumps. There is a small outdoor seating area at the back. The pub is in the centre of town, next to the bus stops and close to the Ffestiniog and Welsh Highland Railway Station. ➳❶♿🚲❤🚌🐾🛜

Spooner's Bar

Harbour Station, LL49 9NF
☎ (01766) 516032 🌐 spoonerspub.co.uk
Purple Moose Cwrw Eryri/Snowdonia Ale; 2 changing beers (sourced nationally; often Bragdy Lleu, Conwy, Cwrw Llyn) Ⓗ

A bar situated in the terminus of the world-famous Ffestiniog Railway and Welsh Highland Railway, with steam trains outside the door most of the year round. At least three ales are served from a changing range of local and national breweries. The bar is next to the café-restaurant and has outdoor seating overlooking the platforms and the scenic coast. Food is served every lunchtime and evening meals Tuesday to Saturday, but check hours out of season. A former local CAMRA Pub of the Year. Q➳❶◖🅰➂(Harbour)🚌🛜

Red Wharf Bay

Ship Inn ✅

LL75 8RJ (off A5025 between Pentraeth and Benllech)
☎ (01248) 852568 🌐 shipinnredwharfbay.co.uk
House beer (by Facer's); 2 changing beers Ⓗ

Red Wharf Bay was once a busy port exporting coal and fertilisers in the 18th and 19th centuries. Previously known as the Quay, the Ship enjoys an excellent reputation for its bar and restaurant, with meals served lunchtimes and evenings. It gets busy with locals and visitors in the summer. The garden has panoramic views across the bay to south-east Anglesey. The resort town of Benllech is two miles away and the coastal path passes the front door. Q➳✿❶◖♿🐾

Rhoscolyn

White Eagle ✅

LL65 2NJ (off B4545 signed Traeth Beach)
☎ (01407) 860267 🌐 white-eagle.co.uk
6 changing beers (often Conwy, Weetwood) Ⓗ

After being saved from closure by new owners some years ago, the pub was renovated and rebuilt with an airy, brasserie-style ambience. It has a fine patio enjoying superb views over Caernarfon Bay and the Llyn Peninsula to Bardsey Island. The nearby beach offers safe swimming with a warden on duty in the summer months. The pub is also close to the coastal footpath. Excellent food is available lunchtimes and evenings; all day during the school holidays. Q➳✿❶◖♿🅰♣P

Tremadog

Union Inn ✅

7 Market Square, LL49 9RB
☎ (01766) 512748 🌐 union-inn.com
1 changing beer Ⓗ

Friendly local in the village square, with two separate cosy bars and a restaurant at the rear. The pub has a policy of using locally sourced produce, and the ale range features mainly local beers. Children are welcome and there are board games available. Excellent food is served in the bar and restaurant. Tremadog was the birthplace of TE Lawrence (Lawrence of Arabia). Frequent bus services pass by. Q➳✿❶◖♿🅰⚑⌂🚌(1A,T2)

Waunfawr

Snowdonia Park

Beddgelert Road, LL55 4AQ
☎ (01286) 650409 🌐 snowdonia-park.co.uk
House beer (by Snowdonia Parc); 5 changing beers (often Snowdonia Parc) Ⓗ

Home of the Snowdonia brewery, this is a popular pub for walkers, climbers and families, with a children's play area. Meals are served all day. The pub adjoins Waunfawr railway station on the Welsh Highland Railway – stop off here before continuing on one of the most scenic sections of narrow gauge railway in the world. There is a large campsite adjacent on the riverside. A former local CAMRA Pub of the Year on several occasions. Q➳✿❍❶◖♿🅰➂♣⚑⌂🚌🐾🛜

Breweries

Anglesey Brewhouse

Unit 12, Pen Yr Orsedd, Industrial Estate Road, Parc Bryn Cefni, Llangefni, LL77 7AW
☎ (01248) 345506 ☎ 07748 650368
🌐 angleseybrewhouse.co.uk

Microbrewery established in 2017 in the centre of Anglesey by a former homebrewer. The brewery relocated to larger premises in 2019 with a 10-barrel plant. Currently producing five canned beers sold direct from the brewery or in shops around North Wales. 🍺

Black Cloak SIBA

🍴 **71 Abergele Road, Colwyn Bay, LL29 7RU** ☎ 07701 031121

Office: Glog Ddu Llangernyw, Abergele, LL22 8PS

A brew-pub opened in 2018 in a former café using a 2.5-barrel plant producing cask and keg beer. The core range and regular specials are usually only available at the Black Cloak. 🍺🔗

Cader

Unit 4, Parc Menter Marian Mawr Enterprise Park, Dolgellau, LL40 1UU
☎ (01341) 388080 ☎ 07546 272372
🌐 caderales.com

Founded in 2012, Cader Ales uses a five-barrel, purpose-built plant to its optimum. The brewery is situated close to the centre of the picturesque market town of Dolgellau. Deliveries are made to the licensed trade in North and Mid-West Wales and beers in cask or bottle are available to the general public direct from the brewery. ‼

Cregennan (ABV 3.8%) GOLD

Gold (ABV 3.8%) GOLD
Machlyd Mawddach (ABV 3.9%) BITTER
Arran Fawddy (ABV 4%) GOLD
Talyllyn Pale Ale (ABV 4.4%) PALE

Conwy

Unit 2, Ty Mawr Enterprise Park, Tan y Graig Road, Llysfaen, LL29 8UE
☎ (01492) 514305 ⊕ conwybrewery.co.uk

☺Conwy started in 2003 and was the first brewery in Conwy for at least 100 years. In 2013, it increased capacity and moved to bigger premises in Llysfaen with its own tap, known as Mash. Around 100 outlets are supplied. Monthly seasonals are available as well as the West Coast range of American-style beers. The brewery has been owned by the Cadman Capital Group since 2021, which also operates 360 Degrees brewery, and is part owner of the Albion Ale House and the Bridge, Conwy. ‼☞♦LIVE♦

Clogwyn Gold (ABV 3.6%) PALE
A full-flavoured golden ale featuring strong citrus fruit flavours throughout. Hoppy bitterness dominates the full mouthfeel and lasting finish.
Welsh Pride (ABV 4%) BITTER
Beachcomber Blonde (ABV 4.2%) BLOND
A pale beer with a citrus taste, initially sweetish with delicate hoppiness in the lingering bitter finish.
Rampart (ABV 4.5%) BROWN
A dark, fruity beer with a sweetish initial taste. Fruit flavours accompanied by the underlying hoppiness continue into the bittersweet aftertaste
San Francisco (ABV 5.5%) IPA
A robust New World IPA with a powerful smack of hops and tropical fruit flavours in the aroma and taste.

Cybi SIBA

Unit 4a, Penrhos Business Park, Holyhead, LL65 2FD
☎ (01407) 769651

Office: O'r Garw, Porthdafarch Road, Holyhead, LL65 2RU ⊕ bragdycybi.cymru

Family-run microbrewery on Holy Island established in 2020 using a 200-litre brewing system producing bottle-conditioned beers for local distribution on Anglesey. In 2021 the plant was relocated and upgraded to produce 1,600 litres in bottle and keg forms. Local ingredients are used in the production of some of the beers; including wild hops, welsh coast kelp and honey. The taproom has occasional tasting evenings. All beers are unfiltered and unpasteurized ☞LIVE♦

Geipel SIBA

Pant Glas, Llangwm, Corwen, LL21 0RN
☎ (01490) 420838 ⊕ geipel.co.uk

Geipel commenced brewing in 2013 producing unpasteurised and unfiltered beers. The brewery specialises in lagers, drawing inspiration from the classic styles of Germany and beyond. Available in keg, KeyKeg and bottle. LIVE.

Lleu SIBA

Penygroes Industrial Estate, Caernarfon, LL54 6DB
☎ 07840 910460 ⊕ bragdylleu.cymru

☺Brewing began in 2014 using a 1.25-barrel plant and was upgraded to six barrels in 2016 to meet demand, and in 2022 moved to larger premises. The four beers are named after Welsh folklore characters of the Mabinogi. ‼☞

Blodeuwedd (ABV 3.6%) GOLD
Lleu (ABV 4%) BITTER
Gwydion (ABV 4.7%) BITTER
Bendigeidfran (ABV 5%) PALE

Llŷn

1 Parc Eithyn, Ffordd Dewi Sant, Nefyn, LL53 6EG
☎ (01758) 721981 ☎ 07792 050134
⊕ cwrwllyn.cymru

☺Brewing began in 2011 in an old converted barn. In 2016 the brewing moved into a new, purpose-built, 15-barrel brewery that includes a taproom and shop. The brewery is based in the seaside town of Nefyn on the Llyn Peninsula and its cask and keg beers and distributed throughout the North West of Wales, with bottled beer distributed throughout Wales. ‼☞♦

Y Brawd Houdini (ABV 3.5%) PALE
Brenin Enlli (ABV 4%) BITTER
A fruity bitter, the initial malty taste leads to a hoppy, bitter aftertaste.
Cwrw Glyndwr (ABV 4%) GOLD
A full-bodied and well-balanced amber beer, quite fruity with a good hoppy finish.
Seithenyn (ABV 4.2%) GOLD
A fruity golden ale with a tangy citrus taste and a dry hoppy finish.
Porth Neigwl (ABV 4.5%) PALE

Mona

Unit 6, Gaerwen Industrial Estate, Gaerwen, Anglesey, LL60 6HR ☎ 07988 698260
✉ info@bragdymona.co.uk

Seven enthusiastic locals got together and set up Mona Brewery, which was launched in 2019. Beers offered from this Porter Installations kit include one cask beer and a range of keg beers.

Pabo (ABV 3.8%) BITTER
A full-bodied and smooth tasting session bitter. Underlying sweet malt flavours complement the big hoppy taste and bitter finish.

Myrddins

Church Street, Barmouth, LL42 1EH
☎ (01341) 388060 ☎ 07732 967853
⊕ myrddinsbrewery.com

Established in 2016 within a café bar in the centre of Barmouth, it relocated to nearby premises in 2018. Now known as Myrddins Tap & Brewery Shop, the brewery is located in Barmouth but not on the same site as the shop. The brewery produces 1,968 litres maximum per week from 12 brew runs available in 4 or 9 gallon casks. ☞♦

Nant SIBA

Y Felin Pentrefoelas, Bettws-Y Coed, LL24 0HU

Cwrw Nant began brewing in 2021 at a 16th century mill that was last operational in 1984. The brew plant was acquired from the former Bragdy'r Nant.

Purple Moose SIBA

Madoc Street, Porthmadog, LL49 9DB
☎ (01766) 515571 ⊕ purplemoose.co.uk

A 40-barrel plant housed in a former iron works in the coastal town of Porthmadog. It has the 'Australia' pub, plus two shops on Porthmadog High Street, the other at

Betws-y-Coed Station. The names of the beers reflect local history and geography. !! ⏛ ♦

Cwrw Eryri/ Snowdonia Ale (ABV 3.6%) GOLD
Golden, refreshing bitter with citrus fruit hoppiness in aroma and taste. The full mouthfeel leads to a long-lasting, dry, bitter finish.

Cwrw Madog/ Madog's Ale (ABV 3.7%) BITTER
Full-bodied session bitter. Malty nose and an initial nutty flavour but bitterness dominates. Well-balanced and refreshing with a dry roastiness on the taste and a good dry finish.

Cwrw Ysgawen/ Elderflower Ale (ABV 4%) SPECIALITY
A pale and refreshing elderflower beer with a good citrus fruit aroma, bittersweet taste, and a zesty, hoppy, mouthwatering finish

Cwrw Glaslyn/ Glaslyn Ale (ABV 4.2%) BITTER
Refreshing light and malty amber-coloured ale. Plenty of hop in the aroma and taste. Good smooth mouthfeel leading to a slightly chewy finish.

Whakahari (ABV 4.3%) BITTER

Ochr Dywyll y Mws/ Dark Side of the Moose (ABV 4.6%) OLD
A dark, complex beer quite hoppy and bitter with roast undertones. Malt and fruit flavours also feature in the smooth taste and dry finish.

Snowdon Craft

Quinton Hazell Enterprise Parc, 55 Glan-y-Wern Road, Mochdre, LL28 5BS
☎ (01492) 545143 ⊕ snowdoncraftbeer.co.uk

☺Snowdon Craft, is located in Mochdre near Llandudno and uses an 18-barrel plant for its latest core range and seasonal beers. Suppling the local area and the Albion in

Conwy which it part owns, also the Johnny Dough's restaurant chain. !! ♦

IPA (ABV 3.6%) IPA
Bitter (ABV 4.2%) BITTER
Lager (ABV 4.3%) SPECIALITY
Summit IPA (ABV 4.8%) PALE
Porter (ABV 5.7%) PORTER

Snowdonia Parc

⛺ **Snowdonia Parc Brewpub & Campsite, Waunfawr, Caernarfon, LL55 4AQ**
☎ (01286) 650409 ⊕ snowdonia-park.co.uk

Snowdonia Parc started brewing in 1998 in a two-barrel brewhouse. The brewing is now carried out by the owner, Carmen Pierce. The beer is brewed solely for the Snowdonia Parc pub and campsite.

Ty Mo

Old Market Hall, Palace Street, Caernarfon, LL55 1RR
☎ 07391 696575

Brewing commenced in 2020 in a 19th century former market hall building using equipment formerly used by the Old Market Brewery. Output is cask, keg and bottle, supplying local pubs and the market hall bar.

Wild Horse SIBA

Unit 4, Cae Bach Builder Street, Llandudno, LL30 1DR
☎ (01492) 868292 ⊕ wildhorsebrewing.co.uk

Small brewery that initially concentrated on supplying keg, bottled and canned beers to local bars and off-licences but now also produces regular but one-off cask ales. All products are unfiltered and unpasteurised. ♦ ✦

Cottage Loaf, Llandudno (Photo: Stuart McMahon)

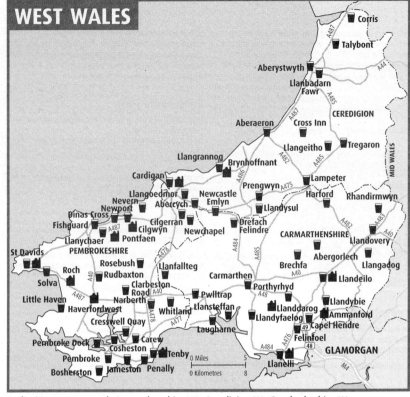

WEST WALES

Authority areas covered: Carmarthenshire UA, Ceredigion UA, Pembrokeshire UA

Aberaeron

Cadwgan Inn

10 Market Street, SA46 0AU (off A487, overlooking harbour)
☎ (01545) 570149
Wye Valley Bitter; 2 changing beers (sourced nationally; often Mantle, Tinworks) ⓗ

Named after the last ship built in the attractive regency town of Aberaeron, this old-style single-bar pub offers a friendly welcome and lively conversation. It is popular for its sports coverage, mainly rugby and racing. Guest beers are from a wide range of small and regional breweries. The paved terraced area at the front is a real suntrap; opposite is a free, but busy, harbourside public car park. Buses T1 and T5 stop nearby from Aberystwyth, Cardigan and Carmarthen. Q❀▲�☷(T1,T5)❀☂

Abercych

Nag's Head

SA37 0HJ (on B4332 between Cenarth and Eglwyswrw)
☎ (01239) 841200 ⊕ nagsheadabercych.co.uk
Mantle Cwrw Teifi; 1 changing beer (sourced locally; often Coles Family, Jennings) ⓗ

A restored old smithy, with a beamed bar, open fires and an attractive riverside garden. The bar area is furnished with collections of old medical instruments, railway memorabilia and timepieces showing the time in various parts of the world. There is also extensive display of beer bottles. The beer range is local, with regional and national guests. Food is sourced locally and includes trout and lamb; Sunday roasts are particularly popular. It is closed on Mondays during winter. ☷❀ᕯᐁᐧ♥P☂

Abergorlech

Black Lion

Abergorlech Road, SA32 7SN
☎ (01558) 685271 ⊕ blacklionabergorlech.co.uk
2 changing beers (sourced regionally; often Evan Evans, Harbwr) ⓗ

Traditional village pub that is also a restaurant and coffee shop. It serves home-made food including cakes, using locally sourced ingredients where possible. Just a few steps from the pub are signposted walks in the Brechfa forest or you can ride the thrilling Brechfa mountain bike trails. Bike-locking facilities are provided in the car park and muddy bikers are always welcome – the 300-year-old stone floor in the bar is easily cleaned! ☷❀◁ᐁＡＰ☷❀☂♫

Aberystwyth

Bottle & Barrel

14 Cambrian Place, SY23 1NT
☎ (01970) 625888 ⊕ bottleandbarrel.cymru
8 changing beers (sourced nationally; often Lucky 7, Polly's)

A mid-terrace bar in the town centre, providing a cosy yet modern atmosphere in which to enjoy a drink. At the front of the building is a relaxed area with comfy armchairs and wooden tables, and at the rear a number of high tables. At the very back the small garden with tables and chairs is a suntrap in the summer. The bar serves two cask ales and 14 keg lines, with a focus on Welsh breweries, plus real cider. There is also an on-site bottle shop. ☷❀ᕯ♣♥☷❀☂

Glengower Hotel L

3 Victoria Terrace, SY23 2DH (on seafront at N end of promenade)

☎ (01970) 626191 ⊕ glengower.co.uk

Mantle Rock Steady, MOHO; Wye Valley Butty Bach; 2 changing beers (sourced regionally; often Ludlow, Purple Moose, Salopian) Ⓗ

A warm and welcoming pub with rooms. Outside seating on its suntrap front terrace offers stunning views over Cardigan Bay; inside is a comfortable, light and airy bar, a quieter dining area, and a large back room. The cask beers and draught ciders on offer are usually sourced from Welsh micros or independent breweries close to the border. Good-quality food is served from all day Monday to Saturday and in the evening on Sunday.
ዄ❀☎🌢⊙⏢🅰️♦🖺(03)♣🛜

Hen Orsaf ✓

Station Buildings, Alexandra Road, SY23 1LH

☎ (01970) 636080

Greene King Abbot; Ruddles Best Bitter; Sharp's Doom Bar; 6 changing beers (sourced nationally; often Evan Evans, Glamorgan) Ⓗ

Award-winning conversion of Aberystwyth's former GWR railway station, which dates from 1924. This excellent Wetherspoon pub offers up to six guest ales, usually including light and dark beers, and often regional brews. Outdoor drinking is on the old station concourse (dogs not allowed) with direct access to Aberystwyth station; buses and taxis are also close by. The pub holds regular real ale festivals. ዄ❀⊙⏢🅰️⇌♦🖺🛜

Ship & Castle

1 High Street, SY23 1JG

☎ 07773 778785

Wye Valley HPA, Butty Bach; 3 changing beers (sourced nationally; often Oakham, Salopian, Tiny Rebel) Ⓗ

Aberystwyth's flagship pub offers microbrewery guest ales from the UK and Ireland. Cider and perry are also available alongside excellent beer in other formats including craft keg (Polly's, Tiny Rebel), bottles and cans. A platter of five third-pint cask ales is available. The well-considered decor reflects the pub's name and history. It gets busy on rugby days, but is always welcoming.
ዄ🅰️⇌♦🖺🛜

Bosherston

St Govan's Country Inn

SA71 5DN

☎ (01646) 661311

Evan Evans Cwrw; 3 changing beers (sourced nationally; often Adnams, Elgood's) Ⓗ

Cosy and comfortable pub with exposed beams, horse brasses and a large stone fireplace with log-burner. Up to four ales from regional and national brewers are available in the summer, when the pub can get busy. The tiny village of Bosherston lies just a short walk from Broad Haven South Beach on the stunning Pembrokeshire coast, and the Bosherston Lily Ponds, renowned for their beauty and varied wildlife.
ዄ❀☎🌢⊙⏢🅰️🖺🛜

Brechfa

Forest Arms

B4310, SA32 7RA (travelling on B4310 from Felingwm direction, on left in front of church)

☎ (01267) 202288 ⊕ forestarms.com

2 changing beers (sourced regionally; often Glamorgan) Ⓗ

Community-focused pub in the centre of an ancient village dating back to the 6th century. It has two bars warmed by a real fire, and separate restaurant/function rooms. Two well-kept real ales are served, reducing to one for winter months. A wide range of freshly cooked meals uses locally sourced food where possible; bookings preferred. Outside is beer garden. Accommodation is available. The Brechfa mountain biking trails are nearby (muddy gear allowed in the pub), as is the River Cothi, where fishing is possible by prior arrangement. ዄ❀☎🌢⊙⏢P❀♣🛜♪

Capel Hendre

King's Head Hotel L

Waterloo Road, SA18 3SF

☎ (01269) 842377

2 changing beers (sourced regionally; often Gower, Zoo) Ⓗ

A village pub tucked away just three miles from M4 junction 49, and a couple of miles from the former mining town of Ammanford. There is a main bar and dining room, with a sliding door leading to a separate snug. It serves two or sometimes three real ales sourced from Wales: Glamorgan, Bluestone and Neath breweries are regular visitors. Outside is a large car park and garden. ዄ❀☎🌢⊙⏢🖺●♦P🖺(128,129)♣🛜♪

Cardigan

Grosvenor

Bridge Street, SA43 1HY SN177459

☎ (01239) 613792

Greene King Abbot; Sharp's Doom Bar; 1 changing beer (sourced nationally) Ⓗ

Situated on the edge of the town centre next to Cardigan Castle and the River Teifi, this large pub offers a good choice of ales, including a selection of bottled beers. The large open-plan bar/lounge provides various areas in which to relax, eat and drink, and there is an extra room upstairs for dining and functions. Good-value food is served lunchtimes and evenings every day. An outdoor patio area overlooks the River Teifi and the revamped quay area. ዄ❀☎🌢⊙⏢🖺♦🖺🛜♪

Carew

Carew Inn ✓

SA70 8SL (off A477 before Pembroke Dock)

☎ (01646) 651267 ⊕ carewinn.co.uk

Brains Rev James Original; Sharp's Doom Bar; 1 changing beer (often Harbwr) Ⓗ

Situated close to Carew's historic Celtic Cross, castle and tidal mill, this former estate pub of the Trollope-Bellew

REAL ALE BREWERIES

Bluestone ✦ Cilgwyn
Cardigan ✦ Brynhoffnant
Coles Family 🍺 Llanddarog
Core of the Poodle Haverfordwest (NEW)
Electro Cardigan
Evan Evans Llandeilo
Felinfoel Llanelli
Gwaun Valley Pontfaen
Harbwr ✦ Tenby
Mantle Cardigan
Old Farmhouse St Davids
Tenby ✦ Tenby
Tinworks ✦ Llanelli
Victoria Inn 🍺 Roch
Zoo Ammanford

family makes an ideal stop-off with its village location and many local attractions. A pine-boarded bar features old photographs of the local area. Outside there is a marquee and a large grassed garden with a children's play area. Local, regional and national guest beers are served, along with home-cooked traditional food with a modern twist. Check winter opening times before visiting. Q⌂♿◐♦🅰♣P🚻♿♪

Carmarthen

Coracle Tavern
1 Cambrian Place, SA31 1QG
☎ (01267) 468180
2 changing beers (sourced regionally; often Glamorgan) Ⓗ
A friendly free house offering a warm welcome to locals and visitors alike, situated in the centre of town, close to the main shopping area. It has a large open-plan bar area with comfy sofas, and a separate seating area upstairs that can be booked for private gatherings. Darts is popular and a number of teams are hosted. Local CAMRA meetings are sometimes held here. ⇌♣🖵

Friends Arms
Old St Clears Road, SA31 3HH (W of town centre at the bottom of Monument Hill B3412)
☎ (01267) 234073
Thornbridge Jaipur IPA; 1 changing beer (sourced regionally; often Gower, Wye Valley) Ⓗ
Excellent local hostelry half a mile from Carmarthen town centre. The cosy and friendly atmosphere and warm welcome are enhanced by two open fires. It is popular with sports fans and has Sky Sports and BT Sports. An annex building can be booked for functions and events. A former local CAMRA Pub of the Year. ⌂♿♣🖵(222,322)♿🌐♪

Hen Dderwen ✅
47-48 King Street, SA31 1BH
☎ (01267) 242050
Greene King Abbot; Ruddles Best Bitter; Sharp's Doom Bar; 4 changing beers (sourced nationally; often Glamorgan, Rhymney) Ⓗ
Terraced town-centre pub named after the local legend of Merlin and an ancient oak tree, depicted throughout the premises. An recent refurbishment introduced a first-floor dining area and extensive roof terrace. Local Welsh ales are always available, as well as a good selection of ales from around the UK, and bottled and canned craft ales. There are beer festivals in the spring and autumn, and a summer cider festival. Food is served all day. ⌂◐♿♿⇌♿🖵🌐

Rose & Crown Hotel
114 Lammas Street, SA31 3AE
☎ (01267) 232050 🌐 roseandcrowncarmarthen.co.uk
Evan Evans Cwrw; 1 changing beer (often Fuller's, Sharp's) Ⓗ
Large town-centre pub, popular both with locals and visitors, with friendly staff and well-kept ale. There is a long bar and numerous segregated drinking areas. Towards the rear of the premises is a large separate restaurant area offering a wide selection of pub food - Sunday lunches are particularly popular. There is large area outside with a heated covered patio and widescreen TV. ♿🏠◐⇌P🖵🌐♪

Stag & Pheasant
34 Spilman Street, SA31 1LQ
☎ (01267) 232040 🌐 stagandpheasant.co.uk
Wadworth 6X; 2 changing beers (sourced nationally; often Glamorgan, Ringwood) Ⓗ

Busy pub on the main thoroughfare in Carmarthen, with a warm and friendly atmosphere that makes it popular for tourists and locals. The landlady has managed to vary the ownership tie away from a large Pubco and has the freedom to select her own choice of ales. The two large TV screens make it a popular venue for watching sports. The pleasant beer garden has outdoor heaters for cold weather. ♿♿⇌♣🖵♿🌐

Cilgerran

Masons Arms 🏆
Cwnce, SA43 2SR
☎ 07989 990461
Mantle Cwrw Teifi; 1 changing beer (sourced locally) Ⓗ
Also known as the Rampin, the Masons Arms is thought to have opened in 1836. It is a small, cosy and friendly village pub, with an open fire (old kitchen range). Many local characters can be found here, contributing to a great atmosphere. Three real ales are served, one changing regularly, usually from a local brewery. Various charity events are held throughout the year, and there is the occasional musical evening. Check winter opening times before visiting. Local CAMRA Pub of the Year 2023. ⌂♿🅰♣P♿

Clarbeston Road

Cross Inn
SA63 4UL (N of railway station)
☎ (01437) 731506
Evan Evans Warrior; Glamorgan Jemimas Pitchfork; 1 changing beer (sourced nationally; often Bluestone) Ⓗ
Multi-roomed village inn well worth seeking out, with stone and wooden floors and original oak beams throughout. The large bar area houses pool, sport TV and a jukebox. There are also two small snugs and a dining room where reasonably priced home-cooked food is served Thursday to Saturday evenings and Sunday lunchtime. Outside are more spacious drinking areas. The beer range comes from regional and national breweries. A beer festival is held in summer. Q⌂♿◐♿⇌♣P🖵♿🌐

Corris

Slater's Arms
Bridge Street, SY20 9SP
☎ (01654) 761324 🌐 slatersarmscorris.co.uk
3 changing beers (sourced nationally; often Big Bog, Purple Moose, Tudor) Ⓗ
Named after what was formerly the main trade of the townsfolk in Corris, this Grade II-listed village pub is popular with locals and visitors. The main bar has some traditional features such as slate flooring and a decorative mantelshelf above a large inglenook fireplace. In winter a blazing log-burner is a welcome sight. A dining area is at the rear. Walkers, families and well-behaved dogs are welcome. Accommodation is available in four en-suite double bedrooms. 🛏️◐🅰♿🖵(34)♿🌐♪

Cosheston

Brewery Inn
SA72 4UD
☎ (01646) 686678 🌐 thebreweryinn.com
2 changing beers (sourced regionally) Ⓗ
A Grade II-listed stone-built free house that was once accommodation for monks, with its own brewhouse

situated in the outbuildings behind – brewing ceased in 1889. The light and airy interior boasts a traditional slate floor and beamed ceiling. To one side is a cosy non-food area where you can enjoy a chat in front of the log fire. Ingredients for the extensive menu are sourced locally and include fresh fish. Check opening hours before visiting in winter. Q ⏰ ❀ ✦ ◑ ◐ ♿ ▲ ♣ P ⌂ ❀ ☂ ♪

Cresswell Quay

Cresselly Arms

SA68 0TE

☎ (01646) 651210

Hancocks HB; Wye Valley Butty Bach; 2 changing beers (sourced locally; often Bluestone, Mantle) ⊞
Situated on the Cresswell River, this 250-year-old, ivy-covered hostelry seems like a throwback to the Georgian age. The homely farm kitchen interior, where a roaring fire burns in the hearth, is a haven for locals and visitors alike. The house beer is complemented by Worthington Bitter dispensed from the barrel by jugs. The pub is accessible by boat from the Milford Haven estuary at high tide, and also lies on a series of interesting walking routes. Q ⏰ ❀ ♿ ▲ ♣ P ⌂ (361) ♪

Cross Inn

Rhos yr Hafod Inn ▼ ᴸ

SY23 5NB (at B4337/B4577 crossroads)

☎ (01974) 272644

2 changing beers (sourced regionally; often Bluestone, Mantle, Tudor) ⊞
Friendly, family-run pub offering a range of guest ales and a warm welcome. The choice of drinking areas includes a front bar, popular in the early evening with lively locals, and a comfortable rear bar. Sunny days can be enjoyed in the roadside drinking area or the large rear garden. It serves two constantly changing ales from Welsh breweries. Varied events are held throughout the year. There is ample parking on both sides of the pub. A local CAMRA Pub of the Year. ⏰ ❀ ♣ P ❀ ☂

Dinas Cross

Freemasons Arms

Spencer Buildings, SA42 0UW (on A487 coast road midway between Fishguard and Newport)

☎ (01348) 811674

Coles Family Llanddarog; Gower Gold ⊞
Traditional sea captains' meeting place in the Pembrokeshire National Park. This pub is conveniently placed for those who enjoy sailing or like to visit attractive beaches and walk the coastal path. It also has the advantage of being on a principal bus route. The main bar has a cosy open fire with a dining area at the side. It has been recently tastefully refurbished and retains its original character. Check winter opening times before venturing forth. Q ⏰ ❀ ◑ ♿ ▲ ♣ P ⌂ (T5) ❀ ☂ ♪

Drefach Felindre

John Y Gwas

Drefach Felindre, SA44 5XG SN354383

☎ (01559) 370469

3 changing beers (sourced nationally; often Brains, Glamorgan, Robinsons) ⊞
Early 19th-century village tavern with a striking yellow and black faùlade, popular with locals and tourists. The cosy interior, heated by a wood-burning stove, features two snugs. The landlord offers a friendly and enthusiastic welcome with three well-kept and changing beers. A wide variety of bottled beers and ciders is also available.

A beer festival, hosting over 10 different ales, is held over the August bank holiday weekend. Food is available every night. ⏰ ❀ ✦ ♣ P ⌂ (460) ❀ ☂ ♪

Red Lion

SA44 5UH (in village centre, 1 mile off A484 Llandysul to Newcastle Emlyn road) SN354388

☎ (01559) 371287

Mantle Cwrw Teifi; 1 changing beer (sourced nationally; often Exmoor) ⊞
A warm welcome awaits at this recently renovated 19th-century pub, located in the small village of Drefach Felindre, near the National Woollen Museum. The interior is mostly open plan, with a separate dining room and a large outside drinking area; note the original tiled entrance porch. The pub is community focused, with regular fundraising events held for charity. The car park is small, but on-street parking is also available.
Q ⏰ ❀ ◑ ♿ ♣ P ⌂ (460) ☂ ♪

Felinfoel

White Lion Inn

Parkview, SA14 8BH (on main A476 in Felinfoel)

☎ (01554) 776644

2 changing beers (sourced nationally; often Gower, Hancocks) ⊞
A family-friendly split-level hostelry with defined drinking and dining spaces, plus a function room. A selection of well-kept real ales is available, and there is a good-value carvery. Quizzes are held on Sunday and Wednesday. Outside are covered and open drinking areas. National cycle and walking paths to the Swiss Valley and beyond are nearby. There is ample parking space on the road. ⏰ ❀ ◑ ♿ ♣ P ⌂ ❀ ☂

Fishguard

Cambrian Inn

Hamilton Street, SA65 9HL (turn off A487 onto Gwaun Valley road)

☎ (01348) 873848 ⊕ cambrianinn.com

Felinfoel Double Dragon; 1 changing beer (often Gwaun Valley) ⊞
Friendly pub that has recently undergone an internal and external makeover. Inside, a log-burner provides warmth on chilly days and there is a comfy leather sofa and armchairs to relax in. It serves two regularly changing real ales, with an emphasis on local breweries. Light meals such as pasta, pizza and pies are available when staffing permits – best to check in advance.
Q ⏰ ♿ ♣ P ⌂ (T5) ❀ ☂

Harford

Tafarn Jem

SA48 8HF

☎ (01558) 650633

1 changing beer (sourced nationally; often Wye Valley) ⊞
Welcoming 19th century pub named after landlady Jemima, previously known as 'Mountain Cottage', which hints at the stunning views. The main interior is open plan with two distinct areas; a comfortable small bar and a larger room with a pool table and seating. Booking is essential for the occasional steak/curry nights. A touring caravan site is located about a mile and a half from the pub, in addition to a glamping site just a quarter of a mile away. ♿ ▲ ♣ P ❀

Jameston

Swanlake Inn

SA70 8QE (backs onto main road)
☎ (01834) 871262
Gower Gold; 1 changing beer (often St Austell) ⌂
A traditional Grade II-listed 16th-century inn that was originally a single-storey cottage. The three main bar areas have some walls that are still wattle and daub, and there is a bread oven by the open fire. An unusual air-duct running from near the bar to the chimney is said to assist the fire to draw. A small panel of reeds, used as a base for plastering, has been uncovered for display. The pub may close early in the week if quiet, so phone ahead to check. ⑤❀◐♣ (349)✿♪

Lampeter

Nag's Head

14 Bridge Street, SA48 7HG
☎ (01570) 218517
2 changing beers (sourced regionally; often Evan Evans, Glamorgan, Gower) ⌂
Town-centre pub that has been refurbished to provide a modern and bright horseshoe-shaped bar area. It is a fun and friendly and pub – with decor to match – and attracts a good mix of locals, students and tourists. It shows most live sports events and has live music every Friday night. Evening basket meals are available Monday to Saturday, and lunch on Sunday. It also offers B&B accommodation. ⑤❀🖚◐🖵❤✿♪

Laugharne

New Three Mariners Inn Ⓛ

Victoria Street, SA33 4SE
☎ (01994) 427426
2 changing beers (sourced locally; often Courage, Evan Evans, Gower) ⌂
Popular locals' pub in the centre of this historic town, only yards from the early 11th-century castle. The pub moved to its current site when the original ale house opposite was converted to a carpentry shop. Two ales are served; one in winter. Evening meals are available and there is a weekly quiz night. Dylan Thomas lived in Laugharne for a number of years and he and his wife Caitlin are buried in the graveyard of St Martin's Church. ⑤❀🖚◐₺♣🖵❤✿

Little Haven

Saint Bride's Inn Ⓛ

St Brides Road, SA62 3UN
☎ (01437) 781266 ⊕ saintbridesinn.co.uk
Sharp's Atlantic; 2 changing beers (sourced locally; often Mantle) ⌂
Family-run pub in the centre of this quaint old fishing village on the Pembrokeshire Coast National Park. It is open all year round, selling a range of Welsh and Pembrokeshire ales. The attractive interior includes a separate dining area, and there are heaters on the patio in the pretty suntrap garden for outdoor drinking. The pub is noted for the ancient well in the cellar. Q⑤❀◐₳P🖵(311,400) ✿

Llanbadarn Fawr

Black Lion

SY23 3RA
☎ (01970) 636632
Wye Valley Butty Bach; 2 changing beers (sourced nationally; often Wye Valley) ⌂

A mile from Aberystwyth, this modernised pub is popular with locals and students alike. The spacious main bar has seating at one end, darts and pool at the other, and a large function room. Quizzes are held every other Friday and pub teams play darts, pool and poker. There is a Sunday carvery and bar meals are served Thursday to Saturday. The large beer garden at the rear has a delightful air of rural seclusion. Q⑤❀◐♣P🖵(526,X47) ❤✿♪

Llandeilo

Hen Vic

82 New Road, SA19 6DF
☎ (01558) 822596
3 changing beers (sourced regionally; often Glamorgan, Mumbles, Oakham) ⌂
A lively locals' pub with a welcome for all who pass through its doors. It was a sports club originally but has been a pub for the past 15 years. Three constantly changing and well-kept beers are always available. There are several large TVs showing sport in the bar and there is a separate pool room. The dining area to the front of the pub has recently had a major refurbishment. ⑤◐≉♣P🖵(X13,281) ❤✿♪

Salutation Inn

33 New Road, SA19 6DF
☎ (01558) 824255
Wye Valley Butty Bach; 2 changing beers (sourced regionally; often Gower, Greene King) ⌂
A locals' pub near the town centre. Friendly staff dispense three well-kept beers. The pub is separated into two areas, with a pool table in one side and a wood fire in the other. It holds an open mic session on a Tuesday as well as live music on most weekends. There is a garden and function area at the rear. The pub has a beer festival in the summer. ❀₵≉♣🖵✿

Llandovery

Whitehall

1 High Street, SA20 0PU
☎ (01550) 721139
Mantle MOHO, Cwrw Teifi; 1 changing beer (sourced nationally) ⌂
Friendly 17th-century pub in the town centre, warmed by cosy log fires in the winter. Three well-kept ales are served, reducing to two in the winter. There is seating at the front of the pub and a beer garden to the rear. A darts league competes on a Thursday evening, and it is home to the Llandovery Vintage Tractor Club. Meals are served but availability at weekends can be limited; booking ahead is recommended. ⑤❀🖚◐≉♣🖵(280,281) ❤✿

Llandybie

Ivy Bush

18 Church Street, SA18 3HZ (100yds from church)
☎ (01269) 850272
Timothy Taylor Landlord; 1 changing beer (sourced regionally; often Exmoor) ⌂
This friendly local has a single bar with two comfortable seating areas. Pub games and quizzes are run weekly and a largescreen TV shows sport. Timothy Taylor Landlord is always on, plus at least one guest beer which changes regularly. The railway station nearby is on the Heart of Wales line. The local birdwatching group hold their meetings here. ⑤❀≉♣P🖵(103,X13)✿♪

Llandyfaelog

Red Lion

SA17 5PR (300yds off A484)
☎ (01267) 267530 ⊕ redlionllandyfaelog.co.uk
Wye Valley Butty Bach; 2 changing beers (sourced nationally; often Butcombe, Glamorgan) ⑪
Popular family-run village hostelry that is genuinely at the heart of its community. A warm welcome and friendly service are offered, along with three well-kept ales. There is a large public bar, a restaurant, a separate family room, and an annexe which hosts concerts and functions. Bar and restaurant meals are available; booking is recommended. Q✿❋❀◑ ♿♣▲🚌(198,X12)🛜

Llandysul

Porth Hotel

Church Street, SA44 4QS SN418407
☎ (01559) 362202 ⊕ porthhotel.co.uk
2 changing beers (sourced locally; often Glamorgan) ⑪
Originally a 17th-century coaching inn and now a family-run village hotel on the banks of the River Teifi. It has bar, restaurant and function room areas. The public rooms still feature the original oak beams and panels. Food and drink is sourced locally, where possible. At the rear of the hotel is a customer car park and a lawned rear garden overlooking the river. It is ideal for access to walks and fishing. ✿❋❀◑♣♠P🚌❀🛜

Llanelli

New Drovers

32-34 Thomas Street, SA15 3JA (just below Thomas Arms Hotel, on opp side; can be hard to spot as there is little to indicate that it is a public house from outside)
☎ 07845 004407
Felinfoel Double Dragon; Fuller's London Pride; 2 changing beers (sourced regionally; often Evan Evans) ⑪
Quirky town-centre pub with no pub sign other than a brass plaque near the door – which makes you feel as if you are entering a solicitor's office. The large open-plan bar area is complemented by a couple of side rooms for quiet drinking. Four real ales are served. It hosts monthly food events – booking essential. The pub enforces a strict over-25s policy, and there is no smoking allowed outside. Closed on Thursday from January to April. Q✿♿🚌♪

Stradey Arms

1 Stradey Road, SA15 4ET
☎ (01554) 753332 ⊕ thestradeyarms.com
Brains Rev James Original; 1 changing beer (sourced nationally) ⑪
Popular pub on the outskirts of town, with a comfortable bar and separate restaurant. The friendly and welcoming staff add to the pleasant ambience. Real ale is served from two handpumps in the bar. A varied menu of freshly prepared food is served during the week, except Sundays when there is a lunchtime carvery. The pub gets busy during sporting events, especially rugby internationals. ✿❋◑♣P🚌❀🛜♪

York Palace ✓

51 Stepney Street, SA15 3YA (opp Town Hall Square Gardens)
☎ (01554) 758609
Greene King Abbot; Ruddles Best Bitter; 7 changing beers (often Glamorgan, Gower, Tomos Watkin) ⑪
A refurbished former picture house retaining much of the original decor. It offers a good selection of beers from

around the world including a choice of bottled and canned craft beers. It also boasts a varied selection of bag in box and bottled ciders, occasionally on handpull. There are two international beer festivals in the spring and autumn each year. There is also a cider festival each summer. The pub also hosts a number of Meet the Brewer sessions throughout the year. Food is served all day. Q◑♿≠❀🚌🛜

Llanfallteg

Plash

SA34 0UN (off A40 at Llanddewi Velfrey)
☎ (01437) 563472 ⊕ theplashinn.co.uk
Wye Valley Butty Bach; 2 changing beers ⑪
At the centre of village life, this welcoming, terrace-style cottage pub has been an inn for more than 180 years. Its guest beers are usually from small, independent breweries. Home-made food using locally sourced ingredients is served, with specials on Wednesday, Thursday and Friday. The pub hosts a quiz night on Tuesday and a folk night, plus a number of other special nights each month. An accessible entrance is to the rear. A former local CAMRA Pub of the Year. Q✿❋◑♿▲♣P❀🛜♪

Llangadog

Red Lion

Church Street, SA19 9AA
☎ (01550) 777228
Glamorgan Jemimas Pitchfork; Gower Power; 1 changing beer (sourced regionally) ⑪
A traditional coaching inn with a history that dates back to the early 1600s. The Grade II-listed building has been refurbished to provide traditional character and charm. You will find a genuinely warm welcome in comfortable and relaxed surroundings. Meals are served lunchtime and evenings, except on Monday and Tuesday, and Sunday when a lunchtime carvery is served. Q✿❋◑♿▲≠♣P🚌🛜

Llangeitho

Three Horse Shoe Inn Ⓛ

SY25 6TW
☎ (01974) 821244
2 changing beers (sourced regionally; often Evan Evans, Glamorgan, Wye Valley) ⑪
A traditional, family-run pub that is the hub of life in this historic village. It has a main bar, dining room, function room and a sunny rear garden with a beautifully built wooden undercover area. The friendly landlord is a keen supporter of real ale and Welsh breweries. Good-value evening meals and Sunday lunch are offered (no food at lunchtime on other days). Pool and darts are played, and there is a monthly open mic night. ✿❋◑♣🚌(585) ❀🛜♪

Llangoedmor

Penllwyndu

B4570, SA43 2LY (on B4570 4½ miles from Cardigan) SN240458
☎ (01239) 682533
Brains Rev James Original; Hancocks HB; 1 changing beer (sourced regionally) ⑪
Old-fashioned alehouse standing at an isolated crossroads where Cardigan's evil-doers were once hanged – the pub sign is worthy of close inspection. The cheerful and welcoming public bar retains its quaintness, with a slate floor and inglenook with wood-burning

stove. Good home-cooked food, including traditional favourites, is available all day in the bar and the separate restaurant. Free live music plays on the third Thursday evening of the month. ⌂☺❀◑♣P♥☺♫

Llangrannog

Pentre Arms Hotel
SA44 6SP (at seaward end of B4321/B4334)
☎ (01239) 654345 ⊕ pentrearms.co.uk
Mantle MOHO; 2 changing beers (often Bluestone, Purple Moose) Ⓗ
Cosy pub in a pretty village on the Wales Coastal Path, with tremendous sea views from the huge window in the bar and the small decking area. Aside from the main bar, there is also a games room (pool, darts) and dining room. Two Welsh real ales are served, three at busier times. Hearty pub food includes lunchtime sandwiches and fresh fish from Easter to October. Live music plays on summer weekends. Dogs are welcome in the bar. B&B accommodation is available. A free car park is half a mile away. ⌂☺❀◑▲♣Ⓟ(552)♥☺♫

Llansteffan

Castle Inn
The Square, SA33 5JG
☎ (01267) 241225
Sharp's Doom Bar; house beer (by Evan Evans); 1 changing beer (often Evan Evans) Ⓗ
A traditional pub committed to real ale, with a relaxing atmosphere and friendly staff. The interior has been completely redecorated and the toilets renovated. There is an open-plan layout but also plenty of cosy corners for customers to relax and unwind in. It hosts a number of local community groups, and provides bar snacks from an uncomplicated menu. There is an outside seating area overlooking the village square where locals and tourists mingle. Q⌂☺❀◑♣♣Ⓟ(227)♥☺

Llanychaer

Bridge End Inn Ⓛ
SA65 9TB (on B4313, 2 miles SW of Fishguard)
☎ (01348) 872545
Evan Evans Cwrw Ⓗ; **1 changing beer (sourced locally; often Gwaun Valley)** Ⓗ/Ⓖ
Known locally as the Bont, this friendly country pub, over 150 years old, nestles in the beautiful Gwaun Valley at a bridging point across the river. The cosy bars are warmed by log fires, and serve mainly local real ales, plus sometimes a guest ale from further afield. The pub features an external water wheel and a pretty garden at the rear. Free snacks are often available on Friday evenings, otherwise no food is served. A former local CAMRA Pub of the Year. Q⌂☺❀▲♣●Ⓟ(345)♥☺

Narberth

Dingle Inn
Jesse Road, SA67 7DP
☎ (01834) 869979 ⊕ dinglecaravanparknarberth.co.uk
2 changing beers (sourced regionally) Ⓗ
Friendly local next to a caravan and camping site, offering plenty of Narberth's distinctive community spirit. Regular customers' preferences guide the selection of beers from the local area and further afield. There is only one handpump so the beer changes frequently. The town boasts a range of specialist shops and attractions, including an award-winning museum, that would be the envy of many larger places. ⌂☺❀◑▲⇌Ⓟ(381)♫

Nevern

Trewern Arms
SA42 0NB (off the A487, 2 miles N of Newport)
☎ (01239) 820395 ⊕ trewernarms.com
3 changing beers (sourced regionally; often Bluestone, Harbwr, Mantle) Ⓗ
A picturesque 16th-century pub deep within a secluded valley astride the banks of the River Nevern, close to St Brynach's Church, noted for its ancient Celtic High Cross, Ogham Stone and Bleeding Yew. The village of Nevern is less than a mile from the beautiful fishing town of Newport. This multi-roomed pub caters for all, from those who just want a drink to large parties and wedding receptions. It is a great place to stay to experience some of the best walks in West Wales. Q⌂☺❀◑&▲♣Ⓟ(T5)♥☺♫

Newcastle Emlyn

Bunch of Grapes ✓
Bridge Street, SA38 9DU
☎ (01239) 711185
Sharp's Sea Fury; 1 changing beer (often Wye Valley) Ⓗ
A Grade II*-listed building dating back to the 17th century, reputed to have been built from the ruins of the nearby 13th-century castle. The pub is at the heart of the community and offers a warm and welcoming place to eat, drink and relax. Its enclosed rear garden has a children's play area and a covered smoking shelter. ⌂☺◑&▲♣●Ⓟ(460) ♥☺♫

Newchapel

Ffynnone Arms Ⓛ
SA37 0EH
☎ (01239) 841800 ⊕ ffynnonearms.co.uk
Wye Valley Butty Bach; 2 changing beers (sourced locally) Ⓗ
A charming traditional 18th-century pub on the borders of three counties: Pembrokeshire, Carmarthenshire and Ceredigion. Local ales are often available, with regional and national beers the rest of the time. Welsh cider is also sold. The landlady prides herself on the food, offering gluten-, dairy- and sugar-free menus, mostly using locally sourced ingredients. Fish & chips is a Wednesday evening special, and the Sunday carvery features beef and pork. Q⌂☺❀◑&♣●PⓇ♫

Newport

Castle Inn Ⓛ ✓
Bridge Street, SA42 0TB
☎ (01239) 820742 ⊕ castleinnpembs.co.uk
Wye Valley Butty Bach; 2 changing beers (sourced locally) Ⓗ
Friendly, popular local in this characterful small town halfway between Cardigan and Fishguard. The attractive bar features some impressive wood paneling. Guest beers are local and regional. Food is served at lunchtimes and in the evening in the dining area. Beer and cider festivals are held on the May and August bank holidays. There is an off-street car park behind the hotel. A wealth of prehistoric remains and the Pembrokeshire Coastal Path add interest to the many local walks. Q⌂☺❀◑&▲♣PⓇ♥☺♫

Pembroke

Old King's Arms Ⓛ
13 Main Street, SA71 4JS

☎ (01646) 683611 ⊕ oldkingsarmshotel.co.uk
Felinfoel Double Dragon; 2 changing beers (sourced locally; often Bluestone, Draught Bass) Ⓗ
Former coaching inn, allegedly the oldest in Pembroke, dating back to around 1520. The hotel bar is a small room with exposed stone walls, beams, and a real fire. Four handpumps dispense local, regional and national beers. There is a separate lounge with a dining area and a separate restaurant with room for larger groups. Locally sourced meat and fish feature on the menus.
Q ☺ ☺ ☜ ◖ ◑ ᕦ ♿ P 🖵 ♨ 🛜

Pembroke Dock

First & Last
London Road, SA72 6TX (on A477)
☎ (01646) 682687
Brains Rev James Original; Sharp's Doom Bar; 1 changing beer Ⓗ
Friendly single-bar local run by the same family for 50 years. Formerly the Commercial, it acquired its more distinctive name in 1991 to reflect its edge-of-town location. An eclectic mix of photos and prints adorn the walls. Guest beers are from local and national breweries, and a menu of good pub fare is offered. There is a popular Sunday evening quiz. The pub is handy for the Cleddau Bridge, giving easy access to Haverfordwest, and is close to the historic dockyard and ferries to Ireland.
☺ ☺ ◑ ⇌ P 🖵 🛜

Penally

Cross Inn
SA70 7PU
☎ (01834) 844665 ⊕ crossinnpenally.co.uk
Sharp's Doom Bar; 2 changing beers (sourced regionally) Ⓗ
Situated in a picturesque village with some well-preserved Georgian and Victorian houses, this pub features military and sporting themes, with shields of regiments stationed in a nearby barracks adorning the walls alongside local pictures. The sporting prowess of the locals is evident from the cups and shields on the trophy shelf. A signed photo and a set of darts used by the legendary Phil 'The Power' Taylor is framed in an alcove. The wood and brick bar leads to the restaurant where food is sometimes available – phone to check in advance. ☺ ☺ ◖ ◑ ᕦ ⇌ ♣ 🖵 (349,358) ♨

Porthyrhyd

Mansel Arms 🍺 ⌞
Banc y Mansel, SA32 8BS (on B4310 between Porthyrhyd and Drefach)
☎ (01267) 275305
5 changing beers (sourced regionally; often Evan Evans, Grey Trees, Rhymney) Ⓗ/Ⓖ
Welcoming 18th-century coaching inn with plenty of traditional character, featuring wood fires in both bars. The landlord encourages customers to taste and experience a variety of flavours, with third-pint measures available. Beers are selected from local and regional brewers. Five ever-changing ales on handpump are usually available Friday to Sunday; always at least three during the week. The pub's cask ale club has regular brewery visits and brewers' speaker/taster events. A local CAMRA Pub of the Year and former Welsh national winner. ☺ ☺ ◑ ♣ ♿ P 🖵 (129) ♨ 🛜 ♫

Prengwyn

Gwarcefel Arms
Prengwyn, SA44 4LU (on crossroads of A475 and B4476) SN424442
☎ (01559) 363126
Sharp's Doom Bar; 1 changing beer (sourced nationally) Ⓗ
Traditional stone-built pub standing at the junction of five roads. There is a main bar with wood-burning stove and pool table, and seating around the walls. A rear snug with cosy seating is open at busier times. The large restaurant serves evening meals and Sunday lunches, and can also cater for functions and private parties. Fish & chips is a speciality. There is a beer garden and ample car parking to the rear. ☺ ☺ ◑ ♣ P 🖵 ♨ 🛜

Pwlltrap

White Lion
SA33 4AT
☎ (01994) 230370 ⊕ whitelion-pwlltrap.co.uk
Greene King Abbot; Shepherd Neame Bishops Finger; Young's London Original; 1 changing beer (sourced nationally; often Courage) Ⓗ
This roadside pub, just outside St Clears, is warm and welcoming, with a real fire in winter. Its oak beams and panelled walls lend it an old-world charm. Four cask beers are available in summer; two in winter. It boasts a large annexe restaurant with good food; takeaway meals are also available. Local teams for pool and darts are hosted and a large TV screen shows regular sporting fixtures. The pub organises a range of events throughout the year. Q ◑ ♿ ♣ P 🖵 (224,322) ♨ 🛜

Rhandirmwyn

Towy Bridge Inn
Rhandirmwyn, SA20 0PE
☎ (01550) 760370
Glamorgan Jemimas Pitchfork; house beer (by Carlsberg-Tetley)
A delightful rural riverside location makes this remote pub worth a visit. The interior is a single room with a table seating area and a bar. Outside is a large covered seating area with views across the river. The pub serves well-kept ales, and the house beer, Towy Ale, is actually the rarely seen Ansells Best Bitter. Home-cooked food is available. The pub is popular with walkers, bikers and cyclists; dogs are welcome. Q ☺ ☺ ᕦ P ♨ 🛜

Rosebush

Tafarn Sinc ✅
SA66 7QU
☎ (01437) 532214 ⊕ tafarnsinc.cymru
3 changing beers (often Gwaun Valley, Harbwr, Sharp's) Ⓗ
Victorian hotel that was built in 1876 to attract tourists to the Preseli mountains, when the Clunderwen to Rosebush railway line was opened. Originally called the Precelly Hotel, it closed in 1992 but was bought by locals, refurbished and renamed Tafarn Sinc. The building features in the history and social life of the area, and its interior is full of olde-worlde character and charm. Its location in the heart of the Preseli Mountains ensures scenic views, whether driving or walking. The hotel is noted for its locally sourced food. ☺ ☺ ◑ ᕦ ♿ P ♨

Rudbaxton

Corner Piece Inn

A40, SA62 5PG (on A40 to Fishguard, 2 miles from Haverfordwest on turning to Spittal)

☎ (01437) 742185

2 changing beers (sourced locally; often Mantle) [H]

The first pub for two miles from Haverfordwest in one direction and Wolf's Castle in the other. It is a cosy three-roomed hostelry serving good ale and food. The owners are enthusiastic about their real ales and offer two changing beers, normally from Mantle. Pie Night is Wednesday and fish night Friday. There is seating and play equipment outside, though the adjacent A40 can be noisy. Q🐴✿◐⛺P🚌(T5)🐾

St Davids

Farmers Arms

14-16 Goat Street, SA62 6RF (down hill to left of square)

☎ (01437) 721666 🌐 farmersstdavids.co.uk

Hancocks HB; house beer (by Felinfoel); 1 changing beer (sourced nationally; often Sharp's) [H]

This traditional three-room city pub is the westernmost in Wales. The top bar is mainly for dining, with a smaller room off (the Coxswains), which is the social meeting place for the St David's lifeboat crew. The Glue Pot bar is where the locals tend to gather around the fire. An outside patio offers views of the cathedral and has a seasonal bar. Winter opening times vary and food may not be available in winter – check beforehand. No. 400 and 404 buses stop nearby in summer.
🐴✿◐♿⛺♣🍏🚌(T11)🐾📶♫

Solva

Ship

15 Main Street, SA62 6UU (on A487)

☎ (01437) 721528 🌐 theshipsolva.co.uk

Banks's Amber Ale; Wye Valley Butty Bach; 1 changing beer (often Wye Valley) [H]

Families are particularly welcome at this traditional pub which features black and white timbers both inside and out. The food offering includes authentic Indian curries in the evening, with free delivery available, and a popular Sunday roast. An outdoor smoking area is covered and heated, and ample parking is available nearby overlooking the picturesque harbour. Winter opening times vary so check before visiting. Former local CAMRA Pub of the Year. 🐴✿🛏◐♿⛺P🚌(T11)🐾📶

Talybont

White Lion/Llew Gwyn

SY24 5ER

☎ (01970) 832245

Banks's Hobgoblin Gold; Wainwright; 1 changing beer (sourced nationally; often Wye Valley) [H]

A proper community pub at the heart of village life. The main slate-floored room is heated by a solid fuel stove with separate games and dining rooms serviced from the central bar. Interesting local memorabilia adorns most of the walls. A popular Sunday lunch is served, and there is an antique shop on the premises. There is a children's playground in the large beer garden. Camper vans are welcome. Bus services in the evening and on Sundays are limited. Q🐴✿🛏◐♿⛺♣P🚌(T2,X28)🐾📶♫

Tenby

Hope & Anchor [L]

St Julian Street, SA70 7AX (head from square towards harbour)

☎ (01834) 842131

Felinfoel Double Dragon; Harbwr M V Enterprise, North Star [H]**, Caldey Lollipop** [G]**; Sharp's Atlantic; 4 changing beers (sourced regionally; often Mantle)** [H]

Set in the old town on the way down to the harbour, this welcoming pub offers four guest beers and ciders. Good food is important and specials supplement the standard menu with fish dishes understandably popular. The convivial atmosphere and interesting local decor make it an excellent place to relax over a beer. Harbwr ales dominate but guest beers appear mainly from Welsh breweries including Evan Evans, Mantle and Purple Moose: Wye Valley sometimes sneaks over the border.
🐴✿◐⛺🚆🥃🚌🐾📶♫

Tregaron

Talbot [L]

The Square, SY25 6JL

☎ (01974) 298208 🌐 ytalbot.com

3 changing beers (sourced regionally; often Evan Evans, Mantle, Wye Valley) [H]

A heritage pub of immense character. It has a front bar with an open fire and huge beams, a snug with an inglenook fireplace, a rear main bar, and a restaurant. Two real ales are served in winter, three in summer from Wales and the Borders, plus real cider from Welsh producers in busier months. Excellent quality food is available in the bars and restaurant; the menu includes local meat, fish and cheese. Outside is a rear patio and large, beautifully landscaped beer garden, with a memorial to the circus elephant that is reputedly buried here. Q🐴✿🛏◐♿♣🍏P🚌(585,588)🐾📶

Whitland

Station House Hotel

St. Johns Street, SA34 0AP

☎ (01994) 240556 🌐 stationhousewhitland.co.uk

5 changing beers (often Felinfoel, Sharp's, Wye Valley) [H]

A warm welcome is always on tap in this friendly family-run pub. It is very much a local pub for all ages and offers something for everyone, including pool and darts teams, plus bingo on Sunday evenings. A small room is available for customers looking for a quiet corner. Five well-kept and ever-changing beers are always offered. The outside drinking area us partly covered, and there are individual covered booths. The pub is only 20 yards from the railway station. Car parking is to the rear.
✿◐🚆♣P🚌🐾📶

Breweries

Bluestone SIBA

Tyriet, Cilgwyn, SA42 0QW

☎ (01239) 820833 🌐 bluestonebrewing.co.uk

⊗ Family-run business established in 2013 on a working farm in the Preseli Hills, within the Pembrokeshire Coast National Park. The 10-barrel brewery is housed in the 300-year-old dairy, and has a visitor facility and office (see website for open times). Outdoor music and other events are held in the summer. Spring water, filtering down through the Preseli Bluestones to the brewery's well, gives the beers a unique taste. Local outlets plus wholesalers around the UK are supplied. Green Key accredited for environmental sustainability. ☛♦LIVE♦

Bedrock Blonde (ABV 4%) BLOND
Stone Cold (ABV 4.2%) PALE
Hammerstone IPA (ABV 4.5%) PALE
Rocketeer (ABV 4.6%) BITTER

Camel

Aberaeron, SA46 0BB ☎ 07539 466105
✉ alistair@cwrwcamel.com

New brewery set up in 2019, using spare capacity at Bluestone (qv). The beers are all unfined and suitable for vegans, and are produced in various forms of packaging. Brewing is currently suspended. **V**

Cardigan (Teifi)

Y Bryn a'r Bragdy, Brynhoffnant, SA44 6EA
☎ (01239) 614974 ☎ 07961 658701

Office: 5a Morgan Street, Cardigan, SA43 1DF
⊕ cardiganbrewery.com

Cardigan Brewery Ltd is a craft microbrewery that was established in 2021 and is part of the Innkeeper (UK) Ltd group of companies. All ales are available in the sister company, trading as the Teifi Waterside Hotel at Poppit, St Dogmaels, Cardigan. Its more traditional ales can be found under the Penlon brand name (bottles only), with the more innovative ales being under the Craft Dai brand, which can be purchased in cask, keg and bottle. LIVE♦

Coles Family

⬗ White Hart Thatched Inn & Brewery, Llanddarog, SA32 8NT
☎ (01267) 275395 ⊕ thebestpubinwales.co.uk

Brewpub based in the White Hart Inn. It uses a one-barrel plant and also produces a cider. Production invariably is for the pub only. ♦

Core of the Poodle (NEW) SIBA

26 Market Street, Haverfordwest, SA61 1NH

New nanobrewery located within a record shop in the town centre. It has produced a number of beers and is working towards a permanent range.

Electro

Unit 19, Parc Teifi, Cardigan, SA43 1EW

Office: Glenydd Cwmin St Dogmaels, Cardigan, SA43 3HF ✉ contact@electrobrewing.com

Artisan brewery with beers first appearing in 2021. Some of the output is one-off cask beers.

Old School Bitter (ABV 4.3%) BROWN

Evan Evans SIBA

1 Rhosmaen Street, Llandeilo, SA19 6LU
☎ (01558) 824455 ⊕ evanevansbrewery.com

> Where village statesmen talked with looks profound
> And news much older than the ale went round.
> **Alfred, Lord Tennyson**

⊠ Evan Evans brews six core beers and an array of seasonal beers. The company owns the Celt craft beer range and produces the unique Fire Island brand of gluten-free bottled beers. Evan-Evans and James Buckley beers form the traditional cask beer range. The Archers brand name is used for occasional beers. The brewery markets its own Redhog Wild Cider that is both gluten free and vegan-friendly. The brewery also bottles its own beer brands as well as bottling for other independent breweries. ‼☛♦LIVE GF

J Buckley Best Welsh Beer (ABV 4%) BITTER
WPA (Welsh Pale Ale) (ABV 4.1%) PALE
Cwrw (ABV 4.2%) BITTER
Wrecker (ABV 4.5%) BITTER
Sea Scape (ABV 4.6%) GOLD
Warrior (ABV 4.6%) BITTER

Felinfoel SIBA

Farmers Row, Felinfoel, Llanelli, SA14 8LB
☎ (01554) 773357 ⊕ felinfoel-brewery.com

Founded in the 1830s, the company is still family-owned and is now the oldest brewery in Wales. The present buildings are Grade II*-listed and were built in the 1870s. It supplies cask ale to half its 84 houses, though some use top pressure dispense, and to approximately 350 free trade outlets. ‼☛♦

Dragon Welsh IPA (ABV 3.6%) IPA
Dragon Stout (ABV 4.1%) STOUT
Double Dragon (ABV 4.2%) BITTER
This pale brown beer has a malty, fruity aroma. The taste is also malt and fruit with a background hop presence throughout. A malty and fruity finish.
Nut Brown Ale (ABV 4.3%) BITTER
Celtic Pride (ABV 4.5%) BITTER
Dragons Heart (ABV 4.5%) BITTER
Welsh ESB (ABV 4.6%) BITTER
Double Dragon Export (ABV 4.7%) BITTER

Gwaun Valley SIBA

Kilkiffeth Farm, Pontfaen, SA65 9TP ☎ 07854 767383
⊕ gwaunvalleybrewery.com

Founded in 2009, this microbrewery produces traditional and experimental ales. It has won many awards since being taken on by homebrewer Nigel Smith in 2019. Ales are available in cask, keg and bottle. Based on a campsite, tourists can hire a holiday cottage, tent or caravan pitches and enjoy folk music sessions once a month. ‼☛

Nutty 'Brown' Mild (ABV 4%) MILD
Traditional Porter (ABV 4.3%) PORTER
Pembrokeshire Best Bitter (ABV 4.5%) BITTER
St Davids Special (ABV 4.6%) GOLD
Cascade (ABV 4.7%) PALE
Cwrw Melyn (ABV 4.7%) BLOND
Cwrw Gwyn (ABV 5.3%) IPA

Harbwr Tenby SIBA

Sargeants Lane, St Julian Street, Tenby, SA70 7BU
☎ (01834) 845797 ⊕ harbwr.wales

Five-barrel brewing plant in an outbuilding of the Harbwr Tap & Kitchen (its associated pub). The beers are available in the pub as well as in the brewery itself, which has a mezzanine bar area overlooking the brewery. Information boards explain the building's history and the brewing process. The brewery offers a tour package named Hops and Hwyl. Beers are found at more than 20 outlets in South Wales. ‼♦♦

M V Enterprise (ABV 4%) PALE
North Star (ABV 4.2%) BITTER
Caldey Lollipop (ABV 4.5%) PALE
RFA Sir Galahad (ABV 4.6%) BITTER
La Nossa Signora (ABV 5%) SPECIALITY

Mantle

Unit 16, Pentood Industrial Estate, Cardigan, SA43 3AG
☎ (01239) 623898 ☎ 07552 609909
⊕ mantlebrewery.com

From start-up in 2013 on a 10-barrel plant, Mantle has become a major player in the West Wales area. Engineer Ian Kimber and his scientist wife Dominique, formerly home brewers, have built a sound reputation for consistent quality. Over 200 outlets are supplied direct with wider distribution via carefully selected wholesalers. ‼☛◆

Rock Steady (ABV 3.8%) GOLD
MOHO (ABV 4.3%) PALE
Cwrw Teifi (ABV 4.5%) BITTER
Dark Heart (ABV 5.2%) PORTER

Old Farmhouse SIBA

Upper Harglodd, St Davids, SA62 6BX

With a planned brewery name of St David's, later changed, Mark and Emma Evans commenced brewing in 2021 in a renovated farmhouse. The brewery uses home-grown grain and its own well water in the process.

St Davids

Grange Porthgain, Haverfordwest, SA62 5BJ

Office: Lecha Farm, SOLVA, Haverfordwest, SA62 6YD

Long-established trading concern which owns a number of pubs in far West Wales. It has no brewery and its range of bottled beers are contract brewed at Felinfoel.

Tenby

Unit 15, The Salterns, Tenby, SA70 8EQ
☎ (01834) 218090 ☎ 07410 169447
⊕ tenbybrewingco.com

Tenby Brewing Co have been brewing a diverse range of full-flavoured beers in South Pembrokeshire since 2015, including pale ales to stouts, and everything in between.

Energy used at the brewery is 90%+ sustainable, with the majority from an onsite solar array. Its taproom is open Friday and Saturday in the spring and summer. The brewery also owns bars at Tap & Tan, Tenby town centre, and Hwb Food Hall, Narberth. KeyKegs are a significant part of the output and cask beers are no longer produced. LIVE ◆

Tinworks SIBA

Unit 20.1, Trostre Industrial Park, Llanelli, SA14 9UU
☎ 07595 841958 ⊕ tinworksbrewery.co.uk

Brewery commenced operations on a rural farm but relocated and upgraded to a 10-barrel kit in 2019. Cask, bottled and keg beers are produced. ☛◆

Cwrw Grav (ABV 3.9%) BITTER
Old Castle Pale (ABV 4.6%) PALE
Marshfield Red (ABV 4.7%) RED
Ashburnham Porter (ABV 5%) PORTER
Dafen IPA (ABV 6.3%) IPA

Victoria Inn

⊟ Victoria Inn, Roch, Haverfordwest, SA62 6AW
☎ (01437) 710426 ☎ 07814 684975
⊕ thevictoriainnroch.com

⊠ A small brewery on the site of the pub which also offers B&B. In addition to the mainstay beers, occasional seasonals are produced. Check website for openings and special events as these may vary according to season. ‼◆

Zoo SIBA

ExCAL House, Capel Hendre Industrial Estate, Ammanford, SA18 3SJ ☎ 07889 592614
⊕ zoo-brew.com

⊠ Zoo Brew was established in 2019. It produces a small range of cask-conditioned and bottled ales. Beer is mainly supplied to local pubs plus home deliveries. The company has recently diversified into distilling.

Amman Eagle (ABV 4.4%) GOLD
Towy Tiger (ABV 5%) BITTER
Merlin's Own (ABV 5.2%) PALE

Spores for thought

Yeast is a fungus, a single cell plant that can convert a sugary liquid into equal proportions of alcohol and carbon dioxide. There are two basic types of yeast used in brewing, one for ale and one for lager. (The yeasts used to make the Belgian beers known as gueuze and lambic are wild spores in the atmosphere).

It is often said that ale is produced by 'top fermentation' and lager by 'bottom fermentation'. While it is true that during ale fermentation a thick blanket of yeast head and protein is created on top of the liquid while only a thin slick appears on top of fermenting lager, the descriptions are seriously misleading. Yeast works at all levels of the sugar-rich liquid in order to turn malt sugars into alcohol. If yeast worked only at the top or bottom of the liquid, a substantial proportion of sugar would not be fermented. Ale is fermented at a high temperature, lager at a much lower one. The furious speed of ale fermentation creates the yeast head and with it the rich, fruity aromas and flavours that are typical of the style. It is more accurate to describe the ale method as 'warm fermentation' and the lager one as 'cold fermentation'.

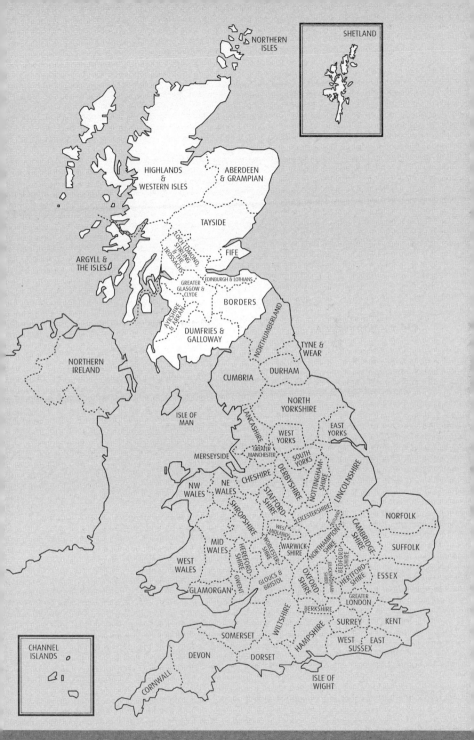

Scotland

Scotland

ABERDEEN & GRAMPIAN

Aberchirder

New Inn

79 Main Street, AB54 7TB
☎ (01466) 780633 ● newinnaberchirder.co.uk
3 changing beers (sourced nationally; often Orkney, Outlandish) Ⓗ
Extensively refurbished during Covid lockdowns, this traditional, friendly inn has wood-burning stoves, candlelit areas and a vintage atmosphere. It offers a changing selection of three quality ales. A separate dining area provides home-made food prepared by the owner/chef using locally sourced produce; the pork pies are highly recommended. Families with children are welcome in the dining room until 9pm and booking is recommended. Closed Monday, opens at 4pm other days. Q❄☎✿☎❶♿P🚃(301,303)♣🎵

Aberdeen

Archibald Simpson ⊘

5 Castle Street, AB11 5BQ (E end of Union S)
☎ (01224) 621365
Belhaven 80/-; Greene King Abbot; Sharp's Doom Bar; 9 changing beers (sourced nationally; often Orkney, Stewart, Windswept) Ⓗ
Wetherspoon pub in the former headquarters of Clydesdale Bank. It is named after local architect Archibald Simpson, who designed many of the city's monumental granite buildings. It has a pillared entrance and retains many original architectural features. The main room is a central hall with a high ceiling and additional seating areas to the side. Twelve handpumps offer beers mainly from Scottish breweries. There is a narrow outside drinking space on the pavement. Beer festivals are held several times a year. Alcohol served from 10am. ❄🎵♿⭐🚃🎵🎵

Blue Lamp

121 Gallowgate, AB25 1BU
☎ (01224) 647472 ● jazzatthebluelamp.com
2 changing beers (sourced regionally; often Cromarty, Orkney) Ⓟ
Time has stood still in this small public bar, where little has changed since the 60s. Next door, the cavernous converted warehouse is a popular music venue hosting the Aberdeen Jazz Festival each March, plus various other jazz events, a folk club, and bands at weekends (for which there may be a charge). Two ales available in lounge, and one in bar. A small, upstairs lounge is available for private functions and small gigs. Opening times midweek may vary but normally 5pm; the lounge is open till 2am at weekends. Closed Sundays.
♿🚃(11,727) 🎵♫

Globe Inn

13-15 North Silver Street, AB10 1RJ (off Golden Square)
☎ (01224) 641171 ⊕ the-globe-inn.com
3 changing beers (sourced regionally; often Cromarty, Stewart, Windswept) ⊞
This convivial open-plan pub reverted to private ownership in 2018 after being run by Belhaven for several years. It now serves up to three beers from a variety of Scottish breweries. Excellent food is served all day. Alfresco drinking and dining can take place in the beer garden, which may be partially covered in inclement weather. HM Theatre and the Music Hall are nearby; reasonably priced en-suite accommodation is available. Alcohol is served from 11am.
ॐ❀⇔∅⏸&⇌❀⏰☂

Grill ★

213 Union Street, AB11 6BA
☎ (01224) 583563 ⊕ thegrillaberdeen.co.uk
4 changing beers (sourced regionally; often Cromarty, Orkney, Windswept) ⊞
With an exquisite interior redesigned in 1926, this is the only pub in the area identified by CAMRA is having a nationally important historic pub interior. It has been part of the McGinty's Group since 2019. The ale pumps are now all in a central position, offering guest beers mainly from various Scottish breweries. The large selection of whiskies has won numerous awards. Bar snacks, including stovies, are available. Musicians appearing at the Music Hall opposite often visit during concert breaks. A former local CAMRA Pub of the Year. ⇌🖵☂

Justice Mill ⬤

423 Union Street, AB11 6DA
☎ (01224) 252410
Belhaven 80/-; Greene King Abbot; Sharp's Doom Bar; 3 changing beers (sourced nationally; often Broughton, Spey Valley, Stewart) ⊞
Long, narrow, dark Wetherspoon pub, with some raised seating near the bar and booths at both the main entrance and the rear entrance on Justice Mil Lane – hence its name. The quiet, family-friendly atmosphere during the day changes to a louder one favoured by many of the younger clientele in the evenings. There is often a DJ playing from 8pm at weekends. The pub has two statement art pieces: a statue of an upside down man and a fire behind glass. Alcohol is served from 11am every day. ॐ⏸&⇌♣🖵☂

Krakatoa

2 Trinity Quay, AB11 5AA (facing quayside at bottom of Market St)
☎ (01224) 587602 ⊕ krakatoa.bar
10 changing beers (sourced regionally; often Cromarty, Swannay, Windswept) ⏸
This historic harbourside bar, owned by the Black Cat Worker Collective, changes character from a friendly, laid-back local to a raucous rock bar on weekend evenings, when there may be a cover charge. The eclectic jukebox is popular with the varied clientele. A wide selection of Scottish ales is served on up to 12 American-style fonts, and a varied selection of Belgian beers and ciders is also available, plus a variety of cocktails. A former local CAMRA City Pub of the Year.
&⇌♣🖵🖩❀☂♫

Prince of Wales ⬤

7 St Nicholas Lane, AB10 1HF (lane opp Marks & Spencer, parallel to Union St)
☎ (01224) 640597 ⊕ princeofwales-aberdeen.co.uk
Greene King IPA, Abbot; 6 changing beers (sourced nationally; often Cromarty, Fyne, Stewart) ⊞

One of the oldest bars in Aberdeen, the Prince has possibly the longest bar counter in the city, a large following of regulars and a friendly atmosphere buzzing with conversation. The bar has been identified by CAMRA as having a nationally important historic pub interior. It offers a varied selection of ales from up to eight pumps, though lately only four at any one time, mostly from Scottish breweries, with tasters for the undecided. Good-value food is served daily including filled rolls. A prize quiz is on Thursday and open mic on Friday. May close earlier if not busy. Q♿⏸⇌🖵☂♫

Queen Vic

126 Rosemount Place, AB25 2YU (approx 10 mins' walk from W end of Union St)
☎ (01224) 638500 ⊕ queenvicaberdeen.co.uk
Timothy Taylor Landlord; 3 changing beers (sourced nationally; often Burnside, Orkney, Windswept) ⊞
A cosy one-room locals' lounge bar, slightly off the beaten track in two converted shops in the Rosemount residential area. Sporting events are frequently shown, when the pub can get extremely busy and noisy. Guest cask ales are mainly from a variety of Scottish breweries. A popular quiz featuring a Play Your Cards Right jackpot is held on Monday evening and live bands play occasionally at weekends. No food is served but online deliveries are allowed. A former local and city CAMRA Pub of the Year.
🖵(3,3A)❀☂♫

St Machar Bar 🏆

97 High Street, Old Aberdeen, AB24 3EN (near Kings College)
☎ (01224) 483079
3 changing beers (sourced regionally; often Cromarty, Orkney, Stewart) ⊞
Located in the photogenic Old Aberdeen conservation area amid the university buildings, this historic pub is frequented by academia and locals alike. The bar features a splendid Thomson Marshall Aulton brewery mirror and an original Devanha one. Usually three beers are available from a variety of Scottish breweries. The pub has a growing reputation as a whisky destination and hosts monthly 'Drams for Bams' tastings. Food is burgers and buckets. The bar is home to a darts team and the university football and rugby teams. Local CAMRA Pub of the Year 2023. ❀⏸♣🖵(20)❀☂

Under the Hammer

11 North Silver Street, AB10 1RJ (off Golden Square)
☎ (01224) 640253 ⊕ underthehammeraberdeen.co.uk
Timothy Taylor Landlord; 3 changing beers (often Black Isle, Cromarty, Orkney) ⊞
Located in a quiet side street near Golden Square, just minutes off Union Street, this popular pub is located in a basement next to Milne's auction house – hence the name. The pub underwent a major refurbishment after being closed for a couple of years, and was reopened in 2021 by the local McGintys pub group. It sells one guest ale from mainly Scottish breweries, and some from local Fierce brewery, in addition to Landlord. Cocktails are also offered. Food consists of sharing platters. Q⏸⇌☂♫

Aboyne

Boat Inn

Charleston Road, AB34 5EL (N bank of River Dee next to Aboyne Bridge)
☎ (01339) 886137 ⊕ theboatinnaboyne.co.uk
3 changing beers (sourced nationally; often Belhaven) ⊞
Popular riverside inn with a food-oriented lounge. Junior diners (and adults) may request to see the model train, complete with sound effects, traverse the entire pub at

picture-rail height upon completion of their meal. The Shed public bar has a recess at the back used for live music nights. Three ales are served in summer, two in winter, usually at least one from Belhaven and another from a local brewery. Breakfast is served. Fifteen twin rooms and a family room are available for overnight stays. Q ⚲ ⊨ ◐ & ▲ ♣ P ✿ 🛜 ♫

Ballater

Alexandra Hotel

12 Bridge Square, AB35 5QJ
☎ (01339) 755376 ⊕ alexandrahotelballater.co.uk
Cairngorm Trade Winds; 2 changing beers (sourced regionally; often Cairngorm) ⊞
Originally built as a private home in 1800, this friendly, family-owned lounge bar became the Alexandra Hotel in 1915. It is popular both with locals and those visiting for bar suppers. Three Cairngorm ales are available in summer; generally just two in winter. Benches outside at the front are ideal for alfresco drinking, and there is a beer garden to the rear. A handy stop-off on your way to Braemar for the Highland Games or on a visit with the royals at Balmoral. ⚲ ✿ ⊨ ◐ & ▲ ♥ (201) ✿ 🛜

Balmoral Bar

1 Netherley Place, AB35 5QE
☎ (01339) 755462
Braemar Pale; 1 changing beer (sourced regionally; often Cairngorm) ⊞
Smart, modern, public bar, situated on a corner opposite the village square in this picturesque Deeside village. Six large screens show sports and news while the adjacent pool room also has two large screens. An old poster on the wall shows the coach timetable from Aberdeen of days gone by. Food is served every day.
⚲ ◐ ▲ ♣ ♥ (201) ✿ 🛜 ♫

Glenaden Hotel

6 Church Square, AB35 5NE
☎ (01339) 755488
2 changing beers (sourced regionally; often Windswept) ⊞
Situated on the far side of this picturesque town square, this small hotel displays a prominent external sign for its Barrel Lounge. It normally serves three beers in busy periods, usually Scottish, mostly from Windswept. Darker ales are apparently favoured by the locals. There is a large function suite and a beer garden at the rear of the hotel. Q ⚲ ✿ ⊨ ◐ ♣ P ♥ (201) ✿ 🛜 ♫

Banchory

Ravenswood Club (Royal British Legion)

25 Ramsay Road, AB31 5TS (up Mount St from A93, then second right)
☎ (01330) 822347 ⊕ banchorylegion.co.uk
2 changing beers (sourced nationally) ⊞
Large British Legion club with a comfortable lounge adjoining the pool and TV room and a spacious function room frequently used by local clubs and societies as well as members. Darts and snooker are popular and played most evenings. The two handpumps offer excellent value and the beer choice is constantly changing. An elevated terrace has fine views of the Deeside hills. Show a copy of this Guide or your CAMRA membership card for entry. ⚲ ✿ ⊨ ◐ & ▲ ♣ P 🛜 ♫

Banff

Market Arms

5 High Shore, AB45 1DB
☎ (01261) 818616
1 changing beer (sourced nationally; often Morland, Ruddles, Timothy Taylor) ⊞
This fine building is one of the oldest in historic Banff, dating back to 1585. The courtyard at the back retains many original features. The long public bar has several fine examples of historic brewery and distillery mirrors. One of the two handpumps always serves a changing beer, with two beers on at weekends and holidays. The impressive upstairs lounge is used mainly for meals. The Banff tourist hub is around the corner. ⚲ ◐ & ▲ ♣ ♥ ✿ 🛜

Braemar

Invercauld Mews

Glenshee Road, AB35 5YR
☎ 07710 596629
Cairngorm Stag, Trade Winds; 2 changing beers (sourced locally; often Braemar, Cairngorm) ⊞
The Mews Bar lies in a separate building behind the Invercauld Hotel and reopened in 2020 after a full refurbishment that restored the bar to the same way it looked when it closed in 2002. Four brand new handpulls were installed, with ales supplied all year round, mainly by Cairngorm brewery plus at least one from the local Braemar brewery. There is substantial outdoor seating on the grass outside. Opening hours may be subject to seasonal change. Q ⚲ & ▲ ♣ P ♥ (201) ✿ 🛜

Craigellachie

Highlander Inn

10 Victoria Street, AB38 9SR (on A95, opp post office)
☎ (01340) 881446 ⊕ whiskyinn.com
3 changing beers (often Orkney, Spey Valley, Windswept) ⊞
Picturesque whisky and cask ale bar on Speyside's Whisky Trail, close to the Speyside Way and twinned with the Highlander Whisky Bar in Tokyo. It offers a fine selection of malt whiskies, including many Japanese ones, plus up to three ales. CRAC (Craigellachir Real Ale Club) meet on the first Wednesday of the month, and its members help to choose the pub's guest ales. An outside decked area with tables and chairs is a delight on a sunny afternoon. ⚲ ✿ ⊨ ◐ ▲ P ♥ (36) 🛜 ♫

Dyce

Spider's Web

19 Station Road, AB21 7BA (near railway station)
☎ (01224) 772092 ⊕ spiderswebpub.co.uk
1 changing beer (sourced nationally; often Caledonian, Orkney) ⊞
Formerly a shop until 1970, and conveniently situated only yards from Dyce railway station, this village pub has a comfy two-level lounge to the left and a separate public bar on the right. One pump serves a varying beer, sometimes Deuchars IPA or one from the Orkney range. Meals are served all day in the lounge, with the menu changing in the early evening. There are regular trains to Aberdeen and Inverurie. ⚲ ◐ ⇌ P ♥ ✿ 🛜 ♫

Elgin

Muckle Cross ✅

34 High Street, IV30 1BU
☎ (01343) 559030

Belhaven 80/-; Greene King Abbot; Sharp's Doom Bar; 6 changing beers (sourced regionally; often Orkney, Windswept) Ⓗ

A typical small Wetherspoon pub converted from what was once a bicycle repair shop. Refurbished in 2018, the pleasant long room has ample seating, a family area and a long bar. Deservedly popular, it can be busy, particularly at weekends. Twelve handpumps (some duplicates) offer a wide range of beers from national and Scottish microbreweries, and ciders are available during the annual cider fest. Two beer festivals are held annually. Q❀🕏⊕🕼🅑♿🚆♣🚌🚪🛈🔌🅿

Ellon

Tolbooth

21-23 Station Road, AB41 9AE (opp public library)
☎ (01358) 721308

3 changing beers (sourced nationally; often Cairngorm, Cromarty, Orkney) Ⓗ

A large pub, popular with all ages, close to the town centre and just a short walk from the bus stops on Market Street. There are separate seating areas on split levels as well as an airy conservatory with barrel tables and a patio garden area for alfresco drinking. Two Scottish and one English guest ale, often Directors or London Pride, are usually available. No food is served. Several National Trust Scotland properties are nearby. Handy for buses to Aberdeen or Peterhead/Fraserburgh. 🕏❀🕼♿🚆🚌♣🛈🔌🎵

Forres

Mosset Tavern Ⓛ

Gordon Street, IV36 1DY
☎ (01309) 672981 ⊕ mossettavern.com

5 changing beers (sourced locally; often Spey Valley, Swannay, Windswept) Ⓗ

Described as 'the country pub in the heart of Forres', this smart, extremely popular Scottish lounge bar/restaurant is situated next to the Mosset burn and pond. Friendly, efficient staff serve ale from a single handpump in the lounge and up to five in the spacious, comfortable public bar, where there are pool tables and large screens showing sport. A large function room is also available, home to the Foot Tapper beer festival in June. Live music plays on Friday evening, and there is a pub quiz every Tuesday. Local CAMRA Country Pub of the Year 2022.
🕏❀🍴⊕🕼♿🚆♣🅿🚪(10) 🛈🔌🎵

Fraserburgh

Elizabethan Bar & Lounge

36 Union Grove, AB43 9PH (10 mins' walk from A90)
☎ (01346) 510464

3 changing beers (sourced regionally; often Kelburn, Windswept) Ⓗ

Set in the middle of a housing estate, with a mock-Tudor exterior, the pub has a public bar, games room with four dartboards and two pool tables, and a lounge bar with a largescreen TV usually featuring sport. The bar has a formidable reputation for offering a wide range of quality ales sourced from throughout the country, and also features an extensive range of malts – the largest collection in the area. The beach, harbour and lighthouse museum are a mile away. A former local CAMRA Pub of the Year. May not open till 5pm midweek.
🕏♿♣🅿🚪🛈🔌🎵

Garlogie

Garlogie Inn

AB32 6RX (B9125 W of Westhill just before B9119 jct)

☎ (01224) 743212 ⊕ garlogieinn.com

1 changing beer (sourced regionally; often Cairngorm) Ⓗ

This roadside inn dates from the early 19th century and has been owned and run by the same family since 1986. Numerous extensions have been added to the original building, forming a large restaurant area. It has a reputation for excellent food – booking advised. Drinkers are welcome in the small bar area, which has a collection of coffee mugs hanging up relating to a variety of football clubs. The one beer is sourced from a variety of local and regional breweries. Drum Castle and Cullerlie stone circle are close by. Q🕏❀🕼♿🅿🛈🎵

Gourdon

Harbour Bar

William Street, DD10 0LW
☎ (01561) 361337

1 changing beer (sourced regionally) Ⓗ

Traditional seafaring decor abounds in this harbourside howff. It has a public bar, a smaller taproom, and a separate pool room with more seating. Nationally sourced beers are offered in winter and local ales during the summer season. An extension to the bar is expected to be finished before this Guide is published. It is handy for the Maggie Law lifeboat museum and next door to the locally renowned Quayside Fish & Chip restaurant.
🕏❀⊕♿♣🅿🚪(747) 🛈🔌🎵

Huntly

Crown Bar

4 Gordon Street, AB54 8AJ
☎ (01466) 792244

Windswept Wolf; 1 changing beer (sourced locally; often Spey Valley) Ⓟ

Bar situated just off the main square in the centre of Huntly. It consists of an original, small, but airy public bar, and a separate lounge, labelled 'Harry's Lounge and Beer Garden', accessed from Richmond Lane. The ale is dispensed from the lounge but is served in either bar. It is served on KeyKeg and like all Windswept beers, is unfined and unfiltered. The small outdoor drinking area closes at 10pm and is accessed from the lounge.
🕏♣🚆♣🚪(10,301) 🛈🔌

Inverurie

Gordon Highlander ✔

West High Street, AB51 3QQ
☎ (01467) 626780

Belhaven 80/-; Greene King Abbot; Sharp's Doom Bar; 4 changing beers (sourced nationally; often Orkney, Strathaven, Windswept) Ⓗ

A fine Wetherspoon conversion of a splendid Art Deco building which used to be the Victoria Cinema. The name refers to a locomotive built at the now defunct Inverurie Locomotive Works and there are many references to this throughout the pub. The famout Gordon Highlander Regiment also features prominently, with displays and a large mural. The books on the shelves are free to borrow, with donations welcome. There are at least three guest ales, the occasional real cider, and the usual Wetherspoon beer festivals. 🕏⊕♿🚆🚪(10,37)🔌

Lossiemouth

Windswept Tap Room

13 Coulardbank Industrial Estate, IV31 6NG
☎ (01343) 814310 ⊕ windsweptbrewing.com/tap-room

2 changing beers (sourced locally; often Windswept) Ⓟ
This small industrial/office unit, converted to a taproom for the brewery next door, has an industrial-chic decor and furniture fashioned from pallets. It is now the only outlet for real ale in Lossiemouth. Two varying cask ales are supplemented by eight KeyKeg beers. Coffee, tea, soft drinks, cakes and snacks are sold, as well as a range of bottled beers and brewery merchandise. The bar is available for private hire and may host the occasional weekend beer festival. Dogs are welcome till 6pm. Onn some days it may only be open for merchandise and takeaway beer; best to check. ❀Ⓟ🚋(33A,33C)📶

Methlick

Ythanview Hotel
Main Street, AB41 7DT
☎ (01651) 806235 ⊕ ythanviewhotel.co.uk
2 changing beers (sourced regionally; often Fyne, Swannay) Ⓗ
Traditional inn in the village centre, home to the Methlick Cricket Club at nearby Lairds. Log fires warm both the lounge bar at the front and the friendly sports-themed public bar at the rear. Beers are exclusively from Scottish micros. The restaurant is renowned for the owner's special chicken curry, and steak night on Thursday is popular. Meals are served all day at weekends. Live music and quiz nights take place on most Saturdays. Haddo House, Tolquhon Castle and Pitmedden Garden are nearby. Closed weekday afternoons.
🛏❀🍴◗♣Ⓟ🚋(290,291)❀📶♪

Newtonhill

Newton Arms
10 Old Mill Road, AB39 3TZ
☎ (01569) 730227
1 changing beer (sourced regionally; often Cromarty, Orkney) Ⓗ
Traditional village local with a classic, dark-wood panelled public bar, featuring 1950s bar counters, intriguing under-counter shelves for drinks and an original Devanha brewery mirror. The lounge at the side has light-wood panelling and tables. Up to two beers may be available in the public bar only, but there is usually just one. No food, but you can bring in a curry from the restaurant next door. There is an east-facing patio to the rear for alfresco drinking. Stagecoach no 7 bus stops close to the pub. 🛏❀♣Ⓟ🚋(7)❀📶♪

Oldmeldrum

Redgarth 🏆
Kirk Brae, AB51 0DJ (signposted off A947)
☎ (01651) 872353 ⊕ redgarth.com
3 changing beers (sourced regionally; often Cromarty, Fyne, Swannay) Ⓖ
Offering a warm welcome and excellent views of the eastern Grampian mountains, the Redgarth celebrates 34 years under the same ownership in January 2024. The emphasis is on excellent beers served on gravity, with three handpumps on the bar to show which ales are available. Extra choice is offered during occasional Brewer in Residence evenings. Meals are served in the bar and in a separate restaurant area. A winner of many CAMRA awards, including local Country Pub of the Year 2023, it retains a strong reputation for its imaginative choice of Scottish beers. Closed afternoons except Sunday. 🛏❀🍴◗Ⓐ♣Ⓟ🚋(35,305)📶♪

Peterhead

Cross Keys ✅
23-27 Chapel Street, AB42 1TH
☎ (01779) 483500
Belhaven 80/-; Greene King Abbot; Sharp's Doom Bar; 3 changing beers (sourced nationally; often Orkney) Ⓗ
A typical Wetherspoon outlet in the centre of a bustling port, close to the local museum where you can learn about the town's maritime history. The pub is named after the chapel dedicated to St Peter that previously stood on the site. The long single room has the bar towards the front and a large seating area at the rear. A sheltered and heated area outside caters for hardy souls and smokers. Children are welcome until 9pm if dining. Alcohol served from 9am. Q🛏❀🍴◗&Ⓐ♣🚻🚋📶

Pitmedden

Craft Bar
Tarves Road, AB41 7NX
☎ (01651) 842049 ⊕ thecraftpitmedden.wordpress.com
2 changing beers (sourced regionally; often Orkney, Spey Valley, Windswept) Ⓗ
A one-room corner pub run by a enthusiastic local CAMRA member. Old church pews provide seating for some of the tables around the walls; other tables have bench seating. Two handpumps serve ales from Scottish breweries, supplemented by a wide variety of KeyKeg beers from UK breweries. There is also a comprehensive range of bottled and canned beer for takeaway in the fridge, with much of the pub taken up as the village off-licence (these may be consumed on the premises for a small fee). Occasional Brewer in Residence evenings are held. Snacks are available. 🛏Ⓐ♣Ⓟ🚋(290, 291)❀📶♪

Portsoy

Shore Inn
Church Street, AB45 2QR (overlooking harbour)
☎ (01261) 842831
2 changing beers (sourced regionally; often Kelburn, Spey Valley, Windswept) Ⓗ
Cosy, comfortable, coastal howff with a warm welcome inside in winter and scenic outdoor views in summer of the oldest harbour on the Moray Coast (it was a location for the 2016 remake of Whisky Galore). The L-shaped room with low ceilings is a fine example of a nautical bar. Expect it to be busy during Boat Festival in early July. Only one beer is normally available in winter months. No food is served. 🛏❀Ⓐ♣❀📶♪

Stonehaven

Marine Hotel
9-10 Shorehead, AB39 2JY (overlooking harbour)
☎ (01569) 762155 ⊕ marinehotelstonehaven.co.uk
7 changing beers (sourced regionally; often Cairngorm, Windswept, Cromarty) Ⓗ
Once the only outlet for Six°North cask ales, it is now often available in some independent pubs. This small harbourside hotel features simple wood panelling in the bar and a rustic lounge with an open fireplace. Seating outside offers a splendid view of the harbour. An ale from Six°North and several varieties from other breweries are served, plus numerous Belgian and up to 18 craft keg beers. Historic Dunnottar Castle is one mile south and the open-air bathing pool one mile north. 🛏❀🍴◗Ⓐ🚻🚋(747,X7)❀📶

Ship Inn

5 Shorehead, AB39 2JY (on harbour front)
☎ (01569) 762617 ⊕ shipinnstonehaven.com
2 changing beers (sourced regionally; often Cromarty, Inveralmond, Orkney) Ⓗ

Built in 1771, this harbour-front hotel has a maritime-themed, wood-panelled bar and a small seating area outside overlooking the water. The long, narrow bar features a mirror from the defunct Devanha brewery. Two beers are available, both usually from the same Scottish brewery, plus a KeyKeg from local Reids Gold, and an extensive range of malt whiskies. A modern restaurant with panoramic harbour views is adjacent to the bar —fish is the speciality and food is served all day at the weekend. Accommodation is available in 11 guest rooms. ♿✿🛏️◐&🅿️ (747,X7)😺🎱

Breweries

Big Fish

c/o 45 Glenury Crescent, Stonehaven, AB39 3LF
✉ info@brewscotland.com

A nomad brewery established in 2017. Collaboration brews form part of the brewery strategy.

Braemar SIBA

Airlie House, Chapel Brae, Braemar, AB35 5YT
☎ 07709 199914 ⊕ brewbraemar.uk

Small brewery founded in 2021 and located next to Hazelnut Patisserie. It produces cask and bottle-conditioned ales using Scottish malt and British hops. Bottled beers are available direct from the brewery.

Oat Stout (ABV 4%) STOUT
Braemar Pale (ABV 4.2%) PALE
Summer Sun (ABV 4.5%) GOLD
80/- (ABV 5%) BITTER

Brew Toon SIBA

72a St Peter Street, Peterhead, AB42 1QB
☎ (01779) 560948 ⊕ brewtoon.co.uk

Established in 2017, beers are brewed in small batches.
🍷

Brewdog

Balmacassie Industrial Estate, Ellon, AB41 8BX
☎ (01358) 724924 ⊕ brewdog.com

Established in 2007 by James Watt and Martin Dickie. Most of the production goes into cans and keg. The first Brewdog brewery outside of Ellon opened in Tower Hill, London, in 2018. Another site opened in 2022 underneath the former Eurostar platforms at Waterloo station, London, and claims to have the largest bar in London. More than 50 bars now exist in the UK. ‼🍽️🍷

Burnside SIBA

Unit 3, Laurencekirk Business Park, Laurencekirk, AB30 1EY
☎ (01561) 377316 ⊕ burnsidebrewery.co.uk

⊠ Burnside began brewing in 2010 using a 2.5-barrel plant and by 2012 had expanded to a 10-barrel plant. It

> Bread is the staff of life, but beer is life itself. **Traditional**

changed ownership in 2018, since when the focus has been on developing a range of cask and bottle-conditioned beers, including new seasonal bottled beers, plus collaborations with local businesses such as Smoke-and-Soul and Figment Coffee. Barrel-aged beers are produced using Fettercairn Distillery casks. Free delivery between Montrose, Banchory, Aberdeen, Dundee and everywhere in-between. It offers brewer experiences.
‼🍽️LIVE

New Tricks (ABV 3.8%) IPA
Lift & Shift (ABV 4%) PALE
Flint's Gold (ABV 4.1%) BITTER
Chain & Anchor (ABV 4.2%) PALE
Lost Shadow (ABV 4.4%) STOUT
Wild Rhino (ABV 4.5%) GOLD
Stone River (ABV 5%) IPA
Sunset Song (ABV 5.3%) BITTER

Clinkstone

The Steading, Seggiecrook, Insch, AB52 6NR ☎ 07583 027179 ✉ info@clinkstonebrewing.com

Farm-based brewery commissioned in mid-2021. Clinkstone Brewing Company uses sustainable natural resources to produce hop-forward beers predominantly available in small pack formats. No real ale.

Copper Fox

c/o 3 Essie Road, Rhynie, AB54 4GF
☎ (01464) 833289 ☎ 07484 386496
⊕ copperfoxbrewery.co.uk

⊠ Copper Fox Brewery Ltd, founded in 2017, is an independently-run, one-man, small batch microbrewery based in Rhynie, Aberdeenshire. Production is exclusively in 330ml bottles, with 10p credit on bottle returns. Beers can be found at farmer's markets in the region and in Westhill. LIVE

Fierce SIBA

Unit 60, Howe Moss Terrace, Dyce, Aberdeen, AB21 0GR
☎ (01224) 035035 ⊕ fiercebeer.com

The multi award-winning Fierce Beer was established by Dave Grant and David McHardy, brewing its first beer in 2016. It produces a range of hoppy, fruity, dark and speciality beers. Production is cask, KeyKeg and cans. Three bars are owned, in Aberdeen, Edinburgh and Manchester. A taproom was opened in 2023. 🍷

Keith

Malcomburn, Mulben, Keith, AB55 5DD
☎ (01542) 488006 ⊕ keithbrewery.co.uk

Formerly known as Brewmeister and established in 2012, the brewery was renamed Keith Brewery in 2015. It moved production to Malcolmburn, Mulben, sharing facilities with Spey Valley Brewery (qv). Keith Brewery is part of the Consolidated Craft Breweries Group ‼🍽️♦LIVE

LabRat

Office: 33 Bernham Avenue, Stonehaven, AB39 2WD
☎ 07542 072774

Commercial nanobrewer Peter Mackenzie started brewing in 2019, producing beers based on international styles.

Mad Bush

Office: 136 Gardner Drive, Aberdeen, AB12 5SA
⊕ madbushbeer.com

Mad Bush Beer is a small brewery based in Aberdeen producing bottled beers.

Quiet

🍴 Woodend Barn, Burn O Bennie, Banchory, AB31 5QA
☎ (01330) 826530 ⊕ buchananfood.com

Quiet Brewery produces bottle-conditioned beers, supplied to Buchanan's Bistro, Banchory. ◆LIVE

Reids Gold

61 Provost Barclay Drive, Stonehaven, AB39 2GE
⊕ reidsgold.com

The brewery was established in 2018. It is a small-batch microbrewery with an average weekly production of five barrels. Beers are unfiltered and unpasteurised and available in cans and mini-kegs.

Six ° North

Reekie House, Aberdeen Road, Laurencekirk, AB30 1AG
☎ (01561) 377047 ☎ 07840 678243
⊕ sixdnorth.co.uk

⊗ Established in 2013, the brewery brews beers in the Belgian tradition, using a purpose-built, 470-hectolitre plant. Depending on beer style, the beers are supplied as cask or keg. ‼◆LIVE

Chopper Stout (ABV 4.1%) STOUT
Roasted coffee malted, with background liquorice.

Spey Valley SIBA

Malcolmburn, Mulben, Keith, AB55 6YH
☎ (01542) 488006 ☎ 07780 655199
⊕ speyvalleybrewery.co.uk

⊗ Founded in 2007, Spey Valley Brewery merged with Keith Brewery in 2018 and is part of the Consolidated Craft Breweries Group, along with Alechemy Brewing (qv). It brews on a 20-barrel plant on a purpose-built site at Mulben. Brewing capacity was increased in 2022. ‼🍺◆

Sunshine on Keith (ABV 3.5%) BITTER
Golden, malt with a light citrus bitter hop. Name is a play on Proclaimers song.
Any Time /Winter time (ABV 4%) BLOND
David's Not So Bitter (ABV 4.4%) BITTER
Light brown with a good mix of malts, hops and red fruits.
Stillman's IPA (ABV 4.6%) SPECIALITY
Amber hoppy bitter with a whisky background.
Spey's Hopper (ABV 5%) SPECIALITY

Spey Stout (ABV 5.4%) STOUT
Excellent name and a good thick dark malty stout with a smoky blackcurrant background.

Speyside

10-11 West Road, Greshop Industrial Estate, Forres, IV36 2GW
☎ (01309) 763041 ⊕ speysidecraftbrewery.com

Based in a traditional whisky-producing area, Speyside Brewery uses the same water that goes into the region's whisky. A number of local outlets are supplied. Following suspension of brewing in 2020 the brewery resumed production in 2023 in bigger premises with a larger 8-hectolitre plant, just yards from its previous home. Beer is available in bottle and membrane keg. ◆

Twisted Ankle

The Old Mill Of Kincraigie, Aboyne, AB34 4TT
☎ 07814 922442
✉ twistedanklebrewco@gmail.com

Twisted Ankle is a small-batch microbrewery situated in the Howe of Cromar, Aberdeenshire, using home grown hops. Beer is available in bottles at local farmers markets in Aboyne and Ballater. It regularly produces cask and bottle-conditioned ale. LIVE

Windswept SIBA

Unit B, 13 Coulardbank Industrial Estate, Lossiemouth, IV31 6NG
☎ (01343) 814310 ⊕ windsweptbrewing.co.uk

Windswept Brewing Co was established in 2012 and is situated near the gates of RAF Lossiemouth. It is run by two CAMRA members who are former Tornado pilots. The brewery has developed to include a bar (open Friday-Saturday), shop (six days a week) and regular tours. Bottle-conditioned beers and small casks can be ordered online and delivered locally. ‼🍺LIVE 🍷

Blonde (ABV 4%) PALE
Smooth, golden, citrus hoppy brew with hints of peach. Slight malty background.
APA (ABV 5%) PALE
Good mix of malts and grapefruited hop throughout. Tangy finish.
Weizen (ABV 5.2%) SPECIALITY
Cloudy wheat beer full of bananas and pear drops with a hint of spices
Wolf (ABV 6%) OLD
Dark, strong tasting, slightly sweet, roasted malty brew with chocolate and a vanilla coffee background and a bitter finish.

Choosing pubs

CAMRA members and branches choose the pubs listed in the Good Beer Guide. There is no payment for entry, and pubs are inspected on a regular basis by personal visits. CAMRA branches monitor all the pubs in their areas, and the choice of pubs for the guide is often the result of democratic vote at branch meetings. However, recommendations from readers are welcomed and will be passed on to the relevant branch: write to Good Beer Guide, CAMRA, 230 Hatfield Road, St Albans, Hertfordshire, AL1 4LW; or send an email to: **gbgeditor@camra.org.uk**

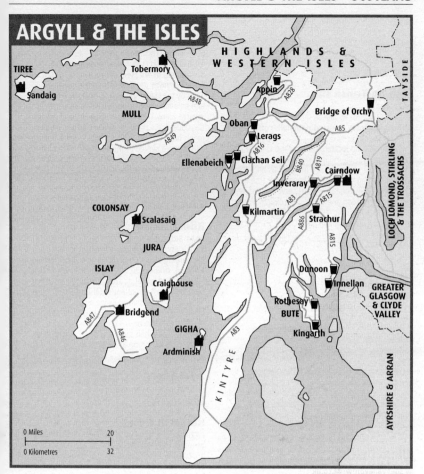

ARGYLL & THE ISLES

[Map of Argyll & the Isles showing locations including Tiree, Sandaig, Tobermory, Mull, Appin, Oban, Lerags, Ellenabeich, Clachan Seil, Bridge of Orchy, Cairndow, Inveraray, Colonsay, Scalasaig, Jura, Kilmartin, Strachur, Islay, Craighouse, Dunoon, Innellan, Bridgend, Rothesay, Bute, Kingarth, Gigha, Ardminish, and surrounding regions: Highlands & Western Isles, Tayside, Loch Lomond, Stirling & The Trossachs, Greater Glasgow & Clyde Valley, Ayrshire & Arran]

0 Miles 20
0 Kilometres 32

Appin

Creagan Inn

Creagan, PA38 4BQ (on A828 ½ mile N of Loch Creran bridge)

☎ (01631) 730250 ∰ creaganinn.co.uk

2 changing beers (sourced regionally; often Fyne) Ⓗ
Originally a ferryman's house, the inn is set in a beautiful location on the shores of Loch Creran. Up to two cask beers are available, one of them from Fyne Ales. Local produce is prominent on the menu, with ever-changing daily specials, and there is a good selection of vegetarian and vegan options. There is a limited bus service from Oban and Fort William. Opening times can vary and the pub sometimes closes over winter – phone ahead.
Q ☰ ✿ ⓓ ♿ P ⍐ (405,918) ♣ 🛜

Bridge of Orchy

Bridge of Orchy Hotel

PA36 4AD

☎ (01838) 400208 ∰ bridgeoforchy.co.uk

Harviestoun Bitter & Twisted; 1 changing beer (sourced regionally) Ⓗ
Situated on the A82, leading north to Glencoe, Fort William and Skye, and with a railway station not far away, this remote hotel is surprisingly accessible. It serves as a convenient resting spot for walkers on the West Highland Way. The bar and lounge at the front are heated by iron stoves and the restaurant to the rear gives a panoramic view of the mountains. Local produce is well represented on the menu. Sometimes closes over winter – phone ahead. ☰ ✿ ⌂ ⓓ ⍐ P ⍐ (915) ♣ 🛜

Cairndow

Fyne Ales Brewery Tap Ⓛ

Achadunan, PA26 8BJ (up side road at head of Loch Fyne)

☎ (01499) 600120 ∰ fyneales.com/visit

Fyne Jarl; 4 changing beers (sourced locally; often Fyne) Ⓗ
Brewery tap and shop in what was originally a farm building. The bar, with its fine polished granite front, sells a range of beers from the brewery along with a full and varied selection of bottled beers. An impressive array of brewing award certificates can be seen above the shelves displaying the beers for sale. Snacks are available

REAL ALE BREWERIES

Bun Dubh 🍺 Sandaig: Isle of Tiree
Colonsay Scalasaig: Isle of Colonsay
Fyne ✦ Cairndow
Gigha Ardminish: Isle of Gigha (NEW)
Islay ✦ Bridgend: Isle of Islay
Jura Isle of Jura: Craighouse
ToBEERmory Tobermory: Isle of Mull (NEW)

at weekends but visitors can bring their own food. The shop is open until 6pm each day, but closed on some public holidays. Q ▷ ☆ & P ♣ 🕯 ♥ 📶

Clachan Seil

Tigh-an-Truish Inn

PA34 4QZ
☎ (01852) 300242 ⊕ tigh-an-truish.co.uk
2 changing beers (sourced nationally; often Fyne, Loch Lomond) ⊞

This charming inn located just over the Clachan Bridge – the 'Bridge over the Atlantic' – is worth a diversion off the A816. The rustic wooden interior has an L-shaped counter with an unusual high bench seat (the Perch). Two handpumps (one in winter) serve Scottish ales. In summer the garden and patio are a delight. A door by the bar leads from the 19th century to the 21st with a recently refurbished dining area. Closed on Mondays and Tuesdays in winter and other opening times can vary – phone ahead. Q ☆ ⇔ ◑ P 🚍 (418) ♥ 📶 ♪

Dunoon

Ingrams ●

21-23 Ferry Brae, PA23 7DJ
☎ (01369) 704141
1 changing beer (sourced nationally; often Belhaven) ⊞

Town-centre corner bar halfway up a steep hill, popular with both locals and tourists. The public bar is small and serves mainly as the pool room. The main bar is the lounge, where the handpump can be found. The ale changes frequently and is often from the Greene King stable. A simple food menu is available, often supplemented with specials. Live music is often performed at weekends. ▷ ◑ ♣ 🚍 📶 ♪

Ellenabeich

Oyster Bar & Restaurant

PA34 4RQ (on the Isle of Seil, overlooking island of Easdale)
☎ (01852) 300121 ⊕ oysterbareasdale.com
2 changing beers (sourced regionally; often Fyne, Loch Lomond) ⊞

A family-run pub by the harbour at the end of a row of low, whitewashed cottages once occupied by workers at the nearby slate quarries, which are now flooded. The ale is generally from Scottish breweries. The small lounge bar opens out to the rear decking area, offering views of Scarba and Jura. Opening times vary according to the season and how busy it is – phone ahead. Q ☆ ◑ & 🚍 (418) ♥ 📶

Innellan

Osborne

44 Shore Road, PA23 7TJ
☎ (01369) 830820 ⊕ theosborneinnellan.co.uk
St Austell Tribute; 2 changing beers (sourced nationally) ⊞

A whitewashed seafront hotel a few miles south of Dunoon, built in 1869. The comfortable bar has a pool table to one side and a cosy lounge with a log fire. At the front is the conservatory dining room, with excellent views across the Firth of Clyde. Any good weather can be enjoyed in a small outdoor area to one side. Unlike most Argyll pubs, beers are mainly from English breweries. ▷ ☆ ⇔ ◑ 🚍 (489) 📶

Inveraray

George Hotel

Main Street East, PA32 8TT
☎ (01499) 302111 ⊕ thegeorgehotel.co.uk
3 changing beers (sourced regionally; often Fyne) ⊞

Attractive hotel developed from two private houses in 1860 by the Clark family who still own it. The restaurants and bars have been completely restored but retain the original ambience, with an abundance of dark wood, flagstone floors throughout and four roaring fires. The meals have an emphasis on quality local produce. Two real ales are served in the cocktail bar and there is one pump in the lively public bar (open from 5pm on weekdays) to one side. Q ▷ ☆ ⇔ ◑ & 🚍 (926,976) ♥ 📶 ♪

Kilmartin

Kilmartin Hotel

PA31 8RQ (on A816 10 miles N of Lochgilphead)
☎ (01546) 510250 ⊕ kilmartin-hotel.com
3 changing beers (sourced regionally; often Loch Lomond, Orkney) ⊞

A pleasant hotel set above Kilmartin Glen, one of Scotland's most important prehistoric sites. The small public bar to one side provides a cosy fireside nook and offers a good selection of whiskies to complement the real ale. Good home-cooked food is available in the evenings and when the bar is open at lunchtime. Children are welcome at meal times and pub games are available. Beers are mainly from Scottish breweries. Opens at 5pm on weekdays in winter. ▷ ☆ ⇔ ◑ & ♣ P 🚍 (421,423) ♥ 📶

Kingarth

Kingarth Hotel

PA20 9LU (on A844 at jct for turn-off to Kilchattan)
☎ (01700) 831662
2 changing beers (sourced nationally; often Fyne, Greene King) ⊞

A friendly welcome awaits you at this rare gem of a pub set in a secluded yet reachable location on the south of the Isle of Bute. Two handpumps supply an ever-changing range of beers from all over Britain. It is popular for relaxed dining. You can enjoy a stroll to Kilchattan Bay and return for a few beers and an alfresco meal under cover on the rear veranda, or at tables on the front patio. ▷ ☆ ⇔ ◑ P 🚍 (490) ♥ 📶

Lerags

Barn Bar

PA34 4SE (2 miles S of Oban on A816, turn right to Cologin Chalets and then first right after about 1 mile)
☎ (01631) 564618 ⊕ cologin.co.uk/the-barn-bar
1 changing beer (sourced locally; often Fyne) ⊞

Cologin farmhouse forms the centre of a range of holiday chalets and lodges in a secluded glen a couple of miles south of Oban. The Barn was originally the cattle byre and some of the slate stalls have been retained to provide the backrest for seating, helping to contribute to the cosy ambience. An enclosed veranda at the front provides extra seating looking over the play area and duck pond. Closed Tuesdays and Wednesdays, hours can vary – phone ahead. Q ▷ ☆ ⇔ ◑ A P ♥ 📶 ♪

Oban

Corryvreckan ●

The Waterfront Centre, Railway Pier, PA34 4LW

☎ (01631) 568910
Belhaven 80/-; Greene King Abbot; Sharp's Doom Bar; 4 changing beers (sourced nationally) ⊞
Conveniently located Wetherspoon named after the famous whirlpool between Jura and Scarba. It is close to the railway and bus stations and the ferry terminal, with views across Oban Bay and the island of Kerrera. The interior has an exposed wood-panelled roof and the layout is open and spacious. A wide range of beers can be found, often from English breweries. The pub is enlivened by much nautical ephemera including a casting of a sea eagle. ⏻❀◑ᴓ⇌🚬🚪🛜

Markie Dans

1 Victoria Crescent, Corran Esplanade, PA34 5PN
☎ (01631) 564448 ⊕ markiedans.co.uk
1 changing beer (sourced regionally; often Fyne) ⊞
Situated in the lower floor of a grand house overlooking Oban Bay, Markie's is a cosy and welcoming locals' pub. A pool table is available most days, but it is moved away when there is entertainment. An intimate snug with three tables off the main bar provides welcome seclusion for a quiet chat. One ale, usually one of Fyne Ales' less common beers, is present and can be enjoyed in their small beer terrace overlooking the bay. ⏻❀◑⇌🚬❀♪

Oban Inn

1 Stafford Street, PA34 5NJ
☎ (01631) 567441 ⊕ obaninn.co.uk
3 changing beers (sourced regionally; often Fyne) ⊞
A traditional corner local by the old harbour pier which originally opened 1790. The public bar retains its dark-wood panelling and stone floors of Easdale slate. Maritime artefacts are displayed on the walls and currency notes from many nations cover the wooden beams. The comfortable lounge upstairs only has real ale on occasion, but it is worth taking a look to admire the stained-glass panels acquired from an Irish monastery. ◑⇌🚬❀🛜♪

Rothesay

Black Bull Inn

3 West Princes Street, PA20 9AF
☎ (01700) 505838 ⊕ blackbullrothesay.co.uk
3 changing beers (sourced regionally; often Fyne, Greene King) ⊞
A popular pub, situated in the centre of the town close to the ferry terminal, opposite the marina and within walking distance of all amenities including the famous Victorian toilets. The pub has two bars and a separate dining area. The front entrance is closed in cold weather so it is worth checking round the back if the pub appears to be closed. Food times vary frequently, so it is best to phone ahead. Closed on Mondays in winter. ◑♣🚪(90,490) 🛜

Macs Bar

14-18 Castlehill Street, PA20 0DA
☎ (01700) 502417
1 changing beer (sourced nationally; often Orkney, Timothy Taylor) ⊞
Occupying the ground floor of a three-storey stone building opposite the entrance to Rothesay Castle, Macs has been in the same family since 1951. The pub is popular with locals but visitors are given a warm welcome. The cramped bar, decorated with Scottish women's football memorabilia, leads to a surprisingly spacious lounge area with leather seating and a design reminiscent of a bar on a ship. There are three dartboards and domino competitions take place. ♣🚪❀♪

Strachur

Creggans Inn 🅛

PA27 8BX (on A815 at N end of village)
☎ (01369) 860279 ⊕ creggans-inn.co.uk
2 changing beers (sourced locally; often Fyne) ⊞
A convenient stopping place along Loch Fyne. MacPhunn's bar, named after a half-hung sheep rustler of yore, is comfortable, with a real fire and plenty of room for dining. Two handpumps offer a changing selection of beers from Fyne Ales. Drinks may be taken to other lounges, the pool room or restaurant, or enjoyed in the garden overlooking the loch. The games room and toilets are decorated with sea charts. Opening times in winter can vary – phone ahead.
Q⏻❀🏠◑◑P🚪(484,486) ❀🛜

Breweries

Bun Dubh SIBA

🏠 Ceabhar, Sandaig, Isle of Tiree, PA77 6XG
☎ (01879) 220684 ☎ 07792 789733
✉ bundubh@gmail.com

Duncan Castling began brewing on his picobrewery in 2016, then catering solely for his restaurant, Ceabhar. The brewery expanded into the adjoining former guesthouse during 2020-2021, with its live beer now available in local hotels. With an enviropunk ethos, all production goes into reusable containers, no bottles or cans, and distribution, though wider, remains exclusive to the island. ♦

Colonsay

The Brewery, Scalasaig, Isle of Colonsay, PA61 7YT
☎ (01951) 200190 ⊕ colonsaybrewery.co.uk

Colonsay began brewing in 2007 on a five-barrel plant. Beer is mainly bottled or brewery-conditioned for the local trade. LIVE

Fyne SIBA

Achadunan, Cairndow, PA26 8BJ
☎ (01499) 600120 ⊕ fyneales.com

☺Fyne Ales has been brewing since 2001 and is situated at the head of Loch Fyne. Expansion has allowed for the production of experimental brews. FyneFest runs annually, celebrating local fare and showcasing other breweries. ‼🍴♦LIVE⦿

Jarl (ABV 3.8%) GOLD
Strong citrus notes, through use of the Citra hop. A light, golden ale that can be drunk in any season.
Maverick (ABV 4.2%) BITTER
Full-bodied, roasty, tawny best bitter. It is balanced, fruity and well-hopped.
Hurricane Jack (ABV 4.4%) GOLD
Vital Spark (ABV 4.4%) PORTER
Avalanche (ABV 4.5%) GOLD
A true golden ale, stunning citrus hops on the nose with fruit balancing a refreshing hoppy taste.
Highlander (ABV 4.8%) BITTER
A full-bodied, bittersweet ale with a good dry hop finish.
Sublime (ABV 6.8%) STOUT
Superior IPA (ABV 7.1%) IPA

Gigha (NEW)

Ardminish, Isle of Gigha ⊕ isleofgighabrewing.co.uk

A microbrewery based on the Isle of Gigha, just off the Kintyre peninsula on the west coast of Scotland.

Islay SIBA

The Brewery, Islay House Square, Bridgend, PA44 7NZ
☎ **(01496) 810014** ✉ **info@islayales.com**

Off the West Coast of Scotland, this is the only brewery on an island famous for its malt whiskies. Islay Ales started brewing in 2004 and continues to use a four-barrel plant. It is situated in converted farm buildings that house a visitor centre and shop, the latter sells clothing plus other merchandise as well as the range of beers. The brewery tap is the only outlet for the brewery's cask-conditioned beers. Bottles are sold across the island in pubs, restaurants and shops. Tours and tastings are offered. ♦♥⚲

Jura

7 Keills Croft, Craighouse, Isle of Jura, PA60 7XG
☎ **07817 456347** ✉ **jurabrewery2017@gmail.com**

Microbrewery that opened in 2021. Jura bottles the majority of its produce with some available in keg.

ToBEERmory (NEW)

11a Main Street, Tobermory, Isle of Mull, PA75 6NU

Brewery and bottle shop on Tobermory harbour front that began brewing in 2021. Handpulls are used to fill growler cans with cask beer. Its beers are also available bottled.

Oban Inn, Oban (Photo: Mig Gilbert / Flickr CC BY-SA 2.0)

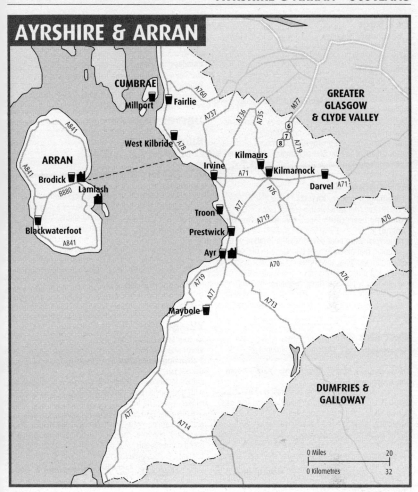

AYRSHIRE & ARRAN

Ayr

Chestnuts Hotel

52 Racecourse Road, KA7 2UZ (on A719, 1 mile S of centre)

☎ (01292) 264393 ⊕ chestnutshotel.com

3 changing beers (often Courage, Fyne, Morland) Ⓗ

A sandstone villa that used to be a synagogue, with a stone bay window, real open fire and timber-beamed, vaulted ceiling displaying an array of whisky water jugs. It offers various seating/dining options and stools at the bar. The quiet, family-run bar has helpful staff and good food (booking advisable at weekends). There is a secure south-facing garden to the side with varied seating, and a car park at the front. The bar is within walking distance of the beach at Seafield. Accommodation is in 10 en-suite rooms. Q ☜ ⊛ 🖾 ◑ ⅁ P 🖵 (9) 🛜

Glen Park Hotel Ⓛ

5 Racecourse Road, KA7 2DG (on corner of Miller Rd)

☎ (01292) 263891 ⊕ theglenparkhotel.co.uk

4 changing beers (sourced locally; often Ayr) Ⓗ

This comfortable lounge bar, in an attractive 1860s B-listed Victorian building, is the brewery tap for Ayr Brewing Company, who operate in the back of the building. The guest ales often include a seasonal from the brewery. Beers are also available to take away from a shop/bar at the rear of the dining room. Bar and restaurant meals are served daily except Monday and Tuesday; booking is advised at weekends. There is outside seating at the front, next to a busy road. ☜ ⊛ 🖾 ◑ ⅁ ≉ P 🖵 (9) 🐾 🛜

Smoking Goat

2A Academy Street, KA7 1HS (just off Sandgate)

☎ (01292) 857137 ⊕ thesmokinggoatayr.com

Fyne Jarl; 1 changing beer (often Fyne) Ⓗ

A basement bar at the entrance to a lane opposite Ayr Town Hall, identified by a sandwich board and a small sign on the wall next to the door. Enter via steep stone stairs and narrow double doors. Tuesday is quiz night, with comedy on the first Thursday of the month, live music on Friday evenings, and DJ night on a Saturday. Wheelchair access is via a ramp to the sunny, upgraded outdoor terrace. Burgers, hotdogs, pizzas, nachos and fries are served. ⊛ ◑ 🖵 (14,585) 🐾 🛜 ↻ ♫

REAL ALE BREWERIES

Arran ⚭ Brodick: Isle of Arran
Arran Botanical Drinks Brodick: Isle of Arran
Ayr Ayr
Seagate Lamlash: Isle of Arran

Twa Dugs

4 Killoch Place, KA7 2EA (across square from railway station)
☎ (01292) 288971
1 changing beer Ⓗ
This lively pub sits on the edge of Burns Statue Square in the centre of town. Real ales are sourced from a wholesaler who supplies beers that are not usually found in other pubs in the area. The wall at the back of the stage is dominated by a large flat-screen TV and live sport is shown. There is a quiz on a Monday, a round-table acoustic session on Tuesday afternoons, acoustic music streamed live on Thursday nights, and live music on Friday, Saturday and Sunday nights. ⇌🚌🕏🛜🎵

Wellingtons Bar

17 Wellington Square, KA7 1EZ
☎ (01292) 262794 ⊕ welliesbar.weebly.com
3 changing beers (often Born, Five Kingdoms, Loch Lomond) Ⓗ
A large Wellington boot advertises the location of this welcoming real ale basement bar. Close to the seafront, bus station and local government offices, it attracts tourists and office workers alike. The Wednesday evening quiz is popular. Three changing ales vary constantly between brewers. Bar food is served, with daily specials on the menu, but check for serving times. 🛏️🏵️⇌🚌🕏🛜

West Kirk ✅

58A Sandgate, KA7 1BX (near bus station)
☎ (01292) 880416
Belhaven 80/-; Greene King Abbot; Sharp's Doom Bar; 6 changing beers Ⓗ
Spacious Wetherspoon serving breakfast and meals all day. This former church retains many original features. The vaulted ceiling is bathed in light, featuring a huge chandelier, and there is a balcony. Toilets are accessed via the pulpit (an accessible toilet is downstairs). Various seating options include stools, chairs and booths. A paved seating area outside on a busy road gets some sun. The news, with subtitles, is usually shown on small TV screens. The pub can be busy on weekends and during Ayr races. Q🛏️🏵️♿♣⇌🚌🛜

Blackwaterfoot: Isle of Arran

Kinloch Hotel

KA27 8ET
☎ (01770) 860444 ⊕ kinloch-arran.com
Ayr Uisge Dubh; 1 changing beer (often Ayr, Belhaven, Greene King) Ⓗ
A hidden gem in a quiet rural village on the west coast of Arran, offering coastal comfort and spectacular scenery. The family hotel has 37 bedrooms, a restaurant and three refurbished bar. Facilities include a heated indoor swimming pool, squash court and a fitness room and sauna. A varied choice of food is on offer, made with local produce, at lunch and dinner. A popular beer festival is held in August. Coffee is available in the lounge from 11.30am.
🛏️🏵️🛌🍴♿▲♣P🚌(322,323) 🕏🛜

Brodick: Isle of Arran

Ormidale Hotel

Knowe Road, KA27 8BY (off A841 at W end of village)
☎ (01770) 302293 ⊕ ormidale-hotel.co.uk
Arran Blonde; 2 changing beers (often Ayr, Caledonian, Kelburn) Ⓗ
A friendly and popular bar at the heart of a large sandstone hotel. It features tables carved in the shape of

the island of Arran, and the boat-shaped bar dispenses fine ales to both locals and visitors alike. One ale in winter increases to three during the summer, with Arran Blonde now a permanent feature. Entertainment includes darts and dominoes on Monday, a music quiz on Tuesday, rock 'n' pop bingo on Wednesday and a general knowledge quiz on Thursday evenings, plus folk nights and summer discos. 🛏️🏵️🛌🍴♣P🚌(322,324) 🕏🛜🎵

Darvel

Black Bull Inn

24 West Main Street, KA17 0AQ
☎ 07860 355736
1 changing beer (often Five Kingdoms, Fyne, Loch Lomond) Ⓗ
Dating from 1840, this former coaching inn retains much of its original character. The bar features a dark wooded gantry offering a wide selection of spirits. Many photographs adorn the pub's interior, reflect the rich history of this former lace town. An open mic session is held on Wednesdays, and live bands play on Saturday evenings. Although there is no permanent kitchen, a variety of food trucks visit by prior arrangement on a regular basis. 🏵️♣P🚌(1,X71) 🕏🛜🎵

Fairlie

Village Inn

46 Bay Street, KA29 0AL
☎ (01475) 560059
1 changing beer (often Kelburn, Loch Lomond, Orkney) Ⓗ
Known locally as the Mudhook, this is a community local with good-value pub food, served in the lounge, conservatory, Fife Room and traditional public bar. The real ale is likely to be a pale beer of around 4% ABV. The pub walls are decorated with photos of Fife yachts, which were built opposite. The pub hosts regular quizzes and board games nights, plus occasional live music and beer festivals. Dogs are welcome in the public bar, and children in other areas if eating. Pub games are available. 🛏️🏵️🛌♿♣P🚌(585) 🕏🛜🎵

Irvine

Auld Brig ✅

15 Fullarton Square, KA12 8EJ (opp Irvine station)
☎ (01294) 277818
Greene King Abbot; Sharp's Doom Bar; 4 changing beers Ⓗ
Wetherspoon outlet next to the west entrance to Rivergate shopping centre. Six of the 12 handpumps dispense a variety of real ales. This large, modern pub has a sloping glass roof providing natural light to the front seating and mezzanine area, which features an art installation made from cotton rope. Also note the wooden doors on the wall and the various old photos. The back downstairs area has the long wooden bar, a tiled floor and subdued lighting. Quiz night is on the first Wednesday of the month. Q🛏️🏵️🛌♿⇌🚌🛜

Kilmarnock

Wheatsheaf Inn ✅

70 Portland Street, KA1 1JG
☎ (01563) 572483
Greene King Abbot; Ruddles Best Bitter; Sharp's Doom Bar; 3 changing beers Ⓗ
A large, modern pub incorporating the frontage of the original Wheatsheaf Hotel, which was an important coaching inn dating from the early 1700s. Robert Burns

was first published in Kilmarnock and may have socialised here with his cronies, including Tam Samson who lived close by. The bar is divided into various seating areas and a quiet corner can be found even when busy. Six handpumps dispense a range of ales. The food is standard Wetherspoon fare. Licensed from 11am.
🏠❀◑&⇌☷�

Kilmaurs

Weston Tavern ⏻

27 Main Street, KA3 2RQ

☎ (01563) 538805 ⊕ westontavern.co.uk

2 changing beers (often Broughton, Sulwath, Theakston) Ⓗ

Housed in the former manse of reformist minister David Smeaton, a contemporary of Robert Burns, this fully refurbished country pub and restaurant has a tiled floor, stone walls and a wood-burning fire. It sits beside the Jougs, a former jailhouse and tollbooth. Two handpumps serve ales from a rotating list of local breweries, often including house beer Kilmaurs Cross by Broughton. The pub holds regular live music and quiz nights. Local CAMRA Pub of the Year 2023.
🏠❀◑&⇌♣P☷(9,13)🐾☂♪

Maybole

Maybole Arms

37 Whitehall, KA19 7DS

☎ (01655) 883173

1 changing beer (often Ayr) Ⓗ

A welcome watering hole for those visiting an area with few real ale pubs. This small, established local inn has a friendly clientele and offers good food from a family-friendly menu. Dogs are permitted, with water and biscuits supplied. A handy stop-off for the nearby Culzean Castle and Country Park, and also a good starting point for visits to the northern end of Galloway Forest Park.
🏠◑Å⇌♣P☷(58,60)🐾☂

Millport: Isle of Cumbrae

Fraser's Bar Ⓛ

9 Cardiff Street, KA28 0AS (opp bus terminus)

☎ (01475) 530518

2 changing beers (often Alechemy, Kelburn, Stewart) Ⓗ

Well maintained and tidy, this pub caters for visitors to the island as well as locals. Buses meet every ferry from Largs and terminate just across the road. Two handpumps serve mostly light-coloured ales, usually including one from a local brewery. Good-value pub food is available lunchtime and early evening. The main bar has an open fire and a fine display of old Clyde steamer photographs. Children are welcome in the rear lounge until 8pm. Q🏠❀◑&♣☷(320)☂

> Burton beer makes me blithe,
> French wine makes me sick.
> I'm devoted to ale,
> And to ale I will stick.
> Henceforth let the grape
> To the barleycorn bow;
> Here's to success to the farmer,
> And God speed the plough.
> **Traditional**

Prestwick

Prestwick Pioneer ✅

87 Main Street, KA9 1JS

☎ (01292) 473210

Greene King Abbot; Ruddles Best Bitter; 6 changing beers Ⓗ

Modern Wetherspoon outlet in a former Woolworths store, named after the first Scottish Aviation Pioneer light aircraft, built in 1947 at the nearby international airport. The pub has an airy feel, with a light-wood decor, and features photographs of early Open Championship golf at Prestwick, and of Elvis at the airport (the only place in the UK where he set foot). Ten handpumps serve local and national ales and food is available. Licensed from 10am. Local CAMRA Pub of the Year 2022.
🏠◑&⇌(Town)☷☂

Troon

McKay's

69 Portland Street, KA10 6QU

☎ (01292) 737372

3 changing beers (often Fyne, Greene King, Timothy Taylor) Ⓗ

A friendly and welcoming single-room town-centre bar with a large CAMRA award-winning beer garden, which is popular on sunny days. The bar hosts local dominoes competitions and shows live sports on TV. Dogs are welcome in the garden only. A former CAMRA Regional Pub of the Year, and a long-standing stalwart of the local real ale scene. 🏠❀&⇌☷(14,10)🐾☂

Number Forty Seven

47 Templehill, KA10 6BQ

☎ (01292) 312814

Cairngorm Wildcat; Morland Old Speckled Hen; 3 changing beers (often Ayr, Five Kingdoms, Greene King) Ⓗ

A long single-room bar which has been attractively refurbished, situated on one of the town's main routes. Five handpulls dispense real ales from Scottish and English breweries, with a discount for over-60s (except when other regular drinks discounts apply). Quiz night is Thursday. There is a pool table, a jukebox and a lot of TVs showing a variety of live sport. The gantry is stocked with a wide selection of different spirits. On Friday and Saturday nights a DJ plays and the bar moves into nightclub mode. &⇌♣☷(14,10)🐾☂

West Kilbride

Twa Dugs

71 Main Street, KA23 9AW

☎ (01294) 822524

2 changing beers (often Ayr, Five Kingdoms, Kelburn) Ⓗ

A popular, well cared for and comfortable pub in Scotland's Craft Town. A variety of real ales from local and national brewers are served from two handpulls. There is regular live music at weekends, a pool table, and frequent quiz nights (usually every second Thu). The pub holds occasional beer festivals. Local CAMRA Pub of the Year 2022. The bus stops at the door, and the railway station is five minutes' walk away. Currently closed Mon/Tues – check for opening times.
&⇌♣☷(585,585A)🐾☂♪

Breweries

Arran SIBA

Cladach, Brodick, Isle of Arran, KA27 8DE
☎ (01770) 302353

Office: Isle of Arran Brewery Guesthouse, Shore Road, Whiting Bay, Isle of Arran, KA27 8PZ
⊕ arranbrewery.com

☺The brewery opened in Brodick in 2000 using a 20-barrel plant with water sourced from the nearby mountains. It has its own in-house bottling plant, shop and taproom. Around 400 outlets around the UK are supplied direct, and via distributors. The brewery owns the rights to the former Devil's Dyke Brewery beers.
‼🏪♦⚗

Guid Ale (ABV 3.8%) GOLD
A golden, refreshing session ale with a delicate balance of malt and fruit.

Dark (ABV 4.3%) BROWN
A well-balanced malty beer, roast and hop in the taste and a dry, bitter finish. A traditional 'Scottish Heavy'.

Sunset (ABV 4.4%) GOLD
A mid-amber summer ale, light-perfumed aroma, good balance of malt, fruit and hops with a pleasant dry finish.

Blonde (ABV 5%) SPECIALITY
A hoppy beer with substantial fruit balance. An aromatic strong golden ale that drinks below its weight.

Brewery Dug (ABV 5.5%) IPA
An American-style IPA with a refreshing citrus body and a dry, lemon zest, bitter finish.

Arran Botanical Drinks

Cladach Beach House, Brodick, KA27 8DE
☎ (01770) 302513 ⊕ arranbotanicaldrinks.com

Formerly known as Arran Gin, Arran Botanical Drinks is located beside the beach at Cladach, Brodick. It has a small brewkit producing a couple of in-house bottle-conditioned and kegged beers using locally foraged ingredients. It has a shop and tastings are available for all its products. 🏪LIVE

Ayr

5 Racecourse Road, Ayr, KA7 2DG ☎ 07834 922142
⊕ ayrbrewingcompany.com

☺Established in 2009, Ayr has a five-barrel plant. Typically, two brew runs are carried out weekly with casks supplied to more than 50 outlets throughout Scotland and England. The beers are also available in bottles, cans and mini casks from the brewery shop,

conveniently located in the neighbouring Glen Park Hotel. 🏪♦V

Leezie Lundie (ABV 3.8%) PALE
A pale golden session ale with hints of grapefruit and a dry, lingering finish.

Uisge Dubh (ABV 3.8%) BITTER

Camboozedoon 25 (ABV 4%) PALE

One Daisy (ABV 4%) PALE

Boing! (ABV 4.1%) BITTER

Jolly Beggars (ABV 4.2%) BITTER
A complex best bitter with plenty of character and lingering malty aftertaste.

Complicated Maisie (ABV 4.3%) BITTER

Rabbie's Porter (ABV 4.3%) PORTER
Award-winning, robust, full-bodied porter with well-balanced toffee, fruity maltiness and a slightly smoky finish.

Siren Song (ABV 5%) PALE

Summer Knitting (ABV 5.3%) BLOND

Ethical

Roddenloft Brewery, Roddenloft, Mauchline, KA5 5HH ⊕ ethicalales.com

Roddenloft Brewery, trading as Ethical Ales, is a Scottish craft brewery producing keg beers from Scottish barleys and British hops, together with Ayrshire water. A number of styles are available from Pilsner to IPA to stout.

Seagate

Seagate, Lamlash, Isle of Arran, KA27 8JN
☎ (01770) 600110 ☎ 07798 854295
⊕ seagatebrewery.co.uk

In 2020 Stephen Sparshott progressed from homebrewing in his kitchen into commercial brewing in a purpose-built shed on the shores of Lamlash Bay. Concentrating on Belgian and Scottish ales, a small range of core beers are brewed on his 30-litre and 50-litre kits, with further ales produced on a separate installation at Arran Botanical Drinks, Cladach, Brodick. All bottled beers are bottle-conditioned. ‼♦LIVE

Rise Above 80/- (ABV 4.5%) BITTER

Moulin D'Or Houblon (ABV 5%) SPECIALITY

RYIPA (ABV 5%) SPECIALITY

Saorsa Blond Ale (ABV 5%) SPECIALITY

Scottie Stout (ABV 5%) STOUT

Return trays

Also known as an Autovac or beer economiser, a return tray is a device that collects beer spilled in the pouring process, recycles it by mixing it with fresh beer, and returns it to the glass.

It can be identified by a stainless steel drip tray below the nozzle on a handpump, with a pipe connected from the bottom of the tray to the draw line of the cask. They are commonly found in use in Yorkshire and parts of south-east Scotland and have been seen in north-east Scotland and north-west England.

A symbol will appear next to entries in the Guide where a return tray is in use on some or all of the beers (see inside cover key).

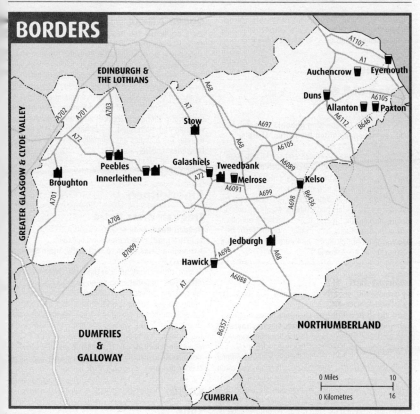

BORDERS

Allanton

Allanton Inn ♟

Main Street, TD11 3JZ (on B6437)
☎ (01890) 818260 ⊕ allantoninn.co.uk
2 changing beers (sourced nationally; often Born, Fyne, Timothy Taylor) Ⓗ

Only six miles from the border, the pub provides a warm welcome to Scotland. An old coaching inn dating back to the 18th centur, it has a bright, airy feel. Quality food is served in the dining rooms. A small bar area, which overlooks the superb beer garden and views of the countryside beyond, may also be used for dining. The bar has an attractive decor with artworks and comfortable cushioned benches. Families are welcome – a children's menu and games are provided. Booking is strongly recommended. Local CAMRA Pub of the Year 2023. Usually closed Tuesday and Wednesday lunchtimes.
Q❄☺♨⌂◑♣P🖵(260) 🛜

Auchencrow

Craw Inn

TD14 5LS (signed from A1)
☎ (01890) 761253 ⊕ thecrawinn.co.uk
2 changing beers (sourced nationally; often Fyne, Loch Lomond, Timothy Taylor) Ⓗ

A friendly and revitalised 18th-century, listed country inn. The real ales are usually from smaller breweries, as can be seen from the numerous pumpclips on show. The cosy front bar has a wood-burning stove and tables for dining and drinking. Excellent home-cooked food is served in the bar and well-appointed restaurant. There is also an additional area with comfy settees and a TV.

Usually closed on Monday and Tuesday, mid-afternoon Wednesday to Friday, and may close early if no custom so check ahead. Q❄☺♨⌂◑♣P🖵(34)🐾🛜

Duns

White Swan Hotel

31-32 Market Square, TD11 3AL
☎ (01361) 883338 ⊕ whiteswan-hotel.co.uk
2 changing beers (sourced locally; often Born, Hadrian Border, Loch Lomond) Ⓗ

Town-centre hotel with a deceptively extensive interior. The bar is a welcoming and comfortable room for locals as well as visitors, with a very friendly and lively clientele. There is a separate dining room, and a function room upstairs for special events. There is a good menu serving great-value meals. Breakfasts and pensioner's lunches on Thursday are especially popular. Children are welcome until 9pm if eating – a children's menu is provided. Alcoholic drinks are served from 11am.
❄⌂◑♣P🖵🐾🛜♪

Eyemouth

Ship Inn

Harbour Road, TD14 5HT
☎ (01890) 751495 ⊕ theshipeyemouth.com
2 changing beers (sourced regionally; often Born, Fyne) Ⓗ

A pleasant, friendly bar and restaurant where families are welcome until 8pm. The decor is modern and airy, with a nod towards the town's seafaring heritage. The varied food menu should have something to suit everyone, including local fish and children's options.

Situated on the quayside, the pub offers views of the harbour and Gunsgreen House. The accommodation is run as a separate business. ⌘❄️✉️◗⏻🧊🅿️❀🐾📶

Galashiels

Hunters Hall ✔
56 High Street, TD1 1SE (N end of centre)
☎ (01896) 759795
Belhaven 80/-; Greene King Abbot; 3 changing beers (sourced nationally; often Broughton, Sharp's, Stewart) 🅷
This former Presbyterian church and school has been sympathetically restored to expose much of the original stonework, high ceiling and the skylight roof panels. Historical photographs of Galashiels decorate the walls. The pub offers typical Wetherspoon fare and caters for families, locals, visitors and students. Meals are available all day and include breakfasts and children's options. Real cider is generally only available during festivals. Opens at 8am but alcoholic drinks are not served until 11am. Q⌘❄️◗⏻🅰️🦽🎐🍴🅿️📶

Salmon Inn
54 Bank Street, TD1 1EP (town centre, opp gardens)
☎ (01896) 752577
Black Sheep Best Bitter; 2 changing beers (sourced nationally; often Born, Caledonian, Timothy Taylor) 🅷
A comfortable, friendly town-centre inn. The single L-shaped room and adjacent standalone bistro is split into three areas, decorated with contemporary photographs of the Galashiels area. The changing real ales are often from smaller breweries. Good home-cooked meals are served all day (except Sun) and families are welcome at lunchtimes. The pub gets quite animated when sporting events are screened on the TV. B&B accommodation is available. ⌘❄️✉️◗⏻🦽🅰️🎐♣️❀🐾📶🎵

Hawick

Bourtree ✔
22 Bourtree Place, TD9 9HL (NE edge of town centre)
☎ (01450) 360450
Belhaven 80/-; Greene King Abbot; 3 changing beers (sourced nationally; often Sharp's, Stewart, Wychwood) 🅷
Built as the Hawick Conservative Club in 1897, this listed building has been stunningly transformed into a Wetherspoon pub. The original badminton and snooker halls form the main area and there are three other quieter sections. Photographs on the walls depict the history of Hawick life. Food is served all day, with breakfast and children's options. Either bingo or a quiz is held on Wednesday evenings. Real cider is generally only available during festivals. Opens at 8am, with alcoholic drinks served from 11am. Q⌘❄️◗⏻🦽♣️🍴🅿️📶

Exchange Bar (Dalton's)
1 Silver Street, TD9 0AD (off SW end of High St)
☎ (01450) 376067
2 changing beers (sourced regionally; often Belhaven, Born, Orkney) 🅷
Tucked away near St Mary's Kirk, the pub used to overlook the Corn Exchange and took its name from that. However, a previous owner was called Dalton and that name has stuck ever since. Popular with locals, this Victorian gem has a bar featuring original dark-wood panelling and ornate cornice work. A comfy back lounge is used for parties, occasional karaoke and Sunday folk sessions. Children are not admitted. ❄️🅰️♣️🎐❀🐾📶🎵

Queen's Head
2-4 Cross Wynd, TD9 9EG
☎ (01450) 367456
3 changing beers (sourced regionally; often Borderlands, Born, First and Last)
This excellent and long-established traditional bar reopened after a 10-year absence in 2022. It welcomes locals and visitors alike and hosts frequent open mic music evenings. Many of the old features such as the spectacular bar gantry, cornices and panelling have been retained and refurbished. It also has an upstairs cocktail lounge. The real ales are generally from local small breweries. Children are not admitted. Usually closed Monday and Tuesday and may close early if quiet. 🅰️♣️🎐(X95,20)❀🐾📶🎵

Innerleithen

Traquair Arms Hotel
Traquair Road, EH44 6PD (B709, off A72)
☎ (01896) 830229 ● traquairarmshotel.co.uk
3 changing beers (sourced nationally; often Stewart, Tempest) 🅷
Elegant 18th-century hotel in the scenic Tweed Valley offering accommodation in 16 en-suite rooms and two self-catering cottages. The comfortable lounge bar features a welcoming real fire and a flagstoned sports bar with log-burner provides a great thawing-out space for mountain bikers, walkers and anglers. A bistro area and separate restaurant offer plenty of room for diners. Meals are served all day at weekends and there is a menu for children. The bar may close earlier if quiet. ⌘❄️✉️◗⏻🦽🅰️♣️🎐🅿️(X62)❀🐾📶🎵

Kelso

1905
Crawford Street, TD5 7DP (off N corner of town square)
☎ (01573) 225556
3 changing beers (sourced regionally; often Born, Firebrick, Stewart) 🅷
Formerly the Red Lion, this pub has a lively atmosphere when events are held, but at other times has a pleasant, peaceful ambience. The main room has a fine wood and plastered vaulted ceiling, wooden panelling and mosaic flooring. Brewery mirrors adorn the walls and are also inlaid into the bar gantry. Other areas with different styling lead off from the bar. Children are not admitted, except for some functions. Often closed on Monday in winter. Q❄️✉️♣️🎐❀🐾📶🎵

Cobbles Freehouse & Dining
7 Bowmont Street, TD5 7JH (off N corner of town square)
☎ (01573) 223548 ● cobbleskelso.co.uk
Tempest Armadillo; 1 changing beer (sourced locally; often Tempest) 🅷
This gastro-pub is often busy with diners but drinkers are also welcome. The decor is bright and welcoming, with a bar warmed by a real fire. Food is served in a dining area throughout the day Monday to Friday, but lunchtime only on Saturday and Sunday. The menu should suit all tastes, including children. The pub is dedicated to Tempest ales,

REAL ALE BREWERIES

Born Jedburgh
Broughton Broughton
Freewheelin' Peebles (brewing suspended)
Stow Stow
Tempest ✦ Tweedbank
Traquair House Innerleithen

with some lined glasses available. Likely to be closed all day Monday and Tuesday and Wednesday lunchtime – other times may vary. ⌂✿🏠🍽👍🛒🖤❄

Rutherfords

38 The Square, TD5 7HL
☎ 07917 824183
4 changing beers (sourced locally; often Cheviot, Firebrick, First and Last) Ⓗ

This tiny shop conversion was the first micropub in Scotland. With no TV or music to distract, it is ideal for a friendly chat or playing board games. The area extends onto the pavement under canopies. The real ales are generally from smaller breweries, with third-pint tasting paddles available. Some simple bar snacks are provided. Children are welcome until 3pm and games are provided. Always check the opening hours as they can be limited, especially in winter. Q⌂✿🏠❤🖤❄♪

Melrose

Burt's Hotel

Market Square, TD6 9PL
☎ (01896) 822285 ⊕ burtshotel.co.uk
Born Amber; Timothy Taylor Landlord; 1 changing beer Ⓗ

An elegant, family-run hotel with colourful window boxes providing a striking appearance in summer. The comfortable lounge bar decor reflects the country sporting interests of many of the clientele. The focus is unashamedly on food, which is excellent in both the bar and restaurant. Those visiting solely for a drink may find space limited at busy times. Children are permitted and a menu provided. The Townhouse opposite has the same owners. Q⌂✿🏠🍽👍🛒🖤❄

George & Abbotsford Hotel

High Street, TD6 9PD (NW of Market Square)
☎ (01896) 822308 ⊕ georgeandabbotsfordmelrose.co.uk
Greene King Abbot; Tempest Armadillo; 2 changing beers (sourced regionally; often Orkney) Ⓗ

A spacious family-run hotel with a comfortable bar and lounges, offering a warm welcome to locals and visitors alike. The real ales come from both sides of the Border. Food features prominently and is served all day; the menu is supplemented with various specials and children's options. The partially covered enclosed suntrap beer garden has plenty of seating. The pub is popular with walkers, cyclists and Melrose rugby supporters, and is a pleasant walk from the rail terminus at Tweedbank. Q⌂✿🏠👍🛒🖤❄♪

Paxton

Cross Inn

Paxton, TD15 1TE (off B6461)
☎ (01289) 384877 ⊕ thecrossinn.co.uk
Timothy Taylor Landlord; 2 changing beers (sourced nationally; often Firebrick, Hadrian Border, Tempest) Ⓗ

A friendly, rejuvenated, 19th-century village local. Its small, welcoming bar is stone-floored, while the attractive larger dining and function area has floorboards and carpeting. At the front is a raised decking area for outside drinking and eating. Food is served all day Saturday and Sunday. The menu, along with daily specials, children's options and Sunday roasts, should appeal to most tastes. Local CAMRA Pub of the Year runner up 2023. Usually closed Monday and Tuesday and mid-afternoons on Wednesday and Thursday. ⌂✿🍽👍🛒🖤(32)❤🖤♪

Peebles

Bridge Inn (Trust)

Portbrae, EH45 8AW
☎ (01721) 720589 ⊕ thebridgeinnpeebles.co.uk
3 changing beers (sourced nationally; often Born, Cromarty, Stewart) Ⓗ

Cheerful, welcoming pub also known as the Trust and once called the Tweedside Inn. The bright, comfortable bar is decorated with jugs, bottles, pictures of old Peebles and displays relating to outdoor pursuits. There is a cosy corner with a log-burner and a small room to the rear with a dartboard. The Gents has superb old fittings. The suntrap patio overlooks the river and hills beyond. Children are not admitted. ✿🏕🛒🖤❄♪

Cross Keys ✓

24 Northgate, EH45 8RS
☎ (01721) 723467
Greene King Abbot; Sharp's Doom Bar; 4 changing beers (sourced nationally; often Broughton, Cairngorm, Harviestoun) Ⓗ

This old coaching inn has a pleasant, rambling, wood-panelled main area with low ceilings and a mix of tables and chairs, as well as booths with bench seating. The serving area is tucked away to the left of the entrance and has high tables and chairs. Steps lead up to the excellent beer garden. Food is available all day – children are permitted if dining. It is likely to open at 7am, with alcoholic drinks served from 11am.
Q⌂✿🏠🍽👍🏕🛒🖤❄

Breweries

Born

Lanton Mill, Jedburgh, TD8 6ST
☎ (01835) 830495 ☎ 07802 416494
⊕ bornintheborders.com

Scotland's original plough-to-pint brewery, it started brewing as Scottish Borders Brewery in 2011, using its own barley, before changing to Born in the Borders Brewery, and then Born Brewery in 2020. Beyond its core range of ales, projects have included the 'Wild Harvest' initiative, which sources locally-foraged ingredients. ‼🍽◆

Blonde (ABV 3.8%) GOLD
Well-balanced hop and malt flavour, with bitterness coming through.
Amber (ABV 4%) BITTER
An amber ale with a balance of malty sweetness and hop bitterness, fruity and easy to drink.
IPA (ABV 4.8%) IPA

Broughton SIBA

Main Street, Broughton, ML12 6HQ
☎ (01899) 830345 ⊕ broughtonales.co.uk

☺Founded in 1979, Broughton Ales was one of the first microbreweries. Broughton has developed since then, and though more than 60% of production goes into bottle for sale in Britain and abroad, it retains a sizeable range of cask ales. It merged with Consolidated Craft Breweries Group in 2022. All beers are suitable for vegetarians and Hopo Lager is certified gluten free.
‼🍽◆GF

Hopo Session IPA (ABV 3.8%) PALE
Dry-hopped pale ale with slightly tart, fruit taste and distinctive tang.
Merlin's Ale (ABV 4.2%) GOLD

A well-hopped, fruity flavour is balanced by malt in the taste. The finish is bittersweet, light but dry.

Hopo 2 Rivers IPA (ABV 4.6%) PALE
Beautifully-hopped, robust bitter with a dry finish.

Wee Jock (ABV 4.6%) BROWN
Pleasant 80/- style. Light fruit and a malty sweetness.

Stout Jock (ABV 4.8%) STOUT

Glasgow Cross IPA (ABV 5%) PALE
A fruity, refreshing IPA with a good body and a pleasant hoppy flavour. A long-lasting bitterness in the finish.

Hopo Proper IPA (ABV 5%) PALE

Old Jock (ABV 6.7%) STRONG
A bold Scotch ale, full-bodied, sweetish and fruity in the finish.

Durty (NEW)

4 Traquair Road, Innerleithen, EH43 6AN
⊕ durtybrewing.com

Durty Brewing produces beers inspired by the landscape of the Scottish Borders, with each beer named after the famous mountain biking trails of the Tweed Valley. Beers are available in cans. ⚘

Freewheelin'

Peebles Hydro, Innerleithen Road, Peebles, EH45 8LX
☎ 07802 175826 ⊕ freewheelinbrewery.co.uk

Freewheelin' began brewing in 2013 and is based in Peebles. It is located in a former joiners shed in the grounds of the Peebles Hydro Hotel. Local spring water is used in the brewing process. Brewing is currently suspended. ‼◆

Stow

Plenploth House, Old Stage Road, Stow, TD1 2SU
☎ 07834 396991 ⊕ dhubrew.com

Stow is a small-batch nanobrewery in the Scottish Borders that produces four core cask beers available in the Borders and the central belt, sold under the name Dhu Brew. The beers, excepting the stout, are also available in can, bottle and keg. There are plans for significant growth over the next 3-4 years, with contract brewing for larger volumes already underway.

Brewed under the Dhu Brew brand name:

IPA (ABV 3.8%) IPA

Sport (ABV 3.8%) BITTER

Red (ABV 4%) RED

Pils (ABV 4.2%) SPECIALITY

Tempest SIBA

Block 11, Units 1 & 2, Tweedbank Industrial Estate, Tweedbank, TD1 3RS
☎ (01896) 759500 ⊕ tempestbrewco.com

Now well established in its premises at Tweedbank, Gavin Meiklejohn's brewery continues to evolve with specialised brews, many using lesser known hop varieties. Cask beers were restricted during Covid (with Armadillo the only ever-present), but many other beers were available in KeyKeg while the brewery remained open throughout, and expanded its bottle and can portfolio. Within the brewery is the shop where regular tap sessions and beer festivals are held. ‼☛◆LIVE⚘

Armadillo (ABV 3.8%) GOLD

Modern Helles (ABV 4.1%) PALE

Elemental Porter (ABV 5.1%) PORTER

Traquair House SIBA

Traquair House, Innerleithen, EH44 6PW
☎ (01896) 830323 ⊕ traquair.co.uk/
traquair-house-brewery

The 18th century brewhouse is based in one of the wings of the 1,000-year-old Traquair House, Scotland's oldest inhabited house. All the beers are oak-fermented and 60% of production is exported. ‼☛◆

Bear Ale (ABV 5%) BITTER
Malty aroma and a complex taste of malts, citrus fruit, sweetness and bitterness, all lasting into the aftertaste.

Reading the runes

There are terms and expressions used in the pub trade that need to be translated into a language understood by consumers.

'Wet pub' doesn't mean the roof leaks but indicates that beer and other alcohols are the main feature, rather than food.

Stillage is a cradle or platform in the pub cellar where casks of beer are stored horizontally while secondary fermentation takes place.

'Barrel behind the bar' is a widely-used description but usually inappropriate as a barrel is a large 36-gallon container, too big to store at bar level. The correct term for a container for real ale is cask and casks come in several sizes: 4-and-a-half gallon pins; nine-gallon firkin; 18-gallon kilderkin; 36-gallon barrels; and 54-gallon hogshead. Hogsheads are rare. Most pubs use firkins and kilderkins these days. If a cask is used at bar level to serve a seasonal beer such as winter ale, it's likely to be a pin.

Beer 'served by gravity' means it comes straight from the cask and is not drawn by a beer engine and handpump.

'Tight sparkler' is a small device containing a mesh that's screwed to the nozzle of a beer engine operated by a handpump on the bar. The sparkler agitates the beer as it enters the glass and creates the tight, thick head of foam sometimes preferred by northern drinkers.

'Cask breather' is a system used by a few brewers to prolong the life of cask beer. Casks are connected to cylinders of carbon dioxide and a demand valve injects gas into the cask as beer is drawn off.

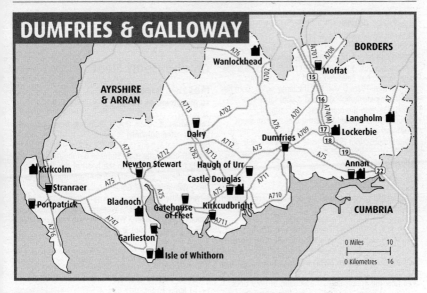

DUMFRIES & GALLOWAY

BORDERS

Wanlockhead

Moffat

15

AYRSHIRE & ARRAN

16

A7

A74(M)

Langholm

17

Dalry

Dumfries

Lockerbie

18

19

Kirkcolm

Newton Stewart

Haugh of Urr

Annan

22

Stranraer

Castle Douglas

Portpatrick

Bladnoch

Kirkcudbright

CUMBRIA

Gatehouse of Fleet

Garlieston

Isle of Whithorn

0 Miles 10

0 Kilometres 16

SCOTLAND

Annan

Blue Bell Inn ♟

10 High Street, DG12 6AG
☎ (01461) 202385
Caledonian Deuchars IPA; 3 changing beers (sourced nationally; often Carlisle, Kelburn) Ⓗ
Former coaching inn with some traditional features, notably the inter-war panelling on the walls and the bar counter. The courtyard to the rear of the pub still has the original stables and provides a pleasant seated area. The pub has an onsite brewery called Motte and Bailey, and their beers are only available here. Annual beer and cider festivals are held. Local CAMRA Pub of the Year and Cider Pub of the Year 2023. ⛲❀Å⇌♣●P🚫(79,383)❀🛜🎵

Castle Douglas

Sulwath Brewery Tap Room Ⓛ

209 King Street, DG7 1DT
☎ (01556) 504525 🌐 sulwathbrewers.co.uk
Sulwath Black Galloway; 5 changing beers (sourced locally; often Sulwath) Ⓗ
The visitor centre for Sulwath brewery is a showcase for the brewery's beers, with four in cask conditioned form, alongside other guest beers on occasion. One keg cider, usually from Westons, is also available. Dried hop bines decorate the walls and old wooden casks of various sizes provide some of the furniture. Brewery tours are available Monday and Friday. Occasionally open on Sunday for special events. Q⛲ÅP🚫❀🛜

Dalry

Clachan Inn

8-10 Main Street, DG7 3UW
☎ (01644) 430241 🌐 theclachaninn.co.uk
3 changing beers (sourced regionally; often Ayr, Five Kingdoms, Fyne) Ⓗ
Pub with a reputation for excellent food, cosy, well-equipped bedrooms and a welcoming atmosphere. The varied menu features daily specials and the kitchen makes good use of local produce. It has an attractive traditional main bar and a relaxing lounge bar, both with warming open log fires in winter, plus a separate restaurant. Three changing beers are sourced regionally;

often Ayr, Five Kingdoms and Fyne Ales. The pub is a handy stop for walkers on the Southern Upland Way. Winter opening hours may vary. Local CAMRA Pub of the Year 2023. Q⛲❀🏠◑⅋Å♣P🚫(520,521)❀🛜

Dumfries

Cavens Arms

20 Buccleuch Street, DG1 2AH
☎ (01387) 252896 🌐 cavensarms.com
Fyne Jarl; Morland Old Speckled Hen; Swannay Orkney IPA; Timothy Taylor Landlord; 4 changing beers (sourced nationally; often Thornbridge) Ⓗ
Busy food-oriented pub that is popular with diners for its range of good-value meals. Drinkers are welcomed in the bar area but seating can be limited during food service times. An outdoor area with covered barn is accessed by stairs or from the Whitesands. It serves five regular beers and three guests which are from a wide range of breweries, including some rarely seen in this locality. Local CAMRA Pub of the Year 2022. ❀◑⅋P🚫🛜

Douglas Arms ♟ Ⓛ

75 Friars Vennel, DG1 2RQ
☎ (01387) 248236
2 changing beers (often Five Kingdoms) Ⓗ
This recently refurbished.traditional town centre bar with a warming fire in winter and a cosy snug is always a popular venue. The choice of available beers, often from smaller less well-known breweries, reflect the care taken by the licensee to give real ale drinkers something different. This pub makes full use of Facebook to inform about its beer choices. Local CAMRA Pub of the Year 2023. ⛲⇌🚫❀🛜🎵

REAL ALE BREWERIES

Borderlands ⚒ Langholm
Five Kingdoms Isle of Whithorn
Lola Rose 🍺 Wanlockhead
Lowland Lockerbie
Motte & Bailey 🍺 Annan
Portpatrick Kirkcolm
Sulwath ⚒ Castle Douglas
Wigtown Bladnoch (NEW)

Fleshers Arms
48 Loreburn Street, DG1 1HJ
☎ (01387) 256461
3 changing beers (often Five Kingdoms) Ⓗ
This popular pub, situated between the station and the town centre, has been reopened by the previous licensee of the Tam O'Shanter. The large single room has modern seating to one side and a pool table in a separate area to the rear. There is occasional live music. The building is reputed to be the oldest in Loreburn Street and was so named because of the proximity to a slaughterhouse that is long gone. ⛲&♣🚐🐾🛜♪

Riverside Bar
Dock Park, DG1 2RY
☎ (01387) 254477
Morland Old Speckled Hen; 3 changing beers (sourced nationally) Ⓗ
The Riverside Bar is an established venue on the Dumfries real ale scene. Comfortable and friendly, it has seating on two levels and a large conservatory. Three outside seating areas include a terrace with open views over the Dock Park and access to walks on both sides of the River Nith. The pub is accessible from the St Michaels area near the Robert Burns Mausoleum or from Dock Park. Guest beers are sourced from throughout the UK. ⛲🐾♣🚐🐾🛜♪

Robert the Bruce ✅
81 Buccleuch Street, DG1 2AB
☎ (01387) 270320
Caledonian Deuchars IPA; Greene King Abbot; Sharp's Doom Bar; 4 changing beers (sourced nationally) Ⓗ
This former Methodist Church, sensitively converted by Wetherspoon, has a relaxed atmosphere and is a popular meeting place in the town centre. There is a pleasant outside seating area to the rear. The pub stands near the site where Robert the Bruce killed John Comyn in 1306 in an incident linked to Scotland's fight for independence. The food menu offers a range of good-value meals served all day, every day. Alcohol is served from 11am. ⛲🐾◑🚆♣P🚐🛜

Tam O'Shanter
113-117 Queensberry Street, DG1 1BH
☎ (01387) 256696
3 changing beers (sourced locally; often Five Kingdoms, Sulwath) Ⓗ
Established in 1630, this 17th-century coaching inn with a connection to Robert Burns has been a mainstay of the Dumfries beer scene for many years. Situated just off the High Street, the pub has been refurbished to an aesthetically pleasing standard without ruining the traditional bar. Brand new toilets for all genders are on the ground floor. The twin-booth snug is lovely, with the stove made into a glass-fronted feature. There is an updated outdoor smoking/vaping area. ⛲🚆♣🐾🛜

Garlieston

Harbour Inn
18 South Crescent, DG8 8BQ
☎ (01988) 600685 🌐 the-harbour-inn.co.uk
House beer (by Greene King); 1 changing beer (often Belhaven, Greene King) Ⓗ
Well-established and well-known pub in the Garlieston area, dating back to 1700. It sits in the village centre with scenic sea views over the bay and is busy all year with locals and holidaymakers. A second handpump was recently installed. The comfortable bar area is friendly and cosy, and pub meals are served lunchtime and evenings. There is a separate restaurant area adjacent to the bar. This is a great place for coastal walking and fishing. Dogs are welcome.
Q⛲🛏◑♣&▲🚐(415,416)🐾🛜♪

Gatehouse of Fleet

Masonic Arms
10 Ann Street, DG7 2HU
☎ (01557) 814335 🌐 masonicarms.co.uk
Caledonian Deuchars IPA; 1 changing beer (sourced locally; often Sulwath) Ⓗ
Built by local Masons in 1785, the pub is situated just off the east end of the main street in Gatehouse of Fleet, a lovely traditional village in the heart of the Stewartry. Exposed beams are a feature in the comfortable bar area, along with a real fire. Good, locally sourced food is served in the bar and in the conservatory and restaurant. There are daily specials, a weekly curry night, and a popular Sunday carvery. Winter opening times may vary. ⛲🐾◑ΔP🚐(431,500)🐾🛜♪

Haugh of Urr

Laurie Arms Hotel
11-13 Main Street, DG7 3YA
☎ (01556) 660246
4 changing beers (sourced nationally; often Caledonian, Fyne) Ⓗ
Welcoming family-run pub and restaurant in a charming, quiet village, popular for its range of beers and freshly cooked food featuring local produce. It has a good village-pub atmosphere, enhanced on winter nights by the warming log fire in the bar. Up to four beers are available, depending on the season, mainly from independent breweries. National Cycle Route Seven passes nearby. Winter opening times may vary, so check before visiting. The pub is on the bus route between Dumfries, Dalbeattie and Castle Douglas. Local CAMRA Pub of the Year 2022. ⛲🐾◑♣P🚐(501)🐾🛜

Isle of Whithorn

Steam Packet Inn Ⓛ ✅
Harbour Row, DG8 8LL (on B7004 from Whithorn)
☎ (01988) 500334 🌐 thesteampacketinn.co.uk
8 changing beers (often Five Kingdoms, Fyne, Kelburn) Ⓗ
Traditional and historic family-run hotel overlooking the harbour, welcoming to all including families and pets. The public bar has stone walls and a multi-fuel stove, and there are pictures of the village and maritime events throughout. Two guest ales from a wide variety of breweries, along with up to six beers from in-house brewery Five Kingdoms, are available in both bars. Bottle-conditioned ales are also stocked. The extensive food menu features local produce.
Q⛲🛏◑ΔP🚐(415,416)🐾🛜

Kirkcudbright

Masonic Arms
19 Castle Street, DG6 4JA
☎ (01557) 330517 🌐 masonic-arms.co.uk
2 changing beers (sourced nationally) Ⓗ
This well-situated, friendly pub has been a firm favourite with real ale enthusiasts for many years. It serves one real ale year round with two in summer months. The well-stocked bar has more than 50 malt whiskies and over 250 gins, as well as a good selection of world beers. There is a smaller back bar and a garden with a smoking area. Q🐾&ΔP🚐🐾🛜♪

Selkirk Arms Hotel ✓

High Street, DG6 4JG

☎ (01557) 330402 ⊕ selkirkarmshotel.co.uk

2 changing beers (sourced nationally; often Five Kingdoms, Sulwath) ⊞

Refurbished 18th-century hotel with a restaurant, bistro and lounge bar, renowned for locally sourced food. The large garden area with tables is popular in summer. Two real ales are available, sometimes three in summer. The bar also features a good selection of malt whiskies and gins. Robert Burns wrote his famous Selkirk Grace at the hotel in 1794. Kirkcudbright is notable for its artistic heritage and houses a number of interesting galleries and museums. Q❀✿☕◗&♿AP🚃❀🕏

Moffat

Famous Star Hotel L

44 High Street, DG10 9EF

☎ (01683) 220156 ⊕ famousstarhotel.co.uk

1 changing beer (sourced regionally; often Greene King, Sulwath) ⊞

The Famous Star Hotel is recognised by the Guinness Book of Records as the narrowest detached hotel in the world. The building is 20 feet wide and 162 feet long but feels much bigger due to the clever use of internal space. It offers excellent service. The Star has at least one beer available all year round. There is a large public bar downstairs with entry at the rear, and a smaller lounge accessed from the front. Moffat is a good base for exploring the Southern Uplands and there are excellent walks nearby. Q❀✿☕◗&♿🚃🕏🎵

Newton Stewart

Creebridge House Hotel

Minnigaff, DG8 6NP (on B7079, E of river)

☎ (01671) 402121 ⊕ creebridge.co.uk

2 changing beers (often Five Kingdoms) ⊞

This traditional country house hotel is set in three acres of gardens and woodland next to the River Cree and close to the town centre. Two ales are available throughout the summer, with one at other times. Food choices are excellent and locally sourced meat, game and fish are served. The bar and lounge areas have real fires. There is also an outdoor bar when weather permits. Dominoes league games are played Tuesday and some charity events are held. Q❀✿☕◗&♿AP🚃(415,500)❀🕏

Portpatrick

Crown Hotel

9 North Crescent, DG9 8SX (facing harbour)

☎ (01776) 810261 ⊕ crownhotelportpatrick.com

2 changing beers (often Five Kingdoms, Sulwath) ⊞

Hotel overlooking the picturesque and historic harbour with views on a clear day across to Ireland. The large, comfortable bar area at the front is adorned with fine pictures and ornaments, and warmed by an open fire. Two regularly changing ales are sourced from breweries across the UK, including the local Five Kingdoms brewery. Live music on Friday and Saturday nights features local and visiting musicians and groups. ✿☕◗&♿(367)❀🕏🎵

Stranraer

Grapes

4-6 Bridge Street, DG9 7HY

☎ (01776) 703386

2 changing beers (often Bowness Bay, Coniston) ⊞

Popular historic public bar, with impressive mirror and gantry, little altered in over 50 years. It has a comfortable refurbished snug bar downstairs, an upstairs Art Deco lounge/function room, and a bright and sunny seated courtyard. Local musicians play in the public bar most Friday evenings, and touring American-style bands often perform in the public bar or upstairs. There is a strong commitment to real ales, often sourced from Cumbria but also from around the UK. A mini beer festival is usually held annually. ✿❀☕&♿🚃(500,358)❀🕏🎵

Breweries

Borderlands

116A High Street, Langholm, DG13 0DH ☎ 07843 896644 ⊕ borderlandsbrewery.co.uk

Brewing in the heart of Langholm, also known as 'The Muckle Toon', Borderlands was founded by Stuart Campbell restoring brewing to the town, yards away from the historic brewery, after a break of over a century. Proudly nestled in the Esk Valley, the brewery is a 2.5-barrel plant brewing in small batches. Three core beers are supplemented by limited editions (all cask, bottle and can). Expanded into a new premises incorporating a taproom in 2022. ✒

Five Kingdoms SIBA

22 Main Street, Isle of Whithorn, DG8 8LF

☎ (01988) 500334 ⊕ fivekingdomsbrewery.com

☺Five Kingdoms was established in 2015 by Alastair Scoular, owner of the Steam Packet Inn, and Brendon Dennett, using a 2.5-barrel plant. It is situated in the harbourside village of Isle of Whithorn, the most southerly point of the Wigtownshire peninsula in Galloway and a tourist and sailing hotspot. It supplies numerous local and Scottish outlets, selected national beer festivals, and the Steam Packet Inn. Brewery tours and expansion are planned. ‼◆LIVE

Bright Idea (ABV 3.8%) PALE
McGregors Mild (ABV 3.8%) MILD
Bitter X Blonde (ABV 4%) GOLD
Hillbillie (ABV 4%) PALE
Rebus (ABV 4%) PALE
Summerisle (ABV 4%) GOLD
Invisible Hand (ABV 4.2%) BROWN
Gatsby (ABV 4.3%) PALE
Private Idaho (ABV 4.5%) PALE
Renton (ABV 4.5%)
Wee McAsh Bitter (ABV 4.5%) BROWN
Prentice (ABV 4.6%) PALE
Calm Before the Storm (ABV 5%) STOUT
Captain Morrison's IPA (ABV 6.5%) STRONG
Dark Storm Stout (ABV 6.9%) STOUT
Such Is Life NEIPA (ABV 6.9%) IPA

Lola Rose

Wanlockhead Inn, Wanlockhead, ML12 6UZ
☎ (01659) 74535 ☎ 07500 663405
⊕ lola-rose-brewery.co.uk

Lola Rose is based in the family-run Wanlockhead Inn, situated in the scenic Lowther Hills of the Scottish Lowlands. Local outlets only are supplied at present. LIVE

Lowland

8 Well Street, Lockerbie, DG11 2EY

☎ (01576) 203999 ☎ 07493 716521
⊕ lowlandbrewery.co.uk

⊠ Brewing began in 2018 using a five-barrel plant. Three regular beers are produced with plans to expand the range as the brewery develops. The brewery is located in converted premises in the town centre and supplies direct to pubs in Dumfries & Galloway, Scottish Borders and north Cumbria. ‼ ☛ ♦

Rabbie's Drouth (ABV 3.8%) PALE
Twa Dugs (ABV 4%) PALE
Golden Eagle (ABV 4.5%) GOLD
Dryfe Blonde (ABV 5%) BLOND

Motte & Bailey

🏠 Blue Bell Inn, 10 High Street, Annan, DG12 6AG
☎ (01461) 202385

⊠ Brewing began in 2018 in the cellar of the Blue Bell Inn, Annan, using equipment from Andrews Ales. Brewing capacity is one barrel. The range varies and is only available at the pub. ☛ ♦

Portpatrick

24 Main Street, Kirkcolm, Stranraer, DG9 0NN
☎ 07713 114844 ✉ portpatrickbrewery@gmail.com

☺The brewery has now been in operation since early 2022. It produces three core beers in both cask (occasional) and bottle conditioned. ♦LIVE

Sulwath SIBA

The Brewery, 209 King Street, Castle Douglas, DG7 1DT
☎ (01556) 504525 ⊕ sulwathbrewers.co.uk

☺Sulwath started brewing in 1995. Its award-winning beers are supplied to around 100 outlets and four

wholesalers as far away as Devon and Aberdeen. The brewery has a popular, fully-licensed taproom.
‼ ☛ ♦LIVE ☂

Cuil Hill (ABV 3.6%) BLOND
Distinctively fruity session ale with malt and hop undertones. The taste is bittersweet with a long-lasting dry finish.

Tri-ball (ABV 3.9%) GOLD
Brewed with three hops, it is fresh, crisp and blond – the ideal session ale.

The Grace (ABV 4.3%) MILD
A refreshing, rich ale with a full-bodied flavour that balances the caramel undertones.

Black Galloway (ABV 4.4%) PORTER
A robust porter that derives its colour from the abundance of chocolate malts.

Criffel (ABV 4.6%) BITTER
Full-bodied beer with a distinctive bitterness. Fruit is to the fore with hops becoming increasingly dominant in the finish.

Galloway Gold (ABV 5%) GOLD
A cask-conditioned lager that will be too sweet for many despite being heavily-hopped.

Knockendoch (ABV 5%) BITTER
Dark, copper-coloured, reflecting a roast malt content, with bitterness from Challenger hops.

Solway Mist (ABV 5.5%) SPECIALITY
A naturally cloudy wheat beer. Sweetish and fruity.

Wigtown (NEW)

Bladnoch, DG8 9AB ⊕ wigtownbrewery.co.uk

Family owned and run, small-batch microbrewery set up by the Kitson family, that first commercially brewed in 2019. Four core beers are available in bottles with limited availability.

Tam O'Shanter, Dumfries (Photo: Stuart McMahon)

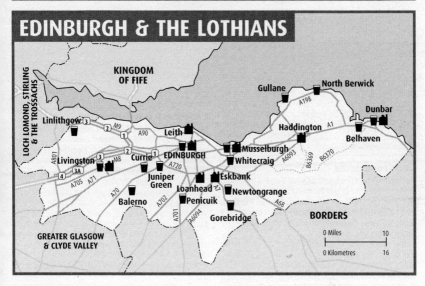

EDINBURGH & THE LOTHIANS

Balerno

Grey Horse
20 Main Street, EH14 7EH (off A70, in pedestrian area)
☎ (0131) 449 2888 ⊕ greyhorsebalerno.com
3 changing beers (sourced regionally; often Fyne, Orkney, Stewart) Ⓗ
Traditional stone-built village pub dating from the 18th century. The cosy public bar retains original features including wood panelling and a fine Bernard's mirror. The pleasant lounge has a more modern feel and there is also a small restaurant. A varied food menu is offered, with lighter options at lunchtime, a children's menu and Chinese specials. Dogs are allowed in the bar, with biscuits and water provided. There is occasional Sunday afternoon music. Often closed Monday and Tuesday lunchtime; no food on those days. Q❄▨❀◗♿➰(44)❀♪

Belhaven

Brig & Barrel
8 High Street, EH42 1NP (1 mile W of Dunbar)
☎ (01368) 866847 ⊕ thebrigandbarrel.com
Harviestoun Schiehallion; 1 changing beer (sourced regionally; often Harviestoun) Ⓗ
The former Masons Arms has a bright comfortable bar overlooking the beer garden, with views of the Lammermuir Hills. It features a small horseshoe counter finished with reclaimed wood and barrels, a smart wooden floor and a real fire in winter. Meals are served all day in summer and Friday to Sunday in winter. The superb beer garden has heated booths as well as tables and chairs. Families are welcome, and a children's menu is provided. Likely to be closed Monday and Tuesday in winter. Q❄▨❀◗▲➰❀🎵♪

Currie

Riccarton Inn
198 Lanark Road West, EH14 5NX
☎ (0131) 449 2230 ⊕ riccartoninn.co.uk
4 changing beers (sourced nationally; often Fyne, Loch Leven, Stewart) Ⓗ
Originally a coaching inn, the comfortable pub has a long central bar with half-timbered walls and contemporary exposed stonework. There are attractive seating areas

including booths next to the bar and a separate restaurant area. Meals are served all day and include children's options. The decking at the front has southerly views to the Pentland Hills and there's a large beer garden at the rear. Handy for the Water of Leith walkway. ❄▨❀◗➰➰(44,45)❀❖

Dunbar

Volunteer Arms
17 Victoria Street, EH42 1HP (near swimming pool)
☎ (01368) 862278 ⊕ volunteerarmsdunbar.co.uk
2 changing beers (sourced nationally; often Cairngorm, Harviestoun, Stewart) Ⓗ
A friendly, traditional locals' pub near the harbour. The cosy wood-panelled bar is decorated with lots of fishing- and lifeboat-oriented memorabilia, interesting photos and a good selection of old pumpclip badges on the ceiling. Upstairs is a restaurant serving an excellent good-value menu with an emphasis on seafood (all day except Wed & Thu). Food is also served downstairs. Families are welcome, with a children's menu and games provided. Q❄▨❀◗▲⇌✦➰➰❀❖♻♪

Edinburgh: Central

Abbotsford Bar & Restaurant ★
3-5 Rose Street, EH2 2PR
☎ (0131) 225 5276 ⊕ theabbotsford.com
Loch Lomond Southern Summit Ⓐ; **Timothy Taylor Landlord** Ⓗ; **5 changing beers (sourced regionally; often Cromarty, Orkney, Swannay)** Ⓗ/Ⓐ
This traditional Scottish bar features a magnificent island bar and gantry in dark mahogany – both fixtures since 1902. The ornate plasterwork and corniced ceiling are outstanding. The room is predominantly furnished with large tables and wooden bench seating. An extensive food menu is available all day in the bar. The separate restaurant is upstairs where real ale can be ordered from downstairs – and children over five are permitted. Return trays are not used on the handpumps.
Q❄▨❀◗⇌(Waverley) ☗(St Andrew Square) ➰❀❖♻

Black Cat
168 Rose Street, EH2 4BA
☎ (0131) 225 3349

2 changing beers (sourced regionally; often Bellfield, Harviestoun, Williams Bros) [H]
A small, single-roomed bar, selectively lit and with pleasant modern styling including a wall-to-wall mirror. An eclectic range of tables, chairs and stools include half-barrels and an upholstered banquette. It is a friendly pub and a lively place to visit, especially when folk musicians arrive. Food is served all day. The two real ales, usually from smaller Scottish breweries, and an extensive range of malt whiskies may be sampled in taster flights. Children are permitted until 8pm. May be open till 3am during the Festival in August. 🐎✿🍴🚊(West End - Princes Street) 🚌🐾📶♫

Guildford Arms

1 West Register Street, EH2 2AA (off E end of Princes St)
☎ (0131) 556 4312 🌐 guildfordarms.com
Fyne Jarl; Loch Lomond Silkie Stout; Stewart Pentland IPA; Swannay Orkney IPA; Timothy Taylor Landlord; 5 changing beers (sourced nationally; often Black Sheep, Cromarty, Newt) [H]
A large establishment built in the golden age of Victorian pub design. The high ceiling, cornices, friezes, window arches and screens are spectacular. There is a large standing area around the canopied bar, and extensive seating areas. The diverse range of real ales includes many from Scottish breweries. Meals and simple bar snacks are available all day, both downstairs and in the noteworthy upstairs gallery restaurant where children over five are permitted.
🐎🍴🚆(Waverley) 🚊(St Andrew Square) 🚌🐾📶↺♫

Jolly Judge 🏆

7 James Court, 493 Lawnmarket, EH1 2PB (in Old Town)
☎ (0131) 225 2669 🌐 jollyjudge.co.uk
4 changing beers (sourced nationally; often Cromarty, Fyne, Tempest) [H]
Comfortable small bar with an attractive painted ceiling, just off the Royal Mile hidden down an Old Town close. Outdoor tables in the close provide extra seating. The real ales are usually from smaller UK-wide breweries. A varying selection of six ciders is also available. This is a welcome spot for refreshment after visiting the castle and other Old Town attractions. Dogs are permitted after 3pm, but no children inside. Local CAMRA Pub of the Year and Cider Pub of the Year 2023.
Q✿🍴🚆(Waverley) 🚊(Princes Street) 🍎🚌🐾📶

Ryrie's

1 Haymarket Terrace, EH12 5EY (1 mile W of centre)
☎ (0131) 337 0550 🌐 ryries.bar
8 changing beers (sourced regionally; often Fyne, Swannay, Timothy Taylor) [H]
A classic Scottish bar in a listed building, tastefully refurbished in 2022, with dark wooden interior, fine bar gantry and stained/leaded glass windows. It is popular with a varied clientele from the local community and those using Haymarket station, and gets busy when Heart of Midlothian are at home. An upstairs lounge is now a cocktail bar and there is a bar annexe down two steps. Traditional Scottish pub meals are served all day. Children are not admitted.
✿🍴🚆(Haymarket) 🚊(Haymarket) 🚌🐾📶↺

Standing Order ✔

62-66 George Street, EH2 2LR
☎ (0131) 225 4460
Belhaven 80/-; Greene King Abbot; Sharp's Doom Bar; 9 changing beers (sourced nationally; often Inveralmond, Stewart) [H]
Designed by David and John Bryce and built in 1874-78 as the head Edinburgh office of the Union Bank, this is now a Wetherspoon pub. The vast main bar has a superb high ceiling and polished granite pillars. There are three smaller rooms with tables for dining, one containing the old Chubb vault. Meals are served all day. It can be busy at peak times. Children are welcome for meals in the family area until 8pm. Alcoholic drinks are served from 9am (11am on Sun).
🐎✿🍴♿🚆(Waverley) 🚊(Princes Street) 🚌📶

Teuchters Bar & Bunker

26 William Street, EH3 7NH (W edge of centre)
☎ (0131) 225 2973 🌐 teuchtersbar.co.uk
Fyne Jarl; Stewart Pentland IPA; Timothy Taylor Landlord; 2 changing beers (sourced regionally; often Born, Broughton, Fyne) [H]
Two cosy but deceptively roomy bars with a rustic feel, wooden beams and original stone walls. Seating includes chunky sofas and chairs around wooden tables. The real ales are usually from smaller Scottish breweries. The gantry has an impressive range of single malt whiskies and an explanation of the pub's name. Meals are served all day from a varied menu with a Scottish emphasis. Children are permitted until 10pm.
🐎🍴♿🚆(Haymarket) 🚊(West End/Princes Street) 🚌🐾📶

Edinburgh: East

Bellfield Brewery Tap Room

46 Stanley Place, EH7 5TB (1 mile E of centre)
☎ (0131) 656 9390 🌐 bellfieldbrewery.com
2 changing beers (often Bellfield)
The taproom is on the brewery site and tours and tastings are available. It has an excellent beer garden with covered booths. The cask ales are usually from Bellfield's standard range but new pilot brews sometimes appear. Bellfield was the UK's first craft brewery dedicated to gluten-free beers and all are certified gluten-free. Food is available on a pop-up basis, with the choice changing every few days. Children are welcome until 9pm. 🐎✿🍴♿🚌🐾📶♫

Edinburgh: North

Clark's Bar

142 Dundas Street, EH3 5DQ (N edge of New Town)
☎ (0131) 556 6677
Cross Borders Heavy; Stewart Jack Back [H]
This tenement bar is popular with locals and office workers. The internal layout is interesting, with two private rooms at the rear. A number of historical brewery mirrors and old photos of the pub adorn the main room. Don't miss the interesting mural on the steep stairs down to the toilets, which shows some former worthies. Children over six are permitted until 9pm. Likely to open at 3pm Monday to Thursday and may close early in winter. 🐎🚌🐾📶

REAL ALE BREWERIES

Alechemy Livingston
Barney's Edinburgh
Belhaven Dunbar
Bellfield ✎ Edinburgh
Campervan ✎ Leith
Cross Borders ✎ Eskbank
Hanging Bat ▮ Edinburgh
Keller ▮ Edinburgh
Newbarns ✎ Leith
Newt Musselburgh
Stewart ✎ Loanhead
Winton ✎ Haddington

Dreadnought

72 North Fort Street, Leith, EH6 4HL (2 miles N of centre)

☎ 07876 351535 ⊕ dreadnoughtpub.com

4 changing beers (sourced nationally; often Brass Castle, Cromarty, Dark Revolution) Ⓗ

A welcoming one-roomed pub with big picture windows, a high ceiling with plaster cornicing, and an attractive old-fashioned bar gantry. A large photograph of HMS Dreadnought hangs on the wall along with other nautical items. The Brass Castle beers are all vegan. No food is served but pizza and burgers can be ordered from local outlets. The TVs are only used for major sports events. Children are not admitted. Likely to be open Monday to Thursday from 4pm, Friday to Sunday from 2pm.

☻▶️Ⓠ(Newhaven) ♣🚌🏠❄️🐾🛜🎵

Foot of the Walk ✅

183 Constitution Street, Leith, EH6 7AA (1 mile N of centre)

☎ (0131) 553 0120

Belhaven 80/-; Greene King Abbot; Sharp's Doom Bar; 2 changing beers (sourced nationally; often Stewart, Williams Bros) Ⓗ

JD Wetherspoon pub attracting a large cross-section of Leith's citizens. Originally the historic, listed, Palace Cinema, it now has a low ceiling hiding the balcony and original decor. The spacious room is broken into discrete areas by waist-high wood panels, and a glass wall lets in light. Food is served all day and children are welcome until 8pm. Disabled access is via the Constitution Street entrance. ☻◀️♿Ⓠ(Foot of the Walk)🚌🛜

Henry Hall's Carriers Quarters

42 Bernard Street, Leith, EH6 6PR (2 miles N of centre)

☎ (0131) 554 4122 ⊕ carriersquarters.co.uk

2 changing beers (sourced regionally; often Fyne, Stewart) Ⓗ

Popular with locals, this small, cosy bar is said to be the oldest pub in the area. The front room contains the bar counter and has a small alcove displaying a series of historical prints depicting life in Leith. The rear room has exposed stone walls and a large fireplace with a welcoming electric stove in winter. The real ales are from Scottish breweries and there is a good selection of malt whiskies. Home-made pizzas are served all day, with a special deal weekday lunchtimes. Children are not admitted. ◀️Ⓠ(Shore)♣🚌❄️🛜🎵

Kay's Bar

39 Jamaica Street West, EH3 6HF (New Town, off India St)

☎ (0131) 225 1858

Fyne Jarl; Timothy Taylor Landlord; Theakston Best Bitter; 3 changing beers (sourced nationally; often Loch Lomond, Stewart, Swannay) Ⓗ

A cosy and convivial pub that retains many features from its days as a Victorian wine merchant. Considering its very small size, it offers an impressive range of real ales. It also has a large collection of malt whiskies. If the front bar is busy, try the small room at the back. Food is available at lunchtime Wednesday to Friday only. Children are not admitted. Edinburgh winner of the CAMRA Real Ale Quality Award 2022. Q◀️♣🚌❄️🛜🔄

Malt & Hops

45 The Shore, Leith, EH6 6QU (1½ miles N of centre)

☎ (0131) 555 0083

Hadrian Border Tyneside Blonde; 7 changing beers (sourced nationally; often Fyne, Swannay) Ⓗ

Old-fashioned single-roomed bar by the Water of Leith dating from 1747. It has a real fire and the walls are bedecked with mirrors, prints and beer-related artefacts.

A large selection of pumpclips, many from long-lost breweries, hang from the ceiling, along with hop bines which are renewed every harvest. The wide variety of real ales has an emphasis towards smaller breweries; beers are listed on the mirror behind the bar. Children are permitted until 6pm. ☻❄️Ⓠ(Shore)🚌🐾🛜🔄🎵

Old Eastway Tap

218 Easter Road, Leith, EH7 5QH (1 mile NE of centre)

☎ (0131) 259 3495 ⊕ oldeastwaytap.co.uk

4 changing beers (sourced locally; often Cross Borders) Ⓗ

Cross Borders brewery's second pub was opened in 2021 with four cask and 16 craft keg lines and was an instant hit with locals. The L-shaped bar is on a split level, and the decor is muted, with relatively low levels of lighting to aid relaxation. Tap takeovers and meet the brewer events are held frequently. Meals consist of various types of hot dogs, mac 'n' cheese, and nachos. Children are not admitted. ☻◀️🍴🚌❄️🎵

Stockbridge Tap

2-4 Raeburn Place, Stockbridge, EH4 1HN (¾ mile N of centre)

☎ (0131) 343 3000

Swannay Island Hopping; 5 changing beers (sourced nationally; often Alechemy, Cross Borders, Cromarty) Ⓗ

A specialist real ale house offering unusual and interesting ales from all over the UK and holding occasional beer festivals. The staff are keen and knowledgeable about the selection. The front area is bright and offers plenty of seating and space for vertical drinking, while the rear has low tables and sofas. Both feature mirrors from lost breweries, including Murray's and Campbell's. A handy stop for those walking the Water of Leith path. Children are not admitted. ♿♣🚌🐾🛜

Teuchters Landing

1C Dock Place, Leith, EH6 6LU (2 miles N of centre)

☎ (0131) 554 7427 ⊕ teuchtersbar.co.uk

Caledonian Deuchars IPA; Fyne Jarl; Timothy Taylor Landlord; 1 changing beer (sourced regionally; often Black Isle, Orkney, Stewart) Ⓗ

Once the waiting room for the Leith to Aberdeen ferry, the attractive front bar has a wood-panelled ceiling edged with tiles featuring Scottish place names from Teuchterland. There are two smaller rooms and a large conservatory opening out on to a pontoon floating on the Water of Leith. The varied food menu is available all day. An excellent selection of malt whiskies is available. Children are permitted in the back rooms. Likely to open at 9.15am; alcoholic drinks are served from 11am. ☻❄️◀️♿Ⓠ(Port of Leith) ♣🍴🚌❄️🛜

Edinburgh: South

Argyle Bar

15 Argyle Place, EH9 1JJ (1 mile S of centre)

☎ (0131) 221 9759

3 changing beers (sourced regionally; often Cross Borders, Fyne, Stewart) Ⓗ

Located on the ground floor of a corner tenement in Marchmont, this small pub has a loyal clientele drawn from locals and the transient student population. It comprises a single room on the ground floor and a basement room where various live and DJ music events are held. The bar has banquette seating along two walls, central tables and chairs, bar stools and large windows overlooking the street. Children are permitted until 8pm. Likely to be closed lunchtimes Monday to Friday. ☻❄️🚌❄️🛜🎵

Bennets of Morningside ✔

1 Maxwell Street, Morningside, EH10 5HT (1½ miles S of centre)

☎ (0131) 447 1903

Stewart Pentland IPA; Timothy Taylor Landlord; house beer (by Hadrian Border); 3 changing beers (sourced nationally; often Cromarty, Fyne, Stewart) ⊞

A cosy, traditional single-room tenement bar in the Morningside area of the city that has been tastefully refurbished. Photographs of old Edinburgh adorn the walls along with some interesting brewery mirrors. The guest ales tend to be from Scotland and north-east England, and one real ale (badged Bennets Ale) is always available. There is a paved outdoor drinking area to the front. Children are not admitted. ✿&♣🖵🏠🎵🛜

Cask & Barrel (Southside)

24-26 West Preston Street, EH8 9PZ (1 mile S of centre)

☎ (0131) 667 0856 ● caskandbarrelsouthside.co.uk

Stewart Jack Back; Swannay Orkney Best; 5 changing beers (sourced nationally; often Cromarty, Fyne, Oakham) ⊞

A modern recreation of a Scottish city tenement bar. The single room, with windows front and back, is divided by a horseshoe bar with a dark-wood gantry adorned with decorative wooden casks. The walls support a fine range of old photos, advertisements and historic brewery and distillery mirrors. Sport is screened on multiple TVs with the sound normally low. This is a good place to try real ales from interesting breweries UK-wide. Children are not admitted. 🖵🛜ひ🎵

Cloisters Bar

26 Brougham Street, EH3 9JH (¾ mile SW of centre)

☎ (0131) 221 9997 ● cloistersbar.com

8 changing beers (sourced nationally; often Black Isle, Stewart, Swannay) ⊞

Established in 1995 in the former All Saints Parsonage, this warm and friendly bar has retained many traditional features. The real ales are generally from interesting breweries UK-wide. Frequent tap takeovers and Meet the Brewer events are held. The wide range of single malt whiskies, gins and rums does justice to the outstanding gantry. Meals are provided by OGs street food and feature burgers, bangers and mash and a roast on Sunday. Children under 16 are not admitted. Q🍴♣🖵🏠🛜ひ

John Leslie ★

45-47 Ratcliffe Terrace, EH9 1SU (1½ miles S of centre)

☎ (0131) 667 7205

Timothy Taylor Landlord; house beer (by Allendale); 4 changing beers (sourced nationally; often Allendale, Belhaven, Stewart) ⊞

Located on the ground floor of a four-storey tenement, this superb pub is divided in two by a fine mahogany counter, gantry with clock and a mirrored snob screen with small 'ticket window' hatches. The bar has an alcove with banquettes while the lounge has three areas, a small snug by the door, an area around the fire and a quieter corner with banquette seating. The elaborate late 19th-century decorative plaster work includes a Lincrusta frieze. Children over two are permitted until 9pm. 🚶♣🖵🏠🛜ひ🎵

Edinburgh: West

Athletic Arms (Diggers) ✔

1-3 Angle Park Terrace, EH11 2JX (1½ miles SW of centre)

☎ (0131) 337 3822

House beer (by Stewart) 🅰; **5 changing beers (sourced nationally; often Fyne, Stewart, Timothy Taylor)** ⊞/🅰

Dating from 1897, this legendary Edinburgh pub is known as the Diggers because of its location between two graveyards. Banquette seating lines the walls and the wooden floor features a compass drawing. Two smaller back rooms, where children are permitted if eating, have further seating and the larger has a dartboard. The pub gets busy when Hearts are playing at home. The pies are outstanding. Return trays (Autovacs) are only used with the tall founts. 🚶♣🖵🏠🛜ひ

Roseburn Bar ✔

1 Roseburn Terrace, EH12 5NG (1½ miles W of centre)

☎ (0131) 337 1067 ● roseburnbar.co.uk

Fyne Jarl; Stewart Pentland IPA; 1 changing beer (sourced nationally; often Cromarty) ⊞

A traditional pub, popular with locals and close to Murrayfield (for rugby) and Tynecastle (for football). It boasts high ceilings and a largely wooden interior, with interesting mirrors and period photos on the walls. There are numerous comfortable booths along the walls and two separate lounge areas. Multiple TVs show sporting events, though the volume is typically kept low. Live music plays on Friday and Saturday evenings. Children are not admitted. &🚆(Murrayfield Stadium)🖵🏠🛜🎵

Winstons ✔

20 Kirk Loan, Corstorphine, EH12 7HD (3 miles W of centre, off St Johns Rd)

☎ (0131) 539 7077 ● winstonslounge.co.uk

Stewart Pentland IPA 🅿; **3 changing beers (sourced regionally; often Harviestoun, Swannay)** ⊞

A comfortable lounge bar in Corstorphine, just over a mile from Murrayfield stadium and half a mile from the zoo. The small, modern building houses a warm and welcoming community pub used by old and young alike, with sports TV and monthly live music. The decor features golfing and rugby themes along with historical photos of Corstorphine. The real ales are usually from a variety of Scottish breweries. Children are not admitted. ✿🖵🏠🛜🎵

Gorebridge

Stobsmill Inn (Bruntons)

25 Powdermill Brae, EH23 4HX (⅓ mile S of centre)

☎ (01875) 820202 ● stobsmill.co.uk

1 changing beer (often Born, Loch Lomond, Stewart) ⊞

This small pub, built in 1866, is now the only pub in Gorebridge. The single-room bar has a long L-shaped counter with a row of bar stools, and an area with tables and chairs, benches, and a large clock. The decor and skylight help to create a bright and welcoming interior. There is another attractive area with tables and chairs and bench seating, and the Brunton Restaurant is downstairs. Entry is restricted to over-21s, unless dining. It is likely to be closed on Tuesday and Wednesday. 🚶✿🍴🚆♣🅿🚌(29,48)🏠🛜🎵

Gullane

Old Clubhouse

East Links Road, EH31 2AF (W end of village, off A198)

☎ (01620) 842008 ● oldclubhouse.com

Timothy Taylor Landlord; 2 changing beers (sourced regionally; often Alechemy, Stewart) 🅿

There is a colonial feel to this pub, with views over the golf links to the Lammermuir Hills. The half-panelled walls are adorned with historic memorabilia and stuffed animals. Caricature figures of the Marx Brothers and Laurel and Hardy look down from the gantry. Food features highly and is served all day, The extensive and varied menu includes simple snacks, vegetarian and children's options and is supplemented with daily specials. Q ♿ ❄ ◐ ♣ 🖵 ❀ 🛜

Juniper Green

Kinleith Mill

604 Lanark Road, EH14 5EN
☎ (0131) 453 3214 🌐 kinleithmill.com
3 changing beers (sourced regionally; often Fyne, Loch Leven, Stewart) Ⓗ

This well-maintained pub and kitchen has a friendly atmosphere and welcomes locals and visitors alike. The large room is decorated with old village pictures and has an island bar counter separating the public bar and the lounge/dining areas. Meals are served all day, with monthly changing specials, and the menu offers children's options. A full range of sports is shown on TVs. Dogs are only allowed in the non-carpeted areas. The rear beer garden has an Astroturf surface and a part-covered decked area. ♿ ❄ ◐ ♣ 🖵 (44,45) ❀ 🛜

Linlithgow

Four Marys ✓

65-67 High Street, EH49 7ED
☎ (01506) 842171
Belhaven 80/-; Greene King Yardbird; 6 changing beers (sourced nationally; often Cromarty, Fyne, Orkney) Ⓗ

Close to Linlithgow Palace, birthplace of Mary Queen of Scots, the building dates back to around 1500 and is named after Mary's four ladies-in-waiting. Initially a dwelling house, the building has had several changes of use over the centuries – it was once a chemists run by the Waldie family whose most famous member, David, helped establish the anaesthetic properties of chloroform in 1847. The pub serves good-quality food and an ever-changing range of real ales from Scottish and English breweries. Q ♿ ❄ ◐ ⇌ ♣ 🖵 ❀ 🛜 ♪

Platform 3 ✓

1A High Street, EH49 7AB
☎ (01506) 847405 🌐 platform3.co.uk
Stewart Pentland IPA; 2 changing beers (sourced regionally; often Fyne, Stewart) Ⓗ

Small, friendly hostelry on the railway station approach. It was originally the public bar of the hotel next door and was renovated in 1998 as a pub in its own right. Look out for the miniature goods train that travels from the station above the bar, with ducks waiting for a train that never arrives. Two Scottish beers are served in addition to the regular ale. It has appeared in this Guide for over 20 years. Dogs are welcomed with biscuits and water. A live train departures board keeps travellers informed. ⇌ ♣ 🖵 ❀ 🛜 ♪

West Port Hotel ✓

18-20 West Port, EH49 7AZ (on A803, ¾ mile W of town centre)
☎ (01506) 847456
2 changing beers (sourced regionally; often Loch Leven) Ⓗ

This hotel at the western end of Linlithgow High Street is a reminder of the western entry or port into Linlithgow, where travellers could rest when the port was barred. Today, this pub and hotel still provides a warm welcome. Food is to the fore, complemented by real ale, usually from Loch Leven brewery. When the sun shines, head to

the spacious rear beer garden. If you feel energetic, the nearby Linlithgow Loch has an enjoyable circular walk. ❀ ⇌ ◐ ♿ P 🖵 ❀ 🛜

Livingston

NewYearField ✓

Designer Outlet, Almondvale Avenue, EH54 6QX
☎ (01506) 420770
Greene King Abbot; 4 changing beers (sourced nationally) Ⓗ

Wetherspoon pub in a large shopping mall next to the bus stances. The interior has a modern design and there is an outdoor patio area with a segregated area for smokers. The pub takes its name from a nearby medieval hunting lodge, where the first hunts of the year took place, and is commemorated by a large sculptured boar's head. Meals are served all day. Children are permitted until 8pm with menu options provided. Alcoholic drinks are not served before 11am. ♿ ❄ ◐ ♿ P 🖵 🛜

Musselburgh

David MacBeth Moir ✓

Bridge Street, EH21 6AG (opp the Brunton)
☎ (0131) 653 1060
Belhaven 80/-; Greene King Abbot; Sharp's Doom Bar; 2 changing beers (sourced nationally; often Broughton, Stewart, Williams Bros) Ⓗ

This Wetherspoon pub, named after a local physician and writer, was converted from a cinema dating back to 1935. Many original features have been beautifully restored. The vast, single-roomed bar has Art Deco styling and artefacts from a cinema background. There is a long bar counter with a good mix of real ales. Food is served all day and families are welcome until 8pm, with children's menu and crayons provided. Likely to open at 8am with alcoholic drinks served from 11am (12.30 Sun). Q ♿ ❄ ◐ ♿ 🛜

Levenhall Arms

10 Ravensheugh Road, EH21 7PP (B1348, 1 mile E of centre)
☎ (0131) 665 3220
Born Blonde; Winton Peelywally; 1 changing beer (sourced regionally) Ⓗ/Ⓐ

A friendly three-roomed hostelry dating from 1830 and close to the racecourse. The lively, cheerfully decorated public bar is half-timber panelled, with a wood effect floor. Dominoes is regularly played and the TV often shows sporting events. A smaller area leads off, with a dartboard and pictures of old local industries. The pleasant lounge, where families are welcome until 8pm, has a hardwood floor and comfortable seating. It now has a second dartboard that is used for matches. ♿ ❄ ♣ ▲ ♣ P 🖵 ❀ 🛜 ♪

Volunteer Arms (Staggs) ♆

81 North High Street, EH21 6JE (behind the Brunton)
☎ (0131) 665 9654
Fyne Jarl; Oakham JHB, Citra, Bishops Farewell, Green Devil; 3 changing beers (sourced nationally; often Fyne, Two by Two, Vocation) Ⓗ

Superb pub run by the same family since 1858. Its bar and snug are traditional, with wooden floors, wood panelling, mirrors from defunct local breweries, and an attractive gantry topped with old casks. The more modern lounge opens at the weekend. Real ales are mostly pale and hoppy but there is always a dark one. Children are permitted until 7.30pm in the lounge and snug. Local CAMRA Pub of the Year 2023, and winner of many previous awards. ♿ ❄ ♣ 🖵 ❀ 🛜 ↻

Newtongrange

Dean Tavern

80 Main Street, EH22 4NA
☎ (0131) 663 2419 ⊕ deantavern.co.uk
1 changing beer (sourced regionally; often Born, Loch Lomond, Stewart) ⊞
Superb pub run by trustees on Gothenburg principles, with profits returned to the local community. The spacious bar was designed to help miners recover from their day in darkness, with roof lights in a high ceiling supported by arched iron beams. There is also the Lamp Room restaurant and a function room with a large mural depicting the town's mining past. Meals are available all day (not Tue). Children are welcome until 8pm if dining.
🛏🐕❶🕽&🔥♿🐾😼🐾🎵

North Berwick

Auld Hoose

19 Forth Street, EH39 4HX (N edge of centre)
☎ (01620) 892692 ⊕ auldhoosenorthberwick.co.uk
Greene King Abbot; Timothy Taylor Landlord; 1 changing beer (sourced regionally; often Broughton, Spey Valley, Williams Bros) ⊞
Built in 1896 and said to be the oldest pub in town, this interesting, high-ceilinged, traditional Scottish drinking shop has been tastefully updated. The bar has bare floorboards around a mahogany bar, carpeted areas and a welcoming atmosphere enhanced by a real fire in winter. The gantry has four carved pillars and supports six old numbered whisky casks. The through lounge, where children are permitted until 8pm, has varied seating, a pool table and pictures of sporting heroes.
🛏♿🔥🖳😼🐾🎵

Nether Abbey Hotel

20 Dirleton Avenue, EH39 4BQ (A198, ¾ mile W of centre)
☎ (01620) 892802 ⊕ netherabbey.co.uk
Fyne Jarl; 3 changing beers (sourced nationally; often Alechemy, Stewart, Williams Bros) ⊞
Family-run hotel in a stone-built villa with a bright, contemporary, open-plan interior. The Fly Half Bar is in a split-level glass extension; large folding doors open out onto an attractive patio. Real ales can be served without sparklers on request. The award-winning restaurant is famed for its freshly cooked and locally sourced food, available daily and served all day Saturday and Sunday. Children are welcome until 8pm (7pm in the bar). Likely to be closed until 4pm Monday to Friday.
🛏🐕❶🕽&🔥♿🖳(124,X5) 😼🐾

Ship Inn

7-9 Quality Street, EH39 4HJ (E edge of centre)
☎ (01620) 890699 ⊕ theshipinnnorthberwick.com
Fyne Jarl; 2 changing beers (sourced nationally; often Bellfield, Greene King, Orkney) ⊞
Friendly, spacious, often lively venue with a wide variety of seating and tables. The bar area has pine floorboards and a tastefully modernised bar and gantry. To the side and rear is a quieter carpeted area (dogs not allowed) and there is maritime artwork throughout. It is popular for food, which is served all day, with good children's, vegetarian, vegan and gluten-free choices. Sparklers can be removed on request. Try the suntrap rear patio garden in the summer. 🛏🐕❶🖳😼🐾🎵

Penicuik

Navaar House Hotel

23 Bog Road, EH26 9BY (¼ mile W of centre)
☎ (01968) 672683 ⊕ navaarhouse.co.uk

Fyne Jarl; 1 changing beer (sourced locally; often Stewart) ⊞
A lively pub with a strong community spirit. The large bar is open plan with a log/coal stove, TV screens and a pool table. A pleasantly decorated bistro serves locally sourced food lunchtimes, evenings, and all day on Saturday and Sunday. Children (menu provided) are permitted in the restaurant only. There is a small lounge by the bistro and pleasant beer garden. The bar opens at 3pm Monday to Friday but drinks can be enjoyed in the bistro and lounge before then. 🛏🐕❶🕽♣🖳😼🐾

Whitecraig

Mercat Bar & Grill

10 Whitecraig Road, EH21 8PG
☎ 0800 124 4112 ⊕ mercatgrill.com
1 changing beer (sourced regionally; often Cross Borders, Stewart, Winton) ⊞
Pleasantly decorated and furnished pub that focuses on food but has a bar area for drinkers. Meals are served all day anywhere in the three linked areas, including the popular conservatory restaurant. The menu offers a good choice of options and is supplemented by daily specials, Sunday roasts, smaller portion options and children's dishes. The real ale may occasionally be from Walkie Talkie brewery. An electric car charging point is provided. Likely to be closed Tuesday and may close early if quiet.
🖳🛏🐕❶&🔥♣🖳😼🐾

Breweries

Alechemy SIBA

5 Rennie Square, Brucefield Industrial Park, Livingston, EH54 9DF
☎ (01506) 413634 ⊕ alechemy.beer

Dr James Davies, a keen traditional brewer and chemist, started brewing in 2012. A 12-barrel plant is used. Beers can be found in shops and pubs across the UK, Sweden and China. Alechemy is now part of the Consolidated Craft Breweries group, which opened its first bar in 2019, the Froth & Flame in Edinburgh. Brewing may be undertaken for other breweries in the group. ◆LIVE

Charisma (ABV 3.7%) PALE
Ritual (ABV 4.1%) PALE
Well-balanced golden ale. A strong hop character, balanced by malt and fruit with a long and dry finish..
10 Storey Malt Bomb (ABV 4.5%) BITTER
Bad Day At The Office (ABV 4.5%) GOLD
RumDMC (ABV 4.8%) SPECIALITY

Barney's SIBA

Summerhall Brewery, 1 Summerhall, Edinburgh, EH9 1PL ☎ 07512 253660 ⊕ barneysbeer.com

The only microbrewery in Edinburgh's city centre, Barney's Beer was founded in 2010 and now brews on the site of the original 1800s Summerhall Brewery. Summerhall is Edinburgh's centre for the arts and science. ◆V

Red Rye (ABV 4.5%) RED
Warming spicy notes from the rye malt create an interesting twist.
Volcano IPA (ABV 5%) PALE
Nice floral aroma to this moderately bitter IPA.

Belhaven

Brewery Lane, Dunbar, EH42 1PE
☎ (01368) 862734 ⊕ belhaven.co.uk

☺Belhaven is Scotland's oldest working brewery, established in 1719. Nestling between the rolling hills of East Lothian and a beautiful bay (the meaning of Belhaven), it brews beers using 100% Scottish malted barley, fresh water from a local source and its own Belhaven yeast. Part of Greene King plc. Now brewing Caledonian beers for Heineken. ‼🍽

80/- (ABV 4.2%) BITTER
St Andrew's Amber Ale (ABV 4.9%) BITTER
A bittersweet beer with lots of body. The malt, fruit and roast mingle throughout with hints of hop and caramel.

Contract brewed for Heineken:
Deuchars IPA (ABV 3.8%) BITTER

Bellfield SIBA

46 Stanley Place, Edinburgh, EH7 5TB
☎ (0131) 656 9390 ⊕ bellfieldbrewery.com

☺Bellfield was established in 2014 and was the UK's first certified gluten-free brewery. It is accredited by Coeliac UK and registered with the Vegan Society. The new site with taproom and all-weather beer garden opened in 2019. ‼♦GFV✦

Lucky Spence Ale (ABV 3.5%) BITTER
Session Ale (ABV 3.8%) PALE
Light citrus tones flavour this balanced bitter.
Lawless Village IPA (ABV 4.5%) PALE
Eighty Shilling (ABV 4.8%) BROWN
Jex-Blake Mosaic IPA (ABV 5.6%) IPA

Campervan SIBA

Unit 4, Bonnington Business Centre, 112 Jane Street, Leith, Edinburgh, EH6 5HG
☎ (0131) 553 3373 ☎ 07786 566000
⊕ campervanbrewery.com

Campervan began brewing in 2016 in a garage and an old campervan (hence the name). The van is still used for some events. A new 10-barrel facility in Leith was opened in 2017. Campervan's Lost in Leith Bar and Fermentaria houses an onsite barrel-ageing project. Campervan returned to cask ale production in 2022 and looked set to extend the range in 2023. LIVE ✦

Hoppy Camper (ABV 4.5%) PALE

Cold Town SIBA

8-10 Dunedin Street, Edinburgh, EH7 4JB
☎ (0131) 221 9978

Second Site: 4 Grassmarket, Edinburgh, EH1 2JU
⊕ coldtownbeer.com

Launched as a microbrewery in an old disused church on Grassmarket in 2018, Cold Town evolved quickly and expanded to a larger site in 2019. The original brewery metamorphosed into a bar and restaurant, Cold Town House, was upgraded and continues to produce some beers on site. Beers available in keg and can. ‼

Cross Borders SIBA

28-1, Hardengreen Industrial Estate, Eskbank, Dalkeith, EH22 3NX
☎ (0131) 629 3990 ⊕ crossborders.beer

⊗ Established in 2016 by childhood friends Jonathan Wilson and Gary Munckton, Cross Borders brews

traditional Scottish ales without pretension. The onsite taproom is open Friday and Saturday. ‼🍽✦

Hop Series Pale (ABV 3.8%) PALE
Notes of citrus on the nose with a balanced bitter finish.
Wee BRAW (ABV 4%) PALE
A fresh, fruity beer with lots of hops creating a great aroma and a lightly bitter aftertaste.
Heavy (ABV 4.1%) BITTER
A malt forward 'heavy', fruity with a slight bitterness not found in a traditional 80/-.
Bill's Beer (ABV 4.2%) PALE
Session IPA, a pale, full flavoured ale with zesty fruits and a clean finish
Porter (ABV 4.2%) PORTER
Flavours of coffee and chocolate come through in the finish of this easily drinkable porter.
Stout (ABV 5%) STOUT
BRAW (ABV 5.2%) PALE
Enticing citrus and tropical notes in the aroma of this juicy, refreshing golden ale.
IPA (ABV 6%) IPA

Edinburgh Beer Factory

The Works, Implement Road, West Barns, Dunbar, EH11 4EQ
☎ (0131) 442 4562 ⊕ edinburghbeerfactory.co.uk

Family-run brewery that was established in 2015. With packaging inspired by Leith-born artist Eduardo Paolozzi the beers are available in bottle, keg and can. Brewing ceased in Edinburgh in 2022, before moving to West Barns, East Lothian. ‼✦

Hanging Bat

🏠 **Hanging Bat Beer Café, 133 Lothian Road, Edinburgh, EH3 9AB**
☎ (0131) 229 0759
⊕ hangingbatbrewco.tumblr.com

⊗ Brewing began in 2012 from within the Hanging Bat bar using a 50-litre brew kit from the United States.

Keller

🏠 **23-27 Broughton Street Lane, Edinburgh, EH39 5NG**
⊕ kellertaproom.com

This in-house brewery operates from a space next to, and visible from, the Keller Taproom. There is also a distillery. The first unfiltered craft lager appeared in mid 2021.

Moonwake SIBA

6a Tower Street, Leith, Edinburgh, EH6 7BY
☎ (0131) 553 6995 ⊕ moonwakebeer.com

Brewing commenced in 2021 from a site close to the Water of Leith using a 35hl three-vessel brew kit. The range of core beers together with seasonal beers, one-offs and collaborations are produced in keg. Beers are also available in can. No real ale. 🍽✦

Newbarns

13 Jane Street, Leith, Edinburgh, EH6 5HE
☎ (0131) 554 4363 ⊕ newbarnsbrewery.com

The four founders moved north from London having worked at Kernel and Siren breweries in the past decade, and opened Newbarns in 2020. Real ale production commenced at the end of 2021. An adjacent taproom was opened in 2022. Collaboration on cask ale with Donzoko, which also brews at the site, has been a recent feature. ✦

Table Beer (ABV 3%) PALE
Pale Ale (ABV 4.8%) PALE
Stout (ABV 5%) STOUT

Newt SIBA

Unit 1, Block 4, Inveresk Industrial Estate,
Musselburgh, EH21 7UL ☎ 07979 905055

Office: 7 / 7 Cornwallis Place, Edinburgh, EH3 6NG
⊕ newtbrew.com

Originally set up at the organic farm, East Coast Organics in Pencaitland, Newt Brew moved in 2021 to new premises at Eskbank, Musselburgh, just outside Edinburgh. Beers are produced in small 100-1,000-litre batches usually using the main 1000-litre kit, or the 200-litre pilot kit for small runs. All beer brewed is certified organic, unfined and vegan. Available in casks and bottles with expansion to cans and kegs planned. LIVE V

Thirsty Dog (ABV 4%) PALE
Cascade Karma (ABV 4.7%) PALE
Organic Pale Ale (ABV 5%) PALE
Sunshine Pale (ABV 5%) PALE
Night Porter (ABV 5.5%) PORTER

Otherworld

27/ 1 Hardengreen Estate, Eskbank, Dalkeith,
EH22 3NX ⊕ otherworldbrewing.com

Otherworld Brewing Ltd was established in 2022 and specialises in producing modern sour and mixed fermentation beers. Available mostly in cans.

Pilot Beer SIBA

4B Stewartfield, Edinburgh, EH6 5RQ
☎ (0131) 561 4267 ⊕ pilotbeer.co.uk

Pilot began brewing in 2013 in an industrial unit in Leith using a five-barrel plant. A move to larger premises has allowed for expansion. Beers are unfined and unfiltered. Almost all output is keg or can but cask-conditioned ale is occasionally available. 🍺

Stenroth

Kenmure Avenue, Edinburgh, EH8 7HD
⊕ stenrothbrewing.co.uk

Founded by partners Kat Drinnan and Jimmy Mehtala in 2019, this home-based, 60-litre nanobrewery produces four core beers.

Stewart SIBA

26a Dryden Road, Bilston Glen Industrial Estate,
Loanhead, EH20 9LZ
☎ (0131) 440 2442 ⊕ stewartbrewing.co.uk

☺Established in 2004 by Steve and Jo Stewart, Stewart Brewing is Edinburgh's original craft brewery and has been innovating and brewing award-winning beers for 20 years, now from a custom-built 20,000 hectolitre brewhouse just outside of Edinburgh. As well as producing a wide range of beers there is a varied retail offering including an onsite Brew-It-Yourself Experience, a well-stocked brewery shop with growler fill station, weekly brewery tours, and a Bar & Pizza Kitchen with cask-conditioned, tank and kegged beers. ‼️🍺♦LIVE 🍴

Jack Back (ABV 3.7%) PALE
A pale hoppy beer with strong citrus and tropical fruit aromas. The taste is light, crisp and refreshing.
Pentland IPA (ABV 3.9%) PALE

A delicately-hopped, deep golden-coloured session ale. The dry bitter taste is well-balanced by sweetness from the malt, and fruit flavours.
Citra Blonde (ABV 4%) BLOND
80/- (ABV 4.4%) MILD
Superb traditional Scottish heavy. The complex profile is dominated by malt with fruit flavours giving the sweetish character typical of this beer style. Hops provide a gentle balancing bitterness that intensifies in the dry finish.
Edinburgh Gold (ABV 4.8%) GOLD
A full-bodied but easy-drinking, continental-style golden ale. Bitterness from the hop character is strong in the finish and complemented in the taste by a little sweetness from malt, and fruit flavours.

Suspect

34 Jane Street, Leith, Edinburgh, EH6 5HD ☎ 07468 436652 ⊕ suspectbrewing.co.uk

A gluten-free brewery set up in the former Liquid Brewing premises. No real ale. GF

Tartan Shark

5 Bangholm Park, Edinburgh, EH5 3BA ☎ 07746 432512 ⊕ tartanshark.co.uk

This self-styled 'smallest brewery in Edinburgh' began production in early 2020. LIVE

Vault City SIBA

Unit 2, A1 Industrial Park, Sir Harry Lauder Road,
Edinburgh, EH15 2QA ⊕ vaultcity.co.uk

Launched as a kitchen brewery in Edinburgh in 2018, Vault City Brewing relocated to share facilities at 71 Brewing in Dundee in 2019 before moving back to Edinburgh. Making fruit-forward, modern sour beers, the monthly Farm to Fermenter series utilises local fruits. Available in bottles and kegs.

Walkie Talky

10 Whitecraig Road, Whitecraig, EH21 8PG
⊕ walkietalkybrewing.com

A craft brewery set up in 2021 by Michael Johnstone and Joel Saunderson amplifying classic beer styles with a post-punk mindset.

Winton

10 Station Yard Industrial Estate, Hospital Road,
Haddington, EH41 3PP
☎ (01620) 826854 ⊕ wintonbrewery.com

After a spell brewing at Top Out (qv), and a site adjacent to Thistly Cross Cider, Winton relocated to Haddington in 2021. It produces a range of beers in keg, cask and can. It took over the Station Yard micropub, Dunbar, in 2020, before opening a taproom in 2022. ✦

Peelywally (ABV 5%) BITTER
Barry Swally (ABV 5.5%) PALE

Yikes (NEW)

13 New Broompark, Granton, Edinburgh, EH5 1RS
⊕ yikesbrew.co

The original plan for Yikes Brew Co was to borrow ideas from the world of soda and add them to fruited sours, however that has now expanded to encompass traditional beers and historic farmhouse brewing. Beers are available canned.

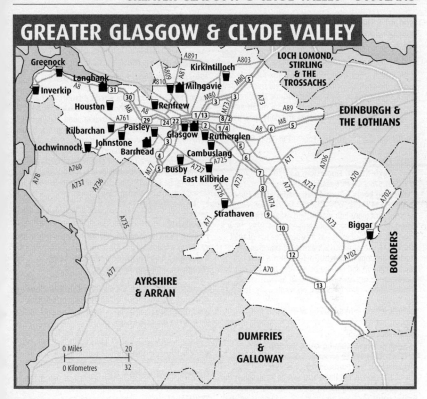

GREATER GLASGOW & CLYDE VALLEY

Biggar

Crown Inn Ⓛ
109-111 High Street, ML12 6DL
☎ (01899) 220116 ● thecrownbiggar.co.uk
6 changing beers (sourced nationally; often Broughton, Stewart) Ⓗ

A pleasant and friendly inn in the centre of this market town, the Crown has hundreds of years of tradition behind it, officially dating from the mid-17th century. The bar area is directly accessed from the street and there is a small quiet room, conservatory and beer garden to the rear. The real ales are mainly from Scottish breweries and these can be served in flights of three third-pints.
ᗩ✿❶🖥(91,101)✿🛜♪

Busby

White Cart ✓
61 East Kilbride Road, G76 8HX
☎ (0141) 644 2711
Greene King IPA, Abbot Ⓗ

A bright, spacious and lively Chef and Brewer pub in the conservation village of Busby, with a large bar and restaurant area and a designated family space. The large outdoor patio area at the front is used as a beer garden and as a restaurant which is popular in the summer. In winter customers can enjoy the roaring fires.
ᗩ✿❶🖥↹🅿🖥✿🛜

Cambuslang

John Fairweather ✓
52-58 Main Street, G72 7EP
☎ (0141) 646 2411

East Kilbride (continued from other column)

Belhaven 80/-; Greene King Abbot; 3 changing beers (sourced nationally; often Broughton, Williams Bros) Ⓗ

An impressive Wetherspoon conversion of the former Savoy cinema, named after the man who designed it. Many original features have been retained and restored, including some of the seats which fold up when you stand. The former ticket office leads to the bar. At the back is an upstairs area where the screen used to be. The pub is watched over by models of movie-goers sitting in the balcony. Outside is a small beer garden.
✿❶♿↹🖥✿🛜

East Kilbride

Hudsons ✓
14-16 Cornwall Way, G74 1JR
☎ (01355) 581040
3 changing beers (sourced nationally; often Black Sheep, Shepherd Neame) Ⓗ

Busy town-centre pub just outside the bus station, near to the entrance of the Princes Mall shopping centre and handy for the cinema complex. There is a central elliptical-shaped bar with comfortable seating around both sides. The real ales are prominently displayed on the curve of the bar as you enter and are usually from English breweries. Several strategically placed TVs show sport. The main toilets are accessed by a spiral staircase.
♿↹✿🛜♪

Glasgow

Babbity Bowster
16-18 Blackfriars Street, Merchant City, G1 1PE
☎ (0141) 552 5055 ● babbitybowster.com

Fyne Jarl; 2 changing beers (sourced nationally; often Broughton, Kelburn) Ⓗ
Named after a Scottish dance, Babbity Bowster is a unique pub/hotel/restaurant tucked away down a side street. The café-style room has three pumps serving beers mainly from Scottish breweries. The furniture is simple and practical, with plain tables and free-standing chairs augmented by wall seating. Outside there is more seating in the secluded beer garden. Fine meals are provided in the restaurant upstairs and daily specials are served in the bar.
❀🛏◑≠(High Street) Ꙩ(St Enoch) P🚌(CB4) ᯤ ♫

Ben Nevis

1147 Argyle Street, Finnieston, G3 8TB
☎ (0141) 576 5204 🌐 thebennevisbar.com
2 changing beers (sourced nationally; often Fyne, Swannay) Ⓗ
A corner tenement pub established around 1880 but closed for a long time before reopening in 1999. Now a small but popular bar, it has a large selection of malt whiskies, some of which appear to be precariously perched on sloping shelves. There is also a range of unusual canned and bottled beers. Ales are chosen from a wide range of breweries, normally at least one is Scottish. There is live folk music on Wednesday, Thursday and Sunday evenings.
❀≠(Exhibition Centre) 🚌(2,3) 🐾ᯤ ♫

Bon Accord 🏆

153 North Street, Charing Cross, G3 7DA
☎ (0141) 248 4427 🌐 bonaccordpub.com
8 changing beers (sourced nationally) Ⓗ
One of the pioneers of the real ale scene in Glasgow, the Bon has been serving quality ales for over 50 years. The wall opposite the bar is adorned with an impressive array of award certificates, including some from CAMRA. The pub's owner is passionate about malt whisky and there are 400 varieties behind the bar to complement the wide choice of real ales. A raised dining area at the rear also hosts quiz and live music nights. Local CAMRA Pub of the Year 2023.
❀◑♿≠(Charing Cross) Ꙩ(St George's Cross) 🚌ᯤ ♫

Counting House ✔

2 St Vincent Place, City Centre, G1 2DH
☎ (0141) 225 0160
Belhaven 80/-; Greene King Abbot; Sharp's Doom Bar; 4 changing beers (sourced nationally) Ⓗ
A busy Wetherspoon conversion of a bank provincial head office in the centre of the city next to George Square. It has many fine features including a central dome and surrounding sculptures. As well as the regular cask beers, there is a wide selection of guest ales, sourced UK wide with many from Scotland. A bottle store in one of the old strong rooms holds a large range of bottled and canned beers. Meet the Brewer events are held regularly.
❀◑♿≠(Queen St) Ꙩ(Buchanan Street) 🚌ᯤ

Crystal Palace ✔

36 Jamaica Street, City Centre, G1 4QD
☎ (0141) 221 2624
Caledonian Deuchars IPA; Greene King Abbot; Sharp's Doom Bar; 8 changing beers (sourced nationally) Ⓗ
Something of an architectural landmark and inspired by London's Crystal Palace, this Wetherspoon pub is in a Victorian iron-framed former furniture house, close to Central station. The building still features the original window arches. There are two large bars, one on each floor, offering different guest beers. The ground floor is slightly larger, with two raised areas at the far side and a more private area behind the stairs. Upstairs is a large hall with basic tables and chairs. The original lift remains operational and serves all floors.
◑♿≠(Central) Ꙩ(St Enoch) 🚌ᯤ

Curlers Rest ✔

256-260 Byres Road, Hillhead, G12 8SH
☎ (0141) 341 0737
Stewart 80/-; house beer (by St Austell); 3 changing beers (sourced nationally; often St Austell, Titanic) Ⓗ
Taking its name from a local curling pond, this quirky city-centre Nicholson's pub was originally a conversion from two 18th-century cottages. The large open-plan pub space is spread over two floors. The house beer is complemented by a range of Scottish and English real ales and a selection of world beers. There is a more limited range served in the upstairs bar with its open fire. Classic pub food is served daily.
◑♿Ꙩ(Hillhead) 🚌(8,90) 🐾ᯤ ♫

Doublet

74 Park Road, Woodlands, G4 9JF
☎ (0141) 334 1982
3 changing beers (sourced nationally; often Broughton, Kelburn, Orkney) Ⓗ
Corner tenement pub in a mock-Tudor style that opened its doors in 1961. The small friendly locals' bar offers real ales from Scottish breweries and the opportunity for good conversation. In addition there is a range of bottled beers and a distinctive lager. The small lounge upstairs to the rear is usually closed at quiet times but it is available for large functions and often used as a music venue.
❀Ꙩ(Kelvinbridge) 🚌🐾ᯤ ♫

Drum & Monkey ✔

91 St Vincent Street, City Centre, G2 5TF
☎ (0141) 221 6636
St Austell Nicholson's Pale Ale; 5 changing beers (sourced nationally; often Stewart) Ⓗ
A corner pub, housed in a former American-style bank, with an opulent marble and wood-panelled interior and ornate ceilings. Convenient for both main railway stations and numerous bus routes, it is usually busy with a varied clientele. Family groups are welcome until 8pm when dining. The large P-shaped central bar features six handpumps, offering a wide variety of different styles from well-known local and national favourites and new emerging breweries.
◑♿≠(Central) Ꙩ(Buchanan Street) 🚌🐾ᯤ ♫

Griffin ✔

266 Bath Street, Charing Cross, G2 4JP
☎ (0141) 332 2833 🌐 thegriffinglasgow.co.uk
Isle of Skye Skye Gold, Skye Red; 2 changing beers (sourced regionally; often Isle of Skye) Ⓗ
A well-known bar, located close to the King's Theatre and Charing Cross rail station. It reopened in 2022 under the ownership of the Isle of Skye brewery. The Griffin is a B-listed building and retains much wood panelling and original features. The front door opens to the main island bar which has two sets of handpumps offering Skye

REAL ALE BREWERIES

Dargavel Langbank
Dookit Glasgow
Drygate ▮ Glasgow
Epochal Glasgow
Glasgow Beer Works Glasgow
Jaw ▮ Milngavie
Kelburn Barrhead
Overtone Glasgow
Simple Things Fermentations Glasgow
West ▮ Glasgow

beers. To the rear is a function room with a separate bar (no real ale), which is often used for comedy and music events. ⌂◑⏃⊞⇌(Charing Cross)⊠(Cowcaddens)⊟☂

Horse Shoe ★ ✓

17-19 Drury Street, City Centre, G2 5AE
☎ (0141) 248 6368 ⊕ thehorseshoebarglasgow.co.uk
4 changing beers (sourced nationally; often St Austell, Stewart) Ⓗ

Dating from 1870, this Victorian pub is recognised by CAMRA as having a nationally important historic pub interior, which includes Scotland's longest bar. The real ales, from a wide selection of breweries, can be found halfway down the bar on the left side. The pub is close to Central station and the main bus routes and gets busy in the evenings and at weekends. Above the bar is a lounge/diner where children are welcome until the evenings when karaoke takes over.
⌂◑⏃⇌(Central) ⊠(Buchanan Street) ⊟☂

Laurieston Bar ★

58 Bridge Street, Tradeston, G5 9HU
☎ (0141) 429 4528
Fyne Jarl; 2 changing beers (sourced locally; often Fyne) Ⓗ

A warm welcome is guaranteed in this unpretentious, characterful corner bar that has remained unchanged for decades. A horseshoe bar is surrounded by formica-top tables, with walls covered in vintage photographs, mirrors and memorabilia. The roomier lounge has a much smaller bar and some unusual artwork on the walls. Pies are served from a 1970s counter-top display unit. It is close to Bridge Street subway station and Glasgow Central and can be busy at weekends. Payment is by cash only. ⇌(Central)⊠(Bridge Street)⊟❀☂

Pot Still

154 Hope Street, City Centre, G2 2TH
☎ (0141) 333 0980 ⊕ thepotstill.co.uk
4 changing beers (sourced regionally; often Kelburn, Loch Lomond, Orkney) Ⓐ

Near both main rail stations and major bus routes, this classic city-centre bar is one of Scotland's leading whisky pubs with a collection of around 750 malts. Four traditional Scottish air founts offer beers, usually from Scotland, but some not often seen in Glasgow. Food of the 'pie and beans' school is available during the day. The main bar area is small but there is a mezzanine level providing additional seating. Tutored whisky tastings can be arranged. ⌂◑⇌(Central)⊠(Buchanan Street)⊟❀☂

Scotia Bar

112-114 Stockwell Street, City Centre, G1 4LW
☎ (0141) 552 8681
4 changing beers (sourced regionally; often Broughton, Orkney) Ⓗ

One of several pubs that claim to be the oldest in Glasgow. It certainly looks the part with its half-timbered frontage, wood panelling, dark wooden benches and low ceilings. It has been a firm fixture on the folk music scene for decades, the likes of Hamish Imlach and Billy Connolly performed here, and there are still regular sessions and live bands. Most of the seating is close to the L-shaped bar, and there is also a cosy snug. Beers are predominantly from Scottish breweries.
⇌(Argyle St) ⊠(St Enoch) ♣⊟❀☂♪

Sir John Moore ✓

260-292 Argyle Street, City Centre, G2 8QW
☎ (0141) 222 1780
Belhaven 80/-; Greene King Abbot; Sharp's Doom Bar; 5 changing beers (sourced nationally; often Oakham, Stewart) Ⓗ

A Wetherspoon pub across the road from Glasgow Central station's (lower level) Hope Street exit. With live departure screens inside, this is an ideal place to wait for a train. It is also handy for breakfast after a night on the sleeper. Converted from several shops into one large room, it has several distinct areas marked with screens and a licensed pavement area. It takes its name from a 19th-century Glasgow-born general whose statue stands in George Square. ⌂◑◑⏃⇌(Central)⊠(St Enoch)⊟☂

Society Room ✓

151 West George Street, City Centre, G2 2JJ
☎ (0141) 229 7560
Belhaven 80/-; Greene King Abbot; Sharp's Doom Bar; 3 changing beers (sourced nationally; often Stewart) Ⓗ

Large Lloyd's No. 1 bar in the city centre, attracting a diverse clientele. The room's low ceiling and lack of windows at the back give it a cavernous feel. The beer choice often features several high-strength beers. In the evening the pub is frequented by a younger crowd, accompanied by loudish background music. At weekends there is music from 5pm, with a DJ from 8pm.
⌂◑◑⏃⇌(Central) ⊠(Buchanan Street) ⊟☂

State Bar

148 Holland Street, Charing Cross, G2 4NG
☎ (0141) 332 2159
House beer (by Stewart); 5 changing beers (sourced nationally; often Oakham) Ⓗ

A regular local CAMRA award winner, this popular town centre pub just off Sauchiehall Street is handy for restaurants and entertainment venues and gets busy at lunchtimes and weekends. It has a traditional island bar. The beer choice includes at least one, and often two, from Oakham and other beers, sometimes unfined, rarely seen in Glasgow. Old pictures and show bills displayed around the walls reflect the pub's proximity to the King's Theatre. There are blues sessions on Tuesdays.
⇌(Charing Cross) ⊠(Cowcaddens) ❀☂↻♪

Tennent's ✓

191 Byres Road, Hillhead, G12 8TN
☎ (0141) 339 7203 ⊕ thetennentsbarglasgow.co.uk
7 changing beers (sourced nationally; often Draught Bass, Stewart, Thornbridge) Ⓗ

One of Glasgow's oldest pubs, dating from 1884, which still retains some of its Victorian finery, with tall columns supporting the high ceilings. The pub is situated on the West End's main street, close to Glasgow University, and is often busy. With its wide selection of real ales, this pub has been listed in the Guide for over 25 years. Food is served all day and sports are shown on several large TVs. There is a separate bar downstairs for live music and functions. ◑◑⏃(Hillhead)⊟❀☂♪

Three Judges ✓

141 Dumbarton Road, Partick, G11 6PR
☎ (0141) 337 3055
9 changing beers (sourced nationally; often Fyne, Orkney) Ⓗ

For over 30 years this traditional corner pub has brought the best new real ales to Glasgow from all over Britain. A wide choice of ales is supplemented with an ever-changing selection of three ciders (one on handpump, two bag in box) although these might not be real. Numerous local CAMRA awards adorn the walls. There is a quiz on Mondays and there are monthly jazz sessions on Sunday afternoons. No food is served but you can bring your own. ⇌(Partick)⊠(Kelvinhall)●⊟❀☂♪

SCOTLAND

Greenock

James Watt ✓
80-92 Cathcart Street, PA15 1DD
☎ (01475) 722640
Greene King Abbot; Sharp's Doom Bar; 4 changing beers ⊞
Situated across the road from Greenock Central station and 200 yards from the bus station, this large open-plan Wetherspoon, in a former post office, is named after one of Greenock's famous sons who improved steam engine technology and has the SI unit of power named after him. The chain's standard value-for-money food is available all day and beer festivals are hosted at various times throughout the year. This pub is an oasis in a beer desert. ⏘ & ≉ (Central) 🛜

Houston

Fox & Hounds 🄻
South Street, PA6 7EN
☎ (01505) 808604 ⊕ foxandhoundshouston.co.uk
Kelburn Goldihops; 4 changing beers (sourced nationally; often Fuller's, Fyne, Kelburn) ⊞
Excellent traditional village pub, established in 1779, with a bar, lounge and restaurant downstairs and cocktail bar upstairs. The downstairs bar has five handpumps and an excellent selection of spirits including 130 whiskies, plus a selection of canned and bottled craft beers. Gastro-pub food is served throughout the pub. There is a pool table upstairs and board game night every Wednesday. An annual beer festival is held on the late May bank holiday weekend. Q ⏘ ❀ ⏘ & ♣ P 🗐 ❀ 🛜

Inverkip

Inverkip Hotel
Main Street, PA16 0AS
☎ (01475) 521478 ⊕ inverkip.co.uk
Fyne Jarl; 1 changing beer (sourced regionally; often Fallen, Fyne) ⊞
Small, family-run hotel set in the heart of a conservation village. It is a short walk from the large Inverkip Marina, making it an ideal staging post for those just messing about on the river or passing through on the way to Largs and the Ayrshire coast. Food options range from snacks through to special occasion dining. All-ticket Battle of the Brewer nights are extremely popular.
❀ ⇆ ⏘ ≉ P 🗐 (578,580) 🛜

Johnstone

Callum's 🄻
26 High Street, PA5 8AH
☎ (01505) 322925
Harviestoun Bitter & Twisted; Kelburn Pivo Estivo; 4 changing beers (often Orkney) ⊞
Popular town-centre pub in an area short of real-ale outlets, offering a friendly welcome and a comfortable atmosphere. A large but unobtrusive TV screen features major sporting events. The restaurant has been recently refurbished and has an extensive menu. A side lounge allows for some relaxation away from the main bar area. There are a wide range of events throughout the year including live music most Saturdays, quiz nights, tribute acts and karaoke. ⏘ ⏘ & ≉ (Strathclyde) 🗐 (36,38) 🛜 ♫

Kilbarchan

Habbies Bar & Grill
25 New Street, PA10 2LN
☎ (01505) 706606

2 changing beers (sourced locally) ⊞
Busy local pub within a conservation village and close to the famous Weaver's Cottage owned by the National Trust for Scotland. Live music plays on most Saturday nights, with an emphasis on supporting local musicians. The beer garden is popular in summer. Live sports are shown on large screens in a separate area. A wide range of food is on offer, including family favourites, steak and curry nights, weekend specials and afternoon teas. The pub is family-friendly, with child-specific drinks and menus. ⏘ ❀ & P 🗐 (38) ♫

Trust Inn
8 Low Barholm, PA10 2ET
☎ (01505) 702401
3 changing beers ⊞
Small, popular, single-roomed pub in the centre of a conservation village, with old village photographs adorning the walls. The excellent bar meal menu and special promotions mean it can be busy at meal times. Children are welcome in the evening until 9pm if dining. Regular live events include music featuring local bands and other entertainment nights are advertised via social media. ⏘ ⏘ 🗐 (38) 🛜 ♫

Kirkintilloch

Kirky Puffer ✓
1-11 Townhead, G66 1NG
☎ (0141) 775 4140
Belhaven 80/-; Sharp's Doom Bar; 4 changing beers (sourced nationally; often Oakham, Theakston, Thornbridge) ⊞
Large community-friendly Wetherspoon pub standing alongside the Forth and Clyde Canal. It features a modern interior with Mackintosh-style wood panelling, and there is an extensive beer garden at the rear. Off the main room is a sizeable family-friendly corner and more secluded alcoves. A wide selection of beers is available, especially for those preferring strong ales. The pub is popular with locals, canal users, and visitors to the Roman Antonine Way. There are frequent buses to Glasgow. ⏘ ❀ ⏘ & 🗐 🛜

Lochwinnoch

Brown Bull
32 Main Street, PA12 4AH
☎ (01505) 843250
Harviestoun Bitter & Twisted; 3 changing beers (sourced nationally; often Cromarty, Fyne, Kelburn) ⊞
More than 200 years old, this family-run pub attracts locals and visitors throughout the year. An ever-changing range of national ales is offered with an emphasis on regional breweries. Ther is rear access to a quirky outdoor seating area and garden with cooperage tools. It hosts quiz nights on Tuesdays and live music monthly. Dogs are welcome. It is close to RSPB Lochwinnoch nature reserve and Castle Semple Visitor Centre and Country Park. Q ⏘ ❀ ⏘ ● 🗐 (X34,X36) ❀ ♫

Milngavie

Jaw Brew Bar 🄻
26 Crossveggate, G62 6RA
☎ 07880 690995 ⊕ jawbrew.co.uk
2 changing beers (sourced locally; often Jaw) ⊞
This two-room micropub opened in 2019 as Jaw Brew's brewery tap. The interior has a rustic feel, with wooden tables and free-standing chairs. As well the cask ales there are four keg beers on tap. Visitors can take home

some of Jaw Brew's beers and also Bardowie gin from the family's own distillery. Conveniently situated by the town's station car park. Q❀♻️P🖾♿♫

Paisley

Bull Inn 🍺 ★ ✅

7 New Street, PA1 1XU

☎ (0141) 849 0472

4 changing beers (sourced regionally; often Kelburn, Loch Lomond) Ⓗ

Established in 1901 and identified by CAMRA as having a nationally important historic pub interior, this is the oldest inn in Paisley. The building retains many original features including stained-glass windows, three small snugs and a spirit cask gantry. It boasts the only original set of spirit cocks left in Scotland. Live sport is regularly shown on large screens in the main bar and also in the snugs. Four changing guest ales are offered, from the likes of Kelburn, Loch Lomond, Orkney and Stewart breweries. ♿≈(Gilmour Street)🖾♿🛜

Last Post 🅛 ✅

2 County Square, PA1 1BN

☎ (0141) 849 6911

Belhaven 80/-; Greene King Abbot; Sharp's Doom Bar; 6 changing beers Ⓗ

Large Wetherspoon converted from the town's main post office. Open-plan in design on two levels, there is plenty of seating and good wheelchair access. The standard Wetherspoon food menu is available. It is next to Gilmour Street railway station and close to the bus station, so is handy for a pint between trains or buses. Six guest ales are usually available. ◑♿≈(Gilmour Street)🖾(9,36)🛜

Northern Way

13-19 Causeyside Street, PA1 1UW

4 changing beers (sourced nationally) Ⓗ

This Northern Way-branded Amber Taverns pub has undergone a massive refurbishment from previous incarnations. It is well-appointed throughout and has several areas that can be isolated for bookings without feeling cut off from the rest of the pub. It serves up to four different ales, primarily from the north of England, and there is also a huge selection of premium gins alongside more traditional drink offerings. Various live sporting events are shown on a number of largescreen TV's. No children allowed. ♿≈(Gilmour Street)🛜

Wee Howff

53 High Street, PA1 2AN

☎ (0141) 887 8299

2 changing beers (sourced nationally; often Kelburn) Ⓗ

The Wee Howff has appeared in over 30 editions of this Guide and is a little piece of heaven in an otherwise crowded area of cheap drinking establishments. A small, traditional pub with a loyal regular clientele, the Howff offers up to three guest ales from around Britain from a quarterly rotating list. It has an open mic night on the first Monday of each month and a pub quiz every Thursday. The jukebox caters for even the most eclectic of tastes. ♿≈(Gilmour Street)🖾(9,36)♿🛜♫

Renfrew

Lord of the Isles ✅

Unit 21 Xscape, Kings Inch Road, PA4 8XQ

☎ (0141) 886 8930

Belhaven 80/-; Greene King Abbot; Sharp's Doom Bar; 3 changing beers (sourced nationally) Ⓗ

Large, purpose-built, lively Wetherspoon pub at the XSite Leisure Complex, with its cinema, crazy golf, rock climbing and much more. Throughout the pub the walls display photographs depicting the history of industry on the River Clyde. The outside seating area is south-facing and a suntrap during warm summer days. The typical JDW menu is available all day and three ever-changing guest ales are on handpump. A short stroll takes you to the shipyard opposite where you can see ships in dock. ♿☺◑♿P🖾🛜

Rutherglen

Ruadh-Ghleann ✅

40-44 Main Street, G73 2HY

☎ (0141) 613 2370

Belhaven 80/-; Greene King Abbot; Sharp's Doom Bar; 3 changing beers (sourced nationally) Ⓗ

Busy Wetherspoon in the town centre taking its name from the Gaelic for Rutherglen. The single room is long and narrow, and is decorated in a contemporary style. The bar is halfway down and there is a family area at the far end leading to the beer garden. There is also a window into the cellar. The beer garden is on two levels and affords a view of the Cathkin Braes when the weather is good. Q♿☺◑♿≈🖾🛜

Strathaven

Weavers ✅

1-3 Green Street, ML10 6LT

☎ 07749 332914

4 changing beers (sourced nationally; often Black Iris, Broughton, Outlandish) Ⓗ

Standing in the centre of the town, the pub has links to the 19th-century weaving industry and has been listed in the Guide for over 25 years. Sympathetically refurbished inside and out in 2022, the single room has modern and comfortable furnishings and is decorated with black and white pictures of film stars. There is an ever-changing range of ales featuring a mix from breweries in the region, and some that are rarely seen in Scotland. A range of imported bottled beers is also available. ♿🖾🛜

Breweries

Boden

Unit 3, 95 Boden Street, Glasgow, G40 3QF ☎ 07511 022231

Launched in 2019, Boden Brewing is a one-man operation based in the east end of Glasgow. Six core beers are available in bottle and keg.

Bungo

50 Moray Place, Glasgow, G41 2DF

🌐 bungobrew.co.uk

A homebrew collective of four members, Ewen, Fin, Michael and Will, turned commercial in 2021. Small-batch production available, mostly in cans, with a range from milk stouts through to lager.

Dargavel SIBA

Mid Glen Farm, West Glen Road, Langbank, PA14 6YL

☎ 07493 854537 ✉ dargavelbrewery@hotmail.com

☺Established in 2021 this is a traditional real ale brewery. Using its own spring water from the initial source of Dargavel Burn located between Kilmacolm and

Langbank, its beers are available in cask and various small pack formats. LIVE

Blonde Belter (ABV 3.6%) BLOND
Peter's Wellies (ABV 4.2%) PALE
Moo-Lin Rouge (ABV 5%) RED
Haud Yer Wheasht (ABV 5.1%) SPECIALITY

Dead End Brew Machine

Office: Flat 1-2, 10 Lawrence Street, Glasgow, G11 5HQ ✉ chris@deadendbrewmachine.com

Dead End Brew Machine produce small batch, artisinal beers specialising in brettanomyces and saccharomycetes blends, augmented with fruit and spices. Beers are available in bottle and can. ♦LIVE

Dookit

Block 3, Unit 1, Tollcross Industrial Estate, Causewayside Crescent, Glasgow, G32 8LJ ☎ 07792 889210 ⊕ dookitbrewing.co.uk

Established in 2020, Dookit originally brewed at Ride Brewing before moving to its own premises in 2022. Beers are available in bottle and keg. LIVE

Drygate

▤ 85 Drygate, Glasgow, G4 0UT
☎ (0141) 212 8810 ⊕ drygate.com

Restaurant, bar and microbrewery, Drygate is a joint venture of Tennent's and Williams Bros, though operationally independent. The onsite brewery began production in 2014. A core range of keg and bottled beers is available. ‼♦

Epochal

Payne Street, Glasgow, G4 0LE ⊕ epochal.co.uk

Gareth Young founded Epochal in 2021. A former winner of the UK National Homebrewing Awards, Gareth spent time with local craft breweries to learn about brewing on a small commercial scale. The brewery specialises in barrel fermentation, with beers available in keg and bottle. LIVE

Glasgow Beer Works SIBA

Block 23, Unit 2, Queenslie Industrial Estate, Glasgow, G33 4JJ
☎ (0141) 258 1661

Office: Pavillion 1, Finnieston Business Park, Minerva Way, Glasgow, G3 8AU ⊕ merchantcitybrewing.com

Established in 2017 as Merchant City Brewing using a 12-barrel plant, Glasgow Beer Works moved and rebranded in 2020. In addition to the core range, small pilot batches and barrel-aged beers are produced. 25 outlets are supplied direct, plus specialist off-licences across central Scotland. A pop-up bar in Osborne Street, beneath the John Byrne mural of Billy Connolly, opened in 2020.

Session Ale (ABV 3.9%) GOLD
Unit 1 Red Ale (ABV 4%) RED
American Pale Ale (ABV 4.7%) PALE
Vienna Lager (ABV 5%) SPECIALITY
IPA (ABV 5.8%) IPA

Hidden Lane

Argyle Street, Finnieston, G3 8ND
☎ (0141) 258 2520 ⊕ hiddenlanebrewery.com

Organic brewery launched in Glasgow in 2019.

Jaw

▤ 26 Crossveggate, Milngavie, G62 6RA
☎ (0141) 237 5840 ⊕ jawbrew.co.uk

An independent, family-run, craft microbrewery from Glasgow. Committed to producing the absolute pinnacle of high quality beer. LIVE

Kelburn SIBA

10 Muriel Lane, Barrhead, G78 1QB
☎ (0141) 881 2138 ⊕ kelburnbrewery.com

⊗ Kelburn is an award-winning family business established in 2002. ‼♦

Goldihops (ABV 3.8%) GOLD
Well-hopped session ale with a fruity taste and a bitter finish.
Pivo Estivo (ABV 3.9%) GOLD
A pale, dry, citrus, hoppy session ale.
Misty Law (ABV 4%) BITTER
Red Smiddy (ABV 4.1%) BITTER
This bittersweet ale predominantly features an intense citrus hop character balanced perfectly with fruity malt.
Dark Moor (ABV 4.5%) MILD
A dark, fruity ale with undertones of liquorice and blackcurrant.
Jaguar (ABV 4.5%) GOLD
A golden, full-bodied ale with undertones of grapefruit and a long lasting citrus, hoppy aftertaste.
Cart Noir (ABV 4.8%) STOUT
Cart Blanche (ABV 5%) GOLD
A golden, full-bodied ale. The assault of fruit and hop camouflages the strength of this easy-drinking ale.

Mains

Office: 45a Alderman Road, Glasgow, G13 3YG
✉ mainsbrewco@gmail.com

Mains is a small-batch brewery, producing farmhouse-inspired beers.

Out of Town

84 Telford Road, Lenziemill Industrial Estate, Cumbernauld, G67 2NJ ⊕ outoftown.co

Originally set up in 2016 by three homebrewers, the brewery was sold and is now part of Consolidated Craft Breweries. Beers may be brewed by Alechemy (qv).

Outlandish

Woodend Hayloft, Birkenshaw Road, Glenboig, Coatbridge, ML5 2QH

Established in 2020, brewing traditional and contemporary craft beers with names inspired by local lingo.

Overtone

Unit 19, New Albion Industrial Estate, Halley Street, Glasgow, G13 4DJ
☎ (0141) 952 7772 ⊕ overtonebrewing.com

Established in 2018, Overtone produce hop-forward craft beers with an emphasis on quality and flavour. It specialises in New England-style IPAs but also brews a number of other styles such as fruit sours and stouts.

Shilling

92 West George Street, Glasgow, G2 1PJ
☎ (0141) 353 1654 ⊕ shillingbrewingcompany.co.uk

Brewing began in 2016 at this pub in the heart of Glasgow. Events including tasting evenings are often held.

Simple Things Fermentations SIBA

The Bakehouse, 6 Hazel Avenue Lane, Glasgow, G44 3LJ
☎ **(0141) 237 2202**
⊕ **simplethingsfermentations.com**

Opened in 2019 using a small 600-litre kit, beer is now produced in can, bottle, keg and cask. All beer is naturally carbonated through re-fermentation in package. ‼LIVE

Spectra

Office: 33 Highfield Drive, Clarkston, G76 7SW
⊕ **spectrabrewing.com**

Former science teacher Alex Cavers launched Spectra Brewing in early 2022. Being a nomad brewery, Alex uses other breweries equipment to produce his American East Coast style beers. Beers are available in cask and can.

Visible Light (ABV 3.9%) PALE
Fundamental DDH IPA (ABV 5.5%) IPA

Tennent Caledonian

Wellpark Brewery, 161 Duke Street, Glasgow, G31 1JD

Home of Tennent's beers. No real ale.

Two Towns Down

47 Back Sneddon Street, Paisley, PA3 2DD
⊕ **twotownsdown.com**

Two Towns Down is a brewing project founded in 2019 by Sandy McKelvie, formerly of Hanging Bat, Fallen, Black Isle and 71 Brewing. Now settled in Paisley, the brewery utilises a 10-hectolitre kit. The cans each feature an example of the famous paisley pattern.

Up Front SIBA

Office: 1 / 1, 27 Skirving Street, Glasgow, G41 3AB
☎ **07526 088973** ⊕ **upfrontbrewing.com**

Founded in 2015 by former homebrewer Jake Griffin, Up Front is a nomad brewery primarily using spare capacity at Overtone Brewing Co (qv), plus that at other local breweries. Predominantly producing canned beers and speciality bottles, cask-conditioned beers are available on rare occasions.

WEST

▤ Binnie Place, Glasgow Green, Glasgow, G40 1AW
☎ **(0141) 550 0135** ⊕ **westbeer.com**

Brewery producing artisan lagers and ales in strict accordance with the German Purity Law of 1516, which also has an onsite beer hall, restaurant and events venue. All beers are unpasteurised. ‼◆

SCOTLAND

Counting House, Glasgow (Photo: Stuart McMahon)

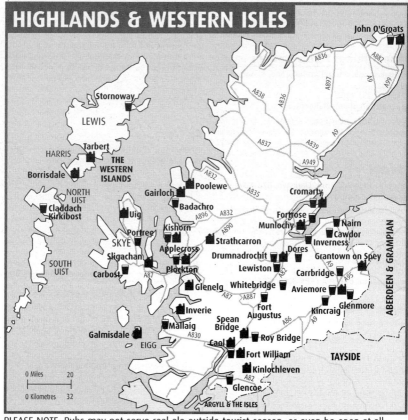

HIGHLANDS & WESTERN ISLES

PLEASE NOTE: Pubs may not serve real ale outside tourist season, or even be open at all. Opening hours may vary all year round. Please contact pubs before intended visit to check.

Applecross

Applecross Inn
Shore Street, IV54 8LR NG70974444
☎ (01520) 744262 ⊕ applecrossinn.co.uk
3 changing beers (sourced locally; often Applecross Craft) ⊞

This remote, multi award-winning inn is reached via a spectacular, hair-raising drive over the steepest road pass in Britain, or by a longer scenic coastal route. Beers come from the local Applecross Craft microbrewery. Renowned for its local seafood and venison, this is a must for foodies. There are additional tables outside, with the Inn-Side-Out Airstream caravan offering light refreshments and takeaways. The inn is a popular stop-off on the North Coast 500. A former local CAMRA Pub of the Year runner-up. ☺☀✎◑⅃&A︎P➗❀⚡❄

Aviemore

Cairngorm Hotel ᴸ
77 Grampian Road, PH22 1PE
☎ (01479) 810233 ⊕ cairngorm.com
Cairngorm Stag, Gold ⊞

Just over the road from the train station and bus stop, this is the first watering hole for many after a long journey. The privately owned Cairngorm Hotel has a warm and familiar feel about it, with comfy seats in the lobby to the bar and seating under cover outside. Although not tied, Cairngorm beers feature on the two handpumps. Largescreen TVs show popular sporting events and there is Scottish entertainment for the many visitors most evenings. Food with a Scottish twist is available much of the day. ☺☀✎◑⅃&A≈P➗❀⚡❄♪

Old Bridge Inn ᴸ
23 Dalfaber Road, PH22 1PU
☎ (01479) 811137 ⊕ oldbridgeinn.co.uk
4 changing beers (sourced locally; often Cairngorm, Caledonian, Windswept) ⊞

Close to the gently flowing River Spey, this gem of a pub off the main drag is worth seeking out. The cosy, intimate inn, converted from a cottage in 1982, is an ideal place to relax after a busy day on the hills, or even just touring the area. Four handpumps offer a mix of local and regional beers. Booking is recommended for the restaurant, with a menu using produce with low food miles (lunch is not served on Wed). Entertainment is laid on most nights. There is a bunkhouse adjacent and self-catering accommodation available. Handy for Strathspey steam railway. ☺☀✎◑⅃&A≈P➗❀⚡❄♪

Winking Owl ᴸ ✅
123 Grampian Road, PH22 1RH (N end of village)
☎ (01479) 812368 ⊕ thewinkingowl.co
6 changing beers (sourced locally; often Cairngorm, Caledonian) ⊞

The Winky has been the brewery tap for the award-winning Cairngorm brewery since 2014, with the 2018 addition of the popular Bothy Bar downstairs. Both offer four Cairngorm and two Caledonian beers, although the Winky is now exclusively a restaurant serving hearty pub

grub. Live music plays in the Bothy. The courtyard's covered seating area is made of upcycled materials and logs. Once a farmhouse, the pub is probably one of the oldest hostelries in Aviemore, where Robert Burns is reported to have breakfasted in 1787.
చ⊛(D&Å⇌P❄🐾🎵

Badachro

Badachro Inn

IV21 2AA (B8056 to Red Point and Badachro) NG781736
☎ (01445) 741255 ⊕ badachroinn.com
2 changing beers (often Cairngorm, Ewebrew) Ⓗ
Badachro Inn is on the south side of Loch Gairloch, with a single bar that remains essentially unchanged. Specialising in seafood, it is a foodies' delight. The decking outside offers an idyllic location to watch the tide ebb and flow in the safe and secure anchorage that the inlet provides. A conservatory also overlooks the inlet. It is more than a three-mile drive from the road itself, but worth it. A unique bar and restaurant in a unique place, you may miss the small sign to the pub on the road out of Gairloch, but you won't miss the big one!
Q⊛☝💬(D&🖵?

Carbost: Isle of Skye

Old Inn

IV47 8SR NG379318
☎ (01478) 640205 ⊕ theoldinnskye.co.uk
3 changing beers (sourced locally; often Cuillin, Isle of Skye) Ⓗ
On the shores of Loch Harport, the Old Inn nestles on the tideline. Outside, trestle tables take advantage of the views that Skye is famous for – there can be no better place to enjoy a pint. The pub is busy year-round with an eclectic mix of outdoor folk, and those touring Skye or visiting the Talisker distillery close by. Seafood is top of the menu, most of it coming from the loch.
Q☝⊛💬(D🐶P🖵❄🎵

Carrbridge

Cairn Hotel Ⓛ

Main Road, PH23 3AS (just off A9 on B9153)
☎ (01479) 841212 ⊕ cairnhotel.co.uk
3 changing beers (sourced regionally; often Cairngorm, Cromarty, Orkney) Ⓗ
The Cairn Hotel is the hub of this small village, with the lure of a warming open fire and excellent gastro-pub style menus. The licensee selects the best cask ales from the Highlands and Islands for his three handpumps, so the pub is deservedly popular both with devoted locals and the many visitors to the area. The 1717 Packhorse Bridge and Landmark Forest Adventure Park are in the village. There are 14 rooms for overnight stays.
☝⊛💬(D🐶P🖵❄?

Cawdor

Cawdor Tavern

The Lane, IV12 5XP NH845500
☎ (01667) 404777 ⊕ cawdortavern.co.uk
Orkney Northern Light, Red MacGregor, Dark Island; 1 changing beer (sourced regionally; often Orkney) Ⓗ
Situated in the conservation village of Cawdor, close to the castle made famous by Shakespeare's Macbeth. The Cawdor Tavern's owners, who took over in 1994, also run the Orkney/Atlas brewery at Quoyloo. Accordingly, up to five handpumps feature their beers. Oak panelling covers the walls of the public areas, including the spacious cosy bar with its water taps for whisky on the bar. The lounge

is mainly for meals and includes a separate baronial dining hall. The tempting menu caters for all tastes and ages, but leave room for pudding!
Q☝⊛(D&🐾P🖵(2,20)?

Claddach Kirkibost: North Uist

Westford Inn Ⓨ

HS6 5EP (2½ miles NW of Clachan on A865)
NF7751066195
☎ (01876) 580653 ⊕ westfordinn.com
3 changing beers (sourced regionally; often Fyne, Isle of Skye) Ⓗ
The owners took on the Westford Inn in 2015 and have turned around its fortunes. The pub is very much the community hub, with live music and an annual beer festival. A second Skye ale is on rotation in winter, with three in summer, as well as a range of bottles and cans. Good-quality food is available to eat in or take away. One of the most remote pubs in the Guide, it is well worth making the effort to visit. Accommodation is available in the Bothy, a former byre. Q☝⊛🖤(D Å🐾P🖵❄?🎵

Cromarty

Fishertown Inn Ⓛ

Church Street, IV11 8XA
☎ (01381) 600988 ⊕ fishertowninn.com
Cromarty Happy Chappy; 2 changing beers (often Cromarty) Ⓗ
A family-run pub providing B&B accommodation and delicious home-made bar meals. A traditional music session is held every second Thursday of the month. The beers are from Cromarty brewery less than three miles away. Just opposite is National Trust for Scotland Hugh Miller's Cottage and Cromarty Courthouse, or take a dolphin spotting tour from the harbour where you can also see the oil rigs in for maintenance. A two-car ferry operates during the summer to Nigg.
Q☝⊛💬(D&🐾P🖵(26,26A)❄?🎵

Dores

Dores Inn Ⓛ

IV2 6TR (on B852) NH59753476
☎ (01463) 751203 ⊕ thedoresinn.co.uk

REAL ALE BREWERIES	
Applecross	Kishorn
Ardgour	Fort William
Black Isle	Munlochy
Cairngorm	Aviemore
Cromarty	Cromarty
Cuillin 🍺	Sligachan: Isle of Skye
Dun 🌾	Glenelg
Ewebrew	Poolewe
Glen Spean	Spean Bridge
Hanging Tree 🍺	Drumnadrochit
Isle of Eigg	Isle of Eigg: Galmisdale
Isle of Harris	Borrisdale
Isle of Skye	Isle of Skye: Uig
John O'Groats	John O'Groats
Knoydart	Inverie
Loomshed 🌾	Tarbert: Isle of Harris
Old Inn 🍺	Gairloch (brewing suspended)
Plockton	Plockton
River Leven	Kinlochleven
Strathcarron	Strathcarron
Two Thirsty Men	Grantown on Spey
Wild Barn	Caol

4 changing beers (sourced regionally; often Cairngorm, Cromarty, Inveralmond) Ⓗ

Set on the shores of Loch Ness, the inn offers excellent monster-spotting opportunities. It is popular all year round, and a must-stop for the views alone. A cosy, wood-finished bar has up to four handpumps offering local and independent ales, plus an occasional English guest. During summer an outdoor bar serves the beer garden. Great food is available all day. Open from 10am, full bar service from 11am (noon on Sun), closed Monday and Tuesday in winter. Free minibus service locally to/from Inverness. Q ❺ ✿ ◐ ▶ 🚪 (301,302) 🏮 🎕

Drumnadrochit

Benleva Hotel Ⓛ

Kilmore Road, IV63 6UH (signed off A82) NH513295
☎ (01456) 450080 🌐 benleva.co.uk
Hanging Tree First Light, Eighty Shillings, Hangmans IPA Ⓗ

The 400-year-old sweet chestnut outside the Benleva was once a hanging tree, hence the name of the brewery in the bothy just outside. The bar in this 300-year-old former manse offers four Hanging Tree beers. Classic home-made dishes have a Scottish twist. Regular music and themed nights are held throughout the year. It is centrally located for touring the Highlands and Loch Ness. ❺ ✿ 🛏 ◐ ▶ Å ♣ P 🚪 🏮 🎕 🎵

Fort Augustus

Lock Inn

Canal Side Road South, PH32 4AU (just off A82)
☎ (01320) 366302 🌐 the-lockinn.co.uk
2 changing beers (often Cairngorm) Ⓗ

Pub situated right next to the flight of locks, with seating outside so you can watch the boats go by. There are usually two ales on. Huge portions of good food are served – the fish & chips with home-made tartar is recommended. Its can be busy during high season, but there is additional seating upstairs. There is an impressive stag's head on the wall in the stairwell with an interesting plaque underneath. ✿ ◐ ▶ Å 🚪

Fort William

Ben Nevis Bar

103 High Street, PH33 6DG
☎ (01397) 702295 🌐 bennevisbarfortwilliam.com
Hanging Tree After Dark, Hangmans IPA; 1 changing beer (sourced locally; often Hanging Tree) Ⓗ

Built in 1806 and under new ownership since 2019, this pleasant two-room traditional locals' pub on the pedestrianised High Street is said to have a resident ghost in the loft. A decked area at the rear gives splendid views of Loch Linnhe. As well as the three ales, over 50 malt whiskies are stocked. A food menu of good, honest pub favourites is available all day. Live music plays at weekends. ❺ ✿ ◐ 👤 ⇌ ♣ 🚪 🏮 🎕 🎵

Ben Nevis Inn Ⓛ

Achintee Road, Claggan, PH33 6TE NN12477293
☎ (01397) 701227 🌐 ben-nevis-inn.co.uk
2 changing beers (sourced locally; often Cairngorm, River Leven) Ⓗ

Traditional 200-year-old stone-built barn at the start of the Ben Nevis mountain path, popular with outdoor enthusiasts. The small bar counter has two handpumps offering local beers. The barn, with long, beer hall-style tables and beckoning stove, is festooned with mountaineering and skiing paraphernalia. This warm, informal and friendly setting is ideal for their regular live

music. A hearty food menu changes daily. The adjacent bunkhouse sleeps 24. Check ahead for opening hours in winter (closed in Nov). Q ✿ 🛏 ◐ ▶ & Å P 🎵

Grog & Gruel Ⓛ

66 High Street, PH33 6AD (on pedestrianised High St)
☎ (01397) 705078 🌐 grogandgruel.co.uk
6 changing beers (sourced locally) Ⓗ

The Grog & Gruel alehouse is busy all day every day with a mix of locals and tourists. Up to six handpumps dispense predominantly local, sometimes regional beers, making it a draw for the real ale connoisseur. The bar menu offers imaginative and interesting food at affordable prices all day. After 5pm the restaurant upstairs opens, offering a wider selection for hungry hill walkers. Open mic features on most Friday evenings. ❺ ◐ 👤 ⇌ ♠ 🚪 🏮 🎕 🎵

Fortrose

Anderson

Union Street, IV10 8SU (corner of High St)
☎ (01381) 620236 🌐 theanderson.co.uk
2 changing beers (sourced nationally; often Cromarty, Inveralmond) Ⓗ

A regular entry since 2005, the Anderson offers well-chosen ales, mostly local or regional, drawn from a 200-year-old cellar. The Whisky Lounge has a single cider handpump and more than 250 single malts. The restaurant has a reputation for excellence and is a popular destination for foodies. Regular music, quiz and special food nights throughout the year. Nine bedrooms are available. Local attractions include the golf course and dolphin watching at Chanonry Point. Closed for about a month before Christmas – phone ahead to check. Q ❺ ✿ 🛏 ◐ & ♣ P 🚪 (26,26A) 🏮 🎕 🎵

Glencoe

Clachaig Inn Ⓛ

Glencoe, PH49 4HX (3 miles SE of village, off A82)
NN12705668
☎ (01855) 811252 🌐 clachaig.com
10 changing beers (sourced locally; often Cairngorm, Loch Lomond, Orkney) Ⓗ

The Clachaig is a must for outdoor enthusiasts and beer aficionados alike, set in a remote location among the spectacular hills and scenery of Glencoe. Having worked up a hunger on the hills, a huge choice of well-kept beers and hearty grub will replenish your energy. There are also more than 400 whiskies and 130 gins. On cooler days, wood-burning stoves keep the three bars and snugs warm. Beer festivals are held during the year and music hosted most weekend evenings. Open fours a day a week in January. ❺ ✿ 🛏 ◐ & ♣ P 🏮 🎕 🎵

Glenmore

Pine Marten Bar & Scran

PH22 1QU (on ski road by Loch Morlich) NH974098
☎ (01479) 861253 🌐 aviemoreski.co.uk
Cairngorm Trade Winds, Black Gold, Wildcat Ⓗ

Though unassuming from the outside, this 'wee snug of a bar' has a welcoming wood-burning stove and a bar topped with three handpumps. The minimalist building is designed to emulate Alpine mountain refuges, and ice axes and skis festoon the walls, along with quirky artefacts from across Europe. The kitchen serves some great grub, and there is also a shop, ski hire and accommodation including glamping pods and a tree house. Live music plays most Friday and Saturday nights. ❺ 🛏 ◐ & Å ♣ P 🚪 🏮 🎕 🎵

Inverness

Castle Tavern Ⓛ

1 View Place, IV2 4SA (top of Castle St)
☎ (01463) 718178 ⊕ castletavern.pub
5 changing beers (sourced regionally; often Cromarty, Isle of Skye, Windswept) Ⓗ

Just a short walk from town, the Castle Tavern is popular with tourists visiting the castle opposite and locals who know their beer. Six handpumps offer an interesting rolling selection, mostly from Scottish independents, and a changing cider. There is plenty of seating inside but the covered canopy area outside is always busy, even in winter, with panoramic views along the River Ness. Bar meals are available all day and the upstairs restaurant opens in the evening. ゐ֍⑪▷ᕁ⏦⇌◗Pꆤ❀ 🛜

Clachnaharry Inn

17-19 High Street, Clachnaharry, IV3 8RB (on A862 Beauly road)
☎ (01463) 239806 ⊕ clachnaharryinn.co.uk
Fyne Jarl; Harviestoun Bitter & Twisted; Inveralmond Ossian; 2 changing beers (sourced nationally; often Cairngorm) Ⓗ

The Clach has featured in the Guide for more than 35 years. The 17th-century coaching inn offers a warm welcome to all, with an open fire some days. Food is available Wednesday to Sunday in both the bar area and the quieter restaurant. Quiz and music nights feature regularly. Outside the occasional train rumbles by, or boat using the Caledonian Canal. Beyond are stunning views of the Beauly Firth and Ben Wyvis, often snowcapped. Qゐ֍⑪▷Aᕁ⏦P몮(28,28A)❀🛜♫

Corriegarth Ⓛ

5-7 Heathmount Road, IV2 3JU
☎ (01463) 224411
Cromarty Happy Chappy; 3 changing beers (sourced nationally; often Fyne) Ⓗ

The Corrie is located in the quiet Crown area of Inverness, just 10 minutes from the town centre. The imposing red sandstone building once did a stint as a club for Navy and RAF officers. Cromarty Happy Chappy, Deuchars and two others from the Punch list are almost always available. There is a large area to sit outside in summer. This busy and popular local has nine boutique en-suite rooms, making it a great place to stay. Qゐ֍⑪▷⑪▷ᕁ⏦P몮❀🛜

King's Highway ✔

72-74 Church Street, IV1 1EN
☎ (01463) 251830
Caledonian Deuchars IPA; Fuller's London Pride; Greene King Abbot; Sharp's Doom Bar; changing beers (sourced nationally) Ⓗ

Situated centrally, this Wetherspoon pub has offered good-value fare since 2001. Up to 10 handpumps feature mainly Scottish beers, many local to the area. A popular meeting point, it is handy for the town's buses and train station. Even when busy, you can always find a quiet place to sit and enjoy a pint. There is now a decked area outside. Accommodation is available. Breakfast is available, with alcoholic drinks served from 11am.
ゐ֍⑪▷ᕁ⏦P몮🛜

Phoenix Ale House Ⓛ

106-110 Academy Street, IV1 1LX
☎ (01463) 240300
10 changing beers (sourced nationally; often Cairngorm, Cromarty, Windswept) Ⓗ

The Phoenix offers a selection of Scottish real ales from up to 10 handpumps. Identified by CAMRA as having a nationally important historic pub interior, the island bar is surrounded by a spittoon – there is even talk of sawdust

returning! The pub is mostly standing only, but it is popular with tourists and those who know their ales. It is now jointly owned with the Indian restaurant next door, where you can enjoy hearty meals all day.
Q⑪▷ᕁ⇌P몮🛜♫

John O'Groats

John O'Groats Brewery & Tap Room

The Last House, KW1 4YR
☎ 07842 401571 ⊕ johnogroatsbrewery.co.uk
4 changing beers (sourced locally; often John O'Groats) Ⓗ

The Last House is the taproom for the adjoining John O' Groats brewery. Situated just metres from the Pentland Firth, it is the most northerly pub and brewery in mainland Britain. Drinkers can sit in the small bar, or in the shop window overlooking the sea and Orkney Isles, or outside on warmer days. Four handpumps serve ales brewed next door, and usually a Highland real cider.
֍Aᕁ⏦P몮(77,80)

Kincraig

Suie Bar Ⓛ

PH21 1NA (on B9152, just off A9) NH829057
☎ (01540) 651788 ⊕ thesuiebar.com
Cairngorm Trade Winds; 2 changing beers (sourced regionally; often Orkney) Ⓗ

It is worth pulling off the busy A9 and following the old road to seek out this wee gem of a country pub. From the outside it does not look much, but inside a warm Highland welcome is accompanied by four handpumps offering Cairngorm and some local Highland beers. A much-loved old stove has been replaced with a more modern, efficient model. The Suie holds a beer festival in late February and hosts music most weekends. Close to the River Spey and Loch Insh, it is also handy for the Kincraig Wildlife Park. Currently only open from 5pm so phone ahead. ֍ᕁ⏦P몮❀🛜♫

Lewiston

Loch Ness Inn

nr Drumnadrochit, IV63 6UW (W of the A82)
☎ (01456) 450991 ⊕ staylochness.co.uk
3 changing beers (sourced regionally; often Cairngorm, Cromarty, Windswept) Ⓗ

Dating from 1838, this traditional inn has rooms and a new bunkhouse. The restaurant is fiercely proud of its ingredients' local provenance. The comfy bar with its welcoming stove has up to three handpumps, offering beers from mainly local breweries, occasionally Applecross. The inn is ideally located for visiting Loch Ness, Urquhart Castle, or even walking the Great Glen Way. A free eight-seater courtesy bus is available for local pick-ups within five miles; call the pub.
ゐ֍⑪▷ᕁ⏦Aᕁ⏦P몮🛜♫

Mallaig

Steam Inn

Davies Brae, PH41 4PU (off top of Station Rd)
☎ (01687) 462002 ⊕ steaminnmallaig.co.uk
2 changing beers (often Isle of Skye) Ⓗ

Hanging baskets adorn the striking frontage of this pub in summer. Inside, there is a wood-burner at one end and an open fire at the other for cooler days. The 20-table beer garden at the rear comes into its own in fine weather. The pub fills up when the Skye/Uist ferry docks in the harbour, or the Hogwarts Express train arrives – both are just a short walk away. An extensive food menu features local seafood, bar food and children's options. Isle of Skye ales are served on handpump.

ᵰ☆⌂◑≡♣P☂❄🛜♪

Nairn

Bandstand 🅛 ✅

Crescent Road, IV12 4NB (E end of town towards beach)
☎ (01667) 452341 ⊕ thebandstandnairn.co.uk
5 changing beers (sourced nationally; often Cairngorm, Cromarty, Orkney) ⊞
Overlooking the green, with its bandstand and the Moray Firth beyond, the bar has five handpumps offering a great selection of local and regional Scottish beers, including the occasional English ale. The pub holds popular spring and autumn beer festivals, said to be the biggest independent events in the UK, which are accompanied by themed food and music acts over three days. The restaurant offers good-value quality food and live music plays at the weekend.

Q ᵰ☆⌂◑♿≡♣P☂❄🛜♪

Havelock

Crescent Road, IV12 4NB
☎ (01667) 455500 ⊕ havelocknairn.co.uk
Cromarty Happy Chappy; 1 changing beer (sourced regionally; often Cromarty) ⊞
The Havelock is a hotel and bar located by the seaside in the popular tourist town of Nairn. The bar has a welcoming, lively and informal atmosphere and dispenses beers from three handpumps. There is regular live music entertainment and karaoke on Sunday.

ᵰ⌂◑♿≡♣P☂🛜♪

Plockton

Plockton Hotel ✅

41 Harbour Street, IV52 8TN NG80293343
☎ (01599) 544274 ⊕ plocktonhotel.co.uk
4 changing beers (often Cromarty, Fyne, Swannay) ⊞
Plockton was the setting for TV's Hamish Macbeth, which is an attraction for visitors to this pretty village, many of whom arrive by train on the picturesque Kyle Line. The bar proudly offers four handpumps dispensing local and regional beers that can be enjoyed on the terrace with views of the sea. The food menu features locally sourced seafood, beef and venison. A real ale and gin festival is held in May. Closed throughout January.

Q ᵰ☆⌂◑♿≡P☂❄🛜♪

Portree: Isle of Skye

Portree Hotel

Somerled Square, IV51 9EH (E side of main square)
☎ (01478) 612511 ⊕ theportreehotel.com
Isle of Skye Skye Gold, Skye Red ⊞
The West Highland Bar at the Portree Hotel is modern but cosy, with comfortable seating booths and a central poseur table next to the bar. It is popular with locals and tourists alike. Two handpumps normally dispense ales from local Isle of Skye brewery, though occasionally something else is on one. Food is available in the next-door restaurant for residents and non-residents, and diners can order drinks from the bar. There may be live music on weekends. ⌂◑🖵♪

Roy Bridge

Stronlossit Inn 🅛

Main Street, PH31 4AG (on A86) NN27228117
☎ (01397) 712253 ⊕ stronlossit.co.uk

3 changing beers (sourced locally; often Cairngorm, Isle of Skye, Orkney) ⊞
The inn's location makes it attractive to those keen on the outdoors, and with the railway station just over the road, you can leave the car at home and arrive by train from Fort William. The train can also take you for a day trip to Corrour, to walk around Loch Ossian. Up to four handpumps serve ales from various Scottish breweries including the local Glen Spean. Great food is available all day, and there are rooms for all budgets. Closed November-February inclusive.

Q ᵰ☆⌂◑♿Å≡♣P☂🛜

Stornoway: Isle of Lewis

Crown Inn ✅

Castle Street, HS1 2BD (close to ferry terminal)
☎ (01851) 703734 ⊕ crownhotelstornoway.com
2 changing beers (sourced nationally; often Caledonian, Inveralmond, Timothy Taylor) ⊞
Located in the centre of Stornoway, minutes' walk from the ferry terminal and bus station, the lounge bar and Harbour View restaurant are accessed via the Crown Hotel while the large public bar, featuring sports TV, pool and weekly live music sessions, has a separate entrance. Both bars sport two handpumps. In 1963 the Crown famously witnessed the 'Cherry Brandy Scandal', when the former Prince of Wales indulged in an underage tipple. An impressive range of over 120 gins is on offer. Opening hours vary seasonally. The restaurant is closed Sunday and Monday. ᵰ⌂◑♣P☂❄🛜♪

Whitebridge

Whitebridge Hotel 🅛

IV2 6UN (on B862 towards SE side of Loch Ness) NH487152
☎ (01456) 486226 ⊕ whitebridgehotel.co.uk
3 changing beers (sourced regionally; often Cairngorm, Cromarty, Orkney) ⊞
Built in 1899 and located on the quieter east side of Loch Ness, this two-star hotel has fishing rights on three local lochs. Inside, the attractive pitch-pine panelled bar features a welcoming wood-burning stove. An adjacent room has a pool table and a separate area for dining. Three ales are usually available, reducing to two or one in winter. The traditional pub food is all home-cooked. The hotel has a green tourism policy.

Q ☆⌂◑♿♣P☂❄🛜

Breweries

Applecross

Russel Yard, Kishorn, Strathcarron, IV54 8XF
⊕ applecrossbrewingcompany.co.uk

Applecross Brewing Co was established in 2016 in the remote wilderness of the Applecross Estate in the Highlands of Scotland. All the beers are available in bottle and cask. The main cask outlet is the famous Applecross Inn.

Applecross (ABV 3.7%) PALE
Sanctuary (ABV 4%) RED
Inner Sound (ABV 4.7%) PORTER

Ardgour SIBA

The Manse, Ardgour, Fort William, PH33 7AH
☎ (01855) 632321 ☎ 07785 763659
⊕ ardgourales.scot

Opening in 2020, eight years after Fergus and Lizzy Stokes bought the crumbling Manse with a view to bringing great beer to Scotland's west coast, this new-build, five-barrel brewery is situated in the village of Ardgour on the edge of the remote Morvern and Ardnamurchan peninsulas. An onsite bakery is also in operation. ♯♠

Eas Geal (ABV 3.4%) PALE
Boc Beag (ABV 3.6%) GOLD
Gobhar Shamhna (ABV 4.1%) RED
Gobhar Odhar (ABV 4.3%) BITTER
Bainne nan Gobhar (ABV 4.5%) STOUT
Boc Ban (ABV 5.1%) BITTER
Boc na Braiche (ABV 6.4%) PALE
Gobhar Reamhar (ABV 6.5%) STOUT

Black Isle SIBA

Old Allengrange, Munlochy, IV8 8NZ
☎ (01463) 811871 ● blackislebrewery.com

⊛Black Isle Brewery was set up in 1998 in the heart of the Scottish Highlands. It expanded substantially in 2011 with a new brewhouse and bottling line. All beers are organic with Soil Association certification. ♯♠♦

Yellowhammer (ABV 3.9%) GOLD
A refreshing, hoppy golden ale with light hop and peach flavour throughout. A short bitter finish.
Red Kite (ABV 4.2%) BITTER
Tawny ale with light malt on the nose and some red fruit on the palate and a hoppy background. Slight sweetness in the taste.
Heather Honey (ABV 4.6%) SPECIALITY
Sweet amber beer brewed with a background mix of organic malt, hops and Highland heather honey.
Porter (ABV 4.6%) PORTER
A hint of liquorice and burnt chocolate on the nose and a creamy mix of malt and fruit in the taste.
Blonde (ABV 5%) BLOND

Cairngorm SIBA

Unit 12, Dalfaber Industrial Estate, Aviemore, PH22 1ST
☎ (01479) 812222 ● cairngormbrewery.com

⊛Cairngorm brews using a 20-barrel plant. Now with its own bottling line, it supplies the free trade as far south as the central belt, and nationally via wholesalers. In 2016, in partnership with the Cobbs Group, it bought the brands of the Loch Ness Brewing Co and now brews selected beers under the Loch Ness brand name. ♯♠♦

Nessies Monster Mash (ABV 4.1%) BITTER
A fine best bitter with plenty of bitterness and malt flavour and a fruity background. Lingering bitterness in the aftertaste with diminishing sweetness.
Stag (ABV 4.1%) BITTER
A good mix of roasted malt, red fruits and hops throughout. This tawny brew also has plenty of malt in the lingering bitter-sweet aftertaste.
Trade Winds (ABV 4.3%) SPECIALITY
Award-winning brew with a strong elderflower and citrus fruity hop nose following on through to the bittersweet finish.
Black Gold (ABV 4.4%) STOUT
Roast malt dominates throughout, slight smokiness in aroma leading to a liquorice and blackcurrant background taste giving it a background sweetness. Very long, dry bitter finish. A worthy Championship winner.
Gold (ABV 4.5%) GOLD
Fruit and hops to the fore with a hint of caramel in this sweetish brew.
Highland IPA (ABV 5%) PALE

Refreshing, light-coloured, citrus American and South Pacific hopped IPA. Some background biscuit and caramel.
Wildcat (ABV 5.1%) BITTER
A full-bodied warming strong bitter. Malt predominates but there is an underlying hop character through to the well-balanced aftertaste. Drinks dangerously less than its 5.1%.

Cromarty SIBA

Davidston, Cromarty, IV11 8XD
☎ (01381) 600440 ● cromartybrewing.co.uk

Family-owned, Cromarty began brewing in 2011 in a purpose-built brewhouse. Many awards have been garnered. Fermenting capacity was increased during 2014 and again in 2015. Its varied portfolio of regular and occasional brews now surpasses 20. A bottling line was commissioned in 2017, a warehouse in 2018, and a canning line in 2019. The brewer is constantly trialling new recipes and collaboration brews. ♯♠♦

Whiteout (ABV 3.8%) SPECIALITY
Happy Chappy (ABV 4.1%) GOLD
An excellent golden ale with plenty of hop character. Floral citric hop aroma with a good bitter taste which increases in aftertaste and balanced with malt.
Red Rocker (ABV 5%) SPECIALITY
Red-coloured rye hop monster with a malty background leading to a bitter finish.
Raptor IPA (ABV 5.5%) IPA
Rogue Wave (ABV 5.7%) IPA
Easy-drinking, strong, peachy, hoppy bitter.
Ghost Town (ABV 5.8%) PORTER
Classic, dark-roasted, malty porter with blackcurrant and liquorice background.
AKA IPA (ABV 6.7%) IPA
Strong IPA with a smooth citrus hoppy taste.

Cuillin SIBA

⬛ **Sligachan Hotel, Sligachan, Carbost, IV47 8SW**
☎ 07795 250808 ● cuillinbrewery.com

⊛The five-barrel brewery opened in 2004 and is situated in central Skye at the foot of the Cuillin mountains. The water from the Cuillins provides a distinctive colour and taste to the ales. Beers are available onsite at the Sligachan Hotel and at several other pubs and hotels on the Isle of Skye. The brewery is open by appointment only in winter (November-March). ♯♦

Dog Falls SIBA

Scaniport, IV2 6DL ● dogfallsbrewing.com

Microbrewery founded by Bob Masson in 2019, Dog Falls brew modern interpretations of international beer styles. Beers are unfined and unfiltered, available mainly in can. V

Dun

Corrary Farm, Glen Beag, Glenelg, IV40 8JX
☎ (01599) 522333 ● dunbrewing.co.uk

⊛Established in 2018, this four-barrel brewery is named after the two neighbouring Iron Age brochs (forts) – Dun Telve and Dun Trodden. Using its own spring water, Soil Association-certified, 100% organic ingredients, and 100% renewable energy, the environmentally-sustainable cask ales are unfiltered and naturally-carbonated. Beers are only available locally at present. ♠♦♢

Ewebrew SIBA

**2 Naast Achnasheen, Poolewe, IV22 2LL ☎ 07494
310317 ⊕ ewebrew.beer**

☺Commissioned in early 2022, Ewebrew is the creation
of James and Jo Struthers. Initially two core beers are
brewed with an ever-evolving range coming on stream.
A self-catering holiday cottage is operated adjacent to
the brewery. **LIVE**

Arctic Convoy (ABV 4.5%) BLOND
Firemore (ABV 5%) BITTER

Glen Spean SIBA

**Tirindrish, Spean Bridge, PH34 4EU ☎ 07511 869958
⊕ glenspeanbrewing.com**

Based in a converted steading, brewing began in 2018.
🍺

Pale Blonde (ABV 3.6%) BLOND
Highbridge IPA (ABV 4%) BITTER
Red Revival (ABV 4.5%) BITTER

Hanging Tree

**▤ Benleva Hotel, Kilmore Road, Drumnadrochit,
IV63 6UH**

☺Hanging Tree began brewing in 2017 using a two-
barrel brew plant in an old bothy in the grounds of the
Benleva Hotel. Named after the 400-year-old chestnut
tree growing in the garden, which was used as the
hanging tree for the local area. Beers are available in the
pub and a few other local outlets.

Isle of Eigg SIBA

Galmisdale, PH42 4RL ⊕ eiggbrewery.com

Crowdfunded during 2020, Isle of Eigg is Scotland's first
cooperative brewery. Having built the brewery and
installed the kit in 2021, production began in 2022. The
brewery uses 100% renewable energy with its water
coming from a natural source, and supports the local
crofting community by reusing its raw materials.

Isle of Harris

**Croft No 6, Borrisdale, HS5 3UE ☎ 07584 354144
⊕ isleofharrisbrewery.com**

Established in 2020, small batch, limited edition beers
are produced in a tiny brewshed overlooking the Sound
of Harris. Beers are bottled and labelled by hand. **LIVE**

Isle of Skye SIBA

**The Pier, Uig, IV51 9XP
☎ (01470) 542477 ⊕ skyeale.com**

☺The Isle of Skye Brewery was established in 1995.
Originally a 10-barrel plant, it was upgraded to 20 barrels
in 2004. ‼🍺♦

Tarasgeir (ABV 4%) SPECIALITY
YP (Young Pretender) (ABV 4%) BITTER
A refreshing amber hoppy grapefruit bitter. Some
sweetness in the taste but continuing into a lingering
bitter finish.
Skye Red (ABV 4.2%) BITTER
A light, fruity nose with a hint of caramel leads to a
hoppy, malty, fruity flavour and a dry, bittersweet finish.
Skye Gold (ABV 4.3%) SPECIALITY
Porridge oats are used to produce this delicious speciality
beer. Nicely-balanced. it has a refreshingly soft lemon,
bitter flavour with an oaty background.

Skye Black (ABV 4.5%) OLD
Full-bodied with a malty richness. Malt holds sway but
there are plenty of hops and fruit to be discovered in its
varied character. A delicious Scottish old ale.
Skye IPA (ABV 4.5%) PALE

John O'Groats

**County Road, John O'Groats, KW1 4YR
☎ (01955) 611220 ☎ 07842 401571**

**2nd Site: Last House, John O'Groats, KW1 4YR
⊕ johnogroatsbrewery.co.uk**

☺Brewing began in 2015 with a four-barrel plant. It is
housed in the old John O'Groats Fire Station almost
opposite its tap, the Seaview Hotel. A second three-
barrel plant is installed in the Last House by the harbour,
which is now a visitor centre complete with shop, bar
and brewery tours. A bottling facility has been added
next to the Fire Station plant. ‼🍺

Swelkie (ABV 4%) BITTER
Slight honey taste in this citrus hoppy brew
Duncansby (ABV 4.2%) BITTER
Deep Groat (ABV 4.8%) STOUT
Nearly black brew full of chocolate and coffee with some
background roast.

Knoydart

**St. Agatha's Chapel & Manse, Inverie, Knoydart,
PH41 4PL ⊕ knoydartbrewery.co.uk**

Knoydart is one of the most remote breweries on
mainland Britain. There are no road links so access is by
ferry, or on foot over mountain passes. Beers are brewed
in part of an old chapel using a 60-litre electric brewery
and a five-barrel plant with four fermenters.

Loomshed

**Unit 3, Lomairt an Obain, Tarbert, Isle of Harris,
HS3 3DS ☎ 07808 098860 ⊕ loomshed.scot**

Brewing commenced in 2019 on the outskirts of Tarbert.
The brewery backs onto the Minch, with views of the
Scottish mainland. An eco-friendly approach to brewing
extends to the onsite taproom. Following a period of
inactivity the brewery resumed production in 2022. ♥

Nessie

Westoaks, Fort William Road, Fort Augusus, PH32 4BH

Set up in 2017 Nessie Brew is a nanobrewery that
markets a range of bottled beers to the tourist trade
around Fort Augustus.

Old Inn

**▤ Old Inn & Brewpub, Flowerdale Glen, Gairloch,
IV21 2BD**

☎ (01445) 712006 ⊕ theoldinn.net

Brewing began in 2010 using a 150-litre plant. Brewing
is currently suspended. ♦

Plockton

**5 Bank Street, Plockton, IV52 8TP
☎ (01599) 544276 ☎ 07823 322043
⊕ theplocktonbrewery.com**

The brewery started trading in 2007 and expanded to a
2.5-barrel plant in 2009. Bottle-conditioned beers are
available and are suitable for vegetarians. ‼♦LIVE

Yarrowale (ABV 4.2%)

Plockton Bay (ABV 4.6%) BITTER

A well-balanced, tawny-coloured premium bitter with plenty of hops and malt which give a bittersweet fruity flavour.

Starboard! (ABV 5.1%) GOLD

A fine fruity golden ale with a light citrus bitterness. Hop and spicy fruit feature in the nose with a smack of grapefruit in the taste. The bitterness holds well into the aftertaste.

Ring Tong (ABV 5.6%) IPA

River Leven SIBA

Lab Road, Kinlochleven, PH50 4SG
☎ (01855) 831519 ⊕ riverlevenales.co.uk

First established in 2011, the brewery is under new ownership from 2023. Beers are produced using the pure Kinlochleven water with no added sugars or unmalted grain.

Blonde (ABV 4%) GOLD

IPA (ABV 4%) PALE

Strathcarron

Arinackaig, Strathcarron, IV54 8YN
☎ (01599) 577236 ⊕ strathcarronbrewery.com

⊗ Brewing since 2016 with a 2.5-barrel plant using its own onsite water supply. All beer is cask and bottle-conditioned, and is usually available on draught at seven or eight local pubs, and in bottles at a dozen or so local shops and restaurants (see website). Bottles available from the website. Labels are available in Gaelic or English. LIVE

Golden Cow (ABV 3.8%) GOLD
Black Cow (ABV 4.2%) STOUT
Red Cow (ABV 4.2%) BITTER
Highland Cow (ABV 5.4%) BITTER

Two Thirsty Men

76 High Street, Grantown on Spey, PH26 3EL
☎ 07779 227795 ⊕ twothirstymen.com

Brewing began in 2016 in a garage at the back of a café bar.

Spey IPA (ABV 3.5%) PALE
No74 (ABV 4.5%) BITTER

Wild Barn

Unit 1, Caol Industrial Estate, Kilmallie Road, Caol, PH33 7PH ☎ 07367 888431
✉ hello@wildbarnbeer.com

Purchased in late 2021, this nanobrewery moved to new premises by the end of 2021. Building from the recipes inherited from the previous Belgian owner, production is currently focused on cans. Trial cask production commenced early in 2023. 🍺

SCOTLAND

Castle Tavern, Inverness (Photo: Matt Kieffer / Flickr CC BY-SA 2.0)

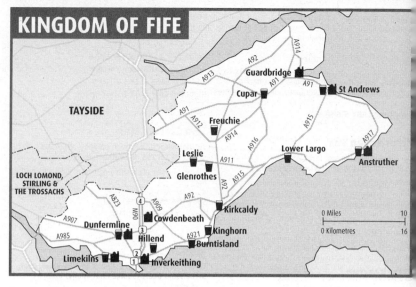

KINGDOM OF FIFE

Anstruther

Bank ✓
23-25 High Street East, KY10 3DQ
☎ (01333) 310189 ⊕ thebank-anstruther.co.uk
3 changing beers (often Morland, Stewart) Ⓗ
Family-run bar and hotel with one of the finest views in Anstruther, where the Dreel Burn merges with the Firth of Forth, lovely while enjoying your evening meal. The Bank offers something for everyone, with freshly produced lunches, bar suppers from local suppliers, and a choice of real ales, draught beers, wines and spirits on offer. The large mature gardens are a suntrap.
⚜🛏🚪(X60,95) ☺ ☎

Dreel Tavern
16 High Street, KY10 3DL
☎ (01333) 279238 ⊕ dreeltavern.co.uk
3 changing beers (sourced nationally; often Adnams, Stewart) Ⓗ
One of Anstruther's most historic buildings, the Dreel Tavern has served the area as a venue for fine food and drinks over the years. This traditional pub is popular with locals, walkers and visitors, and its open fire in winter creates a cosy atmosphere. At the rear is a sunny beer garden overlooking the Dreel Burn, from which the pub takes its name. This family-run pub is becoming renowned for the quality of its locally sourced food.
Q🛏☺◑♣🚪(95,X60) ☺ ☎ ♪

Burntisland

Sands Hotel ✓
Lochies Road, KY3 9JX
☎ (01592) 872230 ⊕ burntislandsands.co.uk
1 changing beer (sourced regionally) Ⓗ
A warm welcome awaits at this family-run hotel by the seafront in this picturesque coastal resort. Burntisland is home to the second oldest Highland Games in the world (1652), held at the end of July, alongside the town's annual summer fairground. The hotel has a choice of restaurants and is renowned for its high teas. The Sands Bar now boasts an outside area in which to relax with friends and family. ☺🛏◑P🚪(7)☺ ☎

Cupar

Boudingait
43 Bonnygate, KY15 4BU
☎ (01334) 208310 ⊕ theboudingaitcupar.co.uk
3 changing beers (sourced regionally; often Harviestoun, Orkney) Ⓗ
Situated in the centre of town is this small, quiet pub with a pleasant atmosphere. The pub is mostly given over to food, though seating is available at the bar. The knowledgeable staff can give advice on the available ales. There is no TV and board games are available for customers to use. The pub is family and dog-friendly.
Q🛏◑&⇌🚪(36,42) ☺ ☎ ♪

Dunfermline

Commercial Inn
13 Douglas Street, KY12 7EB
☎ (01383) 696994
6 changing beers (sourced nationally; often Harviestoun, Orkney, Stewart) Ⓗ
Located in the heart of the town centre, close to the main shopping area, the pub attracts an eclectic clientele and gets busy on match days. Formerly a hotel, this 19th-century listed building is full of character and retains the high ceilings and decorative cornices of that period. A spiral staircase leads down to the lower levels. Local and Regional CAMRA Pub of the Year 2022.
🛏◑⇌(Town) 🚪☺ ☎ ♪

East Port ✓
7 East Port, KY12 7JG
☎ (01383) 736678

changing beers (sourced regionally; often Loch Leven, Loch Lomond, Stewart) ⊞
Located on the high street, just a short distance from the main shopping area, this busy town-centre pub is well worth a visit when out and about in Dunfermline. The interior features wood panelling and a wooden bar and gantry. Giant screens show a variety of sports, and soft background music usually plays. This is also a great place to relax with a few drinks in one the many cosy booths. ☎♿≷(Town)♣🚪🐾🛜

Guildhall & Linen Exchange ✔

79-83 High Street, KY12 7DR
☎ (01383) 625960
8 changing beers (sourced nationally; often Belhaven, Greene King, Stewart) ⊞
This Wetherspoon outlet was originally a guildhall and linen exchange when Dunfermline was synonymous with fine quality table linen. The Category A-listed building is now a split level pub and hotel. The interior is decorated with a mix of modern and Art Deco features and displays numerous pictures highlighting the town's past. In the middle of the busy retail area, this is a great place to stop for a pint and a bite to eat.
☎♿🍴🕭♿≷(Town)🚪🛜

Freuchie

Albert Tavern

2 High Street, KY15 7EX
☎ 07876 178863 ⊕ alberttavern.wixsite.com
5 changing beers (sourced nationally; often Phoenix) ⊞
Small two-roomed pub serving up to five ales and at least two ciders. The bar area is decorated with pumpclips from ales that have been sold previously. On entering, on the right is the lounge furnished with bench seating and with a large TV showing free-to-air sports. The team are always friendly and willing to share their ale knowledge. The pub is a frequent local CAMRA Pub of the Year and Cider Pub of the Year, and a former Scottish Pub of the Year. Q🍴♣🚪(36,42)🐾🛜

Glenrothes

Golden Acorn ✔

1 North Street, KY7 5NA
☎ (01592) 755252
3 changing beers (sourced nationally) ⊞
A large open-plan Wetherspoon pub with a slightly raised seating area at the front. The family area is to the rear of the pub, as well as a quiet space. There are a number of TVs throughout the building, showing a mixture of sports and news. This busy pub caters to all tastes, with themed menus and promotions available most days. Parking is available directly in front of the pub – you must register your car details via the monitored parking system on the bar. ☎♿🍴🕭♿🅿🚪🛜

Hillend

Hillend Tavern 🍸 ✔

37 Main Street, KY11 9ND
☎ (01383) 415391 ⊕ hillendtavern.co.uk
4 changing beers (sourced nationally; often Cromarty, Loch Lomond, Timothy Taylor) ⊞
A community-focused village pub near Dalgety Bay, with cosy log fires, a beer garden and real ales all adding to the friendly and welcoming atmosphere. The Tav, as it is known, has a traditional bar and a spacious area at the rear which is ideal for groups or larger functions. The pub hosts many village events and its live music nights and

two quiz nights each month are well attended. A local CAMRA Pub of the Year and regional runner-up.
☎♿🍴≷(Dalgety Bay)♣🚪(7,87)🐾🛜♫

Kinghorn

Auld Hoose

6-8 Nethergate, KY3 9SY
☎ (01592) 891074
2 changing beers (sourced nationally) ⊞
A traditional two-room pub just off the main street of this popular seaside village. It has a large bar area as you enter and a comfortable lounge at the side. The family-run pub is popular with both locals and visitors, and is an ideal stopping-off point for real ale enthusiasts walking the Fife Coastal Path. Lunches are served daily. It features regular evening events such as live music, karaoke and dominoes, and open mic sessions in the lounge on occasional Sunday afternoons. ◖≷♣🚪(7)🐾🛜

Crown Tavern Ⓛ ✔

55-57 High Street, KY3 9UW
☎ (01592) 891363
2 changing beers (sourced nationally; often St Andrews) Ⓐ
Historically know as the Middle Bar, this two-roomed venue is in the centre of Kinghorn, a short walk from the train station. Very much a community pub, it is a sports bar at heart with a large screen and several smaller screens. Two ales are served from traditional Scottish tall founts, as well as two or three ciders. The pub is a keen LocAle supporter, often serving beer from he nearby St Andrews brewery. Evening events are often held, mainly featuring live music. ≷🚪(7)🐾🛜♫

Kirkcaldy

Betty Nicols

297 High Street, KY1 1JL
☎ (01592) 591408
Fyne Jarl; 1 changing beer (sourced regionally; often Fyne) ⊞
This traditional pub is located in the merchants' quarter of the town's High Street. The interior features vintage patterned titles and comfortable seating, lending it a relaxed, cosy atmosphere. The pub is proud to serve two real ales, often from Fyne Ales, and also offers a selection of bottled beers, wines and spirits. The bistro menu features a range of meals. The pub hosts a regular quiz and other events. Closed Mondays.
☎◖♿≷🚪🐾🛜♫

Harbour Bar

473 High Street, KY1 2SN
☎ (01592) 264270
Oakham Citra; 4 changing beers (sourced nationally; often Greene King, Oakham, Vocation) ⊞
Historic pub dating from 1870, offering a lively atmosphere with live music and quizzes. It serves Belgian food, with a variety of real ales alongside a range of Belgian beers. The building, a former ships chandlers, has been identified by CAMRA as having an interior of regional importance and is one of only a few pubs still with a Jug Bar. Behind the pub, in the old sailmaker's workshop, brewing will commence from late 2023 in the once mothballed Fyfe brewery. Closed Mondays. ☎◖●♣🚪(X60,X27)🐾🛜

Robert Nairn ✔

2-6 Kirk Wynd, KY1 1EH
☎ (01592) 205049

Greene King Abbot; 5 changing beers (sourced nationally; often Belhaven, Oakham, Stewart) ⊞
This Wetherspoon pub is named after a member of the Nairn family, who opened a linoleum factory. The building, a former bank, is just off the town's main pedestrianised area. It has a split-level lounge, and pictures of old Kirkcaldy adorn the walls. The pub's central location, close to the town's Old Kirk, allows it to attract a mixed clientele, who enjoy a wide variety of real ales from six handpumps. ⧉❀⫛❍⇌🚍🛜

Leslie

Burns Tavern
184 High Street, KY6 3DB
☎ (01592) 741345
Timothy Taylor Landlord; 1 changing beer (sourced nationally) ⊞
A traditional tavern that is very much the hub of the community in this former paper-making town. It consists of a public bar and a lounge. The main bar is split into two sections – the lower level with the main bar and the higher area with a pool table. This is a pub where you can sit back, relax and enjoy your pint of Timothy Taylor's Landlord while watching sport on the numerous TVs. Q⧉❀⫛⬩λ♣P🚍(39A)❀

Limekilns

Bruce Arms L
2 Main Street, KY11 3HL
☎ (01383) 872259 ⊕ brucearmslimekilns.co.uk
2 changing beers (sourced nationally; often Fuller's, Inner Bay) ⊞
A warm and welcoming public house in this historic village on the Fife Coastal Path; the original settlement dates back to the 14th century. Stunning views across the Firth of Forth can be admired while enjoying a bite to eat or a quick drink. The pub supports LocAle, and often has a beer or two from local brewery Inner Bay. ⧉❀⫛♣P🚍❀🛜♪

Ship Inn L
Halketts Hall, KY11 3HJ
☎ (01383) 872247 ⊕ the-ship-inn-limekilns.co.uk
3 changing beers (sourced nationally; often Belhaven, Brewshed, Orkney) ⊞
This pub sits on the River Forth, at the west end of this former fishing village, with views of the three bridges spanning the river. The Ship Inn is a family-run venue and prides itself in providing a warm relaxed atmosphere. The pub features in Robert Louis Stevenson's novel Kidnapped, in which two characters were carried across the Forth after an alleged tipple here. Q⧉❀⫛P🚍(6)❀

Lower Largo

Railway Inn L
1 Station Wynd, KY8 6BU
☎ (01333) 320239 ⊕ railwayinnlargo.co.uk
5 changing beers (sourced regionally; often Loch Lomond, Ovenstone109, Stewart) ⊞
The Railway is a friendly and traditional village pub, dating back to 1749. It stands in the shadow of the old railway viaduct, in the picturesque village of Lower Largo. Numerous items of railway memorabilia adorn the walls, the fireplace and the bar counter. In warmer months you can relax outside, with the views of the local harbour, or in the private beer garden. Lunches consisting of pies and toasties are available daily. Q⧉❀⫛🚍(95)❀🛜

St Andrews

Aikmans Bar-Bistro
32 Bell Street, KY16 9UX
☎ (01334) 477425 ⊕ cellarbar.co.uk
3 changing beers (often Belhaven, Kelburn, Kelham Island) ⊞
Located between St Andrews' two main streets, North and South Street, Aikmans is a two-level venue, with the bistro at street level and the cellar bar below. This retro-decorated bar-bistro offers a relaxed atmosphere and is frequented by tourists and students alike, who come to enjoy a quick bite to eat or to sample one of the many ales on offer. Q⫛🚍❀♪

Criterion L ⊘
99 South Street, KY16 9QW
☎ (01334) 474543 ⊕ criterionstandrews.co.uk
House beer (by Stewart); 3 changing beers (sourced nationally; often Loch Lomond, St Andrews, Stewart) ⊞
One of the few family-run pubs in this famous university town, the Criterion was established back in 1874 and is situated on one of the main shopping streets. It is popular with locals, tourists, students and golfers. In addition to the four cask ales, a large selection of whiskies and gins are stocked, and the famous Cri-Pie is served until late. The pub operates a card payment service only. ⧉❀⫛🚍❀🛜♪

Breweries

Beath SIBA
54 Foulford Road, Cowdenbeath, KY4 9AS ☎ 07792 369678 ⊕ beathbrewing.com

⊛Beath began brewing in 2016, originally with a 20-litre capacity upgraded to 100-litre within a few months. There are plans for a further expansion. The beer range varies from week to week. LIVE

Mad World (ABV 4%) PORTER
Are You With Me (ABV 4.5%) BITTER
Ella Ella Ella (ABV 4.5%) SPECIALITY
Funky Town (ABV 5%) BITTER

Black Metal
Unit 20, M90 Commerce Park, Lathalmond, Dunfermline, KY12 0SJ
☎ (0131) 623 3411 ☎ 07711 295385

Office: Flat 10 / 7, Smithfield Street, Edinburgh, EH11 2PQ ✉ info@blackmetalbrewery.com

Black Metal Brewery was established in Edinburgh in 2012 by two old friends; metalheads and inspired brewers. In 2021 operations moved to its own brewing site in Dunfermline. ◆LIVE

Will-o'-the-Wisp (ABV 6%) SPECIALITY
Blood Revenge (ABV 6.6%) SPECIALITY
Yggdrasil (ABV 6.6%) GOLD

Brew Shed
Sandilands, Limekilns, KY11 3JD ☎ 07484 727672 ⊕ brewshedbeers.wordpress.com

Brewing began in 2016 in a tiny brewery behind the owner's house, the first brewery in Limekilns since 1849. Brew Shed Beers revives a tradition of local breweries serving the neighbourhood.

Eden Mill

Main Street, Guardbridge, KY16 0UU ☎ **07786 060013** ⊕ **edenbrewerystandrews.com**

☺The brewery was established in 2012 using a five-barrel plant in part of the former Guardbridge paper mills. In 2014 a new 20-barrel plant and distillery was installed. Brewing is currently suspended. ‼☕LIVE

Futtle

Unit 2, The Bowhouse, St Monans, KY10 2FB ⊕ **futtle.com**

Organic farmhouse brewery producing European-style beers. A 1,000-litre 'coolship' (a shallow, open fermentation vessel), has been installed in the rafters of the brewery.

Inner Bay SIBA

Seacliffe Villa, Hill Street, Inverkeithing, KY11 1AB ⊕ **innerbay.co.uk**

Brewing began in 2016. Inner Bay is a family-run brewery using traditional ingredients and methods producing bottle-conditioned beers in small batches. LIVE

North Sea

15 Primrose Court, Rosyth, KY11 2TE ✉ **info@northseabrewery.co.uk**

A microbrewery based in Rosyth, supplying craft beer locally to Fife, Scotland.

Ovenstone 109 SIBA

Ovenstone Works, Ovenstone, Anstruther, KY10 2RR ☎ **(01333) 311394** ⊕ **ovenstone109.com**

Established in 2018, Ovenstone 109 is a microbrewery in the East Neuk of Fife. The brewer aims to use renewable and sustainable technology in the brewing process.

St Andrews

Unit 7, Bassaguard Business Park, St Andrews, KY16 8AL ☎ **(01334) 208586** ⊕ **standrewsbrewingcompany.com**

Established in 2012 as a four-barrel brewery it was upgraded in 2019 to a thirty-barrel plant producing bottle-conditioned, cask and eco keg beers. In addition to its own three outlets (two in St Andrews, and one in Dundee), beers are supplied to a number of supermarket chains, local retailers and outlets. ‼LIVE

Oatmeal Stout (ABV 4.5%) STOUT
Mocha Porter (ABV 6%) SPECIALITY
Notorious BIPA (ABV 6%) SPECIALITY
Yippie IPA (ABV 6%) IPA

SaltRock SIBA

Lochend Farm, Dunfermline, KY12 0RY ⊕ **saltrockbrewing.co.uk**

SaltRock Brewing began brewing in 2021. Born of a desire to re-awaken a celebration of malt over the hop, it produces malt-forward beers.

SCOTLAND

Hillend Tavern, Hillend (Photo: Stuart McMahon)

LOCH LOMOND, STIRLING & THE TROSSACHS

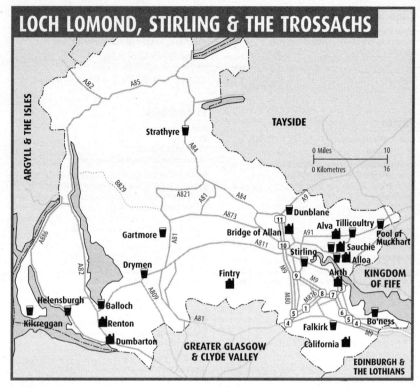

Alloa

Bobbing John ✔

46 Drysdale Street, FK10 1JL

☎ (01259) 222590

Belhaven 80/-; Greene King Abbot; Sharp's Doom Bar; 2 changing beers (sourced regionally; often Harviestoun, Hybrid, Williams Bros) Ⓗ

A Wetherspoon pub in a traditional three-storey sandstone building, purpose built in 1895 for the Alloa Co-operative Society. It is named after Alloa-born John Erskine who created industrial Alloa, developing the town as a coal mining centre. He was twice Secretary of State for Scotland under Queen Anne. However, his frequent changes of political allegiance earned him the nickname 'Bobbing John'. Much of the building's original stonework has been retained and a Victorian shop front reintroduced. It has a warming firepit in the centre. Q❄️🅰️🕙&🍴🚆🚪🐾🎵

Balloch

Tullie Inn Ⓛ ✔

Balloch Road, G83 8SW

☎ (01389) 752052

2 changing beers (sourced locally; often Loch Lomond) Ⓗ

This large establishment by Balloch station, close to the shores of Loch Lomond and the Balloch Castle Country Park, offers rooms, food and up to three real ales. Its modern decor and comfortable sofas give a bright and airy feel. In good weather you can enjoy a drink in the patio running alongside the pub, or in the large raised rear garden. The food menu offers a wide range of meals. Live music is performed occasionally.
❄️🅰️🕙&🚆P🚪🐾🎵♪

Bo'ness

Corbie Inn ♈

84 Corbiehall, EH51 0AS

☎ (01506) 825307 ⊕ corbieinn.co.uk

3 changing beers (sourced nationally; often Cross Borders, Hybrid, Kelburn) Ⓗ

Since 2011 the pub has been run by a family that is passionate about real ale. Up to three ales are available, mainly from Scottish breweries, plus a few English. It has a large lounge area serving fine food. It is very much a community pub involved in local charities and supporter of Bo'ness Real Ale Society's festival. The large, covered beer garden has a pizza oven and a children's play area. Close to the Bo'ness and Kinneil Railway, Bo'ness Motor Museum and the Hippodrome (Scotland's oldest purpose-built picture house). Q❄️🅰️🕙&P🚪🐾🎵

Drymen

Clachan Inn

2 The Square, G63 0BL

☎ (01360) 660824 ⊕ clachaninndrymen.co.uk

REAL ALE BREWERIES

Allanwater 🍺 Bridge of Allan
Devon 🍺 Sauchie
Harviestoun Alva
Loch Lomond ✦ Renton
Mosaik 🍺 Fintry
No Limits Dumbarton (NEW)
Not That California California (NEW)
SLOPEmeisteR Airth
Williams Bros Alloa

2 changing beers (sourced regionally; often Belhaven, Loch Lomond) ⊞
Established in 1734, this free house is the oldest licensed premises in Scotland. It has been recently refreshed, preserving many original features. There are two handpumps (one during winter) dispensing an ever-changing selection of excellent local and Scottish beers. This busy, popular pub offers a warm welcome to visitors, including walkers on the West Highland Way, tourists for Loch Lomond & The Trossachs National Park, and dog owners. Quality food is served all day in the bar and restaurant. ♿⌂✦◖▲☐(309)❀☞

Dunblane

Tappit Hen ✔

Kirk Street, FK15 0AL
☎ (01786) 825226
Greene King IPA; 4 changing beers (sourced regionally; often Cromarty, Fyne, Stewart) ⊞
Taking its name from a type of Scottish pewter drinking vessel, this traditional, friendly, one-room pub was refurbished in 2019 to a high standard. The helpful and knowledgeable staff serve regularly changing beers on four guest pumps. The pub is opposite one of Scotland's oldest cathedrals. The railway station and car parking are both close by. As well as charity and community events, the pub holds a successful real ale festival once a year. Dogs are welcome. ⇌☐❀☞♫

Falkirk

Wheatsheaf Inn ✔

16 Baxters Wynd, FK1 1PF
☎ (01324) 638282 ⊕ wheatsheaffalkirk.co.uk
3 changing beers (sourced nationally; often Cromarty, Hybrid, Loch Lomond) ⊞
Falkirk's oldest public house, dating from the late 18th century, is near the town's famous steeple and is a must-visit venue. It can be found off the High Street via one of the three vennels. Retaining much of its original character, the wood-panelled bar is furnished in traditional style with interesting and historical pub decor. Two guest beers come from breweries in Scotland and England. A recently renovated, secluded suntrap beer garden is at the rear. There is a friendly welcome here from the knowledgeable staff and fellow drinkers. ❀⇌(Grahamston)☐❀☞♫

Gartmore

Black Bull Hub & Pub

Main Street, FK8 3RW
☎ (01877) 382054 ⊕ blackbullgartmore.com
Harviestoun Schiehallion; 1 changing beer (sourced regionally; often Fyne) ⊞
A community-owned pub and hotel that is the village hub. The fine old building is largely unspoilt and comprises a warren of small rooms, including a cosy bar with real fire, two dining rooms and a society meeting room. It is mainly staffed by enthusiastic volunteers, supported by two paid staff. This family- and dog-friendly pub featured on the BBC series Saving Britain's Pubs with Tom Kerridge. Q♿❀⌂◖▲☐(X10A)❀☞♫

Helensburgh

Ashton

74 West Princes Street, G84 8UG
☎ (01436) 675900
Stewart Pentland IPA; 2 changing beers (sourced nationally; often Fyne, Stewart, Timothy Taylor) ⊞

A warm welcome awaits at this genuine local. The bar has been tastefully modernised and decorated with a nautical theme while retaining its original charm. During the work a set of tiles depicting scenes from the Waverley novels was revealed. There is a small room for playing darts. An ever-changing selection of ales from Scottish microbreweries is complemented by quality English beers. Live music is a regular Saturday night feature. ⇌(Central)♣☐(1B,316)❀☞♫

Commodore ✔

112-117 West Clyde Street, G84 8ES
☎ (01436) 676924 ⊕ vintageinn.co.uk
Sharp's Doom Bar; Stewart Jack Back; 1 changing beer (sourced nationally) ⊞
Just a short walk from the station, this bar offers scenic views of the Firth of Clyde and the Gareloch. In addition to the quality real ales there is a wide selection of food in the informal restaurant. In good weather you can enjoy sitting in the popular garden to the front where you might spot sea birds, ships, the wrecked sugar boat, and the occasional submarine. The building was once an inn offering accommodation but the hotel upstairs is now a separate business. ❀◖&P☐(1B)❀

Henry Bell ✔

19-29 James Street, G84 8AS
☎ (01436) 863060
Belhaven 80/-; Greene King Abbot; Sharp's Doom Bar; 4 changing beers (sourced nationally; often Broughton, Stewart) ⊞
Close to the town centre and esplanade, this sympathetic Wetherspoon conversion of an old furniture showroom has now established itself as an important real ale outlet, offering a wide range of ales from across Britain. It is a popular venue with both locals and visitors. The decor is in the style of Charles Rennie Mackintosh. There is a beer garden to the rear. Q❀◖&⇌(Central)☐☞

Kilcreggan

Creggans

Princes Terrace, Shore Road, G84 0JJ
☎ (01436) 842700
2 changing beers (sourced nationally; often Fyne) ⊞
This single-room bar has a wooden floor and a mix of table and chairs, with a pool table and sports TV. It stands opposite the traditional wooden pier which is a calling point for the paddle steamer Waverley and the small passenger ferry to Gourock. Beers are mainly from Fyne Ales but guests from England are sometimes available. Live music plays occasionally. Children are welcome in the front patio, which offers great views of the Firth of Clyde. Pub food is served daily. ❀◖&☐(316)❀☞♫

Pool of Muckhart

Inn at Muckhart ✔

FK14 7JN
☎ (01259) 781324 ⊕ theinnatmuckhart.com
Devon Original (70/-), 24K IPA, Pride ⊞
Single-storey old coaching inn in a picturesque rural village on the south-east edge of the Ochil Hills. It has low ceilings, exposed timber construction and a welcoming open fire, giving a comfortable atmosphere. The pub serves its own Devon Ales, brewed at its sister pub, the Mansfield Arms in Sauchie. The restaurant produces good food and is popular with locals at weekends in winter, and with tourists during the summer, when they can relax in the beer garden. Q♿❀⌂◖▲P☐(202)❀☞

Sauchie

Mansfield Arms ✓

7 Main Street, FK10 3JR (in centre of village, 100yds from main road)
☎ (01259) 722020 ⊕ devonales.com/mansfield-arms
Devon Original 70/- Ⓗ, 24K IPA Ⓗ/Ⓖ, Pride Ⓗ
A traditional two-bar pub and the oldest operating microbrewery in the Wee County. Its four Devon Ales are dispensed from three changing handpumps. The bar is family-owned and run, and popular with the locals who come to enjoy the lively banter and the food served in the comfortable lounge. The beer and food are excellent value for money. The pub is on the Stirling-Alloa circular bus route. Q७❀◑ᵹ♣P�☐❀🌢

Stirling

Allan Park

20 Allan Park, FK8 2QG
☎ (01786) 475336 ⊕ theallanparkstirling.co.uk
Belhaven Deuchars IPA; 2 changing beers (sourced regionally; often Cairngorm) Ⓗ
This historic category B-listed building in centre of Stirling is a fine example of Georgian architecture, also featuring a Roman Doric columned fanlight door. Built in 1880, it was extensively renovated in 2018 to a high standard and now includes a warming wood-burning stove. It operates as a pub, restaurant and coffee shop. Several open-plan rooms and large conservatory serves a wide Scottish menu and three Scottish beers. It is popular with tourists and locals alike. Q७❀🏠◑ᵹ⇌P�☐❀🌢

Birds & Bees

Easter Cornton Road, FK9 5PB (off Causewayhead Rd)
☎ (01786) 473663 ⊕ thebirdsandthebees-stirling.com
3 changing beers (sourced regionally; often Harviestoun, Stow, Williams Bros) Ⓗ
A welcoming converted rustic farmstead, located between the historic Wallace Monument and Stirling Castle, in a residential area on the northern outskirts of town. This award-winning gastro-pub serves locally sourced food, and three handpumps dispense a variety of good-quality Scottish real ales. Two large, award-winning and well-maintained beer gardens feature a permanent barbecue area in the courtyard and a pétanque pitch. This is a popular pub with locals and tourists. Q७❀◑ᵹ♣P�☐(C30)❀🌢

No.2 Baker Street ✓

2 Baker Street, FK8 1BJ
☎ (01786) 448722
Greene King IPA; 3 changing beers (sourced nationally; often Broughton, Harviestoun, Orkney) Ⓗ
A busy, large-windowed Victorian pub in the town centre that is part of the Belhaven/Greene King chain. The interior is open plan with bare floorboards, local paintings and rustic furnishings, creating a traditional atmosphere. It is popular with locals, students and tourists, and holds regular quiz nights, open mic sessions, and live music performances The beer range is a mixture of Belhaven/Greene King and Scottish and English guest ales. Hearty pub food is served. ७❀◑ᵹ⇌�☐🌢♪

Portcullis Hotel

Castle Wynd, FK8 1EG (next to Stirling Castle)
☎ (01786) 472290 ⊕ theportcullishotel.com
2 changing beers (sourced nationally; often Cairngorm, Orkney, Timothy Taylor) Ⓗ
Dating from 1787, this historic B-listed building (originally a grammar school) is now a popular pub/ hotel adjacent to Stirling Castle esplanade. James VI was educated on this site. Exposed stone walls and an open fireplace with ornate surround create a warm welcome in the heart of old Stirling. Frequented by tourists and supported by locals, it is renowned for its food and regularly changing selection of Scottish and English ales. Diners are advised to reserve a table. ७❀🏠◑⇌P�☐🌢

Settle Inn

91 St Marys Wynd, FK8 1BU
3 changing beers (sourced regionally; often Alechemy, Hybrid, Stewart) Ⓗ
Warm, friendly and atmospheric inn whose customers are a mixture of locals, students and tourists. Situated on a hill to/from Stirling Castle, it was built in 1733 and is the oldest pub in Stirling. It lives up to its name: settle down in front of the cosy fire and you may not want to leave (ghosts or no ghosts). There is music on Monday, Wednesday, Friday and Saturday, and a quiz on Sunday. The pub hosts an annual beer festival. Q⇌♣�☐🌢♪

Strathyre

White Stag Inn

Main Street, FK18 8NA
☎ (01877) 384333 ⊕ thewhitestag.co.uk
3 changing beers (sourced regionally; often Fyne, Loch Lomond, MòR) Ⓗ
A cosy, popular pub serving meals in the bar or bistro, all made with local produce. The beers are mainly from small independent Scottish brewers. Dogs and children are welcome in the bar. Hill walking, fishing, golf and water sports are all nearby, and Stirling, Callander and The Trossachs are within easy travelling distance. Accommodation is available on-site. Opening hours are restricted during winter – phone to check. A microbrewery is to open soon. Q७❀🏠Å♣P�☐🌢♪

Tillicoultry

Royal Arms

2 High Street, FK13 6AE
☎ (01259) 753037
3 changing beers (sourced nationally; often JW Lees, Timothy Taylor, Theakston) Ⓗ
Popular drinks-only pub with an enthusiastic owner, catering mainly to locals but welcoming to visitors. It has a dartboard, large sports TVs and a fruit machine. It's furnished with comfortable seating and bar stools plus a Victorian fireplace with log burner. A quieter side room with a small counter is ideal for families. There are three handpumps serving changing beers. ❀♣ᐁ(52,C2)❀🌢

Volunteer Arms

132 High Street, FK13 6DU
☎ (01259) 750368
2 changing beers (sourced nationally; often Greene King, Hybrid) Ⓗ
This friendly and unpretentious corner pub near the main bus stop offers a warm welcome to all. It has a small bar area with ample seating in three distinct bays on two levels. Large TVs cater for sports fans. The pub is a recent and important addition to this growing and thriving local real ale community and has received a local CAMRA Newcomer award. ७♣❀🌢

Breweries

Allanwater

🛢 Queens Lane, Bridge of Allan, FK9 4NY
☎ (01786) 834555 ☎ 07831 224242
⊕ allanwaterbrewhouse.co.uk

⊙Originally named Tinpot and then Wash House, the brewery was established in 2009 using a one-barrel plant. The beer range varies depending on season and demand, which is increasing every year. ‼🍺♦LIVE

Black Wolf

Unit 7c, Bandeath Industrial Estate, Throsk, Stirling, FK7 7NP
☎ (01786) 437187 ⊕ blackwolfbrewery.com

⊙Established in 2005, the brewery is located in a former torpedo factory on the shores of the River Forth. In 2014 the brewery changed its name from Traditional Scottish Ales to Black Wolf and rebranded its beers. All are brewed on demand all year round. The brewery also bottles beers for other breweries. ♦

Devon

🍴 **Mansfield Arms, 7 Main Street, Sauchie, FK10 3JR**
☎ (01259) 722020 ⊕ devonales.com

⊙Named after the nearby River Devon and the former Devon colliery, the brewery was established in 1992 and run by the Gibson family to supply their two pubs, the Mansfield Arms, and the Inn at Muckhart. Beer is also available to the free trade. ‼

Harviestoun SIBA

Alva Industrial Estate, Alva, FK12 5DQ
☎ (01259) 769100 ⊕ harviestoun.com

Harviestoun has grown from one-man brewing in a bucket in the back of a shed, in 1983, to a 60-barrel, multi award-winning brewery today. Now based in Alva, Scotland. ‼🍺♦LIVE

Bitter & Twisted (ABV 3.8%) GOLD
Refreshingly hoppy beer with fruit throughout. A bittersweet taste with a long bitter finish. A golden session beer.

Schiehallion (ABV 4.8%) SPECIALITY
A Scottish cask lager, brewed using a lager yeast and Hersbrucker hops. A hoppy aroma, with fruit and malt, leads to a malty, bitter taste with floral hoppiness and a bitter finish.

Loch Lomond SIBA

Vale of Leven Industrial Estate, Unit 11, Block 2, Renton, G82 3PD
☎ (01389) 755698 ☎ 07891 920213
⊕ lochlomondbrewery.com

⊙Established in 2011 by Fiona and Euan MacEachern. Having reached brewing capacity at its original site in Alexandria, it moved to a new purpose-built 35-hectolitre brewery in Renton in 2019. The site also houses a canning line and taproom. 🍺♦LIVE V🌱

West Highland Way (ABV 3.7%) BITTER
A light ale with fruity flavours.
Bonnie and Blonde (ABV 4%) BITTER
Maris Otter and Caragold malts give a light, refreshing ale and a blend of hops produces a well-rounded citrus flavour.
Southern Summit (ABV 4%) BLOND
The palate is fresh and fruity, with hints of grapefruit and lemon which lead on to a crisp, light bitter finish.
The Ale of Leven (ABV 4.5%) BITTER
An amber ale with spicy citrus aroma and a well-rounded bitterness, it seems to please most palates.
Bonnie 'n' Clyde (ABV 4.6%) BITTER
A wonderful amber ale with a big citrus hit on the nose that follows through to the rich, bitter finish.

Silkie Stout (ABV 5%) STOUT
Award-winning black stout with chocolate-orange spicy notes.
Kessog Dark Ale (ABV 5.2%) BITTER
Dark with warm spicy flavours.
Bravehop Amber IPA (ABV 6%) IPA
Upfront hop bite and lots of sweetness to give balance.
Bravehop Dark IPA (ABV 6%) IPA
A black IPA with upfront hop bite balanced with roasted malt and a long dry bitter finish.

Mosaik

🍴 **Fintry Inn, 23 Main Street, Fintry, G63 0XA**
☎ 07970 473601 ⊕ fintryinn.co.uk/mosaik-brewing

Microbrewery based at the Fintry Inn.

No Limits (NEW)

25 Lime Road, Broadmeadow Industrial Estate, Dumbarton, G82 2RP

A craft nanobrewery, opened in 2022, producing 120-litres per brew, it sells beers direct from the brewery. After four months expansion was marked with the purchase of a new 300-litre fermenter.

Not That California (NEW)

Braeview, California, FK1 2DH ☎ 07972 574949
⊕ notthatcalifornia.com

A microbrewery in the heart of Scotland, in a small village called California. Run by former homebrewers that moved into commercial brewing in 2022, it brews modern takes on traditional styles of beer.

SLOPEmeisteR

Oak House, Airth Castle Estate, Airth, FK2 8JF
☎ 07895 734867 ⊕ slopemeister.com

SLOPEmeisteR started brewing in 2018, initially at Hybrid Brewery in Grangemouth, then setting up a nanobrewery in a garage in Airth. Cask-conditioned beer is supplied to festivals.

Strangers SIBA

Narrowboat Farm, Linlithgow, EH49 6QY
⊕ strangersbrewing.co.uk

Commencing brewing in 2022, Strangers Brewing Co brew hand-crafted beer in small batches. Three core beers are available in cans, as well as seasonal specials that take their flavours from what's growing on the farm and the surrounding Scottish countryside.

Williams Bros SIBA

New Alloa Brewery, Kelliebank, Alloa, FK10 1NT
☎ (01259) 725511 ⊕ williamsbrosbrew.com

⊙A brotherhood of brewers, creating unique beers. Bruce and Scott Williams started brewing Heather Ale in 1988. A range of indigenous, historic ales have been added since. Three cask ales are produced all year round. The ales are regularly found in pubs in Central Scotland. ‼🍺♦

Fraoch Heather Ale (ABV 4.1%) SPECIALITY
The unique taste of heather flowers is noticeable in this beer. A fine floral aroma and spicy taste give character to this drinkable speciality beer.
Birds & Bees (ABV 4.3%) GOLD
Joker IPA (ABV 5%) PALE

JOIN THE CAMRA STORY

People from all walks of life join CAMRA. They're brought together by a love of real ale, cider and perry, the traditions of the pub and a desire to protect them. Be part of the story and seek out your local branch. Keep real ale alive and share tasting notes. Volunteer at a festival or campaign to protect everything you love for the future. Discover the many ways to celebrate our shared passions.

Join as a member from only £30.50† today – as a thank you for being a hero in the CAMRA story, your membership gets you...

Join the
CAMRA story

Real stories, real people, real ale

- A **welcome pack**, including membership card, to help you make the most of your membership

- Access to award-winning, quarterly *BEER* **magazine** and **What's Brewing** online news

- £30* worth of **CAMRA real ale** ** **vouchers**

- Access to the **Real Ale Discount Scheme**, where you receive discounts on pints at over 3,500 participating pubs nationwide

- **Learn & Discover** online resources to help you discover more about beer and brewing

- **Free or reduced entry** to CAMRA beer festivals

- The opportunity to **campaign for great real ale, cider and perry**, and to save pubs under threat from closure

- **Discounts on CAMRA books** including our best-selling *Good Beer Guide*

- Social activities in your local area and **exclusive member discounts online**

Whether you're a dedicated campaigner, a beer enthusiast looking to learn more about beer, or you just love beer and pubs, CAMRA membership is for you. Join us today!

Join the campaign at
camra.org.uk/join

CAMRA, 230 Hatfield Road, St Albans, Herts AL1 4LW.
Tel: 01727 798440 Email: camra@camra.org.uk

Rates and benefits are subject to change.
† Concessionary rates may be lower.
* Joint members receive £40 worth of vouchers.
** real ale, cider and perry, subject to terms and conditions.

Campaign
for
Real Ale

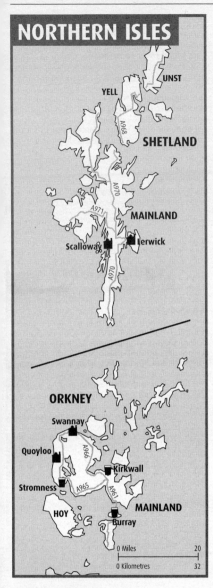

☎ (01856) 873001 ⊕ ayrehotel.co.uk
Swannay Scapa Special Ⓗ
The recently refurbished restaurant and bar is now renamed the Orcadian Restaurant & Bar and has a smart, modern look. Overlooking Kirkwall harbour, the oldest part of the hotel dates back to 1791 and it was a Temperance Hotel between 1885 and 1938. The dining area has a conservatory and booking is strongly advised. Lunches and evening meals use Orkney beef, fish and other produce. The hotel is close to the bus station and ferries to the outer isles of Orkney. ➷🛏◑🌙🕹♣🅿🚃🛜

Helgi's Bar 🍸
14 Harbour Street, KW15 1LE (right by harbour)
☎ (01856) 879293 ⊕ helgis.co.uk
Swannay Scapa Special; 2 changing beers (sourced locally; often Swannay) Ⓗ
Converted from a former shipping office, this small, smart bar has the look of a modern café with wood panelling and a floor of local stone. Special food nights where food is matched with ales are a highlight. Booking for food is recommended. Regular music sessions and a weekly Thursday quiz night are also hosted. Set on the harbourfront where seafood is landed daily, this is a handy place to fill in time before island hopping on the many ferries to outlying parts. Local CAMRA Pub of the Year 2022 and 2023. May close Monday and Tuesday out of season. ◑🕹🚃🛜🎵

Skippers Bar
Bridge Street, KW15 1LE (corner of Harbour St and Bridge St)
☎ (01856) 872232 ⊕ kirkwallhotel.com
Swannay Scapa Special Ⓗ
Skippers Bar is a vibrant bar with multiple TV screens, busy, especially in the evenings, with a mainly youngish clientele. It is part of the Kirkwall Hotel, which overlooks the harbour. The hotel part has a large lounge area with a whisky bar and often hosts functions and wedding parties. Both the lounge and Skippers serve one real ale and you can move between bars via a connecting corridor. 🛏◑♣🐾🛜🎵

St Ola Hotel
Harbour Street, KW15 1LE
☎ (01856) 875090 ⊕ stolahotel.co.uk
Swannay Scapa Special; 1 changing beer (sourced locally; often Swannay) Ⓗ
Built overlooking the harbour on the site of the Inns of Sinclair dating back to the 14th century, the Ola is a short walk from all of Kirkwall's attractions. It has a traditional public bar and the larger lounge to the rear where food is served. Ales are available in both bars along with an extensive range of whiskies. A music session is held from 4pm on Sundays on the last Sunday of the month, and these can be lively during the summer months. A former local CAMRA Pub of the Year. 🕹🛏◑🕹♣🚃🐾🛜🎵

Stromness: Orkney

Ferry Inn
10 John Street, KW16 3AD (directly across from from ferry terminal)
☎ (01856) 850280 ⊕ ferryinn.com

REAL ALE BREWERIES
Lerwick ✦ Lerwick: Shetland
Orkney ✦ Orkney: Quoyloo
Swannay Orkney: Swannay
Wreck Creation Shetland: Scalloway

Burray: Orkney

Sands Hotel
KW17 2SS (follow signs for pier at Burray village)
☎ (01856) 731298 ⊕ thesandshotel.co.uk
Swannay Scapa Special Ⓗ
Overlooking the harbour and South Ronaldsay beyond, the Sands was originally a 19th-century fish store. It is popular with locals and visitors alike. Meals are served in the bar or in the separate restaurant; each have their own menus, specialising in local seafood. Dive boats and yachts can tie up at the pier outside. Kirkwall is eight miles to the north, and the Italian Chapel and Churchill Barriers are within easy reach. Q🛏◑🅿⚓🅿

Kirkwall: Orkney

Ayre Hotel
Ayre Road, KW15 1QX

Swannay Scapa Special; 2 changing beers (sourced locally; often Orkney, Swannay) Ⓗ
An easy walk from the harbour front, the Ferry reopened in 2022 following major refurbishment. It is popular with locals and visitors, including divers who come to Orkney to explore the sunken German fleet at Scapa Flow. Annual folk and blues festivals are held, with a marquee erected outside complete with an ale pump. The pub is handy for buses to Kirkwall and the mainland ferry from Scrabster. Nearby attractions include the Ring of Brodgar and Skara Brae village. A previous local CAMRA Pub of the Year winner. ⚤🌐🔟👤♣️P🏠❄️🐾🎵

Breweries

Lerwick SIBA

Staneyhill, North Road, Lerwick, ZE1 0NA
☎ (01595) 694552 ☎ 07738 948336
⊕ lerwickbrewery.co.uk

Lerwick Brewery was established in 2011 using a 12-barrel plant and sits at the very edge of the North Atlantic. Originally only brewing keg beer, a cask-conditioned range was launched in 2015. 🍴♦️◆

Skipper's Ticket (ABV 4%) BITTER
Azure (ABV 4.3%) GOLD
Refreshing, grapefruity/peachy, hoppy, golden bitter.
Lerwick IPA (ABV 5%) PALE
Grapefruity hoppy bitter with a slight biscuit background.
Tushkar (ABV 5.5%) STOUT
Very good dark brown roasted malty stout with chocolate, coffee and liquorice.

Orkney SIBA

Orkney Brewery, Quoyloo, KW16 3LT
☎ (01667) 404555 ☎ 07721 013227

Office: Sinclair Breweries Ltd, Cawdor, IV12 5XP
⊕ orkneybrewery.co.uk

☺Orkney was established in 1988 in an old village school building. Having incorporated sister brewery Atlas, it moved next door in 2010 to enable an increase in capacity and the completion of an award-winning visitor centre in 2012. 🍴🍺♦️◆

Island Life (ABV 3.7%) GOLD
Light golden citrus hoppy ale with grapefruit and peach flavours leading to a bitter finish.
Raven (ABV 3.8%) BITTER
A well-balanced quaffable bitter. Malty fruitiness and bitter hops last through to the long, dry aftertaste.
Northern Light (ABV 4%) BITTER
A well-balanced clean and crisp amber ale with a good mix of malt, citrus and hops in the taste and an increasing bitter aftertaste.
Red MacGregor (ABV 4%) BITTER
This tawny red ale has a well balanced mix of red fruit, malt and hops. Slight sweetness throughout.

Corncrake (ABV 4.1%) GOLD
A straw-coloured beer with soft citrus fruits and a floral aroma.
Dark Island (ABV 4.6%) MILD
A sweetish roast chocolate malt taste leads to a long-lasting roasted, slightly bitter, dry finish. Has won many awards.
Cliff Edge IPA (ABV 4.7%) PALE
Skull Splitter (ABV 8.5%) BARLEY
An intense velvet malt nose with hints of apple, prune and plum. The hoppy taste is balanced by satiny smooth malt with sweet fruity spicy edges, leading to a long, dry finish with a hint of nut.

Swannay

Birsay, Swannay by Evie, KW17 2NP
☎ (01856) 721700 ⊕ swannaybrewery.com

☺Brewing began in 2006 at the redundant Swannay dairy on Orkney mainland's exposed North-Western tip. Two brewing plants are utilised, a five and a twenty barrel. Founder Rob is assisted by son Lewis plus a further small team of passionate beer lovers. 🍴🍺♦️

Orkney Best (ABV 3.6%) GOLD
A refreshing, light-bodied, low gravity, golden beer bursting with hop, peach and sweet malt flavours. The long, hoppy finish leaves a dry bitterness.
Island Hopping (ABV 3.9%) GOLD
Passionfruit hoppiness with some caramel with a lasting bitter aftertaste.
Dark Munro (ABV 4%) MILD
The nose presents an intense roast hit which is followed by plums and blackcurrant in the mouth. The strong roast malt continues into the aftertaste.
Scapa Special (ABV 4.2%) BITTER
A good copy of a typical Lancashire bitter, full of bitterness and background hops, leaving your mouth tingling in the lingering aftertaste.
Sneaky Wee Orkney Stout (ABV 4.2%) STOUT
Bags of malt and roast with a mixed fruit berry background. Dry bitter finish.
Pale Ale (ABV 4.7%) PALE
Orkney IPA (ABV 4.8%) PALE
A traditional bitter, with light hop and fruit flavour throughout.
Duke IPA (ABV 5.2%) PALE
Good, refreshing, citrus-fruited IPA with background malt.
Orkney Blast (ABV 6%) BITTER
Plenty of alcohol in this warming strong bitter/barley wine. A mushroom and woody aroma blossoms into a well-balanced smack of malt and hop in the taste.

Wreck Creation

Scalloway Public Hall, Berry Road, Scalloway, ZE1 0UJ
☎ (01595) 880884 ✉ wreckcreation@outlook.com

Small-batch microbrewery established in 2021 in Shetland producing two bottled beers. LIVE

Store of good ale

Though it was but about the middle of August, and in some places the harvest hardly got in, we saw the mountains covered with snow, and felt the cold very acute and piercing but we found, as in all these northern counties, the people had a happy way of mixing the warm and the cold together; for store of good ale which flows plentifully in the most mountainous parts of this country seem abundantly to make up for all the inclemencies of the season, or difficulties of travelling.
Daniel Defoe, A Tour Through the Whole Island of Great Britain, 1726

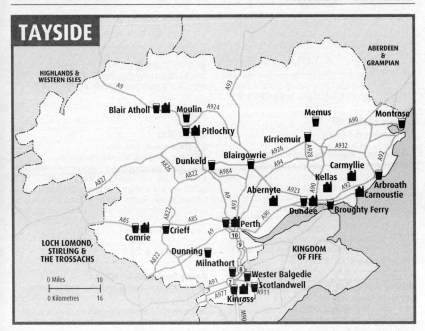

SCOTLAND

Arbroath

Corn Exchange ✓

14 Olympic Centre, Market Place, DD11 1HR
☎ (01241) 432430
Belhaven 80/-; Greene King Abbot; Sharp's Doom Bar; 3 changing beers (sourced nationally; often Stewart) Ⓗ
Located just off the High Street, this Wetherspoon is in the former 19th-century corn exchange. Although it is largely open plan, there are a number of booths providing some privacy. A varied selection of real ales is always available, with alcoholic drinks served from 11am. Boat trips offering fishing or a visit to the 200-year-old Bell Rock lighthouse can be taken from the nearby harbour. ☕️🏠🌓♿🚲🚌🚉🛜

Blair Atholl

Atholl Arms Hotel Ⓛ

PH18 5SG
☎ (01796) 481205 ⊕ athollarmshotel.co.uk
Moulin Light, Braveheart, Ale of Atholl, Old Remedial Ⓗ
The Atholl Arms has a grand and imposing façade in the Victorian Highland style. Its characterful Highland Bothy Bar serves four ales produced by the local Moulin brewery, as well as freshly cooked food served throughout the day. Blair Atholl and the surrounding area are a popular destination for walking, climbing, biking and sightseeing. Off-season Bothy Bar opening hours may be shorter but ales can be brought through to the lounge bar. Q☕️🏠🌓🛏🏕♿🅿️🚉(87,M91)🐕🛜

Blairgowrie

Ericht Alehouse 🍺

13 Wellmeadow, PH10 6ND
☎ (01250) 872469
4 changing beers (sourced nationally) Ⓗ
Classic town-centre pub with a friendly atmosphere. There are two seated areas separated by a well-stocked bar offering a wide range of ever-changing ales and ciders, plus a number of Scottish gins, malts and rums. No food is served but customers are welcome to bring in their own as long as they tidy up after themselves. Local CAMRA Pub of the Year, an award it has won several times during the current landlord's tenure since 1999. Q♣🍴🐕🌓🚌🐕🛜

Fair O'Blair ✓

25-29 Allan Street, PH10 6AB
☎ (01250) 871890
Belhaven 80/-; Greene King Abbot; 4 changing beers (sourced regionally; often Stewart) Ⓗ
Town-centre Wetherspoon run by a real ale enthusiast. It has a small beer garden to the rear on two levels, the lower of which is accessible by wheelchairs. The pub is near the Wellmeadow, the grassy triangular plot that has been a venue for fairs, markets and outdoor entertainment since 1824. ☕️🏠🌓♿♣🚌(57)🛜

Broughty Ferry

Fisherman's Tavern

12-16 Fort Street, DD5 2AD
☎ (01382) 775941 ⊕ fishermanstavern-broughtyferry.co.uk
Greene King IPA; 5 changing beers (sourced nationally; often Belhaven) Ⓗ

REAL ALE BREWERIES

Abernyte Abernyte
Cullach ⚓ Perth
Inveralmond Perth
Law Dundee
Loch Leven ⚓ Kinross
MòR Kellas
Moulin 🍺 Pitlochry
Nat 20 Comrie
Redcastle Carmyllie (brewing suspended)
Shed 35 Carnoustie
Wasted Degrees ⚓ Blair Atholl

Licensed since 1857, this famous pub was originally three fishermen's cottages, later converted into a small hotel. The bar is to the right of the entrance, with a snug on the left, leading to the dining room/lounge, which has a real fire. The lounge to the rear has disabled access from Bell's Lane. This Belhaven/Greene King managed house serves ales from breweries all round the UK. An annual beer festival is held in July. ☻❀⏃◐&⇌❀�⃗♫

Jolly's Hotel ⊘

43A Gray Street, DD5 2BJ
☎ (01382) 734910
Belhaven 80/-; Greene King Abbot; Sharp's Doom Bar; 3 changing beers (sourced nationally) Ⓗ
Named after John Jolly, its proprietor for two decades in the late 19th century, this Wetherspoon hotel has expanded considerably over the years. It features two large areas, one for drinking and dining, the other principally for dining. The numerous handpulls serve a wide selection of ales to a mixed clientele. The TV screens are usually muted. An outdoor patio area has a number of tables. Alcoholic drinks are served from 11am. ☻❀⏃◐&⇌🖵(73) ⏃

Royal Arch Bar ⊘

285 Brook Street, DD5 2DS
☎ (01382) 779741 ⊕ royal-arch.co.uk
3 changing beers (sourced nationally) Ⓗ
A popular locally-owned pub in the centre of the Ferry. There are three TVs in the public bar for the many sports fans, and good-quality meals are served in the Art Deco lounge. Local ales, and some from all over the UK, are served through three handpulls. The gantry in the public bar was rescued previously from the demolished Craigour Bar in Dens Road. ❀◐⇌🖵(73)❀⏃

Ship Inn

121 Fisher Street, DD5 2BR
☎ (01382) 779176 ⊕ theshipinn-broughtyferry.co.uk
Timothy Taylor Landlord; 2 changing beers Ⓗ
The Ship Inn is a traditional free house on the waterfront at Broughty Ferry, with views over the Tay towards Fife. Dating back to 1847, this cosy retreat is atmospheric and interesting, with several nautical features. Usually three well-kept real ales are available. A range of tasty bar meals is on offer and there is a restaurant upstairs. There is pavement seating outside in fine weather. ⏃◐⇌❀⏃

Comrie

Royal Hotel

Melville Square, PH6 2DN
☎ (01764) 679200 ⊕ royalhotel.co.uk
1 changing beer (sourced regionally; often Fyne, Swannay) Ⓗ
The former Bothy Bar reopened in 2021 as the Melville, now described as a casual dining area, café and wine bar. The interior has been modernised, with a blue and bare wood theme, and has a range of furnishings. One real ale is available from the single handpump. It has been run by the same family since 2001. There is a suntrap beer garden to the rear. Q☻❀⏃◐&P🖵(15)❀⏃

Crieff

Tower

81 East High Street, PH7 3JA
☎ (01738) 650050 ⊕ thetowercrieff.com
2 changing beers (sourced regionally; often Hybrid) Ⓗ

Small family-run gastro-pub that welcomes children and dogs. The beams in the bar display some interesting and amusing proverbs and quotations. Outside, a comfortable seating terrace overlooks the secluded beer garden, with great views south to the Ochil Hills and plenty of shelter over tables for rainy days. Attached to the pub are three self-catering apartments. Q☻❀⏃◐P🖵(15)❀⏃

Dundee

Bank Bar

7-9 Union Street, DD1 4BN
☎ (01382) 205037 ⊕ thebankbardundee.com
Fyne Jarl; 3 changing beers (sourced nationally) Ⓗ
A former bank with bare-board floors, wooden furnishings and a series of alcoves with tables, in the tradition of older Scottish city pubs. Three or four ales are usually available and food is served during the day every day. Live music (of various popular kinds) features on most Friday and Saturday nights. It is close to the rail station and local buses. Local CAMRA Pub of the Year 2022. ☻❀◐&⇌🖵❀⏃♫

Counting House ⊘

67-71 Reform Street, DD1 1SP
☎ (01382) 225251
Belhaven 80/-; Greene King Abbot; Sharp's Doom Bar; 3 changing beers (sourced nationally; often Marston's, MòR, Stewart) Ⓗ
This Wetherspoon pub was once a branch of the Royal Bank of Scotland, having first opened as a bank in 1856. It is smaller than most pubs in the chain but still boasts a good selection of ales. It gets busy at weekends, but is a great city-centre location, close to Albert Square and McManus Galleries. Alcoholic drinks served from 11am. ☻❀◐&⇌●🖵(1,18) ⏃

Phoenix

103 Nethergate, DD1 4DH
☎ (01382) 200014
Caledonian Deuchars IPA; Timothy Taylor Landlord; 3 changing beers (sourced nationally; often Greene King, Morland, Orkney) Ⓗ
One of Dundee's oldest pubs, this traditional inn is warm and cosy and has a great atmosphere. Subdued lighting, sturdy wooden tables and chairs, green leather benches and a rare Ballingall brewery mirror give the place character. Five ales are on offer, along with excellent pub food at reasonable prices. The location is handy for the Rep Theatre, Dundee Contemporary Arts and Bonar Hall. ◐⇌🖵(16,73) ❀⏃

Speedwell Bar 🍺 ★ ⊘

165-167 Perth Road, DD2 1AS
☎ (01382) 667783 ⊕ speedwell-bar.co.uk
3 changing beers (sourced nationally) Ⓗ
Built in 1903 for James Speed, this pub is known as Mennie's after the family who ran it for more than 50 years. The L-shaped bar is divided by a part-glazed screen and has a magnificent mahogany gantry and counter, dado-panelled walls and an anaglypta Jacobean-style ceiling. There are usually three ales to choose from. Two seated areas are separate from the bar and there is some outside seating for sunny days. Local CAMRA Pub of the Year 2023. ◐🖵❀⏃♫

Dunkeld

Perth Arms Ⓛ

High Street, PH8 0AJ
☎ (01350) 727270

2 changing beers (often Orkney, Stewart, Wasted Degrees) H
Cosy one-room establishment serving a mix of locals and tourists. This friendly place has been in the same family for almost 50 years and is the area's oldest trading pub, dating back to 1795. Its two handpulls dispense ales that are mostly from Scottish breweries. The beer garden at the back has an area for smokers. ⌂❀⌕◉♪

Dunning

Kirkstyle Inn ✔
Kirkstyle Square, PH2 0RR
☎ (01764) 684248 ⊕ thekirkstyleinn.co.uk
House beer (by Marston's); 2 changing beers (sourced nationally) H
A traditional village inn dating from 1760, overshadowed by the impressive Norman steeple of St Serf's Church, which is home to the ancient Dupplin Cross and other Pictish relics. One or two ales in the cosy public bar come from a variety of Scottish independents, as well as English and Welsh regional breweries. The pub also serves its house ale, Risky Kelt. There is a separate restaurant. ⌂❀✦◉(17)❀♪

Kinross

Loch Leven Brewery Taproom L
Muirs, KY13 8AS
☎ (01577) 864881 ⊕ lochleven.beer
Loch Leven Warrior Queen, Shining Knight, Outlaw King, King Slayer H
Loch Leven's very own taproom and craft beer bottle shop is attached to the brewery and offers a choice of three beers on handpull from its full cask range, plus two keg beers from Cold Town. Loch Leven gins are also featured. Drinks may be consumed indoors or at tables outside. A growler dispenser enables cask beers to be purchased to take home. Bottled beers, brewery gifts and souvenirs may be purchased from the shop. Check in advance for up-to-date opening times. ❀(X56)❀♪

Kirriemuir

Airlie Arms
St Malcolm's Wynd, DD8 4HB
☎ (01575) 218080 ⊕ airliearms.net
2 changing beers (often Burnside, MòR) H
A large, B-listed, 18th-century establishment that has gone from strength to strength since 2015, when it was reopened by a local family following substantial renovatation. Real ale has made a welcome appearance and there are two handpulls on the bar serving a good selection of ales. Food is served at most times in the bar, and the restaurant is open at weekends. Accommodation is also available in 15 en-suite rooms of various sizes. ⌂❀✦◉♣P◉(21)❀

Memus

Drovers Inn
DD8 3TY
☎ (01307) 860322 ⊕ the-drovers.com
Timothy Taylor Landlord; 1 changing beer (often Harviestoun, MòR) H
Located in the rural setting of Memus, just north of Forfar, and handily placed for the Angus Glens, the Drovers is a traditional Scottish Inn with a contemporary look. An old range fire in the bar adds to the atmosphere, especially on a chilly day. Two ales are usually served and excellent food using locally sourced seasonal

produce is available daily. There is a large outdoor dining area under the trees with an adjoining play area for children. Q⌂❀◉P◉❀

Milnathort

Village Inn ♥
36 Wester Loan, KY13 9YH
☎ (01577) 863293
2 changing beers (sourced regionally) H
Friendly local with a semi open-plan interior featuring classic brewery mirrors and local historical photographs. The comfortable lounge area has low ceilings, exposed joists and stone walls, and the bar area is warmed by a log fire. The pub has been family-owned since 1985 and usually serves two beers, mostly locally sourced. Milnathort links some great cycling routes through the Ochils, via Burleigh Castle, to the more leisurely Loch Leven Heritage Trail. Local CAMRA Pub of the Year. ❀✦♣◉(X56)❀♪

Montrose

Market Arms ♥
95 High Street, DD10 8QY
☎ (01674) 673384
2 changing beers (sourced regionally; often Harviestoun, MòR, Orkney) H
Busy town-centre pub providing a comfortable retreat for its wide mix of customers, it was stylishly renovated a few years ago. Two handpulls are sited on a long bar near the entrance in the main open area. Several TVs show live sport, and there is a snug at the front for those wishing to enjoy a quiet pint. Beers are mostly sourced from Scottish breweries. Convenient for visitors to the nearby Montrose Air Station Heritage Centre, at what was the first operational airfield in the UK. Local CAMRA Pub of the Year 2023. ❀✦▲✦◉(X7)❀♪

Moulin

Moulin Inn L
11-13 Kirkmichael Road, PH16 5EH
☎ (01796) 472196 ⊕ moulininn.co.uk
Moulin Light, Braveheart, Ale of Atholl, Old Remedial H
First opened in 1695, the inn is in the oldest part of the Moulin Hotel, situated within the village square at an ancient crossroads just east of Pitlochry. Full of character and charm, it is traditionally furnished and has two log fires. A good choice of home-prepared local fare is available, with a seasonal specials board, along with four Moulin beers, brewed in the old coach house and stables behind the hotel. There is an area outside for dining and drinking in good weather. An ideal base for outdoor pursuits, with several marked walks nearby. Q⌂❀✦◉♣P◉(24,83)❀

Perth

Capital Asset ✔
26 Tay Street, PH1 5LQ
☎ (01738) 580457
Greene King Abbot; Sharp's Doom Bar; 4 changing beers (sourced nationally; often Stewart) H
A Wetherspoon pub in a former savings bank, now managed by a real ale enthusiast. The high ceilings and ornate cornices have been retained and pictures of old Perth adorn the walls of the open-plan lounge which overlooks the River Tay. The large safe from the building's banking days can be found in the family area. A variety of six ales are dispensed, with alcoholic drinks

served from 11am. Food is available all day. Beer festivals twice a year are popular with local ale drinkers. Q❀☺➊◗₤⬤🖵(7) 🛜

Cherrybank Inn
210 Glasgow Road, PH2 0NA
☎ (01738) 624349 ⊕ cherrybankinn.co.uk
Harviestoun Bitter & Twisted; 2 changing beers (sourced nationally; often Belhaven, Fyne, Stewart) Ⓗ
This 250-year-old former drovers' inn has been in the same family for many years and is a popular watering hole and stopover for travellers. Three ales are dispensed in the public bar or from the larger L-shaped lounge. Good bar lunches and evening meals are served. There is a large elevated and covered wooden decking to the rear. The inn has seven en-suite rooms.
❀☺➊⬤P🖵(7,8)❀🛜♪

Old Ship Inn 🍷 ✅
31 High Street, PH1 5TJ (on Skinnergate)
☎ 07956 924767 ⊕ oldshipinnperth.co.uk
3 changing beers (sourced regionally; often Fyne, Harviestoun, Belhaven) Ⓗ
Said to be the oldest pub in Perth, having traded under the same name since 1665. This was the city's oasis for real ale in the 1980s, and now serves one regular beer and two changing ales. A large oil painting of a sailing ship adds interest in the timber-lined bar, which is lightened by a frieze and white-painted ceiling. The upstairs lounge reopened in 2018 after a 20-year closure. Local CAMRA Pub of the Year. ❀♿P🖵(7)❀🛜

Silvery Tay
189 South Street, PH2 8NY
☎ (01738) 321119
1 changing beer (often Stewart) Ⓗ
Conveniently located at the historic South Street Port, this is the first pub you encounter when walking from the train station to the city centre. Real ale was reintroduced in 2019. It is a high-ceilinged, single-room establishment with dark wood panelling and a fine staircase up to the closed first floor. There are a number of alcoved seating areas, giving privacy if desired. ♿🚌🖵❀🛜♪

Twa Tams
79-81 Scott Street, PH2 8JR
☎ (01738) 580948 ⊕ thetwatamsperth.com
2 changing beers (often Loch Lomond, Cromarty) Ⓗ
Perth's premier music pub began its rise in 2019 when it was taken over by the Mad Ferret Band folk duo, whose enthusiasm for real ale is only matched by their passion for music. The atmospheric bar has a beamed low ceiling. Its three handpulls serve at least one real ale and a cider. There is a large outdoor drinking area.
❀☺➊♿🚌⬤🖵(X56)❀♪

Pitlochry

Old Mill Inn
Mill Lane, PH16 5BH
☎ (01796) 474020 ⊕ theoldmillpitlochry.co.uk
4 changing beers (sourced regionally; often Cromarty, Orkney, Wasted Degrees) Ⓗ
A well-run, family-owned establishment in the town centre. Built in the 19th century as a mill, with a mill wheel still driven by the stream – customers can sit beside it when the weather allows. The large bar serves a varied selection of guest ales, and usually has three or four to choose from. ❀☺➊♿🚌⬤P🖵❀🛜♪

Scotlandwell

Well Country Inn
Main Street, KY13 9JA (on A911)
☎ (01592) 840444 ⊕ thewellcountryinn.co.uk
2 changing beers (sourced regionally; often Alechemy, Stewart) Ⓗ
A pleasant country inn that sits below the imposing Bishop Hill on the A911 between Kinross and Glenrothes. Both the village and the pub take their name from the impressive canopied well. The bar is warmed by an open fire in winter. Its real ale often comes from Stewart Brewing. It is close to the Loch Leven Heritage Trail, popular with cyclists and walkers. Accommodation is available in chalets. ☺❀➊♿P❀🛜♪

Wester Balgedie

Balgedie Toll Tavern Ⓛ
KY13 9HE (at jct of A911 and B919)
☎ (01592) 840212 ⊕ balgedietolltavern.com
Harviestoun Bitter & Twisted; Loch Leven Warrior Queen; 1 changing beer (sourced locally; often Inveralmond) Ⓗ
Welcoming country tavern dating from 1534, located where travellers had to break their journey to pay tolls. The oldest part of the building is now the Harness Bar, which features low ceilings, oak beams, horse brasses and wooden settles. There are seating areas on two levels. Cask-conditioned beers from local breweries are served from two handpulls in the lower bar area. A fine selection of meals and bar snacks is available throughout. ☺❀➊♿P🖵(201)❀🛜♪

Breweries

71 Brewing SIBA
36-40 Bellfield Street, Dundee, DD1 5HZ
☎ (01382) 203133 ⊕ 71brewing.com
Brewing began in 2016, producing craft keg and bottled beers. Current production is focused on canning. Collaboration projects are popular with local start-up craft brewers. It is hoped cask-conditioned beers will make a return in 2024. ‼🍺♦

Abernyte
South Latch Farm, Abernyte, PH14 9SU ☎ 07827 715915 ⊕ abernytebrewery.com
Established in 2016, the brewery overlooks the Carse of Gowrie. Brewing features a step mashing process in small batch, producing a range of unfiltered and naturally carbonated craft beers, packaged mainly in bottles. LIVE V

Cullach
50 Princes Street, Perth, PH2 8LJ
⊕ cullachbrewing.co.uk
⊗ The brewery opened in 2019 in an industrial unit on the outskirts of Perth. It moved into a retail unit closer to the town centre allowing a welcoming taproom. Some draught beers are real ale in KeyKeg and some cans are also produced. 🍺LIVE♦

Holy Goat SIBA
Unit 5, Mid Wynd, Dundee, DD1 4JG ⊕ holygoat.beer
Holy Goat is a Dundee-based brewery specialising in the production of mixed fermentation and wood-aged beers. All beers are bottled with some available in can.

Inveralmond SIBA

22 Inveralmond Place, Inveralmond Industrial Estate, Perth, PH1 3TS
☎ (01738) 449448 ⊕ inveralmond-brewery.co.uk

☺Established in 1997, Inveralmond was the first brewery in Perth for more than 30 years. In 2016, it became part of the Innis & Gunn (I&G) family, an independent Scottish brewer based in Edinburgh. I&G makes no real ale but the Inveralmond range continues. ‼☒♦

Ossian (ABV 4.1%) GOLD
Well-balanced best bitter with a dry finish. This full-bodied amber ale is dominated by fruit and hop with a bittersweet character although excessive caramel can distract from this.
Lia Fail (ABV 4.7%) BITTER
The Gaelic name means Stone of Destiny. A dark, robust, full-bodied beer with a deep malty taste. Smooth texture and balanced finish.

Law

Unit 17, Mid Wynd, Dundee, DD1 4JG ☎ 07893 538277 ⊕ lawbrewing.co

Law was established in 2016 and is named after Dundee's most distinctive landmark; the volcano-like slopes of the Law.

Loch Leven SIBA

The Muirs, Kinross, KY13 8AS
☎ (01577) 864881 ⊕ lochleven.beer

Based opposite the Green Hotel, Kinross, the brewery started production in 2017. Four cask-conditioned beers are produced and available throughout Tayside, with availability spreading westwards through Scotland's central belt. ‼☒♦

Warrior Queen (ABV 3.8%) PALE
Shining Knight (ABV 4%) SPECIALITY
Outlaw King (ABV 5%) MILD
King Slayer (ABV 5.2%) OLD

Manual

c/o 36-40 Bellfield Street, Dundee, DD1 5HZ
⊕ manualbrewing.co.uk

Launched in 2018, Manual Brewing Co uses spare capacity at 71 Brewing in Dundee.

MòR

Old Mill, Kellas, DD5 3PD ☎ 07402 900755
⊕ morbeers.co.uk

Established in 2012 and now trading as MòR Beers. Dominic Hughes, an experienced brewer, moved to Scotland from London to take ownership of the brewery in 2018. ‼♦LIVE

MòR Tea Vicar? (ABV 3.8%) BITTER
MòR Ish! (ABV 4.2%) BITTER
MòR Please! (ABV 4.5%) GOLD

Moulin

🏠 **2 Baledmund Road, Moulin, Pitlochry, PH16 5EL**
☎ (01796) 472196

Office: Moulin Hotel, 11-13 Kirkmicheal Road, Moulin, Pitlochry, PH16 5EH ⊕ moulinhotel.co.uk

☺The brewery opened in 1995 to celebrate the Moulin Hotel's 300th anniversary. Two pubs are owned and four outlets are supplied. ‼LIVE

Munro

Devonian Lodge, Logie, Kirriemuir, DD8 5PG
☎ (01575) 572232 ⊕ munrobrewingco.com

A family-owned business founded in 2020 in Kirriemuir, the final resting place of the Scottish mounaineer, Sir Hugh Munro. Beer is available in cans.

Nat 20

Hut 53, Cultybraggan Camp, Comrie, PH6 2AB
☎ 07754 093561

A microbrewery producing traditional ales plus mead, brewed using old family and historic recipes.

Redcastle SIBA

Drummygar Mains, Carmyllie, Arbroath, DD11 2RA
☎ (01241) 860516 ☎ 07967 226357
⊕ redcastlebrewery.co.uk

☒ Established by local farmer John Anderson, brewing began in 2016 on the family farm. The brewery takes its name from the nearby ruined castle at Lunan Bay. The beers are named accordingly with a historic theme. In addition to the 10-barrel plant, the brewery also includes a bottling line. Brewing is currently suspended.

Shed 35

Chapman Drive, Carnoustie, DD7 6DX ☎ 07530 430579 ⊕ shed35brewery.co.uk

Set up by friends Gary Mellon and John Wilson, brewing began in 2016. Although mainly producing bottle-conditioned beers for sale locally at farmers' markets and other outlets in Angus and the surrounding area, the brewery occasionally produces cask beer.

Wasted Degrees SIBA

Unit 11, Sawmill Yard, Blair Atholl, PH18 5TL
⊕ wasteddegrees.com

Owned and established by two graduate brothers, brewing began commercially in 2016 before a move to the current site, in Blair Atholl, in 2018. Production capacity doubled in 2022 and output grew to 35,200 litres, including its first export of cans to Europe. Cask ales are found in local pubs. Taproom open April-October. ‼☒V♦

Atholl Light (ABV 3.2%) PALE
Atholl Gold (ABV 3.5%) GOLD
Drookit Session (ABV 3.9%) PALE

SCOTLAND

World Beer Guide

Roger Protz

The world of beer is on fire!

Traditional brewing countries are witnessing a spectacular growth in the number of beer makers while drinkers in such unlikely nations as France and Italy are moving from the grape to the grain. Innovation in brewing is remarkable. Beer is not simply about ale and lager. Young artisan brewers are pushing the boundaries and are making beers with the addition of herbs, spices, fruit, chocolate, and coffee. Many are ageing beer in oak for additional flavour and character while others, inspired by the Belgian model, are fermenting beers with wild yeasts in the atmosphere. But readers new to beer need not be nervous. The main aim of this guide is to turn the spotlight on the great and often amazing beers being produced by dedicated brewers in every continent. Beer is the world's favourite alcohol. It needs to be revered, respected and, above all, enjoyed.

RRP: £30.00   **ISBN**: 978-1-85249-373-8

For this and other books on beer and pubs, visit CAMRA's online bookshop at **shop1.camra.org.uk** or call 01727 867201.

Discounts are available for CAMRA members.

NORTHERN ISLES

SHETLAND

HIGHLANDS & WESTERN ISLES

ABERDEEN & GRAMPIAN

TAYSIDE

ARGYLL & THE ISLES

LOCH LOMOND, STIRLING & TROSSACHS

FIFE

GREATER GLASGOW & CLYDE

EDINBURGH & LOTHIANS

AYRSHIRE & ARRAN

BORDERS

DUMFRIES & GALLOWAY

NORTHUMBERLAND

TYNE & WEAR

NORTHERN IRELAND

CUMBRIA

DURHAM

ISLE OF MAN

NORTH YORKSHIRE

LANCASHIRE

WEST YORKS

EAST YORKS

MERSEYSIDE

GREATER MANCHESTER

SOUTH YORKS

CHESHIRE

DERBYSHIRE

NOTTINGHAMSHIRE

LINCOLNSHIRE

NW WALES

NE WALES

STAFFORD SHIRE

LEICESTERSHIRE

NORFOLK

SHROPSHIRE

WEST MIDLANDS

WORCESTERSHIRE

NORTHAMPTON SHIRE

CAMBRIDGESHIRE

SUFFOLK

MID WALES

HEREFORDSHIRE

WARWICKSHIRE

BEDFORDSHIRE

BUCKINGHAMSHIRE

HERTFORDSHIRE

WEST WALES

GWENT

GLOUCS & BRISTOL

OXFORD SHIRE

GREATER LONDON

ESSEX

GLAMORGAN

BERKSHIRE

SURREY

KENT

WILTSHIRE

HAMPSHIRE

WEST SUSSEX

EAST SUSSEX

CHANNEL ISLANDS

SOMERSET

DEVON

DORSET

ISLE OF WIGHT

CORNWALL

Northern Ireland
Channel Islands
Isle of Man

Northern Ireland

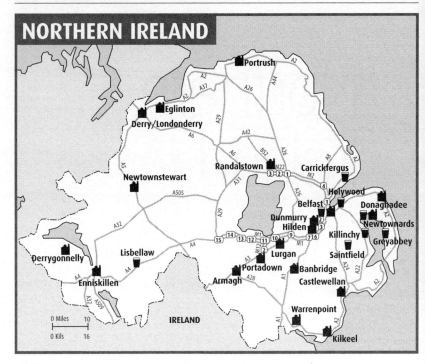

NORTHERN IRELAND

Belfast

Boundary Taproom
310 Newtownards Road, BT4 1HE
🌐 boundarybrewing.coop
Changing beers Ⓚ
The taproom for Boundary brewery is a roomy, contemporary bar housed in part of the Portview Trade Centre. There are 20 craft taps and one cask ale – mainly Boundary's own beers. Fridges stock a range of canned beer and a number of beers from Belgium that can be taken away. Pizza can be brought in from across the road. Q&≉(Titanic Quarter)🏮

Bridge House ✔
37-43 Bedford Street, BT2 7EJ
☎ (028) 9072 7890
Greene King Abbot; Ruddles Best Bitter; Sharp's Doom Bar; changing beers (sourced nationally) Ⓗ
A large and busy Wetherspoon bar close to the city centre. It has a main bar with eight handpumps serving a range of national ales along with a couple of local brews from Whitewater brewery. Upstairs is a restaurant-style floor more suitable for families, and there is a beer garden at the back. It is open for food from 8am, with alcohol available from 11.30am (12.30 on Sun). A former local CAMRA Pub of the Year.
Q♿⛲◑◐♿≉(Great Victoria Street) 🏮🛜

Bullhouse East
442-446 Newtownards Road, BT4 1HJ
☎ (028) 9013 8554 🌐 bullhousebrewco.com
1 changing beer (sourced locally) Ⓗ
A new craft bar, opened in 2022 on the former site of a men's clothing outlet. The 20 taps serve a range of Bullhouse East's beers along with a number from other breweries – phone beforehand to check what is on. It is a bright and cheerful place to drink in, and can get busy. Wood-fired pizza is available in the beer garden.
Q♿&🍔🏮🌮🛜

Crown Liquor Saloon ★ ✔
46 Great Victoria Street, BT2 7BA (opp Europa Hotel and Great Victoria Street station)
☎ (028) 9024 3187
St Austell Nicholson's Pale Ale; 5 changing beers (sourced regionally) Ⓗ
This popular pub is a must-see destination on any visit to the city. Owned by the National Trust and run by Nicholson's, the pub is famous for its magnificent Grade A-listed historic architecture. Its impressive façade is one of the city's most popular photo spots. It serves a mixture of frequently changing local and national ales, including Nicholson's Pale Ale. Additionally, handpulled cider is

REAL ALE BREWERIES
Ards Newtownards
Armagh Armagh
Baronscourt Newtownstewart
Beer Hut Kilkeel
Boundary ◆ Belfast
Bullhouse Belfast
Fermanagh Derrygonnelly
Hercules Belfast
Hilden Hilden
Knockout Belfast
Lacada Portrush
Mashdown Banbridge
McCracken's Portadown
Modest Beer Randalstown
Mourne Mountains Warrenpoint
Norn Iron Dunmurry
Northbound Eglinton
Our Randalstown
Rough Brothers Derry / Londonderry
Sheelin Enniskillen
Spadetown Lurgan (NEW)
Twisted Kettle Donaghadee
Whitewater Castlewellan

permanently available, mainly from Westons. Good food is available in the bar and upstairs. A former local CAMRA Pub of the Year winner. Q ◐◑ ♿ 🚆(Great Victoria St) 🚌

Errigle Inn

312-320 Ormeau Road, BT7 2GE
☎ (028) 9064 1410 🌐 errigle.com
4 changing beers (sourced locally; often Whitewater) [H]
The Errigle's Oak Lounge is a quiet back bar with up to four handpumps mainly serving a range of ales from local breweries, plus occasional national brands. A handpulled cider features regularly, and there are taps dispensing a selection of craft beers. The lounge's opening hours are limited, so check in advance. If you ask at the main bar, staff will bring handpulled drinks in from the lounge. Q ◐◑ ♿ 🚌 📶 ♫

John Hewitt

51 Donegal Street, BT1 2FH (100yds from St Anne's Cathedral)
☎ (028) 9023 3768 🌐 thejohnhewitt.com
Changing beers (sourced locally) [K]
Named after the renowned poet, this busy single-room bar features a large snug and a stage. The pub has become a popular venue for live music and quizzes. It is different from most bars in that it is run by the Belfast Unemployed Resource Centre, and profits go to fund their charitable work. The bar is now run by Boundary brewery and features their own beers, plus those from several other craft breweries. Closed on Mondays.
Q 🔥 ♿ 🚌 ♫

McHughs

29-31 Queens Square, BT1 3FG (near Albert Clock)
☎ (028) 9050 9999 🌐 mchughsbar.com
Whitewater Maggie's Leap IPA [H]
Close to Belfast's Albert Clock landmark, McHughs is a long-established traditional pub. Housed in the city's oldest building, it features a restored old bar which adjoins a more modern public bar with a basement. There is one handpump exclusively dispensing ales from Whitewater Brewery. Good food can be consumed in the bar or in the upstairs restaurant. Sport is a big draw, and folk and traditional music acts perform in the bar and in the basement. Q ◐◑ ♿ 🚆(Central) 🖵 🚌 📶 ♫

Northern Lights

451 Ormeau Road, BT7 3GQ
☎ (028) 9029 0291 🌐 galwaybaybrewery.com
1 changing beer (sourced regionally) [H]
Modern craft beer bar owned by Galway brewery. There are usually 10 beers from the owners, with 10 others from a variety of craft producers. An impressive selection of beer and cider in bottles and cans are also stocked. The single handpump dispenses various cask ales from Irish breweries; phone first to check what is on. Good food is also available. A former local CAMRA Pub of the Year. Q 🔥 ◐◑ ♿ ♣ 🚌 🐾 📶

Sunflower 🏆

65 Union Street, BT1 2JG
☎ (028) 9023 2474 🌐 sunflowerbelfast.com
1 changing beer (sourced locally) [H]
The Sunflower recently celebrated its tenth anniversary as a real ale pub. The downstairs bar features one handpump with ales from local breweries, along with a selection of craft beers. It is one of the few pubs that does not sell Ireland's most famous beverage. Music is a big draw, with acts in the main bar and the lounge upstairs. It has a large beer garden, where pizza is served at the weekend. Local CAMRA Pub of the Year 2023.
✿ ◑ 🚌 🐾 📶 ♫

Woodworkers

20-22 Bradbury Place, BT7 1RS
☎ (028) 9087 1106 🌐 woodworkersbelfast.com
Changing beers (sourced locally) [K]
Based in the south of the city, this craft beer bar is run by the larger Laverys Bar next door. It has three distinct areas known as the Workshop, the Café Bar and the Kickback. Up to 14 regularly changing craft beers feature a mixture of local and national breweries. The beers are in the Workshop area which retains much of the look of its former usage as a woodworking supplies shop.
Q 🔥 ◐◑ ♿ 🚆(Botanic) 🚌 📶

Carrickfergus

Central Bar ✔

13-15 High Street, BT38 7AN (opp Castle)
☎ (028) 9335 7840
Greene King Abbot; Ruddles Best Bitter; Sharp's Doom Bar; 2 changing beers (sourced regionally) [H]
Lively community local with a dedicated clientele. This Wetherspoon pub has a non-nonsense ground-floor public bar and, upstairs, a quieter, family-friendly, loggia-style sitting room with exposed timber trusses, affording inspirational views from its many windows over Belfast Lough and the adjacent 12th-century castle. Handpumps on both levels serve three house beers and guest ales, with local ale from Whitewater Brewery. Alcohol is served from 11.30am (12.30pm on Sun).
Q 🔥 ✿ ◐◑ ♿ 🚆 🚌(563)

Greyabbey

Wildfowler Inn

1 Main Street, BT22 2NE (7 miles S of Newtownards on A20)
☎ (028) 4278 8234 🌐 wildfowlerinn.co.uk
1 changing beer (sourced locally; often Ards) [K]
The Wildfowler is restaurant in a small village on the Ards peninsula. It has pleasant surroundings, both inside and out. Good food is available and the tap on the restaurant's bar dispenses a variety of KeyKeg ale brewed in the nearby Ards brewery. Phone beforehand to check what is on. Drink can be taken in the restaurant without purchasing a meal. There is also a beer garden, and the public bar occasionally opens to host real ale events. Q 🔥 ✿ ◐◑ ♿ P 🚌

Holywood

Dirty Duck Ale House

3 Kinnegar Road, BT18 9JN
☎ (028) 9059 6666 🌐 thedirtyduckalehouse.co.uk
3 changing beers (sourced nationally) [H]
Set by Belfast Lough, not far from Holywood train station, the Dirty Duck has three handpumps. National brands are the mainstay, with occasional local brews. Upstairs is a restaurant with great views and outside there is a ship-shaped beer garden with a retractable roof and its own bar. A collection of pumpclips, plastic ducks and the Rory McIlroy corner are worth seeing. Twice former local CAMRA Pub of the Year. Q 🔥 ✿ ◐◑ ♿ 🚆(Holywood) 📶

Killinchy

Daft Eddy's [L]

Sketrick Island, BT23 6QH (2 miles N of Killinchey at Whiterock Bay)
☎ (028) 9754 1615 🌐 dafteddys.co.uk
1 changing beer (sourced locally; often Whitewater) [H]

A bar, restaurant, and coffee shop situated beside Strangford Lough. Slightly hard to find, it is one of the province's hidden gems. The bar has a handpump with a variety of beers from Whitewater brewery. The restaurant is highly recommended, with food mainly sourced from local producers. Food is also served in Little Eddy's coffee shop. The area is worth visiting to see the remnants of the 12th-century castle and for the great views from Sketrick Island. Q ኈ ⊛ ◑ ₺ P ♣ ☂

Lisbellaw

Dog & Duck Inn

30 Main Street, BT94 5ER
☎ (028) 6638 5371 ⊕ thedogandduckinn.com
1 changing beer (sourced locally) Ⓗ
Located in the village of Lisbellaw, about five miles from Enniskillen, this pub specialises in independent beers, ciders and spirits, with 14 guest taps; which include four traditional cask beer pumps serving real ale and ciders. Locally brewed ales from Inishmacsaint, Hercules and Lacada have featured. Food using locally sourced and seasonal produce is also available. The pub also has its own Brewstillery – Glenwinny – which which will produce whiskey, rum, and beer. Q ኈ ⊛ ➡ ◑ ₺ ♣ ♫

Newtownards

Spirit Merchant ⊘

54-56 Regent Street, BT23 4LP (opp bus station)
☎ (028) 9182 4270
Greene King Abbot; 4 changing beers (sourced nationally) Ⓗ
A roomy one-bar Wetherspoon pub on the main road from Belfast to Newtownards. The name recalls a previous pub that was on the same site. There are five handpumps with a variety of well-kept real ales. There is a variety of areas in which to sit inside, while outside there is a large enclosed beer garden. It is open from 8am but alcohol is only available from 11.30am (12.30pm on Sun). Q ኈ ⊛ ◑ ₺ Å 🚌 (7) ☂

Saintfield

White Horse

49-53 Main Street, BT24 7AB
☎ (028) 9751 1143 ⊕ whitehorsesaintfield.com
Whitewater Copperhead, Maggie's Leap IPA Ⓗ
Modern pub that is a pleasing combination of real ale bar, bistro and pizza joint. The bar is split betwen an eating area and a library-style drinking area with a log stove. There are usually two real ales on from Whitewater brewery, located about 20 miles away. Food is available in the bistro and in the Flaming Crust pizzeria, which is open Thursday, Friday, and Saturday from 5pm (4pm Sat). A former local CAMRA Pub of the Year. Q ኈ ⊛ ◑ ₺ 🚌 (15,215) ♫

Breweries

Ards

34B Carrowdore Road, Greyabbey, Newtownards, BT22 2LX ☎ 07515 558406
✉ ardsbrewing@blackwood34.plus.com

Ards began brewing in 2011 using a 100-litre plant. A five-barrel plant is now in operation, allowing cask production in addition to the increasing range of bottle-conditioned and KeyKeg beers. Very much a local brewery with beers generally only supplied within a 15-mile radius. ♦ LIVE

Citra (ABV 4.8%) GOLD
Scrabo Gold (ABV 4.8%) GOLD
Hip Hop (ABV 5%) BITTER
Pig Island (ABV 5.2%) BITTER

Armagh

28 Drumgraw Road, Armagh, BT60 2AD ☎ 07828 473199

A microbrewery based on the outskirts of Armagh, established in 2016.

Baronscourt

38 Baronscourt Road, Newtownstewart, Omagh, BT78 4EY ☎ 07788 839907
⊕ baronscourtbrewery.com

A family-run, farm-based brewery founded in 2018 nestled at the foot of the picturesque Bessie Bell mountain, close to Harry Avery's Castle, producing high end hand-crafted artisan beer. Brewery waste is directly fed back to livestock or sent to the local anaerobic digester thereby neutralising the carbon footprint.

Beer Hut

14 Binnian Enterprise Park, Kilkeel, BT34 3NA
☎ 07885 566599 ⊕ beerhutbrewing.shop

Microbrewery situated near Kilkeel harbour. Established in a flat pack hut using a 100-litre kit, it has since upscaled twice and now operates using a 1,000-litre plant. Further expansion is planned.

Citra Ella (ABV 4.5%) GOLD
Fluffy Bunny (ABV 5%) SPECIALITY
Wahey IPA (ABV 5.6%) IPA
There's Something in the Water (ABV 6%) IPA
Simcoe Simon (ABV 6.5%) IPA
Ahoy Captain (ABV 7.4%) IPA

Bell's

▣ Deer's Head, 1-3 Lower Garfield Street, Belfast, BT1 1FP
☎ (028) 9043 4655

Brewery within the Deer's Head pub, Belfast.

Boundary SIBA

Unit A5, 310 Portview Trade Centre, Newtownards Road, Belfast, BT4 1HE ⊕ boundarybrewing.coop

Boundary is a cooperative brewery based in Belfast, established in 2014. ♦ ✦

APA (ABV 3.5%) PALE
Export Stout (ABV 7%) STOUT
IPA (ABV 7%) IPA

Bullhouse SIBA

22 Balmoral Road, Belfast, BT12 6QA ☎ 07749 877841 ⊕ bullhousebrewco.com

Bullhouse was set up in 2016 by beer enthusiast and homebrewer William Mayne at his family farm. The brewery has since relocated to Belfast and a new permanent tap has opened at 442-446 Newtownards Road, Belfast.

Road Trip (ABV 4%) GOLD
Small Axe (ABV 4.3%)
Frank the Tank (ABV 5%) SPECIALITY
The Dankness (ABV 5.5%)
Merc Bro (ABV 6.5%) SPECIALITY

Dopey Dick

Office: 4 Custom House Street, Derry, BT48 6AA
☎ **(028) 7141 8920** ✉ **dopeydickderry@gmail.com**

A microbrewery founded in Derry by the proprietors of the Grand Central Bar. Beers can also be found at its sister pub, the Guildhall Taproom. Beers are contract brewed.

Fermanagh

75 Main Street, Derrygonnelly, BT93 6HW
☎ **(028) 6864 1254**

Under the Inishmacsaint brand, Fermanagh Beer Company is a small-scale brewery producing a range of bottle-conditioned beers since 2009. **LIVE**

Heaney Farmhouse

The Wood, 96a Ballymacombs Road, Bellaghy, BT45 8JP ⏚ **heaney.ie**

Founded in 2014. Initially beers were brewed at Boundary Brewing (qv) in Belfast while Mal and Suzy McCay's brewhouse project was being constructed on a farm in Bellaghy, Co Londonderry. In 2019 production began on their 100% renewable powered brewery, which utilises its own water supply. Favourites, seasonal and special beers are available in bottle and can. No real ale. ◆

Hercules

Unit 5b, Harbour Court, Heron Road, Sydenham, Holywood, Belfast, BT3 9HB
☎ **(028) 9036 4516** ✉ **niall@herculesbrewery.com**

The original Hercules Brewing Company, founded in the 19th century, was one of 13 breweries in Belfast at the time. The company has been re-established to produce small batch brews using old brewing traditions. Its output is all under the Yardsman brand name.

Brewed under the Yardsman brand name:
IPA (ABV 4.3%)
Lager (ABV 4.8%)
Belfast Pale Ale (ABV 5.6%) GOLD

Hilden

Hilden House, Grand Street, Hilden, Lisburn, BT27 4TY
☎ **(028) 9266 0800** ⏚ **hildenbrewery.co.uk**

☺Established 1981, Hilden is Ireland's oldest independent brewery. Now in the second generation of family ownership, the beers are widely distributed across the UK. The beers are regularly available in JD Wetherspoon outlets in Northern Ireland. ‼☰◆

Nut Brown (ABV 3.8%) BITTER
Ale (ABV 4%) BITTER
An amber-coloured beer with an aroma of malt, hops and fruit. The balanced taste is slightly slanted towards hops, and hops are also prominent in the full, malty finish.

Barney's Brew (ABV 4.2%) SPECIALITY
Irish Stout (ABV 4.3%) STOUT
Scullion's Irish Ale (ABV 4.6%) BITTER
Twisted Hop (ABV 4.7%) BITTER
Halt (ABV 6.1%) RED

Brewed for College Green Brewery:
Headless Dog (ABV 4.3%) GOLD

Knockout

Unit 10, Alanbrooke Park, Alexander Road, Belfast, BT6 9HB

Founded in 2009 by Joseph McMullan, Knockout produces a range of bottle-conditioned beers. Each brew is usually in small 900-litre batches. **LIVE**

Lacada SIBA

7a Victoria Street, Portrush, BT56 8DL
☎ **(028) 7082 5684** ⏚ **lacadabrewery.com**

Lacada is a co-operative brewery founded in 2015. It produces a wide variety of styles. It is situated on the scenic north coast of Northern Ireland, and each beer is named after a feature of the coast line (along with a picture of the feature on the cans and bottles).

McCracken's

Derryall Road, Portadown, BT62 1PL
⏚ **mccrackensrealale.com**

Currently Co Armagh's only real ale brewery, established in 2018. Producing a range of bottle-conditioned beers. **LIVE**

Mashdown

Castlewellan Road, Banbridge, BT32 4JF

Mashdown began brewing on its own nanobrewery in 2018 with brewing formerly taking place in collaboration with other breweries. Although cask is available on occasion the majority of production is bottled. A range of bottle-conditioned beers, Half Bap Pour, is produced for Commercial Court Inns. **LIVE**

Modest Beer

86 Clonkeen Road, Randalstown, BT41 3JJ
⏚ **modestbeer.co.uk**

Small, independent brewery, originally brewing in a private garage but has now moved to a much larger brewery in Randalstown.

Mourne Mountains SIBA

Milltown East Industrial Estate, Upper Dromore Road, Warrenpoint, BT34 3PN
☎ **(028) 4175 2299**
⏚ **mournemountainsbrewery.com**

Brewing since 2015 with an extensive and varying range of seasonal, special and one-off brews produced throughout the year – some may appear in cask format. Isinglass finings are used in all cask products, except stouts, and so they are not suitable for vegans. Keg, can and bottled beers (not bottle-conditioned) are suitable for vegans. ◆**LIVE V**

Mourne Gold (ABV 4%) GOLD

Norn Iron

Unit 30, The Cutts, Dunmurry, Belfast, BT17 9HN
⏚ **nornironbrewco.com**

Proudly brewing beer on the outskirts of Belfast since 2018 using quality local ingredients.

Northbound

Campsie Industrial Estate, McLean Road, Eglinton, BT47 3XX ☎ **07512 198686**
⏚ **northboundbrewery.com**

Established in 2015, Northbound produce a range of bottle-conditioned beers primarily named after their measurement of bitterness (IBUs). ◆LIVE

O'Connor

12 Lime Road, Faughanvale, Greysteel, BT47 3EH
☎ **07748 004065**

Brewing began in 2013. No real ale.

Ormeau (NEW)

Knock Eden Park, Belfast, BT6 0JF

Launched in 2022 this nanobrewery, based in South Belfast, delivers quality internationally inspired beer at a local level in a sustainable way. Available in can and keg.

Our

86 Clonkeen Road, Randalstown, BT41 3JJ
☎ **(0800) 228 9433**

Energy efficient brewery launched in 2022, which is a passion project from the team at Get Er Brewed, overlooking Lough Neagh.

Out of Office

🛏 **Ulster Sports Club, 96-98 High Street, Belfast, BT1 2BG**
☎ **(028) 9023 0771** ⊕ **outofofficebrewing.co.uk**

Located on the second floor of the Ulster Sports Club, the brewery opened in 2021, producing modern craft beers. The onsite taproom is open Thursday through Sunday. No real ale. ‼◆

Rough Brothers SIBA

Unit 2D, Altnagelvin Industrial Estate, Derry / Londonderry, BT47 2ED

A family-run microbrewery producing handmade beer in Derry/Londonderry. LIVE

Sheelin

178 Derrylin Road, Bellanaleck, Enniskillen, BT92 2BA
☎ **07730 432232** ⊕ **sheelinbrewery.com**

Sheelin was established by brewer and chemist Dr George Cathcart in 2013. Beer is mainly available in bottles.

Spadetown (NEW)

25 Silverwood Industrial Estate, Lurgan, BT66 6LN

Established in Lurgan in 2021, a group of brewers are producing a range of craft beers available in bottle and can and also on draft.

Tilt & Pour (NEW)

Belfast ⊕ tiltnpour.com

After ten years informing and promoting the Northern Ireland beer scene, Tilt & Pour have collaborated with Heaney Farmhouse Brewery to produce its own canned beer.

Twisted Kettle

25 Ballyblack Road East, Donaghadee, BT21 0NA

An independent nanobrewery producing small-batch beers.

Walled City

🛏 **Ebrington Square & Parade Ground, 70 Ebrington Square, Derry, BT47 6FA**
☎ **(028) 7134 3336** ⊕ **walledcitybrewery.com**

Restaurant-based brewery established in Derry in 2015. Beers are brewed onsite, and a member of staff is usually happy to show you around. It now has a taproom too (see social media for opening times). ✦

Whitewater

Lakeside Brae, Clarkhill Road, Castlewellan, BT31 9RH
☎ **(028) 4377 8900** ⊕ **whitewaterbrewery.com**

Established in 1996, Whitewater is now the biggest brewery in Northern Ireland. ‼◆

Copperhead (ABV 3.7%) BITTER
Belfast Black (ABV 4.2%) STOUT
Belfast Ale (ABV 4.5%) BITTER
Maggie's Leap IPA (ABV 4.7%) PALE
Clotworthy Dobbin (ABV 5%) PORTER

Definitions

bivvy – beer
bumclink – inferior beer
bunker – beer
cooper – half stout, half porter
gatters – beer
shant of gatter – glass of beer
half and half – mixture of ale and porter, much favoured by medical students
humming – strong (as applied to drink)
ponge or pongelow – beer, half and half
purl – mixture of hot ale and sugar, with wormwood infused
rot-gut – bad
small beer shandy – gaffs ale and gingerbeer
shant – pot or quart (shant of bivvy – quart of beer)
swipes – soup or small beer
wobble-shop – shop where beer sold without a licence
J C Hotten, The Slang Dictionary, 1887

Channel Islands

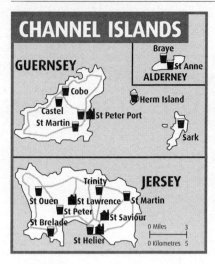

CHANNEL ISLANDS

GUERNSEY

Braye
St Anne
ALDERNEY

Cobo
Herm Island
Castel
St Peter Port
St Martin
Sark

Trinity
JERSEY
St Ouen
St Lawrence
St Martin
St Peter
St Saviour
St Brelade
St Helier

0 Miles 3
0 Kilometres 5

ALDERNEY
Braye

Divers Inn
Braye Street, GY9 3XT
☎ (01481) 822632 ⊕ brayebeach.com
2 changing beers (sourced nationally; often Fuller's, Sharp's) Ⓗ
Traditional pub with a great atmosphere, attached to the Braye Beach Hotel. It serves two real ales and has a good bar menu. The interior features wooden tables, chairs and counter, and is warmed by real fires. Walking through the bar area reveals sea views and a superb outdoor seating space overlooking the beach. Themed and musical events attract locals and visitors alike, and make this a must-visit location when on Alderney.
🛏️🜂♣

St Anne

Georgian House Hotel
54 Victoria Street, GY9 3UF (taxi or uphill walk from harbour; taxi or 20-min walk from airport)
☎ (01481) 822471 ⊕ georgianalderney.com
Butcombe Original, Gold; 1 changing beer (sourced nationally; often Greene King, Morland) Ⓗ
Just up from the town church, the hotel extends a warm welcome to all. There is a pleasant garden, which has an outside bar during the summer months – casks can be found on the counter. Sometimes live music is also featured in the garden area. Meals are served all day (lunchtime only on Sun). During the summer months there is also a real cider. During the winter the two multi-fuel fires make it warm and cosy. 🌥️❀🜂◑&🛏️P🔊

GUERNSEY
Castel

Fleur du Jardin ⚫
Les Grands Moulins, Kings Mills, GY5 7JT
☎ (01481) 257996 ⊕ fleurdujardin.com
Little Big Brew Co. Alan; 2 changing beers (sourced nationally; often Butcombe, Sharp's, Timothy Taylor) Ⓗ
A building of unique charm with two bars – one traditional, small and cosy, attached to the restaurant, the other renovated in a more contemporary style to create a comfortable, relaxing area to enjoy a beer. A door leads to a large covered patio and out to the garden. Menus in both the bar and restaurant feature fresh local produce. The car park can be busy in summer.
Q🌥️🜂❀◑🛏️&P🚃(61)❀

Cobo

Rockmount Restaurant & Bar
Cobo Coast Road, GY5 7HB
☎ (01481) 252778 ⊕ therocky.gg
4 changing beers (often Randalls) Ⓗ
A spacious pub comprising a large lounge bar, a taproom that shows sport on TV and a public bar with a pool table and largescreen TV for sport. The lounge has an emphasis on food, served lunchtimes and evenings, but there are comfy chairs near the fire for drinkers. Five handpumps offer a changing range of beers and you can also try a tasting paddle of different ales.
🌥️❀◑&🛏️P🚃(41,42)❀🎵

Herm Island

Mermaid Tavern ⚫
GY1 3HR (Trident ferry from St Peter Port)
☎ (01481) 750050 ⊕ herm.com/mermaid
House beer (by Liberation); 2 changing beers Ⓗ
A welcoming inn on the beautiful island of Herm, a short trip by ferry from Guernsey. The large courtyard is a popular spot in summer; an open fire adds to the charm in winter. The house beer is Liberation's Herm Island Gold, brewed specially for the island. The pub holds regular themed music and food events, and hosts real ale and cider festivals in June and September.
🌥️❀◑▲♣❀🛏️🎵

St Martin

Les Douvres Hotel
La Fosse, GY4 6ER
☎ (01481) 238731 ⊕ lesdouvres.com
Little Big Brew Co. Alan; 2 changing beers (often Butcombe, Sharp's, Timothy Taylor) Ⓗ
Former 18th-century manor house set in private gardens in St Martin near the south coast, two and a half miles from St Peter Port. Cliff walks and Saints Bay fishing harbour are nearby. A well-maintained, changing range of beers is offered on three handpumps and cask cider during the season. Excellent meals, including pizzas, are served in the bar and separate restaurant. Live music features on Friday night and occasional Wednesdays.
❀🛏️◑🛏️P🚃(81)🎵

St Peter Port

Red Lion
Les Banques, GY1 2RX
☎ (01481) 724042
4 changing beers (often Randalls) Ⓗ
Friendly pub on the northern outskirts of St Peter Port, with two bar areas – a lounge overlooking Belle Greve Bay to the front and a public area at the rear. Gluten-free beer is available in bottles, and real cider is served in

REAL ALE BREWERIES

Bliss 🍺 Jersey: St Helier
Liberation Jersey: St Saviour
Little Big ✒ St Peter Port: Guernsey
Randalls St Peter Port: Guernsey
Stinky Bay Jersey: St Lawrence

summer. Numerous TVs show sport. Meat draws are held on Friday and Saturday evenings. The pub is on several bus routes and the cycle route between St Peter Port and St Sampson. ⏶⏢⏥⏤🍴⏢🐾🛜

Ship & Crown ✅
North Esplanade, GY1 2NB
☎ (01481) 721368
Butcombe Original; Liberation Ale, Herm Island Gold, IPA Ⓗ
Traditional local on the town seafront, with fantastic views of the harbour, neighbouring islands and Castle Cornet. Popular with locals, yachtsman and tourists alike, this is an ideal pub to enjoy a pint and a good meal. It is decorated throughout with photos of local shipwrecks, Guernsey and the pub under German occupation. Up to four handpumps serve Liberation and Butcombe ales, and all major sports events are shown on TV in a friendly and lively atmosphere. Real cider is sometimes available on handpump. The Crown Pier car park is opposite. ⏤🍴🐾🛜

Slaughterhouse
Castle Pier, GY1 1AN
☎ (01481) 712123 ⏥ slaughterhouse.gg
3 changing beers (often Randalls) Ⓗ
Popular harbourside restaurant and pub that offers fine views over Havelet Bay and the harbour from its mezzanine restaurant and upper section of the large outdoor terrace. The Randalls-managed pub serves a changing range of up to six real ales, some from small breweries. Winner of a CAMRA design award in 2019 for its conversion from an abbatoir, hence the name. ⏢⏤🚃🍴

Thomas de la Rue ✅
9 The Pollet, GY1 1WQ
☎ (01481) 714990
Butcombe Original; 1 changing beer (often Liberation) Ⓗ
A traditional town pub in the heart of St Peter Port, overlooking the harbour and Castle Cornet, popular both with locals and tourists. It comprises a main bar with two handpumps serving a rotating selection of Liberation and Butcombe ales. Food ranges from sandwiches to pub classics like burgers and fish & chips. Downstairs is the Front Room bar and terrace, which can be booked for private parties but does not serve real ale. ⏶⏢⏤🅿🚃🛜♪

JERSEY
St Brelade

Old Smugglers Inn ✅
Le Mont du Ouaisne, Ouaisne, JE3 8AW
☎ (01534) 741510 ⏥ oldsmugglersinn.com
Draught Bass; house beer (by Liberation); 2 changing beers (often Marston's, Ringwood, Skinner's) Ⓗ
Perched on the edge of Ouaisne Bay, the Smugglers has been the crown jewel of the Jersey real ale scene for many years. Dating back to when pirates came here to enjoy an ale or two, it is set within granite-built fishermen's cottages with foundations reputedly from the 13th century. Up to four ales are available, including one from Skinner's, and mini beer festivals are regularly held. It is renowned for its good food and fresh daily specials. Q⏶⏤🍴🐾

Trafalgar Inn ✅
Charing Cross, St Aubin, JE3 8AA
☎ (01534) 741334 ⏥ trafalgarinn.je

5 changing beers (often Butcombe, Liberation, St Austell) Ⓗ
Traditional community pub with a nautical theme. There are two bars - the saloon bar at the front and a sports bar with pool, darts and sports TV behind. The handpumps are in the sports bar – beers are regularly rotated but usually include one from Liberation brewery (see website for what's in the cellar). It is popular with local rugby fans, and the Jersey Reds usually come here after Saturday home matches. ⏤♣🚃🐾

St Helier

Biere Atelier
Bath Street, JE2 4ST
☎ (01534) 874059 ⏥ labastille.bar
Purity Pure Gold, Mad Goose, Pure UBU; 1 changing beer (sourced nationally) Ⓗ
Possibly Jersey's first micropub, this single-room bar has a few tables and stools around the walls. The small counter has real ales on handpump and a craft beer wall behind. Popular with office workers, it is fast becoming a destination bar for real ale lovers. It is interconnected with the nearby Bastille restaurant and bar, where the beers are also available. Food from the Bastille can also be enjoyed at tables outside on the pedestrian street. ⏤

Lamplighter Ⓛ ✅
9 Mulcaster Street, JE2 3NJ
☎ (01534) 723119
8 changing beers (sourced nationally) Ⓗ
A traditional pub with a modern feel. The gas lamps that gave the pub its name remain, as does the original antique pewter bar top. An excellent range of up to eight real ales is available - the largest selection on the island - including one from Skinner's. All real ales are served direct from the cellar. A real cider is sometimes also on offer. A repeat winner of local CAMRA Pub of the Year. 🍴🚃🐾🛜

Post Horn Ⓛ ✅
Hue Street, JE2 3RE
☎ (01534) 872853
Butcombe Original; Draught Bass; Liberation Ale, IPA; 1 changing beer (often Liberation) Ⓗ
Busy, friendly pub adjacent to the precinct and five minutes' walk from the Royal Square. Popular at lunchtimes with its own nucleus of regulars, it offers up to four draught ales. The large L-shaped public bar extends into the lounge area where there is an open fire and TV showing sport. A good selection of freshly cooked food is served. There is a large function room on the first floor, a drinking area outside and a public car park nearby. ⏢⏤🐾🛜

Prince of Wales Tavern
8 Hilgrove Street, JE2 4SL
☎ (01534) 737378
Courage Best Bitter; Fuller's London Pride; Ringwood Boondoggle; Sharp's Doom Bar; Wychwood Hobgoblin Gold; 5 changing beers (sourced nationally; often Shepherd Neame) Ⓗ
A traditional pub, next to the historic central market, offering a large selection of up to eight cask ales advertised on blackboards. The Victorian-style interior has a bright and sparkling bar-back that features a large selection of whiskies. No food is served but there are a number of eateries nearby. The beer garden at the rear is a pleasant spot for a relaxing drink. ⏢🍴🐾

St Martin

Royal

La Grande Route de Faldouet, JE3 6UG
☎ (01534) 856289
Courage Directors; Skinner's Lushingtons ⊞; 1 changing beer (often Bombardier) ⊞/ⓖ
Originally a coaching inn, this large country-style hostelry is located at the centre of St Martin, with sizeable public and lounge bars, a restaurant area, and a spacious alfresco area. The interior features traditional furnishings, cosy corners and a real fire in colder months. Owned by Randalls brewery, it serves guest ales from the Marston's, Sharp's and Skinner's stables. Quality food is popular with locals and visitors alike, with a good menu available lunchtimes and evenings (no food Sun eve). ☺✿⊕ⓑ&ⓐ♣Pⓕ(3)❀

St Ouen

Farmers Inn ✔

La Grande Route de St Ouen, JE3 2HY
☎ (01534) 485311
Butcombe Original; Liberation Pale Ale, Herm Island Gold; 2 changing beers (often Liberation) ⊞
Situated in the hub of St Ouen, near the war memorial and parish hall, the rustic Farmers Inn is a typical country inn offering up to three ales as well as a locally made cider when available (usually April to July). Traditional pub food is served in generous portions. Best described as a friendly community local, there is a good chance of hearing Jersey French (Jerriais) spoken at the bar. There is an outside seating area at the front. ☺❿♣ⓕPⓠ

Moulin de Lecq ✔

Le Mont De La Greve De Lecq, Greve de Lecq, JE3 2DT
☎ (01534) 482818 ⊕ moulindelecq.co.uk
Shepherd Neame Spitfire; house beer (by Liberation); 2 changing beers (often Marston's, Skinner's) ⊞
A free house offering a range of real ales, the Moulin is a converted 12th-century watermill, in the valley above the beach at Greve de Lecq. The waterwheel is still in place and the turning mechanism can be seen behind the bar. A restaurant adjoins the mill. The children's play space and a barbecue area are used extensively in the summer. The 120-seat restaurant can be hired for functions. Pool can be played in the second-floor games room. Q☺✿⊕ⓑ&♣ⓕPⓠ❀☂

St Peter

Tipsy

La Route de Beaumont, JE3 7BQ
☎ (01534) 485556 ⊕ thetipsy.co.uk
6 changing beers (sourced nationally; often Castle Rock, Elland, Liberation) ⊞
The Tipsy, formerly the Tipsy Toad, was the site of the original Skinner's brewery before it moved to Cornwall. The friendly pub has been refurbished to provide a main bar with comfortable seating. Six handpumps dispense a rotating selection of ales, including a house beer from Liberation, Tipsy Toad Ale, a 3.8% ABV bitter. The separate restaurant area offers an extensive menu. Outside is a patio with heating. ☺✿⊕ⓑ&Pⓠ(9)❀☂

Trinity

Trinity Arms ⓛ ✔

La Rue es Picots, JE3 5JX
☎ (01534) 864691
Liberation Ale; 1 changing beer (often Butcombe, Liberation) ⊞

Sporting the parish's ancient symbol of the Trinity, this pub, built in 1976, is modern by Jersey's country pub standards but has plenty of character. Owned by the Liberation Group, it is central to village community life. It has recently undergone a full refurbishment and both bars have been merged into one, with a central island bar. Food is served at breakfast, lunchtime and evenings. There is seating outside and a children's play area. ☺✿⊕ⓑ&♣Pⓠ(4)❀☂

SARK
Sark

Bel Air

Harbour Hill, GY10 1SB
☎ (01481) 832052 ⊕ belairinnsark.gg
2 changing beers (often Randalls) ⊞
Located at the top of Harbour Hill, this family-friendly pub is popular with tourists and local residents. Two handpumps serve a changing selection of local and national real ales, and a real cider. Pizza is available from noon until late, to eat in or take away. There is a cosy fire for cold weather and a large garden and courtyard, where barbecues and live music feature during summer weekends. Off-sales are available. Open all day every day. Dog friendly. ☺✿⊕ⓑ&♣❀☂

Mermaid Tavern

Main Street, GY10 1SG
☎ (01481) 832022
Butcombe Original ⊞
Established before WWII, this pub is a little like Sark – an island that harks back to an earlier time. The decor has remained unchanged since the 1960s. Though a locals' pub, the Mermaid extends a warm welcome to visitors. It is child friendly and serves snacks such as pizza and sandwiches on request. There is an outdoor seating area. Darts and pool can be played, in addition to the jukebox and a piano, which is available for spontaneous sing-songs or a dance! ☺♣

Breweries

Bliss

🍺 **4 Wharf Street, St Helier, JE2 3NR**
⊕ blissbrewco.com

Bliss Brew Co was formed during 2019, the first new commercial brewery in Jersey for over a century. A partnership between a talented former homebrewer and a local craft beer bar, it focuses on craft beers mainly served from KeyKeg, tentative steps have been taken in cask. Some beers have been made available in can.

Liberation SIBA

Tregar House, Longueville Road, St Saviour, JE2 7WF
☎ (01534) 764089 ☎ 07911 744568
⊕ liberationgroup.com

⊠ The Liberation Brewery (owned by the Liberation Group, which also owns Butcombe Brewery) is located at Longueville, just outside St Helier. Its multi-award-winning flagship beer Liberation Ale can be found in many of the Group's freehold and partner pubs in the Channel Islands and on the mainland; 39 in Jersey, 17 in Guernsey and three in Alderney and 60 in the UK. ‼🍺♦

Ale (ABV 4%) GOLD
Herm Island Gold (ABV 4.2%) GOLD
IPA (ABV 4.8%) PALE

Little Big SIBA

23 St George's Esplanade, St Peter Port, GY1 2BG
☎ **(01481) 728149** ⊕ **littlebigbrewco.com**

☺Little Big Brew Co was founded in 2020. ‼️🍺♦️✦

Alan (ABV 4%) PALE
Betty (ABV 4%) RED

Randalls

La Piette Brewery, St Georges Esplanade, St Peter Port, GY1 3JG

☎ **(01481) 720134** ⊕ **randallsbrewery.com**

Randalls has been brewing in Guernsey since 1868. The company was bought out in 2006 and moved into a modern, purpose-built brewery in 2008. 19 pubs are owned and a further 70 outlets are supplied. ‼️♦️

Stinky Bay

La Grand Route, St Lawrence, JE3 1NH ☎ **07797 781703** ⊕ **stinkybay.com**

Named after a rugged bay on the North-Western tip of Jersey, Stinky Bay Brewing Co was established in 2017.

Trafalgar Inn, St Brelade, Jersey (Photo: Hugh Llewelyn / Flickr CC BY-SA 2.0)

NI & ISLANDS

Modern British Beer

Matthew Curtis

Over the last two decades beer as we know it has changed, forever. Taking their cues from the craft beer revolution in the US and the resurrection of traditional styles in continental Europe, the brewers of Great Britain and Northern Ireland have carved out a unique and world-leading beer culture.

Matt Curtis tells the story of the evolution of modern British beer, and guides you on a journey around these isles, discovering a beer culture that has a global reach, but which is also local at heart.

'A beauty and a triumph ... An incredibly engaging read.'

CLAIRE BULLEN, Editor-in-Chief *Good Beer Hunting*

'If you're looking for a primer on the best independently produced British beers available today, you're in luck.' WILL HAWKES

'UK brewing is at a crossroads and the definitions Matthew comes up with help illuminate the path forward.' JONNY GARRETT, The Craft Beer Channel

RRP: £15.99   **ISBN**: 978-1-85249-370-7

For this and other books on beer and pubs, visit CAMRA's online bookshop at **shop1.camra.org.uk** or call 01727 867201.

Discounts are available for CAMRA members.

Isle of Man

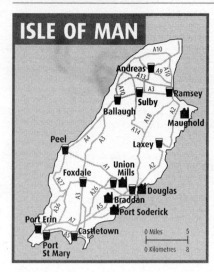

ISLE OF MAN

Andreas

Grosvenor Country Inn 🅻
Andreas Road, IM7 4HE
☎ (01624) 888007
Odin Manx Mild, Laksaa Pale; 2 changing beers (sourced nationally; often Brains, Timothy Taylor) 🄷
The island's most northerly pub is a free house that is popular for both drinking and dining, and is a meeting place for many local groups. Its informal public bar hosts pub games and displays many darts trophies. Quiz nights and musical events are held. Food is offered both to eat in (booking advised), or to take away.
🍽️🅑🛏️🕭👬♿🅟🚗🐾🛜🎵

Ballaugh

Raven 🅻 ⭕
Main Road, IM7 5EG
☎ (01624) 896128
Okell's Bitter; house beer (by Okell's); 1 changing beer (sourced nationally) 🄷
A thriving village-centre pub next to Ballaugh Bridge on the TT course. The pub has a good reputation for food, but drinkers are very much welcome in comfortable surroundings. The pub has its own house beer, Raven's Claw, by Okell's. The outdoor areas are hugely popular, especially during race periods when bikes leap over the bridge. The walls are adorned with many signed photographs of riders. Q🕭🕭👬♿🅐🅟🚗(5,6)🐾🛜

Castletown

Castle Arms 🅻 ⭕
The Quay, IM9 1LD
☎ (01624) 824673
Okell's Manx Pale Ale, Bitter; 1 changing beer (sourced locally) 🄷
Known locally as the Gluepot, this small and characterful two-roomed pub is wedged in between the harbour and the imposing castle. It is thought to date from around 1750 and originally hosted a local garrison. The pub famously features on the Manx £5 note and has long been a favourite for visitors to the town. One of the rooms has a nautical theme, and the other a motorbike theme. Three beers are kept in summer.
Q🛏️🕭🅐🕭♿🅟🚗(1,2)🐾🛜🎵

George Hotel 🅻 ⭕
The Parade, IM9 1LG
☎ (01624) 822533
Okell's Manx Pale Ale, Bitter; 1 changing beer (often Okell's) 🄷
An imposing historic building dating from 1833, in the heart of Castletown town square overlooking the magnificent castle. The George has an increasing reputation for dining and there is a function room to the rear catering for 60 at meal times. The pub is a meeting point for local community groups, including bridge, rotary and a stamp club, as well as others. Eleven rooms for accommodation have been refurbished to a high standard. 🕭🛏️🕭👬♿🕭🅟🚗(1)🐾🛜

Sidings 🅻
Victoria Road, IM9 1EF (next to railway station)
☎ (01624) 823282
Bushy's Castletown Bitter, Bitter; Castle Rock Harvest Pale; Okell's Bitter; 8 changing beers (sourced nationally; often Bowness Bay, Coach House, Copper Dragon) 🄷
Formerly the Duck's Nest, this former ticket office for the Isle of Man Steam Railway has three distinct lounges, a bar area, dining room and live music lounge, plus a games and TV room. Twelve handpumps line the bar, serving four regular Manx ales. The extensive beer garden to the rear is well used in summer. The pub has made no fewer than 44 appearances in the Guide, and is a former local CAMRA Pub of the Year on several occasions. Q🛏️🕭🕭👬♿🕭🅟🚗(1,1A)🐾🛜🎵

Douglas

Albert Hotel ⭕
3 Chapel Row, IM1 2BJ (cllose to bus stands and indoor market)
☎ (01624) 673632 🌐 albertiom.com
Odin Manx Mild; Okell's Bitter; 2 changing beers (sourced locally; often Bushy's, Kaneen's) 🄷
Traditional, immaculately maintained pub close to the island's main sea terminal. It consists of two distinct rooms, with a central bar serving beers from several local breweries. The larger room has seating as well as a pool table and a sports TV. The smaller room to the left of the pub also has TV, plus comfortable seating to the rear and walls adorned with photographs of steam packet vessels.
Q🕭♿🅟🚗🐾🛜🎵

Cat with no Tail 🅻 ⭕
Hailwood Court, Hailwood Avenue, IM2 7EA
☎ (01624) 616364
Okell's Bitter; 3 changing beers (sourced nationally; often Okell's, Timothy Taylor) 🄷
A modern pub serving the Governors Hill housing estate, two miles from central Douglas. The Cat has a public bar with largescreen TVs for sports, as well as pool and darts. The large lounge has a conservatory area popular with families. This leads to an extensive outside seating areas, with a patio and play areas, that looks onto open countryside. The pub usually has up to four ales including two guest beers, which may be different in the two bars.
🛏️🕭🕭👬♿🕭🅟🚗🐾🛜🎵

Old Market Inn Ⓛ

Chapel Row, IM1 2BJ

☎ 07624 381076

2 changing beers (sourced locally; often Bushy's) 🅷

A pub with a loyal following, not least from the many TT fans who visit annually for the island's famous races. The tiny bar serves beers, almost always from Bushys, in the two rooms that are little-changed for many years. The cellars, and those of the adjacent pub, are thought to be some of the oldest surviving manmade structures in Douglas. The pub raises a lot of money for charitable causes. ⇌🖼🛜

Prospect Hotel ⓁⓄ

Prospect Hill, IM1 1ET

☎ (01624) 616773

Okell's Manx Pale Ale, Bitter; 5 changing beers (sourced nationally; often Okell's) 🅷

This pub in the heart of the Douglas finance sector opened in 1857. It has a large open-plan interior, with a bar facing the door and another long bar to the right. There is also a small area to the rear that is often used for meetings of various groups. An impressive eight handpumps are split between the two bars, always with two to three Okell's beers available. Closing times vary on weekday nights. ⇌🍴🖼(3,11)🌸🛜

Queen's Hotel ⓁⓄ

Queens Promenade, IM2 4NL (towards N end of promenade)

☎ (01624) 674438

Okell's Bitter; 3 changing beers (sourced nationally) 🅷

A large Heron and Brearley pub (Okell's), three-quarters of the way along the promenade from the sea terminal. It is popular with tourists in the summer, who come to enjoy the extensive outdoor heated seating areas. Inside are two rooms, one with a pool table and sports TV, and another to the right with more seating. A cider is always available. Q🕑🌸🕐🍴⇌(Derby Castle)♣🍴🖼🛜♪

Rovers Return Ⓛ

11 Church Street, IM1 2AG (on pedestrianised area behind town hall)

☎ (01624) 676459

Bushy's Bitter; 5 changing beers (sourced nationally; often Bushy's) 🅷

An unusual pub that is full of surprises, with an eclectic and fascinating mix of memorabilia adorning the walls. The warren of small rooms include a pool room to the rear and a 'Rovers' room full of Blackburn Rovers memorabilia. The pub's clientele are equally eclectic, judging by the selection on the jukebox. Live music sometimes features. This is a main outlet for Bushy's beer in Douglas. 🍴⇌♣🖼🛜♪

Thirsty Pigeon Ⓛ

38-40 Victoria Street, IM1 2LW

☎ (01624) 675584 ⊕ thirstypigeon.com

Okell's Bitter; 3 changing beers (often Kaneen's, Odin) 🅷

Welcoming open-plan pub that has become one of Douglas's institutions. This former bank serves an eclectic range of beers to an even-more eclectic clientele. The dark wood interior is complemented by button-back seating in dark green with matching bar stools. Casks are taken down the vault cellars via a box lift visible in the corner. The pub is a huge supporter of regular live music, and can be lively at weekends. 🍴🕐⇌🖼🛜♪

Woodbourne Hotel ⓁⓄ

Alexander Drive, IM2 3QF (in the Woodbourne area of Douglas)

☎ (01624) 676754

Okell's Bitter, Manx Pale Ale; 5 changing beers (sourced nationally) 🅷

An imposing Victorian-era pub in the Douglas suburbs. It comprises four rooms: a games and sports room, front bar, and a spacious back bar on a lower level. In the middle there is a former gents-only bar, with a unique set of portraits on the wall featuring customers in former years. As an Okell's pub, it stocks one of the largest ranges of real ales in the island's capital. The pub still holds a meat raffle and raises money for charity, especially guide dogs. Q🌸🕐♣🖼(3)🌸🛜♪

Foxdale

Baltic Inn Ⓛ

1 Glentramman Terrace, IM4 3EE

☎ (01624) 801305 ⊕ balticinn.pub

Okell's Bitter, Manx Pale Ale; 1 changing beer (sourced nationally) 🅷

This much-revived pub is the hub of this former mining village. There are two darts and pool teams, and various local groups use the pub, including a heritage group and local football club. Live music often features and there are two local mhelliahs (an ancient Celtic custom) a year. Rare pictures of the village's mining past adorn the walls, illustrating the scale of its importance to the local economy. Accommodation is available all year.
Q🛏🌸🍴🕐⛺♣🖼(4)🌸🛜♪

Laxey

Queen's Hotel Ⓛ

New Road, IM4 7BP (600yds S of village centre)

☎ (01624) 861195

Bushy's Castletown Bitter, Bitter; Odin Manx Mild, Laksaa Pale, Asgard Bitter; 1 changing beer (sourced locally) 🅷

A large open-plan pub with traditional character and old-fashioned chandeliers. The pub walls feature many photographs of the motorbike races and local village, It supports live music, and has pool, darts and sports TV. An extensive beer garden overlooks the passing Manx Electric Railway trams. A well-supported meat raffle draw is held on Sundays. The small porch area is useful for those wanting to linger with a pint until the very last moment, as the bus stops just outside. 🛏🌸🕐🕐⇌♣🍴P🖼(3,3A)🌸🛜♪

Shore Hotel Ⓞ

Old Laxey Hill, IM4 7DA (follow signs to Old Laxey from Laxey main road)

☎ (01624) 861509 ⊕ shorehotellaxey.im

House beer (by Bushys) 🅷

Built in 1837, the Shore Hotel is situated in a picturesque location in Old Laxey, beside the Laxey River and harbour. The public house was fully refurbished in 2021 and now combines Victorian design with contemporary styling. A boutique hotel and restaurant will be the next phase of the renovation, to be constructed at the rear of the public house. Outside tables and chairs, beside the river, make for a perfect location to enjoy a beer on a summer evening. 🌸🕐⛺⇌(South Cape Halt)♣P🖼🛜

Peel

Miller's T'Ale

33 Michael Street, IM5 1HD

☎ 07624 307356

5 changing beers (sourced nationally) 🅷

The first and only micropub on the Isle of Man. The beers served here are usually different to those available in other local pubs, and have often never been seen on the island before. It also serves craft beers and cider. Events such as Cheese O'Clock Sundays, a Tuesday pub quiz, and bring a board game nights feature regularly. A former local CAMRA Pub of the Year. Q♿🍴🅿🚋(5,6)🐾🐕📶

White House Hotel 🅛 ●
2 Tynwald Road, IM5 1LA (200yds from bus station)
☎ (01624) 842252
Bushy's Bitter; Cross Bay Sunset; Odin Manx Mild, Laksaa Pale; Okell's Bitter; 2 changing beers (sourced nationally) 🅗
A traditional community pub with several rooms and drinking areas, including a small Captain's Cabin bar set slightly lower down. The pub boasts more than half a dozen teams for darts and pool, with many societies and groups meeting here, including bee keepers, choirs, and Manx language groups. The pub has been cask ale stalwart for many years, and is a multiple former local CAMRA Pub of the Year winner. Q🐕♣🍴🅿🚋(5,6)🐾📶♪

Port Erin

Bay Hotel 🅛
Shore Road, IM9 6HL
☎ (01624) 832084 ⊕ bushys.com/the-bay
Bushy's Bitter, Old Bushy Tail; house beer (by Bushy's); 2 changing beers (sourced locally) 🅗
Bushy's flagship pub in the south of the island was brought back to life and extensively refurbished 20 years ago. Set in a spectacular location on Port Erin seafront, the building consists of several rooms, a dining area to the right, and two traditional rooms for drinkers to the left, including a darts area and an open fire in winter. Live music features outside in the summer months. A former local CAMRA Pub of the Year winner.
Q🐕🐾🍴🔌👨‍🦽🚋♣🍴🅿🐾📶♪

Haven 🅛 ●
Station Road, IM9 6AB
☎ (01624) 834030
Okell's Bitter; 1 changing beer (sourced locally) 🅗
Though very much a locals' pub, the Haven is friendly to visitors. There is a large room to the front, with big windows and ample room for live music and pool. Another room to the rear is more often used at quieter times. The pub can get quite lively on summer evenings when bands play. Okell's Bitter is supplemented by a seasonal beer in the summer months. 🚋♣🅿🐾📶♪

Port St Mary

Albert Hotel 🅛
Athol Street, IM9 5DS (opp harbour)
☎ (01624) 832118
Bushy's Bitter; Okell's Bitter; 2 changing beers (sourced nationally; often Kaneen's, Marston's) 🅗
A hidden gem in the heart of this idyllic coastal village. It has a games room and sports bar, a middle bar, and a side room to the right, used more often during peak periods. The pub is open until midnight and is a community hub, with many groups using it for events, including anglers and a local knitting group. A former local CAMRA Pub of the Year. Q🐕👨‍🦽♣🚋(1)📶

Railway Station Hotel 🅛
Station Road, IM9 5LF
☎ (01624) 832494
Bushy's Bitter; Okell's Bitter; 2 changing beers (sourced locally) 🅗
An imposing building in the heart of the countryside yet only a short walk to Port Erin and Port St Mary. It has

several rooms including a games room and another small bar area with a roaring open fire in the winter months. Four well-kept beers are split across the two bars. The pub also operates as a hotel from April to October.
Q🐕🛏👨‍🦽🚋♣🅿(1,2)📶♪

Ramsey

Mitre 🅛
16 Parliament Street, IM8 1AP
☎ (01624) 813045
Okell's Bitter; house beer (by Okell's); 2 changing beers (sourced locally) 🅗
Built in 1840, the Mitre has recently been refurbished to a traditional but high standard throughout. It enjoys excellent views of the working harbour. The pub is a huge supporter of local breweries and their Okell's house beer is always available. Live music is played in the Harbour Bar, and at the weekend in the Cooil Bar, which is popular with younger revellers. A popular Sunday carvery is also served in the Harbour Bar.
◑🚋(Plaza)♣🚋(3,3A)🐾📶♪

Plough 🅛
46 Parliament Street, IM8 1AN
☎ (01624) 813323
Okell's Bitter; 1 changing beer (sourced nationally; often Timothy Taylor) 🅗
In the heart of Ramsey's main street, the recently refurbished Plough stocks a frequently changing guest ale in addition to Okell's Bitter. This small, busy two-roomed pub caters for a mixed clientele, from shoppers taking a break to football fans. The Plough is a proud sponsor of Shennaghys Jiu, a Manx music festival held in Ramsey in March/April, and produces bespoke beer mats to advertise and celebrate the event. 🚋(Plaza)♣🚋📶

Swan 🅛 ●
Lezayre Road, IM8 2LN
☎ (01624) 814236
Okell's Bitter; Dr Okell's IPA; 2 changing beers (sourced locally) 🅗
A family-friendly pub with a spacious beer garden, the Swan is known for its good food and a reservation is recommended at peak periods. This Okell's brewery pub has a public bar and lounge bar, and its location, close to the shops and picturesque working harbour of Ramsey, makes it a favourite place to watch the TT races from the inside of the course. Q🐕🐾◑🚋(Plaza)♣🚋(3)🐾📶♪

Trafalgar Hotel 🍴 🅛 ●
West Quay, IM8 1DW
☎ (01624) 814601
Odin Manx Mild, Rhumsaa Bitter, Laksaa Pale; 3 changing beers (sourced nationally) 🅗
A friendly, welcoming and often busy pub on Ramsey's scenic harbour, now linked with Odin brewery and usually serving its regular beers. Other guest ales are sourced nationally. There is a TV showing sporting events and a real fire during the winter months. Local CAMRA Pub of the Year 2022 and 2023. Close to bus and tram services. 🐾🚋(Plaza)♣🚋🐾📶

Sulby

Ginger Hall 🅛
Ballamanagh Road, IM7 2HB
☎ (01624) 897231
4 changing beers (sourced locally) 🅗
Built in 1818, the Ginger Hall Hotel is so named due to the original licensee brewing his own ginger beer. The pub is next to the TT racing circuit, and a huge TT map is

on the ceiling of the bar area. A real fire is lit in colder months. An impressive beer engine dominates the bar, dispensing the regularly changing beers. Thai food is served, and there is regular live music. Accommodation is available. ⛄🕮✠◖◗ Å♣P💻(5)🐾 📶 ♫

Union Mills

Railway Inn 🛢

Main Road, IM4 4NE
☎ (01624) 853006

Okell's Bitter; 5 changing beers (sourced nationally; often Bushy's, Odin, Kaneen's) 🅷

This three-roomed free-house is one of the rare pubs on the island that serves beer from all five local breweries. The elevated beer garden is perfect for watching the famous TT races or enjoying the summer evenings. The Jeff Astle lounge is a shrine to West Bromwich Albion Football club. A roaring log fire will keep you cosy in the colder months. A former local CAMRA Pub of the Year on a few occasions. Q🕮Å♣P💻🐾📶

Breweries

Bushy's SIBA

Mount Murray Brewery, Mount Murray, Braddan, IM4 1JE
☎ (01624) 661244 🌐 bushys.com

😊Launched in 1986 as a brewpub, Bushy's relocated in 1990 when demand outgrew capacity. Bushy's goes one step further than the Manx Pure Beer Law preferring the German Reinheitsgebot (Pure Beer Law). The brewery hosts a successful festival during the TT period at Villa Marina Gardens, Douglas. Bushy's distributes to many pubs and clubs throughout the Isle of Man. ‼◆

Castletown Bitter (ABV 3.5%) BITTER
Bitter (ABV 3.8%) BITTER
A traditional malty and hoppy beer with good balnace. The fruit lasts through to the bitter finish.
Darkside (ABV 4%) MILD
Mannannan's Cloak (ABV 4%) BITTER
Triskellion (ABV 4%) GOLD
Classic (ABV 4.3%) BITTER
Bramble (ABV 4.4%) SPECIALITY
Buggane (ABV 4.4%) BITTER
Old Bushy Tail (ABV 4.5%) BITTER
Red (ABV 4.7%) RED
Star of India (ABV 5%) PALE

Kaneen's

Kaneens Garage, Main Road, Union Mills, IM4 4AE
☎ 07624 302245 🌐 kaneensbrewery.com

⊗ Launched in 2021, head brewer Peter Kaneen converted a vehicle repair workshop into Kaneen's Microbrewery.

Lhune Airh (ABV 4.8%) PALE
Gentle sweet malt and fruit, with hops present to give bitterness throughout.

Noa (NEW)

🛢 **Peveril Building, Peveril Square, Douglas, IM1 2BS**

Brewing began in 2023. The brewery is based directly opposite the ferry terminal in Douglas. Beers are brewed using leftover sourdough bread from the associated bakehouse as yeast. No cask ale is currently produced. ◆

Odin SIBA

Glen Mona Loop Road, Maughold, IM7 1HJ ☎ 07624 266664

Established in 2019 using the 2.5-barrel brewery from Betteridge's of Hampshire. Founder and brewer Rob Storey brews six core beers in cask. **LIVE**

Manx Mild (ABV 3.4%) MILD
Well-balanced mild, malt and caramel sweetness along with roast bitterness in the taste is followed by a sweeter malty finish.
Rhumsaa Bitter (ABV 3.7%) BITTER
Laksaa Pale (ABV 3.8%) PALE
Asgard Bitter (ABV 4.2%) BITTER
Black Claw (ABV 4.5%) STOUT
Accomplished full-bodied stout, roast builds along with some hop and caramel leads into a lasting slightly drier finish.
Oyster Stout (ABV 4.8%) STOUT

Okell's

Kewaigue, Douglas, IM2 1QG
☎ (01624) 699400 🌐 okells.co.uk

😊Founded in 1874 by Dr Okell, this is the main brewery on the island and moved in 1994 to a new, purpose-built plant at Kewaigue. All the beers are produced under the Manx Brewers' Act. ‼◆

MPA – Manx Pale Ale (ABV 3.6%) PALE
A golden fruity, session beer with background sweetness and a rising hoppy finish.
Bitter (ABV 3.7%) BITTER
Classic traditional bitter with sweet malt and hops in balance. Some fruit and caramel throughout and an even bitter finish.
Dr Okell's IPA (ABV 4.5%) BLOND
A clean, fruity, sweetish bitter with an alcoholic bite.

Radical

Oak Hill, Port Soderick, IM4 1AN ☎ 07624 493304
🌐 radicalbrewing.im

Dr Mike Cowbourne, who was in charge of brewing at Okell's Brewery, has set up this small brewery in his garage. The beers are available to the free trade and the most likely venue to have them is the Falcon Hotel, Port Erin. This brewery only produces pins so no firkins are used and usually there is one brew a week (could be one of four beers).

Ironic Rye (ABV 3.8%) PALE
Radical Bitter (ABV 3.8%) BITTER
Amarillo Dreamin (ABV 4.4%) PALE
SuperNova Sunshine (ABV 4.6%) PALE

By George!

It was my Uncle George who discovered that alcohol was a food well in advance of modern medical thought.

P G Wodehouse, The Inimitable Jeeves

World's Greatest Beers

Pete Brown, Emma Inch, Jonny Garrett, Joe Stange, Lotte Peplow, Roger Protz, Claire Bullen, John Holl

This book is the definitive guide to the 250 best beers in the world today, selected by a panel of eight renowned international beer writers and influencers. Illustrated in full colour throughout, this high-quality book is a must-have for all self-respecting beer lovers.

Each of the 250 beers from around the world is fully explored with a detailed and personal recommendation from one of the well-established beer writers.

About the Contributors
All the contributors to this book are award-winning beer writers and professionals in their field and are based in Europe and the USA. Many of the writers have won awards for their work at home and abroad and they continue to contribute to the exciting and innovative world of beer publishing.

RRP: £17.99   **ISBN**: 978-1-85249-379-0

For this and other books on beer and pubs, visit CAMRA's online bookshop at **shop1.camra.org.uk** or call 01727 867201.

Discounts are available for CAMRA members.

Indexes & Further Information

Places index

London index

*shown on Inner London map

Breweries index

Beers index

These beers refer to those in bold type in the brewery listings (beers in regular production) and so therefore do not include seasonal, special or occasional beers that may be mentioned elsewhere in the text.

Bidon Ampersand 81
Bier Head Liverpool Brewing 689
Biere De Garde Fuddy Duck 496
Big Bad Wolf Lord Conrad's 38
Big Bang Theory Nene Valley 505
Big Boot Tomos & Lilford 741
Big Butty 3P's 461
Big Cat Stroud 345
Big Chief Green Mill 673
    Redemption 151
Big Game Tamworth 407
Big Hard Sun Birch Cottage 462
The Big Lubelski Cerne Abbas 323
Big Nose Kate Tombstone 86
Big Red Ale Crossed Anchors 309
Big Red American Amber Little
    Black Dog 555
The Big Smoke Stout Cat
    Asylum 517
Big Smoke Hive Mind 747
Big Tree Bitter Dunham
    Massey 672
Big Willie Mr Grundy's (Black
    Hole) 463
Billabong Big Bog 688
Bill's Beer Cross Borders 813
Billericay Dickie Billericay 53
Billy Boy Poachers 497
Billy Mill Ale Three Kings 721
Billy No Mates Indigenous 164
Billy's Best Bitter Tollgate 468
Bird Strike Black Box 54
Birds & Bees Williams Bros 837
Bishop's APA Steam Town 193
Bishopric Horsham 272
Bishops Farewell Oakham 38
Bishops Finger Shepherd
    Neame 222
Bison Brown Phipps NBC 505
Bit 'O' 52 Birch Cottage 462
Bit C01n Flipside 517
Bit o' That Don Valley 495
Bitter & Twisted Harviestoun 837
Bitter Brummie Birmingham 434
Bitter Bully Cheddar 362
To the Bitter End Matlock Wolds
    Farm 466
Bitter Entropy Godstone 248
The Bitter Ex Three Brothers 704
Bitter Exe Crossed Anchors 309
Bitter Reality Reality 521
Bitter Seas Northdown 221
Bitter Strikes Back Hartlebury 447
Bitter X Blonde Five Kingdoms 805
Bitter All Nations 389
    Backyard 433
    Big Lamp 719
    Black Hole 463
    Boot (Little) 466
    Brains 738
    Brewsmith 647
    Bridgetown 308
    Bushy's 865
    Cliff Quay 98
    Daleside 554
    Drinkstone 98
    Elmtree 82
    Goose Eye 594
    Grasmere 628
    Hardys & Hansons (Greene
    King) 99
    Hawkshead 628
    Hill Island 703
    Iron Pier 220
    Joseph Holt 673

JW Lees 674
Keswick 629
Kirkstall 594
LAMB 555
Ledbury 382
Nene Valley 505
Okell's 865
Old Pie Factory 416
Otter 311
Quirky 597
Rhymney 747
Roebuck 406
Sandbanks 326
Snowdon Craft 769
Steamin' Billy 480
Tower 407
Uley 346
Vaguely 521
Wold Top 558
Wye Valley 382
Blŵbri Twt Lol 741
Black & Blueberry Beowulf 403
Black Abbots Grafton 518
Black Adder Mauldons 99
Black Angus Porter Craven 553
Black Arrow Battle 258
Black As Yer 'At Glastonbury
    (Parkway) 363
Black Band Porter Kirkstall 594
Black Beauty Porter Vale 174
Black Beauty White Horse 235
Black Bee Mr Bees 99
    Phoenix 675
Black Beerd Newby Wyke 497
Black Boar/Board Break Country
    Life 309
Black Bull Bitter Theakston 557
Black Bull Lager Three B's 650
Black Bull Three B's 650
Black Cat Lady Luck 555
    Moorhouse's 649
Black Celebration Crafty
    Monkey 702
Black Charge Dynamite Valley 286
Black Cherry Mild Kissingate 272
Black Cherry Goldmark 271
Black Claw Odin 865
Black Country Bitter Holden's 436
Black Country Mild Holden's 436
Black Cow Strathcarron 829
    Welland 497
Black Crow Stout Poachers 497
Black Death Fallen Angel 55
Black Dog Porter Drop The
    Anchor 190
Black Dog Elgood's 37
    Loxley 571
Black Dub Wensleydale 557
Black Eagle Eagles Crag 593
Black Fire Towcester Mill 506
Black Flag Mutineers 149
Black Forest Hambleton 554
Black Friday Paradigm 66
Black Galloway Sulwath 806
Black Goddess Meanwood 596
Black Gold Cairngorm 827
    Castle Rock 517
    Copper Dragon 553
    Kent 220
    Stancill 572
Black Hag Cheviot 710
Black Hole Stout Moonshine 38
Black Hole Peakstones Rock 406
Black IPA Incredible 343
    Isca 311

Black Jack Porter Cliff Quay 98
    Milltown 596
Black Knight Ludlow 390
    Rocket 39
Black Lace Tom Herrick's 518
Black Listed IBA Farr Brew 66
Black Llama Broadtown 373
Black Magic IPA Snowhill 650
Black Magic Woman Freestyle 416
Black Mass Abbeydale 568
Black Moor Goose Eye 594
Black Mountain Stout Tudor 748
Black Noise Dorking 247
Black Ops Rother Valley 260
    Taw Valley 313
Black Panther Mill Valley 596
    Panther 85
Black Pearl Milestone 520
Black Pheasant Dark Ale
    Pheasantry 520
Black Pig Wantsum 223
Black Port Blackedge 671
Black Porter Captain Cook 553
Black Prince Porter Bexley 142
Black Prince Olde England
    (Potbelly) 505
    Wantsum 222
Black Ram Stout Kinver 405
Black Road Stout Grey Trees 740
Black Rock Noss Beer Works 311
    Tudor 748
Black Ryeno Crafty Little 532
Black Sabbath Brunswick 463
Black Sail Hesket Newmarket 628
Black Spell Porter Forest, The 342
Black Stag Peak 467
Black Stallion Arundel 270
Black Star Keswick 629
    Phipps NBC 505
Black Sun Potbelly 505
Black Taxi to the Moon Angels &
    Demons (McCanns) 221
Black Troll Tillingbourne 249
Black Volt Shortts 101
Black Wave Vaux 722
Black Widow 8 Sail 494
Black William Adur 270
Black Blackedge 671
    Boss 738
    Castle Eden 702
    Lancaster 648
    Tatton 614
Blackbeerble Stout
    Beerblefish 142
Blackberry Porter Elgood's 37
    Mauldons 99
    S&P 85
Blackbird Pig & Porter 221
Blackeyed Susan Kissingate 272
Blackfoot Brunning & Price
    (Tombstone) 86
Blackhall English Stout
    Hexhamshire 711
Blackheart Stout Yorkshire
    Heart 558
Blackheath Stout Fixed Wheel 435
Blackhorse Brick 143
Blackjack Mild AJ's 433
Blacksmith Handsome 628
Blacksmith's Gold Little
    London 192
Blackwater Mild Crouch Vale 54
Blackwood Grain 83
Blade Prior's Well 521
Blaydon Brick Firebrick 720

BEERS INDEX

Brew Brittania Britt *434*
Brew Springsteen Rock & Roll *437*
Brewers Blend Hanlons *310*
Brewers Gold Blackedge *671*
  Crouch Vale *54*
  Pictish *676*
Brewers Reserve Kent *220*
Brewers Truth Church End *415*
Brewery Dug Arran *798*
Brhubarb Leigh on Sea *55*
Brickworks Bitter Industrial Ales
  (Silver) *468*
Bricky Bang The Elephant *462*
Bridge Best Bitter Bason
  Bridge *361*
Bridge Bitter Burton Bridge *404*
Bridge Copper Ale Bason
  Bridge *361*
Bridge Double Hopped Pale Ale
  Bason Bridge *361*
Bridge Stout Bason Bridge *361*
Bright & Early Wakey Wakey *678*
Bright Black Porter Stubbee *598*
Bright Day Sunbeam *598*
Bright Eyes GPA Dhillon's *435*
Bright Idea Five Kingdoms *805*
Bright Island Northdown *221*
Bright Star Pope's Yard *67*
Bright Fresh Standard *342*
  Otter *312*
Brighton Bier Brighton Bier *258*
Brill Gold Vale *174*
Brim Fell IPA Hesket
  Newmarket *629*
Brisons Bitter Penzance *289*
British Bulldog Westerham *223*
Britt Pop Britt *434*
Broad Water Gold Stow Fen *101*
Broadland Sunrise Humpty
  Dumpty *83*
Broadside Adnams *97*
Broadsword George's *55*
  Tom Herrick's *518*
Brock Bitter Tring *67*
Broken Dream Breakfast Stout
  Siren *165*
Brook Raven Hill *533*
Brother Rabbit Thornbridge *468*
Brown Ale Caps Off *702*
Brown Clough Dancing Duck *464*
Brown Derby Bowler's *36*
Brown's Porter Church Farm *415*
Brune Hawkshead *628*
Brut IPA Peregrine *649*
BS21 Clevedon *362*
Buckden Pike Yorkshire Dales *558*
Buckeye Rooster's *556*
Budding Stroud *345*
Buff Amber Blindmans *361*
Buggane Bushy's *865*
Building Bridges Brewis *710*
Bull Run Bakers Dozen *523*
Bull Village (Hambleton) *554*
Bullion IPA Old Mill *532*
Bullion Freestyle *416*
  Nottingham *520*
Bullseye Langton *479*
Bumble Hole Bitter Olde
  Swan *436*
Bumble Bowland *647*
Bunji Mobberley *613*
Bunk Wakey Wakey *678*
Bunny Chaser Longdog *192*
Bunny Hop Purity *416*
Bunting's Blonde Uttoxeter *407*

Bure Gold Woodforde's *87*
Burke's Special Wincle *614*
Burning Dragon Magic Dragon *760*
Burnthouse Verdant *291*
Bursted Session Bitter Bexley *142*
Burston's Cuckoo Elmtree *82*
Burton Porter Burton Bridge *404*
Business As Usual Derby *464*
Busted Monkey Chapel-en-le-
  Frith *464*
Buster IPA Bowland *647*
Buster Muckle *711*
Buster's Best Flower Pots *191*
Butcher's Bitter Draycott *464*
Butchers Beastly Best Wintrip *448*
Butter Tubs Yorkshire Dales *558*
Butterley Ossett *597*
Butts Pale Ale Ashover *462*
Butty Bach Wye Valley *382*
Buwch Goch Gota (Little Red
  Cow) Twt Lol *741*
Buzz Godstone *248*
Bwgan Brain (Scarecrow) Twt
  Lol *741*
Bwlch Passage Cold Black
  Label *738*
Byker Brown Ale Brinkburn
  Street *719*

C

C Bomb Arbor *340*
C Monster Little Critters *571*
C.O.W Brolly *270*
Cad Leatherbritches *466*
Caerphilly Pale Well Drawn *741*
Caldey Lollipop Harbwr Tenby *780*
Caldi-kolsch Zulu Alpha *748*
Caliburn Tintagel *290*
California Dreaming Hemlock *479*
California Steam Beer
  Draycott *464*
California Wigan Brewhouse *678*
Calm Before the Storm Five
  Kingdoms *805*
Calmer Chameleon Brew York *553*
Camboozedoon 25 Ayr *798*
Cambrian Gold Stonehouse *391*
Cambridge Best Bitter
  Moonshine *38*
Cambridge Bitter Elgood's *37*
Cambridge Gold Elgood's *37*
Cambridge Pale Ale Moonshine *38*
Campfire Hophurst *674*
Candelriggs Drone Valley *465*
Candlewick Torride *469*
Canteen Cowboy Twisted *376*
The Cap Bitter Ampersand *81*
CAPA Elmesthorpe *478*
Capability Brown Rooster's *556*
Cappuccino Stout Titanic *407*
Captain Bob Mighty Oak *55*
Captain Manby Two Rivers *86*
Captain Morrison's IPA Five
  Kingdoms *805*
Captain Smith's Strong Ale
  Titanic *407*
Car Park Cuddle IVO *37*
Caradog Grey Trees *739*
Caramel Stout Grafton *518*
  Tindall *86*
Carfax Horsham *272*
Cariad Bang-On *737*
Carmen Carnival *688*
Carpe Diem Roman Way *506*

Carr Lane Black Label Drone
  Valley *465*
Cart Blanche Kelburn *820*
Cart Noir Kelburn *820*
Cartmel Pale Unsworth's Yard *631*
Cartmel Thoroughbred Unsworth's
  Yard *630*
Cascade IPA Mighty Oak *55*
  Robinsons *676*
Cascade Karma Newt *814*
Cascade Pale Bricknell *532*
Cascade Blackedge *671*
  Gloucester *342*
  Gwaun Valley *779*
  Liverpool Brewing *689*
  Nailmaker *571*
  Saltaire *598*
  Stamps *690*
  Stockport *677*
Cascadia Harbour *287*
Casemate IPA Southsea *193*
Casino Wigan Brewhouse *678*
Cask Ale Mansfield (Banks's) *433*
Cass 2CV Tigertops *599*
Cast Iron Stout Iron Pier *220*
Castle Black Merlin *613*
Castle Gold Tintagel *290*
Castle Hill Dunham Massey *672*
Castle Arundel *270*
Castlerigg Blonde Tirril *630*
Castletown Bitter Bushy's *865*
Cat Nap Barngates *626*
Catbells Hesket Newmarket *629*
Cat's Eyes Darkland *592*
Cathedral Ale Hill Island *703*
Cat's Whiskers Colchester *54*
Caudle Bitter Langton *479*
Causeway Cornish Crown *286*
  Horsham *272*
Cave Man Manning
  (Beartown) *611*
Cavegirl Bitter Kinver *405*
Cavendish Red Roughacre *100*
CCC Chadkirk *672*
Celebration Ale Ulverston *630*
Celebration Maypole *519*
Celestial Love Out There *721*
Cellarman's Stout Moonshine *38*
Celtic Gold Hereford *381*
Celtic Pride Felinfoel *779*
  Sandstone *761*
Cemetery Gates Crafty
  Monkey *702*
Centaurus Stockport *677*
Centennial Bingley *591*
Central Line Red Portobello *150*
Centurion II Corinium *342*
Centurion Pale Ale Parker *649*
Centurion Dow Bridge *478*
Centwealial Milk Stout Weal *408*
Cerberus Stout Fox *83*
Chaff Farm Yard *648*
Chain & Anchor Burnside *789*
Chain Ale Black Country *434*
Chain Reaction Pale Ale Fixed
  Wheel *435*
Chained Oak Peakstones Rock *406*
Chairman Dave Amwell
  Springs *233*
Chalk Stream Ramsbury *374*
  Raven Hill *533*
Challenger Ales of Scilly *285*
  Kingstone *747*
ChamAleon Crafty Little *532*

Columbus Bottle Brook *463*
Come As You Are Nightjar *596*
Comet Newby Wyke *497*
Common Grounds Magic Rock *595*
Common Pale Ale Wimbledon *154*
The Company Consett *702*
Complete Muppetry Two Towers *438*
Complicated Maisie Ayr *798*
Congreve IPA Rocket *39*
Coniston K7 Coniston *627*
Conqueror Windsor & Eton *165*
Conquest Battle *258*
Consett Stout Consett *702*
Consols Mine *288*
Converted Front Row *405*
Cooking Grainstore *523*
Cool Bay Chelmsford *54*
Cool Citra Ainsty *552*
Copper Ale Palmers *325*
Rother Valley *260*
Copper Beacons Brecon (Cold Black Label) *739*
Copper Best Taw Valley *313*
Copper Hop Long Man *260*
Copper Hoppa Wriggle Valley *326*
Copper Jack Grafton *518*
Copper Leaf Wimbledon *154*
Copper Penny Flipside *517*
Copper Plate Irwell Works *674*
Copper 3 Brewers of St Albans *65*
Wrytree *711*
Copperhead Whitewater *854*
Coppernob Tonbridge *222*
Copycat Snowhill *650*
Corbel Eight Arch *324*
Corby Ale Great Corby *628*
Corinium Gold I Corinium *342*
Cormorant Stout Coastline *626*
Corn Du Brecon (Cold Black Label) *739*
Corncrake Orkney *840*
Cornish Best Bitter Castle *286*
St Austell *289*
Cornish Bitter Harbour *287*
Cornish Knocker Skinner's (Goodh) *290*
Cornwall's Pride Tintagel *290*
Corolean Pale Ale Pig Barn *497*
Corvus Squawk *677*
Cosmati Hophurst *674*
Cosmic Black Hole *463*
Cosmonaut Nightjar *596*
Costa Del Salford Irwell Works *674*
Cotswold Best North Cotswold *416*
Cotswold Gold Donnington *342*
Country Bitter McMullen *66*
Country Bumpkin Country Life *309*
Countryman Tonbridge *222*
County Best Exeter *310*
Courthouse Porter New Buildings *479*
Cousin Jack Mine *288*
Coventry Bitter Byatt's *434*
Covert Stealth *375*
Cow Down Stone Daisy *375*
Cowcatcher American Pale Ale East London *145*
Cowgirl Gold Fallen Angel *54*
Cowjuice Milk Stout Breakwater *218*
Coyote Strange Times *677*
Crack Gold Twisted Oak *364*
Crack Hops Twisted Oak *364*
Crackatoa IPA CrackleRock *190*

Cracker Barngates *626*
Quartz *406*
Crackerjack CrackleRock *190*
Craft Pale Boilerhouse (JW Lees) *674*
Crafty Flanker Front Row *405*
Crafty Fox Wily Fox *678*
Crafty Mild Kirkby Lonsdale *629*
Crafty Shag CrackleRock *190*
Crafty Stoat Wibblers *56*
Cragg Bitter Little Valley *595*
Craken Edge Chapel-en-le-Frith *464*
Cranesbill IPA Coastline *626*
Crash on the Hill Black Lodge *688*
Craven Bitter Dark Horse *554*
Craven Pale Ale Craven *553*
Crazy Daze Potbelly *505*
Cregennan Cader *767*
Creme Bearlee Beartown *611*
Crex Squawk *677*
Crib Goch Cold Black Label *739*
Cribyn Brecon (Cold Black Label) *739*
Cricklade Ordinary Bitter (COB) Hop Kettle *374*
Criffel Sulwath *806*
Crimson Rye'd GT *310*
Crispin Ale Mad Cat *220*
Crispin's Ommer Fownes *435*
Crofters FILO *259*
Cromwell Best Milestone *520*
Crooked Hooker Towcester Mill *506*
Crop Circle Hop Back *374*
Cross Stout Four Priests *612*
Crouch Front Row *405*
Crow Black Hattie Brown's *324*
Crow Wobbly *382*
Crowlas Bitter Penzance *288*
Crown & Glory Cheddar *362*
Crown Best Bitter Stockport *677*
Crown Imperial Stout Goacher's *219*
Crows-an-Wra Penzance *289*
Crowstone Leigh on Sea *55*
Cruckhouse New Buildings *479*
Crusader Gold Unsworth's Yard *631*
Crusader Milestone *520*
Cryo Triple Point *572*
Crystal Ship Papworth *38*
Crystal Quartz *406*
Cub Moody Fox *466*
Cuil Hill Sulwath *806*
Cult Leader Anarchy *719*
Cumberland Ale Jennings (Marston's) *406*
Cumbria Way Robinsons *676*
Cumbrian Bitter Carlisle *626*
Cunning Stunt Fuzzy Duck *648*
The Cure Shortts *100*
Cushie Butterfield Firebrick *720*
Cuthberts Fee Bakers Dozen *523*
Cwrw Eryri/ Snowdonia Ale Purple Moose *769*
Cwrw Glaslyn/ Glaslyn Ale Purple Moose *769*
Cwrw Glyndwr Llŷn *768*
Cwrw Gorslas/ Bluestone Bitter Glamorgan *739*
Cwrw Grav Tinworks *780*
Cwrw Gwyn Gwaun Valley *779*
Cwrw Madog/ Madog's Ale Purple Moose *769*
Cwrw Melyn Gwaun Valley *779*

Cwrw Teifi Mantle *780*
Cwrw Ysgawen/ Elderflower Ale Purple Moose *769*
Cwrw Evan Evans *779*
Cwrw'r Afr Serchog (Horny Goat Ale) Twt Lol *741*
Cwrw'r Ddraig Aur Robinsons *676*
Cwtch Tiny Rebel *747*
Cyclops Milton *38*
Cymryd y Pyst Twt Lol *741*

D

Déjà Brewed Snaggletooth *650*
DAD Bang-On *737*
Dafen IPA Tinworks *780*
Daggers Ale Three Daggers *375*
Daggers Blonde Three Daggers *375*
Daggers Edge Three Daggers *375*
Daily Bread Abbeydale *568*
Dainty Eight Arch *324*
Daisy Gold Brightwater *247*
Dale Strider Richmond *556*
Damn Gates Burton *405*
Damned Deceiver Horncastle *496*
Damson Porter Burton Bridge *404*
Dancing Dragonfly Pheasantry *520*
Dancing in the Streets Vale of Glamorgan *741*
Dangerous Brian Guisborough *554*
Dangerous Darren A Bloke Down the Pub (Potbelly) *505*
Danish Dynamite Stonehenge *375*
The Dankness Bullhouse *852*
Danny's Brew Cerne Abbas *323*
Dark Ages Copper Street *323*
Dark Ale Tremethick *291*
Dark Angel Durham *703*
Dark Arts Magic Rock *595*
Dark Denomination Flipside *517*
Dark Destroyer CrackleRock *190*
Dark Drake Dancing Duck *464*
Dark Dunkel Barnaby's *308*
Dark Flagon Wily Fox *678*
Dark Fox Hornes *173*
Dark Habit Guisborough *554*
Dark Heart Mantle *780*
Dark Horse Mild Uttoxeter *407*
Dark Horse Stout Elmtree *82*
Dark Horse Blythe *403*
GT *310*
Hepworth *272*
Keswick *629*
Dark Island Orkney *840*
Dark Knight Hopstar *648*
Tewkesbury *345*
Whitley Bay *722*
Dark Magic Merlin *613*
Dark Masquerade Half Moon *532*
Dark Matter Atom *531*
Bridge *672*
Dark Mild Artefact *97*
Bank Top *671*
Blackedge *671*
Fell *627*
Harvey's *259*
Timothy Taylor *599*
Dark Mode Liverpool Brewing *689*
Dark Moor Kelburn *820*
Dark Munro Swannay *840*
Dark Night Southport *690*
Dark Nights Porter Jolly Sailor *555*
Dark Oatmeal Stout Stockport *677*

Dreigiau'r Diafol (Diablo Dragons) Twt Lol *741*
Dronfield Best Drone Valley *465*
Dronny Bottom Bitter Drone Valley *465*
Drookit Session Wasted Degrees *845*
Drop Bar Pale Ale Tring *67*
Drove Road First & Last *710*
Drover Wishbone *600*
Drover's Return Cotswold Lion *342*
Drovers Arms Yorkshire Dales *558*
Drummer Boy Grey Trees *740*
Dry Bones Wigan Brewhouse *678*
The Dry Road Beeston *81*
Dry Stone Stout Hawkshead *628*
Dryfe Blonde Lowland *806*
DSB – Dolly's Special Beer Urban Island *194*
Dubbel Godstone *248*
Duck Soup Warwickshire *416*
Duffield Amber Tollgate *468*
Duke IPA Swannay *840*
The Duke Ben's *647* Bowler's *36*
The Duke's Return Pig Barn *497*
Dukey's Delight AJ's *433*
Duncansby John O'Groats *828*
Dune Buggy Northdown *221*
Duneham Ale Downham Isle *37*
Dunham Dark Dunham Massey *672*
Dunham Gold Dunham Massey *673*
Dunham Milk Stout Dunham Massey *673*
Dunham Porter Dunham Massey *673*
Dunham Stout Dunham Massey *673*
Dunham XPA Dunham Massey *673*
Dunstable Giant 3 Brewers of St Albans *65*
Durdle Door Dorset (DBC) *324*
Dusky Dark Logan Beck *629*
Dusty Penny Flipside *517*
DV US Deeply Vale *672*
DV8 Deeply Vale *672*
Dynamo Wantsum *223*

E

The Eagle Has Landed Eagles Crag *593*
Eagle of Darkness Eagles Crag *593*
Eagle of Kindness Eagles Crag *593*
The Eagle's Feather Eagles Crag *593*
The Eagle's Jester Eagles Crag *593*
The Eagle's Strike Eagles Crag *593*
EAPA (East Anglian Pale Ale) Humpty Dumpty *83*
Earl de Grey IPA Aitcheson's *531*
Earl Grey Bitter Whim *469*
Earl Grey PA Marble *675*
Earl Grey PA Atlantic *285*
Earls RDA Island *198*
Early-Days Northern Porter Blackjack *671*
Earth Koomor *220*
Earthmover Gold Uttoxeter *407*
Earthmover Uttoxeter *407*
Eas Geal Ardgour *827*

East India Pale Ale Dunham Massey *673* Whitstable *223*
East India Tom Herrick's *518*
East Kent Gold Breakwater *218*
East Star Hop Kettle *374*
Easterly Northdown *221*
Eastern Nights Bollington *612*
Eastgate Weetwood *614*
Easy Life Eight Arch *324*
Easy Pale Citra Stardust *165*
Easy Chadkirk *672*
Eazy Geez Amwell Springs *233*
Ebb & Flow Brewis *710*
Ebb Rock Noss Beer Works *311*
Echo Beach Dovedale *464*
Echo Chamber Alter Ego *462*
Eclipse Clay Brow *647* Navigation *520*
Ed Porter Dove Street *98*
Eddystone South Hams *312*
Edge Hopper Swamp Bog *165*
Edge Kinver *405*
Edinburgh Gold Stewart *814*
Edith Cavell Wolf *87*
Edmonton Best Bitter Beerblefish *142*
Eel River IPA Unsworth's Yard *631*
Eezee Wishbone *600*
Egbert's Stone Copper Street *323*
Egret Great Oakley *504*
Egyptian Cream Nene Valley *505*
Egyptian Goose IPA Thames Side *249*
Eight Million Aldwark Artisan *462*
Eight XT *174*
Eighty Shilling Bellfield *813*
Ein Stein Lymestone *405*
Ekuanot IPA Brewers Folly *323*
El Dorado American Pale Ale Loud Shirt *260*
El Dorado Bridge *672*
Elan Valley Pale Hwgga *753*
Elder Pale Brimstage *688*
Elder Statesman Firebrick *720*
Elderflower Blonde Atlantic *285*
Elderquad Downton *373*
Electric Eye Pale Ale Big Smoke *247*
Electric Landlady Bakers Dozen *523*
Electric Trail Star Wing *101*
Elemental Porter Tempest *802*
Elephant In The Room Bang The Elephant *462*
Elephant Riders Fownes *435*
Elevation Raven Hill *533*
Elevator Guisborough *554*
Eleven APA Blimey! *81*
Elixir Gold Aldwark Artisan *461*
Elizabeth Ale Earl Soham *98*
Ella Ella Ella Beath *832*
Ellensberg Harbour *287*
Elmers Flying Monk *373*
Elsie Mo Castle Rock *517*
Elterwater Gold Langdale *629*
Elysium Amber Ale Chapel-en-le-Frith *464*
Emotional Blackmail Mad Cat *220*
Emotional Support Hamster Nightjar *596*
Emperor Eden River *627*
Empire IPA Spitting Feathers *614*
Empire George's *55*
Emu War Mutineers *149*

Encore Lacons *84*
Endeavour Bingley *591* Captain Cook *553*
Endike Black Aitcheson's *531*
Endless Summer Black Iris *516*
English Ale Tavistock *313*
English Bitter Stardust *165*
English IPA Barnaby's *308* Botley *190*
English Lore Gritchie *374*
English Pale Ale Artefact *97* Castle Eden *702* Woolybutt Brew Shed *533*
English Pale Lakedown *259*
English Standard Yelland Manor *314*
English Stout 4Ts *611*
English Hop Fuzz *219*
Enigma Stealth *375*
Entire Stout Hop Back *374*
Entire Cronx *144* Olde Swan *436*
EPA 100 WHARF *56*
EPA Marston's *406* Pig Iron (Britt) *434* Two Bob *67*
Epic IPA Settle *557*
Epiphany Pale Ale Little *466*
Equator Ridgeside *597*
Equilibrium Consall Forge *404* Deeply Vale *672*
Equinox Aither *516* First & Last *710* Isle of Purbeck *325* Whitley Bay *722*
Eric's ESB Clearwater *308*
Ernest Brightwater *247*
Ernie's Milk Stout Settle *557*
ESB Bason Bridge *361* Fuller's *146* Hop Kettle *374* Tiley's *345*
Essanell Weldon *506*
Essential Treen's *290*
Essex Boys Best Bitter Crouch Vale *54*
Esthwaite Bitter Cumbrian *627*
Estuary Porter Shivering Sands *222*
Et al Beer Ink *591*
ETale Cheviot *710*
Eternal Northern Monk *597*
Ethelfleda Tamworth *407*
Eton Boatman Windsor & Eton *165*
Eve's Drop S&P *85*
Even Keel Keltek *287*
Evening Brown IVO *37*
Evening Star Hop Kettle *374*
Evergreen Serious *676*
Evolution APA Mr Winter's *84*
Evolution Darwin *719* Zulu Alpha *748*
Exam Room Tears Stu Brew *721*
Excalibur Reserve George's *55*
Excalibur George's *55* Merlin *613*
Excelsius Ossett *597*
Excitra Pheasantry *520*
Expedition Ale Clearwater *308*
Expedition Blonde Lord's *595*
Expedition Darwin *719*
Export Light Rhymney *747*
Export Stout Boundary *852*
Export Rhymney *747*
Extra Blonde Quartz *406*
Extra Double Stout Fengate *83*

Fudge Unit Three Fiends *599*
Fuggle Stone Hop Back *374*
Fuggle-Dee-Dum Goddards *197*
Fuggles Eden River *627*
Full Gallop Uttoxeter *407*
Full Measure Porter
 Aitcheson's *531*
Full Moon Chantry *569*
 Hattie Brown's *324*
Full Nelson Hartshorns *465*
 Kelchner *26*
Full Steam Ahead Isle of
 Purbeck *325*
Full Tilt Wriggly Monkey *236*
Full Whack Peerless *689*
Fully Fitted Freight Muirhouse *466*
Fundamental DDH IPA Spectra *821*
Funky Monkey Frome *362*
 Northern Monkey *675*
Funky Town Beath *832*
Funny Farm Blindmans *361*
Furness IPA Townhouse *630*
Fursty Ferret Hall & Woodhouse
 (Badger) *324*
Fusion Hartshorns *465*
Fusioneer Mr Winter's *84*
Fuster Cluck Bang-On *737*
Fyrds Gold Battle *258*

G

Gadds' Black Pearl Ramsgate
 (Gadds') *221*
Gadds' Faithful Dogbolter Porter
 Ramsgate (Gadds') *221*
Gadds' Hoppy Pale Ramsgate
 (Gadds') *221*
Gadds' No. 3 Kent Pale Ale
 Ramsgate (Gadds') *221*
Gadds' No. 5 Best Bitter Ale
 Ramsgate (Gadds') *221*
Gadds' No. 7 Bitter Ale Ramsgate
 (Gadds') *221*
Gadds' Seasider Ramsgate
 (Gadds') *221*
Gadds' SheSells SeaShells
 Ramsgate (Gadds') *221*
Galaxy Australian Pale Ale
 Frome *362*
Galaxy Dream Tindall *86*
Galaxy Hopping Basement
 Beer *341*
Galaxy Bridge *672*
Galloway Gold Sulwath *806*
Gallows Park *150*
Galvy Stout Weldon *506*
Game Changer Facer's *760*
Game Over Leatherbritches *466*
Gamekeeper Wensleydale *557*
Gannet Mild Earl Soham *98*
Garden Kalendar Gilbert
 White's *191*
Garsdale Smokebox Yorkshire
 Dales *558*
Garside Gold Grafton *518*
Gate Hopper Maypole *519*
Gatekeeper Buxton *464*
Gates Burton Ale (GBA) Gates
 Burton *405*
Gatsby Five Kingdoms *805*
Gaucho / Fly Half Twisted *376*
Gem Bath Ales *341*
General Picton Rhymney *747*
Genesis Goody *219*

George Shaw Premium Tipsy
 Angel (4Ts) *611*
George's Best George's *55*
Georgiana Welbeck Abbey *521*
German Ale Altbier Fuddy
 Duck *496*
GFB Hop Back *374*
Ghost Porter Yorkshire Heart *558*
Ghost Ship Adnams *96*
Ghost Ships Whitley Bay *722*
Ghost Town Cromarty *827*
 Twisted Oak *364*
Ghyll Fell *627*
Giggle & Titter Parkway *363*
Gigglemug Bang The Elephant *462*
Gilt Complex Surrey Hills *248*
Gilt Trip Surrey Hills *248*
Ginger Beer Enville *404*
 Fallen Angel *54*
Ginger Brew Bollington *611*
Ginger Ninja Dancing Duck *464*
Ginger Panther Panther *85*
Ginger Stout Angel *433*
Ginger Tinge Stockport *677*
Ginger Weal Angel *408*
GL12 Lucifer *344*
Glacier Beartown *611*
Gladiator Dow Bridge *478*
Gladstone Guzzler Dove Street *98*
Glasgow Cross IPA Broughton *802*
Glitch Electric Bear *362*
Glo in the Dark Twt Lol *741*
Glog Twt Lol *741*
Glorious Devon Isca *311*
Gloucester Gold Gloucester *342*
Glyder Fawr Cold Black Label *738*
GNE Stout Great North Eastern *720*
Go Your Own Way Don Valley *495*
Goat Walk Topsham *314*
Goat's Leap Cheddar *362*
Goat's Milk Church End *415*
Gobble Great Oakley *504*
Gobhar Odhar Ardgour *827*
Gobhar Reamhar Ardgour *827*
Gobhar Shamhna Ardgour *827*
God's Twisted Sister Twisted
 Barrel *437*
Going Off Half-Cocked
 Bespoke *341*
**Gold (Also known as Yella Belly
 Gold)** Batemans *495*
Gold Beacons Brecon (Cold Black
 Label) *739*
Gold Cup Ascot *246*
Gold Dust St Peter's *100*
Gold Muddler Andwell *189*
Gold Rush Blythe *403*
 Cabin *97*
 CrackleRock *190*
 Dynamite Valley *286*
 Lenton Lane *519*
Gold Star Strong Ale Goacher's *219*
Gold Star Phipps NBC *505*
 Shipstone's *521*
 Silhill *437*
Gold 9 Lives *737*
 AJ's *433*
 Ashton *340*
 Backyard *433*
 Bays *308*
 Beech Avenue *759*
 Black Storm *719*
 Bowland *647*
 Brentwood *54*
 Brewsmith *647*

Butcombe *361*
 Cader *768*
 Cairngorm *827*
 Clevedon *362*
 Courtyard *54*
 Dancing Duck *464*
 Davenports *434*
 Exmoor *362*
 FILO *259*
 Gower *739*
 Great North Eastern *720*
 Green Mill *673*
 Isca *311*
 Keswick *629*
 Kingstone *747*
 Ledbury *382*
 Ludlow *390*
 Mersea Island *55*
 Mumbles *740*
 Pumphouse Community *56*
 Ramsbury *374*
 Riviera *312*
 Snowhill *650*
 Stod Fold *598*
 Tatton *614*
 Tewkesbury *345*
 Thwaites *651*
 Triple Point *572*
 Two Bob *67*
 Wild Card *154*
 Wobbly *382*
 Wold Top *558*
 Wrytree *711*
 Wylam *722*
 Yard of Ale *704*
Golden Acre Bexley *142*
Golden Ale Avid *647*
 Chadlington *233*
 Cooper Hill *592*
 Drinkstone *98*
 Isca *311*
 Lister's *272*
 Rhymney *747*
 Tavistock *313*
Golden Bear Wriggle Valley *326*
Golden Best Green Jack *98*
 Jolly Boys *570*
 Timothy Taylor *599*
Golden Bitter Yates' *198*
Golden Boar WHARF *56*
Golden Braid Hopdaemon *220*
Golden Brown Butts *163*
Golden Bud Brampton *463*
Golden Buzzard Leighton
 Buzzard *26*
Golden Cascade Fuzzy Duck *648*
Golden Chalice Glastonbury
 (Parkway) *363*
Golden Citrus Turpin *235*
Golden Close IPA Barsham *81*
Golden Cow Strathcarron *829*
Golden Dart St Annes *390*
Golden Delicious Burton
 Bridge *404*
Golden Eagle Eagles Crag *593*
 Lowland *806*
Golden Embers Inferno *343*
Golden English Ale 3 Brewers of St
 Albans *65*
Golden Fiddle Branscombe *308*
Golden Fleece Cotswold Lion *342*
Golden Gauntlet Castle *285*
Golden Glow Holden's *436*
Golden Goat Little Goat *740*
Golden Goose Goose Eye *594*

Haze Chadkirk 672
Hazed & Confused Loud Shirt 260
Hazy Blonde Ashton 340
Hazy Pale Navigation 520
Three Acre 260
Hazy Vaguely 521
HBA Hattie Brown's 324
HBC Horsham 272
HDA #1 – Ernest Buxton 464
Heacham Gold Fox 83
Head Hunter Sperrin 416
Head Otter 312
Headland Red Wold Top 558
Headlander Southbourne (Poole Hill) 325
Headless Dog College Green (Hilden) 853
Headless RedWillow 613
Headmaster Old School 649
Heads Up Paradigm 66
Heanor Pale Ale Bottle Brook 463
Heart & Soul Vocation 599
Heart Quartz 406
Heartbreak Stout Barefaced 323
Heartland Pennine 556
Hearty Bitter Yorkshire Heart 558
Heathen Abbeydale 568
Heather Honey Black Isle 827
Heavenly Blonde Zest 497
Heavenly Matter Moonshine 38
Heavy on the Chips IVO 37
Heavy Cross Borders 813
Hebden's Wheat Little Valley 595
He's Behind You Thornsett 468
Hedge Monkey Glastonbury (Parkway) 363
Hedgerow Hop Lord Conrad's 37
Hedonism Potbelly 505
Heel Stone Stonehenge 375
Hella Pale St Ives 289
Helles Lager Grasmere 628
Hellhound IPA Clarkshaws 144
Hello Darkness Scarborough 557
Hellstown West Coast IPA Harbour 287
Helm Brewis 710
Helter India Pale Ale Cornish Crown 286
Helvellyn Gold Hesket Newmarket 628
Hen Cloud Wincle 614
Hen Harrier Bowland 647
Henry's Alt Thames Ditton 249
Henry's IPA Wadworth 376
Herald Meanwood 596
Here Comes the Sun Little 466
Hereford Dark Hereford 381
Heresy Bishop Nick 53
Heritage Mild Twisted 375
Heritage Porter RedWillow 613
Heritage XX Firebird 271
Heritage Gentlewood 405
Herkules Hattie Brown's 324
Herm Island Gold Liberation 858
Hermit Crab of Hope Nightjar 596
Heroes Bitter Beowulf 403
Heron Ale Thames Side 249
Hetton Pale Ale Dark Horse 554
Hibernation Stealth 375
Hicks St Austell 289
High Tor Matlock Wolds Farm 466
High Wire Magic Rock 595
Highbridge IPA Glen Spean 828
Highland Cow Strathcarron 829
Highland IPA Cairngorm 827

Highlander Fyne 793
Highway 51 Rooster's 556
Hill Climb Prescott (Hanlons) 310
Hillbillie Five Kingdoms 805
Hillfoot Best Bitter Blue Bee 569
Hills & Holes Kent Pale Bexley 142
Hindmarsh Marble 675
Hinges Chapter 612
Hinkypunk Big Bog 687
Hip Hop Ards 852
Briggs Signature 592
Langham 272
Quirky 597
Historic Porter Hopshackle 496
HLA (Herefordshire Light Ale) Hereford 381
HMS Queen Elizabeth Newby Wyke 497
HMS Quorn Newby Wyke 497
The Hoard Backyard 433
Hobby Horse Rhymney 747
Hobgoblin Gold Wychwood (Banks's) 433
Hobgoblin Ruby Wychwood 236
Hobson's Choice City of Cambridge (Wolf) 87
Hockley Gold Two Towers 438
Hockley Soul McCanns 221
Hocus Pocus Loddon 234
Hodders Panama Grafham 37
Hodgkins Hop Beccles 97
Hodl Ultra Pale Lord's 595
Hoffman Gold Settle 557
Hogget Cotswold Lion 342
Hogsgate Austendyke 495
Holbeach High Street Austendyke 495
Holcombe White Isca 311
Holderness Dark Great Newsome 532
Hole Hearted Fallen Acorn 191
Holistic Paradigm 66
Holmes Stead Farm Yard 648
Holy Cow Bridgehouse 592
Holy Ground Worcester 448
Home Sweet Home Thornsett 468
Homefront Richmond 556
Hometown Pale Roam 312
Honey Ale Atlantic 285
Honey Bee Three B's 650
Honey Blonde Downton 373
Honey Brown Pin-Up 273
Honey Citra IPA Hive Mind 747
Honey Panther Panther 85
Honey Porter Milestone 520
Honey Helmsley 554
Hood Lincoln Green 519
Hoof Farm Yard 648
Hooker Hartlebury 447
Hooky Mild Hook Norton 234
Hooky Hook Norton 234
Hoop Full Circle 720
Hop a Doodle Brew Urban Chicken 469
Hop A Doodle Doo Brewster's 495
Hop Across the Pond Fox 83
Hop Black Wibblers 56
Hop Culture Fine Tuned 362
Hop Devil Rockingham 506
Hop Fusion Maypole 519
Hop Idol Goldmark 271
Hop Kick Mumbles 740
Hop Kitty XT 174
Hop Pocket 1648 258
Hop on the Run Holsworthy 311

Hop Series Pale Cross Borders 813
Hop Star Silhill 437
Hop Stash: Simcoe Nene Valley 505
Hop Till You Drop Derby 464
Hop Tipple Crafty 247
Hop Token: Amarillo Adur 270
Hop Token: Summit Adur 270
Hop Troll Tillingbourne 249
Hop Trotter Potbelly 505
Hop Twister Salopian 390
Hop on Allendale 710
Hop Blackedge 671
Hop On Brew61 446
Hop Deeply Vale 672
Hop On Kings Clipstone 518
Hop Morwell 311
Q Brewery 480
Hopadelic By The Horns 247
Hope & Glory Brentwood 54
Hoperation IPA Arkell's 373
The Hopfather Wye Valley 382
Hophead Brewster's 495
Dark Star (Fuller's) 146
Hopical Kings Clipstone 518
Hopla Left Bank 753
Hopmaster Tamworth 407
Hopnicity Great North Eastern 720
Hopnosis Hopshackle 496
Hopo 2 Rivers IPA Broughton 802
Hopo Proper IPA Broughton 802
Hopo Session IPA Broughton 801
Hoppers Ale Rother Valley 260
Hoppily Ever After Magpie 519
Hoppiness Moor 345
Hopping Toad Castor 37
Hoppit Loddon 234
Hoppy as Funk Chapel-en-le-Frith 464
Hoppy Blonde Aitcheson's 531
Hoppy Camper Campervan 813
Hoppy Hilda Little London 192
Hoppy Jester Magic Dragon 761
Hoppy Little Fish Beerblefish 141
Hoppy Poppy Tamworth 407
Hoppy Red Ale Pig Barn 497
Hops 'n' Honey Skinner's (Goodh) 290
Hopsack Phoenix 675
Hopscotch Old School 649
Hopspur Redemption 151
Hopster Hydes 674
Hoptical Illusion Brass Castle 552
Hoptimystic Hemlock 479
Hopzester Roebuck 406
Horizon Wadworth 376
Hornswoggle Froth Blowers 435
Horny Goat Lord Conrad's 38
Horse & Jockey Full Mash 517
Horse Brass Fresh Standard 342
Horsell Best Thurstons 249
Horsell Gold Thurstons 249
Hotel Barrifornia VOG (Vale of Glamorgan) 741
Hound Handsome 628
Hounded Best Bitter Hairy Dog 271
How Now Brolly 270
Howardian Gold Helmsley 554
Howay in a Manger Mordue (Blue) 719
An Howl Firebrand 286
HPA (Hambrook Pale Ale) Hop Union 343

Jack's Batch 34 Old Mill *532*
Jackdaw Jacaranda *518*
Jaguar Kelburn *820*
Jail Ale Dartmoor *309*
Jaipur IPA Thornbridge *468*
Jake the Snake Mighty Oak *55*
Jamboree East London *145*
James Blonde Kelchner *26*
Jamestown APA Bingley *591*
Jarl Fyne *793*
Jay IPA Magpie *519*
JC Hopstar *648*
Jemimas Pitchfork Glamorgan *739*
Jem's Stout Great Newsome *532*
Jentacular Bakers Dozen *523*
Jericho Blonde Settle *557*
Jerusalem Brampton *463*
Jester Brew 6 Mango IPA
    Goff's *343*
Jester IPA Weetwood *614*
Jester Pale Ale Nailmaker *571*
Jester Big Bog *688*
    Butts *163*
    Stockport *677*
Jet Black Stout Mad Cat *220*
Jet Black Whitby *558*
Jewellery Porter Two Towers *438*
Jex-Blake Mosaic IPA Bellfield *813*
JHB Oakham *38*
Jigfoot Moon Gazer *84*
Jock's Trap Poachers *497*
Joe Solo Pale Ale No Frills Joe *221*
John Barleycorn 8 Sail *494*
John Bull's Best Froth Blowers *435*
Johnny Utah Bad Bunny *462*
Johnsons Blythe *403*
Joined at the Hop Pale Ale Iron
    Pier *220*
Joker IPA Williams Bros *837*
Jolly Beggars Ayr *798*
Jolly Brolly Brown Ale Brolly *270*
Jolly Cascade Blonde Jolly
    Boys *570*
Jolly Collier Porter Jolly Boys *570*
Jolly IPA Jolly Boys *570*
Jorvik Blonde Rudgate *556*
Joshua Jane Ilkley *594*
Jouster Goff's *343*
Joy of Sesh New Bristol *345*
JPR Pale Grey Trees *722*
Ju-bee-lation Three B's *650*
Jubilee IPA Blue Anchor *285*
Jubilee Bewdley *446*
    Kirkby Lonsdale *629*
Judy's Hole Chocolate Porter
    Burwell *36*
Juice Rocket Three Blind Mice *39*
Jumper Moon Gazer *84*
Jumping Frog Pig & Porter *221*
Jumping Jack Flash North
    Cotswold *416*
Jumping Jack Little Goat *740*
Junction 6 Godstone *248*
Junction Sambrook's *151*
Junior Old School *649*
Jurassic Dorset (DBC) *324*
Just Jane Ferry Ales *496*
Just Like Heaven Brewis *710*
Just One More! Nuttycombe *363*
Just Stout Stardust *165*
Justinian Milton *38*

K

K4 Keswick *629*

Kahuna Beartown *611*
Kaldo Chantry *569*
Kaleidoscope Vibrant Forest *194*
Kandata Chapter *612*
Kangaroo Whitley Bay *722*
Karma Citra Wily Fox *678*
Kashmir Salopian *390*
Kazan Twisted Barrel *437*
Kazbek Redemption *151*
Kebab & Calculator Marlix *149*
Keelman Brown Big Lamp *719*
Keepers Gold Hurst *272*
KEN Gan Yam *627*
Ken's Best Bitter Pig Barn *497*
Kennall Vale Pale Dynamite
    Valley *286*
Kennard's Steam Taw Valley *313*
Kent Golding Bitter Kent *220*
Kentish Reserve Whitstable *223*
Kessog Dark Ale Loch Lomond *837*
Khyber Kinver *405*
Kia Kaha! Iâl *760*
Kick-Start Vibrant Forest *194*
Kicker IPA Wigan Brewhouse *678*
Killcat Pale Park *150*
Killer Stout Beowulf *403*
Kilmington Best Wessex *376*
King Billy Bitter Aitcheson's *531*
King Carp Izaak Walton *408*
King George's Bitter Little *466*
King John Andwell *189*
King John's EPA Kings
    Clipstone *518*
King John's Jewels 8 Sail *494*
King Korvak's Saga Fownes *435*
King Neptune Bosun's *591*
King Slayer Humber Doucy *99*
    Loch Leven *845*
King Street Hopshackle *496*
King Keltek *287*
King's Ale Rhymney *747*
Kingdom of Ovingtonia
    Mithril *555*
Kings Crag Muckle *711*
Kings Island Bitter Wickham
    House *497*
Kings Mighty Oak *55*
Kingston Topaz Newby Wyke *497*
Kinky Boots Phipps NBC *505*
Kipling Thornbridge *468*
Kirkstone Gold Tirril *630*
Kirrin Island Hattie Brown's *324*
Kiwi Kick Two Rivers *86*
Kiwi Blackedge *671*
Knee-Buckler IPA Peerless *689*
Knight of the Garter Windsor &
    Eton *165*
Knobbled Horse Blythe *403*
Knock John Shivering Sands *222*
Knockendoch Sulwath *806*
Knocker Up Three*B's *650*
Knocker Upper 3P's *461*
Knowle Spring Timothy Taylor *599*
Kodiak Beartown *611*
Kohatu IPA Brewers Folly *323*
Kokomo Weekday Good
    Chemistry *343*
Kong Gorilla *55*
Kopek Stout Flipside *517*
Kotchin Cronx *144*
Koura Papworth *39*
Kraken Lady Luck *555*
Krakow Angel *433*
KSB (Keswick Special Bitter)
    Keswick *629*

Kumquat May Prior's Well *521*
Kursaal Gold Leigh on Sea *55*
Kursaal Stout Harrogate *554*

L

La Bolsa Coffee Porter Old Mill *532*
La Joll'a Blonde Jolly Boys *570*
La Nossa Signora Harbwr
    Tenby *780*
Lab Session Stu Brew *721*
Lacerta Pope's Yard *67*
Lady Godiva Warwickshire *416*
Lady Marmalade McColl's *703*
Lady of the Lake Glastonbury
    (Parkway) *363*
Lager Brau Potbelly *505*
Lager Snowdon Craft *769*
    Yardsman (Hercules) *853*
Lagonda Marble *675*
Laika Out There *721*
Lakeland Blonde Bowness
    Bay *626*
Lakeland Gold Hawkshead *628*
Lakeland Summit Great Corby *628*
Lakeside MonsteX *479*
Laksaa Pale Odin *865*
Lamanva Verdant *291*
Lamb & Flag Draycott *464*
Lambeth Walk By The Horns *247*
Lambtons Maxim *720*
Lampblack Beer Ink *591*
Lamplight Bitter Big Lamp *719*
Lamplight Porter Longdog *192*
Lancashire Gold Hopstar *648*
Lance Keltek *287*
Lancer Goff's *343*
Land Bier Rigg & Furrow *711*
Landing Gear Black Box *54*
Landlady Dunham Massey *673*
Landlord Dark Timothy Taylor *599*
Landlord Timothy Taylor *599*
Landlords De-Light Lord
    Randalls *519*
Landmark Hafod *760*
Landslide Facer's *760*
Langdale Cumbrian *627*
Langham Special Draught (LSD)
    Langham *272*
Langley Best Leadmill *465*
Langport Bitter Fine Tuned *362*
Langton Spin Peerless *689*
Larksong Mile Tree *38*
The Lash Crooked *553*
The Last Drop Northern
    Monkey *675*
Last Orders Phipps NBC *505*
Laughing Frog 1648 *258*
Laughing Gravy Ulverston *630*
Lavender Honey Wolf *87*
Lawless Village IPA Bellfield *813*
Laxton Original Lord Randalls *519*
Lea Cross Dark St Annes *390*
Leading Lights WHARF *56*
Leap Frog Two by Two *721*
Leaves on the Line George
    Samuel *703*
Ledbury Pale Ale Ledbury *382*
Leezie Lundie Ayr *798*
Legacy Golden Ale Brewpoint
    (Wells & Co) *26*
Legacy Lacons *84*
Legend Dartmoor *309*
    Nottingham *520*
Leggless Jester Cerne Abbas *323*

Legion Dow Bridge *478*
Legra Pale Leigh on Sea *55*
Leila's Lazy Days Leila Cottage (8 Sail) *494*
Leila's One Off Leila Cottage (8 Sail) *494*
Lemon & Ginger Weal Weal *408*
Lemon & Ginger Humpty Dumpty *83*
Lemon Dream Salopian *390*
Lemongrass & Ginger Leatherbritches *466*
Lemonhead Hemlock *479*
Leningrad Chapel-en-le-Frith *464*
Lerwick IPA Lerwick *840*
Let the Dragon See the Wolf Oxford *235*
Level Best Rother Valley *260*
Level Crossing Delphic *163*
Level Up Elusive *163*
Levelling-up Paradigm *66*
Levelly Black Shalford *56*
Levelly Gold Shalford *56*
Leveret Twisted Oak *364*
Leveson Buck Titsey *249*
Leviathan Hopdaemon *220*
LFB (Lunns First Brew) Golden Duck *478*
LGM1 Green Jack *98*
Lhune Airh Kaneen's *865*
Li'l Napoleon Stubborn Mule *677*
Lia Fail Inveralmond *845*
Liberation Suthwyk Ales (Bowman) *190*
Liberator Tindall *86*
Life & Death Vocation *599*
Life on Mars Hammerton *147*
Life Of Riley Wincle *614*
Lifeboat Titanic *407*
Lifeline Brolly *270*
Lifesaver Strong Bitter Mumbles *740*
Lifesaver Salcombe *312*
Lift & Shift Burnside *789*
Ligh Mild Fell *627*
The Light Brigade Ben's *647*
Light No. 2 Harbour *287*
Light Railway Kinver *405*
Light Rale Ashover *462*
Light Harbour *287*
Lighterman Exeter *309*
Lightfoot Theakston *557*
Lightheaded Great British Breworks *554*
Lighthouse IPA Red Rock *312*
Lighthouse Pale Ale New Buildings *479*
Lightning Pale Ale Axholme (Docks) *495*
Lightweights & Gentlemen Irwell Works *674*
Lignum Vitae Grain *83*
Likeley More Bar Tat Red Rose *676*
Lilith's Lust Horncastle *496*
Limehouse Porter Lister's *272*
Limestone Cowboy Iâl *760*
Lincoln Best Poachers *497*
Lincoln Gold Lincolnshire Craft *496*
Lincoln Imperial Ale Small Beer (Black Hole) *463*
Lincoln Red Welland *497*
Lincoln Tank Ale Pheasantry *520*
Lincolnshire Country Bitter Firehouse *496*
Line of Sight Broadtown *373*

Linebacker Leadmill *465*
Lion's Pride Milestone *520*
Lip Smacker Brightwater *247*
Liquid Bread Bakehouse (Warwickshire) *416*
Liquid Gold Goldmark *271*
Liquorice Lads Stout Great Newsome *532*
Lit Beartown *611*
Litehouse Forge *286*
Little Belgium Firebrick *720*
Little Bitter That Brew Foundation (Wincle) *614*
Little Black S Big Hand *759*
Little Bollington Bitter Dunham Massey *672*
Little Dragon Eight Arch *324*
Little Fox Newbridge *436*
Little Hopper Little Critters *571*
Little IPA Liverpool Brewing *689*
Little Jack Old Sawley *467*
Little John Milestone *520*
Little Nipper Brightwater *247*
Little Pearl Brolly *270*
Little Rock IPA Harbour *287*
Little Sharpie Humpty Dumpty *83*
Little Tor Buxton *463*
Little Weed Maypole *519*
Littlemoor Citra Ashover *462*
Liverpool Light Rock the Boat *689*
Liverpool Pale Ale Liverpool Brewing *689*
Liverpool Stout Liverpool Brewing *689*
Llandogo Trow Kingstone *747*
Lleu Lleu *768*
Loaded Bull of the Woods *82*
Local is Lekker Kelchner *26*
Local Treen's *290*
Lock n Load BOA (Brothers of Ale) *446*
Locomotion No. 1 George Samuel *703*
Lode Star Hop Kettle *374*
Lodestar Festival Ale Calvors *97*
Lodona 1862 Bricknell *532*
LOHAG (Land of Hops and Glory) Front Row *405*
Lol! Twt Lol *741*
Lomas Loxley *571*
London Glory Greene King *99*
London Lush London Brewing *148*
London Original Young's (Wychwood) *236*
London Pale Ale Southwark *152*
London Porter Mad Squirrel *66*
Moonface *479*
London Pride Fuller's *146*
London Special Young's (Wychwood) *236*
London Tap New River *66*
London Thunder Rooster's *556*
Lone Rider Tombstone *86*
Lonely Snake Three Blind Mice *39*
Lonesome Pine Ulverston *630*
Long Blonde Long Man *260*
Long Hop Bollington *611*
Long Lane Austendyke *495*
Long Moor Pale Small World *598*
Loop Little *466*
Looper Full Circle *720*
Loophole Clun *389*
Lord Cullens Ruby Elmesthorpe *478*
Lord Have Mercy Draycott *464*

Lord Kitchener Mr Grundy's (Black Hole) *463*
Lord Marples Thornbridge *468*
Lost In Ikea Nightjar *596*
Lost in the Woods Devon Earth *309*
Lost Luggage Black Box *54*
Lost Shadow Burnside *789*
Lotus IPA Ilkley *594*
Lou's Brew Driftwood Spars *286*
Loud Mouth BOA (Brothers of Ale) *446*
Love Monkey Glastonbury (Parkway) *363*
Lovely Nancy Longdog *192*
Lovely Nelly Cullercoats *719*
Lover's Leap Hwgga *753*
Low Tide Southsea *193*
Low Tor Buxton *463*
Loweswater Gold Cumbrian *627*
Lowry Hydes *674*
Loxhill Biscuit Crafty *247*
Loxley Ale Milestone *520*
Lucid Dream Turning Point *557*
Lucifer's Desire Horncastle *496*
Lucky Spence Ale Bellfield *813*
Lucy Strawberry Fields (Big Bog) *688*
Luddite Ale Mill Valley *596*
Lumberjack Brentwood *54*
Lumina Siren *164*
Luminaire Pope's Yard *67*
Lunnys No. 8 Golden Duck *478*
Lupus Lupus Wolf *87*
Lurcher Stout Green Jack *98*
Lush Hopstar *648*
Lushingtons Skinner's (Goodh) *290*
Luvly Little London *192*
Lux Folly *648*
Luxury Porter Chelmsford *54*
Lyme Regis Ammonite Gyle 59 *324*
Lynch Pin Toolmakers *572*

M

M V Enterprise Harbwr Tenby *780*
M&B Brew XI Molson Coors (Brains) *738*
MòR Ish! MòR *845*
MòR Please! MòR *845*
MòR Tea Vicar? MòR *845*
Machlyd Mawddach Cader *768*
Mad Cow Welland *497*
Mad Dogs & Englishmen Irwell Works *674*
Mad Gaz Amwell Springs *233*
Mad Goose Purity *416*
Mad Hatter Weetwood *614*
Mad Jack Ha' First & Last *710*
Mad Jack Papworth *38*
Mad King Sweeney Strange Times *677*
Mad Max Weldon *506*
Mad Monk Digfield *504*
Mad Ruby Leatherbritches *466*
Mad Wolf Wolf *87*
Mad World Beath *832*
Madagascan Vanilla Porter Cornish Crown *286*
Madchester Cream Mighty Medicine *649*
Madre Brolly *270*
Maggie's Leap IPA Whitewater *854*
Maggs' Mild Renegade *164*
Magic Malt Mighty Medicine *649*

Magic Number Carlisle *626*
Magic Potion Bakers Dozen *523*
Magik Keltek *287*
Magnitude Axholme (Docks) *495*
Magnum Mild Muirhouse *466*
Magus Durham *703*
Maharaja IPA Renegade *164*
Mahseer IPA Green Jack *98*
Maid Marian Milestone *520*
Maiden Voyage Bosun's *591*
 Hop Union *343*
Mail Train Stamps *690*
Main Street Best Bitter Downham
 Isle *37*
Main Street Citra Downham Isle *37*
Mainwarings Mild Firehouse *496*
Majestic Mark A Bloke Down the
 Pub (Potbelly) *505*
Major Oak Maypole *519*
Make it Real Pale Little Big
 Dog *496*
Malamute Lord's *595*
Maldon Gold Mighty Oak *55*
Malham Tarn Stout Three
 Peaks *651*
Mallophant Elephant School
 (Brentwood) *54*
Malt Bitter Mumbles *740*
Malten Copper Tipple's *86*
Malthouse Bitter Brancaster
 (Beeston) *81*
Malthouse Acorn *569*
Malty Python Little Critters *571*
Man Up! Manning (Beartown) *611*
Manchester Bitter Marble *675*
Manchester Pale Ale JW Lees *674*
The Mancunian Brightside *672*
Mandarin Candidate Stubborn
 Mule *677*
Mandarina Cornovia Atlantic *285*
Mango Magic Pale Ale
 Nailmaker *571*
Mango Sypian Beowulf *403*
Manhattan Project Nene
 Valley *505*
Manhattan Full Mash *517*
Mannannan's Cloak Bushy's *865*
Manorhouse New Buildings *479*
Mansion Mild Tring *67*
Mantel Buxton *464*
Manx Mild Odin *865*
March Hare Digfield *504*
Marcus Aurelius Milton *38*
Margaret's Field Amber
 Burwell *36*
Mariners Clearwater *308*
Marion Lincoln Green *519*
Market Porter Portobello *150*
 Thornbridge *468*
Mark's Gold Cabin *97*
Marmalade Porter Wold Top *558*
Marmalade Skies Strawberry
 Fields (Big Bog) *688*
Marmalade Fat Cat *83*
Marmoset Blue Monkey *516*
Marquis Brewster's *495*
Marsh Mild Firehouse *496*
Marsh Sunset Romney Marsh *221*
Marsha's Mood S&P *85*
Marshfield Red Tinworks *780*
Marshmallow Unicorn Irwell
 Works *674*
Martello Hop Fuzz *219*
Martyr Bishop Nick *53*

Marvellous Maple Mild
 Brentwood *54*
Mary Celeste Cabin *97*
Mary Jane Ilkley *594*
Marynka Whim *469*
Masala Chai PA Atlantic *285*
Mash City Rocker Rock & Roll *437*
Mash Tun Bitter Leadmill *465*
Masquerade Kelchner *26*
Master Ale Tavistock *313*
Master Brew Shepherd Neame *222*
Mat Black Church Hanbrewery *233*
Matchlock Musket *221*
Matilda's Tears Oxford *235*
Maunsell Shivering Sands *222*
Maverick IPA Brightside *672*
Maverick Deeply Vale *672*
 Fyne *793*
 Vale of Glamorgan *741*
Maximus Maxim *721*
Maybee Maypole *519*
Maybug Kinver *405*
Mayfair Maypole *519*
Mayflower Gold Billericay *53*
Mayflower 8 Sail *494*
 Southwark *152*
Mayfly Bitter Maypole *519*
MC6 – Mash Concentration 6
 Exeter *310*
McFadden Mild Leigh on Sea *55*
McGregors Mild Five
 Kingdoms *805*
Meadowgold Mile Tree *38*
Mean Old Bastard Ben's *647*
Meg's Mild Townhouse *630*
Melford Mild Nethergate *100*
Mellow Yellow Bottle Brook *463*
 Leadmill *465*
Melton Mild Lincolnshire Craft *496*
Memento Mori Strange Times *677*
Memento Siren *164*
Men of Steel Consett *702*
Menacing Dennis
 Summerskills *313*
Menhir Cheviot *710*
Mental Martha Inferno *344*
Meon Valley Bitter Bowman *190*
Meor IPA St Ives *289*
Merc Bro Bullhouse *852*
Mercia IPA Derby *464*
Mercian Shine Beowulf *403*
Merlin's Ale Broughton *801*
Merlin's Gold Merlin *613*
Merlin's Own Zoo *780*
Merlins Muddle Tintagel *290*
Merrie City Atlantic Hop
 Clark's *592*
Merrie City Cascadian Clark's *592*
Merrie City Crystal Gold Clark's *592*
Merry Gentlemen George's *55*
Mersea Mud Mersea Island *55*
Metal Briggs Signature *592*
Metropolis Colchester *54*
 Vibrant Forest *194*
Mew Stone Noss Beer Works *311*
Microball Elusive *163*
Microdose Big Trip *671*
Mid Atlantic Pale Moonface *479*
Mid-Week Bender Nene
 Valley *505*
Midge Maypole *519*
Midnight Bell Leeds (Kirkstall) *595*
Midnight Belle South Oxfordshire
 (SOX) *235*
Midnight Tempter Horncastle *496*

Midsummer Meadow Phipps
 NBC *505*
Mighty Millers Chantry *569*
Mighty Monk Flying Monk *373*
Mild Ale Bathams *433*
Mild Mary Ilkley *594*
Mild Panther Panther *85*
Mild Side Lucifer *344*
Mild Thing Papworth *38*
Mild Banks's *433*
 Buxton *464*
 Davenports *434*
 Hobsons *390*
 Joseph Holt *673*
 Mine *288*
 Penzance *288*
 Shed Beer *650*
 Three Tuns *391*
 Thwaites *651*
 Tindall *86*
 Titanic *407*
Mile Mumbles *740*
Milk Stout Ashover *462*
 Avid *647*
 Bristol Beer Factory *341*
 Fat Cat *83*
 Incredible *343*
 Jolly Sailor *555*
 Pin-Up *273*
 Thurstons *249*
Milk Worm Three Blind Mice *39*
Milky Joe Ridgeside *597*
Milky Way Black Hole *463*
Mill Blonde Mill Valley *596*
Mill Race Towcester Mill *506*
Mill Yard Mild Hawkshead *628*
The Miller's Ale Canterbury
 Ales *218*
Millie George Pennine *556*
Millwright Mild 8 Sail *494*
Mind Bleach Brecon (Cold Black
 Label) *739*
Mind Peroxide Brecon (Cold Black
 Label) *739*
Mine Beer Blindmans *361*
Mine's a Mild Holsworthy *310*
Miner Morwell *311*
Miners Ale Cold Black Label *738*
Miners Imperial Ale Cold Black
 Label *739*
Miners Mild Two Rivers *86*
Minerva Milton *38*
Mines Best Mine *288*
Minnesota North Star American
 Red Ale Draycott *464*
Minotaur Milton *38*
Minstermen Pride Brew York *553*
Mire Big Bog *687*
Mischief Monty's *753*
Misfit Brass Castle *552*
Missenden Pale Malt *173*
Mister Chubb's Renegade *164*
Mister Squirrel Mad Squirrel *66*
Misty Law Kelburn *820*
Misty Mountain Hop Drop The
 Anchor *190*
Mocha Choc Stout Lucifer *344*
Mocha Porter St Andrews *833*
Mockingbird Wheatsheaf *39*
Moderation Malt *173*
Modern Helles Tempest *802*
Moel Famau Ale Hafod *760*
MOHO Mantle *780*
Moletrap Bitter Mauldons *99*
Molly's LoveBeer *235*

North Star Porter Facer's 760
North Star Harbwr Tenby 780
North Wall Hop Kettle 374
Northdown Bitter People's 85
Northern Blonde Brass Castle 552
Northern Brewers People's 85
Northern IPA Hadrian Border 720
Northern Light Orkney 840
Northern Lights Ainsty 552
    Full Mash 517
    Green Mill 673
Northern Pale Ale Three
    Brothers 704
Northern Pale Hadrian Border 720
Northern Soul Briggs
    Signature 592
Northway IPA Firehouse 496
Northwich Pale Ale Hush 612
Norwegian Blue Newark 520
    Parkway 363
Norwich Bitter Fat Cat 83
Nosey Parker Golden Duck 478
    Indigenous 164
Nostrum Amber Aldwark
    Artisan 462
Nostrum Gold Aldwark Artisan 461
Not All Heroes Wear Capes
    Nightjar 596
Not on your Nelly LoveBeer 235
Notorious BIPA St Andrews 833
Notorious D.O.G. Oscars 649
Notorious Bristol Beer Factory 341
Notts Pale Avalanche 504
Now Then Horbury 594
NPA (Netherton Pale Ale) Olde
    Swan 436
NPA (Newark Pale Ale)
    Newark 520
Number 8 Front Row 404
Number One Colchester 54
Nut Brown Ale Felinfoel 779
Nut Brown Hilden 853
    Shipstone's 521
Nut Kin Guisborough 554
Nutcracker Indigenous 164
Nutty 'Brown' Mild Gwaun
    Valley 779
Nutty Ale Cold Black Label 739
Nutty Ambassador Little
    Critters 571
NZ Pale Steam Town 193

O _____

Oak Grain 83
Oaks Barsham 81
Oat Mill Stout Bollington 611
Oat Stout Braemar 789
OatiX Stout Xtreme 39
Oatmeal Stout Brewsmith 647
    Castle Rock 517
    Little Black Dog 555
    Peerless 689
    Southey 152
    St Andrews 833
    Woodcote 448
Obelisk Dunham Massey 672
Objects in Space Ridgeside 597
Oblensky Front Row 405
Oblivion Peakstones Rock 406
Obsidian Draycott 464
    Magic Dragon 761
**Ochr Dywyll y Mws/ Dark Side of
    the Moose** Purple Moose 769
Octane Silverstone 506

Oddfellows Red Aitcheson's 531
Odin Blonde Brightside 672
Odissi Bang The Elephant 462
Off The Hook Hook Norton 234
Off the Lip Papworth 38
Off the Rails Hartlebury 447
Off t'Mill Hopstar 648
OG LoveBeer 235
Old Ale Brolly 270
    Harvey's 259
Old Appledore Country Life 309
Old Barn Twisted Oak 364
Old Bee Three B's 651
Old Brewery Bitter Samuel
    Smith 557
Old Brown Mouse Three Blind
    Mice 39
Old Bushy Tail Bushy's 865
Old Cadger Indigenous 164
Old Carrock Strong Ale Hesket
    Newmarket 629
Old Castle Pale Tinworks 780
Old Chestnut Tonbridge 222
Old Colony 8 Sail 494
Old Crow Porter Digfield 504
Old Dick Suthwyk Ales
    (Bowman) 190
Old Dog Weetwood 614
Old Empire Marston's 406
Old Faithful Tirril 630
Old Forge Bitter Half Moon 532
Old Freddy Walker Moor 345
Old Golden Hen Morland (Greene
    King) 99
Old Growler Nethergate 100
Old Higby Hop Union 343
Old Hooky Hook Norton 234
Old Horizontal Stocks (Welbeck
    Abbey) 521
Old Jailhouse Monty's 753
Old Jock Broughton 802
Old King Coel London Porter
    Colchester 54
Old Knacker Metalhead 711
Old Laund Bitter Reedley
    Hallows 650
Old Leg Over Daleside 554
Old Magic Magic Dragon 760
Old Man Ale Coniston 627
Old Man and the Sea Mighty
    Oak 55
Old Man Long Man 260
Old Market Monk Holsworthy 311
Old Mill Stout Little Eaton (Black
    Hole) 463
Old Moor Porter Acorn 569
Old Oak Bitter Leadmill 465
Old Original Everards 478
Old Peculier Theakston 557
Old Porter Enville 404
Old Prickly Hobsons 390
Old Rasputin Tollgate 468
Old Ric Uley 346
Old Riverport Stout Papworth 38
Old School Bitter Electro 779
Old School Charnwood 478
Old Scrooge Three Tuns 391
Old Scruttock's Bitter Barn
    Owl 233
Old Scruttock's Dirigible Barn
    Owl 233
Old Sea Dog Camerons 702
Old Smithy Porter Settle 557
Old Speckled Hen Morland
    (Greene King) 99

Old Spot Prize Strong Ale Uley 346
Old Stoatwobbler Beeston 81
Old Style Bitter (OSB) Tomos
    Watkin 741
Old Tale Porter Kissingate 272
Old Thumper Ringwood 193
Old Tom Robinsons 676
Old Town Tom FILO 259
Old Wavertonian Spitting
    Feathers 614
Olde Trip Hardys & Hansons
    (Greene King) 99
Oligo Nunk Hollow Stone
    (Shipstone's) 521
Oliver's Island Fuller's 146
Oliver's Light Ale Coniston 627
Omega Cross Bay 648
Omina Piglove 597
Once a Knight Castle 286
One Daisy Ayr 798
One Foot in the Yard Yard of
    Ale 704
One for the Woad Boudicca
    (S&P) 85
One Hop Wonder Battle 258
One Hop Wantsum 223
One Crafty 247
    XT 174
Onslaught Dow Bridge 478
OPA (Organic Pale Ale) Stroud 345
Opaque Reality Wilde Child 599
Oppenchops Northern Whisper 649
Optic Stardust 165
Optimum Deeply Vale 672
Oracle Salopian 390
    Wheatsheaf 39
Orang-A-Tang Gorilla 570
Orange Beacons Brecon (Cold
    Black Label) 739
Orange Wheat Beer Green Jack 98
Orbital Dark Revolution 373
The Ordinary Bitter Anspach &
    Hobday 141
Ordinary Bitter Tiley's 345
Ordinary Pale Tiley's 345
Oregon Pale Weetwood 614
Oregon Trail Elusive 163
Organic Best St Peter's 100
Organic Pale Ale Newt 814
Origin Pale Ale Brewpoint (Wells &
    Co) 26
Origin Dorset (DBC) 324
Original Bitter Davenports 434
    Morland (Greene King) 99
    Tirril 630
Original Blonde White Rose 572
Original Battledown 341
    Brunning & Price (Phoenix) 675
    Butcombe 361
    Hydes 674
    Olde Swan 436
    Shipstone's 521
    Thwaites 651
Orkney Best Swannay 840
Orkney Blast Swannay 840
Orkney IPA Swannay 840
Orsino Newby Wyke 497
Oscar Wilde Mighty Oak 55
Ossian Inveralmond 845
Ostara Big Hand 759
Otakaro NZ Pale Drop The
    Anchor 190
Our Aethel Tamworth 407
Our Best Bitter Farr Brew 66
Our Greatest Golden Farr Brew 66

Pheasant Plucker Bowland 647
    Fuzzy Duck 648
Philanthropist Phil A Bloke Down
    the Pub (Potbelly) 505
Phoenix Gold Byatt's 434
Phoenix IPA Bedlam 270
The Phoenix IPA Drop The
    Anchor 190
Phoenix Pale Logan Beck 629
Phoenix Rising Clarkshaws 144
Phoenix Falstaff 465
    Guisborough 554
    Keltek 287
    Newark 520
Piano Man Blues Draycott 464
Piccadilly Porter Isaac Poad 555
Piddle Piddle 325
Pie In The Sky Old Pie Factory 416
Piffle Snonker Froth Blowers 435
Pig Island Ards 852
Pig on the Wall Black Country 434
Pigeon Ale Xtreme 39
Piggin' Saint Potbelly 505
Pigs Do Fly Potbelly 505
Pigs Ear Uley 346
Pigswill Stonehenge 375
Pike Blackedge 671
    Izaak Walton 408
Pikes Pale Langdale 629
Pilcrow Pale Dorking 247
Pilgrims Ale Barsham 81
Pilot Gig Keltek 287
Pils, Thrills & Bellyaches Stubborn
    Mule 677
Pils Dhu Brew (Stow) 802
Pilsner Barnaby's 308
    Black Storm 719
Pinewoods Pale Ale Harrogate 554
Piney Sleight Cheddar 362
Pink Grapefruit Hambleton 554
Pint Of Avid 647
Pint Marble 675
Pintail Moon Gazer 84
Pioneer Stout Sherfield Village 193
Pirate Bay Cold Black Label 739
Pirate Twisted 376
Pirate's Gold Muirhouse 466
Pirate's Treasure Lady Luck 555
Piston Bob Tydd Steam 39
Pit Black Red Dog 467
Pit Pony Stout Urban Chicken 469
Pit Stop Prescott (Hanlons) 310
Pitch Perfect Fine Tuned 362
Pitch Shifter IPA Goldmark 271
Pitstop Silverstone 506
Pivo Estivo Kelburn 820
PiXie APA Xtreme 39
Pixie Pee Swamp Bog 165
PK3 Stardust 165
Planet Amarillo Harrison's 518
Plastered Pheasant Quantock 363
Plateau Burning Sky 258
Platinum Blonde Byatt's 434
    Mad Cat 220
    Maypole 519
    Milltown 596
Platinum EPA Yorkshire Heart 558
Platinum Blackedge 671
Plato Ridgeside 597
Plautus V Corinium 342
Plockton Bay Plockton 829
Plotline Kettlesmith 374
Ploughman's Lunch 8 Sail 494
Ploughmans Mauldons 99

Plum Porter Elgood's 37
    Harrogate 554
    Nailmaker 571
    St Peter's 100
    Three Peaks 651
    Titanic 407
Plummeth the Hour Old
    Sawley 467
Plymouth Porter Summerskills 313
PMA Moor 345
Poachers Pride Poachers 497
Pocket Rocket Iâl 760
Poco Loco Zulu Alpha 748
POD First Chop 673
Podium Finish Prescott
    (Hanlons) 310
Podsnappery Bang The
    Elephant 462
Poets Tipple Ashover 462
Poison Redscar 556
Poison's Pleasure Red Moon 437
Polar Eclipse Beartown 611
Polar Star Buntingford 65
Polaris True North 572
Polestar Silverstone 506
Polka Hop Sunbeam 598
The Pollinator Hive Mind 747
Polly Donkin Oatmeal Stout
    Cullercoats 719
Polly's Potion Godstone 248
Pommies Revenge Goose Eye 594
Pommy Blonde Botley 190
Pompey Royal Fallen Acorn 191
Pondtail Godstone 248
Pontcanna Pale Well Drawn 741
Pop Up! Cronx 144
Port Jackson Chelmsford 54
Port Nelson Small World 598
Port O' Call Bank Top 671
Port Stout Hanlons 310
Porter Leven Shoals 289
The Porter Anspach & Hobday 141
Porter Black Isle 827
    Black Storm 719
    Bridgehouse 592
    Calverley's 37
    Consett 702
    Cross Borders 813
    Farr Brew 66
    Harbour 287
    Harrison's 518
    Humber Doucy 99
    Larkins 220
    Leatherbritches 466
    Lithic (Cold Black Label) 739
    Loose Cannon 234
    Mile Tree 38
    Quirky 597
    Snowdon Craft 769
    Snowhill 650
    Stancill 572
    Triple Point 572
    Vaguely 521
Porteresque Hophurst 674
Porters Pride Two Rivers 86
Porth Neigwl Llŷn 768
Porth Pilsner St Ives 289
Porthleven Skinner's (Goodh) 290
Portside Teignmouth 313
Post Horn Premium Pale Ale
    Coach House 612
Pothering Fresh Standard 342
Pothole Porter Iâl 760
Potholer Cheddar 362
Potion No. 9 Penzance 288

Pots Bitter Flower Pots 191
Potters' Fields Porter
    Southwark 152
Powder Blue Kissingate 272
Power Gower 739
Powerhouse Porter
    Sambrook's 151
Powick Porter Worcester 448
Próst! Peregrine 649
Practicable and Useful
    Chapter 612
Praetorian Porter Dow Bridge 478
Pragmatic Beermats 516
Prasto's Porter Boudicca (S&P) 86
Pre-Prohibition Cream Ale
    Stubborn Mule 677
Premier Moorhouse's 649
Prentice Five Kingdoms 805
Preservation Castle Rock 517
Pressed Rat & Warthog Triple
    fff 194
Pretoria Wigan Brewhouse 678
Pricky Back Otchan Great
    Newsome 532
Pride & Joy Vocation 599
Pride of England Big Bog 687
Pride of Fulstow Firehouse 496
Pride of Pendle Moorhouse's 649
Pride Pale Farr Brew 66
Pride Front Row 405
Primate Best Bitter Blue
    Monkey 516
Prime Porter Hawkshead 628
Prime Serious 676
Primo Halton Turner 436
Prince Bishop Ale Big Lamp 719
Prior's Pale Prior's Well 521
Priorswell Pale Grafton 518
Priory Gold Prior's Well 521
Priory Pale Gloucester 342
Priory Wood Rauch Burwell 36
Private Idaho Five Kingdoms 805
Progress Pilgrim 248
Prohibition APA Wily Fox 678
Prohibition Kent 220
Project Babylon Pale Ale Gun 259
Prometheus Inferno 344
Promise Ilkley 594
Proof of Concept Harrison's 518
Proper Ansome Clearwater 308
Proper Charlie Parish 479
Proper Grafter Ben's 647
Proper Job St Austell 289
Proper Lager Holsworthy 311
Proper XB Logan Beck 629
Proper Logan Beck 629
Prospect Organic Hepworth 272
Prospect Oxford 235
Pryde Little London 192
PSB Parish 479
Psychotropic Hartshorns 465
Pub Ale: Best Bitter Blackjack 671
Pucks Folly WHARF 56
Pudding Lane Liverpool
    Brewing 689
Puffin Tears Harbour 287
Pugin's Gold Peakstones Rock 406
Pullman First Class Ale
    Hepworth 272
Pulping on your Stereo Nene
    Valley 505
Pulpit Pale Ampersand 81
Pulsar Avalanche 504
Pumphouse Pale Sambrook's 151
Punch Drunk Three Fiends 599

Ribblehead Bitter Settle 557
Riber Gold Matlock Wolds Farm 466
Ribersborg Stout Shivering Sands 222
Rich Ruby Milestone 520
Rider / Three Lions Twisted 375
Ridge Way Raven Hill 533
Ridgeline Kettlesmith 374
Ridgemere Q Brewery 480
Ridgeway Tring 67
Ridley's Rite Bishop Nick 53
Ridware Pale Blythe 403
Riff IPA Clearwater 308
Riggwelter Black Sheep 552
Right to Roam Buxton 464
Ring of Fire Three Kings 721
Ring Tong Plockton 829
Ringmaster Magic Rock 595
Ringneck Amber Ale Pheasantry 520
RIPA Cross Bay 648
Ripper Green Jack 98
Rise Above 80/- Seagate 798
Rising Giant Long Man 260
Rising Star Hop Kettle 374
Ritual Alechemy 812
Riverbed Red New River 66
Rivet Catcher Great North Eastern 720
Riwaka Station Buntingford 65
Road Apple Strong Drinkstone 98
Road Crew Camerons 702
Road Trip Bullhouse 852
Roadie All-Night IPA Signature 152
Roadrunner Bottle Brook 463
Roan Aldwark Artisan 462
Roast Note Stardust 165
Roasted Nuts Rebellion 174
Robbie's Red Adur 270
Robin Goodfellow Papworth 38
Rock & Roll Briggs Signature 592
Rock Ape Poachers 497
Rock Bitter Nottingham 520
Rock Mild Nottingham 520
Rock Steady Bull of the Woods 82
Mantle 780
Rockabilly Shortts 101
Rocket Nun Three Blind Mice 39
Rocket Brunswick 463
Rocketeer Bluestone 779
Rogue Wave Cromarty 827
Rokerite North Pier 703
Rolling Hitch Darwin 720
Rolling Home Red Dog 467
Rolling Maul Snaggletooth 650
Rolling Stone 8 Sail 494
Roman Gold Castor 37
Roman Mosaic Castor 37
Roman Mosaics Weldon 506
Roman Road Towcester Mill 506
Romney Amber Ale Romney Marsh 221
Romney APA Romney Marsh 221
Romney Best Bitter Romney Marsh 221
Romsey Gold Flack Manor 191
Rook Wood Clavell & Hind 341
Room No. 6 Posh Boys 56
Root Thirteen Downlands 271
Ropetackle Golden Ale Adur 270
Rorschach Mr Winter's 84
Rosherville Red Iron Pier 220
Rotten End Shalford 56

Round the Wrekin St Annes 390
Routemaster Red Southwark 152
Royal Oak Bitter Fownes 435
Royal Stag Stout Kings Clipstone 518
RPA (Riviera Pale Ale) Riviera 312
Rubis Horsforth 594
Ruby Duck Fuzzy Duck 648
Ruby Jewel Muirhouse 466
Ruby Mild Harrison's 518
Rudgate 556
Ruby Red St Peter's 100
Ruby Revolution Three Brothers 704
Ruby Ruby Ruby Ruby Crafty Monkey 702
Ruby Sunset Combe 309
Ruby AJ's 433
Quirky 597
Rucked Front Row 405
Rude Best Rude Giant 375
Rude Not To Amwell Springs 233
Rude Pale Ale Rude Giant 375
Rufus Crooked 553
Rum Porter Stamps 690
RumDMC Alechemy 812
Rumour Gower 739
Run Hop Run Rigg & Furrow 711
Rundle Beck Bitter Brewster's 495
Runnen Chapter 612
Running with the Big Dog Six Hills 67
Rupert's Revenge Q Brewery 480
Rush Hour Spitting Feathers 614
Ruskin's Kirkby Lonsdale 249
Russian Rouble Flipside 517
Rustic Tonbridge 222
Rusty Giraffe Welland 497
Rusty Stag Farr Brew 66
Rusty's Ale Godstone 248
Rutland Beast Grainstore 523
Rutland Bitter Grainstore 523
Rutland Osprey Grainstore 523
Rutland Panther Grainstore 523
Rye The Hell Not Chapel-en-le-Frith 464
Ryestone Hornes 173
RYIPA Seagate 798

S

Séance Full Mash 517
S'more Fire Alter Ego 462
S'more Porter Three Brothers 704
SA Gold Brains 738
SA Brains 738
Saaz Pilsner Stardust 165
Sabrina's Dark Ruby Ale Worcester 448
Sabro IPA Brewers Folly 323
Sabro Harrison's 518
Sacrificed Soul Horncastle 496
Saddleback Best Bitter Slaughterhouse 416
Saffron Sun Roughacre 100
Sailing on the 7 C's Navigation 520
St Andrew's Amber Ale Belhaven 813
St Davids Special Gwaun Valley 779
St Edmunds Greene King 99
St George Holsworthy 311
St Leger Gold Stocks (Welbeck Abbey) 521

St Margaret's Ale Pumphouse Community 56
St Mary's Mild Q Brewery 480
Saint Petersburg Imperial Russian Stout Thornbridge 468
Saints Reserve Premium English Ale Roughacre 100
Saison d'Etre Papworth 39
Saison Langham 272
Salcombe Gold Salcombe 312
Salem Porter Batemans 495
Salt Mine Stout Wintrip 448
Saltwick Nab Whitby 558
Salvation Charnwood 478
Salvation! Session IPA Blackjack 671
Samson Maxim 721
San Francisco Conwy 768
Sanctuary Pale Ale Camerons 701
Sanctuary Applecross 826
Sand House Doncaster 569
Sand in the Wind Bottle Brook 463
Sand Martin Hatherland 310
Sand Storm Cold Black Label 738
Sandgrounder Bitter Southport 690
Sandpiper Light Ale Brimstage 688
Sandstone Edge Sandstone 761
Santa Fe Tombstone 86
Saorsa Blond Ale Seagate 798
Sapphire Dancing Duck 464
Saracen Pilgrim 249
Sargeant's Special Ale Uttoxeter 407
Satan Session Bull of the Woods 82
Satan's Fury Horncastle 496
Satan's Little Helper Little Goat 740
Saved by the Bell Bespoke 341
Savinjski Chapel-en-le-Frith 464
Saviour Navigation 520
Sawley Stout Birch Cottage 462
Saxon Bronze Alfred's 189
Saxon Gold Copper Street 323
Saxon Red Ale Parker 649
SaXquatch Xtreme 39
SB Special Old Vicarage 630
SBA Donnington 342
Scafell Blonde Hesket Newmarket 629
Scapa Special Swannay 840
Scapegoat Little Goat 740
Pennine 556
Scaramanga Extra Pale Gun 259
Scarborough Fair IPA Wold Top 558
Scarecrow Bitter Brimstage 688
Scary Hairy Export Leatherbritches 466
Schiehallion Harviestoun 837
Scholar Oxford 235
Schooner Black Dog (Hambleton) 554
Captain Cook 553
Schrodingers Cat Atom 531
Schwarz Rose Horsforth 594
Scottie Stout Seagate 798
Scotts 1816 Copper Dragon 553
Scoundrel Leatherbritches 466
Tydd Steam 39
Scrabo Gold Ards 852
Scramasax Copper Street 323
Scrawler Beer Ink 591
Screaming Dwarf Red Moon 437
Screaming Queen Thames Ditton 249

Techno Briggs Signature *592*
Tedi Boy Poachers *497*
Teeter Chapter *612*
Telegram Neighbourhood *613*
Telegraph Session IPA Crafty
  Monkey *702*
Tell No Tales Bosun's *591*
Tempest Bosun's *591*
Templer Teignmouth *313*
Tempo Wigan Brewhouse *678*
Ten DDH APA Cryo Blimey! *81*
Ten Fifty Grainstore *523*
Tenfoot Yorkshire Brewhouse *533*
Tent Zapato *600*
Tequila Blonde Bridgehouse *592*
Terminus George Samuel *703*
Tern IPA Bowness Bay *626*
Tether Blond Wharfe
  (Hambleton) *554*
Tetherdown Wheat Saison
  Muswell Hillbilly *149*
Tetley Bitter Tetley
  (Camerons) *702*
Tetley Gold Tetley (Camerons) *702*
Tewdric's Tipple Kingstone *747*
Texas Cleggy Whitley Bay *722*
Texas Jack Tombstone *86*
Textbook Old School *649*
THAIPA Hill Island *703*
That Old Rope Chapter *612*
That Teme Valley *447*
There's Something in the Water
  Beer Hut *852*
Thick as Thieves Sperrin *416*
Thieving Rogue Magpie *519*
Third Party Sperrin *416*
Thirst Aid Kit Rock & Roll *437*
Thirst Aid Bang-On *737*
Thirst Celebration Keswick *629*
Thirst of Many GT *310*
Thirst Quencher Keswick *629*
Thirst Rescue Keswick *629*
Thirst Run Keswick *629*
Thirstquencher Spitting
  Feathers *614*
Thirsty Blonde Teignworthy *313*
Thirsty Dog Newt *814*
Thirsty Moon Phoenix *675*
Thirsty Walker Dove Street *98*
Thirteen Blimey! *82*
Thirty Three Brighton Bier *258*
This is the Modern Weal Weal *408*
This Splendid Ale Facer's *760*
This Teme Valley *447*
Thomas Lift Langton *479*
Thomas Sykes Burton Bridge *404*
Thoroughbred IPA Hambleton *554*
Thousand Yard Stare Rooster's *556*
Three & Sixpence Twisted *375*
Three Amigos Snaggletooth *650*
Three Brewers Blonde 3 Brewers
  of St Albans *65*
Three Counties East Anglian Best
  Bitter Roughacre *100*
Three Erics St Annes *390*
Three Swords Kirkstall *594*
Three Tails Boudicca (S&P) *85*
Three XT *174*
ThreeOneSix Grain *83*
Thriller Cappuccino Porter
  Glastonbury (Parkway) *363*
Through & Off Fixed Wheel *435*
Thrupenny Bitter Phipps NBC *505*
Thunderbird Glamorgan *739*

Thunderbridge Stout Small
  World *598*
Thurlton Gold People's *85*
Thurstein Pilsner Coniston *627*
Tick Tock Muirhouse *466*
Tickety-Boo Indigenous *164*
Tickle Muckle *711*
Tidal Pool Northdown *221*
Tidy Bang-On *737*
Tiffield Thunderbolt Great
  Oakley *504*
Tiffin Gold Kirkby Lonsdale *629*
Tiger Rut Millstone *675*
Tiger Tom Ruby Mild Cerne
  Abbas *323*
Tiger Everards *478*
Tigers Tail Milltown *596*
Tight Bar Steward
  Elmesthorpe *478*
Tiller Pin Wishbone *600*
Tilt S&P *85*
Tilted Pieces Chapter *612*
Time Lapse Good Chemistry *343*
Timeline Kettlesmith *374*
Tin Plate Irwell Works *674*
Tinder Box Inferno *343*
Tinderbox IPA Fell *627*
Tinners Tipple Golden Duck *478*
Tiny Pixie Wishbone *600*
Tip Top Citra London Beer Lab *148*
Tipsy Fisherman Steamin' Billy *480*
Tiptoe Stealth *375*
Tiramisu Stout Sussex Small
  Batch *273*
Tiramisu Horbury *594*
Titanium Quantock *363*
Titus Saltaire *598*
Tizzie Whizie Great Corby *628*
TNT IPA Dynamite Valley *286*
Tod's Blonde Little Valley *595*
Tollbridge Porter Old Sawley *467*
Tolly Roger Cliff Quay *98*
Tom Cat Fat Cat *83*
Tom, Dick and Harry Escape *673*
Tom Long Stroud *345*
Tomahawk Exeter *309*
Tommy the Miller Monkey
  House *711*
Tonkoko Brew York *553*
Too Wet To Wo Red Rose *676*
Toon Broon Firebrick *720*
Top Dog Oscars *649*
Top Knot Handsome *628*
Top Notch Brightwater *247*
Top of the Hops Draycott *464*
Topaz Blonde S&P *85*
Topsail Bays *308*
Totty Pot Cheddar *362*
Touch Front Row *405*
Toujours Gyle 59 *324*
Tournament Goff's *343*
Tower Blonde Darkland *592*
Town Crier Hobsons *390*
Towy Tiger Zoo *780*
TPL Brightwater *247*
TPP (The People's Poet)
  Marlix *149*
Trade Star Firebrick *720*
Trade Winds Cairngorm *827*
Traditional (North) Brunning &
  Price (Brightside) *672*
Traditional Ale Larkins *220*
  Tonbridge *222*
Traditional Bitter Old Mill *532*

Traditional Porter Gwaun
  Valley *779*
Traditional Sussex Bitter
  Hepworth *272*
Traditional Butts *163*
Trafalgar Horsham *272*
Tranquility Mr Winter's *84*
Trapper's Hat Bitter Brimstage *688*
Travelling Light George
  Samuel *703*
Trawlerboys Best Bitter Green
  Jack *98*
Treacle Miner's Tipple Red
  Rose *676*
Treehouse Marmalade IPA New
  Buildings *479*
Trembling Rabbit Mild
  Poachers *497*
Trenchman's Hop Godstone *248*
Trent Bridge Inn Ale
  Nottingham *520*
Tri State Bingley *591*
Tri-ball Sulwath *806*
Tribune Roman Way *506*
Tribute St Austell *289*
Trident Scarborough *557*
Trig Point Cheviot *710*
Trigger Musket *221*
Trilogy Three Brothers *704*
Trinity Oxford *235*
  Redemption *151*
Trink Penzance *289*
Trinnacle Millstone *675*
Triple B Grainstore *523*
Triple Blond Peerless *689*
Triple Champion 1648 *258*
Triple Choc Saltaire *598*
Triple Chocolate Stout
  Nailmaker *571*
Triple Goat IPA Hornes *173*
Triple Goat Pale Ale Hornes *173*
Triple Goat Porter Hornes *173*
Triple Hop Xtra-IPA Xtreme *39*
Triple Hop Blue Bee *569*
  Brunswick *463*
Triple S Untapped *748*
Triple XXX Langham *272*
Triskellion Bushy's *865*
Trooper Robinsons *676*
Tropic Ale Kent *220*
Tropical Pale Liverpool
  Brewing *689*
  Navigation *520*
TropicAle Avid *647*
Trout Tickler Poachers *497*
True Grit Millstone *675*
Trumpington Tipple Moonshine *38*
Trunk Koomor *220*
Trusty Steed Bowler's *36*
Try Front Row *405*
Tubthumper 3P's *461*
Tuck Lincoln Green *519*
Tucktonia Drop The Anchor *190*
Tudor Rose Brampton *463*
Tumble Home Cliff Quay *98*
Tumbledown Dick St Annes *390*
Tunnel Vision Godstone *248*
Turbulent Priest Wantsum *223*
Turning Tides Brewis *710*
Tushkar Lerwick *840*
TVO 54 Farm Yard *648*
Twa Dugs Lowland *806*
TwentyFourSeven Rooster's *556*
Twin Falls Small World *598*
Twin Parallel Mr Winter's *84*

West Coast IPA Battledown 341
  Fengate 83
  Phoenix 675
  Steam Town 193
West Coast Pale Ale Silver 468
West Coast Pale Empire 593
West Coast Red Hesket
  Newmarket 629
West Coast Session IPA
  Firebrand 286
West Coast Blackedge 671
West Highland Way Loch
  Lomond 837
West Pier Brighton Bier 258
Westcountry IPA Bridgetown 308
Westward Ho! Summerskills 313
Westway Pale Ale Portobello 150
Wey-Aye P.A. Firebrick 720
Whakahari Purple Moose 769
  Tillingbourne 249
Whapweasel Hexhamshire 711
What the Fox's Hat Church End 415
What Makes Larry Happy Bang
  The Elephant 462
What What? Peregrine 649
WHB (White Horse Bitter) White
  Horse 235
Wheat Ear Full Mash 517
Wheat Storm Inferno 343
Wheelie Pale Fixed Wheel 435
Whernside Pale Ale Three
  Peaks 651
Wherry Woodforde's 87
Whimble Gold Radnorshire 753
Whin Sill Blonde Muckle 711
Whispering Grass Papworth 38
Whistle Belly Vengeance
  Summerskills 313
Whistlin' Dixie Full Mash 517
Whitby Abbey Ale Black Dog
  (Hambleton) 554
Whitby Whaler Whitby 558
White Boar Village
  (Hambleton) 554
White Feather Brunswick 463
White Gold Durham 703
White Hot Consett 702
White Knight Goff's 343
White Lion Empire 593
White Monk Phoenix 675
White Nancy Bollington 611
White Rabbit Rockingham 506
White Rat Ossett 597
White Sea Newby Wyke 497
White Squall Newby Wyke 497
White Star Titanic 407
White Swan Pale Ale Thames
  Side 249
White Witch Moorhouse's 649
White Wolf Deeply Vale 672
  Little Critters 571
White Enville 404
Whiteout Cromarty 827
The Whitfield Citrabolt
  Papworth 38
Whitstable Bay Pale Ale Shepherd
  Neame 222
Wholesome Stout Wye Valley 382
Whoopass Avid 647
Whoosh Untapped 748
Whopper Tamworth 407
Wibbly Wallaby Wincle 614
Wicked Blonde Horncastle 496
Wide to Gauge Broadtown 373

The Wife of Bath's Ale Canterbury
  Ales 218
Wigan Junction Wigan
  Brewhouse 678
Wight Gold Island 198
Wight Knight Island 198
Wight Squirrel Goddards 197
Wild Bill Hiccup Wildcraft 87
Wild Blonde South Hams 312
Wild Boar Slaughterhouse 416
Wild Caribbean Wildcraft 87
Wild Cat IPA Fat Cat 83
Wild Coast Chelmsford 54
Wild Eye P.A. Wildcraft 87
Wild Heaven Arundel 270
Wild Norfolk Wildcraft 87
Wild One Wildcraft 87
Wild Orchid Brightwater 247
Wild Rhino Burnside 789
Wild Ride Wildcraft 87
Wild Stallion Wildcraft 87
Wild Summer Wildcraft 87
Wild Swan Thornbridge 468
Wild Un-Bongo Wildcraft 87
Wild Weekend Wildcraft 87
Wild Wood Twisted Oak 364
  Wildcraft 87
Wild Ennerdale 627
Wildcat Cairngorm 827
Wilde East Coast Pale Ale
  Bedlam 270
Wildern Botley 190
Wildwood Mile Tree 38
Will O the Wisp Big Bog 688
Will-o'-the-Wisp Black Metal 832
William Mucklow's Dark Mild
  Bewdley 446
Wills Neck Quantock 363
Wiltshire Gold Arkell's 373
Wily Ol' Fox WHARF 56
Win-win Paradigm 66
To the Winchester Nightjar 596
Windermere IPA Tirril 630
Windermere Pale Hawkshead 628
Windjammer Padstow 288
Windmill Best Bitter New
  Buildings 479
Windmill Bitter 8 Sail 494
Windmill Stout Birch Cottage 462
Windmill Wheat Two Rivers 86
Windmill Weldon 506
Windrush Ale North Cotswold 416
Windsor Knot Windsor & Eton 165
Windy Miller 8 Sail 494
On The Wing Ampersand 81
Wingding Sociable 447
Wingman Flying Monk 373
Winkle Picker Whitstable 223
Winter Ale Mile Tree 38
Winter Gold Newark 520
Winter Hill Northern Monkey 675
Winter Porter Snowhill 650
Wipeout Little Ox 234
Witch Way Home Wookey 364
Witchfinder General Kinver 405
Withens Pale Little Valley 595
The Wizard Merlin 613
Wizard's Ruin Shadow Bridge 497
Woah Man Manning
  (Beartown) 611
Wobbly Bob Phoenix 675
Wobbly Weasel Firehouse 496
Woild Moild Wolf 87
Woke Paradigm 66
Wolds ESB Stow Fen 101

Wolds Way Wold Top 558
Wolf Ale Wolf 87
Wolf Bite APA Crafty Little 532
Wolf in Sheep's Clothing Wolf 87
Wolf Allendale 710
  Windswept 790
Wolfcatcher Prior's Well 521
Wolfenbrau Darkland 592
Wonderland IPA New Bristol 345
Woodcock's Relish Nene
  Valley 505
Wooden Ships Neptune 689
Woodman Pale Ale Firehouse 496
Woodstock Bull of the Woods 82
Woody's Bark Billericay 53
Woolly Bugger Izaak Walton 408
Worcestershire Sway/ 2857
  Bewdley 446
Worcestershire Way Bewdley 446
Workie Mordue (Blue) 719
World's End Delphic 163
Worth the Wait Beeston 81
Worthington's Bitter Molson Coors
  (Brains) 738
Worthog Green Jack 98
Wotever Next? Teme Valley 447
Wot's Occurring Great Oakley 504
Wotton Hop Project Lucifer 344
WPA (Welsh Pale Ale) Evan
  Evans 779
Wrangler Stonehouse 391
Wrecker Evan Evans 779
Wreckless RedWillow 613
Wrench Shiny 467
WRU IPA Brecon (Cold Black
  Label) 739
Wryneck Rye IPA Thames Side 249
WSB 4Ts 611
Wuffa Beowulf 403
Wybar Hop Shed 447

X

X Mild (Dark) LAMB 555
X Mild LAMB 555
X No. 1 Moonface 479
XB Batemans 495
  Theakston 557
XK Dark Byatt's 434
XL Bitter Burton Bridge 404
XL Mild Burton Bridge 404
XPA Five Points 145
  Tatton 614
  Woodcote 448
Xplorer Pale Ale Xtreme 39
Xporter Xtreme 39
XTRA Fudge Stout Mill Valley 596
XX Crooked 553
XXX Three Tuns 391
XXXB Batemans 495

Y

Y Brawd Houdini Llŷn 768
Yabba Dabba Doo Little Ox 234
Yachtsmans Ale Island 198
Yakima Gold Crouch Vale 54
Yakima Valley Arbor 340
Yammerhouse Northern
  Whisper 649
Yamoto Newby Wyke 497
Yankee Doodle Nanny Little
  Goat 740
Yankee Rooster's 556
Yard Dog Brown Ale Yard of
  Ale 704

Readers' recommendations

Suggestions for pubs to be included or excluded

All pubs are regularly surveyed by local branches of the Campaign for Real Ale to ensure they meet the standards required by the *Good Beer Guide*. If you would like to comment on a pub already featured, or on any you think should be featured, please fill in the form below (or a copy of it), and send it to the address indicated. Alternatively, email **gbgeditor@camra.org.uk**. Your views will be passed on to the branch concerned. Please mark your envelope/email with the county where the pub is, which will help us to direct your comments efficiently.

Pub name:

Address:

Reason for recommendation/criticism:

Pub name:

Address:

Reason for recommendation/criticism:

Pub name:

Address:

Reason for recommendation/criticism:

Your name and address:

Please send to: [Name of county] Section, Good Beer Guide,
230 Hatfield Road, St Albans, Hertfordshire AL1 4LW

Readers' recommendations

Suggestions for pubs to be included or excluded

All pubs are regularly surveyed by local branches of the Campaign for Real Ale to ensure they meet the standards required by the *Good Beer Guide*. If you would like to comment on a pub already featured, or on any you think should be featured, please fill in the form below (or a copy of it), and send it to the address indicated. Alternatively, email **gbgeditor@camra.org.uk**. Your views will be passed on to the branch concerned. Please mark your envelope/email with the county where the pub is, which will help us to direct your comments efficiently.

Pub name:

Address:

Reason for recommendation/criticism:

Pub name:

Address:

Reason for recommendation/criticism:

Pub name:

Address:

Reason for recommendation/criticism:

Your name and address:

Please send to: [Name of county] Section, Good Beer Guide,
230 Hatfield Road, St Albans, Hertfordshire AL1 4LW

HOW BEER IS BREWED

The brewer's art sees raw ingredients transformed into a wide variety of styles of beer. Follow their journey from field to glass with this general look at how beer is brewed.

THE KEY INGREDIENTS OF BEER

While brewers will experiment and make use of the cornucopia of ingredients available to them, there are four key elements most beers have in common: water, yeast, malt and hops, although, increasingly brewers are playing with extra ingredients that impart unusual and exciting flavours, aromas or consistency into a beer. Lactose, and heather, for example, have historically been used as additions, but more and more brewers are now employing honey, flowers, spices, fruits, and even meat in specialty ales.

Differing preparation methods, and varietals can create a spectrum of beer – from the very pale, to the near black; from clean, simple aromas, to deep coffee notes, or a fruity punch on the nose; and gentle, sessionable flavours that comfort the palate, to those that assault and challenge your taste buds.

Some breweries will have their own specific way of doing things, and each brewery set-up is individual, but the process is broadly the same. Use the flow chart overleaf to discover how brewers take the four key ingredients below and use them to create one of the most diverse drinks on the planet.

MALT

The mix of malts used in making a beer contribute to the colour, flavour and strength of the beer. Malted barley is most common, but other grains, such as wheat, oats or rye can be used. Once harvested, maltsters steep barley in water to absorb moisture, then spread it on heated floors or inside rotating drums where it will start to germinate.
It is then kilned to dry. The temperature determines the type of malt produced – from pale, through to black. Common flavours and aromas derived include Ovaltine, oatmeal biscuits, Ryvita, almonds/nuts, honey, butterscotch, caramel, tobacco and vanilla.

HOPS

Hops can be used either as dried whole flowers or ground and compressed into pellets. Hops – via their oils and resins – impart aroma and flavour (including bitterness) into a beer, and are added into the copper/kettle, but can also be added later in the process. 'Dry-hopping', for example, is the process of adding a small amount of hops to a cask before it leaves the brewery en route to the pub, for additional aroma. Delicate aromas that can be destroyed during the boil can be retained in this way. While New World hops have become increasingly popular for their tropical fruit explosion in recent decades, UK hops provide the basis of more traditional beers.

◍ WATER

Water used for the brewing process is called liquor. Pure water can come from springs, bore holes or from the public supply. And while some breweries will treat their water to achieve a certain profile (adding sulphates such as gypsum and magnesium), or to remove potential off-flavour-causing compounds, others have embraced the natural, distinct quality of the local water – such as world-renowned Burton water. This water trickles through bands of gypsum and gives the resulting beer the world-famous, sought-after 'Burton snatch'.

⚗ YEAST

Every brewery will have its own yeast culture and often this will be a closely guarded asset. Yeast are living organisms that consume sugars, turning them into alcohol and carbon dioxide. Traditionally most yeast used in UK beer production would have been 'ale yeast' which rises to the surface during fermentation and is therefore known as 'top-fermenting'. Other commonly-used yeasts are lager yeast, known as 'bottom-fermenting', and wild yeasts which create 'spontaneous fermentation', when beer in open vats is exposed to wild yeast in the air. Yeast produces natural chemical compounds called esters that give off aromas reminiscent of apples, oranges, pear drops, banana, liquorice, molasses and, in especially strong beers, fresh leather.

START

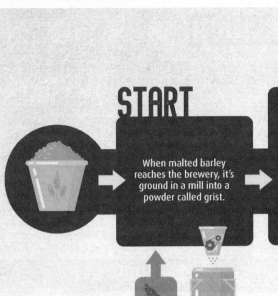

When malted barley reaches the brewery, it's ground in a mill into a powder called grist.

Grist and pure hot water, also called liquor, flow into the mash tun, where the porridge-like mixture of grain and water starts the brewing process.
The mixture is left to stand in the mash tun for around two hours, and during that time enzymes in the malt convert the remaining starch into fermentable sugar.

Malt mill

Mash tun   Liquor tank

Casks have to be vented to allow some of the natural gas to escape. A cask has two openings: a bung at the flat end where a tap is inserted to serve the beer; and a shive hole on top. A soft porous peg of wood, known as a spile or peg, is knocked into the shive, enabling some of the CO_2 to escape. As fermentation dies down, the soft spile is replaced after 24 hours by a hard one that leaves some gas in the cask: this gives the beer its natural sparkle, known as 'condition'.
Inside the cask, finings sink to the bottom, attracting the yeast in suspension.

When the publican is satisfied that the beer has 'dropped bright', plastic tubes or 'lines' are attached to the tap and the beer is drawn by a suction pump activated by a handpump on the bar. Some pubs and beer festivals may serve the beer straight from the cask.

FINISH

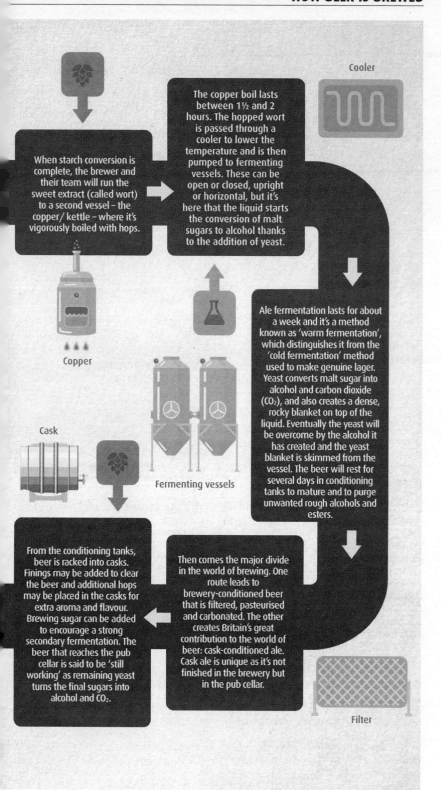

When starch conversion is complete, the brewer and their team will run the sweet extract (called wort) to a second vessel – the copper/ kettle – where it's vigorously boiled with hops.

The copper boil lasts between 1½ and 2 hours. The hopped wort is passed through a cooler to lower the temperature and is then pumped to fermenting vessels. These can be open or closed, upright or horizontal, but it's here that the liquid starts the conversion of malt sugars to alcohol thanks to the addition of yeast.

Cooler

Copper

Cask

Fermenting vessels

Ale fermentation lasts for about a week and it's a method known as 'warm fermentation', which distinguishes it from the 'cold fermentation' method used to make genuine lager. Yeast converts malt sugar into alcohol and carbon dioxide (CO_2), and also creates a dense, rocky blanket on top of the liquid. Eventually the yeast will be overcome by the alcohol it has created and the yeast blanket is skimmed from the vessel. The beer will rest for several days in conditioning tanks to mature and to purge unwanted rough alcohols and esters.

From the conditioning tanks, beer is racked into casks. Finings may be added to clear the beer and additional hops may be placed in the casks for extra aroma and flavour. Brewing sugar can be added to encourage a strong secondary fermentation. The beer that reaches the pub cellar is said to be 'still working' as remaining yeast turns the final sugars into alcohol and CO_2.

Then comes the major divide in the world of brewing. One route leads to brewery-conditioned beer that is filtered, pasteurised and carbonated. The other creates Britain's great contribution to the world of beer: cask-conditioned ale. Cask ale is unique as it's not finished in the brewery but in the pub cellar.

Filter

BREWERIES OVERVIEW

The mayhem goes on. The long shadow cast by Covid, lockdowns and energy and cost-of-living crises has had a shocking impact on pubs and breweries.

In 2022, 97 breweries and some 200 pubs closed. Even more breweries pulled down the shutters in 2023. Pubs continue to shut at a rate of knots – 150 in the first six months of 2023.

A number of independent breweries fought with great tenacity to survive, but in the end had to call in the administrators, overwhelmed by the costs of raw materials, fuel, electricity and gas.

We reported last year that Heineken planned to close the Caledonian Brewery in Edinburgh – famous for its prize-winning Deuchar's IPA. At the same time, the group spent £1 million launching a new lager, Heineken Silver.

In 2023, the Dutch giant said it was promoting Cruzcampo – a 'Spanish' lager brewed in Manchester – with a 'multi-million spend'. While vast amounts of cash are thrown at expensively marketed brands, all Caledonian needed was a minor overhaul, but the money and the will weren't available.

MERGER WOES

The 2022 merger that created the Carlsberg Marston's Brewing Company (CMBC) has resulted in three breweries being closed or sold. The first to go was Jennings in Cumbria. It had twice been saved following floods when Marston's was independent but now Carlsberg is the dominant partner and Jennings, dating from 1828 and brewing such popular beers as Cumberland Ale, has seen the waters close over its head.

In 2017, Marston's bought the Eagle Brewery in Bedford from Charles Wells and continued to produce both ale and lager at the site. But CMBC sold the brewery in November 2022 to the Spanish brewer Estrella Damm and only lager will now be brewed there.

A major blow was the decision by the group to sell Ringwood Brewery and its brands in June 2023. Paul Davies, CMBC's chief executive, said the sale was necessary as the brewery was in a residential area 'which makes expansion difficult and the investment required to bring its capacity up to the level we need to be a viable part of CMBC'.

But when Ringwood moved to the current site in 1986 it occupied part of the former Tunks Brewery that dated from 1876. In other words, Tunks was bigger than Ringwood and

there are no known complaints from residents about having a brewery in their midst. And if Paul Davies is anxious to expand capacity, why is he selling the Ringwood brands as well as the plant? CMBC has 750 outlets for Ringwood beers and those pubs will still need such popular beers as Boondoggle and former Champion Beer of Britain Old Thumper.

The grim truth is that global brewers such as Carlsberg and Heineken have little or no interest in ale and are determined to increase the sale and dominance of their main lager brands.

Carlsberg Marston's have taken the decision to sell the Ringwood brewery in Hampshire

SUCCESS STORIES

There are more positive reports from family-owned breweries with a commitment to ale. Timothy Taylor in Yorkshire reports sales of its beers, including the leading brand Landlord, are ahead of the pre-Covid period. Chief Executive Tim Dewey says that in May 2023 sales were up by 25 per cent compared to May 2019. Landlord is now the second biggest-selling ale brand in Britain after Molson Coors' Doom Bar.

Across the Pennines, Robinsons in Stockport, with a large estate of 249 pubs, similarly reports successful sales of such beers as Unicorn, Cascade and Trooper. It says sales are worth close to £83 million, overtaking pre-Covid levels. It has spent £4 million updating and improving its pubs and plans to buy additional outlets.

In Leicester, Everards, with 154 pubs, says beer sales have recovered well since the end of the pandemic and turnover doubled in 2022.

Hogs Back Brewery in Surrey, which has planted its own hop field, also reports that sales of its beers, including TEA – Traditional English Ale – are back to pre-Covid levels.

BREWERY NEWS

Last year the Guide reported that one of Britain's best-known independent breweries, Kelham Island in Sheffield, founded in 1980, had closed, defeated by rising costs. It has since reopened, bought by a group of beer-loving entrepreneurs, including Jim Harrison and Simon Webster, the founders of Thornbridge Brewery in Bakewell. Kelham Island's beers include Pale Rider, Champion Beer of Britain in 2004: its success kick-started the now insatiable demand for pale, fruity and hoppy ales.

A major shock in 2023 was the announcement that Black Sheep in the Yorkshire Dales had gone into administration. Founded in 1992 by Paul Theakston of the famous Masham brewing dynasty, the brewery seemed impregnable, with impressive sales of its cask beers. But it was overwhelmed by rising costs and it called in administrators. In May 2023 it was sold to the London-based Beal Group, an investment firm that specialises in running businesses in a 'sustainable way'. 150 jobs have been saved and members of the Theakston family remain in charge of the brewery and its visitor centre.

Black Sheep Brewery, Masham, went into administration in 2023

In Cornwall, the much-loved Skinners Brewery in Truro, which closed in 2022, has been bought and reopened and it's hoped that such popular beers as Betty Stogs and Cornish Knocker will be brewed again.

Closures include some long-running family breweries, including Woods in Shropshire, which had made beer for 40 years, and Slaters of Stafford, with 27 years on the clock. Dark Star in West Sussex, dating from 1994, was closed by its owner, the Japanese Asahi group, but its key brands will continue to be brewed by Asahi's main British brewery, Fuller's in West London. Wild Beer in Somerset, which specialised in beers made by spontaneous fermentation, went into administration but its brands were bought by Curious Brewery at Ashford in Kent, doubling its output.

POLICY CHANGES

Appeals to the government to help pubs by tackling the burdens of high business rates and VAT fell on deaf ears. But it did listen to appeals by CAMRA and SIBA, the Society of Independent Brewers, to cut excise duty on draught beer to help pubs combat unfair competition from heavily discounted beer sold in supermarkets. The Chancellor responded by announcing there would be a freeze on draught beer prices from August 2023. At the same time, he brought in more generous rates of Small Brewers Relief. For many years, breweries in the 'squeezed middle' between national producers and small brewers weren't eligible for lower rates of duty but that problem has now been addressed.

POST PANDEMIC

Not all pub closures are the result of the post-pandemic lockdown and rising prices. Whitbread is selling its Beefeater and Brewers Fayre pubs – part of its restaurant and pubs division worth £700 million – in order to grow its Premier Inns sector.

Tenants of the Wellington Pub Company, owned by billionaires David and Simon Reuben, have been forced into bankruptcy by demands for rents owed during lockdown, when their pubs were shut and they had no income.

Such horror stories aside, there's a general feeling among brewers and publicans that there's now more stability where producing and selling beer are concerned.

For consumers, the advice is simple: support the Great British Pub and Great British Beer!

Former editor of The *Good Beer Guide*, Roger Protz is considered one of the leading beer writers in the world, with a long career in journalism and publishing, and having won multiple awards. Roger has authored many books on beer and pubs including *The Family Brewers of Britain*. Follow him on Twitter **@RogerProtzBeer** and **protzonbeer.co.uk**

Closed Breweries

The following breweries have closed or gone out of business since the 2023 Guide was published:

3 Lamps, Swansea, Glamorgan

Acid Brewing Cartel, Glasgow, Greater Glasgow & Clyde Valley

Alphabet, Manchester, Greater Manchester

Amazing, Sandgate, Kent

Anchor House, Plympton, Devon

Anglesey, Carmel, North West Wales

Appleby, Kendal, Cumbria

Artisan, Minchinhampton, Gloucestershire & Bristol

Assembly, Reddish, Greater Manchester

Aurora, Ilkeston, Derbyshire

Autumn, Seaham, Durham

Aye Been, Eyemouth, Borders

Bad Seed, Malton, North Yorkshire

Barnard Castle, Barnard Castle, Durham

Beacon Brauhaus, Lindisfarne, Northumberland

Beat, Lye, West Midlands

Beer Brothers, Bamber Bridge, Lancashire

Bere, Bere Alston, Devon

Black Mountain, Lisburn, Northern Ireland

Black Tor, Christow, Devon

Blonde Brothers, Wylye, Wiltshire

Blueball, Runcorn, Cheshire

Blunt Chisel, Blairadam, Tayside

Boutilliers, Faversham, Kent

Box Steam, Holt, Wiltshire

Brew Shack, Sixpenny Handley, Dorset

Buckland, Bideford, Devon

Burley Street, Leeds, West Yorkshire

Burton Town, Burton upon Trent, Staffordshire

Caffle, Llawhaden, West Wales

Canopy, SE24: Herne Hill, Greater London

Chapeau, Horsham, West Sussex

Coalshed, Caerphilly, Glamorgan

Constellation, Tonbridge, Kent

Craft Brews, Frensham, Surrey

Crafty Cats, St Nicholas Hurst, Berkshire

Crafty Dragon, Pontsticill, Glamorgan

Crankshaft, Leyland, Lancashire

Creaton Grange, Creaton, Northamptonshire

Dark Star, Partridge Green, West Sussex

Dartford Wobbler, South Darenth, Kent

Dawkins, Bristol, Gloucestershire & Bristol

Dent, Dent, Cumbria

Dig, Birmingham: Digbeth, West Midlands

Distant Hills, Glossop, Derbyshire

Dominion, Colchester, Essex

Donkeystone, Greenfield, Greater Manchester

Dovecote, Denbigh, North East Wales

Dowr Kammel, St Breward, Cornwall

Dragonfly/Portobello, W3: Acton, Greater London

Ealing, Brentford, Greater London

East Side, Harold Wood, Essex

Emsworth, Havant, Hampshire

Epic Beers, West Huish, Somerset

Errant, Newcastle upon Tyne, Tyne & Wear

Fable, Great Wakering, Essex

Faking Bad, Prestonpans, Edinburgh & the Lothians

Farmageddon, Comber, Northern Ireland

Federation, Altrincham, Greater Manchester

Ferry, South Queensferry, Edinburgh & the Lothians

Fish Key, Lambley, Nottinghamshire

Fox One, Cwmbran, Gwent

Foxfield, Foxfield, Cumbria

Framework, Leicester, Leicestershire

Friends Arms, Johnstown, West Wales

Ghost, Baildon, West Yorkshire

Gil's, Dinas Powys, Glamorgan

Good Things, Eridge, East Sussex

Goose Island, E1: Shoreditch, Greater London

Greenodd, Greenodd, Cumbria

Greywood, N22: Wood Green, Greater London

Harwich Town, Coggeshall, Essex

Heavy Water, W11: Notting Hill Gate, Greater London

Heritage, Burton upon Trent, Staffordshire

Hildenborough, Hildenborough, Kent

Hopping Mad, Sherington, Buckinghamshire

Hops & Dots, Bishop Auckland, Durham

Hunters, Ipplepen, Devon

Hybrid, Grangemouth, Loch Lomond, Stirling & the Trossachs

Jeffersons, SW13: Barnes, Greater London

Junction, Baildon, West Yorkshire

Kentish Town, NW5: Kentish Town, Greater London

Keystone, Berwick St Leonard, Wiltshire

Lakeland, Ulverston, Cumbria

Lazy Turtle, Hepworth, West Yorkshire

Lennox, Dumbarton, Loch Lomond, Stirling & the Trossachs

Linfit, Linthwaite, West Yorkshire

Lymm, Lymm, Cheshire

Mad Yank, Northwood Hills, Greater London

Madrigal, Hele Bay, Devon

Malvern Hills, Malvern, Worcestershire

Manchester, Manchester, Greater Manchester

Mayflower, Hindley, Greater Manchester

Morton, Coven, Staffordshire

Newcastle, Newcastle upon Tyne, Tyne & Wear

Newtown Park, Bristol, Gloucestershire & Bristol

Nomadic, Leeds, West Yorkshire

North Yorkshire, Warrenby, North Yorkshire

Ogwen, Bethesda, North West Wales

Old Boot, Bacup, Lancashire

Old Dairy, Tenterden, Kent

Old Fountain, EC1V: Old Street, Greater London

Old Spot, Cullingworth, West Yorkshire

One Mile End, E1: Whitechapel, Greater London

One More Than Two, South Shields, Tyne & Wear

Origami, Manchester, Greater Manchester

Outgang, Kinsley, West Yorkshire

Outhouse, Wokingham, Berkshire

Parakeet City, W5: Pitshanger, Greater London

Partizan, SE16: South Bermondsey, Greater London

Philsters, Little Haseley, Oxfordshire

Platform 5, Torquay, Devon

Point Break, Liskeard, Cornwall

Potton, Potton, Bedfordshire

Red Fox, Coggeshall, Essex

Red Shoot, Linwood, Hampshire

Revolutions, Whitwood, West Yorkshire

Ride, Glasgow, Greater Glasgow & Clyde Valley

Riverside, Upper Beeding, West Sussex

Roa Island, Roa Island, Cumbria

Rockin' Robin, Loose, Kent

Ryedale, Sinnington, North Yorkshire

S43, Coxhoe, Durham

Saviour, Hamstead Marshall, Berkshire

Short Stack, E8: Hackney, Greater London

Silver Rocket, Hassocks, West Sussex

Solvay Society, E11: Leytonstone, Greater London

Soul (cuckoo)

South Causey, Durham, Durham

South Lakes, Ulverston, Cumbria

Southbrew, Ringmer, East Sussex

Steel Brew, Plymouth, Devon

Sticklegs, Great Bromley, Essex

To the Moon, Stockport, Greater Manchester

Top Out, Loanhead, Edinburgh & the Lothians

Totally Brewed, Nottingham, Nottinghamshire

Treboom, Shipton-by-Beningbrough, North Yorkshire

Trinity Ales, Gisleham, Suffolk

Tryst, Larbert, Loch Lomond, Stirling & the Trossachs

Turpin's, Burwell, Cambridgeshire

Unity, Northam, Hampshire

Veterans, Coatbridge, Greater Glasgow & Clyde Valley

West End, Leicester, Leicestershire

Wild Beer, Evercreech, Somerset

Witham, Coggeshall, Essex

Yorkshire Coast, Bridlington, East Yorkshire

Future Breweries

The following new breweries have been notified to the Guide and will start to produce beer during 2023/2024. In a few cases they were in production during the summer of 2023 but were too late for a full listing:

Axeljack, Maesteg, Glamorgan

Be: Vito, Cwmbran, Gwent

Bent Barrel, Heanor, Derbyshire

Bottle Monkey, Castletown, Isle of Man

Deirge, Castlederg, Northern Ireland

Firkin, SE13: Lewisham, Greater London

Flame Out, Ross-on-Wye, Herefordshire

Glenwinny, Lisbellaw, Northern Ireland

LuneBrew, Lancaster, Lancashire

On Point, Bristol, Gloucesteshire & Bristol

Reluctant Hero, Leeds, West Yorkshire

Rock Leopard, SE2: Thamesmead, Greater London

Tanant, Pen-y-Garnedd, Mid Wales

Breweries for Sale

The following breweries are reported as being for sale:

Church Aston, Church Aston, Shropshire

Coastal, Crewe, Cheshire

Concrete Cow, Milton Keynes, Buckinghamshire

Hadham, Little Hadham, Hertfordshire

Leeds, Leeds, West Yorkshire

Shropshire Brewer, Longden Common, Shropshire

Slater's, Stafford, Staffordshire

AWARD-WINNING PUBS

The Pub of the Year competition is judged by CAMRA members. Each of the CAMRA branches votes for its favourite pub: criteria include the quality and choice of real ale, atmosphere, customer service, community offering, and value. The pubs listed below are the current winners of the title, look out for the 🏆 next to the entries in the Guide.

ENGLAND

East of England

Bedfordshire
Wellington Arms, Bedford
Stone Jug, Clophill
March Hare, Dunton
Black Lion, Leighton Buzzard

Cambridgeshire
Geldart, Cambridge
Drayman's Son, Ely
King of the Belgians, Hartford
Blue Bell, Peterborough

Geldart, Cambridge

Essex
Victoria Arms, Brentwood
Railway Tavern, Brightlingsea
Finchingfield Lion, Finchingfield
Olde Albion, Rowhedge
Station Arms, Southminster
Endeavour, Springfield
Woodbine Inn, Waltham Abbey
Mile & a Third, Westcliff-on-Sea

Hertfordshire
Lordship Arms, Benington
Land of Liberty, Peace & Plenty, Heronsgate
Woodman, Wild Hill

Norfolk
Ampersand Brew Tap, Diss
New Entertainer, Gorleston
Angel, Larling
White Lion, Norwich

Suffolk
Cock, Brent Eleigh
Fat Cat, Ipswich
Buck, Rumburgh

Greater London

Greater London
Stag & Lantern, E4: Highams Park
Bohemia, N12: North Finchley
Tapping the Admiral, NW1: Camden Town
Royal Oak, SE1: Borough
Sultan, SW19: South Wimbledon
Harp, WC2: Charing Cross

Harp, WC2: Charing Cross, Greater London

Butchers Arms, Balscote, Oxfordshire

Dodo Micropub, W7: Hanwell
Long Haul, Bexleyheath
Hope, Carshalton
Cockpit, Chislehurst
Jolly Coopers, Hampton
Hop Inn, Hornchurch
Watchman, New Malden

South East

Berkshire
Bell Inn, Aldworth
Newtown Pippin, Bracknell
A Hoppy Place Maidenhead, Maidenhead
Alehouse, Reading

Buckinghamshire
Mitre, Buckingham
George Ale House, Great Missenden
Bird in Hand, Princes Risborough

Hampshire
Eight Bells, Alton
Junction Tavern, Gosport
Olaf's Tun, Southampton
Wonston Arms, Wonston

Isle of Wight
Highdown Inn, Totland Bay

Kent
Royston, Broadstairs
Elephant, Faversham
Three Daws, Gravesend
Bouncing Barrel, Herne Bay
Armoury, Linton
Coopers Arms, Rochester
This Ancient Boro', Tenterden
Nelson Arms, Tonbridge
Berry, Walmer

Oxfordshire
Broad Face, Abingdon
Butchers Arms, Balscote
Royal Blenheim, Oxford
George, Sutton Courtenay
King's Arms, Wantage

Surrey
Jolly Coopers, Epsom
Crown, Horsell
Surrey Oaks, Newdigate
Barley Mow, Shepperton

East Sussex
Brickmaker's Alehouse, Bexhill on Sea
Watchmaker's Arms, Hove
King's Arms, Rotherfield

West Sussex
Brewery Shades, Crawley
Wilkes' Head, Eastergate
Five Bells, West Chiltington

Nelson Arms, Tonbridge, Kent

South West

Cornwall
'front, Falmouth

Devon
Globe Inn, Beaford
Queen's Arms, Brixham
Exeter Inn, Chittlehamholt
Thatched House Inn, Exeter
Fortescue Hotel, Plymouth
Walkhampton Inn, Walkhampton

Dorset
White Lion, Broadwindsor
Saxon Bar, Christchurch
Barking Cat Alehouse, Poole

Gloucestershire & Bristol
Sandford Park Alehouse, Cheltenham
Pelican Inn, Gloucester
Bell Inn, Moreton-in-Marsh
Cross House Tavern, Tewkesbury

Somerset
Raven, Bath
Halfway House, Pitney
Siren's Calling, Portishead

Wiltshire
Fox & Goose, Coombe Bissett
Duke of York, Salisbury
Five Bells, Royal Wootton Bassett

West Midlands

Shropshire
Golden Lion, Bridgnorth
Bailey Head, Oswestry
Pheasant Inn, Telford: Wellington

Staffordshire
Swan, Brewood
Devonshire Arms, Burton upon Trent
Arcade, Cannock
Black Lion, Cheddleton
Cat Inn, Enville
Bull's Head, Stoke-on-Trent: Burslem
Borehole, Stone
Tamworth Tap, Tamworth
Night Inn, Uttoxeter

Warwickshire
Lord Nelson Inn, Ansley
Bird in Hand, Austrey
Three Tuns, Henley-in-Arden
Old Bakery, Kenilworth
New Inn, Norton Lindsey
Thirst Edition, Shipston-on-Stour

West Midlands
Swan, Amblecote
Hop & Scotch, Birmingham: Kings Heath
Hops d'Amour, Coventry: City Centre
Pup & Duckling, Solihull
Pretty Bricks, Walsall
Keg & Comfort, Wolverhampton
Bird in Hand, Wordsley

Worcestershire
Weighbridge, Alvechurch
Trumpet Inn, Evesham
Bear & Wolf, Kidderminster
Dragon Inn, Worcester

East Midlands

Derbyshire
Smith's Tavern, Ashbourne
Angels Micro Pub, Belper
Chesterfield Arms, Chesterfield
Falstaff, Derby
Miners Arms, Hundall
Feather Star, Wirksworth

Leicestershire
Wheel Inn, Branston
New Plough Inn, Hinckley
Organ Grinder, Loughborough
Stilton Cheese, Somerby

Lincolnshire
Railway Tavern, Aby
Five Horseshoes, Barholm
Sweyn Forkbeard, Gainsborough
Lord Harrowby, Grantham
Yarborough Hotel, Grimsby
Strugglers Inn, Lincoln

Tamworth Tap, Tamworth, Staffordshire

Northamptonshire
Road to Morocco, Northampton
Wharf Inn, Welford

Nottinghamshire
Just Beer Micropub, Newark
Beer Under The Clock, Retford
Old Coach House, Southwell
Horse & Jockey, Stapleford

Rutland
Grainstore Brewery Tap, Oakham

Yorkshire

Salt Cellar, Saltaire, West Yorkshire

East Yorkshire
Old Ship Inn, Bridlington
Hop & Vine, Hull

North Yorkshire
Harrogate Tap, Harrogate
Countryman's Inn, Hunton
Crown Inn, Manfield
Sun Inn, Pickering
Beer Engine, Skipton
New Inn, Yarm
Phoenix, York

South Yorkshire
Heaven & Ale, Barnsley
Doncaster Brewery Tap, Doncaster
Cutlers Arms, Rotherham
Kelham Island Tavern, Sheffield: Kelham Island

North West

Cheshire
Lodge Inn, Alsager
Cellar, Chester
Castle, Macclesfield
Ferry Tavern, Penketh
Chapter Brewing Tap, Sutton Weaver

Cumbria
Manor Arms, Broughton-in-Furness
Drovers Rest, Monkhill

Lancashire
Crossing, Hest Bank
Swan with Two Necks, Pendleton
Black Horse, Preston
Fifteens of St Anne's, St Anne's-on-the-Sea

Kelham Island Tavern, Sheffield, South Yorkshire

Crossing, Hest Bank, Lancashire

West Yorkshire
West Riding Refreshment Rooms, Dewsbury
Cross Keys, Halifax: Siddal
Riverhead Brewery Tap, Marsden
Travellers Rest, Meltham
Old Cock, Otley
Salt Cellar, Saltaire
Black Rock, Wakefield

Greater Manchester
Beer House, Chorlton-cum-Hardy
Silly Country Bar & Bottle Shop, Droylsden
Brewery Bar, Horwich
Bobbin, Leigh
Molly House, Manchester
Fox & Pine, Oldham
New Oxford, Salford
Petersgate Tap, Stockport
Real Crafty, Wigan

Fifteens of St Anne's, St Anne's-on-the-Sea, Lancashire

Merseyside
Bridewell, Liverpool: City Centre
Turk's Head, St Helens
Red Fox, Thornton Hough

North East

Durham
Grey Horse, Consett
Quakerhouse, Darlington
Old Elm Tree, Durham
Surtees Arms, Ferryhill Station
Golden Smog, Stockton-on-Tees

Tyne & Wear
Microbus, Gateshead
Town Mouse Ale House, Newcastle Upon Tyne: City Centre
Marine, South Shields

WALES

Glamorgan
Flute & Tankard, Cardiff: City Centre
Plough & Harrow, Monknash
Bunch of Grapes, Pontypridd
No Sign Bar, Swansea

Gwent
Queen's Head, Chepstow

Mid Wales
Royal Oak, Pencelli

North-East Wales
Mold Alehouse, Mold
Magic Dragon Brewery Tap, Wrexham

North-West Wales
Adelphi Vaults, Amlwch Port
Albion Ale House, Conwy

West Wales
Masons Arms, Cilgerran
Rhos yr Hafod Inn, Cross Inn (Llanon)
Mansel Arms, Porthyrhyd

SCOTLAND

Aberdeen & Grampian
St Machar Bar, Aberdeen
Redgarth, Oldmeldrum

Ayrshire & Arran
Weston Tavern, Kilmaurs

Borders
Allanton Inn, Allanton

Dumfries & Galloway
Blue Bell Inn, Annan
Douglas Arms, Dumfries

Blue Bell Inn, Annan, Dumfries & Galloway, Scotland

Douglas Arms, Dumfries, Scotland

Edinburgh & the Lothians
Jolly Judge, Edinburgh: Central
Volunteer Arms (Staggs), Musselburgh

Greater Glasgow & Clyde Valley
Bon Accord, Glasgow
Bull Inn, Paisley

Highlands & Western Isles
Westford Inn, Claddach Kirkibost: North Uist

Kingdom of Fife
Hillend Tavern, Hillend

Loch Lomond, Stirling & the Trossachs
Corbie Inn, Bo'ness

Northern Isles
Helgi's Bar, Kirkwall: Orkney

Tayside
Ericht Alehouse, Blairgowrie
Speedwell Bar, Dundee
Village Inn, Milnathort
Market Arms, Montrose
Old Ship Inn, Perth

Sunflower, Belfast, Northern Ireland

OFFSHORE ISLANDS

Northern Ireland
Sunflower, Belfast

Isle of Man
Trafalgar Hotel, Ramsey

Speedwell Bar, Dundee, Tayside, Scotland

ADDITIONAL RESOURCES

The *Good Beer Guide* is also available in digital formats, including a mobile app and a sat-nav Points of Interest (POI) download. Together, these offer the perfect solution to pub-finding on the move. See **shop1.camra.org.uk** for further information.

GOOD BEER GUIDE APP

The *Good Beer Guide* mobile app provides detailed information on the latest Good Beer Guide pubs, breweries and beers wherever you are or wherever you are going. It also provides information for more than 31,000 other real ale pubs all over the UK, collated by CAMRA. Social media integration lets you share your beer experiences with other users and you can record your pub visits, tasted beers and personal reviews. For more information visit **camra.org.uk/gbgapp**

CAMRA'S NATIONAL BEER SCORING SYSTEM

CAMRA's National Beer Scoring System (NBSS) is used by members across the country to help them identify outlets that serve consistently good beer. The system uses a 0–5 scale that can be submitted online. Any member can submit a beer score by visiting **whatpub.com**, logging in as a member and selecting 'Submit Beer Scores' or by using the beer scoring function on the Good Beer Guide app.

The NBSS is also used to select beers for the annual Champion Beer of Britain competition.

See **camra.org.uk/NBSS** for details.

JOIN CAMRA'S GOOD BEER GUIDE PRIVILEGE CLUB

CAMRA members can take advantage of an even bigger discount on the *Good Beer Guide*, and get further benefits, by joining the Good Beer Guide Privilege Club.

- Pay just £12 (RRP £16.99) for your copy, with free p&p
- Receive your copy hot off the press and in advance of other purchasers
- Receive occasional special Club offers and discounts on other CAMRA books and merchandise
- Stay up-to-date every year with the *Good Beer Guide* as everything is taken care of with one simple Direct Debit
- Help to fund CAMRA directly, allowing us to continue to campaign for real ale and community pubs

For further details and to sign up visit **camra.org.uk/gbg-privilege-club** and follow the online instructions.

BOOKS AND MERCHANDISE

CAMRA's online shop is the ideal place to visit for anyone looking for beer- and pub-related books, clothing or merchandise for themselves or fellow beer lovers.

Books on beer, brewing, pubs, and breweries have been exploding onto our bookshelves in more numbers than ever before in recent years. Alongside a rise in the 'craft' beer movement the books on beer have taken on a much more eclectic and varied approach to the subject. Beer and cooking, brewing your own with a myriad of ingredients and the most exotic places to drink beer, have all been covered in one form or another. CAMRA books are keen to embrace this new-found desire to explore the quirky and exciting aspects of beer but with 50 years of publishing and a combined membership life experience of over 9 million years, we are much more inclined to approach these subjects with the long term in mind. As an authority on beer, we are very much concerned with preserving it in its purest form and celebrating the changes and innovations for their benefits.

- Browse the full range of CAMRA Books titles within categories including beer knowledge; beer travel; history & culture, heritage, home brewing and pub walks & travel
- Discover our growing selection of beer-related titles from other publishers
- Shop our expanding range of clothing and merchandise
- Get upcoming CAMRA titles in advance of publication at special pre-order prices
- As a CAMRA member, log in to receive further discounts

Visit us at: **shop1.camra.org.uk**

London's Best Beer, Pubs & Bars

Des De Moor

The essential guide to beer drinking in London, completely revised for 2022. Laid out by area, the book makes it simple to find the best London pubs and bars – serving the best British and world beers – and to explore the growing number of London breweries offering tours, taprooms and direct sales. Features tell you more about London's rich history of brewing and the city's vibrant modern brewing scene. The venue listings are fully illustrated, with detailed information on opening hours, local landmarks, and public transport links to make planning any excursion quick and easy. The book also includes a comprehensive listing of London breweries.

RRP: £16.99   **ISBN**: 978-1-85249-360-8

For this and other books on beer and pubs, visit CAMRA's online bookshop at **shop1.camra.org.uk** or call 01727 867201.

Discounts are available for CAMRA members.

Beer Breaks

Tim Webb

This essential pocket guide to European beer travel features over 30 destinations, all easily accessible from the UK for short break travel.

Each featured city includes a review of the city, with selected tourist highlights, food recommendations, itineraries for first-time visitors, accommodation, and travel options, followed by recommended beer bars, cafés and brewery taps where the reader can experience the best of each city's burgeoning beer scene.

An extensive section on transportation will enable the beer tourists wanting to see more of Europe to link destinations using public transport.

Featured destinations include Barcelona, Berlin, Bristol, Copenhagen, Edinburgh, Madrid, Porto, Tallin, Tel Aviv and Vienna.

RRP: £15.99   **ISBN:** 978-1-85249-364-6

For this and other books on beer and pubs, visit CAMRA's online bookshop at **shop1.camra.org.uk** or call 01727 867201.

Discounts are available for CAMRA members.

Cask
The real story of Britain's unique beer culture

Des De Moor

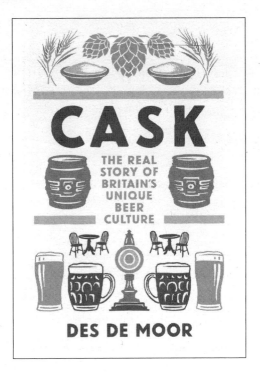

Cask beer played a crucial role in the rise of beer appreciation and remains a unique product, delivering a drinking experience that can't be achieved any other way. But cask no longer enjoys the same priority among beer connoisseurs and brewers that it once did. Its shorter shelf life and need for conscientious cellaring and dispense is part of the problem, but it's also misunderstood by many drinkers and surrounded by myths and half-truths dating from times when beer knowledge was disseminated much less widely.

In this new book, award-winning beer writer Des de Moor introduces the wonders of cask to a new generation of beer drinkers. He explains what distinguishes it from other beer, explores its long and tumultuous history, and examines how it's survived world wars, economic depression and a global pandemic. Cask remains Britain's greatest gift to the world of beer and this book tells us why it's so important.

RRP: £17.99   **ISBN**: 978-1-85249-384-4

For this and other books on beer and pubs, visit CAMRA's online bookshop at **shop1.camra.org.uk** or call 01727 867201.

Discounts are available for CAMRA members.

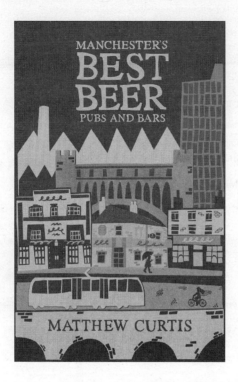

JOIN THE CAMRA STORY

People from all walks of life join CAMRA. They're brought together by a love of real ale, cider and perry, the traditions of the pub and a desire to protect them. Be part of the story and seek out your local branch. Keep real ale alive and share tasting notes. Volunteer at a festival or campaign to protect everything you love for the future. Discover the many ways to celebrate our shared passions.

Join as a member from only £30.50[†] today – as a thank you for being a hero in the CAMRA story, your membership gets you...

- A **welcome pack**, including membership card, to help you make the most of your membership

- Access to award-winning, quarterly *BEER* **magazine** and **What's Brewing** online news

- £30[*] worth of **CAMRA real ale**[**] **vouchers**

- Access to the **Real Ale Discount Scheme**, where you receive discounts on pints at over 3,500 participating pubs nationwide

- **Learn & Discover** online resources to help you discover more about beer and brewing

- **Free or reduced entry** to CAMRA beer festivals

- The opportunity to **campaign for great real ale, cider and perry**, and to save pubs under threat from closure

- **Discounts on CAMRA books** including our best-selling *Good Beer Guide*

- Social activities in your local area and **exclusive member discounts online**

Join the
CAMRA story

Real stories, real people, real ale

Whether you're a dedicated campaigner, a beer enthusiast looking to learn more about beer, or you just love beer and pubs, CAMRA membership is for you. Join us today!

Join the campaign at
camra.org.uk/join

CAMRA, 230 Hatfield Road, St Albans, Herts AL1 4LW.
Tel: 01727 798440 Email: camra@camra.org.uk

Rates and benefits are subject to change.
[†] Concessionary rates may be lower.
[*] Joint members receive £40 worth of vouchers.
[**] real ale, cider and perry, subject to terms and conditions.

Campaign
for
Real Ale